SPECIAL EDITION

USING

Microsoft®

Office Access 2003

Roger Jennings

Pearson Education
800 East 96th Street
Indianapolis, Indiana 46240

Contents at a Glance

Special Edition Using Microsoft Office Access 2003

International Standard Book Number: 0-7897-2952-0

Library of Congress Catalog Card Number: 2003106309

Printed in the United States of America

First Printing: September 2003

07 06 05 9 8 7 6 5

Bulk Sales

Que Publishing offers excellent discounts on this book when ordered in quantity for bulk purchases or special sales. For more information, please contact

U.S. Corporate and Government Sales
1-800-382-3419
corpsales@pearsontechgroup.com

For sales outside of the U.S., please contact

International Sales
international@pearsoned.com

Trademarks

All terms mentioned in this book that are known to be trademarks or service marks have been appropriately capitalized. Que Publishing cannot attest to the accuracy of this information. Use of a term in this book should not be regarded as affecting the validity of any trademark or service mark.

Warning and Disclaimer

Every effort has been made to make this book as complete and as accurate as possible, but no warranty or fitness is implied. The information provided is on an "as is" basis. The authors and the publisher shall have neither liability nor responsibility to any person or entity with respect to any loss or damages arising from the information contained in this book.

Associate Publisher
Michael Stephens

Acquisitions Editor
Loretta Yates

Development Editor
Sean Dixon

Managing Editor
Charlotte Clapp

Project Editor
Andy Beaster

Indexer
John Sleeva

Proofreader
Suzanne Thomas

Technical Editor
Rebecca Riordan

Team Coordinator
Cindy Teeters

Interior Designer
Gary Adair

Cover Designer
Aren Howell

Contents

IV Designing Forms and Reports

VII Programming and Converting Access Applications

Troubleshooting Table of Contents

About the Author

Roger Jennings is an author and consultant specializing in Windows client/server databases and data-centric XML Web services. He was a member of the Microsoft technical beta testing team for all eight editions of Microsoft Access, every release of Visual Basic since version 2.0, and Windows 3.1 and all subsequent Microsoft operating systems. He also was one of the founding members of Microsoft's former Access Insiders group.

Roger's books have more than one million English copies in print and have been translated into more than 20 languages. He is the author of Que's *Special Edition Using Microsoft Access* titles for Access versions 1.0, 1.1, 2.0, 95, 97 (first and second editions), 2000, and 2002, and *Platinum Edition Using Access 97*. He also wrote Que's *Special Edition Using Windows NT Server 4*, *Special Edition Using Windows 2000 Server*, *Unveiling Windows 95*, *Access Hot Tips*, and *Discover Windows 3.1 Multimedia*. For Pearson Education's SAMS imprint, he has written two editions of *Access Developer's Guide* and three editions of *Database Developers Guide with Visual Basic* (for versions 3.0, 4.0, and 6.0). Additionally, he was the series editor for the *Roger Jennings' Database Workshop* titles.

Roger is a contributing editor for Fawcette Technical Publication's *Visual Studio Magazine* and a columnist for *.NET Magazine* (`http://www.fawcette.com/`); his "Database Design" and "SQL Connection" columns and feature articles on Microsoft database technology appear regularly. Roger co-authored with Microsoft's Greg Nelson "A Client/Server Application: From Concept to Reality" Microsoft Tech*Ed presentation and white paper on Access 2.0, which appeared on the Microsoft Developer's Network CD-ROM and in the *Microsoft Developer Network News*. An Access 2003 version of the application described in the white paper is located in the \Seua11\Chaptr14 folder of the accompanying CD-ROM.

Roger has more than 25 years of computer-related experience, beginning with his work on the Wang 700 desktop calculator/computer. He is a principal of OakLeaf Systems, a Northern California software consulting firm, and is the developer of the OakLeaf XML Web Services site (`http://www.oakleaf.ws/`). His OakLeaf U.S. Code of Federal Regulations (CFR) XML Web services demonstration project (`http://www.oakleaf.ws/CFR/`) won the 2001 Microsoft .NET Best Award for horizontal solutions. You can contact Roger at `Roger_Jennings@compuserve.com`.

Dedication

This book is dedicated to my wife, Alexandra.

Acknowledgments

Loretta Yates, acquisitions editor, made sure that I didn't fall too far behind the manuscript submission and author review schedule. Sean Dixon, development editor, contributed to the content and organization of this new edition. Andy Beaster, project editor, worked hard to make sure that all of the components of this edition flowed through the editing process and got to their final destination on time. Media developer Dan Scherf handled production of the accompanying CD-ROM.

Technical editor Rebecca M. Riordan is the author of *Microsoft SQL Server 2000 Programming Step by Step* and *Designing Relational Database Systems* (Microsoft Press). Rebecca has worked as a consultant, systems analyst, and senior technical support engineer. She has completed coursework in database design and analysis at the University of California, Irvine. Rebecca also was a presenter at Microsoft Tech*Ed 1994 and 1995.

Steven Gray and Rick Lievano, authors of *Roger Jennings' Database Workshop: Microsoft Transaction Server 2.0*, created the original version of the Oakmont.mdb database for the CD-ROM as a Microsoft SQL Server 6.5 database.

We Want to Hear from You!

As the reader of this book, *you* are our most important critic and commentator. We value your opinion and want to know what we're doing right, what we could do better, what areas you'd like to see us publish in, and any other words of wisdom you're willing to pass our way.

You can email or write me directly to let me know what you did or didn't like about this book—as well as what we can do to make our books stronger.

Please note that I cannot help you with technical problems related to the topic of this book, and that due to the high volume of mail I receive, I might not be able to reply to every message.

When you write, please be sure to include this book's title and author as well as your name and phone or email address. I will carefully review your comments and share them with the author and editors who worked on the book.

Email: `feedback@samspublishing.com`

Mail: Michael Stephens
Associate Publisher
Sams Publishing
800 East 96th Street
Indianapolis, IN 46240 USA

Reader Services

For more information about this book or others from Sams Publishing, visit our Web site at `www.samspublishing.com`. Type the ISBN (excluding hyphens) or the title of the book in the Search box to find the book you're looking for.

INTRODUCTION

In this chapter

Microsoft Office Access 2003 (version 11.0, called *Access 2003* in this book) is a powerful, robust, and mature 32-bit relational database management system (RDBMS) for creating desktop and client/server database applications that run under Windows XP/2000+. As a component of the Professional and Professional Enterprise editions of Microsoft Office System 2003, Access 2003 has an upgraded user interface that's consistent with the other members of the Office 2003 suite.

Access has vanquished all desktop relational database management system (RDBMS) rivals except Visual FoxPro and FileMaker Pro. The primary reasons for Access's success are its inclusion in Microsoft's productivity suite and its prowess as a rapid application development (RAD) environment for creating industrial-strength database applications. Another contributor to Access's market share is the capability to duplicate on the PC desktop the features of client/server relational database systems, also called SQL databases. Client/server RDBMSs have led the way in transferring database applications from costly mainframes and Unix servers to modestly priced networked PCs. Despite Access's power—and the claims of its erstwhile competitors—this desktop RDBMS is easy for nonprogrammers to use.

Like all members of Office 2003, Access 2003 offers a variety of Internet-related features for creating HTML and XML documents for use on intranets and the Internet. An important feature of Access 2003 is the upgraded version of data access pages (DAP), which is now ready for full deployment on your intranet and—with a few reservations—the Internet. Intranet and Internet users no longer need Office licenses to use the most important DAP features, but they do need to run Windows XP/2000+. You can redistribute the runtime version of the Office Web Components (OWC) 11, which enables full use of the Data Source Control and its navigation bar, plus view-only PivotTable and PivotChart pages. Internet users can automatically download OWC 11 from the Microsoft Web site.

Next in line on the feature list is the inclusion of Microsoft SQL Server 2000 Desktop Edition (MSDE). Graphic table and query designers make creating and modifying SQL Server tables, views, functions, and stored procedures almost as easy as working with Jet tables and queries. Extended properties add lookup fields, subdatasheets, input masks, and other Access accouterments to SQL Server databases.

Microsoft's rallying cry for Windows XP/2000+ and Office 2003 is Total Cost of Ownership (TCO). Ease of use is one of the primary requisites for reducing TCO; Access 2003 includes many wizards and other aids designed for first-time database users. If you're still using Access 97 or 2000, Access 2003 and MSDE alone justify the cost of upgrading to Office 2003. If your goal is to use DAP for viewing and updating data in Internet Explorer 5+, make upgrading from Access 2000 your first priority.

Who Should Read This Book

Special Edition Using Microsoft Office Access 2003 takes an approach that's different from most books about database management applications. This book doesn't begin with the creation of a database for Widgets, Inc., nor does it require you to type a list of fictional customers for the company's new WidgetPlus product line to learn the basics of Access. Instead, this book makes the following basic assumptions about your interest in Microsoft's relational database management system:

- You aren't starting from "ground zero." You now have or will have access via your PC to much of the data that you want to process with a Windows database manager. You've acquired Access and want to learn to use it more quickly and effectively. Or, you might be considering using Access as the database manager for yourself, your department or division, or your entire organization.
- Your existing data is in the form of one or more database, spreadsheet, mailing list, or even plain-text files that you want to manipulate with a relational database management system. Access 2003 can process the most common varieties of these file types, as well as HTML tables, element-centric XML files, Outlook contact lists, Windows SharePoint Services lists, and other tabular data sources.
- If you're planning to use Access 2003 as a front end to a client/server RDBMS, you'll use MSDE or SQL Server 2000 as the back-end database. Access 2003 lets you replicate data between a local copy of MSDE and MSDE or SQL Server on the server.
- If your data is on a mainframe computer, you're connected to that computer by a local area network and a database gateway, or through terminal-emulation software and an adapter card. Alternatively, you download text files from the mainframe to create Jet or SQL Server tables.

If some or all of your data is in the form of ASCII/ANSI text files, or files from a spreadsheet application, you need to know how to create an Access database from the beginning and import the data into Access's own .mdb file structure. If your data is in the form of dBASE, FoxPro, or Paradox files, you can import them directly to Access tables. Access 2002 also lets you link Excel workbook and conventional text files, as well as Outlook and SharePoint lists to Access databases. The capability to link files in their native format lets you synchronize the contents of your database tables with the original source documents. All these subjects receive thorough coverage in this book.

Learning relational database design and management with Access 2003 as the training tool is the quickest and easiest way to upgrade your professional skills. If you're a Web designer, the expertise in client/server database techniques that you gain by working with Access data projects, SQL Server, and data access pages greatly enhances your future employment prospects. Despite the prolonged downturn in the dot-com sector, there's no slack in the demand for unlocking islands of data stored in client/server databases and making the data available as usable business information on corporate intranets.

Access 2003 is a great first step in gaining XML, XML schema (XSD), and XSL transform (XSLT) skills. Most XML-related books and other training materials use trivial examples to illustrate XML and XSL(T) methodology. Access 2003 lets you dynamically generate real-world XML data and schemas, and provides a standard transform to render data in HTML format. Working with the resulting .xsl files and their embedded VBScript is the fastest way to learn practical XSLT techniques for delivering XML data as fully formatted Web pages.

How This Book Is Organized

Special Edition Using Microsoft Office Access 2003 is divided into seven parts arranged in increasing levels of detail and complexity. Each division after Part I, "Getting Acquainted with Access 2003," draws on the knowledge and experience that you've gained in the previous parts, so use of the book in a linear, front-to-back manner through Part IV, "Designing Forms and Reports," is recommended during the initial learning process. After you absorb the basics of working with Jet databases, you progress through upsizing databases to SQL Server 2000. Chapters on Access's new XML and Data Access Pages features follow the SQL Server chapters because some XML and DAP elements depend on MSDE as the data source.

As you progress through the chapters in this book, you create a model of an Access application called Human Resources Actions. In Chapter 5, "Working with Jet Databases and Tables," you create the HR Actions table. In the following chapters, you add new features to the HR Actions application. Be sure to perform the example exercises for the HR Actions application each time you encounter them because succeeding examples build on your previous work. (The accompanying CD-ROM contains sample databases at each stage of the process).

The seven parts of *Special Edition Using Microsoft Office Access 2003* and the topics that they cover are described in the following sections.

Part I: "Getting Acquainted with Access 2003"

The chapters in Part I introduce you to Access and many of the unique features that make Access 2003 the premier desktop database management system.

- Chapter 1, "Access 2003 for Access 97 and 2000/2002 Users: What's New," provides a summary of the most important new features of Access 2003 and a detailed description of each addition and improvement. Much of this chapter's content is of interest primarily to readers who now use Access 97 or 2000 because many of the changes from Access 2000 to Access 2003 are incremental in nature. Readers new to Access, however, benefit from the explanations of why many of these new features are significant in everyday Access 2003 use.
- In Chapter 2, "Building a Simple Desktop and Web Application," you use the Database Wizard to create a database from the standard database templates included with Access 2003. You gain a basic understanding of the standard data-related objects of Access, including tables, forms, reports, pages, and Visual Basic for Applications (VBA) modules. Chapter 2 also introduces you to automating Access operations with VBA Class Modules, the replacement for Access macros, and the Office VBA editor.

- Chapter 3, "Navigating the Access User Interface," shows you how to take best advantage of Access by explaining its toolbar and menu choices and then showing how they relate to the structure of the Access object model. Chapter 4 also shows you how to use Access 2003's new online help system, including the Type a Question for Help text box and the Help task pane that replace Office 2000's intrusive Office Assistant.

PART II: "LEARNING THE FUNDAMENTALS OF JET DATABASES"

Part II is devoted to understanding the design principals of relational databases, creating new Jet tables, adding and editing table data, and integrating Jet tables with other sources of data. Most of the techniques that you learn in Part II also apply to SQL Server tables.

- Chapter 4, "Exploring Relational Database Theory and Practice," describes the process that you use to create relational database tables from real-world data—a technique called normalizing the database structure. The chapter also introduces you to the concepts of key fields, data integrity, and views of tables that contain related data.
- Chapter 5, "Working with Jet Databases and Tables," delves into the details of Jet desktop database tables, shows you how to create tables, and explains how to choose the optimum data types from the many new types that Access offers. Chapter 5 explains how to use subdatasheets and lookup tables to display and edit records in related tables. The chapter also explains how to use the Database Documentor tool included with Access 2003 to create a data dictionary that fully identifies each object in your database.
- Chapter 6, "Entering, Editing, and Validating Jet Table Data," describes how to add new records to tables, enter data in the new records, and edit data in existing records. Using keyboard shortcuts instead of the mouse for editing speeds manual data entry. Adding input masks and data validation rules minimizes the chance for typographic errors when entering new data.
- Chapter 7, "Sorting, Finding, and Filtering Data," shows you how to arrange the data in tables to suit your needs and to limit the data displayed to only that information you want. You learn how to use Find and Replace to search for and alter multiple instances of data in the fields of tables. Chapter 7 further describes how to make best use of the Filter by Form and Filter by Selection features of Access 2003.
- Chapter 8, "Linking, Importing, and Exporting Data," explains how to import and export files of other database managers, spreadsheet applications, and text files downloaded from mainframe or Unix database servers or the Internet. You also learn how use the Access Mail Merge Wizard to create form letters from data stored in Jet tables.

PART III: "TRANSFORMING DATA WITH QUERIES AND PIVOTTABLES"

The chapters in Part III explain how to create Access queries to select the way that you view data contained in tables and how to take advantage of Access's relational database structure to link multiple tables with joins. Part III also covers Access 2003's PivotTable and PivotChart views of query result sets.

- Chapter 9, "Designing Queries for Jet Databases," starts with simple queries you create with Access's graphical Query Design window. You learn how to choose the fields of the tables included in your query and return query result sets from these tables. Examples of Jet SQL generated by the queries that you design let you learn SQL "by osmosis." Chapter 9 shows you how to use the Simple Query Wizard to simplify the design process.
- Chapter 10, "Understanding Jet Operators and Expressions," introduces you to the operators and expressions that you need to create queries that provide a meaningful result. Most Jet operators and expressions are the same as those that you use in VBA programs. You use the Immediate window of the Office 2003 VBA editor to evaluate the expressions that you write.
- In Chapter 11, "Creating Multitable and Crosstab Queries," you create relations between tables, called joins, and learn how to add criteria to queries so that the query result set includes only records that you want. Chapter 11 also takes you through the process of designing powerful crosstab queries to summarize data and to present information in a format similar to that of worksheets.
- Chapter 12, "Working with PivotTable and PivotChart Views," shows you how to manipulate data from multitable queries in the OWC's PivotTable control and then display the results in PivotChart controls. The query design and PivotTable/PivotChart techniques that you learn here also apply to PivotTables and PivotCharts that you embed in Access forms and Data Access Pages.
- Chapter 13, "Creating and Updating Jet Tables with Action Queries," shows you how to develop action queries that update the tables underlying append, delete, update, and make-table queries. Chapter 13 also covers Access 2003's advanced referential integrity features, including cascading updates and cascading deletions.

PART IV: "DESIGNING FORMS AND REPORTS"

The chapters in Part IV introduce you to the primary application objects of Access. (Tables and queries are considered database objects.) Forms make your Access applications come alive with the control objects that you add by using Access 2003's Toolbox. Access's full-featured report generator lets you print fully formatted reports, export or mail report snapshot files, and save reports to files that you can process in Excel 2003 or Word 2003.

- Chapter 14, "Creating and Using Access Forms," shows you how to use Access's Form Wizards to create simple forms and subforms that you can modify to suit your particular needs. Chapter 14 introduces you to the Subform Builder Wizard that uses drag-and-drop techniques to automatically create subforms for you.
- Chapter 15, "Designing Custom Multitable Forms," shows you how to design custom forms for viewing and entering your own data with Access's advanced form design tools.

- Chapter 16, "Working with Simple Reports and Mailing Labels," describes how to design and print basic reports with Access's Report Wizard, and how to print preformatted mailing labels by using the Mailing Label Wizard.
- Chapter 17, "Preparing Advanced Reports," describes how to use more sophisticated sorting and grouping techniques, as well as subreports, to obtain a result that exactly meets your detail and summary data-reporting requirements. Chapter 17 also covers the snapshot technology that lets you distribute Access reports as Outlook email attachments and save reports as snapshot (.snp) files. The Snapshot Viewer lets users without Access view and print email attachments or .snp files.
- In Chapter 18, "Adding Graphs, PivotCharts, and PivotTables," you first learn to use the OLE-based Chart Wizard to create databound graphs and charts based on Jet crosstab queries. PivotCharts are destined to replace conventional Access Charts, so Chapter 18 builds on Chapter 12 by showing you how to add bound PivotTables and Pivot Charts whose data is supplied by the form's data source.

PART V: "UPGRADING TO SQL SERVER DATABASES"

Jet isn't dead, but version 4.0 is Microsoft's last iteration of this venerable desktop database. From Access 2003 on, SQL Server is the preferred desktop or back-end data source for Access applications in Access Data Project (.adp) format. If you're new to client/server RDBMSs, Access 2003 is the ideal learning tool for upgrading your database design and management skills to the requirements of today's job market.

- Chapter 19, "Linking Access Front-Ends to Jet and Client/Server Tables," explains how to use the Upsizing Wizard to migrate from single-file or split (front-end/back-end) Jet applications to SQL Server back-end databases. Retaining the front-end queries and application objects in a Jet (.mdb) file, and using the SQL Server ODBC driver to connect to the server database, minimizes application changes required to take advantage of client/server technology. This chapter also explains how to secure Jet databases with workgroup information (.mdw) files.
- Chapter 20, "Exploring Access Data Projects and SQL Server 2000," introduces you to Access Data Projects. The chapter shows you how to use Access 2003's built-in project designer to create and modify SQL Server tables, views, functions, and stored procedures. Backing up, restoring, copying, and moving SQL Server databases is covered in detail. You also learn how to link other databases, including Jet .mdb files, with OLE DB data providers and how to secure ADP front ends as .ade files.
- Chapter 21, "Moving from Jet Queries to Transact-SQL," provides a formal introduction to ANSI-92 SQL and explains how the Jet and Transact-SQL dialects differ. Special emphasis is given to queries that you can't create in the graphical project designer—such as `UNION` queries and subqueries—and enabling transactions in stored procedures that update two or more tables.

- Chapter 22, "Upsizing Jet Applications to Access Data Projects," explains how to use the Upsizing Wizard to convert existing Jet applications directly to Access data project front ends and SQL Server tables, views, functions, and stored procedures. The Wizard can't upsize Jet crosstab queries, so the chapter explains how to write T-SQL make-table statements to emulate crosstab queries.

Part VI: "Publishing Data to Intranets and the Internet"

The chapters in Part VI explain how to take advantage of Access's new XML features and the upgraded Data Access Pages technology of Access 2002.

- Chapter 23, "Exporting and Importing Data with XML," explains the role of XML in database applications, how Access 2003's ReportML XML schema describes Access objects as an XML data document. The chapter shows you how to take advantage of the Report2HTML4.xsl XML transform to generate HTML pages from tables and queries with the Save As XML option. You learn how to modify Access's standard XSLT files to format the resulting tables and add images to the tables. Exporting conventional Access reports as fully formatted static and live Web reports also receives detailed coverage.
- Chapter 24, "Designing and Deploying Data Access Pages," shows you how to design dynamic Web pages to display and update data on your organization's intranet. The chapter guides your use of the Page Wizard and AutoPage option to create simple pages to display and edit live data. The chapter also covers adding PivotTables and PivotCharts to pages, and deploying pages from file shares or Internet Information Server 5+ virtual directories.
- Chapter 25, "Converting Access Objects to Data Access Pages," explains the benefits and limitations of using the Access 2003's Save As Data Access Page feature to export tables, queries, and reports as preformatted pages. The chapter includes VBScript examples for creating navigation pages to open and pass parameters as cookie crumbs to pages saved from parameter queries and reports based on parameter queries.
- Chapter 26, "Integrating with InfoPath and SharePoint Services," introduces you to these new members of Office System 2003 and their data-related features. You get acquainted with Office InfoPath 2003 form templates by modifying a sample form and then progress to creating a single-view query/data entry form that connects to a Jet or SQL Server table. You learn to export Jet or SQL Server tables to Windows SharePoint Services lists, and how to link the lists to Jet tables (and vice versa). Finally, the chapter shows you how to publish data-bound InfoPath templates to SharePoint forms libraries.

Part VII: "Programming and Converting Access Applications"

The chapters in Part VII assume that you have no programming experience in any language. These chapters explain the principles of writing programming code in VBA. They also show you how to apply these principles to automate Access applications and work directly with ADO `Recordset` objects. XML Web services are destined to play a major role in sharing data between Office and other applications running on a variety of platforms. Thus, Part VII includes an advanced chapter that shows you how to integrate Web services in your Access applications. Part VII also supplies tips for converting Access 97 applications to Access 2003.

- Chapter 27, "Learning Visual Basic for Applications," introduces you to the VBA language with emphasis on using VBA to automate your Access front ends. The chapter describes how to write VBA code to create user-defined functions stored in modules and to write simple procedures that you activate directly from events.
- Chapter 28, "Handling Events with VBA 6.0," describes how to use VBA event-handling subprocedures in class modules to replace the macros used by earlier versions of Access. This chapter explains the events triggered by Access form, report, and control objects, and tells you how to use methods of the `DoCmd` object to respond to events, such as clicking a command button.
- Chapter 29, "Programming Combo and List Boxes," shows you how to take maximum advantage of Access 2003's unique combo and list boxes in decision-support applications. This chapter explains the VBA coding techniques for loading combo box lists and populating text and list boxes based on your combo box selections.
- Chapter 30, "Understanding Universal Data Access, OLE DB, and ADO," explains Microsoft's approach to Jet and SQL Server data connectivity in Office applications, describes how to migrate from Data Access Objects (DAO) to ActiveX Data Objects (DAO), and tells why this direction is important for your new Access projects.
- Chapter 31, "Consuming and Providing XML Web Services," shows you how to write the VBA code to create an XML Web service consumer (client) and how to use Microsoft's SQLXML 3.0 add-on to SQL Server 2000 to publish a Web service from a stored procedure. You learn how to use the Office Web Services Toolkit and its Web Service Reference tool to generate most of the VBA code for the client, which makes connecting to basic Web services practical for non-developers.
- Chapter 32, "Upgrading Access 97 and 2000/2002 Applications to Access 2003," tells you what changes you need to make when you convert your current 32-bit Access database applications and data access pages to Access 2003.

GLOSSARY

The glossary presents a descriptive list of the terms, abbreviations, and acronyms used in this book that you might not be familiar with and that can't be found in commonly used dictionaries.

THE ACCOMPANYING CD-ROM

The CD-ROM that accompanies this book includes Access database files containing tables, forms, reports, HTML pages, VBA and VBScript code, and special files to complement

design examples, and it shows you the expected result. An icon identifies sections that point to chapter files included on the accompanying CD-ROM.

A very large (20MB) database, Oakmont.mdb, is included for optional use with some of the examples in this book. Oakmont University is a fictitious institution in Texas with 30,000 students and 2,300 employees. Databases with a large number of records in their tables are useful when designing applications to optimize performance, so the CD-ROM also includes a version of the Northwind.mdb database, NwindXL19.mdb, that has 21,096 records in the Orders table and 193,280 Order Details records.

The CD-ROM also includes the following Visual Basic 6.0 utility programs:

- *Crosstab Upsizer* (Crosstab.exe) detects conventional and parameterized crosstab queries in Jet .mdb files and automatically generates SQL Server T-SQL stored procedures to emulate the output of the original crosstab query.
- *User Login and Permissions Manager for MSDE 2000* (UserMan.exe) is a tool for establishing SQL Server logins and database user accounts, and assigning user roles for databases or applying specific user permissions to any database object. UserMan fills the MSDE management gap as a result of Microsoft Office Access 2000's SQL Server security management features from Access 2002 and later.

Installing the sample files with the Setup.exe application on the accompanying CD-ROM requires about 150MB of free disk space.

How This Book Is Designed

The following special features are included in this book to assist readers.

If you've never used a database management application, you're provided with quick-start examples to gain confidence and experience while using Access with the Northwind Traders sample database. Like Access, this book uses the *tabula rasa* approach: Each major topic begins with the assumption that you have no prior experience with the subject. Therefore, when a button from the toolbar or control object Toolbox is used, its icon is displayed in the margin.

TIP

> Tips describe shortcuts and alternative approaches to gaining an objective. These tips are based on the experience that the author gained during more than seven years of testing successive alpha and beta versions of Access and Microsoft Office Developer (MOD).

NOTE

> Notes offer advice to help you use Access, describe differences between various versions of Access, and explain the few remaining anomalies that you find in Access 2003.

Jet SQL

The book provides numerous examples of Jet SQL statements for queries and Transact-SQL statements for views, functions, and stored procedures.

XML

Part VI of this book includes sample XML, XSL, and XML Schema documents (XSD) and examples of altering XSL Transforms (XSLT) to modify the presentation of HTML documents.

CAUTION

Cautions are provided when an action can lead to an unexpected or unpredictable result, including loss of data; the text provides an explanation of how you can avoid such a result.

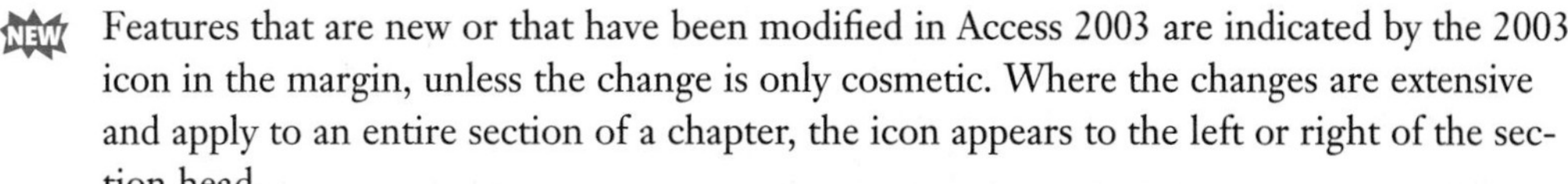

Features that are new or that have been modified in Access 2003 are indicated by the 2003 icon in the margin, unless the change is only cosmetic. Where the changes are extensive and apply to an entire section of a chapter, the icon appears to the left or right of the section head.

Many Access users will upgrade from Access 2000 or Access 97, so the 2002 icon indicates changes that occurred in the upgrade from Access 2000 to 2002.

References to resources available on the Internet—such as World Wide Web Consortium (W3C) Recommendations—are identified by the Web icon.

Cross-references to specific sections in other chapters follow the material that they pertain to, as in the following sample reference:

→ See *"A Section in Another Chapter,"* **p. xxx**.

Most chapters include a "Troubleshooting" section at the end of the tutorial and reference contents. The elements of this section help you solve specific problems—common and uncommon—that you might run into when creating applications that use specific Access features or techniques.

At the end of each chapter is an "In the Real World" section that discusses the relevance of the chapter's content to the realm of production databases, the Internet, and other current computer-related topics that affect Access users and developers. The opinion-editorial (op-ed) style of many of the "In the Real World" sections reflects the author's view of the benefits—or drawbacks—of new Access features and related Microsoft technologies, based on experience with production Access applications installed by several Fortune 500 corporations.

Typographic Conventions Used in This Book

This book uses various typesetting styles to distinguish between explanatory and instructional text, text that you enter in dialogs (set in **bold**), and text that you enter in code-editing windows (set in `monospace` type).

Key Combinations, Menu Choices, and File Names

Key combinations that you use to perform Windows operations are indicated by joining the keys with a plus sign: Alt+F4, for example. In the rare cases when you must press and release a key, and then press another key, the keys are separated by a comma without an intervening space: Alt,F4. Shortcut key combinations appear as Ctrl+*Key*.

Sequences of individual menu items are separated by a comma: Edit, Cut.

File and folder names are initial-letter-capitalized in the text and headings of this book to conform with 32-bit Windows file-naming conventions and the appearance of file names in Windows Explorer.

SQL Statements and Keywords in Other Languages

SQL statements and code examples are set in a special `monospace` font. Keywords of SQL statements, such as `SELECT`, are set in all uppercase. Ellipses (...) indicate intervening programming code that isn't shown in the text or examples.

Square brackets in `monospace` type (`[]`) that appear within Jet SQL statements don't indicate optional items, as they do in syntax descriptions. In this case, the square brackets are used instead of quotation marks to frame a literal string or to allow use of a table and field names, such as `[Order Details]`, that include embedded spaces or special punctuation, or field names that are identical to reserved words in VBA.

Typographic Conventions Used for VBA

This book uses a special set of typographic conventions for references to Visual Basic for Applications keywords in the presentation of VBA examples:

- `Monospace` type is used for all examples of VBA code, as in the following statement:

  ```
  Dim NewArray ( ) As Long
  ReDim NewArray (9, 9, 9)
  ```

- `Monospace` type also is used when referring to names of properties of Access database objects, such as *`FormName`*`.Width`. The captions for text boxes and dropdown lists in which you enter values of properties, such as Source Connect String, are set in this book's regular textual font.

- **`Bold monospace`** type is used for all VBA reserved words and type-declaration symbols, as shown in the preceding example. Standard function names in VBA also are set in **`bold monospace`** type so that reserved words, standard function names, and reserved symbols stand out from variable and function names and values that you assign to variables.

- `Italic monospace` type indicates a replaceable item, as in

  Dim *DataItem* **As String**

- ***Bold italic monospace*** type indicates a replaceable reserved word, such as a data type, as in

  Dim *DataItem* **As** ***DataType***

  DataItem is replaced by a keyword corresponding to the desired VBA data type, such as **String** or **Variant**.

- An ellipsis (…) substitutes for code not shown in syntax and code examples, as in

  If…Then…Else…End If

- Braces ({}) enclosing two or more identifiers separated by the pipe symbol (¦) indicate that you must choose one of these identifiers, as in

  Do {While¦Until}…Loop

  In this case, you must use the **While** or **Until** reserved word in your statement, but not the braces or the pipe character.

- Three-letter prefixes to variable names indicate the VBA data type of the variable, such as `bln` for **Boolean**, `str` for **String**, and `lng` for **Long** (integer).

- Square brackets ([]) enclosing an identifier indicate that the identifier is optional, as in

  Set tbl*Name* = db*Name*.OpenTable(str*TableName*[, blnExclusive])

  Here, the `blnExclusive` flag, if set to **True**, opens the table specified by str*TableName* for exclusive use. `blnExclusive` is an optional argument. Don't include the brackets in any code that you type.

Typographic Conventions Used for VBScript

The few Visual Basic Scripting Edition (VBScript) examples of this book use lowercase `monospace` type for reserved words, a practice that originated in ECMAScript (JavaScript or Microsoft JScript). Variables are in mixed case with a data type prefix, despite the lack of VBScript support for data types other than **Variant**. Object, property, and method names included in the World Wide Web Consortium (W3C) Document Object Model (DOM) standard also are in lower case. Most non-DOM objects, such as `MSODSC.RecordsetDefs()`, use mixed case.

System Requirements for Access 2003

Access 2003 is a very resource-intensive application, as are all other Office 2003 members, including InfoPath. You'll find execution of Access applications on Pentium PCs slower than 166MHz to be impaired, at best. A 300+ MHz Pentium II delivers acceptable performance, but a 667+ MHz Pentium III machine is a more realistic minimum.

Microsoft's somewhat optimistic minimum RAM recommendations for Office System 2003 running under Windows XP (SP1) or Windows 2000 Professional (SP3) is 64MB plus 8MB for each Office component running simultaneously. 128MB plus 16MB per component is a more realistic requirement.

The preceding recommendations don't take into account the RAM required to run SQL Server 2000. Double the realistic RAM recommendations to achieve acceptable performance with MSDE running. All the examples of this book were created and tested under Windows XP Professional (SP-1) or Windows Server running on a 667MHz Intel P-III computer with 384MB RAM.

Standard installation of Office 2003—without SQL Server 2000 or SQL Server Books Online—requires 245MB of free disk space, of which 115MB must be on the system volume. Add another 100MB for SQL Server, and 50MB each for InfoPath and Windows SharePoint Services. From a practical standpoint, you need 500MB or more of free disk space to use Office 2003 effectively. Add another 200MB for the sample files on the accompanying CD-ROM.

Other Sources of Information for Access

Relational database design and SQL, discussed in Chapters 4 and 21, are the subject of myriad guides and texts covering one or both of these topics. Articles in database-related periodicals in print form or on the Internet provide up-to-date assistance in using Access 2003. The following sections provide a bibliography of database-related books and periodicals, as well as a brief description of Web sites and newsgroups of interest to Access users.

Books

The following books complement the content of this book by providing detailed coverage of database design techniques, Structured Query Language, VBA database programming, SQL Server 2000, XML, and HTML:

- *Database Design for Mere Mortals, Second Edition*, by Michael J. Hernandez (Addison-Wesley, ISBN 0-201-75284-0), is a comprehensive guide to sound relational database design techniques for developing productive desktop and client/server databases. The book is platform-agnostic, but the methods that you learn are especially effective for Jet and SQL Server database design.
- *Understanding the New SQL: A Complete Guide*, by Jim Melton and Alan R. Simpson (Morgan Kaufmann Publishers, ISBN 1-55860-245-3), describes the history and implementation of the American National Standards Institute's X3.135.1-1992 standard for the latest official version of Structured Query Language, SQL-92, on which Jet SQL is based. Melton was the editor of the ANSI SQL-92 standard, which consists of more than 500 pages of fine print.
- *SQL Queries for Mere Mortals*, by Michael J. Hernandez and John L. Viescas (Addison-Wesley, ISBN 0-201-43336-2), is your best source for learning to write effective `SELECT` queries in any SQL dialect. The book includes detailed coverage of `JOIN`, `UNION`, `GROUP BY`, `HAVING` and subquery syntax.

- *Database Developer's Guide with Visual Basic 6*, by Roger Jennings (SAMS Publishing, ISBN 0-672-31063-5), covers advanced VBA programming with ADO, Remote Data Service (RDS), hierarchical Recordsets, the PivotTable service, DataCubes, and other developer topics.
- *XML By Example, Second Edition*, by Benoit Marchal (Que, ISBN 0-7897-2504-5), describes the technologies and standards that make up XML. It includes chapters that cover modeling with XML Schema, managing namespaces, using XSL transformations, and applying style with XSL Formatting Objects and Cascading Style Sheets.
- *Special Edition Using HTML 4*, by Molly E. Holzschlag (Que, ISBN 0-7897-2267-4), is an indispensable tutorial and reference for learning the basics of HTML and gaining a full understanding of Dynamic HTML (DHTML) and Cascading Style Sheets (CSS).

Periodicals

The following magazine and newsletter cover Access topics:

- *Access-VB-SQL Advisor Magazine*, published by Advisor Communications International, Inc., is a bimonthly magazine intended to serve Access users and developers. You can supplement your subscription with an accompanying disk that includes sample databases, utilities, and other software tools for Access (`http://advisormedia.com/www/AccessVBSQLAdvisor`).
- *Smart Access* is a monthly newsletter of Pinnacle Publishing, Inc., which publishes several other database-related newsletters. *Smart Access* is directed primarily to developers and Access power users. This newsletter tends toward advanced topics, such as creating libraries and using the Windows API with VBA. A disk is included with each issue (`http://www.smartaccessnewsletter.com/`).

Internet

Microsoft's Web site now is the primary source of new and updated information for Access users and developers. Following are the primary Web sites and newsgroups for Access 2000 users and developers:

- Microsoft's Access page, `http://www.microsoft.com/office/access/`, is the jumping-off point for Access users. It includes links to all related Access 2003 and earlier pages on the Microsoft Web site.
- Microsoft's Access Developer page, `http://msdn.microsoft.com/office/access/`, provides links to information of particular interest to the Access developer community.
- Microsoft's online support home page, `http://support.microsoft.com/support/`, provides links to Microsoft Knowledge Base pages for all its products. For other support options, go to `http://www.microsoft.com/support/`.
- Woody's Office Watch has an Access page at `http://www.woodyswatch.com/access/`. Woody Leonhard and Peter Deegan offer a free Woody's Access Watch (WAW) newsletter.

- Microsoft's `msnews.microsoft.com` news server offers various Access-related newsgroups at `microsoft.public.access.`*`subject`*. When this book was written, there were more than 20 Access subject areas.
- The Usenet `comp.databases.ms-access` newsgroup is an active community of Access users and developers.

PART I

Getting Acquainted with Access 2003

CHAPTER 1

ACCESS 2003 FOR ACCESS 97 AND 2000/2002 USERS: WHAT'S NEW

In this chapter

1

WELCOME TO MICROSOFT OFFICE ACCESS 2003

Access 2003, the eighth iteration of Microsoft's desktop database management system, is a member of the newly christened Microsoft Office System 2003 and sports a new name—*Microsoft Office Access 2003*. Microsoft Office System 2003 includes the core Office 2003 applications—Word, Excel, Access, Outlook, and PowerPoint. The 2003 versions of standalone products, such as FrontPage, Publisher, Visio, and Project, plus the new InfoPath and OneNote applications, also gain Office System membership. On the server side, Windows SharePoint Services—formerly SharePoint Team Services—and SharePoint Portal Server fall under the Office System 2003 umbrella.

The goal of the new Office System brand is to reposition Microsoft's dominant productivity application suite as software to facilitate collaboration between information workers. For example, Access 2003 can export tables or queries and link tables to or from SharePoint lists. InfoPath form templates can connect to Jet or Microsoft SQL Server 2000 Desktop Engine (MSDE) databases directly. Another Microsoft Office System goal appears to be encouraging operating system upgrades—Office System 2003 will install only under Windows 2000 Professional or Server with Service Pack 3 (SP3), Windows XP Home or Professional, or any Windows Server 2003 version. Windows SharePoint Services run under Windows Server 2003 only. Windows NT, 98, 98SE, and Me users can't use any members of Office System 2003.

Whether Microsoft achieves its lofty goals for Office System 2003 upgrades remains to be seen. The Gartner Group, a well-respected information technology research organization, conducted an informal survey during its October 2002 Symposium/ITxpo. Gartner reported that 31 percent of the companies represented used Office 97, 56 percent ran Office 2000 and only 6 percent had installed Office XP. If Gartner's data is representative of the entire Office installed base, close to 90 percent of Access 2003 users will upgrade from Office 97 or 2000. Thus, this chapter begins with a brief description of new Access 2003 features for Access 2002 users and then covers important changes that affect Access 2000 and 97 users who upgrade to Access 2003.

TIP

> If you haven't used an earlier Access version, you might want to skip to the "SQL Server 2000 Desktop Engine Setup" section near the end of this chapter. The succeeding chapters of this book cover in detail all the material presented in this chapter, with the exception of initial SQL Server 2000 setup.

WHAT'S NEW IN ACCESS 2003

The following sections describe Access 2003 features that are new to Access 2002 users, which are few compared to prior version changes. For the first time in Access's history, there's no new database version; like Access 2002, 2003 uses the 2000 file format by default. Saving databases and projects in Access 2002 format is optional.

Macro Security and Jet "Sandbox" Mode

The first change you notice when opening a new or existing Access database or data project is a macro security warning dialog that appears if the database or project contains Access macros or Visual Basic for Applications (VBA) code (see Figure 1.1). The warning is similar to that of other Office members that use VBA as their programming language. Click Yes to enable running an Access application with unsigned code.

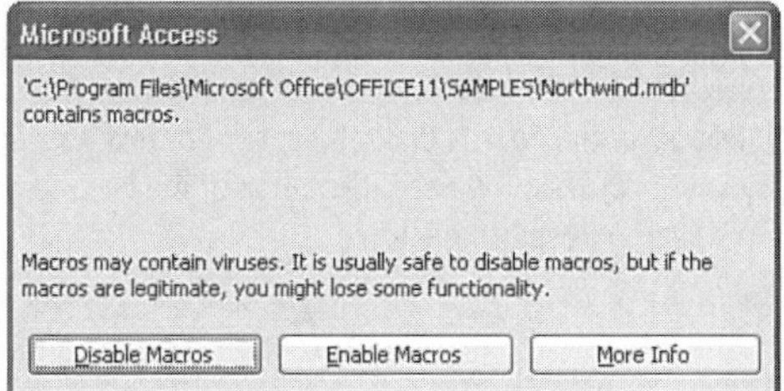

Figure 1.1 Access 2003 has adopted the standard macro security warning of other VBA-enabled Office members.

By default, Access 2003 installs with the Medium security option selected, which lets you choose whether to load a file that contains VBA code and hasn't been digitally signed by a trusted source. The sample Northwind.mdb database and NorthwindCS.adp project aren't digitally signed by Microsoft. To change the security level, choose Tools, Macro, Security to open the Security dialog and select the Low option (see Figure 1.2).

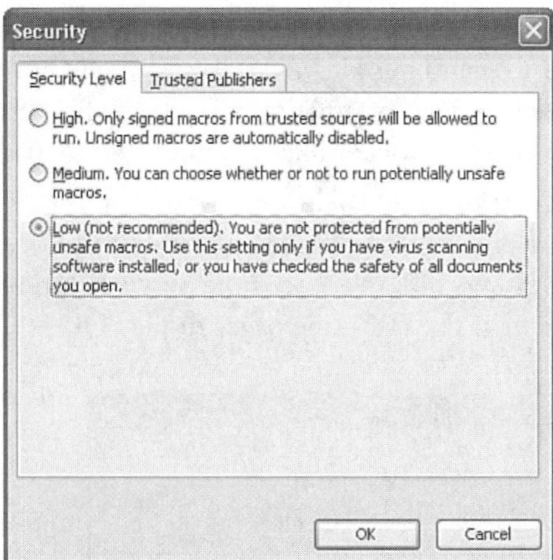

Figure 1.2 Select the Low security option if you want to bypass the macro warning dialog. Other Office applications have implemented macro security in several earlier versions.

TIP

> If the Security choice isn't visible in the Tools, Macro menu, right-click any toolbar, choose Customize, click the Toolbars tab, select the Menu Bar item, and click the Reset button.

1

If you select High, unsigned VBA code won't load and most Access applications will display errors on opening or during their use. Thus, High security isn't a practical option for most users. Medium and High security run Jet in a more secure "sandbox" mode. The term *sandbox* originated with Java applets and means that code in an application, including user-defined functions in queries, can't execute instructions that operate on system-level objects—such as the file system.

NOTE

For more information on sandbox mode in Windows 2002, go to `http://www.microsoft.com`, click the Support link, choose Knowledge Base from the drop-down menu, type **Q294698** in the Search dialog's Search For text box, and click Go. Alternatively, type **sandbox** in the Search text box of the Help task pane, as described in the next section's Search Results page topic.

NEW TASK PANES AND HELP SYSTEM

Like the other Office 2003 members, Access 2003 makes more extensive use of the task pane than the 2002 version. The new task pane relies on an optional Internet connection to Microsoft's Office Online Web site for much of its content, including updated online help files.

Access 2002 had only New File, Clipboard, and Search pages. Access 2003 offers the following task pages:

- **Getting Started**—A welcome page with links to Microsoft's Office Online site, a Search text box, your most recently used (MRU) Access .mdb and .adp files, and a link to the New File page. Clicking the Automatically Update This List from the Web link enables Microsoft to add task pane hyperlinks to Office Online pages.
- **Help**—Replaces Access 2002's HTML help window with a Search text box, a Table of Contents link to the complete Access help contents, links to Office Online help topics, and an Online Content Settings link that opens the Service Options dialog (see Figure 1.3). Check boxes determine if the task pane pages display Office Online content.

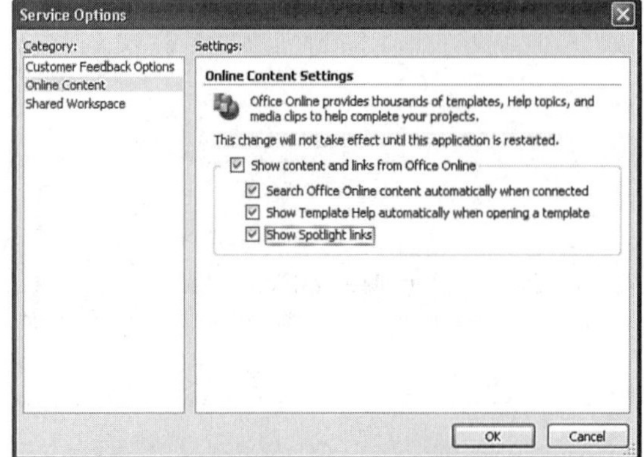

Figure 1.3
The Service Options dialog lets you enable or disable online help and other hyperlinks to Microsoft's Office Online site. You must close and reopen Access for changes to become effective.

➔ To learn more about Access 2003's new online help system, **see** "Using Access Help," **p. 108**.

- **Search Results**—Displays a list of topics returned from an online or offline help search operation. Typing **sandbox** in the Help page's Search text box returns a single topic from the Office Online site (see Figure 1.4, left). Clicking the link displays the help topic (see Figure 1.5, right).

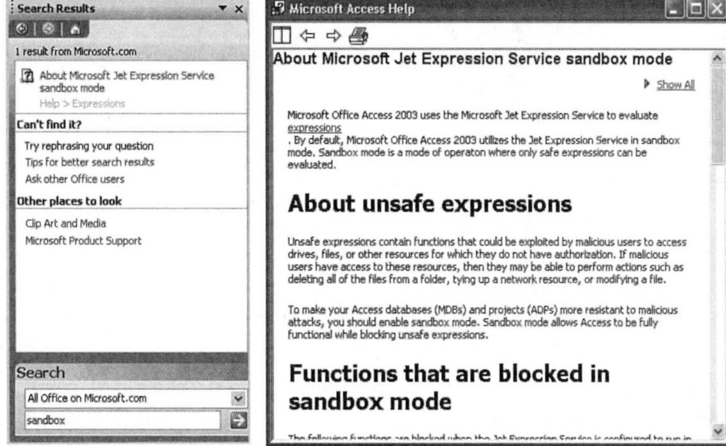

Figure 1.4
The Search Results page displays links to topics matching a help search term (left). Clicking a link opens the help topic window (right).

- **File Search**—Opens the Basic File page that emulates Windows Search Results dialog. Clicking the Advanced File Search lets you specify additional criteria for the search operation.
- **Clipboard**—Displays a list of up to 24 active Office Clipboard items that you can paste to the active Access object.
- **New File**—Displays the standard list of options for creating a new Jet-based application, data access page, or Access data project, or opening an existing file. You can search for Access templates online or click the On My Computer link to open the Templates dialog. If you've used templates to create an application, the page includes a Recently Used Templates list (see Figure 1.5, left).
- **Object Dependencies**—Displays a list of Access objects that have a dependency on the selected item (see Figure 1.5, right). To select the object, right-click an item in the Database window and choose Object Dependencies. Selecting the Objects That I Depend On link reverses the relationships.

➔ For more information on the Object Dependencies feature, **see** "Enabling and Viewing Object Dependencies," **p. 200**.

- **Template Help**—Provides a link to an online template's help topic. The standard set of templates that come with Access 2003 don't include help files.

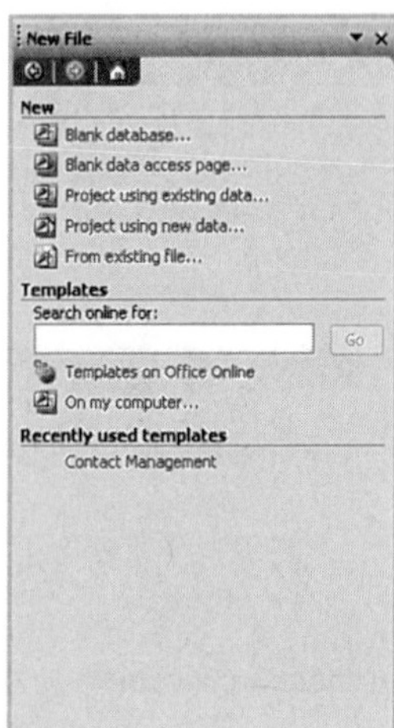

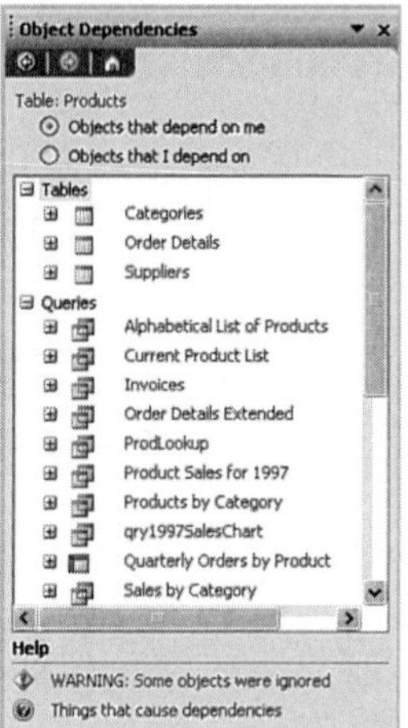

Figure 1.5 The New File page (left) is similar to that of Access 2002, except for the newly added Most Recently Used Template sections. The Object Dependencies page (right) displays a list of Access objects that depend on an object you select in the database window.

Microsoft's move from conventional Windows online help files, such as those provided with Access 97, to an Office-centric HTML-based help system is a controversial topic for long-time Access users. The capability to add and update help topics dynamically at the Office Online site is a definite benefit. The consensus of members of Access newsgroups, however, is that the online help features of Access 2000 and later don't come close to matching the utility of Access 97's help system.

BUILT-IN AND CUSTOM SMART TAGS

Smart tags are pop-up buttons with context menus that execute a predefined set of actions. Access 2003 has the following built-in smart tags:

- **Auto Correct Options**—A button that lets you undo an automatic spelling correction or turn spell-checking off.
- **Error Checking Options**—A button that appears when Access detects an error, such as specifying an input mask that doesn't conform to the size property value of a text field. The action list depends on the nature of the error.
- **Property Options**—A button that appears when you change a property value of a table field and lets you propagate the change to all dependent objects.

Access 2003 lets you attach smart tags to fields of a table or query and controls of a form, report, or data access page. Clicking the build button of the new Smart Tag property of a smart tag-enabled field or control opens a Smart Tags dialog with a list of available Microsoft smart tags.

Following are the three Microsoft smart tags included with Access 2003:

- **Person Name**—Lets you connect to Outlook 2003 and send an email message to a contact, schedule a meeting with a contact, edit the contact information, or add the name to the contact list.

- **Date**—Uses Outlook 2003 to schedule a meeting on or display your calendar for the specified date.
- **Financial Symbol**—Connects to MSN MoneyCentral and lets you obtain a stock quote, report, or recent news about the company.

Microsoft provides a list of a few third-party smart tags that you can add to Access objects. To open the list, click the Smart Tag dialog's More Smart Tags button.

→ To learn more about smart tags in Access 2003, **see** "Activating the Access Property Options Smart Tag," **p. 202** and "Adding an Internet-Based Smart Tag to a Field," **p. 203**.

Office Web Components for Data Access Pages, PivotTables, and PivotCharts

Access 2003 installs Office Web Components versions 10.0 (OWC10) and 11.0 (OWC11). OWC10 provides backward compatibility with Access 2002 data access pages (DAP) and PivotTable and PivotChart views of tables, queries, and forms. OWC10 works with all Windows versions except Windows 95 (and, of course, Windows 3.x). The lack of Access 2000's OWC version 9.0 prevents upgrading DAP you've created in Access 2000.

TIP

If you need to upgrade DAP that you created with Access 2000 to Access 2003, install OWC version 9.0 from the Office 2000 or Office XP CD-ROM. All OWC versions install side by side under Windows XP/2000+.

All new and upgraded DAP use OWC11, which doesn't support viewing DAP with Internet Explorer running under Windows NT, 98, 98SE, or Me. The OWC11 runtime version won't install to these operating systems from the Office 2003 CD-ROM or from the Microsoft download site.

CAUTION

Don't upgrade Access 2000 or 2002 DAP if you must continue to support DAP users whose computers run Windows NT, 98, or Me.

Improvements to XML Data Export and Import Operations

Access 2002 introduced the ability to export data from tables or queries to element-centric XML documents (.xml files) and corresponding schemas in XML Schema 1.0 format (.xsd files). Access 2002 was limited to exporting *flat* XML documents; a flat document doesn't contain nested elements from multiple tables.

Access 2003 lets you export all or selected records of a table and include records from related tables as nested (child) elements. You also can include lookup tables in the document; doing this increases the size of the .xml file dramatically.

1

Another new XML-related feature is the capability to apply an XSLT (Extensible Stylesheet Language Transformations) document (.xsl file) to XML documents you import as new Access tables or append to existing tables. Writing XSLT documents is beyond the scope of this book.

→ For more information Access's XML import/export capabilities, **see** "Exporting Tables and Queries to XML and HTML," **p. 954**.

SUPPORT FOR XML WEB SERVICES

Access power users and developers expected Office 2003 to include built-in support for consuming XML Web services. (The term *consuming* means the ability to connect to and receive data from a Web service; the XML prefix is optional.) Microsoft promotes XML Web services as the *lingua franca* for interoperable data exchange between components of distributed computer systems. Microsoft and IBM have been the primary contributors to industry standards for Web services, and both firms have made large-scale investments in the technology.

Built-in Web service support failed to materialize in the release version of Office 2003, so you must install the current version of the Microsoft Office Web Services Toolkit to avoid writing many lines of VBA code to consume a Web service.

NOTE

The Office XP Web Services Toolkit 2.0 was the current version when this book was written. You can expect future Office 2003 upgrades to the Toolkit. Download and install the current version of the Toolkit from a link on the Microsoft Developer Network's main Microsoft Office page at `http://msdn.microsoft.com/office/`.

Installing the Toolkit and its Web Service Reference Tool adds a Web Service References menu choice to the VBA Editor's Tools menu. The Web Service Reference (WSR) Tool dialog lets you find registered Web services in a public directory (see Figure 1.6). Alternatively, you can type the URL for the known location of a Web service on your intranet or the Internet. When you click the Add button, WSR generates about 95 percent of the code required by your Access application to consume the service.

Figure 1.7 shows a simple form that connects to an address-correction XML Web service, which returns the address in US Postal Service standard format with ZIP and ZIP+4 codes.

NOTE

WSR 2.0 is limited to basic Web services that don't implement forthcoming industry standards—such as WS-Security, WS-Addressing, WS-Routing, and WS-*Whatever*—that have mandatory SOAP headers. Fortunately, the free public Web services you can use for address checking, weather data, and the like don't require headers.

→ To learn more about consuming XML Web services in Access 2003, **see** "Creating an Access Web Service Consumer," **p. 1342**.

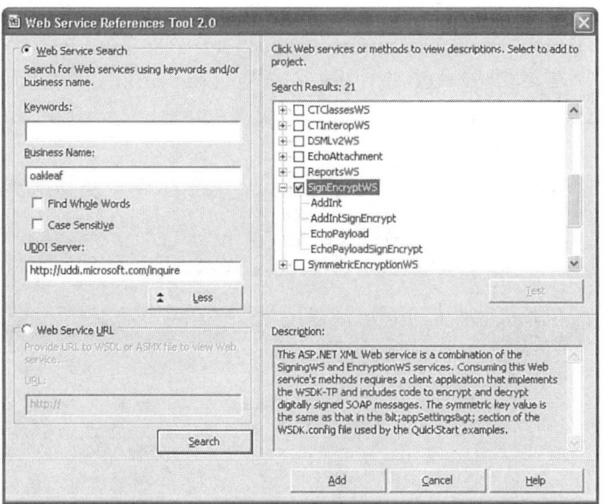

Figure 1.6
This dialog added by the Office XP Web Services Toolkit 2.0 lets you query the public Universal Discovery, Description, and Integration (UDDI) directory for public Web services. Clicking Add generates most of the VBA code to consume the selected Web service.

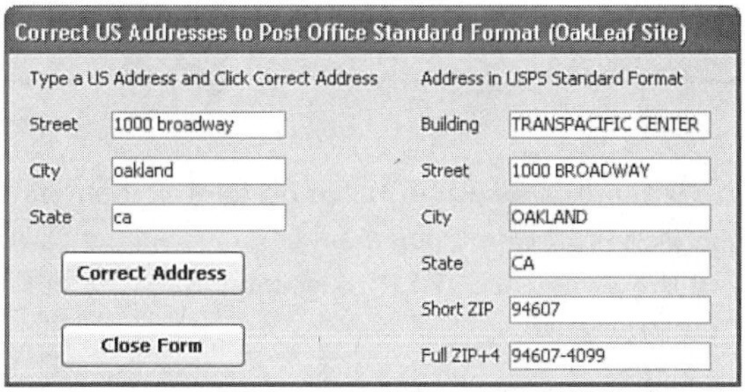

Correct US Addresses to Post Office Standard Format (OakLeaf Site)
Type a US Address and Click Correct Address
Street 1000 broadway
City oakland
State ca
Correct Address
Close Form
Address in USPS Standard Format
Building TRANSPACIFIC CENTER
Street 1000 BROADWAY
City OAKLAND
State CA
Short ZIP 94607
Full ZIP+4 94607-4099

Figure 1.7
This simple Access form consumes the ZipCodeResolver Web service that accepts a US address, city, and state, and returns the complete address in standard US Postal Service format.

DATA DISPLAY AND EDITING WITH INFOPATH

Microsoft Office InfoPath 2003 is a general-purpose, forms-based XML document editor that can connect to Jet or SQL Server data sources. InfoPath forms rely on an XSD schema to define the data structure; InfoPath creates the schema based on the form's design template. An auto-generated XSLT file renders the HTML form. In this respect, working with InfoPath templates and forms resembles the process you use when creating and rendering Access 2003 DAP.

NOTE

> Microsoft includes InfoPath only with the Office 2003 Enterprise edition, but you can purchase InfoPath as a standalone product. Although InfoPath is a member of Office System 2003, it doesn't require any version of Office to be installed on the machine that runs it.

Figure 1.8 shows a simple query and data entry form for the Northwind sample database's Customers table. Selecting a CustomerID value from the drop-down list and clicking Query returns a customer record, which InfoPath stores as an XML document. You edit the customer record—online or offline—and then click Submit to update the table. Clicking New Record lets you add a customer record, and Delete & Submit deletes the current record if it has no dependent records. After you become familiar with designing InfoPath form templates, you can create a similar query and data entry form in less than 30 minutes.

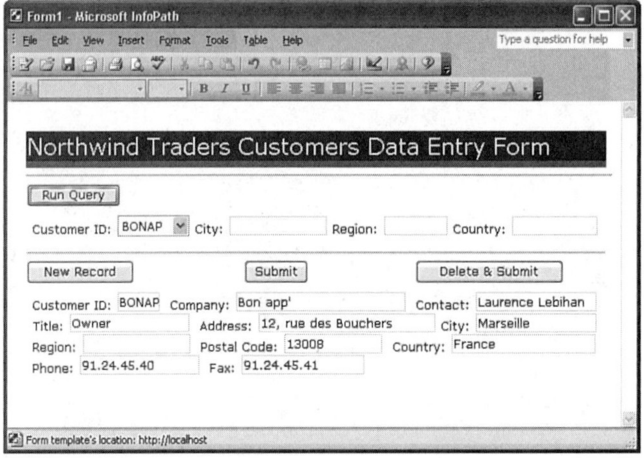

Figure 1.8
InfoPath makes it easy to create templates for Jet or SQL Server query/data entry forms, such as this example. Query, New Record, Submit, and Delete & Submit operations don't require any programming.

Users who open a form without InfoPath installed on their computers see the XML data for the form in Internet Explorer. If you email a form to a recipient without InfoPath, she sees a read-only copy of the form; the XML data accompanies the HTML form as an attachment (see Figure 1.9).

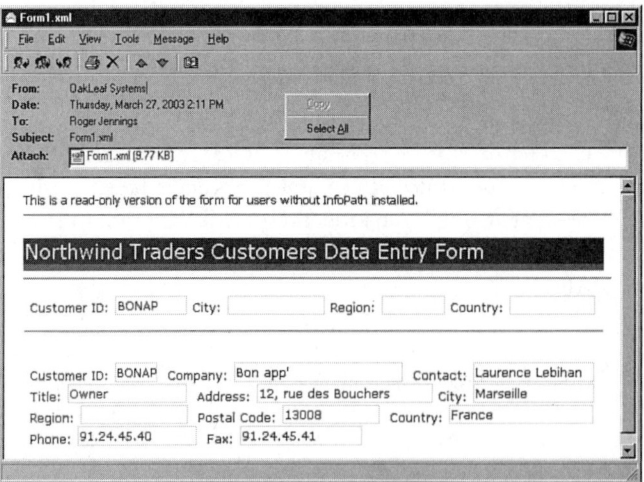

Figure 1.9
Outlook Express running under Windows 98SE displays the email version of Figure 1.8's form. This read-only copy includes the XML data as an attachment but doesn't display the buttons.

InfoPath can submit requests—including parameter values—to basic Web services and display the data returned from the services. The Wizard that generates the Web service connection currently has limitations similar to those of WSR 2.0. In most cases, Web service operations are read-only, but you can connect a single form to another Web service that updates the data.

→ For more detailed information on designing InfoPath templates, **see** "Designing an InfoPath Query and Data Editing Form," **p. 1117**.

COLLABORATION WITH WINDOWS SHAREPOINT SERVICES

Windows SharePoint Services (WSS) is a do-it-yourself portal for facilitating collaboration between members of an organization's teams, workgroups, and small departments. WSS's primary claims to fame are easy installation, management by users, and no per-seat licensing fees. WSS is a no-charge add-on to all versions of Windows Server 2003. WSS didn't make the cut-off date for the April 2003 release of Microsoft's latest server offering, so system administrators must download and install the product from the Windows Update site. Once installed, users of the portal service are expected to manage their WSS sites.

If you have a WSS site on your intranet or a subscription to an Internet-hosted WSS site, you can export Jet or SQL Server tables as shared WSS lists. You can then connect the list to a linked Jet table and synchronize the list's contents between Access applications and WSS. (You can't link SQL Server tables to WSS lists.) Figure 1.10 shows in WSS datasheet view a list imported from Northwind.mdb's suppliers table and linked to a table named Northwind Suppliers in the same database. Changes made to the table in Access or the list in WSS replicate automatically.

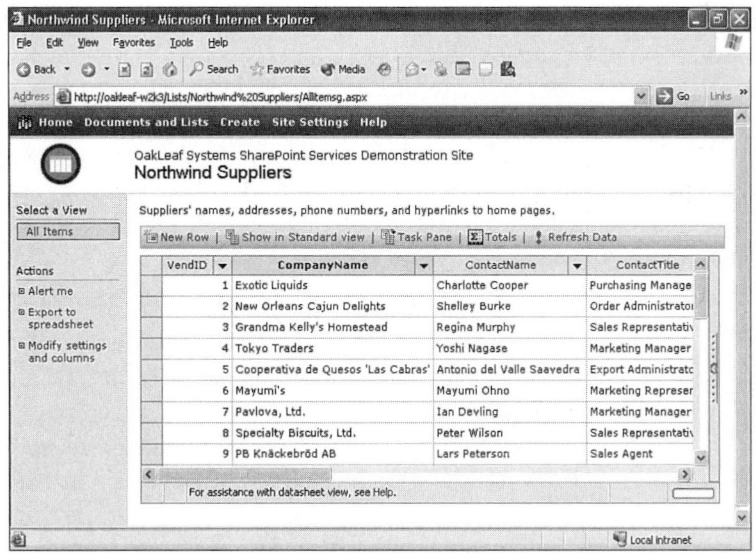

Figure 1.10 The shared Northwind Suppliers list is linked to a Jet table of the same name in Northwind.mdb. Updates propagate from Access to WSS and vice versa.

→ To learn how to create Jet tables linked to SharePoint lists, **see** "Working with Windows SharePoint Services and Access," **p. 1136**.

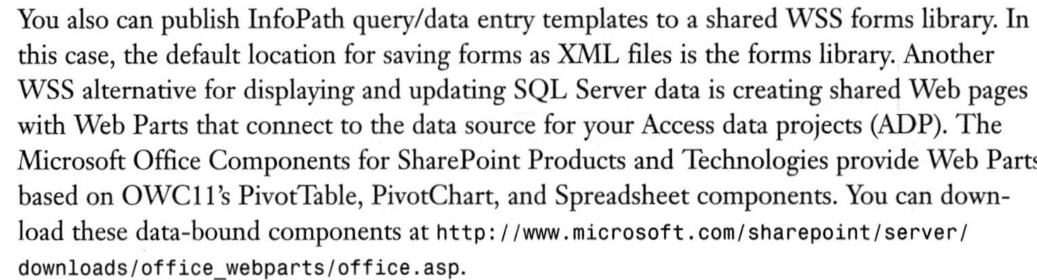

You also can publish InfoPath query/data entry templates to a shared WSS forms library. In this case, the default location for saving forms as XML files is the forms library. Another WSS alternative for displaying and updating SQL Server data is creating shared Web pages with Web Parts that connect to the data source for your Access data projects (ADP). The Microsoft Office Components for SharePoint Products and Technologies provide Web Parts based on OWC11's PivotTable, PivotChart, and Spreadsheet components. You can download these data-bound components at `http://www.microsoft.com/sharepoint/server/downloads/office_webparts/office.asp`.

→ For more information on adding InfoPath templates to shared form libraries, **see** "Publishing Data-Bound InfoPath Templates to WSS," **p. 1142**.

DIRECT DATABASE BACKUP

Prior to Access 2003, backing up Access .mdb and .adp files required closing the open file and performing manual copy and paste operations. Access 2003's Tools, Database Utilities menu has a new choice—Back Up Database. Choosing Back Up Database opens the Save Backup As dialog with the active database name followed by the date as the proposed filename. Clicking Save closes the database, saves the backup file, and reopens the database automatically.

ACCESS 2002 CHANGES TO BASIC ACCESS 2000 FEATURES

Basic features involve the user interface (UI) for viewing and designing Access objects, and the Access (Jet) file system. Most existing Access applications use Jet databases to store traditional Access objects—forms, reports, macros, and modules—and data, and probably will continue to use Jet, despite Microsoft's promotion of the SQL Server 2000 Desktop Engine (MSDE) as the preferred back end for Access applications. Access data projects and data access pages, introduced in Access 2000 with MSDE 1.0, have their own storage systems and don't use Jet .mdb files for object storage. SQL Server is the data source for ADP; DAP can connect to SQL Server or Jet data sources.

→ To learn more about ADP and DAP, **see** "Access Data Projects and SQL Server 2000," **p. 34** and "Data Access Pages Revisited," **p. 40**.

NOTE

> This book uses the term *SQL Server* when referring to any edition of SQL Server 2000, including MSDE. The term *MSDE* indicates a reference that's specific to the Desktop Engine. *MSDE 1.0* is an abbreviation for Access 2000's Microsoft Data Engine version of SQL Server 7.0.

ACCESS 2000 AND 97 FILE COMPATIBILITY

Traditionally, each new version of Access has required an update to the Jet file system; Access 2002 and 2003 are exceptions. Access 2003 and 2002 default to the Access 2000 file format for backward compatibility. You specify Access 2000 or 2002 as the default format for new databases and ADP in the Advanced Page of the Options dialog.

Like Access 2000 and 2002, you can save data-only Access 2003 .mdb files in Access 97 format; saving Access 200x front-end .mdbs containing forms, reports, macros, and modules in Access 97 format isn't practical because Access 2000 and 2002 made extensive changes to these objects and VBA code. Upgrading from Access 2002 to 2003 makes no significant changes to any Access object except DAP.

NOTE

If you're migrating from Access 97 to Access 2003, you must convert your .mdb files to Access 2000 format to open them in Design view. There is no benefit to upgrading directly to Access 2002 format.

Converted front-end .mdbs continue to connect to back-end (data-only) Access 97 .mdbs. Chapter 32, "Upgrading Access 97 and 2000/2002 Applications to Access 2003," covers the Access 97 upgrade process in detail.

The Access 2002 Jet and ADP file formats are intended primarily to improve the performance of very large Access projects. Access 2002 format also supports a few new properties, events, and methods for traditional Access objects and ADP. Access 2000 ignores any Access 2002 format-specific settings you make in the UI. If your VBA code refers to Access 2002-only elements, however, the application won't run under Access 2000 because of differences in the Access type libraries for the two formats. Unless your front-end application is very large or requires Access 2002-only events, methods, properties, or VBA functions, you can continue to use the default Access 2000 format. All examples in this book use Access 2000 format.

➔ For more information on programming elements added by Access 2002 that also applies to Access 2003, **see** "Programmability Enhancements," **p. 43**.

UNDO AND REDO ENHANCEMENTS

DAP; Jet tables and queries; ADP views, functions, and stored procedures; and forms, reports, macros, and modules have a multiple undo and redo feature. Lack of undo capability in DAP Design view was one of the primary complaints about the Access 2000 version of this feature. Changing between most Access views and object types empties the undo stack.

CHOICE OF SUBFORM AND SUBREPORT DESIGN VIEWS

Users of Access 2000 encountered difficulties when editing complex subforms in their parent form's Design view, called *in-situ subform editing*. Access 2002 introduced the option to right-click the subform and choose Subform in New Window from the context menu or choose View, Subform in New Window to edit the subform by the traditional (Access 97 and earlier) method.

ADDED SHORTCUT KEY COMBINATIONS

The four shortcut key combinations added by Access 2002 aren't exciting, but Table 1.1 lists them for the sake of completeness.

TABLE 1.1 SHORTCUT KEYS ADDED IN ACCESS 2002

Key/Combination	View	Action
F4	Design	Opens the *ObjectType* Properties dialog
F7	Form/Report Design	Opens the Choose Builder dialog if the form or report has the focus; opens the code window if the form or report doesn't have the focus
Shift+F7	Form/Report Design	Returns focus to the selected control if the *ControlName* Properties dialog has the focus
Ctrl+> or Ctrl+.	Any	Cycles the view from the current view forward in the view sequence (Design, Form, Datasheet, PivotTable, and PivotChart for forms)
Ctrl+< or Ctrl+,	Any	Cycles the view from the current view backward in the view sequence (PivotChart, PivotTable, Datasheet, Form, and Design for forms)

PIVOTTABLE AND PIVOTCHART VIEWS

Access 2000 introduced the Office Web Components (OWC), which include PivotTable, PivotChart, and Spreadsheet ActiveX controls, for use with Data Access Pages. Access 2002 added PivotTable and PivotChart views of tables, queries, and forms in traditional Access applications, ADP, and DAP. In most cases, PivotTable and PivotChart views use summary or crosstab queries as their data source. Data in conventional relational tables seldom is suited to display in either of these new views. You can specify the default view of a table, query, view, or function to be a PivotTable or PivotChart.

PivotTables let you manipulate a spreadsheet-like view of data by increasing or decreasing the level of detail and filtering the data to reduce the number of rows, columns, or both. You also can rotate (pivot) the view by interchanging rows and columns. The PivotTable's AutoCalc feature lets you generate the equivalent of a Jet crosstab query from detail or summary data and add grand totals to rows and columns. Transact-SQL (T-SQL), SQL Server's query language, doesn't have direct equivalents to the Jet SQL `TRANSFORM` and `PIVOT` statements that generate crosstab queries. You can use PivotTables to emulate Jet crosstab queries in ADP and DAP that use SQL Server as the data source.

→ To learn how to take advantage of PivotTables, **see** "Slicing and Dicing Data with PivotTables," **p. 463**.

By default, PivotTable and PivotChart views of queries you select from the View button's dropdown menu are empty when you open them. You start by selecting the PivotTable view and opening the Field List dialog of the query. Then, drag fields from the Field List to one of four drop zones: Row Fields, Column Fields, Totals or Detail Fields, and Filter Fields. Figure 1.11 illustrates the PivotTable view of the Product Sales for 1997 query of the Northwind sample database. The Dairy Products category is expanded to display sales subtotals for individual products.

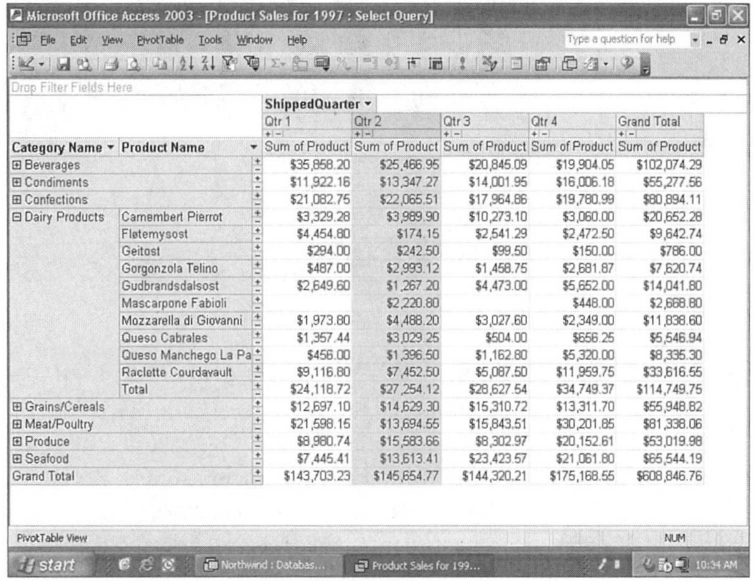

Category Name	Product Name	Qtr 1 Sum of Product	Qtr 2 Sum of Product	Qtr 3 Sum of Product	Qtr 4 Sum of Product	Grand Total Sum of Product
⊞ Beverages		$35,858.20	$25,466.95	$20,845.09	$19,904.05	$102,074.29
⊞ Condiments		$11,922.16	$13,347.27	$14,001.95	$16,006.18	$55,277.56
⊞ Confections		$21,082.75	$22,065.51	$17,964.86	$19,780.99	$80,894.11
⊟ Dairy Products	Camembert Pierrot	$3,329.28	$3,989.90	$10,273.10	$3,060.00	$20,652.28
	Fløtemysost	$4,454.80	$174.15	$2,541.29	$2,472.50	$9,642.74
	Geitost	$294.00	$242.50	$99.50	$150.00	$786.00
	Gorgonzola Telino	$487.00	$2,993.12	$1,458.75	$2,681.87	$7,620.74
	Gudbrandsdalsost	$2,649.60	$1,267.20	$4,473.00	$5,652.00	$14,041.80
	Mascarpone Fabioli		$2,220.80		$448.00	$2,668.80
	Mozzarella di Giovanni	$1,973.80	$4,488.20	$3,027.60	$2,349.00	$11,838.60
	Queso Cabrales	$1,357.44	$3,029.25	$504.00	$656.25	$5,546.94
	Queso Manchego La Pa	$456.00	$1,396.50	$1,162.80	$5,320.00	$8,335.30
	Raclette Courdavault	$9,116.80	$7,452.50	$5,087.50	$11,959.75	$33,616.55
	Total	$24,118.72	$27,254.12	$28,627.54	$34,749.37	$114,749.75
⊞ Grains/Cereals		$12,697.10	$14,629.30	$15,310.72	$13,311.70	$55,948.82
⊞ Meat/Poultry		$21,598.15	$13,694.55	$15,843.51	$30,201.85	$81,338.06
⊞ Produce		$8,980.74	$15,583.66	$8,302.97	$20,152.61	$53,019.98
⊞ Seafood		$7,445.41	$13,613.41	$23,423.57	$21,061.80	$65,544.19
Grand Total		$143,703.23	$145,654.77	$144,320.21	$175,168.55	$608,846.76

Figure 1.11
This PivotTable view of a summary displays total order amounts for product categories, with subtotals for individual products of the Dairy Products categories. In addition to generating subtotals, the AutoCalc feature adds grand totals for rows and columns.

PivotCharts rely on PivotTables to calculate values that display in several chart formats. PivotCharts reflect changes you make to the PivotTable layout and vice-versa. The PivotChart shown in Figure 1.12 corresponds to the PivotTable of Figure 1.11 with the Dairy Products category collapsed. The chart's legend is an extension to the ShippedQuarter filter button.

Interaction between the PivotTable and PivotChart views can confuse users who aren't accustomed to manipulating PivotTables. Using a form or subform bound to a query to display a PivotTable or PivotChart is a better approach than delivering these views of a query directly. You can use form properties to control which views are accessible to the user and add VBA code to limit the extent to which the user can modify the PivotTable. The Sales Analysis form of the NorthwindCS ADP is an example of a simple application that uses a command button to alternate between PivotTable and PivotChart views of a query.

→ To learn how to design PivotCharts, **see** "Formatting and Manipulating PivotCharts," **p. 481** and "Working with PivotChart Forms," **p. 726**.

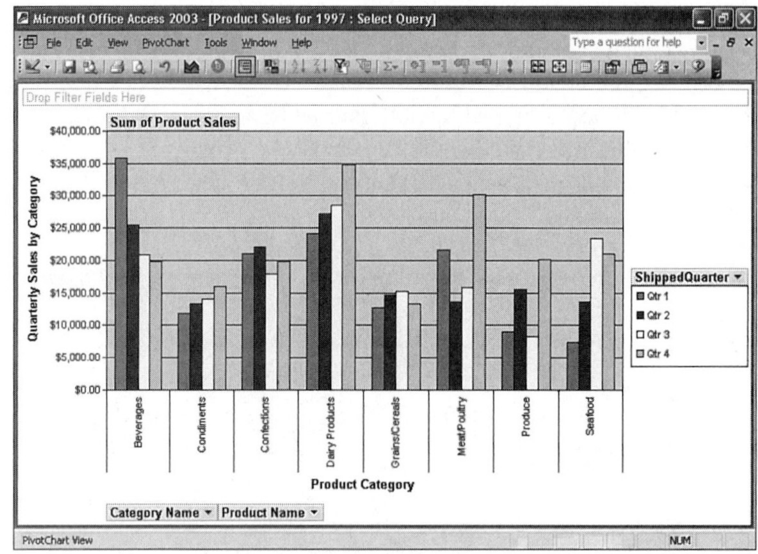

Figure 1.12 Collapsing the Dairy Products category in PivotTable view generates a PivotChart with eight groups of four bars representing quarterly sales of each product category.

ACCESS DATA PROJECTS AND SQL SERVER 2000

It's clear that Microsoft envisions the future of Access as a general-purpose development tool for creating SQL Server-based applications. The inclusion of SQL Server 7.0 Data Engine (MSDE 1.0) with Access 2000 and the upgraded SQL Server 2000 Desktop Engine (MSDE 2000) supplied with Access 2002 and Access 2003's MSDE with Service Pack (SP) 3 provide the benefits of a robust client/server relational database management system (RDBMS) without per-user license fees.

MSDE is a distributable component that you can include with Access runtime applications. Runtime Access applications don't require users to have a copy of Access 200x on their machines, but you must purchase a license for the Access 2003 Developer Extensions, which is part of the Visual Studio Tools for the Microsoft Office System add-on, to create and distribute runtime versions of your applications.

NEW SQL SERVER 2000 FEATURES

Microsoft offers six editions of SQL Server 2000: Enterprise, Standard, Developer, Personal, Windows CE, and MSDE. All SQL Server 2000 versions share the same basic database feature set, but the Personal, Windows CE, and MSDE editions don't include Analysis Services (formerly OLAP Services) for online analytical processing. The next section describes MSDE limitations.

Access 97 users upgrading to Access 2003 ADP must become familiar with Visual Studio 6.0's da Vinci database design tools for SQL Server, which emulate—but don't duplicate—Access's design tools for Jet databases. Members of Visual Studio 6.0, such as Visual Basic 6.0, also use the da Vinci toolset, whose name is derived from the beta version of the tools. After you learn SQL Server terminology for data types and T-SQL syntax for creating views, functions, and stored procedures, working with the da Vinci toolset—also called the project designer—is almost as easy as using Access's Jet design tools.

→ For more information on the da Vinci toolset, **see** "Working with SQL Server Tables in the Project Designer," **p. 810**.

1

NEW 2002 Much of Microsoft's SQL Server 7.0 to 2000 upgrade development effort went into conforming ADP and Jet functionality, which makes it easier for Access users to migrate from Jet to SQL Server back ends. Following is a list of the new SQL Server 2000 features that are of most interest to Access developers:

- *Extended properties* enable SQL Server 2000 to support features previously restricted to Jet databases, such as lookup fields, subdatasheets, master-child table relationships, text for data validation messages, data-entry masks, and column formatting. When you run the Upsizing Wizard to move a Jet database to SQL Server, a new "Creating extended properties" message appears for each table you export.
- *Functions* substitute for views and stored procedures that return a single Recordset. Unlike views, you can specify the name of an inline, table-returning function as the data source for a `SELECT` query. Functions also can return numeric and character (scalar) values.

→ To learn how to write SQL Server functions in T-SQL, **see** "Taking Advantage of In-line Functions," **p. 825**.

- *Updatable views and functions* correspond to updatable Jet queries. The rules for creating updatable Jet queries now apply to data sources for ADP. If the query is updatable in Jet, it's usually updatable in SQL Server.
- *Full Declarative Referential Integrity (DRI)* support for cascading updates and deletions, which finally matches Access's support for enforcing the referential integrity of Jet databases. In a da Vinci Database diagram, you right-click a relationship between two tables of the database, choose Properties to open the Properties dialog for the database, and click the Relationships tab. By default, DRI enforces relationships between primary and foreign key field values for replication, and `INSERT` and `UPDATE` operations. You can enable cascading updates and deletions by marking the two corresponding check boxes (see Figure 1.13).

→ To learn more about SQL Server database diagrams and how they differ from the Jet Relationships window, **see** "Diagramming Table Relationships," **p. 835**.

- *Copying or moving* database (.mdf) and log (.ldf) files to another SQL Server installation (also called an *instance*) is simplified by the new Transfer Database dialog.

→ To learn how to copy or move an SQL Server 2000 database, **see** "Transferring the Project's Database to a Server," **p. 839**.

SQL Server 2000 Desktop Engine

MSDE shares executable code with SQL Server 2000, but Microsoft imposes restrictions on MSDE's use to prevent direct competition with the licensed versions of SQL Server. In the simplest terms, MSDE is a bare-bones, detuned version of SQL Server 2000. The only

administrative tool that MSDE installs is the command-line Osql.exe utility, which replaces Isql.exe of earlier SQL Server versions.

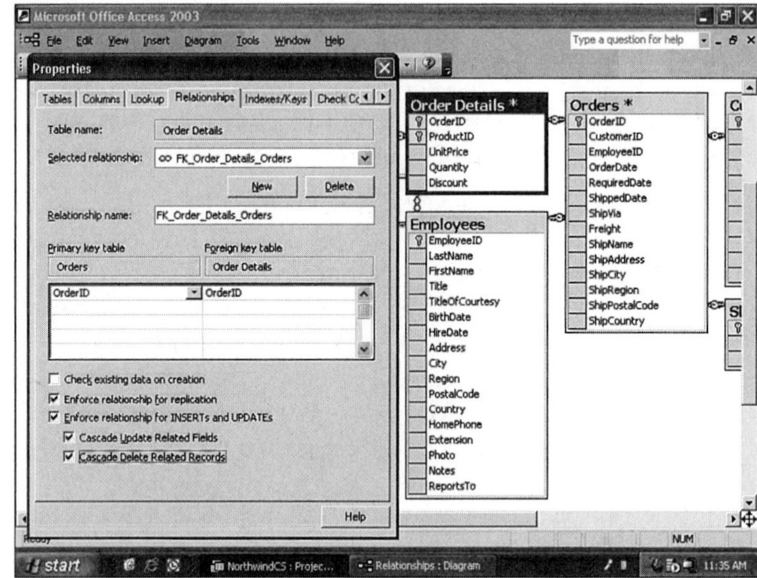

Figure 1.13
The Relationships properties page lets you set DRI properties for a relationship. In this case, referential integrity is enforced for `replication`, `INSERT`, `UPDATE`, and `DELETE` operations, including cascading `UPDATE`s and `DELETE`s.

→ For more information on using the OSQL utility, **see** "Adding User Logins with the OSQL Utility," **p. 776**.

The primary differences between MSDE and SQL Server 2000 Standard Edition are as follows:

- Database files are limited to a maximum size of 2GB. SQL Server database files are limited by the amount of physical disk storage available to the server.

- The Setup.exe program that installs MSDE is silent; the setup dialogs of the prior version no longer appear. You use Control Panel's Services tool, an Administrative Tools menu choice, to change the Windows XP/2000+ account under which the SQL Server and related services run.
- MSDE allows a maximum of five simultaneous batch operations, a number that Microsoft considers acceptable for a shared departmental database. (A *batch operation* is execution of a query, view, function, or stored procedure.) SQL Server 2000's autotuning feature optimizes performance for hundreds or, with the Enterprise Edition, thousands of simultaneous connections. Batch operations execute very quickly on servers having 667-MHz or faster Pentium III+ CPUs and adequate RAM. MSDE can handle at least 25 simultaneous users running a combination of decision support and transaction processing applications.
- The Northwind and pubs sample databases aren't included in MSDE. Access 2002's NorthwindCS ADP includes code that runs a T-SQL script (NorthwindCS.sql) to create the NorthwindCS sample database.

- Installing MSDE doesn't add MSDE 1.0's Msde choice and its submenus to the Programs menu. The only server management tool installed by MSDE is the SQL Server Service Manager.

- SQL Server 2000 supports up to 16 named instances of SQL Server on a single server, but MSDE doesn't. You can install a single named instance of MSDE if you want to continue to use MSDE 1.0 alongside MSDE. Multiple instances of SQL Server are especially useful for application service providers who rent time and storage space to organizations who want to outsource their RDBMS requirements.

→ For instructions on running MSDE 1.0 and 2000 side-by-side on your computer, **see** "Installing a Named Instance of SQL Server 2000," **p. 1386**.

- English Query, a natural-language query generation tool, Analytical Services (OLAP), and Data Mining features aren't included.
- SQL Server 2000 Enterprise Manager and other database management tools, such as Query Analyzer, aren't installed, nor is the Books Online documentation for SQL Server available.

TIP

You can download SQL Server 2000 Books Online (updated for Service Pack 3) from `http://www.microsoft.com/sql/downloads/`. Service Pack (SP) 3 was the latest SP for SQL Server when this book was written.

Microsoft licensing terms for the SQL Server management tools don't permit their use with MSDE unless you have an SQL Server 2000 license.

CHANGES TO ADP FEATURES

Following are the primary differences, excluding the da Vinci toolset features described earlier, between ADP functionality in Access 2000 and 2003:

- A single Queries button replaces the Views and Stored Procedures buttons in the Objects list of the Database window. Access 2003 represents SQL Server functions, views, and stored procedures as query subtypes.
- The Linked Table Wizard lets you link SQL Server databases to other databases for which you have OLE DB providers. Linking creates an SQL Server view of the tables in the linked database. Access 2003 includes support for linking to Jet and other SQL Server databases. If you link to an SQL Server for which you have a per-seat license, you need a CAL for each user of the linked database. If you have the required OLE DB driver, you can link to Oracle, IBM DB2/Informix, Sybase, mySQL, and other client/server RDBMSs.
- The Tools, Database Utilities, Transfer Database and Copy Database commands open wizards to move or copy an MSDE database and its log files from, for example, the local MSDE instance to another computer running any version of SQL Server 2000. These tools replace the missing Msde, Import and Export menu choice of MSDE 1.0.

- You can change your login password if your connection to the database uses SQL Server security, which requires a username and password. You receive a message that you can't change the password if your connection uses integrated Windows security.
- SQL Server Recordsets can serve as the Row Source property of combo and list boxes.
- ADP supports disconnected Recordsets for any ADP object that has Record Source and Row Source properties. A disconnected Recordset is stored locally on the client (cached) and doesn't need to maintain a connection to the database server. Changes made to the cached data when disconnected apply to the database when the client reconnects. You must be proficient in writing VBA code to take advantage of disconnected Recordsets.

TIP

> Using disconnected Recordsets as the Record Source for forms enable MSDE to support substantially more than 25 simultaneous users running ADPs that update SQL Server tables.

→ For an example of VBA code that connects and disconnects Recordsets, **see** "Taking Advantage of Disconnected Recordsets," **p. 1312**.

- MSDE installs with Windows integrated security as the user authentication method. By default, the local Administrator account is the only authorized SQL Server login and database user account. MSDE 1.0's setup program lets you choose between integrated security and SQL Server security. SQL Server security uses a password-protected sa (system administrator) account for database access and administration.

- Access 2000's SQL Server Security and Replication dialogs are missing in Access 2003. Microsoft expects Access users to type arcane T-SQL statements at the OSQL prompt to add user (or group) logins and database user accounts, and then assign permissions to the accounts. Setting up SQL Server replication with OSQL is a thankless—and almost impossible—task.

The lack of graphical MSDE security tools is a serious impediment to widespread adoption of SQL Server as the back-end for Access 2003 client/server front ends. The User Login and Permissions Manager for MSDE 2000 tool, which is located in the \Seua11\UserMan folder of the accompanying CD-ROM, is a Visual Basic 6.0 program that lets you add SQL Server logins and database user accounts, and assign user roles for databases or apply specific user permissions to any database object. You can use the program with any MSDE or SQL Server 2000 instance for which you have system administrator privileges. Figure 1.14 shows the tool's Server Logins/Database Users page.

→ For User Login and Permissions Manager operating instructions, **see** "Securing Projects with the MSDE 2000 Login/User Tool," **p. 936**.

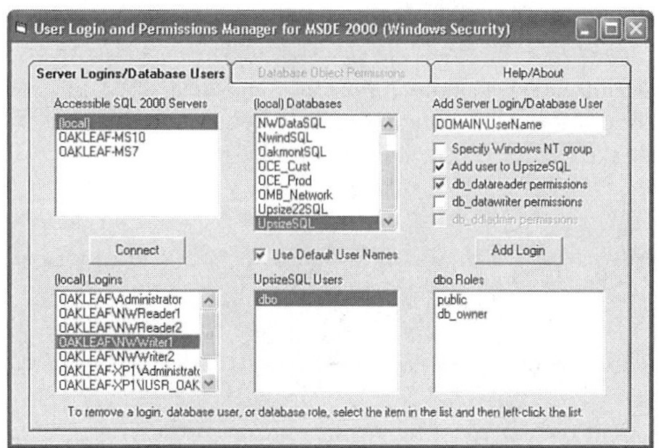

Figure 1.14
This Visual Basic 6.0 program lets you secure your ADP by adding server logins and database user accounts with built-in roles. The Database Object Permissions page lets you set specific permissions for a user account.

Live Web Reports

You can export most Access reports to static XML-based reports, which are formatted to resemble their counterparts in report Preview mode. Static HTML reports are similar to report snapshot (.snp) files that users who don't have Access can open in the Snapshot Viewer; you must update static reports periodically to deliver current information. A *live* report displays current data and eliminates the need to manage the update process.

ADP have the capability to export live Web reports as ASP that run under IIS 5.0+. Exporting the Sales Total by Amount report to XML as Top100Orders with the Live Data and Run from Server options specified generates the live Web report shown in Figure 1.15.

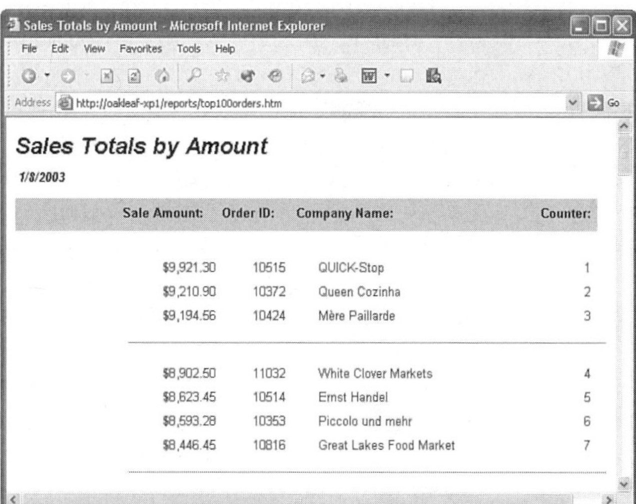

Figure 1.15
The live Web report is a close facsimile of the original Access Sales Total by Amount report, except for the values of the Counter column. Live Web reports don't support the Running Sum property.

1

NOTE

> In Access 2000, Microsoft abandoned the attempt made in Access 97 to generate ASP that emulate Access forms. If you export an Access 200x form to .asp, you get an HTML table containing the entire content of the form's underlying Record Source. Exporting tables or queries to .asp produces the same result.

→ To learn more about creating live Web reports, **see** "Exporting Live Web Reports," **p. 967**.

DATA ACCESS PAGES REVISITED

The objective of DAP is to provide a means of quickly authoring interactive, data-bound Web pages with little or no programming. DAP rely on the OWC's Data Source Control (DSC) to bind other ActiveX Control objects on a page to a Jet or SQL Server database. DAP use a combination of XML, Dynamic HTML (DHTML), and Cascading Style Sheets (CSS) to generate Web pages that permit users to view and update data. IE 5.0+ is required to display DAP; when you open a page in Access 2003, IE's rendering engine displays the content from the page's .htm file.

Access 2000 introduced DAP version 1.0, which most Access developers agree wasn't "fully cooked" when released. DAP version 1.0 suffered from the following shortcomings:

- A clunky design surface made creating attractive DAP very difficult. Aligning controls wasn't easy, and multi-select for controls and table fields wasn't available. As mentioned earlier in the chapter, DAP 1.0 didn't include an undo feature.
- Displaying DAP in client browsers required a license for Office 2000 because Microsoft designated the OWCs as Office products, not redistributable ActiveX Controls. This restriction limited deployment of DAP to corporate intranets with client PCs having Office 2000 installed or, if not installed, an Office 2000 license for the user.
- Unlike Web pages generated by exporting tables, queries, and reports to Run-from-Server ASP, DAP aren't browser-independent. Organizations that standardize on Netscape or Opera browsers, for example, can't deploy DAP.

Access 2003 overcomes most DAP 1.0 problems except for the browser issue, which loses significance as Microsoft increases IE's share of the Web browser market.

SAVE AS DATA ACCESS PAGE

The capability to save Access table, query, form, and report objects to DAP was one of Access 2002's more important new features. It's much easier for new *and* seasoned Access developers to build forms and reports in Access's traditional Design view than in DAP Design view. DAP don't have counterparts for all native Access form and report controls, and DAP use VBScript, not VBA, in event-handling procedures. Only *very* simple forms and reports save intact to DAP. Tables convert quickly to pages, which emulate Access datasheets and let users update table data in the browser. Queries also transform to datasheet-style pages; the page is updatable if the underlying query permits updates.

Following are the primary limitations when exporting Access form and report objects to DAP:

- Subforms and subreports aren't exported. The converter ignores these objects.
- Tab controls in forms aren't supported.
- Combo boxes and list boxes are limited to two bound columns, the second of which displays. The converter ignores additional columns. This is an HTML limitation; HTML dropdown lists and list boxes can display only a single column.
- Control sources that include references with `Forms!` expressions don't convert.
- Input masks and validation functions aren't included, but you can script the validation process with DHTML.
- Subtotals and other aggregate values displayed by text boxes in report Header and Footer sections don't convert, but the workaround to add subtotals isn't difficult.

Chapter 25, "Converting Access Objects to Data Access Pages," shows you how to overcome most of the limitations you encounter when saving reports as DAP. Figure 1.16 shows part of the Inventory By Category report saved as the Inventory.htm data access page.

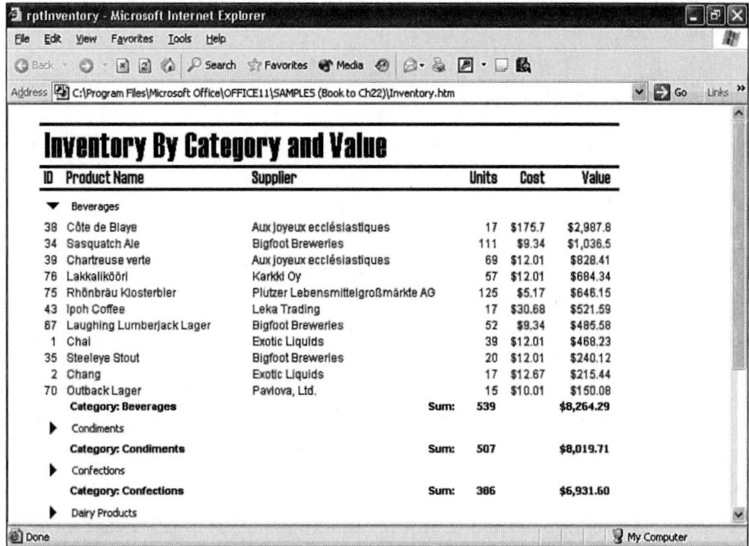

ID	Product Name	Supplier		Units	Cost	Value
	Beverages					
38	Côte de Blaye	Aux joyeux ecclésiastiques		17	$175.7	$2,987.8
34	Sasquatch Ale	Bigfoot Breweries		111	$9.34	$1,036.5
39	Chartreuse verte	Aux joyeux ecclésiastiques		69	$12.01	$828.41
76	Lakkalikööri	Karkki Oy		57	$12.01	$684.34
75	Rhönbräu Klosterbier	Plutzer Lebensmittelgroßmärkte AG		125	$5.17	$646.15
43	Ipoh Coffee	Leka Trading		17	$30.68	$521.59
67	Laughing Lumberjack Lager	Bigfoot Breweries		52	$9.34	$485.58
1	Chai	Exotic Liquids		39	$12.01	$468.23
35	Steeleye Stout	Bigfoot Breweries		20	$12.01	$240.12
2	Chang	Exotic Liquids		17	$12.67	$215.44
70	Outback Lager	Pavlova, Ltd.		15	$10.01	$150.08
	Category: Beverages		**Sum:**	**539**		**$8,264.29**
	Condiments					
	Category: Condiments		**Sum:**	**507**		**$8,019.71**
	Confections					
	Category: Confections		**Sum:**	**386**		**$6,931.60**
	Dairy Products					

Figure 1.16 This conventional Access report saved as a Data Access Page requires several post-conversion modifications to display aggregate values (category units and value subtotals) in the Detail section's footer. Other design changes—such as removal of record navigation controls—make the page more attractive and usable.

OFFICE WEB COMPONENTS LICENSING

Version 11 of the OWCs are freely distributable, that is, you can include the OWCs in a runtime Access application that you create with MOD 11's Package and Deployment

Wizard. Microsoft provides an OWC merge module to add OWCs to the Windows Installer package for runtime applications. A warning page greets DAP recipients who don't have OWC version 11 with an option to download the OWC installer package from the location of your original Office 2003 installation or the `microsoft.com` Web site. As mentioned earlier in the chapter, OWC11 installs only on computers running Windows XP/2000+.

There are no restrictions to the Data Source Control OWC for DAP recipients without an Office 2003 license, but the unlicensed PivotTable, PivotChart, and Spreadsheet controls have the following limitations:

- Users can't drag and drop fields to pivot the table in the UI.
- Filtering with the UI isn't permitted.
- Design changes to PivotCharts, such as changing the chart type, aren't supported.
- Spreadsheet objects are read-only.

NOTE

> **If you're an accomplished VBScript programmer, you can add script to your pages to manipulate the unlicensed PivotTable, PivotChart, and Spreadsheet controls.**

Microsoft's OWC licensing policy is intended to extend the reach of DAP to a much larger audience than Office 2003 users, but the Windows XP/2000+ installation restriction compromises that objective.

New DAP Design View Features

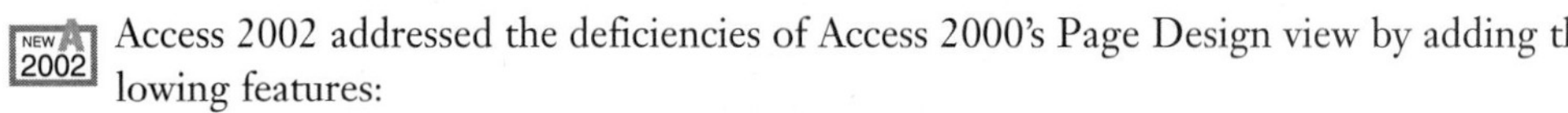

Access 2002 addressed the deficiencies of Access 2000's Page Design view by adding the following features:

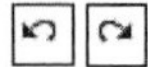

- *Multi-level redo and undo* applies to most design changes.
- *Multi-select for controls* lets you apply size, horizontal and vertical spacing, alignment, and other property settings to a group of controls.
- *Multi-select drag and drop* lets you drag a group of fields from the field list to the page.

- *Banded pages* are updatable if the query is updatable. The AllowAdditions, AllowDeletions, and AllowEdits group-level properties determine users' ability to update data. Auto-indent for group levels is provided, and you can specify common formatting for captions and footers in the Pages page of the Options dialog.

- *AutoSum* lets you add a grand total, subtotal, average, count, or other aggregate value to the section above the detail records. Figure 1.17 shows the Northwind.mdb's Review Orders page. The page has an AutoSum text box in the Header: Orders-OrderDate section that displays a grand total of the ExtendedPrice field of the Order Details Extended query. The Grand Total value is the sum of the Sub Total values for each order received during the specified Order Year.

- *Context menus* let you choose Page, Group Level, Section, or Element properties by right-clicking any region on the page. The context menu also has Clipboard, formatting, and Group Filter choices.
- *Tabular, PivotChart, and Office Spreadsheet options* have been added to the Page Wizard, which automatically generates the basic DAP design you select. You now can bind the Spreadsheet OWC to a table or query.

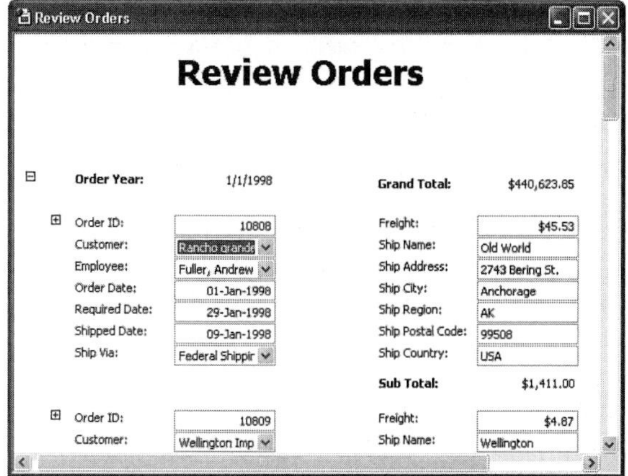

Figure 1.17
The Review Orders page illustrates use of the AutoSum feature to add a Sub Total value for each record in the Detail section and a Grand Total in the header for the Order Year. Data in the text boxes and dropdown lists is updatable.

- *Batch update features* are available for DAP based on SQL Server 2000 data sources.
- *Offline access* to static and updatable pages is provided by local XML data storage and, for updatable pages, SQL Server merge publication. Updatable pages require MSDE on the client and publication enabled on the remote server. The Access 2000 Replication dialog is missing in Access 2002, so you must configure publication with OSQL.
- *Default locations* for the deployment folder and the Office Data Connection (ODC) or Universal Data Link (UDL) files for new DAP are set in the Pages page of the Options dialog.
- *Hyperlink controls* now bind to Jet Hyperlink fields. SQL Server doesn't support Hyperlink fields, so this feature isn't available in DAP bound to SQL Server data sources.

PROGRAMMABILITY ENHANCEMENTS

Every Access upgrade has added new events, properties, and methods, but Access 2003 is an exception. The only programmability enhancements in the Access 2003 upgrade are changes to the `ExportXML` and `ImportXML` methods, and programmatic access to properties associated with smart tags. These topics are beyond the scope of this book. Thus, the following sections, which describe new events, properties, and methods introduced by Access 2002, are intended for Access 97 and 2000 users who upgrade to Access 2003.

The number of new programming elements added by Access 2002 was much fewer than most previous upgrades. For example, the upgrade from Access 97 to 2000 replaced VBA 5.0 with 6.0, and introduced the Office VBA Editor. The VBA 6.0 upgrade added hundreds of new programming elements.

ACCESS 2002 EVENTS FOR FORMS, CONTROLS, AND BATCH UPDATES

Most Access upgrades add new events for forms and controls, which results in Access having unrivaled data-related event granularity. Table 1.2 lists the three events for forms and controls added by Access 2002. Each of these events has its VBA event counterpart, which is shown in parentheses.

TABLE 1.2 EVENTS FOR FORMS AND CONTROLS ADDED BY ACCESS 2002

Event	When the Event Fires
On Undo (`Undo`)	After the user has applied the Undo command to return a control or form to its original (clean) state (the opposite of the On Dirty event)
On Mouse Wheel (`MouseWheel`)	Movement of the mouse wheel (forms only)

ACCESS 2002 PROPERTIES AND THE PRINTERS COLLECTION

One of the most important Access 2002 programming features is the addition of the `Printers` collection, which lets you assign a particular `Printer` object from the collection to print a form or report. Addition of the `Printers` collection and `Printer` object eliminates the cumbersome `PrtDevMode` and `PrtDevNames` programming required by earlier Access versions. Table 1.3 lists the properties added by Access 2002 that apply to forms, reports, and controls. Table 1.4 lists only higher-level Access properties.

TABLE 1.3 PROPERTIES OF FORMS, REPORTS, AND CONTROLS ADDED BY ACCESS 2002

Collection or Property	Purpose
`Application.Printers`	Collection of local and network `Printer` objects accessible to the application
`Form``.Printer`	Assigns a member of the Printers collection to print a form
`Report``.Printer`	Assigns a member of the Printers collection to print a report
`Control``.Recordset`	Binds a `DAO.Recordset` or `ADODB.Recordset` object to a list box or combo box control
`Report``.Recordset`	Binds a `DAO.Recordset` or `ADODB.Recordset` object to a report
`Report``.Shape`	Returns the text of the `Shape` command used to create a grouped report

TABLE 1.4 APPLICATION, PROJECT, AND ACCESS OBJECT PROPERTIES ADDED BY ACCESS 2002

Property	Purpose
`Application.Build`	Returns the Access build number
`Application.BrokenReference`	Returns **True** if the VBA project contains broken references
`CurrentProject.FileFormat`	Returns the version of the Access project
AccessObject`.DateCreated`	Returns the date and time when an Access object (form, report, macro, or module) was created
AccessObject`.DateModified`	Returns the date and time of the last design change to an Access object

METHODS ADDED BY ACCESS 2002

Table 1.5 lists control and form methods added by Access 2002. The `AddItem` and `RemoveItem` methods for Access combo- and list boxes are similar to Visual Basic's methods for these two control types. The two `Move` methods simplify changing the position or altering the size of a control or form.

TABLE 1.5 CONTROL AND FORM METHODS ADDED BY ACCESS 2002

Object.Method	Purpose
Control`.AddItem`	Adds an item specified by a string `Item` value and optional `Index` argument to a combo box or list box. The `RowSourceType` property of the control must be set to `Value List`.
Control`.RemoveItem`	Removes the item specified by the value of the `Index` argument.
Control`.Move`	Sets the `Left`, `Top`, `Width`, and `Height` properties of a control.
Form`.Move`	Sets the `Left`, `Top`, `Width`, and `Height` properties of a form, overriding the `Moveable` property value.

The eight added methods of the Access `Application` object, listed in Table 1.6, let you duplicate with VBA code actions that ordinarily take place in the UI. For example, the ExportXLM and ImportXML methods correspond to the File, Export and File, Get External Data, Import commands with XML Documents (*.xml) specified in the Export or Import dialog.

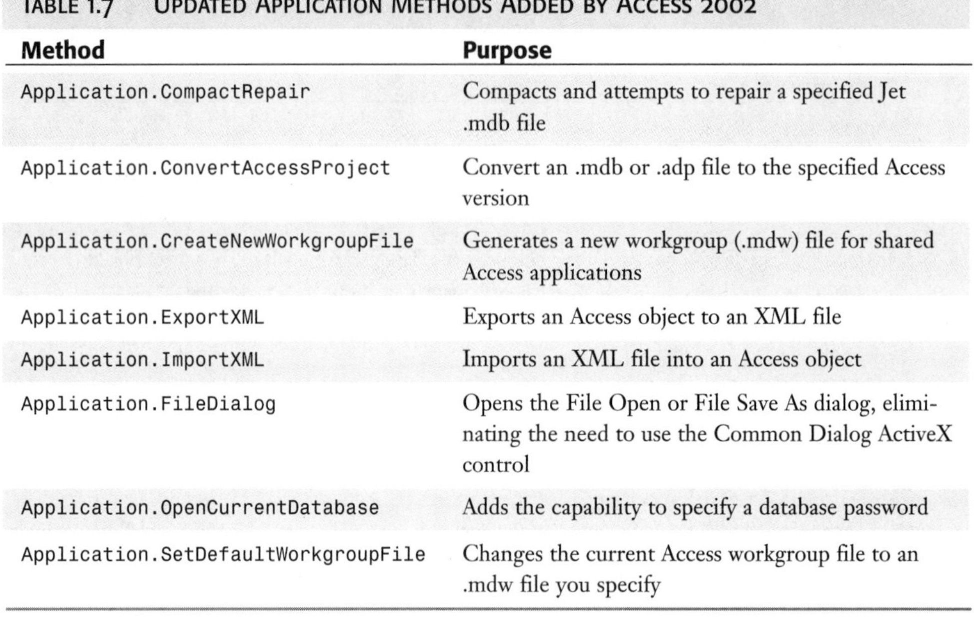

Table 1.7 Updated Application Methods Added by Access 2002

Method	Purpose
`Application.CompactRepair`	Compacts and attempts to repair a specified Jet .mdb file
`Application.ConvertAccessProject`	Convert an .mdb or .adp file to the specified Access version
`Application.CreateNewWorkgroupFile`	Generates a new workgroup (.mdw) file for shared Access applications
NEW `Application.ExportXML`	Exports an Access object to an XML file
NEW `Application.ImportXML`	Imports an XML file into an Access object
`Application.FileDialog`	Opens the File Open or File Save As dialog, eliminating the need to use the Common Dialog ActiveX control
`Application.OpenCurrentDatabase`	Adds the capability to specify a database password
`Application.SetDefaultWorkgroupFile`	Changes the current Access workgroup file to an .mdw file you specify

Visual Basic Functions

Access 2003 queries against Jet databases and VBA code support the nine VBA 6.0 functions added by Office XP listed in Table 1.9. The added `Format...` functions eliminate the need to specify format strings when you use the general-purpose `Format` function in a Jet query or code.

Table 1.9 VBA 6.0 Functions Added by Office XP

Function	Description
`FormatCurrency`	Formats a numeric value with a currency symbol, a specified number of digits after the decimal point, leading digit, negative numbers in parentheses, and digits grouped with a delimiter. By default, the function uses the computer's Regional Settings values for currency.
`FormatDateTime`	Formats a `Date` value in one of four standard date and time representations.
`FormatNumber`	Same as `FormatCurrency` but doesn't display the currency symbol.
`FormatPercent`	Same as `FormatCurrency` but multiplies the value by 100 and adds a trailing % symbol.
`InstrRev`	Searches for the occurrence of a substring within a string value beginning at the end of the string.
`MonthName`	Returns the full or abbreviated name of the month from numeric values 1 through 12.

Function	Description
`Replace`	Returns a string in which a specified substring replaces one or more occurrences of the value's substring.
`StrReverse`	Returns a string with the characters in reverse order.
`WeekdayName`	Returns the full or abbreviated name of the day of the week from numeric values 1 through 7 with the capability to specify the first day of the week.

1

CAUTION

If you use any of these new functions in Jet queries or VBA code, your Access 2003 application saved in Access 2000 format won't run under Access 2000.

SQL SERVER 2000 DESKTOP ENGINE SETUP

The Office 2002 Setup program doesn't include an option to automatically install MSDE. You must install MSDE from the distribution CD-ROM or a network share as the last step in installing Access 2002. MSDE's Setup program is totally automatic and, unlike the prior version 1.0, offers no installation options. You must install MSDE to take advantage of ADP, live Web reports, and other Access 2002 features that require SQL Server instead of Jet 4.0 as their data source.

TIP

Be sure to install MSDE before you open the NortwindCS.adp file. MSDE must be running for NorthwindCS to execute its stored procedure (NorthwindCS.sql) to create the back-end NorthwindCS database.

Following are the decisions that the Setup program makes for you:

- The network protocol is TCP/IP Sockets on port 1433, the standard port for SQL Server.
- The collation (sorting) order is determined by the current locale (regional language) setting of the computer on which you install MSDE. You can't change the collation order without reinstalling MSDE.
- The installation folder is *D*:\Program Files\SQL Server, where *D* is the drive (usually C) on which you installed Office XP. You can't change the installation folder or drive.
- MSDE supports integrated Windows and SQL Server security, but SQL Server security is disabled. The logon account under which you install MSDE, commonly *DOMAIN*\Administrator, and the local Administrators group (BUILTIN\Administrators for Windows 2000+) are members of the System Administrators security role. By default, only the Administrator and other members of the local Administrators group can connect to the MSDE database server.

- The default service account under Windows XP/2000+ is the LocalSystem account. You change the service account with Control Panel's Services tool.

RUNNING THE MSDE SETUP PROGRAM

Choosing the Typical Install or Complete Install option during the Office 2003 installation process copies all Access 2003 components to your local disk. MSDE installation, however, is totally independent from Office System 2003 installation. For example, you can install MSDE on a Windows XP Professional peer server (workstation) in a Workgroup or on a Windows Server 2000+ member server or domain controller and connect your ADP to the remote MSDE server. In this case, you don't need to install MSDE on client machines. The most common initial configuration, however, is to install MSDE on the machine on which you're running Access 2003.

TIP

Office 2003 installs MSDE 2000 with Service Pack 3 (MSDE SP3), which includes protection from the infamous Slammer worm vulnerability. If you're upgrading from Access 2002 and have applied MSDE SP3, you don't need to upgrade. To learn more about the Slammer worm, to `http://www.microsoft.com` and type **Slammer** in the Search For text box.

If you're running MSDE and haven't applied SP3, you are in jeopardy of being infected by and infecting others with the Slammer worm when you connect your computer to the Internet without a firewall that blocks UDP port 1434. One approach is to download and apply SP3, and skip the following steps. The easier method is to upgrade an existing MSDE installation with the code from the Office 2003 CD-ROM.

→ To install a named instance of MSDE so you can run both MSDE 1.0 and 2000 on the same machine, **see** "Installing a Named Instance of SQL Server 2000," **p. 1386**.

→ To upgrade your local instance of MSDE 1.0 to 2000, **see** "Upgrading from MSDE 1.0 to SQL Server 2000," **p. 1384**.

To install MSDE 2000 if you don't have MSDE 1.0 installed, do this:

1. Navigate to the \MSDE2000 folder of the Office System 2003 distribution CD-ROM or a network installation share.
2. Double-click Msde2ks3.exe to open the License Agreement dialog, and click I Agree.
3. In the Installation Folder dialog, accept or change the default location, C:\Sql2ksp3, to extract and copy the installation files to the folder. Click Yes to create the folder (see Figure 1.18). Extracting the files takes about a minute.

TIP

If you want to learn more about SQL Server 2000 SP3, open Sp3readme.htm in your C:\Sql2ksp3\MSDE folder before proceeding.

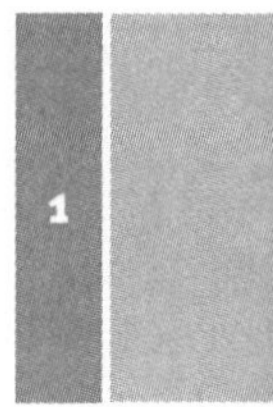

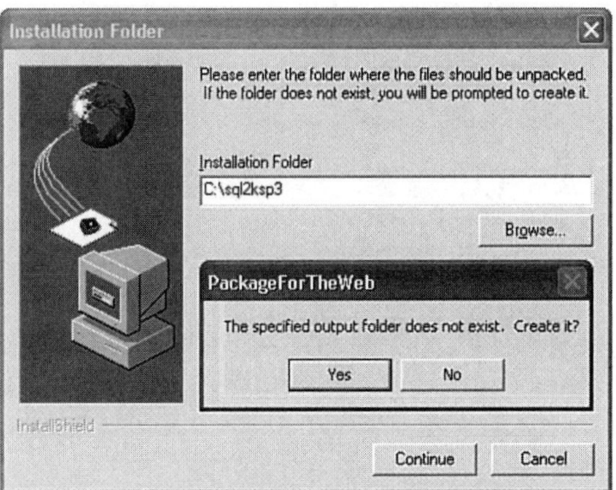

Figure 1.18
You specify the location for the temporary setup files in the second dialog of the initial setup process.

4. Choose Start, Run, type **cmd** in the Open text box, and click OK to open a Command window.
5. Type **cd \sql2ksp3\msde** and press Enter.
6. If you're installing a new instance of MSDE, type **setup.exe blanksapwd=1** (see Figure 1.19).

   If you're upgrading your existing instance of MSDE 2000 to SP3, type **setup.exe /upgradesp setup\sqlrun01.msi blanksapwd=1**. If you assigned a password to the sa account, omit blanksapwd=1 or change 1 to **0**.

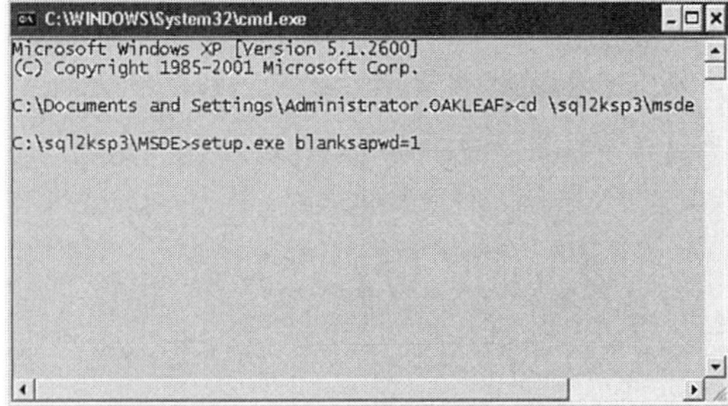

Figure 1.19
Run the extracted Setup.exe with the appropriate command line switches and parameters for initial installation or the SP3 upgrade. The example shown here is for a new MSDE installation.

7. Press Enter to start the installation process. A Windows Installer message appears briefly, followed by a Microsoft SQL Server Desktop Engine dialog, which displays an installation progress bar (see Figure 1.20).
8. Although it's not necessary to do so, it's a good practice to reboot your computer to verify that MSDE starts during boot-up.
9. After Windows XP/2000+ restarts, verify that MSDE is running by observing the small server icon with a green arrow in the taskbar tray. Passing the mouse pointer over the icon displays a "Running - *ServerName* - MSSQLServer" ToolTip.

Figure 1.20
The only messages that appear during MSDE 2000 installation are a brief announcement that Windows installer is starting and a progress dialog. The final setup process requires only a minute or two.

USING SQL SERVICE MANAGER

You use SQL Service Manager to start and stop the SQL Server and SQL Server Agent services. To get acquainted with SQL Service Manager, do this:

1. Double-click the server icon in the taskbar tray to display SQL Server Manager's dialog. Your computer's name appears in the Server list, and SQL Server is the default selection of the Services list.
2. If SQL Server is stopped, click the Start button to start the service. After a few seconds, MSDE starts.
3. If the Auto-start Service When OS Starts check box isn't marked, click the check box (see Figure 1.21).

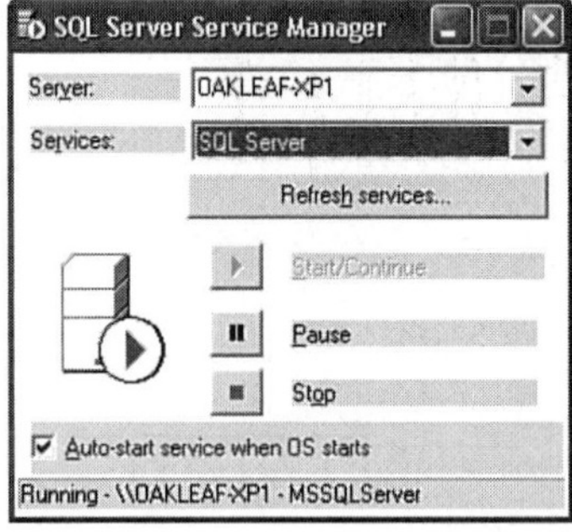

Figure 1.21
You start and stop MSDE with the SQL Service Manager. You must stop MSDE to copy, move, or back up SQL Server data files.

MSDE also installs the SQL Server Agent, which handles scheduled jobs, events, alerts, and SQL Mail notification services, and the Distributed Transaction Controller (DTC). Ordinary ADP don't require the Agent's or DTC's services. Thus, the SQL Server Agent service and DTC don't start automatically.

IN THE REAL WORLD—STILL WAITING FOR "ACCESS .NET"

Many veteran Office users, developers, and book writers expected Office version 11 to be named "Microsoft Office .NET." Microsoft's early promotion of the .NET Framework and Visual Studio .NET involved applying ".NET" to many unrelated products, such as "Windows .NET Server"—now Windows Server 2003—and classifying SQL Server and other back-end applications as ".NET Enterprise Servers." This tactic backfired and caused widespread confusion in information technology circles about what ".NET" meant.

Lack of support for the .NET Framework by every core Office member and most related Office applications is another reason for Office 11's new name—Microsoft Office System 2003. Only Microsoft Office Word 2003 and Excel 2003 have hooks to the .NET Framework. Developers need Visual Studio .NET and the Visual Studio Tools for the Microsoft Office System to write Word and Excel macros in C# or Visual Basic .NET. Access 2003, which might have benefited more than Word and Excel from a .NET connection, is missing the .NET hooks.

In the real world, Access users and developers won't suffer as a result of .NET-less Access 2003. VBA 6.0 is more than adequate for automating Access applications of any size and complexity. Moving from VBA to Visual Basic .NET programming is a transition that imposes a very steep learning curve and the cost of licensing Visual Studio .NET 2003. Whether experienced Word and Excel developers will turn to C# or Visual Basic .NET macro programming is questionable at best.

New XML-related capabilities of Office 2003 members, including Access 2003 and InfoPath 2003, will have a much greater impact on business users and developers than .NET macros. Adoption of XML as the standard format for interchanging data within and between businesses continues to accelerate. During the product lifetime of Office 2003, proficiency with XML documents and schemas, and a working knowledge of XSLT will be mandatory for Access power users and part- or full-time Access developers. Access is an excellent tool for gaining familiarity with XML data documents (called *Information Sets* or *InfoSets*), schemas, and even XSLT. You can polish your data-related XML skills by designing InfoPath form templates that connect to your Jet or SQL Server databases.

The next version of SQL Server—code-named Yukon when this book was written—will extend the realm of XML into the database with a native XML data type. Yukon supports providing XML Web services from within the database, rather than from Internet Information Services. You can expect a Yukon MSDE counterpart to release before the next Office version. Hopefully, Office 2003 licenses will include the right to use the Yukon Desktop Edition. If so, your Access data projects will gain additional XML prowess.

Users of Access 2003 for personal applications or small-business projects probably won't be interested in XML or MSDE features. You just want to get your database up and running as easily and quickly as possible. Access 2003 is unmatched as a rapid application development (RAD) environment for basic data-handling chores. The next chapter proves this claim.

CHAPTER 2

Building a Simple Desktop and Web Application

In this chapter

UNDERSTANDING ACCESS'S APPROACH TO APPLICATION DESIGN

Unlike other members of Microsoft Office System 2003, Access 2003 requires that you build an application to take advantage of the product's power as a database development platform. Word 2003 and Excel 2003 let you automate simple repetitive operations by recording Visual Basic for Applications (VBA) macros. Access 2003 supports a set of macro commands for compatibility with previous versions, but Access macros don't use VBA. Access doesn't capture your mouse clicks and keystrokes and turn them into a series of macro commands or VBA code. It's up to you to design and implement the Access applications you need for your database projects.

A full-scale Access application involves at least the following three basic Access object types:

- Tables that store the data you or others add to the database
- Forms for displaying and entering data, controlling the opening and closing of other forms, and printing reports
- Reports to print detail information, summary information, or both in tables

Most Access applications also use queries to filter, sort, and combine your data, and modules to store VBA code. Access 2003 forms can (and usually do) contain VBA code in a special type of module, called a *Class Module*. All objects that make up your application are stored in a container called a *Database object*, which is a single file with an .mdb extension, such as Northwind.mdb. Access is unique in that it can store an entire database application in a single file. Other desktop databases, such as Microsoft FoxPro, require multiple files to store their objects.

New Access users often find it difficult to "get a grip" on how to start developing a self-contained database application. Dealing with an unfamiliar set of objects tends to intimidate first-time database developers. Fortunately, Microsoft includes with Access 2003 various wizards that guide you, step by step, through complex tasks. One of the most accomplished of the Access wizards is the Database Wizard that creates a typical Access 2003 "starter" application from a set of prefabricated database templates. In this chapter, you use the Database Wizard to create a relatively simple but useful Contact Manager application. Then you explore the objects generated by the Wizard to gain perspective on the relationship of Access objects and learn how they're integrated within a typical Access database application.

If you're upgrading from Access 97 to 2003, the following features introduced by Access 2000 and 2002 are discussed in this chapter:

- *Subdatasheets*, which open when you click a plus sign to the left of the first field in Table Datasheet view. Subdatasheets automatically display records of another table that's related to the current table.
- *Visual Basic for Applications code editor*, which Access 2003 shares with other Office 2003 applications. Access 97 and earlier used its own VBA editing window for code modules.

- *Data access pages (DAP)*, which Access 2000 introduced and Access 2002 made practical for intranet or Internet deployment.

CREATING AN ACCESS APPLICATION FROM A TEMPLATE FILE

When you launch Access 2003, the upgraded Office 2003 task pane appears at the right of the main window with the default Getting Started page active. The Create a New File link at the bottom of this page opens the New File page, which offers you the following options:

- Opening a new (blank) database or data access page (DAP).
- Creating a new Access data project (ADP) connected to an existing or new Microsoft SQL Server Desktop Engine (MSDE) database.
- Creating a copy of a database from an existing Access file.
- Searching for an Access template by keyword or opening the Microsoft Office Templates home page to select a specific template.
- Using the Database Wizard to generate a new database from one of the 10 database templates included with Access 2003. Template files contain the definitions of Table, Form, and Report objects, plus the VBA code required to automate interaction of these objects.

To use the Database Wizard to create a sample application from an Access 2003 template, follow these steps:

1. Choose Programs, Microsoft Office, Microsoft Office Access 2003 from the Start menu to launch Access 2003 with the Getting Started task pane visible. If you don't see the task pane, press Ctrl+F1 or choose View, Toolbars, Task Pane to display it.
2. Click the Create a New File link or click the arrow to the right of Getting Started, and choose New File from the drop-down list.
3. Click the On My Computer link of the Templates group (see Figure 2.1) to open the Templates dialog.
4. Click the Databases tab, if necessary, and select one of the 10 database templates (*.mdz files) to build your new application from (see Figure 2.2). Access stores its templates in the \Program Files\Microsoft Office\Templates\1033 folder. This example uses the Contact Management.mdz template. Click OK to open the File New Database dialog.
5. The Wizard proposes a default database with the name of the template plus a 1 suffix. The default location of the database file is your My Documents folder. Accept the default filename or shorten it to Contacts.mdb (see Figure 2.3). Click Create to generate an empty Jet 4.0 database file (Contacts.mdb) and start the Database Wizard.

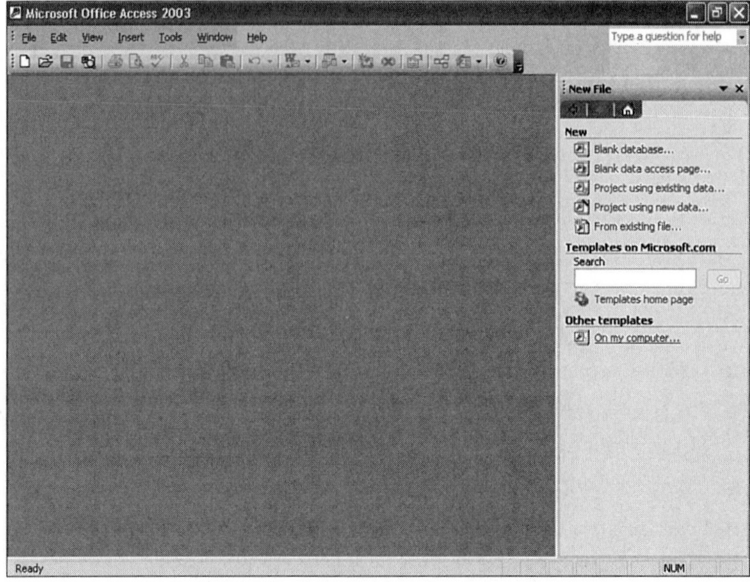

Figure 2.1
Clicking the On My Computer link under the Other Templates heading of the task pane's New File page opens the Templates dialog with the Databases page active.

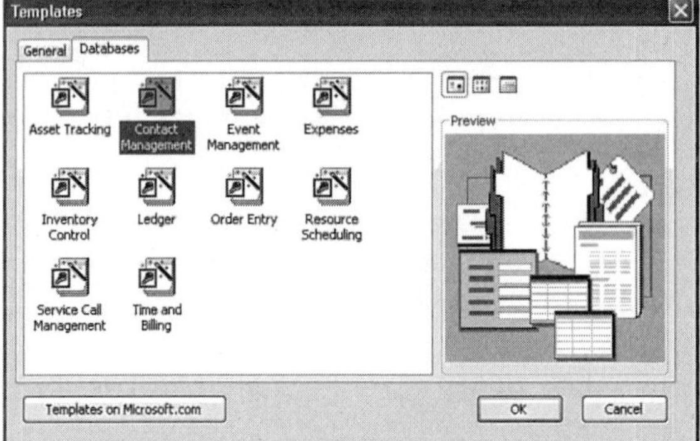

Figure 2.2
Select the Contact Management template in the Databases page of the Templates dialog.

Figure 2.3
Shorten the default database filename, Contact Management1.mdb to Contacts.mdb.

6. The first dialog of the Database Wizard describes the type of information that the new database stores (see Figure 2.4). Click Next to continue.

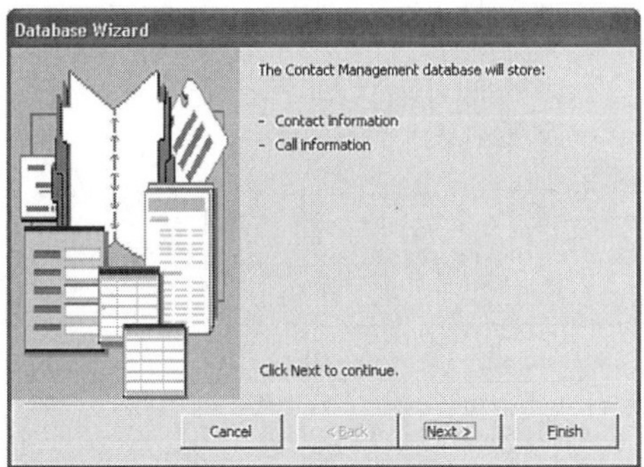

Figure 2.4
The first Database Wizard dialog offers a brief description of the new database.

7. The second Wizard dialog lets you add or remove optional fields to each of the three tables. Optional fields appear in italic type in the list. To add or remove an optional field of the Contact Information table, mark or clear the check box (see Figure 2.5). Mark the Home Phone field and click Next to continue.

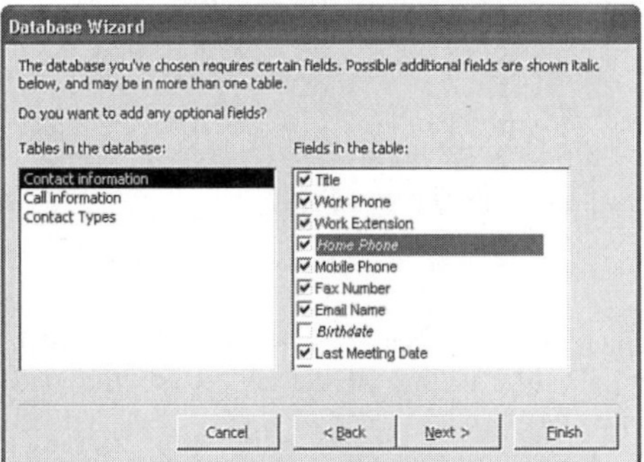

Figure 2.5
Add the optional Home Phone field of the Contact Information table of Contacts.mdb.

NOTE

> You can remove only the optional fields you add. You can't remove the standard set of fields that appear in Roman type; you receive an error message if you try.

8. The third Wizard dialog offers a selection of text colors and background colors or images for the data forms that the Wizard creates. As you select an item in the list, a sample of the style appears in the dialog (see Figure 2.6). Select a form style and click Next to continue.

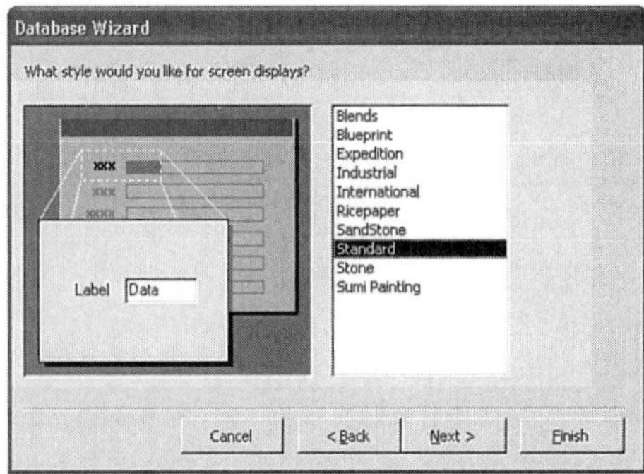

Figure 2.6
Select the text color and background color or image for data-entry forms.

9. The fourth dialog lets you choose a style for printed reports (see Figure 2.7). Pick a report style, such as the conservative Soft Gray and click Next to continue.

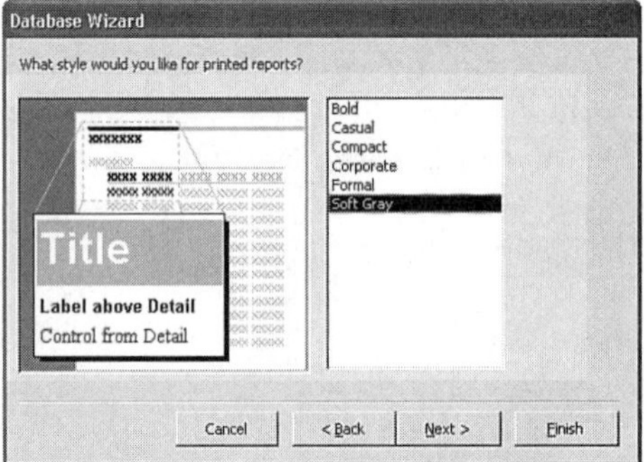

Figure 2.7
Select the header and type styles for reports in the fourth Wizard dialog.

10. You enter the title to appear on your forms and reports in the fifth Wizard dialog (see Figure 2.8). The default title is the name of the template file. Accept or edit the title.

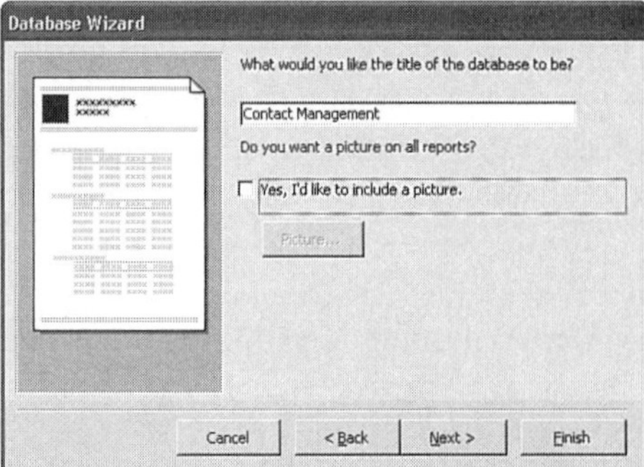

Figure 2.8
Accept the default title to appear on forms and reports.

NOTE

If you have an image of a logo that's of a size suited to the header of your reports and is in one of the 16 graphics file formats supported by Office 2003, mark the Yes, I'd Like to Include a Picture check box. (The logo should be about 80×80 pixels or less.) Click the Picture button to open the Insert Picture dialog. Select the image file and then click OK to insert the image and close the Insert Picture dialog.

11. Click Next to open the final Wizard dialog (see Figure 2.9). With the Yes, Start the Database check box marked, click Finish to add the objects whose properties you've specified to the database file you named in step 4.

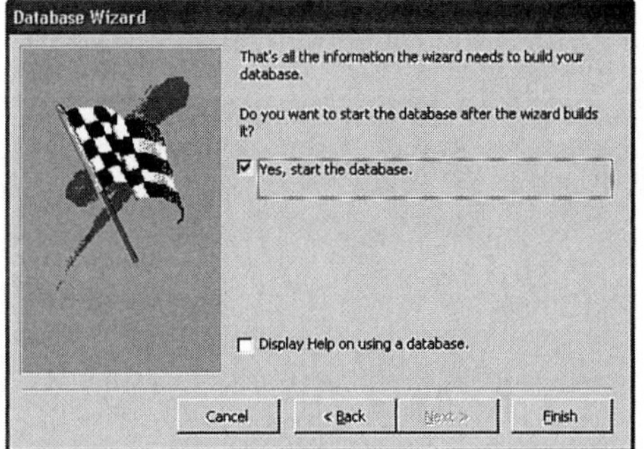

Figure 2.9
Click Finish in the final Database Wizard dialog to start generation of the Contacts.mdb database.

A set of progress bars displays the Wizard's actions. The time required to complete the generation of database objects depends on your CPU's and disk drive's speed; it takes less than 10 seconds to finish the Contact Management database with a 667MHz Pentium III PC and a high-speed fixed-disk drive. After the Wizard completes its work, the Main Switchboard form for the completed Contact Management application appears as shown in Figure 2.10. The Database window, which lets you manually open any of the objects in the Contacts database, is minimized at the bottom left of the display.

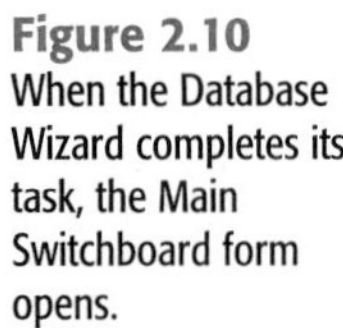

Figure 2.10 When the Database Wizard completes its task, the Main Switchboard form opens.

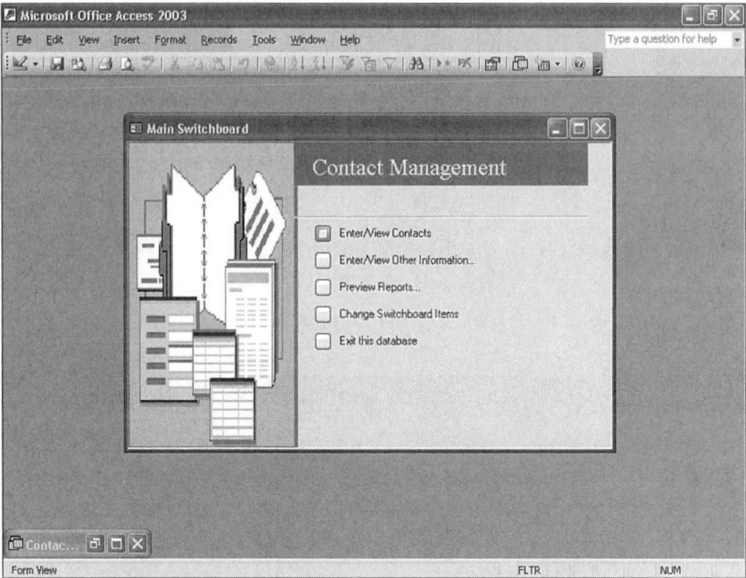

TOURING THE CONTACT MANAGEMENT APPLICATION

The Contact Management application appears complex to most first-time Access users. The Database Wizard generates Table, Form, Report, and Module objects in the new database. The following sections explain the purpose of each object in the context of your new Contact Management application.

TABLE OBJECTS IN THE DATABASE WINDOW

Tables are the foundation of Access databases. To examine some Table objects generated from the Contact Management template by the Database Wizard, do the following:

1. Click the Database window's Restore button to open the Database window in Normal mode. An Outlook-style shortcut bar appears at the left of the list.

NOTE

> By default, Access 2003 saves database files in Access 2000 format for backward compatibility. Using Access 2002 format is advantageous only for very large database applications. For the first time in Access's 10-year history, Access 2003 doesn't introduce a new Jet database file format.

2. Click the Tables shortcut to display a list of the three Create Table... options and the four Table objects in the Contacts database (see Figure 2.11).

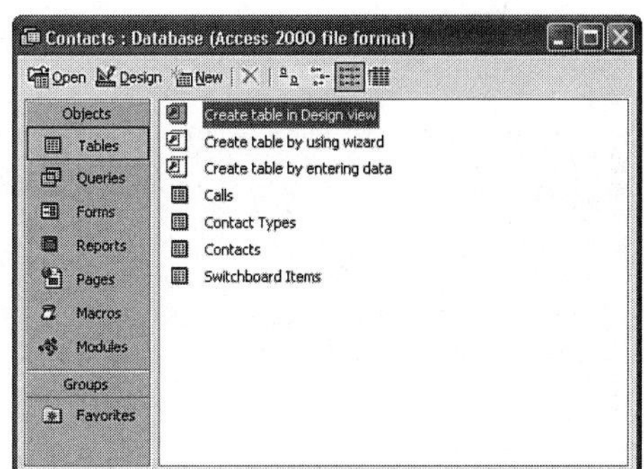

Figure 2.11
The Tables page of the Database window displays the Table objects of Contacts.mdb.

3. Double-click the Contacts item to open the Contacts table in Datasheet view. The fields of the Contacts table correspond to the items in the list of the second Wizard dialog (refer to step 7 in the preceding section). The first field is an AutoNumber field that sequentially numbers the records you add; you can't change the value of an AutoNumber field.

4. Type a test contact entry in the initially visible fields of the Contacts table. When you type in the First Name cell, a pencil symbol appears to the left of the Contact ID cell, indicating an edit in process, and a new row—called the tentative append record in this book—appears below the test contact record (see Figure 2.12). Click in any cell of the tentative append record to save your entry; you must move to another row in the datasheet to assure that entries add to the Contacts table.

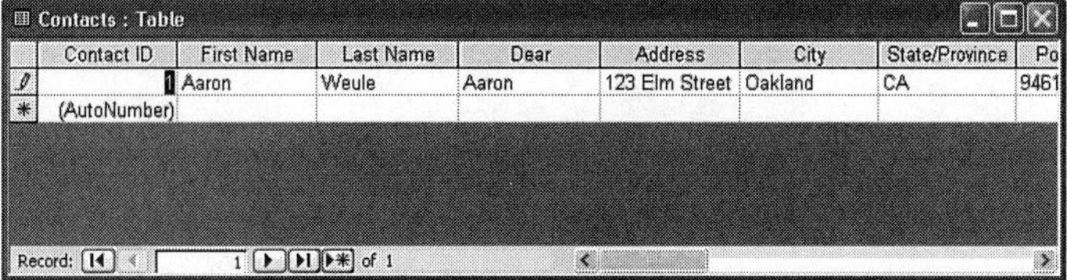

Figure 2.12
The Datasheet view of the Contacts table displays a test entry.

5. Close the Contacts datasheet, return to the Database window, and double-click to open the Contact Types table. In the Contact Type field, type a typical title, such as Executive. Add records with Director, Manager, Supervisor, and Developer as Contact Types. Click in a cell of the first record to save your last entry, and then close the Contact Types window.
6. Reopen the Contacts table, and use the scrollbar to display the rightmost fields. Click the Contact Type ID cell of the first record of the table to display a drop-down list button in the grid. Click the button to open a list with items you added to the Contact Types table and select one of the titles (see Figure 2.13).

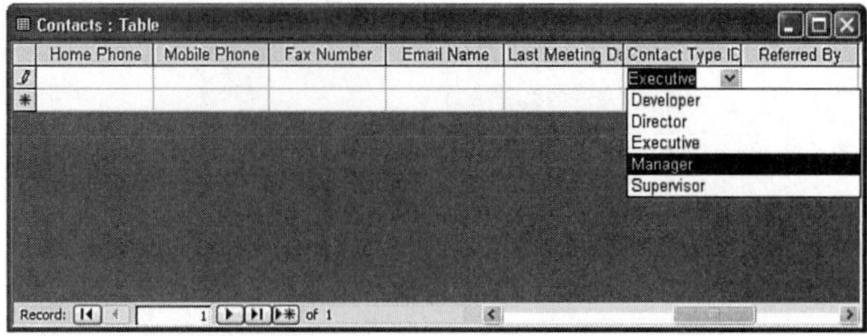

Figure 2.13 The drop-down lookup list of the Contact table's Type ID field displays choices for the field value.

→ If you're not comfortable navigating the interface yet, **see** "Understanding Access's Table Display," **p. 88**.

NOTE

The Contact Type ID field of the Contacts table is related to the Contact Type ID field of the Contact Types table, which contains the numeric values 1 (Executive), 2 (Director), 3 (Manager), and any additional records you added in step 5 of the preceding list. Relations between tables are the foundation of relational database management systems (RDBMSs). The relation between the Contacts and Contact Types tables is called a *many-to-one relationship* because many records in the Contacts table can relate to a single record in the Contact Types table. The Contact Type ID field of the Contacts table, which actually contains numeric value 1 or 2, is called a *lookup field* because it looks up data in the Contact Types table based on the numeric value and substitutes the corresponding text value for the number. You can change the Contact Type ID from Executive to Manager by selecting Manager from the drop-down list.

Additionally, inserting entries from a lookup field is a popular method for avoiding spelling errors and reducing the number of keystrokes for repeated selections.

→ For other ways to use this method of data entry, **see** "Using Lookup Fields in Tables," **p. 412**.

7. Scroll to the first field (ContactID) of the table and click the plus (+) sign at the left of the ContactID field to open a subdatasheet that displays an empty Calls datasheet for your test contact entry. (You might need to click the ContactID field to display the plus sign.) Subdatasheets display records of other tables related to the currently open table. Type entries typical of a phone call in the subdatasheet fields (see Figure 2.14). The Calls table has a many-to-one relationship to the Contacts table.

NOTE

The Calls datasheet has an input mask for the Call Date column, which requires two-digit month, day, and year values. The default display is one- or two-digit months and four-digit years. You must type the date in mm/dd/yy format. This conflict between the input mask and display formats is a known bug that was reported in Access 2000 and hasn't been fixed in later versions.

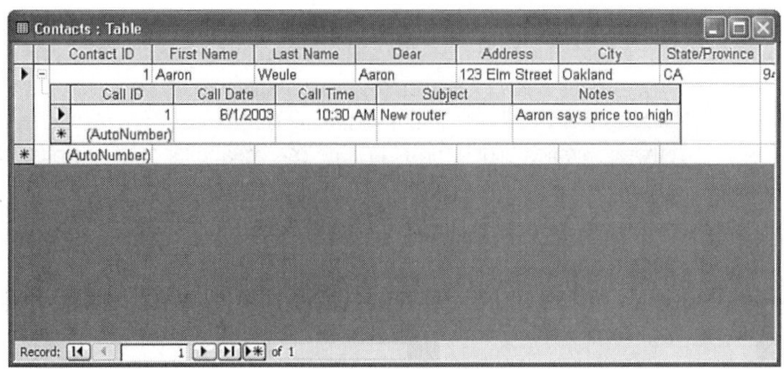

Figure 2.14 The subdatasheet lets you add new records to the related Calls table.

2

8. Choose Tools, Relationships or click the toolbar's Relationships button to display graphically the relations between the Contact Types, Contacts, and Calls tables in Access's Relationships window. Drag down the bottom of the Contacts list to expose the ContactTypeID field (see Figure 2.15).

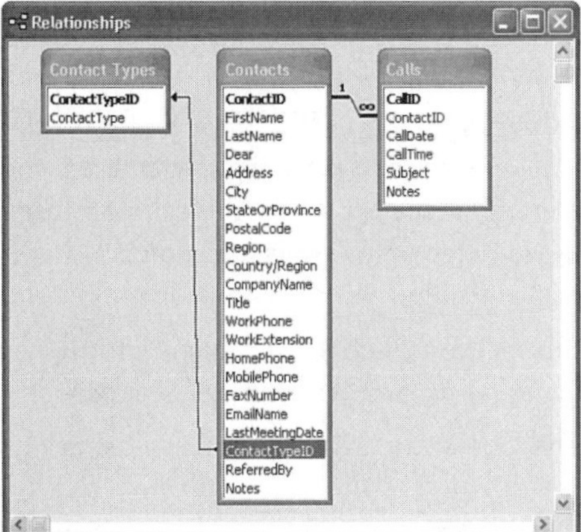

Figure 2.15 The Relationships window shows how the Contact Types, Contacts, and Calls tables of the Contacts.mdb database relate.

NOTE

The line between the ContactTypeID fields of the Contact Types and Contacts tables illustrates a many-to-one relationship. (The arrowhead identifies the "one" table in the relation.) The line between the ContactID fields of the Contacts and Calls tables also indicates a many-to-one relationship. (The infinity symbol, ∞, identifies the "many" side and the 1 represents the "one" side of the relation.) The ContactID line's symbols indicate that Access enforces the referential integrity of the relationship.

→ For details on how relationships and referential integrity protect your data, **see** "Maintaining Data Integrity and Accuracy," **p. 140**.

TIP

The field names in the Relationships window and the field names that appear in the Datasheet views of the corresponding tables aren't the same. The column names in the Datasheet views are captions, which include spaces for readability. The actual field names, which usually don't include spaces, appear in the field lists of the Relationships window.

9. Close the Relationships and Contacts Table windows, saving your layout changes.

THE SWITCHBOARD FORM

The Main Switchboard is the controlling form of the Contact Management application (refer to Figure 2.10). Switchboard forms take the place of the conventional menu choices of conventional Windows applications. Switchboard forms are found in commercial Access applications. The five buttons on the Main Switchboard perform the following functions:

- *Enter/View Contacts* opens the two-page Contacts form.
- *Enter/View Other Information* opens another switchboard that has Enter/View Contact Types and Return to Main Switchboard buttons. The Enter/View Contact Types button opens a small form for adding additional records to the Contact Types table.
- *Preview Reports* opens the Reports Switchboard page, which lets you preview and print an Alphabetical Contact Listing Report or a Weekly Call Summary Report or return to the Main Switchboard. Preview Reports is equivalent to choosing Print Preview from the File menu.
- *Change Switchboard Items* opens the Switchboard Manager form, which lets you customize the Switchboard pages, add a new page, or delete a page.
- *Exit This Database* closes the Contacts database but doesn't shut down Access.

Figure 2.16 shows the relationship between the buttons on the three versions of the Switchboard and the forms and reports that make up the Contact Management application. For clarity, this diagram omits the Call Details Subform, Call Listing Subform, and Report Date Range form. A *subform* is a form that's contained within another form; subforms are unique to Access. Lines between forms and tables with arrows on each end indicate the capability to display and edit table data. Lines between reports and tables have only a single arrow, because reports involve only reading table data.

→ For help building a new subform, **see** "Creating a Basic Transaction-Processing Form with the Form Wizard," **p. 522**.

NOTE

Figure 2.16 shows three individual Switchboard forms. Contact Manager uses records in the Switchboard Items table to customize a single Switchboard form to perform the three functions shown in the diagram.

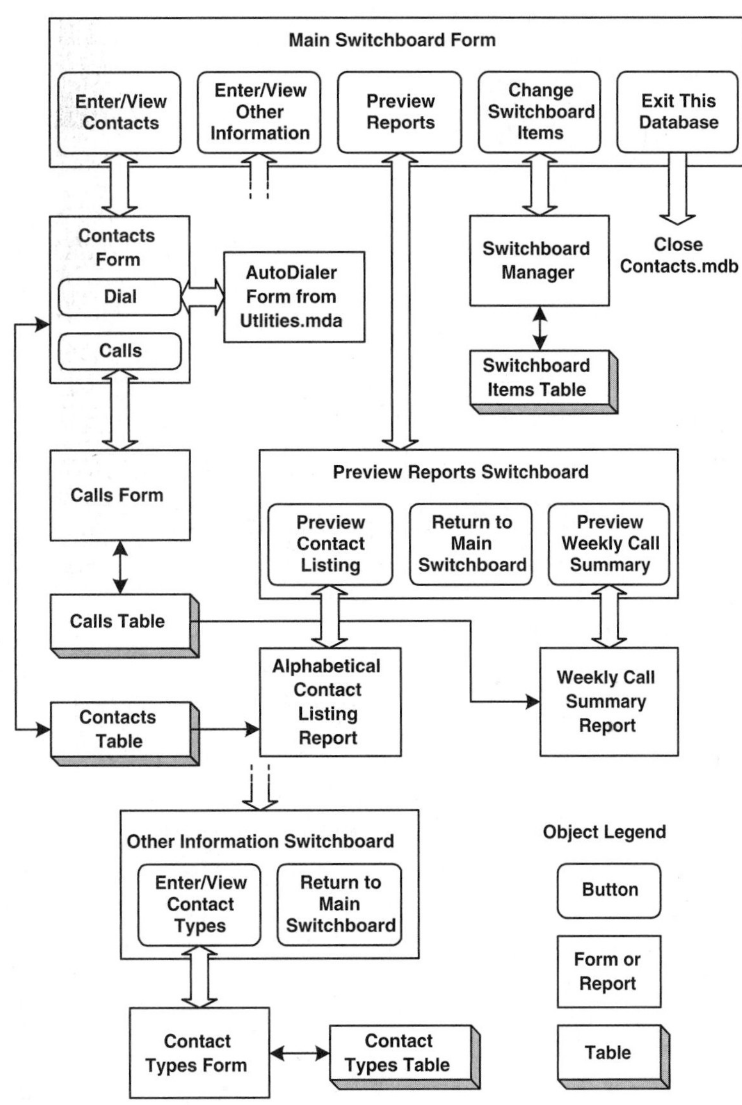

Figure 2.16
This diagram shows the relationship of Switchboard buttons to forms, reports, and tables of the Contact Manager application.

Compared to menu commands, switchboards offer more control over the sequence of user interaction with data display and entry forms. The Main Switchboard acts as a home base that you return to on completion of one or more specific tasks. Simplified navigation of multiple layers of forms is the reason that many Access developers use switchboards or their equivalent for complex applications.

ACCESS FORMS

The following steps introduce you to Access forms and form-based data entry:

1. Close all open Access windows except the Switchboard form and the Database window.

> **NOTE**
>
> If you accidentally closed the Switchboard form, restore the Database window, click the Forms shortcut, and double-click the Switchboard item in the list to open the Main Switchboard.

2. Click the Enter/View Contacts button to open the Contacts form, which displays in text boxes most of the data you entered in the first record of the Contacts table (see Figure 2.17). The record displayed in the form is called the *current record* of the table.

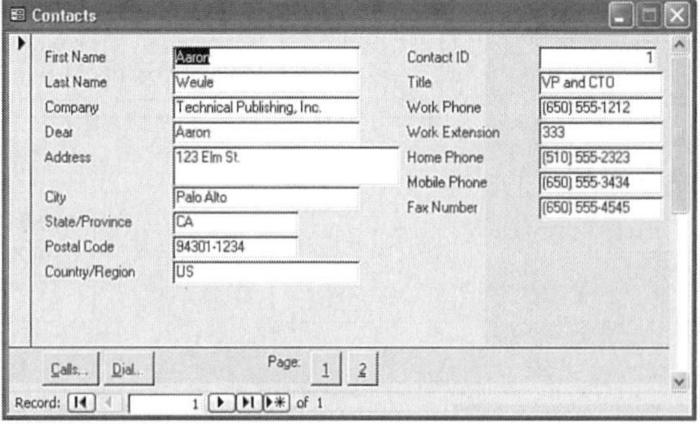

Figure 2.17
On opening, the upper part of the Contacts form displays most of the information for the first record of the Contacts table.

3. Click the Next Record button (with the right-pointing triangle) at the bottom left of the form to display successive records of the Contacts table. If you added only a single Contacts record, the text boxes empty in preparation for adding a new record.
4. Click the First Record button (with the left-pointing triangle and bar) to return to the first record you typed.
5. Click the 2 button to show the bottom part of the form, which displays the data for the remaining fields of the Contacts table. You also can navigate to the bottom of the display with the form's scrollbar. Clicking inside the Notes text box adds a scrollbar to that box (see Figure 2.18). Click the 1 button to return to the top of the form.
6. Press the Tab key 10 times to move the focus to the Work Phone field. (The Tab key is the primary method of navigating through a form's fields.) Click the Dial button to open the AutoDialer form of the Utility.mda library (see Figure 2.19). Clicking the Setup button opens the Windows XP or 2000 Modem Properties sheet. Close the Modem Properties sheet, if you opened it, and then click Cancel to close the AutoDialer form.

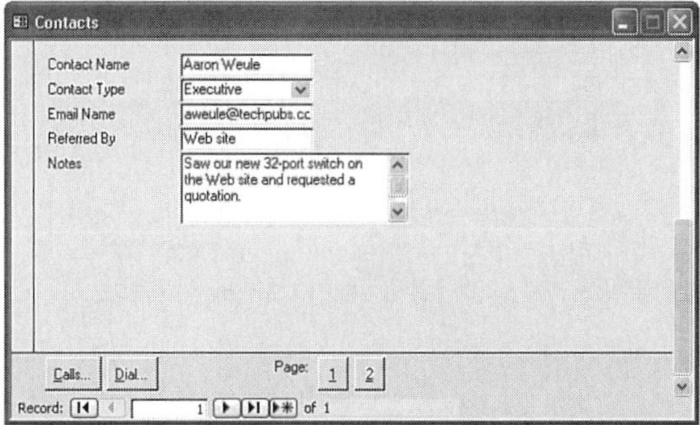

Figure 2.18
Clicking the 2 button moves to the lower part of the Contacts form, which displays additional contact data.

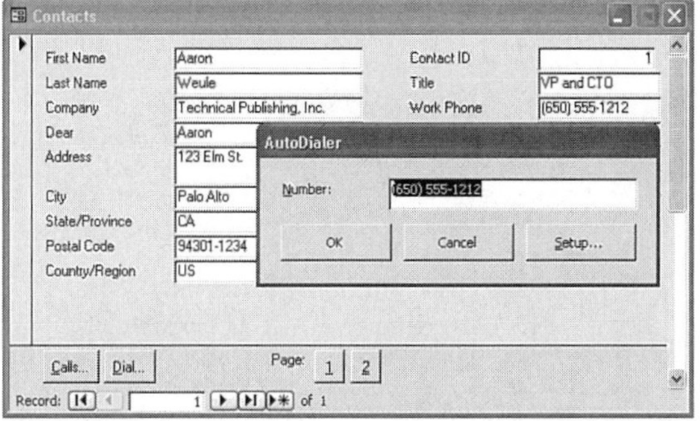

Figure 2.19
The AutoDialer form is a part of the Ultility.mda library database that's attached when you launch Access.

NOTE

AutoDialer uses the Windows XP/2000+ built-in Phone Dialer accessory. AutoDialer detects whether the call is within your local dialing area (set by the Dialing Properties sheet that you open from the Modem Properties sheet). The Phone Dialer prepends the required 1 digit to the area code and telephone number when dialing long distance.

7. Click the Calls button to open the Calls form, which superimposes the Contacts form. The Calls form displays only the records in the Calls table for the contact selected in the Contacts form, a process called *synchronizing forms* (see Figure 2.20). The Calls form must display multiple records, so the Calls form uses a Datasheet view of the Calls table.

8. Add a new Calls record for the Contacts record you entered earlier by clicking the Subject field of the tentative append record and adding some text. When you start typing text, a new tentative append record appears.
9. Click inside the Call Notes text box and type a short transcript of the call (see Figure 2.21). The Call Notes caption and text box are contained in the Call Details Subform.

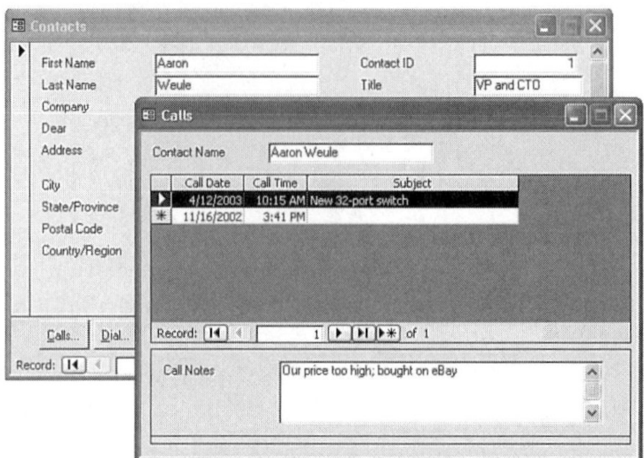

Figure 2.20
The Calls form synchronizes to the active (current) record of the Contacts form.

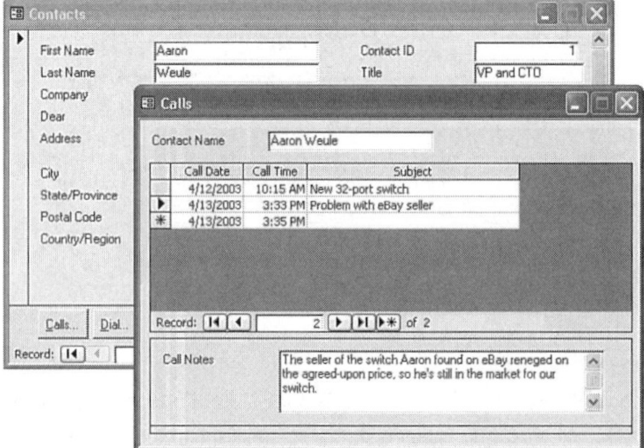

Figure 2.21
A new record added to the Calls form.

10. To delete the record you just added, click the gray record selector button to the left of the Call Date field and press Delete. You receive the warning message shown in Figure 2.22.

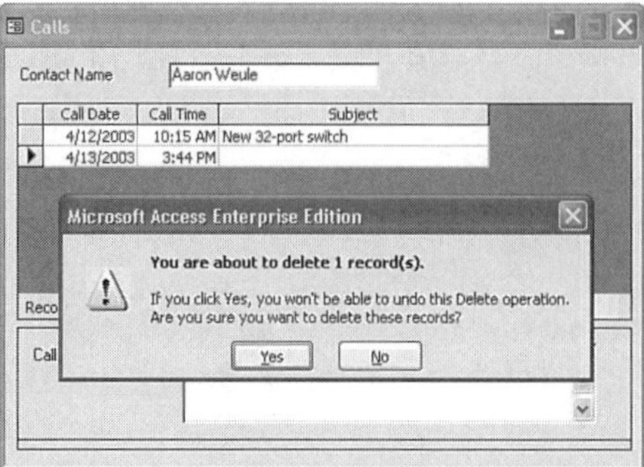

Figure 2.22
You receive a warning message before permanently deleting a record.

NOTE

Office 2003 no longer installs the Office Assistant by default, so conventional windows warning messages replace the Office Assistant's intrusive pop-up window.

11. Close the Calls form to return to the Contacts form.

12. If you want to add a new contact record to the Contacts form, click the Tentative Append record navigation button (also known as the New Record button) to open a form in which only the Contact ID field is filled in by an (AutoNumber) placeholder for the next Contact ID value (see Figure 2.23).

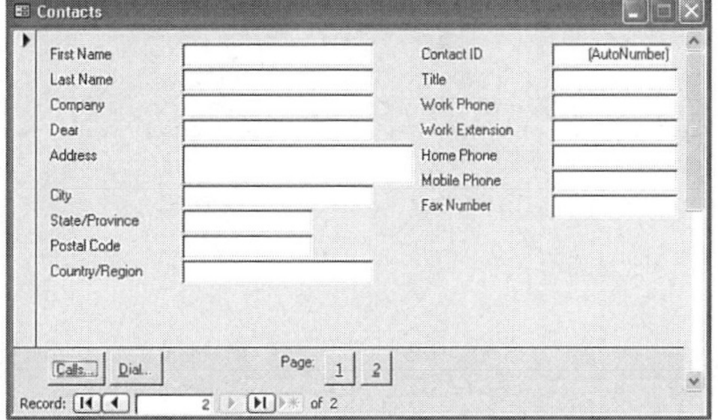

Figure 2.23
Click the tentative append button to add a new record to the Contacts table.

13. Close the Contacts form to return to the Main Switchboard.

NOTE

The Contact ID field uses the AutoNumber field data type, which automatically assigns the next number in sequence to an added record. If you don't enter text in any field and then move the record pointer with the navigation buttons to an active record, the empty record isn't appended.

To delete a record, click the record selector bar at the left of the form and press the Delete key. If you delete a record of the Contacts table that has related records in the Calls table, the related Calls records are deleted simultaneously, a process called *cascading deletions*. The related Calls records are deleted because referential integrity is enforced between the Calls and Contacts tables, and cascading deletions are specified in the properties of the relation in the Relationships window.

Clicking the Enter/View Other Information button regenerates the Forms Switchboard. To add a new contact type, click the Enter/View Contact Types button to open the simple Contact Types form. Like Contact ID, Contact Type ID is an AutoNumber field. Close the Contact Types form and then click the Return to Main Switchboard button to return the Switchboard form to its original status.

ACCESS REPORTS

Reports are one of Access's strongest selling points. The capability to program the generation of complex, fully formatted reports sets Access apart from its competitors, including Microsoft's own Visual Basic. To preview and optionally print the two reports of the Contact Management application, follow these steps:

1. Click the Preview Reports button to generate the Reports Switchboard, and then click Preview the Alphabetical Contact Listing Report to open the small Print Preview window in Normal mode. Fit appears in the toolbar's Zoom list.
2. Type or select 75% in the Zoom list to view almost all the report (see Figure 2.24).

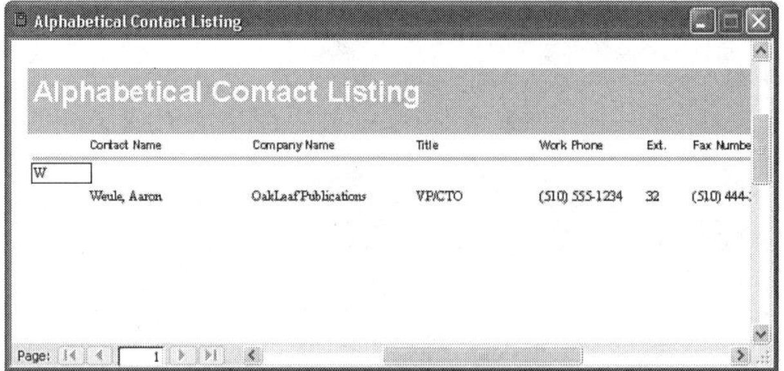

Figure 2.24 The Print Preview window of the Alphabetical Contact Listing report displays the contacts you enter prior to printing the report.

3. To print the report, click the toolbar's Print button.
4. Close the Print Preview window, and click the Restore button of the Switchboard form. Click the Preview the Weekly Call Summary Report button to open the Weekly Call Summary form. The default beginning and ending report dates are for the current system date and the preceding six days.
5. Edit the date in the Begin(ning) Call Date and the Ending Call Date text boxes to a range of dates for which data is available, if necessary. You receive an error message if there are no Call records within the specified date range.

6. Click the Weekly Call Summary form's Preview button to open the report in Print Preview mode (see Figure 2.25).

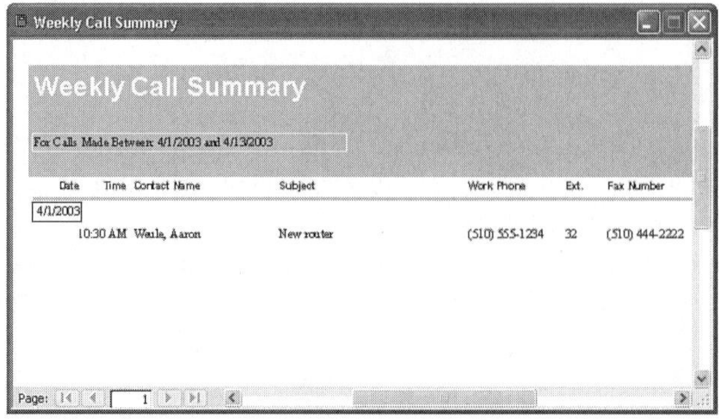

Figure 2.25 The Weekly Call Summary report displays a chronological list of sales calls.

7. Print a copy of the report, if you want, and then close the Print Preview window and click the Return to Main Switchboard button.

ACCESS MODULES

Access modules contain VBA subprocedures and functions that are accessible to VBA code contained in the class module of any form or report. You also can call VBA functions in modules by using the RunCode action of an Access macro. Access 2000 was the first version of Access to take advantage of the shared VBA editor used by other Office applications. The chapters in Part VII, "Programming and Converting Access Applications," focus on writing VBA subprocedures and functions to automate your Access applications.

To see and test a simple example of VBA code for a function, follow these steps:

1. Choose Window, 1 Contacts: Database (Access 2000 File Format) to open the Database window.

2. Click the Modules tab and then double-click the Global Code item in the list to open the Global Code module in the VBA code editor. The Global Code module contains a single function, `IsLoaded` (see Figure 2.26), which returns **`True`** if a specified form is open (loaded) or **`False`** if not.

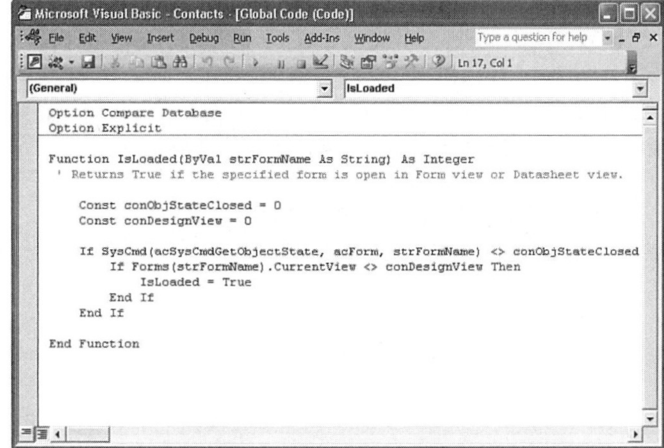

Figure 2.26
The Contact Management template includes VBA code for the `IsLoaded` user-defined VBA function.

3. To test the `IsLoaded` function, press Ctrl+G to open the Immediate window. Type **? IsLoaded("Switchboard")** in the bottom pane of the Immediate window. The VBA debugger returns `-1` (the numeric value of the VBA **`True`** intrinsic constant), indicating that the Switchboard form is open (see Figure 2.27).

4. Close the Immediate window, Alt+Tab over to Access, and minimize the Database window to return to the Main Switchboard.

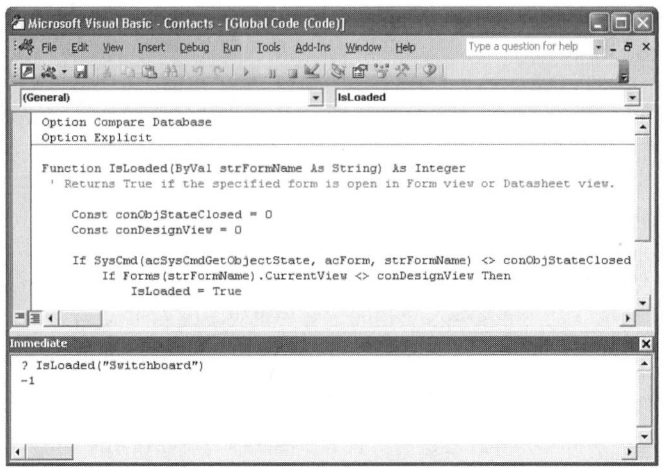

Figure 2.27
The value returned by executing the `IsLoaded` function from the Immediate window depends on the value of the `strFormName` argument you pass and the name of the currently active form.

USING THE SWITCHBOARD MANAGER

The Switchboard Manager lets you modify the navigation process for your application. The following steps delete the Forms Switchboard and substitute a button that opens the Contact Types form directly:

1. Click the Change Switchboard Items button of the Main Switchboard to open the Switchboard Manager dialog.
2. Select the Forms Switchboard item in the Switchboard Pages list (see Figure 2.28) and click the Delete button. When the "Are you sure?" message appears, click Yes.

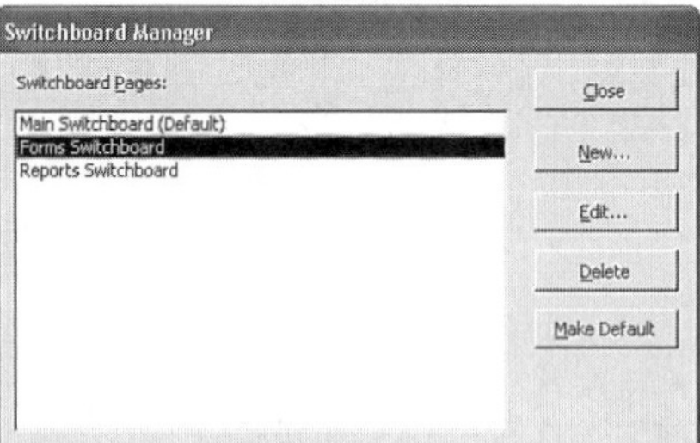

Figure 2.28
Select and delete the Forms Switchboard in the Switchboard Manager.

3. With the Main Switchboard (Default) item selected, click the Edit button to open the Edit Switchboard Page dialog.
4. Select the Enter/View Other Information item in the Items on This Switchboard list (see Figure 2.29) and click Edit to open the Edit Switchboard Item dialog (see Figure 2.30). The Switchboard text box is empty because you deleted the associated switchboard in step 2.

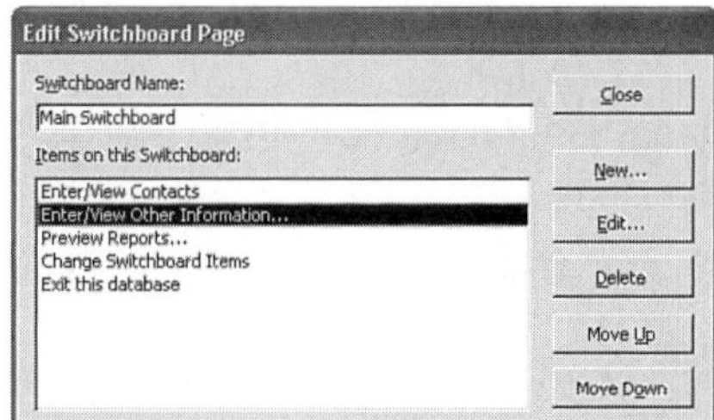

Figure 2.29
Select the Enter/View Other Information item to change the navigation process.

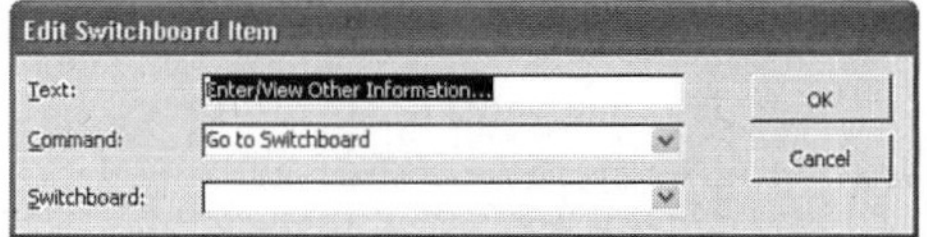

Figure 2.30
The Edit Switchboard Item opens with the default values.

5. Replace the existing content of the Text text box with Enter/View Contact Types, and select Open Form in Edit Mode from the Command drop-down list (see Figure 2.31).

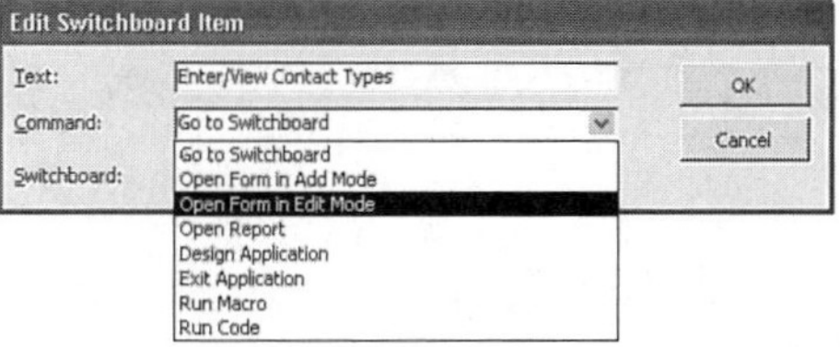

Figure 2.31
Change the entries for the Main Switchboard button to open a form directly.

6. Open the Form drop-down list (which replaces the Switchboard list) and select Contact Types (see Figure 2.32). Click OK to accept the changes and return to the Edit Switchboard Item dialog.

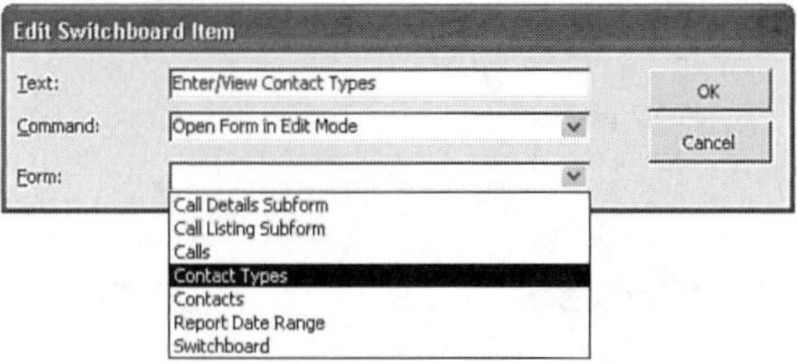

Figure 2.32
Select the form to edit in Edit mode.

7. The Edit Switchboard Item dialog shows the caption change you made in step 5. Click Close to return to the Switchboard Manager dialog and then click Close again to return to the Main Switchboard form. The second button reflects the caption change. Click the Edit/View Contact Types button to test your work.
8. Close the Contact Types form to return to the Main Switchboard.

You can import a Switchboard form and Switchboard Items table created by the Database Wizard into Access applications you create from scratch and then use the Switchboard Manager to modify the original design to suit your navigational needs. Starting with a pre-built switchboard saves a substantial amount of design work and VBA code writing.

→ To import a Switchboard form or other database objects, **see** "Linking and Importing External ISAM Tables," **p. 272**.

2

EXPLORING FORM DESIGN VIEW AND VBA CLASS MODULES

Designing forms and writing VBA code are advanced Access topics, but you can preview the topics covered by later chapters by following these steps:

1. With the Main Switchboard active, click the Design view button at the extreme left of the toolbar to open the Main Switchboard in Design view (see Figure 2.33). The Toolbox, which you use to add controls (text boxes, buttons, and the like) to forms, appears to the left of the Form Design window. If the Toolbox isn't open, click the Toolbox button on the Form Design toolbar.

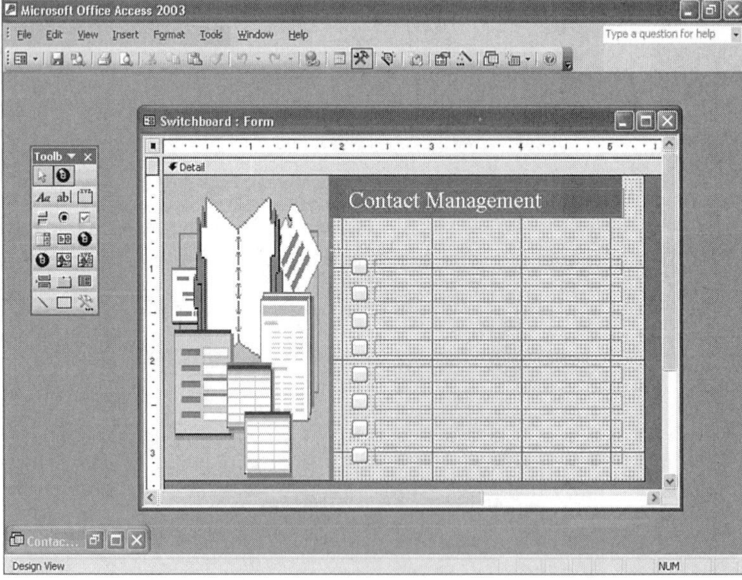

Figure 2.33 Open the Switchboard form in Design view.

2. Press Ctrl+R to select the entire form and then click the toolbar's Properties button to open the Properties window. By default, the Properties window displays all the properties of the selected object—in this case, the form.
3. Click the Data tab to display only the data-related properties of the form (see Figure 2.34). The most important property is the Record Source, which specifies the

Switchboard Items table as the table bound to the form. The Filter property specifies that the form obtains its data from the first record of the Switchboard Items table.

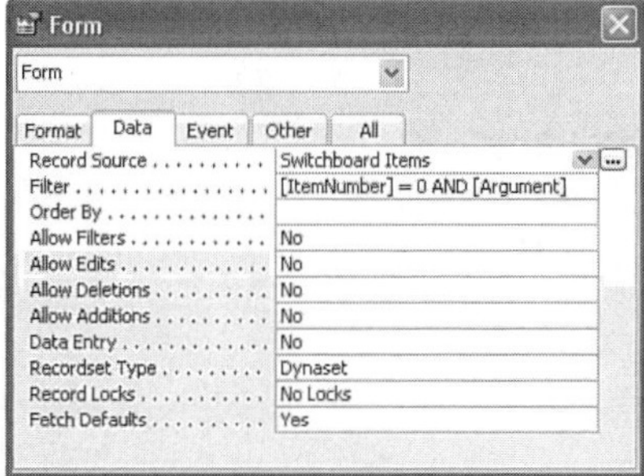

Figure 2.34
The Data page of the Form properties sheet for the Switchboard form displays data-related property values.

4. Click to select the top button (under the C of Contact Management in the Design view of the form). The Properties window displays the properties of Command Button: Option1.
5. Click the Event tab to display the Event properties of Option1 (see Figure 2.35). The =HandleButtonClick(1) value of the On Click event executes the `HandleButtonClick` VBA function when you click the button.

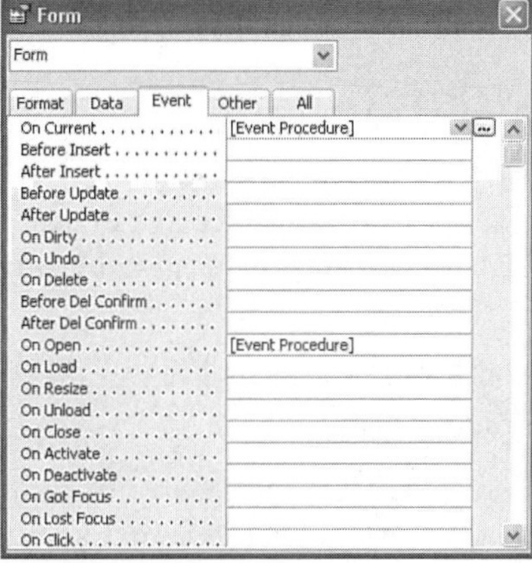

Figure 2.35
The Event page displays a list of the events that Access forms can fire.

6. Click the Code button on the toolbar to display the Contacts—Form_Switchboard (Code) window of the VBA editor. Page down until you see **`Private Function`** `HandleButtonClick(intBtn` **`As Integer`**`)`, as shown in Figure 2.36. The Option1 command button calls this function to handle the On Click event. The (1) suffix of the event value is passed to the function as the value of the `intBtn` argument. Scroll through the code until you reach the **`End Function`** statement, which terminates the `HandleButtonClick` function.

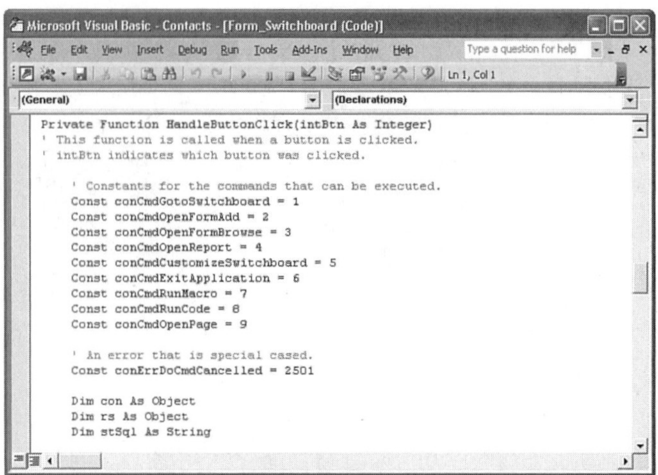

Figure 2.36
The VBA code editor displays the start of the `HandleButtonClick` event-handling function selected in Figure 2.35.

7. Close the VBA editor or press Alt+Tab to return to the Switchboard form and then click the Form view button to return the Switchboard form to its original state. (You might also need to close the Properties window.)

Downloading Templates from the Microsoft Office Update Site

Microsoft's Office Tools on the Web site (`http://office.microsoft.com`) offers a collection of Access 2000 databases (.mdb files) disguised as templates. Most of the templates duplicate the functions of the .mdz template files provided with Access 2003 but have a different main switchboard design. Unlike the built-in Access 2003 templates, the Office Update databases include sample data.

To view the current list of Access 2003 templates and give one of the templates a test run, close any open database and follow these steps:

1. In the New File task pane page, type **Access** in the Search Office Online text box and click Go to display a list of available templates in the Search Result page.
2. Click one of the template names, such as Customer Orders Database to open a Template Preview dialog (see Figure 2.37).
3. Click the Download button to retrieve the template file and open its Main Switchboard (see Figure 2.38).
4. Click the Add or Delete a Customer button to open the form of the same name (see Figure 2.39). The Customers table has four sample records.

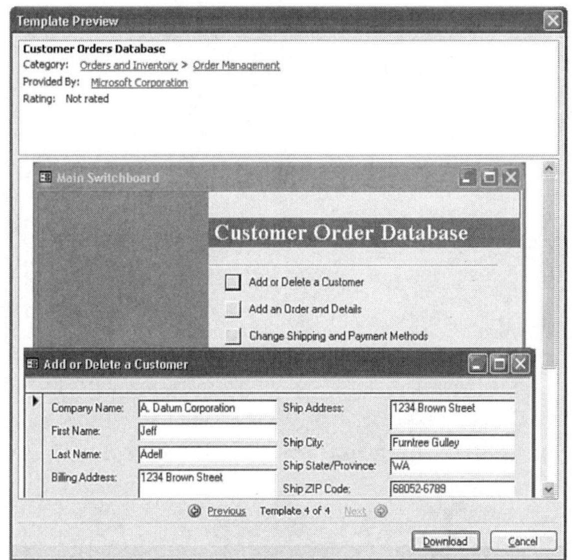

Figure 2.37
Each online template for Access 2003 has a Preview dialog that lets you view all available templates and download the one you want.

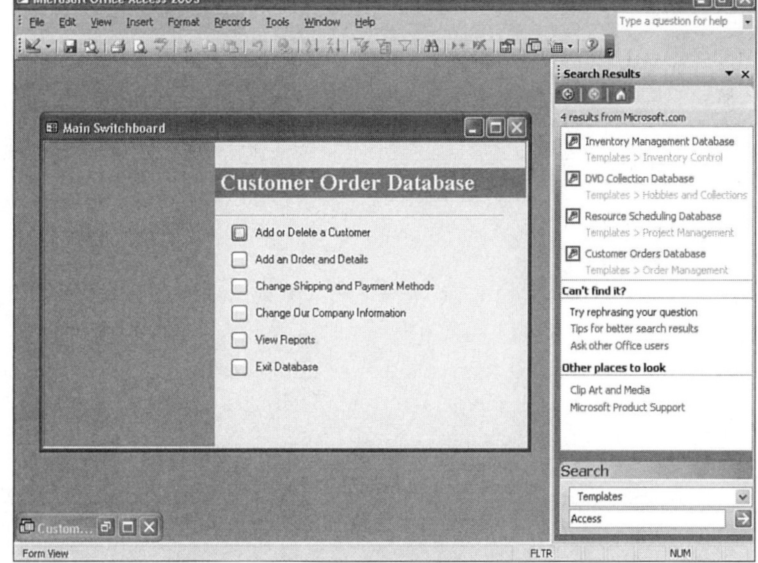

Figure 2.38
The Customer Orders Database template installs a database that resembles the sample Northwind Traders (Northwind.mdb) database and a switchboard with several more options than the Contact Management template.

Add or Delete a Customer

Company Name: A. Datum Corporation
First Name: Jeff
Last Name: Adell
Billing Address: 1234 Brown Street
City: Furntree
State/Province: WA
ZIP Code: 68052-6789
Web site: http://www.adatum.com/
Phone Number: (425) 555-1234
Fax Number: (425) 555-5678
Ship Address: 1234 Brown Street
Ship City: Furntree Gulley
Ship State/Province: WA
Ship ZIP Code: 68052-6789
Phone Number: (425) 555-1234
Delete
Close
Record: 1 of 4

Figure 2.39 The Add or Delete a Customer form has a Web Site field of the Hyperlink data type. All four links point to `http://www.microsoft.com`, not sample Web pages.

5. Close the Add or Delete a Customer form and open the Add Order and Order Details form, which consists of a main form and Order Details subform (see Figure 2.40).

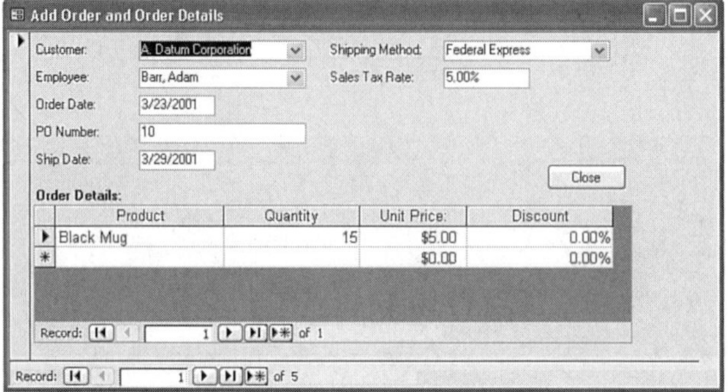

Figure 2.40 The Add Order and Order Details form lets you edit existing orders or add a new order and the order's line items.

SAVING A FORM AS A DATA ACCESS PAGE

Access 2003's data access pages (DAP) feature underwent a major facelift in its second Access 2002 incarnation. One of the most useful additions to DAP is the capability to save a conventional Access form as a Web page. There are serious limitations to the design of forms that you can convert automatically to DAP. Some of the restrictions are due to the limited repertoire of HTML control objects; others relate to problems with forms that depend on a value in another form to supply data. The advantages of DAP as a means of quickly deploying a simple multiuser Jet application on your intranet often outweigh the form design limitations.

→ For a list of the most important limitations in form design for DAP, **see** "Understanding the Limitations of the DAP Conversion Process," **p. 1066**.

Simple forms, such as the Contacts form of Contacts.mdb, convert to DAP satisfactorily, but even they usually require a few design tweaks to optimize their design for the Web. To give Access 2003's Save as DAP function a test run with the Contacts form, follow these steps:

1. Open Contacts.mdb, and click the Enter/View Contacts button of the Main Switchboard to open the Contacts form.
2. Choose File, Save As to open the Save As dialog. Open the As list, and select Data Access Page (see Figure 2.41). Click OK to open the New Data Access Page dialog.

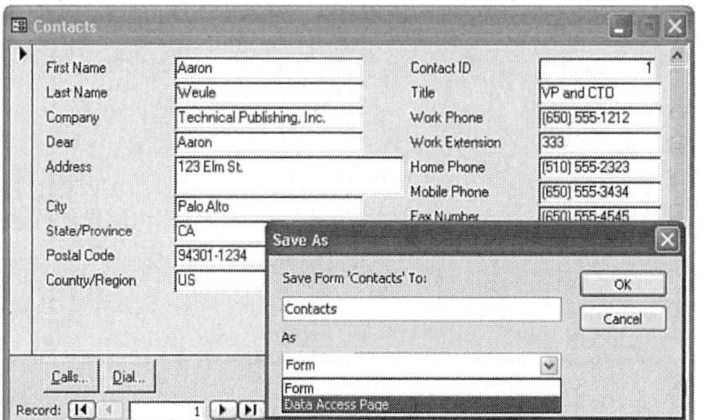

Figure 2.41
Access 2003's Save As dialog can save a table, query, form, or report as a Data Access Page.

3. Accept the default page name, Contacts.htm in the My Documents folder, and click OK to convert the form. When conversion completes, the Contacts page is behind the Contacts and Main Switchboard forms. Click the Contacts page to bring it to the foreground (see Figure 2.42).

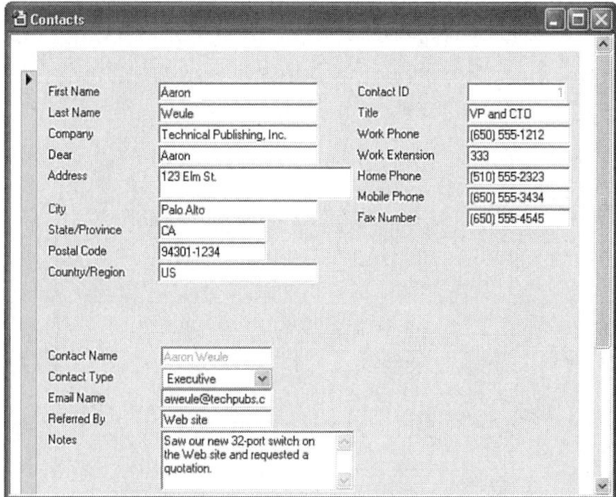

Figure 2.42
The top of the Contacts page appears here in DAP Page view. Data access pages don't support the Page Break control, so there's extra vertical spacing between the controls on the form's pages 1 and 2.

4. Scroll to the bottom of the page to expose the Data Source Control (DSC), a member of the Office Web Components (OWC) that DAP use for record navigation (see Figure 2.43).

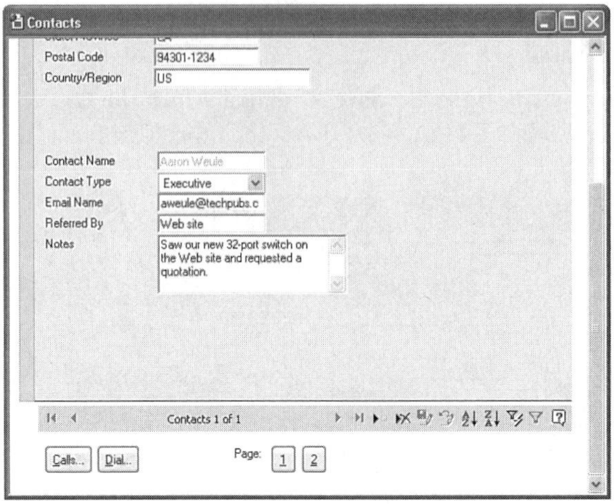

Figure 2.43
The bottom of the Contacts.htm page also has extra space between the page 2 controls and the DSC.

NOTE

> The four command buttons of the original Contacts form appear below the DSC but they don't function. DAP require VBScript or ECMAScript (JavaScript/JScript) event-handling code, but they don't support VBA code.

5. To open the Contacts.htm page in Internet Explorer (IE) 5+, right-click the page's title bar and choose Web Page Preview. Figure 2.44 shows the page after modifying its design to conserve browser space and eliminate nonfunctioning buttons. After you deploy the page to your Web server, multiple users with Office 2003 installed can simultaneously edit existing contacts, add new contact records, or delete obsolete contacts with this page.

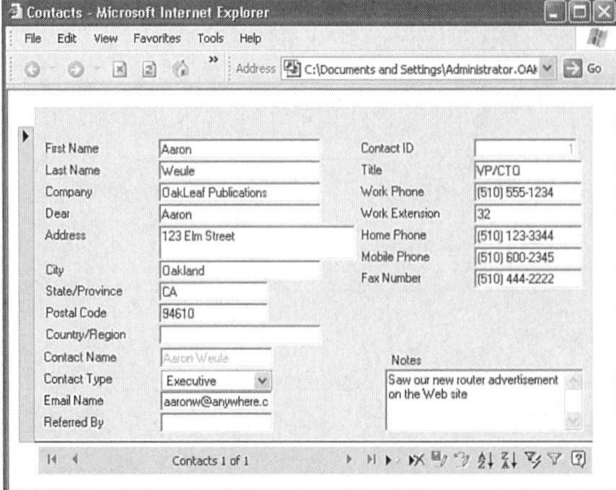

Figure 2.44
Choosing Web Page Preview displays the redesigned Contacts.htm page in IE 6+.

NOTE

To prevent conflicts with the preceding steps, the page shown in Figure 2.43 is saved as Contacts2.htm in the \Seua11\Chaptr02 folder of the accompanying CD-ROM. If you installed the sample files in the default location, Contacts2.htm is in your C:\Program Files\Seua11\Chaptr02 folder.

6. To view the XML, Dynamic HTML (DHTML), and Cascading Style Sheets (CSS) code needed to create typical DAP, close IE 5+, return to the Contacts.htm page, change to Design view, and click the Microsoft Script Editor button on the toolbar. Alternatively, right-click the title bar and choose Microsoft Script Editor. Figure 2.45 shows the Script Editor displaying a fraction of the script required to generate DAP.

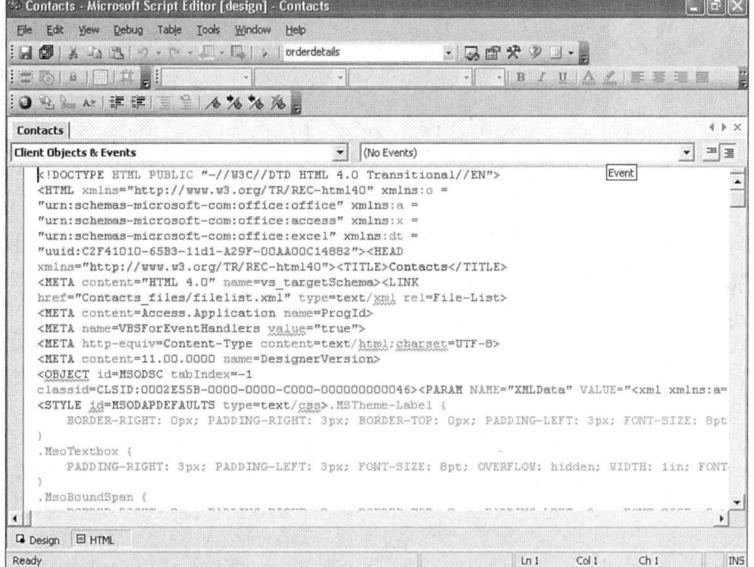

Figure 2.45 The Microsoft Script Editor for DAP corresponds to the Office VBA editor for VBA code in Access modules.

7. Scroll to the bottom of the window to view the nonfunctional VBA code that the Save as DAP process adds to the page for reference. Close the editor to return to Access, and return Contacts to Page view.

It's clear from a cursory inspection of the code shown in Figure 2.45 that writing VBScript to handle page- and control-level events isn't for the faint of heart. Fortunately, VBScript is a subset of VBA; if you gain a solid foundation in writing VBA functions and procedures, adapting to VBScript doesn't require a major effort.

In the Real World—Putting What You've Learned in Perspective

If you're new to Access, many terms used in this chapter might sound like ancient Aramaic. The objective was to give you an overview of some of the most important objects that make up an Access application, the relationships between these objects, and how you assemble the objects you create into self-contained, easily navigable applications. Using the Database Wizard helps you quickly understand the components and comprehend the behavior of a completed Access application. If you're interested in designing an Access inventory management application, for example, use the Inventory Control template to create an elementary sample application. You're likely to find that one of the Database Wizard or downloaded templates bears some resemblance to your intended application. Most Access 2003 templates that appear in the task pane's Search Results page have sample data, which makes it easier to determine if you can use the design as a starting point for the application you intend to create.

If you didn't perform the step-by-step tutorial to create the sample application and Web page of this chapter, not to worry. There's a copy of the Contacts.mdb database and Contacts2.htm in the \Seua11\Chaptr02 folder of the accompanying CD-ROM. Sample databases for most of the chapters are included in corresponding \Seua11\Chaptr## folders.

Data access pages were Access's initial approach to browser-based collaboration on private intranets and the public Internet. You can use Microsoft Office InfoPath 2003 to display and edit data in Access's Jet or MSDE databases. Access 2003's new capability to export tables and queries or link to Windows SharePoint Services (WSS) lists is an alternative database collaboration method. WSS runs only under Windows Server 2003, which is an initial impediment to widespread SharePoint deployment. Unless your organization is an early WSS adopter, DAP is your best bet for creating simple browser-based front ends to Access 2003 and SQL Server 2000 databases. Chapter 24, "Designing and Deploying Data Access Pages," and Chapter 25, "Converting Access Objects to Data Access Pages," show you how to take best advantage of DAP, and Chapter 26, "Integrating with InfoPath and SharePoint Services," describes how to get the most out of InfoPath and WSS with Access 2003 data sources.

The remainder of this book covers each category of Access objects in detail, beginning with Table and Query objects and then progressing to Form and Report objects. By the time you get about halfway through this book, you gain the experience necessary to design your own versions of these objects. The last half of this book deals with advanced topics, such as exporting Access forms and reports to XML-based Web pages, using InfoPath to edit tables of Access databases, generating SharePoint lists from tables and queries, creating data access pages with Spreadsheet, PivotTable, and PivotChart controls, and writing professional-quality VBA code.

CHAPTER 3

Navigating the Access User Interface

In this chapter

UNDERSTANDING ACCESS FUNCTIONS AND MODES

Access, unlike word-processing and spreadsheet applications, is a truly multifunctional program. Although word-processing applications, for example, have many sophisticated capabilities, their basic purpose is to support text entry, page layout, and formatted printing. The primary functions and supporting features of all word-processing applications are directed to these ends. You perform all word-processing operations with views that represent a sheet of paper. Most spreadsheet applications use the row-column metaphor for all their functions. In contrast, Access consists of a multitude of related tools for generating, organizing, segregating, displaying, printing, and publishing data. The following sections describe Access's basic functions and operating modes.

DEFINING ACCESS FUNCTIONS

To qualify as a full-fledged relational database management system (RDBMS), an application must perform the following four basic but distinct functions, each with its own presentation to the user:

- *Data organization* involves creating and manipulating tables that contain data in conventional tabular (row-column or spreadsheet) format, called *Datasheet view* by Access.
- *Table joining and data extraction* uses queries to connect multiple tables by data relationships and create virtual (temporary) tables, called *Recordsets*, stored in your computer's RAM or temporary disk files. Expressions are used to calculate values from data (for example, you can calculate an extended amount by multiplying unit price and quantity) and to display the calculated values as though they were a field in one of the tables.
- *Data entry and editing* require design and implementation of data viewing, entry, and editing forms as an alternative to tabular presentation. A form lets you, rather than the application, control how the data is presented. Most users find forms much easier to use for data entry than tabular format, especially when many fields are involved.
- *Data presentation* requires the creation of reports that you can view, print, or publish on the Internet or an intranet (the last step in the process). Charts and graphs summarize the data for those officials who take the "broad brush" approach.

The basic functions of Access are organized into the application structure shown in Figure 3.1. If you're creating a new database, you use the basic functions of Access in the top-down sequence shown in Figure 3.1. You choose a function by clicking a button in the Datasheet window, except for security and some printing operations, which are menu choices.

NOTE

Figure 3.1 shows queries as the sole data source for forms, pages, and reports. You can base forms, pages, and reports on data from tables, but it's more common to use a query as the data source. In the case of Access Data Pages (ADP), which substitute SQL Server for Jet tables, you ordinarily use views as the data source. An SQL Server view is the direct counterpart of a Jet `SELECT` query. You also can use SQL Server in-line functions and stored procedures as data sources.

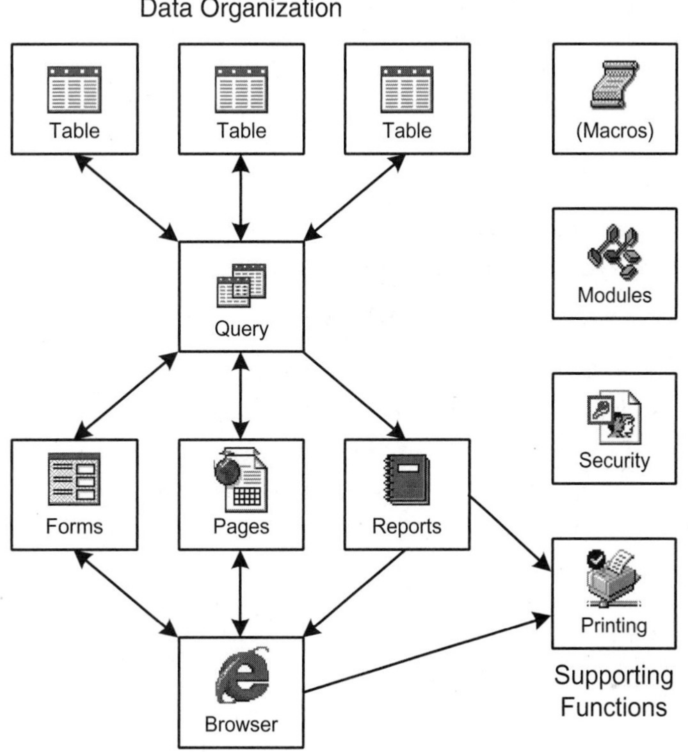

Figure 3.1
This diagram shows the relationship of the basic and supporting functions of Access. Reports have a one-way relationship with other functions, because you can't use a report to modify data.

Five supporting functions apply to all the basic functions of Access:

- *Macros* are sequences of actions that automate repetitive database operations. In Access 97 and earlier versions, macros were a common means of automating database operations. In later versions, macros are supported for backward compatibility only. You use Visual Basic for Applications (VBA) to automate Access 2003 database actions.
- *Modules* are containers for functions and procedures written in the VBA programming language. You use VBA functions to make calculations that are more complex than those that can be expressed easily by a series of conventional mathematical symbols. You run VBA subprocedures by attaching the subprocedure to particular events, such as clicking a command button with the mouse when a form or page is the active object.
- *Security* consists of functions available as menu choices and through VBA subprocedures. In a multiuser environment, where other people use your database application, you can grant access to user groups and individuals, and you can restrict their ability to view or modify objects in the database.
- *Printing* lets you print virtually anything you can view in Access's run mode. Printing is the most common form of distributing reports, but you also can export reports to Web pages or to Snapshot (.snp) files.

- *Publishing* features facilitate distribution of information over corporate intranets and the public Internet as World Wide Web pages. Access 2000 added data access pages (DAP) that let you build applications for displaying and updating data in pages that take advantage of Dynamic HTML (DHTML) and Extensible Markup Language (XML). You also can publish tables, query result sets, forms, and reports by taking advantage of Access 2003's upgraded Save As XML feature.

The terms "open" and "close" have the same basic usage in Access as in other Windows applications but usually involve more than one basic function:

- Opening a database makes its content available to the application through the Database window. You can open only one database at a time in the Access user interface, but you can link tables from Access, client/server, and other desktop databases. You also can open multiple databases with VBA code.

- Opening a table displays a Datasheet view of its contents.

- Opening a SELECT query, the most common query type, opens one or more tables and displays the data specified by the query in Datasheet view. You can change data in the tables associated with the query if the query's Recordset is updatable.

- Opening a form, page, or report automatically opens the table or query that's associated with it. Forms, pages, and reports usually are associated with (called *bound to*) queries rather than to tables.
- Closing a query closes the associated tables.
- Closing a form, page, or report closes the associated query and its tables.

Defining Access Operating Modes

Access has three basic operating modes:

- *Startup* mode lets you compress, convert, encrypt, decrypt, and repair a database by choosing commands from the Tools menu's Database Utilities and Security submenus before opening a database. Most of these commands, some of which are discussed at the end of this chapter, are available only when you don't have a database open. Access lets you convert an open database to another Access version, compact and repair an open database, or backup an open database. The backup feature is new in Access 2003.
- *Design* mode lets you create and modify the structure of tables and queries, develop forms or pages to display and edit your data, and format reports for printing. Access calls design mode Design view.
- *Run* mode displays your table, form, and report designs in individual document windows (the default mode). Run mode is Datasheet view for tables and queries, *Form view* for forms, *Page view* for data access pages (DAP), and *Print Preview* for reports.

You can select design or run mode by choosing command buttons in the Datasheet window, buttons on the toolbar, or commands from the View menu.

OPENING THE NORTHWIND.MDB SAMPLE DATABASE

The Northwind Traders sample database (Northwind.mdb) is the primary Access application used in the examples of this book. The default location for Access databases and other application-related files, such .htm files for Data Access Pages, is the My Documents folder. The \Program Files\Microsoft Office\Office11\Samples folder holds the Access sample files.

To open Northwind.mdb and display its Database window, do the following:

1. Launch Access, if it isn't running.
2. Choose Help, Sample Databases, Northwind Sample Database to open Northwind.mdb and display its splash screen form (see Figure 3.2).

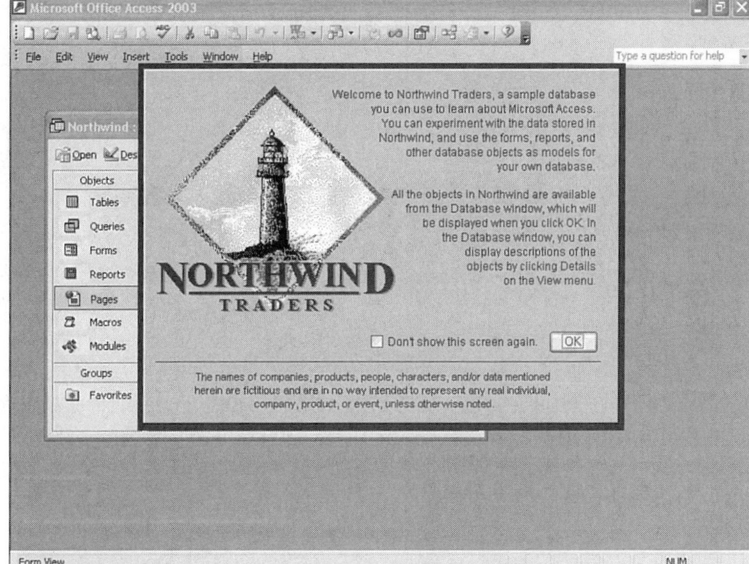

Figure 3.2
When you open Northwind.mdb, code in the Startup module displays the Startup form, unless you mark the Don't Show This Screen Again check box.

3. Mark the Don't Show This Screen Again check box, and click OK to open the Main Switchboard form (see Figure 3.3).
4. Optionally, click the buttons in the View Products and Other Information frame to open four of the sample forms, and try printing one of the sales reports.
5. Close the Main Switchboard form to give the focus to the Database window.

After you open Northwind.mdb for the first time, an entry for the database appears in the most-recently used (MRU) list under the Open heading of the Getting Started task pane. It's quicker to open Northwind.mdb or any other recently used databases from the task pane. If the task pane isn't open, press Ctrl+F1 or choose View, Task Pane to display it.

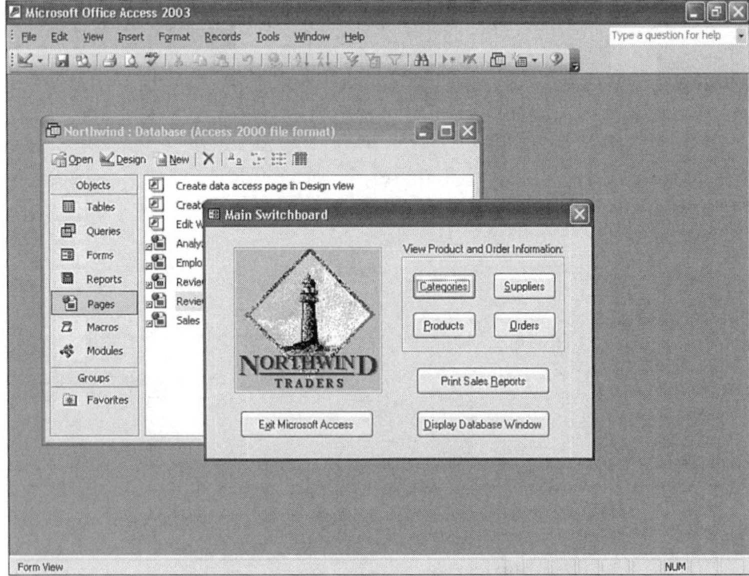

Figure 3.3
The Main Switchboard form lets you view four sample forms or print three types of sales reports.

TIP

> To prevent the Main Switchboard form from appearing each time you open Northwind.mdb, choose Tools, Startup to open the Startup Dialog. Open the Display Form/Page list, select (None), and click OK to close the dialog.

Understanding Access's Table Display

You're probably familiar with the terms for many of the components that comprise the basic window in which all conventional Windows applications run. The presentation of Access windows varies with each basic function that Access performs. Because Part I, "Getting Acquainted with Access 2003," of this book deals almost exclusively with tables, the examples that follow use Table Datasheet view. Figure 3.4 shows Access 2003's display for run-mode operations with tables; Table 3.1 describes the window's Access-related components.

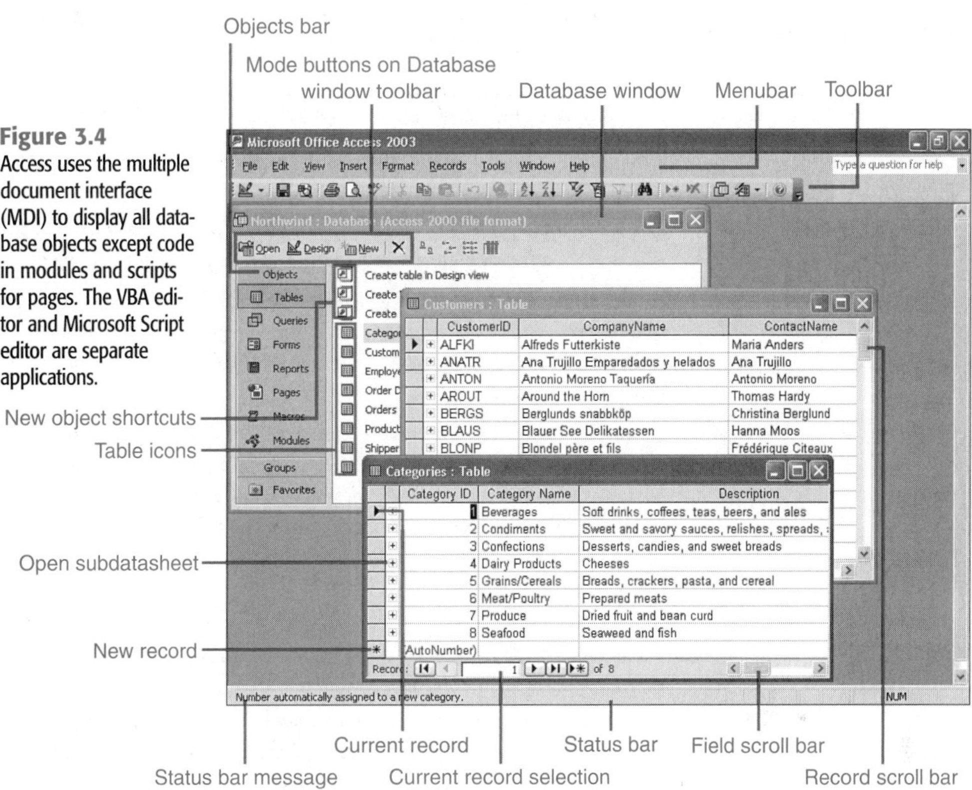

Figure 3.4
Access uses the multiple document interface (MDI) to display all database objects except code in modules and scripts for pages. The VBA editor and Microsoft Script editor are separate applications.

TABLE 3.1 COMPONENTS OF THE ACCESS DISPLAY FOR TABLES

Term	Description
Menu bar	A bar containing Access main menu choices. The specific menu bar choices and the commands in the menus change depending on the object you select and Access's mode. Menu bars and toolbars collectively are called *command bars*.
Toolbar	A bar containing command buttons that duplicate the more commonly used menu choices. The actual number and type of toolbar buttons depend on which basic function of Access you're using.
Database window	The window that selects the active document window's current function. From the database components displayed in the Database window, you select the component (such as a particular table) to display in the documents pane.
Database window toolbar	The toolbar that lets you open or design the currently selected database object, create a new object, delete an object, and control how icons display in the Database window.

continues

TABLE 3.1 CONTINUED

Term	Description
Objects bar	An Outlook-styled bar with shortcuts to lists of database objects.
Mode buttons	Two buttons that determine the operating mode of Access. Open places Access in run mode. Design puts Access in design mode, where you can create or edit tables.
New object	A drop-down list of eight shortcuts to create a new database object.
Current record buttons	A button that indicates a single selected record in the table. When you're editing the current record, the button icon displays a pencil rather than a triangular arrow. The Current Record button also is called the *record selector*.
Record navigation buttons	Buttons that position the record selector to the first, next, previous, and last record number in the table and show the number of the currently selected record. If the table has a key field, the record number reflects the sequence of records in the primary key's sorting order; if there's no primary key in the table, the record number corresponds to the order in which records were physically added to the table.
New record	A button with an asterisk that indicates the location of the next record to be added to a table. Typing data in the new record appends the record to the table and creates another new record. This book calls the new record the *tentative append record*, because the record isn't added until you enter data.
Field scroll bar	The scroll bar that lets you view table fields that are outside the bounds of the document window. Record scroll bars provide access to records located outside the document window.
Open subdatasheet	A click on the plus sign in the square box opens subdatasheet(s) for each record if the table has subdatasheets. Another name for this button is the subdatasheet expand indicator.
Status bar	A bar, located at the bottom of the application window, that displays prompts and indicators, such as the status of the Num Lock key.

THE TOOLBARS IN TABLE DATASHEET VIEW

The buttons that appear in Access's toolbar, and the number of toolbars displayed, change according to the function that Access is currently performing. When you're working with tables in run mode, Access 2000 displays the Table Datasheet and the Formatting (Datasheet) toolbars (see Figures 3.5 and 3.6 in the following sections). The next two sections describe the toolbars that appear in table run mode (Datasheet view). Click the Tables shortcut on the Database window and double click one of the table shortcuts—such as Customers—to follow the text in the next few sections.

NOTE

This chapter concentrates on the toolbars that apply to Table and Query Datasheet and Table Design views. Chapter 14, "Creating and Using Access Forms," describes the toolbars for Form and Form Design views. Chapter 16, "Working with Simple Reports and Mailing Labels," explains the elements of the Report Design and Print Preview toolbars.

THE TABLE DATASHEET TOOLBAR

The Table Datasheet toolbar appears whenever you open an Access table in Datasheet view. Figure 3.5 shows the Table Datasheet toolbar, and Table 3.2 describes the buttons that appear on the toolbar, except those buttons that are common to all Office 2003 applications.

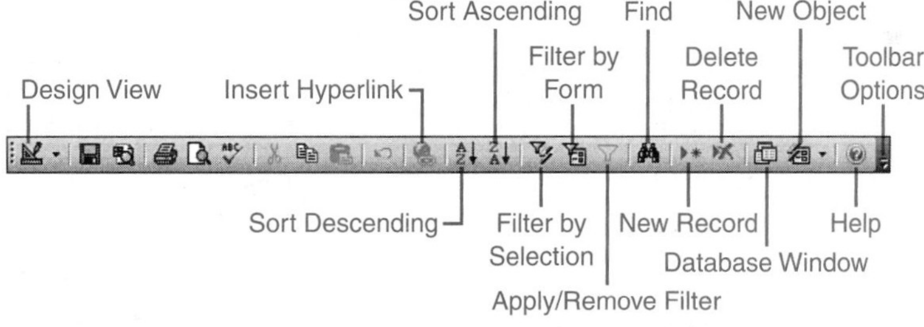

Figure 3.5 Access's Table Datasheet toolbar has the buttons shown here when you open a table in Datasheet view.

NOTE

Toolbar buttons provide shortcuts to traditional selection methods, such as choosing menu commands or selecting command or option buttons in a particular sequence. The Menu Sequence columns of Tables 3.2 and 3.3 list how you can duplicate the effect of clicking a toolbar button by using the menus or the command buttons in the Database window.

TABLE 3.2 APPEARANCE AND FUNCTIONS OF ACCESS-SPECIFIC BUTTONS AND OTHER ELEMENTS OF THE TABLE DATASHEET TOOLBAR

Icon	Toolbar Button	Menu Sequence	Function
	Design View	View, Design View	Changes the table display to design mode, in which you specify the properties of each field of the table.
	Insert Hyperlink	Insert, Hyperlink	Opens the Insert Hyperlink dialog, which lets you add a URL or UNC address to a Hyperlink field in a table.
	Sort Ascending	Records, Sort, Sort Ascending	Sorts the records in ascending order, based on the current field.

continues

TABLE 3.2 CONTINUED

Icon	Toolbar Button	Menu Sequence	Function
	Sort Descending	Records, Sort, Sort Descending	Sorts the records in descending order, based on the current field.
	Filter by Selection	Records, Filter, Filter by Selection	Filters records based on the selected text in a field.
	Filter by Form	Records, Filter, Filter by Form	Lets you type criteria in a datasheet to establish how records are filtered.
	Apply/Remove Filter/Sort	Records, Apply/Remove Filter/Sort	Applies or removes a filter.
	Find	Edit, Find	Displays the Find dialog to locate records with specific characters in a single field or all fields.
	New Record	Edit, Go To, New Record	Selects the tentative append record.
	Delete Record	Edit, Delete	Deletes the active (selected) record.
	Database window	Window, 1	Displays the Database window.
	New Object	Insert, *ObjectType*	Displays a drop-down list from which you choose the type of new object that you want to create: tables, forms, reports, pages, queries, macros, modules or class modules. The first object type in the list is your most recent selection.
	Help	F1	Activates the Access online HTML help system.
	Toolbar Options	View, Toolbars, Customize	Displays a drop-down list from which you can add or remove buttons from the toolbar.

3

THE DATASHEET FORMATTING TOOLBAR

In addition to the Table Datasheet toolbar, you can display the Datasheet Formatting toolbar whenever you open a table in Datasheet view. Choose View, Toolbars, Formatting (Datasheet) to add the toolbar. The buttons in the datasheet formatting toolbar provide shortcuts to various text-formatting commands. In Datasheet view, the text-formatting commands apply to the entire table; you can't format individual cells in Datasheet view. Figure 3.6 shows the Datasheet Formatting toolbar, and Table 3.3 summarizes the action of each button on the toolbar.

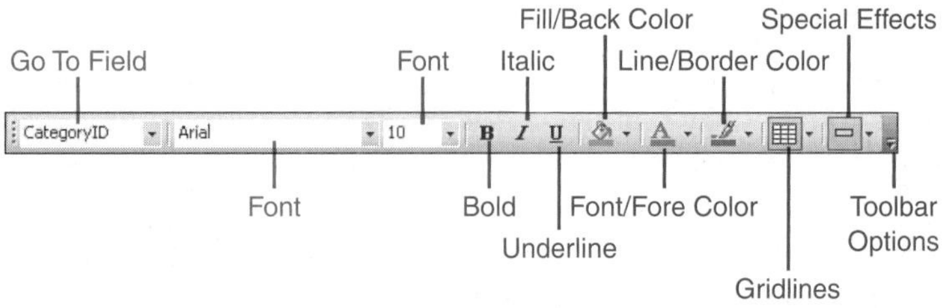

Figure 3.6
Settings you apply from the Datasheet Formatting toolbar apply to all fields and records of the table. Unlike Excel worksheets, you can't format individual cells, rows, or columns.

TABLE 3.3 APPEARANCE AND FUNCTIONS OF BUTTONS AND OTHER ELEMENTS OF THE DATASHEET FORMATTING TOOLBAR

Icon	Toolbar Button	Menu Sequence	Function
CategoryID	Go To Field		Displays a drop-down list from which you can jump quickly to any field in the table
Arial	Font	Format, Font	Lets you select the font (typeface) for text in a table
10	Font Size	Format, Font	Lets you select the size of the text in a table
B	Bold	Format, Font	Turns bold text formatting on and off for the text in a table
I	Italic	Format, Font	Turns italic text formatting on and off for the text in a table
U	Underline	Format, Font	Turns underlining on and off for the text in a table
	Fill/Back Color	Format, Datasheet	Displays a palette of colors from which to choose the background color for the table's data cells
A	Font/Fore Color	Format, Font	Displays a palette of colors from which to choose the color of the text in the table
	Line/Border	Format, Datasheet	Displays a color palette from which to choose the color of the gridlines that surround rows and columns in the table
	Gridlines	Format, Datasheet	Displays four buttons that let you choose which gridlines are shown: horizontal and vertical, vertical only, horizontal only, or none
	Special Effects	Format, Datasheet	Displays three buttons that let you select the cell display style: flat, raised, or sunken

Toolbar Customization

Access uses the resizable, customizable, floating toolbars that have become standard in Microsoft productivity applications such as Excel and Word. In Office 2000 and later, menu bars and toolbars have been combined into a single object, called a *command bar*, and share many features. The primary characteristic that distinguishes a menu bar from a toolbar in Access 2003 (and other Office 2003 applications) is that every application has at least one menu bar, and the menu bar can't be hidden. In all other respects, menu bars and toolbars are the same.

The Toolbars command on the View menu lets you select which toolbars are currently visible. The Toolbars submenu lists those toolbars pertinent to Access's current operating mode. Figure 3.7 shows the Toolbars submenu for Table Datasheet view. A mark at the left of a menu choice indicates that specific toolbar is now displayed. To display or hide a toolbar, click its name in the submenu.

3

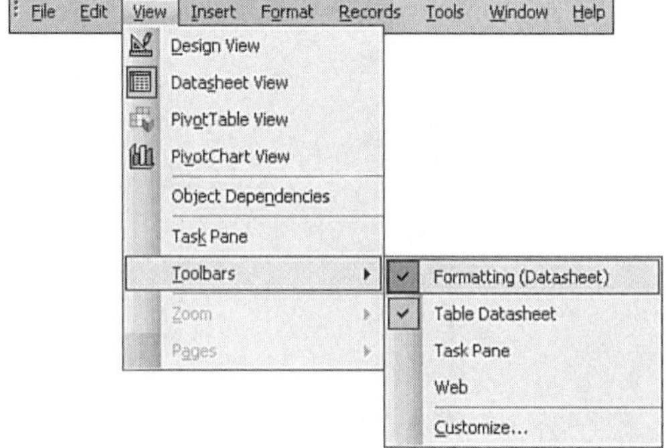

Figure 3.7
Choosing View, Toolbars lets you display or hide toolbars quickly.

The Customize choice on the Toolbars submenu opens the Customize dialog (see Figure 3.8), which lets you display as many toolbars as you want or hide toolbars that Access would otherwise display automatically. To display a toolbar, click the Toolbars tab to display the Toolbars page (if necessary) and then click the box to the left of the toolbar name so that the check box is marked. To hide a toolbar, click the box again to clear it.

TIP

When an Access toolbar is in docked position, it has a fixed width, anchored at its left edge. If you reduce the width of Access's application window by dragging either vertical border inward, the buttons at the docked toolbar's extreme right begin to disappear beyond the application window's right edge. Operating Access in a maximized window with docked toolbars is usually best because you can then easily access all toolbar buttons when you use the default inline horizontal toolbar.

Figure 3.8
The Toolbars page of the Customize dialog lets you add or remove toolbars, but not the main menu bar.

You also can use the Customize dialog to change the viewing options for toolbars. The Options page let you select various toolbar viewing options (see Figure 3.9). If you're using XGA 1,024×768 or higher screen resolution on a small monitor, you might want to mark the Large Icons check box to cause the toolbar button icons to approximately double in size, making them easier to discern and easier to click. The Show ScreenTips on Toolbars check box governs whether Access displays ScreenTips (formerly known as ToolTips), that is, hints on the mouse pointer for toolbar buttons. The Show Shortcut Keys in ScreenTips check box determines whether Access displays the keyboard shortcut (if there is one) as part of the ScreenTip text.

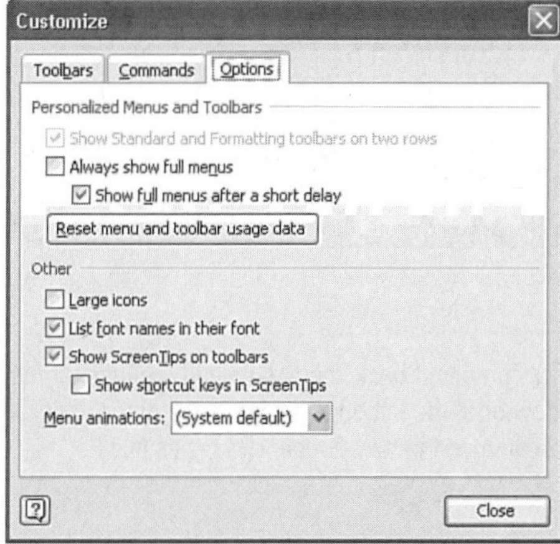

Figure 3.9
The Options page of the Customize dialog controls the Intellimenu, icon size, font display style, ScreenTips, and menu animations.

The List Font Names in Their Font check box, if checked, displays each font name as a sample of the font in lists of fonts. If you clear the check box, font lists use the standard font and display faster. The Always Show Full Menus check box, if cleared, displays only the menu choices that you use on a regular basis, a feature Microsoft calls Intellimenus. The

Show Full Menus After a Short Delay check box governs whether the full Access menu is displayed after you hover your mouse on the menu. The Reset My Usage Data button resets menu, menu usage, and toolbar settings.

Finally, the Menu Animations drop-down list lets you select how Access draws menus onscreen. You might select None (for no special effects when drawing menus), Random (Access randomly chooses an animation effect each time you open a menu), Unfold (the menu unfolds like a fan), Slide (the menu opens like a roller-shade) or Fade as the technique for displaying Access's menus. The entertainment value of the Menu Animations feature is minimal, to be charitable.

In addition to displaying multiple toolbars, you can reshape or reposition the toolbars to suit your own taste. Click a blank area of the toolbar and hold down the left mouse button to drag the toolbar to a new location. The toolbar turns into a pop-up floating toolbar, similar to the toolbox that you use to add control objects to forms and reports. Pop-up toolbars always appear on top of any other windows open in your application.

Figure 3.10 shows three floating command bars: the Table Datasheet toolbar, the Formatting (Datasheet) toolbar, and the Menu Bar. Command bars in their fixed position are called docked command bars, whereas command bars in their pop-up window are referred to as floating command bars. Floating command bars display the Toolbar Options button as part of the title bar. After you change a command bar to a floating command bar (or dock it), Access displays the command bar in that location until you reposition it.

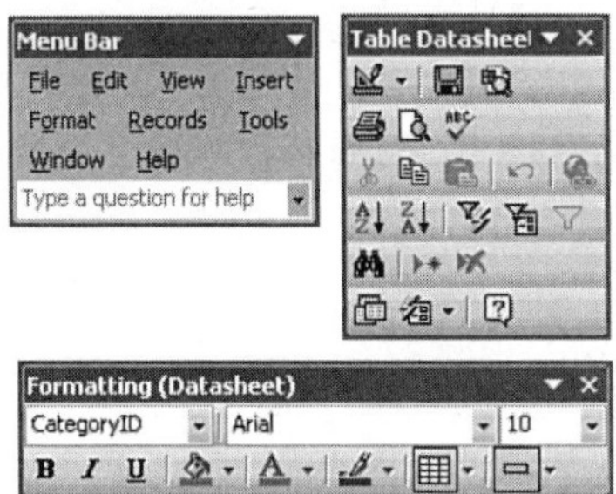

Figure 3.10
You can position command bars anywhere on the screen that suits you.

TIP

> You also can dock command bars (menu bars and toolbars) at the bottom of the Access application window or at the left edge or right edge of the application window. You can quickly redock a command bar by double-clicking its title bar.

Right-Click Shortcut Menus

Another feature that Access 2003 shares with other Microsoft applications, as well as with Windows 98 and Windows 2000/NT, is the shortcut menu that appears when you right-click an Access database object. Shortcut menus (also called pop-up or context menus) present choices that vary depending on the type of object that you click. Figure 3.11 shows the shortcut menu for a field of a table selected by clicking the field name header.

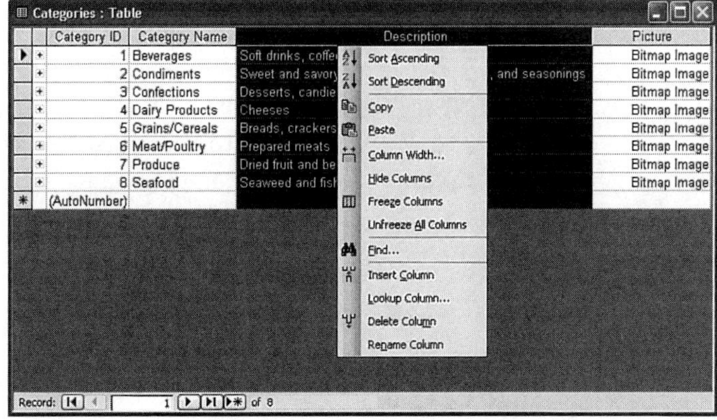

Figure 3.11 Context menus let you choose from a list of actions applicable to the object you right-click.

> **TIP**
>
> Context menus are useful and provide shortcuts to many common tasks. If you're not sure what you can do with an object onscreen, try right-clicking it to see what context menu commands are available.

Using the Function Keys

Access assigns specific purposes to all 12 function keys of the 101-key extended keyboard. Some keys, such as Shift+F4 (which you press to find the next occurrence of a match with the Find dialog), derive from other Microsoft applications—in this case, Word.

Global Function Keys

Windows, rather than Access, uses global function-key assignments, except for F11, Ctrl+F1, and Alt+F1, to perform identical functions in all Windows applications. Table 3.4 lists the global function-key assignments.

Table 3.4 Global Function-Key Assignments

Key	Function
F1	Displays context-sensitive help related to the present basic function and status of Access. If a context-sensitive help topic isn't available, F1 opens the Microsoft Access Help task pane page, which lets you search online help for a keyword or open its table of contents.

continues

TABLE 3.4 CONTINUED

Key	Function
Shift+F1	Adds a question mark to the mouse pointer when hovering over an element that has a description. Place the mouse pointer with the question mark over an object onscreen for which you want more information and then click.
Ctrl+F1	Toggles (alternates) visibility of the task pane in all Office 2003 members.
Ctrl+F4	Closes the active window.
Alt+F4	Exits Access or closes a dialog if one is open.
Ctrl+F6	Selects each open window in sequence as the active window.
F11	Selects the Database window as the active window.
F12	Opens the File Save As dialog.
Shift+F12	Saves your open database; the equivalent of the File menu's Save command.

NEW

3

FUNCTION-KEY ASSIGNMENTS FOR FIELDS, GRIDS, AND TEXT BOXES

Access assigns function-key combinations that aren't reserved for global operations to actions specific to the basic function that you're performing at the moment. Table 3.5 lists the function-key combinations that apply to fields, grids, and text boxes. (To present complete information, this table repeats some information that appears in the previous tables.)

→ For an extensive list of Access shortcut key assignments, **see** "Using Keyboard Operations for Entering and Editing Data," **p. 218**.

TABLE 3.5 FUNCTION KEYS FOR FIELDS, GRIDS, AND TEXT BOXES

Key	Function
F2	Toggles between displaying the caret for editing and selecting the entire field.
Shift+F2	Opens the Zoom box to make typing expressions and other text easier.
F4	Opens a drop-down combo list or list box.
Shift+F4	Finds the next occurrence of a match of the text typed in the Find or Replace dialog, if the dialog is closed.
F5	Moves the caret to the record-number box. Type the number of the record that you want to display.
F6	In Table Design view, cycles between upper- and lower parts of the window. In Form Design view, cycles through the header, body (detail section), and footer.
F7	Starts the spelling checker.

Key	Function
F8	Turns on extend mode. Press F8 again to extend the selection to a word, the entire field, the whole record, and then all records.
Shift+F8	Reverses the F8 selection process.
Ctrl+F	Opens the Find dialog.
Ctrl+H	Opens the Replace dialog.
Ctrl++ (plus sign)	Adds a new record to the database.
Shift+Enter	Saves changes to the active record in the database.
Esc	Undoes changes in the current record or field. By pressing Esc twice, you can undo changes in the current field and record. Also cancels extend mode.

3

SETTING DEFAULT OPTIONS

You can set about 100 options that establish the default settings for Access. (But you aren't likely to want to change default options until you're more familiar with Access 2003.) This book is a reference as well as a tutorial guide, and options are a basic element of Access's overall structure, so this section explains how to change these settings.

NOTE

The Options dialog discussed in this chapter corresponds to the options available using Jet databases and not the Microsoft SQL Server 2000 Desktop Engine (MSDE) used by Access data projects (ADP). See Chapter 20, "Exploring Access Data Projects and SQL Server 2000," for more information on ADP.

You set defaults by choosing Tools, Options to open the Options properties dialog (see Figure 3.12). The options you set on the View, General, Edit/Find, Keyboard, International, and Spelling pages apply to the system as a whole. The Datasheet and Tables/Queries options apply to tables and queries in Datasheet and Design views, respectively. Forms/Reports and Pages options apply to Design view only. Advanced options apply mainly to multiuser database performance.

NOTE

If you're familiar with early Access versions, you might notice the absence of the Module options page. Access 2003 uses the VBA Integrated Design Environment (IDE), so the Module options are found by choosing Tools, Options in the IDE. Using the IDE is one of the subjects of Chapter 27, "Learning Visual Basic for Applications."

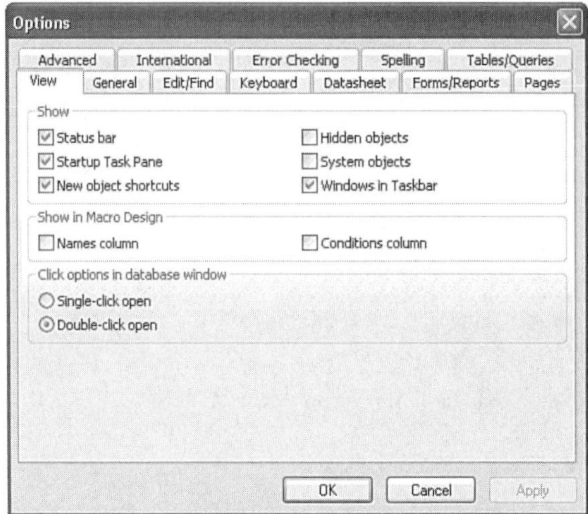

Figure 3.12
The View page of the Options properties dialog sets global option values that apply to all databases you open in Access 2003.

3

Most settings are option buttons and check boxes, although many other items require multiple-choice entries that you select from drop-down lists. In some cases, you must type a specific value from the keyboard. After you complete your changes, click OK to close the properties dialog to save your changes. If you decide not to implement your changes, click Cancel to exit without making any changes. The next few sections and their tables summarize options that affect Access as a whole and those options that affect viewing and printing data in Datasheet view.

Access 2003 uses the Windows Registry to store all default properties for displaying and printing the contents of tables, queries, forms, reports, and modules for each user of Access.

View Options

The View options, as described in Table 3.6, apply to all databases you open. The "Function" column describes the effect of marking a check box or selecting an option.

Table 3.6 View Options for the Access System

Option	Function
Show Group	
Status Bar	Displays the status bar at the bottom of the Access application window (marked by default)
Startup Task Pane	Displays the New File page of the task pane whenever you start Access (marked by default)
New Object Shortcuts	Displays shortcuts for the creation of new objects in the Database window (marked by default)
Hidden Objects	Displays hidden objects in the Database window

Option	Function
Show Group	
System Objects	Displays system objects in the Database window
Windows in Taskbar	Causes the Database window and each open window to display as an icon in the Windows Taskbar (marked by default)
Show in Macro Design Group	
Names Column	Displays the Names column in new macros
Conditions Column	Displays the Conditions column in new macros
Click Options in Database Window Group	
Single-click Open	Lets you open a database object with a single click instead of the conventional double-click
Double-click Open	Requires a double-click to open a database object (the default option)

GENERAL OPTIONS

General options also apply to Access as a whole (see Figure 3.13 and Table 3.7). The settings that you make on the General options page apply to any new objects that you create (tables, forms, and reports) but don't retroactively affect existing objects. For example, changing the print margins on the General page affects reports that you create subsequently, but not any existing reports. To change the print margins of existing objects, you must change each object's individual printing settings in Design view.

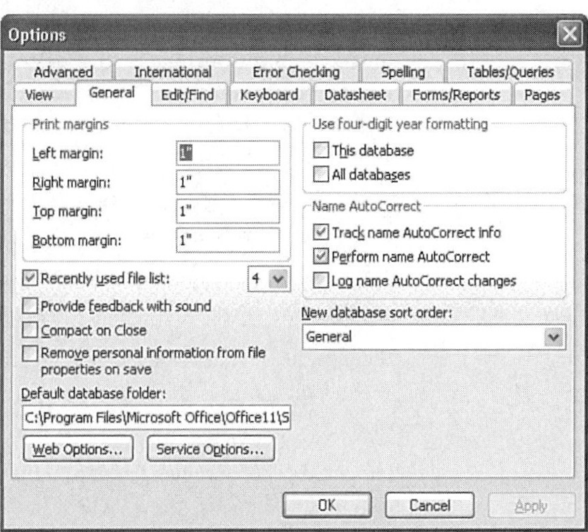

Figure 3.13
The General page includes default printing margins, date formats and Name Autocorrect option settings. In this example, the Default Database Folder has been changed to ...\Microsoft Office\Office11\Samples.

TABLE 3.7 GENERAL OPTIONS FOR THE ACCESS SYSTEM

Option	Function
Print Margins Group	
Left Margin	Establishes the default left margin.
Top Margin	Establishes the default top margin.
Right Margin	Establishes the default right margin.
Bottom Margin	Establishes the default bottom margin.
Use Four-Digit Year Formatting Group	
This Database	Applies four-digit year formatting to all Date/Time fields in the current database.
All Databases	Applies four-digit year formatting to all Date/Time fields in every database you open.
Name AutoCorrect Group	
Track Name AutoCorrect Info	If marked, Access stores information it needs to correct errors caused by renaming database objects. Access only tracks, but does not correct immediately unless Perform Name AutoCorrect is marked.
Perform Name AutoCorrect	If marked, Access repairs naming errors immediately as the name changes occur.
Log Name AutoCorrect Changes	If marked, Access records in the AutoCorrectLog table the changes made to the database to repair naming errors
Individual Settings	
Recently Used File List	If marked, Access maintains a list on the File menu of recently opened databases. The default number of files tracked is four, but this setting can be changed by selecting a number from the list.
Provide Feedback with Sound	If marked, Access generates sound through WAV files to accompany various tasks with Sound.
Compact on Close	If marked, Access automatically compacts and repairs your database, if needed, when you close Access.
Default Database Folder	Changes the default folder for the Open Database dialog. The default folder is the Access working folder, indicated by a period.
 Remove Personal Information from This File	Removes property values relating to individuals, such as Author and Manager, from the text boxes of the Properties dialog for the database.

Option	Function
Individual Settings	
New Database Sort Order	Sets the alphabetical sort order used for new databases. You can change the sort order for an existing database by selecting a different sort-order setting and then compacting the data base by choosing Tools, Database Utilities, Compact and Repair Database.
NEW Web Options	Clicking this button opens the Web Options dialog.
Web Options Dialog General Appearance Group	
Hyperlink Color	Selects the color for hyperlink text that has not been viewed since you opened the database.
Followed Hyperlink Color	Selects the color for hyperlink text that has been viewed since you opened the database.
Underline Hyperlink	If marked, Access displays hyperlink text with an underline.
NEW Service Options	Clicking this button opens the Web Options dialog.
Service Options Dialog Categories	
NEW Online Content	Lets you set the conditions under which Access connects to Microsoft's Office Web site to obtain additional help or download Access templates.
NEW Privacy Settings	Controls your participation in Microsoft's Customer Experience Improvement Program, which collects data about your computer hardware and your use of Access 2003.
NEW Shared Workspace	Controls how Access responds when you link tables from SharePoint Team Services sites and other users update the information. Also determines behavior of Net Meeting shared workspaces.

Margins usually are expressed in inches. If you're using an international version of Access, margin settings are in centimeters. You also can specify margin settings in twips, the default measurement of Windows and Visual Basic for Applications. A *twip* is 1/20 of a printer's point. A point is 1/72 inch, so a twip is 1/1,440 inch.

The 1-inch default margins are arbitrary; you might want to reset them to your preference before printing any forms or reports of your own. Refer to the printer's manual to determine the maximum printable area; the printable area determines the minimum margins that you can use.

Apart from the printing margins, the General option you're most likely to want to change is the default database folder. When you create your own databases, you should store them in a folder dedicated to databases to simplify backup operations. Use My Documents only if the folder is redirected to a server or you have a server-stored user profile, and the server is backed up nightly.

EDIT/FIND OPTIONS

The Edit/Find options affect the behavior of Access's Find feature for tables in either Form view or Datasheet view and when working with VBA code in a module (see Figure 3.14). Table 3.8 summarizes the Edit/Find options and their effects. The options in the Default Find/Replace Behavior group determine the default searching method for the Edit menu's Find and Replace commands. The options in the Confirm group determine which actions Access asks the user to confirm. The final option group in the Edit/Find options page is the Filter by Form Defaults for the current database. These options don't actually affect Access itself, but affect the defaults for the open database.

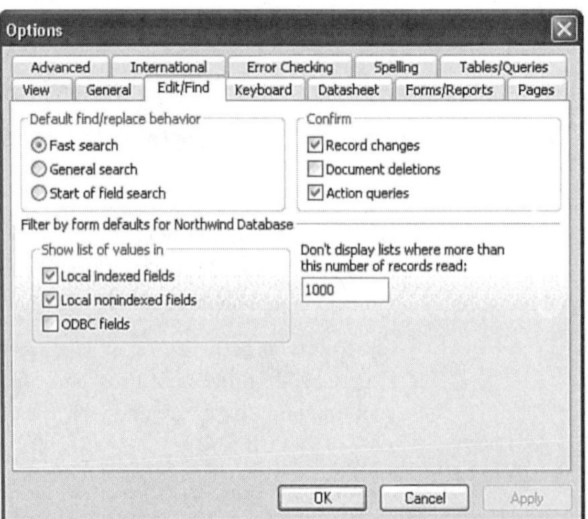

Figure 3.14
The Edit/Find page determines settings for find, find and replace, and filter by form operations. You also specify whether to confirm object and record deletion, and action query execution on this page.

TABLE 3.8 EDIT/FIND OPTIONS FOR THE ACCESS SYSTEM

Option	Function
Default Find/Replace Behavior Group	
Fast Search	Sets the default search method to search in the current field and to match the whole field
General Search	Sets the default search method to search in all fields, matching any part of a field
Start of Field Search	Causes the default search method to search the current field, matching only the beginning of the field

Option	Function
Confirm Group	
Record Changes	Causes Access to request confirmation of any changes that you make to a record
Document Deletions	Causes Access to confirm document (table, query, form, page, or report) deletions
Action Queries	Causes Access to confirm an action query (such as adding or deleting records) before executing the query
Show List of Values Group	
Local Indexed Fields	Includes indexed fields of Jet databases in the list of values that you can use when setting filter-by-form criteria
Local Non-Indexed	Includes non-indexed fields of Jet databases in the list of values that you can use when setting filter-by-form criteria
ODBC Fields	Includes fields from remote tables connected by ODBC in the lists of values that you can use when setting filter-by-form criteria
Individual Setting	
Don't Display Lists	Prohibits the display of filter values Where More Than This whenever the number of items in More Number of Records Read Than This list exceeds the specified number of Records Read

KEYBOARD OPTIONS

Keyboard options are especially important if you're accustomed to a particular type of arrow-key behavior. You probably will want to change keyboard options more than you will change any other options. You alter Keyboard options primarily to expedite keyboard entry of data in Table Datasheet view, so Keyboard options are one of the subjects of Chapter 6, "Entering, Editing, and Validating Jet Table Data."

DEFAULTS FOR DATASHEET VIEW

You use Datasheet view options to customize the display of all query datasheets and new and existing table and new form datasheets (see Table 3.9). As with printing options, to change the display format of existing table and form datasheets, you must edit the appropriate properties of the table or form in Design view. The Datasheet view options that you set don't apply to forms and reports created with Access wizards. Each wizard has its own set of default values. The options in the Default Colors group set the background and foreground colors for text displayed in Datasheet view, whereas the Default Font group's options determine the typeface and text size. The Default Gridlines Showing options determine which gridlines (if any) Access displays in Datasheet view. Finally, the Default Cell Effect options let you select a default style for datasheet cells.

TABLE 3.9 OPTIONS FOR DATASHEET VIEWS

Option	Function
Default Colors Group	
Font	Displays a drop-down list from which you can select the color of the text in new tables, queries, and forms. Access's default font color is black.
Background	Lets you select the background color of cells in Datasheet view. Access's default background color is white.
Gridlines	Lets you select the color of the gridlines displayed in Datasheet view. Access's default gridline color is silver (medium gray).
Default Font Group	
Font	Displays a drop-down list from which you can select the typeface that Access uses to display text in Datasheet view. Access's default font is Arial.
Weight	Displays a drop-down list from which you can select the weight of the text characters displayed in Datasheet view. You can select Normal (the default), Thin, Extra Light, Medium, Semi-bold, Bold, Extra Bold, or Heavy.
Size	Lets you select the default font size, in points. Access's default font size for Datasheet view is 10 points.
Italic	If selected, displays all datasheet text in italic.
Underline	If selected, displays all datasheet text with a single underline.
Default Gridlines Showing Group	
Horizontal	If selected, displays horizontal gridlines (that is, gridlines between rows) in Datasheet view. By default, this option and the Vertical Gridlines option are turned on.
Vertical	If selected, displays vertical gridlines (that is, gridlines between columns) in Datasheet view. You can display vertical and horizontal gridlines by combining the Vertical Gridlines option with the Horizontal Gridlines option.
Default Column Width	Specifies the default column width in inches. Access's default value for this text box setting is 1 inch.
Default Cell Effect Group	
Flat	When selected, displays a data cell as a "flat" cell—that is, the cell has no special shading.
Raised	When selected, adds shadow effects to each data cell so that the cell appears to be raised above the surface of the screen, like a command button.

3

Option	Function
Default Cell Effect Group	
Sunken	When selected, adds shadow effects to each data cell so that the cell appears to be sunken below the surface of the screen.
Individual Settings	
Show Animations	If selected, displays animated cursors and other animation effects. If you have a slow computer, you'll probably want to turn off this option to improve Access's operating speed slightly.
Show Smart Tags on Datasheets	If selected, enables display of the Smart Tags you specify on a table or query datasheet.

Tables/Queries, Forms/Reports, and Pages options are discussed in the chapters that cover the subject of the particular option category. Chapter 14, "Creating and Using Access Forms," describes Access 2003's new Error Checking feature for forms. International options handle right-to-left languages, such as Arabic, and East Asian calendars, and are beyond the scope of this book. Options related to multiuser, DDE, and ODBC features are described in more detail in the chapters devoted to those special topics.

Spelling Options

The Spelling options page is identical to Excel 2003's and is a subset of Word 2003's Spelling and Grammar options page. Spelling options are similar in all Office System 2003 members and there are no Access-specific spelling features.

AutoCorrect smart tags appear by default when you type a combination of characters in the AutoCorrect list during data entry in table Datasheet view and text and combo boxes of forms. You can turn AutoCorrect smart tags (but not the AutoCorrect function) off by clicking the AutoCorrect smart tag, choosing Control AutoCorrect Options to open the AutoCorrect dialog, and clearing the Show AutoCorrect Options Buttons check box. You also can display the AutoCorrect Options dialog by clicking a button on the Spelling Options page. Forms have an AllowAutoCorrect property that lets you disable the AutoCorrect feature in text and combo box entries.

Error Checking Options

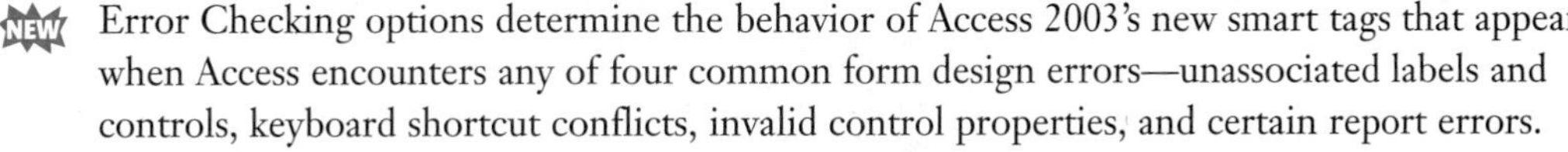

Error Checking options determine the behavior of Access 2003's new smart tags that appear when Access encounters any of four common form design errors—unassociated labels and controls, keyboard shortcut conflicts, invalid control properties, and certain report errors.

→ For more information on error checking smart tags, **see** "Understanding the Role of Access Forms and Controls," **p. 520**.

Advanced Options

The only option on the Advanced page of interest to beginning Access users is the setting of the Default File Format list. By default, Access 2003 creates and saves database files in

Access 2000 format for backward compatibility. If you're designing multiuser front-end applications for users who don't have Access 2003 or 2002 installed, you must continue to use Access 2000 format. Otherwise, you can specify Access 2002 format for new databases, but there is little incentive for doing so. The benefits of the new format accrue only to large database front ends with many complex forms and reports.

The Advanced page also has options that affect multiuser operations, DDE linking and updating, and tables attached by the ODBC feature of the Jet 4.0 database engine. The default values for the other options on the Advanced page are satisfactory for single-user and almost all multiuser applications.

Using Access Help

3

The Access Help system uses HTML help—the Microsoft online help standard introduced by Office 2000. HTML help uses compiled HTML document (.chm) files to replace traditional Windows help files (.hlp) and the familiar Help windows. Version 1.0 of HTML help in Office 2000, like version 1.0 of most Microsoft products, wasn't ready for prime time. Access 2003's online help system offers a few changes to the two previous versions, but still doesn't reach the level of usefulness of Access 97 and earlier online help systems.

The Help Menu

Access's Help menu provides an alternative to using context-sensitive help. Table 3.10 lists the Help menu choices.

Table 3.10 Access's Help Menu Commands

	Choice or Button	Function
	Microsoft Access Help	Opens the Microsoft Access Help task pane page (same as pressing F1 or clicking the Microsoft Access Help button on the toolbar) if the Office Assistant isn't enabled.
NEW	Show/Hide the Office Assistant	Toggles use of the Office Assistant. By default, the Office Assistant is hidden.
	Office on Microsoft.com	Launches Internet Explorer (IE) and opens the Office Online home page.
NEW	Microsoft Access Developer Resources	Launches IE and opens the Microsoft Access home page on the Microsoft Developer Network (MSDN) Web site.
NEW	Contact Us	Launches IE and opens the Contact Us page of the Office Online Web site. The page has technical support and other links, such as to bug report and suggestion forms.
NEW	Sample Databases	Displays submenu choices for opening the Northwind Sample Database and the Northwind Sample Access data project.
NEW	Check for Updates	Launches IE and opens the Office Updates page of the Microsoft Web site.

Choice or Button	Function
Detect and Repair	Opens the Detect and Repair dialog that attempts to repair a damaged Office 2003 installation. This choice does *not* detect damaged .mdb or .adp files and repair them.
Activate Product	Starts the Activation Wizard if you haven't activated Office 2003. Otherwise, a message box states that the product is already activated.
Customer Feedback Options	Opens the Service Options dialog that lets you specify options for Microsoft's Customer Experience Program Options, automatic delivery of Microsoft Office Online content, and Shared Workspace settings for Windows SharePoint Services.
About Microsoft Access	Displays the copyright notice for Microsoft Access, and the name and organization that you entered during setup. The About dialog has an OK button and the following three command buttons.
System Info button	Opens the System Information window that displays information about your computer system, such as how much memory you've installed, processor and BIOS data, amount of remaining disk space, and a list of running applications (see Figure 3.15). Windows 2000's System Information snap-in for the Microsoft Management Console (MMC) displays installation information for Office 2003 components.
Tech Support button	Opens a help topic with links to sources of Microsoft Technical Support for Office 2003 members.
Disabled Items button	Opens the Disable Items dialog, which lists files that prevent Office 2003 from functioning correctly, if any exist.

→ For more information on using the Office Online and Office Update site with Access, **see** "Downloading Templates from the Microsoft Office Update Site," **p. 76**.

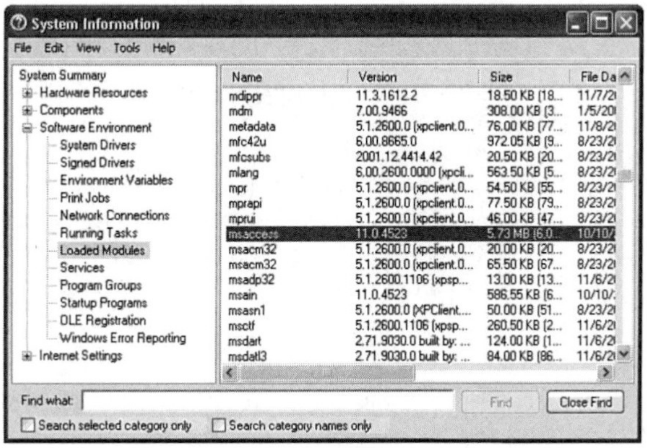

Figure 3.15
The System Information window, shown here running under Windows XP Professional, displays information on your hardware, system settings, and the applications you've opened.

TIP

If you have a serious problem with Access 2003 or other Office 2003 applications, a Microsoft Technical Support representative might request that you send a System Info (MSInfo, .nfo) file for inspection. To create a .nfo file in Windows XP, choose File, Save and supply a filename. In Windows 2000, you can create an .nfo file by opening the System Information snap-in, clicking Action, choosing Save as Information File, and providing a filename.

The .nfo file contains a substantial amount of information about your PC and the programs you've installed, which is needed to troubleshoot major problems, but .nfo files don't included confidential personal or corporate information, such as passwords.

THE ACCESS 2003 HELP TASK PANE AND WINDOW

3

NEW Access 2003 and other Office 2003 members share a common online help system that differs markedly from earlier releases. Access 2003 replaces Access 200x's Help window with a combination of the Help task pane page and a sliding Window that opens to display an HTML help topic page. The traditional index lookup for help topics and the Answer Wizard is gone. What's left is the Type a Question for Help text box at the upper right of Access 2003's window; its equivalent, the Search text box of the Microsoft Access Help task pane page; and the Help page's Table of Contents link for the local help files.

NOTE

Unfortunately, the Office team performed a similar operation on the VBA Editor's help system, which–in previous Access versions–provided more and better assistance than the current incarnation.

Another new Access 2003 "feature"—links to Access- or Office-related content on the Microsoft.com Web site—makes the assumption that all Access users have an always-on Internet connection. When you type a question in the Help or Search text box, you're sent to the Microsoft Web site, not the local online help files. For example, typing **Export Table to Excel** in the text box and pressing Enter returns a set of 30 topic choices from Microsoft.com (see Figure 3.16).

Clicking a likely link in the task pane's Search Results page displays the topic page by downloading it from the Office Online Web site (see Figure 3.17). Depending on the speed of your Internet connection and Microsoft's Web site at the moment, it might take several seconds for the topic to appear.

TIP

To use the local help files, which usually return fewer unrelated entries than the Office Online search, open the Search drop-down list at the bottom of the task pane, and select Offline Help (refer to Figure 3.16). "Export to Excel" returns only 20 offline help links.

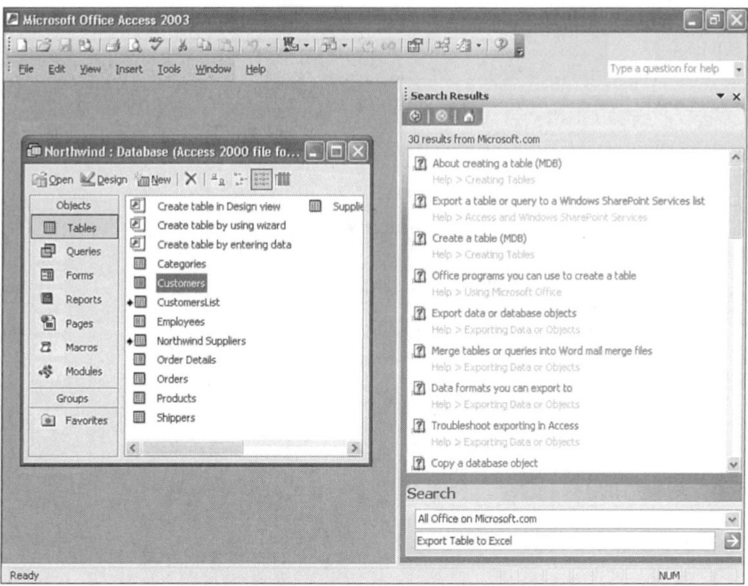

Figure 3.16
Office 2003's help engine usually returns a set of links to possibly-related topics on the Microsoft Web site. In this case, the list displays all topics containing the word "export" and doesn't restrict the list to topics containing "Excel."

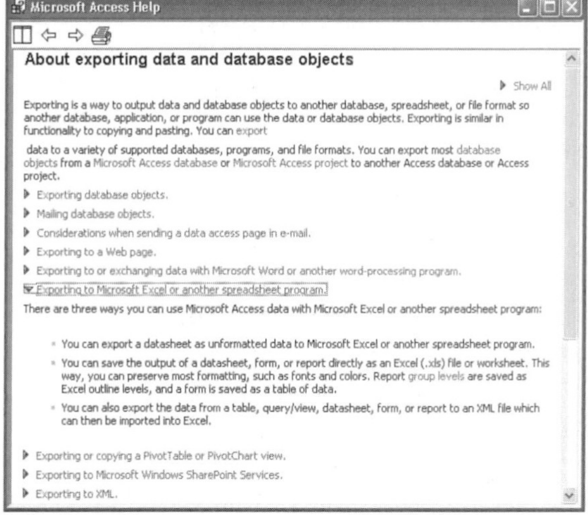

Figure 3.17
Clicking a link in the Search Results page downloads the help topic and displays it in a window. In most cases, the topic explains what you can do but not how to do it.

You're more likely to have better luck clicking the Table of Contents link of the task pane's Microsoft Access Help page to display an expandable list of topics in the Table of Contents task pane. Expand one of the topics to display subtopics, and then click the subtopic to display an HTML page in the sliding (tiled) window (see Figure 3.18).

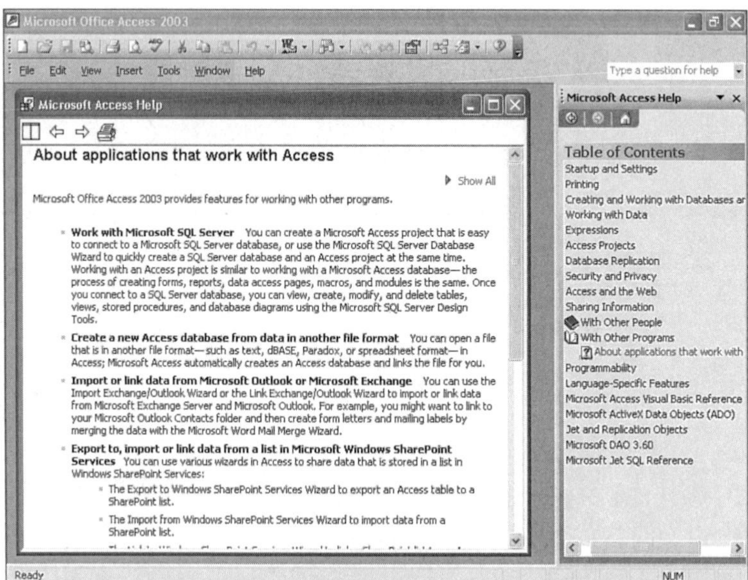

Figure 3.18
Nodes of the task pane's Table of Contents page expand to display links to help topics. Like most other topics, this example lacks specific instruction to perform the tasks.

3

TIP

> If you prefer to use Access 200x-style help windows, navigate to \Program Files\Microsoft Office\Office11\1033 folder (for the U.S. English version) or the folder with the number for your locale. Add desktop shortcuts to the .chm files you use commonly, such as Acmain11.chm–the main Access 2003 help file–and Vbaac11.chm–the Microsoft Access Visual Basic Reference.

USING THE DATABASE UTILITIES

Access 2003 offers the following seven utility functions, which you access by choosing Tools, Database Utilities:

- *Convert Database* lets you change the version of the currently open database to the Access 97, 2000, or 2002 version by saving it as a new .mdb file. The choice corresponding to the current database version is disabled.
- *Compact and Repair Database* checks the database for consistency, repairs problems found, and then compacts it to save disk space. Access automatically replaces the existing database with the compacted or repaired version.
- NEW *Back Up Database* is a new Access 2003 feature that opens the Save Backup As dialog and proposes to save your current database file as *FileName_YYYY-MM-DD*.mdb. Using the backup feature is a bit faster than making a copy with Windows Explorer.
- *Linked Table Manager* tests for the existence of linked .mdb or other types of data files and, if the links aren't valid, lets you change the path to the linked files. This choice is disabled if you don't have a database open.

- *Database Splitter* divides a single-file Access .mdb application with application and data objects into a front-end .mdb file and a back-end Jet database. This choice is disabled if you don't have a database open.
- *Switchboard Manager* creates a new Switchboard form if one isn't present in the current database and lets you edit the new or an existing Switchboard form. This choice also disabled is if you don't have a database open.
- *Upsizing Wizard* lets you move tables and queries from the current Jet database to SQL Server and, optionally, change the .mdb file containing application objects to an Access Data Project (.adp) file.
- *Make MDE File* creates a secure copy of the file, which prevents users from opening objects in Design view and viewing or changing VBA code. This choice is enabled only when no database is open.

If you select one of the utility operations described in the following sections when you don't already have a database open, the operation involves two dialogs. In the first dialog, you select the database in which Access is to perform the operation; in the second dialog, you type the name of the file that the operation is to create. Default file names for new files are Db#.mdb, where # is a sequential number, beginning with 1, assigned by Access.

Compacting and Repairing Databases

After you make numerous additions and changes to objects within a database file—especially additions and deletions of large amounts of data in tables—the database file can become disorganized. When you delete a record, you don't automatically regain the space in the file that the deleted data occupied. You must compact the database to optimize its file size and the organization of data within the tables that the file contains. When you pack an Access file, you regain space only in 32KB increments.

To compact the current database, do the following:

1. Open the database you want to compact.
2. Choose Tools, Database Utilities, Compact and Repair Database. Access immediately closes the database and begins compacting it.

When Access finishes compacting the database, it opens the database and returns you to the Database window. Your compacted database is stored with the same name it had before you compacted it.

If you want, you also can compact a database and save the compacted database in a different database file by following these steps:

1. Close the open database.
2. From the Tools menu, choose Database Utilities, Compact and Repair Database. The Database to Compact From dialog opens, as shown in Figure 3.19.

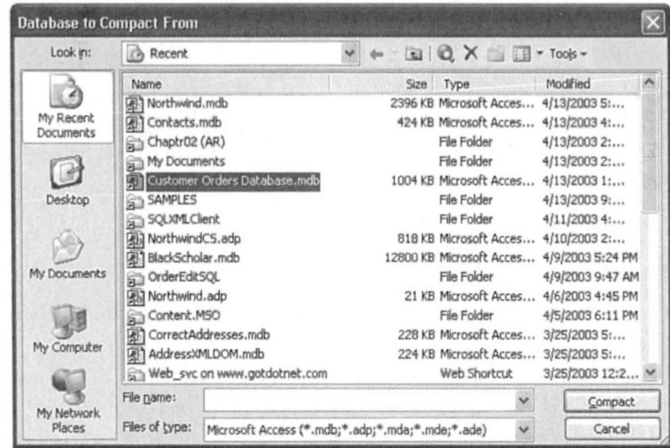

Figure 3.19
The default location for storing Access databases is My Documents. If your source database is stored in another folder, use the Database to Compact From dialog's My Recent Documents option to select it for compacting.

3. Double-click the name of the database file that you want to compact or click the name and then click Compact to open the Compact Database Into dialog.
4. Navigate to the folder you want to save the compacted files in. (This compacted version is saved in the ...\Office10\Samples folder.) You can't save the compacted file to the Recent folder.
5. In the File Name text box, type the name of the new file that is to result from the compaction process (see Figure 3.20). If you choose to replace the existing file with the compacted version, you see a message box requesting that you confirm your choice. Click Save.

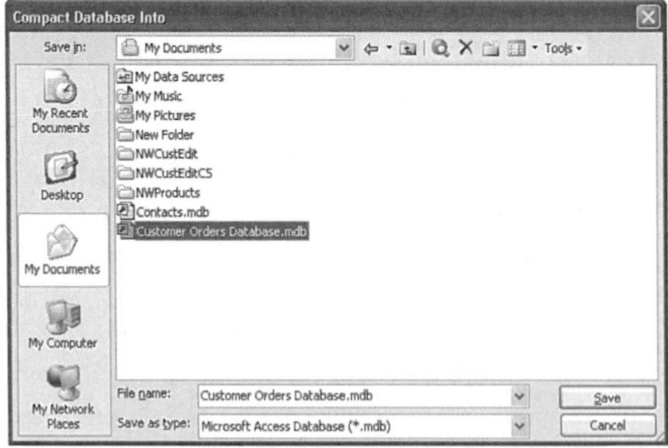

Figure 3.20
If you opened the source file from the History option's list, make sure to navigate to the correct folder to hold the compacted version.

Access then creates a compacted and repaired version of the file. The progress of the compaction is shown in a blue bar in the status bar. If you decide to use the same filename, the new file replaces the source file after compaction.

CAUTION

> If the compaction process fails, your database might be damaged. Databases damaged in the compaction process are unlikely to be repairable. So, you should not use the preceding process to compact the database into a new database with the same name. Do so only after backing up your database by copying it with a different name in the same folder or with its original name in a different folder.

A database can become corrupted as the result of the following problems:

- Hardware problems that occur when writing to your database file, either locally or on a network server
- Accidentally restarting the computer while Access databases are open
- A power failure that occurs after you make modifications to an Access object but before you save the object

Occasionally, a file might become corrupted without Access detecting the problem. This lack of detection occurs most frequently with corrupted indexes. If Access or your application behaves strangely when you open an existing database and display its contents, try compacting and repairing the database.

Periodically compacting and repairing production database files usually is the duty of the database administrator in a multiuser environment, typically in relation to backup operations. You should back up your existing file on disk or tape before creating a compacted version. When you're developing an Access 200x database, you should compact and repair the database frequently. Access 200x databases that are not compacted grow in size much more rapidly during modification than with Access 97 and earlier versions.

TIP

> To compact the current database automatically each time you close it, choose Tools, Options, click the General tab of the Options dialog, and mark the Compact on Close check box of the General page. Access 2000 added the automatic compaction option.

CONVERTING DATABASES TO ACCESS 2002 FORMAT

To convert prior Access version .mdb database files, .MDA library files created with Access 1.x or Access 2.0, and .mda library files created with Access 95 or 97 to the new database format of Access 2002, close any open database. Choose Tools, Database Utilities, Convert Database, To Access 2002 File Format. The process of converting database files from earlier versions of Access database formats to that of Access 2000 or 2002 is almost identical to the second file-compaction process described in the preceding section. The only difference that you'll notice is that the names of the dialogs are Database to Convert From and Database to Convert Into. Chapter 32, "Upgrading Access 97 and 2000/2002 Applications to Access 2003," covers this conversion process in detail.

If you encounter error messages when converting your Access 97 or earlier .mdb file to Jet 3.0 format, see the "Compile Errors in the Convert Database Process" topic of the "Troubleshooting" section near the end of the chapter.

Converting Databases to Access 97 Format

To convert Access 200x data .mdb files to Access 97 format, open the Access 2000 database that you want to convert and then choose Tools, Database Utilities, Convert Database, To Access 97 File Format. Access displays the Convert Database Into dialog. In the File Name text box, type the file name to convert into and then click the Save button.

TIP

> You must have a copy of the Access 97 object libraries on the machine on which you perform the version downgrade, and the libraries must be registered. The easiest way to accomplish this is to install Access 97 on your computer.
>
> You can convert most data-only .mdb files to Access 97 format. Conversion of application objects is likely to result in conversion errors, which can be difficult to fix.

3

Creating .MDE Files

An .mde file is a special version of an Access .mdb file. In an .mde file, all VBA code is stored only in compiled format, and the program source code for that database is unavailable. Also, users can no longer modify forms, reports, queries, or tables stored in that database, although those objects can be exported to other databases. Typically, .mde databases are used to create libraries of add-in wizards; create custom database applications intended for commercial or in-house distribution; and provide templates for forms, reports, queries, and other objects for use in other databases.

You can convert any Access 2002 .mdb database to an .mde file by choosing Tools, Database Utilities, Make MDE File. You must covert files in Access 2000 format to 2002 format to enable the Make MDE File choice. It's uncommon to convert a single-file .mdb to .mde format; .mde files are intended to protect application objects, not data objects. If you have a database open at the time you select this command, Access assumes that you want to save the current open database as an .mde file and immediately displays a Save MDE As dialog. This dialog is essentially the same as any Save As dialog.

TIP

> Access 2000 users can't open an .mde file created from an Access 2002 .mda file. If your secured application must support Access 2000 users, use Access 2000 to create the .mde file.

If you choose Tools, Database Utilities, Make MDE File when no database is open, Access first displays a Database to Save as MDE dialog. Use this dialog to select the .mdb database file that you want to convert to an .mde file.

TIP

> Be sure to save an archive copy of any .mda file you convert to .mde format on a removable disk, and store the archive copy in a safe place. The copy you make in .mde format is permanently altered; you can't restore an .mdb from an .mde file.

TROUBLESHOOTING

INVALID DATABASE LOCKED MESSAGES WHEN COMPILING IN PLACE

You receive the "database that is already opened" message shown in Figure 3.21 when you attempt to compact and repair the currently open database in place.

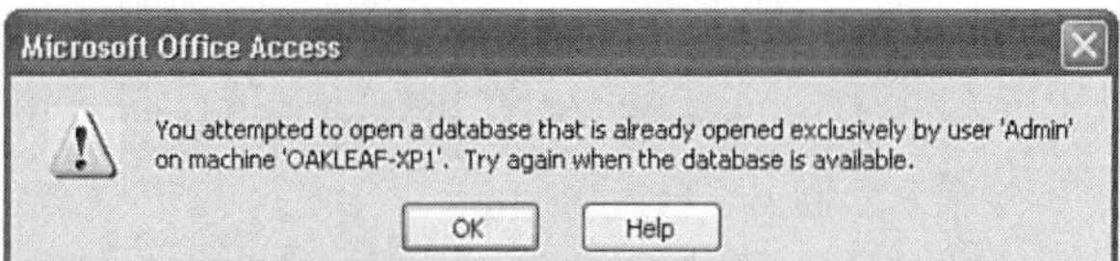

Figure 3.21
This message indicates that the operation you're attempting can't be completed because there's another instance of the database running or an exclusive lock on the database file hasn't been released.

This message occurs if you—or you and another user—have two copies of Access running with the same database open. If you know that you have only a single instance of the database open, the message is the result of a locking bug. In most cases, closing and reopening Access solves the locking problem. If not, you need to reboot Windows and try again.

COMPILE ERRORS IN THE CONVERT DATABASE PROCESS

Error messages appear when converting to Access 200x from early Access versions.

Access 2.0 and earlier were 16-bit applications. The first error message you might receive is "There are calls to 16-bit dynamic-link libraries (.dll) in this application." In this case, you must alter the code of Declare statements to call the current 32-bit equivalents of the 16-bit DLLs. For example, you must change calls to functions in User.dll, Kernel.dll, and Gdi.dll to User32.dll, Kernel32.dll, and Gdi32.dll.

A more common error message when converting Access 2.0, 95, and 97 applications is "There were compilation errors during the enabling or conversion of this database." If you're converting from Access 2.0, many of these errors are likely to arise from Access Basic reserved words and symbol usage that VBA 6.0 doesn't support. Similar problems occur with applications that originated in Access 2.0 or earlier and were converted to Access 9x. In some cases, conversion of earlier application versions to Access 97, and then to Access 2000 format is easier than attempting direct conversion. There's seldom a need to convert Access 97 and earlier files to Access 2002. See Chapter 32 for additional information on conversion issues.

IN THE REAL WORLD—HTML HELP OR HINDRANCE

Many new Access 2003 users are upgrading directly from Access 97. The new feature of Access 2003 that users of Access 97 probably will find most traumatic is the move from the traditional Windows help system (WinHelp32) to HTML Help. Changing to HTML Help violates one of the primary tenets of software development—"If it ain't broke, don't fix it." WinHelp32 was a mature, stable help system that was part of the Windows 9x and Windows NT operating systems, and is supported by Windows 2000 and XP. Fortunately for Access book authors, Microsoft's Office 2003 implementation of HTML help *still* has the hallmarks of a work in progress.

"If it's meant to be read, convert it to HTML" is today's variation on the navy's "If it don't move, paint it" rule. It's a reasonably safe bet that the number of HTML pages on the World Wide Web today exceeds the number of pages of books in the world's library. When it comes to online help, however, most Access 97 developers believe Microsoft took the "If it ain't broke, break it" route.

The move to HTML help was inevitable for the following reasons:

- There are many more Web page designers than help authors. Whether competency in Web page design aids the writing of meaningful help files remains to be seen. Access 2003's online help offers no supporting evidence.
- Hyperlinked, forward and back, Web-style navigation is native to the help system. Windows 3.x's 16-bit WinHelp anticipated many of the navigation features employed by HTML. The WinHelp32 engine in Windows 9x, Me, and NT brought new and useful features to online help.
- HTML help files in their native .htm format can be deployed from a central intranet server or published on the public Web as a software marketing aid. Compiled .htm (.chm) files that work in conjunction with the HTML help engine save disk space and download time.
- Microsoft can update your local help files by downloading (pushing) new, corrected, or expanded topics to your PC. This feature doesn't appeal to many Access users.
- Internet standards—such as Cascading Style Sheets (CSS) and the Document Object Model (DOM)—combined with Dynamic HTML (DHTML) contribute the capability of customizing the look and feel, respectively, of HTML Help pages.
- Scripting with Microsoft JScript or VBScript enables dynamic HTML Help. A DHTML event model and scripting eliminates the need to write custom help DLLs to add new types of action to help files.

- Microsoft saves the time and effort—and thus expense—of converting WinHelp32 .hlp files to HTML for publication on the `www.microsoft.com` Web site.

The real problem with the HTML help in Office 2003 isn't the change in help file format. Primary user complaints are elimination of useful help features—such as context-sensitive (Shift+F1 or What's This?) help and the keyword index—and reliance on a much less than perfect inference engine to generate a relevant help topic list. Rephrasing a question seldom leads to more on-topic hits.

HTML help files combine content and presentation; a primary objective of XML is to separate data and its formatting. Divorcing content from presentation makes it much simpler to update help topics. You can expect future versions of Access and the other Office members to move to XML encoding of help content and use Extensible Stylesheet Language Transformations (XSLT) to format the XML content for display. For example, an XML document (...\Office11\Actoc.xml) generates Access 2003's Table of Contents task pane page. It's likely that *every* Microsoft product from now on will sport XML features to support "rich content." Only time will tell whether XML-based online help will offer any improvement over Access 97's online WinHelp32 system.

PART II

Learning the Fundamentals of Jet Databases

CHAPTER 4

Exploring Relational Database Theory and Practice

In this chapter

MOVING FROM SPREADSHEETS TO DATABASES

Word processing and spreadsheet applications were the engines that drove the early personal computer market. In the early PC days, WordPerfect and Lotus 1-2-3 dominated the productivity software business. Today, almost everyone with a PC uses Microsoft Word and Excel on a daily basis. It's probably a safe bet that there's more data stored in Excel spreadsheets than in all the world's databases. It's an equally good wager that most new Access users have at least intermediate-level spreadsheet skills, and many qualify as Excel power users.

Excel's Data menu offers basic database features, such as sorting, filtering, validation, and data-entry forms. You can quickly import and export data in a variety of formats, including those of database management applications, such as Access. Excel's limitations become apparent as your needs for entering, manipulating, and reporting data grow beyond the spreadsheet's basic row-column metaphor. Spreadsheets basically are list managers; it's easy to generate a simple name and address list with Excel. If your needs expand to contact management and integrating the contact data with other information generated by your organization, a spreadsheet isn't the optimal approach.

The first problem arises when your contacts list needs additional rows for multiple persons from a single company. You must copy or retype all the company information, which generates redundant data. If the company moves, you must search and replace every entry for your contacts at the firm with the new address. If you want to record a history of dealings with a particular individual, you add pairs of date and text columns for each important contact with the person. Eventually, you find yourself spending more time navigating rows and columns than using the data they contain.

4

Contact lists are only one example of problems that arise when attempting to make spreadsheets do the work of databases. Recording medical or biological research data, managing consulting time and billings, organizing concert tours, booking artist engagements, and a myriad of other complex processes are far better suited to database than spreadsheet applications.

Moving to a relational database management system (RDBMS), such as Access, solves duplicate data and navigation problems, and greatly simplifies updating existing information. After you understand the basic rules of relational database design, Access makes creating highly efficient databases quick and easy. Access 2003 has a collection of wizards to lead you step-by-step through each process involved in developing and using a production-grade database application. Unfortunately, there's no "Relational Wizard" to design the database for you.

TIP

> If your goal is learning relational database fundamentals, start with Access 2003. Access is by far the first choice of universities, colleges, trade schools, and computer-training firms for courses ranging from introductory data management to advanced client/server database programming. The reason for Access's popularity as a training platform is its unique combination of initial ease of use and support for advanced database application development techniques.

RELIVING DATABASE HISTORY

Databases form the foundation of world commerce and knowledge distribution. Without databases, there would be no World Wide Web, automatic teller machines, credit/debit cards, or online airline reservation systems. Newsgathering organizations, research institutions, universities, and libraries would be unable to categorize and selectively disseminate their vast store of current and historical information. It's difficult to imagine today a world without a network of enormous databases, many of which probably contain a substantial amount of your personal data that you don't want to be easily available to others.

THE EARLY HISTORY OF DATABASES

The forerunner of today's databases consisted of stacks of machine-readable punched cards, which Herman Hollerith used to record the 1890 U.S. census. Hollerith formed the Computing-Tabulating-Recording Company, which later became International Business Machines. From 1900 to the mid-1950s, punched cards were the primary form of business data storage and retrieval, and IBM was the primary supplier of equipment to combine and sort (collate) punched cards, and print reports based on punched-card data.

NOTE

Jim Gray's article, "Data Management: Past, Present, and Future," which is available as a Microsoft Word document at `http://research.microsoft.com/~gray/DB_History.doc`, offers a more detailed history of data processing systems. Dr. Gray is a senior researcher and the manager of Microsoft's Bay Area Research Center (BARC).

The development of large computer-maintained databases—originally called *databanks*—is a post-World War II phenomenon. Mainframes replaced punched cards with high-capacity magnetic tape drives to store large amounts of data. The first databases were built on the hierarchical and network models, which were well suited to the mainframe computers of the 1950s. Hierarchical databases use parent-child relationships to define data structures, whose diagrams resemble business organization charts or an inverted tree with it's root at the top of the hierarchy. Network databases allow relaxation of the rules of hierarchical data structures by defining additional relationships between data items. Hierarchical and network databases ordinarily are self-contained and aren't easy to link with other external databases over a wide-area network (WAN).

NOTE

Hierarchical databases remain alive and well in the 21st century. For example, data storage for Windows 2000's Active Directory and Microsoft Exchange Server is derived from the hierarchical version of Access's relational Jet databases. The name Jet comes from the original Access database engine called *Joint Engine Technology*.

The Internet's Domain Name System (DNS) is a collection of hierarchical databases for translating character-based Internet domain names into numerical Internet Protocol (IP) addresses. The DNS database is called a *distributed database*, because its data is held by a global network of thousands of computers.

Early databases used batch processing for data entry and retrieval. Keypunch operators typed data from documents, such as incoming orders. At night, other operators collated the day's batch of punched cards, updated the information stored on magnetic tape, and produced reports. Many smaller merchants continue to use batch processing of customer's credit-card purchases, despite the availability of terminals that permit almost instantaneous processing of credit- and debit-card transactions.

THE RELATIONAL DATABASE MODEL

Dr. E. F. Codd, an employee of IBM Corporation, published "A Relational Model of Data for Large Shared Databanks" in a journal of the Association for Computing Machinery (ACM) in June 1970. A partial copy of the paper is available at `http://www.acm.org/classics/nov95/`. Dr. Codd's specialty was a branch of mathematics called set theory, which includes the concept of *relations*. He defined a relation as a named set of *tuples* (records or rows) that have *attributes* (fields or columns). One of the attributes must contain a unique value to identify each tuple. The common term for relation is a *table* whose presentation to the user is similar to that of a spreadsheet.

NOTE

> This book uses the terms *field* and *record* when referring to tables, and *columns* and *rows* when discussing data derived from tables, such as the views and query result sets described later in this chapter.

Relational databases solve a serious problem associated with earlier database types. Hierarchical and network databases define sets of data and explicit links between each data set as parent-child or owner-member, respectively. To extract information from these databases, programmers had to know the structure of the entire database. Complex programs in COBOL or other mainframe computer languages are needed to navigate through the hierarchy or network and extract information into a format understandable by users.

Dr. Codd's objective was to simplify the process of extracting formatted information and make adding or altering data easier by eliminating complex navigational programming. During the 1970s, Dr. Codd and others developed a comparatively simple language, Structured Query Language (SQL), for creating, manipulating, and retrieving relational data. With a few hours of training, ordinary database users could write SQL statements to define simple information needs and bypass the delays inherent in the database programming process. SQL, which was first standardized in 1985, now is the *lingua franca* of database programming, and all commercial database products support SQL.

NOTE

> The most recent SQL standard, SQL-92, was published by the American National Standards Institute (ANSI) in 1992. Few, if any, commercial relational database management systems (RDBMSs) today fully support the entire SQL-92 standard.

RDBMS competitors have erected an SQL Tower of Babel by adding non-standard extensions to the language. For example, Microsoft's Transact-SQL (T-SQL) for SQL Server, which is the subject of Chapter 21, "Moving from Jet Queries to Transact-SQL," has many proprietary keywords and features. Oracle Corporation's Oracle: SQL and PL/SQL dialects also have proprietary SQL extensions.

CLIENT/SERVER AND DESKTOP RDBMSS

In the early database era, the most common presentation of data took the form of lengthy reports processed by centralized, high-speed impact printers on fan-folded paper. The next step was to present data to the user on green-screen video terminals, often having small printers attached, which were connected to mainframe databases. As use of personal computers gained momentum, terminal emulator cards enabled PCs to substitute for mainframe terminals. Mainframe-scale relational databases, such as IBM's DB2, began to supplement and later replace hierarchical and network databases, but terminals continued to be the primary means of data entry and retrieval.

Oracle, Ingres, Informix, Sybase, and other software firms developed relational databases for lower-cost minicomputers, most of which ran various flavors of the Unix operating system. Terminals continued to be the primary data entry and display systems for multiuser Unix databases.

The next step was the advent of early PC-based flat-file managers and relational database management systems (RDBMSs). Early flat-file database managers, typified by Jim Button's PCFile for DOS (1981) and Claris FileMaker for Macintosh (1988) and Windows (1992), used a single table to store data and offered few advantages over storing data in a spreadsheet. The first desktop RDBMSs—such as dBASE, Clipper, FoxBase, and Paradox—ran under DOS and didn't support SQL. These products later became available in multiuser versions, adopted SQL features, and eventually migrated to Windows. Access 1.0, which Microsoft introduced in November 1992, rapidly eclipsed its DOS and Windows competitors by virtue of Access's combination of native SQL support, versatility, and ease of use.

NOTE

Microsoft celebrated Access's 10th birthday with a "Happy Anniversary Microsoft Access" subsite at `http://www.microsoft.com/office/access/10years/default.asp`. You can open a Macromedia Flash animated timeline that describes the new features in each of Access's seven prior versions. There's also a link to "war stories" told by long-time Access developers, who Microsoft calls "Access Heroes."

PC-based desktop RDBMSs are classified as shared-file systems, because they store their data in conventional files that multiple users can share on a network. One of Access's initial attractions for users and developers was its capability to store all application objects—forms, reports, and programming code—and tables for a database application in a single .mdb file.

FoxPro, dBASE, Clipper, and Paradox require a multitude of individual files to store application and data objects. Today, almost all multiuser Access applications are divided into a front-end .mdb file, which contains the application objects and links to a back-end database that holds the data. Each user has a copy of the front-end .mdb and shares connections to a single back-end .mdb on a peer Windows XP/2000 workstation, or Windows 2000+ server.

Client/server RDBMSs have an architecture similar to Access's front-end/back-end shared-file multiuser configuration. What differentiates client/server from shared-file architecture is that the RDBMS on the server handles most of the data processing activity. The client front end provides a graphical user interface (GUI) for data entry, display, and reporting. Only SQL statements and the specific data requested by the user pass over the network. Client/server databases traditionally run on network operating systems, such as Windows 2000+ or Unix, and are much more robust than shared-file databases, especially for applications in which many users make simultaneous additions, changes, and deletions to the database. All commercial data-driven Web applications use client/server databases.

Since version 1.0, Access has had the capability to connect to client/server databases by linking their tables to a Jet database. Linking lets you treat client/server tables almost as if they were native Jet tables. Linking uses Microsoft's widely accepted Open Database Connectivity (ODBC) standard, and Access 2003 includes an ODBC driver for SQL Server and Oracle databases. You can purchase licenses for ODBC drivers that support other Unix RDBMSs, such as Sybase or Informix, from the database supplier or third parties. Chapter 19, "Linking Access Front-Ends to Jet and to Client/Server Databases," describes the process of linking Jet and SQL Server databases. Although Chapter 19 uses SQL Server 2000 for its examples, the linking procedure is the same—or at least similar—for other client/server RDBMSs.

NOTE

Prior to Access 2000, Jet was Access's standard database engine, so the terms *Access database* and *Jet database* were interchangeable. Microsoft now considers SQL Server to be its *strategic* RDBMS, which means that SQL Server gets continuing development funds and Jet doesn't. Jet 4.0, which is included with Access 2003, is the final version and is headed toward retirement. To reflect this change, this edition uses the terms *Jet database* and *SQL Server* database. Unless otherwise noted, *SQL Server* refers to all versions except the Windows CE edition.

Access data projects (ADP) and the Microsoft SQL Server 2000 Desktop Engine (MSDE) combine to make Access 2003 a versatile tool for designing and testing client/server databases, and creating advanced data entry and reporting applications. You can start with a conventional Jet database and later use Access's Upsizing Wizard to convert the .mdb file(s) to an .adp file to hold application objects and an SQL Server 2000 back-end database. Access 2003's Upsizing Wizard incorporated many improvements to the Access 2000 and earlier versions, but Access 2003's Wizard is the same as 2002's. Despite the upgraded wizardry, you're likely to need to make changes to queries to accommodate differences between Jet 4.0 and SQL Server 2000.

→ For an example of differences between Jet and SQL Server SQL syntax that affects the upsizing process, **see** "Displaying Data with Queries and Views," **p. 142**.

The ability to save ADP forms and, especially, reports to data access pages (DAP) greatly simplifies delivering up-to-date information over corporate intranets. ADP rely on SQL Server and don't directly support Oracle or other client/server databases. Fortunately, you can link SQL Server to other client/server databases. Instead of ODBC drivers, SQL Server requires OLE DB drivers to link to other databases. Section VI, "Publishing Data to Intranets and the Internet," shows you how to take advantage of client/server ADP and DAP.

DEFINING THE STRUCTURE OF RELATIONAL DATABASES

Relational databases consist of a collection of self-contained, related tables. Tables typically represent classes of physical objects, such as customers, sales orders, invoices, checks, products for sale, or employees. Each member object, such as an invoice, has its own record in the invoices table. For invoices, the field that uniquely identifies a record, called a *primary key [field]*, is a serial invoice number.

Figure 4.1 shows Access's Datasheet view of an Invoices table, which is based on the Northwind.mdb sample database's Orders table. The InvoiceNo field is the primary key. Values in the OrderID, CustomerID, EmployeeID, and ShipperID fields relate to primary key values in Northwind's Orders, Customers, Employees, and Shippers tables. A field that contains values equal to those of primary key values in other tables is called a *foreign key [field]*.

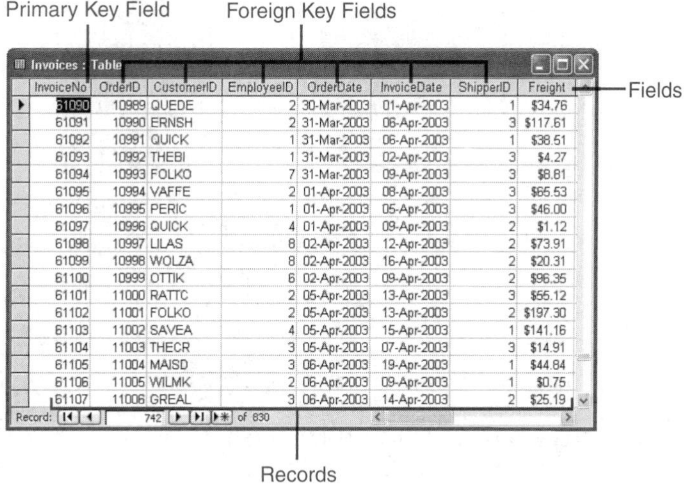

InvoiceNo	OrderID	CustomerID	EmployeeID	OrderDate	InvoiceDate	ShipperID	Freight
61090	10989	QUEDE	2	30-Mar-2003	01-Apr-2003	1	$34.76
61091	10990	ERNSH	2	31-Mar-2003	06-Apr-2003	3	$117.61
61092	10991	QUICK	1	31-Mar-2003	06-Apr-2003	1	$38.51
61093	10992	THEBI	1	31-Mar-2003	02-Apr-2003	3	$4.27
61094	10993	FOLKO	7	31-Mar-2003	09-Apr-2003	3	$8.81
61095	10994	VAFFE	2	01-Apr-2003	08-Apr-2003	3	$65.53
61096	10995	PERIC	1	01-Apr-2003	05-Apr-2003	3	$46.00
61097	10996	QUICK	4	01-Apr-2003	09-Apr-2003	2	$1.12
61098	10997	LILAS	8	02-Apr-2003	12-Apr-2003	2	$73.91
61099	10998	WOLZA	8	02-Apr-2003	16-Apr-2003	2	$20.31
61100	10999	OTTIK	6	02-Apr-2003	09-Apr-2003	2	$96.35
61101	11000	RATTC	2	05-Apr-2003	13-Apr-2003	3	$55.12
61102	11001	FOLKO	2	05-Apr-2003	13-Apr-2003	2	$197.30
61103	11002	SAVEA	4	05-Apr-2003	15-Apr-2003	1	$141.16
61104	11003	THECR	3	05-Apr-2003	07-Apr-2003	3	$14.91
61105	11004	MAISD	3	06-Apr-2003	19-Apr-2003	1	$44.84
61106	11005	WILMK	2	06-Apr-2003	09-Apr-2003	1	$0.75
61107	11006	GREAL	3	06-Apr-2003	14-Apr-2003	2	$25.19

Figure 4.1
This simple Invoices table was created from the Northwind Orders table and doesn't take advantage of Access's extended properties, such as the field captions, lookup fields, and subdatasheets in the Datasheet view of the Orders table.

→ To learn more about primary keys in Access tables, **see** "Selecting a Primary Key," **p. 193**.

If you need information about a particular invoice or set of invoices, you open the Invoices table and search for the invoice(s) by number (InvoiceNo) or another attribute, such as a customer code (CustomerID), date (ShippedDate), or range of dates. Unlike earlier database models, the user can access the Invoices table independently of its related tables. No database navigation programming is needed. A simple, intuitive SQL statement, `SELECT * FROM Invoices`, returns all the data in the table. The asterisk (*) represents a request to display the contents of all fields of the table.

REMOVING DATA REDUNDANCY WITH RELATIONSHIPS

The Invoices table of Figure 4.1 is similar to a spreadsheet containing customer billing information. What's missing is the customer name and address information. A five-character customer code (CustomerID) identifies the each customer to whom the invoice is directed. The CustomerID values in the Invoices table match CustomerID values in a modified version of Northwind's Customers table (see Figure 4.2). Matching a foreign key with a primary key value often is called a lookup operation. Using a key-based lookup operation eliminates the need to repeatedly enter name, address, and other customer-specific data in the Invoices table. In addition, if you change the customer's address, the change applies to all past and future invoices.

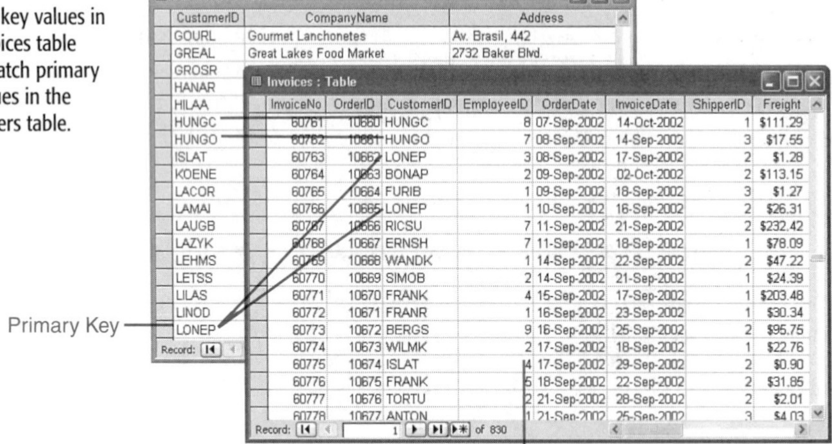

Customers : Table

CustomerID	CompanyName	Address
GOURL	Gourmet Lanchonetes	Av. Brasil, 442
GREAL	Great Lakes Food Market	2732 Baker Blvd.
GROSR		
HANAR		
HILAA		
HUNGC		
HUNGO		
ISLAT		
KOENE		
LACOR		
LAMAI		
LAUGB		
LAZYK		
LEHMS		
LETSS		
LILAS		
LINOD		
LONEP		

Invoices : Table

InvoiceNo	OrderID	CustomerID	EmployeeID	OrderDate	InvoiceDate	ShipperID	Freight
60761	10660	HUNGC	8	07-Sep-2002	14-Oct-2002	1	$111.29
60762	10661	HUNGO	7	08-Sep-2002	14-Sep-2002	3	$17.55
60763	10662	LONEP	3	08-Sep-2002	17-Sep-2002	2	$1.28
60764	10663	BONAP	2	09-Sep-2002	02-Oct-2002	2	$113.15
60765	10664	FURIB	1	09-Sep-2002	18-Sep-2002	3	$1.27
60766	10665	LONEP	1	10-Sep-2002	16-Sep-2002	2	$26.31
60767	10666	RICSU	7	11-Sep-2002	21-Sep-2002	2	$232.42
60768	10667	ERNSH	7	11-Sep-2002	18-Sep-2002	1	$78.09
60769	10668	WANDK	1	14-Sep-2002	22-Sep-2002	2	$47.22
60770	10669	SIMOB	2	14-Sep-2002	21-Sep-2002	1	$24.39
60771	10670	FRANK	4	15-Sep-2002	17-Sep-2002	1	$203.48
60772	10671	FRANR	1	16-Sep-2002	23-Sep-2002	1	$30.34
60773	10672	BERGS	9	16-Sep-2002	25-Sep-2002	2	$95.75
60774	10673	WILMK	2	17-Sep-2002	18-Sep-2002	1	$22.76
60775	10674	ISLAT	4	17-Sep-2002	29-Sep-2002	2	$0.90
60776	10675	FRANK	5	18-Sep-2002	22-Sep-2002	2	$31.85
60777	10676	TORTU	2	21-Sep-2002	28-Sep-2002	2	$2.01
60778	10677	ANTON	1	21-Sep-2002	25-Sep-2002	3	$4.03

Record: 1 of 830

Figure 4.2 Foreign key values in the Invoices table must match primary key values in the Customers table.

TIP

> Using derived key values, such as alphabetic codes for CustmerID, is no longer in favor among database designers. Most designers now use automatically generated numerical key values—called Jet AutoNumber or SQL Server `identity` fields. The Northwind Orders and Products tables, among others, have primary keys that use the AutoNumber data type.
>
> Another method of generating unique keys is by use of Globally Unique Identifiers(GUIDs), which also are called Universally Unique Identifiers (UUIDs). GUIDs are 16-byte computed binary numbers that are guaranteed to be unique locally and universally; no other computer in the world will duplicate a GUID. SQL Server's `uniqueidentifier` data type is a GUID. You can't select a GUID data type in Access's Table Design mode, but Jet uses internally-generated GUIDs for data replication.

The Invoices table also connects with other tables, which contain information on orders, sales department employees, and the products ordered. Connections between fields of related tables having common values are called *relationships* (not relations). Figure 4.3 shows Access's Relationships window displaying the relationships between the Invoices table and the other tables of the Northwind sample database.

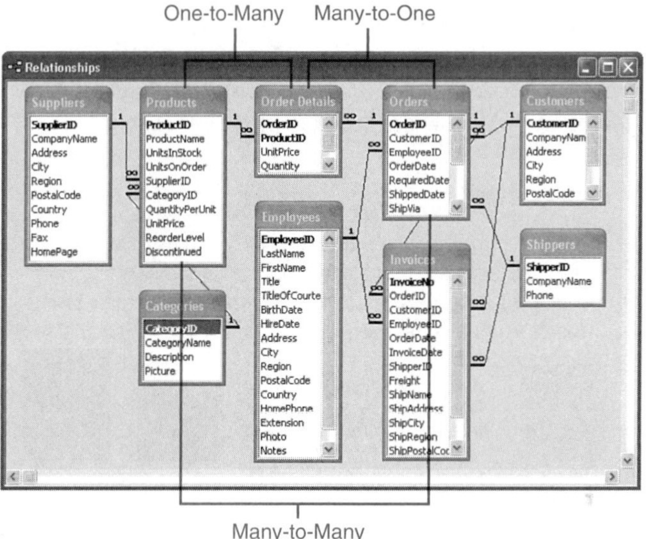

Figure 4.3 Access's Relationships window displays the relationships between the tables of the Northwind sample database, plus the added Invoices table. Every relationship between these tables is one-to-many. The many-to-many relationship between Products and Orders is an indirect relationship.

Relationships come in the following three flavors:

- *One-to-many* relationships represent connections between a single primary key value (the "one" side) and multiple instances of the same value in the foreign key field (the "many" side). One-to-many relationships commonly are identified by the number one and the infinity (∞) symbol, as in Figure 4.3. All the direct relationships between the tables in Figure 4.3 are one-to-many. One-to-many—also called many-to-one—relationships are by far the most common.
- *One-to-one* relationships connect primary key values in two tables. You might think that the relationship between the Orders and Invoices tables could be one-to-one, but an order requires more than one invoice if one or more items are backordered and then shipped later. One-to-one relationships are uncommon.
- *Many-to-many* relationships require three tables, one of which is called a *linking table*. The linking table must have two foreign keys, each of which has a many-to-one relationship with a primary key in two related tables. In the example of Figure 4.3, the Order Details table is the linking table for the many-to-many relationship between the Orders and Products tables. Many-to-many relationships also are called indirect relationships.

There are many other indirect relationships between the tables shown in Figure 4.3. For example, there is a many-to-many relationship between the Suppliers and Orders tables. In this case, the Products and Order Details act as linking tables between the Suppliers and Orders tables.

The Relationships window displays the names of primary key fields in a boldface font. Notice in Figure 4.3 that the OrderID and ProductID field names are bold. The OrderID and ProductID fields comprise a *composite primary key*, which uniquely identifies an order line item. You can't repeat the same combination of OrderID and ProductID; this precaution makes sense for products that have only one stock-keeping unit (SKU), such as for Aniseed Syrup, which comes only in a carton of 12 550-ml bottles.

NOTE

> The one-product-entry-per-order restriction prevents shared use of the Order Details table as an invoice line items table. If you short-ship an order item on one invoice, you can't add another record to the Order Details table when you ship the remaining quantity of the item. Microsoft didn't add an Invoices table for Northwind Traders, probably because of the complexity of dealing with backorders and drop-shipments.

The OakmontSQL.mdf sample database file in the \Seua2003\Oakmont folder of the accompanying CD-ROM has structure that differs from that of Northwind.mdb, but the design principals of the two databases are similar. OakmontSQL is an SQL Server 2000 database for use with ADP. ADP use a special set of tools—called the *project designer* or *da Vinci toolset* in this book—for designing and managing SQL Server databases.

The Oakmont model is a course enrollment database for a college. Figure 4.4 shows the Database Diagram window for the OakmontSQL database. The SQL Server Diagram window is similar to the Relationships window for Access's traditional Jet databases. The key and infinity symbols at the ends of each line represent the one and many sides, respectively, of the one-to-many relationships between the tables. Jet and SQL Server databases store information on table relationships as an object within the database file.

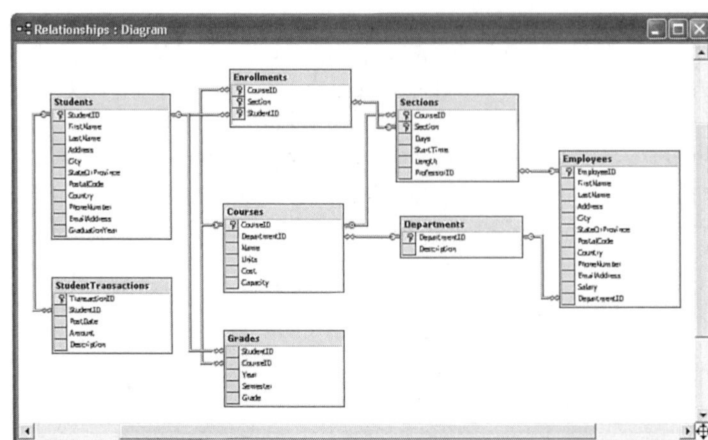

Figure 4.4 The SQL Server Database Diagram window for the OakmontSQL database shows one-to-many relationships between primary key fields (identified by key symbols) and foreign key fields (infinity symbols).

This book uses the Jet 4.0 and SQL Server 2000 versions of the Northwind and Oakmont sample databases in almost all examples. The tables of the Oakmont database have many more records than the Northwind tables. The large number of records in the Oakmont database makes it better suited than Northwind for predicting the performance of production Jet and SQL Server database applications.

CONFORMING TO TABLE DESIGN RULES

Designing tables for relational databases follows a formalized procedure called *normalization*. Dr. Codd described the complete normalization process in his 1972 paper, "Further Normalization of the Data Base Relational Model." This paper isn't an easy read; it's steeped in the language of set theory and relational algebra. The sections that follow explain in common English the application of the normalization process to Access's Northwind database.

You normalize tables in a series of steps called *normal forms*. Applying the normalization process is necessary to move spreadsheet-style data to relational tables. You also employ the normalization rules when designing a new database or analyzing existing databases. In specific cases, however, you might need to depart from strict adherence to normalization rules to retain a history of data values that change over time or to improve performance of a large database.

FIRST NORMAL FORM

First normal form requires tables to be flat and have no repeating or potentially repeating fields or groups of fields. A flat table is one in which every record has the same number of fields. In addition, a single field cannot contain multiple data values. Repeating fields must be moved to a related table. The first normal form is the most important of the normalization steps. If all your tables don't meet the rules of first normal form, you are in *big* trouble.

Northwind's Customers and Suppliers tables violate the no repeating fields rule. If a customer or supplier has more than one person involved in the ordering process, which is likely, the table would need repeating pairs of fields with different names, such as ContactName2 and ContactTitle2 or the like. To conform the Customers and Suppliers tables to first normal form, you must create two new tables, CustPers(sonel) and SuppPers(sonel) for example, to hold contact records. Including contact names in the Customers and Suppliers tables also violates third normal form, which is the subject of the later "Third Normal Form" section.

The ContactName field also violates the rule against multiple data values in a single field by combining given and family names. This isn't a serious violation of first normal form, but it's a good database design practice always to identify persons by given and family names in separate fields. When you create the new CustPers and SuppPers tables, separate the ContactName field into two fields, such as LastName and GivenName, which can include initials. You can then use a code similar to that for CustomerID for the ContactID field. For this example, the ContactID code is the first character of GivenName and the first four characters of LastName. Alternatively, you could assign an AutoNumber value to ContactID.

Figure 4.5 shows the first 19 of the 91 records of the CustPers table generated from the Customers table. The CustomerID field is required for a many-to-one relationship with the Customers table. Additional fields, such as Suffix, TitleOfCourtesy, Email(Address), Phone, and Fax, make the individual contact records more useful for creating mailing lists and integration with other applications, such as Microsoft Outlook.

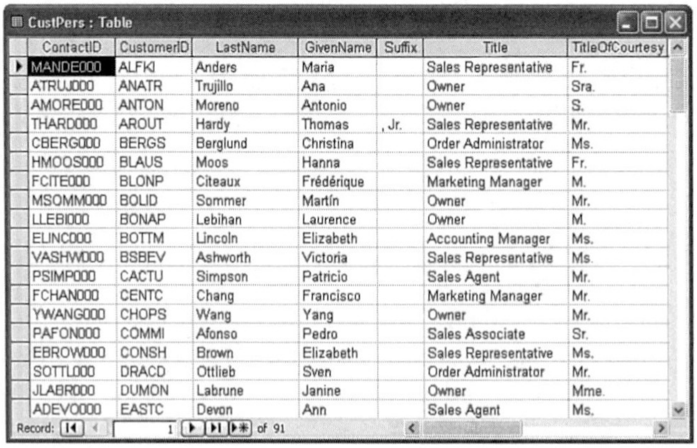

Figure 4.5
You extract data for records of the CustPers table from the ContactName and ContactTitle fields of the Customers table. Separating given and last names simplifies generating a ContactID code to identify each record.

CustPers : Table

ContactID	CustomerID	LastName	GivenName	Suffix	Title	TitleOfCourtesy
MANDE000	ALFKI	Anders	Maria		Sales Representative	Fr.
ATRUJ000	ANATR	Trujillo	Ana		Owner	Sra.
AMORE000	ANTON	Moreno	Antonio		Owner	S.
THARD000	AROUT	Hardy	Thomas	, Jr.	Sales Representative	Mr.
CBERG000	BERGS	Berglund	Christina		Order Administrator	Ms.
HMOOS000	BLAUS	Moos	Hanna		Sales Representative	Fr.
FCITE000	BLONP	Citeaux	Frédérique		Marketing Manager	M.
MSOMM000	BOLID	Sommer	Martín		Owner	Mr.
LLEBI000	BONAP	Lebihan	Laurence		Owner	M.
ELINC000	BOTTM	Lincoln	Elizabeth		Accounting Manager	Ms.
VASHW000	BSBEV	Ashworth	Victoria		Sales Representative	Ms.
PSIMP000	CACTU	Simpson	Patricio		Sales Agent	Mr.
FCHAN000	CENTC	Chang	Francisco		Marketing Manager	Mr.
YWANG000	CHOPS	Wang	Yang		Owner	Mr.
PAFON000	COMMI	Afonso	Pedro		Sales Associate	Sr.
EBROW000	CONSH	Brown	Elizabeth		Sales Representative	Ms.
SOTTL000	DRACD	Ottlieb	Sven		Order Administrator	Mr.
JLABR000	DUMON	Labrune	Janine		Owner	Mme.
ADEVO000	EASTC	Devon	Ann		Sales Agent	Ms.

Record: 1 of 91

TIP

You don't need to retype the data to populate the CustPers and SuppPers tables. You can use Access to import the data from an Excel worksheet or text file, or use Access action (append and update) queries to handle this chore.

→ For more information on importing from Excel, **see** "Importing and Linking Spreadsheet Files," **p. 284**.

→ To learn how to use Access action queries, **see** "Creating Action Queries to Append Records to a Table," **p. 497**.

Figure 4.6 shows the Relationships window with the CustPers and SuppPers tables added to the Northwind database and their many-to-one relationships with the Customers and Suppliers tables, respectively.

Second Normal Form

Second normal form requires that data in all non-key fields be fully dependent on the value of a primary key. The objective of second normal form is to avoid data redundancy in your tables.

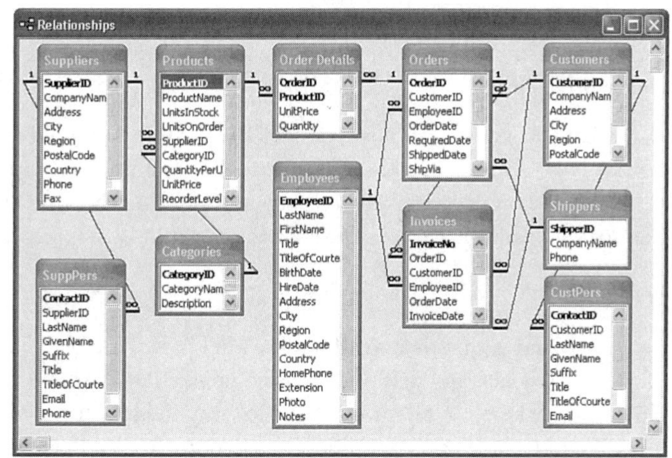

Figure 4.6 The Relationships window displays the many-to-one relationships between the Customers and CustPers tables and the Suppliers and SuppPers tables.

Only Northwind's Order Details linking table (see Figure 4.7) has a composite primary key (OrderID + ProductID). The UnitPrice field appears to violate the second normal form, because UnitPrice is a field of the Products table. UnitPrice values added to the Order Details table are dependent on the ProductID component of the composite primary key and not the OrderID component, so UnitPrice data is not *fully dependent* on the primary key. On first glance, the UnitPrice field appears to be redundant data. If you change the unit price of a product, it would appear that you would need to alter the UnitPrice value in every Order Details record for the product.

Order Details : Table

OrderID	ProductID	UnitPrice	Quantity	Discount
10248	11	$14.00	12	0%
10248	42	$9.80	10	0%
10248	72	$34.80	5	0%
10249	14	$18.60	9	0%
10249	51	$42.40	40	0%
10250	41	$7.70	10	0%
10250	51	$42.40	35	15%
10250	65	$16.80	15	15%
10251	22	$16.80	6	5%
10251	57	$15.60	15	5%
10251	65	$16.80	20	0%
10252	20	$64.80	40	5%
10252	33	$2.00	25	5%
10252	60	$27.20	40	0%
10253	31	$10.00	20	0%
10253	39	$14.40	42	0%
10253	49	$16.00	40	0%

Record: 1 of 2155

Figure 4.7 The Order Details linking table has a composite primary key consisting of the OrderID and ProductID fields.

The Order Details table is an example of a situation in which you *must* retain what appears to be redundant information to maintain the integrity of historical data. Prices of products vary over time, so the price of a particular product is likely to change for orders placed on different dates. If the price of a product changes between the order and shipping (invoice) dates, the invoice reflects a different amount than the order. Despite "Prices are subject to change without notice" boilerplate, customers become incensed if the invoice price is greater than the order price.

Eliminating the UnitPrice field from the Order Details table and looking up its value from the current price in the Products table also can cause accounting errors and distortion of historical reports based on bookings and sales data. Removing the UnitPrice data also violates the rules for the fifth normal form, explained later in this chapter.

THIRD NORMAL FORM

Third normal form requires that data in all non-key fields of the table be fully dependent on the value of the primary key and describe only the object that the table represents. In other words, make sure that the table doesn't include non-key fields that relate to some other object or process and includes non-key fields for descriptive data that isn't contained in another related table.

As mentioned in the "First Normal Form" section, including contact information in the Customers and Products table violates third normal form rules. Contacts are persons, not customer or supplier organizations and deserve their own related table that has attributes related to individuals.

Other examples of a common third normal form violation are the UnitsInStock and UnitsOnOrder fields of the Products table (see Figure 4.8). These fields aren't fully dependent on the primary key value nor do they describe the object; they describe how many of the product you have now and how many you might have if the supplier decides to ship your latest order. In a production order-entry database, these values vary over time and must be updated for each sale of the product, each purchase order issued to the product's supplier, and each receipt of the product. Purchases, receipts, and invoices tables are the most common source of the data on which the calculations are based.

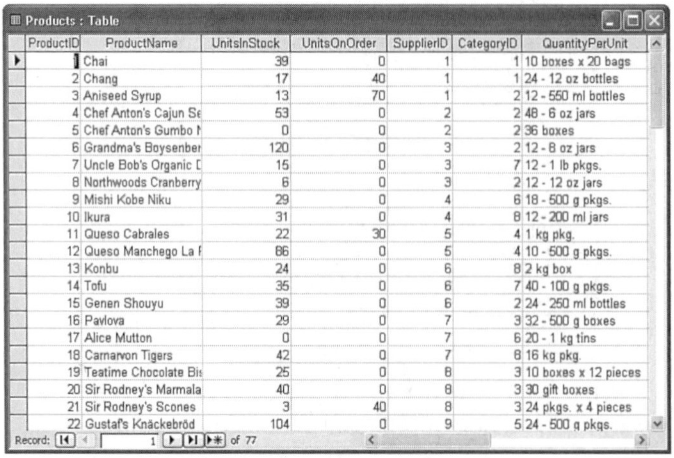

Figure 4.8
The Products table's UnitsInStock and UnitsOnOrder values must be calculated from data in tables that record purchases, receipts, and shipments of products.

Products : Table

ProductID	ProductName	UnitsInStock	UnitsOnOrder	SupplierID	CategoryID	QuantityPerUnit
1	Chai	39	0	1	1	10 boxes x 20 bags
2	Chang	17	40	1	1	24 - 12 oz bottles
3	Aniseed Syrup	13	70	1	2	12 - 550 ml bottles
4	Chef Anton's Cajun Se	53	0	2	2	48 - 6 oz jars
5	Chef Anton's Gumbo M	0	0	2	2	36 boxes
6	Grandma's Boysenber	120	0	3	2	12 - 8 oz jars
7	Uncle Bob's Organic D	15	0	3	7	12 - 1 lb pkgs.
8	Northwoods Cranberry	6	0	3	2	12 - 12 oz jars
9	Mishi Kobe Niku	29	0	4	6	18 - 500 g pkgs.
10	Ikura	31	0	4	8	12 - 200 ml jars
11	Queso Cabrales	22	30	5	4	1 kg pkg.
12	Queso Manchego La P	86	0	5	4	10 - 500 g pkgs.
13	Konbu	24	0	6	8	2 kg box
14	Tofu	35	0	6	7	40 - 100 g pkgs.
15	Genen Shouyu	39	0	6	2	24 - 250 ml bottles
16	Pavlova	29	0	7	3	32 - 500 g boxes
17	Alice Mutton	0	0	7	6	20 - 1 kg tins
18	Carnarvon Tigers	42	0	7	8	16 kg pkg.
19	Teatime Chocolate Bis	25	0	8	3	10 boxes x 12 pieces
20	Sir Rodney's Marmala	40	0	8	3	30 gift boxes
21	Sir Rodney's Scones	3	40	8	3	24 pkgs. x 4 pieces
22	Gustaf's Knäckebröd	104	0	9	5	24 - 500 g pkgs.

Record: 1 of 77

Including UnitsInStock and UnitsOnOrder fields isn't a serious violation of the normalization rules, and it's not uncommon for product-based tables of order entry databases to include calculated values. The problem with calculated inventory values is the need to process a potentially large number of records in other tables to obtain an accurate current value.

TIP

> If you're designing an order-entry database, make sure to take into account committed inventory. Committed inventory consists of products in stock or en route from suppliers for which you have unfulfilled orders. If you decide to include inventory information in a products table, add a UnitsCommitted field.

FOURTH NORMAL FORM

Fourth normal form requires that tables not contain fields for two or more independent, multi-valued facts. Loosely translated, this rule requires splitting tables that consist of lists of independent attributes. The Northwind and Oakmont databases don't have an example of a fourth normal form violation, so the following is a fabricated example.

One of the objectives of human resources departments is to match employee job skills with job openings. A multinational organization is likely to require a combination of specific job skills and language fluency for a particular assignment. A table of job skill types and levels exists with entries such as JP3 for Java Programmer—Intermediate, as well as language/fluency with entries such as TE5 for Telagu—Very Fluent. Thus, the HR department constructs an EmplSkillLang linking table with the following foreign key fields: EmployeeID, SkillID, and LanguageID.

The problem with the linking table is that job skills and language fluency are independent facts about an employee. The ability to speak French has nothing to do with an employee's ability to write Java code. Thus the HR department must split (decompose) the three-field table into two two-field linking tables: EmplSkills and EmplLangs.

FIFTH NORMAL FORM

Fifth normal form involves further reducing redundancy by creating multiple two-field tables from tables that have more than two foreign keys. The classic example is identifying independent sales agents who sell multiple products or categories of products for different companies. In this case, you have a table with AgentID, CompanyID, and ProductID or CategoryID. You can reduce redundancy—at the risk of making the database design overly complex—by creating three two-field tables: AgentCompany, CompanyProduct (or CompanyCategory), and AgentProduct (or AgentCategory). Database developers seldom attempt to normalize designs to fifth normal form because doing so requires adding many addition small tables to the database.

CHOOSING PRIMARY KEY CODES

All Northwind and Oakmont tables use codes for primary key values, as do almost all production databases. The critical requirement is that the primary key value is unique to each record in the table. Following are some tips, many with online resources, to aid in establishing primary key codes:

- Many types of tables—such as those for storing information on sales orders, invoices, purchase orders, and checks—are based on documents that have consecutive serial numbers, which are obvious choices for unique primary key values. In fact, most database designs begin with collecting and analyzing the paper forms used by an organization. If the table itself or programming code generates the consecutive number, make sure that every serial number is present in the table, even if an order is canceled or voided. Auditors are *very* suspicious of invoice and purchase order registers that skip serial numbers.

TIP

> AutoNumber primary key values work well for serially-numbered documents if you don't allow records to be deleted. Adding a true-false (Boolean) field named Deleted and setting the value to true is one approach. This technique complicates queries against the tables, so you should consider moving deleted records to another table. Doing this lets you write a query to reconstruct all records for audit purposes.

4

- Packaged retail products sold in the United States have a globally unique 10-digit or longer Uniform Product Code (UPC). The UPC identifies both the supplier and the product's SKU. The Uniform Code Council, Inc. (`http://www.uc-council.org/`) assigns supplier and product ID values, which are combined into linear bar codes for automated identification and data capture (AIDC). The European Article Number (EAN) is coordinated with the UPC to prevent duplication. The UPC/EAN code is a much better choice than Microsoft's serially assigned number for the ProductID field.
- Books have a 10-digit International Standard Book Number (ISBN) code that's unique throughout the world and, in North America, a UPC. ISBNs include a publisher prefix and book number, assigned to U.S. publishers by the U.S. ISBN Agency (`http://www.bowker.com/standards/home/isbn/us/isbnus.html`). ISBN Group Agencies assign code for other countries. Canada has separate agencies for English- and French-language books. Either a UPC or ISBN field is suitable for the primary key of a North American books database, but ISBN is preferred if the code is for books only.
- The North American Industry Classification System (NAICS, pronounced "nakes") is replacing the U.S. Standard Industrial Classification (SIC) for categorizing organizations by their type of business. A six-digit primary key code for 18,000 classifications replaces the four-digit SIC code. Five of the six digits represent codes for classifications common to the United States, Canada, and Mexico. You can view a text file or purchase a CD-ROM of the NAICS codes and their SIC counterparts at `http://www.naics.com/`.

- The U.S. Postal Service offers Address Information Systems (AIS) files for verifying addresses and corresponding ZIP/ZIP+4 codes. For more information on these files, go to `http://www.usps.com` and click the Address Quality link.
- Social Security Numbers (SSNs) for U.S. residents are a possible choice for a primary key of an Employees table, but their disclosure compromises employee's privacy. Large numbers of counterfeit Social Security cards having identical numbers circulate in the United States, making SSN even less attractive as a primary key field. The Oakmont database uses fictitious nine-digit SSNs for EmployeeID and StudentID fields. Most organizations assign each employee a sequential serial number.

Specifying a primary key for tables such as CustPers isn't easy. If you use the five-character code based on first- and last names for the primary key, you encounter the problem with potential duplication of CustomerID codes discussed earlier. In this case, however, common last names—Jones, Smith, and Anderson for example—quickly result in duplicate values. Creating a composite primary key from CustomerID and ContactID doesn't work; doing this increases the number of new contacts you can add for a company before inevitable duplicates occur. One approach is similar to that for CustomerID values: Add two or three zeros to the ContactID values, which provides for future name duplications and doesn't require a composite primary key. As you detect duplicate key values, add 1 to the numeric suffix of the key. In most cases, it's easier to use an AutoNumber key for all ID values.

Figure 4.9 shows the final design of the modified Northwind database with the added contact details tables. The tables of this database are included on the accompanying CD-ROM as Nwind04.mdb in the \Seua2003\Chaptr04 folder.

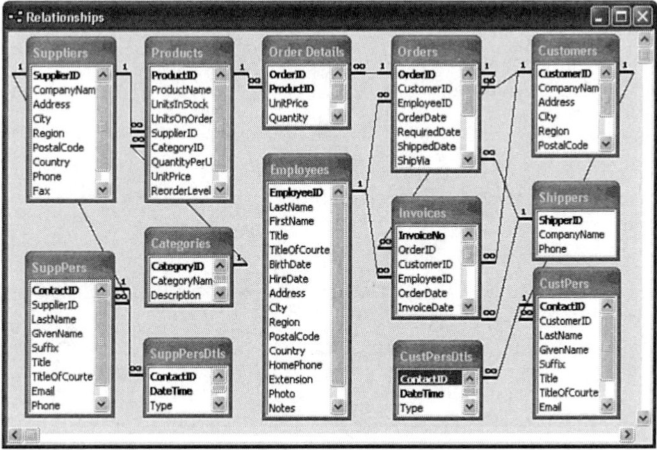

Figure 4.9
The final design of the expanded Northwind database with customer and supplier contact details tables added.

The modified Northwind database doesn't qualify as a full-fledged customer relationship management (CRM) system, but the design is sufficiently flexible to serve as the model for a sales and purchasing database for a small-sized wholesale or retail concern.

MAINTAINING DATA INTEGRITY AND ACCURACY

When you add, modify, or delete table data, it's important that the additions and changes you make to the data don't conflict with the normalization rules that you used to create the database. One of the most vexing problems facing users of large RDBMs is "unclean data." Over time, data-entry errors and stray records accumulate to the point where obtaining accurate historical information from the database becomes difficult or impossible. Software vendors and database consultants have created a major-scale "data cleansing" business to solve the problem. You can avoid the time and expense of retroactive corrections to your data by taking advantage of Jet and SQL Server features that aid in preventing errors during the data-entry process.

REFERENTIAL INTEGRITY

Maintaining referential integrity requires strict adherence to a single rule: *Each foreign key value in a related table must correspond with a primary key value in a base (primary) table*. This rule requires that the following types of modifications to data be prevented:

- Adding a record on the many side of a one-to-many relationship without the existence of a related record on the one side of the relationship, for example, adding a record to the Orders table with a CustomerID value of BOGUS when no such customer record exists in the Customers table
- Deleting a record on the one side of a one-to-many relationship without first deleting all corresponding records on the many side of the relationship, for example deleting Around the Horn's Customers record when the Orders table contains records with AROUT as the CustomerID value
- Changing the value of a primary key field of a base table on which records in a related base or linking table depend, such as changing AROUT to ABOUT in the CustomerID field of the Customers table
- Changing the value of a foreign key field in a linking table to a value that doesn't exist in the primary key field of a base table, for example changing AROUT to ABOUT in the CustomerID field for OrderID 10355

NOTE

You also must avoid changing the primary keys of or deleting one of two tables in a one-to-one relationship.

A record in a related table that doesn't have a corresponding foreign key value in the primary key of a base table is called an *orphan record*. For example, if the CustomerID value of a record in the Orders table is ABCDE and there's no ABCDE value in the CustomerID primary key field of the Customers table, there's no way to determine which customer placed the order.

Jet and SQL Server 2000 databases offer the option of automatically enforcing referential integrity when adding or updating data. Cascading updates and deletions are optional. If you specify cascading updates, changing the value of a primary key of table makes the identical change to the foreign key value in related tables. Cascading deletions delete all related records with a foreign key that corresponds to the primary key of a record in a base table that you want to delete.

→ To learn more about enforcing referential integrity in Jet databases, **see** "Establishing Relationships Between Tables," **p. 189** and "Cascading Updates and Deletions," **p. 192**.

ENTITY INTEGRITY AND INDEXES

When you add new records to a base table, entity integrity assures that each primary key value is unique. Jet and SQL Server ensure entity integrity by adding a no-duplicates index to the field you specify for the primary key. If duplicate values exist when you attempt to designate a field as the primary key, you receive an error message. You receive a similar error message if you enter a duplicate primary key value in the table.

→ For more information on Jet indexes, **see** "Adding Indexes to Tables," **p. 194**.

Indexes also speed searches of tables and improve performance when executing SQL statements that return data from fields of base and related tables.

DATA VALIDATION RULES AND CHECK CONSTRAINTS

Data-entry errors are another major source of "unclean data." In the days of punched-card data entry, keypunch operators typed the data and verifiers, who usually worked during the succeeding shift, inserted the cards in a punched-card reader and repeated the keystrokes from the same source document. This process detected typographical errors, which the verifier corrected. Keypunch operators had no visual feedback during data entry, so typos were inevitable; video display terminals didn't arrive until the mainframe era.

NOTE

Keypunch operators kept their eyes on the source documents, which gave rise to the term *heads-down data entry*. The term continues in common use to describe any data-entry process in which the operator's entire working day is spent adding or editing database records as quickly as possible.

Rekeying data leads to low productivity, so most data-entry applications support data validation rules designed to detect attempts to enter illegal or unreasonable values in fields. An example of a validation rule is preventing entry of a shipping date that's earlier than the order date. The rule is expressed as an inequality: ShipDate >= OrderDate, which returns False if the rule is violated. Similarly, UnitPrice > 0 prevents accidentally giving away a line item of an order.

Jet tables and fields have a Validation Rule property that you set to the inequality expression. SQL Server calls validation rules *check constraints*. Both Jet and SQL Server have a Validation Text property for which you specify the text to appear in an error message box when the entry violates the rule or constraint. It's a more common practice when working with client/server databases to validate data in the front-end application before sending the entry to the back-end server. Detecting the error on the server and returning an error message requires a *roundtrip* from the client to the server. Server round trips generate quite a bit of network traffic and reduce data-entry efficiency. One of the objectives of client/server front-end design is to minimize server round-tripping.

→ To learn more about Jet's validation methods, **see** "Validating Data Entry," **p. 227**.

TRANSACTIONS

A database transaction occurs when multiple records in one or more tables must be added, deleted, or modified to complete a data-entry operation. Adding an order or invoice that has multiple line items is an example of a transaction. If an order or invoice has five line items, but a network or database problem prevents adding one or more item records, the entire order or invoice is invalid. Maintaining referential integrity prevents adding line item records without a corresponding order or invoice record, but missing item records don't violate integrity rules.

Transaction processing (TP, also called *online transaction processing*, OLTP) solves the missing line item problem. Requiring TP for order entry, invoice processing, and similar multi-record operations enforces an all-or-nothing rule. If every individual update to the tables' records occur, the transaction succeeds (*commits*); if any update fails, changes made before the failure occurs are reversed (*rolled back*). Transaction processing isn't limited to RDBMSs. Early mainframe databases offered TP and transaction monitors. IBM's Customer Information and Control System (CICS, pronounced "kicks") was one of the first transaction processing and monitoring systems and remains in widespread use today.

4

Jet and SQL Server databases offer built-in TP features. Jet has a Use Transactions property that you set to Yes to require TP for updates. SQL Server traditionally requires writing T-SQL statements—`BEGIN TRANS`, `COMMIT TRANS`, and `ROLLBACK TRANS`—to manage transactions, but Access 2003's ADP forms have a new Batch Updates property that lets you enforce transactions without writing complex T-SQL statements. You also can specify automatic batch updating for DAP connected to SQL Server databases.

→ For a brief description of the new batch update feature, **see** "Changes to ADP Features," **p. 37**.

DISPLAYING DATA WITH QUERIES AND VIEWS

So far, this chapter has concentrated on designing relational databases and their tables, and adding or altering data. SQL `SELECT` queries return data to Access, but you don't need to write SQL statements to display data in forms or print reports from the data. Access has built-in graphical tools to automatically write Jet SQL for Jet databases and T-SQL for SQL Server databases. Access's query tools use a modern implementation of *query-by-example* (QBE, an IBM trademark). QBE is a simple method of specifying the tables and columns to view, how the data is sorted, and rows to include or exclude.

NOTE

> As mentioned earlier in the chapter, *fields* become *columns* and *records* become *rows* in a query. This terminology is an arbitrary convention of this book and not related to relational database design theory. The reason for the change in terminology is that a query's rows and columns need not–and often do not–represent data values stored in the underlying tables. Queries can have columns whose values are calculated from multiple fields and rows with aggregated data, such as subtotals and totals.

Linking related tables by their primary and foreign keys is called *joining* the tables. Early QBE programs required defining joins between tables; specifying table relationships automatically defines joins when you add records from two or more related Jet or SQL Server tables.

Figure 4.10 is an example of Access's QBE implementation for Jet databases, called Query Design view. You add tables to the query, in this case, Northwind's Customers, Orders, and Employees tables. As you add the tables, join lines indicate the relationships between them. You drag the field names for the query columns from the table lists in the upper pane to the Field row of the lower pane. You also can specify the name of a calculated column (Salesperson) and the expression to create the column values ([FirstName] & " " & [LastName]) in the Field row. The brackets surrounding FirstName and LastName designate that the values are field names.

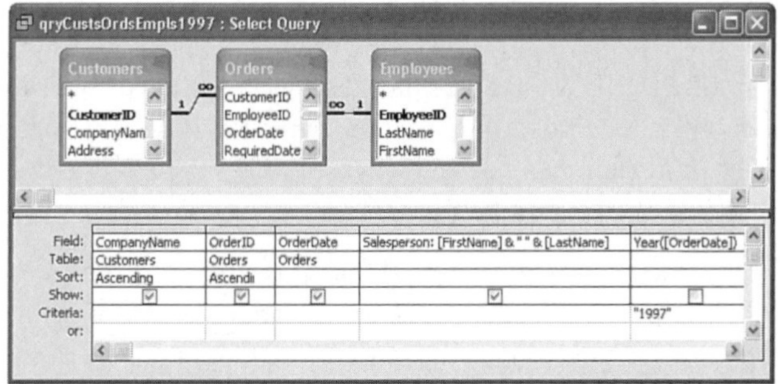

Figure 4.10
Access's Query Design view for Jet databases uses graphical QBE to create queries you can store in the database.

Selecting Ascending or Descending in the Sort column orders the rows in left-to-right column priority. You can restrict the display to a particular set of values by adding an expression in the Criteria column.

Running the query returns the result set, part of which is shown by Figure 4.11. You can save the query for later reuse as a named Jet `QueryDef`(inition) object in the database.

Figure 4.11
These are the first 16 of the 408 rows of the query result set returned by executing the query design of Figure 4.10.

qryCustsOrdsEmpls1997 : Select Query

CompanyName	Order ID	Order Date	Salesperson
Alfreds Futterkiste	10643	25-Aug-1997	Michael Suyama
Alfreds Futterkiste	10692	03-Oct-1997	Margaret Peacock
Alfreds Futterkiste	10702	13-Oct-1997	Margaret Peacock
Ana Trujillo Emparedados y helados	10625	08-Aug-1997	Janet Leverling
Ana Trujillo Emparedados y helados	10759	28-Nov-1997	Janet Leverling
Antonio Moreno Taquería	10507	15-Apr-1997	Robert King
Antonio Moreno Taquería	10535	13-May-1997	Margaret Peacock
Antonio Moreno Taquería	10573	19-Jun-1997	Robert King
Antonio Moreno Taquería	10677	22-Sep-1997	Nancy Davolio
Antonio Moreno Taquería	10682	25-Sep-1997	Janet Leverling
Around the Horn	10453	21-Feb-1997	Nancy Davolio
Around the Horn	10558	04-Jun-1997	Nancy Davolio
Around the Horn	10707	16-Oct-1997	Margaret Peacock
Around the Horn	10741	14-Nov-1997	Margaret Peacock
Around the Horn	10743	17-Nov-1997	Nancy Davolio
Around the Horn	10768	08-Dec-1997	Janet Leverling

Record: 1 of 408

Jet SQL

Access QBE automatically converts query design of Figure 4.10 into the following Jet SQL statement:

```
SELECT Customers.CompanyName, Orders.OrderID, Orders.OrderDate,
         [FirstName] & " " & [LastName] AS Salesperson
   FROM Employees
      INNER JOIN (Customers
         INNER JOIN Orders
         ON Customers.CustomerID = Orders.CustomerID)
      ON Employees.EmployeeID = Orders.EmployeeID
   WHERE ((Year([OrderDate])="1997"))
   ORDER BY Customers.CompanyName, Orders.OrderID;
```

4

It's obvious that using QBE is much simpler than writing `SELECT` queries to concatenate field values, join tables, establish row selection criteria, and specify sort order. Access's Jet QBE features are powerful; many developers use Access to generate the SQL statements needed by Visual Basic, C++, and Java programs.

The da Vinci QBE tool for creating T-SQL views is similar to the Jet Query Design view, but has an additional pane to display the T-SQL statement as you generate it. You add tables to the upper pane and drag field names to the Column cells of the middle pane. An SQL Server view is the client/server equivalent of a Jet QueryDef. Like Jet QueryDefs, you can execute a query on an SQL Server view.

Despite their common ANSI SQL-92 heritage, SQL Server won't execute most Jet SQL statements and vice-versa. Copying the preceding Jet SQL statement to the Clipboard and pasting it into the SQL pane of the query designer for the NorthwindCS sample database doesn't work. The da Vinci designer does its best to translate the Jet SQL flavor into T-SQL when you paste, but you receive errors when you try to run the query.

T-SQL

T-SQL uses `+` rather than `&` to concatenate strings, uses a single quote (') as the string delimiter, and requires a numerical instead of a string criterion for the `YEAR` function. Here's the T-SQL version of the preceding Jet SQL statement after tweaking the `SELECT` and `WHERE` clauses:

```
SELECT TOP 100 PERCENT dbo.Customers.CompanyName,
      dbo.Orders.OrderID, dbo.Orders.OrderDate,
      dbo.Employees.FirstName + ' ' +
      dbo.Employees.LastName AS Salesperson
   FROM dbo.Employees
      INNER JOIN dbo.Customers
         INNER JOIN dbo.Orders
         ON dbo.Customers.CustomerID = dbo.Orders.CustomerID
      ON dbo.Employees.EmployeeID = dbo.Orders.EmployeeID
   WHERE (YEAR(dbo.Orders.OrderDate) = 1997)
   ORDER BY dbo.Customers.CompanyName, dbo.Orders.OrderID
```

The `TOP 100 PERCENT` clause is needed to permit an `ORDER BY` clause in a view; prior to adding the `TOP` keyword in SQL Server 7.0, creating sorted views wasn't possible. The `dbo.` prefix to table and field names is an abbreviation for database owner, the default owner for all SQL Server databases you create as a system administrator. The only change to the `WHERE` clause is removal of the double-quotes surrounding 1997. Figure 4.12 shows the design of the T-SQL query generated by pasting the preceding statement into the da Vinci query pane.

→ For more information on the da Vinci toolset, **see** "Exploring SQL Server Views," **p. 819**.

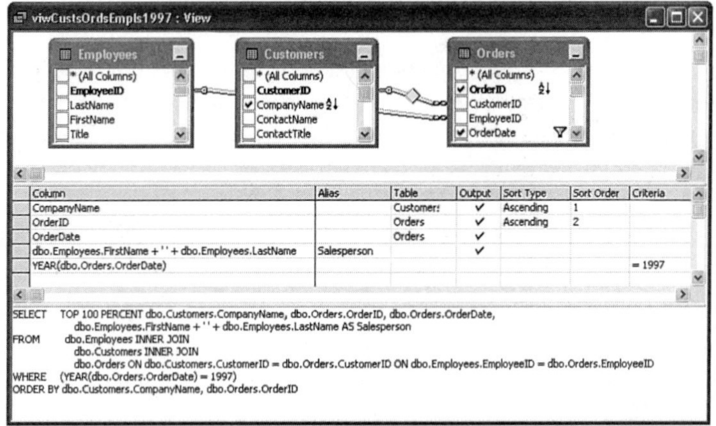

Figure 4.12
Pasting a Jet SQL statement into Access's version of the da Vinci query design tool and making a few minor changes to the T-SQL statement results in an SQL Server view equivalent to the Jet query of Figure 4.10.

NOTE

Access 2003 automatically creates the NorthwindCS database the first time you open the NorthwindCS.adp file after installing MSDE from the distribution CD-ROM.

→ For detailed instructions on installing MSDE and NorthwindCS.adp, **see** "SQL Server 2000 Desktop Engine Setup," **p. 47** and "Exploring the NorthwindCS Sample Project," **p. 808**.

NEW Figure 4.13 shows the SQL Server view of the query design of Figure 4.12 and the preceding T-SQL statement. The only difference between the view and the Jet query result set is the format of the OrderDate column, which is Short Date for SQL Server and Medium

Date for Jet. You can change the date display by selecting an entry from the Format list on the Columns page of the view's Properties dialog.

viwCustsOrdsEmpls1997 : View

CompanyName	OrderID	OrderDate	Salesperson
Alfreds Futterkiste	10643	8/25/1997	Michael Suyama
Alfreds Futterkiste	10692	10/3/1997	Margaret Peacock
Alfreds Futterkiste	10702	10/13/1997	Margaret Peacock
Ana Trujillo Emparedados y helados	10625	8/8/1997	Janet Leverling
Ana Trujillo Emparedados y helados	10759	11/28/1997	Janet Leverling
Antonio Moreno Taquería	10507	4/15/1997	Robert King
Antonio Moreno Taquería	10535	5/13/1997	Margaret Peacock
Antonio Moreno Taquería	10573	6/19/1997	Robert King
Antonio Moreno Taquería	10677	9/22/1997	Nancy Davolio
Antonio Moreno Taquería	10682	9/25/1997	Janet Leverling
Around the Horn	10453	2/21/1997	Nancy Davolio
Around the Horn	10558	6/4/1997	Nancy Davolio
Around the Horn	10707	10/16/1997	Margaret Peacock
Around the Horn	10741	11/14/1997	Margaret Peacock
Around the Horn	10743	11/17/1997	Nancy Davolio
Around the Horn	10768	12/8/1997	Janet Leverling
Around the Horn	10793	12/24/1997	Janet Leverling
B's Beverages	10471	3/11/1997	Andrew Fuller
B's Beverages	10484	3/24/1997	Janet Leverling
B's Beverages	10538	5/15/1997	Anne Dodsworth

Record: 1 of 408

Figure 4.13
This Access Datasheet view of an SQL Server view is identical to the Jet version of Figure 4.11, with the exception of the display format of the OrderDate column.

PARTITIONING DATABASES

4

A single relational database can contain a set of tables that represent every tangible object with which an organization deals. It's more common, however, to create individual databases that relate to specific organizational functions—typically sales, manufacturing, finance, and human resources. Each database is owned and managed by its department, and other departments only have access to specific fields of selected tables. For example, the sales department's order entry system must associate salespersons with their orders, but doesn't need access to employees' personnel information maintained by the human resources department.

As mentioned earlier, Jet databases let you link table data stored in other Jet, desktop, and client/server databases. Linked tables can reside on any computer to which you have a network connection and security permissions to read and, optionally, update the data. In the case of an employees table, you might find it necessary to split the table to prevent linked access to confidential employee information. Splitting a base table for linking is one of the few instances in which you use a one-to-one relationship.

SQL Server 2000 lets you link multiple servers, which provides access to every database stored on the linked server, including table and view objects, for which you have appropriate SQL Server permissions. You can write T-SQL *distributed queries* to return data from more than one database. SQL Server's *Distributed Transaction Coordinator* (DTC) enables transactions to include tables in more than one database. You also can link Windows 2000+ Server's Active Directory (AD) to an SQL Server database by using the OLE DB Provider for Microsoft Directory Services. The capability to integrate data about users, security groups, organizational units, domains, and other AD objects into Access applications is a useful feature for medium- to large-size organizations.

→ For brief introduction to linking Jet and SQL Server databases, **see** "Linking Remote Servers," **p. 842**.

Another method of distributing information between multiple databases is called *replication*. Replication periodically updates a copy of selected data in another database; updates occur only for changes that have occurred since the last replication. Replication is an ideal method for providing mobile users with tables containing the data they need while disconnected from the network. Partial database replicas let you replicate a particular set of columns or rows of a table, which eliminates the need for multiple tables to restrict distribution of confidential information. Conventional Access replication only supports Jet databases but lets you replicate application design changes in addition to data.

SQL Server replication uses the publish-subscribe model and works only with data. SQL Server 2000 can replicate data to and from Jet 4.0 databases by using merge replication. Database administrators (DBAs) often use one-way snapshot replication to provide department-level Access developers with subscriptions to the information they require from corporate databases. The advantage of snapshot replication is that users of the departmental database don't need permission to connect to the corporate database. ADP use SQL Server replication and don't permit using Jet replication to update application objects.

NOTE

Access replication for Jet databases and SQL Server replication are advanced database topics and are beyond the scope of this book. You should, however, be aware of replication options when you make the decision between creating a conventional Jet application or SQL Server-based ADP.

IN THE REAL WORLD—WHEN AND WHY LEARN RELATIONAL THEORY?

A corollary of the Law of Preservation of Matter is: "Everything Has to be Somewhere." Most books about Microsoft Access deal with relational database design theory in the first few chapters, and this latest of the eight editions of *Special Edition Using Microsoft Office Access* is no exception. Prior editions categorized this subject as an "Advanced Access Technique" that appeared toward the end of the book.

Understanding relational database design requires familiarity not only with the objects that make up the database, but with the use of these objects. After you're comfortable with table and query basics, have a feeling for form and report design, and gained an introduction to Web-based database applications, you're probably better prepared to delve into the arcana of relational algebra, such as normalization rules. That's why the previous editions didn't include this chapter in the first part of the book.

After you've gained experience working with the sample relational databases in Access and this book, their design appears intuitive and entirely logical. Experienced database designers envision even the most complex business processes as collections of related tables. So, it's somewhat surprising to many that Dr. Codd's relational database theory originated in 1970, well after the development of complex network and hierarchical architectures. If you're embarking on the road to relational database development, however, you're not likely to find database design topics at all intuitive.

An argument in favor of moving the relational database design topic to the beginning of the book is that many readers decide to use Access to accomplish a specific task that involves creating a special-purpose database. In this case, you advance through the book's chapters using the sample databases as examples rather than learning models. If you're using Access as a learning tool, starting with database design and implementation also makes the structure and relationships of the tables in the sample databases of the book more meaningful.

Increasing sales of desktop and client/server RDBMSs has spawned a multitude of books—ranging from introductory tutorials to graduate-level texts—on relational database design theory and practice. Michael J. Hernandez' *Database Design for Mere Mortals*, Second Edition (Addison-Wesley, ISBN 0-201-75284-0), subtitled "A Hands-On Guide to Relational Database Design," is an excellent resource for folks who want more than this chapter offers in the way of database design guidance. Mike and John L. Viescas, a well-known Access writer and developer, are co-authors of *SQL Queries for Mere Mortals* (Addison-Wesley, ISBN 0-201-143336-2), which delivers thorough coverage of SQL SELECT queries for Access and SQL Server users.

You need a basic knowledge of relational database design techniques to understand the structure of XML documents and schemas generated from Access tables and queries. XML is today's *lingua franca* for interchanging data between systems, not just productivity applications. Almost all software publishers offer XML document import and export, and most support XML schema definition (XSD) language.

Access 2003's upgraded XML export feature generates XML documents and corresponding XML schemas from multiple, related tables. (Access 2002 was limited to exporting flat XML documents from a single table or query). For example, you can export all or selected (contiguous) records of the Orders table and specify that the XML document and its schema includes all related Order Details records (see Figure 4.14). You also can export lookup tables that supply data for subdatasheets, but doing this can greatly increase the size of your XML document.

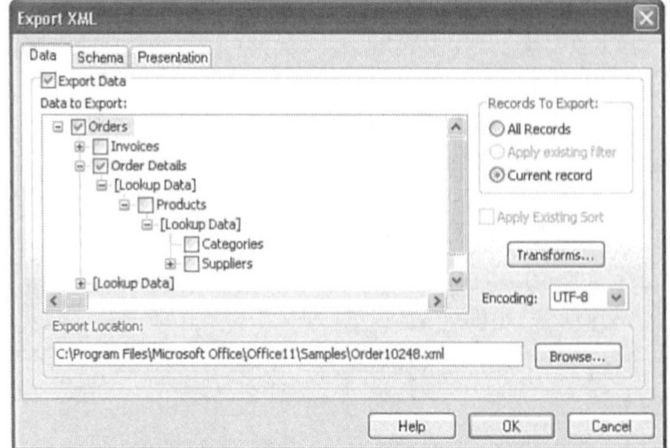

Figure 4.14
Access 2003's new Export XML dialog lets you generate a hierarchical XML document that includes elements for records in base (Orders) and related (Order Details) tables.

→ For more information on Access 2003's new XML export features, **see** "Exporting Tables and Queries to XML and HTML," **p. 954**.

The XML elements for the Order Details records are called *child nodes* of the Order *parent node* (see Figure 4.15). The `noNamespaceSchemaLocation="OrdersOrderDetails.xsd"` attribute specifies the schema file associated with the document and is assumed to be in the same folder. The `xmlns:od="urn:schemas-microsoft-com:officedata"` XML namespace declaration indicates that the document originated from an Office 2002 or 2003 member.

Figure 4.15 This exported XML document for the first Order record in the Northwind Orders database includes child nodes for its three Order Details records, only one of which is visible here. Spaces aren't allowed in XML element names, so Access and SQL Server substitute _X0020_ for spaces in table and field names.

The exported XML schema contains a complete description of the relationship between the tables and their fields (see Figure 4.16). Access 2003's XML schema generation feature depends on information from the Relationships window. You can use the schema to import the XML document into other XML-enabled Office 2003 members automatically, because the schema also includes the `xmlns:od="urn:schemas-microsoft-com:officedata"` namespace declaration. For example, if you import the Order10248.xml document into an empty Access 2003 database, the document/schema combination generates new Orders and Order Details tables, creates indexes, and establishes the relationship between the tables. Importing the sample document into Excel 2003 automatically generates an Excel list that displays data from the three Order Details records with duplicated Orders data in each row.

NOTE

Copies of Order10248.xml, OrdersOrderDetails.xsd, an XML worksheet with an imported list (ExportXML.xls), and a Word 2003 document created from Order10248.xml are in the \Seua2003\Chaptr04 folder of the accompanying CD-ROM.

4

```
<?xml version="1.0" encoding="UTF-8" ?>
- <xsd:schema xmlns:xsd="http://www.w3.org/2001/XMLSchema"
    xmlns:od="urn:schemas-microsoft-com:officedata">
  - <xsd:element name="dataroot">
    - <xsd:complexType>
      - <xsd:sequence>
          <xsd:element ref="Orders" minOccurs="0"
            maxOccurs="unbounded" />
        </xsd:sequence>
      </xsd:complexType>
    </xsd:element>
  - <xsd:element name="Orders">
    - <xsd:annotation>
      - <xsd:appinfo>
          <od:index index-name="PrimaryKey" index-key="OrderID"
            primary="yes" unique="yes" clustered="no" />
          <od:index index-name="CustomerID" index-
            key="CustomerID" primary="no" unique="no"
            clustered="no" />
          <od:index index-name="CustomersOrders" index-
            key="CustomerID" primary="no" unique="no"
            clustered="no" />
          <od:index index-name="EmployeeID" index-
            key="EmployeeID" primary="no" unique="no"
            clustered="no" />
          <od:index index-name="EmployeesOrders" index-
            key="EmployeeID" primary="no" unique="no"
            clustered="no" />
```

Figure 4.16
The XML schema for Figure 4.15's document, only a small part of which is shown here, contains all the information needed by Access 2003 to generate new Orders and Order Details tables in another database and populate the tables with the contents of the associated XML document.

→ For the details of importing XML documents into Access and other Office 2003 members, **see** "Importing XML Data to Tables," **p. 983**.

If you're serious about getting the most out of Access 2003, consider purchasing a copy of Mike's book or browse the bookstore shelves for titles on relational database design. Your investment will pay handsome dividends when you're able to create the optimum design to start, instead of attempting to restructure a badly designed database after it's grown to 20 or 30 tables containing thousands—or millions—of rows.

CHAPTER 5

Working with Jet Databases and Tables

In this chapter

UNDERSTANDING JET DATABASE FILES

The traditional name for an .mdb file that stores Access application, data objects, or both is *Access database*. As other database programming tools, such as Visual Basic, began using data-only .mdb files, *Jet database* became the preferred designation for files containing only tables and queries. Access is only one of many Microsoft applications and programming tools that take advantage of the Jet database engine. Jet 4.0, which Access 2000 and 2002 also use, is the latest *and last* Jet version. Access 2002 was the first Access upgrade that didn't introduce a new Jet version or require converting existing .mdb files into a new format to enable changing the design of database objects. Access 2003's default database version remains Access 2000 format.

Microsoft's determination to make SQL Server the database engine of choice for Access 2003 and all future Access versions is another reason for changing from Access to Jet terminology for applications that use .mdb and related files. Access 2000 and 2002 store application objects—forms, reports, macros, and modules—in a new compound file format called a *DocFile*. Conventional Access applications store the application object DocFile within the .mdb file. Access Data Projects (ADP), which now represent the preferred approach to designing Access applications that connect to SQL Server databases, store the DocFile directly on disk as an .adp file. Combining ADP front ends with SQL Server back-end databases eliminates the need to periodically compact .mdb files and occasionally repair corrupted Jet databases. The chapters of Part V, "Upgrading to SQL Server 2000 Databases," cover designing ADP and SQL Server databases.

TIP

> Using ADP and SQL Server databases for simple, single-user Access applications is overkill. You don't need the power of SQL Server 2000 for mailing list, contact management, or similar projects. Creating applications that use Jet to store your data is easier than designing and managing SQL Server databases. Thus, the beginning chapters of this book deal exclusively with Jet databases.
>
> If you intend to create multiuser applications, which let several users update the database simultaneously, seriously consider using Access's no-charge version of SQL Server 2000 Desktop Engine (MSDE) to store the data. Use SQL Server for any databases whose content is vital to the continued success–or existence–of an organization, such as sales orders, invoices, and accounts receivable. Access 2003 includes an Upsizing Wizard that greatly simplifies moving from Jet to SQL Server databases. So, you can start with Jet and then move to SQL Server as you become proficient in database application design.

References in earlier chapters to the advantages of Jet's single-file approach to database storage don't take into account the other types of files associated with Jet databases. Access requires a workgroup information file to open an .mdb file and automatically creates record-locking information files for open databases. The following sections briefly describe the additional types of files used by conventional Access (Jet) applications.

JET WORKGROUP INFORMATION FILES

In addition to database files with the .mdb extension, Access uses a default security database file called the *workgroup file* and named System.mdw. In early versions of Access, this file was named System.mda and called the *system file*. The location of System.mdw depends on your operating system. Windows XP, the operating system used for most of the examples of this book, and Windows 2000 store System.mdw in the \Documents and Settings*LogonID*\ My Documents\Application Data\Microsoft\Access folder. The LogonID folder name is the logon you used when installing Office 2003 on your computer—usually the local Administrator account. If you're a member of a Windows NT/2000+ domain, the *LogonID* folder is *DOMAIN.UserName*.

TIP

> To determine the location of System.mdw on your computer, open a database, and choose Tools, Security, Workgroup Administrator to open the Workgroup Administrator dialog, which displays the local path to the file.

System.mdw contains information about the following:

- Names of users and groups of users who can open a Jet database. Access's default username is Admin with an empty password, which lets you open Jet databases without providing a username and password in a logon dialog.
- User passwords and a unique binary code, called a Security ID (SID), that identifies the current user to Access.
- An optional Workgroup ID (WID) that uniquely identifies the workgroup. The default System.mdw file doesn't have a WID.

5

The default System.mdw file is the same for every initial Access installation. Access runs and lets you open unsecured databases without having System.mdw on your machine.

CAUTION

> If you decide to secure your Admin account with a password or apply security to database objects in an .mdb file, make a backup of System.mdw or another .mdw file you create with the Workgroup Administrator and save it in a secure location. If you delete your workgroup file or it becomes corrupted, you won't be able to open secure .mdb files.

JET RECORD-LOCKING INFORMATION FILES

When you open an .mdb or other types of Access-related Jet files, Jet automatically creates a record-locking file having the same name as the database but with an .ldb extension. The purpose of the .ldb file is to maintain for multiuser applications a list of records that each user currently is updating. The .ldb file prevents data corruption when two or more users simultaneously attempt to change data in the same record. The presence of an .ldb file also prevents two or more users from saving design changes to the same database. If you open a database that another user has open with an object in design mode, you receive a message that you can't save any changes you make. The same restriction applies if you have the same database open in two instances of Access. When all users or instances of Access close the .mdb file, Jet deletes the .ldb file.

JET ADD-IN (LIBRARY) DATABASES

Another category of Access database files is *add-ins*, also called *libraries*. Add-ins are Access databases—usually with an .mda or .mde extension to distinguish them from user databases—that you can link to Access by choosing Tools, References in the VBA editor's menu, or through the Add-In Manager, which you access by choosing Tools, Add-Ins from Access's main menu. The Add-In Manager also lets you add another class of extensions to Access called *COM Add-ins*.

When you link an Access add-in, all elements of the library database are available to you after you open Access. The Access 2003 wizards that you use to create forms, reports, graphs, and other application objects are stored in a series of Access add-in database files: Acwzlib.mde, Acwztool.mde, and Acwzmain.mde. Access 2003 also installs add-in data files, which have an .mdt extension. The standard Access wizards don't appear in the Add-In Manager's dialog. Add-in databases are an important and unique feature of Access; third-party firms provide useful libraries to add new features and capabilities to Access.

CREATING A NEW JET DATABASE

If you have experience with relational database management systems, you might want to start building your own database as you progress through this book. In this case, you need to create a new database file at this point. If database management systems are new to you, however, you should instead explore the sample databases supplied with Access and on the accompanying CD-ROM as you progress through the chapters of this book. Before you design your first database, review the principles outlined in Chapter 4, "Exploring Relational Database Theory and Practice." Then return to this section and create your new database file.

To create a new Jet database in Access 2000 format, follow these steps:

1. If you aren't already running Access, launch it and skip to step 3.

2. If Access is running and the task pane isn't visible, press Ctrl+F1 or choose View, Task Pane to display the Getting Started page. Click the Create a New File link under the Open heading to display the New File page.
3. Click the Blank Database item under the task pane's New heading on the New File page to open the File New Database dialog (see Figure 5.1).

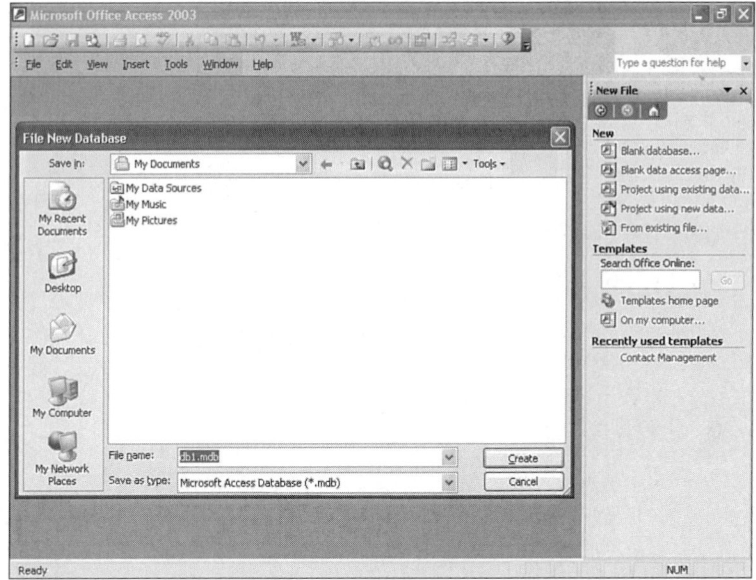

Figure 5.1
Clicking the Blank Database link in the New File page of the task pane opens the File New Database dialog with db1.mdb as the default database name and My Documents as its location.

NOTE

> Access supplies the default file name, db1.mdb, for new databases, and proposes to save the database in your My Documents folder. If you've previously saved a database file as db1.mdb in the current folder, Access supplies db2.mdb as the default.

4. In the File Name text box, type a file name for the new database. Use conventional file-naming rules; you can use spaces and punctuation in the name, but doing so isn't a recommended practice. You don't need to include an extension in the file name; Access automatically supplies the .mdb extension.
5. Click Create or press Enter to create the new Jet database file.

5

→ For more about file and object naming conventions, **see** "In the Real World—Database Strategy and Table Tactics," **p. 215**.

If a database was open when you created the new database, Access closes open windows displaying database objects, the Database window, and the task pane. Then the Database window for the new database opens.

All Office 2003 applications use DocFiles to store their data and share similar *FileName* Properties dialogs, which open when you choose File, Database Properties (see Figure 5.2). Each new Jet 4.0 database occupies 96KB of disk space when you create it. Most of the 96KB is space consumed by hidden system tables for adding the information necessary to specify the names and locations of other database elements that the database file contains.

Figure 5.2
The *FileName* Properties dialog for .mdb files has five tabbed pages that contain properties similar to the DocFiles created by other Office 2003 applications.

EXPLORING THE PROPERTIES OF TABLES AND FIELDS

Before you add a table to a database that you've created or to one of the sample databases supplied with Access, you need to know the terms and conventions that Access uses to describe the structure of a table and the fields that contain the table's data items. With Access, you specify property values for tables and fields.

Properties of Jet tables apply to the table as a whole. You enter properties of tables in text boxes of the Table Properties window (see Figure 5.3), which you display by clicking the toolbar's Properties button in Table Design view. Setting table property values is optional unless you have a specific reason to override the default values.

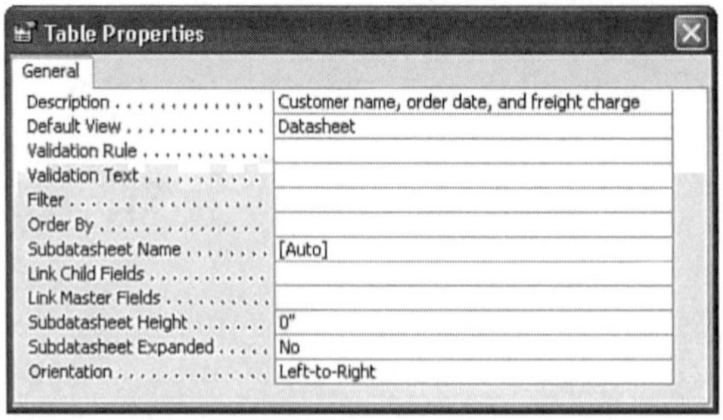

Table Properties

General

Description	Customer name, order date, and freight charge
Default View	Datasheet
Validation Rule	
Validation Text	
Filter	
Order By	
Subdatasheet Name	[Auto]
Link Child Fields	
Link Master Fields	
Subdatasheet Height	0"
Subdatasheet Expanded	No
Orientation	Left-to-Right

Figure 5.3
The Table Properties dialog for Northwind.mdb's Orders table uses default values for all but the Description property.

Following are brief descriptions of some of the 12 properties of Access 2003's Jet tables. The properties related to subdatasheets are detailed in the next section.

- *Description* is a text explanation of the table's purpose. If you choose View, Details, the Database window displays this description. This description also is useful with a data dictionary, which you use to document databases and database applications.

- *Default View* lets you select from Datasheet, PivotTable, and PivotChart views of a table, a feature introduced by Access 2002. The default selection is Datasheet view. PivotTable and PivotChart views of tables seldom are meaningful. Chapter 12, "Working with PivotTable and PivotChart Views," describes how to design queries that optimize the usefulness of these two views.
- *Validation Rule* is an expression (formula) used to establish domain integrity rules for more than one field of the table. The Validation Rule expression that you enter here applies to the table as a whole, instead of to a single field. Validation rules and domain integrity are two of the subjects of Chapter 6, "Entering, Editing, and Validating Jet Table Data."

→ For more information on validation rules for tables, **see** "Adding Table-Level Validation Rules with the Expression Builder," **p. 230**.

- *Validation Text* specifies the text of the message box that opens if you violate a table's Validation Rule expression.
- *Filter* specifies a constraint to apply to the table whenever it's open. Filters restrict the number of records that appear, based on selection criteria you supply. Chapter 7, "Sorting, Finding, and Filtering Data," discusses filters.

→ To learn more about filters, **see** "Filtering Table Data," **p. 249**.

- *Order By* specifies a sort(ing) order to apply to the table whenever it's opened. Chapter 7 also explains sort orders. If you don't specify a sort order, records display in the order of the primary key, if a primary key exists. Otherwise, they appear in the order in which you enter them. The "Working with Relations, Key Fields, and Indexes" section, later in this chapter, discusses primary key fields.

→ For the details of applying sort order to a table, **see** "Sorting Table Data," **p. 242**.

5

- *Orientation*, another Access 2002 property, lets you specify right-to-left display of data in languages such as Hebrew and Arabic. Orientation is an Access-only data display property, and doesn't affect how Jet stores the data.

NOTE

> SQL Server 2000 has a new *extended properties* feature to support special Jet and Access table and field properties, such as subdatasheets and lookup fields. The Table Properties dialog differs greatly from Access's version, but Table Design view of SQL Server's da Vinci toolset—also called the project designer—is similar to Access's Jet Table Design view.

TABLE PROPERTIES FOR SUBDATASHEETS

Access 2000 introduced subdatasheets to display sets of records of related tables in nested datasheets. You can use subdatasheets in the Datasheet view of tables and queries, and also in forms and subforms. Access, not Jet, implements subdatasheets. Figure 5.4 illustrates

Northwind.mdb's Orders table in Datasheet view with a subdatasheet opened to display related records from the Order Details table. The Orders Details (child) table has a many-to-one relationship with the Orders (master) table. To open a subdatasheet, click the + symbol adjacent to a record selection button.

Figure 5.4
Opening a subdatasheet displays records of the child table (Order Details) that are related to the selected record in the master table (Orders).

Orders : Table

Order ID	Customer	Employee	Order Date	Required Date	Shipped Date
10248	Wilman Kala	Buchanan, Steven	04-Jul-1996	01-Aug-1996	16-Jul-1996

Product	Unit Price	Quantity	Discount
Queso Cabrales	$14.00	12	0%
Singaporean Hokkien Fried Mee	$9.80	10	0%
Mozzarella di Giovanni	$34.80	5	0%
*	$0.00	1	0%

Order ID	Customer	Employee	Order Date	Required Date	Shipped Date
10249	Tradição Hipermercados	Suyama, Michael	05-Jul-1996	16-Aug-1996	10-Jul-1996
10250	Hanari Carnes	Peacock, Margaret	08-Jul-1996	05-Aug-1996	12-Jul-1996
10251	Victuailles en stock	Leverling, Janet	08-Jul-1996	05-Aug-1996	15-Jul-1996
10252	Suprêmes délices	Peacock, Margaret	09-Jul-1996	06-Aug-1996	11-Jul-1996
10253	Hanari Carnes	Leverling, Janet	10-Jul-1996	24-Jul-1996	16-Jul-1996
10254	Chop-suey Chinese	Buchanan, Steven	11-Jul-1996	08-Aug-1996	23-Jul-1996
10255	Richter Supermarkt	Dodsworth, Anne	12-Jul-1996	09-Aug-1996	15-Jul-1996
10256	Wellington Importadora	Leverling, Janet	15-Jul-1996	12-Aug-1996	17-Jul-1996
10257	HILARIÓN-Abastos	Peacock, Margaret	16-Jul-1996	13-Aug-1996	22-Jul-1996
10258	Ernst Handel	Davolio, Nancy	17-Jul-1996	14-Aug-1996	23-Jul-1996
10259	Centro comercial Moctezuma	Peacock, Margaret	18-Jul-1996	15-Aug-1996	25-Jul-1996
10260	Old World Delicatessen	Peacock, Margaret	19-Jul-1996	16-Aug-1996	29-Jul-1996
10261	Que Delícia	Peacock, Margaret	19-Jul-1996	16-Aug-1996	30-Jul-1996
10262	Rattlesnake Canyon Grocery	Callahan, Laura	22-Jul-1996	19-Aug-1996	25-Jul-1996
10263	Ernst Handel	Dodsworth, Anne	23-Jul-1996	20-Aug-1996	31-Jul-1996

Record: 1 of 3

→ If you're not familiar with relationships between tables, **see** "Removing Data Redundancy with Relationships," **p. 130**.

The following table properties apply to subdatasheets:

- *Subdatasheet Name* determines whether and how subdatasheets display data in related records. The default value is [Auto], which automatically adds subdatasheets for records linked from a related table that has a many-to-one relationship with the open table. You also can select a name from a list of the database's tables and queries. A value of [None] turns off subdatasheets in the master table.
- *Link Child Fields* specifies the name of the linked field of the related (subordinate) table whose records appear in the subdatasheet. You don't need to specify a value if the Subdatasheet Name property value is [Auto] and a many-to-one relationship exists with the master table.
- *Link Master Fields* specifies the name of the linking field of the master table, if you specify a Subdatasheet Name value.
- *Subdatasheet Height*, if supplied, specifies the maximum height of the subdatasheet. A value of 0 (the default) allows the subdatasheet to display all related records, limited only by the size of the master datasheet or subdatasheet.
- *Subdatasheet Expanded* controls the initial display of the subdatasheet. Setting the value to Yes causes the datasheet to open with all subdatasheets expanded (open).

NOTE

> You can nest subdatasheets within other subdatasheets. For example, the Customers table has an Order table subdatasheet that, in turn, has an Order Details table subdatasheet.

→ For information on how to create a subdatasheet for a table, **see** "Adding Subdatasheets to a Table or Query," **p. 419**.

FIELD PROPERTIES

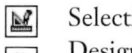

Selecting a table in the Database window and clicking the Design button opens the Table Design window. You assign each field of a Jet table a set of properties. You specify values for the first three field properties in the Table Design grid, the upper pane of the Table Design window shown in Figure 5.5. The primary key of the Customers table is the CustomerID field, indicated by a small key symbol in the field selection button. You set the remaining property values in the Table Design window's lower pane, Field Properties.

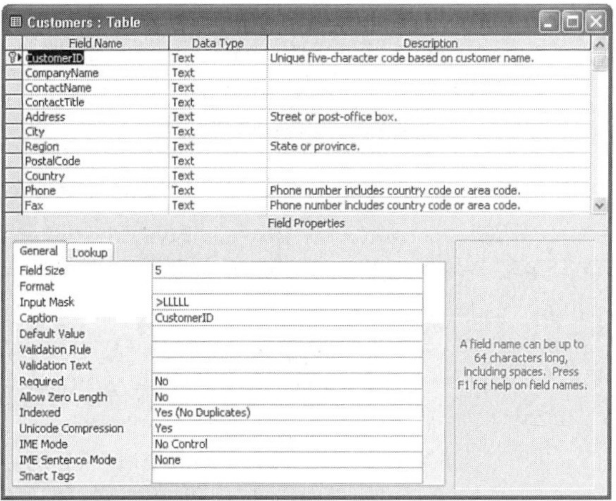

Figure 5.5 Northwind.mdb's Customers table's CustomerID field is designated the primary key field. All fields of the Customer tables are of the Text data type.

→ If you're not familiar with the term *primary key*, **see** "Defining the Structure of Relational Databases," **p. 129**.

The following list summarizes the properties you set in the Table Design grid:

- *Field Name*—You type the name of the field in the Table Design grid's first column. Field names can be as long as 64 characters and can include embedded (but not leading) spaces and punctuation—except periods (.), exclamation marks (!), and square brackets ([]). Field names are mandatory, and you can't assign the same field name to more than one field in the same table. It's good database programming practice not to include spaces or punctuation characters in field names. (Substitute an underscore (_) for spaces or use uppercase and lowercase letters to improve the readability of field names.) Minimizing the length of field names conserves resources.

- *Data Type*—You select data types from a drop-down list in the Table Design grid's second column. Data types include Text, Memo, Number, Date/Time, Currency, AutoNumber, Yes/No, OLE Object, Hyperlink, and Lookup Wizard. (The Lookup Wizard is an Access feature, not a data type). Choosing a data type is the subject of the next section.
- *Description*—You can enter an optional description of the field in the text box in the Table Design grid's third column. If you add a description, it appears in the status bar at the lower left of Access's window when you select the field for data entry or editing. Description is a special property of Jet and SQL Server 2000 databases and is for informative purposes only.
- *Primary Key*—To choose a field as the primary-key field, select the field by clicking the field-selection button to the left of the Field Name column, and then click the Primary Key button on the toolbar.

Depending on the specific data type that you choose for a field, you can set additional properties for a table field. You set these additional properties on the General page of the Table Design window's Field Properties pane by selecting from drop-down or combo lists or by typing values in text boxes. You use the Field Properties pane's Lookup page to set the control type for lookup fields on forms—list box, combo list, and so on. Chapter 15, "Designing Custom Multitable Forms," describes how to use lookup fields.

The following list summarizes the General field properties of Jet tables:

- *Field Size*—You enter the field size for the Text data type in this text box. (See the "Fixed-Width Text Fields" section later in this chapter to learn how to select a text field size.) For most Numeric data types, you determine the field size by selecting from a drop-down list. The Decimal data type requires that you type values for Precision and Scale. Field size doesn't apply to the Date/Time, Yes/No, Currency, Memo, Hyperlink, or OLE Object data type.
- *Format*—You can select a standard, predefined format in which to display the values in the field from the drop-down combo list that's applicable to the data type that you selected (except Text). Alternatively, you can enter a custom format in the text box (see "Custom Display Formats" later in this chapter). The Format property doesn't affect the data values; it affects only how these values are displayed. The Format property doesn't apply to OLE Object fields.
- *Precision*—This property appears only when you select Decimal as the data size of the Number data type. Precision defines the total number of digits to represent a numeric value. The default is 18, and the maximum value is 28 for Jet .mdb files.
- *Scale*—Like Precision, this property appears only for the Decimal data size selection. Scale determines the number of decimal digits to the right of the decimal point. The value of Scale must be less than or equal to the Precision value.
- *Decimal Places*—You can select Auto or a specific number of decimal places from the drop-down combo list, or you can enter a number in the text box. The Decimal Places

property applies only to Number and Currency fields. Like the Format property, the Decimal Places property affects only the display, not the data values, of the field.

- *Input Mask*—Input masks are character strings, similar to the character strings used for the Format property, that determine how to display data during data entry and editing. If you click the Builder button for a field of the Text, Currency, Number, or Date/Time field data type, Access starts the Input Mask Wizard to provide you with a predetermined selection of standard input masks, such as telephone numbers with optional area codes.
- *Caption*—If you want a name (other than the field name) to appear in the field name header button in Table Datasheet view, you can enter an alias for the field name in the Caption list box. The restrictions on field name punctuation symbols don't apply to the Caption property. (You can use periods, exclamation points, and square brackets, if you want.)
- *Default Value*—By entering a value in the Default Value text box, you specify a value that Access automatically enters in the field when you add a new record to the table. The current date is a common default value for a Date/Time field. (See "Setting Default Values of Fields" later in this chapter for more information.) Default values don't apply to fields with AutoNumber or OLE Object field data types.
- *Validation Rule*—Validation rules test the value entered in a field against criteria that you supply in the form of a Jet expression. Unlike table-level validation rules, the field validation expression operates only on a single field. The Validation Rule property isn't available for fields with AutoNumber, Memo, or OLE Object field data types.

→ For an example of applying field-level validation rules, **see** "Adding Field-Level Validation Rules," **p. 228**.

- *Validation Text*—You enter the text that is to appear in the status bar if the value entered does not meet the Validation Rule criteria.
- *Required*—If you set the value of the Required property to Yes, you must enter a value in the field. Setting the Required property to Yes is the equivalent of typing Is Not Null as a field validation rule. (You don't need to set the value of the Required property to Yes for fields included in the primary key because Jet doesn't permit Null values in primary-key fields.)
- *Allow Zero Length*—If you set the value of the Allow Zero Length property to No and the Required property to Yes, the field must contain at least one character. The Allow Zero Length property applies to the Text, Memo, and Hyperlink field data types only. A zero-length string ("") and the Null value aren't the same.
- *Indexed*—From the drop-down list, you can select between an index that allows duplicate values or one that requires each value of the field to be unique. You remove an existing index (except from a field that is a single primary-key field) by selecting No. The Indexed property is not available for Memo, OLE Object, or Hyperlink fields. (See "Adding Indexes to Tables" later in this chapter for more information on indexes.)
- *New Values*—This property applies only to AutoNumber fields. You select either Increment or Random from a drop-down list. If you set the New Values property to

Increment, Access generates new values for the AutoNumber field by adding 1 to the highest existing AutoNumber field value. If you set the property to Random, Jet generates new values for the AutoNumber field by producing a pseudo-random long integer.

The "Gaps in AutoNumber Field Values" element of the "Troubleshooting" section near the end of the chapter discusses issues when you delete records from a table that has an AutoNumber field.

- *Unicode Compression*—Unicode is a method of encoding characters in multiple alphabets with two bytes, instead of the conventional single-byte ASCII or ANSI representation. Ordinarily, the use of two-byte encoding doubles the space occupied by values typed in Text, Memo, and Hyperlink fields. The first Unicode character of languages using the Latin alphabet is 0. If Unicode compression is set to Yes, the default value, Jet stores all Unicode characters with a first-byte value of 0 in a single byte.

- *IME Mode* and *IME Sentence Mode*—These two properties apply only to fields having Text, Memo, and Hyperlink data types. IME is an abbreviation for Office 2003's Input Method Editor, which governs the method of inputting characters of East Asian languages. IME Sentence Mode is applicable only to the Japanese language. A discussion of IME features is beyond the scope of this book.

- *Smart Tags*—You can add smart tags, which usually link Internet resources to a specific field. For example you can add a Financial Symbol smart tag to a Jet table field containing New York Stock Exchange or NASDAQ stock symbols to let users select from stock quotes, company reports, and recent company news from the MSN Money Central Web site. Access 2003 also uses a smart tag to apply changes in a property value to dependent database objects.

→ For details on Access 2003's use of smart tags to propagate field property value changes to other database objects, **see** "Working with Object Dependencies and Access Smart Tags," **p. 200**.

5

As illustrated later in this chapter, adding the first example table, HRActions, to the Northwind.mdb database, requires you to specify appropriate data types, sizes, and formats for the table's fields.

CHOOSING FIELD DATA TYPES, SIZES, AND FORMATS

You must assign a field data type to each field of a table, unless you want to use the Text data type that Jet assigns by default. One principle of relational database design is that all data in a single field consists of one data type. Jet provides a much wider variety of data types and formats from which to choose than most other PC database managers. In addition to setting the data type, you can set other field properties that determine the format, size, and other characteristics of the data that affect its appearance and the accuracy with which numerical values are stored. Table 5.1 describes the field data types that you can select for data contained in Jet tables.

TABLE 5.1 FIELD DATA TYPES AVAILABLE IN JET 4.0

Information	Data Type	Description of Data Type
Characters	Text	Text fields are most common, so Access assigns Text as the default data type. A Text field can contain as many as 255 characters, and you can designate a maximum length less than or equal to 255. Access assigns a default length of 50 characters.
Characters	Memo	Memo fields ordinarily can contain as many as 65,535 characters. You use them to provide descriptive comments. Access displays the contents of Memo fields in Datasheet view. A Memo field can't be a key field.
Numeric Values	Number	Several numeric data subtypes are available. You choose the appropriate data subtype by selecting one of the Field Size property settings listed in Table 5.2. You specify how to display the number by setting its Format property to one of the formats listed in Table 5.3.
	AutoNumber	An AutoNumber field is a numeric (Long Integer) value that Jet automatically fills in for each new record you add to a table. Jet can increment the AutoNumber field by 1 for each new record, or fill in the field with a randomly generated number, depending on the New Values property setting that you choose. The maximum number of records in a table that can use the AutoNumber field with the Long Integer size is slightly more than two billion.
	Yes/No	Logical (Boolean) fields in Access use numeric values: –1 for Yes (True) and 0 for No (False). You use the Format property to display Yes/No fields as Yes or No, True or False, On or Off, or –1 or 0. (You can also use any nonzero number to represent True.) Logical fields can't be key fields but can be indexed.
	Currency	Currency is a special fixed format with four decimal places designed to prevent rounding errors that would affect accounting operations in which the value must match to the penny.
Dates and Times	Date/Time	Dates and times are stored in a special fixed format. The date is represented by the whole number portion of the Date/Time value, and the time is represented by its decimal fraction. You control how Access displays dates by selecting one of the Date/Time Format properties listed in Table 5.3.

continues

TABLE 5.1 CONTINUED

Information	Data Type	Description of Data Type
Large Objects (Binary Data)	OLE Object	Includes bitmapped and vector-type graphics, and other BLOBs (binary large objects), such as waveform audio files and video files. You can't assign an OLE Object field as a key field, nor can you include an OLE Object field in an index. Clicking an OLE Object in Datasheet view opens the object in its editing application.
Web Addresses	Hyperlink	Hyperlink fields store Web page document addresses. A Web address stored in the Hyperlink field can refer to a Web page on the Internet or one stored locally on your computer or network. Clicking a Hyperlink field in datasheet view causes Access to start your Web browser and display the referenced Web page. Choose Insert, Hyperlink to add a new hyperlink address to a Hyperlink field. Hyperlink is an Access, not a Jet, data type.
Related Data	Lookup Wizard	Lookup Wizard isn't a legitimate data type; it's a property of a field. Selecting Lookup Wizard starts the Lookup Wizard to add a lookup feature to the table. Most lookup operations execute a query to obtain data from a field of a related table.

→ To learn how to use the Lookup Wizard, **see** "Using Lookup Fields in Tables," **p. 412**.

5

NOTE

The OLE Object field data type is unique to Access; other applications that use Jet designate the OLE Object field data type as *Binary* or *Long Binary*. When you add an OLE object, such as a bit-mapped graphic from Windows Paint or a Word document, Access adds a special header, which identifies the source application, to the binary graphics data. Other applications can't read data from OLE Object fields you create in Access. OLE Object fields won't upsize to SQL Server 2000, because SQL server's `image` fields don't support the OLE Object data type.

CHOOSING FIELD SIZES FOR NUMERIC AND TEXT DATA

The Field Size property of a field determines which data type a Number field uses or how many characters fixed-length text fields can accept. Field Size properties are called subtypes to distinguish them from the data types listed in Table 5.1. For numbers, you select a Field Size property value from the Field Size drop-down list in the Table Design window's Field Properties pane (see Figure 5.6).

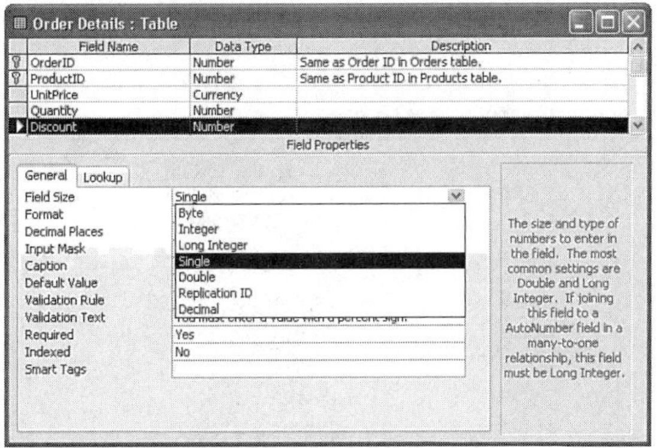

Figure 5.6
You can select one of seven Field Size (data subtype) property values for fields having a Number data type from the drop-down list.

SUBTYPES FOR NUMERIC DATA

The Number data type of the previously shown Table 5.1 isn't a fully specified data type. You must select one of the subtypes from those listed in Table 5.2 for the Field Size property to define the numeric data type properly. To select a data subtype for a Number field, follow these steps:

1. Select the Data Type cell of the Number field for which you want to select the subtype.
2. Click the Field Size text box in the Field Properties window. You also can press F6 to switch windows, and then use the arrow keys to position the caret within the Field Size text box.
3. Click the drop-down arrow to open the list of choices shown previously in Figure 5.6. You can also press the F4 key to open the list.
4. Select the data subtype. (Table 5.2 describes data subtypes.) When you make a selection, the list closes.

After you select a Field Size property, you select a Format property from those listed in Table 5.3 (later in this chapter) to determine how to display the data. Table 5.2 includes the Currency data type because it also can be considered a subtype of the Number data type.

Regardless of how you format your data for display, the number of decimal digits, the range, and the storage requirement remains that specified by the Field Size property.

NOTE

These data types are available in Visual Basic for Applications 6.0. VBA includes all the data types listed in Table 5.2 as reserved words. You can't use a reserved data type word for any purpose in VBA functions and procedures other than to specify a data type.

TABLE 5.2 SUBTYPES OF THE NUMBER DATA TYPE DETERMINED BY THE FIELD SIZE PROPERTY

Field Size	Decimals	Range of Values	Bytes
Decimal	28 places	–10^-28 to 10^28 –1	14
Double	15 places	–1.797 * 10^308 to +1.797 * 10^308	8
Single	7 places	–3.4 * 10^38 to +3.4 * 10^38	4
Long Integer	None	–2,147,483,648 to +2,147,483,647	4
Integer	None	–32,768 to 32,767	2
Byte	None	0 to 255	1
Replication ID	None	Not applicable	16
Currency	4 places	–922337203685477.5808 to +922337203685477.5808	8

➔ For more information on VBA reserved words for data types, **see** "Data Types and Database Objects in VBA," **p. 1159**.

As a rule, you select the Field Size property that results in the smallest number of bytes that encompasses the range of values you expect and that expresses the value in sufficient precision for your needs. Mathematical operations with Integer and Long Integer proceed more quickly than those with Single and Double data types (called floating-point numbers) or the Currency and Date/Time data types (fixed-point numbers). Microsoft added the Decimal data subtype for conformance with the SQL Server decimal data type.

5

TIP

Always use the Decimal data type for fractional values—such as percentages—that you intend to use for calculating Currency or other Decimal values. The Order Details table's Discount field uses the Jet Single data type, which is notorious for causing rounding errors in decimal calculations.

NOTE

You can apply the Replication ID field size to Number or AutoNumber fields. A replication ID is a specially formatted 32-character (16-byte) hexadecimal number (values 0 through 9 and A through F) surrounded by French braces. The more common name for a replication ID is *globally unique identifier* (GUID, pronounced "goo id" or "gwid"). A typical GUID looks like {8AA5F467-3AF5-4669-B4CB-5207CDC79EF4}. GUID values, which Windows calculates for you, supposedly are unique throughout the world. If you apply the Replication ID field size to an AutoNumber field, Access automatically adds a GUID value for each row of the table.

FIXED-WIDTH TEXT FIELDS

You can create a fixed-width Text field by setting the value of the Field Size property. By default, Access creates a 50-character-wide Text field. Enter the number, from 1 to 255, in the Field Size cell corresponding to the fixed length that you want. If the data you import to the field is longer than the selected field size, Access truncates the data; so, you lose the far right characters that exceed your specified limit. You should enter a field length value that accommodates the maximum number of characters that you expect to enter in the field.

NOTE

The terms fixed-width and fixed-length have two different meanings in Access. Even if you specify a fixed-width for a field of the Text field data type, Access stores the data in the field in variable-length format. Thus, setting the Length value to 255 for all Text fields has no effect on the ultimate size of the database file.

SELECTING A DISPLAY FORMAT

You establish the Format property for the data types that you select so that Access displays them appropriately for your application. You select a format by selecting the field and then clicking the Format text box in the Field Properties window. Figure 5.7 shows the choices that Access offers for formatting the Long Integer data type. You format Number, Date/Time, and Yes/No data types by selecting a standard format or creating your own custom format. The following sections describe these two methods.

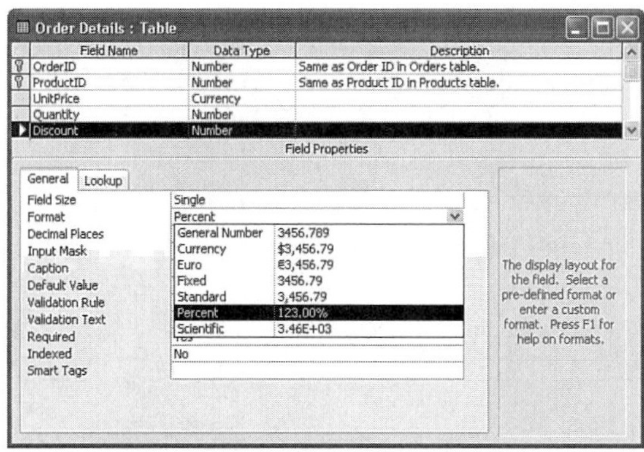

Figure 5.7 You can apply one of seven numeric display formats to fields of the Number Data type and the Long Integer subtype. Access 2000 added the Euro format.

5

STANDARD FORMATS FOR NUMBER, DATE/TIME, AND YES/NO DATA TYPES

Access provides 18 standard formats that apply to the numeric values in fields of the Number, Date/Time, and Yes/No data types. Format is an Access, not a Jet, field property. The standard formats shown in Table 5.3 should meet most of your needs.

TABLE 5.3 STANDARD DISPLAY FORMATS FOR ACCESS'S NUMBER, DATE/TIME, AND YES/NO DATA TYPES

Data Type	Format	Appearance
Number	General Number	1234.5
	Currency	$1,234.50
	Euro	£1,234.50
	Fixed	12345 or 12345.00 depending on Decimal Places setting
	Standard	1,234.50
	Percent	0.1234 = 12.34%
	Scientific	1.23E+03
Date/Time	General Date	3/1/99 4:00:00 PM
	Long Date	Thursday, March 1, 2003
	Medium Date	1-Mar-2003
	Short Date	3/1/2003
	Long Time	4:00:00 PM
	Medium Time	04:00 PM
	Short Time	16:00
Yes/No	Yes/No	Yes or No
	True/False	True or False
	On/Off	On or Off
	None	–1 or 0

Microsoft's Year 2000 (Y2K) compliance features include an Access 2000 addition to the General page of the Options dialog (Tools menu). The Use Four-Digit Year Formatting frame has two check boxes: This Database and All Databases. Marking either check box changes Date/Time field formatting as shown in Table 5.4. Long Date and Time formats don't change; the formatting shown in the Access 2003 Default column is based on the standard Windows Short Date format, m/d/yy.

TABLE 5.4 A COMPARISON OF ACCESS 2003 DEFAULT AND FOUR-DIGIT YEAR FORMATTING

Date/Time Format	Access 2003 Default	With Four-Digit Year
General Date (default)	1/15/03 10:10 AM	1/15/2003 10:10 AM
Short Date	1/15/03	1/15/2003
Long Date	Friday January 15, 2003	Friday January 15, 2003
Medium Date	15-Jan-03	15-Jan-2003
Medium Time	10:10 AM	10:10 AM
mm/dd/yy	01/15/03	01/15/2003

Marking the This Database check box sets a flag in the current database, so the formatting changes apply only to the current database. Marking the All Databases check box adds a Registry entry to your PC, so opening any Jet database in Access forces four-digit year formatting.

TIP

Access's Short Date (m/d/yy and mm/dd/yy) formats for the English (United States) locale default to two-digit years unless you change the default date format of Windows or set the Four-Digit Year Formatting option(s). Two-digit year presentation isn't Y2K compliant. To make the Windows short date format Y2K compliant for most applications, open Control Panel's Regional and Language Options tool, click the Customize button and the Date tab, and check the Short Date setting. If the Short Date style is M/d/yy, change it to M/d/yyyy.

The Null Value in Jet Tables

Fields in Jet tables can have a special value, Null, which is a new term for most spreadsheet users. The Null value indicates that the field contains no data at all. Null is similar but not equivalent to an empty string (a string of zero length, "", often called a null string). For now, the best synonym for Null is no entry or unknown.

The Null value is useful for determining whether a value has been entered in a field, especially a numeric field in which zero values are valid. The next section and the later "Setting Default Values of Fields" section use the Null value.

Custom Display Formats

To display a format that's not a standard format in Access, you must create a custom format. You can set a custom display format for any field type, except OLE Object, by creating an image of the format with combinations of a special set of characters called placeholders (see Table 5.5). Figure 5.8 shows an example of a custom format for date and time. If you type **mmmm dd, yyyy - hh:nn** as the format, the date 03/01/01 displays as March 1, 2001 - 00:00. Access automatically adds double quotes around the comma when you save the table.

Except as noted, the sample numeric value that Table 5.4 uses is `1234.5`. Bold type distinguishes the placeholders that you type from the surrounding text. The resulting display is shown in `monospace` type.

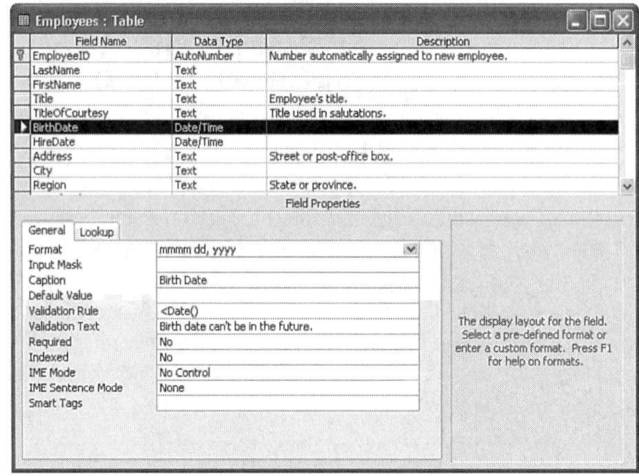

Figure 5.8
If one of the standard Format property values doesn't meet your needs, you can type a string to represent a custom format in the Format text box.

TABLE 5.5 PLACEHOLDERS FOR CREATING CUSTOM DISPLAY FORMATS

Placeholder	Function
Empty string	Displays the number with no formatting. Enter an empty string by deleting the value in the Format field of the Field Properties pane.
0	Displays a digit if one exists in the position, or a zero if not. You can use the **0** placeholder to display leading zeros for whole numbers and trailing zeros in decimal fractions. **00000.000** displays `01234.500`.
#	Displays a digit, if one exists in the position. The **#** placeholder is similar to **0**, except that leading and trailing zeros aren't displayed. **#####.###** displays `1234.5`.
$	Displays a dollar sign in the position. **$###,###.00** displays `$1,234.50`.
.	Displays a decimal point at the indicated position in a string of **0** and **#** placeholders. **##.##** displays `1234.5`.
%	Multiplies the value by 100 and adds a percent sign in the position shown with **0** and **#** placeholders. **#0.00%** displays 0.12345 as `12.35%` (12.345 is rounded to `12.35`).
,	Adds commas as thousands separators in strings of **0** and **#** placeholders. **###,###,###.00** displays `1,234.50`.
E- e-	Displays values in scientific format with the sign of exponent for negative values only. **#.####E-00** displays `1.2345E03`. 0.12345 is displayed as `1.2345E-01`.
E+ e+	Displays values in scientific format with the sign of exponent for positive and negative values. **#.####E+00** displays `1.2345E+03`.
/	Separates the day, month, and year to format date values. Typing **mm/dd/yyyy** displays `03/06/2003`. (You can substitute hyphens for virgules to display `03-06-2003`.)

Placeholder	Function
m	Specifies how to display months for dates. **m** displays 1, **mm** displays 01, **mmm** displays Jan, and **mmmm** displays January.
d	Specifies how to display days for dates. **d** displays 1, **dd** displays 01, **ddd** displays Mon, and **dddd** displays Monday.
y	Specifies how to display years for dates. **yy** displays 01; **yyyy** displays 2003.
:	Separates hours, minutes, and seconds in format time values. **hh:mm:ss** displays 02:02:02.
h	Specifies how to display hours for time. **h** displays 2; **hh** displays 02. If you use an **AM/PM** placeholder, **h** or **hh** displays 4 PM for 16:00 hours.
n	Minutes placeholder for time. **n** displays 1; **nn** displays 01. **hhnn "hours"** displays 1600 hours.
s	Seconds placeholder for time. **s** displays 1; **ss** displays 01.
AM/PM	Displays time in 12-hour time with AM or PM appended. **h:nn AM/PM** displays 4:00 PM. Alternative formats include **am/pm**, **A/P**, and **a/p**.
@	Indicates that a character is required in the position in a Text or Memo field. You can use **@** to format telephone numbers in a Text field, as in **@@@-@@@-@@@@** or **(@@@) @@@-@@@@**.
&	Indicates that a character in a Text or Memo field is optional.
>	Changes (custom display format) placeholder> all text characters in the field to uppercase.
<	Changes all text characters in the field to lowercase.
*	Displays the character following the asterisk as a fill character for empty spaces in a field. **"ABCD"*x** in an eight-character field appears as ABCDxxxx.

The Format property is one of the few examples in Access in which you can select from a list of options or type your own entry. Format uses a true drop-down combo list; lists that enable you to select only from the listed options are drop-down lists. The comma is a nonstandard formatting symbol for dates (but is standard for number fields). When you create nonstandard formatting characters in the Field Properties window, Access automatically encloses them in double quotation marks.

When you change Format or any other property field, and then change to Datasheet view to view the result of your work, you must first save the updated table design. The confirmation dialog shown at the top of Figure 5.9 asks you to confirm any design changes. Clicking No returns you to Table Design view. If you want to discard your changes, close Table Design view and click No when asked if you want to save your changes (see Figure 5.9, bottom).

Figure 5.9
Changing from Design to Datasheet view after making changes to the table's design displays the upper message box. If you close the table in Design view, the lower message box gives you the option of saving or discarding changes, or returning to Table Design view.

If you apply the custom format string **mmmm dd", "yyyy** (refer to Figure 5.8) to the BirthDate field of the Employees table, the BirthDate field entries appear as shown in Figure 5.10. For example, Nancy Davolio's birth date appears as December 08, 1968. The original format of the BirthDate field was dd-mmm-yyyy, the format also used for the HireDate field. The BirthDate caption property value appears in the heading row.

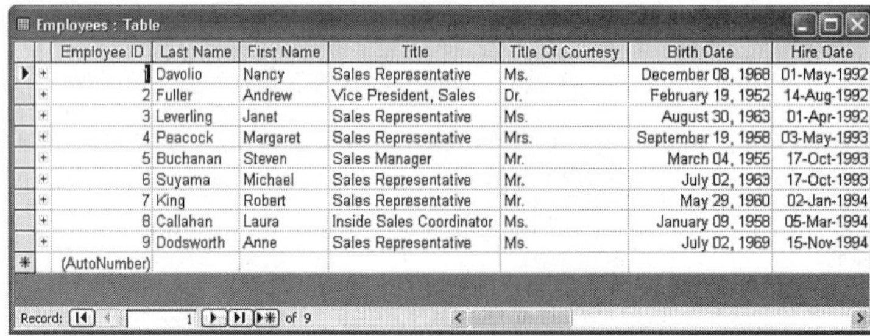

Employees : Table

Employee ID	Last Name	First Name	Title	Title Of Courtesy	Birth Date	Hire Date
1	Davolio	Nancy	Sales Representative	Ms.	December 08, 1968	01-May-1992
2	Fuller	Andrew	Vice President, Sales	Dr.	February 19, 1952	14-Aug-1992
3	Leverling	Janet	Sales Representative	Ms.	August 30, 1963	01-Apr-1992
4	Peacock	Margaret	Sales Representative	Mrs.	September 19, 1958	03-May-1993
5	Buchanan	Steven	Sales Manager	Mr.	March 04, 1955	17-Oct-1993
6	Suyama	Michael	Sales Representative	Mr.	July 02, 1963	17-Oct-1993
7	King	Robert	Sales Representative	Mr.	May 29, 1960	02-Jan-1994
8	Callahan	Laura	Inside Sales Coordinator	Ms.	January 09, 1958	05-Mar-1994
9	Dodsworth	Anne	Sales Representative	Ms.	July 02, 1969	15-Nov-1994
(AutoNumber)						

Record: 1 of 9

Figure 5.10
The BirthDate field of the modified employees table displays the effect of applying **mmmm dd", "yyyy** as the custom date/time format.

You must expand the width of the BirthDate field to accommodate the additional characters in the Long Date format. You increase the field's width by dragging the field name header's right vertical bar to the right to display the entire field. Access displays the time of birth as 00:00 because the decimal fraction that determines time is 0 for all entries in the BirthDate field.

The following is an example that formats negative numbers enclosed in parentheses and replaces a Null entry with text:

```
$###,###,##0.00;$(###,###,##0.00);0.00;"No Entry Here"
```

The entries 1234567.89, –1234567.89, 0, and a Null default value appear as follows:

```
$1,234,567.89
$(1,234,567.89)
0.00
No Entry Here
```

Using Input Masks

Access 2003 lets you restrict entries in Text fields to numbers or to otherwise control the formatting of entered data. Access 2003's Input Mask property is used to format telephone numbers, Social Security numbers, ZIP codes, and similar data. Table 5.6 lists the placeholders that you can use in character strings for input masks in fields of the Text field data type.

Table 5.6 Placeholders for Creating Input Masks

Placeholder	Function
Empty string	No input mask
0	Number (0–9) required; sign (+/–)not allowed
9	Number (0–9) or space optional; sign (+/-) not allowed
#	Number (0–9) or space optional (a space if nothing is entered)
L	Letter (A–Z) required
?	Letter (A–Z) not required (a space if nothing is entered)
A	Letter (A–Z) or number (0–9) required
a	Letter (A–Z) or number (0–9) optional
&	Any character or a space required
C	Any character or a space optional
Password	Displays the characters you type as asterisks (***...) to prevent others from viewing the entry
. , : ; / ( )	Literal decimal, thousands, date, time, and special separators
>	All (input mask) placeholder> characters to the right are converted to uppercase
<	All characters to the right are converted to lowercase
!	Fills the mask from right to left
****	Precedes the other placeholders to include the literal character in a format string

For example, typing **\(000") "000\-0000** as the value of the Input Mask property results in the appearance of (___) ___-____ for a blank telephone number cell of a table. Typing **000\-00\-0000** creates a mask for Social Security numbers, ___-__-____. When you type the telephone number or Social Security number, the digits that you type replace the underscores.

NOTE

> The \ characters (often called escape characters) that precede parentheses and hyphens specify that the character that follows is a literal, not a formatting character. If the format includes spaces, enclose the spaces and adjacent literal characters in double quotation marks, as shown for the telephone number format.

Access includes an Input Mask Wizard that opens when you move to the Input Mask field for the Text or Date/Time field data type and click the Builder (...) button at the extreme right of the text box. Figure 5.11 shows the opening dialog of the Input Mask Wizard, which lets you select from 10 common input mask formats.

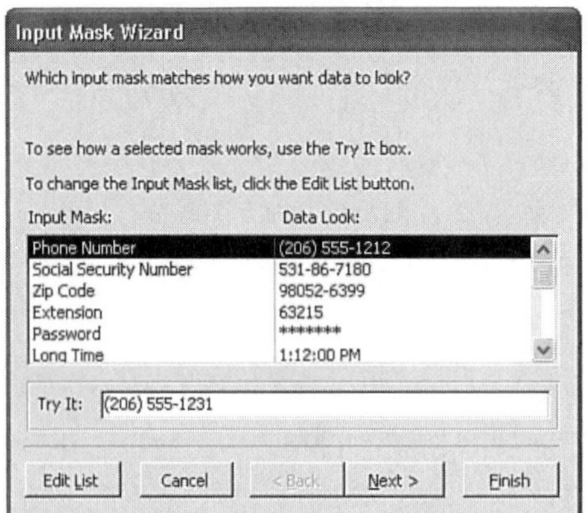

Figure 5.11
The Input Mask Wizard lets you select one of 10 preset formats to specify a fixed data entry pattern for the selected field. In the second wizard dialog, you can add a custom format.

5

WORKING WITH THE NORTHWIND TRADERS SAMPLE DATABASE

One fundamental problem with books about database management applications is the usual method of demonstrating how to create a "typical" database. You are asked to type fictitious names, addresses, and telephone numbers into a Customers table. Next, you must create additional tables that relate these fictitious customers to their purchases of various widgets in assorted sizes and quantities. This process is unrewarding for readers and authors, and few readers ever complete the exercises.

Therefore, this book takes a different track. Access includes a comprehensive—but outdated—sample order-entry database, Northwind Traders. Rather than create a new database at this point, you create a new table as an addition to the Northwind Traders database. Adding a new table minimizes the amount of typing required and requires just a few entries to make the table functional. The HRActions table you add later demonstrates many elements of relational database design. Before you proceed to create the HRActions table, try the quick example of adding a new contact-tracking table to the Northwind Traders sample database in the following section.

USING THE TABLE WIZARD TO ADD A NEW TABLE

Access includes various wizards that simplify the creation of new database objects. Access 2003 includes a Table Wizard that you can use to create new tables based on prefabricated designs for 25 business-oriented and 20 personal-type tables. Many of the business-oriented table designs are based on tables contained in Northwind.mdb or the tables created by the Database Wizard based on one of the database templates.

→ To review using the Database Wizard to create a contacts table, **see** "Creating an Access Application from a Template File," **p. 55**.

The Table Wizard serves as an excellent introduction to the use of Access wizards in general, if you didn't complete the example application in Chapter 2, "Building a Simple Desktop and Web Application." Follow these steps to add a new Jet CustContacts table to Northwind.mdb and add a CustomerID field on which to create a many-to-one relationship with Northwind.mdb's Customers table:

1. If the Employees table is open, close it to make the Database window active. Alternatively, click the Database Window button of the toolbar.

2. Double-click the Create Table by Using Wizard item in the Database window's Tables list to open the first Table Wizard dialog.
3. Accept the default Business option to display a list of tables for business use in the Sample Tables list, and click the Contacts entry to display the predetermined set of field names for the new table in the Sample Fields list.
4. Select the ContactID field, and click the > button to add the field from the Sample Fields list to the Fields in My New Table list.

NOTE

> The >> button adds all fields from the Sample Fields list, the < button removes a single selected field from the Fields in My New Table list, and the << button removes all the fields in the Field in My New Table list.

5. Repeat step 1–4 for the FirstName, LastName, Dear, Title, WorkPhone, WorkExtension, HomePhone, MobilePhone, FaxNumber, EmailName, LastMeetingDate, ContactTypeID, ReferredBy, and Notes fields. The Table Wizard's dialog now appears as shown in Figure 5.12.
6. Scroll to the top of the Fields in the My New Table list and select ContactID. Then select Customers in the Sample Tables list, select CustomerID in the Sample Fields list, and click the > button to add the CustomerID field below the ContactID field.
7. Click Next to display the second Table Wizard dialog in which you select the name for your new table, and specify how to determine the table's primary-key field. Type **CustContacts** in the text box, and then select the No, I'll Set the Primary Key option (see Figure 5.13).

5

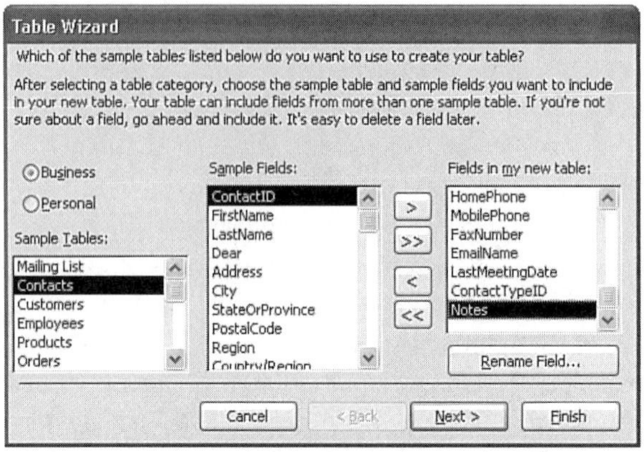

Figure 5.12
The first Table Wizard dialog lets you select the table category, the sample table type, and the fields of the select table type to add to the new table.

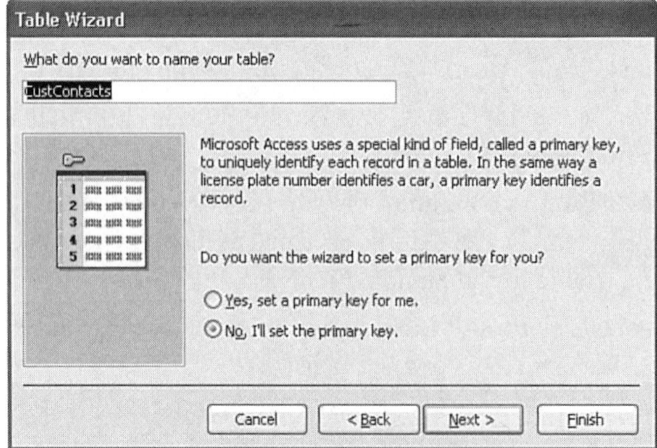

Figure 5.13
The second Table Wizard dialog lets you rename the table and choose whether to let the Wizard or you specify the primary-key field.

8. Click Next to display the third dialog in which you select the primary-key field and its data type. Accept the ContactID and Consecutive Numbers… (AutoNumber) default values determined by the Table Wizard.
9. Click Next to open the Table Wizard's relationships dialog (see Figure 5.14). Scrolling the list shows that the Wizard hasn't detected a relationship with another table in the Northwind database.

TIP

In any wizard, you can always redo a step by clicking the Back button until you return to the step that you want to redo.

NOTE

The data type of the CustomerID field of the Contacts table is Long Integer and the CustomerID field of the Customers table is Text. So, the Wizard correctly doesn't automatically detect a relationship between these two fields. If the names and data types of the related fields are the same, the Wizard automatically detects the relationship.

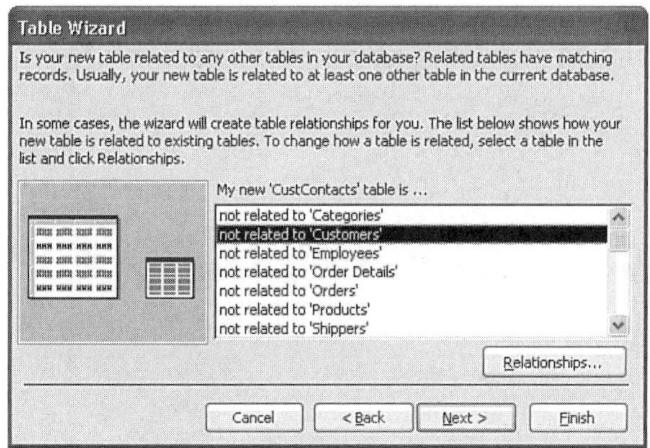

Figure 5.14 The Wizard doesn't find the related table (Customers) automatically in the fourth dialog.

10. Click Next to display the final Wizard dialog. Select the Modify the Table Design option (see Figure 5.15), and click the Finish button to display the new table in Design view.

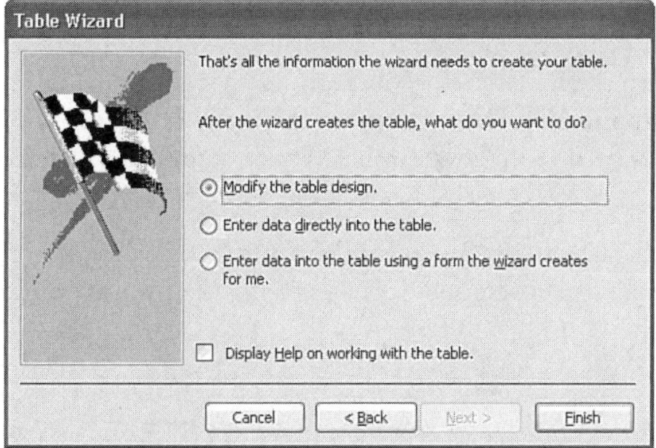

Figure 5.15 The last Table Wizard dialog offers the options of opening the table in Datasheet or Design view, or generating a data-entry form.

11. Select the Data Type cell of the CustomerID field, open the list, and select Text to match the data type of the CustomerID field of the Customers table.
12. In the General page of the properties pane, type **5** in the Field Size text box to match the length of the CustomerID field of the Customers table. Set the Required value to Yes and the Allow Zero length value to No, because CustomerID is a foreign key field and must contain a CustomerID value from the Customers table (see Figure 5.16).
13. After you finish reviewing the design of your new CustContacts table, close the table and save your design changes.

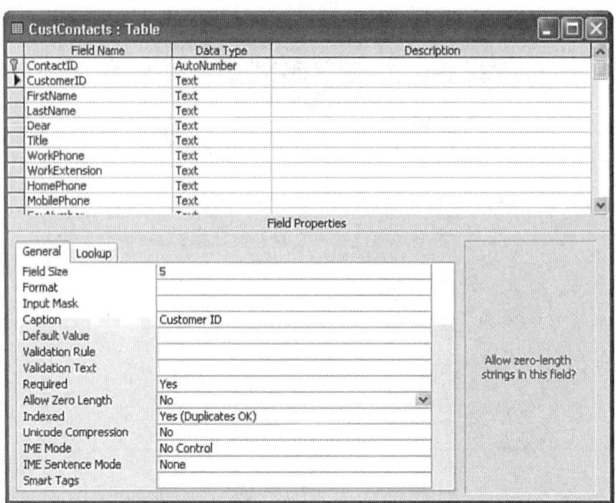

Figure 5.16 To establish a one-to-many relationship between the CustomerID fields of the Customers and CustContacts tables, the field data types must be the same (Text). Setting the Field Size property value to the same length as the primary key field of the related table is optional for text fields, but is a good database design practice. The Field size property for related Number fields must match.

You can use the Table Wizard to create a table similar to CustContacts for supplier contacts (SuppContacts). In the preceding step 6, select the CustomerID field, click the Rename Field button to open the Rename Field dialog, and change the field name from CustomerID to **SupplierID**. The data type of the SupplierID field of Northwind's Suppliers table is Long Integer, so the Table Wizard automatically detects and adds the relationship between the SupplierID fields of the Suppliers and SuppContacts tables.

The Nwind05.mdb database in the \Seua11\Chaptr05 folder of the accompanying CD-ROM includes the CustContacts and SuppContacts tables, which you can import into Northwind.mdb.

PREPARING TO ADD A TABLE RELATED TO THE EMPLOYEES TABLE

Northwind.mdb includes the Employees table that provides information typical of personnel tables maintained by human resources departments. The following sections explain how to add a new table to the Northwind database that is related to the Employees table and called HRActions. The HRActions table is a record of hire date, salary, commission rate, bonuses, performance reviews, and other compensation-related events for employees. Because HRActions is based on information in the Employees table, the first step is to review the Employees table's structure. In Chapter 6, you add validation rules to the HRActions table and enter records in the table.

With the Database window active, you can open the Design view of an existing table in the following ways:

- Right-click the entry for the Employees table in the Database window's list and choose Design View from the context menu (the quickest method).
- Select the table in the list and click Design in the Database Window's toolbar.

- Select the table in the list, click Open in the Database Window's toolbar, and then click the Design view button of the Table Datasheet toolbar (the slowest method.)

Figure 5.17 shows the Employees table in Design view. The fields grid in the figure shows properties for only 11 of the 17 fields of the table. Scroll down to display the properties of the remaining six fields.

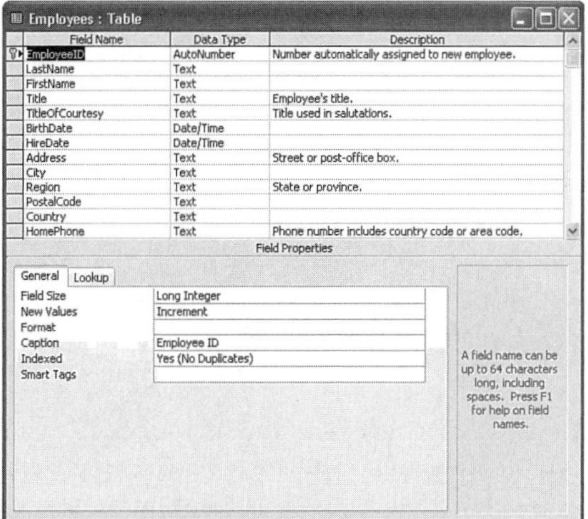

Figure 5.17 Design view of the Employees table displays most of the table's fields in the upper grid pane. The most important field is the primary key, EmployeeID, on which the new table's relationship depends.

Designing the HRActions Table

Designing the HRActions table is typical of the process you go through when you create a set of relational tables for almost any purpose. Rather than add fields for entries—such as salary, commission rate, and bonuses—to the Employees table, you should place employee remuneration data in a table of its own, for the following reasons:

- Multiple HRActions are taken for individual employees over time. If you add these actions to records in the Employees table, you have to create many additional fields to hold an arbitrary number of HRActions. If, for example, quarterly performance reviews are entered, you would need to add a new field for every quarter to hold the review information. In this situation, spreadsheet applications and flat-file managers encounter serious difficulties.
- HRActions usually are considered confidential information and are made accessible only to a limited number of people. Although you can design forms that don't display confidential information, restricting permission to view an entire table is a more secure approach.

- You can identify employees uniquely by their EmployeeID numbers. Therefore, records for entries of HRActions can be related to the Employees table by an EmployeeID field. This feature eliminates the necessity of adding employee names and other information to the records in the HRActions table. You link the Employees table to the HRActions table by the EmployeeID field, and the two tables are joined; they act as though they are a single table. Minimizing information duplication to only what is required to link the tables is your reward for choosing a relational, rather than a flat-file, database management system.
- You can categorize HRActions by type so that any action taken can use a common set of field names and field data types. This feature makes the design of the HRActions table simple.

The next step is to start the design of the HRActions table. Chapter 4 discusses the theory of database design and the tables that make up databases. Because the HRActions table has an easily discernible relationship to the Employees table, the theoretical background isn't necessary for this example.

Determining What Information the Table Should Include

Designing a table requires that you identify the type of information the table should contain. Information associated with typical human resources department actions might consist of the following items:

- *Important dates*—The date of hire and termination, if applicable, are important dates, but so are the dates when the employer adjusts salaries, changes commission rates, and grants bonuses. You should accompany each action with the date when it was scheduled to occur and the date when it actually occurred.
- *Types of actions*—Less typing is required if HRActions are identified by a code character rather than a full-text description of the action. This feature saves valuable disk space, too. First-letter abbreviations used as codes, such as H for hired, T for terminated, and Q for quarterly review, are easy to remember.
- *Initiation and approval of actions*—As a rule, the employee's supervisor initiates a personnel action, and the supervisor's manager approves it. Therefore, the table should include the supervisor's and manager's EmployeeID number.
- *Amounts involved*—Salaries are assumed to be bimonthly based on a monthly amount, hourly employees are paid weekly, bonuses are quarterly with quarterly performance reviews, and commissions are paid on a percentage of sales made by the employee.
- *Performance rating*—Rating employee performance by a numerical value is a universal, but somewhat arbitrary, practice. Scales of 1 to 9 are common, with exceptional performance ranked as 9 and candidacy for termination as 1.
- *Summaries and comments*—The table should provide for a summary of performance, an explanation of exceptionally high or low ratings, and reasons for adjusting salaries or bonuses.

NOTE

> Fields containing a code for pay type–salary, hourly, commission–and bonus eligibility would be useful additions to the Employees table. You could use such codes to validate amount entries in the HRActions table.

If you're involved in personnel management, you probably can think of additional information that the table might include, such as accruable sick leave and vacation hours per pay period. The HRActions table is just an example; it isn't meant to add full-scale human resources application capabilities to the database. The limited amount of data described serves to demonstrate several uses of the new table in this and subsequent chapters.

ASSIGNING INFORMATION TO FIELDS

After you determine the types of information—called data attributes or just attributes—to include in the table, you must assign each data entity to a field of the table. This process involves specifying a field name that must be unique within the table. Table 5.7 lists the candidate fields for the HRActions table. Candidate fields are written descriptions of the fields proposed for the table. Data types are logically derived from the type of value described. Table 5.8 add specifics for the data types.

TABLE 5.7 CANDIDATE FIELDS FOR THE HRACTIONS TABLE

Field Name	Data Type	Description
EmployeeID	Number	The employee to whom the action applies. EmployeeID numbers are assigned based on the EmployeeID field of the Employee table (to which the HRActions table is related).
ActionType	Text	Code for the type of action taken: H is for hired; Q, quarterly review; Y, yearly review; S, salary adjustment; R, hourly rate adjustment; B, bonus adjustment; C, commission rate adjustment; and T, terminated.
InitiatedBy	Number	The EmployeeID number of the supervisor who initiates or is responsible for recommending the action.
ScheduledDate	Date/Time	The date when the action is scheduled to occur.
ApprovedBy	Number	The EmployeeID number of the manager who approves the action proposed by the supervisor.
EffectiveDate	Date/Time	The date when the action occurred. The effective date remains blank if the action has not occurred.

continues

5

TABLE 5.7 CONTINUED

Field Name	Data Type	Description
HRRating	Number	Performance on a scale of 1–9, with higher numbers indicating better performance. A blank (Null value) indicates no rating; 0 is reserved for terminated employees.
NewSalary	Currency	The new salary per month, as of the effective date, for salaried employees.
NewRate	Currency	The new hourly rate for hourly employees.
NewBonus	Currency	The new quarterly bonus amount for eligible employees.
NewCommission	Percent	The new commission rate for commissioned salespersons, some of whom might also receive a salary.
HRComments	Memo	Abstracts of performance reviews and comments on actions proposed or taken. The comments can be of unlimited length. The supervisor and manager can contribute to the comments.

TIP

Use distinctive names for each field. This example precedes some field names with the abbreviation HR to associate–or establish relations–with field names in other tables that might be used by the human resource department.

5

CREATING THE HRACTIONS TABLE

Now you can put to work what you've learned about field names, data types, and formats by adding the HRActions table to the Northwind Traders database. Table 5.8 shows the field names, taken from Table 5.7, and the set of properties that you assign to the fields. Fields with values required in a new record have an asterisk (*) following the field name. The text in the Caption column substitutes for the Field Name property that is otherwise displayed in the field header buttons.

TABLE 5.8 FIELD PROPERTIES FOR THE HRACTIONS TABLE

Field Name	Caption	Data Type	Field Size	Format
EmployeeID*	ID	Number	Long Integer	General Number
ActionType*	Type	Text	1	>@ (all uppercase)
InitiatedBy*	Initiated By	Number	Long Integer	General Number
ScheduledDate*	Scheduled	Date/Time	N/A	mm/dd/yyyy

Field Name	Caption	Data Type	Field Size	Format
ApprovedBy	Approved By	Number	Long Integer	General Number
EffectiveDate	Effective	Date/Time	N/A	Short Date
HRRating	Rating	Number	Byte	General Number
NewSalary	Salary	Currency	N/A	Standard
NewRate	Rate	Currency	N/A	Standard
NewBonus	Bonus	Currency	N/A	Standard
NewCommission	% Comm	Number	Single	#0.0
HRComments	Comments	Memo	N/A	(None)

NOTE

You must set the EmployeeID field's Field Size property to the Long Integer data type, although you might not expect Northwind Traders to have more than the 32,767 employees that an integer allows. The Long Integer data type is required because the AutoNumber field data type of the Employees table's EmployeeID field is a Long Integer. Later in this chapter, the "Working with Relations, Key Fields, and Indexes" section explains why EmployeeID's data type must match that of the Employees table's EmployeeID number field.

To add the new HRActions table to the Northwind database, complete the following steps:

1. Close the Employees table, if it's open, to return to the Database window.
2. Click the Tables shortcut of the Database window, if it isn't selected, and double-click the Create Table in Design View item. Access enters design mode, opens a blank grid, and selects the grid's first cell. The General page of the lower properties pane is empty for a new table with no fields.
3. Type **EmployeeID** as the first field name, and press Tab to accept the field name and move to the Data Type column. Access adds the default field type, Text.
4. Click to open the Data Type list (see Figure 5.18) and select Number. Alternatively, type **N**[**umber**] in the list. Typing characters that unambiguously match an item in the drop-down list selects the item.

NOTE

Another selection alternative in drop-down lists is to use Alt+down arrow to open the list, press the up- or down-arrow keys to make the selection, and then press Enter.

5. Press F6 to move to or click Field Size text box in the Field Properties window. Access has already entered Long Integer as the value of the default Field Size property for a Number field.

5

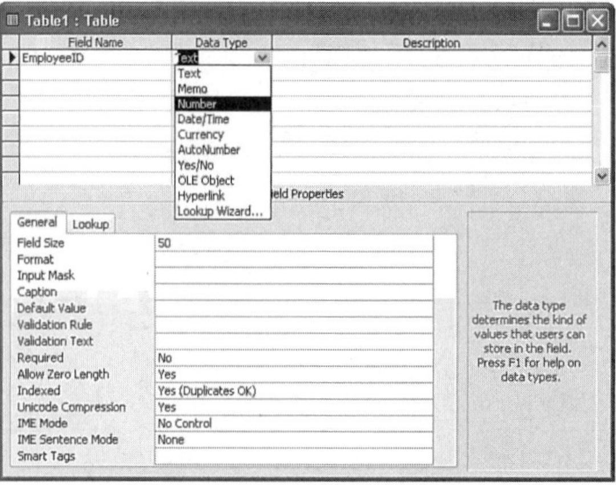

Figure 5.18
The Data Type list lets you select from one of the nine Jet/Access data types or the Lookup Wizard. If you type a text value in a Data Type cell, the value must match the first character or two of one of the entries in the drop-down list.

NOTE

> Whenever you create a new Number type field, Access enters Long Integer in the Field Size property as the default. Because the EmployeeID field should be a Long Integer, you don't need to set the Field Size property for this field and can skip to step 8; continue with steps 6 and 7 when you enter the other fields from Table 5.8.

6. For Number data types other than Long Integer, select from the list the appropriate Field Size value from Table 5.8, or type the first letter of one of the values of the list, such as **B**[**yte**] or **S**[**ingle**]. For Text fields, type the maximum number of characters.
7. Press the down-arrow key or click to select the Format text box, and type **G**[**eneral**], or select General Number from the list (see Figure 5.19).

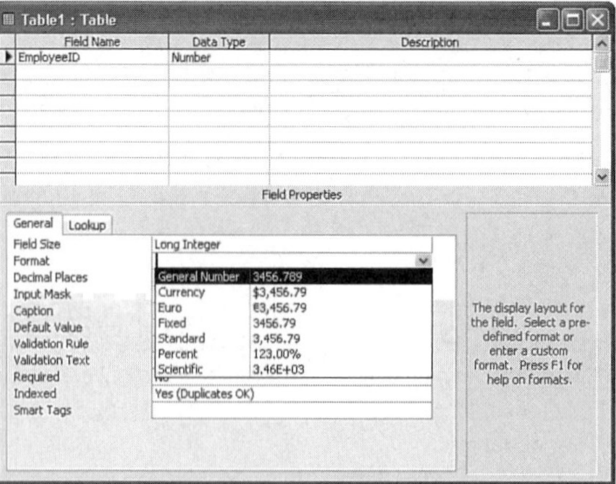

Figure 5.19
Select one of the seven standard number formats from the list or type a format string in the Format text box. The General Number format applies if you don't set the Format property value.

8. Press the down-arrow key, or select the Caption text box, and type **ID** as the caption. ID is used as the Caption property to minimize the column width necessary to display the EmployeeID number.
9. Press the down-arrow key four times, bypassing the Default Value, Validation Rule, and Validation Text properties, and type **Y** in the Required text box. Typing **Y**[**es**] or **N**[**o**] is an alternative to selecting Yes or No in the drop-down list.

NOTE

> When entering a Text field with the Required property set to Yes, set the Allow Zero Length property value to No.

10. Press F6 to return to the Table Design grid.

TIP

> Add descriptions to create prompts that appear in the status bar when you are adding or editing records in run mode's Datasheet view. Although descriptions are optional, it's good database design practice to enter the field's purpose if its use isn't obvious from its Field Name or Caption property.

11. Press Enter to move the caret to the first cell of the next row of the grid.
12. Repeat steps 3 through 11, entering the values shown in Table 5.8 for each of the 11 remaining fields of the HRActions table. N/A (not applicable) means that the entry in Table 5.8 doesn't apply to the field's data type.

Your Table Design grid should now look similar to the one shown in Figure 5.20, with the exception of the optional Description property values. You can double-check your properties entries by selecting each field name with the arrow keys and reading the values shown in the property text boxes of the Field Properties window.

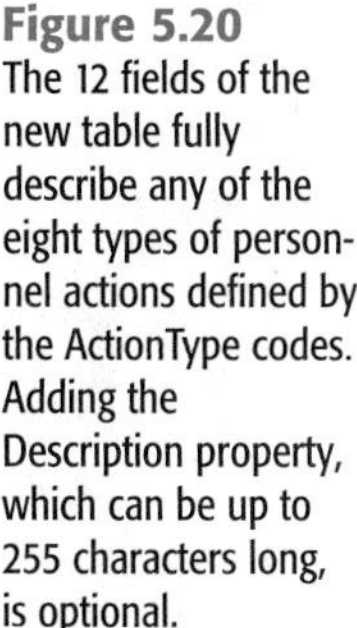

Figure 5.20 The 12 fields of the new table fully describe any of the eight types of personnel actions defined by the ActionType codes. Adding the Description property, which can be up to 255 characters long, is optional.

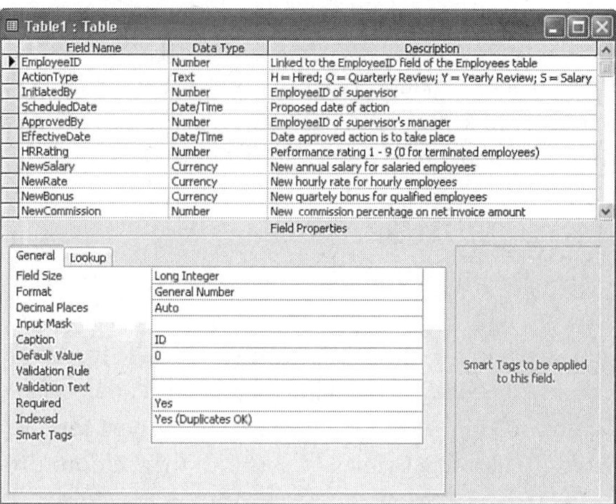

Click the Datasheet view toolbar button to return to Datasheet view in Run mode to view the results of your work. Click Yes when the "Do you want to save the table now?" message opens (see Figure 5.21, top). The Save As dialog opens, requesting that you give your table a name and suggesting the default table name, Table1. Type **HRActions**, as shown in Figure 5.21 (middle), and press Enter or click OK.

At this point, Access displays a dialog informing you that the new table does not have a primary key (see Figure 5.21, bottom). You add primary keys to the HRActions table later in this chapter, so click No in this dialog.

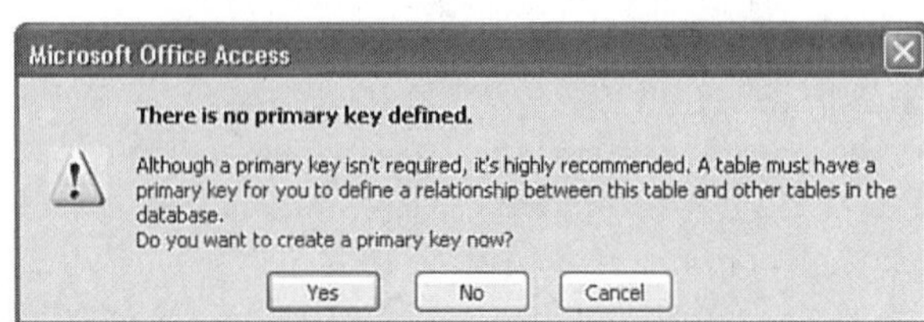

Figure 5.21
When you change the view of a new table that doesn't have a primary key to Datasheet, these three messages appear in sequence.

Your table opens in Datasheet view, with its first default record. To view all the fields of your new table, narrow the field name header buttons by dragging to the left the right vertical bar that separates each header. When you finish adjusting your fields' display widths, the HRActions table appears in Datasheet view (see Figure 5.22). Only the tentative append record (a new record that Access adds to your table only if you enter values in the cells) is present. You have more property values to add to your HRActions table, so don't enter data in the tentative append record at this point. If you close the table, a message asks if you want to save your table layout changes. Click Yes.

CREATING A TABLE DIRECTLY IN DATASHEET VIEW

If you're a complete database novice and under pressure to create database tables immediately, Access lets you create tables directly in Datasheet view. When you create a table in Datasheet view, Access displays an empty table with a default structure of 20 fields and 30 empty records. You then enter data directly into the table. When you save the table, Access analyzes the data you entered and attempts to select a data type for each field that matches the data. Creating tables in datasheet view is a shortcut that seldom produces a satisfactory result.

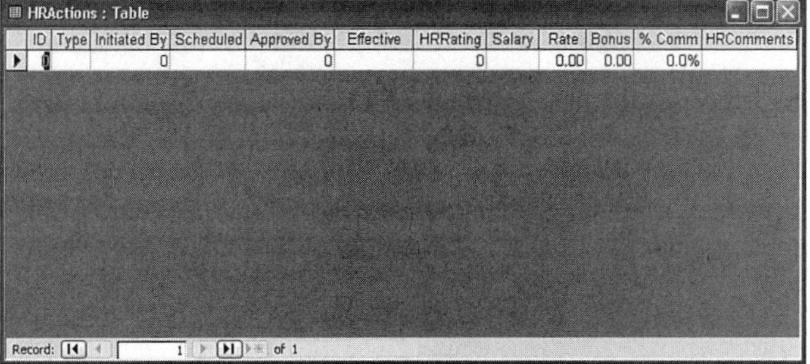

Figure 5.22 Adjust the display width of the fields in Datasheet view so all fields appear without scrolling the window. Specifying a Decimal Places property value of 1 results in the 0.0% default entry in the % Comm field.

SETTING DEFAULT VALUES OF FIELDS

Access assigns Number and Currency fields a default value of 0; all other field types are empty by default. (Notice that the tentative append record in Figure 5.22 has zeros entered in all the Number and Currency fields.) You can save data-entry time by establishing default values for fields; in some cases, Access's default values for Number and Currency fields might be inappropriate, and you must change them. Table 5.9 lists the default values you should enter for the HRActions table's fields.

TABLE 5.9 DEFAULT FIELD VALUES FOR THE HRACTIONS TABLE

Field Name	Default Value	Comments
EmployeeID	**Null**	0 is not a valid Employee ID number, so you should remove Access's default.
ActionType	**Q**	Quarterly performance reviews are the most common personnel action.
InitiatedBy	**Null**	0 is not a valid Employee ID number.
ScheduledDate	**=Date()**	This expression enters today's date from the computer system's clock.
ApprovedBy	**Null**	0 is not a valid Employee ID.
EffectiveDate	**=Date()+28**	This expression enters today's date plus four weeks.
HRRating	**Null**	In many cases, a rating doesn't apply. A 0 rating is reserved for terminated employees.
NewSalary NewRate NewBonus NewCommission	**Null**	If a salary, hourly rate, bonus, or commission has no change, no entry should appear. 0 would indicate no salary, for example.
HRComments	No Entry	Access's default is adequate.

5

If you don't enter anything in the Default Value text box, you create a Null default value. It's a better database design practice to be explicit when overriding default values, so you replace 0 values with **Null**. You can use Null values for testing whether a value has been entered into a field. Such a test can ensure that users have entered required data.

You use expressions, such as `=Date()+28` to enter values in fields, make calculations, and perform other useful duties, such as validating data entries. Expressions are discussed briefly in the next section and in much greater detail in Chapter 10, "Understanding Jet Operators and Expressions." An equal sign must precede expressions that establish default values.

To assign the new default values from those of Table 5.9 to the fields of the HRActions table, complete these steps:

1. Click the View button of the Datasheet toolbar. Access selects the first field of the table.
2. Press F6 to switch to the Field Properties window, move the caret to the Default Value text box, and type **Null** for the default value of the EmployeeID field.
3. Press F6 to switch back to the Table Design grid. Move to the next field and press F6 again.
4. Add the default values for the 10 remaining fields having the default entries shown in Table 5.9, repeating steps 1 through 3. For example, after selecting the Default Value text box for the ActionType field, type **Q** to set the default value; Access automatically surrounds Q with double quotes.

5. After completing your default entries, click the View button of the Table Design toolbar, and click Yes when asked if you want to save the table. The HRActions table appears in Datasheet view with the new default entries you assigned (see Figure 5.23).

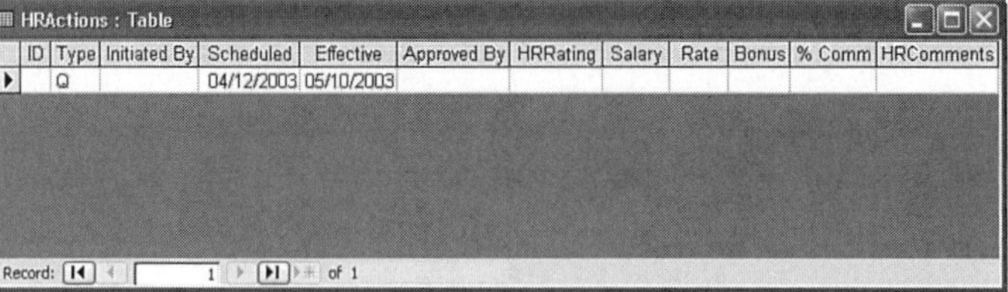

Figure 5.23
Datasheet view of the HRActions table confirms the changes you make to the Default Value property of the fields.

The Nwind05.mdb database in the \Seua11\Chaptr05 folder of the accompanying CD-ROM includes the HRActions table, which you can import into Northwind.mdb.

WORKING WITH RELATIONS, KEY FIELDS, AND INDEXES

Your final tasks before adding records to the HRActions table are to determine the relationship between HRActions and an existing table in the database, assign a primary-key field, and add indexes to your table.

ESTABLISHING RELATIONSHIPS BETWEEN TABLES

Many records in the HRActions table apply to a single employee whose record appears in the Employees table. A record is created in HRActions when the employee is hired, and a record is created for each quarterly and yearly performance review. Also, any changes made to bonuses or commissions other than as the result of a performance review are added, and employees might be terminated. Over time, the number of records in the HRActions table is likely to be greater by a factor of 10 or more than the number of records in the Employees table. Thus, the records in the new Personnel table have a many-to-one relationship with the records in the Employees table. Establishing the relationships between new and existing tables when you create a new table enables Access to enforce the relationship when you use the tables in queries, forms, pages, and reports.

Access requires that the two fields participating in the relationship have exactly the same data type. In the case of the Number field data type, the Field Size property of the two fields must be identical. You cannot, for example, create a relationship between an AutoNumber type field (which uses a Long Integer data type) and a field containing Byte, Integer, Single, Double, or Currency data. (You can create a relationship between fields having AutoNumber and Long Integer data types only.) On the other hand, Access lets you relate two tables by text fields of different lengths. Such a relationship, if created, can lead to strange behavior when you create queries, which is the subject of Part III, "Transforming Data with Queries and PivotTables." As a rule, the relationships between text fields should use fields of the same length.

Access uses a graphical Relationships window to display and create the relationships among tables in a database. To establish the relationships between two tables with Access's Relationships window, using the Employees and HRActions tables as an example, follow these steps:

5

1. Close the Employees and HRActions tables, and click the Relationships button of the main Access toolbar or choose Tools, Relationships to open the Relationships window (see Figure 5.24).

2. Click the Show Table button of the toolbar or choose Relationships, Show Table to open the Show Table dialog (see Figure 5.25).
3. For this example, add the HRActions table to the Relationships window by double-clicking the HRActions entry in the Tables list, or by clicking the entry to select it and then clicking the Add button. Click the Close button.
4. Drag the bottom of the Relationships window to make room to display the fields of the HRActions table. Move the HRActions table object under the Products table object, and drag the bottom of the HRActions table object to expose all its fields.

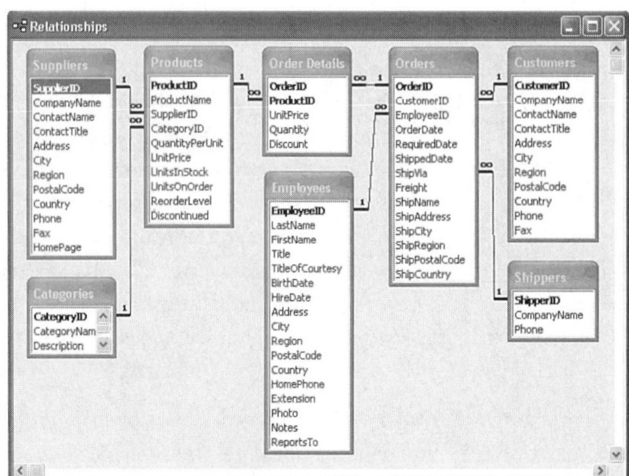

Figure 5.24 The Relationships window for the Northwind.mdb database displays lines representing the one-to-many relationships between the original sample tables. The 1 symbol indicates the "one" side and the infinity (∞) symbol indicates the "many" side of one-to-many relationships. Bold type identifies primary-key fields.

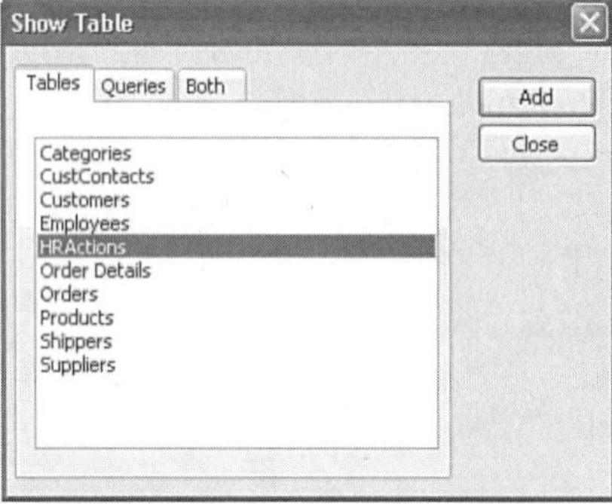

Figure 5.25 The Tables page of the Show Table dialog displays a list of all tables in the database. If you added the CustContacts and SuppContacts tables with the Table Wizard earlier in the chapter, these tables also appear in the list.

5. The relationship of the HRActions table to the Employees table is based on the HRActions table's EmployeeID field (the foreign key) and the Employees table's EmployeeID field (the primary key). Click the Employees table's EmployeeID field and, holding the left mouse button down, drag it to the HRActions table's EmployeeID field. Release the mouse button to drop the field symbol on the EmployeeID field. The Edit Relationships dialog opens (see Figure 5.26).

6. Click the Join Type button to display the Join Properties dialog shown in Figure 5.27. You are creating a one-to-many join between the Employees table's EmployeeID field (the one side) and the HRActions table's EmployeeID field (the many side). You want to display all Employee records, even if one or more of these records don't have a corresponding record in HRActions. To do so, select option 2 in the Join Properties dialog. Click OK to close the dialog and return to the Relationships dialog.

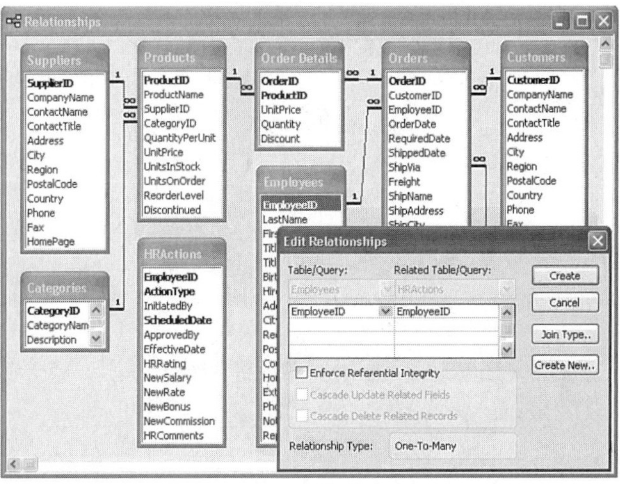

Figure 5.26 Establishing a relationship by dragging a field symbol from one table object to another opens the Edit Relationships dialog. By default, the name of the table with a primary-key field appears in the Table/Query list and the other table appears in the Related Table/Query list. In this case, Access automatically detects a one-to-many relationship.

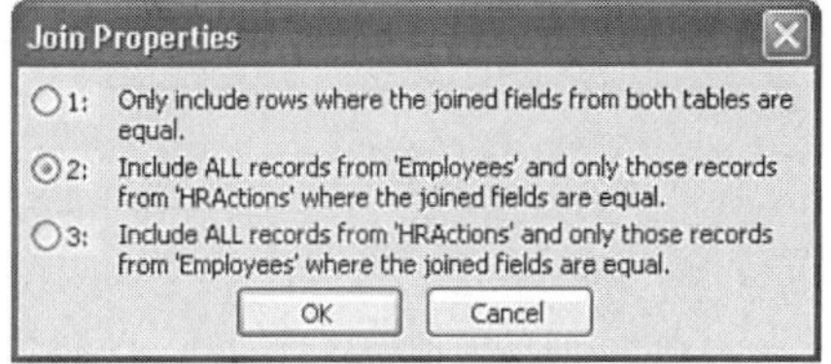

Figure 5.27 The Join Properties dialog lets you specify one of three types of one-to-many joins for the relationship. Option 1 is called an `INNER JOIN` by SQL, 2 is a `LEFT OUTER JOIN`, and 3 is a `RIGHT OUTER JOIN`.

7. The Edit Relationships dialog offers the Enforce Referential Integrity check box so that you can specify that Access perform validation testing and accept entries in the EmployeeID field that correspond only to values present in the Employees table's EmployeeID field. This process is called enforcing (or maintaining) referential integrity. (The following section discusses referential integrity.) The relationship between these two tables requires enforced referential integrity, so make sure to select this check box (see Figure 5.28).

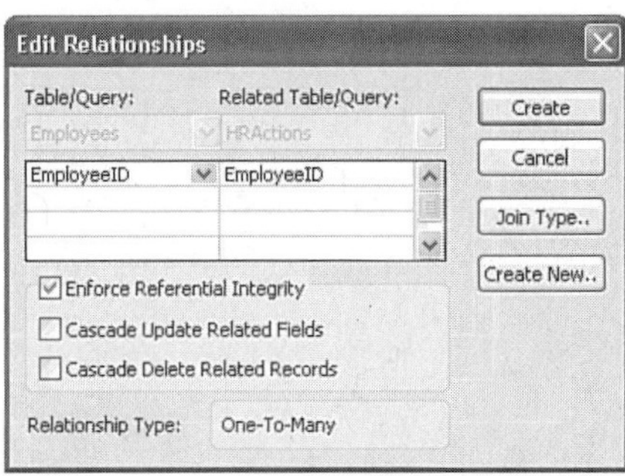

Figure 5.28 Marking the Enforce Referential Integrity check box ensures that values you enter in the HRActions table's EmployeeID field have corresponding values in the EmployeeID field of the Employees table.

NOTE

> Access automatically maintains referential integrity of tables by providing check boxes you can mark to cause cascading updates to, and cascade deletions of, related records when the primary table changes. The following section discusses cascading updates and deletions. Access enables the cascade check boxes only if you elect to enforce referential integrity.

8. Click the Create button to accept the new relationship and display it in the Relationships window (see Figure 5.29).

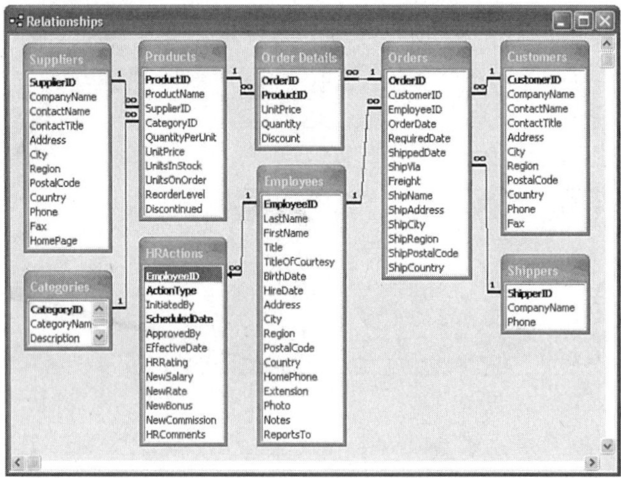

Figure 5.29 The Relationships window displays the newly added one-to-many relationship between the Employees and HRActions table.

9. Close the Relationships window and return to the Database window. Click Yes when asked to confirm that you want to save the layout changes to the Relationships diagram.

Access uses the relationship that you've created when you design queries and design forms, pages, and reports that use data in the HRActions table. Access 2000 introduced the File, Print Relationships menu command, which gives you a convenient means of printing the relationships. In Access 97, the Print Relationships command was provided as an add-in.

CASCADING UPDATES AND DELETIONS

Access's cascading deletion and cascading update options for tables with enforced referential integrity makes maintaining referential integrity easy: Just mark the Cascade Update Related Fields and Cascade Delete Related Records check boxes. In this case, marking the Cascade Update Related Fields check box is unnecessary, because you can't change the value of the AutoNumber EmployeeID field of the Employees table. You can delete records in the Employees table, so marking the Cascade Delete Related Records check box prevents orphan records—records without a corresponding record from appearing in the Employees table—in the HRActions table.

NOTE

Automatically enforcing referential integrity is usually, but not always, good database design practice. An example of where you would not want to employ cascade deletions is between the EmployeeID fields of the Orders and Employee tables. If you terminate an employee and then attempt to delete the employee's record, you might accidentally choose to delete the dependent records in the Orders table. Deleting records in the Orders table could have serious consequences from a marketing and accounting standpoint. (In practice, however, you probably would not delete a terminated employee's record.)

SELECTING A PRIMARY KEY

You don't need to designate a primary-key field for a table that is never used as a primary table. A *primary table* is the term used in this book to designate a table that contains information representing an object, such as a person or an invoice, and only one record uniquely associated with that object. The HRActions table can qualify as a primary table because it identifies an object—in this case, the equivalent of a paper form representing the outcome of two actions: initiation and approval. HRActions, however, probably wouldn't be used as a primary table in a relationship with another table.

Using a primary key field is a simple method of preventing the duplication of records in a table. Access requires that you specify a primary key if you want to create a one-to-one relationship or to update two or more tables at the same time. (Chapter 11, "Creating Multitable and Crosstab Queries," covers this subject.)

5

The primary table participating in relationships that you set with the Relationships window must have a primary key. Access considers a table without a primary-key field an oddity; therefore, when you make changes to the table and return to Design view, you might see a message stating that you haven't created a key field. (Access 2000 and later asks only once whether you want to add a primary-key field.) Related tables can have primary-key fields and often do. A primary-key field is useful for preventing the accidental addition of duplicate records.

You can create primary keys on more than one field. In the case of the HRActions table, a primary key that prevents duplicate records must consist of more than one field. If you establish the rule that no more than one type of personnel action for an employee can be scheduled for the same date, you can create a primary key that consists of the EmployeeID, ActionType, and ScheduledDate fields. When you create a primary key, Access creates an index based on the primary key.

To create a multiple-field primary key, called a *composite primary key*, and a primary-key index for the HRActions table, follow these steps:

1. Open the HRActions table in Design view.
2. Click the selection button for the EmployeeID field.
3. Ctrl+click the selection button for the ActionType field. In most instances, when you Ctrl+click a selection button, you can make multiple selections.
4. Ctrl+click the selection button for the ScheduledDate field.
5. Click the Primary Key toolbar button. Symbols of keys appear in each previously selected field, indicating their inclusion in the primary key.
6. To verify the sequence of the fields in the primary key, click the toolbar's Index button to display the Indexes dialog shown in Figure 5.30. Access automatically added the first EmployeeID index, which duplicates the Primary Key index on the EmployeeID field.

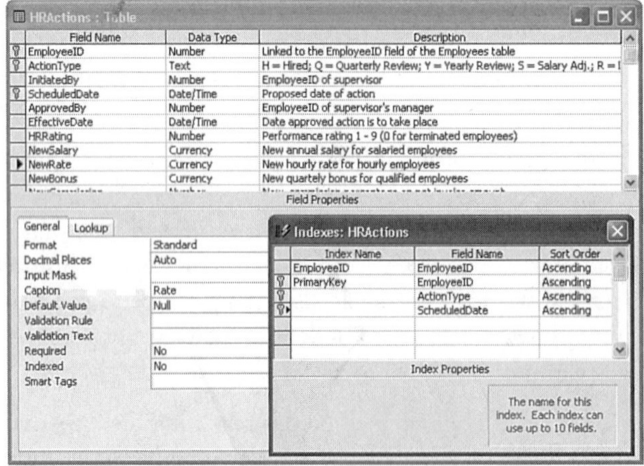

Figure 5.30
The three fields of the HRActions table's composite primary key have indexes. You can delete the extra EmployeeID index.

7. To delete the extra EmployeeID index, select the index row and press Delete.
8. Close the Indexes dialog, and press Ctrl+S to save your table design changes.

You now have a multiple-field primary key and a corresponding index to the HRActions table that precludes the addition of records that duplicate records with the same primary key value.

ADDING INDEXES TO TABLES

Although Access creates an index on the primary key, you might want to create an index on some other field or fields in the table. Indexes speed searches for records that contain specific types of data. For example, you might want to find all HRActions that occurred in a given period and all quarterly reviews for all employees in ScheduledDate sequence. If you have many records in the table, an index speeds up the searching process. A disadvantage of multiple indexes is that data-entry operations are slowed by the time it takes to update the additional indexes. You can create as many as 32 indexes for each Jet table, and 5 of those can be of the multiple-field type. Each multiple-field index can include as many as 10 fields.

TIP

> You should add only indexes you need to improve search performance. Each index you add slows the addition of new records, because adding a new record requires an addition to each index. Similarly, editing indexed fields is slower, because the edit updates the record and the index. When you create relationships between tables, Access automatically creates a hidden index on the related fields, if the index doesn't already exist. Hidden indexes count against the 32-index limit of each table. If an extra index appears in the Indexes dialog, as occurred for the HRActions table, see the "Extra Indexes Added by Access" item in the "Troubleshooting" section near the end of this chapter.

To create a single-field index for the HRActions table based on the EffectiveDate field, and a multiple-field index based on the ActionType and the ScheduledDate fields, follow these steps:

1. Select the EffectiveDate field by clicking its selection button.
2. Select the Indexed text box in the Field Properties window.
3. Open the Indexed drop-down list by clicking the arrow button or pressing Alt+down arrow (see Figure 5.31).

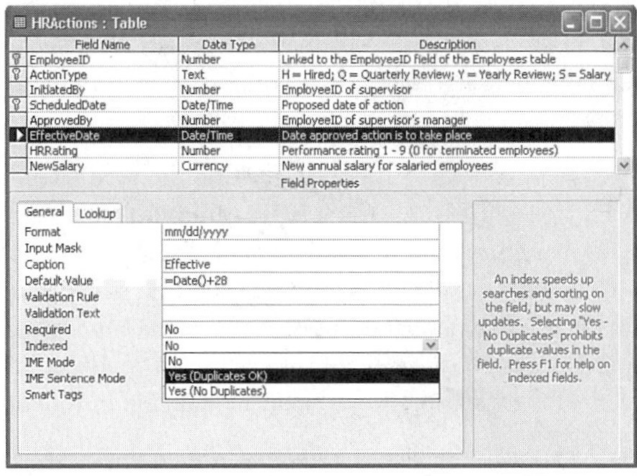

Figure 5.31 You can add an index on a single field by setting the value of the Indexed property to Yes (Duplicates OK) or Yes (No Duplicates).

4. In this case, duplicate entries on the same date are likely, so select Yes (Duplicates OK) and close the list. You can create only a single-field index with this method.

5. Click the Indexes button. The Primary Key and EffectiveDate indexes already created appear in the list boxes. Type **ActionTypeEffDate** as the name of the composite index, and then select ActionType in the Field Name drop-down list. Move the caret to the next row of the Field Name column and select ScheduledDate to create a multiple-field index on these two fields (see Figure 5.32).

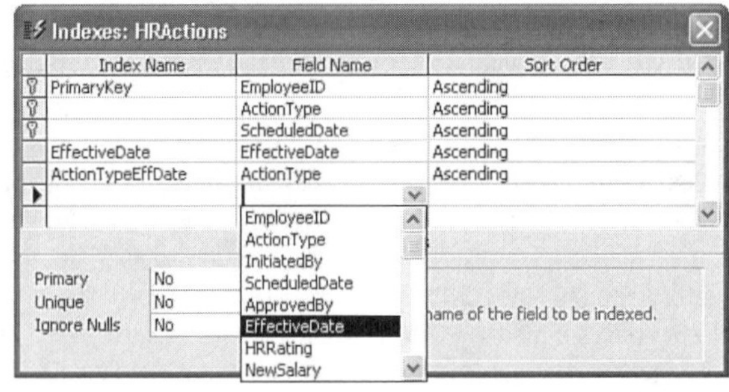

Figure 5.32
You add multiple-field indexes in the Indexes dialog.

6. In the Ignore Nulls row of the Index Properties pane for the EffectiveDate field, select Yes so that records without an EffectiveDate value aren't included in the index.

7. Click the Datasheet View button, and click Yes to save your design changes.

You now have three indexes for the Primary Key table: the index automatically created for the primary key, the single-key index on EffectiveDate, and the multiple-key index on ActionType and ScheduledDate.

ALTERING FIELDS AND RELATIONSHIPS

When you're designing a database, you often discover that you must alter the original choices you made for the sequence of fields in a table, data types, or relationships between tables. One reason for adding substantial numbers of records to tables during the testing process is to discover any necessary changes before putting the database into daily use.

5

You can change formats, validation rules and text, lengths of Text fields, and other minor items in the table by changing to design mode, selecting the field to modify, and making the changes in the property boxes. Changing data types can cause a loss of data, however, so be sure to read the later "Changing Field Data Types and Sizes" section before you attempt to make such changes. Changing the data type of a field that participates in a relationship with another table requires that you delete and, if possible, recreate the relationship. Changing relationships between tables is considered a drastic action if you have entered a substantial amount of data, so this subject is also covered later in "Changing Relationships Between Tables."

NOTE

> Access 2000 introduced the Name AutoCorrect feature. Renaming a database object in previous versions required you to search manually through all objects of your database and change all references to the renamed objects. The Name AutoCorrect feature handles the corrections for you; when you open a database object, Access scans and fixes discrepancies. New databases you create in Access 2003, whether in 2000 or 2002 file format, have this feature turned on by default. Databases you convert from previous versions require you to turn on Name AutoCorrect by choosing Tools, Options, and then

> marking the Track Name AutoCorrect Info and Perform Name AutoCorrect check boxes on the General page of the Options dialog.
> Track Name AutoCorrect must be enabled to view object dependencies and enable table field property change propagation, but Perform Name AutoCorrect isn't required.

➔ To learn how field property value changes propagate to dependent database objects, **see** "Working with Object Dependencies and Access Smart Tags," **p. 200**.

Rearranging the Sequence of Fields in a Table

If you're typing historical data in Datasheet view, you might find that the sequence of entries isn't optimum. You might, for example, be entering data from a printed form with a top-to-bottom, left-to-right sequence that doesn't correspond to the left-to-right sequence of the corresponding fields in your table. Access makes rearranging the order of fields in tables a matter of dragging and dropping fields where you want them. You can decide whether to make the revised layout temporary or permanent when you close the table.

To rearrange the fields of the HRActions table, follow these steps:

1. Click the View button. Rearranging the sequence of fields is the only table design change you can implement in Access's Datasheet view.
2. Click the field name button of the field you want to move. This action selects the field name button and all the field's data cells.
3. Hold down the left mouse button while over the field name button. The mouse pointer turns into the drag-and-drop symbol, and a heavy vertical bar marks the field's leftmost position. Figure 5.33 (top) shows the ScheduledDate field being moved to a position immediately to the left of the EffectiveDate field.
4. Move the vertical bar to the new position for the selected field and release the mouse button. The field assumes the new position shown in Figure 5.33 (bottom).

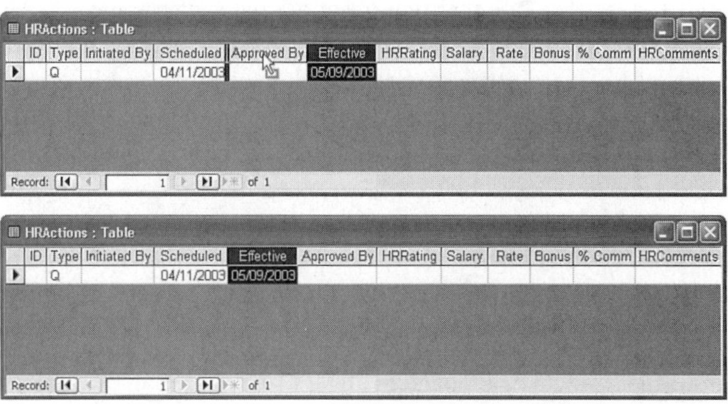

Figure 5.33
In Datasheet view, you can rearrange the left-to-right sequence of a table's fields without changing their sequence in Design view. These two windows illustrate dragging the Effective(Date) field to the left of the Approved By field.

5. When you close the HRActions table, you see the familiar Save Changes message box. To make the modification permanent, click Yes; otherwise, click No.

Rearranging the field sequence in Datasheet view doesn't change their order in Design view's fields grid. To reposition fields in Design view, click the select button of the row of the field you want to move and then drag the row vertically to a new location. Changing the position of a table's field doesn't change any of the field's other properties.

CHANGING FIELD DATA TYPES AND SIZES

You might have to change a field data type as the design of your database develops or if you import tables from another database, a spreadsheet, or a text file. If you import tables, the data type automatically chosen by Access during the importation process probably won't be what you want, especially with Number fields. Chapter 8, "Linking, Importing, and Exporting Data," discusses importing and exporting tables and data from other applications. Another example of altering field properties is changing the number of characters in fixed-length Text fields to accommodate entries that are longer than expected, or converting Text to Memo fields.

CAUTION

Before making changes to the field data types of a table that contains substantial amounts of data, back up the table by copying or exporting it to a backup Access database. If you accidentally lose parts of the data contained in the table (such as decimal fractions) while changing the field data type, you can import the backup table to your current database. Chapter 8 covers the simple and quick process of exporting Jet tables. After creating a backup database file, you can copy a table to Windows Clipboard and then paste the table to the backup database. The later section "Copying and Pasting Tables" discusses Clipboard operations.

→ For details on propagating field property value changes to dependent database objects, **see** "Working with Object Dependencies and Access Smart Tags," **p. 200**.

NUMERIC FIELDS

Changing a data type to one that requires more bytes of storage is, in almost all circumstances, safe; you don't sacrifice your data's accuracy. Changing a numeric data type from Byte to Integer to Long Integer to Single and, finally, to Double doesn't affect your data's value because each change, except for Long Integer to Single, requires more bytes of storage for a data value. Changing from Long Integer to Single and Single to Currency involves the same number of bytes and decreases the accuracy of the data only in exceptional circumstances. The exceptions can occur when you are using very high numbers or extremely small decimal fractions, such as in some scientific and engineering calculations.

On the other hand, if you change to a data type with fewer data bytes required to store it, Jet might truncate your data. If you change from a fixed-point format (Currency) or floating-point format (Single or Double) to Byte, Integer, or Long Integer, any decimal fractions in your data are truncated. Truncation means reducing the number of digits in a number to fit the new Field Size property that you choose. If you change a numeric data type from

Single to Currency, for example, you might lose your Single data in the fifth, sixth, and seventh decimal places (if any exists) because Single provides as many as seven decimal places and Currency provides only four.

You can't convert any field type to an AutoNumber-type field. You can use the AutoNumber field only as a unique record identifier; the only way you can enter a new value in an AutoNumber field is by appending new records. You can't edit an AutoNumber field. When you delete a record in Access, the AutoNumber values of the higher-numbered records are not reduced by 1.

Text Fields

You can convert Text fields to Memo fields without Jet truncating your text. You can't add indexes to Memo fields, so any index(es) on the converted Text field disappear. Jet won't let Memo fields participate in relationships.

Converting a Memo field to a Text field truncates characters beyond the 255-character limit of Text fields. Similarly, if you convert a variable-length Text field to a fixed-length field, and some records contain character strings that exceed the length you chose, Jet truncates these strings.

Conversion Between Number, Date, and Text Field Data Types

Jet makes many conversions between Number, Date, and Text field data types for you. Conversion from Number or Date to Text field data types does not follow the Format property that you assigned to the original data type. Numbers are converted with the General Number format, and dates use the Short Date format. Jet is intelligent in the methods it uses to convert suitable Text fields to Number data types. For example, it accepts dollar signs, commas, and decimals during the conversion, but ignores trailing spaces. Jet converts dates and times in the following Text formats to internal Date/Time values that you then can format the way you want:


```
1/4/2003 10:00 AM
04-Jan-03
January 4
10:00
10:00:00
```

Changing Relationships Between Tables

Adding new relationships between tables is a straightforward process, but changing relationships might require you to change data types so that the related fields have the same data type. To change a relationship between two tables, complete the following steps:

1. Close the tables involved in the relationship.

2. If the Database window is not active, click the Database Window button, or choose Window, 1 Database.

3. Display the Relationships window by clicking the Relationships button of the toolbar or by choosing Tools, Relationships.

4. Click the join line that connects to the field whose data type you want to change. When you select the join line, the line becomes darker (wider).
5. Press Delete to clear the existing relationship. Click Yes when the message box asks you to confirm your deletion.
6. If you intend to change the data type of a field that constitutes or is a member field of the primary table's primary key, delete all other relationships that exist between the primary table and every other table to which it is related.
7. Change the data types of the fields in the tables so that the data types match in the new relationships.
8. Re-create the relationships by using the procedure described earlier in the section "Establishing Relationships Between Tables."

Working with Object Dependencies and Access Smart Tags

NEW In earlier versions of Access, changing a table field's property value—such as the Format or Input Mask specification—often wreaked havoc on other Access form and report objects that depend on the field. Typically, you bind form and report control objects, such as text boxes, to fields of a table or query. In Access terminology, the control objects *inherit* the properties of the underlying table fields.

NOTE

> Technically, control objects don't support inheritance as defined by standards for object-oriented programming. Instead, control objects contain a copy of the property values of the source field. The copied properties aren't automatically updated when you change the source field's property values.

5

Enabling and Viewing Object Dependencies

Access 2003 offers a new feature, called *object dependencies*, which enables field property change propagation to dependent objects, such as queries, forms and reports. Before you can use change propagation, you must generate dependency data for your database. The version of Northwind.mdb included with Access 2003 doesn't have the required hidden object dependency table. To enable the object dependency feature in Northwind.mdb, do this:

1. Close all open Northwind objects except the Database window.
2. Select a table, such as HRActions, in the Database window, and choose View, Object Dependencies or right-click the table entry and choose Object Dependencies.
3. Click OK in the message box that asks if you want to update object dependencies (see Figure 5.34).

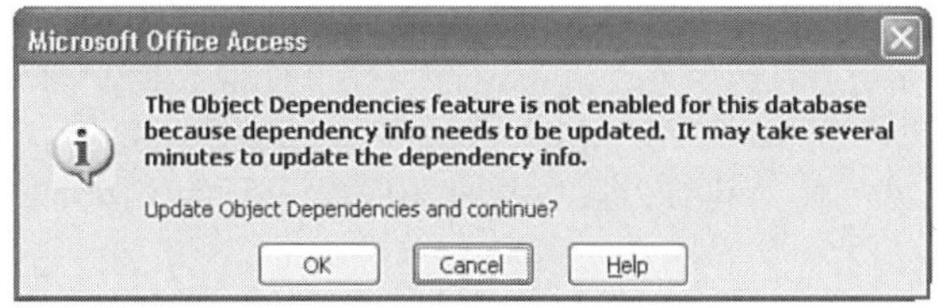

Figure 5.34 Before you can display object dependencies, you must generate a hidden dependency table for the current database.

After a few seconds, the task pane displays the dependencies for the selected table, HRActions for this example. The Employees table depends on the HRActions table because of the relationship you created in the earlier "Establishing Relationships Between Tables" section (see Figure 5.35). Some types of objects, such as union queries (Query: Customers and Suppliers by City) and SQL-specific queries (Query: Products Above Average Price), don't support dependency tracking, so they are ignored. When you select the Objects That I Depend On option, the Employees table appears, but the Ignored Objects node disappears from the list.

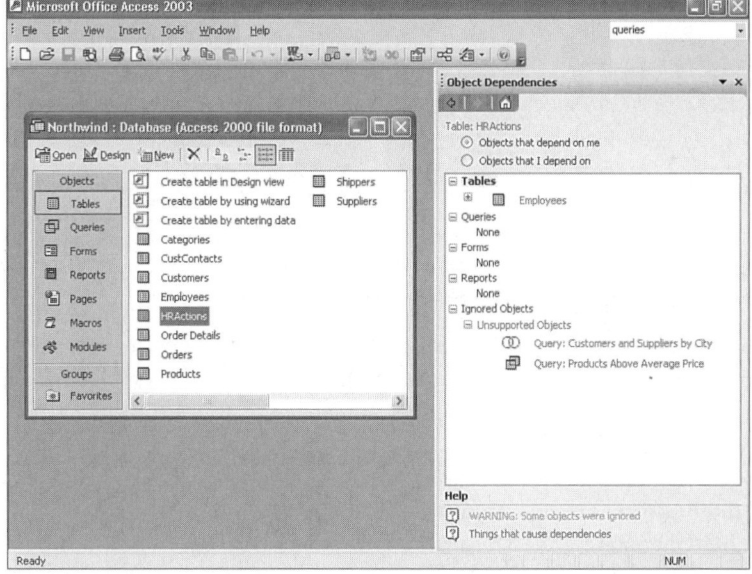

Figure 5.35 The Employees table depends on the HRActions table, and vice-versa, because of the one-to-many relationship between the EmployeeID fields of the two tables.

NOTE

> Field property change propagation doesn't apply to changing the Name property of a field. Access 2000+'s Name AutoCorrect feature propagates field name changes. As mentioned earlier in the "Altering Fields and Relationships" section, Track Name AutoCorrect must be enabled to generate object dependency data and enable viewing of dependencies in the task pane.

At this point, no queries, forms, or reports depend on the HRActions table. To view multiple object dependencies, select the Customers table and choose View, Dependencies. One table, three queries, five forms, and a report depend on the Customers table (see Figure 5.36). Click the + symbol for a dependent object to display that object's dependencies in a tree view.

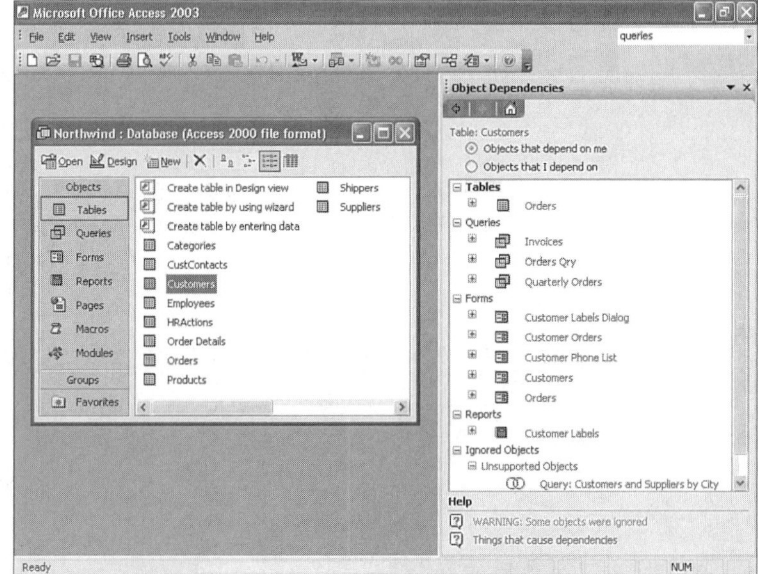

Figure 5.36
Multiple Access objects depend on the Customers table. The Orders table has even more dependencies than the Customers table.

ACTIVATING THE ACCESS PROPERTY OPTIONS SMART TAG

5

Access uses a special-purpose Property Options smart tag to propagate altered field property values. To activate this smart tag, open the Customers table in Design view, temporarily change the Input Mask property value from >LLLLL to **>LLLL**. When you move the cursor to the Caption field, the smart tag icon appears to the left of the property value text box (see Figure 5.37). Moving the mouse pointer over the icon changes its color, exposes a drop-down arrow and adds a Property Update Options screen tip. Clicking the arrow opens the single option—Update Input Mask Everywhere CustomerID is Used. Don't click the option in this case; return the Input Mask property to its original value, which causes the smart tag option to disappear. Close the table without saving your changes.

TIP

If you click the option, you must repeat the process with **>LLLLL** as the Input Mask to return the objects to their original condition.

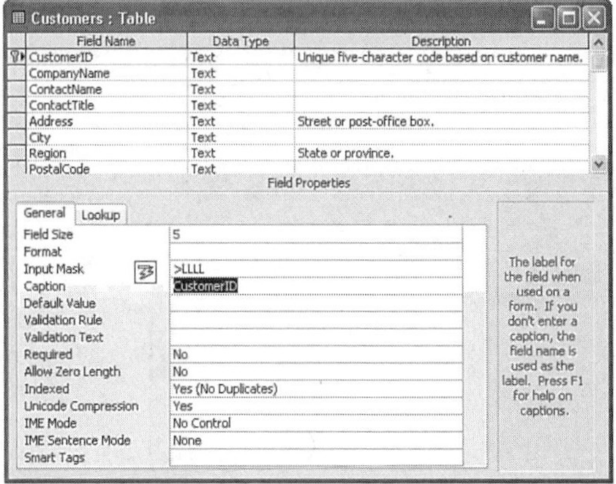

Figure 5.37
Changing the value of a table field property and moving the cursor to a different property displays the Access Property Options smart tag icon.

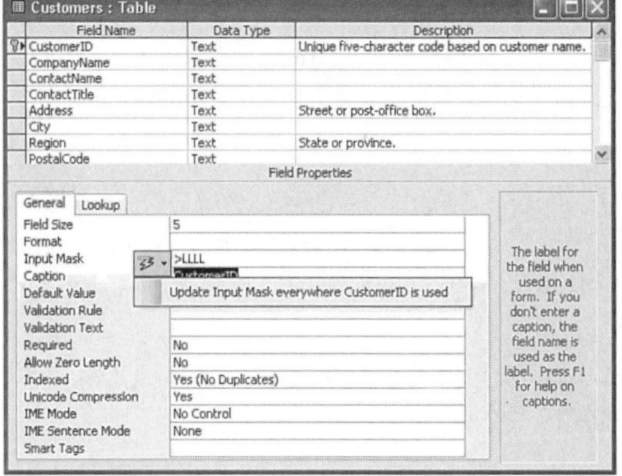

Figure 5.38
Opening the Property Options' dropdown list displays the single option that updates dependent objects with the altered property value.

NOTE

> The object dependencies feature and Property Options smart tags aren't available in Access data projects (ADP) or data access pages (DAP).

ADDING AN INTERNET-BASED SMART TAG TO A FIELD

Access 2003 also supports smart tags linked to Web pages. The only Web-based smart tag included with the product is Financial Symbol, which links to stock quotes, company reports, and recent company news from MSN MoneyCentral. To give this smart tag a test drive, do the following:

1. Create a new table with a field named Symbol and, optionally, another field named Company.
2. Select the Symbol field, move the cursor to the Smart Tags property's text box and click the builder button to open the Smart Tags dialog.

3. Mark the Financial Symbol check box (see Figure 5.39), and click OK to add "urn:schemas-microsoft-com:office:smarttags#stockticker" as the SmartTags property's value.

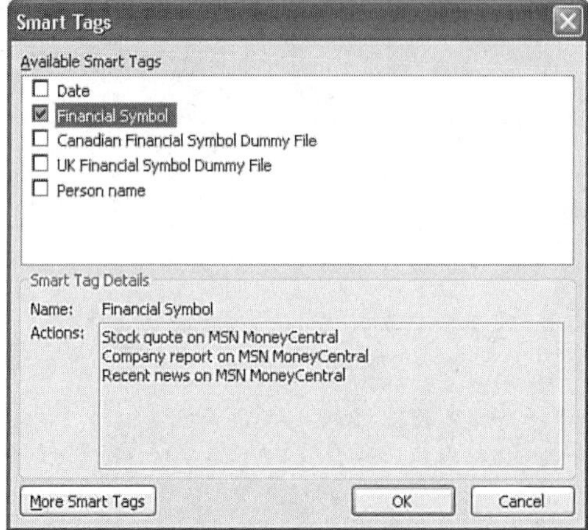

Figure 5.39 Records in a table with a Smart Tag property value specified for a field have an identifier in the lower right corner of the field and display a smart tag icon when selected.

4. Change to Datasheet view, and add a few NASDAQ and New York Stock Exchange stock symbols to the Symbols field. As you add symbols, a triangular marker is present at the bottom right of the cell and a smart tag information icon appears adjacent to the cell.

5. Move the mouse pointer over the icon, and click the arrow to open the Smart Tag Options list (see Figure 5.40).

5

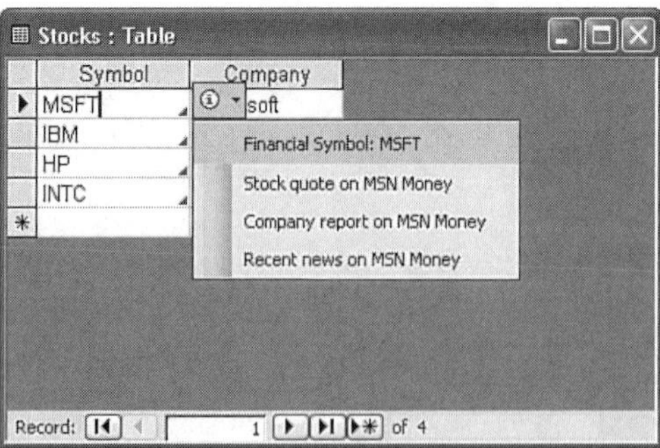

Figure 5.40 Selecting the smart tag icon and opening its dropdown list displays the available smart tag actions.

6. Select one of the options—Stock Quote on MSN MoneyCentral for this example—to open the specified Web page (see Figure 5.41).

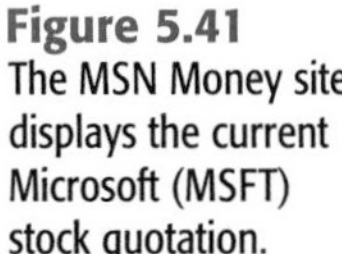

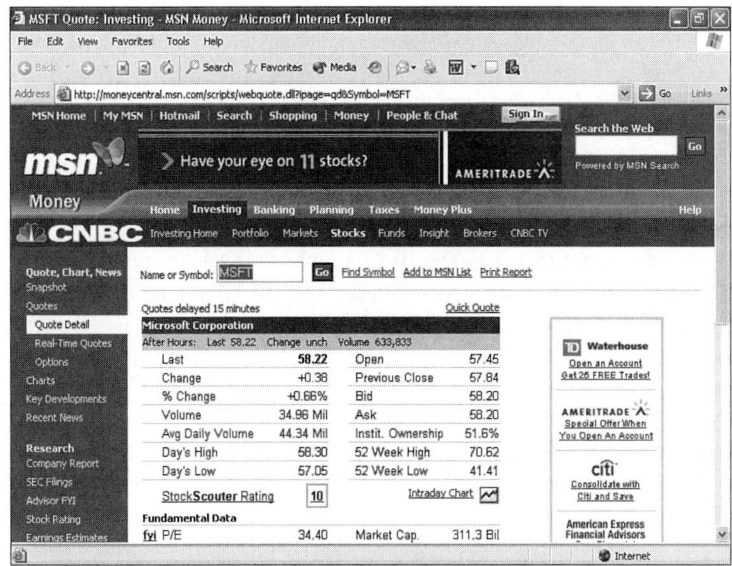

Figure 5.41
The MSN Money site displays the current Microsoft (MSFT) stock quotation.

Custom smart tags, such as Financial Symbol, are defined by XML documents. The `urn:schemas-microsoft-com:office:smarttags#stockticker` property value is the Universal Resource Name (urn) for the custom smart tag `type` attribute value. The corresponding custom smart tag is defined by the Stocks.xml document in Windows XP's \Program Files\Common Files\Microsoft Shared\Smart Tag\Lists\1033\ folder (for the U.S. English locale). Navigate to and double-click Stocks.xml to open the document in Internet Explorer (see Figure 5.42). The three <FL:action> elements define the action options you see when opening the list (refer to Figure 5.40).

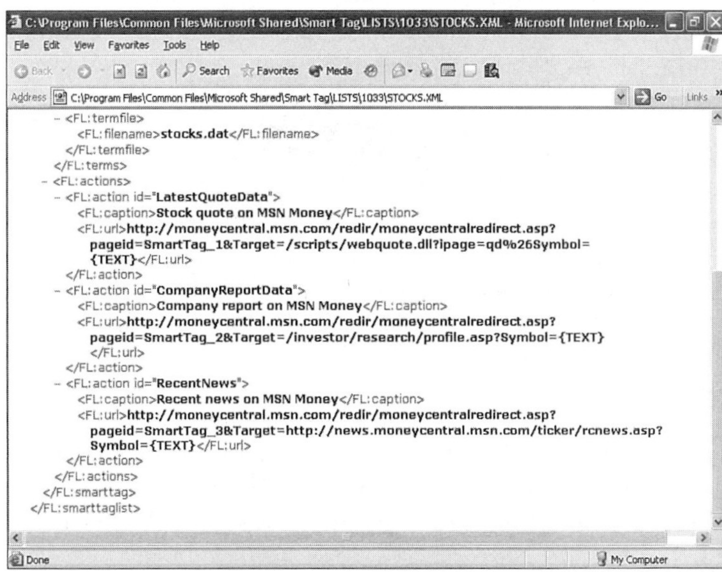

```
C:\Program Files\Common Files\Microsoft Shared\Smart Tag\LISTS\1033\STOCKS.XML - Microsoft Internet Explo...
Address C:\Program Files\Common Files\Microsoft Shared\Smart Tag\LISTS\1033\STOCKS.XML
  - <FL:termfile>
      <FL:filename>stocks.dat</FL:filename>
    </FL:termfile>
  </FL:terms>
- <FL:actions>
  - <FL:action id="LatestQuoteData">
      <FL:caption>Stock quote on MSN Money</FL:caption>
      <FL:url>http://moneycentral.msn.com/redir/moneycentralredirect.asp?
        pageid=SmartTag_1&Target=/scripts/webquote.dll?ipage=qd%26Symbol=
        {TEXT}</FL:url>
    </FL:action>
  - <FL:action id="CompanyReportData">
      <FL:caption>Company report on MSN Money</FL:caption>
      <FL:url>http://moneycentral.msn.com/redir/moneycentralredirect.asp?
        pageid=SmartTag_2&Target=/investor/research/profile.asp?Symbol={TEXT}
        </FL:url>
    </FL:action>
  - <FL:action id="RecentNews">
      <FL:caption>Recent news on MSN Money</FL:caption>
      <FL:url>http://moneycentral.msn.com/redir/moneycentralredirect.asp?
        pageid=SmartTag_3&Target=http://news.moneycentral.msn.com/ticker/rcnews.asp?
        Symbol={TEXT}</FL:url>
    </FL:action>
  </FL:actions>
 </FL:smarttag>
</FL:smarttaglist>
Done                                                    My Computer
```

Figure 5.42
These elements of the Stocks.xml document generates the fixed list (FL) for the MSN Money Financial Symbols smart tag.

NOTE

Creating custom smart tags is beyond the scope of this book. If you want to learn more about Microsoft smart tag technology, go to `http://msdn.microsoft.com` and search for "smart tag" with the double-quotes included in the search term.

COPYING AND PASTING TABLES

To copy a complete table or records of a table to the Windows Clipboard, use the same methods that apply to most other Windows applications. (Using the Clipboard to paste individual records or sets of records into a table is one of the subjects of the next chapter.) You can copy tables into other databases, such as a general-purpose backup database, by using the Clipboard.

To copy a table to another Access database, a destination database must exist. To create a backup database and copy the contents of the HRActions table to the database, follow these steps:

1. Activate the Database window.

2. Click the Tables tab, if necessary, to display the list of tables.
3. Select the table that you want to copy to the new database.

4. Click the Copy button on the toolbar, press Ctrl+C, or choose Edit, Copy.

   If you plan to copy the table to your current database, skip to step 7.
5. If you've created a destination backup database, choose File, Open Database to open the database; then skip to step 7.

6. To create a backup database, choose Tools, Database Utilities, Back Up Database to open the Save Backup As dialog. Accept the default filename, or name the new database Backup.mdb or another appropriate filename.

7. Click the Paste button on the toolbar, press Ctrl+V, or choose Edit, Paste to open the Paste Table As dialog (see Figure 5.43).

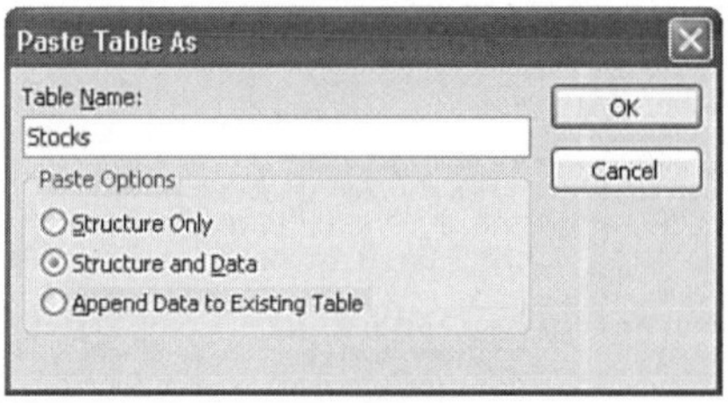

Figure 5.43
The Paste Table As dialog lets you paste a backup copy of a table into the current or another database.

8. You have three options for pasting the backup table to the destination database. The most common choice is Structure and Data, with which you can create a new table or replace the data in a table with the name you enter in the Table Name text box. You can also paste only the structure and then append data to the table later by selecting

Structure Only, or append the records to an existing table of the name that you enter. For this example, accept the default: Structure and Data.

9. Your current or backup database now has a copy of the table that you selected, and the name you entered appears in the Database window. You can save multiple copies of the same table under different names if you're making a series of changes to the table that might affect the integrity of the data that it contains.

To delete a table from a database, select the table name in the Database window and then press Delete. A confirmation message appears. Click Yes to delete the table forever. You can't choose Edit, Undo after deleting a table.

USING THE TABLE ANALYZER WIZARD

Access 2003's Table Analyzer Wizard detects cells containing repeated data in table columns and proposes to create two new related tables to eliminate the repetition. This wizard uses the Lookup Wizard, described in Chapter 11 to create the relationship between the two new tables. After the Wizard creates the new related tables, *NewName* and *Lookup*, your original table is renamed to *TableName*_OLD, and the Wizard creates a one-to-many `INNER JOIN` query named *TableName* to return a result set that duplicates the Datasheet view of the original table. So, you need not change the references to *TableName* in your Access application objects.

The *Lookup* table must have a valid primary-key field to provide unambiguous association of a single record in the Lookup table with a foreign key field in the *NewName* table. One of the problems associated with repetitious data is data-entry errors, such as occasional misspelling of a company name or an address element in *Lookup*. The Table Analyzer Wizard detects and displays instances of minor mismatches in repeated cell values, such as a missing apostrophe, for correction. If such errors aren't corrected, the *Lookup* table includes spurious, almost-duplicate entries that violate the rules of table normalization. 5

Northwind.mdb's Orders table has a set of fields for shipping addresses. The data in these fields is the same for every order placed by each customer with three exceptions: order numbers 10248, 10249, and 10260. Shipping addresses comprise the bulk of the data in the Orders table, so removal of duplicate shipping information greatly reduces the size of the Orders table. Placing shipping addresses in a lookup table also offers the opportunity to streamline the data-entry process.

NOTE

> The Access 97 and 2000 versions of the Table Analyzer Wizard had several bugs that resulted in error messages or spurious typographical error entries. The Access 2003 version corrects the problems.

To demonstrate use of the Table Analyzer Wizard to eliminate duplicate shipping address information in the Orders table of Northwind.mdb, follow these steps:

1. Use the Clipboard method—described in the preceding section—to create a copy of the Orders table named SalesOrders in the Northwind.mdb database. Working with a copy prevents making changes to Northwind.mdb's sample tables that would affect later examples in this book.
2. Launch the Table Analyzer Wizard by choosing Tools, Analyze, Table.
3. Skip the two introductory dialogs by clicking the Next button twice to reach the Table Selection dialog shown in Figure 5.44.

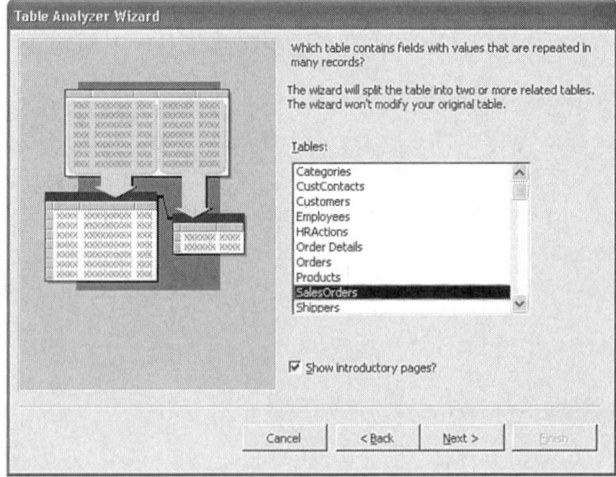

Figure 5.44
Select the table to analyze in the third Table Analyzer Wizard dialog.

4. Select the table with the duplicated data in the Tables list box, the SalesOrders table for this example, and clear the Show Introductory Pages? check box. Click Next to continue.
5. You want to choose the fields for the *Lookup* table, so select the No, I Want To Decide option, and click Next. The Wizard displays a list of fields in the SalesOrders table renamed to Table1.
6. Click to select in the Table1 field list the first of the fields with duplicated information, ShipName; then press Shift and click the last of the fields to move, ShipCountry (see Figure 5.45).
7. Holding the left mouse button down, drag the selected fields from the field list to an empty area to the right of the Table1 list. When you release the mouse button, the wizard creates a new field list for proposed Table1 with a many-to-one relationship between Table1 and Table2. The relationship is based on a lookup field in Table1 and a Generated Unique ID (AutoNumber) field in Table2. An input box opens to rename Table1; type **ShipAddresses** in the Table Name text box (see Figure 5.46). Click OK to close the input box.

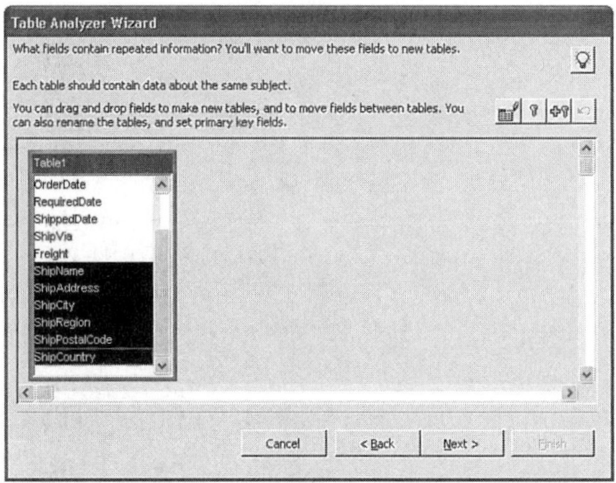

Figure 5.45
Select the fields with the duplicate data to move to a new lookup table. For this example, the fields to select begin with "Ship."

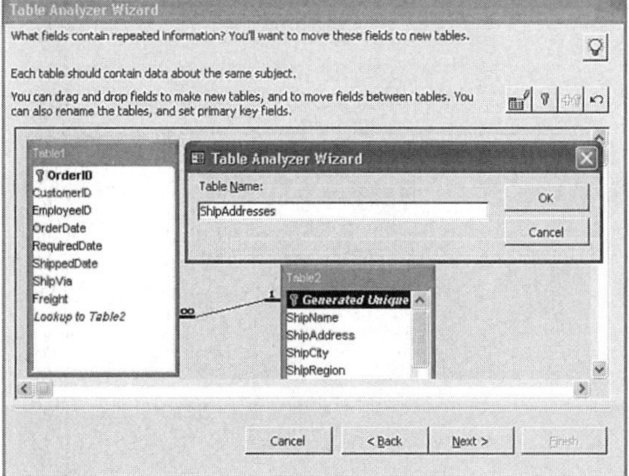

Figure 5.46
The Wizard designs a lookup table to contain the fields moved from the source table, and opens an input box in which you assign a name to the lookup table.

8. CustomerID is a better choice than an AutoNumber field for the initial primary-key field of ShipAddresses, because there's currently only one correct ShipAddress per customer in the Orders table. Click and drag the CustomerID field from the Table1 field list to the ShipAddresses field list. With the CustomerID field selected in the ShipAddresses field list, click the Set Unique Identifier button (the one with the key icon only). The Generated Unique ID field disappears and the CustomerID field becomes the primary key for the proposed ShipAddress table (see Figure 5.47). Click Next to continue.
9. If the Wizard detects a misspelling of an entry in the lookup table, it opens a Correcting Typographical Errors...dialog. The Wizard bases the value in the Correction column on the frequency of exact duplication of records. In this case, the Wizard has detected two ShipAddress values for Old World Delicatessen (see Figure 5.48). Click the Next Key >>> button.

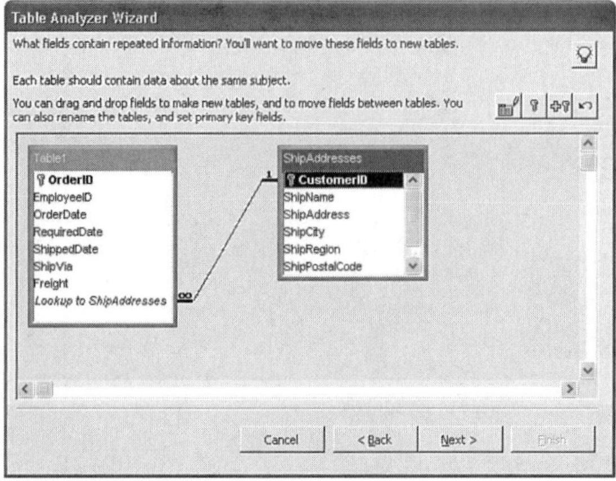

Figure 5.47
Specify the CustomerID field as the primary key for the ShipAddresses lookup table.

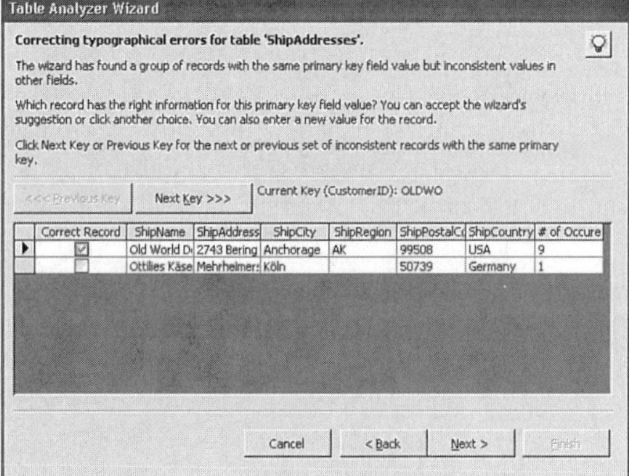

Correct Record	ShipName	ShipAddress	ShipCity	ShipRegion	ShipPostalC	ShipCountry	# of Occure
☑	Old World D	2743 Bering	Anchorage	AK	99508	USA	9
☐	Ottilies Käse	Mehrheimer	Köln		50739	Germany	1

Figure 5.48
The Wizard detects and proposes to correct a misspelled shipping address, which actually reflects a second shipping address. Two additional records have different shipping addresses, which call for shipment to a destination other than the customer's billing address.

10. Click the Next Key >>> button three times to view the three additional records (10260 for OLDWO, 10249 for TRADH, and 10248 for WILMK) with different shipping addresses. Shipping information in the three records later reverts to the values selected in the check boxes, because the Wizard can't handle multiple shipping addresses for a single primary key value.
11. Click Next and the Wizard proposes to create a query, in this case named SalesOrders, that substitutes for the original SalesOrders table. Accept the default Yes, Create the Query option. Clear the Display Help check box to prevent two wizard Help screens from appearing when you complete the operation.
12. Click Finish to create the SalesOrders query, and acknowledge the "Here is the query…" message to open the SalesOrders query.
13. Select the Lookup to ShipAddresses field and click the down-arrow button to open the lookup list, which displays the shipping addresses extracted from the SalesOrders table

(see Figure 5.49). Notice that the list has only one entry for ALKFI, proving that the wizard corrected the spelling error.

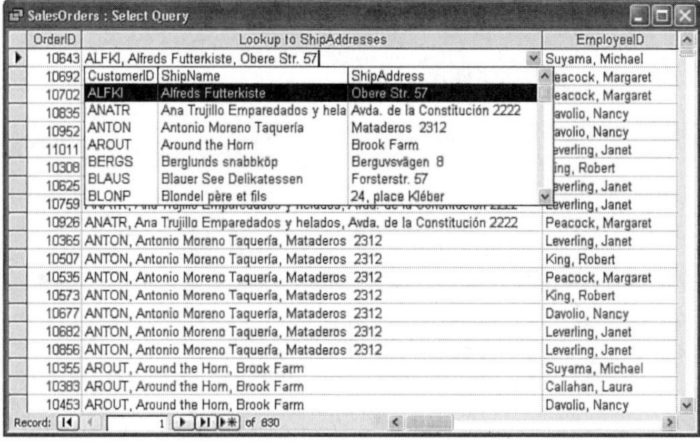

Figure 5.49
The SalesOrders query, which replaces the SalesOrders table, has a lookup field from which you can select a shipping address for the order.

The Wizard has renamed the original SalesOrders table as SalesOrders_OLD, and substitutes the SalesOrders query for the SalesOrders table. The Nwind05.mdb database in the \Seua10\Chaptr05 folder of the accompanying CD-ROM includes the tables and query created in the preceding steps.

TIP

Extracting the duplicate shipping address information from the copy of the Orders table to a new ShipAddresses table is helpful to demonstrate use of the Table Analyzer Wizard. But the preceding example isn't practical in the real world, where individual customers might have several shipping addresses. You're likely to find this wizard better suited for extracting duplicate information from spreadsheets you import into Access tables than from existing relational tables.

To make the ShipAddresses table useful, you must add a field, such as ShipToID, to identify multiple shipping addresses for a single customer. Assign a value of 0 for the ShipToID field for the default shipping information created by the wizard. Additional shipping addresses for a particular CustomerID are numbered 1, 2, 3, ... You need to redesign forms that specify shipping addresses to allow adding new ShipAddresses records for customers. You must change the primary key to a composite primary key consisting of CustomerID + ShipToID, and you must use VBA code to create successive ShipToID values automatically for a particular CustomerID.

NOTE

If you want to return Northwind.mdb to its original state, open the Database window, and delete the SalesOrders query plus the SalesOrders_OLD, Table1, and ShipAddress tables.

GENERATING A DATA DICTIONARY WITH THE DATABASE DOCUMENTER

After you've determined the individual data entities that make up the tables of your database and have established the relationships between them, the next step is to prepare a preliminary written description of the database, called a *data dictionary*. Data dictionaries are indispensable to database systems; an undocumented database system is almost impossible to administer and maintain properly. Errors and omissions in database design often are uncovered when you prepare the preliminary data dictionary.

When you've completed and tested your database design, you prepare the final detailed version of the data dictionary. As you add new forms and reports to applications or modify existing forms and reports, update the data dictionary to keep it current. Even if you're making a database for your personal use, a simplified version of a data dictionary pays many dividends on the time invested.

Access 2003's Database Documenter creates a report that details the objects and values of the properties of the objects in the current database. You can also use Office Links to export the report as a rich-text format (RTF) file (Publish It with Microsoft Word) or in Excel business interchange file format (BIFF) file (Analyze It with Microsoft Excel).

In many cases, Documenter tells you more than you want to know about your database; the full report for all objects in Northwind.mdb, for example, requires about 400 printed pages. Most often, you only want to document your tables and, perhaps, you queries to create a complete data dictionary. The following steps show you how to create a data dictionary for the table objects (only) of Northwind.mdb:

1. Open the database you want to document, Northwind.mdb for this example, and choose Tools, Analyze, Documenter to open Documenter's tabbed dialog.
2. Click the tab for the type of database object(s) you want to document. Current Database and Tables are the most common data dictionary objects, so click the Current Database Tab.
3. Mark the Properties and Relationships check boxes, or click Select All (see Figure 5.50), and click the Tables tab.

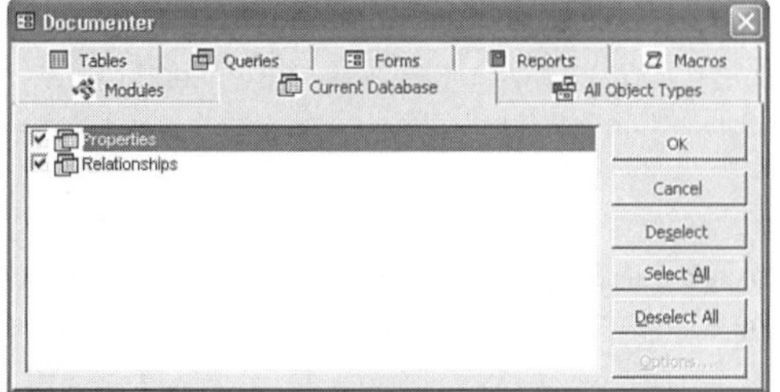

Figure 5.50 Mark both the Properties and Relationships check boxes to list database properties and generate simple diagrams of table relationships.

4. Mark the check boxes of the tables to analyze, Employees and HRActions for this example (see Figure 5.51), and click the Options button to open the Print Table Definition dialog.

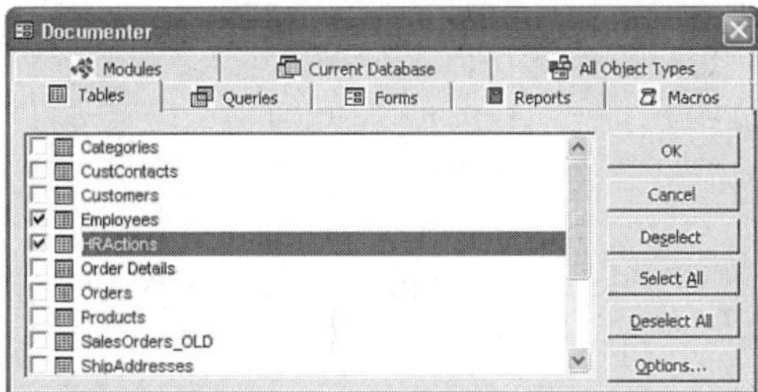

Figure 5.51
Select a couple of tables to give the Documenter a test run.

5. Northwind.mdb isn't a secure database, so clear the Permissions by User and Group check box. The default options for fields and indexes specify the full gamut of information on these objects (see Figure 5.52). Click OK to close the dialog.

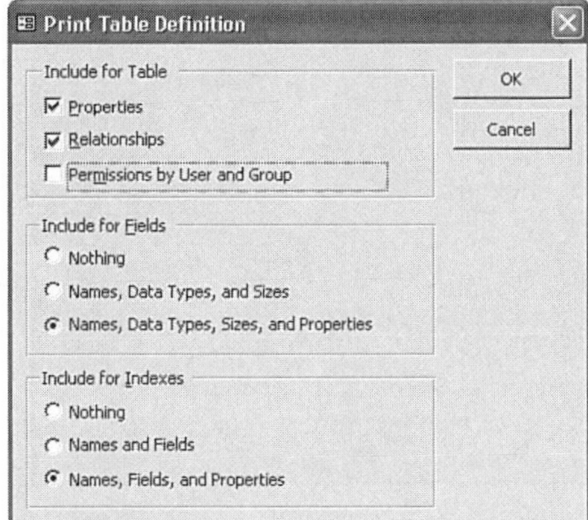

Figure 5.52
The Print Table Definition dialog lets you specify the amount of detail the report contains for tables.

5

6. Click OK to close the Documenter dialog and start the report generation process. After a few seconds, page 1 of an 17-page report opens in Print Preview mode.
7. Click the Print Preview window to display the report at 100% scale and expand the size of the window to display the full width of the report (see Figure 5.53). For this example, the Employees table is the report's first object.
8. Scroll the report to review the remainder of page 1, and then click the next page button to display additional fields of the Employees table and the HRActions table.
9. Database properties appear at the end of the report. Navigate to page 15 to view the first page of the Database section of the report. Pages 16 through 18 of the example report display simplified entity-relationship (E-R) diagrams for the database's relationships (see Figure 5.54).

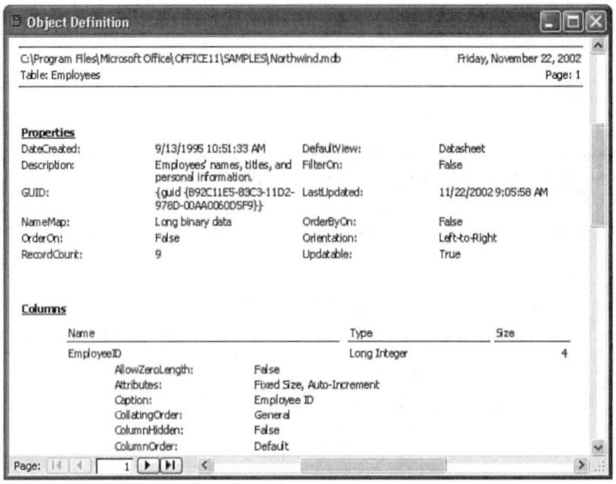

Figure 5.53
Properties of tables and their fields appear at the beginning of Documenter's report.

Object Definition

C:\Program Files\Microsoft Office\OFFICE11\SAMPLES\Northwind.mdb — Friday, November 22, 2002
Table: Employees — Page: 1

Properties

DateCreated:	9/13/1995 10:51:33 AM	DefaultView:	Datasheet
Description:	Employees' names, titles, and personal information.	FilterOn:	False
GUID:	{guid {B92C11E5-83C3-11D2-978D-00AA0060D5F9}}	LastUpdated:	11/22/2002 9:05:58 AM
NameMap:	Long binary data	OrderByOn:	False
OrderOn:	False	Orientation:	Left-to-Right
RecordCount:	9	Updatable:	True

Columns

Name		Type	Size
EmployeeID		Long Integer	4
AllowZeroLength:	False		
Attributes:	Fixed Size, Auto-Increment		
Caption:	Employee ID		
CollatingOrder:	General		
ColumnHidden:	False		
ColumnOrder:	Default		

Page: 1

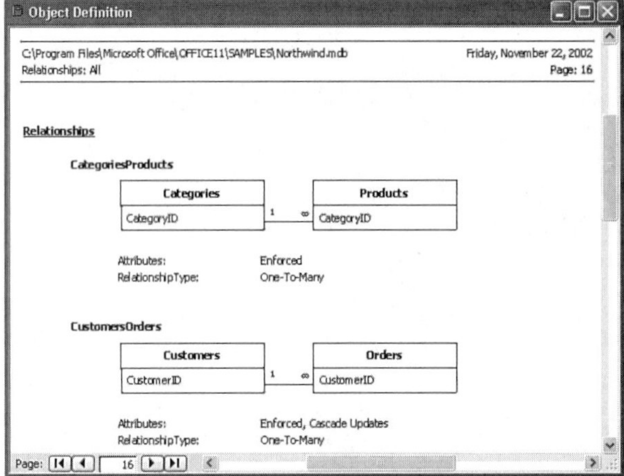

Figure 5.54
Documenter's Current Database, Relationships option generates Spartan entity-relationship diagrams for all tables in the database, regardless of the tables you select to document.

5

10. Click the Print button on the main toolbar to print the report, or click the OfficeLinks button to create a doc_rptObjects.rtf or doc_rptObjects.xls file in the My Documents folder. Word or Excel opens automatically to display the exported file.

11. Right-click the report and choose Send To, Mail Recipient (as Attachment) to open the Send dialog in which you can choose one of eight formats, including HTML, Report Snapshot, and XML. Alternatively, choose Export, to open the Export Report dialog, and save the file in one of the supported formats.

→ For more information on emailing or exporting reports, **see** "Mailing Report Snapshots," **p. 696** and "Exporting Static Reports as XML," **p. 965**.

Documenting other types of objects in your database follows the same method outlined in the preceding steps. The ability to send Documenter reports by email simplifies keeping others involved in the database design project up to date on changes.

TROUBLESHOOTING

GAPS IN AUTONUMBER FIELD VALUES

When I accidentally add a new record to a table with an AutoNumber field and then delete it, the next record I add has the wrong AutoNumber value--increment of 2 instead of 1.

That's the major drawback of AutoNumber fields, especially when the AutoNumber field value corresponds to a physical record, such as an invoice or check number. The AutoNumber feature offers no simple method of replacing an incorrect record that you delete from the table. The best approach, which insures that your table is auditable, is to never delete a record from a table with an AutoNumber field. Instead, type **VOID** in an appropriate field, and add an explanation (if there's a field available to do so).

EXTRA INDEXES ADDED BY ACCESS

After I specified a primary key on a field containing the characters "ID", an additional index appeared for the field.

In many cases, Access automatically specifies a primary key and index on fields whose names contain the characters "ID", "key", "code", and "num" when you create or import tables. This behavior is controlled by the contents of the AutoIndex on Import/Create text box of the Tables/Queries page of the Options dialog (from the Tools menu). When you change the primary-key field(s), the old index remains. You can safely delete the automatically added index.

IN THE REAL WORLD—DATABASE STRATEGY AND TABLE TACTICS

In warfare, strategy defines the objective; tactics specify the battlefield methods to achieve the strategic objective. Carl von Clauswitz' *On War* is the seminal 19th century study of strategy and tactics of modern warfare. Niccolo Machiavelli's *The Art of War* and Che Guevera's *On Guerilla Warfare* provide earlier and later takes, respectively, on the subject. Designing strategic databases and laying out the tables that comprise the database shouldn't—but often does—involve open or guerilla hostilities between the participants.

As a database and table designer, try to remain on the side of your product's consumers; you might win a battle or two, but the consumers (users) ultimately will win the war. This is especially true when the consumers control your database implementation budget. Interview database users to determine their workflow and what information is important to the activities for which they're responsible. Keep your consumers in the loop as you develop the database structure. Provide users with periodic copies of the data dictionary or a printed copy of the Relationships table as you make database and table design changes. It's a good idea, however, to minimize the amount of detail in the Documenter reports you send to others involved in the database design process.

Table and field naming is an important database design tactic. There are several schools of thought on naming conventions for tables and fields, but most Access developers agree on one rule: Don't add spaces to table or field names. Northwind.mdb contains only one table, Order Details, with a space in its name, and none of the current Northwind.mdb tables have spaces in field names. Despite the fact that SQL Server 7.0 and later accommodate this dubious feature introduced by Access 1.0, don't use spaces in database, table, or field names. When you export tables or queries to XML documents, spaces in field or table names result in ugly element names, such as `<Order_x0020_Details>`, in which `_x0020_` replaces the space. Use a mixture of upper- and lower-case letters to make names more readable.

Many developers use "tbl" as a table name prefix for consistency with other Access object type identification prefixes, such as "frm" for forms, "dap" for pages, and "rpt" for reports. Using a table object identifier prefix is uncommon in real-world production databases, because tables are the core objects of a database. Using table names that identify the source document or object of the table, such as "Orders", "Invoices", "Products", and the like is a good database design practice. Use plural nouns when naming tables, because tables contain multiple instances of the objects they represent.

Some database administrators (DBAs) use a short prefix for field names that identify the table that contains the fields. A field name prefix indicates to developers the source of the field without the necessity of having to refer to a database diagram or a table field list. Another benefit of adding a prefix based on a table name is avoidance of duplicate names in primary-key and foreign-key pairs. If you choose this approach, a logical prefix for the fields of the HRActions table would be "hra."

Some Access developers add a prefix to field names—such as "dat" (for Date/Time) or "txt" (for Text)—that specifies the Jet data type, following the generally accepted convention for adding a data type prefix to VBA variable and constant names. This practice is becoming less common as more developers work interchangeably with Jet and MSDE/SQL Server databases. Corresponding Jet and SQL Server data type names aren't necessarily the same; conflicts between Jet-based prefixes and SQL Server prefixes can cause confusion when upsizing Jet databases to SQL Server 2000.

CHAPTER 6

Entering, Editing, and Validating Jet Table Data

In this chapter

Entering Data in Access Tables

Ease of data entry is a primary criterion for an effective database development environment. Most of your Access database applications probably will use forms for data entry. In many instances, however, entering data in Table Datasheet view is quicker than using a form, especially during the database development cycle. For example, it's a good idea to test your proposed database structure before you commit to designing the forms and reports. Although the Name AutoCorrect feature introduced by Access 2000 reduces discrepancies, changing table and field names or altering relationships between tables after you create a collection of forms and reports can involve a substantial amount of work.

To test the database design, you must enter test data. In this instance, using Table Datasheet view to enter data makes more sense than using a form. Even if you import data from another database type or from a spreadsheet, you probably need to edit the data to make it compatible with your new application. The first part of this chapter concentrates on data entry and editing methods.

Another important factor in a database development environment is maintaining the integrity of your data. Entity integrity rules limit the data you enter in fields to a particular range or set of valid values.

Like earlier versions, Access 2003 lets you enforce entity integrity rules (often called *business rules*) at the field and table levels. You enforce entity integrity (also called *domain integrity*) by entering expressions as the value of the Validation Rule property of fields and tables. This chapter shows you how to use simple expressions for domain integrity validation rules. After you master Jet/VBA operators and expressions in Chapter 10, "Understanding Jet Operators and Expressions," you can write complex validation rules that minimize the possibility of data entry errors in your Jet tables.

Using Keyboard Operations for Entering and Editing Data

Access is mouse-oriented, as are most Windows applications, but keyboard equivalents are available for the most common actions. One reason for providing keyboard commands is that constantly shifting the hand from a keyboard to a mouse and back can reduce data-entry rates by more than half. Shifting between a keyboard and mouse can also lead to or aggravate *repetitive stress injury* (RSI), of which the most common type is *carpal tunnel syndrome* (CTS).

Keyboard operations are as important in a data-entry environment as they are in word-processing applications. Consequently, the information concerning key combinations for data entry appears here instead of being relegated to fine print in an appendix. The data-entry procedures you learn in the following sections prove useful when you come to the "Testing Field and Table Validation Rules" section near the end of the chapter.

CREATING A WORKING COPY OF NORTHWIND.MDB

If you want to experiment with the keyboard operations described in the following sections, work with a copy of the Northwind.mdb database. By using a copy, you don't need to worry about making changes that affect the sample database. An easy way to make a copy of Northwind.mdb is to save a copy with a different name in the Access 2002 file format.

TIP

This chapter uses the HRActions table for data entry and validation examples. If you didn't create the HRActions table in the preceding chapter, choose File, Get External Data, Import, and import the HRActions table from the location where you saved the CD-ROM files, typically C:\Program Files\Seua11\Chaptr05. After you import the table, choose Tools, Relationships, add the HRActions table, and create a one-to-many relationship between the EmployeeID fields of the Employees and HRActions table. Nwind05.mdb only contains tables and a single query.

To create a copy of Northwind.mdb in Access 2002 format, follow these steps:

1. With the Access 2000 version of Northwind.mdb open, close all windows except the Database window.
2. Choose Tools, Database Utilities, Convert Database, To Access 2002 Format to open the Convert Database Into dialog. Unless you've changed the Default Database Folder property in the General Page of the Options dialog, the default location for saving the copy is My Documents.
3. You can accept the default file name (Db1.mdb) in the Filename text box, or you can type a more descriptive name, such as **Nwind2002.mdb**, in the Filename text box, and then click Save. Acknowledge the message that states that Access 2000 and earlier users can't open the database.

4. Click the Open button on the toolbar to display the Open dialog, and double-click the new .mdb file to open it.

SETTING DATA-ENTRY OPTIONS

Most keyboard operations described in the following sections apply to tables and updatable queries in Datasheet view, text boxes on forms, and text boxes used for entering property values in Properties windows and in the Field Properties grid of Table Design view. In the examples, the Arrow Key Behavior property is set to Next Character rather than the default Next Field value. When the Arrow Key Behavior property is set to Next Field, the arrow keys move the cursor from field to field. Data-entry operators accustomed to mainframe terminals or DOS applications probably prefer to use the Next Character setting.

To modify the behavior of the arrow keys and the Tab and Enter keys, choose Tools, Options and click the Keyboard tab to display the keyboard options settings (see Figure 6.1). Table 6.1 lists the available options with the default values. These keyboard options let you emulate the behavior of the data-entry keys of mainframe terminals.

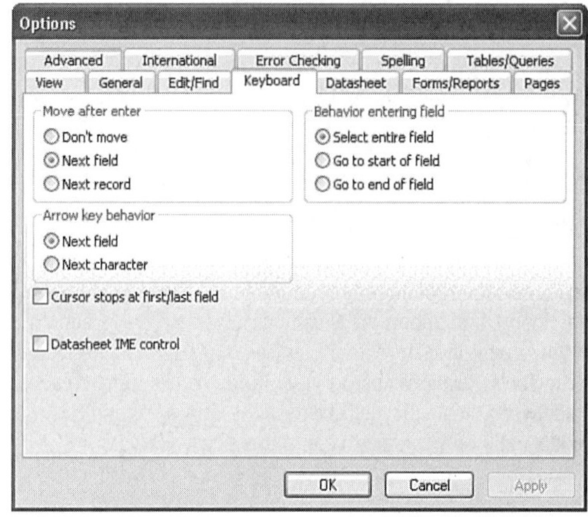

Figure 6.1
The settings you specify on the Keyboard page of the Options dialog apply to all databases you open, because they're stored in your computer's Registry.

TABLE 6.1 KEYBOARD OPTIONS FOR ALL ACCESS DATABASES

Option	Function
Move After Enter Group	
Don't Move	When this option is selected, the cursor remains in the current field when you press Enter.
Next Field (default)	When this option is selected, the cursor moves to the next field when you press Enter. Use this setting to duplicate dBASE and its clones' behavior.
Next Record	When this option is selected, the cursor moves down the column to the next record when you press Enter.
Arrow Key Behavior Group	
Next Field (default)	If this option is selected, pressing the right- or left-arrow keys moves the cursor to the next field.
Next Character	If this option is selected, pressing the right- or left-arrow keys moves the cursor to the previous or next character in the same field. Use this setting if you want to duplicate the behavior of mainframe terminal or xBase applications.
Behavior Entering Field Group	
Select Entire Field (default)	When this option is selected, the entire field's contents are selected when you use the arrow keys to move the cursor into the field.
Go to Start of Field	Selecting this option causes the cursor to move to the beginning of the field when you use the arrow keys to move the cursor into the field.

Option	Function
Behavior Entering Field Group	
Go to End of Field	Selecting this option causes the cursor to move to the end of the field when you use the arrow keys to move the cursor into the field. Use this setting to duplicate mainframe terminal and xBase behavior.
Individual Settings	
Cursor Stops at First/Last field	Marking this check box keeps the cursor from moving to another record when the left or right arrow keys are pressed and the cursor is in the first or last field of the record.
NEW Datasheet IME Control	Enables the Input Method Editor (IME) for entering data in East Asian languages (Windows XP and 2003 only).

USING DATA-ENTRY AND EDITING KEYS

Arrow keys and key combinations in Access are, for the most part, identical to those used in other Windows applications. The F2 key, used for editing cell contents in Excel, has a different function in Access—F2 toggles between editing and select mode. (*Toggle* means to alternate between two states.) In the editing state, the cursor indicates the insertion point in the field; the key combinations shown in Table 6.2 are active. If the field or any character in the field is selected (indicated by a black background with white type), the editing keys behave as indicated in Table 6.3.

TABLE 6.2 KEYS FOR EDITING FIELDS, GRIDS, AND TEXT BOXES

Key	Function
F2	Toggles between displaying the cursor for editing and selecting the entire field. The field must be deselected (black text on a white background) and the cursor must be visible for the keys in this table to operate as described.
End	Moves the cursor to the end of the field in a single-line field or the end of the line in a multiple-line field.
Ctrl+End	Moves the cursor to the end of a multiple-line field.
←	Moves the cursor one character to the left until you reach the first character in the line.
Ctrl+←	Moves the cursor one word to the left until you reach the first word in the line.
Home	Moves the cursor to the beginning of the line.
Ctrl+Home	Moves the cursor to the beginning of the field in multiple-line fields.

continues

TABLE 6.2 CONTINUED

Key	Function
Backspace	Deletes the entire selection or the character to the left of the cursor.
Delete	Deletes the entire selection or the character to the right of the cursor.
Ctrl+Z or Alt+Backspace	Undoes typing, a replace operation, or any other change to the record since the last time it was saved. An edited record is saved to the database when you move to a new record or close the editing window.
Esc	Undoes changes to the current field. Press Esc twice to undo changes to the current field and to the entire current record, if you edited other fields.

TABLE 6.3 KEYS FOR SELECTING TEXT IN FIELDS, GRIDS, AND TEXT BOXES

Key	Function
Text Within a Field	
F2	Toggles between displaying the cursor for editing and selecting the entire field. The field must be selected (white type on a black background) for the keys in this table to operate as described.
Shift+→	Selects or deselects one character to the right.
Ctrl+Shift+→	Selects or deselects one word to the right. Includes trailing spaces.
Shift+←	Selects or deselects one character to the left.
Ctrl+Shift+←	Selects or deselects one word to the left.
Next Field	
Tab or Enter	Selects the next field if the default Next Field option is selected.
Record	
Shift+spacebar	Selects or deselects the entire current record.
↑	Selects the first field in the preceding record when a record is selected.
↓	Selects the first field in the next record when a record is selected.
Column	
Ctrl+spacebar	Toggles selection of the current column.
←	Selects the first field in the column to the left (if a column is selected and a column is to the left).

Key	Function
Fields and Records	
F8	Turns on Extend mode. You see "EXT" in the status bar. In Extend mode, pressing F8 extends the selection to the word, then the field, then the record, and then all the records.
Shift+F8	Reverses the last F8.
Esc	Cancels Extend mode.

Operations that select the entire field or a portion of the field, as listed in Table 6.3, generally are used with Windows Clipboard operations.

TIP

> Selecting an entire field and then pressing Delete or typing a character is a quick way to rid the field of its original contents.

USING KEY COMBINATIONS FOR WINDOWS CLIPBOARD OPERATIONS

In Table Datasheet view, the Clipboard is used primarily for transferring Access data between applications, such as copying data to an Excel worksheet or a Word table. However, you can also use the Clipboard for repetitive data entry. Access lets you select a rectangular block of data cells in a table and copy the block to the Clipboard. To select a block of cells, follow these steps:

1. Position the mouse pointer at the left edge of the top-left cell of the block you want to select. The cursor (a mouse pointer shaped like an I-beam until this point) turns into a cross similar to the mouse pointer for Excel worksheets.
2. Drag the mouse pointer to the right edge of the bottom-right cell of the desired block.
3. The selected block appears in reverse type (white on black, also called reverse video). Release the mouse button when the selection meets your requirement.
4. Press Ctrl+C to copy the selected block to the Clipboard.

Figure 6.2 shows a selected block of data in the Customers table. You can copy data blocks but can't cut them.

Table 6.4 lists the key combinations for copying or cutting data to and pasting data from the Clipboard.

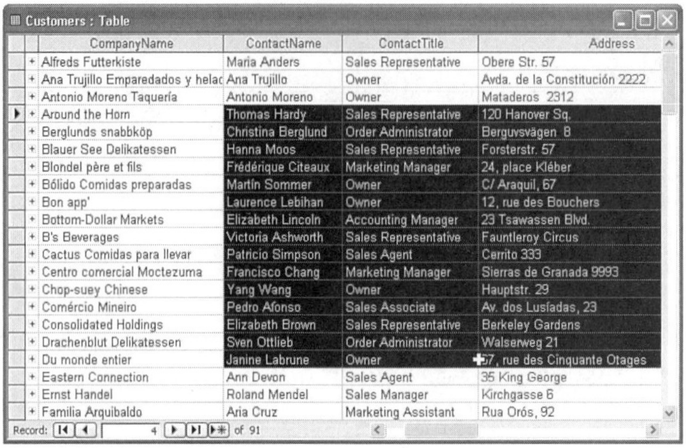

Customers : Table

CompanyName	ContactName	ContactTitle	Address
Alfreds Futterkiste	Maria Anders	Sales Representative	Obere Str. 57
Ana Trujillo Emparedados y helac	Ana Trujillo	Owner	Avda. de la Constitución 2222
Antonio Moreno Taquería	Antonio Moreno	Owner	Mataderos 2312
Around the Horn	Thomas Hardy	Sales Representative	120 Hanover Sq.
Berglunds snabbköp	Christina Berglund	Order Administrator	Berguvsvägen 8
Blauer See Delikatessen	Hanna Moos	Sales Representative	Forsterstr. 57
Blondel père et fils	Frédérique Citeaux	Marketing Manager	24, place Kléber
Bólido Comidas preparadas	Martín Sommer	Owner	C/ Araquil, 67
Bon app'	Laurence Lebihan	Owner	12, rue des Bouchers
Bottom-Dollar Markets	Elizabeth Lincoln	Accounting Manager	23 Tsawassen Blvd.
B's Beverages	Victoria Ashworth	Sales Representative	Fauntleroy Circus
Cactus Comidas para llevar	Patricio Simpson	Sales Agent	Cerrito 333
Centro comercial Moctezuma	Francisco Chang	Marketing Manager	Sierras de Granada 9993
Chop-suey Chinese	Yang Wang	Owner	Hauptstr. 29
Comércio Mineiro	Pedro Afonso	Sales Associate	Av. dos Lusíadas, 23
Consolidated Holdings	Elizabeth Brown	Sales Representative	Berkeley Gardens
Drachenblut Delikatessen	Sven Ottlieb	Order Administrator	Walserweg 21
Du monde entier	Janine Labrune	Owner	67, rue des Cinquante Otages
Eastern Connection	Ann Devon	Sales Agent	35 King George
Ernst Handel	Roland Mendel	Sales Manager	Kirchgasse 6
Familia Arquibaldo	Aria Cruz	Marketing Assistant	Rua Orós, 92

Record: 4 of 91

Figure 6.2
You can select a rectangular block of data to copy to the Clipboard, and paste the block to cells of an Excel worksheet or Word table.

Table 6.4 Key Combinations for Windows Clipboard Operations

Key	Function
Ctrl+C or Ctrl+Insert	Copies the selection to the Clipboard.
Ctrl+V or Shift+Insert	Pastes the Clipboard's contents at the cursor's location.
Ctrl+X or Shift+Delete	Copies the selection to the Clipboard and then deletes it. This operation also is called a cut. You can cut only the content of a single cell you select with the cursor.
Ctrl+Z or Alt+Backspace	Undoes your last Cut, Delete, or Paste operation.

Tip

To create a new table from the copied block, click the Create Table by Entering Data option in the Database window and choose Edit, Paste Append to add the block to the table. Pasting the records to the table doesn't add the field names, so you must replace the default Field1...Field*n* names in Table Design view.

6

Using Shortcut Keys for Fields and Text Boxes

Shortcut keys minimize the number of keystrokes required to accomplish common data-entry tasks. Most shortcut key combinations use the Ctrl key with other keys. Ctrl+C, Ctrl+V, and Ctrl+X for Clipboard operations are examples of global shortcut keys in Windows. Table 6.5 lists shortcut keys for field and text box entries.

Tip

Ctrl+' or Ctrl+" are the most important of the shortcut keys for entering table data. The ability to copy data from a field of the preceding record into the same field of a new record is a welcome timesaver.

TABLE 6.5 SHORTCUT KEYS FOR TEXT BOXES AND FIELDS IN TABLES

Key	Function
Ctrl+; (semicolon)	Inserts the current date
Ctrl+: (colon)	Inserts the current time
Ctrl+' (apostrophe) or Ctrl+" (double quote)	Inserts the value from the same field in the preceding record
Ctrl+Enter	Inserts a newline character (carriage return plus line feed, CRLF) in a text box
Ctrl++ (plus)	Adds a new record to the table
Ctrl+– (minus)	Deletes the current record from the table
Shift+Enter	Saves all changes to the current record

TIP

Emulating the data-entry key behavior of a mainframe terminal or DOS database application can make a major difference in the acceptance of your database applications by data-entry operators with years of experience with mainframe and DOS database applications.

ADDING RECORDS TO A TABLE

When you open an updatable table in Datasheet view, the last row is an empty placeholder for a new record, called the *tentative append record* in this book. (An *updatable table* is one whose data you can add to or edit.) An asterisk in the last record selection button in the datasheet indicates the tentative append record. Record selection buttons are the gray buttons in the leftmost column of Table Datasheet view. If you open a database for read-only access, the tentative append record doesn't appear. Tables attached from other databases can also be read-only. The updatability of attached tables is discussed in Chapter 8, "Linking, Importing, and Exporting Data."

TIP

To go to the tentative append record of a table quickly, press Ctrl++ (plus).

When you press Ctrl++ or place the cursor in a field of the tentative append record, the record selection button's asterisk symbol turns into the selected (current) record symbol. When you add data to a field of the selected tentative append record, the selected record symbol changes to the edit symbol (a pencil), and a new tentative append record appears in the row after your addition. Figure 6.3 shows a new record in the process of being added to the Customers table. The CustomerID field has an Input Mask property value (>LLLLL)

that requires you to enter five letters, which are capitalized automatically as you enter them. The input mask changes the cursor from an I-beam to a reverse-video block.

Figure 6.3
The CustomerID field of Northwind's Customers table has an input mask that requires exactly five letters and automatically capitalizes the letters as you enter them.

Customers : Table

CustomerID	CompanyName	ContactName	ContactTitle	
SIMOB	Simons bistro	Jytte Petersen	Owner	Vinbæltet 34
SPECD	Spécialités du monde	Dominique Perrier	Marketing Manager	25, rue Lauriston
SPLIR	Split Rail Beer & Ale	Art Braunschweiger	Sales Manager	P.O. Box 555
SUPRD	Suprêmes délices	Pascale Cartrain	Accounting Manager	Boulevard Tirou, 2
THEBI	The Big Cheese	Liz Nixon	Marketing Manager	89 Jefferson Way
THECR	The Cracker Box	Liu Wong	Marketing Assistant	55 Grizzly Peak F
TOMSP	Toms Spezialitäten	Karin Josephs	Marketing Manager	Luisenstr. 48
TORTU	Tortuga Restaurante	Miguel Angel Paolino	Owner	Avda. Azteca 123
TRADH	Tradição Hipermercados	Anabela Domingues	Sales Representative	Av. Inês de Castr
TRAIH	Trail's Head Gourmet Provisioners	Helvetius Nagy	Sales Associate	722 DaVinci Blvd.
VAFFE	Vaffeljernet	Palle Ibsen	Sales Manager	Smagsløget 45
VICTE	Victuailles en stock	Mary Saveley	Sales Agent	2, rue du Comme
VINET	Vins et alcools Chevalier	Paul Henriot	Accounting Manager	59 rue de l'Abbay
WANDK	Die Wandernde Kuh	Rita Müller	Sales Representative	Adenauerallee 90
WARTH	Wartian Herkku	Pirkko Koskitalo	Accounting Manager	Torikatu 38
WELLI	Wellington Importadora	Paula Parente	Sales Manager	Rua do Mercado,
WHITC	White Clover Markets	Karl Jablonski	Owner	305 - 14th Ave. S
WILMK	Wilman Kala	Matti Karttunen	Owner/Marketing Assist	Keskuskatu 45
WOLZA	Wolski Zajazd	Zbyszek Piestrzeniew	Owner	ul. Filtrowa 68
XYZ				

Record: 92 of 92

➔ To review how input masks work, **see** "Using Input Masks," **p. 173**.

To cancel the addition of a new record, press the Esc key twice. Pressing Esc once cancels the changes you made to the current field. You might not need to press Esc twice, but doing so guarantees canceling the record addition.

SELECTING, APPENDING, REPLACING, AND DELETING TABLE RECORDS

You can select a single record or a group of records to copy or cut to the Clipboard, or to delete from the table, by the following methods:

- To select a single record, click its record selection button.
- To select a contiguous group of records, click the first record's selection button and then drag the mouse pointer along the record selection buttons to the last record of the group.
- Alternatively, to select a group of records, click the first record's selection button and then Shift+click the last record to include in the group. You can also press Shift+↓ to select a group of records.

You can't use Ctrl+click to select discontiguous records.

NOTE

> You can cut groups of records to the Clipboard, deleting them from the table, but you can't cut data blocks. A group of records includes all fields of one or more selected records. A data block consists of a selection in a table datasheet that doesn't include all fields of the selected rows. The Edit, Cut command is enabled for groups of records and disabled for data blocks.

You can cut or copy and append duplicate records to the same table (if appending the duplicate records doesn't cause a primary-key violation) or to another table. You can't cut records from a primary table that has dependent records in a related table if you enforce referential integrity. The following methods apply to appending or replacing the content of records with records stored in the Clipboard:

- To append records from the Clipboard to a table, choose Edit, Paste Append. (No shortcut key exists for Paste Append.)
- To replace the content of a record(s) with data from the Clipboard, select the record(s) whose content you want to replace and then press Ctrl+V. Only the number of records you select or the number of records stored in the Clipboard (whichever is fewer) is replaced.

To delete one or more records, select those records and press Delete. If deletion is allowed, a message box asks you to confirm your deletion, if you haven't cleared the Confirm Record Changes text box on the Edit/Find page of the Options dialog. You can't undo deletions of records.

VALIDATING DATA ENTRY

The data entered in tables must be accurate if the database is to be valuable to you or your organization. Even the most experienced data-entry operators occasionally enter incorrect information. To add simple tests for the reasonableness of entries, add short expressions as a Validation Rule in the General page of Table Design view's Field Properties pane. If the entered data fails to pass your validation rule, a message box informs the operator that a violation occurred. You can customize the error message by adding the text as the value of the Validation Text property. Validating data maintains the entity integrity of your tables.

6

Expressions are a core element of computer programming. Jet lets you create expressions without requiring that you be a programmer, although some familiarity with a programming language is helpful. Expressions use the familiar arithmetic symbols `+`, `-`, `*` (multiply), and `/` (divide). These symbols are called operators because they operate on (use) the values that precede and follow them. These operators are reserved symbols in VBA. The values operated on by operators are called *operands*.

You (greater than) operator> can also use operators to compare two values; the `<` (less than) and `>` (greater than) symbols are examples of comparison operators. **`And`**, **`Or`**, **`Is`**, **`Not`**,

`Between`, and `Like` are called logical operators. (`Between` and `Like` are Jet, not VBA, operators, so they don't appear in bold type). Comparison and logical operators return only **`True`**, **`False`**, and no value (the **`Null`** value). The **`&`** operator combines two text entries (character strings or just strings) into a single string. To qualify as an expression, at least one operator must be included. You can construct complex expressions by combining the different operators according to rules that apply to each operator involved. The collection of these rules is called *operator syntax*.

→ To learn more about Access operators, **see** "Understanding the Elements in Expressions," **p. 357**.

Data validation rules use expressions that result in one of two values: **`True`** or **`False`**. Entries in a data cell are accepted if the result of the validation is true and rejected if it's false. If the data is rejected by the validation rule, the text you enter as the Validation Text property value appears in a message box. Chapter 10 explains the syntax of Jet validation expressions.

NOTE

SQL Server substitutes `CHECK` constraints for the Validation Rule property. As with Jet, `CHECK` constraints can apply at the table or field level. The Jet Expression Service lets you use VBA functions, such as **`UCase`**`()`, in validation rules. SQL Server requires use of Transact-SQL (T-SQL) functions for `CHECK` constraints. Chapter 21, "Moving from Jet Queries to Transact-SQL," explains how to translate Jet/VBA functions into T-SQL functions.

ADDING FIELD-LEVEL VALIDATION RULES

Validation rules that restrict the values entered in a field and are based on only one field are called *field-level validation rules*. Table 6.6 lists the simple field-level validation rules used for some fields in the HRActions table you created in Chapter 5, "Working with Jet Databases and Tables."

6

TABLE 6.6 VALIDATION CRITERIA FOR THE FIELDS OF THE HRACTIONS TABLE

Field Name	Validation Rule	Validation Text
EmployeeID	**>0**	Please enter a valid employee ID number.
ActionType	**In("H","Q", "Y","S","R", "B","C","T")**	Only H, Q, Y, S, R, B, C, and T codes are valid.
Initiated By	**>0**	Please enter a valid supervisor ID number.
ScheduledDate	**Between Date()-5475 And Date()+365**	Scheduled dates can't be more than 15 years ago or more than 1 year from now.
ApprovedBy	**>0 Or Is Null**	Enter a valid manager ID number or leave blank if not approved.
EffectiveDate	None	
HRRating	**Between 0 And 9 Or Is Null**	Rating range is 0 for terminated employees, 1 to 9, or blank.

Field Name	Validation Rule	Validation Text
NewSalary	None	None.
NewRate	**>5.5 Or Is Null**	Hourly rate must be more than the minimum wage.
NewBonus	None	None.
NewCommission	**<=0.1 or Is Null**	Commission rate can't exceed 10%.
HRComments	None	None.

NOTE

You must allow ScheduledDate values as early as 1992 to accommodate the hire dates in the first two records of the Employees table. Microsoft hasn't updated Northwind.mdb data since releasing Access 2000. The last OrderDate in the Orders table has remained May 6, 1998 in the last three Access versions.

TIP

The `In` operator simplifies expressions that otherwise would require multiple `Or` operators. For example, using the `Or` operator for the Validation Rule property value of the ActionType field requires typing **"H" Or "Q" Or "Y" Or "S" Or "R" Or "B" Or "C" Or "T"**, which has many more characters.

In their present form, the validation rules for fields that require employee ID numbers can't ensure that a valid ID number is entered. You could enter an EmployeeID number that isn't present in the Employees table. A validation rule for the EmployeeID field could test the EmployeeID number field of the Employees table to determine whether the EmployeeID number is present. You don't need to create this test because the rules of referential integrity perform this validation for you. Validation rules for InitiatedBy and ApprovedBy require tests based on entries in the Employees table.

→ To review referential integrity rules, **see** "Working with Relations, Key Fields, and Indexes," **p. 188**.

To add the validation rules of Table 6.6 to the HRActions table, follow these steps:

1. Open the HRActions table, if it isn't already open, by double-clicking its name in the Database window's tables list.

2. Click the Design View button. The EmployeeID field is selected.
3. Press F6 to switch to the Field Properties window, and then move to the Validation Rule text box.
4. Type **>0** and move to the Validation Text text box.
5. Type **Please enter a valid employee ID number.** The text scrolls to the left when it becomes longer than can be displayed in the text box. To display the beginning of the text, press Home. Press End to position the cursor at the last character. Figure 6.4 shows your entries in the Field Properties text boxes.

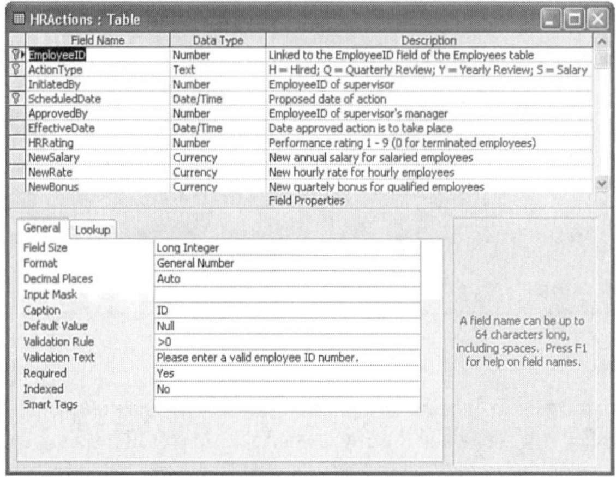

Figure 6.4
The Field Properties pane displays the first Validation Rule and Validation Text property values entered from the data in Table 6.6.

6. Press F6 to switch back to the Table Design grid. Move to the next field and press F6.
7. Enter the validation rule and validation text for the seven remaining fields listed in Table 6.6 that use data-entry validation, repeating steps 4 through 6.

You test your validation rule entries later in the "Testing Field and Table Validation Rules" section.

ADDING TABLE-LEVEL VALIDATION RULES WITH THE EXPRESSION BUILDER

One field, EffectiveDate, requires a validation rule that depends on ScheduledDate's value. The effective date of the personnel department's action shouldn't be before the scheduled date for the review that results in the action. You can't refer to other field names in a Jet validation rule expression; instead, you add such validation rules in the Table Properties window. Validation rules in which the value of one field depends on a previously entered value in another field of the current record are called *table-level validation rules*.

The following steps add a table description and create a table-level validation rule for the EffectiveDate field:

1. Click the Properties toolbar button to display the Table Properties dialog.
2. Type **Human Resources Department Actions** in the Description text box (see Figure 6.5).

3. In the Validation Rule text box, click the ellipsis (Builder) button to display the Expression Builder dialog. The current table, HRActions, is selected in the lefthand list, and the fields of the table appear in the center list.
4. Double-click EffectiveDate in the center list to place [EffectiveDate] in the Expression Builder's text box at the top of the dialog. Square brackets surround field names to distinguish them from literal (string) values.

Table Properties
General
Description .... Human Resources Department Actions
Default View .... Datasheet
Validation Rule ....
Validation Text ....
Filter ....
Order By ....
Subdatasheet Name .... [Auto]
Link Child Fields ....
Link Master Fields ....
Subdatasheet Height .... 0"
Subdatasheet Expanded ..... No
Orientation .... Left-to-Right

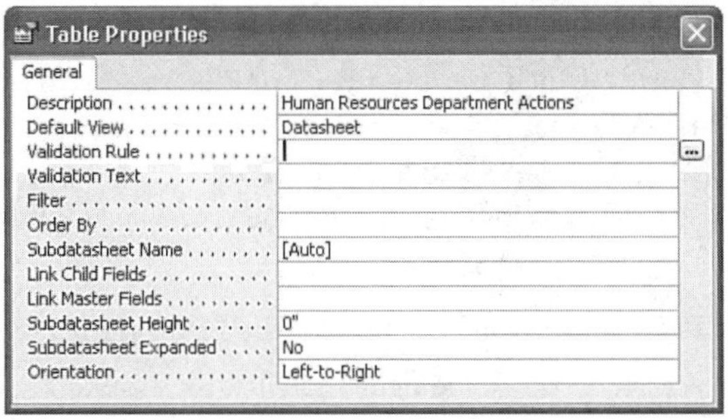

Figure 6.5
When you move the cursor to the Validation Rule row of the Table Properties dialog, the ellipsis button appears so you can open the Jet Expression Builder.

5. Type **>=** in the text box and double-click ScheduledDate in the center list to add [ScheduledDate] to the expression.
6. To accept a blank entry if the effective date of the personnel action isn't scheduled, add **Or [EffectiveDate] Is Null** to the expression, which appears as shown in Figure 6.6.

Expression Builder
[EffectiveDate]>=[ScheduledDate] Or [EffectiveDate] Is Null
OK
Cancel
Undo
+ - / * & = > < <> And Or Not Like ( )
Paste
Help
HRActions
Functions
Constants
Operators
EmployeeID
ActionType
InitiatedBy
ScheduledDate
ApprovedBy
EffectiveDate
HRRating
NewSalary
NewRate
NewBonus
NewCommission
<Value>

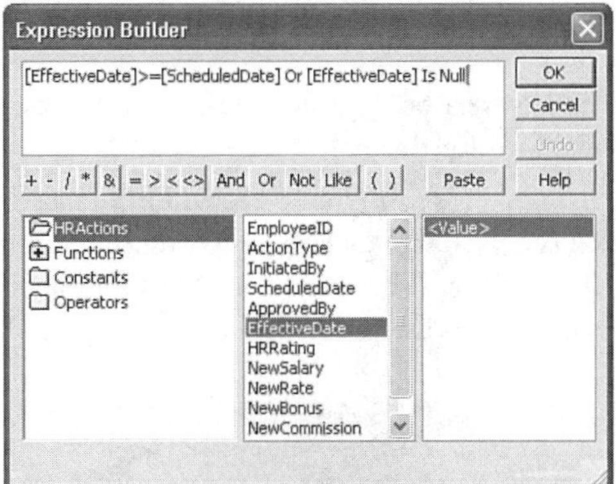

Figure 6.6
You can use the Jet Expression Builder to generate more complex expressions for use as table-level validation rules.

7. Click OK to add the table-level validation rule and close the Expression Builder dialog.
8. In the Validation Text text box, type **Effective date must be on or after the scheduled date**. Your Table Properties window appears as shown in Figure 6.7.

Table Properties
General
Description .... Human Resources Department Actions
Default View .... Datasheet
Validation Rule .... [EffectiveDate]>=[ScheduledDate] Or [EffectiveDate] Is Null
Validation Text .... Effective date must be on or after the scheduled date.
Filter ....
Order By ....
Subdatasheet Name .... [Auto]
Link Child Fields ....
Link Master Fields ....
Subdatasheet Height .... 0"
Subdatasheet Expanded ..... No
Orientation .... Left-to-Right

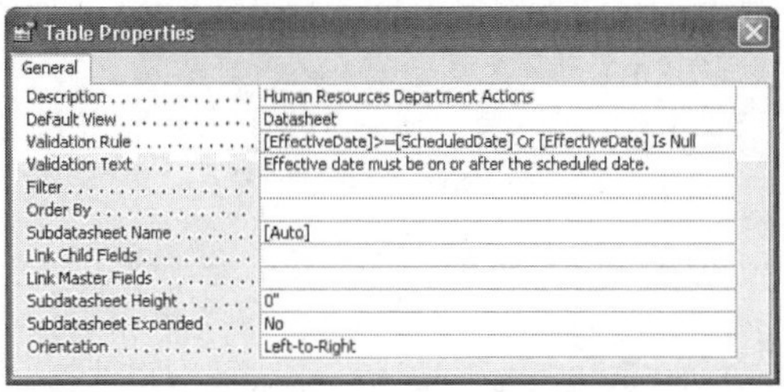

Figure 6.7
Closing the Expression Builder adds the expression of Figure 6.6 as the Validation Rule property value of the table.

9. Close the Table Properties dialog.

ADDING A SIMPLE LOOKUP LIST TO THE ACTIONTYPE FIELD

Lookup tables require queries, which are the subject of this book's Part III, "Transforming Data with Queries and PivotTables." However, you can add a lookup list to the table by adding a set of values that's similar to a validation expression. You create a lookup list by selecting the field the list applies to in Table Design view, and specifying property values in the Lookup page of the Field Properties pane.

To add a combo box lookup list to the ActionType field of the HRActions table, do this:

1. In Design view, select the ActionType field and click the Lookup tab in the Field Properties pane.
2. Open the Display Control list and select Combo Box or List Box. This example uses a combo box.
3. Open the Row Source Type list and select Value List.
4. Accept the first column (1) default in the Bound Column list, and type **2** in the Column Count text box. The value list needs code and description columns.
5. In the Column Widths text box type **0.3";1.2"**, and in the List Width text box type **1.5"**.
6. Type **Y**(es) in the Limit to List text box. Limiting entries to the list's items is equivalent to the validation rule you added for this field.
7. Return to the Row Source property and type **H;Hired;Q;Quarterly Review;Y;Yearly Review;S;Salary Adj.;R;Hourly Rate Adj.;B;Bonus Adj.;C;Commission Adj.;T;Terminated** in the text box. The semicolons separate the entries that add in pairs to create the list. Your lookup list design appears as shown in Figure 6.8.

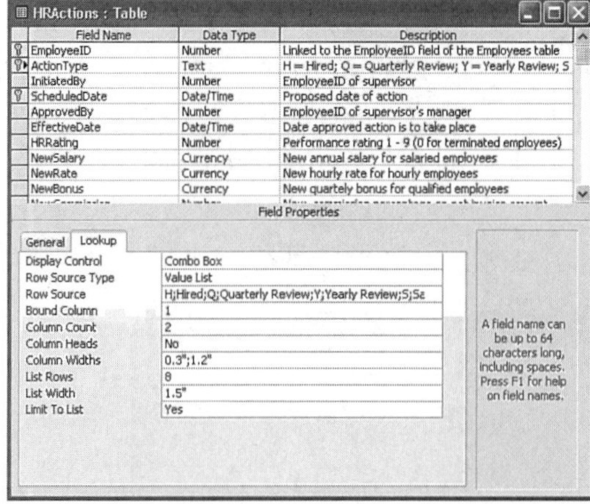

Figure 6.8
You create lookup lists by specifying a combo box or list box, and setting its properties in the Lookup page of the Field Properties pane.

8. Return to Datasheet view and save your design changes.
9. Press Tab to move to the ActionType field and press F4 to open the lookup list (see Figure 6.9).

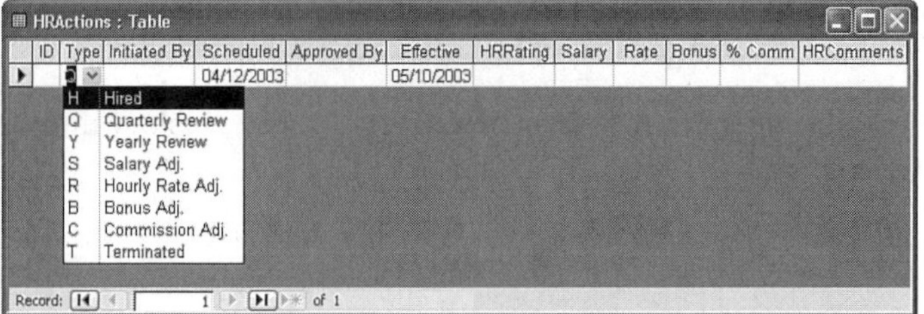

Figure 6.9
The lookup list for ActionType codes has a description for each of the eight valid codes.

Lookup lists are handy for adding codes and other field values that seldom, if ever, change. When entering data, you can use the lookup list or type the code letter; the latter is considerably faster. You must keep lookup lists up to date and, if multiple tables use the same list, update each table's list manually. Lookups from tables, which you create with queries, are one of the topics of Chapter 11, "Creating Multitable and Crosstab Queries," are the preferred method for creating lookup tables. You can use a single lookup table for all tables that need the table's lookup values.

ADDING RECORDS TO THE HRACTIONS TABLE

Now you can test your work in creating the HRActions table and check whether Access is enforcing domain integrity. Table 6.7 shows the initial entries for each employee of Northwind Traders. The dates are based on values in the Employees table's HireDate field. No Rating entries appear in Table 6.7 because ratings don't apply to newly hired employees.

TABLE 6.7 FIRST NINE ENTRIES FOR THE HRACTIONS TABLE

Employee ID	Action Type	Initiated By	Scheduled Date	Approved By	Effective Date	New Salary	HRComment
1	H	1	05/01/1992	1	05/01/1992	2,000	Hired
2	H	1	08/14/1992	1	08/14/1992	3,500	Hired
3	H	1	04/01/1992	1	04/01/1992	2,250	Hired
4	H	2	05/03/1993	2	05/03/1993	2,250	Hired
5	H	2	10/17/1993	2	10/17/1993	2,500	Hired
6	H	5	10/17/1993	2	10/17/1993	4,000	Hired
7	H	5	01/02/1994	2	01/02/1994	3,000	Hired
8	H	2	05/05/1994	2	05/05/1994	2,500	Hired
9	H	5	11/15/1994	2	11/15/1994	3,000	Hired

Entering historical information in a table in Datasheet view is a relatively fast process for experienced data-entry operators. This process also gives you a chance to test your default entries and Format properties for each field. You can enter bogus values that don't comply with your validation rules to verify that your rules are operational.

To add the first nine historical records to the HRActions table with the data from Table 6.7, follow these steps:

1. Click the Datasheet button to return to Datasheet view, if necessary. The cursor is positioned in the EmployeeID field of the default first record.
2. Enter the EmployeeID of the employee. Press Enter, Tab, or the right-arrow key to move to the next field and to add a new default blank record to the view but not to the table's content.
3. Type **H** in the Type field or select H from the lookup list, and move to the next field.
4. Type the numeric value of 1 or greater for the InitiatedBy field. (You need a value in this field for each employee because of the field's validation rule.) Move to the next field.
5. Type the ScheduledDate entry. You don't need to delete the default date value; typing a new date replaces the default value. Then press Enter, Tab, or the right-arrow key.
6. Type the ApprovedBy value and move to the next field.
7. Type the EffectiveDate entry, and skip the HRRating field.
8. Type the NewSalary of the monthly salary at the time of hiring, and skip the NewRate, NewBonus, and NewCommission fields.
9. Type **Hired** or any other comment you care to make in the HRComments field. Move to the EmployeeID field of the next default blank record.
10. Repeat steps 2 through 9 for eight more employees in Table 6.7.

When you complete your entries, the HRActions table appears as shown in Figure 6.10. If you skipped any of the example procedures in this chapter, an updated version of the Nwind05.mdb database with the data entered for you is in your \Program Files\Seua11\Chaptr06 folder. As mentioned early in the chapter, importing the HRActions table required adding a one-to-many relationship to the Employees table. If you don't add the relationship, some validation tests in the next section won't behave as expected.

6

Figure 6.10 The HRActions tables contains initial entries for the nine employees of Northwind Traders.

HRActions : Table

ID	Type	Initiated By	Scheduled	Approved By	Effective	HRRating	Salary	Rate	Bonus	% Comm	HRComments
1	H	1	05/01/1992	1	05/01/1992		2,000				Hired
2	H	1	08/14/1992	1	08/14/1992		3,500				Hired
3	H	1	05/03/1993	1	05/03/1993		2,250				Hired
4	H	2	05/03/1993	2	05/03/1993		2,250				Hired
5	H	2	10/17/1993	2	10/17/1993		2,500				Hired
6	H	5	10/17/1993	2	10/17/1993		4,000				Hired
7	H	5	01/02/1994	2	01/02/1994		3,000				Hired
8	H	2	05/05/1994	2	05/05/1994		2,500				Hired
9	H	5	11/15/1994	2	11/15/1994		3,000				Hired
	Q		04/12/2003		05/10/2003						

Record: 10 of 10

TESTING FIELD AND TABLE VALIDATION RULES

You can experiment with entering table data and testing your validation rules at the same time. Testing database applications often requires much more time and effort than creating them. The following basic tests are required to confirm your validation rules:

- *Referential integrity.* Type **25** in the EmployeeID field and **2** in the InitiatedBy field of the default blank record (number 10) and then press the up-arrow key. Pressing the up-arrow key tells Access that you're finished with the current record and to move up to the preceding record with the cursor in the same field. Access then tests the primary-key integrity before enabling you to leave the current record. If you haven't turned on the Office Assistant, the message box shown in Figure 6.11 appears; otherwise the Assistant delivers the message. Click OK and press Escape to abandon the entry.

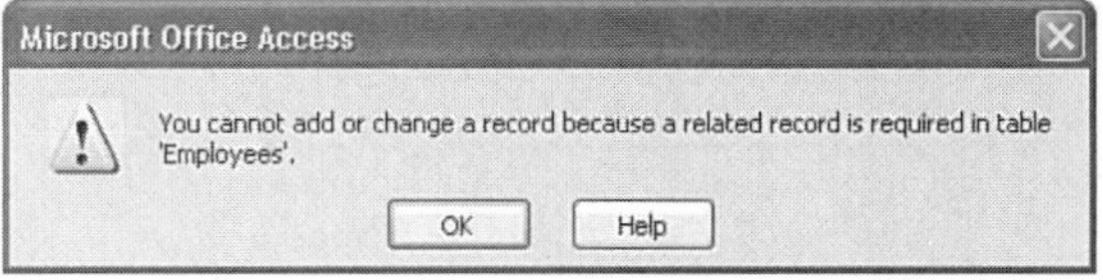

Figure 6.11
If you violate referential integrity rules by typing an EmployeeID value without a corresponding record in the Employees table, this message appears.

- *No duplicates restriction for primary key.* In the record just added, attempt to duplicate exactly the entries for record 9, and then press the up-arrow key. You see the message box shown in Figure 6.12, if you've turned off the Assistant. Click OK and press Escape to cancel the entry.

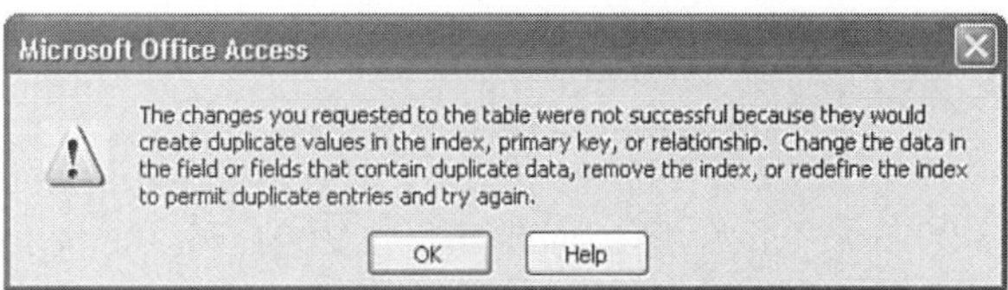

Figure 6.12
If you duplicate the values of another record in the EmployeeID, ActionType, and ScheduledDate fields, you receive an error message because a primary key duplication occurs.

- *ActionType validation.* Type **x** and press the right-arrow key to display the message that appears if you added the lookup list and set the Limit To List property value to Yes (see Figure 6.13, top). Otherwise, the message box with the validation text you entered for the ActionType field appears (see Figure 6.13, bottom). Click OK and press Escape to abandon the entry.

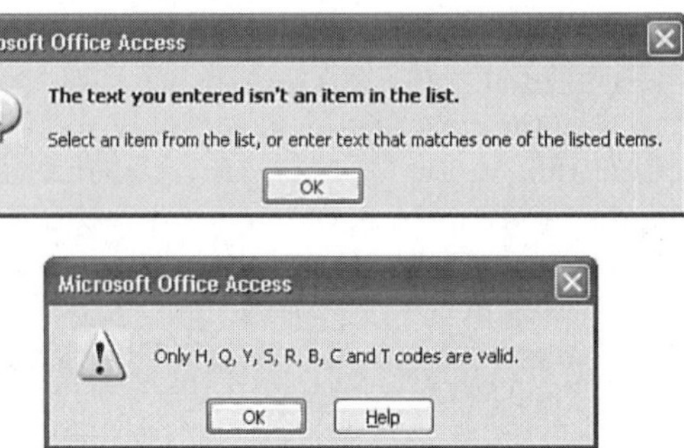

Figure 6.13
The error message for a lookup list with the Limit To List restriction set responds to an entry error with the upper message. If the Limit To List restriction is missing or you didn't add a lookup list, the Validation Text message appears.

- *Employee ID validation in the InitiatedBy field.* Type **q** and move to the InitiatedBy field. When the cursor leaves the ActionType field, the q changes to Q because of the > format character used. Type **0** (an invalid employee ID number), and press the right-arrow key to display the message box shown in Figure 6.14. Click OK or press Enter.

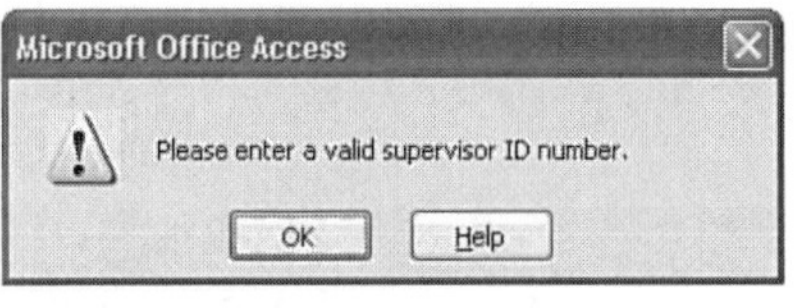

Figure 6.14
Typing 0 in the InitiatedBy field violates the >0 Validation Rule and displays the Validation Text.

Continue with the testing. Type a date, such as **1/31/2001**, for the ScheduledDate, and type a date one day earlier (such as **1/30/2001**) for the EffectiveDate to display the error message boxes with the validation text you entered. (You must move the cursor to a different record to cause the table-level validation rule to be applied.) Enter a valid date after the test. To edit a field, rather than retype it, press F2 to deselect the entire field and display the cursor for editing. F2 toggles selection and editing operations.

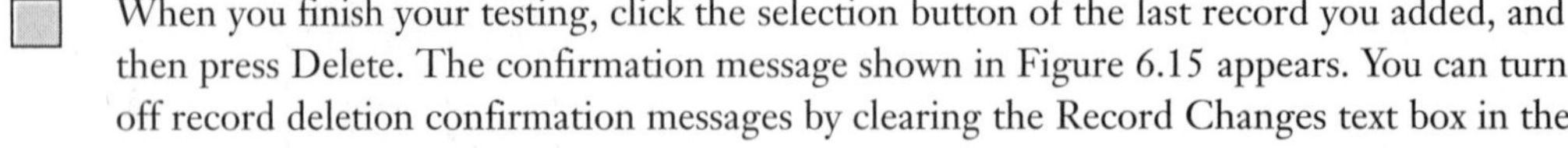

When you finish your testing, click the selection button of the last record you added, and then press Delete. The confirmation message shown in Figure 6.15 appears. You can turn off record deletion confirmation messages by clearing the Record Changes text box in the

Confirm group of the Options dialog's Edit/Find page. Why this option group is located on the Edit/Find page is a mystery.

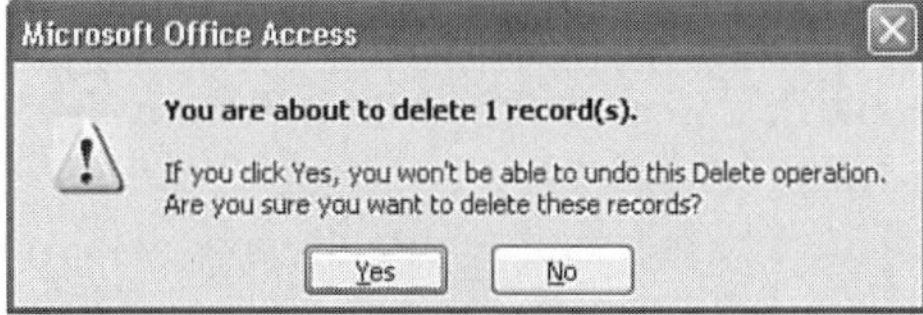

Figure 6.15
Unless you turn off confirmation of record deletion, this message appears when you delete a record.

TROUBLESHOOTING

FIELD PROPERTY VALUES CAUSE PASTE FAILURES

Access beeps when I attempt to paste data into a cell.

The paste operation would violate a domain or referential integrity rule, usually the Field Size property value. For instance, if you attempt to paste more than five characters into the CustomerID field of the Customers table, the paste operation fails without an error message. Make sure that the cells or blocks of cells you paste conform to Field Size and other data validation rules.

MULTIPLE RECORD SELECTION CAUSES SILENT PASTE FAILURES

Nothing happens when I try to paste data into a cell.

Selecting multiple records, then attempting to paste the records into a single cell, even the first cell of the tentative append record, results in a silent paste failure. Access limits multiple-record insert operations to the Edit, Paste Append command.

ERROR MESSAGES FROM VALIDATION ENFORCEMENT

Error messages appear when I enter data in fields with validation rules.

Edit or re-enter the data to conform to the data types and validation rules for the field. Error messages that appear when you enter the data correctly indicate that something is amiss with your validation rules. In this case, change to design mode and review your validation rules for the offending fields against those listed in Table 6.6. You might want to remove the validation rule temporarily by selecting the entire expression and cutting it to the Clipboard. (You can paste the expression back into the text box later.) Return to Run mode to continue with your entries.

IN THE REAL WORLD—HEADS-DOWN DATA ENTRY

This chapter's tables that list key combinations to expedite data entry make dull reading, at best. *Special Edition Using Microsoft Office Access 2003* serves as both a tutorial and a reference, and references must be comprehensive. Detailed lists of *Access 11* features and their functions, no matter how tedious the list or the features and functions, are unavoidable. There have been no significant changes to data entry key definitions since Access 2.0.

You probably won't appreciate the benefits of Access's data entry shortcut keys until you must type a large amount of table data in a Datasheet view. Clearly, it's preferable to import existing data, taking advantage of Access's flexible data import features described in Chapter 8. Almost everyone, however, faces the inevitable chore of typing table data, such as testing entries for a new database.

COMPARING HEADS-DOWN KEYPUNCH DATA ENTRY WITH ACCESS'S DATASHEET VIEW

In the days of supremacy of mainframe computers, most of which were less powerful than today's PCs, IBM 026 or 029 keypunch operators generated decks of 80-column punched cards from stacks of source documents. Keypunch operators often received piecework wages, based on the number of cards they produced; salaried operators usually had to fill a daily quota. The eyes of keypunch operators were focused eight hours per day on the top document of a stack, giving rise to the term "heads-down data entry."

NOTE

> If you've never seen a punched card machine, there's a picture of an IBM 029 keypunch at `http://info.ox.ac.uk/ctitext/history/keypnch.html`. Ed Thelen, a computer historian, has posted a 34-page history of punched card computing at `http://ed-thelen.org/comp-hist/CBC-Ch-04.pdf`.

Datasheet view of a table or updatable query is the simplest and quickest means for heads-down addition of large numbers of records to tables. The need to scroll horizontally to expose more than the first few columns of a wide table, such as that for a customer name and address list, makes Datasheet entry a bit more cumbersome. If you're a good typist, using shortcut keys for column navigation quickly becomes second nature.

Datasheet view for adding related records was cumbersome in previous versions of Access, so most developers are accustomed to creating data entry form-subform pairs, described in Chapter 15, "Designing Custom Multitable Forms." Access 11, however, offers subdatasheets that let you add multiple related records almost as effortlessly as adding single records to base tables. The major shortcoming of subdatasheets is that expanding the subdatasheet requires a mouse click on the + symbol. Moving between heads-down keyboard data entry and mouse operations greatly reduces data-entry operator productivity.

REPLACING THE PUNCHED CARD VERIFYING STEP

Verifying data to preserve domain integrity was a critical step in the keypunch process. The most common method of data verification, sometimes called validation, was retyping the original data to determine if the second typing pass matched the first. Clearly, this approach isn't practical in Datasheet view, although you could implement punched-card verification with a simple form and some VBA code to compare the two sets of entries.

Data verification and validation aren't synonymous. *Verification* attempts to eliminate typographic errors by duplication, whereas *validation* primarily tests data entry conformance to a fixed set of rules. The more clever you become in writing well-defined Access Validation Rules, the better the overall accuracy of the input data. Although form-level validation is more flexible, field- and table-level validation applies to data you enter with any form that's bound to the table. So, you avoid having to recreate validation operations in each of the multiple forms that permit table data entry. The most annoying thing about field- and table-level validation is having to repeatedly close Validation Text message boxes that describe data entry errors.

Where Not to Use Datasheet Entry

Datasheet entry works well for "punching" standard documents on a routine basis. Datasheet entry isn't suited to ad hoc situations, such as taking telephone orders or reservations, or other activities that involve lookup operations on related tables. The "In the Real World—The Art of Form Design" section of Chapter 14, "Creating and Using Access Forms," describes some of the features of a typical Access data-entry form designed for heads-down telephone order taking. A single form with list and text boxes, and a subform that appears and disappears in concert with the current operating mode lets the operator quickly find an existing customer's record, list the customer's past and current orders, and add a new order with multiple line items. The form is designed expressly for keyboard-only operations to eliminate the transition to and from a mouse or trackball.

CHAPTER 7

SORTING, FINDING, AND FILTERING DATA

In this chapter

Understanding the Role of Sorting and Filtering

Microsoft Access provides a variety of sorting and filtering features that make customizing the display data in Table Datasheet view a quick and simple process. Sorting and filtering records in tables is useful when you use data to create a mailing list or print a particular set of records.

Access also includes versatile search and replace facilities that let you locate every record that matches a value you specify and then, optionally, change that value. Using the Search features, you can quickly locate values even in large tables. Search and replace often is needed when you import data from another database or a worksheet, which is the primary subject of the next chapter.

Access's sorting, filtering, searching, and replacing features actually are implemented behind-the-scenes by queries that Access creates for you. When you reach Part III, "Transforming Data with Queries and PivotTables," you'll probably choose to implement these features in Access's graphical Query Design window. Learning the fundamentals of these operations with tables, however, makes queries easier to understand. You also can apply filters to query result sets, use the find feature with queries in Datasheet view, and use search and replace on the result sets of updatable queries.

NOTE

> The last significant change to Access's sort, filter, find, and replace features occurred in Access 2000 with the addition of Filter by Form. In Access 2003, these features behave identically when applied to Jet tables in conventional applications and SQL Server tables in Access data projects (ADP).

Sorting Table Data

By default, Access displays records in the order of the primary key. If your table doesn't have a primary key, the records display in the order in which you enter them. Access uses sorting methods to display records in the desired order. If an index exists on the field in which you sort the records, the sorting process for large tables is quicker. Access automatically uses indexes, if indexes exist, to speed the sort in a process called *query optimization*.

The following sections show how to use Access's sorting methods to display records in the sequence you want. The Customers table of Northwind.mdb is used for most examples in this chapter because it's typical of a table whose data you might want to sort.

7

NOTE

> You can use the 15MB Oakmont.mdb database, which has a 30,000-record Students table, to evaluate sorting operations on large tables. If you haven't installed all the sample files from the accompanying CD-ROM, copy Oakmont.mdb from the \Seua10\Oakmont folder to your working folder. Right-click the Explorer entry for the copy of Oakmont.mdb, choose Properties, and clear the Read-Only check box in the Attributes group.

FREEZING DISPLAY OF A TABLE FIELD

If the table you're sorting contains more fields than you can display in Access's Table Datasheet view, you can freeze one or more fields to make viewing the sorted data easier. Freezing a field makes the field visible at all times, regardless of which other fields you display by manipulating the horizontal scroll bar.

NOTE

> This example and those that follow use field names, rather than column header names (captions). The Microsoft developers added spaces when two nouns make up a field name, such as Company and Name, are extended–and, in this case, superficial–properties of fields.

To freeze the CustomerID and CompanyName fields of the Customers table, follow these steps:

1. Open the Customers table in Datasheet view.
2. Click the field header button of the CustomerID field to select the first field.
3. Shift+click the CompanyName field header button. Alternatively, you can drag the mouse from the CustomerID field header to the CompanyName field header to select the first and second fields.
4. Choose Format, Freeze Columns.

When you scroll to fields to the right of the frozen columns, your Datasheet view of the Customers table appears as shown in Figure 7.1. A solid vertical line replaces the half-tone gridline between the frozen and thawed (selectable) fields.

Customers : Table

Customer ID	Company Name	City	Region	Postal Code	Country
ALFKI	Alfreds Futterkiste	Berlin		12209	Germany
ANATR	Ana Trujillo Emparedados y helados	México D.F.		05021	Mexico
ANTON	Antonio Moreno Taquería	México D.F.		05023	Mexico
AROUT	Around the Horn	London		WA1 1DP	UK
BERGS	Berglunds snabbköp	Luleå		S-958 22	Sweden
BLAUS	Blauer See Delikatessen	Mannheim		68306	Germany
BLONP	Blondel père et fils	Strasbourg		67000	France
BOLID	Bólido Comidas preparadas	Madrid		28023	Spain
BONAP	Bon app'	Marseille		13008	France
BOTTM	Bottom-Dollar Markets	Tsawassen	BC	T2F 8M4	Canada
BSBEV	B's Beverages	London		EC2 5NT	UK
CACTU	Cactus Comidas para llevar	Buenos Aires		1010	Argentina
CENTC	Centro comercial Moctezuma	México D.F.		05022	Mexico
CHOPS	Chop-suey Chinese	Bern		3012	Switzerland
COMMI	Comércio Mineiro	São Paulo	SP	05432-043	Brazil
CONSH	Consolidated Holdings	London		WX1 6LT	UK

Record: 1 of 91

Figure 7.1
The CustomerID and CompanyName fields of this Datasheet view of the Customers table are frozen.

TIP

> If you frequently freeze columns, add the Freeze Columns button from the Datasheet collection to your Datasheet toolbar.

→ To learn how to customize your toolbars, **see** "Customizable Toolbars," **p. 574**.

SORTING DATA ON A SINGLE FIELD

Access provides an easy way to sort data in the Datasheet view, called a Quick Sort. Simply click the field name button of the field you want to use to sort the table's data and click either the Sort Ascending or the Sort Descending icon on the toolbar. In mailing lists, a standard practice in the United States is to sort the records in ascending ZIP code order. This practice often is also observed in other countries that use postal codes. To Quick Sort the Customers table in the order of the Postal Code field, follow these steps:

1. Select the PostalCode field by clicking its field header button.
2. Click the Sort Ascending (A–Z) button of the toolbar or choose Sort and then Sort Ascending from the Records menu.

Your Customers table quickly is sorted into the order shown in Figure 7.2.

Customers : Table

Customer ID	Company Name	City	Region	Postal Code	Country
HUNGO	Hungry Owl All-Night Grocers	Cork	Co. Cork		Ireland
WOLZA	Wolski Zajazd	Warszawa		01-012	Poland
QUICK	QUICK-Stop	Cunewalde		01307	Germany
QUEDE	Que Delícia	Rio de Janeiro	RJ	02389-673	Brazil
RICAR	Ricardo Adocicados	Rio de Janeiro	RJ	02389-890	Brazil
MORGK	Morgenstern Gesundkost	Leipzig		04179	Germany
GOURL	Gourmet Lanchonetes	Campinas	SP	04876-786	Brazil
ANATR	Ana Trujillo Emparedados y helados	México D.F.		05021	Mexico
CENTC	Centro comercial Moctezuma	México D.F.		05022	Mexico
ANTON	Antonio Moreno Taquería	México D.F.		05023	Mexico
PERIC	Pericles Comidas clásicas	México D.F.		05033	Mexico
TORTU	Tortuga Restaurante	México D.F.		05033	Mexico
COMMI	Comércio Mineiro	São Paulo	SP	05432-043	Brazil
FAMIA	Familia Arquibaldo	São Paulo	SP	05442-030	Brazil
HANAR	Hanari Carnes	Rio de Janeiro	RJ	05454-876	Brazil
QUEEN	Queen Cozinha	São Paulo	SP	05487-020	Brazil

Record: 1 of 91

Figure 7.2 Access's Quick Sort feature works on a single field or multiple fields in left-to-right sequence. This Datasheet is sorted on the PostalCode field.

SORTING DATA ON MULTIPLE FIELDS

Although the sort operation in the preceding section accomplishes exactly what you specify, the result is less than useful because of the variants of postal-code formats used in different countries. What's needed here is a multiple-field sort: first on the Country field and then on the PostalCode field. You can select the Country and the PostalCode fields to perform the multicolumn sort. The Quick Sort technique, however, automatically applies the sorting priority to the leftmost field you select, Postal Code. Access offers two methods of handling this problem: reorder the field display or specify the sort order in a Filter window. Follow these steps to use the reordering process:

→ Filters are discussed later in this chapter; **see** "Filtering Table Data", **p. 249**.

1. Select the Country field by clicking its field header button.
2. Hold down the left mouse button and drag the Country field to the left of the PostalCode field. Release the left mouse button to drop the field in its new location.

3. Shift+click the header button of the PostalCode field to select the Country and PostalCode fields.

4. Click the Sort Ascending button on the toolbar or choose Sort and then Ascending from the Records menu.

The sorted table, shown in Figure 7.3, now makes much more sense. A multiple-field sort on a table sometimes is called a *composite sort*.

Figure 7.3 Rearrange the fields to use Quick Sort on multiple fields in left-to-right sequence. Changing the sequence of fields in Datasheet view affects the display—but not the design—of the table.

Customers : Table

Customer ID	Company Name	City	Region	Country	Postal Code
RANCH	Rancho grande	Buenos Aires		Argentina	1010
OCEAN	Océano Atlántico Ltda.	Buenos Aires		Argentina	1010
CACTU	Cactus Comidas para llevar	Buenos Aires		Argentina	1010
PICCO	Piccolo und mehr	Salzburg		Austria	5020
ERNSH	Ernst Handel	Graz		Austria	8010
MAISD	Maison Dewey	Bruxelles		Belgium	B-1180
SUPRD	Suprêmes délices	Charleroi		Belgium	B-6000
QUEDE	Que Delícia	Rio de Janeiro	RJ	Brazil	02389-673
RICAR	Ricardo Adocicados	Rio de Janeiro	RJ	Brazil	02389-890
GOURL	Gourmet Lanchonetes	Campinas	SP	Brazil	04876-786
COMMI	Comércio Mineiro	São Paulo	SP	Brazil	05432-043
FAMIA	Familia Arquibaldo	São Paulo	SP	Brazil	05442-030
HANAR	Hanari Carnes	Rio de Janeiro	RJ	Brazil	05454-876
QUEEN	Queen Cozinha	São Paulo	SP	Brazil	05487-020
TRADH	Tradição Hipermercados	São Paulo	SP	Brazil	05634-030
WELLI	Wellington Importadora	Resende	SP	Brazil	08737-363

Record: 1 of 91

Removing a Table Sort Order and Thawing Columns

After you freeze columns and apply sort orders to a table, you might want to return the table to its original condition. To do so, Access offers you the following choices:

- To return the Datasheet view of an Access table with a primary key to its original sort order, select the field(s) that comprise the primary key (in the order of the primary key fields), and click the Sort Ascending button.
- To return to the original order when the table has no primary key field, close the table without saving the changes and then reopen the table.
- To thaw your frozen columns, choose Format, Unfreeze All Columns.
- To return the sequence of fields to its original state, drag the fields you moved back to their prior positions or close the table without saving your changes.

If you make substantial changes to the layout of the table and apply a sort order, it's usually quicker to close and reopen the table. (Don't save your changes to the table layout.)

Finding Matching Records in a Table

To search for and select records with field values that match (or partially match) a particular value, use Access's Find feature. To find Luleå (a relatively large city in northern Sweden close to the Arctic Circle) in the City field, follow these steps:

1. In the Customers table, select the field (City) you want to search by clicking its header button or by placing the cursor in that field.

2. Click the toolbar's Find button or choose Edit, Find to display the Find and Replace dialog (see Figure 7.4). You can also display this dialog by pressing Ctrl+F. The dialog opens with the Find page active by default.

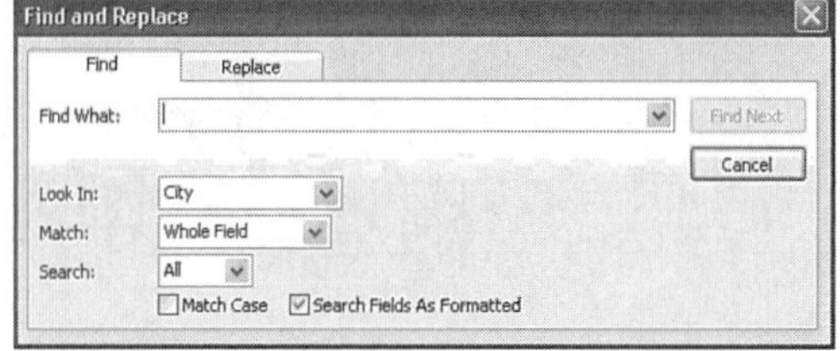

Figure 7.4
The Find and Replace dialog opens with the name of the selected field in the Look In list of the Find page. The Find Next button is disabled until you type an entry in the Find What text box.

NOTE

> If you select the field by clicking the field header button rather than by selecting all characters of a value in the field, the Find What value defaults to the datasheet's first cell value in the field or the last find criterion you chose.

3. Type the name of the city (**Lulea**) in the Find What text box (see Figure 7.5). The Find Next command button is enabled. The default values of the Match and Search lists are satisfactory at this point. Matching case or format is not important here, so clear the Search Fields As Formatted check box.

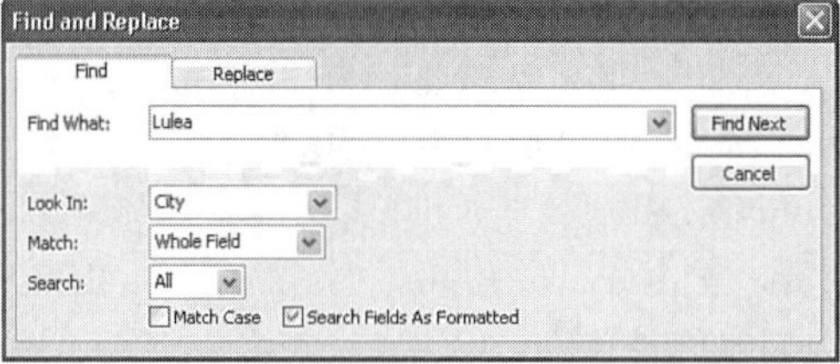

Figure 7.5
A Whole Field match is selected by default, so type the entire value (Lulea for this example) to find in the Find What text box.

4. Click the Find Next button. If you don't have a Scandinavian keyboard, Access displays the message box shown in Figure 7.6. Click OK to dismiss the message box.

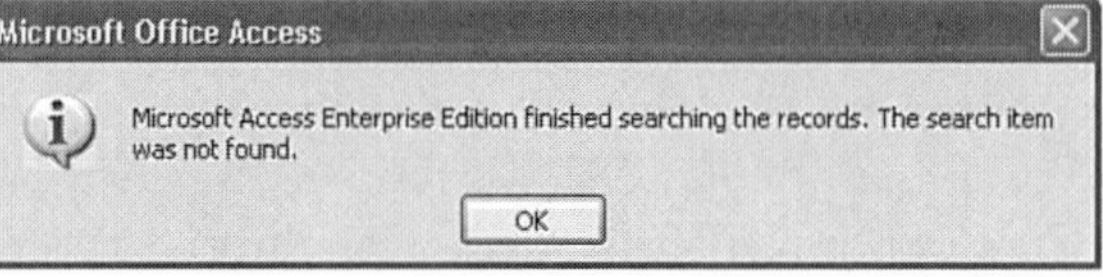

Figure 7.6
If the Find feature doesn't find a match for your entry, you receive a "not found" message.

The "not found" message indicates that the Find feature didn't locate a match in the City field of the entire table. Access missed your entry because the Scandinavian diacritical ° is missing over the "a" in Lulea. In the ANSI character set, "a" has a value of 97, and "å" has a value of 229.

TIP

> To enter international (extended) characters in the Find What text box, type the English letters and then use the Windows XP or Windows 2000 Character Map (Charmap.exe) applet to find and copy the extended character to the Clipboard. (Don't worry about choosing the correct font.) Paste the character into the Find What text box at the appropriate location.

If the letters preceding an extended character are sufficient to define your search parameter, follow these steps to find Luleå:

1. Type **Lule**, omitting the a, in the Find What text box.
2. Select Start of Field from the Match drop-down list.
3. Click the Find Next button. Access finds and highlights Luleå in the City field (see Figure 7.7).

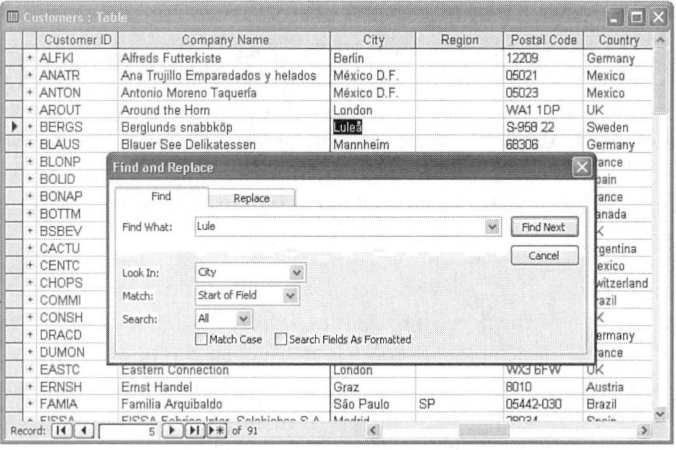

Figure 7.7
Omitting the special Scandinavian character from the search and using the Start of Field search option finds Luleå.

You also can find entries in any part of the field. If you type **ule** in the Find What text box and choose Any Part of Field from the Match drop-down list, you get a match on Luleå. However, you could also match Thule, the location of the Bluie West One airfield (also known as Thule Air Force Base) in Greenland. (There's no actual entry for Thule in the Customers table.)

7

TIP

> You can search all fields of the table for a match by opening the Look In list and selecting *Tablename*: Table. Searching all fields in a table for a matching entry is usually much slower than searching a single field, especially if you have an index on the field being searched. Unless you specify the Any Part of Field Match option, Access uses the index to speed the searching operation.

Following is a list of the options available in the Find dialog:

- To specify a case-sensitive search, mark the Match Case check box.
- To search by using the field's format, mark the Search Fields as Formatted check box. This way you can enter a search term that matches the formatted appearance of the field, such as (510) 555-1212, rather than the native (unformatted) value (5105551212), if you applied a Format property value to the field. Using the Search Fields as Formatted option slows the search operation because indexes aren't used.
- To find additional matches, if any, click the Find Next button. If the Search option is set to Down, clicking the Find Next button starts the search at the current position of the record pointer and searches to the end of the table.
- To start the search at the last record of the table, select Up in the Search drop-down list.

REPLACING MATCHED FIELD VALUES AUTOMATICALLY

The Find and Replace dialog's Replace page lets you replace values selectively in fields that match the entry in the Find What text box. To open the dialog with the Replace page active, choose Edit, Replace or press Ctrl+H. The shortcut key combination for the Edit menu's Replace command is Ctrl+H, which is the same for Microsoft Word and most other Office members.

The entries to search for Luleå and replace with Lulea appear in Figure 7.8. If you performed the search in the preceding section, select Customers:Table from the Look In drop-down list, click the Find Next button, and then click the Replace button for those records in which you want to replace the value. You can do a bulk replace in all matching records by clicking the Replace All button. Unlike Word and Excel, you can't undo search and replace operations in Jet (or SQL Server) tables. Before making replacements, a message box opens to request that you confirm the pending changes.

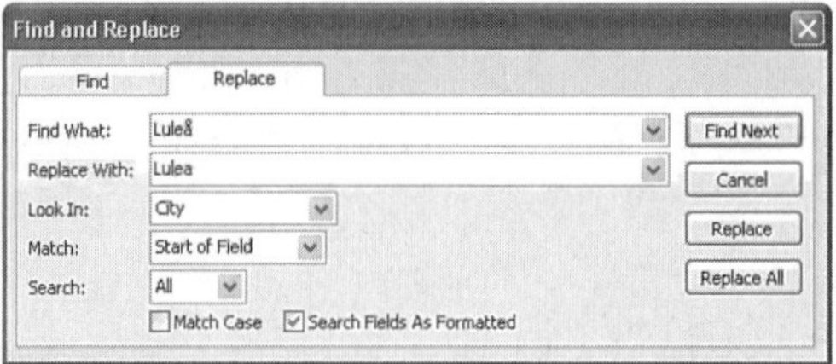

Figure 7.8
Click the Replace tab, type a replacement value in the Replace With text box, and then click Find Next and Replace for each match or Replace All for all occurrences of the Find What value.

FILTERING TABLE DATA

Access lets you apply a filter to specify the records that appear in the Datasheet view of a table or a query result set. For example, if you want to view only those customers located in Germany, you use a filter to limit the displayed records to only those whose Country field contains the text Germany. Access gives you four different ways to apply filters to the data in a table:

- *Filter by Selection* is the fastest and simplest way to apply a filter. You establish the filter criteria by selecting all or part of the data in one of the table's fields; Access displays only records that match the selected sample. With Filter by Selection, you can filter records based only on criteria in a single field of the table.
- *Filter Excluding Selection* functions opposite to Filter by Selection—all records except those matching the selection appear when you apply the filter.

- *Filter by Form* is the second fastest way to apply a filter. You enter the filter criteria into a blank datasheet form of the table; Access displays records that match the combined criteria in each field. Use Filter by Form to quickly filter records based on criteria in more than one field.

- *Advanced Filter/Sort* is the most powerful type of filter. With an advanced filter/sort, you can make an Access filter do double duty because you also can add a sort order on one or more fields. The Advanced Filter/Sort icon doesn't appear on the toolbar.

FILTERING BY SELECTION

Creating a Filter by Selection is as easy as selecting text in a field. When you apply the filter, Access uses the selected text to determine which records to display. Table 7.1 summarizes which records are displayed, depending on how you select text in the field. In all cases, Access applies the filter criteria only to the field in which you have selected text. Filter by selection lets you establish filter criteria for only a single field at one time.

TABLE 7.1 HOW SELECTED TEXT AFFECTS FILTER BY SELECTION

Selected Text	Filter Effect
Entire field	Displays only records whose fields contain exactly matching values
Beginning of field	Displays records in which the text at the beginning of the field matches the selected text
End of field	Displays records in which the text at the end of the field matches the selected text
Characters anywhere in field	Displays records in which any part of the field matches the selected text

To create a Filter by Selection on the Customers table (displaying only those customers located in Germany), follow these steps:

1. If necessary, open the Customers table in Datasheet view and use the scroll bars to make the Country field visible in the Table window.
2. Select all the text in the Country field of the first record in the Customers table. (This entry should be Germany.)

3. Click the Filter by Selection toolbar button or choose Records, Filter, Filter by Selection. Access applies the filter as shown in Figure 7.9.

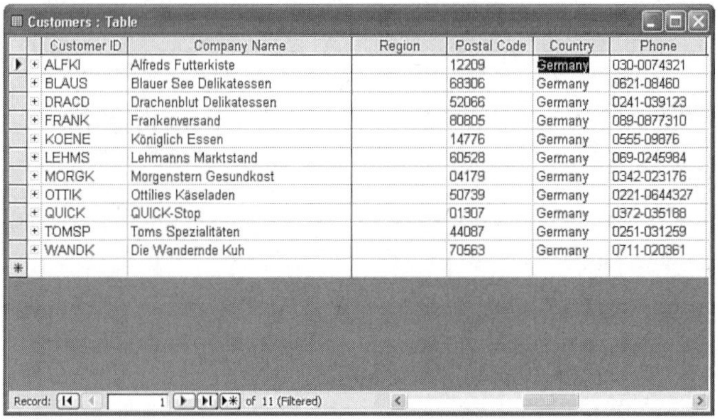

Figure 7.9
Applying "Germany" as a selection filter results in the filtered Datasheet view shown here.

Customers : Table

Customer ID	Company Name	Region	Postal Code	Country	Phone
ALFKI	Alfreds Futterkiste		12209	Germany	030-0074321
BLAUS	Blauer See Delikatessen		68306	Germany	0621-08460
DRACD	Drachenblut Delikatessen		52066	Germany	0241-039123
FRANK	Frankenversand		80805	Germany	089-0877310
KOENE	Königlich Essen		14776	Germany	0555-09876
LEHMS	Lehmanns Marktstand		60528	Germany	069-0245984
MORGK	Morgenstern Gesundkost		04179	Germany	0342-023176
OTTIK	Ottilies Käseladen		50739	Germany	0221-0644327
QUICK	QUICK-Stop		01307	Germany	0372-035188
TOMSP	Toms Spezialitäten		44087	Germany	0251-031259
WANDK	Die Wandernde Kuh		70563	Germany	0711-020361

Record: 1 of 11 (Filtered)

Notice that the Apply Filter toolbar button is now displayed in active status (a contrasting background color), indicating that a filter is being applied to the table, and the ToolTip changes to Remove Filter. The legend (Filtered) also is added to the record selection and status bar at the bottom of the Table window. To remove the filter, click the activated Apply Filter button.

TIP

Use the Find and Replace dialog to quickly locate the first record of a group you're interested in filtering and then apply a Filter by Selection.

As mentioned previously, you can also apply a Filter by Selection based on partially selected text in a field. Figure 7.10 shows the Customers table with a different Filter by Selection applied—this time, only the letters "er" in the Country field were selected. You must remove the previous filter before applying a new filter for the entire table, rather than the filtered records.

Customers : Table

	Customer ID	Company Name	Region	Postal Code	Country	Phone
+	ALFKI	Alfreds Futterkiste		12209	Germany	030-0074321
+	BLAUS	Blauer See Delikatessen		68306	Germany	0621-08460
+	CHOPS	Chop-suey Chinese		3012	Switzerland	0452-076545
+	DRACD	Drachenblut Delikatessen		52066	Germany	0241-039123
+	FRANK	Frankenversand		80805	Germany	089-0877310
+	KOENE	Königlich Essen		14776	Germany	0555-09876
+	LEHMS	Lehmanns Marktstand		60528	Germany	069-0245984
+	MORGK	Morgenstern Gesundkost		04179	Germany	0342-023176
+	OTTIK	Ottilies Käseladen		50739	Germany	0221-0644327
+	QUICK	QUICK-Stop		01307	Germany	0372-035188
+	RICSU	Richter Supermarkt		1203	Switzerland	0897-034214
+	TOMSP	Toms Spezialitäten		44087	Germany	0251-031259
+	WANDK	Die Wandernde Kuh		70563	Germany	0711-020361
*						

Record: 1 of 13 (Filtered)

Figure 7.10
Selecting only a part of the field—in this case the letters "er"—displays records containing the partial selection in any part of the field.

TIP

> You can apply a Filter by Selection to more than one field at a time. For example, after applying a Filter by Selection to display only those customers in Germany, you could then move to the City field and apply a second Filter by Selection for Berlin. The resulting table would include only those customers in Berlin, Germany. An easier way to apply filters based on more than one field value is to use a Filter by Form, described in the "Filter by Form" section coming up.

USING THE FILTER FOR OPTION

The Filter For option is a quick method for applying a filter to a single field. To use the Filter For feature, do this:

1. Right-click the field on which you want to filter the table, and choose the Filter For text box in the context menu.
2. In the text box, type the value you want to filter on, such as **USA** for the Country field of the Customers table, and press Enter to apply the filter.

To remove the filter, right-click anywhere in the Datasheet window and choose Remove Filter/Sort. Alternatively, click the toolbar's Remove Filter/Sort button. Use this shortcut to remove any filter you've applied to the table.

FILTERING BY FORM

Filtering by form is slightly more complex than filtering by selection because it lets you filter records based on criteria in more than one field at a time. For example, you saw in the preceding section how to use a Filter by Selection to view only those customers in Germany. To further limit the displayed records to those customers located in Berlin, Germany (and not Berlin, New Hampshire), use a Filter by Form.

In a Filter by Form, Access displays a blank form for the table (see Figure 7.11). This window is called a form to distinguish it from the Table Datasheet window, although it's not the same as the data-entry forms discussed later in this book. You can combine criteria in a Filter by Form with a logical **Or** operator or a logical **And** operator. For example, you can filter the Customers table to display only those customers in the United States or Canada. As another example, you could filter the Customers table to display only those customers in the United States and in ZIP codes beginning with the digit 9 (such as 94609 or 90807).

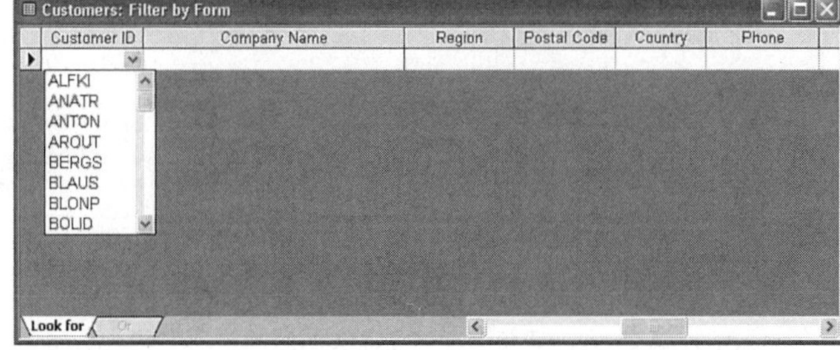

Figure 7.11
The Filter by Form variation of Datasheet view has a single row in which you add filter criteria. Each field has a drop-down list of values you can choose for the filter.

TIP

> Verify that all the fields of the filter form are empty before designing a new filter. The last filter expression you apply appears in the filter form when you open it. For instance, the Country field contains `Like "*er*"` if you tested the partial selection example in the preceding section.

To create a Filter by Form on the Customers table to display only those customers in the United States or Canada, follow these steps:

1. If necessary, open the Customers table in Datasheet view.

2. Click the Filter by Form toolbar button or choose Records, Filter, Filter by Form to display the Filter by Form window (refer to Figure 7.11).
3. Make the Country field visible in the Filter by Form window if necessary. (The CustomerID and CompanyName fields in the figures have been frozen, as described previously in this chapter.)
4. Click inside the Country field and open the Country list box, or press F4. The drop-down list contains all the unique values in the Country field.
5. Select Canada in the list box, as shown in Figure 7.12. Access automatically adds the quotation marks around the value you select and enters it into the Country field form box.
6. Click the Or tab at the bottom of the Filter by Form window. Access combines criteria that you enter on separate tabs in the Filter by Form window with a logical **Or** operator. When you add an **Or** operator, a tab for another **Or** operator appears.
7. Click the arrow to open the Country list box or press F4. Select USA from the drop-down list (see Figure 7.13).

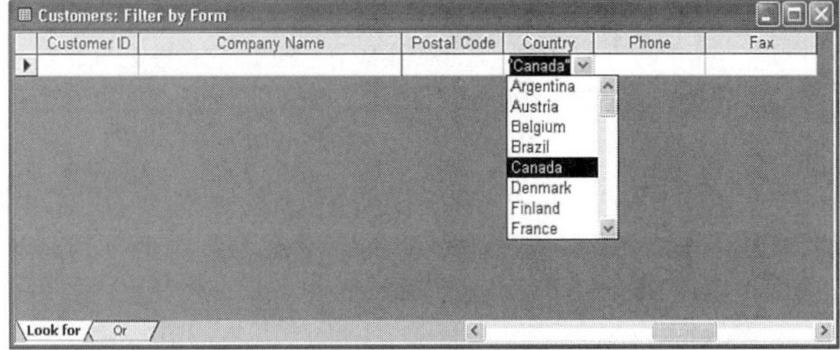

Figure 7.12
The drop-down list in the Filter by Form datasheet lets you select a single criterion on which to filter the field.

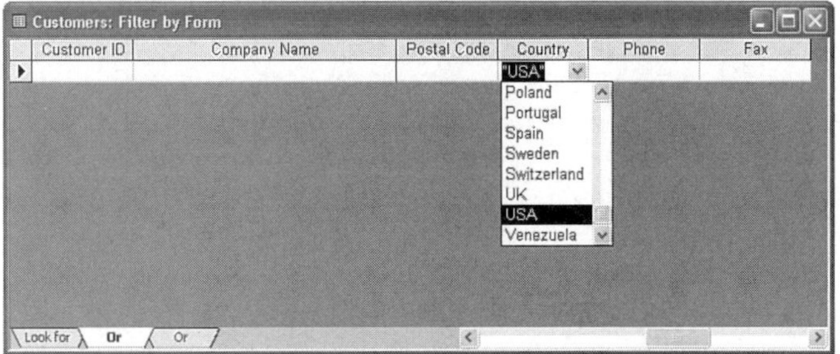

Figure 7.13
Clicking the Or tab of the Filter by Form window opens another empty row in which you can select another criterion. Each time you add an Or criterion, an additional disabled Or tab appears at the bottom of the window.

8. Click the Apply Filter button. Access applies the new filter to the table, displaying the records shown in Figure 7.14.

Figure 7.14
The Customers table in Datasheet view displays the result of applying the "Canada" Or "USA" filter.

Customers : Table

Customer ID	Company Name	Postal Code	Country	Phone	Fax
BOTTM	Bottom-Dollar Markets	T2F 8M4	Canada	(604) 555-4729	(604) 555-3745
GREAL	Great Lakes Food Market	97403	USA	(503) 555-7555	
HUNGC	Hungry Coyote Import Store	97827	USA	(503) 555-6874	(503) 555-2376
LAUGB	Laughing Bacchus Wine Cellars	V3F 2K1	Canada	(604) 555-3392	(604) 555-7293
LAZYK	Lazy K Kountry Store	99362	USA	(509) 555-7969	(509) 555-6221
LETSS	Let's Stop N Shop	94117	USA	(415) 555-5938	
LONEP	Lonesome Pine Restaurant	97219	USA	(503) 555-9573	(503) 555-9646
MEREP	Mère Paillarde	H1J 1C3	Canada	(514) 555-8054	(514) 555-8055
OLDWO	Old World Delicatessen	99508	USA	(907) 555-7584	(907) 555-2880
RATTC	Rattlesnake Canyon Grocery	87110	USA	(505) 555-5939	(505) 555-3620
SAVEA	Save-a-lot Markets	83720	USA	(208) 555-8097	
SPLIR	Split Rail Beer & Ale	82520	USA	(307) 555-4680	(307) 555-6525
THEBI	The Big Cheese	97201	USA	(503) 555-3612	
THECR	The Cracker Box	59801	USA	(406) 555-5834	(406) 555-8083
TRAIH	Trail's Head Gourmet Provisioners	98034	USA	(206) 555-8257	(206) 555-2174
WHITC	White Clover Markets	98128	USA	(206) 555-4112	(206) 555-4115

Record: 1 of 16 (Filtered)

NOTE

Access stores the last filter you applied as the value of the table's Filter property. To view the filter value, change to Table Design view and click the Properties button to open the Properties window for the table. For the preceding example, the filter value is ((Customers.Country="Canada")) OR ((Customers.Country="USA")). The parenthesis pairs are superfluous for this filter.

7

You can also combine filter criteria in a logical **And** operator by entering criteria in more than one field on the same tab of the Form window. For example, you want to filter the Orders table to find all orders handled by Nancy Davolio and shipped to France. You easily can use a Filter by Form to do so, as the following example shows:

1. Open the Orders table and freeze the OrderID, Customer, and Employee fields. Then position the ShipCountry field so that it's visible (see Figure 7.15). Freezing the fields isn't an essential step, but it makes setting up the filter and viewing the filtered data easier.

Figure 7.15
Simplify the filtering process by freezing the first three fields of the Orders table.

Orders : Table

Order ID	Customer	Employee	Ship Country
10248	Wilman Kala	Buchanan, Steven	France
10249	Tradição Hipermercados	Suyama, Michael	Germany
10250	Hanari Carnes	Peacock, Margaret	Brazil
10251	Victuailles en stock	Leverling, Janet	France
10252	Suprêmes délices	Peacock, Margaret	Belgium
10253	Hanari Carnes	Leverling, Janet	Brazil
10254	Chop-suey Chinese	Buchanan, Steven	Switzerland
10255	Richter Supermarkt	Dodsworth, Anne	Switzerland
10256	Wellington Importadora	Leverling, Janet	Brazil
10257	HILARIÓN-Abastos	Peacock, Margaret	Venezuela
10258	Ernst Handel	Davolio, Nancy	Austria
10259	Centro comercial Moctezuma	Peacock, Margaret	Mexico
10260	Old World Delicatessen	Peacock, Margaret	Germany
10261	Que Delícia	Peacock, Margaret	Brazil
10262	Rattlesnake Canyon Grocery	Callahan, Laura	USA
10263	Ernst Handel	Dodsworth, Anne	Austria
10264	Folk och fä HB	Suyama, Michael	Sweden
10265	Blondel père et fils	Fuller, Andrew	France
10266	Wartian Herkku	Leverling, Janet	Finland
10267	Frankenversand	Peacock, Margaret	Germany
10268	GROSELLA-Restaurante	Callahan, Laura	Venezuela

Record: 1 of 830

2. Click the Filter by Form toolbar button to display the Filter by Form window.
3. Click the Clear Grid toolbar button or choose Edit, Clear Filter to clear any previous filter criteria from the Filter by Form grid.
4. Use the drop-down list in the EmployeeID field to select Davolio, Nancy, and then use the drop-down list in the ShipCountry field to select France. You must manually add quotes around a text criterion that includes a comma (see Figure 7.16).

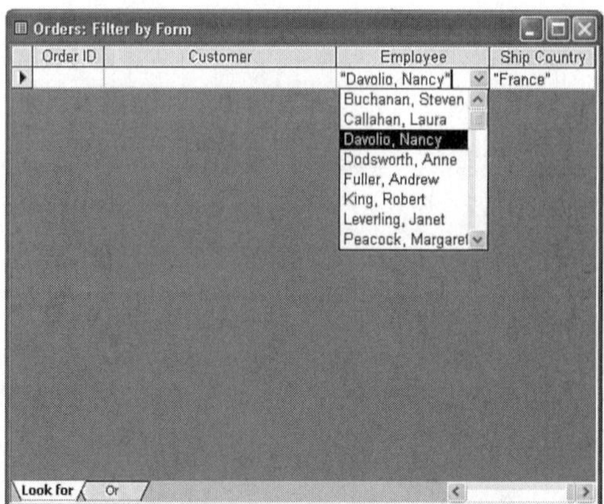

Figure 7.16
The criterion in the EmployeeID field is based on the lookup field that displays the LastName and FirstName values from the Employees tables, separated by a comma and space. Matching a composite criterion requires surrounding the value with quotes.

5. Click the Apply Filter button. Access applies the new filter to the table, displaying the records shown in Figure 7.17. This filter shows only those records for orders that were handled by Nancy Davolio and shipped to France.

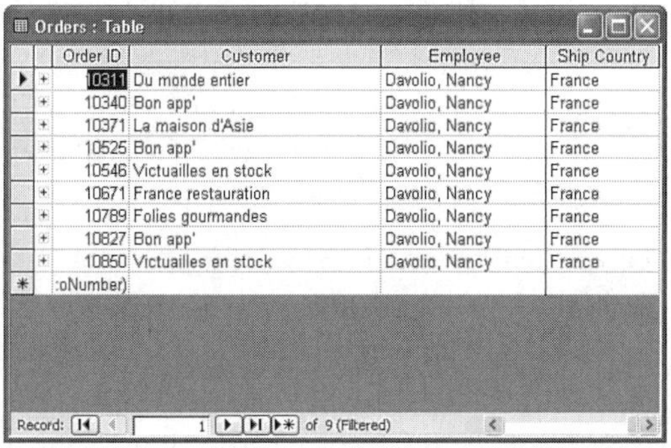

Figure 7.17
The EmployeeID and Country filter criteria shown in Figure 7.16 result in the following Datasheet view of the Orders table.

Orders : Table

Order ID	Customer	Employee	Ship Country
10311	Du monde entier	Davolio, Nancy	France
10340	Bon app'	Davolio, Nancy	France
10371	La maison d'Asie	Davolio, Nancy	France
10525	Bon app'	Davolio, Nancy	France
10546	Victuailles en stock	Davolio, Nancy	France
10671	France restauration	Davolio, Nancy	France
10789	Folies gourmandes	Davolio, Nancy	France
10827	Bon app'	Davolio, Nancy	France
10850	Victuailles en stock	Davolio, Nancy	France
:oNumber)			

Record: 1 of 9 (Filtered)

TIP

> You also can apply the Filter by Form feature to Access forms that are bound to tables or queries. With forms that display field values in text boxes, clicking the Filter by Form button clears the text boxes and adds the Look For and Or tabs to the bottom of the form. You type search value(s) in the appropriate text box(es) for the `And` operator, `Or` operator, or both.

If Access doesn't return the records you expected, try the solution in the "Troubleshooting" section at the end of the chapter.

APPLYING ADVANCED FILTERS AND SORT ORDERS

Filters in Access, as mentioned previously, are queries in disguise, and provide a useful introduction to single-table Access queries, the subject of Chapter 9, "Designing Queries for Jet Databases." Creating an advanced filter/sort is much like creating a query, with some basic differences, as follows:

- The Show Table dialog doesn't appear.
- The SQL button is missing from the toolbar, so you can't display the underlying SQL statement.
- The Show row is missing from the Filter Design grid.

Filters are limited to using one table or query that Access automatically specifies when you enter Filter Design view. You can save a filter you create as a query or load a filter from a query, but Access has no provision for saving a filter as a filter. The following sections describe how to add criteria to filter records and to add a sort order in the Filter Design window.

NOTE

SQL Server tables opened in ADP don't support Jet's advanced filter/sort function.

ADDING A MULTIFIELD SORT AND COMPOUND FILTER CRITERIA

In its default configuration, the Datasheet toolbar doesn't have an Advanced Filter/Sort button. Instead, you start the advanced filter/sort operation by choosing Records, Filter, Advanced Filter/Sort. To create a filter on the Orders table (which provides more records to filter than the Customers table), follow these steps:

1. Close and reopen the Orders table in Datasheet view—without saving changes—to clear filter or sort criteria you applied previously.
2. Choose Records, Filter, Advanced Filter/Sort to display the Filter window (see Figure 7.18). The default filter name, Filter1, is concatenated with the table name to create the default name of the first filter, OrdersFilter1. The Field List window for the Orders table appears in the upper pane of the Filter window.

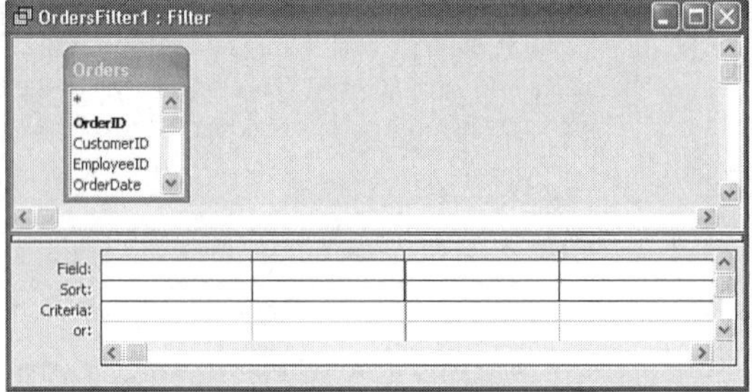

Figure 7.18 The Filter window is similar to the Query Design window, but doesn't have Table or Show rows in the lower pane's grid.

TIP

The Datasheet toolbar doesn't have an Advanced Filter/Sort command button in its default configuration, but you can customize the Datasheet toolbar to add an Advanced Filter/Sort button.

➔ To add the Advanced Filter/Sort button to your toolbar, **see** "Customizable Toolbars," **p. 574**.

3. One field that you might want to use to sort or limit displayed records is OrderID. Click it in the field list in the upper pane and drag it to the first column of the Field row of the Filter Design grid in the lower pane. (When your mouse pointer reaches the lower pane, the pointer turns into a field symbol.) Alternatively, double-click the OrderID field to add it to the grid.
4. Repeat step 3 for other fields on which you want to sort or establish criteria. Candidates are CustomerID, ShipCountry, ShipPostalCode, OrderDate, and ShippedDate.

7

5. To check the sorting capabilities of your first advanced filter, add an ascending sort to the ShipCountry and ShipPostalCode fields by selecting Ascending from that field's Sort cell. Your Filter Design window appears as shown in Figure 7.19.

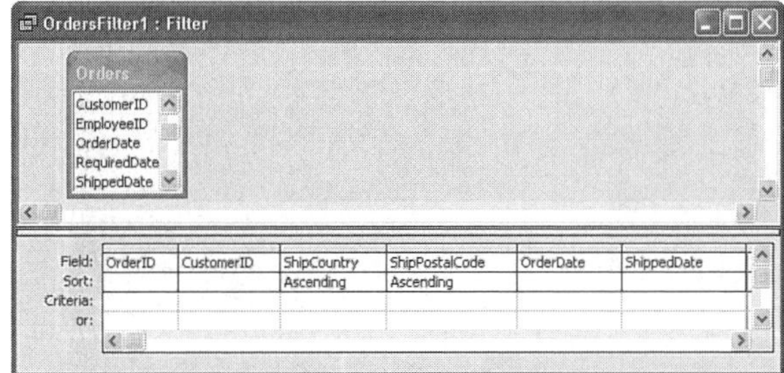

Figure 7.19
The grid of the Filter Design window has ascending sorts specified for the ShipCountry and ShipPostalCode fields.

6. Click the Apply Filter toolbar button or choose Filter, Apply Filter/Sort.

7. Use the horizontal scroll bar of the datasheet to reveal the ShipCountry and ShipPostalCode fields. Your sorted table appears as shown in Figure 7.20.

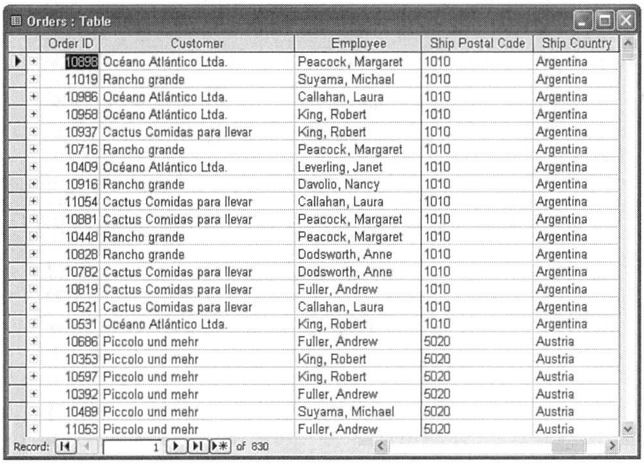

Orders : Table

Order ID	Customer	Employee	Ship Postal Code	Ship Country
10898	Océano Atlántico Ltda.	Peacock, Margaret	1010	Argentina
11019	Rancho grande	Suyama, Michael	1010	Argentina
10986	Océano Atlántico Ltda.	Callahan, Laura	1010	Argentina
10958	Océano Atlántico Ltda.	King, Robert	1010	Argentina
10937	Cactus Comidas para llevar	King, Robert	1010	Argentina
10716	Rancho grande	Peacock, Margaret	1010	Argentina
10409	Océano Atlántico Ltda.	Leverling, Janet	1010	Argentina
10916	Rancho grande	Davolio, Nancy	1010	Argentina
11054	Cactus Comidas para llevar	Callahan, Laura	1010	Argentina
10881	Cactus Comidas para llevar	Peacock, Margaret	1010	Argentina
10448	Rancho grande	Peacock, Margaret	1010	Argentina
10828	Rancho grande	Dodsworth, Anne	1010	Argentina
10782	Cactus Comidas para llevar	Dodsworth, Anne	1010	Argentina
10819	Cactus Comidas para llevar	Fuller, Andrew	1010	Argentina
10521	Cactus Comidas para llevar	Callahan, Laura	1010	Argentina
10531	Océano Atlántico Ltda.	King, Robert	1010	Argentina
10686	Piccolo und mehr	Fuller, Andrew	5020	Austria
10353	Piccolo und mehr	King, Robert	5020	Austria
10597	Piccolo und mehr	King, Robert	5020	Austria
10392	Piccolo und mehr	Fuller, Andrew	5020	Austria
10489	Piccolo und mehr	Suyama, Michael	5020	Austria
11053	Piccolo und mehr	Fuller, Andrew	5020	Austria

Record: 1 of 830

Figure 7.20
The sorted ShipCountry field is to the left of the sorted ShipPostalCode field in Query Design view, so the table is sorted first by country and then by postal code. Applying an Advanced Filter/Sort doesn't require repositioning the fields in Datasheet view.

8. Click the Filter Design window or choose Records, Filter, Advanced Filter/Sort to edit the filter criteria.

9. Type **USA** in the Criteria row of the ShipCountry field to limit records to those orders shipped to an address in the United States. Access automatically adds quotes around "USA".

10. Click the Apply Filter button on the toolbar and scroll to display the sorted fields. Only records with destinations in the United States appear, as shown in Figure 7.21.

7

Orders : Table

	Order ID	Customer	Employee	Ship Postal Code	Ship Country
+	10624	The Cracker Box	Peacock, Margaret	59801	USA
+	10775	The Cracker Box	King, Robert	59801	USA
+	11003	The Cracker Box	Leverling, Janet	59801	USA
+	10271	Split Rail Beer & Ale	Suyama, Michael	82520	USA
+	10385	Split Rail Beer & Ale	Davolio, Nancy	82520	USA
+	10369	Split Rail Beer & Ale	Callahan, Laura	82520	USA
+	10349	Split Rail Beer & Ale	King, Robert	82520	USA
+	10821	Split Rail Beer & Ale	Davolio, Nancy	82520	USA
+	10432	Split Rail Beer & Ale	Leverling, Janet	82520	USA
+	10974	Split Rail Beer & Ale	Leverling, Janet	82520	USA
+	10329	Split Rail Beer & Ale	Peacock, Margaret	82520	USA
+	10756	Split Rail Beer & Ale	Callahan, Laura	82520	USA
+	10678	Save-a-lot Markets	King, Robert	83720	USA
+	10748	Save-a-lot Markets	Leverling, Janet	83720	USA
+	10757	Save-a-lot Markets	Suyama, Michael	83720	USA
+	10815	Save-a-lot Markets	Fuller, Andrew	83720	USA
+	10607	Save-a-lot Markets	Buchanan, Steven	83720	USA
+	10393	Save-a-lot Markets	Davolio, Nancy	83720	USA
+	10722	Save-a-lot Markets	Callahan, Laura	83720	USA
+	10398	Save-a-lot Markets	Fuller, Andrew	83720	USA
+	10714	Save-a-lot Markets	Buchanan, Steven	83720	USA
+	10713	Save-a-lot Markets	Davolio, Nancy	83720	USA

Record: 1 of 122 (Filtered)

Figure 7.21 Adding "USA" in the Criteria row under the ShipCountry field filters the Datasheet view to display orders destined for the United States only.

USING COMPOSITE CRITERIA

You can apply composite criteria to expand or further limit the records that Access displays. Composite criteria are applied to more than one field. To display all orders from the Orders table that were received on or after 1/1/1997 with destinations in North America, extend the exercise in the preceding section and try the following:

1. Click to display the Filter Design window.
2. Type **Canada** in the second criteria row of the ShipCountry field and **Mexico** in the third row; then move the cursor to a different cell. When you add criteria under one another, the effect is to make the criteria alternative—that is, combined by a logical `Or` operator.
3. Open the Sort list for the PostalCode field and select (not sorted) to remove the sort. Open the Sort list for the OrderDate field and select Ascending.
4. Type **>=#1/1/1997#** in the first criteria line of the OrderDate field. When you add criteria on the same line as another criterion, the criteria is additive (a logical `And` operator)—that is, orders placed on or after 1/1/1997. The # symbols indicate to Jet that the enclosed value is of the Date/Time data type.
5. Press F2 to select the date entry you made in step 3 and then press Ctrl+C to copy the expression to the Clipboard. Position the cursor in the second row of the OrderDate field and press Ctrl+V to add the same expression for Canada. Repeat this process to add the date criterion for Mexican orders. Your Filter Design grid now appears as shown in Figure 7.22.

NOTE

> You must repeat the date criterion for each country criterion because of a limitation in constructing SQL statements from Jet query grids, which is discussed shortly.

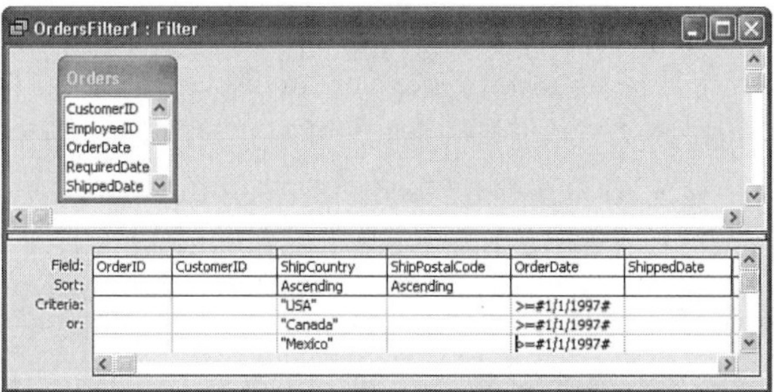

Figure 7.22
The design of this composite filter restricts the display to orders received in 1997 and later destined for North America.

6. Click the Apply Filter button to display your newly filtered datasheet (see Figure 7.23, which has the field sequence rearranged and is scrolled to show the three countries).

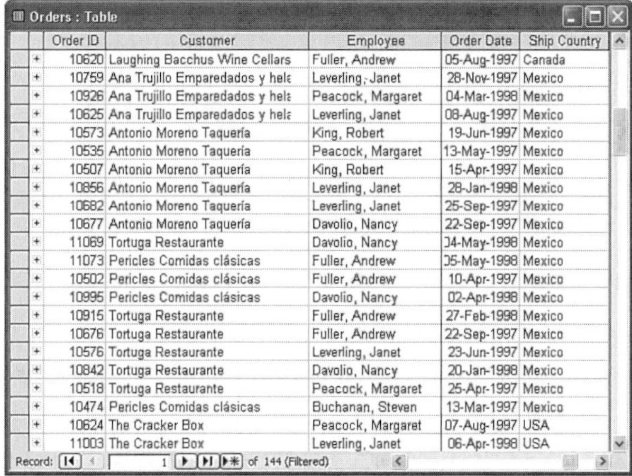

Orders : Table

Order ID	Customer	Employee	Order Date	Ship Country
10620	Laughing Bacchus Wine Cellars	Fuller, Andrew	05-Aug-1997	Canada
10759	Ana Trujillo Emparedados y hel	Leverling, Janet	28-Nov-1997	Mexico
10926	Ana Trujillo Emparedados y hel	Peacock, Margaret	04-Mar-1998	Mexico
10625	Ana Trujillo Emparedados y hel	Leverling, Janet	08-Aug-1997	Mexico
10573	Antonio Moreno Taquería	King, Robert	19-Jun-1997	Mexico
10535	Antonio Moreno Taquería	Peacock, Margaret	13-May-1997	Mexico
10507	Antonio Moreno Taquería	King, Robert	15-Apr-1997	Mexico
10856	Antonio Moreno Taquería	Leverling, Janet	28-Jan-1998	Mexico
10682	Antonio Moreno Taquería	Leverling, Janet	25-Sep-1997	Mexico
10677	Antonio Moreno Taquería	Davolio, Nancy	22-Sep-1997	Mexico
11069	Tortuga Restaurante	Davolio, Nancy	04-May-1998	Mexico
11073	Pericles Comidas clásicas	Fuller, Andrew	05-May-1998	Mexico
10502	Pericles Comidas clásicas	Fuller, Andrew	10-Apr-1997	Mexico
10995	Pericles Comidas clásicas	Davolio, Nancy	02-Apr-1998	Mexico
10915	Tortuga Restaurante	Fuller, Andrew	27-Feb-1998	Mexico
10676	Tortuga Restaurante	Fuller, Andrew	22-Sep-1997	Mexico
10576	Tortuga Restaurante	Leverling, Janet	23-Jun-1997	Mexico
10842	Tortuga Restaurante	Davolio, Nancy	20-Jan-1998	Mexico
10518	Tortuga Restaurante	Peacock, Margaret	25-Apr-1997	Mexico
10474	Pericles Comidas clásicas	Buchanan, Steven	13-Mar-1997	Mexico
10624	The Cracker Box	Peacock, Margaret	07-Aug-1997	USA
11003	The Cracker Box	Leverling, Janet	06-Apr-1998	USA

Record: 1 of 144 (Filtered)

Figure 7.23
This Datasheet view of the Orders table has the filter of Figure 7.22 applied. The field sequence has been rearranged to permit viewing the OrderDate and ShipCountry fields.

→ To become more familiar with the power of selecting data with criteria, **see** "Using the Query Design Window," **p. 334**.

SAVING YOUR FILTER AS A QUERY AND LOADING A FILTER

Access doesn't have a persistent Filter object. A persistent database object is one you create that's stored as a component of your database's .mdb file. Persistent database objects appear as items in one of the list views of the Database window. A filter is equivalent to a single-table query, so Access lets you save your filter as a `QueryDef` (query definition) object. Access saves the names of the filters associated with each table in the system tables of your database when you save a filter as a query. This feature is the principal advantage of using a filter rather than a query when only a single table is involved.

7

To save your filter and remove the filter from the Orders table, follow these steps:

1. Choose Records, Filter, Advanced Filter/Sort to display the Filter Design window if it isn't already displayed or click the toolbar button if you have customized your menu.

2. Click the Save as Query toolbar button or choose File, Save As Query to display the Save as Query dialog.
3. Enter a descriptive name—such as fltOrdersNorthAmerica—for your filter in the Query Name text box. Using the flt prefix distinguishes the filters you save from conventional queries (see Figure 7.24).

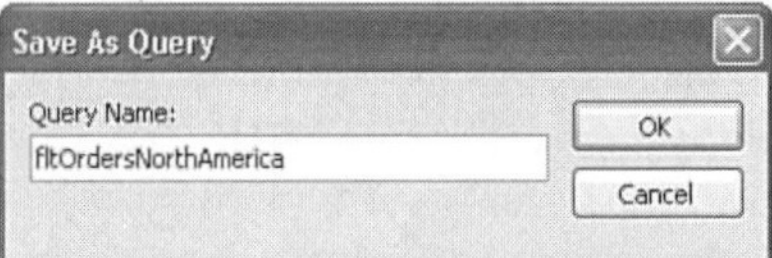

Figure 7.24 Use a descriptive name when saving the filter as a `QueryDef` object.

4. Click OK to save the filter and close the Filter window.

5. Click the Remove Filter toolbar button to remove the filter from the Orders datasheet.
6. A filter remains in memory while the table it applies to is open. To close the filter, close the Orders table, without saving changes.

Re-applying a filter from the filter you saved as a query requires the following steps:

1. Reopen the Orders table in Datasheet view.
2. Choose Records, Filter, Advanced Filter/Sort to open the Filter Design window with the default OrdersFilter1 filter.
3. Click the Load from Query toolbar button or choose File, Load from Query to open the Applicable Filter dialog (see Figure 7.25). You use the Applicable Filter dialog to select the filter you want if you've saved more than one filter for the table.

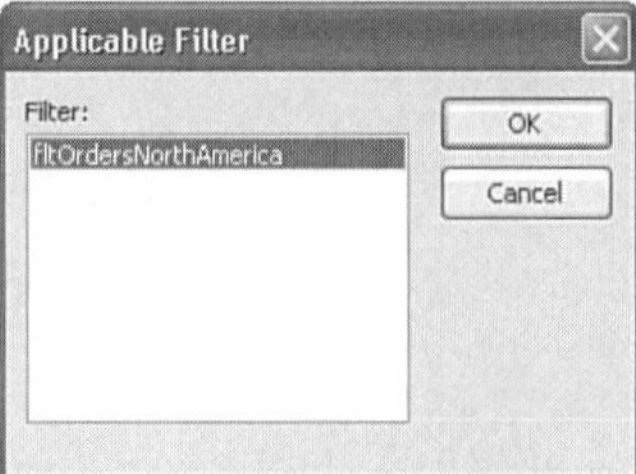

Figure 7.25 Clicking the Load from Query toolbar button opens the Applicable Filter dialog from which you can select the filter to apply to the table.

4. Double-click the fltOrdersNorthAmerica filter to load the saved query into the Filter window.

5. Click the Apply Filter toolbar button to display the resulting filtered set in the Orders datasheet.

TIP

> To remove a filter saved as a query so it doesn't appear in the Applicable Filters list, delete the query in the Database window's query list.

APPLYING A SAVED QUERY AS A FILTER

An alternative to the preceding steps is to execute the saved filter as query. You execute a query the same way you open a table:

1. Close the Orders table.
2. Click the Database window's Queries shortcut to list the saved queries.
3. Double-click the fltOrdersNorthAmerica item. The datasheet of the fltOrdersNorthAmerica: Select Query window that appears is similar to the datasheet you created in step 5 of the preceding operation, except that the fields appear in the original order of the table design.

4. Click the Design view toolbar button to display the query design (see Figure 7.26). Fields in which no selection criteria or sort order are entered don't appear in the Query Design grid.

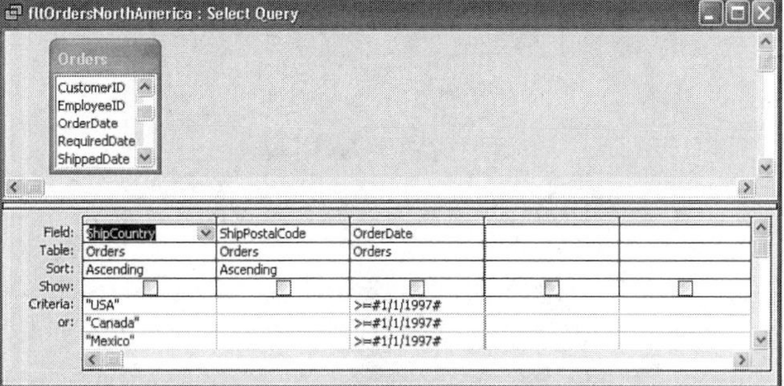

Figure 7.26
The Query Design view of a filter is similar to the Filter Design view, but adds Table and Show rows to the grid.

CUSTOMIZING TABLE DATASHEET VIEW

To customize the appearance of Table Datasheet view, you can hide the fields you don't want to appear in your datasheet, change the height of the record rows, eliminate the gridlines, and select a different font for your display. The following list describes each option for customizing Table and Query Datasheet views:

- *To hide a field*, select it by clicking its header or placing the cursor in the column for the field. Then choose Format, Hide Columns.
- *To show a hidden field*, choose Format, Unhide Columns to display the Unhide Columns dialog (see Figure 7.27). A mark next to the field name in the Column list indicates fields appearing in Datasheet view. Click the check box to the left of the field name to toggle between hiding and showing the field.

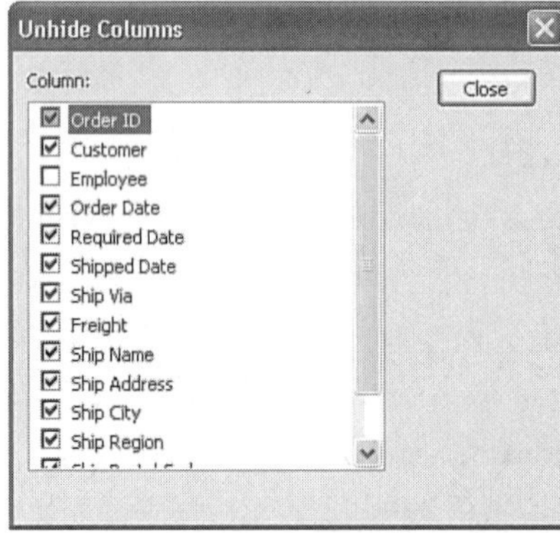

Figure 7.27
The Unhide Columns dialog lets you specify the fields that appear in Table Datasheet view.

- *To change the font used to display and print the datasheet*, use the Font drop-down list on the Formatting toolbar (if it's displayed) or choose Format, Font to display the Font dialog. The appearance of the Font dialog depends on your operating system; Figure 7.28 shows Windows 2000's Font dialog.

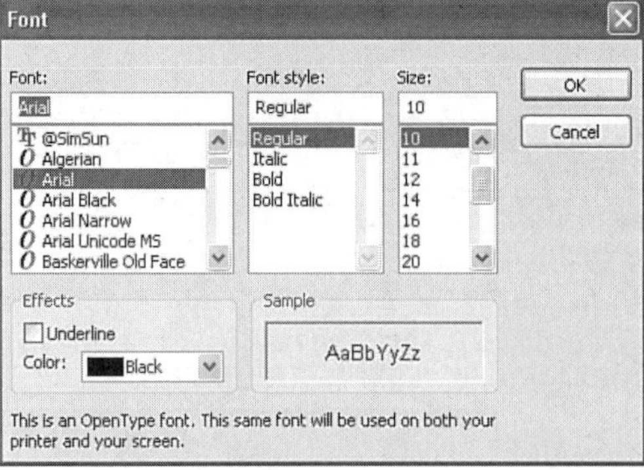

Figure 7.28
Windows XP's Font dialog identifies new OpenType fonts with an italic letter O and traditional TrueType fonts with two Ts.

- *To remove gridlines from the display and printed versions of the datasheet*, use the Gridlines drop-down list on the Formatting toolbar or choose Format, Datasheet. If you use the Gridlines drop-down list, Access displays a palette of four gridline display choices: Both, Horizontal, Vertical, and None; click the button corresponding to the gridline display you want. If you use the Format menu, Access displays the Datasheet

Formatting dialog, shown in Figure 7.29, which contains check boxes for the horizontal and vertical gridlines. Select or clear the check boxes for the desired gridline display.

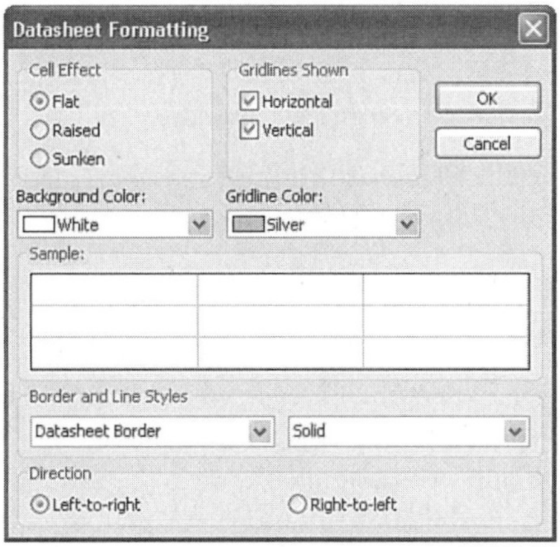

Figure 7.29
The Datasheet Formatting dialog lets you apply special effects, control the appearance of gridlines, and select background and gridline colors.

- *To change the height of the rows as displayed and printed,* position the mouse pointer at the bottom edge of one of the record selector buttons. The pointer turns into a double-headed arrow (see Figure 7.30). Drag the bottom edge of the button to adjust the height of all the rows. Alternatively, choose Format, Row Height and set the height in points in the Row Height dialog. (Multiply the size of your font by about 1.25 to obtain normal row spacing; printers call 10-point type with 12-point spacing "10 on 12.")

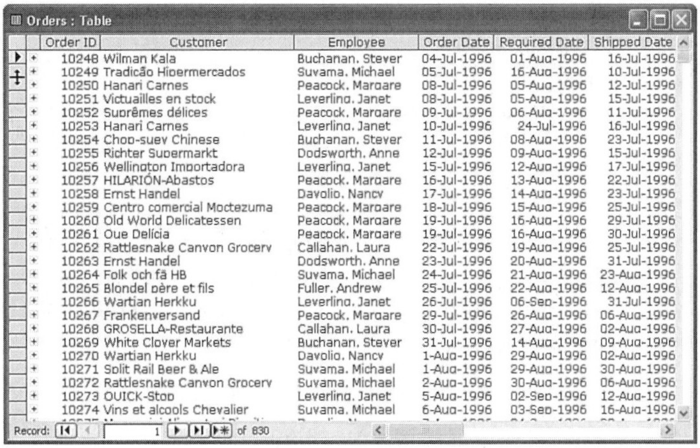

Figure 7.30
This customized Datasheet View uses a 9-point Verdana type and no gridlines. You adjust line spacing, shown here between the second and third record selection buttons, by dragging the double-headed arrow up or down.

- *To change the width of the field columns to accommodate a larger font,* choose Format, Column Width and then click the Best Fit button to let Access determine the size of your columns. You might need to adjust individual column widths by dragging the right edge of the field header with the mouse.

COPYING, EXPORTING, AND MAILING SORTED AND FILTERED DATA

A common use for filters and customized datasheets is to export the filtered and sorted records to another application, such as Microsoft Excel or Word. Several methods for exporting filtered and custom-formatted records are available:

- Copy the entire datasheet to the Clipboard and then paste the datasheet into the other application as a table or a range of cells. Hidden fields don't appear, and formatting (font, font attributes, and row height) is preserved.
- Use the Export feature to export the datasheet to an Excel worksheet (.xls) or a Rich Text Format (.rtf) file for Word or other Windows word-processing applications. (Choose File, Export, and then select the file type you want in the Export Table '*TableName*' To dialog's Save as Type drop-down list of the Save Table In dialog.) Save As/Export preserves the attributes you use to customize the filtered and sorted data when you choose Excel format. Hidden fields, however, appear when you open the resulting file in any version of Excel.

- Use the OfficeLinks toolbar button or choose Tools, Office Links, Analyze It with MS Excel to save the filtered or sorted data in an Excel worksheet; choose Tool, Office Links, Publish It with MS Word to save the data as an RTF document. Whether you choose to Analyze It or Publish It, Access starts Excel or Word with the exported document displayed.

- Use the toolbar button or choose Tool, Office Links, Merge It with MS Word to create form letters with Microsoft Word.
- Choose File, Send To to send the file as an attachment to an email message. Hidden fields don't appear, but formatting isn't preserved in some types of messages.

NOTE

If you make the Database window the active window and choose File, Export, the entire content of the table is exported regardless of the filter you added.

NEW The next chapter provides complete descriptions of Access's traditional data export features, including exporting filtered and sorted tables to Microsoft Word mail-merge documents. Chapter 23, "Exporting and Importing Data with XML," and Chapter 26, "Collaborating with SharePoint Team Services 2.0," describe Access 2003's new data export/import features.

TROUBLESHOOTING

FILTER BY FORM DOESN'T FIND THE EXPECTED RECORDS

Either too few records or records extraneous to the filter appear when using Filter by Form.

Access keeps your last filter settings for a table until you close the table. If you've applied a different filter—whether through filter by selection or filter by form earlier in your current work session—Access might be applying additional filter criteria that you're not expecting. Right-click the datasheet, and choose Remove Filter/Sort to clear all previous filter criteria and ensure that the new filter criteria you enter are the only ones in effect. Alternatively, choose Records, Remove Filter/Sort from the main Access menu.

IN THE REAL WORLD—COMPUTER-BASED SORTING AND SEARCHING

Donald E. Knuth's *Sorting and Searching*, volume 3 of his *The Art of Computer Programming* series, is the seminal work on computer algorithms (programs) to perform sorts and searches. Dr. Knuth is Professor Emeritus of The Art of Computer Programming at Stanford University. Addison-Wesley published the first edition of Sorting and Searching in 1973. There's a good probability that every student who was granted a computer science degree during and after the mid-1970s has a well-worn copy of Knuth's classic text. Knuth updated *Sorting and Searching* with a second edition in mid-1998; the book remains required reading for assembly-language programmers, but you need a good foundation in combinatorial mathematics and set theory to fully understand the contents.

THE INFLUENCE OF COMPUTER POWER ON KNUTH'S APPROACH

As Knuth points out in the first page of the chapter on sorting, a better term to describe the process is "ordering." (The 724-page book has only two chapters: Chapter 6, "Sorting," and Chapter 7, "Searching.") Structured Query Language (SQL) takes Knuth's advice and uses `ORDER BY` clauses to define sort sequences. One of the dictionary definitions of the verb "to sort" is "to arrange according to characteristics," and the definition of "order" includes "arrange" as a synonym.

Both *sort* and *order* infer that the process physically moves records; this was the case in the 1970s, a period when punched cards were the dominant means of computer data entry and storage. The advent of magnetic tape drives eliminated the need for punched card sorting and collating machines, but sorting still required individual records be rewritten to tape in the chosen order. Decks of punched cards and magnetic tape use sequential access, so sorting by merging expedites searching—assuming that records matching your search criteria appear early in the deck or tape. Thus the "Sorting" chapter precedes "Searching," as it does in this book's chapter. Searching is the foundation for all filtering operations.

NOTE

SQL Server's *clustered indexes* physically order records in the order of the primary key to speed execution of multitable queries. When you export Jet tables to SQL Server with Access 2003's Upsizing Wizard, the Wizard automatically creates a clustered index on the primary key field.

Today's PCs are far more powerful than the largest mainframe computers of the 1970s. Multi-gigabyte fixed disk drives in PC clients dwarf the storage capabilities of tape and multi-spindle disk drives of the 1970s and early 1980s. When you apply a sort order to a Jet table or query, records don't change position; Access displays the table records in the desired sequence. If you have plenty of RAM, all the record resequencing occurs in memory because Jet picks those records needed to populate the visible rows of the datasheet, plus some additional records to make page down operations go faster. When Jet runs out of RAM, temporary disk files store the overflow. It's no longer necessary to optimize searching by prior sorting; the brute force approach (searching a random-order file) usually is fast enough for files of moderate (10,000 records) to even large size (1 million or more records).

KNUTH AND INDEXES

Two Russian mathematicians, G. M. Adelson-Velski and E. M. Landis, proposed a balanced binary tree indexing structure in 1963. In a balanced binary tree structure, the length of the search path to any ordered record is never more than 45% longer than the optimum. Jet, like most other desktop RDBMSs, has a balanced binary tree (B-tree) structure; a Jet primary key index orders the records.

One of Knuth's other contributions to computer science is his analysis of binary tree searching on ordered tables. An ordered table's records are physically or logically organized in alphabetic or numeric order by the key field being searched. Binary tree searches optimize the searching process by minimizing the number of comparisons required to zero in on the record(s) with the desired value. Knuth went into great detail on "hashing" algorithms that create a set of unique values to identify each record. Hashing greatly speeds searching on the key field of tables when the key field comprises more than a few characters. The "hash tables" of early databases are called indexes today. SQL Server 2000 still generates temporary hash tables when needed to speed query processing.

When you search on a field that isn't ordered, called a secondary key, search efficiency drops rapidly for large tables. The early approaches used in the 1970s, including a process called combinatorial hashing, have given way to secondary indexes on unordered keys, such as postal codes in a table in which the primary key is a customer name or code. Each secondary key you add decreases the speed at which you can insert new records because of the need to maintain and rebalance the trees of the indexes. Despite the performance of today's PC clients and servers, it's still a good idea to minimize the number of secondary indexes on tables used for online transaction processing (OLTP).

It isn't necessary to understand the underlying details of hashing and balanced B-tree indexes to take full advantage of Access's searching and sorting features. Familiarity with the surprisingly efficient methods used in the early days of computing, however, offers a useful perspective on the dramatic improvements in database design and implementation that has occurred in the 30 years since Knuth published the first edition of *Searching and Sorting*.

CHAPTER 8

Linking, Importing, and Exporting Data

In this chapter

MOVING DATA FROM AND TO OTHER APPLICATIONS

Undoubtedly, every personal computer user has data that can be processed through database-management techniques. Any data that a computer can arrange in tabular form—even tables in word-processing files—can be converted to database tables. The strength of a relational database management system (RDBMS) lies in its capability to handle large numbers of individual pieces of data stored in tables and to relate the pieces of data in a meaningful way.

PC users turn to RDBMSs when the amount of data created exceeds a conventional productivity application's capability to manipulate the data effectively. A common example is a large mailing list created in Microsoft Word. As the number of names in the list increases, using Word to make selective mailings and maintain histories of responses to mailings becomes increasingly difficult. An RDBMS is the most effective type of application for manipulating large lists.

One strong point of Access is its capability to transform existing database tables, spreadsheets, and text files created by other DOS and Windows applications into the Jet .mdb format—a process known as importing a file. Access can export (create) table files in any format in which it can import the files, including Extensible Markup Language (XML) files.

NOTE

> This chapter doesn't include use of Access 2003's new XML import/export features for intranet- and Internet-based database applications. Chapter 23, "Importing and Exporting Data with XML," covers these topics.

Access can link a database table file created by Access or another RDBMS to your current Jet database; Access then acts as a database front end. Because Access has a linking capability, it can use a file created by another RDBMS in its native form. This capability is far less common in other desktop and client/server RDBMSs. When you link a database table from a different RDBMS, you can display and, in many cases, update the linked table as though it were an Access table contained in your .mdb file. If the file containing the table is shared on a network, others can use the file with their applications while it's linked to your database.

The capability to link files is important for two reasons: It lets you connect to multiple Jet databases, and you can create new applications in Access that can coexist with applications created by other database managers. Access 2003 also can link Outlook contacts, tasks, and calendar folders, as well as Outlook Express mail. Outlook 2003 also lets you import and export folders to and from Jet 4.0 tables.

This chapter deals primarily with what are known as desktop database-development applications—a term that distinguishes them from client/server RDBMSs, such as Microsoft SQL Server, IBM DB2, Oracle, and Sybase databases. Client/server RDBMSs are designed specifically for use with networked clients and—except for the Microsoft (SQL Server) Desktop Edition (MSDE)—require you to have an application server, such as

Windows 2000/2003 Server, to run the RDBMS and store the database files. Chapter 19, "Linking Jet Applications to Client/Server Tables," covers use of conventional Access (Jet) front ends with client/server back ends.

NOTE

> This chapter uses conventional Jet 4.0 databases for its examples, but most of the import and export operations described in this chapter also work with Access data projects (ADP) and SQL Server tables. You also can establish links to Jet 4.0 databases and other client/server RDBMSs with the ADP Link Table Wizard. Chapter 20, "Exploring Access Data Projects and SQL Server 2000," describes SQL Server's linking and export/import features.

Working with Tables in Other Database File Formats

Access and other Microsoft programming platforms, such as Visual Studio 6.0 and—increasingly—Visual Studio .NET, dominate today's database front-end development market. Thus the importance of Access's import/link support for legacy desktop database files has decreased as use of Paradox, dBASE, and FoxPro have declined, especially for new projects. Paradox, dBASE, Clipper, and FoxPro now qualify as *legacy* data formats, although today's diehard Visual FoxPro programmers certainly would argue this point.

Conventional desktop database development applications maintain each table in an individual file. Each file contains a header followed by the data. A *header* is a group of bytes that provides information on the file's structure, such as the names and types of fields, number of records in the table, and file length. When you create a table file in dBASE, Visual FoxPro, or Paradox, for example, the file contains only a header. As you add records to the file, the file size increases by the number of bytes required for one record, and the header is updated to reflect the new file size and record count.

Desktop RDBMSs create a variety of supplemental files, some of which are required to import, link, or export RDBMSs:

- Visual FoxPro and dBASE .dbf files store memo-type data in a separate .dbt file. If a FoxPro or dBASE table file contains a memo field, the .dbt file must be available. If the .dbt file is missing, you can't import or link dBASE or Visual FoxPro tables that contain a memo field.
- Use of .ndx (dBASE III), .mdx (dBASE IV+), or .idx or .cdx (FoxPro) index files is optional. You always should use index files when you have them. If you don't link the index files when you link an indexed .dbf table file, modifications you make to the linked tables aren't reflected in the index, which causes errors to occur when you try to use the indexed tables with dBASE. Linking an indexed dBASE table requires the Borland Database Engine (BDE) described in the following Caution.

8

- Paradox stores information about the primary-key index file (.px) in the associated table (.db) file; the .px file for the .db file must be available for Access to open a Paradox .db file for updating. Access links the .px file automatically if it exists. Like dBASE, Paradox stores memo-type data in a separate file with a .mb extension. Linking an indexed Paradox table also requires the BDE.

TIP

You must have exclusive access to the dBASE file when you first create the link; multiuser (shared) access is supported thereafter. For more information see the "Using dBASE Data with Access 2002 and Jet" Knowledge Base topic at `http://support.microsoft.com/default.aspx?scid=kb;EN-US;290867`.

Office 2003 installs Jet 4.0 Service Pack 7, which doesn't support multiuser access to Paradox files; you must have exclusive access to the Paradox file whenever you have the linked file open. See the "Using Paradox Data with Access 2002 and Jet" at `http://support.microsoft.com/default.aspx?scid=kb;EN-US;286246`.

CAUTION

You can't attach dBASE 7-8 or Paradox indexes to linked .dbf or .db files unless you have the Borland Database Engine (BDE) from Borland (formerly Inprise) Corporation installed on your computer. The inability to attach indexes means that any records you add or in which you change values of indexed fields no longer are accessible from dBASE 7-8 or Paradox applications that rely on table indexes. (Almost all commercial dBASE and Paradox applications use indexes.)

You need the BDE to export or create read or write links to Paradox 7-8 and dBASE 7-8 files. You can obtain more information on the BDE, which is included with the Delphi 4.0 development platform, at `http://info.borland.com/devsupport/bde/`. If you have a BDE version earlier than 5.01, you can obtain a no-charge upgrade to version 5.1.1 at `http://info.borland.com/devsupport/bde/bdeupdate.html`.

All supplemental files must be in the same folder as the related database file to be used by Access.

TIP

Create a new folder to store the tables you import or export. The default folder for exporting and importing files is \My Documents in all current Windows operating systems. If you intend to import or export a large number of files, change the Default Database Folder entry in the General page of the Options dialog (choose Tools, Options).

DEALING WITH PC DATABASE FILES

Access can import and export, subject to the preceding limitations, the following types of database table files used by the most common PC database managers:

- **dBASE .dbf table and .dbt memo files as well as dBASE III .ndx and dBASE IV, 5.0, and 7.0 .mdx index files**—dBASE III+ files are a common denominator of the PC

RDBMS industry. Most PC RDBMSs and all common spreadsheet applications can import and export .dbf files; the most popular formats are dBASE III and IV. Some of these RDBMSs can update existing .ndx and .mdx index files, and a few RDBMSs can create these index files. Access 2003 links and exports .ndx and .mdx indexes only if you have the BDE installed. You must have version 5.01+ of the BDE to import, export, or link dBASE 7.0/8.0 tables. When this book was written, the current version was 5.1.1.

- **Visual FoxPro .dbf table and .dbc database container files**—Access 2003 requires the Microsoft Visual FoxPro ODBC driver (VFPODBC.dll) for import and link operations. Prior to OLE DB and ActiveX Data Objects (ADO), Open Database Connectivity (ODBC) was Microsoft's preferred technology for connecting to client/server databases and other data sources.

NOTE

Windows 2000 installs VFPODBC.dll as a component of Microsoft Data Access Components (MDAC) 2.5, but Windows XP and .NET Server install MDAC 2.6, which doesn't include the Visual FoxPro driver. You can download and run version 6.01.8629 of the FoxPro ODBC driver installer (Vfpodbc.msi) from `http://msdn.microsoft.com/vfoxpro/downloads/addons/odbc.asp`. This version, which is the latest (and final) FoxPro ODBC driver that Microsoft offers, has serious limitations when exporting Jet tables to FoxPro .dbf or .dbc files. You receive an "Error -7778" message if you attempt to use a file data source. The Microsoft Knowledge Base article at `http://support.microsoft.com/support/kb/articles/q212/8/86.asp` confirms the problem.

If you use a Machine data source, the filename and all field names must be eight characters or less, and field names can't contain spaces. The Knowledge Base article at `http://support.microsoft.com/support/kb/articles/q237/8/19.asp` has more information on this issue.

- **Paradox 3.x, 4.x, 5.x, 7.x, and 8.x .db table, .mb memo, and .px primary-key files**—Access 2003 supports importing and exporting Paradox 3.x, 4.x, and 5.x .db and .mb files. Access doesn't generate .px files when you export a .db file. You can link Paradox 3-5 files with or without .px indexes, but if you don't have a .px index, the linked table won't open in Datasheet view.

NOTE

If you work in a multiuser environment, you must have exclusive access to the file you intend to import. No one else can have this file open when you initiate the importing process, and everyone else is denied access to the file until you close the Import dialog.

CAUTION

Make sure that you work on a backup, not on the original copy of the linked file, until you're certain that your updates to the data in the linked table are valid for the existing database application.

LINKING AND IMPORTING EXTERNAL ISAM TABLES

ISAM is an acronym for indexed sequential access method, the architecture used for all desktop RDBMS tables. To link or import a dBASE or Paradox file as a table in Access 2000 or 2002 file format, follow these steps:

> **NOTE**
>
> Linking an external file to an Access database was referred to as attaching a table in Access 95 and earlier. Don't confuse linking an external file to an Access database with OLE Object field links to image or sound files; when you link an external file, you just give Access information about the external file necessary to open, read, and modify the data in that file.

1. If you have a test database that you can use for this procedure, open it, and skip to step 4.
2. If you don't have a test database, create a sample to use throughout this chapter. Click the Blank Database link of the task pane's New File page to display the File New Database dialog.
3. Navigate to the folder in which to store the new database, type a name, such as LinkTest.mdb, in the Filename text box and click Create. Access creates and tests the new database.
4. In this example, you link an external table to the database. Choose File, Get External Data, Link Tables or click the Link icon to open the Link dialog; the Link dialog is a variation of your operating system's Open dialog. If you choose File, Get External Data, Import, the Import dialog opens.
5. Open the Files of Type drop-down list to select the file type you want to link, as shown in Figure 8.1. (If you have a Paradox table with a primary key index to link, select Paradox. Otherwise, select dBASE III, dBASE IV, DBase 5, or another database type as appropriate to the format of your table file.)

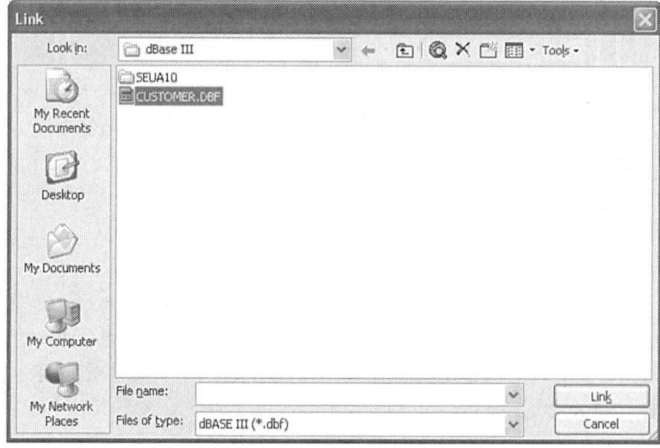

Figure 8.1
Navigate to the folder that holds the database file to link and select the type of database file in the drop-down list.

Power Tools

NOTE

The \Seua11\Chaptr08 folder of the accompanying CD-ROM has subfolders that contain example dBASE III and IV, FoxPro 6, Paradox, and text files that you can import or link to your test database. All examples in this chapter assume that you've installed the sample database files to C:\Program Files\Seua11\Chaptr## folders and that the read-only attribute of the files isn't set.

6. Double-click the name of the table you want to link or import (or click the name to select it and then click the Link button). Access supplies the standard extensions for dBASE and Paradox table files.
7. If the Paradox file you choose is encrypted and requires a password to decrypt it, the Password Required dialog opens. Type the password and press Enter.
8. After you successfully link or import the file, a dialog confirms this operation (see Figure 8.2). If you link more than one table with the same name, Access automatically appends a sequential digit to the table name. If a memo or other related file is missing, you receive an error message at this point.

Figure 8.2
This message box confirms the linking process.

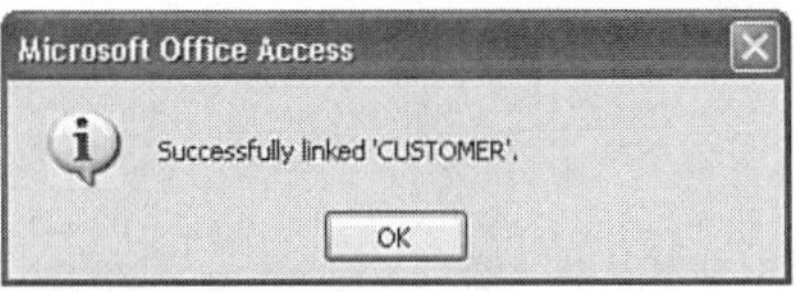

NOTE

The Link (or Import) dialog remains open at this point. If you want to link or import additional external tables to this database (most Paradox and xBase databases consist of several separate table files), repeat steps 6 through 9 for all the files you want to link or import. If you're linking external Access tables, you can select all the tables you want to link at once by clicking each one.

9. In the Link dialog, click Close. The table(s) you linked or imported now are listed in the Database window. If you linked a file, Access adds an icon that shows the type of database table and an arrow to indicate the table is linked. Figure 8.3 illustrates linked dBASE CUSTOMER, Paradox Employee, and dBASE EMPLOYEE1 tables. Access added the "1" suffix, because the Paradox Employee table was present before adding the dBASE EMPLOYEE table.
10. Double-click the entry for the table you linked to display the records in Table Datasheet view (see Figure 8.4).

NOTE

Images stored in the sample Employee.mb file in the ...\Chaptr08\Paradox folder are in Access OLE Object format, so you can open the images in Windows Paint by double-clicking a Bitmap Image cell.

Figure 8.3
Linked tables are identified in the Database window by an icon for the file type (dB for dBASE and Px for Paradox) with an arrow to represent the link.

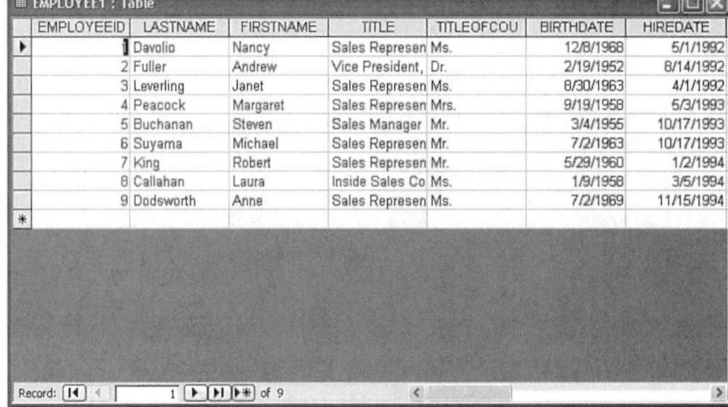

EMPLOYEE1 : Table

EMPLOYEEID	LASTNAME	FIRSTNAME	TITLE	TITLEOFCOU	BIRTHDATE	HIREDATE
1	Davolio	Nancy	Sales Represen	Ms.	12/8/1968	5/1/1992
2	Fuller	Andrew	Vice President,	Dr.	2/19/1952	8/14/1992
3	Leverling	Janet	Sales Represen	Ms.	8/30/1963	4/1/1992
4	Peacock	Margaret	Sales Represen	Mrs.	9/19/1958	5/3/1993
5	Buchanan	Steven	Sales Manager	Mr.	3/4/1955	10/17/1993
6	Suyama	Michael	Sales Represen	Mr.	7/2/1963	10/17/1993
7	King	Robert	Sales Represen	Mr.	5/29/1960	1/2/1994
8	Callahan	Laura	Inside Sales Co	Ms.	1/9/1958	3/5/1994
9	Dodsworth	Anne	Sales Represen	Ms.	7/2/1969	11/15/1994

Record: 1 of 9

Figure 8.4
The EMPLOYEE1 table is linked from a pair of dBASE III tables—EMPLOYEE.DBF and EMPLPLOYEE.DBT. The EMPLOYEE.DBT file contains the data for the Notes field and doesn't appear in the Database window.

After you link an external file as a table, you can use it almost as though it were a table in your own database. If you don't have the BDE installed, linked dBASE 5 and later and all Paradox tables are read-only. A general limitation is that you can't change the structure of a linked table: field names, field data types, or the Field Size properties. There is no limitation on changing the structure or properties of an imported table.

NOTE

> Although you can't change field properties for linked tables, you can change the name of the attached table within this database only. Select the link, press F2, and type the new name for the table. The name for the table (called an alias) is changed only in the current Access database and not in the native database.

LINKING VISUAL FOXPRO TABLES WITH ODBC

You can use the ODBC drivers provided with Office 2003 to link Visual FoxPro databases or tables to Jet databases. Data source is a synonym for database when you use the ODBC Application Programming Interface (API) to link tables.

TIP

Windows 2000 installs 32-bit Excel, FoxPro, Paradox, Access, dBASE, and Text file ODBC drivers, plus the SQL Server and Oracle client/server drivers. As mentioned in the earlier "Dealing with PC Database Files" section, Windows XP doesn't install the FoxPro ODBC driver.

The ODBC Data Source Administrator Control Panel tool is installed by the Windows operating system. Windows XP/2000+ call the ODBC Manager's icon *Data Sources (ODBC)*, which you find in Control Panel's Administrative Tools folder. You can determine which drivers are installed by clicking the Drivers tab of the Administrator dialog.

Follow these steps to link Visual FoxPro 6.0 table(s) to an Access database via ODBC:

1. With an Access database open, choose File, Get External Data, Link Table to display the Link dialog (refer to Figure 8.1).
2. Select ODBC Databases in the Files of Type drop-down list. Access closes the Link dialog and displays the Select Data Source dialog. If you want to create a file to define a data source (except for FoxPro tables) that you can share with others, accept the default File Data Source page. This example uses a Machine Data Source installed by the Visual FoxPro ODBC driver, so click the Machine Data Source tab.
3. Select Microsoft Visual FoxPro Tables (for a .dbf file) in the Data Source Name (DSN) list, and click OK to open the Configure Connection dialog. If you want to link tables from a .dbc file, select the Visual FoxPro Database DSN, as shown in Figure 8.5, and click OK to close the dialog.

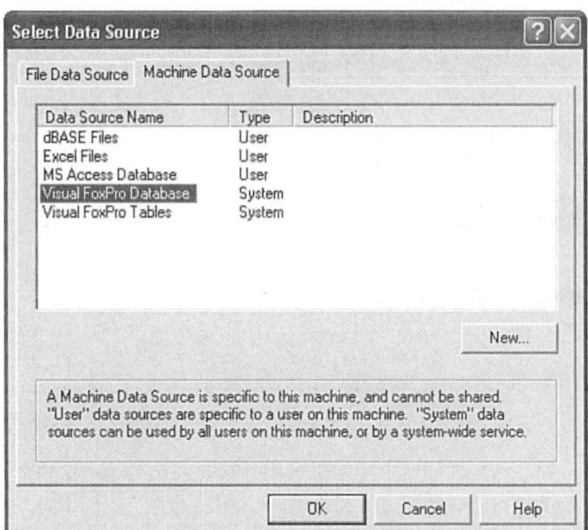

Figure 8.5
Select the ODBC driver for the type of database to link from the list of drivers installed on your machine.

NOTE

If you haven't installed the FoxPro ODBC driver, you will receive a Visual FoxPro ODBC Error message at this point.

4. If you chose the Visual FoxPro Database DSN, select the Visual FoxPro Database (.DBC) option, click Browse to open the Select Database dialog, navigate to the folder containing the .dbc file, and select the file in the list (see Figure 8.6).

   Otherwise Accept the Free Table Directory, and click Browse to display the Select Directory Containing Free Tables dialog. If necessary, use the Drives and Directories lists to navigate to the folder in which your FoxPro files are stored in the Folders list. In either case, click Open and OK to display the Link Tables dialog.

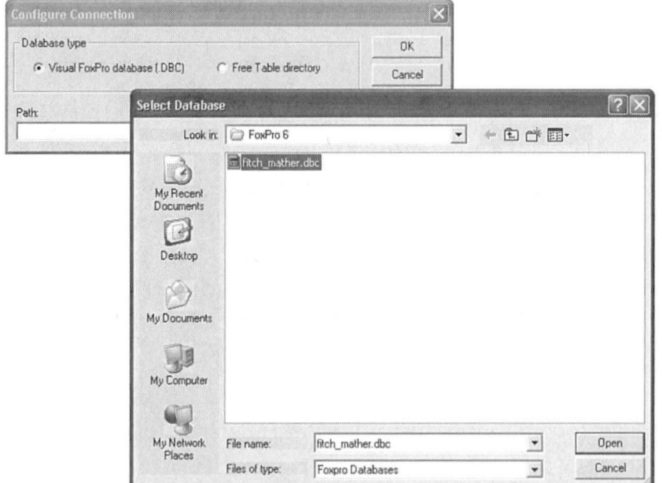

Figure 8.6
Select the .dbc file or the folder containing the FoxPro .dbf file(s) to configure the ODBC connection with the Office 2003 FoxPro driver.

5. The Link Tables dialog lists the FoxPro tables in the folder you selected in step 4. Click each table name to select it, or click Select All. After you select all the tables that you want to link (see Figure 8.7), click OK.

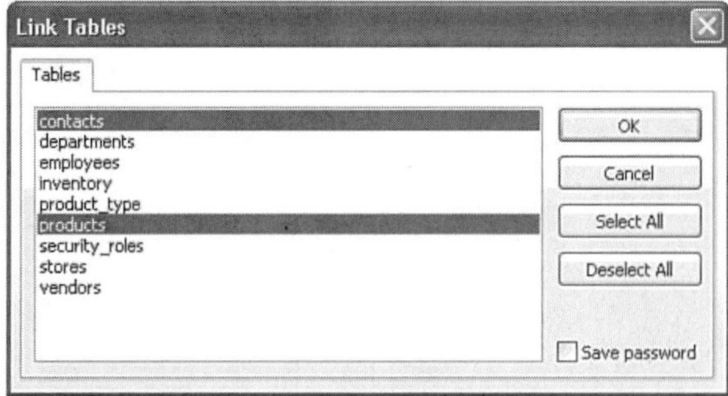

Figure 8.7
The Link Tables dialog lists all FoxPro tables in the folder or in a .dbc container file. Select the table(s) you want to link to your Jet database, and click OK.

6. If any of the table(s) you selected don't have a primary-key index, the Select Unique Record Identifier dialog opens. If you want to update the data in the ODBC-linked table without a primary-key index, you must select a field (or combination of fields) that creates a unique record identification for each row in the table—essentially, you

create a surrogate primary key for the linked table. To select a field, click it, and then click OK. In the example in Figure 8.8, the primary-key field of the customers table is customerid.

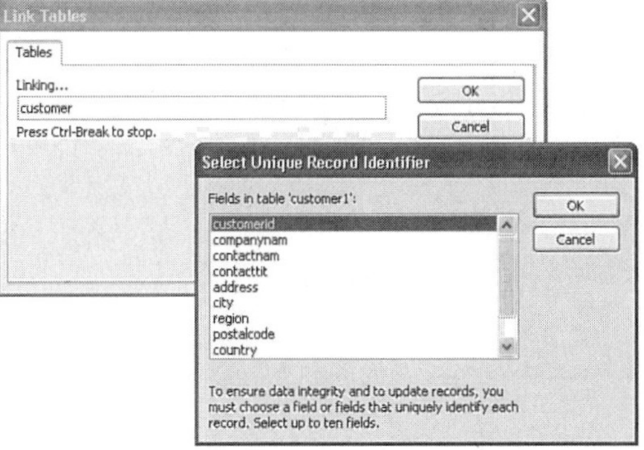

Figure 8.8
If the folder with the tables or the .dbc file doesn't include a primary-key index for any of the tables you select to link, you must select a field to act as a surrogate primary key in the Select Unique Identifier dialog.

NOTE

> All FoxPro 6.0 tables in the \Program Files\Seua10\Chaptr08\FoxPro 6 folder have primary key indexes, so the Select Unique Record dialog doesn't appear when you link these tables.

Your linked Visual FoxPro tables appear in the Database window (with the ODBC globe turned to display Africa), as shown in Figure 8.9. Any table linked by ODBC displays the globe icon. Double-click the table icon to display your newly linked Visual FoxPro table (see Figure 8.10). By default, Visual FoxPro table and field names appear in lowercase. The maximum length of a FoxPro or dBASE field name is 10 characters.

Figure 8.9
The FoxPro contacts and products files are linked to the Jet database. The two dBASE tables and the Paradox table have been renamed in this figure.

Figure 8.10 The linked FoxPro products table is updatable, as indicated by the tentative append (*) record at the end of the table records.

products : Table

product_id	product_sku	product_name	product_brand	product_type_id	product_desc	product_retail_p
17		Captain's Mate	Captain Barbeq	1	Gas rectangular	159.95
18		Captain's Cooke	Captain Barbeq	1	Two burner gas	199.95
19		Captain's Kitche	Captain Barbeq	1	Two burner grill	249.95
20		Wire Composte	The Terra Firma	1	Heavy-gauge wi	59.95
21		Compost Bucke	The Terra Firma	1	Under-the-sink (	10.95
22		Wooden Worm	The Terra Firma	1	Top opening wo	99.95
23		Circular Compo:	The Terra Firma	1	Plastic, circular	59.95
24		Compost Bags	The Terra Firma	1	10 Biodegradab	49.95
25		Box rack	Trey Research	3	Steel box pot ra	179
26		Hook rack	Trey Research	3	Steel hook pot r	309
27		Lake 4	Lakes & Sons	3	Four pc. cookse	150
28		Lake 3	Lakes & Sons	3	Three pc. cooks	80
29		Adirondack Cha	Enchantment L	1	Adirondack Cha	160
30		Hexagonal picni	Enchantment L	1	Hexagonal picni	170
31		Pot Set #1	Main Street Ma	3	4 pc. Cookset	159
32		Pot Set #2	Main Street Ma	3	5 pc. Cookset	140
33		Pot Rack #1	Main Street Ma	3	6 pc. Cookset	180
34		Pot Rack #2	Main Street Ma	3	7 pc. Cookset	190
35		Lawn Chair	Northwind Trade	1	Cedar lawn chai	155
36		Table and Awni	Northwind Trade	1	Mahogany lawn	400
*						

Record: 1 of 36

Access detects problems with linked or imported tables that might cause errors when you try to use the tables with Access. Importing and linking errors are the subject of the "Troubleshooting" section near the end of this chapter.

DEALING WITH IMAGES IN EXTERNAL DATABASE FILES

Most database managers designed for Windows include some form of graphics field data type. Early versions of Paradox, for example, provide a special field data type for graphics; later versions support OLE objects. Although early versions of dBASE lack a field data type for graphics, third-party software firms publish applications that let you store images in dBASE memo fields. Various add-on applications for desktop RDBMSs let programmers display and edit graphic images. The images usually are in individual files, but a few third-party applications continue to place images in memo files.

When you try to import or link desktop database files containing images or other binary data, you might receive an error message that the memo file is corrupted or that you can't import the .db or .dbf file that contains the offending memo or graphics field. In rare cases—usually involving tiny images—you can import the .dbf and .dbt files, but you see random characters in the Access memo field. With Paradox tables, the graphics or binary fields disappear from the table.

The simplest approach to dealing with graphics files missing from imported tables is to convert the individual files to Graphic Interchange Format (.gif) or Joint Photographic Experts Group (.jpg) format, and then use Windows Paint to import the images into an OLE Object field. The following procedure uses the employees table imported from the fitch_mather.dbc FoxPro 6 database of the preceding section, and the nine bitmap files, Empid1.bmp–Empid9.bmp, in the \Program Files\Microsoft Office\Office 10\Samples folder.

TIP

> The Empid#.bmp files are relatively small, but .bmp files of large images with 24-bit or 32-bit color depth can become very large. Using .gif or .jpg format to compress the images before you insert them in an OLE Object field saves a substantial amount of disk space.

To add an OLE Object field and images from files to an imported (or new) table, do this:

1. Open the table in Design view, select the field below the location for the new OLE Object field, and press Insert to add an empty field. This example uses the employees table imported from the FoxPro Fitch&Mather.dbc database.
2. Type the Field Name, **emp_photo** for this example, and select OLE Object as the Data Type (see Figure 8.11).

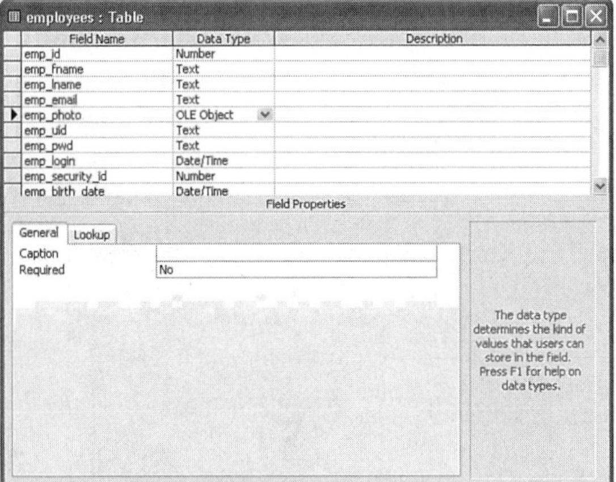

Figure 8.11
Add an OLE Object field to the imported table to hold image data in OLE 2.0 format or to create a link to external image files.

3. Return to Datasheet view; saving the design changes, right-click the OLE Object cell in the first row, and choose Insert Object to open the Microsoft Access (formerly Insert Object) dialog.
4. Select the Create From File option, click Browse to open the Browse dialog, and navigate to the folder that contains your image files (\Program Files, Microsoft Office\Office 10\Samples for this example).
5. Double-click the image file you want to embed in the field (Empid1.bmp for the first image), which adds the well-formed path to the file in the text box (see Figure 8.12).

NOTE

> Instead of embedding the image in the database, you can create a link to the image's source file by selecting the Link check box. Linking reduces the size of the .mdb file, but requires a permanent path to the source image files. If a network server stores the image files, the path might change. If this happens, you receive an error when attempting to open the linked file.

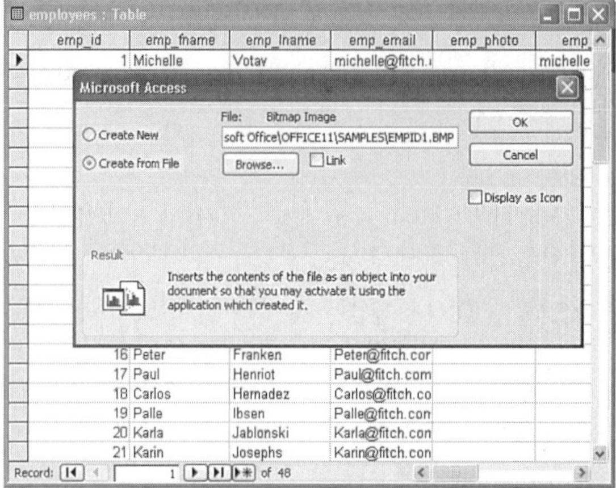

Figure 8.12
By default, the bitmap data is included in the OLE Object field. Select the Link check box to maintain the image data in the source .gif, .jpg, or .bmp files.

6. Click OK to embed or link the image, which adds a Bitmap Image value to the cell. Double-click the cell to open the image in Windows Paint (see Figure 8.13). You can edit the image in Paint; Access automatically saves your changes when you close Paint and return to the table.

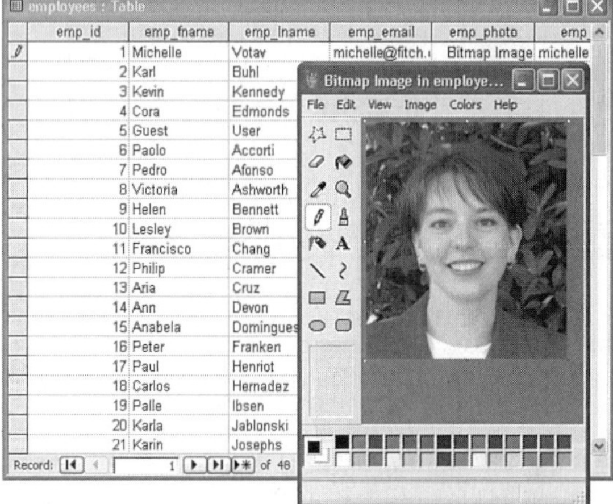

Figure 8.13
Double-clicking a Bitmap Image cell opens the image for editing in Windows Paint. If you've associated a different OLE 2.0-compliant application to the file type, the image opens in that application.

7. Repeat steps 4, 5, and 6 for each image to add, selecting the row appropriate to the image file.

The employees table of the LinkTest.mdb database in the \Seua10\Chaptr08 folder of the accompanying CD-ROM includes several embedded bitmap images.

CONVERTING FIELD DATA TYPES TO JET DATA TYPES

When you import or link a file, Access reads the header of the file and converts the field data types to Access data types. Access usually is successful in this conversion because it offers a greater variety of data types than most of the other widely used PC RDBMSs. Table 8.1 shows the correspondence of field data types between dBASE, Paradox, and Access files.

TABLE 8.1 FIELD DATA TYPE CONVERSION BETWEEN ACCESS AND OTHER RDBMSS

dBASE III/IV/5	Paradox 3.x, 4.x, 5.0	Access
Character	Alphanumeric	Text (Specify Size property)
Numeric, Float*	Number, Money, BCD*	Number (Double) Number (Single) Number (Byte)
	Short Number Long Number AutoIncrement	Number (Integer) Number (Long) AutoNumber
Logical	Logical	Yes/No
Date	Date, Time, Timestamp*	Date/Time
Memo	Memo, Formatted Memo, Binary* OLE	Memo OLE Object

**Sometimes two types of field data, separated by commas, are shown within a single column in Table 8.1. When Access exports a table that contains a data type that corresponds with one of the two field data types, the first data type is assigned to the field in the exported table. The Float data type is available only in dBASE IV and 5.*

TIP

> If you're importing tables, you can change the field data type and the Field Size property to make them more suitable to the type of information contained in the field. When you change a data type or Field Size, however, follow the precautions noted in Chapter 5, "Working with Jet Databases and Tables."
>
> Remember that you can't change the field data type or Field Size property of linked tables. You can, however, use the Format property with imported or linked tables to display the data in any format compatible with the field data type of imported or linked files. You can change any remaining properties that are applicable to the field data type, such as validation rules and text. By using the Caption property, you can give the field a new and more descriptive name.

→ To review field properties of Jet databases, **see** "Choosing Field Data Types, Sizes, and Formats," **p. 162**.

8

Using the Linked Table Manager Add-in to Relink Tables

Moving linked files to another folder or logical drive causes the existing links to break. Access provides an add-in assistant known as the Linked Table Manager to simplify relinking tables.

If you move a Jet, dBASE, FoxPro, or Paradox file that provides a table linked to a Jet 4.0 database, choose Tools, Database Utilities, Linked Table Manager. The Linked Table Manager's window lists all tables linked to the database. The list also displays the path to the database containing the linked table(s) at the time the link was created, with the exception of the path to files or databases linked by ODBC. Click the check box of the file(s) whose location(s) might have changed (see Figure 8.14).

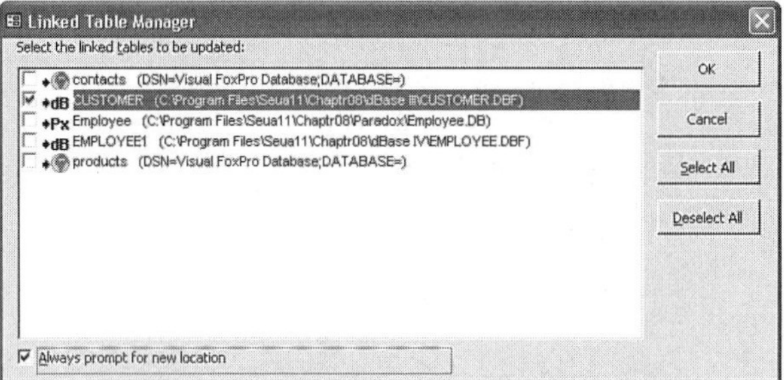

Figure 8.14
The Linked Table Manager handles recreating links to tables or databases that have moved since you created the original links to a Jet database.

TIP

> You also can view the path to the folder containing a linked table by opening the linked table in Design view, opening the Table Properties window, and scrolling through the contents of the Description text box.

Click OK to display the Select New Location of *TableName* dialog shown in Figure 8.15. (If your linked files haven't moved, Mark the Always Prompt for New Location check box to open the dialog.) Navigate to the folder where the table or database is located; then double-click the new link reference and close the dialog. If Access successfully refreshes the table links, it displays a dialog saying so; click OK to close the success message dialog. Click the Close button of the Linked Table Manager to close the add-in.

NOTE

> If you select a table linked by ODBC, the ODBC Manager's Select Data source dialog opens so you can recreate the data source for the linked table or database.

TIP

> The Linked Table Manager can refresh links only for tables that have been moved to another disk or folder–the table must have the same name. If the linked table's file was renamed, you must delete the table link from your Access database and relink the table under its new name.

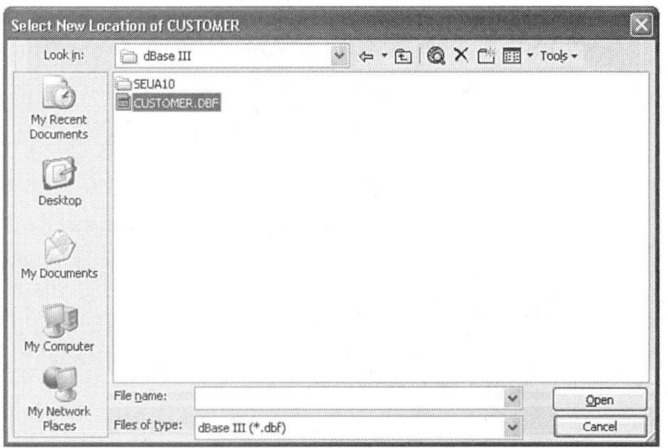

Figure 8.15
The Select New Location of *TableName* dialog lets you substitute another folder or database file for the broken link.

IMPORTING VERSUS LINKING DATABASE FILES AS TABLES

The preceding examples demonstrate the differences between the behavior of Access with linked and imported database files. You should link tables contained in another database file if any of the following conditions exist:

- You use another RDBMS to modify the file in any way.
- The database or file is resident on another computer, such as a server, and its size is larger than fits comfortably on your fixed disk.
- You observe the recommended database application development practice of maintaining separate .mdb files for tables and your application's objects.

You should import a table when one of the following conditions exists:

- You've decided on Access as your database development platform and have mothballed existing dBASE, Paradox, or FoxPro applications.
- You're developing an application and want to use data types or Field Size properties different from those Jet has chosen for a linked table.
- You or the users of your application don't have online access to the required database files and can't link them.
- You want to use a primary-key field different from the field specified in a desktop database or client/server table. This situation can occur when the structure of one or more of the files you plan to use seriously violates one or more of the normalization rules described in Chapter 4, "Exploring Relational Database Theory and Practice."
- You need Access to allow duplicate values in your table when a primary-key field of a linked table precludes duplicate values.

In most cases, importing a table is a one-way process. After you import and modify the table, it's unlikely that applications in the source RDBMS will be able to use an exported version of the modified table.

8

IMPORTING AND LINKING SPREADSHEET FILES

Access can import files created by spreadsheet and related applications, such as project management systems, in the following formats:

- Excel 3, 4, 5, 7, 9x, and 200x .xls files as well as task and resource files created by Microsoft Project in .xls format. A single ISAM driver handles the import of all Excel formats.
- Lotus 1-2-3 .wks (Release 1 and Symphony), .wk1 (Release 2), and .wk3 (Release 3 and later), and .wj* files created by the DOS version of Lotus. Most spreadsheet applications can export files to at least one of these Lotus formats.

NOTE

> You can use OLE to embed or link charts created by Microsoft Excel and stored in files with an .xlc extension. Copy the contents of the file to the Windows Clipboard from Excel. Choose Edit, Paste to embed or link (via OLE) the chart in a field of the OLE Object type; then display the chart on a form or print it on a report as an unbound object. Similarly, you can embed or link most views displayed in Microsoft Project, which also uses the Microsoft Graph applet; the exceptions are task and resource forms and the Task PERT chart.

CREATING A TABLE BY IMPORTING AN EXCEL WORKSHEET

Figure 8.16 illustrates the preferred format for Excel and other spreadsheet applications for importing to Access and other RDBMS tables. Most spreadsheet applications refer to this format as a database. The names of the fields are typed in the first row and the remainder of the database range consists of data. The type of data in each column must be consistent within the database range you select.

CAUTION

> All cells that comprise the worksheet range to be imported into an Access table must have frozen values. Frozen values substitute numeric results for the Excel expressions used to create the values. When cells include formulas, Access imports the cells as blank data cells. Freezing the values causes Access to overwrite the formulas in the spreadsheet that has the frozen values. If the range to import includes formulas, save a copy of your .xls file with a new name.
>
> Open the new workbook, select the worksheet and range to import, and freeze the values by pressing Ctrl+C. Choose Edit, Paste Special, select the Values option, and click OK. Save the new worksheet by its new name and use this file to import the data.

TIP

> You get an opportunity to assign field names to the columns in the worksheet during the importation process, although the process is easier if you add field names as column headings first.

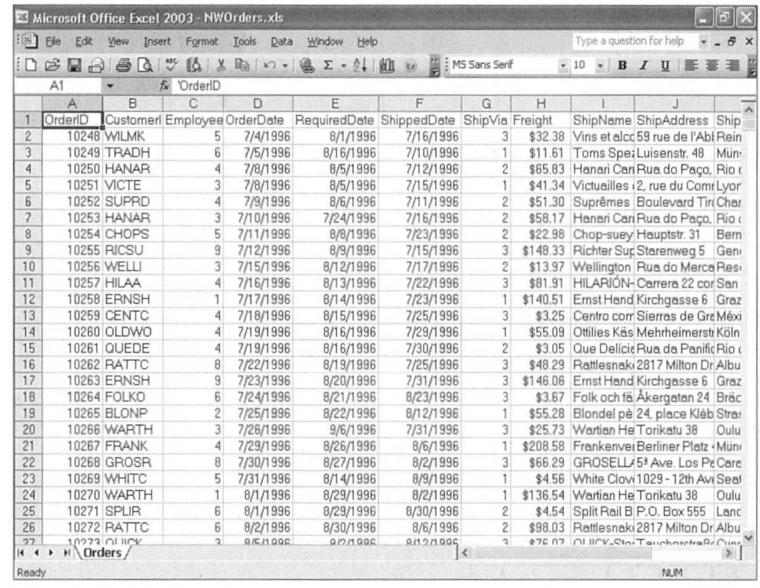

	A	B	C	D	E	F	G	H	I	J	
1	OrderID	Customerl	Employee	OrderDate	RequiredDate	ShippedDate	ShipVia	Freight	ShipName	ShipAddress	Ship
2	10248	WILMK	5	7/4/1996	8/1/1996	7/16/1996	3	$32.38	Vins et alcc	59 rue de l'Abl	Rein
3	10249	TRADH	6	7/5/1996	8/16/1996	7/10/1996	1	$11.61	Toms Spe:	Luisenstr. 48	Mün:
4	10250	HANAR	4	7/8/1996	8/5/1996	7/12/1996	2	$65.83	Hanari Cari	Rua do Paço,	Rio (
5	10251	VICTE	3	7/8/1996	8/5/1996	7/15/1996	1	$41.34	Victuailles	2, rue du Comr	Lyor
6	10252	SUPRD	4	7/9/1996	8/6/1996	7/11/1996	2	$51.30	Suprêmes	Boulevard Tir	Char
7	10253	HANAR	3	7/10/1996	7/24/1996	7/16/1996	2	$58.17	Hanari Cari	Rua do Paço,	Rio (
8	10254	CHOPS	5	7/11/1996	8/8/1996	7/23/1996	2	$22.98	Chop-suey	Hauptstr. 31	Bern
9	10255	RICSU	9	7/12/1996	8/9/1996	7/15/1996	3	$148.33	Richter Sup	Starenweg 5	Gen
10	10256	WELLI	3	7/15/1996	8/12/1996	7/17/1996	2	$13.97	Wellington	Rua do Merca	Res
11	10257	HILAA	4	7/16/1996	8/13/1996	7/22/1996	3	$81.91	HILARIÓN-	Carrera 22 cor	San
12	10258	ERNSH	1	7/17/1996	8/14/1996	7/23/1996	1	$140.51	Ernst Hand	Kirchgasse 6	Graz
13	10259	CENTC	4	7/18/1996	8/15/1996	7/25/1996	3	$3.25	Centro com	Sierras de Gra	Méxi
14	10260	OLDWO	4	7/19/1996	8/16/1996	7/29/1996	1	$55.09	Ottilies Käs	Mehrheimerstr	Köln
15	10261	QUEDE	4	7/19/1996	8/16/1996	7/30/1996	2	$3.05	Que Delícia	Rua da Panific	Rio (
16	10262	RATTC	8	7/22/1996	8/19/1996	7/25/1996	3	$48.29	Rattlesnak	2817 Milton Dr	Albu
17	10263	ERNSH	9	7/23/1996	8/20/1996	7/31/1996	3	$146.06	Ernst Hand	Kirchgasse 6	Graz
18	10264	FOLKO	6	7/24/1996	8/21/1996	8/23/1996	3	$3.67	Folk och fä	Åkergatan 24	Bräc
19	10265	BLONP	2	7/25/1996	8/22/1996	8/12/1996	1	$55.28	Blondel pè	24, place Kléb	Stra
20	10266	WARTH	3	7/26/1996	9/6/1996	7/31/1996	3	$25.73	Wartian He	Torikatu 38	Oulu
21	10267	FRANK	4	7/29/1996	8/26/1996	8/6/1996	1	$208.58	Frankenve	Berliner Platz	Mün
22	10268	GROSR	8	7/30/1996	8/27/1996	8/2/1996	3	$66.29	GROSELL/	5ª Ave. Los Pa	Care
23	10269	WHITC	5	7/31/1996	8/14/1996	8/9/1996	1	$4.56	White Clov	1029 - 12th Av	Sea
24	10270	WARTH	1	8/1/1996	8/29/1996	8/2/1996	1	$136.54	Wartian He	Torikatu 38	Oulu
25	10271	SPLIR	6	8/1/1996	8/29/1996	8/30/1996	2	$4.54	Split Rail B	P.O. Box 555	Lanc
26	10272	RATTC	6	8/2/1996	8/30/1996	8/6/1996	2	$98.03	Rattlesnak	2817 Milton Dr	Albu

Figure 8.16
This Excel 2003 worksheet was created by exporting the Orders table to a workbook file. The worksheet serves as an example for importing a worksheet to an Access table.

To prepare the data in an Excel spreadsheet for importation into a Jet table, follow these steps:

1. Launch Excel and then open the .xls file that contains the data you want to import.
2. Add field names above the first row of the data you plan to export (if you haven't done so). Field names can't include periods (.), exclamation points (!), or square brackets ([]). You can't have duplicate field names. If you include improper characters in field names or use duplicate field names, you see an error message when you attempt to import the worksheet.
3. If your worksheet contains cells with data you don't want to include in the imported table, select the range that contains the field names row and all the rows of data needed for the table. In Excel, choose Insert, Name, Define and then name the range.
4. If the worksheet cells include expressions, freeze the values as described in the caution preceding these steps.
5. Save the Excel file (use a different filename if you froze values) and exit Excel to conserve Windows resources for Access, if you're short on RAM.

Now you're ready to import worksheets from the Excel workbook file, NWOrders.xls for this example. (NWOrders.xls is located in the \Seua11\Chaptr08 folder of the accompanying CD-ROM). To import the prepared data from an Excel spreadsheet into an Access table, follow these steps:

1. Open the database you want to add the new table to. The Database window must be active before you can import a file.

2. Choose File, Get External Data, Import to open the Import dialog, select Microsoft Excel (*.xls) in the Files of Type drop-down list, and navigate to the folder that contains the .xls file with the worksheet to import (see Figure 8.17).

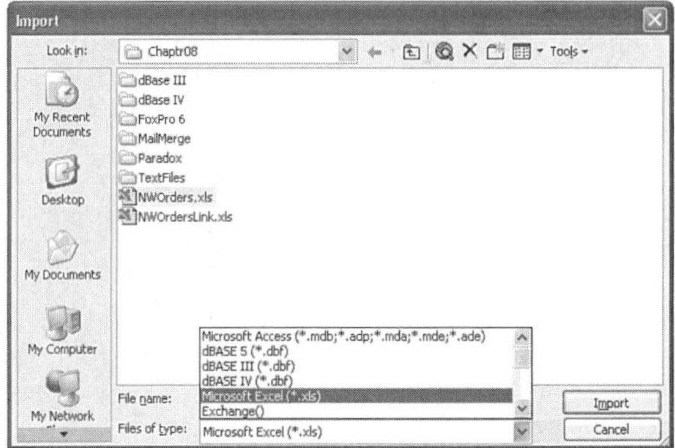

Figure 8.17 Navigate to the folder, select Microsoft Excel (.xls) in the Files of Type list, and select the worksheet to import.

3. Double-click the name of the Excel workbook that contains the spreadsheet you want to import (you also can click the filename to select it and then click Import). Access invokes the Import Spreadsheet Wizard (see Figure 8.18).

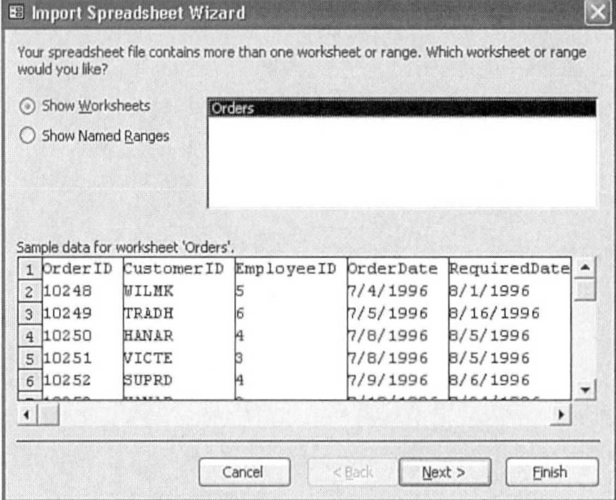

Figure 8.18 The first dialog of the Import Spreadsheet Wizard lets you select multiple worksheets or named ranges to import as tables.

4. If you're importing an entire worksheet, select the Show Worksheets option; if you're importing a named range, select the Show Named Ranges option. The Import Spreadsheet Wizard lists the worksheets or named data ranges, depending on the option you select in the list box in the upper-right corner of the Wizard's opening dialog.
5. Select the worksheet or the named data range that you want to import in the list box. The Import Spreadsheet Wizard shows a sample view of the data in the worksheet,

Orders in the NWOrders.xls workbook for this example, or the named range at the bottom of the dialog.

6. Click Next to move to the second dialog of the Spreadsheet Import Wizard, shown in Figure 8.19.

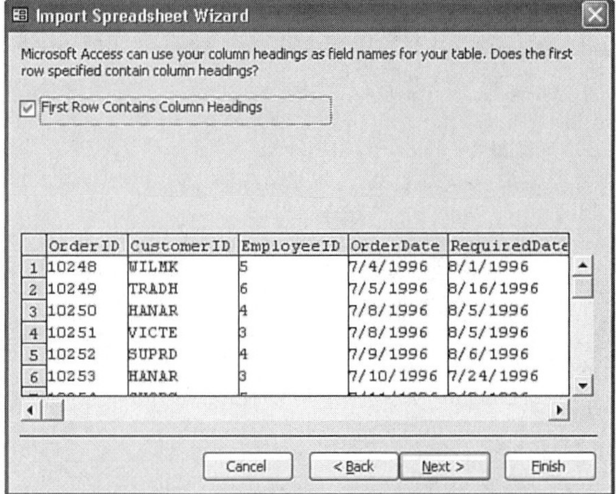

Figure 8.19
The Wizard's second dialog lets you specify whether the first row of the worksheet or named range contains column headings.

7. If the first row of your spreadsheet data contains the field names for the imported table, select the First Row Contains Column Headings check box. (In most cases, the Wizard detects the headings and marks the check box for you). Click Next to continue with the third step; the Import Spreadsheet Wizard displays the dialog shown in Figure 8.20.

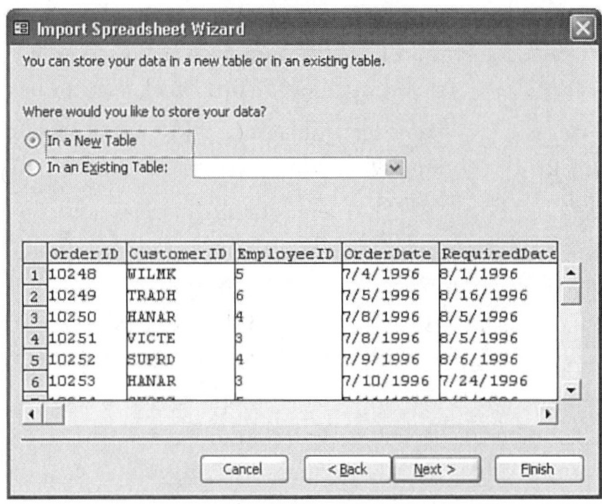

Figure 8.20
The third dialog lets you choose between creating a new table or appending the rows in the worksheet or range to an existing table. If you select the latter option, the existing table must have the same structure as the appended data.

8. If you want to create a new table to hold the imported spreadsheet data, select the In a New Table option. To add the imported data to an existing table, select the In an Existing Table option and select the table you want to add the imported data to in the drop-down list. Click Next to continue with the fourth step; the Import Spreadsheet Wizard displays the dialog shown in Figure 8.21.

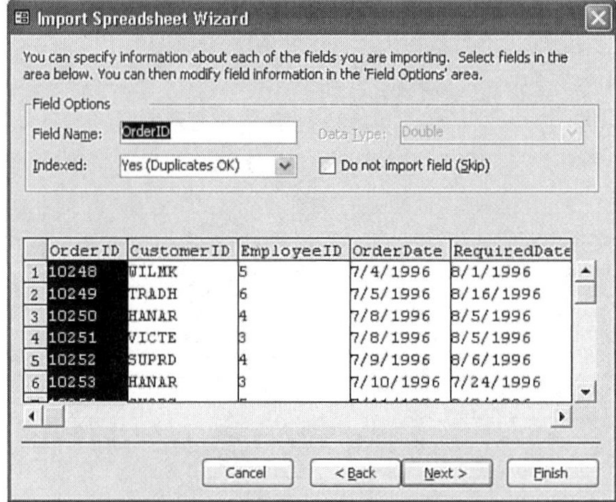

Figure 8.21
The fourth Wizard dialog lets you edit the field name, specify an index, or skip a field. For unknown reasons, you can't change the field data type in this version of the Wizard.

> **NOTE**
>
> If you elect to add the imported data to an existing table, the Import Spreadsheet Wizard skips over all intervening steps and goes immediately to its final dialog, described in step 14.

9. If you want to exclude a column from the imported database, select the column by clicking it, select the Do Not Import Field (Skip) check box, and skip to step 12.
10. The Import Spreadsheet Wizard lets you edit or add the field names for the spreadsheet columns; click the column whose name you want to edit or add and then type the name in the Field Name text box.
11. If you want Access to index this field, choose the appropriate index type in the Indexed list box; you can choose No, Yes (Duplicates OK), or Yes (No Duplicates).
12. Repeat steps 9, 10, and 11 for each column in the worksheet or data range that you import. When you're satisfied with your options for each column, click Next to move to the fifth dialog.
13. Select the Let Access Add Primary Key option to have Access add an AutoNumber field to the imported table; Jet fills in a unique number for each existing row in the worksheet that you're importing. Select the Choose My Own Primary Key option and select the primary-key field in the drop-down list if you know you can use a column in the worksheet or data range as a primary key for the imported table. The OrderID

column is the primary-key field for this example (see Figure 8.22). If this imported table doesn't need a primary key, select the No Primary Key option.

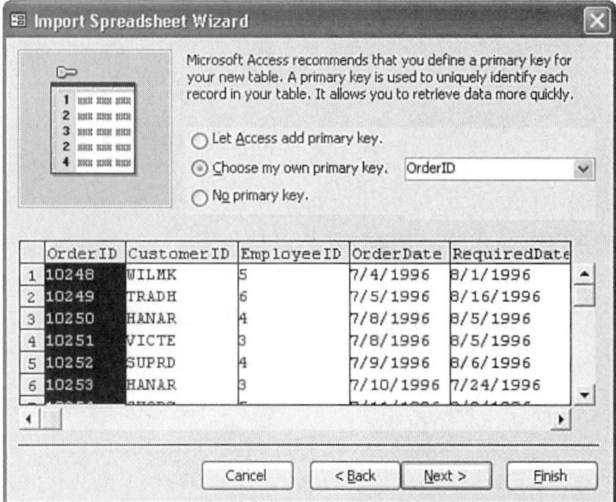

Figure 8.22
If the data you're importing contains a column with a unique value to identify each row, select the Choose My Own Primary Key option and the column name with the unique data.

14. Click Next to move to the final dialog of the Import Spreadsheet Wizard (see Figure 8.23). Type the name of the new table, Orders for this example, in the Import to Table text box; Access uses the name of the worksheet or data range as the default table name. If you want to use the Table Analyzer Wizard to split the imported table into two or more related tables, select the I Would Like a Wizard to Analyze My Table After Importing the Data check box.

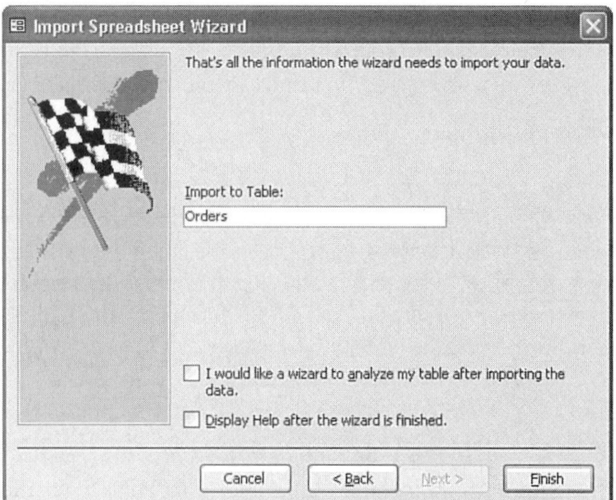

Figure 8.23
The final Wizard dialog lets you rename the table and, optionally, run the Table Analyzer Wizard on the table data after the import operation completes.

8

TIP

You can use the Table Analyzer Wizard at any time on any table by choosing Tools, Analyze, Table.

➔ To review use of the Table Analyzer Wizard to move duplicate data to a related table, **see** "Using the Table Analyzer Wizard," **p. 207**.

15. Click Finish to complete the importing process. Access closes the Import Spreadsheet Wizard and imports the data. When Access completes the import process without errors, it displays the message shown in Figure 8.24. Click OK to dismiss the message.

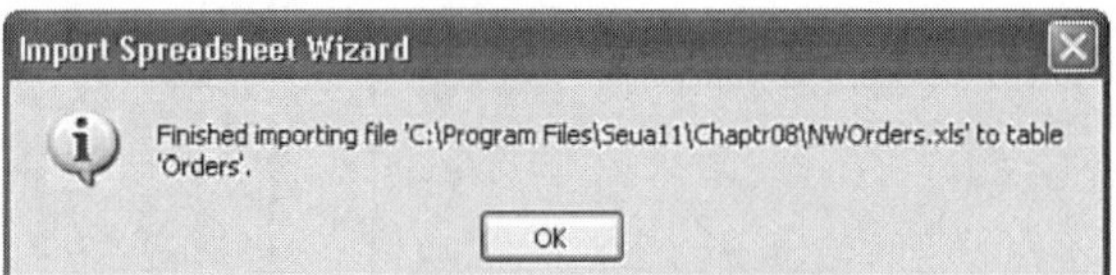
Import Spreadsheet Wizard
Finished importing file 'C:\Program Files\Seua11\Chaptr08\NWOrders.xls' to table 'Orders'.
OK

Figure 8.24
This message confirms the spreadsheet import process succeeded.

The Import Spreadsheet Wizard analyzes approximately the first 20 rows of the spreadsheet you are importing and assigns data types to the imported fields based on this analysis. If every cell in a column has a numeric or date value, the columns convert to Number and Date/Time field data types, respectively. If a column contains mixed text and numbers, the Wizard converts the column as a text field. If, however, a column contains numeric data in the first 20 rows (the rows that the Wizard analyzes) and then has one or more text entries, the Wizard doesn't convert these rows.

If the Wizard encounters cell values that it can't convert to the data type that it assigned to the imported field, Access creates an Import Errors table with one record for each error. You can review this table, select the records in which the errors are reported, and fix them. A better approach, however, is to correct the cells in the spreadsheet, resave the file, and import the corrected data.

TIP

The Import Spreadsheet Wizard doesn't display an error message when it encounters inconsistent field data types; it just creates the Import Errors table. You must look in the Database window to see whether the Import Errors table is present. After you resolve the import errors, make sure that you delete the Import Errors table so that you can more easily detect errors the next time you import a spreadsheet or other external file.

The Database window now contains a new table with the name you accepted or edited in the final dialog of the Import Spreadsheet Wizard. If you import another file with the same name as your worksheet or named range, the Wizard asks if you want to overwrite the existing table.

To verify that you obtained the desired result, double-click the name of the imported table in the Database window to display the new table in Datasheet view. Figure 8.25 illustrates a part of the Jet table created from the Orders worksheet in the NWOrders.xls spreadsheet file shown in Figure 8.16. The table *appears* to be identical to the Orders table of Northwind.mdb from which it was exported, with the exception of the CustomerID, EmployeeID, and ShipVia lookup fields.

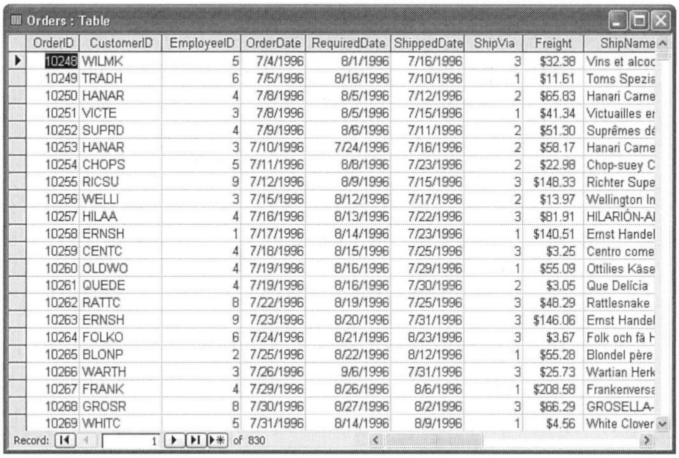

Figure 8.25 The Orders table imported from the Excel worksheet appears to be identical to the Northwind Orders table from which it was created—but it isn't.

Orders : Table

OrderID	CustomerID	EmployeeID	OrderDate	RequiredDate	ShippedDate	ShipVia	Freight	ShipName
10248	WILMK	5	7/4/1996	8/1/1996	7/16/1996	3	$32.38	Vins et alcoc
10249	TRADH	6	7/5/1996	8/16/1996	7/10/1996	1	$11.61	Toms Spezia
10250	HANAR	4	7/8/1996	8/5/1996	7/12/1996	2	$65.83	Hanari Carne
10251	VICTE	3	7/8/1996	8/5/1996	7/15/1996	1	$41.34	Victuailles er
10252	SUPRD	4	7/9/1996	8/6/1996	7/11/1996	2	$51.30	Suprêmes dé
10253	HANAR	3	7/10/1996	7/24/1996	7/16/1996	2	$58.17	Hanari Carne
10254	CHOPS	5	7/11/1996	8/8/1996	7/23/1996	2	$22.98	Chop-suey C
10255	RICSU	9	7/12/1996	8/9/1996	7/15/1996	3	$148.33	Richter Supe
10256	WELLI	3	7/15/1996	8/12/1996	7/17/1996	2	$13.97	Wellington In
10257	HILAA	4	7/16/1996	8/13/1996	7/22/1996	3	$81.91	HILARIÓN-AI
10258	ERNSH	1	7/17/1996	8/14/1996	7/23/1996	1	$140.51	Ernst Handel
10259	CENTC	4	7/18/1996	8/15/1996	7/25/1996	3	$3.25	Centro come
10260	OLDWO	4	7/19/1996	8/16/1996	7/29/1996	1	$55.09	Ottilies Käse
10261	QUEDE	4	7/19/1996	8/16/1996	7/30/1996	2	$3.05	Que Delícia
10262	RATTC	8	7/22/1996	8/19/1996	7/25/1996	3	$48.29	Rattlesnake
10263	ERNSH	9	7/23/1996	8/20/1996	7/31/1996	3	$146.06	Ernst Handel
10264	FOLKO	6	7/24/1996	8/21/1996	8/23/1996	3	$3.67	Folk och fä H
10265	BLONP	2	7/25/1996	8/22/1996	8/12/1996	1	$55.28	Blondel père
10266	WARTH	3	7/26/1996	9/6/1996	7/31/1996	3	$25.73	Wartian Herk
10267	FRANK	4	7/29/1996	8/26/1996	8/6/1996	1	$208.58	Frankenversa
10268	GROSR	8	7/30/1996	8/27/1996	8/2/1996	3	$66.29	GROSELLA-
10269	WHITC	5	7/31/1996	8/14/1996	8/9/1996	1	$4.56	White Clover

Record: 1 of 830

To display the .xls file data types that the Wizard chose, click the Design view toolbar button. Figure 8.26 shows the structure of the new Orders table. The Wizard incorrectly applied the Jet Double data type to the OrderID and EmployeeID fields, which you should change to the Long Integer data type. The Wizard correctly detected that the Currency data type applies to Freight field, because of the dollar-sign prefix of data in the worksheet column.

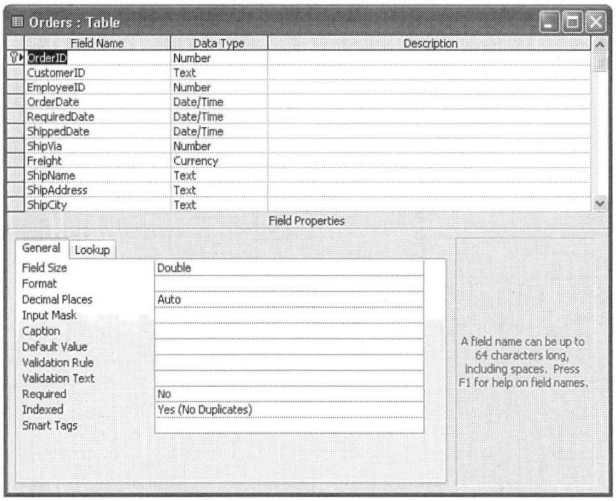

Figure 8.26 The Import Spreadsheet Wizard isn't omniscient. It chose the wrong Jet data type (Double) for the OrderID and EmployeeID columns.

Orders : Table

Field Name	Data Type	Description
OrderID	Number	
CustomerID	Text	
EmployeeID	Number	
OrderDate	Date/Time	
RequiredDate	Date/Time	
ShippedDate	Date/Time	
ShipVia	Number	
Freight	Currency	
ShipName	Text	
ShipAddress	Text	
ShipCity	Text	

Field Properties

General | Lookup

Field Size	Double
Format	
Decimal Places	Auto
Input Mask	
Caption	
Default Value	
Validation Rule	
Validation Text	
Required	No
Indexed	Yes (No Duplicates)
Smart Tags	

A field name can be up to 64 characters long, including spaces. Press F1 for help on field names.

8

TIP

> Don't use the Double (or Single) data type for primary-key fields. These data types require floating-point arithmetic to determine their values, which is subject to rounding errors. Relationships based on floating-point values might fail because of these rounding errors. In addition, multitable queries having relationships based on Double (or Single) fields usually exhibit very poor performance.

LINKING EXCEL WORKSHEETS

Prior to Access 2000, you could link Excel worksheets with either the ISAM or ODBC driver; Access 2003 doesn't permit use of the ODBC driver to link Excel worksheets. Like RDBMS tables, the advantages of linking an Excel worksheet are that you always work with the latest version of the worksheet, and you can alter worksheet cell values from within Access. The primary beneficiaries of linked Excel worksheets are die-hard spreadsheet users who aren't willing to move to database applications. The principal problem with linked worksheets is that you can't change the data type of fields used as primary keys.

Linking an Excel spreadsheet uses a truncated version of the Import Spreadsheet Wizard renamed to the Link Spreadsheet Wizard. To link an Excel worksheet to a Jet 4.0 table, do the following:

1. Open the database to which you want to link the worksheet, if necessary, and choose File, Get External Data, Link Tables to open the Link dialog. Select Microsoft Excel (*.xls) from the Files of Type list.
2. Navigate to the folder containing the worksheet you want to link, select the folder, and click Link to open the Link Spreadsheet Wizard (see Figure 8.27).

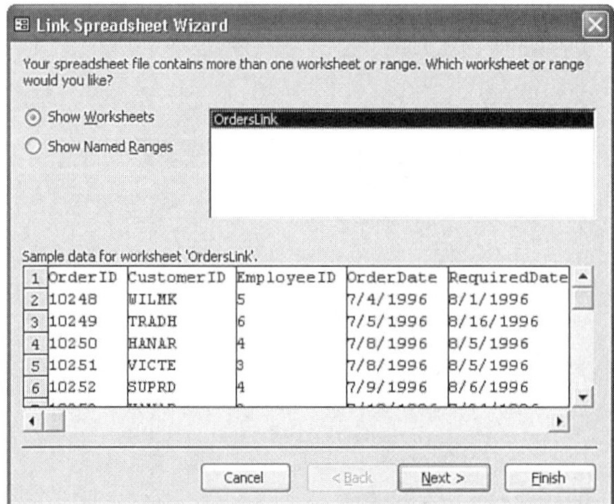

Figure 8.27
The Link Spreadsheet Wizard's first dialog lets you select a worksheet or named range to link to a Jet database.

3. Select the worksheet or named range to link, the NWOrdersLink.xls sample worksheet for this example, and then click the Next button.
4. The Wizard automatically detects that the first row contains column headings. If the Wizard guesses incorrectly, mark or clear the First Row Contains Column Headings check box. Click Next to continue.
5. The Wizard proposes the name of the worksheet as the table name. Change the table name if you want, click Finish, and then click OK to link the table. The linked table is identified in the Database window by an Excel icon and an arrow (see Figure 8.28).

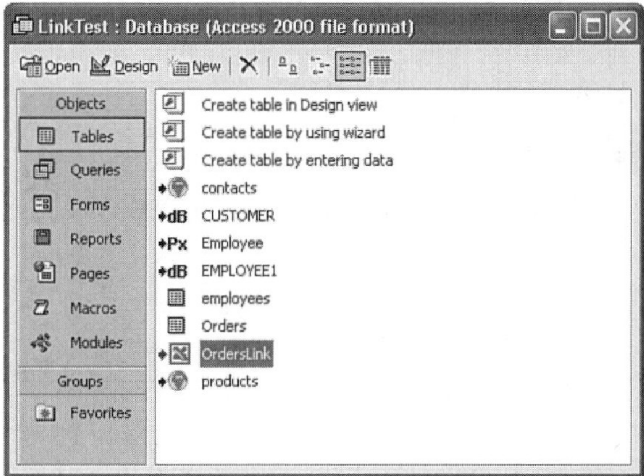

Figure 8.28 Worksheets or ranges linked to Jet databases display the Excel icon with a link-identifier arrow.

6. Open the linked table in Design view, clicking OK to acknowledge that you can't change the design of a linked table. Unfortunately, the Wizard again makes the wrong data type choice (Double) for the OrderID and EmployeeID columns.

The Linked Table Manager lets you fix broken links to worksheets.

WORKING WITH MICROSOFT OUTLOOK AND EXCHANGE FOLDERS

Microsoft Outlook 2003 lets you import data from and export data to a wide range of file types, including Jet 4.0 databases. For example, you can export data to a variety of file types and import Internet-standard VCARD, iCalendar, or vCalendar files. Outlook's import capability is far more eclectic than that of Access; you can import from the ACT! and ECCO personal information manager (PIM) applications, Lotus Organizer, and Schedule+ files.

TIP

> If you want to put data from ACT!, ECCO, Organizer, or Sidekick into Access 2003, importing to Outlook and exporting to Access is the best alternative unless you have versions of these applications that handle exporting to Jet 4.0 databases.

8

Access 2000 added the Exchange/Outlook Wizard for linking to the contents of Outlook's private and Exchange's public folders. The following two sections show you how to export, import, and link Contacts folders. The Contacts folder is most commonly used with databases; working with other folders follows a similar course.

NOTE

You must have the Outlook Import/Export engine installed to try the examples in the following two sections. If you haven't installed the engine, you receive a "Would you like to install it now?" message after you specify the action you want to take.

The following Outlook 2003 examples use personal folders. If you have Microsoft Exchange 2000+ running under Windows 2000 or 2003 Server, your results might differ, depending on your Outlook settings, Exchange Server configuration, or both.

Importing and Exporting Jet 4.0 Tables with Outlook

To use Outlook to import an Access table to an Outlook 2003 contacts folder, do the following:

1. Open Outlook and select the folder you want to import to. (Create a new empty contacts subfolder, Northwind for this example, when you're testing import and export operations.)
2. Choose File, Import and Export to open the Import and Export Wizard. Select Import from Another Program or File in the Choose an Action to Perform list (see Figure 8.29), and click Next.

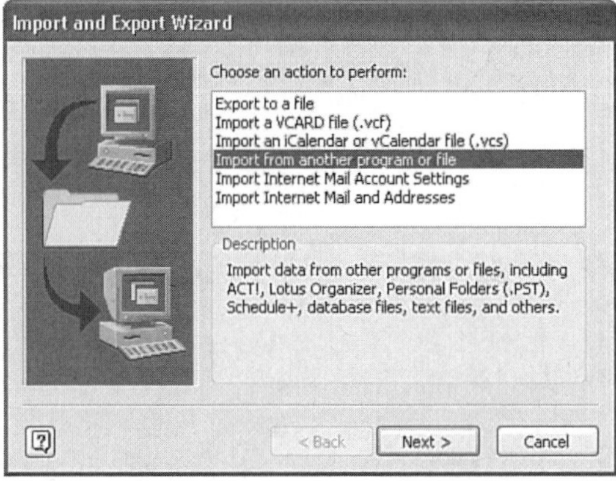

Figure 8.29
Select Import from Another Program or File in the first dialog of Outlook's Import and Export Wizard.

3. Select Microsoft Access in the Import a File dialog (see Figure 8.30), and click Next.
4. In the second Import a File dialog, click Browse to open the Browse dialog, and then navigate to and select the .mdb file that contains the table you want to import. This example uses Northwind.mdb's Customers table. Select an option for handling duplicates, and then click Next (see Figure 8.31).

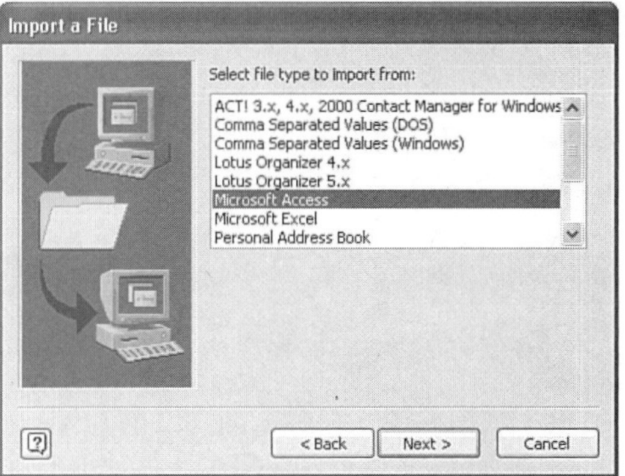

Figure 8.30
Select Microsoft Access in the second Wizard dialog.

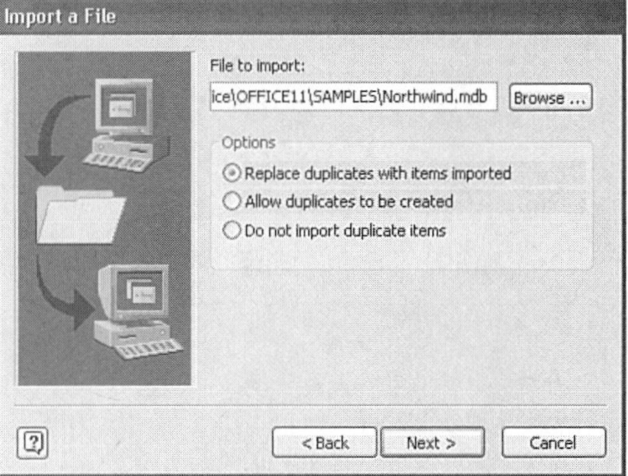

Figure 8.31
Navigate to the database you want to import the contact data from, and select Replace Duplicates with Items Imported to assure your Outlook contact information is up to date.

TIP

Make sure the.mdb file you intend to import the data from is closed at this point. If the .mdb file is open, you receive an error message when you attempt to complete the next step.

5. The destination folder you specified in step 1 is selected in the Import a File dialog (see Figure 8.32). If you didn't select a folder, you must do so at this point. Click Next.
6. Mark the Import *TableName* into the *FolderName* option for the table to import (Customers, for this example).
7. Click Map Custom Fields to open the Map Custom Fields dialog, and drag the fields you want to include in the Northwind list from the left list (the From category) to the appropriate Outlook field name in the right list (the To category), as shown in see Figure 8.33. Fields that you don't drag to the right list aren't included in the new Contacts folder.

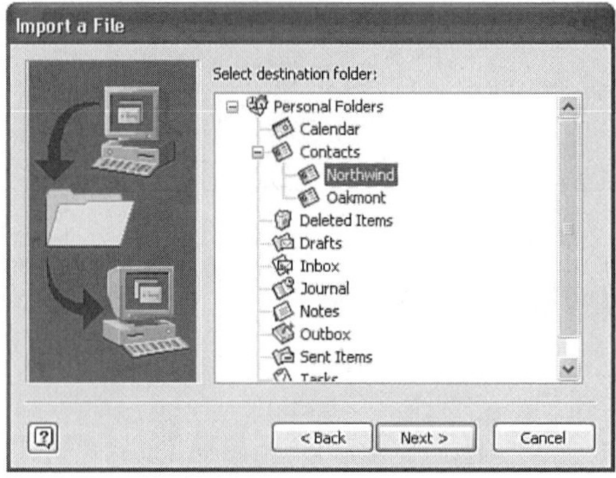

Figure 8.32
Verify the destination folder in the fourth Wizard dialog. In this case, the folder is created in the Contacts folder of your Personal Folders.

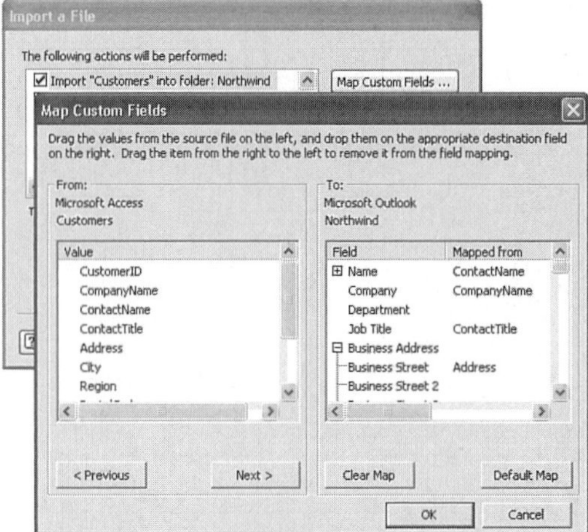

Figure 8.33
Drag field names from the Jet source table to the corresponding Outlook fields.

8. Click OK to close the Map Custom Fields dialog; then click Finish to close the Import File dialog and complete the import process. When the records are imported, Outlook automatically displays them (see Figure 8.34).
9. To add the company name to the contacts list, right-click an empty area of the contacts list, and choose Show Fields to open the Show Fields dialog. Drag the Company item from the Available Fields to the Show These Fields in This Order list below the File As item (see Figure 8.35). Click OK to complete the addition.

TIP

> Alternatively, choose View, Current View, Detailed Address Cards to display the contact items with field name prefixes, such as Full Name:, for each field.

Figure 8.34
Outlook's Contacts folder by default displays the contact name and company address, but not the company name.

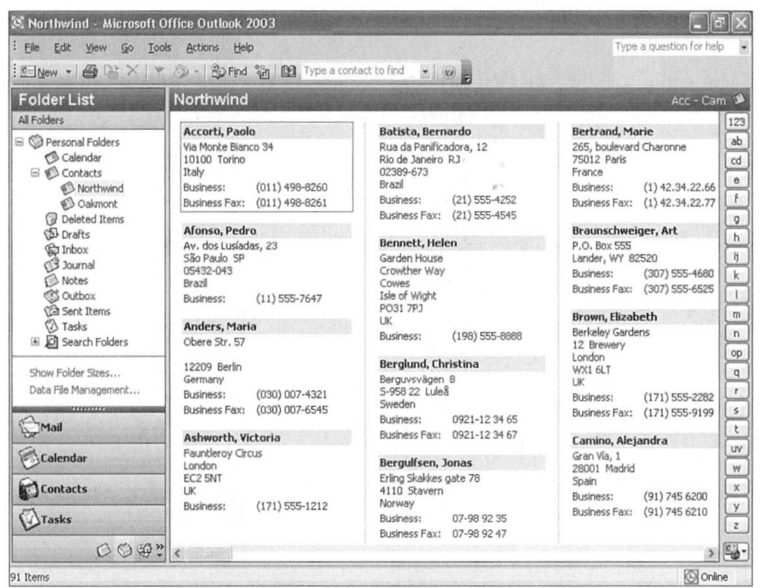

Figure 8.35
Use the Show Fields dialog to add additional fields to the contact list's display.

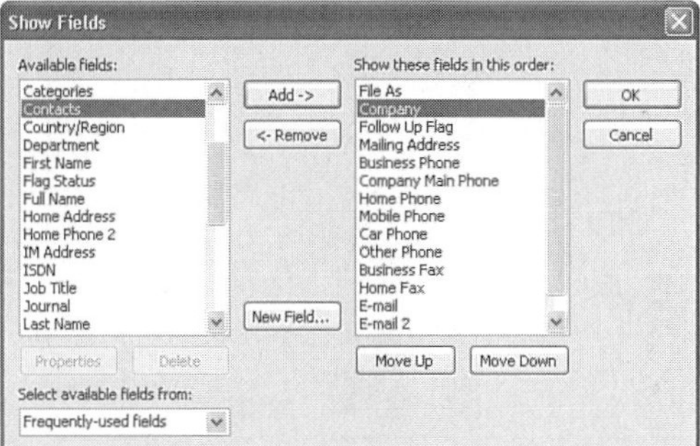

Exporting Contacts or other Outlook records to an Access table with the Outlook Import and Export Wizard follows the pattern of the preceding steps. Select the folder to export, choose File, Import and Export, select Export to a File, Microsoft Access, and confirm the folder selection. Then specify the destination .mdb file, and export the records to a table with the name of the folder or a name you specify.

TIP

> The better approach is to use Access's Import Exchange/Outlook version of Outlook's Export Wizard. The Access Wizard's method of selecting the fields to import is simpler than Outlook's Export Wizard.

8

Linking with the Exchange/Outlook Wizard

The Exchange/Outlook Wizard provides the capability of linking records in Outlook or Exchange folders to Jet 4.0 table(s). Linking is a better option than importing because your Access table always is up-to-date with information entered in Outlook, and vice-versa.

To link a Contacts folder to a Jet table, follow these steps:

1. Open the database you want to link the Outlook folder to and choose File, Get External Data, Link Tables to open the Link dialog.
2. Select Outlook() or Exchange() in the Files of Type list to open the Link Exchange/Outlook Wizard. This example uses Outlook().
3. Expand the nodes as necessary to open the folder to link. This example uses the Oakmont contacts subfolder.

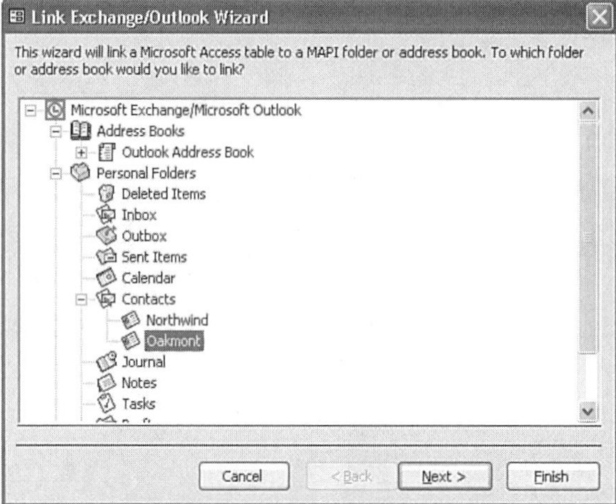

Figure 8.36
Select the folder to link in the Link Exchange/Outlook Wizard's first dialog.

4. Click Next to open the second (and last) Wizard dialog, in which you accept the folder name as the table name, or change it to your liking, **Oakmont** for this example.
5. Click Finish to link the table, and acknowledge the "Finished linking" message. Your linked table appears in the Database window, identified by an envelope icon with an adjacent arrow (see Figure 8.37).

6. Open the linked table in Datasheet view. The rows appear in first name order and many contacts fields are empty. Select each empty column and choose Format, Hide Columns, and apply a sort on the Last field to improve readability (see Figure 8.38). Tables linked to Exchange address lists aren't updatable. Tables linked to personal and public folders are updatable, even without a primary-key field, but your account must have permissions to make changes to Exchange public folders.

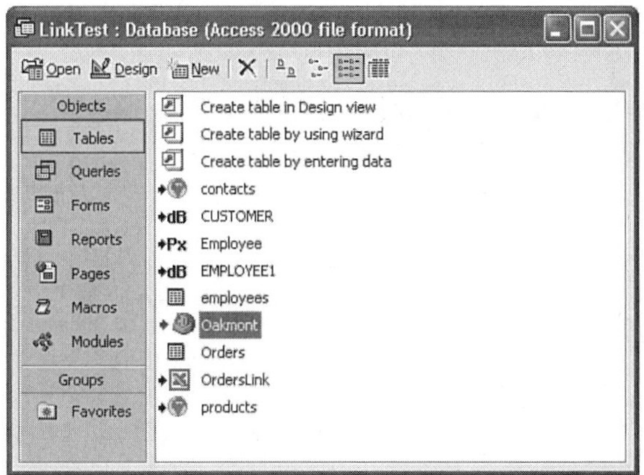

Figure 8.37
An envelope icon with an arrow identifies Linked Exchange folders.

Oakmont : Table

First	Last	Department	Address	Display name	File As
Dave	Abele	Music	Music Building, Room 256	Prof Dave Abele	Abele, Dave
John	Ableman	Music	Delivery to home address only	Prof John Ablen	Ableman, John
Mara	Abu	Music	Delivery to home address only	Prof Mara Abu	Abu, Mara
Mary	Abushanab	Music	Music Building, Room 822	Prof Mary Abus	Abushanab, Ma
Jeff	Acevedo	Music	Music Department Office	Jeff Acevedo	Acevedo, Jeff
Boyd	Adams	Music	Music Building, Room 552	Prof Boyd Adan	Adams, Boyd
Kirt	Adamson-Wooc	Music	Music Building, Room 466	Prof Kirt Adams	Adamson-Woo
Dean	Adank	Music	Music Building, Room 692	Dean Lynn Adai	Adank, Dean L
Mark	Adkins	Music	Music Department Office	Mark Adkins	Adkins, Mark
Greg	Alani	Music	Music Department Office	Greg Alani	Alani, Greg
Rian	Alawadhi	Music	Music Department Office	Rian Alawadhi	Alawadhi, Rian
Rick	Albelo	Anthropology	Liberal Arts Building, Room 9	Prof Rick Albelc	Albelo, Rick
Eric	Albers	Anthropology	Delivery to home address only	Prof Eric Albers	Albers, Eric
Dale	Albertson	Anthropology	Liberal Arts Building, Room 2	Prof Dale Albert	Albertson, Dale
Andy	Albrecht	Anthropology	Anthropology Department Offi	Andy Albrecht	Albrecht, Andy
Paul	Albright	Music	Delivery to home address only	Prof Paul Albrig	Albright, Paul
Paul	Alfadhel	Anthropology	Delivery to home address only	Prof Paul Alfadh	Alfadhel, Paul
Mark	Alford	Anthropology	Liberal Arts Building, Room 3	Prof Mark Alforc	Alford, Mark
Chad	Al-Ghanem	Anthropology	Delivery to home address only	Prof Chad Al-Gh	Al-Ghanem, Ch
John	Aliski	Music	Delivery to home address only	Prof John Aliski	Aliski, John
Dean	Allen	Anthropology	Liberal Arts Building, Room 8	Dean Greg Aller	Allen, Dean Gr

Record: 1 of 1649

Figure 8.38
The linked Oakmont table contains fields whose data is stored in an Outlook contacts folder.

TIP

> Exchange 2000 uses Active Directory to store recipient data, so you can link to the Global Address List, which is shown in Figure 8.36. If all users on a Windows 2000+ Server network are mailbox-enabled (not just mail-enabled), a link to the Global Address List provides a link to information about every network user.

The response of linked Exchange public folders to changes, sorts, and other operations is slower than linked Jet database tables because a local temporary link table (JET*xxxx*.tmp) acts as an intermediary between Jet and Exchange. Mail API (MAPI) translation to Windows 2000 or .NET Server Active Directory and network delays also contribute to slower operation.

8

NOTE

A copy of the data imported from the Exchange Global Address List folder of the sample `oakmont.edu` domain is included in the LinkTest.mdb database in the \Seua11\Chaptr08 folder of the accompanying CD-ROM. Fields with no data have been skipped in the table.

IMPORTING TEXT FILES

If the data you want to import into a Jet table was developed in a database management system, word processor, or other application that can't export the data as a .dbf, .wk?, or .xls file, you need to create a text file in one of the text formats supported by Access. Most DOS- and Windows-compatible data files created from data stored by mainframes and mini-computers, and files generated from nine-track magnetic tapes are text files.

Access refers to the characters that separate fields as delimiters or separators. In this book, the term delimiter refers to characters that identify the end of a field; *text identifiers* refers to the single and double quotation marks that you can use to distinguish text from numeric data.

Table 8.2 details the text formats that Access supports for import and export operations.

TABLE 8.2 TEXT FILE FORMATS SUPPORTED BY ACCESS 2003

Format	Description
Comma-delimited text files (also called CSV files)	Commas separate (delimit) fields. The newline pair, carriage-return (ASCII character 13), and line feed (ASCII character 10), separate records. Some applications enclose all values within double quotation marks, a format often called *mail-merge*, to prevent commas in a field value from erroneously specifying the end of the field. Other applications enclose only text (strings) in quotation marks to differentiate between text and numeric values, the standard format for files created by the xBase command `COPY TO` *`FILENAME`* `DELIMITED`.
Tab-delimited text files (also called TAB files)	These files treat all values as text and separate fields with tabs. Records are separated by newline pairs. Most word-processing applications use this format to export tabular text.
Space-delimited files	Some text files use spaces to separate fields in a line of text. The use of spaces as delimiter characters is uncommon because it can cause what should be single fields, such as street addresses, to be divided inconsistently into different fields.
Fixed-width text files (usually called TXT or ASCII files)	Access separates (parses) the individual records into fields based on the position of the data items in a line of text. Newline pairs separate records, and every record must have exactly the same length. Spaces pad the fields to a specified fixed width. Fixed width is the most common format for data exported by mainframes and minicomputers on nine-track tape.

NOTE

Text files in three of these formats (CSV, TAB, and TXT) derived from Northwind.mdb's Orders table are located in the \Seua11\Chaptr08\TextFile folder of the accompanying CD-ROM.

USING THE IMPORT TEXT WIZARD

To import any of the text file types listed in Table 8.2, you follow a procedure similar to the procedure for importing any external data into Access. To import a text file, follow these steps:

1. Open the database you want to import the text file into and make the Database window active.
2. Choose File, Get External Data, Import to open the Import dialog.
3. Select Text Files (*.txt, *.csv, *.tab, or *.asc) in the Files of Type drop-down list. Use the Look In drop-down list to select the folder that contains the text file you want to import and double-click the text file's name. Access starts the Import Text Wizard (see Figure 8.39), which is similar to Excel's Wizard of the same name.

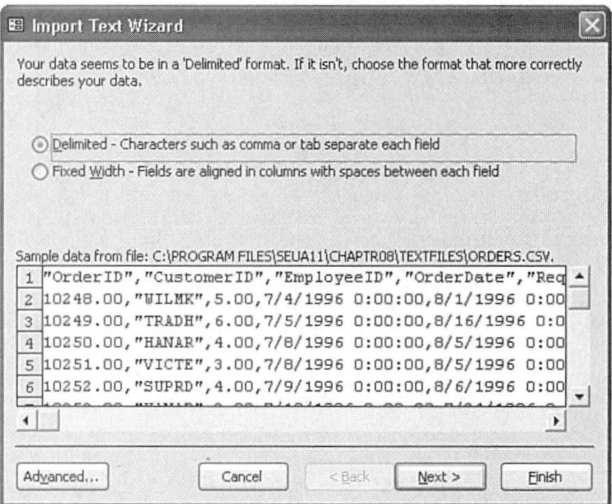

Figure 8.39
The first dialog of the Import Text Wizard lets you select between delimited (the default) or fixed-width files, and displays sample data from the file. The two decimal zeros in the OrderID column aren't present in the sample Orders.csv text data.

4. Select the Delimited option to import a delimited text file or select Fixed Width to import a fixed-width text file. The Import Text Wizard displays a sample of the text file's contents in the lower portion of the dialog to help you determine the correct file type. Figure 8.39 shows a comma-delimited text file being imported. Click Next to proceed to the next step in the Import Text Wizard.

   If you selected Delimited as the file type, the Import Text Wizard displays the dialog shown in Figure 8.40; if you selected the Fixed Width option for the Orders.txt file, the Wizard displays the dialog in Figure 8.41.

Figure 8.40
The Wizard's second dialog gives a preview of the table to be created on importing the Orders.csv text file.

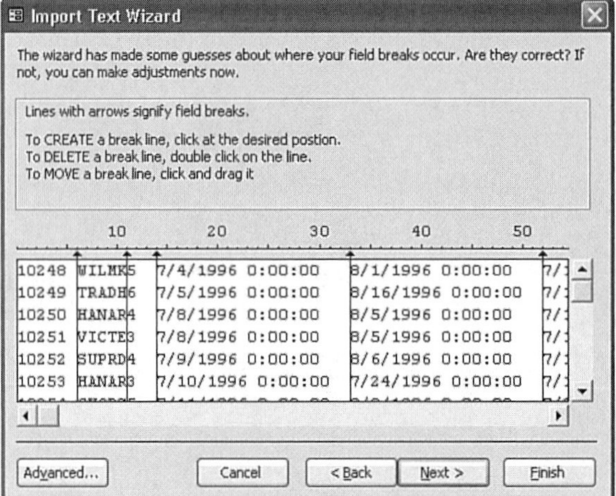

Figure 8.41
If you import from the fixed-width Orders.txt, the second dialog lets you define field boundaries. The Wizard doesn't detect the EmployeeID field, so you must add a break after the five-character CustomerID field.

5. If you're importing a delimited text file, accept the default or select the delimiter character that separates fields in the table (most delimited files use the tab separator). If the text file you're importing uses a text qualifier other than double quotation marks, type it in the Text Qualifier text box. If the first line in the text file contains field names (such as the column headings in a spreadsheet file), select the First Row Contains Field Names check box. Click Next to move to the next step of the Import Text Wizard.
6. If you're importing a fixed-width text file, the Import Text Wizard analyzes the columns and makes an approximation about where the field breaks lie. Scan through the sample data at the bottom of the dialog; if the field breaks aren't in the right place, there are too many field breaks, or there aren't enough field breaks, you can add, delete, or move the field breaks that the Import Text Wizard suggests. To move a field

break, drag it with the mouse. To remove a field break, double-click it. To add a field break, click at the desired location. When you're satisfied with the field break arrangement, click Next to continue.

7. The Wizard opens the dialog shown in Figure 8.42. Choose the In a New Table option to create a new Access table for the imported text file. Choose the In an Existing Table option to add the data in the text file to an existing database table; then select the table you want to add the data to in the accompanying drop-down list. Click Next to continue. (If you selected the In an Existing Table option, the Import Text Wizard skips directly to its final step, step 10 of this procedure.)

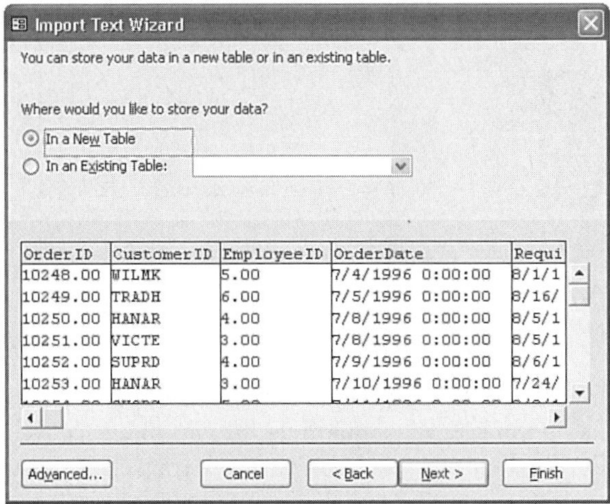

Figure 8.42
The third Wizard dialog lets you select between creating a new table and appending the data to an existing table.

CAUTION

The Wizard matches fields from left to right when you import a text file into an existing table. You must make sure that the data types of the fields in the imported text file match those in the Jet table; otherwise, the added data values aren't inserted into the correct fields. In most cases, you end up with many import errors in the Import Errors table. If you're not certain that the format of your input data exactly matches the format of the desired table, you can choose the In a New Table option and then place your data in the existing table with an append query, as discussed in Chapter 13, "Creating and Updating Jet Tables with Action Queries."

8. The fourth Wizard dialog lets you edit field names, choose whether to use index and what kind to use for each field, and adjust each field's data type (see Figure 8.43). To set the options for a field, click the field column at the bottom of the dialog to select it; you then can edit the field name, select an index method in the Indexed drop-down list, and select the data type for the field in the Data Type drop-down list. Select the Do Not Import Field (Skip) check box if you don't want to import the selected field column.

The OrderID, EmployeeID, and ShipVia column require the Long Integer data type to conform to the original table design, and a No Duplicates index selection is appropriate for the OrderID primary-key field. When you're satisfied with your field settings, click Next.

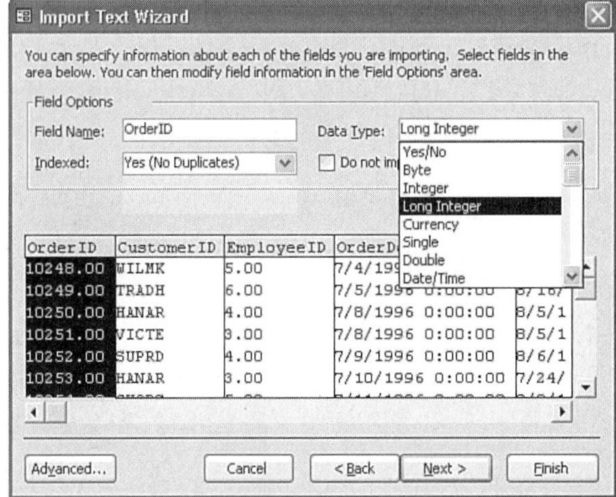

Figure 8.43
The fourth dialog lets you change or assign field names, alter data types, specify indexes, and skip fields.

9. The Wizard displays the dialog in Figure 8.44. Choose the appropriate option for the primary key: allow Access to add a new field with an automatically generated primary key, select an existing field to use as a primary key yourself, or import the table without a primary key. For this example OrderID is the primary key. Click Next.

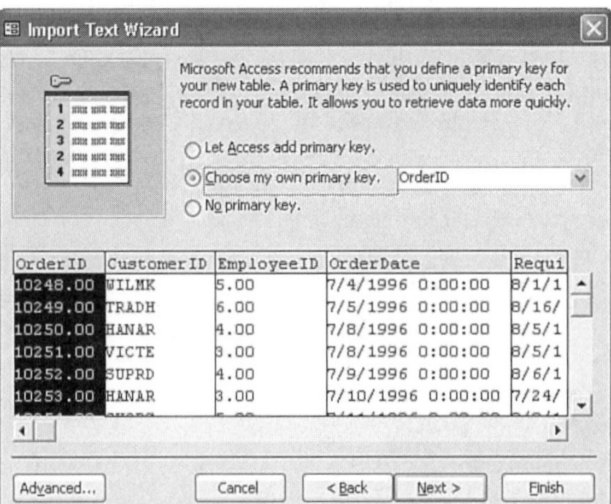

Figure 8.44
The fifth dialog offers three primary key choices. For the Orders table, select Choose My Own Primary Key option and the OrderID field as the primary key. Notice that the change to the Long Integer data type of the OrderID field isn't reflected in the Wizard's display.

10. The Wizard displays its final dialog with the filename of the text file or the existing table you specified in step 7 as the default table name (refer to Figure 8.23). Edit the table name, or type a different table name, if you want. Click Finish to import the text file.

The Import Text Wizard imports the text file and displays a success message. As with other import operations, Access creates an Import Errors table to document any errors that occurred during the import process and displays a message informing you that errors occurred.

Setting the Import Text Wizard's Advanced Options

You're likely to find that you import text data from the same text file more than once or that you have several text files with the same format. A typical situation in many corporations is that data from the company's mainframe computer system is provided to desktop computer users in the form of a text file report. Frequently, reports are delivered over the network in a text file, using the same name for the text file each time. You can use the Import Text Wizard's advanced options to configure Access to import a text file with a specific set of options and save the option values so that you don't have to go through every step in the Wizard every time you import the text file.

Every dialog of the Import Text Wizard has an Advanced button. Clicking this button displays the *TableName* Import Specification dialog that shows all the Import Text Wizard settings in a single dialog and allows you to select a few options, such as date formatting, that don't appear in the regular Import Text Wizard dialogs. If you select the Delimited option and the text file includes field names, the Customers Import Specification dialog has the options and field grid shown in Figure 8.45. Settings in the Data Type and Indexed columns reflect the changes suggested in Figure 8.43.

Figure 8.45
The Orders Import Specification dialog for the sample Orders.csv text file lets you create a template for future import of text files in the same format.

If you select the Fixed-Width option for a file without field names in the first record, the dialog has the options and field grid shown in Figure 8.46. For the Orders.txt sample file, type the field names, specify the data types, and set the indexes as shown previously in Figure 8.45.

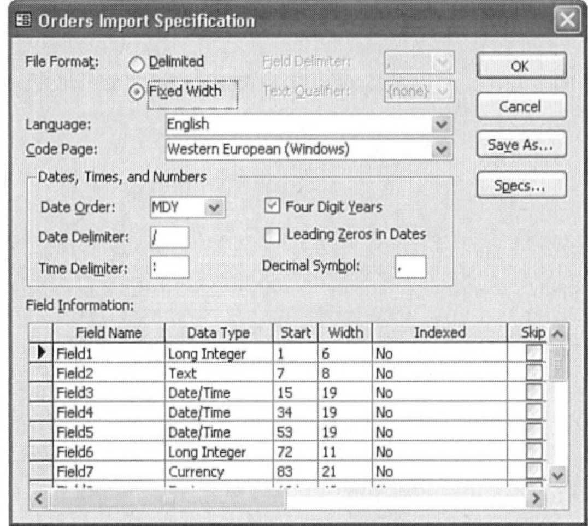

Figure 8.46
The Orders Import Specification dialog for a fixed-width table without field names in the first row assigns default Field# field names.

You can select the following options in the *TableName* Import Specification dialog:

- **File Format**—Use these option buttons to choose which type of text file format you're importing: delimited or fixed width. The file format you select determines which additional options are available.
- **Field Delimiter**—Use this drop-down list to select the symbol that delimits fields in the text file. This option is disabled for fixed-width text files.
- **Text Qualifier**—Use this drop-down list to select the symbol that marks the beginning and end of text strings in the text file. This option is disabled for fixed-width text files.
- **Language and Code Page**—Use these lists to handle localized text files.
- **Date Order**—If the data in the text file uses a European or other date format that varies from the month-day-year format typical in the United States, select the appropriate date order in the Date Order drop-down list.
- **Date Delimiter and Time Delimiter**—Type the symbol used to separate the month, day, and year in a date in the Date Delimiter text box; type the symbol used to separate hours, minutes, and seconds in the Time Delimiter text box. For example, in the United States, the date delimiter is the virgule (/) character, and the time delimiter is the colon (:).
- **Four Digit Years**—Mark this check box if the dates in the text file use four digits for the year, such as 8/28/1999.

- **Leading Zeros in Dates**—Mark this check box if the dates in the text file have leading zeros, such as 08/09/1999.
- **Decimal Symbol**—Type the symbol used for the decimal separator in numeric values in the text box. In the United States, the decimal symbol is the period (.), but many European nations use a comma (,).
- **Field Information**—The appearance of this grid depends on the file format you select. For a delimited text file, the Field Information grid lets you edit field names, select the field's data type and indexing, and specify whether to skip the field in importing (refer to Figure 8.45). For a fixed-width text file, the Field Information grid lets you perform the same operations but adds specifications for the starting column and width of each field (refer to Figure 8.46).
- **Save As**—Click this button to display the Save Import/Export Specification dialog. By typing a name for the specification and clicking OK, you can save the file import settings for later use.
- **Specs**—Click this button to display the Import/Export Specifications dialog (see Figure 8.47). Select a previously saved specification and click OK to use import settings that you defined previously.

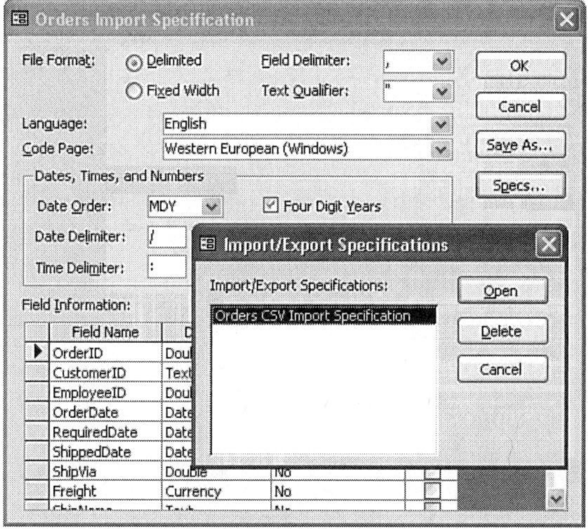

Figure 8.47
The Import/Export Specifications dialog lets you select a set of saved import specifications to apply when importing a text file. This figure illustrates the import specification for the sample Orders.txt fixed-width file.

The LinkTest.mdb sample database in the \Seua10\Chaptr08 folder of the accompanying CD-ROM includes the two import specifications shown in Figure 8.47.

TIP

If you even suspect that you'll need to import the same or a similar text file, save the import specification in your database with a descriptive name. You can edit the specification in the Wizard and resave it, if necessary.

USING THE ACCESS MAIL MERGE WIZARD

Access 2003's Mail Merge Wizard can help you create a new main merge document or employ an existing main merge document from which to create form letters. The Mail Merge Wizard uses a table or a query as the data source for the merge data file. The sections that follow describe two methods of creating a form letter:

- Using the Mail Merge Wizard to create a new main merge document whose merge data source is a Jet table
- Using an existing main merge document with a merge data source from a Jet table with a filter or a select query

Access 2000 and earlier used Dynamic Data Exchange (DDE) to send mail merge data to Word. Access 2003 uses an OLE DB data source to generate mail-merge documents. OLE DB and Automation is a much more reliable method of interapplication communication than DDE. Using OLE DB also lets you take advantage of Word's filter and sort features, which were unavailable from documents created with earlier versions of the Mail Merge Wizard.

CREATING AND PREVIEWING A NEW FORM LETTER

When you first try a new wizard, it's customary to create a new object rather than use the wizard to modify an existing object, such as a main merge document. The following steps use the Mail Merge Wizard to create a new main merge document from records in the Customers table of Northwind.mdb:

1. Open Northwind.mdb, if necessary, and select the Customers table in the Database window.
2. Click the arrow beside the Office Links button to open the drop-down menu and select Merge It with Microsoft Word to launch the Microsoft Word Mail Merge Wizard.

3. Select the Create a New Document and Then Link the Data to It option (see Figure 8.48) to create a new main merge document using fields from the Customers table.

Figure 8.48
The Mail Merge Wizard's only dialog lets you use an existing merge document (the default) or create a new document.

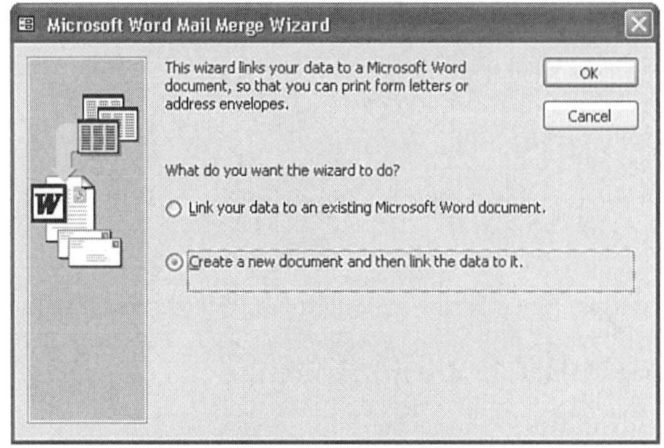

4. Click OK to launch Word 2003, if it isn't running. Word opens a new mail merge main document, Document1, and displays the Mail Merge page of the task pane.

5. Click the Insert Merge Fields button to verify the available fields from the Customers table in the Insert Merge Field dialog, as shown in Figure 8.49. Click Cancel to close the dialog, and close the task pane.

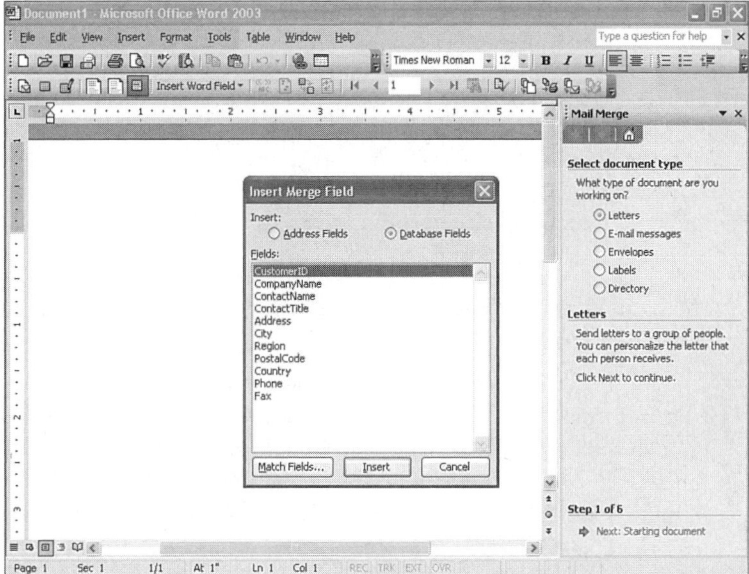

Figure 8.49
When you start the mail merge process, Word opens with the Mail Merge menu and task pane page active. The Insert Merge Field dialog confirms that you selected the correct table as the merge data source.

TIP

Click the Show/Hide button on Word's toolbar to display end-of-paragraph marks. Choose Tools, Options, and mark the options on the View page to show space characters, tab characters, and other document symbols that are usually hidden. All figures of Word 2003 in these sections were captured with the Show/Hide button active.

6. With the cursor at the top of the document, choose Insert, Date and Time to display the Date and Time dialog; choose any date format you want, mark the Update Automatically check box, and click OK to add a date field to the main document.

7. Add two blank lines, click the Insert Merge Fields button to display the list, and double-click to insert the CompanyName, Address, City, Region, PostalCode, ContactName, and ContactTitle fields from the Customers table to create the address section of the main document. Format the field names, which insert in a single line in Word's Normal view, as shown in Figure 8.50.

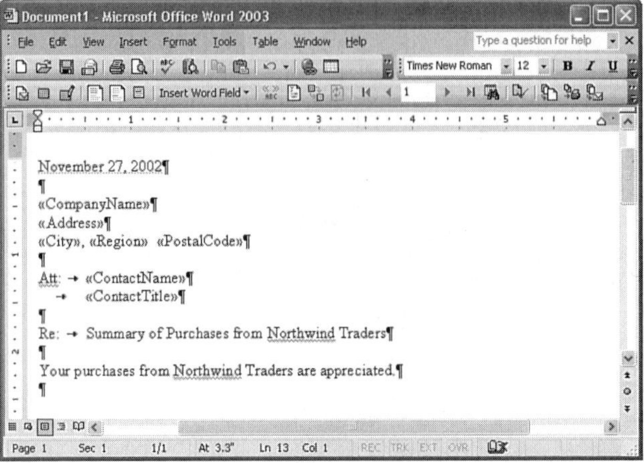

Figure 8.50
Arrange merge fields in letter format after you insert them.

8. Click the View Merged Data button of the Mail Merge toolbar to preview the appearance of the first of your form letters.

9. The form letters go only to customers in the United States, so you should check the address format for United States addresses. Click the Find Entry button on the toolbar to open the Find Entry dialog, type **USA** in the Find text box, and select Country from the This Field list. Click Find Next to find the first U.S. record. Alternatively, type **32** in the Go To Record text box of the toolbar, and press enter. The preview of the form letter for Great Lakes Food Market appears as shown in Figure 8.51.

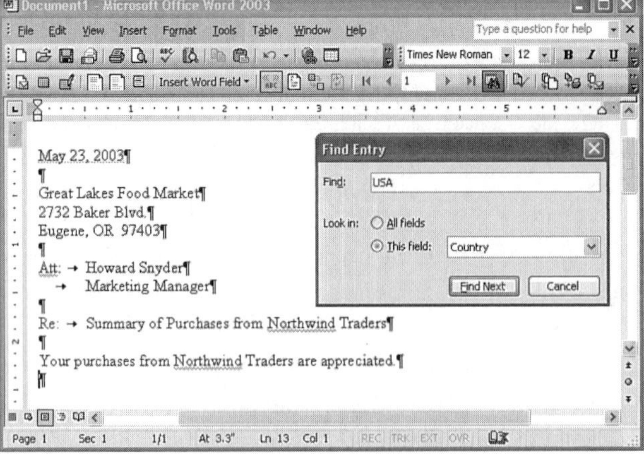

Figure 8.51
After clicking the View Merged Data toolbar button, use the Find Entry dialog to locate the record for the first U.S. customer.

10. To send letters to U.S. customers only, click Word's Mail Merge Recipients button to open the eponymous dialog with the current record selected. Open the Country field's list and choose (Advanced…), as shown in Figure 8.52 to specify a Word filter on the Country field.

Figure 8.52
Word 2003's Mail Merge Recipients dialog lets you choose how to filter and sort the data source for mail merge documents.

NEW 2002

11. In the Filter dialog, select the Country field, if necessary, accept the default Equal To comparison, and type **USA** in the Compare To text box (see Figure 8.53). You can create complex filters by adding additional criteria and selecting And or Or to determine the filter logic. Click the Sort tab, select PostalCode in the Sort By list, and click OK to close the dialog.

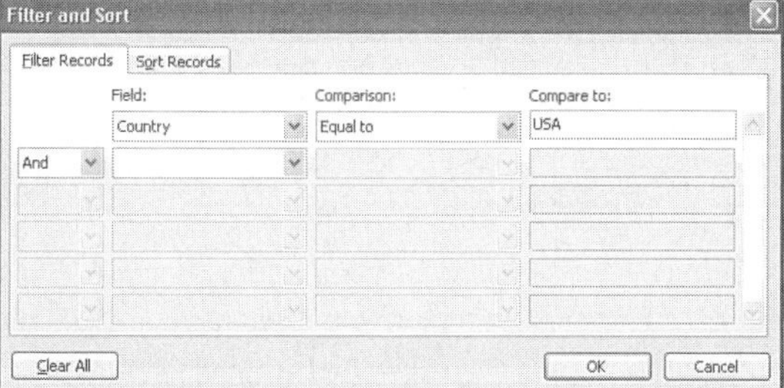

Figure 8.53
The Filter page of the Filter and Sort dialog lets you specify expressions and criteria on which to filter the data source.

12. Applying a filter marks for inclusion only those records that meet the filter criterion (see Figure 8.54). Click OK to close the dialog.

Figure 8.54
The Wizard marks and sorts the set of filtered records in preparation for generating the mail-merge documents.

13. The filtered list is applied to the mail-merge document. Click the Next Record button to display only the U.S. records in sequence.

14. Click the Merge to New Document button to open the dialog of the same name. Accept the All (records) option, and click OK to generate the Letters1 document that contains the 13 letters to U.S. customers (see Figure 8.55).

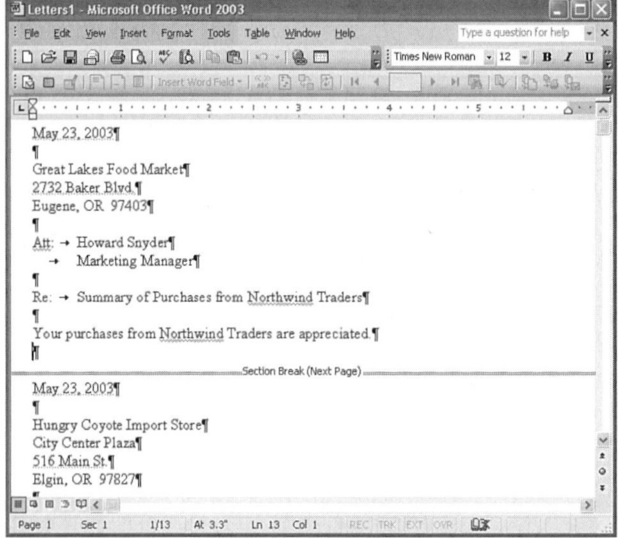

Figure 8.55
The merge document contains a letter for each of the 13 U.S. customers in the filtered list.

15. Close Letters1 and save it with a descriptive name, such as **USCustomersLetters.doc**, and do the same for Document1, the main merge document (**USCustomersMerge.doc**).

The two documents created in the preceding steps are located in the \Seua10\Chaptr08\MailMerge folder of the accompanying CD-ROM. The merge document doesn't save the filter, so you must reestablish the filter when opening the main merge document.

USING AN EXISTING MAIN MERGE DOCUMENT WITH A NEW DATA SOURCE

After you create a standard main merge document, the most common practice is to use different data sources to create form letters by addressee category. Word main merge documents store database and table connection data, and retain filter settings. Using Access filters or queries to restrict the recipient list usually is more convenient than performing the same operation in Word.

Take the following steps to use the main mail-merge document you created in the preceding section, USCustomersMerge.doc, with a data source based on a filter for the Customers table:

1. In Access, open the Customers table in Datasheet view, and click the toolbar's Filter by Form button.
2. Scroll to the Country field, open the field list and select USA.
3. Click the Apply Filter button to filter the table data and display only U.S. customers.
4. Choose Records, Filter, Advanced Filter/Sort to open the Filter Design window, which displays the filter criterion you applied in step 2. Drag the PostalCode field to the second column, and select an Ascending sort (see Figure 8.56).

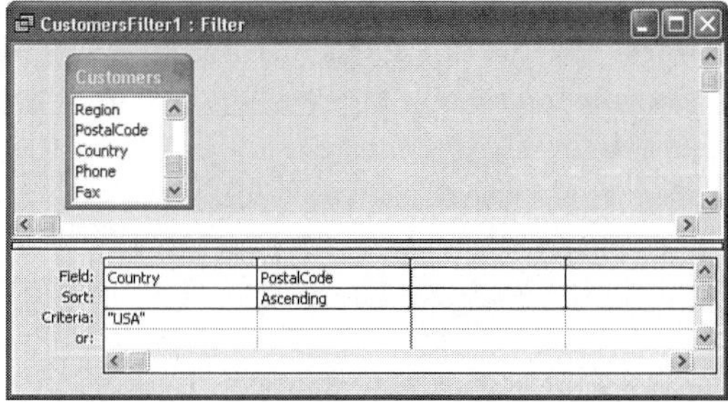

Figure 8.56
The Filter Design window opened by the Advanced Filter Sort command displays the filter for the Customers table with an ascending sort on the PostalCode field.

→ To review use of Access's Advanced Filter/Sort feature, **see** "Applying Advanced Filters and Sort Orders," **p. 255**.

5. Choose File, Save As Query, give your filter a descriptive name, such as **fltUSCustomers**, and click OK.

6. Close the Filter window and the Customers table, and click the Queries shortcut of the database window.
7. Double-click the filter item, fltUSCustomers for this example, to open the query result set and test the filter. Close the Query Datasheet window.

8. Click the Merge It with Microsoft Word button to launch the Mail Merge Wizard. With the Link Your Data to an Existing Microsoft Word Document option marked (the default), click OK to open the Select Microsoft Word Document dialog.
9. Navigate to and double-click your main merge document, USCustomersMerge.doc for this example, in the file list. After a few seconds, Word opens, and Access's title bar flashes. Minimize Word to expose the message box, shown in Figure 8.57. Click Yes to change to the new data source.

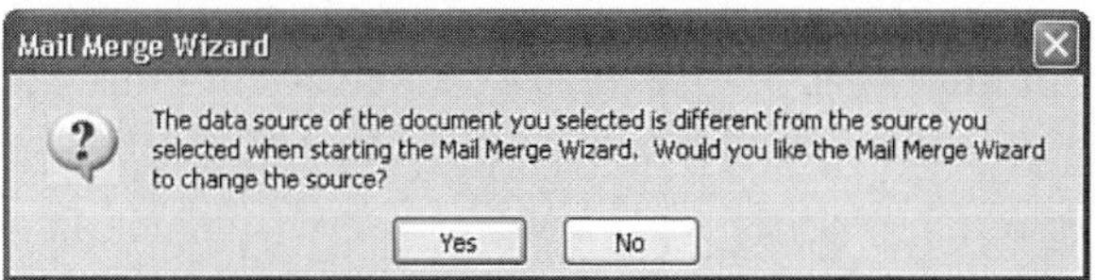

Figure 8.57
When you change the data source for a main merge document, Word opens a message box.

10. If Word can't resolve the data source type, the Confirm Data Source dialog opens to verify use of an OLE DB data source for the Jet query. Accept the default OLE DB Database Files, and click OK to continue in Word.

TIP

> If you attempt to connect to an open document, you receive a "File in Use" error message. Click Cancel, and then click OK when the "Command Failed" error message appears. Close the merge document, and try again.

11. Restore Word and confirm that the filter is the new merge data source—[fltUSCustomers] in "Northwind.mdb"—in the task pane's Mail Merge page (see Figure 8.58). Double-check the list by clicking the Mail Merge Recipients button. Only the filtered records appear in the list. Click OK to close the list.

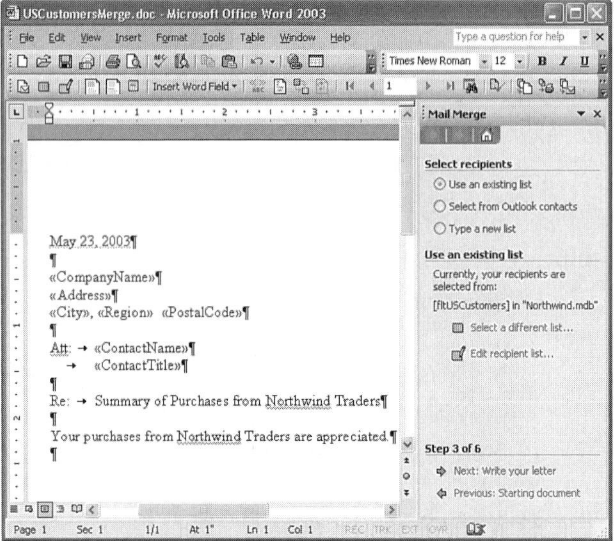

Figure 8.58
The Mail Merge task pane page confirms the document is using the fltUSCustomers filter.

12. You can merge the main document and data source directly to the printer, spam the customers via email, send faxes, or create a series of form letters in a new document, which is identical to the sample document you created in the preceding section.

If you close Word at this point, be sure to save your changes to the main mail-merge document.

EXPORTING TABLES TO WORD AND EXCEL

The OfficeLinks toolbar button shortcuts the process of exporting tables or query result sets to Word tables and Excel worksheets. Select the table or query to save in the Database window, open the OfficeLinks list, and then do either of the following:

- Select Publish It with Microsoft Word to generate a Rich Text Format (.rtf) filenamed for the table or query and display the table in Word (see Figure 8.59). The .rtf format embeds formatting instructions and data for text, images, and other objects. Most word processing applications, including WordPad, can open .rtf files.

- Select Analyze It with Microsoft Excel to generate a workbook (.xls) filenamed for the table or query and display worksheet in Word (see Figure 8.60).

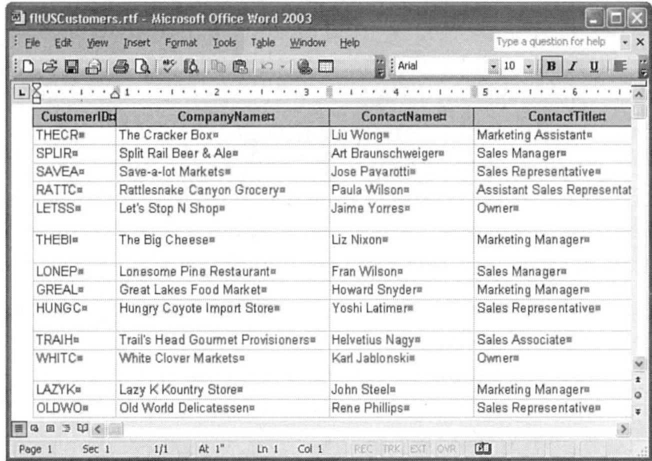

CustomerID	CompanyName	ContactName	ContactTitle
THECR	The Cracker Box	Liu Wong	Marketing Assistant
SPLIR	Split Rail Beer & Ale	Art Braunschweiger	Sales Manager
SAVEA	Save-a-lot Markets	Jose Pavarotti	Sales Representative
RATTC	Rattlesnake Canyon Grocery	Paula Wilson	Assistant Sales Representat
LETSS	Let's Stop N Shop	Jaime Yorres	Owner
THEBI	The Big Cheese	Liz Nixon	Marketing Manager
LONEP	Lonesome Pine Restaurant	Fran Wilson	Sales Manager
GREAL	Great Lakes Food Market	Howard Snyder	Marketing Manager
HUNGC	Hungry Coyote Import Store	Yoshi Latimer	Sales Representative
TRAIH	Trail's Head Gourmet Provisioners	Helvetius Nagy	Sales Associate
WHITC	White Clover Markets	Karl Jablonski	Owner
LAZYK	Lazy K Kountry Store	John Steel	Marketing Manager
OLDWO	Old World Delicatessen	Rene Phillips	Sales Representative

Figure 8.59 Choosing Publish It with Microsoft Word exports a .rtf file of the selected table or query object and opens Word.

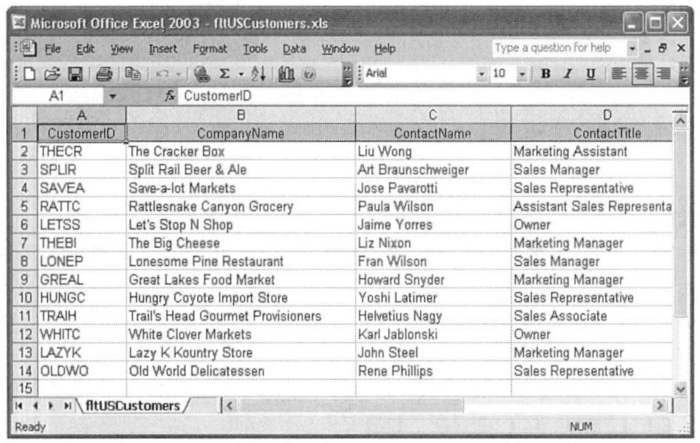

	A	B	C	D
1	CustomerID	CompanyName	ContactName	ContactTitle
2	THECR	The Cracker Box	Liu Wong	Marketing Assistant
3	SPLIR	Split Rail Beer & Ale	Art Braunschweiger	Sales Manager
4	SAVEA	Save-a-lot Markets	Jose Pavarotti	Sales Representative
5	RATTC	Rattlesnake Canyon Grocery	Paula Wilson	Assistant Sales Representa
6	LETSS	Let's Stop N Shop	Jaime Yorres	Owner
7	THEBI	The Big Cheese	Liz Nixon	Marketing Manager
8	LONEP	Lonesome Pine Restaurant	Fran Wilson	Sales Manager
9	GREAL	Great Lakes Food Market	Howard Snyder	Marketing Manager
10	HUNGC	Hungry Coyote Import Store	Yoshi Latimer	Sales Representative
11	TRAIH	Trail's Head Gourmet Provisioners	Helvetius Nagy	Sales Associate
12	WHITC	White Clover Markets	Karl Jablonski	Owner
13	LAZYK	Lazy K Kountry Store	John Steel	Marketing Manager
14	OLDWO	Old World Delicatessen	Rene Phillips	Sales Representative
15				

Figure 8.60 Choosing Analyze It with Microsoft Excel exports an .xls file of the object and opens the worksheet in Excel.

In both cases, Access stores the exported files in your My Documents folder. The process doesn't permit you to specify the location of the exported files.

8

EXPORTING DATA TO WEB SERVERS

Access 2003 has the capability to export data from tables and queries in the following Web-enabled formats:

- *HTML Documents (*.html; *.htm)* for static display of data in pages delivered from any Web server. Exporting as HTML is the simplest process.
- *Microsoft Active Server Pages (*.asp)* for dynamic display of data in browser-independent Web pages delivered from Internet Information Server (IIS) 3+. You must specify an OLE DB or ODBC data source and other parameters to export data to an .asp file.
- *Microsoft IIS 1-2 (*.htx: *.idc)* for dynamic display of data in a format determined by a *Filename*.htx template file. The *Filename*.idc file defines an Internet data connection and an SQL query to generate the data for the page. You must specify an ODBC data source and other parameters to export data to a .htx/.idc file pair. This option is available only for Access data projects (ADP) with SQL Server databases; Access version 2000 and earlier supported this option for Jet databases. This format is obsolete and isn't secure.
- NEW SharePoint Team Services() to export a table to a list on a Windows SharePoint Services (WSS) server. Chapter 26, "Integrating with InfoPath and SharePoint Services," explains how to take advantage of Access 2003's new WSS list export and linking features.
- NEW *XML Documents (*.xml)* for use with applications that can parse and transform XML to HTML or text. As mentioned near the beginning of this chapter, Chapter 23 covers the use of Access 2003's new XML import/export features for intranet- and Internet-based database applications.

Only brief descriptions for the use of the first two formats of the preceding list is provided here, because saving tables or queries as data access pages (DAP) is a much more effective method of delivering dynamic data to browsers.

SAVING AN .HTM FILE TO A WEB SERVER

If a standard HTML table is adequate for presentation of your data, exporting a table as an HTML file is the simplest process. Access writes the HTML code for you, but you can use Notepad or any other HTML editor to modify the page design.

To export a table (Customers for this example) to an HTML table and display it in Internet Explorer (IE) 5.0+, do this:

1. Select the table in the Database window, and choose File, Export to open the Export Table 'Customers' To dialog.

2. In the Save As Type list, select HTML Documents (*.html;*.htm) which adds Customers as the default filename. Be sure to check the Save Formatted check box next to the Export button.

3. Navigate to the folder that stores your Web pages. The default folder for IIS is \Inetpub\wwwroot. If you don't have a Default.htm page in the folder, you can make the table the default page for the server or a subfolder by naming the file **Default.htm**. Click Export to open the HTML Output Options dialog.

4. Accept the default entries in the HTML Output dialog. An HTML template isn't required, and default HTML encoding works with all PC browsers. Click OK to create the .htm file.

5. Launch IE and type ***servername*[/*filename*.html]** in the Address bar. If the Web server is running on your computer, you can use **localhost[/*filename*.html]** as the URL. The `/Filename.html` element of the address is required if you didn't specify Default.htm as the filename. IE adds the `http://` prefix for you and opens the table (see Figure 8.61). In this example, the server is the local computer and the file is Default.htm.

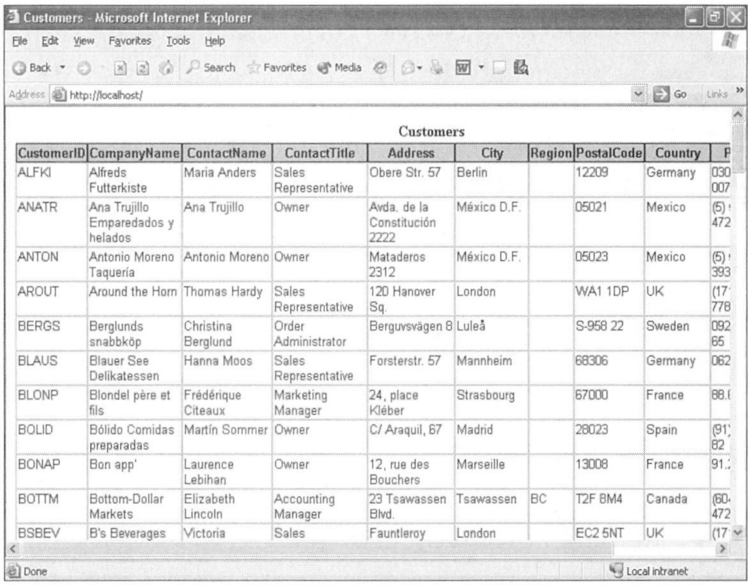

Customers

CustomerID	CompanyName	ContactName	ContactTitle	Address	City	Region	PostalCode	Country	P
ALFKI	Alfreds Futterkiste	Maria Anders	Sales Representative	Obere Str. 57	Berlin		12209	Germany	030 007
ANATR	Ana Trujillo Emparedados y helados	Ana Trujillo	Owner	Avda. de la Constitución 2222	México D.F.		05021	Mexico	(5) 472
ANTON	Antonio Moreno Taquería	Antonio Moreno	Owner	Mataderos 2312	México D.F.		05023	Mexico	(5) 393
AROUT	Around the Horn	Thomas Hardy	Sales Representative	120 Hanover Sq.	London		WA1 1DP	UK	(17 778
BERGS	Berglunds snabbköp	Christina Berglund	Order Administrator	Berguvsvägen 8	Luleå		S-958 22	Sweden	092 65
BLAUS	Blauer See Delikatessen	Hanna Moos	Sales Representative	Forsterstr. 57	Mannheim		68306	Germany	062
BLONP	Blondel père et fils	Frédérique Citeaux	Marketing Manager	24, place Kléber	Strasbourg		67000	France	88.
BOLID	Bólido Comidas preparadas	Martín Sommer	Owner	C/ Araquil, 67	Madrid		28023	Spain	(91) 82
BONAP	Bon app'	Laurence Lebihan	Owner	12, rue des Bouchers	Marseille		13008	France	91.
BOTTM	Bottom-Dollar Markets	Elizabeth Lincoln	Accounting Manager	23 Tsawassen Blvd.	Tsawassen	BC	T2F 8M4	Canada	(60 472
BSBEV	B's Beverages	Victoria	Sales	Fauntleroy	London		EC2 5NT	UK	(17

Figure 8.61 The HTML table Access exports won't win Web-design awards, but it's better than the HTML default format that appears if you forget to mark the Save Formatted check box.

Pages generated by exporting data from a table or query contain static data. To keep a page's data current, you must periodically re-export the table or query.

NOTE

You also can import data from standard HTML tables saved as an .htm file to an Access table. In the Files of Type list of the Import dialog, choose HTML Documents (*.html;*.htm).

EXPORTING TABLES TO ACTIVE SERVER PAGES

Active Server Pages overcome the need for periodic refreshing of static .htm pages by generating *dynamic pages*. Dynamic pages read the table data or execute a query to return the specified data each time a user opens a page. Access 2003's ASP export feature for tables and queries requires an ODBC data source for the database before you export the table. If you don't have a System or File DSN for the database, you must create one.

TIP

> Use ASP, not HTML, to make data from tables and queries available to intranet or Internet users in a basic tabular format. ASP requires more server resources than HTML pages when many users open the page simultaneously, but the advantage of providing current data outweighs the server load issue.

To create an ODBC data source and export Northwind.mdb's Suppliers table to ASP, do the following:

1. From Control Panel, launch the ODBC Administrator tool from the Administrative Tools subfolder of Control Panel in Windows XP/2000.
2. Click the System DSN tab to create a data source that's available regardless of who's logged on to the Web server, and click the Add button (the New button in Windows 2000) to open the Create New Data Source dialog.
3. Select the Microsoft Access Driver (*.mdb) in the Name list, and click Finish to open the ODBC Microsoft Access Setup dialog.
4. Type a short name, **NwindJet** for this example, in the Data Source Name text box and an optional description of the data source in the Description text box.
5. Click Select to open the Select Database dialog, navigate to Northwind.mdb in the ...\Office11\Samples folder, and double-click the file in the Database Name list to close the dialog. The ODBC Microsoft Access Setup dialog appears as shown in Figure 8.62. Northwind.mdb isn't secured, so you don't need to specify a system database (workgroup file).

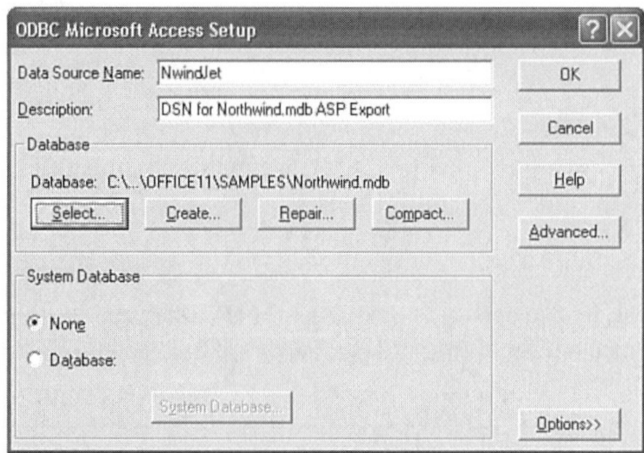

Figure 8.62
Create a new ODBC System DSN for the database that contains the table or query to generate the page's data.

6. Click OK twice to close the two dialogs.

7. Select the table to export, Suppliers for this example, in the Database window, and choose File, Export to open the Export Table 'Suppliers' To dialog.
8. Select Microsoft Active Server Pages (*.asp) in the Save As Type list, accept or change the default filename (Suppliers), and click Export to open the Microsoft Active Server Pages Export Options dialog.
9. Skip the HTML Template text box, and type the name of the ODBC DSN you specified in step 4 in the Data Source Name text box. The database isn't secured, so you can skip the User to Connect As and Password for User text boxes.
10. Type **http://** followed by the name of your Web server, **localhost** for this example, in the Server URL text box. Type a nominal value, such as **5** (minutes), in the Session Timeout (Min) text box (see Figure 8.63). Click OK to export *Filename*.asp to the ...wwwroot folder of the specified server.

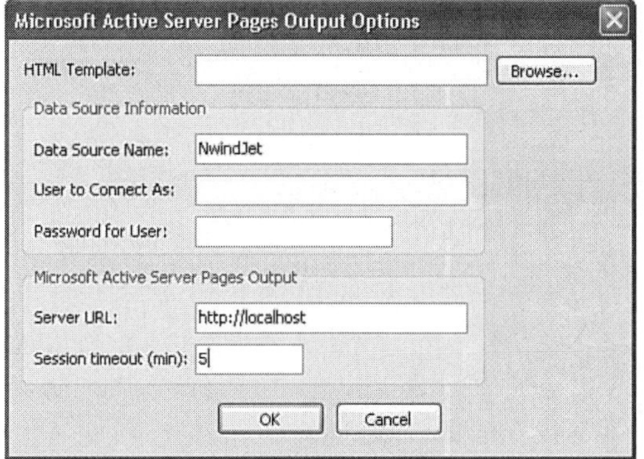

Figure 8.63 Exporting a simple ASP from a table of an unsecured database requires specifying only the ODBC DSN, the URL of the server, and a session timeout value.

11. Close Access, launch IE, and type **http://*servername*/*filename*.asp** in the Address text box. Press Enter to display the table (see Figure 8.64). If you don't close Access before opening the ASP page, you receive an HTTP 500.100 ASP "file in use" error.

NOTE

None of the hyperlinks in the Homepage field that refer to pages "(on the World Wide Web)" work, because ODBC or the generated ASP script doesn't translate the hyperlink field for Web pages to the required `<a href:... ></a>` format.

Exported ASP contain standard VBScript code to open a connection to the specified database with the OLE DB data provider for ODBC. An SQL statement, `SELECT * FROM [tablename]`, opens an Active Data Objects (ADO) Recordset of the table, and a loop structure populates the table rows with the contents of the Recordset. To view the ASP code, navigate to the server's ...\wwwroot folder and open the .asp file you exported in Notepad. Figure 8.65 shows most of the VBScript code for the Suppliers.asp page.

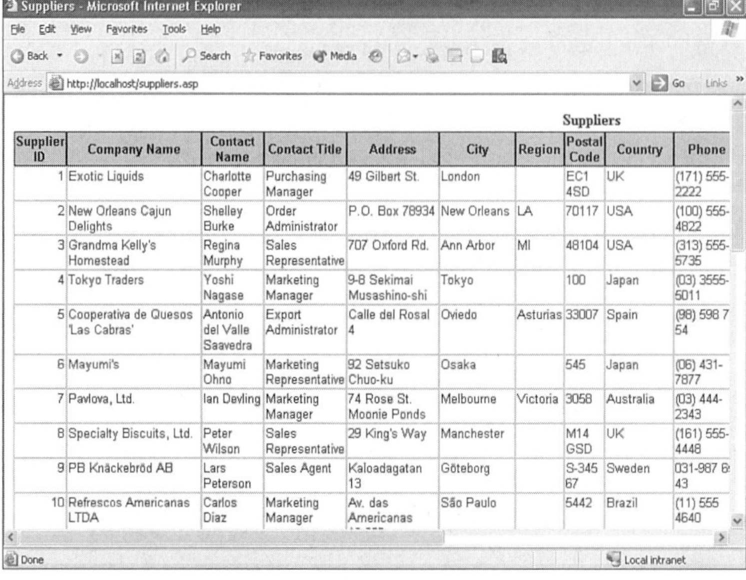

Suppliers

Supplier ID	Company Name	Contact Name	Contact Title	Address	City	Region	Postal Code	Country	Phone
1	Exotic Liquids	Charlotte Cooper	Purchasing Manager	49 Gilbert St.	London		EC1 4SD	UK	(171) 555-2222
2	New Orleans Cajun Delights	Shelley Burke	Order Administrator	P.O. Box 78934	New Orleans	LA	70117	USA	(100) 555-4822
3	Grandma Kelly's Homestead	Regina Murphy	Sales Representative	707 Oxford Rd.	Ann Arbor	MI	48104	USA	(313) 555-5735
4	Tokyo Traders	Yoshi Nagase	Marketing Manager	9-8 Sekimai Musashino-shi	Tokyo		100	Japan	(03) 3555-5011
5	Cooperativa de Quesos 'Las Cabras'	Antonio del Valle Saavedra	Export Administrator	Calle del Rosal 4	Oviedo	Asturias	33007	Spain	(98) 598 7 54
6	Mayumi's	Mayumi Ohno	Marketing Representative	92 Setsuko Chuo-ku	Osaka		545	Japan	(06) 431-7877
7	Pavlova, Ltd.	Ian Devling	Marketing Manager	74 Rose St. Moonie Ponds	Melbourne	Victoria	3058	Australia	(03) 444-2343
8	Specialty Biscuits, Ltd.	Peter Wilson	Sales Representative	29 King's Way	Manchester		M14 GSD	UK	(161) 555-4448
9	PB Knäckebröd AB	Lars Peterson	Sales Agent	Kaloadagatan 13	Göteborg		S-345 67	Sweden	031-987 6 43
10	Refrescos Americanas LTDA	Carlos Diaz	Marketing Manager	Av. das Americanas	São Paulo		5442	Brazil	(11) 555 4640

Figure 8.64 Tables or queries exported to ASP have the same table format as those Access exports as static HTML pages.

```
<HTML>
<HEAD>
<META HTTP-EQUIV="Content-Type" CONTENT="text/html;charset=windows-1252
<TITLE>Suppliers</TITLE>
</HEAD>
<BODY>
<%
Session.timeout = 5
If IsObject(Session("NwindJet_conn")) Then
    Set conn = Session("NwindJet_conn")
Else
    Set conn = Server.CreateObject("ADODB.Connection")
    conn.open "NwindJet","",""
    Set Session("? NwindJet_conn") = conn
End If
%>
<%
If IsObject(Session("Suppliers_rs")) Then
    Set rs = Session("Suppliers_rs")
Else
    sql = "SELECT * FROM [Suppliers]"
    Set rs = Server.CreateObject("ADODB.Recordset")
    rs.Open sql, conn, 3, 3
    If rs.eof Then
        rs.AddNew
    End If
    Set Session("Suppliers_rs") = rs
End If
%>
<TABLE BORDER=1 BGCOLOR=#ffffff CELLSPACING=0><FONT FACE="Arial" COLOR=
```

Figure 8.65 Access uses a component from Microsoft FrontPage to generate the VBScript code to establish the connection to the database and generate the Recordset to populate the table rows.

→ For more information on exporting Access tables in XML format, **see** "Exporting Tables and Queries to XML and HTML," **p. 954**.

EXPORTING TABLE DATA AS TEXT FILES

Exporting a table involves a sequence of operations similar to importing a file with the same format. To export a table as a comma- or tab-delimited file that you can use as a merge file with a variety of word-processing applications, complete these steps:

1. Select the table you want to export in the Database window, and choose File, Export to open the Export Table '*Tablename*' To dialog.
2. Select Text Files (*.txt;*.csv;*.tab;*.asc) in the Save as Type drop-down list. Use the Save In drop-down list to select the drive and folder in which you want to store the exported file, type a name and extension for the exported file in the Filename text box, and then click Save to start the Text Export Wizard.

8

NOTE

Using the Text Export Wizard, including its advanced options, is the same as using the Import Text Wizard described in the "Importing Text Files" section earlier in the chapter, except that the result is an external text file instead of an Access table. You save and reuse export specifications by the method described for import specs.

When exporting a text file, the Text Export Wizard doesn't have a step to edit field names or select field data types; these options aren't relevant when exporting data.

3. Follow the procedures as though you were importing a text file. Figure 8.66 shows the Customers table exported as a tab-separated text file from the Northwind.mdb database and displayed in Windows Notepad.

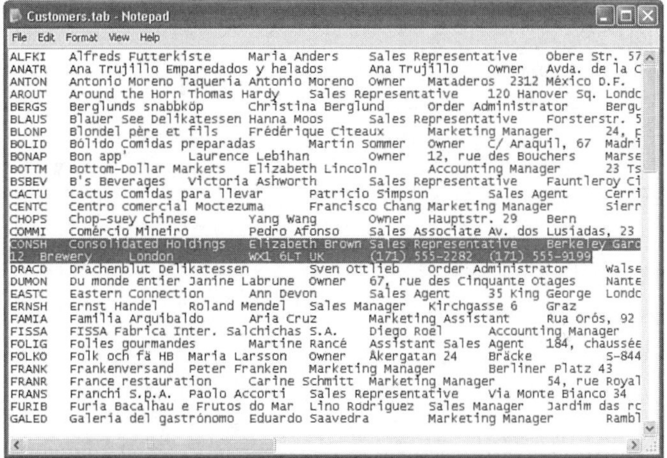

Figure 8.66
The two highlighted records of tab-separated text file demonstrates the problem that arises when fields contain newline pairs to, for instance, create multiline display of address data.

CAUTION

The two highlighted lines in Figure 8.66 are a single record from the Access table that was split into two text records during the export process. A newline pair is included in the Address field of the record for Consolidated Holdings. The purpose of the newline pair is to separate a single field into two lines: Berkeley Gardens and 12 Brewery. Use of newline pairs within fields causes many problems with exported files. Use of embedded newline pairs in text fields is a bad database design practice. Use two address fields if you need secondary address lines.

The records in files created by Access are exported in the order of the primary key. Any other order you might have created is ignored. If you don't assign primary-key fields, the records are exported in the sequence in which you entered them into the table.

EXPORTING DATA IN OTHER FILE FORMATS

In addition to text and Web-based formats, you can export data to any other file format that Access can import. Access supports exports to the following file formats:

- Excel .xls files (versions 3.0 through 11).
- Lotus 1-2-3 .wk? files.
- Paradox 3.x, 4.x, 5.0, 7.x, and 8.x; versions 7.x and 8.x require the BDE.
- dBASE III/III+, IV, 5.0, and 7.0; version 7.0 requires the BDE.
- Any format supported by an installed ODBC driver, including client/server databases. Exporting Visual FoxPro files is subject to the limitations described earlier in the chapter.

TROUBLESHOOTING

THE INCORRECT PASSWORD DIALOG

I received a "Can't decrypt file" message, even though the file isn't encrypted.

If you type a wrong password or just press Enter, Access informs you that it can't decrypt the file. You do, however, get another opportunity to type the password or click Cancel to terminate the attempt.

THE NULL VALUE IN INDEX DIALOG

I get a "Can't have Null value in index" message.

Occasionally, older Paradox .px index files don't have an index value for a record; when this situation occurs, you see a warning dialog with the message "Can't have Null value in index." Usually, you can disregard the message and continue linking or importing the file. The offending record, however, might not appear in the table; fixing the file in Paradox and starting over is better than ignoring the message.

THE MISSING MEMO FILE DIALOG

A "Cannot locate the requested Xbase memo file" message appears.

Both dBASE and Paradox use additional memo files to store the data from memo fields in a particular table. dBASE memo files have the .dbt file type, and Paradox memo files have the .mb file type. Access correctly decides that it can't import or link an external table if it can't open the table's associated memo file—either because the memo file doesn't exist, isn't in the same folder as the table with which it is associated, or contains nontext data.

IMPORTING FIXED-WIDTH TEXT FILES

When importing tables created from fixed-width text files, many errors occur.

You probably miscalculated one or more of the starting positions of a field. Locate the first field name with a problem; the names following it usually have problems, too. Close all open tables. From the Database window, select the table you imported and press Delete. If you have an Import Errors table, delete it, too. You can't delete an open table. Perform the importation process again and reposition the field breaks in the Import Text Wizard. Remember that the Wizard analyzes only the first 20 lines of the text file, so the guesses it makes about where to position the field breaks might be incorrect and might not allow enough room for the actual width of a field.

IN THE REAL WORLD—MICROSOFT GIVETH AND MICROSOFT TAKETH AWAY

Microsoft bundles a raft of no-additional-charge features in Windows XP/2000+ but there's no free lunch at the export/import counter when you upgrade from Access 97 to Access 2003. The most controversial issue is restriction of Office 2003 to running under Windows XP, 2000 Professional or Server, or Server 2003. Long-standing dBASE and Paradox import, export, and linking features disappeared in Access 2000, and even Microsoft's Visual FoxPro was slighted by losing its ISAM driver, while gaining limited import/export support with an ODBC driver that has known defects. These defects weren't corrected in Access 2003 and, because VFPODBC.dll is officially in Microsoft "maintenance" mode, never will be fixed.

Microsoft taketh away Windows 9x/Me compatibility and desktop database connectivity features, but giveth links to Outlook and Exchange folders, Windows Sharepoint Services, and InfoPath 2003 plus enhanced XML import/export operations. Fair bargain? Probably, because it's a good bet that more Access users are interested in Outlook/Exchange features than full xBase/Paradox/FoxPro support. These early desktop databases are on their way out. If Jet, in Microsoft's terms, is "not strategic," support for other desktop RDBMSs must be even lower on Microsoft's database totem pole. Unlike Visual Basic 6.0, Visual Basic .NET, and C#, Visual FoxPro's xBase dialect isn't a general-purpose Windows programming language.

NEW It remains to be seen if Access 2003's new XML import/export features score an immediate hit with Access power users and developers. For most current Access users, XML is more likely to be abbreviated as ineXplicable Munging Language. XML, however, is destined to replace text files and other intermediary formats—such as Excel's Business Interchange File Format (BIFF) and RTF—for interapplication communication and data exchange between systems. For example, you can export XML data from one or more Access tables and open the XML file in Excel as a formatted worksheet.

NOTE

One of the meanings of the term *munge* is converting data from one format to another, sometimes imperfectly. Early versions of Access used a function named `BIFFMunge` for Excel import/export. The Free On-Line Dictionary of Computing site offers a brief etymology of munge at `http://wombat.doc.ic.ac.uk/foldoc/foldoc.cgi?munge`.

Microsoft's.NET technology relies almost entirely on XML messaging and Web services based on the Simple Object Access Protocol (SOAP) for application integration and cross-platform communication. Use of Access 2003 with XML Web services is the subject of Chapter 31, "Creating and Consuming XML Web Services." One of the more promising uses of XML by Access 2003 is exporting live (dynamic), formatted reports from ADP. XML reports from Jet tables remain static in Access 2003, so live Jet reports are restricted to tables created with ASP. As noted in Chapter 1, "Access 2003 for Access 97 and 2000/2002 Users—What's New," Access 2003 is a great platform for becoming proficient in working with data-related XML Infosets, XSD schema, and XSL/T transformation style sheets.

The improved DAP features added by Access 2002 are certain to result in DAP replacing tables and queries exported as HTML or ASP. Banded pages, such as the Inventory by Category and Value page shown in Figure 8.67, are much easier for users to navigate than a 91-row table. Licensing policies for the Office Web Components (OWC) now make DAP practical for Internet as well as intranet applications. Unlike Office 2000's OWC, users no longer need an Office license to view DAP in IE 5+; if the Office 2003 version of OWC isn't installed on a user's PC, the download from the Microsoft Web site is automatic.

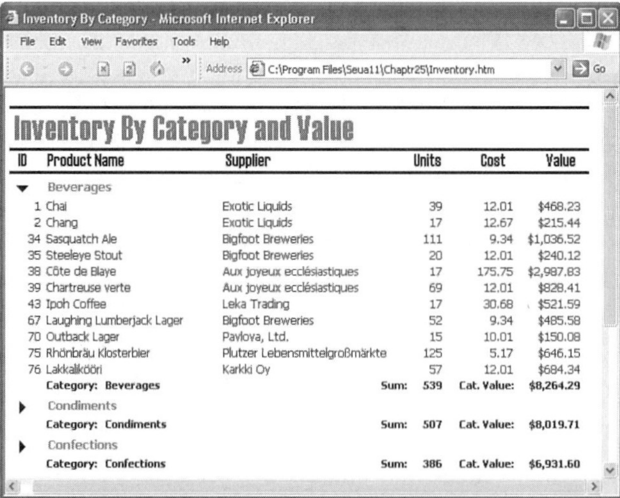

Inventory By Category and Value

ID	Product Name	Supplier	Units	Cost	Value
	Beverages				
1	Chai	Exotic Liquids	39	12.01	$468.23
2	Chang	Exotic Liquids	17	12.67	$215.44
34	Sasquatch Ale	Bigfoot Breweries	111	9.34	$1,036.52
35	Steeleye Stout	Bigfoot Breweries	20	12.01	$240.12
38	Côte de Blaye	Aux joyeux ecclésiastiques	17	175.75	$2,987.83
39	Chartreuse verte	Aux joyeux ecclésiastiques	69	12.01	$828.41
43	Ipoh Coffee	Leka Trading	17	30.68	$521.59
67	Laughing Lumberjack Lager	Bigfoot Breweries	52	9.34	$485.58
70	Outback Lager	Pavlova, Ltd.	15	10.01	$150.08
75	Rhönbräu Klosterbier	Plutzer Lebensmittelgroßmärkte	125	5.17	$646.15
76	Lakkalikööri	Karkki Oy	57	12.01	$684.34
	Category: Beverages	**Sum:**	**539**	**Cat. Value:**	**$8,264.29**
	Condiments				
	Category: Condiments	**Sum:**	**507**	**Cat. Value:**	**$8,019.71**
	Confections				
	Category: Confections	**Sum:**	**386**	**Cat. Value:**	**$6,931.60**

Figure 8.67 This modified version of a Microsoft design for a Data Access Page illustrates the advantage of banding for displaying read-only data from lengthy tables.

On the whole, Microsoft gaveth more in Access 2003 than they tooketh away from Access 97. Hopefully, the new features added in Access 2000, 2002, and 2003 will convince more users and developers to migrate from the still all-time favorite version—Access 97.

Transforming Data with Queries and PivotTables

CHAPTER 9

Designing Queries for Jet Databases

In this chapter

9

INTRODUCING JET QUERIES

Queries are an essential tool in any database management system. You use queries to select records, and add, update, and delete records in tables. Most often you use queries to select specific groups of records that meet criteria you specify. You can also use queries to combine information from different tables, providing a unified view of related data items. In this chapter, you learn the basics of creating your own select queries, including specifying selection criteria and using the results of your queries to generate reports and create new tables. You create queries using more than one table in Chapter 11, "Creating Multitable and Crosstab Queries," after you learn the details of how to use operators and create expressions in Chapter 10, "Understanding Jet Operators and Expressions."

This chapter covers queries that apply to Jet databases and to client/server databases, such as SQL Server, that you link to a conventional Access front-end .mdb file. When you link client/server tables to an Access front end, your application uses the Jet query engine to process the back-end data. Jet has its own dialect of SQL, called Jet SQL, which, for the most part, conforms to the ANSI SQL-92 standard but has several extensions that aren't included in SQL-92. All query techniques you learn in Part III, "Transforming Data with Queries and PivotTables," apply to Jet databases and client/server tables linked to an Access front end that stores application objects—queries, forms, reports, and modules—in an .mdb file.

In contrast, Access data projects (ADP) use SQL Server's query engine. ADP offers three types of queries—views, functions, and stored procedures—and uses the SQL Server design tools, called the *da Vinci toolset* in this book, for designing queries. (Microsoft used the da Vinci codename for the toolset during its beta cycle, and it stuck). SQL Server uses Transact-SQL (T-SQL), another flavor of SQL-92 that has many proprietary extensions to the language. Most of the Jet SQL `SELECT` query examples in this chapter also work for creating ADP views. Chapter 21, "Moving from Jet Queries to Transact-SQL," provides detailed coverage of SQL-92 topics and explains the differences between Jet SQL and T-SQL.

Jet SQL

The chapters of Part III include examples and brief explanations of the SQL statements the Jet query engine generates from your graphical query designs. The objective of these examples is to encourage learning "SQL by osmosis," a process similar to learning a foreign language by immersion rather than from a grammar textbook. By the time you complete Chapter 13, "Creating and Updating Jet Tables with Action Queries," you'll have a working knowledge of basic SQL syntax.

TRYING THE SIMPLE QUERY WIZARD

The Simple Query Wizard is aptly named; it's capable of generating only trivial select queries. If you don't have a numeric or date field in the table on which you base the query, the Wizard has only two dialogs—one to select the table(s) and fields to include and the other to name the query. Following are the characteristics of the Simple Query Wizard:

- You can't add selection criteria or specify the sort order of the query.
- You can't change the order of the fields in the query; fields always appear in the sequence in which you add them in the first Wizard dialog.
- If one or more of your selected fields is numeric, the Wizard lets you produce a summary query that shows the total, average, minimum, or maximum value of the numeric field(s). You also can include a count of the number of records in the query result set.
- If one or more of your selected fields is of the Date/Time data type, you can specify summary query grouping by date range—day, month, quarter, or year.

TIP

Use Crosstab queries for grouping records with numeric values, especially when you're interested in returning a time series, such as multiple monthly, quarterly, or yearly totals or averages. Crosstab queries deliver greatly enhanced grouping capability and show the query result set in a much more readable format compared to that delivered by the Simple Query Wizard. Chapter 11 shows you how to take maximum advantage of Jet SQL's powerful crosstab queries.

CREATING A SIMPLE SELECT QUERY

Northwind.mdb's Orders table has a Currency and several Date/Time fields, so it's the best choice for demonstrating the Simple Query Wizard. To give the Wizard a test drive with the Orders table, do the following:

1. Display Northwind.mdb's Database window and click the Queries shortcut.
2. Double-click the Create Query by Using Wizard shortcut to open the Simple Query Wizard's first dialog.
3. Select Table: Orders in the Tables/Queries list. All fields of the Orders table appear in the Available Fields list.
4. Select the OrderID field in the Available Fields list and click the right-arrow (>) button to add OrderID to the Selected Fields list and remove it from the Available Fields list. Alternatively, you can double-click the field to add to the query.
5. Repeat step 4 for the CustomerID, OrderDate, and Freight fields. The first Wizard dialog appears as shown in Figure 9.1.
6. Click Next to open the second Wizard dialog that lets you select between detail and summary queries. Accept the Detail option (see Figure 9.2).
7. Click Next to open the final dialog (see Figure 9.3). Rename the query to **qryOrders1** or the like, and click Finish to display the query result set in Datasheet view (see Figure 9.4).

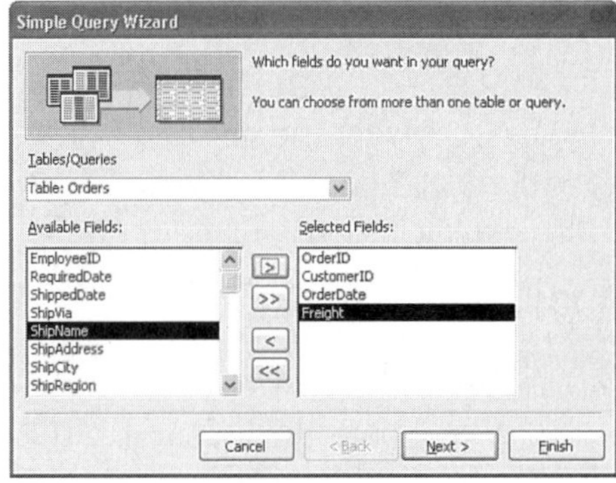

Figure 9.1
You select the source of the query—either a table or a query—in the first dialog of the Simple Query Wizard.

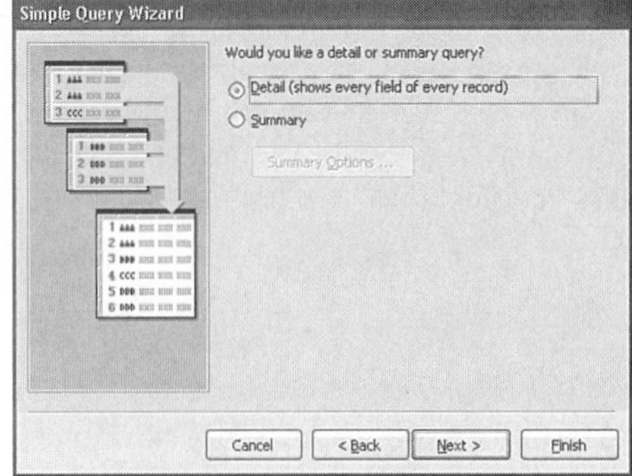

Figure 9.2
The second Wizard dialog, which appears only for data sources with numeric or date fields, gives you the option of displaying all records or generating a summary query.

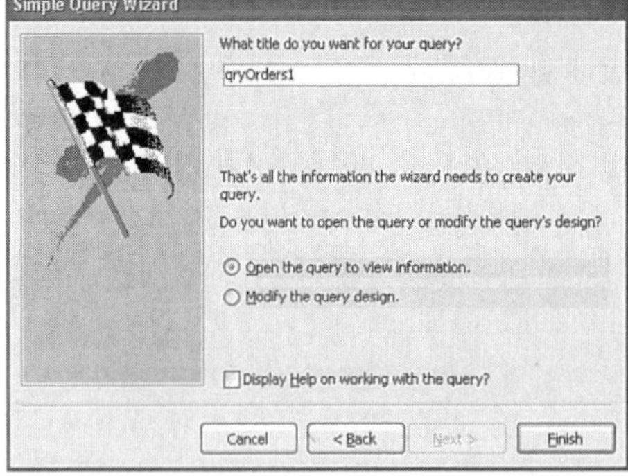

Figure 9.3
The final Wizard dialog lets you name the query. This book uses a naming convention, called Hungarian notation, which adds a two- or three-letter prefix (qry for queries) to Jet object names, except names of tables.

SQL

8. Open the toolbar's View button and choose SQL View from the list to open the SQL window, which displays the Jet SQL version of the query (see Figure 9.5). Alternatively, press Ctrl+> to move from Datasheet to SQL view.
9. Close the SQL window and save your changes if you altered the query's layout.

qryOrders1 : Select Query

Order ID	Customer	Order Date	Freight
10248	Wilman Kala	04-Jul-1996	$32.38
10249	Tradição Hipermercados	05-Jul-1996	$11.61
10250	Hanari Carnes	08-Jul-1996	$65.83
10251	Victuailles en stock	08-Jul-1996	$41.34
10252	Suprêmes délices	09-Jul-1996	$51.30
10253	Hanari Carnes	10-Jul-1996	$58.17
10254	Chop-suey Chinese	11-Jul-1996	$22.98
10255	Richter Supermarkt	12-Jul-1996	$148.33
10256	Wellington Importadora	15-Jul-1996	$13.97
10257	HILARIÓN-Abastos	16-Jul-1996	$81.91
10258	Ernst Handel	17-Jul-1996	$140.51
10259	Centro comercial Moctezuma	18-Jul-1996	$3.25
10260	Old World Delicatessen	19-Jul-1996	$55.09
10261	Que Delícia	19-Jul-1996	$3.05
10262	Rattlesnake Canyon Grocery	22-Jul-1996	$48.29
10263	Ernst Handel	23-Jul-1996	$146.06
10264	Folk och fä HB	24-Jul-1996	$3.67
10265	Blondel père et fils	25-Jul-1996	$55.28
10266	Wartian Herkku	26-Jul-1996	$25.73
10267	Frankenversand	29-Jul-1996	$208.58

Record: 1 of 830

Figure 9.4
The Wizard's query result set substitutes captions for the field names you selected in steps 4 and 5, and the customer name for the CustomerID lookup field. Queries inherit table properties, such as captions and lookup fields, from the data source.

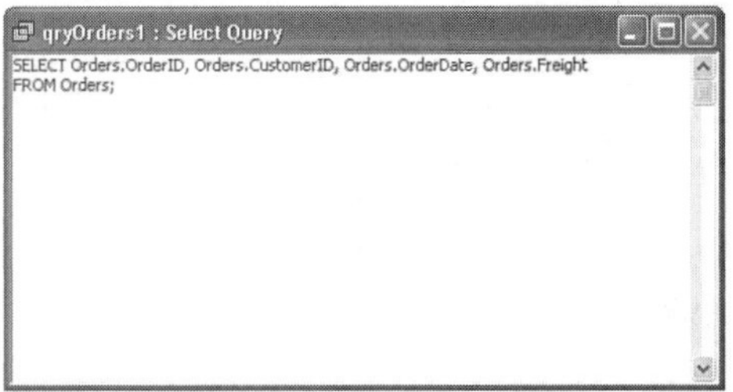

qryOrders1 : Select Query

```
SELECT Orders.OrderID, Orders.CustomerID, Orders.OrderDate, Orders.Freight
FROM Orders;
```

Figure 9.5
The SQL window displays the Jet SQL statement that the Simple Query Wizard generated from your selections in steps 4–6.

Jet SQL

The `SELECT Orders.OrderID, Orders.CustomerID, Orders.OrderDate, Orders.Freight FROM Orders;` statement generated by the Wizard is an example of a simple SQL `SELECT` query. The `Orders.` prefixes specify the query's source table name.

The `SELECT` keyword indicates that the query returns records; by tradition, SQL keywords in Jet and T-SQL are capitalized. Field lists contain field names, separated by commas. The `FROM` clause, `FROM` *`tablename`*, specifies the query's data source. Jet SQL uses the semicolon to indicate the end of a query; like the square brackets, the semicolon isn't necessary if the query includes only one complete SQL statement.

If you want to test the Simple Query Wizard's capability to base a query on another query and check the Wizard's summary query capabilities, do the following:

1. Return to the Database window and double-click the Create Query by Using Wizard shortcut to open the Simple Query Wizard's first dialog. Select Query: qryOrders1 or Orders Qry in the Tables/Queries list.

NOTE

Jet calls a query whose source is a query, rather than a table, a *nested query*. You sometimes see the term *subquery* incorrectly applied to a nested query. A subquery is an SQL statement for a query within a query.

2. Add only the OrderDate and Freight fields to the Selected Fields list.

TIP

Include only the field(s) by which the data is grouped (OrderDate) and the numeric value(s) to be summarized in a summary query. If you add other fields, such as OrderID, every record appears in the summary query, and you don't obtain the summary you're seeking.

3. Click Next to open the second Wizard dialog (refer to Figure 9.2). Select the Summary option and then click Summary Options to open the identically named dialog. Mark the Avg check box to calculate the average freight cost and mark the Count Records in Orders Qry check box to add a column with the record count for the group (see Figure 9.6).

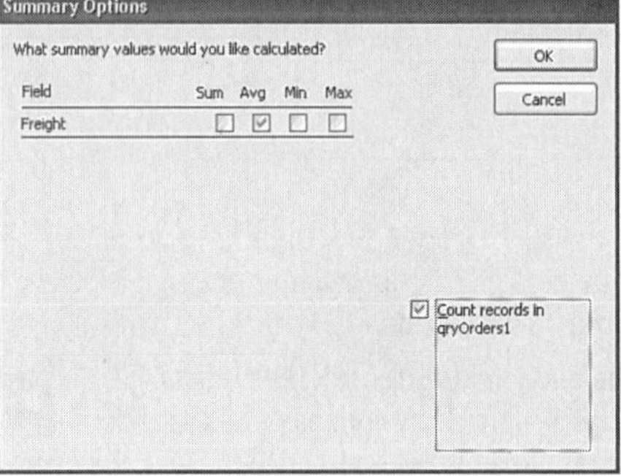

Figure 9.6 If you select a Summary query, you must specify one of the functions in the Summary Options dialog.

4. Click OK to return to the second Wizard dialog and then click Next to move to the third Wizard dialog. The Wizard has detected the OrderDate Date/Time field and offers you the choice of date grouping; select Quarter (see Figure 9.7).
5. Click Next to open the last Wizard dialog and replace the default query name, Orders Qry Query, with a more descriptive name, such as **qryOrdersSummary**.
6. Click Finish to execute the summary query. The query result set appears as shown in Figure 9.8. Open the SQL window to display the SQL statement that generates this considerably more complex query (see Figure 9.9).

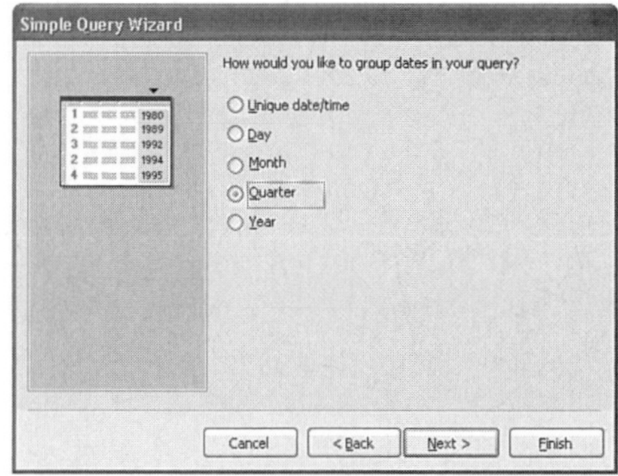

Figure 9.7 Summary queries with a field of the Date/Time data type open an additional Wizard dialog that lets you group the result set by a date interval.

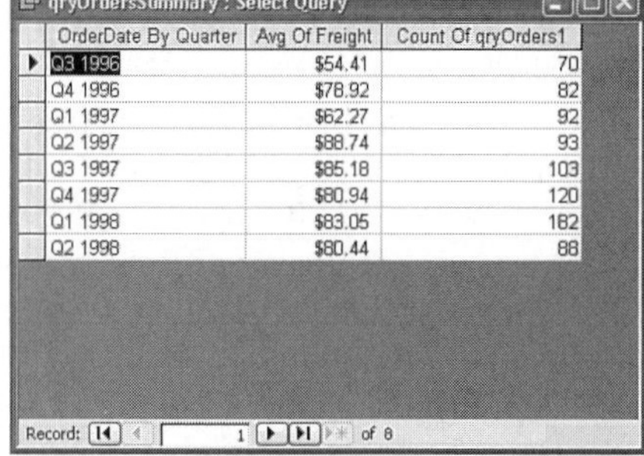

OrderDate By Quarter	Avg Of Freight	Count Of qryOrders1
Q3 1996	$54.41	70
Q4 1996	$78.92	82
Q1 1997	$62.27	92
Q2 1997	$88.74	93
Q3 1997	$85.18	103
Q4 1997	$80.94	120
Q1 1998	$83.05	182
Q2 1998	$80.44	88

Figure 9.8 The query result set displays the average freight charge and number of orders for each quarter within the range of dates for which data is available.

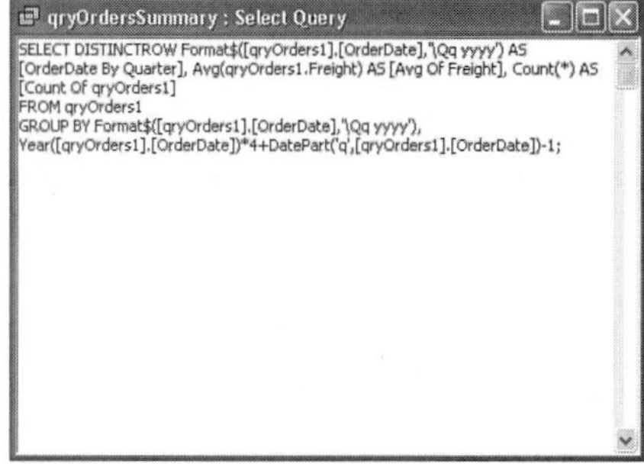


```
SELECT DISTINCTROW Format$([qryOrders1].[OrderDate],"\Qq yyyy') AS
[OrderDate By Quarter], Avg(qryOrders1.Freight) AS [Avg Of Freight], Count(*) AS
[Count Of qryOrders1]
FROM qryOrders1
GROUP BY Format$([qryOrders1].[OrderDate],"\Qq yyyy'),
Year([qryOrders1].[OrderDate])*4+DatePart('q',[qryOrders1].[OrderDate])-1;
```

Figure 9.9 The SQL statement for the Wizard's summary query belies the simplicity of the steps required to create the query.

For problems with attempted updates to a summary query, see the "Non-Updatable Summary Queries" topic of the "Troubleshooting" section near the end of the chapter.

Jet SQL

The SQL statement for the summary query, which is a bit advanced for this point in your SQL learning curve, requires formatting for better readability:

```
SELECT DISTINCTROW
   Format$([qryOrders1].[OrderDate],'\Qq yyyy')
      AS [OrderDate By Quarter],
   Avg(qryOrders1.Freight) AS [Avg Of Freight],
   Count(*) AS [Count Of qryOrders1]
FROM qryOrders1
GROUP BY Format$([qryOrders1].[OrderDate],'\Qq yyyy'),
   Year([qryOrders1].[OrderDate])*4+
   DatePart('q',[qryOrders1].[OrderDate])-1;
```

`DISTINCTROW` is a Jet SQL keyword that isn't required in this query. The `Format$` function determines the appearance of the first column (Q# *YYYY*). `AS` specifies the caption (alias) for the column. `Avg` is the aggregate function you selected in step 3. `Count(*)` adds the third column to the result set. Jet treats queries as if they were tables, so the `FROM` clause specifies the source query. `GROUP BY` is the clause that specifies the date grouping range you chose in step 4 to calculate the values in the second column.

Square brackets (`[ ]`) surround query column names–such as `OrderDate by Quarter`–that have spaces or punctuation symbols, which aren't permitted by the SQL-92 specification. In some cases, the Jet query analyzer adds square brackets where they're not needed, as in `[qryOrders1].[OrderDate]`.

`Avg`, `Year`, `DatePart`, and `Format$` are VBA functions executed by the Jet expression service. The next chapter shows you how to apply these functions to queries. SQL-92 and T-SQL don't include `DISTINCTROW` and VBA functions, but do support the `COUNT` function.

Summary queries—more commonly called aggregate queries—are a common element of decision-support applications that deliver time-based trend data to management. Aggregate queries also are the foundation for graphical data analysis, which is one of the subjects of Chapter 12, "Working with PivotTable and PivotChart Views." PivotTables and PivotCharts must be based on queries to present meaningful information. PivotTables have built-in aggregation features, so you can use detail queries as PivotTable data sources.

Using the Query Design Window

The Simple Query Wizard has limited usefulness, so the better approach is to design your queries from scratch in Access's graphical Query Design window. The Query Design window is one of Access's most powerful features.

To devise a simple query that lets you customize mailing lists for selected customers of Northwind Traders, for example, follow these steps:

1. Double-click the Create Query in Design View shortcut to open the Query Design window. The Show Table dialog is superimposed on the Query Design window, as shown in Figure 9.10. The tabbed lists in the Show Table dialog let you select from all existing tables, all queries, or a combination of all tables and queries. You can base a new query on one or more previously entered tables or queries.

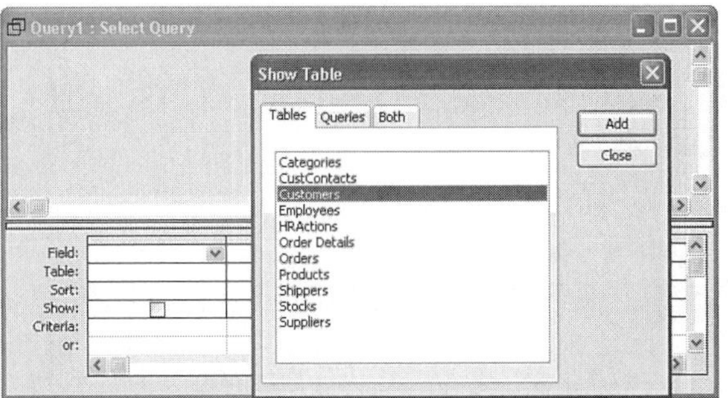

Figure 9.10
When you open a new query in Design view, the Show Table dialog lets you select from lists of tables, queries, or both to designate the new query's data source.

NOTE

If you select a table in the Tables page of the Database window, and then click the New Object toolbar button and select Query from the drop-down menu, Access automatically places the selected table in the Query Design window, without displaying the Show Tables dialog.

2. This example uses only tables in the query, so accept the default selection of Tables. Click (or use the ↓ key to select) Customers in the Show Table list to select the Customers table and then click the Add button. Alternatively, double-click Customers to add the table to the query. You can use more than one table in a query by choosing another related table from the list and choosing Add again. This example, however, uses only one table. After selecting the tables that you want to use, click Close.

The Fields list for the Customers table appears at the left in the upper pane of the Query Design window, and a blank Query Design grid appears in the lower pane. The Fields list displays all the names of the fields of the Customers table, but you must scroll to display more than five entries with the default Fields list size. The asterisk (*) item at the top of the list is a shortcut symbol for adding all table fields to the query.

SELECTING FIELDS FOR YOUR QUERY

After you add a table from the Show Table dialog, the next step is to decide which of the table's fields to include in your query. Because you plan to use this query to create a customer mailing list, you must include the fields that make up a personalized mailing address.

To select the fields to include in the Query Design grid, do this:

1. When you open the Query Design window, the cursor is located in the Field row of the first column. Click the List Box button that appears in the right corner of the first column or press Alt+↓ to open the Field Names list (see Figure 9.11).
2. Select the ContactName field as the first field header of the query or use the ↓ key to highlight the name and press Enter. The Field list in the lower pane closes.

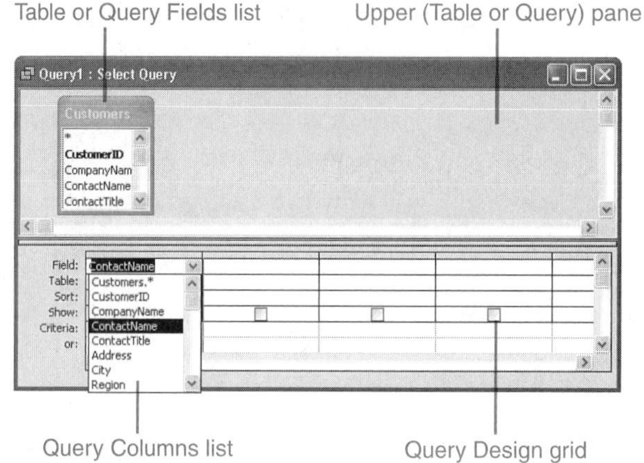

Figure 9.11
One way to add a field to your query is to select it in the drop-down query fields list of the Query Design grid.

3. Move the cursor to the second column by using the → or Tab key. Double-click CompanyName in the Customers Field list in the upper pane to add CompanyName as the second field of your query. Double-clicking entries in the upper pane's list is the second method that Access provides to add fields to a query.
4. Access offers a third method of adding fields to your query: the drag-and-drop method. To use the drag-and-drop method to add the Address, City, Region, PostalCode, and Country fields to columns 3 through 7, first select the fields. In the Customers Field list of the upper pane's Query Design window, click Address, and then Shift+click Country. Alternatively, select Address with the ↓ key, hold the Shift or Ctrl key, and press the ↓ key four more times. You've selected the Address, City, and Region fields, as shown in the Customers field list of Figure 9.12.

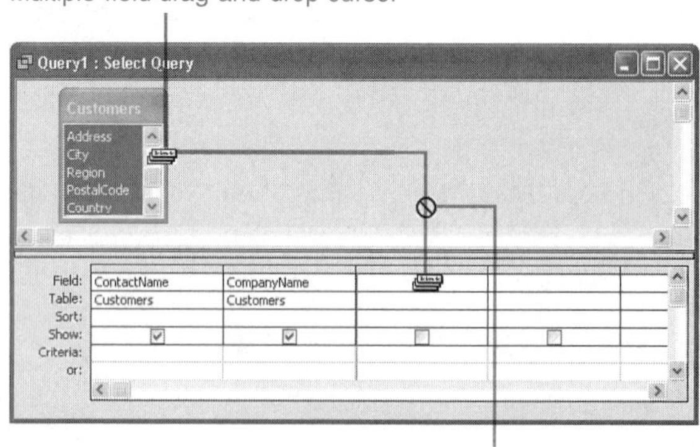

Figure 9.12
You also can select multiple fields in the table fields list and drag them to the Fields row of the Query Design grid.

5. Position the mouse pointer over the selected fields and click the left mouse button. Your mouse pointer turns into a symbol representing the three selected field names (after you drag the mouse a bit). Drag the symbol for the three fields to the third column of your query's Field row, as shown in Figure 9.12, and release the left mouse button.

> **NOTE**
>
> Access adds the five fields to your query, in sequence, starting with the column in which you drop the symbol. When the mouse pointer is in an area where you can't drop the fields, it becomes the international Do Not Enter symbol shown in the upper pane of the Query Design window of Figure 9.12.
>
> The Query Design grid in the lower pane displays four columns (in the default width) in a normal Query Design window. This query uses seven fields, so you need to drag the edges of the Query Design window to increase the width of the grid's display to expose two additional empty fields.

6. To reduce the columns' width, drag the divider of the grid's header bars to the left. Click the scroll-right button (on the horizontal scroll bar at the bottom of the window) or drag the scroll bar slider button to the right to expose the remaining fields. Your Query Design window appears as shown in Figure 9.13.

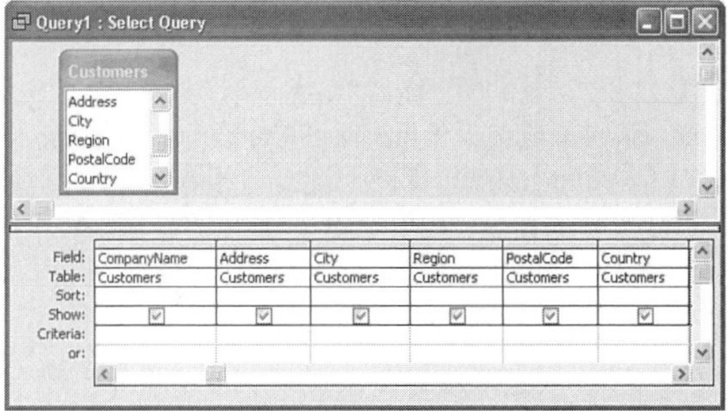

Figure 9.13 Reduce the width of the columns so Design view displays all columns in your current display resolution (800×600 in this book).

7. Click the Datasheet View toolbar button to execute the query. Alternatively, click the Run toolbar button to run your query against the Customers table.

You haven't yet entered any selection criteria in the Criteria row of the Query Design grid, so your query result set in the Customers table displays all records. These records appear in the order of the primary key index on the CustomerID field because you haven't specified a sorting order in the Sort row of the Query Design grid. (The values in the CustomerID field are alphabetic codes derived from the Company Name field.) Figure 9.14 shows the result of your first query after adjusting the width of the fields.

Query1 : Select Query

Contact Name	Company Name	Address	City	Region	Postal Code	Country
Maria Anders	Alfreds Futterkiste	Obere Str. 57	Berlin		12209	Germany
Ana Trujillo	Ana Trujillo Empar	Avda. de la Cons	México D.F.		05021	Mexico
Antonio Moreno	Antonio Moreno Ta	Mataderos 2312	México D.F.		05023	Mexico
Thomas Hardy	Around the Horn	120 Hanover Sq.	London		WA1 1DP	UK
Christina Berglund	Berglunds snabbkö	Berguvsvägen 8	Luleå		S-958 22	Sweden
Hanna Moos	Blauer See Delikat	Forsterstr. 57	Mannheim		68306	Germany
Frédérique Citeaux	Blondel père et fils	24, place Kléber	Strasbourg		67000	France
Martín Sommer	Bólido Comidas pr	C/ Araquil, 67	Madrid		28023	Spain
Laurence Lebihan	Bon app'	12, rue des Bou	Marseille		13008	France
Elizabeth Lincoln	Bottom-Dollar Marl	23 Tsawassen E	Tsawassen	BC	T2F 8M4	Canada
Victoria Ashworth	B's Beverages	Fauntleroy Circu	London		EC2 5NT	UK
Patricio Simpson	Cactus Comidas p	Cerrito 333	Buenos Aires		1010	Argentina
Francisco Chang	Centro comercial M	Sierras de Gran	México D.F.		05022	Mexico
Yang Wang	Chop-suey Chines	Hauptstr. 29	Bern		3012	Switzerland
Pedro Afonso	Comércio Mineiro	Av. dos Lusíada	São Paulo	SP	05432-043	Brazil
Elizabeth Brown	Consolidated Holdi	Berkeley Garder	London		WX1 6LT	UK
Sven Ottlieb	Drachenblut Delika	Walserweg 21	Aachen		52066	Germany
Janine Labrune	Du monde entier	67, rue des Cinq	Nantes		44000	France

Record: 1 of 91

Figure 9.14
The initial query design in Datasheet view displays the seven selected fields of all records in the Customers table.

SELECTING RECORDS BY CRITERIA AND SORTING THE DISPLAY

The mailing for which you're creating a list with your sample query is to be sent to U.S. customers only, so you want to include in your query only those records that have USA in the Country field. Selecting records based on the values of fields—that is, establishing the criteria for the records to be returned (displayed) by the query—is the heart of the query process.

Take the following steps to establish criteria for selecting the records to make up your mailing list:

1. Click the Design View toolbar button.
2. To restrict the result of your query to firms in the United States, type **USA** in the Criteria row of the Country column. Entering a criterion's value without preceding the value with an operator indicates that the value of the field must match the value you type. You don't need to add quotation marks to the expression; Access adds them for you (see the Country column in Figure 9.15).
3. Click the Show check box in the Country column to clear the check mark that appeared when you added the column. After you deactivate the Show check box, the Country field doesn't appear when you run your query. If you don't deactivate a Show check box, that field in the query appears in the query's result by default.
4. Move the cursor to the Postal Code column's Sort row and press Alt+↓ to display the sorting options for that field: Ascending, Descending, and (Not Sorted). Select the Ascending option to sort the query by Postal Code from low codes to high. At this point, the Query Design grid appears as shown in Figure 9.15.
5. Click the Datasheet View or Run button on the toolbar to display the result of the criterion and sorting order.

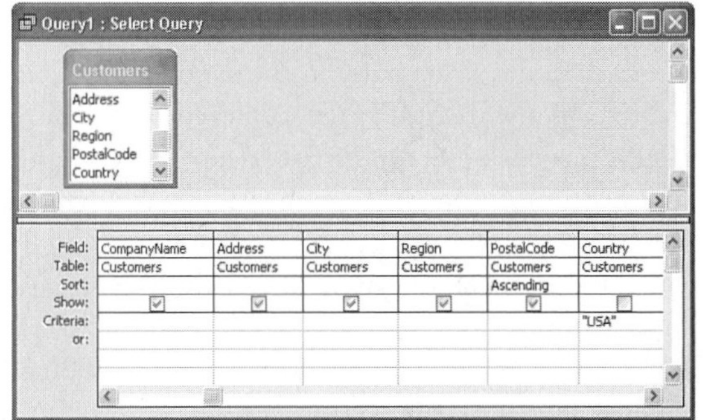

Figure 9.15
Add the USA criterion, hide the Country column, and apply an ascending sort order to the PostalCode column to complete the mailing list query.

Figure 9.16 shows the query result set that Jet refers to as an *updatable Recordset* (also called a Jet *Dynaset*), which is indicated by the tentative append (*) in the last (empty) row of the query result set. A `Recordset` object is a temporary table stored in your computer's memory; it's not a permanent component of the database file. You can edit the data in any visible fields of the underlying table(s) in Query Datasheet view if your Recordset is updatable.

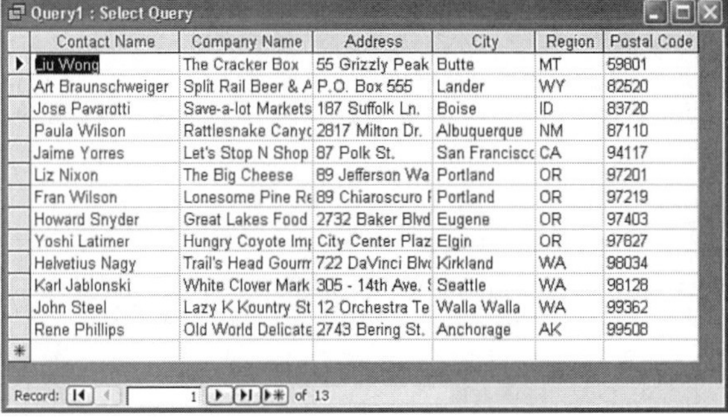
Query1 : Select Query

Contact Name	Company Name	Address	City	Region	Postal Code
Liu Wong	The Cracker Box	55 Grizzly Peak	Butte	MT	59801
Art Braunschweiger	Split Rail Beer & A	P.O. Box 555	Lander	WY	82520
Jose Pavarotti	Save-a-lot Markets	187 Suffolk Ln.	Boise	ID	83720
Paula Wilson	Rattlesnake Canyo	2817 Milton Dr.	Albuquerque	NM	87110
Jaime Yorres	Let's Stop N Shop	87 Polk St.	San Francisco	CA	94117
Liz Nixon	The Big Cheese	89 Jefferson Wa	Portland	OR	97201
Fran Wilson	Lonesome Pine Re	89 Chiaroscuro R	Portland	OR	97219
Howard Snyder	Great Lakes Food	2732 Baker Blvd	Eugene	OR	97403
Yoshi Latimer	Hungry Coyote Imp	City Center Plaz	Elgin	OR	97827
Helvetius Nagy	Trail's Head Gourm	722 DaVinci Blvd	Kirkland	WA	98034
Karl Jablonski	White Clover Mark	305 - 14th Ave. S	Seattle	WA	98128
John Steel	Lazy K Kountry St	12 Orchestra Te	Walla Walla	WA	99362
Rene Phillips	Old World Delicate	2743 Bering St.	Anchorage	AK	99508

Record: 1 of 13

Figure 9.16
Datasheet view displays the mailing list query's updatable result set (Recordset).

If you encounter problems with updating query result sets, see the "Missing Required Fields" topic of the "Troubleshooting" section near the end of the chapter.

Jet SQL

The SQL statement for a sorted `SELECT` query with a criterion is much simpler than the statement of the preceding example:

```
SELECT Customers.ContactName, Customers.CompanyName,
   Customers.Address, Customers.City, Customers.Region,
   Customers.PostalCode
FROM Customers
WHERE (((Customers.Country)="USA"))
ORDER BY Customers.PostalCode;
```

The `WHERE` clause specifies the selection criterion and the `ORDER BY` clause determines the sort order. `ASC[ENDING]` is the default sort order; `DESC[ENDING]` performs a reverse sort. SQL-92 permits abbreviation of the directional keywords. Access adds multiple sets of unneeded parentheses to the `WHERE` clause; if you remove them all, the query executes correctly.

PREVENTING UPDATES TO THE QUERY RESULT SET

You can edit any of the values in the seven columns of the query and, theoretically, add new records because the tentative append record appears in the last row of the query and the new record navigation button is enabled. You can't add a new record, however, because the query doesn't include the primary key field (CustomerID). If you attempt to add a new record, you receive the message shown in Figure 9.17. You must press Esc to delete all characters you typed in any field of the tentative append record.

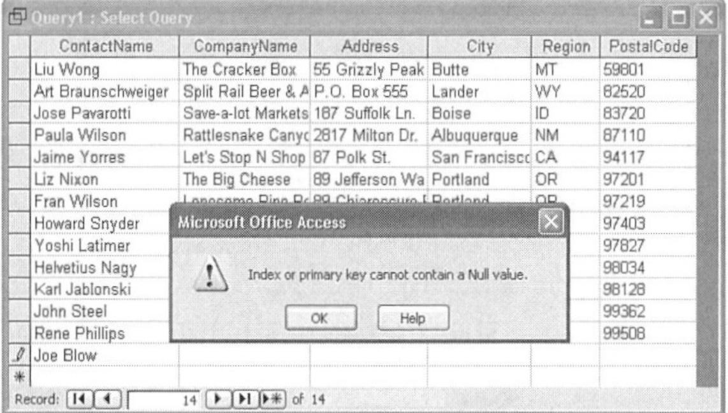

Figure 9.17
If you attempt to add a new record to the query, you receive the message shown here because you can't add a value for the primary key field, CustomerID.

The message that appears to a user of your query who attempts to add a new record is confusing, because most database users don't know what "primary key" or "null" value means. It's good database design practice to prevent users from attempting operations they can't complete, so you should designate the query as not updatable by changing the query type to a Jet *Snapshot*. The terms *Dynaset* and *Snapshot* refer to the cursor type of the query; a Dynaset has an *updatable cursor* and a Snapshot has a *read-only cursor*. A *cursor* is what RDBMSs use to navigate, read, and—if the cursor is updatable—update the rows returned by the query and add a new row.

To change the type of cursor, which doesn't affect the SQL statement for the query, do this:

1. Click the Design View button on the toolbar to return to Query Design view.
2. Right-click in an empty area in the upper Query Design pane, and choose Properties to open the Query Properties dialog.
3. Select the Recordset Type text box, open the drop-down list, and choose Snapshot (see Figure 9.18).

4. Return to Datasheet view to verify that the tentative append record is missing and the new record navigation button is disabled (see Figure 9.19).
5. Press Ctrl+S, choose File, Save, or close the query, type a name for the query in the text box, **qryCustomersUSA** for this example, and click OK to save the query.

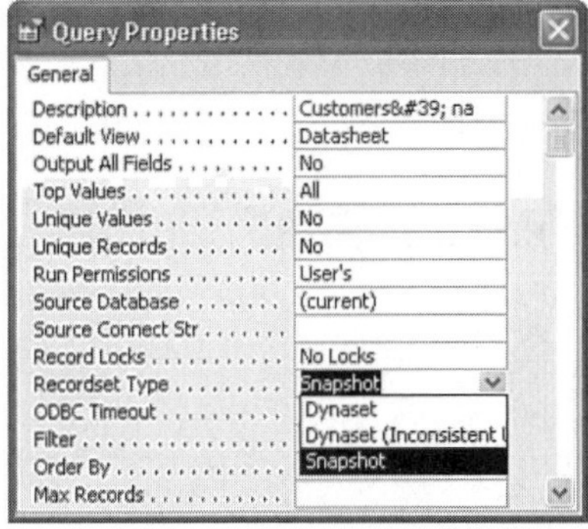

Figure 9.18
Open the Query Properties dialog and select Snapshot as the value of the Recordset Type property to create a read-only query result set.

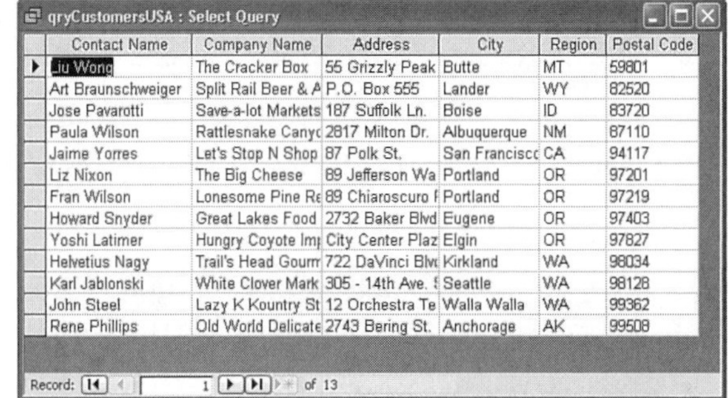
qryCustomersUSA : Select Query

Contact Name	Company Name	Address	City	Region	Postal Code
Liu Wong	The Cracker Box	55 Grizzly Peak	Butte	MT	59801
Art Braunschweiger	Split Rail Beer & A	P.O. Box 555	Lander	WY	82520
Jose Pavarotti	Save-a-lot Markets	187 Suffolk Ln.	Boise	ID	83720
Paula Wilson	Rattlesnake Canyo	2817 Milton Dr.	Albuquerque	NM	87110
Jaime Yorres	Let's Stop N Shop	87 Polk St.	San Francisco	CA	94117
Liz Nixon	The Big Cheese	89 Jefferson Wa	Portland	OR	97201
Fran Wilson	Lonesome Pine Re	89 Chiaroscuro R	Portland	OR	97219
Howard Snyder	Great Lakes Food	2732 Baker Blvd	Eugene	OR	97403
Yoshi Latimer	Hungry Coyote Imp	City Center Plaz	Elgin	OR	97827
Helvetius Nagy	Trail's Head Gourm	722 DaVinci Blvc	Kirkland	WA	98034
Karl Jablonski	White Clover Mark	305 - 14th Ave. S	Seattle	WA	98128
John Steel	Lazy K Kountry St	12 Orchestra Te	Walla Walla	WA	99362
Rene Phillips	Old World Delicate	2743 Bering St.	Anchorage	AK	99508

Record: 1 of 13

Figure 9.19
The read-only Snapshot query doesn't have a tentative append record and the new record button is disabled.

When you save the query, the Northwind.mdb file saves only the design specifications of the query, not the values that the query contains. The query design specification is called a `QueryDef` object. When you open the query, Jet executes the query and displays the result set in Datasheet view.

CREATING MORE COMPLEX CRITERIA

To limit your mailing to customers in a particular state or group of states, you can add a Criteria expression to the Region or PostalCode field. To restrict the mailing to customers in California, Oregon, and Washington, for example, you can specify that the value of the PostalCode field must be equal to or greater than 90000. Alternatively, you can specify that Region values must be CA, OR, and WA.

Follow these steps to restrict your mailing to customers in California, Oregon, and Washington:

1. Open the query, and click the Design View toolbar button.
2. Move to the Region column and type CA in the first criterion row of the Region column. Access adds the quotation marks around CA (as it did when you restricted your mailing to U.S. locations with the USA criterion).

3. Press the ↓ key tzo move to the next criterion row in the Region column. Type **OR** and then move to the third criterion row and type **WA**. Your query design now appears as shown in Figure 9.20. Access also adds the required quotation marks to these criteria.

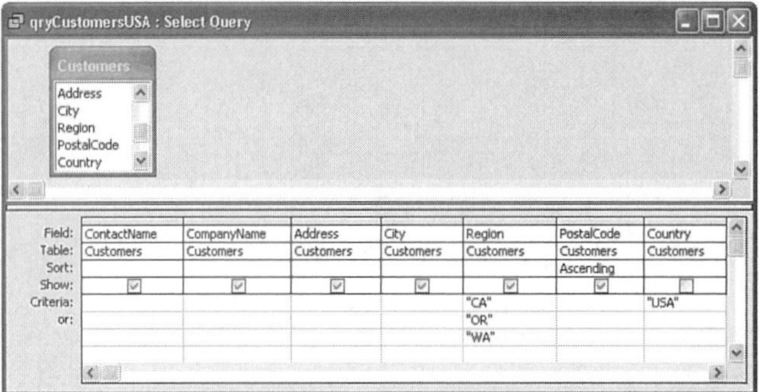

Figure 9.20
You can further restrict records returned by the query with additional criteria in the Region field.

4. Click the Datasheet View or Run toolbar button. The query result set appears as shown in Figure 9.21.

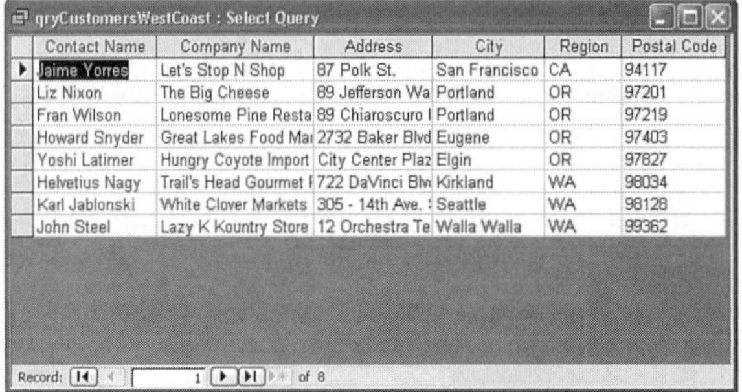

Contact Name	Company Name	Address	City	Region	Postal Code
Jaime Yorres	Let's Stop N Shop	87 Polk St.	San Francisco	CA	94117
Liz Nixon	The Big Cheese	89 Jefferson Wa	Portland	OR	97201
Fran Wilson	Lonesome Pine Resta	89 Chiaroscuro I	Portland	OR	97219
Howard Snyder	Great Lakes Food Ma	2732 Baker Blvd	Eugene	OR	97403
Yoshi Latimer	Hungry Coyote Import	City Center Plaz	Elgin	OR	97827
Helvetius Nagy	Trail's Head Gourmet I	722 DaVinci Blv	Kirkland	WA	98034
Karl Jablonski	White Clover Markets	305 - 14th Ave.	Seattle	WA	98128
John Steel	Lazy K Kountry Store	12 Orchestra Te	Walla Walla	WA	99362

Figure 9.21
The query result set with the additional criteria include only records for the three West Coast states.

After you type a criterion on the same line as a previously entered criterion in another field, only those records that meet both criteria are selected for display. In the preceding example, therefore, records with Region values equal to CA and Country values equal to USA, and records with Region values of OR and WA are displayed.

Jet SQL

The SQL statement that includes the additional criteria is

```
SELECT Customers.ContactName, Customers.CompanyName,
   Customers.Address, Customers.City, Customers.Region,
   Customers.PostalCode
FROM Customers
WHERE (((Customers.Region)="CA") AND ((Customers.Country)="USA"))
   OR (((Customers.Region)="OR")) OR (((Customers.Region)="WA"))
ORDER BY Customers.PostalCode;
```

Again, Access adds many superfluous parentheses, but the first element of the `WHERE` clause requires a single pair in the `(Customers.Region ="CA" AND Customers.Country)="USA")` expression.

To be displayed, records for `Region` values `OR` and `WA` need not have `Country` values equal to `USA`, because the `USA` criterion is missing from the OR and WA rows. This omission doesn't affect the selection of records in this case, because all `OR` and `WA` records also are `USA` records. Thus the `WHERE` clause can be simplified to `WHERE Customers.Region="CA" OR Customers.Region="OR" OR Customers.Region="WA"`. If you edit the SQL statement accordingly, the query result set is the same.

9

CHANGING THE NAMES OF QUERY COLUMN HEADERS

You can substitute a query's field header names with column header names of your choice—a process called aliasing—but only if the header name hasn't been changed by an entry in the field Caption property of the table. If yours is a U.S. firm, for example, you might want to change Region to State and PostalCode to ZIP. (Canadian firms might want to change only Region to Province.)

As demonstrated in the following example, you can't change the PostalCode field for queries based on the Customers table because the PostalCode field previously has been changed (aliased) to Postal Code by the Caption property for the field. You can, however, make the change to the Region field because this field isn't aliased at the table level.

TIP

If you already have a main document for mail merge operation, substitute the main merge document's merge field names for the table's field header names in your query.

→ For more information on merging data with documents, **see** "Using the Access Mail Merge Wizard," **p. 308**.

NOTE

Field names in queries that have been altered by use of the Caption property in the source table can't be aliased, so don't use the Caption property of table fields. If you want to display different field headers, use a query for this purpose. In a client/server RDBMS, such a query is called an SQL `VIEW`. Aliasing field names in tables rather than in queries isn't considered a generally accepted database design practice.

To change the query column header names, perform the following steps:

1. Click the Design View button on the toolbar. Then place the cursor in the Field column containing the field header name that you want to change—in this case, the Region column.
2. Press F2 to deselect the field; then press Home to move the cursor to the first character position.
3. Type the new name for the column and follow the name with a colon (with no spaces) as in **State:**. The colon separates the new column name that you type from the existing

table field name, which shifts to the right to make room for your addition. The result, in this example, is State: Region.

4. Use the arrow key to move to the PostalCode field and repeat steps 2 and 3, typing **ZIP**: as that header's new name. The result is ZIP: PostalCode.
5. Change the column header for the ContactName field to **Contact**; change the column header for the CompanyName field to **Company**.
6. Delete the three criteria ("CA" Or "OR" Or "WA" criterion you added to the SQL statement described in the preceding section) from the State: Region column so that all records for the United States appear (see Figure 9.22). If you altered the SQL statement, add the Country field to the grid, clear the Show check box, and add **USA** as the criterion.

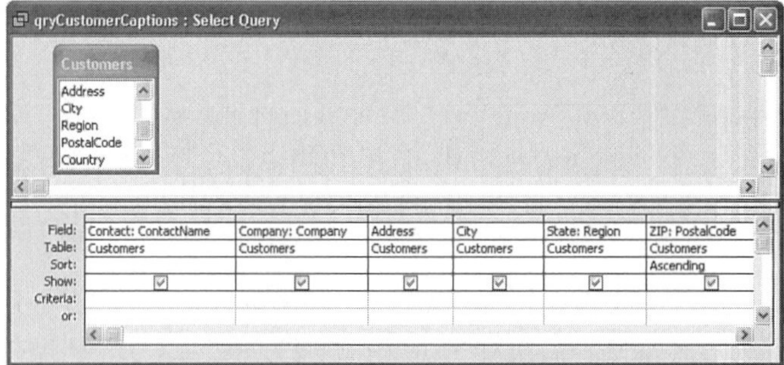

Figure 9.22 This query design attempts to assign aliases to field names that have Caption property values assigned at the table level.

7. Click the Run or Datasheet View button on the toolbar to execute the query. Observe that only the Region column header is changed to State; the other columns are unaffected by the alias entry (see Figure 9.23).

qryCustomersUSA : Select Query

Contact Name	Company Name	Address	City	State	Postal Code
Liu Wong	The Cracker Box	55 Grizzly Peak	Butte	MT	59801
Art Braunschweiger	Split Rail Beer & A	P.O. Box 555	Lander	WY	82520
Jose Pavarotti	Save-a-lot Markets	187 Suffolk Ln.	Boise	ID	83720
Paula Wilson	Rattlesnake Cany	2817 Milton Dr.	Albuquerque	NM	87110
Jaime Yorres	Let's Stop N Shop	87 Polk St.	San Francisc	CA	94117
Liz Nixon	The Big Cheese	89 Jefferson Wa	Portland	OR	97201
Fran Wilson	Lonesome Pine Re	89 Chiaroscuro I	Portland	OR	97219
Howard Snyder	Great Lakes Food	2732 Baker Blvd	Eugene	OR	97403
Yoshi Latimer	Hungry Coyote Im	City Center Plaz	Elgin	OR	97827
Helvetius Nagy	Trail's Head Gourm	722 DaVinci Blv	Kirkland	WA	98034
Karl Jablonski	White Clover Mark	305 - 14th Ave.	Seattle	WA	98128
John Steel	Lazy K Kountry St	12 Orchestra Te	Walla Walla	WA	99362
Rene Phillips	Old World Delicate	2743 Bering St.	Anchorage	AK	99508

Record: 1 of 13

Figure 9.23 The table's Caption property value overrides alias names assigned by the query. Only the Region field, which doesn't have a caption, is aliased to State in this example.

8. Choose File, Save As, and save your query with the name **qryUSMailList**.

Jet SQL

The SQL statement that attempts to rename all query columns is

```
SELECT Customers.ContactName AS Contact,
   Customers.CompanyName AS Company,
   Customers.Address, Customers.City,
   Customers.Region AS State,
   Customers.PostalCode AS ZIP
FROM Customers
WHERE (((Customers.Country)="USA"))
ORDER BY Customers.PostalCode;
```

Although the SQL statement renames four fields, only the `Customer.Region` field receives a renamed column.

TIP

To make field aliasing in queries operable, in Table Design view delete the entry in the Caption field for each aliased field of the table. Deleting these entries makes the aliases you entered in the preceding example work as expected.

PRINTING YOUR QUERY AS A REPORT

You often use queries to print quick, ad hoc reports. Access 2003 lets you print your report to a printer, a Microsoft Word .rtf (rich-text format) file, an Excel worksheet .xls file, a DOS .txt (text) file, or as an attachment to an e-mail message. You also can publish a query to a Web server. The table export procedures described in the preceding chapter also apply to queries.

Previewing your query table's appearance to see how the table will appear when printed is usually a good idea. After you determine from the preview that everything in the table is correct, you can print the finished query result set in various formats.

To preview a query result set before printing it, follow these steps:

1. In Query Datasheet view, click the Print Preview toolbar button. A miniature version of the query table appears in Report Preview mode.
2. Position the Zoom pointer (the magnifying glass cursor) anywhere on the table and click the left mouse button or the Zoom button above the window to view the report at approximately the scale at which it will print.
3. Use the vertical and horizontal scroll bar buttons to position the preview in the window (see Figure 9.24).

NOTE

Field width in the query table is based on the column width that you last established in Run mode. You might have to drag the right edge of the field header buttons to the right to increase the columns' width so that the printed report doesn't truncate the data. If the query data's width exceeds the available printing width (the paper width minus the width of the left and right margins), Access prints two or more sheets for each page of the report.

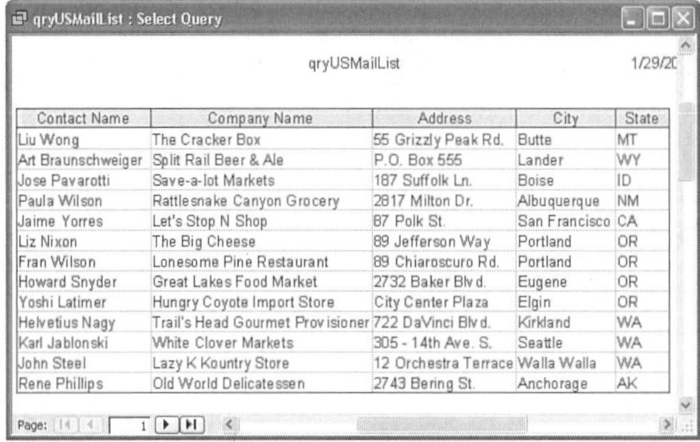
qryUSMailList : Select Query

qryUSMailList 1/29/20

Contact Name	Company Name	Address	City	State
Liu Wong	The Cracker Box	55 Grizzly Peak Rd.	Butte	MT
Art Braunschweiger	Split Rail Beer & Ale	P.O. Box 555	Lander	WY
Jose Pavarotti	Save-a-lot Markets	187 Suffolk Ln.	Boise	ID
Paula Wilson	Rattlesnake Canyon Grocery	2817 Milton Dr.	Albuquerque	NM
Jaime Yorres	Let's Stop N Shop	87 Polk St.	San Francisco	CA
Liz Nixon	The Big Cheese	89 Jefferson Way	Portland	OR
Fran Wilson	Lonesome Pine Restaurant	89 Chiaroscuro Rd.	Portland	OR
Howard Snyder	Great Lakes Food Market	2732 Baker Blvd.	Eugene	OR
Yoshi Latimer	Hungry Coyote Import Store	City Center Plaza	Elgin	OR
Helvetius Nagy	Trail's Head Gourmet Provisioner	722 DaVinci Blvd.	Kirkland	WA
Karl Jablonski	White Clover Markets	305 - 14th Ave. S.	Seattle	WA
John Steel	Lazy K Kountry Store	12 Orchestra Terrace	Walla Walla	WA
Rene Phillips	Old World Delicatessen	2743 Bering St.	Anchorage	AK

Page: 1

Figure 9.24
You can quickly print a query by clicking the Print Preview toolbar button and clicking the table to zoom it to approximately the print scale.

4. Right-click the Print Preview window and choose Page Setup to open the Page Setup dialog shown in Figure 9.25. If necessary, click the Margins tab to display the Margins page.

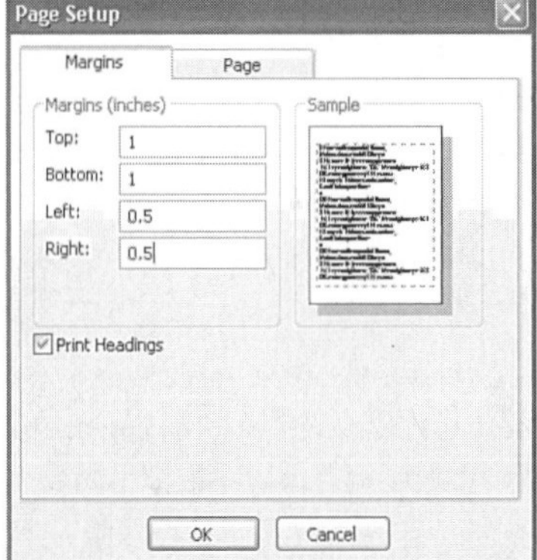

Figure 9.25
The Margins page of the Print Setup dialog lets you change printing margins from the default 1-inch values. The Page page has orientation, paper size and source, and printer selection options.

5. Enter any changes that you want to make to the margins; mark the Print Headings check box if you want to print the field header names. Click the Page tab to change the print orientation, paper size or source, or printer. Then click OK to return to Print Preview.

6. Click the Print toolbar button to print your query report.

CREATING OTHER TYPES OF QUERIES

Access lets you create the following four basic types of queries to achieve different objectives:

- *Select* queries extract data from one or more tables and display the data in tabular form.

- *Crosstab* queries summarize data from one or more tables in the form of a spreadsheet. Such queries are useful for analyzing data and creating graphs or charts based on the sum of the numeric field values of many records.

- *Action* queries create new database tables from query tables or make major alterations to a table. Such queries let you add or delete records from a table or make changes to records based on expressions that you enter in a query design.
- *Parameter* queries repeatedly use a query and make only simple changes to its criteria. The mailing list query that you created earlier is an excellent candidate for a parameter query because you can change the criterion of the Region field for mailings to different groups of customers. When you run a parameter query, Access displays a dialog to prompt you for the new criterion. Parameter queries aren't actually a separate query type because you can add the parameter function to select, crosstab, and action queries.

Chapter 11 and Chapter 13 explain how to create each of the four query types. Creating a table from the mailing list query to export to a mail merge file is an example of an action query. In fact, this is the simplest example of an action query and also the safest because make-table queries don't modify data in existing tables. A make-table query creates a new table from your query result set.

→ To review the use of tables for Word mail merge operations, **see** "Using the Access Mail Merge Wizard," **p. 308**.

CREATING AND USING A SIMPLE MAKE-TABLE ACTION QUERY

To create a table from your mailing list query, you first must convert the query from a select to an action query. Follow these steps to make this change:

1. Open your mailing list query in Query Design view and choose Query, Make-Table Query. (You can access the Query menu only in Query Design view.) Alternatively, click the Query Type toolbar button and select Make-Table Query to open the Make Table dialog.
2. In the Table Name text box, type a descriptive table name for your query table, such as **tblUSMailList** (see Figure 9.26).

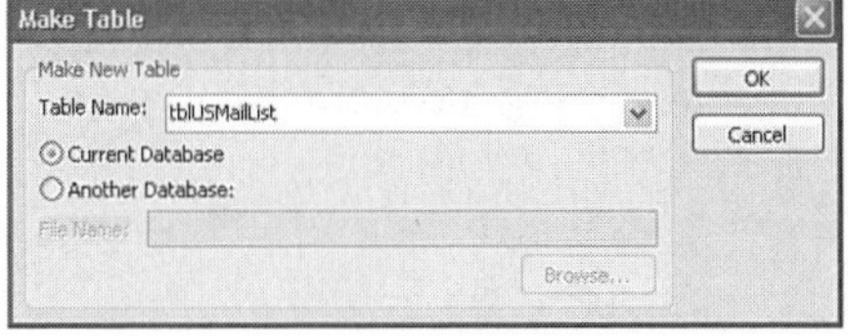

Figure 9.26 Specify the table name for your make-table query. When creating a table with a query, it's a good practice to use the tbl prefix to identify the table as one created by a query.

NOTE

> The Make Table dialog lets you define your query table's properties further in several ways. You can add the table to the Northwind database by choosing the Current Database option (the default). You also can pick the Another Database option to add the table to a different database that you specify in the File Name text box.

9

3. Click OK. Access converts your select query to the make-table type of action query.
4. Save your make-table query with a new name and close it. The query's icon in the Database window now is prefixed by an exclamation point, which indicates that the query is an action query.

Jet SQL

The SQL statement for the make-table query is

```
SELECT Customers.ContactName AS Contact,
   Customers.CompanyName AS Company,
   Customers.Address, Customers.City,
   Customers.Region AS State, Customers.PostalCode AS ZIP
INTO tblUSMailList
FROM Customers
WHERE (((Customers.Country)="USA"))
ORDER BY Customers.PostalCode;
```

The clause that differentiates the make-table query from the select query from which it's derived is `INTO tblMailList`. The `INTO` clause lets you specify the table name.

Now that you've converted your query from a select query to an action query, you can create a new U.S. mailing list table. To create the table, follow these steps:

1. Run the newly converted action query table to create your mailing list by double-clicking its name in the Queries page of the Database window. Acknowledge the message that asks you to confirm that the table, if it exists, will be overwritten, and acknowledge another warning about the number of rows to be "pasted" to the new table (see Figure 9.27).

Figure 9.27 Access displays two warning messages before your make-table query creates the table if you haven't cleared the Action Queries and Record Changes text boxes on the Edit/Find page of the Options dialog.

2. Click the Tables Object shortcut in the Database window. Access adds the new tblUSMailList table to the list of tables in the Northwind database.
3. Double-click the tblUSMailList item to open the table. Its contents are identical to the contents of the Datasheet view of the make-table query.

After you create the new table, you can export its data to any of the other file formats supported by Access. To do so, use any of the methods described in Chapter 8, "Linking, Importing, and Exporting Data."

ADDING A PARAMETER TO YOUR MAKE-TABLE QUERY

A simple modification to your mailing list query lets you enter a selection criterion, called a parameter, from a prompt generated by Access. Parameterized queries are very useful for generating custom tables for Word mail-merge operations. You can use the same merge specifications with different tables to generate multiple lists for selected regions or types of recipients.

→ For more information on parameterized queries, **see** "Designing Parameter Queries," **p. 440**.

To create a parameterized SELECT query, follow these steps:

1. Close the tblUSMailList table and then click the Queries shortcut in the Database window.

2. Right-click the qryUSMailList query that you created earlier in the chapter, and choose Design View to display your make-table action query in design mode.
3. Type **[Enter the state code:]** in the first criterion row of the State: Region column, as shown in Figure 9.28. The enclosing square brackets indicate that the entry is a prompt for a parameter when you run the action query.

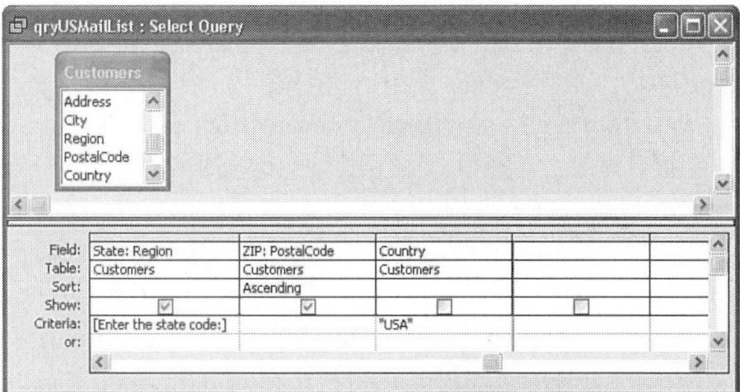

Figure 9.28
Adding a criterion enclosed in square brackets creates a prompt for a value to filter the query result set.

4. Choose File, Save As, and save your query with a new name, such as **qryStateMailList**.
5. Change to Datasheet view. Access opens the Enter Parameter Value dialog, which contains the prompt for you to enter the state criterion. Type **WA** for this example (see Figure 9.29), and click OK to display the parameter query result set (see Figure 9.30).

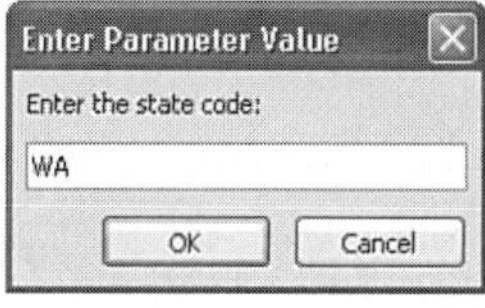

Figure 9.29
The Enter Parameter dialog includes the prompt you added as the criterion of the field for which a value is required.

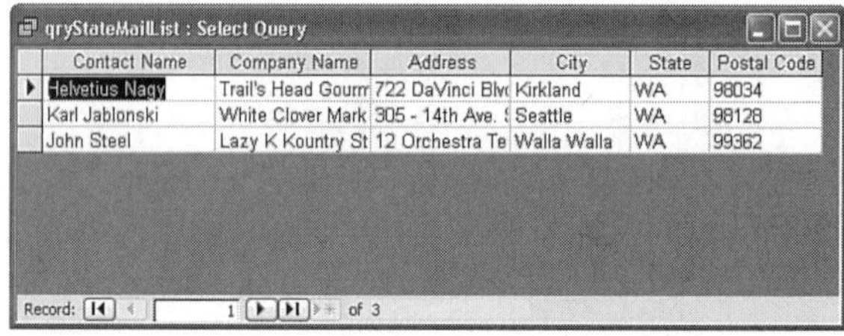

Contact Name	Company Name	Address	City	State	Postal Code
Helvetius Nagy	Trail's Head Gourn	722 DaVinci Blvc	Kirkland	WA	98034
Karl Jablonski	White Clover Mark	305 - 14th Ave. S	Seattle	WA	98128
John Steel	Lazy K Kountry St	12 Orchestra Te	Walla Walla	WA	99362

Figure 9.30
This query result set illustrates the effect of applying a parameter to a SELECT query.

Jet SQL

The Jet SQL statement for the parameterized make-table query is

```
SELECT Customers.ContactName AS Contact,
   Customers.CompanyName AS Company,
   Customers.Address, Customers.City,
   Customers.Region AS State, Customers.PostalCode AS ZIP
INTO tblUSMailList
FROM Customers
WHERE (((Customers.Region)=[Enter the state code:])
   AND ((Customers.Country)="USA"))
ORDER BY Customers.PostalCode;
```

The first `Customers.Region)=[Enter the state code:]` criterion of the `WHERE` clause specifies the prompt and opens the Enter Parameter Value dialog. This syntax is Jet-specific and isn't supported by SQL-92 or T-SQL. ADP use SQL Server functions to return parameterized query result sets.

Access doesn't limit you to using a single parameter. For example, you can replace the "USA" criterion for the Country field with [Enter the country name:], and drag the Country column to the left of the Region column so the country prompt occurs first. In the case of the Orders table, however, you encounter a problem with countries such as Germany and the UK that don't have entries in Region columns. See the "Problems with Null Values in Parameter Fields" of the next section for more information on this issue.

TROUBLESHOOTING

MISSING REQUIRED FIELDS

I created a query that shows the tentative append record, but when I try to add a new record, I receive a "The field 'FieldName' can't contain a Null value because the Required property is set to True" error message. I don't want FieldName in the query.

You must include in your query result set all columns whose Required property value is set to Yes. This means, of course, that each of these fields must have a value typed in it. A unique primary key value is required to add a new record to any table with a primary key. For example, attempting to add a new record to a query on the Customers table that doesn't include CustomerID and CustomerName columns fails, because CustomerID is the primary key and CustomerName is a required field of the table.

NON-UPDATABLE SUMMARY QUERIES

I can't update data in my summary query.

Summary queries aggregate data, so there's no direct relationship between the content of a query row and records in the underlying table(s). This means that there's no way for changes to aggregate values (dates, totals, averages, and the like) to propagate back to the table records. If you want to fudge the figures, change your select summary query to a make-table summary query, and then alter the data in the new table.

PROBLEMS WITH NULL VALUES IN PARAMETER FIELDS

When I enter an empty parameter value to return records without an entry in the specified field, the query returns no records.

You must edit the Jet SQL statement for the query to include an `OR FieldName IS NULL` expression to the `WHERE` clause to return records for fields with missing values. For example, in a query against the Orders table with Region and Country parameters, you must add `OR Customers.Region IS NULL` to return records for Germany and other countries whose Region values are missing. Following is the SQL statement that corrects the missing records for Germany problem:

```
SELECT Customers.ContactName AS Contact,
   Customers.CompanyName AS Company,
   Customers.Address, Customers.City,
   Customers.Region AS State,
   Customers.PostalCode AS ZIP
INTO tblUSMailList
FROM Customers
WHERE Customers.Country=[Enter the country name:]
   AND (Customers.Region=[Enter the state code:]
   OR Customers.Region IS NULL)
ORDER BY Customers.PostalCode;
```

In the preceding SQL statement, non-essential parentheses added by Access (not Jet) have been removed. The parentheses surrounding the `(Customers.Region=[Enter the state code:] OR Customers.Region IS NULL)` expression are required to group the two condition expressions into a single criterion. This issue exemplifies the importance of learning SQL while you're gaining experience with query design.

IN THE REAL WORLD—OPTIMIZING QUERY DESIGN

The objective of select query design is to convert raw data to useful information. The design of decision-support queries in production database applications is a combination of art and science.

THE ART OF QUERY DESIGN

An artful query design returns the result set in the format that's most meaningful to the recipient. For example, a query that displays orders sorted by customer and uses the customer code for identification might be understandable by a salesperson, but not management. Salespeople are likely to know the codes for their particular customers. Few sales or marketing managers, however, are capable of memorizing hundreds or thousands of codes. This is especially true if the codes are numeric, rather than based on the first few letters of customers' names, as is the case for the Northwind Customers table.

Access's table lookup feature propagates to queries; when you specify CustomerID as a query column for the Orders table, a table lookup against Customers automatically substitutes CompanyName for CustomerID in the query result set. On the other hand, database purists object to displaying tables with embedded lookup queries that disguise the actual design of the table.

Another aspect of the art of query design is appropriate left-to-right and top-to-bottom ordering of query columns. If your summary query is a time series—such as qryOrdersSummary that you created in the "Trying the Simple Query Wizard" section at the beginning of the chapter—the Order Date column is the most important, so it appears in the leftmost column. If you're writing Access applications for others, make sure to interview prospective users to determine their column presentation priorities. Use drag and drop to optimize the relative position of columns in Datasheet view.

Most recent data probably is what users want, so applying a descending sort on the Order Date column aids information usability. You can quickly apply a descending sort on a date column in Datasheet view by right-clicking the field-name header, and choosing Sort Descending from the context menu.

Apply intuition and inductive reasoning when designing decision-support queries. Access makes it easy to alter the presentation of your queries in Datasheet view. As in music, painting, dance, and the other performing and pictorial arts, practice and experimentation are the keys to query artistry. This is especially true when you design queries that act as the data source for PivotTables and PivotCharts.

THE SCIENTIFIC SIDE OF QUERY DESIGN

The scientific part of query design is optimizing query performance. All production database applications deliver query result sets over some type of network, usually a Local Area Network (LAN) but often a Wide Area Network (WAN), such as the Internet. The performance of queries executed over LANs—and, especially WANs—is dependent on a multitude of factors, the most important of which is the network connection, followed by the amount of network traffic. Although broadband Internet access is becoming more widespread, most Internet users still connect with dial-up modems. Even if you're writing queries for execution on a single PC, plan ahead for networking your application.

The tables of the Northwind.mdb sample database contain far fewer records than you find in typical production databases, and thus aren't representative of the databases behind real-world applications. The nine-person Northwind Traders sales force produced only 830 orders over a span of almost two years, indicating a serious lack of sales productivity. If you have 15MB of disk space to spare, install the Oakmont.mdb database from the \Seua11\Oakmont folder of the accompanying CD-ROM and run test queries against its tables. To better emulate network performance, install Oakmont.mdb on a file-sharing server and link the tables to a new .mdb file on your client PC. The Students table has about 30,000 rows, which is more typical of a production customers table. The Enrollments table has 50,000 records.

With networked data, smaller definitely is better. Limit the data returned by your query to only that required by your application's immediate need. It's especially necessary to restrict the amount of data you send to modem-connected mobile users, whether they dial into your LAN or get their data over the Internet. You minimize the amount of data sent "over the wire" to database users' PCs in two ways—setting precise criteria and limiting the number of columns.

Setting precise criteria minimizes the number of rows sent to the client PC. For example, restrict initial queries against large tables—such as those containing orders or invoices—to provide only the current month's or week's orders. Create separate "last month," "this quarter," and "last quarter" queries for users who need historical data. Jet's query-expression service lets you write queries that automatically roll over when the month or quarter changes.

There's seldom a reason to include all fields (by using the field list's * choice) in a query. Include in the initial query only those fields necessary to provide the basics. For example, you might want to include the ShipName column in a query on the Orders table to identify the customer, but don't include the ShipAddress, ShipCity, ShipRegion, ShipPostalCode, and ShipCountry columns in management reports. Only salespeople and shipping departments need detailed destination data. Salespeople only need shipping information for their particular accounts, so you can use EmployeeID as a criterion to limit the number of records that have large text fields.

Don't include OLE Object (usually images) or Memo fields in initial queries unless they're absolutely essential. Access doesn't automatically retrieve these data types unless the user double-clicks an OLE Object cell or moves the cursor to a Memo field, but data in OLE Object and Memo fields often is very large. A modem-connected user who accidentally double-clicks a 1MB high-resolution image won't be happy when his computer is tied up for several minutes downloading unwanted data. If some users require either of these field data types, create a special query for them.

The science of query design requires detailed analysis and deductive reasoning. Keep these basic query design rules in mind as you progress through the remaining chapters of the "Transforming Data with Queries and PivotTables" part of this book.

CHAPTER 10

UNDERSTANDING JET OPERATORS AND EXPRESSIONS

In this chapter

WRITING EXPRESSIONS FOR QUERY CRITERIA AND DATA VALIDATION

Chapter 6, "Entering, Editing, and Validating Jet Table Data," briefly introduced you to operators and the expressions that use them when you added validation rules to table fields. Chapter 9, "Designing Queries for Jet Databases," touched on expressions again when you devised selection criteria for the query that you created. Expressions play an important role in all the chapters that follow.

Much of this chapter is devoted to describing the VBA functions available to Jet 4.0 for dealing with data of the Numeric, Date/Time, and Text field data type. Functions play important roles in every element of Access, from validation rules for tables and fields of tables to the control of program flow with VBA. You use functions when creating queries, forms, reports, and even more extensively when writing VBA and VBScript code. To use Access 2003 effectively, you must know what functions are available to you and how to use functions and operators effectively.

10

NOTE

> As mentioned in earlier chapters, the Jet expression service enables Jet 4.0 to take advantage of most VBA 6.0 functions in validation rules for Jet tables. You use VBA 6.0 functions to set criteria and format fields of queries against Jet databases and client/server databases attached to Access front-end .mdbs.
> Access data projects (ADP), which use the SQL Server query processor, don't support VBA/Jet functions and use different characters for some operators. You must use corresponding Transact-SQL (T-SQL) built-in functions, where available, for `CHECK` constraints, `VIEW` column formatting, `WHERE` clause criteria, and elsewhere. T-SQL built-in functions aren't the same as SQL Server functions, which are more properly called *user-defined functions*.

If you're upgrading to Access 2003 from Access 97 or earlier, here's a list of the new functions and features introduced by Access 2000 that are germane to this chapter:

- **`MonthName`** and **`WeekdayName`** functions return a string containing the localized (language- or locale-dependent) name of a month and day.
- **`Filter`**, **`InstrRev`**, **`Join`**, **`Replace`**, **`Split`**, and **`StrReverse`** are new string manipulation functions.
- **`Round`** returns a numeric value rounded to the specified number of decimal places.
- VBA 6.0 adds four specialized **`Format...`** functions: **`FormatCurrency`**, **`FormatDateTime`**, **`FormatNumber`**, and **`FormatPercent`** that you can substitute for the generic **`Format`** function in VBA code and, as of Access 2002, in queries.
- The VBA Editor, common to all VBA-enabled Office 200x and 2003 members, replaces the Module window of Access 97 and earlier.

- Access 2003 calls the Debug window of Access 97 and earlier the *Immediate* window, but you still press Ctrl+G (Debug) to open it. You use the VBA Editor's Immediate window in this chapter to experiment with expressions and functions.

Access 2003, which continues to use VBA 6.0, adds no new functions to Access 200x.

NOTE NEW

> Access 2003's new macro security feature—called Jet *sandbox mode*—proscribes the use of unsafe VBA expressions. Here's how Microsoft describes unsafe expressions: "Unsafe expressions contain methods or functions that could be exploited by malicious users to access drives, files, or other resources for which they do not have authorization." None of the functions of this chapter are blocked unless they are used to supply the default value of a text box control on a form, report, or data access page.

T-SQL

This chapter provides brief descriptions of the SQL Server Transact-SQL (T-SQL) substitutes for Jet/VBA operators and functions, where equivalent or similar operators and functions exist. Chapter 21, "Moving from Jet Queries to Transact-SQL," provides more detailed information on differences between T-SQL and Jet query syntax.

UNDERSTANDING THE ELEMENTS OF EXPRESSIONS

An *expression* is a statement of intent. If you want an action to occur after meeting a specific condition, your expression must specify that condition. To select records in a query that contains ZIP field values of 90000 or higher, for example, you use the expression

```
ZIP >= 90000
```

if the ZIP field has a numeric data type.

Arithmetic calculations are expressions also. If you need an ExtendedAmount field in a query, for example, use

```
ExtendedAmount: Quantity * UnitPrice
```

as the expression to create calculated values in the data cells of the ExtendedAmount column.

To qualify as an expression, a statement must have at least one operator and at least one literal, identifier, or function. In some cases, such as simple query criteria and field-validation rules, the equals operator (=) is inferred. The following list describes these elements:

- *Operators* include the familiar arithmetic symbols `+`, `-`, `*` (multiply), and `/` (divide), as well as many other symbols and abbreviations. Some operators are specific to Access or SQL, such as the `Between`, `In`, `Is`, and `Like` operators.

- *Literals* consist of values that you type, such as **12345** or **ABCDE**. Literals are used most often to create default values and, in combination with field identifiers, to compare values in table fields and query columns.
- *Identifiers* are the names of objects in Access (such as forms and reports) or Jet (such as fields in tables) that return distinct numeric or text values. The term *return*, when used with expressions, means that the present value of the identifier is substituted for its name in the expression. For example, the field name identifier CompanyName in an expression returns the value (a firm name) of the CompanyName field for the currently selected record. Access has five predefined named constants that also serve as identifiers: **`True`**, **`False`**, `Yes`, `No`, and **`Null`**. Named constants and variables that you create in Access VBA also are identifiers.
- *Functions* return a value in place of the function name in the expression, such as the `Date`... and `Format`... functions, which are used in the examples in Chapter 9. Unlike identifiers, most functions require you to supply an identifier or value as an argument enclosed by parentheses. Later in this chapter, the "Functions" section explains functions and their arguments.

10

When literals, identifiers, or functions are used with operators, these combinations are called *operands*. The following sections explain these four elements of expressions more thoroughly.

NOTE

Expressions in this book appear in `monospace` type to distinguish expressions from the explanatory text. Operators, including symbolic operators, built-in functions, and other reserved words and symbols of VBA, are set in **`monospace bold`** type. (VBA reserved words appear in blue color in the Code-Editing window of modules.) SQL operators and names of Access objects are set in `monospace` type; by convention, SQL-92 reserved words are capitalized.

OPERATORS

Access and VBA provide six categories of operators that you can use to create expressions:

- *Arithmetic* operators perform addition, subtraction, multiplication, and division.
- *Assignment* and *comparison* operators set values and compare values.
- *Logical* operators deal with values that can only be true or false.
- *Concatenation* operators combine strings of characters.
- *Identifier* operators create unambiguous names for database objects so that you can assign the same field name, for example, in several tables and queries.
- Other operators, such as the `Like`, `Is`, `In`, and `Between` operators, simplify the creation of expressions for selecting records with queries.

Operators in the first four categories are available in almost all programming languages. Identifier operators are specific to Access; the other operators of the last category are provided only in RDBMSs that create queries based on SQL. The following sections explain how to use each of the operators in these categories.

ARITHMETIC OPERATORS

Arithmetic operators operate only on numeric values and must have two numeric operands, with the following exceptions:

- When the minus sign (-) changes the sign (negates the value) of an operand. In this case, the minus sign is called the *unary minus*.
- When the equal sign (=) assigns a value to an Access object or a VBA variable identifier.

Table 10.1 lists the arithmetic operators that you can use in Access expressions.

TABLE 10.1 ARITHMETIC OPERATORS

Operator	Description	Example
+	Adds two operands	`Subtotal + Tax`
-	Subtracts two operands	`Date - 30`
- (unary)	Changes the sign of an operand	`-12345`
*	Multiplies two operands	`Units * UnitPrice`
/	Divides one operand by another	`Quantity / 12.55`
\	Divides one integer operand by another	`Units \ 2`
`Mod`	Returns the remainder of division by an integer	`Units Mod 12`
^	Raises an operand to a power (exponent)	`Value ^ Exponent`

Jet/VBA operators are identical to operators used by all versions of BASIC. If you aren't familiar with BASIC programming, the following operators need further explanation:

Operator	Description
\	The integer division symbol is the equivalent of "goes into," as used in the litany of elementary school arithmetic: 3 goes into 13 four times, with 1 leftover. When you use integer division, operators with decimal fractions are rounded to integers, but any decimal fraction in the result is truncated.
`Mod`	An abbreviation for modulus, this operator returns the leftover value of integer division. Therefore, 13 Mod 4, for example, returns 1.
^	The exponentiation operator raises the first operand to the power of the second. For example, `2 ^ 4`, or two to the fourth power, returns `16 (2*2*2*2)`.

These three operators seldom are used in business applications but often occur in VBA program code.

T-SQL

SQL Server supports all Jet/VBA operators, except ^ (exponentiation). T-SQL substitutes % for **Mod**.

Assignment and Comparison Operators

Table 10.1 omits the equal sign associated with arithmetic expressions because in Access you use it in two ways—neither of which falls under the arithmetic category. The most common use of the equal sign is as an assignment operator; = assigns the value of a single operand to an Access object or to a variable or constant. When you use the expression `= "Q"` to assign a default value to a field, the equal sign acts as an assignment operator. Otherwise, = is a comparison operator that determines whether one of two operands is equal to the other.

10

Comparison operators compare the values of two operands and return logical values (**True** or **False**) depending on the relationship between the two operands and the operator. An exception is when one of the operands has the **Null** value. In this case, any comparison returns a value of **Null**. Because **Null** represents an unknown value, you cannot compare an unknown value with a known value and come to a valid **True** or **False** conclusion.

Table 10.2 lists the comparison operators available in Access.

Table 10.2 Comparison Operators

Operator	Description	Example	Result
<	Less than	`123 < 1000`	**True**
<=	Less than or equal to	`15 <= 15`	**True**
=	Equal to	`2 = 4`	**False**
>=	Greater than or equal to	`1234 >= 456`	**True**
>	Greater than	`123 > 123`	**False**
<>	Not equal	`123 <> 456`	**True**

The principal uses of comparison operators are to create validation rules, to establish criteria for selecting records in queries, to determine actions taken by macros, to create joins using the SQL-89 `WHERE` and SQL-92 `JOIN` clauses, and to control program flow in VBA.

Logical Operators

Logical operators (also called *Boolean* operators) are used most often to combine the results of two or more comparison expressions into a single result. Logical operators can combine only expressions that return the logical values **True**, **False**, or **Null**. With the exception of **Not**, which is the logical equivalent of the unary minus, logical operators always require two operands.

Table 10.3 lists the Jet/VBA logical operators.

TABLE 10.3 LOGICAL OPERATORS

Operator	Description	Example 1 Example 2	Result 1 Result 2
`And`	Logical and	`True And True` `True And False`	`True` `False`
`Or`	Inclusive or	`True Or False` `False Or False`	`True` `False`
`Not`	Logical not	`Not True` `Not False`	`False` `True`
`Xor`	Exclusive or	`True Xor False` `True Xor True`	`True` `False`

The logical operators **`And`**, **`Or`**, and **`Not`** are used extensively in Access expressions and SQL statements; in SQL statements these operators are uppercase, as in `AND`, `OR`, and `NOT`. **`Xor`** is seldom used in Jet or VBA. **`Eqv`** (equivalent) and **`Imp`** (implication) are rarely seen, even in programming code, so Table 10.3 omits these two operators.

T-SQL

T-SQL has conventional `AND`, `OR`, and `NOT` logical operators. **`Xor`** is supported by the `^` bitwise comparison operator. Other T-SQL bitwise operators are `&` (bitwise and) and `¦` (bitwise or).

CONCATENATION OPERATORS

Concatenation operators combine two text values into a single string of characters. If you concatenate `ABC` with `DEF`, for example, the result is `ABCDEF`. The ampersand (**`&`**) is the preferred concatenation operator in VBA and Jet. Concatenation is one of the subjects of "The Variant Data Type in Jet and VBA" section later in the chapter.

TIP

Don't use the + symbol to concatenate strings in queries or Jet SQL. In Jet SQL and VBA, + is reserved for the addition of numbers; **`&`** concatenates literals and variables of any field data type. The **`&`** operator performs implicit type conversion from numbers to text; the **`&`** operator treats all variables as character strings. Thus `1234 & 5678` returns `12345678`, not `6912`.

T-SQL

T-SQL uses the + symbol for string concatenation. The SQL-92 specification, however, designates two vertical bars (pipe symbols) as the official concatenation operator, as in `'String1' ¦¦ 'String2'`. The string concatenation symbol is one of the least consistent elements of common flavors of SQL.

IDENTIFIER OPERATORS

Earlier versions of Access used identifier operators, `!` (the exclamation point, often called the *bang* operator) and `.` (the period, called the *dot* operator in VBA). As of Access 2000, the period replaces the bang operator, which Access 2003 continues to support for backward compatibility. The period operator performs the following operations:

- Combine the names of object classes and object names to select a specific object or property of an object. For example, the following expression identifies the Personnel Actions form:

  ```
  Forms.HRActions
  ```

  This identification is necessary because you might also have a table called HRActions.
- Distinguish object names from property names. Consider the following expression:

  ```
  TextBox1.FontSize = 8
  ```

  `TextBox1` is a control object, and `FontSize` is a property.
- Identify specific fields in tables, as in the following expression, which specifies the CompanyName field of the Customers table:

  ```
  Customers.CompanyName
  ```


T-SQL

T-SQL uses the bang operator (`!`) as an alternative to `NOT`, as in `!`< (not less than) and !> (not greater than). This usage isn't compliant with SQL-92.

OTHER OPERATORS

The remaining Jet operators are related to the comparison operators. These operators return **`True`** or **`False`**, depending on whether the value in a field meets the chosen operator's specification when used in a `WHERE` clause criterion. A **`True`** value causes a record to be included in a query; a **`False`** value rejects the record. When you use these operators in validation rules, entries are accepted or rejected based on the logical value returned by the expression.

Table 10.4 lists the four other operators used in Access queries and validation rules.

TABLE 10.4 OTHER OPERATORS

Operator	Description	Example
`Is`	Used with **`Null`** to determine whether a value is **`Null`** or **`Not Null`**	`Is` **`Null`** `Is` **`Not Null`**
`Like`	Determines whether a string value begins with one or more characters (for `Like` to work properly, you must add a Jet (DOS) wild card, `*` or one or more ?s)	`Like "Jon*"` `Like "FILE????"`

Operator	Description	Example
`In`	Determines whether a string value is a member of a list of values	`In("CA", "OR", "WA")`
`Between`	Determines whether a numeric or date value lies within a specified range of values	`Between 1 And 5`

You use the wildcard characters `*` and `?` with the `Like` operator the same way that you use them in DOS. The `*` (often called *star* or *splat*) takes the place of any number of characters. The `?` takes the place of a single character. For example, `Like "Jon*"` returns **True** for values such as Jones or Jonathan. Like `"*on*"` returns **True** for any value that contains on. `Like "FILE????"` returns **True** for `FILENAME`, but not for `FILE000` or `FILENUMBER`. Wildcard characters can precede the characters that you want to match, as in `Like "*son"` or `Like "????NAME"`.

T-SQL

T-SQL supports the `IS`, `LIKE`, `IN`, and `BETWEEN` logical operators, as described in Table 10.4. However, T-SQL uses the single quote (`'`) as the string identifier, rather than Jet's default double quote (`"`).

Except for `Is`, the operators in this other category are equivalent to the SQL reserved words `LIKE`, `IN`, and `BETWEEN`. Jet includes these operators to promote compatibility with SQL. You can create each of these operators by combining other VBA operators or functions. `Like "Jon*"` is the equivalent of VBA's `InStr(Left(FieldName, 3), "Jon")`; `In("CA", "OR", "WA")` is similar to `InStr("CAORWA", FieldName)`, except that matches would occur for the ambiguous `AO` and `RW`. `Between 1 And 5` is the equivalent of `>= 1 And <= 5`.

TIP

Always use `Between...And`, not the >= and <= comparison operators, to specify a range of dates. You must repeat the field name when using the comparison operators, as in `DateValue >= #1/1/1999# And DateValue <= #12/31/1999#`. `Between` syntax is shorter and easier to understand, as demonstrated by `DateValue Between #1/1/1999# And #12/31/1999#`.

LITERALS

VBA provides three types of literals that you can combine with operators to create expressions. The following list describes these types of literals:

- *Numeric* literals are typed as a series of digits, including the arithmetic sign and decimal point if applicable. You don't have to prefix positive numbers with the plus sign; Access assumes positive values unless the minus sign is present. Numeric literals can include `E` or `e` and the sign of the exponent to indicate an exponent in scientific notation—for example, `-1.23E-02`.

- *Text* (or *string*) literals can include any printable character, plus unprintable characters returned by the `Chr` function. The `Chr` function returns the characters specified by a numeric value from the ANSI character table (similar to the ASCII character table) that Windows uses. For example, `Chr(9)` returns the Tab character. Printable characters include the letters A through Z, numbers 0 through 9, punctuation symbols, and other special keyboard symbols such as the tilde (~). VBA expressions require that you enclose string literals within double quotation marks (""). Combinations of printable and unprintable characters are concatenated with `&`. For example, the following expression separates two strings with a newline pair:

  ```
  "First line" & Chr(13) & Chr(10) & "Second line"
  ```

  `Chr(13)` is the carriage return (CR), and `Chr(10)` is the line-feed (LF) character; together they form the newline pair. VBA has a constant `vbCrLf`, which you can substitute for `Chr(13) & Chr(10)`.

  When you enter string literals in the cells of tables and Query Design grids, Access adds the quotation marks for you. In other places, you must enter the quotation marks yourself.

- *Date/Time* VBA/Jet literals are enclosed within number or pound signs (#), as in the expressions `#1-Jan-1980#` or `#10:20:30#`. If Access detects that you're typing a date or time in one of the standard Jet Date/Time formats into a Design grid, it adds the enclosing pound signs for you. Otherwise, you must type the # signs.

10

T-SQL

T-SQL numeric literals are identical to Jet's, but, as mentioned earlier, string (character) literals are enclosed between single quotes (`'string'`). T-SQL doesn't have a Date/Time identifier; you must supply date values as quoted strings in one of the standard formats that T-SQL recognizes, such as `'3/15/2003'`.

IDENTIFIERS

An identifier usually is the name of an object; databases, tables, fields, queries, forms, and reports are objects in Access. Each object has a name that uniquely identifies that object. Sometimes, to identify a subobject, an identifier name consists of a family name (object class) separated from a given name (object name) by a bang symbol or a period (an identifier operator). The family name of the identifier comes first, followed by the separator and then the given name. SQL uses the period as an object separator. An example of an identifier in an SQL statement is as follows:

```
Customers.Address
```

In this example, the identifier for the Address field object is contained in the Customers table object. `Customers` is the family name of the object (the table), and `Address` is the given name of the subobject (the field). In VBA, however, you use the `.` symbol to separate table names and field names. (The period separates objects and their properties.) If an identifier contains a space or other punctuation, enclose the identifier within square brackets, as in this example:

```
[Order Details].Quantity
```

You can't include periods or exclamation points within the names of identifiers; `[Unit.Price]`, for example, isn't allowed.

In simple queries that use only one table, you can omit the *`TableName.`* prefix. You use identifiers to return the values of fields in form and report objects. Chapters 14 through 18 cover the specific method of identifying objects within forms and reports.

T-SQL

T-SQL uses the period to separate table and field names, but adds an *ownername* prefix (usually `dbo` for database owner) to the table name, as in `dbo.Customers.Address`. SQL Server 7.0+ also encloses table names having spaces or other SQL-illegal punctuation with square brackets `[ ]`.

FUNCTIONS

Functions return values to their names; functions can take the place of identifiers in expressions. One of the most common functions used in VBA/Jet expressions is **`Now`**, which returns to its name the date and time from your computer's system clock. If you type **`Now`** as the Default Value property of a table's Date/Time field, for example, `3/15/2003 9:00` appears in the field when you change to Datasheet view (at 9:00 a.m. on March 15, 2003).

VBA defines about 150 individual functions. The following list groups functions by purpose:

- *Date and time* functions manipulate date/time values in fields or Date/Time values that you enter as literals. You can extract parts of dates (such as the year or day of the month) and parts of times (such as hours and minutes) with date and time functions.
- *Text-manipulation* functions are used for working with strings of characters.
- *Data-type conversion* functions enable you to specify the data type of values in numeric fields instead of depending on Access to pick the most appropriate data type.
- *Mathematic and trigonometric* functions perform on numeric values operations that are beyond the capability of the standard Access arithmetic operators. You can use simple trigonometric functions, for example, to calculate the length of the sides of a right triangle (if you know the length of one side and the included angle).
- *Financial* functions are similar to functions provided by Lotus 1-2-3 and Microsoft Excel. They calculate depreciation, values of annuities, and rates of return on investments. To determine the present value of a lottery prize paid out in 25 equal yearly installments, for example, you can use the PV function.
- *General-purpose* functions don't fit any of the preceding classifications; you use these functions to create Access queries, forms, and reports.

- *Other* functions include those that perform dynamic data exchange (DDE) with other Windows applications, domain aggregate functions, Jet SQL aggregate functions, and functions used primarily in VBA programming.

Only the first three groups of functions commonly are used in Jet queries; Chapters 27 through 31 offer examples of the use of some of members of the last four function groups.

USING THE IMMEDIATE WINDOW

When you write VBA programming code in a module, the Immediate window is available to assist you in debugging your code. You also can use the module's Immediate window to demonstrate the use and syntax of functions.

To experiment with some of the functions described in the following sections, open the Northwind.mdb database and perform these steps:

1. Click the Modules shortcut in the Database window.
2. Double-click the Utility Functions module to open it in the VBA Editor. If you haven't changed the docking options for the VBA Editor, the Immediate window appears at the bottom of the Editor's window. Otherwise, press Ctrl+G to open the Immediate window.
3. Type **? Now** in the Immediate window (see Figure 10.1) and press Enter. The date and time from your computer's clock appear on the next line. The **?** is shorthand for the VBA `Print` statement (which displays the value of a function or variable) and must be added to the `Now` function to display the function's value.

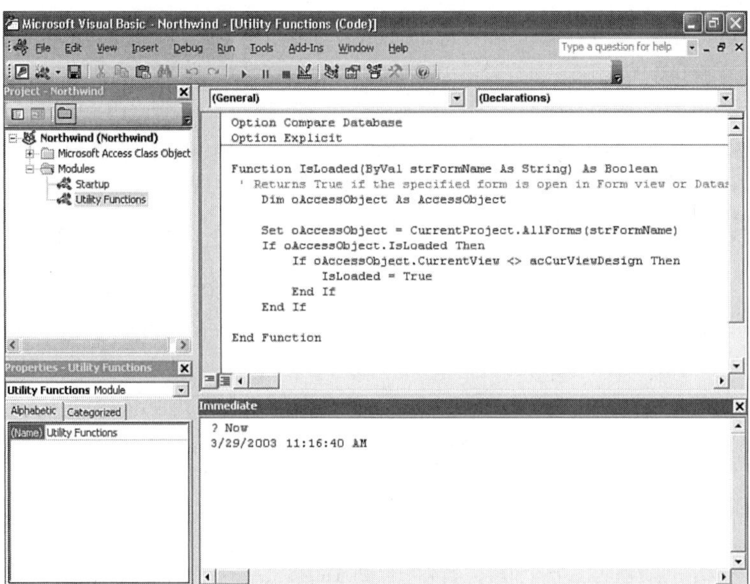

Figure 10.1
The VBA editor's Immediate window lets you quickly test the return values of VBA functions.

TIP

> If you neglected to precede the function entry with **?** or **Print**, an error message appears, indicating that the VBA editor expected you to type a statement or an equal sign. Click OK and type **?** before the function name in the Immediate window. Press End to return the cursor to the end of the line and then press Enter to retry the test.

4. To reposition the Immediate window more easily, click its title bar and drag the window to a central area of your display where it remains undocked.

GETTING HELP AS YOU WRITE QUERIES

As you type in your functions in the Immediate window, Access displays an Autocompletion screen tip, showing the function's name and its complete argument list. You must type a space or opening parenthesis after the function name to make the Autocompletion screen tip appear. An argument list is the list of information that you specify for the function to work on—for example, if you use the **Sqr** function to compute the square root of a number, you must supply a number inside the function's parentheses. Figure 10.2 shows the screen tip for the **Sqr** function. You can turn this feature on and off by choosing Tools, Options and marking or clearing the Auto Quick Info option on the Editor page.

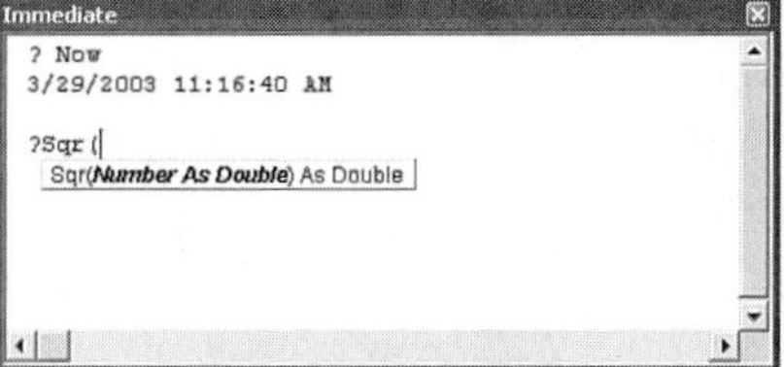

Figure 10.2
Typing a function in the Immediate window displays the VBA Autocompletion screen tip before you add required arguments for the function.

TIP

> Obtain online help for a function by placing the cursor within the function name and pressing F1 to display the Visual Basic Reference topic for the function (see Figure 10.3).

NOTE

> If you specified Install on First Use, rather than Run from My Computer, for Access and VBA help files, you receive an "Installing components for Microsoft Access" message. In this case, you must have the distribution CD-ROM available or have access to a networked Office 2002 installation share to install the required HTML help files.

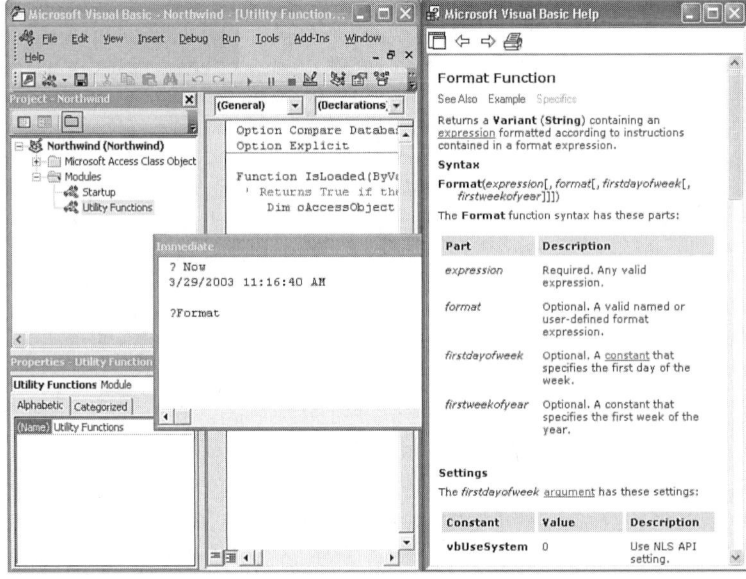

Figure 10.3 Positioning the cursor within the name of a function and pressing F1 opens the Microsoft Visual Basic Help window and displays the online help topic for the function.

If you click an enabled Example link in any function Help window, the window displays an example of the function used in Access VBA code. These examples show the syntax of the functions and appropriate arguments. The examples, however, usually aren't applicable to the function's use in a Jet query or validation rule. Figure 10.4 illustrates the examples for the VBA **`Format`** function.

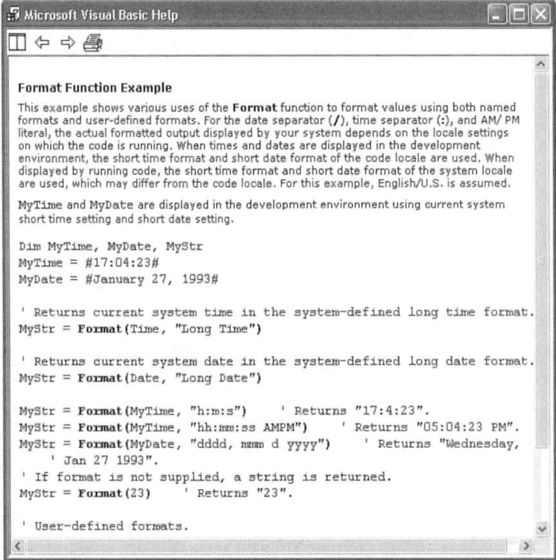

Figure 10.4 Most examples of VBA function syntax apply to writing VBA code, not formatting the columns of Jet query result sets.

THE Variant DATA TYPE IN JET AND VBA

Variant is a special data type unique to Visual Basic dialects. The **Variant** data type enables you to concatenate values that ordinarily have different data types, such as an integer and a character string, which otherwise would result in an error. The capability to concatenate different data types is called *turning off data-type checking*. The **Variant** data type also lets you use operands with data of different types, such as adding **Integer** and **Double** values. Internally, Jet handles all data in tables and queries as **Variant** data.

The **Variant** data type enables you to concatenate field values of tables and queries that have dissimilar data types without using VBA's data-type conversion functions such as **Str**. (**Str** converts numeric values to the **String** data type.) The **Variant** data type simplifies expressions that combine field values to create concatenated indexes. The **Variant** data type also enables you to use the **&** symbol to concatenate values of different data types.

Table 10.5 lists the 16 common subtypes of the **Variant** data type of VBA 6.0, along with the names of the intrinsic Visual Basic constants, vb*Constant*, corresponding to the **Variant** subtype value. In addition to the Access intrinsic constants, VBA provides its own set of intrinsic constants, which are prefixed with vb. Access intrinsic constants are prefixed with ac. Intrinsic constants, which you use primarily when writing VBA code, are one of the subjects of Chapter 30, "Understanding Universal Data Access, OLE DB, and ADO."

TABLE 10.5 SUBTYPES OF THE Variant DATA TYPE

Subtype	Constant	Corresponds To	Stored As
0	(None)	Empty (uninitialized)	Not applicable
1	vbNull	**Null** (no valid data)	Not applicable
2	vbInteger	**Integer**	2-byte integer
3	vbLong	**Long**	4-byte long integer
4	vbSingle	**Single**	4-byte single-precision floating point
5	vbDouble	**Double**	8-byte double-precision floating point
6	vbCurrency	**Currency**	4-byte fixed point
7	vbDate	**Date/Time**	8-byte double-precision floating point
8	vbString	**String**	Conventional string variable
9	vbObject	**Object**	Automation object
10	vbError	**Error**	Error data type (error number)
11	vbBoolean	**Boolean**	**True** or **False** values only
12	vbVariant	**Variant**	Used with **Variant** arrays

continues

TABLE 10.5 CONTINUED

Subtype	Constant	Corresponds To	Stored As
13	vbDataObject	Special	Non-Automation object
17	vbByte	**Byte**	Numeric value from 0–255
8192	vbArray	**Array**	Used with **Variant** arrays

You can concatenate **Variant** values with **Variant** subtypes 1 through 8 listed in Table 10.5. You can concatenate a subtype 8 **Variant** (**String**) with a subtype 5 **Variant** (**Double**), for example, without receiving the Type Mismatch error message displayed when you attempt this concatenation with conventional **String** (text) and **Double** data types. Access returns a value with the **Variant** subtype corresponding to the highest subtype number of the concatenated values. This example, therefore, returns a subtype 8 (**String**) **Variant** because 8 is greater than 5, the subtype number for the **Double** value. If you concatenate a subtype 2 (**Integer**) value with a subtype 3 (**Long**) value, Access returns subtype 3 **Variant** data.

10

T-SQL

SQL Server 2000 supports the `sql_variant` data type, which can store any SQL Server data type except `text` (Memo), `ntext` (Unicode or national text), `image` (long binary), `timestamp`, and `sql_variant` data. Concatenation rules for `sql_variant` values differ from Jet/VBA **Variants**.

Distinguishing between the empty and **Null Variant** subtypes is important. Empty indicates that a variable you created with VBA code has a name but doesn't have an initial value. Empty applies only to VBA variables (see Chapter 27, "Learning Visual Basic for Applications"). **Null** indicates that a data cell doesn't contain an entry. You can assign the **Null** value to a variable, in which case the variable is initialized to the **Null** value, **Variant** subtype 1.

FUNCTIONS FOR DATE AND TIME

Access offers a variety of functions for dealing with dates and times. If you've used Visual Basic, you probably recognize most of the functions applicable to the Date/Time field data types shown in Table 10.6. VBA has several Date/Time functions, such as **DateAdd** and **DateDiff**, to simplify the calculation of date values. **MonthName** and **WeekdayName** functions are new to VBA 6.0.

TABLE 10.6 ACCESS FUNCTIONS FOR DATE AND TIME

Function	Description	Example	Returns
Date	Returns the current system date and time as a subtype 7 date **Variant** or a standard date **String** subtype 8.	**Date**	3/15/2003 03-15-2003

Function	Description	Example	Returns
DateAdd	Returns a subtype 7 date with a specified number of days ("d"), weeks ("ww"), months ("m"), or years ("y") added to the date.	**DateAdd**("d",31, #3/15/2003#)	4/15/2003
DateDiff	Returns an **Integer** representing the difference between two dates using the d/w/m/y specification.	**DateDiff**("d", Date, #3/15/2003#)	116 (assuming Date = 11/19/2002)
DatePart	Returns the specified part of a date such as day, month, year, day of week ("w"), and so on, as an **Integer**.	**DatePart**("w", #3/17/2003#)	2 (Monday)
DateSerial	Returns a subtype 7 **Variant** from year, month, and day arguments.	**DateSerial** (2003, 3, 15)	3/15/2003
DateValue	Returns a subtype 7 **Variant** that corresponds to a date argument in a character format.	**DateValue** ("**15-Mar-2003**")	3/15/2003
Day	Returns an **Integer** between 1 and 31 (inclusive) that represents a day of the month from a Date/Time value.	**Day**(**Date**)	15 (assuming that the date is the 15th of the month)
Hour	Returns an **Integer** between 0 and 23 (inclusive) that represents the hour of the Date/Time value.	**Hour**(#2:30 PM#)	14
Minute	Returns an **Integer** between 0 and 59 (inclusive) that represents the minute of a Date/Time value.	**Minute**(#2:30 PM#)	30
Month	Returns an **Integer** between 1 and 12 (inclusive) that represents the month of a Date/Time value.	**Month**(#15-Jul-98#)	7
MonthName	Returns the full or abbreviated name of a month from the month number (1 to 12). If you omit the second argument, the function returns the full name.	**MonthName**(10, False) **MonthName**(10, True)	October Oct

continues

TABLE 10.6 CONTINUED

Function	Description	Example	Returns
Now	Returns the date and time of a computer's system clock as a **Variant** of subtype 7.	**Now**	3/15/2003 11:57:28 AM
Second	Returns an **Integer** between 0 and 59 (inclusive) that represents the second of a Date/Time value.	**Second(Now)**	28
Time	Returns the time portion of a Date/Time value from the system clock.	**Time**	11:57:20 AM
TimeSerial	Returns the time serial value of the time expressed in hours, minutes, and seconds.	**TimeSerial**(11, 57, 20)	11:57:20 AM
TimeValue	Returns the time serial value of the time (entered as the **String** value) as a subtype 7 **Variant**.	**TimeValue**("11:57")	11:57
Weekday	Returns day of the week (Sunday = 1) corresponding to the date as an **Integer**.	**Weekday**(#3/15/2003#)	7
WeekdayName	Returns the full or abbreviated name of the day from the day number (0 to 7). Setting the second argument to **True** abbreviates the name. A third optional argument lets you specify the first day of the week.	**WeekdayName**(4, False) **WeekdayName**(4, True)	Wednesday Wed
Year	Returns the year of a Date/Time value as an **Integer**.	**Year**(#3/15/2003#)	2003

T-SQL

When you use the Upsizing Wizard to convert a conventional Access application with a Jet database to an Access Data Project with an SQL Server database, the Wizard converts the following Jet/VBA Date/Time functions to their T-SQL equivalents:

Jet/VBA Function	SQL Server Function
Date	CONVERT(datetime, CONVERT(varchar, GETDATE( ))
DateAdd( )	DATEADD( )
DateDiff( )	DATEDIFF( )

Jet/VBA Function	SQL Server Function
DatePart( )	DATEPART( )
Day( )	DATEPART(dd, *date*)
Hour( )	DATEPART(hh, *time*)
Minute( )	DATEPART(mi, *time*)
Now	GETDATE( )
Second( )	DATEPART(ss, *time*)
Weekday( )	DATEPART(dw, *date*)
Year( )	DATEPART(yy, date)

The Wizard doesn't convert Jet/VBA Functions not included in the preceding list. You must manually correct conversion failures.

10

TEXT-MANIPULATION FUNCTIONS

Table 10.7 lists the functions that deal with the Text field data type, corresponding to the **String** VBA data type. Most of these functions are modeled on BASIC string functions.

TABLE 10.7 FUNCTIONS FOR THE String DATA TYPE

Function	Description	Example	Returns
Asc	Returns ANSI numeric value of a character as an Integer	**Asc**("C")	67
Chr	Returns character corresponding to the numeric ANSI value as a String	**Chr**(67) **Chr**(10)	C (line feed)
Format	Formats an expression in accordance with appropriate format strings	**Format**(**Date**, "dd-mmm-yyyy")	15-Mar-2003
InStr	Returns the position of one string within another as a **Long**	**InStr**("ABCD", "C")	3
InStrRev	Returns the position of one string within another as a **Long**, counting from the end of the string	**InStrRev**("ABCD", "C")	2

continues

TABLE 10.7 CONTINUED

Function	Description	Example	Returns
Join	Generates a String from a one-dimension array consisting of strings (spaces separate the array strings)	`Join(astrArray)`	Depends on array's contents
LCase	Returns the lowercase version of a string	`LCase("ABCD")`	abcd
Left	Returns the leftmost characters of a string	`Left("ABCDEF", 3)`	ABC
Len	Returns the number of characters in a string as a **Long**	`Len("ABCDE")`	5
LTrim	Removes leading spaces from a string	`LTrim(" ABC")`	ABC
Mid	Returns a part of a string, beginning at the character position specified by the second argument	`Mid("ABCDE", 2, 3)`	BCD
Replace	Replaces occurrences of a specified substring in a string	`Replace("ABCDE", "BC", "YZ")`	AYZDE
Right	Returns the rightmost characters of a string	`Right("ABCDEF", 3)`	DEF
RTrim	Removes trailing spaces from a string	`RTrim("ABC ")`	ABC
Space	Returns a string consisting of a specified number of spaces	`Space(5)`	
Split	Returns an array of substrings based on a separator character (the default is a space)	`Split("ABC DEF")`	(0)ABC (1)DEF
Str	Converts the numeric value of any data type to a string	`Str(123.45)`	123.45

Function	Description	Example	Returns
`StrComp`	Compares two strings for equivalence and returns the integer result of the comparison	`StrComp("ABC", "abc")`	0
`String`	Returns a string consisting of specified repeated characters	`String(5, "A")`	AAAAA
`StrReverse`	Returns a string whose characters are reversed	`StrReverse("ABCDE")`	EDCBA
`Trim`	Removes leading and trailing spaces from a string	`Trim(" ABC ")`	ABC
`UCase`	Returns the uppercase version of a string	`UCase("abc")`	ABC
`Val`	Returns the numeric value of a string in a data type appropriate to the argument's format	`Val("123.45")`	123.45

NOTE

VBA includes two versions of many functions that return String variables—one with and one without the BASIC-language **$** String type identification character. This book doesn't use type identification characters in queries, so the second form of the function is omitted from the tables in this chapter. In VBA code, adding the **$** suffix to functions that return strings gives slightly better performance.

T-SQL

The Upsizing Wizard converts the following Jet/VBA text-manipulation functions to their T-SQL equivalents:

Jet/VBA Function	SQL Server Function
`Asc( )`	`ASCII( )`
`Chr( )`	`CHAR( )`
`LCase( )`	`LOWER( )`
`Len( )`	`DATALENGTH( )`
`LTrim( )`	`LTRIM( )`
`Mid( )`	`SUBSTRING( )`
`Right( )`	`RIGHT( )`
`RTrim( )`	`RTRIM( )`

Jet/VBA Function	SQL Server Function
Space( )	SPACE( )
Str( )	STR( )
UCase( )	UCASE( )

Functions included in Table 10.7 but not in this list cause conversion errors. T-SQL doesn't support the Jet/VBA **Format** or **Format...** functions.

Figure 10.5 shows Immediate window examples of common string-manipulation functions. The Immediate window is particularly valuable for learning exactly how these functions behave with different types of literal values.

```
? Asc("C")
 67
? chr(67)
C
? Format(Date, "dd-mm-yyyy")
15-03-2003
? Left("ABCDE", 3)
ABC
? Mid("ADBDE", 3, 2)
BD
? Right("ABCDE", 2)
DE
? StrReverse("ABCDE")
EDCBA
? UCase("abcde")
ABCDE
? Lcase("ABCDE")
abcde
```

Figure 10.5
Use the Immediate window to verify the syntax of the VBA functions you plan to include in Jet queries or validation rules.

You can use the new localized **Format...** functions of VBA 6.0 in Jet 4.0 queries, if you provide numeric values for the functions' arguments. For example, you must substitute the numeric values shown for the vb... constants of the **FormatDateTime** function. Following is the syntax for the **Format...** functions:

- **FormatCurrency**(*NumericValue*[, *DigitsAfterDecimal* [, *IncludeLeadingDigit* [, *ParensForNegativeNumbers* [, *GroupDigits*]]]]) returns a value formatted with the localized currency symbol, including the Euro. With the exception of *NumericValue*, the arguments are optional. If *IncludeLeadingDigit* is **True**, fractional values are prefixed with `$0` in North America. Setting *GroupDigits* to **True** applies the group delimiter, comma (as in `$1,000`) for North America.
- **FormatDateTime**(*DateValue*[, *NamedFormat*]) returns a date string whose format depends on the value of *NamedFormat*. Valid values of *NamedFormat* are `vbGeneralDate` (`0`), `vbLongDate` (`1`), `vbShortDate` (`2`), `vbLongTime` (`3`), or `vbShortTime` (`4`). Figure 10.6 illustrates the use of the **FormatDateTime** and other **Format...** functions.

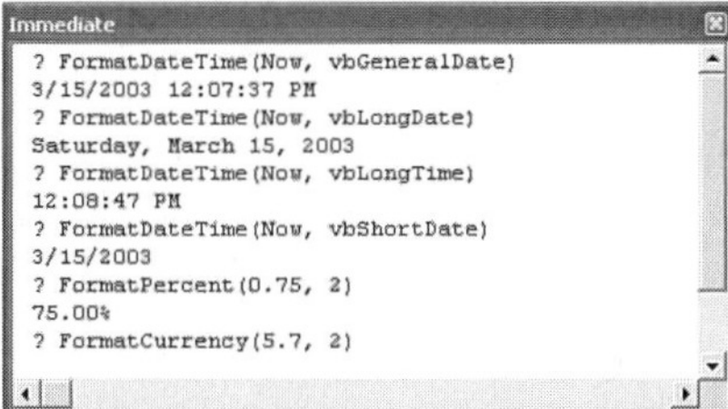

Immediate
? FormatDateTime(Now, vbGeneralDate)
3/15/2003 12:07:37 PM
? FormatDateTime(Now, vbLongDate)
Saturday, March 15, 2003
? FormatDateTime(Now, vbLongTime)
12:08:47 PM
? FormatDateTime(Now, vbShortDate)
3/15/2003
? FormatPercent(0.75, 2)
75.00%
? FormatCurrency(5.7, 2)

Figure 10.6
The Immediate window displays examples of the use of the VBA 6.0 `Format...` functions.

- **`FormatNumber`**`(`*`NumericValue`*`[, `*`DigitsAfterDecimal`*` [, `*`IncludeLeadingDigit`*` [, `*`ParensForNegativeNumbers`*` [, `*`GroupDigits`*`]]]])` returns the same values as **`FormatCurrency`**, but without the currency symbol.
- **`FormatPercent`**`(`*`NumericValue`*`[, `*`DigitsAfterDecimal`*` [, `*`IncludeLeadingDigit`*` [, `*`ParensForNegativeNumbers`*` [, `*`GroupDigits`*`]]]])` returns the same values as **FormatNumber**, but multiplies *`NumericValue`* by 100 and adds a trailing `%` symbol.

NUMERIC, LOGICAL, DATE/TIME, AND STRING DATA-TYPE CONVERSION FUNCTIONS

You can assign a particular data type to a numeric value with any of the data-type conversion functions. After you freeze (or coerce) a data type with one of the numeric data-type conversion functions, you cannot concatenate that data type with the **`String`** data type.

Table 10.8 lists the 11 numeric data-type conversion functions of Access 2003. The `NumValue` argument in the Syntax column can be any numeric or **`String`** value. However, if you use a **`String`** value as the argument of a numeric-type conversion function, the first character of the argument's value must be a digit, a dollar sign, a plus symbol, or a minus symbol. The most commonly used conversion function in queries is **`CCur`**.

TABLE 10.8 DATA-TYPE CONVERSION FUNCTIONS FOR NUMERIC, TIME/DATE, AND STRING VALUES

Function	Syntax	Description
`CBool`	**`CBool`**`(`*`NumValue`*`)`	Converts a numeric value to the **`Boolean`** (**`True`** or **`False`**) data type
`CByte`	**`CByte`**`(`*`NumValue`*`)`	Converts a numeric value to the **`Byte`** (0–255) data type
`CCur`	**`CCur`**`(`*`NumValue`*`)`	Converts a numeric value to the **`Currency`** data type
`CDate`	**`CDate`**`(`*`NumValue`*`)`	Converts a numeric value to a **`Date`** value (**`CDate`** replaces **`CVDate`**, which is obsolete)
`CDbl`	**`CDbl`**`(`*`NumValue`*`)`	Converts a numeric value to the **`Double`** data type
`CInt`	**`CInt`**`(`*`NumValue`*`)`	Converts a numeric value to the **`Integer`** data type

continues

TABLE 10.8 CONTINUED

Function	Syntax	Description
CLng	**CLng**(*NumValue*)	Converts a numeric value to the **Long** integer data type
CSng	**CSng**(*NumValue*)	Converts a numeric value to the **Single** data type
CStr	**CStr**(*varValue*)	Converts a **Variant** value to the **String** data type
CVar	**CVar**(*NumValue*)	Converts a numeric value to a **Variant** data type
CVErr	**CVErr**(*NumValue*)	Converts a valid error number to create user-defined errors
Nz	Nz(var*FieldValue*[, *ReturnValue*]	Converts a **Null** value to 0 or a zero-length string, depending on the context of use

T-SQL

The Upsizing Wizard converts the following Jet/VBA data type conversion functions to their T-SQL equivalents:

Jet/VBA Function	SQL Server Function
CCur(*NumValue*)	CONVERT(money, *NumValue*)
CDbl(*NumValue*)	CONVERT(float, *NumValue*)
CInt(*NumValue*)	CONVERT(smallint, *NumValue*)
CLng(*NumValue*)	CONVERT(int, *NumValue*)
CSng(*NumValue*)	CONVERT(real, *NumValue*)
CStr(*NumValue*)	CONVERT(varchar, *NumValue*)
CDate(*NumValue*)	CONVERT(datetime, *NumValue*)
CVDate(*NumValue*)	CONVERT(datetime, *NumValue*)

Functions included in Table 10.8 but not in this list cause conversion errors.

The Nz (Null-to-zero) function accepts only a **Variant** *varFieldValue* argument. Nz returns non-**Null** **Variant** argument values unchanged. When used in a Jet query, Nz returns an empty string ("") for **Null** argument values, unless you specify 0 or another literal, such as "Null" as the value of the optional *ReturnValue* argument. The Jet expression service supplies the Nz function; it's not a VBA reserved word, so it doesn't appear in bold type.

TIP

Use Nz to format the result sets of your crosstab queries, replacing **Null** values with 0. When you execute a crosstab query—such as quarterly product sales by region—cells for products with no sales in a region for the quarter are empty. Empty cells might mislead management into believing information is missing. Applying the Nz function puts a 0 in empty cells, which eliminates the ambiguity.

Intrinsic and Named Constants

As noted earlier in this chapter, VBA and Access have many predefined intrinsic constants. The names of these constants are considered keywords because you cannot use these names for any purpose other than returning the value represented by the names, such as -1 for **True** and Yes, and 0 for **False** and No. (**True** and Yes are Access synonyms, as are **False** and No, so you can use these pairs of values interchangeably in Access, but not in VBA.) As noted throughout the chapter, **Null** indicates a field without a valid entry. **True**, **False**, and **Null** are the most commonly used VBA intrinsic constants.

T-SQL

T-SQL uses 1 for TRUE and 0 for FALSE. Conversion between -1 for **True** and 1 for TRUE succeeds because **True** accepts any non-0 number as **Not False**. The Upsizing Wizard converts Jet **Boolean** fields to the SQL Server bit data type.

Symbolic constants, which you define, return a single, predetermined value for the entire Access session. You can create named constants for use with forms and reports by defining them in the declarations section of an Access VBA module. Chapter 27 describes how to create and use symbolic (named) constants.

→ To find the constants that are built into Access, **see** "Symbolic Constants," **p. 1167**.

Creating Jet Expressions

Chapter 6 uses several functions to validate data entry for most fields in the HRActions table. Chapter 9 uses an expression to select the country and states to be included in a mailing-list query. These examples provide the foundation on which to build more complex expressions that define more precisely the validation rules and query criteria for real-world database applications.

→ To review examples using functions to restrict data-entry values, **see** "Validating Data Entry," **p. 227**.

→ For information on how to enter expressions in a query, **see** "Selecting Records by Criteria and Sorting the Display," **p. 338**.

The sections that follow provide a few examples of typical expressions for creating default values for fields, validating data entry, creating query criteria, and calculating field values. The examples demonstrate the similarity of syntax for expressions with different purposes. Part IV of this book, "Designing Forms and Reports," provides additional examples of expressions designed for use in forms and reports; Part VII, "Programming and Converting Access Applications," explains the use of expressions with Access VBA code.

Expressions for Creating Default Values

Expressions that create default field values can speed the entry of new records. Assigning values ordinarily requires you to use the assignment operator (=). When entering a default value in the properties pane for a table in design mode, however, you can enter a simple literal. An example is the `Q` default value assigned to the ActionType field of the HRActions table in Chapter 5, "Working with Jet Databases and Tables." In this case, Access (not Jet) infers the `=` assignment operator and the quotation marks surrounding the `Q`. You often can use shorthand techniques when typing expressions because Access infers the missing characters. If you type **= "Q"**, you achieve the same result.

You can use complex expressions for default values if the result of the expression conforms to or can be converted by Access to the proper field data type. You can type `= 1` as the default value for the ActionType field, for example, although `1` is a numeric value and ActionType has the Text data type. The **`Variant`** data type used for all Jet data operations permits this action.

T-SQL

The Upsizing Wizard converts Jet default values to SQL Server default values, if the expression for the default value contain functions that have T-SQL equivalents.

10

→ To review using the assignment operator to assign a default value, **see** "Setting Default Values of Fields," **p. 187**.

EXPRESSIONS FOR VALIDATING DATA

The HRActions table uses several expressions to validate data entry. The validation rule for the EmployeeID field is `> 0`; the rule for the ApprovedBy field is `> 0 Or Is Null`. The validation rule for the EmployeeID field is equivalent to the following imaginary in-line VBA **`IIf`** function:

```
IIf(DataEntry > 0, EmployeeID = DataEntry,
    MsgBox("Please enter a valid employee ID number."))
```

Jet tests *`DataEntry`* in the validation rule expression. If the validation expression returns **`True`**, the value of *`DataEntry`* replaces the value in the current record's field. If the expression returns **`False`**, a message box displays the validation text that you added. **`MsgBox`** is a function used in VBA programming to display a message box onscreen. You can't type the imaginary validation rule just described as a property value; Jet infers the equivalent of the imaginary **`IIf`** expression after you add the Validation Rule and Validation Text property values with entries in the two text boxes for the EmployeeID field.

You might want to change the validation expression `"H" Or "Q" Or "Y" Or "S" Or "R" Or "B" Or "C" Or "T"`, which you use to test the ActionType field, to a function. The **`In`** function provides a simpler expression that accomplishes the same objective:

```
In("H", "Q", "Y", "S", "R", "B", "C", "T")
```

Alternatively, you can use the following table-level validation expression:

```
InStr("HQYSRBCT",[ActionType]) > 0
```

`Instr` returns the position of the second argument's character(s) within the first argument's characters. If `ActionType` is `Q`, the preceding example returns `2`. Both **`In`** and **Instr** expressions give the same result, but you can use **InStr** only for table-level validation because one of its arguments refers to a field name. Thus, the **In** function provides the better solution.

T-SQL

The Upsizing Wizard converts Jet default values to SQL Server default values, if the expression for the default value contain functions that have T-SQL equivalents.

Expressions for Query Criteria

When creating Chapter 9's qryStateMailList query to select records from the states of California, Oregon, and Washington, you type **CA**, **OR**, and **WA** on separate lines; Access adds the equal sign and double quotes around the literals for you. A better expression is **In**("CA", "OR", "WA"), entered on the same line as the ="USA" criterion for the Country field. This expression corrects the failure to test the Country field for a value equal to USA for the OR and WA entries.

→ If you're not sure how multiple criteria should look in the grid, **see** "Creating More Complex Criteria," **p. 341**.

You can use a wide range of other functions to select specific records to be returned to a query table. Table 10.9 shows some typical functions used as query criteria applicable to the Northwind Traders tables. (Table 10.9 uses 1997 as the year value, because 1997 has a full calendar year of data in the Northwind.mdb tables.)

Table 10.9 Typical Expressions Used as Query Criteria

Field	Expression	Records Returned
Customers Table		
Country	**Not** "USA" **And Not** "Canada"	Firms other than those in the United States and Canada
Country	**Not** ("USA" **Or** "Canada")	Firms other than those in the United States and Canada; the parentheses apply the condition to both literals
CompanyName	Like "[N-S]*"	Firms with names beginning with N through S
CompanyName	Like S* **Or** Like V*	Firms with names beginning with S or V (Access adds quotation marks for you)
CompanyName	Like "*shop*"	Firms with shop, Shop, Shoppe, or SHOPPING in the firm name
PostalCode	>=90000	Firms with postal codes greater than or equal to 90000, including codes that begin with alphabetic characters

continues

TABLE 10.9 CONTINUED

Field	Expression	Records Returned
Orders Table		
OrderDate	`Year([OrderDate]) = 1997`	Orders received in 1997
OrderDate	`Like "*/*/1997"`	Orders received in 1997; using wild cards simplifies expressions
OrderDate	`Like "1/*/1997"`	Orders received in the month of January 1997
OrderDate	`Like "1/?/1997"`	Orders received from the 1st to the 9th of January 1997
OrderDate	`Year([OrderDate]) = 1997 And DatePart("q", [OrderDate]) = 1`	Orders received in the first quarter of 1997
OrderDate	`Between #1/1/1997# And #3/31/1997#`	Orders received in the first quarter of 1997
OrderDate	`Year([OrderDate]) = 1997 And DatePart("ww", [OrderDate])= 10`	Orders received in the 10th week of 1997
OrderDate	`>= DateValue("1/15/1997")`	Orders received on or after 1/15/1997
ShippedDate	`Is Null`	Orders not yet shipped
Order Subtotals Query		
Subtotal	`>= 5000`	Orders with values greater than or equal to $5,000
Subtotal	`Between 5000 And 10000`	Orders with values greater than or equal to $5,000 and less than or equal to $10,000
Subtotal	`< 1000`	Orders less than $1,000

The wildcard characters used in `Like` expressions simplify the creation of criteria for selecting names and dates. As in the Windows Search dialog and DOS, the asterisk (*) substitutes for any legal number of characters, and the question mark (?) substitutes for a single character. When a wildcard character prefixes or appends a string, the matching process loses case sensitivity, if case-sensitivity is specified.

T-SQL

As mentioned earlier in the chapter, T-SQL substitutes `%` for `*` and _ (underscore) for `?`. `%` and _ comply with ANSI SQL-92.

If you want to match a string without regard to case, use the following expression:

```
UCase(FieldName) = "FIELDNAME"
```

ENTERING A QUERY CRITERION AND ADDING A CALCULATED FIELD

To experiment with query criteria expressions with tables from the Northwind.mdb database and add a calculated field value, follow these steps:

1. Click the Queries shortcut of the Database window and then double-click the Create Query in Design View shortcut to open the Query Design window and the Add Tables dialog.
2. Double-click the Customers, Orders, and Order Details tables in the Tables list of the Show Table dialog, and then click Close. The CustomerID fields of the Customers and Orders tables and the OrderID fields of the Orders and Order Details tables are joined; joins are indicated by a line between the fields of the two tables. (Chapter 11, "Creating Mulitable and Crosstab Queries," covers joining multiple tables.)

NOTE

> The Order Details table, which has Quantity, UnitPrice and Discount fields, is required to calculate the total amount of each order.

3. Add the CompanyName, PostalCode, and Country fields of the Customers table to the query. You can add fields by selecting them from the Field drop-down list in the Query Design grid, by clicking a field in the Customers field list above the grid and dragging the field to the desired Field cell in the grid, or by double-clicking a field in the Customers field list above the grid.
4. Add to the query the OrderID, ShippedDate, and Freight fields of the Orders table. Use the horizontal scroll bar slider under the Query Design grid to expose additional field columns as necessary. Place the cursor in the Sort row of the OrderID field, open the Sort list box, and select Ascending Sort. Add an Is Not Null criterion for the ShippedDate column to return only orders that have shipped.

Σ

5. Click the Totals button of the toolbar or choose View, Totals to add the Total row to the Query Design grid. The default value, Group By, is added to the Total cell for each field of your query. The Query Design view appears as shown in Figure 10.7.

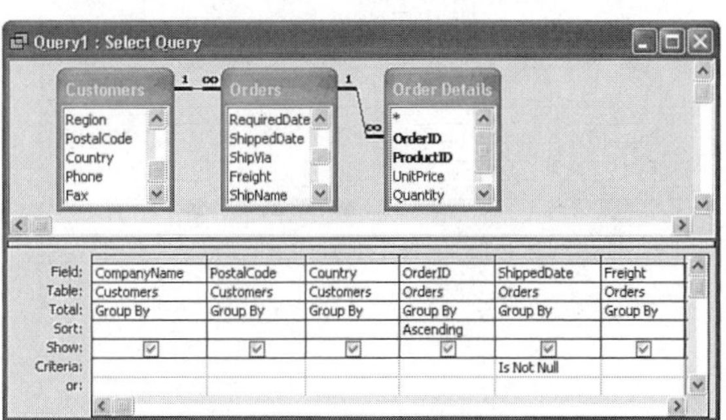

Figure 10.7
This multitable summary query has joins between the Customer and Orders, and the Orders and Order Details tables.

NOTE

> The query requires Group By because the Order Details table has multiple rows for most orders. If you don't specify Totals, the query returns a row for each Order Details record.

6. Click the Run button on the toolbar to test the result of the interim query design, which returns 809 rows (see Figure 10.8).

Query1 : Select Query

Company Name	Postal Code	Country	Order ID	Shipped Date	Freight
Wilman Kala	21240	Finland	10248	16-Jul-1996	$32.38
Tradição Hipermercados	05634-030	Brazil	10249	10-Jul-1996	$11.61
Hanari Carnes	05454-876	Brazil	10250	12-Jul-1996	$65.83
Victuailles en stock	69004	France	10251	15-Jul-1996	$41.34
Suprêmes délices	B-6000	Belgium	10252	11-Jul-1996	$51.30
Hanari Carnes	05454-876	Brazil	10253	16-Jul-1996	$58.17
Chop-suey Chinese	3012	Switzerland	10254	23-Jul-1996	$22.98
Richter Supermarkt	1203	Switzerland	10255	15-Jul-1996	$148.33
Wellington Importadora	08737-363	Brazil	10256	17-Jul-1996	$13.97
HILARIÓN-Abastos	5022	Venezuela	10257	22-Jul-1996	$81.91
Ernst Handel	8010	Austria	10258	23-Jul-1996	$140.51
Centro comercial Moctezuma	05022	Mexico	10259	25-Jul-1996	$3.25
Old World Delicatessen	99508	USA	10260	29-Jul-1996	$55.09
Que Delícia	02389-673	Brazil	10261	30-Jul-1996	$3.05
Rattlesnake Canyon Grocery	87110	USA	10262	25-Jul-1996	$48.29

Record: 1 of 809

Figure 10.8 Design view of the interim query design of Figure 10.7 verifies that only one record appears for each order because of the addition of the Group By expression in the Total row.

7. Return to Design view, and scroll the grid so that the Freight column appears. Click the selection bar above the Field row to select the Freight column, and press the Insert key to add a new column.
8. Type **Amount: CCur([UnitPrice]*[Quantity]*(1–[Discount]))** in the new column's Field cell. This expression calculates the net amount of each line item in the Order Details table and formats the column as if the field data type were `Currency`. The next section discusses how to use expressions to create calculated fields.
9. Move the cursor to the Total row of the new column and press F4 to open the drop-down list. Select Sum from the list (see Figure 10.9). The Sum option totals the net amount for all the line items of each order in the Orders table. In the next chapter, you learn the details of how to create queries that group data.

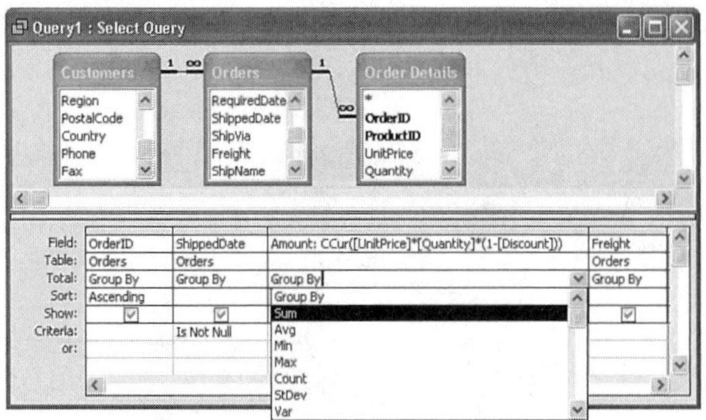

Figure 10.9 The calculated Amount column supplies the total net amount of the line items of the Order Details records for each Order.

➔ For other ways you can manipulate results from queries, **see** "Making Calculations on Multiple Records," **p. 435**.

TIP

> The Total row for all the other columns of the query shows Group By. Make sure that you mark the Show check box so that your new query column appears when you run the query.
>
> Don't make an entry in the Table row of your new query column; if you do, you receive an error message when you run the query.

10. Click the Run or Datasheet View button on the toolbar to run your new query. Your query appears as shown in Figure 10.10. The Amount column contains the total amount of each order, which is net of any discounts.

Query1 : Select Query

Company Name	Postal Code	Country	Order ID	Shipped Date	Amount	Freight
Wilman Kala	21240	Finland	10248	16-Jul-1996	$440.00	$32.38
Tradição Hipermercados	05634-030	Brazil	10249	10-Jul-1996	$1,863.40	$11.61
Hanari Carnes	05454-876	Brazil	10250	12-Jul-1996	$1,552.60	$65.83
Victuailles en stock	69004	France	10251	15-Jul-1996	$654.06	$41.34
Suprêmes délices	B-6000	Belgium	10252	11-Jul-1996	$3,597.90	$51.30
Hanari Carnes	05454-876	Brazil	10253	16-Jul-1996	$1,444.80	$58.17
Chop-suey Chinese	3012	Switzerland	10254	23-Jul-1996	$556.62	$22.98
Richter Supermarkt	1203	Switzerland	10255	15-Jul-1996	$2,490.50	$148.33
Wellington Importadora	08737-363	Brazil	10256	17-Jul-1996	$517.80	$13.97
HILARIÓN-Abastos	5022	Venezuela	10257	22-Jul-1996	$1,119.90	$81.91
Ernst Handel	8010	Austria	10258	23-Jul-1996	$1,614.88	$140.51
Centro comercial Moctezuma	05022	Mexico	10259	25-Jul-1996	$100.80	$3.25
Old World Delicatessen	99508	USA	10260	29-Jul-1996	$1,504.65	$55.09
Que Delícia	02389-673	Brazil	10261	30-Jul-1996	$448.00	$3.05
Rattlesnake Canyon Grocery	87110	USA	10262	25-Jul-1996	$584.00	$48.29

Record: 1 of 809

Figure 10.10 Datasheet view confirms that the Amount column totals the net amount of each line item for an order.

Using the Expression Builder to Add Query Criteria

After creating and testing your query, you can apply criteria to limit the number of records that the query returns. You can use Access's Expression Builder to simplify the process of adding record-selection criteria to your query. To test some of the expressions listed in Table 10.9, follow these steps:

1. Click the Design View button on the toolbar to change to Query Design mode.
2. Place the cursor in the Criteria row of the field for which you want to establish a record-selection criterion.

3. Click the Build button on the toolbar to display the Expression Builder's window. Alternatively, you can right-click the Criteria row and then choose Build from the pop-up menu.
4. In the Expression text box at the top of Expression Builder's window, type one of the expressions from Table 10.9. Figure 10.11 shows the sample expression `Like "*shop*"` that applies to the Criteria row of the Company Name column. You can use the Like button under the expression text box as a shortcut for entering `Like`.

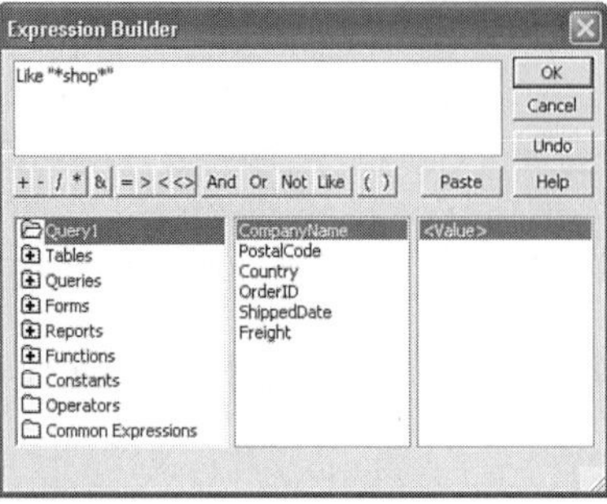

Figure 10.11 You can use the Expression Builder to add simple or complex expressions as WHERE clause criteria.

5. Click OK to return to the Query Design grid. The Expression Builder places the expression that you built in the field where the cursor is located (see Figure 10.12).

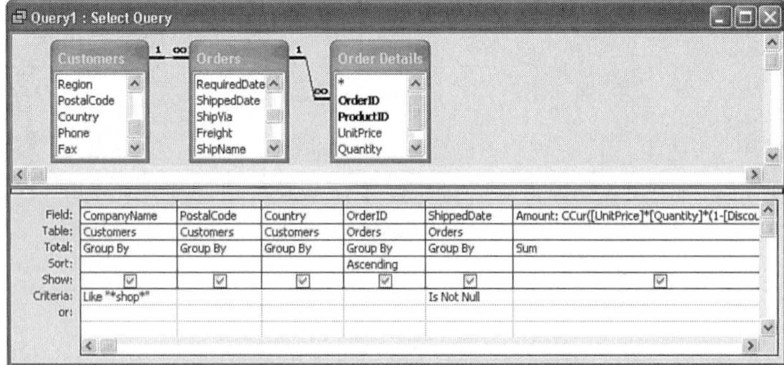

Figure 10.12 The expression you create in the Expression Builder applies to the field you selected when opening the Builder.

6. Click the Run button on the toolbar to test the expression. The query result for the example in Figure 10.12 appears as shown in Figure 10.13.

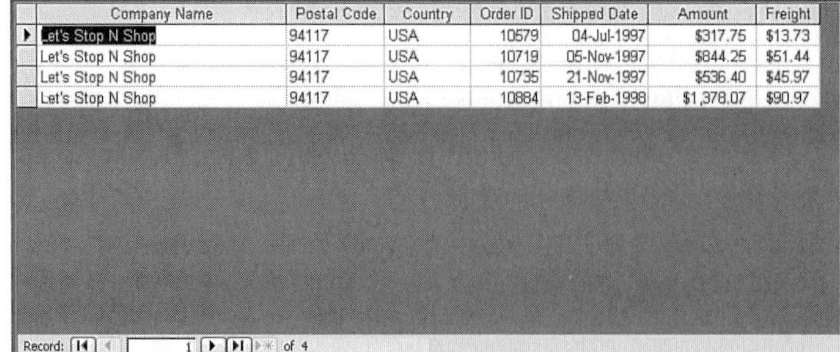

Company Name	Postal Code	Country	Order ID	Shipped Date	Amount	Freight
Let's Stop N Shop	94117	USA	10579	04-Jul-1997	$317.75	$13.73
Let's Stop N Shop	94117	USA	10719	05-Nov-1997	$844.25	$51.44
Let's Stop N Shop	94117	USA	10735	21-Nov-1997	$536.40	$45.97
Let's Stop N Shop	94117	USA	10884	13-Feb-1998	$1,378.07	$90.97

Figure 10.13 The `Like "*shop*"` expression displays records only for customers whose names contain "shop", "Shop", or "SHOP".

7. Return to Query Design mode; then select and delete the expression by pressing the Delete key.

8. Repeat steps 2 through 7 for each expression that you want to test. When you test expressions using Date/Time functions, sort the OrderDate field in ascending order. Similarly, sort on the Amount field when queries are based on amount criteria. You can alter the expressions and try combinations with the implied **And** condition by entering criteria for other fields in the same row. Access warns you with an error message if you make a mistake in an expression's syntax.
9. After you finish experimenting, save your query with a descriptive name, such as **qryInvoiceAmount**.

The preceding query and its underlying tables are included in Chaptr10.mdb sample file, located in the \Seua10\Chaptr10 folder of the accompanying CD-ROM.

Jet SQL

The Jet SQL statement for the qryOrderAmount query is

```
SELECT Customers.CompanyName, Customers.PostalCode,
   Customers.Country, Orders.OrderID, Orders.ShippedDate,
   Sum(CCur([UnitPrice]*[Quantity]*(1-[Discount]))) AS Amount,
   Orders.Freight
FROM (Customers
   INNER JOIN Orders
      ON Customers.CustomerID = Orders.CustomerID)
   INNER JOIN [Order Details]
      ON Orders.OrderID = [Order Details].OrderID
GROUP BY Customers.CompanyName, Customers.PostalCode, Customers.Country,
   Orders.OrderID, Orders.OrderDate, Orders.Freight
   HAVING (((Customers.CompanyName) Like "*shop*") AND
      ((Orders.ShippedDate) Is Not Null))
ORDER BY Orders.OrderID;
```

The `Sum(`**`CCur`**`([UnitPrice]*[Quantity]*(1-[Discount]))) AS Amount` expression combines the Sum aggregate operation you specified (refer to Figure 10.9) with the expression you typed to define the calculated Amount column.

Each `INNER JOIN...ON` clause defines the joins between two tables; `JOIN` clauses are one of the subjects of the next chapter.

You might think that the `GROUP BY` clause includes more fields than required and only the `Orders.OrderID` field is required for grouping. One of the Total aggregate functions *must* appear in each column of a grouped query.

The `HAVING` clause for grouped rows is the equivalent of the `WHERE` clause for individual rows.

If the Jet or SQL Server query designer throws an error when you attempt to run a query with aggregate functions, check the "Troubleshooting" section near the end of this chapter.

The SQL Server Version of a Query

If you've installed MSDE2002 to support ADP, you can run the Upsizing Wizard on the Chaptr10.mdb database to create the SQL Server version of the tables and qryOrderAmount query. Chapter 22, "Upsizing Jet Applications to Access Data Projects," provides detailed examples of the upsizing process.

→ For instructions on how to install MSDE2000 from the Office 2003 distribution CD-ROM, **see** "SQL Server 2000 Desktop Engine Setup," **p. 47**.

The Chaptr10.mdb database that the accompanying CD-ROM installs in your \Program Files\Seua11\Chaptr10 folder contains the Customers, Orders, and Order Details tables and the qryInvoiceAmount query you created in the preceding section. To upsize the Chaptr10.mdb database to an SQL Server Chaptr10SQL database and a Chaptr10CS.adp project, do this:

1. Verify that the Chaptr10.mdb file doesn't have the Read-Only attribute applied, and then open it in Access.
2. Choose Tools, Database Utilities, Upsizing Wizard to start the upsizing process.
3. Accept the default Create New Database option in the first Wizard dialog, and click Next.
4. In the second dialog, accept the default Use Trusted Connection to use your Administrator logon account for MSDE. Click Next.
5. In the third dialog, click the >> button to add all three tables to the SQL Server database, and click Next.
6. In the fourth and fifth dialogs, accept the defaults, and click Next.
7. In the sixth and last dialog, accept the default Open the New ADP File option, and click Finish to upsize the database. After a minute or so, depending on the speed of your computer, the Chaptr10CS.adp project opens and displays an eight-page Upsizing Wizard report.
8. Close the report to return to the Database window, click the Queries shortcut, and double-click the query, which the Wizard upsizes to an SQL Server 2000 (user defined) function. The Datasheet view of the query is identical to that of the Jet version of the query (refer to Figure 10.10).

9. Click the Design button to open the da Vinci Filter Design window. The three tables and the joins between them appear in the upper pane. Field definitions, including the calculated Amount field definition, appear in the lower pane.

10. Click the SQL toolbar button to display the filter's T-SQL statement. Adjust the position of the table windows and the depths of the three panes as shown in Figure 10.14.

T-SQL

The The T-SQL statement for the qryInvoiceAmount function (without a WHERE criterion on the Customers column) is

```
SELECT TOP 100 PERCENT dbo.Customers.CompanyName, dbo.Customers.PostalCode,
   dbo.Customers.Country, dbo.Orders.OrderID, dbo.Orders. ShippedDate,
   SUM(CONVERT(money, (dbo.[Order Details].UnitPrice * dbo.[Order
Details].Quantity) *
      (1 - dbo.[Order Details].Discount))) AS Amount, dbo.Orders.Freight
FROM  dbo.Customers
   INNER JOIN dbo.Orders
```

```
      ON dbo.Customers.CustomerID = dbo.Orders.CustomerID
   INNER JOIN dbo.[Order Details]
      ON dbo.Orders.OrderID = dbo.[Order Details].OrderID
GROUP BY dbo.Customers.CompanyName, dbo.Customers.PostalCode,
   dbo.Customers.Country, dbo.Orders.OrderID, dbo.Orders.OrderDate,
   dbo.Orders.Freight
HAVING (dbo.Orders.ShippedDate IS NOT NULL)
ORDER BY dbo.Orders.OrderID
```

The SQL statement is similar to that of the Jet query, but substitutes `CONVERT(money— )` for Jet's **`CCur`** function. The `TOP 100 PERCENT` prefix is required to permit an `ORDER BY` clause in a view or function. The `dbo.` prefix identifies the default database owner.

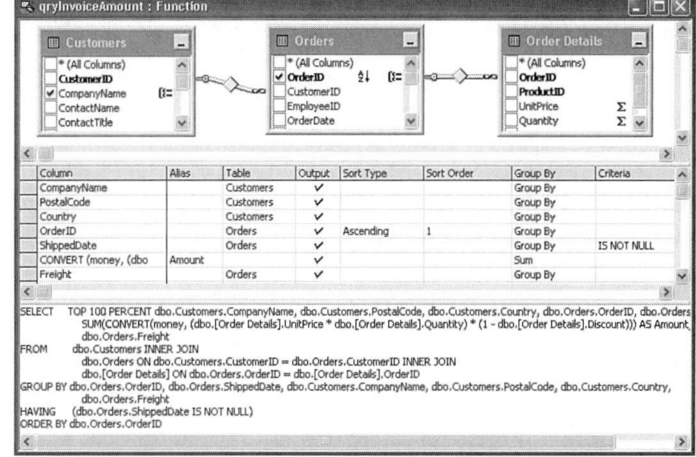

Figure 10.14
The da Vinci Design view of a filter, one of SQL Server's three choices for generating query result sets, has a three-pane window.

Expressions for Calculating Query Field Values

The three preceding sections demonstrate that you can use expressions to create new, calculated fields in query tables. Calculated fields display data computed based on the values of other fields in the same row of the query table. Table 10.10 shows some representative expressions that you can use to create calculated query fields. Notice that Jet field names must be enclosed with square brackets when typed in the Query Design window.

Table 10.10 Typical Expressions to Create Calculated Query Fields

Column Name	Expression	Values Calculated
TotalAmount	`[Amount] + [Freight]`	Sum of the OrderAmount and Freight fields
FreightPercent	`100 * [Freight]/[Amount]`	Freight charges as a percentage of the order amount

continues

TABLE 10.10 CONTINUED

Column Name	Expression	Values Calculated
FreightPct	**Format**([Freight]/[Amount], "Percent")	Freight charges as a percentage of the order amount, but with formatting applied
SalesTax	**Format**([Amount] * 0.08, "$#,###.00")	Sales tax of 8 percent of the amount of the order added with a display that's similar to the **Currency** data type

NOTE

T-SQL doesn't support the VBA **Format** function, and the Upsizing Wizard won't generate views or functions from Jet queries that use this function.

To create a query containing calculated fields, follow these steps:

1. In Query Design view, move to the first blank column of the qryInvoiceAmount query. Type the column name shown in Table 10.10, followed by a colon and then the expression:

```
Total Invoice: [Amount]+[Freight]
```

NOTE

If you don't type the field name and colon, Access provides the default `Expr1` as the calculated field name.

2. Place the cursor in the Total cell of the calculated field and select Expression from the drop-down list. If you don't select Expression, your query opens a Parameters dialog or returns an error message when you attempt to execute it.
3. Move to the next empty column, type the following expression, and add the Expression aggregate (see Figure 10.15):

```
Freight Pct: Format([Freight]/[Amount],"Percent")
```

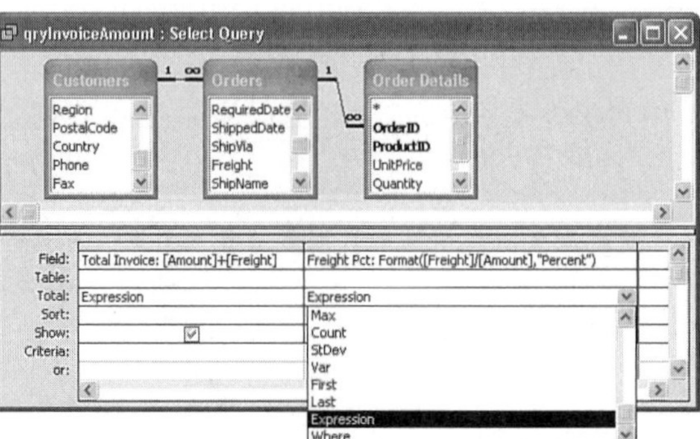

Figure 10.15 Type one of the expressions of Table 10.10 to add an additional calculated column. The example shown here calculates Total Invoice and Freight Pct column values from another calculated column, Amount, and a table field, Freight.

To avoid this error, see "Query Expressions Fail to Execute" in the "Troubleshooting" section at the end of the chapter.

4. Remove the Like "*shop*" criterion from the CompanyName column.
5. Run the query. The result set for the query with the added calculated fields appears as shown in Figure 10.16.

Figure 10.16
Datasheet view displays the query result set of the design shown in Figure 10.15.

qryInvoiceAmount : Select Query

Postal Code	Country	Order ID	Shipped Date	Amount	Freight	Total Invoice	Freight Pct
21240	Finland	10248	16-Jul-1996	$440.00	$32.38	$472.38	7.36%
05634-030	Brazil	10249	10-Jul-1996	$1,863.40	$11.61	$1,875.01	0.62%
05454-876	Brazil	10250	12-Jul-1996	$1,552.60	$65.83	$1,618.43	4.24%
69004	France	10251	15-Jul-1996	$654.06	$41.34	$695.40	6.32%
B-6000	Belgium	10252	11-Jul-1996	$3,597.90	$51.30	$3,649.20	1.43%
05454-876	Brazil	10253	16-Jul-1996	$1,444.80	$58.17	$1,502.97	4.03%
3012	Switzerland	10254	23-Jul-1996	$556.62	$22.98	$579.60	4.13%
1203	Switzerland	10255	15-Jul-1996	$2,490.50	$148.33	$2,638.83	5.96%
08737-363	Brazil	10256	17-Jul-1996	$517.80	$13.97	$531.77	2.70%
5022	Venezuela	10257	22-Jul-1996	$1,119.90	$81.91	$1,201.81	7.31%
8010	Austria	10258	23-Jul-1996	$1,614.88	$140.51	$1,755.39	8.70%
05022	Mexico	10259	25-Jul-1996	$100.80	$3.25	$104.05	3.22%
99508	USA	10260	29-Jul-1996	$1,504.65	$55.09	$1,559.74	3.66%
02389-673	Brazil	10261	30-Jul-1996	$448.00	$3.05	$451.05	0.68%
87110	USA	10262	25-Jul-1996	$584.00	$48.29	$632.29	8.27%
8010	Austria	10263	31-Jul-1996	$1,873.80	$146.06	$2,019.86	7.79%

Record: 1 of 809

6. Repeat steps 3 through 5 for the remaining examples in Table 10.10.

You use the **`Format`** function with your expression as its first argument to display the calculated values in a more readable form. When you add the percent symbol (%) to a format expression or specify "Percent" as the format, the value of the expression argument multiplies by 100 and the percent symbol preceded by a space appends to the displayed value.

If you run into a "Can't evaluate expression" or "Wrong data type" error, check the "Troubleshooting" section near the end of this chapter.

TIP

Use the **`Format`** function with custom percent formatting if you want fewer or more decimal places. For example, if you only want one digit to the right of the decimal separator, substitute `FreightPct: Format([Freight]/[Amount],"#0.0%")` for the standard formatting in the preceding example. Adding the `%` symbol to the format string automatically multiplies the value argument by 100.

Avoid the use of the **`Format`** or **`Format`**... functions in tables you plan to upsize to SQL Server. T-SQL doesn't support these two functions.

TROUBLESHOOTING

QUERY EXPRESSIONS FAIL TO EXECUTE

When attempting to execute a query that contains an expression, a "Can't evaluate expression" or "Wrong data type" message box appears.

The "Can't evaluate expression" message usually indicates a typographic error in naming a function or an object. Depending on the use of the function, an Enter Parameter Value dialog might appear if the named object does not exist. The "Wrong data type" message is most likely to occur as a result of attempting to use mathematic or trigonometric operators with values of the Text or Date/Time field data types. If your expression refers to a control contained in a form or report, the form or report must be open when you execute the function.

AGGREGATE QUERIES THROW ERRORS

I receive a "You tried to execute a query that does not include the specified expression 'ExpressionName' as part of an aggregate function" message when I attempt to run my aggregate query.

An aggregate function is missing from the Totals row of one of the columns. You must select Group By, Expression, or an aggregate function—such as Sum, Avg, Min, Max, or Where—for each column of your query. For T-SQL Queries, the da Vinci toolset's "ADO Error: Column 'dbo.*TableName.ColumnName*' is invalid in the select list because it is not contained in either an aggregate function or the GROUP BY clause" error message is more explicit.

TWO-DIGIT YEARS TURN INTO FOUR DIGITS IN QUERY CRITERIA

When I type Between #1/1/03# and #12/31/03# in the Criteria cell of Query Design view, Access changes my entry to Between #1/1/2003# and #12/31/2003#.

Windows XP and 2000—and the Office applications that run under these operating systems—are year 2000 (Y2K) compliant. By default, earlier versions of Access running under Windows 9x and Me drop the century digits when creating Jet SQL statements to execute queries, regardless of the formatting applied to the underlying table—mm-ddd-yyyy for all date fields in Northwind.mdb. Windows XP and 2000 define the short date format as having four-digit years. It's a good data entry practice to require typing four-digit years by adding the appropriate input mask (99/99/0000) with the Input Mask Wizard.

IN THE REAL WORLD—THE ALGEBRA OF ACCESS EXPRESSIONS

A junior high school algebra class provides most students their first introduction to abstract mathematics. Expressions (algebraic formulas) are crucial to the majority of decision-support queries you design, as well as presentation of calculated data in form and report text boxes and other text-based controls. The colon following the column name of a calculated expression is the equivalent of an equal sign; in mathematical terms, `Amount: CCur([UnitPrice]*[Quantity]*(1-[Discount]))` is the equivalent of `curAmount = CCur(sngUnitPrice*intQuantity*(1-sngDiscount))` in VBA.

Similarly, functions that convert data types and format query columns also are important to forms and reports. The classic definition of a function is this: If when X is given, Y is determined, then Y is a function of X. For example, in `Price: Format([UnitPrice], "#,##0.00")`, the value of the UnitPrice field (X) uniquely determines the value of the calculated Price (Y) column. The fact that queries can have calculated and specially formatted columns is one of the reasons this book uses the term column with queries and field for tables.

In most cases, it's a good design practice to base forms and reports on queries with precalculated and preformatted columns, rather than calculating and formatting values for individual text boxes. It's quicker and easier to check your expressions in the query result set, and you don't need to add expressions or formatting (or both) to every text box, subform, and other control that displays the data.

The only drawback of this approach is that calculating and formatting columns of queries with a large number of rows slows performance, but usually only slightly. For instance, formatting the nine-digit StudentID column of the 45,000-record StudentTransactions table of the Oakmont.mdb database with the `ID: Left([StudentID], 3) & "-" & Mid([StudentID], 4, 3) & "-" & Right([StudentID], 3)` expression causes an imperceptible effect on query execution speed. Bear in mind, however, that adding calculated columns to queries against networked databases increases the amount of data sent "over the wire." Calculated columns slow networked query execution by the proportion of characters added per row, as does applying formatting that increases the number of characters per column. The alternative is to perform calculations and add formatting by customized controls on Access forms.

Expressions and, to a lesser extent, functions play a major role in query criteria. When you type a criterion—such as `CA`—in the query design grid, Access converts the criterion to a valid Jet SQL expression, in this case `WHERE FieldName = "CA"`. In this example, the equal sign is the identity operator. Another use for the identity operator is in creating joins using SQL `WHERE` clauses, as in `WHERE Table2.PrimaryKey = Table1.ForeignKey`. SQL Server required the use of `WHERE` syntax to define joins prior to adopting the SQL-92 JOIN syntax in SQL Server 6+.

You can perform logical operations on query result sets with the **`IIf`** (inline **`If`**) function, whose arguments can contain other functions. For instance, the equivalent of the `Province: Nz([Region], "None")` expression is `Province: IIf(IsNull([Region]),"None",[Region])`. You must use the **`IIf`** function in Data Access Pages (DAP), the subject of Chapter 25, "Designing and Deploying Data Access Pages," because the `Nz` function isn't marked "safe for scripting."

CHAPTER 11

Creating Multitable and Crosstab Queries

In this chapter

INTRODUCING JOINS ON TABLES

Your purpose in acquiring a license for Access is undoubtedly to take advantage of its relational database management capabilities. To do so, you must be able to link related tables based on key fields that have values in common—a process called *joining tables*. Chapter 9, "Designing Queries for Jet Databases," and Chapter 10, "Understanding Jet Operators and Expressions," showed you how to create simple queries based on a single table. If you tried the examples in Chapter 10, you generated a multiple-table query when you joined the Order Details table to the Orders table and the Customers table to create the query for testing expressions. The first part of this chapter deals exclusively with queries created from multiple tables that are related through joins.

This chapter provides examples of queries that use each of the four basic types of joins that you can create in Access's Query Design view: inner joins, outer joins, self-joins, and theta joins. It also shows you how to take advantage of `UNION` queries that you can't create in Access's Query Design. The chapter also briefly covers subqueries, which you can substitute for nested Jet queries. Chapter 13, "Creating and Updating Jet Tables with Action Queries," presents typical applications for and examples of four types of action queries: update, append, delete, and make-table.

11

Some of the sample queries in this chapter use the HRActions table that you created in Chapter 5, "Working with Jet Databases and Tables." If you didn't create the HRActions table and have installed the sample databases from the accompanying CD-ROM, choose File, Get External Data, Import, and import the HRActions table from \Program Files\Seua11\Chaptr05\Nwind05.mdb or ...\Chaptr11\Joins11.mdb, which includes all the examples of this chapter.

→ For a detailed description of the HRActions table, **see** "Designing the HRActions Table," **p. 179**.

TIP

> Read this chapter and create the sample queries sequentially, as the queries appear in text. The sample queries of this chapter build on queries that you create in earlier sections.

If you're upgrading from Access 97 to 11, the following features added by Access 2000 apply to the subject matter of this chapter:

- New Query Properties—Subdatasheet Name, Link Child Fields, Link Master Fields, Subdatasheet Height, and Subdatasheet Expanded—control the behavior of subdatasheets in query result sets.
- You can print the contents of the Relationships window. When the Relationships window has the focus, choosing File, Print Relationships creates a report from the contents of the Relationships window and then displays the report in Print Preview mode for subsequent printing.

Access 2002 introduced *extended properties* of SQL Server 2000 tables, which let you specify lookup field and subdatasheet properties in Access Data Projects. Extended properties establish parity between Datasheet views of Jet and SQL Server tables and queries.

→ For a brief list of these extended properties, **see** "Access Data Projects and SQL Server 2000," **p. 34**

JOINING TABLES TO CREATE MULTITABLE QUERIES

Before you can create joins between tables, you must know which fields are related by common values. As mentioned in Chapter 5, assigning identical names to primary-key and foreign-key fields in different tables that contain related data is a common practice. This approach, used by Microsoft when creating the Northwind sample database, makes determining relationships and creating joins among tables easier. The CustomerID field in the Customers table and the CustomerID field in the Orders table, for example, are used to join orders with customers. A join between tables requires that one field in each table have a common set of values—CustomerID codes for this example.

Figure 11.1 shows the structure of the Northwind.mdb database with a graphical display of the relationships between the tables. Access indicates relationships with lines between field names of different tables. Bold type indicates primary-key fields. Each relationship usually involves at least one primary-key field. Relationships define *potential* joins between tables, but it's not necessary to have a predefined relationship to create a join.

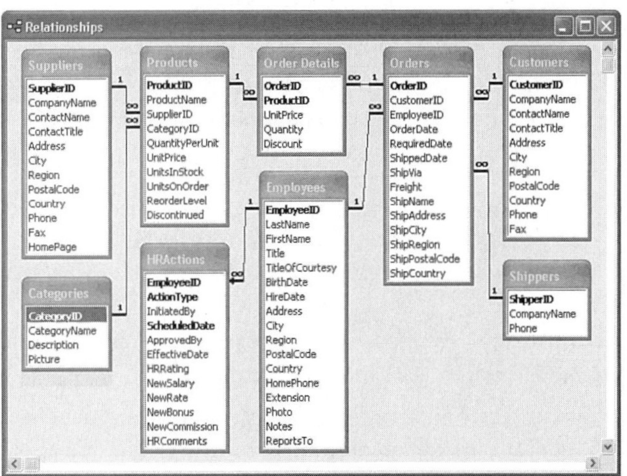

Figure 11.1 The Relationships window displays the relationships between primary keys and foreign keys in the Northwind database with the HRActions table added. Tables with composite primary keys (such as Order Details and HRActions) show each field of the primary key in bold type.

You can display the structure of the joins between the tables in Access 2003's Northwind database by giving the Database window the focus (press F11) and then clicking the Relationship button on the toolbar or by choosing Tools, Relationships. The 1 above the line that shows the join between two tables in Figure 11.1 indicates the "one" side of a one-to-many relationship; the infinity symbol ([is]) indicates the "many" side.

You can choose between displaying only the direct relationships for a single table (the Show Direct Relationships button on the toolbar) or all relationships for all tables in a database (the Show All Relationships button). All tables of Northwind.mdb appear by default when you open the Relationships window of the Northwind sample database. In this case, clicking the Show Direct Relationships button has no effect.

TIP

> To show relationships for only one table, click the Clear Layout toolbar button, click the Show Table button to display the Show Table dialog, select the table to display in the Tables list, and then click Add and Close. Click the Show Direct Relationships button to display the relationships for the selected table. Clearing the layout of the Relationships windows doesn't affect the underlying relationships between the tables. The Show Direct Relationships feature is useful primarily with databases that contain many related tables. Close the Relationships window and don't save the changes.

Access supports four types of joins in the Query Design window:

- *Inner joins* are the most common join for creating select queries. The most common type of an inner join is a *natural join* (also called an equi-join), which displays all the records in one table that have corresponding records in another table. The correspondence between records is determined by identical values (`WHERE` *`field1`* `=` *`field2`* in SQL) in the fields that join the tables. In most cases, joins are based on a unique primary-key field in one table and a foreign-key field in the other table in a one-to-many relationship. If none of the table's records that act as the many side of the relationship has a field value that corresponds to a record in the table of the one side, the corresponding records in the one side don't appear in the query result.

NOTE

> Access automatically creates natural joins between tables if the tables share a common field name that's a primary key of one of the tables.

- *Outer joins* display records in one member of the join, regardless of whether corresponding records exist on the other side of the join.
- *Self-joins* relate data within a single table. You create a self-join in Access by adding to the query a duplicate of the table (Access provides an alias for the duplicate), and then you create a join to the field(s) of the duplicate table.
- *Theta joins* relate data by using comparison operators other than `=`. Theta joins include not-equal joins (<>) used in queries designed to return records that don't have corresponding values. It's easier to implement theta joins by `WHERE` criteria rather than by the SQL `JOIN` reserved word. The Query Design window doesn't indicate theta joins by drawing lines between field names.

The 15.5MB Oakmont.mdb database, in the \Seua11\Oakmont folder of the accompanying CD-ROM, has a circular set of relationships. Open Oakmont.mdb, either from the CD-ROM or from a copy on your fixed disk, and then click the Relationships button to open the Relationships window (see Figure 11.2). Courses are one-to-many related to Courses, Departments are one-to-many related to Courses, and Employees are one-to-many related to Sections. You also can see a circular relationship between Courses, Enrollments, Students, Grades, and Courses. Oakmont.mdb is useful when you want to test the performance of queries with a large number of records. The fictitious Oakmont University in Navasota, Texas, has about 30,000 students, 2,320 employees, and offers 1,770 sections of 590 courses in 14 academic departments.

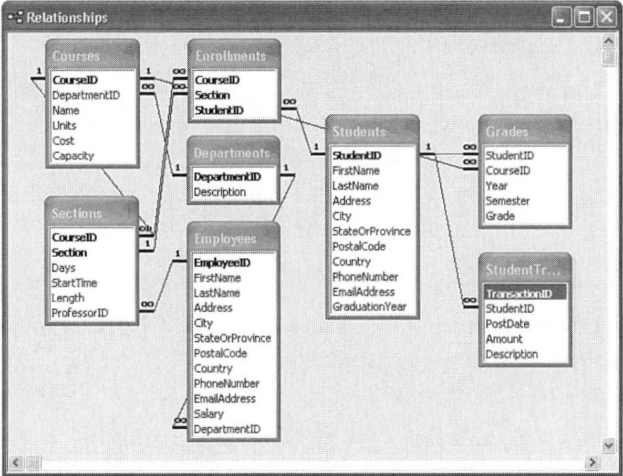

Figure 11.2
The Oakmont.mdb database has a circular set of relationships between the Courses, Enrollments, Students, Grades, and Course tables.

Creating Conventional Single-Column Inner Joins

Joins based on one column in each table are known as *single-column inner equi-joins*. The following list details the basic rules for designing a database that lets you use simple single-column inner equi-join for all queries:

- Each table on the one side of the relationship must have a primary key with a No Duplicates index to maintain referential integrity. Access automatically creates a No Duplicates index on the primary-key field(s) of a table.
- Many-to-many relationships, such as the relationship of Orders to Products, are implemented by an intermediary table (in this case, Order Details) having a one-to-many relationship (Orders to Order Details) with one table and a many-to-one relationship (Order Details to Products) with another.
- Duplicated data in tables, where applicable, is extracted to a new table that has a primary-key, no-duplicates, one-to-many relationship with the table from which the duplicate data is extracted. Using a multicolumn primary key to identify extracted data uniquely often is necessary because individual key fields might contain duplicate data.

The combination (also known as concatenation) of the values of the key fields, however, must be unique. Access 2003's Table Analyzer Wizard locates and extracts most duplicate data automatically.

→ For more information on Make-Table queries, **see** "Creating New Tables with Make-Table Queries," **p. 490**.

→ If you're not sure how to create relationships, **see** "Establishing Relationships Between Tables," **p. 189**.

All joins in the Northwind database, shown earlier by the lines that connect field names of adjacent tables in Figure 11.1, are single-column inner joins between tables with one-to-many relationships. Figure 11.2 illustrates the two-column relationship between the CourseID and SectionID fields of the Sections and Enrollments tables. Access uses the ANSI SQL-92 reserved words `INNER JOIN` to identify conventional inner joins, and `LEFT JOIN` or `RIGHT JOIN` to specify outer joins.

Among the most common uses for queries based on inner joins is matching customer names and addresses with orders received. You might want to create a simple report, for example, that lists the customer name, order number, order date, and amount. To create a conventional one-to-many, single-column inner join query that relates Northwind's customers to their orders, sorted by company and order date, follow these steps:

1. With Northwind.mdb open, close all windows except the Database window.

2. Click the Queries shortcut of the Database window and then double-click the Create Query in Design View shortcut. Access displays the Show Table dialog superimposed on an empty Query Design window.

3. Select the Customers table from the Show Table list and click the Add button. Alternatively, you can double-click the Customers table name to add the table to the query. Access adds the Field Names list for Customers to the Query Design window.
4. Double-click the Orders table in the Show Table list and then click the Close button. Access adds to the window the Field Names list for Orders, plus a line that indicates a join between the CustomerID fields of the two tables. Access creates the join automatically because Access found a relationship to the CustomerID field (a foreign key) in the Orders table.
5. To identify each order with the customer's name, select the CompanyName field of the Customers table and drag the field symbol to the Field row of the Query Design grid's first column.
6. Select the OrderID field of the Orders table and drag the field symbol to the second column's Field row. Drag the OrderDate field to the third column. Your query design appears as shown in Figure 11.3.
7. Click the Run or Datasheet view button to display the result of the query, the Recordset shown in Figure 11.4. Notice that the field headers of the query result set show the captions for the table fields, which include spaces, rather than the actual field names, which don't have spaces.

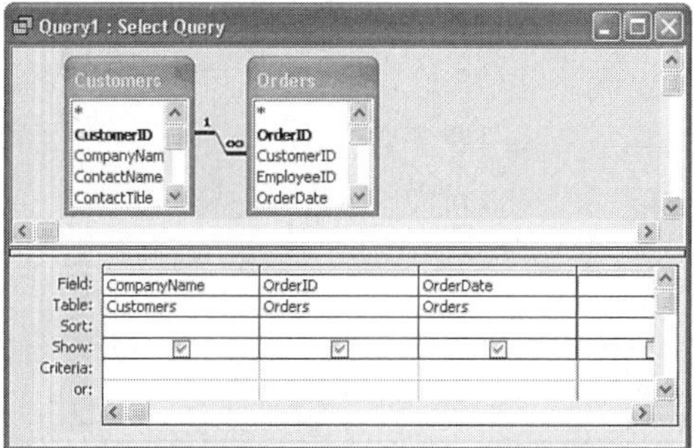

Figure 11.3 Access automatically creates the inner join on the CustomerID field between the Customers and Orders table.

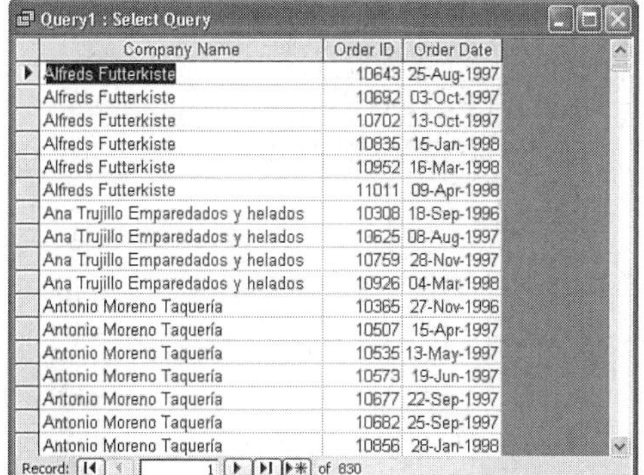

Company Name	Order ID	Order Date
Alfreds Futterkiste	10643	25-Aug-1997
Alfreds Futterkiste	10692	03-Oct-1997
Alfreds Futterkiste	10702	13-Oct-1997
Alfreds Futterkiste	10835	15-Jan-1998
Alfreds Futterkiste	10952	16-Mar-1998
Alfreds Futterkiste	11011	09-Apr-1998
Ana Trujillo Emparedados y helados	10308	18-Sep-1996
Ana Trujillo Emparedados y helados	10625	08-Aug-1997
Ana Trujillo Emparedados y helados	10759	28-Nov-1997
Ana Trujillo Emparedados y helados	10926	04-Mar-1998
Antonio Moreno Taquería	10365	27-Nov-1996
Antonio Moreno Taquería	10507	15-Apr-1997
Antonio Moreno Taquería	10535	13-May-1997
Antonio Moreno Taquería	10573	19-Jun-1997
Antonio Moreno Taquería	10677	22-Sep-1997
Antonio Moreno Taquería	10682	25-Sep-1997
Antonio Moreno Taquería	10856	28-Jan-1998

Figure 11.4 The Datasheet view of the query design of Figure 11.3 displays the three fields added to the grid.

SPECIFYING A SORT ORDER AND TOP VALUES LIMIT

Access displays query result sets in the order of the index on the primary-key field, unless you specify sorting on another field or a different sort direction on the primary key field. If more than one column represents a primary-key field, Access sorts simple query result sets in left-to-right key-field column precedence. Because CompanyName is the leftmost primary-key field, the query result set displays all orders for a single company in order-number sequence. You can override the primary-key display order by adding a sort order to the query. For example, if you want to see the most recent orders first, you can specify a descending sort by the order date.

→ For more information on primary-key indexes, **see** "Adding Indexes to Tables," **p. 194**.

You can use the Top Values option to limit the number of rows returned by the query to those that are likely to be of most interest. For this example with a descending sort, only the most recent orders are relevant. Minimizing the number of rows returned by a query is especially important with client/server queries against large tables or when creating networked applications for remote users having slow dial-up connections.

To add this sort sequence and row limit to your query, follow these steps:

1. Click the Design View button.
2. Place the cursor in the Sort row of the Order Date column of the Query Design grid and click the arrow or press Alt+↓ to open the drop-down list.
3. Select Descending from the drop-down list to specify a descending sort on date—latest orders first (see Figure 11.5).

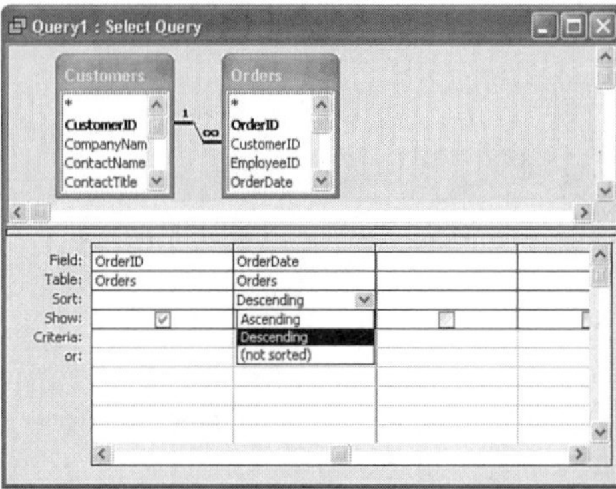

Figure 11.5 Add a descending sort on the OrderDate field to display the latest orders first.

4. Open the Top Values list of the toolbar and select 5%. Adding a Top Values constraint doesn't affect the Query Design grid.
5. Click the Run button or the View button to display the query result set with the new sort order and row limit (see Figure 11.6).

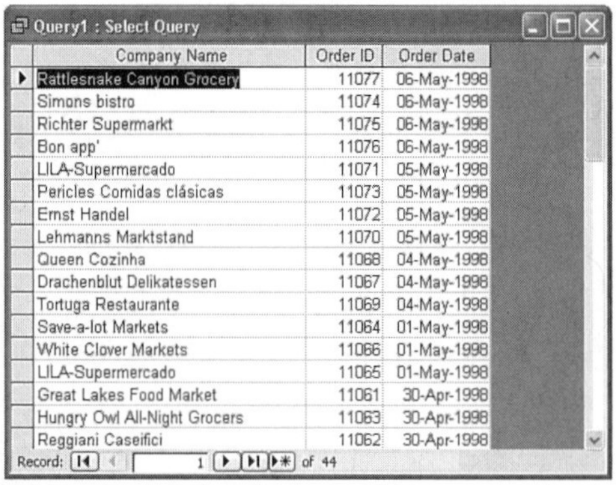

Query1 : Select Query

Company Name	Order ID	Order Date
Rattlesnake Canyon Grocery	11077	06-May-1998
Simons bistro	11074	06-May-1998
Richter Supermarkt	11075	06-May-1998
Bon app'	11076	06-May-1998
LILA-Supermercado	11071	05-May-1998
Pericles Comidas clásicas	11073	05-May-1998
Ernst Handel	11072	05-May-1998
Lehmanns Marktstand	11070	05-May-1998
Queen Cozinha	11068	04-May-1998
Drachenblut Delikatessen	11067	04-May-1998
Tortuga Restaurante	11069	04-May-1998
Save-a-lot Markets	11064	01-May-1998
White Clover Markets	11066	01-May-1998
LILA-Supermercado	11065	01-May-1998
Great Lakes Food Market	11061	30-Apr-1998
Hungry Owl All-Night Grocers	11063	30-Apr-1998
Reggiani Caseifici	11062	30-Apr-1998

Record: 1 of 44

Figure 11.6 Orders appear in descending date sequence in this Datasheet view. With 5% set in the Top Values list, the query returns only 44 rows.

6. Open the View list button on the toolbar, and choose SQL View to open the SQL window, which displays the Jet SQL statement for the query.

Jet SQL

The Jet SQL statement for the sorted query with the Top Values limit is

```
SELECT TOP 5 PERCENT Customers.CompanyName,
   Orders.OrderID, Orders.OrderDate
FROM Customers
   INNER JOIN Orders
   ON Customers.CustomerID=Orders.CustomerID
ORDER BY Orders.OrderDate DESC;
```

The `INNER JOIN Orders` clause specifies a join with the Customers table, and the `ON Customers.CustomerID=Orders.CustomerID` qualifier names the joined fields.

A pre-SQL-92 alternative method for creating joins is to use the `WHERE` clause to specify a join. If you edit the SQL statement as follows, you achieve the same result:

```
SELECT TOP 5 PERCENT Customers.CompanyName,
   Orders.OrderID, Orders.OrderDate
FROM Customers, Orders
WHERE Customers.CustomerID=Orders.CustomerID
ORDER BY Orders.OrderDate DESC;
```

Using `WHERE` clauses to specify `INNER`, `LEFT`, and `RIGHT JOIN`s no longer is common practice, because result sets created by `WITH` clauses aren't updatable.

DESIGNING NESTED QUERIES

Jet lets you use a saved query (`QueryDef` objects) in lieu of that query's tables (`TableDef` objects) in other queries. The only significant difference between these two objects from a query design standpoint is that queries don't have primary keys. Prior to executing the top-level query, Jet executes the `QueryDef` objects of lower-level (nested) queries, and then creates the join with other tables.

To add a saved query, Northwind.mdb's sample Order Subtotals query for this example, as a nested query in the customer/orders query you created in the preceding section, do this:

1. Return to Query Design view and click the Show Table button to open the dialog.
2. Click the Queries tab of the Show Tables dialog, double-click the Order Subtotals entry in the list, and click Close.
3. Double-click the Subtotal column of the Order Subtotals query to add it to the grid. Optionally, double-click the Freight field of the Orders table to add a Freight column to the query (see Figure 11.7). The join line represents a one-to-one relationship between the OrderID fields of the Orders table and the Order Subtotals query.
4. Click the Run button to display the result set (see Figure 11.8).

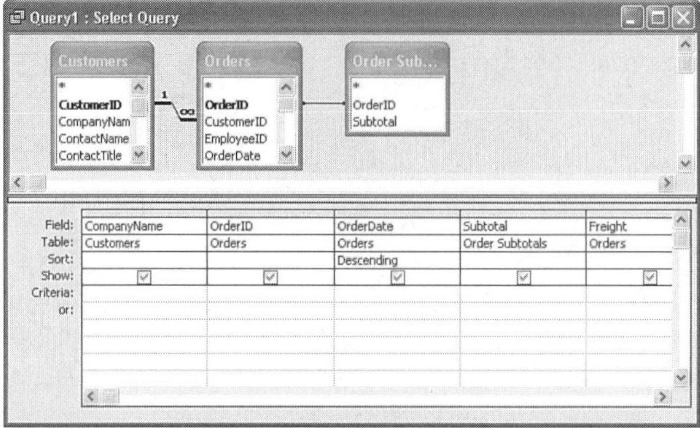

Figure 11.7
Adding a query instead of a table as a query data source adds a relationship between columns and fields of the same name. In this case, the relationship is one-to-one.

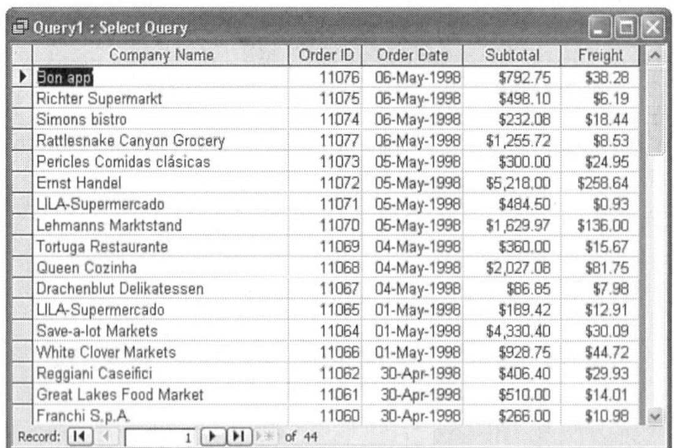

Query1 : Select Query

Company Name	Order ID	Order Date	Subtotal	Freight
Bon app'	11076	06-May-1998	$792.75	$38.28
Richter Supermarkt	11075	06-May-1998	$498.10	$6.19
Simons bistro	11074	06-May-1998	$232.08	$18.44
Rattlesnake Canyon Grocery	11077	06-May-1998	$1,255.72	$8.53
Pericles Comidas clásicas	11073	05-May-1998	$300.00	$24.95
Ernst Handel	11072	05-May-1998	$5,218.00	$258.64
LILA-Supermercado	11071	05-May-1998	$484.50	$0.93
Lehmanns Marktstand	11070	05-May-1998	$1,629.97	$136.00
Tortuga Restaurante	11069	04-May-1998	$360.00	$15.67
Queen Cozinha	11068	04-May-1998	$2,027.08	$81.75
Drachenblut Delikatessen	11067	04-May-1998	$86.85	$7.98
LILA-Supermercado	11065	01-May-1998	$189.42	$12.91
Save-a-lot Markets	11064	01-May-1998	$4,330.40	$30.09
White Clover Markets	11066	01-May-1998	$928.75	$44.72
Reggiani Caseifici	11062	30-Apr-1998	$406.40	$29.93
Great Lakes Food Market	11061	30-Apr-1998	$510.00	$14.01
Franchi S.p.A.	11060	30-Apr-1998	$266.00	$10.98

Record: 1 of 44

Figure 11.8
The query design of Figure 11.7 adds the Order Subtotals' Subtotal column and the optional Freight field of the Orders table.

5. Choose Tools, Relationships, to open the Relationships window, click the Show Tables button, click the Queries tab, double-click the Orders Subtotals item in the list, and click Close. Unlike the Query Design process, Access doesn't automatically display the relationship between queries and tables.
6. Drag the OrderID field from the Orders table and drop it on the OrderID column of the Orders Subtotals column to display the Edit Relationships dialog (see Figure 11.9). You can't enforce referential integrity between tables and queries. Click OK to close the dialog.
7. Close the Relationships window, and save the layout changes. Then close your query, and save it with a descriptive name, such as **qryOrderAmountsRecentTop5%**.

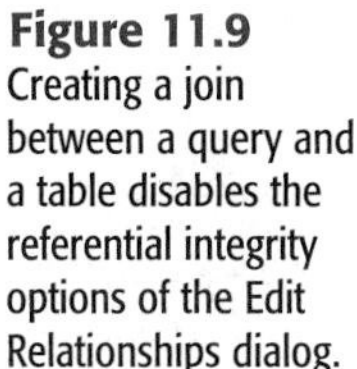

Figure 11.9 Creating a join between a query and a table disables the referential integrity options of the Edit Relationships dialog.

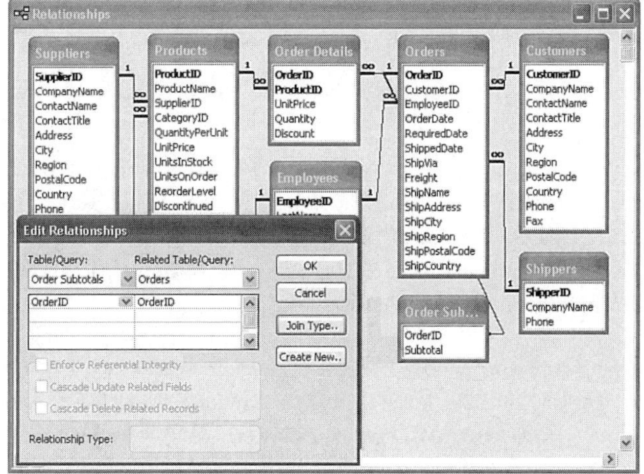

Jet SQL

The Jet SQL statement for the nested query is

```
SELECT TOP 5 PERCENT Customers.CompanyName, Orders.OrderID,
   Orders.OrderDate, [Order Subtotals].Subtotal, Orders.Freight
FROM Customers
   INNER JOIN (Orders
      INNER JOIN [Order Subtotals]
      ON Orders.OrderID = [Order Subtotals].OrderID)
   ON Customers.CustomerID = Orders.CustomerID
ORDER BY Orders.OrderDate DESC;
```

Square bracket pairs (`[ ]`)surround table or query names having spaces or SQL-illegal punctuation. Indenting the `INNER JOIN` statements at the same level as the `ON` prepositions makes the syntax easier to understand.

CREATING QUERIES FROM TABLES WITH INDIRECT RELATIONSHIPS

You can create queries that return indirectly related records, such as the categories of products purchased by each customer. You must include in the queries each table that serves as a link in the chain of joins. If you're designing queries to display the categories of products purchased by each customer, for example, include each of the tables that link the chain of joins between the Customers and Categories tables. This chain includes the Customers, Orders, Order Details, Products, and Categories tables. You often need indirect relationships for data analysis queries.

> **TIP**
>
> Queries with indirect relationships are especially useful to create PivotTable and PivotChart views of data. Several of the next chapter's PivotTable and PivotChart examples use this and related queries as data sources.

11

To create a query that you can use to analyze customers purchases by category, which requires specifying fields of indirectly related records, follow these steps:

1. In the Queries list of the Database window, click the Create Query in Design View shortcut.
2. Add the Customers, Orders, Order Details, Products, and Categories tables to the query, in sequence; then click the Close button of the Add Table dialog. Access automatically creates a chain of joins between Customers and Categories based on relationships between the primary-key field of each intervening table and the identically named foreign-key field in the adjacent table.

> **TIP**
>
> As you add tables to the Query Design window, the table field lists might not appear in the upper pane. Use the upper pane's vertical scroll bar to display the "hidden" tables. You can drag the table field lists to the top of the upper pane and then rearrange the field lists to match the appearance of the upper pane of Figure 11.10.

3. Double-click the CompanyName and CategoryName fields from the Customers and Categories tables, to add them to the first two columns of the grid.
4. In the Field row of the third column, type **Amount: CCur([Order Details].[UnitPrice]*[Quantity]*(1-[Discount]))** to calculate the net amount of the purchase of each line item in the Orders Details table (see Figure 11.10).

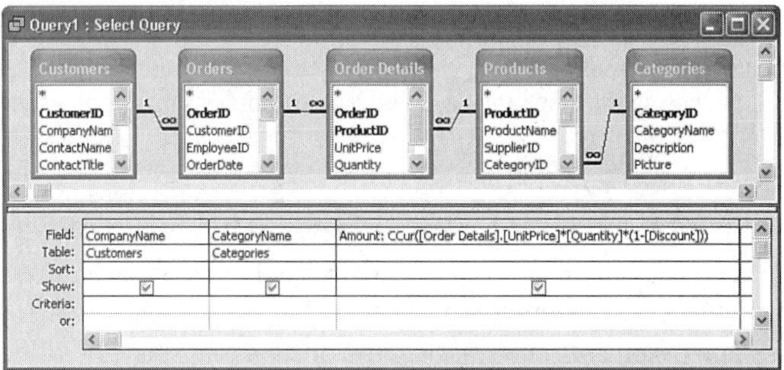

Figure 11.10 The query design shown here calculates the net purchases of each product by every customer.

5. Click the Run button to test the query at this intermediate point of the design (see Figure 11.11). The query returns 2,155 rows, which is the number of records in the Order Details table.

Figure 11.11
The Datasheet view of the query design of Figure 11.10 has too much detail to be usable for sales analysis of product categories.

Query1 : Select Query

Company Name	Category Name	Amount
QUICK-Stop	Beverages	$518.40
Rattlesnake Canyon Grocery	Beverages	$259.20
Lonesome Pine Restaurant	Beverages	$288.00
Die Wandernde Kuh	Beverages	$183.60
Pericles Comidas clásicas	Beverages	$172.80
Chop-suey Chinese	Beverages	$183.60
Queen Cozinha	Beverages	$144.00
La maison d'Asie	Beverages	$345.60
Princesa Isabel Vinhos	Beverages	$216.00
Lehmanns Marktstand	Beverages	$576.00
Wartian Herkku	Beverages	$122.40
Tortuga Restaurante	Beverages	$180.00
Mère Paillarde	Beverages	$360.00
Du monde entier	Beverages	$54.00

Record: 1 of 2155

6. Return to Design view and click the Totals button to group the data by CategoryName and CustomerName, and generate total sales by category for each customer. Apply an ascending sort to the CategoryName column, and select Sum from the drop-down list in the Group By row of the Amount column (see Figure 11.12).

Figure 11.12
To reduce the amount of detail, group the records by the CustomerName and CategoryName fields, and calculate the sum of the Amount column.

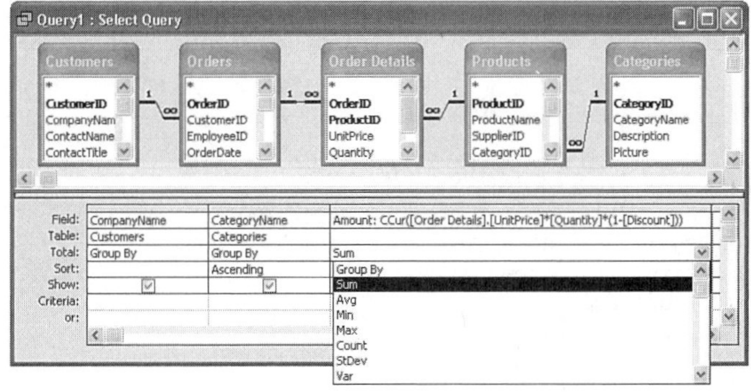

7. Run the query to display the summary (aggregated) result set, which now contains 598 records (see Figure 11.13). 598 records are too many for most people to analyze by inspection.

Figure 11.13
This summary query result set totals product sales by category and customer to reduce the number of rows from 2,155 to 598.

Query1 : Select Query

Company Name	Category Name	Amount
Alfreds Futterkiste	Beverages	$553.50
Ana Trujillo Emparedados y helados	Beverages	$60.00
Antonio Moreno Taquería	Beverages	$1,759.00
Around the Horn	Beverages	$1,227.00
Berglunds snabbköp	Beverages	$8,298.68
Blauer See Delikatessen	Beverages	$342.00
Blondel père et fils	Beverages	$3,975.92
Bólido Comidas preparadas	Beverages	$310.00
Bon app'	Beverages	$2,275.90
Bottom-Dollar Markets	Beverages	$1,762.75
B's Beverages	Beverages	$1,845.00
Cactus Comidas para llevar	Beverages	$1,091.00
Chop-suey Chinese	Beverages	$685.50
Consolidated Holdings	Beverages	$152.00
Die Wandernde Kuh	Beverages	$2,146.85
Drachenblut Delikatessen	Beverages	$247.20
Du monde entier	Beverages	$194.00

Record: 1 of 598

8. Return to Query Design view, open the Field list of the first column, substitute **Country** for CustomerName to reduce the number of records to 165, and run the query (see Figure 11.14).

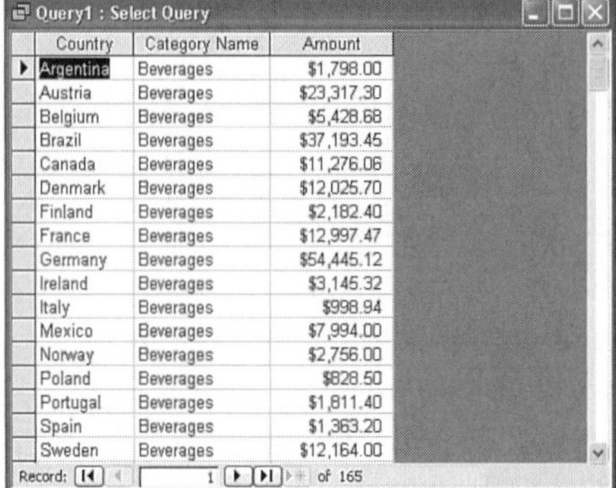
Query1 : Select Query

Country	Category Name	Amount
Argentina	Beverages	$1,798.00
Austria	Beverages	$23,317.30
Belgium	Beverages	$5,428.68
Brazil	Beverages	$37,193.45
Canada	Beverages	$11,276.06
Denmark	Beverages	$12,025.70
Finland	Beverages	$2,182.40
France	Beverages	$12,997.47
Germany	Beverages	$54,445.12
Ireland	Beverages	$3,145.32
Italy	Beverages	$998.94
Mexico	Beverages	$7,994.00
Norway	Beverages	$2,756.00
Poland	Beverages	$828.50
Portugal	Beverages	$1,811.40
Spain	Beverages	$1,363.20
Sweden	Beverages	$12,164.00

Record: 1 of 165

Figure 11.14
Aggregating sales by country and category displays 165 records. If customers in all 21 countries had made purchases in all eight categories, the result set would have 168 records.

9. Close the Query and save it as **qryOrdersByCountryAndCategory**.

Jet SQL

The Jet SQL statement for the aggregate query is

```
SELECT Customers.Country, Categories.CategoryName,
   Sum(CCur([Order Details].[UnitPrice]*
   [Quantity]*(1-[Discount]))) AS Amount
FROM (Categories
   INNER JOIN Products
      ON Categories.CategoryID = Products.CategoryID)
   INNER JOIN ((Customers INNER JOIN Orders
      ON Customers.CustomerID = Orders.CustomerID)
   INNER JOIN [Order Details]
      ON Orders.OrderID = [Order Details].OrderID)
      ON Products.ProductID = [Order Details].ProductID
GROUP BY Customers.Country, Categories.CategoryName
ORDER BY Categories.CategoryName;
```

If you write SQL statements for queries with several joins instead of using Access's graphical query design window, it's easier to use a pre-SQL-92 `WHERE` clause to define the joins, as in:

```
SELECT Customers.Country, Categories.CategoryName,
   Sum(CCur([Order Details].UnitPrice*
   [Quantity]*(1-[Discount]))) AS Amount
FROM Customers, Orders, [Order Details], Products, Categories
WHERE Categories.CategoryID=Products.CategoryID
   AND Customers.CustomerID=Orders.CustomerID
   AND Orders.OrderID=[Order Details].OrderID
   AND Products.ProductID=[Order Details].ProductID
GROUP BY Customers.Country, Categories.CategoryName
ORDER BY Categories.CategoryName;
```

The two preceding SQL statements produce the same result set, but using the WHERE clause causes the join lines to disappear from the Query Design pane. Notice that the WHERE clause elements are identical to the ON elements. Updatability isn't a factor in this case, because aggregate queries aren't updatable.

Queries that use SQL aggregate functions are the foundation of Jet crosstab queries. Access data projects (ADP) don't support crosstab queries, because T-SQL lacks the Jet SQL reserved words needed to create crosstabs directly. Instead, ADP use PivotTables to display aggregate query result sets in crosstab format.

→ For more information on summary queries, **see** "Using the SQL Aggregate Functions," **p. 435**.

→ To learn more about crosstab queries, **see** "Creating Crosstab Queries," **p. 442**.

TIP

Access's graphical Query Design features are much more comprehensive than those included with Windows programming languages, such as Visual Basic 6.0 or Visual Basic .NET. If you're a Visual Basic programmer (or plan to learn Visual Basic to create database front ends for Jet databases), use Access to write your programs' Jet SQL statements. SQL Server is the production back end preferred by most Visual Basic programmers, but Jet remains an effective database engine for storing and manipulating local data on Windows clients.

CREATING MULTICOLUMN INNER JOINS AND SELECTING UNIQUE VALUES

You can't have more than one join between a pair of tables, but you can have joins on multiple fields. You might, for example, want to create a query that returns the names of customers who have the same billing and shipping addresses. The billing address is the Address field of the Customers table, and the shipping address is the ShipAddress field of the Orders table. Therefore, you need to match the CustomerID fields in the two tables and Customers.Address with Orders.ShipAddress. This task requires a multicolumn inner join.

To create this example of an address-matching, multicolumn inner join, follow these steps:

1. Open a new query in Design view.
2. Add the Customers and Orders tables to the query and close the Add Tables dialog. Access creates the join on the CustomerID fields.
3. Click and drag the Address field of the Customers table's Field List box to the ShipAddress field of the Orders table's Field List box. This creates another join criterion, indicated by the new line between Address and ShipAddress (see the top pane of Figure 11.15). The new join line between Address and ShipAddress has dots at both ends, indicating that the join is between a pair of fields that doesn't have a specified relationship, the same field name, or a primary-key index.

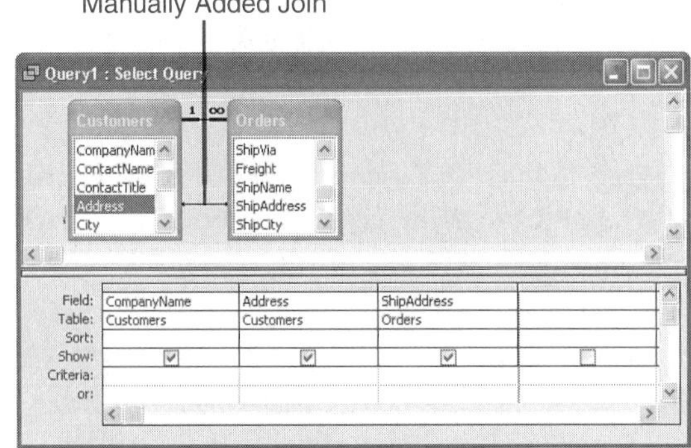

Figure 11.15 This query has an inner join on two fields. You must manually add join criteria between fields with dissimilar names.

4. Drag the Customers table's CompanyName and Address fields to the Field row of the first and second query columns and then drop the fields. Drag the Orders table's ShipAddress field to the query's third column and drop the field in the Field row (refer to the lower pane of Figure 11.15).

5. Click the Run button. Figure 11.16 shows the query's result set.

11

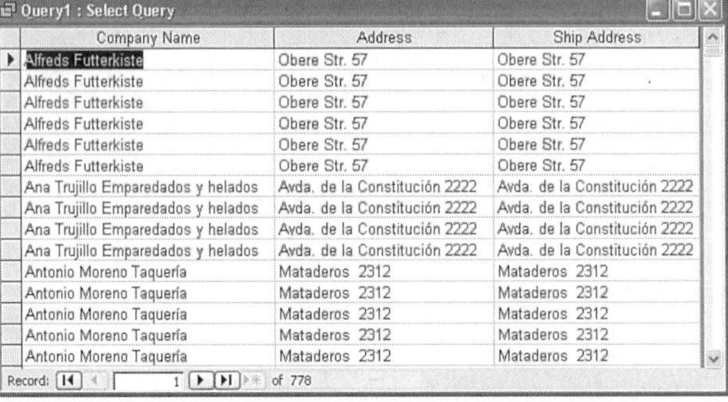

Query1 : Select Query

Company Name	Address	Ship Address
Alfreds Futterkiste	Obere Str. 57	Obere Str. 57
Alfreds Futterkiste	Obere Str. 57	Obere Str. 57
Alfreds Futterkiste	Obere Str. 57	Obere Str. 57
Alfreds Futterkiste	Obere Str. 57	Obere Str. 57
Alfreds Futterkiste	Obere Str. 57	Obere Str. 57
Alfreds Futterkiste	Obere Str. 57	Obere Str. 57
Ana Trujillo Emparedados y helados	Avda. de la Constitución 2222	Avda. de la Constitución 2222
Ana Trujillo Emparedados y helados	Avda. de la Constitución 2222	Avda. de la Constitución 2222
Ana Trujillo Emparedados y helados	Avda. de la Constitución 2222	Avda. de la Constitución 2222
Ana Trujillo Emparedados y helados	Avda. de la Constitución 2222	Avda. de la Constitución 2222
Antonio Moreno Taquería	Mataderos 2312	Mataderos 2312
Antonio Moreno Taquería	Mataderos 2312	Mataderos 2312
Antonio Moreno Taquería	Mataderos 2312	Mataderos 2312
Antonio Moreno Taquería	Mataderos 2312	Mataderos 2312
Antonio Moreno Taquería	Mataderos 2312	Mataderos 2312

Record: 1 of 778

Figure 11.16 The result set displays records for all orders in which billing and shipping addresses are the same.

6. To eliminate the duplicate rows, you must use the Unique Values option of the Query Properties window. To display the Query Properties window, click the Design View button, and then double-click an empty area in the Query Design window's upper pane. (If the title bar of the Properties window displays Field Properties or Field List, click an empty area in the Query Design window's upper pane so that the title bar displays Query Properties.) Alternatively, right-click an empty region of the upper pane and select Properties from the pop-up menu.

7. By default, both the Unique Records query property and the Unique Values property are set to No. Open the Unique Values list and select Yes (see Figure 11.17). Setting the Unique Values property to Yes adds the ANSI SQL reserved word `DISTINCT` to the query. Close the Query Properties window.

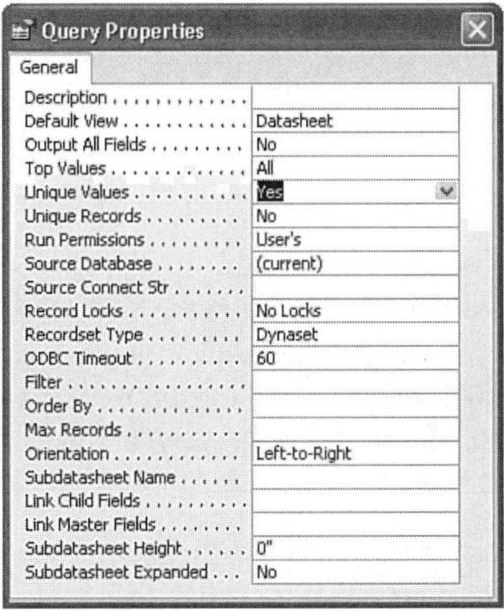

Figure 11.17 Setting the Unique Values property to Yes adds the `DISTINCT` qualifier to the query to display only rows that have different contents.

TIP

Alternatively, you can change the property settings for the Unique Records and Unique Values properties by double-clicking their text boxes in the Properties window. All properties with Yes/No values let you toggle their value by double-clicking.

8. Click the Run button. The result set no longer contains duplicate rows, as shown in Figure 11.18.

Query1 : Select Query

Company Name	Address	Ship Address
Alfreds Futterkiste	Obere Str. 57	Obere Str. 57
Ana Trujillo Emparedados y helados	Avda. de la Constitución 2222	Avda. de la Constitución 2222
Antonio Moreno Taquería	Mataderos 2312	Mataderos 2312
Berglunds snabbköp	Berguvsvägen 8	Berguvsvägen 8
Blauer See Delikatessen	Forsterstr. 57	Forsterstr. 57
Blondel père et fils	24, place Kléber	24, place Kléber
Bólido Comidas preparadas	C/ Araquil, 67	C/ Araquil, 67
Bon app'	12, rue des Bouchers	12, rue des Bouchers
Bottom-Dollar Markets	23 Tsawassen Blvd.	23 Tsawassen Blvd.
B's Beverages	Fauntleroy Circus	Fauntleroy Circus
Cactus Comidas para llevar	Cerrito 333	Cerrito 333
Centro comercial Moctezuma	Sierras de Granada 9993	Sierras de Granada 9993
Comércio Mineiro	Av. dos Lusíadas, 23	Av. dos Lusíadas, 23
Consolidated Holdings	Berkeley Gardens	Berkeley Gardens
Die Wandernde Kuh	Adenauerallee 900	Adenauerallee 900

Record: 1 of 84

Figure 11.18 This result set demonstrates the effect of adding the `DISTINCT` qualifier to a query.

9. Click the Close Window button to close the query, and save it as **qryShipBillAddresses** for use later in the chapter.

Because most of the orders have the same billing and shipping addresses, a more useful query is to find the orders for which the customer's billing and shipping addresses differ. You can create a not-equal join for this purpose by changing the `(Customers.Address = Orders.ShipAddress)` criterion to `(Customers.Address <> Orders.ShipAddress)`. If you make this change, Access displays an error message in Query Design view.

If you encounter the Enter Parameter dialog when attempting to execute the preceding query, see the "Missing Objects in Queries" member of the "Troubleshooting" section near the end of this chapter.

USING LOOKUP FIELDS IN TABLES

Access 2003's lookup feature for table fields lets you substitute drop-down list boxes or list boxes for conventional field text boxes. The lookup feature is a one-to-many query that Access automatically creates for you. The lookup feature lets you provide a list of acceptable values for a particular field. When you select the value from the list, the lookup feature automatically enters the value in the field of the current record. You can specify either of the following two types of lookup field:

- In a field that contains foreign-key values, a list of values from one or more fields of a related base table. The purpose of this type of lookup field is to add or alter foreign-key values, preserving relational integrity by assuring that foreign-key values match a primary-key value. A relationship must exist in the Relationships window between the tables to define a field as containing a foreign key.

  As an example, the Orders table of Northwind.mdb has two foreign-key fields: CustomerID and EmployeeID. The lookup feature of the CustomerID field displays the CompanyName field value from the Customers table in a drop-down list. The EmployeeID field displays the LastName and FirstName fields of the Employees table, separated by a comma and space (see Figure 11.19).

11

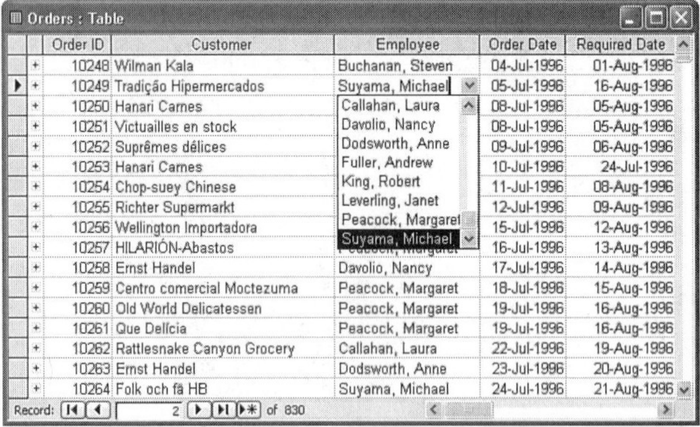

Orders : Table
Order ID | Customer | Employee | Order Date | Required Date
10248 Wilman Kala | Buchanan, Steven | 04-Jul-1996 | 01-Aug-1996
10249 Tradição Hipermercados | Suyama, Michael | 05-Jul-1996 | 16-Aug-1996
10250 Hanari Carnes | 08-Jul-1996 | 05-Aug-1996
10251 Victuailles en stock | 08-Jul-1996 | 05-Aug-1996
10252 Suprêmes délices | 09-Jul-1996 | 06-Aug-1996
10253 Hanari Carnes | 10-Jul-1996 | 24-Jul-1996
10254 Chop-suey Chinese | 11-Jul-1996 | 08-Aug-1996
10255 Richter Supermarkt | 12-Jul-1996 | 09-Aug-1996
10256 Wellington Importadora | 15-Jul-1996 | 12-Aug-1996
10257 HILARIÓN-Abastos | 16-Jul-1996 | 13-Aug-1996
10258 Ernst Handel | Davolio, Nancy | 17-Jul-1996 | 14-Aug-1996
10259 Centro comercial Moctezuma | Peacock, Margaret | 18-Jul-1996 | 15-Aug-1996
10260 Old World Delicatessen | Peacock, Margaret | 19-Jul-1996 | 16-Aug-1996
10261 Que Delícia | Peacock, Margaret | 19-Jul-1996 | 16-Aug-1996
10262 Rattlesnake Canyon Grocery | Callahan, Laura | 22-Jul-1996 | 19-Aug-1996
10263 Ernst Handel | Dodsworth, Anne | 23-Jul-1996 | 20-Aug-1996
10264 Folk och fä HB | Suyama, Michael | 24-Jul-1996 | 21-Aug-1996
Callahan, Laura
Davolio, Nancy
Dodsworth, Anne
Fuller, Andrew
King, Robert
Leverling, Janet
Peacock, Margaret
Suyama, Michael
Record: 2 of 830

Figure 11.19 A query against the Employees table generates the lookup list of the Orders table's EmployeeID field.

- In any field except a single primary-key field, a list of fixed values from which to select. Field lists are equivalent to validation rules that specify allowable field values, so a fixed lookup list isn't appropriate in this case.

You can add a new lookup field in either Table Design or Table Datasheet view; however, in Design view you can add the lookup feature only to an existing field. In Datasheet view, only the combo box control is displayed, even if you specify a list box control. You can display a combo box or a list box on a form that is bound to a table with lookup fields. In practice, the drop-down list (a combo box with the Limit to List property set to Yes) is the most common type of lookup field control. The following sections describe how to add foreign-key and fixed-list lookup features to table fields.

ADDING A FOREIGN-KEY DROP-DOWN LIST WITH THE LOOKUP WIZARD

The HRActions table you created in earlier chapters of this book is a candidate for a lookup field that uses a foreign-key drop-down list. If you didn't create and populate the HRActions table, you'll find it in the \Seua10\Chaptr06\Nwind06.mdb database on the accompanying CD-ROM. Import the HRActions table into Northwind.mdb.

TIP

> Before using the imported HRActions table, open it in Design view, select the InitiatedBy field, and delete the General Number value from the Format property. If you don't remove the Format property, lookup fields with text values are right-justified, which is inconsistent with the justification of other text fields.

Follow these steps to use the Lookup Wizard to change two fields of the HRActions table to lookup fields:

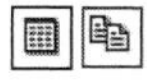

1. In the Database window, select the HRActions table and press Ctrl+C to copy the table to the Clipboard.

2. Press Ctrl+V to display the Paste Table As dialog. Type a name for the copy, such as **tblHRLookup**, and click the OK button to create the copy with the structure and data.

3. Open the table copy in Design view and select the InitiatedBy field. Click the Lookup tab to display the current lookup properties; a text box control has no lookup properties. Open the Data Type drop-down list and select Lookup Wizard (see Figure 11.20) to open the first dialog of the Lookup Wizard.

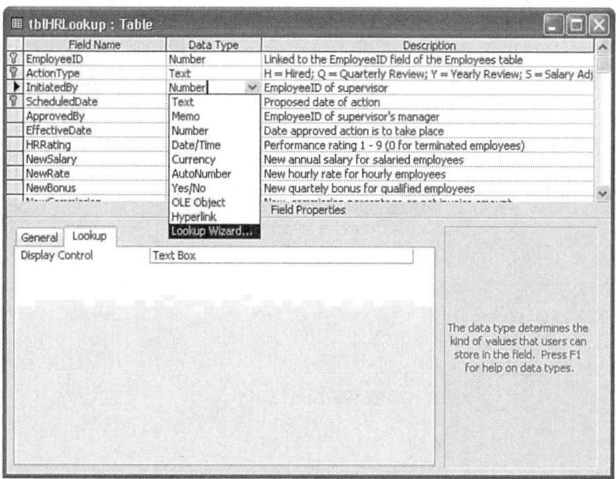

Figure 11.20 You start the Lookup Wizard from the Data Type field of the Table Design grid, despite the fact that Lookup Wizard isn't a Jet data type.

4. You want the field to look up values in another table (Employees), so accept the first (default) option (see Figure 11.21). Click Next to open the Lookup Wizard's second dialog.

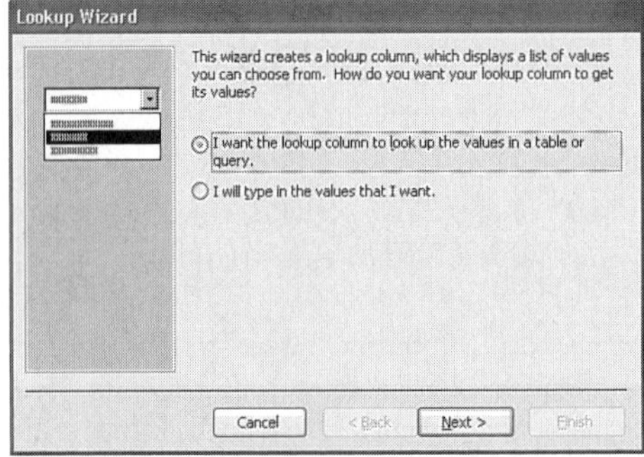

Figure 11.21 The first Lookup Wizard dialog has options for the two types of lookup fields.

5. With the View Tables option enabled, select the Employees base table to which the InitiatedBy field is related (see Figure 11.22). Click Next to display the third dialog.

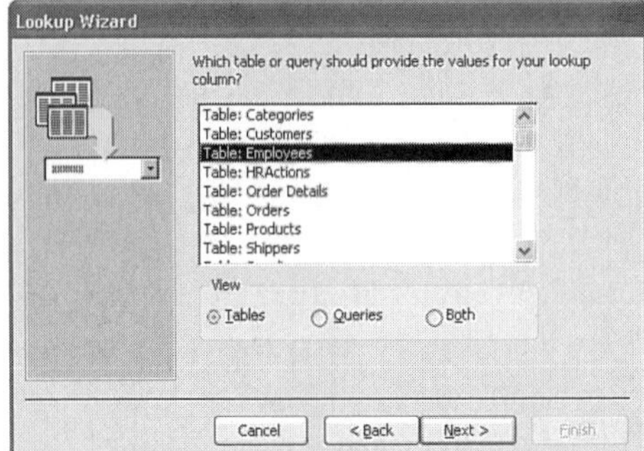

Figure 11.22 The second Wizard dialog asks you to select the table to provide data for the lookup columns.

6. Click the > button three times to add the EmployeeID, LastName, and FirstName fields to your lookup list (see Figure 11.23). You must include the base table primary-key field that's related to your foreign-key field. Click Next for the fourth dialog.

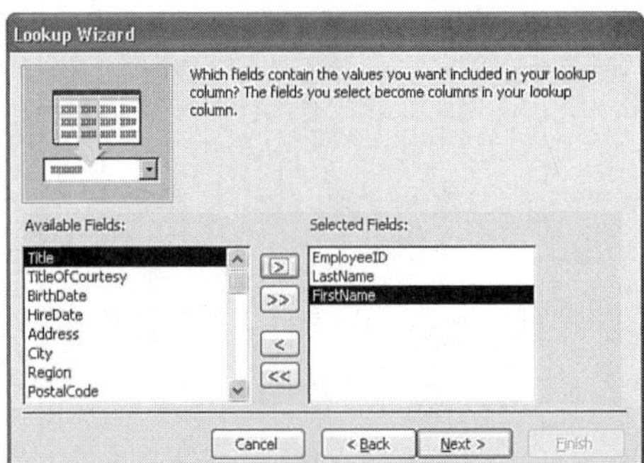

Figure 11.23 The third dialog requests you to specify the fields to include in the lookup list. You must include the table's primary-key field.

7. The fourth dialog lets you sort the list by up to four fields. In this case, you don't need to apply a sort order, so click Next to open the fifth dialog.
8. Adjust the widths of the columns to display the first and last names without excessive trailing whitespace. The Wizard determines that EmployeeID is the key column and recommends hiding the key column by marking the check box (see Figure 11.24). Accept the recommendation, and click Next to display the fifth and final dialog.

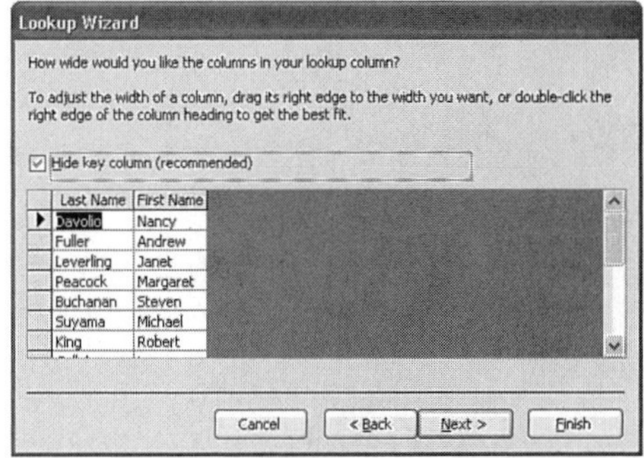

Figure 11.24
Verify the fields to appear in the lookup list, and adjust the column widths to suit the data.

9. Accept the default InitiatedBy as the label for the lookup field in the text box of the final Wizard dialog. The label you specify doesn't overwrite an existing Caption property value. Click Finish to complete the Wizard's work.
10. Click Yes when the message asks whether you want to save the table design. Your new lookup field properties appear as shown in Figure 11.25. The simple Jet SQL query statement created by the Wizard as the Row Source property is `SELECT [Employees].[EmployeeID], [Employees].[LastName], [Employees].[FirstName] FROM [Employees];`.

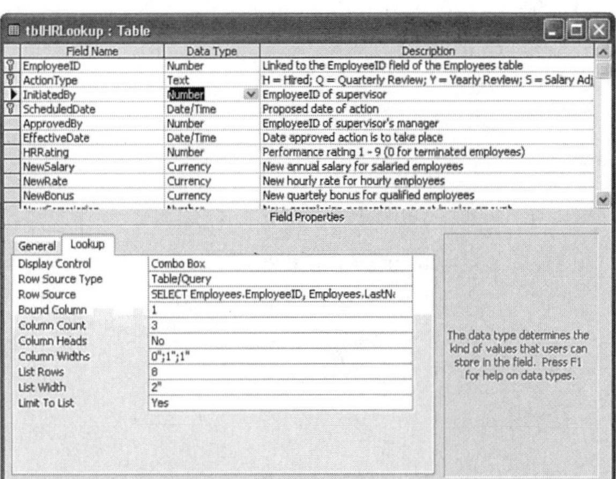

Figure 11.25
The Lookup page of the InitiatedBy field displays the lookup list property values added by the Wizard.

TIP

Preceding step 6 adds fields in their table order, but you can add fields with the Lookup Wizard in any order you prefer. Alternatively, you can rearrange columns by editing the Row Source property's SQL statement after you create the lookup list.

11. Click the View button. Only the first visible column of the list appears in the Initiated By column. With the cursor in the Initiated By column, open the drop-down list to display the Wizard's work (see Figure 11.26).

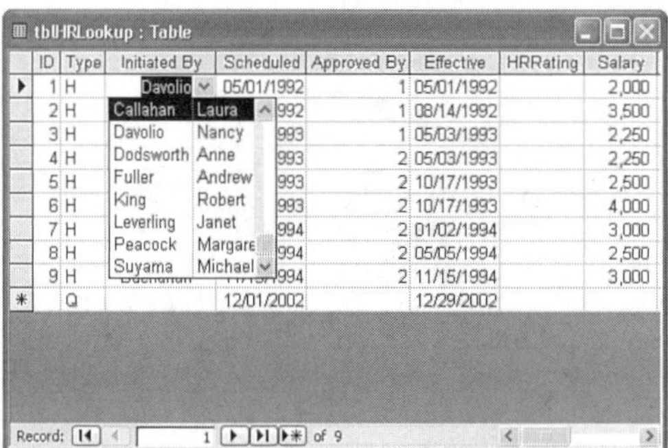

Figure 11.26 The lookup list of the InitiatedBy field has LastName and FirstName columns. Some FirstName values are truncated, because the column width setting didn't compensate for the width of the vertical scroll bar. The last names in the InitiatedBy field are right-justified if you don't remove the Format property value from the field.

12. To change the SQL statement to open a single-column, alphabetized LastName, FirstName list, return to Design view, select the Row Source property of the InitiatedBy field in the Lookup page, and press Shift+F2 to open the Zoom dialog. Edit the SQL statement as follows:

```
SELECT Employees.EmployeeID,
   Employees.LastName & ", " & Employees.FirstName
FROM Employees
ORDER BY LastName, FirstName;
```

Click OK to close the Zoom dialog.

13. Change the value of the Column Count property to **2** and the Column Widths property to **0";1.3"**. Optionally, change the List Rows value to **9** to accommodate Northwind's nine employees without a vertical scroll bar. Click View, and then click Yes to save your changes, and open the lookup list to verify your changes (see Figure 11.27).

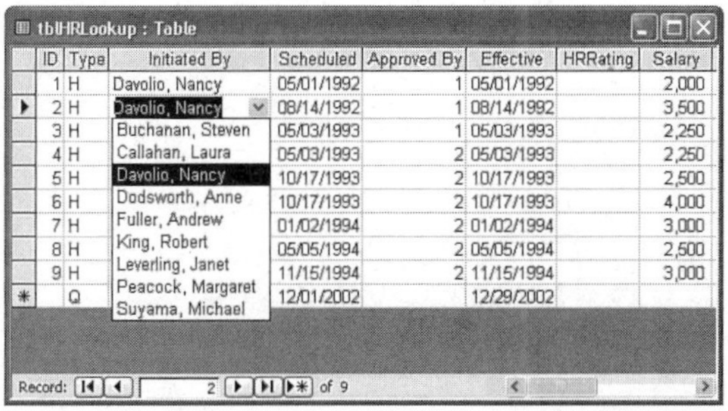

Figure 11.27
A single-column lookup list, like that used for the EmployeeID of the Orders table, is better suited to selecting peoples' names.

tblHRLookup : Table

ID	Type	Initiated By	Scheduled	Approved By	Effective	HRRating	Salary
1	H	Davolio, Nancy	05/01/1992	1	05/01/1992		2,000
2	H	Davolio, Nancy	08/14/1992	1	08/14/1992		3,500
3	H	Buchanan, Steven	05/03/1993	1	05/03/1993		2,250
4	H	Callahan, Laura	05/03/1993	2	05/03/1993		2,250
5	H	Davolio, Nancy	10/17/1993	2	10/17/1993		2,500
6	H	Dodsworth, Anne	10/17/1993	2	10/17/1993		4,000
7	H	Fuller, Andrew	01/02/1994	2	01/02/1994		3,000
8	H	King, Robert	05/05/1994	2	05/05/1994		2,500
9	H	Leverling, Janet	11/15/1994	2	11/15/1994		3,000
	Q	Peacock, Margaret	12/01/2002		12/29/2002		
		Suyama, Michael					

Record: 2 of 9

TIP

Make sure to correct the lookup field's name to the original value if the Lookup Wizard changes it. The Wizard changes the field name if it isn't the same as the base table's field name. Although Name AutoCorrect can handle field name changes, it's a much better database design practice to freeze the names of tables and fields. Change table and field names during the development process only if absolutely necessary.

→ If you need a list of the properties of the combo box control created by the Wizard, **see** "Adding Combo and List Boxes" **p. 596**.

ADDING A FIXED-VALUE LOOKUP LIST TO A TABLE

You add the alternative lookup feature—a fixed list of values—using the Lookup Wizard in much the same way as you created the foreign-key lookup list in the preceding section. To add a fixed-list lookup feature to the ActionType field of your copy of the HRActions table, follow these steps:

1. In Design view, select the ActionType field, open the Data Type list, and select Lookup Wizard to launch the Wizard.
2. In the first Lookup Wizard dialog, select the I Will Type in the Values That I Want option and click the Next button.
3. In the second Lookup Wizard dialog, type 2 in the Number of Columns text box and press the Tab key to create the second list column.
4. Type **H, Hired**; **Q, Quarterly Review**; **Y, Yearly Review**; **S, Salary Adj.**; **R, Hourly Rate Adj.**; **B, Bonus Adj.**; **C, Commission Adj.**; **T, Terminated** in the Col1 and Col2 columns of eight rows. (Don't include the commas or semicolons.) Adjust the width of the columns to suit the entries (see Figure 11.28). Click the Next button to display the Wizard's third dialog.
5. The ActionType field uses single-character abbreviations for the type of HRActions, so select Col1 as the "field that uniquely identifies the row." (The ActionType field doesn't uniquely identify the row; Col1 contains the single-character value that you want to insert into the field.) Click the Next button to display the fourth and final Wizard dialog.

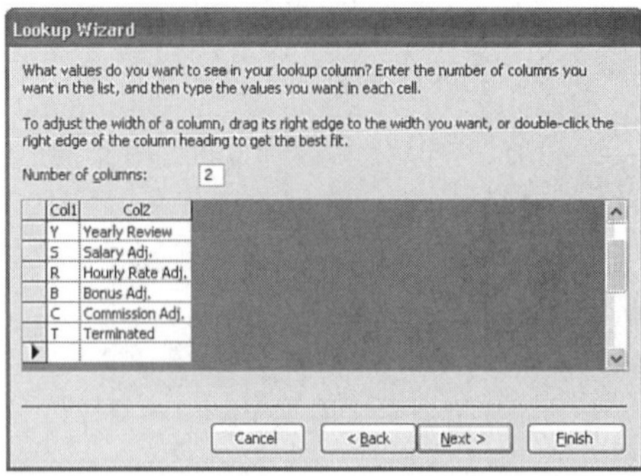

Figure 11.28
Specify the number of columns and type values in the second Wizard dialog for a lookup value list.

6. Accept ActionType as the label for your column and click the Finish button. The lookup properties for the ActionType field appear as shown in Figure 11.29. The Row Source Type is Value List. The Row Source contains the following values:

```
"H";"Hired";"Q";"Quarterly Review";"Y";"Yearly Review";
"S";"Salary Adj.";"R";"Hourly Rate Adj.";"B";
"Bonus Adj.";"C";"Commission Adj.";"T";"Terminated"
```

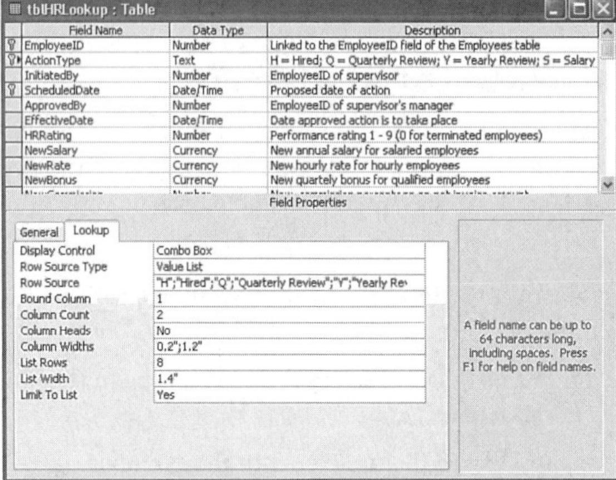

Figure 11.29
Compare the Lookup properties page for a lookup value list with that for a lookup list based on a related table (refer to Figure 11.25).

7. Click the View button and save the changes to your table. Place the cursor in the Type column, and open the fixed value list to check the Wizard's work (see Figure 11.30).

8. If you don't want the abbreviation to appear in the drop-down list, change the first entry of the Column Widths property value to 0.

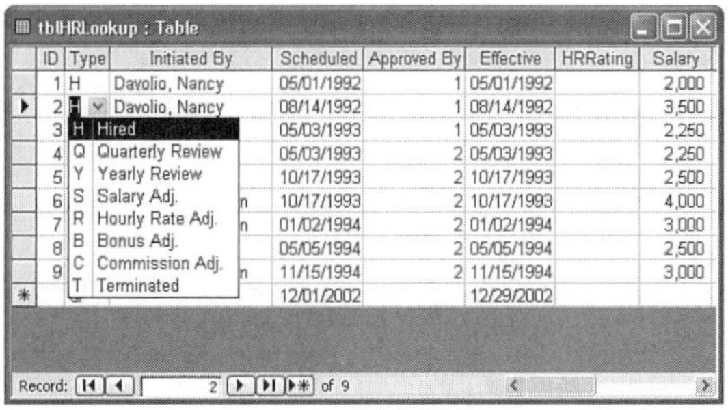

Figure 11.30 Datasheet view displays the fixed-value lookup list for the ActionType field.

TIP

To remove the lookup feature from a field, select the field, click the Lookup tab, and choose Text Box from the Display Control drop-down list.

NOTE

The lookup feature has generated controversy among seasoned database developers. Relational database purists object to embedding queries as table properties. Another objection to the use of foreign-key, drop-down lists is that it is easy for uninitiated users to inadvertently change data in a table after opening the list. Access 2003's lookup feature, however, is a useful tool, especially for new database users.

ADDING SUBDATASHEETS TO A TABLE OR QUERY

Subdatasheets are closely related to lookup fields, but serve a different purpose. *Subdatasheets* display related table values in an embedded datasheet, whereas lookup fields display base table values in a combo box or list box. Both of these Access features depend on the equivalent of one-to-many queries; the difference between the queries is that the many side of a subdatasheet is a related table, whereas a lookup field uses a query against a related table to supply the many side values.

You also can cascade subdatasheets to display related data of multiple joined tables, a feature not applicable to lookup fields, but a table or query can't have more than one subdatasheet. Figure 11.31 illustrates the Customers table displaying the Orders subdatasheet for Alfreds Futterkiste with embedded sub-subdatasheets that display Order Details records.

→ For more information on subdatasheets, **see** "Table Properties for Subdatasheets," **p. 157**.

CAUTION

Editing data in subdatasheets can lead to serious data-entry errors. For example, if you use the Order Details subdatasheet to change an entry in the Product field, the UnitPrice value doesn't change to correspond to the price for the new product. Subdatasheets are an interesting feature, but should only be used to view, not edit, vital business data.

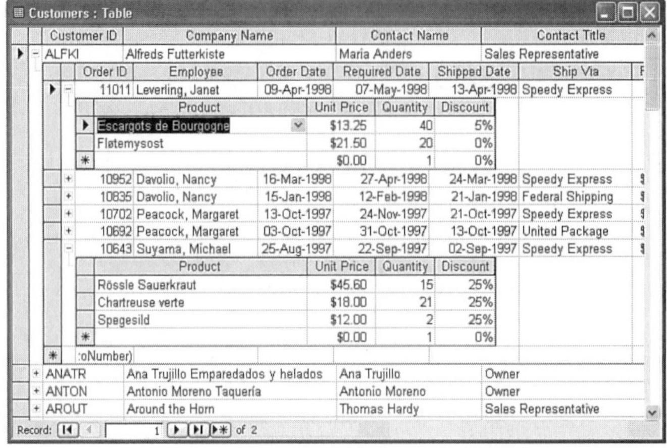

Figure 11.31
The Customers table has a two-level subdatasheet hierarchy. Note the + and - column at the left of both the Customers and Orders subdatasheets.

TABLE SUBDATASHEETS

Some of the tables of Northwind.mdb already have subdatasheets; Employees doesn't. To add an HRActions subdatasheet to the Employees table, follow these steps:

1. Verify in the Relationships window that a relationship exists between the EmployeeID fields of the HRActions and Employees tables.
2. Open the Employees table in Datasheet view.
3. Click one of the + symbols in the first column of the Employees datasheet to open the Insert Subdatasheet dialog.

TIP

> If the + symbols aren't present, choose Insert, Subdatasheet to open the Insert Subdatasheet dialog.

4. Select the HRActions table in the list. The EmployeeID foreign-key field of the HRActions table appears in the Link Child Fields drop-down list and the EmployeeID field of the Employees table appears in the Link Master Fields list (see Figure 11.32). The The HRAction table is included in the Relationships window; the relationship supplies the default values for the two drop-down lists.

NOTE

> The Link Master Fields and Link Child Fields values create a one-to-many join on the specified fields.

5. Click OK to add the subdatasheet and close the dialog. The subdatasheet for the selected record opens automatically.

Figure 11.32 Clicking the + symbol in a row of a table that doesn't have a subdatasheet opens the Insert Subdatasheet dialog.

6. Click one or two of the + symbols in the Employees datasheet to display the newly added subdatasheets (see Figure 11.33).

Employees : Table

Employee ID	Last Name	First Name	Title	Title Of Courtesy	Birth Date	Hire Dat
1	Davolio	Nancy	Sales Representative	Ms.	08-Dec-1968	01-May-1

Type	Initiated By	Scheduled	Approved By	Effective	HRRating	Salary	Rate	Bonus	% Comm	HRComments
	1	05/01/1992	1	05/01/1992		2,000				Hired
Q		04/01/2003		04/29/2003						

Employee ID	Last Name	First Name	Title	Title Of Courtesy	Birth Date	Hire Dat
2	Fuller	Andrew	Vice President, Sales	Dr.	19-Feb-1952	14-Aug-1

Type	Initiated By	Scheduled	Approved By	Effective	HRRating	Salary	Rate	Bonus	% Comm	HRComments
H	1	08/14/1992	1	08/14/1992		3,500				Hired
Q		04/01/2003		04/29/2003						

Employee ID	Last Name	First Name	Title	Title Of Courtesy	Birth Date	Hire Dat
3	Leverling	Janet	Sales Representative	Ms.	30-Aug-1963	01-Apr-1

Type	Initiated By	Scheduled	Approved By	Effective	HRRating	Salary	Rate	Bonus	% Comm	HRComments
H	1	05/03/1993	1	05/03/1993		2,250				Hired
Q		04/01/2003		04/29/2003						

Employee ID	Last Name	First Name	Title	Title Of Courtesy	Birth Date	Hire Dat
4	Peacock	Margaret	Sales Representative	Mrs.	19-Sep-1958	03-May-1

Type	Initiated By	Scheduled	Approved By	Effective	HRRating	Salary	Rate	Bonus	% Comm	HRComments
H	2	05/03/1993	2	05/03/1993		2,250				Hired
Q		04/01/2003		04/29/2003						

Employee ID	Last Name	First Name	Title	Title Of Courtesy	Birth Date	Hire Dat
5	Buchanan	Steven	Sales Manager	Mr.	04-Mar-1955	17-Oct-1
6	Suyama	Michael	Sales Representative	Mr.	02-Jul-1963	17-Oct-1
7	King	Robert	Sales Representative	Mr.	29-May-1960	02-Jan-1
8	Callahan	Laura	Inside Sales Coordinator	Ms.	09-Jan-1958	05-Mar-1
9	Dodsworth	Anne	Sales Representative	Ms.	02-Jul-1969	15-Nov-1

Record: 1 of 1

Figure 11.33 Only one HRActions record exists for each employee at this point.

7. Change to Table Design view and click the Properties button to display the Table Properties window. The selections you make in the Insert Subdatasheet dialog appear in the subdatasheet-related properties of the table (see Figure 11.34).

NOTE

> The child (foreign-key) field, EmployeeID, doesn't appear as a column of the subdatasheet. When you add a new record in the subdatasheet, Access automatically inserts the primary-key value of the selected base-table record into the related record. In this case, Access adds the EmployeeID value from the Employees field to the EmployeeID value of the HRActions table.

continues

continued

> The default value of the Subdatasheet Name property for new tables you create is [Auto], which adds the column of boxed + symbols to a new table datasheet. To open the Add Subdatasheet dialog for a new table, choose Insert, Subdatasheet. Alternatively, you can set the subdatasheet properties directly in the Table Properties window. To remove a subdatasheet, set the Subdatasheet Name property value to [None]. If you remove a subdatasheet from a table, setting Subdatasheet Name to [Auto] displays the boxed + symbols and lets you add a new subdatasheet in Datasheet view.

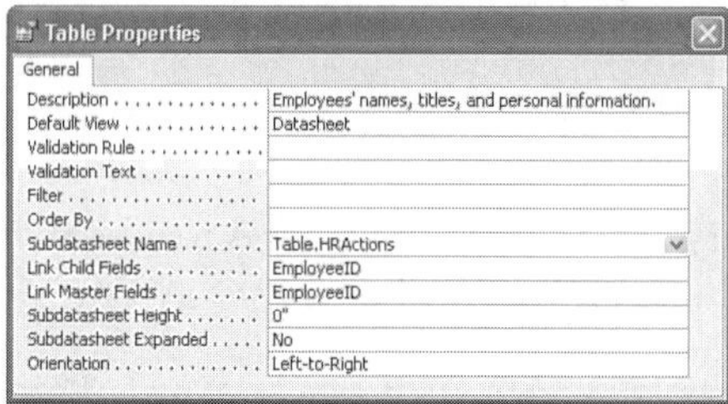

Figure 11.34 You also can add a subdatasheet by opening the Table Properties window and selecting a table or query from the Subdatasheet name list.

QUERY SUBDATASHEETS

If you don't want your subdatasheet to display all the related table's columns, you must design a simple select query with only the desired fields and then use the query to populate the subdatasheet. As an example, you can minimize the width of the Orders subdatasheet of the Customers table by doing the following:

1. In Design view, create a simple `SELECT` query that includes only the OrderID, CustomerID (required for the master-child join), OrderDate, ShippedDate, and ShippedVia fields of the Orders table.
2. Double-click the top pane to open the Query Properties window, and set the Recordset Type property to Snapshot. Selecting Snapshot creates a read-only subdatasheet to prevent editing. Close the query and save it as **qryShortOrders**.
3. Open the Customers table in Design view, open the Table Properties window, and select Query.qryShortOrders from the Subdatasheet Name list. CustomerID remains the value of the linked fields.
4. Return to Datasheet view, saving your changes. The expanded subdatasheet appears as shown in Figure 11.35, without the + sign column. The query is read-only, so the subdatasheet has no tentative append record and you can't edit the data.
5. In Design view, create another select query that includes all fields (*) of the Order Details table. Open the Query Properties window, set the Recordset Type property value to Snapshot, close the windows, and save the query as **qryShortOrderDetails**.

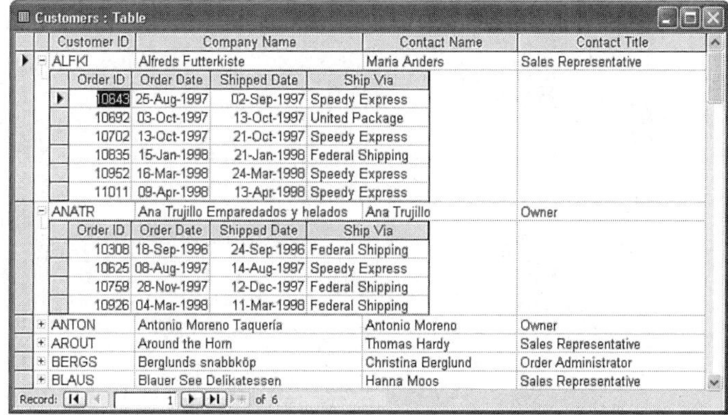

Figure 11.35
Use a Snapshot query to create a read-only subdatasheet.

6. Close the Customers table, open qryShortOrders in Design view, right-click an empty area of the upper pane, and choose Properties to open the Query Properties window.
7. Select Query.qryOrderDetails in the Subdatasheet Name field and then type **OrderID** in the two Link...Fields text boxes (see Figure 11.36). You must type the field names because you haven't established a relationship between the query and table in the Relationships window.

11

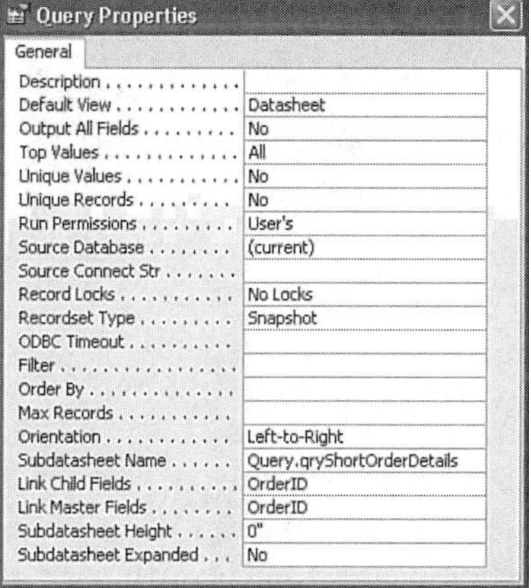

Figure 11.36
After adding Query.qryOrderDetails as the value of the Subdatasheet Name property, you manually set the Link Child Fields and Link Master Fields property values.

8. Run the query and then expand one or more of the subdatasheets to test your work (see Figure 11.37).
9. Close qryShortOrders, save your changes, open the Customers table, and display the subdatasheets. The new version of the Customers table appears as shown in Figure 11.38. You can open the Products list, but you can't change the value of the Product column.

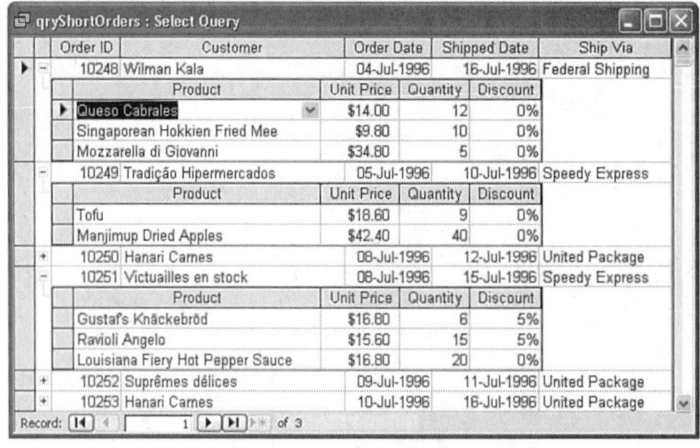

Figure 11.37
The read-only qryShortOrders query has a read-only query subdatasheet based on qryOrderDetails.

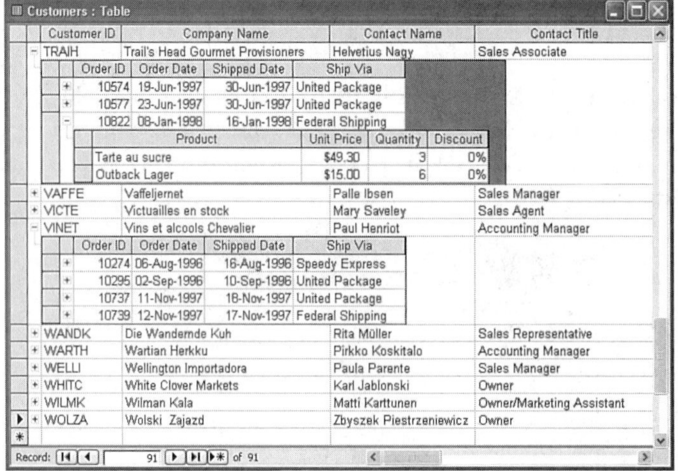

Figure 11.38
The subdatasheet and sub-subdatasheet are read-only, but the Customers table continues to have read-write attributes, as indicated by its tentative append record.

OUTER, SELF, AND THETA JOINS

The preceding sections of this chapter described the inner join, which is the most common type of join in database applications. Jet also lets you create three other joins: outer, self, and theta. The following sections describe these three less-common types of joins, which also apply to SQL Server views, functions, and stored procedures.

CREATING OUTER JOINS

Outer joins let you display the fields of all records in a table participating in a query, regardless of whether corresponding records exist in the joined table. Jet lets you choose between left and right outer joins.

A left outer join query displays all records in the first table your specify, regardless of whether matching records exist in second table. For example `Table1 LEFT JOIN Table2` displays all records in `Table2`. Conversely, a right outer join query displays all records in the second table, regardless of a record's existence in the first table. Records in the second table without corresponding records in the first table usually, but not necessarily, are orphan records; these kinds of records can have a many-to-one relationship to another table.

To practice creating a left outer join to detect whether records are missing for an employee in the HRActions table, follow these steps:

1. Open the Employees table and add a record for a new (bogus) employee. You need only add values for the LastName and FirstName fields.
2. Open a new query and add the Employees and HRActions tables.
3. Drag the EmployeeID field symbol to the EmployeeID field of HRActions to create an inner join between these fields if Access doesn't create the join automatically.
4. Select and drag the LastName and FirstName fields of the Employees table to columns 1 and 2 of the Query Design grid. Select and drag the ActionType and ScheduledDate fields of the HRActions table to columns 3 and 4.
5. Click the line joining EmployeeID with EmployeeID to select it, as shown in Figure 11.39. The thickness of the center part of the line increases to indicate the selection. (In Figure 11.39, the two Field List boxes are separated so that the thin section of the join line is apparent.)

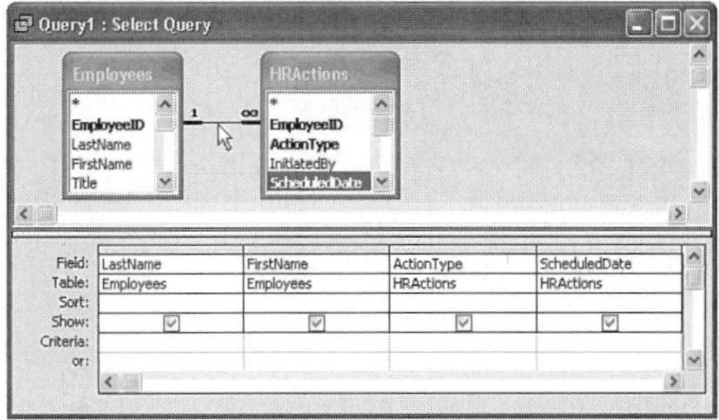

Figure 11.39
Double-clicking the thin region of the join line opens the Join Properties dialog.

6. Double-click the thin section of the join line to open the Join Properties dialog. (Double-clicking either of the line's thick sections displays the Query Properties window.) Type 1 is a conventional inner join, type 2 is a left join, and type 3 is a right join.
7. Select a type 2 join—a left join—by selecting option 2 (see Figure 11.40). Click OK to close the dialog.

NOTE

> Access adds an arrowhead to the line that joins EmployeeID and EmployeeID. The direction of the arrow, left to right, indicates that you've created a left join between the tables, assuming that you haven't moved the field lists from their original position in the table.

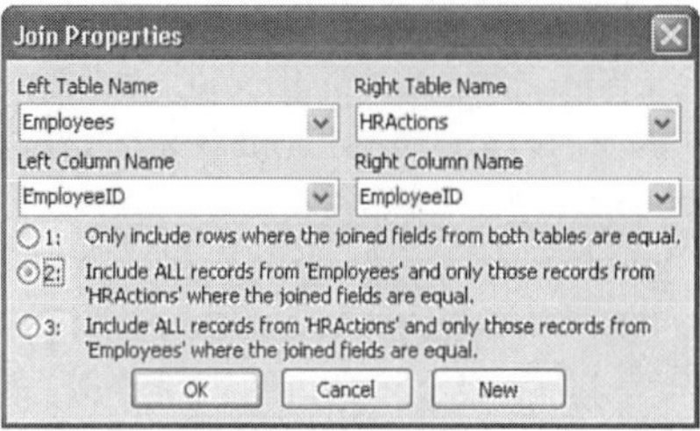

Figure 11.40
Select the option for a type 2 join, which includes all records in the left table and only those records of the right table where the two column values match.

8. Click the Run button to display the result of the left join query. In Figure 11.41, the employee you added without a record in the HRActions table appears in the result table's last active row. (Your query result set might differ, depending on the number of entries that you made when creating the HRActions table.)

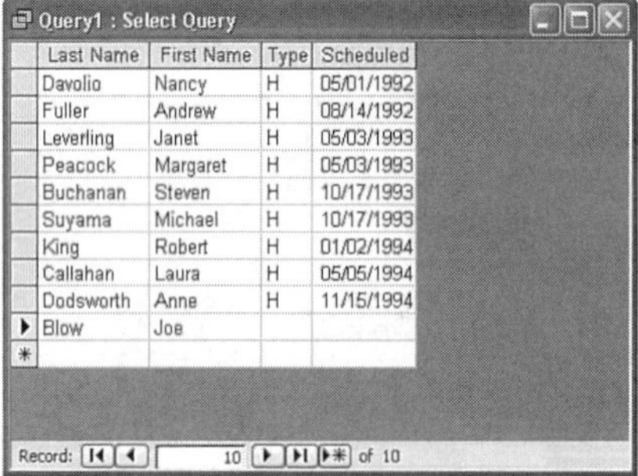

Last Name	First Name	Type	Scheduled
Davolio	Nancy	H	05/01/1992
Fuller	Andrew	H	08/14/1992
Leverling	Janet	H	05/03/1993
Peacock	Margaret	H	05/03/1993
Buchanan	Steven	H	10/17/1993
Suyama	Michael	H	10/17/1993
King	Robert	H	01/02/1994
Callahan	Laura	H	05/05/1994
Dodsworth	Anne	H	11/15/1994
Blow	Joe		

Figure 11.41
A record for EmployeeID 10 with no HRActions record(s) appears in this left outer join.

9. Close, but don't save, the query, and then delete the bogus record in the Employees table.

If you could add an HR department action for a nonexistent EmployeeID (referential integrity rules for HRActions table prevent you from doing so), a right join would show the invalid entry with blank employee name fields.

CREATING SELF-JOINS

Self-joins relate values in a single table. Creating a self-join requires that you add a copy of the table to the query and then add a join between the related fields. An example of self-join use is to determine whether supervisors have approved HRActions that they initiated, which is prohibited by the imaginary personnel manual for Northwind Traders.

To create this kind of self-join for the HRActions table, follow these steps:

1. Open a new query and add the HRActions table.
2. Add another copy of the HRActions table to the query by clicking the Add button again. Access names the copy HRActions_1. Close the Show Tables dialog.

3. Drag the original table's InitiatedBy field to the copied table's ApprovedBy field. The join appears as shown in the upper pane of Figure 11.42.

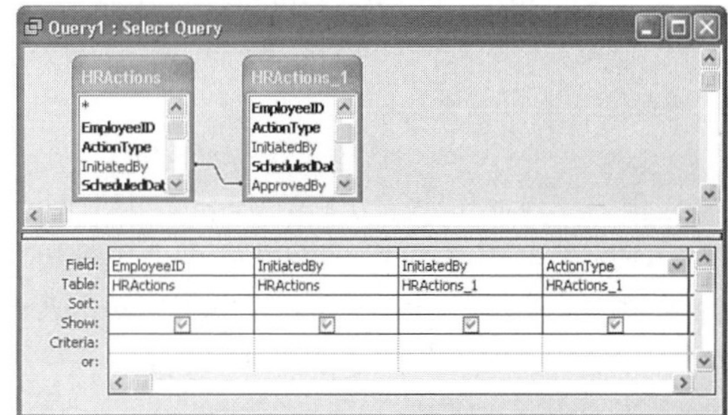

Figure 11.42 A self-join returns rows for which values of two fields in the same table are equal.

4. Drag the EmployeeID and InitiatedBy fields of the original table, and the ApprovedBy and ActionType fields of the copy of the HRActions table, to the Field row of columns 1–4, respectively, of the Query Design grid.

5. With self-joins, you must specify that only unique values are included. (If you don't specify unique values, the query returns every row.) Click the Properties toolbar button or double-click an empty area in the Query Design window's upper pane, set the value of the Query Properties window's Unique Values property to Yes, and close the Query Properties window.

6. Click the Run button to display the records in which the same employee initiated and approved an HR department action, as shown in Figure 11.43. In this case, EmployeeID 1 (Nancy Davolio) was the first employee; EmployeeID 2 (Andrew Fuller) is a vice-president and can override personnel policy. (Your results might differ, depending on the entries you made in the HRActions table.)

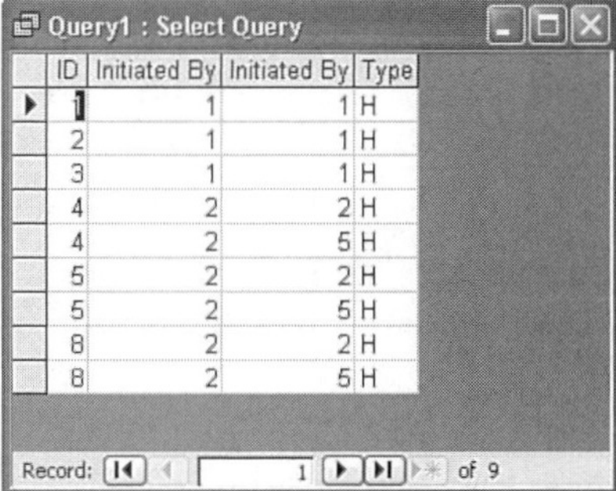
Query1 : Select Query

ID	Initiated By	Initiated By	Type
1	1	1	H
2	1	1	H
3	1	1	H
4	2	2	H
4	2	5	H
5	2	2	H
5	2	5	H
8	2	2	H
8	2	5	H

Record: 1 of 9

Figure 11.43 This datasheet displays the result set of the design of Figure 11.42. If you don't set the Unique Values property to Yes, the result set has 27 rows.

CREATING NOT-EQUAL (THETA) JOINS WITH CRITERIA

Most joins are based on fields with equal values, but sometimes you need to create a join on unequal fields. Joins that you create graphically in Access are restricted to conventional equi-joins and outer joins. You can create the equivalent of a not-equal theta join by applying a criterion to one of the two fields you want to test for not-equal values.

Finding customers that have different billing and shipping addresses, as mentioned previously, is an example in which a not-equal theta join is useful. To create such a join, follow these steps:

1. Create a new query and add the Customers and Orders tables.
2. Select the Customers table's CompanyName and Address fields and the Orders table's ShipAddress field. Drag them to the Query Design grid's first three columns.
3. Type **<>Customers.Address** in the Criteria row of the ShipAddress column. The Query Design window appears as shown in Figure 11.44.

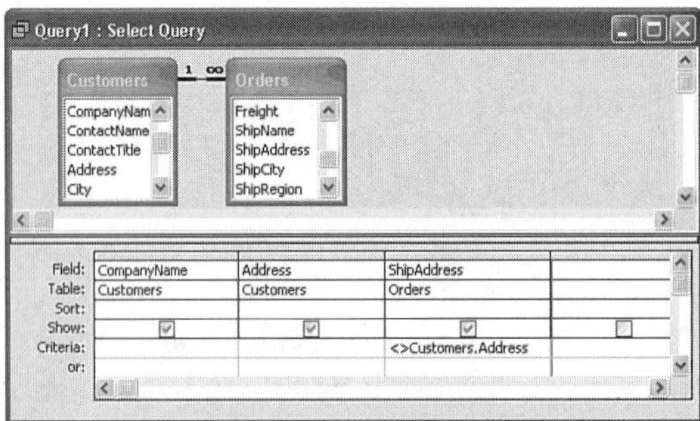

Figure 11.44 Not-equal joins require a not-equal (<>) WHERE clause criterion to establish the join.

NOTE

Typing **<>Orders.ShipAddress** in the Address column gives the same result as <>Customers.Address.

4. Click the Properties toolbar button or double-click an empty area in the Query Design window's upper pane to open the Query Properties window and set the value of the Unique Values property to Yes. Otherwise, the query returns a record for every order with a different ship address.
5. Run the query. Only the records for customers that placed orders with different billing and shipping addresses appear, as shown in Figure 11.45.
6. Click the Close Window button and save your query if you want.

NOTE

As mentioned in the earlier "Creating Multicolumn Inner Joins and Selecting Unique Values" section, you can create a theta-join by changing the operator of a equi-join criterion from = to <>. If you do this, you receive an error message every time you open the query in Design view.

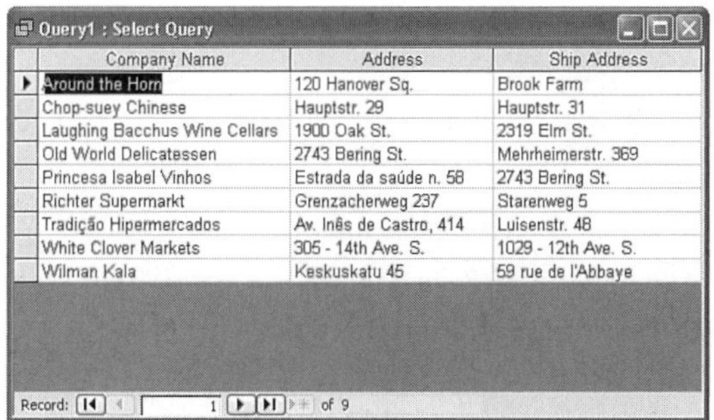

Query1 : Select Query

Company Name	Address	Ship Address
Around the Horn	120 Hanover Sq.	Brook Farm
Chop-suey Chinese	Hauptstr. 29	Hauptstr. 31
Laughing Bacchus Wine Cellars	1900 Oak St.	2319 Elm St.
Old World Delicatessen	2743 Bering St.	Mehrheimerstr. 369
Princesa Isabel Vinhos	Estrada da saúde n. 58	2743 Bering St.
Richter Supermarkt	Grenzacherweg 237	Starenweg 5
Tradição Hipermercados	Av. Inês de Castro, 414	Luisenstr. 48
White Clover Markets	305 - 14th Ave. S.	1029 - 12th Ave. S.
Wilman Kala	Keskuskatu 45	59 rue de l'Abbaye

Record: 1 of 9

Figure 11.45 The result set of the not-equal join displays customers with different shipping and billing addresses. If you don't set the Unique Values property to Yes, the query returns 51 rows.

UPDATING TABLE DATA WITH QUERIES

Queries you create with the Unique Values property set to Yes to add the ANSI SQL `DISTINCT` modifier to the SQL statement aren't updatable. If you set the Unique Records property, instead of the Unique Values property, to Yes, some queries are updatable because Unique Records substitutes Jet SQL's `DISTINCTROW` modifier for `DISTINCT`.

T-SQL

T-SQL doesn't support Jet SQL's `DISTINCTROW` modifier and the rules that determine the updatability of SQL Server views and table-returning, user-defined functions differ from those of Jet. Chapter 21, "Moving from Jet Queries to Transact-SQL," covers updatability issues with SQL Server views and functions. Recordsets returned by SQL Server stored procedures aren't updatable.

Unique Records queries create Recordset objects of the updatable Dynaset type. You can't update table data with a query unless you see the tentative (blank) append record (with the asterisk in the select button) at the end of the query result table. The next few sections describe the conditions under which you can update a record of a table included in a query. The following sections also discuss how to use the Output Field Properties window to format query-data display and editing.

NOTE

> You can't set both the Unique Values and Unique Records properties to Yes—these choices are mutually exclusive. In Access 2003, the default setting of both the Unique Values and Unique Records properties is No.

CHARACTERISTICS THAT DETERMINE WHETHER YOU CAN UPDATE A QUERY

Adding new records to tables or updating existing data in tables included in a query is a definite advantage in some circumstances. Correcting data errors that appear when you run the query is especially tempting. Unfortunately, you can't append or update records in many queries that you create. The following properties of a query prevent you from appending and updating records:

- The Unique Values property is set to Yes in the Query Properties window.
- The Recordset Type property is set to Snapshot in the Query Properties window.
- Self-joins are used in the query.
- Jet SQL aggregate functions, such as `Sum()`, are employed in the query. Crosstab queries, for example, use SQL aggregate functions.
- The query has three or more tables with many-to-one-to-many relationships. Most queries with indirect relationships fall in this category.
- No primary-key field(s) with a unique (No Duplicates) index exist for the one table in a one-to-many relationship.

When designing a query to use as the basis of a form for data entry or editing, make sure that none of the preceding properties apply to the query.

TIP

> You can't edit data returned by a query with three or more tables in Query Datasheet view, unless the query is one-to-many-to-many, but you can update values in other types of three-table queries in forms and data access pages (DAP) that are bound to the query. To make the query updatable with forms and DAP, set the Recordset Type property value to Dynaset (Inconsistent Updates).

11

If none of the preceding properties apply to the query or any table within the query, you can append records to and update fields of queries in the following:

- A single-table query
- Both tables in a one-to-one relationship
- The many table in a one-to-many relationship or the most-many table in a one-to-many-to-many relationship
- The one table in a one-to-many relationship if none of the fields of the many table appear in the query

Updating the one table in a one-to-many query is a special case in Access. To enable updates to this table, follow these steps:

1. Add to the query, the primary-key field or fields of the one table and additional fields to update. You don't need to add the primary-key field if its Jet data type is AutoNumber.
2. Add the foreign key field or fields of the many table that correspond to the key field or fields of the one table; this step is required to select the appropriate records for updating.
3. Add the criteria to select the records for updating to the fields chosen in step 2.
4. Click the Show box so that the many table fields don't appear in the query.

After following these steps, you can edit the nonkey fields of the one table. You can't, however, alter the values of key fields that have relationships with records in the many table, unless you specify Cascade Update Related Fields in the Relationships window's Edit Relationships dialog for the join. Otherwise, such a modification violates referential integrity.

By adding lookup fields to tables, you often can avoid writing one-to-many queries and precisely following the preceding rules to make such queries updatable. For example, the Orders table, which includes three lookup fields (CustomerID, EmployeeID, and ShipVia), is updatable. If you want to allow updates in Datasheet view (called *browse updating*), using lookup fields is a simpler approach than creating an updatable query. Most database developers, however, consider simple browse updating to be a poor practice because of the potential for inadvertent data-entry errors. As mentioned earlier, browse updating with lookup fields is especially prone to data-entry errors.

➔ For more discussion of the browse-mode method and other alternatives, **see** "In the Real World—Alternatives to Action Queries," **p. 514**.

TAKING ADVANTAGE OF ACCESS'S ROW FIX-UP FEATURE

Access queries and SQL Server views have a row fix-up feature (called AutoLookup by Access) that fills in query data when you add a new record or change the value of the foreign key of a many-side record. To take advantage of row fix-up, your query must include the foreign-key value, not the primary-key value of the join.

Northwind Traders' Orders Qry is an example of a query that uses row fix-up. Orders Qry includes every field of the Customers and Orders tables, *except* the CustomerID field of the Customers table. To demonstrate row fix-up, do the following:

1. Open the Orders Qry in Datasheet view, and scroll to the tentative append record. Alternatively, press Ctrl+End, Home, and [da] to avoid the scrolling exercise.
2. Tab to the Customer column, open the lookup list, which is bound to the CustomerID field of the Customers table, and select a customer for a new order. The edited record symbol replaces the asterisk and the datasheet adds a new tentative append row.
3. Scroll the columns to the right until you reach the Address column, which displays the Address field of the Customers table. Row fix-up automatically enters data from the Customer table's record for the selected customer (see Figure 11.46).
4. Press Esc to cancel the new record addition.

Row fix-up is more useful for forms that are bound to a query than for queries that update data in Datasheet view. Orders Qry is the data source for the sample Orders form. When you add a new order with this form, row fix-up automatically updates its customer data.

Columns from Orders Table — Columns from Customers Table

Orders Qry : Select Query

Order ID	Customer	Employee	Address	City	Region	Postal Code
11032	White Clover Markets	Fuller, Andrew	305 - 14th Ave. S.	Seattle	WA	98128
11066	White Clover Markets	King, Robert	305 - 14th Ave. S.	Seattle	WA	98128
10248	Wilman Kala	Buchanan, Steven	Keskuskatu 45	Helsinki		21240
10615	Wilman Kala	Fuller, Andrew	Keskuskatu 45	Helsinki		21240
10673	Wilman Kala	Fuller, Andrew	Keskuskatu 45	Helsinki		21240
10695	Wilman Kala	King, Robert	Keskuskatu 45	Helsinki		21240
10873	Wilman Kala	Peacock, Margaret	Keskuskatu 45	Helsinki		21240
10879	Wilman Kala	Leverling, Janet	Keskuskatu 45	Helsinki		21240
10910	Wilman Kala	Davolio, Nancy	Keskuskatu 45	Helsinki		21240
11005	Wilman Kala	Fuller, Andrew	Keskuskatu 45	Helsinki		21240
10374	Wolski Zajazd	Davolio, Nancy	ul. Filtrowa 68	Warszawa		01-012
10611	Wolski Zajazd	Suyama, Michael	ul. Filtrowa 68	Warszawa		01-012
10792	Wolski Zajazd	Davolio, Nancy	ul. Filtrowa 68	Warszawa		01-012
10870	Wolski Zajazd	Buchanan, Steven	ul. Filtrowa 68	Warszawa		01-012
10906	Wolski Zajazd	Peacock, Margaret	ul. Filtrowa 68	Warszawa		01-012
10998	Wolski Zajazd	Callahan, Laura	ul. Filtrowa 68	Warszawa		01-012
11044	Wolski Zajazd	Peacock, Margaret	ul. Filtrowa 68	Warszawa		01-012
11078	Alfreds Futterkiste		Obere Str. 57	Berlin		12209
:oNumber)						

Record: 831 of 831

Figure 11.46 Row fix-up automatically adds data from the table on the one side of a one-to-many relationship when you add a new row. The first three columns of the datasheet are frozen to demonstrate row fix-up when adding a new record to the Orders table.

FORMATTING DATA WITH THE QUERY FIELD PROPERTIES WINDOW

The display format of data in queries is inherited from the format of the data in the tables that underlie the query. You can override the table format by using the **Format**(*ColumnName*, *FormatString*) function to create a calculated field. In this case, however, the column isn't updatable.

Access provides an easier query column formatting method: the Field Properties window, which you can use to format the display of query data. You also can create an input mask to aid in updating the query data. To open the Field Properties window, place the cursor in the Field cell of the query column that you want to format, and then click the Properties button of the toolbar. Figure 11.47 shows the Field Properties window for the OrderDate column of the Orders Qry. Specifying formats in queries lets you alter the column's display format without affecting the display of table fields.

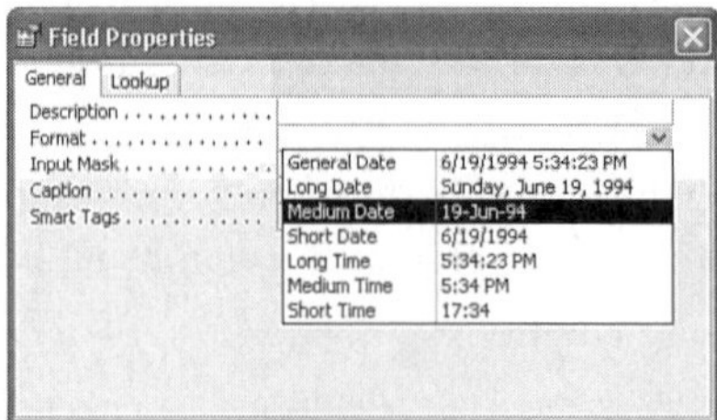

Figure 11.47 Access's Medium Date format (dd-mmm-yy) doesn't comply with Y2K requirements. To specify a four-year Medium Date format for all Windows operating systems, assign the dd-mmm-yyyy format.

By default, Access 2003's General Date, Long Date, and Short Date formats display four-digit years, which is required for Year 2000 (Y2K) conformance. (Four-digit years is the default for Windows XP and 2000.) You can alter the default Short Date or Long Date format in text boxes of the Date page of Control Panel's Customize Regional Options dialog. (Windows 2000's tool is called Regional Options.) Systemwide settings specify the General Date, Long Date, and Short Date formats, but don't affect the Medium Date style. To obtain a four-digit year display with Medium Date format, you must type the Format descriptor string—**dd-mmm-yyyy**—in the Format text box. Most sample tables in Northwind.mdb have the custom dd-mmm-yyyy format applied.

NOTE

> The format symbol for month in the [Customize] Regional Options dialog is "M", not "m", which is the systemwide symbol for minutes. Access and VBA use "n" for minutes.

TIP

> Always use the default Short Date and Long Date systemwide formats. Don't depend on users to change their default formats. If you want to specify two-digit day and month values, for example, use a custom date format, such as mm/dd/yyyy.

The Field Properties window displays the following subset of the properties that apply to a query's fields:

- *Description* lets you enter the text to appear in the status bar when the user selects the field in Datasheet view.
- *Format* lets you control the appearance of the data in Datasheet view, such as Short Date.
- *Input Mask* lets you specify the format for entering data, such as 99/99/0000. (To create an input mask that is appropriate for the field data type, click the ellipsis button to open the Input Mask Wizard.)

→ For more information on the Input Mask Wizard and a listing of placeholders, **see** "Using Input Masks," **p. 173**.

- *Caption* lets you change the query column heading, such as Received, for the Order Date column.

- Smart tags are a new feature of Access 2003 that enable links to Web-based resources and perform other operations, such as propagating changes to field or column properties to dependent forms and reports.

→ To learn more about smart tags, **see** "Working with Object Dependencies and Access Smart Tags," **p. 200**.

Each of the preceding query properties follows the rules described in Chapter 5 for setting table field properties. Adding a value (Received) for the Caption property of a query against the Orders table is the equivalent of adding a column alias by typing Received: as a prefix in the OrderDate column's Field cell. Adding a Caption property value, however, doesn't change the SQL statement for the query. The value of the Input Mask property need not correspond exactly to the value of the Format property, but input mask characters don't appear if you try to use a Short Date mask with a Medium Date format you apply in the query.

TIP

> **Add captions to queries, not tables. Table Datasheet view should display field names rather than captions to conform to good database design principles. Unfortunately, the tables in Northwind.mdb don't conform to this recommendation.**

For example, the Received (OrderDate) column in Figure 11.48, which shows the effect of setting the property values shown in the preceding list, has a single-digit (no leading zero) month and day for the Short Date display format, which overrides the mm/dd/yyyy format of the table field. The input mask (99/99/0000;0;_) permits updating with one-digit or two-digit months and days. Adding or editing a single-digit or two-digit entry gives the same result. Most typists prefer to enter a consistent number of digits in a date field.

Figure 11.48
This query uses m/d/yyyy display format and a 90/90/0000 input mask to allow month and date entries as single- or two-digit values.

Orders Qry : Select Query

Order ID	Customer	Employee	Received
10643	Alfreds Futterkiste	Suyama, Michael	3_/25/1997
10692	Alfreds Futterkiste	Peacock, Margaret	10/3/1997
10702	Alfreds Futterkiste	Peacock, Margaret	10/13/1997
10835	Alfreds Futterkiste	Davolio, Nancy	1/15/1998
10952	Alfreds Futterkiste	Davolio, Nancy	3/16/1998
11011	Alfreds Futterkiste	Leverling, Janet	4/9/1998
10308	Ana Trujillo Emparedados y hel	King, Robert	9/18/1996
10625	Ana Trujillo Emparedados y hel	Leverling, Janet	8/8/1997
10759	Ana Trujillo Emparedados y hel	Leverling, Janet	11/28/1997
10926	Ana Trujillo Emparedados y hel	Peacock, Margaret	3/4/1998
10365	Antonio Moreno Taquería	Leverling, Janet	11/27/1996
10507	Antonio Moreno Taquería	King, Robert	4/15/1997
10535	Antonio Moreno Taquería	Peacock, Margaret	5/13/1997
10573	Antonio Moreno Taquería	King, Robert	6/19/1997

Record: 1 of 830

If your query has tables linked to dBASE, FoxPro, or other non-Access tables and you can't update records in or add records to the query result set, see "Queries with Linked Tables Aren't Updatable" in the "Troubleshooting" section near the end of this chapter.

MAKING ALL FIELDS OF TABLES ACCESSIBLE

Most queries you create include only the fields you specifically choose. To choose these fields, you either select them from or type them into the drop-down combo list in the Query Design grid's Field row, or you drag the field names from the field lists to the appropriate cells in the Field row. You can, however, quickly include all fields of a table in a query. Access provides the following three methods for including all fields of a table in a query:

- Double-click the field list title bar of the table to select all fields in the field list and then drag the field list to the Query Design grid. Each field appears in a column of the grid.

- Drag the asterisk (*) to a single Query Design grid column. To sort on or apply selection criteria to a field, drag the field to the Query Design grid and clear the Show check box for the field.
- Set the Output All Fields property value in the Query Properties sheet to Yes to add with asterisks all fields of all tables to the grid.

MAKING CALCULATIONS ON MULTIPLE RECORDS

One of SQL's most powerful capabilities is obtaining summary information almost instantly from specified sets of records in tables. Summarized information from databases is the basis for virtually all management information systems (MIS) and business intelligence (BI) projects. These systems or projects usually answer questions: What are our sales to date for this month? or How did last month's sales compare with the same month last year? To answer these questions, you must create queries that make calculations on field values from all or selected sets of records in a table. To make calculations on table values, you must create a query that uses the table and employ Jet's SQL aggregate functions to perform the calculations.

USING THE SQL AGGREGATE FUNCTIONS

11

Summary calculations on fields of tables included in query result tables use the SQL aggregate functions listed in Table 11.1. These are called aggregate functions because they apply to groups (aggregations) of data cells. The SQL aggregate functions satisfy the requirements of most queries needed for business applications.

TABLE 11.1 SQL AGGREGATE FUNCTIONS

Function	Description	Field Types
`Avg()`	Average of values in a field	All types except Text, Memo, and OLE Object
`Count()`	Number of Not Null in a field	All field typesvalues
`First()`	Value of a field ofsthe first record	All field type
`Last()`	Value of a field ofthe last record	All field types
`Max()`	Greatest value in field	All numeric data types and Text
`Min()`	Least value in field	All numeric data types and Text
`StDev()`, `StDevP()`	Statistical standard deviation of values in a field	All numeric data types
`Sum()`	Total of values in a field	All numeric data types
`Var()`, `VarP()`	Statistical variation of values in a field	All numeric data types

`StDev()` and `Var()` evaluate population samples. You can choose these functions from the drop-down list in the Query Design grid's Total row. (The Total row appears when you click the Totals button on the toolbar or choose View, Totals.) `StDevP()` and `VarP()` evaluate populations and must be entered as expressions. If you're familiar with statistical principles, you recognize the difference in the calculation methods of standard deviation and variance for populations and samples of populations. The following section explains the method of choosing the SQL aggregate function for the column of a query.

T-SQL

ANSI SQL and most SQL (client/server) databases support the equivalent of Access SQL's `Avg()`, `Count()`, `First()`, `Last()`, `Max()`, `Min()`, and `Sum()` aggregate functions as `AVG()`, `COUNT()`, `FIRST()`, `LAST()`, `MAX()`, `MIN()`, and `SUM()`, respectively. T-SQL also provides equivalents of Jet's `StdDev()`, `StdDevP()`, `Var()`, and `VarP()` functions with the same names.

MAKING CALCULATIONS BASED ON ALL RECORDS OF A TABLE

Managers, especially sales and marketing managers, are most often concerned with information about orders received and shipments made during specific periods of time. Financial managers are interested in calculated values, such as the total amount of unpaid invoices and the average number of days between the invoice and payment dates. Occasionally, you might want to make calculations on all records of a table, such as finding the historical average value of all invoices issued by a firm. Usually, however, you apply criteria to the query to select specific records that you want to total.

Access considers all SQL aggregate functions to be members of the Totals class of functions. You create queries that return any or all SQL aggregate functions by clicking the Totals button (with the Greek sigma, Σ, which represents summation) on the toolbar.

Follow these steps to apply the five most commonly used SQL aggregate functions to the sample Order Subtotals query:

1. Open a new query and add the Order Subtotals query.
2. Drag the OrderID column to the first new query column and then drag the Subtotal column four times to the adjacent column to create four Subtotal columns.
3. Click the Totals button to add the Totals row.
4. Move to the Total row of the OrderID column and press Alt+↓ to display the drop-down list of SQL aggregate functions. Choose Count as the function for the OrderID column, as shown in Figure 11.49.
5. Move to the first Subtotal column, open the list, and choose Sum from the Total drop-down list. Repeat the process, choosing Avg for the second Subtotal column, Min for the third, and Max for the fourth.

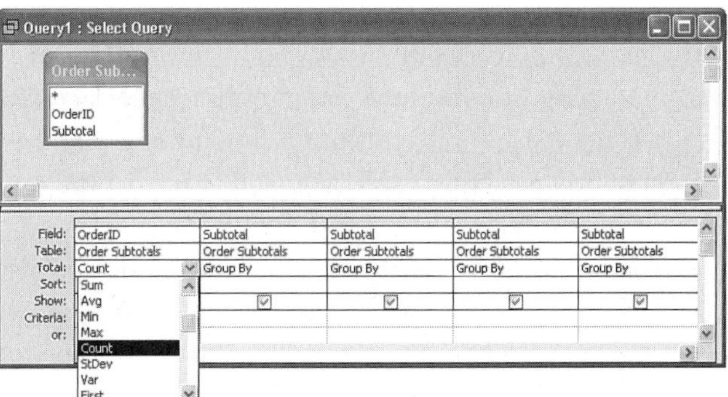

Figure 11.49 You apply the Count() function to one of the rows of the query that has a value in every row to obtain the total number of rows returned by the query. The OrderID column is the logical choice for counting.

6. Place the cursor in the OrderID field and click the Properties button on the toolbar (or right-click in the Count field and then click Properties in the pop-up menu) to display the Field Properties window. Type **Count** as the value of the Caption property.
7. Repeat step 6 for the four Subtotal columns, typing **Sum**, **Average**, **Minimum**, and **Maximum** as the values of the Caption property for the four columns, respectively. (You don't need to set the Format property, because the Subtotal column is formatted as Currency.)
8. Click Run to display the query's result. The query design doesn't have fields suitable for row-restriction criteria, so the result shown in Figure 11.50 is for the whole table.

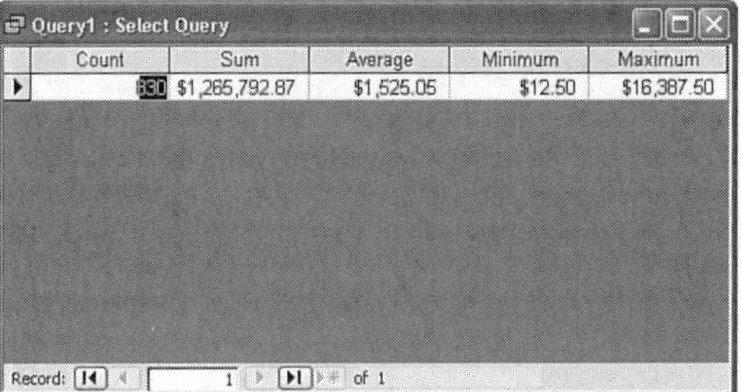

Figure 11.50 The datasheet displays the five SQL aggregate values for all records of the Orders table.

9. Save your query with a descriptive name, such as **qryOrdersAggregates**, because you use this query in the two sections that follow.

MAKING CALCULATIONS BASED ON SELECTED SETS OF ROWS OR RECORDS

The preceding sample query performed calculations on all orders received by Northwind Traders that were entered in the Orders table. Usually, you are interested in a specific set of records—a range of dates, for example—from which to calculate aggregate values. To restrict the calculation to orders that Northwind received in March 1998, follow these steps:

1. Return to Query Design view and add the Orders table to the qryOrdersAggregates query. Access automatically creates the join on the OrderID fields. If you didn't create this query, you can import it from the Join11.mdb sample database.
2. Drag the OrderDate field onto the OrderID column to add OrderDate as the first column of the query. You need the OrderDate field to restrict the data to a range of dates.
3. Open the Total drop-down list in the OrderDate column and choose Where to replace the default Group By. Access deselects the Show box of the OrderDate column.
4. In the OrderDate column's Criteria row, type **Like "3/*/1998"** to restrict the totals to orders received in the month of March 1998 (see Figure 11.51). When you use the Like criterion, Access adds the quotation marks if you forget to type them.

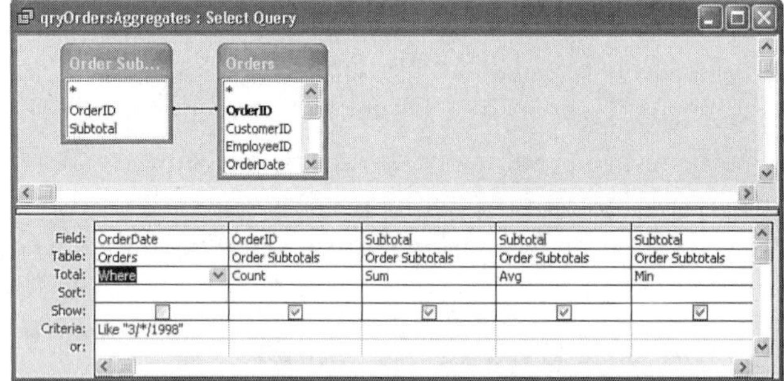

Figure 11.51 The OrderDate field of the Orders table is needed to restrict the aggregate data to orders received within a specified period, March 1998 in this case.

11

TIP

The examples of this chapter use Jet `Like "{m¦*}/{d¦*}/yyyy"` expressions as shorthand for `Between #mm/dd/yyyy# And #mm/dd/yyyy# WHERE` clause date constraints. Current versions of the Microsoft Data Access Components and the Jet OLE DB driver don't recognize `Like "*/*/yyyy"` and similar `Like` expressions. If you plan to copy Jet SQL statements to Visual Basic 6.0 or Visual Basic .NET programs, use the `Between...And` operator, not `Like` for dates.

5. Click the Run button on the toolbar to display the result for orders received during the month of March 1998 (see Figure 11.52).

You can create a more useful grouping of records by replacing the field name with an expression. For example, you can group aggregates by the year and month (or year and quarter) by grouping on the value of an expression created with the Format function. The following steps produce a sales summary record for each month of 1997, the most recent year for which 12 months of data are available in the Orders table:

1. Return to Query Design view, and then click the header bar of the query's OrderDate column to select the first column. Press the Insert key to add a new, empty column to the query.

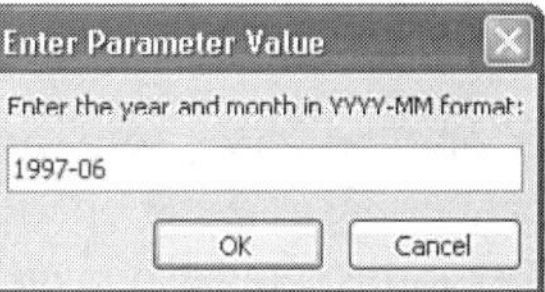

Figure 11.52
This datasheet shows the effect of adding a date criterion, in this case, orders received in March 1998.

2. Type **Month: Format([OrderDate],"yyyy-mm")** in the first (empty) column's Field row. (You use the "yyyy-mm" format so that the records group in date order. For a single year, you also can use "m" or "mm", but not "mmm", because "mmm" sorts in alphabetic sequence starting with Apr.)
3. Change the Where criterion of the OrderDate column to **Like "*/*/1997"** to return a full year of data. Your query design appears as shown in Figure 11.53.

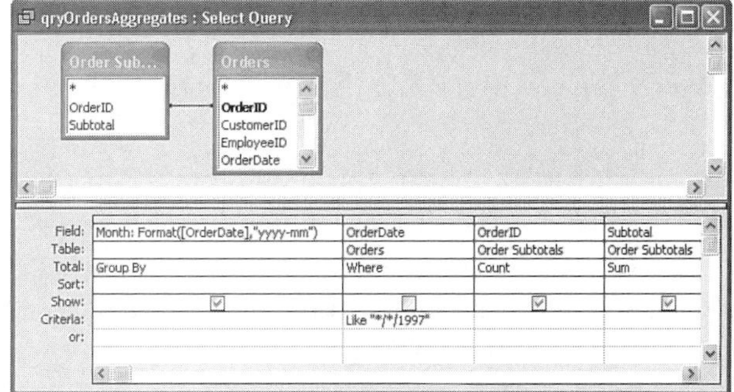

Figure 11.53
This query design returns a row containing aggregate values of orders received in each month of 1997.

4. Click Run to display the result of your query (see Figure 11.54). The query creates sales summary data for each month of 1997.

qryOrdersAggregates : Select Query

Month	Count	Sum	Average	Minimum	Maximum
1997-01	33	$61,258.06	$1,856.30	$49.80	$11,188.40
1997-02	29	$38,483.63	$1,327.02	$174.90	$4,924.13
1997-03	30	$38,547.21	$1,284.91	$147.00	$10,495.60
1997-04	31	$53,032.95	$1,710.74	$136.80	$9,921.30
1997-05	32	$53,781.28	$1,680.67	$110.00	$10,191.70
1997-06	30	$36,362.79	$1,212.09	$155.00	$2,944.40
1997-07	33	$51,020.83	$1,546.09	$23.80	$6,475.40
1997-08	33	$47,287.66	$1,432.96	$55.80	$5,510.59
1997-09	37	$55,629.24	$1,503.49	$45.00	$5,256.50
1997-10	38	$66,749.23	$1,756.56	$93.50	$10,164.80
1997-11	34	$43,533.79	$1,280.41	$52.35	$4,529.80
1997-12	48	$71,398.41	$1,487.47	$12.50	$6,635.27

Record: 1 of 12

Figure 11.54
The datasheet displays aggregate rows for each month of 1997.

5. Choose File, Save As and save the query under a different name, such as **qryMonthlyOrders1997**, because you modify the query in the next section.

Designing Parameter Queries

If you expect to run a summary or another type of query repeatedly with changes to the criteria, you can convert the query to a parameter query. Parameter queries—which Chapter 9 explained briefly—enable you to enter criteria with the Enter Parameter Value dialog. Access prompts you for each parameter. For the qryMonthlyOrders1997 query that you created in the preceding section, the only parameter likely to change is the range of dates for which you want to generate the product sales data. The two sections that follow show you how to add a parameter to a query and specify the data type of the parameter.

Adding a Parameter to the Monthly Sales Query

To convert the qryMonthlyOrders1997 summary query to a parameter query, you first create prompts for the Enter Parameter Value dialog that appears when the query runs. You create parameter queries by substituting the text with which to prompt the user, enclosed within square brackets, for actual values. Follow these steps:

1. Open in Design view the qryMonthlyOrders1997 query that you created in the preceding section.

2. With the cursor in the Month column's Field row, press F2 to select the expression in the Field cell. Then press Ctrl+C to copy the expression to the Clipboard.

3. Move the cursor to the OrderDate column's Field row and press F2 to select OrderDate. Then press Ctrl+V to replace OrderDate with the expression used for the first column.
4. Move to the OrderDate column's Criteria cell and replace Like "*/*/1997" with **[Enter the year and month in YYYY-MM format:]** (see Figure 11.55).

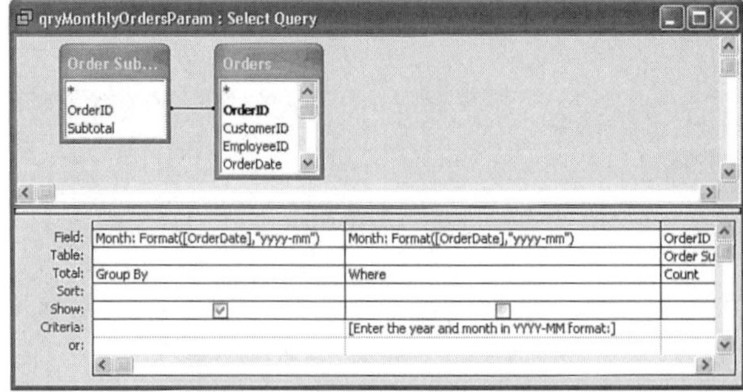

Figure 11.55 Specify the same format for the parameter column as that of the grouping column, and add the prompt for the Enter Parameter dialog.

5. Choose File, Save As, and save the query as **qryMonthlyOrdersParam**.
6. Click the Run button. The Enter Parameter Value dialog opens with the label that you assigned as the value of the criterion in step 4.
7. Type **1997-06** in the text box to display the data for June 1997, as shown in Figure 11.56.

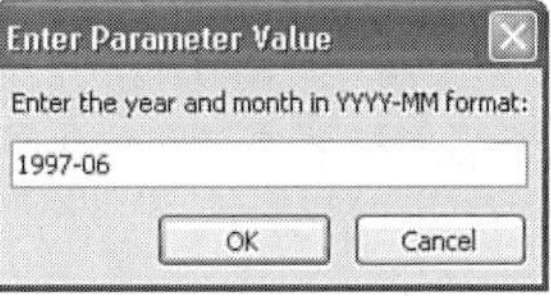

Figure 11.56
You must type the parameter exactly as shown in the Enter Parameter Value dialog's prompt to return rows.

8. Click OK to run the query. The result appears as shown in Figure 11.57.

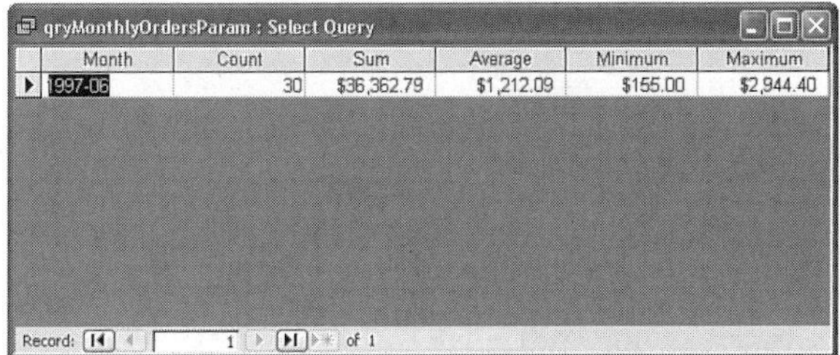

Figure 11.57
This datasheet shows the result of the parameter value entered in step 7.

SPECIFYING THE PARAMETER'S DATA TYPE

The default field data type for parameters of Access queries is Text. If the parameter creates a criterion for a query column of the Date/Time or Number field data type, you must assign a data type to each entry that is made through an Enter Parameter Value dialog. Data types for values entered as parameters are established in the Query Parameters dialog. If you have more than one parameter, you can establish the same or a different data type for each parameter.

11

NOTE

> The data type for the prompt of the qryMonthlyOrdersParam query's parameter is Text (the default), not Date/Time. Thus you don't need to apply a data type specification for the query.

Follow these steps to demonstrate adding an optional data type specification to a parameter:

1. Return to Design view, use the mouse to select the prompt text only in the Month column's Criteria cell (omit the square brackets and colon character), and copy the text of the prompt to the Clipboard by pressing Ctrl+C.
2. Choose Query, Parameters to display the Query Parameters dialog.

3. To insert the prompt in the Parameter column of the dialog, place the cursor in the column and press Ctrl+V. The prompt entry in the Parameter column must match the prompt entry in the Criteria field exactly; copying and pasting the prompt text ensures an exact match. Don't include the square brackets in the Parameter column.

4. Press Tab to move to the Data Type column, press Alt+[da] to open the Data Type drop-down list, and select Date/Time (see Figure 11.58). Click Cancel to close the dialog without adding the Date/Time data type, because it isn't applicable to this query.

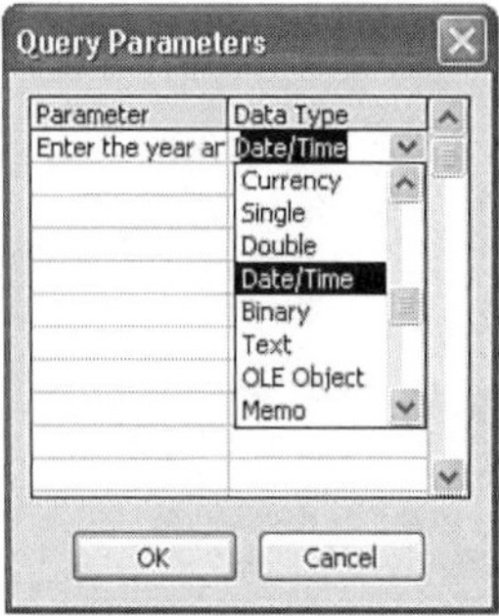

Figure 11.58
Select the data type for the parameter's prompt from the Data Type list in the Query Parameters dialog.

5. If you applied the Date/Time data type to the qryMonthlyOrdersParam query, reopen the Query Parameters dialog and delete the prompt text, which also deletes the data type entry.

11

TIP

> Complete your query design and testing before you convert any type of query to a parameter query. Using fixed criteria with the query maintains consistency during the testing process. Furthermore, you can make repeated changes between Design and Run view more quickly if you don't have to enter one or more parameters in the process. After you finish testing the query, edit the criteria to add the prompt for the Enter Parameter Value dialog.

The parameter-conversion process described in this section applies to all types of queries that you create if one or more of the query columns includes a criterion expression. The advantage of the parameter query is that you or a user of the database can run a query for any range of values—in this case, dates—such as the current month to date, a particular fiscal quarter, or an entire fiscal year.

Creating Crosstab Queries

Crosstab queries are summary queries that let you determine exactly how the summary data appears onscreen. Crosstab queries rotate the axis of the datasheet and display the equivalent of repeating fields (often called *buckets*) in columns. Thus the datasheet displayed by a crosstab query doesn't conform to first normal form. Crosstab queries are closely related to Excel PivotTables and PivotTables you create with the PivotTable control of the Office Web Components (OWC). PivotTable and PivotChart views of queries are the subject of the next chapter.

→ For more information on PivotTables, **see** "Slicing and Dicing Data with PivotTables," **p. 463**.

With crosstab queries, you can perform the following operations:

- Specify the field that creates labels (headings) for rows by using the Group By instruction
- Determine the fields that create column headers and the criteria that determine the values appearing under the headers
- Assign calculated data values to the cells of the resulting row-column grid

---

T-SQL

As mentioned earlier in the chapter, SQL Server doesn't support crosstab queries directly, so you ordinarily use PivotTables to display an equivalent to a Jet crosstab query. You can, however, write T-SQL stored procedures to emulate Jet crosstab queries. The "In the Real World—Crosstab Queries" section at the end of this chapter describes a Visual Basic 6.0 application that generates T-SQL stored procedures from Jet crosstab queries.

The following list details the advantages of using crosstab queries:

- You can display a substantial amount of summary data in a compact datasheet that's familiar to anyone who uses a spreadsheet application or columnar accounting form.
- The summary data is presented in a datasheet that's ideally suited for creating graphs and charts automatically with the Access Chart Wizard.
- Designing queries to create multiple levels of detail is quick and easy. Queries with identical columns but fewer rows can represent increasingly summarized data. Highly summarized queries are ideal to begin a drill-down procedure by instructing the user, for example, to click a Details button to display sales by product.

Using crosstab queries imposes only one restriction: You can't sort your result table on calculated values in columns. You can't, therefore, create a crosstab query that ranks products by sales volume. Columns are likely to have values that cause conflicts in the sorting order of the row. You can choose an ascending sort, a descending sort, or no sort on the row label values in the `GROUP BY` field, which usually is the first column.

Using the Wizard to Generate a Quarterly Product Sales Crosstab Query

Access's Crosstab Query Wizard can generate a crosstab query from a single table, but an individual table seldom contains data suitable as the data source for a crosstab query. If you need more than one table to get the result you want from the Wizard, which is almost always the case, you must design a query specifically for crosstab presentation.

Follow these steps to create a query and then use the Crosstab Query Wizard to generate a result set that shows quarterly sales by product for the year 1997:

1. Create a new query in Design view and add the Orders table and Order Details Extended query. Drag the OrderDate field of the Orders table and the ProductID, ProductName, and ExtendedPrice fields of the Order Details Extended query to the grid. Add **Like "*/*/1997"** as the criterion of the OrderDate field to restrict the data to a single year (see Figure 11.59).

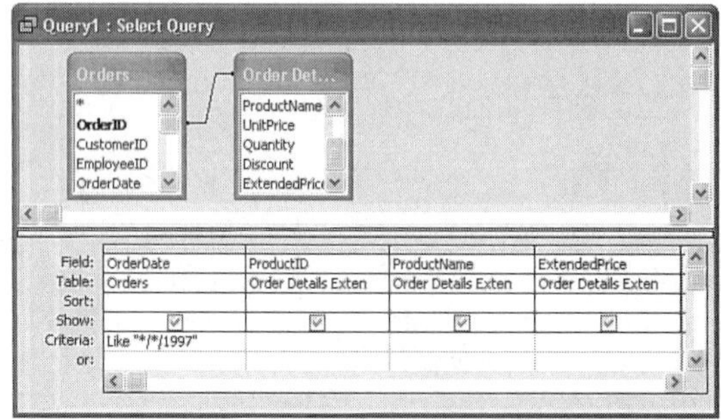

Figure 11.59
The source query for the first crosstab query is based on the sample Orders table and Order Details Extended query.

2. With the ProductID field selected, click the Properties button, click the Lookup tab, and select Text Box in the Display Control to revert from the ProductName lookup to the numeric ProductID value. Click Run to verify your design (see Figure 11.60).

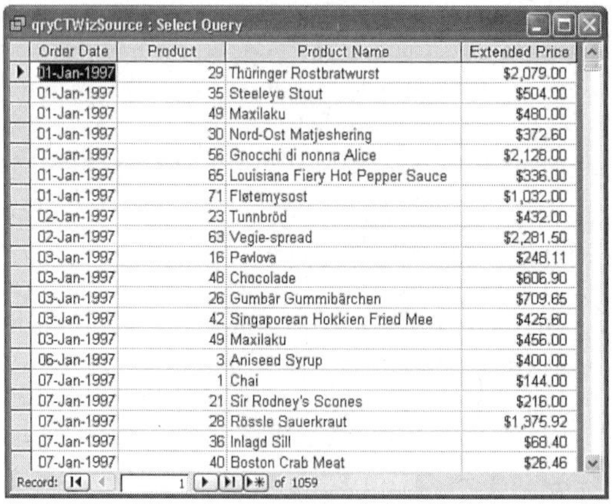

qryCTWizSource : Select Query

Order Date	Product	Product Name	Extended Price
01-Jan-1997	29	Thüringer Rostbratwurst	$2,079.00
01-Jan-1997	35	Steeleye Stout	$504.00
01-Jan-1997	49	Maxilaku	$480.00
01-Jan-1997	30	Nord-Ost Matjeshering	$372.60
01-Jan-1997	56	Gnocchi di nonna Alice	$2,128.00
01-Jan-1997	65	Louisiana Fiery Hot Pepper Sauce	$336.00
01-Jan-1997	71	Fløtemysost	$1,032.00
02-Jan-1997	23	Tunnbröd	$432.00
02-Jan-1997	63	Vegie-spread	$2,281.50
03-Jan-1997	16	Pavlova	$248.11
03-Jan-1997	48	Chocolade	$606.90
03-Jan-1997	26	Gumbär Gummibärchen	$709.65
03-Jan-1997	42	Singaporean Hokkien Fried Mee	$425.60
03-Jan-1997	49	Maxilaku	$456.00
06-Jan-1997	3	Aniseed Syrup	$400.00
07-Jan-1997	1	Chai	$144.00
07-Jan-1997	21	Sir Rodney's Scones	$216.00
07-Jan-1997	28	Rössle Sauerkraut	$1,375.92
07-Jan-1997	36	Inlagd Sill	$68.40
07-Jan-1997	40	Boston Crab Meat	$26.46

Record: 1 of 1059

Figure 11.60
This datasheet displays the first few rows of the result set from the design of Figure 11.59, which has a row for each Order Details item for orders received in 1997.

3. Close and save the query as **qryCTWizSource**.

4. Click the Database window's New button to open the New Query dialog and double-click the Crosstab Query Wizard to open the Wizard's first dialog.

5. Select the Queries option and then select qryCTWizSource from the list (see Figure 11.61). Click Next.

Figure 11.61 Select the data source, usually a query, in the first Crosstab Query Wizard dialog.

6. Double-click the ProductID column to move ProductID from the Available Fields to the Selected Fields list. Do the same for the ProductName column. The second Wizard dialog appears as shown in Figure 11.62. Click Next.

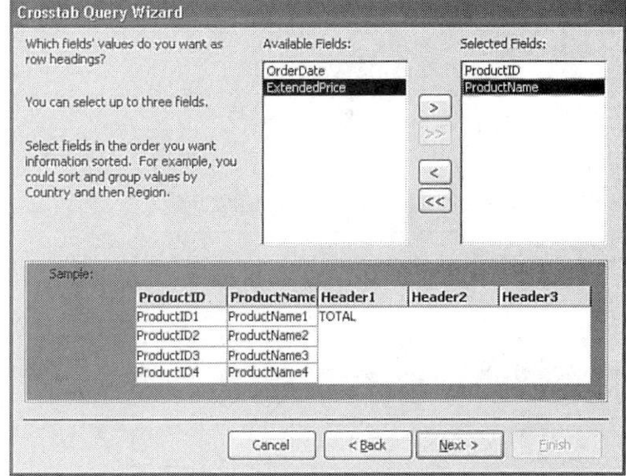

Figure 11.62 Select the query columns to appear as row headers in the second Wizard dialog.

7. Accept the default OrderDate field for the column headings (see Figure 11.63). Click Next.
8. Select Quarter as the date interval for the columns (see Figure 11.64). Click Next.
9. Select Sum as the aggregate function to total sales for each quarter. Leave the Yes, Include Row Sums check box marked to include a column that shows the total sales for the four quarters (see Figure 11.65). Click Next.
10. In the final Wizard dialog, type **qry1997QuarterlyProductOrdersCT** as the name of the query and click Finish to display the crosstab query result set (see Figure 11.66).

Figure 11.63
Specify the query column that provides the column headers in the third Wizard dialog.

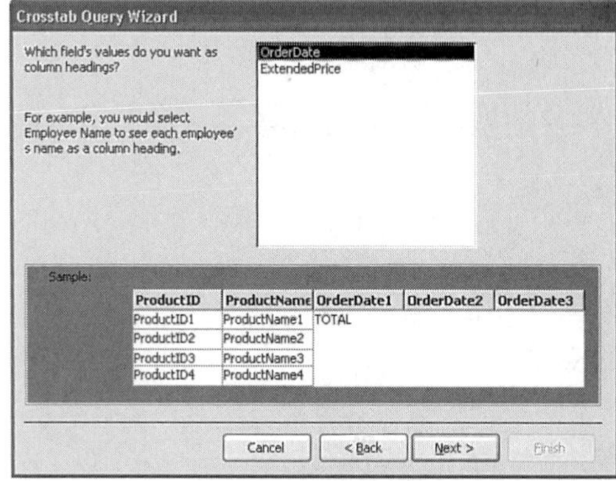

Figure 11.64
Specify the date interval in the fourth dialog's list. This dialog appears only if you specify a date field for row or column headings.

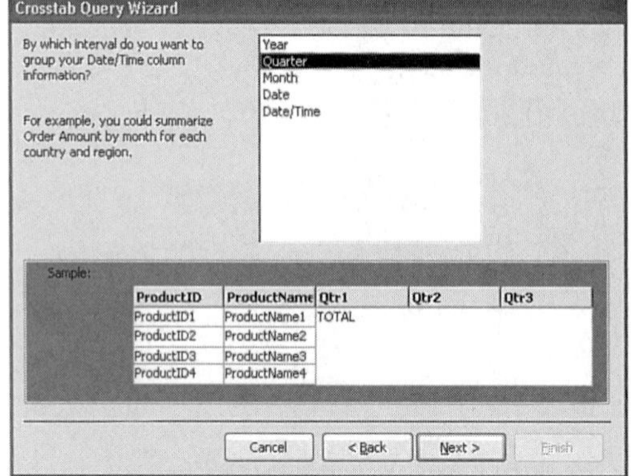

11

Figure 11.65
You can specify any aggregate function to summarize the numeric data for the crosstab query.

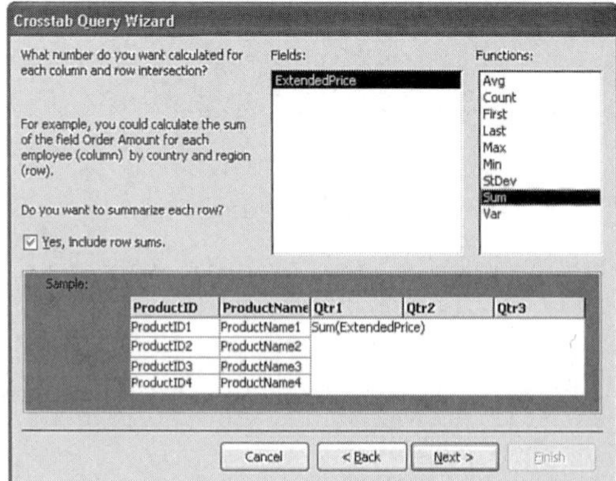

qry1997QuarterlyProductOrdersCT : Crosstab Query

Product	Product Name	Total Of Extend	Qtr 1	Qtr 2	Qtr 3	Qtr 4
1	Chai	$4,887.00	$705.60	$878.40	$1,174.50	$2,128.50
2	Chang	$7,038.55	$2,435.80	$228.00	$2,061.50	$2,313.25
3	Aniseed Syrup	$1,724.00	$544.00	$600.00	$140.00	$440.00
4	Chef Anton's Cajun Seasoning	$5,214.88	$225.28	$2,970.00	$1,337.60	$682.00
5	Chef Anton's Gumbo Mix	$373.62			$288.22	$85.40
6	Grandma's Boysenberry Spread	$2,500.00			$1,750.00	$750.00
7	Uncle Bob's Organic Dried Pears	$9,186.30	$1,084.80	$1,575.00	$2,700.00	$3,826.50
8	Northwoods Cranberry Sauce	$4,260.00		$1,300.00		$2,960.00
9	Mishi Kobe Niku	$6,935.50	$1,396.80	$1,319.20	$3,637.50	$582.00
10	Ikura	$9,935.50	$1,215.20	$688.20	$4,212.90	$3,819.20
11	Queso Cabrales	$6,911.94	$1,630.44	$2,756.25	$504.00	$2,021.25
12	Queso Manchego La Pastora	$8,335.30	$456.00	$1,396.50	$4,962.80	$1,520.00
13	Konbu	$812.94	$13.44	$168.00	$469.50	$162.00
14	Tofu	$6,234.48	$1,432.20	$2,734.20	$1,318.27	$749.81
15	Genen Shouyu	$1,474.82		$331.70	$1,143.12	

Record: 1 of 77

Figure 11.66 The crosstab query has rows for each of the 77 products sold by Northwind traders.

11. Change to Design view to check the query the Query Wizard based on the original qryCTWizSource query. Open the list in one of the cells of the added Crosstab row to view the choices for each field of the query (see Figure 11.67).

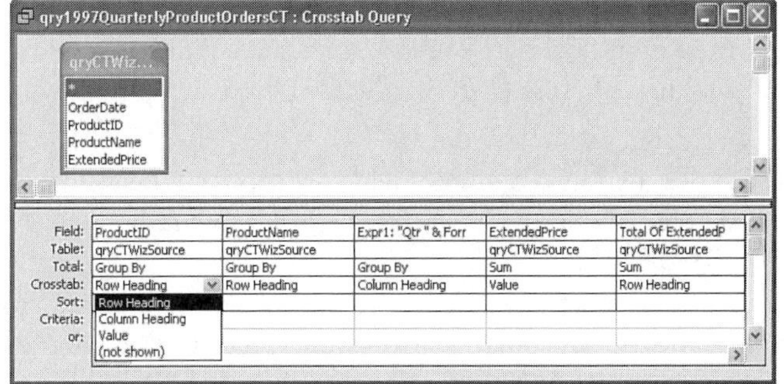

Figure 11.67 Crosstab queries have an additional row, Crosstab, in the grid.

The Crosstab row choices—Row Heading, Column Heading, Value, and (Not Shown)—determine the location of field values in the crosstab datasheet.

Jet SQL

The Jet SQL statement for the crosstab query is

```
TRANSFORM Sum(qryCTWizSource.ExtendedPrice) AS SumOfExtendedPrice
SELECT qryCTWizSource.ProductID, qryCTWizSource.ProductName,
   Sum(qryCTWizSource.ExtendedPrice) AS [Total Of ExtendedPrice]
FROM qryCTWizSource
GROUP BY qryCTWizSource.ProductID, qryCTWizSource.ProductName
PIVOT "Qtr " & Format([OrderDate],"q");
```

The Jet SQL `PIVOT` and `TRANSFORM` reserved words generate the crosstab query result set. The expression following `TRANSFORM` defines the numeric values for the matrix. The `SELECT` field list supplies the row headings and values. The `PIVOT` expression defines the column headings and acts as an extension to the `GROUP BY` expression. The `"q"` format string specifies a quarterly date interval.

DESIGNING A MONTHLY PRODUCT SALES CROSSTAB QUERY

You can bypass the Query Wizard by manually designing a crosstab query from scratch. To create a typical crosstab query in Query Design view that displays products in rows and the monthly sales volume for each product in the corresponding columns, follow these steps:

1. Open a new query and add the Products, Order Details, and Orders tables to the query.
2. Drag the ProductID and ProductName fields from the Products table to the query's first two columns and then drag the OrderDate field of the Orders table to the third column.

3. Choose Query, Crosstab Query. The title bar of the query changes from Query1: Select Query to Query1: Crosstab Query. The Crosstab row is added to the Query Design grid.
4. Open the drop-down list of the ProductID column's Crosstab row and select Row Heading. Repeat this process for the ProductName column. These two columns provide the required row headings for your crosstab. A crosstab query must have at least one row heading.
5. Open the Total drop-down list of the OrderDate column and select Where. Type **Like "*/*/1997"** in this column's Criteria row to restrict the query to orders received in 1997.
6. Move to the next (empty) column's Field row and type the following:

   ```
   Sales: Sum([Order Details].[Quantity]*[Order Details].[UnitPrice]*(1-[Order
   Details].[Discount]))
   ```

   Move to the Total row, choose Expression from the drop-down list, and then choose Value from the Crosstab row. The expression calculates the gross amount of the orders received for each product that populates your crosstab query's data cells. (You must specify the Orders Detail table name; if you don't, you receive an "Ambiguous field reference" error message.)

7. Click the Properties button to open the Field Properties window for the Sales column and select Currency as the Format property of the column.
8. In the next (empty) column's Field row, type **Format([OrderDate], "mmm")**. Access adds a default field name, Expr1:. Accept the default because the Format function that you added creates the column names, the three-letter abbreviation for the months of the year ("mmm" format), when you run the query. The months of the year (Jan through Dec) are your column headings, so move to the Crosstab row and choose Column Heading from the drop-down list. The design of your crosstab query appears as shown in Figure 11.68.
9. Click Run to execute the query (see Figure 11.69).

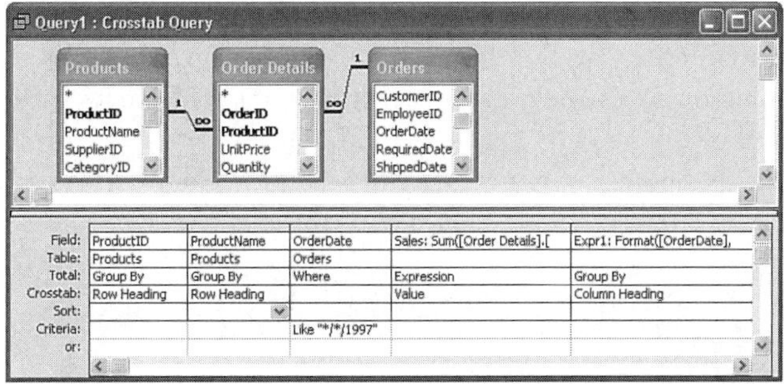

Figure 11.68 This crosstab query design displays order amounts for products by month.

Query1 : Crosstab Query

Product ID	Product Name	Apr	Aug	Dec	Feb	Jan
1	Chai	$576.00	$652.50			$489.60
2	Chang	$228.00	$1,871.50	$1,505.75	$733.40	$912.00
3	Aniseed Syrup			$180.00		$400.00
4	Chef Anton's Cajun Seasoning	$935.00	$748.00			
5	Chef Anton's Gumbo Mix		$288.22			
6	Grandma's Boysenberry Spread		$1,750.00			
7	Uncle Bob's Organic Dried Pears	$1,275.00	$1,050.00	$1,126.50	$364.80	
8	Northwoods Cranberry Sauce	$1,300.00		$960.00		
9	Mishi Kobe Niku	$1,319.20				$1,396.80
10	Ikura	$471.20	$418.50	$1,612.00	$744.00	
11	Queso Cabrales		$210.00	$1,601.25	$685.44	$504.00
12	Queso Manchego La Pastora		$1,162.80		$456.00	
13	Konbu	$60.00	$66.30	$102.00		$8.64
14	Tofu	$1,627.50	$558.00	$279.00		$1,209.00
15	Genen Shouyu	$176.70				
16	Pavlova	$872.50		$1,483.25	1,023.73	$248.11
17	Alice Mutton			$3,480.75	$312.00	$2,355.60
18	Carnarvon Tigers	$1,406.25	$5,100.00	$1,875.00		

Record: 1 of 77

Figure 11.69 The "mmm" format string for months sorts the columns by month name, not month number.

11

Notice that the crosstab query result contains a major defect: The columns are arranged alphabetically by month name rather than in calendar order. You can solve this problem by using fixed column headings, which you learn about in the following section.

USING FIXED COLUMN HEADINGS WITH CROSSTAB QUERIES

Access uses an alphabetical or numerical sort on row and column headings to establish the sequence of appearance in the crosstab query result table. For this reason, if you use short or full names for months, the sequence is in alphabetic rather than calendar order. You can correct this problem by assigning fixed column headings to the crosstab query. Follow these steps to modify and rerun the query:

→ To review the ways Access lets you manipulate dates and time, **see** "Functions for Date and Time," **p. 370**.

1. Return to Query Design view and click the Properties button on the toolbar, or double-click an empty area in the Query Design window's upper pane. The Query Properties window contains an option that appears only for crosstab queries: Column Headings.

2. In the Column Headings text box, type the three-letter abbreviations of all 12 months of the year. You must spell the abbreviations of the months correctly; data for months with spelling mistakes doesn't appear. You can separate entries with commas or semicolons, and you don't need to type quotation marks, because Access adds them (see Figure 11.70). Spaces are unnecessary between the Column Headings values. After you complete all 12 entries, close the Query Properties window.

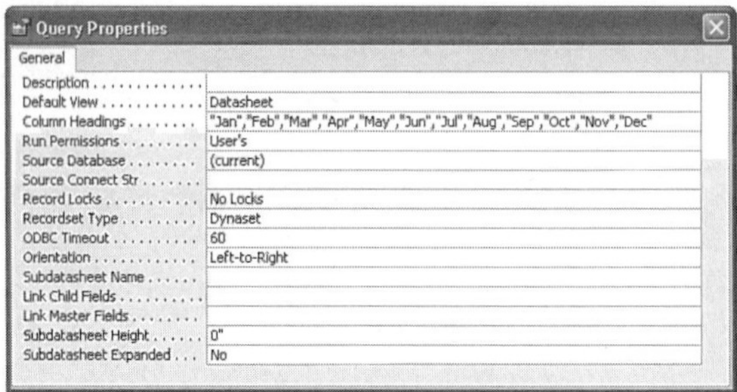

Query Properties

General

Description	
Default View	Datasheet
Column Headings	"Jan","Feb","Mar","Apr","May","Jun","Jul","Aug","Sep","Oct","Nov","Dec"
Run Permissions	User's
Source Database	(current)
Source Connect Str	
Record Locks	No Locks
Recordset Type	Dynaset
ODBC Timeout	60
Orientation	Left-to-Right
Subdatasheet Name	
Link Child Fields	
Link Master Fields	
Subdatasheet Height	0"
Subdatasheet Expanded	No

Figure 11.70 Add month names separated by semicolons to the Column Headings property of crosstab queries.

3. Click Run. Now the result table, shown in Figure 11.71, sorts the months in numeric order, although you can see only January through May in the figure. (Scroll to the right to see the remaining months.)

Query1 : Crosstab Query

Product ID	Product Name	Jan	Feb	Mar	Apr	May
1	Chai	$489.60		$216.00	$576.00	$122.40
2	Chang	$912.00	$733.40	$790.40	$228.00	
3	Aniseed Syrup	$400.00		$144.00		$600.00
4	Chef Anton's Cajun Seasoning			$225.28	$935.00	$2,035.00
5	Chef Anton's Gumbo Mix					
6	Grandma's Boysenberry Spread					
7	Uncle Bob's Organic Dried Pears		$364.80	$720.00	$1,275.00	$300.00
8	Northwoods Cranberry Sauce				$1,300.00	
9	Mishi Kobe Niku	$1,396.80			$1,319.20	
10	Ikura		$744.00	$471.20	$471.20	$62.00
11	Queso Cabrales	$504.00	$685.44	$441.00		$1,832.25
12	Queso Manchego La Pastora		$456.00			$1,396.50
13	Konbu	$8.64		$4.80	$60.00	$108.00
14	Tofu	$1,209.00		$223.20	$1,627.50	
15	Genen Shouyu				$176.70	
16	Pavlova	$248.11	1,023.73	$663.72	$872.50	$1,334.92
17	Alice Mutton	$2,355.60	$312.00			$2,718.30
18	Carnarvon Tigers			$1,500.00	$1,406.25	

Record: 1 of 77

Figure 11.71 Adding the fixed column headers eliminates the sorting problem with the month columns.

TIP

If your crosstab datasheet differs from that of Figure 11.71, check whether you properly entered the fixed column headings in the Query Properties window. A misspelled month causes Access to omit the month from the query result set; if you specified "mmmm" instead of "mmm", only May appears.

4. Choose File, Save As and save the query with an appropriate name, such as **qry1997MonthlyProductOrdersCT**.

You can produce a printed report quickly from the query by clicking the Print Preview button on the toolbar and then clicking the Print button.

TIP

> You might want to use fixed column headings if you use the Group By instruction with country names. Users in the United States will probably place USA first, and Canadian firms will undoubtedly choose Canada as the first entry. If you add a record with a new country, you must remember to update the list of fixed column headings with the new country value. Fixed column headings have another hidden benefit: they usually make crosstab queries operate more quickly.

Jet SQL

The Jet SQL statement for the crosstab query with fixed column headings is

```
TRANSFORM Sum([Order Details].[Quantity]*[Order Details].[UnitPrice]*
   (1-[Order Details].[Discount])) AS Sales
SELECT Products.ProductID, Products.ProductName
FROM Orders
   INNER JOIN (Products
      INNER JOIN [Order Details]
      ON Products.ProductID = [Order Details].ProductID)
   ON Orders.OrderID = [Order Details].OrderID
WHERE (((Orders.RequiredDate) Like "*/*/1997"))
GROUP BY Products.ProductID, Products.ProductName
PIVOT Format([OrderDate],"mmm")
   In("Jan","Feb","Mar","Apr","May","Jun",
   "Jul","Aug","Sep","Oct","Nov","Dec");
```

The only significant differences between the preceding SQL statement and that for the quarterly crosstab query is the lack of a grand total column for each product, the change of the date interval (`"mmm"` instead of `"q"`), and the addition of the `In( )` function with the fixed column names list as its argument.

If you want to add a grand totals column, add to the field list of the `SELECT` statement **`, Sum(Sales) AS [Total Orders]`**, return to Design view, select the Grand Total column, and set its Format property to Currency. The added column appears in Figure 11.72.

11

Query1 : Crosstab Query

Product ID	Product Name	Total Orders	Jan	Feb	Mar	Apr
1	Chai	$4,887.00	$489.60		$216.00	$576.00
2	Chang	$7,038.55	$912.00	$733.40	$790.40	$228.00
3	Aniseed Syrup	$1,724.00	$400.00		$144.00	
4	Chef Anton's Cajun Seasoning	$5,214.88			$225.28	$935.00
5	Chef Anton's Gumbo Mix	$373.62				
6	Grandma's Boysenberry Spread	$2,500.00				
7	Uncle Bob's Organic Dried Pears	$9,186.30		$364.80	$720.00	$1,275.00
8	Northwoods Cranberry Sauce	$4,260.00				$1,300.00
9	Mishi Kobe Niku	$6,935.50	$1,396.80			$1,319.20
10	Ikura	$9,935.50		$744.00	$471.20	$471.20
11	Queso Cabrales	$6,911.94	$504.00	$685.44	$441.00	
12	Queso Manchego La Pastora	$8,335.30		$456.00		
13	Konbu	$812.94	$8.64		$4.80	$60.00
14	Tofu	$6,234.49	$1,209.00		$223.20	$1,627.50
15	Genen Shouyu	$1,474.82				$176.70
16	Pavlova	$8,663.42	$248.11	1,023.73	$663.72	$872.50
17	Alice Mutton	$17,604.60	$2,355.60	$312.00		
18	Carnarvon Tigers	$15,950.00			$1,500.00	$1,406.25

Record: 1 of 77

Figure 11.72
You can add a Total Orders column by adding `Sum(Sales) AS [Total Orders]` to the column list of the `SELECT` statement. You must specify the Currency format of the column in the Field Properties window.

WRITING UNION QUERIES AND SUBQUERIES

`UNION` queries and queries that include subqueries require you to write Jet SQL statements. Union is one of the three choices of Query Design view's Query, SQL Specific menu. There is no menu choice for subquery. The following sections provide general syntax examples for writing `UNION` and subqueries, and provide simple Jet SQL examples. The general syntax examples use the same format as those of Chapter 21, "Moving from Jet Queries to Transact-SQL," for T-SQL statements.

USING UNION QUERIES TO COMBINE MULTIPLE RESULT SETS

`UNION` queries let you combine the result set of two or more `SELECT` queries into a single result set. Northwind.mdb includes an example of a `UNION` query, which has the special symbol of two overlapping circles, in the Database window. You can create `UNION` queries only with SQL statements; if you add the `UNION` keyword to a query, the Query Design Mode button on the toolbar and the query design choices of the View menu are disabled.

The general syntax of `UNION` queries is as follows:

```
SELECT select_statement
   UNION SELECT select_statement
     [GROUP BY group_criteria]
     [HAVING aggregate criteria]
  [UNION SELECT select_statement
     [GROUP BY group_criteria]
     [HAVING aggregate criteria]]
  [UNION. . .]
  [ORDER BY column_criteria]
```

The restrictions on statements that create `UNION` queries are the following:

- The number of fields in the *`field_list`* of each `SELECT` and `UNION SELECT` query must be the same. You receive an error message if the number of fields is not the same.

- The sequence of the field names in each *`field_list`* must correspond to similar entities. You don't receive an error message for dissimilar entities, but the result set is likely to be unfathomable. The field data types in a single column need not correspond; however, if the column of the result set contains both numeric and Jet Text data types, the data type of the column is set to Text.
- Only one `ORDER BY` clause is allowed, and it must follow the last `UNION SELECT` statement. You can add `GROUP BY` and `HAVING` clauses to each `SELECT` and `UNION SELECT` statement if needed.

The sample Customers and Suppliers by City query is a `UNION` query that combines rows from the Customers and Suppliers tables. When you open a `UNION` query, Query Design view is disabled.

To create a new `UNION` query, click the Database window's New button, select Design view, close the Show Table dialog, choose Query, SQL Specific, Union query to open the SQL window, and type the SQL statement.

Jet SQL

SQL

The Jet SQL statement for a slightly modified version of the Customers and Suppliers by City query is

```
SELECT City, CompanyName, ContactName,
   CustomerID AS Code, "Customer" AS Relationship
FROM Customers
UNION SELECT City, CompanyName, ContactName,
   SupplierID, "Supplier"
FROM Suppliers
ORDER BY City, CompanyName;
```

The syntax of the preceding SQL statement illustrates the capability of `UNION` queries to include values from two different field data types, Text (CustomerID) and Long Integer (SupplierID), in the single, aliased Code column (see Figure 11.73).

11

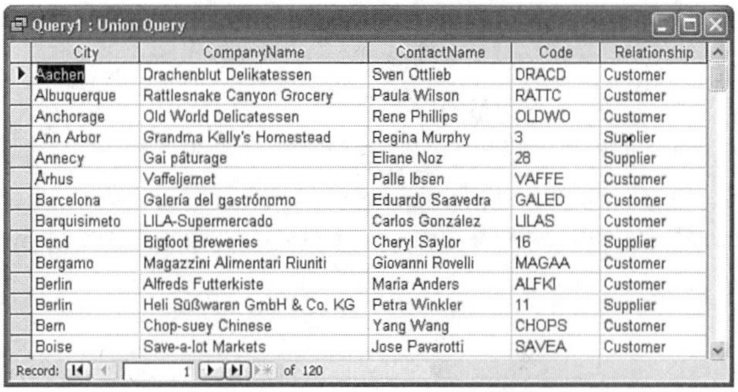

Query1 : Union Query

City	CompanyName	ContactName	Code	Relationship
Aachen	Drachenblut Delikatessen	Sven Ottlieb	DRACD	Customer
Albuquerque	Rattlesnake Canyon Grocery	Paula Wilson	RATTC	Customer
Anchorage	Old World Delicatessen	Rene Phillips	OLDWO	Customer
Ann Arbor	Grandma Kelly's Homestead	Regina Murphy	3	Supplier
Annecy	Gai pâturage	Eliane Noz	28	Supplier
Århus	Vaffeljernet	Palle Ibsen	VAFFE	Customer
Barcelona	Galería del gastrónomo	Eduardo Saavedra	GALED	Customer
Barquisimeto	LILA-Supermercado	Carlos González	LILAS	Customer
Bend	Bigfoot Breweries	Cheryl Saylor	16	Supplier
Bergamo	Magazzini Alimentari Riuniti	Giovanni Rovelli	MAGAA	Customer
Berlin	Alfreds Futterkiste	Maria Anders	ALFKI	Customer
Berlin	Heli Süßwaren GmbH & Co. KG	Petra Winkler	11	Supplier
Bern	Chop-suey Chinese	Yang Wang	CHOPS	Customer
Boise	Save-a-lot Markets	Jose Pavarotti	SAVEA	Customer

Record: 1 of 120

Figure 11.73 The Code column of this `UNION` query demonstrates Jet's capability to combine values of two different data types. T-SQL `UNION` queries require compatible data types in a column.

You also can use `UNION` queries to add `(All)` or other explicit options to a query result set when populating combo and list boxes. As an example, the following SQL statement adds `(All)` to the query result set for a combo box used to select orders from a particular country or all countries:

```
SELECT Country FROM Customers
   UNION SELECT "(All)" FROM Customers
ORDER BY Country;
```

The parentheses around `(All)` causes it to sort at the beginning of the list; the ASCII value of `"("` is 40 and `"A"` is 65. Automatic sorting of combo and list box items uses the ASCII value returned by the VBA **`Asc`** function.

➔ To create a query that returns all rows from joined tables, **see** "Using the tblShipAddress Table in a Query," **p. 506**.

➔ To update a table by substituting a string for a specified value, **see** "Using the tblShipAddress Table with `UNION` Queries," **p. 508**.

➔ For examples of using a `UNION` query to add an (All) item to a drop-down list, **see** "Adding an Option to Select All Countries or Products," **p. 1244**.

IMPLEMENTING SUBQUERIES

Access traditionally has used nested queries to emulate the subquery capability of ANSI SQL, because early Jet versions didn't support subqueries. Access 2003 lets you write a `SELECT` query that uses another `SELECT` query to supply the criteria for the `WHERE` clause. Depending on the complexity of your query, using a subquery instead of nested queries often improves performance. The general syntax of subqueries is as follows:


```
SELECT field_list
   FROM table_list
   WHERE [table_name.]field_name
      IN (SELECT select_statement
  [GROUP BY group_criteria]
     [HAVING aggregate_criteria]
  [ORDER BY sort_criteria]);
```

Jet SQL

Following the Jet SQL statement for a subquery that returns names and addresses of Northwind Traders customers who placed orders between January 1, 1997, and June 30, 1997:

```
SELECT CompanyName, ContactName, ContactTitle, Phone
FROM Customers
WHERE CustomerID IN
   (SELECT CustomerID FROM Orders
    WHERE OrderDate BETWEEN #1/1/1997# AND #6/30/1997#);
```

The `SELECT` subquery that begins after the `IN` predicate returns the CustomerID values from the Orders table against which the CustomerID values of the Customers table are compared. Be sure to surround the subquery with parentheses.

Unlike `UNION` queries, you can create a subquery in Query Design view. You type **IN**, followed by the `SELECT` statement as the criterion of the appropriate column, enclosing the `SELECT` statement within the parentheses required by the `IN` predicate. Figure 11.74 shows the query design with part of the `IN (SELECT...)` statement in the Criteria row of the Customer ID column. Figure 11.75 shows the result set returned by the SQL statement and the query design.

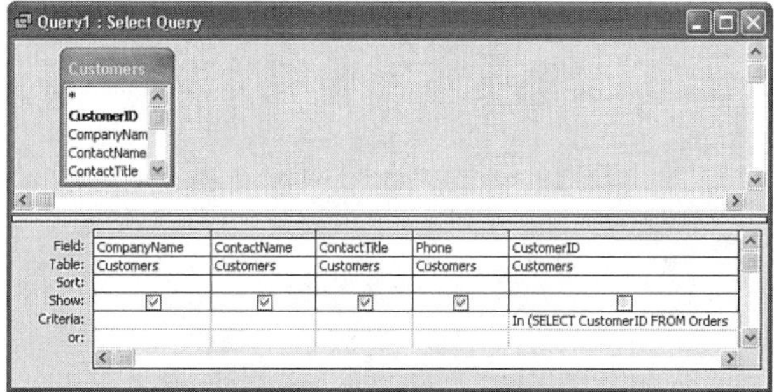

Figure 11.74
You can create the base query in Access's Query Design view, but you must type the `IN` predicate and the subquery's `SELECT` statement in the Criteria row of the grid.

Company Name	Contact Name	Contact Title	Phone
Antonio Moreno Taquería	Antonio Moreno	Owner	(5) 555-3932
Around the Horn	Thomas Hardy	Sales Representative	(171) 555-7788
Berglunds snabbköp	Christina Berglund	Order Administrator	0921-12 34 65
Blauer See Delikatessen	Hanna Moos	Sales Representative	0621-08460
Blondel père et fils	Frédérique Citeaux	Marketing Manager	88.60.15.31
Bon app'	Laurence Lebihan	Owner	91.24.45.40
Bottom-Dollar Markets	Elizabeth Lincoln	Accounting Manager	(604) 555-4729
B's Beverages	Victoria Ashworth	Sales Representative	(171) 555-1212
Cactus Comidas para llevar	Patricio Simpson	Sales Agent	(1) 135-5555
Chop-suey Chinese	Yang Wang	Owner	0452-076545
Comércio Mineiro	Pedro Afonso	Sales Associate	(11) 555-7647
Consolidated Holdings	Elizabeth Brown	Sales Representative	(171) 555-2282
Eastern Connection	Ann Devon	Sales Agent	(171) 555-0297
Ernst Handel	Roland Mendel	Sales Manager	7675-3425

Record: 1 of 73

Figure 11.75
This datasheet displays the result set of the subquery design of Figure 11.74.

CREATING QUERIES FROM TABLES IN OTHER DATABASES

Access's Query Properties window includes two properties that let you create a query based on tables contained in a database other than the current database. The database that you open after you launch Access is called the *current database*. Databases other than the current database commonly are called *external databases*. The use of these two properties is as follows:

- The value of the Source Database property for desktop databases is the path to the external database and, for Jet databases, the name of the database file. To run a query against tables contained in the Oakmont.mdb sample database from the accompanying CD-ROM, replace (current) in the Source Database text box with the following, as shown in Figure 11.76:

  C:\Program Files\Seua10\Oakmont\Oakmont.mdb

  You must have installed the sample files from the CD-ROM in the default C:\Program Files\Seua11 folder for this connection string to work.

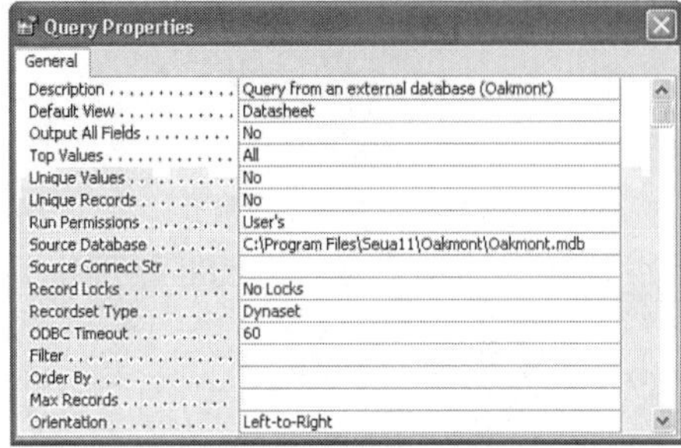

Figure 11.76 Specify the full path to the external database as the value of the Source Database property.

- The value of the Source Connect Str property depends on the type of external database being used. If your external Jet database isn't secure, leave the Source Connect Str text box empty; otherwise, type **UID=*UserID*;PWD=*Password*** to specify the user ID and password needed to open the external database. For other desktop databases, you type the product name, such as Paradox 3.5 or dBASE IV. ODBC data sources require the complete ODBC connect string.

Running a query against an external database is related to running a query against linked tables. When you link tables, the data in the tables is available at any time that your application is running. When you run a query against an external database, the connection to the external database is open only while your query is open in Design or Datasheet view. A slight performance penalty exists for running queries against an external database—each time that you run the query, Jet must make a connection to open the database. The connection is closed when you close the query.

After you specify the external database, its tables appear in the Show Table dialog's list. Figure 11.77 illustrates a query design based on tables in the external Oakmont.mdb sample database. Figure 11.78 shows the result of executing the query design of Figure 11.77.

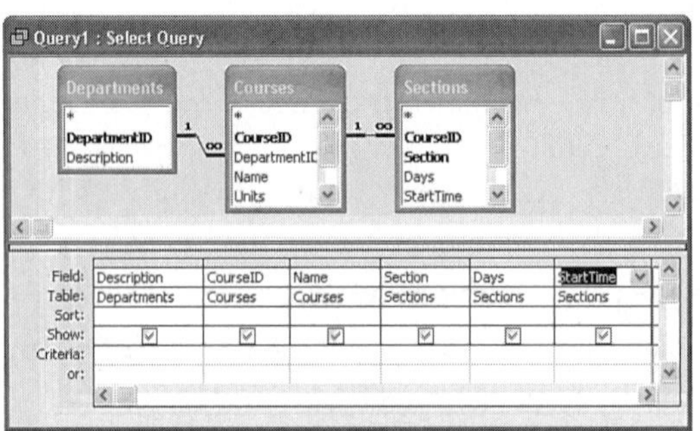

Figure 11.77 Design view of a query in an external Jet database is the same as for a query against tables in the current database. You can create joins between external and current database tables, but you can't enforce referential integrity.

Query1 : Select Query

Description	CourseID	Name	Section	Days	StartTime
Anthropology	ANTHRO110	Introduction to Cultural Anthropology	1	MWF	10:00
Anthropology	ANTHRO110	Introduction to Cultural Anthropology	2	TTh	17:00
Anthropology	ANTHRO110	Introduction to Cultural Anthropology	3	MWF	15:00
Anthropology	ANTHRO120	Introduction to Archaeology	1	MWF	11:00
Anthropology	ANTHRO120	Introduction to Archaeology	2	TTh	17:00
Anthropology	ANTHRO120	Introduction to Archaeology	3	MWF	18:00
Anthropology	ANTHRO130	Introduction to Human Evolution	1	MWF	11:00
Anthropology	ANTHRO130	Introduction to Human Evolution	2	TTh	11:00
Anthropology	ANTHRO130	Introduction to Human Evolution	3	MWF	16:00
Anthropology	ANTHRO140	Evolution of Monkeys and Apes	1	MWF	9:00
Anthropology	ANTHRO140	Evolution of Monkeys and Apes	2	TTh	14:00
Anthropology	ANTHRO140	Evolution of Monkeys and Apes	3	MWF	16:00
Anthropology	ANTHRO150	Evolution of Human Adaptation	1	MWF	11:00
Anthropology	ANTHRO150	Evolution of Human Adaptation	2	TTh	9:00
Anthropology	ANTHRO150	Evolution of Human Adaptation	3	MWF	13:00
Anthropology	ANTHRO160	Evolution of Human Sexuality	1	MWF	9:00
Anthropology	ANTHRO160	Evolution of Human Sexuality	2	TTh	9:00

Record: 1 of 1770

Figure 11.78 This datasheet displays the result set of the query of Figure 11.77 against the external Oakmont.mdb database.

NOTE

The Joins11.mdb database in the \Seua11\Chaptr10 folder of the accompanying CD-ROM includes all the sample queries of this chapter.

TROUBLESHOOTING

MISSING OBJECTS IN QUERIES

When I run my query, an Enter Parameter Value dialog appears that asks me to enter a value. I didn't specify a parameter for the query.

The Enter Parameter Value dialog appears when the Jet engine's query parser can't identify an object specified in the query or evaluate an expression. Usually, the Enter Parameter Value dialog appears because of a typographic error. Intentionally creating parameter queries is the subject of this chapter's "Designing Parameter Queries" section.

QUERIES WITH LINKED TABLES AREN'T UPDATABLE

I can't create an updatable one-to-many query with my linked dBASE or FoxPro tables despite the fact that my query displays only fields from the many side of the relationship.

You must specify (or create) primary-key indexes for each dBASE or FoxPro table that participates in the query. The field or fields that you choose must uniquely identify a record; the index doesn't allow duplicate values. Delete the attachment to the dBASE or FoxPro tables and then reattach the table with the primary-key indexes. Make sure that you specify which index is the primary-key index in the Select Unique Record Identifier dialog that appears after you attach each table.

Also, make sure that you don't include the field of the many-side table on which the join is created in the query. If you add the joined field to the field list, your query isn't updatable.

In the Real World—Optimizing Multitable Queries

Chapter 9's "In the Real World—Optimizing Query Design" section discusses the art and science of query design to optimize the presentation of information and query performance. The single-table query design recommendations apply equally to multitable queries.

This chapter is one of the longest in the book because of the importance of multitable SELECT and SQL aggregate queries in production database applications. Joins are fundamental to relational databases. You're likely to find that more than 75% of the queries you create require at least one join, and a substantial percentage need two or more joins.

Subdatasheets

Access 2003's subdatasheet feature is useful for browse-mode editing of related tables, but not much else. Browse-mode is a term for editing table data in a datasheet. As mentioned earlier in the chapter, it's easy for inexperienced users and data-entry operators to make errors when editing datasheets, so minimize or eliminate updatable datasheets and subdatasheets in production Access applications. Instead, use multitable forms—the subject of Chapter 15, "Designing Custom Multitable Forms"—that display a single record of the base table in the main form and show related records in a subform.

NOTE

> Browse-mode editing operations in multiuser and client/server environments are the bane of database administrators (DBAs) because they require multiple database connections and create a substantial amount of network traffic.

→ For more discussion of the browse-mode method and other alternatives, **see** "In the Real World—Alternatives to Action Queries," **p. 514**.

Aggregate Queries

Aggregate queries generate summary data that's critical for decision-support analysis. Aggregate queries offer quick and easy totaling of orders, sales, and other financial data for one or more time periods. Aggregation methods create large-scale data warehouses and smaller data marts, which are used in online analytical processing (OLAP) applications. Experience with SQL aggregation techniques is a necessity for understanding OLAP methodology.

TIP

> Apply "reasonableness" tests against every summary query you design. Testing becomes increasingly important as the significance of data to others grows. It's very embarrassing to find that you provided data for 1998 when your manager needed 1999 information. Become familiar with trends in the summary data generated by your queries, and compare new query result sets with previous values. If the comparison shows unexpected changes (good or bad), run a simple summary query for one or two periods to verify your data. If the summary data still fails the reasonableness test, you must review the underlying detail data (called drilling down). Familiarity with the detail data you summarize is job insurance when your manager says the "numbers don't look right to me."

Crosstab Queries

Most executives prefer the crosstab formats for time series and other comparative financial analyses. Access's Crosstab Query Wizard does a respectable job of generating simple crosstab queries for you. Designing crosstab queries that are more complex than the Wizard can handle requires that you first gain experience writing conventional summary queries.

One of the primary issues with Jet crosstab queries is that the Jet SQL reserved words, `PIVOT` and `TRANSFORM`, both of which you need to generate crosstab queries, aren't available in SQL Server's T-SQL or any other client/server SQL dialect. Thus you can't automatically upsize Access 2003 Jet applications that include crosstab queries to ADP with the Upsize Wizard. (You can't automatically upsize `UNION` queries, either.) ADP substitute SQL Server views for select queries; you create views by writing T-SQL `SELECT` queries for views, functions, or stored procedures. ADP are the subject of Chapter 20.

If your data source is a client/server RDBMS, you can use linked server tables with the Crosstab Query Wizard. Alternatively, you can generate the summary query on the server with an Access passthrough query, and then use the Jet query result set as the data source for the crosstab query. Passthrough queries, which are more network-efficient than linked tables, are one of the subjects of Chapter 19.

An alternative—and more interesting approach—is generating crosstab queries with SQL Server stored procedures. The Visual Basic 6.0 CrosstabUpsizer application, which you install by running \Seua11\Crosstab\Setup.exe on the accompanying CD-ROM, translates most Jet crosstab queries to a combination of SQL Server views, tables, and stored procedures. Figure 11.79 shows the result set of a view, table, and stored procedure generated from a slightly modified version of the qry1997QuarterlyProductOrdersCT query you created in this chapter.

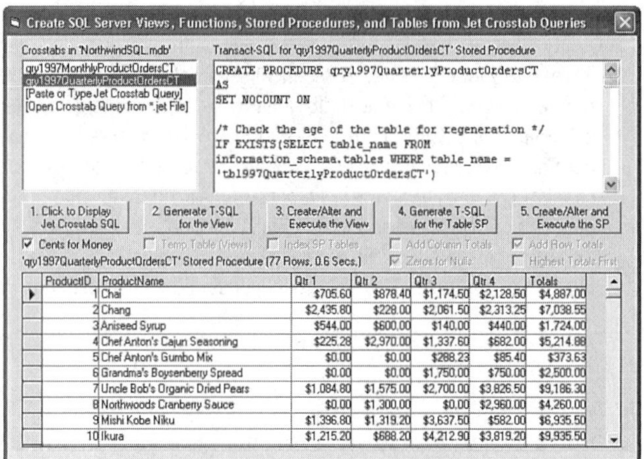

Figure 11.79
The Visual Basic 6.0 CrosstabUpsizer program (Crosstab.exe) detects Jet crosstab queries in a database and generates SQL Server views, tables, and stored procedures that emulate the Jet queries.

The wizard-like CrosstabUpsizer offers more options than Access 2003's Crosstab Query Wizard—you can round values to the nearest dollar, add row and column totals for crossfooting, and determine how often to update the crosstab data. Avoiding the aggregate calculation process by storing crosstab data in a table that's updated periodically minimizes resource consumption and speeds execution greatly, especially when the query is based on source tables with thousands of rows. The "Upsize Jet Crosstab Queries" article from *Visual Studio Magazine* (`http://www.fawcette.com/archives/premier/mgznarch/vbpj/2001/10oct01/sqlpro0110/rj0110/rj0110-1.asp`) explains the project's design principles. You can download the project and its source code from a link on page 1 of the article.

CHAPTER 12

Working with PivotTable and PivotChart Views

In this chapter

Understanding the Role of PivotTables and PivotCharts

PivotTables and PivotCharts are powerful tools for summarizing detailed data stored in Jet or SQL Server databases. Like crosstab queries, PivotTables present data generated by aggregate queries in a spreadsheet-like format that's familiar to all accounting and management personnel. PivotTable views deliver to Access users the benefits of Excel worksheets without having to launch Excel to manipulate the data. PivotChart views automatically render PivotTable views as line, bar, or area charts. PivotTables and PivotCharts accomplish the primary objective of decision-support front ends—converting online transaction processing (OLTP) data to usable information.

Office 2000 introduced the Microsoft Office PivotTable 9.0 ActiveX control—a lightweight version of the Excel 2000 PivotTable—and the Chart 9.0 control, a substitute for the Microsoft Graph OLE server application. Microsoft designed these two controls primarily for use with data access pages (DAP) and intranet applications, but you also could insert them in Access forms or reports. The original PivotTable and Chart controls were members of the Office 2000 Web Components (OWC) 9.0, which required an Office 2000 license and Internet Explorer (IE) 5+ for users to view them. These licensing restrictions made Access 2000's DAP unsuitable for public consumption via the Internet. Other deficiencies in Access 2000's DAP implementation limited their deployment on private intranets.

NOTE

Office XP changed the licensing terms for its updated OWC 10; the new terms also apply to Access 2003. Users of runtime Access 2003 applications and DAP who don't have Office 2003 licenses automatically download the runtime version of OWC 11 from the Microsoft Web site. Using the runtime version of OWC, however, limits user modification of the PivotTable view. Internet users still need IE 5+ to view PivotTables in DAP, but IE's increasing share of the browser market makes this a less onerous problem. Chapter 24, "Designing and Deploying Data Access Pages," covers the ramifications of read-only DAP for users without OWC licenses.

PivotTables replace embedded Excel PivotTables, and PivotCharts supplement or replace Access charts embedded by the Chart Wizard. Excel PivotTables require a local copy of Excel.exe and the Chart Wizard needs Office 2002's Graph.exe to act as Object Linking and Embedding (OLE) 2+ servers. Internet protocols and Web browsers don't support OLE. If you subscribe to Microsoft's Internet-centric view of the world, original Excel PivotTables and OLE-based charts are obsolete. In the real world, Office PivotTables outperform their earlier Excel counterparts, but conventional Access charts you create with the Chart Wizard have several features that PivotCharts don't offer.

→ To add charts or graphs to forms with the Chart Wizard, **see** "Using the Chart Wizard to Create an Unlinked Graph," **p. 704**.

Access 2002 added two new views to tables, queries, and forms: PivotTable and PivotChart. These views are available in conventional (Jet) Access applications and Access data projects (ADP). PivotTables and PivotCharts are interdependent; when you design a PivotChart view, you create a corresponding PivotTable view, and vice-versa. You can't restrict tables and queries to specific views—such as PivotTable, PivotChart, or both—but you can set the default view. You can set the default view and limit views of forms to include or exclude Pivot... views.

The behavior of the PivotTable and PivotChart views of forms is identical to those of tables or queries. You can use the AutoForm: PivotTable and AutoForm: PivotChart Wizards to create these views of forms from a table or query you specify. Northwind.mdb's sample Sales Analysis form, for example, alternately displays PivotChart and PivotTable form views of a query in a subform.

Forms, reports, and DAP can contain OWC PivotTable and PivotCharts as conventional ActiveX control objects. You can set the properties of these controls in forms and reports with Visual Basic for Applications (VBA). You use VBScript or ECMAScript (JavaScript) to program PivotTable and PivotChart controls in DAP. You can't, however, program these two controls in PivotTable or PivotChart views of tables, queries, or forms.

NOTE

> The limitations of PivotTable and PivotChart views might cause you to wonder why this chapter is in Part III, "Transforming Data with Queries and PivotTables," rather than in Part IV, "Designing Forms and Reports," or Part VI, "Publishing Data to Intranets and the Internet." The reason is that well-designed queries–usually based on multiple tables–are fundamental to generating meaningful data for presentation in PivotTables and PivotCharts. The query and view design techniques you learn in this chapter apply equally to PivotTables and PivotCharts contained in conventional Access and ADP forms, as well as in DAP.

SLICING AND DICING DATA WITH PIVOTTABLES

PivotTables closely resemble Access crosstab query datasheets, which are one of the main topics of Chapter 11, "Creating Multitable and Crosstab Queries." Both PivotTables and crosstab queries employ aggregate functions—sum, average, count, standard deviation, variance, and the like—to summarize data, but PivotTables can handle the entire aggregation process. This enables PivotTables to selectively display the detail data behind subtotals and grand totals.

Crosstab queries are limited to creating row-by-row subtotals, with optional row (but not column) totals. PivotTables not only provide subtotals but also supply grand totals for rows and columns, plus crossfoot totals. *Crossfooting* is an accounting term for testing the accuracy of a set of numerical values by comparing grand totals calculated by row and by column. One of the primary advantages of PivotTables over crosstab datasheets is that the user, not the database developer who designed the query, can control data presentation.

PivotTables let you swap axes and apply filters to the underlying data. Like Jet filters for tables and queries, you can use PivotTable filters to remove extraneous or unneeded data from the current view.

TIP

> Substitute PivotTables for crosstab queries when your data presentation needs crossfooting or you want to apply sophisticated report formatting to the presentation. It's usually much faster to use PivotTable features to generate row totals, subtotals, and grand totals than it is to use crosstab queries. Another advantage of PivotTables is that users can set the amount of detail information that appears in the report and then generate their own graphs or charts from the data.

CREATING THE QUERY FOR A SAMPLE PIVOTTABLE VIEW

Queries designed for users who are accustomed to using Excel PivotTable should offer a high degree of flexibility for slicing and dicing the data. For example, sales and marketing managers are likely to want to explore the total value of orders received each quarter by salesperson, customer, product, country, or any combination of these selection criteria. Thus, your query must supply more than the ordinary amount of data to the PivotTable.

TIP

> Don't assign Caption property values to fields of tables you intend to use with queries for PivotTables and PivotCharts. You can't override the Caption property with query aliases in Access 2003.
>
> To override the Caption property value in aggregate queries, apply a function to the field that doesn't change its values, such as **`Trim`** for text fields and **`Round`** for numeric fields. Alias the column with an `AS Caption` modifier. This workaround causes conventional `SELECT` queries to not be updatable, but most PivotTables are based on aggregate queries, which aren't updatable under any condition.

12

→ For more information the Caption property issue, **see** "Changing the Names of Query Column Headers," **p. 343**.

One of the most common forms of PivotTables displays time-series data, such as orders or sales by quarter for one or more years. To design a time-series query that supplies the underlying data for a PivotTable to display the quarterly value of orders by salesperson and country, do the following:

1. Open a new query in Design view in Northwind.mdb or your working copy of the database.
2. Add the Employees and Orders tables, and the Order Subtotals query.
3. Drag the LastName field of the Employees table to the query grid, followed in order by the ShipCountry and OrderDate fields of the Orders table, and the Subtotal field of the Order Subtotals query.

4. Add a **Between #1/1/1997# And #12/31/1997#** criterion to the OrderDate column to restrict the data to the last full year for which order data exists in Northwind.mdb. Clear the Show check box for this column.

5. Drag the OrderDate field from the Orders table to create a new column to the left of the existing OrderDate field. Replace the content of the Field cell of this column with **1997 Quarter: Format([OrderDate],"q")** to create a calculated column to display the number of the calendar quarter in which the order was received.

6. Place the cursor at the beginning of the LastName field, and replace LastName with **Name: Trim(LastName)** to add an alias to the field. Replace ShipCountry with **Country: Trim(ShipCountry)** and add an **Orders:** alias to the Subtotals field. Your query design appears as shown in Figure 12.1.

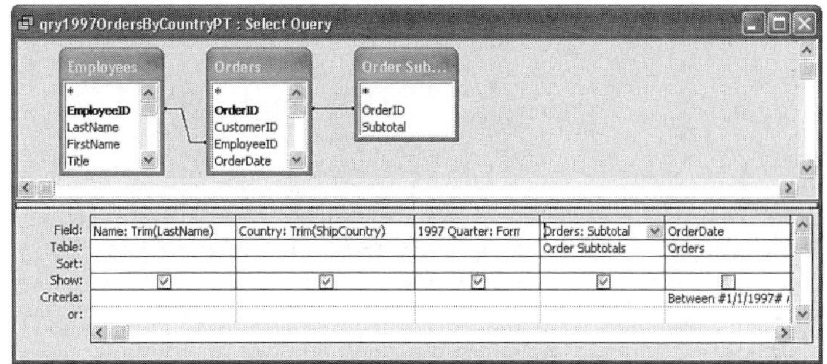

Figure 12.1
This query design provides detail data suitable for analyzing employee sales by country.

7. Run the query to check your work (see Figure 12.2), and save the query as **qry1997OrdersByCountryPT**.

Figure 12.2
The Datasheet view of the query design of Figure 12.1 shows the altered field captions and lists the 408 orders received by Northwind Traders in 1997.

Query1 : Select Query

Name	Country	1997 Quarter	Orders
Davolio	UK	1	$3,063.00
Davolio	USA	1	$3,868.60
Callahan	Austria	1	$2,713.50
Peacock	Austria	1	$855.01
Fuller	Italy	1	$1,591.25
Davolio	Venezuela	1	$400.00
King	Brazil	1	$1,830.78
Fuller	Germany	1	$1,194.00
Callahan	France	1	$1,622.40
Leverling	Argentina	1	$319.20
Leverling	Canada	1	$802.00
Dodsworth	Canada	1	$966.80
Callahan	Finland	1	$334.80
Leverling	France	1	$2,123.20
Fuller	Brazil	1	$224.83
Leverling	USA	1	$102.40
Callahan	Finland	1	$720.00

Record: 1 of 408

DESIGNING THE PIVOTTABLE VIEW OF THE SAMPLE QUERY

Click the PivotTable View button in the toolbar; the main Access toolbar changes to the PivotTable toolbar. An empty PivotTable view opens with the PivotTable Field List window active and empty Filter Fields, Column Fields, Row Fields, and Totals or Detail Fields drop zones (see Figure 12.3).

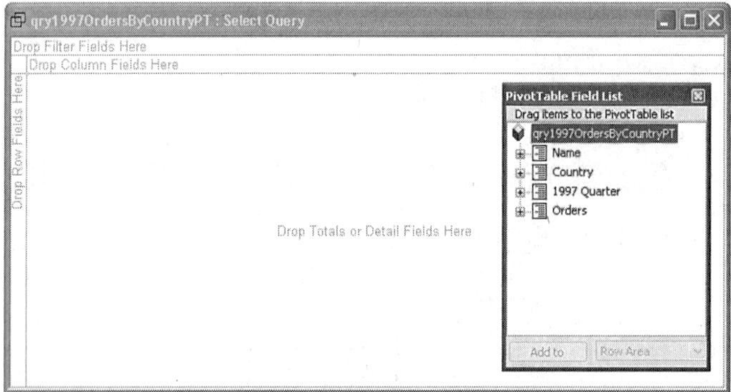

Figure 12.3
When you open a new PivotTable view of a table or query, the field list of the source table or query has the focus.

> **TIP**
>
> If the PivotTable Field List isn't visible, click the Field List button on the toolbar.

You drag fields from the PivotTable Field List to the appropriate drop zone, as follows:

- **Column Fields**—Usually hold date-based fields to create a left-to-right time series. If you're not creating a time-series PivotTable, you can select any appropriate field of the table or query. As a rule, the field having the fewest number of rows belongs in columns.
- **Row Fields**—Hold one or more fields that display data by attribute(s). Adding row fields lets you increase the degree of detail displayed by the PivotTable. Increasing the amount of detail data shown is called *drilling down* or *drill-down*.
- **Totals or Detail Fields**—As the central area of the empty PivotTable, these fields display the crosstabulated data. This drop area accepts only fields having numeric values or fields for which you only want to display a count of records.
- **Filter Fields**—One or more optional fields that let you restrict the number of fields that appear in columns, rows, or both. In most cases, you filter data by column or row fields, not fields dropped in the Filter Fields zone. (A field can appear only in one drop zone of a PivotTable.)

GENERATING THE INITIAL PIVOTTABLE

To create the initial PivotTable view of the qry1997OrdersByCountryPT query, do the following:

1. Drag the 1997 Quarter field to the Column Fields drop zone. As the field symbol enters the drop zone, a blue border appears (see Figure 12.4). When you drop the field by releasing the mouse button, a 1997 Quarter filter button appears on the first row, and four columns display quarter numbers 1 through 4. PivotTables automatically add a Grand Total column to the right of the last column you add from the field list.

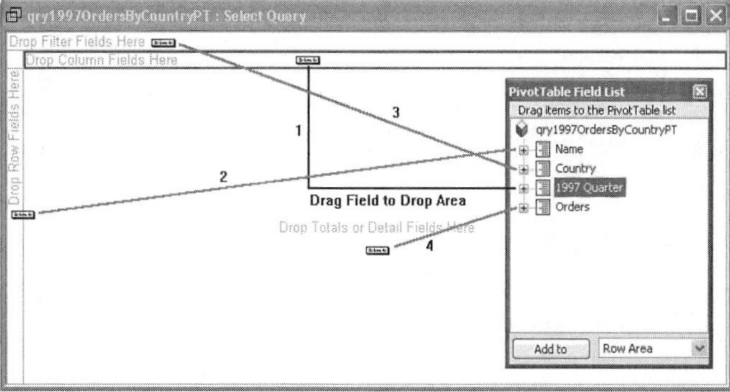

Figure 12.4 When you drag a field from the PivotTable Field List to a drop zone, the drop zone gains a thicker blue border.

2. Drag the Name field to the Row Fields drop zone, the Orders field to the Totals or Detail Fields drop zone, and the Country field to the Filter Fields drop zone. The PivotTable appears with the rows displaying detail values, as shown in Figure 12.5.

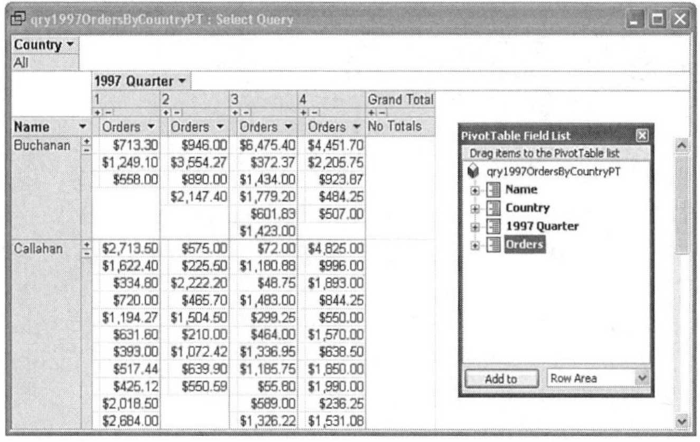

Name	1 Orders	2 Orders	3 Orders	4 Orders	Grand Total No Totals
Buchanan	$713.30	$946.00	$6,475.40	$4,451.70	
	$1,249.10	$3,554.27	$372.37	$2,205.75	
	$558.00	$890.00	$1,434.00	$923.87	
		$2,147.40	$1,779.20	$484.25	
			$601.83	$507.00	
			$1,423.00		
Callahan	$2,713.50	$575.00	$72.00	$4,825.00	
	$1,622.40	$225.50	$1,180.88	$996.00	
	$334.80	$2,222.20	$48.75	$1,893.00	
	$720.00	$465.70	$1,483.00	$844.25	
	$1,194.27	$1,504.50	$299.25	$550.00	
	$631.60	$210.00	$464.00	$1,570.00	
	$393.00	$1,072.42	$1,336.95	$638.50	
	$517.44	$639.90	$1,185.75	$1,850.00	
	$425.12	$550.59	$55.80	$1,990.00	
	$2,018.50		$589.00	$236.25	
	$2,684.00		$1,326.22	$1,531.08	

Figure 12.5 After dragging the four fields to the locations shown here, the default PivotTable view includes detail values for rows. In this case, the amount of each order obtained by the salesperson appears in the expanded quarter columns.

12

3. You can't identify the countries for the orders in the columns, so drag the Country field from the Filter Fields drop zone to the Name button to group the orders by country. Close the PivotTable Field list.

4. Click the Name button to select it, and click the Bold button on the Formatting toolbar to increase the contrast of the selected column (see Figure 12.6).

Figure 12.6 Moving the Country field from the Filter Fields to the right of the Name field displays the orders for each country.

qry1997OrdersByCountryPT : Select Query

Drop Filter Fields Here

		1997 Quarter				
		1	2	3	4	Grand Total
Name	Country	Orders	Orders	Orders	Orders	No Totals
Buchanan	Belgium	$713.30	$946.00	$1,434.00		
	Brazil			$372.37 $1,779.20		
	France				$484.25	
	Germany		$3,554.27 $2,147.40	$1,423.00	$923.87	
	Mexico	$1,249.10				
	Portugal	$558.00				
	Sweden			$601.83		
	USA		$890.00	$6,475.40	$4,451.70 $2,205.75 $507.00	
	Total					
Callahan	Argentina		$225.50			
	Austria	$2,713.50	$550.59		$2,158.00	
	Brazil	$1,194.27 $1,472.00			$550.00 $236.25 $1,531.08	

TIP

> If the Formatting toolbar isn't visible, choose View, Toolbars, Formatting (PivotTable/PivotChart) to add it.

12

Reducing the Level of Detail and Adding Grand Totals

Including amounts for each order in the PivotTable shows excessive detail. One approach for this example is to alter the query design to an aggregate (summary) query and group the individual orders by salesperson, country, and quarter.

To modify the query, regenerate the PivotTable data, and add grand totals, do this:

1. Change to Design view.

2. Click the Totals button to group the query data by LastName, ShipCountry, and 1997 Quarter.

3. Open the Total cell for the Subtotal column and choose Sum as the SQL aggregate function. Open the OrderDate field and select Where. Your modified aggregate query design appears as shown in Figure 12.7.

4. Run the query to verify the design (see Figure 12.8).

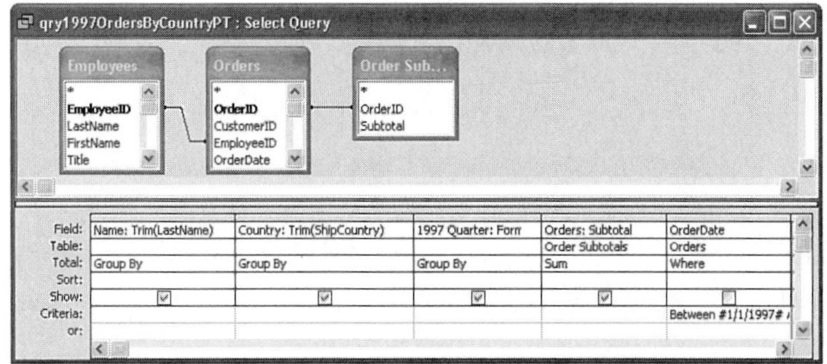

Figure 12.7 Change the query design to an aggregate query to sum individual orders by LastName, ShipCountry, and 1997 Quarter columns.

qry1997OrdersByCountryPT : Select Query

Name	Country	1997 Quarter	Orders
Buchanan	Belgium	1	$713.30
Buchanan	Belgium	2	$946.00
Buchanan	Belgium	3	$1,434.00
Buchanan	Brazil	3	$2,151.57
Buchanan	France	4	$484.25
Buchanan	Germany	2	$5,701.67
Buchanan	Germany	3	$1,423.00
Buchanan	Germany	4	$923.87
Buchanan	Mexico	1	$1,249.10
Buchanan	Portugal	1	$558.00
Buchanan	Sweden	3	$601.83
Buchanan	USA	2	$890.00
Buchanan	USA	3	$6,475.40
Buchanan	USA	4	$7,164.45
Callahan	Argentina	2	$225.50

Record: 1 of 251

Figure 12.8 The result set of the query design has 251 records; the original query had 408 records (refer to Figure 12.2).

5. Return to PivotTable view, which now displays the summary data.

qry1997OrdersByCountryPT : Select Query

Drop Filter Fields Here

		1997 Quarter				
		1	2	3	4	Grand Total
Name	Country	Orders	Orders	Orders	Orders	No Totals
Buchanan	Belgium	$713.30	$946.00	$1,434.00		
	Brazil			$2,151.57		
	France				$484.25	
	Germany		$5,701.67	$1,423.00	$923.87	
	Mexico	$1,249.10				
	Portugal	$558.00				
	Sweden			$601.83		
	USA		$890.00	$6,475.40	$7,164.45	
	Total					
Callahan	Argentina		$225.50			
	Austria	$2,713.50	$550.59		$2,158.00	
	Brazil	$2,666.27			$2,317.33	
	Canada		$639.90		$638.50	
	Denmark			$48.75		
	Finland	$4,131.80				
	France	$2,047.52		$1,015.05		

Figure 12.9 Converting the PivotTable source query to an aggregate query results in a PivotTable with a single value for the total amount of orders from each country.

6. To add Grand Total values, click one of the Orders buttons to select all the Quarter columns, click the AutoCalc button, and select Sum from the aggregate functions list.

Adding Grand Totals also adds Totals and Sum of Orders items to the PivotTable Field List and totals rows to each Country entry (see Figure 12.10). Close the PivotTable Field List.

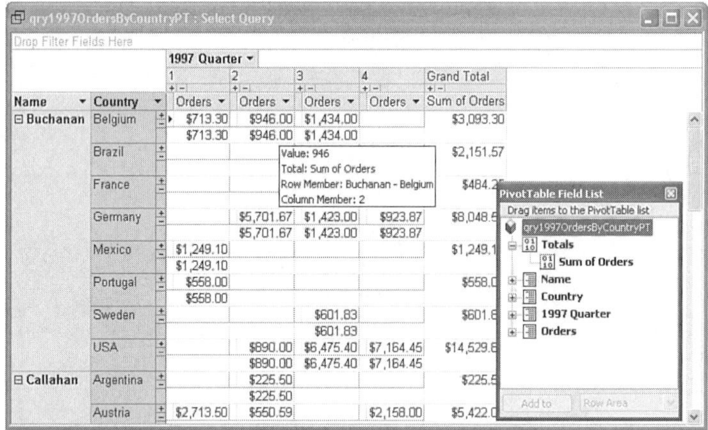

Figure 12.10 Adding Grand Totals to the PivotTable also adds Sum of Order totals to the Country entries.

7. Click the Country button and click Hide Details to display only a single Sum of Orders value for each employee and country. The PivotTable now displays only a single row per country for each employee. Countries from which the employee obtained no orders during the year don't appear.
8. With the Country field selected, click the Subtotals button to add a Totals row for each employee (see Figure 12.11).

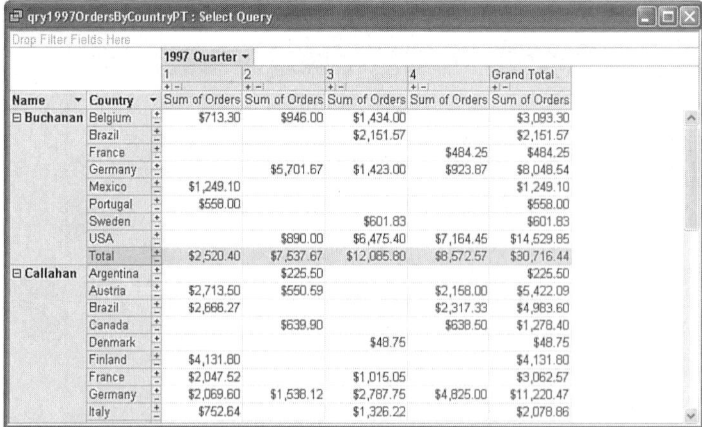

Figure 12.11 Hiding detail rows and adding subtotals for each employee results in a more meaningful PivotTable presentation of your data. Bold formatting is applied to the Total label for emphasis.

9. Click the Name button to select the column, and click the Collapse button to remove Country values for the employees and display the summary entries for all employees

without scrolling (see Figure 12.12). Clicking the adjacent Expand and Collapse buttons toggles display of detail columns.

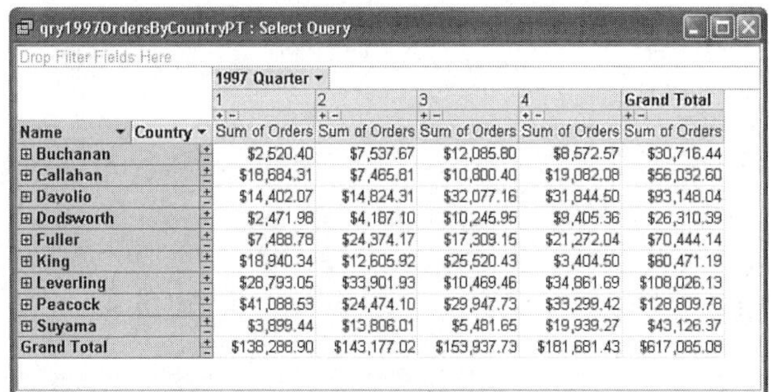

qry1997OrdersByCountryPT : Select Query

Drop Filter Fields Here

		1997 Quarter				
		1	2	3	4	Grand Total
Name	Country	Sum of Orders	Sum of Orders	Sum of Orders	Sum of Orders	Sum of Orders
Buchanan		$2,520.40	$7,537.67	$12,085.80	$8,572.57	$30,716.44
Callahan		$18,684.31	$7,465.81	$10,800.40	$19,082.08	$56,032.60
Davolio		$14,402.07	$14,824.31	$32,077.16	$31,844.50	$93,148.04
Dodsworth		$2,471.98	$4,187.10	$10,245.95	$9,405.36	$26,310.39
Fuller		$7,488.78	$24,374.17	$17,309.15	$21,272.04	$70,444.14
King		$18,940.34	$12,605.92	$25,520.43	$3,404.50	$60,471.19
Leverling		$28,793.05	$33,901.93	$10,469.46	$34,861.69	$108,026.13
Peacock		$41,088.53	$24,474.10	$29,947.73	$33,299.42	$128,809.78
Suyama		$3,899.44	$13,806.01	$5,481.65	$19,939.27	$43,126.37
Grand Total		$138,288.90	$143,177.02	$153,937.73	$181,681.43	$617,085.08

Figure 12.12 Collapsing the Name column eliminates the Country field detail and displays summary data only. Bold formatting is applied to the two Grand Totals labels.

TIP

You can expand the display for a single employee by clicking the small Show/Hide Details (+) button to the left of the employee's name. The Show/Hide Details button toggles the + and - states.

FILTERING PIVOTTABLE CATEGORY VALUES

Worldwide sales data probably satisfies top management, but regional managers might want to display only orders received from a particular area, such as North America, Europe, or Scandinavia. By default, all field values appear in PivotTable rows or columns and are included in all calculated values, such as totals.

You can filter the PivotTable to display only selected values of a category field, such as Country, by following these steps:

1. Expand the PivotTable display to include the field on which you want to filter. For this example, select the Name field, and click the Expand button to display the Countries column. (You might need to reopen the Field list to access the Name column.)
2. Click the arrow of the field button to filter, Country for this example, in order to open the field value list. The list contains an item for each field value.
3. Click the (All) check box to deselect all fields.
4. Mark the check boxes of the field values you want to include—Canada, Mexico, and USA for this example.
5. Click OK to close the list and apply the filter.

Figure 12.13 illustrates the sample PivotTable with only the Canada, Mexico, and USA fields selected. To return to displaying all fields, open the list and click the (All) check box.

12

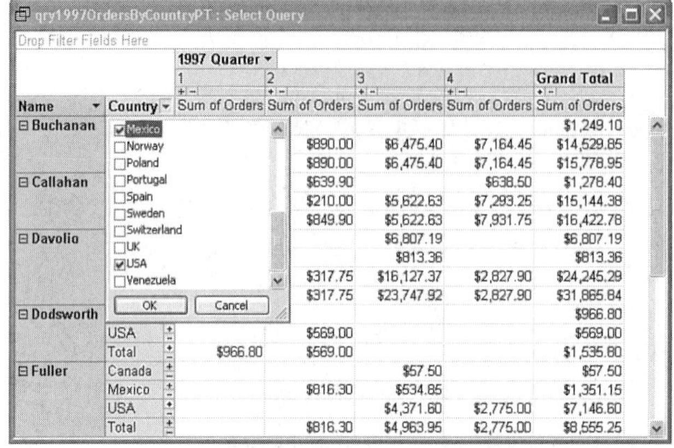

Figure 12.13 This filtered PivotTable view restricts the visible values to orders received from Canada, Mexico, and the USA.

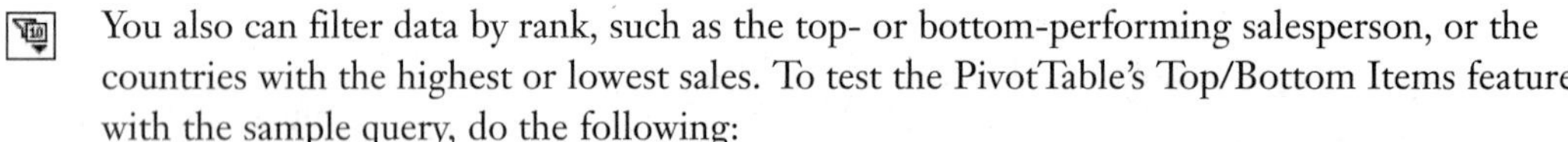

You also can filter data by rank, such as the top- or bottom-performing salesperson, or the countries with the highest or lowest sales. To test the PivotTable's Top/Bottom Items feature with the sample query, do the following:

1. Select the Name column, click the Show Top/Bottom Items button, choose Show Only the Top, and choose 1 from the submenu. The PivotTable displays data only for Janet Leverling, the top salesperson for North America orders.
2. Click the Show Top/Bottom Items button, choose Show Only the Bottom, and choose 1 from the submenu. The PivotTable shows Anne Dodsworth occupies the lowest rung on the North America sales ladder.
3. Remove the filter on the Names column by clicking the Show Top/Bottom Items button and choosing Show All.

TIP

Use the AutoFilter toolbar button to toggle between filtered and unfiltered display quickly.

4. Select the Country column, click the Show Top/Bottom Items button, choose Show Only the Top, and choose 2 from the submenu. The PivotTable displays data for Germany and the USA for all employees (see Figure 12.14).
5. Remove the filter on the Country column by clicking the Show Top/Bottom Items button and choosing Show All.

If you select Other in the list of values, the Properties dialog opens to the Filter and Group page, where you can set custom filtering options by numeric or percentage rank.

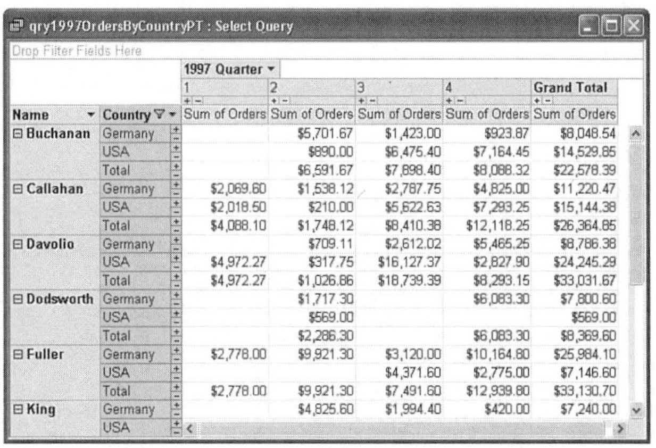

qry1997OrdersByCountryPT : Select Query

Drop Filter Fields Here

Name	Country	1997 Quarter 1 Sum of Orders	2 Sum of Orders	3 Sum of Orders	4 Sum of Orders	Grand Total Sum of Orders
Buchanan	Germany		$5,701.67	$1,423.00	$923.87	$8,048.54
	USA		$890.00	$6,475.40	$7,164.45	$14,529.85
	Total		$6,591.67	$7,898.40	$8,088.32	$22,578.39
Callahan	Germany	$2,069.60	$1,538.12	$2,787.75	$4,825.00	$11,220.47
	USA	$2,018.50	$210.00	$5,622.63	$7,293.25	$15,144.38
	Total	$4,088.10	$1,748.12	$8,410.38	$12,118.25	$26,364.85
Davolio	Germany		$709.11	$2,612.02	$5,465.25	$8,786.38
	USA	$4,972.27	$317.75	$16,127.37	$2,827.90	$24,245.29
	Total	$4,972.27	$1,026.86	$18,739.39	$8,293.15	$33,031.67
Dodsworth	Germany		$1,717.30		$6,083.30	$7,800.60
	USA		$569.00			$569.00
	Total		$2,286.30		$6,083.30	$8,369.60
Fuller	Germany	$2,778.00	$9,921.30	$3,120.00	$10,164.80	$25,984.10
	USA			$4,371.60	$2,775.00	$7,146.60
	Total	$2,778.00	$9,921.30	$7,491.60	$12,939.80	$33,130.70
King	Germany		$4,825.60	$1,994.40	$420.00	$7,240.00
	USA					

Figure 12.14 The PivotTable's Top/Bottom Items feature lets you filter items by the value rank. Germany and the USA rank by order amount as the top two countries.

INCREASING THE LEVEL OF DETAIL FOR DRILL-DOWN

The preceding section demonstrates the capability to reduce to a manageable level the amount of detail information displayed by PivotTable. Total amounts of the orders obtained by employees for each country might satisfy the vice-president of sales, but sales managers and salespersons might want to review values of individual orders. Commissioned salespersons want order number and date information to ensure that all orders they book are assigned to them.

Providing additional drill-down information requires you to modify the underlying sample query and regenerate the value data, as follows:

1. Return to Query Design view.
2. Click the Totals button to remove the Totals row and eliminate data grouping.
3. Drag the OrderID and OrderDate fields of the Orders table field list to the right of the LastName field. (The column sequence isn't important.)

4. Return to PivotTable view, and click the Field List button to display the PivotTable Field List, which now has Order ID, Order Date, Order Date by Week, and Order Date by Month items added.
5. Drag the Order ID field to the immediate left of the Orders button. Drag the Order Date field to the immediate right of the Order ID button (see Figure 12.15), and close the PivotTable Field List. If the Order… fields aren't in the correct sequence, drag their buttons to the proper relative position.
6. Click the Hide Details button to reduce the PivotTable's level of detail.

TIP

Be judicious when increasing the detail level of PivotTables by eliminating grouping in your query. The later "Optimizing Performance of PivotTables" section describes performance problems that result from large query result sets.

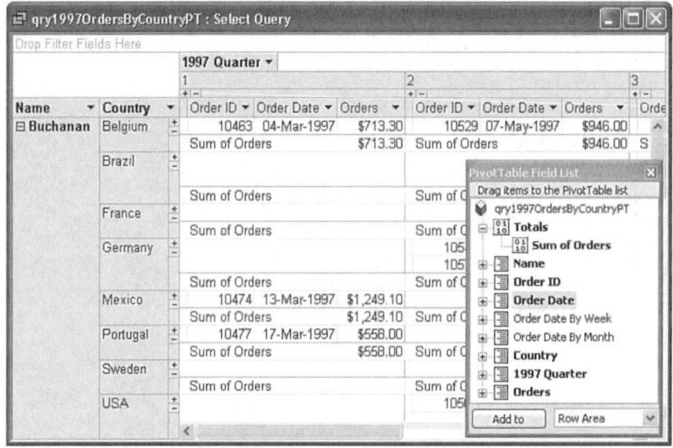

Figure 12.15
The PivotTable now displays Order ID and Order Date values for each order.

CHANGING FILL/BACKGROUND AND TEXT COLORS

You can increase the contrast of the PivotTable's display or emphasize elements by changing their color with the Fill/Back Color tool of the PivotTable Format toolbar. (The background color of column and row header buttons is much darker under Windows 2000 than Windows XP.) For example, you can remove the gray tint from the Name, Country, and Quarter lists by selecting each field in sequence, clicking the Fill/Back Color tool, and choosing white in the color picker (see Figure 12.16). Alternatively, you can apply a new color scheme to the display.

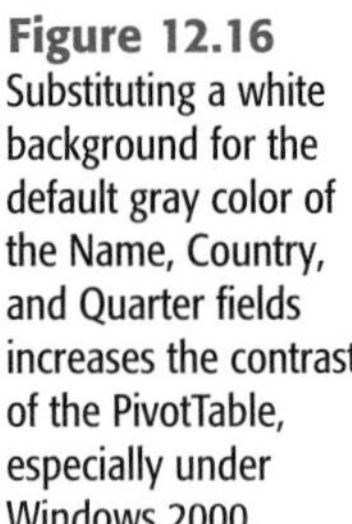

Figure 12.16
Substituting a white background for the default gray color of the Name, Country, and Quarter fields increases the contrast of the PivotTable, especially under Windows 2000.

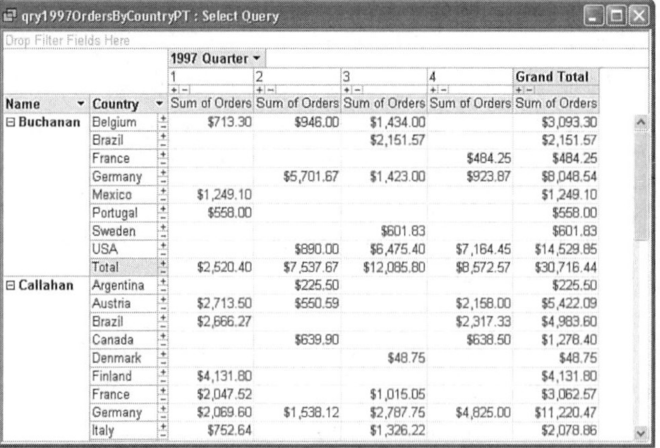

qry1997OrdersByCountryPT : Select Query

Drop Filter Fields Here

Name	Country	1997 Quarter 1 Sum of Orders	2 Sum of Orders	3 Sum of Orders	4 Sum of Orders	Grand Total Sum of Orders
Buchanan	Belgium	$713.30	$946.00	$1,434.00		$3,093.30
	Brazil			$2,151.57		$2,151.57
	France				$484.25	$484.25
	Germany		$5,701.67	$1,423.00	$923.87	$8,048.54
	Mexico	$1,249.10				$1,249.10
	Portugal	$558.00				$558.00
	Sweden			$601.83		$601.83
	USA		$890.00	$6,475.40	$7,164.45	$14,529.85
	Total	$2,520.40	$7,537.67	$12,085.80	$8,572.57	$30,716.44
Callahan	Argentina		$225.50			$225.50
	Austria	$2,713.50	$550.59		$2,158.00	$5,422.09
	Brazil	$2,666.27			$2,317.33	$4,983.60
	Canada		$639.90		$638.50	$1,278.40
	Denmark			$48.75		$48.75
	Finland	$4,131.80				$4,131.80
	France	$2,047.52		$1,015.05		$3,062.57
	Germany	$2,069.60	$1,538.12	$2,787.75	$4,825.00	$11,220.47
	Italy	$752.64		$1,326.22		$2,078.86

EXCHANGING PIVOTTABLE AXES AND CATEGORY HIERARCHIES

The term PivotTable derives from the capability to exchange (pivot) the x- (horizontal) and y- (vertical) axes of the table. PivotTables also let you exchange the hierarchy of category columns, which often is more useful than pivoting the table. If you're more interested in sales by country than by employee, drag the sample PivotTable's Country button to the left of the Name button. The All Orders values now represent quarterly sales by country (see Figure 12.17).

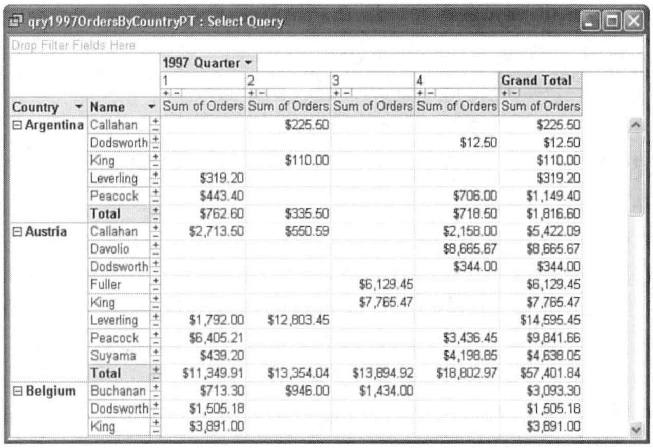

Figure 12.17
Interchanging the Country and Names fields recalculates the PivotTable to display values for quarterly sales by country. Details are hidden with the Hide Details button in this example.

qry1997OrdersByCountryPT : Select Query

Drop Filter Fields Here

		1997 Quarter				
		1	2	3	4	Grand Total
Country	Name	Sum of Orders	Sum of Orders	Sum of Orders	Sum of Orders	Sum of Orders
Argentina	Callahan		$225.50			$225.50
	Dodsworth				$12.50	$12.50
	King		$110.00			$110.00
	Leverling	$319.20				$319.20
	Peacock	$443.40			$706.00	$1,149.40
	Total	$762.60	$335.50		$718.50	$1,816.60
Austria	Callahan	$2,713.50	$550.59		$2,158.00	$5,422.09
	Davolio				$8,665.67	$8,665.67
	Dodsworth				$344.00	$344.00
	Fuller			$6,129.45		$6,129.45
	King			$7,765.47		$7,765.47
	Leverling	$1,792.00	$12,803.45			$14,595.45
	Peacock	$6,405.21			$3,436.45	$9,841.66
	Suyama	$439.20			$4,198.85	$4,638.05
	Total	$11,349.91	$13,354.04	$13,894.92	$18,802.97	$57,401.84
Belgium	Buchanan	$713.30	$946.00	$1,434.00		$3,093.30
	Dodsworth	$1,505.18				$1,505.18
	King	$3,891.00				$3,891.00

TIP

If you accidentally drag the field out of the PivotTable window, which removes the field from the PivotTable, open the Field List and drag the missing field to the proper location.

Interchanging the axes lets you view the data from a different perspective. In many cases, users want data presented in a familiar format. For example, the sales manager might be accustomed to comparing the quarter-by-quarter performance of his or her salespeople with quarterly data in rows, not columns. To exchange the Name and 1997 Quarter axes, drag the Name button to its original position (left of the Country button), drag the 1997 Quarter button to the left of the Name button, and then drag the Name button to the empty Column Fields drop zone. Optionally, drag the Country field to the Filter Fields drop zone (see Figure 12.18).

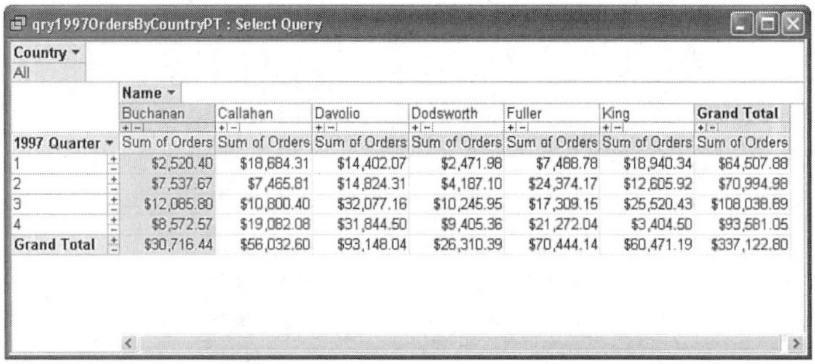

Figure 12.18
Rotating the axes of a PivotTable lets you conform data presentation to users' preference. In this example, the Employees field includes only the first six employees in the filter list.

qry1997OrdersByCountryPT : Select Query

Country: All

	Name						
	Buchanan	Callahan	Davolio	Dodsworth	Fuller	King	Grand Total
1997 Quarter	Sum of Orders	Sum of Orders	Sum of Orders	Sum of Orders	Sum of Orders	Sum of Orders	Sum of Orders
1	$2,520.40	$18,684.31	$14,402.07	$2,471.98	$7,488.78	$18,940.34	$64,507.88
2	$7,537.67	$7,465.81	$14,824.31	$4,187.10	$24,374.17	$12,605.92	$70,994.98
3	$12,085.80	$10,800.40	$32,077.16	$10,245.95	$17,309.15	$25,520.43	$108,038.89
4	$8,572.57	$19,082.08	$31,844.50	$9,405.36	$21,272.04	$3,404.50	$93,581.05
Grand Total	$30,716.44	$56,032.60	$93,148.04	$26,310.39	$70,444.14	$60,471.19	$337,122.80

12

Setting PivotTable Property Values

The Properties dialog has four pages of PivotTable property settings for active elements. Right-click a field, and choose Properties to open the dialog. Following are brief descriptions of the purpose of each page:

- **Format**—Lets you select a field name, and select the font name, size, color, attributes (bold, italic, underlined), and justification (left, right, and centered). You also can set the background color, column width, and sort the column or row in ascending (default) or descending order. The value in the Select list determines the field to which properties you set in the Filter and Group and Captions pages applies (see Figure 12.19, left).
- **Filter and Group**—Enables customer top/bottom value filtering of the field you select on the Format page. If you have ungrouped items in a field, you can use the Grouping controls to aggregate them (see Figure 12.19, right).

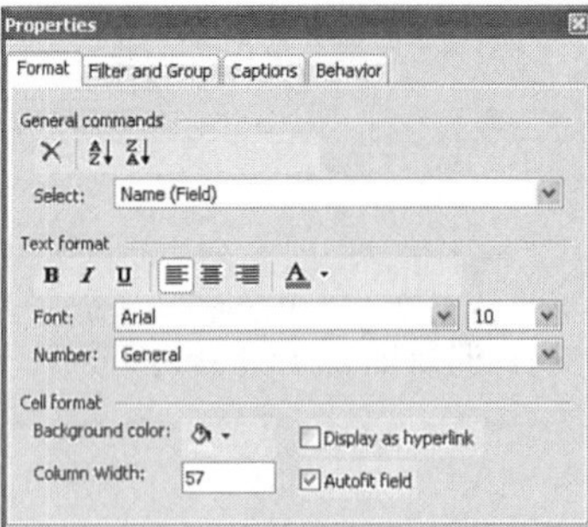

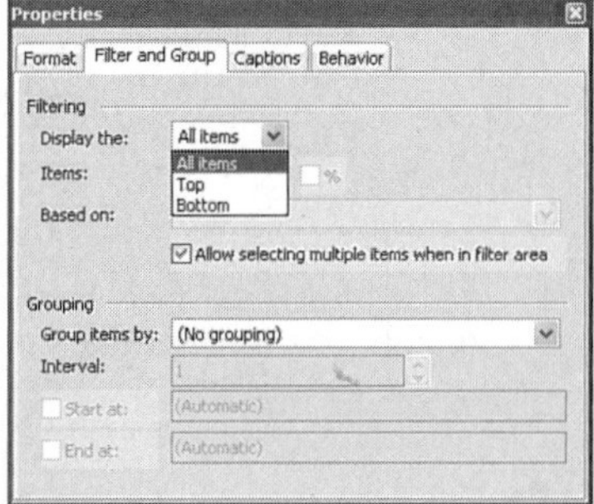

Figure 12.19
The Format (left) page's Select value determines the field to which the settings of the Filter and Group (right) and Captions pages apply.

- **Captions**—Lets you change the caption for the field you selected in the Format page. For example, you can change Sum of Orders caption to All Orders, Order ID to Number, and Order Date to Date. The captions page also has a list of uninteresting property values (see Figure 12.20, left).
- **Behavior**—Options apply to the entire PivotTable. You can hide the Show/Hide Details buttons of fields and the drop zones. In the case of the PivotTable of the sample query, you can hide the Filter Fields drop zone, because there is no suitable field available to drop in the zone. PivotTable views of tables and queries don't have a title bar or built-in toolbar, so two of the check boxes are disabled (see Figure 12.20, right). PivotTable view of forms have a title bar. When you add PivotTables to DAP, the title bar and toolbar appear in Design view and in the browser, unless otherwise specified.
- **Report**—These options also apply to the entire PivotTable. The Report page only appears when you right-click an empty region of the PivotTable. The most important options are Always Display Empty Rows and Empty Columns. Marking either of these check boxes generates a row or column, regardless of whether a value is present. Accept the default options, unless you have a good reason to do otherwise.

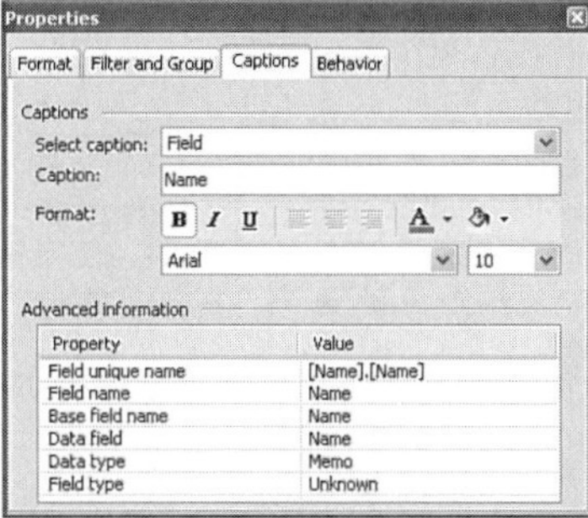

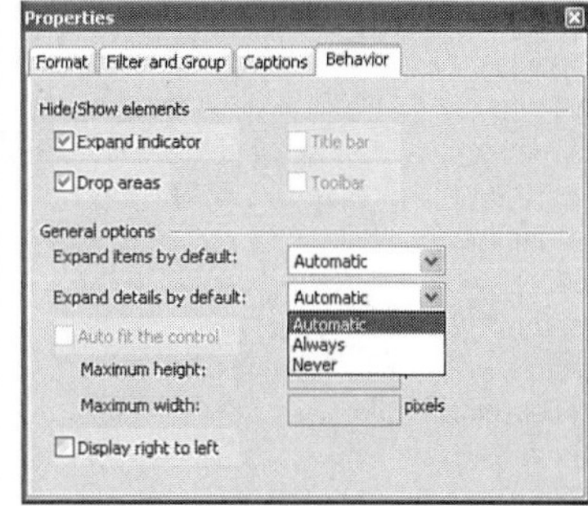

Figure 12.20
The most important feature of the Captions page (left) is the ability to change the caption of any PivotTable field. The options you set in the Behavior page (right) apply to all fields.

If you right-click an empty area of the PivotTable and choose Properties, only the Captions, Report, and Behavior pages appear. In this case, the Captions page lets you change captions for the four drop zones and the title bar.

TIP

> To make PivotTable view the default for your query, change to Design mode, open the Query Properties dialog, and change the Default View property value to PivotTable.
>
> To print a PivotTable, choose File, Print in PivotTable view. You might need to widen the columns slightly to print Grand Total columns correctly.

EXPORTING THE PIVOTTABLE TO EXCEL

You can export the PivotTable as a *FileName*.htm file, together with supporting .xml, .htm, and .css files, to a pseudo-PivotTable in an Excel workbook. This isn't a very exciting feature, because the process exports the data as a static XML rowset (Cachedata.xml in the ...*FileName*_files folder). The temporary workbook is read-only and doesn't update as the underlying data from the query changes.

Click the Export to Microsoft Excel button to generate the PivotTable workbook. Figure 12.21 shows the default view of the PivotTable exported to Sheet1 of a workbook with the Excel PivotTable toolbar and PivotTable Field List displayed. Excel's PivotTable toolbar is similar to Access's. Sheet 2 contains data exported by the source query of the PivotTable, which Excel translates from the Cachedata.xml file.

Clicking Excel's Chart Wizard button automatically generates a PivotChart from the PivotTable. To create a readable chart, select the Name button and click the Hide Detail button to eliminate the Country detail data before you click the Chart Wizard button. Otherwise, the chart is impossible to decipher. Figure 12.22 shows the PivotChart created from the collapsed PivotTable.

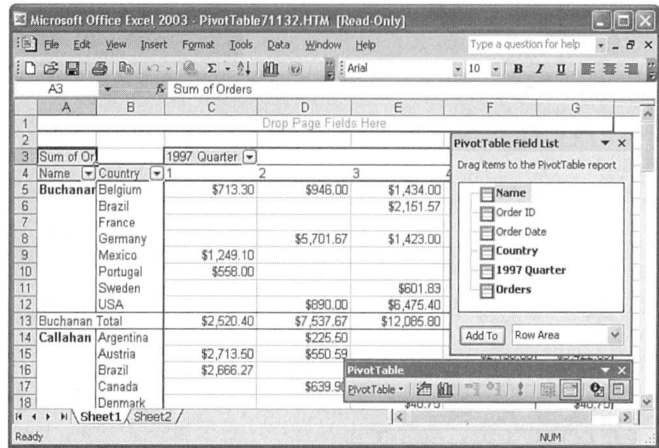

Figure 12.21 This Excel workbook was created by exporting the sample PivotTable from the earlier "Increasing the Level of Detail for Drill-Down" section. The PivotTable can't display detail data, so double-clicking a value opens a new worksheet to display the detail behind the entry.

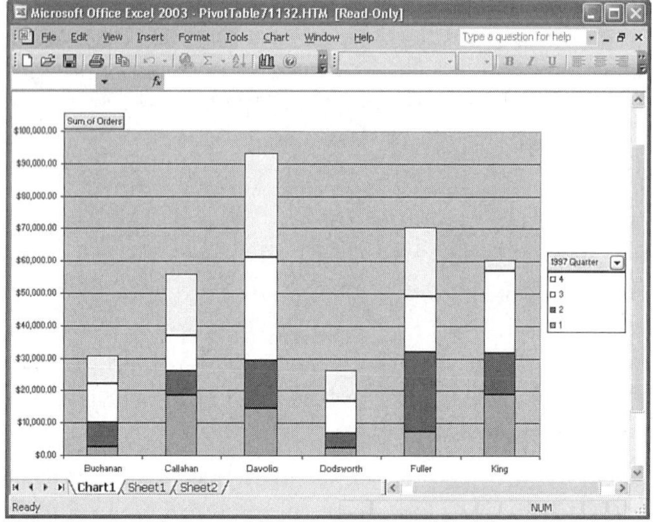

Figure 12.22 The Excel Chart Wizard displays in another worksheet a PivotChart based on each row and column displayed in the PivotTable.

12

NOTE

The files required to create the Excel workbook described in this section are included in the \Seua11\Chaptr12 folder of the accompanying CD-ROM. Double-click the 1997OrdersByEmployee&CountryPT.htm file to open a static PivotTable in IE 5+. Opening the *PivotTableName*.htm file of a PivotTable saved as a Web page adds an Edit with Microsoft Excel button to IE's toolbar. The drop-down list also lets you select Edit with Notepad, which displays the HTML code, or Edit with Microsoft Word, which generates a table.

OPTIMIZING PERFORMANCE OF PIVOTTABLES

The first and most important rule of PivotTables is *Minimize the number of rows returned by queries that you intend to use as the data source for PivotTable views.* Jet returns only the first 100 rows of the query result set to the initial Datasheet view, so response is almost instantaneous for a default Dynaset-type query without `GROUP BY` or other operations that require operations on the entire result set. The Jet database engine retrieves additional rows as you scroll the datasheet. Unfortunately, PivotTables don't take advantage of Jet's incremental row retrieval feature.

The Oakmont.mdb sample database has a sufficient number of records to bring a PivotTable view to its knees with a simple query. For example, you might want to analyze tuition revenue by student graduation year and course. The average Oakmont student is enrolled in only two courses, so the query returns 59,996 rows. The objective of the query is to return total revenue and an enrollment count for all sections of each of the 590 courses offered by the college, and to summarize the data by academic department. In theory, the PivotTable's AutoCalc feature should be able to total the revenue and count the number of enrollment records. Figure 12.23 shows the initial design of a query that's capable of providing the required data.

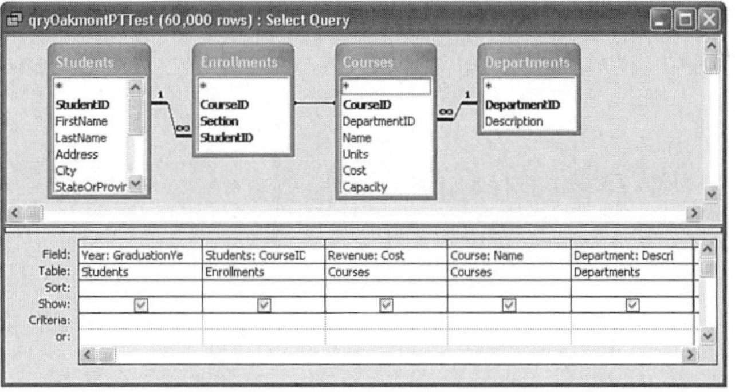

Figure 12.23
This sample query against four tables of the Oakmont.mdb database returns 59,996 rows.

NOTE

The three qryOakmontPTTest sample queries (60,000, 2,350, and 52 Rows) discussed in this section are included in the PivotOM.mdb database in the \Seua11\Chaptr12 folder of the accompanying CD-ROM. You must install the Oakmont.mdb database from the CD-ROM to its default location, C:\Program Files\Seua11\Oakmont, for these queries to execute from the default linked tables. If you've installed Oakmont.mdb to another location, choose Tools, Database Utilities, Linked Table Manager, and change the links to the correct path before attempting to open a table or query.

→ To review how to use the Linked Table Manager, **see** "Using the Linked Table Manager Add-in to Relink Tables," **p. 282**.

Opening a local copy of the 60,000-row query design of Figure 12.23 in an empty PivotTable view takes 15 seconds or more on a fast computer (a 667MHz Pentium III system with 512MB RAM and an Ultra-DMA66 drive running Windows XP Professional). This delay occurs every time you move from Query Datasheet or Design view to PivotTable view, because all rows of the query must be loaded into the PivotTable to compute totals. An equal delay occurs between PivotTable and PivotChart views. If the Oakmont.mdb file is on a network server, opening the PivotTable view can take at least a minute and consume a large part (or all) of the network's available bandwidth. Clicking Show Details requires about about a minute to regenerate the PivotTable view.

If you're using large Jet tables shared from a network server and experience performance problems with PivotTables, see the "PivotTable Performance Problems with Networked Tables" topic of the "Troubleshooting" section near the end of this chapter.

If the opening delay doesn't sufficiently deter you, dropping fields of this query to rows or columns can consume 100% of your CPU cycles and take even longer. If you don't select Hide Details beforehand, dropping the Year field on the Column Fields zone takes a minute or two for the four year (2001 through 2004) columns to appear. Clicking Hide Details and dropping the Year field takes only a few seconds to display the columns. With details hidden, dropping Department on the Row Fields zone, and Revenue and Students on the Totals and Detail Fields zone takes only a few seconds to regenerate totals (see Figure 12.24).

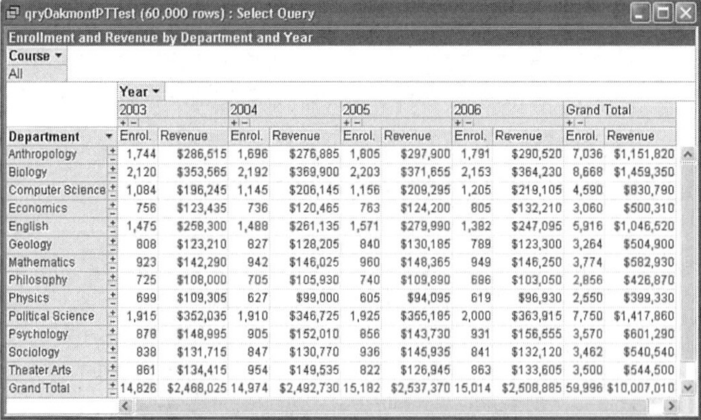

qryOakmontPTTest (60,000 rows) : Select Query

Enrollment and Revenue by Department and Year

Course: All

	Year: 2003		2004		2005		2006		Grand Total	
Department	Enrol.	Revenue	Enrol.	Revenue	Enrol.	Revenue	Enrol.	Revenue	Enrol.	Revenue
Anthropology	1,744	$286,515	1,696	$276,885	1,805	$297,900	1,791	$290,520	7,036	$1,151,820
Biology	2,120	$353,565	2,192	$369,900	2,203	$371,655	2,153	$364,230	8,668	$1,459,350
Computer Science	1,084	$196,245	1,145	$206,145	1,156	$209,295	1,205	$219,105	4,590	$830,790
Economics	756	$123,435	736	$120,465	763	$124,200	805	$132,210	3,060	$500,310
English	1,475	$258,300	1,488	$261,135	1,571	$279,990	1,382	$247,095	5,916	$1,046,520
Geology	808	$123,210	827	$128,205	840	$130,185	789	$123,300	3,264	$504,900
Mathematics	923	$142,290	942	$146,025	960	$148,365	949	$146,250	3,774	$582,930
Philosophy	725	$108,000	705	$105,930	740	$109,890	686	$103,050	2,856	$426,870
Physics	699	$109,305	627	$99,000	605	$94,095	619	$96,930	2,550	$399,330
Political Science	1,915	$352,035	1,910	$346,725	1,925	$355,185	2,000	$363,915	7,750	$1,417,860
Psychology	878	$148,995	905	$152,010	856	$143,730	931	$156,555	3,570	$601,290
Sociology	838	$131,715	847	$130,770	936	$145,935	841	$132,120	3,462	$540,540
Theater Arts	861	$134,415	954	$149,535	822	$126,945	863	$133,605	3,500	$544,500
Grand Total	14,826	$2,468,025	14,974	$2,492,730	15,182	$2,537,370	15,014	$2,508,885	59,996	$10,007,010

Figure 12.24
This PivotTable performs grouping and aggregation operations on a 60,000-row query result set. Performing these operations in the PivotTable can take a long time.

The solution to the preceding performance hit is to use Jet's Totals (Group By) feature to reduce the number of query rows. Grouping by year, course, and department; counting Enrollments records; and summing the Cost field of the Courses table lets the Jet query engine—instead of the PivotTable—handle the initial aggregation (see Figure 12.25).

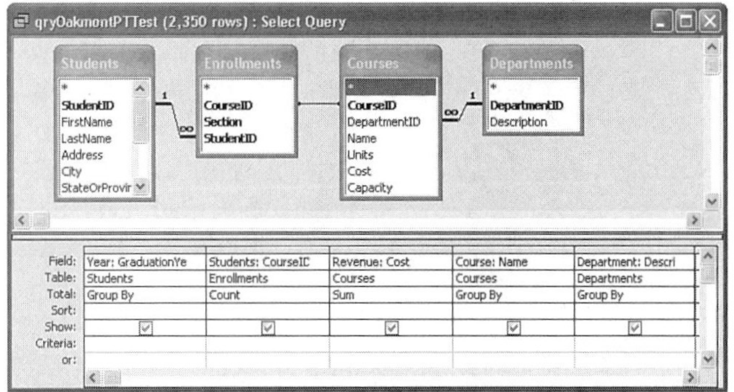

Figure 12.25 Adding a GROUP BY expression to the query and summing the enrollment count and tuition revenue in the Jet query reduces the number of query rows from 59,996 to 2,348.

The PivotTable—identical to that shown earlier in Figure 12.24—better digests the result set of the aggregate query, which now contains 2,348 rows. Jet takes only about five seconds to execute this query from a local database, and the same PivotTable view opens in a bit more than five seconds. The detail data is consolidated by the query, so the Show Detail/Hide Detail toggle operation is almost instantaneous. Reducing the number of rows of the local query result set, however, doesn't reduce network traffic if you're connected to a remote database.

If you don't need detail enrollment and revenue data for each course, you can speed PivotTable operations by removing the Course: Name field from the query design of Figure 12.25 to return only 52 rows. Execution of the Jet query with 52 rows takes about the same time as for 2,348 rows, but PivotTable operations are almost instantaneous.

FORMATTING AND MANIPULATING PIVOTCHARTS

When you define a PivotTable view, you also automatically generate a corresponding PivotChart view of tables, queries, and forms. Access links PivotTable and PivotChart views, so there's no need for a Chart Wizard to specify the initial design. For example, open the PivotTable view of the qry1997OrdersByCountryPT sample query you created in the "Creating the Query for a Sample PivotTable View" section near the beginning of the chapter and collapse the Name category, if Country fields are visible. Choose PivotChart view to open the chart, as shown in Figure 12.26.

ADDING LEGENDS, AXIS TITLES, AND FILTERS

Following are some of the PivotChart property values you can alter to change the format of PivotCharts and filter the data presented:

- **Legends**—The default PivotChart style is Clustered Column; each column of each category—quarterly sales columns for the Name category for this example—is color coded. Clicking the Show Legend button on the toolbar toggles the legend below the 1997 Quarters field button.

- **Axis titles**—Titles for the x- and y-axes of the sample chart are missing. To add axis titles, right click the axis title, choose Properties to open the Properties dialog, and click the Format page. You can change the font, size, and attributes, and type the title in the Caption text box.
- **Category filters**—Filters on category fields limit the chart's display to selected values. As you change filter values, the chart automatically reformats the display and changes the scale of the y-axis to optimize the display. Adding filters to category fields also affects the PivotTable view.

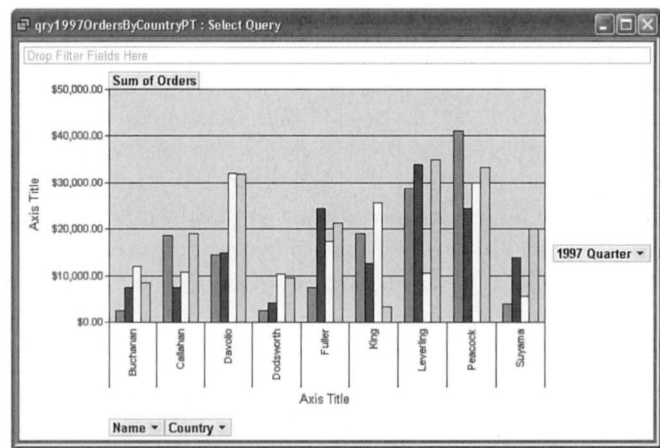

Figure 12.26
The PivotTable automatically creates a PivotChart view of the qry1997OrdersByCountryPT sample query. Be sure to minimize the amount of category detail in the PivotTable before opening a PivotChart.

Figure 12.27 shows the legend and axis titles added, and filters applied to the Name and Country categories. Axis totals and a legend have been added. X-axis category values rotate 90 degrees counterclockwise if their width fits the divisions.

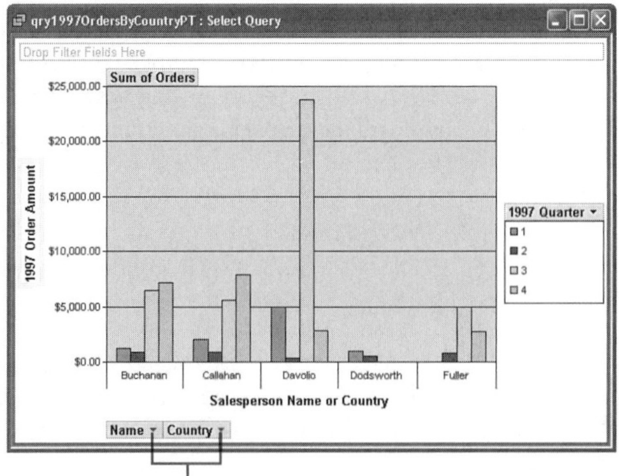

Figure 12.27
The sample PivotChart displays totals of North American orders for the first five employees.

TIP

Remove filters applied to category fields as soon as you no longer need them. The only visible feedback that a filter is applied is a change to the color of the small arrows from black to blue, which isn't readily apparent. Accidentally leaving a filter in place when changing the chart's layout can lead to interpretation errors.

ALTERING CATEGORY PRESENTATION

PivotCharts have Filter Fields and Category Fields drop zones similar to those of PivotTables, and field buttons corresponding to those of the source PivotTable. An additional field button, All Orders for this example, represents the PivotTable's values displayed by the chart, called a *series*. You can change category presentation by dragging category fields to the Filter Fields drop zone and changing the chart's display as follows:

- **Coalesce clusters to totals**—To display total sales for each employee for the year 1997, drag the 1997 Quarter button to the Filter Fields drop zone (see Figure 12.28). The y-axis scale changes to reflect the larger totals.

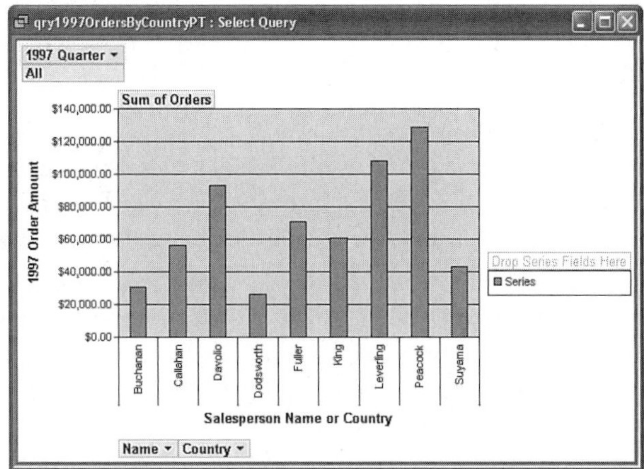

Figure 12.28 Dragging a category field button to the Filter Fields drop zone changes the clustered columns to a single total column for each category.

NOTE

Filter Field buttons indicate that a filter is applied by changing the All label to the filter selection. If you select more than one filter criterion, the label displays "(multiple items)."

- **Replace Categories**—Drag the Name button to the Filter Fields drop zone to display total 1997 sales for each country (see Figure 12.29). Passing the mouse pointer over the chart's bars opens a ScreenTip, which displays detail data.

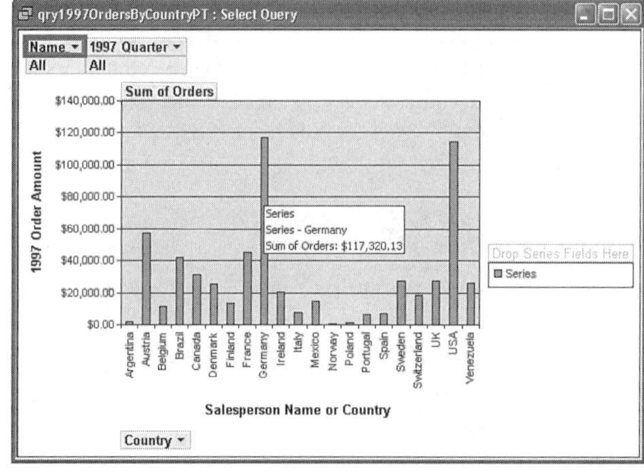

Figure 12.29 Dragging the leftmost (primary) category field button to the Filter Fields drop zone displays data for the remaining category button.

TIP

If you accidentally drag a field button outside the PivotChart's window and remove it from the PivotChart (and the PivotTable), open the Field List and drag the field to the appropriate drop zone.

- **Remove excessive detail**—When you return the Name and 1997 Quarter fields to their original locations—the Category and Series Fields drop zones, respectively—the category axis of the chart becomes an unreadable jumble. To remove the Country bars from the chart, select the Name button and click the Collapse button on the toolbar or right-click the chart, and choose Collapse from the context menu.
- **Drill down into a category**—The Drill Into toolbar button or context menu choice lets you display the second (or lower) level of detail for a category. To display sales by country for a single salesperson, right-click the name in the category axis and choose Drill Into to display sales by country and quarter for the person (see Figure 12.30). To return to the original chart format, right-click the name, and choose Drill Out. Drill Into and Drill Out menu choices and toolbar buttons are enabled only when you select a category item.

CHANGING THE CHART TYPE

PivotCharts come in a remarkable variety of types and styles, ranging from the default Clustered Column to Radar, which displays values relative to a centerpoint (as in the radar display of an airport approach control facility). To change the chart's style, click outside the chart area, and click the Chart Type button on the toolbar to open the Properties dialog to the Type page. Click one of the styles to preview the chart's appearance. Figure 12.31 shows the sample chart type changed from Clustered to Stacked Column. Choosing a 100% Stacked Column style changes the y-axis units to percent.

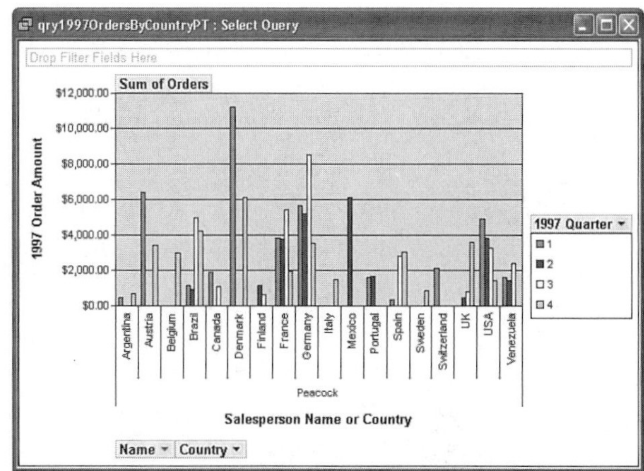

Figure 12.30 Selecting a primary category item in the x-axis, such as Peacock, and clicking the toolbar's Drill Into button displays secondary category values—in this case, sales for Margaret Peacock by country and quarter.

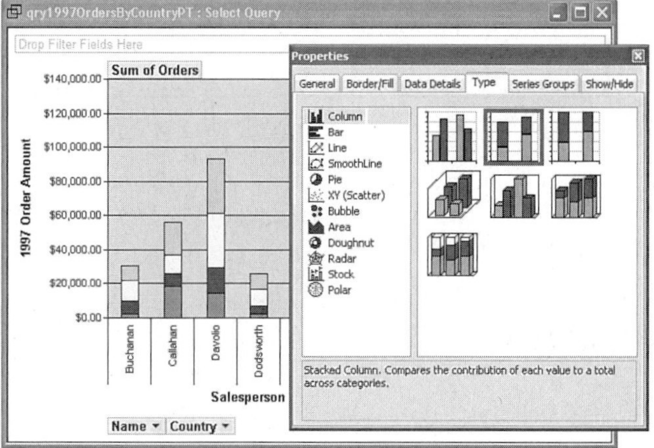

Figure 12.31 Column charts are one of 12 types you can select from the Types page of the Properties dialog. Each type has between 2 and 10 styles, and most types offer 3D versions.

TIP

> Don't change to a 100% Stacked Column—or any other 100%... style—unless you specifically need this style. When you return to another style, the format of the y-axis values change to General Number. You then must select the values, click the Format tab, and reset the numeric format.

The most useful formats for conventional PivotCharts are as follows:

- **Stacked Column charts**—Display contribution of series elements, such as quarters, to a total value. ScreenTips display the numeric value of each element of the column but, unfortunately, not the total value.
- **Bar charts**—Rotate the axes 90 degrees counterclockwise, offer the same styles as Column charts.

- **Stacked Area charts**—Better suited to time-series data, such as monthly, quarterly, or yearly categories. Figure 12.32 shows a Stacked Area chart from a slightly modified (monthly) version of the sample query. Unlike Stacked Bar or Column charts, ScreenTips of stacked area charts don't display numeric values.

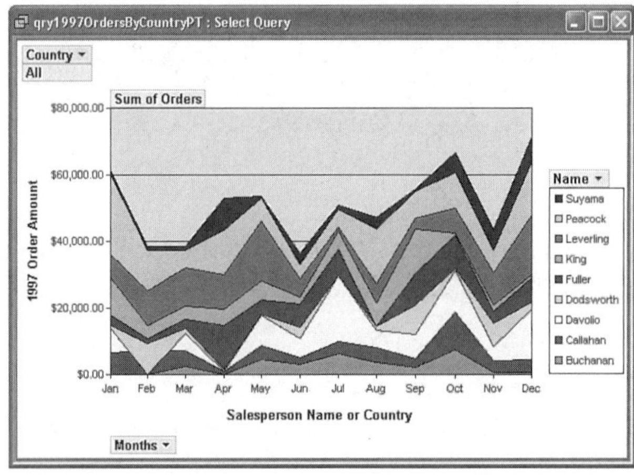

Figure 12.32 This Stacked Area chart displays the month-to-month trend of each employee's contribution to total sales order value.

The qry1997OrdersByCountryPT sample query and the completed PivotChart and PivotTable are included in the Pivot.mdb sample database located in the \Seua11\Chaptr12 folder of the accompanying CD-ROM.

TROUBLESHOOTING

PIVOTTABLE PERFORMANCE PROBLEMS WITH NETWORKED TABLES

When I link large back-end tables on a network server as the data source for PivotTables, I experience serious deterioration in performance.

Opening PivotTables based on aggregate queries against remote Jet tables requires moving all affected rows of the underlying tables across the network, because the query that performs the aggregation runs on your local computer. In a lightly loaded 100BaseT network, the added opening time for a PivotTable isn't a serious issue. If your network uses 10BaseT media or you're connected to a hub (not a switch), and the network has a substantial amount of traffic, aggregate queries against large tables can slow dramatically. For historical (static) data, consider converting the aggregate query to a make-table query, and changing the data source to the table. Using a table with fewer rows also helps solve performance problems that result from overtaxed server disk drives.

If you upsize your application to SQL Server, queries run as views, functions, or stored procedures on the server, not the client PC. One of the primary advantages of client/server RDBMSs, such as SQL Server, is that only query result sets move across the network.

IN THE REAL WORLD—VISUALIZING DATA

Database developers, who deal with tables and query result sets on a daily basis, tend to forget that consumers of their products aren't necessarily fond of tabular data. Having to scan—let alone digest—reams of tabular data, whether on paper or PC monitor, is one of the curses of the cubicle.

Management executives primarily are interested in trends and exceptions. Only when trends go the wrong way or exceptions hit the bottom line are suits (middle management) or pinstripes (top execs, bankers, eastern venture capitalists) likely to be interested in detail data. Well-designed PivotTables let users control the amount of detail displayed, subject to the performance issues that result from using very large data sets to provide multiple drill-down levels. PivotChart's Drill Into and Out feature makes drill-down simple enough for management types to use.

THE PERILS OF PIVOT MANIPULATION

Before the advent of PivotTables and PivotCharts, application programmers had to design individual forms or write complex VBA code to let users slice and dice data according to their preferences. PivotTables and PivotCharts in Access forms and DAP let users choose the fields to display, change category hierarchies, and swap axes. The problem with this approach, of course, is that users who aren't familiar with PivotTables and PivotCharts get into trouble and call for help. After a few calls from users who've lost field buttons, it's tempting to lock down the view by clearing all the check boxes except ScreenTips in the Show/Hide page of the PivotChart's Properties dialog.

A better alternative to lockdown is user education. PivotTables are the cornerstone of Microsoft's approach to delivering crosstabs from SQL Server and other client/server tables linked to SQL Server databases. As Digital Dashboards and Web Parts for delivering Web-based information become more popular, you can expect PivotCharts to play an important role in all data-intensive presentation formats. Design an illustrated Web page that shows users how to work with PivotTables and PivotCharts in general. Add a link to the page on your DAP or forms that use these views. Writing a Web page is far easier and faster than designing a full-fledged online help file.

MEANING, SIGNIFICANCE, AND VISUALIZATION

Data becomes information when one grasps the meaning and significance of the data. Well-designed charts and graphs based on summary queries make the data contained in millions of rows of transactional tables meaningful. The significance of information is in the eye of the beholder. If your bonus is based on sales, trends in sales determine much of your income; if you're a profit-sharing participant, the bottom line counts the most. As noted at the beginning of the chapter, time-series graphs and charts are most common, because spotting trends and taking action based on trends is one of management's primary responsibilities. Trends inherently are historical in nature; regression analysis and other statistical methods enable projecting historical performance to the future with varying degrees of risk. In many cases, the experienced eye of a seasoned executive can better project future trends than the most sophisticated statistical algorithms.

Data visualization, the foundation of graphs based on queries, is more of an art than a science. Edward R. Tufte's self-published 1983 classic, *The Visual Display of Quantitative Information*, is still a bestseller—at least by computer book standards. Tufte's sequel, *Envisioning Information* (1990), deals primarily with cartography. The final volume of the trilogy, *Visual Explanations: Images and Quantities, Evidence and Narrative* (1997), covers presentation of dynamic data. Tufte describes his three books as "pictures of numbers, pictures of nouns, and pictures of verbs." Anyone designing Access graphs and charts for any purpose other than entertainment should own a copy of *The Visual Display of Quantitative Information*. After you become acquainted with Tufte's seminal work, you're very likely to acquire his other two books.

Management by Trend Exception

Most managers and executives suffer from information overload. One of the approaches to making information delivered to management more effective is to flag situations in which performance falls outside of the expected or budgeted range. Multiline graphs, which present actual versus projected performance, are especially useful for flagging poor or exceptional results at the region, department, division, or corporate level. Regression methods often are more useful in actual-versus-budgeted graphs, because extrapolated trend lines that cross budget lines in the wrong direction are immediately visible to the most harried executive. Adding budgetary data usually requires nested queries, views, or functions to combine summary results from transaction data and presummarized budget data.

CHAPTER 13

Creating and Updating Jet Tables with Action Queries

In this chapter

Getting Acquainted with Action Queries

Action queries create new tables or modify the data in existing tables. Access offers the following four types of action queries:

- *Make-table* queries create new tables from the data contained in query result sets. One of the most common applications for make-table queries is to create tables that you can export to other applications or that summarize data from other tables. A make-table query provides a convenient way to copy a table to another database. In some cases, you can use make-table queries to speed the generation of multiple forms and reports based on a single, complex query.

- *Append* queries add new records to tables from the query's result set.

- *Delete* queries delete records from tables that correspond to the rows of the query result set.

- *Update* queries change the existing values of fields of table records that correspond to rows of the query result set.

By default, new queries you create are select queries. After opening a new or existing query in Design view, you can change its type to one of the four action queries by making a selection from the Query menu.

NOTE

Access data projects (ADP) offer the same Query menu choices for action queries when you create a new stored-procedure query. Stored procedures have an additional type of append query, called an *Append Values* procedure, which lets you add a new record with values you type in the da Vinci Query Design grid. SQL Server functions and views don't support make-table queries.

This chapter shows you how to create each of the four types of Jet action queries and how to use Access's cascading deletions and cascading updates of related records. Cascading deletions and cascading updates are covered here because these referential-integrity features are related to delete and update action queries, respectively.

13

TIP

Always make a backup copy of a table that you intend to modify with an action query. Changes made to table data with action queries are permanent; an error can render a table useless. Invalid changes made to a table with an action query containing a design error often are difficult to detect.

Creating New Tables with Make-Table Queries

In the following sections, you learn how to use a make-table query to create a new table, tblShipAddresses, for customers that have different shipping and billing addresses. This process enables the deletion of the tblShipAddresses data that, in most of the records in the Orders table, duplicates the address data in the Customers table. Removing duplicated data to new tables is an important step when you're converting data contained in a flat (nonrelational) database to a relational database structure. You can use the Table Analyzer Wizard, described in Chapter 5, "Working with Jet Database and Tables," to perform an operation similar to that described in the following sections. Removing duplicated data manually, however, is one of the best methods of demonstrating how to design make-table queries.

➔ To use a wizard to remove duplicate data, **see** "Using the Table Analyzer Wizard," **p. 207**.

A modification of the query that you created in the "Creating Not-Equal Theta Joins with Criteria" section of Chapter 11, "Creating Multitable and Crosstab Queries," generates the data for the new tblShipAddresses table. Make-table queries are especially useful in converting flat-file tables that contain duplicated data, including tables created by spreadsheet applications, to relational form.

NOTE

Completed versions of most sample queries in this chapter are included in the Action13.mdb database located in the \Seua11\Chaptr13 folder of the accompanying CD-ROM.

DESIGNING AND TESTING THE SELECT QUERY

To create the new tblShipAddresses table from the data in the Orders table, you first must build the following SELECT query:

1. Open your working copy of Northwind.mdb, create a new select query, and add the Customers and Orders tables to it.
2. Drag the CustomerID field from the Customers table and drop it in the query's first column. The CustomerID field links the tblShipAddresses table to the Orders table.
3. Drag the ShipName, ShipAddress, ShipCity, ShipRegion, ShipPostalCode, and ShipCountry fields from the Orders table and drop them in columns 2–7, respectively. You use these fields, in addition to CustomerID, to create the new tblShipAddresses table.

To add criteria to select only those records of the Orders table in which the ShipName doesn't match the CompanyName or the ShipAddress doesn't match the Customers table's address, do this:

1. In the ShipName column's first Criteria row, type the following:

   <>[Customers].[CompanyName]
2. In the next row of the ShipAddress column, type the following:

   <>[Customers].[Address]

3. Finally, to ensure against the slight possibility that the same address might occur in two different cities, in the third row of the ShipCity column, type this:

   <>[Customers].[City]

NOTE

> Each not-equal criterion must be on a separate Criteria row to specify the OR operator for the three criteria. Multiple criteria on the same row use the AND operator. If you add the three criteria in the previous steps to the same row, the sample query returns only three records.

4. Double-click an empty area in the Query Design window's upper pane to open the Query Properties window. Open the Unique Values drop-down list, select Yes, and close the Query Properties window. The query design appears as shown in Figure 13.1.

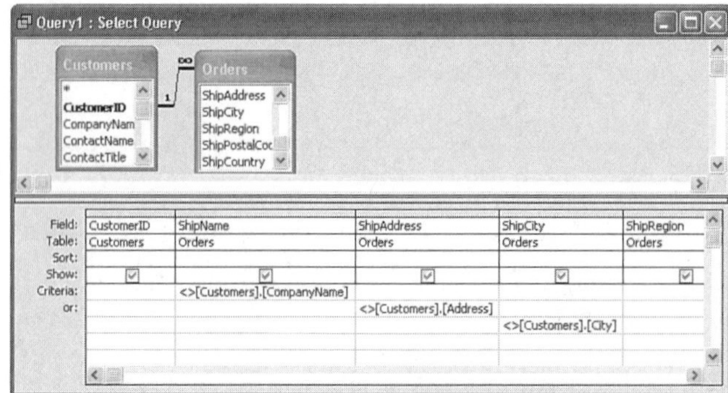

Figure 13.1
The design of the tblShipAddresses make-table query requires that the not-equal criteria be added on separate rows of the grid.

5. Click Run to execute the select query and test the result (see Figure 13.2).

Query1 : Select Query

Customer ID	Ship Name	Ship Address	Ship City	Ship Region	Ship Postal Code
AROUT	Around the Horn	Brook Farm	Colchester	Essex	CO7 6JX
CHOPS	Chop-suey Chinese	Hauptstr. 31	Bern		3012
GALED	Galería del gastronómo	Rambla de Cataluña, 23	Barcelona		8022
LAUGB	Laughing Bacchus Wine Cellars	2319 Elm St.	Vancouver	BC	V3F 2K1
OLDWO	Ottilies Käseladen	Mehrheimerstr. 369	Köln		50739
PRINI	Old World Delicatessen	2743 Bering St.	Anchorage	AK	99508
RICSU	Richter Supermarkt	Starenweg 5	Genève		1204
TRADH	Toms Spezialitäten	Luisenstr. 48	Münster		44087
WHITC	White Clover Markets	1029 - 12th Ave. S.	Seattle	WA	98124
WILMK	Vins et alcools Chevalier	59 rue de l'Abbaye	Reims		51100
WOLZA	Wolski Zajazd	ul. Filtrowa 68	Warszawa		01-012

Record: 1 of 11

Figure 13.2
The query design of Figure 13.1 returns 11 rows of shipping addresses that differ from the customers' billing addresses.

JET SQL

If you don't add the Unique Values property, which adds the `DISTINCT` qualifier to the query's `SELECT` statement, the query returns a row for each order with a different shipping address. Following is the Jet SQL statement for the preceding query, with unneeded parentheses and square brackets removed for readability:

```
SELECT DISTINCT Customers.CustomerID, Orders.ShipName,
   Orders.ShipAddress, Orders.ShipCity, Orders.ShipRegion,
   Orders.ShipPostalCode, Orders.ShipCountry
FROM Customers
   INNER JOIN Orders
   ON Customers.CustomerID = Orders.CustomerID
WHERE Orders.ShipName<>Customers.CompanyName
   OR Orders.ShipAddress<>Customers.Address
    OR Orders.ShipCity<>Customers.City;
```

CONVERTING THE SELECT QUERY TO A MAKE-TABLE QUERY

Now that you've tested the select query to make sure that it creates the necessary data, create the table from the query by following these steps:

1. Return to Query Design view and choose Query, Make-Table Query to open the Make Table dialog. Type the name of the table, tblShipAddresses, in the Table Name text box (see Figure 13.3), and click OK.

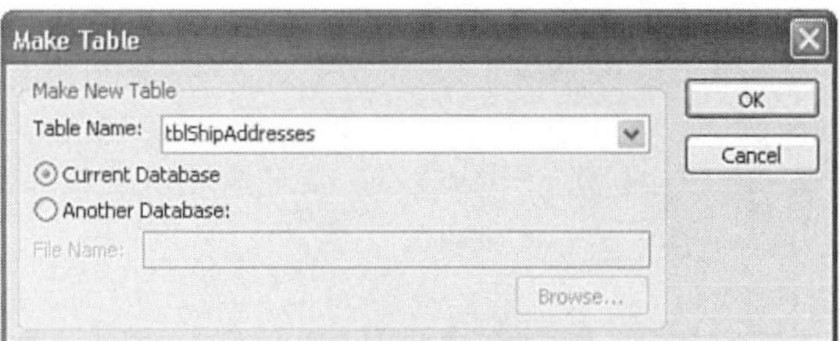

Figure 13.3
The Make Table dialog lets you type a new name for the table or select an existing table to replace with new data.

2. Click Run. A message confirms the number of records that you are about to add to the new table. Click Yes to create the new table.
3. Close and save your query with an appropriate name, such as **qryMTtblShipAddresses**.
4. Press F11 to activate the Database window, click the Table shortcut, and open the new tblShipAddresses table. The records appear as shown in Figure 13.4.

tblShipAddresses : Table

CustomerID	ShipName	ShipAddress	ShipCity	ShipRegion	ShipPostalCode	ShipCountry
AROUT	Around the Horr	Brook Farm	Colchester	Essex	CO7 6JX	UK
CHOPS	Chop-suey Chin	Hauptstr. 31	Bern		3012	Switzerland
GALED	Galería del gast	Rambla de Cata	Barcelona		8022	Spain
LAUGB	Laughing Bacch	2319 Elm St.	Vancouver	BC	V3F 2K1	Canada
OLDWO	Ottilies Käselad	Mehrheimerstr.	Köln		50739	Germany
PRINI	Old World Delic	2743 Bering St.	Anchorage	AK	99508	USA
RICSU	Richter Superm	Starenweg 5	Genève		1204	Switzerland
TRADH	Toms Spezialitä	Luisenstr. 48	Münster		44087	Germany
WHITC	White Clover Ma	1029 - 12th Ave	Seattle	WA	98124	USA
WILMK	Vins et alcools	59 rue de l'Abba	Reims		51100	France
WOLZA	Wolski Zajazd	ul. Filtrowa 68	Warszawa		01-012	Poland

Record: 1 of 11

Figure 13.4
Caption property values of a make-table query don't propagate to the newly created table. Compare the field names of this table with the query result set of Figure 13.2.

Now complete the design of the new tblShipAddresses table by following these steps:

1. Change to Table Design view. The table's basic design is inherited from the Field Name and Data Type properties of the fields of the tables used to create the new table. The tblShipAddresses table doesn'tinherit the primary-key assignment from the Customers table's CustomerID field.
2. Choose the CustomerID field, open the Indexed property drop-down list, and choose the Yes (Duplicates OK) value. Indexing improves the performance of queries when you have multiple ShipAddresseses for customers.
3. The CustomerID, ShipName, ShipAddress, ShipCity, and ShipCountry fields are required, so set the value for each of these fields' Required property to Yes, and the Allow Zero Length property to No.
4. Many countries don't have values for the ShipRegion field, and a few countries don't use postal codes, so verify that the Allow Zero Length property is set to Yes for the ShipRegion and ShipPostalCode fields.

JET SQL

The only difference between the select and make-table queries is the addition of the `INTO` *`tablename`* clause that specifies the name of the new table to create. Following is the Jet SQL statement for the sample make-table query:

```
SELECT DISTINCT Customers.CustomerID, Orders.ShipName,
   Orders.ShipAddress, Order's.ShipCity, Orders.ShipRegion,
   Orders.ShipPostalCode, Orders.ShipCountry
INTO tblShipAddresses
FROM Customers
   INNER JOIN Orders
   ON Customers.CustomerID = Orders.CustomerID
WHERE Orders.ShipName<>Customers.CompanyName
   OR Orders.ShipAddress<>Customers.Address
   OR Orders.ShipCity<>Customers.City;
```

This query and the preceding query are SQL-92 and T-SQL compliant. You can copy and paste either query into the SQL pane of the da Vinci stored procedure design window, save the query, and execute it. The da Vinci toolset, also called the Project Designer, adds SQL Server's `dbo.` (database owner) prefix to each table name before creating the stored procedure.

→ For more information on using the da Vinci toolset to create T-SQL stored procedures, **see** "Examining Stored Procedures," **p. 828**.

ESTABLISHING RELATIONSHIPS FOR THE NEW TABLE

Now you must complete the process of adding the new table to your database by establishing default relationships and enforcing referential integrity so that all records in the tblShipAddresses table have a corresponding record in the Customers table. Access's graphical Relationships window makes this process simple and intuitive. To establish the relationship of tblShipAddresses and the Customers table, follow these steps:

1. Close the tblShipAddresses table. Answer Yes when asked whether you want to save changes to the table's design and answer Yes again when asked whether you want to apply the new data integrity rules to the table. Press F11 to make the Database window active.
2. Click the Relationships button on the toolbar or choose Tools, Relationships to open the Relationships window.
3. Click the Show Table button and double-click the tblShipAddresses table to add the table to the Relationships window; then close the Show Table dialog. Move the tblShipAddresses field list to the lower-right position shown in Figure 13.5.

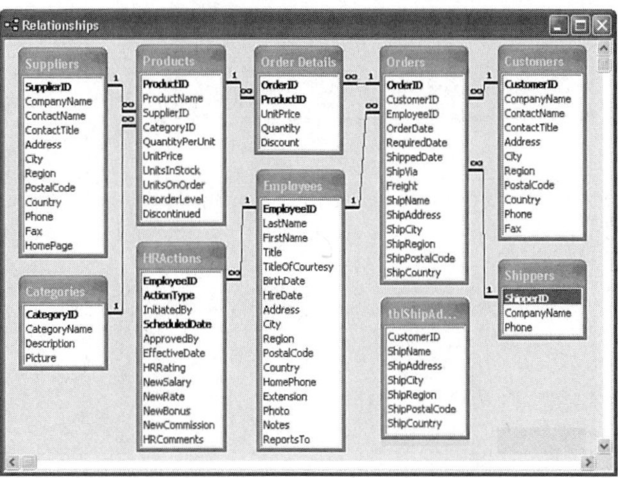

Figure 13.5 Add the new tblShipAddresses table to the Relationships window.

4. Click the Customers table's CustomerID field, drag the field symbol to the tblShipAddresses table's CustomerID field, and drop the symbol to open the Edit Relationships dialog.

TIP

> The direction in which you drag the field is important to support changes you make later in the chapter. The field that you select to drag appears in the Table/Query list (the one side of the relationship), and the field on which you drop the dragged field appears in the Related Table/Query list (the many side of the relationship).

5. Mark the Enforce Referential Integrity check box. Access sets the default relation type, One-To-Many, which is the correct choice for this relation. Access also establishes a conventional `INNER JOIN` as the default join type, so in this case you don't need to click the Join Type button to display the Join Properties window.
6. Select the Cascade Update Related Fields and Cascade Delete Related Records check boxes to maintain referential integrity automatically (see Figure 13.6).

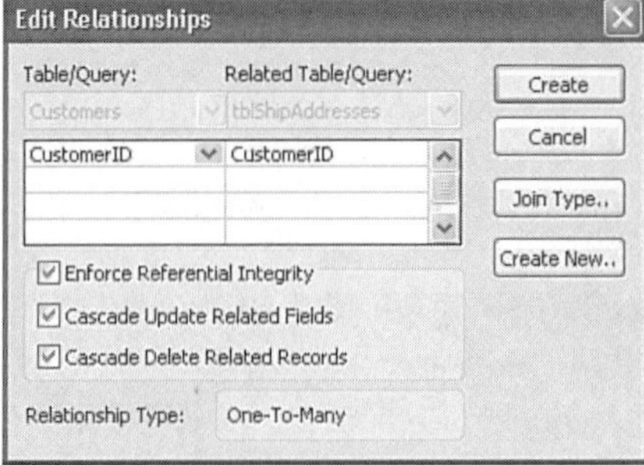

Figure 13.6 Establish a one-to-many relationship between the Orders and tblShipAddresses tables and specify cascade updates and deletions to maintain referential integrity of the tblShipAddresses table.

7. Click the Create button in the Edit Relationships dialog to close it. Your Relationships window appears as shown in Figure 13.7.

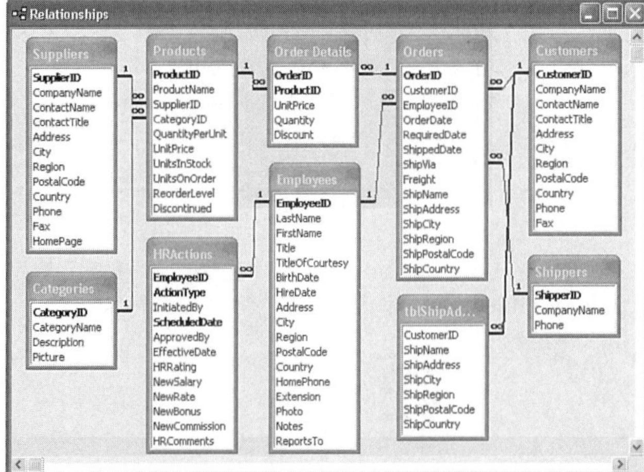

Figure 13.7 An infinity ([is]) symbol indicates the many-to-one relationship of the tblShipAddress table with the Customers table.

8. Close the Relationships window and click Yes to save your changes.

USING THE NEW TBLSHIPADDRESSES TABLE

The purpose of creating the new tblShipAddresseses table is to eliminate the data in the Orders table that duplicates information in the Customers table. The additional steps that you must take to use the new table include the following:

- You need a new Number (Long Integer) field, ShipToID, for the tblShipAddresses and Orders tables. In the Orders table's ShipToID field, you can have a 0 value to indicate that the shipping and billing addresses are the same. You then assign a sequential number to each tblShipAddresses for each customer. (In this case, the value of the ShipToID field is 1 for all records in tblShipAddresses.) By adding the ShipToID field to the tblShipAddresses table, you can create a composite primary key on the CustomerID and ShipToID fields.
- Don't delete fields that contain duplicated data extracted to a new table until you confirm that the extracted data is correct and modify all the queries, forms, and reports that use the table. You use the update query described later in this chapter to assign the correct ShipToID field value for each record in the Orders table. After you verify that you've assigned the correct value of the ShipToID field, you can delete the duplicate fields.
- Add the new table to any queries, forms, reports, or VBA procedures that require the extracted information.
- Change references to fields in the original table in all database objects that refer to fields in the new table.

During this process, you have the opportunity to test the modification before deleting the duplicated fields from the original table. Making a backup copy of the table before you delete the fields also is a low-cost insurance policy.

CREATING ACTION QUERIES TO APPEND RECORDS TO A TABLE

A make-table query creates the new table structure from the structure of the records that underlie the query. Only the fields of the records that appear in the Datasheet view of the query are added to the new table's structure. If you design and save a tblShipAddresses table before extracting the duplicated data from the Orders table, you can use an append query to add the extracted data to the new table.

13

To remove and then append records to the tblShipAddresses table, for example, follow these steps:

1. Open the tblShipAddresses table in Datasheet view, choose Edit, Select All Records, and then press the Delete key to delete all the records from the table. Click Yes when asked to confirm the deletion and then close the table.

2. Open your make-table query, qryMTtblShipAddresses, from the Database window in Design view.

> **TIP**
>
> Take extra care when designing action queries not to execute the query prematurely. If you double-click the query in the Database window or open the query in Datasheet view, you run the make-table query.

3. Choose Query, Append Query or use the Query Type toolbar icon and specify an append query. The Append dialog—a renamed version of the Make Table dialog—opens with tblShipAddresses as the default value in the Table Name drop-down list.
4. Click OK to close the Append dialog and add the Append To row to the Query Design grid (see Figure 13.8).

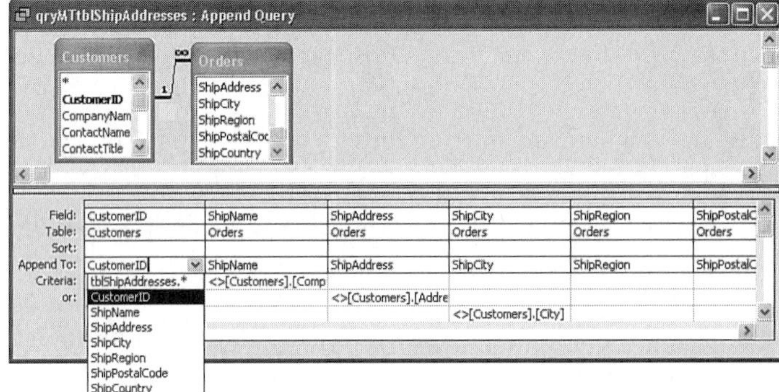

Figure 13.8 Changing a select or make-table query adds an Append To row to the grid. You can specify appending values to a field by opening the Append To list for the query field and selecting the field name.

> **TIP**
>
> To append data to a table, the field names of the query and of the table you are appending the records to must be identical, or you must specify the field of the table that the append query column applies to. Access doesn't append data to fields in which the field name differs by even a single space character. The Query Design grid for append queries has an additional row, Append To (shown in Figure 13.8), that Access attempts to match by comparing field names of the query and the table. Default values appear in the Append To row of columns for which a match occurs. If a match doesn't occur, open the Append To row's drop-down list and select the destination table's field.

5. Click Run to execute the append query. A message box displays the number of records that the query will append to the table. Click Yes to append the records, and then save the query.
6. Open the tblShipAddresses table to verify that you've added the 11 records.

If you can't add a primary key on a table you've appended new records to, see the "Appending Records Causes Primary Key Problems" topic of the "Troubleshooting" section near the end of the chapter.

Jet SQL

Append queries—more commonly called `INSERT` queries—add an `INSERT INTO` *`tablename(field list)`* clause to the `SELECT` statement. The field list argument is what lets you append data to a field with a different name. Following is the SQL statement for the `INSERT` version of the make-table query:

```
INSERT INTO tblShipAddresses ( CustomerID, ShipName,
   ShipAddress, ShipCity, ShipRegion, ShipPostalCode, ShipCountry )
SELECT DISTINCT Customers.CustomerID, Orders.ShipName,
   Orders.ShipAddress, Orders.ShipCity, Orders.ShipRegion,
   Orders.ShipPostalCode, Orders.ShipCountry
FROM Customers
   INNER JOIN Orders
   ON Customers.CustomerID = Orders.CustomerID
WHERE Orders.ShipName<>Customers.CompanyName
   OR Orders.ShipAddress<>Customers.Address
   OR Orders.ShipCity<>Customers.City;
```

Like the select and make-table versions, the Jet SQL statement is SQL-92 compliant, so the preceding statement also executes as an SQL Server stored procedure.

You can't append records containing values that duplicate those of the primary key fields or other fields with no-duplicates index in existing records. If you try to do so, a message box indicates the number of records that cause key-field violations. Unlike the paste append operation, however, Access doesn't create a Paste Errors table that contains the unappended records.

DELETING RECORDS FROM A TABLE WITH AN ACTION QUERY

Often you might have to delete records from a table. For example, you might want to delete records for canceled orders or for customers that have made no purchases for several years. Deleting records from a table with a delete query is the reverse of the append process. You create a select query with all fields (using the * choice from the field list) and then add the individual fields to be used to specify the criteria for deleting specific records. If you don't specify any criteria, Access deletes all the table's records when you convert the select query into a delete query and run it against the table.

TIP

> It's a good practice to run a select query to display the records that you are about to delete and then convert the select query to a delete query.

To give you some practice at deleting records—you stop short of actual deletion in this case—suppose that Northwind Traders' credit manager has advised you that Austrian authorities have declared Ernst Handel (CustomerID ERNSH) insolvent and that you are to cancel and delete any orders from Ernst Handel not yet shipped. To design the query that selects all of Ernst Handel's open orders, follow these steps:

1. Open a new query in Design view and add the Orders table to it.
2. Drag the * (all fields) item from the field list to the Field cell of the query's first column.
3. Drag the CustomerID field to the second column's Field cell. You need this field to select a specific customer's record. The fields that make up the query must be exactly those of the Orders table, so clear the Show box to prevent the CustomerID field from appearing in the query's result twice. This field is already included in the first column's * indicator.
4. In the CustomerID field's Criteria cell, type **ERNSH** to represent Ernst Handel's ID.
5. A Null value in the ShippedDate field indicates orders that have not shipped. Drag the ShippedDate field from the field list to the third column's Field cell. Click the Show box to prevent the ShippedDate field from appearing in the select query's result twice, because the * in the first column also includes that field.
6. In the ShippedDate field's Criteria cell, type **Is Null**. To ensure that you delete only records for Ernst Handel *and* only those that have not been shipped, you must place this criterion on the same line as that of the CustomerID field (see Figure 13.9).

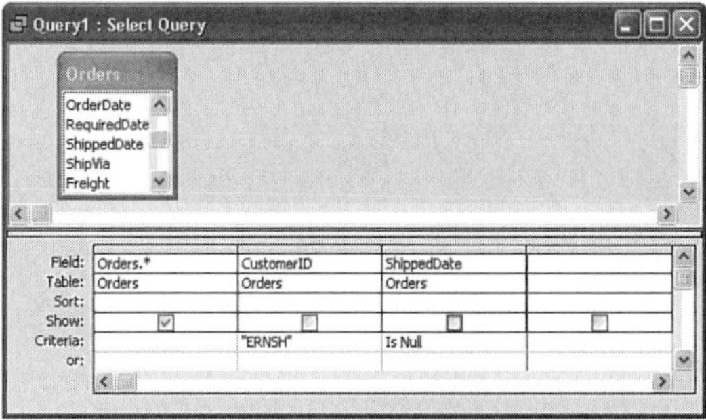

Figure 13.9
The test select query design returns all unshipped orders for CustomerID equal to ERNSH.

7. Run the select query to display the records to delete when the delete query runs (see Figure 13.10).

To proceed with the simulated deletion, which would delete the Order Details records for the two orders, follow these steps:

1. Click the toolbar's Database Window button to activate the Database window and then click the Tables button to display the table list. Create a copy of the Orders table by clicking the Orders table entry and pressing Ctrl+C to copy the table to the Clipboard. Press Ctrl+V to open the Paste Table As dialog. Type **tblOrders** as the name of the new table copy, and press Enter.

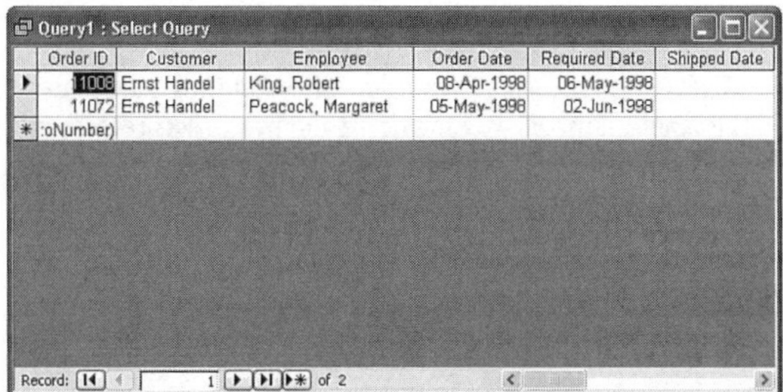

Figure 13.10
The select query displays the two orders for Ernst Handel that haven't been shipped.

2. Repeat step 1 for the Order Details table, naming it **tblOrderDetails**. These two tables are backup tables in case you actually delete the two records for Ernst Handel. The relationship between the Orders table and its related Order Details table specifies Cascade Delete Related Fields but not Cascade Update Related Fields.

3. Open your select query in design mode and choose Query, Delete Query. Access then replaces the select query grid's Sort and Show rows with the Delete row, as shown in Figure 13.11. The From value in the Delete row's first column, Orders.*, indicates that Access will delete records that match the Field specification from the Orders table. The Where values in the remaining two cells indicate fields that specify the deletion criteria.

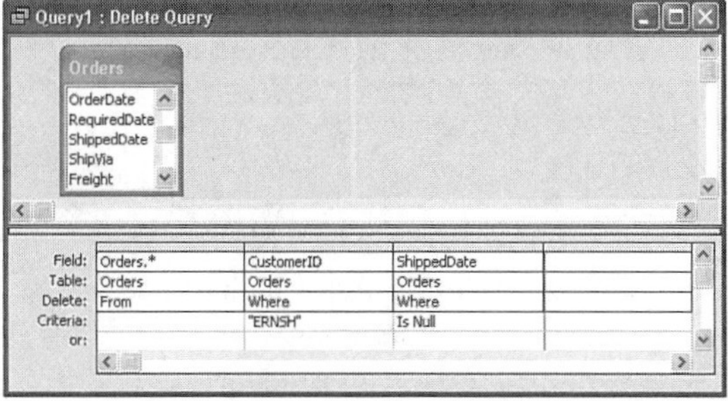

Figure 13.11
Specifying a delete query adds a Delete row to the grid that identify From and Where fields.

4. Click the Run button. A message box asks you to confirm the deletion of the rows. Click No to prevent the deletion.
5. Close, and save your query if you want.

NOTE

Deleting records in a *one* table when records corresponding to the deleted records exist in a related *many* table violates the rules of referential integrity; the records in the *many* table would be made orphans. In this situation, referential integrity is enforced with cascading deletions for the Order Details and Orders table. If you delete the two ERNSH records, Jet first deletes the corresponding Order Detail records and then deletes the Orders records.

13

continues

continued

By default, Access uses a transaction when applying action queries to multiple tables. In this example, if the query can't delete the two Orders records and their seven related Order Details records, the transaction is rolled back, and no deletions occur. Otherwise, the transaction commits and permanently deletes all base and related records. If you set the action query's Use Transactions property value to No, the query deletes any records it can without violating referential integrity rules.

If you accidentally delete records for Ernst Handel, reverse the process that you used to make the backup tables: copy the backup tables—tblOrders and tblOrderDetails—to Orders and Order Details, respectively. You use the tblOrders table in the following section.

Jet SQL

Following is the Jet SQL statement for the sample delete query:

```
DELETE Orders.*, Orders.CustomerID, Orders.ShippedDate
   FROM Orders
WHERE Orders.CustomerID="ERNSH"
   AND Orders.ShippedDate) Is Null;
```

The field list is optional for delete queries, but you must have at least one field in the field list to satisfy the Jet query designer. If you delete the field list in SQL view, the query executes, but won't open in Query Design view.

Like all other Jet action queries, the Jet SQL and T-SQL statements are identical.

UPDATING VALUES OF MULTIPLE RECORDS IN A TABLE

Update queries change the values of data in a table. Such queries are useful when you must update field values for many records with a common expression. For example, you might need to increase or decrease the unit prices of all products or products within a particular category by a fixed percentage.

To see how an update query works, you perform some of the housekeeping chores discussed earlier in the chapter that are associated with using the tblShipAddresses table. To implement this example, you must have created the tblShipAddresses table, as described in the "Creating New Tables with Make-Table Queries" section earlier in this chapter.

NOTE

If you didn't create the tblShipAddresses table and you've installed the sample files from the accompanying CD-ROM, you can import this table from the \Program Files\Seua11\Chaptr13\Action13.mdb database.

ADDING A SHIPTOID FIELD TO THE TBLORDERS TABLE

You must modify the tblOrders and tblShipAddresses tables to include a field for the ShipToID code that relates the two tables. To add the ShipToID field to the tblOrders table, do this:

1. Open the tblOrders table in Design mode. If you didn't create the tblOrders table as a backup table for the example of the preceding section, do so now.
2. Select the ShipVia field by clicking the selection button and then press Insert to add a new field between ShippedDate and ShipVia. (Access inserts fields in tables above the selected field.)
3. Type **ShipToID** as the field name, select Number as the field data type, and accept the default Long Integer as the field's Field Size. Set the Required property value to Yes. Access automatically adds a Duplicates OK index to fields whose names end with "ID". You don't need an index on this field, so set the Indexed property value to No. The table design pane appears as in Figure 13.12, which shows the new ShipToID field selected.

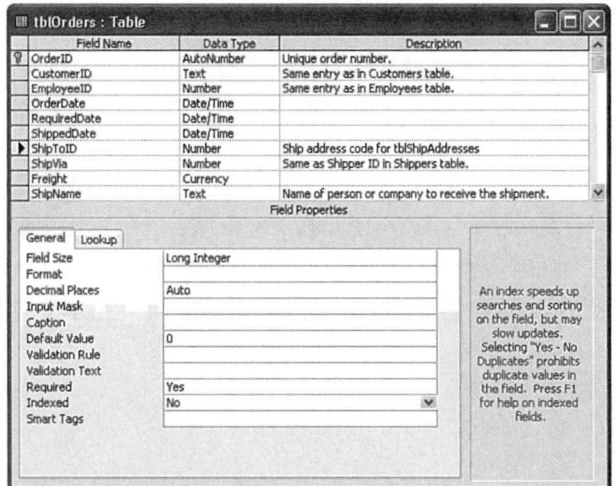

Figure 13.12
Add the ShipToID field as the foreign key for a relationship with the ShipToID field you add to the tblShipAddress table.

4. Close the tblOrders table and save the changes to your design. You changed the domain integrity rules when you added the Required property, so a message box asks whether you want to test domain integrity. Click No to avoid the test, which would fail because no values have been added to the ShipToID field.

13

ADDING A SHIPTOID FIELD AND COMPOSITE PRIMARY KEY TO THE TBLSHIPADDRESSES TABLE

Now add the ShipToID field and establish a composite primary key for the tblShipAddresses table by doing the following:

1. Open the tblShipAddresses table in Datasheet view.
2. Click the ShipName field header and choose Insert, Column to add a Field1 field between the CustomerID and the ShipName fields.
3. Type **1** in the Field1 cell for each record of the tblShipAddresses table.

4. Change to design mode and change the name of Field1 to **ShipToID**. Access detects from your data entries that the field should be a Number field and assigns Long Integer as the default Field Size property value. Change the value of the Required property to Yes.
5. Click the CustomerID field and Shift+click the ShipToID field to select both fields.
6. Click the toolbar's Primary Key button to create a composite primary key on the CustomerID and ShipToID fields. Your table design appears as shown in Figure 13.13.

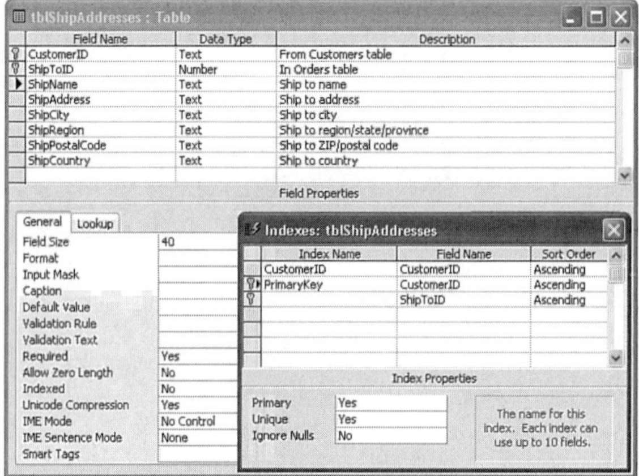

Figure 13.13 The ShipToID and CustomerID fields comprise a composite primary key of the tblShipAddresses table.

7. Close the tblShipAddresses table. This time you test the changes that you made to the table, so click Yes when the Data Integrity Rules message box opens.

Writing Update Queries to Add Foreign-Key Values to the tblOrders Table

To indicate where the orders were shipped, you must update the ShipToId field in tblShipAddresses. The value 1 indicates a shipping address other than the customer's address; the value 0 indicates the order is shipped to the customer's billing address. You can accomplish this by running an update query:

1. Create a new query and add the Customers and tblOrders tables to it. Relationships haven't been specified between the two tables, so the join line between the tables doesn't have one-to-many symbols.

2. Drag the tblOrders table's ShipName and ShipAddress fields to the first two columns of the Query Design grid.
3. Type **<>[Customers].[CompanyName]** in the first Criteria row of the ShipName column and **<>[Customers].[Address]** in the second Criteria row of the ShipAddress column. (Prior tests show that you don't need to test the City, PostalCode, and Country fields.) Your query design appears as shown in Figure 13.14.

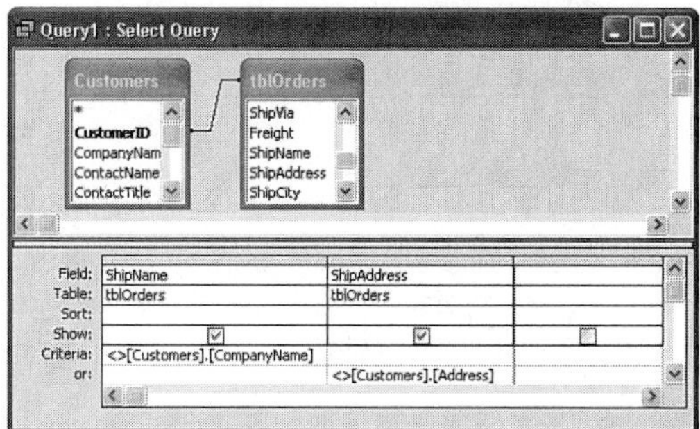

Figure 13.14 This query design, which is similar to qryMTShipAddresses, returns all orders for which the ship to name or ship to address differs from the billing data.

4. Run the query to verify that you have correctly selected the set of records to be updated. In this case, you *don't* specify Unique Values, because you must change every tblOrders record that meets the query criteria.

After ensuring that you've selected the appropriate records of the tblOrders table for updating, 64 rows for the sample query, you're ready to convert the select query to an update query by following these steps:

1. Return to Query design mode and drag the tblOrders table's ShipToID field to the query's first column.
2. Choose Query, Update Query. A new Update To row replaces the Sort and Show rows of the select Query Design grid.
3. In the ShipToID column's Update To cell, type **1** to set ShipToID's value to 1 for orders that require the use of a record from the tblShipAddresses table. The Update Query Design grid appears as shown in Figure 13.15. The Update To cells of the remaining fields are blank, indicating that Jet is not to update values in these fields.
4. Run the update query. A message box indicates the number of records to be updated, 64 for this example. Click Yes to continue.
5. Click the Database Window button and open the tblOrders table. Check a few records to see that you correctly added the ShipToID value of 1.
6. Close and save the update query, if desired.

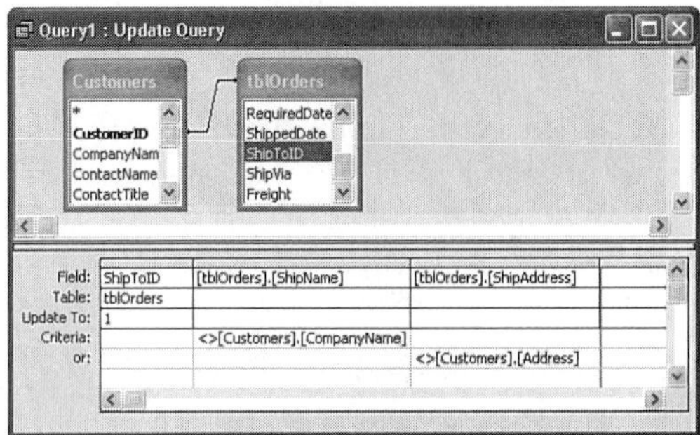

Figure 13.15 Type the value (1) for the update to the ShipToID field of records that require a join to a record in the tblShipAddresses table.

Jet SQL

Update queries substitute `UPDATE` for `SELECT`, and a `SET` list for the `SELECT` field list. An update query can set multiple field values by additional, comma-separated *`TableName.FieldName = Value`* statements. Following is the Jet SQL statement for the sample update query:

```
UPDATE Customers
   INNER JOIN tblOrders
      ON Customers.CustomerID = tblOrders.CustomerID
   SET tblOrders.ShipToID = 1
WHERE tblOrders.ShipName<>[Customers].[CompanyName]
   OR tblOrders.ShipAddress<>[Customers].[Address];
```

The Jet SQL and T-SQL statements are identical.

Finally, you must add 0 values to the ShipToID cells of records that have the same shipping and billing by following these steps:

1. Create a new query, and add only the tblOrders table.
2. Drag the ShipToID field to the query's first column and choose Query, Update Query.

3. Type **0** in the Update To row and **Is Null** in the Criteria row. Before running the query, check it in Datasheet view; all fields should be empty.
4. When you're sure the query is correct, click Run to replace Null values in the ShipToID column with 0.

After you check the tblOrders table to verify the result of your second update query, you can change to Table Design view and safely delete the ShipName, ShipAddress, ShipCity, ShipRegion, ShipPostalCode, and ShipCountry fields from the table.

Using the tblShipAddress Table in a Query

When you join the tblOrders and tblShipAddresses tables in a query to regenerate the appearance of the original Orders table, you must specify a `LEFT OUTER JOIN` on the CustomerID and ShipToID fields of the tables to return all tblOrders records, not just those with records in the tblShipAddresses table.

To create a query that returns all rows of the tblOrders table with empty Ship... fields for records with 0 ShipToID values, do the following:

1. Open a new query, and add the tblOrders and tblShipAddresses tables.
2. Double-click the caption of the tblOrders field list in the upper pane to select all fields, and drag the selected fields to the grid. Add an ascending sort to the OrderID column.
3. Click the ShipName field in the tblShipAddresses field list, Shift+click the ShipCountry field, and drag the selected fields to the right of the Freight field in the grid.
4. In the upper pane, drag the CustomerID field of tblOrders and drop it on the CustomerID field of tblShipAddresses to create an `INNER JOIN`. Do the same for the ShipToID fields. As with earlier examples of this chapter, the direction in which you drag the field symbol (the same direction as the other join, left-to-right) is important. Your query design appears as shown in Figure 13.16. The query grid is scrolled to the right to show the first two fields from the tblShipAddresses table.

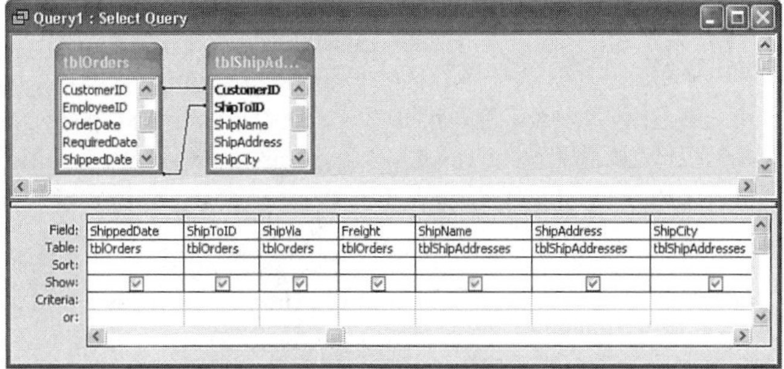

Figure 13.16
This query design has INNER JOINs between tblOrders and tblShipAddresses, so the query returns only rows for which records exist in the tblShipAddresses table.

5. Select and then double-click the join line between the CustomerID fields to open the Join Properties dialog. Select option 2, a `LEFT OUTER JOIN`, and click OK. Specifying this join adds a right-pointing arrow to the join line.
6. Repeat step 5 for the ShipToID field (see Figure 13.17). Both joins must be `LEFT OUTER JOIN`s to return all tblOrders records.

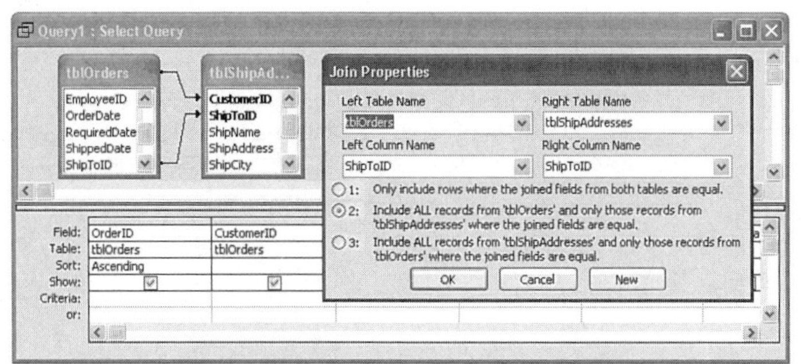

Figure 13.17
Specifying a `LEFT (OUTER) JOIN` (option 2) in the Join Properties dialog adds an arrow to the join line.

13

7. Run the query to verify that records for orders with and without ship addresses appear (see Figure 13.18). Save the query as **qryLOJtblOrders** or a similar name, but don't close it.

Figure 13.18
This Datasheet view of the query result set from the design of Figure 13.17 returns all orders. The first two columns are frozen.

Query1 : Select Query

Order ID	Customer	ShipToID	Ship Via	Freight	ShipName	ShipAddress	ShipCity
10248	Wilman Kala	1	Federal S	$32.38	Vins et alcools	59 rue de l'Abba	Reims
10249	Tradição Hipermerc	1	Speedy E	$11.61	Toms Spezialitä	Luisenstr. 48	Münster
10250	Hanari Carnes	0	United Pa	$65.83			
10251	Victuailles en stock	0	Speedy E	$41.34			
10252	Suprêmes délices	0	United Pa	$51.30			
10253	Hanari Carnes	0	United Pa	$58.17			
10254	Chop-suey Chinese	1	United Pa	$22.98	Chop-suey Chin	Hauptstr. 31	Bern
10255	Richter Supermarkt	1	Federal S	$148.33	Richter Superm	Starenweg 5	Genève
10256	Wellington Importa	0	United Pa	$13.97			
10257	HILARIÓN-Abastos	0	Federal S	$81.91			
10258	Ernst Handel	0	Speedy E	$140.51			
10259	Centro comercial M	0	Federal S	$3.25			
10260	Old World Delicate	1	Speedy E	$55.09	Ottilies Käselad	Mehrheimerstr.	Köln
10261	Que Delícia	0	United Pa	$3.05			
10262	Rattlesnake Canyo	0	Federal S	$48.29			
10263	Ernst Handel	0	Federal S	$146.06			

Record: 1 of 830

Using the tblShipAddress Table with UNION Queries

If you want to substitute "Same as Bill To" or the like as the Ship To address on invoices for those orders in which the value of the ShipToID field is 0, you can either write VBA code or a `UNION` query to accomplish this task; however, the latter approach is much simpler.

→ To review creating `UNION` queries, **see** "Using `UNION` Queries to Combine Multiple Result Sets," **p. 452**.

To quickly write the SQL statement for a `UNION` query that adds a text value—Same as Bill To—to the ShipName field for 0 ShipToID values, do this:

1. Open the SQL view of qryLOJtblOrders, select the entire SQL statement, and press Ctrl+C to copy it the Clipboard. Close the query.

2. Open a new query, close the Show Table dialog, and select SQL View from the View button to open the SQL window. Delete the `SELECT;` fragment.
3. Press Ctrl+V to paste the SQL statement to the window.
4. Replace `LEFT` in `LEFT JOIN` with **`INNER`** to return only the rows with values in the tblShipAddresses table.
5. Delete the trailing semicolon of the pasted text, press Enter twice, and type the following `UNION SELECT` statement as shown here:

```
UNION SELECT tblOrders.OrderID, tblOrders.CustomerID,
   tblOrders.EmployeeID, tblOrders.OrderDate, tblOrders.RequiredDate,
   tblOrders.ShippedDate, tblOrders.ShipToID, tblOrders.ShipVia,
tblOrders.Freight,
   "Same as Bill To", " ", " ", " ", " ", " "
FROM tblOrders
WHERE tblOrders.ShipToID = 0;
```

Your SQL window appears as shown in Figure 13.19. The five space values (" ",) in the added statement are required because both components of the UNION query result set must have the same number of columns.

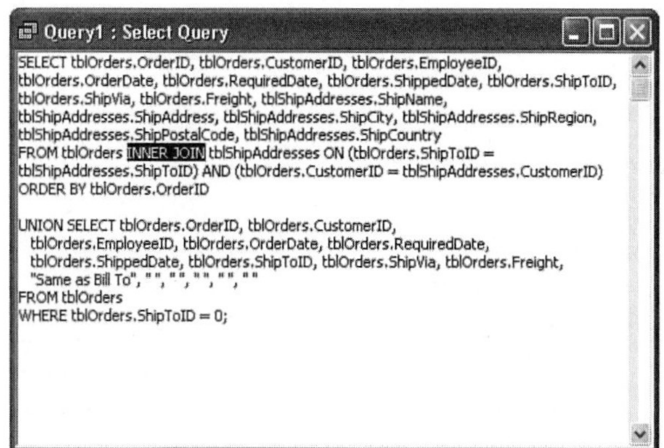

Query1 : Select Query

```
SELECT tblOrders.OrderID, tblOrders.CustomerID, tblOrders.EmployeeID,
tblOrders.OrderDate, tblOrders.RequiredDate, tblOrders.ShippedDate, tblOrders.ShipToID,
tblOrders.ShipVia, tblOrders.Freight, tblShipAddresses.ShipName,
tblShipAddresses.ShipAddress, tblShipAddresses.ShipCity, tblShipAddresses.ShipRegion,
tblShipAddresses.ShipPostalCode, tblShipAddresses.ShipCountry
FROM tblOrders INNER JOIN tblShipAddresses ON (tblOrders.ShipToID =
tblShipAddresses.ShipToID) AND (tblOrders.CustomerID = tblShipAddresses.CustomerID)
ORDER BY tblOrders.OrderID

UNION SELECT tblOrders.OrderID, tblOrders.CustomerID,
  tblOrders.EmployeeID, tblOrders.OrderDate, tblOrders.RequiredDate,
  tblOrders.ShippedDate, tblOrders.ShipToID, tblOrders.ShipVia, tblOrders.Freight,
  "Same as Bill To", " ", " ", " ", " ", " "
FROM tblOrders
WHERE tblOrders.ShipToID = 0;
```

Figure 13.19 This SQL statement consists of a copy of the SELECT query of the preceding example with an INNER instead of a LEFT JOIN and a UNION SELECT statement to add the rows with the 0 ShipToID values.

TIP

> You can save some typing by copying the tblOrders... elements of the field list after the UNION SELECT statement.

5. Run the query to verify that the result set contains the Same as Bill To values in the ShipName column (see Figure 13.20). Save the query as **qryUQtblOrdersShipTo**.

Query1 : Union Query

OrderID	CustomerID	ShipToID	ShipVia	Freight	ShipName	ShipAddress
10248	WILMK	1	3	$32.38	Vins et alcools Chevalier	59 rue de l'Abb:
10249	TRADH	1	1	$11.61	Toms Spezialitäten	Luisenstr. 48
10250	HANAR	0	2	$65.83	Same as Bill To	
10251	VICTE	0	1	$41.34	Same as Bill To	
10252	SUPRD	0	2	$51.30	Same as Bill To	
10253	HANAR	0	2	$58.17	Same as Bill To	
10254	CHOPS	1	2	$22.98	Chop-suey Chinese	Hauptstr. 31
10255	RICSU	1	3	$148.33	Richter Supermarkt	Starenweg 5
10256	WELLI	0	2	$13.97	Same as Bill To	
10257	HILAA	0	3	$81.91	Same as Bill To	
10258	ERNSH	0	1	$140.51	Same as Bill To	
10259	CENTC	0	3	$3.25	Same as Bill To	
10260	OLDWO	1	1	$55.09	Ottilies Käseladen	Mehrheimerstr.
10261	QUEDE	0	2	$3.05	Same as Bill To	
10262	RATTC	0	3	$48.29	Same as Bill To	

Record: 1 of 830

Figure 13.20 The UNION query Jet SQL statement of Figure 13.18 returns the expected result set. (The first two columns are frozen).

The Query Datasheet view of a Jet query you generate from an SQL statement differs from queries you create in the Access query designer. Queries based on SQL statements that Access can't display in Query Design view don't inherit table properties, such as captions and lookup fields.

13

Jet SQL

You can regenerate an exact duplicate of the original Orders table that has ship to addresses for each order with the following lengthy SQL statement:

```
SELECT tblOrders.OrderID, tblOrders.CustomerID, tblOrders.EmployeeID,
   tblOrders.OrderDate, tblOrders.RequiredDate, tblOrders.ShippedDate,
   tblOrders.ShipToID, tblOrders.ShipVia, tblOrders.Freight,
tblShipAddresses.ShipName,
   tblShipAddresses.ShipAddress, tblShipAddresses.ShipCity,
   tblShipAddresses.ShipRegion, tblShipAddresses.ShipPostalCode,
   tblShipAddresses.ShipCountry
FROM tblOrders
   INNER JOIN tblShipAddresses
      ON (tblOrders.ShipToID = tblShipAddresses.ShipToID)
         AND (tblOrders.CustomerID = tblShipAddresses.CustomerID)

UNION SELECT tblOrders.OrderID, tblOrders.CustomerID, tblOrders.EmployeeID,
   tblOrders.OrderDate, tblOrders.RequiredDate, tblOrders.ShippedDate,
   tblOrders.ShipToID, tblOrders.ShipVia, tblOrders.Freight,
Customers.CompanyName, Customers.Address, Customers.City, Customers.Region,
   Customers.PostalCode, Customers.Country
FROM tblOrders
   INNER JOIN Customers
      ON (Customers.CustomerID = tblOrders.CustomerID)
WHERE tblOrders.ShipToID = 0;
```

You can save time by copying the basic structure of the first `SELECT` statement to the `UNION SELECT` statement, changing `tblShipAddresses`... field names to corresponding `Customers`... field names, and altering the `INNER JOIN` statement to join the `Customers` and `tblOrders` tables on the `CustomerID` field. (The name of this query is qryUQtblOrdersShipTo; Figure 13.21 shows its query result set.)

Figure 13.21 You can produce a query result set that's an exact duplicate of the original Orders table with a UNION query that returns Bill To addresses from the Customer table.

Query1 : Union Query

OrderID	CustomerID	ShipToID	ShipVia	Freight	ShipName	ShipAddress
10248	WILMK	1	3	$32.38	Vins et alcools Chevalier	59 rue de l'Abbaye
10249	TRADH	1	1	$11.61	Toms Spezialitäten	Luisenstr. 48
10250	HANAR	0	2	$65.83	Hanari Carnes	Rua do Paço, 67
10251	VICTE	0	1	$41.34	Victuailles en stock	2, rue du Commerce
10252	SUPRD	0	2	$51.30	Suprêmes délices	Boulevard Tirou, 255
10253	HANAR	0	2	$58.17	Hanari Carnes	Rua do Paço, 67
10254	CHOPS	1	2	$22.98	Chop-suey Chinese	Hauptstr. 31
10255	RICSU	1	3	$148.33	Richter Supermarkt	Starenweg 5
10256	WELLI	0	2	$13.97	Wellington Importadora	Rua do Mercado, 12
10257	HILAA	0	3	$81.91	HILARIÓN-Abastos	Carrera 22 con Ave. Carlos So
10258	ERNSH	0	1	$140.51	Ernst Handel	Kirchgasse 6
10259	CENTC	0	3	$3.25	Centro comercial Moctezuma	Sierras de Granada 9993
10260	OLDWO	1	1	$55.09	Ottilies Käseladen	Mehrheimerstr. 369
10261	QUEDE	0	2	$3.05	Que Delícia	Rua da Panificadora, 12
10262	RATTC	0	3	$48.29	Rattlesnake Canyon Grocery	2817 Milton Dr.
10263	ERNSH	0	3	$146.06	Ernst Handel	Kirchgasse 6
10264	FOLKO	0	3	$3.67	Folk och fä HB	Åkergatan 24
10265	BLONP	0	1	$55.28	Blondel père et fils	24, place Kléber

Record: 1 of 830

13

Testing Cascading Deletion and Cascading Updates

When you delete a record in a primary or base table on which records in a related table depend, cascading deletion automatically deletes the dependent records. Similarly, if you modify the value of a table's primary-key field and a related table has records related by the primary-key field's value, cascading updates changes the value of the related foreign-key field for the related records to the new primary-key field value.

Cascading deletions and cascading updates are special types of action queries that the Jet engine executes for you. The following three sections show you how to use Jet's cascading deletion and cascading updates features with a set of test tables copied from the Orders and Order Details tables of Northwind.mdb.

CREATING THE TEST TABLES AND ESTABLISHING RELATIONSHIPS

When experimenting with database features, you should work with test tables rather than live data. As mentioned in the note at the beginning of this chapter, using copied test tables is particularly advisable when the tables are participants in action queries. The remaining sections of this chapter use the two test tables, tblOrders and tblOrderDetails, that you created in preceding sections:

1. Open the tblOrders table in Table Design view.
2. Change the field data type of the OrderID field from AutoNumber to Number and make sure that the Field Size property is set to Long Integer. (This change is necessary to test cascading updates in the next section.)
3. Close tblOrders and save your changes.

Cascading deletions and updates require that you establish a default relationship between the primary and related tables, and enforce referential integrity. To add both cascading deletions and updates to the tblOrderDetails table, follow these steps:

1. If you haven't created tblOrderDetails, use the Clipboard to copy the Order Details table to tblOrderDetails.

2. Click the Relationships button to display the Relationships window.
3. Scroll right to an empty area of the Relationships window.

4. Click the toolbar's Show Table button to display the Add Table dialog. Alternatively, right-click the upper pane of the Query window and choose Show Table.
5. Double-click the tblOrders and tblOrderDetails items in the list, and then close the Show Table dialog.
6. Click and drag the OrderID field of tblOrders to the tblOrderDetails table's OrderID field to establish a one-to-many join on the OrderID field and open the Relationships dialog.
7. Mark the Enforce Referential Integrity check box, which enables the two cascade check boxes.
8. Mark the Cascade Update Related Fields and Cascade Delete Related Records check boxes, as shown in Figure 13.22.

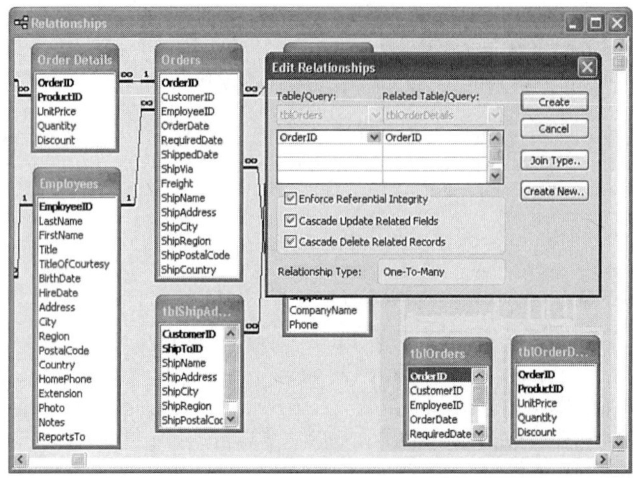

Figure 13.22 Add Jet's Cascade Update Related Fields and Cascade Delete Related Records features to automatically maintain the tblOrderDetails table's referential integrity.

9. Click Create to make your changes to the join effective and close the Relationships window. Click Yes when Access asks if you want to save your changes to the window's layout.

If you receive an error message when you click the Create button, see the "Access Won't Create a Jet Relationship to a New Table" topic of the "Troubleshooting" section near the end of the chapter.

TESTING CASCADING DELETION

To try cascading deletion with the test tables, follow these steps:

1. Open the tblOrders and tblOrderDetails tables in Datasheet view.
2. Click the surface of the tblOrders datasheet to make it the active window and then click a record-selection button to pick an order in tblOrders to delete.
3. Press the Delete key to tentatively delete the selected records and the related order's line-item records in tblOrderDetails.
4. A message asks you to confirm the deletion. Click Yes to delete the records.

To verify that you've deleted the related records, you can scroll to the related record or records for the order that you deleted in the tblOrderDetails table. If you opened tblOrderDetails in step 1, the data cell values for the deleted related records are replaced with #Deleted. (These values aren't saved with the table.)

TESTING CASCADING UPDATES

Cascading updates to the foreign-key field of records that depend on a primary-key value that you want to change in a primary table is a valuable Jet feature. Performing updates of primary-key values while enforcing referential integrity is not a simple process; Chapter 5 briefly discusses the problems associated with performing such updates manually. To see how Jet takes the complexity out of cascading updates, follow these steps:

1. With the tblOrders and tblOrderDetails windows open, size and position the two datasheets as shown in Figure 13.23. Then click the surface of the tblOrders datasheet to make it the active window. Positioning the two table datasheet windows as shown in Figure 13.23 enables you to see the cascading updates in the tblOrderDetails window as they occur.
2. Change the value of the OrderID cell of the first record to the order number that you deleted in the preceding section. Alternatively, change the value of the OrderID cell to a value, such as **20000**, that's outside the range of the values of the test table.
3. Move the cursor to another record to cause the cascading update to occur. You immediately see the changes in the OrderID foreign-key field of the related dependent records (see Figure 13.23).

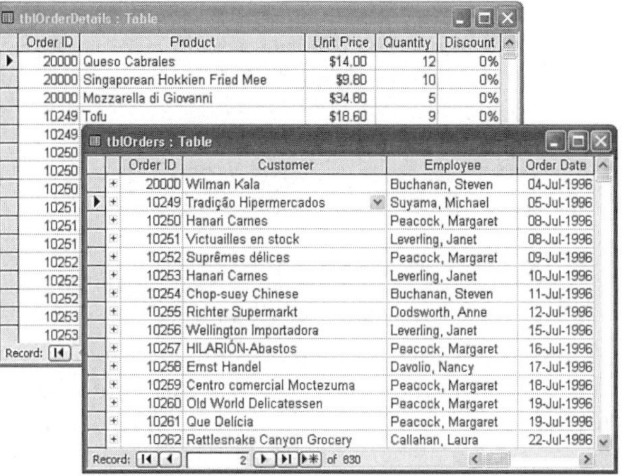

Figure 13.23
Changing the OrderID value in the base table automatically changes the OrderID values of related records, if you specify cascading updates.

No confirmation message appears when you execute a cascading update, because the effect is reversible. If you make an erroneous entry that causes an undesired cascading update, you can change the entry to its original value by reentering the original or the correct value manually.

Troubleshooting

Appending Records Causes Primary Key Problems

After appending records to an existing table, I can't create a primary key on the table.

The Unique Values Only test that you specify in the Query Properties window applies only to the query, not to the table to which you append the records. If possible, create a primary key for the destination table before appending records. For example, if you want to preclude the possibility of appending duplicate records to the tblShipAddresses table, you must first create the composite primary key, discussed in the "Using the New tblShipAddresses Table" section, which creates a No Duplicates index on the primary key, and then append the records.

Access Won't Create a Jet Relationship to a New Table

When I try to enforce referential integrity, I get a "Can't create relationship to enforce referential integrity" message.

You dragged the field symbols in the wrong direction when you created the relationship. The related (to-many) table is in the Table/Query list and the primary (one-to) table is in the Related Table/Query list. Close the Edit Relationships dialog, click the thin area of the join line to select the join, and then press the Delete key to delete the join. Make sure that you drag the field name that you want from the primary table to the related table. Alternatively, you can make these changes in the Edit Relationships dialog.

In the Real World—Alternatives to Action Queries

Microsoft calls any Jet query that alters table data an action query; the more common name is *update query*, as in updating the database. With Jet, however, there's a good reason to distinguish graphical action queries from the update queries used in online transaction processing (OLTP). Access's graphical action queries are intended primarily for bulk operations—adding, altering, or deleting large numbers of records in a single operation. OLTP usually deals with a single record or a few related records per operation. Creating a new Access action query each time you must update a single record clearly is an inefficient process, even if you add a parameter to designate the record you want to update or delete.

NOTE

> The sections that follow deal with advanced Access topics, which are covered in detail by chapters later in this book. In the real world, production databases reside on a file or application server and multiple users connect their client PC's front-end applications to networked client/server (MSDE or SQL Server) databases. Chapter 19, "Linking Access Front-Ends to Jet and Client/Server Tables," and Chapter 20, "Exploring Access Data Projects and SQL Server 2000," deal with client/server databases. The purpose of this "In the Real World" episode is to demonstrate the many options that Jet and SQL Server offer for executing action queries and their equivalents.

BROWSE-MODE UPDATING

Browse-mode table editing in Datasheet view is the obvious alternative to action queries when you need to add, alter, or delete only one or a few records. In the real world of networked multiuser databases, however, database administrators (DBAs) discourage or prohibit browse-mode editing because browsing usually requires multiple database connections for a single client PC and generates a substantial amount of network traffic.

Further, multiuser browse-mode editing often results in contention problems when two users attempt to edit the same record. Jet's optimistic record-locking approach minimizes such conflicts, but resolving which user's edit of a record is correct often requires manual intervention by the DBA or a supervisor. DBAs, especially, don't like to get involved with table-level contention issues. DBAs suffer perpetual contention with information technology managers and chief financial officers.

FORM-BASED UPDATING

Form-based updates are the most common approach for production Access applications using Jet databases. Designing Access forms for OLTP applications is the subject of the next two chapters. Typically, the main form displays field values of a single record, for example an invoice, in text boxes. Data from related tables, such as invoice line items, appear in a multirow subform. Conventional Access form-based updating, however, is a variation on the browse-mode datasheet updating process. The client PC maintains at least one connection to the database tables while the editing application is open and generates a significant amount of network traffic during the editing process.

The primary advantage of form-based over datasheet updating is that you can add to the form VBA code that resolves contention issues with error-handling procedures. An even better approach to contention problems is to write VBA code that takes advantage of the data-related events of ActiveX Data Objects (ADO). You must be a fluent VBA programmer, however, to write effective event-handling subprocedures for Access's form Recordsets.

UPDATING WITH SQL STATEMENTS

Sending SQL `INSERT` (append), `UPDATE`, or `DELETE` queries over the network to the database server is a much more efficient process than browse-mode editing with datasheets or forms. You send an SQL `SELECT` query to the database to retrieve only the record(s) you need, disconnect from the database, edit the records, open a connection, send one of the three types of SQL update queries, and then close the connection. Following is a typical T-SQL statement to add a new order with three line items to the Orders and Order Details tables of the NorthwindCS SQL Server database:

```
INSERT INTO Orders
   VALUES(11093, 'KOENE', 1,
      '5/15/1998', '6/1/1998', NULL, 3, NULL,
      'Königlich Essen',
      'Maubelstr. 90',
      'Brandenburg', '', '14776',
      'Germany')
```

```
INSERT INTO [Order Details]
   VALUES(11093, 24, 4.5, 24, 0)
INSERT INTO [Order Details]
   VALUES(11093, 36, 19, 36, 0)
INSERT INTO [Order Details]
   VALUES(11093, 42, 9.8, 12, 0)
```

The preceding SQL INSERT statement contains a substantial amount of text overhead, but executes very quickly over a network connection. You can quickly convert the statement into an SQL Server transaction by adding a BEGIN TRANS[ACTION] prefix and a COMMIT [TRANS[ACTION]] suffix. Wrapping the statement in a transaction assures that either all INSERT operations succeed or the entire operation fails and no change occurs to either of the tables. Adding TRANS[ACTION] statements qualifies the operation for OLTP. Chapter 21, "Moving from Jet Queries to Transact-SQL," describes T-SQL TRANSACTION syntax.

Another update alternative is to use an ADO 2.7 disconnected Recordset object to retrieve and update Jet or SQL Server 2000 records. The advantage of disconnected Recordset objects is that ADO handles most of the disconnecting and reconnecting chores for you. Disconnected Recordsets also let you edit multiple groups of records, and then send only the changes to the database with the UpdateBatch method. Sending only the changes is especially efficient for UPDATE operations.

→ For an example of the VBA code for batch update operations, **see** "Taking Advantage of Disconnected Recordsets," **p. 1312**.

UPDATING WITH SQL SERVER STORED PROCEDURES

The fastest and by far the most efficient method of updating is by using a parameterized stored procedure with a client/server database, such as SQL Server 2000. A stored procedure is a precompiled query that's similar to a stored Jet query (called a QueryDef object). Chapter 21 shows you how to write T-SQL parameterized stored procedures. SQL Server 2000—and thus MSDE2000—execute stored procedures faster than prior SQL Server versions.

You send the new values to add or change as stored procedure parameters. It's a common practice to write separate stored procedures for INSERT, UPDATE, and DELETE operations. DBAs greatly appreciate developers who take full advantage of stored procedures. Well-written stored procedures let DBAs spend more of their time contending with management, instead of putting out fires started by contentious OLTP users.

PART IV

DESIGNING FORMS AND REPORTS

CHAPTER 14

Creating and Using Access Forms

In this chapter

UNDERSTANDING THE ROLE OF ACCESS FORMS AND CONTROLS

Access forms create the user interface to your tables. Although you can use Table view and Query view to perform many of the same functions as forms, forms offer the advantage of presenting data in an organized and attractive manner. You can arrange the location of fields on a form so that data entry or editing operations for a single record follow a natural left-to-right, top-to-bottom sequence. You can limit the number of fields that appear on the form, and allow or prevent editing of specific field values. A properly designed form speeds data entry and minimizes operator keying errors.

Forms are constructed from a collection of individual design elements called *controls* or *control objects*. An Access form consists of a window in which you place the following classes of Access controls:

- *Bound controls* display the data from the table or query that serves as the data source of the form. Access's native bound controls include text boxes, combo and list boxes, subforms, and object frames for graphics. You can bind many Microsoft and third-party ActiveX controls to a form's data source. For example, you can bind the PivotTable, PivotChart, and Spreadsheet controls of the Office Web Components (OWC) to the data source of your form.
- *Unbound dynamic controls*, also called *calculated controls*, can display data from sources other than the table or query that serves as the data source for the form. For example, you can use an unbound text box to display the current date and time.
- *Unbound static controls* display, for example, fixed-text labels and logo graphics.

In most cases, you base an Access form on a table or query, which you specify during the initial form design step, to serve as the master data source for your form. This chapter concentrates on creating bound forms with dynamic text-based controls and subforms. A *subform* is another form contained within a form. The primary use of subforms is to display detail data from a table or query that has a many-to-one relationship with the form's master data source. The ease with which you can link the data in forms and subforms is one of Access's most important advantages over other database front-end platforms, such as Visual Basic 6.0 and Visual Studio .NET.

Access 2003 adds the following new features for forms:

- *Smart tags* for form controls. If you specify a smart tag for a table field, the smart tag appears in controls bound to that field. The Show Smart Tags on Forms check box of the Forms/Reports page of the Options dialog determines whether smart tags assigned to table fields appear on forms. Alternatively, you can add smart tags to form text boxes, combo boxes, and other dynamic controls.

→ To learn how to apply smart tags to table fields, **see** "Adding an Internet-Based Smart Tag to a Field," **p. 203**.

14

- *Object dependencies* of forms. The Object Dependencies task pane page displays objects that the form depends on, such as tables, queries, and subforms. You also can show objects that depend on the form, such as queries that use form control values as WHERE clause criteria.

→ For more information on object dependencies, **see** "Enabling and Viewing Object Dependencies," **p. 200**.

- *Form error autocorrection.* AutoCorrect's new On Object UI error-checking pop-up buttons indicate the following errors on forms: unassociated labels, invalid or duplicate accelerator key assignments, circular references, and duplicate option (radio button) values.
- *Property value change propagation for forms based on Jet tables and queries.* Changes to the following property values of table fields propagate to bound controls of forms and subforms: Description, Format, Decimal Places, Input Mask, IME Mode, IME Sentence Mode, Smart Tags, Column Heads, Column Widths, List Rows, List Width, and Limit To List. When a field property value changes, an Access smart tag lets you choose whether to accept or reject the change to the bound control.

→ To enable property change propagation, **see** "Activating the Access Property Options Smart Tag," **p. 203**.

- *Windows XP themes for controls.* If you want users to be able to apply custom Windows XP themes for form controls, you can enable this feature by marking the Use Windows Themed Controls on Forms check box of the Options dialog's Forms/Reports page. The examples of this chapter don't use XP themes for controls.
- *Combo box list sorting.* The Combo Box Wizard has an added sorting step.

NEW 2002

Access 2002 added PivotTable and PivotChart views of a bound form's master data source. These two form views are identical to those based on Jet or SQL Server queries and are described in Chapter 12, "Working with PivotTable and PivotChart Views." Access 2002 also added about 30 form events. These events primarily are of interest to developers writing VBA event-handling code, and aren't germane to the graphical form design techniques covered in this or the next chapter.

If you're upgrading from Access 97 to Access 2003, following are the form-related features added by Access 2000:

- *Subdatasheets in subforms* let you display lower levels of one-to-many relationships in datasheet-style subforms.

NEW 2002

- *In-site subform editing* enables simultaneous design mode editing of forms and subforms. The Design view of the subform appears within the region you assign to the Subform view in Run mode. Access 2002 added the Subform in New Window menu choice, which lets you temporarily disable in-situ subform editing.

- *Name AutoCorrect* automatically updates your forms and underlying queries for changes to object names, such as altering the name of a field in a table. To take advantage of Name AutoCorrect, you must mark the Track Name AutoCorrect Info check box on the General page of the Options dialog before making changes.
- *Control grouping* lets you define a group of controls that you can relocate as a single element.
- *Form view editing* lets you change many properties of controls without changing to Design view.
- *Justified and Vertical Alignment* options for labels improve the appearance of forms and reports.
- *Added graphics formats* let forms apply Web-standard .gif and .jpg files, plus additional graphics file formats, as background images for forms.

NOTE

> The form design techniques you learn in this chapter also apply to designing forms of Access Data Projects (ADP), one of the subjects of Chapter 20, "Exploring Access Data Projects and SQL Server 2000." Forms for ADP are identical in almost all respects to forms that use Jet tables or queries as data sources. The primary differences are ADP's connection to the SQL Server data source (instead of a native Jet connection) and Access's method of storing the forms in an .adp file (rather than in an .mdb file).

CREATING A BASIC TRANSACTION-PROCESSING FORM WITH THE FORM WIZARD

The content and appearance of your form depend on its use in your database application. Database applications fall into two basic categories:

- *Transaction-processing* applications add new records to tables, or edit or delete existing records. Transaction-processing applications require write access to (permissions for) the tables that are linked to the form.
- *Decision-support* applications supply information as graphs, tables, or individual data elements but don't allow the user to add or edit data. Decision-support applications require only read access to the tables that are linked to the form.

The form that you create in this example is typical of transaction-processing forms used to add new records to the many side of a one-to-many relationship. Adding line items to an invoice is an example of when a form of this kind—called a *one-to-many form*—is necessary. The objective of the HRActions form is to add new records to the HRActions table or let you edit the existing records.

Maintaining a record of employee performance reviews and actions resulting from the reviews is one of the primary responsibilities of personnel departments. For organizations with more than a few employees, a database is an effective tool for recording dates on which employees were hired, promoted, demoted, or terminated, and the justification for actions taken. This information often critical in the defense of wrongful termination or other litigation brought by disgruntled former (or even current) employees. Human resources—the more politically correct term for personnel—databases also can handle scheduling of periodic reviews and aid in assuring that managers or supervisors handle their human resources (HR) responsibilities in a timely manner.

If you didn't add records to the HRActions table when you created it in Chapter 5, "Working with Jet Databases and Tables," you can add them with the HRActions form you create in the following sections with the assistance of Access's Form Wizard. If you didn't create the HRActions table, you can import it from the Forms14.mdb database in the \Seua11\Chaptr14 folder of the accompanying CD-ROM.

TIP

If you import the HRActions table from Forms14.mdb, make sure to establish a one-to-many relationship between the Employees and HRActions table, as described in Chapter 5.

→ If you need help for creating or altering relationships, **see** "Establishing Relationships between Tables," **p. 189**.

The easiest way to create a form and subform combination is with the Access Form Wizard. The Form Wizard lets you create forms (with or without subforms) that contain fields from one or more tables or queries. The Form Wizard creates the basic design of the form and subform and adds text box controls to display and edit the values of data fields.

To create the HRActions form in Northwind.mdb with the Form Wizard, follow these steps:

1. Click the Forms shortcut of the Database window and then click the New button to open the New Form dialog.
2. Select Form Wizard from the list in the New Form dialog. (The Design View choice opens a blank form in Design view).

NOTE

The various AutoForm choices automatically create forms with the specified layouts: Columnar, Tabular, and Datasheet. The Chart Wizard choice invokes the Chart Wizard to add a graph or chart (not a PivotChart) to your form, and the PivotTable Wizard choice helps you create a form based on an Excel PivotTable report, not an OWC PivotTable. Using the Chart Wizard is one of the subjects of Chapter 18, "Adding Graphs, PivotCharts, and PivotTables."

14

→ For an example of how the Chart Wizard is used, see "Using the Chart Wizard to Create an Unlinked Graph," **p. 706**.

3. The drop-down list at the bottom of the New Form dialog lists the existing tables and queries that can serve as a source of data for a form. For this example, select the Employees table (see Figure 14.1).

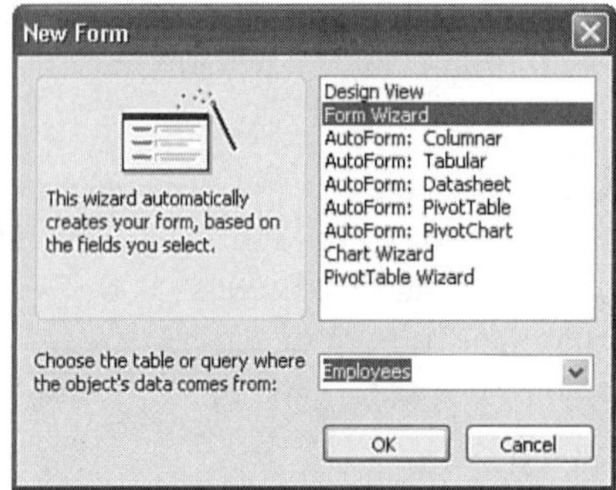

Figure 14.1
The New Form dialog displays initial selections for the HRActions form.

4. Click OK, and Access displays the first dialog of the Form Wizard.
5. Click to select the EmployeeID field in the Available Fields list, and then click the > button to move the EmployeeID field from the Available Fields list to the Selected Fields list. Alternatively, you can double-click the field name to move it.
6. Repeat step 5 for the LastName, FirstName, and Title fields of the Employees table so that you can edit data in these fields (see Figure 14.2).

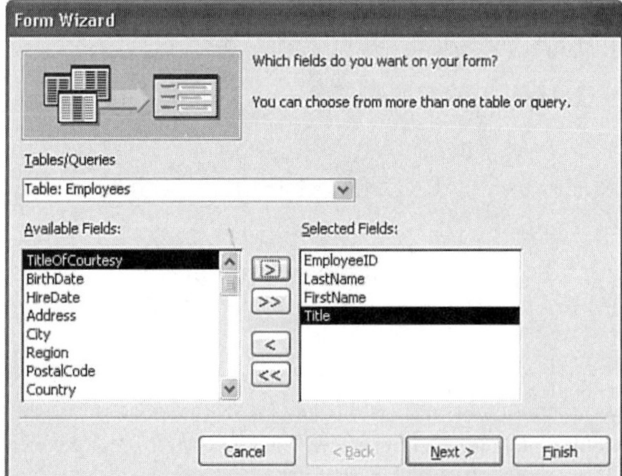

Figure 14.2
Select the Employees fields to display in your form. The EmployeeID field is an AutoNumber field, so you can't edit its value.

7. Open the Tables/Queries drop-down list, and select the HRActions table to serve as the data source for the subform. The Available Fields list changes to show the available fields in the HRActions table.
8. Click the >> button to copy all fields from the Available Fields list to the Selected Fields list.

NOTE

> If you haven't established a one-to-many relationship between the Employees and HRActions table, you receive an error message at this point. When you acknowledge the error message, the Relationships window opens. Add the relationship between EmployeeID fields of the two tables and close the Relationships window. You must then click Cancel, and start over from step 1.

TIP

> It's easy to change the sequence of location of form fields from the default—the order of fields in the table proposed by the Wizard and added by clicking the >> button. Select the first field and click > to position it at the upper-left corner of the form. Select each field and then click > to add the remaining fields in the sequence you want. If you've added many fields to a form, but decide to change your layout, it's often faster to delete the newly created form, and then start over with the Wizard.

9. The EmployeeID field from the HRActions table is included in the Selected Fields list, but you don't need to include it in the subform. The form determines the current Employees record. Select the HRActions.EmployeeID field in the list of Selected Fields and then click the < button to remove this field from the Selected Fields list (see Figure 14.3). When you remove the HRActions.EmployeeID field, it returns to the Available Fields list. The EmployeeID field that remains in the Selected Fields list is from the Employees table.

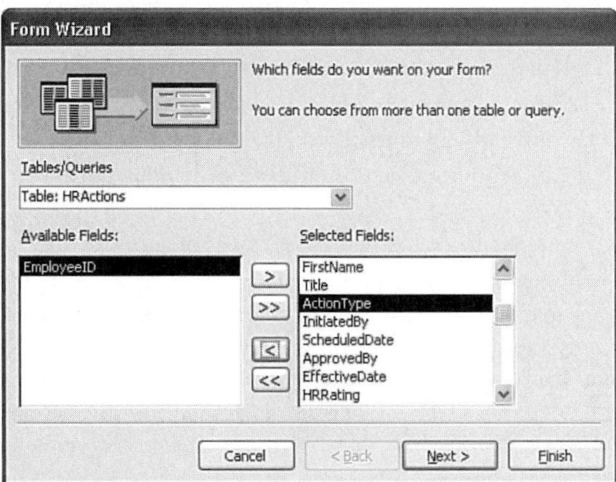

Figure 14.3 Add all HRActions fields except the HRActions. EmployeeID field to provide subform fields.

10. Click Next to display the Form Wizard's second dialog, which is shown in Figure 14.4.

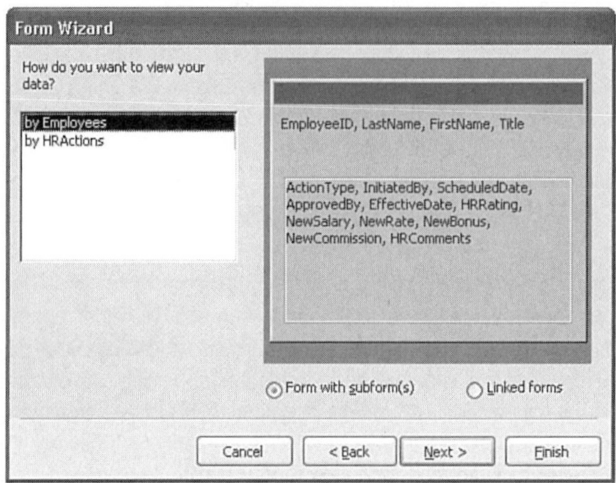

Figure 14.4
The Form Wizard sets default values for a form-subform relationship based on the one-to-many relationship of the Employees and HRActions tables.

TIP

Verify in the second Wizard dialog that the fields you specified in the first dialog appear in the proper form or subform location. The picture in the upper-right area of the Form Wizard dialog shows the fields of the master form (from the Employees table), with a sunken frame that lists the fields of the subform (from the HRActions table). If you realize that you made an error—or if you change your mind about something—and you're on a later step of the Form Wizard, you can click the Back button to return to and modify your previous choices. You can also click Cancel at any time to abort the form-creation process and return to the Database window.

11. The fields you've selected to appear on the form come from two different tables, so the Form Wizard asks how you want to view the data. Because you want to view the data by employee, with the employee's human resources action data in a subform, accept By Employees (the default) and make sure that the Form with Subform(s) option is selected (refer to Figure 14.4).

NOTE

In one-to-many forms, the subform needs to be linked to the main form so that all records displayed in the subform are related to the current record displayed in the main form. The Form Wizard obtains the information it needs to link the main form and subform from a join in the Relationships window (in this case, between the Employees table and the HRActions table).

12. Click Next to open the third Wizard dialog, which asks you to select the layout style for the subform. Clicking different options gives you a preview thumbnail in the dialog. Select the Tabular option (see Figure 14.5). This option creates a subform that displays the data from the HRActions table in a tabular format that is similar to Datasheet view but has a structure in which you can change the formatting (colors, column headings, and so on).

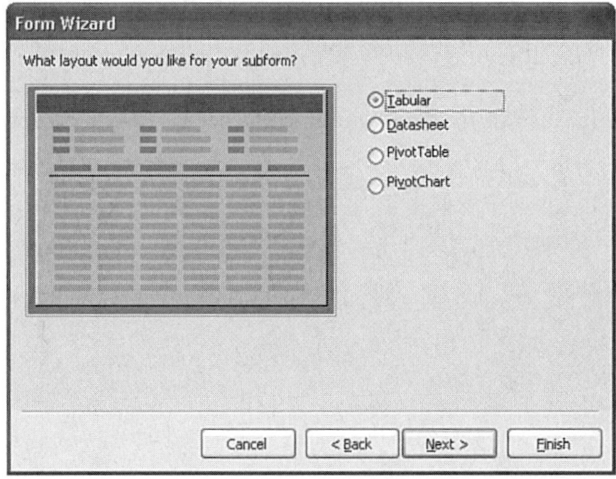

Figure 14.5
Select a tabular layout for the HRActions form and subform to allow specifying custom formatting and other property values for the subform fields.

NOTE

Access 2002 added to the Wizard two new display options—PivotTable and PivotChart for the subform. Chapter 18 shows you how to use the Form Wizard to generate PivotTable and PivotChart subforms.

13. Click Next to move to the fourth Wizard dialog, which asks you to select a style for the new form. The Access Form Wizard has several predefined styles. Because the sample form you're creating is for use by a data-entry operator and doesn't require special effects to decorate the form's background, accept the Standard default (see Figure 14.6).

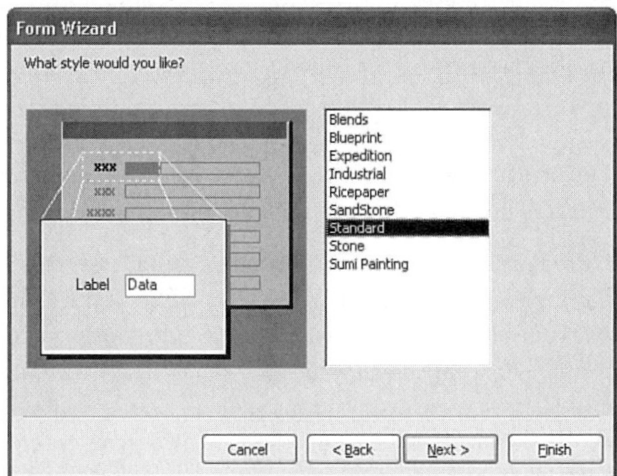

Figure 14.6
Select a predefined form style in the Form Wizard's fourth dialog. The conservative Standard style is the best choice for most data-entry forms.

14. Click Next to open the last Form Wizard dialog, which asks you to type a name for the master form and subform. Type **frmHRActions** in the Form text box and

sbfHRActions in the Subform text box (see Figure 14.7). Accept the default Open the Form to View or Enter Information option, and then click Finish to complete your form. (If you want Access to display help for working with your completed form, select the Display Help on Working with the Form? check box before you click Finish.)

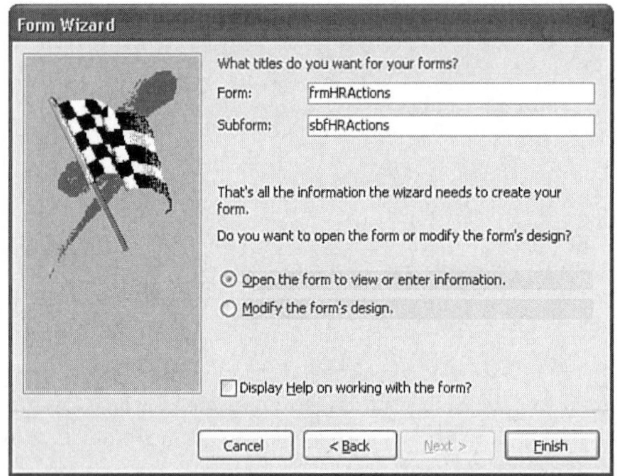

Figure 14.7
Type a name for the main form and its subform. Access developers commonly use *frm* and *sbf* prefixes for forms and subforms, respectively.

TIP

> Access suggests default names for the form and any subforms; but the default names seldom are appropriate to production databases. When naming forms, make sure to specify names that are indicative of what the form really does. Also, unless you intend to use the subform with other forms, make sure that you include the name of the main form (or an abbreviation) in the name of your subform so that the relationship between the form and subform is evident. Using standard Access naming conventions–*frm* and *sbf* prefixes for forms and subforms, respectively–is the approach used by most Access developers. You later can set the Caption property value of the form to a name meaningful to users.

The Form Wizard creates and automatically saves the form and subform with the names you specified in the last dialog, and then opens the form (see Figure 14.8).

On the main form, the Form Wizard creates a single column of text boxes—each with an associated label—for entering or editing data values in three of the four fields from the Employees table that you selected for the master form. The subform contains all the fields from the HRActions table (except the EmployeeID field) arranged in a tabular layout. Access uses the fields' Caption property values as default text box labels and also as column headings for the tabular subform. Access adds the name that you entered for the subform as the label for the subform container.

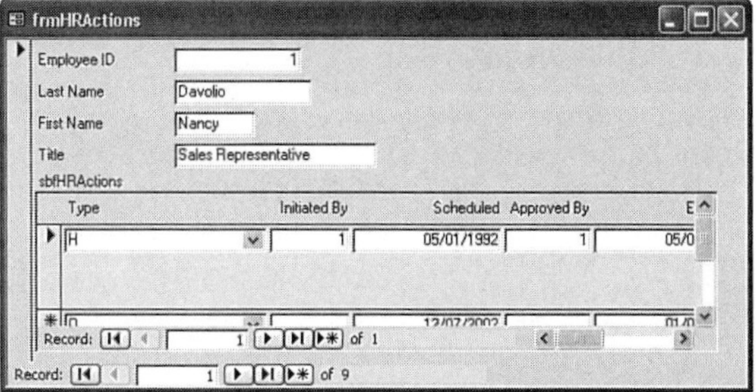

Figure 14.8
The basic frmHRActions form created by the Form Wizard is the starting point of the final form-design process.

In Figure 14.8, notice that the Effective Date and the remaining fields of the HRActions table are partially or completely obscured, and scroll bars appear in the subform area. The subform is larger than the area created for it in the main form, so Access automatically adds scroll bars to let you access all data displayed in the subform. The subform's record navigation buttons let you scroll all records related to the current record of the main form.

The basic form as created by the Form Wizard needs many cosmetic adjustments to the layout of the main form and, especially, the subform. The remaining discussions and exercises in this chapter show you how to modify forms created with the Form Wizard; you can apply these form-editing skills when you create your own forms from scratch, as described in the next chapter.

TIP

No matter how adept you become at designing Access forms, using the Form Wizard to create the basic form design saves you time.

USING THE FORM DESIGN WINDOW

To modify the design of the form you create with the Wizard, click the View button on the toolbar to open the Form Design window (see Figure 14.9, where the height of the form has been increased). The floating window that appears in Form Design mode contains an undocked toolbar, called the *Toolbox*, that lets you place new control elements on a form. Using the Toolbox to add new control elements to the form is covered in the next chapter. For this exercise, hide the Toolbox by clicking the Toolbox button on the Forms toolbar or by clicking the Close Window button in the upper-right corner of the Toolbox.

NOTE

Access usually shows the Toolbox automatically whenever you enter Form Design mode. If you've manually closed the Toolbox, Access doesn't automatically display it the next time you open the Form Design window. To display the Toolbox, click the Toolbox button on the Forms toolbar, or choose View, Toolbox.

The frmHRActions form lets you experiment with methods of modifying forms and their contents, which are described in the following sections.

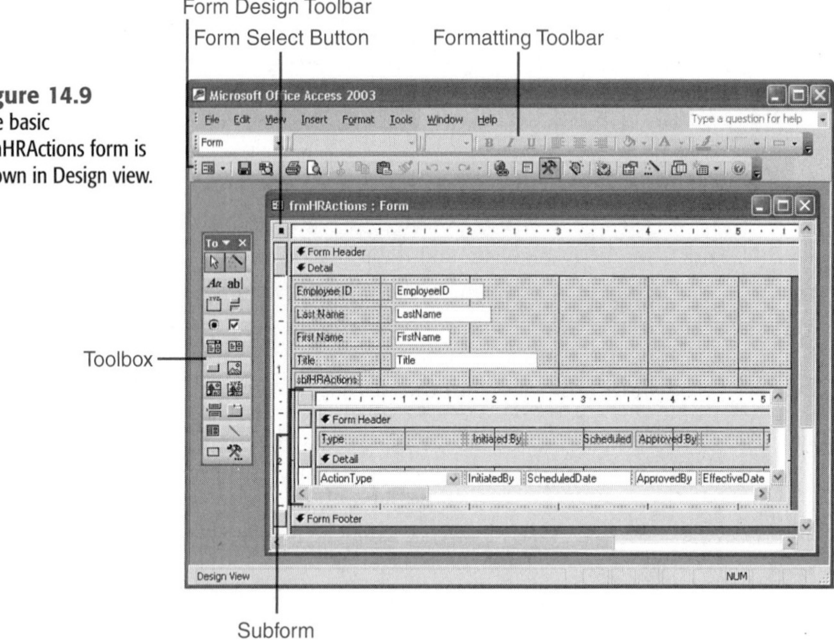

Figure 14.9
The basic frmHRActions form is shown in Design view.

TIP

Use the Form Select button to select the entire form when a section or control is the currently selected object. Clicking the Form Select button is much faster than choosing Edit, Select Form. It's even faster, however, to press Ctrl+R.

Elements of the Form Design Window

Access divides forms into five sections: Form Header, Page Header, Detail, Page Footer, and Form Footer. Page Headers and Footers are optional, and don't appear in Figure 14.9. The Form Design window includes the following basic elements:

- The Form Design toolbar contains buttons that are shortcuts for menu selections in Form Design mode. The functions of the buttons and their equivalent menu choices are listed in tables in the next section, "Form Design Toolbar Buttons and Menu Choices."
- The Formatting toolbar contains buttons that are shortcuts for color, text, border, and various other formatting options. The functions of the formatting buttons and their equivalent menu choices are listed in tables in the next section.
- Vertical and horizontal rulers help you determine the size and placement of objects on the form.

TIP

The rulers are calibrated in inches for the U.S. version of Access and in centimeters for versions of Access that are supplied to countries where the metric system is used. To change from U.S. to metric units, open Control Panel's Regional Settings or Options tool, click the Number tab, and change the Measurement System setting from U.S. to Metric.

- The top of the Form Footer bar represents the bottom of the form. You can click and drag this bar to a new location. Margins are important when you are designing a subform to fit within a rectangle of a predetermined size on the main form.
- Vertical and horizontal scroll bars let you view those parts of the form that are outside the boundaries of the form window.
- A Form Header bar defines the height of the form's header section. The bar appears only if you choose to add a header and footer to your form, or you create the form with the Form Wizard. The Form Header section contains static text, graphic images, and other controls that appear at the top of the form. The Form Header appears only on the first page of a multipage form; subsequent printed pages of forms display an optional Page Header. (Page Headers and Footers don't display in Form view; Page Headers and Footers apply only when you print forms.) You add Form and Page Headers by choosing View, Form Header/Footer and View, Page Header/Footer, respectively.
- A Form Detail bar divides the Form Header from the rest of the form. Form controls that display data from your tables and queries, plus static data elements such as labels and logos, are on the Form Detail bar.
- A Form Footer bar defines the height of the Form Footer section. The Form Footer section is similar in function to the Form Header section. If you print a multipage form, the Form Footer appears only at the bottom of the last page; optional Page Footers appear at the bottom of preceding printed pages.

NOTE

Although the form shown previously in Figure 14.9 has both Form Header and Form Footer sections, neither section takes up any space on the form—that's why the Form Header bar touches the Detail bar, and the Form Footer bar touches the bottom margin of the form. Even though no text or other information is in the header and footer areas, the Form Wizard adds these two elements to the form automatically. When you create a new, blank form without using the Form Wizard, header and footer sections aren't added automatically.

You delete Form Header and Form Footer sections by choosing View, Form Header/Footer to clear the menu check mark. Similarly, you delete Page Headers for printed forms, by choosing View, Page Header/Footer.

NOTE

> If a header or footer section contains any text or other form controls when you try to delete it, Access displays a dialog warning that you are about to lose the contents of the header and footer.

FORM DESIGN TOOLBAR BUTTONS AND MENU CHOICES

The Form Design toolbar of Access 2003 contains several buttons that apply only to the design of forms. You select color and font options from the Format toolbar. Table 14.1 lists the function and equivalent menu choice for each of the Form Design toolbar buttons that are specific to Access 2003. The buttons that relate to text and color formatting are described in the following section, "The Formatting Toolbar."

TABLE 14.1 STANDARD FORM-RELATED TOOLBAR BUTTONS IN FORM DESIGN VIEW

Button	Menu Choice	Function
	View, Form View	Displays the form in Run mode (clicking the arrow at the right of this button displays a drop-down list that lets you select Datasheet view).
	File, Save	Saves the current form.
	File, Search	Opens the Basic Search task pane.
	File, Print	Prints with the current printer settings all records in the table using the onscreen form to format the printed data.
	File, Print Preview	Selects Print Preview to display how your form appears if printed. You can print the form from the Print Preview window.
	Edit, Cut (Ctrl+X)	Copies selected controls to the Clipboard and deletes them from the form.
	Edit, Copy (Ctrl+C)	Copies selected controls to the Clipboard for duplication.
	Edit, Paste (Ctrl+V)	Pastes controls on the Clipboard to the active section of the form.
	None	Invokes the Format Painter and copies formatting from selected objects to another object of similar type.
	Edit, Undo	Undoes the changes you made to the form in last to first order.

Button	Menu Choice	Function
	Edit, Redo	Redoes the undoes you made to the form in sequence.
	Insert, Hyperlink	Inserts a new Hyperlink control or lets you edit an existing Hyperlink control.
	View, Field List	Displays a list of the fields in the query or table that's the data source for the main form.
	View, Toolbox	Displays or closes the Toolbox.
	Format, AutoFormat	Applies your choice of several predefined form formats, including formatting for the back ground bitmap of a form, text fonts, and color settings.
	View, Code	Opens the VBA Editor for the code behind the active form.
	View, Properties	Displays the Properties window for one of the two sections of the form when you click the section bars, for the entire form after you click the Form Select button, or for a control when you select it.
	None	Displays the Build Wizard for the selected object or property in the form. This button is enabled only if Access has a Builder for the selected item.
	None	Creates a new object (Table is the default). Click the arrow at the right of this button to see a drop-down list of the objects you can create. You can't run AutoForm or AutoReport in Form Design view.

NOTE

Multiple Undo and Redo operations in Form, Report, and Table Design view were new in Access 2002. In previous versions, Undo and Redo were limited to a single design change.

Figure 14.10 shows the Form Design window after adding Page Headers and Footers to the form and clicking the Properties button with the EmployeeID text box selected.

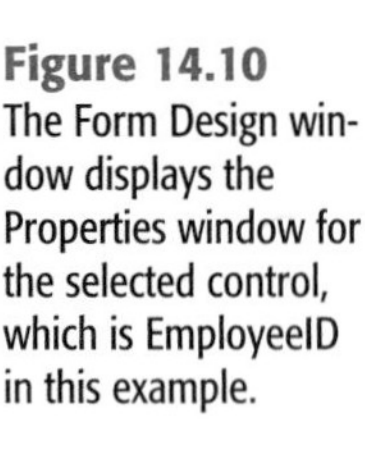

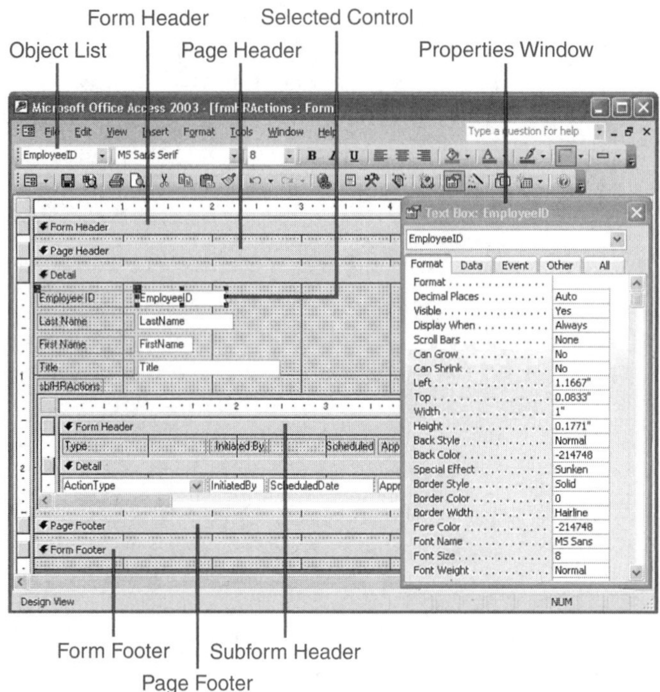

Figure 14.10
The Form Design window displays the Properties window for the selected control, which is EmployeeID in this example.

THE FORMATTING TOOLBAR

Access displays in Form and Report Design view shortcut buttons and drop-down lists for all text formatting, line, color, and cell effects options on a separate toolbar: the Formatting toolbar. The Object list at the extreme left of the Formatting toolbar displays the name of the currently selected object on the form and lets you rapidly select another object on the form by selecting its name in the list. In Figure 14.10, the EmployeeID text box is the currently selected object, so the Font and Font Size lists are enabled.

Table 14.2 lists the function of each text-formatting button in Form Design view and its equivalent property setting.

TABLE 14.2 TOOLBAR BUTTONS FOR TEXT CONTROLS IN FORM DESIGN MODE

Button	Function	Property and Value
B	Sets text style to bold (the default for titles and labels).	Font Weight = Bold
I	Sets italic text style.	Font Italic = Yes

Button	Function	Property and Value
	Sets underline text style.	Font Underline = Yes
	Left-justifies text within border.	Text Align = Left
	Centers text horizontally within border.	Text Align = Center
	Right justifies text within border.	Text Align = Right
	Displays a color palette from which you choose the background color for the selected object.	Back Color = *number*
	Displays a color palette from which you choose the color of the text in the selected object.	Fore Color = *number*
	Displays a color palette from which you choose the color for the border of the selected object.	Border Color = *number*
	Displays a drop-down list from which you choose the width of the selected object's borders. You can select a hairline width or widths ranging from 1 to 6 points.	Border Width = *width*
	Displays a drop-down list from which you choose a special effect for how the selected object is displayed. You can choose Flat, Raised, Sunken, Etched, Shadowed, or Chiseled.	Special Effect = *name*

SETTING FORM APPEARANCE PROPERTIES

Access offers an extraordinary number of formatting properties that you can use to customize the appearance of your forms and the control objects they contain. You also can apply most of the property settings described in the following sections to subforms.

DEFAULT VALUES FOR FORMS

You can change some of the default values used in the creation of all forms by choosing Tools, Options and clicking the Forms/Reports tab (see Figure 14.11). You can create a form to use as a template and replace the standard (Normal) template, and you can determine how objects are displayed when chosen. The effects of these options are described in the sections that follow. The options that you or other Access users choose in the Options dialog are saved for each user ID in the MSysOptions table of the current System.mdw workgroup system file.

You can change the default values for the current form, section, or controls by choosing the object and then changing the default values displayed in the Properties window for that object. You can also use the AutoFormat feature to quickly apply a predefined format to all controls in the form. The next section describes using AutoFormat to change a form's appearance, and subsequent sections describe ways to change the format of text or controls manually on a form.

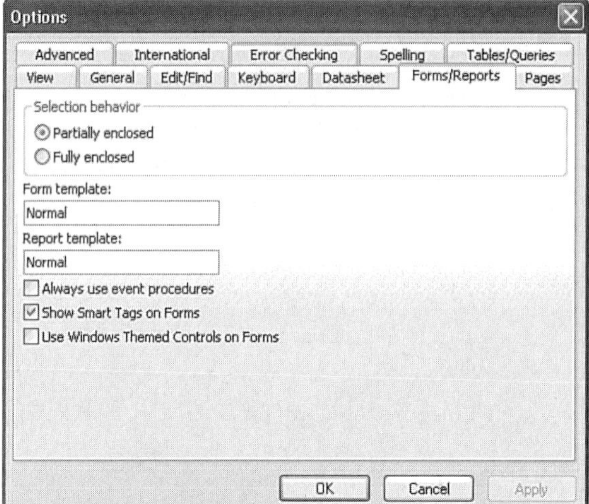

Figure 14.11
You can change default values in the Forms/Reports page of the Options dialog.

TIP

Check the title bar of the Properties window before you change property values to make sure the selected object is the one whose properties you want to change. It's a common practice to leave the Properties window open as you alter the form design, and the selected object might not be the object you intend.

Access 2002 added a drop-down list to the Properties window that lets you select any object on the form or report. Selecting objects from the list in the Properties window is faster than selecting from the Object list on the toolbar.

14

USING AUTOFORMAT

AutoFormat lets you apply a predefined format to an entire form with only a few mouse clicks. Access 2003 comes with several predefined formats, and you also can create your own formats for use with AutoFormat. The AutoFormat dialog is similar to the third Form Wizard (form layout) dialog described earlier in the chapter.

APPLYING AN AUTOFORMAT

To apply a format to a form with AutoFormat, follow these steps:

1. Press Ctrl+R or click the Form Select button to apply your AutoFormat selection to the entire form. If you select a control or other object, AutoFormat is applied only to the selected object.

2. Click the toolbar's AutoFormat button to open the AutoFormat dialog shown in Figure 14.12.

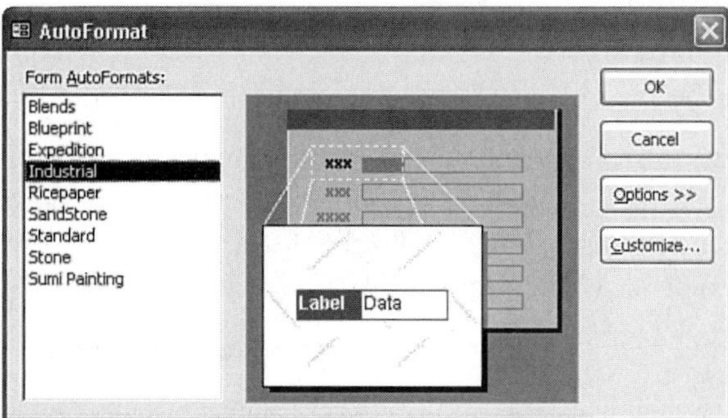

Figure 14.12 Use the AutoFormat feature to apply a predefined format to an entire form or a section of a form.

3. Click to select the format you want to use in the Form AutoFormats list; a preview of the format you select appears in the window in the center of the dialog.
4. Click OK to apply the format to the form. Figure 14.13 shows the frmHRActions form after the Industrial format has been applied.
5. Change the style to the original Standard format you selected when creating the form, if you want. You can't undo initial application of an AutoFormat.

The AutoFormat dialog, when expanded by clicking the Options button, lets you omit the application of font, color, or border style information to your form when you apply the AutoFormat. Deselect the check box for the elements of the AutoFormat that you don't want AutoFormat to apply to your form.

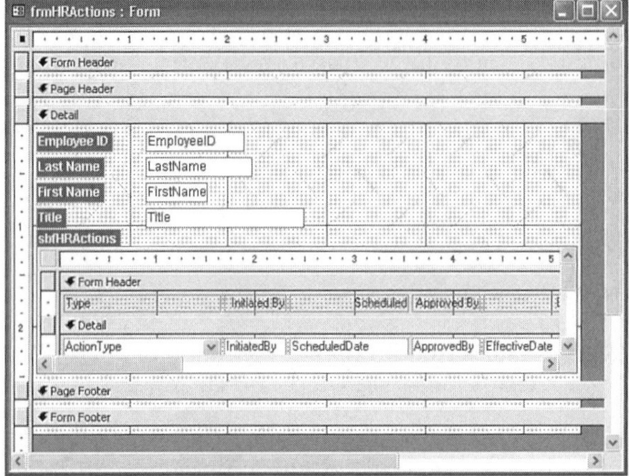

Figure 14.13
The frmHRActions form has the Industrial format (a tread-plate pattern) applied to the main form. Applying this format also changes label formatting (refer to Figure 14.12).

CREATING AND CUSTOMIZING AUTOFORMATS

The predefined AutoFormat styles might not suit your tastes, or you might want to create AutoFormat styles specific to your company or application.

Applying formatting to a form through an AutoFormat style is by far the easiest way to create standardized forms for your database application—especially because the Form Wizard uses the same format style list as the AutoFormat feature. In other words, any AutoFormat you create also becomes available in the Form Wizard dialog.

To create a new AutoFormat or customize an existing one, follow these steps:

1. Create a form and alter its appearance (using the techniques described in the next five sections of this chapter) so that the form has the font, border, background picture, and other options adjusted exactly the way you want them for your new or customized AutoFormat.
2. Click the AutoFormat button to display the AutoFormat dialog. If you want to modify an existing AutoFormat, select it in the Form AutoFormats list now.
3. Click the Customize button to display the Customize AutoFormat dialog shown in Figure 14.14.

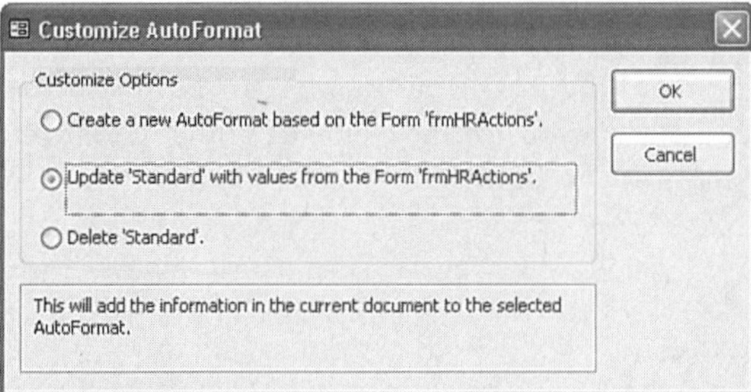

Figure 14.14
The Customize AutoFormat dialog is used to create, modify, or delete an AutoFormat.

4. Select the Create a New AutoFormat Based on the Form *formname* option, or the Update *formatname* with Values from the Form *formname* option to create or modify an AutoFormat, respectively. (Deleting AutoFormats is covered in the next section.)
5. Click OK. If you're creating a new AutoFormat, the New Style Name dialog opens. Type an appropriate name for your new AutoFormat and click OK. Access creates or updates the AutoFormat and returns you to the AutoFormat dialog.
6. Click Close to close the AutoFormat dialog.

DELETING AUTOFORMATS

If you've created your own AutoFormats, you might want to delete an AutoFormat that you no longer use. To delete an AutoFormat, follow these steps:

1. Open any form in Design view.
2. Click the AutoFormat button to display the AutoFormat dialog.
3. Click to select the AutoFormat you want to delete in the Form AutoFormats list and then click the Customize button. Access displays the Customize AutoFormat dialog (refer to Figure 14.14).
4. Select the Delete *formname* option and click OK. Access deletes that AutoFormat from the list.

TIP

Be sure to select the correct AutoFormat for deletion before you click OK. Access doesn't ask for confirmation when you delete an AutoFormat.

5. Click Close to close the AutoFormat dialog.

CHANGING AN OBJECT'S COLORS

You select object colors through the buttons on the Formatting toolbar, as well as through property settings that are accessible through the Properties window of the form and individual objects on the form. The following sections describe how to use the Formatting toolbar controls and the Property dialog to change background and foreground colors of form sections and control objects, as well as border properties of control objects.

BACKGROUND COLORS

The background color (Back Color property) of a form section (Header, Detail, or Footer) applies to all areas of that section except areas occupied by control objects that don't have a transparent background. The default background color of all sections of forms created by the Form Wizard depends on the specific form style you choose when you create the form; the Standard format scheme used to create the frmHRActions form, for example, is the Windows system color for 3D Objects (the default is light gray).

The 40 default color choices on the palette displayed by the Fill/Back Color toolbar button are standard colors of Windows XP/2000 in 256+ color mode. If you're creating a form that you intend to print, a dark or deeply textured background will not only be distracting but will also consume substantial amounts of printer toner. Data-entry operators often prefer a light gray background rather than a colored, or textured background. Colored and textured backgrounds tend to distract users.

If you've selected a picture as the background for a form—or used an AutoFormat style that includes a background picture, such as the International style of Northwind.mdb's Customers form—then any changes you make in the background color of the form are hidden by the overlying picture.

To change the background color of a section of a form, follow these steps:

1. Click an empty area within the section of the form (Header, Detail, or Footer) whose background color you want to change. Alternatively, click the section's header bar. This step selects the appropriate section.
2. Click the Fill/Back Color button on the toolbar to display the color palette.
3. Click the box that contains the color you want to use.

Because the background color of each form section is independent, you must repeat the process if you want to change the color for other sections of your form. The Transparent button of the Fill/Back Color palette is disabled when a form section is chosen because a transparent background color isn't applicable to forms.

You choose the background color for a control object, such as a label, just as you do for a form. In most cases, the chosen background color of labels is the same as that of the form, so click the Transparent button to allow the background color to appear. The default value of the Back Color property of text boxes is white so that text boxes (and the data they contain) contrast with the form's background color.

CHANGING THE BACKGROUND BITMAP

You can use a bitmap picture as the background for a form. Unlike background colors, of which you can have several, you select a single bitmap picture for the entire form. Access 2003 comes with a few bitmap pictures that it uses in the AutoFormat formats—International, for example, uses the Globe.wmf graphics file (stored in the Program Files\Microsoft Office\Office11\Bitmaps\Styles folder) as the background for the form. You can use any .bmp, .dib, .emf, .gif, .ico, .jpg, .pcx, .png, or .wmf graphics file as a background for a form. Access 2000 added the capability to use compressed .gif, .jpg, .pcx, and .png files.

TIP

> Forms with bitmap graphics as a background can look dramatic and, therefore, are best suited for decision-support forms intended for management personnel. (Management types are known to prefer form over substance.) For accurate, high-speed data entry, keep your transaction-processing forms visually simple so that users can easily distinguish data fields on the form and easily read text labels.

You set or remove a form's background bitmap through the Properties window of the form; you can also specify several viewing and formatting properties for the background picture. Follow these steps to set the background picture properties of a form:

1. Open the form in Design view if necessary.

2. Click the Form Select button.
3. If the Properties window isn't already open, click the Properties button on the toolbar to display this window.
4. Click the Format tab in the Properties window and scroll down to the end of the Format properties list to view the various Picture properties: Picture, Picture Type, Picture Size Mode, Picture Alignment, and Picture Tiling. These properties and their effects are described in the list following these numbered steps.
5. Specify the path to the graphics file in the Picture text box, and set the various Picture properties until you're satisfied with the appearance of the form. As you change each property, results of the change become immediately visible on the form. Figure 14.15 illustrates use of a .gif image of a book cover as the background for the detail section of a form.

Figure 14.15
A bitmap from a scan of a book cover creates the background for this form.

6. Optionally, close the Properties window.

The following list summarizes form properties related to the background picture, available choices for each property, and the effects of each choice:

- The Picture property contains the folder path and file name of the graphics file that Access uses as the form's background. You can either type the folder path and file name directly in the Picture property text box, or use the Builder to help you select the background graphics file. To use the Builder, click the Picture property field to select that field and then click the Build button that appears next to the text box. Access opens the Insert Picture dialog; navigate to the location and select the graphics file to use, as shown in Figure 14.16.

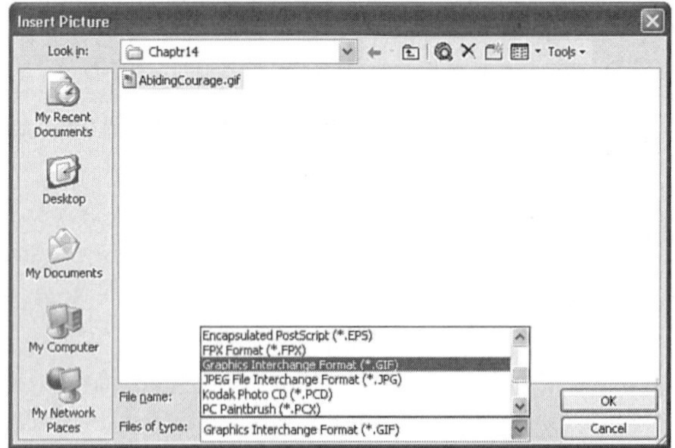

Figure 14.16
Use the Insert Picture dialog to select a graphics file for a form's background.

TIP

To remove a background picture, delete the entry in the Picture text box and click Yes when asked if you want to remove the picture from the form.

- The Picture Type property specifies the method that Access uses to attach the background picture to the form. You can select either Embedded or Linked as the picture type. Use the Embedded picture type, especially if you intend to distribute your database application; the resulting form is self-contained and doesn't rely on the presence of external files that might be moved or deleted. If you have many forms that use the same background bitmap graphic, linking the background picture can save some disk space.
- The Picture Size Mode property controls how Access sizes the background picture. The available choices are Clip, Stretch, and Zoom. Clip causes Access to display the picture at its full size behind the form; if the picture is larger than the form, the picture is clipped to fit the form. If the picture is smaller than the form, the form's own background color shows in any part of the form background not covered by the picture. Stretch causes Access to stretch the picture vertically and horizontally to match the size of the form; the Stretch option permits distortions in the picture. Zoom causes Access to magnify the picture, without distortion, to fit the size of the form.

- The Picture Alignment property controls where Access positions the background picture. The available choices are Top-left (aligns the upper-left corner of the picture with the upper-left corner of the form window), Top-right (aligns the upper-right corner of the picture with the upper-right corner of the form window), Center (places the picture in the center of the form window), Bottom-left (aligns the lower-left corner of the picture with the lower-left corner of the form), Bottom-right (aligns the lower-right corner of the picture with the lower-right corner of the form), and Form Center (centers the picture on the form).

TIP

To ensure that a background picture is displayed relative to the form, rather than the form's window, select Form Center as the value for the Picture Alignment property.

- The Picture Tiling property has two permissible values: Yes or No. Tiling means that the picture is repeatedly displayed to fill the entire form or form window (if the Picture Alignment property is set to Form Center, the tiling fills just the form).

Now that you know how to adjust the background picture and colors of a form, the next section describes how to adjust the foreground colors and border properties of the form and objects on the form.

Foreground Color, Border Color, and Border Style

You might set the foreground color, border color, and border width through buttons on the Formatting toolbar or directly in the Properties window for a selected control. To set a border style (solid style or a variety of dashed-line styles), you must set the property directly in the Properties window.

Foreground color (the Fore Color property) is applicable only to control objects. (The Font/Fore Color button on the toolbar is disabled when you select a form section.) Foreground color specifies the color for the text in labels and text boxes. The default value of the Fore Color property is black. You choose border colors for control objects that have borders by using the Line/Border Color toolbar button.

The Special Effects button of the Formatting toolbar lets you simulate special effects for control objects, such as a raised or sunken appearance. The Line/Border Width button allows you to control the width of the border of controls. The Formatting toolbar buttons were listed earlier in this chapter in Table 14.2.

To set a control's foreground color, border width, or border color by using the Formatting toolbar buttons, first click the control whose properties you want to change and then click the arrow to the right of the toolbar button for the property you want to change. Click the color or line width you want for the control.

To set a control's foreground color, border width, border color, or border style in the Properties window, first select the control whose properties you want to change by clicking it. If necessary, open the Properties window by clicking the Properties button on the toolbar. Click the Format tab in the Properties window and then scroll to the text box for the property you want to change. Most of the border properties are selected from drop-down lists; color properties require you to type a number that represents the desired color in Windows 98/Me or Windows 2000/NT color notation. (Windows color notation is too complex to explain here; the easiest way to enter color values is with the toolbar buttons or by using the color Builder described in the following section, "Creating Custom Colors with the Color Builder.")

Creating Custom Colors with the Color Builder

If you aren't satisfied with one of the predefined colors for your form sections or control objects, you can specify your own custom colors by following these steps:

1. Place the cursor in the Back Color, Fore Color, or Border Color text box of the Properties window for a form section or control.
2. Click the Builder button to open the Color dialog. The basic form of this dialog enables you to choose from a set of 48 colors. If one of these colors suits your taste, click the color square and then click OK to assign that color as the value of the property, and close the dialog. If you want a custom color, proceed to step 3.
3. Click the Define Custom Colors button to expand the Color dialog to include the Hue/Saturation and Luminance windows, as shown in Figure 14.17.

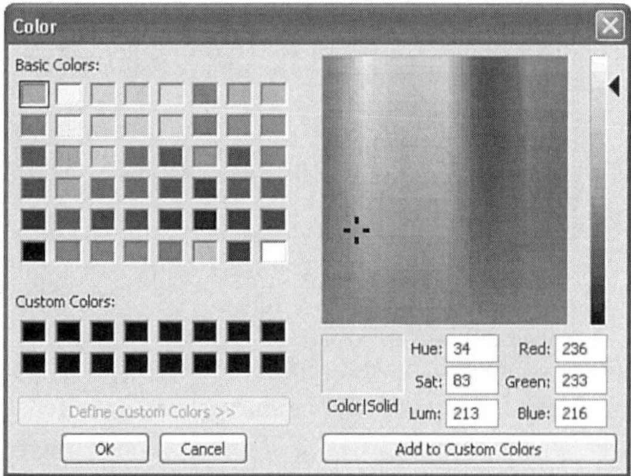

Figure 14.17 Define a custom color in the expanded Color dialog.

4. Click and drag the cursor within the square Hue/Saturation area to choose the color you want.
5. Click and drag the arrow at the right of the rectangular luminance area while observing the Color block; release the mouse button when the Color block has the luminance (brightness) value you want.

6. Click Add to Custom Colors to add your new color to the first of the 16 custom color blocks.
7. Click the new custom color block to select it. Click OK to add this color value to the property, and close the Color dialog.

In 256-color VGA mode, any colors you choose or create, other than the standard Windows 256-color palette, are simulated by a dithering process. Dithering alternates pixels of differing colors to create the usually imperfect illusion of a solid color.

SELECTING, EDITING, AND MOVING FORM ELEMENTS AND CONTROLS

The properties that apply to the entire form, to the five sections of the form, and to each control object on the form are determined by the values shown in the Properties window. To view the Properties window for a control, select the control by clicking anywhere on its surface; then click the Properties button on the toolbar. Alternatively, right-click the control and choose Properties from the pop-up menu.

The following list describes how to select and display the properties of form sections and control objects:

- **Header section only**—To select the Form Header, click the Form Header or Page Header bar. The set of properties you work with applies only to the Form Header or Page Header section.
- **Detail section only**—To select the Detail section, click the Detail bar. You get a set of properties similar to those of the Form Header section, but all of these apply to the Detail section.
- **Footer section only**—To select the Footer section, click the Form Footer or Page Footer bar. A set of properties identical to the header properties is available for the footer sections. A Form Footer appears only if a Form Header has been added. The same applies to Page Headers and Footers.
- **Control object (or both elements of a control with an associated label)**—Click the surface of the control to select the control. Each type of control has its own set of properties. Displaying the properties of multiple-control objects is the subject of the section "Selecting, Moving, and Sizing a Single Control" later in this chapter.

CHANGING THE SIZE OF THE FORM HEADER AND FORM FOOTER

You can change the height of a form section by dragging the Form Header, Page Header, Detail, Page Footer, or Form Footer bar vertically with the mouse. When you position the mouse pointer at the top edge of a section divider bar, it turns into a line with two vertical arrows. You drag the pointer with the mouse to adjust the size of the section above the mouse pointer.

The height of the Detail section is determined by the vertical dimension of the window in which the form is displayed, less the combined heights of all the header and footer sections that are fixed in position. When you adjust the vertical scroll bar, only the Detail section scrolls.

SELECTING, MOVING, AND SIZING A SINGLE CONTROL

When you select a control object by clicking its surface, the object is enclosed by a shadow line with an anchor rectangle at its upper-left corner and seven smaller, rectangular sizing handles (see Figure 14.18).

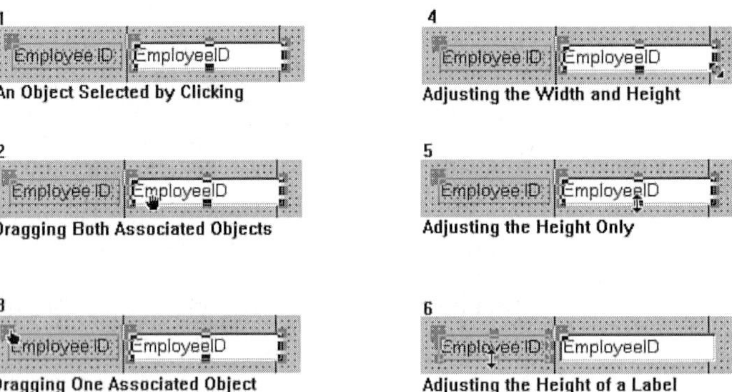

Figure 14.18 The appearance of selection or sizing handles and the mouse pointer depend on the moving or sizing operation in progress.

NOTE

Most controls have attached labels. When you select one of these objects, the label and object are selected as a unit.

Selecting and deselecting controls is a toggling process. *Toggling* means repeating an action with the effect of alternating between On and Off conditions. The Properties, Field List, and Toolbox buttons on the toolbar—as well as their corresponding menu choices—are toggles. The Properties window, for example, appears and disappears if you repeatedly click the Properties button.

The following choices are available for moving or changing the size of a control object (the numbers correspond to the numbers in Figure 14.18):

1. *To select a control* (and its associated label, if any), click anywhere on its surface.

TIP

If you have trouble selecting a small control, such as a thin line (particularly one that is adjacent to a section bar), you can select the control using the Object drop-down list on the toolbar or in the drop-down list at the top of the Properties window.

2. *To move the control* (and its associated label, if any) to a new position, move the mouse pointer within the outline of the object at any point other than the small resizing handles or the confines of a text box (where the cursor can become an editing cursor). The mouse pointer becomes a hand symbol when it's on an area that you can use to move the entire control. Press and hold down the left mouse button while dragging the hand symbol to the new location for the control. An outline of the control indicates its position as you move the mouse. When the control is where you want it to be, release the mouse button to drop the control in its new position.

TIP

If the control doesn't have an associated label, you can drag the control's anchor handle at the upper-left corner to move the control.

3. *To separately move the elements of a control that has an associated label*, position the mouse pointer on the anchor handle in the upper-left corner of the control that you want to move. The mouse pointer becomes a hand with an extended finger. Click and drag the individual element to its new position and then release the mouse button.
4. *To simultaneously adjust the width and height of a control*, click the small sizing handle at any of the three corners of the outline of the control. The mouse pointer becomes a diagonal two-headed arrow. Click and drag this arrow to a new position and then release the mouse button.
5. *To adjust only the height or width of the control*, click the sizing handle on one of the horizontal or vertical surfaces of the outline. The mouse pointer becomes a vertical or horizontal two-headed arrow. Click and drag this arrow to a new position and then release the mouse button.
6. *To adjust the height or width of the label only*, select the label as described in step 3, and then adjust the label's dimensions.

ALIGNING CONTROLS TO THE GRID

The Form Design window includes a grid that consists of one-pixel dots with a default spacing of 24 to the inch horizontally and 24 to the inch vertically. When the grid is visible, you can use the grid dots to assist in maintaining the horizontal and vertical alignment of rows and columns of controls. Even if the grid isn't visible, you can cause controls to "snap to the grid" by choosing Format, Snap to Grid. This menu command is a toggle, and when Snap to Grid is active, the menu choice is checked. Whenever you move a control while Snap to Grid is active, the upper-left corner of the object jumps to the closest grid dot.

You can cause the size of control objects to conform to grid spacing by choosing Format, Size, To Grid. You also can make the size of the control fit its content by choosing Format, Size, To Fit.

TIP

> If Snap to Grid is on and you want to locate or size a control without reference to the grid, press and hold the Ctrl key while you move or resize the control.

Toggling the View, Grid menu command controls the visibility of the grid; by default, the grid is visible for all new forms. If the grid spacing is set to more than 24 per inch or 10 per centimeter, the dots aren't visible. For "non-metrified" users, better values are 10 per inch for Grid X and 12 per inch for Grid Y. This grid dot spacing is optimum for text controls that use the default 8-point MS Sans Serif font. To change the grid spacing for a form, follow these steps:

1. Click the Form Select button or press Ctrl+R to select the entire form.
2. Click the toolbar's Properties button to open the Properties window.
3. Click the Format tab, and then scroll through the list until the Grid X and Grid Y properties are visible.
4. Change the value of Grid X to 10 dots per inch (dpi) and Grid Y to 12 dpi, or change both values to 16 (if you want controls to align with inch ruler ticks). Metrified users are likely to prefer a value of 10 for both Grid X and Grid Y.

SELECTING AND MOVING MULTIPLE CONTROLS

You can select and move several objects at a time by using one of the following methods:

- *Enclose the objects with a selection rectangle.* Begin by clicking the surface of the form outside the outline of a control object. Press and hold down the mouse button while dragging the mouse pointer to create an enclosing rectangle that includes each of the objects you want to select (see Figure 14.19). Release the mouse button. You can now move the group of objects by clicking and dragging the anchor handle of any one of them.

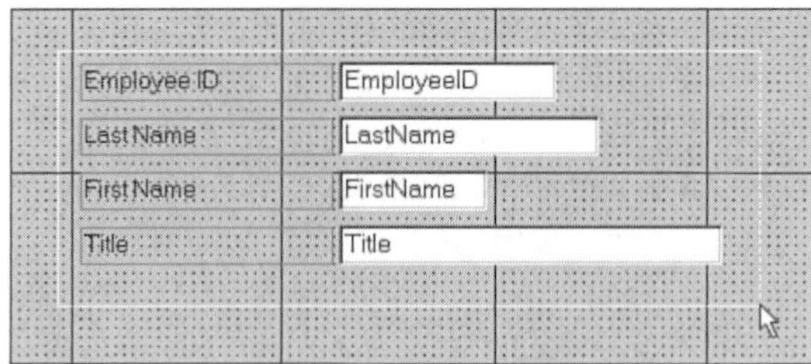

Figure 14.19
Selecting a group of objects by dragging a selection rectangle.

- *Click to select one object; then hold down the Shift key while you click to select the next object.* You can repeat this step as many times as necessary to select all the objects you want.
- *To remove a selected object from a group,* hold down the Shift key and click the object with the mouse to deselect it. To deselect an entire group, click any inactive area of the form. An inactive area is an area outside the outline of a control.

14

- *To create a group of the multiselected objects*, choose Format, Group. The selection rectangle permanently encloses the objects, which lose their individual selection rectangles. Choose Format, Ungroup to remove the group attribute from the enclosed objects.

If you select or deselect a control with an associated label, the label is selected or deselected along with the control. You can change some property values—such as font size and foreground or background color—of all multiply-selected controls.

NOTE

> The selection rectangle selects a control if any part of the control is included within the rectangle. This behavior is unlike many drawing applications in which the entire object must be enclosed to be selected. You can change the behavior of Access's selection rectangle to require full enclosure of the object by choosing Tools, Options; selecting the Forms/Reports tab (refer to Figure 14.11); and changing the value of the Selection Behavior option from Partially Enclosed to Fully Enclosed.

ALIGNING A GROUP OF CONTROLS

You can align selected individual controls, or groups of controls, to the grid or each other by choosing Format, Align and completing the following actions:

- To fine-adjust the position of a control by the width of a single pixel, select the control and press Ctrl+*Arrow*.
- To align a selected control (or group of controls) to the grid, choose To Grid from the submenu.
- To adjust the positions of controls within a selected columnar group so that their left edges fall into vertical alignment with the leftmost control, choose Left from the submenu.
- To adjust the positions of controls within a selected columnar group so that their right edges fall into vertical alignment with the right edge of the rightmost control, choose Right from the submenu.
- To align rows of controls at their top edges, choose Top from the submenu.
- To align rows of controls at their bottom edges, choose Bottom from the submenu.

Your forms have a more professional appearance if you take the time to align groups of controls vertically and horizontally.

TIP

> To quickly select a group of controls in a column or row, click within the horizontal or vertical ruler. This shortcut selects all controls intersected by the vertical or horizontal projection of the arrow that appears when you move the mouse within the ruler.

USING THE WINDOWS CLIPBOARD AND DELETING CONTROLS

All conventional Windows Clipboard commands apply to control objects. You can cut or copy a selected control or group of controls to the Clipboard. After that, you can paste the control or group to the form using Edit menu commands and then relocate the pasted control or group as desired. Access uses the Windows keyboard shortcut keys: Ctrl+X to cut, Ctrl+C to copy selected controls to the Clipboard, and Ctrl+V to paste the Clipboard contents. The traditional Shift+Delete, Ctrl+Insert, and Shift+Insert commands perform the same operations.

You can delete a control by selecting it and then pressing Delete. If you accidentally delete a label associated with a control and Edit, Undo doesn't solve the problem, do the following: select another label, copy it to the Clipboard, select the control the label needs to be associated with, and paste the label to the control.

CHANGING THE COLOR AND BORDER STYLE OF A CONTROL

As mentioned earlier in this chapter, the default color for the text and borders of controls is black. Borders are one pixel wide (called hairline width). Some objects, such as text boxes, have default borders. Labels have a gray background color by default, but a better choice for the default label color would have been transparent. Transparent means that the background color of the object under the control (the form section, in this case) appears within the control except in areas of the control that are occupied by text or pictures.

You control the color and border widths of a control from the Line/Border Color and Line/Border Width buttons on the Formatting toolbar. You must select a border style directly in the Properties window.

To change the color or border width of a selected control or group of controls, follow these steps:

1. Select the control(s) whose color or border width you want to change.
2. Click the arrow of the Fill/Back Color toolbar button to open the color palette pop-up window. Click the color square you want or click the Transparent button to make the background transparent.
3. Click the arrow of the Line/Border Color toolbar button to open the color palette pop-up window, where you change the border color for any selected control with borders.
4. Click the arrow of the Line/Border Width toolbar button to open the border width pop-up window, where you change the thickness of the border for any selected control whose borders are enabled.
5. Click the arrow of the Font/Fore Color toolbar button to open the color palette pop-up window, where you change the color of the text of selected controls.

14

NOTE

> The general practice for Windows data-entry forms is to indicate editable elements with borders and clear backgrounds. Still, some popular software uses reverse video as the default to indicate editable text. You can create the effect of reverse video by choosing black or another dark color for the fill of a text box control and a light color for its text. If you decide to implement reverse text, remember that reverse text is more difficult to read than normal text, so consider using a larger font and adding the bold attribute to ensure legibility.

To set the border style, you must select the Border Style property directly in the Properties window, as explained earlier in this chapter.

CHANGING THE CONTENT OF TEXT CONTROLS

You can edit the content of text controls by using conventional Windows text-editing techniques. When you place the mouse pointer within the confines of a text control and click the mouse button, the mouse pointer becomes the Windows text-editing cursor that you use to insert or delete text. You can select text by dragging the mouse over it or by holding down Shift and moving the cursor with the arrow keys. All Windows Clipboard operations are applicable to text within controls. Keyboard text selection and editing techniques using the arrow keys in combination with Shift are available, also.

If you change the name of a field in a text box and make an error naming the field, you receive a "#Name?" error message in the offending text box when you select Run mode. Following is a better method of changing a text box with an associated label:

1. Delete the existing field control by clicking to select it and then pressing Delete.
2. Click the Field List button in the Properties bar to display the Field List dialog.
3. Scroll through the entries in the list until you find the field name you want.
4. Click the field name to select it; then drag the field name to the location of the deleted control. Release the mouse button to drop the new name.
5. Close the Field List dialog when you're finished.

You can relocate and resize the new field caption and text box (or edit the caption) as necessary.

USING THE FORMAT PAINTER

The Format Painter lets you quickly copy the format of any control on the form to any other control on the form. The Format Painter copies only those formatting properties that are relevant to the control on which you apply the Format Painter. To use the Format Painter, follow these steps:

1. Select the control with the formatting you want to copy.

2. Click or double-click the Format Painter button on the toolbar; the mouse cursor changes to a pointing arrow with a paintbrush icon attached to it. (Double-clicking "locks" the Format Painter on. Double-click the Format Painter button only if you want to copy the formatting to more than one control.)
3. Click any control that you want to copy the formatting to; the Format Painter copies all relevant formatting properties to this control. If you didn't double-click the Format Painter button, the Format Painter turns itself off after copying the formatting properties to one control.
4. If you locked the Format Painter on by double-clicking its button, you can repeat step 3 as many times as you want. Click the Format Painter button again to turn off the Format Painter.

Typically, you use the Format Painter to quickly set the formatting properties for field text labels, or in any situation where selecting several controls by dragging a selection rectangle seems undesirable. By locking the Format Painter, it's easy to format several controls one after another.

Rearranging the HRActions Form

The objective of the following procedure is to rearrange the controls on the frmHRActions form so that all the elements on the form (and its subform) are completely visible in the form window. Another objective is to optimize the position of the fields for data entry. After you complete the following steps, your main form with its embedded subform appears as shown in Figure 14.20.

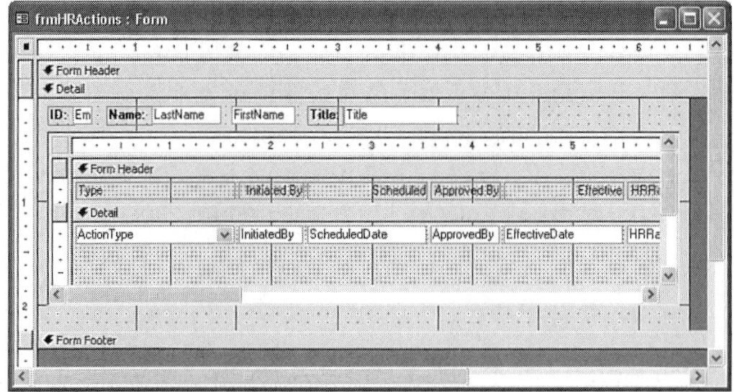

Figure 14.20 The frmHRActions form appears as shown here after relocating and resizing its control objects. You modify the subform design in the next section.

14

Setting Properties of the Main Form

To change the color of form objects and rearrange the controls of the frmHRActions form to correspond with the positions shown in Figure 14.20, follow these steps:

1. Close the frmHRActions form, and don't save any changes you made in the preceding sections.
2. Select frmHRActions from the Forms list in the Database window and click the Design button.
3. Expand the Form Design window to add working room. Alternatively, click the Maximize window button to maximize the Form Design window.
4. Click the Form Select button, and then click the Properties button on the toolbar.
5. Click the Format tab of the Properties window and then scroll through the properties list until you see Grid X and Grid Y. Change the Grid X property to 10 and the Grid Y property to 12. (Metric users might prefer a 5×5 grid, providing 2mm resolution.)
6. Close the Properties window by clicking the Properties button again.
7. Drag the right margin of the form from its present position (5.5 inches) to 6.5 inches.
8. Delete the FirstName label (click the label and then press Delete). Select the FirstName field and drag it to a position to the right of the LastName field (refer to Figure 14.20).
9. Edit the LastName label to **Name:**, the EmployeeID label to **ID:**, and the Title label to **Title:**.
10. Resize the labels and their text boxes to suit their content and reduce the space between each text box and its label. At this point, you must estimate the required width of the text box.
11. Click and drag the LastName, FirstName, and Title text boxes and their associated labels to the positions shown in Figure 14.20.
12. Delete the sbfHRActions field label (the size and content of the subform is sufficient to identify it) and drag the subform control to a position below the FirstName and LastName fields (refer to Figure 14.20).
13. Click and drag the Form Footer bar to approximately 2.5 inches. (Alternatively, you can type the Detail section's height directly in the Height property on the Format sheet of the Properties window.) At present, the dimensions of your form are 6.5×2.5 inches.
14. Resize the sbfHRActions subform control on the form so that its left, right, and bottom edges are one grid mark inside the edges of the form (this makes the sbfHRActions subform control about 6.25×1 7/8 inches).

15. Click the text label of the EmployeeID field to select it and then click the Bold and Align Right buttons on the Formatting toolbar to make the text label bold and right-justified.

16. Double-click the Format Painter button on the toolbar (remember that this step locks the Format Painter).
17. In turn, click the text labels for all the remaining controls on the form to apply the formatting with the Format Painter.

18. Click the Format Painter button on the toolbar again to turn off the Format Painter.

19. Select the form, and click the Properties button. Click the Data tab, and set the Allow Additions and Allow Deletions properties to No. Setting these property values to No prevents you from adding or deleting employee records in this form. You can, however, edit employee names, which might change as the result of a marriage (or divorce).

20. Click the Format tab, set the Record Selectors, Allow Datasheet View, Allow PivotTable View, and Allow PivotChart View property values to No.

21. Click the Save button (or press Ctrl+S) to save your changes to the frmHRActions form, and close the Properties window.

You might need to adjust the sizes of some controls individually to make their appearance consistent with other controls. When you complete your rearrangement, click the Form View button to review your work. In particular, you might need to adjust the width of the LastName and FirstName text boxes to accommodate data in Employees table.

If you encounter problems when you open the form in Form view, see the "Form Problems" topic of the "Troubleshooting" section near the end of the chapter.

Setting the Properties of a Subform

You can learn about modifying the properties of a subform by working with the subform that's used to create the history of prior HRActions for an employee. In this example, editing or deleting entries using the subform isn't allowed, but you can add new entries. The subform needs to be modified so that all its columns are readable without horizontal scrolling. When you complete the following steps, the sbfHRActions subform appears as shown in Figure 14.21.

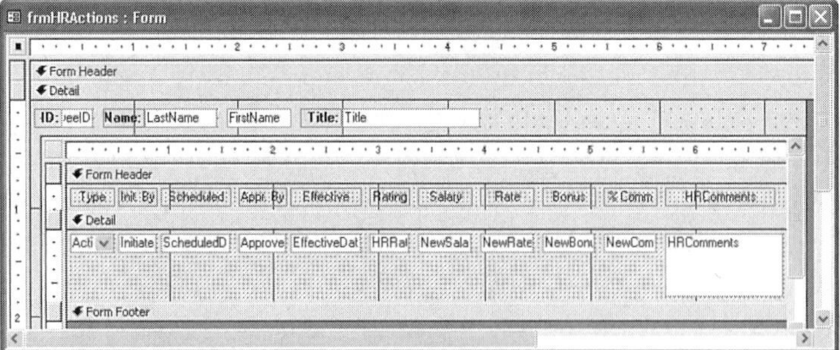

Figure 14.21 The sbfHRActions subform in the frmHRActions form appears as shown here after modifying its field sizes and overall dimensions.

TIP

Although you can use the in-situ subform editing feature to alter the design of a subform, in most cases it's easier to use the traditional method of subform design modification. In-situ editing is better suited for changing subform property values than for altering subform dimensions.

To change the properties of the sbfHRActions subform, follow these steps:

1. Right-click the sbfHRActions subform and choose Subform in New Window from the context menu. The new subform window, a feature added by Access 2002, replaces the in-situ subform.

> **TIP**
>
> When you close a subform that's been opened in its own window, the in-situ subform disappears from Form Design view. To regain the in-situ version, click Form view and then Form Design view.

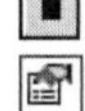

2. Select the form and use the Properties window to make sure that the Grid X and Grid Y properties are both set to 24. In this case, the finer grid lets you make more precise changes to the size of subform controls. Close the Properties window.
3. Using the same techniques you used when working with the main form, resize the label boxes in the Form Header section of the form so that they match what you see in Figure 14.21. Use the Format Painter to center the text in every text label in the Form Header section.
4. Adjust the field text boxes in the Detail section of the form to line up with the headings in the Form Header section (see Figure 14.22).

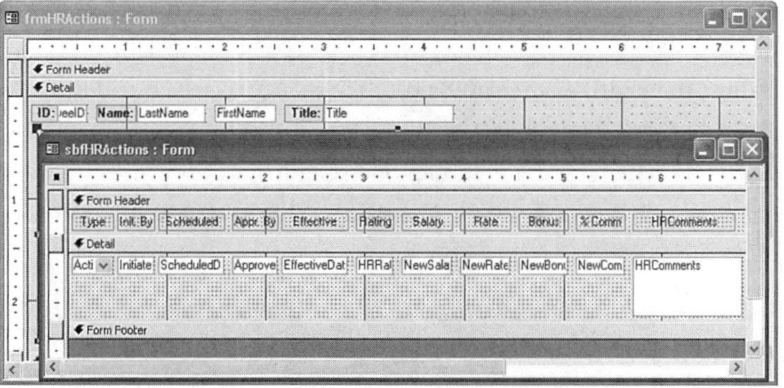

Figure 14.22
Choosing New Window from the context menu opens the subform in a windows superimposed on the Form Design view. Adjust the widths of the subform's labels and fields as shown here.

> **TIP**
>
> As you make changes to the subform, click the Save button on the toolbar to save them. It's frustrating to spend several minutes adjusting the positions and formatting of fields, and then lose your changes by an inadvertent error.

5. Drag the right edge of the form to the left until the form is one grid width wider than fields (about 7 1/2 inches) and then drag the Form Footer upward so that the Detail section is about 5/8 inches high.

6. With the subform window active, click Form Select button and the Properties button on the toolbar to display the Properties window for the subform.
7. Click the Data tab in the Properties window so that the Allow Edits, Allow Deletions, and Allow Additions properties are visible.
8. Set the Allow Edits and Allow Deletions property values to No; this setting prevents the user from editing or deleting earlier Personnel Action records displayed in this subform.

NOTE

> You can set the Data Entry property to Yes to achieve a result that is similar to setting the Allow Edits and Allow Deletions property to No and the Allow Additions property to Yes. When you set the Data Entry property to Yes, however, only the tentative new record appears–no prior entries appear in the subform.

9. Save your changes, close the sbfHRActions subform, and close and reopen the form in Design view.

TIP

> You must close and reopen the main form to make changes you apply to a subform in the window appear in Form view. The form embeds a copy of the subform; the embedded copy doesn't change until you close and reopen the form.

10. Adjust the width of the subform to about 7 3/8 inches, and drag the right margin of the form to the right edge of the subform.
11. Save your changes, close and re-open the form in Form view, and restore the form window if its maximized. Then, choose Windows, Size to Fit Form. Your form appears as shown in Figure 14.23.

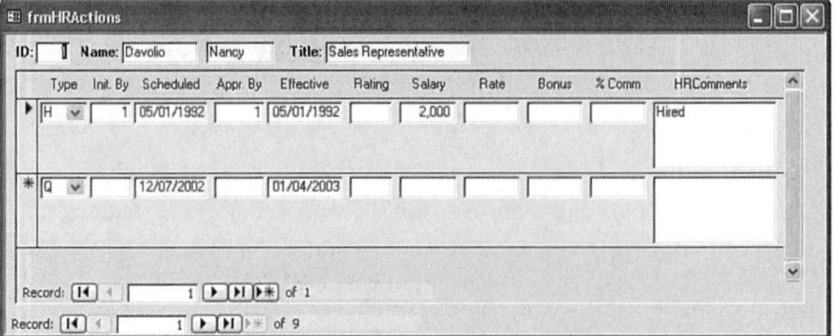

Figure 14.23 The completed frmHRActions and sbfHRActions forms in Form view display a single HRActions record for Northwind Traders' first employee.

Notice in Figure 14.23 that there's no horizontal scroll bar and that the appearance and visibility of fields and column headings in the subform have improved. By changing the size of the subform control in the main form and resizing the subform to fit completely within the subform control (allowing room for the vertical scroll bar), the subform fits completely in the main form. Notice also the tentative append record that's visible as the second record in the subform.

If problems occur when you attempt to add a new subform record for an employee, see the "Subform Problems" topic of the "Troubleshooting" section near the end of the chapter.

USING TRANSACTION-PROCESSING FORMS

As noted near the beginning of this chapter, the purpose of transaction-processing forms is to add new records to, delete records from, or edit data in one or more tables that underlie the form. The sections that follow describe how to add new records to the HRActions table with the frmHRActions form.

TOOLBAR BUTTONS IN FORM VIEW

The toolbar buttons of Form view are the same as those for tables in Datasheet view. For example, the Find button serves the same purpose for forms in Run mode as it does for tables and queries. You type characters in the Find dialog using wildcards if needed. When you execute the search, Access displays the first record that matches your entry if a match is found.

The Sort Ascending, Sort Descending, Filter by Selection, and Filter by Form buttons work the same way in Form view as they do in Datasheet view. Using these filter buttons is described in Chapter 7, "Sorting, Finding, and Filtering Data." Sorting specified in the form overrides the sort criteria of the primary query used as the source of the data (if your form is based on a query, rather than directly on one or more tables). The filter or sort criteria you specify don't take effect until you click the Apply Filter/Sort button or make the equivalent Records, Apply Filter/Sort menu choice.

NOTE

Some toolbar buttons are disabled as a result of your form design or its property values. For example, the Delete Record button is disabled when the frmHRActions form is open because you've set the Allow Deletions property value to No for the both form and subform. The Add Record button is disabled when you select the main form and enabled when you select the subform.

14

USING THE HRACTIONS FORM

Forms you create with the Form Wizard use the standard record-navigation buttons located at the bottom of the form. The record-navigation buttons perform the same functions with forms as they do with tables and queries. You can select the first or last records in the table or query that is the source of data for your main form, or you can select the next or previous record. Subforms include their own set of record-selection buttons that operate independently of the set for the main form.

NOTE

If you didn't create the frmHRActions form in the preceding sections of this chapter, the form, subform, and HRActions table are included in the Forms14.mdb database in your \Program Files\Seua11\Chaptr14 folder.

Navigation between the text boxes used for entering or editing data in the form is similar to navigation in queries and tables in Datasheet view except that the up-arrow and down-arrow keys cause the cursor to move between fields rather than between records. Accept the values you've entered by pressing Enter or Tab.

APPENDING NEW RECORDS TO THE HRACTIONS TABLE

In Datasheet view of a table or query, the last record in the datasheet is provided as a tentative append record (indicated by an asterisk on the record-selection button). If you enter data in this record, the data automatically is appended to the table and Access starts a new tentative append record. Forms also provide a tentative append record, unless you set the Allow Additions property value for the form to No.

The following comments apply to adding HRAction records with the frmHRActions form:

- Because data from the Employees table is included in the main form, the ID number, name, and title of the employee appear in the text boxes on the main form. Your form design lets you edit the LastName, FirstName, and Title data, although these fields are incorporated in the table (Employees) on the one side of a one-to-many relationship. The editing capability of a form is the same as that for the underlying table or query that serves as its source unless you change the form's editing capabilities by setting the form's Allow Editing property and other related properties.
- After you add a new record to the HRActions table, you can't delete or edit it, because the Allow Edits and Allow Deletions property values are set to No.

TIP

When experimenting with adding records to the HRActions table, temporarily set the subform's Allow Edits and Allow Deletions property values to Yes.

14

- If you added an entry for the chosen employee ID when you created the HRActions table in Chapter 5, the entry appears in the subform's fields. The subform's data display is linked to the data in the main form through the one-to-many relationship between the Employees table and the HRActions table. The subform only displays records from the HRActions table whose EmployeeID fields match the value of the EmployeeID field of the record currently displayed by the main form.

To append a new record to the HRActions table and enter the required data, follow these steps:

1. Open the frmHRActions form if it isn't already open or click the Form View button if you're in Design view. Data for the first record of the Employees table—with the matching data from the corresponding record(s) in the HRActions table—appears in the text-box controls of your form.

2. Access places the cursor in the first text box of the main form, the ID text box. The first example uses Steven Buchanan, whose employee ID is 5, so do the following: Click the Find button on the toolbar to open the Find dialog, type **5** in the Find What text box, make sure that the Look In control is set to ID, and click Find First. Access displays the Employees table data for Steven Buchanan in the main form and his HRActions records in the subform. Click Cancel to close the Find dialog.

NOTE

Alternatively, click the Next Record button of the lower set of navigation buttons four times to open the record for Mr. Buchanan.

TIP

If you change the value of the AutoNumber ID field, for instance to 5, you receive a "Field can't be updated" message when you move the cursor to another field. Press Esc to cancel the change. (Typing the original value generates the same message.)

You can prevent editing of this or any other field of a form or subform by changing the Locked property of the field's text box to Yes.

3. Click in the Type field of the tentative append record in the subform. If the tentative append record in the subform isn't visible, click in any field in the subform and then click the New Record button on the toolbar to move to the tentative append record at the end of the existing HRActions table entries for Steven Buchanan.
4. Type a valid HRAction type (**H**, **Q**, **Y**, **S**, **R**, **B**, **C**, or **T** because of the field's validation rule) in the Type text box. (If you added the lookup list to the Action field, you can select the type code from the list.) Default date values appear in the Scheduled and Effective fields. In this example, you bring Steven Buchanan's HRActions records up-to-date by adding quarterly performance review information. Press Tab or Enter to accept the default Type value and move the cursor to the next data-entry text box, Initiated By.
5. Mr. Buchanan reports to the vice president of sales, Andrew Fuller, whose employee ID is 2. Type 2 in the Initiated By text box and press Enter.

NOTE

The pencil symbol, which indicates that you're editing a record, replaces the triangle at the top of the Record Selector bar to the left of the record that you are entering. The Description property you entered for the field in the table underlying this query appears in the status bar and changes as you move the cursor to the next field. (To change a previous entry, press Shift+Tab, or use the up- and down-arrow keys to maneuver to whichever text box contains a value you want to change.)

6. Mr. Buchanan was hired on 10/17/1993, but Northwind Traders had no human resources (HR) department to maintain HR data until mid-1998, so type **10/17/1998** in the Scheduled field.
7. Because Mr. Fuller is a vice-president, he has the authority to approve salary increases. Type Mr. Fuller's employee ID, **2**, in the Approved By text box and then press Enter to move the cursor to the next field.
8. The effective date for salary adjustments for Northwind Traders is the 1st or 15th day of the month in which the performance review is scheduled. Type the appropriate date in the Effective text box.
9. You can type any number from **0** (terminated) to **9** (excellent) in the Rating text box, which reflects the employee's performance.
10. You can be as generous as you want with the salary increase that you enter in the Salary text box. The value of the Salary field is a new monthly salary, not an incremental value.
11. In the Comments multiline text box to the right of the New Amount field, add any comments you care to make concerning how generous or stingy you were with this salary increase. The multiline text box includes a scroll bar that appears when the cursor is within the text box.

12. When you complete your entries, Access stores them in a memory buffer but doesn't add the new record to the HRActions table. You can add the record to the table by choosing Records, Save Record; clicking the New Record button; or changing the position of the record pointer with the Previous or Next record selector button. If you want to cancel the addition of a record, press Esc twice.
13. Repeat steps 3 through 12 to add a few additional records.

TIP

]If you click the New Record button on the toolbar (or the Next Record selector button) to select the tentative append record, and then decide that you don't want to add any more data, click the Previous Record button to make sure this new record is not added to the table. If the table has required fields without default values, however, you must enter a value for each required field, and then delete the added record. Deleting records requires setting the subform's Allow Deletions property value to Yes.

When adding a record, your form appears like the one shown in Figure 14.24. Each record for an employee appears in the subform datasheet in the order of the primary key fields of the HRActions table.

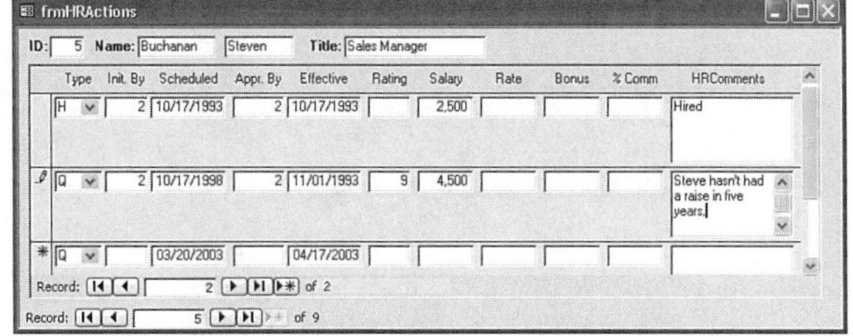

Figure 14.24
The frmHRActions form appears as shown here after appending a new subform record for an employee.

MODIFYING THE PROPERTIES OF A FORM OR CONTROL AFTER TESTING

The entries you added and edited gave you an opportunity to test your form. Testing a form to ensure that it accomplishes the objectives you have in mind usually takes much longer than creating the form and the query that underlies it. During the testing process, you might notice that the order of the fields isn't what you want or that records in the subform aren't displayed in an appropriate sequence. The following two sections deal with modifying the properties of the form and subform control.

CHANGING THE ORDER OF FIELDS FOR DATA ENTRY

The order in which the editing cursor moves from one field to the next is determined by the Tab Order property value of each control. The Form Wizard established the tab order of the controls when you first created the form. The default Tab Order property of each field is assigned, beginning with the value 0, in the sequence in which you add the fields. Because the Form Wizard created a single-column form, the order of the controls in HRActions is left to right, top to bottom. The tab order originally assigned doesn't change when you relocate a control.

To change the sequence of entries—for example, to match the pattern of entries on a paper form—follow these steps:

1. Change to Form Design view.
2. Choose View, Tab Order to display the Tab Order dialog shown in Figure 14.25. The order of entry is shown by the sequence of field names in the Custom Order list. (In this example, changing the sequence of the entries is unnecessary because the sequence is logical, even after moving the controls to their present locations on the HRActions form.)

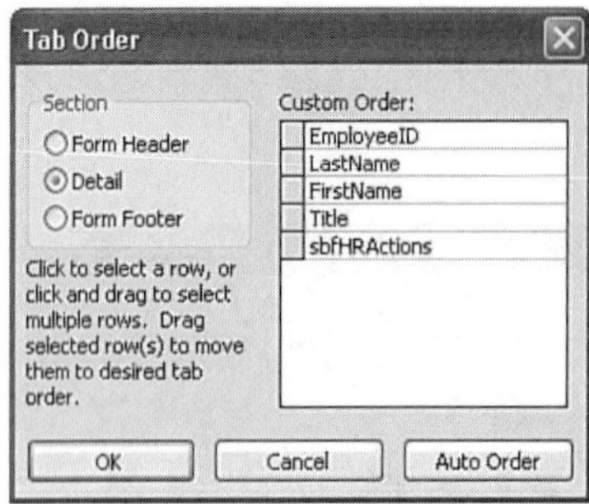

Figure 14.25 Change the sequence of data-entry fields with the Tab Order dialog.

3. Click the Auto Order button if you want to reorder the entry sequence going left to right across each row of fields, and then top to bottom.
4. Drag any control to a new location by clicking the button at the left of its name and dropping it wherever you want it to be in the sequence.
5. Click OK to implement the changes you made; click Cancel to retain the original entry sequence.

NOTE

> Using the Auto Order button to change the tab order of fields on a form also changes the left-to-right order of the table fields in Datasheet view to correspond to the Auto Order field sequence. Datasheet and other views of the frmHRActions form has been disabled, which you can prove by opening the View button's menu.

Removing Fields from the Tab Order

Access lets you set the value of the Tab Stop property to No to prevent controls from receiving the focus in the tab order. To remove a control from the tab order, select the control, open the Properties window, select Other, and change the value of the Tab Stop property to No. You can't edit the EmployeeID field, so set the Tab Stop property to No for this control.

NOTE

> Setting the Tab Stop property's value to No doesn't disable a given control, but it removes the control from the tab sequence. As a result, the control can't be selected by pressing the Tab key, but can still be selected by clicking it with the mouse.

TROUBLESHOOTING

FORM PROBLEMS

I can't add a new record to a form or subform that's bound to a Jet query.

The most likely cause of this problem is that the query you're using as the record source for the form or subform isn't updatable. Run the query and verify that the tentative append record appears after the last record with data. If the tentative append record is present in the datasheet and not in the form or subform, then you might have accidentally set the Allow Additions property value to No.

The text boxes on my form are empty, the Next and Previous record navigation buttons are disabled, and the First and Last record buttons don't work.

You accidentally set the Data Entry property of the form to Yes. Setting the Data Entry property permits adding new records, but prevents the user from seeing existing records. Why the First and Last buttons are enabled is a mystery. This problem also occurs with subforms and often results from selecting the form instead of the subform when setting the Data Entry property value.

No controls appear on my form in Form view.

You've set the Allow Additions property to No, and accidentally set the Data Entry property of the form to Yes. In this case, subforms don't appear on the form. There have been many requests by Access users and developers to display an error message when you specify these mutually-exclusive property values. (New Access users have been known to panic after having spent several hours designing a form and then seeing their work disappear in Form view.) The problem also applies to subforms but isn't as dramatic.

SUBFORM PROBLEMS

The subform I added to the main form doesn't change its data when I move the main form's record pointer with the navigation buttons.

You didn't create the required link between the main form and the subform in the Data page of the main form's Properties window, or the link is broken as the result of changing a table or query name.

Select the subform container of the main form (not the subform itself) by clicking the edge of the subform in Form Design view, open the Properties window, and click the Data tab. Click the Builder button to open the Subform Field Linker dialog, and add or correct the field names of the linked tables or queries.

IN THE REAL WORLD—THE ART OF FORM DESIGN

Creating an effective form design for data entry requires a unique combination of graphic design and programming skills. Whether your goal is to develop Access front ends for Jet or

SQL Server databases, or to design Data access pages (DAP) that run over an intranet, the basic methodology of form design is the same. Large database-development projects usually begin with a detailed specification for the database, plus a set of descriptions of each data display and entry form. Small- to medium-sized organizations, however, seldom have the resources to develop an all-encompassing specification before embarking on a project. If your objective is to develop from-scratch Access forms for decision-support or online transaction processing (OLTP) applications, keep in mind the guidelines of this and the following chapter's "Real World" sections.

UNDERSTAND THE AUDIENCE

Your first task is to determine how your Access application fits into the organization's business processes. If the application is for decision support, determine its audience. Most executives want a broad-brush, organization-wide view of the data, which usually entails graphical presentation of the information. Generating graphs is the primary topic of Chapter 18 and one of the topics of Chapter 12. Managers commonly request graphs or charts for trend analysis, together with tabular summary information for their area of responsibility. PivotTables, described in Chapter 12, let managers "slice and dice" the data to present multiple views of the data. Supervisors need detailed information to handle day-to-day employee performance and productivity issues. Thus, your decision-support application is likely to require several forms, each tailored to the information needs of users at different levels in the organization's hierarchy.

OLTP front ends require a different design approach than decision-support applications. For heads-down OLTP—typified by telephone order or reservation applications—keyboard-only data entry in a single form is the rule. One of the primary objectives of OLTP form design is minimizing operator fatigue; tired operators tend to enter inaccurate data. OLTP forms need to be simple, fast, and easily readable. Easy reading implies larger-than-standard fonts—at least 10 points—and subdued form colors. Designing forms in which the field sequence is in the order that the data entry operator expects, such as finding or adding customer information before entering an order, is especially important for telephone order entry forms.

DESIGN IN CLIENT MONITOR RESOLUTION

You might have a 19-inch or larger 1,280×960 monitor and a 3D graphics accelerator with 32-bit color depth, but it's not very likely that all the users of your Access application are so fortunate. In the Access 2.0 era, designing for 640×480 resolution was the rule; in those days, most laptop and many desktop PCs had standard 256-color VGA displays. Today, most laptop and all desktop PCs support at least 800×600 (SVGA) resolution and 24-bit color depth. When designing your forms for SVGA resolution, switch to 800–600 display mode, even if you have a 21-inch monitor. Make sure to test your form designs with the 15-inch monitors that organizations commonly assign to data-entry operators.

If your application must support mobile users having a variety of laptop and notebook hardware, make sure to check for adequate contrast and text readability on laptop and notebook PCs with 12-inch displays.

STRIVE FOR CONSISTENCY AND SIMPLICITY

Microsoft's goal for the Office suite is visual and operational consistency between members. Design your Access decision support-forms to emulate the "look and feel" of other Office XP members, especially Microsoft Excel. It's a likely bet that most decision-support users are familiar with Excel.

Simplicity is the watchword when designing OLTP forms. Provide only the elements—forms, subforms, and controls—required for data-entry operators to get their work done. Above all, attempt to design a single form that handles all aspects of the OLTP process, if possible. Opening a new form for each step in the data entry process causes visual discontinuities that lead to operator fatigue. Substitute visually simple list boxes for read-only datasheets; show and hide the list boxes with VBA code to minimize screen clutter. Chapter 29, "Programming Combo and List Boxes," shows you how to take full advantage of combo and list boxes in decision-support and OLTP applications.

Figure 14.26 shows the single form of an Access demonstration OLTP application, A11oltp.mdb, in order lookup mode. A11oltp.mdb originated as a Microsoft Tech*Ed presentation for designers of Access 2.0 client/server OLTP front ends for SQL Server 6.0. The application has been upgraded for each succeeding Access and SQL Server version. Typing the first letter or two of a customer name in the Bill To text box and pressing Return opens a list box of customer matches. This process speeds determination of whether the customer's data is present in the database.

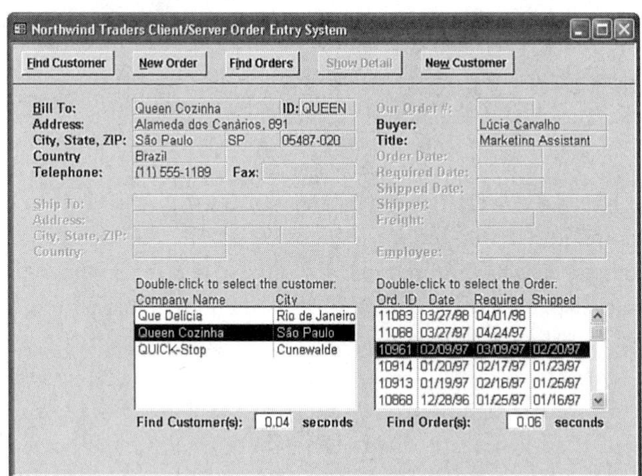

Figure 14.26 This demonstration OLTP application uses a single form for heads-down entry of telephone orders and order status reporting. The time values below the list boxes compare performance between Jet and client/server operating modes. Client/server mode for the Microsoft Data Engine isn't enabled in this version.

NOTE

> A version of A11oltp.mdb that's restricted to use of a linked Jet database, A11data.mdb is included in the \Seua11\Chaptr14 folder of the accompanying CD-ROM. The application expects to find A11data.mdb in your C:\Program Files\Seua11\Chaptr14 folder after installing the sample applications from the CD-ROM to the default location. If you installed the book's sample files to another location, acknowledge the two error messages that appear when you open the database. Then open the Database window, and choose Tools, Database Utilities, Linked Table Manager to change the path to A11data.mdb.

Select the customer in the left list box with the down-arrow key and press Enter to open the right text box. Use the down-arrow key to select an existing order to review from this text box. Pressing Enter again fills the Ship To information text boxes and shows a list box of order line items (see Figure 14.27). Each command button and data field group has a shortcut key to eliminate the need for mouse operations.

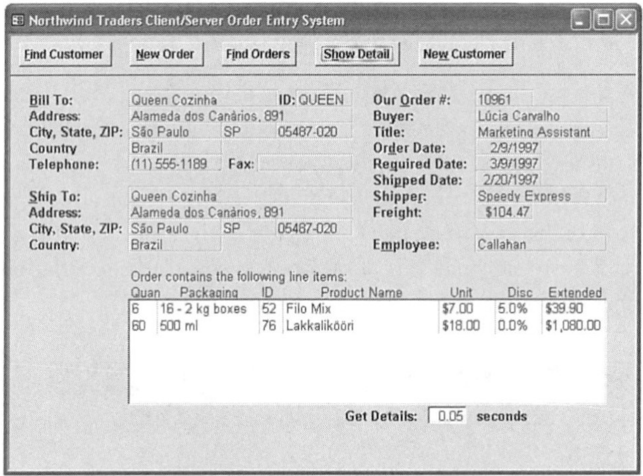

Figure 14.27 Selecting a customer and order in the two list boxes shown in Figure 14.26 adds information from the Orders and Order Details tables to the form.

To add a new order for a customer, press Alt+N to replace the Order Details list box with a subform for adding line items. Mark the Same as Bill To checkbox, type a value in the Required Date field, select a Shipper and Employee, and then type a quantity and product ID value in the first two fields of the subform. When you tab past the ID field, a lookup operation completes the Product Name, Packaging, and Unit Price fields, and calculates the Extended (amount). If you add a discount, the Extended value updates automatically (see Figure 14.28). Use screen tips to prompt inexperienced operators for appropriate entries, as shown for the Quan[tity] subform field in Figure 14.28. Pressing Alt+A or clicking Add New Order adds the order and its line items to the Orders and Order Details tables, and displays the result in the Order Details list box.

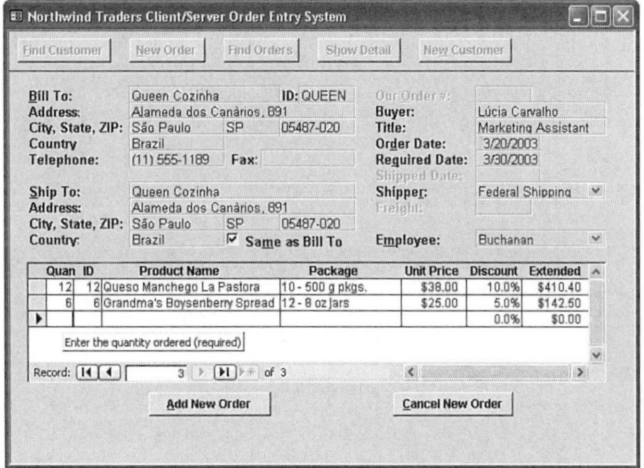

Figure 14.28
It's easy to add line items in the subform, because VBA code automatically completes the entries after you make quantity and product ID entries.

The A11oltp.mdb application is almost a full-fledged order entry system; the only missing element is the ability to edit existing orders that haven't been shipped. Give the application a test drive to sharpen your data-entry skills in subforms, and consider layouts similar to A11oltp.mdb when you design forms for production use.

CHAPTER 15

Designing Custom Multitable Forms

In this chapter

15

EXPANDING YOUR FORM DESIGN REPERTOIRE

The controls that the Form Wizard adds to the forms it creates are only a sampling of the 17 native control objects offered by Access 2003. *Native controls* are built into Access; you also can add various ActiveX controls to Access forms. Until now, you used the Form Wizard to create the labels, text boxes, and subform controls for displaying and editing data in the HRActions table. These three controls are sufficient to create a simple transaction-processing form.

The remaining 14 controls described in this chapter let you take full advantage of the Windows graphical user environment. You add controls to the form by using the Access Toolbox. List and combo boxes increase data-entry productivity and accuracy by letting you select from a list of predefined values instead of requiring you to type the value. Option buttons, toggle buttons, and check boxes supply values to Yes/No fields. You can place option buttons, toggle buttons, and check boxes in an option group. Inside an option group, the control you click sets the numeric Value property of the option group control. The Image control supplements the Bound and Unbound Object Frame controls for adding pictures to your forms. Page breaks determine how forms print. Access 2003's tab control lets you create tabbed forms to display related data on forms and subforms in a space-saving and more clearly organized fashion. Command buttons usually execute VBA event-handling procedures.

NOTE

> The form-design techniques you learn in this chapter also apply to Access Data Projects (ADP). ADP forms are identical to conventional Access forms, except that the forms and controls bind to objects in SQL Server 2000—not Jet 4.0—databases.

UNDERSTANDING THE ACCESS TOOLBOX

The Access Toolbox is based on the Toolbox that Microsoft first created for Visual Basic. Essentially, the Access Toolbox is a variety of toolbar. You select one of the 20 buttons that appear in the Toolbox to add a native control—represented by that tool's symbol—to the form. Selecting a tool lets you select a control, enable or disable the Control Wizards, or add a Microsoft or third-party ActiveX control to the form. When you create a report, the Toolbox serves the same purpose—although tools that require user input, such as combo boxes, seldom are used in reports.

CONTROL CATEGORIES

Three control object categories apply to Access forms and reports:

- *Bound controls* are associated with a field in the data source for the form or subform. Binding a control means connecting the control to a data source, such as a field of a table or a column of a query, which supplies the current value to or accepts an updated value from a control. Bound controls display and update values of the data cell in the associated field of the currently selected record. Text boxes are the most common bound control. You can display the content of graphic objects or play audio files embedded in a table with a bound OLE object. You can bind toggle buttons and check boxes to Yes/No fields. Option button groups bind to fields with numeric values. All bound controls have associated labels that display the Caption property of the field; you can edit or delete these labels without affecting the bound control.
- *Unbound controls* display data you provide that is independent of the form's or subform's data source. You use the image or unbound OLE object control to add a drawing or bitmapped image to a form. You can use lines and rectangles to divide a form into logical groups or simulate boxes used on the paper form. Unbound text boxes are used to enter data that isn't intended to update a field in the data source but is intended for other purposes, such as establishing a value used in an expression. Some unbound controls, such as unbound text boxes, include labels; others, such as unbound OLE objects, don't have labels. Labels also are unbound controls.
- *Calculated controls* use expressions as their source of data. Usually, the data source expression includes the value of a field, but you also can use values created by unbound text boxes in calculated control expressions.

THE ACCESS TOOLBOX

The Toolbox appears only in Design view for forms and reports, and it appears only if you click the Toolbox button on the toolbar or toggle the View, Toolbox menu choice. When the Toolbox is visible, the Toolbox menu choice is checked; Figure 15.1 shows the Toolbox in its default mode—a two-column floating toolbar. You can select one of the 17 controls and three other buttons, whose names and functions are listed in Table 15.1.

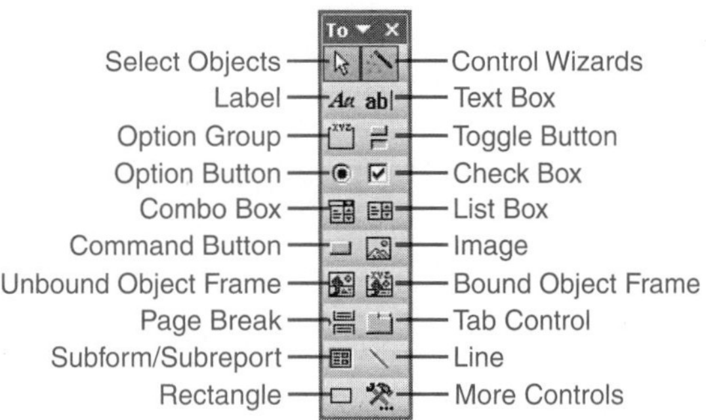

Figure 15.1
The Access Toolbox lets you add 17 different native controls to forms and reports.

TABLE 15.1 NAMES AND FUNCTIONS OF ACCESS TOOLBOX BUTTONS

Tool	Name	Function
	Select Objects	Changes mouse pointer to the Object Selection tool. Deselects a previously selected tool and returns the mouse pointer to normal selection function. Select Objects is the default tool when you open the Toolbox.
	Control Wizards	Turns the Control Wizards on and off. Control Wizards aid you in designing complex controls, such as option groups, list boxes, and combo boxes.
Aa	Label	Creates a box that contains fixed descriptive or instructional text.
ab|	Text Box	Creates a box to display and allow editing of a data value and also creates a corresponding label, which you can choose to delete.
XYZ	Option Group	Creates a frame of adjustable size in which you can place toggle buttons, option buttons, or check boxes. Only one of the objects within an object group frame can be selected. When you select an object within an option group, the previously selected object is deselected.
	Toggle Button	Creates a button that changes from On to Off when clicked. The On state corresponds to Yes (–1), and the Off state corresponds to No (0). When used within an option group, toggling one button On toggles a previously selected button Off. You can use toggle buttons to let the user select one value from a set of values.
	Option Button	Creates a round button (originally called a *radio button*) that changes from the Off to On state when you select it. Option buttons are most commonly used within option groups to select between values in a set in which the choices are mutually exclusive.
	Check Box	Creates a check box that toggles On and Off. Multiple check boxes should be used outside option groups so that you can select more than one check box at a time.
	Combo Box	Creates a combo box with an editable text box where you can enter a value, as well as a list from which you can select a value from a set of choices.
	List Box	Creates a drop-down list box you can select a value from. A list box is the list portion of a combo box.

Tool	Name	Function
	Command Button	Creates a command button that, when clicked, triggers an event that can execute an Access VBA event-handling procedure.
	Image	Displays a static graphic on a form or report. This is not an OLE image, so you can't edit it after placing it on the form.
	Unbound Object Frame	Adds an OLE object created by an OLE server application, such as Microsoft Chart or Paint, to a form or report.
	Bound Object Frame	Displays the content of an OLE field of a record if the field contains a graphic object. If the field contains no graphic object, the icon that represents the object appears, such as the Sound Recorder's icon for a linked or embedded .wav file.
	Page Break	Causes the printer to start a new page at the location of the page break on the form or report. Page breaks don't appear in form or report Run mode.
	Tab Control	Inserts a tab control to create tabbed forms. (The tab control looks like the tabbed pages you've seen in the Properties windows and dialogs throughout this book.) Pages of a tab control can contain other bound or unbound controls, including subform/subreport controls.
	Subform/Subreport	Adds a subform or subreport to a main form or report, respectively. The subform or subreport object you intend to add must exist before you use this control.
	Line	Creates a straight line that you can size and relocate. You can change the color and width of the line by using the Formatting toolbar buttons or the Properties window.
	Rectangle	Creates a rectangle that you can size and relocate. The border color, width, and fill color of the r ectangle are determined by selections from the palette.
	More Controls	Clicking this tool opens a scrolling list of ActiveX controls that you can use in your forms and reports. The ActiveX controls available through the More Controls list aren't part of Access; ActiveX controls are supplied as .ocx or .dll files with Office 2003, Visual Basic, and various third-party tool libraries.

Using controls in the design of reports is discussed in Chapter 16, "Working with Simple Reports and Mailing Labels" and Chapter 17, "Preparing Advanced Reports." Using command buttons to execute VBA code is covered in Part VII of this book, "Programming and Converting Access Applications."

ACCESS'S CONTROL WIZARDS, BUILDERS, AND TOOLBARS

Access provides a number of features to aid you in designing and using more complex forms. Three of these features—Control Wizards, Builders, and customizable toolbars—are described in the three sections that follow.

ACCESS CONTROL WIZARDS

Much of the success of Access is attributable to the Form Wizard, Report Wizard, and Chart Wizard that simplify the process of creating database objects. The first wizard appeared in Microsoft Publisher, and most of Microsoft's productivity applications now include a variety of wizards. Chapter 14, "Creating and Using Access Forms," introduced the Form Wizard; the Report Wizard is discussed in Chapter 16 and the Chart Wizard is described in Chapter 18, "Adding Graphs, PivotCharts, and PivotTables." In this chapter, you're introduced to a Control Wizard each time you add a control for which a wizard is available.

ACCESS BUILDERS

Builders are another feature that makes Access easy to use. You use the Expression Builder, introduced in Chapter 5, "Working with Jet Databases and Tables," to create expressions that supply values to calculated controls on a form or report. The Query Builder creates the Jet SQL or Transact-SQL statements you need when you create list boxes or combo boxes whose Row Source property is an SQL statement that executes a select query. The Query Builder is described in the "Using the Query Builder to Populate a Combo Box" section near the end of this chapter.

CUSTOMIZABLE TOOLBARS

The preceding chapters demonstrated that Access toolbars include many shortcut buttons to expedite designing and using Access database objects. Access 2003, like most other contemporary Microsoft applications, lets you customize the toolbars to your own set of preferences. Access stores customized toolbar preferences in System.mdw. Toolbars that you create yourself, called *command bars*—are stored in a hidden system table—MSysCmdbars—in each database.

By default, the Toolbox is a floating toolbar. To anchor the Toolbox, also called *docking* the toolbar, follow these steps:

1. Press and hold down the mouse button while the mouse pointer is on the Toolbox's title bar, and drag the Toolbox toward the Form Design toolbar. When the Toolbox reaches the toolbar area, the dotted outline changes from a rectangle approximately the size of the Toolbox into a wider rectangle only as high as a toolbar.
2. Release the mouse button to change the Toolbox to an anchored toolbar positioned below the standard Form Design toolbar.

TIP

> You can anchor or dock a toolbar to any edge of Access's main window. Press and hold down the mouse button on an empty area of the toolbar (not covered by a button), and drag the toolbar until its outline appears along the left, right, or bottom edge of the window. If you drop the toolbar within the confines of Access's main window, it becomes a floating toolbar. In addition, double-clicking the title bar automatically docks a toolbar to its last docked position.

ADD OR DELETE TOOLBARS

You can add or delete buttons from toolbars with the Customize Toolbars dialog. To add form design utility buttons to the Toolbox toolbar (whether it's docked or floating), do the following:

1. Choose View, Toolbars, Customize to display the Customize dialog. Alternatively, click the down arrow of the Toolbox's title bar, choose Add or Remove Buttons from the context menu, and select Customize from the button list.

TIP

> You can also open the Customize dialog by right-clicking any part of a toolbar and choosing Customize from the context menu.

2. Click the Commands tab, and select Form/Report Design from the Categories list. The optional buttons applicable to form design operations appear in the Commands list, as shown in Figure 15.2.
3. The most useful optional buttons for form design are control alignment and sizing buttons. Click and hold down the mouse button on the Align to Grid command, drag this button to the Toolbox toolbar, and drop it to the right of the Rectangle button. The right margin of the Toolbox toolbar expands to accommodate the new button (if you customize the Toolbox while it's floating, the window expands to accommodate the new button). You can drag the Align to Grid button slightly to the right to create a gap between the new button and the Rectangle button.

Figure 15.2
Add Align to Grid and other Form/Report Design toolbar buttons to the Toolbox with the Customize dialog.

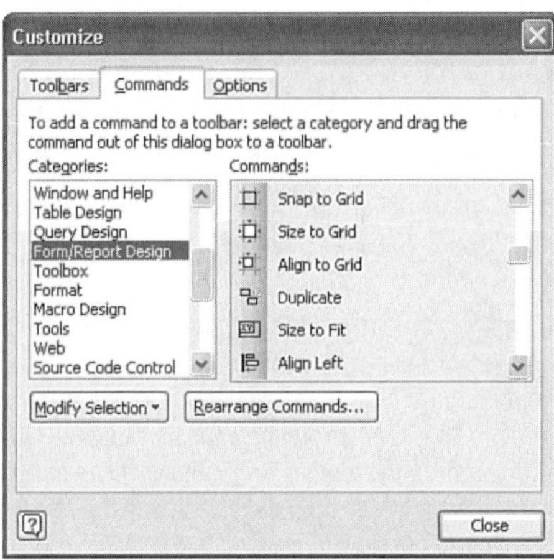

4. Repeat step 3 for the Size to Fit, Size to Grid, and Align Left commands, dropping each button to the right of the preceding button. You now have four new and useful design buttons available in your Toolbox.The Customize dialog for toolbars provides the following additional capabilities:

- To remove buttons from the toolbar, open the Customize dialog; click and drag the buttons you don't want, and drop them anywhere off the toolbar.
- To reset the toolbar to its default design, open the Customize dialog, and click the Toolbars tab. In the Toolbars list, select the toolbar you want to reset, and click the Reset button. A message box asks you to confirm that you want to abandon any changes you made to the toolbar.
- To create a button that opens or runs a database object, open the Customize dialog, display the Commands page, and scroll the Categories list to display the All *Objects* items. When, for example, you select All Tables, the tables of the current database appear in the Commands list. Select a table name, such as Employees, and drag the selected item to an empty spot on a toolbar. The ScreenTip for the new button displays Open Table 'Employees'. (If you select All Macros and drag a macro object to the toolbar, the button you add runs the macro when clicked.)
- To substitute a different image for the picture on the buttons, open the Customize dialog. Right-click the button you want to change (on the toolbar, not in the Customize dialog) to display the button shortcut menu. Click Change Button Image to display the Change Button Image dialog. Click one of the images offered. To edit the button's image, click Edit Button Image.
- To create a new empty toolbar that you can customize with any set of the supplied buttons you want, open the Customize dialog and select Utility 1 or Utility 2 on the Toolbars page. If there's space to the right of an existing toolbar, the empty toolbar

appears in this space. Otherwise, Access creates a new toolbar row for the empty toolbar. The Utility 1 and Utility 2 toolbars and the changes you make to them are available in any Access database you open.

- To create a custom toolbar that becomes part of your currently open database, open the Customize dialog and click New on the Toolbars page. The New Toolbar dialog appears, requesting a name for the new toolbar (Custom 1 is the default). Access creates a new floating tool window to which you add buttons from the Commands page of the Customize dialog. You can anchor the custom tool window to the toolbar, if you want.
- To delete a custom toolbar, open the Customize dialog, select the custom toolbar on the Toolbars page, and click the Delete button. You are requested to confirm the deletion. The Delete button is disabled when you select one of Access's standard toolbars in the list.

As mentioned earlier, custom toolbars to which you assign names become part of your database application and are stored in the current database file; they are available only when the database in which you store them is open. Built-in Access toolbars that you customize are stored in System.mdw and are available in any Access session.

Using the Toolbox to Add Label and Text Controls

Using the Form Wizard or the AutoForm feature of Access 2003 simplifies the generation of standard forms for displaying and updating data in tables. Creating forms from scratch in Form Design view by adding controls from the Toolbox provides much greater design flexibility than automated form generation. The examples in this chapter use the HRActions table that you created in Chapter 5, and a query, qryHRActions, which you create in the next section.

→ For more information on creating the data source for this chapter and establishing the correct relationships, **see** "Creating the HRActions Table," **p. 182**.

Tip

If you haven't created the HRActions table, you can import it from the Forms15.mdb database in your \Program Files\Seua11\Chaptr15 folder or from the \Seua10\Chaptr15 folder of the accompanying CD-ROM.

Creating the Query Data Source for the Main Form

The HRActions table identifies employees uniquely by their sequential ID numbers, located in the EmployeeID field. As before, you need to display the employee's name and title on the form to avoid entering records for the wrong person. The form design example in this chapter uses a one-to-many query to provide a single source of data for the new, custom HRActions form.

To create the HRActions query that serves as the data source for your main form, follow these steps:

1. Close any open Northwind forms, click the Tables shortcut in the Database window, and select HRActions in the table list.

2. Click the New Object: Query toolbar button to open the New Query dialog, and click OK with Design View selected to open Query1 with the HRActions table added. (Don't worry if your query's name contains a different number.)

3. Click the Show Table toolbar button to open the Show Table dialog, and add the Employees table to your query. Click the Close button to close the Show Table dialog.
4. If you defined relationships for the HRActions table as described in Chapter 5, the upper pane of the query window appears as shown in Figure 15.3. The line connecting the two tables indicates that a many-to-one relationship exists between the EmployeeID field in the HRActions table and the EmployeeID field of the Employees table.

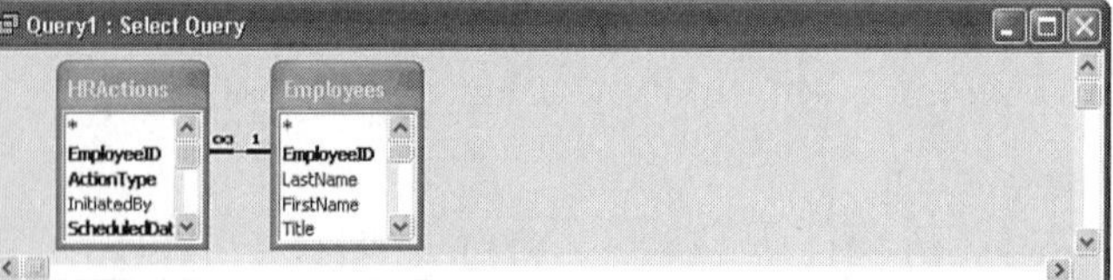

Figure 15.3 The upper pane of the Query Design window displays the many-to-one relationship between the Employees and HRActions tables.

TIP

> If you didn't define any relationships, the join line doesn't appear. In this case, you need to drag the EmployeeID field from the HRActions field list to the EmployeeID field of the Employees field list to create a join between these two fields.

5. Click the * field of the HRActions table, and then drag and drop it in the first column of the Query Design grid. This adds all the fields of the HRActions table to your query.
6. From the Employees table, click and drag the LastName, FirstName, Title, HireDate, Extension, ReportsTo, and Notes fields to columns 2 through 8 of the Query grid, respectively, as shown in Figure 15.4.
7. To simplify finding an employee, click the Sort row of the LastName column and select an Ascending sort.
8. Click the Run toolbar button to check your work, and then close the new query. Click Yes when the message box asks if you want to save the query.
9. In the Save As dialog, name the query **qryHRActions** and click OK.

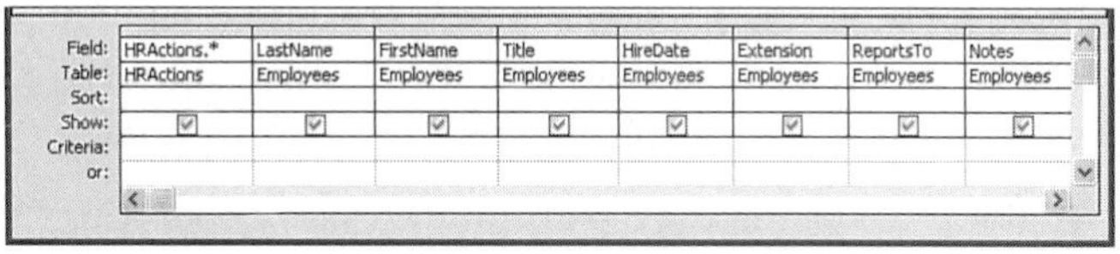

Field:	HRActions.*	LastName	FirstName	Title	HireDate	Extension	ReportsTo	Notes
Table:	HRActions	Employees	Employees	Employees	Employees	Employees	Employees	Employees
Sort:								
Show:	☑	☑	☑	☑	☑	☑	☑	☑
Criteria:								
or:								

Figure 15.4
The query includes all fields (*) from the HRActions table and seven fields from the Employees table.

Now that you've created the query that provides a unified data source for the main form, you're ready to begin creating your custom multitable form.

CREATING A BLANK FORM WITH A HEADER AND FOOTER

When you create a form without using the Form Wizard, Access opens a default blank form to which you add controls that you select from the Toolbox. To open a blank form to begin duplicating the form you created with the Form Wizard in Chapter 14, do the following:

1. In the Database window, click the Forms shortcut, and click the New button to open the New Form dialog.
2. With the default Design view selected in the upper list of the New Form dialog, select qryHRActions in the lower drop-down list (see Figure 15.5). Click OK.

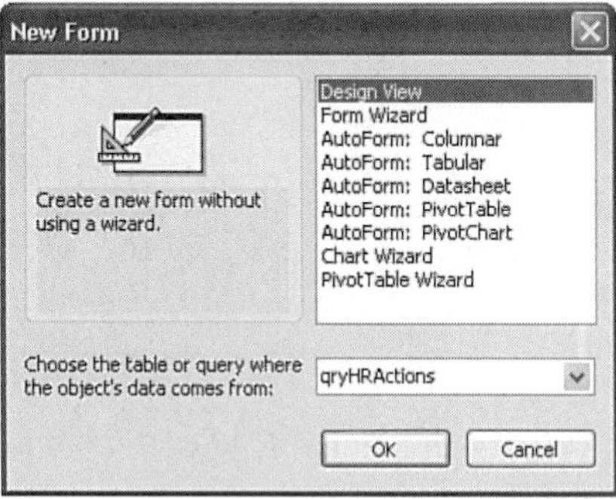

Figure 15.5
Select qryHRActions as the data source for the new form in the New Form dialog.

3. Access creates a new blank form with the default title Form1. By default, the Toolbox and the field list for the qryHRActions query open. Click the Maximize button of the Form Design window to expand the form to fill the document window.

TIP

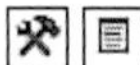

If the Toolbox or field list isn't visible, click the appropriate button on the Form Design (top) toolbar. If the grid doesn't appear on the form, choose View, Grid.

4. Choose View, Form Header/Footer to add a header and footer to the form.

15

The default width of blank forms is 5 inches. The default height of the Form Header and Footer sections is 0.25 inch, and the height of the Detail section is 2 inches. To adjust the height of the form's Detail section and the width of the form, do this:

1. Place the mouse pointer on the top line of the Form Footer bar. The mouse pointer becomes a double-headed arrow with a line between the heads. Hold down the left mouse button and drag the bar to create a Detail section height of about 3.0 inches, measured by the left vertical ruler. The active surface of the form, which is gray with the default 24×24 grid dots, expands vertically as you move the Form Footer bar downward, as shown in Figure 15.6.

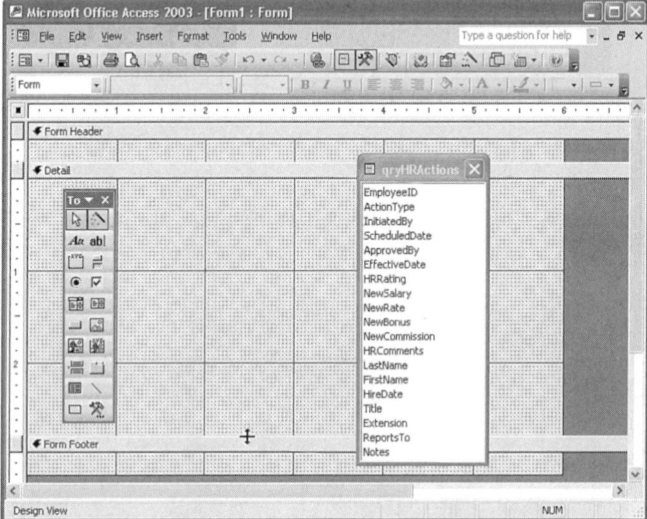

Figure 15.6
When you drag a section header or margin, the mouse pointer changes to a line with a double-headed arrow.

2. Minimize the Form Footer section by dragging the bottom margin of the form to the bottom of the Form Footer bar.

3. Drag the right margin of the form to 6 inches as measured by the horizontal ruler at the top of the form.

Adding a Label to the Form Header

The label is the simplest control in the Toolbox to use. By default, labels are unbound and static, and they display only the text you enter. Static means that the label retains the value you originally assigned as long as the form is displayed, unless you change the Caption value with VBA code. To add a label to the Form Header section, complete the following steps:

1. Click the Toolbox's Label button. When you move the mouse pointer to the form's active area, the pointer becomes the symbol for the Label button, combined with a

crosshair. The center point of the crosshair defines the position of the control's upper-left corner.

2. Locate the crosshair at the upper-left of the Form Header section. Press and hold down the left mouse button while you drag the crosshair to the position for the lower-right corner of the label (see Figure 15.7).

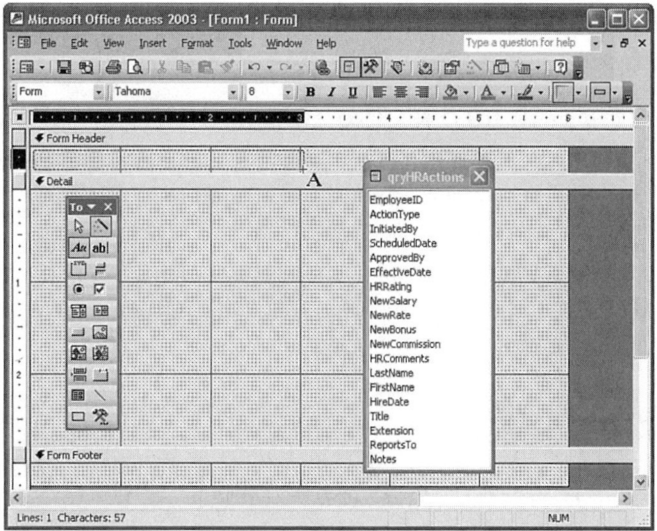

Figure 15.7
Drag the symbol for the control, a label in this example, from the upper left to the lower right to define a rectangle that represents the size of the control.

NOTE

As you drag the crosshair, the outline of the container for the label follows your movement. The number of lines and characters that the text box can display in the currently selected font appears in the status bar.

3. If you move the crosshair beyond the bottom of the Form Header section, the Form Header bar moves to accommodate the size of the label after you release the left mouse button. When the label is the size you want, release the mouse button.

4. The mouse pointer becomes the text-editing cursor inside the outline of the label. Type **Human Resources Action Entry** as the text for the label, and click anywhere outside the label to finish its creation. If you don't type at least one text character in a label after creating it, the box disappears the next time you click the mouse.

5. Choose File, Save, and type the name **frmHRActionEntry** in the Form Name text box of the Save As dialog. Click OK.

➔ For tips on manipulating elements of a form, **see** "Selecting, Moving, and Sizing a Single Control," **p. 546**.

You use the basic process described in the preceding steps to add most of the other types of controls to a form. (Some Toolbox buttons, such as the graph and command buttons, launch a Control Wizard to help you create the control if the Control Wizards button is activated.)

After you add the control, you use the anchor and sizing handles described in Chapter 14 to move the control to the desired position and to size the control to accommodate the content. The location of the anchor handle determines the Left (horizontal) and Top (vertical) properties of the control. The sizing handles establish the control's Width and Height property values.

FORMATTING TEXT AND ADJUSTING TEXT CONTROL SIZES

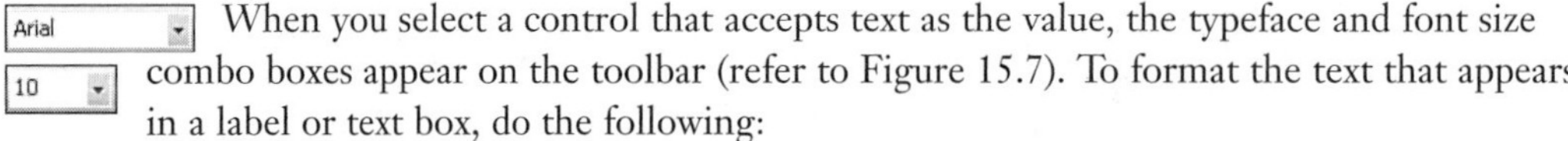

When you select a control that accepts text as the value, the typeface and font size combo boxes appear on the toolbar (refer to Figure 15.7). To format the text that appears in a label or text box, do the following:

1. Click the Human Resources Action Entry label you created in the preceding section to select the label. If the Properties window isn't open, click the Properties toolbar button. Alternatively, double-click the unselected label.

NOTE

> Access 2002 added a drop-down list to the Properties window that lets you select any object on the form or report. Selecting objects from the Properties window's list is faster than selecting from the toolbar's Object list.

2. Open the Font list on the Formatting toolbar and select the typeface family you want. Tahoma is Access 2003's default font. (MS Sans Serif was the default typeface in Access 97 and earlier.)

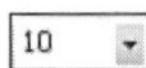

3. Open the Font Size list and select 14 points.

4. Click the Bold attribute button on the toolbar.

5. The size of the label you created probably isn't large enough to display the larger font. To adjust the size of the label to accommodate the content of the label, click the Size to Fit button—if you added it to the Toolbox—or choose Format, Size, To Fit. Access resizes the label's text box to display the entire label; if necessary, Access also increases the size of the Form Header section.

TIP

> The two Format commands–Size, To Grid and Size, To Fit–work slightly differently, depending on whether one or more controls are selected. If one or more controls are selected when you execute one of the sizing commands, the command is applied to the selected control(s). If no controls are selected, the chosen sizing command applies as the default to all objects you subsequently create, move, or resize.

When you change the properties of a control, the new values are reflected in the Properties window for the control, as shown in Figure 15.8. If you move or resize the label, you see the label's Left, Top, Width, and Height property values change in the Properties window. You usually use the Properties window to change the property values of a control only if a toolbar button or menu choice isn't available.

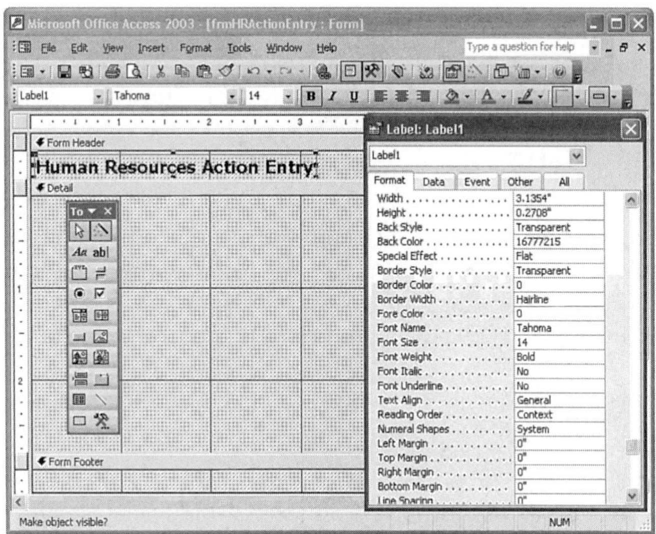

Figure 15.8
The Properties window reflects changes you make to the property values of a control with toolbar controls.

NOTE

You can select different fonts and the Bold, Italic, and Underline attributes (or a combination) for any label or caption for a control. Good design practices dictate use of a single font family, such as Tahoma, for all controls on a form. If the PC running your Access application doesn't have the font family you specified, Windows selects the closest available match—usually Arial for sans serif fonts. Changes you make to the formatting of data in controls doesn't affect the data's display in Datasheet view.

TIP

Change the default format of a control, such as a label, by doing this: Select the control in the toolbox and click the Properties button or press F4 to open the Default *ControlName* window. Click the Format tab and change the property values—such as Font Name, Font Size, and Font Weight—to apply a standard format to the new labels or other controls you add.

15

CREATING BOUND AND CALCULATED TEXT BOXES

Following are the most common attributes of Access text boxes:

- *Single-line text boxes* usually are bound to controls on the form or to fields in a table or query.
- *Multiline text boxes* usually are bound to Memo field types and include a vertical scroll bar to allow access to text that doesn't fit within the box's dimensions.
- *Calculated text boxes* obtain values from expressions that begin with = (equal sign) and are usually a single line. Most calculated text boxes get their values from expressions that manipulate table field or query column values; but the =Now expression to supply the current date and time also is common. Calculated text boxes are unbound and read-only. You can't edit the value displayed by a calculated text box.
- *Unbound text boxes* can be used to supply values—such as limiting dates—to Access VBA procedures. As a rule, an unbound text box that doesn't contain a calculation expression can be edited.(An unbound text box control can be set to inhibit editing, but doing so negates the control's purpose in most cases.)

The following sections show you how to create the first three types of text boxes.

ADDING BOUND TEXT BOXES

The most common text box used in Access forms is the single-line bound text box that makes up the majority of the controls for the frmHRActions form of Chapter 14. To add a bound text box do the following:

1. If necessary, click the Field List button on the toolbar to redisplay the field list.
2. Click and drag the EmployeeID field in the field list window to the upper-left corner of the form's Detail section. When you move the mouse pointer to the active area of the form, the pointer becomes a field symbol, but no crosshair appears. (Notice that Access creates two controls with this action: the text box and its label control.) The position of the field symbol indicates the upper-left corner of the text box, not the label, so drop the symbol in the approximate position of the text box anchor handle, as shown in Figure 15.9.
3. Drag the text box by the anchor handle closer to the ID label, and decrease the box's width.

4. Small type sizes outside a field text box are more readable when you turn the Bold attribute on. Select the ID: label and click the Bold button.

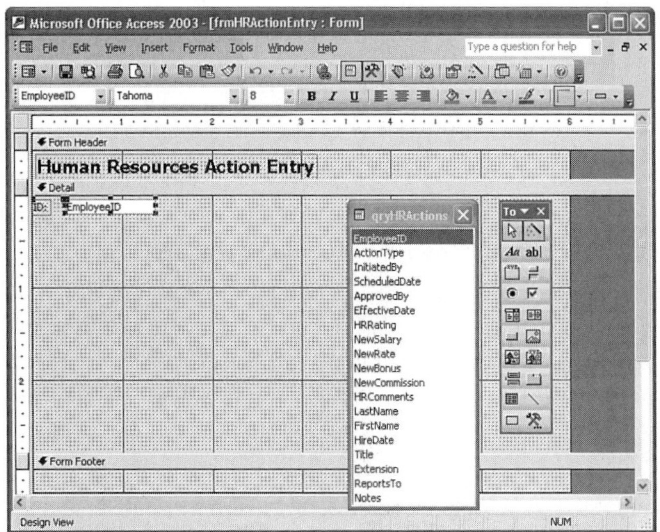

Figure 15.9
Add a bound text box control by dragging the field name to the position where you want the text box to appear.

NOTE

When Access creates a label for a text box that's associated with a form control, the bound object's name is the value for the text label. If the form control is bound to a table object, such as a field, that has a Caption property (and the Caption property isn't empty), Access combines the value of the Caption property with a colon suffix (the colon is a default you can inhibit) as the default value for the text label of the bound form control. When you created the HRActions table in Chapter 5, you set the Caption property for each field name. The EmployeeID field has a Caption property set to ID, so the label for the text box bound to the EmployeeID field is also ID plus a colon.

5. Drag the HRComments field from the list box to the form about 0.75 inch below the ID label, delete the label, and resize the text box to about 1×2 inches, as shown later in Figure 15.10. When you add a text box bound to a memo field, Access automatically sets the Scrollbars property to Vertical, and they appear when the memo is longer than the text box space or you place the cursor in the text box.
6. Press Ctrl+S to save your work.

When you drag fields from the Field list in this manner, you automatically create a bound control. By default, however, all controls you add with the Toolbox are *unbound* controls. You can bind a control to a field by creating an unbound control with a tool and and selecting a field in the Control Source property dropdown list (reach the Control Source list by clicking the Data tab in the Properties window for the control).

ADDING A CALCULATED TEXT BOX AND FORMATTING DATE/TIME VALUES

You can display the result of all valid Access expressions in a calculated text box. An expression must begin with = and can use VBA functions to return values. To create a calculated text box that displays the current date and time, do the following:

1. Close the Properties window, click the Text Box tool in the Toolbox, and draw an unbound text box at the right of the Form Header section of the form.

2. Edit the label of the new text box to read **Date/Time:**, and relocate the label so that it is adjacent to the text box. Apply the Bold attribute to the label.
3. Type **=Now** in the text box to display the current date and time from your computer's system clock; Access adds a trailing parentheses pair for you. Adjust the width of the label and the text box to accommodate the approximate length of the text.

4. Change to Form view and inspect the default date format, MM/DD/YYYY HH:MM:SS AM/PM for North America.

5. To delete the seconds value, open the Properties window for the text box, and click the Format tab. Select the Format property and type **mm/dd/yyyy hh:nn ampm** in the text box.

Your reformatted Date/Time text box appears as shown in Figure 15.10. Access lets you alter properties of text boxes and other controls in Form *and* Form Design views. When you change the focus to another control, the format string, mm/dd/yyyy hh:nn ampm for this example, properly reformats the text box.

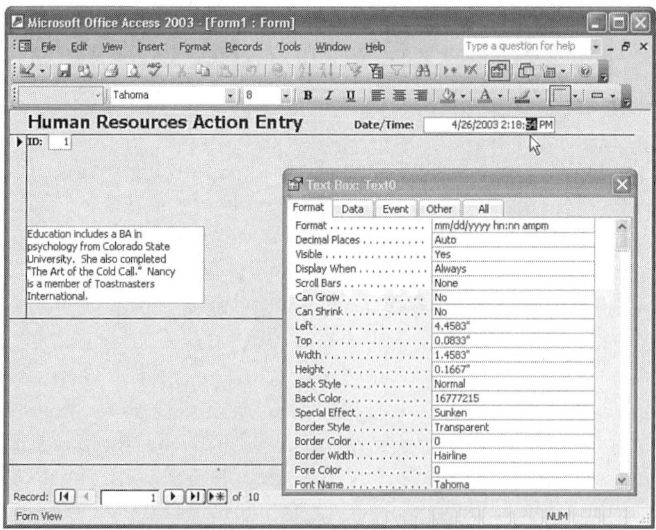

Figure 15.10
The format string you specify for a text box doesn't apply when the Properties window for the text box is open in Form or Form Design view until you change the focus.

NOTE

> When you return to Design view, the Human Resources Action Entry label you added to the form header has an error correction flag. An error correction flag is a small green triangle in the top left corner of the control. The "Accepting or Declining Control Error Correction" section, which follows shortly, describes dealing with error correction on forms.

USING THE CLIPBOARD WITH CONTROLS

You can use the Windows Clipboard to make copies of controls and their properties. As an example, create a copy of the Date/Time control using the Clipboard by performing the following steps:

1. Return to Form Design mode and select the unbound Date/Time control and its label by clicking the field text box. Both the label and the text box are selected, as indicated by the selection handles on both controls.

2. Copy the selected control to the Clipboard by pressing Ctrl+C.

3. Click the Detail bar to select the Detail section, and paste the copy of the control below the original version by pressing Ctrl+V.(Access pastes the control into the top-left corner of the section, so you'll need to reposition it.)
4. Click the Format property in the Properties window for the copied control, and select Long Date from the drop-down list.

5. To check the appearance of the controls you've created, click the View button on the toolbar.

6. Return to Design view and delete the added Date/Time text box and label. To do so, enclose both with a selection boundary created by dragging the mouse pointer across the text boxes from the upper-left to the lower-right corner. Press Delete. (You need the Date/Time text box only in the Form Header section for this form.)

ACCEPTING OR DECLINING CONTROL ERROR CORRECTION

After you add a text box control to the form header section, Access 2003's new control error correction feature becomes evident in Form Design view. The Human Resources Action Entry label sports a green flag in its upper left corner. When you select a control with an error flag, the error checking smart tag icon—a diamond-shaped sign with an exclamation point—appears to the right of the control.

When you pass the mouse pointer over the icon, an error message screen tip describing the problem appears—in this case: "This is a new label and is not associated with a control." Clicking the icon's arrow opens the following list (see Figure 15.11):

- *Error description*—New Unassociated Label for this example.

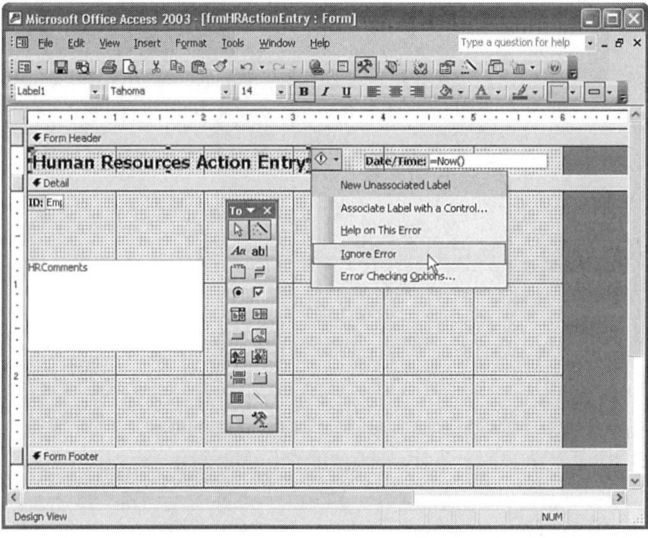

Figure 15.11 When you add an unbound label control that's not associated with a text box, Access 2003 flags the control for error correction and offers these selections to ignore or correct the purported error.

- *Corrective action(s)*—Associate Label with Control for this example, which opens a list of text box(es) in the section to which the label can be associated.
- Help on This Item opens a Microsoft Access Help window with the topic relating to the error.
- Ignore Error removes the flag from the selected control.
- Error Checking Options lets you specify the errors to be flagged or turn off error checking (see Figure 15.12). Clearing the New Unassociated Labels check box and clicking Apply removes the flag from the selected control. Clicking OK with a check box cleared prevents further error checking for the selection.

Figure 15.12 The error checking Options dialog lets you specify the types of errors to be flagged by this new feature.

Adding new unassociated labels is a common task, so removing this error check is a good form and report design practice. Changes you make in the error checking Options dialog apply to all databases.

15

CHANGING THE DEFAULT VIEW AND OBTAINING HELP FOR PROPERTIES

A form that fills Access's Design window might not necessarily fill the window in Run mode. Run mode might allow the beginning of a second copy of the form to appear. A second copy appears if the Default View property has a value of Continuous Forms. Forms have the following five Default View property values from which you can choose:

- *Single Form* displays one record at a time in one form.
- *Continuous Forms* displays multiple records, each record having a copy of the form's Detail section. You can use the vertical scroll bar or the record selection buttons to select which record to display. Continuous Forms view is the default value for subforms created by the Form Wizard.
- *Datasheet* displays the form fields arranged in rows and columns.

- *PivotTable* displays an empty PivotTable design form, unless you've previously designed the PivotTable.

- *PivotChart* displays an empty PivotChart design form, unless you've previously designed the PivotChart.

NOTE

> PivotTable and PivotChart views of the data source for a form seldom are useful. These views require aggregate values, which are uncommon except in decision-support forms. Rather than use a PivotTable or PivotChart view of the data, add these controls to a form. Chapter 18 describes how to add PivotTable and PivotChart controls to forms.

To change the form's Default View property, do the following:

1. Click the View button on the toolbar to return to Form Design view, if necessary.

2. Press Ctrl+R or choose Edit, Select Form.

3. Click the Properties button if the Properties window isn't visible. Click the Format tab.
4. Click the Default View property and open the list.
5. Select the value you want for this property for the current form. For this exercise, select Single Form (the default) from the list.
6. While Default view is selected, press F1 to open the Help window for the Default View property. This Help window also explains how the Default View and Views Allowed properties relate to each another.

NOTE

> The vertical scroll bar disappears from the form in Run mode if a single form fits within its multiple document interface (MDI) child window.

You can verify your changes, if any, to the Default View property by clicking the View button to review the form's appearance.

15

ADDING OPTION GROUPS WITH THE WIZARD

Option buttons, toggle buttons, and check boxes ordinarily return only Yes/No (–1/0 or True/False) values when used by themselves on a form. These three controls also can return Null values if you change the TripleState property value to Yes. Individual bound option button controls are limited to providing values to Yes/No fields of a table or query. When you place any of these controls within an option group, however, the buttons or check boxes can return a number you specify for the value of the control's Option Value property.

The capability to assign numbers to the Option Value property lets you use one of the preceding three controls inside an option group frame for assigning values to the HRRating field of the HRActions table. Option buttons are most commonly used in Windows applications to select one value from a limited number of values.

The Option Group Wizard is one of three Control Wizards that take you step-by-step through the creation of complex controls. To create an option group for the HRRating field of the HRActions table with the Option Group Wizard, follow these steps:

1. Click the Control Wizards tool to turn on the wizards if the toggle button isn't On (the default value).

NOTE

Access's toggled Toolbox (and toolbar) buttons indicate the On (True) state by a border with a colored background under Windows XP or a white background under Windows 2000. This differs from toggle buttons on forms, which use a very light gray background and a sunken effect to indicate the On (pressed) state. Background colors differ if you've applied a Windows XP desktop theme.

2. Click the Option Group tool, position the pointer where you want the upper-left corner of the option group, and click the mouse button to display the first dialog of the Option Group Wizard.
3. For this example, type five of the nine ratings in the Label Names datasheet (pressing Tab, not Enter): **Excellent**, **Good**, **Acceptable**, **Fair**, and **Poor** (see Figure 15.13). Click Next.

Figure 15.13
Type the caption for each option button of the option group in the first dialog of the Option Group Wizard.

15

TIP

You can specify accelerator keys in the captions of your option buttons by placing an ampersand (**&**) before the letter to be used as an accelerator key. Thereafter, pressing Alt in combination with that letter key selects the option when your form is in Run mode. To include an ampersand in your caption, type **&&**.

4. The second dialog lets you set an optional default value for the option group. Select the option named Yes, the Default Choice Is, and open the drop-down list. Select Good, as shown in Figure 15.14, and click Next. If you need to, you can return to any previous step by clicking Back one or more times.

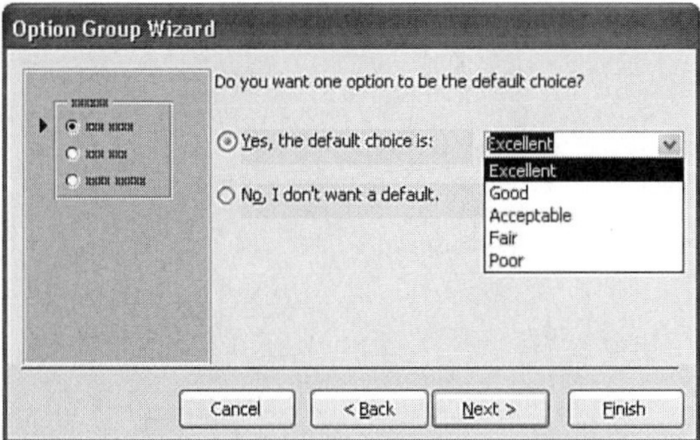

Figure 15.14
Select a default value in the second Option Group Wizard dialog.

5. The third dialog of the Option Group Wizard provides for the assignment of option values to each option button of the group. The default value is the numbered sequence of the buttons. Type **9**, **7**, **5**, **3**, and **1** in the five text boxes, as illustrated in Figure 15.15, and click Next.

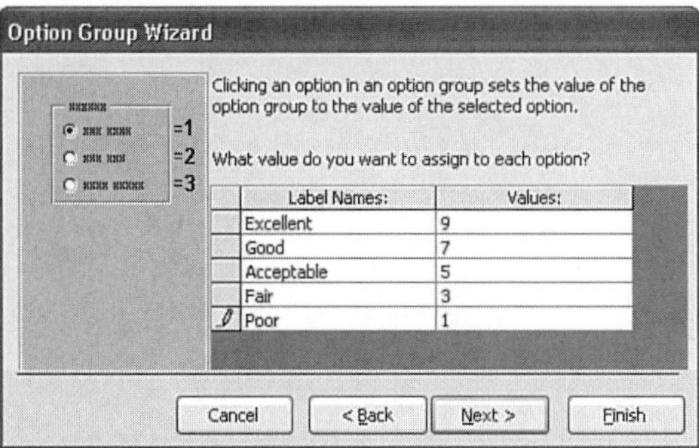

Figure 15.15
Assign a numeric value to each option button in the group. In Form view, clicking an option button assigns its value to the option frame.

15

NOTE

> The domain integrity rule for the HRRating field provides for nine different ratings. Nine option buttons, however, occupy too much space on a form, so this example uses only five of the nine ratings. (Only 5 of the 9 options are included here for the sake of simplicity. In the real world, you wouldn't just eliminate options because there are too many.)

6. The fourth Wizard dialog lets you bind the option group to a field of a table or a column of a query that you specified as the Record Source property value of the bound form. Select the HRRating column of the qryHRActions query to which your form is bound (see Figure 15.16). Click Next.

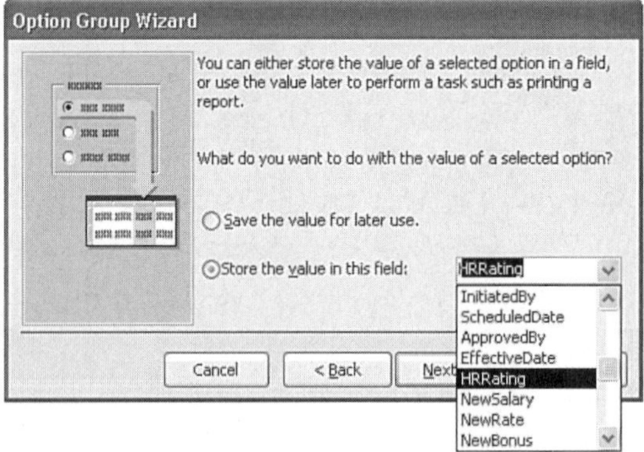

Figure 15.16
Bind the option group value.

7. The fifth dialog lets you determine the style of the option group, as well as the type of controls (option buttons, check boxes, or toggle buttons) to add to the option group. You can preview the appearance of your option group and button style choices in the Sample pane. For this example, select Option Buttons and Sunken (see Figure 15.17). The sunken effect matches the default effect applied to text boxes.

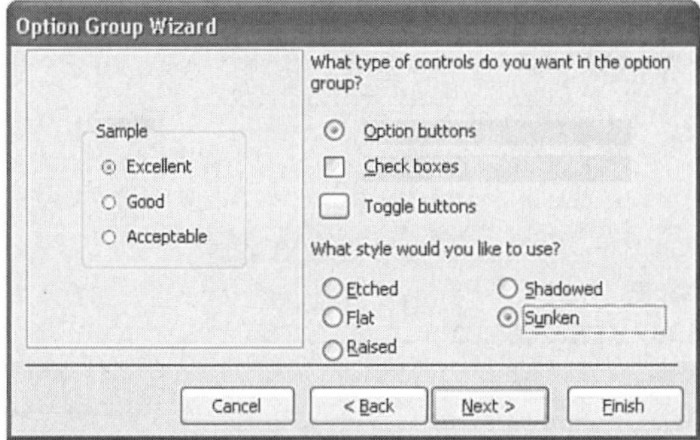

Figure 15.17
The fifth Wizard dialog lets you choose the option frame's control type and appearance.

NOTE

> Check boxes are an inappropriate choice for controls in an option group. Windows programming standards reserve multiple check boxes for situations in which more than one option choice is permissible.
>
> The sunken and raised styles of option groups, option buttons, and check boxes are applicable only to control objects on forms or option groups with a Back Color property other than white.

8. The last dialog provides a text box for entering the Caption property value of the label for the option group. Type **Rating**, as shown in Figure 15.18, and click Finish to let the Wizard complete its work.

Figure 15.18 Add the caption for the option group in the last Wizard dialog.

9. Open the Properties dialog for the option frame, and assign the frame a name, **fraRating** for this example. Figure 15.19 shows the completed Rating option group and its properties window in Form Design view.

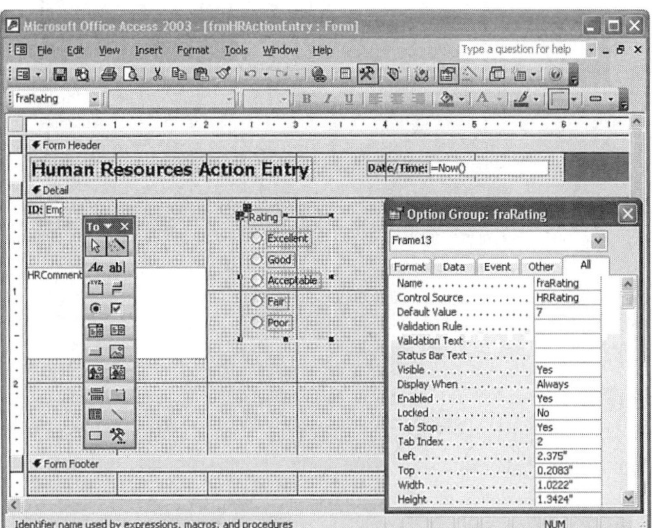

Figure 15.19 The Properties dialog for the fraRating option frame displays the property values assigned by the Wizard.

TIP

> Name the controls you add to identify their use, rather than accepting Access default value for the Name property. This book uses object-naming conventions that consist of a three-letter, lowercase abbreviation of the object type–*fra* for frames, *txt* for text boxes, *frm* for forms, and the like–followed by a descriptive name for the control. Using a consistent object naming convention makes it much easier to write (and later interpret) VBA code for automating your application.
>
> Access 2000 added the capability to change property values in Form view. However, you can change the Name property value of an object only in Form Design view.

→ For more information on Access and VBA naming conventions, **see** "Typograhpic and Naming Conventions Used for VBA," **p. 1152**.

To test your new bound option group, select the Text Box tool and drag the HRRating field from the field list to the form to add a text box that's bound to the HRRating column. Figure 15.20 shows the option group in Form view with the Bold attribute applied to the option group label and the Rating text box added. Click the option buttons to display the rating value in the text box. Although your entry on the form tentatively updates the value onscreen, the value in the table doesn't change until you move the record pointer or change the view of the form. Press Ctrl+S to save your form.

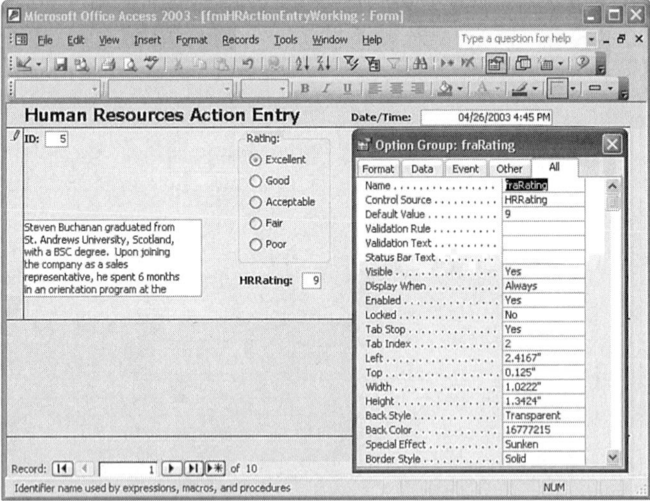

Figure 15.20 Clicking an option button displays its value in the HRRating text box and makes a tentative change to the HRRating field of the current record of the HRActions table.

CHANGING ONE CONTROL TYPE TO ANOTHER

Access lets you "morph" a control of one type to become a control of a compatible type. You can change an option button to a check box, for example, or you can change a toggle button to an option button. You can't, however, change a text box to an object frame or other control with a different field data type. To change a control to a different type, follow these steps:

1. In the form's Design view, select the control whose type you want to change.
2. Choose Format, Change To to see a submenu of form control types. Only the submenu choices for control types that are compatible with the selected control are enabled.
3. Select the control type you want from the submenu. Access changes the control type.

USING THE CLIPBOARD TO COPY CONTROLS TO ANOTHER FORM

Access's capability of copying controls and their properties to the Windows Clipboard lets you create controls on one form and copy them to another. You can copy the controls in the header of a previously designed form to a new form and edit the content as necessary. The form that contains the controls to be copied need not be in the same database as the destination form in which the copy is pasted. This feature lets you create a library of standard controls in a dedicated form that is used only for holding standard controls. If your library includes bound controls, you can copy them to the form, and then change the field or column to which they're bound.

The Date/Time calculated text box is a candidate to add to Chapter 14's frmHRActions form. You might want to add a Time/Date text box to the Form Header or Detail section of all your transaction forms. To add the Date/Time control to the frmHRActions form, assuming both forms are in the same database, do the following:

1. With the frmHRActionEntry form open, click the Design View button, and select the Date/Time control and its label by clicking the text box.
2. Press Ctrl+C to copy the selected control(s) to the Clipboard.
3. Press Alt+W, 1 and open the frmHRActions form from the Database window in Design view.
4. Click the Detail section selection bar, and press Ctrl+V. A copy of the control appears in the upper-left corner of the Detail section.
5. Position the mouse pointer over the copied text box so that the pointer becomes a hand symbol.
6. Hold down the mouse button and drag the text box and its label to a position to the right of the Title label and text box.

7. Click Form view to display the modified frmHRActions form (see Figure 15.21).
8. Return to Form Design view, click the Save button to save your changes, and close the frmHRActions form.

If you receive an error message when the focus moves to controls you've copied to another form, see "Error Messages on Copied Controls" in "Troubleshooting" near the end of this chapter.

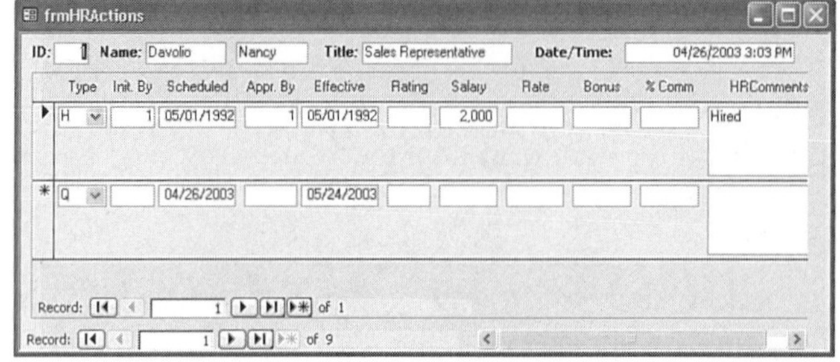

Figure 15.21
Copying a previously formatted control and its label from one form to another saves design time.

Adding Combo and List Boxes

Combo and list boxes both serve the same basic purpose by letting you pick a value from a list, rather than type the value in a text box. These two kinds of lists are especially useful when you need to enter a code that represents the name of a person, firm, or product. You don't need to refer to a paper list of the codes and names to make the entry. The following list describes the differences between combo and list boxes:

- *Combo boxes* consume less space than list boxes in the form, but you must open these controls to select a value. You can allow the user to enter a value in the text box element of the drop-down combo list or limit the selection to just the members in the drop-down list. If you limit the choice to members of the drop-down list (sometimes called a pick list), the user can still use the text box to type the beginning of the list value—Access searches for a matching entry. This feature reduces the time needed to locate a choice in a long list.
- *List boxes* don't need to be opened to display their content; the portion of the list that fits within the size of the list box you assign is visible at all times. Your choice is limited to values included in the list.

In most cases, you bind the combo or list box to a field so that the choice updates the value of this field. Two-column controls often are the most common. The first column contains the code that updates the value of bound field, and the second column contains the name associated with the code. A multiple-column list is most useful when assigning supervisor and manager employee ID numbers to the InitiatedBy and ApprovedBy fields in the frmHRActionEntry form, for example.

Using the Combo Box Wizard

Designing combo boxes is a more complex process than creating an option group, so you're likely to use the Combo Box Wizard for every combo box you add to forms. Follow these steps to use the Combo Box Wizard to create the cboInitiatedBy drop-down list that lets you select from a list of Northwind Traders' employees:

1. Open the frmHRActionEntry form (that you created and saved earlier in this chapter) from the Database window in Form Design view if it isn't presently open.

2. Click the Control Wizards button, if necessary, to turn on the wizards.

3. Click the Combo Box tool in the Toolbox. The mouse pointer turns into a combo box symbol while on the active surface of the form.

4. Click the Field List button to display the Field List.
5. Drag the InitiatedBy field to a position at the top and rightmost edge of the form's Detail section, opposite the EmployeeID field (look ahead to Figure 15.26). The first Combo Box Wizard dialog opens.
6. You want the combo box to look up values in the Employees table, so accept the default option (see Figure 15.22). Your selection specifies Table/Query as the value of the Row Source Type property of the combo box. Click Next.

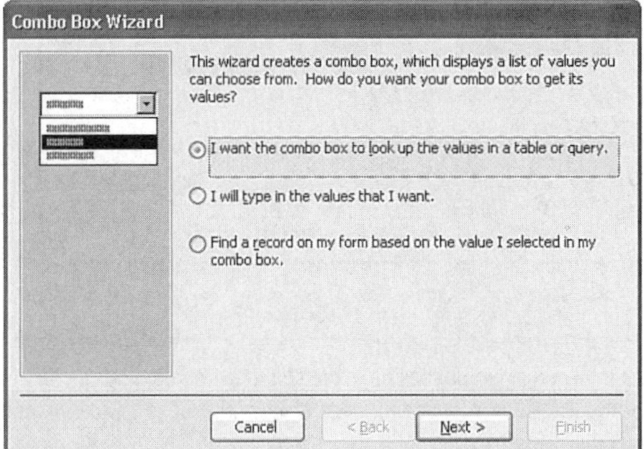

Figure 15.22 The first Combo Box Wizard dialog lets you select the type of combo box to create. This example uses a lookup-type combo box.

7. In the second Wizard dialog, select Employees from the list of tables (see Figure 15.23), and click Next.

Figure 15.23 Select the table or query to provide the list items of the combo box in the Wizard's second dialog. Use a base table, Employees for this example, to assure that the list doesn't contain multiple entries for a single lookup value.

8. For this example, the combo box needs the EmployeeID and LastName fields of the Employees table. EmployeeID is the field that provides the value to the bound column of the query, and your combo box displays the LastName field. EmployeeID is selected in the Available Fields list by default, so click the > button to move EmployeeID to the Selected Fields list. LastName is then selected automatically, so click the > button again to move LastName to the Selected Fields list. Your Combo Box Wizard dialog appears as shown in Figure 15.24. This selection generates the Jet SQL `SELECT` query that serves as the value of the combo box's Row Source property and populates its list. Click Next.

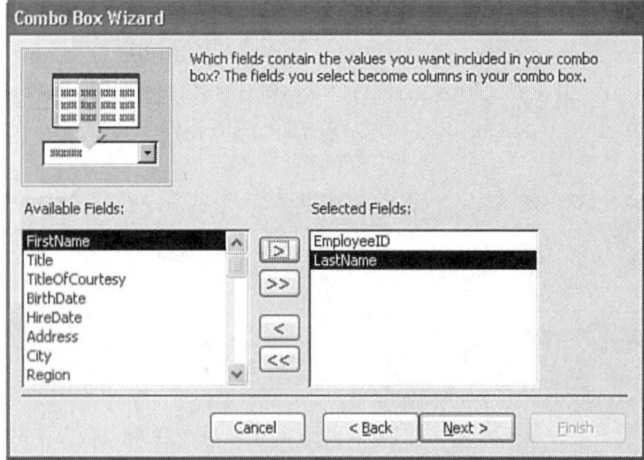

Figure 15.24
In the third Wizard dialog, add the bound column and one or more additional columns to display in the combo box list.

TIP

If two or more employees have the same last name, add the FirstName field to the combo list. Unlike conventional combo and list boxes, Access controls can display multiple columns.

9. Access 2003 adds a new sorting dialog to the Combo Box Wizard. To sort the list by last name, open the first list and select the LastName field (see Figure 15.25). Selecting a sort on one or more fields adds an `ORDER BY` clause to the combo box's `SELECT` query.

10. The fifth dialog displays the list items for the combo box. Access has successfully determined that the EmployeeID field is the key field of the Employees table and has assumed (correctly) that the EmployeeID field binds the combo box.

NOTE

The Hide Key Column check box is selected by default; this option causes Access to hide the bound column of the combo box. You've selected two columns for the combo box, but only one column (the LastName field) displays in the combo box's list. The EmployeeID column is hidden and used only to supply the data value for the InitiatedBy field.

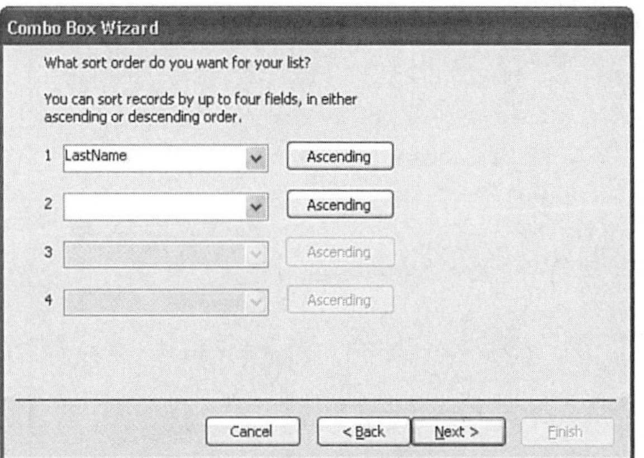

Figure 15.25
In the new Wizard sorting dialog, select the field(s) on which to apply an ascending or descending sort. Clicking an Ascending button toggles an Descending or Ascending sort.

11. Resize the LastName column by dragging the right edge of the column to the left—you want the column wide enough to display everyone's last name but not any wider than absolutely necessary (see Figure 15.26). Click Next.

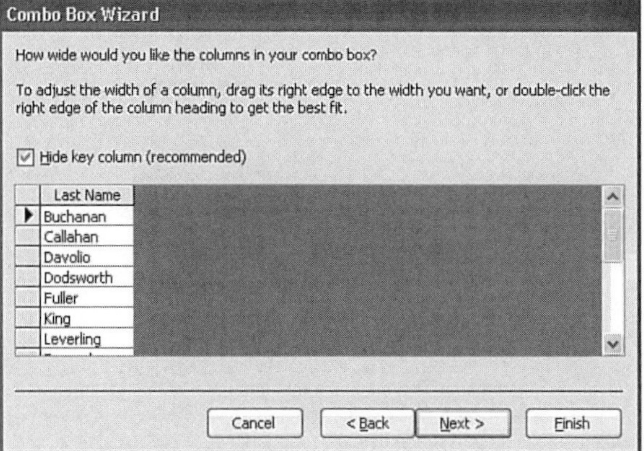

Figure 15.26
The Wizard queries the combo box's data source (the Employees table) and displays the control's list items. Double-click the right edge of the list to size the list's width to fit the list items.

NOTE

Resizing the list width doesn't accomplish its objective in Access 2003 or the previous two versions. The Wizard adds a combo box of the size you created when dragging the tool on the form, regardless of the width you specify at this point.

12. Your combo box updates the InitiatedBy field the EmployeeID value corresponding to the name you select. You previously specified that the Control Source property is the InitiatedBy column when you dragged the field symbol to the form in step 5. The Combo Box Wizard uses your previous selection as the default value of the Control Source property (see Figure 15.27), so accept the default by clicking the Next button to display the sixth and final dialog.

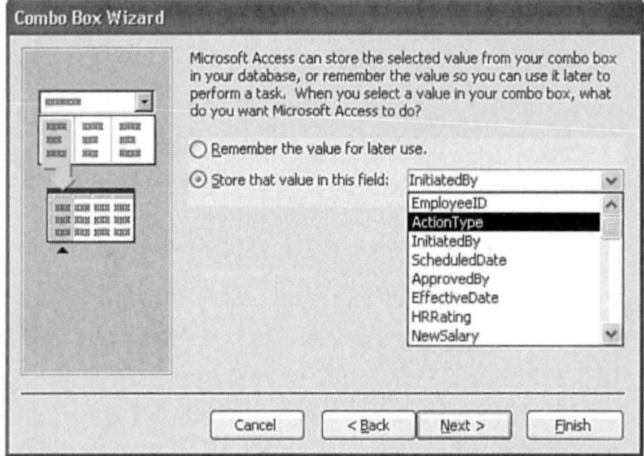

Figure 15.27
The fifth Wizard dialog specifies the column of the query to be updated by the combo box selection.

13. The last dialog lets you edit the label associated with the combo box (see Figure 15.28). Type **Initiated by:** and click Finish to add the combo box to your form.

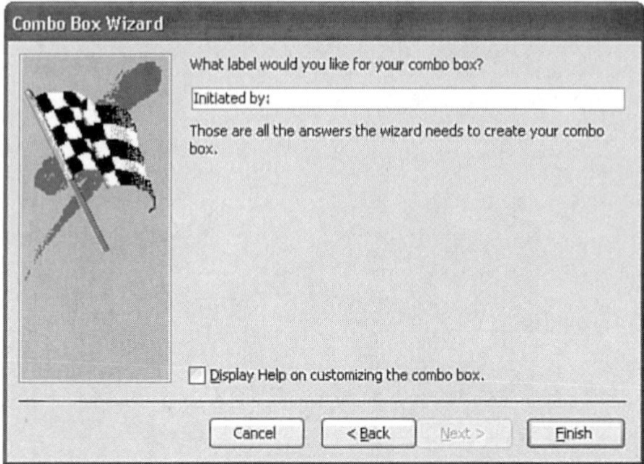

Figure 15.28
Type the label caption for the combo box in the sixth and last Wizard dialog.

14. Apply the bold attribute to the combo box label, and adjust the width and position of the label. Open the Properties window for the combo box, and change its name to **cboInitiatedBy**. Figure 15.29 shows the new combo box in Form Design view.

NOTE

> The Row Source property is the SQL `SELECT` statement that fills the combo box's list. Specifying a Column Width value of 0 hides the first column. The Description property of the EmployeeID field provides the default Status Bar Text property value.

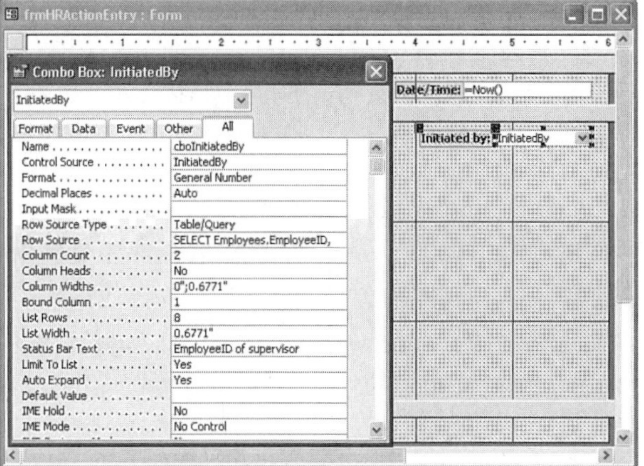

Figure 15.29
The Combo Box Wizard sets the property values for the combo box.

15. Change to Form view to test your combo box. Change the Initiated by value to another person, and then use the navigation buttons to move the record pointer and make the change permanent. Return to the original record, and verify that the combo box is bound to the InitiatedBy field (see Figure 15.30).

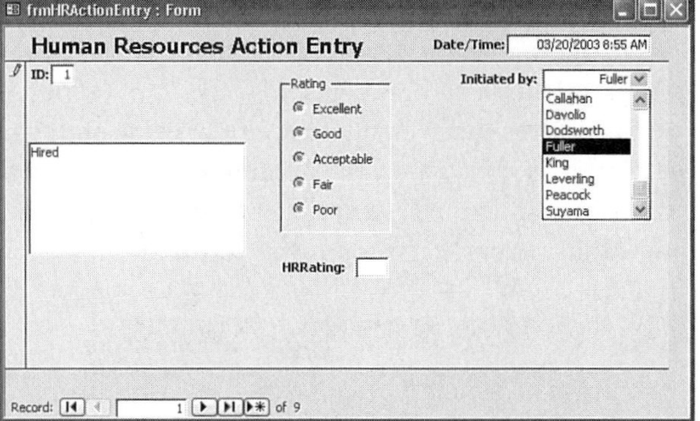

Figure 15.30
The combo box in Form view displays a list with the default maximum of eight items. You can change the depth of the list by specifying a different value for the List Rows property.

Jet SQL

The Jet SQL statement generated by the Combo Box Wizard for cboInitiatedBy is

```
SELECT Employees.EmployeeID, Employees.LastName
FROM Employees
ORDER BY [LastName];
```

TIP

If you don't use the Wizard to generate the combo box, you can select an existing table or query to serve as the Row Source for the combo box.

USING THE QUERY BUILDER TO POPULATE A COMBO BOX

If the Row Source Type property for a combo box is Table/Query, you can substitute a custom SQL statement for a named table or query as the value of the Row Source property. For either tables or queries, you can choose only the fields or columns you want for the text box, eliminating the need to hide columns. In addition, you can specify a sort order for the list element of your combo box and specify criteria to limit the list.

To invoke Access's Query Builder and create an SQL statement for populating a manually added Approved by combo box, follow these steps:

1. Return to or open frmHRActionEntry in Design view, and click to disable the Toolbox's Control Wizards button to add the combo box manually. Click the Field List button, if necessary, to display the field list.

2. Click the Combo Box button in the Toolbox, and then drag the ApprovedBy field to add a new combo box under the Initiated By combo box you added in the preceding section. Select the new control and open the Properties window if necessary.

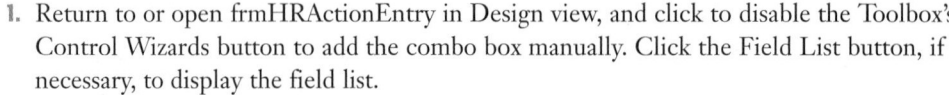

3. Select the Row Source property, and click the Build button to launch the Query Builder. The Query Builder window is identical in most respects to the Query Design window, but its title and behavior differ.
4. Add the Employees table to the query, and then close the Show Table dialog. Drag the EmployeeID, LastName, and Title fields to the Query Design grid.
5. You want an ascending sort on the LastName field, so select Ascending in the Sort check box. Only presidents, vice-presidents, managers, and supervisors can approve HR actions, so type **Like *President*** in the first Criteria row of the grid's Title column, **Like *Manager*** in the second, and **Like *Supervisor*** in the third. Access adds the quotation marks surrounding the Like argument for you. Clear the Show check box of the Title column. Your query design appears as shown in Figure 15.31.

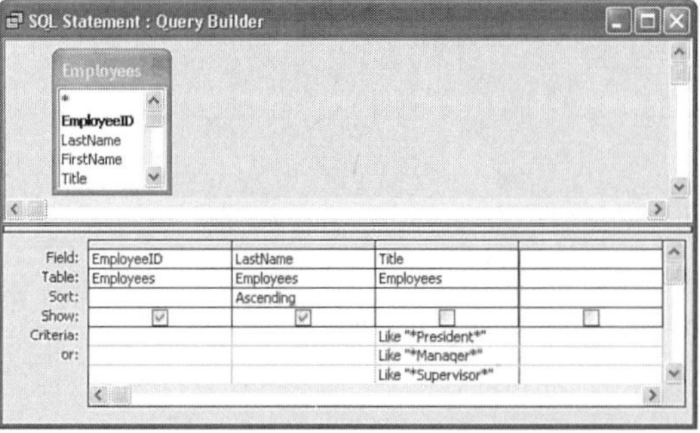

Figure 15.31
This query design limits its approval to employees whose titles include President, Manager, or Supervisor.

TIP

Test the results of your query by clicking the Run button on the toolbar. Access executes the query and displays a Datasheet view of the query's results. For this example, only Mr. Buchanan and Dr. Fuller meet the criteria.

6. Close the Query Builder. The message box shown in Figure 15.32 appears to confirm your change to the Row Source property value, instead of asking if you want to save your query. Click Yes and the SQL statement derived from the graphical Query Design grid becomes the value of the Row Source property.

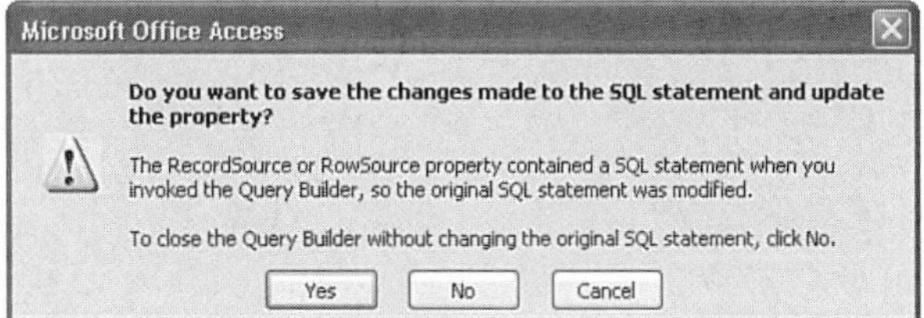

Figure 15.32
This query design supplies the corresponding Jet SQL statement as the value of the combo box's Row Source property.

7. In the combo box's Properties window, change the name of the combo box to **cboApprovedBy**. Change the Column Count property value to **2** and type **0.2;0.8** in the Column Widths text box. You specify column widths in inches, separated by semicolons, Access adds the units—double quotes (") for inches—to the widths. (Metrified users specify column widths in cm.) Finally, change the Limit to List value to **Yes**.

TIP

You can display only the LastName field in the combo box, making the combo box similar in appearance to that for the InitiatedBy field, by setting the first Column Width value to **0**.

8. Change the label caption to **Approved by:** and apply the Bold attribute.

9. Switch to Form view to test the effect of adding the sort (the `ORDER BY` clause) and criteria (the `WHERE` clause) to the query (see Figure 15.33). Press Ctrl+S to save your form changes.

Jet SQL

The Jet SQL statement generated by the Query Builder is

```
SELECT Employees.EmployeeID, Employees.LastName
FROM Employees
WHERE (((Employees.Title) Like "*President*")) OR
      (Employees.Title) Like "*Manager*") OR
      (Employees.Title) Like "*Supervisor*"))
ORDER BY Employees.LastName;
```

Jet SQL uses the DOS and UNIX `*` and `?` wildcards for all characters and a single character, respectively. T-SQL requires the ANSI SQL wildcards `%` and `_`, and surrounds character strings with a single-quote rather than double-quotes. The table name prefixes aren't needed, and the parentheses in the `WHERE` clause are superfluous.

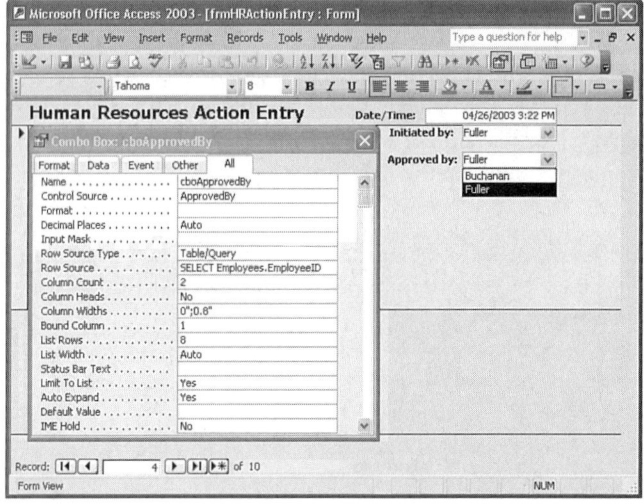

Figure 15.33 The combo box list contains items for employees whose titles comply with the Like criteria.

T-SQL

The simplified T-SQL equivalent of the preceding Jet SQL statement for ADP is

```
SELECT EmployeeID, LastName
FROM dbo.Employees
WHERE Title LIKE '%President%' OR
      Title LIKE '%Manager%' OR
      Title LIKE '%Supervisor%'
ORDER BY LastName
```

The `dbo.` prefix–called the *schema* component of the table name–in the preceding statement is optional, but is a common practice in T-SQL statements.

It's a more common practice for ADP to use SQL Server 2000 views, stored procedures, or table-returning functions to provide the Row Source for forms, combo boxes, and list boxes.

CREATING A COMBO BOX WITH A LIST OF STATIC VALUES

Another application for list boxes and combo boxes is picking values from a static list of options that you create. A drop-down list to choose a Rating value saves space in a form compared with the equivalent control created with option buttons within an option group. As you design more complex forms, you find that display "real estate" becomes increasingly valuable.

The option group you added to the frmHRActionEntry form provides a choice of only 5 of the possible 10 ratings. To add a drop-down list with the Combo Box Wizard to allow entry of all possible values, do the following:

1. Change to Form Design view, and click the Control Wizards button in the Toolbox to enable the Combo Box Wizard.
2. Open the Field List window, and then click the Combo Box tool in the Toolbox. Drag the HRRating field symbol to a position underneath the cboApprovedBy combo box you added previously.
3. In the first Wizard dialog, select the I Will Type in the Values That I Want option (refer to Figure 15.22), and then click Next to open the second dialog.
4. The Rating combo box requires two columns: The first column contains the allowable values of HRRating, 0 through 9, and the second column contains the corresponding description of each rating code. Type **2** as the number of columns.
5. Access assigns value-list Row Source property values in column-row sequence; you enter each of the values for the columns in the first row and then do the same for the remaining rows. Type **9 Excellent**, **8 Very Good**, **7 Good**, **6 Average**, **5 Acceptable**, **4 Marginal**, **3 Fair**, **2 Sub-par**, **1 Poor**, **0 Terminated** (use the Tab key and don't type the commas).
6. Set the widths of the columns you want by dragging the edge of each column header button to the left, as shown in Figure 15.34. If you don't want the rating number to appear, drag the left edge of column 1 fully to the left to reduce its width to 0. When you've adjusted the column widths, click Next to open the third dialog.

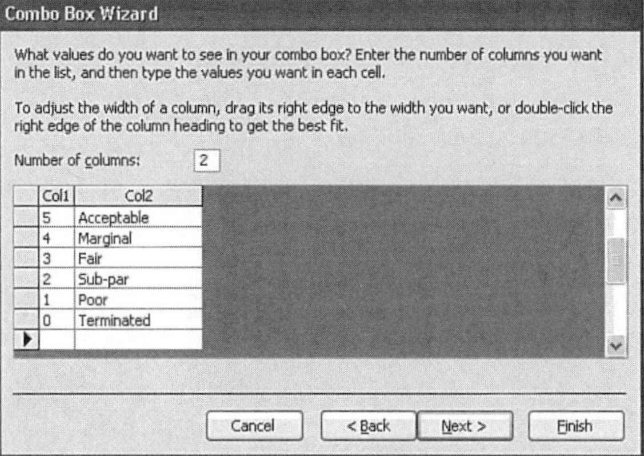

Figure 15.34
Type the values for the two columns in the list, and then adjust the column widths to suit the list's contents.

7. Select Col1, the HRRating code, as the bound column for your value list—that is, the column containing the value you want to store or use later (see Figure 15.35); this column must contain unique values. Click Next to open the fourth dialog.

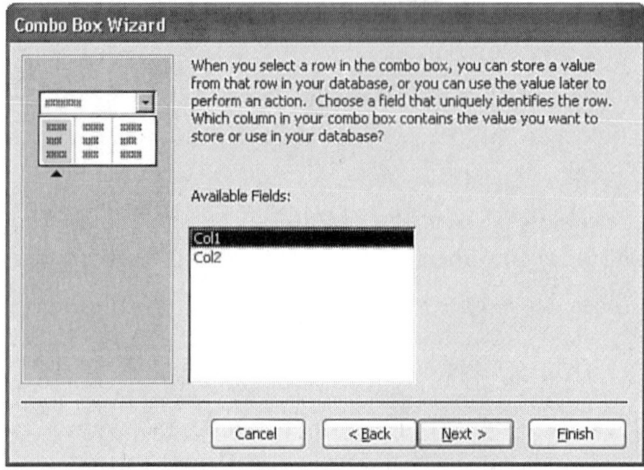

Figure 15.35
Select the column that contains the unique value to identify the rows of the list, in most cases, Col1.

8. Accept the default value (the HRRating column) in the fourth dialog, and click Next to open the final dialog of the Combo Box Wizard.

9. Type **Rating:** as the label for the new combo box control, apply the Bold attribute to the label, and then click Finish to complete the combo box specification and return to Form Design view.

10. Open the Properties window for the combo box, change the Name to **cboRating**, and then click the Data tab in the Properties window. Set Limit to List to Yes to convert the drop-down combo to a drop-down list. Quickly review the Row Source property. Notice that the Wizard has added semicolons between the row entries, and quotation marks to surround the text values in the Row Source property. You use this format when you enter list values manually.

11. Change to Form view. The open Rating static-value combo box and its Properties window appear as shown in Figure 15.36.

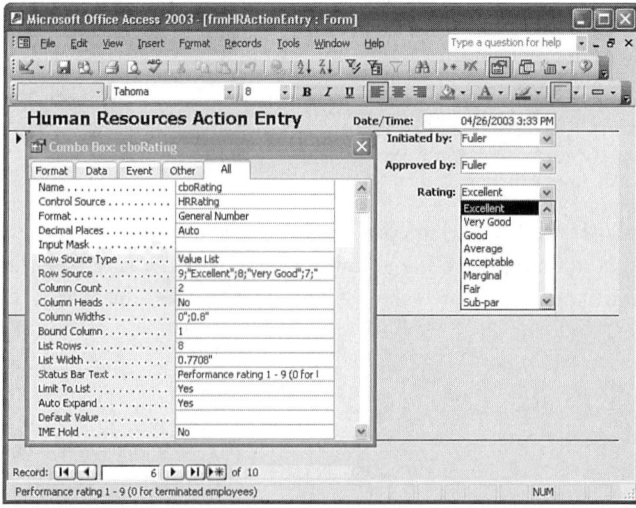

Figure 15.36
The value-list version of the cboRating combo box closely resembles the cboApprovedBy combo box.

Another opportunity to use a static-value combo box is as a substitute for the Type text box. Several kinds of performance reviews exist: Quarterly, Yearly, Bonus, Salary, Commission, and so on, each represented by an initial letter code.

TIP

You can improve the appearance of columns of labels and associated text, list, and combo boxes by right-aligning the text of the labels and left-aligning the text of the boxes. Select all the labels in a column with the mouse, and click the Align Right button on the toolbar. Then select all the boxes and click the Align Left button.

CREATING A COMBO BOX TO FIND SPECIFIC RECORDS

The Combo Box Wizard includes a third type of combo list box that you can create—a combo list that locates a record on the form based on a value you select from the list. You can use this type of combo box, for example, to create a Find box on the frmHRActionEntry form that contains a drop-down list of all last names from the Employees table. Thus, you can quickly find HRActions records for employees.

To create a combo box that finds records on the form based on a value you select from a drop-down list, follow these steps:

1. Change to Design view, and click the Control Wizards button in the Toolbox, if necessary, to enable the Combo Box Wizard.

2. Click the Combo Box tool in the Toolbox, and then click and drag on the surface of the form's Detail section to create the new combo box in a position underneath the cboRating combo box you created previously. Release the mouse, and the first Combo Box Wizard dialog appears. When you don't drag a column name to the form, you create an unbound combo box.
3. Select the Find a Record on My Form Based on the Value I Selected in My Combo Box option, and click Next (refer to Figure 15.22).
4. In the second Wizard dialog, scroll the Available Fields list until the LastName field is visible. Click to select this field, and then click the > button to move it to the Selected Fields list (see Figure 15.37). Click Next to open the third dialog.

TIP

When creating a combo box to find records, select only one field. The combo box won't work for finding records if you select more than one field for the combo box's lists.

If the record source contains more than one person with the same last name, you need to add a calculated FullName query column to use the find-record combo box version. For this example the expression to create a FullName query column is `FullName: [LastName] & ", " & [FirstName]`.

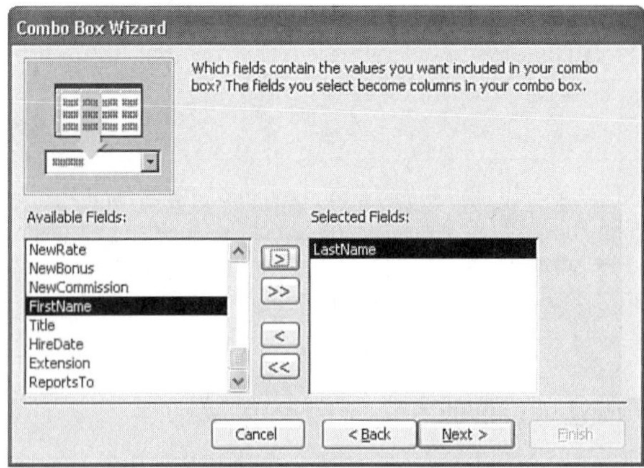

Figure 15.37 Select the name of the field to search in the Available Fields list, and click > to add the entry to the Selected Fields list.

5. The Combo Box Wizard now displays a list of the field values from the column you just selected. Double-click the right edge of the LastName column to get the best column-width fit for the data values in the column, and then click Next to go to the fourth and final step of the Wizard.

B

6. Type **Find:** as the label for the new combo box, and then click Finish to complete the new combo box control. After applying the bold attribute to the label and adjusting its size, your form appears as shown in Figure 15.38.

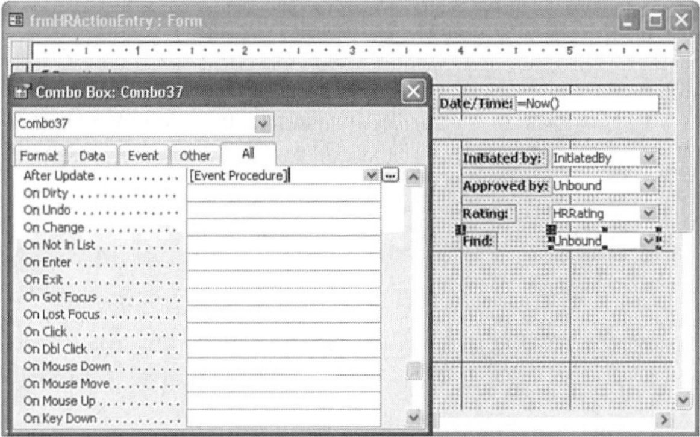

Figure 15.38 The record-finding version of the combo box uses an event procedure to move the record pointer to the first record matching the combo box selection.

CAUTION

> Don't change the name of the new combo box at this point. If you change the name at this point, the Find combo box won't work in Form view.

7. Click the Form View button on the toolbar to display the form. The open Find: combo box appears as shown in Figure 15.39.
8. Press Ctrl+S to save your work so far.

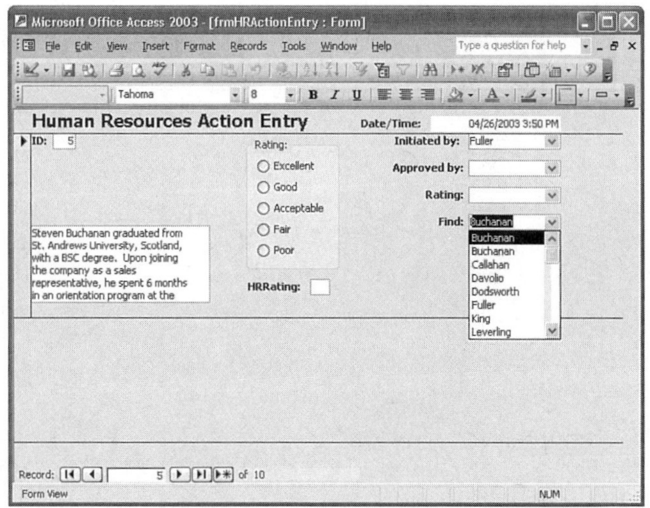

Figure 15.39 The combo box finds the records for last name Buchanan. If you have more than one record for an employee, multiple instances of the LastName value appear in the list at this point.

TIP

Always use unbound combo box controls for record selection. If you bind a record-selection combo box to a field, the combo box updates field values with its value.

When you create this type of combo box, the Combo Box Wizard automatically creates a VBA event subprocedure for the After Update property of the combo box (refer to the Property window in Figure 15.35). An event subprocedure is a VBA procedure that Access executes automatically whenever a particular event occurs—in this case, updating the combo box. Chapter 27, "Learning Visual Basic for Applications," describes how to write Access VBA code and Chapter 28, "Handling Events with VBA 6.0" describes how to write event-handling subprocedures.

To view the event procedure code that the Wizard created for your new combo box, change to Design view, open the Properties window for the Name: combo box, click the Events tab in the window, select the After Update property text box, and then click the Build button. Access opens the VBA Editor window shown in Figure 15.40. After you've looked at the code, close the VBA Editor and return to Design view.

To use a combo box of this type, select a value from the list. As soon as you select the new value, Access updates the combo box's text box, which then invokes the VBA code for the After Update event procedure. The VBA code in the After Update procedure finds the first record in the form's Recordset with a matching value and displays it. You can use this type of combo box only to find the first matching record in a Recordset.

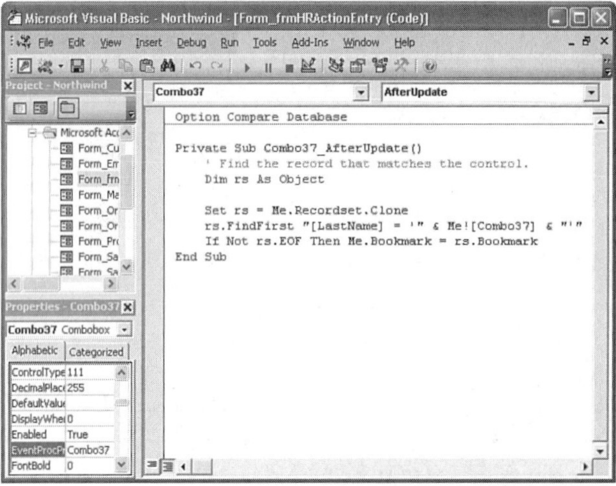

Figure 15.40
The Combo Box Wizard generates the `Combo37_AfterUpdate` VBA subprocedure to find the record.

TIP

> If you change the name of the combo box to comply with the naming convention mentioned earlier, you must also change the name of the VBA procedure. For example, replace the two instances of `Combo37` in the VBA code shown in Figure 15.40 with **cboFind**, close the VBA code editor, then change the Name property value of the combo box to **cboFind**, and finally set the After Update event's value to [Event Procedure].
>
> Name AutoCorrect, which is enabled by default in the General Page of the Options dialog, doesn't change the names of VBA event procedures to correspond to changes of object names, or vice-versa.

Because the field on the form is based on the LastName column of the form's underlying query, you see an entry in the list for every last name entry in the Recordset produced by the qryHRActions query. If, for instance, more than one Personnel Action record exists for Steve Buchanan, Buchanan appears in the combo list as many times as there are records for him. If an employee doesn't have a record in the qryHRActions query result set, the name doesn't appear in the list. To display a unique list of all employee last names, change the Row Source property to obtain the LastName field values for the combo box list through an SQL statement based on a query from the Employees table.

To change the Row Source property, follow the procedure you learned in the "Using the Query Builder to Populate a Combo Box" section, earlier in this chapter: Open the Properties window of the Name: combo box, click the Data tab, select the Row Source text box, and then open the Query Builder. Change the query so that it uses the LastName field of the Employees table, add an ascending sort, as shown in Figure 15.41, and change the Limit to List property value to Yes.

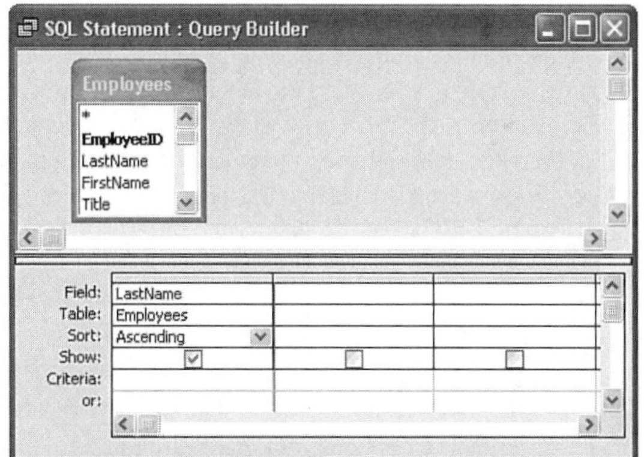

Figure 15.41 Changing the Row Source of the combo box to a query against the Employees table eliminates duplicate items in the Find: combo box.

USING BOUND OBJECT FRAMES

Access OLE Object fields let you embed or create a link to graphic images, sound or video files, or any other type of object for which you have an OLE 2.0 server installed and registered on your computer. OLE Object fields are unique to Access, and other applications (such as Visual Basic) can't directly read the data the fields contain. Access adds a special "OLE wrapper" to the data that identifies the OLE 2.0 server used to create and display or play the data.

The tab control that you add later in the chapter includes a bound object frame to display a photo for each employee. To use a bound object frame, you must add a field of the OLE Object type to the Employees table, and then insert the images from the files into the Employees table. The sections that follow describe how to add an OLE Object field to a table, insert objects into the field, and test displaying bitmap objects in a temporary bound object frame.

NOTE

Storing images in OLE Object fields isn't considered a good database design practice, especially if you expect to handle a large number of images. This isn't an issue, however, with the nine Northwind employee photos that are used in the following example.

ADDING AN OLE OBJECT FIELD TO THE EMPLOYEES TABLE

The Employees table of early versions of Access used an OLE Object field to hold employee photos, and the Employees form displayed the images in a bound object frame. Access 2002 changed the Photo field to a field of the Text data type, which contains the names of individual bitmap files—EmpID1.bmp through EmpID9.bmp—stored in the ...\Office10\Samples folder. The Employees form contains VBA code to display the appropriate image in an image control.

15

NOTE

> Microsoft's objective in substituting linked .bmp files for embedded bitmaps isn't clear. The reason might have been to make the Employees table compatible with SQL Server, which doesn't support OLE Object fields. However, the Categories table has a Picture OLE Object field. Even less clear is the reason for using the .bmp format, which consumes much more storage space than a compressed image format, such as Graphics Interchange Format (.gif) or Joint Photographic (Experts) Group (.jpg).

To add a new OLE Object field to the Employees table, do this:

1. Close the frmHRActionEntry form and any open queries against the Employees table.
2. In the Database window, create a backup copy of the Employees table by selecting it, pressing Ctrl+C, and then pressing Ctrl+V. Type a name for the backup, such as **Employees_Orig**, in the Paste Table As dialog, and click OK.
3.  Open the Employees table in Design view, and select the Notes field.
4. Press Insert to add a new field, type **PhotoOLE** as the field name, and set the Field data type to OLE Object.
5.  Change to Datasheet view, and save your change to the table design.

EMBEDDING OR LINKING IMAGES IN AN OLE OBJECT FIELD

Embedding the object's data is safer than creating an OLE link to the object's source file, because someone might move the source files. Linking the source files doesn't save space in the database, because the OLE Object field stores the last version of the image, called its *presentation*. Linking assures that modifications to the image's source file appear when you display the image in a bound object frame. This example uses embedded data from the nine sample EmpID?.bmp files, but the process is identical for any file type that has an association with an OLE 2.0 server.

To embed or link the sample bitmap files to the PhotoOLE field, do this:

1.  With the Employees table open in Datasheet view, navigate to the PhotoOLE field of the first record.
2. Right-click the PhotoOLE cell and choose Insert Object to open a Microsoft Access dialog with an Object Type list, which includes all OLE 2.0 servers registered by your computer (see Figure 15.42).
3. Select the Create from File option, click Browse, and navigate to the \Program Files\Microsoft Office\Office 11\Samples folder.
4. Double-click Empid1.bmp in the folder to add the file to the File: Bitmap Image text box (see Figure 15.43). If you want to link, rather than embed, the data, click Link before clicking OK.

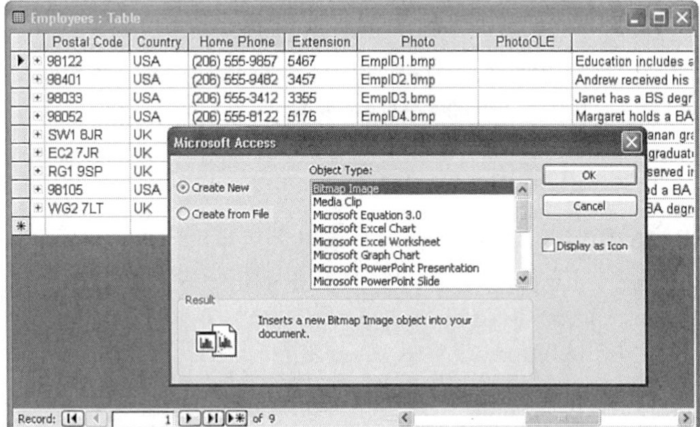

Figure 15.42
Right-clicking an OLE Object field and choosing Insert Object opens a dialog with a list of registered OLE 2.0 servers.

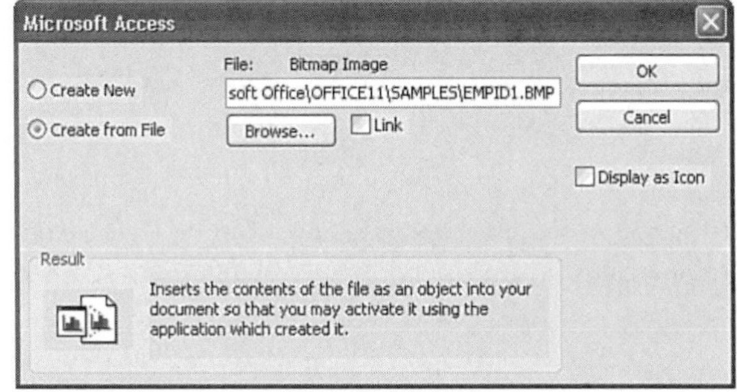

Figure 15.43
Selecting the Create from File option changes the dialog to provide a text box to enter the name of the file to embed or link.

5. Move to each of the remaining eight records in succession, repeating steps 2, 3, and 4 to add Empid2.bmp through Empid9.bmp to the PhotoOLE field.

6. After you've added all nine bitmaps, double-click one of the Bitmap Image cells to display the image in Microsoft Paint (see Figure 15.44).

Figure 15.44
Double-clicking a cell of an OLE Object field opens the object in its OLE 2.0 server, in this case Microsoft Paint.

NOTE

> If .bmp files are associated with another OLE 2.0 server on your computer, such as Adobe Photoshop, the associated server opens. Microsoft Paint is the default server for .bmp files, if another application hasn't assumed this role.

DISPLAYING OLE OBJECT BITMAPS IN A BOUND OBJECT FRAME

Bound object frames display or play OLE objects in a form, and print bitmap and vector-based images in reports. To add a temporary bound object frame to the frmHRActionEntry form that displays the bitmap objects in the PhotoOLE field of the query, do the following:

1. Close the Employees table, if it's open, and open qryHRActions in Query Design view.
2. Drag the PhotoOLE field from the Employees table to the empty column to the right of the Notes column of the grid. Close and save your changes.

3. Open frmHRActionEntry in Form Design view, and display the Toolbox and Field List.

4. Click the Bound Object Frame control in the Toolbox, and drag the PhotoOLE field from the Field List near the upper right corner of the fraRatings option frame.
5. Adjust the size of the bound object frame to about 1.5×1.7 inches.

6. Change to Form view, and open the Properties window. The default Size Mode property of the control is Clip, so a cropped image of an employee photo opens in the frame (see Figure 15.45).

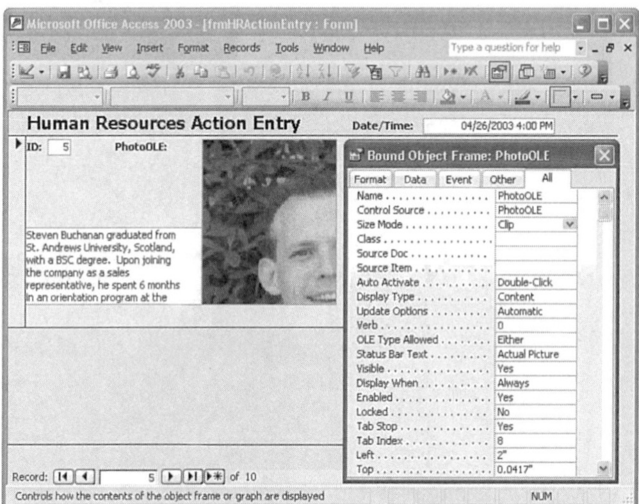

Figure 15.45 When you open a bitmapped or other image in a bound object frame, the default mode is Clip. Clip displays a cropped version of the full-size image.

TIP

> If the employee photo doesn't appear in the bound object frame, close the form, save your changes, and reopen it in Form view.

7. Change the Size Mode property value to Zoom, which sizes the image to fit within the frame but doesn't change its aspect ratio—the ratio of width to height (see Figure 15.46). Stretch mode expands both the width and height of the image to fit the frame, which can result in distortion of the image.

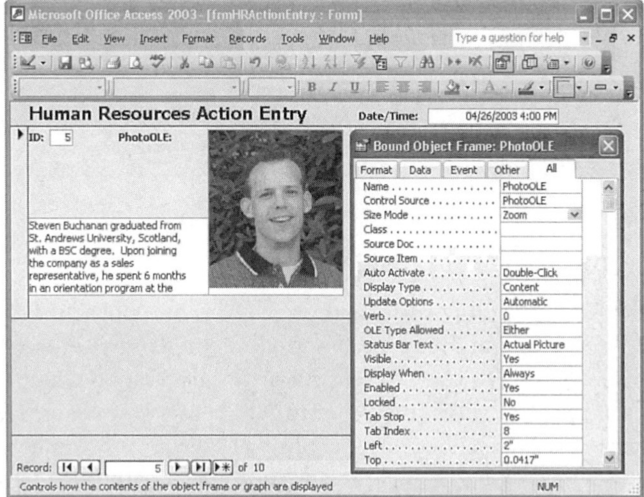

Figure 15.46
Change the Size Mode property value from Clip to Zoom to fit the image within the frame without changing the image's aspect ratio.

8. Double-click the image to edit the bitmap *in situ* with Windows Paint. Paint's menu is grafted to Access's menu, the Paint toolbox opens to the left of the form, an OLE activation border surrounds the Clip mode version of the image, and Paint's palette appears at the bottom of the form (see Figure 15.47).
9. Click outside the image to deactivate the object, then right-click the frame, and choose Bitmap Image Object, Open to open the object in a linked instance of Paint. It's usually easier to edit images in the server's window than in the smaller in-situ frame.
10. To prevent users from activating the image with a double-click, click the Other tab (in the Properties window), and set the Auto Activate property value to Manual.

11. After you've experimented with the bound object frame, return to Form Design view and delete the frame.

The process for adding a static image to an unbound object frame control is similar to that for a bound object frame. You add the unbound frame to the form, right click the frame, and choose Insert Object to add the static image to the control. Charts you create with the Office Chart Wizard in Chapter 18 display in an unbound object frame, but you also can store copies of static charts in an OLE Object field.

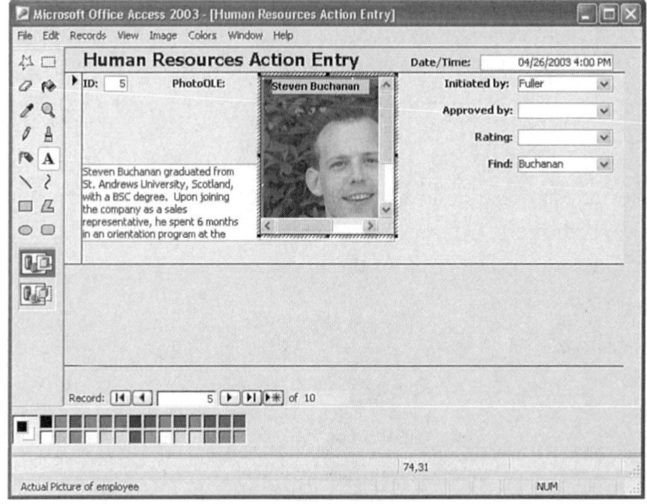

Figure 15.47 Activating the image with a double-click enables in-situ editing of the object with the designated OLE 2.0 server.

WORKING WITH TAB CONTROLS

The tab control lets you easily create multipage forms in a tabbed dialog, similar to the tabbed pages you've seen in the Properties window, in the Options dialog, and elsewhere in Access. The tab control is a very efficient alternative to creating multipage forms with the Page Break control. You can use the tab control to conserve space onscreen and show information from one or more tables. The sections that follow show you how to add images to a new OLE object field of the Employees table, add a tab control to a form, and display images in a bound image control on a tab control page. You also learn to set the important properties of the tab control as a whole, as well as the properties of individual pages of the tab control.

ADDING THE TAB CONTROL TO A FORM

To add a tab control to the frmHRActionEntry form, follow these steps:

1. Click the Design View button on the toolbar if the frmHRActionEntry form isn't already in Design view. No wizard for the tab control exists, so the status of the Control Wizards button doesn't matter.

2. Click the Tab Control tool in the Toolbox; the mouse cursor changes to the Tab Control icon while it's over the active surface of the form.
3. Click and drag on the surface of the form's Detail section to create the new tab control near the bottom center of the form (see Figure 15.48).

15

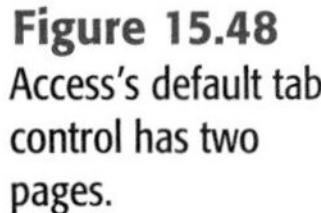

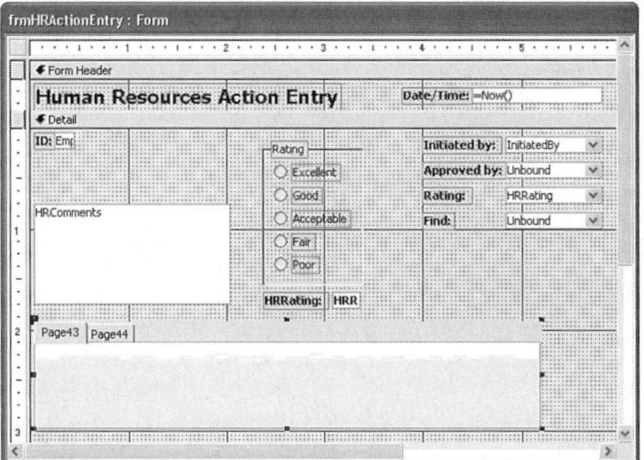

Figure 15.48 Access's default tab control has two pages.

By default, Access creates a tab control with two pages. Each page's tab displays the name of the page combined with a sequential number corresponding to the number of controls you placed on your form in this work session. The next few sections describe how to change the page tab's caption, add or delete pages in the tab control, add controls to the pages, and set the page and tab control properties.

ADDING TAB CONTROL PAGES

Depending on the data you want to display and how you want to organize that data, you might want to include more than two pages in your tab control. To add a page to a tab control, follow these steps:

1. In Design view, right-click the tab control to open the context menu.
2. Choose Insert Page; Access inserts a new page in the tab control to the right of the last page.

CHANGING THE PAGE ORDER

Because Access adds a new page only after the last page, it isn't possible to add a new page at the beginning or middle of the existing tab pages. As a result, if you want the new tab control page to appear in another location in the tab control, you must change the order of pages in the tab control. You might also want to change the order of tab control pages as you work with and test your forms—in general, you should place the most frequently used (or most important) page at the front of the tab control.

To change the order of pages in a tab control, follow these steps:

1. Right-click one of the tabs and choose Page Order to open the Page Order dialog shown in Figure 15.49.

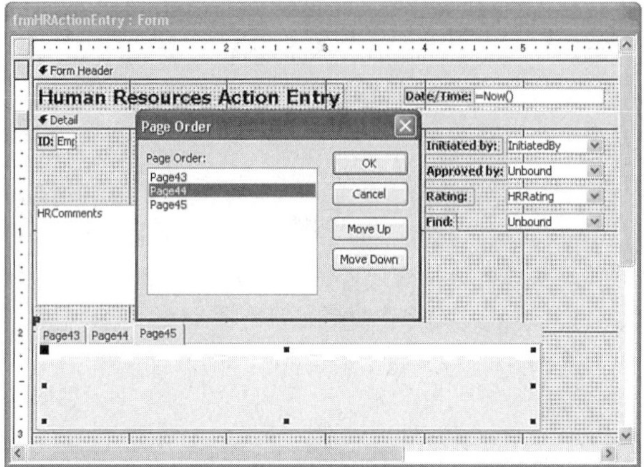

Figure 15.49
Change the left-to-right sequence of the tabs with the Page Order dialog.

2. In the Page Order list, select the page whose position you want to change.
3. Click the Move Up or Move Down buttons, as appropriate, until the page is in the position you want.
4. Repeat steps 3 and 4 until you have arranged the tab control pages in the order you want, and then click OK to close the Page Order dialog and apply the new page order to the tab control.

Deleting a Tab Control Page

At some point, you might decide that you don't want or need a page in a tab control. The frmHRActionEntry form needs only two pages in its tab control. If you added a page to the tab control by following the steps at the beginning of this section, you can delete a page from the tab control by following this procedure:

1. Right-click the page tab of the page you want to delete; Access brings that page to the front of the tab control.
2. Choose Delete Page; Access deletes the currently selected tab control page.

Setting the Tab Control's Properties

Two sets of properties govern the appearance and behavior of a tab control. A set of properties exists for the entire tab control, and a separate set of properties exists for each page in the tab control. The following list summarizes the important properties of the tab control and its pages; the remaining property settings for the tab control and its pages are similar to those you've seen for other controls (height, width, color, and so on):

- *Caption* is a text property, which controls the text that appears on the page's tab and applies to individual tab control pages only. If this property is empty (the default), then the page's Name property is displayed on the page's tab.

- *MultiRow* is a Yes/No property, which applies to the tab control as a whole and determines whether the tab control can display more than one row of tabs. (The Options dialog, reached by choosing Tools, Options, is an example of a multirow tabbed dialog.) The default setting is No; in this case, if there are more tabs than fit in the width of the tab control, Access displays a scroll button in the tab control. If you change this property to Yes and there are more page tabs than will fit in the width of the tab control, Access displays multiple rows of tabs.
- *Picture* displays an icon in any or all the page tabs. You can use any of Access's built-in icons or insert any bitmapped (.bmp) graphics file as the page's tab icon.
- *Style* applies to the tab control as a whole and controls the style in which the tab control's page tabs are displayed. The default setting, Tabs, produces the standard page tabs you're accustomed to seeing in the Properties window and in various dialogs in Access and Windows. Two other settings are available: Buttons and None. The Buttons setting causes the page tabs to be displayed as command buttons in a row across the top of the tab control. The None setting causes the tab control to omit the page tabs altogether. Use the None setting if you want to control which page of the tab control has the focus with command buttons or option buttons located outside the tab control. However, using command buttons external to the tab control to change pages requires writing Access VBA program code. You should use the default Tabs setting unless you have a specific reason for doing otherwise—using the Tabs setting ensures that the appearance of your tab controls is consistent with other portions of the Access user interface. Using this setting also saves you the effort of writing VBA program code.
- *Tab Fixed Height* and *Tab Fixed Width* apply to the tab control as a whole and govern the height and width of the page tabs in the control, respectively. The default setting for these properties is 0. When these properties are set to 0, the tab control sizes the page tabs to accommodate the size of the Caption for the page. If you want all the page tabs to have the same height or width, enter a value (in inches or centimeters, depending on your specific version of Access) in the corresponding property text box.

To display the Properties window for the entire tab control, right-click the edge of the tab control, and choose Properties from the resulting context menu. Alternatively, click the edge of the tab control to select it (clicking the blank area to the right of the page tabs is easiest), and then click the Properties button on the toolbar to display the Properties window.

To display the Properties window for an individual page in the tab control, click the page's tab to select it, and then click the Properties button on the toolbar to display the page's Properties window.

The tab control in the frmHRActionEntry form uses one page to display current information about an employee: the employee's job title, supervisor, company telephone extension, hire date, and photo. The second tab control page displays a history of that employee's HRActions in a subform you add later in the chapter.

Follow these steps to set the Caption property for the frmHRActionEntry form's tab control:

15

1. Open the frmHRActionEntry form, and change to Form Design view, if necessary.
2. Click the first page of the tab control to select it, and then click the Properties button on the toolbar to display that page's Properties window.
3. Click the Format tab, if necessary, to display the Format properties for the tab control page.
4. Type **Employee Info** in the Caption property's text box.
5. Click the Other tab and change the Name property value to **pagEmployeeInfo**.
6. Click the second page of the tab control to select it; the contents of the Property dialog change to show the properties of the second tab control page. Click the Format tab.
7. Type **History** in the Caption property text box for the second page of the tab control, type **pagHistory** in the Name property of the Other page, and close the Properties window.
8. Click outside the tabbed region to select the entire tab control, and type **tabHRAction** as the name of the control.

Figure 15.50 shows the tab control with both page captions set and the first page of the tab control selected. Notice that the sizing handles visible in the tab control are inside the control—this position indicates that the page, not the entire control, is currently selected. When the entire tab control is selected, the sizing handles appear on the edges of the tab control.

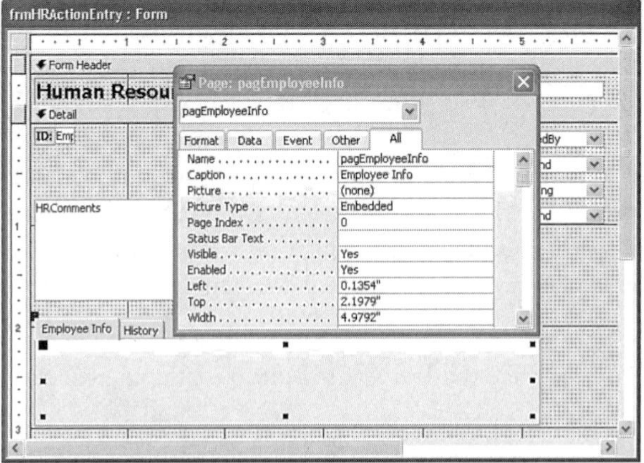

Figure 15.50
Set the Page properties by clicking the tab of one of the pages. Click the empty area to the right of the tabs to set the properties of the entire tab control.

PLACING OTHER CONTROLS ON TAB PAGES

You can place any of Access's 16 other types of controls on the pages of a tab control—labels, text boxes, list boxes, even subforms. To add a control of any type to a tab control's page, follow this procedure:

15

1. In Design view, click the page tab you want to add the control to; Access selects the page and brings it to the front of the tab control.
2. Add the desired control to the tab control's page using the techniques presented earlier in this chapter for creating controls on the main form.

Alternatively, you can copy controls from the same or another form and paste them into the tab control's pages by using the same techniques you learned for copying and pasting controls on a form's Detail and Header/Footer sections. You can't drag controls from the form's Detail or Header/Footer sections onto the tab control's page or vice-versa.

As you proceed with the examples in this chapter and complete the frmHRActionEntry form, you place various bound and unbound controls on the pages of the tab control.

OPTIMIZING THE FORM'S DESIGN

The preceding sections of this chapter have shown you how to use Toolbox controls without regard to positioning the controls to optimize data entry operations. In this section, you add more controls from the qryHRActions query's field list to the main form's Detail section and the Company Info page of the tab control. You place new controls for adding or editing fields of the HRActions table on the main form, and relocate the controls you added earlier into a logical data-entry sequence. The Employee Info page of the tab control displays reference data from the Employees table. Multi-page tab controls are especially effective for displaying data that's related to the entries you make on the main form.

To add and rearrange the forms controls to optimize data entry, follow these steps (look ahead to Figure 15.51 for control placement and formatting):

1. Return to Design view, if necessary, and delete the Rating option group and the HRRating text box. When you delete an option group, you automatically delete the option buttons within the frame.

2. Click the Field List button on the toolbar to open the Field List dialog if it isn't already open.
3. Drag the LastName field from the Field List to a position to the right of the ID field text box. Edit the field's label to read **Name:**.
4. Drag the FirstName field from the Field List to a position to the right of the LastName field; delete the FirstName field's label.
5. Drag the ActionType field from the Field List to a position at the right of the FirstName field to add a combo box.

6. Repeat step 5 for the ScheduledDate, EffectiveDate, NewSalary, and NewBonus fields (see Figure 15.51 for field positioning and sizing). You must move the InitiatedBy, ApprovedBy, HRRating, and Name text boxes that you placed on the form earlier in this chapter.
7. Resize the HRComments field so that it's underneath the EmployeeID and name fields (see Figure 15.51). Next, resize the tab control so that it fills the width of the form and extends from an area below the HRComments field to the bottom of the form. The tab control needs to be as large as possible to display as much data as possible in the sub-form that you add later to its second page.
8. Click the first tab of the tab control to bring it to the front, and then drag the Title field from the Field List to a position near the top-left corner of the Company Info page.
9. Repeat step 8 for the ReportsTo, Extension, and HireDate fields (see Figure 15.51 for field placement).
10. Drag the PhotoOLE field onto the right side of the tab control's first page, and delete its label (the fact that this field displays a photo of the employee is enough to identify the field). Size and position the Photo field at the right edge of the tab control's page; you might need to resize the tab control and the form after inserting the Photo field.
11. Right-click the PhotoOLE field, and choose Properties to display its Properties window, click the Format tab, and select the Size Mode property's text box. Select Zoom from the drop-down list to have the employee photo scaled down to fit the photo field's size.

TIP

Use the Format Painter to format the text labels of the fields.

→ For more information on creating a uniform appearance with the Format Painter, **see** "Using the Format Painter," **p. 551**.

12. Drag the Notes field onto the bottom left side of the tab control's first page and delete its label.
13. Use the techniques you learned in Chapter 14 to move, rearrange, and change the label formats to match the appearance of Figure 15.51. (All labels are bold, sized-to-fit, and right-aligned.)
14. Change the Format property value of the ScheduledDate and EffectiveDate text boxes to **mm/dd/yyyy** to assure Y2K compliance, and change the Format property value of the Salary and Bonus text boxes to **$#,##0** to add a dollar sign.
15. To replace number with text in the Type, ApprovedBy, and Rating combo boxes, change the Column Widths property value from 0.2";0.8" to **0";0.8"**.

16. Click the Select Form button or press Ctrl+R, and set the Caption property value of the form to **Human Resources Action Entry**.

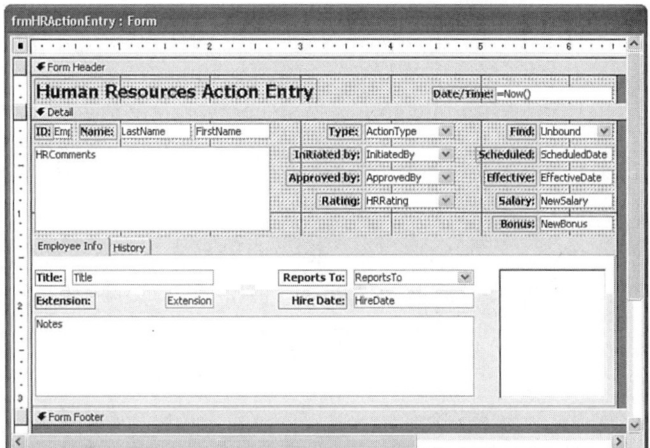

Figure 15.51
Here's the final design of the form with new controls and formatting.

17. Press Ctrl+S to save your changes, and test your new and modified controls by changing to Form view (see Figure 15.52).

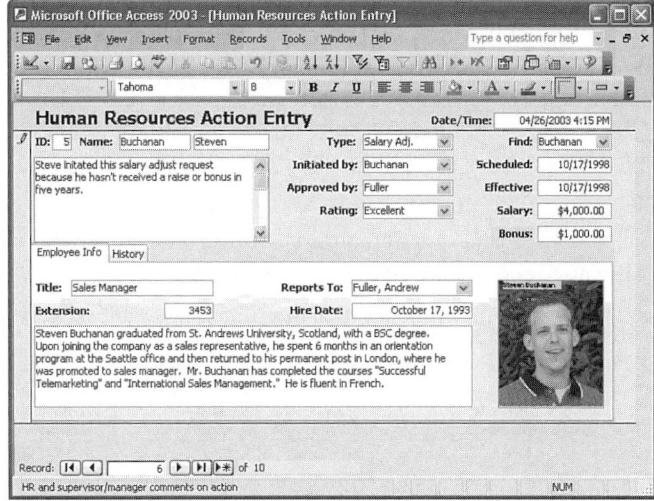

Figure 15.52
The form is now complete, except for the addition of a subform to the History page of the tab control.

ADDING A HISTORY SUBFORM TO A TAB CONTROL PAGE

The frmHRActionEntry form needs a subform to display the history of HRActions for the employee displayed in the main part of the form. The HRActions table provides the data source for the subform. Access's Subform/Subreport control offers a Subform Wizard, which lets you quickly add a new subform. The Subform Wizard of prior Access versions added a datasheet-style subform; the Access 2002 Subform Wizard added a columnar subform, despite the image of a tabular subform in the Wizard's first dialog. This change rendered the Access 2002 Subform Wizard useless for all but very specialized applications. Access 2003's Subform Wizard lets you add an existing form as a subform, as described in the following sections.

CREATING A MODIFIED HRACTIONS SUBFORM

If you didn't create the sbfHRActions subform in the preceding chapter, import the sbfHRActions subform from your \Program Files\Seua11\Chaptr14\Forms14.mdb database.

Follow this drill to adapt the sbfHRActions subform for use on the History page of the tab control:

1. Select sbfHRActions in the Forms page of the Database window, and press Ctrl+C and Ctrl+V to create a copy of the subform named **sbfHRActionsTab** and open it in Design view.
2. Delete the HRComments header and text box.
3. Right-click the ActionType combo box, and choose Change To, Text Box.
4. Shift-click to select the ActionType, InitiatedBy, ApprovedBy, and HRRating text boxes, and click the toolbar's Center button to center the text and labels.
5. To minimize the height of the subform's header select all labels and drag them to the top of the Form header section. Click the Bold button of the Formatting toolbar to apply the bold attribute to all labels. Drag the Detail section bar up to the bottom of the labels.
6. Select all text boxes and drag them to the bottom of the Detail bar. Drag the Form Footer bar up to the bottom of the text boxes.
7. Reduce the width of the subform to about 5.75 inches, and save your changes (see Figure 15.53).

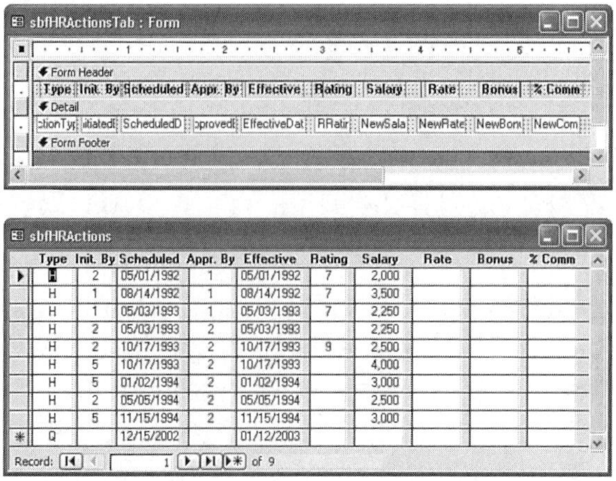

Figure 15.53
Form Design and Form views show the changes you make to the layout for the sbfHRActionsTab subform.

15

ADDING THE SBFHRACTIONSTAB SUBFORM WITH THE WIZARD

To add the sbfActionsTab subform to the History page of the tab control with the Subform Wizard, do the following:

1. With the Wizards activated, open frmHRActionEntry in Design view, click the History tab of the tab control, and select the Subform/Subreport tool in the toolbox.
2. Drag the mouse pointer icon, which assumes the shape of the Subform/Subreport tool, to the History page. The icon changes to a pointer when you reach the active region of the History page, which changes from white to black.
3. Release the mouse to open the Subform Wizard's first dialog.
4. Select the Use an Existing Form option and select sbfHRActionEntryTab in the list (see Figure 15.54). Click Next.

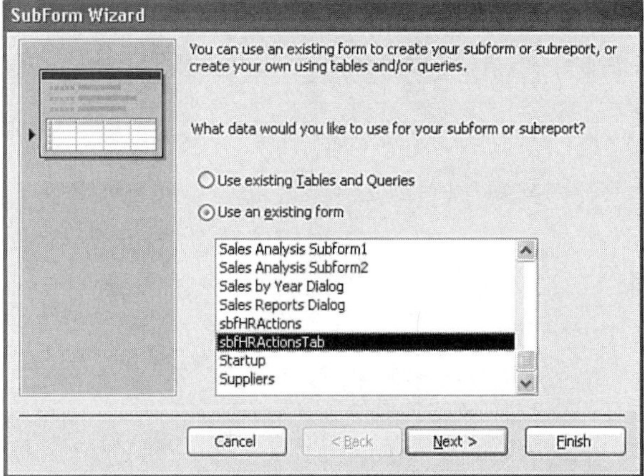

Figure 15.54 The Subform Wizard's first dialog lets you select the existing form to use as a subform.

5. In the second Wizard dialog, accept the Choose from a List option and the Show HRActions for Each Record in qryHRActions Using Employee[ID] (see Figure 15.55). Click Next.
6. Accept sbfHRActionEntryTab as the name of the subform, and click Finish to dismiss the Wizard.
7. Delete the label and adjust the size of the subform to occupy most of the available area of the History page (see Figure 15.56).
8. Change to Form view, select Buchanan in the Find list, and click the History tab to display the hired entry for Steven Buchanan and a tentative append record (see Figure 15.57).

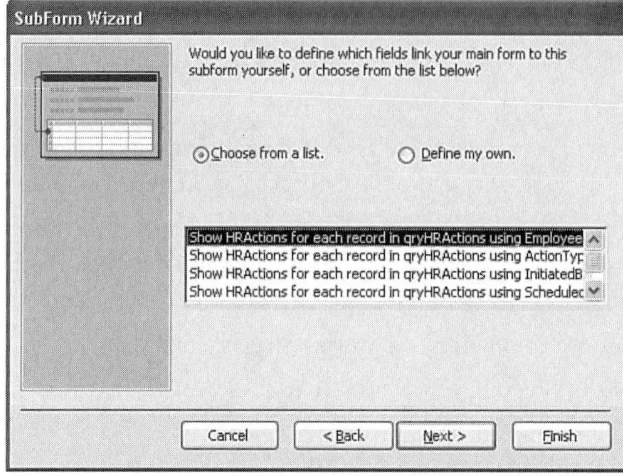

Figure 15.55 The second dialog is where you specify values of the LinkChildFields and LinkMasterFields property value, EmployeeID for this example.

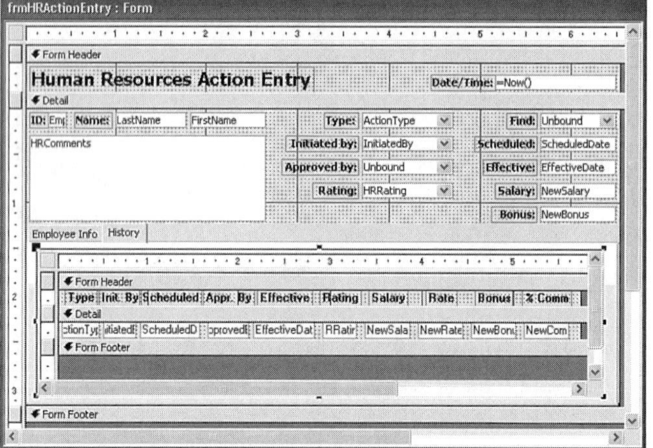

Figure 15.56 After the Wizard adds the subform, adjust its dimensions to suit the active area of the tab control's page.

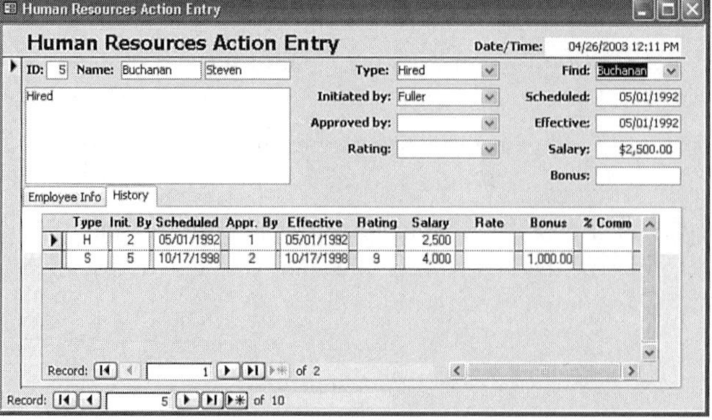

Figure 15.57 Form view with the History page selected displays HRActions record(s) for the employee selected in the Find combo box.

NOTE

The frmHRActionEntry and sbfHRActionEntryTab forms, the qryHRActions query, the HRActions table, and the Employees table with the added PhotoOLE field are included in the \Seua11\Chaptr15\Forms15.mdb database on the accompanying CD-ROM.

15

MODIFYING THE DESIGN OF CONTINUOUS FORMS

The default design of the History page's subform as created by the Subform Wizard lets you edit records of the HRActions table. The term History implies read-only access to the table in the tab control. Therefore, you should alter the properties of the subform to make the form read-only and remove unnecessary controls. For example, the vertical scroll bar lets you display any HRActions record for the employee, so you don't need record navigation buttons, nor do you need record selectors.

Access 2003's in-situ subform editing feature lets you change many of the properties of subforms with the main form open in Design view. Unfortunately, you can't change property values, such as Record Selectors and Navigation Buttons, that affect the structure of the subform. Therefore, you must change the design of the subform independently of its main form container. Access 2003 has a command—Subform in New Window—that provides a shortcut for changing subform properties.

To further optimize the design of the sbfHRActionEntryTab subform, follow these steps:

1. Return to Design view, click the History tab, select and right-click the subform, and choose Subform in New Window to open sbfHRActionEntryTab in Design view, and then click the Properties button to display the properties of the subform.
2. In the Format page of the Properties window, set Scroll Bars to Vertical Only, Record Selectors to No, and Navigation Buttons to No.
3. In the Data page, set the Recordset Type to Snapshot. Doing so has the same effect as setting Allow Edits, Allow Deletions, and Allow Additions to No. Your subform is now read-only because all snapshot-type Recordsets are read-only.
4. Select all text boxes and set the Tab Stop property to No for the group. Close the subform and save your changes.
5. In the now-empty History page, reduce the width of the subform and the tab control by about 1/8-inch to reflect removal of the Record Selector buttons. You can reduce the width of the subform container only when the subform isn't open for in-situ editing.
6. In the main form, select the tab control, and set it's Tab Stop property to No. Do the same for the LastName and FirstName text boxes.
7. Set the tab order by choosing View, Tab Order to open the Tab Order dialog. Click Auto Order to set the tab order of the controls for which the Tab Order property is Yes. The default control tab order is top-right to bottom-left. Click OK to close this dialog.

8. Return to Form view and click the History tab to verify your changes to the subform (see Figure 15.58).

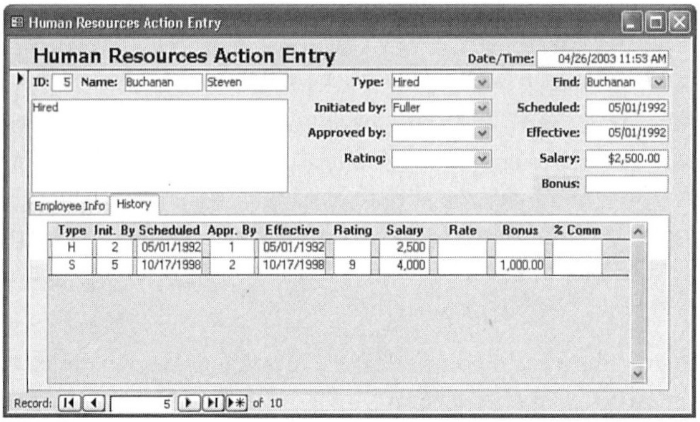

Figure 15.58
Form view reflects subform linking on the EmployeeID field and the changes you made to the design and dimensions of the subform.

TIP

> Removing text boxes and other controls from the tab order that you seldom or can't edit speeds data entry. To further optimize data entry, set the Tab Stop property of all controls on both pages of the tab control to No. Labels don't have a tab stop control; if you multi-select all controls on a page, use Shift+Click to deselect the labels to set Tab Stop to No for all other controls.

ADDING NEW RECORDS IN THE HRACTIONENTRY FORM

Unlike Chapter 14's frmHRActions form, the Record Source for the main frmHrActionEntry form is a query. The query design takes advantage of Access' row fix-up feature when you add a new record to the HRActions table in the form. Row fix-up works in this case, because the source of the qryHRActions query's EmployeeID column is the HRActions table.

→ For a review of row fix-up in one-to-many queries, **see** "Taking Advantage of Access's Row Fix-Up Feature," **p. 431**.

To add a new record to the HRActions table, do the following:

1. Open frmHRActionEntry in Form view, and click the tentative append (new) record button to add a new record. All data disappears from the form.
2. Type a number (other than 1, the default) in the [Employee]ID text box; for this example type **5**. Press Tab or Enter to add data in the query columns from the Employees table and default values from the HRActions table to the form's controls (see Figure 15.59).

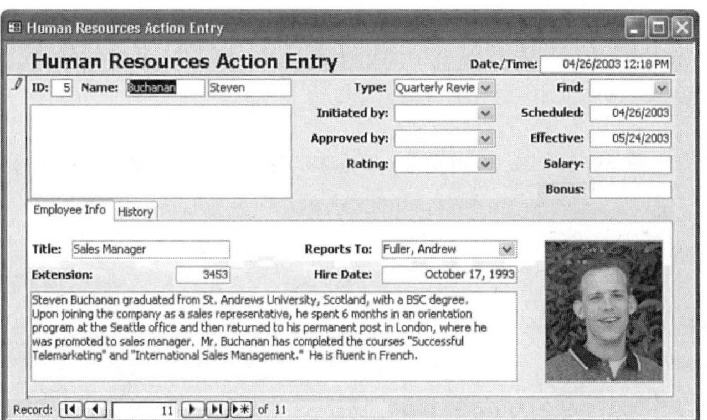

Figure 15.59
Adding a new record and typing an employee ID in the ID text box fills the form with employee data and default values from the qryHRActions query.

3. Make selections in the combo boxes, change the default dates, if necessary, and add a note regarding the action. Choose Records, Save Record or, if your cursor isn't in the Notes multi-line text box, press Shift+Enter to save the record (see Figure 15.60). Shift+Enter in a multi-line text box adds a newline character and doesn't save the record.

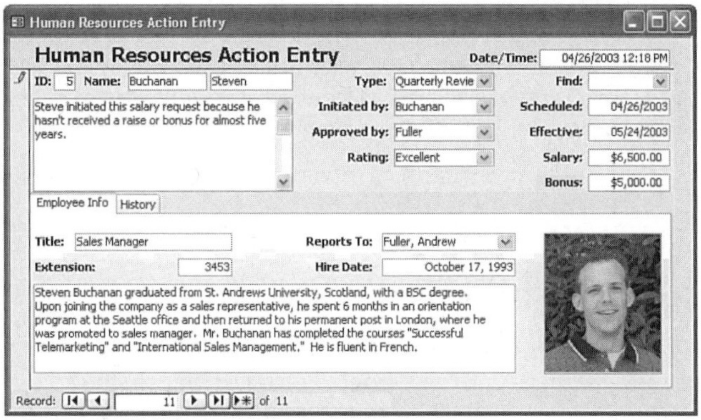

Figure 15.60
Completing the record addition requires only a few combo box selections, changes to dates, and an optional note.

4. Verify that you added the record correctly by selecting the employee for whom you added the action—in this case Steve Buchanan—in the Find combo box. Click the History tab to display the employees entries (see Figure 15.61). The History subform's snapshot Recordset must be refreshed to display the added record.

At this point in its development, frmHRActionEntry would be dangerous to release for use by data entry operators. For example, all fields in the main form are updatable. Thus, an operator could change the FirstName, LastName, and other values of the Employees table, as well as the EmployeeID for an existing HRActions record. You can set the Locked property to Yes for all controls linked to the Employees table, but you can't lock the

EmployeeID text box that's required to specify the EmployeeID of a new record. You can control the locked status of form controls by adding VBA event-handling code for the form's Before Insert and After Insert events.

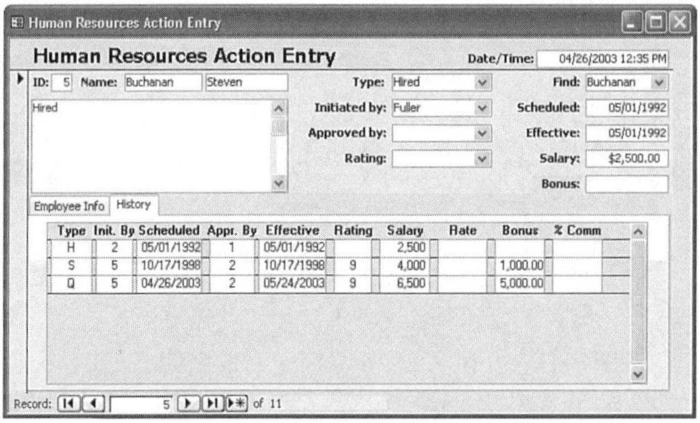

Figure 15.61
After you refresh the History subform by selecting the employee in the Find combo box, the newly added record appears.

TIP

You can make frmHRActionEntry safe for data entry operators by setting the Data Entry property of the form to Yes. Specifying Data Entry prevents operators from viewing existing records and only allows them to enter new records. In this case, you must change the Recordset Type property value of the subform to Dynaset, and set the AllowEdits, AllowDeletions, and AllowAdditions property values to Yes. Otherwise, the added record won't appear in the History subform.

OVERRIDING THE FIELD PROPERTIES OF TABLES

Access uses the table's property values assigned to the fields as defaults. The form or subform inherits these properties from the table or query on which the form is based. You can override the inherited properties, except for the Validation Rule property, by assigning a different set of values in the Properties window for the control. Properties of controls bound to fields of tables or queries that are inherited from the table's field properties are shown in the following list:

- Format
- Decimal Places
- Status Bar Text
- Validation Rule
- Validation Text
- Default Value
- Typeface characteristics (such as Font Name, Font Size, Font Bold, Font Italic, and Font Underline)

Values of field properties that you override with properties in a form apply only when the data is displayed and edited with the form. You can establish validation rules for controls bound to fields that differ from properties of the field established by the table, but you can only narrow the rule. The table-level validation rule for the content of the HRType field, for example, limits entries to the letters H, Q, Y, S, R, B, C, and T. The validation rule you establish in a form can't broaden the allowable entries; if you add F as a valid choice by editing the validation rule for the HRType field to `InStr("HQYSRBCTF",[HRType])>0`, you receive an error when you type F.

However, you can narrow the range of allowable entries by substituting `InStr("SQYB",[HRType])>0`. Notice that you can use expressions that refer to the field name in validation-rule expressions in forms; such expressions aren't permitted in field-level validation-rule expressions in Access 2003.

ADDING PAGE HEADERS AND FOOTERS FOR PRINTING FORMS

Access lets you add a separate pair of sections, Page Header and Page Footer, that appear only when the form prints. You add both of these sections to the form at once by choosing View, Page Header/Footer. The following list shows the purposes of Page Headers and Footers:

- Page Header sections enable you to use a different title for the printed version. The depth of the Page Header can be adjusted to control the location where the Detail section of the form is printed on the page.
- Page Footer sections enable you to add dates and page numbers to the printed form.

Page Header and Page Footer sections appear only in the printed form, not when you display the form onscreen in Form view. Figure 15.62 shows the frmHRActionEntry form in Design view with Page Header and Page Footer sections added.

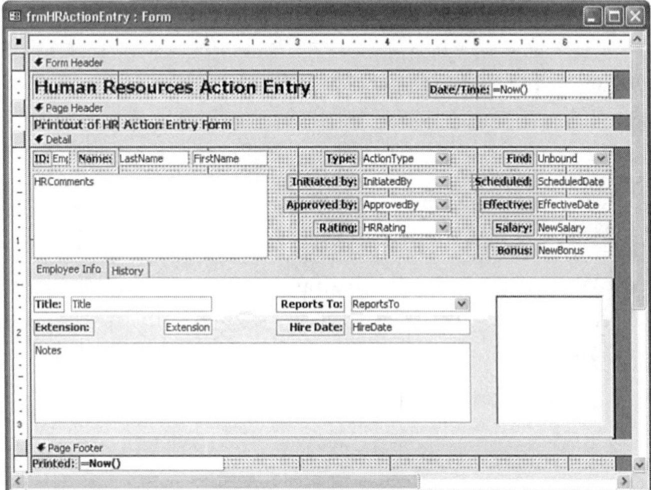

Figure 15.62 Page Headers and Page Footers appear when you print the form, but not in Form view.

With the Display When (Format) property of the Properties window for the Form Header and Form Footer sections, you can control whether these sections appear in the printed form. In Figure 15.62, the Form Header duplicates the information in the Page Header (except for the Date/Time label and text box), so you might not want to print both. To control when a section of the form prints or is displayed, perform the following steps:

1. Double-click the title bar of whichever section of the form you want to change; this opens the related Properties window. (The Page Header and Page Footer sections don't have a Display When property; these sections appear only when printing.)
2. Click the Format tab if the formatting properties aren't already showing. Click to drop down the Display When list.
3. To display but not print this section in Form view, select Screen Only.
4. To print but not display this section, select Print Only.

TROUBLESHOOTING

ERROR MESSAGES ON COPIED CONTROLS

A control copied to another form throws error messages whenever that control gets the focus.

When you copy a control to a form that uses a data source different from the one used to create the original control, you need to change the Control Source property to correspond with the field the new control is to be bound to. Changing the Control Source property doesn't change the Status Bar Text, Validation Rule, or Validation Text properties for the new control source. You must enter the appropriate values manually.

IN THE REAL WORLD—ACCESS WIZARDRY

Access 1.0 had only a few wizards; Access 2003 has 46, the same number as Access 2002. Microsoft defines a wizard as "A Microsoft Access tool that asks you questions and creates an object according to your questions." The "Wizards, add-ins, and Builders in Microsoft Access 2003" online help topic lists 51 wizards, but four items in the list—Documentor, Macro-To-Module Converter, Subform/Subreport Field Linker, and Switchboard Manager—don't carry the Wizard suffix and are better classified as utilities.

Form-related wizards are the most numerous. The following nine wizards, listed in alphabetical order, assist you in creating custom forms:

- *AutoForm* Wizard automatically generates a form. Access 2002 added PivotTable and PivotChart types.
- *AutoFormat Wizard* applies a specific format to a form.
- *Chart Wizard* adds to a form a graph or chart bound to a table or query.

- *Combo Box Wizard* generates one of three classes of bound and unbound combo box controls on a form.
- *Command Button Wizard* adds a command button control.
-  *Form Wizard* generates a new form. Access 2002 added the capability to generate a PivotTable or PivotChart form.
- *Option Group Wizard* adds a group of option buttons.
- *Subform/Subreport Field Linker* creates or alters links between a main form and subform.
- *Subform/Subreport Wizard* adds a new subform.

One of the reasons that Access 2003 has the largest wizard population of all Office 2003 applications is that Access is the most complex of the Office 2003 members—from both the user and developer standpoint. Access's complexity, compared with Word, Excel, PowerPoint, and Outlook, undoubtedly is the reason that Microsoft doesn't include Access 2003 in the Standard or Small Business editions of Office 2003. The omission of Access from the Small Business edition is surprising, because establishing and maintaining databases is crucial for almost every enterprise, regardless of size.

Wizards are classified as Access add-ins, which also include Builders, menu add-ins, and a new class of Component Object Model (COM) add-ins. The standard set of wizards and builders that come with Access appear in the `HKEY_LOCAL_MACHINE\Software\Microsoft\Office\11.0\Access\Wizards` key of the Registry. Figure 15.63 shows the top-level Registry keys for the Control and Form Wizards used in this and the preceding chapter. Microsoft classifies Access Builders as Property Wizards in the Registry.

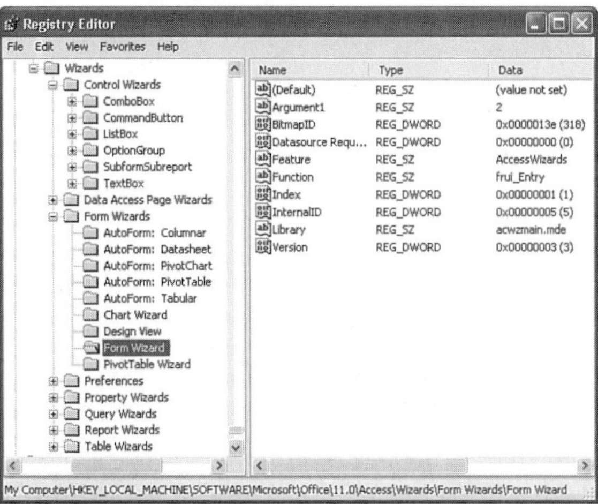

Figure 15.63
The Registry includes keys for each Access wizard and Builder.

Most of the wizards are contained in the Acwzmain.mde file in your ...\Office11 folder; the Acwztool.mde Advanced Wizards file includes the Add-In Manager and some Builders; and Acwzlib.mde holds the Import/Export Wizards. You can open the Acwz... .mde files in Access 2003, but you can't make changes to objects. It's unfortunate that Microsoft uses the .mde format to prevent viewing the wizard VBA code; Access wizards are excellent examples of VBA power programming in action.

CHAPTER 16

Working with Simple Reports and Mailing Labels

In this chapter

16

Understanding the Relationship Between Forms and Reports

The final product of most database applications is a report. Access combines data from tables, queries, and—in some cases—forms to produce a report that you can print for people who need or request it. One of Access's major selling points is its capability to generate fully formatted reports easily and quickly. No other report generator application has even come close to rivaling Access's flexible report-generation capabilities.

With the expansion of email and the growth of intranets and the Internet, it's becoming more common for people to read and, when necessary, print their own reports. Access offers the following methods of distributing paperless reports:

- *Report Snapshots* are self-contained files that you can send as an email attachments with Outlook, Outlook Express, or any other Windows email program. Users must have a local copy of the freely distributable Snapshot Viewer application to open and print the reports, which are exact replicas of the conventional Access report. You can provide copies of the Snapshot Viewer to users or they can download the Viewer from the Microsoft Web site.

→ For more information on Report Snapshots, **see** "Mailing Report Snapshots," **p. 696**.

- *Static Web reports* apply an Extensible Stylesheet Language Transformations (XSLT) document to an Extensible Markup Language (XML) file to generate an HTML 4.0 simulation of the original report. You can export static—also called *snapshot*—Web reports to a Web server from conventional (Jet) applications or Access data projects (ADP). Recipients print the report from the browser.

- *Live Web reports* are similar to static XSL/XML Web reports, but deliver current data by executing an Active Server Pages (ASP) or HTML template query against SQL Server when opening the page in a browser. Live Web reports were one of the most important new features of Access 2002.

→ To learn more about static and live Web Reports, **see** "Exporting Static Reports as XML," **p. 965** and "Exporting Live Web Reports," **p. 967**.

Some reports consist of a single page, such as an order acknowledgment, invoice, graph, or chart. Multipage Access reports—typified by catalogs, general ledgers, and financial statements—are more common than the single-page variety. A multipage report is analogous to a continuous form that's been optimized for printing.

Most methods of creating Access forms, which you learned about in Chapter 14, "Creating and Using Access Forms," and Chapter 15, "Designing Custom Multitable Forms," also apply to reports. The following list details the principal differences between reports and forms:

- Reports are intended for printing only and, unlike forms, aren't designed for display in a window. When you view an 8 1/2×11-inch report in the default Print Preview, its content usually isn't legible. In the zoomed (full-page) view, only a part of the report might be visible in the Print Preview or Layout Preview window, depending on the resolution of your monitor.

- You can't change the value of the underlying data for a report with a control object from the toolbox as you can with forms. With reports, Access disregards user input from combo boxes, option buttons, check boxes, and the like. The primary controls you use on forms are labels and text boxes. You can use a check box to indicate the value of field of the Yes/No (Boolean) data type.
- Reports don't provide a Datasheet view. Only Print Preview, Layout Preview, and Report Design views are available. Layout Preview provides a quick view of the form without displaying all its data.
- In multicolumn reports, the number of columns, the column width, and the column spacing are controlled by settings in the Printer Setup dialog, not by controls that you add or properties that you set in Design view.

Access reports share many characteristics of forms, including the following:

- *Report Wizards* create the three basic kinds of reports: single-column, groups/totals, and mailing labels. You can modify as necessary the reports that the Report Wizard creates. The function of the Report Wizard is similar to that of the Form Wizard discussed in Chapter 14.
- *Sections* include report headers and footers, which appear once at the beginning and at the end of the report, and page headers and footers, which print at the top and bottom of each page. The report footer often is used to print grand totals. Report sections correspond to similarly named form sections.
- *Group* sections of reports, as a whole, comprise the equivalent of the Detail section of forms. Groups often are referred to as *bands*, and the process of grouping records is known as *banding*. You can add Group Headers that include a title for each group, and Group Footers to print group subtotals. You can place static (unbound) graphics in header and footer sections and bound graphics within group sections.
- *Controls* are added to reports from the Access toolbox and then moved and sized with their handles. Reports support embedded bitmaps, OLE objects, such a graphs and charts you create with MSGraph.exe, and ActiveX controls, such as the PivotChart and PivotTable.
- *Subreports* can be incorporated into reports the same way you add subform controls within main forms.

CATEGORIZING TYPES OF ACCESS REPORTS

Reports created by Access fall into six basic types, also called layouts, that are detailed in the following list:

- **Single-column reports**—List in one long column of text boxes the values of each field in each record of a table or query. A label indicates the name of a field, and a text box to the right of the label provides the values. Access's AutoReport feature can create a single-column report with a single click of the toolbar's AutoReport button. You seldom use single-column reports because the format wastes paper.
- **Tabular reports**—Provide a column for each field of the table or query and print the value of each field of the records in rows under the column header. If you have more columns than can fit on one page, additional pages print in sequence until all columns are printed; then the next group of records is printed. The AutoReport feature also can create a tabular report automatically.
- **Multicolumn reports**—Created from single-column reports by using the "newspaper" or "snaking" column approach of desktop-publishing and word-processing applications. Information that doesn't fit in the first column flows to the top of the second column, and so on. The format of multicolumn reports wastes less paper, but the uses are limited because the column alignment is unlikely to correspond with what you want.
- **Groups/totals reports**—The most common kind of report. Access groups/totals reports summarize data for groups of records and then add grand totals at the end of the report.
- **Mailing labels**—A special kind of multicolumn report that prints names and addresses (or other multifield data) in groups. The design of the stock adhesive label on which you are printing determines how many rows and columns are on a page.
- **Unbound reports**—Contain subreports based on unrelated data sources, such as tables or queries.

The first five types of reports use a table or query as the data source, as do forms. These kinds of reports are said to be bound to the data source. The main report of an unbound report isn't linked to a table or query as a data source. The subreports contained by an unbound report, however, must be bound to a data source.

CREATING A GROUPING REPORT WITH THE REPORT WIZARD

This section shows you how to use the Report Wizard to create a grouping report based on data in the Products and Suppliers tables of the Northwind Traders sample database. (Like the Form Wizard, the Report Wizard lets you create reports that contain data from more than one table without first creating a query.) This report displays the quantity of each specialty food product in inventory, grouped by product category.

NOTE

> The process of designing an Access data projects (ADP) report is, for the most part, identical to that for conventional Access reports based on Jet 4.0 data sources. The difference is that ADP use an SQL Server table, view, function, or stored procedure as the data source for the report. ADP doesn't support some Jet features, such as domain aggregate functions, but the workarounds for ADP limitations are relatively simple. Chapter 22, "Upsizing Jet Applications to Access Data Projects," describes the principal workarounds required when migrating from Jet applications to ADP.

Creating an inventory report begins with modifying the basic report created by the Report Wizard. The process of creating a basic report with the Report Wizard is similar to the process that you used to create a form with a subform in Chapter 14. An advantage of using the Report Wizard to introduce the topic of designing Access reports is that the steps for this process are parallel to the steps you take when you start with a default blank report. Chapter 17, "Preparing Advanced Reports," explains how to start with a blank report and create more complex reports.

To create an Inventory by Category report in Northwind.mdb, follow these steps:

1. Click the Reports shortcut in the Database window and then click the New button. Access displays the New Report dialog. The New Report dialog lets you choose one of three report wizards, two AutoReport styles, and Design view.
2. Like forms, reports require a data source, which can be a Jet table or query, or an ADP table, view, function, or stored procedure. For this example, select the Products table from the choices offered in the New Report dialog's drop-down list (see Figure 16.1). Select Report Wizard from the list in the dialog's right side and click OK to open the Report Wizard's first dialog.

Figure 16.1 Select a table or query as the data source for your report, and then choose the Report Wizard in the New Report dialog.

TIP

> You can bypass the New Report dialog and open the Wizard directly by double-clicking the Create Report by Using Wizard shortcut in the Database window. In this case, you select the report's data source in the first Wizard dialog.

3. The fields that you select to display represent columns of the report. You want the report to print the product name and supplier so that users don't have to refer to another report to associate codes with names. The fields from the Products table that you need for this report are CategoryID, ProductID, ProductName, SupplierID, and UnitsInStock. With the > button, select these fields in sequence from the Available Fields list. As you add fields to the Selected Fields list, Access removes the field names from the Available Fields list. Alternatively, you can double-click the field name in the Available Fields list to move the field name to the Selected Fields list. The fields appear from left to right in the report, based on the top-to-bottom sequence in which the fields appear in the Selected Fields list.

4. To demonstrate how the Wizard deals with reports that bind to more than one table, add the CompanyName field from the Suppliers table. Open the Tables/Queries drop-down list and select Table: Suppliers.

TIP

> You can retrace your steps to correct an error by clicking the Back button whenever it is enabled. The Finish button accepts all defaults and jumps to the end of the Wizard, so you shouldn't use this button until you're familiar with the Report Wizard's default selections.

5. Instead of presenting the supplier name as the report's last field, you want the report's CompanyName column to follow the SupplierID report column. Select the SupplierID field in the Selected Fields list. Now select the CompanyName field from the Available Fields list and click the > button. Access moves the CompanyName field from the Available Fields list and inserts the field into the Selected Fields list (see Figure 16.2). Click Next.

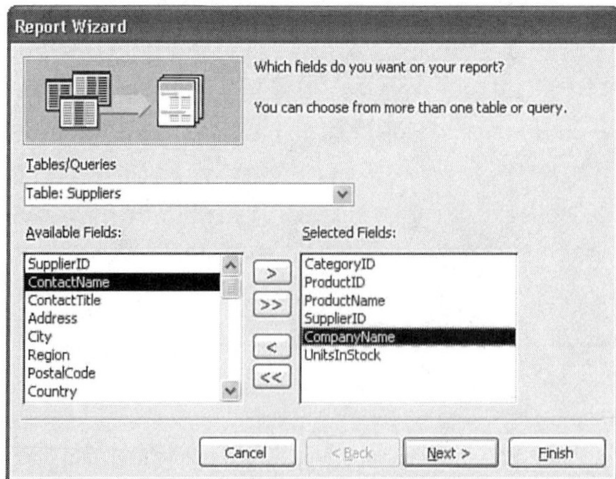

Figure 16.2
After selecting the fields from the primary table, select the SupplierID field, and add the CompanyName field of the Suppliers table in the first Wizard dialog.

NOTE

The purpose of adding the CompanyName field of the Suppliers table is to demonstrate how the Wizard handles the design of reports based on more than one table. If you don't add the CompanyName field, the Wizard dialog of step 6 doesn't appear. The SupplierID field of the Products table is a lookup field, so CompanyName appears in lieu of the numeric SupplierID value. You remove the duplicate field when you modify the report later in the chapter.

6. The Report Wizard asks how you want to view the data in the report. Notice the Show Me More Information button near the left center of the Wizard dialog. Click this button to display the first of a series of hint dialogs for the Report Wizard. If you click the Show Me Examples option, Access displays additional hint screens. These screens use examples from the Sales Reps, Customers, and Orders tables to show you the different groupings that the Report Wizard can automatically add to the report. Click the Close button repeatedly until you return to the Report Wizard dialog shown in Figure 16.3.

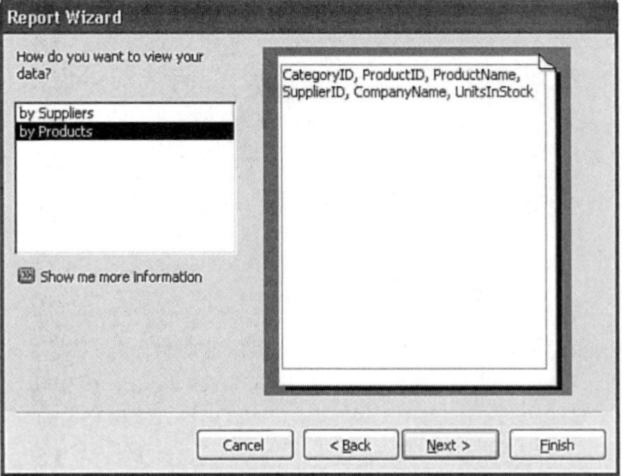

Figure 16.3 Select the Products table as the basis for your Report in the second Wizard dialog.

7. For this report, you select your own groupings. Accept the default By Products item in the list and click Next to continue.
8. The Report Wizard asks whether you want to add any grouping levels to the report. Select the CategoryID field in the list and click the > button to establish the grouping by the Products' category, as shown in Figure 16.4.
9. Click the Grouping Options button to open the Grouping Intervals dialog shown in Figure 16.5. By changing the grouping interval, you can affect how Access groups data in the report. For numeric fields, you can group items by 10s, 50s, 100s, and so on. For text fields, you can group items based on the first letter, the first three letters, and so on. The Wizard checks the field data type and suggests appropriate grouping intervals.

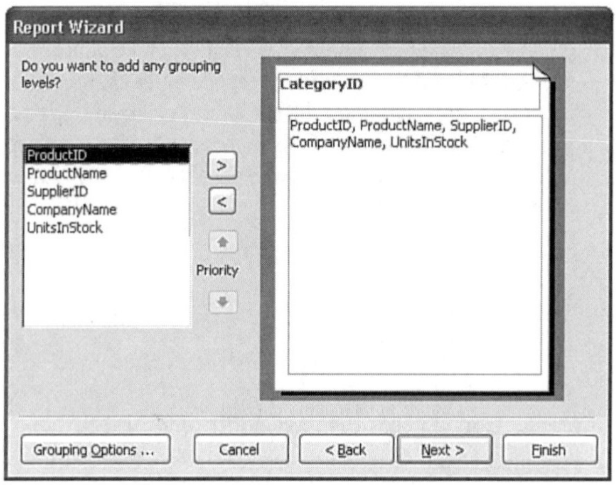

Figure 16.4 Specify the field on which you want to group your report in the third Wizard dialog.

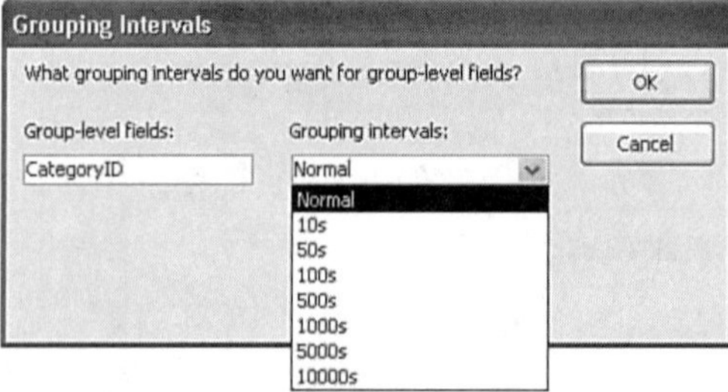

Figure 16.5 The Normal option groups numeric fields by individual values. You also have the option to group numeric fields by seven ranges of values.

TIP

If your application uses a text-coding scheme, such as BEVA for alcoholic beverages and BEVN for nonalcoholic beverages, you can combine all beverages in a single group by selecting 1st 3 Characters from the Grouping Intervals list. Access 2003 provides this option for numeric fields and for fields of the Text data type.

→ For additional methods of grouping data by characters in the field, **see** "Grouping and Sorting Report Data," **p. 678**.

10. This report doesn't require any special grouping interval, so accept Normal in the Grouping Intervals list, click OK to return to the Report Wizard, and click Next.
11. You can sort the records within groups by any field that you select (see Figure 16.6), with up to four different sorted fields. The dialog doesn't offer CategoryID as a choice because the records already are grouped on this field, and the field on which the grouping is based is sorted automatically by the table's primary key. Select ProductID in the first drop-down list.

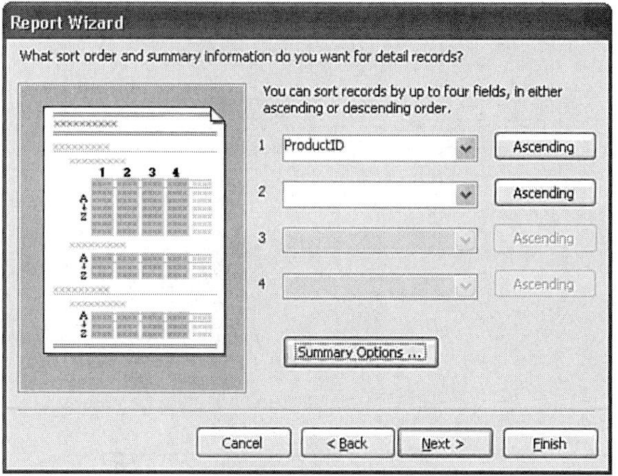

Figure 16.6
In the fourth Wizard dialog, select the field on which to sort records within the group you specified in the third dialog.

NOTE

By default, the sort order is ascending; if you want a descending sort order, click the button to the right of the drop-down list. (This button is a toggle control; click it again to return to an ascending sort.)

12. Click the Summary Options button to display the Summary Options dialog. If you want to add summary information to a report column, you set the options for that column in this dialog. The Report Wizard lists all the numeric fields on the report that aren't AutoNumber fields and offers you check boxes to select a Sum, Average, Minimum, and Maximum for that report column. Depending on the check boxes that you select, the Report Wizard adds those summary fields to the end of the report.
13. The Show option group lets you select whether the report shows the summary fields only or the full report with the summary fields added at the end of each group and at the end of the report. For this report, select the Sum and Avg check boxes for the UnitsInStock field, the Detail and Summary option, and the Calculate Percent of Total for Sums check box (see Figure 16.7). The Calculate Percent of Total for Sums check box displays the group's total as a percentage of the grand total for all groups. Click OK to return to the Report Wizard dialog, and click Next.
14. The Wizard asks you to select a layout for your report. The window on the left shows a preview of the layout style that you select; click each of the six option buttons to check the layouts. For this report, select Stepped in the Layout option group (see Figure 16.8).

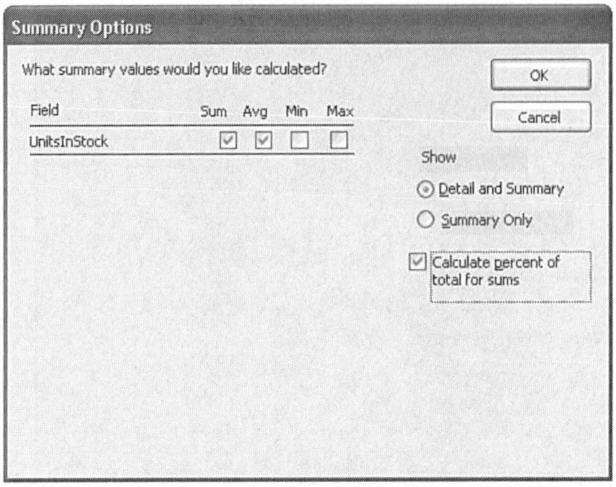

Figure 16.7
The Summary Options dialog lets you add to your report values based on calculations on numeric fields (other than AutoNumber fields).

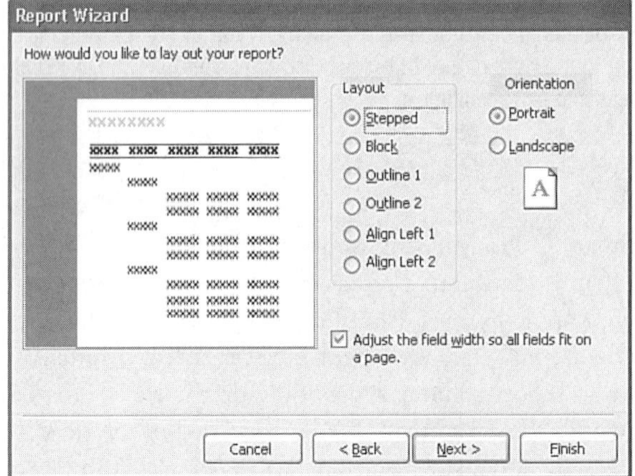

Figure 16.8
The Stepped report layout is the most common choice for reports with a few columns. You can increase the number of columns per page by choosing one of the Align Left layouts.

15. By default, the Report Wizard selects the Adjust the Field Width So All Fields Fit on a Page check box. As a rule, you should select this option to save paper and make your report more legible. In the Orientation option group, you select the report's printing orientation. Make sure that you select the default Portrait option. Click Next.

TIP

> When you restrict field widths to fit all fields on a page, fields with long lines of text often are truncated in the final report. You can adjust field widths in Report Design view to accommodate long text lines or change to multiline text boxes.

16. Select one of the predefined report styles for your report. The window on the left shows a preview of the selected style (see Figure 16.9). (You can customize or create your own styles for the Report Wizard to use. This activity is described in the "Using

AutoFormat and Customizing Report Styles" section later in this chapter.) Select the Compact style to reserve the maximum space for detail columns, and then click Next to display the final Report Wizard dialog.

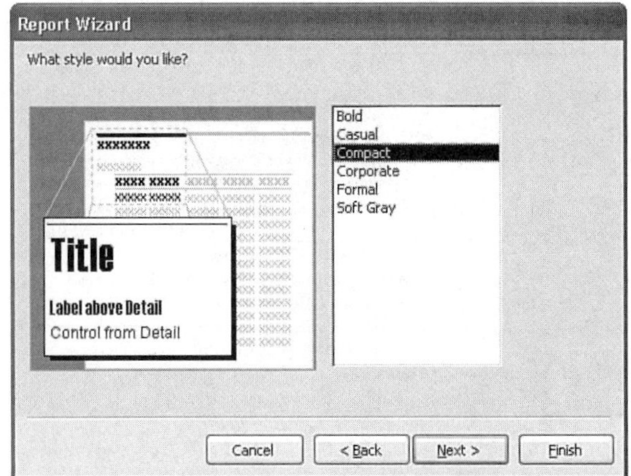

Figure 16.9
Choose one of the six predefined printing styles for the report.

17. Type **rptInventoryByCategory** as the title for the new report; the Report Wizard uses this title as the name of the saved report it creates (see Figure 16.10). Select the Preview the Report option, and click Finish to complete your report specification. The Report Wizard creates the report and displays it in Print Preview mode.

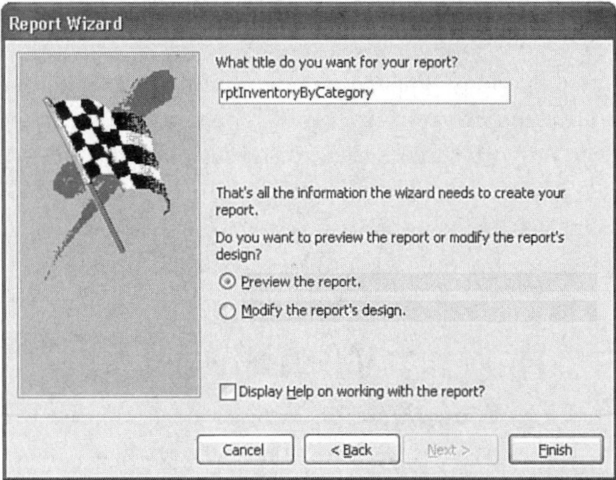

Figure 16.10
Type the name to save your report under in the last Wizard dialog. You change the report's caption to "Inventory by Category" later in the chapter.

Figure 16.11 shows the basic report that the Report Wizard creates, which has some major design deficiencies that you correct in the sections that follow. Use the vertical and horizontal scroll bars to position the preview as shown. When you're finished previewing the report, close it.

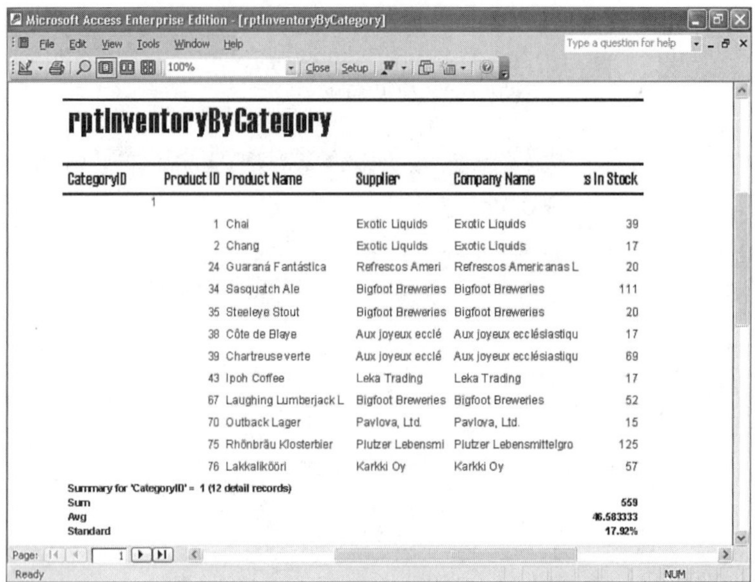

Figure 16.11
The report generated by the Wizard doesn't provide space to display the full heading for the Units in Stock caption in the page header.

TIP

Unlike Access's record navigation text boxes, Print Preview's Page text box shows only the current report page. To obtain a page count, the Access report engine must paginate the report; pagination can take a considerable period of time for very long reports. To display the total number of report pages in the Pages text box, click the Last Page button (arrow and bar) at the bottom of the Print Preview window.

With a few design modifications, you can obtain a finished report with the information necessary to analyze Northwind's current inventory. The modifications correct obvious defects in the Wizard-designed report, such as the excess width of the CategoryID column, cut-off names in the Product Name column, duplication of the Supplier and Company Name columns, and the truncated Units in Stock heading. You make these changes in the "Modifying a Basic Wizard Report" section later in this chapter.

USING ACCESS'S REPORT WINDOWS

The windows that you use to design and run Access reports are easier to use than the windows that you use for other basic Access functions. To open an existing Access report, such as the rptInventoryByCategory report you just created and closed, click the Reports shortcut in the Database window and then select a report name from the Database window. If you click the Design button or the New button to create a new report, the Design view toolbar appears with the buttons listed in Table 16.1.

TABLE 16.1 ACCESS-SPECIFIC TOOLBAR BUTTONS IN REPORT DESIGN MODE

Button	Menu Choice	Function
	View, Print Preview or File, Print Preview	Selects Print Preview to display how your report appears when printed. You can print the report from the Print Preview window.
	Not applicable	Prints the report without displaying the Print dialog. Access prints the report using the current printer settings.
	Insert, Hyperlink	Inserts a new Hyperlink control or allows you to edit an existing Hyperlink control.
	View, Field List	Displays a list of fields in the query or table that is the main report's data source.
	View, Toolbox	Displays or closes the toolbox.
	View, Sorting and Grouping	Displays the Sorting and Grouping dialog in which you can establish the structure of reports and the order in which the report presents the data.
	Format, AutoFormat	Applies your choice of several predefined report formats, including g for the text fonts and color settings.
	View, Code	Opens the VBA Editor window in which you can edit event-handling code.
	View, Properties	Displays the Properties window for the entire report, the sections of the report when you click the section divider bars, or the properties of a control when a control is selected.
	Not applicable	Displays a Build Wizard for the selected object or property in the report. This button is enabled only if Access has a Builder for the selected item.
	Window, 1 Database	Displays the Database window.
	Not applicable	Creates a new object. Click the arrow to the right of this button to see a drop-down list of objects that you can create.
	Help, Microsoft Help Access Help	Opens the Microsoft Window to the Answer Wizard page.

Many of the buttons listed in Table 16.1 serve the same purposes for both forms and reports. As is the case for Form Design mode, the Formatting toolbar's buttons for formatting text are enabled only when a control object that can contain text is selected. The Formatting toolbar for reports is identical to the Formatting toolbar for forms.

➔ For a list of the formatting icons and their uses, **see** Table 14.2 in "The Formatting Toolbar," **p. 534**.

If you double-click the name of an existing report or click the Preview button in the Database window, the report displays in Print Preview mode, which is the default view for reports. Table 16.2 lists the toolbar's buttons in Print Preview mode.

16

TABLE 16.2 STANDARD TOOLBAR BUTTONS IN REPORT PRINT PREVIEW MODE

Button	Menu Choice	Function
	Not applicable	Prints the report without displaying the Print dialog. The report is printed using the current printer settings.
	View, Zoom	Toggles between full-page and full-size (100%) views of the report. Clicking the mouse when its pointer appears as the magnifying glass symbol produces the same effect.
	View, Pages, One Page	Displays one full page.
	View, Pages, Two Pages	Displays two full pages.
	View, Pages, Four Pages	Displays a palette from which you can select several multiple-page views of the report.
100%	View, Zoom	Changes the size of the view from 10% to 1,000% or fits the report to the current size of the window.
Close	Not applicable	Closes the Print Preview window.
Setup	File, Page Setup	Displays the Page Setup dialog.
	Tools, OfficeLinks	Displays a drop-down list of shortcut commands for Microsoft Office Links: Publish It with Microsoft Word, and Analyze It with Microsoft Excel. (Merge It with Microsoft Word is disabled.)

USING AUTOFORMAT AND CUSTOMIZING REPORT STYLES

The AutoFormat toolbar button works the same way for reports as for forms. Chapter 14 contains a detailed, step-by-step explanation of how to use Access's AutoFormat button and how to customize the predefined AutoFormat styles or create your own AutoFormat styles.

→ To apply an AutoFormat style to a report or define or customize a report AutoFormat style, **see** "Using AutoFormat," **p. 537**.

TIP

> Access stores styles for reports and forms separately, so you must create separate AutoFormat styles for your reports. As with forms, to create an AutoFormat style for customized reports, first create a report that contains controls that are formatted for your new style. Click the AutoFormat button on the toolbar, and then click the Customize button in the AutoFormat dialog to customize the format. Choose a naming convention for report AutoFormat styles, such as rptSalesAF or rptFinanceAF.

MODIFYING A BASIC WIZARD REPORT

The Report Wizard tries to create the optimum final report in the first pass. Usually, the Wizard comes close enough to a finished product that you spend far less time modifying a Wizard-created basic report than creating a report from the default blank template.

In the following sections, you use Access's report design features to make the rptInventoryByCategory report more attractive and easier to read.

DELETING, RELOCATING, AND EDITING EXISTING CONTROLS

The first step in modifying the Wizard's report is to modify the existing controls on the report. You don't need to align the labels and text boxes precisely during the initial modification; the "Aligning Controls Horizontally and Vertically" section later in this chapter covers control alignment. To create space for additional controls on the report, follow these steps:

1. Open rptInventoryByCategory in Report Design mode, if it's not already open.

2. Click the Select Report button to select the entire report, and click the Properties button to open the Report properties window.
3. Change the Format page's Caption property value to **Inventory by Category**.
4. Click the label at the top of the page and make the same change. Your report now appears as shown in Figure 16.12.
5. The SupplierID and CompanyName fields are redundant in this report because the SupplierID field is a lookup field. Select the Company Name label in the Page Header section, hold down the Shift key, and click the CompanyName field in the Detail section. Press Delete to remove the field and label from the report. (Don't worry about aligning the fields and labels yet.)

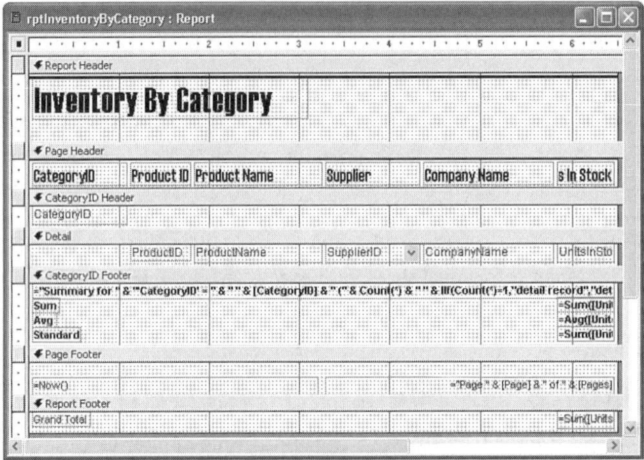

Figure 16.12
Change the Caption property value of the report and the top label to "Inventory by Category".

6. This report is more useful if you include the dollar value of both the inventory and number of units on hand. To accommodate one or two additional columns, you must compress the fields' widths. CategoryID occupies a column, but you can display this column's content in the CategoryID footer (or header) without using the extra column space. Select and delete the CategoryID label from the Page Header section; do the same for the CategoryID text box from the CategoryID Header section (see Figure 16.13).
7. For this report, you'll put the CategoryID name in the footer section of the group. Drag the Detail section bar upward to eliminate the space occupied by the CategoryID Header, and drag the Page Header up to reduce the space below the report caption. Your report now appears as shown in Figure 16.13.

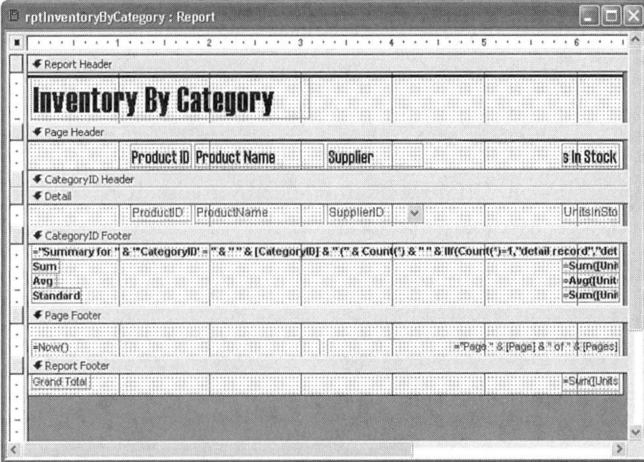

Figure 16.13
Delete the CategoryID label and text box in the Page Header and Detail sections of the report, and remove unnecessary vertical whitespace.

8. All Page Header labels, Detail text boxes, and Totals text boxes in the CategoryID Footer and Report Footer sections must move to the left as a group. Click the Product ID label to select it and then press and hold down Shift. Click the remaining Page Header labels, each of the Detail text boxes, the three summary field text boxes in the CategoryID Footer section, and the Grand Total text box in the Report Footer section (for a total of 12 controls). Now release Shift.

TIP

Enclosing the 12 controls by dragging a rectangle around them doesn't work in this case. There's a hidden line that, when selected, prevents dragging the fields to the left.

9. Position the mouse pointer over the Product ID label at a location where the pointer turns into the graphic of a palm of a hand. Hold down the left mouse button and drag the selected fields to the left margin. Your report appears as shown in Figure 16.14.

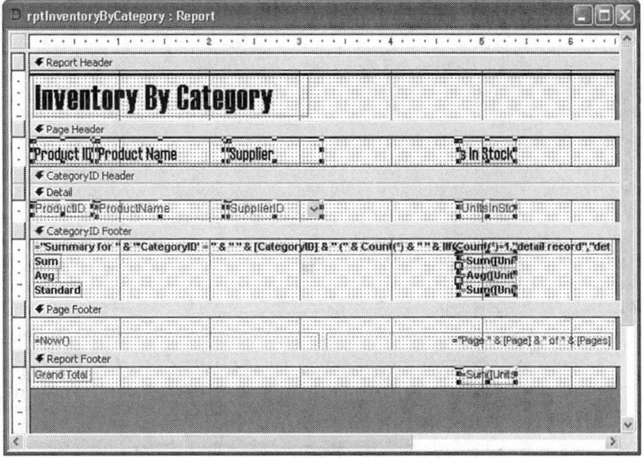

Figure 16.14
Move the group of selected controls to the extreme left of the report.

10. You can more easily edit and position the labels if you left-justify them. Click a blank area of the report to deselect the group, select all Page Header labels, and click the Align Left button on the toolbar.

11. Edit the Product ID label to read ID and edit the Units In Stock label to read only **Units**. Select all labels in the Page Header and choose Format, Size, To Fit. Resize the widths of the ProductID and UnitsInStock text boxes in the Detail section to match the width of the labels in the Page Header. Relocate the labels to provide more space for the Product Name and Supplier columns and gain additional space on the right side of the report, as shown in Figure 16.15.

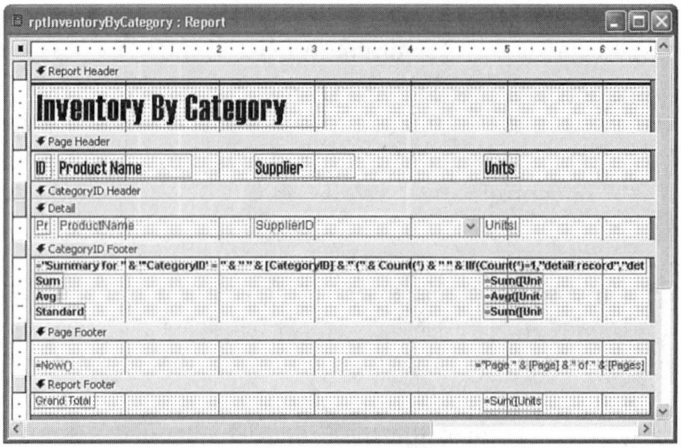

Figure 16.15
After editing the Page Header labels and resizing a few fields, your report design appears as shown here.

12. By default, the Report Wizard adds to the CategoryID Footer a calculated field (visible in Figure 16.15). The calculated field displays the group's field name (CategoryID) and value to help identify the group footer's summary fields. For example, for CategoryID 1, the calculated field displays the following in Print Preview mode:

    ```
    Summary for 'CategoryID' = 1 (12 detail records)
    ```

    For this report, you want a more explicit description of the product category—more than just the CategoryID number. Delete the Category ID Footer's calculated field that starts with `="Summary for"` for now; you replace it in the next few steps. As usual, save your changes frequently.

TIP

> Not every table that you use in your reports will have lookup fields, nor is it necessarily desirable to create lookup fields for all numeric code fields (such as CategoryID and SupplierID). If you want to display a looked-up value for a field that isn't defined as a lookup field, you use Access's domain aggregate function, `DLookUp`, to find values from another table that correspond to a value in one of the report's fields. For example, to display both the actual CategoryID number and the CategoryName in the CategoryID Footer of the Inventory by Category report, you can use the `DLookUp` function to display the text of the CategoryName field from the Categories table, and a bound text field to display the CategoryID number from the Products table. The expression you use is
>
> ```
> =DLookUp("[CategoryName]","Categories","[CategoryID] =
> Report!CategoryID") & " Category"
> ```
>
> `[CategoryName]` is the value that you want to return to the text box. Categories is the table that contains the CategoryName field. `[CategoryID] = Report!CategoryID` is the criterion that selects the record in the Categories table with a CategoryID value that is equal to the value in your report's CategoryID text box. The Report identifier is necessary to distinguish between the CategoryID field of the Categories table and a control object of the same name. (`Report!` is necessary in this example because Access has automatically named the report's CategoryID text box control as CategoryID.) Remember that the `DLookUp` function isn't available in ADP reports.

PRINTING THE LOOKUP FIELD OF A TABLE

To add a new field to display the CategoryName field in the CategoryID footer, and complete the redesign of the report, do the following:

1. For this report, the Avg field is unnecessary, so delete it and its label.
2. Add a bound text box to identify the subtotal in the CategoryID Footer section. Click the Field List button on the toolbar. Select CategoryID from the list in the Field List window.
3. Click and drag the field symbol mouse pointer about a half inch from the left margin of the CategoryID Footer in place of the text box you deleted. Because the CategoryID field is a lookup field, it displays with a drop-down list button for the field box. When printed or displayed in Print Preview, this field shows the CategoryID name rather than the numeric code. Click the Field List button on the toolbar to close the Field List window.
4. Select the label of the CategoryID field that you just placed, press Shift and select the text box, and then use the Font and Size drop-down lists on the Formatting toolbar to set both controls' font to Arial and size to 8 points. Choose Format, Size, To Fit to adjust the size of the controls, and then drag the controls to the top of the Category ID Footer section. Figure 16.16 shows the new bound CategoryID field in place of the calculated field that you deleted in step 11 in the previous "Deleting, Relocating, and Editing Existing Controls" section.

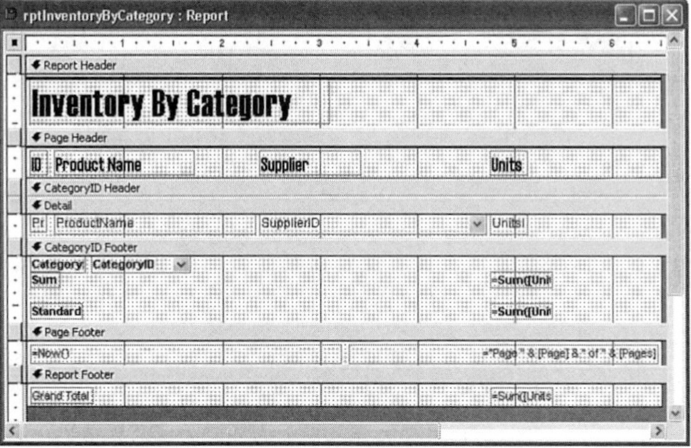

Figure 16.16
Replace the calculated field in the CategoryID Footer with the CategoryID lookup field.

5. Drag the two calculated fields (=`Now` and =`"Page..."`) in the Page Footer section until they are one grid mark away from the top of the Page Footer section. Drag the Report Footer bar upward to reduce the Page Footer's height.
6. Click and drag the `=Sum([UnitsInStock])/[UnitsInStock]` text box from its present location below the `=Sum([UnitsInStock])` text box to a position at the top of the

CategoryID Footer, near the Center of the page. Then drag the Standard label to the left of the text box you moved, and change its caption to **Percent:** (look ahead to Figure 16.17).

7. Drag the `=Sum([UnitsInStock])` field up to the bottom of the CategoryID footer and the Sum label to the left of the text box you moved, and add a colon (:) after Sum for consistency. Move the right edge of the text box to align with right edge of the UnitsInStock text box. Move up the Page Footer divider bar to reduce the footer's depth (again, look ahead to Figure 16.17).

> **TIP**
>
> To differentiate between calculated field text boxes that show only the first few characters of the expression, temporarily increase their width. Shift+F2 doesn't open the Zoom window for report text boxes, and there's no Zoom choice in the text boxes' context menu.

B

8. Select the Grand Total label and text box in the Report Footer section and move the text box to align its right edge with the right edge of the text boxes above it. Your final report design appears as shown in Figure 16.17. Press Ctrl+S to save your report design.

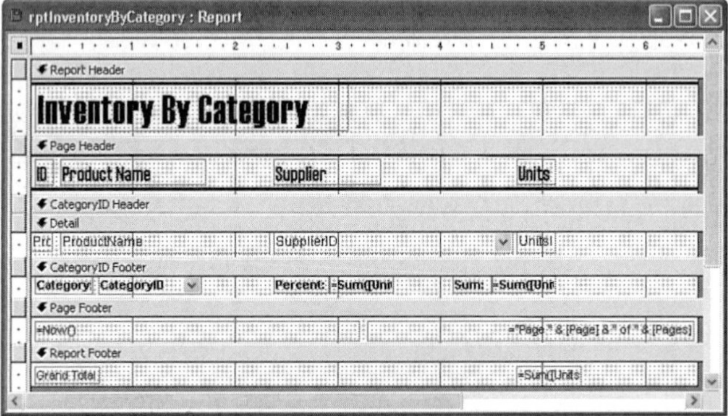

Figure 16.17 At this point, the design of the Inventory by Category report is ready for a test run.

If you get a blank page after each page when you print or preview a report, see the suggestion in "Eliminating Empty Pages" in the "Troubleshooting" section near the end of this chapter.

To check the progress of your work, periodically click the Print Preview button to display the report prior to printing. Figure 16.18 shows your Inventory by Category report in Print Preview mode.

> **TIP**
>
> If two-digit product codes appear in the report as 01 instead of their correct values, increase the width of the ProductID text box slightly.

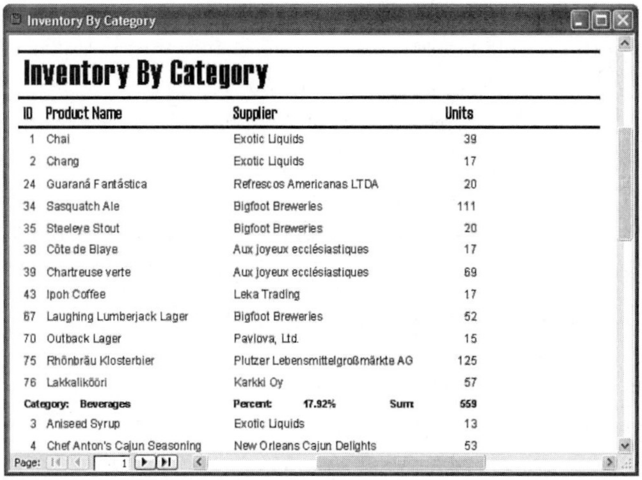

Figure 16.18
Print Preview displays the report design of Figure 16.17 at actual size (100% zoom).

Adding Calculated Controls to a Report

Calculated controls are useful in reports. You use calculated controls to determine extended values, such as quantity times unit price or quantity times cost. Now you have enough space at the right of the report to add two columns: one for the UnitPrice field and one for the extended inventory value, which is UnitPrice multiplied by UnitsInStock. The following subsections explain how to provide the data for and add these controls.

Changing the Report's Record Source

You created the Inventory by Category report by selecting fields directly from the Products and Suppliers tables in the Report Wizard. Therefore, the Record Source property for the report as a whole is an SQL statement that selects only the fields that you chose initially in the Report Wizard. Although you can add fields to the report by creating unbound text box controls and using the Expression Builder to create an expression to retrieve the desired value, it's a more straightforward process to create a query to select the desired fields and then substitute the new query as the report's data source. You also can specify record-selection criteria in a query.

Jet SQL

Following is the Jet SQL statement generated by the Report Wizard:

```
SELECT Products.CategoryID, Products.ProductID,
   Products.ProductName, Products.SupplierID,
   Suppliers.CompanyName, Products.UnitsInStock
FROM Suppliers INNER JOIN Products
   ON Suppliers.SupplierID=Products.SupplierID;
```

Northwind.mdb's Products table includes some products that have been discontinued. Inventory reports shouldn't include counts and valuations of products that no longer are available for sale.

TIP

> Alternatively, you can use the Filter and Filter On property values on the Data page of the report's Properties window to prevent discontinued products from inclusion in the report. Another approach would be to add a `WHERE NOT Discontinued` clause to the Record Source SQL statement. As a rule, however, it's easier to troubleshoot report problems if you use a query as the Record Source property of the report. The query lets you quickly preview the result set on which your report is based.

To create a query that eliminates discontinued products from the result set, follow these steps:

1. Open a new query in Design view by clicking the Queries shortcut in the Database window and then double-clicking the Create Query in Design View shortcut.
2. Double-click the Products table in the Show Table dialog and then close the dialog.
3. Drag * from the field list to the first column of the query.
4. Drag the Discontinued field to the query grid's second column.
5. Clear the Show check box for the Discontinued field and then type **False** in the Discontinued field's first Criteria row.
6. If you want to list products alphabetically by ProductName, add the ProductName field and select an ascending sort (see Figure 16.19). Alternatively, you can specify ProductName in the Order By list and set the Order By On property value to Yes.

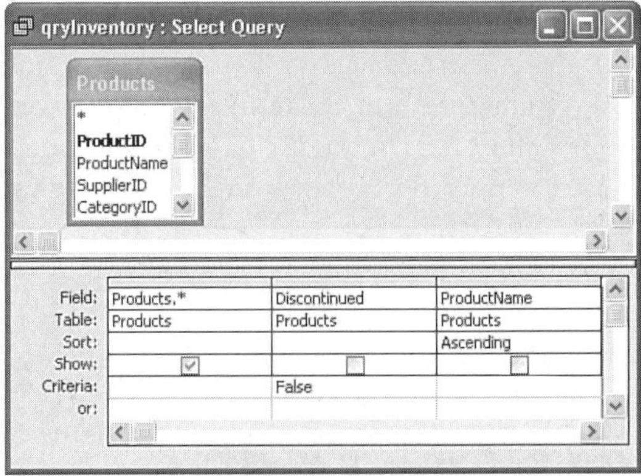

Figure 16.19 This query prevents the Inventory by Category report from including discontinued products.

7. Run the query to test your work, close the Query window, and save your changes using the name **qryInventory**.

TIP

> You don't need to add the Suppliers table to the query because the SupplierID field of the Products table supplies the CompanyName lookup value to the table.

To change the report's Record Source property value to the new query, follow these steps:

1. Open the Inventory by Category report in Report Design view, and press Ctrl+R or click the Select Report button to select the report.

2. Click the toolbar's Properties button to open the report's Properties window. Then click the Data tab to display the report's data properties.
3. Click the Record Source text box and then use the drop-down list to select the qryInventory query as the report's new Record Source property (see Figure 16.20).

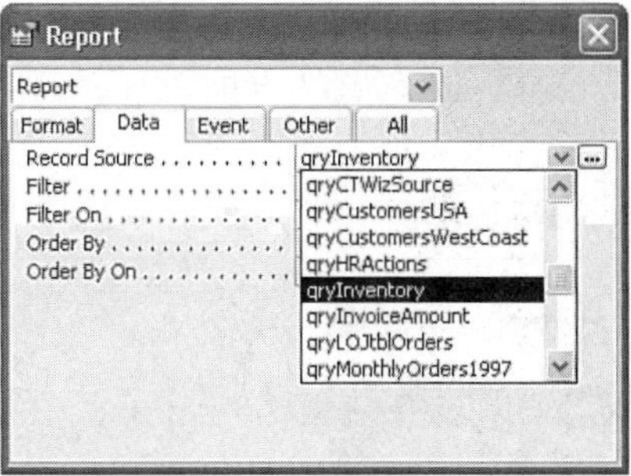

Figure 16.20 Replace the Wizard-generated SQL statement with the new query to serve as the Data Source property value for the report.

4. Check the report in Print Preview mode, and then save the changes to the report.

ADDING THE CALCULATED CONTROLS

Now that you've changed the report's record source, you have easy access to the UnitPrice field that you need for adding the calculated Cost and Value fields to the report. UnitPrice is the selling price of the product, not its cost to Northwind Traders. For this example, assume that Northwind Traders sells its goods at a uniform markup of 50%. In retailing terminology, this means that a product costing $1.00 sells for $1.50, and the inventory value is 66.7% of the UnitPrice value. Thus the text box expression for the cost of the product is `=[UnitPrice]*0.667` and the value is `=[UnitsInStock]*[UnitPrice]*0.667`.

To add the Cost and Value calculated fields to the report, follow these steps:

1. Return to Design view, and click the Toolbox button on the toolbar to display the Access toolbox if it isn't already displayed.

2. Click the Label tool in the toolbox and place the label to the right of the Units label in the Page Header section. Type **Cost** as the caption.

3. Add another label to the right of Cost and type **Value** as the caption.
4. If necessary, change the font and size to match the other labels in the Page Header. (Access automatically sets the font name, but not the size, bold, or other font attributes.)

5. Click the Text Box tool, and add two unbound text boxes in the Detail section under the new labels. Delete the attached labels, and align the right edge of the text boxes under the right edge of the Page Header labels.

TIP

> A faster method of adding text boxes and labels is to select both the label and the text box, and then press Ctrl+C and Ctrl+V to superimpose a copy that has an associated label over the existing controls. Drag the copy to its new location.

6. Select the new Cost text box, open the Properties window, click the Data tab, and type **=[UnitPrice]*0.667** in the Control Source text box (see Figure 16.21).

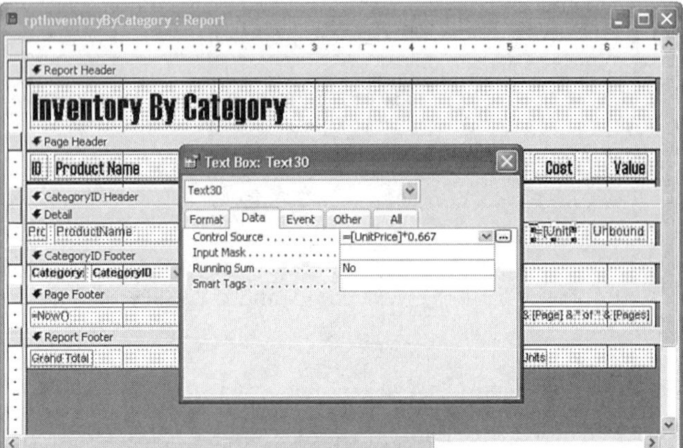

Figure 16.21
Type as the Data Source property value the expression for the value to print in the calculated field text box.

7. Select the Value text box, click the Data tab, and type **=[UnitsInStock]*[UnitPrice]*0.667** as the expression. Change to Print Preview to check your work.

TIP

> A good way to enter long, complex expressions is to click the Builder button to open the Expression Builder, which provides a larger text box in which to type the expression.

8. Return to Design view, drag the Percent label and text box to the left, and change the label caption to % **Cat. Units**.

9. Repeat steps 5 and 6 to add a calculated text box in the CategoryID Footer section under the Value label, but type **=Sum([UnitsInStock]*[UnitPrice]*0.667)** as the subtotal expression and don't delete the label. Click the Bold button on the toolbar to set the Font Weight property to Bold. In the Properties window, click the Other tab and then set this text box's Name property as **txtCatValue**. Type **Value:** as the name of the label and change the font to 8-point Arial bold.

10. Repeat step 9 to create the grand total value text box with the **=Sum([UnitsInStock]*[UnitPrice]*0.667)** expression in the Report Footer section. In the Other page of the Properties window, set this text box's Name property as **txtTotalValue**. Change the Font Size to 8 points, set the Font Weight to Bold, and delete the associated label. Also apply the Bold attribute to the Grand Total label.

11. Add another unbound text box to the right of the % Cat. Units text box in the CategoryID Footer section. Type **=[txtCatValue]/[txtTotalValue]** as the value of the Control Source property and set the Format property's value to Percent and the Font Weight to Bold. Change the label caption to **Value** and conform the font. The report design at this point appears as shown in Figure 16.22. Press Ctrl+S to save your report.

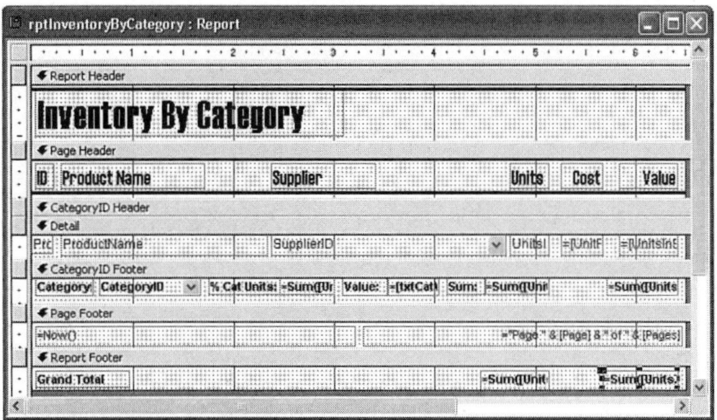

Figure 16.22 The enhanced report design with added Cost, Value, Cat(egory) Value, and Grand Total Value calculated fields.

If a Parameters dialog appears when you test your report in Preview mode, see the "Unexpected Parameters Dialogs" topic of the "Troubleshooting" section near the end of the chapter.

12. Click Print Preview to check the result of your additions. Use the vertical scroll bar, if necessary, to display the category subtotal. The next section describes how you can correct any values that are not aligned properly and the spacing of the Detail section's rows.

13. Click the Bottom of Report page selector button to display the grand totals for the report (see Figure 16.23). The record selector buttons become page selector buttons when you display reports in Print Preview mode.

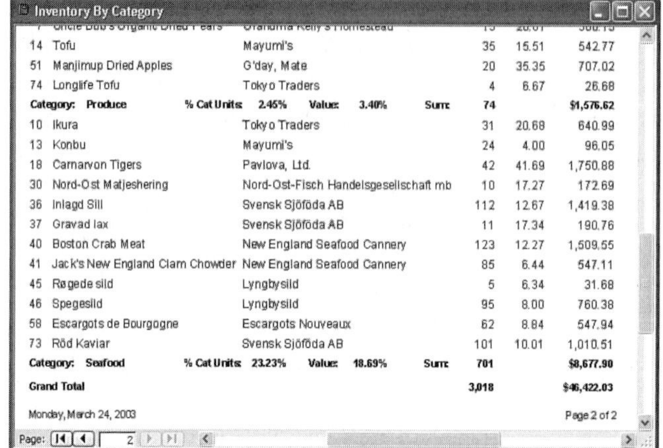

Figure 16.23 The last page of the report displays grand totals for units and inventory values.

Aligning and Formatting Controls and Adjusting Line Spacing

The exact alignment of label and text box controls is more important on reports than it is on forms because in the printed report any misalignment is obvious. Formatting the controls further improves the report's appearance and readability.

The spacing of the report's rows in the Detail section is controlled by the section's depth. Likewise, you can control the whitespace above and below the headers and footers by adjusting the depth of their sections and the vertical position of the controls within the sections. To create a professional-looking report, you must adjust the controls' alignment and formatting as well as the sections' line spacing.

Aligning Controls Horizontally and Vertically

You align controls by first selecting the rows to align and then aligning the columns. Access provides several control-sizing and alignment options to make the process easier. To size and align the controls that you created, follow these steps:

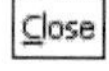

1. If you still have the Inventory by Category report in Print Preview, click the Close button to return to Design view.
2. You can simultaneously adjust the height of all text boxes to fit the font used for their contents. Press Ctrl+A or choose Edit, Select All to select all the controls in the report.
3. Choose Format, Size, To Fit to adjust the height of the selected controls. Access adjusts all the controls to the proper height. To deselect all the controls, click a blank area of the report.
4. Select all labels in the Page Header sections. Choose Format, Align, Top. This process aligns the tops of each selected label with the uppermost selected label. Click a blank area of the report to deselect the labels.

5. Select all text boxes in the Detail section and repeat step 4 for the text boxes.
6. Select the labels and text boxes in the CategoryID Footer and Report Footer sections and repeat step 4.
7. Select all controls in the Units column. Choose Format, Align, Right so that Access aligns the column to the right edge of the text farthest to the right of the column. Then click the Align Right button on the toolbar to right-align the contents of the labels and text boxes. (The first part of this step aligns the controls themselves to the rightmost control, and the second part right-aligns the text or data displayed by the selected controls.)
8. Select all controls in the Cost column and repeat step 7.
9. Select all controls in the Values column (except the Page Footer text box) and repeat step 7.
10. Click Print Preview to display the report with the improved alignment of rows and columns.

Formatting Controls

As shown previously in Figure 16.22, you must revise the formatting of several controls. In particular, the default General Number format for Cost and Value fields results in a varying number of digits after the decimal point. Cost and Value fields should be formatted with thousands separators, and category and grand totals need currency symbols to conform to North American standard accounting practices.

To change the Format property of these fields, follow these steps:

1. Click the Print Preview toolbar's Close button to return to Design view.
2. Double-click the Detail section's Cost text box to open its Properties window, and then click the Format tab of the Properties window.
3. In the Format text box, select Standard. This format specifies two decimal places and adds thousands separators without a currency symbol.
4. Select the Values text box and repeat step 3. The Detail section doesn't require dollar signs.
5. Select each of the three text boxes in the units column, and type **#,##0** as the value of the Format property to add thousands separators to these fields.
6. Select the txtCatValue in the CategoryID Footer. Click the Properties window's Format tab and type **$#,##0.00** in the Format field. Accountants use dollar signs to identify subtotals and totals in ledgers.

TIP

> If you select Currency formatting instead of typing $#,#00.00 to add a dollar sign to the value, your totals don't align. Currency formatting offsets the number to the left to provide space for the parentheses that accountants use to specify negative monetary values.

7. Select the txtTotalValue text box in the Report Footer and repeat step 6 for the grand total values.

10 U 8. The grand total values in the Report Footer are the report's most important element, so increase the font size to 9 points, and apply the underline attribute to the text box.

9. Click the toolbar's Print Preview button to check your formatting modifications. Click the Bottom of Report page selector button to display the last page of the report (see Figure 16.24).

16

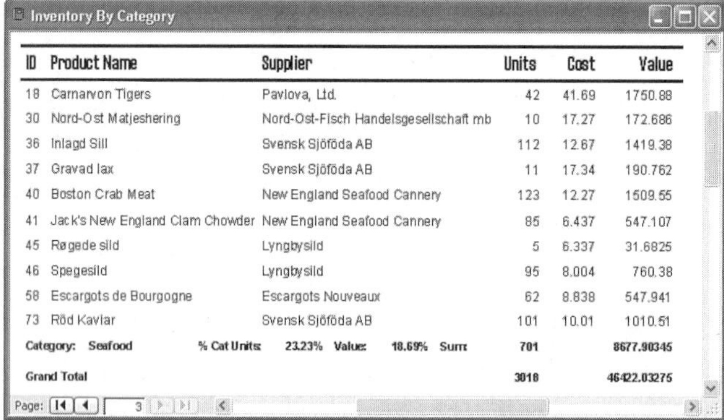

Inventory By Category

ID	Product Name	Supplier	Units	Cost	Value
18	Carnarvon Tigers	Pavlova, Ltd.	42	41.69	1750.88
30	Nord-Ost Matjeshering	Nord-Ost-Fisch Handelsgesellschaft mb	10	17.27	172.686
36	Inlagd Sill	Svensk Sjöföda AB	112	12.67	1419.38
37	Gravad lax	Svensk Sjöföda AB	11	17.34	190.762
40	Boston Crab Meat	New England Seafood Cannery	123	12.27	1509.55
41	Jack's New England Clam Chowder	New England Seafood Cannery	85	6.437	547.107
45	Røgede sild	Lyngbysild	5	6.337	31.6825
46	Spegesild	Lyngbysild	95	8.004	760.38
58	Escargots de Bourgogne	Escargots Nouveaux	62	8.838	547.941
73	Röd Kaviar	Svensk Sjöföda AB	101	10.01	1010.51
Category:	Seafood	% Cat Units: 23.23% Value: 18.69% Sum:	701		8677.90345
Grand Total			3018		46422.03275

Page: 3

Figure 16.24
Right-aligning and applying appropriate formats to numeric values gives your report a professional appearance.

You might need to increase the width of the text boxes to accommodate the added thousands separators and, where applicable, the currency symbol.

ADJUSTING LINE SPACING

In the Page Header section, the controls are placed further apart than is necessary, and the depth of the controls in the Report Header section is out of proportion with the size of the text. The line spacing of the remainder of the report's sections is satisfactory, but you can also change this spacing. Minimizing line spacing allows you to print a report on fewer sheets of paper.

TIP

> You might have to return to Design view and adjust the width or position of the Cat(egory) and Grand Totals text boxes to align these values with those for the individual products.

To change the spacing of the report's Page Header and Detail sections, follow these steps:

Close 1. Click Print Preview's Close button to return to Design view.

2. Select all the labels in the Page Header and move the group to the top of the section.

3. Click the bottom line of the Page Header and move the line to the bottom of the text boxes. (To select the line, you might need to move the CategoryID Header section downward temporarily.)
4. Click a blank area of the report and then move the CategoryID Header section to two grid dots below the line.
5. Drag the CategoryID Footer section up to the bottom of the Detail section's text boxes.
6. Click the toolbar's Report View button to check the Page Header depth and line spacing of the Detail section. The spacing shown in Figure 16.25 is close to the minimum that you can achieve. You can't reduce a section's line spacing to less than that required by the tallest text box or label by reducing the section's Height property in the Properties box. If you try this approach, Access rejects the entry and substitutes the prior value.

Figure 16.25
The report shows the effect of adjusting the depth of the Report Header, Page Header, and Detail sections.

Inventory By Category

Inventory By Category

ID	Product Name	Supplier	Units	Cost	Value
1	Chai	Exotic Liquids	39	12.01	468.23
2	Chang	Exotic Liquids	17	12.67	215.44
34	Sasquatch Ale	Bigfoot Breweries	111	9.34	1,036.52
35	Steeleye Stout	Bigfoot Breweries	20	12.01	240.12
38	Côte de Blaye	Aux joyeux ecclésiastiques	17	175.75	2,987.83
39	Chartreuse verte	Aux joyeux ecclésiastiques	69	12.01	828.41
43	Ipoh Coffee	Leka Trading	17	30.68	521.59
67	Laughing Lumberjack Lager	Bigfoot Breweries	52	9.34	485.58
70	Outback Lager	Pavlova, Ltd.	15	10.01	150.08
75	Rhönbräu Klosterbier	Plutzer Lebensmittelgroßmärkte AG	125	5.17	646.16
76	Lakkalikööri	Karkki Oy	57	12.01	684.34
Category:	**Beverages**	**% Cat Units: 17.86% Value: 17.80% Sum:**	**539**		**$8,264.30**
3	Aniseed Syrup	Exotic Liquids	13	6.67	86.71
4	Chef Anton's Cajun Seasoning	New Orleans Cajun Delights	53	14.67	777.72
6	Grandma's Boysenberry Spread	Grandma Kelly's Homestead	120	16.68	2,001.00
8	Northwoods Cranberry Sauce	Grandma Kelly's Homestead	6	26.68	160.08
15	Genen Shouyu	Mayumi's	39	10.34	403.20
44	Gula Malacca	Leka Trading	27	12.97	350.28

Page: 1

7. Click the Zoom button on the toolbar to display the report in full-page view. (Clicking the mouse when the pointer is the magnifying glass symbol has the same effect as clicking the Zoom button. Alternate clicks toggle between full-size and full-page views).
8. Click Ctrl+S to save your changes.

The Inventory by Category report is included on the accompanying CD-ROM as Report16.mdb in the \Seua11\Chaptr16 folder.

ADJUSTING MARGINS AND PRINTING CONVENTIONAL REPORTS

Clicking the One Page button in Report view shows the report as it would print using Access's default printing margins of 1 inch on the top, bottom, and sides of the report (see

Figure 16.26). In the Print Setup dialog, you can adjust the printed version of the report. The procedure for printing a report applies to printing the data contained in tables and queries as well as single-record or continuous forms.

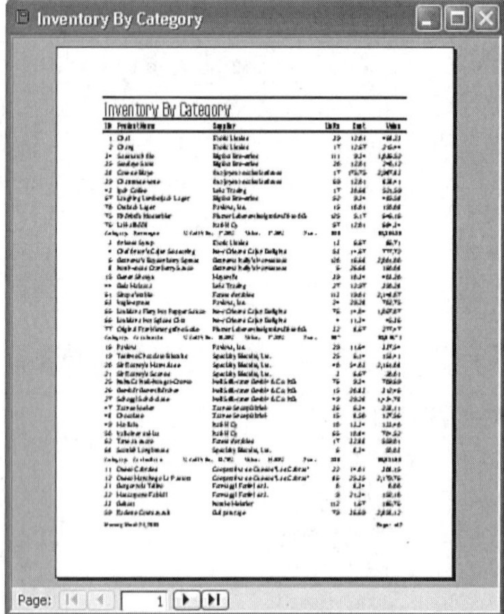

Figure 16.26
One Page view shows the report with the default one-inch printing margins.

To change the printing margins for a report, follow these steps:

1. Choose File, Page Setup to open the Page Setup dialog.
2. The Page Setup dialog is similar to the Print and Page Setup dialogs of other Windows applications, with a section for printing margins included. To increase the amount of information on a page, decrease the top and bottom margins. By selecting the Print Data Only check box, you can print only the data in the report; the Report and Page Headers and Footers don't print.
3. In the Left text box, type **1.5** to specify a 1.5-inch left margin and type **0.5** in the Right text box. In the Top, and Bottom text boxes, type **0.75** (see Figure 16.27). Click OK to see a One Page view of the report with the revised margins (see Figure 16.28).

TIP

> The printing margins that you establish for a report in the Page Setup dialog apply to the active report only; each report has a unique set of margins. When you save the report, Access saves its margin settings.

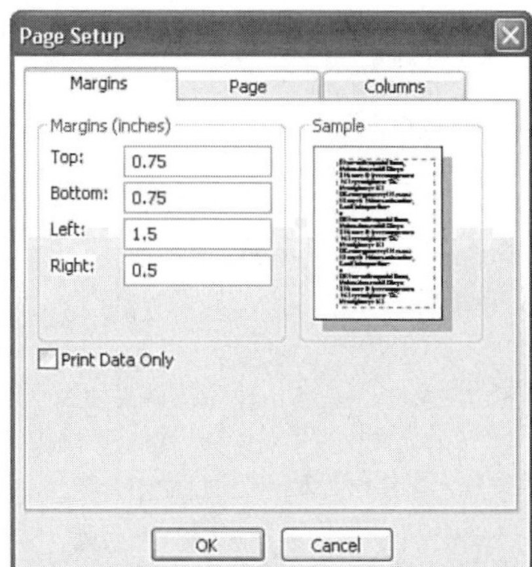

Figure 16.27
The Page Setup dialog lets you set margins and other property values for printing reports, forms, datasheets, and other Access objects.

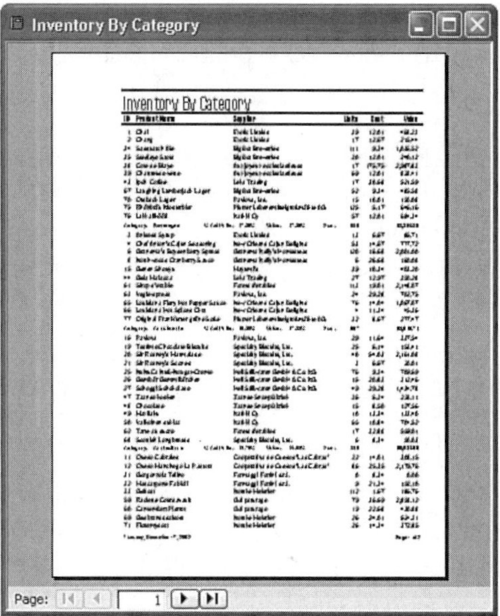

Figure 16.28
The One Page preview shows the effect of applying the margin settings shown in Figure 16.27.

4. To print the report, click the Print button. Access immediately prints the report using the current printer options. If you want to change the selected printer, page orientation, graphics quality, or other printer options, choose File, Print. The standard Print dialog appears for the printer specified in Windows as the default printer. Figure 16.29 shows, for example, the Print dialog for a networked Brother laser printer.

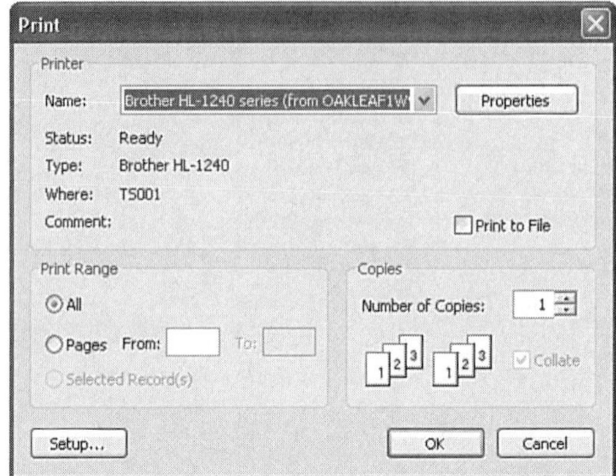

Figure 16.29
The Print dialog lets you select the printer, pages to print, number of copies, and collation sequence.

5. You can print all or part of a report or print the report to a file for later printing; you can also select the number of copies to print. By choosing the Properties button, you can change the parameters that apply to the printer you are using. Click OK to print the report.

The Page Setup dialog (refer to Figure 16.27) includes a Page tab that lets you select the paper size and orientation. The dialog also includes a Columns page that allows you to establish specifications for printing mailing labels and other multiple-column reports. The "Printing Multicolumn Reports as Mailing Labels" section describes these specifications and how you set them.

PREVENTING WIDOWED RECORDS WITH THE GROUP KEEP TOGETHER PROPERTY

Access includes a property for groups, Keep Together, which prevents widowed records from appearing at the bottom of the page. Depending on your report section depths, you might find that only a few records of the next group (called widowed records) appear at the bottom of the page. The report designs shown in Figures 16.26 and 16.28 have six and nine widowed records at the bottom of the first report page.

You can force a page break when an entire group doesn't fit on a page by following these steps:

1. With the report in Design view, click the Sorting and Grouping button to open the Sorting and Grouping dialog.
2. Select the field with the group symbol in the selection button that corresponds to the group that you want to keep together. In this example, select CategoryID.
3. Open the Keep Together drop-down list and select Whole Group, as shown in Figure 16.30.

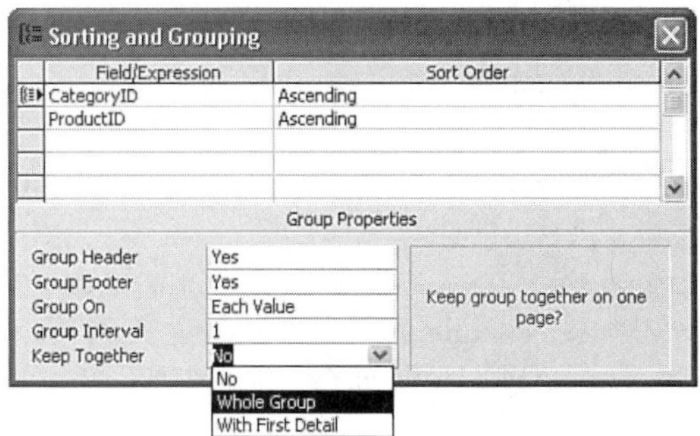

Figure 16.30 Select the group to keep together (CategoryID), and select Whole Group.

4. Close the Sorting and Grouping dialog and click Print Preview to see the result of applying the group Keep Together property.

TIP

> If you want to delete or add a Group Header or Footer singly (rather than in pairs), select Yes or No in the appropriate property field of the Sorting and Grouping dialog.

The Report Wizard makes the other entries in the Sorting and Grouping dialog for you. The next chapter describes how to use the Sorting and Grouping dialog to design reports without the aid of the Wizard.

PRINTING MULTICOLUMN REPORTS AS MAILING LABELS

Access lets you print multicolumn reports. You can create a single-column report with the Report Wizard, for example, and then arrange the report to print values from the Detail section in a specified number of columns across the page. The most common application of multicolumn reports is the creation of mailing labels.

CREATING A MAILING LABEL WITH THE LABEL WIZARD

You can create mailing lists with the Label Wizard, or you can start with a blank form. The Label Wizard's advantage is that it includes the dimensions of virtually every kind of adhesive label for dot-matrix or laser printers made by the Avery Commercial Products division and several other North American and overseas manufacturers. You select the product number of the label that you plan to use, and Access determines the number of columns, rows per page, and margins for the report's Detail section. You also can customize the Label Wizard for labels with unusual sizes or those produced by manufacturers who aren't included in the Wizard's repertoire. Several other manufacturers include a note that indicates the corresponding Avery label number.

To create a report with the Label Wizard, do this:

1. In the Reports page of the Database window, click New to open the New Report dialog.
2. Select Customers as the data source for the labels, select Label Wizard in the list, and click OK to open the first Wizard dialog.
3. If you're using Avery labels, select the product code. Otherwise, select the manufacturer in the list, and select the product code. Accept the Sheet Feed option if you're using laser-printer labels (see Figure 16.31). Click Next.

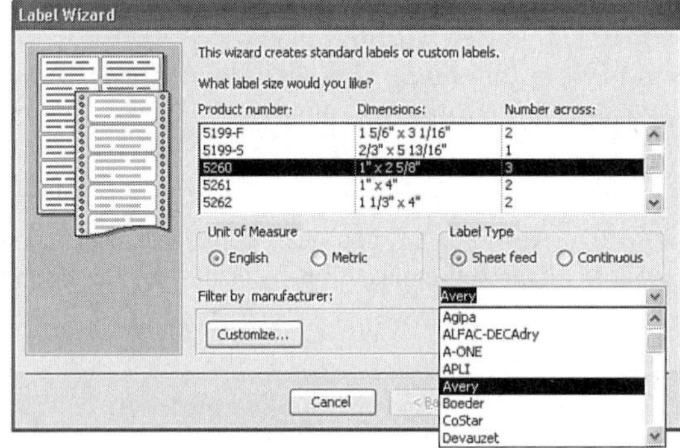

Figure 16.31
The first dialog of the Label Wizard lets you select a manufacturer and then a label size available from the manufacturer.

4. In the second Wizard dialog, select the font family, size, and weight for the label. The defaults—8-point Arial light—make the labels hard to read. This example uses 9-point Courier New medium (see Figure 16.32). Click Next.

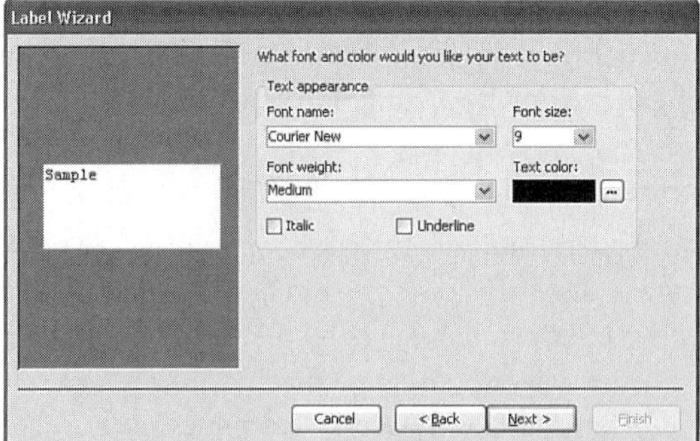

Figure 16.32
Specify the printer font and its attributes in the second Wizard dialog.

5. In the third Wizard dialog, select the field of the record source for the label's first row—ContactName for this example—and click the > button to add it to the Prototype Label text box. Press Enter to add a new line.
6. Repeat step 4 for the CompanyName and Address fields.

7. Select City, press >, and add a comma and a space.
8. Select Region, press >, add two spaces, select PostalCode, and press >. Your Prototype label appears as shown in Figure 16.33.

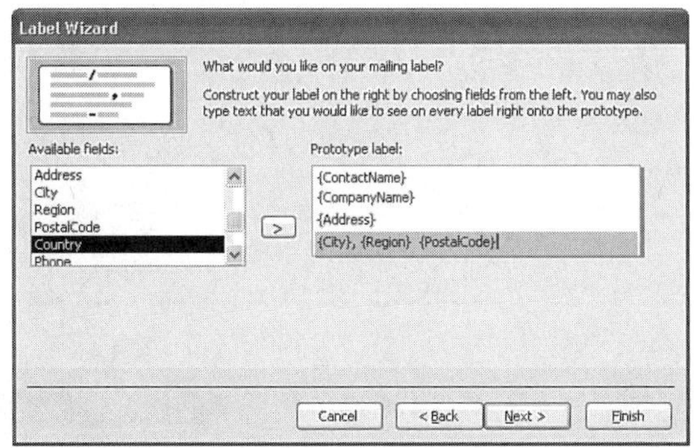

Figure 16.33
The Prototype Label text box displays the label design as you add fields from the Available Fields list.

9. If the mailing is international, add an additional line for the Country field.

NOTE

Although the Avery 5160 label has sufficient depth to add the Country field in 9-point type, the Wizard doesn't let you add more than four lines.

10. Click Next and specify the fields on which to sort the labels. If you added the Country field, double-click Country in the Available fields list. Double-click PostalCode (see Figure 16.34). Click Next.

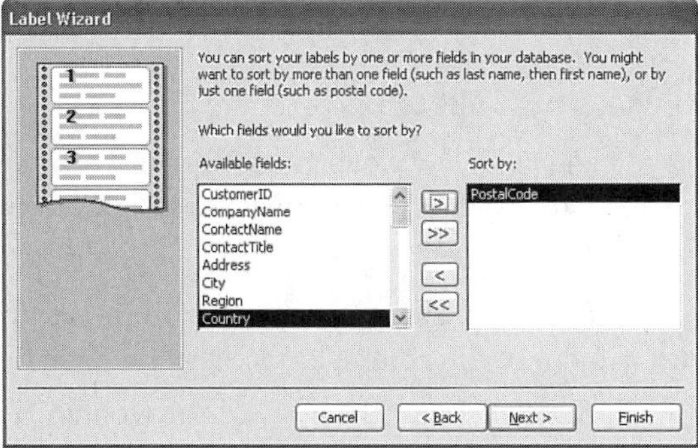

Figure 16.34
Specify the sort order for the labels in the fourth Wizard dialog.

11. In the fifth Wizard dialog, type a name for the report, such as **rptCustomerLabels**, and click Finish to display the labels in Print Preview.

In many cases, you receive the error message shown in Figure 16.35 prior to opening the report in Print Preview. The error message for the preceding example is due to the Wizard's miscalculation of column widths, which you correct in the next section. Click OK to dismiss the message and display the labels in Print Preview (see Figure 16.36).

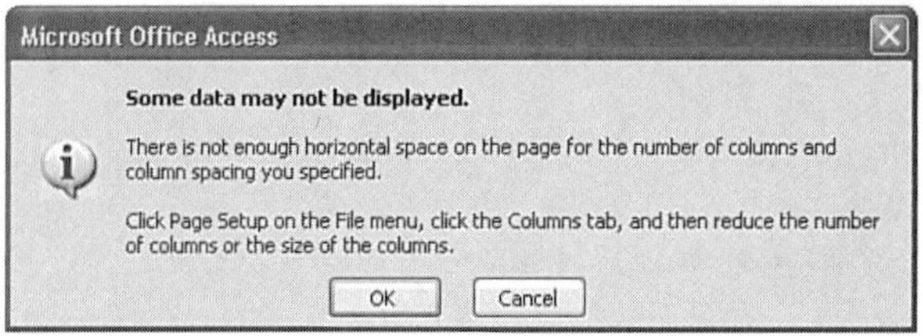

Figure 16.35 This error message occurs when using Avery 5160 labels, because the Wizard's page layout settings require a page width of 8.625 inches.

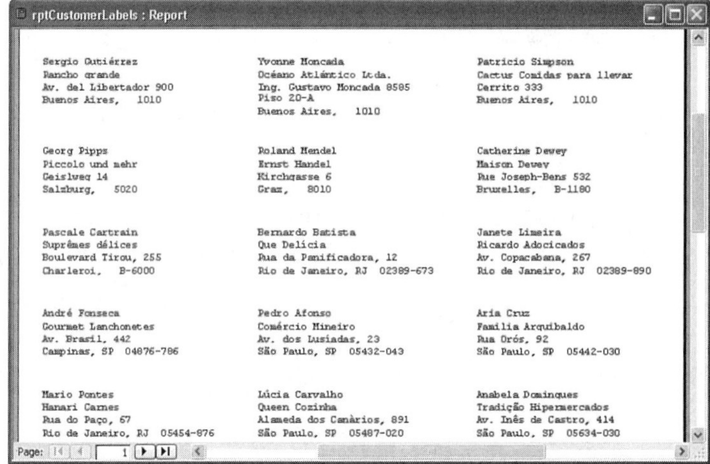

Figure 16.36 Print Preview in maximized window mode shows the first few labels. Type **88** or **90** in the Zoom box to check the top and side margins if your monitor is set to 800×600 resolution.

MODIFYING AN EXISTING MAILING LABEL REPORT

The Wizard doesn't let you add a line for Country, so you must alter the design of the report manually. To add the Country field to the label you created in the preceding section, do the following:

1. Change to Report Design view, press Ctrl+A to select all the text boxes, and move them up within one grid dot of the bottom of the Detail section header.
2. Click outside the text boxes to deselect them, select the ContactName text box, press Ctrl+C and Ctrl+V to add a copy of the text box to the Detail section.
3. Move the added text box directly under the `Trim([City]`... text box.

4. With the added text box selected, click Properties to open the Properties window, click the Data tab, and select Country in the Control Source list.

5. If you didn't add Country as the first sorting field in the fourth Wizard dialog, click the Sorting and Grouping button to open the dialog of the same name, select PostalCode, press Insert, and add Country above Postal Code in the Field/Expression list, and close the dialog.
6. To prepare for fixing the Wizard's column width miscalculation, press Ctrl+A to select the text boxes and move them one grid dot to the left.
7. Click the Select Report button, click the Format tab of the Properties window, and replace the 2.625 Width property value with **2.583**. When you move the cursor to another text box, 2.583 becomes 2.5826. Your modified design appears as shown in Figure 16.37.

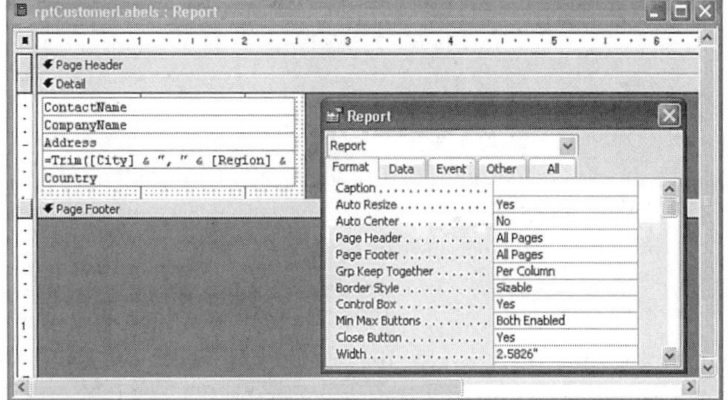

Figure 16.37 The modified label report design has the Country field added, text boxes relocated, and the width reduced.

NOTE

Following is the explanation of the 2.583-inch width for the label report: The Control Wizard calculates the required page width in inches as follows: 0.25 (left margin) + 3 * 2.625 (label width) + 2 * 0.125 (column spacing) + 0.25 (right margin) = 8.625. (In some cases, the right margin is 0.30, but you can change that to 0.25). You need to reduce the width of the labels so the page width is 8.5 or less. Dividing 0.125 by 3, rounding up to 0.042, and subtracting from 2.625 results in a required width of 2.583.

The result of the preceding calculation isn't perfect, because you need to take into account the reduced column width in setting the column spacing.

8. Click Print Preview and zoom the report to 100% scale. Verify that label spacing is consistent. In this example, the label for Yvonne Moncada has an extra address line. The added line pushes down labels below the row with the extra line, which results in a print registration error (see Figure 16.38). Registration errors of this type are cumulative, so if more than one row of a label page has an extra line the registration problem becomes serious.

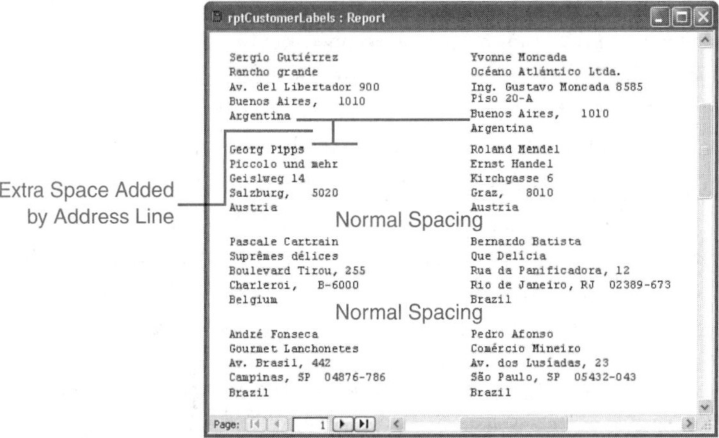

Figure 16.38
The increased space between the first and second lines of the labels is due to an extra line in the Address field of the label for Yvonne Moncado.

NOTE

> If the right margin is set to 0.25, you don't receive the error message shown in Figure 16.35. If you receive the message, choose File, Page Setup to open the Page Setup dialog, and set the right margin value to 0.25.

9. To correct the spacing problem, return to Design view, select the Details section's header bar, open the Properties window, click the Format tab, and set the Can Grow property value to No. Preventing the detail section from expanding results in all rows having the same spacing (compare Figure 16.39 with Figure 16.38).

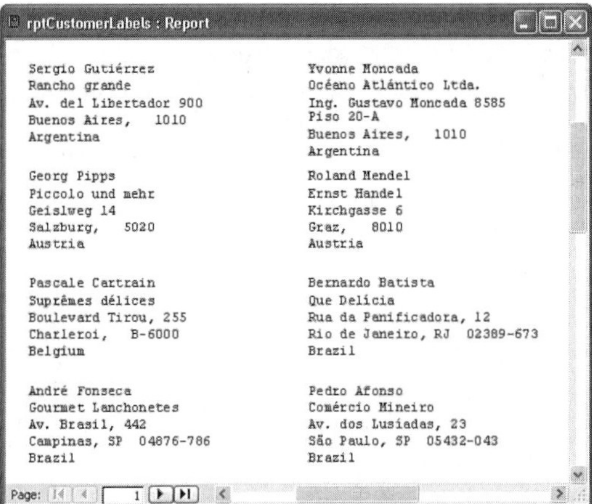

Figure 16.39
Setting the Can Grow property value of the Detail section of the label report prevents print registration problems. The space between the first and second rows is now the same as that between other rows.

10. Press Ctrl+S to save your design changes, change to Print Preview, and print a sample of all pages on plain paper. If your labels appear to print correctly, print the first page on label stock for a test. If registration is correct, print the remaining pages.

NOTE

> Tests with Avery 5160 labels and a Brother HL-1440 laser printer demonstrate that the left, top, and bottom margins set by the Wizard are satisfactory. You can fit six lines of 9-point type on a one-inch deep label.

The Page Setup dialog lets you tweak the Wizard's settings and your adjustments to improve label printing registration. You specify the number of columns in a row and the number of rows on a page by selecting settings in the Columns page of the Page Setup dialog, as shown in Figure 16.40. This dialog opens when you choose File, Page Setup in either Print Preview or Report Design view. The Label Wizard sets these values for you automatically and they change when you set new printing-related property values, but you might need to tweak them for the label stock or printer you use.

Figure 16.40
The Columns page of the Page Setup dialog lets you set the printing properties for reports using newspaper (snaking) columns. You also can change the column spacing and width, and the height (depth) of the labels.

The dialog's text boxes, check boxes, and option buttons let you set the following printing properties:

- The Number of Columns property sets the number of labels across the page. In this example, this property is set to 3, so the labels print three across.

NOTE

> The Left and Top margin settings (which you set on the Margins tab of the Page Setup dialog) specify the position at which Access prints the upper-left corner of the first label on the page. For most laser and inkjet printers, these values can't be less than about 0.25 inches. Labels designed for laser and inkjet printers are die cut so that the marginal areas remain on the backing sheet when you remove the individual labels.

- Row Spacing and the Height property determine the number of labels that fit vertically on a page and the vertical distance between successive labels. If you set Row Spacing to 0, the depth of your Detail section determines the vertical spacing of the labels.
- Column Spacing specifies the position of the left edge of columns to the right of the first column.
- The Width property in the Column Size group overrides the left margin, and the Height property overrides the bottom margin that you establish in Report Design view only if you clear the Same as Detail check box.
- The Down, Then Across option causes the labels to print in snaking column style. The first column is filled from top to bottom, then the second column is filled from top to bottom, and so on.
- The Across, Then Down option, the default for Wizard-created labels, causes the labels to print in columns from left to right and then in rows from the top to the bottom of the page. This setting is preferred for mailing labels because it wastes less label stock when using continuous-feed printers to print on stock with more than one label across.

NOTE

> You might have to make minor alignment adjustments because the upper-left corner of the printer's image and the upper-left corner of the paper might not correspond exactly.

The rptCustomerLabels report is included in Report16.mdb fn the accompanying CD-ROM in the \Seua11\Chaptr16 folder.

TROUBLESHOOTING

ELIMINATING EMPTY PAGES

When previewing or printing a report, Access displays or prints a blank page after each page with data.

If a report's width becomes greater than the net printable width (the paper width minus the sum of the left and right margins), the number of report pages doubles. Columns of fields that don't fit a page's width print on a second page, similar to the printing method used by spreadsheet applications. If you set your right margin beyond the right printing margin or if the right edge of any control on the report extends past the right printing margin, the added pages often are blank. Change the printing margins or reduce the width of your report so that it conforms to the printable page width. (See the section "Adjusting Margins and Printing Conventional Reports" earlier in this chapter.)

Unexpected Parameters Dialogs

A Parameters dialog appears when changing to report Preview mode, but the query to which the report is bound doesn't have parameters.

You misspelled one or more objects—usually text box or query field names—in expressions for text boxes or other controls that use calculated values. Click Cancel and verify that the expression in the Record Source property for each text box or other control on the report contains valid object names.

In the Real World—The Ephemeral Paperless Office

Business magazines of the 1980s and early 1990s touted the forthcoming "paperless office." Articles envisioned scanning incoming documents, storing the images in disk files, and handling all document processing on PC workstations. Document imaging and storage system vendors introduced a wide range of expensive hardware to support the paperless office concept. A new breed of consultants arrived on the scene to develop the workflow systems required to integrate document-processing hardware with existing business processes. Document imaging, workflow, and portal-based collaboration systems have become a multi-billion dollar industry.

Automotive and other large firms developed electronic document interchange (EDI) to process orders, invoices, and payments electronically. Email became a top contender to eliminate ever-growing piles of interoffice memos. Now large and small organizations alike are replacing complex EDI systems and their high-cost private (called *value-added*) networks with XML documents, XML Schema Definition (XSD) language, XSLT transformations, and the Internet.

XML-based business-to-business (B2B) communication was one of the hot topics of the late 1990's dot-net boom. Despite the subsequent decline of stock market valuation of firms at the bleeding edge of the erstwhile business-to-consumer (B2C) revolution, B2B transactions with standards-based XML Web services promise to replace B2C e-commerce as a major source of revenue for an army of software vendors and consultants. Much of Microsoft's .NET Framework and Visual Studio .NET marketing effort is directed to early adopters of XML Web services. Office 2003 isn't immune to Web services propaganda, as demonstrated by Chapter 31, "Creating and Consuming XML Web Services."

Paperless office is an oxymoron—the most popular PC peripheral component continues to be the printer. Sales of printer paper continue to grow at better than 10% per year, and the market for copiers and fax machines shows no signs of a significant slowdown. According to Hewlett-Packard, 90% of information in 1997 was stored on paper and 10% was in digital format; by 2004, HP estimates that paper-based storage will drop to 30%, with digital files holding 70%. The total amount of stored information doubles every four years or so. Thus, HP projects a continuing increase in the demand for printers and paper, and printers continue to deliver HP's highest margins.

Beginning with version 1.0, one of Access's strongest selling points has been its versatile, integrated report-printing capabilities. The report event model lets you write VBA code to customize report generation. Most other database front-end development platforms have add-on report generators, such as Crystal Decisions' Crystal Reports. Visual Basic 6.0's Report Designer, which replaces prior versions' Crystal Reports add-on, doesn't even come close to offering the rich feature set of Access 2003 reports. Visual Studio .NET 1.0 lacks an integrated report designer and relies on a "Lite" add-on version of Crystal Reports.

As this chapter demonstrates, designing and implementing informative, attractive reports can be a tedious process. Exact alignment and proper formatting of labels, text boxes, lines, and other report controls is far more important to reports than forms. Spending the time needed to make reports concise and graphically appealing is worthwhile, especially when you consider that paper reports most likely are destined for management. Cubicle operatives now fulfill most of their information needs electronically.

There have been surprisingly few changes to Access's report printing engine over the years, and Access 2003 incorporates no new report design features. (Microsoft released Report Snapshots, one of the subjects of the next chapter, as an add-in for Access 97.) Access 2002 delivered the capability to export live and static reports in XML format for Web distribution. Chapter 23, "Exporting and Importing Data with XML," covers XML Web reports in detail.

CHAPTER 17

PREPARING ADVANCED REPORTS

In this chapter

CREATING REPORTS FROM SCRATCH

Access 2003's Report Wizard can create reports that you can use "as is" or modify to suit most of your database reporting requirements. In many cases, however, you must create reports that are more complex than or different from those offered by the Report Wizard. For example, you might have to apply special grouping and sorting methods to your reports. Including subreports within your reports requires that you start from a blank report form instead of using the Report Wizard. Like subforms, subreports use master-child relationships to provide detail information, such as the orders placed by each customer by year, quarter, or month.

Reports make extensive use of unbound fields having calculated values. To understand fully the process of designing advanced Access reports independently of the Report Wizard, you must be familiar with VBA and Jet functions, which are two of the subjects of Chapter 10, "Understanding Jet Operators and Expressions." You also must understand the methods that you use to create and design forms, which are covered in Chapters 14, "Creating and Using Access Forms," and 15, "Designing Custom Multitable Forms." Reports make extensive use of Jet functions such as `Sum()` and VBA expressions such as `="Subtotal of" & [FieldName] & ":"`. If you skipped Chapters 10, 14, or 15, you might want to refer to the appropriate sections of those chapters whenever you encounter unfamiliar subjects or terminology in this chapter.

17

NOTE

The report design techniques you learn in this chapter apply, for the most part, to Access data projects (ADP). The queries on which you base reports in ADP must conform to Transact-SQL syntax. For example, you can't use Jet SQL's `TRANSFORM...PIVOT` statements to create ADP reports based on crosstab queries. You also can't include Jet-specific functions, such as `DLookup()` that are provided by the Jet expression service. Chapter 22, "Upsizing Jet Applications to Access Data Projects," describes the workarounds you need to adapt Jet-based reports to ADP.

GROUPING AND SORTING REPORT DATA

Most reports you create require that you organize the data into groups and subgroups in a style similar to the outline of a book. The Report Wizard lets you establish the initial grouping and sorting properties for your data, but you might want to rearrange your report's data after reviewing the Report Wizard's first draft.

The Sorting and Grouping dialog (see Figure 17.1) lets you modify these report properties in design mode. The sections that follow modify the Inventory by Category report that you created in the preceding chapter. The sorting and grouping methods described here, however, apply to any report that you create. To display the dialog, open the report in Design view and click the toolbar's Sorting and Grouping button.

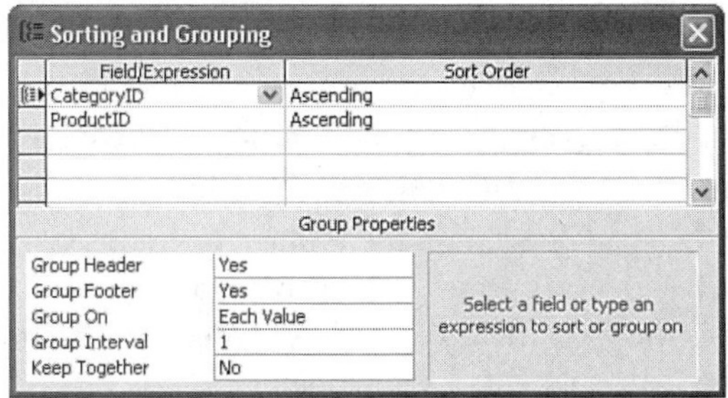

Figure 17.1
Use the Sorting and Grouping dialog to classify and sort your reports by numeric or alphabetic values.

Property values you set in the Sorting and Grouping dialog determine the fields or expressions on which Access is to group the products, up to a maximum of 10 fields or expressions. You can sort the groups and grouped data in ascending or descending order, but you must select one or the other; "unsorted" isn't an option. The small Sorting and Grouping icon in the selection button at the left of the window indicates that Access uses the field or expression in the adjacent column to group the records.

17

GROUPING DATA

The method that you use to group data depends on the type of data in the field you plan to group. You can group by categories, in which case a unique value must represent each category. You can group data by a range of values, which usually are numeric but also can be alphabetic. You can use the data in a field to group the report rows, or you can substitute an expression as the basis for the grouping.

NOTE

Reports demonstrating the grouping examples of the following sections are included in the Report17.mdb database in the \Seua10\Chaptr17 folder of the accompanying CD-ROM.

GROUPING BY NUMERIC VALUES

When you told the Report Wizard in the preceding chapter to use CategoryID as the field by which to group, you elected to group by a numeric value. You can alter the grouping sequence easily by using the Sorting and Grouping dialog. For example, you can group the inventory report by SupplierID to aid in comparing the inventory turnover rate of products from multiple suppliers. The report you create in the later "Working from a Blank Report" section provides some insight into inventory turnover by product category, not by supplier.

→ To review the Report Wizard process, **see** "Creating a Grouping Report with the Report Wizard," **p. 638**.

To group the Inventory by Category report by SupplierID, do the following:

1. If you don't already have it open, open the rptInventoryByCategory report in Design view, and save the report as **rptInventoryBySupplier**. Change the title text box and report Caption property value to **Inventory by Supplier**.

2. Click the Sorting and Grouping icon on the toolbar, open CategoryID's drop-down list, and select SupplierID as the first group field. When you change the group field, Access automatically renames the Group Header and Footer sections from CategoryID to SupplierID. Close the Sorting and Grouping dialog.
3. Delete the CategoryID lookup list in the SupplierID Footer section; CategoryID isn't appropriate to the new grouping.

4. Open the Field List and drag the SupplierID field to the SupplierID Footer section, and drop it in the position formerly occupied by CategoryID. SupplierID is a lookup field, so the new control for the field is a drop-down list.
5. Delete the label and position the SupplierID list at the top left of the Footer. Remove the % Cat. Units label and text box to make room for the long CompanyName values displayed by the SupplierID list. Widen the SupplierID control to about 2.5 inches, apply the Bold attribute, and change the font size of all controls in the SupplierID Footer section to 9 points (see Figure 17.2).

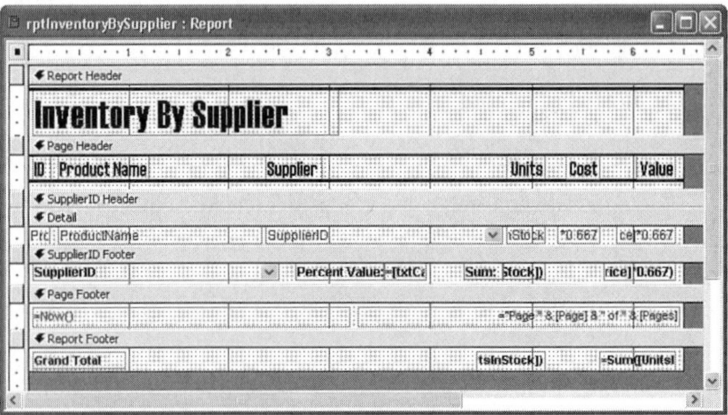

Figure 17.2 You can quickly repurpose an existing report by changing its Group By property value and making minor design changes to the new report.

6. Save your design changes, and open the report in Print Preview (see Figure 17.3).

Grouping by Alphabetic Code Characters

If you use a systematic code for grouping, you can group by the first five or fewer characters of the code field. With an expression, you can group by any set of characters within a field. To group by the second and third digits of a code, for example, use the following expression:

```
=Mid([FieldName], 2, 2)
```

Figure 17.3 The Supplier column in the repurposed inventory report is redundant, but doesn't detract from the overall value of the report.

Inventory By Supplier

Inventory By Supplier

ID	Product Name	Supplier		Units	Cost	Value
1	Chai	Exotic Liquids		39	12.01	468.23
2	Chang	Exotic Liquids		17	12.67	215.44
3	Aniseed Syrup	Exotic Liquids		13	6.67	86.71
Exotic Liquids		**Percent Value 1.66%**	**Sum:**	**69**		**$770.39**
4	Chef Anton's Cajun Seasoning	New Orleans Cajun Delights		53	14.67	777.72
65	Louisiana Fiery Hot Pepper Sauce	New Orleans Cajun Delights		76	14.04	1,067.07
66	Louisiana Hot Spiced Okra	New Orleans Cajun Delights		4	11.34	45.36
New Orleans Cajun Delights		**Percent Value 4.07%**	**Sum:**	**133**		**$1,890.14**
6	Grandma's Boysenberry Spread	Grandma Kelly's Homestead		120	16.68	2,001.00
7	Uncle Bob's Organic Dried Pears	Grandma Kelly's Homestead		15	20.01	300.15
8	Northwoods Cranberry Sauce	Grandma Kelly's Homestead		6	26.68	160.08
Grandma Kelly's Homestead		**Percent Value 5.30%**	**Sum:**	**141**		**$2,461.23**
10	Ikura	Tokyo Traders		31	20.68	640.99
74	Longlife Tofu	Tokyo Traders		4	6.67	26.68
Tokyo Traders		**Percent Value 1.44%**	**Sum:**	**35**		**$667.67**
11	Queso Cabrales	Cooperativa de Quesos 'Las Cabras'		22	14.01	308.15
12	Queso Manchego La Pastora	Cooperativa de Quesos 'Las Cabras'		86	25.35	2,179.76
Cooperativa de Quesos 'Las Cabras'		**Percent Value 5.36%**	**Sum:**	**108**		**$2,487.91**

Page: 1

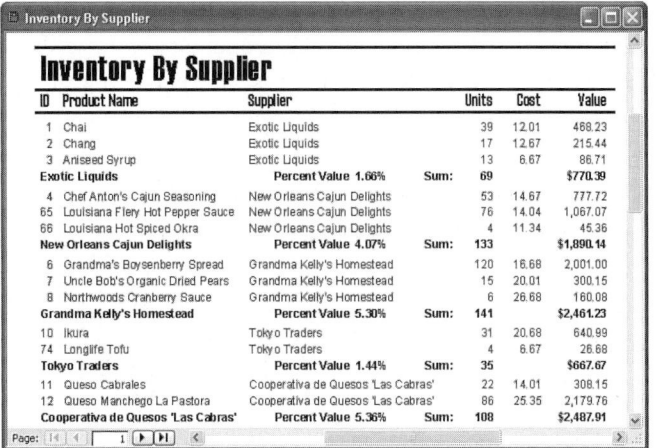

Mid's first numeric argument is the position of the starting character on which to group, and the second is the number of characters to use for grouping.

Grouping with Subgroups

If your table or query contains appropriate data, you can group reports by more than one level by creating subgroups. The Employee Sales by Country report (one of the Northwind Traders sample reports), for example, uses groups (Country) and subgroups (the employee's name—the actual group is a VBA expression that combines the FirstName and LastName fields—to organize orders received within a range of dates. Open the Employee Sales by Country report in Design view to view the additional section created by a subgroup. Change to Print Preview, and type **1/1/1996** and **12/31/1998** as the values of the Beginning Date and Ending Date Enter Parameter Value dialogs to view all orders.

Using a Function to Group by Range

You often must sort reports by ranges of values. (If you opened the Employee Sales by Country report, close it and reopen the rptInventoryByCategory report in Design mode.) If you want to divide the Inventory by Category report into a maximum of nine sections—each beginning with a three-letter group of the alphabet (A through C, D through F, and so on) based on the ProductName field—the entries in the Sorting and Grouping dialog should look like the entries in Figure 17.4.

Alphabetic grouping demonstrates a grouping bug that's been present since Access 2.0. VBA's `=Asc([ProductName])` function returns the ASCII (numeric) value of the first character of its string argument, the ProductName field. You set the Group On specification to Interval and then set the Group Interval to 3. This setup *theoretically* groups the data into names beginning with A through C, D through F, and so on. You must add an ascending sort on ProductName to assure alphabetic sorting within the group (see Figure 17.5). You delete all text boxes in the Group Footer because subtotals by alphabetic groups aren't significant. Although of limited value in this report, an alphabetic grouping often is useful for formatting long, alphabetized lists to assist readers in finding a particular record.

Sorting and Grouping

Field/Expression	Sort Order
=Asc([ProductName])	Ascending
ProductName	Ascending

Group Properties

Group Header	Yes
Group Footer	Yes
Group On	Interval
Group Interval	3
Keep Together	No

Select a field or type an expression to sort or group on

Figure 17.4 Set the Group By properties to those shown here to group product names by a three-initial-letter interval.

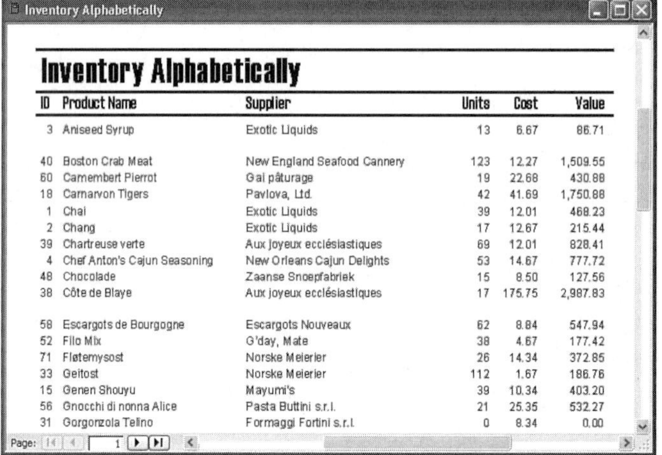

Inventory Alphabetically

ID	Product Name	Supplier	Units	Cost	Value
3	Aniseed Syrup	Exotic Liquids	13	6.67	86.71
40	Boston Crab Meat	New England Seafood Cannery	123	12.27	1,509.55
60	Camembert Pierrot	Gai pâturage	19	22.68	430.88
18	Carnarvon Tigers	Pavlova, Ltd.	42	41.69	1,750.88
1	Chai	Exotic Liquids	39	12.01	468.23
2	Chang	Exotic Liquids	17	12.67	215.44
39	Chartreuse verte	Aux joyeux ecclésiastiques	69	12.01	828.41
4	Chef Anton's Cajun Seasoning	New Orleans Cajun Delights	53	14.67	777.72
48	Chocolade	Zaanse Snoepfabriek	15	8.50	127.56
38	Côte de Blaye	Aux joyeux ecclésiastiques	17	175.75	2,987.83
58	Escargots de Bourgogne	Escargots Nouveaux	62	8.84	547.94
52	Filo Mix	G'day, Mate	38	4.67	177.42
71	Fløtemysost	Norske Meierier	26	14.34	372.85
33	Geitost	Norske Meierier	112	1.67	186.76
15	Genen Shouyu	Mayumi's	39	10.34	403.20
56	Gnocchi di nonna Alice	Pasta Buttini s.r.l.	21	25.35	532.27
31	Gorgonzola Telino	Formaggi Fortini s.r.l.	0	8.34	0.00

Figure 17.5 A bug in Access's interval grouping process when using a VBA expression causes grouping by A, B to D, E to G, and so on. This bug has been present since Access 2.0.

GROUPING ON DATE AND TIME

If you group data on a field with a Date/Time data type, Access lets you set the Sorting and Grouping dialog's Group On property to Year, Qtr (quarter), Month, Week, Day, Hour, or Minute. To group records so that values of the same quarter for several years print in sequence, type the following in the Field/Expression column of the Sorting and Grouping dialog:

```
=DatePart("q",[FieldName])
```

→ For a full listing of ways you can sort by date or time, **see** "Functions for Date and Time," **p. 370**.

SORTING DATA GROUPS

Although most data sorting within groups is based on the values contained in a field, you also can sort by expressions. When compiling an inventory evaluation list based on the original Inventory by Category report, the products with the highest extended inventory value are the most important. The report's users might want these products listed first in a group. This decision requires sorting the records within groups on the expression `=[UnitsInStock]*[UnitPrice]`, which is similar to the expression that calculates the report's Value column. (You don't need to account for the constant markup multiplier when sorting.) A descending sort is necessary to place the highest values at the top of the report. Figure 17.6 shows the required entries in the Sorting and Grouping dialog.

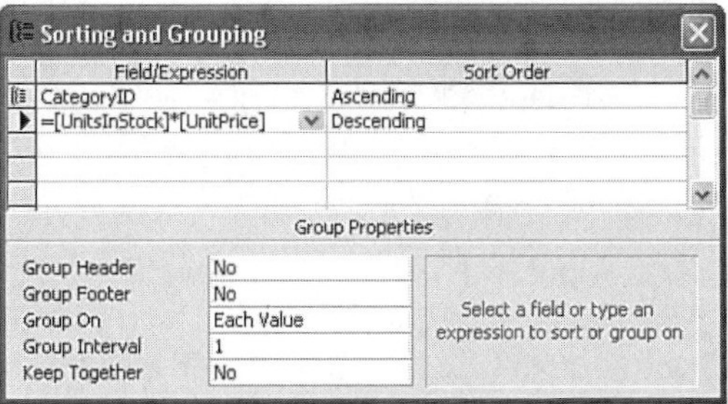

Figure 17.6 The expression in the second row of the Sorting and Grouping dialog places items with the largest inventory value at the top of each CategoryID group.

The descending sort on the inventory value expression results in the report shown in Figure 17.7. As expected, the products with the highest inventory value appear first in each category.

Inventory by Category and Value

Inventory By Category and Value

ID	Product Name	Supplier	Units	Cost	Value
38	Côte de Blaye	Aux joyeux ecclésiastiques	17	175.75	2,987.83
34	Sasquatch Ale	Bigfoot Breweries	111	9.34	1,036.52
39	Chartreuse verte	Aux joyeux ecclésiastiques	69	12.01	828.41
76	Lakkalikööri	Karkki Oy	57	12.01	684.34
75	Rhönbräu Klosterbier	Plutzer Lebensmittelgroßmärkte AG	125	5.17	646.16
43	Ipoh Coffee	Leka Trading	17	30.68	521.59
67	Laughing Lumberjack Lager	Bigfoot Breweries	52	9.34	485.58
1	Chai	Exotic Liquids	39	12.01	468.23
35	Steeleye Stout	Bigfoot Breweries	20	12.01	240.12
2	Chang	Exotic Liquids	17	12.67	215.44
70	Outback Lager	Pavlova, Ltd.	15	10.01	150.08
Category: Beverages	**% Cat Units: 17.86%**	**Value: 17.80% Sum:**	**539**		**$8,264.30**
61	Sirop d'érable	Forêts d'érables	113	19.01	2,148.07
6	Grandma's Boysenberry Spread	Grandma Kelly's Homestead	120	16.68	2,001.00
65	Louisiana Fiery Hot Pepper Sauce	New Orleans Cajun Delights	76	14.04	1,067.07
4	Chef Anton's Cajun Seasoning	New Orleans Cajun Delights	53	14.67	777.72
63	Vegie-spread	Pavlova, Ltd.	24	29.28	702.75
15	Genen Shouyu	Mayumi's	39	10.34	403.20
44	Gula Malacca	Leka Trading	27	12.97	350.28
77	Original Frankfurter grüne Soße	Plutzer Lebensmittelgroßmärkte AG	32	8.67	277.47

Page: 1

Figure 17.7 The grouping and sorting properties shown in Figure 17.6 result in a report that places emphasizes on the most important elements within a group.

17

WORKING FROM A BLANK REPORT

Usually, the fastest way to set up a report is to use the Report Wizard to create a basic report and then modify the basic report as described in Chapter 16, and previous sections of this chapter. If you're creating a report style that the Wizard can't handle or a report containing a subreport, however, modifying a standard report style created by the Report Wizard could take longer than creating a report by using the default blank report that Access provides.

USING A REPORT AS A SUBREPORT

The report you design in the following sections includes information about total monthly orders for products by category. Comparing the monthly orders to the inventory level of a category allows the report's user to estimate inventory turnover rates. This report serves two purposes—a primary report and a subreport within another report. You add the Monthly Orders by Category report as a subreport of the Inventory by Category report in the "Incorporating Subreports" section later in this chapter.

To create a report to use as the Monthly Orders by Category subreport (rpt1997MonthlyCategoryOrders) in the section of this chapter, "Adding and Deleting Sections of Your Report," you need to base the subreport on a query, qry1997MonthlyProductOrdersCT, adapted for this purpose.

A copy of the qry1997MonthlyProductOrdersCT query is included in the Report17.mdb database in the \Seua10\Chaptr17 folder of the accompanying CD-ROM.

→ To review how to create this crosstab query, **see** "Designing a Monthly Product Sales Crosstab Query," **p. 448**.

To modify the query for this subreport, follow these steps:

1. Close any open report(s) and click the Queries shortcut in the Database window.

2. Open the qry1997MonthlyProductOrdersCT query in Design view.
3. In the grid, change the first column's field name from ProductID to CategoryID by opening the Field drop-down list and clicking the CategoryID field name. You need the CategoryID field to link with the CategoryID field in the qryInventory query that the Inventory by Category report uses as its data source.
4. Delete the ProductName column. The modified query appears as shown in Figure 17.8.

5. Choose File, Save As and name the modified query **qry1997MonthlyCategoryOrdersCT**. Click Run to check the query. Your query result set appears as shown in Figure 17.9.

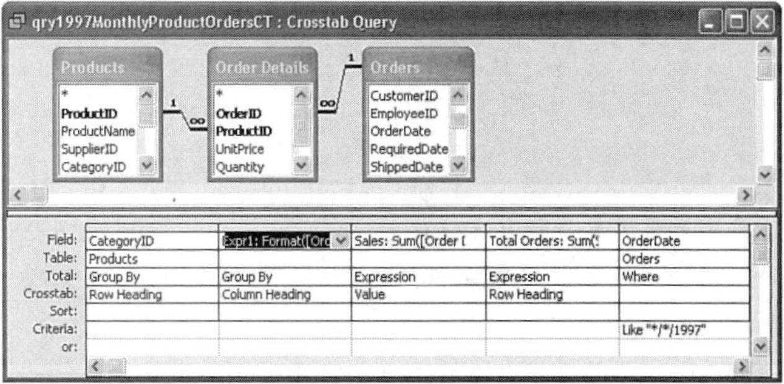

Figure 17.8 The query for inventory analysis uses RequiredDate rather than OrderDate to more accurately reflect the date on which an order became a sale.

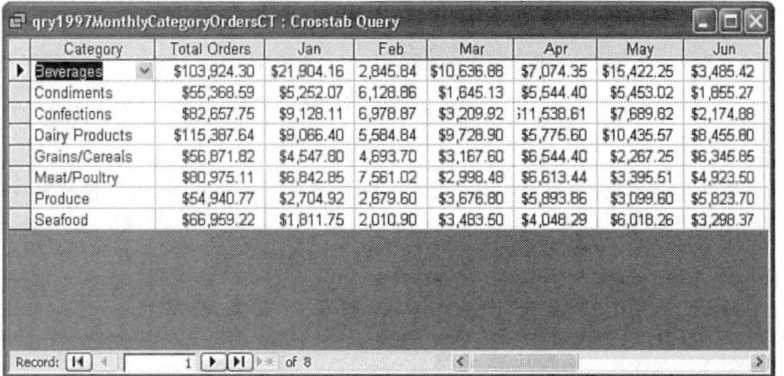

Category	Total Orders	Jan	Feb	Mar	Apr	May	Jun
Beverages	$103,924.30	$21,904.16	2,845.84	$10,636.88	$7,074.35	$15,422.25	$3,485.42
Condiments	$55,368.59	$5,252.07	6,128.86	$1,645.13	$5,544.40	$5,453.02	$1,855.27
Confections	$82,657.75	$9,128.11	6,978.87	$3,209.92	;11,538.61	$7,689.82	$2,174.88
Dairy Products	$115,387.64	$9,066.40	5,584.84	$9,728.90	$5,775.60	$10,435.57	$8,455.80
Grains/Cereals	$56,871.82	$4,547.80	4,693.70	$3,167.60	$6,544.40	$2,267.25	$6,345.85
Meat/Poultry	$80,975.11	$6,842.85	7,561.02	$2,998.48	$6,613.44	$3,395.51	$4,923.50
Produce	$54,940.77	$2,704.92	2,679.60	$3,676.80	$5,893.86	$3,099.60	$5,823.70
Seafood	$66,959.22	$1,811.75	2,010.90	$3,483.50	$4,048.29	$6,018.26	$3,298.37

Record: 1 of 8

Figure 17.9 The query includes a Grand Total column that's useful for calculating inventory turns (total yearly sales divided by inventory value).

6. Open the New Object drop-down list on the toolbar, and select Report from the list to open the New Report dialog.
7. Access automatically selects qry1997MonthlyCategoryOrdersCT as the query on which to base the report. Select Design View from the list and click OK. Access opens the default blank report shown in Figure 17.10.

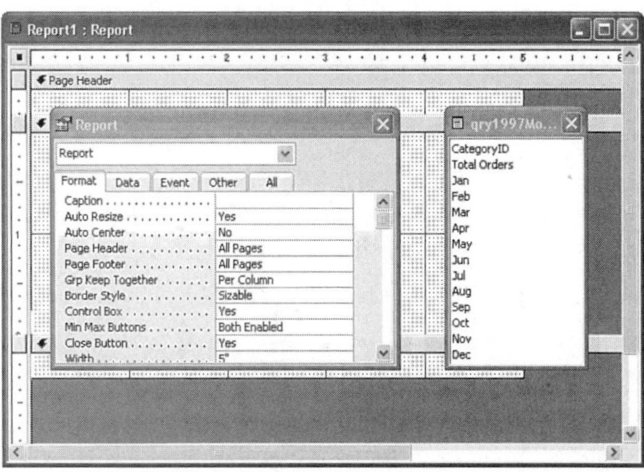

Figure 17.10 This blank report is the starting point for the subreport you add to the Inventory by Category report later in the chapter.

CREATING THE MONTHLY SALES BY CATEGORY REPORT

The crosstab query that acts as the Monthly Sales by Category report's data source is closely related to a report, but the crosstab query doesn't include detail records. Each row of the query consists of subtotals of sales for a category for each month of the year. One row appears below the inventory value subtotal when you link the subreport (child) to the main (master) report, so this report needs only a Detail section. Each detail row, however, requires a header label to print the month. The CategoryID field is included so that you can verify that the data is linked correctly.

To complete the Monthly Sales by Category report (and later a subreport), follow these steps:

1. In the blank report you opened in the preceding section, remove the default Page Header and Page Footer sections by choosing View, Page Header/Footer to clear the toggle check mark. This subreport only requires a Detail section. By default, blank reports have 24×24 grid dots, and Snap to Grid is selected.

2. Drag the right margin of the Detail section to the right so that the report is about 6 3/8 inches wide.
3. Click the toolbar's Sorting and Grouping button to display the dialog, and select CategoryID as the field to use to sort the data with a standard ascending sort. Close the Sorting and Grouping dialog.
4. Click the toolbar's Field List button, if necessary, select CategoryID, and drag its field symbol to the Detail section.
5. Click the CategoryID label and relocate the label to the upper left of the Detail section directly over the CategoryID combo box. (CategoryID appears as a combo box, not a text box, in Report Design view because CategoryID is a lookup field.) Adjust the depth of the label and text boxes so that each equals 0.2 inches (four grid dots), and adjust the width to 1 inch. Edit the label's text to **Category**.
6. Click and drag the field list's Jan field to 1/8 inch (three dots) to the right of the CategoryID field. Move the label to the top of the section, adjacent to the right border of the field to its left. Move the text box under the label. Adjust the label and text box depth to four dots and the width to 16 dots (3/4 inch). Edit the label's text to delete the colon.
7. Repeat step 6 for the month fields of Feb through Jun, separating the fields by 1/8 inch. The report design now appears as shown in Figure 17.11.
8. Click each month label while holding down the Shift key so that you select all six labels (but only the labels).
9. Click the toolbar's Bold button to add the bold attribute to the labels. Then click the Center button to center the labels above the text boxes.
10. Select the CategoryID text box and the label, and click the Bold button.

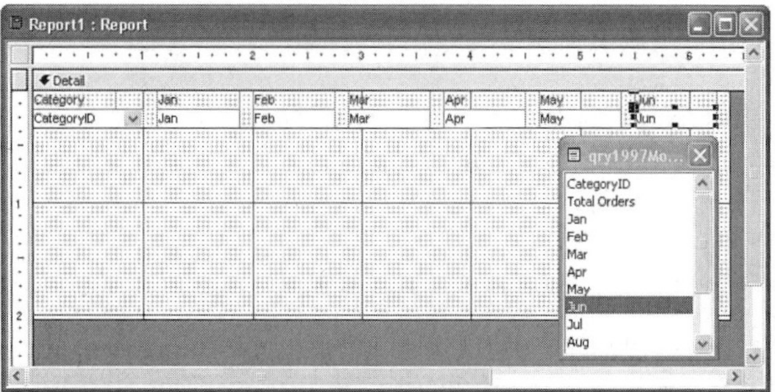

Figure 17.11 Start the report design by adding the CategoryID field and the Jan through Jun fields of the query to the first row of labels and text boxes.

11. Select each of the six month text boxes, and click the Right button to right-align the dollar amounts.

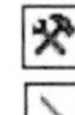

12. If the Toolbox isn't visible, click the Toolbox button on the toolbar. Click the Line tool and add a line at the top edge of the labels. Drag the line's right-end handle to the right edge of the Jun text box.

13. With the line you added selected, click the drop-down list of the Line/Border Width button on the toolbar and click the 1-point line thickness button.
14. Repeat steps 12 and 13 for another identical line but add the new line under the labels (and above the text boxes).
15. Drag the Detail section's margins to within two dots of the bottom and right edge of the controls. The report's design appears as shown in Figure 17.12.

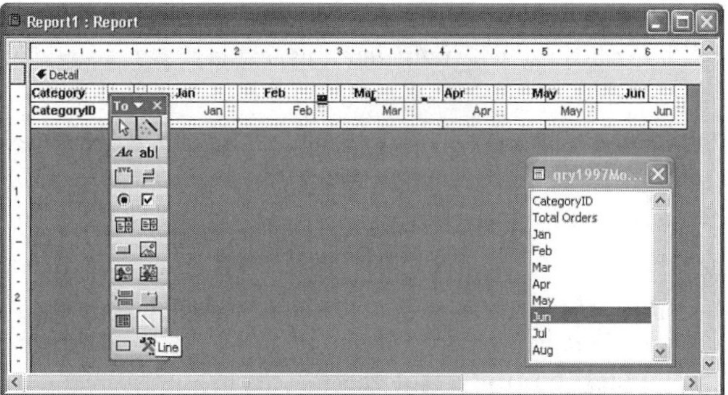

Figure 17.12 Format and align the labels, align the text boxes, and add two one-point lines to dress up the report.

16. Click Print Preview to verify the design (see Figure 17.13).
17. Press Ctrl+S and type **rpt1997MonthlyCategoryOrders** as the report's name.

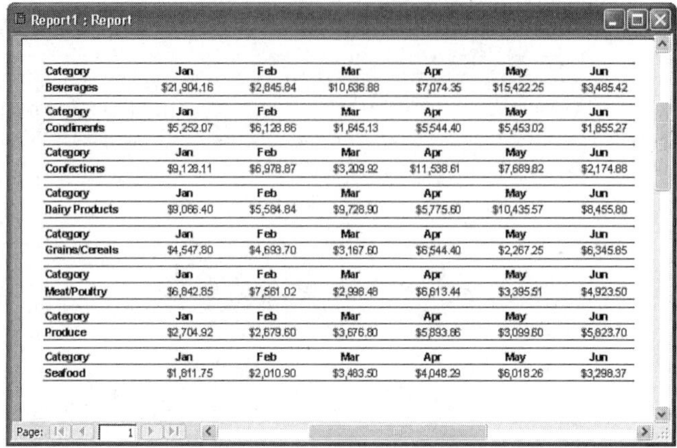

Figure 17.13
Confirm the first phase of the report's design in Print Preview.

17

To add the remaining months of the year and the Grand Total field to your report, follow these steps:

1. To accommodate another row of labels and text boxes, increase the depth of the Detail section by dragging the bottom margin down about 1 inch.
2. Press Ctrl+A or choose Edit, Select All to select all the controls in the Details section.
3. Press Ctrl+C to copy the labels, text boxes, and lines to the Clipboard.
4. Press Ctrl+V to paste a copy of the labels and text boxes to the Detail section.
5. Move this copy directly under the original labels and text boxes.
6. Click a blank area of the report to deselect the controls; then select and delete the new CategoryID text box. When you delete this text box, you also delete the associated label.
7. Edit both the labels and text boxes to display Jul through Dec. (Access automatically resizes the labels to fit the new text value and automatically sets the text boxes' Control Source property to match the field name you type into the text box.)
8. Open the field list, if necessary, and add the Total Orders field and label in place of the second CategoryID field and label you deleted in step 6. Change the label caption to Year Total, select the label and text box, and apply the Bold attribute. Adjust the width of the label and text box to 16 grid dots (3/4 inch).
9. Press Ctrl+A to select all the controls, and choose Format, Align, To Grid to correct any minor alignment discrepancies.
10. Drag the bottom margin up to within two dots of the bottom of the text boxes in the second row. Figure 17.14 shows the final report design.
11. Click Print Preview to display the double-row report (see Figure 17.15).

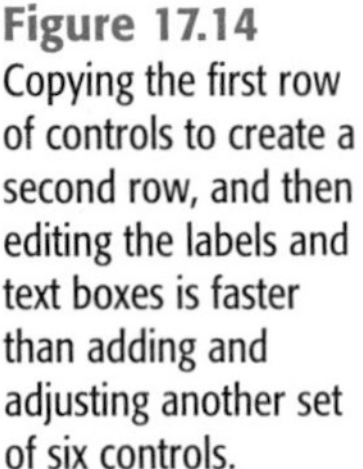

Figure 17.14
Copying the first row of controls to create a second row, and then editing the labels and text boxes is faster than adding and adjusting another set of six controls.

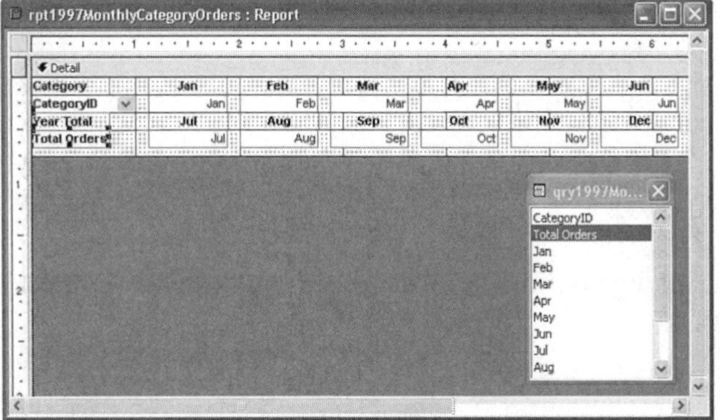

Figure 17.15
Print Preview displays the report design of Figure 17.14.

rpt1997MonthlyCategoryOrders : Report

Category	Jan	Feb	Mar	Apr	May	Jun
Beverages	$21,904.16	$2,845.84	$10,636.88	$7,074.35	$15,422.25	$3,485.42
Year Total	Jul	Aug	Sep	Oct	Nov	Dec
$103,924.30	$7,889.22	$5,836.92	$5,726.70	$8,374.90	$3,851.00	$10,876.65
Category	Jan	Feb	Mar	Apr	May	Jun
Condiments	$5,252.07	$6,128.86	$1,645.13	$5,544.40	$5,453.02	$1,855.27
Year Total	Jul	Aug	Sep	Oct	Nov	Dec
$55,368.59	$6,519.83	$4,220.02	$3,575.18	$6,565.91	$3,784.67	$5,824.20
Category	Jan	Feb	Mar	Apr	May	Jun
Confections	$9,128.11	$6,978.87	$3,209.92	$11,538.61	$7,689.82	$2,174.88
Year Total	Jul	Aug	Sep	Oct	Nov	Dec
$82,657.75	$6,462.60	$7,105.63	$6,708.59	$7,800.70	$5,081.85	$8,778.15
Category	Jan	Feb	Mar	Apr	May	Jun
Dairy Products	$9,066.40	$5,584.84	$9,728.90	$5,775.60	$10,435.57	$8,455.80
Year Total	Jul	Aug	Sep	Oct	Nov	Dec
$115,387.64	$12,387.35	$6,826.55	$11,420.30	$12,869.00	$12,992.47	$9,844.85
Category	Jan	Feb	Mar	Apr	May	Jun
Grains/Cereals	$4,547.80	$4,693.70	$3,167.60	$6,544.40	$2,267.25	$6,345.85
Year Total	Jul	Aug	Sep	Oct	Nov	Dec
$56,871.02	$4,457.80	$5,415.25	$5,371.47	$3,031.00	$5,787.35	$5,242.35

Page: 1

12. Close the rpt1997MonthlyCategoryOrders report and save the changes.

The technique of copying controls to the Clipboard, pasting copies to reports, and then editing the copies is often faster than creating duplicate controls that differ from one another only in the text of labels and the field names of bound text boxes.

INCORPORATING SUBREPORTS

Reports, like forms, can include subreports. Unlike the Form Wizard, however, the Report Wizard offers no option for automatically creating reports that include subreports. You can add subreports to reports that you create with the Report Wizard, or you can create subreports from blank reports, like you did in the earlier section, "Working from a Blank Report."

ADDING A LINKED SUBREPORT TO A BOUND REPORT

If a main report is bound to a table or query as a data source and the subreport's data source can be related to the main report's data source, you can link the subreport's data to the main report's data.

To add and link the rpt1997MonthlyCategoryOrders report as a subreport to the Inventory by Category report, for example, follow these steps:

1. Open the original version of the rptInventoryByCategory report from Chapter 16 in Design view.
2. Drag down the top of the Page Footer border to make room for the subreport in the CategoryID Footer section (about 0.5 inch).

3. Click the toolbar's Database Window button. If the Database window is maximized, click the Restore button.
4. Click and drag the small Report icon from the left of the rpt1997MonthlyCategoryOrders report to a location inside the CategoryID Footer section. The caret becomes an arrow with a plus (+) sign inside a square. Position the tip of the arrow one dot to the right of the left margin and one dot below the bottom of the CategoryID text box.
5. When you release the right mouse button, Access adds a subreport control, which displays the subreport in Design view within a frame for in-site editing. Delete the subreport's label (see Figure 17.16).

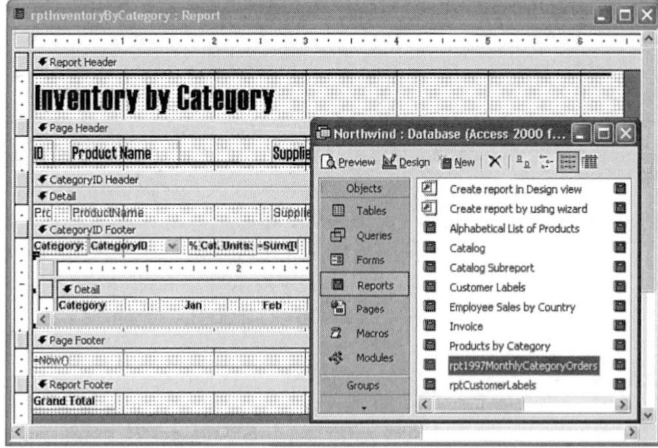

Figure 17.16 Drag a report's icon to a section of another report and drop it to automatically add the subreport.

6. Adjust the CategoryID Footer's depth to provide about 0.1-inch margins above and below the section's controls.

7. You need to link the data in the subreport to the data of the main report so that only the sales data corresponding to a specific group's CategoryID value appears in the CategoryID footer section. Select the subreport control's frame—*not the subreport inside the frame*—and click the Properties button to display the subreport's Properties window. Click the Data tab, and click the Builder button of the Link Child Fields property's text box or the Link Master Fields text box to open the Subreport Field Linker dialog (see Figure 17.17).

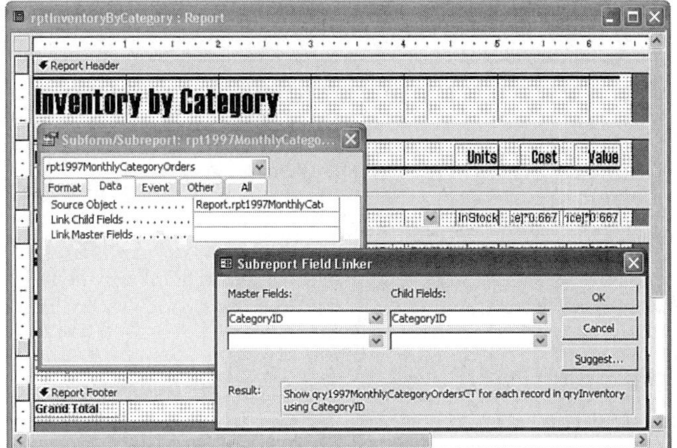

Figure 17.17 Be sure to select the frame, which displays the sizing handles, when you click the Properties button to create the link. If the sizing handles aren't visible, the Data page doesn't display the two Link... text boxes.

8. If the link is correct, click OK to close the Subreport Field Linker dialog, and then close the Properties window.

9. Click the toolbar's Print Preview button to display the report in the full-size view. The subreport appears as shown at the bottom of Figure 17.18. Click the page selector buttons to view other parts of the subreport to confirm that the linkage is correct.

Inventory by Category

Inventory by Category

ID	Product Name	Supplier	Units	Cost	Value
1	Chai	Exotic Liquids	39	12.01	468.23
2	Chang	Exotic Liquids	17	12.67	215.44
34	Sasquatch Ale	Bigfoot Breweries	111	9.34	1,036.52
35	Steeleye Stout	Bigfoot Breweries	20	12.01	240.12
38	Côte de Blaye	Aux joyeux ecclésiastiques	17	175.75	2,987.83
39	Chartreuse verte	Aux joyeux ecclésiastiques	69	12.01	828.41
43	Ipoh Coffee	Leka Trading	17	30.68	521.59
67	Laughing Lumberjack Lager	Bigfoot Breweries	52	9.34	485.58
70	Outback Lager	Pavlova, Ltd.	15	10.01	150.08
75	Rhönbräu Klosterbier	Plutzer Lebensmittelgroßmärk	125	5.17	646.16
76	Lakkalikööri	Karkki Oy	57	12.01	684.34

Category: Beverages % Cat. Units: 17.86% Value: 17.80% Cat. Units: 539 Cat. Value: $8,264.30

Category	Jan	Feb	Mar	Apr	May	Jun
Beverages	$21,904.16	$2,845.84	$10,636.88	$7,074.35	$15,422.25	$3,485.42
Year Total	**Jul**	**Aug**	**Sep**	**Oct**	**Nov**	**Dec**
$103,924.30	$7,889.22	$5,836.92	$5,726.70	$8,374.90	$3,851.00	$10,876.65

ID	Product Name	Supplier	Units	Cost	Value
3	Aniseed Syrup	Exotic Liquids	13	6.67	86.71
4	Chef Anton's Cajun Seasoning	New Orleans Cajun Delights	53	14.67	777.72

Page: 1

Figure 17.18 The appropriate rows of the linked subreport print below the text boxes in the CategoryID Footer section.

10. Choose File, Save As, and save the modified report as **rptInventoryByCategoryWith1997Sales.**

You can add and link several subreports to the main report if each subreport has a field in common with the main report's data source.

TIP

> You can use calculated values to link main reports and subreports. Calculated values often are based on time–months, quarters, or years. To link main reports and subreports by calculated values, you must create queries for both the main report and subreport that include the calculated value in a field, such as Month or Year. You create the calculated field in each query by using the corresponding Access date function, `Month` or `Year`. To group by quarters, select Interval for the Group On property and set the value of the Group Interval property to 3. You can't use Qtr as the Group On property because the calculated value lacks the Date/Time field data type.

17

If you receive an error message when you try to create a link between the main report and subreport, turn to "Link Expression Errors," in the "Troubleshooting" section at the end of this chapter.

USING UNLINKED SUBREPORTS AND UNBOUND REPORTS

Most reports that you create use subreports that are linked to the main report's data source. You can, however, insert independent subreports within main reports. In this case, you don't enter values for the Link Child Fields and Link Master Fields properties. The subreport's data source can be related to or completely independent of the main report's data source.

Figure 17.19 illustrates the effect of including an unlinked subreport in a main report. The figure shows a part of page 1 of the rpt1997MonthlyCategoryOrders subreport within the rptInventoryByCategoryWith1997Sales report after deleting the CategoryID values of the Link Child Fields and Link Master Fields properties, prior to saving the report with a new name. Notice that without the link, the subreport displays all records instead of just those records related to the particular category in which the subreport appears. You might need to set the CategoryID Footer section's Keep Together property to No to display the subform on the first page. The Keep Together property is one of the subjects of the "Controlling Page Breaks and Printing Page Headers and Footers" section later in the chapter.

You can add multiple subreports to an unbound report if all the subreports fit on one page of the report or across the page. In the latter case, you can use the landscape printing orientation to increase the available page width. To create an unbound report with previously created multiple subreports, follow these steps:

1. Click the Reports shortcut in the Database window, if necessary, and then click the New button to display the New Report dialog.
2. Keep the text element of the combo box for the New Report dialog's data source blank, select Design View in the list, and then click OK. This action creates an unbound report.

Inventory by Category with 1997 Sales

43	Ipoh Coffee	Leka Trading	17	30.68	521.59
67	Laughing Lumberjack Lager	Bigfoot Breweries	52	9.34	485.58
70	Outback Lager	Pavlova, Ltd.	15	10.01	150.08
75	Rhönbräu Klosterbier	Plutzer Lebensmittelgroßmärk	125	5.17	646.16
76	Lakkalikööri	Karkki Oy	57	12.01	684.34

Category: Beverages % Cat. Units: 17.86% Value: 17.80% Cat. Units: 539 Cat. Value: $8,264.30

Category	Jan	Feb	Mar	Apr	May	Jun
Beverages	$21,904.16	$2,845.84	$10,636.88	$7,074.35	$15,422.25	$3,485.42
Year Total	**Jul**	**Aug**	**Sep**	**Oct**	**Nov**	**Dec**
$103,924.30	$7,889.22	$5,836.92	$5,726.70	$8,374.90	$3,851.00	$10,876.65
Category	**Jan**	**Feb**	**Mar**	**Apr**	**May**	**Jun**
Condiments	$5,252.07	$6,128.86	$1,645.13	$5,544.40	$5,453.02	$1,855.27
Year Total	**Jul**	**Aug**	**Sep**	**Oct**	**Nov**	**Dec**
$55,368.59	$5,519.83	$4,220.02	$3,575.18	$6,565.91	$3,784.67	$5,824.20
Category	**Jan**	**Feb**	**Mar**	**Apr**	**May**	**Jun**
Confections	$9,128.11	$6,978.87	$3,209.92	$11,538.61	$7,689.82	$2,174.88
Year Total	**Jul**	**Aug**	**Sep**	**Oct**	**Nov**	**Dec**
$82,657.75	$6,462.60	$7,105.63	$6,708.59	$7,800.70	$5,081.85	$8,778.15
Category	**Jan**	**Feb**	**Mar**	**Apr**	**May**	**Jun**
Dairy Products	$9,066.40	$5,584.84	$9,728.90	$5,775.60	$10,435.57	$8,455.80
Year Total	**Jul**	**Aug**	**Sep**	**Oct**	**Nov**	**Dec**
$115,387.64	$12,387.35	$6,826.55	$11,420.30	$12,869.00	$12,992.47	$9,844.85
Category	**Jan**	**Feb**	**Mar**	**Apr**	**May**	**Jun**
Grains/Cereals	$4,547.80	$4,693.70	$3,167.60	$6,544.40	$2,267.25	$6,345.85

Page: 1

Figure 17.19 Removing the link between the master and child fields causes each instance of the CategoryID Footer section to display all rows of the subreport.

3. Click the toolbar's Database Window button to display the Database window and then drag the Report icon for the first subreport to the blank form's Detail section.

4. Drag the Report icon for the second subreport to the blank form's Detail section. If the two subreports fit vertically on one page, place the second below the first. If either subreport requires more than a page, place the second subreport to the right of the first. In this case, you must add column labels for the subreports in the main report's Page Header section so that each page identifies the columns.

TIP

You can also add subreports to a report by using the Toolbox's subform/subreport tool. Use the procedures for adding subforms that you learned in Chapter 15.

CUSTOMIZING DE NOVO REPORTS

Most of the preceding examples in this chapter are based on a standard report structure and template you chose when creating the Inventory by Category report in Chapter 16. When you start a report from scratch, you must add sections required by your reports, set up printing parameters, and, if the number of records in the data source is large, consider limiting the number of detail rows to supply only the most significant information.

ADDING AND DELETING SECTIONS OF YOUR REPORT

When you create a report from a blank template or modify a report created by the Report Wizard, add new sections to the report by using the following guidelines:

17

- To add Report Headers and Footers as a pair, choose View, Report Header/Footer.
- To add Page Headers and Footers as a pair, choose View, Page Header/Footer.
- To add a Group Header or Footer to a report with a Group By value specified, click the Sorting and Grouping button on the toolbar and set the Group Header or Group Footer property value, or both to Yes.

Figure 17.20 shows a blank report, with the headers and footers for each section that you can include in a report. (Although Figure 17.20 shows only one group, you can add up to 10 group levels to your report.)

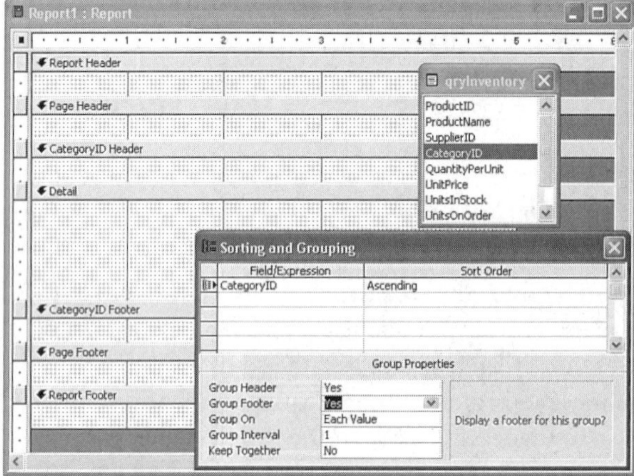

Figure 17.20
A report with a single Group By property value has a total of seven sections.

If you group the data in more than one level (group, subgroup, sub-subgroup), you can add a Group Header and Footer for each level of grouping. This action adds to your report another pair of sections for each subgroup level.

You delete sections from reports by using methods similar to those that you use to create the sections. To delete unwanted sections, use the following guidelines:

- To delete the Detail section or an individual Report Header, Report Footer, Page Header, or Page Footer section, delete all controls from the section, and then drag the divider bar up so that the section has no depth. To delete a Report Footer, drag the report's bottom margin to the Report Footer border. These actions do not actually delete the sections, but sections with no depth do not print or affect the report's layout.
- To delete Report Headers and Footers as a pair, choose View, Report Header/Footer. If the Report Header or Footer includes a control, a message box warns you that you will lose the controls in the deleted sections.
- To delete Page Headers and Footers as a pair, choose View, Page Header/Footer. A warning message box appears if either section contains controls.

- To delete a Group Header or Footer, click the Sorting and Grouping button and set the Group Header or Group Footer property's value to No.

TIP

> Page and Report Headers and Footers that incorporate thin lines at the upper border of the header or footer can be difficult to delete individually. To make these lines visible, choose Edit, Select All to add sizing anchors to the lines. Hold down the Shift key and click the controls that you want to save to deselect these controls. Then press the Delete key to delete the remaining selected lines.

CONTROLLING PAGE BREAKS AND PRINTING PAGE HEADERS AND FOOTERS

The Force New Page and Keep Together properties of the report's Group Header, Detail, and Group Footer sections control manual page breaks. To set these properties, double-click the group's section header to display the section's Properties window. Force New Page causes an unconditional page break immediately before printing the section. If you set the Keep Together property to Yes and insufficient room is available on the current page to print the entire section, a page break occurs and the section prints on the next page.

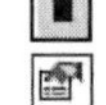

To control whether Page Headers or Footers print on the first, last, or all pages of a report, press Ctrl+R or click the Select Report button, and then click the Properties button. You then select the Page Headers and Page Footers option in the Format page of the Properties window (see Figure 17.21).

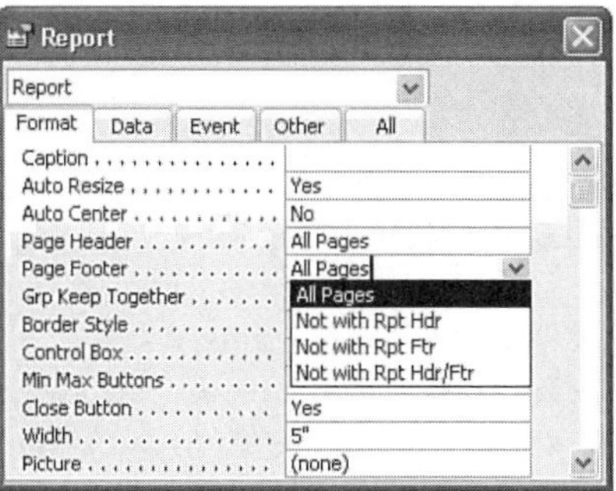

Figure 17.21 Specify when Page Headers or Page Footers appear in the report in the Form Page of the Report Properties window.

ADDING OTHER CONTROLS TO REPORTS

Access places no limit on the Toolbox controls that you can add to reports. So far, the controls that you've modified or added have been limited to labels, text boxes, lines, and the combo boxes that Access places automatically for fields configured as lookup fields. These four kinds of controls are likely to comprise more than 90% of the controls used in the reports you create. Controls that require user interaction, such as lists and combo boxes, can be used in a nonprinting section of the report, but practical use of these controls in reports is limited. The following list describes other controls that you might want to add to reports:

- **Bound object frames**—Print the contents of the OLE Object field data type, including bound charts you design in the next chapter. An OLE object can be a still or animated graphic, a video clip, CD audio track, or even MIDI music. Reports are designed only for printing, so animated graphics, video, and sound are inappropriate for reports.

- **Unbound object frames**—Display OLE objects created by OLE server applications, such as the Graph Wizard, Windows Paint, Microsoft Word, or Excel. Usually, you place unbound objects in the report's Form Header or Form Footer section, but you can add a logo to the top of each page by placing the image object in the Page Header section. A graph or chart created by the Chart Wizard is a special kind of unbound OLE object; you can't create a bound chart with the Wizard.
- **ActiveX controls**—Similar to objects within unbound object frames. You can add PivotTables and PivotCharts to reports, but you must establish the design parameters for the PivotTable or PivotChart before printing.

- **Lines and rectangles (also called shapes)**—Add graphic design elements to reports. Lines of varying widths can separate the sections of the report or emphasize a particular section.

- **Check boxes and option buttons**—Can be used to indicate the values of Yes/No fields or within group frames to indicate multiple-choice selections. Group frames, option buttons, and check boxes used in reports indicate only the value of data cells and do not change the values. Reports seldom use option or toggle buttons.

Adding graphs in bound and unbound object frames and placing PivotTables and PivotCharts in reports are subjects covered in Chapter 18, "Adding Graphs, PivotCharts, and PivotTables."

Reducing the Length of Reports

A report's properties or controls don't limit the number of rows of detail data that a report presents. One way of minimizing detail data is to write a `TOP N` or `TOP N PERCENT` query using Jet or Transact-SQL. Chapter 21, "Moving from Jet Queries to Transact-SQL" has examples of the use of `SELECT TOP N [PERCENT]` statements. All rows of a table or query appear somewhere in the report's Detail section, if the report includes a Detail section with at least one control. To include only a selected range of dates in a report, for example, you must base the report on a query with the criteria necessary to select the Detail records or apply a filter to the report. If the user is to select the range of records to include in the report, use a parameter query as the report's data source.

Mailing Report Snapshots

Outlook or Outlook Express lets you send a report as a Report Snapshot attachment to a message. Microsoft released Report Snapshots (.snp) as an add-in for Access 97; the Report Snapshot feature is built into later Access versions. The advantage of a Report Snapshot is that recipients don't need Access to view the reports. If recipients don't have the Snapshot viewer (Snapview.exe and Snapview.hlp) installed, they must obtain it from the Microsoft Web Site at `http://support.microsoft.com/support/kb/articles/q175/2/74.asp`.

> **NOTE**
>
> You can also publish your reports as HTML pages to make them available on the Internet or your company's intranet. Part VI, "Publishing Data to Intranets and the Internet," of this book describes using HTML and Extensible Markup Language (XML) in Access 2003.

SENDING A REPORT SNAPSHOT WITH OUTLOOK

To send a report in Snapshot format, follow these steps:

1. Make sure that your email client (Outlook or Outlook Express) and current profile is operational. You must have a functioning email system to export a report Snapshot.
2. In the Database window, select a report. You don't need to open the report to send it.
3. Choose File, Send To, Mail Recipient (As Attachment) to open the Send dialog.
4. Select Snapshot Format from the Select Format list (see Figure 17.22). Click OK to close the Send dialog. (You might be prompted to identify your email system at this point.) Access creates the attachment file and opens your email application. The attachment icon appears in the body of the message.

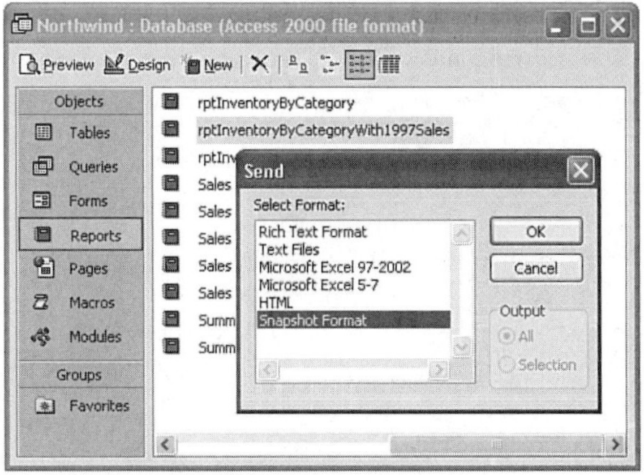

Figure 17.22 Select Snapshot Format in the Send dialog and click OK to generate the .snp file and open your email application with the file as an attachment.

> **NOTE**
>
> NEW
>
> Access 2002 added separate email formats for Excel 5-7 and 97-2002, plus new Data Access Page and XML email formats to the Select Formats list of the Send dialog. Access 2003 removed Data Access Page and XML Format from the Send list.

4. Complete the message (see Figure 17.23) and send it to the recipient. To test the Snapshot Viewer, send the message to yourself.

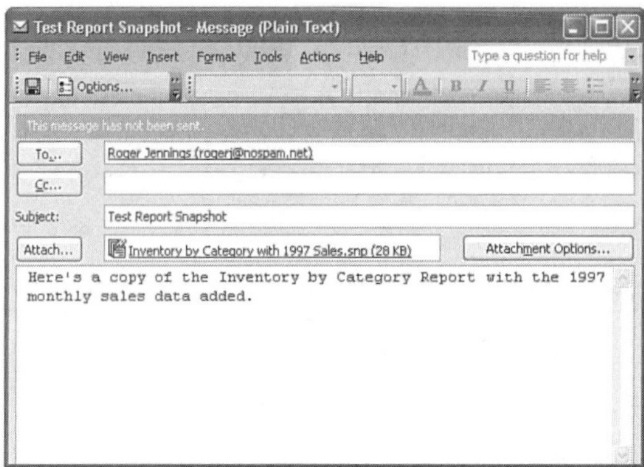

Figure 17.23
This message includes the rptInventoryByCategoryWith1997Sales report attachment.

Alternatively, you can select the report in the Database window, and then choose File, Export, select Snapshot Format (*.snp) in the Save As Type list, and click OK to create the Snapshot file. This approach lets you change the file name of the report snapshot. In this case, you must add the snapshot as an attachment to a message you create in Outlook or Outlook Express.

VIEWING AND PRINTING THE REPORT SNAPSHOT

To emulate a recipient's viewing and printing a copy of the report Snapshot attached to an email message, follow these steps:

1. Send the message to yourself, and then open the message in an email client, such as Outlook 2003 (see Figure 17.24).

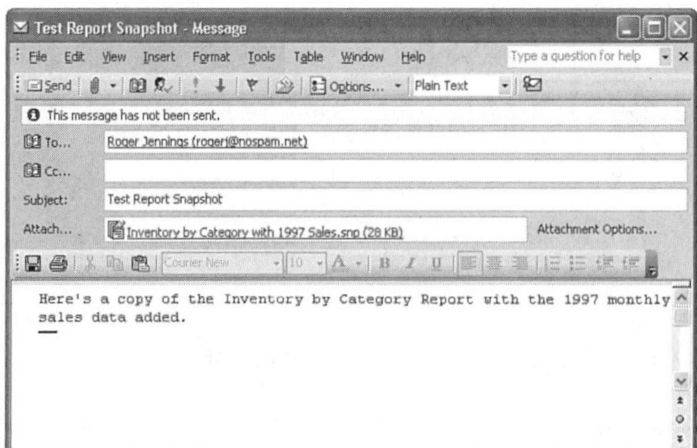

Figure 17.24
This is the message of Figure 17.23 opened in Outlook 2003 running under Windows XP.

2. Double-click the *ReportName*.snp icon to display the Opening Mail Attachment dialog.
3. Select the Open option; then click OK to open Snapshot Viewer and display the first page of the report (see Figure 17.25).

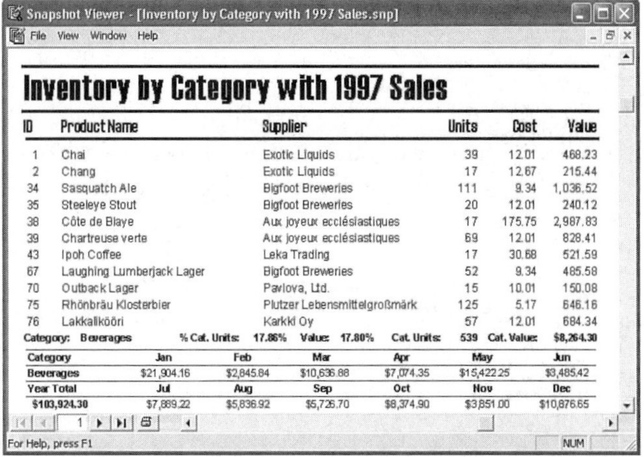

Inventory by Category with 1997 Sales

ID	Product Name	Supplier	Units	Cost	Value
1	Chai	Exotic Liquids	39	12.01	468.23
2	Chang	Exotic Liquids	17	12.67	215.44
34	Sasquatch Ale	Bigfoot Breweries	111	9.34	1,036.52
35	Steeleye Stout	Bigfoot Breweries	20	12.01	240.12
38	Côte de Blaye	Aux joyeux ecclésiastiques	17	175.75	2,987.83
39	Chartreuse verte	Aux joyeux ecclésiastiques	69	12.01	828.41
43	Ipoh Coffee	Leka Trading	17	30.68	521.59
67	Laughing Lumberjack Lager	Bigfoot Breweries	52	9.34	485.58
70	Outback Lager	Pavlova, Ltd.	15	10.01	150.08
75	Rhönbräu Klosterbier	Plutzer Lebensmittelgroßmärk	125	5.17	646.16
76	Lakkalikööri	Karkki Oy	57	12.01	684.34

Category: Beverages % Cat. Units: 17.86% Value: 17.80% Cat. Units: 539 Cat. Value: $8,264.30

Category	Jan	Feb	Mar	Apr	May	Jun
Beverages	$21,904.16	$2,845.84	$10,636.88	$7,074.35	$15,422.25	$3,485.42
Year Total	**Jul**	**Aug**	**Sep**	**Oct**	**Nov**	**Dec**
$103,924.30	$7,889.22	$5,836.92	$5,726.70	$8,374.90	$3,851.00	$10,876.65

Figure 17.25 Snapshot Viewer displays an exact clone of the emailed report.

4. To print the report Snapshot, choose File, Print.

If you receive an error message when you try to open the Snapshot on another computer, check the "Report Snapshots Won't Open" topic in the following "Troubleshooting" section.

TROUBLESHOOTING

LINK EXPRESSION ERRORS

Attempting to create a link between the main report and subreport causes a "Can't evaluate expression" error message.

The most likely cause is that you are trying to create a master-child (or, more properly, parent-child) link with an incompatible data type. Parent-child linkages are similar to joins of queries that use the `WHERE` *`SubreportName.FieldName`* `=` *`ReportName.FieldName`* criterion. As with joins, the data types of the linked fields of tables or columns of queries must be identical. You can't, for example, link a field of the Text data type with a field of the Integer data type, even if your text field contains only numbers. If you use an expression to create the link, the data type that the expression returns must match the field value. You can use the data type conversion functions described in Chapter 10 to change the data type that the expression returns to that of the linked field. For example, you can link a text field that contains numbers to a field of the Long Integer data type by entering `=CLng(TextField)` as the linking value.

REPORT SNAPSHOTS WON'T OPEN

Selecting the Open It option in the Opening Mail Attachment dialog results in a "The Managed Software Installer failed to install the program associated with this file" or similar error message.

The most likely cause of this error is that SnapView.exe is missing from your or the recipient's PC. In this case, open Control Panel, and double-click the Add/Remove Programs icon to open the Add/Remove Programs dialog. Select Microsoft Office XP, and click Add/Remove to open the Microsoft Office Maintenance Mode dialog. Click Change to open the installer's Microsoft Office XP Setup dialog, and select the Add or Remove Features option. Click Next and expand the Microsoft Access for Windows node, set Snapshot Viewer to Run from My Computer, and click Update.

NOTE

> The Snapshot Viewer hasn't changed since the version supplied as an Access 97 add-in. Prior versions of the Snapshot viewer are compatible with Access 2003 reports.

If Snapview.exe is present, you have a Registry problem—the association between the .snp file extension and SnapView.exe is missing. In this case, repeat the preceding Add/Remove Programs process to enter Office 2003 Maintenance Mode, but click the Repair Office button instead of the Add or Remove Features button.

IN THE REAL WORLD—THE ART OF REPORT DESIGN

Designing reports that deliver useful information in a graphically appealing format is a challenge. The challenge becomes acute when you're faced with the prospect of designing a complex report, such as a physician's patient history, that derives its information from multiple related tables. In the case of a patient history, some of the tables contain memo fields with large blocks of formatted text that describe diagnosis and treatment. Specialists often want reports that print from OLE Object fields or linked graphics files, embedded images generated from digital cameras, scanned photographs, or single-frame captures from a video camera. Most physicians also need billing reports that conform to state and federal government agency standards, as well as health insurers' requirements.

Fortunately, Access 2003's report engine and graphical Report Design mode can handle just about any report format imaginable. Report generation flexibility is one of the primary reasons that database developers haven't abandoned Access for Visual Basic 6.0 or Visual Basic .NET, which offer a more traditional approach to programming structure and form design than Access. Many developers use Automation to generate custom Access reports from Jet and SQL Server databases managed by Visual Basic 6.0 and .NET programs.

NEW 2002

One of the most interesting new features added by Access 2002 was the capability to export static and live Web reports, as mentioned at the beginning of Chapter 16. When you select an Access report, choose the static option, and export it in XML format, Access generates a well-formed XML document in ReportML format. Exporting a live report, which requires an Access data project, the server generates an Active Server Pages (.asp) file, which sends the report to the browser. Live Web reports reflect the current state of the underlying data.

ReportML uses Access-specific tags to specify properties (attributes) of the Access object—typically a report or form—and inserts property (attribute) values within the tags. An XSLT transform converts the XML document to HTML for presentation in a browser. Unlike report Snapshots, the ReportML-based presentation isn't an exact clone of the reports, because HTML doesn't support the precise formatting capabilities of conventional Access reports. Chapter 23, "Exporting and Importing Data with XML," provides an expanded description of the XML features of Access 2003.

NOTE

> Access 2002's ReportML became the foundation for Word 2003's WordML and Excel 2003's ExcelML formats.

It's impossible for two chapters of reasonable length to cover every feature of the Access report engine in detail. This chapter and its predecessor provide only an introduction to report design and demonstrate the basic elements of reports and subreports. Complete coverage of Access's reporting capabilities, including the use of VBA to respond to report events and set printer properties, would fill a book of 500 pages or more.

CHAPTER 18

Adding Graphs, PivotCharts, and PivotTables

In this chapter

GENERATING GRAPHS AND CHARTS WITH MICROSOFT GRAPH

Microsoft Graph 11—called *MSGraph* in this book—is a 32-bit, OLE 2.0 mini-server application (Graph.exe) that's identical to Access 2002's Graph.exe, Access 2000's Graph9.exe and Access 97's Graph8.exe. An OLE mini-server is an application that you can only run from within an OLE container application, such as Access 2003. Word 2003 and Excel 2003 also use MSGraph, which originated as the charting component of Microsoft Excel 5.0. Microsoft encourages use of the PivotChart control for new Access applications, but there's no "PivotChart Wizard" to lead you through the steps to design a PivotChart. The AutoForm: PivotChart option generates a databound form with a PivotChart that you must configure manually, as described in Chapter 12, "Working with PivotTable and PivotChart Views," and in more detail in the "Working with PivotChart Forms," section near the end of this chapter.

The sections that follow describe how to use Access's Chart Wizard to add graphs and charts to conventional (Jet) Access 2003 forms and reports. Access data projects (ADP) don't support the Chart Wizard, which generates a Jet crosstab query to use as its final data source. As mentioned in Chapter 11, "Creating Multitable and Crosstab Queries," SQL Server doesn't support the Jet SQL `TRANSFORM` and `PIVOT` keywords for crosstab queries. Sections later in the chapter describe how to add bound PivotChart and PivotTable controls to Jet- and SQL Server-based forms and reports.

CREATING THE QUERY DATA SOURCE FOR THE GRAPH

Most graphs required by management are the time-series type. Time-series graphs track the history of financial performance data, such as orders received, product sales, gross margin, and the like. Time-series graphs usually display date intervals (months, quarters, or years) on the horizontal x-axis—sometimes called the *abscissa*—and numeric values on the vertical y-axis—also called the *ordinate*.

CHOOSING DATA SOURCES FOR SUMMARY QUERIES

In smaller firms, the numerical data for the y-axis comes from tables that store entries from the original documents (such as sales orders and invoices) that underlie the summary information. Queries sum the numerical data for each interval specified for the x-axis.

Detail data for individual orders or invoices, such as that found in the sample Order Details table, often is called a line-item source. Because a multibillion-dollar firm can accumulate millions of line-item records in a single year, larger firms usually store summaries of the line-item source data in tables; this technique improves the performance of queries. Summary data often is referred to as *rolled-up data* or, simply, *rollups*. Rollups of data on mainframe computers often are stored in client/server databases running under Unix or Windows 2000+/NT to create data warehouses or data marts.

Although rolling up data from relational tables violates two of the guiding principles of relational theory—don't duplicate data in tables and don't store derived data in tables—databases consisting solely of rolled-up data are very common. As you move into the client/server realm with ADP and SQL Server, you're likely to encounter many rollup tables derived from production online transaction-processing (OLTP) databases.

NOTE

> The Developer, Standard, and Enterprise Editions of Microsoft SQL Server 2000 include Microsoft Analysis Services, formerly called OLAP services. OLAP is an acronym for online analytical processing, which manipulates multidimensional data from production databases. OLAP can operate directly on OLTP databases, but it's more common to roll up online data into OLAP data structures, often called *cubes*, and then perform analysis on the cubes.

Designing a Query Based on OLTP Tables

Northwind Traders is a relatively small firm that receives very few orders, so it isn't necessary to roll up line-item data to obtain acceptable query performance on a reasonably fast (Pentium III or better) computer. The Chart Wizard handles time-series grouping for you, so you don't need to base your chart on a crosstab query.

To create a summary query designed specifically for use with the Chart Wizard, follow these steps:

1. In the Database window, open a new query in Design view, and add the Categories, Products, Order Details, and Orders table to the query.
2. Drag the CategoryName field of the Categories table to the first column.
3. Enter the expression

```
Amount: CCur([Order Details].[UnitPrice]*[Order Details].[Quantity]*
(1 -[Order Details].[Discount]))
```

   in the second column's Field row.

NOTE

> The `CCur` VBA function is required to change the field data type to Currency when applying a discount calculation.

TIP

> With the cursor in the Field row of the second column, press Shift+F2 to open the Zoom window to make entering the preceding expression easier.

4. Drag the ShippedDate field of the Orders table to the third column. Add an ascending sort on this column.

5. Add the criterion **Between #1/1/1997# And #12/31/1997#** to the ShippedDate column to include only orders shipped in 1997. This example uses the year 1997 instead of 1998 because data is available for all 12 months of 1997.

6. Save your query with the name **qry1997SalesChart** (see Figure 18.1).

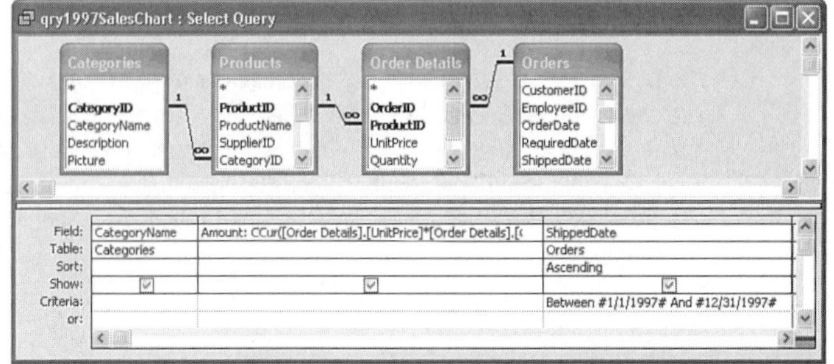

Figure 18.1
This query calculates the net value of all Northwind orders shipped in 1997 classified by product category.

7. Click the Run button to test your query (see Figure 18.2), and then close it.

qry1997SalesChart : Select Query

Category Name	Amount	Shipped Date
Dairy Products	$1,440.00	01-Jan-1997
Produce	$648.72	02-Jan-1997
Confections	$68.00	02-Jan-1997
Dairy Products	$230.40	03-Jan-1997
Beverages	$285.00	03-Jan-1997
Produce	$585.90	03-Jan-1997
Confections	$58.80	03-Jan-1997
Confections	$1,307.25	03-Jan-1997
Dairy Products	$320.00	03-Jan-1997
Seafood	$48.00	03-Jan-1997
Confections	$394.00	03-Jan-1997
Seafood	$241.92	03-Jan-1997
Meat/Poultry	$1,650.60	03-Jan-1997
Dairy Products	$583.80	06-Jan-1997
Grains/Cereals	$288.00	06-Jan-1997
Dairy Products	$1,032.00	06-Jan-1997
Confections	$600.00	08-Jan-1997
Condiments	$145.60	08-Jan-1997

Record: 1 of 1042

Figure 18.2
The query returns a row for each date on which an order was shipped and provides the total amount of the sale for the product categories.

The design of the qry1997SalesChart query is a typical sample data source for time-series graphs and charts you generate with MSGraph as well as PivotCharts.

USING THE CHART WIZARD TO CREATE AN UNLINKED GRAPH

It's possible to create a graph or chart by choosing Insert, Object and selecting Microsoft Graph Chart in the Object Type list, but the Chart Wizard makes this process much simpler. You can use the Chart Wizard to create two different classes of graphs and charts:

- *Unlinked* (also called nonlinked) line graphs display a line for each row of the query. You can also create unlinked stacked column charts and multiple-area charts.

- *Linked* graphs or charts are bound to the current record of the form in which they are contained and display only a single set of values from one row of the table or query at a time.

This section shows you how to create an unlinked line graph based on a query. The "Changing the Graph to a Chart" section describes how to use MSGraph to display alternative presentations of your data in the form of bar and area charts. In the later "Creating a Linked Graph from a Jet Crosstab Query" section, you generate a graph that's linked to a specific record of a query result set.

To create an unlinked graph that displays the data from the qry1997SalesChart query, follow these steps:

1. Click the Database window's Forms shortcut, click New, select Chart Wizard in the list box, and select qry1997SalesChart in the drop-down list (see Figure 18.3). Click OK to launch the Chart Wizard.

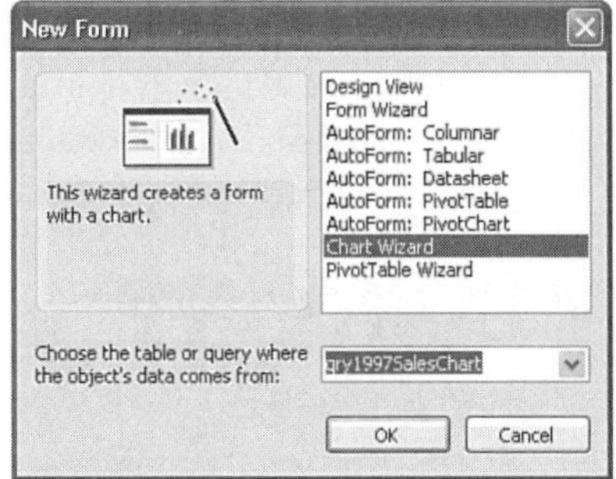

Figure 18.3
Select the Chart Wizard in the New Form list, and select the query for the graph or chart in the drop-down list.

2. In the first Wizard dialog, click the >> button to add all three fields to your graph (see Figure 18.4). Click Next to move to the second dialog.

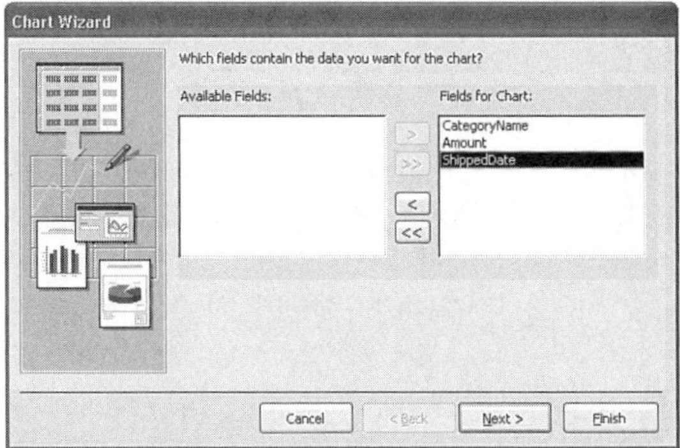

Figure 18.4
Time-series charts require at least date and value columns (ShippedDate and Amount, respectively). Creating a multiple-line chart requires a classification field (CategoryID) to provide the data for each line.

3. Click the Line Chart button, shown selected in Figure 18.5. Click Next.

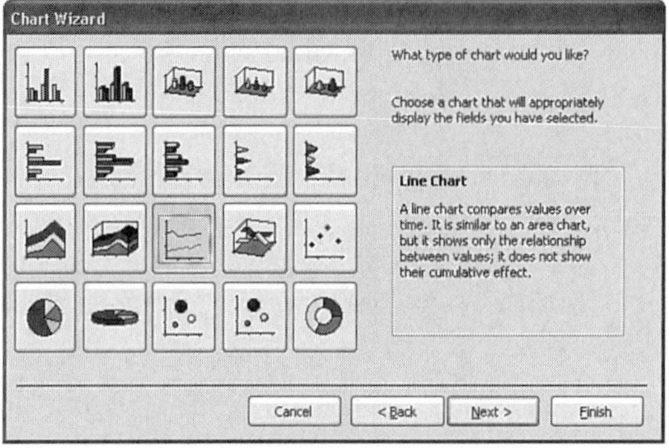

Figure 18.5
A line graph is the best initial choice for data presentation, because lines make it easy to determine whether the data meets reasonableness tests.

> **NOTE**
>
> This book uses the term *graph* when the presentation consists of lines, and chart for formats that use solid regions—such as bars, columns, or areas—to display the data.

4. The Wizard designs a crosstab query based on the data types of the query result set. In this case, the Chart Wizard makes a mistake by assuming you want months in the legend box and product categories along the graph's horizontal x-axis (see Figure 18.6).

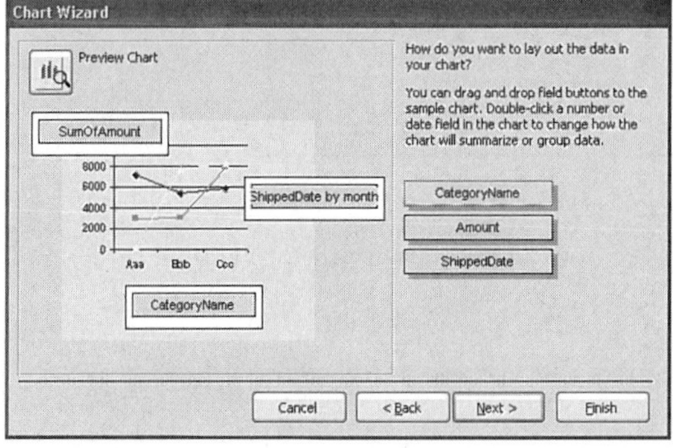

Figure 18.6
Time-series graphs and charts almost always plot time on the horizontal axis, but the Chart Wizard's initial design puts classifications (CategoryName) on the x-axis.

5. You want the categories in the legend and the months of 1997 across the x-axis. Drag the CategoryName button from the right side of the dialog to the drop box under the legend to the right of the chart, and drag the ShippedDate button to the drop box under the x-axis. The button title, partly obscured, is ShippedDate by Month (see Figure 18.7).

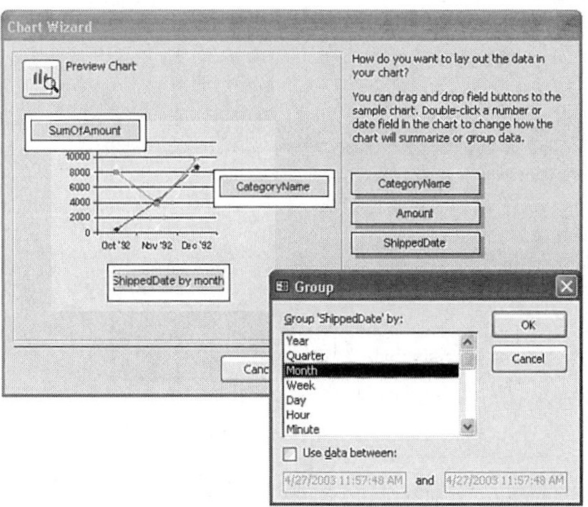

Figure 18.7
Drag the date column button from the right to the x-axis and the classification column button to the legend. The Wizard's default time-series interval is month.

TIP

You can double-click the ShippedDate by Month button and select from a variety of `GROUP BY` date criteria, ranging from Year to Minute, and specify an optional range of dates (refer to Figure 18.7). Marking the Use Date Between check box lets you add a `WHERE` *`DateValue`* `BETWEEN` *`#StartDate#`* `AND` *`#EndDate#`* clause to the crosstab query's SQL statement.

18

6. Click the Preview Chart button to display an expanded—but not full-size—view of your graph. The size relationship between objects in Chart Preview isn't representative of your final graph or chart. Click Close.
7. Click the Next button to go to the fourth and final Chart Wizard dialog. Type **1997 Monthly Sales by Category** in the text box to add a title to your graph. Accept the default Yes, Display a Legend option to display the Category legend (see Figure 18.8).

Figure 18.8
The last Wizard dialog's default options are satisfactory for most graphs and charts. If your source query doesn't have a classification column, you don't need a legend.

8. Accept the remainder of the defaults, and click Finish to display the initial graph layout in Form view (see Figure 18.9).

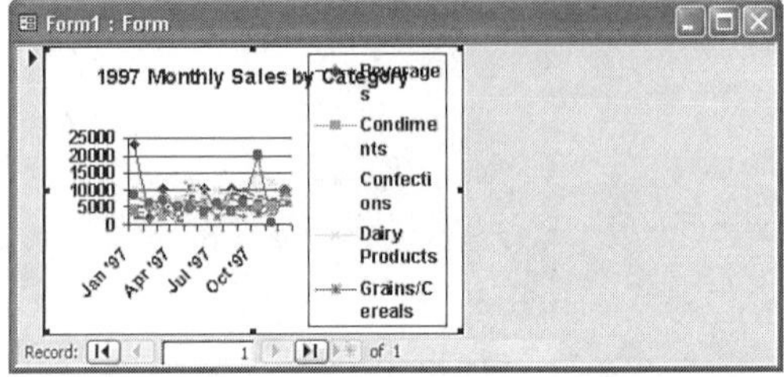

Figure 18.9
The Wizard makes a poor guess at the size of the form and the unbound object frame needed to display the elements the Wizard generates.

NOTE

> In the miniature version of the graph illustrated by Figure 18.9, some month labels are missing and the legend crowds the graph and label. You fix these problems in the next section of this chapter, "Modifying the Design Features of Your Graph."

9. Click the Design View button and increase the size of your graph to at least 5.5 inches wide by 3.5 inches high (see Figure 18.10).

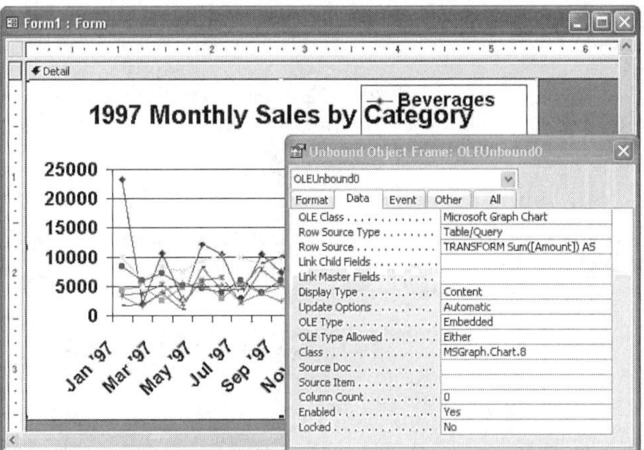

Figure 18.10
The Data page of the unbound object frame that contains the chart lets you check the crosstab query's SQL statement and set the Enable and Locked properties. Graph.exe's version number is 11, but the Class version (8) hasn't changed since Office 97.

10. Click the Data tab of the Properties dialog, and make sure the Enabled property value of the unbound object frame (OLEUnbound0) is set to Yes and the Locked Property is set to No (the defaults).

11. The chart is in an unbound object frame, so you don't need form adornments for record manipulation. Select the form, click the Format tab of the Properties window, and set the Scroll Bars property of the form to Neither, the Record Selectors to No, and the Navigation Buttons to No.

12. Use the sizing handles of the unbound object frame to create a 1/8-inch form border around the frame. Leaving a small form area around the object makes the activation process more evident.
13. Save your form with a descriptive name, such as **frm1997SalesByCategoryChart**. Return to Form view in preparation for changing the size and type of your graph.

Jet SQL

The Wizard writes the following Jet crosstab query to generate the data for the chart:

```
TRANSFORM Sum([Amount]) AS [SumOfAmount]
   SELECT (Format([ShippedDate],"MMM 'YY"))
   FROM [qry1997SalesChart]
   GROUP BY (Year([ShippedDate])*12 + Month([ShippedDate])-1),
      (Format([ShippedDate],"MMM 'YY"))
PIVOT [CategoryName];
```

The `GROUP BY` clause permits display of monthly data for multiple years, which isn't applicable to the example query. The `Format` expression generates x-axis labels, such as Jan '97.

SQL Server's T-SQL doesn't support Jet SQL's `TRANSFORM...PIVOT` statements, so you can't use the Chart Wizard with ADP. You can, however, write T-SQL statements to emulate a crosstab query, so it's possible to use the Insert Object approach to adding a MSGraph chart or graph to forms of ADP.

→ For an example of the SQL Server equivalents of Jet crosstab queries, **see** "Emulating Jet Crosstab Queries with T-SQL," **p. 918**.

TIP

> When you complete your design, set the value of the Enabled property for the form to No so that users of your application can't activate the graph and alter its design. It's also a good practice to set the values of the Allow Datasheet, PivotTable, and PivotChart View properties to No.

MODIFYING THE DESIGN FEATURES OF YOUR GRAPH

Graph.exe is an OLE 2.0 mini-server, so you can activate MSGraph in place and modify the design of your graph. MSGraph also supports *Automation*, which lets you use VBA code to automate design changes. This section shows you how to use MSGraph to edit the design of the graph manually, as well as how to change the line graph to an area or column chart.

To activate your graph and change its design with MSGraph, follow these steps:

1. Display the form in Form view and then double-click the graph to activate MSGraph in place, which opens a Datasheet window that displays the values returned by the crosstab query (see Figure 18.11). A diagonally hashed border surrounds the graph; MSGraph's menus replace or supplement those of Access 2003. (The activation border is missing from the left and top of the object frame if you didn't create some additional space on the form around the object frame in step 12 of the preceding section.)

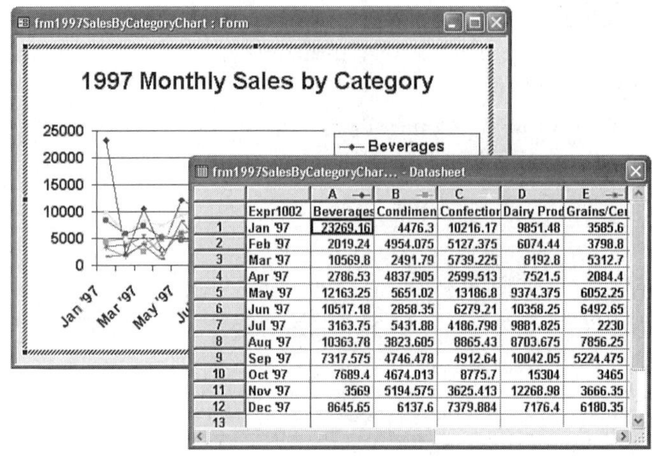

Figure 18.11 Activating the unbound object frame grafts MSGraph's menu commands to Access's and opens the Datasheet window.

> **NOTE**
>
> Menu commands of an OLE server or mini-server added to those of the container application are called *grafted menus* or *object menus*. The process that adds the menu commands is called *menu negotiation*.

2. Change the type family and font size of your chart's labels and legend to better suit the size of the object. Double-click the graph title to open the Format Chart Title dialog. Click the Font tab, set the size of the chart title to 12 points (see Figure 18.12), clear the Auto Scale check box, and then click OK to close the dialog.

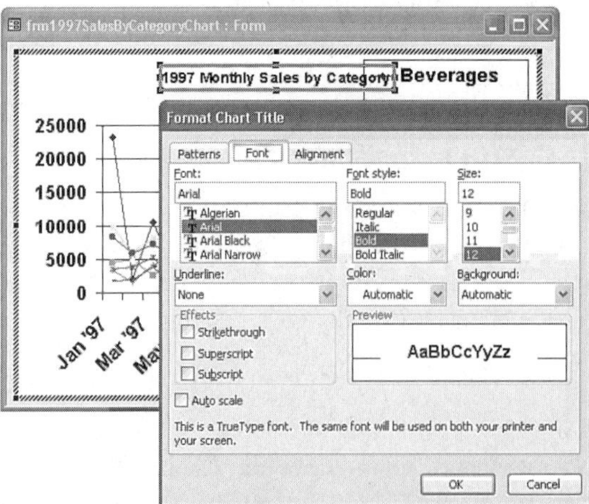

Figure 18.12 MSGraph has properties dialogs for most of its objects, including chart titles, legends, and axes. Reduce the font size of the Chart Title object to 12 points, and clear the Auto Scale check box to retain the font size regardless of the object frame's dimensions.

3. Double-click the legend to open the Format Legend dialog, set the size of the legend font to 9 points, and clear the Auto Scale check box.

4. The y-axis labels should be smaller and formatted as currency, so double-click one of the labels on the y-axis to display the Format Axis dialog. Set the font size to 9 points, and clear the Auto Scale check box.
5. Click the Number tab, select Currency in the Category list, and enter **0** in the Decimal Places text box (see Figure 18.13). Click OK to close the Format Axis dialog.

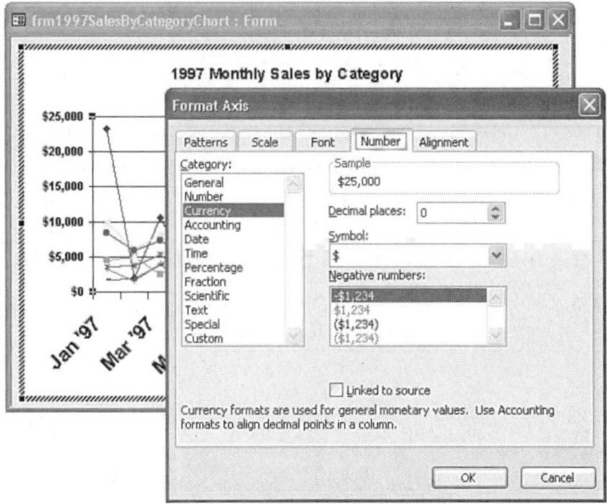

Figure 18.13 Reduce the font size of the y-axis labels to 9 points and apply currency formatting in the Format Axis dialog.

6. The default font size for axis labels at a graph size of 6.5×3.5 inches is 15.25 points, which causes MSGraph to label the x-axis diagonally. Double-click the x-axis and change its font size to 9 points, also clearing the Auto Scale check box. Click OK to close the dialog and apply the new format.
7. Resize the elements of the graph to take maximum advantage of the available area within the unbound object frame. Click the Chart Title and drag it to the top of the frame. Click an empty area in the graph to select the Plot Area, which adds a shaded rectangle around the region, and increase its size.
8. Click the form region outside the graph to deactivate MSGraph, and then save your changes. Your line graph now appears as shown in Figure 18.14.

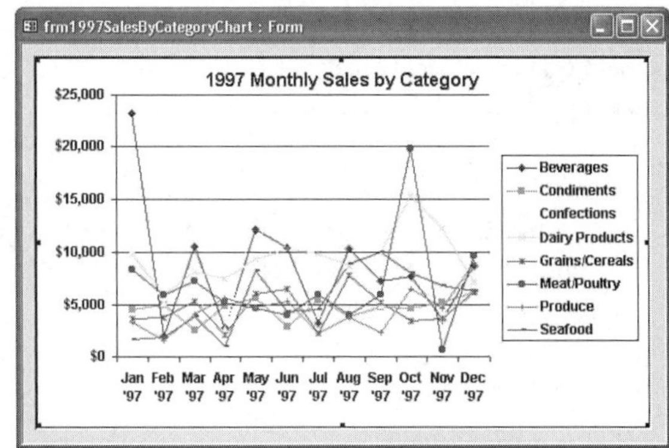

Figure 18.14 The modified graph design corrects the poor choices the Wizard makes for title, axis, and legend font sizes.

Depending on the use of the graph or chart, consider increasing its size to increase the accuracy of data interpretation for users. If you plan to print the chart, you can increase the width to about 6.5 inches and the height to about 4.5 inches without changing the default printing margins. You can save vertical space by deleting the chart title and changing the form's Caption property to that of the deleted title. The figures in the following sections reflect these design changes.

CHANGING THE GRAPH TO A CHART

You might want to change the line graph to some other type of chart (such as area or stacked column) for a specific purpose. Area charts, for example, are especially effective as a way to display the contribution of individual product categories to total sales. To change the line graph to another type of chart, follow these steps:

1. Double-click the graph to activate it and then choose Chart, Chart Type to open the Chart Type dialog with the Standard Types page active.
2. Select Area in the Chart Type list (see Figure 18.15).

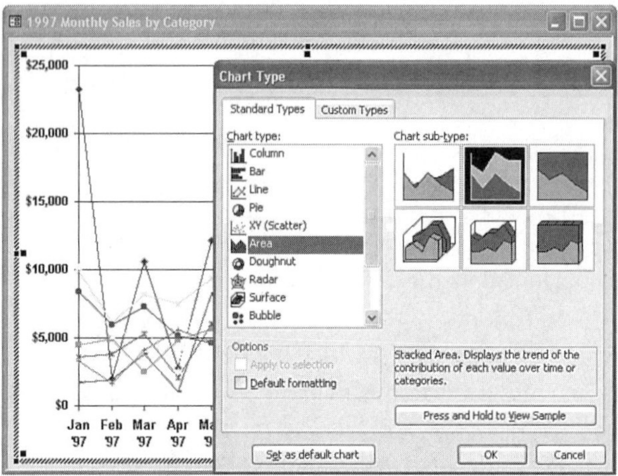

Figure 18.15
MSGraph's Chart Type dialog offers many more choices of chart and graph styles than the Chart Wizard.

TIP

> You can preview your chart by clicking and holding down the left mouse button on the Press and Hold to View Sample button.

3. Select the stacked area chart as the Chart Sub-type (the middle chart in the first row—refer to Figure 18.15). Click OK to change your line graph into an area chart, as shown in Figure 18.16. The contribution of each category appears as an individually colored area, and the top line segment represents total sales.

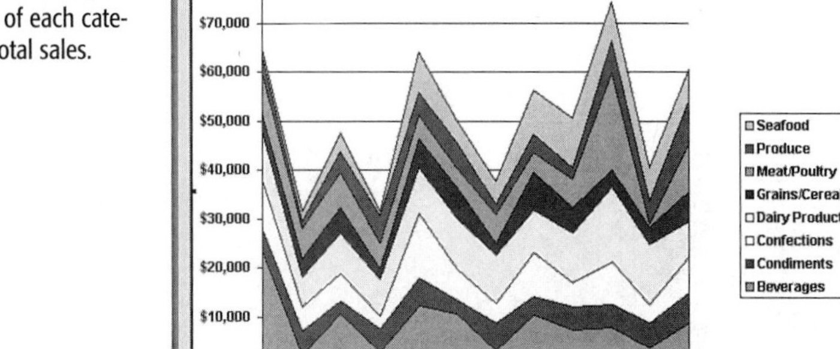

Figure 18.16 The stacked area chart shows the contribution of each category to total sales.

4. To convert the area chart into a stacked column chart, choose Chart, Chart Type to display the Standard Types page of the Chart Type dialog. Select Column in the Chart Type list, and then select as the Chart Sub-Type the stacked column chart shown selected in Figure 18.17).

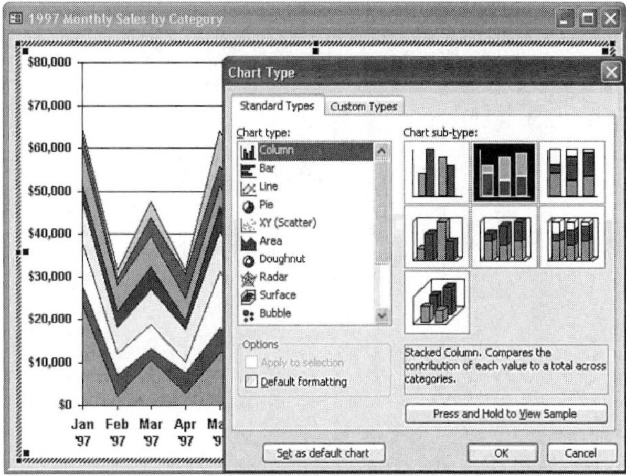

Figure 18.17 You can select a 3D stacked column chart, but conventional 2D column charts are easier to interpret.

5. Click OK to close the Chart Type dialog. Your stacked column chart appears as shown in Figure 18.18.
6. Another subtype of the area chart and stacked column chart is the percentage distribution chart. To create a distribution-of-sales graph, repeat steps 4 and 5 but select the 100% Stacked Column picture (the third thumbnail in the top row) with equal column heights as the Chart Sub-type. Click OK to close the Chart Type dialog.

18

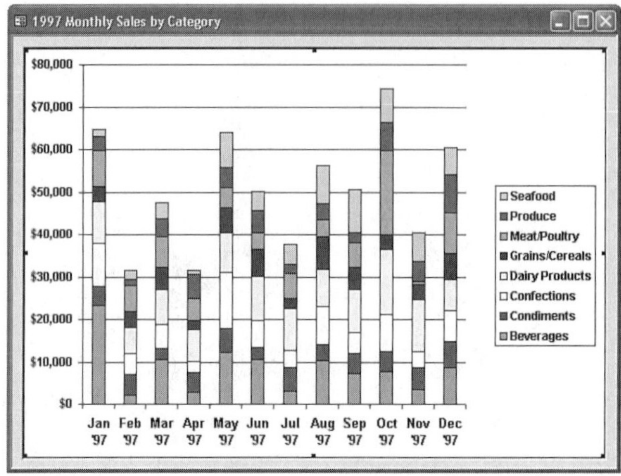

Figure 18.18 A stacked column chart is a less-dramatic alternative to a stacked area chart.

7. Because you previously set the format of the y-axis to eliminate the decimals, you need to change the format of the y-axis manually to Percentage. Double-click the y-axis to open the Format Axis dialog and click the Number page (refer to Figure 18.13). Select Percentage in the Category list, make sure that Decimal Places is set to 0, and then click OK to apply the format. Your chart appears as shown in Figure 18.19.

18

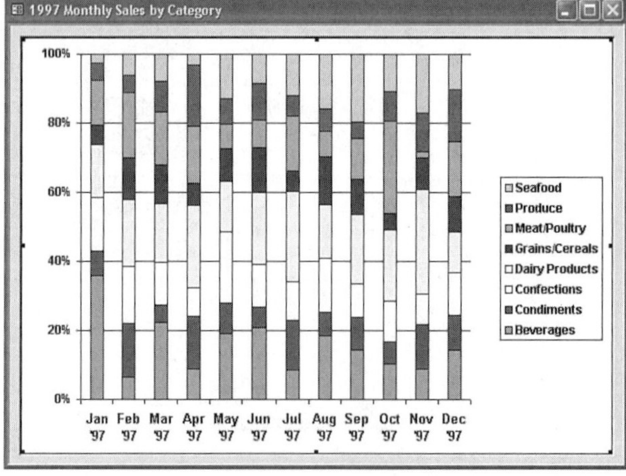

Figure 18.19 A 100% stacked column shows the distribution of sales by category.

8. Change the Chart Type back to a line graph in preparation for the linked graph example of the later section, "Creating a Linked Graph from a Jet Crosstab Query." Change the y-axis format to Currency, click inside the form region outside the object frame to deactivate the graph, and then save your form.

Of the four types of charts demonstrated, most users find the area chart best for displaying time-series data for multiple values that have meaningful total values.

PRINTING GRAPHS OR CHARTS IN REPORTS

The process of adding an unbound MSGraph object to an Access report is identical to that for forms. Unless all your users have access to a color printer, you should select a line graph subtype that identifies data points with a different symbol for each category. For area and stacked column charts, a series of hatched patterns differentiate the product categories. The Custom Types page of the Chart Types dialog offers a selection of B&W... chart types specifically designed for monochrome printers.

You can save a form created by the Chart Wizard to a report by choosing File, Save As, and selecting Report in the Save As dialog. It's almost as easy to create a new report and copy the form's unbound object frame to it, which also demonstrates how to add a graph to an existing report. Follow these steps:

1. Open the form with the graph or chart in Design view, select the unbound OLE object frame, and press Ctrl+C to copy the control to the Clipboard. For this example, copy frm1997SalesByCategoryChart's OLEUnbound0 object.

2. Click the New Object button, and choose Report to open the New Report dialog. Optionally, select the data source for the report, in this case qry1997SalesChart. Click OK to open the new report in Design view.
3. Choose View, Report Header/Footer to add Header and Footer sections to the report. If you plan to add fields to the Detail section, you usually add the chart or graph to the report Footer section. Otherwise, choose View, Page Header/Footer to eliminate these sections, close up the Detail and Report Footer sections of the report, and select the Report Header section.
4. Press Ctrl+V to paste the graph or chart to the selected section.
5. Adjust the height and width of the unbound object frame within the printing limits of the page. Optionally, move the object frame down, and add a label with a report title. Alternatively, you can add a chart title.
6. Double-click the object frame to activate the object, close the Datasheet window, and choose Chart, Chart Type to open the Chart Type dialog.
7. Click the Custom Types tab, and choose B&W Area to change the style to an area chart with hatching (see Figure 18.20).

8. Click OK to apply the style. Click the Report Header bar to deselect the graph and click Print Preview to display the chart, which has a gray background, regular (not-bold) text, and unformatted y-axis labels (see Figure 18.21). Click Close to return to Design view.

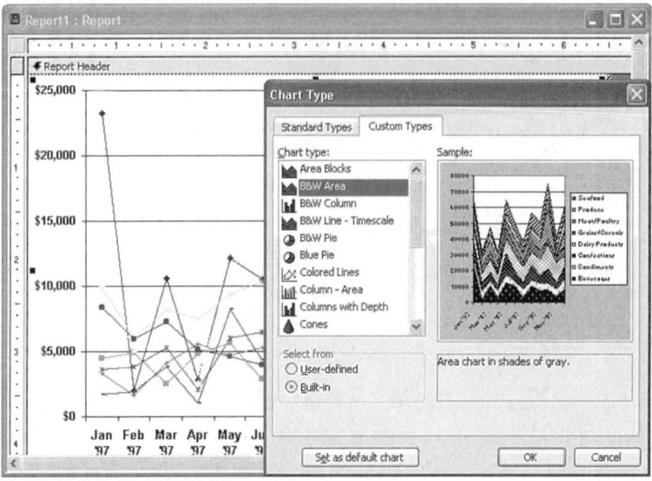

Figure 18.20
The B&W Area style is a better selection for printing (in most cases) than B&W Column, which includes a data table.

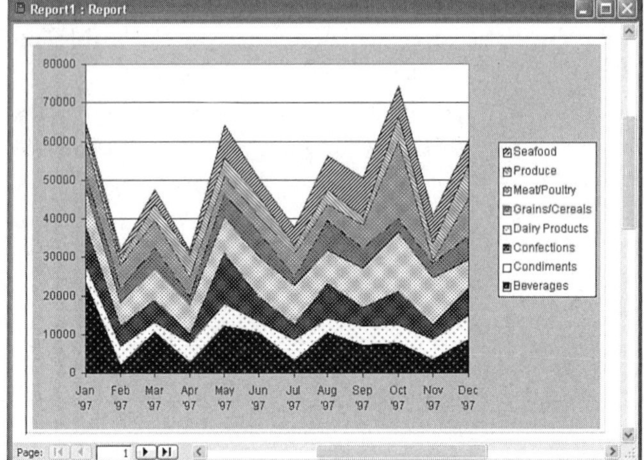

Figure 18.21
Selecting a different chart style removes much of the formatting you applied to the copied chart.

9. To remove the gray background, which consumes toner or ink but doesn't contribute to readability, double-click the object frame to activate it. Right-click the gray region, and choose Format Chart Area to open the dialog of the same name. On the Patterns page, select the None option in the Area frame to make the background transparent, and click OK.

10. Double-click the y-axis labels to open the Format Axis dialog, click the Number tab, select Currency, set Decimal Places to 0, and click OK.

11. Click the Report Header bar to deactivate the object, and open the Properties window for the object frame (OLEUnbound0 for this example).
12. Click the Format tab, and set the Border Style property value to Transparent.

NOTE

Selecting the None option in the Border frame of the Format Chart Area dialog's Patterns page doesn't remove the default border of the object frame.

13. Select the Report, and set the Caption property value to **1997 Monthly Sales by Category**.

14. Click the Print Preview button to display your modified report design (see Figure 18.22). You can't activate the chart object for editing in Print Preview mode.

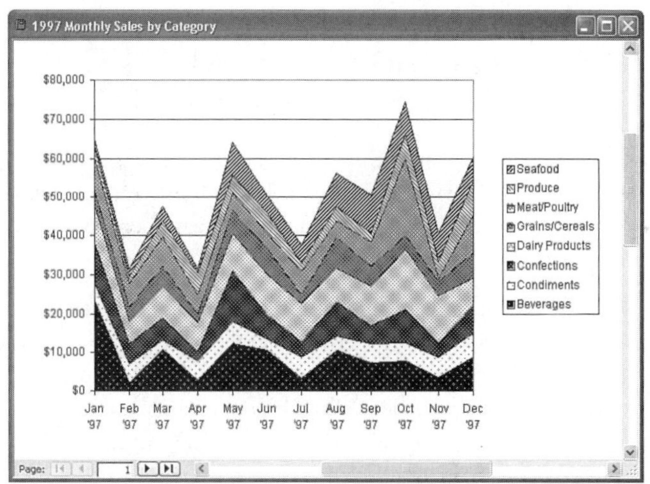

Figure 18.22 Monochrome reports use hatching and shading to differentiate areas by classification. Unfortunately, many laser printers don't distinguish dark regions, such as Confections and Beverages in this example.

15. Save your report with a descriptive name, such as **rpt1997SalesByCategoryChart** for this example.

You can increase the printed width of the graph by returning to Design view and double-clicking the Legend to open the Format Legend dialog. Click the Placement tab, and select the Bottom option. Optionally, click the Format tab and select the None option in the Border frame. Figure 18.23 shows the report with the relocated legend.

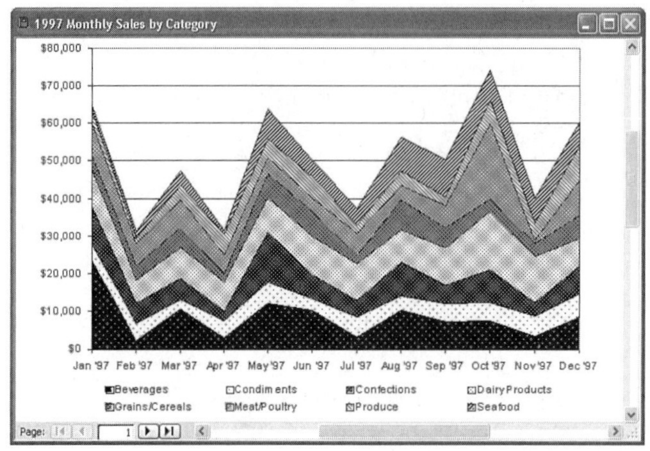

Figure 18.23
Relocating the legend to the bottom of a report (or form) lets you increase the printed (or displayed) width of the chart.

CREATING A LINKED GRAPH FROM A JET CROSSTAB QUERY

Access's Chart Wizard is quite parochial: It insists on creating a crosstab query for you. After you've created a chart with the Chart Wizard, however, you can change the graph's Row Source property value to specify a previously created crosstab query of your own design.

Linked graphs or charts display a succession of graphical representations of related data. Linked graphs are useful for delivering more detailed information than bar or area charts can impart. For example, it's difficult to interpret trends for sales of product categories in a stacked area chart. Linked graphs let you drill down into the data behind summary charts and add features to aid data interpretation—such as trendlines. Linked graphs are one of Access 2003's most powerful features.

For this linked graph example, you create the qry1997SalesChartCT crosstab query and use the query as the Row Source of the unbound object frame to complete the linked graph example in the following section. The linked graph example doesn't work with the crosstab query created by the Chart Wizard in the preceding steps. The Chart Wizard's crosstab query result set has months in rows and categories in columns.

DESIGNING THE CROSSTAB QUERY FOR THE GRAPH

To create the qry1997SalesChartCT query from qry1997SalesChart, follow these steps:

1. Create a new query in Design view, add the qry1997SalesChart query, and choose Query, Crosstab Query.
2. Drag the CategoryName field to the first column of the query and select Row Heading in the Crosstab row.

3. Alias the CategoryName field by typing **Categories:** at the beginning of the Field text box.
4. Type the expression **Month:Format([ShippedDate], "mmm")** into the second Fields cell to use three-letter month abbreviations. Then, select Column Heading in the Crosstab cell.
5. Drag the Amount field to the third column, set the Total cell to Sum, and set the Crosstab cell to Value (see Figure 18.24).

Figure 18.24
A Jet crosstab query for a linked graph requires specifying a Row Heading, Column Heading, and Value in the Crosstab row of the query design grid.

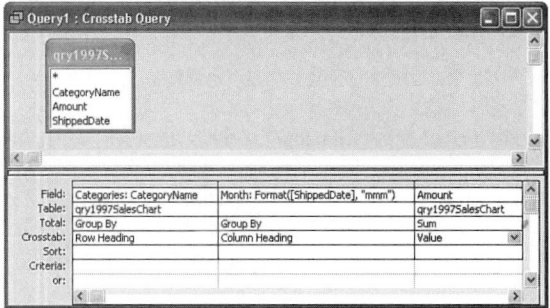

6. Double-click an empty region of the upper query pane to open the Query Properties sheet. In the Column Headings text box, type the 12 month abbreviations, **Jan,...Dec**, separated by commas to arrange the columns in date, not alphabetic, sequence. Access adds the quotes around the month abbreviations for you (see Figure 18.25).

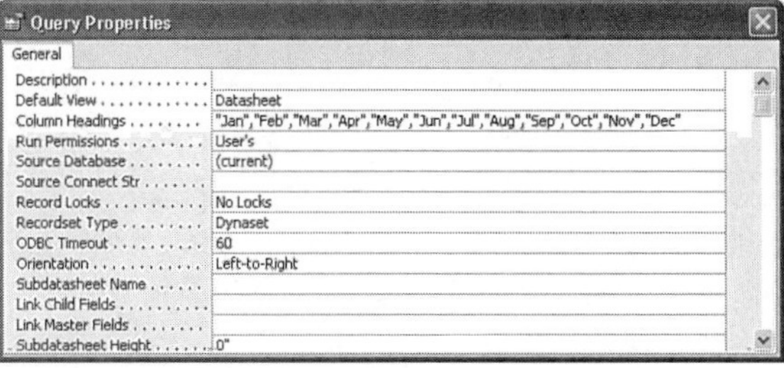

Figure 18.25
In the Query Properties dialog, add a comma-separated list of column headings that correspond to your crosstab query's Format expression for the Column Heading values.

7. Save your query as **qry1997SalesChartCT**.
8. Click the Run button to check your query result set (see Figure 18.26).

qry1997SalesChartCT : Crosstab Query

Category Name	Jan	Feb	Mar	Apr	May
Beverages	$23,269.16	$2,019.24	$10,569.80	$2,786.53	$12,163.25
Condiments	$4,476.30	$4,954.08	$2,491.79	$4,837.91	$5,651.02
Confections	$10,216.17	$5,127.38	$5,739.23	$2,599.51	$13,186.80
Dairy Products	$9,851.48	$6,074.44	$8,192.80	$7,521.50	$9,374.38
Grains/Cereals	$3,585.60	$3,798.80	$5,312.70	$2,084.40	$6,052.25
Meat/Poultry	$8,365.45	$5,958.30	$7,274.40	$5,130.24	$4,597.91
Produce	$3,288.54	$1,587.60	$4,104.60	$5,613.06	$4,695.60
Seafood	$1,693.76	$1,922.65	$3,829.00	$1,023.30	$8,254.15

Record: 1 of 8

Figure 18.26 This Jet crosstab query provides the value of the Row Source property for the linked graph.

Jet SQL

The crosstab query for the linked chart differs from that created by the Chart Wizard for an unlinked chart or graph. Following is the Jet SQL statement for the linked chart's data source:

```
TRANSFORM Sum(qry1997SalesChart.Amount) AS SumOfAmount
SELECT qry1997SalesChart.CategoryName AS Categories
FROM qry1997SalesChart
GROUP BY qry1997SalesChart.CategoryName
PIVOT Format([ShippedDate],"mmm")
   In ("Jan","Feb","Mar","Apr","May","Jun",
       "Jul","Aug","Sep","Oct","Nov","Dec");
```

The primary difference between the two queries is the `GROUP BY` clause, which groups the data by the CategoryName column, rather than by a date expression. In this case, the `In` predicate is required to return the monthly data in date–instead of alphabetic–order.

18

ASSIGNING THE CROSSTAB QUERY AS THE GRAPH'S ROW SOURCE

The next stage in the process is to take advantage of your existing MSGraph design by changing its data source from the Chart Wizard's Jet SQL statement to the new crosstab query. Do the following:

1. Open frm1997SalesByCategoryChart in Form view, select the chart's object frame (OLEUnbound0), and open its Properties window.
2. Open the Row Source list box, and select qry1997SalesChartCT as the value of the Row Source property. The graph displays category labels on the x-axis and month labels in the legend.
3. Double-click to activate the graph, and choose Data, Series in Rows from Access's menu. Verify that your line graph appears the same as the graph that the Chart Wizard created in the earlier "Modifying the Design Features of Your Graph" section (refer to Figure 18.14).

If you're having trouble getting labels into the correct location, see "Reversing the X-Axis and Legend Labels" in the "Troubleshooting" section at the end of this chapter.

LINKING THE GRAPH TO A SINGLE RECORD OF A TABLE OR QUERY

You create a linked graph or chart by setting the values of the MSGraph object's Link Child Fields and Link Master Fields properties. The link is similar to that between a form and subform. A linked graph displays the data series from the current row of the table or query that serves as the Record Source of the form. As you move the record pointer with the record navigation buttons, the graph is redrawn to reflect the data values in the selected row.

To change the frm1997SalesByCategoryChart form to accommodate a linked graph, follow these steps:

1. Change to Form Design view, click the Select Form button, and then click the Properties button to open the Properties window for the form.
2. Click the Data tab, open the Record Source list box, and select qry1997SalesChartCT as the value of the Record Source property of the form, which binds the form to the crosstab query.
3. Your form needs record-navigation buttons for a linked graph or chart, so click the Format tab and set the value of the Navigation Buttons property to Yes.
4. Select the unbound object frame (OLEUnbound0) and then click the Data tab. Verify that qry19971997SalesChartCT is the Row Source for the chart. Type **Categories** as the value of the Link Child Fields and Link Master Fields properties (see Figure 18.27). Disregard the "Can't build a link between unbound forms" error messages that might appear after typing the Link Child Fields value.

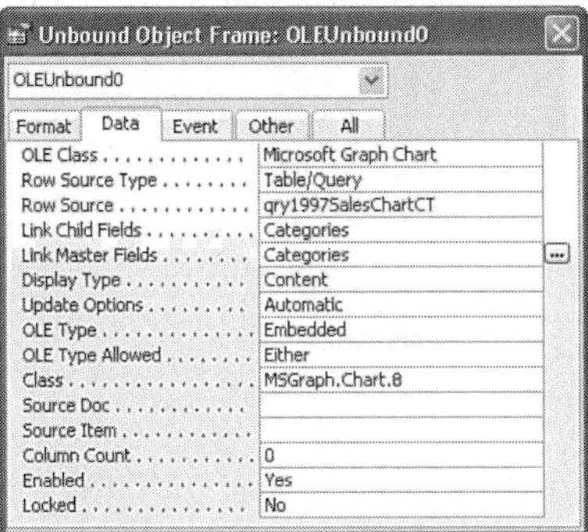

Figure 18.27 Type the column name of the field on which to link the graph and the form in the Link Master Fields and Link Child Fields text boxes. You can't use the Builder button to create the link; you receive an error message if you try.

NOTE

Using this technique, you create the link between the current record of the form and the row of the query that serves as the Row Source property of the graph (through the aliased Categories column of the query).

5. To test your linked graph, click the Form View button. If (in the earlier "Changing the Graph to a Chart" section) you saved the line graph version of the form, your graph initially appears as shown in Figure 18.28.

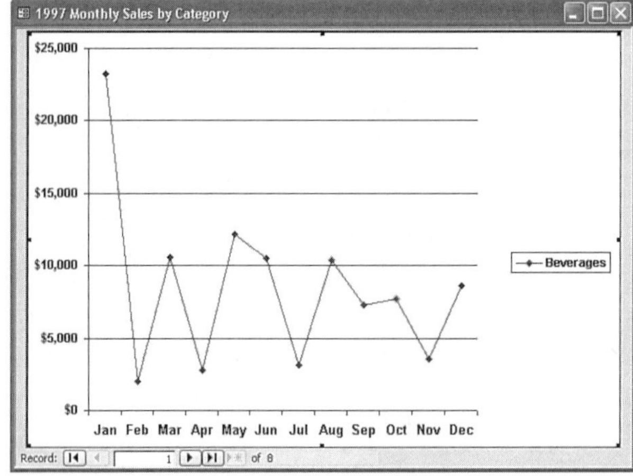

Figure 18.28
The linked graph displays a single line and legend entry for each of the eight product categories.

18

6. The single line appears a bit anemic for a graph of this size, so double-click the graph to activate it in place. Right-click the line with all data points selected, and choose Format Data Series to display the Format Data Series dialog. Click the Patterns tab, select the Custom option, open the Weight drop-down list, and choose the thickest line it offers. Optionally, change the color from Automatic to a color from the pick list.
7. To change the data-point marker, select the Custom option, open the Style drop-down list, and select the square shape. Use the drop-down lists to set the Foreground and Background colors of the marker to automatic to add solid markers of the color complementary to the line. Optionally, increase the size of the markers by a couple of points (see Figure 18.29). Click OK to close the dialog and implement your design changes.
8. Double-click the legend box to open the Format Legend dialog. On the Patterns page, click the None option in the Border frame to remove the border from the legend. Click the Font tab, turn the Bold attribute on, and change the font size to 11 points. Click OK to close the dialog and apply your modification to the legend.
9. To use your enhanced legend as a title for the chart, click and drag the legend to a location above the graph. Click the plot area to display the chart's sizing handles; drag the middle sizing handle to the right to increase the width of the plot area (see Figure 18.30).

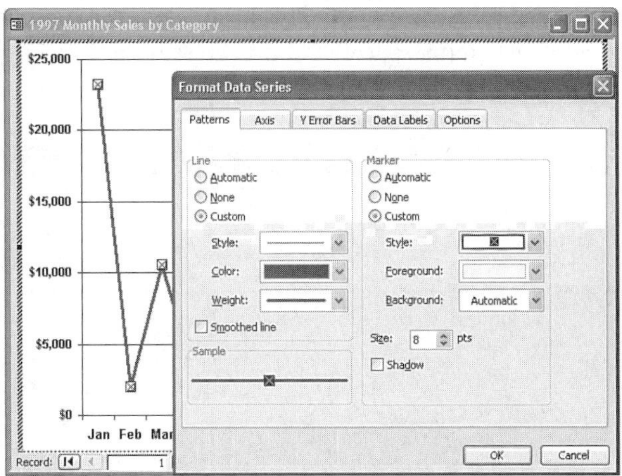

Figure 18.29 The Format Data Series dialog lets you change the thickness and color of the graph's line, add and format data markers, and change the line segment to a continuous curve between data points (called *smoothing*, which is shown later in Figure 8.31).

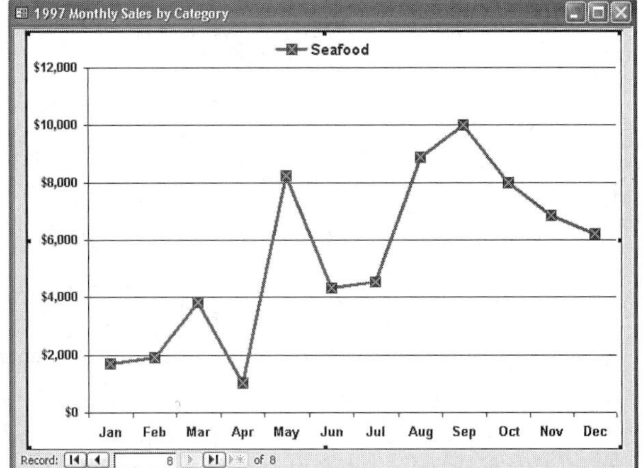

Figure 18.30 This graph is reformatted with increased line thickness, added data points, and a modified legend to act as the chart title.

10. Click the record navigation buttons to display a graph of the sales for each of the eight categories. As you change categories, notice that the y-axis scale changes. The maximum range for the Beverages category is $25,000, while that for Condiments is $7,000.

11. To add a trendline to your graph, activate the graph, and choose Chart, Add Trendline to open the Add Trendline dialog. Accept the default Linear trendline on the Type page, and click the Options tab. Select the Custom option and type a legend for the trendline, such as **1997 Sales Trend**, and click OK.

12. To remove the sizing handles from the Form view of the deactivated object, change to Design view, select the object frame, and open the Properties window. Click the Data tab, and change the Enabled property value to No and Locked to Yes. (You can't change Locked to Yes in Form view.) Changing these two property values prevents users from

activating the graph. With the Smoothed Line check box of the Data Series dialog marked, your modified graph appears in Form view as shown in Figure 18.31. Refer to Figure 18.29 for setting the Smoothed Line option.

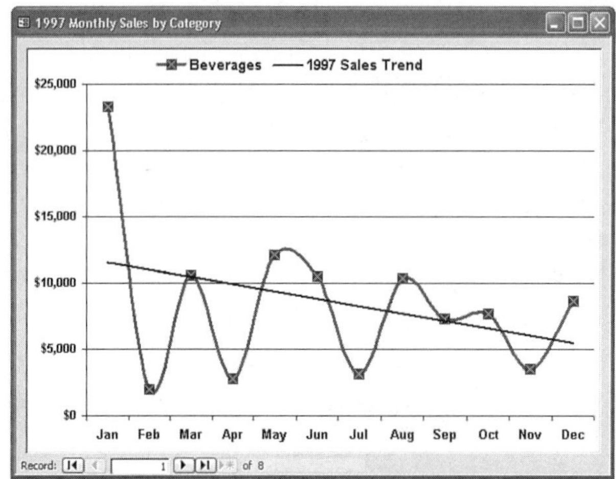

Figure 18.31 Adding a trend line to the graph aids interpretation of the data. Smoothing the data series line implies the existence of additional data points between those in the Datasheet, such as the slower decline from May to June.

11. Choose File, Save As, and then save your bound graph form with a new name, such as **frm1997SalesByCategoryChartLinked**.

WORKING WITH PIVOTCHART FORMS

Microsoft promotes Office System 2003 PivotCharts as a substitute for MSGraph OLE Objects for a good (marketing) reason: MSGraph requires a crosstab query or equivalent and, as mentioned earlier, SQL Server's T-SQL doesn't support crosstab queries directly. If you want to add graphs or charts to ADP, PivotCharts are the least-effort answer. The same is true if you anticipate upsizing your Jet databases to SQL Server and upgrading conventional Access objects to ADP forms and reports.

The sections that follow describe how to use PivotCharts to emulate the unlinked and linked MSGraph objects you created in the preceding sections of this chapter. The example PivotCharts use the qry1997SalesChart query, because the Jet SQL and T-SQL versions of the query are identical. The PivotTable created from the query acts as the data source for the PivotChart by handling the data restructuring ordinarily accomplished by Jet SQL `PIVOT...TRANSFORM` statements.

→ To review PivotChart design basics, **see** "Formatting and Manipulating PivotCharts," **p. 481**.

USING AUTOFORM TO CREATE A PIVOTCHART FORM

PivotCharts don't have the formatting flexibility of MSGraph objects, but they let you duplicate most MSGraph chart types satisfactorily. To generate a stacked area PivotChart based on the qry1997SalesChart query, do the following:

1. Click the Forms shortcut in the Database window, and then click the New button to open the New Form dialog. Select AutoForm: PivotChart in the list, and select the query to serve as the data source for the form. This example uses the qry1997SalesChart query (see Figure 18.32). Click OK to open the PivotChart view of the new form with the Chart Field List superimposed on the empty chart.

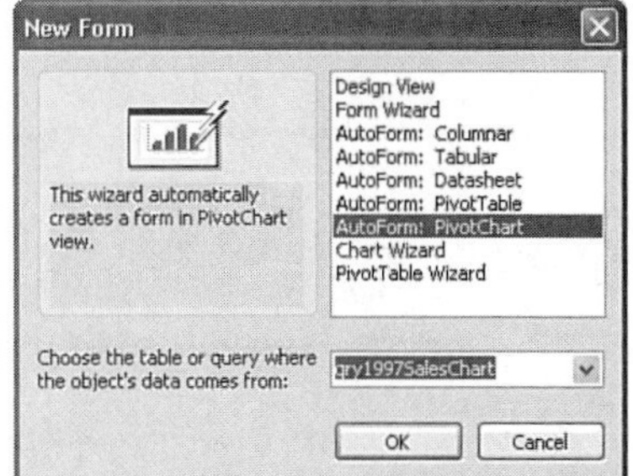

Figure 18.32
The quickest way to create a PivotChart form is to use the New Form dialog's AutoForm: PivotChart option.

2. Drag the Amount field from the Chart Field List to the Drop Data Fields Here zone and the CategoryName field to the Drop Series Fields Here zone. Each product category is a member of Series 1 of the PivotChart.

NOTE

> The PivotChart detects the currency format of the Amount query column and applies standard currency formatting to the y-axis. Unlike MSGraph, you can't remove the two digits after the decimal point without writing a considerable amount of VBA code.

3. Expand the Field List's ShippedDate By Month node and drag the Months field to the Drop CategoryFields Here node. The default chart type is the conventional (not stacked) column version, so Months has one column for each product category (see Figure 18.33).

4. Click the Chart Type button to open the Type page of the Properties dialog. Select the Area chart type and click the Stacked Area subtype to emulate the MSGraph chart you created in the "Changing the Graph to a Chart" section early in the chapter (see Figure 18.34). (If the button is disabled, select the chart to enable it.)

18

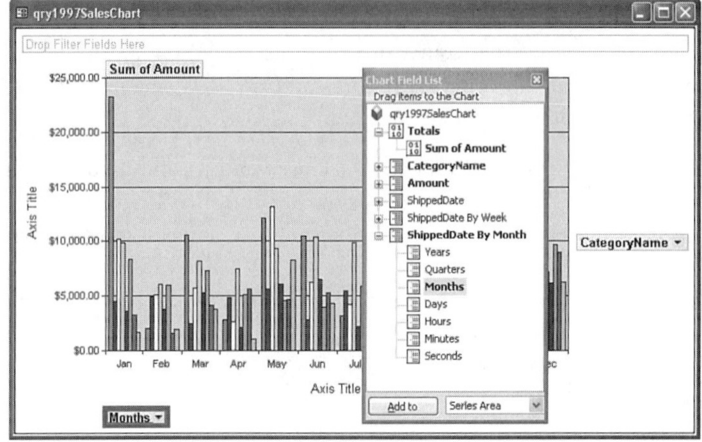

Figure 18.33 Adding value, category (classification), and series fields (columns) from the qry1997SalesChart query generates this default multiple column chart.

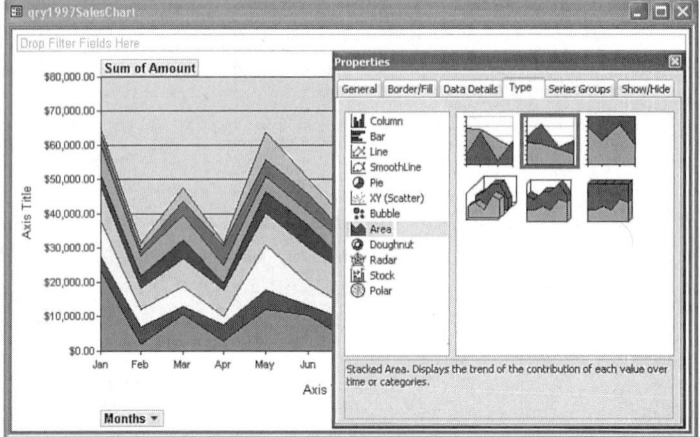

Figure 18.34 The PivotChart's Stacked Area chart type is almost identical to that of MSGraph 10. Notice that the month abbreviations are centered under—instead of between—the x-axis value markers.

5. Click the Show/Hide tab and clear all check boxes except Screen Tips and Commands and Options Dialog Box. Removing the field buttons prevents users from rearranging the chart.

NOTE

"Commands and Options" was the original name of the Properties dialog. Microsoft's developers overlooked changing the caption of the check box.

6. With the Properties dialog open, click the y-axis line, and then click the Format tab. Change the font size to 9 points, and apply the Bold attribute to the labels.
7. Repeat step 6 for the x-axis labels.

8. Select in the General page's list the Value Axis 1 Title, click the Format tab, and delete its Caption property value. Do the same for the Category Axis 1 Title.
9. Optionally, select the Legend, and change the Position to Bottom. (If the Legend isn't visible, choose PivotChart, Show Legend).

10. Change to Form Design view, click the Form Selector button, open the Form properties window, click the Format tab, and type **1997 Monthly Sales By Category** as the value of the Caption property. Your PivotChart in Form view now appears as shown in Figure 18.35.

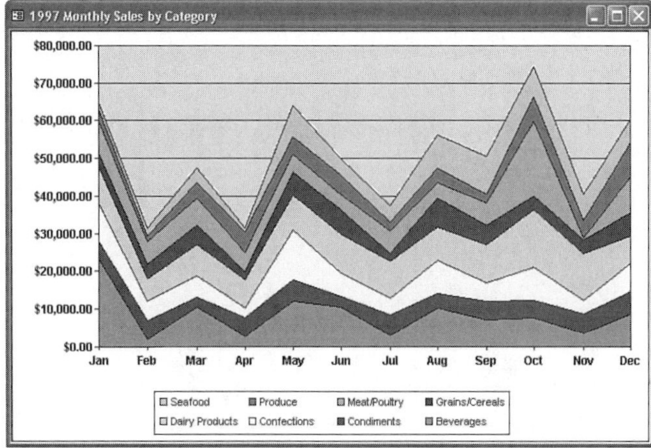

Figure 18.35 With the exception of the two decimal digits of the y-axis labels, this PivotChart successfully emulates the MSGraph stacked area chart shown earlier in Figure 18.16.

11. In Form Design view, open the form's Properties window again and set Allow Form View, Allow Datasheet View, and Allow PivotTable View property values to No. Restricting the view of the form is important because it keeps users from being confused by extraneous views of nonmeaningful data.
12. Save your form with a descriptive name, such as **sbf1997SalesPivotChart**, and close it. You apply the **sbf** prefix because you use the PivotChart form as subform in the next section.

NOTE

> PivotChart forms don't have a Window, Size to Fit Form menu command in Form view. As you change the dimensions of the form, the PivotChart expands or contracts accordingly.

USING THE PIVOTCHART FORM AS A SUBFORM

The PivotChart view of a form prevents you from altering the overall design of the form. For instance, you can't add a visible page header/footer or add extra space to the detail section in which to place a label for a chart title. To achieve form layout flexibility, use the PivotChart form as a subform by following these steps:

1. Click the New Object button and choose Form to open the New Form dialog. Accept the default Design view, leave the table/query list empty, and click OK.
2. Expand the Detail section of the form to accommodate a chart or graph of reasonable size, approximately 6.5 inches wide by 4.5 inches deep for this example.
3. Open the Toolbox, and make sure the Control Wizards button is selected.
4. Select the Subform/Subreport tool, and draw a subform container of moderate size. When you release the mouse, the SubForm Wizard opens.
5. In the first SubForm Wizard dialog, select the Use an Existing Form option, and select the PivotChart form to use as the subform. For this example, select the sbf1997SalesPivotChart you created in the preceding section (see Figure 18.36). Click Next.

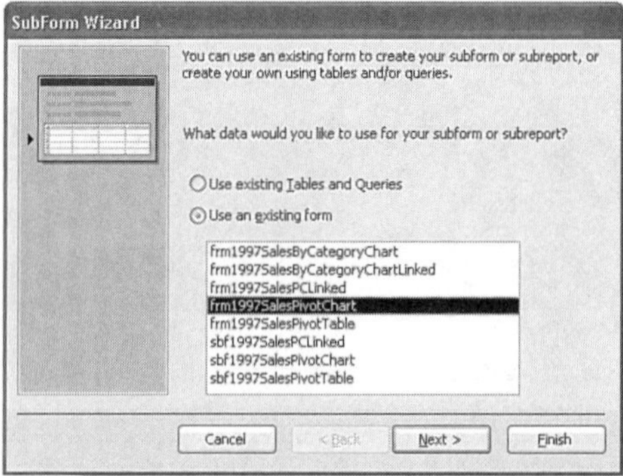

Figure 18.36
In the first SubForm Wizard dialog, select the PivotChart form you saved to serve as a subform of the new form you opened.

6. Accept the default name for the subform container and its label in the last Wizard dialog, and click Finish to add the subform, which has a default size of about 3.5×0.5 inches. Disregard the appearance of the Form Header/Footer and Detail sections in Form Design view; PivotChart forms don't display these sections in Form view.
7. Use the sizing handles to expand the subform to within about 3/8 inch from the top, and 1/8 inch or so from the left, right, and bottom edges of the form.

8. Change to Form view to verify that the subform displays the PivotChart (see Figure 18.37).

TIP

> If the subform opens in Form or Datasheet view, you forgot to disable all but PivotChart view in step 11 of the preceding section.

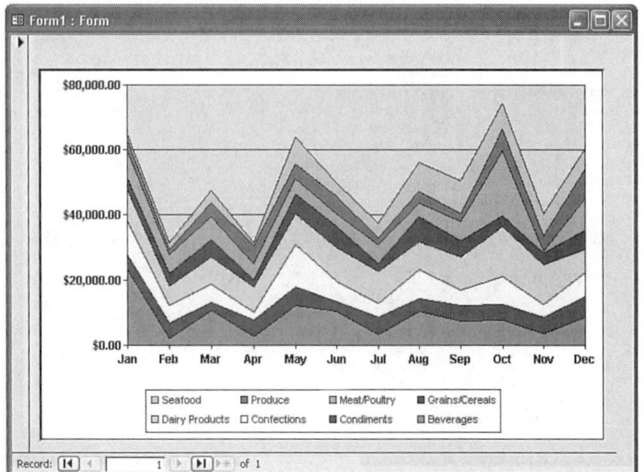

Figure 18.37
Perform a quick check of the initial appearance of your PivotChart subform to verify that it opens in PivotChart view.

9. Return to Form Design mode, and open the Properties window. On the Format page, set the Caption property value to **1997 Monthly Sales By Category**, Allow Datasheet View to No, Allow PivotTable View to No, Allow PivotChart View to No, Scroll Bars to Neither, Record Selectors to No, and Navigation Buttons to No.

10. Add a label above the subform to serve as a chart title (see Figure 18.38)

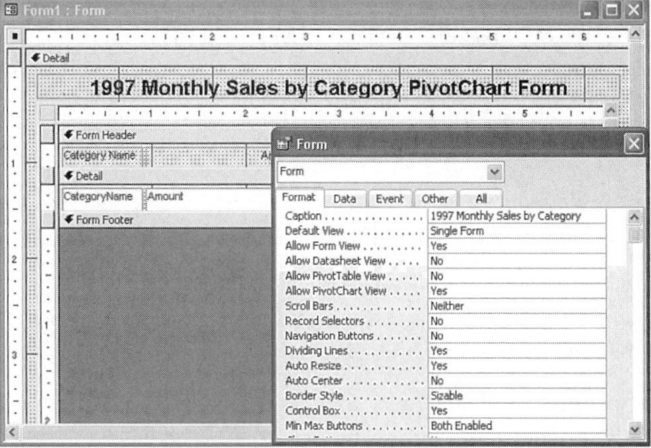

Figure 18.38
Here's the final design of the form/subform combination to display the unlinked PivotChart.

11. Select the subform, and set the Border Style property value to Transparent. When you return to Form view, the form/subform combination appears as shown in Figure 18.39.

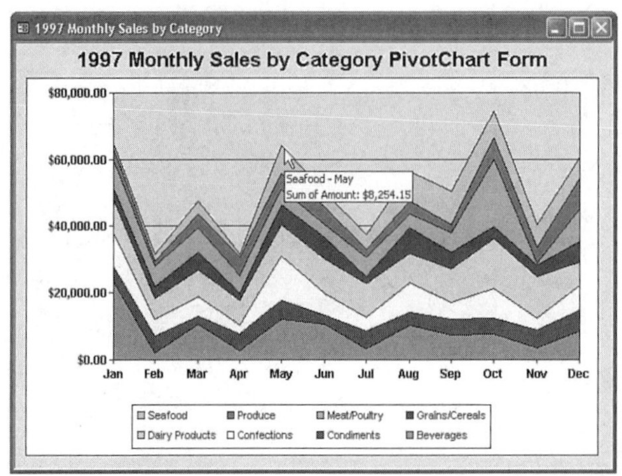

Figure 18.39 Adding the PivotChart form as a subform adds flexibility to form layout, and also enables conversion of the combination to a linked graph. Placing the mousepointer on a data point shows a ScreenTip with the series name and value.

12. Save your form with the usual descriptive name, **frm1997SalesPivotChart** for this example, and close it.

18

TIP

Use the design process described in this and the preceding section to create a report/subreport combination for printing. You can select a set of textures for the individual data series members of the PivotChart if your users need to print black-and-white reports.

You can print the form to color printers, but you might not be pleased with the initial aspect ratio of the chart. By default, the chart expands vertically to fill the entire printable area of the page. To retain the aspect ratio, set the Format page's Can Grow property value to No.

Linking the PivotChart to the Main Form's Current Record

Creating a linked PivotChart isn't as simple as the method described in the earlier "Creating a Linked Graph from a Jet Crosstab Query" section. The basic steps required to link a PivotChart form/subform combination are as follows:

1. Bind the form to a table or query that you can link to the query that provides the data source for the subform and its graph or chart.
2. Set the values of the Link Master Fields and Link Child Fields properties to the common fields of the main form and subform data sources.
3. Add Record Navigation buttons to the main form.
4. Modify the form and PivotChart design to take advantage of chart linking.

The following two sections describe how to modify copies of the form and PivotChart subform you created in the preceding two sections to link a graph to the Categories table.

CLONING A LINKED PIVOTCHART FORM/SUBFORM PAIR

Take the following steps to create renamed copies of the form and subform, and link them:

1. Make a copy of the sbf1997SalesPivotChart subform, and name it **sbf1997SalesPCLinked**. (Right-click the original subform in the Database window, and choose Save As to quickly create the copy.)

2. Open the subform copy in Form view, click the Chart Type button, and select Line or Smoothline in the Chart Type Dialog's list. Click the first subtype, a standard line graph, and then close and save changes to the subform. Changing the chart to a graph verifies that you're using the correct subform when you make changes to the main form.

3. Make a copy of the frm1997SalesPivotChart as **frm1997SalesPCLinked**, and open the copy in Form Design view.

4. Open the Properties dialog for the form, click the Data tab, and set the Record Source property to the Categories table. The CategoryName field of Categories table links to the CategoryName column of the subform's qry1997SalesChart data source.
5. Set the Allow Filters, Allow Edits, Allow Deletions, and Allow Additions property values to No to create a read-only (decision-support) form.
6. Click the Format tab and set the value of the Navigation Buttons property of the form to Yes.
7. Right-click the label at the top of the form, and choose Change To, Text Box to replace it with a text box of the same size. Click the Data tab and set the Control Source property to **="1997 Sales for " & [CategoryName]**, and the Locked property value to Yes.
8. To emulate a label with a text box, click the Format tab and set the text box's Back Style property value to Transparent.
9. Click the edge of the subform to select the subform container, click the Data tab, and select sbf1997SalesPCLinked as the Source Object property value.

10. Click the Builder button of the Link Master Fields property text box to open the Subform Field Linker dialog. If CategoryName isn't selected in both the Master Fields and Child Fields lists, select that field (see Figure 18.40). Click OK.

11. Click Form view to display the linked line graph. Navigate the Recordset to verify that the category name in the caption and the legend track one another (see Figure 18.41). Close the form/subform combination, and save your changes.

TWEAKING THE DESIGN OF THE PIVOTCHART SUBFORM

After you've verified that linking is working, you can delete the legend to devote more space on the form to the graph. Like MSGraph objects, you can change the line (series member) formatting properties and add trendlines to PivotCharts. However, the process is much more tedious than that for linked MSGraph objects, because you must alter each member of the series.

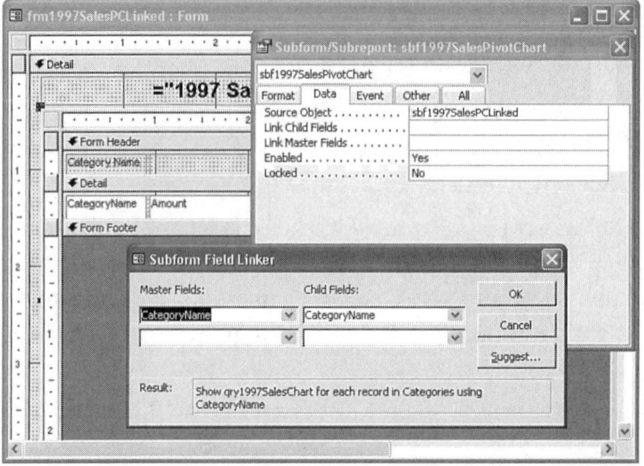

Figure 18.40 Use the Subform Field Linker to set the Link Master Fields and Link Child Fields property values.

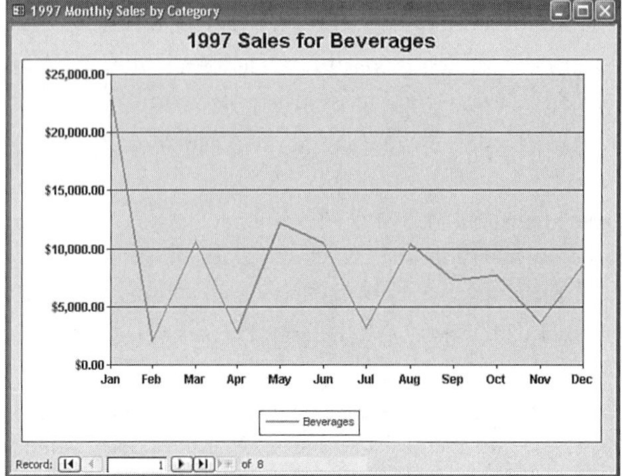

Figure 18.41 The linked PivotChart subform resembles the linked MSGraph object shown earlier in Figure 18.28.

To delete the legend, increase the line thickness, and add a trendline to a series member, do this:

1. Open the sbf1997SalesPCLinked form in Form view, right-click an empty area of the graph, and choose Properties to open the Properties dialog for the Chart Workspace. Be sure to open the subform, not the main form.

2. In the Select list, choose Legend, and click the Delete button to remove the Legend, which isn't necessary for a linked graph.
3. Open the Select list and choose Beverages to select the first series member. In the General Page, click the Add Trendline button (the middle button below the Add line) to add a linear trendline to the graph.
4. Click the Line/Marker tab, and set the Weight property to thick.

5. Return to the General page, and select the added Beverages Trendline 1. Click the Trendline tab and clear the Display Equation and Display R-squared Value check boxes.
6. Press Ctrl+S to save your final changes, and close the subform.
7. Open the frm1997SalesPCLinked form in Form view to check your design changes (see Figure 18.42).

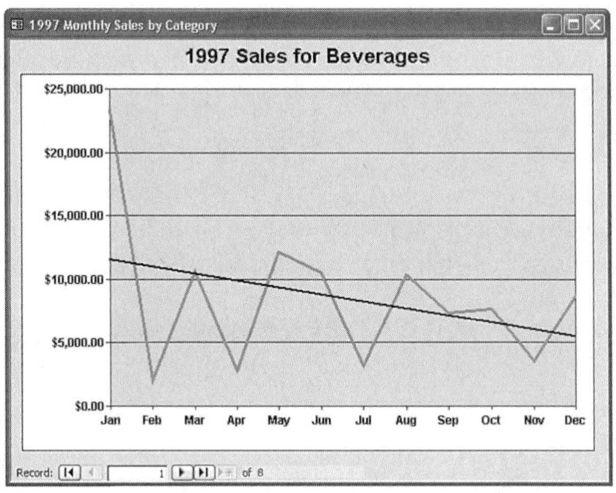

Figure 18.42 Thickening the PivotChart's series line and adding a trendline duplicates the final MSGraph linked chart of the earlier Figure 18.31, except for the data points and line smoothing.

NOTE

The final versions of the forms and subforms you create in this chapter are included in the Charts18.mdb sample database, which is located in the \Seua11\Chaptr18 folder of the accompanying CD-ROM.

PERSISTING LINKED PIVOTCHART PROPERTIES WITH VBA CODE

A defect in the PivotChart Web Component causes the PivotChart to lose the design changes you made in the preceding section when you move the record pointer with the Navigation buttons. This problem appeared in Access 2002 and persists in Access 2003. You must add VBA code to reapply the properties for each category's graph. The code behind the frm1997SalesPCLinked form of the Charts18.mdb sample database performs the following functions:

- Changes the number format of the y-axis labels from Currency to the custom $#,##0 format, which removes the unnecessary decimal digits.
- Sets the scale of all graphs to $25,000 so users aren't misled by scale changes when comparing results of categories with different maximum sales values for the year.
- Establishes a thick line weight.

- Adds a trendline and hides the equation and R-squared text.
- Changes the color of the trendline from black to red and the weight to thick.

NOTE

> The Access 2003 prerelease version used to write this book has a bug in the setup program that omits the required reference to Microsoft Office Web Components 11.0. This reference must be present to persist the linked PivotChart properties.
>
> If this reference is missing from the Visual Basic editor's References list, click Browse, navigate to the \Program Files\Common Files\Microsoft Shared\Web Components\11 folder and double-click OWC11.dll to add it to your Access project.

Figure 18.43 shows frm1997SalesPCLinked form of Charts18.mdb with formatting applied by the Form_Current event handler. To view the VBA code, with the form open in Design view, click the toolbar's Code button to open the VBA editor.

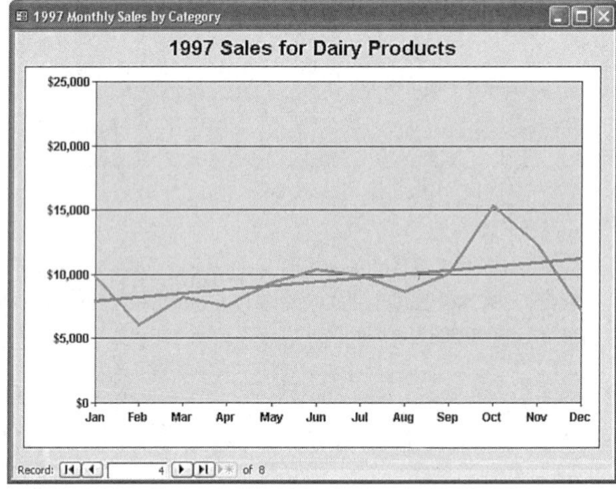

Figure 18.43 Code in the Form_Current event handler of Charts18.mdb's frm1997SalesPCLinked form applies the linked PivotChart formatting changes shown here.

→ For the details of adding VBA formatting code for PivotCharts, **see** "Using the On Current Event to Set Linked PivotChart Properties," **p. 1223**.

SUBSTITUTING OR ADDING A PIVOTTABLE IN A FORM

PivotCharts rely on an underlying PivotTable to supply data to the chart or graph. Thus, it's easy to alter a form or subform to display a PivotTable instead of a PivotChart. For example, you can open the sbf1997SalesPivotChart subform in design view and change its AllowPivotChartView property value to No, AllowPivotTableView to Yes, and DefaultView to PivotTable.

When you open frm1997SalesPivotChart, the PivotTable appears as shown in Figure 18.44. Months are row headings and product categories are column headings, so you might want to pivot the table to correspond to the graph layout. In this case, you must mark the Field Buttons/Drop Zones check box on the PivotChart Property dialog's Show/Hide page to enable pivoting when you change to PivotTable view.

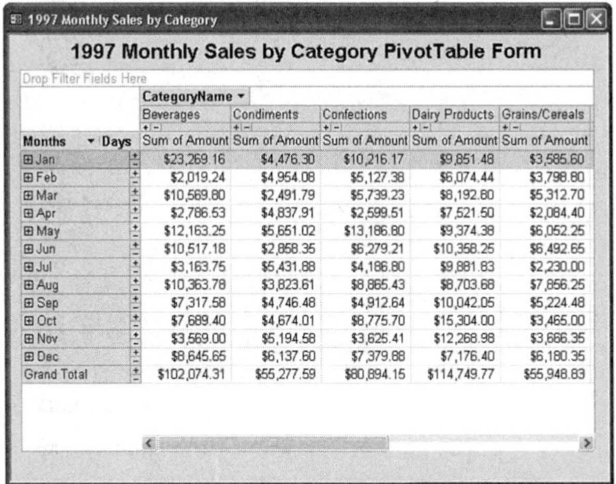

Months / Days	Beverages Sum of Amount	Condiments Sum of Amount	Confections Sum of Amount	Dairy Products Sum of Amount	Grains/Cereals Sum of Amount
Jan	$23,269.16	$4,476.30	$10,216.17	$9,851.48	$3,585.60
Feb	$2,019.24	$4,954.08	$5,127.38	$6,074.44	$3,798.80
Mar	$10,569.80	$2,491.79	$5,739.23	$8,192.80	$5,312.70
Apr	$2,786.53	$4,837.91	$2,599.51	$7,521.50	$2,084.40
May	$12,163.25	$5,651.02	$13,186.80	$9,374.38	$6,052.25
Jun	$10,517.18	$2,858.35	$6,279.21	$10,358.25	$6,492.65
Jul	$3,163.75	$5,431.88	$4,186.80	$9,881.83	$2,230.00
Aug	$10,363.78	$3,823.61	$8,865.43	$8,703.68	$7,856.25
Sep	$7,317.58	$4,746.48	$4,912.64	$10,042.05	$5,224.48
Oct	$7,689.40	$4,674.01	$8,775.70	$15,304.00	$3,465.00
Nov	$3,569.00	$5,194.58	$3,625.41	$12,268.98	$3,666.35
Dec	$8,645.65	$6,137.60	$7,379.88	$7,176.40	$6,180.35
Grand Total	$102,074.31	$55,277.59	$80,894.15	$114,749.77	$55,948.83

Figure 18.44
To substitute this PivotTable for a PivotChart, change the Allow...View and Default View property values on the Format page of the PivotChart subform.

Another approach is to create individual PivotTable and PivotChart subforms. You can locate an additional PivotTable subform below the PivotChart. Alternatively, you can add a command button and VBA event-handling code to alternate between the two subforms as the Source Object property value of the subform container. Northwind.mdb's sample Sales Analysis form uses this method to alternately display Sales Analysis Subform1 and Sales Analysis Subform2.

To examine the Sales Analysis approach, open the form in Design view, and click the Code button to display the `btnEdit_Click` event handler's code.

TIP

> Access 2003's PivotTable Wizard is an alternative to the AutoForm: PivotTable choice. The second dialog lets you select a data source for the PivotTable and specify the fields available. The AutoForm: PivotTable's Field list does the same. It's easier to use AutoForm: PivotTable to generate a PivotTable form from a query.

TROUBLESHOOTING

REVERSING THE X-AXIS AND LEGEND LABELS

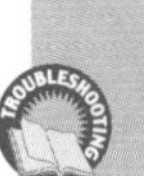

After changing the Row Source property of a chart to the qry1997SalesChartCT crosstab query, the product categories appear in the chart as the x-axis labels, and the month abbreviations appear in the legend.

In the example in the "Assigning the Crosstab Query as the Graph's Row Source" section, you didn't change to Series in Rows in step 3. Crosstab queries you design can have the legend values (representing a series of lines) as column headers or row headers. If your x-axis and legend labels are wrong, activate the chart, choose Data, and then choose either Series in Columns or Series in Rows to make the change.

CONNECTING A PIVOTCHART (MICROSOFT OFFICE CHART 11.0) OR PIVOTTABLE (MICROSOFT OFFICE PIVOTTABLE 11.0) ACTIVEX CONTROL

Using Insert Object to add a PivotChart or PivotTable ActiveX control to a form or report, and setting up the Microsoft.Jet.OLEDB.4.0 provider to connect to the current database results in a Data Link Error message.

When you have an Access object open in Design view, the Jet database is locked in the read-only state to prevent others from modifying objects simultaneously. The lock prevents opening the second connection to the database, which is required to support the ActiveX control version of these objects. This problem doesn't occur with ADP, because you can establish multiple simultaneous connections to SQL Server in Design view. The only advantage to the ActiveX control version of the PivotChart or PivotTable control, however, is that you don't need to add a subform to add design elements to the form. The downside is that your ADP requires additional connections to SQL Server to support each PivotChart or PivotTable.

IN THE REAL WORLD—A HOBSON'S CHOICE: MSGRAPH OBJECTS VERSUS PIVOTCHARTS

Webster's New Collegiate Dictionary defines a Hobson's choice as an "apparently free choice with no real alternative." You are free to continue to use MSGraph with Jet databases and Jet SQL crosstab queries. MSGraph is a mature and stable product with no significant bugs. Its precursors date back to Excel 5.0, and MSGraph is backward-compatible with the Access 97, 2000, and 2002 versions. If you intend to use VBA to customize MSGraph objects, however, be prepared for a long learning curve. MSGraph's object model is the epitome of obfuscation. Check `http://msdn.microsoft.com/library/officedev/odeomg/deovrmicrosoftgraph2000.htm` for an object model diagram of MSGraph 9.0. Compare the MSGraph object model with the PivotChart object model at `http://msdn.microsoft.com/library/en-us/owcvba10/html/octocChartWorkspaceObjectModel.asp`.

General-purpose OLE 2.0 objects created by mini-servers, such as MSGraph, are endangered species because Web browsers, including IE, don't support them directly. You can open a Word document or Excel spreadsheet in IE and display an embedded MSGraph chart because Word and Excel are OLE 2.0 full servers and act as the graph's container. The catch is that you must have Microsoft Office installed to open the Word or Excel document, plus MSGraph (which Office installs automatically) to view the embedded graph or chart.

The Access 2003 runtime version includes a redistributable runtime version of Graph.exe; the runtime version's design features are disabled.

PivotCharts and their underlying PivotTables are ActiveX controls, so they're Web-enabled and programmable with VBScript or JavaScript, as well as with VBA when they're used in conventional Access forms and reports. The hierarchy of the PivotChart object model is much simpler and more straightforward than that of MSGraph. PivotTables accept XML-encoded data, so they fit into Microsoft's .NET framework. PivotTables—and thus PivotCharts—also can manipulate DataCubes generated by SQL Server's Analysis (OLAP) Services. You can expect Microsoft to enhance these versatile controls in subsequent Office upgrades. MSGraph is in maintenance mode and Microsoft provides it only for backward compatibility; there won't be any additions to its current feature set or changes to its object model.

NEW 2002 Office 2000's license restrictions on Office Web Components (OWC) 9.0 prevented Access developers from using PivotCharts and PivotTables in runtime Access applications. (MOD10 includes the runtime versions of both MSAccess.exe and MSGraph.exe). OWC version 9.0 required users to have Office 2000 installed to open a form or report containing a PivotTable or PivotChart. Office XP changed the licensing terms. The Office 2003 OWC license lets you distribute OWC 11.0 with your runtime applications for users who don't have Office 11 installed. This policy is similar to that for Graph.exe. Alternatively, users of Web-enabled Access applications can download the OWC from Microsoft's Web site; the download is automatic if OWC11.dll isn't present and registered on the user's computer.

The only difference between the licensed and distributable behavior of OWC 11.0 is lack of design-mode features in the latter. For instance, users can't alter the field complement of PivotTables or perform pivoting operations, but expansion/contraction and setting filters are permitted. This is more of an issue with PivotTables than with PivotCharts; most applications set the properties of PivotCharts either in the Properties dialog for the object or with VBA code.

There's no "real alternative" to PivotCharts in the new Access 11 applications you create or, as mentioned early in the chapter, for existing applications you upgrade to ADP and SQL Server. The workaround for the lack of SQL Server crosstab queries described in Chapter 22's "Emulating Jet Crosstab Queries with T-SQL" section is a short-term approach. Dedicate your graph and chart learning investment to PivotCharts; MSGraph is a dead end.

PART V

UPGRADING TO SQL SERVER DATABASES

CHAPTER 19

Linking Access Front-Ends to Jet and Client/Server Tables

In this chapter

Creating Multiuser Access Applications by Linking Tables

A single .mdb file that contains Access *application objects* (forms, reports, macros, and VBA code modules) and Jet data objects (tables and queries) is one of Access's strongest selling points. Other desktop database management applications—such as Visual FoxPro and Visual Basic—require multiple files for a single database application. The obvious advantage of a single .mdb file for a complete Access application is simplicity. You can deploy your application by copying its .mdb file to another computer that has Access 2003 installed.

Sharing your Access application with other users in a Windows XP workgroup or Windows 2000/2003 Server domain requires separating the application objects from database objects. It's *theoretically* possible for multiple users to simultaneously share a single .mdb application on a network or use Windows 2000+ Server's Terminal Services to run multiple instances of the application. In practice, however, application response time and network traffic issues make the single .mdb approach impractical for all but the simplest database projects. Another disadvantage of the single .mdb approach is that making changes to any Access object by opening it in Design mode prevents other users from using the object.

Making your Access application accessible to more than one user at a time requires dividing the application into *front-end* and *back-end* components. For Jet databases, the front end contains all application elements plus queries; the back end contains only Jet tables. If you upsize your Access application to the Microsoft SQL Server Desktop Engine (MSDE) or SQL Server 2000, Jet queries become back-end SQL Server views, functions, or stored procedures. In either case, front-end components *link* to the back-end database objects. The linking process for Jet tables is similar to that for linking dBASE or Paradox files; linking MSDE 2000 tables parallels linking Visual FoxPro files with an Open Database Connectivity (ODBC) driver.

→ To review the table linking process, **see** "Linking and Importing External ISAM Tables," **p. 272** and "Linking Visual FoxPro Tables with ODBC," **p. 274**.

NOTE

Sections later in the chapter cover upsizing Jet tables to MSDE or one of the four SQL Server 2000 editions–Personal, Developer, Standard, or Enterprise. This chapter uses *SQL Server 2000* to refer to MSDE and any of the SQL Server 2000 editions, except when discussing features that are specific to MSDE 2000.

Multiuser Access applications require that each user have a copy of the front-end .mdb file and network access to the back-end .mdb file or SQL Server 2000. Alternatively, users can run multiple front-end Terminal Server sessions. You can share Jet back ends in a peer-to-peer Windows XP or 2000 Professional workgroup environment or within a Windows 2000/.NET Server domain. Providing network access to MSDE 2000 in a Windows XP or 2000 workgroup environment requires modifying MSDE 2000's security settings. For workgroups, linked Jet back ends are simpler to implement.

Deploying multiuser Access applications requires establishing security and user permissions for front-end application and back-end data objects. You secure and assign permissions for Access front ends and links to back ends with the User-Level Security Wizard and other tools you access from the Tools, Security menu. Front-end security is identical for Jet and SQL Server back ends, so sections near the end of this chapter cover the User-Level Security Wizard and other security tools. Securing back-end .mdb files requires setting individual user or group permissions for the shared .mdb file. For example, you should be the only person who can delete, move, or copy the back-end .mdb file. File-level permissions apply only to Jet back ends, so this very important topic comes early in the chapter.

→ To learn more about user-level security, **see** "Applying User-Level Security to Access Front-Ends," **p. 783**.

NOTE

> The following sections describe creating and securing back-end databases shared by a Windows 2000 Server domain controller or member server. The process for sharing files with Windows NT 4.0 Server or Windows XP Professional workgroup member is similar, but the share and file security settings differ. The examples assume that you're familiar with creating file shares, have an administrative account for the server, and know how to manage Windows XP or 2000 local users and groups.

Creating Linked Jet Tables with the Database Splitter

You use the Database Splitter utility to create a conventional multiuser Access/Jet application from a copy of the application's single .mdb file.

NOTE

> The following example assumes that you haven't applied user-level security settings to the single-file application's Jet tables. Applying user-level security to tables of a single-user application is uncommon. If you've applied these settings, you must copy the System.mdw file for the application to the file share and designate it as the Workgroup Information File for the back-end .mdb file. All users must have Read permission for the System.mdw copy.

→ To review System.mdw basics, **see** "Jet Workgroup Information Files," **p. 153**.

→ For more information on changing the Workgroup Information File, **see** "Establishing Your Own Admins Name, Password, and PID," **p. 783**.

Take the following steps to create and link the back-end database to the front-end application objects:

1. If the computer on which you're running Access 2003 has a network connection to a server or another workstation, create a share on the server or another workstation in your workgroup to store the back-end .mdb file. The server or other workstation doesn't need to have Office 2003 installed to share the back-end file. Otherwise, add a new folder to store the shared back end .mdb file on your client machine.

2. If you're splitting a production database, create and use a copy of the database. This example uses a copy of the Northwind.mdb sample database named NWClient.mdb.
3. Open the Jet database to split, and choose Tools, Database Utilities, Database Splitter to open the utility's first and only dialog (see Figure 19.1).

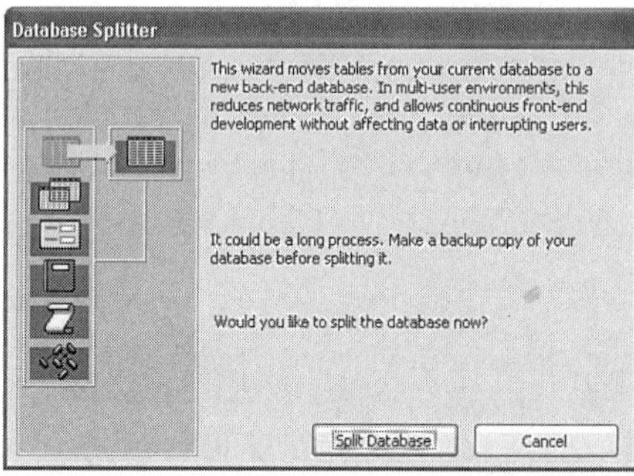

Figure 19.1
The Database Splitter utility has only a single dialog.

4. Click the Split Database button to open the Create Back-End Database dialog. The default name of the back-end .mdb is the front-end name with a _be suffix. Change the name to whatever you want; this example uses NWData.mdb as the name.
5. Navigate to the server share (or local folder, if you're not using a network server). This example uses the Northwind share on the OAKLEAF-MS10 member server of the OAKLEAF Windows 2000 domain (\\OAKLEAF-MS10\Northwind), which also runs SQL Server 2000 (see Figure 19.2).

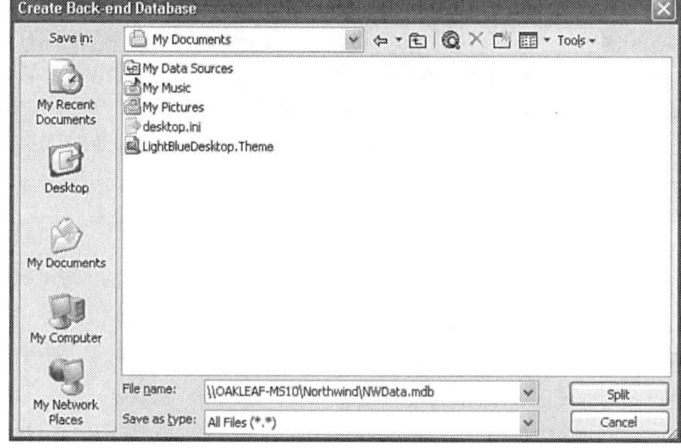

Figure 19.2
Specify a share on a workstation or server in your Windows 2000/.NET domain or another workstation in your Windows XP/2000 Professional workgroup.

TIP

Assigning the Uniform Naming Convention (UNC) name—*//SERVERNAME/ShareName*—to connect to the server share is a better practice than allocating a local logical drive letter to the share. Users can delete or change the drive letter assignment. You can use Access security to prevent users from changing the UNC link to the back-end file.

6. Click the Split Button to create the new back-end database and move the tables to it. Click OK to acknowledge the completion message. The links to the back-end tables appear in the front-end application as shown in Figure 19.3.

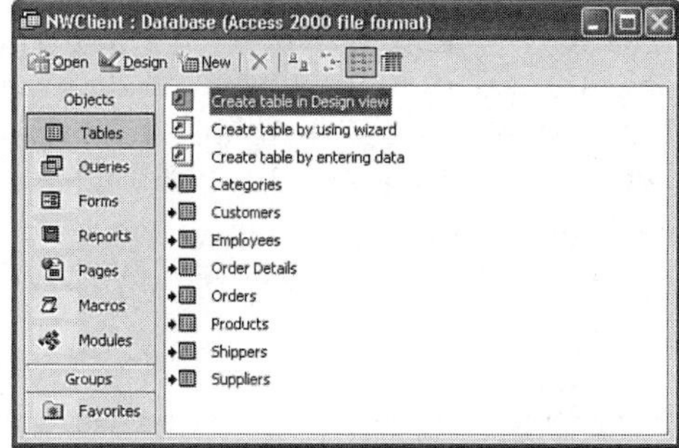

Figure 19.3
The table icons of the Database window gain an arrow to indicate that they're linked to the back-end .mdb file.

7. Verify that the linked tables are operational by opening each table in sequence and navigating to the last record to assure that the tables are updatable.

8. Open one of the tables in design view. You receive a message that some properties of linked tables can't be modified in Design view. Click Yes and then click the Properties button to open the Table Properties window. The Description property value defines the link to the back-end .mdb file (see Figure 19.4).

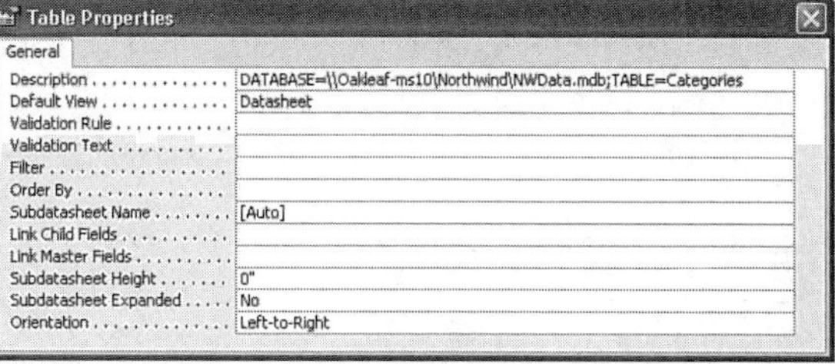

Figure 19.4
The Description property value of the linked table contains the linking information.

9. Run a few queries, and open the forms and reports to verify that the application objects behave as expected with the linked tables.

ESTABLISHING NETWORK SHARE AND FILE SECURITY FOR THE BACK END

The first step after you share a back-end database is to set share and file permissions on the .mdb file. Until you remove Full Control permissions of the share and file for ordinary users, your back-end database might be vulnerable to deletion, copying or moving by any network user who has access to the server. The degree of vulnerability depends on permissions assigned to the logical drive or directory in which you create the shared folder. By default, the share and its files inherit permissions assigned to the parent drive or folder.

Windows 2000's default share permissions give the Everyone group Full Control; Windows XP and Windows .NET server assign no permissions to the Everyone group. This section's examples assume that the Everyone group has no default or inherited permissions for the share or the back-end .mdb file.

All users of your front-end application need Read and Modify permissions for the share, and Read, Write, Create, and Delete permissions for the folder. These permissions enable the first user to create the .ldb locking file (NWData.ldb for this example) when opening the .mdb file during login and the last user to delete the file when logging off the application. You can assign permissions to groups or users; this example assigns permissions to two users in the `oakleaf.org` Windows 2000 domain: NWReader1 and NWWriter1.

> **NOTE**
>
> The locking file contains the computer name and Access security name—such as Admin—of each person who has an active link to the back-end .mdb file. This file can contain up to 255 records, which is Access's limit for concurrent database users.

Following are the steps required to secure the network share and the NWData.mdb file:

1. Log on to the server with an account that has local Administrator privileges.
2. In Explorer, right-click the shared folder (Northwind) and choose properties to open the *FolderName* Properties dialog. Click the Sharing tab, and then click the Permissions button to open the Permissions for *ShareName* dialog.
3. Add the groups or users to the Name list and allow them Read and Change permissions (see Figure 19.5). You need Change permissions for the share to enable all users to create and delete the .ldb file. Click OK to close the Permissions dialog.

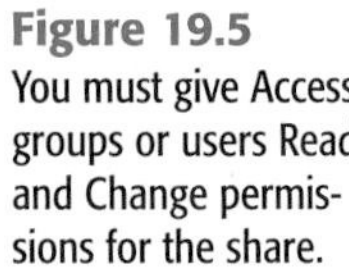

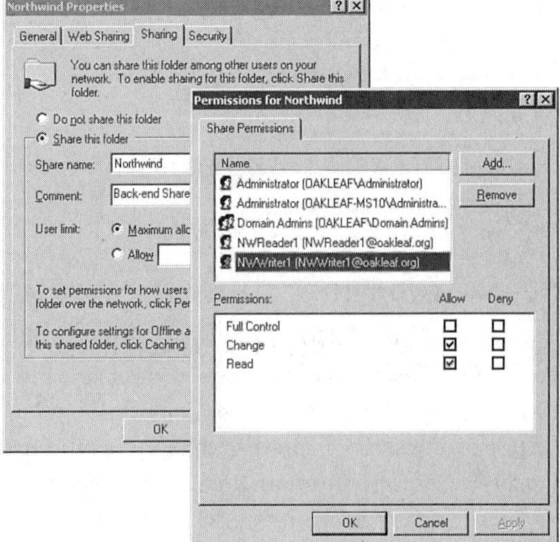

Figure 19.5
You must give Access groups or users Read and Change permissions for the share.

4. Click the Security tab, add the groups or users to the folder Permissions list and allow them Modify permission, which enables all permissions except Full Control (see Figure 19.6). Click OK twice to save your changes and close the Permissions and Security dialogs.

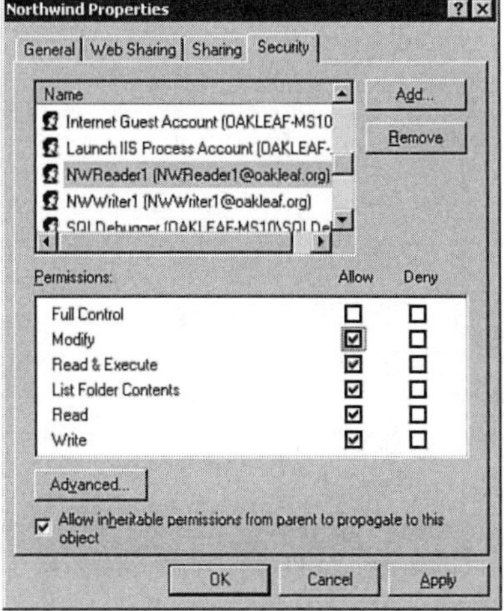

Figure 19.6
Access users or groups must have Modify permission for the shared folder, even if Write permissions aren't required.

5. Right-click the back-end .mdb file and choose Properties to open the *FileName*.mdb Properties dialog. Clear the Allow Inheritable Permissions from Parent to Propagate to This Object check box to prevent users from inheriting the Modify permission. Clearing the check box displays a Security message. Click Remove to clear all permission check boxes.
6. Add at least the local Administrators group and grant this group Full Control permission. You might want to grant Full Control privileges to other administrative accounts and groups. 19
7. Add groups or users who need read-write access to the tables (NWWriter1 for this example), and grant the accounts Read and Write permissions for the file (see Figure 19.7).
8. Add groups or users who need read-only access to the tables (NWReader1 for this example) and grant the accounts Read permissions for the file.
9. If you've applied user-level security to the tables copy the System.mdw file for the application to the share, give all users Read permission for System.mdw. Then open the back-end database in Access, and use the Workgroup Administrator to specify the local copy of System.mdw as the workgroup file.
10. Click OK to apply the file permissions and close the Security dialog.

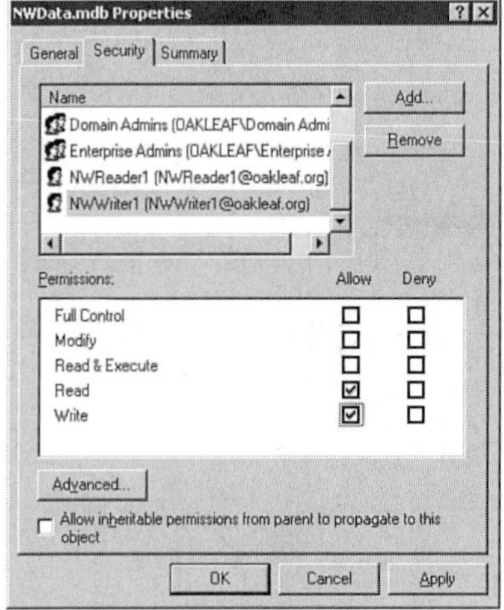

Figure 19.7 Access data entry users require Read and Write privileges for the back-end database file. Others should be granted Read privilege only.

> **TIP**
>
> You can grant all users read-write permissions for the back-end .mdb file and use Access security to prevent read-only users modifying the file. In this case, Access read-only users who have permission to create new front-ends can gain read-write access to the table. Restricting write permission to authorized users provides an additional layer of security for your back-end database.

Your back-end database files are now secured against inadvertent or intentional deletion or modification by non-administrators.

Verifying Back-End Database Network Security

After you secure the back-end .mdb file, you must assign non-administrative users to the Windows XP or 2000 Power Users group. Members of the default Users group have read-only permissions for Access 2003. It's also a good practice to verify your security settings work by following these steps:

1. Log on to the computer running the front-end with your administrative account and add the users you created to the local Power Users group.
2. Log off and log on with the read-only account (NWReader1) and launch Access. The Office 2003 setup program runs to add Registry settings and a workgroup file (System.mdw) for the new user.
3. Open a table from the front-end application (NWClient) and verify that the tentative append record is missing, which verifies that the back-end database is read-only for this user.
4. Log off and log on with the read-write account (NWWriter1) and launch Access. The Office 2003 setup program runs again for the new user.

5. Open a table in the front-end client and verify that the tentative append record is present, which confirms that back-end data is updatable.
6. Finally, log off and log on with an account that's a member of the Power Users group but doesn't have permissions for the back-end share or file.
7. Attempt to open a table in the front-end client. You receive a message that the table is locked by another user or you need permission to view the data.

Shared Jet back-end databases are satisfactory for Access multiuser applications that support up to about 25 concurrent users with five or fewer making simultaneous data changes. In this case, you can skip the following sections about SQL Server and implement user-level security for your front-end. If your application involves heavy-duty online transaction processing (OLTP) or the data is vital to the economic survival of your organization, you should consider linking to an SQL Server back end.

CAUTION

NEW

After you split a database, Access 2003's new Tools, Database Utilities, Back Up Database command backs up the front end only. Unless you have automated nightly backup for the server or workstation that shares the back-end data, you must back up the data .mdb file manually. Backing up the .mdb file requires administrative access to the server or workstation.

TIP

As an administrator, you can open the back-end data .mdb in Access and take advantage of Access 2003's database backup and compact/repair utilities. For the preceding example, you would open \\OAKLEAF-MS10\Northwind\NWData.mdb.

EVALUATING THE BENEFITS OF MIGRATING TO CLIENT/SERVER DATABASES

Modern client/server databases, typified by Microsoft SQL Server 2000, provide a much more *reliable* and *scalable* data storage environment than shared-file databases, such as Jet. The vast majority of production databases used by all but very small organizations follow the client/server model. Oracle currently claims the lion's share of the client/server relational database management system (RDBMS) business, but IBM, Microsoft, and Sybase each own significant market share.

Client/server technology offloads much of the data-processing workload to the server. When an RDBMS client instructs the server to execute an SQL `SELECT *` statement having `WHERE` clause criteria, only those rows that meet the criteria pass over the network to the client. If you replace `*` with an explicit field list, the RDBMS only populates query columns that correspond to the specified fields. Minimizing the amount of data transmitted to the client saves costly network bandwidth and improves performance, especially for remote users who access the database over low-speed connections.

Another advantage of migrating from conventional multiuser Jet applications to client/server back-end databases is elimination of routine compact/repair operations to remove deleted records from Jet tables. When you delete records from a table, Jet marks the records as deleted but doesn't remove them from the table. You must compact the database periodically to remove deleted records and regain the disk space they occupy. Using a client/server back end also eliminates the Jet database locking problems that often occur after a power outage or unscheduled shutdown when users are in the process of making changes to Jet tables.

CLIENT/SERVER RELIABILITY AND SCALABILITY BENEFITS

Reliability—also called *availability* in this context—is the most important property of a production database. The goal of most database administrators is to assure that the database is available to users at least 99.9% of the time. 99.9% (called "three nines") availability means that the database has a maximum downtime of 7.3 hours per month. Four nines reduces downtime to about 45 minutes per month, and five nines to five minutes per year. Achieving 99.99% or better database availability requires very costly server clusters, but it's reasonable to expect at least three nines from SQL Server 2000 running under Windows 2000 Server.

Database scalability primarily is hardware-related. You can increase the number of concurrent users without suffering a performance slowdown by increasing the amount of RAM, CPU speed, and number of CPUs in the server(s). Unlimited-use licenses for most RDBMSs are based on the number of CPUs. You can compare licensing costs of Oracle, SQL Server, and IBM DB2 for different software editions, and server CPU and CPU speed configurations at `http://www.microsoft.com/sql/productinfo/pricecomparison.htm`.

SQL SERVER 2000 DESKTOP ENGINE FEATURES AND LIMITATIONS

19

SQL Server 2000 Desktop Engine (called *MSDE 2000* when referring specifically to this version of SQL Server 2003 with Service Pack 3) running under Windows 2000/2003 Server and the NTFS file system has the same level of reliability as SQL Server Standard or Enterprise Edition running on one machine. You can achieve similar reliability when running MSDE 2000 under Windows XP or 2000 Professional, if you dedicate the machine to running MSDE and don't use the machine to run desktop applications. The source code of MSDE 2000 is identical to that of other SQL Server 2000 editions; the scalability limitations applied to the freely distributable Desktop Engine don't affect its reliability.

TIP

> One of the advantages of running MSDE 2000 or other SQL Server editions under Windows 2000/2003 Server is the capability to manage the server from a Windows XP, 2000, NT, 9x, or Me workstation by running Terminal Services in administrative mode.
>
> You don't need to install Active Directory on the Windows 2000/2003 Server to run MSDE 2000 or other SQL Server 2000 versions. If your network uses Active Directory, installing MSDE 2000 on a member server, not a domain controller, devotes more of the server's available resources to database management and improves performance.

Microsoft limits the scalability of MSDE 2000 by restricting it to using a single CPU, regardless of how many processors you plug into your multiprocessing server or workstation. The Access 2003 help file states that MSDE 2000 "also limits database size and user workload." The maximum size of any MSDE 2000 database is 2GB, and MSDE 2000 "is designed and optimized for use on smaller computer systems, such as a single-user computer or small workgroup server." MSDE can't act as a transactional replication publisher, but this limitation isn't likely to affect most Access users and developers.

NOTE

As mentioned earlier, shared Jet databases have a fixed limit of 255 concurrent users. MSDE 2000 has a limit of five simultaneous batch operations, which translates to five users executing queries simultaneously. The sixth and higher concurrent users' queries are held in a queue pending completion of previous operations. There's no limit on the number of simultaneously connected clients. Windows 2000 and XP Professional have a fixed maximum of 10 inbound (client) connections, so the maximum number of simultaneous networked users connected to MSDE 2000 running under either of these operating systems is 10.

A much more serious limitation of Access 2003 is the lack of management tools for MSDE 2000. Access 2000's data projects provided a Tools, Security, Database Security command to let you add user logins and set user-level database permissions for the MSDE 1.0 version of SQL Server 7.0 with a set of dialogs. Microsoft removed this feature, which used elements of SQL Server 7.0's Enterprise Manager, from Access 2002 and MSDE 2000. Instead, Microsoft recommends use of the OSQL.exe command-line utility to add SQL Server user accounts, but provides no online help for OSQL with Access 2003. OSQL's arcane Transact-SQL (T-SQL) syntax for adding server logins and database permissions with SQL Server system stored procedures requires the command-line skills of a UNIX or Linux administrator.

NOTE

SQL Server 2000 Developer, Standard, and Evaluation editions include Enterprise Manager. The Developer Edition license, however, is restricted to development projects. Microsoft takes the position that you cannot use the Evaluation or Developer Edition's Enterprise Manager and other SQL Server tools with MSDE 2000 databases.

CHOOSING A CLIENT/SERVER MIGRATION STRATEGY

Prior to the introduction of Access 2000, linking was the only method of migrating Access applications from Jet tables to client/server databases. The primary advantage of linking client/server tables is that the Jet 4.0 database engine running on the client processes your

Jet SQL queries. Thus, crosstab queries continue to execute as expected, and you can use MSGraph objects in your forms and reports. Linked client/server tables let you take advantage of Jet passthrough queries to send Transact-SQL (T-SQL) statements directly to SQL Server, PL/SQL to Oracle, or any other SQL dialect to your RDBMS. The downside of linking is that you lose the efficiency of server-side query processing, which is one of the most important features of client/server RDBMSs. The sections that follow describe Access 2003 options for moving to SQL Server databases.

NOTE

> You create passthrough queries by opening a new query in Design view, closing the Show Table dialog, and choosing Query, SQL-Specific, Pass-Through to open an empty Query1: SQL Pass-Through Query window. In the window, type the query's SQL statement in the SQL dialect of the server, and then close the window and save the query. When you execute the query, Jet sends the SQL statement to the linked database for execution. If the SQL statement returns rows, the query result set opens in Datasheet view.

MIGRATING JET APPLICATIONS TO SQL SERVER WITH THE UPSIZING WIZARD

Access 2003 supports the following three automated migration—called *upsizing*—scenarios from conventional Jet applications to SQL Server:

- **Splitting, upsizing, and linking a single-user Jet database**—If your .mdb file contains application objects (queries, forms, pages, reports, modules, macros, or any combination) and data objects (tables), you can split and upsize the tables, and link the application objects to the server tables in a single process. An example of this scenario is upsizing Northwind.mdb.
- **Upsizing and linking a multiuser Jet application**—If you've used the Database Splitter utility to segregate application and data objects into front-end and back-end .mdb files, respectively, you upsize only the front-end .mdb file. Upsizing the back-end .mdb doesn't work directly; you receive a "Can't find *TableName*" error message when you attempt to open the upsized linked table in the front-end application's Datasheet view or in a form or report.
- **Upsizing a Jet application to an Access Data Project**—This scenario moves your Jet tables to SQL Server and attempts to update your queries to T-SQL stored procedures. Chapter 22, "Upsizing Jet Applications to Access Data Projects," describes this upsizing method and how to overcome problems with Jet queries that T-SQL can't handle.

TIP

> Use MSDE 2000 as the back end for all new multiuser Access applications you create. Microsoft will continue to upgrade SQL Server; what you see now is what you get in the future with Jet 4.0. There will be no further updates or upgrades to Jet. This chapter covers use of the Database Splitter tool to create Jet back ends only to demonstrate how to convert existing Jet back ends to SQL Server 2000.

You use the Access 2003 Upsizing Wizard—which works only with SQL Server 6.5 (having SP5 installed), 7.0, or 2000—for the preceding three scenarios, but this chapter focuses only on the first two. The client/server examples in this book use MSDE 2000 as the server, but most examples also accommodate all SQL Server 7.0 editions, including the original version of MSDE. None of the examples have been tested with SQL Server 6.5 or 7.0.

SQL Server enforces referential integrity by triggers or declarative referential integrity (DRI), if specified in the Relationships window for the Jet tables. Jet uses DRI, which conforms to ANSI-92 SQL syntax, and DRI is the preferred approach for SQL Server 2000 databases. SQL Server 2000 also supports Jet's cascading updates and deletions; SQL Server 7.0 doesn't. No version of SQL Server has a field data type that corresponds to Jet's Hyperlink data type, so the Wizard converts Hyperlink fields to plain text.

➔ For a brief description of SQL Server 2000's feature set, **see** "New SQL Server 2000 Features," **p. 34**.

NOTE

Access 2003 doesn't include SQL Server 2000's Books Online documentation. Microsoft has published an online version of updated SQL Server 2000 documentation at `http://www.microsoft.com/sql/techinfo/productdoc/2000/books.asp`.

Exporting Tables to Other RDBMSs

Access uses the Open Database Connectivity application programming interface (ODBC API) to link conventional Access (.mdb) front ends to client/server RDBMSs. Office 2003 installs ODBC drivers for SQL Server and Oracle databases. If you're using Oracle, IBM DB2, Sybase, Informix, or another RDBMS as your application's data source, you can't use the Upsizing Wizard to automate the table export and linking process. You must manually export (copy) your Jet tables to the RDBMS and then link the RDBMS tables to your Jet front end.

➔ For an introduction to the ODBC table-linking process, **see** "Linking Visual FoxPro Tables with ODBC," **p. 274**.

NOTE

Linking to databases of an RDBMS other than SQL Server or Oracle requires a vendor-supplied or third-party ODBC driver. You can't use an OLE DB data provider to link client/server tables to Jet front ends.

An alternative to linking tables in "foreign" databases to Jet front ends is to use the *linked server* feature of SQL Server 2000. Linking a server–other than another SQL Server instance–requires an OLE DB data provider for the linked server. Linking servers to SQL Server 2000 is required to use ADP with other RDBMSs.

➔ For more information on linking other RDBMSs to SQL Server, **see** "Linking Remote Servers," **p. 842**.

Migrating tables and linking to databases other than SQL Server involve the following basic steps:

1. You or your organization's database administrator (DBA) must create the database, and you must have permissions to create, read, and write to objects in the database.
2. Back up the Jet database, and verify the integrity of the backup.
3. Use Access's File, Export command to export the Jet tables to the new database.
4. Use the RDBMS's management tools to add indexes, default values, and validation rules, and enforce referential integrity between the tables. Add cascading updates and deletions, if the RDBMS supports them (most do).
5. Rename the existing Jet tables, and use the File, Get Existing Data, Link command to establish links to the database tables.
6. Delete the existing Jet tables after you confirm that the linked tables operate properly and have been backed up on the server.

TIP

Microsoft has reported many issues with exporting and linking Oracle tables to Access 2002 applications, many of which also apply to Access 2003. To review the known problems, search the Microsoft Knowledge Base (KB) with Access 2002 selected in the My Search Is About list and type **Oracle** in the My Question Is text box; then repeat the process with Access 2003 as the product. You can reach the Knowledge Base Search page quickly by opening the Support menu and choosing Knowledge Base on the Microsoft home page (`http://www.microsoft.com`).

19

UPSIZING A SINGLE-FILE APPLICATION TO SQL SERVER 2000

If you've created a single-file Jet application and want to make it available to your colleagues who have Access 200x installed, the Upsizing Wizard makes the process easy and fast. You must, of course have installed MSDE 2000 from the distribution CD-ROM or have access to another version of SQL Server 2000 before you can upsize your application. If your application is secured, you must have full (Admins) permissions for the Jet tables. All the examples of this chapter assume you are logged in to the Jet database as the Admin user, with or without a password.

→ For instructions on how to install MSDE 2000, **see** "SQL Server 2000 Desktop Engine Setup," **p. 47**.

TIP

For a production application, install MSDE 2000 from the distribution CD-ROM on the production server, if you don't intend to create the new database on an existing installation of SQL Server 2000 Standard or Enterprise Edition. The network name of the server–called its NetBIOS name–is embedded in the Description property value of each table.

If you specify the local instance of MSDE 2000 installed on your client computer, you must change the property value—called the ODBC connection string—to reflect the NetBIOS name change when you move the database to a production server. Making this change isn't a simple process; you must update each link manually or use a VBA subprocedure to regenerate the links to the new server.

→ For details on the required subprocedure, **see** "Changing the Link Connection String with a VBA Subprocedure," **p. 767**.

MODIFYING TABLE PROPERTIES TO ASSURE SUCCESSFUL UPSIZING

The Upsizing Wizard has several limitations, most of which are imposed by SQL Server 2000 or earlier. In some cases, the upsizing process fails silently, and the final upsizing report doesn't indicate the reason for the failure.

Following is a check list of modifications you must make to your tables—and a few other recommendations—to assure upsizing success:

- **Validation rule and default value expressions**—T-SQL can't handle many Jet-specific or VBA expressions that establish default field values, or table- or field-level validation rules. In such cases, the Upsizing Wizard won't create the SQL Server table. You must remove the offending expressions and run the Upsizing Wizard again to link only the missing tables. Then you must rewrite the expressions to comply with T-SQL syntax rules using the da Vinci toolset or SQL Server Enterprise Manager.

NOTE

Chapter 21, "Moving from Jet Queries to Transact-SQL," includes examples of T-SQL expressions you can use for default values and validation rules, and shows you how to use the da Vinci toolset to change the property values of SQL Server tables and fields.

- **Hidden tables**—If you've applied the Hidden attribute to any of the tables you want to upsize, the Wizard ignores the hidden tables during the upsizing process.
- **Fields added by Jet replication**—If you've implemented Jet replication, you must remove all replication system fields from the tables before upsizing. Tables with replication fields don't upsize.

TIP

Replication fields have a `dbSystemField` attribute applied, which prevents you from deleting them in Table Design view. Microsoft Knowledge Base article Q153526, "ACC: How to Make a Replicated Database a Regular Database," has links to two downloadable wizards for removing replication system fields from Access 95 and 97 tables. Michael Kaplan's Trigeminal Software Web site, `http://www.trigeminal.com/`, has a TSI Access 2000 Un-Replicator for Jet 4.0 and a TSI Replication System Fields Utility for Jet 3.5x and 4.0. Both utilities work with Access 2003 if your database uses the default Access 2000 format.

- **Tables without unique indexes**—You can update a Jet table that doesn't have a Unique Values Only index, but SQL Server tables require a unique index for updatability. Make sure all tables have a unique index. Add an AutoNumber field to the table if you can't create a unique index from the data in the table. (AutoNumber fields become `integer` fields with the `identity` property in SQL Server tables.) The unique index doesn't need to be a primary key.
- **Related fields with unequal Field Size property values**—Jet lets you create relations on Text fields having different sizes, but SQL Server doesn't. The tables upsize, but the Wizard doesn't establish the relationship between them. Make sure that the size of the primary- and foreign-key field pair is the same in both related tables. Specify the longer of the two size values to prevent inadvertently truncating data.
- **Very large tables**—During addition of data to an upsized table, SQL Server adds entries to the transaction log file. If you have a very large table and are short on disk space, the combination of the table and log file might exceed the free space on the destination disk. Make sure that the destination drive has free space greater than three times your .mdb file size.

TIP

Microsoft has published a "Using the Access 2002 Upsizing Tools" whitepaper, which you can download from Knowledge Base article Q294407. The whitepaper hadn't been updated for Access 2003 when this book was written. Search the Knowledge base at `http://search.support.microsoft.com/kb/c.asp` with Access 2003 as the product and **upsizing tools** as the text to find the updated version.

19

RUNNING THE UPSIZING WIZARD

Following are the steps to upsize a simple, single-file Jet application with the Upsizing Wizard:

1. Make a backup copy of the Jet database to upsize, and verify that the backup copy works.
2. Open the original database file, but don't open any database objects. This example uses Nwind.mdb, a modified copy of the Access 2000 version of the Northwind.mdb database with images embedded in the Photo field of the Employees table and the Employees form imported from Access 2000's Northwind.mdb file.

→ For an explanation of how to embed the EmpID#.bmp bitmap files in an OLE Object field, **see** "Dealing with Images in External Database Files," **p. 278**.

NOTE

The Nwind.mdb database used for this example is included as Nwind19.mdb in the \Seua11\Chaptr19 folder of the accompanying CD-ROM. Nwind19.mdb includes the VBA subprocedure required to change the server name when you move the SQL Server database from one machine to another.

3. Choose Tools, Database Utilities, Upsizing Wizard to start the upsizing process.
4. Accept the default Create a New Database option in the first Wizard dialog (see Figure 19.8), and click Next.

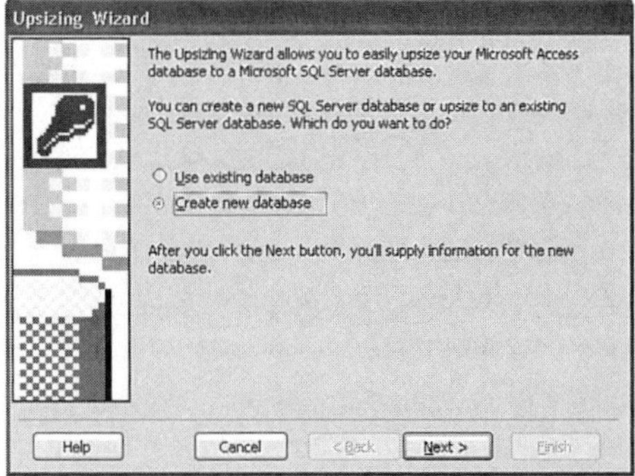

Figure 19.8
The first Upsizing Wizard dialog lets you add your tables to an existing database or create a new database. You create a new SQL Server database unless you're running the Wizard to upsize a table that wasn't upsized because of an error.

5. In the second Wizard dialog, open the What SQL Server Would You Like... list, and select the name of a production server or peer workstation server that has MSDE 2000 installed. This example uses MSDE 2000 installed on a Windows 2000 member server (OAKLEAF-MS10). The client computer (OAKLEAF-XP1) runs Office 2003 under Windows XP Professional.

NOTE

> If you're upsizing a sample database to become familiar with the process, you can select (local) or the NetBIOS name of your computer.

19

6. If the target SQL Server is running under Windows XP/2000+/NT, the Use Trusted Connection check box is enabled (see Figure 19.9). MSDE 2000 installs by default with Windows authentication only enabled, which prevents use of the sa (system administrator) login and SQL Server-based security.

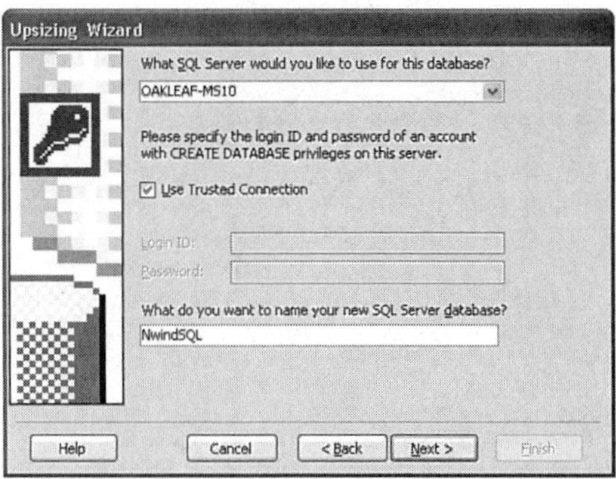

Figure 19.9
The second Wizard dialog requires you to select the machine running SQL Server, specify the authentication method for your connection, and provide a name for the new database.

NOTE

> A Trusted Connection to SQL Server uses Windows .NET/2000/NT authentication for database connections, and is the *much* preferred method of managing client/server database security.
>
> Using Windows NT/2000+ authentication requires that your logon account has at least `CREATE DATABASE` privileges for SQL Server. A member of the local Administrators group of the machine running SQL Server (BUILTIN\Administrators) has system administrator (sa) rights for the server and all databases by default.

7. Accept the default database name, the name of your .mdb file with an "SQL" suffix, or change it to a name you like better. Don't use spaces or punctuation symbols in the name; doing so violates generally accepted database naming practices. Click Next.
8. After a brief delay, the third Wizard dialog opens with a list of the tables in the Jet database in the Available Tables list. Click the >> button to export all the tables to SQL Server (see Figure 19.10). If you want to retain temporary or local tables on the client, select the table(s) and click the < button to move them from the Export to SQL Server list back to the Available Tables list. Click Next.

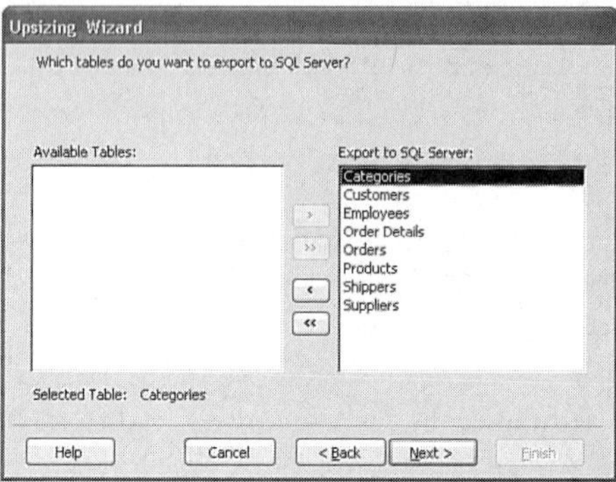

Figure 19.10
The only Jet tables you should retain in the front-end application are temporary tables or local tables that you use to set user preferences.

9. In the fourth Wizard dialog, accept the default options unless you have a specific reason for doing otherwise (see Figure 19.11). Click Next.

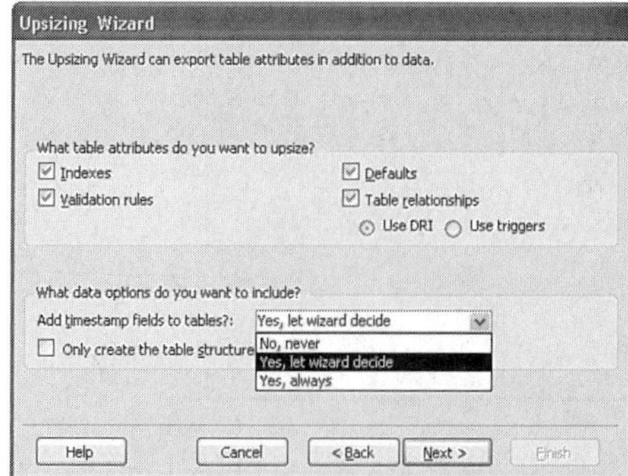

Figure 19.11
The fourth Wizard dialog proposes the most common set of options for the upsizing process.

NOTE

As mentioned earlier in the chapter, SQL Server's DRI features are preferred over triggers to enforce referential integrity. Prior to SQL Server 7.0, triggers were the only method of enforcing referential integrity.

SQL Server can use optional timestamp fields to determine quickly whether large Memo and OLE Object fields (SQL Server `ntext` fields) have been updated. The size of the bitmap and text data in the example database is relatively small, so timestamp fields aren't needed. If your Jet table includes lengthy Memo fields or OLE Object fields contain large images or other data, select the Yes, Let The Wizard Decide choice in the Add Timestamp Fields to Tables list.

10. In the fifth Wizard dialog, select the Link SQL Server Tables to Existing Application option (see Figure 19.12). If you accept the default No Application Changes option, you must manually link the tables to your database front-end application. Click Next to open the final Wizard dialog and click Finish to start the upsizing process.

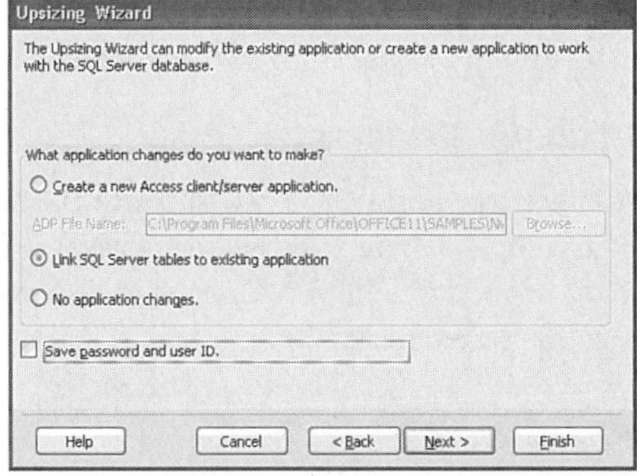

Figure 19.12
Be sure to select the Link SQL Server Tables to Existing Application option to have the Wizard handle the table-linking process for you.

NOTE

The Save Password and User ID check box only applies to SQL Server security, which isn't enabled by default. Even if you could save your administrative logon name and password, doing so would breach security rules–users would be able to impersonate your administrative account to gain full control over the SQL Server instance.

11. A progress indicator dialog appears for a period that depends on the size of the tables, the speed of your computer and, if the database is remote, network and server performance. After the Wizard completes its task, an Upsizing Wizard Report appears in Print Preview. Click the report to zoom to 100% scale and review its contents (see Figure 19.13).

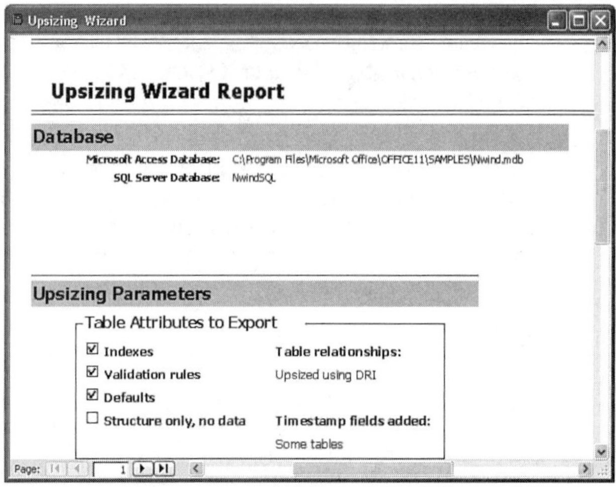

Figure 19.13
After the Wizard updates and links the table, it generates a report summarizing the upsizing process. Look for errors and "not upsized" entries. (The report for upsizing the example Nwind.mdb database is 15 pages long.)

12. Print the report, if you want, and then close the Upsizing Wizard window. The Wizard saves the report as a Snapshot file (*FileName*.snp) in the front-end application's folder.

VERIFYING THE UPSIZING AND LINKING PROCESS

The Wizard renames your Jet tables by adding a "_local" suffix to the table name and adds links—identified by the ODBC symbol—to the SQL Server tables (see Figure 19.14). When you pass the mousepointer over a linked table item, a ScreenTip displays in a single line part of the ODBC connection string for the database.

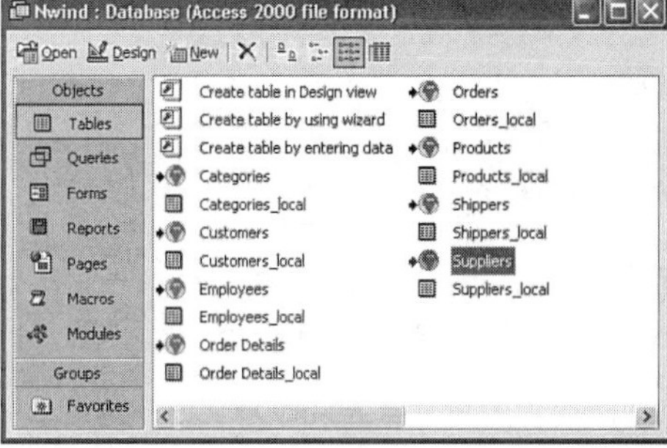

Figure 19.14
The Database window displays linked tables with the original Jet table names and the Jet tables renamed with a "_local" suffix.

If some tables don't upsize to SQL Server, indicated by a missing link entry for the tables, see the "Jet Tables Fail to Upsize" topic of the "Troubleshooting" section at the end of the chapter.

After you've verified that all required server tables have links, do the following to confirm that the tables are operable with your front end:

1. Open the front-end forms and reports to verify that the upsizing process completed satisfactorily.

2. Verify in Form or Table Datasheet view that default values, formats, input masks, field and table validation rules, and other special property values you've specified for tables have upsized successfully. SQL Server 7.0 doesn't support extended properties, so display formats, input masks, and other Jet-specific properties aren't updated. Also, verify by the presence of the tentative append record that the tables are updatable.
3. If your tables have lookup fields, subdatasheets, or both, verify that these extended property features work as they did in the Jet tables.
4. Open the upsized tables in Design view, and acknowledge the message that warns you that you can't change some table properties. Check the data type of a Jet Hyperlink field, which changes to a Jet Memo field (see Figure 19.15). Jet Memo fields upsize to SQL Server's `ntext` (Unicode text) data type. No version of SQL Server supports the Allow Zero Length property, so this value is No for all fields, regardless of your original setting. The upsize_ts field is the `timestamp` field added by the Upsizing Wizard.

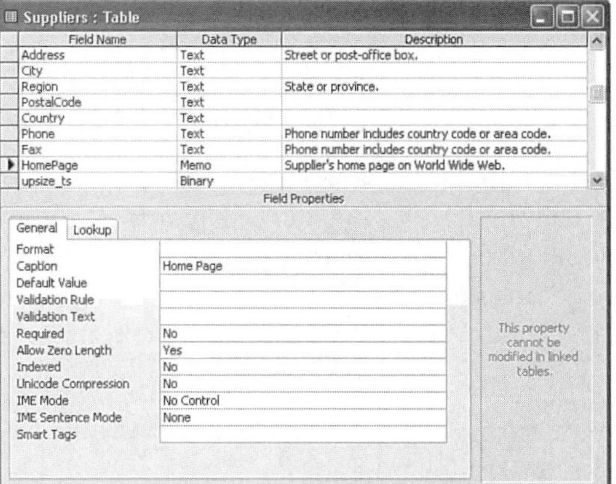

Figure 19.15 Upsizing Jet Hyperlink fields results in a change to the SQL Server data type (ntext) that corresponds to a Jet Memo field. Design view of a linked SQL Server database displays Jet, not SQL Server, field data types.

5. Right-click the Table Design view window, and choose Properties to open the Table Properties dialog with the Description text box selected. Press Shift+F2 to open the Zoom dialog to view the full connection string for the table. Figure 19.16 shows the connection string for the Suppliers table with the Zoom dialog's font size changed to 10 points and newline characters added to format the string for readability.
6. Execute every `SELECT` query to make sure the Wizard hasn't modified the query and rendered it inoperable. Don't execute action queries that update table values. Some queries—such as Northwind.mdb's Sales by Year query—require entering parameter values.
7. Open the Relationships window. Upsized tables lose their relationships, and you must depend on SQL Server's DRI to maintain referential integrity. To make creating new queries easier, re-establish the relationships between the tables. (Referential integrity options are disabled in the Edit Relationships window for client/server tables.)

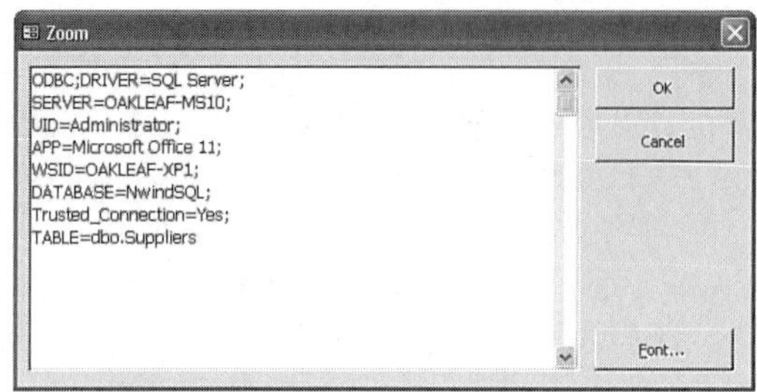

Figure 19.16
The Zoom dialog displays a formatted version of the ODBC connection string for the Suppliers table.

After you've verified the success of the upsizing process, you can safely delete the …_local tables, if you made a backup of your application.

To return a test application to its original condition, delete the links to the table, and rename the Jet tables by removing the _local suffix.

UPSIZING AN APPLICATION WITH LINKED TABLES

As mentioned earlier in the chapter, the process for upsizing Access front-ends with linked Jet tables is identical to that for upsizing single-file applications. You run the Upsizing Wizard from the front-end .mdb. The Wizard connects to the shared .mdb back-end and generates the SQL Server tables from the linked Jet database. This example uses the NWClient.mdb front end and NWData.mdb back end you created at the beginning of the chapter.

To create an SQL Server database on your local machine that you move to a production server later in the chapter, do the following:

1. Make backup copies of NWClient.mdb and NWData.mdb, if you haven't done this.
2. Open the NWClient.mdb front end, start the Upsizing Wizard, accept the default Create New Database option in the first dialog, and click Next.
3. In the second Wizard dialog, specify (local) as the SQL server, accept NWDataSQL as the name of the database, and click Next.
4. In the third dialog, select all tables, and in the fourth dialog, accept the defaults.
5. In the fifth dialog, make sure to select the Link SQL Server Table to Existing Application option and clear the Save Password and User ID check box. Click Next and Finish to upsize the linked tables.
6. Verify the upsizing process with the methods described in the preceding section.

EXAMINING THE ODBC TABLE CONNECTION STRING

When you choose the Create a New Database option in the first Upsizing Wizard dialog, the ODBC connection string for each table contains all the information Jet needs to connect to the server and link each table (refer to Figure 19.16). This type of ODBC connection doesn't require you to create a named ODBC user or system data source (user or system DSN), or a file data source to establish the connection. Using a DSN-less connection simplifies the process of making your linked-table application available to users, because they don't need a user or system DSN on their computer or a link to a file data source on the server.

A DSN-less ODBC connection string consists of the following elements, separated by semicolons:

- `ODBC` designates the connection as using the ODBC API.
- `Driver=SQL Server` specifies the current version of the SQL Server ODBC driver on the user's machine.
- `SERVER=`*`SERVERNAME`* designates the NetBIOS computer name of the machine running the instance of SQL Server with the upsized database. In a Windows 2000/.NET domain, the NetBIOS name often is called the *downlevel* name of a computer.
- `UID=`*`UserName`* specifies the network logon ID for your administrative account.
- `PWD=`*`Password`* is present only when you specify SQL Server security during the MSDE 2000 installation process or by changing a Registry entry after installation. Using Windows authentiation is recommended strongly, because it's integrated with Windows networking, and is more secure and easier to administer than SQL Server's username/password security approach.
- `APP=Microsoft Office 11` is for information only.
- `WSID=`*`COMPUTERNAME`* is the NetBIOS name of your computer (workstation ID) and is for information only.
- `DATABASE=`*`DatabaseName`* designates the name of the upsized database.
- `Trusted_Connection=`*`Yes`* specifies use of Windows 2000/NT authentication; *`No`* or a missing entry specifies SQL Server security.
- `TABLE=dbo.`*`TableName`* specifies the SQL Server table and its owner prefix. The default prefix is `dbo`, which is the abbreviation for the system administrator (sa) as the object's owner (database owner).

NOTE

> The `dbo.`*`TableName`* element isn't present in the `Connect` property value of the link's `TableDef` object. (Jet local or linked tables are members of the database's `TableDefs` collection). Access appends `TABLE=` and the `SourceTableName` property value of the `TableDef` to the Description property value.

If you select the Use an Existing Database in the first Upsizing Wizard dialog, you must use an existing—or create a new—machine or file data source. If one of your tables won't upsize, you must run the Wizard again to create the table and add the link to existing database. If you delete a link and must restore it, you must choose File, Get External Data, Link

Tables, select ODBC Databases( ) in the Files of Type list, and select or create the DSN to use.

→ To learn how to create a temporary or permanent ODBC DSN, **see** "Linking Client/Server Tables Manually," **p. 770**.

NOTE

> When you use the Link Tables command to link a table, the link name gains a dbo_ prefix. Delete the prefix to enable existing Access objects to connect to the table.

In either case, your tables end up with a combination of conventional and DSN-less convention strings. If you don't change the `Connect` property of the `TableDef` object to specify a DSN-less connection, all users of your application must add the ODBC DSN to their computer or have access to a server share holding a file data source.

The standard DSN for an SQL Server table replaces the `Driver=SQL Server` element with `DSN=DataSourceName`, and `SERVER=SERVERNAME` element with `Description=OptionalText` in the Description and `Connect` property values. Otherwise, the elements of the connection string are the same as in the preceding DSN-less connection list. The `ChangeServer` VBA subprocedure, which is described in the later "Changing the Link Connection String with a VBA Subprocedure" section, also changes DSN to DSN-less connections.

Moving the Upsized Database to Another Server

If you upsize the database on a local instance of MSDE 2000 and then decide to move the database to another server, be prepared to add a substantial amount of VBA code to your project to regenerate the links. There's no Access wizard or utility to automatically change the `SERVER=SERVERNAME` element of a DSN-less connection string for each linked table.

19

CAUTION

> Don't try to use the Linked Table Manager database utility to change the server name in a DSN-less connection string. The Linked Table Manager requires an ODBC user or system DSN, or a file data source, instead of modifying the current DSN-less connection string. If you use the Linked Table manager to change the link, you must set up a machine DSN on each user's computer or create a file data source on the server and specify the Uniform Naming Convention (UNC) path to the file in the connection string. The `ChangeServer` procedure requires at least one DSN-less connection to change DSN connections.

Moving or Copying the SQL Server Database Files

You can move or copy an SQL Server database from one machine to another by any of the following methods:

- Create a temporary New Project (Existing Data), connect to the SQL Server database, and choose Tools, Database Utilities, Transfer Database to install the database on the new SQL Server 2000 instance. The original database is retained. This is the simplest and most foolproof method.

→ For an example of using the Transfer Database command to move an SQL Server database, **see** "Transferring the Project's Database to the Server," **p. 839**.

- Use SQL Enterprise Manager's Copy Database Wizard to copy or move the database to the new SQL Server instance. (Access 2003 uses the Copy Database Wizard to transfer the database.) This approach requires a licensed copy of Enterprise Manager.
- Close all connections to the database, stop SQL Server on the source computer, and use Explorer to copy the *DatabaseName*.mdf (database) and *DatabaseName*.ldf (log file) from the \Program Files\Microsoft SQL Server\MSSQL\Data folder to the same folder on the new server. After copying the files, create a temporary New Project (Existing Data). In the DataLink Properties dialog, select the Attach a Database File as a Database Name option, specify the database name and the *DatabaseName*.mdf file, which must be on the same machine as the SQL Server instance you specify.

CHANGING THE LINK CONNECTION STRING WITH A VBA SUBPROCEDURE

After you've moved the linked tables to the new server, you face the challenge of changing the `SERVER=SERVERNAME` element of the DSN-less connection string to the new server name. Properties of linked table definitions, which Jet calls `TableDefs`, are read-only. You can't persist changes to the Description property value of a linked table. If you alter the server name in the connection string of the Description property, and close and save your changes to the table design, the connection string doesn't change.

Nwind19.mdb in the \Seua11\Chapt19 of the accompanying CD-ROM contains a modChangeServer module with a single VBA subprocedure, `ChangeServers`. You can use this procedure to change the connection string to point to the new server or change a DSN connection string to the DSN-less type. To add the modChangeServer and its subprocedure to your front-end .mdb, choose File, Get External Data, Import, and import the module from Nwind19.mdb. The following example uses NWClient.mdb, upsized to your local computer in the earlier "Upsizing an Application with Linked Tables" section. Running the example requires you to have a networked computer running SQL Server.

→ To review the process for working with VBA modules, **see** "Using the Immediate Window," **p. 366**.

To run the ChangeServer subprocedure in an application that has tables linked to SQL Server and the modChangeServer module installed, do this:

1. Click the Modules shortcut inNWClient.mdb's Database window, and double-click modChangeServer to open the VBA editor with the ChangeServer subprocedure active.

19

2. Press Ctrl+G to open the Immediate window. Type **Call ChangeServer("*CurrentServerName*", "*NewServerName*")**. For this example, the procedure call is **Call ChangeServer("OAKLEAF-XP1", "OAKLEAF-MS10")** (see Figure 19.17). If you haven't copied or moved the tables to another server, use the current workstation or server name as the value of both arguments.

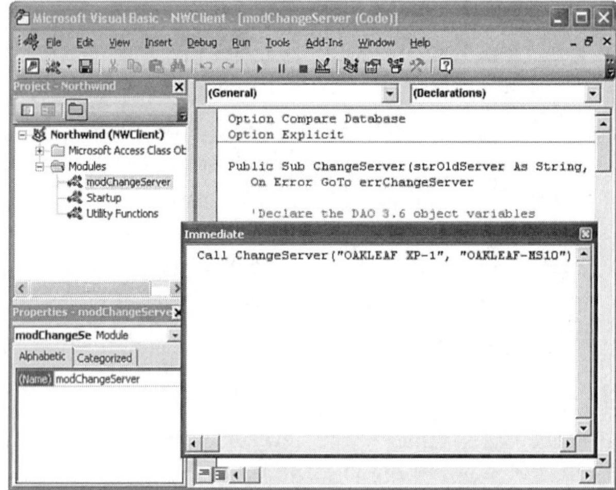

Figure 19.17 Call the ChangeServer subprocedure with two literal string arguments: the current server name followed by the destination server.

3. Press Enter to execute the procedure. The first stage of the procedure creates an array of the new connection data for each linked table, and displays a message asking you to confirm the change (see Figure 19.18, top).

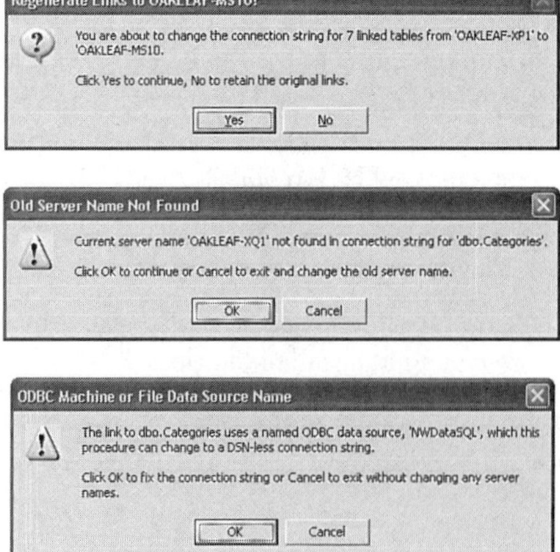

Figure 19.18 You see one of these three messages, depending on your argument values and whether you've added a link with a DSN data source.

NOTE

> If you type the wrong value for the *`CurrentServerName`* argument, you receive the middle message shown in Figure 19.18. If you've added links with a DSN connection, you see the bottom message. If you only want to change DSN to DSN-less connections, type the current server name as the value of both `ChangeServer` arguments.

4. After a second or more, depending on the speed of your machine and the network, a **`Debug`**`.Print` statement confirms all new connection strings in the Immediate window (see Figure 19.19).

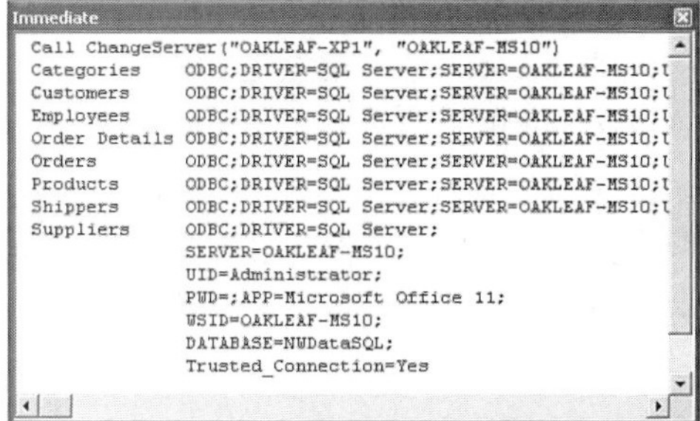

Immediate
Call ChangeServer("OAKLEAF-XP1", "OAKLEAF-MS10")
Categories ODBC;DRIVER=SQL Server;SERVER=OAKLEAF-MS10;
Customers ODBC;DRIVER=SQL Server;SERVER=OAKLEAF-MS10;
Employees ODBC;DRIVER=SQL Server;SERVER=OAKLEAF-MS10;
Order Details ODBC;DRIVER=SQL Server;SERVER=OAKLEAF-MS10;
Orders ODBC;DRIVER=SQL Server;SERVER=OAKLEAF-MS10;
Products ODBC;DRIVER=SQL Server;SERVER=OAKLEAF-MS10;
Shippers ODBC;DRIVER=SQL Server;SERVER=OAKLEAF-MS10;
Suppliers ODBC;DRIVER=SQL Server;
SERVER=OAKLEAF-MS10;
UID=Administrator;
PWD=;APP=Microsoft Office 11;
WSID=OAKLEAF-MS10;
DATABASE=NWDataSQL;
Trusted_Connection=Yes

Figure 19.19
The Immediate window displays the new connection strings for the links.

If you type a nonexistent server name as the second argument value, or the database isn't present on the destination server you specify, you receive the two error messages shown in Figure 19.20. The upper message from SQL Server appears after about 30 seconds of inactivity. Clicking OK opens an SQL Server Login dialog. Click Cancel to dismiss the dialog, and display the procedure's error message (see Figure 19.20, bottom). Click OK to cancel execution and leave the connection strings unaffected.

Figure 19.20
These two error messages appear in sequence if you type an invalid destination server name.

Microsoft SQL Server Login

Connection failed:
SQLState: '01000'
SQL Server Error: 53
[Microsoft][ODBC SQL Server Driver][DBNETLIB]ConnectionOpen (Connect()).
Connection failed:
SQLState: '08001'
SQL Server Error: 17
[Microsoft][ODBC SQL Server Driver][DBNETLIB]SQL Server does not exist or access denied.

OK

Error Creating Link to 'OAKLEAF-MS11'

Unable to create a test ODBC link to the 'NWDataSQL' database of the 'OAKLEAF-MS11' server.

Error Number: 3059
Description: Operation canceled by user.

Please verify the name you used for the destination server.

OK

NOTE

`ChangeServer` creates a test connection to the destination server to prevent deleting the first existing link. The properties of linked `TableDef` objects are read-only, so the existing link must be deleted before adding the new `TableDef`.

LINKING CLIENT/SERVER TABLES MANUALLY

As mentioned in the earlier "Examining the ODBC Table Connection String" section, you must create an ODBC data source when you use the Upsizing Wizard with an existing SQL Server database. You also must create a DSN when you manually export Jet tables to an RDBMS other than SQL Server, and then link the tables to your Jet front end. The number and appearance of the dialogs varies according to the ODBC driver you use to make the connection to the existing database on the RDBMS.

After you create the DSN, you can use the upsizing Wizard to add new tables to an SQL Server database. For other RDBMSs, you must manually export your Jet tables to the database. You use the same DSN to export the data from and attach the tables to your Jet front end.

CREATING THE ODBC DATA SOURCE

To create a DSN for any RDBMS for which you've installed an ODBC 2.x or 3.x driver, do the following:

1. Launch Control Panel's ODBC Data Source Administrator tool. Under Windows XP and 2000, the Data Sources (ODBC) icon is in Control Panel's Administrative Tools subfolder. The Administator opens with the User DSN page active.

NOTE

If you select the Use Existing Database option in the first Upsizing Wizard dialog, the Wizard opens the Select Data Source dialog.

2. If you're preparing a temporary data source for addition of tables to an SQL Server database you created with the Upsizing Wizard, you can create a User or System DSN on your workstation. Otherwise, click the File DSN tab and navigate to a server share for which users of your application have at least read access.
3. Click the Add button to open the Create New Data Source dialog, and select the driver for the RDBMS with the database for your application (see Figure 19.21). This example uses the SQL Server driver installed by Office 2003 running under Windows XP.

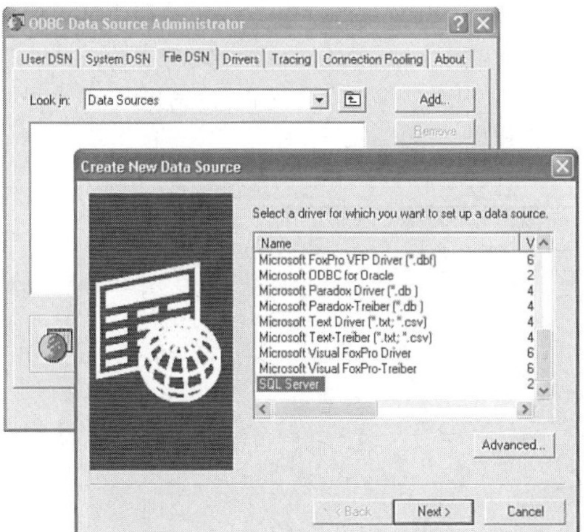

Figure 19.21
Select the ODBC driver for your RDBMS in the Create New Data Source dialog. Don't set Advanced properties, unless the driver vendor instructs otherwise.

4. Click Next to open the second Create New Data Source dialog, and type the UNC path and name of the data source file, **\\OAKLEAF-MS10\Northwind\NWDataSQL.dsn** for this example. The standard extension for DSN files is, not surprisingly, *dsn*.

> **TIP**
>
> The default location for file DSN's is the \Program Files\Common Files\ODBC\Data Sources on your computer. The best location for the file DSN for an upsized multiuser application is the share in which you placed the Jet back-end database. Use UNC's `\\ServerName\ShareName` network path format, not a mapped drive, to specify the file location.

5. Click Next to confirm your initial settings and then Click Finish to open the first driver-specific dialog—Create a New Data Source to SQL Server in this case.
6. Type a description of the DSN, and open the Server list to select the RDBMS server, OAKLEAF-MS10 for this example (see Figure 19.22).

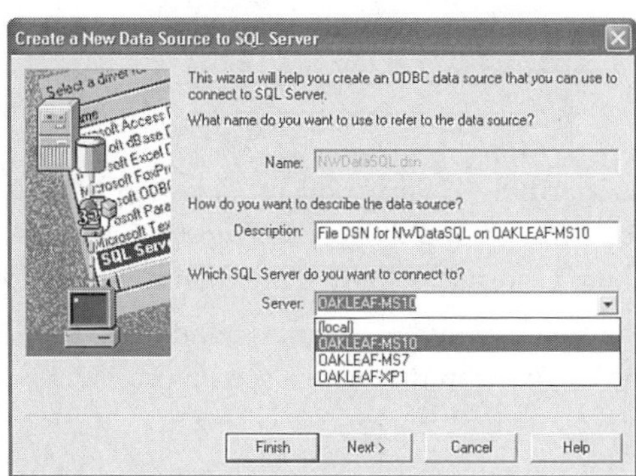

Figure 19.22
The first driver-specific dialog for the SQL Server driver lets you add a description of the DSN and specify the server name.

7. Click Next to open the second driver-specific dialog. For SQL Server, accept the default Windows NT Authentication option (see Figure 19.23). Alternatively, select With SQL Server Authentication..., which requires a user account and password having at least `CREATE DATABASE` privileges.

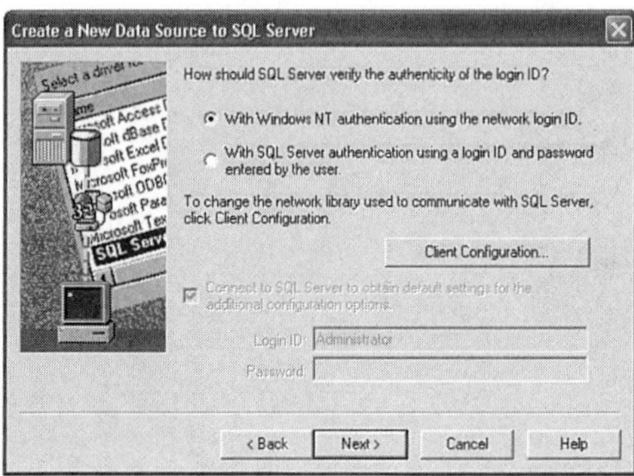

Figure 19.23
The SQL Server driver's second dialog lets you select the authentication method. The default client configuration is TCP/IP. Click the Client Configuration button to open a dialog that lets you add additional network protocols, such as IPX/SPX or Named Pipes, if you need them.

8. Click Next to make a temporary connection to the server. Mark the Change the Default Database To check box, open the drop-down list, and select the database name, NwindSQL for this example. Accept the default Use ANSI... settings (see Figure 19.24).

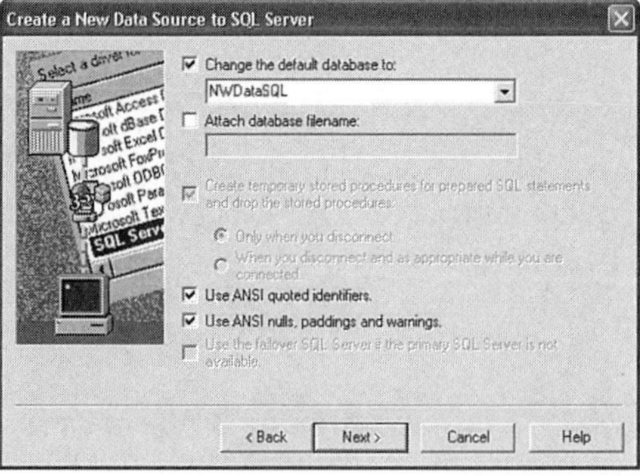

Figure 19.24
Select the database for the DSN in the third SQL Server-specific dialog.

9. Click Next to open the fourth SQL Server dialog. The single default option, Perform Translation for Character Data, is satisfactory for most DSNs. Specify logging options only if you need to debug performance problems when using the DSN.

10. Click Finish to display a summary of your settings, and click Test Data Source to confirm connectivity to the database on the server (see Figure 19.25).

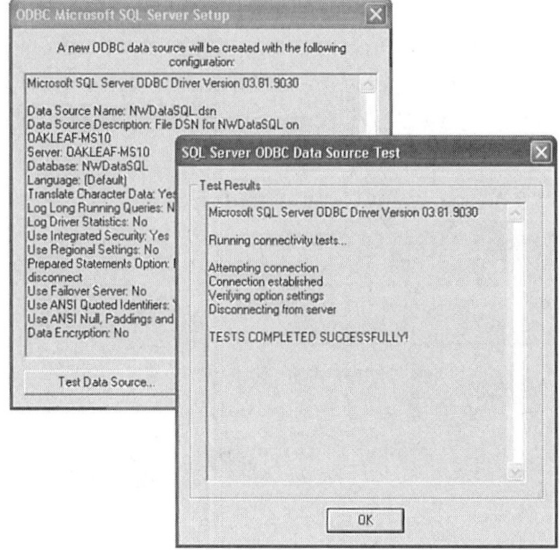

Figure 19.25 The final step when configuring an SQL Server ODBC data source is to test connectivity to the specified database.

11. Click OK twice to save the file DSN, and then click OK to close the ODBC Administrator tool.

NOTE

> If you use a temporary user or system DSN to add table(s) to a new SQL Server database you created with the Upsizing Wizard, run the `ChangeServer` subprocedure, described in the earlier "Changing the Link Connection String with a VBA Subprocedure" section, to change to DSN-less connections for added tables.

EXPORTING JET TABLE DATA TO THE RDBMS

Manually exporting Jet tables to an ODBC-connected client/server database is a straightforward process, but the manual export procedure creates only the basic table structure with a simple `CREATE TABLE` statement and then populates the table with an `INSERT` statement for each row. Unlike the Upsizing Wizard, exporting a table doesn't establish primary keys, add indexes, or enforce referential integrity with DRI. You or the DBA must handle these tasks after exporting all tables.

Following are the steps to export Jet tables to RDBMSs other than SQL Server:

1. Open the .mdb file containing the Jet tables to export, Northwind.mdb for this example.
2. Choose File, Export to open the Export '*TableName*' To dialog.
3. Select ODBC Databases( ) in the Files of Type list, which closes the Export dialog and opens the Export dialog with *TableName* in the Export *TableName* To text box (see Figure 19.26, top).

19

4. Click OK to open the Select Data Source dialog with the File DSN page active. If you specified a default folder for file DNSs in step 3 of the preceding section, the file you created appears in the list. If not, navigate to the server share in which you stored the DSN. Select the file (see Figure 19.26, bottom), and click OK to close the dialog and start the export process.

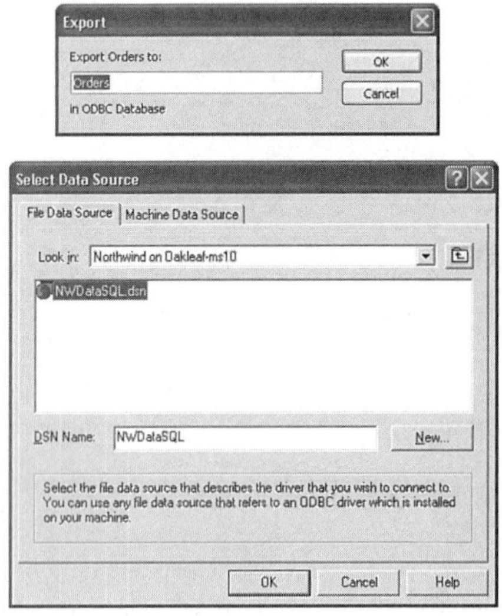

Figure 19.26 When you select ODBC Databases( ) in the Export dialog's Files of Type list, the Export dialog (top) opens. Clicking OK opens the ODBC Administrator's Select Data Source dialog.

5. Repeat steps 2–4 for each table to export. You don't need to wait for the export process to complete before selecting another table to export.
6. Use the RDBMSs toolset to specify primary-key fields, add indexes, and establish referential integrity to emulate—as closely as possible—your original Jet database.

DBAs use SQL Server Enterprise Manager (commonly called *EntMan*) to perform step 6's operations for SQL Server databases. Alternatively, you can add SQL Server indexes and create relationships (called constraints) by opening an Access data project for the database. The process for adding indexes and other table accouterments is tedious when upsizing many tables, so use the Upsizing Wizard for all Jet export operations to SQL Server.

ATTACHING THE EXPORTED TABLES

Attaching the tables to your front-end application with the file DSN follows the same process as that described for FoxPro databases in Chapter 8, "Linking, Importing, and Exporting Data." Unfortunately, you can't use the Linked Table Manager to change front-end links from an .mdb file to a .dsn file.

To attach the client/server tables you exported, do this:

1. Open the front-end .mdb, and choose File, Get External Data, Link Tables to open the Link dialog.

2. Select ODBC Databases( ) in the Files of Type list to open the File DSN page of the Select Data Source dialog.
3. Navigate to and double-click the *FileName*.dsn file to open the Link Tables dialog.
4. Multi-select the tables to attach to the front-end .mdb file. Figure 19.27 shows the eight upsized SQL Server Northwind tables and a tblOrders table selected.

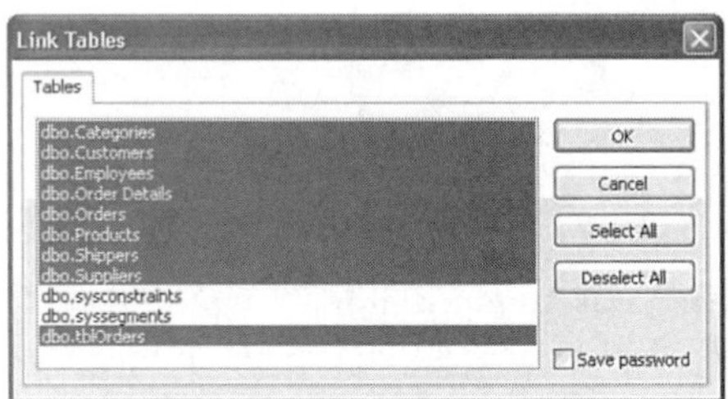

Figure 19.27
Select in the Link Tables dialog each exported table to attach to the front end.

5. If you specified Windows authentication when you created the DSN, the Save Password check box should be cleared. Most Windows NT versions of client/server RDBMSs accommodate Windows authentication. For RDBMS-based security, you can mark the Save Password check box if you didn't use sa (or its equivalent) as the account when you created the DSN. Click OK to begin the linking process.
6. If Jet can't determine the primary-key field(s) of linked tables, the Select Unique Record Identifier dialog opens for each table (see Figure 19.28). Select the key field(s) for the table; if you click cancel, the table won't be updatable.

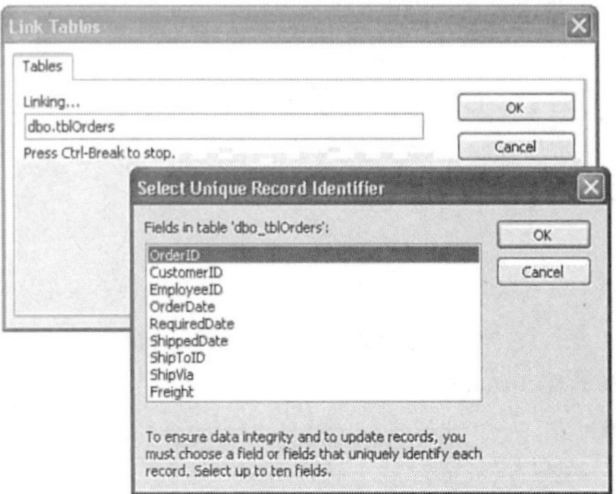

Figure 19.28
Specify the name(s) of the primary-key field(s) if Jet can't detect a table's primary key.

7. The prefix of the attached table names depend on the RDBMS's table naming conventions. As mentioned earlier in the chapter, SQL Server tables gain a dbo_ prefix. Temporarily rename the original tables or links, and then rename the new ODBC links to remove the prefix.

19

8. Open the Relationships windows to verify all tables are present and that every table has key field(s) identified by a bold font. Reestablish the relationships between the primary- and foreign-key fields of the tables.
9. Check all queries for proper execution, and make sure your forms and reports operate as before.

After you've verified that all's well with the attached tables, you can delete the renamed Jet tables or their links.

ADDING USER LOGINS WITH THE OSQL UTILITY

Users who aren't members of the local Administrators group of the machine hosting SQL Server don't have access to the linked databases you created in the preceding sections. When you log on to the front-end .mdb with a non-administrative Windows account you receive an SQL Server "Connection failed" error message (see Figure 19.29, top). Clicking OK opens an inoperative SQL Server Login dialog (see Figure 19.29, bottom). At this point, your only option is to click Cancel to display the original error message, click OK to open the dialog, and then click Cancel again.

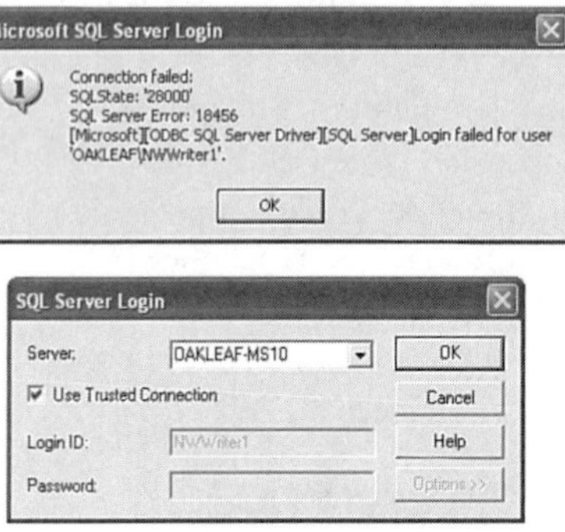

Figure 19.29
A user without an SQL Server login receives the following two messages when attempting to open an upsized table or front-end objects, such as queries, that are bound to upsized tables.

NOTE

> If you marked the Save Password and User ID check box when upsizing the tables, you receive a different pair of error messages: "ODBC-call failed" and "Can't open table in datasheet view."

OSQL lets you execute T-SQL statements, which include the `EXEC[UTE]` statement for stored procedures. Installing SQL Server generates a large number of *system stored procedures*, which apply to all server databases. You use OSQL to execute several of these system stored procedures, which have an `sp_` prefix, to add server logins and database permissions for users or groups. It's more common to add Windows 2000/.NET security groups for database access, but adding individual user accounts is appropriate when you only have a few users.

You use the following system stored procedures to add or revoke logins and permissions for users or groups in the default `public` server role:

- `sp_grantlogin` *`'DOMAIN\LogonID'`* to add a login with Windows authentication. *`LogonID`* can be the name of a user or group. If you're running MSDE 2000 on your local computer that's not a member of a Windows 2000/.NET domain, omit *`DOMAIN\`*. Execute `sp_revokelogin` with the same argument to remove the login.
- `sp_grantdbaccess` *`'login'`*, *`'UserOrGroupName'`* gives the user or group access to the current database. Ordinarily, you specify *`LogonID`* as the value of *`login`*. You set the current database with the `USE` *`'databasename'`* statement. Executing `sp_revokedbaccess` with the same arguments revokes database access.
- `sp_addrolemember` *`'RoleName'`*, *`'login'`* assigns the user or group to a predefined or custom role in the current database, such as `db_reader` or `db_writer`. Revoking database access removes that user from all database role(s).

By default, members of the `public` server role have no database permissions.

The following example adds with OSQL two logins—NWReader1 and NWWriter1— on a remote SQL Server (OAKLEAF-MS10) for the two members of the local Power Users group that have file-level permissions for the linked NWData.mdb back-end. NWReader1 receives read-only permissions (the `db_datareader` role) and NWWriter1 receives read-write permissions (`db_datareader` and `db_datawriter`) to the NWDataSQL database. You can use either a remote or local version of the NWDataSQL database.

→ If you didn't create the two Power User accounts, **see** "Establishing Network Share and File Security for the Back End," **p. 747**.

→ If you didn't create the NWDataSQL database, **see** " Upsizing an Application with Linked Tables," **p. 746**.

Follow these steps and refer to Figure 19.30 to add the logins and permissions for the two users:

1. Log on with an administrative account to the machine running SQL Server, open a command prompt, and type **osql -E** to start OSQL and display a numbered prompt (1>). Press enter after each instruction.
2. Type **EXEC sp_grantlogin 'OAKLEAF\NWReader1'** and type **GO** to execute the instruction and add the login. OSQL confirms the operation or returns an error message.
3. Type **EXEC sp_grantlogin 'OAKLEAF\NWWriter1'** and type **GO**.
4. Type **USE NWDataSQL** and **GO** to make NWDataSQL the current database. Note that no single quotes surround NWDataSQL, which is the name of a database object.
5. Type **EXEC sp_grantdbaccess 'OAKLEAF\NWReader1', 'NWReader1'** and **GO** to grant NWReader1 access to the NWDataSQL database.
6. Type **EXEC sp_grantdbaccess 'OAKLEAF\NWWriter1', 'NWWriter1'** and **GO**.
7. Type **EXEC sp_addrolemember 'db_datareader', 'NWReader1'** and **GO** to add NWReader1 to the read-only role. Do the same for NWWriter1.

8. Type **EXEC sp_addrolemember 'db_datawriter', 'NWWriter1'** and GO to enable NWWriter1 in the read-write roles.
9. Type **quit** to exit OSQL.
10. Log on to the NWClient.mdb front-end workstation with the NWReader1 account and open a table, such as Categories. The tentative append record is present, but you receive an "ODBC - insert on a linked table 'Categories' failed" error message when you attempt to add a new record to the table.
11. Log off and log on with the NWWriter1 account, and verify that you can add a new record to one of the tables and delete the added record.

```
Command Prompt - osql -E
Microsoft Windows 2000 [Version 5.00.2195]
(C) Copyright 1985-2000 Microsoft Corp.

D:\Documents and Settings\Administrator.OAKLEAF>cd\

D:\>osql -E
1> EXEC sp_grantlogin 'OAKLEAF\NWReader1'
2> GO
Granted login access to 'OAKLEAF\NWReader1'.
1> EXEC sp_grantlogin 'OAKLEAF\NWWriter1'
2> GO
Granted login access to 'OAKLEAF\NWWriter1'.
1> USE NWDataSQL
2> GO
1> EXEC sp_grantdbaccess 'OAKLEAF\NWReader1', 'NWReader1'
2> GO
Granted database access to 'OAKLEAF\NWReader1'.
1> EXEC sp_grantdbaccess 'OAKLEAF\NWWriter1', 'NWWriter1'
2> GO
Granted database access to 'OAKLEAF\NWWriter1'.
1> EXEC sp_addrolemember 'db_datareader', 'NWReader1'
2> GO
'NWReader1' added to role 'db_datareader'.
1> EXEC sp_addrolemember 'db_datareader', 'NWWriter1'
2> GO
'NWWriter1' added to role 'db_datareader'.
1> EXEC sp_addrolemember 'db_datawriter', 'NWWriter1'
2> GO
'NWWriter1' added to role 'db_datawriter'.
1> quit

D:\>_
```

Figure 19.30 This series of T-SQL commands in the OSQL utility add two logins, database access, and database user permissions for the linked NWDataSQL database.

19

TIP

If you have a large number of users or groups that need access to several databases, you can write a T-SQL script in Notepad or your favorite text editor, and then run the script with the `OSQL -E -q -i` *`Path\Script`*`.sql [-o` *`Path\Result`*`.sql]` command. The `-q` parameter causes OSQL to remain open after execution; `-i` specifies the T-SQL script file. The optional `-o` parameter specifies an output file that includes the commands and responses.

PASSWORD-PROTECTING ACCESS FRONT-ENDS

All production database applications should have at least some level of security applied. The minimum level of security is password-protecting the front end .mdb file. The problem with password protection is that users can open any Access object—except password-protected VBA code—in Design view and make changes to the front end. The only method of preventing unauthorized design changes to a password-protected .mdb file is to distribute the front end as an .mde file or supply a runtime version of your application, which requires the Access 2003 Developer Extensions' runtime version of MSAccess.exe, which was included with the Microsoft Office Developer Edition (MOD) for earlier Office versions. Creating an .mde version from a copy of your front-end .mdb file or use of runtime Access prevents users from opening any object in Design view. As a general rule, don't password-protect or create .mde versions of back-end .mdb files. Instead, use share- and file-level security, as described in the earlier "Establishing Network Share and File Security for the Back End" section, apply user-level security, or both.

➔ For more information about user-level security, **see** "Applying User-Level Security to Access Front-Ends," **p. 783**.

CAUTION

> **Don't password-protect back-end .mdbs whose data you intend to replicate. Jet replication fails with password-protected databases. SQL Server back ends use publish/subscribe replication, which relies on Windows or SQL Server security.**

Providing your application's users with a password-protected .mde version of your front-end database is the simplest method to achieve nominal security. You set only the initial password for the .mdb precursor of the .mde file; users can change the password of an .mde file. This means that everyone running your front-end can unset the password, which can compromise security. You or your network administrator can minimize security breaches by requiring network users to change their logon passwords periodically. Changing logon passwords doesn't require changes to file-based or SQL Server security parameters for the back end.

Adding a Database Password

To password-protect a front-end .mdb file, do this:

1. Close the database if it's open, and store an unprotected backup copy of the front end on a secure medium, such as a recordable or rewritable CD, or floppy disk. Most front-end .mdbs will fit on a 1.44MB floppy disk. Use the backup copy if you forget the password. This copy also serves as the backup for an .mde version.
2. Choose File, Open to display the Open dialog.
3. Select the file to protect, and click the arrow to the right of the Open button to display a list of Open... options (see Figure 19.31). Choose Open Exclusive to open the file for exclusive use.
4. Choose Tools, Security, Set Database Password to open the dialog of the same name. If you didn't open the file for exclusive use in step 3, you receive an error message.
5. Type and confirm the password in the two text boxes (see Figure 19.32), click OK, and close the database.

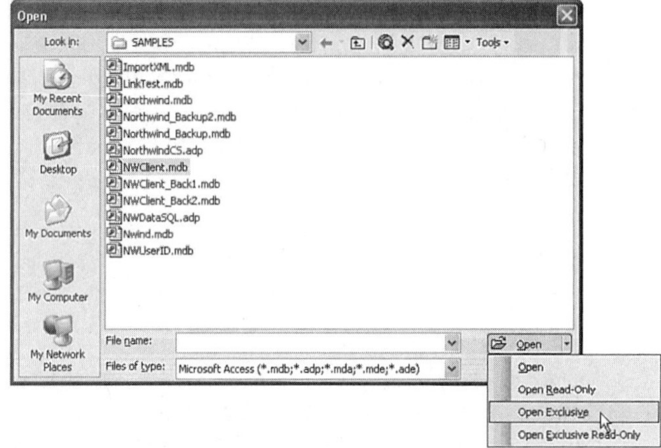

Figure 19.31
Use the Open button's list to open the .mdb file in exclusive mode. You need exclusive access to change the database password.

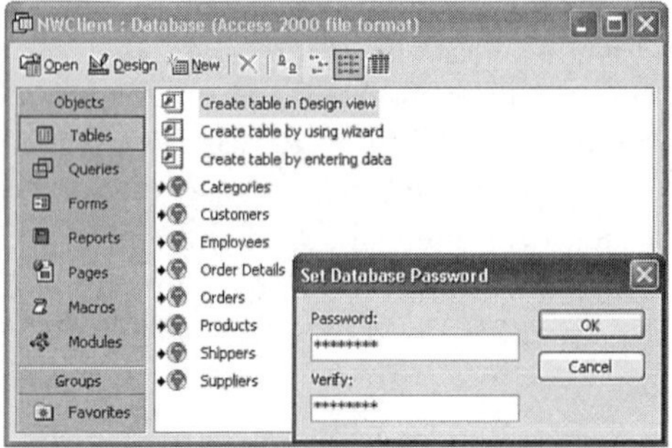

Figure 19.32
Type and confirm the front-end password in the Set Database Password text boxes. For maximum security, use a combination of upper- and lower-case letters, numbers, and allowed punctuation characters. You can't use the following characters in a password: " \ [ ] : | < > + = ; , . ? *.

6. Reopen the .mdb file, type the password in the Password Required dialog's Enter Database Password text (see Figure 19.33), and click OK.

To remove the password, repeat steps 2–4, but choose Unset Database Password in step 4. Type the password again in the text box and click OK.

Password-Protecting VBA Code

Access 2000 introduced password protection for VBA 6.0 code in conventional and Class Modules. You don't need to password-protect VBA code if you convert your front end to an .mde file, which compiles your source code and removes it from the .mde file. *Class Modules* (also called *Microsoft Access Class Objects*) hold the VBA code behind forms and reports. You might want to protect your VBA code against modification by users who have design privileges for the front end.

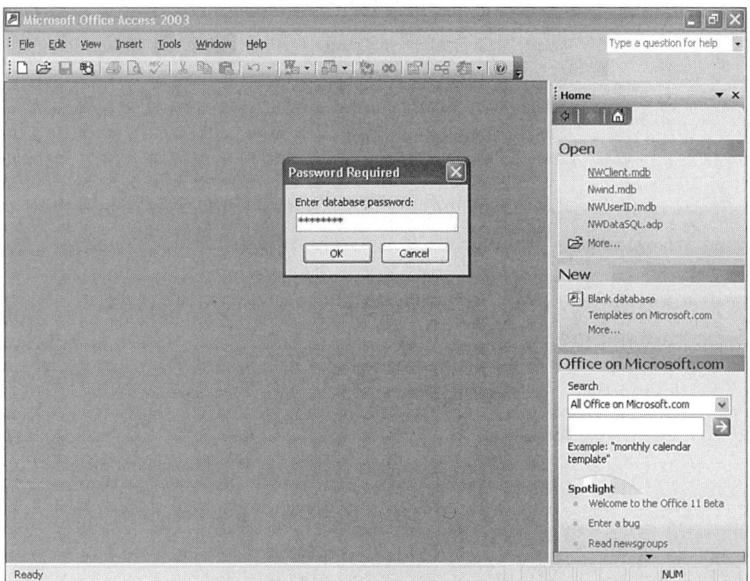

Figure 19.33
Users must type the database-specific password to open the front end. Password protecting a database doesn't prevent users from making design changes or other modifications to database objects.

You can prevent users from viewing or modifying the VBA code in your entire front end by taking the following steps:

1. Open any module, form, or report in Design view, and click the Code button of the form or report to open the VBA editor. Exclusive access isn't necessary to password-protect VBA code.
2. Choose Tools, *ProjectName* Properties to open the *ProjectName* Properties dialog, and click the Protection tab.
3. Mark the Lock Project for Viewing check box, and type and confirm a password in the two text boxes (see Figure 19.34). Click OK.

19

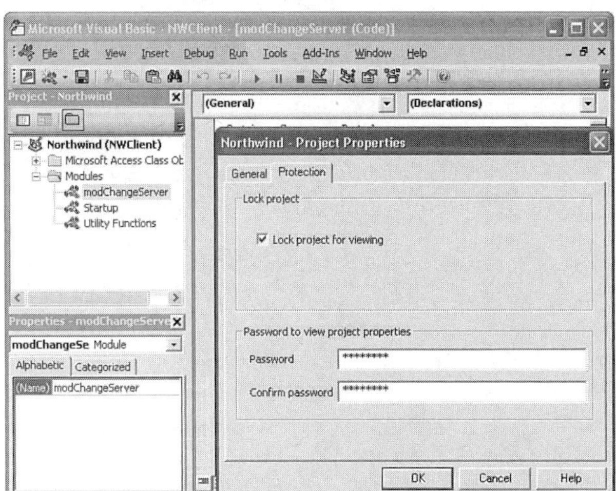

Figure 19.34
Prevent front-end users from viewing and modifying your VBA code behind forms and reports and in modules by password-protecting the code for the entire project.

TIP

Don't use the same or a similar password for the VBA code and the database. The database password will be the first choice of curious users. More determined users will try variations on the database password, such as adding a numeric suffix.

4. Close and reopen the database, and then repeat step 1. Type the password in the *ProjectName* Password dialog, and click OK.

To remove the VBA code password, repeat steps 1 and 2, clear the Lock Project for Viewing check box, and click OK.

NOTE

You can't apply user-level security to Access 200x VBA 6.0 modules, because VBA modules no longer are Access objects, despite the fact that the code is stored in the .mdb file. The VBA 6.0 editor is the same for all Office 2003/2000 components. Access 97 and earlier versions have an Access-specific version of the VBA editor.

CREATING AND TESTING AN .MDE FRONT-END

As mentioned earlier, .mde files provide a quick way to protect your front ends from modification by users. Users can't add, delete, or view in design mode forms, reports, and modules. Users have unrestricted access to tables and queries, which means they can wreak havoc on their own copy of the program by deleting links to tables, rewriting queries, and performing other mischief. Applying user-level security is the only means of securing local and linked tables, and preserving the integrity of queries and macros (if you use macros).

Creating an .mde file from an .mdb front end is a one- or two-step process. If you created your front-end database in the default Access 2000 format, you must choose Tools, Database Utilities, Convert Database, To Access 2002 Format and specify a different name for your front end, such as NWClient2002.mdb. This action, of course, restricts use of your MDB file to users with Access 2002 or later.

Open your Access 2002 front-end .mdb file and choose Tools, Database Utilities, Make MDE File to open the Save MDE As dialog. Accept the default MdbFileName.mde or rename the file. Click Save to create the new .mde file. Open the .mde file and verify user restrictions for tables, forms (see Figure 19.35), reports, and modules. Users might be able to open the Visual Basic Editor but can't view source code, because creating the .mde file removes the source code.

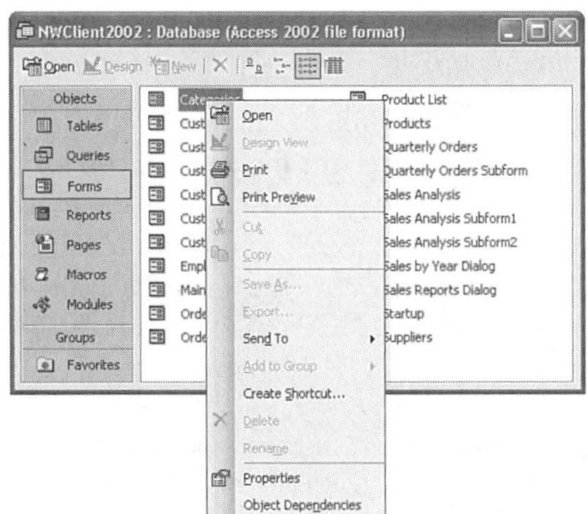

Figure 19.35 The context menu for a form illustrates user restrictions by disabled choices. Unfortunately, there are no user restrictions for tables, queries, and macros other than Add to Group.

APPLYING USER-LEVEL SECURITY TO ACCESS FRONT-ENDS

Descriptions of Access's user- and group-based security design range from labyrinthine to inscrutable. In reality, the Jet-based security model closely resembles that of Windows .NET/2000/NT and early versions of SQL Server. You create groups having particular sets of permissions for Access objects, and then add individual users to the groups. Unlike SQL Server and Windows versions of other client/server RDBMSs, Jet-based security doesn't integrate with Windows authentication.

ESTABLISHING YOUR OWN ADMINS NAME, PASSWORD, AND PID

Access has two levels of security: user level and file level. The user-level security system requires each user of Access to enter a username and a password to start Access. You establish file-level security for back-end .mdbs through the network operating system, and grant users permissions to access shared folders. If the server's file system is NTFS, you can grant permissions for individual files, as described in the earlier "Establishing Network Share and File Security for the Back End" topic. Network administrators usually manage server folder- and file-level security.

User-level security for multiuser Jet front ends requires a shared System.mdw workgroup file that contains user and group names, user passwords, and security identifiers (SIDs). You can use a shared System.mdw file to hold user and group accounts for multiple secured databases.

→ To review System.mdw basics, **see** "Jet Workgroup Information Files," **p. 153**.

Establishing user-level security for Jet front ends involves the following basic steps, which are covered later in this section in more detail:

1. Add a copy of the current System.mdw file to a network share for which you have Read and Change permissions. You can change the file name, if you want. If you're using linked Jet tables, place the .mdw file in the same folder as the backend .mdb file. If you want the .mdw file to control permissions for multiple front and back ends, create a back-end database folder hierarchy, and store the .mdw file at the top level. All Windows groups or users must have Read permission for the .mdw file.

TIP

> To find the location of the current System.mdw file, choose Tools, Security, Workgroup Administrator to open the Workgroup Administrator dialog. The Workgroup label contains the well-formed path to the current (default, in this case) workgroup file.

2. Connect to the shared .mdw file, and activate the logon procedure for Access. This action requires that you add a password for the Admin user. To remain Admin, you need not complete the remaining steps, but your only security is your password.
3. Create a new account for yourself as a member of the Admins group.
4. Log on to Access using your new Admins user account.
5. Remove the default Admin user account from the Admins group. The Admins group should include entries for active database administrators only. You can't remove the Admin user from the Users group.
6. Run the User-Level Security Wizard to create a secured version of the front-end .mdb. If you're using a Jet back end, you have the option to create a secured copy of the data .mdb file. The Wizard changes the ownership of all Access objects from the Admin user to the Admins account you use when starting Access.

If you forget the username or password you assigned to yourself after deleting the Admin user, you can't log on to Access. So before you begin the following procedure, make a floppy disk backup copy of the System.mdw file in use and any database files that you created or modified while using the default System.mdw. Most back-end .mdbs won't fit on a floppy disk, so use a higher-capacity removable disk drive or burn and test a CD-R or CD-RW disc. In this case, you must restore the original version of the System.mdw file. Then you might not be able to open the database files with which the original version of the System.mdw file is associated unless you restore the backed-up versions. For this reason, it's not a common practice to apply user-level security to back-end .mdb files. You can however, apply user-level security to the links.

CAUTION

> Don't use the Northwind.mdb database in your ...\Office10\Samples folder for the examples that follow. You should preserve Northwind.mdb and the System.mdw file in the original state. Use the NWClient.mdb file created earlier in this chapter with the Database Splitter, or make a copy of Northwind.mdb for a user-level security trial run. If you've password-protected the front-end .mdb file, open it in Exclusive mode and remove the password.

TIP

> You don't need to open a database to add or modify user accounts. All user account information is stored in System.mdw, which Access automatically opens when launched. Only members of the Admins group can open System.mdw in Access's database window.

Creating a Shared System.mdw File and Activating Logon for the Admin User

A password for the Admin user is necessary to activate Access's logon procedure. To activate the logon procedure for Access, complete the following steps:

1. Copy System.mdw to the shared folder on the server, which can be a machine running Windows NT/2000/.NET Server or a peer server running Windows XP or 2000 Professional. For this example, the server share is \\OAKLEAF-MS10\Northwind on a Windows 2000 member server with Read and Modify permissions.

TIP

> Alternatively, you can create a new workgroup file with the Workgroup Administrator tool.

19

2. If you're running Windows NT/2000+/XP, set permissions on the *System*.mdw file which give users read-only access and database owners (you and other Access developers) at least Read and Write permissions.
3. Choose Tools, Security, Workgroup Administrator to open the dialog, which displays the path to your current System.mdw file.
4. Click Join to open the Workgroup Information File dialog, and type the UNC path to and the name of the shared *System*.mdw file you copied in step 1 (see Figure 19.36). For this example, the shared file is \\OAKLEAF-MS10\Northwind\Northwind.mdw.
5. Click OK three times to make the change, acknowledge the confirmation message, and close the Workgroup Administrator dialog.
6. Choose Tools, Security, User and Group Accounts to open the User and Group Accounts properties dialog (see Figure 19.37). You are logged on as Admin, a member of the Admins and Users group, by default.

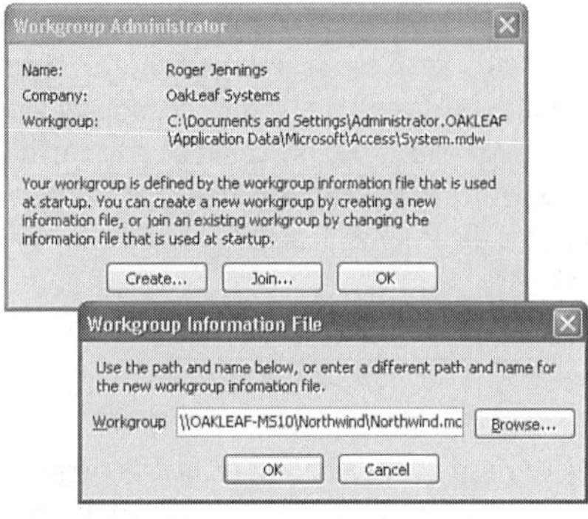

Figure 19.36
Click Join in the Workgroup Administrator, and then type in the Workgroup Information File dialog the full UNC path to the new *System*.mdw in the shared folder (Nortwind.mdw for this example).

Figure 19.37
The User and Group Accounts dialog displays Access's default user (Admin) and groups (Admins and Users).

7. Click the Change Logon Password tab, press the Tab key to bypass the Old Password text box (this enters the equivalent of an empty password), and type a difficult-to-guess password, such as **Xy8zW3ab**, in the New Password text box. Passwords are case sensitive, so Xy8zW3ab is a different password from xy8zw3ab.

8. Type the password in the Verify text box to test your entry, as shown in Figure 19.38. Access 2003's verification test is case sensitive, unlike some of its predecessors. Click OK to close the dialog and save the new password in the .mdw file.
9. Exit Access and launch it again, and then open the front-end database. The Admin account is password-protected, so the Logon dialog appears.

NOTE

> Versions prior to Access 2000 required you to log on to start Access after applying user-level security. After you log onto a database, you can open—without a logon step—other databases for which your username and password are valid.

Figure 19.38 With the Old Password text box empty, type your new password twice and click OK to assign a password to the Admin account. Workgroup passwords have the same character limitations as database passwords.

10. The initial default logon ID is your computer's network or Windows logon ID, if you've assigned it. Type **Admin** in the Logon dialog's Name text box, press Tab, and type the password exactly as you typed it in step 3 (see Figure 19.39). Press Enter or click OK. If you type the password correctly, Access continues the startup procedure.

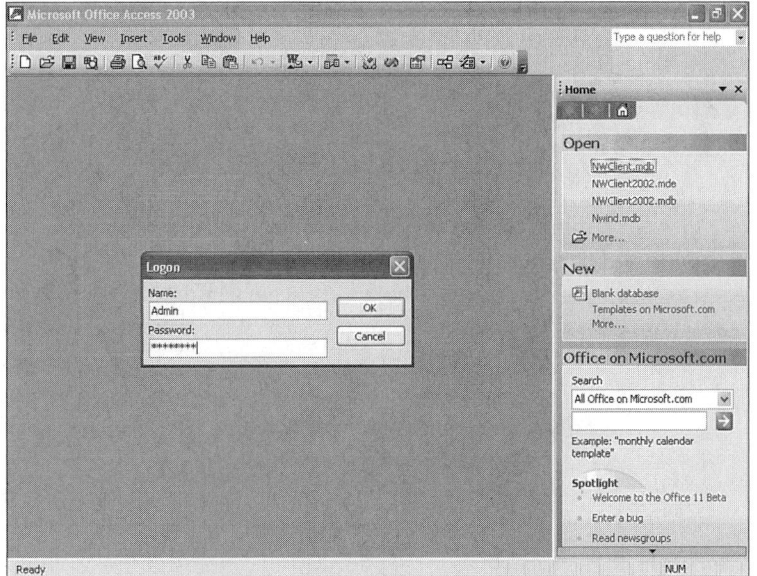

Figure 19.39 In Access 2000 and later, the Logon dialog appears when you open a database with user-level security applied.

Creating Your New Account in the Admins Group

To add your new user account in the Admins group, do the following:

1. Choose Tools, Security, User and Group Accounts to display the User and Group Accounts properties dialog.
2. Click the New button to open the New User/Group dialog.

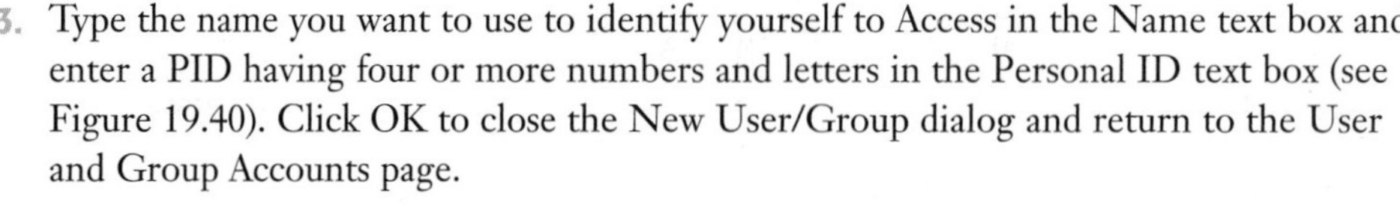

3. Type the name you want to use to identify yourself to Access in the Name text box and enter a PID having four or more numbers and letters in the Personal ID text box (see Figure 19.40). Click OK to close the New User/Group dialog and return to the User and Group Accounts page.

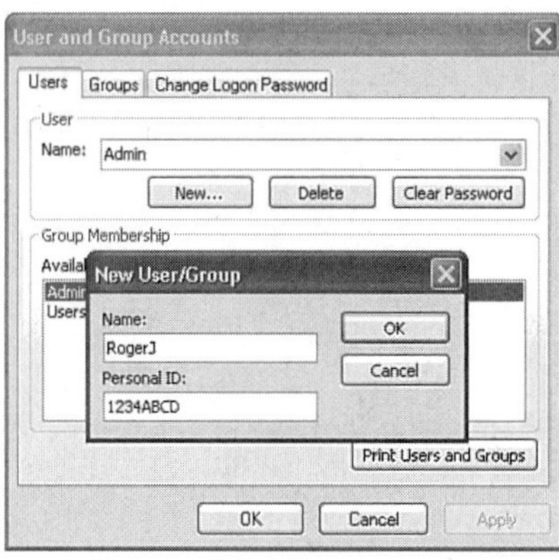

Figure 19.40
A new user account requires a logon Name and Personal ID code.

NOTE

The PID, with the Name entry, uniquely identifies your account. This precaution is necessary because two people might use the same logon name; the Name and PID values are combined to create a no-duplicates index on the Users table in the shared System.mdw file.

4. This is a critical step. Select Admins in the Available Groups list and click the Add button to add the Admins group to your new username (see Figure 19.41). If you fail to do this, you can't later remove the Admin account from the Admins group. (Access requires that there be at least one member of the Admins group in each system database file.)

Figure 19.41
Be sure to add your new administrative user account to the Admins group. Adding a new Admins user also adds the account to the Users group.

NOTE

> When you log on with your new username, you can't see the names of the last databases you opened as Admin when you choose File, Open. Prior database selections are specific to each user.

5. You don't enter a password for the new user at this time because you still are logged onto Access as Admin. Click OK to close the User and Group Accounts properties sheet, and then exit Access.
6. Open the front end, type your new username in the Logon dialog, and press Enter or click OK. Don't enter a password because you have an empty password at this point. Usernames aren't case sensitive; Access considers NewAdmin and newadmin to be the same user.
7. Choose Tools, Security, User and Group Accounts, select your new username from the Name drop-down list, and click the Change Logon Password tab. Press Tab to bypass the Old Password text box and type the password you plan to use until it's time to change your password (to maintain system security). Verify your password, and then press Enter or click OK to close the Password sheet.
8. Close Access, reopen the front end, and log on with your new username and password. This step verifies that your new Admins username and password are valid.
9. Choose Tools, Security, User and Group Accounts. Open the Users list of the User and Group Accounts page and select your new username from the list. Verify for the last time that you're a member of the Admins and Users group.
10. Open the Users list again and select the Admin user. Select Admins in the Member Of list; then click Remove. Admin remains a member of the Users group, as shown in Figure 19.42. Click OK to close the properties dialog.

Figure 19.42 Delete the default Admin user's membership in the Admins group in preparation to secure a database previously created with this account.

You use the same procedure to add other users as members of the default Admins or Users group or of new security groups you create. You have not fully secured the open database because the Admin user still has full permissions for the objects in the database as a result of being the database owner when creating the objects. The Admin user also is the owner of sample databases and Data Access Pages (DAP) included with Access.

TIP

Write down and save your PID and the PID of every user you add to the workgroup for future reference. Usernames and PIDs aren't secure elements, so you can safely keep a list without compromising system security. This list, however, should be accessible only to database administrators. You need a user's PID so that the user can be recognized as a member of another workgroup when the need arises.

TAKING ADVANTAGE OF THE USER-LEVEL SECURITY WIZARD

You can change the ownership of and permissions for all the objects in a database for which you have Administer permissions by importing all the database objects into a new database you create with a user ID other than Admin. Access 2.0 first made it easy to import all the database objects from one .mdb file into another .mdb file with its Import Database Add-In. Access 2000 introduced a greatly enhanced Security Wizard, which goes the Import Database Add-In one better by letting you choose the database objects to secure in a long series of steps. One of the primary benefits of the Security Wizard is that you can add groups, users, and assign object permission in a series of linked dialogs.

Don't use the Security Wizard with the Northwind.mdb database in your ...\Office11\Samples directory. Use the NWClient.mdb and NWData.mdb files you created earlier in this chapter with the Database Splitter, and use the *System*.mdw file and new database account you added in the previous two sections.

19

To give the Security Wizard a test drive with a front-end .mdb, follow these steps:

1. Re-launch Access, if necessary, open the database to secure, NWClient.mdb for this example, and log on with your new user ID that includes Admins group membership.
2. Choose Tools, Security, User-Level Security Wizard to display the Security Wizard's opening dialog. Accept the default Modify My Current Workgroup Information File, unless you have a particular reason for creating a new .mdw file (see Figure 19.43). Click Next to open the second Wizard dialog.
3. By default, the Wizard secures all objects in the database. Click the appropriate tab that corresponds to the class of database objects that you don't want to make secure, and then clear the check box for the individual object. If you want to secure all database objects, accept the Wizard's default (see Figure 19.44). Click Next to proceed to the third Wizard dialog.

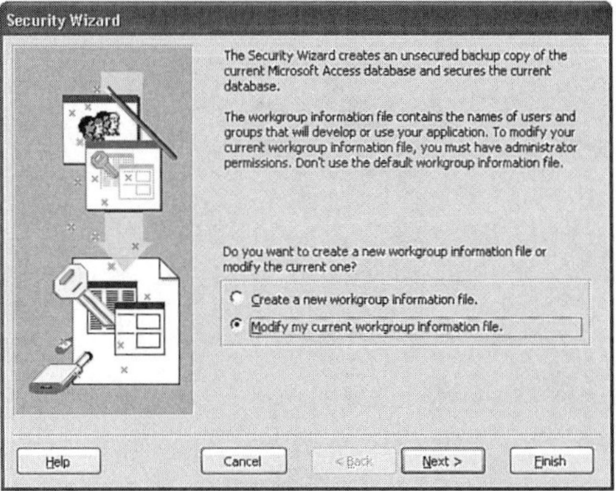

Figure 19.43 The first User-Level Security Wizard dialog gives you the opportunity to create a new System.mdw file.

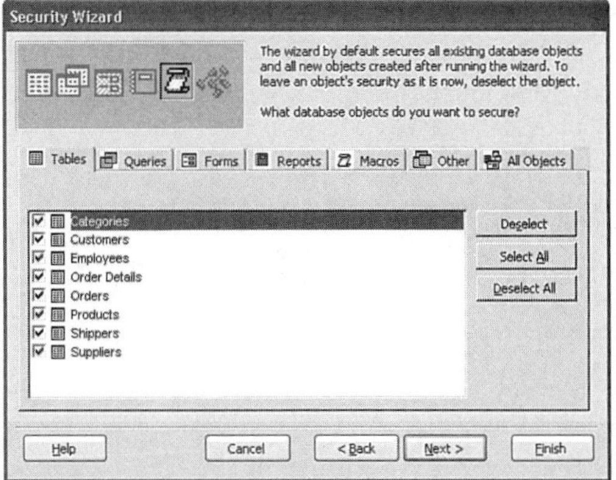

Figure 19.44 If you don't want to secure all objects in your database, clear the check boxes for those objects to remain unsecured in the second Wizard dialog.

NOTE

NWClient.mdb contains only links to SQL Server or Jet back-end tables, not the tables themselves. However, permissions you apply to the links to Jet or SQL Server back ends are enforced on the link. For example, if a group has read-only privileges for a link to an SQL Server table, the members of the group don't see the tentative append record in Table or Query Datasheet view, nor can they update data in the table, even if they have `sp_datawriter` privileges for the database.

The Access 2002 version of the Wizard lets you password protect the VBA code in your project at this point. To password-protect your code, use the procedure described in the earlier "Password-Protecting VBA Code" section.

4. The Wizard offers a collection of predefined groups with a specific set of access permissions appropriate to the group. Text within the Group Permissions frame describes the object permissions for each group. The Wizard adds the groups you specify in this dialog to the current .mdw file. Mark the check boxes of the groups to gain permissions for the tables of NWDataSQL or NWData.mdb (see Figure 19.45). Click Next.

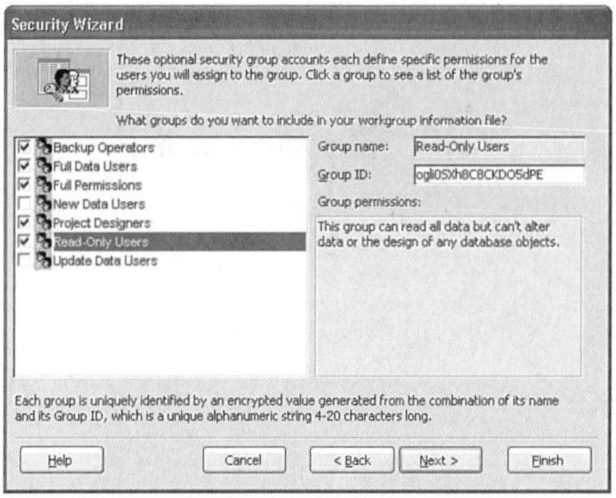

Figure 19.45
Mark the check boxes for the default security groups you want to include in the System.mdw file. The six groups shown here are the most useful.

5. By default, members of the Users group have full permissions for all objects until you secure them. Accept No, the Users Group Should Not Have Any Permissions, unless you have a very specific reason for doing otherwise (see Figure 19.46). Click Next to continue with the Security Wizard's task.

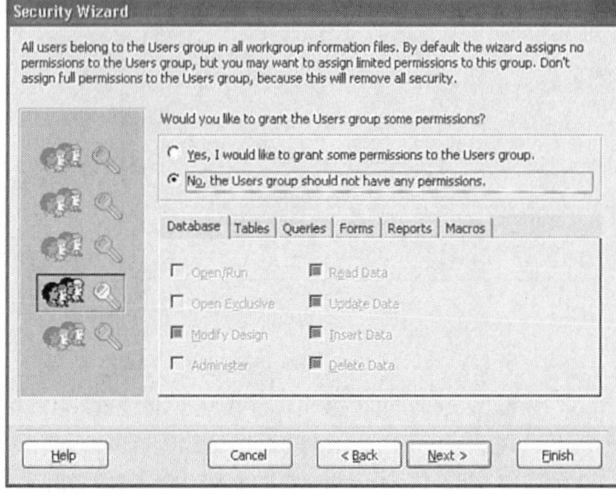

Figure 19.46
The groups you specified in earlier step 4 eliminate the need for the default Users group, which includes all user accounts you add. To prevent permissions from being inherited from the Users group, remove all the group's permissions.

6. Another feature of the User-Level Security Wizard is the ability to add new users to your .mdw file during the securing process. Type the name of a new user in the User Name text box and provide a password, which appears in the clear in the Password text box (see Figure 19.47). Click the Add This User to the List button. Add a test user account with the name of each group account, such as **BackupTest**, **FullDataTest**, and the like, with a common password. (The Password text box in this case doesn't substitute asterisks for password characters.) Add user accounts for users of your production database at this point, such as **NWReader1** and **NWWriter1**. Click Next when you've finished adding users.

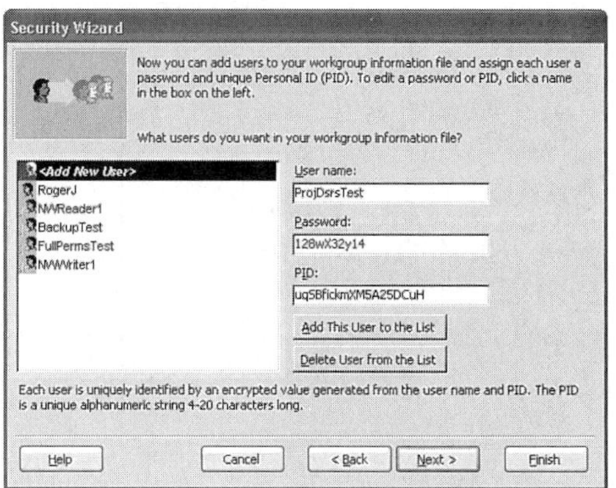

Figure 19.47
Add production database users and a test user account for the groups you selected in step 5. The test user accounts let you verify that the Wizard applies security as advertised in the Group Permissions frame.

7. You can assign or remove (except from Users) group memberships of all users in your workgroup file (see Figure 19.48). Accept the default Select a User and Assign the User to Groups option. Assign each of the test user and the production accounts you added to the appropriate security group you select from the drop-down list. For example, make NWReader1 a member of the Read-Only Users group and NWWriter1 a member of the Full Data Users group. After making group assignments, click Next to open the last Wizard dialog.

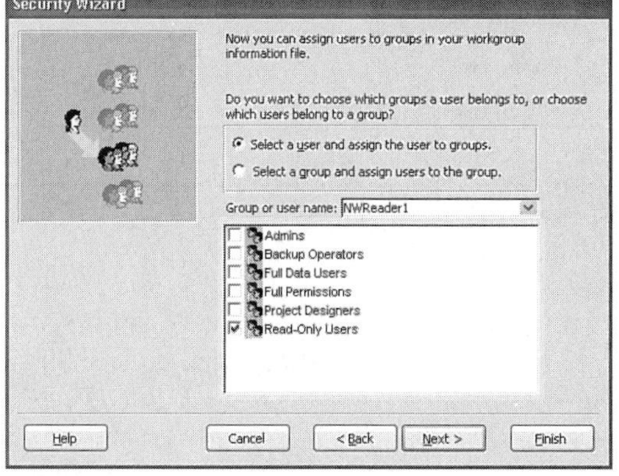

Figure 19.48
Adding test and production users and their passwords in the Wizard dialog is faster than adding them with the User and Group Accounts properties dialog.

19

8. The Wizard secures the current database, and creates a unsecured backup database copy in the process. The default name of the backup file is *DatabaseName*.bak (see Figure 19.49).
9. Click Finish to put the Security Wizard to work. After a few seconds, the "One-step Security Wizard Report" shown in Figure 19.50 opens, indicating successful creation of the new secure database. The report for the NWClient.mdb front end is three pages long. Close the report.

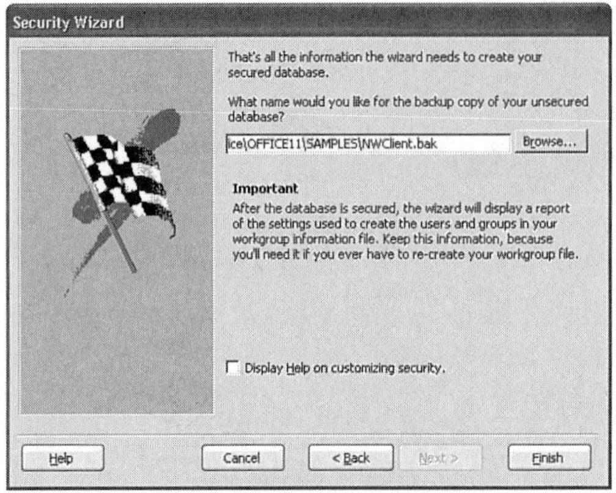

Figure 19.49
Accept or change the name of the unsecured backup file the Wizard creates when you click Finish.

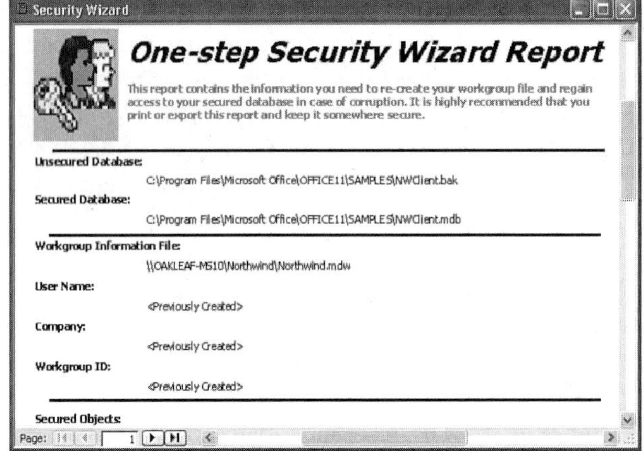

Figure 19.50
The Wizard's report includes a list of the objects secured and the names, passwords, and group membership of users you added.

10. Closing the report opens a message box asking whether you want to save a Report Snapshot (.snp) file that you can view with the Access Snapshot viewer. Take the Wizard's advice to store a copy of the report in a secure place for future reference. (You should also print a copy now.) Click Yes to create and view *DatabaseName*.snp, which is identical to the report created in the preceding step.

TIP

> Copy the *DatabaseName*.snp file to a floppy disk saved in a secure location, and then delete the .snp file from your fixed disk. The printed report and .snp file includes the logon IDs and passwords you assigned to test and production users. Users should change their passwords periodically; unlike Windows NT/2000+, Access doesn't store password expiration intervals.

19

11. Close the .snp file window. The Wizard has added new users and assigned object permissions. You can confirm the Wizard's work in the User and Group Accounts and User and Group Permissions dialogs. Object permissions are the subject of the later "Changing Database Group and User Permissions" section.
12. If you didn't do so in step 3, apply password protection to the VBA code in your front end using the procedure described in the earlier "Password-Protecting VBA Code" section.
13. Log on with the test user accounts you created in step 6, change the accounts' workgroup file to the shared, secure copy, and verify the privileges of each user. If your version of NWClient.mdb links to the NWDataSQL SQL Server database, notice that the tables no longer have a tentative append record when you log on as the NWReader1 user.

NOTE

> The Access 97 version of the Security Wizard automatically encrypted front-end and back-end .mdb files. It's not a common practice to encrypt front ends, so Access 2003 doesn't encrypt .mdb files that don't contain tables. When you apply user-level security to back-end .mdb databases, encryption is automatic.

The owner of all the objects in the new database is the user ID you entered when you opened the source database. Only members of the Admins, Full Permissions, and Project Designers groups have design access of any kind to the newly secured database. You should provide the VBA code password to other members of the Admins group and to all Project Designers.

NOTE

> This chapter uses the term user ID to identify users of Access. Internally, Access uses a system ID (SID) to identify users. The SID is a value that Access computes from the user ID, password, and PID. The SID is stored in the MSysUsers table of System.mdw as an encrypted binary value in a field of the Binary (`varbinary`) data type.

SECURING JET BACK-END DATABASES

If you use Jet as the database back end, you might want to secure the back-end tables against exploration by unauthorized users. All users need read/write access to the shared folder, but only groups having the authority to update tables need write permissions for the back-end .mdb. For this example, NWWriter1 has Read and Write access to NWData.mdb and could open it and change its design with Access.

1. Open the back-end .mdb file with the new account you added with Admins permissions.

2. Repeat steps 2–12 of the preceding procedure. You must specify the same groups you specified in step 4, but you don't need to add users to the groups in step 7.
3. Close Access, and reopen the front-end .mdb file with the test user accounts to verify appropriate read-only and read/write access to the encrypted back-end Jet database.

You can run the User-Level Security Wizard multiple times to alter permissions for either front-end or back-end databases.

CHANGING DATABASE GROUP AND USER PERMISSIONS

After you design your hierarchy of permissions and add initial user groups and users with the User-Level Security Wizard, you can change individual group and user permissions, and ownership for each of the objects in your database. Only members of the Admins group can alter permissions for Groups or Users or reassign ownership of objects. The Permissions check boxes that are enabled depend on the type of object you choose. Open/Run, for example, is enabled only for database, form, report, and macro objects.

TIP

> If you have a large number of users who need different permissions for application and table objects, prepare a checklist for group permissions and the group membership of users. Excel is useful for creating this type of checklist. Keep a printed copy of the checklist with the snapshot file you printed when running the Security Wizard.

To change the object permissions for a user or group, do the following:

1. As a member of the Admins group, open the database for which permissions are to be granted or revoked with the appropriate workgroup system database active. For this example, you've decided to grant Admins permissions for forms and reports to the Project Designers group. (Pages and modules don't use Jet security.)
2. Choose Tools, Security, User and Group Permissions to open the User and Group Permissions dialog.
3. Users is the default option, which displays the permissions for individual users. Select the user account, ProjDesrsTest for this example.
4. Open the Object Type drop-down list and select the type of database object whose permissions you want to change, Forms to start.
5. Select the specific object to which the new permissions will apply in the Object Name list. Permissions currently granted to the group are shown by a mark in the Permissions check boxes. To select all objects, click the first item in the list, press the Shift key, and then click the last item in the list. Including <New *ObjectType*> in your multiple selection is optional.

NOTE

> When you make a multiple selection in the Object Name list, all check boxes change to the unknown state indicated by a gray mark in each box.

6. Mark the Administer check box to give the ProjDsrsTest account the right to change object permissions. When you make multiple selections, you might need to click the check box twice to make a selection effective. Your Permissions page appears as shown in Figure 19.51. The account inherits the four ...Data permissions from the Project Designers group permissions for tables, so these permission don't need changing.

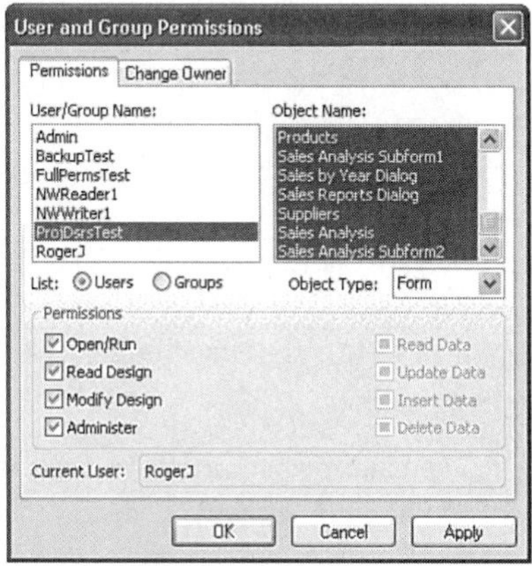

Figure 19.51 Grant or revoke special permissions for database objects to users or groups with the User and Group Permissions dialog. Individual account permissions don't appear for other users, because the users inherit all permissions from group membership.

7. Click the Apply button to make the new permissions effective for the selected database object(s).
8. Repeat steps 4–7 for each database object and object type whose user permissions you want to change.

The Change Owner page of the User and Group Permissions dialog lets you assign ownership of objects to another user. By default, the owner of an object is the account under which the object was created. When you run the User-Level Security Wizard, the account you use becomes the owner of all objects.

TROUBLESHOOTING

JET TABLES FAIL TO UPSIZE

I receive error messages during the upsizing process, and some tables don't upsize.

The most common cause of failure is the presence of complex Jet or VBA expressions in table or field validation rules. SQL Server has counterparts for many Jet query expressions, but only a few for VBA functions. SQL Server 2000's extended properties accommodate Jet input masks, data display formatting, subdatasheets, and lookup fields. The Upsizing

Wizard, however, handles a surprisingly broad range of validation rules. For example, you can upsize with no difficulty the Forms14.mdb application whose HRActions table has several table and field validation rules.

If you adhere to the recommendations in the "Modifying Table Properties to Assure Successful Upsizing" section near the middle of this chapter, there little probability of encountering table upsizing failures.

MSDE Performance Problems

Performance of my multiuser Jet applications is significantly slower after upsizing the tables to MSDE 2000 or other SQL Server 2000 editions.

If your MSDE 2000 back end appears to be running out of steam as you add more users, the first step is to optimize your queries to minimize the amount of data returned to the client. Revisit all queries with `SELECT *` statements to determine whether you need all columns returned. For example, don't include the shipping address fields of Northwind.mdb's Orders table in your query if you're only interested in order dates or customer billing information. Avoid Jet-specific or VBA expressions in `WHERE` clause criteria, because the server must return all records for processing by the Jet expression service. Both Jet and SQL Server support `SELECT TOP` *n* `[PERCENT]` queries, but ODBC doesn't. Thus the server must return all records to the client for `TOP` *n* processing by Jet.

Try to design your form queries with `WHERE` clause criteria that return fewer than 100 rows. Such queries require only a single connection to the server.

After you've streamlined your queries, the next step is to add RAM. Minimum RAM for reasonable performance with five or fewer users is 128MB for Windows XP or 2000 Professional, and 256MB for Windows 2000 or .NET Server (without Active Directory installed). Start with at least 384MB RAM if your Windows 2000/.NET Server running MSDE is a domain controller. MSDE will run under Windows NT 4.0 Workstation or Server with 128MB of RAM. Double the amount of RAM if you experience a slowdown in performance due to disk page swapping as you add more users.

If some—but not all—users experience performance problems, check their client PCs for adequate RAM to run Office 2003 or the Access 2003 runtime version. The "System Requirements for Access 2003" section of the Introduction lists the RAM requirements for Office 2003. Network connectivity between the client and server also can be a problem; solving networking issues is beyond the scope of this book.

Invalid Path Errors Occur when Users Open a Secured Jet Database

After changing the location of the workgroup file to a network share, users encounter "'d:\path\filename.mdw' isn't a valid path" messages.

You specified a logical drive mapped to the share, instead of the UNC path (*ServerName**ShareName**System*.mdw) to the .mdw file. You can't depend on users to assign specific logical drive letters to a share. Always use UNC to specify the location to the .mdw file.

IN THE REAL WORLD—THE (ALMOST) FREE LUNCH

Controversy over the future of conventional shared-file multiuser Jet applications continues unabated among Access developers and Microsoft marketers. The shared-file, "Jet is alive and well" axis insists that Jet is a viable back end for workgroup-size online transaction processing (OLTP) applications. The "Jet is dead" cabal, whose membership is dominated by SQL Server marketing folks, consider MSDE to be Microsoft's "strategic database" for Office applications and SQL Server 2000 to be the natural back-end choice for everyone else, including users of hand-held devices running Windows CE. Regardless of the rhetoric, you can't beat the price of MSDE; it's free.

Shared-file proponents tend to favor traditional Data Access Objects (DAO), a mature technology now in its final version (3.6). Members of the MSDE/SQL Server clan justifiably promote OLE DB and ActiveX Data Objects (ADO) as being where the action is for database connectivity. OLE DB and ADO are designed to support Web-based applications; DAO isn't. ADP use OLE DB and ADO to connect to SQL Server. Microsoft's .NET framework is centered on SQL Server and an enhanced version of ADO called ADO.NET, and you can expect major changes to Access when Microsoft finally gets around to releasing the next version of Office. Access versus *Next* undoubtedly will toll the death knell for new Jet-based applications and DAO.

The reality is that multiuser Jet does run out of steam in heavy-duty OLTP applications having many simultaneous users. The point at which concurrency and file corruption problems begin to appear in Jet back-end databases depends on a variety of factors. Each upgrade to Jet has improved multiuser reliability, but many developers still consider 20 to 30 simultaneous updating users to be the practical limit for Jet 4.0. The absolute maximum number of concurrent user connections to any Jet database is 255. Thus Jet isn't a serious contender for an e-commerce orders database on a highly trafficked Web site. The 1GB maximum table size and 32-index limit (including indexes created by relationships) makes Jet impractical for use in data marts and warehouses of medium or larger scope.

Jet offers the advantage of easy conversion from single-user, single-file mode to shared-file multiuser mode. The Database Splitter utility makes the transition automatic. Descriptions of the Jet security system range from Byzantine to Machiavellian, but Jet security is easier to manage than SQL Server security, especially when using OSQL. You would probably be surprised to learn how many production SQL Server databases installed with mixed (Windows authentication and SQL Server security) have run unsecured for months or years with the default sa as the username and no password. Access's User-Level Security Wizard takes most of the pain out of securing front-end and back-end .mdb files.

If you seek multiuser simplicity in a small Windows XP workgroup environment, shared-file Jet probably is your best bet. For more sizable projects, linking Jet front ends to MSDE under Windows 2000+ Server—followed ultimately by a transition to a full version of SQL Server—is the natural choice. Jet security applies to SQL Server links, but doesn't secure the back-end database itself against marauding members of the local Administrators group that have a copy of SQL Server Enterprise Manager.

MSDE is substantially more robust than Jet, especially for OLTP. You don't need to periodically compact SQL Server files as users edit and delete records. MSDE offers automated backup and restore operations and provides a transaction log that you can use to return restored tables to their exact state at the time of a crash. Although Microsoft claims to "tune" MSDE for five simultaneous users, tests indicate that MSDE running under Windows 2000 Server can support many more than five clients.

If you're starting an Access project from scratch, and you expect more than about 20 users to update database tables simultaneously, seriously consider starting directly with ADP. Although you can use the Access Upsizing Wizard to convert a conventional Access application to ADP, the upsizing process isn't bulletproof. You must rewrite Jet queries that contain Access-specific reserved words and functions missing from the Wizard's bag of tricks. You save time in the short and long run by conforming to SQL Server's T-SQL dialect when you design your queries. Chapter 22, "Upsizing Jet Applications to Access Data Projects," describes typical workarounds for Jet queries that won't upsize to T-SQL.

Your free lunch ticket expires when you must upgrade your server from MSDE 2000 to the $4,995 SQL Server 2000 Standard Edition for a single processor. To mitigate the pain of SQL Server license costs, Microsoft gives you a free copy of SQL Server Analysis (formerly OLAP) Services. Of course, the SQL Server folks hope you'll build data marts so large that they require their own dedicated server cluster (and thus pairs of even more costly SQL Server 2000 Enterprise Edition licenses).

TIP

If you're thinking about upgrading from MSDE 2000 and will have less than 50 users for a year or two, consider Microsoft's $1,299 Small Business Server (SBS) with five Client Access Licenses (CALs). SBS includes Windows 2000 Server, SQL Server 2000, Exchange 2000 Server, and the Internet Security and Acceleration (ISA) Server 2000. Additional CALs are $44 each in groups of five. Make sure your server has at least 512MB RAM because all services must run on the same box. Go to `http://www.microsoft.com/sbserver/` for more details. When this book was written, Microsoft hadn't announced licensing terms or pricing for the Windows Server 2003 SBS version.

CHAPTER 20

EXPLORING ACCESS DATA PROJECTS AND SQL SERVER 2000

In this chapter

MOVING ACCESS TO THE CLIENT/SERVER MODEL

Access 2003's Access data projects (ADP), also called Microsoft Access projects or Access client/server applications, let you connect to the Microsoft SQL Server 2000 Desktop Engine (MSDE) with Service Pack (SP) 3 on your PC; on a peer server running Windows XP or 2000 Professional, or NT 4.0 Workstation with SP 4+; or on a network server running Windows 2003/2000/NT 4.0 Server. You also can connect to networked SQL Server 6.5 with SP 5, 7.0, and 2000 databases. As in the previous chapters of this book, the term *SQL Server* refers to any of these three SQL Server versions, plus MSDE 1.0 and 2000. *SQL Server 2000* is used when discussing new features that aren't supported by its predecessors.

NOTE

> Office 2003 is limited to installation under Windows XP and 2000+, but you can install MSDE 2000 on PCs running Windows NT 4.0 Professional or Server, and even Windows Me or 98. MSDE installed under Windows Me or 98 uses SQL Server (login ID and password) security. This book's examples use MSDE running under Windows XP Professional or Windows 2000 Server with integrated Windows authentication.

Following are the most important characteristics of ADP:

- Like upsized Jet applications, ADP rely on SQL Server tables, but they don't use .mdb files to store database front-end forms, reports, and other application objects. ADP store application objects in a single .adp compound document file (docfile).
- Unlike upsized Jet front-end .mdbs, the .adp file doesn't contain queries; SQL Server stores `SELECT` queries as views. A view is a precompiled SQL `SELECT` query, which replaces conventional Access `SELECT` queries saved as Jet `QueryDef` (query definition) objects.
- SQL Server stored procedures replace Jet action queries. Like views, stored procedures are precompiled queries, but stored procedures aren't limited to `SELECT` queries. Stored procedures are especially efficient at processing `INSERT`, `UPDATE`, and `DELETE` operations, and managing transactions.
- Project tool windows substitute for Jet's Table and Query Design windows. The da Vinci windows perform functions similar to—but differ in layout from—their Jet counterparts. Table and Query Datasheet views are almost identical to those for Jet back ends.
- NEW 2002 SQL Server 2000 offers *user-defined functions (UDFs)*, which you can use to return the equivalent of a table to an ad-hoc query, view, or stored procedure. User-defined functions support SQL Server's new *linked servers* feature to connect to other client/server RDBMSs, Active Directory, Index Service, and Exchange 2000's Web folders. For example, you can connect ADP to an Oracle database linked to MSDE. You also can use UDFs to return scalar (character or numeric) values.

- SQL Server 2000 uses *extended properties* to support Jet's lookup field and subdatasheet features, so you don't lose these capabilities when migrating to the client/server model. Extended properties also support input masks, captions, and data display formatting. SQL Server includes system stored procedures to add, read, and remove custom extended properties from the database.
- SQL Server 2000 has its own panoply of new Extended Markup Language (XML) features, which are independent of those offered by Access 2003. For example, you can write an XML file that contains a query and add an XML Stylesheet Language transform (XSL/T) to return data directly from SQL Server to a fully formatted table in a Web page.
- ADP dispense with Jet, Open Database Connectivity (ODBC), and Data Access Objects (DAO), substituting OLE DB data providers and ActiveX Data Objects (ADO) for database connectivity and data manipulation, respectively. OLE DB and ADO are the subjects of Chapter 30, "Understanding Universal Data Access, OLE DB, and ADO."
- You design ADP in Access's standard Form and Report views and use the standard Toolbox to add native Access and ActiveX controls to forms and reports. You can import Access objects—other than tables and queries—from existing Jet databases.

You can use the Upsizing Wizard to convert a conventional Access .mdb application to an Access project, instead of retaining the Jet front end. In the ADP environment, you also can create DAP bound to SQL Server databases. Access 2003 lets you convert simple forms and reports you design in the ADP environment to DAP.

ADP are best suited to the following types of Access 2003 applications:

- Front ends to new or existing SQL Server databases. Access 2003 is an effective rapid application development (RAD) tool for client/server front ends.
- Applications that you expect to upsize to SQL Server 2000 Standard or Enterprise Edition in the near future or even long term. Microsoft has made it easy to migrate ADP from MSDE on your PC to SQL Server running under Windows 2000+/NT Server. Using ADP, rather than Jet, assures a quick and seamless transition from a local MSDE database to SQL Server 2000 or its successor—codenamed "Yukon" when this book was written.
- Projects that use two-way SQL Server 2000 replication, rather than Jet-to-Jet or Jet-to-SQL Server replication, to synchronize multiple copies of the database. SQL Server replication is more robust and flexible than the Jet version.

Users of your Access project must have Access 2000 or 2002 installed, unless you use the Access 2003 runtime version to create a distributable version of your ADP. The runtime version of MSAccess.exe is a member of the Access 2003 Developer Extensions. If your Access project requires a local SQL Server database, users also must install MSDE. If the application connects to an SQL Server 6.5, 7.0, or 2000 database (not the Desktop editions), users must have the requisite client licenses for Windows 2000+/NT Server and SQL Server.

TIP

You can use a local Jet database with ADP client applications, but you must write VBA code to connect to the local database and manipulate its contents. You can use either DAO or ADO to make the connection to the local .mdb, but using ADO is much more efficient. If you use DAO to connect to the local .mdb file, clients must load both DAO and ADO, which consumes additional resources.

UNDERSTANDING THE ROLE OF SQL SERVER AND ADP

Microsoft's announcement in mid-1995 that Access 2000 would include an "alternate database" led to a flurry of "Jet is dead" pronouncements in the computer press. These stories gained credence when members of the SQL Server 2000 team described their forthcoming product as "Microsoft's strategic database direction." The reality is that Jet obituaries are very premature. Jet plays a major role in more than 25 Microsoft products, and variants of the Jet database engine serve as the message store for Microsoft Exchange. Jet is likely to be alive and well, at least through the first few years of the twenty-first century.

Regardless of Jet's prospects for long-term survival, there's a definite trend toward the use of client/server back ends when database reliability is the primary objective. Production Web-based applications require client/server back ends for security and scalability. Thus, SQL Server 2000 will play an increasingly important role as even small firms migrate database applications to intranets and the Internet. You can expect Microsoft to add new ADP features to future releases, but don't look for any upgrades to Jet.

SQL SERVER EDITIONS, LICENSING, AND FEATURES

SQL Server 2000 comes in Evaluation, Windows CE, Desktop (MSDE), Personal, Developer, Standard, and Enterprise editions. The Standard and Enterprise editions run only under Windows 2000+/NT Server, and the Personal edition is restricted to use on workstations. MSDE is licensed only for a "stand-alone desktop device," and is intended to run under Windows 98, Windows NT 4.0 Workstation (with SP4 or later applied), Windows XP or 2000 Professional, or Windows 2000+/NT Server. Unlike Access 2000's version of MSDE (sometimes called MSDE 1.0), you can't install MSDE 2000 under Windows 95.

NOTE

Links from Microsoft's SQL Server Web pages at `http://www.microsoft.com/sql/` offer product and licensing information for all SQL Server 2000 editions. The "Appropriate Uses of MSDE" page at `http://www.microsoft.com/sql/howtobuy/msdeuse.asp` has questions and answers regarding your rights—or more accurately, lack of rights—when using MSDE in production projects.

All SQL Server editions, except Windows CE, share a common code base, and data files are fully interchangeable between the versions. All editions use Transact-SQL (T-SQL), which includes many extensions to ANSI-92 SQL. The primary difference between MSDE and the other SQL Server 2000 editions (except Windows CE) is that MSDE doesn't include the SQL Server Enterprise Manager, which provides graphic tools for creating and managing databases and executing T-SQL queries. MSDE installs OSQL.exe, which lets you run T-SQL statements and execute stored procedures from a command prompt, but there's no online help for using OSQL. Access 2003 provides the graphic tools you need to create and modify MSDE databases, but not to manage MSDE user logins and database permissions.

→ For an example of using OSQL to add logins and database permissions to MSDE, **see** "Adding User Logins with the OSQL Utility," **p. 776**.

NOTE

> Access 2003 doesn't include Access 2000's Tools, Security, Database Security menu choice, which opens the SQL Server Security dialog to let you set permissions on a project's database. In the absence of an SQL Server 2000 license, you can't use the Enterprise Manager tools with MSDE 2000.

Microsoft designed SQL Server 2000 for ease of installation and minimum maintenance. Unlike version 6.5 and earlier, you don't need to create fixed-size .dat files (devices) to hold SQL Server objects. SQL Server 2000 uses the NTFS or—less commonly—FAT32 file system to store all its objects. Files expand or contract automatically as tables grow or shrink, and you don't need to compact SQL Server databases to regain disk space after large-scale deletions, such as those that occur when you archive noncurrent data. SQL Server 2000 databases are self-tuning, so you don't need to be an accomplished database administrator (DBA) to get maximum performance from MSDE.

Benefits and Drawbacks of Access Data Projects

Chapter 19, "Linking Access Front-Ends to Jet and Client/Server Tables," describes the benefits of moving multiuser applications from shared-file to client/server back ends. There's little controversy among application developers that client/server architecture ultimately will replace all shared-file databases for production applications.

The benefits of moving from Jet front ends with linked client/server databases to ADP aren't so clear-cut. The newer OLE DB and ADO technology is more flexible and efficient than ODBC and Jet's Data Access Objects (DAO). ADO is compatible with scripting languages—such as VBScript and JScript—for Web applications, but DAO isn't. All application objects in the project share a single OLE DB connection to SQL Server, and consume inconsequential server resources when they're idle. Jet applications usually require multiple, active connections to the back-end server.

OLE DB and ADO don't offer dramatic performance improvements over Jet, ODBC, and DAO for databases having tables with a 100,000 rows or fewer. However, connecting projects directly to SQL Server lets you take advantage of precompiled views and stored procedures that do offer improved server response, especially with databases having tables with a very large number of records. If you expect your databases ultimately to grow to hundreds of thousands or millions of rows, your best bet is to connect directly to SQL Server with ADP.

ADP are best viewed as an advanced form and report engine for SQL Server. Unlike Jet, which can connect to any client/server RDBMS having an ODBC 2+ driver, ADP connect only to SQL Server. If you need to connect to an IBM DB2, Informix, Oracle, or Sybase RDBMS, you must set up SQL Server views on linked server tables. Using ADP requires a long-term commitment to SQL Server for your production databases.

➔ To learn how to link SQL Server to other data sources, **see** "Linking Remote Servers," **p. 842**.

Access is unsurpassed as a RDBMS instructional tool, and ADP with MSDE combine to form an ideal method of learning up-to-date client/server database design and programming techniques. If your goal is to become proficient in managing client/server RDBMSs in general—and SQL Server in particular—ADP is a far better choice than working with linked Jet tables.

Getting Acquainted with Access Data Projects

Microsoft designed ADP as the entry point for building Access front ends for client/server database back-ends. ADP also offer the opportunity for Access users and first-time developers to gain insight into the benefits and drawbacks of client/server computing. Technically, ADP aren't limited to use with SQL Server. As mentioned earlier, it's possible to link other RDBMS servers to SQL Server 2000. This chapter's content is limited to creating ADP that connect to MSDE and other SQL Server 2000 editions. The following two sections are of interest primarily to readers who are upgrading from Access 97 or 2000 to Access 2003. Access 2003 makes no significant changes to Access 2002 ADP.

Access 2000 Features Added for SQL Server 7.0 Conformance

Previous releases of Access required modifications to assure compatibility with the then-current version of SQL Server. Providing an upgrade path to ADP required Access 2000 to add the following features to support SQL Server 7.0:

- **Unicode support for localization**—Unicode defines a two-byte character set for all languages supported by Windows 98, Me, NT, and 2000. Using two bytes per character for all languages eliminates the need for double-byte character set (DBCS) installation for pictographic languages, such as Chinese and Korean. Jet uses *Unicode compression* to minimize the increase in the size of databases having large, text-heavy tables. MSDE lets you choose between conventional code pages and Unicode, but doesn't offer Unicode compression.

- **Decimal data type**—Jet 4.0's Decimal data type corresponds to the SQL Server `decimal` numeric data type that lets you set specific `precision` and `scale` values. The `precision` is the maximum number of digits in the number; `scale` is the maximum number of digits to the right of the decimal point. Jet 4.0's maximum precision or scale is 28, which is the default maximum precision for MSDE and SQL Server; MSDE and SQL Server support `precision` or `scale` up to 38, but you must start MSDE or SQL Server with the `/p` command line parameter to get the extra 10 digits.
- **ANSI SQL conformance**—Jet 4.0 offers two SQL syntax flavors—a new version more compliant with ANSI-92 and T-SQL, and a backward-compatible (legacy) version that supports prior versions of Access, Jet, and VBA. You can set SQL Server Compatible Syntax (ANSI 92) for the current database by choosing Tools, Options, and opening the Tables/Queries page.

CAUTION

Specifying SQL Server Compatible Syntax for existing Jet databases causes all queries that use Jet wildcard characters (`*` and `?`) to fail. T-SQL and ANSI-92 SQL use `%` to represent all characters and _ to represent a single character.

You must use ANSI-92 wildcards in queries you execute from VBA code in ADP, but it isn't necessary to mark the SQL Server Compatible Syntax check box to do this.

NEW SQL SERVER 2000 FEATURES TO SUPPORT ACCESS 2002 AND 2003 ADP

Chapter 1, "Access 2003 for Access 97 and 2000/2002 Users: What's New," includes descriptions of new SQL Server 2000 features that apply to ADP, so the following list provides only a brief summary:

- *Extended properties* support lookup fields, subdatasheets, master-child table relationships, text for data validation messages, data-entry masks, and column formatting.
- *Functions* complement views and stored procedures that return Recordsets. You can bind forms, reports, and pages to tables returned by functions.
- *Updatable, sortable views and functions* correspond to updatable Jet QueryDef objects. If you add a `TOP 100 PERCENT` modifier to the `CREATE VIEW` or `CREATE FUNCTION` statement, you can sort the view or function with an `ORDER BY` clause.
- *Cascading updates and deletions* bring SQL Server's declarative referential integrity features to parity with Jet 4.0.
- *Copying or moving databases* is simplified by SQL Server's Copy Database Wizard. ADP provide similar capabilities when you choose Tools, Database Utilities, Copy Database or Transfer Database.

Later sections of this chapter cover all the preceding new features. The emphasis of this chapter is on the ADP user interface. The next chapter, "Moving from Jet Queries to Transact-SQL," delves into the T-SQL code that supports these features.

→ For additional details on items in the preceding list, **see** "New SQL Server 2000 Features," **p. 34**.

EXPLORING THE NORTHWINDCS SAMPLE PROJECT

Access 2003 includes a sample project, NorthwindCS.adp, which emulates Northwind.mdb. NorthwindCS.adp uses a T-SQL script, NorthwindCS.sql, to create a new MSDE database. A *T-SQL script* is a text file containing a series of T-SQL queries and other instructions to be executed by SQL Server. You must have MSDE installed or network access to another SQL Server 2000 instance to run the NorthwindCS project. The term *instance* refers to a particular installation of SQL Server 2000, because SQL Server 2000 lets you install more than one server on a single machine.

Follow these steps to install the NorthwindCS database on your local computer:

1. Open the NorthwindCS.adp project in the ...\Office11\Samples folder. If you haven't started MSDE, VBA code in the Startup module starts MSDE for you.
2. The first time you open the project, you receive the message shown in Figure 20.1. Click OK to run the NorthwindCS.sql script on your local MSDE instance.

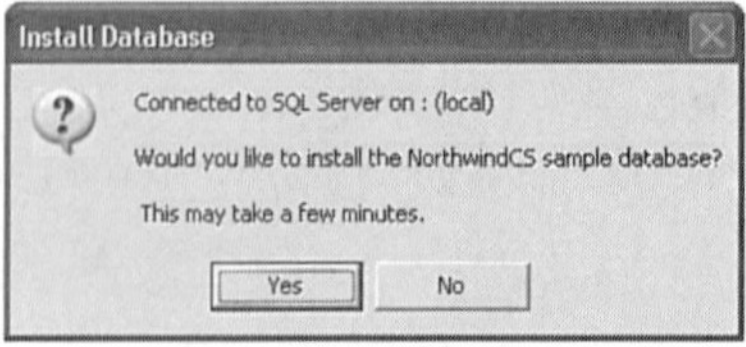

Figure 20.1
You receive an Install Database message when opening NorthwindCS.adp for the first time after installing MSDE from the Office 2003 distribution CD-ROM.

3. After a few seconds, you receive a "Created database on SQL Server" message. Click OK to close the message and open the Northwind Traders splash screen.
4. Mark the Don't Show This Screen Again check box, click OK to get rid of the splash screen, and close the Main Switchboard. The Database window's Tables page appears as shown in Figure 20.2.

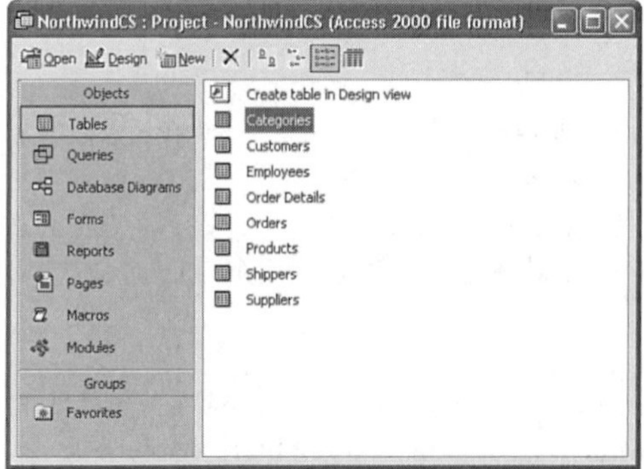

Figure 20.2
Table3 icons for the SQL Server database don't have the link arrow of Jet front ends linked to SQL Server with ODBC.

The Database window pages for Access Data Projects differ considerably from the conventional Access Database window with linked table connections. The most important alterations are as follows:

- *Tables* stored in SQL Server databases appear in the Tables page as though they are local tables. The right-pointing arrow symbol, which indicates a linked table of any type, including client/server tables, is missing. Opening an SQL Server table, such as Orders, in Datasheet view displays the same lookup fields and subdatasheet views as its Jet counterpart.

- *Queries* replaces Access 2000's Views and Stored Procedures items in the Objects list. The Access 2003 Queries page displays saved views, functions, and stored procedures (see Figure 20.3).

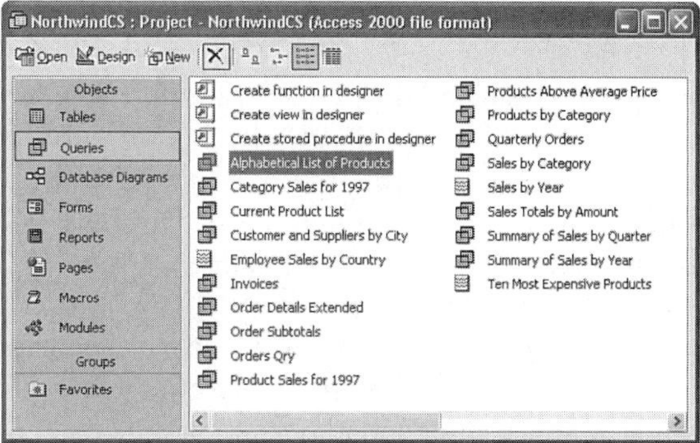

Figure 20.3 The Queries page includes all views, functions, and stored procedures in the SQL Server database. The NorthwindCS database created by NorthwindCS.sql doesn't include functions.

- *Views* (in the Queries page) use the Access select query symbol, because view most closely correspond to simple Jet QueryDefs.

- *Functions* (in the Queries page) that return tables are similar to views, but support parameters.

T-SQL

Views and functions require an explicit field list to support SQL Server's extended properties. If your query contains `SELECT * FROM TableName`, subdatasheets and lookup fields don't appear in the view or function. Recordsets returned by stored procedures don't support extended properties.

- *Stored Procedures* (in the Queries page) execute parameterized and action queries as precompiled Transact-SQL statements. Stored procedures provide a substantial performance improvement over direct execution of complex SQL statements.

- *Database Diagrams* serve the same purpose as Access relationships (and have the same icon) but differ considerably in their visual presentation.

The remaining Access application objects—forms, reports, pages, macros, and modules—are identical, with a few exceptions, to the corresponding objects of conventional Access applications that employ .mdb files for storage. The exceptions primarily are minor changes to form and report properties; as an example, you can set the Record Source property of a form or report to a view, function, or stored procedure.

NOTE

> The primary difference between the Access 97 and 2000 or 2002 file structure is that Access 200x stores all application objects (forms, reports, pages, macros, and modules) in individual streams of a single compound document file, called a *docfile*. A conventional Access application saves its application object docfile within the application .mdb; an Access Project stores its docfile directly on disk as an .adp file.

Working with SQL Server Tables in the Project Designer

ADP use a set of client/server graphical design tools called the *da Vinci toolset* during their development. Microsoft calls da Vinci *MS Design Tools*, but the most common name for Access's implementation of the toolset is the *project designer*. Access's project design mode lets you alter the structure of tables, relationships, views, functions, and stored procedures directly from the user interface. SQL Server and other client/server RDBMSs rely on SQL `CREATE`, `ALTER`, and `DROP` statements for design changes. The project designer executes the SQL statements for your design changes each time you confirm saving changes when exiting design mode. The ability to alter the design of the equivalent to linked tables, unavailable in prior versions of Access, is an important feature of projects.

NOTE NEW

> The SQL panes of Access 2003's product designer don't include the `CREATE VIEW¦FUNCTION¦PROC[EDURE] AS` *`Name`* component of the T-SQL statement to create a new object. The project designer adds a `CREATE`... statement for a new object or an `ALTER`... statement for an existing object when sending the command to SQL Server.

The Visual Studio .NET and 6.0 members also use the da Vinci toolset for client/server database design. Thus, the project designer brings Access 2003 into conformance with other Microsoft application design platforms, at least for client/server databases.

NOTE

> Access data projects are an excellent learning aid and prototyping tool for large-scale client/server database projects. You can quickly and easily create new MSDE databases, add tables, establish relationships, design views, and write stored procedures in the project designer. Creating data-enabled forms, reports, and HTML pages with Access 2003 is a much faster process than that of other design platforms. After you've tested your prototype MSDE database design, you can deploy the .mdf and .ldf files directly to SQL Server running under Windows .NET/2000/NT Server.

Tables appear in conventional Access Datasheet view (see Figure 20.4). Date values appear in short date format, and money (Currency) fields default to the currency format you specify in the Currency page of Control Panel's Regional Settings tool.

Orders : Table

OrderID	Customer Name	Employee Name	OrderDate	RequiredDate	ShippedDate
10643	Alfreds Futterkiste	Suyama, Michael	8/25/1997	9/22/1997	9/2/1997

ProductID	UnitPrice	Quantity	Discount
Rössle Sauerkraut	$45.60	15	0.25
Chartreuse verte	$18.00	21	0.25
Spegesild	$12.00	2	0,25
Spegesild	$0.00	1	0

Spegesild
Zaanse koeken
Chocolade
Maxilaku
Valkoinen suklaa
Manjimup Dried Apples
Filo Mix
Perth Pasties

OrderID	Customer Name	Employee Name	OrderDate	RequiredDate	ShippedDate
1		Peacock, Margaret	10/3/1997	10/31/1997	10/13/1997
1		Peacock, Margaret	10/13/1997	11/24/1997	10/21/1997
1		Davolio, Nancy	1/15/1998	2/12/1998	1/21/1998
1		Davolio, Nancy	3/16/1998	4/27/1998	3/24/1998
1		Leverling, Janet	4/9/1998	5/7/1998	4/13/1998
1		King, Robert	9/18/1996	10/16/1996	9/24/1996
[illegible]	Ana Trujillo Emparedados y he	Leverling, Janet	8/8/1997	9/5/1997	8/14/1997
10759	Ana Trujillo Emparedados y he	Leverling, Janet	11/28/1997	12/26/1997	12/12/1997
10926	Ana Trujillo Emparedados y he	Peacock, Margaret	3/4/1998	4/1/1998	3/11/1998
10365	Antonio Moreno Taquería	Leverling, Janet	11/27/1996	12/25/1996	12/2/1996
10507	Antonio Moreno Taquería	King, Robert	4/15/1997	5/13/1997	4/22/1997
10535	Antonio Moreno Taquería	Peacock, Margaret	5/13/1997	6/10/1997	5/21/1997
10573	Antonio Moreno Taquería	King, Robert	6/19/1997	7/17/1997	6/20/1997
10677	Antonio Moreno Taquería	Davolio, Nancy	9/22/1997	10/20/1997	9/26/1997
10682	Antonio Moreno Taquería	Leverling, Janet	9/25/1997	10/23/1997	10/1/1997

Record: 3 of 3

Figure 20.4
The Datasheet view of NorthwindCS's Orders table demonstrates use of SQL Server extended properties.

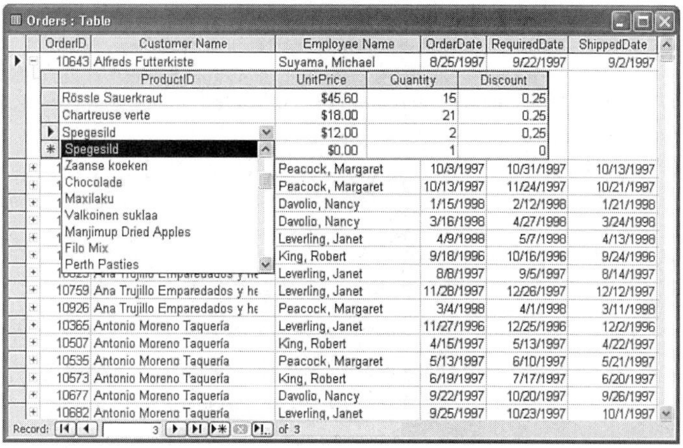

PROJECT DESIGNER'S TABLE DESIGN VIEW

Table Design view differs dramatically from that of tables linked through Jet. Figure 20.5 shows the Orders table in the Access 2003 project designer, which differs from Access 2000's designer. Four basic column properties—Column Name, Data Type, Length, and Nulls—plus an extended property—Description—appear in the columns grid, and the Columns and Lookup properties pages display additional property values for the selected column. Property labels and text boxes are enabled only for those properties that are applicable to the column's data type. After you become familiar with the table-creation features of the project designer, you'll find that adding new SQL Server tables is almost as easy as creating new Jet tables.

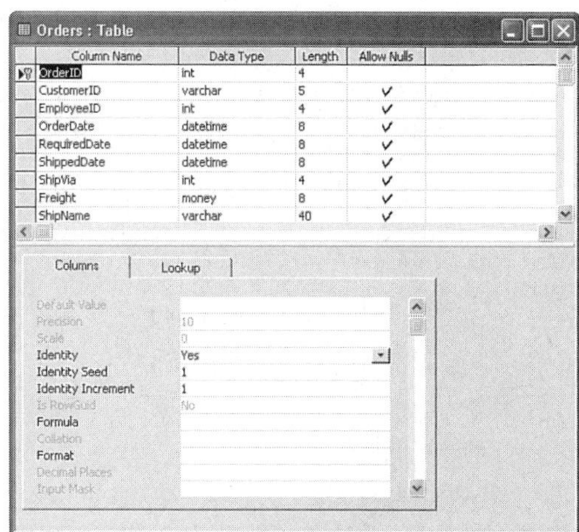

Column Name	Data Type	Length	Allow Nulls
OrderID	int	4	
CustomerID	varchar	5	✓
EmployeeID	int	4	✓
OrderDate	datetime	8	✓
RequiredDate	datetime	8	✓
ShippedDate	datetime	8	✓
ShipVia	int	4	✓
Freight	money	8	✓
ShipName	varchar	40	✓

Figure 20.5
Access 2003's project designer Table Design view has some features in common with Jet's Table Design view for local and attached client/server tables. NorthwindCS.sql doesn't propagate Description property values to NorthwindCS tables.

20

SQL Server data type names are in lowercase, a holdover from Microsoft SQL Server's origin as the PC version of Sybase SQL Server for Unix. Table 20.1 lists the names and the correspondence of each project designer grid and the Columns properties page values you set in Access's Table Design grid and General properties page for Jet.

NOTE

Client/server databases commonly substitute the term column for field; this book uses field for tables and column for query result sets, views, functions, and data-returning stored procedures.

TABLE 20.1 A COMPARISON OF PROJECT DESIGNER AND JET TABLE PROPERTIES

Property	Correspondence to Jet Table Properties
Column Name	Same as Jet's Field Name. Spaces are permitted in SQL Server column names, but aren't recommended.
Data Type	Same as the combination of Jet's Data Type and Field Size, except data types use SQL Server terminology.
Length	Same as Jet's Field Size for text fields, except that `char` columns are fixed length.
Allow Nulls	The inverse of Jet's Required property; a check mark (the default) allows null values in fields.
Description	Same as Jet's Description property (an extended property)
Default Value	Same as Jet's Default Value.
Precision	Applicable primarily to numeric or decimal fields; specifies the total number of digits of the column (the precision property of int(eger) and money fields is fixed).
Scale	Applicable to numeric or decimal fields; specifies the number of digits to the right of the decimal point (the scale of money fields is fixed at 4).
Identity	Equivalent to Jet's AutoNumber field data type with Increment as the New Values property; Yes specifies that an int (same as Jet's Long Integer) field automatically creates a new value when appending a record. (SQL Server doesn't support Jet's Random option for AutoNumber fields.)
Identity Seed	Specifies the starting value of a field with the identity property set.
Identity Increment	Specifies the increment between successive identity values (usually 1).
Is RowGuid	Yes specifies that the row contains a globally unique identifier (GUID, pronounced "goo id") used primarily in conjunction with timestamp fields for replication. Jet has no direct counterpart.
Formula	For tables, the expression (formula) for creating a computed column value; Jet has no equivalent table property.
Collation	Sets the collating (sorting) sequence for character column; the default value is `<database default>`. Jet has no equivalent property.

20

Property	Correspondence to Jet Table Properties
Format	Lets you select a predefined display format from a drop-down list (extended property); same as Jet's Format property.
Decimal Places	Lets you select Auto or from 0 to 6 characters after the decimal point (extended property); same as Jet's Decimal Places property.
Input Mask	Lets you type a format string, such as **>LLLLL** for uppercase letters, or open the Input Mask Wizard to generate the string (extended property); same as Jet's Input Mask property.

The Lookup properties page (see Figure 20.6) lets you specify extended property values that are identical to those of Jet's Lookup page. The Row Source property value for a lookup field can be an SQL Server table, view, or function, or a value or field list.

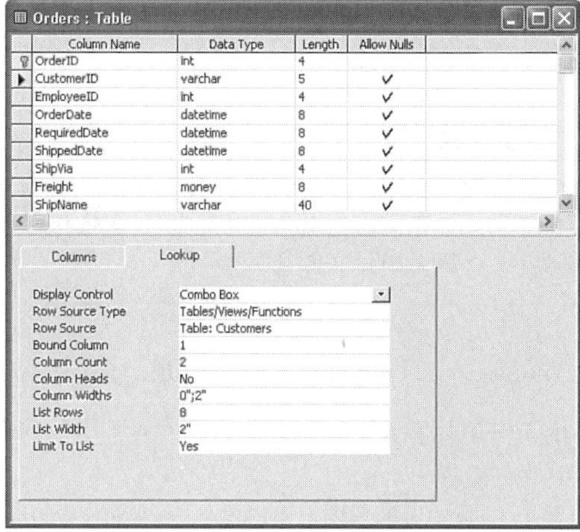

Figure 20.6 SQL Server extended properties in the Lookup properties page correspond exactly to Jet's Lookup properties.

THE TABLE PROPERTIES DIALOG

The table Properties dialog for SQL Server tables also differs greatly from Jet's table properties dialog, and is a modified version of the Access 2000 designers dialog. In Table Design view, click the Properties button on the toolbar to open the new Properties dialog, which has five pages—Table, Relationships, Indexes/Keys, Check Constraints, and Data. Access 2002 added the Check Constraints and Data pages. You set extended property values for Jet table and field properties that aren't included in Table 20.1 and the Lookup Properties page in pages of the Properties dialog.

THE TABLES PROPERTIES PAGE

Figure 20.7 shows the Tables page of the Properties dialog for the Order Details table. The Order Details table is used for this and the following sections because this table has several unique properties.

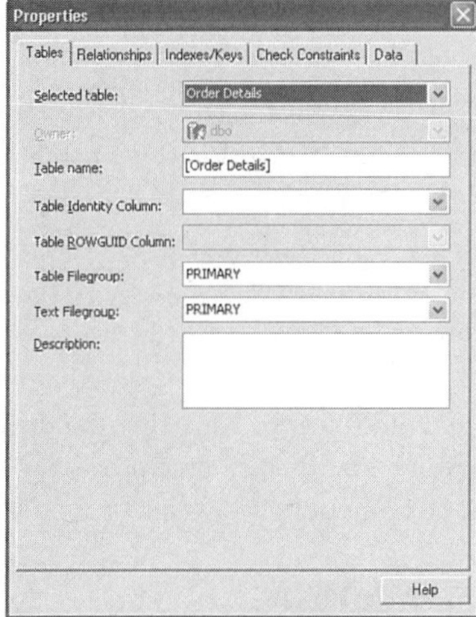

Figure 20.7
The Tables page only displays a few of the properties of the selected table.

> **NOTE**
>
> The Properties dialog doesn't have OK, Apply, or Cancel buttons. As you make changes on the four pages, the SQL statements to alter the properties accumulate in a cache. When you close the Table Design window or click the Datasheet View button, message boxes offer you the options of saving the table design or abandoning the changes.

Following are brief descriptions of the elements on the Tables page:

- **Selected Table**—Although Selected Table is a drop-down list, you can only select the currently open table from the list.
- **Owner**—The default database owner (dbo) appears here as a read-only value.
- **Table Name**—ANSI SQL doesn't allow table names with spaces or punctuation (except underscores), so field names containing illegal characters must be enclosed between square brackets.

> **NOTE**
>
> Microsoft opened a Pandora's box by allowing Jet databases to include spaces and other nonalphanumeric symbols in database, table, and field names. The Northwind.mdb developers finally removed spaces from field names in Access 9x, but the space remains in the Order Details table name. Access developers have complained long and loudly, but to no avail, about Microsoft's continuing use of spaces in Access object names.

- **Table Identity Column**—You can assign the `identity` property to a field from a drop-down list of field with numeric data types.
- **Table ROWGUID Column**—If enabled, you can specify a field to contain automatically generated GUIDs. (Refer to the Is RowGuid property in Table 20.1.)

- **Table Filegroup and Text Filegroup**—SQL Server 2000 lets DBAs create multiple operating system files for a single (usually very large) table. DBAs also can assign SQL Server `text` fields, the equivalent to Jet's Memo data type, to their own filegroup. Users of MSDE aren't likely to need to create filegroups.
- **Description**—You can add a text description of the table as the value for this extended property, which corresponds to Jet's table Description property.

NOTE

> Check Constraints, which appeared on the Tables page of Access 2000's Properties dialog, has been relocated to the new Check Constraints page.

THE RELATIONSHIPS PAGE

Figure 20.8 shows the Relationships page of the Order Details table. Table relationships established by SQL DRI statements also appear in the Database Diagram for the database, which is the subject of the later "Diagramming Table Relationships" section. Many of the properties on this page have counterparts in Jet's Edit Relationships dialog.

→ To review Jet's Edit Relationships dialog, **see** "Establishing Relationships Between Tables," **p. 189**.

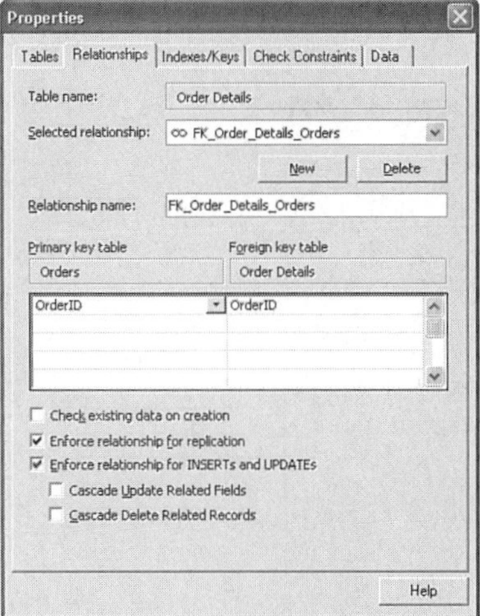

Figure 20.8 The two fields of the primary composite key of the Order Details table have foreign-key (FK) relationships with the primary keys of the Orders and Products table.

Following are descriptions of the Relationship page's elements:

- **Selected Relationship**—The Order details table has a composite primary key (OrderID and ProductID). These two fields have a foreign-key (`FK`) relationship with the Orders table's OrderID field and the Product table's ProductID field, respectively. The list box opens to select the `FK_Order_Details_Products` relationship.

- **Relationship Name**—SQL Server automatically names the keys as `FK_TableName_FieldName`.
- **Primary Key Table and Foreign Key Table, and fields lists**—Table names are read-only, except when you click Add to create a new relationship. The field lists are similar to those of Jet's Edit Relationships dialog.
- **Check Existing Data on Creation**—If you mark this check box, data in the table is tested for relational integrity when you add a new relation. Jet always tests existing data when establishing a new relationship.
- **Enforce Relationship for Replication**—Marking this check box requires replicated copies of the table to enforce the relationship. Jet doesn't have this property.
- **Enforce Relationship for INSERTs and UPDATEs**—This check box has the same effect as marking Jet's Enforce Referential Integrity check box.

- **Cascade Update Related Fields and Cascade Delete Related Records**—These two check boxes correspond to Jet's check boxes of the same names.

THE INDEXES/KEYS PAGE

Figure 20.9 shows the Indexes/Keys page for the Order Details table, which displays the table's primary key by default. This page bears only a faint resemblance to Jet's Indexes dialog.

Figure 20.9 The Indexes/Keys page for the Order Details table displays the properties of the composite, clustered primary key.

Following are descriptions of the controls on the Indexes/Keys page:

- **Selected Index**—Open the list to select an index on the table. Order Details has a primary-key (composite) and a foreign-key index (on ProductID). The Type label changes, depending on the type of index you select: Primary Key, Index, or Unique Constraint.

- **Index Name**—SQL Server names indexes as `PK_TableName` for the primary key and IX_*TableName* for other indexes. You can rename the index, if you want. (The `ProductID` index doesn't have the `IX_` prefix.)
- **Column Name and Order**—These two list fields correspond to the Field Name and Sort Order columns of Jet's Indexes dialog.
- **Index Filegroup**—This list is enabled only when adding a new index. Like text filegroups, it's uncommon to create a special filegroup for MSDE indexes.
- **Create UNIQUE, Constraint, Index, and Ignore Duplicate Key**—These check boxes and options determine index properties when creating a new index. Create `UNIQUE` is equivalent to Jet's No Duplicates modifier. SQL Server lets you choose to enforce unique values with a `CHECK` constraint or an index; Jet relies on an index. The Ignore Duplicate Key property applies only to bulk insert operations, which aren't common for MSDE databases.
- **Create as CLUSTERED**—This check box causes SQL Server to physically order the table records by the primary-key value. Clustered indexes improve performance of `INSERT` and `DELETE` operations. It's a common practice to specify a clustered index on each table's primary key to improve database performance.
- **Fill Factor and Pad Index**—If records aren't added to the table in the order of the primary key, adding some empty space (usually 10% to 20%) to the index page can improve `INSERT` performance. Pad Index reserves empty space (two rows) in clustered tables.
- **Do Not Automatically Recompute Statistics**—Marking this check box speeds creation of indexes on large tables at the possible expense of query performance.

- **Validation Text**—This extended property sets the text of the error message you receive when attempting to `INSERT` or `UPDATE` a value that conflicts with the `UNIQUE` constraint. Jet has built-in message text for attempted violation of the No Duplicates rule.

THE CHECK CONSTRAINTS PAGE

Figure 20.10 shows the Check Constraints page for the Order Details table. Access 2002 moved the constraint property settings to their own page and added a Validation Text property.

20

Following are descriptions of the elements of the Check Constraints page:

- **Selected Constraint**—`CHECK` constraints are the SQL Server equivalent of Jet table- and field-level validation rules. You can specify multiple `CHECK` constraints; the Order Details table has three `CHECK` constraints—`CK_Discount`, `CK_Quantity`, and `CK_UnitPrice`—which you select from the drop-down list.
- **Constraint Name**—This text box lets you rename the default name assigned by SQL Server, `CK_FieldName`.

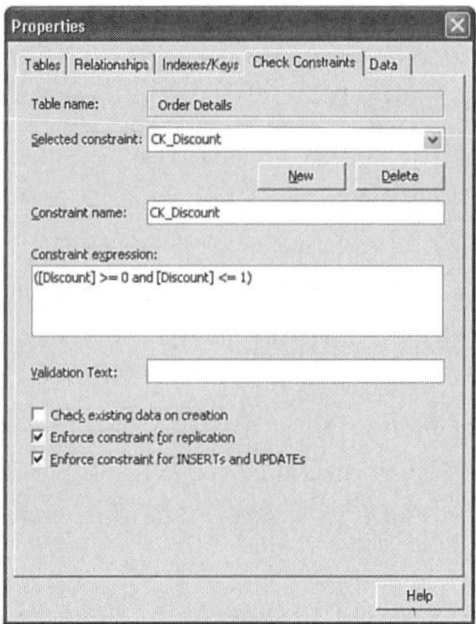

Figure 20.10
The Check Constraints page lets you establish the equivalent of Jet Validation Rule and Validation Text properties.

- **Constraint Expression**—The `CHECK` expression must evaluate to `TRUE` or `FALSE`. You add new constraints by clicking the New button and typing the expression and name in the text boxes.

- **Validation Text**—This extended property sets the text of the error message you receive when attempting to `INSERT` or `UPDATE` a value that conflicts with the selected constraint. The property corresponds to Jet's Validation Text property.
- **Constraint properties**—You can test existing data for conformance to constraints, enable constraints for data addition and updates, and apply constraints to replicated data with the three check boxes at the bottom of the page.

THE DATA PAGE

Figure 20.11 shows the Data page for the Order Details table. All elements on this page are SQL Server extended properties that provide ADP counterparts of Jet table features, such as subdatasheets.

20

TIP

Avoid setting Jet-specific table features and properties, such as subdatasheets, lookup fields, links for subforms and subreports, Filter, and Order By in new ADP. These features and properties are intended to support upsizing Jet tables to SQL Server and have no counterparts in ANSI SQL. Browse-mode editing in Datasheet view with subdatasheets and lookup fields isn't recommended for production client/server applications because this type of editing increases the probability of data-entry errors. To prevent subdatasheet open buttons from appearing in Datasheet view, set the Subdatasheet Name property to [None].

> Use views with `WHERE` criteria and `TOP 100 PERCENT...ORDER BY` statements to avoid use of the Filter and Order By properties. Filter and Order By property values, as well as sort orders and filters applied by toolbar buttons, are applied by Access to the locally cached copy of the table's Recordset, also called a *local snapshot.*

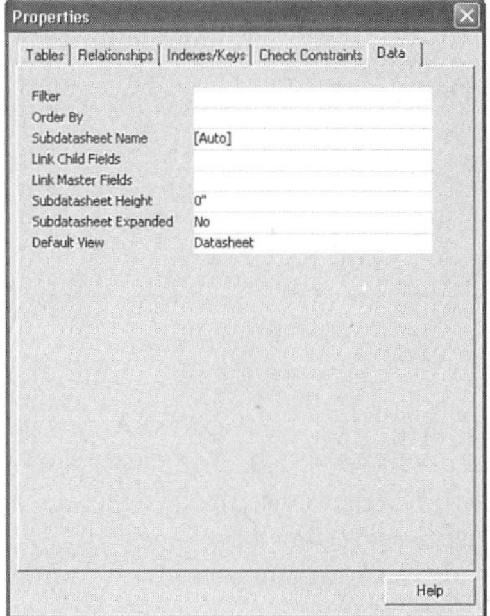

Figure 20.11
The Data page has a collection of extended properties to support upsizing existing Jet tables.

EXPLORING SQL SERVER VIEWS

Like tables, views open in conventional Access datasheets. Figure 20.12 shows the Order Details Extended view, which is almost identical to the Jet version. The Expr1 column duplicates the ProductID column, a minor fault in the NorthwindCS.sql script. Although the new project designer has an extended Format property for columns, the script doesn't set this property value, nor does it set the Caption property. Access 2003 continues to display the Discount field as a decimal fraction, instead of a percentage. The Datasheet View toolbar for views is identical to that for Jet queries. Like tables, the Sort Ascending, Sort Descending, Filter by Form, Filter by Selection, and Find buttons of the toolbar operate on the locally cached copy (snapshot) of the view's Recordset, not the view itself.

Figure 20.12
NorthwindCS's Order Details Extended view has a spurious Expr1 column, doesn't format the Discount column as percent, and doesn't emulate the Jet version by setting the Caption property for the columns.

Order Details Extended : View

OrderID	ProductID	ProductName	UnitPrice	Quantity	Discount	ExtendedPrice	Expr1
10248	Queso Ca	Queso Cabrales	$14.00	12	0	$168.00	11
10248	Singapore	Singaporean Ho	$9.80	10	0	$98.00	42
10248	Mozzarell:	Mozzarella di G	$34.80	5	0	$174.00	72
10249	Tofu	Tofu	$18.60	9	0	$167.40	14
10249	Manjimup	Manjimup Dried	$42.40	40	0	$1,696.00	51
10250	Jack's Ne	Jack's New Eng	$7.70	10	0	$77.00	41
10250	Manjimup	Manjimup Dried	$42.40	35	0.15	$1,261.40	51
10250	Louisiana	Louisiana Fiery	$16.80	15	0.15	$214.20	65
10251	Gustaf's K	Gustaf's Knäcke	$16.80	6	0.05	$95.76	22
10251	Ravioli An	Ravioli Angelo	$15.60	15	0.05	$222.30	57
10251	Louisiana	Louisiana Fiery	$16.80	20	0	$336.00	65
10252	Sir Rodne	Sir Rodney's Ma	$64.80	40	0.05	$2,462.40	20
10252	Geitost	Geitost	$2.00	25	0.05	$47.50	33
10252	Camembe	Camembert Pie	$27.20	40	0	$1,088.00	60
10253	Gorgonzol	Gorgonzola Teli	$10.00	20	0	$200.00	31
10253	Chartreus	Chartreuse verte	$14.40	42	0	$604.80	39
10253	Maxilaku	Maxilaku	$16.00	40	0	$640.00	49
10254	Guaraná F	Guaraná Fantás	$3.60	15	0.15	$45.90	24
10254	Pâté chin	Pâté chinois	$19.20	21	0.15	$342.72	55
10254	Longlife T	Longlife Tofu	$8.00	21	0	$168.00	74
10255	Chang	Chang	$15.20	20	0	$304.00	2
10255	Pavlova	Pavlova	$13.90	35	0	$486.50	16

Record: 1 of 2155

NOTE

The Data properties page of ADP forms and reports has two properties–Server Filter and Server Filter by Form–added by Access 2002. These properties let you apply a server-side filter to a table, view, or function instead of the cached Recordset for the form or report. Using server-side filters minimizes the amount of data sent to the client, which reduces network traffic and improves performance.

SQL Changing to Design view opens the graphical view designer, the structure of which resembles the Access query designer. The primary difference between the two designers is a 90-degree rotation (transposition) of the axes of the design grid. Click the SQL button of the toolbar to display the SQL statement that creates the view (see Figure 20.13). The upper diagram pane displays field lists for each table with a symbolic join. The key symbol indicates the primary-key field(s) and the infinity symbol ([if]) specifies the foreign-key field. Primary-key field(s) of the tables appear in bold type.

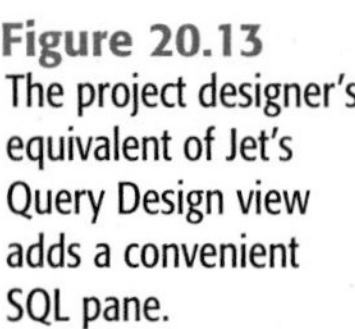

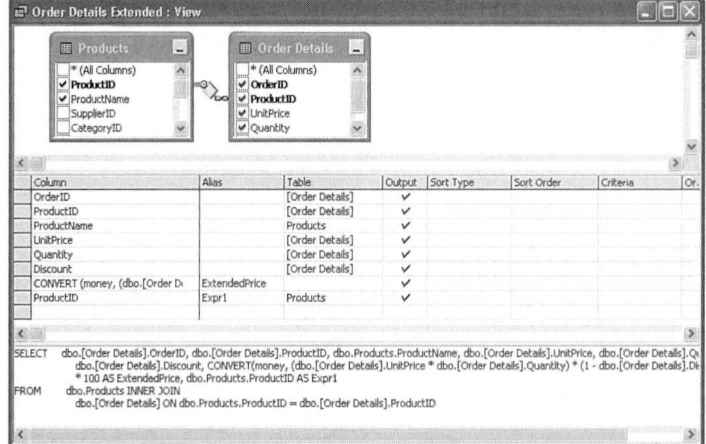

Figure 20.13
The project designer's equivalent of Jet's Query Design view adds a convenient SQL pane.

The view designer adds the following five design-related buttons to the toolbar:

- *Diagram* toggles the display of the diagram in the upper pane. You specify the type of join in a properties sheet.

- *Grid* toggles the display of the column information, which is where you alias columns, select the source table for the column, specify whether column data appears in the view, and add a `TOP 100 PERCENT` modifier, `ORDER BY` clause, or `WHERE` criteria.

- *SQL* toggles the lower text box that displays the Transact-SQL statement that generates the view.

- *Verify SQL Syntax* runs a grammar check on the SQL statement but doesn't execute the query to create the view.
- *Group By* adds a `GROUP BY` expression that includes every member of the `SELECT` statement's field list. Group By properties let you add a `ROLLUP`, `CUBE`, or `ALL` modifier for complex aggregation.

The SQL statement for the Order Details Extended view illustrates substitution of the SQL `CONVERT` function for VBA's **`CCur`** function to change the data type of the calculated `ExtendedPrice` column to `money`. Access 2002 added the `dbo` schema prefix to provide three of the four elements of SQL Server's four-part naming convention. Linked databases require use of three-part names to resolve duplicate table and field names in local and linked servers.

The complete SQL `SELECT` statement—without the extra Expr1 field—for the view is as follows:

```
SELECT dbo.[Order Details].OrderID, dbo.[Order Details].ProductID,
   dbo.Products.ProductName, dbo.[Order Details].UnitPrice,
   dbo.[Order Details].Quantity, dbo.[Order Details].Discount, CONVERT(money,
   (dbo.[Order Details].UnitPrice * dbo.[Order Details].Quantity) *
   (1 - dbo.[Order Details].Discount) / 100) * 100 AS ExtendedPrice
FROM dbo.Products INNER JOIN dbo.[Order Details]
   ON dbo.Products.ProductID = dbo.[Order Details].ProductID
```

To explore adding new tables and setting `JOIN` properties, do the following:

1. Move the Products and Order Details tables to the right to make room for the addition of the field list of the Suppliers table.

2. Click the Add Table button to open the Add Table dialog, which has Tables, Views, and Functions pages. On the Tables page, select Suppliers and click Add to add an `INNER JOIN` between the `SupplierID` fields (see Figure 20.14).
3. Close the Add Table dialog, and click the SupplierID and CompanyName check boxes of the Suppliers table to add the columns to the view.
4. Right-click the join line between the Suppliers and Products tables, and choose Properties to open the Join Properties dialog. You select the type of join from a drop-down list of the available operators. Mark the All Rows from Suppliers check box to

create a RIGHT OUTER JOIN, which squares the left side of the diamond join symbol (see Figure 20.15). (Marking both check boxes creates a FULL OUTER JOIN; the join symbol becomes a square. Scroll the SQL pane to read the JOIN changes to the view's SQL statement).

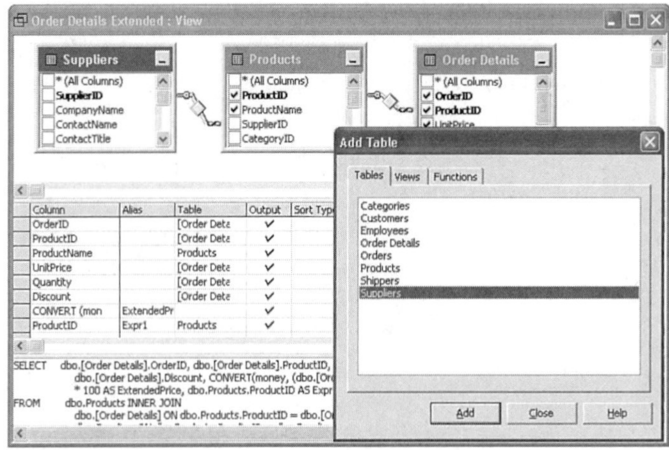

Figure 20.14
The process of adding a new table and its columns to a view is similar to that for Access QueryDefs.

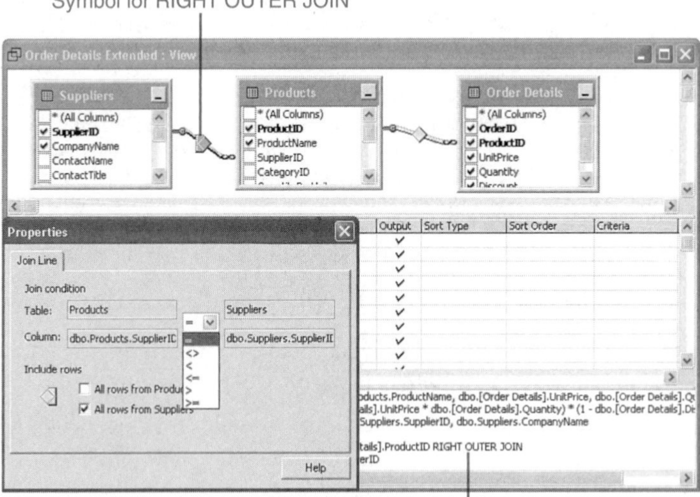

Figure 20.15
The Properties dialog for JOINs in a view offers the same functions as Jet's Join Properties dialog in a different format. SQL Server adds the capability to specify the JOIN operator.

20

5. Clear the All Rows from Suppliers and All Rows from Products check boxes if you marked them, and close the Join Properties dialog. Click the Group By button to add a GROUP BY clause containing all columns, which adds Group By symbols to fields selected in the field lists. Like Jet Totals queries, tabbing or selecting the Group By cell

for each column lets you choose Group By, Sum, Avg, Min, Max, Count, Expression, Where, and many additional SQL Server-specific options from a drop-down list (see Figure 20.16).

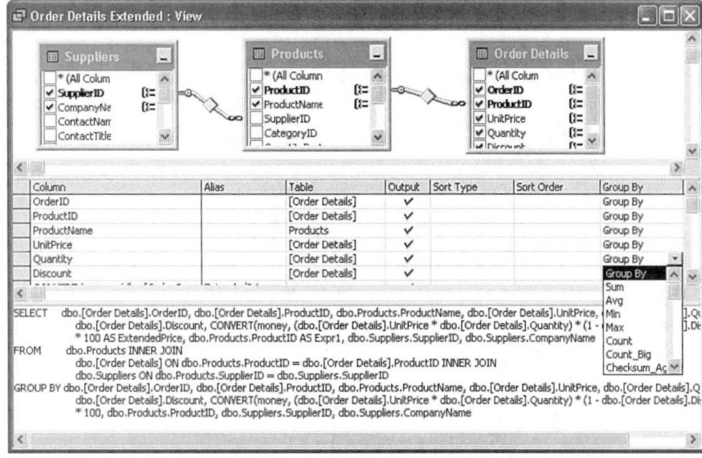

Figure 20.16 Clicking the toolbar's Group By button adds a Group By column to the design grid and a `GROUP BY` clause to the `SELECT` statement. The effect is similar to specifying a Jet Totals query.

6. Click the toolbar's Properties button or right click the window and choose Properties to open the Properties dialog for views, which differs from the original Access 2000 version (see Figure 20.17). On the View page, you can add the `DISTINCT` qualifier to eliminate duplicate rows; specify `CUBE`, `ROLLUP`, or `ALL` extensions to the `GROUP BY` clause; and specify a `TOP n [PERCENT]` view by marking the TOP check box, typing the ***n*** value in the text box, and marking the PERCENT, WITH TIES, or both check boxes. You also can add text to the extended Description and SQL Comment properties.

Figure 20.17 Access 2003's View Properties dialog adds many more properties to the simple, single-page version of Access 2000's project designer.

NOTE

> Many of the properties on the View page have counterparts in Jet's Query Properties dialog. The other property values of the View page—such as Bind to Schema and Update Using View Rules—require familiarity with T-SQL, the subject of the next chapter.

7. Click the Columns tab, and select the Discount column in the Column Name text box. The enabled labels indicate extended properties whose values you can set for the specific field data type, such as Description, Format, Decimal Places, and Caption for most numeric data types (see Figure 20.18). Close the Properties dialog.

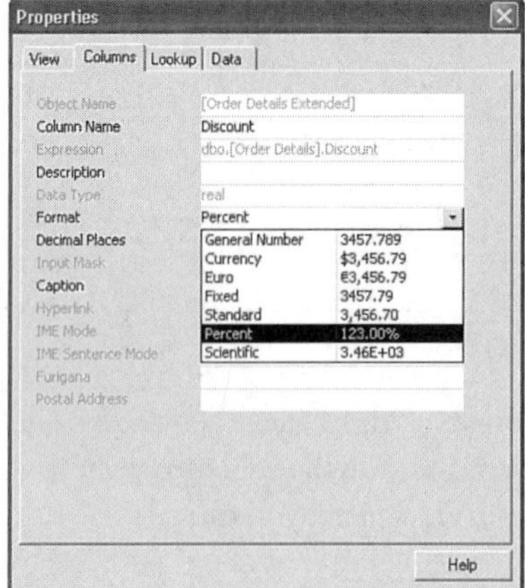

Figure 20.18
The Columns page lets you set additional extended property values.

NOTE

> The Lookup and Data pages of a view have the same set of properties as those for tables.

8. Click the Verify SQL Syntax button on the toolbar to check the changes you made in the preceding steps. You receive a message box confirming the statement's validity. Deliberately introducing an error results in a message providing the approximate location of the mistake. Figure 20.19 illustrates the message that occurs if you delete the left bracket from the second instance of `[Order Details]` in the query's SQL pane and click Verify SQL Syntax.
9. Close the view designer and don't save the changes you made. Modifications to the database are temporary until you close the designer or run the query and elect to save changes.

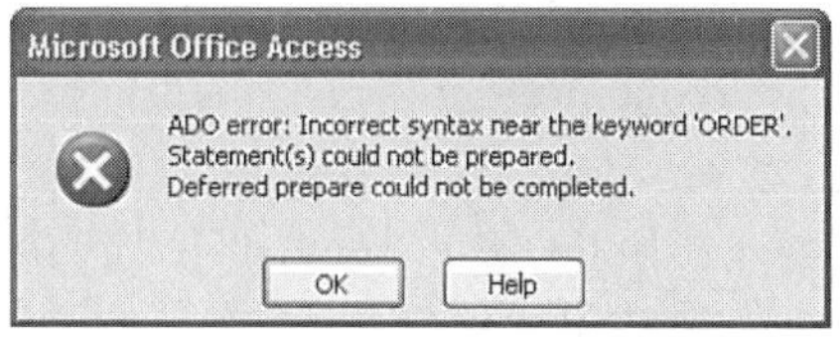

Figure 20.19 You receive an error message if the SQL Server query parser detects incorrect syntax. In this case, the parser interprets 'Order' as the SQL keyword ORDER because of a missing left bracket.

TAKING ADVANTAGE OF IN-LINE FUNCTIONS

SQL Server 2000's in-line functions let you emulate Jet's parameterized queries. Views don't accept parameters, but you can choose between table-returning functions and stored procedures. Functions and stored procedures accept one or more input parameters, which can emulate Jet parameters. One of the advantages of a parameterized function is that it can substitute for a table name in the `FROM` clause of a `SELECT` query.

→ To review Jet parameterized queries, **see** "Designing Parameter Queries," **p. 440**.

CREATING A PARAMETERIZED TABLE-RETURNING FUNCTION

NorthwindCS doesn't include a function, so do the following to create a new parameterized in-line function:

1. In the Database window's Queries page, click New to open the New Query dialog (see Figure 20.20). The choices in the list differ considerable from those of Jet and Access 2000's version.

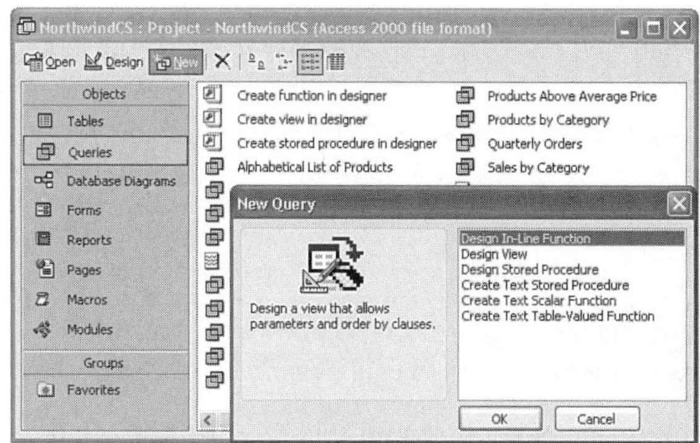

Figure 20.20 The New Query dialog for ADP gives you the choice between using the project designer (Design...) or typing T-SQL statements in a text editor window (Text...).

2. Double-click the Design In-Line Function item to open Function1 in Design view with the Add Table dialog active.
3. Select the Orders table, click Add, and close the Add Table dialog.

20

4. Mark the OrderID, CustomerID, OrderDate, RequiredDate, and ShippedDate check boxes of the field list to add these columns to the grid. Add an ascending sort on the OrderDate column.

5. To add date-based input parameters to the OrderDate field, type the Jet version of a pair of date parameters—**BETWEEN [Start Date] AND [End Date]**—in its Criteria cell (see Figure 20.21). In this case, the square brackets specify an input parameter, *not* that the parameter names include a space. When you tab past the cell, the statement changes to T-SQL parameter syntax—`BETWEEN @Start_Date AND @End_Date`. T-SQL doesn't permit spaces in parameter names.

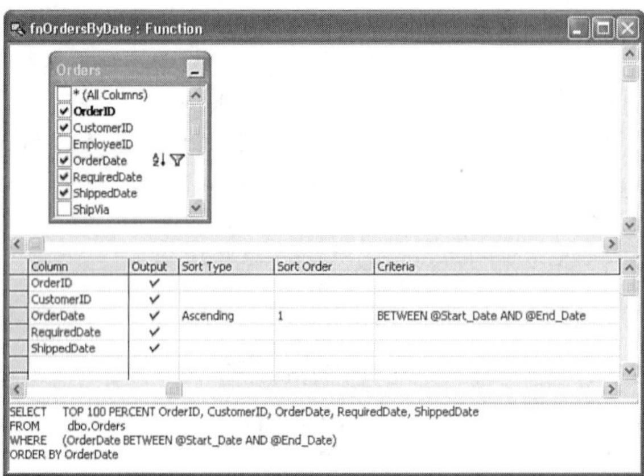

Figure 20.21
Specifying function parameters is similar to adding Jet query parameters.

6. Click the Run button, click Yes when asked whether you want to save your query, type a name for the function—such as **fnOrdersByDate**—in the Save As dialog, and click OK.

7. A slightly modified version of the Jet Enter Parameter Value dialog opens for the `Start_Date` parameter. Type **1/1/1997** and click OK to open the `End_Date` dialog. Type **12/31/1997** and click OK to view the result set of the function in Datasheet view (see Figure 20.22).

ADDING DEFAULT VALUES FOR THE INPUT PARAMETERS

NEW 2002 A feature added to the Access 2002 project designer is support for parameter default values. Jet's Enter Parameter Value dialog doesn't support default values.

To add default values for the `Start_Date` and `End_Date` parameters, do this:

1. Return to Design view, click the properties button or right-click the window and choose Properties to open the function's Properties dialog.

2. Click the Function Parameters tab to display a list with the two parameter names and their data type (`datetime`).

fnOrdersByDate : Function

OrderID	Customer Name	OrderDate	RequiredDate	ShippedDate
10400	Eastern Connection	1/1/1997	1/29/1997	1/16/1997
10401	Rattlesnake Canyon Grocery	1/1/1997	1/29/1997	1/10/1997
10402	Ernst Handel	1/2/1997	2/13/1997	1/10/1997
10403	Ernst Handel	1/3/1997	1/31/1997	1/9/1997
10404	Magazzini Alimentari Riuniti	1/3/1997	1/31/1997	1/8/1997
10405	LINO-Delicateses	1/6/1997	2/3/1997	1/22/1997
10406	Queen Cozinha	1/7/1997	2/18/1997	1/13/1997
10407	Ottilies Käseladen	1/7/1997	2/4/1997	1/30/1997
10408	Folies gourmandes	1/8/1997	2/5/1997	1/14/1997
10409	Océano Atlántico Ltda.	1/9/1997	2/6/1997	1/14/1997
10410	Bottom-Dollar Markets	1/10/1997	2/7/1997	1/15/1997
10411	Bottom-Dollar Markets	1/10/1997	2/7/1997	1/21/1997
10412	Wartian Herkku	1/13/1997	2/10/1997	1/15/1997
10413	La maison d'Asie	1/14/1997	2/11/1997	1/16/1997
10414	Familia Arquibaldo	1/14/1997	2/11/1997	1/17/1997
10415	Hungry Coyote Import Store	1/15/1997	2/12/1997	1/24/1997
10416	Wartian Herkku	1/16/1997	2/13/1997	1/27/1997
10417	Simons bistro	1/16/1997	2/13/1997	1/28/1997
10418	QUICK-Stop	1/17/1997	2/14/1997	1/24/1997
10419	Richter Supermarkt	1/20/1997	2/17/1997	1/30/1997
10420	Wellington Importadora	1/21/1997	2/18/1997	1/27/1997
10421	Que Delícia	1/21/1997	3/4/1997	1/27/1997

Record: 1 of 408

Figure 20.22
Datasheet view of the function confirms the `Start_Date` parameter works. Scroll to the bottom of the datasheet to check for the `End_Date` parameter.

3. Type the default values for the two parameters in the default column. As you move to the second parameter, the first default value is enclosed by single quotes (see Figure 20.23).

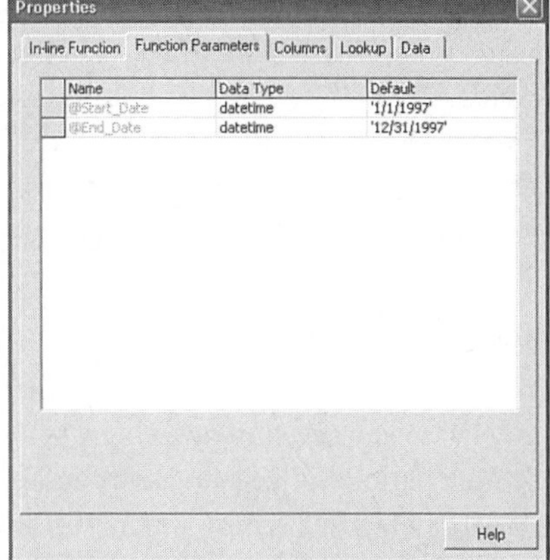

Figure 20.23
The Function Parameters page is blank, unless you add input parameters by the procedure in the preceding section. Add default values for the parameters in the Default column.

NOTE

SQL Server accepts only character values for dates. The default delimiter for T-SQL character values is the single quote or apostrophe ('). Jet's # delimiter doesn't apply to T-SQL date values.

20

4. Click the Run button, save your changes, and open the drop-down list of the `Start_Date` Enter Parameter Value dialog and select <DEFAULT> (see Figure 20.24). The other option is <NULL>, which passes a `NULL` value to the parameter. Stored

procedures and functions often include T-SQL code to act on `NULL` parameter values. Click OK to display the `End_Date` Enter Parameter Value dialog.

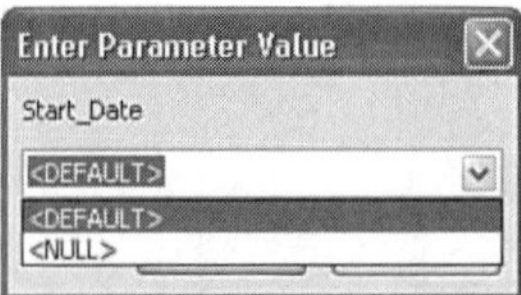

Figure 20.24 Enter Parameter Value dialogs for functions and stored procedures have a drop-down list from which you can select a previously specified default or a `NULL` value.

5. Select <DEFAULT>, and then click OK in the `End_Date` Enter Parameter Value dialog to open the function's datasheet.

EXAMINING STORED PROCEDURES

NEW 2002 Access 2003's project designer lets you create many common types of stored procedures without writing any T-SQL code. This new feature provides parity between Jet and SQL Server action queries, because you can create make-table, update, append values, and delete queries in the designer, instead of writing T-SQL in the text editor. (Access 2000's project designer opened the text editor for new and existing stored procedures.) Like Jet `UNION` queries, you must write SQL Server `UNION` queries for views, functions, and stored procedures in the text editor. The project designer doesn't have a Query, SQL Specific, Union menu choice.

NorthwindCS includes only parameterized `SELECT` stored procedures, which you create using the same process as that for parameterized in-line functions. Open one or more of the sample stored procedures in Design view to see the similarity between the grid and T-SQL statements for stored procedures. Simple parameterized in-line functions are updatable in Datasheet view; stored procedures—parameterized or not—aren't updatable.

20

CREATING AND EXECUTING MAKE-TABLE AND UPDATE STORED PROCEDURES

To give the project designer a test run with make-table and update queries, do this:

1. Click New in Database window's Queries page to open the New Query dialog, and double-click the Design Stored Procedure item.

2. Double-click the Orders item in the Add Table dialog, close the dialog, and click the SQL button. By default, a `SELECT` query skeleton statement opens in the SQL pane. Mark the * (All Columns) check box.

3. Choose Query, Make-Table Query or click the Query Type button, and choose Make-Table Query to open the Make Table dialog. Type a table name, such as **tblOrders**, in the text box, and click OK to create a `SELECT dbo.Orders.* INTO dbo.tblOrders FROM dbo.Orders` statement (see Figure 20.25).

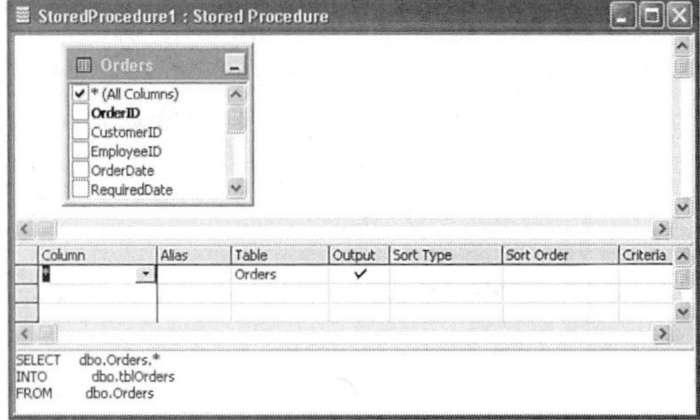

Figure 20.25 The process of creating a make-table stored procedure is identical to that for creating a Jet make-table query.

> **NOTE**
>
> It's an SQL Server convention to use two-letter object type prefixes for views (`vw`), stored procedures (`sp` or `xp`), and functions (`fn`). Microsoft and many developers add an underscore, especially when naming objects with the even more traditional all lowercase convention. However, adding an underscore to the `sp` or `xp` prefixes conflicts with SQL Server's use of `sp_` for system stored procedures and `xp_` for extended stored procedures. It's not common to prefix table names with `tb` or `tb_`, but `tmp` or `tmp_` often precedes temporary table names. The examples of this chapter use the `tbl` prefix for consistency with the Jet tables you created in earlier chapters.

4. Click the Run button, and save your stored procedure as **spMakeTable**. After SQL Server stores and executes the stored procedure, a message confirms that the stored procedure executed, but didn't return any records. Click OK, and then close the project designer.

> **NOTE**
>
> 
>
> The new tblOrders table you created has a structure that's identical to the Orders source table, including the Identity property of the OrderID field. Make-table queries don't set a primary-key field, so the tblOrder table isn't updatable in Datasheet view. (SQL Server tables require a primary key for the cursor-based updates used by datasheets, but not for updates by stored procedures.)
>
> To add a primary-key field, open tblOrders in Design view, select the OrderID field, click the Primary Key button on the toolbar, close the table, and save the changes.

5. Repeat steps 1 and 2, but use the tblOrders table you just created to avoid making changes to the sample Orders table.

6. Choose Query, Update Query to change the grid and skeleton `UPDATE dbo.tblOrders SET` statement to the make-table syntax.
7. Mark the OrderDate, RequiredDate, and ShippedDate check boxes of the field list to add the fields to the `SET` statement, which defines the fields to be updated and their new values. Pencil icons in the check boxes indicate a pending `UPDATE` operation.
8. Type **OrderDate + 365**, **RequiredDate + 365**, and **ShippedDate + 365** in each column's corresponding New Value cell to add a year to date values. Type **not null** in the Criteria cell of the ShippedDate row to prevent an attempt to add a year to a `NULL` value. The designer changes the entry to `NOT IS NULL`, and adds the `WHERE NOT ShippedDate IS NULL` criterion (see Figure 20.26).

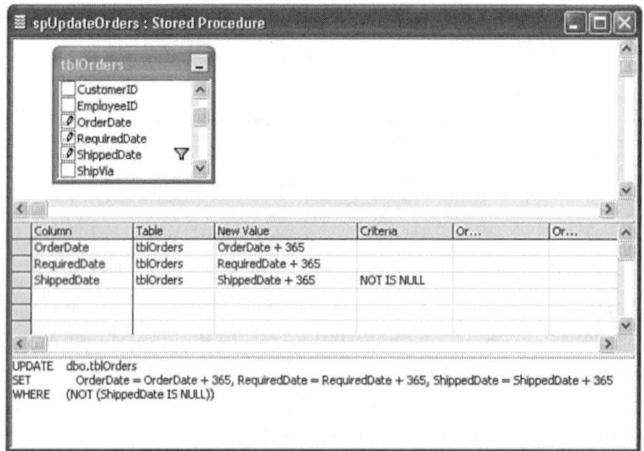

Figure 20.26
Stored procedures that update table values also follow Jet's methodology.

NOTE

Like the Jet query designer, the project designer adds multiple parenthesis pairs to the `WHERE` clause. Parentheses aren't required for simple criterion, but are needed to specify the application sequence of operators–such as `AND`, `OR`, and `NOT`–in complex `WHERE` clauses.

9. Click the Verify SQL Syntax button, click OK to dismiss the syntax confirmation message, and click the Run button. Save the stored procedure as **spUpdateOrders**. Click OK to dismiss the execution confirmation message, and close the project designer.
10. Open tblOrders from the Database window, not by changing to Datasheet view of the designer, to verify the updates. Changing to Datasheet view executes the stored procedure again, which adds another year to the dates.

CAUTION

Jet UPDATE queries post a warning message that indicates the number of rows to be changed, if you haven't cleared the Confirm Record Changes check box of the Option dialog's Edit/Find page. You receive no warning when you execute a stored procedure that updates tables.

NOTE

The IS NOT NULL criterion appears on the same line as ShippedDate, which implies that the criterion only applies to that column and that the query would update the OrderDate and RequiredDate columns for orders with missing ShippedDate values. This is not the case. The criterion applies to all columns included in the SET statement. To update all dates, you need to run two queries–one for OrderDate and RequiredDate and one for ShippedDate.

ADDING RECORDS WITH APPEND STORED PROCEDURES

To execute an append (INSERT INTO) stored procedure you need a table with the same structure as the source table. For example, if you use tblOrders as the source table, you need a new empty table with the same structure as tblOrders. Create a new copy of the Orders (not the tblOrders) table by selecting Order, pressing Ctrl+C, Ctrl+V, typing **tblOrdersEmpty**, and selecting Structure Only in the Paste Table dialog.

DEALING WITH IDENTITY FIELDS

The tblOrders and tblOrdersEmpty tables have a field of the int data type with the Identity property set to Yes, which is equivalent to a Jet AutoNumber field. You have the following choices when appending new records to a table that has an Identity field:

- Change the Identity property value in the target table to No. This approach lets you append records with the source table's value in the former identity column. (You can use SELECT * FROM *SourceTable* in the SELECT INTO statement.) After you append the records, you can set the Identity property to Yes. You don't need to change the Identity Seed property value from the default (1).
- Change the Identity Seed value to the same starting number as the records you're appending (10248 for tblOrders), or to another value to renumber the records consecutively. In this case, you specify all except the identity field in the SELECT field list.

NOTE

It's much easier to change the identity starting value for an SQL Server table than the initial value of a Jet AutoNumber field.

Follow these steps to prepare for testing the second of the preceding choices:

1. Open the tblOrdersEmpty table in Design view, select the OrderID column, and change the Identity Seed value to any number you want. This example uses **1010248**, which represents a change to increase the number of digits for order numbering without renumbering the significant five digits of older orders. (Unfortunately, you can't use 010248, because the leading zero is stripped when you save the table design.)

2. Click Table Datasheet view, save your design changes, and verify that tblOrdersEmpty displays the (AutoNumber) default in the only (empty) record.
3. Close the table. If you leave the table open, the appended records don't appear until you close and reopen it.

CREATING THE APPEND QUERY

To append and renumber records from the tblOrders table, do the following:

1. Click New in the Database window's Queries page, double-click Design Stored Procedure, add tblOrders to the default `SELECT` query, and click the SQL button.
2. Mark each field name check box for the CustomerID through the ShipName fields but omit ShippedDate and Freight, and then choose Query, Append Query to open the Choose Target Table for Insert Results dialog (see Figure 20.27).

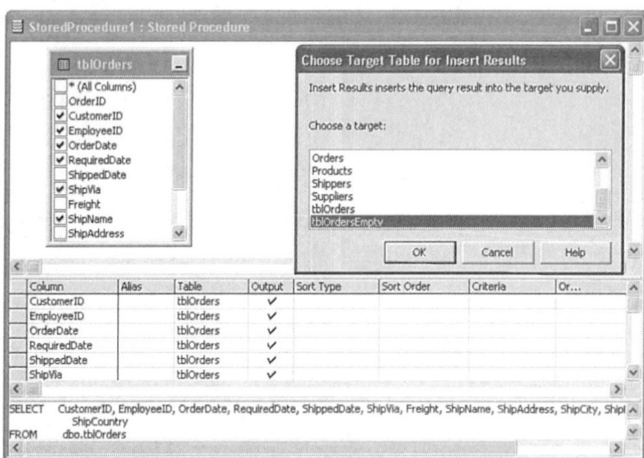

Figure 20.27 You must specify the target table for append queries. The Choose Target Table for Insert Results dialog is a redesigned version of Jet's Append dialog.

3. Select the tblOrdersEmpty table in the list, and click OK to change the grid layout to the append query format, and add the `INSERT INTO` *`TableName`* `(`*`FieldList`*`)` statement to the query (see Figure 20.28). The check box icons change to plus (+) signs.

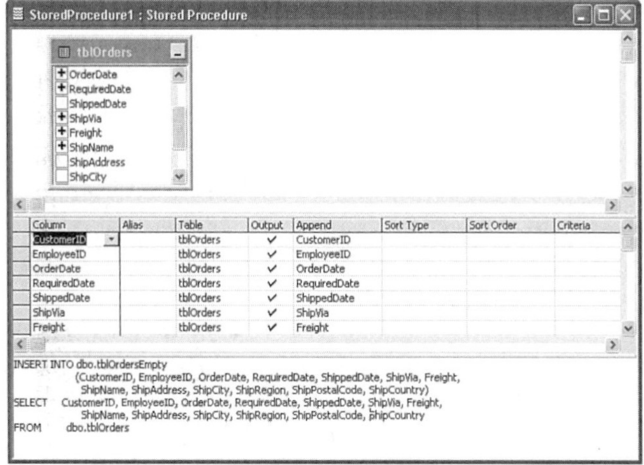

Figure 20.28 The grid for an append query has columns corresponding to the Jet append query design grid's rows.

4. Click Run, save your stored procedure as **spAppendOrders**, and acknowledge the execution confirmation message.
5. Open the table with the appended records to confirm the renumbering process (see Figure 20.29).

tblOrdersEmpty : Table

OrderID	CustomerID	EmployeeID	OrderDate	RequiredDate	ShipVia
1010248	VINET	5	7/4/1997	8/1/1997	3
1010249	TOMSP	6	7/5/1997	8/16/1997	1
1010250	HANAR	4	7/8/1997	8/5/1997	2
1010251	VICTE	3	7/8/1997	8/5/1997	1
1010252	SUPRD	4	7/9/1997	8/6/1997	2
1010253	HANAR	3	7/10/1997	7/24/1997	2
1010254	CHOPS	5	7/11/1997	8/8/1997	2
1010255	RICSU	9	7/12/1997	8/9/1997	3
1010256	WELLI	3	7/15/1997	8/12/1997	2
1010257	HILAA	4	7/16/1997	8/13/1997	3
1010258	ERNSH	1	7/17/1997	8/14/1997	1
1010259	CENTC	4	7/18/1997	8/15/1997	3
1010260	OTTIK	4	7/19/1997	8/16/1997	1
1010261	QUEDE	4	7/19/1997	8/16/1997	2
1010262	RATTC	8	7/22/1997	8/19/1997	3
1010263	ERNSH	9	7/23/1997	8/20/1997	3
1010264	FOLKO	6	7/24/1997	8/21/1997	3
1010265	BLONP	2	7/25/1997	8/22/1997	1
1010266	WARTH	3	7/26/1997	9/6/1997	3
1010267	FRANK	4	7/29/1997	8/26/1997	1

Record: 1 of 830

Figure 20.29 The appended records have one million added to the original order number.

Stored procedures have an append values query option that Jet doesn't offer. An append values query lets you add one record at a time (perform an `INSERT`) with a stored procedure. Practically speaking, append values queries are only useful as parameterized stored procedures; in most cases, you supply the parameter values with VBA code.

To test-drive an append values query with the tblOrdersEmpty table, do this:

1. Close the table, open a new stored procedure, and add the tblOrdersEmpty table to it.

2. Mark the check boxes for the fields, except the OrderID field, that are valid when entering an order. ShippedDate and Freight, for example, don't receive values until the order goes out the door, assuming that your organization complies with generally accepted accounting practices (GAAPs).
3. Choose Query, Append Values Query to change the grid to a Column and Value list.
4. Type appropriate values in each of the Value cells. You must type a value into each cell; use `NULL` to specify a value that's unknown or not applicable. Character identifiers are added automatically to ...`char` and `datetime` fields. Typing the values adds them to the query's `VALUES` list, with a `CONVERT` function added for `datetime` fields (see Figure 20.30).

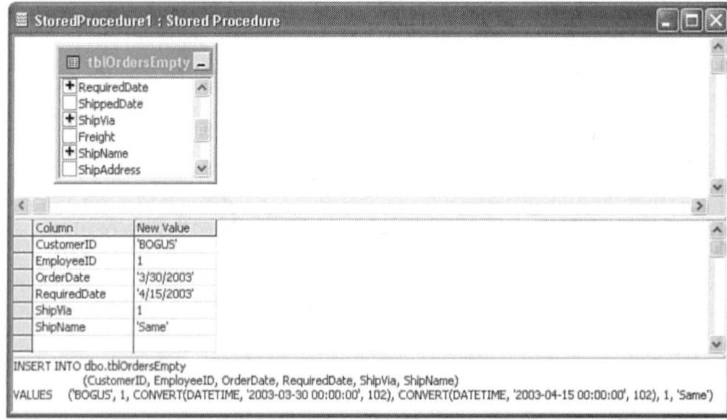

Figure 20.30 Append value stored procedures let you add a single record with values you type in the grid. Without parameters, stored procedures of this type aren't very useful.

5. Click Run, save your stored procedure as **spAppendBogusOrder** or the like, acknowledge the confirmation message, close the procedure, and open the table to verify the appended order.

Deleting Table Records

Delete queries saved as stored procedures without parameters aren't much more useful than append value queries. To create a simple parameter query to delete older records from the tblOrdersEmpty or tblOrders table, run the following drill:

1. Create a new stored procedure, and add tblOrdersEmpty to it.
2. Choose Query, Delete Query to set up the grid, add a skeleton `DELETE FROM` *`TableName`* statement, and change the * (All Columns) item's icon to the delete symbol.
3. Drag the column(s) on which to establish deletion criterion—ShippedDate for this example—to the grid.
4. Type the parameter criterion, **<=@Delete_Date**, in the Criteria column.
5. ShippedDate is `NULL` for some orders, so drag a second copy of ShippedDate to the grid, and type **NOT IS NULL** in the Criteria column. The stored procedure design appears as shown in Figure 20.31.

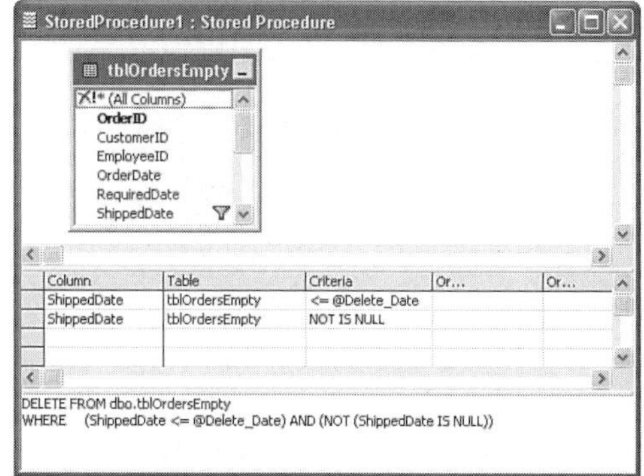

Figure 20.31
The query for this stored procedure that deletes older records requires compound criteria.

6. Click Run, save the stored procedure as **spDeleteParam** or similar, and type a date that's valid for the table to delete records for shipments on or before the date.

DIAGRAMMING TABLE RELATIONSHIPS

Selecting the Database Diagrams shortcut and double-clicking the Relationships item opens the Relationships diagram, derived from Jet's Relationships window. Click the arrow to the right of the Zoom Modes Drop-down button and select the percentage that displays all tables without scrolling (see Figure 20.32).

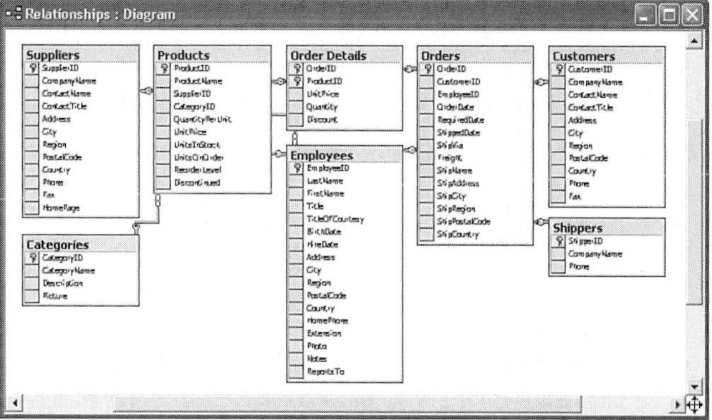

Figure 20.32
The Relationships database diagram displays the same information as Jet's Relationships window in a different format.

You can do the following in the Relationships diagram:

- Modify the properties of any table in the database, including adding and deleting fields, or changing the properties of fields. Right-clicking the table header opens a versatile context menu with 18 choices. Choosing Column Properties expands the selected table window to display a reduced-size version of Table Design view (see Figure 20.33). Choose Column Name to return to the default view.

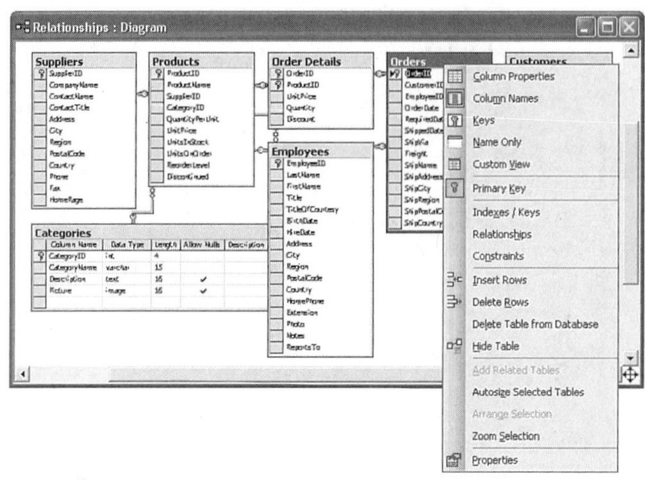

Figure 20.33 You can display column properties (shown here for the Categories table) or make one of 17 other choices from the database diagram's context menu.

- Add or drop tables of the database. You can also start with a new SQL Server database, and then add all the required tables, fields, and relationships in the window.
- View and alter relationships between tables by right-clicking the join line and choosing Properties.
- Hide tables. Hiding a table also causes relationship symbols connecting the table to disappear.
- Print the diagram. If the size of the diagram exceeds the maximum paper size of your printer, you must cut and paste several sheets to obtain a complete diagram.

BACKING UP AND RESTORING DATABASES

Unlike Jet databases, which you back up by a manual copying process, ADP have a built-in snapshot copy process. The best feature of the ADP backup process is that you don't need exclusive access to the database; you can generate a backup while you and other users are connected to the database.

TIP

> Use SQL Server Enterprise Manager to back up large databases to tape manually or automatically. Access's backup and restore features are limited to creating conventional disk files on fixed or removable media. If you intend to back up to a CD-R or CD-RW drive, make a fixed-disk copy and then burn the CD-ROM from the disk copy.

To create a snapshot backup of your project's current database (NorthwindCS for this example), do the following:

1. Choose Tools, Database Utilities, Backup SQL Database to open the Backup dialog.

2. Accept or change the proposed name of the backup file. By default, SQL Server backup files use the name of the database followed by a sequential number and a .dat extension—NorthwindCS1.dat for this example (see Figure 20.34).

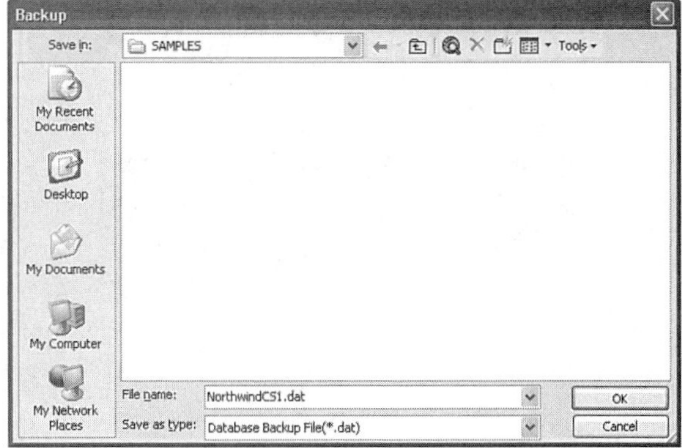

Figure 20.34
Use the backup feature to quickly create live snapshot backups of your project's database.

3. Navigate to a backup folder, preferably on a network server or a second local physical drive. When you click OK, you receive the message shown in Figure 20.35.

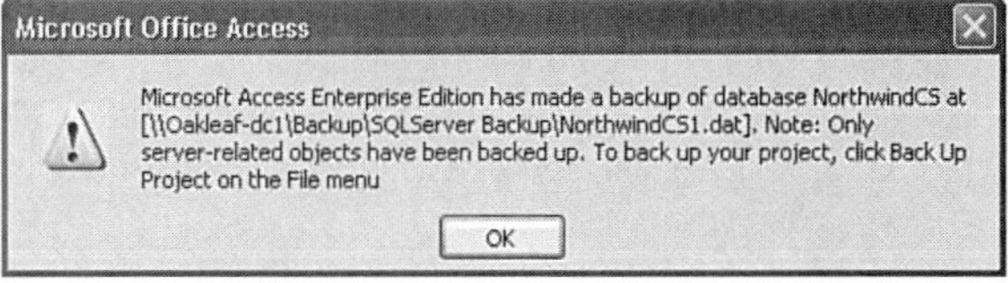

Figure 20.35
This message confirms creation of the snapshot backup and suggests backing up your .adp file by making a conventional copy.

You restore a backup .dat file when, for instance, you accidentally delete a table or other database object. You can't restore a database while you or users are connected to it.

To perform a restore, do the following:

1. Choose Tools, Database Utilities, Restore SQL Database. You receive the message shown in Figure 20.36.

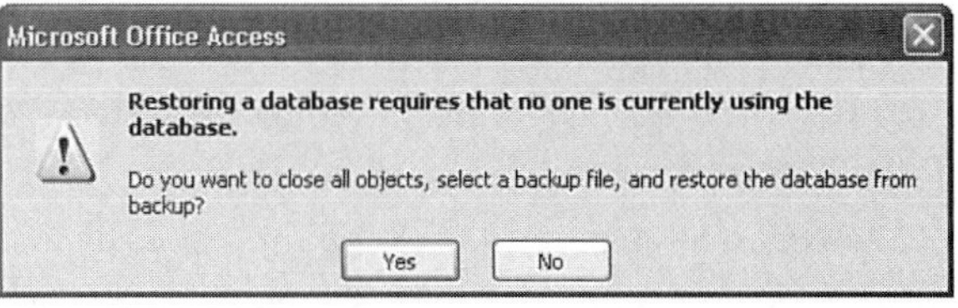

Figure 20.36
This message indicates that you can't perform a live restore of a database. All connections to the database must be closed before proceeding.

2. Click Yes to dismiss the message, navigate to the backup file, select it, and click OK. Your project disconnects from the database, and the message box shown in Figure 20.37 appears after a delay that depends on the size of the database and network performance.

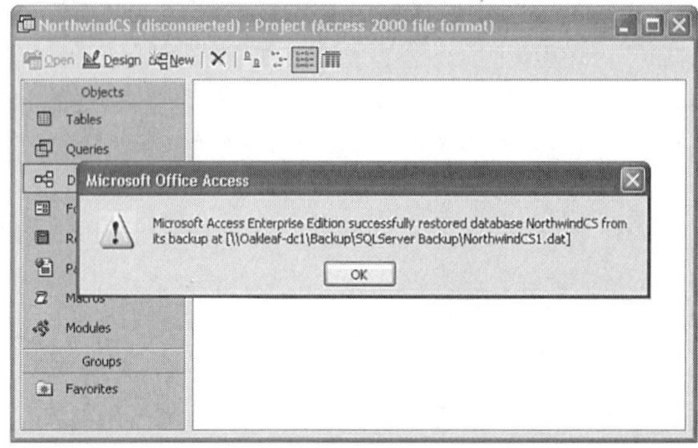

Figure 20.37
Restoring a database from a .dat backup copy requires temporarily disconnecting the project from the database.

3. Click OK to acknowledge the message, and automatically reconnect to the restored database.

TIP

> If you receive the message shown in Figure 20.38, other users have open connections to the database or there's a spurious lock on the database. If no other users are connected, you might be able to remove the lock by stopping and starting SQL Server with SQL Server Service Manager. In most cases, however, you must reboot the machine for the restore operation to succeed.

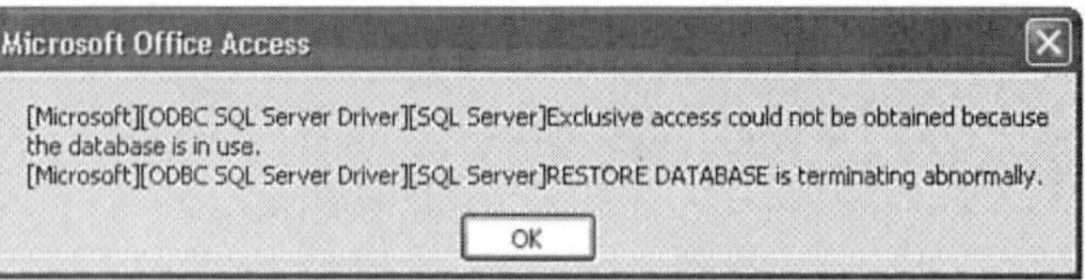

Figure 20.38
This message indicates that there are open connections or a residual lock on the database.

If you need to restore the .adp and .dat files as the result of a catastrophic failure, such as a crashed fixed disk, do this:

1. Copy the .adp file from the backup and open it in the disconnected state.
2. Restored the database, as described in the preceding three steps. Your project remains disconnected from the database.
3. Choose File, Connection to open the Data Link Properties dialog.
4. Accept the default (local) server name, and select the restored database in the Select the Database on the Server list (see Figure 20.39).

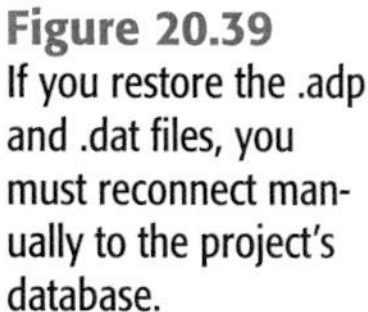

Figure 20.39
If you restore the .adp and .dat files, you must reconnect manually to the project's database.

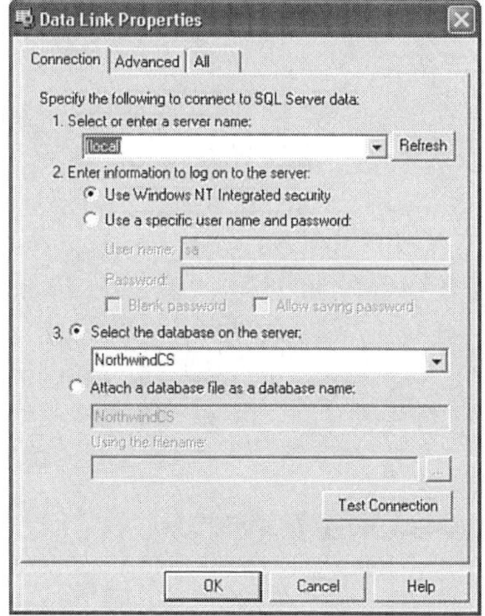

5. Click Test Connection to verify your settings, and click OK to reconnect your project to the restored database.

Transferring the Project's Database to a Server

Access 2002 adds two new choices to the ADP Tools, Database Utilities menu—Transfer Database and Copy Database File. The Transfer Database choice uses SQL Server 2000's Data Transformation Service to create a copy of the current database on another machine running SQL Server. The most common use for this utility is to place a database you've developed into production on a workgroup server. Transfer Database is a live copying process; you don't need to disconnect from the current database.

To copy your project's database to a server, do the following:

1. Choose Tools, Database Utilities, Transfer Database to open the Transfer Database Dialog.
2. Select the destination server—OAKMONT-DC1 for this example—in the drop-down list (see Figure 20.40).
3. If you're transferring the database to a Windows 98/Me machine, you must specify a username and password for SQL Server security. (A password is required only if you've secured the sa account.) Otherwise, accept the default integrated Windows security.
4. Click Next and then Finish to start the transfer process, which displays a progress dialog (see Figure 20.41).

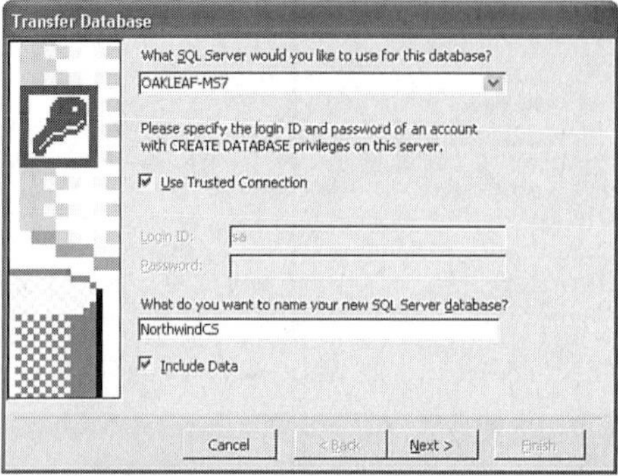

Figure 20.40
Specify the target server for the current database in Transfer Database dialog.

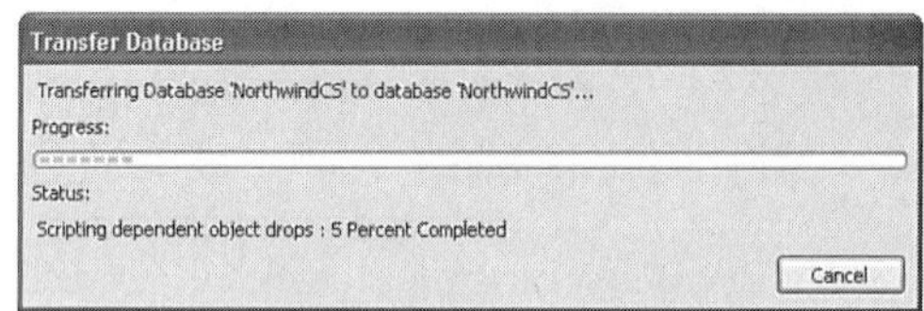

Figure 20.41
This progress dialog displays each step in the Transfer Database operation.

5. When the transfer process completes, your project remains connected to the local (original) database.

The Copy Database File choice copies the database files to the location you specify. When you make this choice, the message shown in Figure 20.42 opens. If you click OK, the Open dialog appears to let you make a copy of the SQL Server database (.mdf) file in another location that you can attach to SQL Server.

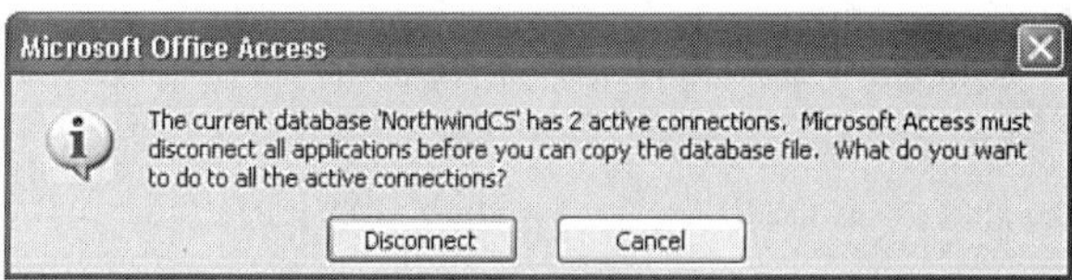

Figure 20.42
Before you can copy the project's database file to another location, you must close all connections to the database.

Connecting to a Remote SQL Server Database

To connect to an SQL Server database on a production server, such as the database you transferred in the preceding section, do this:

1. Choose File, Connection, to open the Data Link Properties dialog.
2. Open the Select Server or Enter a Server Name drop-down list and select the NetBIOS name of the server (see Figure 20.43). If the server doesn't appear in the list, type its name in the list's text box.

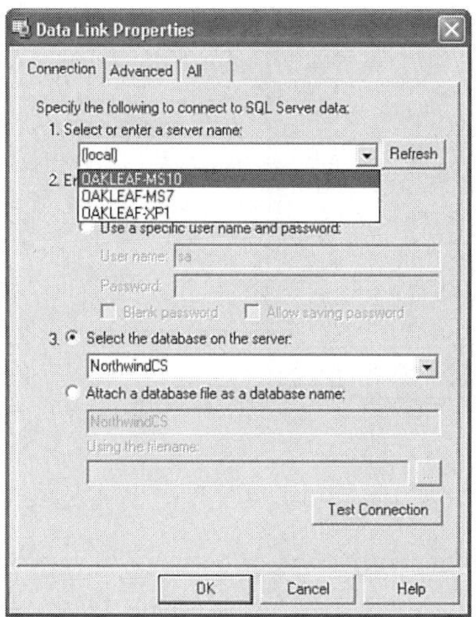

Figure 20.43 All instances of SQL Server on machines running Windows 2000 or NT appear in the server name list. On a client running Windows 98/Me, you must type the NetBIOS name of the server.

3. If you're connecting with Access 2000 or 2002 from a machine running Windows 98/Me, select Use a Specific User Name and Password to connect to the server, and type the logon ID (**sa**, unless you've added SQL Server accounts) and password, if the account is secured. Otherwise, accept the default Use Windows NT Integrated Security option.
4. Select the database name, and click Test Connection.
5. Click OK to connect to the remote SQL Server database.

NOTE

If you used the Copy Database File Feature to copy an .mdf file, you can attach the copied file to your local instance of SQL Server, as shown in Figure 20.44. This process emulates SQL Server Enterprise Manager's capability to attach .mdf files, but you aren't connected to a remote SQL Server. (Only the file is remote.)

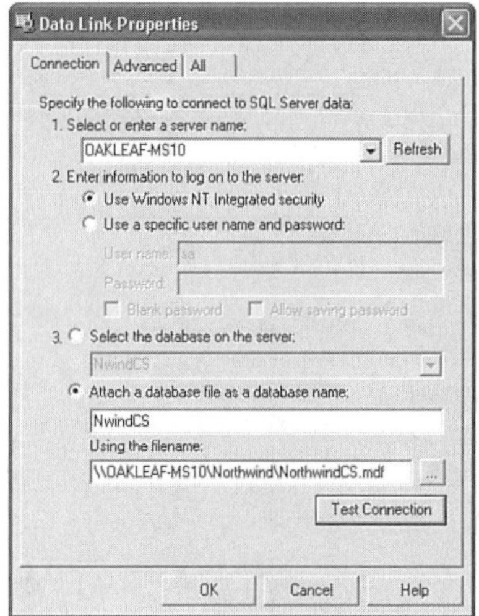

Figure 20.44
If you need to attach an SQL Server .mdf file to a database, you can do so by selecting the Attach a Database File as a Database Name option, typing the database name to use, and navigating to the location of the file.

LINKING REMOTE SERVERS

Access 2003's Linked Table Wizard lets you use SQL Server 2000's new *linked servers* feature to gain access to remote instances of SQL Server, other client/server RDBMSs, and Jet databases. Linking a Jet database provides access to tables linked from Excel worksheets, text files, and other indexed-sequential access method (ISAM) databases, such as dBASE and Paradox. Alternatively, you can link via the Open Database Connectivity (ODBC) API to data sources for which you have current ODBC drivers. You also can link data sources that don't return traditional tabular data—such as Windows 2000 Active Directory, documents indexed by the Microsoft Indexing Service, and Exchange 2000 Web folders.

Linked servers require an OLE DB data provider for the data source. Depending on the data source type and location, as well as the capabilities of the OLE DB provider, the linked tables are read/write or read-only. Office Data Connector (.odc) files store linked table definitions. By default, Access 2003 stores .odc files in your My Documents\My Data Sources folder, the physical location of which depends on your operating system. The following sections describe two scenarios that use the Link Table Wizard to define the links. Your Access project must be connected to a local SQL Server instance to use the Link Table Wizard.

LINKING A JET 4.0 DATABASE

The easiest way to test-drive a linked server is to link a Jet 4.0 database with the Microsoft Jet 4.0 OLE DB provider. To create read-only views of tables from a linked, unsecured Jet database in ADP quickly, do this:

1. Open the NorthwindCS.adp project, if it isn't already open, with the connection to the database on your local instance of MSDE.

2. Choose File, Get External Data, Link Tables to open the Link Table Wizard's first dialog, which offers the option of creating a linked server or using T-SQL's `OpenRowset` function to create a temporary connection to a database (see Figure 20.45). Accept the default Linked Server option, and click Next to open the Select Data Source dialog.

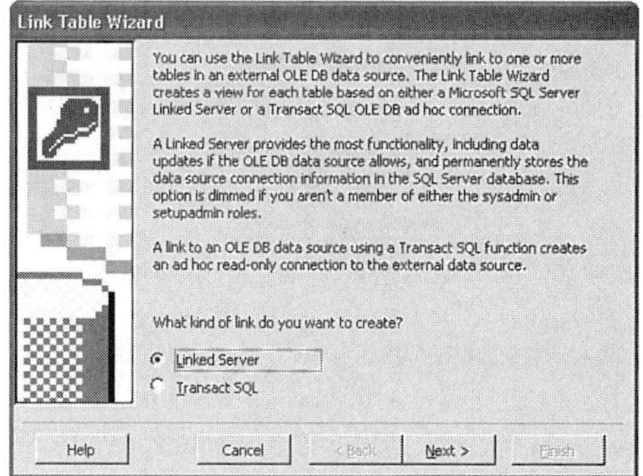

Figure 20.45
The first dialog of the Link Table Wizard briefly describes SQL Server's linked server feature and the difference between a linked server and an ad hoc connection to a remote data source.

3. You can select existing .odc, .mdb, .mde, .adp, .ade, and a variety of other file types from the files of type list. For this example, navigate to your \Program Files\Microsoft Office\Office11\Samples folder, select Northwind.mdb (see Figure 20.46), and click Open.

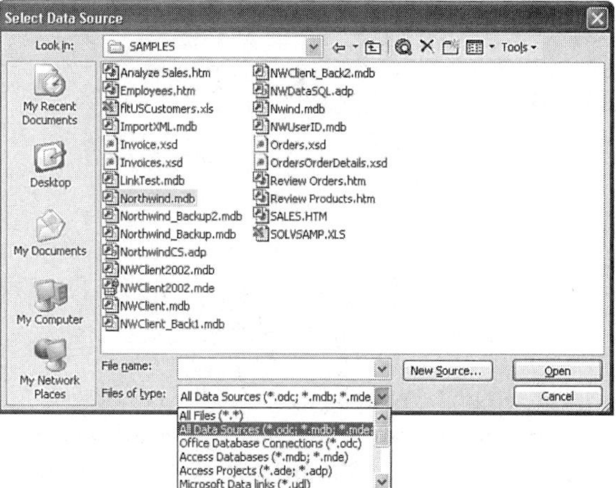

Figure 20.46
The Select Data Source dialog lets you select a data source from a variety of file types. Scroll the Files of Type list to expose more data source types you can specify.

4. In the second Wizard dialog, double-click the tables you might want to link existing SQL Server tables to in the Available Tables list. (The Tables list also includes Jet QueryDefs disguised as views.) For this example, double-click each of the eight original tables of Northwind.mdb (see Figure 20.47). Click Next and then Finish to add the linked server definition to the current SQL Server database.

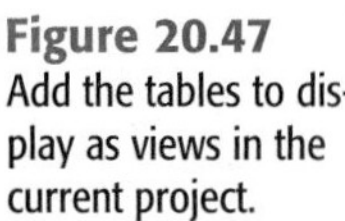

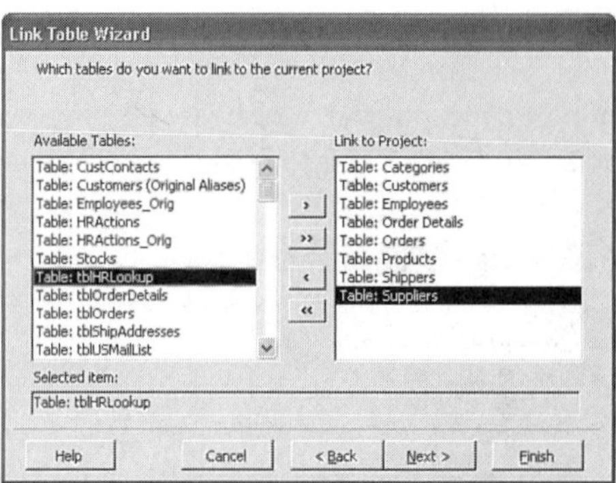

Figure 20.47
Add the tables to display as views in the current project.

5. Click the Queries shortcut in the Database window to display views the Wizard added (see Figure 20.48). The default names for linked views use the *DatabaseName__TableName* format; two underscores separate the object names.

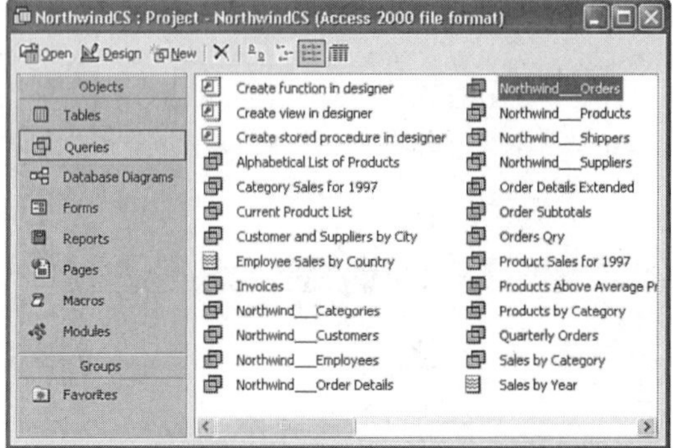

Figure 20.48
Views over linked Jet tables appear in the Queries page of the Database window after the Wizard creates the linked table definition in the local database.

6. Double-click one of the links, such as Northwind__Orders to display the data. The view's columns appear in alphabetical order (see Figure 20.49). The disabled New Record button indicates that the view is read-only.

Datasheets of views created against remote Jet tables linked to SQL Server aren't updatable, despite the fact that the underlying tables' key fields are identified by a bold font in Design view. You can, however, use T-SQL `UPDATE`, `INSERT`, and `DELETE` statements or stored procedures to update the linked Jet tables.

LINKING A REMOTE SQL SERVER DATABASE

The advantage of using an .odc file is that all members of Office XP can use the .odc file to connect to an SQL Server data source. You can copy the .odc file you create to a server share for access by other users. The files are coded in HTML and contain an XML representation of the connection string, which specifies the remote database.

Northwind___Orders : View

CustomerID	EmployeeID	Freight	OrderDate	OrderID	RequiredDate	ShipAddress	ShipCity
WILMK	5	$32.38	7/4/1996	10248	8/1/1996	59 rue de l'Abba	Reims
TRADH	6	$11.61	7/5/1996	10249	8/16/1996	Luisenstr. 48	Münster
HANAR	4	$65.83	7/8/1996	10250	8/5/1996	Rua do Paço, 6	Rio de Janeiro
VICTE	3	$41.34	7/8/1996	10251	8/5/1996	2, rue du Comm	Lyon
SUPRD	4	$51.30	7/9/1996	10252	8/6/1996	Boulevard Tirou,	Charleroi
HANAR	3	$58.17	7/10/1996	10253	7/24/1996	Rua do Paço, 6	Rio de Janeiro
CHOPS	5	$22.98	7/11/1996	10254	8/8/1996	Hauptstr. 31	Bern
RICSU	9	$148.33	7/12/1996	10255	8/9/1996	Starenweg 5	Genève
WELLI	3	$13.97	7/15/1996	10256	8/12/1996	Rua do Mercado	Resende
HILAA	4	$81.91	7/16/1996	10257	8/13/1996	Carrera 22 con	San Cristóbal
ERNSH	1	$140.51	7/17/1996	10258	8/14/1996	Kirchgasse 6	Graz
CENTC	4	$3.25	7/18/1996	10259	8/15/1996	Sierras de Gran	México D.F.
OLDWO	4	$55.09	7/19/1996	10260	8/16/1996	Mehrheimerstr.	Köln
QUEDE	4	$3.05	7/19/1996	10261	8/16/1996	Rua da Panifica	Rio de Janeiro
RATTC	8	$48.29	7/22/1996	10262	8/19/1996	2817 Milton Dr.	Albuquerque
ERNSH	9	$146.06	7/23/1996	10263	8/20/1996	Kirchgasse 6	Graz
FOLKO	6	$3.67	7/24/1996	10264	8/21/1996	Åkergatan 24	Bräcke
BLONP	2	$55.28	7/25/1996	10265	8/22/1996	24, place Klébe	Strasbourg
WARTH	3	$25.73	7/26/1996	10266	9/6/1996	Torikatu 38	Oulu
FRANK	4	$208.58	7/29/1996	10267	8/26/1996	Berliner Platz 4	München
GROSR	8	$66.29	7/30/1996	10268	8/27/1996	5ª Ave. Los Pal	Caracas

Record: 1 of 830

Figure 20.49
Views over linked Jet tables are read-only in Datasheet view and columns appear in alphabetical order by name.

To create an .odc file to link a remote SQL Server database to your local copy of MSDE, do the following:

1. Open the Select Data Source dialog as described in steps 1 and 2 of the preceding section.
2. Double-click the +New SQL Server Connection.odc item in the My Data Sources folder to open the Data Connection Wizard's Connect to Database Server dialog.
3. Type the NetBIOS name of the server—**OAKLEAF-MS10** for this example—in the Server Name text box, and accept the default Use Windows 2000 Security option (see Figure 20.50). Click Next.

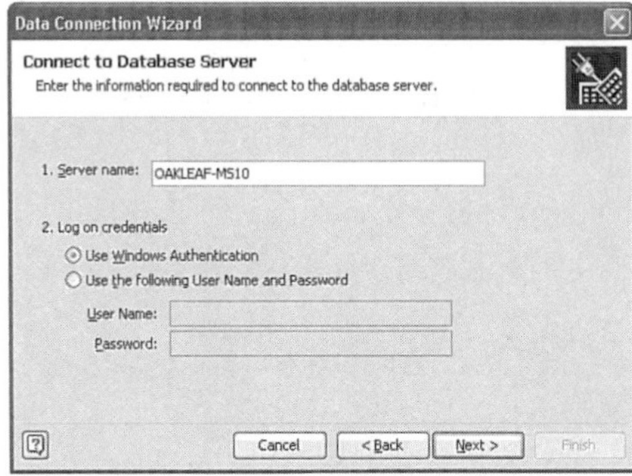

Figure 20.50
The Link Table Wizard calls the Connection Wizard to create a new Office Data Connector (.odc) file that defines the connection to the remote server.

20

4. In the Select Database and Table dialog, open the Select the Database... list and select the database on the remote server. OAKLEAF-MS10 has SQL Server Standard Edition installed, which includes a sample Northwind database (see Figure 20.51). Click Next.

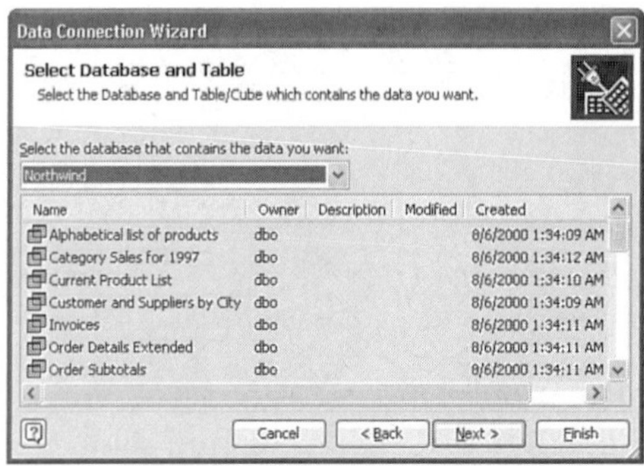

Figure 20.51
Select the database of the remote server in the second Connection Wizard dialog. The list of tables is read-only.

5. In the Save Data Connection File and Finish dialog, accept the default *SERVERNAME DatabaseName*.odc file name and My Data Sources location, or click Browse to open the File Save dialog, and specify a different name, location, or both. Type an optional description of the .odc file (see Figure 20.52), and click Finish to return to the Link Table Wizard.

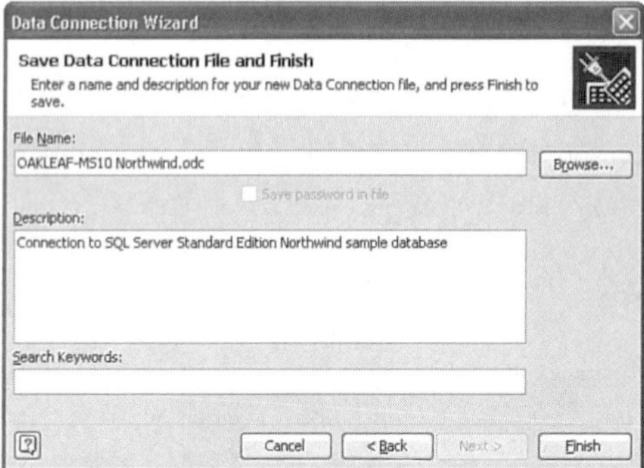

Figure 20.52
Specify the name of the .odc file and add a description in the third Connection Wizard dialog.

6. Double-click the tables that you might want to use in the Available Tables list (see Figure 20.53). Click Finish to add views to the Queries page of the Database window.

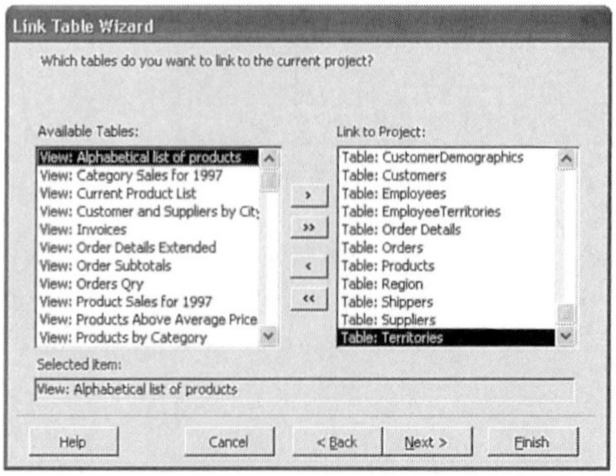

Figure 20.53
The Wizard generates views for each table or view you add to the Link to Project list. All tables are accessible from T-SQL SELECT statements.

7. The Database window displays the views in SQL Server four-part name format, *SERVER_Database_Schema_Table*; underscores replace the periods used when referring to the tables in T-SQL statements (see Figure 20.54).

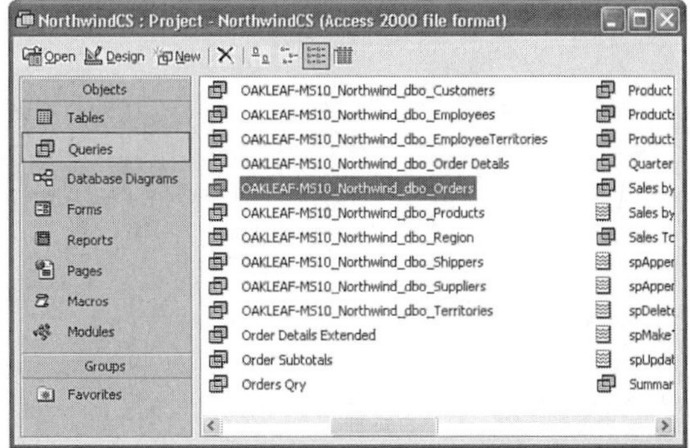

Figure 20.54
Views over linked SQL Server tables use a modified SQL Server four-part naming convention for tables. (Underscores replace periods between object names.)

8. Double-click one of the tables to display the data. Unlike linked Jet tables, the columns of views against SQL Server tables appear in the original order (see Figure 20.55). The Datasheet view isn't updatable, because the current version of the SQL Server OLE DB provider doesn't support the Unique Rows property of linked SQL Server tables.

Figure 20.55
Like linked Jet tables, Datasheet views of remote SQL Server tables are read-only.

OAKLEAF-MS10_Northwind_dbo_Orders : View

OrderID	CustomerID	EmployeeID	OrderDate	RequiredDate	ShippedDate	ShipVia
10248	VINET	5	7/4/1996	8/1/1996	7/16/1996	3
10249	TOMSP	6	7/5/1996	8/16/1996	7/10/1996	1
10250	HANAR	4	7/8/1996	8/5/1996	7/12/1996	2
10251	VICTE	3	7/8/1996	8/5/1996	7/15/1996	1
10252	SUPRD	4	7/9/1996	8/6/1996	7/11/1996	2
10253	HANAR	3	7/10/1996	7/24/1996	7/16/1996	2
10254	CHOPS	5	7/11/1996	8/8/1996	7/23/1996	2
10255	RICSU	9	7/12/1996	8/9/1996	7/15/1996	3
10256	WELLI	3	7/15/1996	8/12/1996	7/17/1996	2
10257	HILAA	4	7/16/1996	8/13/1996	7/22/1996	3
10258	ERNSH	1	7/17/1996	8/14/1996	7/23/1996	1
10259	CENTC	4	7/18/1996	8/15/1996	7/25/1996	3
10260	OTTIK	4	7/19/1996	8/16/1996	7/29/1996	1
10261	QUEDE	4	7/19/1996	8/16/1996	7/30/1996	2
10262	RATTC	8	7/22/1996	8/19/1996	7/25/1996	3
10263	ERNSH	9	7/23/1996	8/20/1996	7/31/1996	3
10264	FOLKO	6	7/24/1996	8/21/1996	8/23/1996	3
10265	BLONP	2	7/25/1996	8/22/1996	8/12/1996	1
10266	WARTH	3	7/26/1996	9/6/1996	7/31/1996	3
10267	FRANK	4	7/29/1996	8/26/1996	8/6/1996	1
10268	GROSR	8	7/30/1996	8/27/1996	8/2/1996	3

Record: 1 of 1130

20

The .odc file you saved in step 5 is an XML file with an HTML wrapper. To view the .odc file in Internet Explorer 5+, navigate to your My Documents\My Data Sources folder, and double-click the .odc file. The browser displays the table name, schema, and type (TABLE or VIEW) in a PivotTable control (see Figure 20.56). Figure 20.57 shows the first part of the source code of the OAKMONT-DC1 Northwind.odc file.

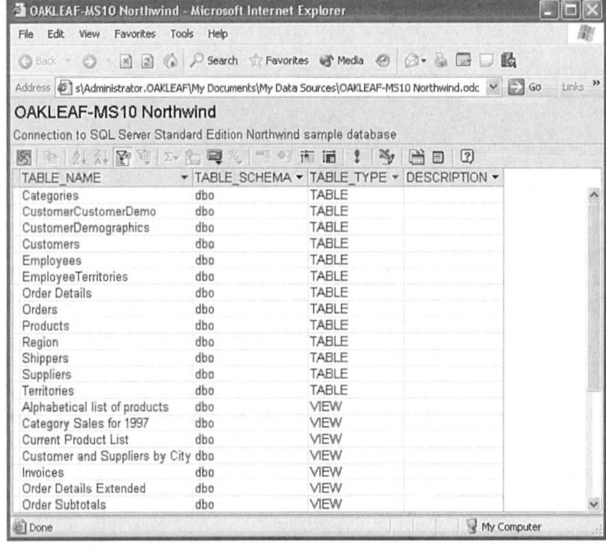

OAKLEAF-MS10 Northwind

Connection to SQL Server Standard Edition Northwind sample database

TABLE_NAME	TABLE_SCHEMA	TABLE_TYPE	DESCRIPTION
Categories	dbo	TABLE	
CustomerCustomerDemo	dbo	TABLE	
CustomerDemographics	dbo	TABLE	
Customers	dbo	TABLE	
Employees	dbo	TABLE	
EmployeeTerritories	dbo	TABLE	
Order Details	dbo	TABLE	
Orders	dbo	TABLE	
Products	dbo	TABLE	
Region	dbo	TABLE	
Shippers	dbo	TABLE	
Suppliers	dbo	TABLE	
Territories	dbo	TABLE	
Alphabetical list of products	dbo	VIEW	
Category Sales for 1997	dbo	VIEW	
Current Product List	dbo	VIEW	
Customer and Suppliers by City	dbo	VIEW	
Invoices	dbo	VIEW	
Order Details Extended	dbo	VIEW	
Order Subtotals	dbo	VIEW	

Figure 20.56 Office Database Connector (.odc) files display in a PivotTable all tables and views in the remote database.

```
<html>

<head>
<meta http-equiv=Content-Type content="text/x-ms-odc; charset=utf-8">
<meta name=ProgId content=ODC.Database>
<meta name=SourceType content=OLEDB>
<meta name=Catalog content=Northwind>
<xml id=docprops><o:DocumentProperties
  xmlns:o="urn:schemas-microsoft-com:office:office"
  xmlns="http://www.w3.org/TR/REC-html40">
  <o:Description>Connection to SQL Server Standard Edition Northwind sample
database</o:Description>
 </o:DocumentProperties>
</xml><xml id=msodc><odc:OfficeDataConnection
  xmlns:odc="urn:schemas-microsoft-com:office:odc"
  xmlns="http://www.w3.org/TR/REC-html40">
  <odc:Connection odc:Type="OLEDB">
   <odc:ConnectionString>Provider=SQLOLEDB.1;Integrated Security=SSPI;Persist
Security Info=True;Data Source=OAKLEAF-MS10;Use Procedure for Prepare=1;Auto
Translate=True;Packet Size=4096;Workstation ID=OAKLEAF-XP1;Use Encryption for
Data=False;Tag with column collation when possible=False;Initial
Catalog=Northwind</odc:ConnectionString>
   <odc:CommandType>Table</odc:CommandType>
  </odc:Connection>
 </odc:OfficeDataConnection>
</xml>
<style>
<!--
    .ODCDataSource
    {
    behavior: url(dataconn.htc);
    }
-->
</style>
```

Figure 20.57 Notepad displays the first few lines of the XML source code for the OAKMONT-DC1 Northwind.odc file. The `<odc:connectionstring>...</odc:connectionstring>` tags enclose the connection string definition (attributes) for the remote server.

Securing Your Project as an .ade File

When you distribute Access projects to users, the only security you can apply on the client side is compiling the project to an encoded .ade file. Like .mde files, projects stored in .ade format prevent users from making design changes to the front end and gaining access to your VBA source code. When you use the default integrated Windows authentication for the back-end SQL Server database, which is the recommended configuration for SQL Server, you can't apply password protection to the project. Windows authentication prevents users who haven't been assigned server logins and database permissions from opening the project's connection to the server.

➔ To learn how to use OSQL to add logins and database permissions to MSDE, **see** "Adding User Logins with the OSQL Utility," **p. 776**.

NOTE

> The Database window's Design and New shortcuts for tables and queries are enabled for all .mde users. Users need SQL Server permissions to create or alter tables, views, functions, and stored procedures. Like .mde files, macros aren't protected from design changes in .ade files.

To create an .ade version of your .adp file, follow the same procedure as described in Chapter 19 for creating a .mde from a .mda file:

1. Create an archive of the .adp file on removable media and then make a backup copy with a different name. Most .adp files fit on a high-density diskette.
2. If your .adp file uses Access 2000 format, you must convert the backup copy to Access 2002 format before creating the .ade file. Only users with Access 2003 or 2002 installed can open the file.

TIP

> Use Access 2000 to create .ade files for Access 2000 users. You can't create an Access 2000-compatible .ade file in Access 2003.

3. Open the backup copy, and then choose Tools, Database Utilities, Make ADE File to open the Save ADE As dialog.
4. Type the name of the .ade file to save in the File Name text box, and click Save to create the .ade file.

NOTE

> Database Creations, Inc. offers an Access Project Security Manager (APSM) add-in to enable user-level security for ADP application objects—forms, reports, and controls on forms. APSM has features similar to the User-Level Security Wizard for Jet-based front-ends. For more information on APSM, which requires enabling SQL Server security for server logins and database permissions, go to `http://www.databasecreations.com/`.

TROUBLESHOOTING

REMOTE DATABASE CONNECTION PROBLEMS

Access hangs or throws an error message when I attempt to connect my project to an instance of SQL Server running on a server.

There are many causes for connection failures to remote databases, the most obvious being network problems. Verify that you can connect to the server PC and open server shares with Explorer. If you can connect to a server share but not the database, and your network runs NetBEUI and TCP/IP protocols, you probably have a TCP/IP problem. Use Control Panel's Network tool, disable the NetBEUI protocol, and verify the TCP/IP settings for your network interface card (NIC).

In the Real World—Strategic Database Schizophrenia

Microsoft has invested a substantial amount of developer time and energy in making the transition from Jet to SQL Server more palatable to Access users and developers. Computer press columnists—especially ZD Net's David Coursey—have derided Access as difficult to use. The simpler alternatives these pundits propose are flat-file managers, not RDBMSs. Designing and managing a relational database for business or even personal use isn't a simple task, but Access's success is in no small part due to the fact that it was easier to use than its early desktop database competitors, such as dBASE, FoxPro, Clipper, and Paradox. Wizards made tasks like creating basic forms and reports a relatively simple process. Of course, inclusion in the Microsoft Office Professional suite was another major factor in the demise of most competitive desktop RDBMSs.

Access 2003's improved user interface for designing SQL Server database objects, and easy addition of parameters to functions and stored procedures bring ADP close to parity with Jet's Table and Query Design views. The Link Table Wizard makes connecting SQL Server to other OLE DB-enabled data sources easier than using ODBC and Jet. The obvious problem with views over linked tables is their lack of updatability in Datasheet view. Forms bound to SQL Server with Jet linked-table views remain read-only. The first page of the Link Table Wizard states: "A Linked Server provides the most functionality, including data updates if the OLE DB data source allows...." Microsoft's failure to correct this defect in Access 2003 is difficult to fathom.

MSDE's lack of even rudimentary menu-based or graphical database management tools makes ordinary database administration chores difficult for developers and next to impossible for ordinary Access users. Using OSQL for server and database management requires familiarity with T-SQL data definition and data security language commands, plus experience executing SQL Server 2000 system stored procedures. The demise of Access 2000's basic tools for administering SQL Server security was a definitive step in the wrong direction for Microsoft's "strategic database." Only minimal developer effort would have been required to upgrade Access 2000's tools to Windows authentication for MSDE 2000. Thus, it's fair to conclude that ADP and MSDE 2000 are tactical, not strategic features of Access 2003.

NOTE

The MSDE User Manager utility (UserMan.exe) is a Visual Basic 6.0 program that uses SQL Server Data Management Objects (SQLDMO) to manage server logins and database permissions for MSDE 2000. The setup program to install UserMan.exe and its source code is in the \Program Files\Seua11\UserMan folder of the accompanying CD-ROM.

→ To learn more about the MSDE User Manager utility, **see** "Securing Projects with the MSDE 2000 Login/User Tool," **p. 936**.

Most users of MSDE in medium-sized and larger concerns probably will migrate to SQL Server 2000 Standard Edition when putting ADP into full-scale production, fulfilling Microsoft's strategic objective in providing MSDE with Access 2003. The $4,995 price tag for an unlimited-user license for the Standard edition undoubtedly will deter small firms from upgrading. The performance of MSDE, however, is likely to meet the needs of most small- to medium-sized businesses.

TIP

Small firms with 50 users or fewer should consider licensing Microsoft Small Business Server (SBS) 2000. SBS 2000 includes Windows 2000 Server, SQL Server 2000 Standard Edition, Exchange 2000 Server, and Internet Security and Acceleration Server 2000 (formerly Proxy Server). A server and five client licenses costs US$1,499 and 20 additional client licenses cost US$999. (SBS 2000 is limited to a total of 50 users.) All Access 2003 clients that connect to or replicate with the SQL Server instance must have a client license. For more information on SBS 2000, go to `http://www.microsoft.com/sbserver/`.

Where SQL Server 2000 shines is in ease of installation, maintenance, and administration. You can run medium-sized SQL Server 2000 installations without a trained DBA, and you'll probably find that SQL Server 2000 databases require less maintenance attention than shared-file Jet back ends. Unlike Jet, SQL Server 2000 databases are largely self-tuning and self-managing. Choosing the optimum set of indexes for server tables traditionally has been a hit-or-miss operation based on DBA intuition. If you have Enterprise Manager, SQL Server's Profiler and Index Tuning Wizard analyze table usage, and the Wizard recommends the fields to index. This is an especially important feature for databases having usage patterns that change significantly over time.

If you decide to stick with Jet front ends linked to MSDE 2000, instead of moving to ADP, you gain most of the advantages of SQL Server 2000 without the pain and suffering of rewriting complex Jet applications for ADP compliance. Query performance won't match that of views and stored procedures, but your crosstab queries execute without modification, and all Jet and VBA query functions remain intact. If MSDE provides the database back end, just create a simple Access project that connects to the SQL Server database to manage occasional table modifications.

CHAPTER 21

Moving from Jet Queries to Transact-SQL

In this chapter

UNDERSTANDING THE ROLE OF SQL IN ACCESS 2003

This chapter describes Structured Query Language (SQL), the grammar of the language, and SQL Server's dialect of ANSI-92 SQL called Transact-SQL (T-SQL). Earlier chapters have demonstrated how Access translates queries you build in its Query Design view into Jet SQL statements. Jet SQL is another SQL dialect that closely resembles T-SQL, but Jet SQL lacks T-SQL's support for views and its extensions for functions, stored procedures, and linked servers. Jet SQL is unique in its support for VBA functions—such as **CCur**() and **DatePart**()—in queries. T-SQL has equivalents to many VBA functions, but the usage syntax differs.

SQL (usually pronounced "sequel" or "seekel," but more properly "ess-cue-ell") is the common language of client/server database management. The principal advantage of SQL is that it's standardized—you can use a common set of SQL statements with all SQL-compliant database-management systems. The first U.S. SQL standard was established in 1986 as ANSI X3.135-1986. The current version is ANSI X3.135-1992, usually known as SQL-92. ANSI is an acronym for the American National Standards Institute. X3.135 is the code name for the ANSI subcommittee that's responsible for editing and publishing SQL standards documentation. The corresponding International Standards Organization (ISO) standard is ISO/IEC 9075:1992.

SQL is an application language for relational databases, not a system or programming language. SQL is a set-oriented language, not a procedural language like VBA. ANSI SQL includes neither a provision for program flow control (branching and looping) nor keywords to create data-entry forms and print reports. Publishers of ANSI SQL-compliant RDBMSs are free to extend the language if the basic ANSI commands are supported in accordance with the standards. Unlike standards (called *recommendations*) for HTML, XML, and other Web-related languages coordinated by the World Wide Web Consortium (W3C), updates to ANSI SQL are few and far between. The latest standard is SQL-99 (called *SQL3* during the seven-year standards process), which supports hierarchical, network, and other database models, not just relational databases.

NOTE

SQL-99 hasn't generated much interest among RDBMS vendors or purchasers. When this book was written, searching the Microsoft Web site with SQL-99, SQL-1999, and similar combinations returned only a few valid hits. According to Microsoft's Richard Waymire, an SQL Server product manager, "...SQL3 was only finalized after most of our development work was done for this [SQL Server 2000] release."

An SQL background helps you understand the query process, and design more efficient Jet SQL and T-SQL queries. You need a basic knowledge of SQL to write subqueries and UNION queries and for any application that uses VBA to generate Recordsets for populating list and combo boxes. Simple examples of Jet SQL and T-SQL are presented in other chapters in this book. These examples demonstrate what occurs behind the scenes when you create a query using either of Access's visual Query by Example (QBE) tools. QBE is the original name for pre-Windows query tools that emulate query-design grids in text-only displays. Almost all graphical query-design tools are based on early QBE techniques.

You probably can use Jet's Query Design window to generate the SQL statements for 90% or more of the queries you need to support conventional Access applications. (You must write `UNION` and pass-through queries in the SQL window.) The graphical project designer (also called the da Vinci toolset) is likely to cover 75% or so of your query needs for Access Data Projects (ADP); you must write the remaining 25% in T-SQL. T-SQL offers many additional features, such as `IF...ELSE` and `WHILE` statements for flow control within queries. Taking advantage of most of the features of SQL Server 2000 requires at least the ability to modify T-SQL statements you create with the project designer.

TIP

> Learn SQL by osmosis. Each time you design a query in Jet's Query Design view or the project designer for ADP, open the SQL window or pane and read the underlying SQL statement. The relationship between the SQL statement and graphic query design is evident for simple queries. As you advance to more complex queries with joins and aggregate functions, carefully compare the SQL statement with the contents of the QBE grid. Over time, you'll find that SQL lives up to its original name, SEQUEL–Structured *English* Query Language.

UNDERSTANDING SQL GRAMMAR

When you learn the grammar of a new language, it's helpful to categorize the vocabulary of the language by usage and then into the familiar parts of speech. SQL commands, therefore, first are divided into six usage categories:

- *Data Query Language (DQL)* consists of commands that obtain data from tables and determines how the results of the retrieval are presented. The `SELECT` command is the principal instruction in this category.
- *Data Manipulation Language (DML)* provides `INSERT` and `DELETE` commands, which add or delete entire rows, and the `UPDATE` command, which changes the values of data in specified columns within rows.
- *Transaction Processing Language (TPL)* includes `BEGIN TRAN[SACTION]`, `COMMIT [TRAN[SACTION]¦WORK]`, and `ROLLBACK [TRAN[SACTION]¦WORK]`, which group multiple DML operations. If one DML operation of a transaction fails, the preceding DML operations are canceled (rolled back). Jet 4.0 SQL and T-SQL implement `BEGIN TRANSACTION`, `COMMIT TRANSACTION¦WORK`, and `ROLLBACK TRANSACTION¦WORK`; only T-SQL supports the `TRAN` abbreviation.
- *Data Definition Language (DDL)* includes `CREATE¦ALTER TABLE`, `ADD¦ALTER COLUMN`, and `CREATE VIEW` instructions that define the structure of tables and views. DDL commands also are used to modify tables and to create and delete indexes. The keywords that

implement declarative referential integrity (DRI) are used with DDL statements. Jet SQL and T-SQL support the `[CREATE¦ALTER] TABLE` and `[CREATE¦ALTER} INDEX` instructions; T-SQL offers non-ANSI `ALTER VIEW`, `[CREATE¦ALTER] FUNCTION`, and `[CREATE¦ALTER] PROCEDURE` statements.

- *Cursor Control Language (CCL)* can select a single row of a query result set for processing. Cursor control constructs, such as `UPDATE WHERE CURRENT`, are handled by ADO's cursor engine or the Jet database engine, so these commands aren't discussed in this chapter.
- *Data Control Language (DCL)* performs administrative functions that grant and revoke privileges to use the database, such as `GRANT` and `REVOKE`, a set of tables within the database, or specific SQL commands. DCL sometimes is called *Data Security Language*.

Keywords that make up the vocabulary of SQL are identified further in the following categories:

- *Commands*, such as `SELECT`, `EXECUTE`, `CREATE`, and `ALTER`, are verbs that cause an action to be performed.
- *Qualifiers*, such as `WHERE`, limit the range of values of the entities that constitute the query.
- *Clauses*, such as `ORDER BY`, modify the action of an instruction.
- *Predicates*, such as `IN`, `ALL`, `ANY`, `SOME`, `LIKE`, and `UNIQUE`, are expressions that test facts about data values. Predicates can return a `TRUE`, `FALSE`, or, in some cases, `NULL` (unknown) result. These three values are SQL keywords.
- *Operators*, such as =, <, or >, compare values and specify joins with a `WHERE` clause or `JOIN` syntax. Jet SQL and T-SQL use `JOIN` syntax by default. Operators also are called *comparison predicates*.
- *Group aggregate functions*, such as `COUNT()`, `MAX()`, and `MIN()`, return a single result for a set of values.
- *Data type conversions functions* change values from one data type to another. `CAST()` and `CONVERT()` are the most commonly-used conversion functions.
- *Utility functions* return values determined by expressions. You can use `NULLIF()`, for example, to return a `NULL` value if the function's expression evaluates to `TRUE`. Date/time and string manipulation functions also fit into the utility category.

→ For more information on the relationship between VBA and T-SQL utility functions, **see** "VBA Functions That Upsize to SQL Server Functions," **p. 917**, and "VBA Functions That You Must Manually Convert to Related SQL Server Functions," **p. 917**.

- *Other keywords* (or reserved words) modify the action of a clause or manipulate cursors that are used to select specific rows of queries. The T-SQL `FOR XML [AUTO¦RAW¦EXPLICIT]` modifier, for example, returns an XML document or subdocument instead of a conventional Recordset from a `SELECT` query. `FOR XML` isn't included in ANSI SQL.

NOTE

SQL keywords usually are capitalized, but the keywords aren't case sensitive. The uppercase convention is used in this book, and SQL keywords are set in monospace type. You use parameters, such as *column_list*, to define or modify the action specified by keywords. Names of replaceable parameters are printed in lowercase italicized monospace type.

ANSI SQL defines *reserved words*, such as SELECT, and *nonreserved words*, such as DATA and FORTRAN. *Keywords* include both reserved and nonreserved words. All the keywords used in this chapter are reserved words; you can't use a reserved word as the name of an object, such as a table.

WRITING SELECT QUERIES IN SQL

The heart of SQL is the SELECT statement used to return a specified set of records from one or more tables. The following lines of syntax are used for an SQL SELECT statement that returns a virtual query table (called a result set, usually a Recordset object) of all or selected columns (fields) from all or qualifying rows (records) of a source table:

```
SELECT [ALL¦DISTINCT¦DISTINCTROW] [TOP n [PERCENT]] select_list
   FROM table_names
  [WHERE search_criteria]
  [ORDER BY column_criteria [ASC¦DESC]]
```

The following list shows the purpose of the elements in this basic select query statement:

- SELECT is the basic command that specifies a query. The *select_list* parameter determines the fields (columns) that are included in the result table of the query. When you design a graphical query, the *select_list* parameter is determined by the fields you add to the Fields row in the Query grid. Only those fields with the Show check box marked are included in the *select_list*. Multiple field names are separated by commas.

  The optional ALL, DISTINCT, and *DISTINCTROW* qualifiers determine how rows are handled. ALL specifies that all rows are to be included, subject to subsequent limitation. DISTINCT eliminates rows with duplicate data in both Jet SQL and T-SQL. *DISTINCTROW* is a Jet SQL keyword, similar to T-SQL's DISTINCT, that eliminates duplicate rows but also enables you to change values in the query result set. T-SQL doesn't support *DISTINCTROW*, so the preceding is the only example in this chapter that includes this qualifier.

  The optional TOP *n* [PERCENT] modifier limits the query result set to returning the first *n* rows or *n* percent of the result set prior to the limitation. TOP and PERCENT are Jet SQL and T-SQL, not ANSI SQL, keywords. You use the TOP modifier to speed display when you want to display only the most significant rows of a query result set. TOP 100 PERCENT, which returns all rows, is required to create SQL Server views that you can sort with the ORDER BY clause.

- FROM *table_name* specifies the name or names of the table or tables that form the basis for the query. The *table_name* parameter is created in QBE by the selections you make in the Add Table dialog. If fields from more than one table are included in the *select_list*, each table should be specified in the *table_name* parameter. You must prepend table names to field names that are present in both tables (see the following Caution). Commas separate the names of multiple tables.

- WHERE *search_criteria* determines which records from the select list are displayed. The *search_criteria* is an expression with a predicate, such as LIKE or = for text fields, or a numeric operator, such as <, > or >=, for fields with numeric values. The WHERE clause is optional; if you don't add a WHERE clause, the query returns all the rows from the table specified by FROM *table_name*.
- ORDER BY *column_criteria* specifies the sorting order of the result set. Like the WHERE clause, ORDER BY is optional. You can specify an ascending or descending sort by the optional ASC or DESC keywords. If you don't specify a sort direction, ascending is the default.

CAUTION

> If you add fields from two or more tables and don't join the tables by a WHERE *Table1.Field1* = *Table2.Field2* clause or a JOIN statement, the statement returns a combination of all rows of all tables, called a *Cartesian product*. Executing such a statement against tables on a remote machine can generate enough traffic to bring a network to its knees. ADP datasheets have a default maximum of 10,000 rows to prevent an accidental Cartesian product from consuming all SQL Server resources for a substantial period.

Using SQL Punctuation and Symbols

In addition to the comparison operators used for expressions, SQL uses commas, periods, semicolons, and colons as punctuation. The following list of symbols and punctuation is used in T-SQL, which follows ANSI standards, and Jet SQL; differences between the two SQL dialects are noted where appropriate:

- **Commas**—Used to separate members of lists of parameters, such as multiple field names, as in Name, Address, City, ZIP.
- **Square brackets**—Square brackets surrounding field names are required only when the field name includes spaces or other symbols—including punctuation—not allowed by ANSI SQL, as in [Order Details]. Square brackets also must surround names you assign in the grid to input parameters for Jet queries.
- **Periods**—Separate named objects of a subordinate class. For example, if fields of more than one table are involved in the query, a period is used to separate the table name from the field name, as in [Order Details].OrderID. Four-part names of linked tables in FROM statements use the *Server.Database.Schema.Table* format.

21

→ For an example of linked tables and four-part names, **see** "Linking a Remote SQL Server Database," **p. 844**.

- **String identifiers (also called delimiters)**—Designate literal character values. ANSI SQL requires the single quote symbol (') to enclose literal string values. You can use the double quote (") or the single quote symbol to enclose literal values in Jet SQL statements. Using the single quote makes writing SQL statements in VBA easier. For backward compatibility with SQL Server 7.0 and earlier, T-SQL interprets the double quote as a square bracket.
- **Wildcards**—Differ in Jet and ANSI SQL. ANSI SQL uses `%` and `_` symbols as the wildcards for the `LIKE` statement, rather than the `*` (asterisk) to specify zero or more characters and `?` to specify a single character in Jet SQL. The Jet wildcards correspond to the wildcards used in specifying DOS group file names.
- **Date/time identifier**—Jet also requires the `#` symbol to enclose date/time values in expressions. ANSI SQL accepts date values in a variety of character formats enclosed by single quotes. Jet also uses the `#` wildcard for the `LIKE` statement to represent any single digit. ANSI SQL doesn't support use of the `#` symbol in queries.
- **`:` and `@` identifiers for variables**—ANSI SQL uses `:` as a prefix to identify variables that receive parameter values (sometimes called *host variables*). T-SQL uses `@` for conventional variables (including variables to receive parameter values) and `@@` for variables whose values SQL Server supplies, such as `@@IDENTITY`, which returns the current value of the identity column of a table. Jet SQL handles input parameters by an entirely different method, and doesn't support declaring variables in SQL statements.
- **`!` (the exclamation mark or bang symbol)**—Synonym for `NOT` in ANSI SQL. ANSI (not equal) operator> SQL uses `!=` for not equal; T-SQL and Jet SQL use <>, but T-SQL also supports `!=`.

As the preceding list demonstrates, relatively minor differences exist in the availability and use of punctuation and symbols between ANSI and Jet SQL. These minor differences, however, can cause a major difference in the behavior of Jet and SQL Server

TRANSLATING SQL STATEMENTS INTO QBE DESIGNS

When you create a `SELECT` query in Query Design mode, Access translates the graphical query design into a Jet SQL `SELECT` statement. Similarly, the project designer for ADP generates T-SQL from your selections in the fields list and entries in the designer grid. The SQL translation operation is bidirectional; when you type an SQL statement into Jet's SQL window or the SQL pane of the project designer, the graphical QBE view changes. Jet queries make you change from Query Design to SQL view. Clicking the Check SQL Syntax button updates the designer's top and middle panes.

> **TIP**
>
> If you want to compare Jet and SQL Server QBE translation directly, open two instances of Access 2003—one with Northwind.mdb as the current database and the other with NorthwindCS.adp as the current project.

➔ If you haven't run NorthwindCS.adp to create the NorthwindCS MSDE database, **see** "Exploring the NorthwindCS Sample Project," **p. 808**.

CREATING JET QUERY DESIGNS

To generate Jet query designs (`QueryDef` objects) from SQL statements in Northwind.mdb, do this:

1. In the Queries page of the Database window, double-click the Create Query in Design View shortcut to open a new query in Design view.
2. Close the Show Table dialog, and click the SQL view button to open the Query1: Select Query SQL window. The window opens with a default `SELECT;` query fragment.
3. Type the SQL statement in the window (see Figure 21.1 and the following Jet SQL box), and select Design view to display the graphical version of the query.

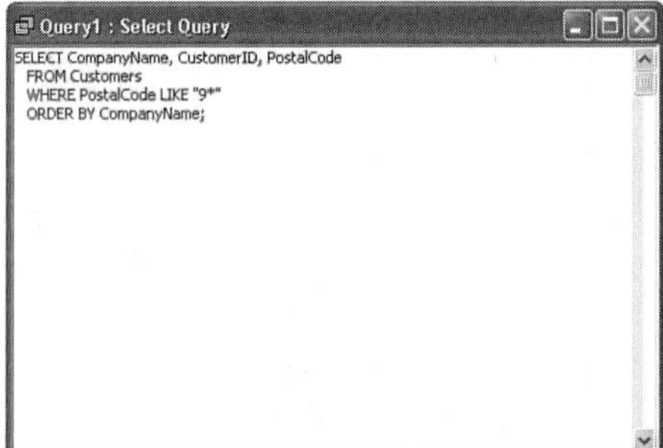

Figure 21.1
Type the SQL statement in Jet's SQL window. Unfortunately, the standard font size is 8 points, which makes reading what you type difficult in high-resolution modes. You can't change the font size.

4. Click Run to display the result of your query in Datasheet view.

Saving the queries is optional. To generate a new query, delete the SQL text and start over.

Jet SQL

The following lines are an example of a simple Jet SQL query statement using default character identifiers and the `*` wildcard:

```
SELECT CompanyName, CustomerID, PostalCode
   FROM Customers
   WHERE PostalCode LIKE "9*"
   ORDER BY CompanyName;
```

Jet SQL terminates statements by adding a semicolon immediately after the last character on the last line. If you don't type the semicolon, Access's query parser adds it for you.

NOTE

> Examples of SQL statements in this book are formatted to make the examples more readable. Access doesn't format its Jet SQL statements. When you enter or edit SQL statements in the SQL window, formatting these statements so that commands appear on individual lines makes the SQL statements more intelligible. Indented lines indicate continuation of a preceding line or a clause that is dependent on a keyword in a preceding line. Use Ctrl+Enter to insert newline pairs (the carriage return and new line characters, CrLf) before SQL keywords. Jet SQL and T-SQL ignore spaces and newline pairs (called *whitespace*) when processing the SQL statement.

The preceding Jet SQL statement creates the query design shown in Figure 21.2.

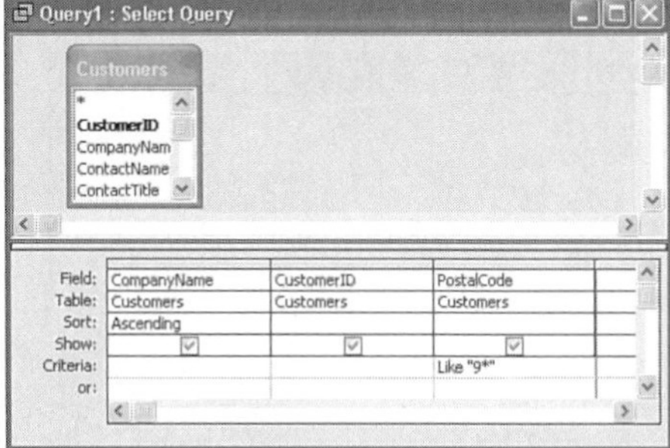

Figure 21.2
The Jet SQL statement of Figure 21.1 creates this simple query design. The Jet query parser causes changes you make in the SQL window to appear immediately in the Query Design window.

WORKING WITH SQL SERVER VIEWS

Views are SQL Server's most common incarnation of `SELECT` queries, but you also can return query result sets from in-line functions and stored procedures. To create a view from an SQL statement in the project designer for ADP, do this:

1. In the Queries page of the Database window, double-click the Create View in Designer shortcut to open a new view.

2. Close the Add Table dialog, and click the SQL button to add the SQL text pane. The pane contains a default `SELECT...FROM` fragment.
3. Type the SQL statement in the pane. If you use the preceding Jet SQL query, the designer automatically adds the `TOP 100 PERCENT` to accommodate the ORDER BY clause, but it's a good practice to add the modifier yourself. You must change `LIKE "9*"` to `LIKE '9%'` to comply with T-SQL syntax (see Figure 21.3).

4. Click Check SQL Syntax, and acknowledge the syntax verification message, to display the QBE version of the query in the top two panes (see Figure 21.4). Clicking either of the QBE panes also refreshes them.

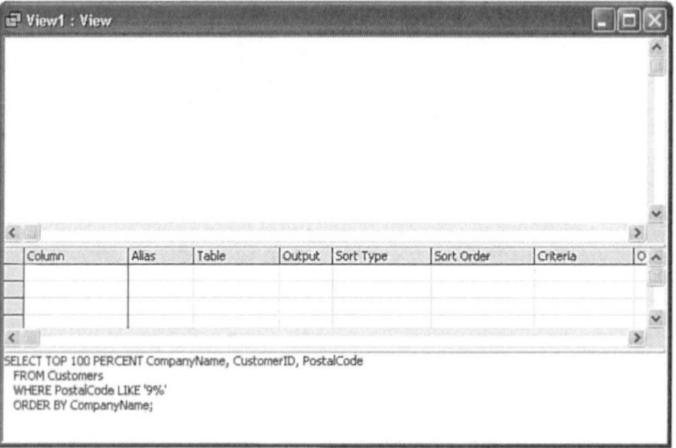

Figure 21.3
This T-SQL query requires `TOP 100 PERCENT` to support the `ORDER BY` clause and use of T-SQL compliant string identifiers and wildcards.

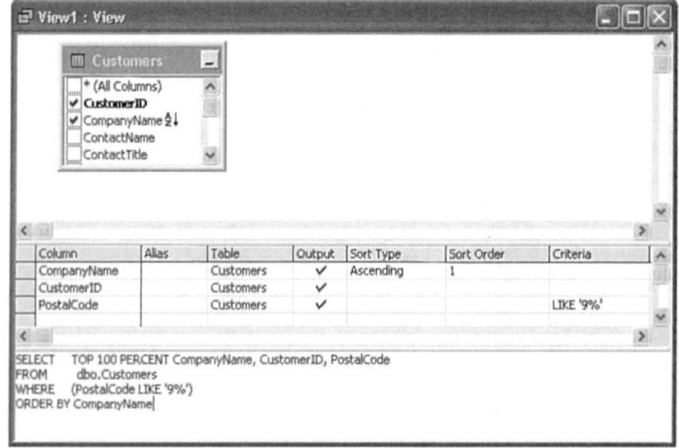

Figure 21.4
When you check the SQL syntax, the project designer reformats the SQL statement, adds the `dbo.` (schema) prefix to table name(s), and adds parentheses to the `WHERE` clause.

5. Click Run to display the result of your query in Datasheet view (see Figure 21.5). Unlike Jet, you must save the view to the SQL Server database before you can execute it.

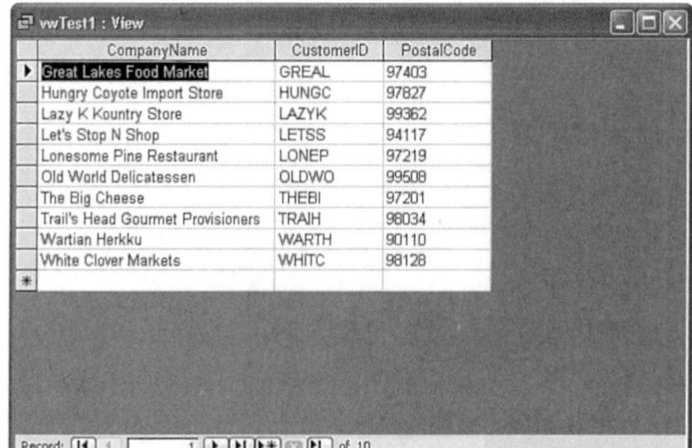

Figure 21.5
The query result set of the view design of Figure 21.4 is updatable, as indicated by the empty tentative append record.

If you copy or type the preceding Jet SQL statement into the project designer's SQL pane without making the changes described in step 3, and then click the Check SQL Syntax button, you receive an "ADO error: Invalid column name '9*'" error message, because SQL Server's query parser interprets the double-quotes as a column identifier. Changing double- to single-quotes eliminates the error message, adds `TOP 100 PERCENT`, changes the statement's format, and removes the trailing semicolon. When you execute the SQL statement, the view has no rows because T-SQL doesn't recognize the * wildcard and interprets the `LIKE` predicate as the two-character string '9*'. Change `*` to `%`, and the view returns the expected Recordset.

T-SQL

Following is the T-SQL statement corresponding to the earlier Jet SQL version, with the required changes in bold type:

```
CREATE VIEW vwTest1 AS
SELECT TOP 100 PERCENT CompanyName, CustomerID, PostalCode
   FROM Customers
   WHERE PostalCode LIKE '9%'
   ORDER BY CompanyName
```

The project designer's SQL pane hides the required `[CREATE¦ALTER] VIEW view_name AS` statement.

USING THE SQL AGGREGATE FUNCTIONS AND WRITING IN-LINE FUNCTIONS

If you want to use the aggregate functions to determine totals, averages, or statistical data for groups of records with a common attribute value, you add a `GROUP BY` clause to your SQL statement.

TIP

T-SQL queries that use the `SUM()` aggregate function and `GROUP BY` clauses are the first step in the laborious process of emulating Jet crosstab queries with T-SQL.

→ For instructions on how to emulate crosstab queries with T-SQL, **see** "Emulating Jet Crosstab Queries with T-SQL," **p. 918**.

You can further limit the result of the `GROUP BY` clause with the optional `HAVING` qualifier:

```
SELECT [ALL¦DISTINCT] [TOP n [PERCENT]]
      aggregate_function(field_name) AS alias_name
     [, select_list]
   FROM table_names
  [WHERE search_criteria]
   GROUP BY group_criteria
     [HAVING aggregate_criteria]
  [ORDER BY column_criteria]
```

The *`select_list`* includes the *`aggregate_function`* with a *`field_name`* as its argument. The field used as the argument of an aggregate function must have a numeric data type. The following list describes the additional required and optional SQL keywords and parameters to create a `GROUP BY` query:

- AS *alias_name* assigns a caption to the column. The caption is created in an Access query by the alias:*aggregate_function(field name)* entry in the Field row of the Query grid.
- GROUP BY *group_criteria* establishes the column(s) on which the grouping is based. In this column, GROUP BY appears in the Totals row of the Query grid. The GROUP BY clause is required for aggregate queries.
- HAVING *aggregate_criteria* applies one or more criteria to the column that contains the *aggregate_function*. The *aggregate_criteria* of HAVING is applied after the grouping is completed. The HAVING clause is optional.
- WHERE *search_criteria* operates before the grouping occurs; at this point, no aggregate values exist to test against *aggregate_criteria*. Access substitutes HAVING for WHERE when you add criteria to a column with the *aggregate_function*. The WHERE clause is optional, but seldom is missing from an aggregate query.

Jet queries and SQL Server views that use aggregate functions aren't updatable.

TIP

Current releases of most client/server RDBMSs support the ANSI SQL AS *alias_name* construct. Early versions of SQL Server, Sybase System 10+, and IBM DB2, as examples, substitute a space for the AS keyword, as in SELECT *field_name alias_name*, ... (SQL Server 7+ accepts either AS or a space.) Some ODBC drivers for these databases use special codes (called escape syntax) to change from Jet/ANSI use of AS to the space separator. If you use ADO with VBA or Jet SQL pass-through queries with some client/server RDBMSs, you might need to use the space separator, not the AS keyword.

Jet SQL

The following Jet GROUP BY query is written in ANSI SQL, except for the # symbols that enclose date and time values:

```
SELECT TOP 100 PERCENT ShipRegion,
      SUM(Freight) AS [Total Freight]
   FROM Orders
   WHERE ShipCountry='USA'
      AND OrderDate BETWEEN #1/1/1997# AND #12/31/1997#
   GROUP BY ShipRegion
   HAVING SUM(Freight)>=100
   ORDER BY SUM(Freight) DESC
```

The query returns a result set that consists of two columns: ShipRegion (states) and the totals of Freight for any shipping region where the total freight charges for that region is greater than or equal to 100 in 1997. The result set is sorted in descending order. The TOP 100 PERCENT modifier isn't required for Jet ORDER BY clauses, but doesn't affect performance.

Figure 21.6 illustrates the Jet Query Design view for the preceding SQL statement.

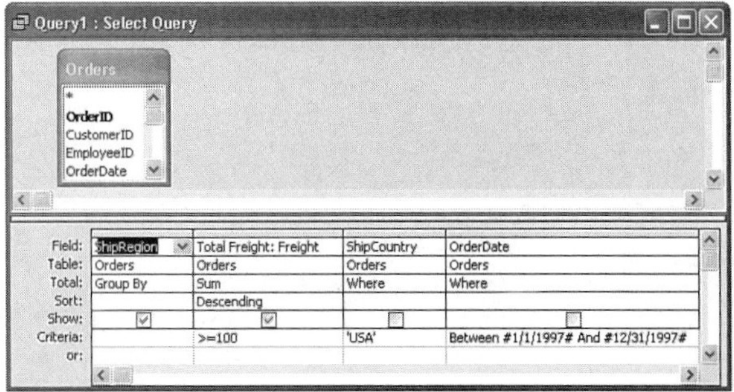

Figure 21.6
The only clue to the presence of a `HAVING` criterion is the `>=100` criterion in the aggregate (Sum) column in Jet Query Design view.

The Jet query design of Figure 21.6 returns seven rows with ShipRegion and Total Freight columns. If you remove the `HAVING` expression, the result set has eight rows.

If you encounter an Enter Parameter dialog when you attempt to run a Jet SQL query, see "Unexpected Enter Parameter Dialogs" of the "Troubleshooting" section near the end of the chapter.

Table-valued functions can substitute for or augment views. To create an SQL Server in-line table-valued function from an SQL statement, do this:

1. In the Queries page of NorthwindCS's Database window, click New Query to open the New Query dialog.
2. Double-click Design In-line Function to open the Function1: Function window and the Add Table dialog.

3. Close the Add Table dialog, and click the SQL button to add the SQL pane.
4. Type the following T-SQL statement in the SQL pane.

T-SQL

You also must substitute single-quotes for the # date/time delimiters of the Jet SQL query to create the following T-SQL version:

```
SELECT TOP 100 PERCENT ShipRegion,
      SUM(Freight) AS [Total Freight]
   FROM Orders
   WHERE ShipCountry='USA'
      AND OrderDate BETWEEN '1/1/1997' AND '12/31/1997'
   GROUP BY ShipRegion
   HAVING SUM(Freight)>=100
   ORDER BY SUM(Freight) DESC
```

5. Click the Check SQL Syntax button to verify the syntax and populate the upper two panes of the project designer (see Figure 21.7).

21

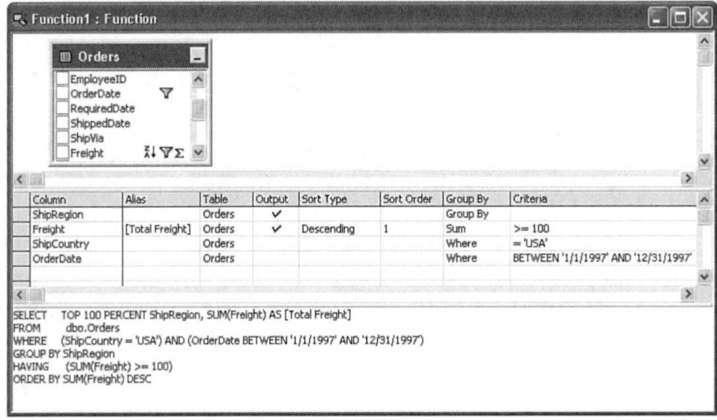

Column	Alias	Table	Output	Sort Type	Sort Order	Group By	Criteria
ShipRegion		Orders	✓			Group By	
Freight	[Total Freight]	Orders	✓	Descending	1	Sum	>= 100
ShipCountry		Orders				Where	= 'USA'
OrderDate		Orders				Where	BETWEEN '1/1/1997' AND '12/31/1997'

Figure 21.7 Other than the name in the designer's title bar, in-line table-valued functions appear identical in the project designer to a view with the same SQL statement.

6. Click the Run button and save your function with a descriptive name, such as **fn1997Freight**.

Datasheet view of the result set returned by the function is identical to that of the Jet query, with the exception of the name.

TIP

> Use in-line table-valued functions instead of stored procedures to generate the equivalent of a parameterized view. Result sets returned by simple table-valued `SELECT` functions are updatable in Datasheet view. SQL Server views don't support parameters, and the Recordsets returned by stored procedures aren't updatable.

→ To review adding parameters to in-line functions, **see** "Creating a Parameterized Table-Returning Function," **p. 825**.

CREATING JOINS WITH SQL

Joining two or more tables with the Jet query designer or the project designer uses the ANSI-92 `JOIN...ON` structure that specifies the table to be joined and the relationship between the fields on which the `JOIN` is based:

```
SELECT [ALL¦DISTINCT]select_list
   FROM
   table_name [INNER¦LEFT [OUTER]¦RIGHT [OUTER]]¦FULL [OUTER]]
      JOIN join_table ON join_criteria
  [table_name [INNER¦LEFT [OUTER]¦RIGHT [OUTER]]¦FULL [OUTER]]
      JOIN join_table ON join_criteria]
  [WHERE search_criteria]
  [ORDER BY column_criteria]
```

The following list describes the elements of the `JOIN` statement:

21

- `table_name [INNER¦LEFT [OUTER]¦RIGHT [OUTER]]¦ JOIN` *`join_table`* specifies the name of the table that's joined with other tables listed in *`table_name`*. When you specify a self-join by including two copies of the field list for a single table, the second table is distinguished from the first by adding an underscore and a digit to alias the table name.

> **NOTE**
>
> One of the four types of joins, `INNER`, `FULL`, `LEFT`, or `RIGHT` must precede the `JOIN` statement in Jet queries, but `INNER` is optional in T-SQL. `INNER` specifies an inner join; `LEFT` specifies a left outer join; `RIGHT` specifies a right outer join. The `OUTER` qualifier for `LEFT` and `RIGHT JOINs` is optional. `OUTER` is optional for `FULL` joins.

- `ON` *`join_criteria`* specifies the two fields to be joined and the relationship between the joined fields. One field is in *`join_table`* and the other is in a table that's included in *`table_names`*. The *`join_criteria`* expression usually contains an equal sign (=) comparison operator and returns a true or false value. Other comparison operators, such as `If`, and the value of the expression is true, the record in the joined table is included in the query.

The number of `JOIN` statements you can add to a query usually is the total number of tables participating in the query minus one. You can create more than one `JOIN` between a pair of tables, but the result often is difficult to predict.

Jet SQL

The following Jet SQL statement, which was created in Query Design view, defines `INNER JOINs` (also called natural joins) between the Orders, Order Details, Products, and Categories tables:

```
SELECT Orders.OrderID, Products.ProductName,
   Categories.CategoryName
FROM Categories INNER JOIN
       (Products INNER JOIN
          (Orders INNER JOIN
          [Order Details] ON Orders.OrderID =
       [Order Details].OrderID) ON Products.ProductID =
     [Order Details].ProductID) ON Categories.CategoryID =
         Products.CategoryID
```

The result set returns a list of products and their category for every order. You can copy this SQL statement from the Jet SQL window into the project designer for a view, table-valued function, or stored procedure to generate the same result set.

If you copy the preceding SQL statement to the SQL pane of an SQL Server view or function and click Check SQL Syntax, the designer adds the `dbo.` prefix to all table and field references, reformats the SQL statement, and reverses the left-to-right order of the tables in the top pane. Figure 21.8 shows the T-SQL version with additional manual formatting of the `JOIN` statements to clarify the nesting of the `JOIN` and `ON` elements of the query.

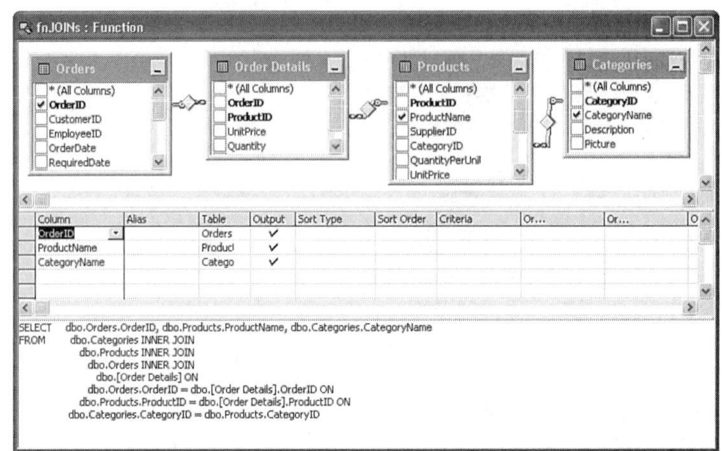

Figure 21.8
Multiple, nested `JOIN` statements aren't easy to write from scratch or read after you've defined them. If you omit the optional `INNER` prefixes, the SQL Server query parser inserts them when you test the syntax.

You can create joins in ANSI SQL with the `WHERE` clause, using the same expression to join the fields as that of the `ON` clause in the `JOIN` command. It's much simpler to write SQL statements using `WHERE` clauses to create relationships than to employ the `JOIN` syntax. Queries using `WHERE` clauses to create joins, however, aren't updatable.

Jet SQL

The following ANSI SQL-89 statement returns the same result set as the preceding Jet SQL statement in Figure 21.8, except that the result set isn't updatable:

```
SELECT Orders.OrderID, Products.ProductName,
      Categories.CategoryName
   FROM Orders, [Order Details], Products, Categories
   WHERE Orders.OrderID = [Order Details].OrderID
      AND Products.ProductID = [Order Details].ProductID
      AND Categories.CategoryID = Products.CategoryID;
```

In versions of SQL Server prior to 7.0, you could specify joins only with `WHERE` clauses.

T-SQL

If you type or copy the preceding Jet SQL statement into the project designer and then click Check SQL Syntax, the query parser insists on converting the `WHERE` clause to `INNER JOIN` structures:

```
SELECT dbo.Orders.OrderID, dbo.Products.ProductName,
dbo.Categories.CategoryName
FROM INNER JOIN dbo.[Order Details]
        ON dbo.Orders.OrderID =
           dbo.[Order Details].OrderID
     INNER JOIN dbo.Products
        ON dbo.[Order Details].ProductID =
           dbo.Products.ProductID
     INNER JOIN dbo.Categories
        ON dbo.Products.CategoryID =
           dbo.Categories.CategoryID
```

In this case, however, the JOINs aren't nested, which makes them easier to read. If you remove the "optional" INNER qualifiers, the query parser inserts them when you check the syntax or save the view.

If you want to preserve WHERE clause join syntax in a T-SQL query, you must write the query in a query execution tool, such as the SQL Server Client Tools' Query Analyzer. Alternatively, you can save your query as an SQL script and execute it with MSDE's OSQL command-line tool. In this case, you must prefix the T-SQL statement with CREATE VIEW *ViewName* AS or CREATE FUNCTION *FunctionName* AS to create the view or function. You execute the view or function with a SELECT * FROM *ViewOrFunctionName* statement.

→ For a brief explanation of the use of OSQL, **see** "Adding User Logins with the OSQL Utility," **p. 778**.

USING UNION QUERIES

UNION queries let you combine the result set of two or more SELECT queries into a single result set. Northwind.mdb includes an example of a UNION query, Customers and Orders by City, which has the special symbol of two overlapping circles, in the Database window. The NorthwindCS database doesn't include a corresponding view. You can create Jet and SQL Server UNION queries only with SQL statements. The general syntax of UNION queries is as follows:

```
SELECT select_statement
   UNION SELECT select_statement
     [GROUP BY group_criteria]
     [HAVING aggregate criteria]
  [UNION SELECT select_statement
     [GROUP BY group_criteria]
     [HAVING aggregate criteria]]
  [UNION...]
  [ORDER BY column_criteria]
```

The restrictions on statements that create UNION queries are the following:

- The number of fields in the *field_list* of each SELECT and UNION SELECT query must be the same. You receive an error message if the number of fields isn't the same.
- The sequence of the field names in each *field_list* must correspond to similar entities. You don't receive an error message for dissimilar entities, but the result set is likely to be unfathomable. In Jet UNION queries, the field data types in a single column need not correspond; if the column of the result set contains Jet numeric and text data types, the data type of the column is set (coerced) to Text. T-SQL doesn't support automatically coercing dissimilar data types in a single column.
- Only one ORDER BY clause is allowed, and it must follow the last UNION SELECT statement. You can add GROUP BY and HAVING clauses to each SELECT and UNION SELECT statement if needed.

21

The following SQL statement creates a UNION query combining rows from the Customers and Suppliers tables:

```
SELECT TOP 100 PERCENT City, CompanyName,
      ContactName, 'Customer' AS Relationship
   FROM Customers
UNION SELECT TOP 100 PERCENT City, CompanyName,
      ContactName, 'Supplier'
   FROM Suppliers
ORDER BY City, CompanyName
```

The preceding statement, which illustrates adding a field (Relationship) with a constant value (Customer) in each row, is valid in Jet SQL and T-SQL. Enclosing an element of a field list in single quotes defines it as a constant value. `TOP 100 PERCENT` in each `SELECT` statement is required for use of the `GROUP BY` clause in T-SQL.

Jet SQL

You can alter the preceding statement to include the CustomerID and SupplierID fields in a Jet SQL query, as follows:

```
SELECT TOP 100 PERCENT City, CustomerID AS Code, CompanyName,
      ContactName, 'Customer' AS Relationship
   FROM Customers
UNION SELECT TOP 100 PERCENT City, SupplierID AS Code, CompanyName,
      ContactName, 'Supplier'
   FROM Suppliers
ORDER BY City, CompanyName
```

The syntax of the SQL statement illustrates the capability of Jet `UNION` queries to include values from two different field data types, Text (CustomerID) and Long Integer (SupplierID), in the single, aliased Code column. SQL Server won't execute this query.

T-SQL

You must use the T-SQL `CAST()` or `CONVERT()` function to conform dissimilar data types to a single data type for a column returned by a `UNION` query. Use the `CAST()` function as shown in the following example:

```
SELECT TOP 100 PERCENT City, CustomerID AS Code,
      CompanyName, ContactName,
      'Customer' AS Relationship
   FROM Customers
UNION SELECT TOP 100 PERCENT City,
       CAST(SupplierID AS varchar(5)) AS Code,
       CompanyName, ContactName, 'Supplier'
   FROM Suppliers
ORDER BY City, CompanyName
```

You can't convert five-character CustomerID values to integers, but you can convert integer SupplierID values to a string. You must know the target SQL Server data type (`varchar(5)`, a 5-character variable length character field in this example) to use `CAST()`. `CAST()` is the most common replacement for the VBA type conversion functions, such as **`CCur()`**. Open the table (Customers) in Design view to obtain the SQL Server data type for the `CAST()` function.

21

After clicking Check SQL Syntax with a `UNION` query statement in the project designer's SQL pane and acknowledging the syntax check, a "Query Definitions Differ" error message appears. In some cases, the error message occurs before the syntax verification message. These error messages appear because the project designer can't represent `UNION` queries graphically; you can ignore them by clicking Yes in the Query Definitions Differ dialog.

Figure 21.9 shows the Datasheet view of the preceding T-SQL query. Datasheet view of the equivalent Jet query is identical, except for the title bar caption. `UNION` queries, like queries returning SQL aggregate functions, aren't updatable.

Figure 21.9
The result set for the Jet SQL and T-SQL versions of the `UNION` query against the Customers and Suppliers tables is the same.

vwUnion : View

City	Code	CompanyName	ContactName	Relationship
Aachen	DRACD	Drachenblut Delikatessen	Sven Ottlieb	Customer
Albuquerque	RATTC	Rattlesnake Canyon Grocery	Paula Wilson	Customer
Anchorage	OLDWO	Old World Delicatessen	Rene Phillips	Customer
Ann Arbor	3	Grandma Kelly's Homestead	Regina Murphy	Supplier
Annecy	28	Gai pâturage	Eliane Noz	Supplier
Århus	VAFFE	Vaffeljernet	Palle Ibsen	Customer
Barcelona	GALED	Galería del gastrónomo	Eduardo Saavedra	Customer
Barquisimeto	LILAS	LILA-Supermercado	Carlos González	Customer
Bend	16	Bigfoot Breweries	Cheryl Saylor	Supplier
Bergamo	MAGAA	Magazzini Alimentari Riuniti	Giovanni Rovelli	Customer
Berlin	11	Heli Süßwaren GmbH & Co. KG	Petra Winkler	Supplier
Berlin	ALFKI	Alfreds Futterkiste	Maria Anders	Customer
Bern	CHOPS	Chop-suey Chinese	Yang Wang	Customer
Boise	SAVEA	Save-a-lot Markets	Jose Pavarotti	Customer
Boston	19	New England Seafood Cannery	Robb Merchant	Supplier
Bräcke	FOLKO	Folk och fä HB	Maria Larsson	Customer
Brandenburg	KOENE	Königlich Essen	Philip Cramer	Customer
Bruxelles	MAISD	Maison Dewey	Catherine Dewey	Customer
Buenos Aires	CACTU	Cactus Comidas para llevar	Patricio Simpson	Customer
Buenos Aires	OCEAN	Océano Atlántico Ltda.	Yvonne Moncada	Customer
Buenos Aires	RANCH	Rancho grande	Sergio Gutiérrez	Customer
Butte	THECR	The Cracker Box	Liu Wong	Customer

Record: 1 of 120

TIP

Use `UNION` queries to add (All) or other options when populating combo and list boxes. As an example, the following SQL statement adds (All) to the query result set for a combo box used to select orders from a particular country or all countries:

```
SELECT TOP 100 PERCENT Country FROM Customers
   UNION SELECT '(All)'
   FROM Customers
ORDER BY Country;
```

The parentheses around `(All)` causes it to sort at the beginning of the list; the ASCII value of "(" is 40 and "A" is 65. Automatic sorting of combo and list box items uses the ASCII value returned by the VBA **`Asc`** function.

→ For examples of using a `UNION` query to add an (All) item to a combo box, **see** "Adding an Option to Select All Countries or Products," **p. 1244**.

IMPLEMENTING SUBQUERIES

Early versions of Access used nested queries to emulate the subquery capability of ANSI SQL. (A *nested query* is a query executed against the result set of another query. Similarly, a *nested view* executes against another view.) Jet SQL and T-SQL let you write a SELECT query that uses another SELECT query to supply the criteria for the WHERE clause. Depending on the complexity of your query, using a subquery instead of nested queries often improves performance, especially with SQL Server. The general syntax of subqueries is as follows:

```
SELECT [TOP 100 PERCENT] field_list
   FROM table_list
   WHERE [table_name.]field_name
      IN (SELECT [TOP 100 PERCENT] select_statement
            [GROUP BY group_criteria]
            [HAVING aggregate_criteria]
            [ORDER BY sort_criteria])
  [ORDER BY sort_criteria]
```

T-SQL

Following is the T-SQL statement for a sample subquery that returns names and addresses of Northwind Traders customers who placed orders between January 1, 1997, and June 30, 1997:

```
SELECT TOP 100 PERCENT Customers.ContactName,
      Customers.CompanyName, Customers.ContactTitle,
      Customers.Phone
   FROM Customers
   WHERE Customers.CustomerID
      IN (SELECT Orders.CustomerID
            FROM Orders
            WHERE Orders.OrderDate
               BETWEEN '1/1/1997' AND '6/30/1997')
   ORDER BY Customers.CompanyName
```

The SELECT subquery that begins after the IN predicate returns the CustomerID values from the Orders table against which the CustomerID values of the Customers table are compared. The only difference between Jet SQL and T-SQL syntax for subqueries is delimiter characters.

Unlike UNION queries, Jet Query Design view and the project designer support graphical design of subqueries. You type IN, followed by the SELECT statement as the criterion of the appropriate column, enclosing the SELECT statement within the parentheses required by the IN predicate. Figure 21.10 shows the view design generated by the preceding T-SQL statement; Figure 21.11 shows the result set.

NOTE

The simple subquery design of Figure 21.10 offers no benefit over a conventional query that has an INNER JOIN between the Customers and Orders table and the WHERE clause applied to the query result set. Subqueries are most commonly used when the subquery's SQL statement is much more complex than that of this example.

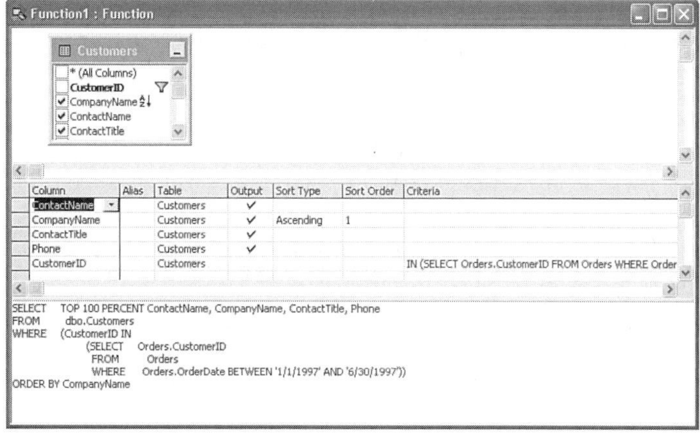

Figure 21.10 The subquery specified for the `IN` predicate appears in the Criteria cell of the field name designated in the `WHERE` clause of the project designer (shown here) and Jet's Query Design view.

fnSubQuery : Function

ContactName	CompanyName	ContactTitle	Phone
Antonio Moreno	Antonio Moreno Taquería	Owner	(5) 555-3932
Thomas Hardy	Around the Horn	Sales Representative	(171) 555-7788
Victoria Ashworth	B's Beverages	Sales Representative	(171) 555-1212
Christina Berglund	Berglunds snabbköp	Order Administrator	0921-12 34 65
Hanna Moos	Blauer See Delikatessen	Sales Representative	0621-08460
Frédérique Citeaux	Blondel père et fils	Marketing Manager	88.60.15.31
Laurence Lebihan	Bon app'	Owner	91.24.45.40
Elizabeth Lincoln	Bottom-Dollar Markets	Accounting Manager	(604) 555-4729
Patricio Simpson	Cactus Comidas para llevar	Sales Agent	(1) 135-5555
Yang Wang	Chop-suey Chinese	Owner	0452-076545
Pedro Afonso	Comércio Mineiro	Sales Associate	(11) 555-7647
Elizabeth Brown	Consolidated Holdings	Sales Representative	(171) 555-2282
Rita Müller	Die Wandernde Kuh	Sales Representative	0711-020361
Ann Devon	Eastern Connection	Sales Agent	(171) 555-0297
Roland Mendel	Ernst Handel	Sales Manager	7675-3425
Aria Cruz	Familia Arquibaldo	Marketing Assistant	(11) 555-9857
Martine Coquard	Folies gourmandes	Assistant Sales Agent	20.16.10.16
Maria Larsson	Folk och fä HB	Owner	0695-34 67 21
Paolo Accorti	Franchi S.p.A.	Sales Representative	011-4988260
Peter Franken	Frankenversand	Marketing Manager	089-0877310

Record: 1 of 73

Figure 21.11 This datasheet displays the result set of the view with the subquery design of Figure 21.10. Data such as ContactName is updatable, but you can't add new records to the Customers table because the primary-key field (CustomerID) isn't present.

WRITING ACTION QUERIES AND STORED PROCEDURES

Data Manipulation Language (DML) commands are implemented by action queries: append, update, delete, and make-table. Jet uses QueryDefs for action queries; ADP require stored procedures or functions to support `INSERT`, `UPDATE`, `DELETE`, and `SELECT...INTO` statements. This section shows the standard syntax for each type of action query, which is identical in Jet SQL and T-SQL.

Append queries use the following syntax:

```
INSERT INTO dest_table
   SELECT [ALL¦DISTINCT] select_list
   FROM source_table
  [WHERE append_criteria]
```

21

If you omit the WHERE clause, specified field values of all records of *source_table* are appended to *dest_table*. The *source_table* must exist and have columns that correspond to those you specify in *select_list*.

→ For an example of a stored procedure that appends records, **see** "Adding Records with Append Stored Procedures," **p. 831**.

UPDATE queries use the SET command to assign values to individual columns:

```
UPDATE table_name
   SET column_name = value [, column_name = value[,…]]
  [WHERE update_criteria]
```

Separate multiple *column_name = value* entries by commas if you want to update the data in more than one field. If you omit the WHERE clause, the SET expression acts on every record of the table, which probably isn't your intention.

Jet SQL and T-SQL support the ANSI SQL VALUES keyword for adding records to or updating tables the hard way (specifying the value of each column of each record). The later "Taking Advantage of Transactions in Stored Procedures" section has a T-SQL statement that uses the VALUES approach.

DELETE queries take the following form:

```
DELETE FROM table_name
  [WHERE delete_criteria]
```

If you omit the optional WHERE clause in a DELETE query, you delete all records from *table_name*.

→ To review creating DELETE stored procedures in the project designer, **see** "Deleting Table Records," **p. 834**.

Make-table queries use the following syntax:

```
SELECT [ALL¦DISTINCT] select_list
   INTO new_table
   FROM source_table
  [WHERE append_criteria]
```

To copy the original table, substitute an asterisk (*) for *select_list* and omit the optional WHERE clause. Data types and sizes in the *new_table* are the same as those of the *source_table*. If your SQL Server *source_table* has a computed column, the corresponding column in the *new_table* contains the computed values, not the expression used to compute the column.

→ For an example of a simple make-table stored procedure, **see** "Creating and Executing Make-Table and Update Stored Procedures" **p. 828**.

21

You can execute any of the preceding SQL statements directly against Jet or SQL Server tables from VBA code and an ActiveX Data Objects (ADO) Connection object. Using VBA code to execute SQL statements directly, rather than designing stored procedures for action queries—or views and functions to return Recordsets—is an option for ADP. Chapter 30, "Understanding Universal Data Access, OLE DB, and ADO," provides examples of generating and executing SQL statements with VBA code.

SPECIFYING PARAMETERS FOR CRITERIA AND UPDATE VALUES

When you design Jet queries or stored procedures to update table data, you specify parameters to supply values to WHERE clause criteria and, for INSERT and UPDATE queries, field values. If you specify the data type for input parameters, Jet adds a PARAMETERS declaration that precedes the SQL statement. The sequence of the parameter values in the declaration determines the order in which the Enter Parameter Value dialogs appear.

Jet SQL

The Jet SQL statement for a typical Jet parameterized UPDATE query for the quantity field of the Order Details table is

```
PARAMETERS [Type Order Number] Long,
           [Type Product Code] Long,
           [Type New Quantity] Short;
UPDATE [Order Details]
   SET [Order Details].Quantity =
       [Enter New Quantity]
   WHERE [Order Details].OrderID =
            [Type Order Number] AND
         [Order Details].ProductID =
            [Type Product Code];
```

The semicolon at the end of the PARAMETERS declaration indicates the start of an independent SQL statement.

T-SQL uses variables to store parameter values; SQL Server identifies user variables by an @ prefix. T-SQL supports input and output parameters, and return values; this section deals only with input parameters, which are by far the most common type.

T-SQL

Following is an example of standard T-SQL syntax to create a parameterized UPDATE stored procedure:

```
CREATE PROCEDURE tsql_edititems
  (@OrderID int,
   @ProductID int,
   @Quantity smallint)
AS UPDATE [Order Details]
SET Quantity = @Quantity
WHERE OrderID = @OrderID AND
   ProductID = @ProductID
```

Parentheses surrounding the three parameter declarations are optional.

If you type the entire statement into the project designer's SQL pane, you receive an error when you click Verify SQL Syntax. The designer wants only the UPDATE statement with the variables. To avoid the error message, open the New Query dialog, choose Create Text Stored Procedure, and replace the SQL window's skeleton CREATE PROCEDURE statement with the preceding code.

21

The right side of the SET expression, = @Quantity, appears in the New Value cell of the Quantity row of the project designer's grid. The WHERE clause variables appear as = @OrderID and = @ProductID in the Criteria column. Unlike Jet parameters, you can't change the sequence of appearance of the Enter Parameter Value dialogs by rearranging the rows of the grid; the dialog to enter the UPDATE variable always opens first.

NOTE

When you execute the preceding UPDATE query, you receive a "The stored procedure executed successfully, but did not return records" message no matter what values you type in the three parameter dialogs (including nothing). Stored procedures that update tables should include T-SQL code to test for parameter value entry errors, especially when you execute them interactively. The "Programming Stored Procedures" topic of SQL Server Books Online has an example of a test for a missing (NULL) parameter value. If you don't clear the Confirm Action Queries check box on the Option dialog's Edit/Find page, Jet action queries display the number of rows that will be affected by execution. The Confirm Record Changes check box values don't apply to execution of T-SQL stored procedures or functions.

TAKING ADVANTAGE OF TRANSACTIONS IN STORED PROCEDURES

Unless you specify otherwise, Jet automatically uses transaction processing when updating data in multiple tables with a single SQL statement. SQL Server requires explicit declaration of the beginning of the transaction and its end. When you write a T-SQL statement that makes changes to more than one table, wrap the statement with BEGIN TRAN[SACTION] and COMMIT TRAN[SACTION] statements, as illustrated by the following simple example.

T-SQL

This simple DELETE stored procedure uses a transaction to assure that the Order Details table doesn't end up with orphan records after deleting the parent Orders record:

```
CREATE PROCEDURE tsql_delorder
   @OrderID int
AS
BEGIN TRAN
   DELETE FROM [Order Details]
      WHERE OrderID = @OrderID
   DELETE FROM Orders
      WHERE OrderID = @OrderID
COMMIT TRAN
```

If you want to create the preceding stored procedure, choose Create Text Stored Procedure (not Design Stored Procedure) in the New Query dialog.

The following stored procedure is one of several that were used to create the NwindXL19.mdb files for Chapter 19, "Linking Access Front-Ends to Jet Client/Server Tables." The AddOrders.adp application adds four stored procedures to a modified copy of the NorthwindCS database, including the preceding example. The only modification to the copy of the database is removal of the IDENTITY attribute from the OrderID field of the

Orders table to permit adding and deleting records while adding records that have consecutive order numbers. Instead of an identity column, the procedure checks for the last OrderID value and adds 1 for the new order number.

T-SQL

This sample stored procedures adds a new order to an Orders table (which doesn't have an `identity` field), and then adds the first line item for the order to the Order Details table:

```
CREATE PROCEDURE tsql_addorder
   @CustID varchar(5),
   @EmpID int,
   @OrdDate datetime,
   @ReqDate datetime,
   @ShipVia int,
   @ShipName varchar(40),
   @ShipAddr varchar(60),
   @ShipCity varchar(15),
   @ShipReg varchar(15) = NULL,
   @ShipZIP varchar(10) = NULL,
   @ShipCtry varchar(15),

   @ProdID int,
   @Price money,
   @Quan int,
   @Disc real

AS DECLARE @OrderID int

SET NOCOUNT ON
BEGIN TRAN
   SELECT @OrderID = MAX(OrderID) FROM Orders
   SELECT @OrderID = @OrderID + 1
   INSERT Orders
      VALUES(@OrderID, @CustID, @EmpID,
        @OrdDate, @ReqDate, NULL, @ShipVia,
        NULL, @ShipName, @ShipAddr, @ShipCity,
        @ShipReg, @ShipZIP, @ShipCtry)
   INSERT [Order Details]
      (OrderID, ProductID, UnitPrice, Quantity, Discount)
      VALUES(@OrderID, @ProdID, @Price, @Quan, @Disc)
COMMIT TRAN
SET NOCOUNT OFF
IF @@error = 0
   RETURN @OrderID
ELSE
   RETURN 0
```

Don't even *think* about typing this or similar stored procedures into the SQL pane of the project designer. The designer can't handle even moderately complex stored procedures. Instead, type the stored procedures in the windows opened by the Create Text Stored Procedure selection in the project designer's New Query dialog.

Following are brief descriptions of the new T-SQL elements in the preceding example:

- The `@ShipReg varchar(15) = NULL` and `@ShipZIP varchar(10) = NULL` parameter declarations have default `NULL` values to accommodate addresses that don't have a `ShipRegion` or `PostalCode` value. Unlike Jet parameters, you can assign default values to T-SQL parameters.
- The `DECLARE @OrderID int` statement creates an internal `@OrderID` variable to return the order number to the VBA subprocedure that calls the stored procedure and supplies the parameter values.
- The two `SELECT` statements obtain the last `OrderID` value, and add 1 to specify the new value.
- `SET NOCOUNT ON` eliminates a roundtrip to the server to report the number of records affected.
- The two `INSERT` statements illustrate different methods of using the `VALUES` function. The first example doesn't include a field list, so the comma-separate list of values must correspond to the sequence of fields in the table. The second example includes a field list that defines the sequence for the following `VALUES` list.
- `SET NOCOUNT OFF` is optional, but is included here as a good stored procedure programming practice (GSPPP).
- The `IF @@error` conditional statement assigns the new `@OrderID` value to the `RETURN` value if the transaction commits (`@@error = 0`). `@@error` is an SQL Server system variable that returns a nonzero value when an execution error is encountered. The `RETURN` value is `0` if the transaction fails. Error handling is one of the primary uses for T-SQL's flow-control structures.

This section's example appears complex, but it pales in comparison with stored procedures and SQL scripts that are used in production databases. For an example of a truly complex script, make a copy of ...\Office10\Samples\NorthwindCS.sql as NorthwindCS.txt, and then open it in Notepad. Go to the end of the file, and then Page Up to view the `INSERT` statements that Microsoft generated to populate the Suppliers and Products tables.

NOTE

> Use the NorthwindCS.txt copy to prevent making inadvertent changes to NorthwindCS.sql. Much of NorthwindCS.txt's 670KB is devoted to binary data for the bitmaps stored in the OLE Object field of the Categories table. Access 2000's NorthwindCS.sql was even larger (1.4MB), because it included data for the larger bitmaps of the Employees table's Photo field.

WORKING WITH TABLES IN ANOTHER DATABASE

Access lets you open only one database at a time unless you write code to open another table with a VBA function or subprocedure, or specify a linked server. However, you can use Jet SQL's `IN` predicate with a make-table, append, update, or delete query to create or modify tables in another database. ANSI SQL doesn't support the IN reserved word as a modifier for SELECT...INTO statements.

Jet SQL

Following is a sample SQL statement to create a copy of Northwind.mdb's Customers table in another Jet database:

```
SELECT *
   INTO Customers
   IN 'c:\Databases\Illwind.mdb'
FROM Customers
```

You receive an error message if the Customers table exists in the target database or if the path or file name is invalid.

The project designer uses SQL Server three-part names to specify tables in another database of the SQL Server instance to which you're connected. Three part names use the *Database.Schema.Table* format; for most RDBMSs, the *Schema* element is the database owner name—dbo for SQL Server. For example, the three-part name for the Customers table of the NorthwindCS database is NorthwindCS.dbo.Customers.

NOTE

> Three-part names are a shortened version of the four-part names you use to refer to tables in a linked database. The missing fourth element is the *ServerName* prefix that you would need to add to specify a table in a linked database.

→ To review linking tables from Jet databases or SQL Server databases on other machines, **see** "Linking Remote Servers," **p. 842**.

SQL Server's default database is master, which the setup program creates during the installation process. You can use the master database as a temporary destination for tables you copy by SELECT...INTO statements.

T-SQL

Following is a simple T-SQL statement for a stored procedure that creates a copy of NorthwindCS's Customers table in the master database:

```
SELECT dbo.Customers.*
   INTO master.dbo.Customers
FROM dbo.Customers
```

You receive an error message if the Customers table exists in the target database or if you don't have CREATE TABLE permission for the target database. You also receive an error if you don't add the dbo. prefix to both instances of Customers.

After you create the table in the other database, you can create a view, function, or stored procedure with tables in both databases. To create a view between the Customers table in the master database and the Orders table in the NorthwindCS database, do the following:

1. Create a new view or function in the project designer and add the Customers and Orders tables from NorthwindCS.
2. Mark the check boxes for a couple of fields from each table—CustomerID, CompanyName, OrderID, and OrderDate for this example.
3. Open the SQL pane and add the prefix **`master.`** to each instance of `dbo.Customers`.

4. Click Check SQL Syntax to verify your T-SQL modifications. The Customers field list adds an arrow and (master) to its title bar, and the join line loses its key and [if] symbols (see Figure 21.12).

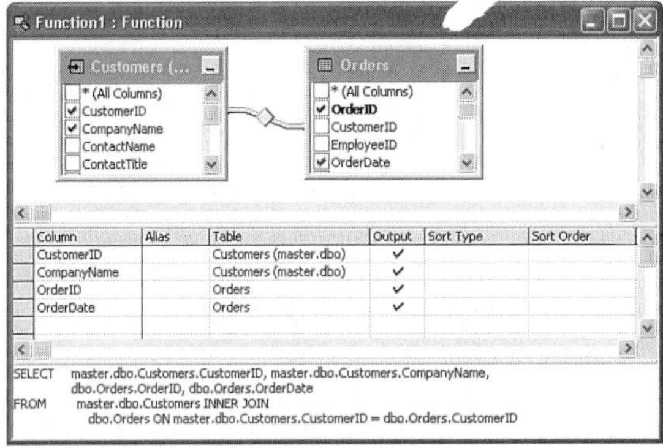

Figure 21.12
JOINs between tables in different databases don't display symbols representing relationships.

You lose the benefit of referential integrity enforcement between tables in different databases, because the relationships between tables are defined only within a single database. Views across multiple databases aren't updatable in Datasheet view, but you can write functions or stored procedures to perform `INSERT`, `UPDATE`, and `DELETE` operations. Production stored procedures that update tables in multiple databases require a substantial amount of additional code to protect tables against violation of referential integrity rules.

NOTE

Transactions across linked SQL Server databases are managed by the Distributed Transaction Coordinator (DTC), which all versions of SQL Server install during the setup process. Operations on multiple databases running on a single SQL Server instance use a single OLE DB connection and don't employ DTC.

CREATING TABLES WITH ANSI-92 DDL

You can create new tables in your current database with DDL reserved words, which are identical for Jet 4.0 and SQL Server 7.0+. Using SQL to create new tables is of primary interest to developers, not users, of Access applications because it's much easier to create new tables with the Jet or SQL Server graphical table design tools than writing the equivalent DDL statements. In some cases, such as emulating Jet crosstab queries with T-SQL stored procedures, however, you must create tables with SQL statements.

NOTE

> Jet supports ANSI-92 DDL statements only in VBA code and requires use of the OLE DB provider for Jet 4.0 to establish an `ADODB.Connection` object to the Jet database. You must add references in the VBA editor to the Microsoft ActiveX Data Objects 2.7 Library (Msado15.dll) and Microsoft ADO Ext. 2.7 for DDL and Security (Msadox.dll) to support Jet 4.0 DDL. Chapter 28 explains how to add these references in the VBA editor.

Following is a brief description of the basic ANSI SQL-92 DDL syntax for creating, altering, and dropping (deleting) tables and related objects:

- `CREATE TABLE` *`table_name`* `(`*`field_name data_type`* `[(`*`field_size`*`)][,` *`field_name data_type...`*`])` creates a new table with the fields specified by a comma-separated list. Properties of fields are space delimited, so you need to enclose entries for field names with spaces in square brackets (`[]`). For Jet SQL, the *`data_type`* can be any valid Jet SQL field data type, such as `TEXT(`*`field_size`*`)` or `INTEGER`. T-SQL accepts any valid SQL Server data, such as `int`, `datetime`, `nvarchar(`*`field_size`*`)`, and `text`. (The default field *`data_type`* for Jet is `Text` and for SQL Server is `char`. The default `field_size` argument value is 50 characters for Jet and SQL Server.)

TIP

> If you don't specify a *`data_type`* for a field, the default values for *`data_type`* and *`field_size`* apply. You can change the default field data type and size in the Tables/Queries page of the Options dialog for Jet and ADP.

NOTE

> If you use the Jet `TEXT` modifier without a *`field_size`* argument (in parentheses), Jet interprets `TEXT` as the Memo field data type for conformance to SQL Server's `text` data type. Jet SQL includes many new data type modifiers, such as `CHARACTER`, `VARCHAR`, `NATIONAL CHAR`, `NATIONAL CHAR VARYING`, and others for localization and Unicode preferences. The corresponding SQL Server data types are `char`, `varchar`, `nchar`, and `nvarchar`.

- `CONSTRAINT` *`constraint_name`* `{PRIMARY KEY¦UNIQUE¦REFERENCES` *`foreign_table`* `[(`*`foreign_field`*`)]}` establishes DRI for the table. Jet and SQL Server create an index on the field name that precedes the expression. You can specify the index as the `PRIMARY KEY` or as a `UNIQUE` index. SQL Server lets you specify `[CLUSTERED¦NONCLUSTERED]` for a `PRIMARY KEY` or `UNIQUE` index. You also can establish a relationship between the field and the field of a foreign table with the `REFERENCES` *`foreign_table`* `[`*`foreign_field`*`]` entry. (The `[`*`foreign_field`*`]` item is required if the *`foreign_field`* is not a primary-key field.)

21

- `CHECK (expression)` creates an additional constraint that's similar to but more flexible than Jet's table-level validation. The expression argument can compare values obtained from other tables by means of a `SELECT` statement.
- `CREATE [UNIQUE] INDEX index_name ON table_name (field_name [ASC¦DESC][, field_name [ASC¦DESC], ...]) [WITH {PRIMARY¦DISALLOW NULL¦IGNORE NULL}]` creates an index on one or more fields of a table. If you specify the `WITH PRIMARY` modifier, `UNIQUE` is assumed (and not required). You can only create one primary-key index/constraint on a table. `DISALLOW NULL` prevents the addition of records with `NULL` values in the indexed field; `IGNORE NULL` doesn't index records with `NULL` *field_name* values.
- `ALTER TABLE` lets you add new fields (`ADD COLUMN field_name...`) or delete existing fields (`DROP COLUMN field_name...`).
- `ALTER COLUMN table_name (field_name data_type [field_size])` lets you change the properties of a single column.
- `DROP COLUMN column_name ON table_name` deletes the column from a table specified by *table_name*.
- `DROP INDEX index_name ON table_name` deletes the index from a table specified by *table_name*.
- `DROP TABLE table_name` deletes a table from the database.

The syntax examples of the preceding list, other than `DROP COLUMN`, `DROP INDEX`, and `DROP TABLE`, cover only the basic syntax common to Jet and SQL Server objects. The "Data Definition Language" topic under the "Microsoft Jet SQL Reference" node of online help's Contents pane provide more complete syntax examples. For a full description of T-SQL's `CREATE TABLE` statement, search for **CREATE TABLE** in the Index pane of SQL Server Books Online.

USING SQL STATEMENTS WITH FORMS, REPORTS, AND CONTROLS

If you create many forms and reports based on queries, views, or stored procedures, the query list in your Database window can become cluttered. The clutter becomes worse as you add queries, views, or functions to populate list and combo boxes. You can use SQL queries you write or copy from the SQL dialog in place of the names of query or view objects as the data source for forms, reports, and lists. After you verify proper operation of the object whose data source you changed, delete the corresponding object from your database. You can use Jet SQL or T-SQL statements for the following purposes:

21

- Record Source property of forms and reports. Substitute the SQL query text for the name of the query in the Record Source text box.
- Row Source property in lists and drop-down combo lists on a form. Using an SQL statement rather than a query or view object can give you greater control over the sequence of the columns in your list.

- Value of the SQL property of a `QueryDef` object or the `strSource` argument of the `OpenRecordset` method in VBA code for Jet databases. You use SQL statements extensively as property and argument values when programming applications with VBA, especially for SQL pass-through queries.

- `Source` property of a `DAO.Recordset` object specified as the `Recordset` property of a Access form, report, or control. The capability to bind Access objects to `DAO.Recordset` objects was new in Access 2002.
- `Source` property of an `ADODB.Recordset` object specified as the `Recordset` property of a form, report, or control. Access 2000 introduced the capability to bind Access form and report objects to ADO Recordsets. Access 2003 ADP can use disconnected Recordsets to minimize active connections to the database.

You can create and test your Jet SQL statement in Query Design view or the project designer's SQL pane for views. You can copy unformatted Jet SQL statements directly to the Clipboard. Paste text of T-SQL statements formatted by the project designer into Notepad, remove the formatting (with WordWrap on), and copy the unformatted text to the Clipboard. Paste the text into the text box for the property or into your VBA module. Then close the test query or view design without saving it.

TROUBLESHOOTING

UNEXPECTED ENTER PARAMETER DIALOGS

When I try to execute a query from my SQL statement, an Enter Parameter Value dialog appears.

You misspelled one of the table names in your ***`table_list`***, one of the field names in your ***`field_list`***, or both. If the Jet engine's query parser can't match a table name or a field name with those specified in the `FROM` clause, Jet assumes that the entry is a parameter and requests its value. Check the spelling of the database objects in your SQL statement. (If you misspell an SQL keyword, you usually receive a syntax error message box.)

IN THE REAL WORLD—SQL AS A SECOND LANGUAGE

It's tempting to use Jet's Query Design view or the project designer to generate all SQL statements behind the scenes. Graphical QBE bypasses the need to learn *two* languages—SQL and VBA—to become a proficient Access or Visual Basic 6.0 database developer. The reality is that you ultimately must master both SQL and VBA, because the two languages are inextricably intertwined in all nontrivial Access database front ends to Jet and SQL Server databases. SQL is the *lingua franca* of all relational databases, just as VBA is the common programming language of Microsoft Office, Visual Basic 6.0, Visio, and many third-party applications. A future version of Access is likely to accommodate programming in Visual Basic .NET and C#, which means another language or two to learn.

NOTE

> SQL is the foundation for several Microsoft query-language extensions, including SHAPE syntax for generating hierarchical Recordsets and Multidimensional Expressions (MDX) for DataCubes and the PivotTable Service for online analytical processing (OLAP) with Microsoft Analysis Services (formerly OLAP Services and Decision Support Services). As more organizations adopt the Standard or Enterprise editions of SQL Server 2000, which include Analysis Services, data warehouses will become commonplace in medium-sized enterprises, and smaller firms will set up data marts.

If English is your native language, make SQL your second tongue and VBA your third. Access is an exceptionally valuable tool for mastering Jet SQL and T-SQL. If your plans include becoming proficient in client/server database technology, concentrate on ADP and T-SQL.

CHOOSING BETWEEN VIEWS, STORED PROCEDURES, AND IN-LINE FUNCTIONS

Database administrators (DBAs) traditionally have used views or stored procedures for delivering production data to front-end applications. Recordsets returned by views can be updatable, but updating table data through views isn't a common practice in production environments. Views are restricted to a single `SELECT` statement and don't accept parameter values to supply `WHERE` clause and `GROUP BY` criteria.

Stored procedures can return Recordsets, perform table update operations, or both. Stored procedures can—and usually do—have parameters to which you can assign default values. If you omit parameter value(s) in the `EXECUTE sp`*`ProcName`*`(`*`param1`*`, `*`param2`*`, …)` statement, the parameter assumes the default value(s). Stored procedures have the additional capability to execute T-SQL procedural code within `BEGIN…END` blocks and return multiple Recordsets. Recordsets returned by stored procedures aren't updatable.

In-line, table-valued functions combine features of views and stored procedures. These functions return a value of the `table` data type; thus, you can specify a function name in the `FROM` clause of an SQL statement. Table values returned by functions are updatable if the function has a single `SELECT` statement. Functions also accept parameters with optional default values. In this case, however, you must substitute the `DEFAULT` keyword to use the default values as in `SELECT * FROM fn`*`FunctionName`*`(`*`param1`*`, DEFAULT, …)`.

Access's project designer hides the T-SQL `[CREATE¦ALTER] FUNCTION` statement required to create or modify an in-line, table-valued function. Here's the statement that creates the example of this chapter's "Implementing Subqueries" section:

```
CREATE FUNCTION dbo.fnSubQuery()
   RETURNS TABLE
   AS RETURN (
   SELECT TOP 100 PERCENT ContactName,
      CompanyName, ContactTitle, Phone
      FROM dbo.Customers
```

```
WHERE (CustomerID IN
   (SELECT Orders.CustomerID
      FROM Orders
      WHERE Orders.OrderDate BETWEEN '1/1/1997'
         AND '6/30/1997'))
ORDER BY CompanyName)
```

The RETURNS TABLE modifier defines the function's data type as table. The AS RETURN statement encloses the SQL statement within parenthesis and delivers the result set. Datasheet view of the function indicates that its table is updatable. You can change values in any of the four columns, but you can't add records because the required CustomerID column is missing from the function's result set.

Microsoft claims that the performance of in-line table-valued functions is about the same as views or stored procedures. Thus, execution speed isn't a deciding factor in the selection process. If you need the equivalent of a Jet parameterized SELECT query, use an in-line function. Otherwise, views and in-line functions offer the same functionality. Stored procedures and dynamic SQL are your best choices for updating tables.

COMPARING DYNAMIC T-SQL WITH PRE-COMPILED QUERY OBJECTS

You can avoid creating pre-compiled views, in-line functions, and stored procedures by executing dynamic (also called ad hoc) T-SQL statements directly. In this case, SQL Server's query optimizer performs the following steps:

1. Parses the T-SQL statement to determine conformance to T-SQL syntax rules and verify the existence of named database objects. Clicking the Verify SQL Syntax button performs this step.
2. Translates named database objects to ID values. For example, table, view, or function names become object IDs, and column names become column IDs.
3. Generates an optimized query execution plan that takes full advantage of table indexes for JOINs and WHERE and GROUP BY criteria.
4. Compiles the optimized query.
5. Executes the compiled query.

Views, functions, and stored procedures execute steps 3 and 4 only when you create or modify them. When you execute the compiled query object, SQL Server's query processor skips steps 3 and 4. Depending on the complexity of your query and its underlying table(s), generating the optimized execution plan and compiling the query can consume a significant amount of server resources.

Fortunately, SQL Server caches the compiled ad hoc query for re-use. Repeated execution of identical ad hoc T-SQL statements also skips steps 3 and 4. In most cases, the query processor recognizes minor changes to WHERE clause and GROUP BY criteria and reuses the cached query.

MAKING CUSTOM QUERIES EASY FOR USERS

One of the most common applications for dynamic SQL statements that you create with VBA code is generating the WHERE clause constraints for SELECT query statements. You base the WHERE clause on user selections from one or more drop-down lists. To analyze orders, for example, users make selections in Product, Region, Employee, Start Date, and End Date (dimension) drop-down lists. The query typically returns aggregate values based on the dimensions.

The simplified VBA code for a dynamic T-SQL WHERE clause is

```
strWhere = "WHERE Products.ProductID = " & cboProduct.Value & _
   " AND Customers.Region = '" & cboRegion.Value & _
   "' AND Employees.EmployeeID = '" & cboEmployee.Value & _
   "' AND Orders.OrderDate BETWEEN '" & cboStartDate.Value & _
   "' AND '" & cboEndDate.Value & "'"
```

You populate each list from the appropriate field(s) of a base table, and add an (All) item with a UNION query. When the user selects (All) you eliminate the corresponding WHERE clause constraint, as in:

```
strWhere = "WHERE "
If cboProduct.Value <> "(All)" Then
   strWhere = Products.ProductID = " & cboProduct.Value & _
End If
...
```

NOTE

> One of the first large-scale client/server applications for Access—originally created in version 1.1—used this approach to emulate Analysis Services before the term OLAP was invented. Users selected their dimension values in list boxes, which generated pass-through SQL statements in IBM's DB2 dialect to return aggregated values to temporary Jet tables stored on the client PCs. The temporary tables served as the source for a Jet crosstab query that provided the data source for forms, reports, and graphs.

CHAPTER 22

Upsizing Jet Applications to Access Data Projects

In this chapter

22

TAKING A HARD LOOK AT THE UPSIZING PROCESS

Upsizing a Jet application to an SQL Server and an Access project is a drastic operation. The Upsizing Wizard banishes all vestiges of Jet from your application. As a general rule, the probability of initial upsizing success is inversely proportional to the size and complexity of your Jet-based Access application. If you've designed your Jet applications with upsizing in mind, the likelihood of upsizing success greatly increases. It's a safe bet, however, that only a small percentage of existing Jet applications were designed with ease of upsizing as a design parameter.

Following are the basic steps that the Upsizing Wizard takes when you select the New Database option in the first Wizard dialog and the Create a New Access Client/Server Application option in the fifth dialog:

- Create a new SQL Server database. By default, the new database is the name of the existing database with an "SQL" suffix.
- Copy the structure of Jet tables to new tables in the database, and add the data to the tables.
- Add indexes to the tables.
- Add extended properties to the tables and set the values of properties.
- Create a view for each Jet `SELECT QueryDef` object that doesn't have a `GROUP BY` clause in the database window's Queries page.
- Create an in-line, table-valued function for each Jet `SELECT QueryDef` object that has a `GROUP BY` clause in the Queries page.
- Create an in-line, table-valued function for parameterized `SELECT` queries.
- Create a stored procedure for each action `QueryDef` object in the Queries page.
- Create a new project (.adp) file with a connection to the new SQL Database.
- Copy all Jet forms, subforms, reports, subreports, pages, macros, and modules in the .mdb file to the new .adp file. The source files for Data access pages (DAP) must be local (not deployed on a Web server) in order for the Wizard to change the connection string in the .htm file. The Wizard makes no changes to VBA code behind forms or reports, or in modules. DAP that use relative connection strings, such as Northwind.mdb, won't upsize if you're running Windows XP Service Pack (SP) 1 Internet Explorer 6.0 SP1.

Upsizing tables, queries, and Jet SQL statements is subject to the limitations described in sections later in this chapter. This chapter covers upsizing conventional single-file and front-end/back-end Jet applications. Chapter 24, "Designing and Deploying Data Access Pages," discusses issues with upsizing DAP to SQL Server data sources.

PREPARING TO UPSIZE YOUR JET APPLICATIONS

There are two basic approaches to increasing the probability of a fully successful upsizing operation:

- **Trial and error**—Run the Wizard early and often to determine the scope of the additional effort necessary to upsize your Jet application successfully. If you have very large tables, you can use the structure-only option to minimize upsizing time. Read the Upsizing Wizard's report, make the changes necessary to upgrade missing objects, and try again.
- **Planned migration**—Make changes to the Jet tables, queries, and application objects to minimize the likelihood of upsizing problems. For example, convert your VBA code that uses Data Access Objects (DAO) to ActiveX Data Objects (ADO) that use the OLE DB data provider for Jet. Thoroughly test your changes.

If your Jet application is relatively simple or in the early development stage and doesn't include VBA code that has reference to any version of DAO, the trial-and-error method might be your best choice. The most efficient upsizing method usually is a combination the two approaches.

TIP

> Replace all instances of `Like` expressions for date constraints in Jet query `WHERE` clauses with `Between...And` expressions. For example, change `Like "*/*/1997"` to `Between #1/1/1997# And #12/31/1997#`. The Wizard upsizes `Like "*/*/1997"` to `LIKE '%/%/1997'`, but the upsized query returns no rows in the project designer.

UPSIZING WITH THE TRIAL-AND-ERROR APPROACH

An initial test of the Upsizing Wizard lets you see how much work is in store to upsize your application. For a complex Jet application, the test drive might convince you to abandon a full-fledged upsizing operation and use SQL Server tables linked to your Jet front end. In this case, Chapter 19, "Linking Access Front-Ends to Jet and Client/Server Tables," describes the quick and easy way to gain most of the advantages of an SQL Server back end.

If you don't have a production Jet application to test and you've created the queries, forms, and reports used as examples in the preceding chapters in a copy of Northwind.mdb, you have a good starting point for determining what types of Jet objects the Upsizing Wizard can handle without modification.

NOTE

> If you didn't perform all the exercises, Upsize22.mdb in the \Seua11\Chaptr22 folder of the accompanying CD-ROM contains most of the example objects created in Chapters 5 through 19. `Between...And` replaces instances of `Like` expressions in the Upsize22.mdb queries.

TIP

> Set Access 2003's macro security level to Low before starting the upsizing process. If you specify Medium as the security level, the you must click the Enable Macros button for each application object that the Wizard copies to the project file.

To give the Upsizing Wizard a test drive with a new SQL Server database, do the following:

1. Create a backup copy of the database you plan to upsize, unless you're using the Upsize22.mdb sample database. You can upsize either a single-file or split (front-end/back-end) application. The upsizing process doesn't affect the source .mdb file under ordinary circumstances, but there's always the chance of an extraordinary occurrence.
2. Log on to the database as a member of the Admins group. You don't need full Admins authority, but you do need at least Read Data and Read Design permissions for all objects in the source database(s).
3. If any Jet database table or query objects are hidden, choose Tools, Options; click the View tab; and mark the Hidden Objects check box in the Show frame of the Options dialog. To upsize the hidden objects, select Window, Unhide to open the Unhide Window dialog. Then, select the window(s), and click OK to unhide them.
4. Choose Tools, Database Utilities, Upsizing Wizard to open the Wizard's first dialog. Accept the default Create a New Database option, and click Next.
5. In the second Wizard dialog, accept the default (local) server for MSDE or open the list box and specify the NetBIOS computer name of the machine running SQL Server.
6. If you're logged on as a Windows user having administrative privileges for the destination SQL Server, mark the Use Trusted Connection check box. Alternatively, use sa or your assigned SQL Server administrator login ID and type your password, if the server uses SQL Server security. By default, MSDE2000 requires a trusted connection, which uses Windows integrated security for authentication.
7. Accept or change the name of the new SQL Server database. This example uses **UpsizeSQL** as the database name (see Figure 22.1). Click Next.
8. In the third Wizard dialog, click the >> button to move all tables from the Available Tables to the Export to SQL Server list (see Figure 22.2). The HRActions table and all tables with a tbl prefix are sample tables created in earlier chapters. Click Next.

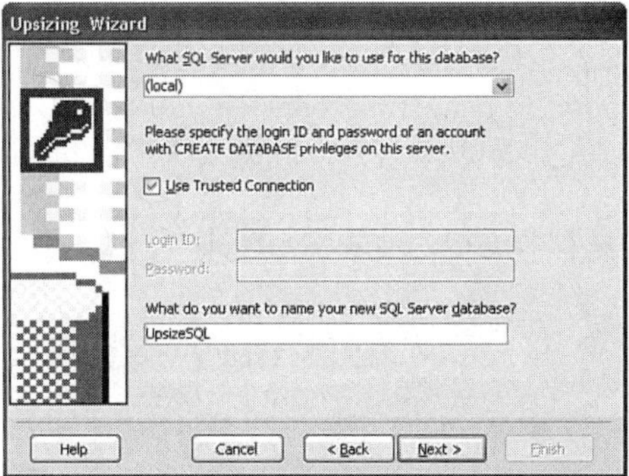

Figure 22.1
Specify (local) or the NetBIOS name of the computer running SQL Server, the type of authentication (integrated Windows or SQL Server), and the name of the new SQL Server database in the second Wizard dialog.

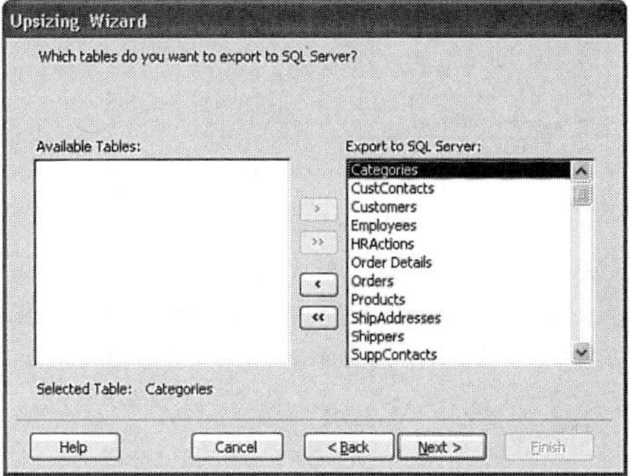

Figure 22.2
Select all Jet tables for upsizing, unless you have a good reason to do otherwise.

9. In the fourth dialog, accept the defaults for table attributes, and select Yes, Let the Wizard Decide in the Add Timestamp Fields to Tables list. Unless you have tables with more than a 100,000 or more records, don't mark the Only Create the Table Structure; Don't Upsize Any Data check box (see Figure 22.3). Click Next.

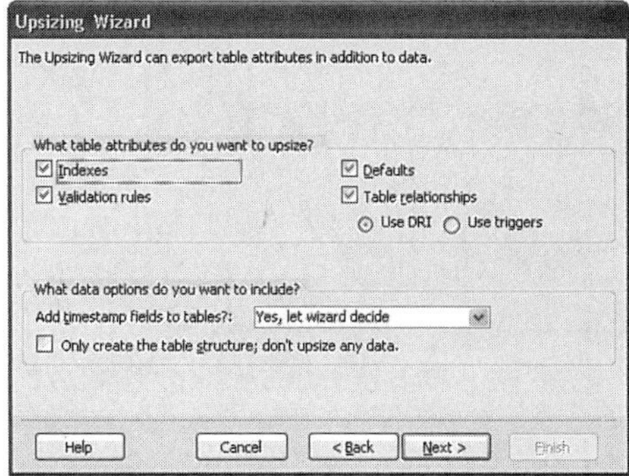

Figure 22.3
Default table attributes are satisfactory for most upsizing operations, but it's a good practice to let the Wizard add `timestamp` fields to upsized tables with Jet Memo and OLE Object fields.

10. The fifth dialog offers the choices of creating a new project or linking SQL Server tables to the Jet application. Select the Create a New Access Client/Server Application option. The Wizard proposes to name the front-end file *MdbName*CS.adp. For this initial example, the name is UpsizeSQL.adp (see Figure 22.4). Click Next.

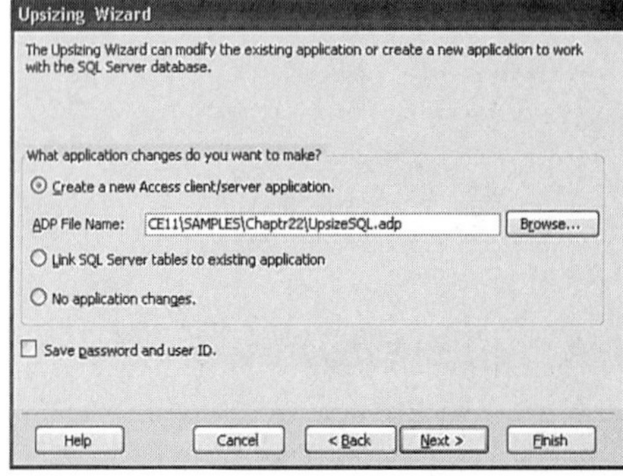

Figure 22.4
Specify a new Access project and give the .adp file a name in the fifth Wizard dialog.

TIP

> Clear the Save Password and User ID box if you want to maintain the security of your back-end database. Default integrated Windows security lets you control database access by the user's group membership in a Windows 2000+/NT domain. If you specified SQL Server security in step 5, users must type their pre-assigned login ID and password to connect to the database.

→ To learn more about granting users access to your upsized database, **see** "Securing Projects with the MSDE 2000 Login/User Tool," **p. 936**.

11. Accept the Open the New ADP File option and click Finish to start the upsizing operation.

The Wizard begins the upsizing process and displays a progress dialog (see Figure 22.5).

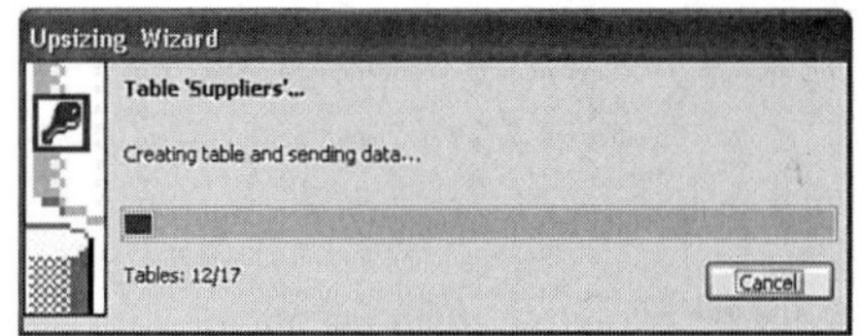

Figure 22.5
The progress dialog briefly describes each Upsizing Wizard operation. The width of the progress bar is based on the number of objects upsized, not the time required for upsizing.

NOTE

The Wizard reports that it's adding triggers to the tables, regardless of whether you specify the default Use DRI (declarative referential integrity) or Use Triggers option in the fourth Wizard dialog.

After the Wizard copies the table structures, data, and extended properties, you receive a series of error messages when the Wizard starts upsizing DAP. Figure 22.6 illustrates a typical DAP error message, which occurs because the Wizard can't handle DAP that use relative paths for their data source. Click OK after reading each message to complete the upsizing process.

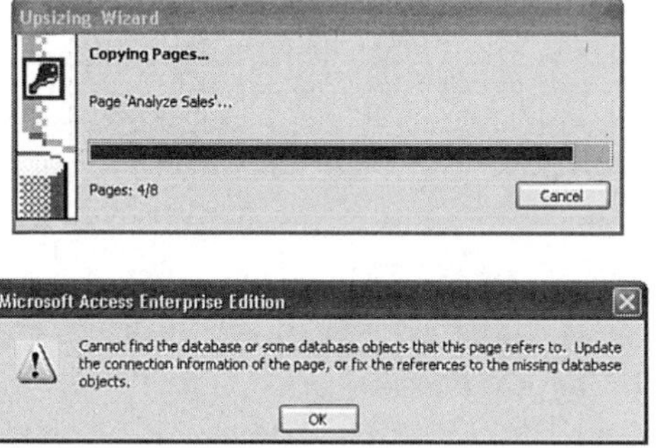

Figure 22.6
Northwind.mdb's sample data access pages fail to upsize under Windows XP SP1 because their use of a relative path (Northwind.mdb, instead of C:*FullPath*\Northwind.mdb) prevents opening the PageName.htm file.

When the Wizard completes copying forms and other application objects, which is a much slower process than copying other objects (except large tables), the Upsizing Wizard Report opens. Upsizing Upsize22.mdb takes about 10 minutes on a moderately fast (833-MHz Pentium III) computer. The report snapshot file (Upsize22.snp) for initial upsizing of Upsize22.mdb is 43 pages, of which pages 32–43 contain results for queries. (Your page numbers might differ.) Figure 22.7 illustrates results for two successfully upsized queries. The Wizard uses SQL Server quoted (`"..."`) identifiers for object names with spaces instead of the more conventional square bracket (`[...]`) pairs.

TIP

Look for the Wizard's upsizing report snapshot files in Access's default database folder, which you specify on the General page of the Options dialog, not in the working folder that contains the source .mdb or destination .adp file.

NOTE

Access 2003's Upsizing Wizard can handle Jet `UNION` queries; Access 2000 and earlier Wizard versions could not. The strange-appearing `' ' AS "__ __"` column identifiers are required, because SQL Server requires the result set of the `UNION SELECT` statement to return the same number of columns as the initial `SELECT` result set, even if the columns are empty.

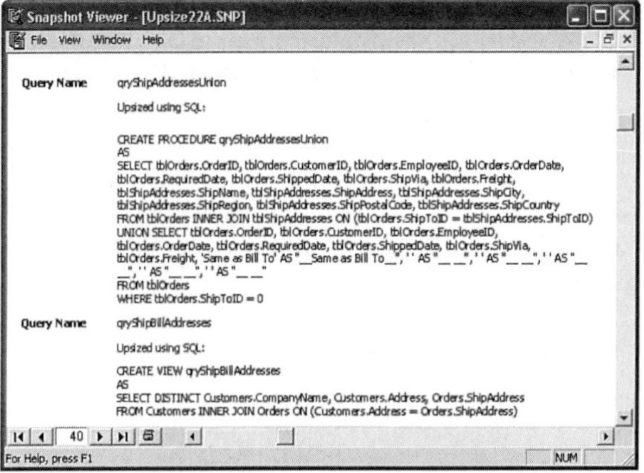

Figure 22.7
Report elements for a `UNION` query upsized to a stored procedure and a simple `SELECT` query upsized to a view.

Following are the Upsizing Wizard's limitations and initial workarounds, where available, based on the report for the initial test run with Upsize22.mdb:

- The Wizard doesn't remove Jet SQL's `DISTINCTROW` reserved word or convert it to T-SQL's `DISTINCT` modifier. Access 95 and earlier automatically added `DISTINCTROW` to all `SELECT` queries, so this problem is likely to occur only with seasoned Jet applications. The "Jet's `DISTINCTROW` and T-SQL's `DISTINCT` Keywords" section later in the chapter compares the difference in effect of these two modifiers on query result sets. Changing `DISTINCTROW` to `DISTINCT` solves this problem, but might have side effects, such as making the query result set not updatable. You seldom need the `DISTINCT` modifier; if you do, add it to the upsized query when you test it.
- The Wizard won't upsize Jet crosstab queries, because SQL Server doesn't support Jet's SQL's `PIVOT` and `TRANSFORM` key words. The workaround for this problem isn't simple, as demonstrated in the later "Emulating Jet Crosstab Queries with T-SQL" section.
- The Wizard bails out when it encounters VBA reserved words, such as **`Format`**, for which T-SQL has no direct equivalent. The qry1997OrdersByCountryPT, qryMonthlyOrders1997, qryMonthlyOrdersParam, qryMonthlySales1997, qryOrderAmount, and Sales by Year queries use the **`Format`** function. The initial workaround for these queries is to remove the function and its format definition string to verify that the unformatted query is upsizable. If `WHERE`, `GROUP BY`, or `ORDER BY` clauses use the **`Format`** function, the query result set won't be valid.
- Nested queries fail to upsize when the source query (also called the outer query) won't upsize. Fixing the outer query solves the problem, if the nested (inner) query that's specified in the `FROM` clause can be upsized.
- Jet `SELECT` and action queries that use the `IN` predicate to specify another .mdb file won't upsize. The four qryOakmont… queries can't be upsized, because the `IN` predicate specifies the Oakmont.mdb file. The only workaround is to upsize the

Oakmont.mdb database, and then write queries that use three-part SQL Server names to specify tables in the OakmontSQL database.

→ For more information on three-part names, **see** "Working with Tables in Another Database," **p. 878**.

- Action queries with parameters don't upsize. `SELECT` queries with parameters upsize to in-line, table-valued functions with parameters. Parameterized `SELECT` queries with spaces in the parameter names, such as qryStateMailList, don't upsize.

→ To review in-line functions that use parameters, **see** "Creating a Parameterized Table-Returning Function," **p. 825**.

- The Wizard fails to upsize queries with column alias names that are SQL Server reserved words. For example, `OrderDate AS Date` or `CostPerUnit AS Cost` as a member of a field list prevents upsizing the query. In most cases, surrounding reserved words with `[...]` delimiters—as in `OrderDate AS [Date]`—solves the problem.
- The Wizard won't upsize queries that aren't executable because of a table- or field-naming error. The tblOrders table doesn't have Ship... fields, so upsizing qryUQtblOrders1 fails. The SalesOrders query fails because Table1 is missing. Delete test queries or action queries you ran once to modify tables.

Modifying complex queries to work around upsizing problems is a tedious process, especially if you have a large number of queries that fail. Be sure to test each query whose Jet SQL statement you modify to verify the changes you make. Deleting crosstab and other queries that the Wizard can't upsize is optional.

Running a Second Upsizing Pass

After performing the first set of query fixes and temporary workarounds, you must run the Upsizing Wizard again. The sample Upsize22A.mdb file has most of the fixes described in the preceding section.

To make a second upsizing pass from scratch, do the following:

1. Close all open objects in the new .adp file except the Database window.
2. Choose Tools, Database Utilities, Drop SQL Database. A message box asks you to confirm dropping the current database (UpsizeSQL for this example).
3. Click Yes to drop SQL Server's reference to the database files and delete the corresponding .mdf and .ldf files. Your database disconnects, and the Tables and Queries pages of the Database window empty.
4. Close the project, and use Windows Explorer to delete the .adp file you created (UpsizeSQL.adp for this initial example).
5. Open Upsize22.mdb (or whatever file you're upsizing) and repeat steps 4–11 of the earlier "Performing an Initial Test of the Upsizing Process" section.

Table 22.1 is a scorecard for the Upsizing Wizard's successive passes on the Upsize22.mdb and Upsize22A.mdb queries. The numbers in the Pass 2 column reflect modification or deletion after the first pass of queries that the Wizard won't attempt to upsize. (Upsize22a.mdb generates the Pass 2 data).

TABLE 22.1 SUCCESS AND FAILURE OF UPSIZE22.MDB QUERIES IN TWO TRIALS WITH THE UPSIZING WIZARD

Query Upsize Status	Pass 1	Pass 2
Successfully upsized	29	46
Failed (`DISTINCTROW`)	13	0
Failed (`PIVOT...TRANSFORM`)	5	0
Failed (VBA **`Format`** function)	5	0
Failed (missing source query)	4	0
Failed (tables in another database)	4	0
Failed (missing field or table)	2	0
Failed (mishandled parameter)	1	0
Failed (other reasons)	1	2

At this point, only two of Upsize22.mdb's queries fail to upsize, so it's not an efficient use of your time to attempt to modify the Jet SQL statements and rerun the Upsizing Wizard. The better approach is to correct the remaining problems in the new project, UpsizeCS.adp, which is used in the following examples.

NOTE

When you click the Check SQL Syntax button or save the upsized view, function, or stored procedure, the SQL Server query parser adds the `dbo.` prefix to each table name in the T-SQL statement.

CORRECTING WIZARD ERRORS

The first of the two queries that fail to upsize for "other reasons" is qry1997OrderDataPT. This nested query, which requires the Order Details Extended query as a data source, is intended as the data source for a PivotTable to display quarterly or monthly orders by employee and category. Figure 22.8 shows the upsizing report entry for the query. This error relates to the decision by the Upsizing Wizard's developers to upsize Jet queries with `ORDER BY` clauses to in-line, table-valued functions instead of views with the `TOP 100 PERCENT` modifier. The Jet Order Details Extended query upsizes to a view, but the Wizard doesn't handle references to functions correctly.

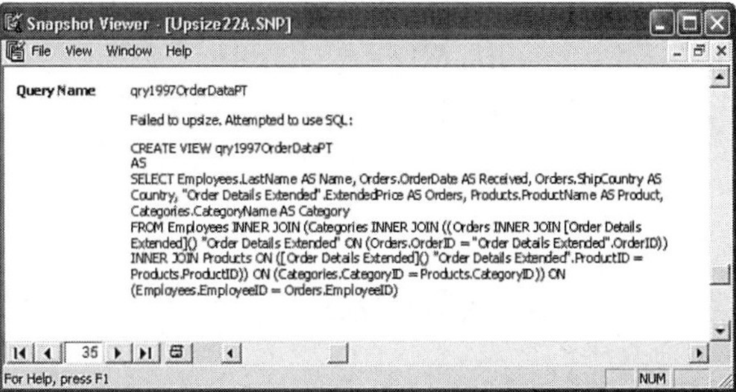

Figure 22.8
Failure to upsize the qry1997OrderDatePT query results from the `[Order Details Extended]() "Order Details Extended"` fragments.

Jet SQL

The Jet SQL version of the qry1997OrderDataPT query is

```
SELECT Employees.LastName AS Name,
      Orders.OrderDate AS [Date],
      Orders.ShipCountry AS Country,
     [Order Details Extended].ExtendedPrice AS Orders,
      Products.ProductName AS Product,
      Categories.CategoryName AS Category
FROM Employees
   INNER JOIN (Categories
      INNER JOIN ((Orders
         INNER JOIN [Order Details Extended]
         ON Orders.OrderID =
               [Order Details Extended].OrderID)
            INNER JOIN Products
            ON [Order Details Extended].ProductID =
               Products.ProductID)
   ON Categories.CategoryID = Products.CategoryID)
         ON Employees.EmployeeID = Orders.EmployeeID;
```

The Wizard erroneously translates the `FROM` clause of the Jet SQL statement to

```
FROM Employees
   INNER JOIN (Categories
      INNER JOIN ((Orders
         INNER JOIN [Order Details Extended]()
            "Order Details Extended"
         ON Orders.OrderID =
              "Order Details Extended".OrderID)
            INNER JOIN Products ON [Order Details Extended]()
            "Order Details Extended".ProductID =
               Products.ProductID)
   ON Categories.CategoryID = Products.CategoryID)
      ON Employees.EmployeeID = Orders.EmployeeID
```

The error is mixing delimiter types in the statement that calls the Order Details Extended function. Changing `[Order Details Extended]()` to `"Order Details Extended"()` solves the problem. The nested query failed to upsize, so you can't just edit the T-SQL for the query. Following is what you must do to fix the problem:

22

- Replace the Order Details Extended function with a view. Copy the T-SQL statement of the function to the Clipboard, delete the function, create a new view in the project designer, and paste the T-SQL statement in the view's SQL pane. The nested query didn't upsize, so you must copy the original Jet SQL Statement to the Clipboard, create a new view, and paste the text to the SQL pane of the view.

T-SQL

The T-SQL for the view of the Order Details Extended query is

```
SELECT TOP 100 PERCENT dbo.[Order Details].OrderID,
   dbo.[Order Details].ProductID,
   dbo.Products.ProductName,
   dbo.[Order Details].UnitPrice,
   dbo.[Order Details].Quantity,
   dbo.[Order Details].Discount,
   CONVERT(money, (dbo.[Order Details].UnitPrice *
      dbo.[Order Details].Quantity) *
      (1 - dbo.[Order Details].Discount) / 100) *
      100 AS ExtendedPrice
      AS ExtendedPrice
FROM dbo.Products
   INNER JOIN dbo.[Order Details]
      ON dbo.Products.ProductID =
         dbo.[Order Details].ProductID
ORDER BY dbo.[Order Details].OrderID
```

You can remove `/ 100` and `* 100` without affecting the values in the ExtendedPrice column.

- Copy the original Jet SQL Statement to the Clipboard, create a new view, and paste the text to the SQL pane of the view.

Alternatively, you can use the existing function as the inner query and modify the outer query. Add the function name with empty parentheses to the INNER JOIN element as follows: `INNER JOIN` **`[Order Details Extended]()`** `[Order Details Extended]`. (Square bracket delimiters work if you don't combine them with double-quote delimiters.) If you use `AS` to explicitly declare the alias, clicking Check SQL Syntax removes it.

The better of the two preceding options is to change the function to a view, because multiple nested queries or the Record Source property value of forms and reports might depend on the source query.

The qryCTWizSource view illustrates the importance of testing each successfully upsized object in the project designer to verify the correctness of column names and data values. The qryCTWizSource view upsizes, but contains an upsizing error—in this case a spurious alias for the ProductID column. Following is the offending SELECT statement's column list with the bad alias in bold:

```
SELECT dbo.Orders.OrderDate,
   [Order Details Extended].ProductID
      AS [_Order Details Extended.ProductID_],
   [Order Details Extended].ProductName,
   [Order Details Extended].ExtendedPrice
```

Remove the alias and the view executes correctly.

22

CONFORMING COMPUTED COLUMNS TO THE ANSI SQL STANDARD

Jet SQL lets you use the value of one computed column as a source for another computed column. It's common to use such compound-computed columns to store values that include sales or value-added taxes.

Jet SQL

The following sample field list with multiple aliased computed columns works when you use Jet SQL but fails with T-SQL:

```
SELECT OrderTotal * 0.06 AS StateTax,
   OrderTotal * 0.01 AS CountyTax,
   OrderTotal * 0.005 AS CityTax,
   StateTax + CountyTax +
      CityTax AS Taxes,
   OrderTotal + Taxes AS InvoiceTotal
FROM Orders
```

The ANSI-92 SQL standard requires that each member of the `SELECT` column list must have an unambiguous reference to a field of a table specified in the `FROM` clause. The computed `Taxes` column of the preceding example fails this test, because it's defined only in the query and not in the table, so SQL Server's query parser won't compile the statement.

Figure 22.9 shows the error message the query parser returns when the Upsizing Wizard encounters the Jet qryOrderAmount query, which computes freight cost as a percentage of the order amount for each order. (The **`Format()`** function to display percent was removed from the query prior to upsizing.) This query uses the VBA **`CCur`** function to convert the Jet data type of the Amount from Double to Currency.

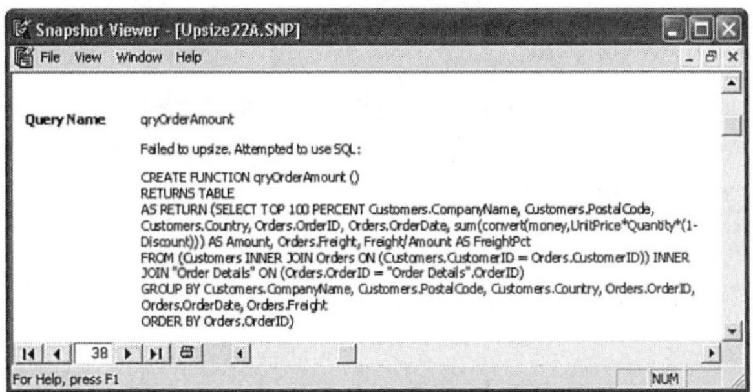

Figure 22.9
The qryOrderAmount query fails to upsize to a function, because the FreightPct column is dependent on the computed Amount column.

Jet SQL

The Jet SQL statement for the qryOrderAmount query is

```
SELECT Customers.CompanyName,
       Customers.PostalCode, Customers.Country,
       Orders.OrderID, Orders.OrderDate,
       Sum(CCur([UnitPrice]*[Quantity]*
          (1-[Discount]))) AS Amount,
       Orders.Freight, [Freight]/[Amount] AS FreightPct
FROM (Customers
       INNER JOIN Orders
          ON Customers.CustomerID = Orders.CustomerID)
       INNER JOIN [Order Details]
          ON Orders.OrderID = [Order Details].OrderID
GROUP BY Customers.CompanyName, Customers.PostalCode,
   Customers.Country, Orders.OrderID,
   Orders.OrderDate, Orders.Freight
ORDER BY Orders.OrderID;
```

The column definition that conflicts with ANSI SQL is in bold type.

You can correct the problem in the source query by substituting the `Sum...AS Amount` aggregate statement for the `[Amount]` value in the second computed column. If you correct the source query, you must rerun the Upsizing Wizard. It's faster to create a new view in the project designer by doing the following:

1. Copy the Jet SQL statement of the source query to the Clipboard.

2. Create a new view in the upsized project, click the SQL button, and paste the statement to the SQL pane.

3. Substitute the T-SQL `CONVERT` or `CAST` function for VBA type conversion statements, if they are used in value expressions. For this example, the `CAST(`*`Expression`*` AS money)` function substitutes for the VBA **`CCur`**`(`*`Expression`*`)` function.

4. Temporarily remove the element of the column definition that prevents compiling the view, `/[Amount]` for this example. Click Check SQL Syntax to verify your changes. The project designer automatically adds `TOP 100 PERCENT` to accommodate the `ORDER BY` clause (see Figure 22.10).

5. Substitute the expression of the calculated column for the alias name you deleted. For this example, `/ SUM((dbo.[Order Details].UnitPrice * dbo.[Order Details].Quantity) * (1 - dbo.[Order Details].Discount))` substitutes for `/[Amount]`. The `CAST` function isn't required here because the column value is a decimal fraction, not a monetary amount.

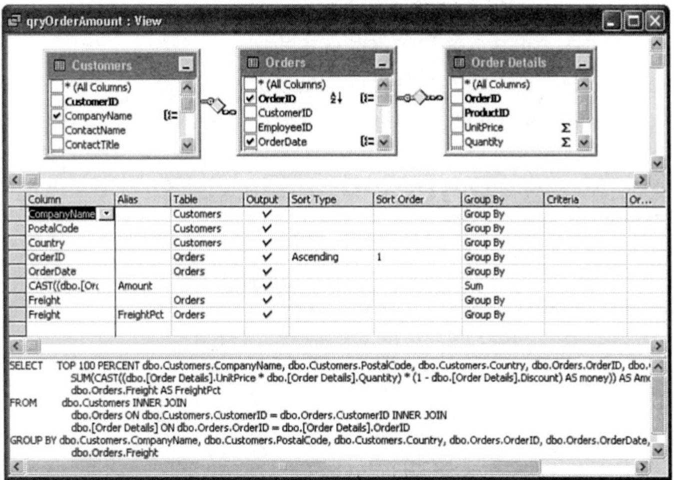

Figure 22.10
The first step in conforming a Jet SQL query with computed column values based on aliased columns is to substitute T-SQL functions for unsupported VBA functions and test the result without the offending aliased value.

T-SQL

The final T-SQL statement for the qryOrderAmount view is

```
SELECT TOP 100 PERCENT dbo.Customers.CompanyName,
     dbo.Customers.PostalCode, dbo.Customers.Country,
     dbo.Orders.OrderID, dbo.Orders.OrderDate,
     SUM(CAST((dbo.[Order Details].UnitPrice *
        dbo.[Order Details].Quantity) *
       (1 - dbo.[Order Details].Discount) AS money)) AS Amount,
     dbo.Orders.Freight,
     dbo.Orders.Freight /
        SUM((dbo.[Order Details].UnitPrice *
        dbo.[Order Details].Quantity) *
       (1 - dbo.[Order Details].Discount)) AS FreightPct
FROM dbo.Customers
    INNER JOIN dbo.Orders
       ON dbo.Customers.CustomerID =
          dbo.Orders.CustomerID
    INNER JOIN dbo.[Order Details]
       ON dbo.Orders.OrderID =
          dbo.[Order Details].OrderID
GROUP BY dbo.Customers.CompanyName,
    dbo.Customers.PostalCode, dbo.Customers.Country,
    dbo.Orders.OrderID, dbo.Orders.OrderDate,
    dbo.Orders.Freight
ORDER BY dbo.Orders.OrderID
```

6. Verify your changes, and save the view with the original query name, **qryOrderAmount** for this example.

7. Run the view and verify that the result set is identical to that of the original Jet Query. In this case, the FreightPct column is formatted as money, because the extended Format property value for the computed column is `$#,##0.00;($#,##0.00)`. The

computed FreightPct column inherits this format from the upsized Jet format applied to the Freight column of the Orders table.

8. To change the format of the FreightPct column, right click anywhere in the project designer window, and choose Properties to open the Properties dialog for the view. Click the Columns tab, select FreightPct from the Column Name list, and select Percent from the Format list (see Figure 22.11). Extended property values apply only to Access objects, such as datasheets.

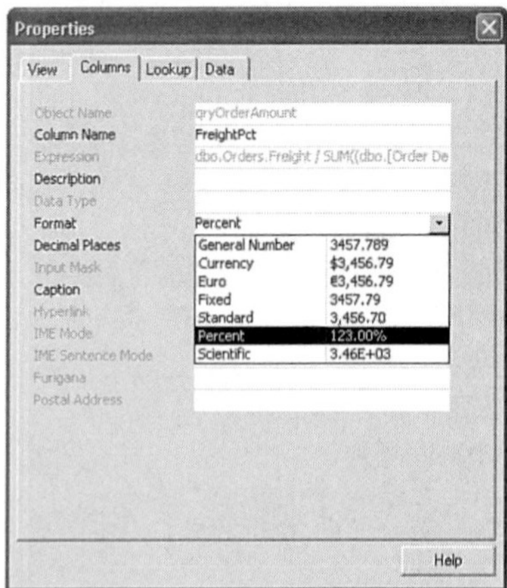

Figure 22.11 Set the extended Format property value of columns you want to display as percentages in Datasheet view. Format property values override the default display of SQL Server formatted data types, such as `money`, `smallmoney`, and `datetime`. You also can specify the number of decimal digits the datasheet displays by setting the value of the Decimal Places property.

9. Close the Properties dialog, save the change to the view, and rerun the view. Figure 22.12 shows the resulting datasheet with the column sequence rearranged to match that of the column list.

qryOrderAmount : View

Company Name	Postal Code	Country	Order ID	Order Date	Amount	Freight	FreightPct
Wilman Kala	21240	Finland	10248	04-Jul-1996	$440.00	$32.38	7.36%
Tradição Hipermercac	05634-030	Brazil	10249	05-Jul-1996	$1,863.40	$11.61	0.62%
Hanari Carnes	05454-876	Brazil	10250	08-Jul-1996	$1,552.60	$65.83	4.24%
Victuailles en stock	69004	France	10251	08-Jul-1996	$654.06	$41.34	6.32%
Suprêmes délices	B-6000	Belgium	10252	09-Jul-1996	$3,597.90	$51.30	1.43%
Hanari Carnes	05454-876	Brazil	10253	10-Jul-1996	$1,444.80	$58.17	4.03%
Chop-suey Chinese	3012	Switzerland	10254	11-Jul-1996	$556.62	$22.98	4.13%
Richter Supermarkt	1203	Switzerland	10255	12-Jul-1996	$2,490.50	$148.33	5.96%
Wellington Importado	08737-363	Brazil	10256	15-Jul-1996	$517.80	$13.97	2.70%
HILARIÓN-Abastos	5022	Venezuela	10257	16-Jul-1996	$1,119.90	$81.91	7.31%
Ernst Handel	8010	Austria	10258	17-Jul-1996	$1,614.88	$140.51	8.70%
Centro comercial Moc	05022	Mexico	10259	18-Jul-1996	$100.80	$3.25	3.22%
Old World Delicatess	99508	USA	10260	19-Jul-1996	$1,504.65	$55.09	3.66%
Que Delícia	02389-673	Brazil	10261	19-Jul-1996	$448.00	$3.05	0.68%
Rattlesnake Canyon (	87110	USA	10262	22-Jul-1996	$584.00	$48.29	8.27%
Ernst Handel	8010	Austria	10263	23-Jul-1996	$1,873.80	$146.06	7.79%
Folk och fä HB	S-844 67	Sweden	10264	24-Jul-1996	$695.63	$3.67	0.53%
Blondel père et fils	67000	France	10265	25-Jul-1996	$1,176.00	$55.28	4.70%
Wartian Herkku	90110	Finland	10266	26-Jul-1996	$346.56	$25.73	7.42%
Frankenversand	80805	Germany	10267	29-Jul-1996	$3,536.60	$208.58	5.90%

Record: 1 of 830

Figure 22.12 Datasheet view of the upsized qryOrderAmount query confirms that it's identical to the result set of the original Jet version.

NOTE

Access saves column widths and other datasheet properties you change in Datasheet view, but doesn't save changes you make to the sequence of columns. When you close and reopen the view, the column sequence reverts to the original sequence.

TIP

To force the datasheet column sequence to conform to that of the column list, create a stored procedure instead of a view. You can quickly create the stored procedure version of a view by copying the view's T-SQL statement, and pasting it into the SQL pane of a new stored procedure.

DEALING WITH FUNCTIONS THAT REFER TO VALUES OF ACCESS CONTROL OBJECTS AND OTHER OBSCURE ISSUES

Jet queries accept values returned by Access objects, such as bound text, combo, and list boxes. For example, the Invoices Filter query uses the value of the OrdersID text box of the Orders form as the `WHERE` clause criterion to filter the Invoices query.

Dealing with the Invoices Filter demonstrates three important rules for testing upsized projects:

- **Don't trust the Wizard**—Despite the known inability of the Wizard to upsize Jet queries that refer to Access object values, the Wizard attempts to do so and creates inoperable functions or stored procedures in the SQL Server database. Compare the execution behavior of every upsized query with its Jet counterpart in the source .mdb.
- NEW **Find and test each Access object that relies on an upsized query**—If you have a large number of application objects, this process is challenging. Take advantage of the Object Dependencies task pane to find references to the query.

TIP

Alternatively, export a Database Documenter report to a .rtf or .txt file, and use the Find feature of Word or your text editor to locate references to specific query names.

- **Verify whether query upsizing issues are the source of apparent form or report malfunction**—This example demonstrates that the upsized Invoices Filter and Invoices queries require you to modify the Orders form and the associated Invoice report.

→ To review use of the Database Documenter, **see** "Generating a Data Dictionary with the Database Documenter," **p. 212**.

This section addresses upsizing a specific set of objects, but the process described typifies the hurdles you face when upsizing even a relatively simple set of interdependent database and application objects.

Jet SQL

The Jet SQL statement for the Invoices Filter query (after changing `DISTINCTROW` to `DISTINCT`) is

```
SELECT DISTINCT Invoices.*
FROM Invoices
WHERE (((Invoices.OrderID)=
   Forms!Orders![OrderID]));
```

T-SQL

The Upsizing Wizard treats the `Forms!Orders![OrderID]` element of the `WHERE` clause as a conventional input parameter:

```
SELECT DISTINCT dbo.Invoices.*
FROM dbo.Invoices
WHERE (OrderID = @Forms_Orders__OrderID_)
```

The Wizard replaces Access's bang (`!`) object separator and square bracket (`[]`) delimiters with underscores (_), so there are two underscores between Orders and OrderID, and another underscore following OrderID. The parameter naming problem is moot for this example, because a parameterized function won't work in the context by which it's called in the Orders form.

SPELUNKING APPLICATION OBJECTS FOR QUERY REFERENCES

It's not easy to determine how the Orders form employs the Invoices Filter query, because it doesn't—and shouldn't—appear as a value of the Filter property in the Data page of the Properties dialog for the Orders form or Orders Subform. The Print Invoice button of the Orders form executes a VBA event handler, `PrintInvoice_Click`, to print an invoice for the currently selected order; event-handling code calls the Invoices Filter. Clicking the Print Invoice button opens a "The column prefix 'Customers' doesn't match with [sic] a table name or alias name used in the query" message.

The reference to the Invoices Filter is in the VBA code behind the Orders form. Following is the code for `PrintInvoice_Click` event handler:

```
Sub PrintInvoice_Click()
' This code created by Command Button Wizard.
On Error GoTo Err_PrintInvoice_Click

   Dim strDocName As String

   strDocName = "Invoice"
   ' Print Invoice report, using Invoices Filter query to print
   ' invoice for current order.
   DoCmd.OpenReport strDocName, acViewNormal, "Invoices Filter"

Exit_PrintInvoice_Click:
  Exit Sub

Err_PrintInvoice_Click:
   ' If action was cancelled by the user,
   ' don't display an error message.
```

```
    Const conErrDoCmdCancelled = 2501
    If (Err = conErrDoCmdCancelled) Then
        Resume Exit_PrintInvoice_Click
    Else
        MsgBox Err.Description
        Resume Exit_PrintInvoice_Click
    End If
End Sub
```

NOTE

> Working with VBA code is the subject of Part VII of this book, "Programming and Converting Access Applications," so including code examples at this point might appear to be premature. If you're considering upgrading existing Access applications to SQL Server, however, it's a reasonable assumption that you have at least some familiarity with VBA.

The `DoCmd.OpenReport strDocName, acViewNormal, "Invoices Filter"` instruction opens the Invoice report, and applies the Invoices Filter to the report before printing. The data source for the Invoice report is the Jet Invoices query, which the Wizard has upsized to an inoperative view. Before attempting to change the event-handler code to print a single invoice, however, test the Report to determine whether it works with T-SQL view. Not surprisingly, it doesn't work, but the incorrectly upsized Invoices Filter isn't the culprit.

CORRECTING DUPLICATE COLUMN NAMES IN VIEWS

To detect the source of the "column prefix" problem and correct it, do the following:

1. In the Reports page of the Database window, double-click the Invoice report. You receive the "column prefix" error message, which indicates the problem is related to the upsized Invoices query.

   TIP

   > Unlike Jet queries, SQL Server views don't support table prefixes to resolve ambiguous references to columns having the same name. T-SQL doesn't permit duplication of column names, so it aliases a duplicate name with a numeric suffix.

2. Change to Report Design view, and find the controls bound to duplicate column names. The `CompanyName` field is common to the Customers and Shippers tables. Views don't support table names, so delete the `Customers.` and `Shippers.` prefixes from the text boxes adjacent to the Bill To and Ship Via labels.

3. Open the Invoices view in Design view to find the aliased `CompanyName` field, which is associated with the Shippers table. Change the `CompanyName1` alias to the more descriptive **`ShipperName`** (see Figure 22.13). Save your change.

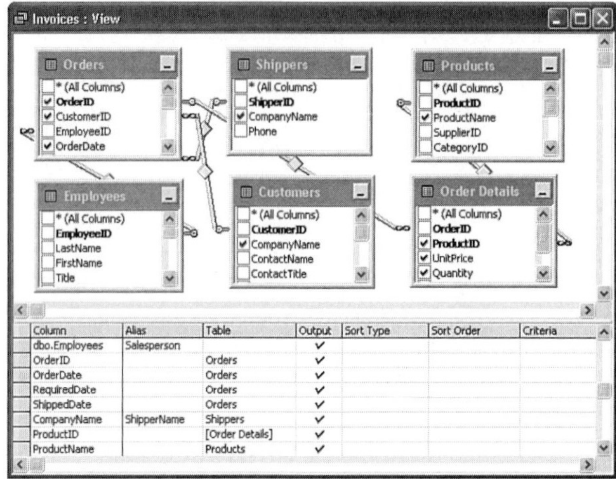

Figure 22.13
T-SQL views require unique column names, so the Wizard generates an alias for duplicate column names in the `SELECT` list. Changing the `CompanyName1` alias to `ShipperName` clarifies the view's output.

TIP

Don't confuse captions with aliases. Captions are extended properties; aliases appear in the SQL `SELECT` statement's field list. The Wizard has upsized Jet Caption property values to extended properties of the view, so Company Name appears as the caption for both the CompanyName and ShipperName columns. To avoid Datasheet view confusion, open the Properties dialog for the query, change the Caption property value of the column to **Shipper Name**, and save the change.

4. Return to the Invoice report and change the name of the CompanyName text box under the ShipVia label from CompanyName to **ShipperName** (see Figure 22.14).

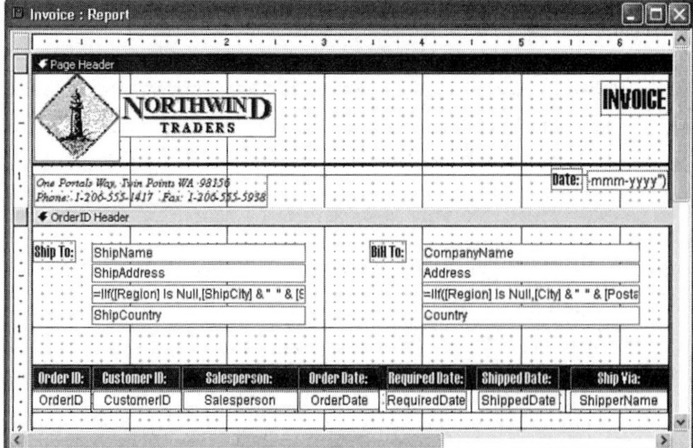

Figure 22.14
Changing the alias of a column of a view requires a corresponding change to the name of all application objects that are bound to the column.

5. Change to Print Preview view to verify that your changes work properly (see Figure 22.15). Close the Invoices report and save the changes.

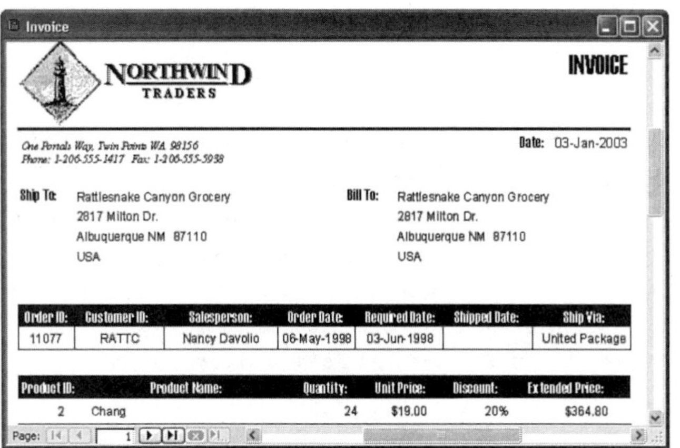

Figure 22.15 Opening the Invoice report in Print Preview demonstrates that your changes to the report and its view data source correct the initial problem.

6. Reopen the Orders form, if you closed it, and click the Print Invoices button. Be prepared to quickly click the Cancel button, because this operation now prints an invoice for every order.

NOTE

> Printing every invoice instead of printing no invoice or displaying an error message is unexpected behavior. No argument value is passed as a parameter to the Invoices Filter function, so you would expect the Enter Parameter Value dialog to appear. All invoices are printed because the `DoCmd.OpenReport` method disregards the filter if it can't open it, instead of displaying an error message.

REMOVING REFERENCES TO THE INVOICES FILTER FROM THE ORDERS FORM

Applying filters saved as query objects is a holdover from the early days of Access when macros were popular for automating applications. There's no simple method of modifying the Invoices Filter to enable its use in this scenario, and it's much more efficient to specify a filter in the VBA code that opens the Invoice report.

The syntax of the `OpenReport` method of the Access-specific `DoCmd` object is

```
DoCmd.OpenReport strReportName, [intMode,
   [strFilterName, [strWHERECondition,
   [intWindowMode, [varOpenArguments]]]]]
```

All the arguments except `strReportName` are optional. In this case, you delete the reference to the Invoices Filter as the `strFilterName` argument, and supply a `strWHERECondition` argument value to provide the OrderID value of the current order to the Invoices report. The `strWHERECondition` value is a valid `WHERE` clause without the `WHERE` keyword.

To fix the `DoCmd.OpenReport` statement of the `PrintInvoice_Click` event handler, do the following:

1. Open the Orders form in Design view, and click the Code button to open the VBA editor.
2. Scroll to the `DoCmd.OpenReport...` line of the `PrintInvoice_Click` subprocedure.
3. Delete `"Invoices Filter"` argument value, but not the preceding comma.
4. Add **, "OrderID = " & CStr(Me.OrderID.Value)** to the line (see Figure 22.16). The two commas between `acViewNormal` and `"OrderID...` are required. The **`CStr`** function converts the **`Variant`** OrderID value of the **`Long`** (`Integer`) type to a **`String`** variable. **`Me`** is a self-reference to the report. Use of **`Me`** and `Value` is optional, but is good VBA programming practice. The entire `DoCmd.OpenReport` statement is

```
DoCmd.OpenReport strDocName, acViewNormal, ,
   "OrderID = " & CStr(Me.OrderID.Value)
```

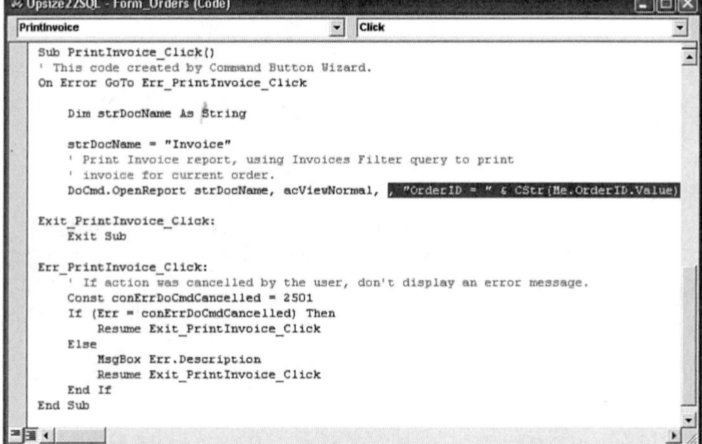

Figure 22.16
Add the highlighted code to the `DoCmd.OpenReport` instruction after deleting the reference to the Invoices Filter view.

> **TIP**
>
> If you want to display the report in Print Preview mode before printing, change the `acViewNormal` Access constant to `acViewPreview`.

5. Return to the Orders form, click Form view, and click the Print Invoice button. If you change the mode, the invoice for the selected order appears in the Print Preview window; otherwise, the default printer prints the invoice.
6. Close the Orders form and save your changes.

If you judge the amount of work required to upsize a relatively simple set of interrelated queries and application objects to be daunting, consider abandoning the upsizing process and linking SQL Server tables to your Jet application.

UPSIZING JET SQL STATEMENTS EXECUTED BY FORMS, REPORTS, AND CONTROLS

Many Access developers use SQL `SELECT` statements, instead of saved (persistent) queries, to supply the record source for bound forms, reports, and controls on forms and reports. Tracking down problems with application objects that execute SQL statements directly is even more of a challenge than fixing objects that refer to SQL Server views, functions, and stored procedures. Unlike the Access 2000 version, Access 2003's Upsizing Wizard doesn't attempt to convert Jet SQL statements used as the values of Record Source and Row Source properties to SQL Server views or stored procedures.

Northwind.mdb—and thus Upsize22.mdb—includes an example of a form (Sales Analysis) that fails to open as a result of a Jet SQL keyword (`DISTINCTROW`) that T-SQL doesn't support. When you double-click the Sales Analysis form, an "Invalid SQL Statement" message opens, which advises you to "Check the server filter on the form record source." The advice is bogus because the Server Filter property value of the form is empty.

The culprits in this case are the Sales Analysis form's two alternating subforms—Sales Analysis Subform1 and Sales Analysis Subform2. Both subforms have SQL statements as the value of the Record Source property. Unfortunately, the Microsoft developers added `DISTINCTROW` to the `SELECT` statement, which renders the SQL statement unusable in a project.

TIP

> **Don't use Jet's `DISTINCTROW` or T-SQL's `DISTINCT` qualifier unless you have a specific reason to do so. The majority of `SELECT` queries used as the record source for forms and reports don't return duplicate rows. You might need the `DISTINCT` qualifier, however, to preclude duplicate values when populating combo and list boxes from queries having joins.**

To correct problems with SQL statements that serve as the record source for bound objects, do this:

1. Open the form or report in Design view, click Properties to open the Properties window for the object, and click the Data tab. For this example, open Sales Analysis Subform1 (see Figure 22.17).

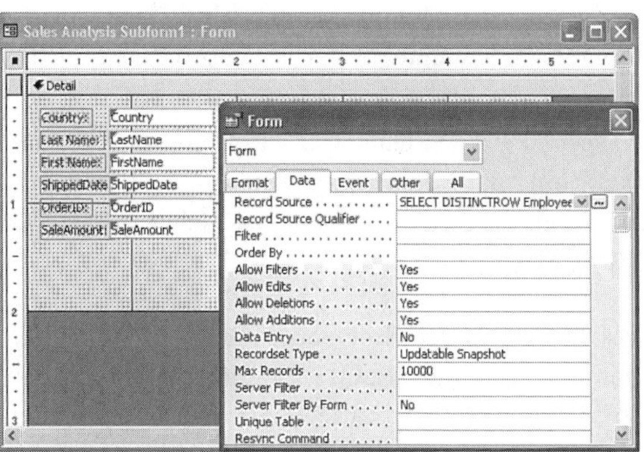

Figure 22.17 Sales Analysis Subform1 has a superfluous `DISTINCTROW` modifier in the `SELECT` statement for the form's Record Source Property. Why Microsoft's developers added this modifier is a mystery.

NOTE

Access smart tags identify each text box with a green triangle. Passing the mouse pointer over the smart tag displays a "This control has an invalid control source. The smart tag opens to provide a list of options to fix the control, but it's the form, not the control, that has Record Source property problem.

2. If the Record Source property has an SQL statement as its value, remove the `DISTINCTROW` modifier, if presenent, and click the Builder button to open the project designer's SQL Statement: Query window.
3. If the problem with the SQL statement isn't immediately evident, click the Check SQL Syntax button, which opens an error message that *might* assist in locating the errant element.
4. Use of `DISTINCTROW` is the obvious problem in this example, so delete it, and click the Check SQL Syntax button. After deleting `DISTINCTROW`, the project designer's window appears as shown in Figure 22.18.

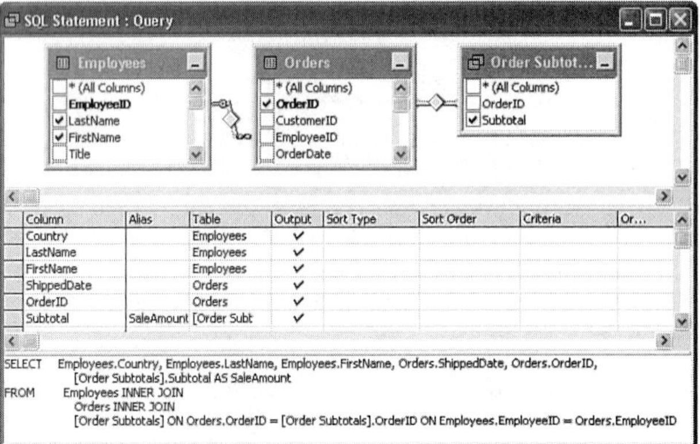

Figure 22.18
Clicking the Builder button of the Record Source property's text box opens the project designer's SQL Statement: Query window. The Diagram and Grid panes don't open until you click Check SQL Syntax.

5. Close the project designer, click Yes to save your changes, close the Properties window, and close the form or report, again saving your changes.
6. For this example, repeat step 1 for the Sales Analysis Subform2 form, delete `DISTINCTROW` from the SQL statement in the Record Source text box, close the Properties window and the form, and save your changes.
7. Test the form to verify that the changes you made to the SQL statements don't lead to incorrect values. Compare the data values displayed by the upsized form with that of the original Jet version. Figure 22.19 shows that deleting `DISTINCTROW` doesn't affect the data of the subform's PivotTable.

The preceding process also applies to Row Source property value of list boxes, combo boxes, and most other objects bound to SQL statements. An exception is the Row Source property of `Chart` objects you create with the Chart Wizard. The later "Emulating Jet

Crosstab Queries with T-SQL" section shows you how to handle T-SQL's lack of crosstab query capability.

Years	Quarters	Buchanan Total Sales	Callahan Total Sales	Davolio Total Sales	Dodsworth Total Sales	Fuller Total Sales	King Total Sales	Grand Total Total Sales
1996	Qtr3	$3,058.82	$11,040.00	$8,892.48	$4,364.30	$4,143.60	$1,686.00	$33,185.20
	Qtr4	$14,608.38	$8,120.70	$21,969.28	$5,530.22	$13,667.86	$13,546.16	$77,442.60
	Total	$17,667.20	$19,160.70	$30,861.76	$9,894.52	$17,811.46	$15,232.16	$110,627.80
1997	Qtr1	$3,237.12	$19,992.23	$17,885.83	$966.80	$11,434.38	$15,108.34	$68,624.70
	Qtr2	$6,647.68	$8,686.73	$15,925.56	$5,692.28	$22,136.67	$16,437.92	$75,526.84
	Qtr3	$12,975.81	$9,650.00	$32,394.94	$5,285.05	$16,148.80	$20,263.93	$96,718.53
	Qtr4	$8,572.58	$18,625.08	$29,644.07	$12,468.76	$21,448.29	$8,017.00	$98,775.78
	Total	$31,433.19	$56,954.04	$95,850.40	$24,412.89	$71,168.14	$59,827.19	$339,645.85
1998	Qtr1	$19,481.90	$27,030.85	$26,350.99	$31,513.21	$36,882.56	$19,757.48	$161,016.99
	Qtr2	$210.00	$20,697.10	$34,214.23	$10,629.45	$36,907.62	$24,802.41	$127,460.81
	Total	$19,691.90	$47,727.95	$60,565.22	$42,142.66	$73,790.18	$44,559.89	$288,477.80
Grand Total		$68,792.29	$123,842.69	$187,277.38	$76,450.07	$162,769.78	$119,619.24	$738,751.45

Figure 22.19 The upsized PivotTable form displays data that's identical to its Jet counterpart in Upsize22.mdb or Northwind.mdb.

COMPARING ANSI-92 SQL, T-SQL, AND JET SQL

Jet SQL and T-SQL don't include many of the approximately 200 keywords incorporated in the ANSI standard for SQL-92. Most of the common SQL keywords missing from Jet's implementation are provided by the expressions you create with operators, built-in functions, or user-defined functions you write in Access's VBA flavor. Understanding the similarities and differences between Jet and ANSI-92 SQL is important when you upsize Jet applications to ADP. This knowledge is even more important if you take the "planned migration" route, described near the beginning of the chapter, to upsizing your database front ends.

ANSI-92 SQL RESERVED WORDS IN JET SQL

Access doesn't support all the ANSI SQL keywords with identical reserved words in the Jet SQL language, but each update to Jet converges on the SQL-92 standard, as does each successive version of SQL Server. In this chapter, keywords are defined as the commands and functions that make up the vocabulary of the ANSI SQL language. Jet SQL commands and functions are referred to here as reserved words to distinguish them from ANSI SQL.

The tables in the following two sections also are intended to acquaint readers who are familiar with ANSI or similar implementations of SQL in other RDBMSs or database front-end applications with the Access implementation of Jet SQL and SQL Server 2000's version of T-SQL. If you haven't used any version of SQL, the tables demonstrate that SQL is a relatively sparse language, having far fewer keywords compared to programming languages such as VBA, and that Jet SQL is even more sparse. Jet SQL has few reserved words to learn. T-SQL implements most ANSI-92 keywords and has many useful additions to ANSI-92 SQL.

22

JET SQL RESERVED WORDS CORRESPONDING TO ANSI SQL AND T-SQL KEYWORDS

Access supports the ANSI SQL and T-SQL keywords listed in Table 22.2 as identical reserved words in Jet SQL. Don't use these reserved words as the names of tables, fields, or variables. The reserved words in Table 22.2 appear in all capital letters in the SQL statements Access creates for you when you design a query or when you add a graph to a form or report. Reserved words marked with an asterisk were introduced by Access 2000 and are accessible only from VBA code and, if you're using ActiveX Data Objects (ADO), require a reference to the Microsoft ADO Ext. 2.x for DDL and Security library (Msadox.dll).

TABLE 22.2 RESERVED WORDS COMMON TO ANSI-92 SQL, JET SQL, AND T-SQL

ADD	ALIAS	ALL
ALTER	ANY	AS
ASC	AVG	BEGIN*
BETWEEN	BY	CHECK*
COLUMN*	COMMIT*	CONSTRAINT
COUNT	CREATE	DELETE
DESC	DISALLOW*	DISTINCT
DROP	EXISTS	FOREIGN
FROM	HAVING	IN
INDEX	INNER	INSERT
INTO	IS	JOIN
KEY	LEFT	LIKE
MAX	MIN	NOT
NULL	ON	OR
ORDER	OUTER	PARAMETERS
PRIMARY*	PROCEDURE	REFERENCES
RIGHT	ROLLBACK*	SELECT
SET	SOME*	TRANSACTION*
UNION	UNIQUE	UPDATE
VALUE	VALUES	VIEW
WHERE		

The keywords that relate to data types, `CHAR[ACTER]`, `FLOAT`, `INT[EGER]`, and `REAL`, aren't included in Table 22.2 because Jet SQL uses a different reserved word to specify these SQL data types (refer to Table 22.4 later in this chapter). The comparison operators (=, <, <=, >, and =>) are common to both ANSI SQL and Jet SQL. Access and T-SQL substitute the <> operator for ANSI SQL's not-equal (`!=`) operator.

As in ANSI SQL, the IN reserved word in Jet SQL can be used as an operator to specify a list of values to match in a WHERE clause or the result set of a subquery.

JET FUNCTIONS AND OPERATORS USED IN PLACE OF ANSI SQL KEYWORDS

Table 22.3 shows reserved words in Jet SQL that correspond to ANSI SQL keywords but are operators or functions used in Jet SQL expressions. Jet doesn't use ANSI SQL syntax for aggregate functions; for example, you can't use the `SUM(DISTINCT *field_name*)` or `AVG(DISTINCT *field_name*)` syntax of ANSI SQL. Jet distinguishes between its use of the `Sum()` aggregate function and the SQL implementation, `SUM()`, by initial letter capitalization. Expressions that use operators such as **And** and **Or** are enclosed in parentheses in Jet SQL statements; Jet SQL uses uppercase AND and OR when criteria are added to more than one column.

TABLE 22.3 JET SQL RESERVED WORDS THAT SUBSTITUTE FOR ANSI SQL KEYWORDS

Jet SQL	ANSI SQL	Jet SQL	ANSI SQL
And	AND	Max()	MAX()
Avg()	AVG()	Min()	MIN()
Between	BETWEEN	Not	NOT
Count()	COUNT()	Null	NULL
Is	IS	Or	OR
In	IN	Sum()	SUM()
Like	LIKE		

The Wizard upsizes Jet SQL Like expressions for DateTime values to the ANSI SQL LIKE operator, as mentioned near the beginning of this chapter. For example WHERE *DateColumn* Like "*/*/1997" upsizes to WHERE *DateColumn* LIKE '%/%/1997'. (The next section discusses differences between Jet and ANSI SQL wildcard characters.) T-SQL statements containing LIKE constraints for columns of the datetime datatype fail to return rows. If you attempt to edit the LIKE expression, you receive a "Your entry cannot be converted to a valid date time value" message. This use of LIKE is valid in T-SQL; T-SQL statements containing LIKE datetime constraints work fine in the SQL Query Analyzer or from OSQL. The problem with LIKE datetime expressions in the project designer appears to stem from the SQL Server OLE DB provider (SQLOLEDB).

The Jet IsNull() function that returns **True** (–1) or **False** (0), depending on whether IsNull()'s argument has a Null value, has no equivalent in ANSI SQL and isn't a substitute for IS NULL or IS NOT NULL qualifiers in WHERE clauses.

Jet SQL doesn't support distinct aggregate function references, such as AVG(DISTINCT *field_name*); the default DISTINCTROW qualifier added to the SELECT statement by Jet serves this purpose.

22

JET SQL RESERVED WORDS, OPERATORS, AND FUNCTIONS NOT IN ANSI SQL

Jet SQL contains a number of reserved words that aren't ANSI SQL keywords (see Table 22.4). Most of these reserved words define Jet data types; some reserved words have equivalents in ANSI SQL and T-SQL, and others don't. You use Jet DDL reserved words to establish or modify the properties of tables and columns. Jet SQL's `DISTINCTROW` modifier is described in the following section. Jet uses `PIVOT` and `TRANSFORM` to create the crosstab queries that are unique to Jet databases.

TABLE 22.4 JET SQL RESERVED WORDS NOT IN ANSI SQL

Jet SQL	ANSI SQL	Category	Purpose
`BINARY`	No equivalent	DDL	Not an official Jet field data type
`BOOLEAN`	No equivalent	DDL	Jet Yes/No field data type
`BYTE`	No equivalent	DDL	Byte field data type, 1 byte integer
`CURRENCY`	No equivalent	DDL	Jet Currency field data type
`DATETIME`	No equivalent	DDL	Jet Date/Time field data type
`DISTINCTROW`	No equivalent	DQL	Updatable Jet `Recordset` objects
`DOUBLE`	`REAL`	DDL	High-precision decimal numbers
`LONG`	`INT[EGER]`	DDL	Long Integer field data type
`LONGBINARY`	No equivalent	DDL	OLE Object field data type
`LONGTEXT`	`VARCHAR`	DDL	Memo field data type
`OWNERACCESS`	No equivalent	DQL	Run with owner's privileges parameters
`PIVOT`	No equivalent	DQL	Used in crosstab queries
`SHORT`	`SMALLINT`	DDL	Integer field data type, 2 bytes
`SINGLE`	No equivalent	DDL	Single-precision real number
`TEXT(n)`	`CHAR[ACTER]`	DDL	Text field data type
`TRANSFORM`	No equivalent	DQL	Creates crosstab query
&	|| (two pipe symbols)	DQL	String concatenation
? (`LIKE` wildcard)	_ (wildcard)	DQL	Single with `LIKE` character
* (`LIKE` wildcard)	% (wildcard)	DQL	Zero or more characters
# (`LIKE` wildcard)	No equivalent	DQL	Single digit, 0–9
# (date specifier)	No equivalent	DQL	Encloses date/time values
<> (not equal)	!=	DQL	Jet uses ! as an object name separator

Jet provides four statistical aggregate functions that aren't incorporated in ANSI SQL. These functions are listed in Table 22.5.

TABLE 22.5 AGGREGATE SQL FUNCTIONS IN JET SQL BUT NOT ANSI SQL

Jet Function	Category	Purpose
`StdDev()`	DQL	Standard deviation of a population sample
`StdDevP()`	DQL	Standard deviation of a population
`Var()`	DQL	Statistical variation of a population sample
`VarP()`	DQL	Statistical variation of a population

JET'S DISTINCTROW AND ANSI SQL'S DISTINCT KEYWORDS

Jet SQL's `DISTINCTROW` reserved word that follows the SQL `SELECT` keyword causes Jet to eliminate duplicated rows from the query's result. The effect of `DISTINCTROW` is especially dramatic in queries used to display records in tables that have indirect relationships. As mentioned earlier in the chapter, you're likely to encounter `DISTINCTROW` in Jet queries created prior to Access 97.

`DISTINCTROW` is related to, but not the same as, the `DISTINCT` keyword in ANSI SQL. Both words eliminate duplicate rows of data in query result tables, but they differ in execution. `DISTINCT` in ANSI SQL eliminates duplicate rows based only on the values of the data contained in the rows of the query, from left to right. You cannot update values from multiple-table queries that include the keyword `DISTINCT`.

`DISTINCTROW` eliminates duplicate rows based on the content of the underlying table, regardless of whether additional field(s) that distinguish records in the table are included. `DISTINCTROW` allows values in special kinds of multiple-table `Recordset` objects to be updated.

NOTE

> You can use the Unique Table property value of a form's record source to make most one-to-many queries updatable. Specify the name of the table on the many side of the relationship as the value of the Unique Table property.

To distinguish between these two keywords, assume that you have a table with a LastName field and a FirstName field and only 10 records, each with the LastName value, Smith. Each record has a different FirstName value. You create a query that includes the LastName field, but not the FirstName field. `DISTINCTROW` returns all 10 Smith records because the FirstName values differ in the table. `DISTINCT` returns one record because the FirstName field that distinguishes the records in the table is absent in the query result table.

Versions before Access 97 included the default reserved word `DISTINCTROW` unless you purposely replaced it with the `DISTINCT` keyword by using the Query Properties dialog's Unique Values Only option. The Jet Query Properties dialog sets the default value of the

Unique Values (`DISTINCT`) and Unique Rows (`DISTINCTROW`) properties to No. Don't specify Unique Rows in Jet queries you intend to upsize to ADP.

JET AND CORRESPONDING SQL SERVER DATA TYPES

SQL Server has more data types than those specified by the ANSI-92 standard (refer to Table 22.2). For example, ANSI-92 doesn't require conforming RDBMSs to support Unicode characters. Jet 4.0 and SQL Server both support Unicode data types; SQL Server identifies Unicode data type by an `n` (for National Character) prefix.

The Upsizing Wizard automatically converts Jet data types to corresponding SQL Server 2000 data types. Table 22.6 lists Jet data types, the SQL Server data type to which the Wizard converts the Jet data type, and SQL Server data types that are related to the upsized data type. Parentheses enclose SQL Server property or extended property values that must be set to emulate Jet data types.

TABLE 22.6 JET 4.0 DATA TYPES, DIRECTLY CORRESPONDING, AND RELATED SQL SERVER 2000 DATA TYPES

Jet Data Type	Upsizes To	Related Data Types
Yes/No	`bit`	
Number (Byte)	`tinyint`	
Number (Integer)	`smallint`	
Number (Long Integer)	`int`	
Number (Single)	`real`	
Number (Double)	`float`	
Number (Decimal)	`decimal`	`numeric`
Number (Replication ID) (GUID)	`uniqueidentifier`	
AutoNumber	`int (Identity)`	
Currency	`money`	`smallmoney`
Date/Time	`datetime`	`smalldatetime`
Text(*n*)	`nvarchar(`*n*`)`	`varchar(n)`
Hyperlink	`ntext (Hyperlink)`	
Memo	`ntext`	`text`
OLE Object	`image`	

Jet doesn't have data types that correspond to SQL Server's `bigint`, `char`, `nchar`, `sql_variant`, `user-defined`, `varchar`, and `varbinary` data types.

VBA Functions That Upsize to SQL Server Functions

T-SQL has many functions that correspond to VBA functions that you commonly use in Jet queries. Table 22.7 lists the VBA functions that the Upsizing Wizard converts to their T-SQL counterparts. The table doesn't include the SQL functions listed earlier in Tables 22.2 and 22.3. You can safely use these VBA functions in Jet queries that you plant to upsize to SQL Server.

Table 22.7 VBA Functions That the Wizard Automatically Converts to T-SQL Functions

Ccur	**Hour**	**Right$**
Cdbl	**Lcase$**	**Right**
Chr$	**Lcase**	**Rtrim$**
Chr	**Left**	**Second**
Cint	**Len**	**Space$**
Clng	**Ltrim$**	**Str$**
Csng	**Mid$**	**Ucase$**
Cstr	**Mid**	**Ucase**
Cvdate	**Minute**	**Weekday**
Day	**Month**	**Year**

VBA Functions That You Must Manually Convert to Related SQL Server Functions

The Upsizing Wizard doesn't automatically convert the VBA functions listed in Table 22.8 into the corresponding T-SQL functions that perform similar or identical operations. In most cases, the reason the Wizard doesn't perform the translation is minor syntax differences. Eliminate, if possible, or minimize use of these functions in Jet queries you plant to upsize.

Table 22.8 VBA Functions That the Wizard Automatically Does Not Convert to T-SQL Functions

VBA Function	T-SQL Function	VBA Function	T-SQL Function
Asc	ASCII	**Lower**	LOWER
Date	GETDATE	**Now**	GETDATE
DateAdd	DATEADD	**Space**	SPACE
DateDiff	DATEDIFF	**Str**	STR
DatePart	DATEPART	**String**	REPLICATE
Format	DATENAME	**StrReverse**	REVERSE
Instr	CHARINDEX		

The **Format** function is one of the most commonly used VBA functions in Jet queries, and DATENAME only handles one of many possible **Format** expressions.

→ For examples of the use of T-SQL DATEPART, DATENAME, DATEDIFF, and GETDATE functions, **see** "The Better Approach for Dynamic *and* Static Data—Stored Procedures," **p. 923**.

TIP

> SQL Server 2000 Books Online has the standard syntax for T-SQL functions and examples of their use. Click the Index tab and type the function name in the text box to open the Transact-SQL Reference topic for the function. The "Date and Time Functions" topic has links to all functions that accept or return date or time values. If you haven't downloaded the updated SQL Server 2000 Books Online, you can find it at `http://www.microsoft.com/sql/techinfo/productdoc/2000/books.asp`.

EMULATING JET CROSSTAB QUERIES WITH T-SQL

Regardless of your upsizing strategy, you must roll your own T-SQL equivalents of Jet crosstab queries to provide the data source for upsized charts you created with Microsoft Graph and the Chart Wizard. Your only alternative is to convert all graphs and charts to PivotCharts and recreate their source queries.

Jet SQL

This is the generalized Jet SQL syntax for crosstab queries:

```
TRANSFORM aggregate_function(field_name) [AS alias]
SELECT [ALL¦DISTINCT] select_list
   FROM table_name
   PIVOT Format(field_name),"format_type")
  [IN (column_list)]
```

TRANSFORM defines a crosstab query, and PIVOT specifies the GROUP BY characteristics plus the fixed column names specified by the optional IN predicate.

→ To review Jet crosstab query design, **see** "Creating Crosstab Queries," **p. 442**.

SQL Server 2000 Books Online calls crosstab queries "cross-tab reports" and equates cross-tab reports with PivotTables. The example creates a trivial result table with explicit numeric values for four quarters of two years. Unfortunately, the topic doesn't show you how to write a stored procedure that emulates the capabilities of Jet's crosstab queries.

The frm1997SalesByCategoryChart form you created in Chapter 18, "Adding Graphs, PivotCharts, and PivotTables," has a generic crosstab SQL statement that the Chart Wizard generates from the query you specify as the data source for the chart. The Chart Wizard stores the crosstab SQL statement as the value of the Row Source property of the chart. The Upsizing Wizard upsizes this form, but when you try to open it, you receive an error message that the SQL statement exceeds a maximum length of 128 characters. When you click OK, another error message appears with possible causes of the problem. The fundamental problem—repeated several times earlier in this and preceding chapters—is that T-SQL doesn't support the Jet SQL TRANSFORM and PIVOT keywords.

You must find a way to deliver the data to the chart in the appropriate format. The following sections describe two methods of emulating the result set of crosstab queries in ADP.

THE PRAGMATIC APPROACH FOR STATIC DATA—CHEAT

If your chart or graph displays historical data that isn't subject to revision, you can save considerable time and effort by creating an SQL Server table from the output of the crosstab query the Chart Wizard generates.

> **TIP**
>
> Check with your organization's chief financial or executive officer before committing to a static version of historical financial data. Retroactive revision of prior financial data—sometimes involving several years of data—became increasingly common in 2001 and later.

CREATING A WORKSHEET FROM THE CROSSTAB QUERY RESULT SET

Cheating by creating a static table isn't as straightforward as you might expect. You use an Excel worksheet as an intermediary in the process. To create the initial worksheet, do the following:

1. Open the original Jet version of the form with a graph or chart created by the Chart Wizard. This example uses the frm1997SalesByCategoryChart form you created in Chapter 18. A copy of this form is included in Upsize22.mdb; this example uses the copy.

2. Change to Design view, right-click the unbound object frame, usually OLEUnbound0, and choose Properties to open the object's Properties window.

3. Click the Data tab, select the entire SQL statement in the text box of the Row Source property, and copy the statement to the Clipboard.

4. Open a new query in Design view, close the Show Table dialog, and click the SQL view button.

Jet SQL

Following is the Jet SQL statement for the Record Source of frm1997SalesByCategoryChart's OLEUnbound0 unbound object frame:

```
TRANSFORM Sum([Amount]) AS [SumOfAmount]
   SELECT (Format([ShippedDate],"MMM 'YY"))
   FROM [qry1997SalesChart]
   GROUP BY (Year([ShippedDate])*12 +
      Month([ShippedDate])-1),
     (Format([ShippedDate],"MMM 'YY"))
PIVOT [CategoryName];
```

The crosstab query uses the qry1997SalesChart query, which upsizes successfully.

→ To review the process for creating the graph, **see** "Generating Graphs and Charts with Microsoft Graph," **p. 704**.

5. Paste the SQL statement into the SQL window, and click Run to verify the data returned. Figure 22.20 shows the query result set from the example chart.

Query1 : Crosstab Query

Expr1002	Beverages	Condiments	Confections	Dairy Products	Grains/Cereals	Meat/Poultry	Produce	Seafood
Jan 97	$23,269.16	$4,476.30	$10,216.17	$9,851.48	$3,585.60	$8,365.45	$3,288.54	$1,693.76
Feb 97	$2,019.24	$4,954.08	$5,127.38	$6,074.44	$3,798.80	$5,958.30	$1,587.60	$1,922.65
Mar 97	$10,569.80	$2,491.79	$5,739.23	$8,192.80	$5,312.70	$7,274.40	$4,104.60	$3,829.00
Apr 97	$2,786.53	$4,837.91	$2,599.51	$7,521.50	$2,084.40	$5,130.24	$5,613.06	$1,023.30
May 97	$12,163.25	$5,651.02	$13,186.80	$9,374.38	$6,052.25	$4,597.91	$4,695.60	$8,254.15
Jun 97	$10,517.18	$2,858.35	$6,279.21	$10,358.25	$6,492.65	$3,966.40	$5,275.00	$4,335.96
Jul 97	$3,163.75	$5,431.88	$4,186.80	$9,881.83	$2,230.00	$5,924.20	$2,198.70	$4,527.81
Aug 97	$10,363.78	$3,823.61	$8,865.43	$8,703.68	$7,856.25	$4,005.74	$3,771.00	$8,878.50
Sep 97	$7,317.58	$4,746.48	$4,912.64	$10,042.05	$5,224.48	$5,913.57	$2,333.28	$10,017.26
Oct 97	$7,689.40	$4,674.01	$8,775.70	$15,304.00	$3,465.00	$19,871.04	$6,540.40	$7,985.63
Nov 97	$3,569.00	$5,194.58	$3,625.41	$12,268.98	$3,666.35	$655.50	$4,609.71	$6,853.60
Dec 97	$8,645.65	$6,137.60	$7,379.88	$7,176.40	$6,180.35	$9,675.31	$9,002.50	$6,222.58

Record: 1 of 12

Figure 22.20 Datasheet view of the chart's crosstab query shows the tabular data structure required to populate the chart's datasheet.

TIP

> Changing the crosstab query type to a make-table query doesn't create a table with the crosstab structure. However, you can use the crosstab query as the data source for a make-table query. Another approach is to save the crosstab query and export its result set to a worksheet, but copying the cells to a worksheet is faster, especially if you have many upsized charts to fix.

6. Press Ctrl+A to select all records in the datasheet, and press Ctrl+C to copy the cell values to the Clipboard.
7. Launch Excel 97 or later with a new workbook. With the cursor in cell A1, press Ctrl+V to paste the cells to Sheet1.

TIP

> If you want to use the crosstab table as a record source for other queries in the project, select the columns with numerical data, and format the cells as Number or Currency.

8. Rename Sheet1 to identify the table (**tbl1997SalesByCategoryChart** for this example), and save the workbook with a descriptive name, such as **JetCrosstabs.xls** (see Figure 22.21).
9. Repeat steps 1–8 for each form or report that contains a Wizard-created chart. In step 7, use the saved workbook and add a new worksheet to store the additional query result set copies.
10. Close the workbook. You can't import the worksheet data if the workbook is open.

The JetCrosstabs.xls workbook is included in the \Seua10\Chaptr22 folder of the accompanying CD-ROM. The three worksheets have cells formatted as Text, Number, and Currency.

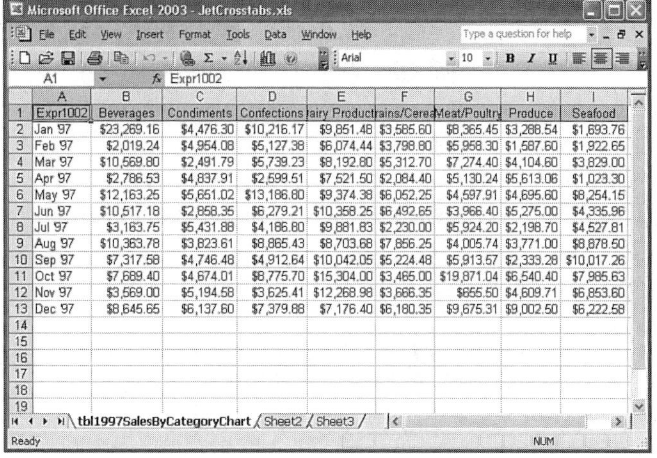

	A	B	C	D	E	F	G	H	I
1	Expr1002	Beverages	Condiments	Confections	airy Product	rains/Cerea	Meat/Poultry	Produce	Seafood
2	Jan '97	$23,269.16	$4,476.30	$10,216.17	$9,851.48	$3,585.60	$8,365.45	$3,288.54	$1,693.76
3	Feb '97	$2,019.24	$4,954.08	$5,127.38	$6,074.44	$3,798.80	$5,958.30	$1,587.60	$1,922.65
4	Mar '97	$10,569.80	$2,491.79	$5,739.23	$8,192.80	$5,312.70	$7,274.40	$4,104.60	$3,829.00
5	Apr '97	$2,786.53	$4,837.91	$2,599.51	$7,521.50	$2,084.40	$5,130.24	$5,613.06	$1,023.30
6	May '97	$12,163.25	$5,651.02	$13,186.80	$9,374.38	$6,052.25	$4,597.91	$4,695.60	$8,254.15
7	Jun '97	$10,517.18	$2,858.35	$6,279.21	$10,358.25	$6,492.65	$3,966.40	$5,275.00	$4,335.96
8	Jul '97	$3,163.75	$5,431.88	$4,186.80	$9,881.83	$2,230.00	$5,924.20	$2,198.70	$4,527.81
9	Aug '97	$10,363.78	$3,823.61	$8,865.43	$8,703.68	$7,856.25	$4,005.74	$3,771.00	$8,878.50
10	Sep '97	$7,317.58	$4,746.48	$4,912.64	$10,042.05	$5,224.48	$5,913.57	$2,333.28	$10,017.26
11	Oct '97	$7,689.40	$4,674.01	$8,775.70	$15,304.00	$3,465.00	$19,871.04	$6,540.40	$7,985.63
12	Nov '97	$3,569.00	$5,194.58	$3,625.41	$12,268.98	$3,666.35	$655.50	$4,609.71	$6,853.60
13	Dec '97	$8,645.65	$6,137.60	$7,379.88	$7,176.40	$6,180.35	$9,675.31	$9,002.50	$6,222.58

Figure 22.21
This Excel 2003 worksheet serves as the data source for a new SQL Server table you can use as the Row Source for the upsized frm1997SalesByCategoryChart form.

IMPORTING THE WORKSHEET TO AN SQL SERVER TABLE

Do the following to import the workbook data to SQL Server for your project and enable forms and reports that include charts:

1. Open the project that contains the upsized form with the inoperable chart, UpsizeCS.adp for this example.
2. Choose File, Get External Data, Import, to open the Import dialog, and choose Microsoft Excel (.xls) in the Files of Type list. Navigate to the location of the workbook you saved, and double-click the file to start the Import Spreadsheet Wizard.
3. In the first Wizard dialog, select the worksheet for the SQL Server table to create, and click Next.
4. In the second dialog, mark the First Row Contains Column Headings check box, and click Next.
5. In the third dialog, accept the In a New Table option (see Figure 22.22), and click Next.

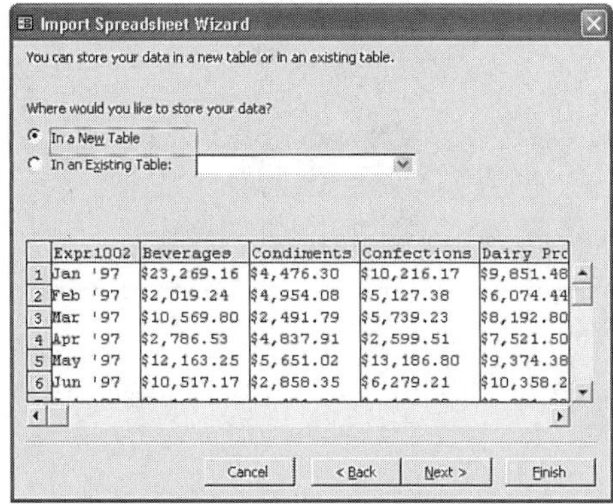

	Expr1002	Beverages	Condiments	Confections	Dairy Pro
1	Jan '97	$23,269.16	$4,476.30	$10,216.17	$9,851.48
2	Feb '97	$2,019.24	$4,954.08	$5,127.38	$6,074.44
3	Mar '97	$10,569.80	$2,491.79	$5,739.23	$8,192.80
4	Apr '97	$2,786.53	$4,837.91	$2,599.51	$7,521.50
5	May '97	$12,163.25	$5,651.02	$13,186.80	$9,374.38
6	Jun '97	$10,517.17	$2,858.35	$6,279.21	$10,358.2

Figure 22.22
Importing the crosstab worksheet with the Import Spreadsheet Process is quick, because you accept all default values. You can speed the process by clicking Finish after selecting the worksheet in the first Wizard dialog.

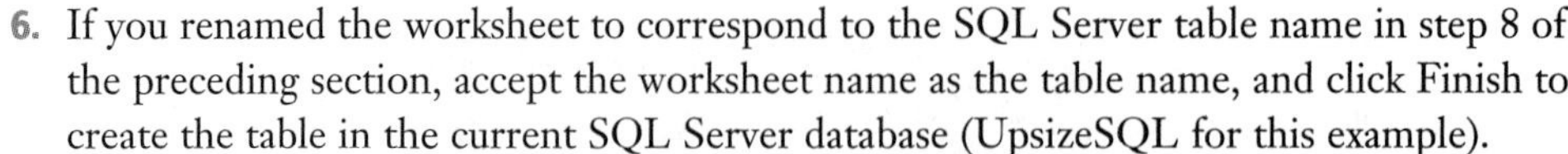

6. If you renamed the worksheet to correspond to the SQL Server table name in step 8 of the preceding section, accept the worksheet name as the table name, and click Finish to create the table in the current SQL Server database (UpsizeSQL for this example).

7. Click OK to clear the confirmation message and then open the new SQL Server table to verify the import process, and check the data types in Design view.
8. Right-click the chart and choose Properties to open the Properties window for the unbound object frame. (The presentation of the graph in Design view is static.)
9. Click the Data tab, open the Row Source list, and select the imported table corresponding to the crosstab query to replace (see Figure 22.23).

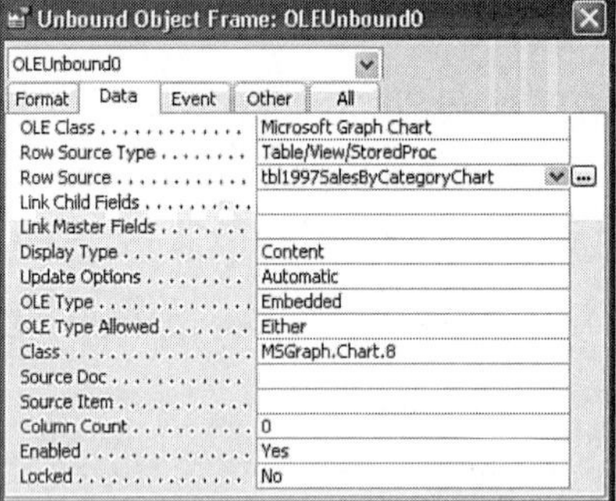

Figure 22.23 Specify the new SQL Server table you created as the value of the Row Source property of the chart.

10. Close the Properties window, and change to Form or Report view to test the data source. Figure 22.24 shows the upsized frm1997SalesByCategoryChart form.

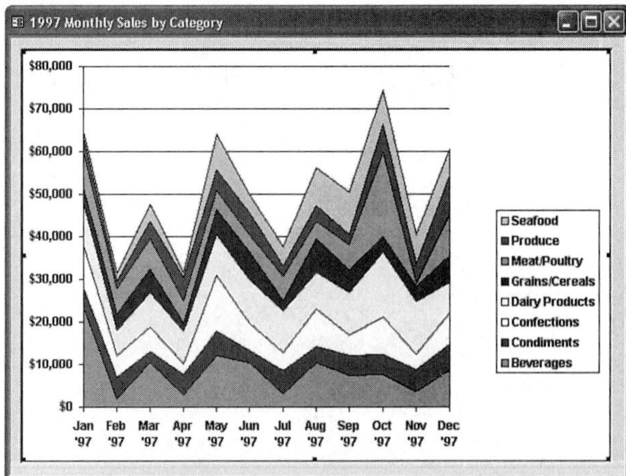

Figure 22.24 The upsized 1997 Monthly Sales by Category form is identical to its Jet counterpart.

11. Repeat steps 2–10 for each worksheet in your crosstab workbook.

MODIFYING THE TABLE TO ACCOMMODATE A LINKED CHART

Linked charts require that the crosstab table column names for the Link Master Fields and Link Child Fields correspond. Forms having linked charts usually specify the name of a table or query as the Record Source for the form and a crosstab query as the Row Source for the chart.

→ To review linking graphs, **see** "Creating a Linked Graph from a Jet Crosstab Query," **p. 720**.

Using the upsized frm1997SalesByCategoryChartLinked form you created in Chapter 18 as an example, follow these steps to fix linked MSGraph objects:

1. Open the form in Design view, right-click the graph, open the Properties window, and click the Data tab.
2. Verify that the table(s) that provide the Record Source property of the form and the Row Source property of the chart have the fields specified by the Link Master Fields and Link Child Fields properties.

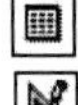

3. The linking field of tbl1997SalesByCategoryChart table is Expr1002 (refer to Figure 22.21), so open the table in Design view and change the name of the first field to **Categories**. (Nonlinked graphs don't use the field name of the first column.)
4. Specify the table as the Row Source for the chart.
5. If the form uses a crosstab query as its Record Source, change the Record Source property value to the name of the crosstab table, tbl1997SalesByCategoryChart in this case.
6. Verify that the linked form behaves and appears identically to the original Jet version, and save your changes.

THE BETTER APPROACH FOR DYNAMIC *AND* STATIC DATA—STORED PROCEDURES

Creating crosstab tables from the contents of datasheets isn't a generally accepted programming practice, so this section describes how to emulate the Jet SQL crosstab statement for the Record Source of frm1997SalesByCategoryChart's OLEUnbound0 unbound object frame. The primary advantage of a table-creating stored procedure is that the table is based on live—not static—data. A secondary benefit is that a single parameterized stored procedure can handle multiple time periods, such as years, that you specify by the parameter value.

There are two basic steps to the stored procedure approach:

- **Design a view that returns the values you need for the table**—For this example, the values are 8 category names, 12 month names in MMM 'YY format, and total sales amounts for each category by month. The upsized qry1997SalesChart view is the starting point for the final view design. The view takes advantage of T-SQL's `DATENAME` and `DATEPART` functions to create the formatted month names and sort them in calendar order.
- **Write a stored procedure that creates the crosstab table from the view's output**—This is the step that involves the most effort. You use a series of `CREATE TABLE`, `INSERT`

`[INTO]`, and multiple `UPDATE` statements to create and populate the table. A `SELECT * FROM` *`tablename`* statement at the end of the stored procedure code delivers the table's data to the chart.

TIP

> Substitute ActiveX PivotCharts for MSGraph OLE charts in your new Jet applications. Relatively simple views, functions, or stored procedures serve as the data source for PivotCharts and their underlying PivotTables in ADP. The Chart Wizard isn't available within ADP because it depends on Jet crosstab queries.

MODIFYING THE UPSIZED QRY1997SALESCHART VIEW

The upsized qry1997SalesChart view returns one record with the total sale amount of products in a category for each date on which a product shipped in 1997. The total number of records returned by the query is about 1,042. You must group the records to return totals for each category by month. You also must change the format of the grouped field to correspond with that generated by the Chart Wizard.

Following are the steps to modify UpsizeCS.adp's qry1997SalesChart view:

1. Open the view in Design view, and click the SQL button to open the SQL pane. Adjust the position of the field lists and the depth of the panes.
2. Click the Group By button, change the Group By criterion of the aliased Amount column to Sum, and the ShippedDate column to Where. Making this change adds another ShippedDate entry to the columns list (see Figure 22.25).

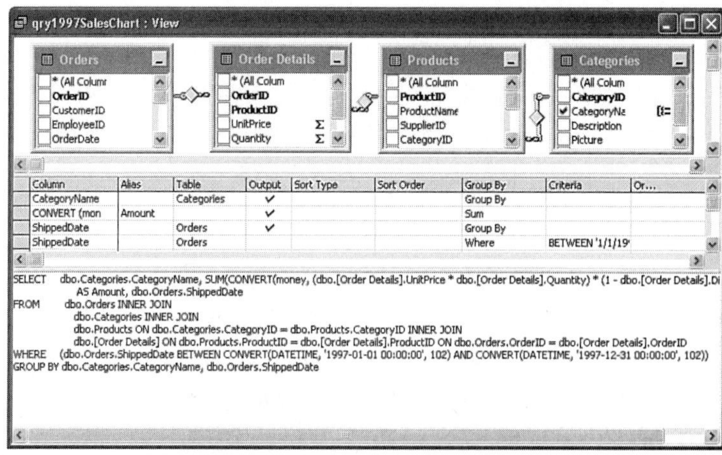

Figure 22.25 The upsized qry1997SalesChart adds the `dbo.` prefix to all table and column names, and translates the VBA `CCur` function to `CONVERT(money,` *`ColumnValue`*`)`. Initial grouping is based on the values or the CategoryName and ShippedDate columns.

3. Grouping by month, not by individual shipping date is required and you need the MMM 'YY format. Modify the ShippedDate column with the Group By setting as follows:

```
LEFT(DATENAME(month, dbo.Orders.ShippedDate), 3) + ' ''' +
   SUBSTRING(DATENAME(year, dbo.Orders.ShippedDate), 3, 2)
```

T-SQL

`DATENAME(month, DateTimeField)` returns the full name of the month. The `LEFT` function returns the three-letter month abbreviation.

T-SQL uses the + symbol for string concatenation. The `' '''` expression adds a space and apostrophe after the month abbreviation. (An *escape sequence* of two apostrophes displays `'`.)

The `SUBSTRING(Expression, 3, 2)` function returns the last two digits of the year (`97` for this example).

---

4. Replace the added Expr1 alias with **Month** in the Alias column.
5. A numeric month value is required to sort the output of the view by Category and calendar (not alphabetic) month. Add the following new column definition:

   ```
   DATEPART(month, dbo.Orders.ShippedDate)
   ```

T-SQL

`DATEPART([month|quarter|year], DateTimeField)` returns the numeric value of the time period.

---

6. Replace the added Expr1 alias with **MonthNum** in the Alias column.
7. Specify an Ascending sort on the CategoryName column and another Ascending sort on the MonthNum column. Adding the `GROUP BY` clauses automatically adds `TOP 100 PERCENT` to the `SELECT` statement. Your view design appears as shown in Figure 22.26.

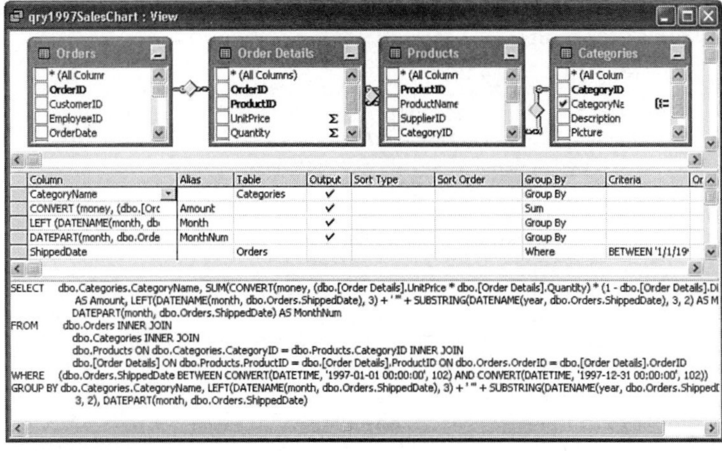

Figure 22.26 The final design of the qry1997SalesChart view illustrates the complexity of T-SQL statements with fully qualified table and field identifiers.

8. Click Check SQL Syntax to verify your changes, and run the view—saving your changes—to display its output (see Figure 22.27).

qry1997SalesChart : View

Category Name	Amount	Month	MonthNum
Beverages	$23,269.16	Jan 97	1
Beverages	$2,019.24	Feb 97	2
Beverages	$10,569.80	Mar 97	3
Beverages	$2,786.53	Apr 97	4
Beverages	$12,163.25	May 97	5
Beverages	$10,517.18	Jun 97	6
Beverages	$3,163.75	Jul 97	7
Beverages	$10,363.78	Aug 97	8
Beverages	$7,317.58	Sep 97	9
Beverages	$7,689.40	Oct 97	10
Beverages	$3,569.00	Nov 97	11
Beverages	$8,645.65	Dec 97	12
Condiments	$4,476.30	Jan 97	1
Condiments	$4,954.08	Feb 97	2
Condiments	$2,491.79	Mar 97	3
Condiments	$4,837.91	Apr 97	4
Condiments	$5,651.02	May 97	5
Condiments	$2,858.35	Jun 97	6
Condiments	$5,431.88	Jul 97	7
Condiments	$3,823.61	Aug 97	8
Condiments	$4,746.48	Sep 97	9

Record: 1 of 96

Figure 22.27
The output of the modified qry1997SalesChart view provides the required 96 rows of source data for the stored procedure.

Jet SQL

Following is the full T-SQL statement for the modified view:

```
SELECT TOP 100 PERCENT dbo.Categories.CategoryName,
   SUM(CONVERT(money, (dbo.[Order Details].UnitPrice *
   dbo.[Order Details].Quantity) *
  (1 - dbo.[Order Details].Discount))) AS Amount,
   LEFT(DATENAME(month, dbo.Orders.ShippedDate), 3) +
   ' ''' + SUBSTRING(DATENAME(year,
   dbo.Orders.ShippedDate), 3, 2) AS Month,
   DATEPART(month, dbo.Orders.ShippedDate) AS MonthNum
FROM dbo.Orders
   INNER JOIN dbo.Categories
      INNER JOIN dbo.Products
         ON dbo.Categories.CategoryID =
            dbo.Products.CategoryID
      INNER JOIN dbo.[Order Details]
         ON dbo.Products.ProductID =
            dbo.[Order Details].ProductID
         ON dbo.Orders.OrderID =
            dbo.[Order Details].OrderID
WHERE (dbo.Orders.ShippedDate BETWEEN
   CONVERT(DATETIME, '1997-01-01 00:00:00', 102) AND
   CONVERT(DATETIME, '1997-12-31 00:00:00', 102))
GROUP BY dbo.Categories.CategoryName,
      LEFT(DATENAME(month, dbo.Orders.ShippedDate), 3) +
      ' ''' + SUBSTRING(DATENAME(year,
      dbo.Orders.ShippedDate), 3, 2),
   DATEPART(month, dbo.Orders.ShippedDate)
ORDER BY dbo.Categories.CategoryName,
   DATEPART(month, dbo.Orders.ShippedDate)
```

The `CONVERT(DATETIME, '1997-01-01 00:00:00', 102)` expression changes the standard SQL Server date format to the ANSI yyyy.mm.dd standard without the time data. Specifying 101 as the second argument value returns the U.S. m/d/yyyy format.

Writing the spCategoriesCT Stored Procedure

Creating the crosstab table from the modified qry1997SalesChart view with a stored procedure isn't a piece of cake. After you understand the basic principles involved, however, it's easy to clone the sample design to accommodate a variety of crosstab scenarios. You also learn how to write `INSERT INTO` and `UPDATE` statements to create nontraditional table structures that don't conform to the rules of relational databases. The table you create in this section is akin to a spreadsheet and isn't a legitimate base table because it has repeating category columns.

The stored procedure to create the crosstab table must accomplish the following tasks:

- Create a table structure with field names and data types that correspond to those of the Jet query result set. For this example, the first field contains row headers (month names and years). The remaining field names represent column headers (categories) and contain total sales amounts.

> **NOTE**
>
> Recreating a new table requires that you drop (delete) the existing table; otherwise you receive a "table exists" error message. The first instruction in your stored procedure must test for the presence of the table.

- Append a row to the table for each row header with an `INSERT INTO` *`table_name`* `(`*`field_name(s)`*`) SELECT DISTINCT` *`field_name(s)`* `FROM` *`view_name`* statement.
- Update amount values for each of the column headers with an `UPDATE` statement that uses a `SELECT` query to supply the values for all rows.
- Execute a `SELECT * FROM` *`TableName`* query against the table to deliver the crosstab Recordset to the graph.

The example stored procedure you write in the following steps isn't *scalable*. Each time someone runs the procedure, it creates a new table. If many users run the procedure simultaneously, locks on the table being deleted and recreated might return errors. You can overcome this problem by using SQL Server's temporary tables, which you specify by adding a `#` prefix to the table name. The tempdb database holds temporary tables, which SQL Server creates for each user and drops when the user closes her database connection. Using temporary tables, however, complicates the stored procedure code. There's an alternative approach to increase performance in the later "Improving Application Scalability and Performance" section.

To create the spCategoriesCT procedure in the UpsizeSQL sample project, do this:

1. In Upsize22.adp, click the Create Stored Procedure in Designer shortcut to open the Stored Procedure1 window. Close the Add Table dialog, and click the SQL button to add the SQL pane.

2. Replace the default `SELECT FROMskeleton` beginning at the `/*` line with the following statements:

```
SET NOCOUNT ON

IF EXISTS(SELECT table_name
   FROM information_schema.tables
   WHERE table_name = 'tbl1997CT')
DROP TABLE tbl1997CT
```

T-SQL

`SET NOCOUNT ON` prevents the procedure from returning row (`RecordsAffected`) counts to the client. The `IF EXISTS...DROP TABLE` conditional statement removes the table, if it exists in the database.

---

3. Click the Run button, type **spCategoriesCT** in the Save As text box, and click OK. Click Yes to close the Query Definitions Differ message and save your SQL statements. The stored procedure designer handles only conventional `SELECT` queries.
4. Acknowledge the message that the stored procedure executed but returned no records. The project designer window changes to a free-form text editing window, and designer-related buttons disappear from the toolbar. The View button adds an SQL view, which is the same as that for Jet SQL queries.
5. Reformat the initial statement as shown in Figure 22.28. The `ALTER PROCEDURE spCategoriesCT AS` statement lets you edit and recreate the procedure.

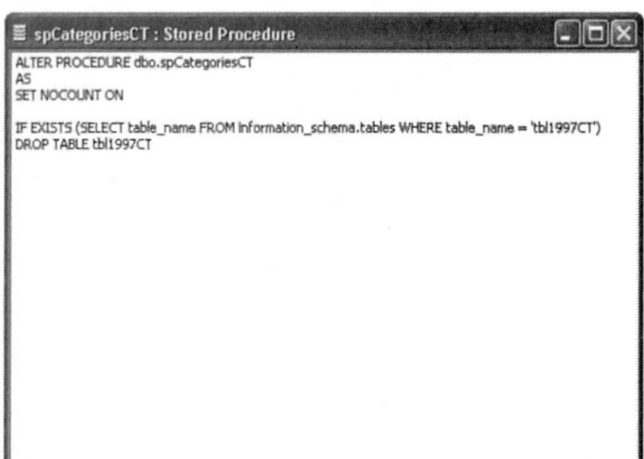

Figure 22.28 Adding any T-SQL statement other than a `SELECT` query in the project designer's SQL pane requires typing the full T-SQL statement in a free-text editing window.

6. Add the following table definition statement after the `DROP TABLE` statement to create a table with a structure similar to that of the table described in the earlier "Modifying the Table to Accommodate a Linked Chart" section:

```
CREATE TABLE tbl1997CT (Categories nvarchar(25),
   Beverages money, Condiments money, Confections money,
   [Dairy Products] money, [Grains/Cereals] money,
   [Meat/Poultry] money, Produce money, Seafood money)
```

7. Click the Run button to create the table and click OK to close the message box.

8. In the Tables page of the Database window, open the tbl1997CT table to check the column headings. The table doesn't have a primary key assigned, so there's no tentative append record and only the field header buttons are present.

9. Return to the spCategoriesCT window, and add the following INSERT statement, which adds 12 records to the table with values for the Categories field:

```
INSERT INTO tbl1997CT (Categories)
   SELECT DISTINCT Month
   FROM qry1997SalesChart
```

T-SQL

The (Categories) field is required to assign values of the view's Month column to the table's Category field. You don't need to add dbo.tablename. or dbo.viewname. prefixes to the field or column names, because there are no duplicate object names in this example.

10. Run the procedure again, and reopen the table in Datasheet view to check the result of the INSERT operation.

TIP

A SELECT * FROM tbl1997CT after the last statement you add to the procedure automatically opens the Datasheet view of the table when you run the procedure.

11. Add the following statement to replace NULL values in the Beverages field with corresponding values from the source query:

```
UPDATE tbl1997CT SET Beverages = Amount
FROM qry1997SalesChart
WHERE CategoryName = 'Beverages'
   AND Categories = Month
```

NOTE

The join you create between the table and view with the Categories = Month expression of the WHERE clause is important. If you don't join the table and view, Amount values in records 2–12 add to the table in random order. (The first record is correct for all fields.) This is unexpected behavior, because the view is ordered such that records *should* update in calendar order.

12. Test the result of the added UPDATE statement (see Figure 22.29) and then add seven more UPDATE statements for the remaining product categories. Replace Beverages with the category name for each column. Surround field names having spaces or virgules (/) with square brackets except when in WHERE clause references (see Figure 22.30).

Figure 22.29
The INSERT statements of steps 9 and 11 add values for the first two columns to the table.

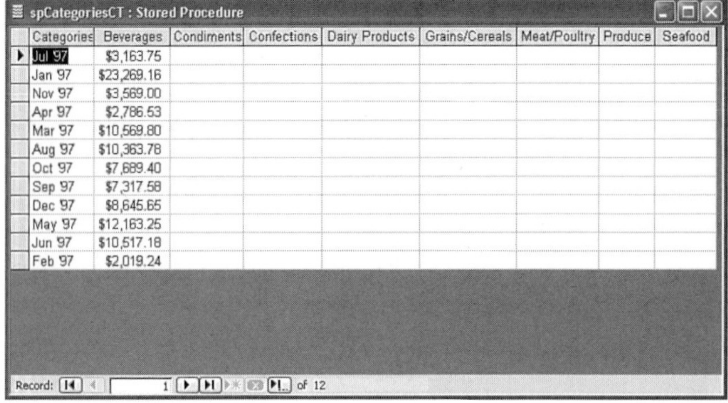

Categories	Beverages	Condiments	Confections	Dairy Products	Grains/Cereals	Meat/Poultry	Produce	Seafood
Jul 97	$3,163.75							
Jan 97	$23,269.16							
Nov 97	$3,569.00							
Apr 97	$2,786.53							
Mar 97	$10,569.80							
Aug 97	$10,363.78							
Oct 97	$7,689.40							
Sep 97	$7,317.58							
Dec 97	$8,645.65							
May 97	$12,163.25							
Jun 97	$10,517.18							
Feb 97	$2,019.24							

TIP

To save typing the additional seven INSERT statements, see the note at the end of the next section.

Figure 22.30
The last step in writing the stored procedure is to write seven more UPDATE statements to add values to the Condiments...Seafood fields.

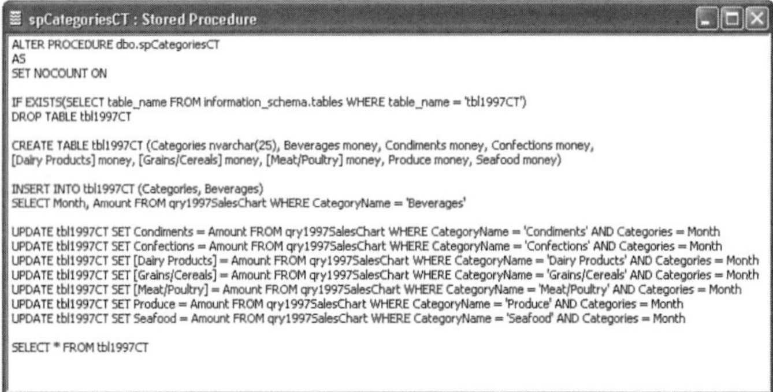


```
ALTER PROCEDURE dbo.spCategoriesCT
AS
SET NOCOUNT ON

IF EXISTS(SELECT table_name FROM information_schema.tables WHERE table_name = 'tbl1997CT')
DROP TABLE tbl1997CT

CREATE TABLE tbl1997CT (Categories nvarchar(25), Beverages money, Condiments money, Confections money,
[Dairy Products] money, [Grains/Cereals] money, [Meat/Poultry] money, Produce money, Seafood money)

INSERT INTO tbl1997CT (Categories, Beverages)
SELECT Month, Amount FROM qry1997SalesChart WHERE CategoryName = 'Beverages'

UPDATE tbl1997CT SET Condiments = Amount FROM qry1997SalesChart WHERE CategoryName = 'Condiments' AND Categories = Month
UPDATE tbl1997CT SET Confections = Amount FROM qry1997SalesChart WHERE CategoryName = 'Confections' AND Categories = Month
UPDATE tbl1997CT SET [Dairy Products] = Amount FROM qry1997SalesChart WHERE CategoryName = 'Dairy Products' AND Categories = Month
UPDATE tbl1997CT SET [Grains/Cereals] = Amount FROM qry1997SalesChart WHERE CategoryName = 'Grains/Cereals' AND Categories = Month
UPDATE tbl1997CT SET [Meat/Poultry] = Amount FROM qry1997SalesChart WHERE CategoryName = 'Meat/Poultry' AND Categories = Month
UPDATE tbl1997CT SET Produce = Amount FROM qry1997SalesChart WHERE CategoryName = 'Produce' AND Categories = Month
UPDATE tbl1997CT SET Seafood = Amount FROM qry1997SalesChart WHERE CategoryName = 'Seafood' AND Categories = Month

SELECT * FROM tbl1997CT
```

13. If you didn't add `SELECT * FROM tbl1997CT` earlier, do it now, and click Run to display the final result of your stored procedure (see Figure 22.31).

If the datasheet doesn't open when you run the procedure, see the "Stored Procedures Don't Return the Expected Recordset" topic of the "Troubleshooting" section near the end of the chapter.

To test the stored procedure with the frm1997SalesByCategoryChart form in UpsizeCS.adp, change the Row Source property of the chart from tbl1997SalesByCategoryChart to **spCategoriesCT**. The graph duplicates that with the copied table as its Row Source.

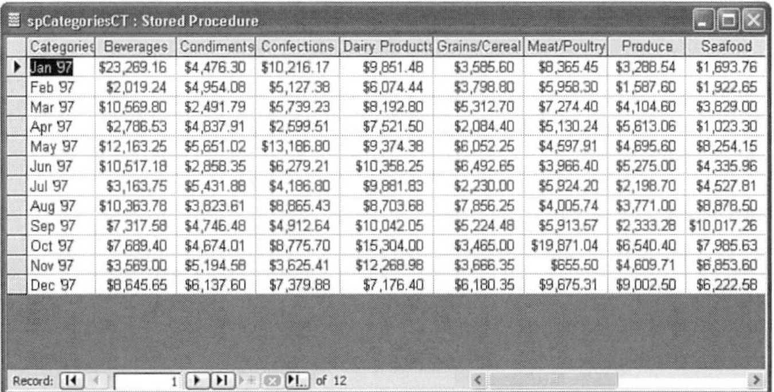

spCategoriesCT : Stored Procedure

Categories	Beverages	Condiments	Confections	Dairy Products	Grains/Cereal	Meat/Poultry	Produce	Seafood
Jan 97	$23,269.16	$4,476.30	$10,216.17	$9,851.48	$3,585.60	$8,365.45	$3,288.54	$1,693.76
Feb 97	$2,019.24	$4,954.08	$5,127.38	$6,074.44	$3,798.80	$5,958.30	$1,587.60	$1,922.65
Mar 97	$10,569.80	$2,491.79	$5,739.23	$8,192.80	$5,312.70	$7,274.40	$4,104.60	$3,829.00
Apr 97	$2,786.53	$4,837.91	$2,599.51	$7,521.50	$2,084.40	$5,130.24	$5,613.06	$1,023.30
May 97	$12,163.25	$5,651.02	$13,186.80	$9,374.38	$6,052.25	$4,597.91	$4,695.60	$8,254.15
Jun 97	$10,517.18	$2,858.35	$6,279.21	$10,358.25	$6,492.65	$3,966.40	$5,275.00	$4,335.96
Jul 97	$3,163.75	$5,431.88	$4,186.80	$9,881.83	$2,230.00	$5,924.20	$2,198.70	$4,527.81
Aug 97	$10,363.78	$3,823.61	$8,865.43	$8,703.68	$7,856.25	$4,005.74	$3,771.00	$8,878.50
Sep 97	$7,317.58	$4,746.48	$4,912.64	$10,042.05	$5,224.48	$5,913.57	$2,333.28	$10,017.26
Oct 97	$7,689.40	$4,674.01	$8,775.70	$15,304.00	$3,465.00	$19,871.04	$6,540.40	$7,985.63
Nov 97	$3,569.00	$5,194.58	$3,625.41	$12,268.98	$3,666.35	$655.50	$4,609.71	$6,853.60
Dec 97	$8,645.65	$6,137.60	$7,379.88	$7,176.40	$6,180.35	$9,675.31	$9,002.50	$6,222.58

Record: 1 of 12

Figure 22.31 The table created by the spCategoriesCT procedure is almost identical to that created by copying the Jet crosstab query result set shown in Figure 22.20. The only difference is the name of the first field, which has been changed to Categories to support the sample linked chart.

With a linked graph, you can use the stored procedure as the Record Source property of the form, but not as the Row Source property of the graph. If you change both record sources to the stored procedure, the link between the master and child fields fails, and the graph displays a line for every category. To solve this problem, change the Record Source property value of the form to **spCategoriesCT** and the Row Source property value of the chart to **tbl1997CT**. Opening the form executes the stored procedure to update the table. Using the table as the Row Source for the chart also improves performance, because the procedure doesn't execute each time you change the category.

Improving Application Scalability and Performance

Opening the frm1997SalesByCategory chart with a stored procedure as the chart's data source is noticeably slower than with a table. On the 667MHz Pentium III machine with 256MB RAM running Windows 2000 Server used to create the examples of this chapter, the difference is about a second. If your SQL Server machine is slower, has less RAM, or serves many simultaneous users, executing the stored procedure can incur a greater performance hit.

You can solve the scalability issues raised in the preceding section and improve the performance of forms based on table-creating stored procedures by recreating the table only when required by changes to the table's source data. For example, updating sales data once per day might be sufficient. In this case, you need to compare the last creation date and time with the current system date, and skip the table-creation process if the difference is, say, less than 12 hours. SQL Server's `DATEDIFF` function can compute the difference in hours between the time the table was last created and the system time returned by the `GETDATE` function.

To prevent creating a new table when the existing table is less than 12 hours old, do this:

SQL

1. In SQL view of the spCatetoriesCT procedure, add the following lines after `SET NOCOUNT ON`:

```
IF EXISTS(SELECT table_name
   FROM information_schema.tables
   WHERE table_name = 'tbl1997CT')
```

22

```
BEGIN
   DECLARE @tabletime datetime
   SET @tabletime = (SELECT crdate FROM sysobjects
      WHERE name = 'tbl1997CT')
   IF DATEDIFF(hh, @tabletime, GETDATE()) < 12
      GOTO shortcut
END
```

2. Add the following label above the `SELECT * FROM tbl1997CT` statement:

   `shortcut:`

3. Run the procedure to save your changes and click Run again to test the speed of opening the datasheet from the stored procedure.

T-SQL

Following is a brief explanation of the new T-SQL statements in the preceding example:

`BEGIN...END` defines a block of code that executes if the `IF` condition is satisfied.

`DECLARE @tabletime datetime` declares a local variable of the datetime data type.

`SET @tabletime = (SELECT...)` sets the value of the variable to the `crdate` (creation date and time) of the existing table. The `sysobjects` table holds the properties of all objects in the current database.

`DATEDIFF(hh, @tabletime, GETDATE())` returns the difference in hours between the current system time and the existing table.

`GOTO shortcut` causes execution to jump to the `shortcut:` label, which returns the result set from the existing table to the graph.

The two preceding sections demonstrate the power and flexibility of SQL Server stored procedures. After you become familiar with T-SQL's additional reserved words for use in stored procedures, writing more complex stored procedures to enforce business rules and perform sophisticated data-validation operations is the next step. Many developers use middle-tier Component Object Model (COM) components between the client and server (called *three-tier architecture*) to validate data and enforce business rules. Well-written stored procedures, however, are much simpler to create and maintain and often provide better performance than middle-tier COM components.

NOTE

> Text files containing the T-SQL code for the modified qry1997SalesChart view (vwChart.txt) and the spCategoriesCT stored procedure (spChart.txt) are included in the \Seua11\Chaptr22 folder of the accompanying CD-ROM. If you didn't perform the preceding exercises, open the file in Notepad, copy the text to the Clipboard, and paste the statement to the SQL pane of a new view or stored procedure.

Running the Jet Crosstab Upsizer

The Visual Basic 6.0 Crosstab Upsizer program (Crosstab.exe), which you install from the \Seua11\Crosstab folder of the accompanying CD-ROM, automates generation of the view or function and stored procedure that are required to emulate a Jet crosstab query. The program connects to the .mdb file that contains the crosstab queries and the upsized SQL Server database. You must install Crosstab.exe and its associated files on a computer running Access 2003.

NOTE

You can learn more about the Crosstab Upsizer and download its source code from *Visual Studio Magazine*'s "Upsize Jet Crosstab Queries" article at `http://www.fawcette.com/archives/premier/mgznarch/vbpj/2001/10oct01/sqlpro0110/rj0110/rj0110-1.asp`.

The help files—CTHelp.doc and CTHelp.txt—provide detailed descriptions for using the Crosstab Upsizer, so the following is a brief example of its use with the Upsize22.mdb file and UpsizeSQL database.

To install and test-drive the Crosstab Upsizer, do the following:

1. Run Setup.exe from your \Program Files\Seua11\Crosstabs folder to install the required files and Programs menu shortcuts. By default, the program installs in the \Program Files\CrosstabUpsizer folder.
2. Choose Program Files, Crosstab Upsizer, Crosstab Upsizer to open the logon dialog. Type the path to the .mdb file or click the ... button to browse for the .mdb file. The default is C:\Program Files\Seua11\Chaptr22\Upsize22.mdb.
3. If your .mdb file is secure, specify the workgroup file in the SystemDB text box or browse for it. Type your user name and password for the .mdb file.
4. Accept the (LOCAL) default or type the SQL Server name in the Instance text box and specify the upsized database name. By default, the program uses Windows security to connect to the database (see Figure 22.32).

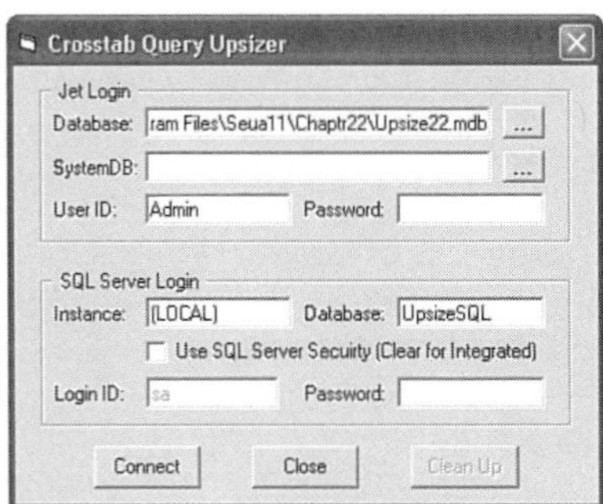

Figure 22.32 Specify the source .mdb file and your Jet credentials, and the SQL Server instance and database in the login dialog.

5. Click Connect to connect to the .mdb file and database and open the main Upsizer form with a list of the crosstab queries in the .mdb file. Click one of the queries in the

list to display its SQL statement in the text box and result set in the grid (see Figure 22.33). If the crosstab query requires parameters, an input box requests parameter value(s). (Use 1996, 1997, or 1998 for the qryQuarterlyOrdersByProductParam query.)

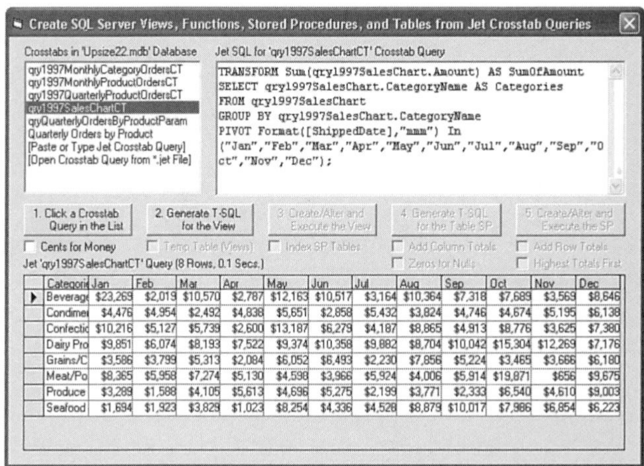

Figure 22.33
Selecting a crosstab query in the list retrieves its SQL statement, executes the query, and displays the data in a grid.

6. Click Generate T-SQL for the View to write the SQL statement for the aggregate values query. If the query has parameters, the Upsizer generates an in-line, table valued function.

> **TIP**
>
> If your crosstab query doesn't include a `CCur()` function for currency, wrap the view's value field expression with a T-SQL `CONVERT(money, *expression*)` function.

7. Click Create/Alter and Execute the View to display the query result set in the grid. Mark Cents for Money if you want decimal currency values, and re-execute the query (see Figure 22.34).
8. Click Generate T-SQL for the Table SP to display the proposed SQL statement to generate the table from the view result set. If you want to include column totals, row totals, or both, mark the check boxes and click Generate again. The grid displays properties of the table fields (see Figure 22.35).
9. Click Create/Alter and Execute the SP to display the crosstab results in the grid. The values duplicate those of Figure 22.33, and include row and column (crossfoot) totals (see Figure 22.36).

The Crosstab Upsizer can't process every Jet crosstab query automatically, so you might need to edit the T-SQL statements for the view/function or stored procedure to obtain the desired result.

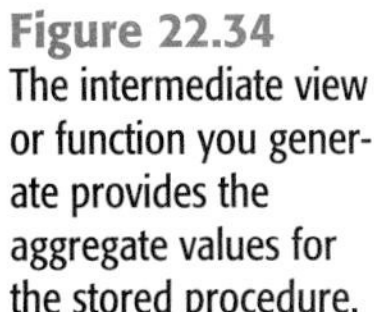

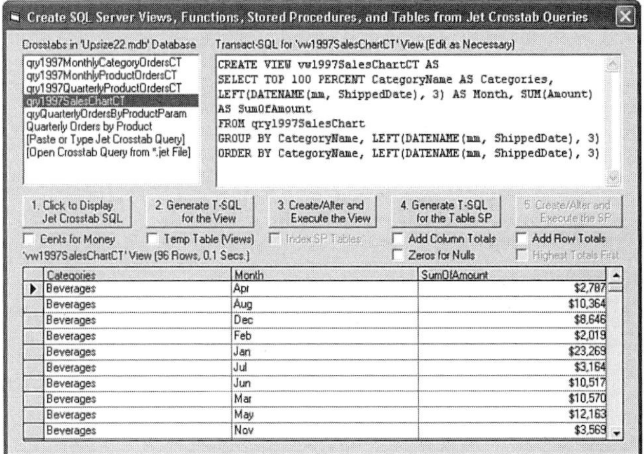

Figure 22.34
The intermediate view or function you generate provides the aggregate values for the stored procedure.

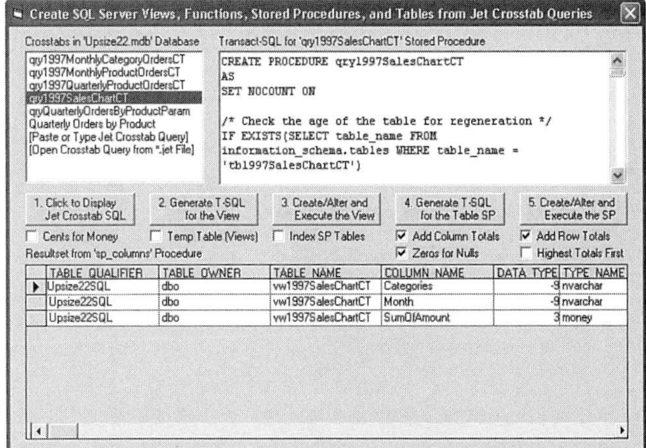

Figure 22.35
The table that stores the crosstab data is named for the view that creates it.

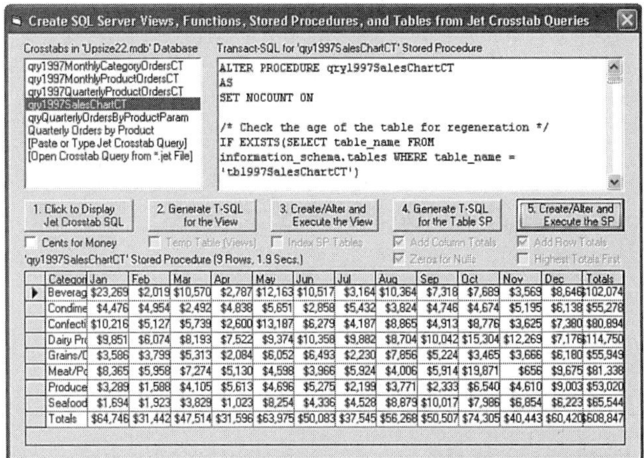

Figure 22.36
The T-SQL stored procedure emulates the Jet crosstab query and includes optional row and column totals.

22

CAUTION

> If you uninstall the Crosstab Upsizer, you might receive a "Shared File" message. If you see this message *do not* remove any shared files.

Securing Projects with the MSDE 2000 Login/User Tool

Adding password protection and converting your upsized project to an encoded (.ade) file doesn't provide security for your back-end SQL Server database. You must provide groups or individual users logins to the server and permissions to read and update specific tables. Issuing a long series of OSQL statements at the command prompt is time-consuming and prone to error. Writing an OSQL script to add logins and permissions is an alternative, but isn't an easy task.

→ For more information on creating .ade files and using the OSQL utility, **see** "Securing Your Project as an .ade File," **p. 848** and **see** "Adding User Logins with the OSQL Utility," **p. 776**.

The MSDE User Manager utility (UserMan.exe) is a Visual Basic 6.0 program that uses SQL Server Data Management Objects (SQLDMO) to manage server logins and database permissions for MSDE 2000. (The MSDE 2000 setup program installs SQLDMO.dll.) UserMan.exe supports Windows authentication only, because Windows authentication is more secure than SQL Server security. UserMan.exe lets you assign groups or users to predefined SQL Server roles—such as `db_datareader` and `db_datawriter`—grant specific object permissions, or both. Users or groups must have Windows accounts before you can add SQL Server logins for them.

Like the Crosstab Upsizer, the MSDE User Manager utility has a detailed help file, so the following steps demonstrate basic functionality:

1. Run Setup.exe from your \Program Files\Seua11\UserMan folder. By default, the program installs in your \Program Files\MSDE User Manager folder and adds an Programs, MSDE User Manager shortcut.
2. If your or your network administrator haven't established Windows accounts for your project's users, do this now. If your computer isn't on a network, add a few local test users to the built-in Power Users group.
3. Choose Programs, MSDE User Manager to open the utility's single form, which displays in the upper left list all SQL Server instances that are accessible to your computer. For this example, the (local) server is OAKLEAF-XP1 in the OAKLEAF domain. (Click the Help tab for detailed instructions.)
4. Select a server instance in the list and click Connect to open a connection and fill the *ServerName* Logins and *ServerName* Databases lists.

5. Click an item in the *ServerName* Databases list to display its user accounts in the *DatabaseName* Users list. For this example, the UpsizeSQL database has only the `sysadmin` user (dbo). Click dbo to display the sysadmin roles in the *UserName* Roles list (see Figure 22.37). All users are a member of the `public` role.

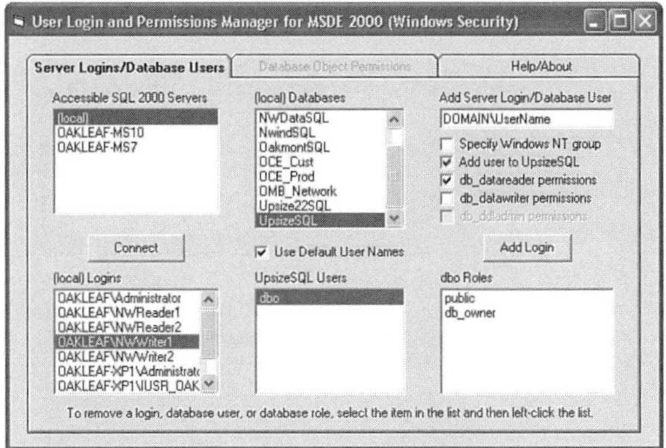

Figure 22.37
The MSDE User Manager utility has lists of server instances, logins for the selected instance, databases, database users, and user roles.

6. Type the group or user name preceded by the domain, local computer name, or BUILTIN for Windows XP/2000 built-in groups in the text box and click Add Login. If the login name is valid and you've marked the Add User to *DatabaseName* check box, the program adds the login to the server and creates a user account in the specified database. If you type an existing login correctly, a message box gives you the option of adding a user account for the login. This example adds a user account for the NWWriter1 account with `db_datareader` and `db_datawriter` roles.
7. Select the new user in the *DatabaseName* Users list to enable the Database Object Permissions tab, and click the tab to display a page with lists of tables, views, stored procedures, and user-defined functions.
8. Click an object to display current permissions for the user in the *ObjectName* Permissions list, which shows permissions inherited from the user's predefined roles (see Figure 22.38). NWWriter1 has implicit permissions for read-write table operations, but not References (DRI). You can add or remove References (DRI) by marking or clearing the only enabled check box.
9. The db_datareader and db_datawriter roles don't have implicit permissions to execute stored procedures. Thus you must grant execute permissions for each stored procedure to each group or user of an upsized project (see Figure 22.39).
10. Repeat steps 6 through 9 to add more logins, database users, and their object permissions.

Closing the form closes the connection to the server instance.

The MSDE User Manager isn't a replacement for SQL Server's Enterprise Manager, but it fulfills the basic role of Access 2000's Database Security tool.

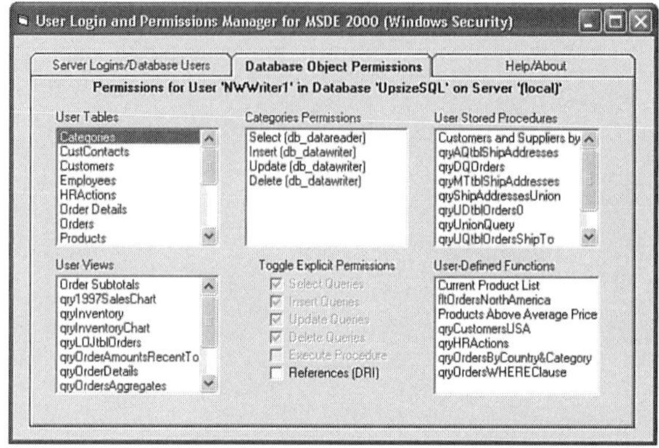

Figure 22.38
The Database Object Permissions page displays inherited permissions and permissions you add by marking enabled check boxes.

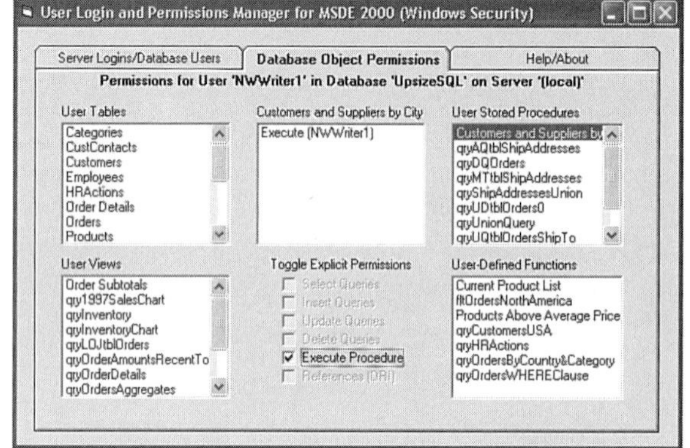

Figure 22.39
Be sure to grant explicit execute permissions for all SELECT stored procedures to read-only and read-write users.

NOTE

Visual Studio Magazine's "Manage MSDE Security" article, which describes the Visual Basic 6.0 and Visual Basic .NET versions of the utility, is at `http://www.ftponline.com/vsm/2003_06/magazine/columns/databasedesign/`.

TROUBLESHOOTING

STORED PROCEDURES DON'T RETURN THE EXPECTED RECORDSET

My `SELECT * FROM TableName` *statement at the end of a stored procedure that includes* `INSERT [INTO]`, `UPDATE`, *or* `DELETE` *statements doesn't return any rows.*

You forgot to add `SET NOCOUNT ON` as the first statement of your procedure. T-SQL and VBA can handle combinations of multiple return values and Recordsets from a stored procedure, but ADP can't. If you don't add `SET NOCOUNT ON`, the server returns the number of records affected for each operation, which generates an unneeded data transfer from the server to the client. In the case of the spCategoriesCT procedure, the server returns 10 values before sending the Recordset. Unless you're using VBA code to execute the query and need the `RecordsAffected` values returned after execution, always make `SET NOCOUNT ON` the first statement of your stored procedures.

IN THE REAL WORLD—STRATEGIC OR NOT?

ADP and SQL Server represent Microsoft strategic migration path to client/server applications. Only those technologies that Microsoft deems *strategic* receive significant development funding. As an example, when Microsoft decided in 1998 that SQL Server was its *strategic* database, Jet development ground to an immediate halt with the release of Access 2000. Jet 4.0 is the end of the line for this venerable database engine, other than for Windows CE developers. (The Windows CE version of SQL Server is based on Jet technology.)

Similarly, Data Access Objects (DAO) and Open Database Connectivity (ODBC) aren't strategic; DAO is terminal at version 3.6 and, when this book was written, the last update to the ODBC page on Microsoft's Web site (`http://www.microsoft.com/data/odbc/default.htm`) was March 17, 1999. Microsoft Data Access Components (MDAC), which include ActiveX Data Objects (ADO) and OLE DB, *are* strategic, but not as strategic as .NET. Office 2003 installs MDAC 2.7. You can expect MDAC to receive a few updates, whereas Jet, DAO, and ODBC languish in maintenance-only purgatory. Most of Microsoft's data connectivity efforts are directed to the .NET Framework and Visual Studio .NET.

Circumstances might dictate that you upgrade your Access application from Jet to SQL Server. A common reason for upsizing is that your application has become critical to the continued success of your organization, so management wants to put it under the aegis of the information technology (IT) department. In this case, you and the IT department must decide whether to link the Jet application to the server or upsize the front-end .mdb to an .adp. Most linked Jet applications consume several simultaneous ODBC connections per user to SQL Server, although ADP consume only one or two. Poorly designed Jet queries can require the server to send thousands of rows to clients when only one or a few rows suffice for the application. If your application has many users, it's likely that the SQL Server database administrator(s) will insist on the more efficient .adp approach.

If you're using Access as a RDBMS learning tool, and want to expand your weltanschauung from the desktop to the client/server world, Access 2003 is your best bet. The project designer makes it easy to design views, functions, and stored procedures based on `SELECT` statements. After you've mastered the transition from Jet SQL to T-SQL, you can experiment with writing increasingly complex stored procedures from scratch. Like a working knowledge of VBA, expertise in stored-procedure programming boosts your career potential. What's more, unlike the transition from Visual Basic 6.0 to Visual Basic .NET, T-SQL in the next version of SQL Server, codenamed "Yukon" when this book was written, is certain to be fully backward-compatible with SQL Sever 2000.

PART VI

Publishing Data to Intranets and the Internet

CHAPTER 23

Exporting and Importing Data with XML

In this chapter

Adopting XML as a Data Interchange Format

Microsoft's primary selling point for Office 2003 is the capability of Word, Excel, and Access to export and import documents and data in Extensible Markup Language (XML) 1.0. Structured documents and relational data stored as XML files can be exchanged between multiple business applications running under different operating systems. Interchangeability is the driving force behind the wide-spread adoption of XML as the 21st-century standard for sharing information.

Microsoft's stated goal for Office 2003 is to make XML an "open standards" alternative to proprietary Microsoft file formats. For example, Access can import structured XML documents—such as resumes, employee performance review, or expense reports—prepared in Word 2003 to relational data stored in a Jet or SQL Server database. The key to the document import process is a consistent document structure that's defined by a *schema*. (The next section defines XML schemas). Access interprets the schema to determine the tables and fields in which to store the data contained in the document's elements. The same schema supports exporting the documents back to Word.

Excel 2002 provided a few XML features and Access 2002 introduced importing and exporting XML-encoded data to and from Jet and SQL Server tables. Access 2002 was limited to import/export of flat (non-relational) data. Access 2003 now handles hierarchical XML representations of relational data. This new feature lets you export documents from related tables to create multiple tables from a single XML document and schema. In some cases, you can append records to multiple tables from an XML document.

This chapter begins with definitions of important XML terms and then covers the use of XML documents exported by Access to generate HTML documents for deployment on intranets and the Internet. Sections at the end of the chapter describe exporting and importing XML data documents, generating and using XML schemas, and transforming XML data with custom XSLT files.

TIP

> If you're only interested in the end result and want to defer learning the underpinnings of Access 2003's XML features, skip to the "Exporting Static Reports as XML" section.

Gaining an XML Vocabulary

SQL has formal grammar rules that depend on the structure of relational databases. XML has a hierarchical structure based on Standard Generalized Markup Language (SGML) for formatting text documents. XML-related "programming" languages, which manipulate XML documents, have a very complex grammar. Before you can begin to interpret—not to mention write and manipulate—XML documents, you need to know a few basic XML terms.

NOTE

> The quotes around "programming" in the preceding paragraph are to contrast procedural code that you write in VBA or other familiar programming languages with XML code that manipulates XML documents. XML document-manipulation code, written in Extensible Stylesheet Language Transformations (XSLT), deals with the entire document as a single "chunk." An example near the end of this chapter illustrates the use of VBScript code to process XML data documents with XSLT.

Following are brief definitions of XML-related terms used in this and the following two chapters; some definitions include simple XML examples:

- **XML document**—Any document that follows all XML syntax rules is a *well-formed* document. An XML document must have a least one pair of tags that define the document root (`<root>...</root>`) and usually has an *XML header*. The tags can have any name, but the case must match; unlike HTML, XML is case-sensitive. In this and the following chapters, an XML document is assumed to be a document containing Jet 4.0 or SQL Server 2000 data, with or without an embedded *XML schema*. XML data documents usually carry an .xml extension; by default, Access names exported data files *TableName*.xml or *QueryName*.xml.
- **Element**—An element is a unit of an XML document that's enclosed between a pair of tags, as in `<tag>element</tag>`. Elements can be—and almost always are—nested within other elements to form a hierarchical document structure.
- **Attribute**—An attribute is a `name="value"` pair that follows the first tag name of an element, as in `<tag attribName="attribValue">...</tag>`. Attributes usually represent properties of an element.
- **XML header**—The `<?xml version="1.0" ?>` header technically is optional, but all XML documents should include the header, which usually specifies the encoding method, as in `<?xml version="1.0" encoding="UTF-8" ?>`. UTF-8 is an abbreviation for Universal Character Set Transformation Format 8-bit, a transformation of 16-bit Unicode that's supported by most Web browsers.
- **Well-formed**—A well-formed document is one that an XML parsing tool, such as the MSXML parser included with IE 5+, can display without reporting syntax errors (for instance, `<ROOT>...</root>`). Well-formed isn't the same as *validated*.

XML

Following is an example of the simplest well-formed XML data document that conveys some information:

```
<?xml version="1.0" encoding="UTF-8" ?>
<dataroot>
   This is data.
</dataroot>
```

If you type the preceding text in Notepad and save the file as **Simple.xml**, you can open it in IE 5+. IE's XML parser color codes XML elements: The first line is blue, tags are brown, and values (This is data.) are black and bold face.

- **Validated**—The original definition of a validated XML document is one that conforms to a predefined Document Type Definition (DTD), which is a holdover from SGML, on which XML (and HTML) is based. DTDs use an arcane syntax and are very difficult to write. An *XML schema* is more appropriate than a DTD for data documents, but is at least equally difficult to compose. Fortunately, Access generates the schemas for the XML documents you export. All XML document examples in this and the following chapters are well-formed and many are validated against XML schemas during import processing.
- **XML schema**—Schemas are metadata (data about data) that describe the structure of a table, query result set, or database. The content of Access's Relationships window is an example of a partial schema for a database. The schema is partial because field data types of the tables are missing. XML schemas define the structure of XML documents and the types of data they contain. For data documents, schemas include field data type definitions and, if a query returns data from more than one table, a description of the relationship between the tables. Access names exported schema files *TableName*.xsd or *QueryName*.xsd.

NOTE

Schemas exported by Access 2003 conform to the W3C's final recommendation of May 2, 2001, for XML Schema 1.0 (`http://www.w3.org/TR/xmlschema-0/` for Part 0: Primer). The accepted file extension for schemas conforming to this to the recommendation is .xsd.

Early SQL Server 2000 XML features and ActiveX Data Objects (ADO) 2.1+ use a Microsoft-designed schema called XML Data Reduced (XDR). ADO Recordsets saved to .xml files incorporate XDR schemas and use the *attribute-centric* format. When saved as schema files, the accepted file extension is .xdr.

- **XML namespace**—XML namespaces associate element and attribute names with a unique identifier to avoid tag-name ambiguity. The namespace attribute (`xmlns`) usually—but not necessarily—has a unique Uniform Resource Identifier (URI) as its value. There's a recent recommendation for XML Namespace attribute names and values at `http://www.w3.org/TR/1999/REC-xml-names-19990114/`.

XML

The following header and namespace declaration appears at the beginning of each XML data document/schema pair you export from an Access 2003 table or query:

```
<?xml version="1.0" encoding="UTF-8" ?>
<dataroot xmlns:od="urn:schemas-microsoft-com:officedata"
xmlns:xsi="http://www.w3.org/2001/XMLSchema-instance"
xsi:noNamespaceSchemaLocation="TableOrQueryName.xsd">
```

Namespaces for the entire document are declared as attributes of the document root. Access doesn't use the `od` (`officedata`) element type when exporting XML data documents; `od` appears in schemas. The `xmlns:xsi=`... line specifies a URI to indicate that the document has an associated schema. The `xsi:noNamespaceSchemaLocation=` line asserts that the document's data elements are defined by the specified XML schema file: *`TableOrQueryName`*`.xsd`. If the location doesn't have a path or an `http://...` URL, the .xsd file must be in the same folder as the .xml file.

- **Element-centric**—XML documents that contain a single value, such as a number or a block of text, within an element are called element-centric. XML data documents exported by Access are element-centric. Element-centric XML typically stores table data in *`<row>`* elements with *`<column>value</column>`* subelements.

XML

The shortest XML document that you can generate by exporting an Access object is the Shippers.xml file:

```
<?xml version="1.0" encoding="UTF-8" ?>
<dataroot xmlns:od="urn:schemas-microsoft-com:officedata"
   xmlns:xsi="http://www.w3.org/2001XMLSchema-instance"
   xsi:noNamespaceSchemaLocation="Shippers.xsd">
  <Shippers>
     <ShipperID>1</ShipperID>
     <CompanyName>Speedy Express</CompanyName>
     <Phone>(503) 555-9831</Phone>
  </Shippers>
  <Shippers>
     <ShipperID>2</ShipperID>
     <CompanyName>United Package</CompanyName>
     <Phone>(503) 555-3199</Phone>
  </Shippers>
  <Shippers>
     <ShipperID>3</ShipperID>
     <CompanyName>Federal Shipping</CompanyName>
     <Phone>(503) 555-9931</Phone>
  </Shippers>
</dataroot>
```

Each sub-element (child) of the Shippers (parent) element consists of a single-valued piece of data that represents field values from the Shippers table.

- **Attribute-centric**—XML documents with multi-valued elements are called attribute-centric. For data documents, the attribute name usually is the field or column name, and the value is a text representation of the field value.

XML

Following is an edited version of the attribute-centric XML document for the Shippers table, which is created by saving an ADO Recordset in an XDR-related format:

```
<xml xmlns:rs='urn:schemas-microsoft-com:rowset'
   xmlns:z='#RowsetSchema'>
   <rs:data>
      <z:row ShipperID='1' CompanyName='Speedy Express' Phone='(503) 555-9831'/>
      <z:row ShipperID='2' CompanyName='United Package' Phone='(503) 555-3199'/>
      <z:row ShipperID='3' CompanyName='Federal Shipping' Phone='(503) 555-9931'/>
   </rs:data>
</xml>
```

continues

continued

Attribute-centric XML can hold the data for an entire row of a table or query result set in a single element. In this case, a set of `z:row` elements nest within an single `rs:data` element for the entire Recordset. The attribute-value pairs are `FieldName='value'`. Single- or double-quotes must enclose text values. (XML documents created by saving ADO Recordsets in XML format include the schema as a separate set of elements. The schema elements are removed from the preceding XML code.)

23

- **XML style sheets**—Extensible Stylesheet Language (XSL) can serve two purposes: defining the presentation of an XML document and transforming one XML document into another XML document with a different structure or into HTML. The most common use of XML style sheets is transforming XML data documents into HTML. XSLT is the language in which you—or more likely others at this point—write XML style sheets. Style sheets are stored in files that carry an .xsl extension (.xslt also is used).

NOTE

The October 2001 W3C recommendation for Extensible Stylesheet Language (`http://www.w3.org/TR/xsl/`) was current when this book was written. XSLT 1.0's finale recommendation of November 1999 is at `http://www.w3.org/TR/xslt.html`.

XSLT isn't limited to manipulating XML data documents. The only requirement is that the data processed by XSLT be structured as a tree of tagged nodes, starting with a root node, progressing through sub-nodes, and terminating in leaf nodes. A leaf node contains only text, although the text can comprise hundreds or thousands of lines of, for instance, VBScript code.

MOVING FROM ACCESS TO XML-BASED WEB FRONT-ENDS

One of the primary objectives of Access is to render data in an organized, easily readable format. Datasheets, subdatasheets, and lookup fields are quite effective for displaying and editing the raw relational data stored in Jet and SQL Server tables. Access queries, forms, reports, PivotTables, and PivotCharts transform your raw data into usable information. The downside of using Access 2003 front-end applications to display information and edit data is that data consumers must run Access 2003 on their machines. With the exception of front-ends that use VBA code to implement disconnected Recordsets, each user must maintain at least one permanent connection to the back-end database while running the front-end application. Permanent connections limit the number of simultaneous users to 255 in the case of Jet; SQL Server (and MSDE) connections aren't limited, but each connection consumes server resources.

→ For more information on disconnected Recordsets, **see** "Taking Advantage of Disconnected Recordsets," **p. 1312**.

Microsoft Office is ubiquitous, but Access isn't; most Office licenses are the Standard Edition that doesn't include Access. Further, industry analysts report that—when this book was written—about 60% of the estimated 150 million Office installations were version 97 or earlier. Making your Access 2003 front end accessible to all Windows XP/2000 users requires using the Access 2003 Developer Extensions' Package Wizard to create a Windows installer (.msi) package of runtime Access 2003 and your application's .mdb/.mde or .adp/.ade front end.

Almost every PC user has a Web browser installed, and the majority—perhaps as many as 90%—of the PCs in the world run Internet Explorer (IE). Users of Windows 95+ who don't have the latest IE version can download it themselves at no charge. Thus viewing and editing Jet or SQL Server data in IE is an attractive alternative to distributing heavyweight runtime Access packages. Office 2003's requirement for Windows XP/2000 makes browser-based operations the only alternative for Windows Me, 98, and 95 users or those whose computers run Linux or Macintosh operating systems. XML plays a crucial role in Microsoft's approach to moving from conventional form-based multiuser Access applications to browser-based views of data in tables and Data access pages (DAP).

NOTE

> This chapter assumes that you have a basic understanding of HTML, including code for generating formatted HTML tables. Familiarity with VBScript or ECMAScript is helpful for one section of this chapter, but isn't a necessity.

Making the Transition to Stateless Front-Ends

Conventional browser-based viewing and editing operations are said to be *stateless*, because successive operations don't depend on the outcome (state) of previous activities. Stateless applications don't depend on a continuous network connection for a session. Viewing or editing a page establishes a temporary connection to the Web server that lasts only as long as it takes to send a page request or data and receive a new or updated page from the server. Statelessness plays a very important role in determining how browsers interact with Jet and SQL Server data.

NOTE

> The Web itself is stateless, but some applications—such as Web-based credit-card purchases—require maintaining some state information until the transaction completes or is abandoned. State information can be maintained on the client browser—typically in the form of a cookie—and on the Web server as a `Session.State` or similar object property.

The stateless nature of the Web is responsible for its scalability from tens of thousands of simultaneous users during its early stages to hundreds of millions today. The number of users that can connect simultaneously to a static Access Web page is limited only by your Web server's hardware and the available bandwidth of its Internet or intranet connection. The performance of the back-end data engine influences the scalability of live Access Web pages.

SEPARATING DATA FROM PRESENTATION WITH XML

HTML is a language designed primarily to determine the presentation of text and graphic data for rendering by Web browsers. The Cascading Style Sheets (CSS) and Document Object Model (DOM) extensions to HTML enable browsers to modify (rerender) Web pages locally. One of the primary problems with HTML is that HTML combines the representation of data with the data itself. For example, conventional HTML tables contain both formatting and text data values for cells. To change the data values, you must regenerate the entire page and its table, which requires a round-trip to the sever. You can use DHTML to minimize round-tripping, but the data remains enmeshed in presentation code.

The objective of XML is to abstract (separate and condense) data and its structure from presentation of the data. In the general case, structured data can be any content—a book, musical score, collection of images, or single news story. Structure is determined by the type of content—for example, chapter, section, paragraph, and figure for books. The basic requirement is that all data within an XML document adhere to the predefined structure that's defined by its XML schema.

TIP

For a brief and somewhat whimsical introduction to XML, read Bert Bos's "XML in 10 points" at `http://www.w3.org/XML/1999/XML-in-10-points`.

In this book, data is restricted to the content of rows and columns of tables or query result sets, which can include text, numbers, images, sound, or video material stored in Jet OLE Object or SQL Server image fields. The structure of the data is determined by the table design and relationships between the tables, if more than one table is involved. XML stores tabular data as a structured text document and uses tags to specify the names of data elements. XML documents generated by query result sets are simple and easily readable in a browser with an XML parser, such as IE 5+. To represent data in related tables, XML uses a hierarchical structure of nested elements that use tags to identify the source tables. Today's ultimate destination of the content of most XML documents is a Web browser, which requires transformation of XML data to formatted HTML code. The examples of this chapter use sets of XML data documents and XML style sheets to deliver Web pages from Access tables and queries.

NOTE

Ultimately, the destination of most XML documents will be server-based applications, not Web browsers. XML Web services, which are the subject of Chapter 31, "Creating and Consuming XML Web Services," represent only one aspect of server-to-server transfer of XML documents.

Unlike basic HTML, which uses a standardized set of embedded tags (such as `<p>...</p>` for a paragraph and attributes (`href="http://www.whatever.com/somepage.htm"`) to define visible objects on or pointers to a Web page, you can define your own tags and attributes to specify (delimit) data. The XML 1.0 specification (`http://www.w3.org/TR/2000/REC-xml`) defines only one tag with an attribute—`<?xml version="1.0" ?>`. Exporting data from tables or query result sets generates tags and, in some cases, attribute names, from the table and field names.

UNDERSTANDING THE ROLE OF ACCESS'S REPORTML

Access 2003 installs two formidable style sheets: RPT2DAP.xsl and RPT2HTML4.xsl in your ...\Office11\AccessWeb folder. ReportML is a Microsoft specification for the representation of Access objects—tables, queries, forms, and reports, as well as the controls on forms and reports—in a well-formed XML data document. The RPT2DAP.xsl style sheet transforms ReportML to DAP; RPT2HTML4.xsl transforms ReportML to HTML 4.0 code that renders a Web page. Tables and queries export to HTML tables; forms export as continuous forms. Simple reports export a page that closely emulates a report snapshot.

Access 2003's ReportML generates .xsl, and .htm, files, which IE 6+ processes by creating two `MSXML.DOMDocument` ActiveX objects to render the Web page. Alternatively, ReportML can generate .asp files to deliver HTML from the server. `MSXML` is the type library for Microsoft's XML parser—version 5.0 when this book was written. `DOMDocument` is the W3C DOM XML Class. DOM is the application programming interface (API) for valid HTML documents and well-formed XML documents. The W3C specification of November 2000 is for DOM version 2.0 (`http://www.w3.org/TR/DOM-Level-2-Core/`).

Figure 23.1 is a diagram of the processes involved and the files created when you export an Access 2003 table, query, form, or report object to XML. The diagram is for XSL presentation of the object by an .htm file processed by the client (the default). Creating an .xsd schema file is optional; ReportML doesn't use the schema information. Sections later in this chapter describe how elements of ReportML contribute to the .xsl file for the exported object.

TIP

If you want to inspect the temporary *ObjectName*_report.xml file generated by AccessWeb.dll, add the following Registry key:

```
HKEY_CURRENT_USER\Software\Microsoft\Office\11.0\Access\ReportML
```

To add the key automatically, double-click the ReportML.reg file in the \Seua11\Chaptr23 folder of your \Program Files folder or the accompanying CD-ROM.

The following two examples illustrate how the code in the *ObjectName*.htm and *ObjectName*.asp files use the `transformNode` method to apply the style sheet to the XML data document.

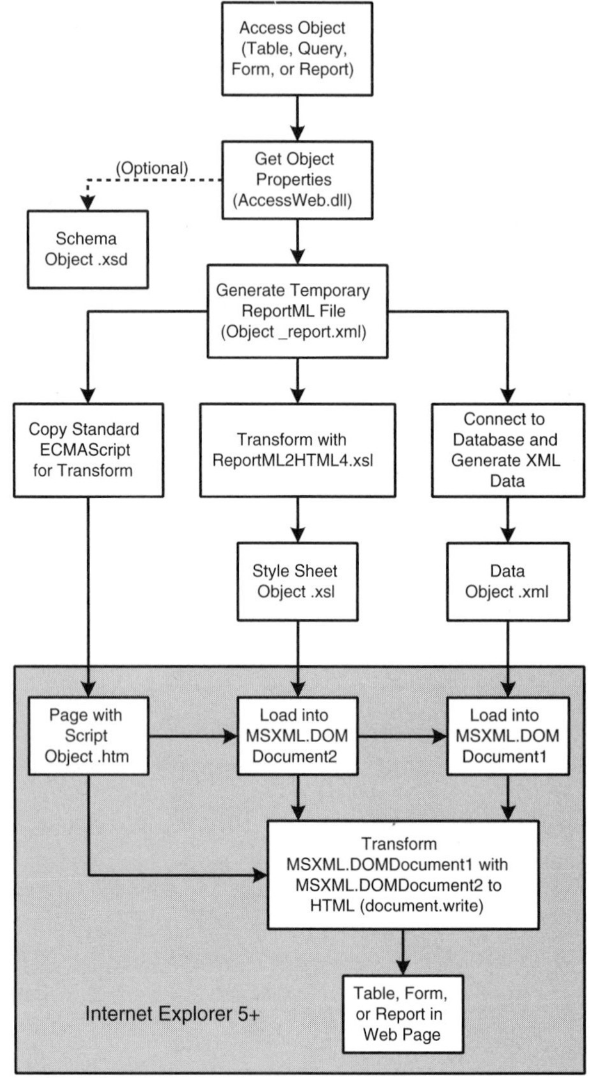

Figure 23.1
This diagram outlines the steps involved in generating in IE 6+ a static Web page from an Access table, query, form, or report object.

VBScript

Following is the VBScript for the vwUnion.htm file, which loads the vwUnion.xml and vwUnion.xsl files as data and style sheet streams into two `MSXML.DOMDocument` objects. The `Document.Write(objData.TransformNode(objStyle))` instruction generates the HTML elements to display the table. IE 6+ running on the client handles the document processing.

```
<HTML xmlns:signature="urn:schemas-microsoft-com:office:access">
<HEAD>
<META HTTP-EQUIV="Content-Type" CONTENT="text/html;charset=UTF-8"/>
</HEAD>
<BODY ONLOAD="ApplyTransform()">
</BODY>
```

```
<SCRIPT LANGUAGE="VBScript">
   Option Explicit

   Function ApplyTransform()
      Dim objData, objStyle
      Set objData = CreateDOM
      LoadDOM objData, "vwUnion.xml"
      Set objStyle = CreateDOM
      LoadDOM objStyle, "vwUnion.xsl"

      Document.Open "text/html","replace"
      Document.Write objData.TransformNode(objStyle)
   End Function

   Function CreateDOM()
      On Error Resume Next
      Dim tmpDOM
      Set tmpDOM = Nothing
      Set tmpDOM = CreateObject("MSXML2.DOMDocument.5.0")
      If tmpDOM Is Nothing Then
         Set tmpDOM = CreateObject("MSXML2.DOMDocument.4.0")
      End If
      If tmpDOM Is Nothing Then
         Set tmpDOM = CreateObject("MSXML.DOMDocument")
      End If
      Set CreateDOM = tmpDOM
   End Function

   Function LoadDOM(objDOM, strXMLFile)
      objDOM.Async = False
      objDOM.Load strXMLFile
      If (objDOM.ParseError.ErrorCode <> 0) Then
         MsgBox objDOM.ParseError.Reason
      End If
   End Function
</SCRIPT>
</HTML>
```

With the exception of the .xml and .xsl file names, the code for all .htm files you generate by exporting Access objects is identical.

VBScript

The following VBScript in the vwUnion.asp file generates the `MSXML2.DOMDocument.5.0` objects on the Web server and delivers browser-agnostic HTML code for the table to the client browser. The `Session.CodePage = 65001` line shown in bold type makes extended ASCII/ANSI characters appear correctly in the table. `65001` is the UTF-8 code page.

```
objData.async = false

if (false) then
   Set objDataXMLHTTP = Server.CreateObject("Microsoft.XMLHTTP")
   objDataXMLHTTP.open "GET", "", false
   objDataXMLHTTP.setRequestHeader "Content-Type", "text/xml"
   objDataXMLHTTP.send
```

continues

continued

```
      objData.load(objDataXMLHTTP.responseBody)
   else
      objData.load(Server.MapPath("vwUnion.xml"))
   end if

   Set objStyle = CreateDOM
   objStyle.async = false
   objStyle.load(Server.MapPath("vwUnion.xsl"))
   Session.CodePage = 65001

   Response.ContentType = "text/html"
   Response.Write objData.transformNode(objStyle)

   Function CreateDOM()
      On Error Resume Next
      Dim tmpDOM

      Set tmpDOM = Nothing
      Set tmpDOM = Server.CreateObject("MSXML2.DOMDocument.5.0")
      If tmpDOM Is Nothing Then
         Set tmpDOM = Server.CreateObject("MSXML2.DOMDocument.4.0")
      End If
      If tmpDOM Is Nothing Then
         Set tmpDOM = Server.CreateObject("MSXML.DOMDocument")
      End If

      Set CreateDOM = tmpDOM
   End Function
   %>
```

Processing the documents on the Web server is resource-intensive, so it's a good practice to specify server-side processing for static pages only if you need to support browsers that can't process .xml and .xsl files.

EXPORTING TABLES AND QUERIES TO XML AND HTML

Access 97 and later can export tables and queries directly to simple, semi-formatted HTML tables. You have the choice of exporting static HTML pages or using Active Server Pages (ASP) to base the page content on a query that executes against a Jet or SQL Server database. The format of static pages is fixed, but you can alter the formatting of ASP-generated pages by editing HTML `BORDER`, `COLOR`, `BGCOLOR`, `BORDERCOLOR`, and other table attribute values in the .asp file.

→ To review conventional HTML and ASP export procedures, **see** "Exporting Data to Web Servers," **p. 316**.

Access 2003's XML table and query export feature generates a plain-vanilla, static HTML table. Fortunately, you can dress up the table by editing the XSL code that transforms the XML data to HTML. (Why the Access XML developers didn't emulate with XSL the more attractive conventional HTML export format is a mystery.) The later "Reformatting HTML Tables and Adding Page Elements" section shows you how to alter the style sheet to format the table to your liking.

➔ To generate a dynamic (live) HTML table from an SQL Server database, **see** "Using SQL Server 2000's HTTP Query Features," **p. 976**.

Do the following to create an HTML page by exporting a table or query as XML:

1. Right-click the table or query to export, and choose Export to open the Export *ObjectType* '*ObjectName*' To dialog. This example uses vwUnion, which is a modified version of NorthwindCS.adp's Customers and Suppliers view.

NOTE

> The XMLXSL23.mdb sample database in the \Seua11\Chaptr23 folder of the accompanying CD-ROM includes Jet versions of vwUnion and the other tables and queries for the examples of this chapter. To use SQL Server, which is recommended as the data source for all production XML and Web applications, upsize XMLXSL23.mdb to an SQL Server database (XMLXSL23SQL) and an Access project (XMLXSL23CS.adp).

➔ To review the upsizing process, **see** "Upsizing with the Trial and Error Approach," **p. 889**.

23

2. Scroll to the end of the Save As Type list, and select XML (*.xml). Click Export to open the Export XML dialog.
3. Mark the Presentation of Your Data (XSL) to add an XSL style sheet (*ObjectName*.xsl) to the XML data (*ObjectName*.xml) and schema (*ObjectName*.xsd) files in the current folder (see Figure 23.2). The default settings generate separate data and schema files.

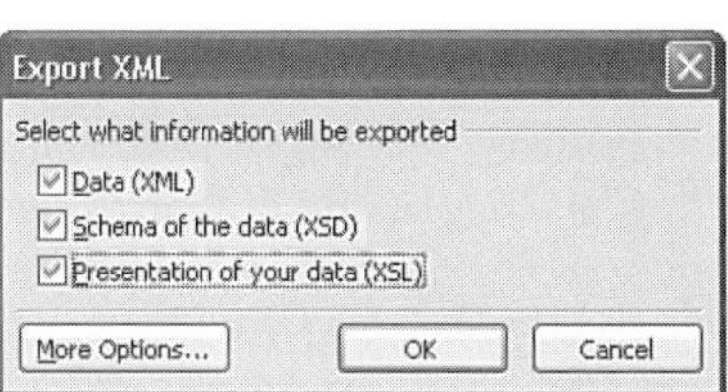

Figure 23.2
The basic version of the Export XML dialog generates the selected XML file types in the same folder as the .mdb or .adp file. Mark the Presentation of Your Data (XSL) check box to create .xsl and .htm files.

4. Click OK to start the export process, which takes only a few seconds for the small query result set generated by vwUnion. In addition to the three files mentioned in step 3, specifying a style sheet generates an *ObjectName*.htm file.

5. Open Explorer, navigate to the folder containing the .mdb or .adp, and double-click the *ObjectName*.htm file— ...\Office11\Samples\vwUnion.htm for this example—to open the page in IE 6.0+ (see Figure 23.3).

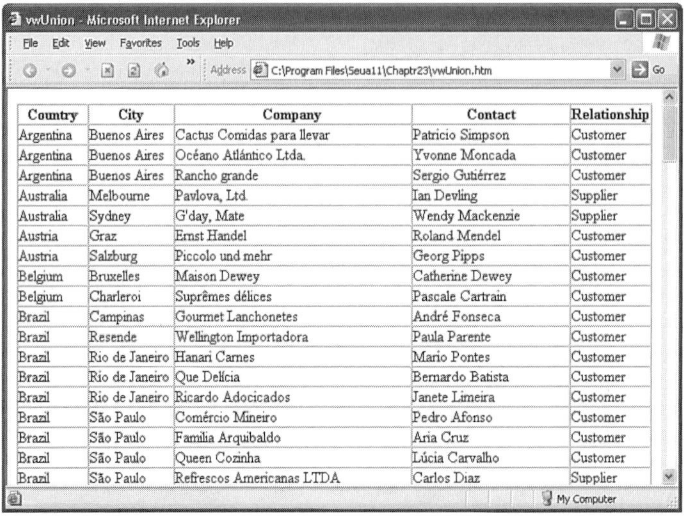

Country	City	Company	Contact	Relationship
Argentina	Buenos Aires	Cactus Comidas para llevar	Patricio Simpson	Customer
Argentina	Buenos Aires	Océano Atlántico Ltda.	Yvonne Moncada	Customer
Argentina	Buenos Aires	Rancho grande	Sergio Gutiérrez	Customer
Australia	Melbourne	Pavlova, Ltd.	Ian Devling	Supplier
Australia	Sydney	G'day, Mate	Wendy Mackenzie	Supplier
Austria	Graz	Ernst Handel	Roland Mendel	Customer
Austria	Salzburg	Piccolo und mehr	Georg Pipps	Customer
Belgium	Bruxelles	Maison Dewey	Catherine Dewey	Customer
Belgium	Charleroi	Suprêmes délices	Pascale Cartrain	Customer
Brazil	Campinas	Gourmet Lanchonetes	André Fonseca	Customer
Brazil	Resende	Wellington Importadora	Paula Parente	Customer
Brazil	Rio de Janeiro	Hanari Carnes	Mario Pontes	Customer
Brazil	Rio de Janeiro	Que Delícia	Bernardo Batista	Customer
Brazil	Rio de Janeiro	Ricardo Adocicados	Janete Limeira	Customer
Brazil	São Paulo	Comércio Mineiro	Pedro Afonso	Customer
Brazil	São Paulo	Familia Arquibaldo	Aria Cruz	Customer
Brazil	São Paulo	Queen Cozinha	Lúcia Carvalho	Customer
Brazil	São Paulo	Refrescos Americanas LTDA	Carlos Diaz	Supplier

Figure 23.3 The HTML table created from the .xml,.xsl, and .htm files won't win any design awards.

> **TIP**
>
> If your goal is simply to deliver the output of a table or query to a single static Web page, use conventional HTML or ASP export. Exporting static data as XML is overkill in this case. The example of the preceding section is the starting point for gaining an understanding how .xml, .xsd, and .xsl files interact to create an .htm file.

Analyzing the Exported XML Schema and Data

As mentioned earlier in the chapter, the primary purpose of XML is to enable interchange of information between multiple applications that run on different operating systems. The capability of XML data to pass through corporate or personal firewalls lets you exchange selected data from your Jet or SQL Server databases with other organizations over the Internet. A major benefit of extracting the data as an XML file is that allowing outsiders to connect to your database isn't required to obtain needed information.

By default, XML data is Unicode (UTF-8) text; the data document isn't aware of the data type of the table fields or query columns that generate the text. If you create an XML data document from a table or query that includes fields of the Jet DateTime or SQL Server `datetime` data type, such as the Northwind or NorthwindCS Orders table, the date elements appear in XSD `dateTime` data type format as

```
<OrderDate>1996-07-04T00:00:00</OrderDate>
<RequiredDate>1996-08-01T00:00:00</RequiredDate>
<ShippedDate>1996-07-16T00:00:00</ShippedDate>
```

XSD's `dateTime` text format is well suited to sorting, but isn't easily readable in a table. Thus the recipient's XSL code must have access to the schema of the table or query to determine how to interpret and, if necessary, transform the data. The XML schema, which you can embed in the XML data file or save as an independent .xsd file, supplies the field data type and other field or column properties. Any application—such as Access 2003—that supports XSD can either import the data directly to a table or use XSLT to transform the schema attributes, such as `sqlSType="varchar"`, to name-value pairs for the target RDBMS, such as Oracle or IBM DB2.

TIP

> Don't embed the schema in the .xml data document you send to others. The XML applications used by your recipients might not be able to handle embedded schema. Send the .xsd schema file with the first transmission of the .xml document, and then send updates to the data as individual .xml files.

The vwUnion.xsd Schema File

Listing 23.1 shows the content of the vwOrders.xsd file you exported in the preceding section with indenting applied for easier reading. The schema defines the XML data as a `complexType` that contains a `sequence` of six `simpleType` column elements. Column elements that may be empty have a `minOccurs="0"` attribute. The combination of the `od:sqlSType="varchar"` attribute and `<xsd:maxLength value="15"/>` element, for example, define a `varchar(15)` data type. Each named element of the associated XML data file has a corresponding `<xsd:element name="name">… </xsd:element>` entry in the XSD schema file.

Listing 23.1 The XML Schema for the vwUnion View Contained in vwUnion.xsd

```
<?xml version="1.0" encoding="UTF-8"?>
<xsd:schema xmlns:xsd="http://www.w3.org/2001/XMLSchema"
            xmlns:od="urn:schemas-microsoft-com:officedata">
   <xsd:element name="dataroot">
      <xsd:complexType>
         <xsd:choice maxOccurs="unbounded">
            <xsd:element ref="vwUnion"/>
         </xsd:choice>
      </xsd:complexType>
   </xsd:element>
   <xsd:element name="vwUnion">
      <xsd:annotation>
         <xsd:appinfo/>
      </xsd:annotation>
      <xsd:complexType>
         <xsd:sequence>
            <xsd:element name="Country" minOccurs="0"
                  od:jetType="text" od:sqlSType="varchar">
               <xsd:simpleType>
                  <xsd:restriction base="xsd:string">
                     <xsd:maxLength value="15"/>
                  </xsd:restriction>
               </xsd:simpleType>
            </xsd:element>
```

continues

LISTING 23.1 CONTINUED

```
            <xsd:element name="City" minOccurs="0"
                  od:jetType="text" od:sqlSType="varchar">
               <xsd:simpleType>
                  <xsd:restriction base="xsd:string">
                     <xsd:maxLength value="15"/>
                  </xsd:restriction>
               </xsd:simpleType>
            </xsd:element>
            <xsd:element name="Company" od:jetType="text"
                  od:sqlSType="varchar">
               <xsd:simpleType>
                  <xsd:restriction base="xsd:string">
                     <xsd:maxLength value="40"/>
                  </xsd:restriction>
               </xsd:simpleType>
            </xsd:element>
            <xsd:element name="Contact" minOccurs="0"
                  od:jetType="text" od:sqlSType="varchar">
               <xsd:simpleType>
                  <xsd:restriction base="xsd:string">
                     <xsd:maxLength value="30"/>
                  </xsd:restriction>
               </xsd:simpleType>
            </xsd:element>
            <xsd:element name="Relationship" od:jetType="text"
                  od:sqlSType="varchar"
               <xsd:simpleType>
                  <xsd:restriction base="xsd:string">
                     <xsd:maxLength value="8"/>
                  </xsd:restriction>
               </xsd:simpleType>
            </xsd:element>
         </xsd:sequence>
      </xsd:complexType>
   </xsd:element>
</xsd:schema>
```

The schema for a table with a variety of data types is more interesting than that for a view having only `text/varchar` data types. Figure 23.4 shows IE 6.0 displaying the `xsd:appinfo` node of the schema for the Orders table. This node specifies the properties of the indexes on the Orders table; the node is empty in the code of listing 23.1 because the view isn't indexed. (You need SQL Server 2000 Enterprise Edition to generate indexed views.) Export the Orders table to XML and specify a schema file, open the Orders.xsd file in IE 5+, and scroll to the `xsd:element` nodes for fields to see how SQL Server data types map to the predefined `xsd` data types.

THE VWUNION.XML DOCUMENT FILE AND ITS CDATA SECTIONS

Figure 23.5 shows IE 6.0 displaying the vwUnion.xml file's XML `dataroot` root element, its namespace attributes, and the elements of the first two rows. The XML code for all rows of the view has a consistent structure.

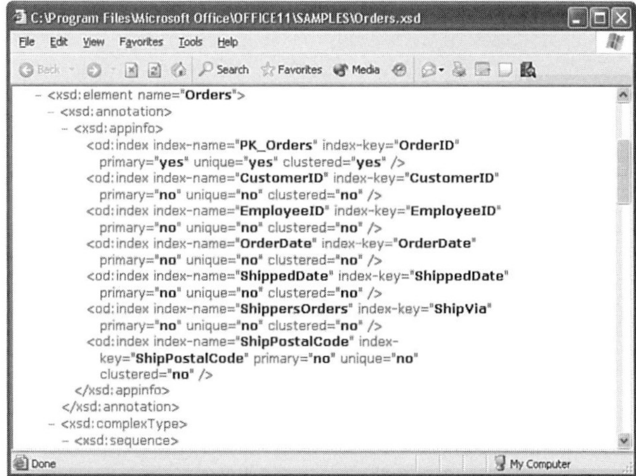

Figure 23.4
The XSD schema for NortwindCS's Orders table includes the properties of the table's indexes.

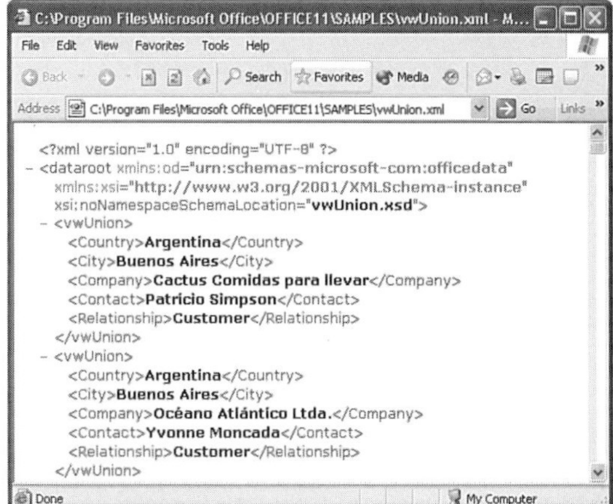

Figure 23.5
IE 6.0's built-in style sheet improves readability of XML data documents by indenting the sub-nodes (sub-trees). If the XML document is malformed, an "XML page cannot be displayed" message occurs at the location of the error.

If you choose View, Source to open the file in Notepad, scroll to the second row for Australia, you see the following line:

```
<Company><![CDATA[G'day, Mate]]></Company>
```

There are 17 occurrences of `CDATA` in the file: 16 element values include an apostrophe (`'`) and one has an ampersand (`&`).

A `CDATA` (character data) section permits inclusion of characters that XML interprets as delimiters or large blocks of text that contain special characters or formatting that doesn't conform to XML syntax rules. For example, XML interprets the apostrophe in `G'day` as a value delimiter. The `![CDATA[`*`free text`*`]]` format is required to ensure that the XML parser doesn't inadvertently interpret ordinary data as `CDATA`. A common use for `CDATA` sections is to contain binary data for bitmaps and scripting code in XSLT.

NOTE

> Microsoft uses `CDATA` sections to handle illegal characters, but it's more common to use conventional HTML literals, such as `'` for apostrophe and `&` for ampersand. Substituting `<Company>G'day, Mate></Company>` for `<Company><![CDATA[G'day, Mate]]></Company>` works just as well.

SPELUNKING THE VWUNION_REPORT.XML AND VWUNION.XSL FILES

If you apply the Registry key described in the tip at the end of the earlier "Understanding the Role of Access's ReportML" section, the ReportML data file is preserved when you export an Access object. Figure 23.6 shows the first few lines of the vwUnion_report.xml file. *ObjectName*_report.xml files exemplify XML's ability to represent software objects by a set of custom tags and element values. ReportML has several hundred tag definitions for the properties and events of all Access objects. vwUnion_report.xml uses only the ReportML elements that relate to table or query properties.

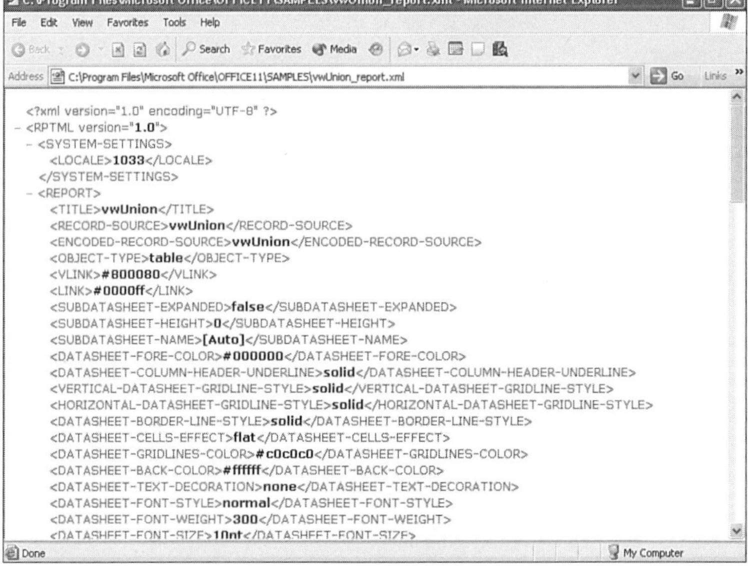

Figure 23.6
If you save the *ObjectName*_report.xml file, you can read every property value of the Datasheet view of the table or query. It's easy to translate most of the tag names to datasheet properties set in the Access UI.

The RPT2HTML4.xsl transform, which generates the vwUnion.xsl stylesheet from vwUnion_report.xml, disregards the `DATASHEET` property elements; these elements emulate the behavior of a datasheet when you save tables or queries as DAP. Following are the important lines in vwUnion_report.xml:

```
<CONNECTION-STRING>
   PROVIDER=SQLOLEDB.1;INTEGRATED SECURITY=SSPI;
   PERSIST SECURITY INFO=FALSE;INITIAL CATALOG=XMLXSL32SQL;
   DATA SOURCE=(local)
</CONNECTION-STRING>
<DATA-MODEL>
```

```
    <ROW-SOURCE id="vwUnion" type="view">
        <COMMAND-TEXT>
            <![CDATA[SELECT * FROM "vwUnion"]]>
        </COMMAND-TEXT>
        <FIELD id="Country" datatype="200" size="15"/>
        <FIELD id="City" datatype="200" size="15"/>
        <FIELD id="Company" datatype="200" size="40"/>
        <FIELD id="Contact" datatype="200" size="30"/>
        <FIELD id="Relationship" datatype="200" size="8"/>
    </ROW-SOURCE>
</DATA-MODEL>
```

AccessWeb.dll uses the `<CONNECTION-STRING>`, `<ROW-SOURCE>`, and `<COMMAND-TEXT>` values to connect to the XMLXSL32SQL database, retrieve a Recordset from the vwUnion view, save it as an XML data document, and add the field names and data types as attributes of `<FIELD>` elements. The `datatype="200"` attribute specifies a `varchar` field with its length having the value of the `size` attribute.

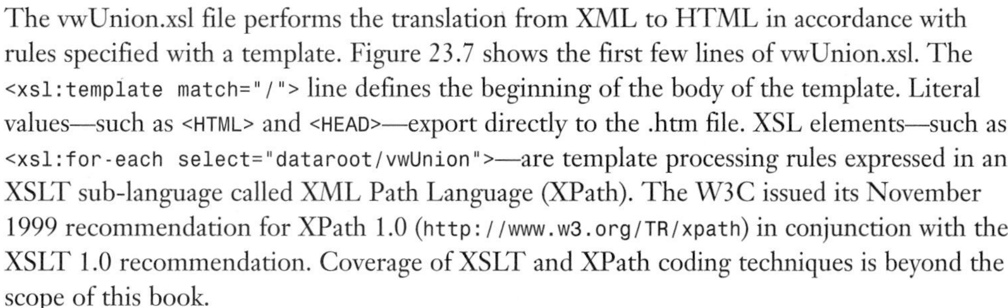

The vwUnion.xsl file performs the translation from XML to HTML in accordance with rules specified with a template. Figure 23.7 shows the first few lines of vwUnion.xsl. The `<xsl:template match="/">` line defines the beginning of the body of the template. Literal values—such as `<HTML>` and `<HEAD>`—export directly to the .htm file. XSL elements—such as `<xsl:for-each select="dataroot/vwUnion">`—are template processing rules expressed in an XSLT sub-language called XML Path Language (XPath). The W3C issued its November 1999 recommendation for XPath 1.0 (`http://www.w3.org/TR/xpath`) in conjunction with the XSLT 1.0 recommendation. Coverage of XSLT and XPath coding techniques is beyond the scope of this book.

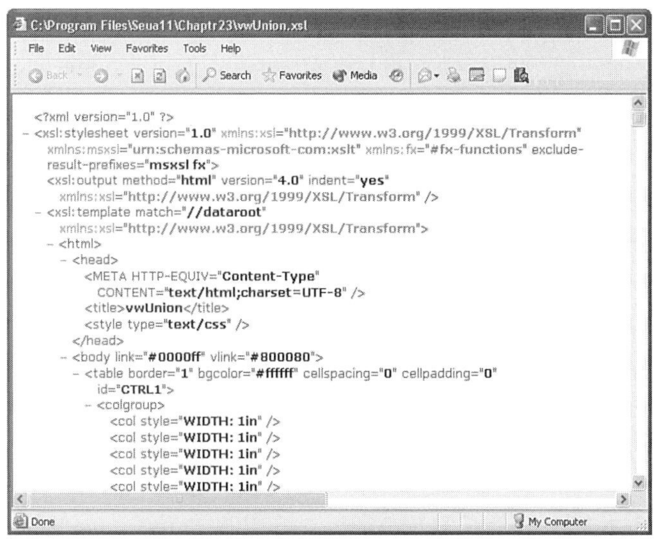


```
  <?xml version="1.0" ?>
- <xsl:stylesheet version="1.0" xmlns:xsl="http://www.w3.org/1999/XSL/Transform"
    xmlns:msxsl="urn:schemas-microsoft-com:xslt" xmlns:fx="#fx-functions" exclude-
    result-prefixes="msxsl fx">
    <xsl:output method="html" version="4.0" indent="yes"
      xmlns:xsl="http://www.w3.org/1999/XSL/Transform" />
  - <xsl:template match="//dataroot"
      xmlns:xsl="http://www.w3.org/1999/XSL/Transform">
    - <html>
      - <head>
          <META HTTP-EQUIV="Content-Type"
            CONTENT="text/html;charset=UTF-8" />
          <title>vwUnion</title>
          <style type="text/css" />
        </head>
      - <body link="#0000ff" vlink="#800080">
        - <table border="1" bgcolor="#ffffff" cellspacing="0" cellpadding="0"
            id="CTRL1">
          - <colgroup>
              <col style="WIDTH: 1in" />
              <col style="WIDTH: 1in" />
              <col style="WIDTH: 1in" />
              <col style="WIDTH: 1in" />
              <col style="WIDTH: 1in" />
```

Figure 23.7 The vwUnion.xsl style sheet starts with the declaration of a template for generating HTML. A collection of VBScript functions that return values to XPath expressions are located in a CDATA section at the end of the file.

TIP

If you're interested in learning more about XSLT, Microsoft offers a comprehensive XSLT Developer's Guide. Search for **"XSLT Developer's Guide"** at `http://msdn.microsoft.com/` to find the latest version.

REFORMATTING HTML TABLES AND ADDING PAGE ELEMENTS

23

Fortunately, you don't need to master XSL/XSLT and XPath to improve the formatting of the default table style. Basic knowledge of HTML is all you need to change the table design and add other elements to the page.

NOTE

You might find it simpler to create Access reports with a design that emulates an HTML table, and save the report design as XML. Working with XSLT-generated HTML tables, however, lets you apply your HTML authoring skills to create custom pages that comply with specific Web site design standards. You also can apply the techniques you learn in the following two sections to the much more complex .xsl files of exported Access reports.

APPLYING STYLE TO TABLE AND TEXT ELEMENTS

If you have an organization-wide style for displaying tabular information—such as phone directories and other data that's suited to a simple list—you can conform the design of exported tables and queries by altering the HTML code of the *ObjectName*.xsl stylesheet.

To change the title, font, border, and background color of the table header and rows in the style sheet, using vwUnion.xsl as an example, do this:

1. Make a backup copy of *ObjectName*.xsl in case you run into problems you can't fix easily.
2. Open *ObjectName*.xsl in Notepad, and change the text between the `<title>...</title>` tags to a more descriptive name—**Customers and Suppliers by Country and City** for this example.
3. Add the following lines after the `<style type="text/css"></style>` line to specify Verdana or Arial font with a height of 12 pixels, set medium gray as the background color for the table header, and specify light gray for the table rows:

```
<style>TH, TR, P { font-family: verdana, arial; font-size: 12px } </style>
<style>TH { background-color: #CCCCCC } </style>
<style>TR { background-color: #EEEEEE } </style>
```

4. Save the .xsl file, open *ObjectName*.htm in IE 5+ to test your changes, and then close the .htm file.

TIP

> Clicking IE's Refresh button doesn't regenerate the HTML. You must close and reopen the page because the `<SCRIPT event=onload for=window>` event handler of the .htm file executes only when you load the file.

5. To specify a small transparent border around each table cell and increase the height of the rows, including the header, change the `<table border=...` line to:

```
<table border="0" bgcolor="#ffffff" cellspacing="2" cellpadding="2" id="CTRL1>
```

6. Repeat step 4 to check your HTML syntax.

   Figure 23.8 illustrates the effect of the preceding changes. 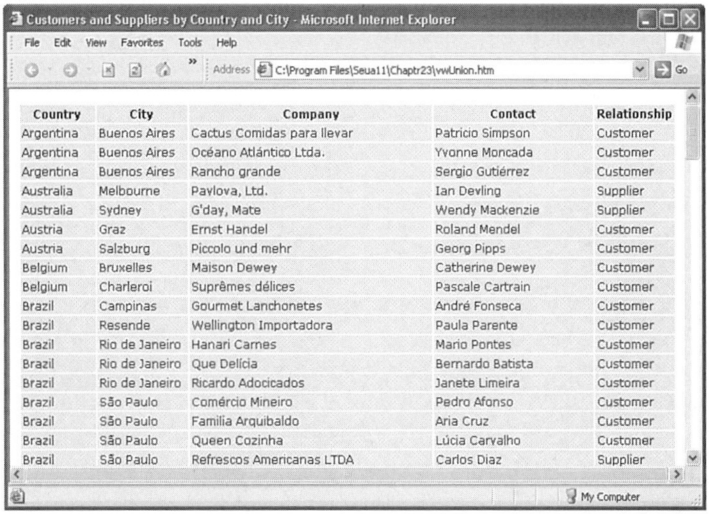

Figure 23.8
Adding a few styles and changing HTML border attributes modernizes the table's appearance.

Customers and Suppliers by Country and City - Microsoft Internet Explorer

Country	City	Company	Contact	Relationship
Argentina	Buenos Aires	Cactus Comidas para llevar	Patricio Simpson	Customer
Argentina	Buenos Aires	Océano Atlántico Ltda.	Yvonne Moncada	Customer
Argentina	Buenos Aires	Rancho grande	Sergio Gutiérrez	Customer
Australia	Melbourne	Pavlova, Ltd.	Ian Devling	Supplier
Australia	Sydney	G'day, Mate	Wendy Mackenzie	Supplier
Austria	Graz	Ernst Handel	Roland Mendel	Customer
Austria	Salzburg	Piccolo und mehr	Georg Pipps	Customer
Belgium	Bruxelles	Maison Dewey	Catherine Dewey	Customer
Belgium	Charleroi	Suprêmes délices	Pascale Cartrain	Customer
Brazil	Campinas	Gourmet Lanchonetes	André Fonseca	Customer
Brazil	Resende	Wellington Importadora	Paula Parente	Customer
Brazil	Rio de Janeiro	Hanari Carnes	Mario Pontes	Customer
Brazil	Rio de Janeiro	Que Delícia	Bernardo Batista	Customer
Brazil	Rio de Janeiro	Ricardo Adocicados	Janete Limeira	Customer
Brazil	São Paulo	Comércio Mineiro	Pedro Afonso	Customer
Brazil	São Paulo	Familia Arquibaldo	Aria Cruz	Customer
Brazil	São Paulo	Queen Cozinha	Lúcia Carvalho	Customer
Brazil	São Paulo	Refrescos Americanas LTDA	Carlos Diaz	Supplier

7. To prevent accidentally overwriting your changes when updating the XML data document, save the .xsl files with a new name—**CityList.xsl** for this example.

TIP

> Select All Files in Notepad's Save As Type list and UTF-8 in the Encoding list when saving XSL, HTML, and XML files. When saving changes with Ctrl+S, you don't need to alter the Save As Type and Encoding selections.

8. Open the .htm file in Notepad, and change the file name argument value in the `LoadDOM objStyle, "vwUnion.xsl"` line to **CityList.xsl**.
9. Save the edited .htm file with a different name—**CityList.htm** for this example—so you don't accidentally overwrite it.
10. Open the new .htm file in IE 6+ to verify the changes you made to the .htm script.

NOTE

> HTML is very forgiving of some coding errors, such as inverting the sequence of closing tags, but XLST isn't. Missing HTML tags or failure to add closing tags in the correct sequence in XSLT causes IE 5+ to display an error message.

ADDING A TABLE HEADER AND INTRODUCTORY TEXT

Adding elements to the style sheet is even easier than modifying existing elements. For example, to add a full-width table caption above the field names and a couple of lines of text to the page, do this:

1. Reopen the .xsl file—CityList.xsl for this example—in Notepad.
2. Insert the following three lines below the `<tbody>` line (before the first `<tr>` element) to add the full-width table header.

```
<tr>
<th colspan="5">Northwind Customers and Suppliers by Country and City</th>
</tr>
```

3. Insert the following two lines after the `<body link="#0000ff" vlink="#800080">` line:

```
<P align="center"><B>Northwind Traders - Confidential - For Internal Use
Only</B></P>
<P align="center">This list is updated every weekday at 2:00 a.m.</P>
```

4. Save the .xsl file, and reopen the .htm file to check you work (see Figure 23.9).

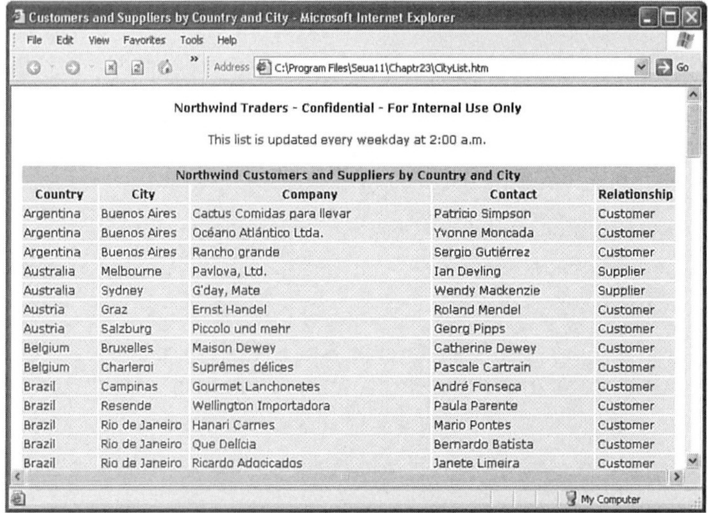

Northwind Customers and Suppliers by Country and City				
Country	City	Company	Contact	Relationship
Argentina	Buenos Aires	Cactus Comidas para llevar	Patricio Simpson	Customer
Argentina	Buenos Aires	Océano Atlántico Ltda.	Yvonne Moncada	Customer
Argentina	Buenos Aires	Rancho grande	Sergio Gutiérrez	Customer
Australia	Melbourne	Pavlova, Ltd.	Ian Devling	Supplier
Australia	Sydney	G'day, Mate	Wendy Mackenzie	Supplier
Austria	Graz	Ernst Handel	Roland Mendel	Customer
Austria	Salzburg	Piccolo und mehr	Georg Pipps	Customer
Belgium	Bruxelles	Maison Dewey	Catherine Dewey	Customer
Belgium	Charleroi	Suprêmes délices	Pascale Cartrain	Customer
Brazil	Campinas	Gourmet Lanchonetes	André Fonseca	Customer
Brazil	Resende	Wellington Importadora	Paula Parente	Customer
Brazil	Rio de Janeiro	Hanari Carnes	Mario Pontes	Customer
Brazil	Rio de Janeiro	Que Delícia	Bernardo Batista	Customer
Brazil	Rio de Janeiro	Ricardo Adocicados	Janete Limeira	Customer

Figure 23.9
Only a few additional lines of HTML code in the .xsl file add the title text and full-width header line shown here.

DEPLOYING EXPORTED XML FILE SETS TO A WEB SERVER

One advantage of exporting Access objects to static XML data documents is that their file sets are self-contained. Presentation of the data as a Web page isn't dependent on access to a Jet or SQL Server data source. Thus you can simply copy or move the .xml, .xsl, and .htm or .asp files for any exported Access object to the default \Inetpub\wwwroot of Internet Information Server (IIS) 5+ or a virtual directory you dedicate to delivering XML-based pages. Client computers must have IE 6+ installed to render the .htm files locally; specify server-side processing with ASP to support all browsers.

It's not necessary to copy static .xml/.xsl/.htm file sets to a Web server to make them accessible to others on a network. If you share the folder that holds the file set, others can open the .htm file by specifying the path and file name in IE 6+'s Open text box. Clients must have IE 6+ installed to process the .xsl file on the client. If you need interoperability with IE 5.5 or earlier, use the conventional HTML or ASP export process.

EXPORTING STATIC REPORTS AS XML

Despite it's name, Microsoft's primary objective for ReportML was to generate DAP from Access query and form objects with RPT2DAP.xsl. Data access pages don't support subforms, so RPT2HTML4.xsl doesn't support subreports. In this respect, exporting reports as XML exhibits the same limitation as early Access versions experienced when exporting reports with subreports to Word and Excel.

NOTE

You can export forms to XML, but doing this isn't very rewarding. Subforms don't export, and the resulting Web page contains an instance of the form for each record of the table or query the form is bound to. Save forms bound to multi-row Recordsets to DAP.

➔ To learn more about exporting forms to DAP, **see** "Saving Forms as DAP," **p. 1082**.

The Invoice report is most graphically interesting of the sample reports of Northwind.mdb and NorthwindCS.adp that don't have a subreport. ReportML.xml and RPT2HTML4.xsl create a remarkably accurate representation of the Invoice report. The only problem with exporting the Invoice report as XML is that the resulting Invoice.xml file includes the data for all 2,155 rows of the Invoices query or view and is almost 2MB in size. The code of Invoice.xsl must process 26 elements for each of the 2,155 rows to generate the HTML to display the data. Depending on the speed of your computer, it can take more than a minute to open the resulting Web page on your computer.

TIP

> Avoid exporting reports based on large query result sets, especially static reports. XML files are much larger than the resulting HTML files, and the entire XML file must be sent to the client for processing a static report. As mentioned earlier, processing a live Web report on the server and sending HTML to the client is very resource intensive, so keep your live Web reports as short as possible.

To create an Invoice report from single order and export it as XML from Northwind.mdb, do the following:

1. Open the Invoice report in design view, open the Property window for the report, click the Data tab, and temporarily change the Record Source property value to Invoices Filter.

2. Change to Print Preview and type a valid OrderID value in the Enter Parameter Value dialog. (**11077** is a good choice because it has many line items). Close the report and save your changes.
3. In the Reports page of the Database window, right-click the Invoice item and choose Export to open the Export Report 'Invoice' To dialog.
4. Open the Save As Type list, scroll to the bottom, and choose XML Documents (*.xml). Access proposes the name of the report as the file name. Click Export to open the Export XML dialog.
5. Mark the Data (XML) and Presentation of Your Data (XSL) check boxes to save Invoice.xml, Invoice.xsl, and Invoice.htm in the ...\Office10\Samples folder and the two small bitmaps—NameLogo.bmp and PictureLogo.bmp—in the Images subfolder. Exporting a schema is optional.
6. Click OK to close the Export XML dialog. After a second or two, the Enter Parameter Value dialog opens. Type the OrderID value and click OK.

7. Open Explorer, navigate to the ...\Office10\Samples folder, and double-click Invoice.htm to display the page in IE 6.0 (see Figure 23.10). It takes a second or two for IE 6.0 to create and modify the two `DOMDocument` objects.

You can't export reports that contain Microsoft Graph objects; use report snapshots to display them. Reports that incorporate PivotChart, or PivotTable views in subreports don't export because of the no-subreport restriction. If you try exporting these types of reports, you receive a "Microsoft Access was unable to export the data" message.

Following are some additional restrictions on exporting reports with RPT2HTML4.xsl:

- Running Sum, Can Grow, and Can Shrink properties aren't supported.
- You can't export reports that use snaking (newspaper) columns.
- SQL aggregates (`SUM`, `AVG`, and so on) that return `NULL` values don't evaluate correctly.

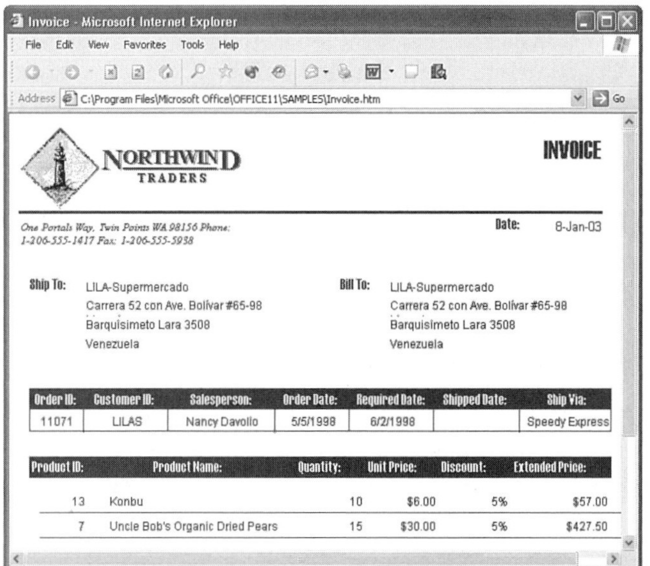

Figure 23.10 The Invoice page generated by the three files exported from the modified Invoice report is a close replica of the Access original.

Use DAP to deliver Web pages that include PivotChart or PivotTable controls, or have features that RPT2HTML4.xsl doesn't support. Alternatively, make snapshot files available on your Web site for these reports.

TIP

Type **report snapshot** in the Ask a Question box, press Enter, and double-click the Publish a Report Snapshot to the Web topic to display the instructions for exporting .snp files to your Web server and authoring Web pages to display them.

If you encounter an error when attempting to open the .htm file for an exported report page, see the "Problems Exporting Reports to HTML" topic of the "Troubleshooting" section near the end of the chapter.

EXPORTING LIVE WEB REPORTS

Exporting live Web reports assures that users have up-to-the-minute data. Live Web reports execute a query against an SQL Server table, view, function, or stored procedure when users open the *ReportName*.htm or *ReportName*.asp file that's generated by the export process. Live Web reports are well-suited for displaying current sales and inventory data, as well as summaries of hourly or daily Web site statistics. An advantage of live Web reports is that you don't need to periodically refresh the .xml file that provides the report's data; live Web reports obtain their data directly from SQL Server in XML format.

NOTE

> Only ADP connected to SQL Server 2000 databases can export live Web reports. Live Web reports issue an SQL Server HTTP query to a designated database. SQL Server 7.0 and earlier don't support HTTP queries, which also are called URL queries.

Exporting live Web reports or running SQL Server 2000 HTTP queries, the subject of the later "Using SQL Server 2000's HTTP Query Features "section, requires installation of the following applications and services:

23

- Any version of SQL Server 2000 for which you have a valid license that covers the intended use. MSDE requires an Office XP license for the machine on which it's installed. The database server can run on the machine running IIS or any other computer on the network.
- IIS 5.0+ and IE 5.0+ installed by Windows XP/2000 Professional and Windows 2000+ Server. Windows XP installs IE 6.0+ and Windows Server 2003 installs IE 6.0+ and IIS 6.0.
- IIS Virtual Directory Management for SQL Server, a component of the SQL Server 2000 Client Tools installed from an SQL Server edition other than the Desktop Engine. IIS Virtual Directory Management for SQL Server is the user interface for the Internet Services API (ISAPI) extension (filter) for SQL Server (Sqlisapi.dll).

NOTE

> The SQL Server 2000 Client Tools are required to enable most XML features of SQL Server 2000 Evaluation Edition, including installation and removal of the SQLXML 3.0 Web download. SQLXML 3.0 installs an advanced version of IIS Virtual Directory Management for SQL Server that's required for creating XML Web Services from SQL Server 2000 stored procedures. Chapter 31 describes how to use the SQLXML 3.0 version.
>
> SQL Server 2000 Trial Software (downloadable) and Evaluation Edition (CD-ROM) also include the Client Tools. You can learn more about these products at `http://www.microsoft.com/sql/evaluation/trial/`.

SETTING UP THE IIS VIRTUAL DIRECTORY FOR THE DATABASE

You can export live Web reports from ADP without configuring SQL Server support for IIS, but you can't test the results by executing the exported *ReportName*.htm or *ReportName*.asp file until you do.

CAUTION

> When you run the SQL Server 2000 setup program, don't install SQL Server 2000. You only need the Client Tools. In the initial screen, click SQL Server Components and Install Data Base Server to start the Installation Wizard. Some editions permit installing only the client tools to the local computer running Windows XP/2000 Professional.

The Installation Configuration page of the Setup Wizard is where you select the installation type. Be sure to select the Client Tools Only option on this page. On the Select Components page, clear all but the Management Tools check box. Be prepared to wait a few minutes while the Wizard installs the required files.

The basic steps to add the IIS virtual directory for an SQL Server database are as follows:

1. Add a subfolder to your ...\Wwwroot folder that you specify as the virtual directory for SQL Server HTTP queries against a specific database. The subfolder name must be the same as the database name, NorthwindCS for this example.
2. Use the IIS Virtual Directory Management for SQL Server MMC snap-in to configure the virtual directory.
3. Export the report to XML using the expanded version of the XML Export dialog, placing the XML and XSL files in the ...\Wwwroot folder or another subfolder, such as ...\Wwwroot\Reports.

Following are the detailed steps to configure IIS 5.0+ for SQL server HTTP queries against the NorthwindCS database:

1. Create the \Inetpub\Wwwroot\NorthwindCS folder.
2. Create an \Inetpub\Wwwroot\Reports folder to place live Web reports in their own folder.
3. Choose Start, Programs, Microsoft SQL Server, Configure SQL Server Support for IIS to open the IIS Virtual Directory Management for SQL Server snap-in.
4. Expand the *ServerName* node—OAKLEAF-XP1 for this example, and select the Default Web Site. The snap-in's right pane displays an empty list with Virtual Directory Name, SQL Server, and Database Name column headers.
5. Right-click the right pane, and choose New, Virtual Directory to open the General Page of the New Virtual Directory Properties dialog.
6. Type a name for the virtual directory, which must have the same name as the SQL Server database (as mentioned earlier). Use **NorthwindCS** for this example.
7. Click Browse to open the Browse for Folder dialog, select the ...\wwwroot\NorthwindCS folder, and click OK (see Figure 23.11).

NOTE

The third Microsoft mystery of this chapter is why the developers of the SQL ISAPI filter decided to specify a height of 600+ pixels for the dialog, when 480 pixels easily would suffice.

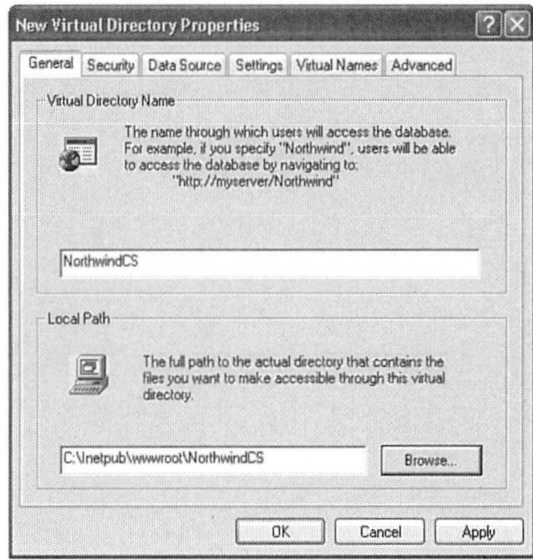

Figure 23.11 Name the new virtual directory as the database name and the path to its physical folder in the General page of the New Virtual Directory Properties dialog.

8. Click the Security tab and select the Use Windows Integrated Authentication option. To permit anonymous Web access to SQL Server, you must grant the IUSER_*SERVERNAME* account an SQL Server login and at least public rights on the NorthwindCS database. A later section describes how to set up Web access permissions for the database.

CAUTION

> MSDE 2000 installs with Windows authentication as the default. If you specify SQL Server security with a login ID and password, both values can become accessible to unauthorized users as clear text in the .htm or .asp file.

9. Click the Data Source tab, type the NetBIOS name of the computer (OAKLEAF-XP1) in the SQL Server text box, and select NorthwindCS in the Database list (see Figure 23.12).

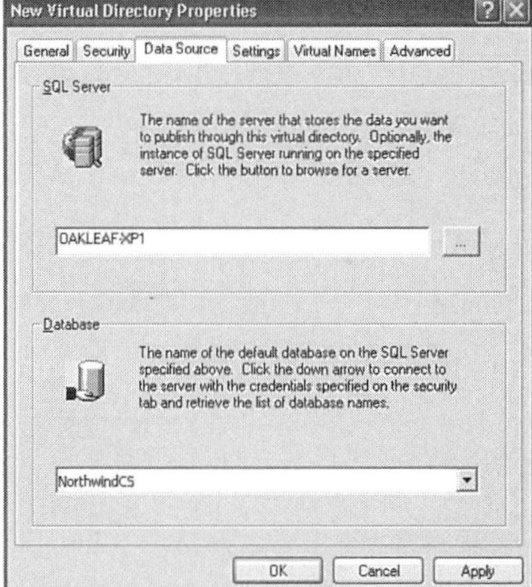

Figure 23.12 Specify the SQL Server instance name, and designate the database for the virtual directory in the Data Source page.

10. Click the Settings Tab and mark the Allow URL Queries check box (see Figure 23.13). The .htm and .asp execute HTTP (URL) queries against the database. (Template queries are permitted by default.)

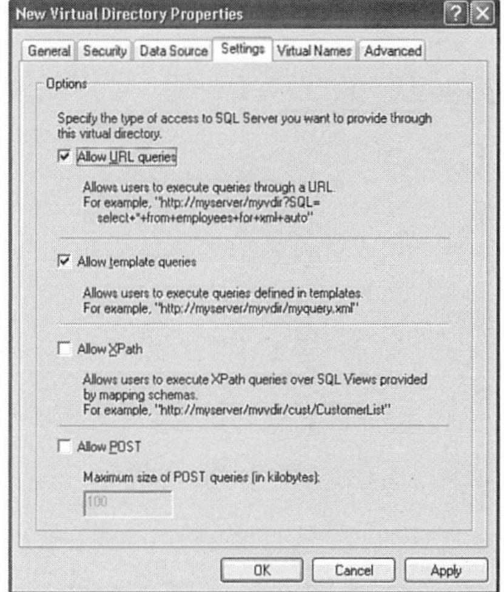

Figure 23.13
Mark the Allow URL Queries check box to permit the exported .asp (or .htm) file to send HTTP queries to the server.

11. Click the Virtual Names tab, and click the New button to open the Virtual Name Configuration dialog.
12. Type Templates as the Virtual Name, and select Template in the Type list.
13. Click the browse button to open the Browse for Folder dialog, navigate to and select the folder you added in step 1, and add **\Templates** to the path (see Figure 23.14). Click Save to return to the Virtual Names page (see Figure 23.15).

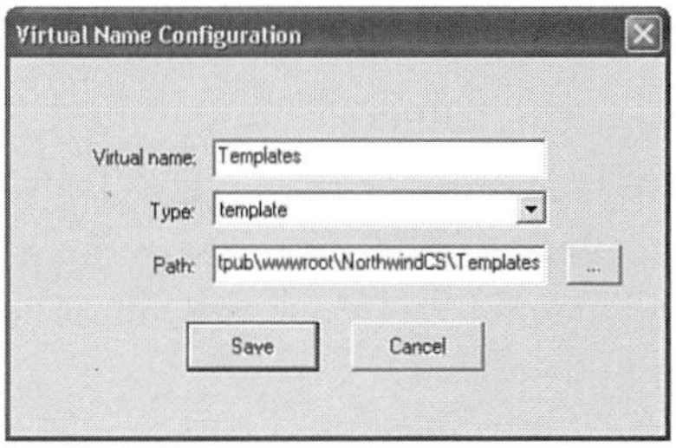

Figure 23.14
The Templates folder you specify at this point is used for custom HTTP queries that you create later in the chapter.

14. Click OK to save your settings, close the dialog, and add the new virtual directory to the IIS Virtual Directory Management for SQL Server snap-in's right pane (see Figure 23.16).

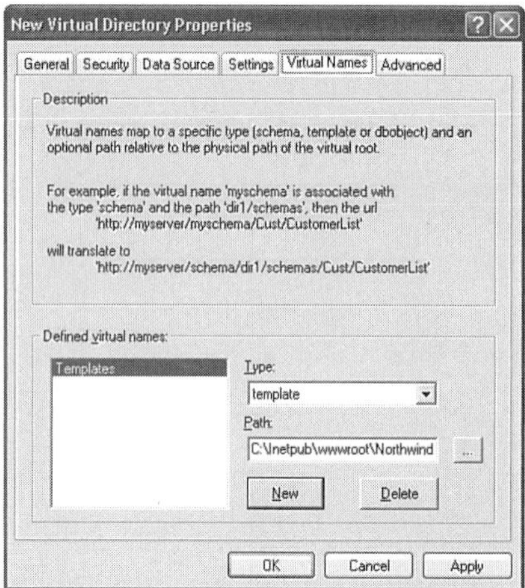

Figure 23.15
The Virtual Names page displays a list of the names of folders you create for templates, database objects, or schemas.

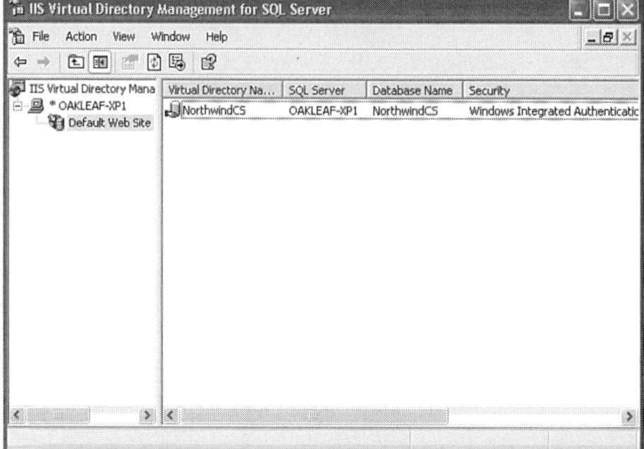

Figure 23.16
You can add as many virtual directories as you have SQL Server databases on your network, or add multiple virtual directories for a single database.

MODIFYING THE SALES TOTALS BY AMOUNT VIEW

A modified version of the Sales Totals by Amount report to provide a report of the 100 largest orders received by Northwind Traders is a good candidate for export as a live Web report. Removing the view's existing limitation to 1997 orders allows newly received orders that meet the `TOP 100` test to appear in the report.

TIP

> You can't export a report having an SQL statement with `JOIN`s between tables as the value of the Record Source property. To work around this problem, copy the SQL statement to a view, function, or stored procedure and specify one of these objects as the Record Source property value.

Modify the view for the live Web report in the following steps:

1. Open NorthwindCS.adp, and choose File, Connection to open the Data Link Properties dialog. If the server name is (local), type the NetBIOS name of the computer (OAKLEAF-XP1 for this example), click Test Connection, and then click OK to save the changes.
2. Open the Sales Totals by Amount view in Design view.
3. Change the `BETWEEN...` criterion of the ShippedDate column to **`NOT IS NULL`** to include only orders that have shipped.
4. Remove the `>2500` criterion of the Subtotal column to make all rows accessible.
5. Add a Descending sort type to the Subtotal column to place the highest-valued orders at the top of the query result set.
6. Right click the upper pane and choose Properties to open the View page of the Properties dialog.
7. Clear the Percent check box to return the first 100 rows, and close the Properties dialog. Figure 23.17 shows the reformatted view design.

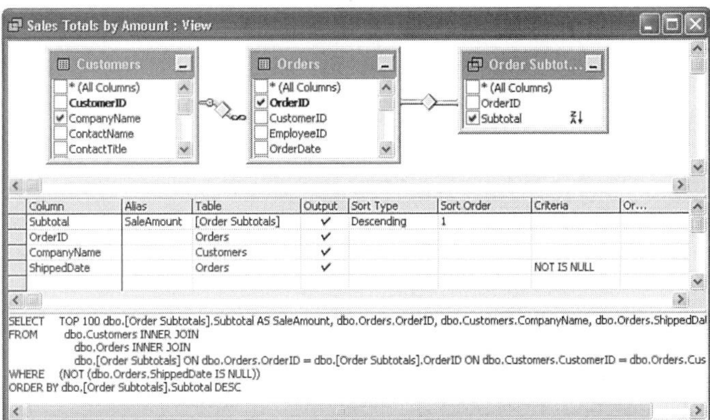

Figure 23.17
The modifications to the Sales Totals by Amount view return 100 orders having the highest sales value.

8. Click Run and save your changes to the view. 100 shipped orders appear in descending order of their total amount (see Figure 23.18).
9. Close the view and open the Sales Totals by Amount report to confirm that it displays correctly. Close the report, because you can't export the report when it's open in Print Preview.

Sales Totals by Amount : View

OrderID	SaleAmount	CompanyName	ShippedDate
10865	$16,387.50	QUICK-Stop	2/12/1998
10981	$15,810.00	Hanari Carnes	4/2/1998
11030	$12,615.05	Save-a-lot Markets	4/27/1998
10889	$11,380.00	Rattlesnake Canyon Grocery	2/23/1998
10417	$11,188.40	Simons bistro	1/28/1997
10817	$10,952.84	Königlich Essen	1/13/1998
10897	$10,835.24	Hungry Owl All-Night Grocers	2/25/1998
10479	$10,495.60	Rattlesnake Canyon Grocery	3/21/1997
10540	$10,191.70	QUICK-Stop	6/13/1997
10691	$10,164.80	QUICK-Stop	10/22/1997
10515	$9,921.30	QUICK-Stop	5/23/1997
10372	$9,210.90	Queen Cozinha	12/9/1996
10424	$9,194.56	Mère Paillarde	1/27/1997
11032	$8,902.50	White Clover Markets	4/23/1998
10514	$8,623.45	Ernst Handel	5/16/1997
10353	$8,593.28	Piccolo und mehr	11/25/1996
10816	$8,446.45	Great Lakes Food Market	2/4/1998
10360	$7,390.20	Blondel père et fils	12/2/1996
11017	$6,750.00	Ernst Handel	4/20/1998
10776	$6,635.27	Ernst Handel	12/18/1997
10607	$6,475.40	Save-a-lot Markets	7/25/1997

Record: 1 of 100

Figure 23.18
The datasheet confirms your modifications to the view.

EXPORTING THE SALES TOTALS BY AMOUNT REPORT

To export the live Web report to the Reports subfolder you created in the preceding section, do this:

1. Choose File, Export to open the Export Report "Sales Totals by Amount" As dialog, select XML(*.xml) in the Save As Type list, and navigate to the \Inetpub\wwwroot\Reports subfolder, if you added it.
2. Replace the report name in the File Name text box with **Top100Orders**, and click Export. (Spaces in the file name require users to type a URL with spaces, which isn't a recommended practice.)
3. Click the More Options button to expand the Export XML dialog, and select the Live Data option in the Data page.
4. NEW Specify `http://`*`COMPUTERNAME`*`/DatabaseName` as the URL for the virtual directory in the adjacent text box—`http://OAKLEAF-XP1/NorthwindCS` for this example.
5. Click the Browse button to open the Browse dialog, navigate to the folder containing the exported files, \Inetpub\wwwroot\Reports for this example, and click OK. The Export XML dialog's Data page appears, as shown in Figure 23.19.
6. Click the Presentation tab and select the Client (HTML) option in the Run From frame to send XML and XSL documents to Web clients for processing by IE 6+. Live reports don't support Active Server Pages.
7. Repeat step 4 to place Top100Orders.xsl in the virtual directory subfolder (see Figure 23.20).
8. Click OK to export the live Web report to the folder you specified in step 1.
9. Open IE, type **http://*servername*[/*folder*]/Top100Orders.htm** in the Address box, and press Return to display the live report (see Figure 23.21).

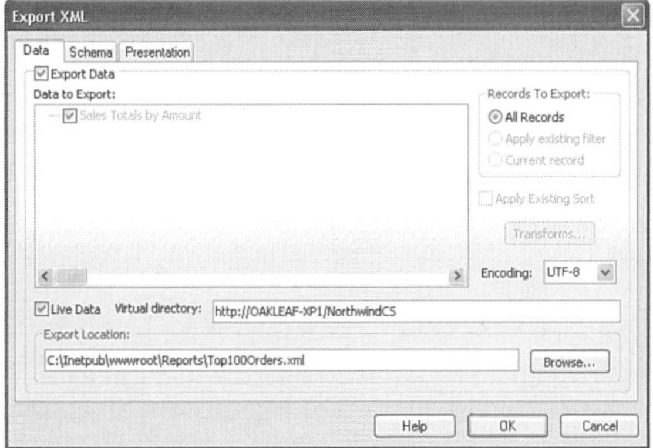

Figure 23.19
Specify the Live Data option, set the Virtual Directory for the database, and set the Export Location to the subfolder for the virtual directory for the exported live report files.

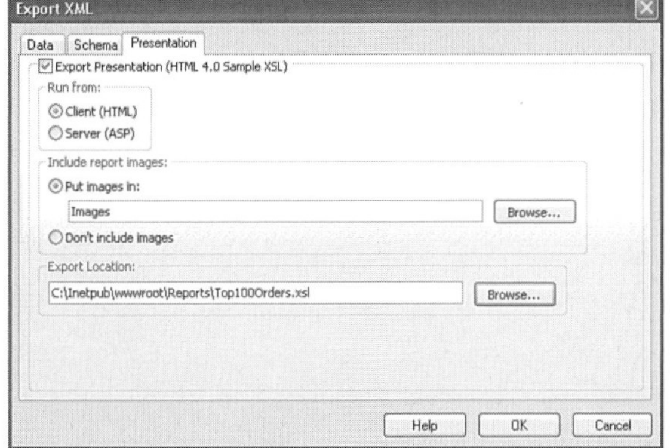

Figure 23.20
Select the Client (HTML) option in the Presentation page to deliver the data document and transform to client browsers.

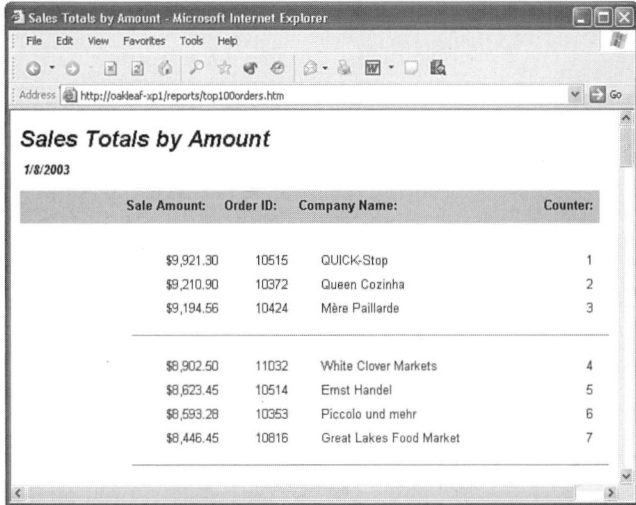

Figure 23.21
The live Web page is a close facsimile of the original Access report, except for the values of the Counter column.

If your report has defects, see the "Problems with Live Web Reports" topic of the "Troubleshooting" section near the end of the chapter.

The RPT2HTML4.xsl style sheet faithfully emulates the appearance of simple Access reports, except for the Counter values incremented by the Running Sum property value of Over All. As mentioned in the earlier "Exporting Static Reports as XML" section, RPT2HTML4.xsl doesn't support the Running Sum property.

23

USING SQL SERVER 2000'S HTTP QUERY FEATURES

You can use SQL Server 2000's HTTP (URL) query features independently of Access to return XML data documents to XML-enabled browsers. Template queries can combine an XML template document, which includes the SQL statement for the query and a custom XSL file to deliver a formatted HTML table.

NOTE

The following three sections provide only a brief description of HTTP and template queries. The "Accessing SQL Server Using HTTP" and "Executing SQL Statements Using HTTP" topics of SQL Server Books Online offers more detailed information on the types and syntax of HTTP queries that SQL Server 2000 offers.

RETURNING XML DOCUMENTS FROM HTTP QUERIES

HTTP queries append `?sql=` and a T-SQL query to the URL for the \Inetpub\www-root\NorthwindCS SQL server virtual directory you established in the earlier "Setting Up the IIS Virtual Directory for the Database" section. As noted earlier, you can type or paste the complete URL into IE's Address text box for a quick test that returns raw XML data to a Web page.

The `http://oakleaf-xp1/NorthwindCS?sql=SELECT+*+FROM+%22Sales+Totals+by+Amount%22+for+xml+auto,elements&root=dataroot` URL that the Top100Orders.htm page sends to SQL Server is a typical example of an HTTP query. Following are the elements of the HTTP query:

- `?sql=` specifies that the following URL components are a T-SQL statement.
- `+` symbols substitute for spaces in the SQL statement.
- `%22` identifiers surround table, view, function, or stored procedure names that contain spaces.
- `for+xml+auto` (the T-SQL `FOR XML AUTO` modifier) specifies that the data is to be returned as an XML data document.
- `elements` specifies element-centric XML, which is required by Access. If you don't add the `elements` modifier, the query returns attribute-centric XML.
- `&root=dataroot` generates a well-formed XML document by adding `<dataroot>…</dataroot>` tags to the XML data.

NOTE

> One application for ad hoc HTTP queries is generating XML data from selections users make in an HTML FORM. Assembling the selections into an HTML query, however, requires a substantial amount of script.

To test drive the preceding HTTP query, do this:

1. Open the Top100Orders.htm file in Notepad, and turn Word Wrap off.
2. Select the URL in the text—starting with `http://` and ending with `dataroot`—and copy the URL to the Clipboard. (Don't include the trailing quote or the `, false` argument of the `objDataXMLHTTP.open` method.)
3. Open IE, paste the URL to the Address box, and press Enter to display the element-centric XML data (see Figure 23.22). The XML data document forms the `MSXML.DOMDocument`, which you can manipulate with XSLT and VBScript or ECMAScript.

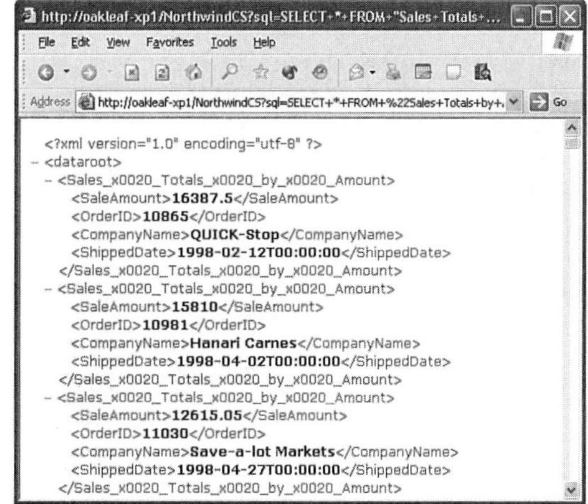

Figure 23.22 This element-centric XML data illustrates use of the hexadecimal `_0x0020_` literal that substitutes for spaces in element names. SQL server `datetime` values return in XSD `dateTime` text format.

4. Choose View, Source to open the unformatted stream of XML data in Notepad, select All Files in the Files of Type list, accept the default UTF-8 encoding, and save the file as **Top100SQL.xml** in your working folder, typically ...\Office11\Samples (not the ...\wwwroot\Reports folder).

You import the Top100SQL.xml file to an Access table in the later "Importing XML Data to Tables" section.

USING SQL SERVER TEMPLATE QUERIES

Typing a lengthy T-SQL query in IE's Address box isn't a piece of cake, so Microsoft provides a template feature that lets you pass conventional T-SQL statements to the server.

Using a template hides the SQL statement from the HTML source and prevents users from executing ad hoc queries.

TIP

You must clear the Allow URL Queries check box on the Settings page of the *VirtualDirectoy* Properties page for the SQL Server virtual directory to prevent users or Web pages from executing HTTP queries.

23

Templates are XML documents that you store in a subfolder of the SQL Server virtual directory for the target database you created in the earlier "Setting Up the IIS Virtual Directory for the Database" section. You added the Templates virtual name, but not the Templates subdirectory. Navigate in Explorer to \Inetpub\wwwroot\NorthwindCS and add a Templates subfolder to store the template files you create in the following sections.

WRITING AND EXECUTING A SIMPLE XML TEMPLATE FILE

A template is a well-formed XML document with the standard XML header, a `<dataroot>…</dataroot>` tag pair that declares the SQL Server XML namespace (`xml-sql`), and an `<sql:query>…</sql:query>` tag pair to enclose the SQL statement, which you write in ordinary T-SQL. You don't add the `&root=dataroot` argument because the template adds `<dataroot…>` with an `xmlns:sql` namespace attribute value.

XML

The XML content of the template file for the Top100Orders query is

```
<?xml version='1.0' encoding='UTF-8'?>
<dataroot xmlns:sql='urn:schemas-microsoft-com:xml-sql'>
   <sql:query>
      SELECT * FROM [Sales Totals by Amount] FOR XML AUTO, ELEMENTS
   </sql:query>
</dataroot>
```

Executing a template file requires a URL with the following format:

`http://servername/virtualdirectory/virtualname/template.xml`

To create the Top100Orders.xml template in the virtual name folder and execute the template query from IE, do this:

1. Open Notepad, type the preceding XML text, and save the file as **Top100Test.xml** in your virtual name folder—...\wwwroot\NorthwindCS\Templates for this example.

NOTE

If you don't want to type the XML yourself, Top100Test.xml is included in the \Seua11\Chaptr23 folder of the accompanying CD-ROM.

2. Launch IE and type **http://*servername*/northwindcs/templates/top100test.xml** as the URL. The template returns an XML data document that's identical to that for the HTTP query in the earlier "Returning XML Documents from HTTP Queries" section (refer to Figure 23.22).

You also can execute stored procedures and specify parameter values with HTTP template queries. The SQL Server Books Online topics mentioned earlier have syntax examples.

APPLYING A STYLE SHEET TO XML DATA FROM TEMPLATE QUERIES

HTTP query templates can specify a style sheet, which—unfortunately—you must write from scratch. A minor addition to the template's XML code specifies the name of the associated XSL file. In this case, you process the default attribute-centric XML delivered by the `FOR XML AUTO` modifier.

XML

The XML template document–Top100Test.xml–for the Top100Orders query must be modified as shown below and saved as Top100.xml for use with a template style sheets named Top100.xsl:

```
<?xml version='1.0' encoding='UTF-8'?>
<ROOT xmlns:sql='urn:schemas-microsoft-com:xml-sql'
   sql:xsl='/Top100.xsl'>
   <sql:query>
      SELECT OrderID, CompanyName, CONVERT(nvarchar, ShippedDate, 101)
      AS ShippedDate, CONVERT(nvarchar, SaleAmount, 1) AS SaleAmount
      FROM [Sales Totals by Amount] FOR XML AUTO
   </sql:query>
</ROOT>
```

The `sql:xsl='/Top100.xsl'` attribute specifies the name of the XSLT file that generates the HTML code. (The Top100.x?? file names prevent overwriting Top100Orders.x??.) Unlike Access XML style sheets, which use the `Format` function to format date and currency values, you must use T-SQL's `CONVERT` or `CAST` functions to deliver pre-formatted text to the stylesheet. The example template style sheet expects attribute-centric XML data, so the `ELEMENTS` modifier isn't present.

The structure of the XSLT code for template style sheets is similar to that described in the earlier "Reformatting HTML Tables and Adding Page Elements" section, but considerably simpler. No script is required to process the XPath expressions. Code in the preceding style sheets generated by RPT2HTML4.xsl "walks the DOMDocument tree" sequentially. In this case, the XSLT processes the XML data as a single "chunk."

XSL

The following XSLT code in Top100.xsl generates a formatted table from the attribute-centric XML that the Top100.xml template generates

```
<?xml version='1.0' encoding='UTF-8'?>
<xsl:stylesheet xmlns:xsl='http://www.w3.org/TR/WD-xsl' >
   <xsl:template match = '*'>
      <xsl:apply-templates />
```

continues

continued

```
   </xsl:template>
   <xsl:template match = 'Sales_x0020_Totals_x0020_by_x0020_Amount'>
      <TR>
         <TD align="center"><xsl:value-of select = '@OrderID' /></TD>
         <TD><xsl:value-of select = '@CompanyName' /></TD>
         <TD align="right"><xsl:value-of select = '@ShippedDate' /></TD>
         <TD align="right">$<xsl:value-of select = '@SaleAmount' /></TD>
      </TR>
   </xsl:template>
   <xsl:template match = '/'>
      <HTML>
         <HEAD>
            <STYLE>TH, TR, P { font-family: verdana, arial; font-size: 12px }
➥</STYLE>
            <STYLE>TH { background-color: #CCCCCC } </STYLE>
            <STYLE>TR { background-color: #EEEEEE } </STYLE>
         </HEAD>
         <BODY>
            <P><B>SQL Server Query: </B>
            SELECT OrderID, CompanyName, CONVERT(nvarchar, ShippedDate, 101) AS
            ShippedDate, CONVERT(nvarchar, SaleAmount, 1) AS SaleAmount
            FROM [Sales Totals by Amount] FOR XML AUTO</P>
            <CENTER>
            <TABLE Border = '0'>
               <TR><TH colspan='4'>SQL Server 2000 HTTP Template Query</TH></TR>
               <TR>
                  <TH>OrderID</TH>
                  <TH>CompanyName</TH>
                  <TH>ShippedDate</TH>
                  <TH>SaleAmount</TH>
               </TR>
               <xsl:apply-templates select = 'ROOT' />
            </TABLE>
            </CENTER>
         </BODY>
      </HTML>
   </xsl:template>
</xsl:stylesheet>
```

The `<xsl:value-of-select = '@ColumnName' />` expressions return the column values of the specified column to the four HTML `<TD>...</TD>` elements. The `<xsl:apply-templates select = 'ROOT' />` expression merges the first `<TR>...</TR>` blocks in the code with the HTML code for the title and table header.

Use the following URL to execute template/style sheet pairs:

`http://servername/virtualdirectory/virtualname/template.xml?contenttype=text/html.`

Omitting the `?contenttype=text/html` argument returns the HTML code generated by the style sheet instead of a formatted page.

Top100.xml and Top100.xsl are included in the \Seau10\Chaptr23 folder of the accompanying CD-ROM. To give the sample files a test run, do the following:

1. Copy the Top100.xml and Top100.xsl files from the CD-ROM or your \Program Files\Seua11\Chaptr23 folder to the Templates virtual name subfolder of your SQL Server virtual directory— ...\Wwwroot\NorthwindCS\Templates for the examples of this chapter.

2. Launch IE and type **http://*servername*/northwindcs/templates/top100.xml?content-type=text/html** in the Address box, and press Enter. The T-SQL statement of the template file and the formatted table appear as shown in Figure 23.23.

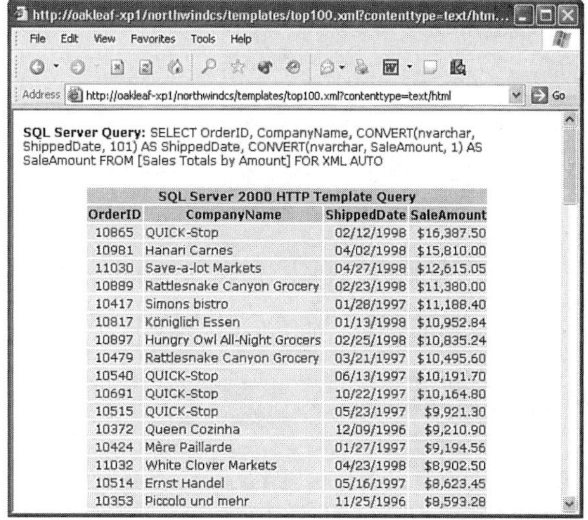

SQL Server Query: SELECT OrderID, CompanyName, CONVERT(nvarchar, ShippedDate, 101) AS ShippedDate, CONVERT(nvarchar, SaleAmount, 1) AS SaleAmount FROM [Sales Totals by Amount] FOR XML AUTO

SQL Server 2000 HTTP Template Query			
OrderID	**CompanyName**	**ShippedDate**	**SaleAmount**
10865	QUICK-Stop	02/12/1998	$16,387.50
10981	Hanari Carnes	04/02/1998	$15,810.00
11030	Save-a-lot Markets	04/27/1998	$12,615.05
10889	Rattlesnake Canyon Grocery	02/23/1998	$11,380.00
10417	Simons bistro	01/28/1997	$11,188.40
10817	Königlich Essen	01/13/1998	$10,952.84
10897	Hungry Owl All-Night Grocers	02/25/1998	$10,835.24
10479	Rattlesnake Canyon Grocery	03/21/1997	$10,495.60
10540	QUICK-Stop	06/13/1997	$10,191.70
10691	QUICK-Stop	10/22/1997	$10,164.80
10515	QUICK-Stop	05/23/1997	$9,921.30
10372	Queen Cozinha	12/09/1996	$9,210.90
10424	Mère Paillarde	01/27/1997	$9,194.56
11032	White Clover Markets	04/23/1998	$8,902.50
10514	Ernst Handel	05/16/1997	$8,623.45
10353	Piccolo und mehr	11/25/1996	$8,593.28

Figure 23.23 Formatting of the HTML table generated by the SQL Server HTTP template query and style sheet is similar to that of the tables you created earlier in the chapter.

TIP

> If you see strange characters when the page opens in IE, right-click the page and select Encoding, Unicode (UTF-8) to correct the problem.

SETTING UP IIS 5.0 AND SQL SERVER 2000 FOR WEB ACCESS

Installing IIS 5.0 under Windows XP and 2000 sets the authentication methods for the Default Web Site to Anonymous Access, Digest Authentication (for Active Directory), and Integrated Windows authentication (see Figure 23.24).

On an intranet, users ordinarily connect to the Web server with integrated Windows security having credentials provided by their Windows 2000+ account, and don't need anonymous access. If you clear the Anonymous Access check box, Internet users having a user account in a Windows 2000+ domain can connect to the Web server by completing a login dialog with their user ID, password, and down-level (NetBIOS) domain name for Windows authentication (see Figure 23.25). Only network access is required to view static pages whose source is an XML document.

Figure 23.24
The default Authentication Methods settings for IIS 5.0's Default Web Site allow all but Basic (clear text) authentication.

Figure 23.25
A Windows 98 user attempting to connect to your Web site via the Internet receives this dialog if you specify integrated Windows security. The IP address in this figure has been altered.

If you're running Windows XP Professional or 2000+ Server behind a firewall, you might need to mark the Digest Authentication for Windows Domain Servers check box in the Authentication Methods dialog for your Web site. Using Digest Authentication is less secure than Windows 2000+ login, but much more secure than Basic (clear text) authentication.

CAUTION

XML or HTML data you send over the Internet to authenticated users isn't secure. Hackers easily can intercept the data, which travels across the Internet as plain text. To maintain data security, set up a secure virtual private network (VPN) for users with Point-to-Point Tunneling Protocol (PPTP) for Windows 98/Me or Layer2 Tunneling Protocol (L2TP). L2TP requires running Windows 2000+ on the server and Windows XP/2000 on the clients. When users log in to your intranet through a VPN, they can use conventional `http://servername/...` addresses to connect to the Web server.

Live Web reports and HTTP queries of any type require IIS to connect to SQL Server. Integrated Windows authentication succeeds for users having SQL Server logins on the destination server and appropriate permissions for the database.

→ To review how to set up SQL Server logins, user accounts, and permissions for individual databases, **see** " Securing Projects with the MSDE 2000 Login/User Tool," **p. 936**.

When anonymous users connect to your Web site over the Internet, they use the default interactive user (IUSR_*SERVERNAME*) account created when you installed IIS. By default, IIS creates and maintains the password for IUSR_*SERVERNAME*, which is a member of Domain Users under Windows 2000+ server. If you grant anonymous access to your Web site, visitors can open .htm and .asp files for static tables and reports that have XML data sources. Data in XML files stored in a Web site folder having anonymous access are available for the whole world to see or hack. If the IUSR_*SERVERNAME* account has an SQL Server login, a database user account, and at least read permission for database objects, anyone can read live reports and execute template queries against the database.

23

NOTE

NorthwindCS's `public` database role, which includes all database user accounts, grants full permissions for all database objects. Granting *any* permissions to the `public` role violates generally-accepted database security standards.

Granting anonymous visitors access to your SQL Server database(s) to run live Web reports or HTTP queries can result in serious security breaches. Use XML documents as the data source to provide anonymous Web access to tables, query result sets, and static Web reports if you *must* support anonymous visitors.

IMPORTING XML DATA TO TABLES

Most of this chapter is devoted to exporting XML documents from Access 2003 and SQL Server 2000. Access 2003 also can import well-formed, element-centric XML data documents to new tables or append data to existing tables. Access's 2002's XML import feature was limited to XML files having elements from a single table or query. If you wanted to import order and line item data, for example, you needed an XML data document for each table. To maintain referential integrity, you had to append the orders document and then the line items document in separate operations.

NEW Access 2003's new import XML dialog lets you import data to multiple tables from a single XML document and its XML schema. If you don't have an .xsd file for the document, Access 2003 infers the structure of the document and can create a schema for it. Another new Access 2003 XML feature is the capability to create empty related tables from an XML schema (.xsd) document. You also can transform the XML data during import with custom .xsl files.

The ability to generate tables from XML schema and import XML data to Jet and SQL Server tables will become increasingly important as Microsoft and other software publishers, as well as many industries, move to XML as the preferred method of interchanging data. Most current standards for XML business documents provide XML schemas to validate instances of the documents.

IMPORTING A FLAT XML DATA DOCUMENT

This simple example uses the Top100SQL.xml document file you created in the earlier "Returning XML Documents from HTTP Queries" section from the Sales Totals by Amount view. If you didn't save the Top100SQL.xml file, there's a copy in the \Seua11\Chaptr23 folder of the accompanying CD-ROM.

To import the Top100SQL.xml document to a new table and append another set of records to the table, do this:

1. Open a database or project that doesn't have the Sales Totals by Amount query or view. The XMLXSL23.mdb sample database or, if you created it, the XMLXSL23.adp project is a good candidate. ADP are used in this and the following examples.
2. Choose File, Get External Data, Import to open the Import dialog, select XML (*.xml, *.xsd) in the Files of Type list, and navigate to the location where you saved the Top100SQL.xml file.
3. Double-click the Top100SQL.xml file to close the Import dialog and open the new Import XML dialog, which displays the name of the source query as a Tables subnode. Expand the Sales Totals by Amount node to display the view columns.
4. Click the Options button to expand the dialog and display the three Import Options shown in Figure 23.26. For an initial test, accept the default Structure and Data option.

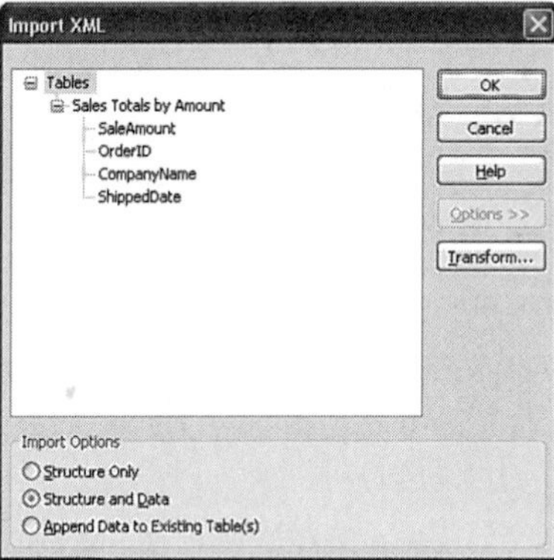

Figure 23.26 The new Import XML dialog displays the name of the source table or view from which you created the data document and its fields or columns.

5. Click OK to create the table with the imported values. Click OK to acknowledge the "Finished importing…" message, and press F5 to refresh the Database window if the new table isn't present.
6. Open the new Sales Totals by Amount table in Datasheet view, which displays SQL Server's default XML text formats for all fields, because you don't have a schema for the XML file (see Figure 23.27).

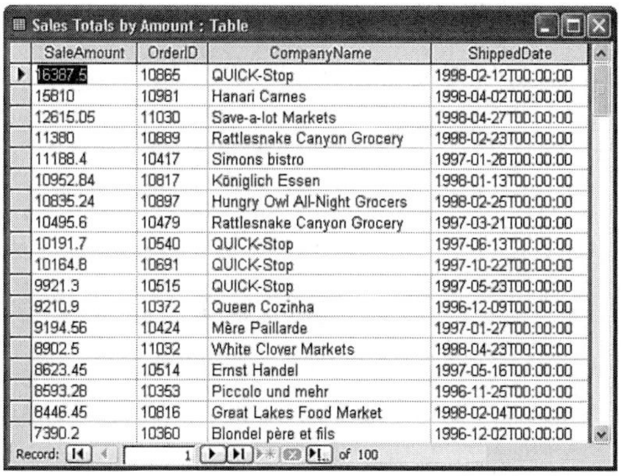

Figure 23.27
The imported table consists of four text fields having the default text format. Datasheet view of the table is the same in Jet and ADP.

Sales Totals by Amount : Table

SaleAmount	OrderID	CompanyName	ShippedDate
16387.5	10865	QUICK-Stop	1998-02-12T00:00:00
15810	10981	Hanari Carnes	1998-04-02T00:00:00
12615.05	11030	Save-a-lot Markets	1998-04-27T00:00:00
11380	10889	Rattlesnake Canyon Grocery	1998-02-23T00:00:00
11188.4	10417	Simons bistro	1997-01-28T00:00:00
10952.84	10817	Königlich Essen	1998-01-13T00:00:00
10835.24	10897	Hungry Owl All-Night Grocers	1998-02-25T00:00:00
10495.6	10479	Rattlesnake Canyon Grocery	1997-03-21T00:00:00
10191.7	10540	QUICK-Stop	1997-06-13T00:00:00
10164.8	10691	QUICK-Stop	1997-10-22T00:00:00
9921.3	10515	QUICK-Stop	1997-05-23T00:00:00
9210.9	10372	Queen Cozinha	1996-12-09T00:00:00
9194.56	10424	Mère Paillarde	1997-01-27T00:00:00
8902.5	11032	White Clover Markets	1998-04-23T00:00:00
8623.45	10514	Ernst Handel	1997-05-16T00:00:00
8593.28	10353	Piccolo und mehr	1996-11-25T00:00:00
8446.45	10816	Great Lakes Food Market	1998-02-04T00:00:00
7390.2	10360	Blondel père et fils	1996-12-02T00:00:00

Record: 1 of 100

7. Change to Table Design view.
8. If you're using a Jet database, change the data type of the SaleAmount field to Currency and the OrderID field to Number, Long Integer. A Jet database won't accept a change of the ShippedDate field, because Jet can't handle the ISO 8601 YYYY-MM-DDThh:mm:ss format designed by the XML Schema Part 2: Datatypes specification for the `dateTime` data type. You must have a schema that specifies the dateTime data type for the DateTime field to import dates successfully.

   For an SQL Server database, change the data type of the SaleAmount field to `money`, OrderID to `int`, and ShippedDate to `datetime` (see Figure 23.28). Not surprisingly, SQL Server *can* handle ISO 8601. Optionally, change the Length property for CompanyName to 40.

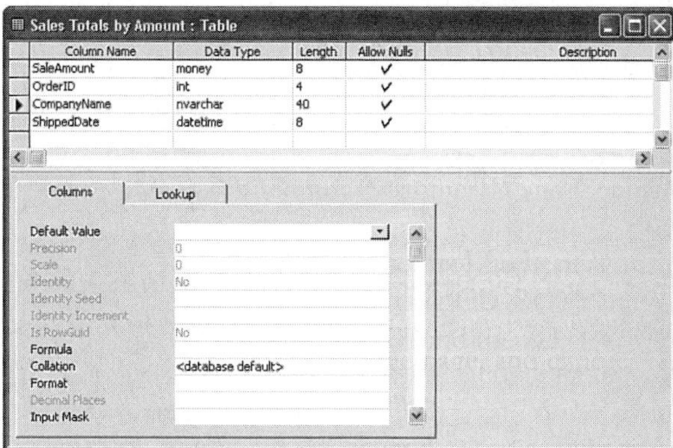

Figure 23.28
Change SQL Server field data types to those appropriate for the type of data in each column. You also can rearrange the sequence of the fields, if you want.

9. Return to Datasheet view, save your changes, and acknowledge the warning message about field data sizes. For an SQL Server table, the Validation Warnings message opens (see Figure 23.29). Figure 23.30 shows the modified SQL Server table in Datasheet view. Click Yes to acknowledge that data might be lost by changes to field data sizes.

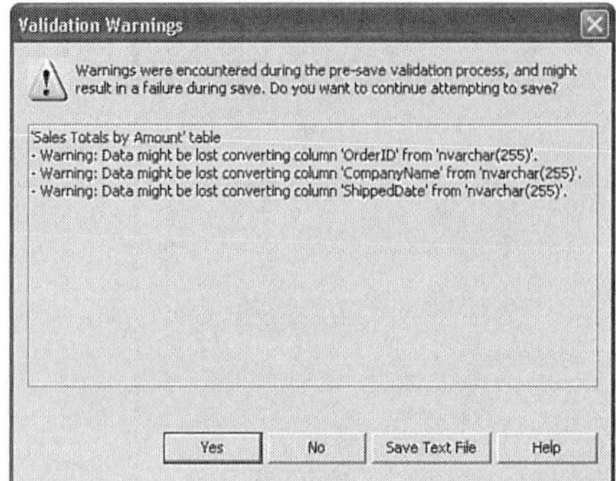

Figure 23.29
This SQL Server warning message advises that data might be lost as a result of shortening the field length from `nvarchar(255)` to `int` or `datetime`, but not `money`. The Save Text File button saves a text file of the warnings, not the data.

23

CAUTION

> Don't disregard a warning message that states that rows will be lost. This message occurs when Jet or SQL Server can't handle the data type change. Cancel the operation and return the data type for the field to Text or `nvarchar`.

Sales Totals by Amount : Table

SaleAmount	OrderID	CompanyName	ShippedDate
$16,387.50	10865	QUICK-Stop	2/12/1998
$15,810.00	10981	Hanari Carnes	4/2/1998
$12,615.05	11030	Save-a-lot Markets	4/27/1998
$11,380.00	10889	Rattlesnake Canyon Grocery	2/23/1998
$11,188.40	10417	Simons bistro	1/28/1997
$10,952.84	10817	Königlich Essen	1/13/1998
$10,835.24	10897	Hungry Owl All-Night Grocers	2/25/1998
$10,495.60	10479	Rattlesnake Canyon Grocery	3/21/1997
$10,191.70	10540	QUICK-Stop	6/13/1997
$10,164.80	10691	QUICK-Stop	10/22/1997
$9,921.30	10515	QUICK-Stop	5/23/1997
$9,210.90	10372	Queen Cozinha	12/9/1996
$9,194.56	10424	Mère Paillarde	1/27/1997
$8,902.50	11032	White Clover Markets	4/23/1998
$8,623.45	10514	Ernst Handel	5/16/1997
$8,593.28	10353	Piccolo und mehr	11/25/1996
$8,446.45	10816	Great Lakes Food Market	2/4/1998
$7,390.20	10360	Blondel père et fils	12/2/1996
$6,750.00	11017	Ernst Handel	4/20/1998
$6,635.27	10776	Ernst Handel	12/18/1997
$6,475.40	10607	Save-a-lot Markets	7/25/1997

Record: 1 of 100

Figure 23.30
SQL Server successfully changes the data types of three fields; Jet can't change the ShippedDate data type from Text to DateTime.

11. Test the ability of your redesigned table to accept updates from XML data documents having the same structure. Close the table, and repeat steps 2–5, except select the Append Data to Existing Table(s) option in step 4.
12. Open the table in Datasheet view, verify that the table now has 200 rows, and the appended records (101 and greater) appear the same as the first 100. You can disregard "Not all your data was imported..." error messages, if they occur, after verifying the new row count value.

NOTE

SQL Server tables imported from XML documents are read only in datasheet view, because they lack a unique record identifier (primary key). You can edit any Jet table imported from an XML document.

Importing hundreds of thousands of records as XML to populate tables isn't likely to replace SQL Server's bulk copy process (BCP), which uses conventional tab- or comma-delimited, or fixed-width text files. BCP data import is much faster than XML import, and conventional text files are much smaller than XML data files for the same number of records. XML import is better suited to making incremental additions to tables. Access 2003 XML import feature makes adding records to SQL Server tables considerably easier than using BCP or SQL Server's Data Transformation Service (DTS).

NOTE

SQLXML, an add-on to SQL Server mentioned earlier in the chapter, offers a high-speed XML bulk load feature and supports XML updategrams for `INSERT`, `UPDATE`, and `DELETE` operations with XML documents. To download SQLXML, which adds a SQLXML choice to your Programs menu, go to `http://www.microsoft.com/sql/downloads/default.htm`. You must have the SQL Server Client Tools installed to run SQLXML's setup program. SQLXML 3.0 SP 1 was current when this book was written.

IMPORTING DATA WITH AN XML SCHEMA

Access can import XML schema in XSD format to create an empty table to which you append XML data that conforms to the schema. If the schema contains `od:jetType="`*`datatype`*`"` and `od:sqlSType="datatype"` attributes, the schema specifies the Jet or SQL Server field data types when you create the empty table.

To export and then import the schema and then add data for the Sales Totals by Amount table to an Jet or SQL Server database, do this:

1. With the Sales Totals by Amount table selected in the Database window, choose File, Export, select XML (*.xml) in the Files of Type list, change the file name to **TopOrdersSQL**, and click Export.
2. In the Export XML dialog, clear the Data (XML) and mark the Schema of the Data (XSD) options, and click OK to export TopOrdersSQL.xsd.
3. Choose File, Get External Data, Import, and double-click the TopOrdersSQL.xsd item to open the XML Import dialog.
4. Click OK to import the schema and data, and acknowledge the "Finished importing…" message.

5. Open the empty table in Design view to verify that the data types are the same as those you specified in the preceding section.

6. Return to Datasheet view, and append the 100 records from the Top100SQL.xml data document to confirm the validity of the imported schema.

Sending XML schema and data documents over the Internet to create and populate Jet and, especially, SQL Server tables is simpler than other alternatives. Many firewalls now reject email enclosures in non-text formats such as Jet .mdb and SQL Server .mdf files. XML documents are text files, so they pass through firewalls with no problems.

EXPORTING AND IMPORTING DATA IN RELATED TABLES

Access 2003's new capability to export data and schemas from related tables lets you generate hierarchical XML documents. The documents contain elements from a base table, such as Orders, and child elements from corresponding records in the related table. Access-specific schemas define the table structures and relationships. Access 2003 also lets you limit the export to a selected record or apply the current filter, and offers the option to export lookup data.

EXPORTING RELATED TABLES AND THEIR SCHEMA

To test-drive exporting related tables with a single record from the Orders table and related records from the Order Details table, do the following:

1. Open NorthwindCS.adp's Orders table in Datasheet view and select the first order (10248).
2. Choose File, Export, select XML Documents (*.xml), type **Order10248** in the File Name text box, and click Export All to open the Export XML dialog. In this case, Export All is a misnomer.
3. Accept the defaults, and click More Options to expand the Export XML dialog and display the Orders and Order Details tables. Expand the nodes to display related lookup tables, and mark the Order Details table for export (see Figure 23.31).

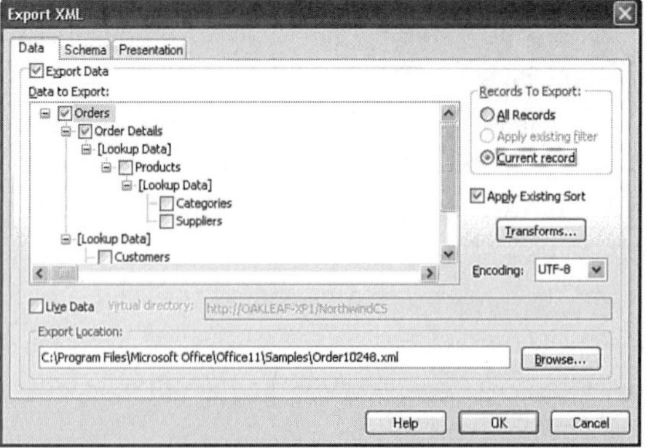

Figure 23.31
Access 2003's enhanced Export XML dialog displays the table you select for export and its directly related table, if any. Lookup Data nodes disclose other related tables.

NOTE

> Exporting all Orders, Order Details, and lookup tables creates a 978MB XML file. Exporting lookup tables adds every record of the lookup tables to the end of the XML file. Images in the categories table are stored with *Base64* encoding in `CDATA` elements. Base64 encoding translates binary bytes to combinations of the 64 printable low-order ASCII text characters.

4. Click OK to export the Order10248.xml and Order10248.xsd files.
5. Open Order10248.xml in IE to verify that the three Order Details line items are present as child elements of the order.
6. Open Order10248.xsd in IE and explore the schema that defines the two tables, indexes, and primary and foreign keys.

The `<keyref… />` node at the end of Order12048.xsd establishes the relationship (a primary-foreign key constraint) between the two tables with the following elements:

```
<xsd:keyref refer="Orders_FK_Order_Details_Orders"
      name="Order_x0020_Details_OrderID">
   <xsd:selector xpath="."/>
<xsd:field xpath="OrderID"/>
```

The schema uses XPath expressions to specify the relationship between the OrderID fields of the Order Details and Orders tables.

NOTE

> XPath is a W3C recommendation for XML Path Language 1.0 (`http://www.w3.org/TR/xpath`). XPath is a very complex language for navigating XML documents during transformation with XSLT. XPath 2.0, which is even more complex than XPath 1.0, and XSLT 2.0 were in the working draft stage when this book was written.

RECREATING AND POPULATING RELATED TABLES

You can recreate the Orders and Order Details tables in another database from Order12048.xml and Order12048.xsd, but it's more interesting to import all NorthwindCS tables into a new database. Including the lookup tables lets you verify that all relationships are present.

The following example recreates the NorthwindCS database from OrdersAll.xml and OrderAll.xsd. You create OrdersAll.xml by marking the check box for every table and exporting the XML document and schema, as mentioned in the preceding section's note.

To import all tables from NorthwindCS from OrdersAll, do the following:

1. Create a new Access data project named OrdersCS.adp with a new SQL Server database named OrdersSQL. Alternatively, create Orders.mdb.

2. Choose File, Get External Data, Import, select XML (*.xml;*.xsd), and open OrdersAll.xml. The Import XML dialog displays Tables subnodes for the eight tables (see Figure 23.32)

Figure 23.32 The Import XML dialog displays subnodes for all tables in NorthwindCS. Expanding the nodes shows the tables' fields.

23

3. Click OK to import the tables, which takes a minute or two depending on the speed of your computer.

4. Open the imported tables in Datasheet view to confirm their resemblance to the source tables.

NOTE

The schemas that Access 2003 generates don't include application-specific annotations to describe SQL Server or Jet extended properties, such as captions and lookup data. Subdatasheets appear because the default value of the Subdatasheet Name property is [Auto]. You must add lookup data manually.

5. Click Database Diagrams in the Database window, and then click the Create Database Diagram in Designer shortcut to open Diagram1 and the Add Table dialog.
6. Click Add 8 times to add all tables to the designer and close the Add Table dialog. Closing the add table dialog adds the relationship lines between the table fields (see Figure 23.33).

NOTE

If you import the tables to a Jet database, Access automatically performs steps 5 and 6.

7. Close the designer and save the diagram with an appropriate name.

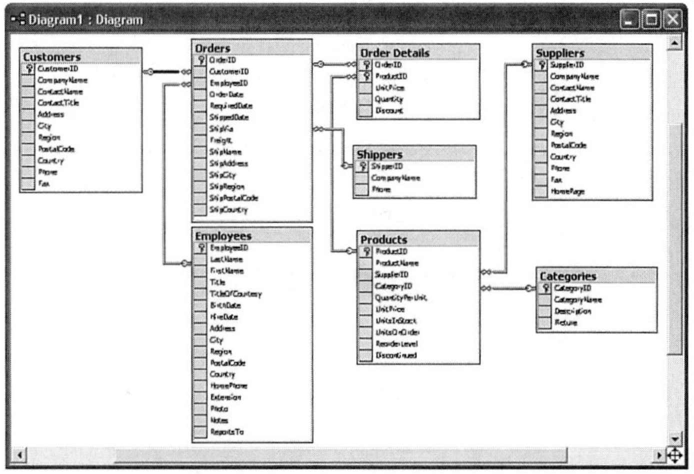

Figure 23.33 Adding the imported tables to a database diagram displays the relationships between primary and foreign keys.

Appending XML data to tables with SQL Server `identity` columns or Jet AutoNumber fields doesn't work. Only SQL Server or Jet can update these fields. If you edit Order10248 to eliminate the values of the <OrderID> element or remove the element entirely, records in the ImportErrors table state that the table wasn't imported and data wasn't inserted. You must use SQL Server updategrams to insert XML data in one or more tables. Updategrams, which SQLXML 3.0 installs and documents, are beyond the scope of this book.

Applying Custom XSL Transforms to XML Data

ReportML and the .xsl files it generates handle the most common use of XSLT—generating Web pages from your Access data. As mentioned earlier in the chapter, XSLT also can transform one class of XML documents to another. For example, you can apply XSLT to transform an XML data document to the format required by the Office Web Components (OWC) 11 Spreadsheet control.

Access doesn't include in the Export XML dialog the capability to specify a custom .xsl file to process exported XML documents. By adding a small amount of VBA code to your Access application, however, you can apply a transform when importing or exporting XML documents. Access 2003's `Application.ExportXML` and `Application.ImportXML` methods handle export/import operations, and the new `Application.TransformXML` method applies a custom transform.

NOTE

> A macro warning message opens when the VBA code executes the `Application.TransformXML` method, because the transform contains VBScript code. This message appears with macro security set to Low or Medium. Click Yes to dismiss the message.

The frmXMLSS11 form of the XMLXSL23.mdb sample database in the \Seua11\Chaptr23 folder includes VBA code that uses custom XSLT in the Top100SS.xsl file to transform element-centric XML data to an XML data document for the OWC Spreadsheet control. Figure 23.34 shows frmXMLSS11 in Form view displaying data generated from a modified version of the Sales Totals by Amount query named Top100. XMLXSL23.mdb also includes frmXMLSS10—an Office XP and OWC10 version of the form. The frmXMLSS10 form substitutes a custom VBA procedure for the Application.TransformXML method.

23

Figure 23.34
The OWC11 Spreadsheet control displays XML data that's exported to element-centric XML and transformed to Spreadsheet namespace requirements.

NOTE

The ossTop100 Spreadsheet control of frmXMLSS expects to find its source Top100Data.xml, Top100SS.xsl, and Top100SS.xml files in the application folder. If you receive an error message when you open either frmXMLSS10 or frmXMLSS11, copy the three files from ...\Seua11\Chaptr23 to the project's application folder.

When you click the Regenerate Spreadsheet Data, the VBA code behind frmXMLSS transforms the data with Top100SS.xsl to the `urn:schemas-microsoft-com:office:spreadsheet` namespace, and recreates the Top100SS.xml document. Excel 2003 uses the same namespace, so you can export the XML data from the control to an Excel worksheet by clicking the Export to Microsoft Excel button.

NOTE

Providing a VBA code listing before you reach Part VII, "Programming and Converting Access Applications," might appear premature. The purpose of the listing here is to demonstrate the similarity of the VBA code to that of the VBScript and ECMAScript in the .asp and .htm files described earlier in the chapter.

Listing 23.2 is the VBA code for the command button (`cmdLoadSS`) Click event and the generic `TransformXML` subprocedure that creates to DOM documents and applies the `transformNode` method, as described in the earlier "Understanding the Role of Access's ReportML" and "Analyzing the Exported XML Files" sections. You can use the `TransformXML` subprocedure in any application for which you have the appropriate .xsl file.

Listing 23.2 VBA Code to Export and Transform an XML Data Document to the OWC Spreadsheet Namespace

```
Option Compare Database
Option Explicit

Private Sub cmdLoadSS_Click()
   Dim strTransform As String
   Dim strSource As String
   Dim strOutput As String
   Dim strPath As String

   strPath = CurrentProject.Path
   'Export the XML data from the query

   'Specify input, transform, and output file names
   strSource = strPath & "\Top100Data.xml"
   strTransform = strPath & "\Top100SS.xsl"
   strOutput = strPath & "\Top100SS.xml"

   'Transform the data to Office Web Control Spreadsheet format

   Application.TransformXML strSource, strTransform, strTarget
End Sub
```

Figure 23.35 shows IE 6.0 displaying part of the XSLT in the Top100SS.xsl file, which is a derivative of the XSLT generated by Access 2002's ReportML. The urn:schemas-microsoft-com:office:spreadsheet namespace has a <Workbook><Worksheet><Table><Row><Cell><Data>…</Data></Cell></Row></Table></Worksheet></Workbook> hierarchy. <Workbook>…</Workbook> is the root element, which corresponds to the <dataroot>…</dataroot> element of Access XML data documents.

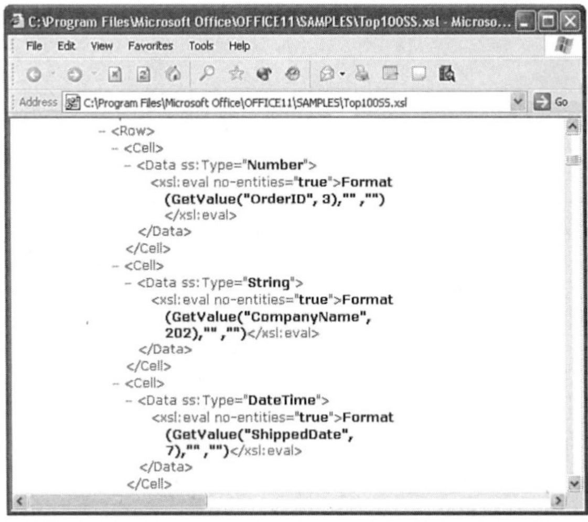

Figure 23.35 XML data that uses the …office:spreadsheet namespace has a deeper hierarchy than Access XML data. The <Row> element is a child of the <Workbook><Worksheet><Table> parent element.

TIP

Monitor Microsoft's Office Update Web site (`http://officeupdate.microsoft.com/welcome/access.asp` or choose Help, Office on the Web) for Access Add-Ins and new or updated XSLT files for transforming Access 2003 XML data documents to Microsoft and other industry-standard XML namespaces. You also can expect many third parties to offer useful XSLT files that handle the generic element-centric XML exported by Access 2003.

TROUBLESHOOTING

PROBLEMS EXPORTING REPORTS TO HTML

My reports having missing fields, incorrect calculated values, incorrectly formatted numbers, or all three problems.

You're likely to encounter problems exporting even moderately complex reports to HTML with RPT2HTML4.xsl. For example, rptInventoryByCategory.htm, which you create by exporting Chapter 16's rptInventoryByCategory report, is missing category names, has the wrong category percentage values, and the category total value has too many decimal places. Currency formatting is missing from all dollar values (see Figure 23.36).

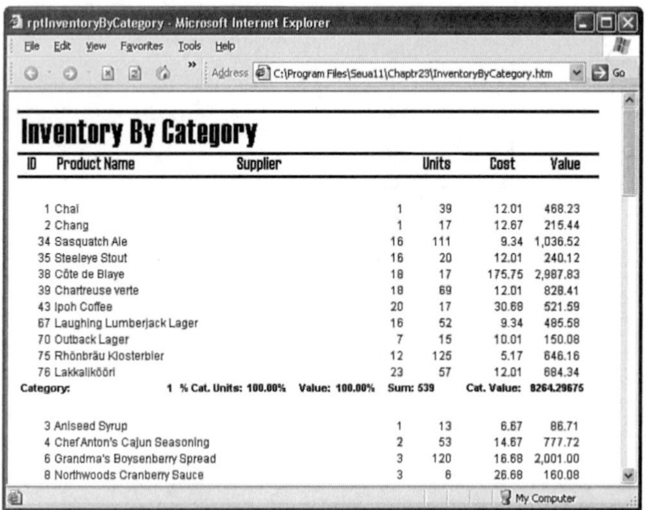

Figure 23.36 Complex reports exported to XML don't format currency data correctly and have problems with calculated field values.

This report, for example, uses Jet's `DLookup` function to return the Category name value; Jet expressions don't work in Web reports. (In Access 2002, `DLookup` and other unsupported functions threw script errors.) You can create a modified version of the report that doesn't include problematic calculated text box values. However, the modified Web report's content is less valuable than the original.

TIP

> When you design reports specifically for export to Web pages, export and test the report's .htm file repeatedly as you add controls. The simpler the expression you use to populate text box controls, the more likely your report page will open without an error.

PROBLEMS WITH LIVE WEB REPORTS

Users receive "access denied" errors when they attempt to open a live Web report on our intranet.

If you specify integrated Windows security for the connection to the project's SQL Server database, which is the recommended choice, users must have an SQL Server login or be a member of a Windows NT/2000+ security group having an SQL Server login for the instance having the source database. You also must grant individual users or groups `db_datareader` permission for the database. It's also a good practice to specify a default database for users and groups; otherwise the default is master. Never grant ordinary users permissions on the master or any other system database.

IN THE REAL WORLD—WHY LEARN XML?

It's unlikely to be evident to casual or even power users of Access 2003 how the new XML features will make their life easier or more productive. This is especially true for users who don't intend to export data or move their Access front ends to an intranet or the Internet. If you fall in that category, this and the remaining chapters of Part VI, "Publishing Data to Intranets and the Internet," might not pique your interest.

If your current or intended career involves databases, however, a full understanding of the roles of XML, XSD, XSLT, and XPath will prove to be a critical skill. The amount of Web content delivered from databases will continue to increase in future, so HTML authors and Web page designers need to be conversant with—if not proficient in—XML and its derivatives. Document-literal XML Web services are XML documents that rely on an embedded schema to describe their payload. Thus, creating and consuming XML Web services requires XML and XSD skills.

Becoming proficient in data-related XML (often called XML Infosets) and, especially, XSLT coding is more challenging than becoming a journeyman VBScript, ECMAScript, VBA, or Visual Basic .NET programmer. Expect a learning curve similar to that for Java or Microsoft's C# language, but not as steep as that for C++. Books are a good starting point, but there's no substitute for working with the complex, real-world data and schemas that many XML texts avoid. Access 2003 is a great source of simple to moderately complex XML documents for gaining an understanding of XML schema language and XSLT coding.

An efficient and satisfying method for learning real-world XSLT is to start with the .xsl presentation files that RPT2HTML4.xsl generates for exported tables and queries. Once you've mastered modifying these relatively simple files, try rolling your own .xsl files to turn attribute-centric SQL Server template queries into formatted HTML tables. (The `xml-sql` namespace expects attribute-centric XML data.) If you're script-enabled, try adopting ReportML's approach to customizing the formatting of HTML data—including adding `<A href=http://www...>...</A>` tags to open pages having other tables that contain related data. Script is a great way to overcome XSLT's lack of variables with values you can change during the transformation process. (XSLT variables are better described as constants.)

The greatest obstacle to the learning-by-writing process is the lack of production-grade debugging tools for XSLT, especially XSLT code that executes scripted functions. Opening .xsl files in IE 6+ only confirms that the XSLT is well formed. Here's hoping that Microsoft or another enterprising software vendor comes up with a combination authoring-debugging tool that's more effective than today's XSLT editors.

CHAPTER 24

Designing and Deploying Data Access Pages

In this chapter

Moving to a New Access Form Model

Data access pages (DAP) are a radical departure from traditional Access database applications. Unlike other Access objects stored in .mdb or .adp files, Access stores DAP in Dynamic HTML (DHTML) files with a standard .htm extension. DAP that appear when you click the Database window's Pages shortcut—such as the sample pages installed by Office 2003's setup program—represent links to the corresponding .htm files. The Review Products and Review Orders page items, for example, are links to the Review Products.htm and Review Orders.htm files in your ...\Office11\Samples folder.

Users view DAP in Internet Explorer (IE) 5+, so they don't need a copy of Access 2003, nor do you need to distribute a runtime version of your DAP. Users can run DAP from a local copy of the required files, which you can send as an email attachment, or from a file or Web server. However, Access 2003 DAP rely on members of the Office Web Components (OWC) 11 for data connection, navigation, and presentation. Users without an Office 2003 license can download the runtime version of OWC 11 from the Microsoft Office Update Web site. The OWC 11 runtime version lets users display data in PivotTable, PivotChart, and Spreadsheet controls, but it freezes their presentation, except PivotTable filters and expand/collapse operations. Clients must have an Office 2003 license to manipulate these three controls; users can't pivot a PivotTable or change the chart type of a PivotChart without an Office 2003 license.

24

NOTE

DAP include a script to detect the Web browser in use on the client PC opening the page. If the client doesn't have IE 5+ installed, the page displays a "Click here to install the latest version of Internet Explorer" message and a link to Microsoft's Internet Explorer site.

If the client PC running Windows 2000 SP3 or Windows XP doesn't have OWC 11 installed, a message opens with a link to download the Web components from the Microsoft Office Update site. (OWC11 won't install under Windows Me, 98, 98SE, or 95.) OWC 11 installs side-by-side with Office 2000's OWC 9 and Office XP's OWC 10, so Office 2000 and XP applications aren't affected by adding OWC 11.

Access 2002 delivered an upgraded page designer for DAP. Like the project designer for SQL Server objects, the page designer is a design-mode tool that automatically generates code. The project designer generates T-SQL statements to create or modify SQL Server objects. The page designer generates DHTML code when you add or modify control objects on the page. Access 2003's page designer differs greatly from Access's Form Design view. The page designer has its own page toolbar and a Toolbox of DHTML-compliant controls, some of which emulate native Access controls for forms and reports. The most notable omissions in the page Toolbox are the Subform/Subreport and Tab Control tools. DAP don't support subforms, subreports, or tab controls because HTML has no direct counterpart of these components.

→ For a list of new and improved DAP features introduced by Access 2002, **see** "Data Access Pages Revisited," **p. 40**.

Combining Report and Form Features in DAP

Many new Access users—and even some seasoned Access experts—have a difficult time getting a grip on the architecture and design methodology of DAP. DAP combine some of the features of forms and reports; for example, DAP make use of report-like grouping methods (called *banding*) to replace subforms. Grouping lets you easily add subtotals and grand totals to a hierarchy of nested sections that contain the bands. Like conventional data-bound Access forms and subforms, each hierarchy level has a default record navigation control. You expand and contract the levels' sections by clicking the boxed plus or minus signs at the left of the page. Figure 24.1 shows a modified version of the sample Review Orders.htm page in IE 6.0.

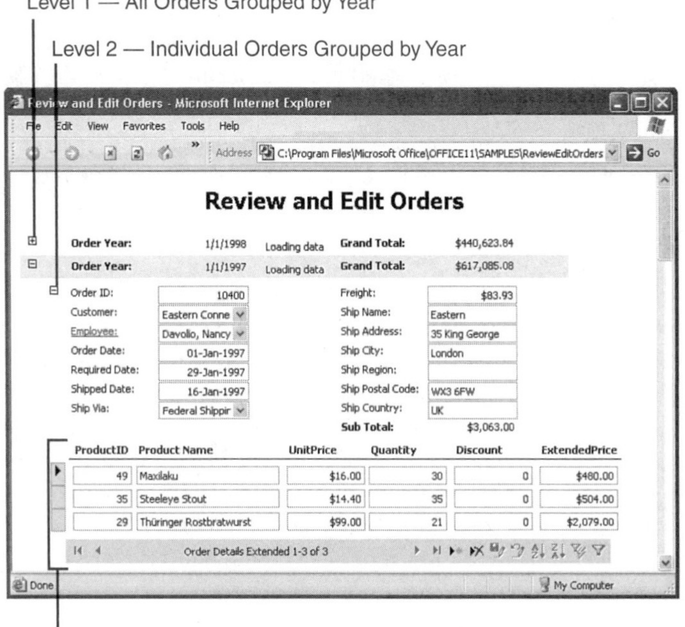

Figure 24.1 This slightly modified version of the Review Orders.htm page has a three-level section grouping hierarchy. The Order Details level shows all line items for the selected order and emulates a datasheet with record selector buttons. Each level has an HTML version of the default record navigation buttons of a form, as well as Save, Undo, Sort Ascending, Sort Descending, Filter by Selection, and Apply Filter buttons.

NOTE

> Generating grand totals for each year's orders and calculating subtotals for each order delay opening Northwind.mdb's Review Orders.htm page. The page must download `Recordsets` for the entire Orders and Order Details tables before displaying the outer section.

The Review and Edit Orders page has a live connection to Northwind.mdb, so you can edit all but two field values shown in the text boxes of Figure 24.1. The OrderID field is read-only because it has the AutoNumber Jet field type, and ProductName is a read-only lookup field from the Products table. If you change a ProductID value and click the Save button of the Order Details Extended navigation control, the Product Name value changes accordingly. Other values, such as UnitPrice and ExtendedPrice, don't change, so editing real order data in this page would be dangerous.

TIP

> To open the sample Review Order page in IE 5+, launch Explorer, navigate to your ...\Office11\Samples folder, and double-click the Review Orders.htm file. The Review and Edit Orders page shown in Figure 24.1 has only minor layout modifications to Northwind.mdb's sample page.

Substituting Multiple Pages for MDI Forms

Access forms are multiple-document interface (MDI) child windows of the main Access parent window. You use command buttons—such as those of the Main Switchboard sample form—to execute `DoCmd.OpenForm` and `DoCmd.Close` methods in VBA *`ButtonName_Click`* event-handling code. Browsers use the single-document interface (SDI) model. HTML frames emulate some MDI features, but the page designer doesn't support frame set editing. You can't open a page with a frame set in Page Design view, but you can use FrontPage 2003 to design the frame set to display the pages. Access 2003 supports embedded frames (<IFRAME> elements) in pages.

DAP use hyperlinks or command buttons to navigate within applications that require multiple pages. The Employee: label of the Review Orders.htm page is formatted as a hyperlink when you open the page in IE 5+, but it doesn't have a `<A href="http://www.`*`wherever`*`.com"></A>` HTML anchor tag pair. Instead, a VBScript event handler for the `onclick` event of the `EmployeeID1` label applies the `window.showModalDialog` method to open the Employees.htm page, as illustrated by Figure 24.2. The main page creates a cookie to pass the EmployeeID filter value (2) from the lookup list to the Employees.htm page, which displays the Employees record for Nancy Davolio. Opening the Employees.htm file with the VBScript event handler instead of a URL eliminates the need to deploy the pages to your Web server to enable navigation by hyperlinks.

Figure 24.2 Clicking the hyperlink-formatted Employee: label opens the Employees.htm page as a modal Web Page Dialog, which emulates an Access pop-up form. Code in the main page creates a cookie to pass the EmployeeID value as a filter on the dialog's Employees `Recordset`.

The navigation controls of the Employees Web Page Dialog illustrate substitution of labels for the page's default record navigation buttons. You also can substitute buttons or custom graphic images.

NOTE

Clicking the Employee label opens the Employees page in either Access Page view or IE. VBScript code in the Review Orders page detects whether the page is open in Page view or in IE 5+. The code applies the blue color and underline attributes to the label text only if you open the page in IE 5+.

CONNECTING TO THE BACK-END DATABASE

By default, DAP use DHTML Data Binding to ActiveX Data Object (ADO) `Recordsets`, which the page automatically generates from server-based Jet or SQL Server tables or queries. The page designer creates a connection string based on current Jet database for an .mdb file or the SQL Server database for the project's .adp file. Alternatively, you can establish the database connection with an Office Data Connector (.odc) file. The page either links to or embeds the contents of the .odc file in an `<OBJECT>.../<OBJECT>` declaration within the `<HEAD>` element to serve as the connection string for the Microsoft Office Data Source Control (MSODSC), a member of OWC 11. MSODSC makes the connection to the database that you specify in the .odc file when you open the page in IE 5+ or Access Page view. DAP also support Office 2000 Uniform Data Locator (.udl) files for backward compatibility.

→ To review how to create an .odc file, **see** "Linking a Jet 4.0 Database," **p. 842**.

CAUTION

Use SQL Server databases with integrated Windows security as the data source for production DAP on your intranet. Users of your pages can display the source code of your pages by choosing View, Source in IE. The default connection string for Jet database files and—if you use SQL Server security—SQL Server databases includes the login ID and password in plain text. You can prevent the password from appearing if you clear the Allow Saving Password check box in the Data Link Properties' Connection page. In this case, viewing the page requires entering the password for the login ID that you specify.

Linking an .odc file to provide the data source lets you specify a common connection for all pages that use the data .mdb file or SQL Server database. The location and name of the file, however, are visible in the page's source code. If users can gain access to the .odc file that contains a password, database security is compromised.

Binding to server-side data sources requires an active database connection to each client. DAP are stateful unless you write script to use a disconnected `Recordset`. The general rule is to avoid stateful intranet and Internet applications, which consume Web and database server resources. Minimizing the number of concurrent active connections is especially important with MSDE, which starts closing the throttle when more than five batch operations occur simultaneously.

→ For additional background on the statefulness issue, **see** "Making the Transition to Stateless Front-Ends," **p. 949**.

→ To learn more about disconnected `Recordsets`, **see** "Taking Advantage of Disconnected `Recordsets`," **p. 1312**.

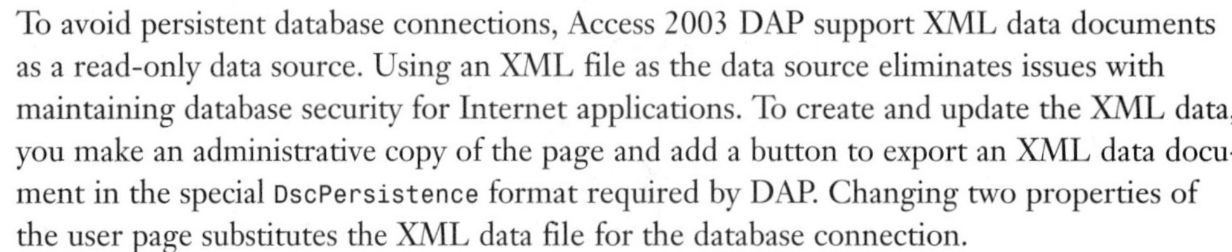

To avoid persistent database connections, Access 2003 DAP support XML data documents as a read-only data source. Using an XML file as the data source eliminates issues with maintaining database security for Internet applications. To create and update the XML data, you make an administrative copy of the page and add a button to export an XML data document in the special `DscPersistence` format required by DAP. Changing two properties of the user page substitutes the XML data file for the database connection.

UNDERSTANDING ACCESS'S DYNAMIC HTML IMPLEMENTATION

If you're new to authoring dynamic Web pages, you first must grasp the terminology used by DAP. Internet-related terminology is replete with three- to five-letter acronyms (TLA and 5LA) that belie the complexity of the underlying technology. If you're conversant with DHTML basics, skip to the "Getting Acquainted with Page and Page Design Views" section. If you've worked with DAP in Access 2000 or 2002, you can move ahead to the "Modifying the Design of AutoPage DAP" section.

Dynamic HTML doesn't currently have the status of an Internet standard, so DHTML implementations vary among browser publishers and versions. In this book, an Internet standard is defined as a World Wide Web Consortium (W3C) Recommendation or an Internet Engineering Task Force (IETF) Request for Comment (RFC). Most of today's W3C and IETF standards represent consensus among the groups' voting members—vendors plus a few governments and universities—not the Internet community as a whole.

TECHNOLOGIES SUPPORTING DHTML AND DAP

The following is a brief list of the W3C Internet standards and proprietary Microsoft technologies that provide the foundation for Microsoft's implementation of DHTML and its use of DAP:

- **Document Object Model (DOM) 2.0**— a W3C recommendation adopted on November 13, 2000. The complete set of recommendations is available at `http://www.w3.org/DOM/`. DOM consists of a Core component (DOM Core) that supports Extensible Markup Language and provides the underpinnings for DOM's HTML component (DOM HTML). Other components include Views, Style, Events, Traversal-Range, and HTML; the HTML component was a working draft when this book was written. Microsoft's "Dynamic HTML Overview" article, at `http://msdn.microsoft.com/workshop/author/dhtml/dhtmlovw.asp` offers a brief introduction to the relationship between DOM and DHTML.

- **Extensible Markup Language (XML) 1.0**—a W3C Recommendation dated February 1998. As mentioned earlier, DAP use XML for embedding database connection strings and as a read-only data source. You also can embed XML data in DAP as an *XML data island*.

➔ For more information on XML 1.0, **see** " Gaining an XML Vocabulary," **p. 944**.

- **Cascading Style Sheets (CSS)**—a W3C standard for specifying the onscreen presentation and printed format of HTML documents without the need to invent new HTML formatting tags. CSS rules let you specify the exact location of elements, such as blocks of text or images, as well as the color, type family, and font of text. The W3C adopted the CSS, Level 2 (CSS2), Recommendation in May 1998; you can read the complete W3C Recommendation at `http://www.w3.org/TR/REC-CSS2/`. DHTML lets you change CSS rules on the fly to specify the properties of an object in response to events, such as passing the mouse pointer over a headline or clicking a block of text. IE 5+ and Netscape 6+ support CSS Level 1 to a varying extent. Microsoft stated objective for IE 6.0 is to support "all the properties, values, and features in the CSS, Level 1 (CSS1) specification."
- **DHTML Behaviors**—Microsoft's approach to separating scripting code from HTML content. DHTML Behaviors let you store scripting code in HTML Component (.htc) files. Separating script from HTML content makes the page source code easier to read and lets you reuse standard event-handling procedures, such as highlighting text. Users must have IE 5+ installed to enable DHTML Behaviors on client PCs. DAP let you specify an .htc file as the value of the `Behavior` property of page objects.
- **OLE DB and ActiveX Data Objects (ADO) 2.1+**—components that provide the underlying database connectivity for DHTML data binding and DAP. The Office 2003 setup program installs ADO 2.7. Chapter 30, "Understanding Universal Data Access, OLE DB, and ADO," explains these two related data access technologies.

Fortunately, you don't need to fully understand the object models and syntax of the preceding technologies or possess HTML design skill to generate DAP with Access 2003. To modify the behavior or extend the usefulness of DAP, however, you must be at least conversant with VBScript or ECMAScript/JScript code.

NOTE

> The examples in this and the next chapter use VBScript because of its similarity to VBA, which is the subject of Chapter 27, "Learning Visual Basic for Applications." VBScript is a subset of VBA, and many of the basic programming techniques described in Chapter 27 also apply to VBScript. Among commercial browsers, only IE supports VBScript. IE 5+ is required to create and display DAP, so the use of VBScript in place of the more widely supported ECMAScript isn't an issue in this case.

24

DOM HTML AND DHTML

DOM HTML describes elements of conventional HTML Web pages as a collection of predefined hierarchical objects based on W3C-standard HTML tags. Listing 24.1 shows the HTML source for a simple three-column, three-row table with row-column (RnCn) text in each cell.

LISTING 24.1 HTML SOURCE FOR A THREE-COLUMN, THREE-ROW TABLE

```
<html>
<head>
<title>New Page 1</title>
</head>

<body>
<table border="1" width="100%">
  <tr>
    <td width="33%">R1C1</td>
    <td width="33%">R1C2</td>
    <td width="34%">R1C3</td>
  </tr>
  <tr>
    <td width="33%">R2C1</td>
    <td width="33%">R2C2</td>
    <td width="34%">R2C3</td>
  </tr>
  <tr>
    <td width="33%">R3C1</td>
    <td width="33%">R3C2</td>
    <td width="34%">R3C4</td>
  </tr>
</table>
</body>
</html>
```

Figure 24.3 illustrates the object hierarchy of the HTML elements defined by Listing 24.1. Like the master-child relationships of forms and subforms, DOM defines parent-child(ren) relationships between objects and properties, which can also be collections of objects. The <HTML> tag defines the document parent object; the document object has a child <HEAD> element, which contains <META> and <TITLE> children; and a <BODY> element (body object), which contains all other elements of the page. The <TABLE> element contains a collection of <TR> row elements, each of which contains a <TD> data or column collection. Microsoft's DOM for the HTML that creates pages is much more complex than this example.

NOTE

> Microsoft's DHTML documentation and this chapter use the terms "element" (HTML tag pair) and "object" interchangeably.

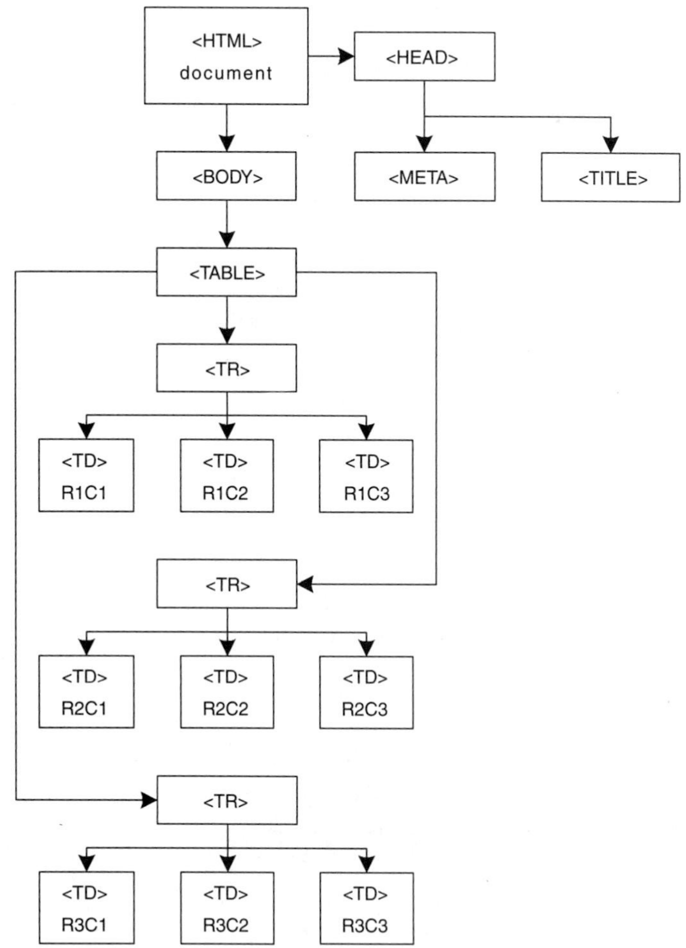

Figure 24.3 This diagram depicts the DOM object model for the table created by the HTML code of Listing 24.1.

DOM HTML also defines an event model for objects. The event model lets Web page authors specify what occurs when a page loads in your browser or when you click an element. Event-handling code, written in a scripting language, specifies the action taken when an event occurs. An object must have a unique `Id` property value, similar to the `Name` property of Access controls, to connect event-handling code to the object.

Getting Acquainted with Page and Page Design Views

Northwind.mdb includes a few sample .htm files to demonstrate simple DAP design techniques. With Northwind.mdb open, click the Database window's Pages shortcut to display the list of sample pages. Double-click the page name in the Database window's list to open a page in Page view. Page view uses IE 5+'s XML parser and HTML engine to display the page in a window similar to that for displaying conventional Access forms. The Page View menu substitutes for the Form View menu when you open a DAP.

TIP

> Clients require IE 5.5+ to take advantage of some of the features of Access 2003 DAP, such as multiselecting controls in Page Design view. For maximum security, IE 6+ is recommended for all DAP clients. Users can download the latest version of IE from the Internet Explorer page (`http://www.microsoft.com/windows/ie/`). Version 6.0 SP1 was current when this book was written.

The Review Products Page

The majority of DAP that you design probably will be read-only pages for displaying summary data, detail data, or both. Northwind.mdb's simplest read-only sample page is Review Products, shown in Page view in Figure 24.4, which displays records of the Products table grouped by the first letter of the product name. The black arrows for expanding and collapsing individual bands—called *section siblings*—are one of six symbols that you can choose in the properties window for the Expand/Collapse object (`MsoExpandCollapse`, which is one of OWC 11's ActiveX controls).

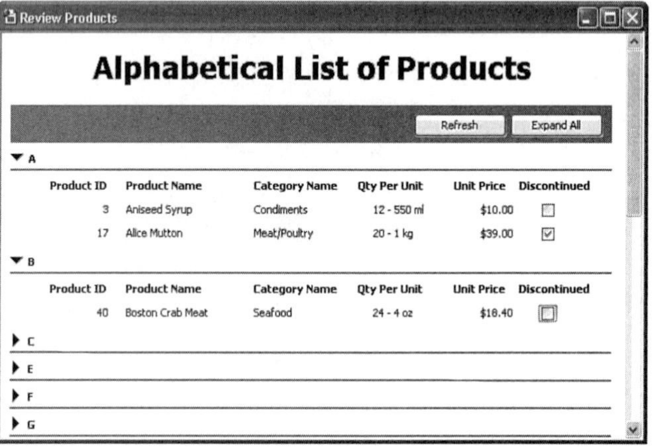

Figure 24.4 The Review Products page is an expandable list of products grouped alphabetically by the ProductName field of the Products table. Black arrows replace the standard Access expand/collapse icons (boxes with +/– symbols).

With the page in normal (not maximized) view, right-click the page's title bar, choose Web Page Preview to open Review Products.htm in IE. Click the Expand All button to execute VBScript code that expands each section sibling to display a list of all Northwind products (see Figure 24.5). The expanded page emulates a conventional Access report that users can print. Pages designed for viewing in a browser, however, aren't optimized for printing. The Review Products page has an excessive amount of vertical whitespace between sibling sections and product data. If you want to generate a page for printing, the better approach is to design an Access report and save it as a page. Chapter 25, "Converting Access Objects to Data Access Pages," explains how to take advantage of Access 2003's Save as Data Access Page feature.

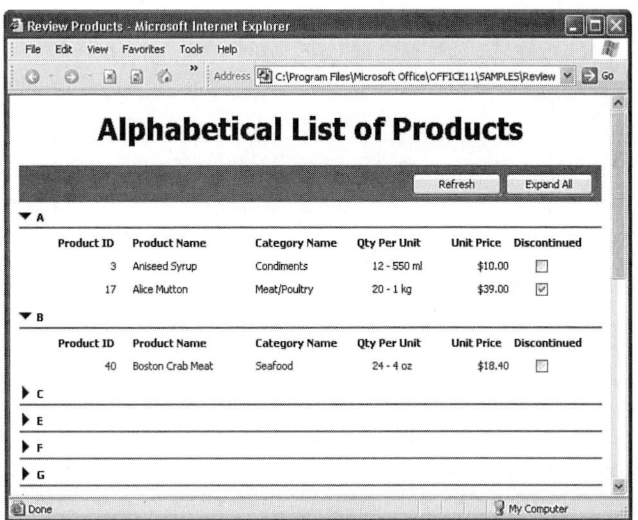

Figure 24.5 The Review Products page opened in IE 6.0+ is identical to Access's Page view. Page view uses IE's rendering engine (often called Trident, its beta name) to execute the DHTML code that generates the page. When you click Expand All, VBScript code changes the button's caption to Collapse All.

Choose View, Source in IE to open Notepad with a copy of the DHTML and XML code, and turn on Word Wrap (see Figure 24.6). The five `xmlns:...` lines in the `<HTML...` tag define Office XML namespaces used by DAP; `xmlns:dt...` is the namespace for standard field data types. Code in the `<OBJECT` tag specifies the `id` of the Data Source Control as `MSODSC` and the Globally Unique Identifier (GUID) of the control in the Registry as its `ClassID` value. Attribute/value pairs in the `<a:ConnectionString>` element fully define the Jet OLE DB provider's connection to the Northwind.mdb database. The content of the `<a:ConnectionString>...</a:ConnectionString>` element is identical to that of an .odc file for a local connection to Northwind.mdb. As mentioned earlier in the chapter, the connection string displays the `User ID` (the default is `Admin` for Jet) and, if the database is secure, the user `Password` or `Database Password` in clear text.

NOTE

> Escaped characters in the XML code make reading the connection string difficult. `
` represents carriage-return/line-feed pairs for formatting; `""` represents empty double-quotes (`""`, `""` in HTML).

```
<!DOCTYPE HTML PUBLIC "-//W3C//DTD HTML 4.0 Transitional//EN">
<HTML xmlns="http://www.w3.org/TR/REC-html40" xmlns:o =
"urn:schemas-microsoft-com:office:office" xmlns:x =
"urn:schemas-microsoft-com:office:excel" xmlns:a =
"urn:schemas-microsoft-com:office:access" xmlns:dt =
"uuid:C2F41010-65B3-11d1-A29F-00AA00C14882"><HEAD><TITLE>Review
Products</TITLE><LINK
href="Review%20Products_files/filelist.xml" type=text/xml rel=File-List>
<META content=2230 name=Version>
<META content=1033 name="Language Code">
<META content=Access.Application name=ProgId>
<META name=VBSForEventHandlers VALUE="TRUE">
<META http-equiv=Content-Type content="text/html; charset=windows-1252">
<META content=11.00.0000 name=DesignerVersion>
<META content="HTML 4.0" name=vs_targetSchema>
<OBJECT id=MSODSC tabIndex=-1
classid=CLSID:0002E55B-0000-0000-C000-000000000046><PARAM NAME="XMLData"
VALUE="<xml
xmlns:a=&quot;urn:schemas-microsoft-com:office:access&quot;>&#13;&#10;
<a:DataSourceControl>&#13;&#10;  <a:OWCVersion>11.0.0.4523
</a:OWCVersion>&#13;&#10;
<a:ConnectionString>Provider=Microsoft.Jet.OLEDB.4.0;User ID=Admin;Data
Source=C:\Program Files\Microsoft
Office\Office11\Samples\Northwind.mdb;Mode=Share Deny None;Extended
Properties=&amp;quot;&amp;quot;;Persist Security Info=False;Jet OLEDB:System
database=&amp;quot;&amp;quot;;Jet OLEDB:Registry Path=&amp;quot;&amp;quot;;Jet
OLEDB:Database Password=&amp;quot;&amp;quot;;Jet OLEDB:Engine Type=0;Jet
OLEDB:Database Locking Mode=1;Jet OLEDB:Global Partial Bulk Ops=2;Jet
OLEDB:Global Bulk Transactions=1;Jet OLEDB:New Database
Password=&amp;quot;&amp;quot;;Jet OLEDB:Create System Database=False;Jet
OLEDB:Encrypt Database=False;Jet OLEDB:Don't Copy Locale on Compact=False;Jet
OLEDB:Compact Without Replica Repair=False;Jet
OLEDB:SFP=False</a:ConnectionString>&#13;&#10;
<a:MaxRecords>10000</a:MaxRecords>&#13;&#10;  <a:GridX>24</a:GridX>&#13;&#10;
```

Figure 24.6
The <HEAD> section of the DHTML code for DAP sets up the Data Source Control (MSODC) to connect to the specified Jet or SQL Server database. The highlighted `<OBJECT...` line is the start of the XML code to establish the database connection.

It's clear from the complexity of the XML source code shown in Figure 24.6 that few, if any, Access users or developers will attempt to edit the XML elements in Notepad or any other HTML editor. The page designer automatically generates the underlying XML and HTML source code when you open a new page, and it alters the code as you add or modify objects in Page Design view. When you edit or move an object, the DAP Designer alters the HTML code within the division (`<DIV>...</DIV>`) that contains the object. (`<DIV>` elements are near the end of the file.) DAP use CSS to fix the relative position of each visible object on the page. The position reference point is the upper-left corner of the section in which the object appears.

VBScript for the `onclick` event of the page's two command buttons appears immediately below the end (`</STYLE>`) of the CSS style definitions for standard page objects, including a Navigation control that's not present on this page. Clicking the `cmdRefresh` button applies the `Requery` method to the first and only data page (`DataPages.Item(0)`) of the Data Source Control. The second VBScript block expands or contracts the section siblings, depending on their state, which is stored in the caption (`innerText` property) of the `cmdExpandCollapse` button (see Figure 24.7).

Page Design View

As mentioned early in the chapter, Page Design view differs dramatically from Form Design view. To explore the new and upgraded features of the page designer, do this:

1. Open Review Products or any other Northwind.mdb sample page in Page Design view.

2. Click the Field List button to open the Field List, if it doesn't open by default. The Field List ordinarily docks to the right edge of the designer's window and resembles a task pane (see Figure 24.8). Unlike the task pane, you can undock the Field List.

Figure 24.7
This VBScript code expands or collapses all sections of the Review Products page. The state of the page is maintained by the value of the `innerText` property of the `cmdExpandCollapse` button.

```
<SCRIPT language=vbscript event=onclick for=cmdExpandCollapse>
<!--
dim sect, dap, i
dim vButton
vButton = document.all.cmdExpandCollapse.innerText
if (vButton = "Expand All") then
                cmdExpandCollapse.innerText = "Collapse All"
                set dap=msodsc.datapages(0)
                set sect=dap.firstsection
                while not sect is nothing
                    If not sect.isexpanded and sect.type = 2 then
                        sect.expand
                    end if
                    set sect=sect.nextsibling
                Wend

        elseif (vButton = "Collapse All") then
                cmdExpandCollapse.innerText = "Expand All"
                set dap=msodsc.datapages(0)
                set sect=dap.firstsection
                while not sect is nothing
                    If sect.isexpanded and sect.type = 2 then
                        sect.collapse
                    end if
                    set sect=sect.nextsibling
                Wend
        else
        msgbox "The button text is not valid."
end if

-->
</SCRIPT>
```


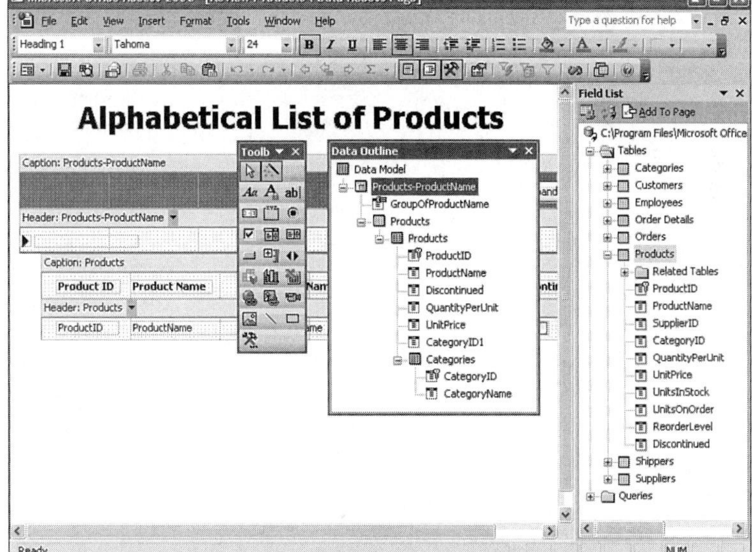

Figure 24.8
The Review Products page is open in Page Design view with the page Toolbox, Field List, and Data Outline windows visible.

NOTE

> The Field List has nodes for every table and query of the source database. Expanding a table node reveals the table's fields; if the table has predefined relationships with other tables, the node has a Related Tables subnode.

3. Click the Data Outline button to open the Data Outline floating window. The Data Outline windows displays the hierarchical structure of the page's sections and control objects.

THE PAGE DESIGN TOOLBAR

The Page Design view toolbar has many buttons in common with the Form Design view toolbar. The most welcome addition for Access 2000 page designers are the added Undo and Redo buttons, which have a drop-down list that lets you undo or redo multiple changes. Table 24.1 describes the Page Design toolbar buttons that don't have a counterpart in the Form Design toolbar. Table 24.1 also includes a menu choice that isn't present in Form Design view. Single-menu commands identified by an asterisk (*) are choices of the form's context menu.

TABLE 24.1 PAGE DESIGN VIEW TOOLBAR BUTTONS AND A MENU COMMAND THAT AREN'T PRESENT IN FORM DESIGN VIEW

	Name	Menu Command	Description
	Email	File, Send To	Sends a copy of the page embedded in the text of a message or as an attachment, or sends a link to the page on a server share.
	Promote	Promote*	Moves the selected section higher in the section hierarchy.
	Group by Table	Group by Table*	Lets you group by the primary key of the table on the one side of a one-to-many relationship. Group by Table works with pages that have two or more related tables or queries with fields from multiple tables.
	Demote	Demote*	Moves the selected section lower in the section hierarchy.
	AutoSum	None	Lets you select from SQL aggregate functions to add a control to display the sum, average, minimum, maximum, count, or standard deviation of numeric values within a section or group of sections.
	Field List	View, Field List	Opens the Field List.
	Data Outline	View, Data Outline	Opens the Data Outline windows that display the hierarchical data model of the page.

	Name	Menu Command	Description
	Microsoft Script Editor	View, HTML Source	Opens the Microsoft Script Editor and displays the DHTML code of the form.
	None	Format, Theme	Opens the Theme dialog, from which you can select a style sheet from one of the 65 designs installed by Office 2003 setup or available from the distribution CD-ROM.

The Page Toolbox

The Page Toolbox has 24 buttons; 12 of the buttons correspond to those of the Form/Report Toolbox. The Label, Text Box, Option Group, Check Box, Dropdown List, List Box, Image, Line, and Rectangle buttons generate the DHTML version of native Access controls. The Select Objects, Control Wizards, and More Controls buttons perform identical functions to the corresponding button in the Form/Report Toolbox. Table 24.2 describes the Toolbox buttons specific to DAP.

Table 24.2 Page Toolbox Buttons That Don't Have a Counterpart in the Form Toolbox

	Name	Description
	Bound Span	Adds a `<SPAN>` element with a label and text box
	Scrolling Text	Adds a DHTML multiline text box (`marquee`) to the page
	Expand	Adds an Expand/Collapse button to a section
	Record Navigation	Adds the standard record navigation bar to a section
	Office PivotTable	Adds an OWC PivotTable control to the page
	Office Chart	Adds an OWC PivotChart control to the page
	Office Spreadsheet	Adds an OWC Spreadsheet control to the page
	Hyperlink	Opens the Insert Hyperlink dialog to add a file-based or conventional navigational hyperlink

continues

TABLE 24.2 CONTINUED

	Name	Description
	Image Hyperlink	Opens the Insert Picture dialog in which to select a graphic file, followed by the Insert Hyperlink dialog to specify the target page
	Movie	Opens the Insert Video dialog in which you can select an .avi, .mov, .mpg, .mpg, or .asf file to run in a simplified version of the Windows Media Player installed on the client

The process of adding Toolbox controls to the page is the same as that for forms and reports. You also can drag table, query, or field nodes from the Field List to the section to create bound objects. When you drag a table or query node to the section, the Layout Wizard dialog opens to enable selection of the page layout or the OWC control to display the data.

24

FIELD LIST BUTTONS

The Field List has the three buttons described in Table 24.3.

TABLE 24.3 BUTTONS ON THE FIELD LIST TOOLBAR

	Name	Description
	Page Connection Properties	Opens the Data Link Properties dialog to change database connection settings
	Refresh Field List	Queries the database and updates the field list
	Add to Page	Lets you make multiple selections in the Field List and add the objects to the page section in a single operation

THE MICROSOFT SCRIPT EDITOR

Unlike IE, which uses Notepad to display HTML source code, the designer uses the Microsoft Script Editor (formerly HTML Source Editor) derived from that of Visual Studio 6.0. Clicking the Microsoft Script Editor button or choosing View, HTML Source opens the Script Editor, if you installed it during the Office 2003 setup process. Otherwise, a message box appears that asks if you want to install it. The Script Editor defaults to a color-coded HTML source window with docked Document Outline and Project Explorer windows (see Figure 24.9). The Project Explorer refers only to the currently active page, so close it to expand the area of the source window.

Many of the features of the Script Editor don't apply to DAP, so most of the default toolbar buttons are disabled. The Script Editor has its own Toolbox, which is useful only for creating HTML pages from scratch. Online help topics for the Script Editor aren't very useful for working with DAP, but the HTML Reference Help and VBScript Help topics provide a wealth of information on the DHTML object model and scripting. Most of the help topics are links to pages on the Microsoft Developer Network (MSDN) Web Workshop site.

CAUTION

> Don't make any changes in the Script Editor to the code created by the page designer. For DAP, the Script Editor is intended for adding or editing VBScript or JScript–Microsoft's implementation of ECMAScript–only. If you change the page designer code, your page is likely to display errors or fail to open in Page or Page Design view. If you make an accidental change to page-designer code, close the Script Editor and don't save the changes.

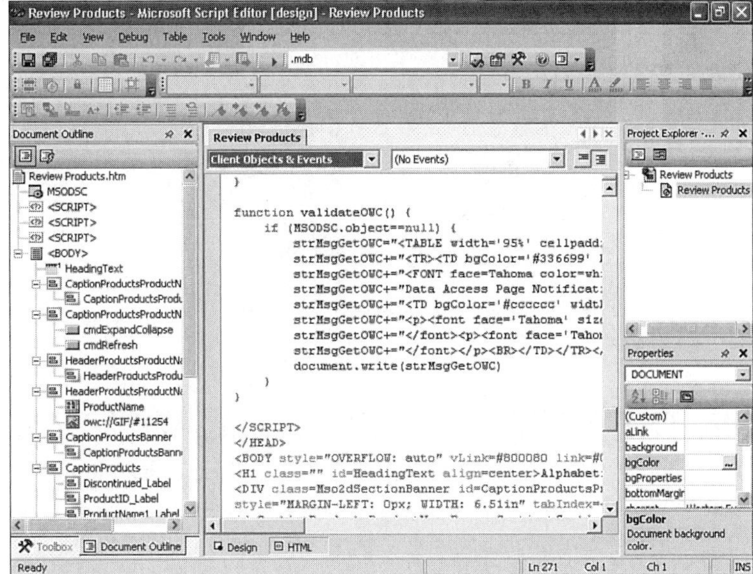

Figure 24.9
All HTML-enabled Office 2003 applications use the Microsoft Script Editor, which is shown here with Word Wrap off and the Document Outline and Project Explorer windows open.

The following is a list of three of the Script Editor features that are useful when working with DAP:

- Limit the editor to displaying script by choosing View, Show Script Only, or by clicking the Script Only View button on the editor's toolbar. Script Only view prevents you from making inadvertent changes to page-designer code and speeds up fixing your scripts.
- Display a Document Outline window by choosing View, Other Windows, Document Outline or by pressing Ctrl+Alt+T. This window has a node for every object in your page; expanding a node displays a list of the events fired by the object. Double-clicking an event item inserts a VBScript event-handler stub for the event.
- Open an Object Member list by typing the `id` of an object—such as `MSODSC`—and the object separator (a period). The Object Member list displays all properties and methods of the object. Double-clicking a member adds the name at the cursor location.

Figure 24.10 shows the Script Editor in Script Only view with an event-handling stub for the `MSODSC` control's `Current` event and the Object Member list for the `MSODSC` object. The `MSODSC.Current` event corresponds to the On Current event of a bound Access form.

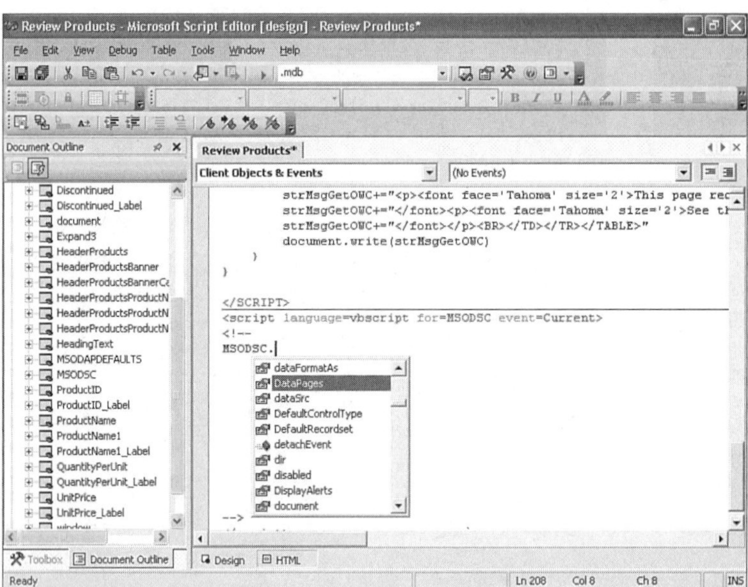

Figure 24.10 The Script Editor page is configured to display the document outline with the `MSODSC` control node expanded to display the control's event repertoire. The control's events duplicate those for a bound Access form and have additional events that apply only to pages.

USING THE PAGE WIZARD TO CREATE SIMPLE DAP

The Page Wizard is the quickest route to creating DAP from multiple related tables. The Page Wizard lets you specify individual table fields for multiple record groupings. In this case, you group products by their category.

To generate a page to display related records from the Categories, Products, and Suppliers tables, do the following:

1. With the Pages shortcut selected in the Database window for Northwind.mdb, double-click the "Create Data Access Page by Using Wizard" shortcut to open the first Page Wizard dialog.
2. In the Tables/Queries list, select Table: Categories, and then double-click CategoryName in the Available Fields list to add the field to the Selected Fields list.
3. Repeat step 2, adding the ProductID, ProductName, and UnitPrice fields of the Products table, and the CompanyName field of the Suppliers table to the Selected Fields list (see Figure 24.11).
4. Click Next to open the second Wizard dialog for grouping levels. Grouping levels in DAP are similar to those for Access reports. Select the CategoryName field on which to group Products records (see Figure 24.12), and click Next to open the third Wizard dialog.

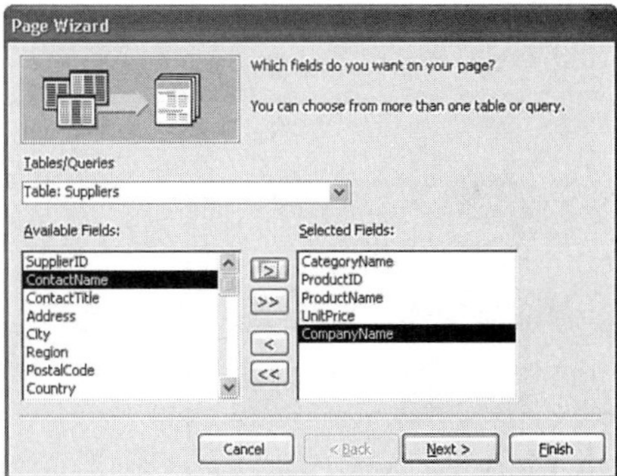

Figure 24.11 Add the CategoryName, ProductID, ProductName, UnitPrice, and CompanyName fields from the Categories, Products, and Suppliers tables in the first Page Wizard dialog.

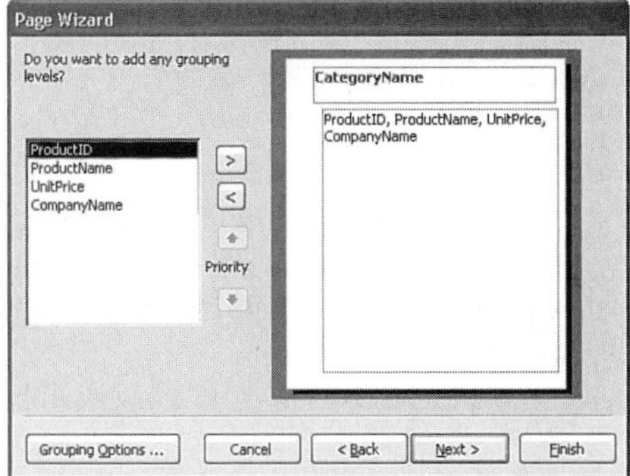

Figure 24.12 The Page Wizard's grouping dialog is identical to the Report Wizard's second dialog. This report uses the CategoryName field to group product records.

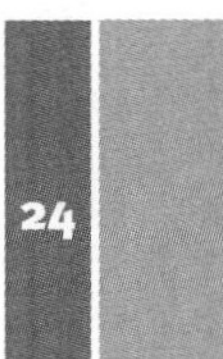

5. Open the first sort order drop-down list and select ProductName for an alphabetic sort on the names of products within the selected category (see Figure 24.13). Click Next to open the final Wizard dialog.

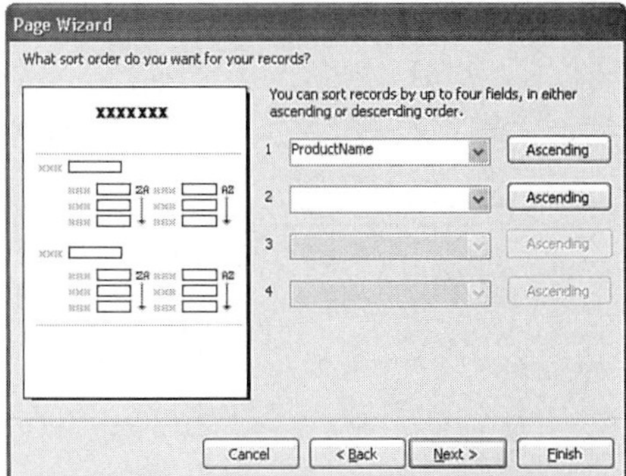

Figure 24.13 The third Page Wizard dialog duplicates the Report Wizard's sorting dialog.

6. Type an appropriate title, such as **Products and Suppliers by Category**, in the text box. Accept the default Modify the Page's Design option, and mark the check box titled Do You Want to Apply a Theme to Your Page? (see Figure 24.14).

Figure 24.14 The last Page Wizard offers the option to apply a standard theme to your page.

TIP

If you marked Microsoft Office, Office Tools, Themes as Not Available when installing Office 2003, clear the Do You Want to Apply a Theme to Your Page? check box. You receive a non-fatal error message if the Wizard can't find themes on your fixed disk or load them from the CD-ROM.

7. Click Finish to initiate creation of the page. After a few seconds of disk activity, the Theme dialog appears with the default Straight Edge item selected. Choose Profile (see Figure 24.15) or another theme that you like better.

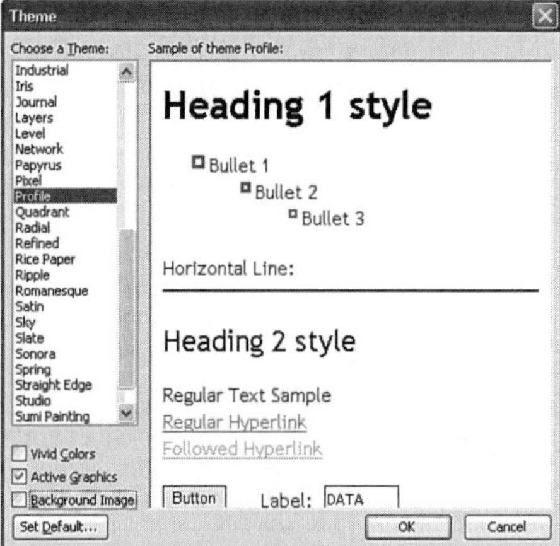

Figure 24.15 Profile is one of many themes that Office 2003 installs by default. The Background Image check box is cleared to remove the patterned background.

NOTE

> Profile without a background is one of the more conservative themes in the list; most themes in the Choose a Theme list are additional themes that load on first use. You can make Profile the theme for successive pages by clicking Set Default and clicking Yes to close the Set Default Themes message box.
>
> Themes are a set of CSS with predefined fonts and background graphics. Marking the Active Graphics check box enables bullet images to change when clicked. Marking the Vivid Colors check box changes the heading and button colors from black to red. Clearing the Background Image check box removes the background bit map.

8. Click OK to close the Theme dialog and display your new page in Design view.
9. Replace Click Here and Type Title Text line with the title that you chose in step 6 (see Figure 24.16).

Figure 24.16 You must add the page title manually to complete the initial design. The space between the title and the first header holds an empty text block.

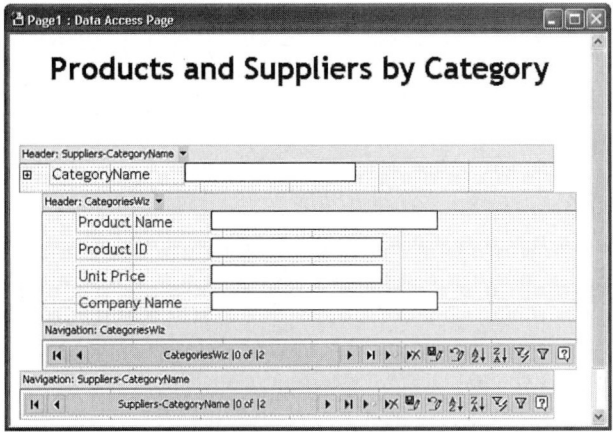

10. Click the Page View button to execute the page's source code and emulate its appearance in IE 5.5. Click the Expand button to display the first record of the Beverages category (see Figure 24.17).

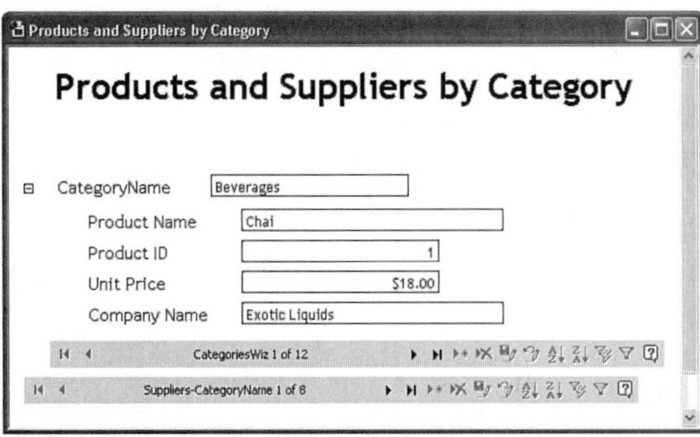

Figure 24.17 The plain-vanilla, columnar pages that the Wizard creates won't win any graphic design awards. The CategoriesWiz and Suppliers–CategoryName <SPAN> elements in the navigation controls could use a bit of improvement also.

11. Save the page with an appropriate name, such as **ProductsAndSuppliersByCategory**.htm, in your working or ...\Office\Samples folder.

> **NOTE**
>
> If you receive "A link to this Data Access Page could not be created because the database cannot be exclusively locked" error, close any other DAP open in IE or Notepad, and then save the page.

12. Acknowledge the warning message about the use of absolute paths for page files (see Figure 24.18).

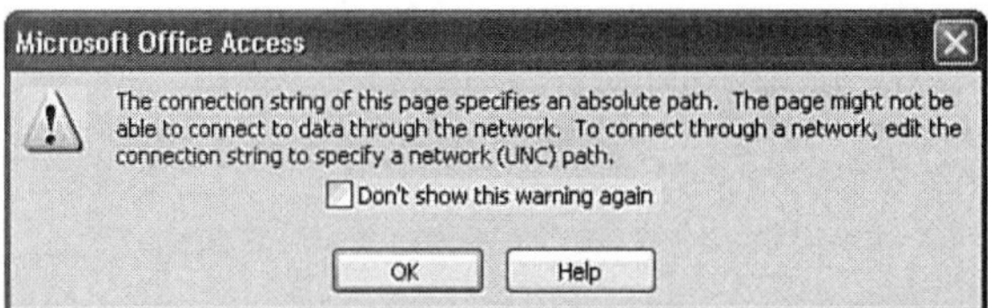

Figure 24.18
This warning message appears when you save a page with a connection to a Jet .mdb file in your working folder.

MAKING DAP UPDATABLE

By default, DAP aren't updatable. To make the innermost section updatable, you must specify the table that supplies the section's data as the UniqueTable property value. Change to Design view, right-click inside the CategoriesWiz section, and choose Section Properties to open the Section: HeaderCategoriesWiz properties dialog. Click the Data tab and select Products from the UniqueTables list (see Figure 24.19).

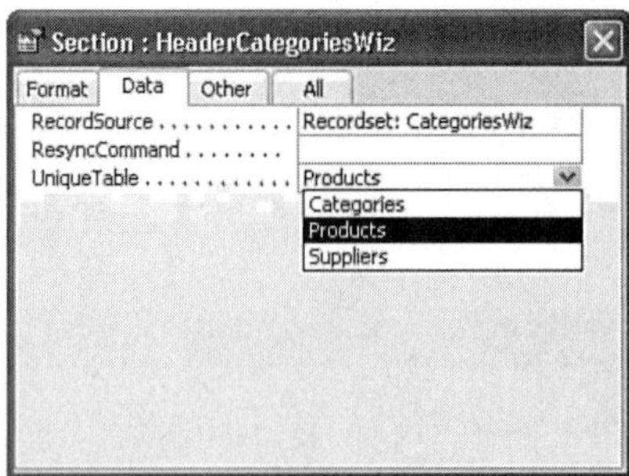

Figure 24.19
Making fields in the Products table updatable requires specifying Products as the value of the UniqueTable property.

TIP

> Be judicious when enabling updates with DAP. Anyone with a copy of the page that has the UniqueTables property value set can wreak havoc on a back-end Jet database. The default connection string uses your Admin account or the account you created in the Admins group for a secure database. Secure your Jet back-end or use SQL Server tables with integrated Windows authentication for any page you want to make updatable by authorized users.

EXPLORING CSS FILES IN THE PAGE'S SUBFOLDER

When you save DAP that have themes applied, Access creates a subfolder named *PageName*_files—ProductsAndSuppliersByCategory_files, for this example—that stores the theme style sheets (.css files), the graphics files (.gif or .jpg files), and a list of the files (filelist.xml) for the page (see Figure 24.20). Double-clicking filelist.xml displays its text in IE 5.5 (see Figure 24.21).

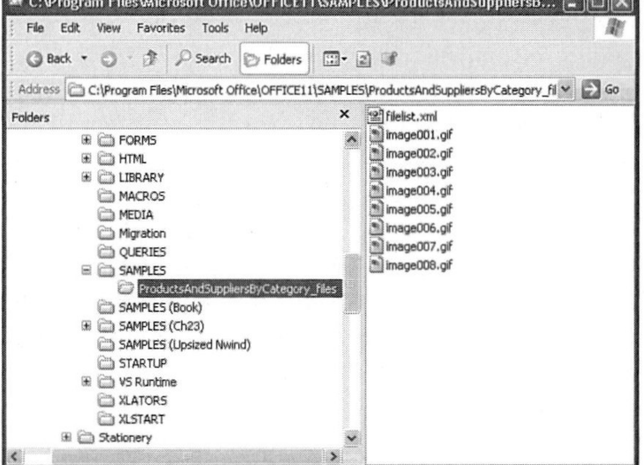

Figure 24.20
The *PageName*_files subfolder stores the XML file list, CSS files, and .gif images for the page theme that you select. If you select (No Theme) in the Theme dialog's Choose a Theme list, Access doesn't create the subfolder.

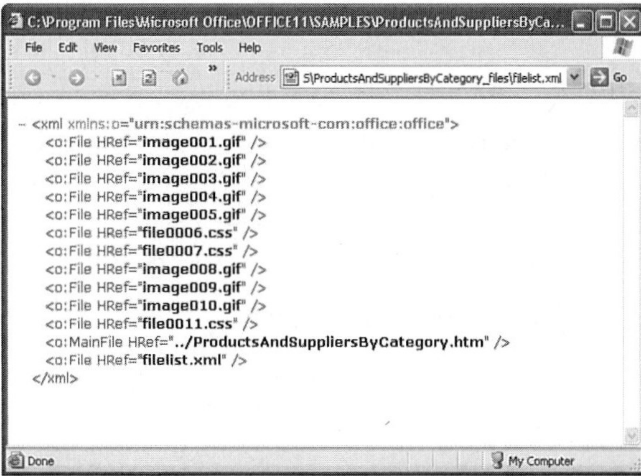

Figure 24.21
The filelist.xml file is a well-formed XML document that lists the sequentially numbered files for the selected page theme.

→ For the definition of a well-formed XML document and other XML-related terms, **see** "Gaining an XML Vocabulary," **p. 944**.

NOTE

> The link from the MainFile to filelist.xml is relative. If you relocate *PageName*.htm, you must also relocate the *PageName*_files subfolder and its contents to the folder containing *PageName*.htm. Double-click .css files to open them in the Microsoft Development Environment (another name for the Script Editor) or FrontPage 2003; .gif files usually open in Microsoft Photo Editor. Installing other Microsoft and third-party software, however, often changes file associations.

See the "DAP Lose Their Style" topic in the "Troubleshooting" section near the end of the chapter for the symptoms of lost filelist.xml and .css files.

24

The ProductsAndSuppliersByCategory.htm page and its subfolder are located in the \Seua11\Chaptr24 folder of the accompanying CD-ROM. The data source for this chapter's Jet examples is C:\Program Files\Seua11\Chaptr24\Data24.mdb. If you've installed the files from the CD-ROM in a different location, you must open the .htm files in Notepad and change the `Data Source` property value to the correct path (refer to Figure 24.6).

TIP

> To prevent the default theme that you chose from applying to all DAP that you create, open a page that uses the default theme in Page Design view. Then choose Format, Theme, select (No Theme) in the Choose a Theme list, and click the Set Default button. Click Yes to confirm your action, and close the page without saving the changes to preserve the page's theme. If you want to remove the theme from your page and use the designer's default formatting, save the changes.

Using AutoPage to Create Columnar DAP

Access 2003's AutoPage feature generates a simple DAP from tables or queries. If all you need is a simple page that displays one record at a time, AutoPage is the fastest approach. To test the AutoPage feature, do the following:

1. Click the Database window's Pages shortcut, if necessary, and click the New button to open the New Data Access Page dialog.
2. Select AutoPage: Columnar in the list and select a table or query in the drop-down list. This example uses the Quarterly Orders by Product query (see Figure 24.22).
3. Click OK to generate the page. After a second or two, depending on the speed of your PC, the page opens in Page view without a title (see Figure 24.23). If you specified a default theme when testing the Page Wizard, the default theme is applied automatically to your page.

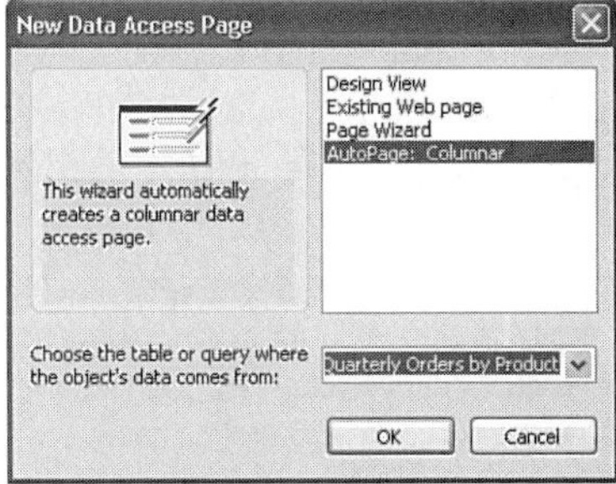

Figure 24.22
The New Data Access Page dialog offers choices similar to those of the New Form dialog.

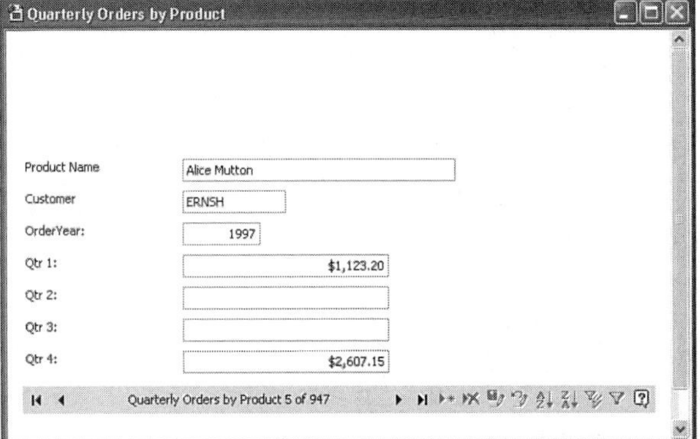

Figure 24.23
The AutoPage: Columnar choice generates a simple page with a single navigation control for the table or query that you select.

24

NOTE

The Quarterly Orders by Product page is read-only because its underlying summary query is read-only. All queries that return aggregate values, such as Jet crosstab queries, are read-only.

4. Save the page as **QuarterlyOrdersByProduct.htm** in your working folder, and acknowledge the warning message.

NOTE

Microsoft's sample DAP have filenames that include spaces. Spaces in production Web page filenames are uncommon and can cause problems with some Web servers and browsers. DAP require IE 5+ for viewing and usually run from a Microsoft Web server, so spaces in file names aren't fatal. It's a good HTML programming practice, however, to remove spaces or other nonstandard punctuation (except hyphens) from .htm file names.

Field labels in Access 2003 DAP display the caption of the underlying table; Access 2000 uses field names for the caption. The Product Name and Customer labels use the Caption property and don't have added colons. The remaining fields are query column names (without Caption property values) and have colons. The reason for omitting colons from Caption-based labels is a mystery.

NOTE

> The Quarterly Orders by Product query displays the CompanyName field of the Customers table in the Customer column of Datasheet view, but not in the Customer field of your AutoPage. Customer is a lookup field; lookup fields don't propagate to pages that you create with the Page Wizard or AutoPage feature. When you drag lookup fields from the Field List to a section, however, a lookup field substitutes a drop-down list for the standard text box. Access 2002 introduced automatic support for lookup fields by DAP.

Using the Record Navigation Control's Filter and Sort Features

Filtering by selection and sorting with the record navigation control is similar to using the filter and sort buttons of the toolbar in Datasheet view. The Quarterly Orders by Product query returns 947 rows, so filtering by Customer is useful to display a subset of the data for a single customer. You can also perform an ascending or descending sort on any field or column, and you can combine filters and sorting.

Sorting and filtering records in DAP follows a pattern similar to that for conventional Access datasheets, forms, and reports. To experiment with the record navigation control's filter and sort features with the Quarterly Orders by Product page, do the following:

1. Click the Customer column's text box to select the field, and then click the Filter by Selection button. When you apply a filter, the Toggle Filter Button changes to the depressed state. If you selected the first record for ANTON (Antonio Moreno Taqueri[as]a), the filter returns 13 records, as illustrated by Figure 24.24.

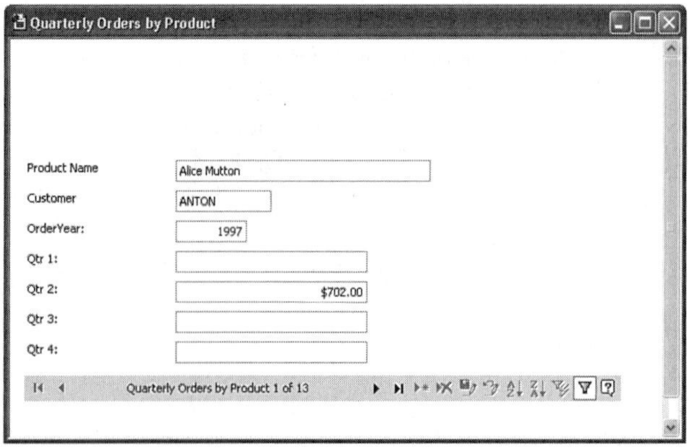

Figure 24.24 Applying Filter by Selection to the underlying `Recordset` limits the records displayed in the section to the records that have the same value as the on you select in a text box. Test the filter by clicking the Last button.

2. Click the Toggle Filter Button to remove the filter. The caption of the Record Navigation control confirms that the original 947 records are accessible.

3. Click one of the Qtr field text boxes, and then click the Sort Descending button to display the largest dollar value of an order in that quarter of 1997. After you apply a sorting sequence, the sort buttons are disabled until you select another field. Figure 24.25 shows the result of a descending sort on the Qtr 1 column.

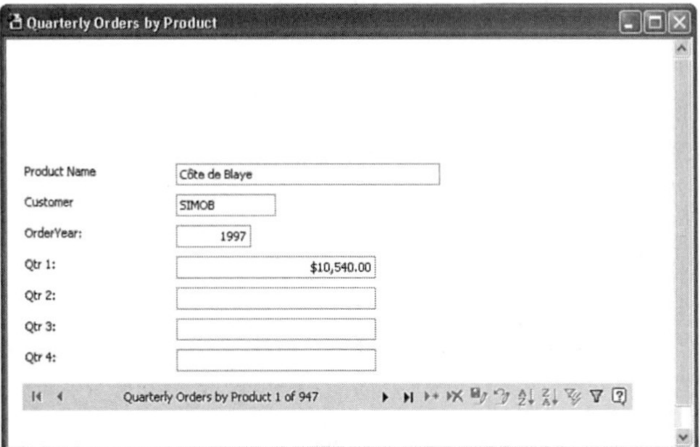

Figure 24.25
Sorting operations on alphabetic and numeric fields of a page are identical to that for Datasheet or Form view. Why a customer in Copenhagen would purchase this much French wine from a U.S. firm is the second unsolved mystery of this chapter.

4. Click to select the ProductName field, and then click the Apply Filter button to restrict the active records to a single product, Co[af]te de Blaye, for this example.

5. Click the Qtr 2 field text box, apply a descending sort, and click the Last and First record buttons to display the largest order for the selected product in 1997Q2.

NOTE

Provide a hyperlinked help page for users of your DAP who don't have experience with Access filtering and sorting techniques. You can write your help pages with any HTML editing tool, such as FrontPage 2003. If only a brief explanation is required, you can add the text to the empty header element of the page.

MODIFYING THE DESIGN OF AUTOPAGE DAP

The AutoPage feature seldom formats DAP satisfactorily, so you should optimize the size and location of the fields to conform to the form design standards discussed in the chapters of Part IV, "Designing Forms and Reports." The process of resizing and moving controls on DAP, however, differs significantly from that of conventional Access forms and reports.

The following are the basic procedures for resizing, relocating, and editing controls and sections of DAP:

- *Resize an element* by clicking it once to display eight sizing handles. When you pass the mouse pointer over a sizing handle, the mouse pointer changes from a pointer or an I-beam to a two-headed arrow (see Figure 24.26). Drag the arrow in the direction of the change that you want to make.

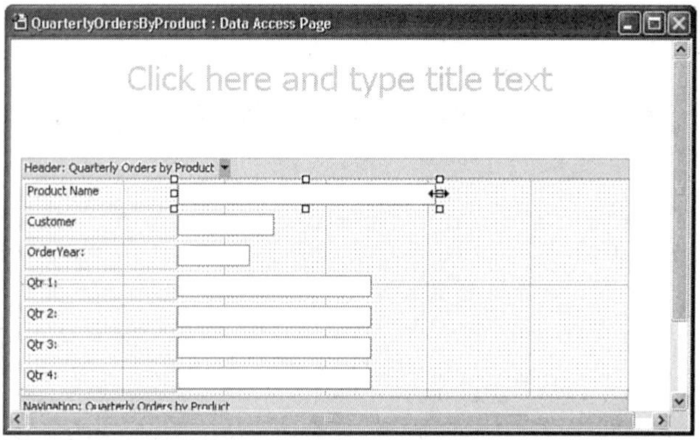

Figure 24.26
Sizing page controls is similar to the methods used for form and report controls, but the sizing handles differ in appearance.

- *Move an element* by clicking it once to select it, and then position the mouse pointer adjacent to the element, where the pointer turns into a four-headed arrow but is not positioned on a sizing handle. Drag the element to its new location.

NOTE

NEW

The Access 2003 DAP designer lets you multiselect and group controls if you have IE 5.5+ installed.

- *Move a label* independently of its associated (parent) text box by clicking and dragging it. If you click and drag a text box, the (child) label follows the movement of the text box.

NOTE

When moving a text box with a child label, move the parent text box to the desired location, and then move the label independently of the text box.

- *Change the caption* of a label or the default text of a text box by clicking the element twice in succession—once to select it and then again to edit its content. In edit mode, a diagonally hatched border surrounds the element (see Figure 24.27). Double-clicking an element opens its *ObjectType*: *ElementName* window.
- *Set the font attributes and alignment* of label captions and text box contents by selecting the element and clicking the appropriate button of the Format (Page) toolbar, which closely resembles the Format toolbar for Access forms and reports.

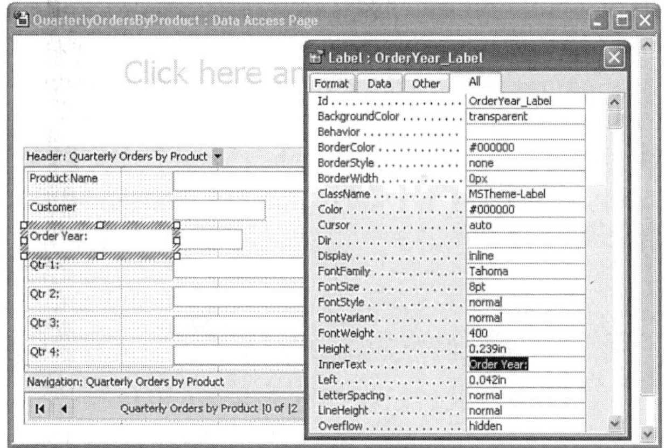

Figure 24.27 Editing a label element requires selecting it and then clicking it a second time to edit its content. Most control objects have a much larger number of properties than their native Access control counterparts.

- *Change the depth or width of a section* by clicking its header to expose the section's sizing rectangles, and then drag the sizing rectangle in the appropriate direction. The minimum size of a section is the size required to encompass all its elements.
- *Alter the property values of an element* by double-clicking the element to open its *ObjectName*: *ElementName* window, which is the DAP equivalent of Access's Properties window (refer to Figure 24.27).

NOTE

> The "DOM HTML and DHTML" section earlier in the chapter noted that every element (object) of a DHTML page must have a unique `Id` property value. In most cases, the DAP Designer adds the `Id` property value, such as `OrderYear_Label` or `Qtr1_Label`, for you. `Id` values shouldn't include spaces or punctuation other than hyphens or underscores, so Qtr 1: shortens to `Qtr1`. (Some `Id` values created by AutoForm include spaces.)

To improve the design of your columnar AutoPage and learn to set custom page and object properties, follow these steps:

1. In Page Design view, a previously hidden element appears for the title of your page. The dynamic elements of the page appear in two sections: Header and Navigation.
2. Click the default title and type a title for the page, such as **1997 Quarterly Orders by Product**.
3. Press the down arrow key, if necessary, to move the empty text region below the title. Type a brief description of what the viewer can do with the page.
4. Make room for a new Customer drop-down list by moving the existing Customer text box and label to the right.

5. Drag the CustomerID field of the Quarterly Orders by Product source query from the Field List to the original location of the Customer field controls to create a new label and drop-down list. Adjust the location of the controls, and widen the list to match the Product Name text box.

6. Double-click the drop-down list to open the Drop-down List: CustomerID window, click the Other tab, and double-click the Disabled property to change the value to True (see Figure 24.28). Disabling the list prevents users from attempting to change the CustomerName value.

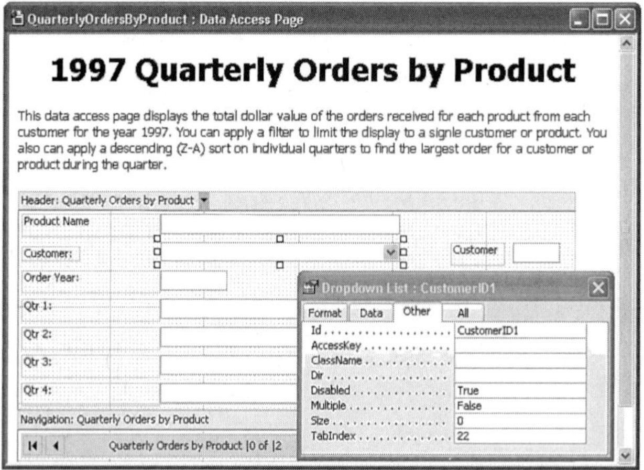

Figure 24.28 Only drop-down lists display the lookup value of table fields, so you must disable the list to prevent users from attempting to change the customer name.

NOTE

You retain the original Customer label and text box so that users can filter on the CustomerID value. You can't filter on the value in a disabled control.

7. Change the Qtr 1:...Qtr 4: label captions to **Quarter 1...Quarter 4**, and right-align the labels. Change the caption of the CustomerID text box from Customer: to **Customer Code:**. Change the name of the OrderYear label to **Year:** and right-align it.

8. Select all controls and apply the Bold attribute.

9. Adjust the size of the Year and Quarter text boxes and labels, and reposition them on two lines with the labels above the text boxes (see Figure 24.29).

10. Select the Header section and drag the height-sizing rectangle close to the bottom of the Order Year and Quarter text boxes. (Look ahead to Figure 24.31 for positioning.)

11. Optionally, add a gray background to match the background color of the navigation control. Right-click the page and choose Page Properties to open the Page: Quarterly Orders by Product window's Format page, and replace `#ffffff` (the code for white) with **gainsboro** (a named color) as the `BackgroundColor` property value.

12. If you change the background color, right-click the navigation control bar and then choose Object Properties to open the Table: QuarterlyOrdersbyProductNavigation window. In the Format page, replace `gainsboro` with **#ffffff** as the BackgroundColor property value (see Figure 24.29).

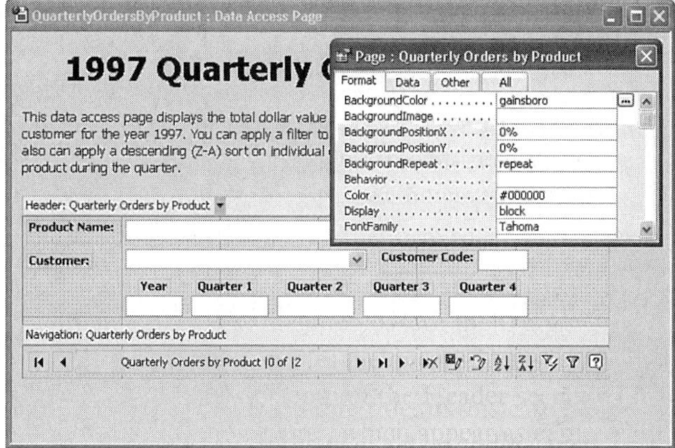

Figure 24.29 Relocating columnar labels and changing background colors gives your page a form-like appearance.

13. Press Ctrl+S to save the page, and change to Page view to check the result of your work (see Figure 24.30). Changing to Page view clears the undo/redo stack.

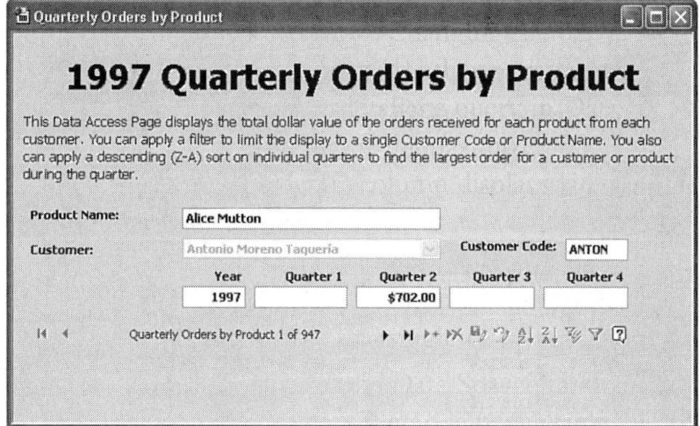

Figure 24.30 Page view displays the result of your redesign. Open the View button list and choose Web Page Preview to display the page in IE 6.0.

TIP

> Save your DAP frequently during the modification process. Saving changes doesn't clear the undo/redo stack. To check you work, choose Web Page Preview instead of changing to Page view. Viewing the page in IE 6+ doesn't clear the undo/redo stack.

ALTERING RECORD NAVIGATION CONTROL ELEMENTS

The four record-editing buttons of the record navigation control are disabled because the underlying ADO `Recordset` is read-only. The Help button leads to information that might confuse users. Thus, you should eliminate these buttons from the page. Deleting the buttons doesn't affect the navigation control. Changing the caption of the label from the name of the underlying query to Record Number makes the purpose of the buttons more evident.

NOTE

The Access 2000 (OWC 9) version of the navigation control required changing navigation control property values to hide buttons. Access 2002 made removing and adding navigation buttons much simpler.

To remove the New (Record), Delete (Record), Save (Edits), Undo (Edits), and Help buttons, and change the label of the record navigation control, do the following:

1. In DAP design mode, select the New button and press Delete. As you delete buttons, the the remaining buttons adjust their position to fill the empty space.
2. Repeat step 1 for the Delete, Save, Undo, and Help buttons.
3. Double-click the Quarterly Orders by Product label to open its properties window, click the Data tab, and change the first instance of the Quarterly Orders by Product element of the `RecordsetLabel` property value to **Record Number**, as shown in Figure 24.31. (Don't make changes to the `¦0 of ¦2` elements.)

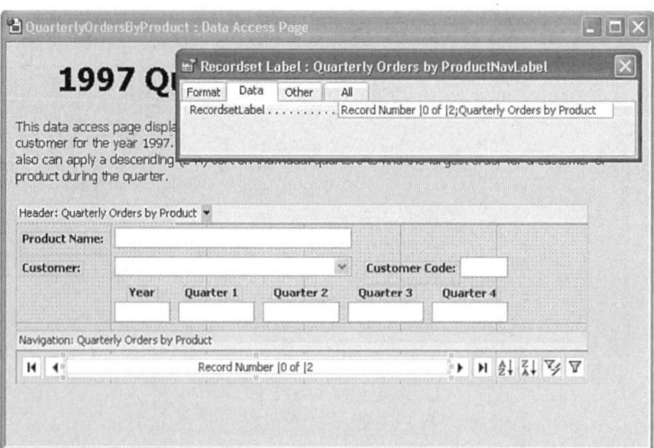

Figure 24.31
Deleting disabled buttons and changing the `Recordset` label caption improves the usability of the page.

4. Click the region below the navigation control, which defaults to an HTML paragraph (`<P>...</P>`) element and, optionally, add instructions for users who are new to DAP.
5. Open the View menu or right-click the page's title bar and choose Web Page Preview to display the modified navigation bar and added text in IE 6+ (see Figure 24.32). If

you have unsaved changes, a message box opens when you change to Web Page Preview. Click Yes to save the changes.

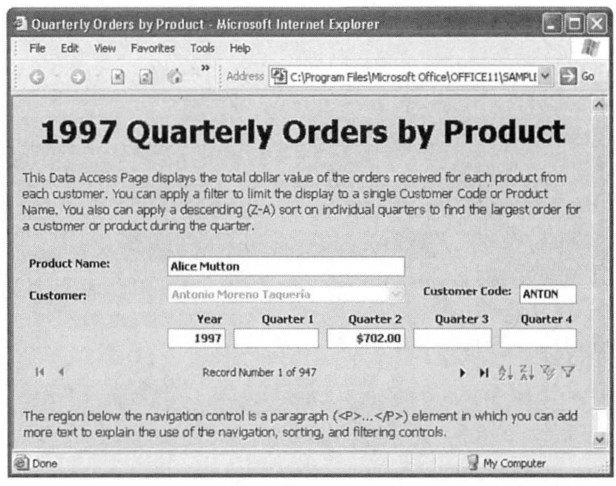

Figure 24.32 Selecting Web Page Preview from the View button list displays the page with the simplified navigation control and added text in IE 6+.

TIP

> Take full advantage of the default text elements of DAP to add instructions for using your pages. By tradition, Web pages contain substantial amounts of text, but forms don't. Adding text instructions to the page–rather than in a hyperlinked help document–is a convenience that most users appreciate. As you become more familiar with DHTML programming, you can add VBScript code to your page to display or hide the explanatory text.

Substituting SPAN Elements for Navigation Buttons

Access 2002 introduced pages that let you substitute text (`<SPAN>`) elements or your own graphic images for navigation control buttons. Navigation control buttons have special `ClassName` property values—`MsoNavFirst`, `MsoNavPrevious`, `MsoNavNext`, and `MsoNavLast`—to identify them as navigation elements. You can assign additional elements as navigation controls or replace the existing graphics.

NOTE

> The following procedure for replacing standard navigation buttons with text labels also shows you how to copy controls and move them from one section of the page to another.

To substitute text labels for the navigation controls, do the following:

1. Return to Page Design view, and drag the bottom of the Header section down to make room for a row of labels.

2. Open the Toolbox, select the Label tool, and draw the label at the bottom left of the Header section.

3. Type **First** as the caption, apply the Bold attribute, and adjust the size of the label to fit the text.

4. Double-click the new label to open the Label: Label6 properties window, and click the Other tab. Change the `Id` property value to **navFirst** and the `ClassName` to **MsoNavFirst**. When you change the `ClassName`, the label becomes a `<SPAN>` element (see Figure 24.33).

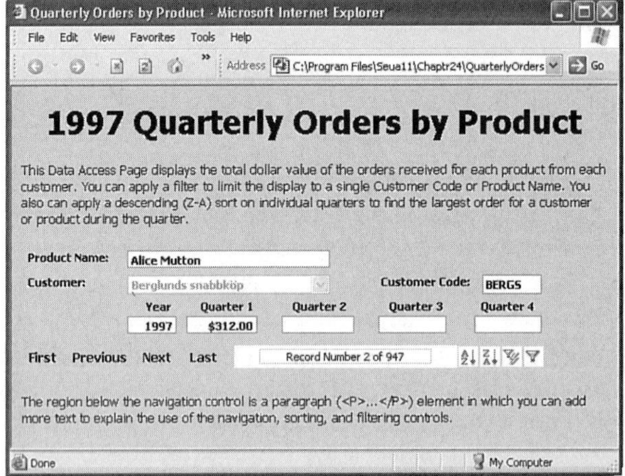

Figure 24.33 Making a label a member of the `MsoNav...` class changes the label to a `<SPAN>` element. It's a good practice to apply `Id` naming conventions similar to those recommended for form controls.

5. Click the Format tab, open the `Cursor` property's list, and select `hand`. If you don't change the cursor type, the cursor defaults to an I-beam. Setting the cursor to `hand` indicates an active control.

6. Change to Page view and verify that the new span control behaves as expected by clicking the Last button and then the First span.

7. Return to Page Design view and select the First control. Press Ctrl+C and Ctrl+V to create a copy of the control, and drag the copy to the right of the First control.

8. Change the caption to Previous, double-click the control, and change the `Id` property to **navPrevious** and the `ClassName` to **MsoNavPrevious**.

9. Repeat steps 7 and 8 to add a `navNext` control as `MsoNavNext` and a `navLast` control as `MsoNavLast`.

10. Change to Page view and test the added span controls.

11. Return to Page Design view and delete the First, Prev, Next, and Last navigation buttons. Then drag the left edge of the navigation bar to the right to make room for the span controls.

12. Select all the added span controls, and press Ctrl+X to remove them from the Header section. Select the Navigation section, and press Ctrl+V to paste the controls.
13. Drag the bottom of the Header section up, adjust the spacing between the controls, and then change to Web Page Preview (see Figure 24.34).

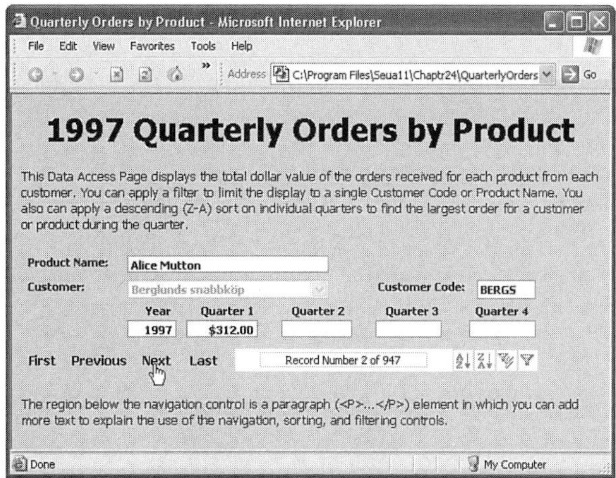

Figure 24.34
Web Page Preview displays the hand cursor when the mouse pointer hovers on the replacement <SPAN> navigation controls.

The completed QuarterlyOrdersByProduct.htm page is located in the \Seua11\Chaptr24 folder of the accompanying CD-ROM.

STARTING A SINGLE-LEVEL PAGE FROM SCRATCH

The Page Wizard and AutoPage have a limited repertoire of page design features, so creating a DAP from scratch or from an existing Web page is an alternative when you want custom page features or to create a DAP to update table values.

Opening new DAP by double-clicking the Create a Data Access Page in Design View item opens the page designer with a page that has the default `<TITLE>` and `<H1>` text elements, as well as a single unbound section that's 6 inches wide and 2 inches deep for the U.S. (1033) locale. You use the Field List to bind the page to a `Recordset` through a record navigation control and add text box and drop-down list controls for lookup fields to the page. Alternatively, you can display data in bound span controls.

CREATING A TABULAR PAGE FROM A TABLE OR QUERY

The Layout Wizard generates a reasonably attractive tabular page that you can easily customize to meet your graphic design preferences or organization-wide standards.

TIP

> As noted earlier in the chapter, tables with lookup fields require drop-down lists to display lookup values. If the table or query for your tabular page has lookup fields, create a new query based on the original table or query with a join to the source table of the lookup data. Add the lookup field to the query's field list, and change the Display Control property value for the original lookup column to Text Box.

To create the starting point of a sample report-type page from a table without lookup fields, do the following:

1. With Pages active in the Database window, double-click the Create a Data Access Page in Design View shortcut. You might receive a message that you can't open pages that you create with Access 2003 in Access 2000's Page Design view (see Figure 24.35). Mark the Don't Show This Warning Again check box, and click OK to open the empty page. Open the Toolbox and verify that the Control Wizard button of the Toolbox is depressed.

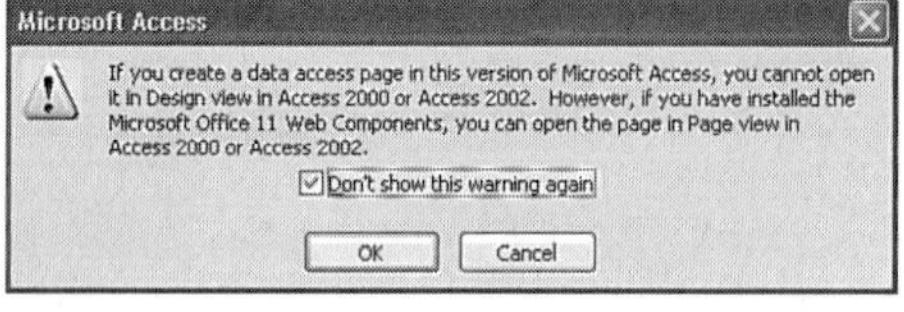

Figure 24.35 This warning message appears each time that you open a new page in Design view if you don't mark the check box.

2. Click the Field List button if the Field List isn't visible, and drag a table or query node to the extreme left of the empty section. This example uses the Suppliers table. The section border turns blue as you drag the icon into the section. When you release the mouse, the Layout Wizard's single dialog opens.
3. Select the Tabular layout (see Figure 24.36), and click OK to generate the standard page design. (If you've specified a default theme, the design applies the theme's style sheet).

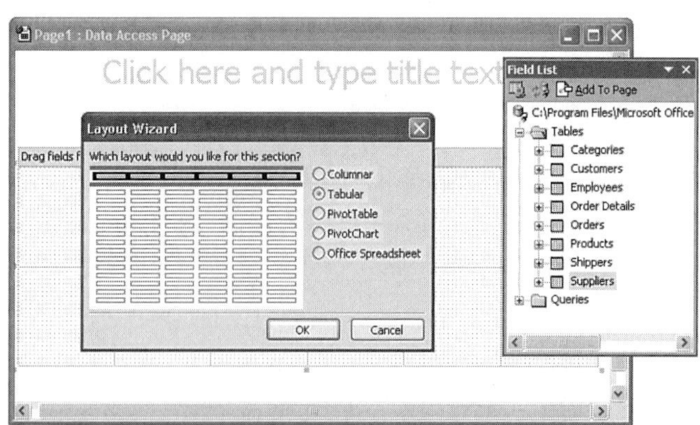

Figure 24.36 The Layout Wizard lets you select between columnar and tabular table or query layouts, or add a Spreadsheet, PivotTable, or PivotChart to the page. Wizards usually have multiple dialogs; this "Wizard" dialog is better named "Select Layout."

4. Add a title and, optionally, text in the default <H1> section. If the text is short, click Center to center the text under the title.

5. Change to Page view to display the initial layout. Figure 24.37 shows the default page design for the Suppliers table. The Wizard generates text boxes of equal width for all fields.

Supplier ID	Company Name	Contact Name	Contact Title	Address	City
1	Exotic Liquids	Charlotte Cooper	Purchasing	49 Gilbert St.	London
2	New Orleans	Shelley Burke	Order	P.O. Box 78934	New Orleans
3	Grandma Kelly's	Regina Murphy	Sales	707 Oxford Rd.	Ann Arbor
4	Tokyo Traders	Yoshi Nagase	Marketing	9-8 Sekimai	Tokyo
5	Cooperativa de	Antonio del Valle	Export	Calle del Rosal 4	Oviedo
6	Mayumi's	Mayumi Ohno	Marketing	92 Setsuko	Osaka
7	Pavlova, Ltd.	Ian Devling	Marketing	74 Rose St.	Melbourne
8	Specialty Biscuits,	Peter Wilson	Sales	29 King's Way	Manchester
9	PB Knäckebröd AB	Lars Peterson	Sales Agent	Kaloadagatan 13	Göteborg
10	Refrescos	Carlos Diaz	Marketing	Av. das	São Paulo

Figure 24.37 The standard tabular page layout places field captions in a Caption section and uses text boxes to permit editing data. The default `Recordset` type is an updateable snapshot.

6. Scroll to the right to display Web hyperlinks that the Wizard adds in a bound span with no column caption.

SETTING GROUP-LEVEL PROPERTY VALUES

The Suppliers table has only 29 records, so it's more convenient for users to display all records instead of navigating in the default groups of 10. When you display all records on a page, there's no need for a navigation control. In addition, you probably don't want users to change the suppliers. You make changes that affect the grouped data in the GroupLevel: *TableOrQueryName* properties window.

To display all records, remove the navigation control, and prevent editing Suppliers data, do this:

1. Return to Page Design view, right-click the page, and choose Group Level Properties to open the GroupLevel: Suppliers window.
2. Set the `AllowAdditions`, `AllowDeletions`, and `AllowEdits` property values to False to prevent edits to the data.
3. Optionally, change the `AlternateRowColor` property value to **silver**. If you make this change, adjust the depth of the Header section to provide the same spacing above and below the text boxes.

4. Open the `DataPageSize` property's list and select All to display all records in a single page.
5. Set the `RecordNavigationSection` property value to False to remove the record navigation control (see Figure 24.38).

Figure 24.38 The GroupLevel properties window lets you set property values that apply to all records in the group.

6. Change to Page view to check your work so far (see Figure 24.39).

Figure 24.39 This double-exposure shows the first six and last three rows of the modified Suppliers list. Setting `AllowEdits` to False has the same effect as setting the Locked property of Access or Visual Basic text boxes to True.

REPLACING TEXT BOXES WITH BOUND SPAN CONTROLS

Bound span controls are a more logical choice for a read-only form than text box controls. As mentioned earlier in the chapter, DAP don't offer an automated method for changing control types. To change the control type created when dragging fields from the Field List, you must change the `DefaultControlType` property value of the page from Text Box to Bound Span.

To replace the text boxes in the Header section with bound span controls, do this:

1. Change to Page Design view, right-click the page, and choose Page Properties to open the Page: Page1 properties window.
2. Click the Data tab and change the DefaultControlType property value to Bound Span.
3. While you have the properties window open, click the Other tab and change the Title property value to **Northwind Suppliers List**. Close the properties window.
4. Delete all the text boxes in the header section. As you delete the text boxes, the captions disappear. Reduce the width of the Header section to about 6.25 inches. (Reducing the width of the Header section also shrinks the Caption section.)

5. Expand the Suppliers node of the Field List, and drag the SupplierID field to the extreme left of the Header section. The tabular format adds the bound span control to the Header section and adds the label to the Caption section. Change the label text to **ID**, and decrease the width of the label and span.
6. Repeat step 5 for each of the fields that you need in the list. Adjust the width of the span and label to accommodate the approximate length of the field's data.

7. Optionally, select all the text boxes and apply the Bold attribute. A bold font makes the data more readable if you applied the silver color to alternate rows.
8. The list is more useful if you sort by company name, not ID number, so open the GroupLevel: Suppliers properties window and specify CompanyName as the value of the DefaultSort property (see Figure 24.40).

Figure 24.40
Replacing text boxes with span controls improves the appearance of the form and requires less vertical space per row. Sorting on the CompanyName field improves the usability of the list.

9. Choose File, Save As, and save your page as **Suppliers List**; save the file as **SuppliersList.htm**, and then open it in Web Page Preview (see Figure 24.41). Click OK to acknowledge the absolute path warning message.

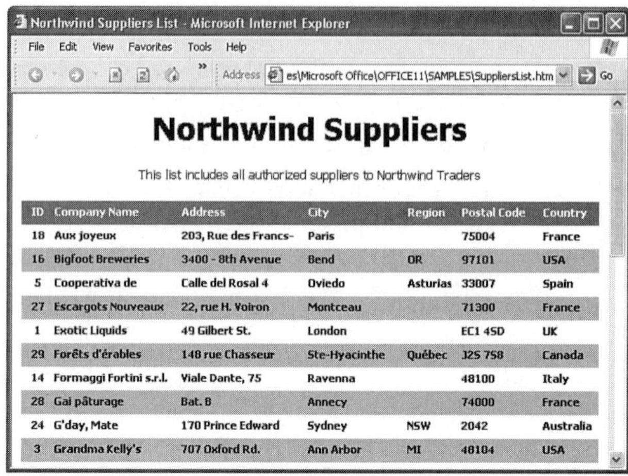

Figure 24.41 Web Page Preview shows the result of this section's redesign.

Publishing limits preclude listing all the property values of page objects; most objects have many more properties than their native Access counterparts. The preceding sections are only an introduction to customizing the content and design of DAP.

TIP

Experiment freely with changes to Page, Group Level, Object, and Element properties. It's easy to undo changes that aren't what you intend.

The completed SuppliersList.htm page is located in the \Seua11\Chaptr24 folder of the accompanying CD-ROM.

Adding Bound Office Web Controls to DAP

The Layout Wizard offers options to add a Spreadsheet, PivotTable, or ChartControl when you drag a table or query node from the Field List. The following three sections describe how to create pages that display the graphic OWCs.

NOTE

Users who install the OWC 11 runtime version are limited to a subset of the features of the three components described in the following sections. If you're a VBScript expert, you can write scripts to perform operations that aren't accessible by unlicensed users. To learn more about scripting OWC 11 objects, start at `http://msdn.microsoft.com/library/officedev/offstrt/aboutoffice.htm`, click Show TOC, and look for Office 11 Developer Documentation.

DISPLAYING A TABLE OR QUERY RESULT SET IN AN OFFICE SPREADSHEET CONTROL

The Office Spreadsheet control offers an alternative to tabular text boxes for interacting with table or query data in a page. Unlike the OWC 9 version of the Spreadsheet control, Access 2003's OWC 11 version binds to a table or query. The spreadsheet control also lets you display calculated data based on numeric and date columns, but this feature (and the AutoSum feature) isn't available when the sheet is bound. Another useful feature is the capability to export the spreadsheet data as an Excel 2003 worksheet that you can save to a file and manipulate offline.

> **NOTE**
>
> The Spreadsheet control's AutoFilter feature is based on the PivotTable and PivotChart approach, so users are likely to find the Spreadsheet filter more intuitive than the filter-by-selection method of the navigation control. Sorting the sheet, however, requires instructions for users who aren't familiar with Excel's sorting methods.

To add a Spreadsheet control to a page, using the Quarterly Orders by Product crosstab query as a read-only example, do the following:

1. With Pages active in the Database window, double-click the Create a Data Access Page in Design View item. If you didn't mark the Don't Show This Warning Again check box in a previous example, click OK to open the empty page.
2. Drag the Quarterly Orders by Product query from the Field list to the empty page section. In the Layout Wizard's dialog, select Office Spreadsheet, and click OK to add the control to the page.
3. Type a title for the page. To conserve vertical space on the page, set the font size to 18 points and delete the <H1> section below the title.
4. Expand the width and depth of the section and the control to display all seven columns and 12 or more rows. The Spreadsheet control uses field names—not Caption values—in the first row of the sheet (see Figure 24.42).

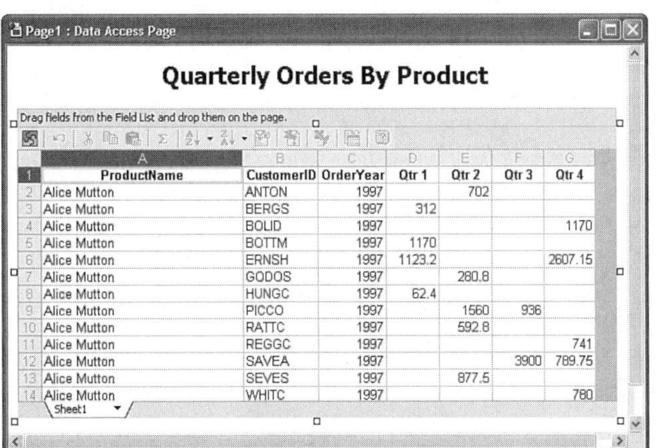

	A	B	C	D	E	F	G
1	ProductName	CustomerID	OrderYear	Qtr 1	Qtr 2	Qtr 3	Qtr 4
2	Alice Mutton	ANTON	1997		702		
3	Alice Mutton	BERGS	1997	312			
4	Alice Mutton	BOLID	1997				1170
5	Alice Mutton	BOTTM	1997	1170			
6	Alice Mutton	ERNSH	1997	1123.2			2607.15
7	Alice Mutton	GODOS	1997		280.8		
8	Alice Mutton	HUNGC	1997	62.4			
9	Alice Mutton	PICCO	1997		1560	936	
10	Alice Mutton	RATTC	1997		592.8		
11	Alice Mutton	REGGC	1997				741
12	Alice Mutton	SAVEA	1997			3900	789.75
13	Alice Mutton	SEVES	1997		877.5		
14	Alice Mutton	WHITC	1997				780

Figure 24.42 You must resize the default section and Spreadsheet control width and height to display all columns from the query and a reasonable number of rows.

5. Change to Page view to test the bound Spreadsheet control's feature set. You can't add new columns to a bound Spreadsheet control, and changes that you make to cell values don't propagate to the underlying tables because crosstab queries can't be updated.

6. To format the order values as currency, select the Qtr 1…Qtr 4 columns, click the Commands and Options button (above the center of the OrderYear column) to open the dialog's Format page, and select Currency in the Number Format list (see Figure 24.43). Return to Design view and adjust the width of the spreadsheet control to accommodate the wider currency columns.

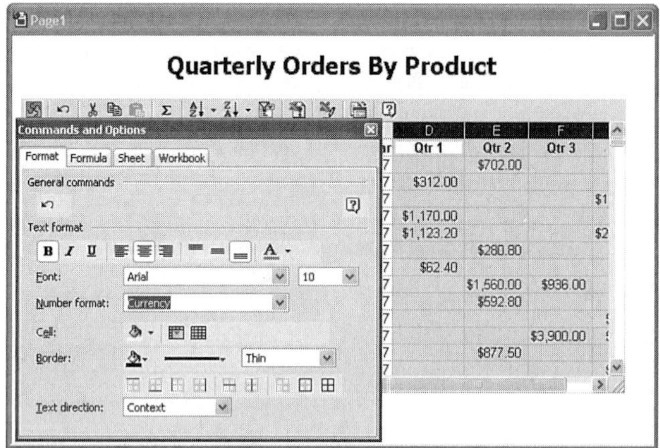

Figure 24.43 The Spreadsheet control doesn't recognize the Jet Currency format of the Qtr… columns, so you must format them manually.

7. To test the AutoFilter feature, return to Page view and click the AutoFilter button to add drop-down buttons to each column. Open the list for a column—CustomerID, for this example—clear the (Show All) check box, and select one or more CustomerID values on which to filter (see Figure 24.44). The capability to filter on multiple-column values is an enhancement to the Filter by Selection feature of tabular pages.

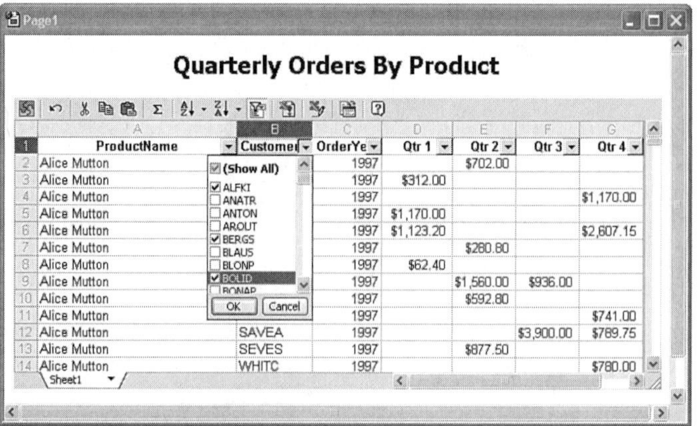

Figure 24.44 The AutoFilter feature lets you multiselect filter values in one or more columns.

8. Click OK to apply the filter, which results in the sheet shown in Figure 24.45. When a filter is applied, the AutoFilter button is in the depressed state, column numbers aren't consecutive, and the color of the column numbers is blue.

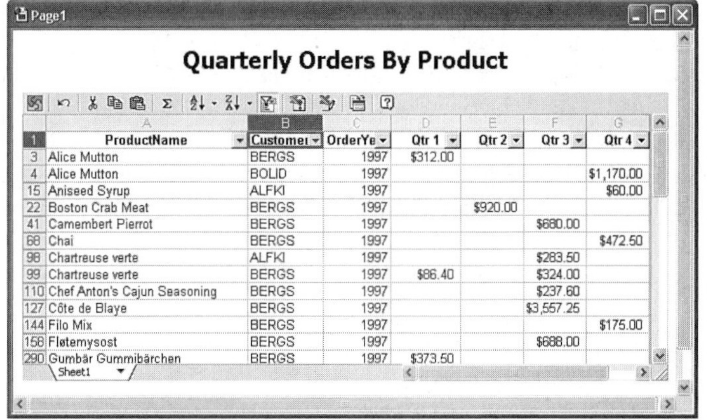

Figure 24.45
The AutoFilter on state is evident from the nonconsecutive column numbers and the on (depressed) state of the AutoFilter button.

9. Click the AutoFilter button to remove the filter.

10. To sort the sheet by one of the columns, click the arrow to the right of the Sort button to open the column selection list. Moving the mouse pointer onto the context menu selects the entire sheet (see Figure 24.46).

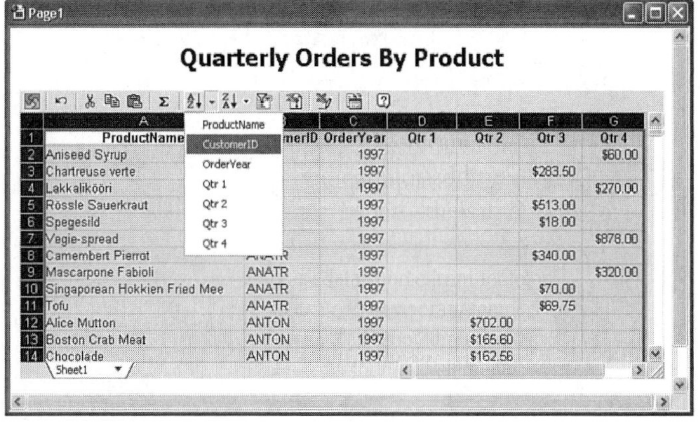

Figure 24.46
Opening the drop-down Sort button automatically selects all cells of the sheet below the field header row. Choosing a column sorts the sheet.

TIP

> Don't select a column and click Sort Ascending or Sort Descending. Doing this sorts the column values independently of the other columns. Fortunately, clicking Undo restores the data to its original order.

11. Click the Undo button to return the sheet its original unsorted state.

You can't use the AutoSum feature or calculate new values in the bound sheet, but you can copy the sheet to a new unbound sheet that lets you add columns and rows. By default, the Spreadsheet control has three sheets, but you can add or delete sheets in the Worksheet page of the Commands and Options dialog. (The third Microsoft mystery of this chapter is why this dialog isn't named "Office Spreadsheet Properties.")

TIP

> If you want to save your Spreadsheet page with a name other than Page1, do it now. When you save a page, only the bound sheet is preserved. The unbound sheet that you add in the following procedure is lost when you save the page.

To copy Sheet1 to Sheet2 and AutoSum the columns and rows, do this:

1. Press Ctrl+ A to select all rows and columns of Sheet1, and press Ctrl+C to copy the cells to the Clipboard.
2. Click the Sheet1 tab and select Sheet2 from the pop-up list.
3. With cell A1 selected, press Ctrl+V to copy Sheet1 to Sheet2.
4. Select the columns and rows to total—D2:G948, for this example—and click the AutoSum button, which creates column but not row totals (see Figure 24.47).

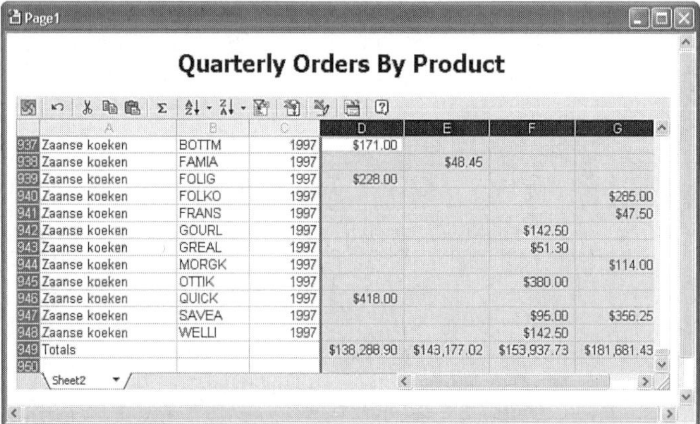

Figure 24.47
The AutoSum feature totals selected columns but not rows.

5. To crossfoot the sheet with row totals, type the formula to sum the individual row values—**=SUM(D2:G2)**, for this example—in another cell of the row (H2), and copy the formula to the remaining rows.

Unfortunately, AutoSum values don't update when you apply AutoFilter, which limits the usefulness of the AutoFilter feature. You can add command buttons or other controls to the form and write VBScript event handlers to automate Spreadsheet operations. The object model of the Spreadsheet control isn't simple, and writing VBScript to manage sheets is more difficult than creating VBA procedures to manipulate PivotTables and PivotCharts of Access forms.

There's no Save button on the Spreadsheet's toolbar, so you can't save Sheet2 and reopen it in the user interface. The only direct method for persisting the data is to export the sheets to an Excel workbook. When you click the Export to Microsoft Excel button, Excel opens a read-only OWCSheet*Number*.xml file with an unbound version of Sheet1 and any other unbound sheets that you added.

You can save a read-write version of the exported file in XML Spreadsheet (*.xml) format or in any other format supported by Excel 2003. Set the `XMLURL` property value of the Spreadsheet control to the file name, QuarterlyOrdersSS.xml for this example. When you specify an `XMLURL` value, the control loads data from the XML file instead of the table or query. The XML file for the workbook with the two worksheets created in the preceding example, QuarterlyOrders.xml has a size of almost 1MB; the .xls version is 226KB. It takes a second or two to load the Spreadsheet control with a large XML file.

CREATING A PIVOTTABLE PAGE

Dragging a table or query node from the Field List to an empty section of a page and selecting PivotTable in the Layout Wizard dialog adds a bound but featureless PivotTable to the section. Unlike Access PivotTable view or PivotTables that you add to forms, the toolbar and drop zones are missing from the default PivotTable control when you add it to a page.

NOTE

> Chapter 12, "Working with PivotTable and PivotChart Views," and Chapter 18, "Adding Graphs, PivotCharts, and PivotTables," explain how to manipulate PivotTable data. The examples in this section and the following section on PivotCharts use the data from the qry1997OrdersByCountryPT sample query that you created in Chapter 12. This query is included in the Data24.mdb database in the \Seua11\Chaptr24 folder of the accompanying CD-ROM. Import the query to Northwind.mdb, or work from the Data24.mdb sample database.

To add a PivotTable based on the qry1997OrdersByCountryPT query, do this:

1. Double-click the Create Data Access Page in Design View item and click the Field List button if the Field List isn't open.
2. Expand the Field List's Queries node, and drag the qry1997OrdersByCountryPT query to the top left of the empty section. Select the Layout Wizard's PivotTable option, and click OK to add a bare-bones PivotTable control. Add a title to the page, reduce its font size, and delete the `<H1>` element to conserve vertical space.
3. Expand the size of the PivotTable to about 3×7 inches to start, right-click the PivotTable, and choose Commands and Options to open the eponymous dialog.

NOTE

The Commands and Options dialog is the full version of the Properties dialog for Access PivotTable view and PivotTables that you add to forms and reports. The Properties dialog doesn't have Protection or Data Source pages.

4. Click the Behavior tab and mark the Drop Areas and Toolbar check boxes to add these features to the control (see Figure 24.48). The Expand Indicator check box is marked by default.

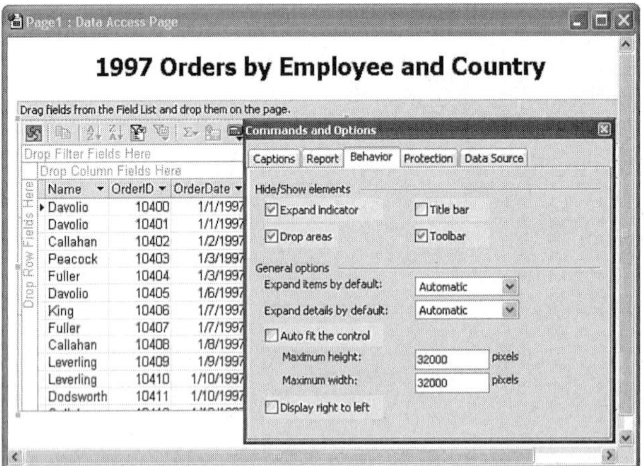

Figure 24.48 Add the drop areas and toolbar to the PivotTable control on the Behavior page of the Commands and Options dialog.

CAUTION

Don't mark the Auto Fit the Control check box. If you do, the height of the page expands to display all rows of the PivotTable. It isn't easy to recover by reducing the height of the section and the control in the user interface.

TIP

If you accidentally expand the control and its section, right-click the PivotTable, select Object Properties, and change the Format page's Height property value to **2in**. Click the section header and change its Height value to **2in**.

5. Select the Orders column, click the Format tab, and change the Number format to Currency. Then close the Commands and Options dialog.
6. Choose File, Save As, and type a descriptive name—such as **1997 Orders by Employee and Country (Pivot Table)**, for this example—in the Save As dialog. Click OK to open the Save As Data Access Page dialog. Type a simpler name for the page file—such as 1997OrdersByCountry.htm—and click Save. Click OK to acknowledge the warning message.

7. Double-click the control to activate it for layout changes, and drag the Country header to the Drop Row Fields Here drop zone. Drag the Name header to the Drop Column Fields Here drop zone, and drag the Quarter header to the drop Filter Fields Here drop zone.

8. Select the Orders header, and click the AutoCalc button and choose Sum to generate Sum of Orders rows.

9. Click the Hide Details button to display only the Sum of Orders values (see Figure 24.49).

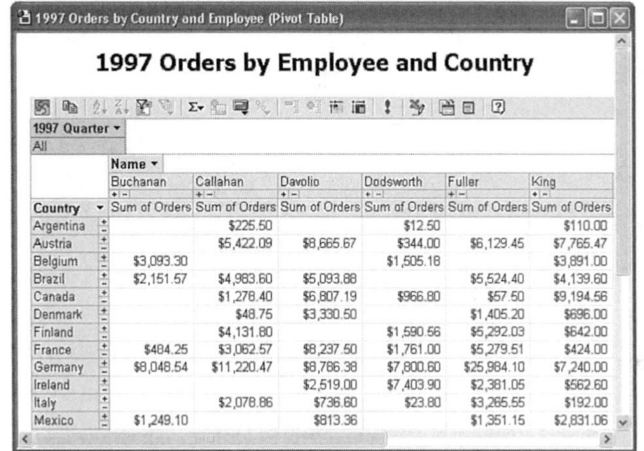

1997 Orders by Country and Employee (Pivot Table)

1997 Orders by Employee and Country

1997 Quarter: All

Country	Buchanan Sum of Orders	Callahan Sum of Orders	Davolio Sum of Orders	Dodsworth Sum of Orders	Fuller Sum of Orders	King Sum of Orders
Argentina		$225.50		$12.50		$110.00
Austria		$5,422.09	$8,665.67	$344.00	$6,129.45	$7,765.47
Belgium	$3,093.30			$1,505.18		$3,891.00
Brazil	$2,151.57	$4,983.60	$5,093.88		$5,524.40	$4,139.60
Canada		$1,278.40	$6,807.19	$966.80	$57.50	$9,194.56
Denmark		$48.75	$3,330.50		$1,405.20	$696.00
Finland		$4,131.80		$1,590.56	$5,292.03	$642.00
France	$484.25	$3,062.57	$8,237.50	$1,761.00	$5,279.51	$424.00
Germany	$8,048.54	$11,220.47	$8,786.38	$7,800.60	$25,984.10	$7,240.00
Ireland			$2,519.00	$7,403.90	$2,381.05	$562.60
Italy		$2,078.86	$736.60	$23.80	$3,265.55	$192.00
Mexico	$1,249.10		$813.36		$1,351.15	$2,831.06

Figure 24.49
A diplay of the Sum of Orders values.

10. At this point, it's safe to allow the PivotTable to expand as necessary to display all data. Right-click the control, choose Commands and Options, click the Behavior tab, mark the Auto Fit the Control check box, and accept the default values.

TIP

> Allowing the control to expand to accommodate detail data prevents users from needing to scroll both the browser and the control. Be sure not to click the Show Details button in Page Design view.

11. Press Ctrl+S to save your changes, and open the page in Page view or Web Page Preview. Figure 24.50 shows the page open in IE 6.0 after you click the Show Details button.

The page persists changes that you make to the layout of the PivotTable in Page Design view, but not in Page view or Web Page Preview. Users who don't have an Office 2003 license can apply filters and hide or show details, but they can't alter the layout of the PivotTable.

24

Figure 24.50
IE 6.0 displays part of the PivotTable page with detail cells for individual orders.

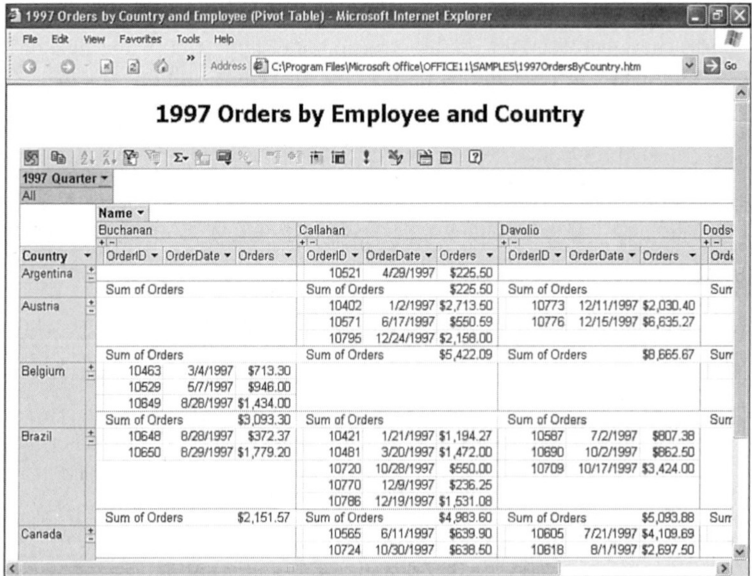

USING THE CHART WIZARD TO BIND AN OFFICE CHART TO THE PIVOTTABLE LIST

The final step in the process is to add an Office Chart control to the page and bind the chart to the PivotTable list. To generate the Chart, do the following:

1. Return to Page Design view and increase the height of Section: Unbound to about 11 inches.

TIP

> Setting the Height property of the SectionUnbound object is easier than dragging the bottom of Section: Unbound in the page designer. Right-click the page and select Section Properties to open the Object: SectionUnbound properties sheet. In the Format list, scroll to the Height property and type the new value in inches (**11in**). You also can type a pixel value, such as **750px**.

2. Click the Toolbox button of the Page Design toolbar, and click to select the Office Chart control.
3. Draw a small chart, and then expand the graph to occupy the remaining vertical space of Section: Unbound. Increase the width to about 7 or 8 inches.
4. Right-click the chart and choose Data to open the Data Source page of the Commands and Options dialog. Select the Data from the Following Web Page option and the default PivotTable: PivotTable0 item in the list. A clustered column chart whose data source is the Pivot Table appears behind the dialog (see Figure 24.51).

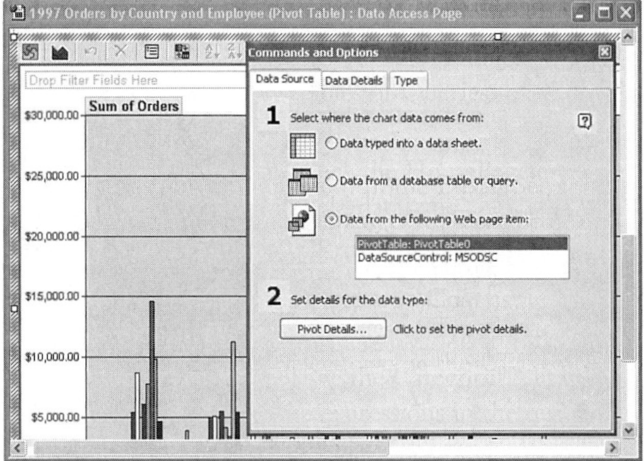

Figure 24.51
The default chart type is a clustered column, which displays a bar for each employee's sales in each country.

5. Click the Chart Type button, and select the stacked column chart type, which is highlighted in Figure 24.52.

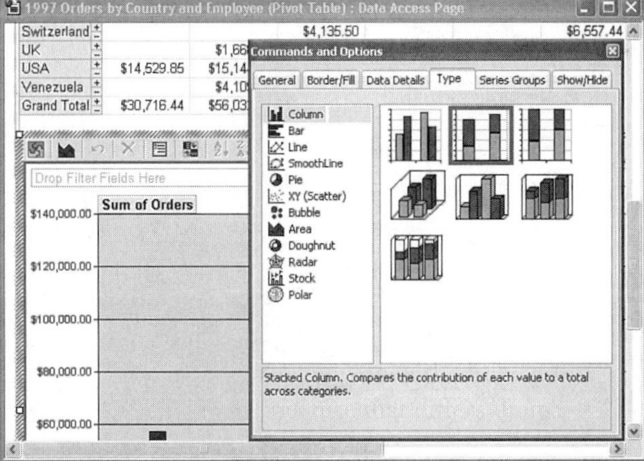

Figure 24.52
The selected stacked column chart is more readable than the clustered column type.

6. Right-click an empty area of the chart, and choose Commands and Options to open the General page of the dialog with the Chart Workspace object selected. Click the Add Legend button to add a legend for the color of employees' bars (see Figure 24.53).

7. Press Ctrl+S to save your changes. Open the page in Web Page Preview, and click the By Row/By Column button to display the data with employee names instead of countries on the x-axis (see Figure 24.54).

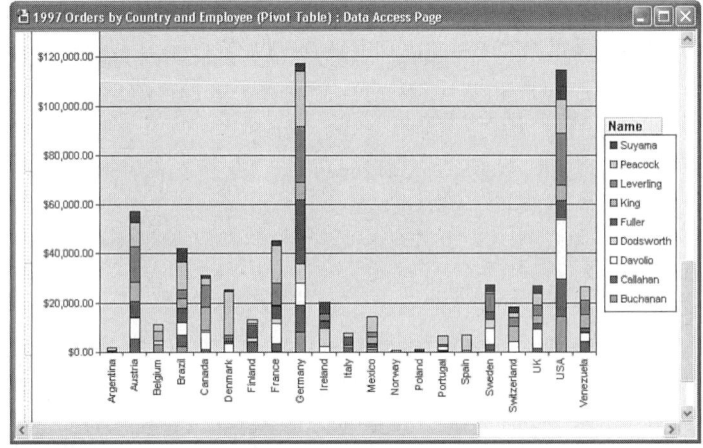

Figure 24.53
Add a legend so that users can decipher the sales contribution by each employee.

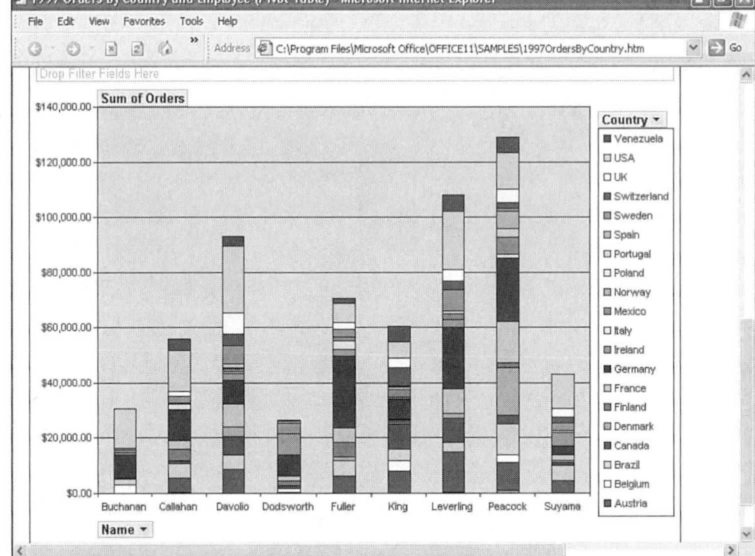

Figure 24.54
Clicking the By Row/By Column button changes the x-axis from countries to employee names. If you want employee names to be the default, you must make the change in Page Design view.

LOCKING DOWN THE LAYOUT OF PIVOTTABLES AND PIVOTCHARTS

By default, PivotTables give users with Office 2003 licenses unlimited ability to alter the design properties of the PivotTable, except changing the data source. You can restrict user manipulation of the PivotTable by clearing one or more check boxes on the Protection page of the Commands and Options dialog. If the data source for the PivotTable is a table or an updateable query, clear the Edit Detail Data, Insert New Detail Rows check box, and Delete Detail Rows check box (see Figure 24.55). PivotTable data entry is prone to typographic errors, and—unlike Access forms—there's no easy method to validate updates. It's also a good idea to clear the View the Commands and Options Dialog Box in Run Mode check box to prevent users from making design changes that lead to help-desk support requests.

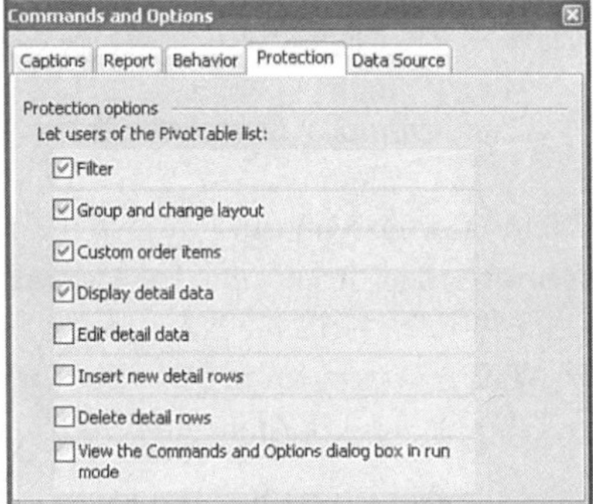

Figure 24.55
The PivotTable's Commands and Options dialog in Page Design view has a Protection page on which you can specify the changes that users can make to the PivotTable.

NOTE

The Commands and Options pages differ in Page Design and run mode. (Run mode is Page view or the page opened in IE 5.5+.) The Protection and Data Source tabs aren't visible in run mode. Changes that users make to page layout in run mode don't persist after they close the page.

PivotCharts bound to PivotTables have fewer default design options than PivotTables. You restrict user design changes on the Show/Hide page of the Commands and Options dialog of the PivotChart. The data displayed by the PivotChart depends on the PivotTable, so you can simplify the PivotChart presentation by clearing the Field Buttons/Drop Zones and Toolbar check boxes (see Figure 24.56). When you apply a filter to the PivotTable, for example, the data changes in the PivotTable and PivotChart.

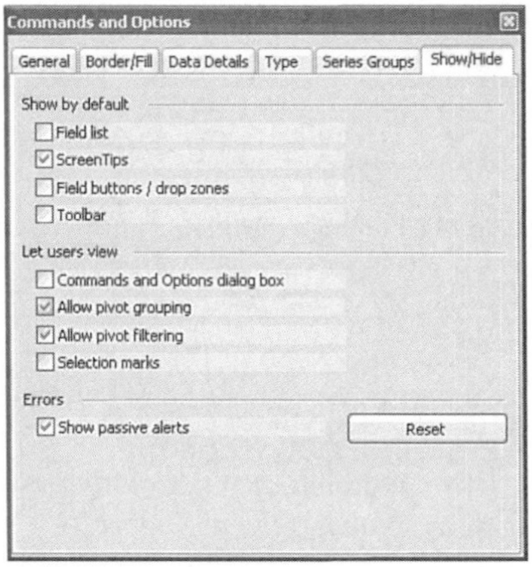

Figure 24.56
Hide the PivotChart's toolbar and field buttons to prevent users from attempting to change the PivotChart layout.

TIP

> Adjust the vertical position of the PivotChart below the PivotTable by dragging the height selection handle up or down, not by moving the entire PivotChart. Moving the PivotChart results in an annoying flashing of the display. After you verify the new position in Page view, adjust the bottom height selection handle to restore the original PivotChart dimension.

When you remove the toolbar and field buttons, you can improve the appearance of the chart by eliminating its border. To remove the border, click the Commands and Options dialog's Border/Fill tab, click the Color button to open a color picker menu, and click the None button. Figure 24.57 shows the PivotChart open in IE, with Qtr 1, country, and employee filters applied to the PivotTable and the border removed from the PivotChart.

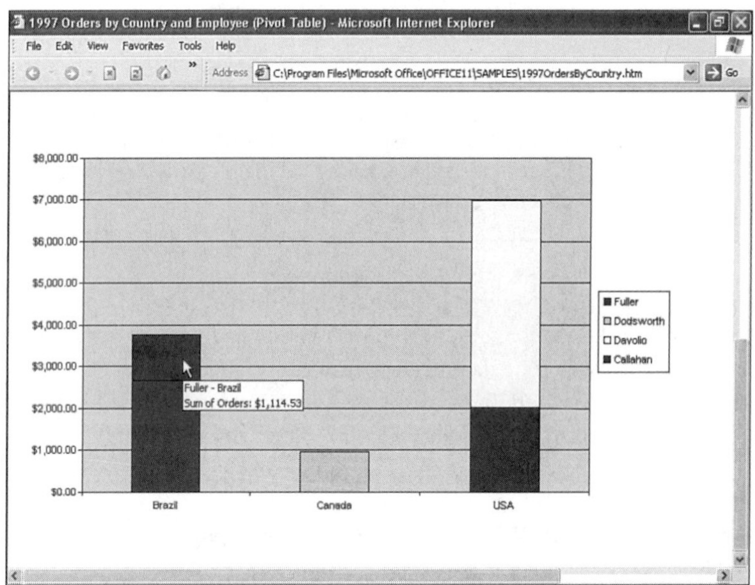

Figure 24.57 Data displayed by PivotCharts bound to PivotTables reflects filters applied to the PivotTable. ToolTips are important because some filters display column stacks of the same color for multiple values.

NOTE

> When you filter the rows of a PivotTable, the space formerly occupied by the missing rows appears as an empty region between the PivotTable and PivotChart.

Generating a Grouped Page

Grouped pages display records of related tables in a set of hierarchical page sections, each of which has its own Record Navigation control (refer to Figure 24.1, at the beginning of the chapter). The section hierarchy is based on the relationships between the sections' tables, as displayed in the Field List. You use the Field List to add individual text boxes to display field values from the base and related tables.

Creating a Three-Level Hierarchical Grouped Page Structure

The first step in designing a grouped page is to create the group structure. Follow these steps to establish a basic three-level grouped hierarchy from the Customers, Orders, and Order Details table:

1. Open a new page in Design view, open the Field List, and expand the Customers table node. Type **Customers-Orders-Order Details** as the title, reduce the font size, and delete the empty <H1> element.
2. Drag the CustomerID field to the Section: Unbound region. The Section: Unbound caption changes to Header: Customers, and a NavigationSection: Customers appears at the bottom of the page. When you drag a field from the Field List at this point, the Layout Wizard's dialog doesn't open.
3. Adjust the size of the CustomerID text box to accommodate the five-character CustomerID value. Apply the Bold attribute to the label, and adjust its size.
4. With the CustomerID text box selected, click the Promote button of the toolbar to add an Expand control to the section and create an additional Header: Customers section. Header: Customers changes to Header: Customers-CustomerID.
5. Expand the Field List's Related Tables and Orders nodes, and drag the OrderID field to the Header: Customers section. Select the Columnar option in the Layout Wizard dialog, and click OK to add an OrderID text box. The section name changes to Header: Orders (see Figure 24.58).

24

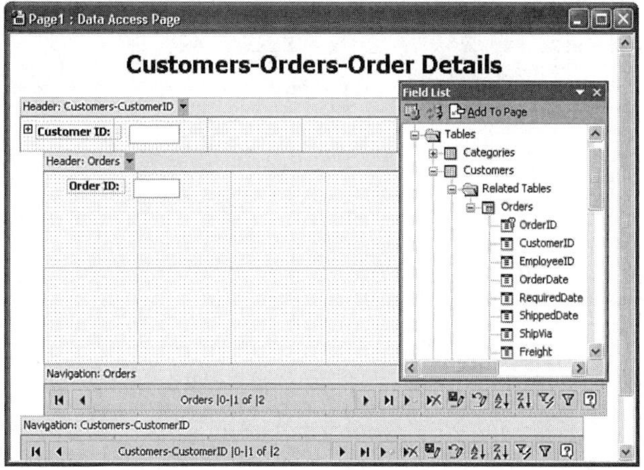

Figure 24.58 Promoting the first level of the hierarchy and dragging the OrderID field from the related Orders table creates the second level.

TIP

> Be sure to select tables at the second and lower levels of the hierarchy from the Field List's Related Tables node to preserve the relationships between the tables in your page.

6. Select the OrderID text box, and click the Promote button. Header: Orders changes to Header: Orders-OrderID, and a new Header: Orders section is added to the page.
7. Scroll in the Field List to the Orders table node, expand its Related Tables node, and expand the Order Details node.
8. Drag the UnitPrice field to the Orders-OrderID section, leaving room for a label and text box to its left. Accept the Columnar default, and click OK to close the Layout Wizard. The section name changes to Header: Order Details. (Don't drag the ProductID field to the section; ProductID is a lookup field, which opens the Combo Box Wizard.)
9. Drag the Quantity, and Discount fields to the Header: Order Details section.
10. In the Field List, open the Order Details Node, expand its Related Tables node, and expand the Products node. Drag the ProductID field to the left of the UnitPrice field, and click OK to close Layout Wizard dialog.
11. Drag the ProductName and QuantityPerUnit fields under the first row of labels and text boxes, and then reduce the height of the Order Details section.
12. Apply bold formatting to the labels, and adjust the size and location of the newly added labels and text boxes (see Figure 24.59).

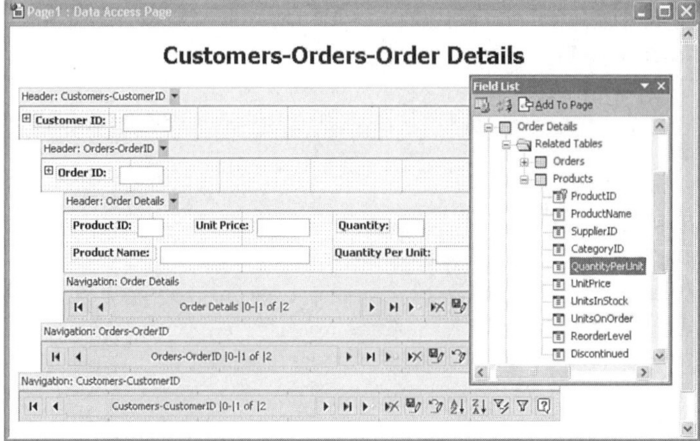

Figure 24.59
The Order Details section includes fields from the Order Details table and the related Products table.

13. Change to Page view to check your work so far. Click the Expand control of the Customers section to display the first five OrderID values for ALKFI, and expand one of the OrderIDs (see Figure 24.60).
14. Choose File, Save As, and give the shortcut a readable name, such as **Orders and Details by Customer**. Save your page with a shorter file name, such as **CustomersOrdersDetails.htm**, and acknowledge the warning message.

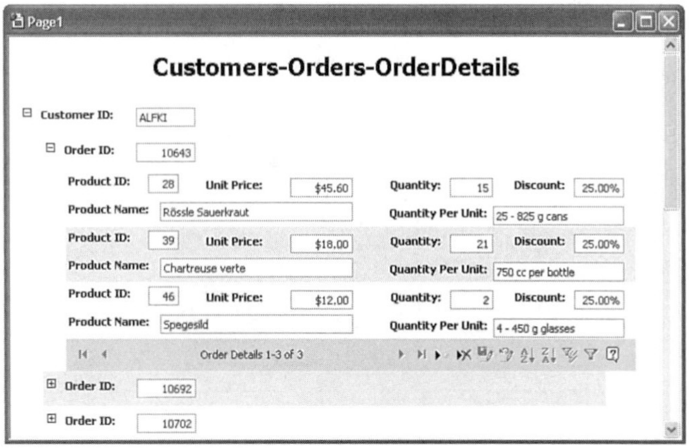

Figure 24.60
An example of the OrderIDs page.

Page1

Customers-Orders-OrderDetails

Customer ID: ALFKI

Order ID: 10643

Product ID: 28 Unit Price: $45.60 Quantity: 15 Discount: 25.00%
Product Name: Rössle Sauerkraut Quantity Per Unit: 25 - 825 g cans
Product ID: 39 Unit Price: $18.00 Quantity: 21 Discount: 25.00%
Product Name: Chartreuse verte Quantity Per Unit: 750 cc per bottle
Product ID: 46 Unit Price: $12.00 Quantity: 2 Discount: 25.00%
Product Name: Spegesild Quantity Per Unit: 4 - 450 g glasses

Order Details 1-3 of 3

Order ID: 10692

Order ID: 10702

ADDING FIELDS AND CAPTIONS

Moving labels to captions increases the number of text boxes that you can place on a single line. Adding fields to existing grouping sections requires an approach that differs from adding fields to a detail section. If you drag an additional field from the table node to the grouping section, the text box displays CountOf*FieldName*, not *FieldName* values. To add text boxes to display additional fields, you must add an unbound text box from the Toolbox and then bind the text box to the field in the Data page of the text box's properties window.

To make the grouped page more readable and informative by removing the default alternate row color, moving some labels to captions, and adding more fields to the existing headers, do the following:

1. Return to Page Design view, right-click the Customers-CustomerID header, and choose Group Level Properties. In the All page, type **white** as the value of the `AlternateRowColor` property. Do the same for the Orders-OrderID and Order Details groups.
2. Move the labels and text boxes in the Customers-CustomerID and Orders-OrderID headers up one grid dot, and then move the bottom of the headers to equalize the top and bottom margins. (Press Ctrl when dragging the bottom of the header to inhibit the snap-to-grid feature.) Delete ID from the CustomerID label.
3. Click the Navigation: Order Details bar and change the `BackgroundColor` property value from `gainsboro` to **white**. Do the same for the Orders-OrderID and Order Details sections.

4. Open the Toolbox, and select the Text Box control. Draw a text box to the right of the CustomerID text box, and delete its label.
5. With the added text box selected, click the Other tab and type **txtCompanyName** as the `Id` value. Click the Data tab, open the `ControlSource` list, and select CompanyName (see Figure 24.61). When you close the list, the property value changes to `GroupOfCompanyName1: CompanyName`.

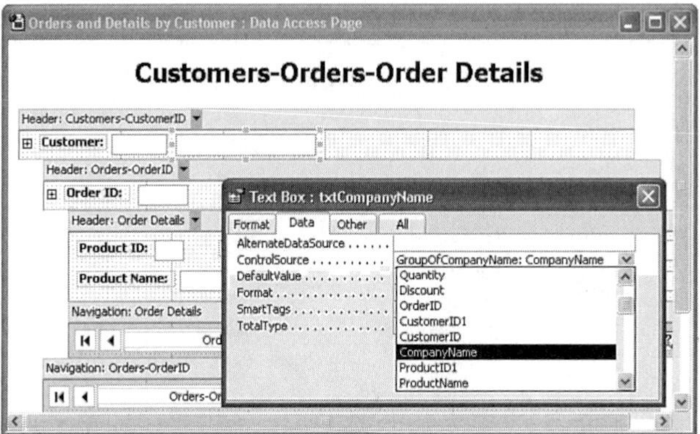

Figure 24.61
Adding text boxes to display field values to group sections requires using the Toolbox to add an unbound text box and then setting the `ControlSource` property value of the text box to the desired field.

B

6. Repeat step 4 for the City and Country fields, but don't delete the labels. Type **City:** and **Country:** as the label captions, and apply the bold attribute.
7. Repeat step 5 for the two text boxes, naming them **txtCity** and **txtCountry**, and setting the `ControlSource` property value to City and Country, respectively.

TIP

> Check your work frequently as you add bound text boxes. If the result in Web Page Preview is what you want, save the page.

8. Following the same procedure, add Order Date:, Shipped Date:, and Ship Via: labels and text boxes to the Orders-OrderID section. For Ship Via, select CompanyName1 under the ShipperID field as the `ControlSource` property value.
9. Right-click the Order Details section header, and choose Caption to add the default caption section above the header.
10. Change the Product ID: label caption to ID, and remove the colons from the other labels.
11. Select all the labels, and press Ctrl+X to remove them from the Header section. Click the Caption: Order Details header, and press Ctrl+V to add the labels to the caption.
12. Arrange the caption labels and header text boxes, and decrease the depth of the Header: Order Details section, as shown in Figure 24.62. Then save the page.
13. Open the page in IE 6+ to test your work (see Figure 24.63).

TWEAKING A READ-ONLY PAGE DESIGN

The following are a few minor design changes that improve the overall appearance of the page and make the order selection process more usable:

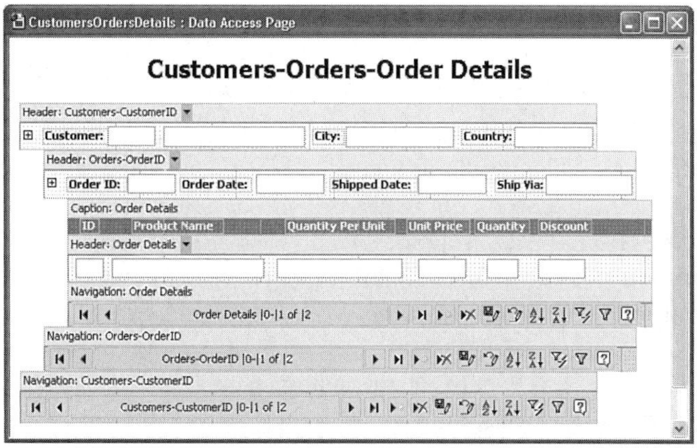

Figure 24.62
The redesigned Order Details section conserves vertical space on the page.

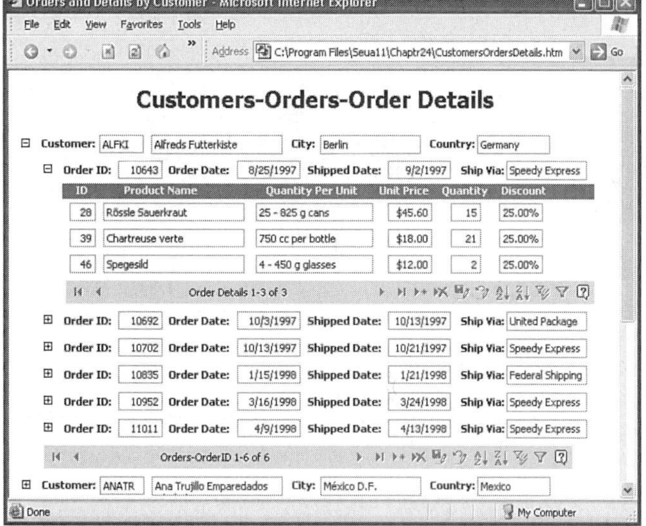

Figure 24.63
Design changes to the three-level hierarchy achieve the goals of providing additional information on customers, orders, and line items.

1. The text of labels isn't aligned vertically with the contents of text boxes. Select all labels in the Header: Customers-CustomerID section, press Ctrl, and press the ↓ key to move the labels down a pixel at a time. (Pressing the Ctrl+*ArrowKey* combination moves selected objects one pixel at a time in any direction.)
2. Changing the label color to steel blue—the default named color for caption sections—reduces the contrast of the page. With the labels selected, click the Properties button and replace the default `#000000` (black) value of the `Color` property to **steelblue**.
3. Repeat steps 1 and 2 for the labels of the Orders-OrderID section.
4. Order data is more useful if you sort orders in descending date sequence. To change the sort order of the Orders: OrderID section, right-click the section, choose Group Level Properties, and add a space and **Desc** to the value of the `DefaultSort` property.

5. If you don't have many line items per order and orders per customer, which is the case for Northwind Traders, set the Group Level `DataPageSize` property value to `All` and set `RecordNavigationSection` to `False` for the Orders-OrderID and Order Details headers.
6. You can edit records only in nongrouped sections—in this case, the Header: Order Details section. The ProductID, ProductName, and QuantityPerUnit values come from the Products table, so it's not feasible to add or edit records with this configuration. Open the Group Level Properties window for this section, and set the `AllowAdditions`, `AllowDeletions`, and `AllowEdits` property values to `False`. Set `DataPageSize` to `All` and `RecordNavigationSection` to `False`.

Figure 24.64 shows the effect of the preceding changes in Page view. The final version of the CustomersOrdersDetails.htm page is in the \Seua11\Chaptr24 folder of the accompanying CD-ROM.

Figure 24.64 The final tweaking process involves sorting the orders in descending date sequence, removing the navigation bars for orders and line items, and vertically aligning the text of labels and text boxes.

DEPLOYING PAGES FOR NETWORK ACCESS TO JET DATA SOURCES

Up to this point, you've ignored the warning messages that recommend placing the data source for your pages in a shared network folder and substituting the UNC path and file name for the default file name—in this case, Northwind.mdb.

Following are the steps to deploy pages to a network share:

1. If the pages' data source is a shared back-end database, skip to step 4.
2. Create a network share for the source database back end. All users of the share must have read-write access to the share and its files so that they can add records to the .ldb lock file.

3. If you haven't done so already, use the Database Splitter tool to move the back-end .mdb to the share. This example uses a split copy of Northwind.mdb with the front end named Pages24.mdb and the back-end named Data24.mdb. Data24.mdb is located in a \\OAKLEAF-MS10\PageData share on a Windows 2000 member server. Pages24.mdb is in the ...\Office11\Samples folder.

→ To review creating a front-end/back-end application, **see** "Creating Linked Jet Tables with the Database Splitter," **p. 745**.

TIP

Alternatively, use the Upsizing Wizard to create an SQL Server 2000 back-end database and convert the front end to an Access project. As noted in the "Moving from Jet to SQL Server Page Data Sources" section near the end of the chapter, using SQL Server as the data source for a DAP doesn't involve significant differences in the design process. Deploying a DAP with a SQL Server database is simpler than a shared Jet back end because you don't need to create a server share for the database.

4. If you specified the UNC path to the .mdb file in step 3, skip to step 6. Otherwise, in the front-end .mdb, choose Tools, Database Utilities, Linked Table Manager, which has the well-formed path to the folder in which you created the back-end .mdb. Click Select All, mark the Always Prompt for New Location check box, and click OK to open the Select New Location of *FirstTableName* dialog.

5. Type the UNC path to the file—**\\OAKLEAF-MS10\PageData\Data24.mdb**, for this example—in the File Name text box, and click OK to substitute the UNC path. (Alternatively, navigate to the network share in My Network Places or Network Neighborhood.) After a few seconds, a message confirms the new links to the tables (see Figure 24.65). Click OK twice.

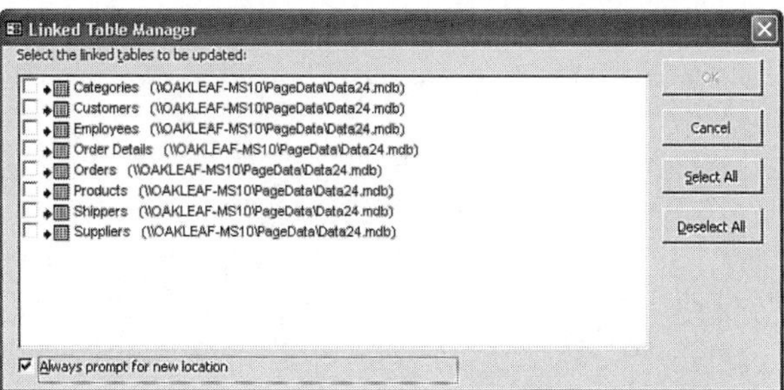

Figure 24.65 Use the Linked Table Manager to change from a fixed, well-formed path to the UNC path of the back-end database.

6. If any page uses a query as its data source, open the back-end .mdb file, choose File, Get External Data, Import, and then import the required queries from your front-end .mdb file. If you're in doubt about which queries are required, import all queries.

7. Open the first page of the front-end .mdb in Page Design view, right-click the title bar, and choose Page Connection. If the Data Link Properties dialog doesn't open, choose Page Properties, click the Data tab, and select the `ConnectionString` property. Then click its Builder button to open the Connection page of the Data Link Properties dialog.
8. Delete the existing path and replace the entry with the UNC path that you specified in step 5. If the back-end database is secure, complete the User Name and Password text boxes for a user account with at least Read Definitions and Read Data permissions for the back end.

9. Click Test Connection to verify the path and copy the path in the text box to the Clipboard. Click OK to update the `ConnectionString` property value, and change to Page view to verify the connection. Press Ctrl+S to save the page.
10. If you want to update the design of the page on the server rather than in your working directory, choose File, Save As; change the name of the link to ***PageLinkName* (Server)**, for example; and click OK. In the File Name text box, type the UNC path to the server location, which need not be the same share as the back-end database, and the original name of the .htm file. When you click OK, a message box opens asking if you want to make the share the default location for all pages. Unless you have a reason not to do so, click Yes.
11. Close the page and repeat steps 7–9 or 10 for each additional page that you want to make accessible to network users. In step 8, paste the UNC path into the text box. If you don't save the pages to a server share, you must manually save copies of the pages to the page share at this point.

TIP

> If your pages deliver images, you must copy the bitmap files to the server page share manually. If pages rely on static XML data sources, you also must copy the .xml files to the page share.

12. Test the pages from a network client by logging on to the client with a test account that has ordinary user privileges. (Don't use a network administrator account.) Launch IE 5+ on the client, choose File, Open, and then click Browse to navigate to the server share with the page files. Double-click one of the files, and click OK to test the page. (The client must have OWC 11—licensed or runtime—installed to fully open the page.)

If you encounter a problem connecting to the data source for your page when you deploy DAP on a production server, see the "DAP Clients Can't Find the Jet Data Source" topic of the "Troubleshooting" section near the end of the chapter.

Users with runtime OWC 11 licenses experience no difference in working with pages that don't use Spreadsheet, PivotTable, or PivotChart controls. For example, the sample

CustomersOrdersDetails.htm page behaves alike in the runtime and licensed OWC versions. Filter buttons of PivotTables open read-only filter lists, which makes filtering data impossible. Runtime users must expand and collapse rows and columns manually because the Expand All and Collapse All buttons are disabled. The only buttons enabled on the PivotTable toolbar are About, Refresh, and Help. When you click the Help button, the "About view-only mode for Office Web Components" topic opens.

DELIVERING PAGES ON AN INTRANET OR THE INTERNET

Most organizations prefer to deploy browser-based applications on their intranet rather than by opening shared .htm pages. Using conventional `http://servername/virtualdirectory/pagename.htm` URLs is more convenient for users, and connecting through IIS 5.0+ is more secure than opening .htm files from read-write shares that contain or allow access to the data .mdb file.

TIP

> Add a Default.htm page to the folder with descriptive links to the pages. The Default.htm page also is a good location for instruction on using the pages or links to help pages.

If you want to enable private or public Internet access to pages, you must consider the security ramifications of potentially exposing your databases to hackers. Internet security issues are beyond the scope of this book, but make sure that the databases to which you allow public access contain no confidential information.

ENABLING INTRANET ACCESS

To enable intranet access to your pages with IIS 5.0, do the following:

1. In the Internet Information Services snap-in, right-click the node for your intranet and choose New, Virtual Directory to start the Virtual Directory Wizard. This example uses OAKLEAF-MS7 running IIS 5.0 under Windows 2000 Server as the Web server. Click Next.
2. In the Virtual Directory Alias dialog, type a name for the directory, such as **DataPages**. Click Next.
3. In the Web Site Content Directory dialog, type the path to the shared folder for the pages that you created in the preceding section. If the page folder is shared from another server, type its UNC path— **\\OAKMONT-MS10\DataPages**, for this example. Click Next.
4. If you specified a share on another server, in the User Name and Password dialog, type your credentials to access the share with at least read-write permissions. Click Next.
5. The Access Permissions dialog has Read and Run Scripts (such as ASP) user permissions enabled by default. If your pages allow data updates, mark the Write check box. Click Next and Finish to create the new DataPages virtual directory. Files in the directory appear in the Name pane of the snap-in (see Figure 24.66).

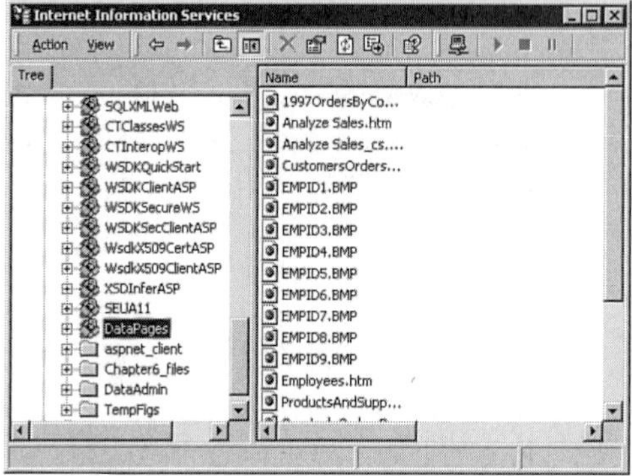

Figure 24.66
When you create an IIS 5+ virtual directory that points to a server share, the files in the share appear in Internet Services Manager's snap-in.

6. On a network client, type the URL for a page— **http://OAKLEAF-MS7/DataPages/1997OrdersByCountry.htm** for this example—to test the virtual directory.

TIP

> If you want to distribute the OWC 11 runtime files from your intranet server, add a virtual directory that points to the Office 11 installation files folder. You must change the `href=` attribute value to the URL for the installation files, such as `<A href='http://*servername*/*virtualdirectoryname*/files/owc/setup.exe'>`.

ENABLING PRIVATE OR PUBLIC INTERNET ACCESS

If you deploy pages on a Web server connected to the Internet, mobile users can access them from any location. By default, IIS 5+ enables integrated Windows security for Internet access. Users with Windows NT/2000+ accounts can open the page by providing their username, password, and domain in the Enter Network Password dialog. Almost all Web servers are protected by firewalls that restrict external connections to HTTP and HTTPS traffic. If your Web server is behind a firewall that doesn't support database connections with ADO, the procedures of this section won't work. Your best bet in this case is to set up a VPN for authenticated users to connect to shared .htm files.

NOTE

> Three-tier data access using Remote Data Services (RDS) in a three-tier configuration is required for Web servers protected by a firewall and to maintain database security, especially with SQL Server. Setting up RDS is beyond the scope of this book, but Microsoft provides detailed instructions in the white paper, "Deploying Data Access Pages on the Internet or Your Intranet." Knowledge Base article Q286327 has a link to the download location for the white paper. The white paper is based on Access 2002 and IIS, but the procedures described apply without change to Access 2003.

When a remote user attempts to open a page without having changed the default IE 6+ security settings, the two messages shown in Figure 24.67 appear.

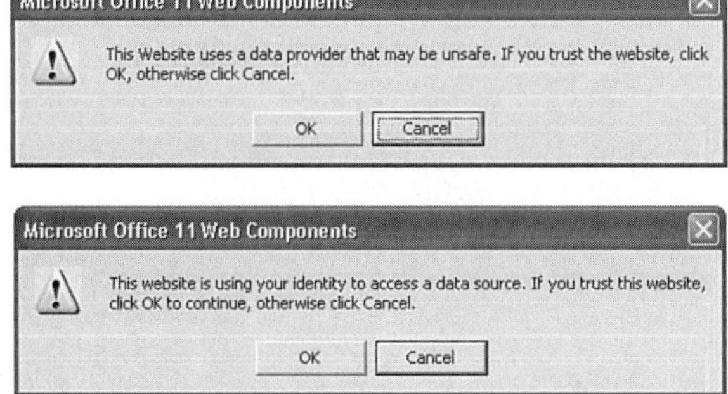

Figure 24.67
IE 6.0 displays these two warning messages when you open DAP deployed to the Internet. You must change your IE 6.0 security settings to avoid them.

To change IE 6.0 security settings to permit users to open a DAP on the Internet, do this:

1. Open the Security page of IE's Internet Options dialog.
2. Click the Trusted Sites icon, and click the Sites button to open the Trusted Sites dialog.
3. Clear the Require Server Verification (https:) for All Sites in This Zone check box.
4. Type the site address—`http://www.`*`whatever`*`.com/` and click Add (see Figure 24.68). This example uses the OakLeaf Web server.

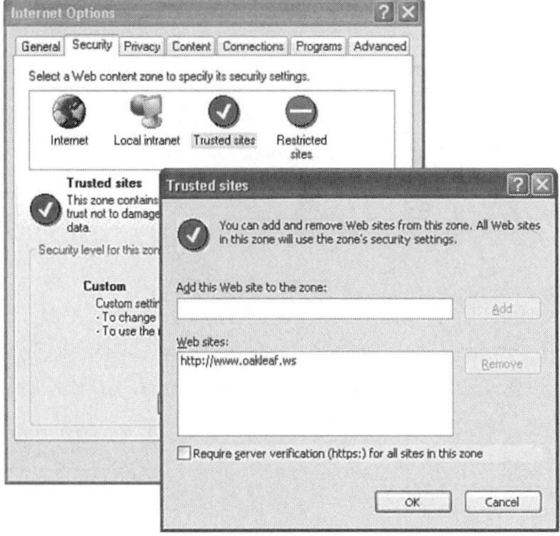

Figure 24.68
Clear the server verification check box and type the URL or IP address of the Web server.

5. Click OK twice to close the dialogs, and click Refresh in the browser to test your changes.

CAUTION

Granting Internet access to DAP by anonymous users creates a serious security risk to your data.

To grant public Internet access to your page on a Web server that's not behind a firewall, do this:

1. Open the *VirtualDirectory* Properties dialog's Directory Security page.
2. Click the Edit button in the Anonymous Access and Authentication Control frame.
3. Mark the Anonymous Access check box, and click OK twice to save the changes.

Internet clients must download and install the OWC 11 runtime to view your DAP.

Moving from Jet to SQL Server Page Data Sources

24

Creating a DAP with SQL Server 2000 as the data source follows the same process as DAP that connect to Jet 4.0 databases. The only difference is that you create the page in an .adp file instead of an .mdb file, and you use views, functions, or stored procedures in place of Jet queries.

The NorthwindCS.adp project doesn't include sample DAP, but you can convert existing pages to work with SQL Server 2000 databases that contain the tables and queries on which your pages depend. The most common approach is to import the *PageName*_cs.htm files, which the Upsizing Wizard creates, into an Access project, but you also can change the data source for pages linked in an .mdb file.

To import sample pages based on Northwind.mdb tables and queries into NorthwindCS.adp as an example, do the following:

1. Open NorthwindCS.adp and click the Database window's Pages shortcut. Alternatively, open the .mdb file for the page, open the page to convert in Page Design view, and skip to step 4.
2. Click the Edit Web Page That Already Exists shortcut to open the Locate Web Page dialog.
3. Double-click any sample *PageName*_cs.htm file in the ...\Office11\Sample folder—such as Review Products.htm—to close the dialog and open the page in Page Design view. Using the *PageName*_cs.htm file prevents overwriting the original *PageName*.htm file.
4. Right-click the page's title bar, choose Page Properties to open the Page: *PageName* window, and click the Data tab.

NOTE

> Importing the page into a project doesn't alter the `ConnectionString` property value that points to the pages Jet data source—...\Samples\Northwind.mdb, for this example.

5. Click the Builder button to open the Data Link Properties dialog, and click the Provider tab.
6. Select Microsoft OLE DB Provider for SQL Server in the list, and click the Next button.
7. In the Select or Enter a Server Name text box type the name of the server or select the SQL Server instance from the drop-down list. This example uses the OAKLEAF-XP1 instance.
8. Select the Integrated Windows Security option.
9. Select NorthwindCS in Select the Database on the Server list, click Test Connection, and click OK to dismiss the "Test connection succeeded" message.
10. Click OK to close the dialog and change the `ConnectionString` property value to point to the NorthwindCS database.
11. Change to Page view and confirm that the page behaves as expected.
12. Choose File, Save As, and accept or change the default link name. Click OK to open the Save As Data Access Page dialog.

TIP

> Change the page name in the Save As dialog if you're using the.mdb file to avoid overwriting the original link.

13. Give the page a different name—such as **ReviewProductsSQL.htm**—to avoid overwriting the original version, and click Save to save the page with the SQL Server connection.

TIP

> If you've deployed Jet back-end databases specifically for use as data sources for DAP, use the Upsizing Wizard to create a new SQL Server database from the tables and queries of the .mdb file.

TROUBLESHOOTING

DAP LOSE THEIR STYLE

My page opens with the default font (Times New Roman), default colors (black and white), and no background image.

You moved the page's PageName.htm file to another folder, but you didn't move the associated PageName_files folder to the folder containing the .css files, which define the page's styles. When DHTML pages can't find their .css files, you don't receive an error message. Always move the PageName.htm file and the associated PageName_files folder as a pair.

DAP Clients Can't Find the Jet Data Source

I receive an "Unable to initialize the data provider" or "FilePathName is not a valid path" message when I try to run the DAP that I deployed on the network.

The connection string for the Jet data source of your page(s) is incorrect. The connection string includes the well-formed (complete) path to the associated .mdb file. When the client executes the DAP from the file or Web server, the location of the shared .mdb file specified by the XML `<a:ConnectionString>` element is incorrect. You must use Uniform Naming Convention (UNC) paths to specify the path, as in *ServerName**ShareName*\ *FileName*.mdb. The fastest method to correct this problem is to make a backup copy and open the offending DAP .htm file in Notepad. Search for `<a:Connect`, and substitute ***ServerName**ShareName*** for the `C:\FolderName\` path in the connection string. Save your changes, and retest the page from a network client.

In the Real World—Is the Third Time a Charm for DAP??

NEW "Microsoft gets it right the third time" is an industry adage that dates from the release of Windows 3.0 and was confirmed by IE 3.0. Microsoft appears to have gotten DAP right—or at least very close to right—on the second pass in Access 2002. Access 2002 solved the serious design-time problems that plagued users who attempted to create Access 2000 DAP without the undo/redo feature. Access 2003 DAP offer undo/redo, multiple control selection and alignment, and other features that bring page layout operations close to the standard established by conventional forms and reports. The primary change to Access 2003 DAP is the operating system restriction of OWC 11. Users running Windows operating systems earlier than Windows 2000 can't view DAP. Users running Windows NT, Me, 98SE, 98, or 95 are out of luck.

If you're an Access 2000 power user or developer, one reason to adopt version 3.0 of DAP as a means of delivering data over your intranet—and, with reservation, the Internet—is the availability of the runtime installation for OWC 11. Access 2000's DAP 1.0 weren't accessible by users who didn't have Office 2000 installed. The relatively low upgrade and adoption rate of Office 2000 and XP resulted in very limited deployment of production DAP. If you need to support Windows Me or earlier clients, however, stick with the Access 2002 version. Providing the runtime version makes view-only DAP accessible to anyone willing to install OWC 11 on their Windows XP or 2000 PC. Access 2002's OWC 10 doesn't have this operating system limitation.

The belt-tightening associated with the economic downturn that occurred when this book was written has caused many large and small organizations to scale back their investments in internal and external Web technology. Expenditure reductions don't mean that the demand for delivery of accurate and up-to-date data over corporate intranets has decreased. Instead, CEOs and CIOs demand more information faster, but at lower development cost. It's doubtful that any current Web-based technology can come close to matching the rapid application deployment (RAD) velocity of DAP. The Save As DAP feature, described in the next chapter, lets you convert existing simple Access objects—primarily queries and reports—to intranet-ready pages in less than a minute.

TIP

> One of the complaints often heard about DAP is that they're limited to use with Jet and SQL Server databases. That's true for the connection, but you can connect to a Jet .mdb that uses client/server tables linked by ODBC, the subject of Chapter 19, "Linking Access Front-Ends to Jet and Client/Server Tables." Another approach is to use SQL Server linked tables, one of the subjects of Chapter 20, "Exploring Access Data Projects and SQL Server 2000." This means that your pages can use as an underlying data source Oracle, IBM DB2, Sybase, Informix, or any other RDBMS that has an ODBC or OLE DB driver.

Users who haven't upgraded to Office 2003 Standard Edition or higher won't be able to pivot or filter the PivotTables or change the type of a PivotChart without some programming effort on your part. Most page recipients, however, likely will be intimidated by field buttons and drop zones. The vast majority of information on intranets and public Web sites is meant to be read—not manipulated. The capability to drill down into view-only PivotTables is probably adequate for most users. There's no limit, however, on programming access to Spreadsheet, PivotTable, and PivotTable features in runtime OWC 11. If your customers (users) want more control over pages, brush up your VBScript or ECMAScript skills.

The upshot of this section is that DAP probably are the most compelling "new" feature of Office 2003 for Office 97 and 2000 users—SharePoint Team services, smart tags, and upgraded XML features notwithstanding. Businesses tend to upgrade to alternate Office releases, and many organizations have Office 97 installed. Microsoft hasn't devoted significant marketing effort to Access since Tod Nielsen spearheaded the release of version 2.0. Here's hoping that Office Access 2003 regains the attention that it deserves from the Redmond marketing machine.

CHAPTER 25

Converting Access Objects to Data Access Pages

In this chapter

Understanding the Limitations of the DAP Conversion Process

Access 2003's Save As Data Access Page feature is available for table, query, form, and report objects in conventional Jet .mdb files and ADP. Be forewarned—Save As DAP has a limited repertoire and stumbles when you try to save most Northwind.mdb or Northwind.adp sample form and report objects as pages. On the other hand, Save As DAP is the quickest and easiest way to create simple data entry pages for tables and to display query result sets in a browser. Saving PivotTable and PivotChart views of aggregate queries as pages is the most expeditious method of delivering data analysis pages to intranet users.

NOTE

SharePoint Team Services 2.0 lists that you import from or link to Jet or SQL server tables and queries are similar in function to data objects saved as DAP. Chapter 26, "Collaborating with SharePoint Team Services 2.0," describes how to create static and updatable lists from Jet and SQL Server 2000 tables and queries.

25

Like the Save As XML feature described in Chapter 23, "Exporting and Importing Data with XML," Save As DAP relies on ReportML to extract the property values of Access objects. The Save As DAP feature substitutes RPT2DAP.xsl for RPT2HTML4.xsl and transforms the intermediate XML data in ReportML format to the combination of XML and DHTML code used by DAP. RPT2DAP.xsl shares most of RPT2HTML4.xsl's limitations on support for native Access controls. The most important of the excluded objects are subform, subreport, tab, and bound and unbound object frame controls. You can use HTML inline frames (`<IFRAME>` elements) and VBScript code to emulate form/subform combinations, but transforming an existing Access form object to a main page and the subform to a page in an embedded frame usually doesn't succeed. Few conventional bound Access forms are suited to saving as pages directly. If you can adapt the page to a banded design, subordinate sections with navigation controls sometimes can take the place of subforms.

→ To download a Wizard that generates DAP with inline frames for subforms and subreports, **see** "In the Real World—Enhancing Data Access Page Design," **p. 1098**.

TIP

The "Embed an Existing Page in a Data Access Page" article at `http://msdn.microsoft.com/library/en-us/dnacc2k2/html/odc_embedpage.asp` explains how to add an inline HTML frame (`<IFRAME>`) and use a server filter to emulate a form/subform combination.

Saving reports as pages is a mixed bag. Even simple reports require design tweaks to generate attractive, usable pages. An exception is Northwind.mdb's Invoice report; it transforms to an almost-identical representation of the original. The only missing element is the

DatePrinted value in the Page Header section, which involves a very simple fix. For more complex reports that include subtotals and grand totals, plan on spending at least an hour or two making page design changes. If your reports print calculated values other than standard aggregates of field values, be prepared to write VBScript event-handling code to generate the values.

NOTE

> The chapter requires familiarity with basic HTML authoring techniques, but you don't need to be a professional Web page designer. Some of the examples include simple VBScript procedures for page navigation and passing parameters from one page to another. You don't need to be an experienced VBScript programmer to follow this chapter's examples.

SAVING TABLES AS DATA ENTRY PAGES

Saving a table as a page is the simplest Save As DAP operation. For example, do the following to save the Suppliers table as a Suppliers.htm page:

1. In the Tables page of Northwind.mdb's Database window, right-click the Suppliers table and choose Save As to open the Save As dialog.
2. Change Copy of Suppliers to **Suppliers**, and select Data Access Page (see Figure 25.1). Click OK to open the New Data Access Page dialog.

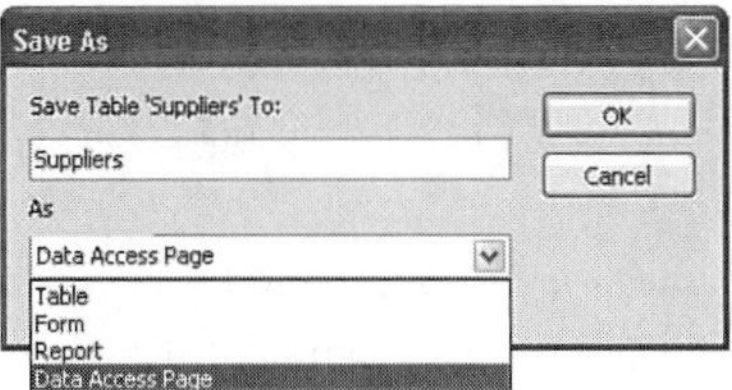

Figure 25.1
Name the page for the table, and choose Data Access Page in the Save As dialog.

3. Accept Suppliers.htm as the file name, and click OK to create the file in the current folder.
4. After a second or two, the Suppliers page opens in Page view with a caption, data-entry, standard page navigation section (see Figure 25.2).

Opening HTML elements;table cell values> a page in IE 6+ or Page view generates an ADO `Recordset` object of the updateable snapshot type over the entire table. Specially formatted text boxes (HTML <TEXTAREA> elements) contain cell values of the table.

Following are the default display and editing characteristics of a table saved as a page:

- The datasheet layout determines the column widths of the page. If the table has a lookup field, the column width of the field is expanded, but the foreign key value—not the lookup field value—appears in the column.

- Clicking a field caption sorts the underlying `Recordset` in ascending order of the field values. For example, clicking Company Name sorts the records in alphabetic order. To restore the original sequence, click the Supplier ID column.
- The default record navigation control displays 10 records at a time.
- `Recordset` navigation progresses by 10-record groups and uses the First, Previous, Next, and Last buttons.
- Record-selector buttons are bitmap images stored in the Office Web Components (OWC) Data Source control (MSODSC). When you select a record by clicking the record-selector button, the black arrow changes to white and the background changes to a darker shade of gray.
- The Tab key navigates from left to right by column and the top to bottom by row. Fields with locked values—such as Jet AutoNumber fields—aren't tab stops. When you reach the last column of the last visible row, the focus changes to the navigation control buttons. Pressing Tab when the focus is on the last navigation control moves to the first editable column of the first row.
- The ↓ and ↑ keys don't navigate rows in the current columns. You can assign key names as the value of the `AccessKey` property of a text box to enable navigation by Alt+*Key* down—but not up—the rows of the specified column. The later "Streamlining Data Entry" section describes how to set `AccessKey` values for columns.
- The Tab key positions the insertion point after the last character of an editable cell. You must manually select the entire field (press Shift+Home or Shift+↑) if you want the text that you type to replace—rather than extend—the existing value.
- Jet Hyperlink fields display the text but not the link; thus, Jet hyperlinks aren't operable. This is the opposite of the behavior of Hyperlink fields that you add to DAP from the Field List.
- Field- and table-level validation rules for Jet tables and `CHECK CONSTRAINT`s for SQL Server tables work as expected, and referential integrity rules are enforced. For example, attempting to delete a Supplier record that has dependent records in the Products table displays the messages shown in Figure 25.3.

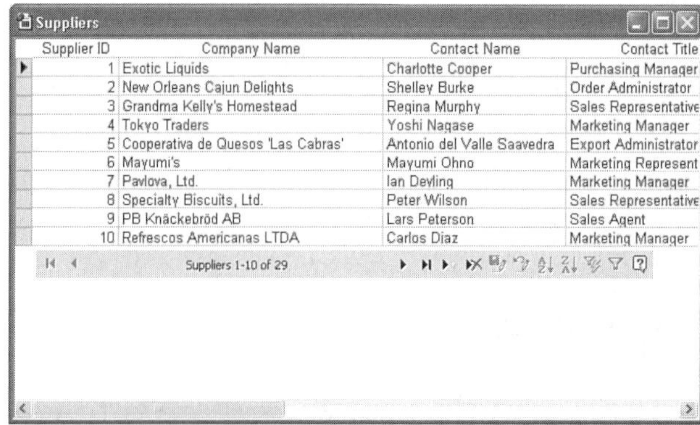

Figure 25.2 Page view of a table saved as a page is a reasonably close rendition of datasheet view, considering the limitations of HTML. The Suppliers datasheet uses default formatting, which displays a plain-vanilla page.

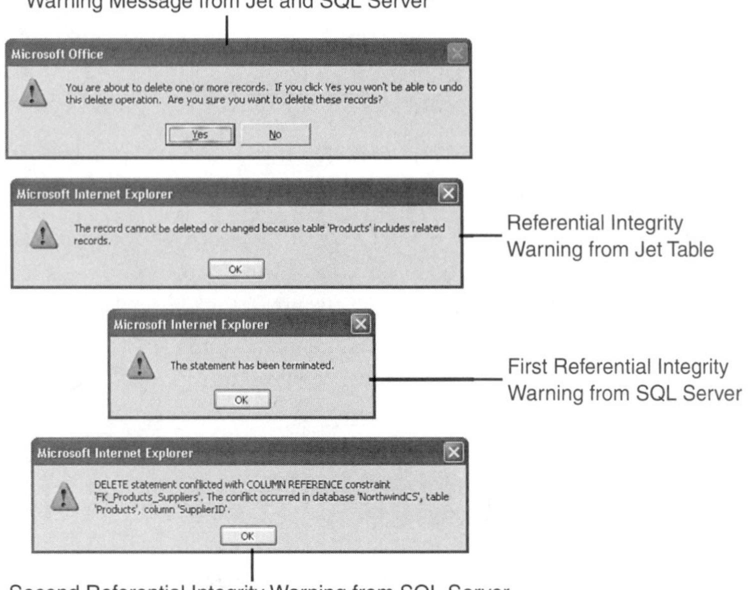

Figure 25.3 Users receive a warning message before deleting a record. If deleting the record violates referential integrity rules, a single message from Jet or two messages from SQL server explain the reason for denying the deletion operation.

- The Input Mask property of fields is ignored. You must write VBScript event-handling code to implement after-entry input masks, such as the >LLLLL mask for the CustomerID field of the Customers table. For this example, the event handler must apply the `ucase` function to the entry, test for the correct number of characters, and use the `asc` function to verify that only letters are present.

TIP

For a VBScript workaround for lack of Input Mask capability in pages, see the "ACC2002: Data Access Page Ignores Underlying Table's Input Mask" Knowledge Base article at `http://support.microsoft.com/support/kb/articles/Q299/0/09.ASP`.

Web pages aren't as effective as Access datasheets for bulk data-entry operations because keyboard shortcuts for editing operations—such as copying field values from the preceding row—aren't available in IE.

Enhancing the Page's Appearance

A few simple design changes can dress up the table-based page and improve the usefulness of the display. The following sections offer suggestions for making table-based pages resemble the style of pages that you create in Page Design view or that the Layout Wizard creates for you.

Adding Heading Elements with the Script Editor

Unlike pages that you create from scratch, pages saved from datasheets don't have empty <H1> and <H2> elements for adding a heading and explanatory text to the table. Adding elements to table-based pages requires adding HTML code with the Script Editor.

→ To review use of the Microsoft Script Editor, **see** "The Microsoft Script Editor," **p. 1012**.

To add <H1> and, optionally, <H2> elements, do the following:

1. With the Suppliers page open, change to Page Design view and click the Microsoft Script Editor button to open the source window for your page.
2. By default, the Script Editor adds HTML tag names in lower case, which conforms to XHTML standards; RPT2DAP.xsl generates upper-case tag names. To change the tag name case, choose Tools, Options, to open the Options dialog. Expand the Text Editor and HTML nodes, and select Format.
3. Select Uppercase in the Generated HTML list. If you want to make your changes more evident, mark the Tag Start: Before and Tag End: After check boxes (see Figure 25.4). Click OK to close the Options dialog.

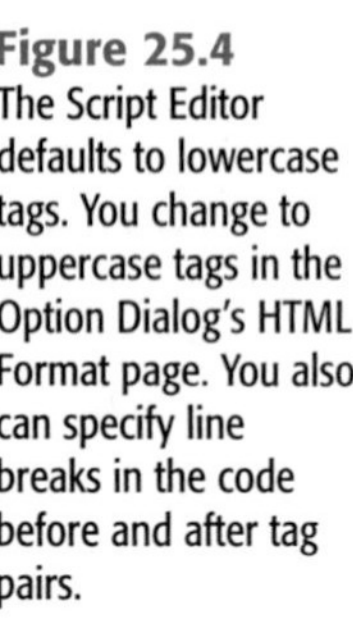

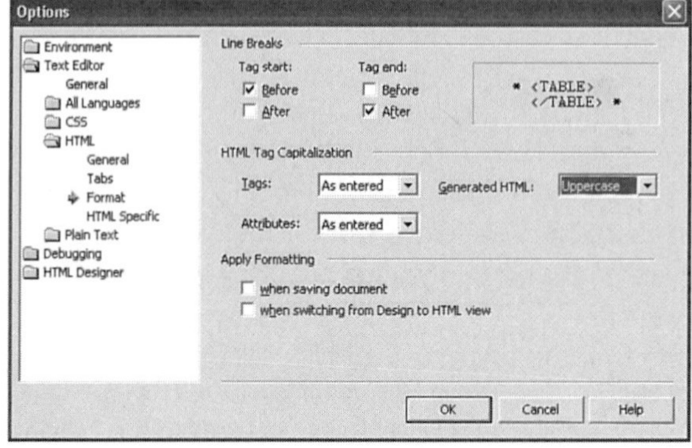

Figure 25.4 The Script Editor defaults to lowercase tags. You change to uppercase tags in the Option Dialog's HTML Format page. You also can specify line breaks in the code before and after tag pairs.

TIP

You can reduce toolbar clutter by choosing View, Toolbars, and toggling the Design, Formatting, and Text Editor toolbars off. Only the Standard toolbar is useful for the HTML editing examples in this chapter.

4. After the <TITLE> tag, change Suppliers to **Suppliers Table Data Entry**.
5. Press Ctrl+F to open the Find dialog, type **body**, and press Alt+F twice to locate the <BODY> tag that follows the </HEAD> tag.
6. Move to the end of the line, and press Enter to create a new line.

7. Type **<h2**, which opens the HTML statement-completion window and selects the H2 item. Double-click H2 and type **>** to create an `<H2></H2>` tag pair. Type the title that you added in step 4 between the tag pair as the heading for the form. As you add the HTML content, Page Design view displays the changes.

8. Optionally, add a `<P></P>` tag element;adding to table-based pages> element;adding to table-based pages> pair with explanatory text after the heading. To center the lines, type a **<CENTER>** tag before the `<H2>` element, and type **</CENTER>** after the `</P>` element. Remove the extra `</CENTER>` and `<CENTER>` tags that the statement completion feature adds (see Figure 25.5), and close the Script Editor.

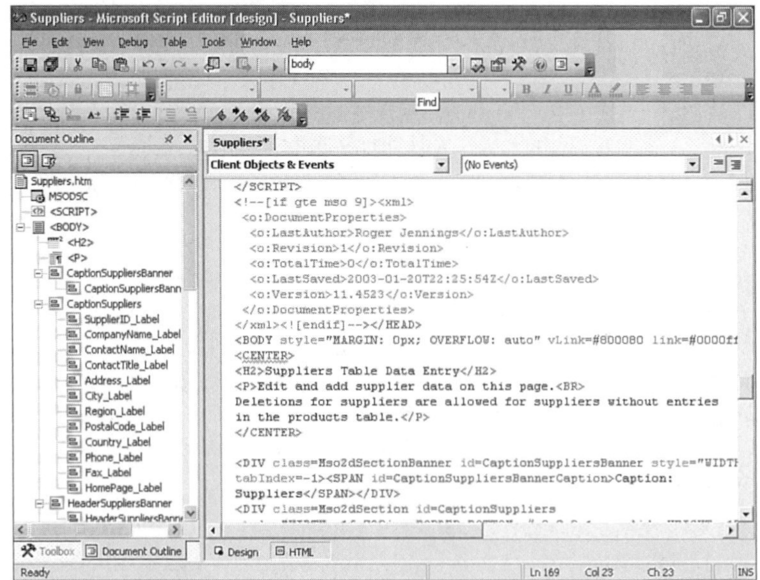

Figure 25.5 The HTML code between the `<CENTER>` and `</CENTER>` tags adds an 18-point heading and a text paragraph to the page.

> **TIP**
>
> Close the Script Editor before making further changes in Page Design view. If you leave the Script Editor open it's difficult–and sometimes impossible–to alter control positions or sizes.

9. Return to Access, select all captions, and click the Bold button. Press Ctrl+S to save your changes.

10. Change element;adding to table-based pages> element;adding to table-based pages> to Page view to check your work so far (see Figure 25.6).

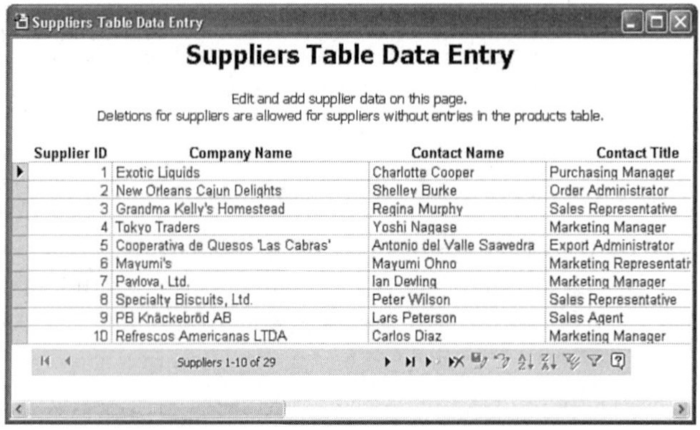

Figure 25.6
The added HTML code of Figure 25.5 provides the heading and text shown here. After you add the elements, you can edit their text in Page Design view.

NOTE

> If you've specified a default theme, the styles of the theme determine the color, font, and size attributes of the elements that you add. Otherwise, the attributes default to the standard style for DAP.

MODIFYING FIXED PAGE LAYOUT AND DESIGN ELEMENTS

A few additional design changes make the page more attractive and make the appearance conform to the DAP that you created from scratch in Chapter 25, "Designing and Deploying Data Access Pages." The sections of DAP that you save from Access objects have fixed positions and dimensions, so you must change section property values to alter the overall design of the page.

To make the form-based design of saved datasheets resemble the standard format of the other pages you've created, using the Suppliers.htm page as an example, do the following:

1. Return to Page Design view, and double-click the Caption: Suppliers section heading to open its properties window.
2. Change the `BackgroundColor` property value to **steelblue** and the Height to **25px**.

3. Select all the captions, open the Fore/Font Color picker, and click the white square.
4. With all captions selected, drag the captions down one grid dot.
5. Change the Supplier ID caption to ID and decrease its width to fit the text.
6. Decrease the width of the Supplier ID text box to match the width of the ID caption, and select and drag the remaining text boxes to the left. Dragging the text boxes also drags the labels.
7. The Home Page hyperlink field isn't functional in the Suppliers page, because the page link isn't present. Delete the field and its caption.

8. The width of the active area of the page is set by the fixed `Width` property of the record navigation section. Double-click the NavigationSuppliers section, and set the `Width` property value to **13.75in**.

9. To add a small margin around the page elements, open the Script Editor and change the `<BODY style="MARGIN: 0px` attribute to **17px**.

10. Press Ctrl+S to save the edits, close the Script Editor, and change to Page view to review your work (see Figure 25.7).

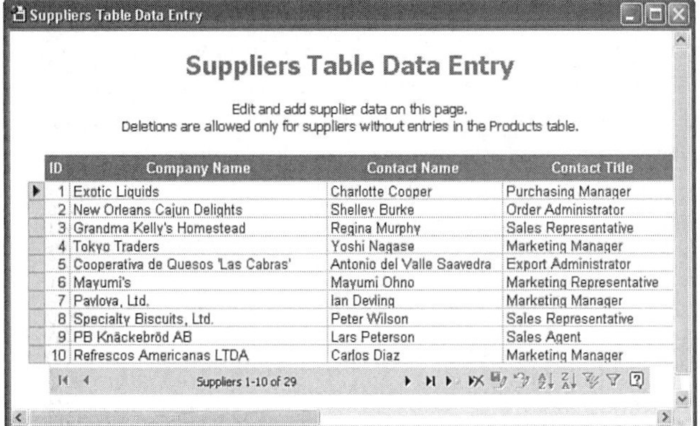

Figure 25.7 Adding a background color to the caption, reducing the width of the Supplier ID column, and adding a margin improves the appearance of the page.

STREAMLINING DATA ENTRY

The width of the sections exceeds the visible page widths on ordinary monitors, so editing values in more than one row of columns that aren't visible is a painfully slow process. Tabbing through columns and then rows causes the display to flash, which leads to data-entry operator fatigue. To navigate by rows of a particular column, you add `AccessKey` property values to each updateable field.

Access key column navigation is limited to the number of rows displayed by the Header section. The 10-row default creates a page that resembles a form more than a Web page. Forms usually have about a 4:3 width-to-height aspect ratio to avoid scrolling the form, but users are accustomed to scrolling Web pages vertically. Displaying more rows of the table in a group aids navigation, especially when combined with column access keys.

To add and test `AccessKey` values for the columns of the sample Suppliers.htm page and increase the number of rows on the page, do this:

1. In Page Design view, double-click the Company Name text box to open the Text Box: CompanyName window.

2. Click the Other tab and type **1** as the `AccessKey` value. Alternatively, type a letter that's easier to reach with a thumb or finger on the Alt key.

3. Select each text box in sequence, and specify a different `AccessKey` value. This example uses 1, 2, 3, … 0 for the 10 active fields of the Suppliers table. (SupplierID is an AutoNumber or `identity` field, so it isn't active.)
4. Right-click the page and choose Group Level Properties to open the Group Level: Suppliers window, and set the `DataPageSize` property value to a larger number. Select `All` if you want to scroll the entire `Recordset`.
5. Press Ctrl+S to save your changes, and then open the page in Web Page Preview. Click the Company Name header to sort the page by company.
6. Press Alt+5 (or the letter that you chose) to move the insertion point to the end of the City name in the first row (see Figure 25.8). Pressing the same key combination repeatedly scrolls the City column. When you reach the last row of a list that's less deep than IE's window, the insertion point returns to the first row of the City column. Otherwise the insertion point returns to the first row of the page.

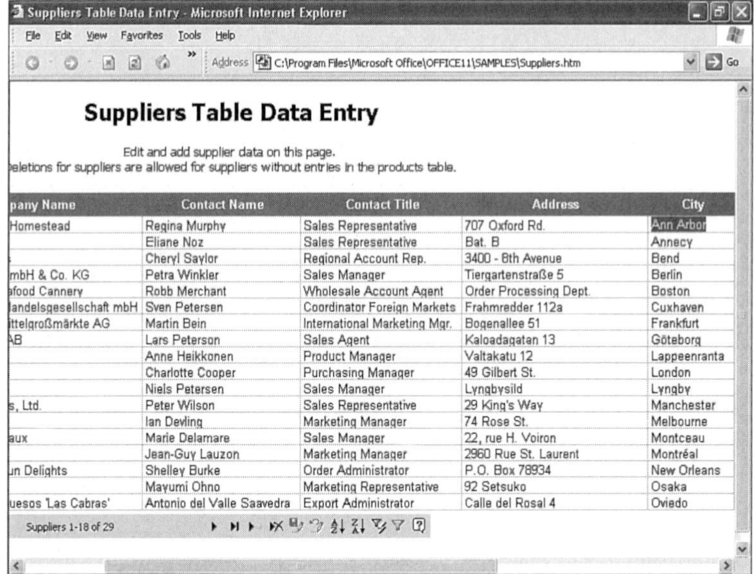

Figure 25.8 You can sort the page by clicking a column heading or selecting a column and clicking the A-Z or Z-A buttons. This view is sorted by city. Pressing Alt+*AccessKey* navigates horizontally to the designated column and then vertically through the rows.

Unfortunately, you can't freeze fields to make the Supplier ID and Company Name field visible while you edit other fields.

It's a good practice to delete buttons in the *PageName*Navigation section that aren't necessary for data entry. For example, the Help button opens the "About Data Access Pages" help topic; installing the Office Web Components (OWC) 11 runtime on client PCs adds this help file. The help file contains more information than most data-entry operators need. Depending on your application, you might want to remove the filter buttons. To remove a button, in Page Design view, select the button and press Delete. Removing unneeded buttons also improves page performance.

→ To make the data entry page available to users, **see** "Delivering Pages on an Intranet or the Internet," **p. 1057**.

If you encounter problems opening the page from a networked computer other than the one on which you're designing the page, see the "Data Source Problems" topic of the "Troubleshooting" section near the end of the chapter.

SAVING QUERIES AS READ-ONLY PAGES

Saving query datasheets as DAP is an alternative to creating the live Web reports described in Chapter 23. If the query is updateable, you can edit the result set by the methods described in the preceding section. In most cases, however, pages based on queries are read-only, even if the result set is updateable.

Datasheets with special formatting preserve the format by changing the Cascading Style Sheet (CSS) style for text boxes. For an example, save the Customers and Suppliers by City `UNION` query to a page that closely resembles the query's Datasheet view. To make the entire text box visible, you must increase the depth of the Header section from 17 to about 21 pixels and then expand the depth of text boxes, which appear as command buttons in Page Design view. On the whole, special effects applied to datasheets are less than special in pages.

DESIGNING THE QUERY LAYOUT FOR DAP

If you intend to save a query as a page, it's faster to change the column captions, when possible, and the column widths in Datasheet view. Changing the default Medium Date to Short Date format makes date columns consistent with other pages that use MM/DD/YYYY format. Figure 25.9 shows a sample Jet qryOrdersPage query in Datasheet view; column widths are minimized to ensure full display within IE 6+ maximized 800×600 monitor resolution. Applying a descending sort on the OrderID column displays latest orders first.

qryOrdersPage : Select Query

Order I	Company Name	Order	Ship	Amount	Freight	Company Name
11077	Rattlesnake Canyon Grocery	05/06/1998		$1,255.72	$8.53	United Package
11076	Bon app'	05/06/1998		$792.75	$38.28	United Package
11075	Richter Supermarkt	05/06/1998		$498.10	$6.19	United Package
11074	Simons bistro	05/06/1998		$232.08	$18.44	United Package
11073	Pericles Comidas clásicas	05/05/1998		$300.00	$24.95	United Package
11072	Ernst Handel	05/05/1998		$5,218.00	$258.64	United Package
11071	LILA-Supermercado	05/05/1998		$484.50	$0.93	Speedy Express
11070	Lehmanns Marktstand	05/05/1998		$1,629.97	$136.00	Speedy Express
11069	Tortuga Restaurante	05/04/1998	05/06/1998	$360.00	$15.67	United Package
11068	Queen Cozinha	05/04/1998		$2,027.08	$81.75	United Package
11067	Drachenblut Delikatessen	05/04/1998	05/06/1998	$86.85	$7.98	United Package
11066	White Clover Markets	05/01/1998	05/04/1998	$928.75	$44.72	United Package
11065	LILA-Supermercado	05/01/1998		$189.42	$12.91	Speedy Express
11064	Save-a-lot Markets	05/01/1998	05/04/1998	$4,330.40	$30.09	Speedy Express
11063	Hungry Owl All-Night Grocers	04/30/1998	05/06/1998	$1,342.95	$81.73	United Package
11062	Reggiani Caseifici	04/30/1998		$406.40	$29.93	United Package
11061	Great Lakes Food Market	04/30/1998		$510.00	$14.01	Federal Shipping
11060	Franchi S.p.A.	04/30/1998	05/04/1998	$266.00	$10.98	United Package

Record: 1 of 830

Figure 25.9 Adjusting column widths, captions, and formatting of queries before you save the page minimizes redesign effort. For orders, it's usually preferable to set the default sort order to descending.

25

When you save the query as a page, RPT2DAP.xsl might transform the design incorrectly. In this case, the Order ID caption doesn't fit the allotted space, so the caption and all rows have a two-line depth (see Figure 25.10).

Figure 25.10 RPT2DAP.xsl interprets the insufficient width for the Order ID caption as requiring an increase in the depth of the rows.

Current Orders

Order ID	Company Name	Order	Ship	Amount	Freight	Company Name
11077	Rattlesnake Canyon Grocery	05/06/1998		$1,255.72	$8.53	United Package
11076	Bon app'	05/06/1998		$792.75	$38.28	United Package
11075	Richter Supermarkt	05/06/1998		$498.10	$6.19	United Package
11074	Simons bistro	05/06/1998		$232.08	$18.44	United Package
11073	Pericles Comidas clásicas	05/05/1998		$300.00	$24.95	United Package
11072	Ernst Handel	05/05/1998		$5,218.00	$258.64	United Package
11071	LILA-Supermercado	05/05/1998		$484.50	$0.93	Speedy Express
11070	Lehmanns Marktstand	05/05/1998		$1,629.97	$136.00	Speedy Express
11069	Tortuga Restaurante	05/04/1998	05/06/1998	$360.00	$15.67	United Package

The solution to this problem is to change Order ID to **ID** in the caption, and delete the Order ID text in the first text box of the header. (Field names aren't necessary in Page Design view of text boxes.) You don't need record-selector buttons for a read-only query, so right-click the page, choose Group Level Properties, and set the `RecordSelector` property value to `False`. After making design changes similar to those recommended in the preceding two sections, your page appears as shown in Figure 25.11. The New, Save, Undo, and Help buttons are deleted because the query result set is read-only.

Figure 25.11 Design changes for table-based pages described earlier have been applied to the query-based page shown here. When you remove the record-selector buttons, the left border of the text box for the first column is missing.

Current Orders

ID	Customer	Order	Ship	Amount	Freight	Ship By
11077	Rattlesnake Canyon Grocery	05/06/1998		$1,255.72	$8.53	United Package
11076	Bon app'	05/06/1998		$792.75	$38.28	United Package
11075	Richter Supermarkt	05/06/1998		$498.10	$6.19	United Package
11074	Simons bistro	05/06/1998		$232.08	$18.44	United Package
11073	Pericles Comidas clásicas	05/05/1998		$300.00	$24.95	United Package
11072	Ernst Handel	05/05/1998		$5,218.00	$258.64	United Package
11071	LILA-Supermercado	05/05/1998		$484.50	$0.93	Speedy Express
11070	Lehmanns Marktstand	05/05/1998		$1,629.97	$136.00	Speedy Express
11069	Tortuga Restaurante	05/04/1998	05/06/1998	$360.00	$15.67	United Package
11068	Queen Cozinha	05/04/1998		$2,027.08	$81.75	United Package
11067	Drachenblut Delikatessen	05/04/1998	05/06/1998	$86.85	$7.98	United Package
11066	White Clover Markets	05/01/1998	05/04/1998	$928.75	$44.72	United Package
11065	LILA-Supermercado	05/01/1998		$189.42	$12.91	Speedy Express
11064	Save-a-lot Markets	05/01/1998	05/04/1998	$4,330.40	$30.09	Speedy Express
11063	Hungry Owl All-Night Grocers	04/30/1998	05/06/1998	$1,342.95	$81.73	United Package
11062	Reggiani Caseifici	04/30/1998		$406.40	$29.93	United Package
11061	Great Lakes Food Market	04/30/1998		$510.00	$14.01	Federal Shipping
11060	Franchi S.p.A.	04/30/1998	05/04/1998	$266.00	$10.98	United Package
11059	Ricardo Adocicados	04/29/1998		$1,838.00	$85.80	United Package

TIP

As an alternative to setting all margins at once by changing the `<BODY style="MARGIN: 0px` attribute value, you can change individual margins on the Format page of the Page: *PageName* window. Set the `MarginLeft` and `MarginTop` property values to **17px** (or more).

To add a left border to the text boxes in the Header section, double-click the text box with the missing border—in this case, ID—to open its properties window. Delete the last `#000000` value of the `BorderColor` property and delete the last `none` value of `BorderStyle`.

TIP

> To minimize active connections to the database, open the Page: *PageName* properties sheet, click the Data tab, and use the `RecordsetType` property's list box to change the default `dscUpdateableSnapshot` to `dscSnapshot`.

The qryOrdersPage query and a Current Orders link to the CurrentOrders.htm page are in the Data25.mdb file located in the \Seua11\Chaptr25 folder of the accompanying CD-ROM.

WORKING WITH PARAMETERIZED QUERIES

Users opening pages based on queries download the entire query result set to a local `Recordset`, unless you add a `TOP` *n* modifier or a `WHERE` clause to limit the number of rows. Alternatively, you can add a parameter to the query to limit the `Recordset` size. For this example, the parameter is the earliest order date to view. To avoid errors that result from not typing the parameter value in the exact date format, add a hidden OrderDate column and type **>=[Enter Earliest Order Date (M/D/YYYY)]** or the like in the Criteria row of the query. (Keep your parameter captions short for pages.)

25

Jet SQL

The Jet SQL statement for the qryOrdersPageParam parameter query used in the following sections is:

```
PARAMETERS [Enter Earliest Order Date (M/D/YYYY)] DateTime;
SELECT Orders.OrderID, Customers.CompanyName,
   Format([OrderDate],"mm/dd/yyyy") AS [Order],
   Format([ShippedDate],"mm/dd/yyyy") AS Ship,
   [Order Subtotals].Subtotal AS Amount,
   Orders.Freight, Shippers.CompanyName
FROM Shippers
   INNER JOIN (Customers
      INNER JOIN (Orders
         INNER JOIN [Order Subtotals]
         ON Orders.OrderID = [Order Subtotals].OrderID)
      ON Customers.CustomerID = Orders.CustomerID)
   ON Shippers.ShipperID = Orders.ShipVia
WHERE (((Orders.OrderDate)>=[Enter Earliest Order Date]))
ORDER BY Orders.OrderID DESC;
```

SUPPLYING PARAMETER VALUES IN THE ENTER PARAMETERS DIALOG

When you open the page in Page View or Web Page Preview, a nonstandard Enter Parameters dialog appears first. The dialog can accommodate about 12 parameter values, but the Name list doesn't expand to accommodate fully descriptive parameter captions. Figure 25.12 shows the Enter Parameters dialog for the CurrentOrdersParam.htm page.

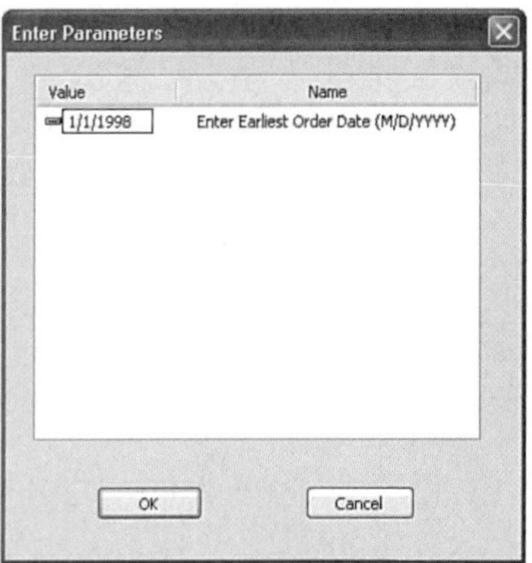

Figure 25.12
A single parameters dialog replaces one or more Access Enter Parameter Value dialogs. The first Microsoft mystery of this chapter is why the parameter names are centered instead of left-justified in the list.

Typing the required value and clicking OK (or pressing Enter twice) sends the parameter value(s) to Jet and opens the page. If you don't enter a value and click OK, no rows appear. If you click Cancel, the page opens with #Name? values in a single row. The parameter entry procedure is the same for SQL Server parameterized stored procedures and table-returning functions.

TIP

> If you copy the parameterized query with a different name—such as qryOrdersParam—and use Save As to save the link and page with a different link and .htm file name, you must change the `RecordSource` property value on the Data page of the Section: Navigation*QueryName* window to point to the parameterized query. Open the `RecordSource` list, and scroll to the Procedure: items—not Query: items—to find the new parametized query (see Figure 25.13). The Procedure: prefix applies to Jet parameterized queries and SQL Server stored procedures with parameters.

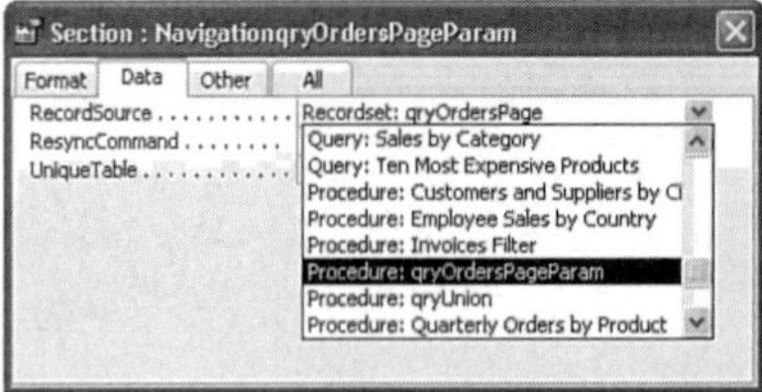

Figure 25.13
When you change the `RecordSource` property from a conventional query to a parameterized query, select the query name from the items with the Procedure: prefix.

The qryOrdersPageParam query and a Current Orders (Param) link to the CurrentOrdersParam.htm page are in the Data25.mdb file located in the \Seua11\Chaptr25 folder of the accompanying CD-ROM.

Passing Filter Criteria from One Page to Another with Cookies

The Enter Parameters dialog isn't user-friendly, and it limits the explanation of the required parameter entry to a few words. A better alternative is an initial page in which users type one or more parameter values in text box(es), and then click a button or a label formatted as a hyperlink to open a second page that displays the data. The `onClick` event handler of the button or label writes a cookie with the parameter names and values, and then opens the other page. The second page retrieves the cookie and passes the values as query parameter values or the criterion value for the DataSourceControl's `ServerFilter` property. One of the advantages of using an initial page is that you can provide a default value for the parameter in a text box.

NOTE

> The DataSourceControl's `ServerFilter` property is similar to the `Filter` property of a table or query. The `Filter` property downloads the entire Recordset and then applies the filter on the client. Applying a `ServerFilter` downloads only those records that meet the filter criterion, which minimizes network traffic and speeds response time.

Cookies are a means for passing variable values between conventional HTML forms. Cookies are `Name=Value` pairs—called *crumbs*—separated by semicolons. Cookies can contain up to 20 crumbs. Unless you add an `expires=datetime` crumb, a cookie ordinarily stays in memory only while the browser is open. In Access, the cookie stays in memory while the page is open in Page or Page Design view. Cookies are properties of the browser's `document` object; you create a cookie with a VBScript `document.cookie = "Name=Value"` statement and retrieve it with a `strVariable = document.cookie` statement. Obtaining the value of a crumb requires parsing the cookie with VBScript string-manipulation functions. VBScript doesn't support all Jet/VBA string-manipulation functions; those that VBScript does support—with a few exceptions—use the same syntax as their Jet/VBA counterpart.

NOTE

> Like VBA, VBScript isn't case sensitive. Web programmers use a variety of capitalization styles when writing VBScript code. A common style is to use lower case for VBScript key words and object, property, and method names defined by the Document Object Model. Mixed case is used for variable names and other object names–such as `MSODSC.RecordsetDefs` for the `RecordsetDefs` collection of the Microsoft Office Data Source Control. This book uses mixed case for VBScript.
>
> VBScript has only one data type–**`Variant`**. The VBScript examples of this chapter use variable-type prefixes–such as `dat` for date and `str` for character variables–for consistency with the VBA code that you encounter in Part VII, "Programming and Converting Access Applications."

You can create the initial page in the Access page designer or any other HTML editor, such as FrontPage 2003. The initial page might include navigation buttons or labels for several related pages. Figure 25.14 shows a simple navigation form with links to the CurrentOrders.htm and CurrentOrdersCookie.htm pages.

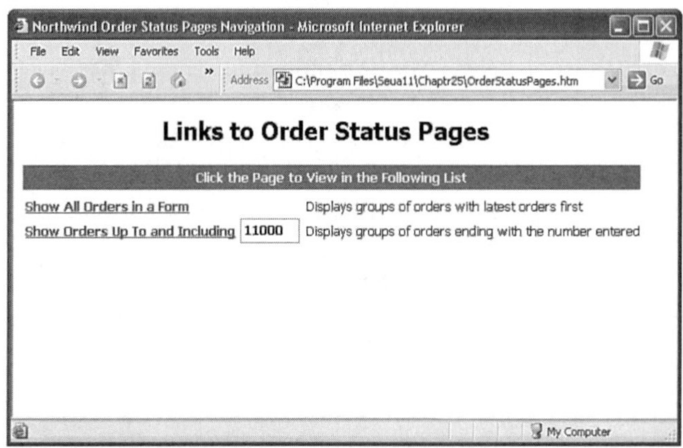

Figure 25.14 OrderStatusPages.htm is an unbound navigation page that has a link to CurrentOrders.htm and a text box for entering the earliest order parameter required when clicking the link to the CurrentOrdersCookie.htm page.

TIP

When you deploy a navigation page with links to other pages, create a virtual directory for it and all related pages in Internet Information Server (IIS). Rename the navigation page to Default.htm. Users enter `http://`*`servername`*`/`*`directoryname`*`/` to open Default.htm; *filename.htm* isn't required.

25 The hyperlinks of the navigation page of Figure 25.14 are formatted labels (`blue` color, underlined). The Show All Orders in a Form link's `onClick` event handler contains the following VBScript code to open the CurrentOrders.htm page:

```
<SCRIPT language=vbscript event=onclick for=lnkAllOrders>
<!--
   dim strURL
   strURL = "CurrentOrders.htm"
   window.navigate(strURL)
-->
</SCRIPT>
```

NOTE

The preceding event-handler code is typical for links or buttons on pages that perform navigation functions similar to that of Northwind.mdb's Main Switchboard form.

The Show Orders Up To and Including... link (`lnkLatestOrders`) points to CurrentOrdersCookie.htm and has a text box (`txtEndDate`) that contains a default value appropriate for the range of the latest orders in the Northwind.mdb Orders table. The following code illustrates how to create the parameter cookie (`LastOrder=11000`) before opening the CurrentOrdersCookie.htm page.

```
<SCRIPT language=vbscript event=onclick for=lnkLatestOrders>
<!--
   Dim strURL
```

```
    Dim lngLastORder
    Const strParam1 = "LastOrder"

    strURL = "CurrentOrdersCookie.htm"
    lngLastOrder = txtLastOrder.value
    document.cookie = strParam1 & "=" & lngLastOrder
    window.navigate(strURL)
-->
</SCRIPT>
```

The following VBScript added to the CurrentOrdersCookie.htm page reads the cookie, extracts the date from the cookie text, and adds a `ParameterValues` object to the `MSODSC.RecordsetDefs` collection.

```
<SCRIPT language=vbscript event=BeforeInitialBind(varParams) for=MSODSC>
<!--
    Dim lngLastOrder
    Dim strCookie

    strCookie = document.cookie
    If Len(strCookie) > 0 Then
       'Extract the date from the cookie
       lngLastOrder = Mid(strCookie, InStr(strCookie, "LastOrder=") +10)
       If InStr(lngLastOrder, ";") Then
          'Remove trailing cookie name-value pairs
          lngLastOrder = Left(lngLastOrder, InStr(lngLastOrder, ";") - 1)
       End If
       MSODSC.RecordsetDefs("qryOrdersPage").ServerFilter = "OrderID >= " &
lngLastOrder
    Else
       MSODSC.RecordsetDefs("qryOrdersPage").ServerFilter = "OrderID >= 11050"
    End If
-->
</SCRIPT>
```

→ To review the syntax of the `Mid` and `InStr` functions, which is the same in VBA and VBScript, **see** "Text-Manipulation Functions," **p. 373**.

For an alternative and more complex VBScript example for passing query parameters between pages, search for "Passing Parameters to a Data Access Page" (include the quotes) at `http://msdn.microsoft.com`.

The OrderStatusPages.htm, CurrentOrders.htm, and CurrentOrdersCookie.htm files are in the \Seua11\Chaptr25 folder of the accompanying CD-ROM. To test passing a parameter with a cookie, open OrderStatusPages.htm in IE and then click the Display Latest Orders... link.

TIP

Don't attempt to pass a cookie value to another page in Page view; both pages must run in IE to share the cookie. The preceding code substitutes a constant OrderID value (11050) to prevent an error or downloading the entire Recordset.

25

If your navigation page's link opens an empty page whose data source is a parameterized query, see the "Parameter Naming and Cookie Parsing Problems" topic of the "Troubleshooting" section near the end of the chapter.

Saving Forms as DAP

The ReportML transform isn't named FormML for a good reason—saving forms as DAP has severe form design limitations. Most forms have subforms, tab controls, or other objects that ReportML ignores. For example, saving Northwind.mdb's sample Employees form as a page results in colorful—but empty—Caption: Employees and Header: Employees sections. Saving the Customer Phone List form creates a page with elements for the form header, detail, and footer section. The Caption section has an extra line of field-name captions, and the 26 command buttons to filter the records are missing from the option group below the navigation control (see Figure 25.15). Loss of the command buttons isn't a major issue because the form relies on Access macros to filter the detail records.

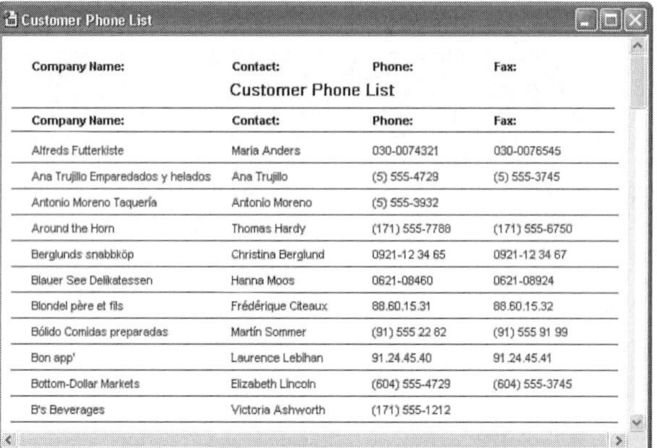

Customer Phone List

Company Name:	Contact:	Phone:	Fax:

Customer Phone List

Company Name:	Contact:	Phone:	Fax:
Alfreds Futterkiste	Maria Anders	030-0074321	030-0076545
Ana Trujillo Emparedados y helados	Ana Trujillo	(5) 555-4729	(5) 555-3745
Antonio Moreno Taquería	Antonio Moreno	(5) 555-3932	
Around the Horn	Thomas Hardy	(171) 555-7788	(171) 555-6750
Berglunds snabbköp	Christina Berglund	0921-12 34 65	0921-12 34 67
Blauer See Delikatessen	Hanna Moos	0621-08460	0621-08924
Blondel père et fils	Frédérique Citeaux	88.60.15.31	88.60.15.32
Bólido Comidas preparadas	Martín Sommer	(91) 555 22 82	(91) 555 91 99
Bon app'	Laurence Lebihan	91.24.45.40	91.24.45.41
Bottom-Dollar Markets	Elizabeth Lincoln	(604) 555-4729	(604) 555-3745
B's Beverages	Victoria Ashworth	(171) 555-1212	

Figure 25.15 Saving to DAP forms that generate simple lists usually works, but you must tweak the page design in most cases.

Saving a form (or a report) that has a Class Module saves the VBA code as a comment block between `BEGIN VBA CODE` and `END VBA CODE` comments (see Figure 25.16). The purpose of saving the code in the script is to aid you when rewriting the code in VBScript, if possible.

NOTE NEW

> Access 2003 doesn't let you save unbound forms as DAP. Access 2002 could save unbound forms, such as Main Switchboard, to non-functional replicas.

Following are a few types of forms that you can save as DAP with varying degrees of success:

1. Simple forms without subforms, such as the Customer Phone List. Bound combo boxes used for lookup and other operations are empty. Bound subforms display all records from the underlying table or query.

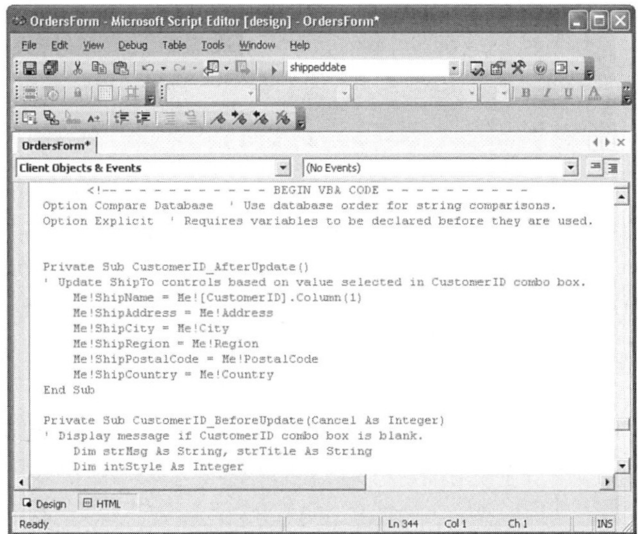

Figure 25.16
The Script Editor displays the VBA code that you can use as a reference when attempting to emulate the form's actions with VBScript.

2. Subforms that contain bound PivotTable or PivotChart objects. For example, the sbf1997SalesPivotChart subform that you created in Chapter 18, "Adding Graphs, PivotCharts, and PivotTables," retains all its properties when saved as a page. You must specify the Default View property as PivotTable or PivotChart to create the correct version of the page. Replace the missing caption supplied by the parent form with a title (see Figure 25.17).

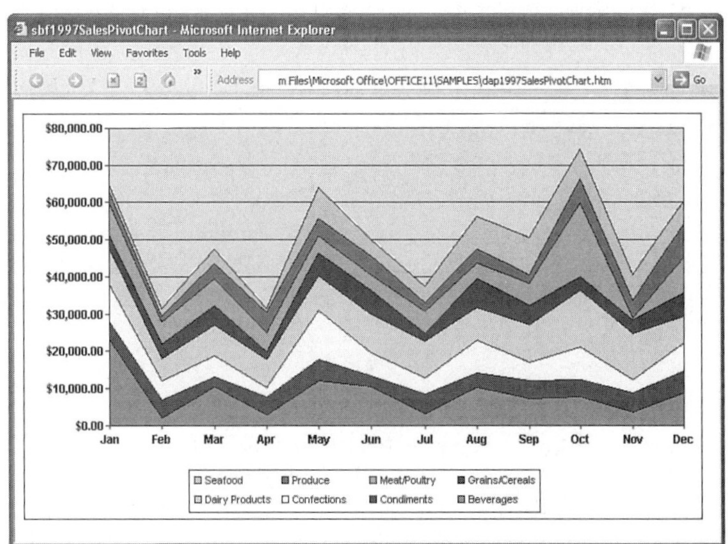

Figure 25.17
PivotChart views of forms or subforms save correctly as pages. A page saved from Chapter 18's sbf1997SalesPCLinked graph displays eight lines instead of the single line specified by the link to the frm1997SalesPCLinked form.

3. Bound pop-up forms and dialogs that don't contain unsupported controls. Pop-up forms and dialogs are better displayed as Web Page Dialogs—such as the Employees.htm page opened by the Review Orders.htm page.

SAVING REPORTS AS DAP

RPT2DAP.xsl does a better job saving simple reports than saving forms as pages. Grouping levels in reports transform to `GroupLevelx` page sections with a navigation control; detail sections also gain a navigation control. Grouped sections are collapsed by default.

Following is a list of the most commonly used features of reports that don't survive the Save As process:

- Subreports—like subforms—are ignored. You must modify the resulting page—such as by adding an embedded inline frame containing a page—to emulate subreports.
- VBA code in the report's Class Module appears in the script as a comment block.
- You can't group by expressions that aren't supported by the Group On property of the report's group. The Alphabetic List of Products report handles the report's `=Left([ProductName],1)` grouping expression correctly because the report's Group On property value is set to Prefix Characters in the Sorting and Grouping dialog.
- Aggregate values in the outermost grouping section move below the navigation control in the navigation section. Text boxes lose their `ControlSource` property value when moved to this section.
- Aggregate value expressions in section footers don't work. You receive an error message if your report includes text boxes to display the result of aggregate expressions, such as `=Sum([FieldName])`.
- Expressions in the report's group headers and footers aren't supported.
- You can't add bound controls to a caption.
- The Can Grow and Can Shrink properties are ignored.

The restriction on subreports and loss of VBA code in Class Modules makes it difficult or impossible to save complex reports as useful DAP. Only 3 of the 11 sample Northwind reports—Alphabetical List of Products, Invoice, and Products By Category—save as readable pages.

MODIFYING THE ALPHABETICAL LIST OF PRODUCTS PAGE

The Alphabetical List of Products report is simple enough for RPT2DAP.xsl to convert without modifying the report before the transformation. The resulting page, however, requires many modifications to improve its appearance and usefulness. The design changes that you make to this report are typical for many simple reports saved as DAP.

To save the Alphabetical List of Products to a page, do the following:

1. In the Database window's Reports page, right-click Alphabetical List of Products and choose Save As to open the Save As dialog.
2. Delete Copy Of in the text box, select Data Access Page in the As list, and click OK to open the New Data Access Page dialog.
3. Shorten the file name of the page to **ProductList.htm**, click Yes to enable scripts, and click OK to open Page view of the transformed report. Expand one or more of the sections to verify the presence of detail records (see Figure 25.18).

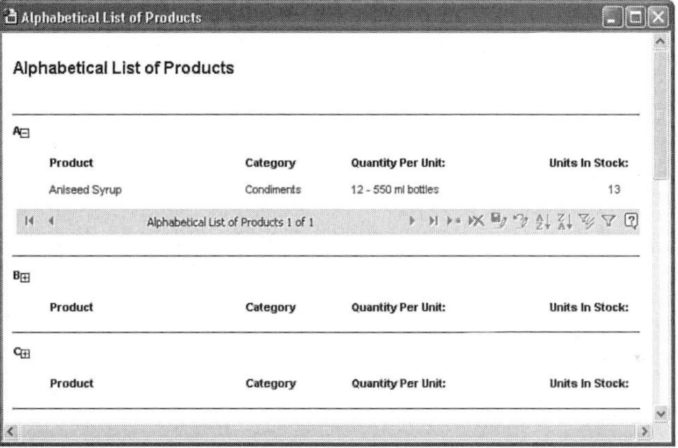

Figure 25.18
The Alphabetical List of Products report creates a page with a navigation control for each group. It's obvious that this page needs a makeover for viewing in a browser.

4. Change to Page Design view, and start redesign by dragging the empty text box below the title to the right of the title. Drag the caption labels from the Header: GroupLevel0 to the Caption: GroupLevel0 section to prevent repetition in every group level, and delete the colon suffix. Drag the line to under the captions, and drag the bottom of the Caption section to just below the line. Look ahead to Figure 25.19 for control positioning.

TIP

> As you make changes to the page, switch to Web Page Preview to check your work. Opening the page in IE 6+ doesn't clear the undo stack when you save changes.

5. Navigation controls aren't appropriate unless the page has many rows in each section, which isn't the case with this page. Right-click in the Header: GroupLevel0 section, and clear the Record Navigation check box. Do the same for the Header: Alphabetical List of Products section.

TIP

Use Ctrl+*ArrowKey* or Ctrl+Shift+*ArrowKey* to make fine adjustments to the position of the controls.

6. In the Header: GroupLevel0 section, move the text box to the right of the Expand control. Double-click the Expand control, click the Other tab, and change the `Src` property value to `Black Arrow`. Drag the bottom of the section to the bottom of the text box.
7. Drag the bottom of the Header: Alphabetical List of Products to the bottom of the text boxes.
8. In the Footer: GroupLevel0 section, move the line up a few pixels, delete the empty text box in the footer, and drag the bottom of the section up.
9. Optionally, change the font of the labels and text boxes to match the font used in other DAP—Tahoma, for the examples in this book. The design at this point appears as shown in Figure 25.19.

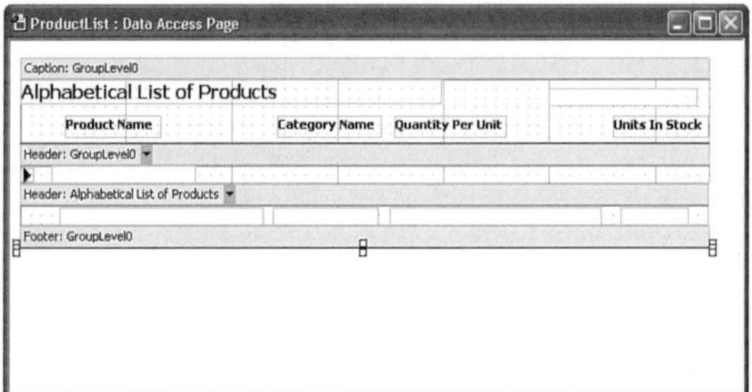

Figure 25.19 The page design changes shown here make the transformed report appear more like a conventional page.

25

10. To add a date to the empty text box in the Caption section, double-click the text box, click the Data tab of its properties window, and type **=Date()** in the `DefaultValue` text box. Right-align the text, add the bold, and remove the italic attribute.

NOTE

Setting the Format property value has no effect on the date display in Page view.

11. The width of the QuantityPerUnit field is larger than required, so you can add the Unit Price field to the left of the Units in Stock field. Decrease the width of the text box to two grid dots wider than the Quantity per Unit label. Open the Field List and the Toolbox, select the Bound Span control, and drag the UnitPrice field to the right of the shortened text box. Move the **Price** label to above the new field.

TIP

> Use bound span controls instead of text boxes wherever possible to improve page performance. If you add a text box, you must change the format of the text box to prevent its borders from appearing on the page.

12. Change to Web Page Preview to display the redesigned report in IE (see Figure 25.20).

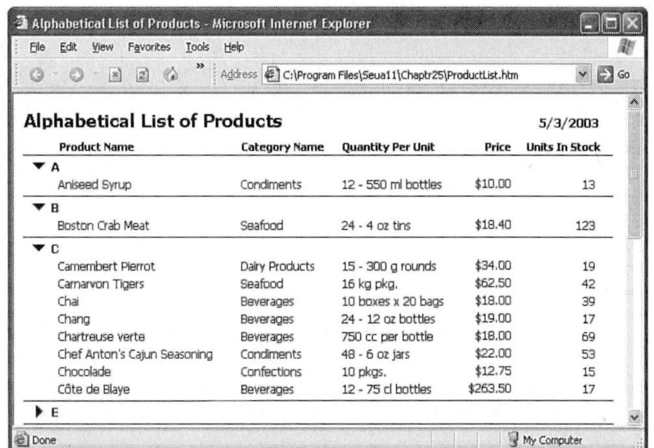

Figure 25.20 Page view of the redesigned page resembles the sample Review Products page but doesn't repeat captions.

The Alphabetical List of Products link to the ProductList.htm page is in the Data25.mdb file located in the \Seua11\Chaptr25 folder of the accompanying CD-ROM.

USING A `ServerFilter` TO DISPLAY A SINGLE INVOICE PAGE

The Invoice report is an example of a report that you can save to a page without a major design change. An Invoice page also is a candidate for addition to the OrderStatusPages.htm page with the order number—the same as the invoice number—passed by a cookie.

CREATING AND MODIFYING THE INVOICE PAGE DESIGN

To transform the Invoice report to an Invoice.htm page and modify its design, do this:

1. Right-click the Invoice report item in the Database window, choose Save As, and change the name to **Invoice**. Then select Save As Data Access Page, click OK, and click Yes to dismiss the warning message, if it appears, to save the page as Invoice.htm.
3. Click the Expand control above the Ship To label to display the Order Details items. Verify that the Subtotal and Total amounts calculate correctly.
4. Change to Page Design view, and double-click the `DatePrinted` text box. Click the Data tab of the properties window, and type **=Date()** as the temporary `DefaultValue` property value.

5. You don't need navigation controls for this page, so right-click Header: GroupLevel0 and clear the Record Navigation check box. Do the same for the Header: Invoices Filter.
6. Right-click Header: GroupLevel0 again and select Group Level Properties. Double-click the `ExpandByDefault` property to change its value from False to True. Delete the Expand control under the Header: GroupLevel0. Save your changes.
7. Open the page in Web Page Preview to verify the design changes in IE (see Figure 25.21) and then close IE.

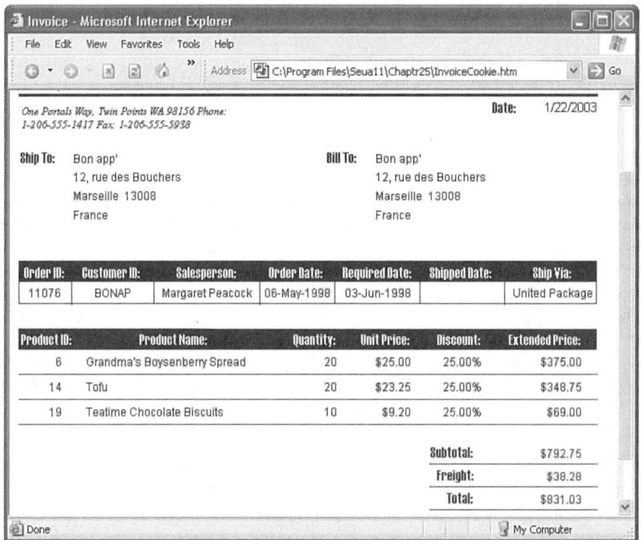

Figure 25.21 The modified Invoice page has the Expand and record navigation controls removed and the missing Date value added.

Adding the VBScript Code to Accept the Invoice Number Cookie

If you created the OrderStatusPages.htm navigation page in the earlier "Passing Filter Criteria from One Page to Another with Cookies" section, you can add a line to the page to navigate to a specific invoice. This section demonstrates how to reuse VBScript code that you added to the CurrentOrdersCookie.htm page in the Invoices.htm page.

To add the VBScript required to accept a cookie value from the OrderStatusPages.htm page, do the following:

1. In the Database window, select the Invoice page and save it as **Invoice (Cookie)** with **InvoiceCookie.htm** as the page file name.
2. Select the Current Orders (Cookie) item and click the Microsoft Script Editor button to open the Script Editor for the CurrentOrdersCookie.htm page.
3. Scroll to and select the `<SCRIPT>...</SCRIPT>` block for the `BeforeInitialBind` event, copy it to the Clipboard, close the Script Editor, and close the page.

4. In Page Design view of the InvoiceCookie.htm page, click the Microsoft Script Editor button, go to the same location in page (after the `<![endif]-->` tag, press Enter, and paste the script block.
5. Change all instances of `lngLastOrder` to **`lngInvoiceNum`**, `+ 10` to **`+11`**, two instances of qryOrdersPage to Invoices and, >= to = (see Figure 25.22).

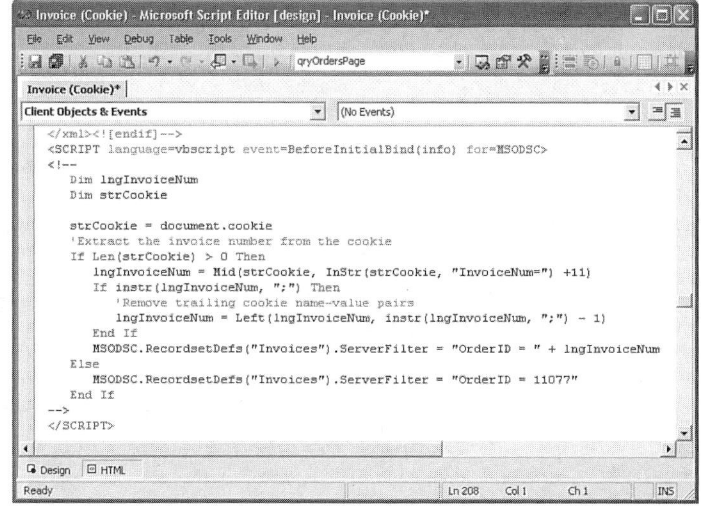

Figure 25.22 Reusing VBScript code from another page saves time. Only minor modifications are required to CurrentOrdersCookie.htm code to display a single invoice.

6. Save your script changes.

You can verify that the `ServerFilter` works by opening InvoiceCookie.htm in IE and verifying display of the default order 11077.

CHANGING THE DATEPRINTED VALUE TO THE SHIPPING DATE

The Invoice report displays the system date in the DatePrinted span. Ordinarily, the invoice date is the date shipped, although some firms have been known to issue invoices for products not shipped or services not rendered. To comply with generally accepted accounting practices (GAAP), the invoice date should be blank if the goods haven't been shipped. Failure to use the shipping date as the invoice date is another Microsoft mystery.

The solution to this problem is to set the `innerText` property of the page's `DatePrinted` span to the `innerText` property of the `ShippedDate` text box. The VBScript code to make the change is simple and illustrates how to write event handlers for the Date Source Control. MSODSC has many more events than the ActiveX Data Object (ADO) `Recordset`; most of the events have equivalents in bound Access forms.

To make the change to the `ShippedDate` span, do this:

1. With Script Editor open with the Invoice.htm page, navigate to a position above or below the cookie script that you added in the preceding section. Add an empty line between the `</SCRIPT>` and `</BODY>` tags.

25

2. With the insertion point on the empty line, choose MSODC in the Object (Client Object & Events) list, open the Event list, and select DataPageComplete to add an event-handling stub.
3. `MSODSC` events require a parameter placeholder, even if the event doesn't return a value to the parameter. Add **(varParam)** to the `event=DataPageComplete` argument to make the event handler work.
4. Add a `DatePrinted.value = ShippedDate.value` statement. The complete event handler code is

```
<SCRIPT language=vbscript event=DataPageComplete(varParam) for=MSODSC>
<!--
   DatePrinted.value = ShippedDate.value
-->
</SCRIPT>
```

5. Save your changes, close the Script Editor, and close the page.

You can't test your addition to the script until you complete the next section.

ADDING A LINK TO OPEN THE INVOICE PAGE

25

Adding a link for the Invoice.htm page to the OrderStatusPages.htm page is similar to adding the link to the CurrentOrdersCookie.htm page in the earlier "Passing Filter Criteria from One Page to Another with Cookies" section. You copy the existing link, text box, and label, change their `Id` values, and add a modified copy of the VBScript code for the new link's `onClick` event.

To add the link to the Invoice.htm page, do this:

1. Open Order Status Pages in Page Design view, and select the link, text box, and label. Press Ctrl+C and Ctrl+V to create a copy.
2. Change the text of the link and label, and reduce the width of the text box. Type a default order number in the text box (see Figure 25.23).

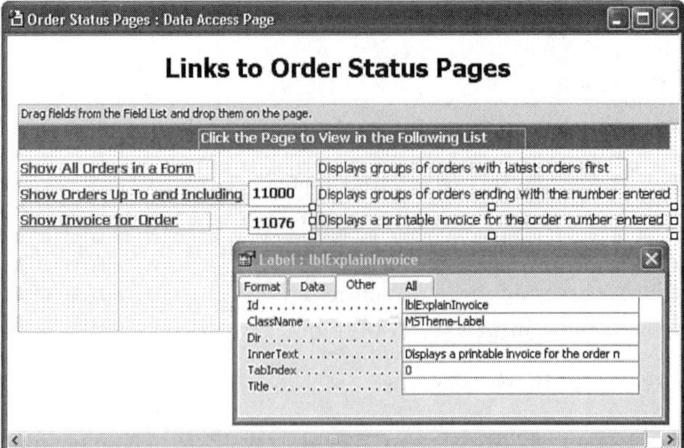

Figure 25.23 Add links to other pages in the Order Status Pages page by copying and editing preceding links.

3. Double-click the link, click the Other tab of the properties window, and change the `Id` property value to **lnkInvoice**. Select the text box and change its `Id` to **txtInvoice**, and change the `Id` of the label to **lblExplainInvoice**, as shown in Figure 25.23.

4. Open the Script Editor, and copy and paste the VBScript block for `lnkLatestOrders`. Edit the event handler code as follows:

```
<SCRIPT language=vbscript event=onclick for=lnkInvoice>
<!--
   dim strURL
   dim lngInvoice
   const strParam1 = "InvoiceNum"

   strURL = "InvoiceCookie.htm"
   lngInvoice = txtInvoice.value
   document.cookie = strParam1 & "=" & lngInvoice
   window.navigate(strURL)
-->
</SCRIPT>
```

5. Save your changes, close the Script Editor, and open the page in Web Page Preview. Click the three links to test the code that you added in this section and the preceding section.

The Invoice link to the InvoiceCookie.htm page is in the Data25.mdb file located in the \Seua11\Chaptr25 folder of the accompanying CD-ROM.

SAVING THE INVENTORY BY CATEGORY REPORT TO A PAGE

The Inventory by Category report (rptInventoryByCategory) that you created in Chapter 16, "Working with Simple Reports and Mailing Labels," is a candidate for conversion to a page. This report illustrates problems that you encounter with aggregate values in group footer sections—the mysterious error message shown in Figure 25.24 appears during the transformation process. It's a common practice to use text boxes with aggregate functions in report group footers, so you're likely to see this message often. Loosely translated, the error message means that RPT2DAP.xsl doesn't translate `=Sum([FieldName])` expressions into the required GroupOf*FieldName* function for section aggregates.

When you click OK to acknowledge the message, the page opens with #Name? as values of aggregate text boxes. Clicking the Expand button to display rows of the detail section opens an "Operation is not allowed when the object is closed" message (see Figure 25.25). The Category name is missing because pages don't display lookup field values. You can't put aggregates in the outermost footer, so there's no Grand Total value. To create a page that you can modify to comply with page design rules, you must delete the text box expressions and then save the modified report as a page.

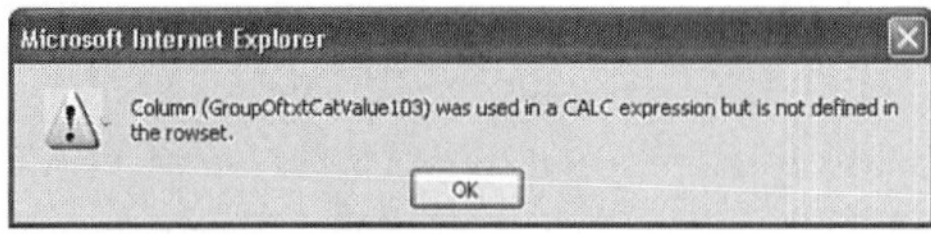

Figure 25.24
This error message appears when the report that you save as a page has an aggregate expression in a group footer.

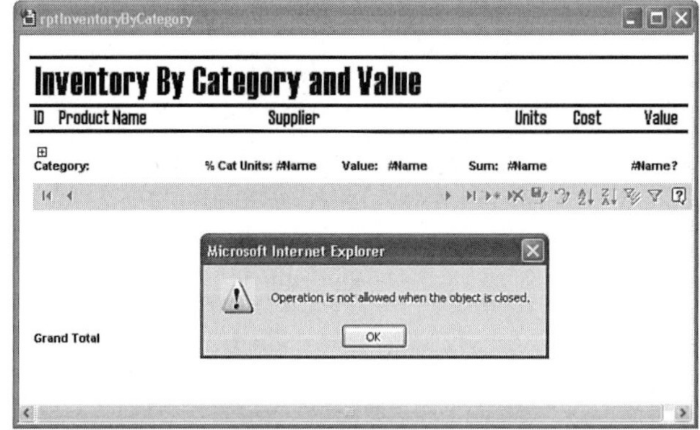

Figure 25.25
After acknowledging the error shown in Figure 25.24, the page opens with errors and missing elements. Another error message appears when you click the Expand control.

25

Modifying the Source Query to Supply Required Field Values

For this example, substituting CategoryName and supplier CompanyName values for lookup fields requires redesigning the source query—qryInventory, for this example. You must also supply fields to replace the calculated Cost and Value columns because the page section Value aggregates depend on field values. The once-simple qryInventory query requires a total makeover. Fortunately, the required changes to the query don't affect the design of the original rptInventoryByCategory report.

Jet SQL

The SQL statement for the modified qryInventory query is:

```
SELECT Products.ProductID, Products.ProductName, Products.QuantityPerUnit,
   Products.UnitPrice, CCur(0.667*[UnitPrice]) AS Cost, Products.UnitsInStock,
   CCur([UnitsInStock]*[Cost]) AS [Value], Categories.CategoryID,
   Categories.CategoryName, Suppliers.SupplierID, Suppliers.CompanyName
FROM Suppliers INNER JOIN (Categories
   INNER JOIN Products
      ON Categories.CategoryID = Products.CategoryID)
      ON Suppliers.SupplierID = Products.SupplierID
WHERE (((Products.Discontinued)=False));
```

The modified qryInventory query is in the \Seua11\Chaptr25\Data25.mdb file.

CREATING AND MODIFYING THE SOURCE REPORT FOR THE PAGE

To permit saving the sample report as a page and to simplify the page redesign process, do the following:

1. Save a copy of rptInventoryByCategory as rptInventory.

2. Open rptInventory in Report Design view. In the Detail Section, right-click the SupplierID drop-down list and choose Change To, Text Box. Replace SupplierID with **CompanyName** as the Control Source value.
3. Delete the expression in the Cost field, and type **Cost** as the field name. Do the same for the Value text box, but type **Value**.
4. In the CategoryID footer section, change the CategoryID list to a text box, and delete the CategoryID field name. Delete the expressions in the remaining four text boxes in the CategoryID footer. All text boxes display Unbound as their value.
5. Delete the two text boxes in the Page Footer section, and move the Report Footer section up. Your redesigned source report appears as shown in Figure 25.26.

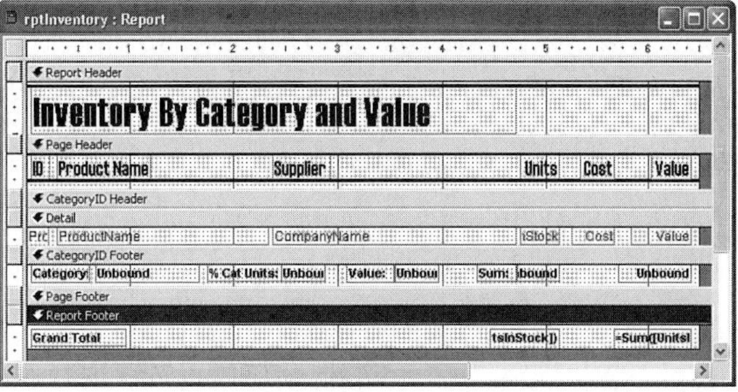

Figure 25.26 The changes shown here are required to eliminate errors when transforming the report to a page and to specify the columns to display from the modified source query.

6. Change to Print Preview to check your work. Close rptInventory and save your changes.
7. Right-click rptInventory in the Database window, choose Save As, and save the report as the Inventory page with Inventory.htm as the file name.
8. Click an Expand control to display the initial version of the Inventory.htm page (see Figure 25.27). Click OK to acknowledge "The DefaultSort property is invalid" message.

REMOVING THE NAVIGATION CONTROLS AND ADDING A CATEGORY CAPTION

The Inventory page has only eight categories and a few products per category, so you don't need navigation controls on the form. If you retain the Header: GroupLevel0 section and the Expand controls for the group, instead of expanding all groups by default, a CategoryName caption adjacent to the Expand control aids readability.

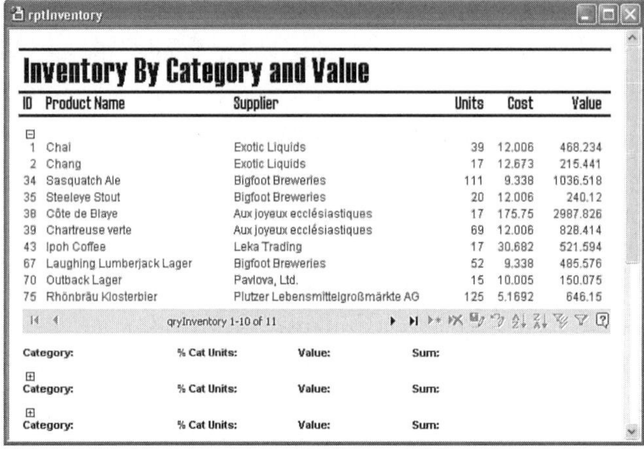

Figure 25.27 Deleting the expressions in the source report's text box and changing the data source of the text boxes results in this initial page design.

To make the initial design changes to the page, do this:

1. Change to Page Design view. Right-click Header: GroupLevel0, and clear the Record Navigation check box. Do the same for the Header: qryInventory section.

2. Double-click the Expand control, click the Other tab, and change the `Src` property value to `Black Arrow`.

3. Open the Toolbox, select the Bound Span control, and draw the control adjacent to the right of the Expand control. Delete the added label.
4. Double-click the control, click the Data tab, open the `ControlSource` list, and select `CategoryName`. The `ControlSource` property value changes to `GroupOfCategoryName: CategoryName`.
5. If you want to retain the Category label and `CategoryID` text box in the Footer: GroupLevel0 section, double-click the text box and set its `ControlSource` property to `CategoryName`. In this case, the property value becomes `GroupOfCategoryName1: CategoryName`.
6. If you change the `ControlSource` property value of the `CategoryID` text box or delete it, you must change the value of the `DefaultSort` property of the `GroupLevel0` group properties. For this example, the original value is `[GroupOfCategoryID98] ASC`, but this field no longer exists in the Field List. Right-click the section, choose Group Level Properties, and set the `DefaultSort` property value to **[GroupOfCategoryName] ASC**.

TIP

Be sure to change the `DefaultSort` property when deleting or changing transformed text boxes on which group sorting depends. If you don't, you receive "The DefaultSort property is invalid" messages when changing to Page view. The `DefaultSort` property value must match a GroupOf*FieldName* item in the Field List.

7. The offending `DefaultSort` property value that raises the error on expanding a group is `DESC` with no field name for GroupLevel: Query Inventory. Change `DESC` to **[Value] DESC** to fix the problem.

8. If the font name for the new controls that you've added isn't the same as the existing controls, conform the fonts in other than the Caption: GroupLevel0 section. Tahoma is the font used for most of the examples in this book.

9. Change to Page view to check your work so far (see Figure 25.28).

Figure 25.28 Removing navigation controls, adding a CategoryName caption, and making other minor changes improve the usability of the form.

rptInventory

Inventory By Category and Value

ID	Product Name	Supplier	Units	Cost	Value
▼ Beverages					
38	Côte de Blaye	Aux joyeux ecclésiastiques	39	12.01	$468.23
34	Sasquatch Ale	Bigfoot Breweries	17	12.67	$215.44
39	Chartreuse verte	Aux joyeux ecclésiastiques	111	9.34	$1,036.52
76	Lakkalikööri	Karkki Oy	20	12.01	$240.12
75	Rhönbräu Klosterbier	Plutzer Lebensmittelgroßmärkte AG	17	175.75	$2,987.83
43	Ipoh Coffee	Leka Trading	69	12.01	$828.41
67	Laughing Lumberjack Lager	Bigfoot Breweries	17	30.68	$521.59
1	Chai	Exotic Liquids	52	9.34	$485.58
35	Steeleye Stout	Bigfoot Breweries	15	10.01	$150.08
2	Chang	Exotic Liquids	125	5.17	$646.15
70	Outback Lager	Pavlova, Ltd.	57	12.01	$684.34
Category: Beverages	**% Cat Units:**	**Value:**	**Sum:**		
▶ Condiments					
Category: Condiments	**% Cat Units:**	**Value:**	**Sum:**		
▶ Confections					
Category: Confections	**% Cat Units:**	**Value:**	**Sum:**		
▶ Dairy Products					

ADDING CATEGORY SUBTOTALS AND GRAND TOTALS TO THE PAGE

Adding subtotals and grand totals to pages differs considerably from the method that you use for reports. The AutoSum feature makes replacing the missing group subtotals and grand totals easy.

To replace the report's missing subtotals and grand totals, do the following:

1. Select the UnitsInStock text box in the Header: qryInventory section, and click AutoSum to add a new label and `SumOfUnitsInStock` text box in the Footer: GroupLevel0 section. Delete the label and the original text box, and drag the `SumOfUnitsInStock` text box to the right of the Sum: label.

2. Repeat step 1 for the text box under the Value label. Move the SumOfValue text box to the right of the Cat. Value label.

3. Delete the % Cat. and Value label and text boxes in the Footer: GroupLevel0 section. Programming calculated text box values is beyond the scope of this chapter. Drag the Category label and text box to the right.

4. Select the `SumOfUnitsInStock` text box, and click AutoSum to add a Footer: qryInventory-SumOfUnitsInStock section and a `SumOfSumOfUnitsInStock` text box. Delete the associated label. Align the left and right edges of the Footer section with the sections above it.

25

5. Repeat step 3 for the `SumOfValue` text box, and then adjust the positions of the text boxes under the `Units` and `Value` text boxes.
6. Select the Grand Total: label, and press Ctrl+X to cut it to the Clipboard. Delete the unnamed footer section where the Grand Total: label was located.
7. Select the Footer: qryInventory-SumOfUnitsInStock section, and press Ctrl+V to paste the label. Figure 25.29 shows the final design in Page Design view.

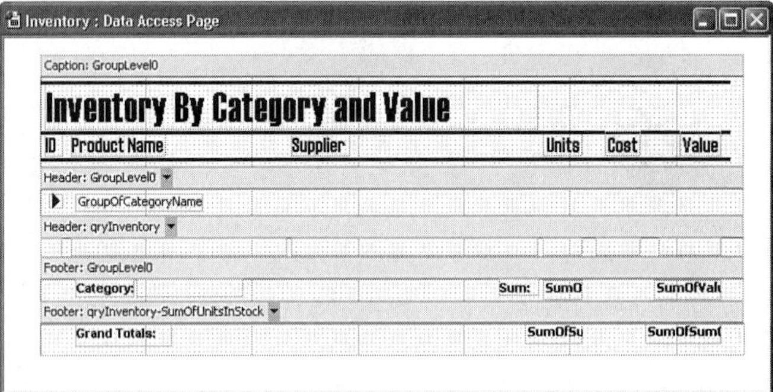

Figure 25.29 The final design of the Inventory.htm page includes units and value subtotals by category, as well as grand totals for all categories.

8. Open the report in Web Page Preview to display the summary version of the page (see Figure 25.30).

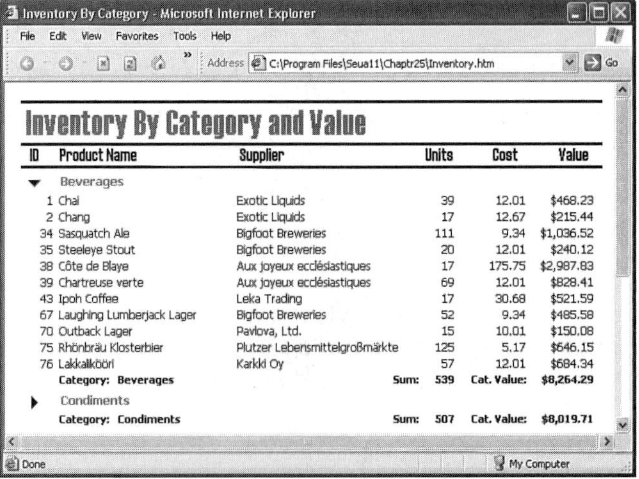

Figure 25.30 Web Page Preview displays the eight subtotals and grand totals for units in stock and inventory value.

The Inventory link to the Inventory.htm page is in the Data25.mdb file located in the \Seua11\Chaptr25 folder of the accompanying CD-ROM.

TROUBLESHOOTING

DATA SOURCE PROBLEMS

A "Microsoft Web Components could not open the database C:\Path\FileName.mdb" message appears when I try to open a page from another machine on the network.

The most likely cause of this problem is that you forgot to change the `ConnectionString` property for the Jet 4.0 data source of the page from the default well-formed path to the UNC *ServerName**ShareName**FileName*.mdb format. On the design computer, open the page in Design view, right-click the page, and choose Page Properties. Click the Data tab, select the `ConnectionString` property, and press Shift+F2 to open the connection string in the Zoom box. Change the `DataSource=` element of the connection string to the UNC path to the share and file.

Another possibility is that the UNC connection string is invalid or the user doesn't have read or read/write permissions for the share. In this case, check the capability of the client to browse the *ShareName* folder named in the error message.

PARAMETER NAMING AND COOKIE PARSING PROBLEMS

When I click the link on the navigation page to open a page that requires a query parameter value, the Enter Parameters dialog opens.

The name that you supplied as the first (parameter name) argument of the `MSODSC.RecordsetDefs("QueryName").parametervalues.Add` method statement doesn't match the name specified in the query design grid. If you're query expects a conventional input parameter, open the query in Design view, copy the [*ParameterName*] element to the Clipboard, and paste it into the Script Editor. (Don't forget to add the surrounding double-quotes.)

When I click the link on the navigation page to open a page that requires a query or filter parameter value, the page opens with an empty Recordset.

The most likely cause of this problem is an error in the length argument of the `mid` function used to parse the cookie. For example, if you substitute `9` or less for `10` in the `lngLastOrder = Mid(strCookie, InStr(strCookie, "LastOrder=") +10)` statement, the parameter value passed to the query or filter begins with `=`, which is invalid for a date value. Count the number of characters in the name element of the cookie carefully to ensure that you're passing the correct value to the parameter.

If the preceding issue isn't the problem, temporarily add a message box (`MsgBox`) statement with the variable name as the `Prompt` argument. For example, to check what the preceding line of script returns, add a `MsgBox lngLastOrder` statement after the line. When you've diagnosed the problem, add an apostrophe (`'`) in front of `msgbox` to comment out the statement. It's also a good idea to add a temporary `MsgBox strCookie` statement to check the crumbs while debugging your cookie-parsing code.

IN THE REAL WORLD—ENHANCING DATA ACCESS PAGE DESIGN

Much of the content of this chapter concentrates on the lack of support by DAP for common Access form and report designs and control objects. Observations about Save As DAP features that work as expected might be classified as damnation by faint praise. There are workarounds for unsupported objects—such as subforms and subreports—but most workarounds aren't elegant, require VBScript programming expertise, and often need additional HTML code. In most cases, what you see in Access isn't what you get in pages without a considerable amount of work on your part. Bear in mind, however, that creating a datasheet-style data entry Web page, for example, isn't a piece of cake in any authoring tool. This is especially true if you need to implement the equivalent of the Undo, Sort..., and Filter... buttons of the navigation control.

Third-party Access developers have the opportunity to improve on the basic functionality of the Save as DAP feature. For example, Michael Kaplan and Julianne Lee of Trigeminal Software, Inc. (TSI) developed a Form/Report to Data Access Page Wizard that overcomes many Save As DAP limitations. For example, the TSI Wizard handles most subforms and subreports, which open in an inline frame (`<IFRAME>`), and generates working drop-down lists (see Figure 25.31). The TSI Wizard is an Access add-in library (FrmRpt2Dap.mde) that you can download from `http://www.trigeminal.com/frmrpt2dap.asp`. Installation instructions are at `http://www.trigeminal.com/frmrpt2dap_readme.asp`. Data25.mdb in the \Seua11\Chaptr25 folder of the accompanying CD-ROM includes the Orders and Orders Subform pages generated by the TSI Wizard. The pages have minor design modifications, and the VBScript in the Orders.htm page has been altered to enable opening the subform directly from the Orders Subform.htm file.

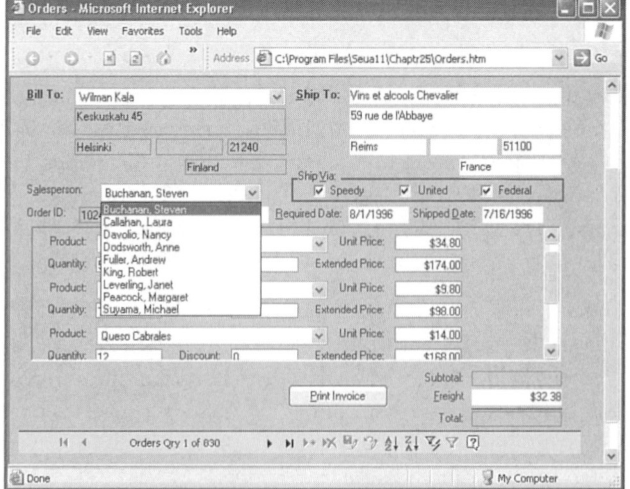

Figure 25.31
Trigeminal Software, Inc.'s Form/Report to Data Access Page Wizard populates combo boxes and displays subforms in an inline frame.

Most of Microsoft's development investment in the upgrade from Office 2002 to Office 2003 is devoted to XML-related features. Microsoft's promotion of the .NET Framework for XML Web services has shifted the company's development focus to XML file generation manipulation by Office System 2003 members and Visual Studio .NET projects. Data access pages rely on HTML, which has a very limited repertoire of native control objects compared to conventional Windows applications. The capability to save complex Access objects to pages is, to a major extent, constrained by HTML 4.0 limitations. "If your only tool is HTML, everything looks like a `<TABLE>`, `<TEXTAREA>`, or `<SPAN>`" oversimplifies the issue but remains a valid aphorism.

Browser users are accustomed to crude Web-based data-entry forms and less-than-lightning response times, but they do expect attractive, consistent page graphics. The appearance of your pages is likely to be more important to executive and management types than their content or performance. Web page form over function priorities of nonusers is one of the reasons why this chapter and the preceding two chapters emphasize design changes to make pages more attractive. If your employer has a organization-wide page layout with standard logos, colors, fonts, and other design attributes, make sure that your DAP conform.

CHAPTER 26

INTEGRATING WITH INFOPATH AND SHAREPOINT SERVICES

In this chapter

WORKING WITH INFOPATH FORMS

Microsoft Office InfoPath 2003—called XDocs during its early beta period—is a forms-based XML document generation and editing application. InfoPath's primary application is producing structured data from common business forms, such as expense reports, employee performance reviews, vendor evaluations, time cards, and sales call reports. The structure of the data is defined by an underlying XML schema, which validates users' entries in the form's controls—text boxes, option buttons, drop-down lists, and check boxes. When you design a form from scratch, InfoPath generates the schema for you. InfoPath also can infer a schema from an existing XML document. These features mean that you don't need to be an XML expert to produce useful data entry and editing forms with InfoPath 2003.

InfoPath forms share many of the features of Access's data access pages (DAP), such as a design surface on which you place controls that are bound to an underlying data source. InfoPath, however, is self-contained and doesn't rely on the Office Web Components for data binding, record navigation, and editing. You display and edit data in InfoPath sections or repeating sections, which correspond to Access's bound forms and subforms. DAP and InfoPath use VBScript or JScript event handlers to customize form behavior.

InfoPath 2003 binds to the following types of data sources:

- Jet tables or queries
- SQL Server tables, views, table-returning functions, and stored procedures
- XML documents stored as .xml files
- Document/literal XML Web services

→ For a definition of document/literal XML Web services, **see** "SOAP Message Formats," **p. 1336**.

26

This is an Access 2003 book, so the InfoPath form you create later in this chapter connects to Jet .mdb files or SQL Server 2000 databases with OLE DB and ActiveX Data Objects (ADO). InfoPath automates the form generation process for ADO Recordsets, which means that you don't need to be a full-fledged InfoPath developer or programmer to take advantage of this new Microsoft Office member. Displaying and updating relational data, however, won't be InfoPath 2003's primary application for most organizations. InfoPath's most common use probably will be creating and editing XML data documents. Thus, this chapter begins with an overview of basic form completion and design techniques for common XML business documents.

Another promising InfoPath application is providing a simple user interface for basic XML Web services. Web services initially were intended for server-to-server communication. A recent trend is employing Web services to deliver business information from databases as messages containing structured XML documents. InfoPath 2003 can handle forms-based data display and database updates with simple XML Web services.

NOTE

NEW

InfoPath 2003 shares the limitations of the Web Service Reference (WSR) 2.0 tool for enabling applications to consume XML Web services. For example, InfoPath can't handle XML Web services you create from the SQL Server 2000 parameterized stored procedures in Chapter 31, "Consuming and Providing XML Web Services."

→ To learn more about WSR 2.0, **see** "Creating an Access Web Service Consumer," **p. 1342**.

GETTING ACQUAINTED WITH INFOPATH FORMS

InfoPath 2003 offers a set of sample templates for common business forms, just as Access 2003 includes templates for a variety of useful business-related databases. The sample templates let you experiment with InfoPath form features such as hidden (optional) sections, drop-down lists populated by a secondary data source, and expanding lists. Drop-down lists correspond to Access's bound combo boxes; the secondary data source is equivalent to the Row Source property. An expanding list emulates an Access subform.

To give InfoPath a test drive with a sample form, do the following:

1. Launch Microsoft Office InfoPath 2003, which opens by default with the Fill Out a Form task pane active.
2. Click the More Forms task pane link to open the Forms dialog, select a form to fill in (see Figure 26.1), and click OK to display the form—Change Order for this example. The first form you open from any template is Form1. Optionally, press Ctrl+F1 to redisplay the task pane.

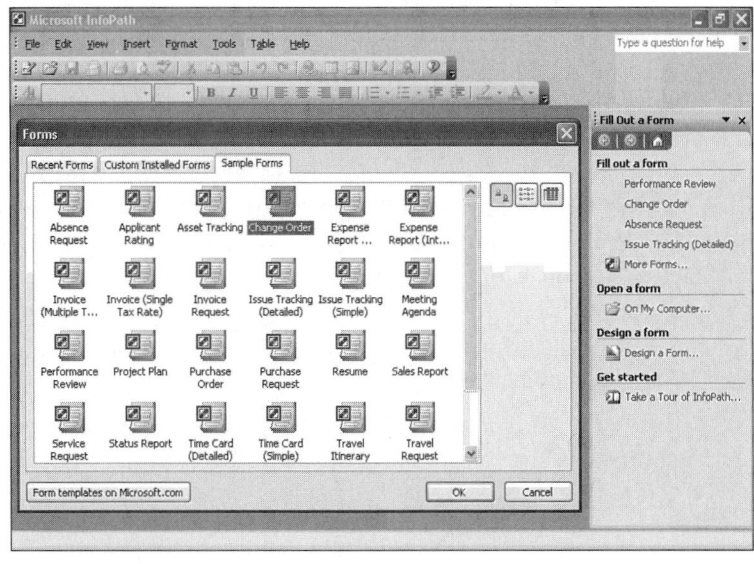

Figure 26.1
InfoPath offers 25 sample business forms and associated schemas that you can alter to suit your requirements. All sample forms share a common design pattern.

3. Type sample data in the form. A dashed rectangle surrounds fields contained in form sections. Some sections are optional, as indicated by a ↓ button to the left of the heading (see Figure 26.2).

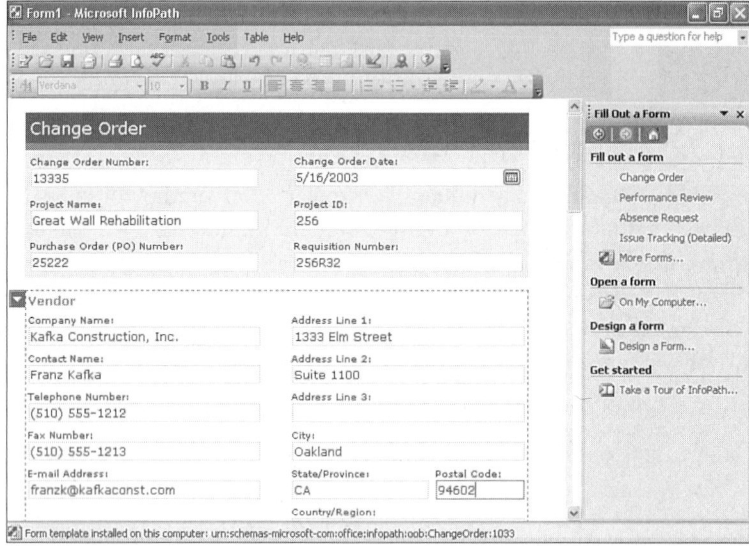

Figure 26.2
As you fill in the form, a blue border identifies the active text box. A blue dashed line surrounds individual sections; optional sections have a button that lets you delete them from the form.

NOTE

> Despite the Remove *SectionName* drop-down menu choice, you can't remove some subsections because doing so violates the schema's requirements.

4. Continue completing the form until you reach the Reason for Change section. Click the ↓ button to open the section's drop-down menu and select Remove Reason for Change. When you remove an optional section, an orange circle with a → icon and a Click Here to Insert the *SectionName* Section caption replaces the hidden section.
5. Open the Currency list to select a currency from the 100 or so choices. A secondary data source populates the currency list for all forms.
6. Remove the Detailed List of Changes section and type a description and value in the Itemized Changes list. JScript code behind the form maintains running totals of Cost and Hours.
7. With the first entry in the Detailed List of Changes selected, press Ctrl+Enter or open the list's drop-down menu, and select Insert Below to add a new line to the section. When you add new Cost and Hours values, the totals update (see Figure 26.3).

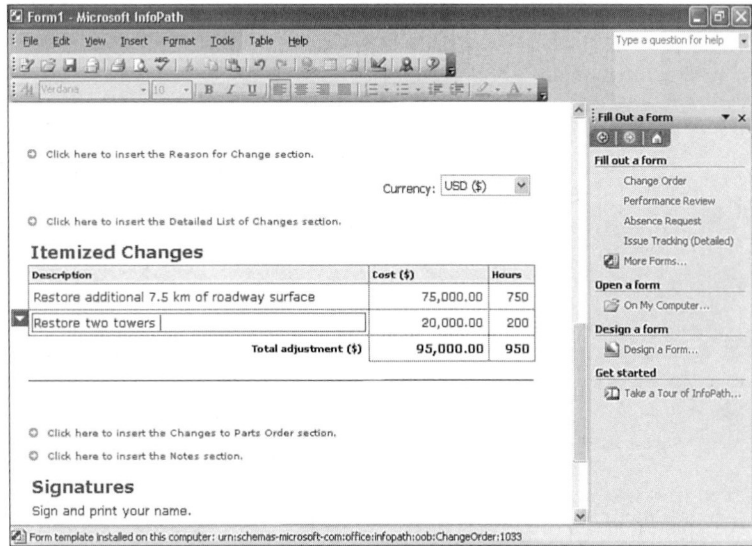

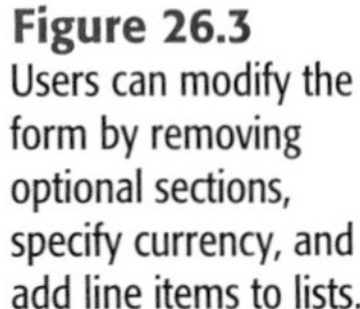

Figure 26.3
Users can modify the form by removing optional sections, specify currency, and add line items to lists.

8. Press Ctrl+S to save the form. If you store the form in My Documents specify a memorable name, such as ChangeOrder1.xml. By default, saving the form doesn't close it.

The XML document you create when saving a form contains a set of processing instructions (PIs), which are highlighted in Figure 26.4. These instructions cause Internet Explorer (IE) 6+ to launch InfoPath, if necessary, and open the form in the template specified by the Universal Resource Name: `urn:schemas-microsoft-com:office:infopath:oob:ChangeOrder:1033`. Thus, you must use Notepad or another text editor to read the XML form document.

26

```
<?xml version="1.0" encoding="UTF-8"?><?mso-infoPathSolution PIVersion="0.9.0.0"
name="urn:schemas-microsoft-com:office:infopath:oob:ChangeOrder:1033"
solutionVersion="1.0.0.1" productVersion="11.0.4920" ?><?mso-application
progid="InfoPath.Document"?><co:changeOrder
xmlns:co="http://schemas.microsoft.com/office/infopath/2003/sample/ChangeOrder"
xmlns:my="http://schemas.microsoft.com/office/infopath/2003/myXSD"
xmlns:xhtml="http://www.w3.org/1999/xhtml" xml:lang="en-us">
	<co:date
xmlns:xsi="http://www.w3.org/2001/XMLSchema-instance">2003-05-16</co:date>
	<co:changeOrderNumber>13335</co:changeOrderNumber>
	<co:purpose></co:purpose>


<co:requester><co:name><co:prefix></co:prefix><co:givenName></co:givenName><co:mid
dleName></co:middleName><co:surname></co:surname><co:suffix></co:suffix><co:single
Name>Roger
Jennings</co:singleName></co:name><co:address><co:line1></co:line1><co:line2></co:
line2><co:line3></co:line3><co:line4></co:line4><co:city></co:city><co:stateProvin
ce></co:stateProvince><co:postalCode></co:postalCode><co:country></co:country></co
:address><co:identificationNumber></co:identificationNumber><co:emailAddressPrimar
y>Roger_Jennings@compuserve.com</co:emailAddressPrimary><co:emailAddressSecondary>
</co:emailAddressSecondary><co:telephoneNumberWork>(510)
555-2345</co:telephoneNumberWork><co:telephoneNumberHome></co:telephoneNumberHome>
<co:telephoneNumberCell></co:telephoneNumberCell><co:telephoneNumberPager></co:tel
ephoneNumberPager><co:faxNumber>(510)
555-2346</co:faxNumber><co:jobTitle></co:jobTitle><co:officeLocation></co:officeLo
cation><co:department></co:department><co:webSite></co:webSite><co:ftpSite></co:ft
pSite></co:requester><co:vendor>
		<co:name>Kafka Construction, Inc.</co:name>
		<co:address>
			<co:line1>1333 Elm Street</co:line1>
			<co:line2>Suite 1100</co:line2>
			<co:line3></co:line3>
			<co:line4></co:line4>
			<co:city>Oakland</co:city>
```

Figure 26.4
The XML form document includes the two processing instructions, which are shown highlighted in Notepad. The `co` (...`ChangeOrder`) namespace qualifies all form element names with a `co:` prefix.

The remainder of the form document consists of optional elements defined by the form's underlying schema(s). Many elements are empty because the form doesn't contain text boxes or other controls bound to these elements.

NOTE

All files for the ChangeOrder1 form and its template are located in the \Seua11\Chaptr26\ChangeOrder1 folder of the accompanying CDROM. If you don't have InfoPath installed, you can inspect the files in IE or Notepad.

If you encounter an "InfoPath cannot create a new, blank form" error when you attempt to open the form, see the "Changing the Publishing Point of an InfoPath Template" topic of the "Troubleshooting" section near the end of this chapter.

Exporting and Mailing InfoPath Forms

In addition to saving the form, you can export the form as a single *FormName*_View 1.mht Web page or to an Excel 2003 worksheet by choosing File, Export To. The .mht page is a read-only replica of the completed form. Command buttons that execute InfoPath's built-in operations—such as Run Query, New Record, and Submit—or custom scripted functions don't appear on .mht pages.

The Export to Excel Wizard lets you create a new workbook from the form's XML data. To save the form data in Excel, do the following:

1. Choose File, Export to, Microsoft Excel to start the Wizard. Click Next.
2. Select the Form Fields and This Table or List option, and select the table(s) or list(s). For this example, the only list is Itemized Changes Entry (see Figure 26.5). Click Next.

26

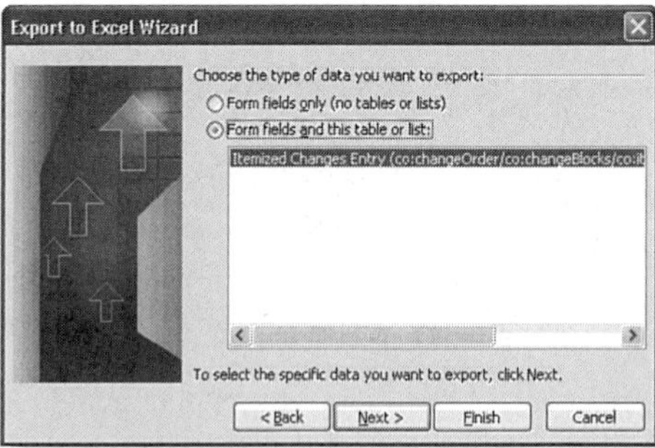

Figure 26.5 The second Export to Excel Wizard dialog lets you add data from form tables or lists to the worksheet.

3. The third Wizard dialog selects all elements that have values for export (see Figure 26.6). Deselect any items you don't want to include and click Next.

Figure 26.6 Select the fields you want to include as worksheet columns in the third Wizard dialog.

4. In the last Wizard dialog, accept the Export Data from This Form Only, unless you've saved other forms from the same template.
5. Click Finish to generate the worksheet, which contains a headings row and the two rows that represent the two items you added to the Itemized Changes Entry list (see Figure 26.7).

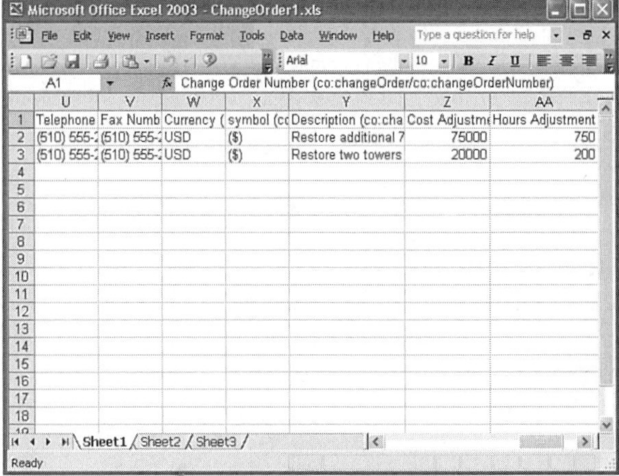

Figure 26.7 Rows of worksheets generated from InfoPath forms that include lists display all form fields as columns.

The obvious benefit of exporting InfoPath forms to Excel is the ability to summarize data from multiple forms based on a single template. You can use Access's import or link table features to create flat tables from the summary worksheet.

→ To review the process for importing or linking Excel files, **see** "Importing and Linking Spreadsheet Files," **p. 284**.

Choosing File, Send to Mail Recipient lets you email a copy of the form to one or more recipients (see Figure 26.8). If the recipient has InfoPath installed, she can edit the form and pass it on to others. Users without InfoPath receive a read-only form copy that's identical to the .mht Web page.

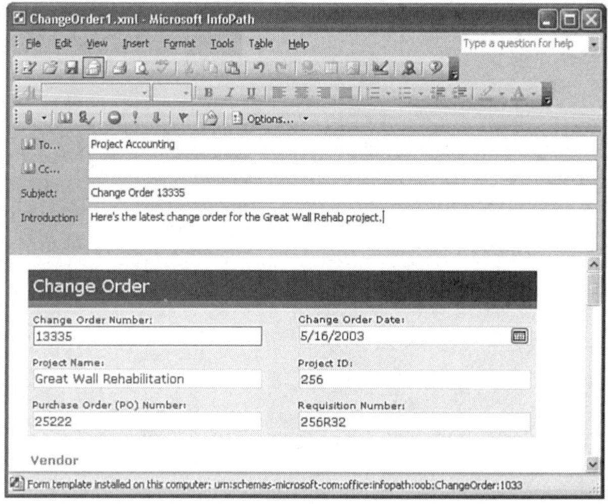

Figure 26.8
You can send a completed form to email recipients for review or further processing. Only recipients with InfoPath installed can edit the form.

NOTE

> Most of the sample forms have signature blocks at the bottom of the page, which apply to printed forms only. InfoPath has a Tools, Digital Signatures menu choice that opens a dialog to let the originator digitally sign the form to prove its authenticity. Others in the approval workflow can add their digital signatures to authenticate the form's status.

Designing and Deploying Form Templates

InfoPath's template design mode is quite similar to Access's DAP Design view. The primary difference is InfoPath's substitution of task pane panels for the data source's Field List and the Tool Box. You create and deploy a data-bound template in later sections, so the following sections describe how to modify a sample template, save the template as an *TemplateName*.xsn file, and publish the solution file to a shared folder for others to use. Sections near the end of the chapter show you how to export form templates to a SharePoint Services site.

Modifying a Sample InfoPath Template

The sample Change Order template is a good choice for exploring InfoPath's design mode because it warrants modification to ensure that the resulting forms created by users are consistent. For example, you might want to make some optional sections mandatory and remove others from the form. The schema includes fields that don't appear on the form and might be useful to include, such as a supplier ID number. You also can provide default values for fields, such as the two members of the Currency group. The following sections describe how to make these typical design modifications.

CHANGING THE PROPERTIES OF SECTIONS

To make initial modifications to the Change Order template's optional sections, do the following:

1. If InfoPath isn't loaded and displaying the Change Order form, follow steps 1 and 2 of the earlier "Getting Acquainted with InfoPath Forms" to open the form.

2. Click the toolbar's Design This Form button to change to template design view. The template name changes to Template1 in the title bar and the Design Tasks task pane opens.
3. Pass the mouse pointer over the text boxes to display the data source, in this case the name of an element defined by the form's XML schema (see Figure 26.9).

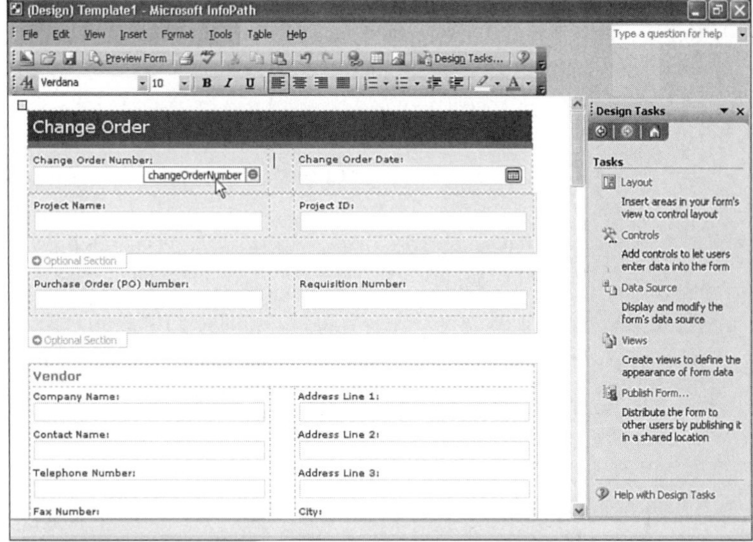

Figure 26.9 Passing the mouse pointer over a bound control in design mode displays the field (element) name defined by the underlying XML schema.

4. Right-click the Optional Section tab of the first optional section (Project Information), and choose Section Properties to open the Section Properties dialog.

> **TIP**
>
> Press Ctrl+Z to undo any inadvertent changes or deletions in the following steps.

5. Clear the Allow Users to Delete This Section check box to make the section mandatory (see Figure 26.10). Click OK to change Optional Section to Section.

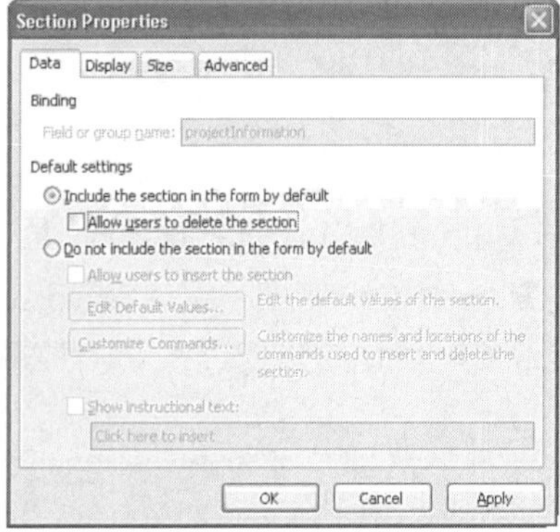

Figure 26.10
You control the default visibility of sections and whether sections are optional on the Data page of the Section Properties dialog.

6. Repeat steps 4 and 5 for the Purchase Order Information, Vendor, Requester, and Itemized Changes. For Itemized Changes select the Include the Section in the Form by Default option.
7. Click the Optional Section tab to select the Reason for Changes section, and press Delete to remove it from the form. Press Delete again to remove the extra vertical space.
8. Repeat step 7 for the remaining Optional Sections—Detailed List of Changes, Changes to Parts Order, and Notes.
9. Click anywhere in the Signatures table to display a selection square at the upper-left corner. (Signatures isn't a section because it's not bound to the form's schema.) Click the square to select the entire table and press delete to remove it.
10. Click the toolbar's Preview Form button to emulate form view. Scroll to the bottom of the form to verify removal of optional sections and the Signatures table.
11. Click the Close Preview button to return to template design mode.

The preceding modifications ensure that all users prepare identical forms for analysis in an Excel worksheet.

USING THE DATA SOURCE LIST TO REPLACE A FORM FIELD

The task pane's Data Source pane provides a tree view of the schema's elements. Many elements don't have bound controls on the form. The Vendor section has three address lines but is missing a supplier ID number. This section explains how to add a field to a section's table, change the font size of the data entry text box, and remove a field from a section table.

To replace Address Line 3 with an `identificationNumber` value, do the following:

1. Click the Data Source link in the Design Tasks pane to view the schema.
2. Scroll to and expand the `vendor` node to display its child nodes.

3. Select the `identificationNumber` element (field) and drag the insertion point to the immediate left of the "A" in the Address Line 1: caption. This step adds an Identification Number: caption and a text box above Address Line 1.
4. Select the new text box and change the font size from 8 to 10 points to equal the font size of the other text boxes on the form.
5. Select the `line3` text box and press delete to remove it. Unlike Access, deleting an InfoPath text box doesn't delete its label.
6. Select the Address Line 3: caption and its trailing line feed and press delete. Your form design appears, as shown in Figure 26.11.

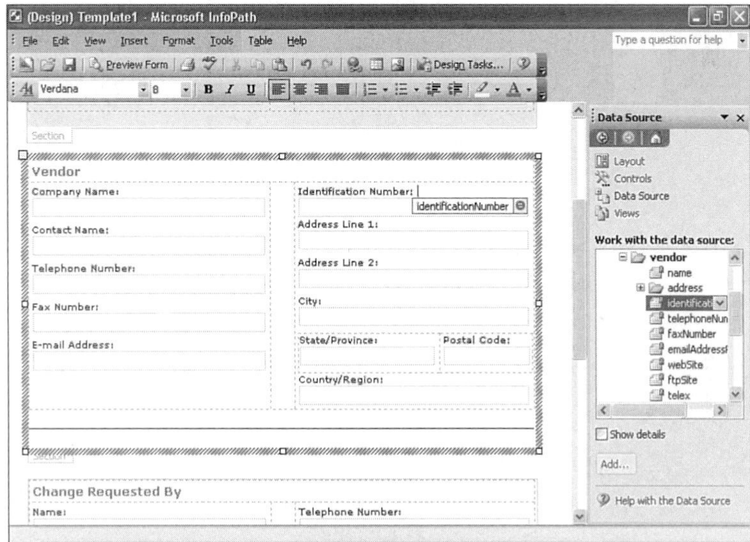

Figure 26.11 The Identification Number caption and related text box replace the Address Line 3 element.

7. Press Ctrl+S to open a dialog, click Save, and save the form template file as ChangeOrder.xsn in My Documents or elsewhere. Don't close the template.

Saving sample Template1 as a form template file changes the name in the title bar to (Design) *FileName*.

SETTING DEFAULT FIELD VALUES

The Currency list box opens with the value of the first element of the currencies.xml file—Select. The currencies.xml file is the secondary data source for the Currency list. Setting a default value for your locale's currency name and symbol eliminates the need for users to set the currency value each time they complete a new form.

To set a default currency name and value, do the following:

1. In the data source list, scroll to and expand the `currency` node.
2. Right-click the `name` field and choose Properties to open the Field or Group Properties dialog.
3. Type the currency name—**USD** for this example—in the Default Value text box (see Figure 26.12). Click OK.

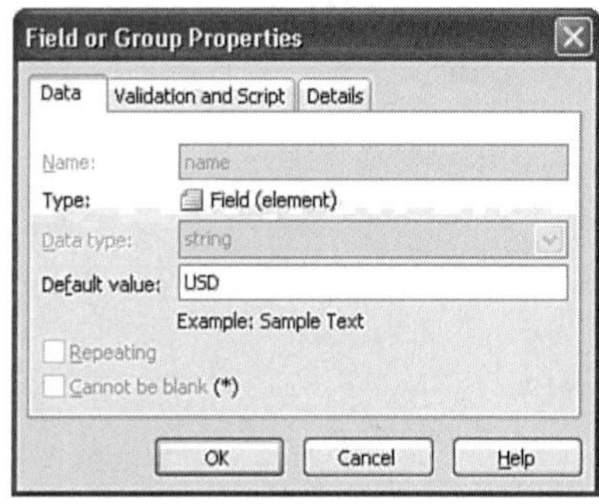

Figure 26.12 Set default values for a selected field in the Field or Group Properties dialog. You also can establish validation rules for fields.

4. Repeat steps 2 and 3, but specify the `symbol` field and type **($)**.
5. Click Preview Form and scroll to the Currency list and verify that "USD ($)" appears and that ($) follows the Cost header of the Itemized Charges list.
6. Press Ctrl+S to save your design changes.

26

JScript code behind the form sets today as the value of the Change Order Date text box when you open the form. Unlike Access, default values of elements must be constants.

Publishing Form Templates

You can publish form templates to a file share, SharePoint form library, or Web site. This example publishes to a file share; you publish the data-bound example that you create later in the chapter to a SharePoint site.

To publish the ChangeOrder.xsn template to a file share, do this:

1. Create a share on your computer and assign appropriate share permissions to groups or users. For this example, the share is the InfoPath folder of the computer used to write this chapter.

2. With the template open in design mode, choose File, Publish to start the Publishing Wizard. Click Next to bypass the Welcome dialog.
3. In the second dialog, accept the default To a Shared Folder on This Computer or on a Network option (see Figure 26.13). Click Next.

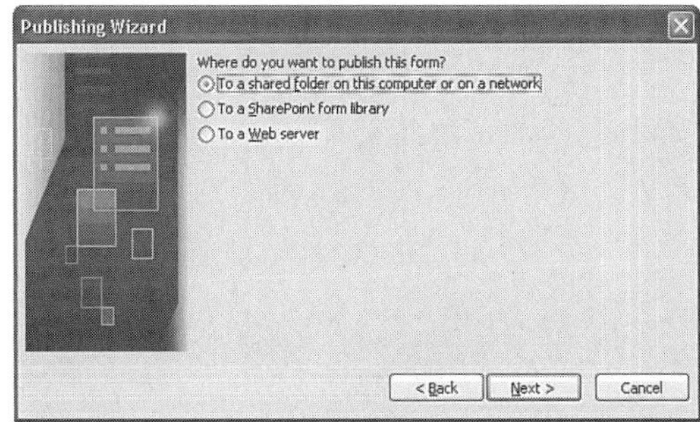

Figure 26.13 You select the location for the published form in the second Publishing Wizard dialog.

4. In the third dialog, type the UNC path to the share you created in step 1 (see Figure 26.14). Click Next to confirm the location, and click Finish to publish the template.

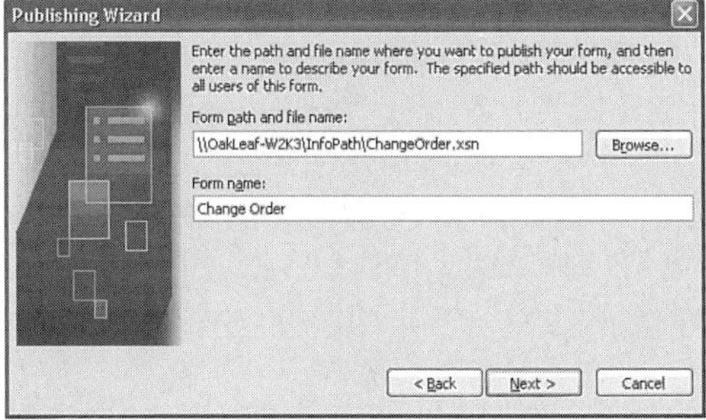

Figure 26.14 Specify the UNC path and file name for published form template.

After publication, the Wizard offers the opportunity to send messages that notify users of the location of the form.

Exploring the Contents of Form Template Files

The form template (originally XDocs solution) files you save with the .xsn extension are compressed archives, which Microsoft calls CAB (for *cabinet*) files. You can open .xsn files in WinZip 8.1 SR1+ or a similar compression utility and extract the files, but you can't add or replace archive files (see Figure 26.15).

Following are brief descriptions of files included in the example ChangeOrder.xsn archive:

- **manifest.xsf** is an XML file that lists the other files required by the template and, if your form connects to an Access or SQL Server database, the OLE DB connection string for the database. Every .xsn file has one manifest.xsf file of the Microsoft InfoPath Form Definition File type. You can open a form from manifest.xsf, make design changes, and save the form as an .xsn file with its original file name.

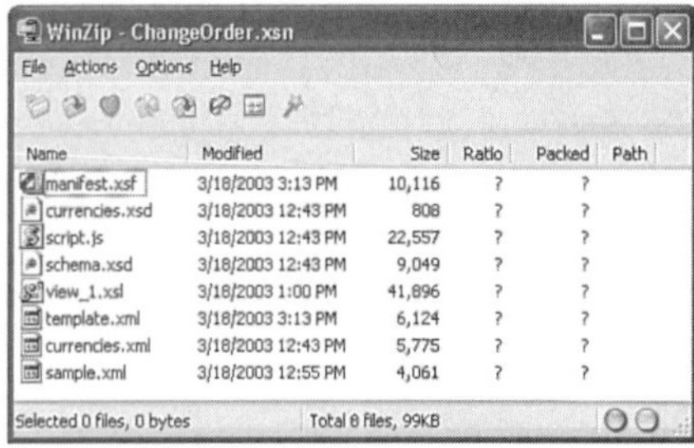

Figure 26.15
WinZip 8.1 SR1 shows the files in the .xsn archive, but the Add toolbar button and File menu choice are disabled.

- **schema.xsd** is the underlying XML schema for the form. All forms require schema.xsd; some forms have more than one schema. For example, forms bound to a database table require schema1.xsd and schema2.xsd to define the ADO Recordset for query and data display views.
- **template.xml** is an XML document that serves as a template for forms you complete. All elements of template.xml are empty, which is another way of saying the elements contain no text. Every .xsn file has a template.xml file.
- **view_1.xsl** is an XSL Transformations (XSLT) file that generates the Extensible HTML (XHTML) code to enable display of the form in a browser. Every .xsn file has at least one .xsl file but the file name(s) might differ. If the form has more than one view, there's an .xsl file for each view of the data.
- **sample.xml** is a version of template.xml with shorthand notation for empty elements—`<co:singleName/>` instead of `<co:singleName></co:singleName>`. Forms bound to an ADO Recordset have a sampledata.xml file with empty attribute values.
- **script.js** is present only if your forms contain JScript event-handling code. All templates you save from InfoPath sample forms contain script.js. If you choose VBScript as the default scripting language, script.vbs replaces script.js.
- **currencies.xml** and **currencies.xsd** are the XML document and schema, respectively, for the secondary data source that fills the Currencies list. The .xsn file must contain the .xml and .xsd files for each secondary data source of your form that relies on XML documents. You also can specify Access or SQL Server tables and queries as secondary data sources.

To extract all files from an .xsn archive, choose File, Extract Form Files, specify the folder that contains the .xsn archive in the Browse for Folder dialog, and click OK.

CREATING AN ABBREVIATED CURRENCIES DATA SOURCE

You can author your own XML file to serve as the secondary data source for a drop-down list or connect to a lookup table or query. In this respect, InfoPath lists resemble Access combo boxes quite closely. You also can modify an existing XML file to better suit the purpose of the list.

The Currency list contains entries for most of—if not all—the world's currencies. Do the following to create a short list of the currencies that your organization is willing to use in transactions:

1. Create a copy of currencies.xml as commoncurs.xml, and currencies.xsd as commoncurs.xsd. XML documents used as secondary data files require a corresponding .xsd file.
2. Open commoncurs.xml in Notepad and delete the elements for currencies that you don't want to appear in the list. Figure 26.16 shows a file that includes 14 common North American, European, Scandinavian, and Asian currencies.

Figure 26.16
This short version of the currencies.xml file has elements for 14 common currencies. The small rectangular symbols represent two byte currency symbols that don't display in NotePad.

commoncurs.xml - Notepad

File Edit Format View Help

```
<?xml version="1.0" encoding="UTF-8"?>
<!-- _lcid="1033" _version="" -->
<!-- _LocalBinding -->
<currencies>
        <currency name="" symbol="" display="Select..." /><!--
_locID@display="xdsln_cur_display" _locComment="{StringCategory=TXT}" -->
        <currency name="CAD" symbol="$" display="CAD ($)" />
        <currency name="CHF" symbol="SFr." display="CHF (SFr.)" />
        <currency name="CNY" symbol="▯" display="CNY (▯)" />
        <currency name="DKK" symbol="kr" display="DKK (kr)" />
        <currency name="EUR" symbol="€" display="EUR (€)" />
        <currency name="GBP" symbol="£" display="GBP (£)" />
        <currency name="HKD" symbol="HK$" display="HKD (HK$)" />
        <currency name="JPY" symbol="¥" display="JPY (¥)" />
        <currency name="KRW" symbol="▯" display="KRW (▯)" />
        <currency name="MXN" symbol="$" display="MXN ($)" />
        <currency name="NOK" symbol="kr" display="NOK (kr)" />
        <currency name="RUR" symbol="p." display="RUR (p.)" />
        <currency name="SEK" symbol="kr" display="SEK (kr)" />
        <currency name="USD" symbol="$" display="USD ($)" />
</currencies>
```

3. Press Ctrl+S to save the edited file and close Notepad.

CHANGING A SECONDARY DATA SOURCE

You can substitute a modified XML document for the original version, but removing the original XML file and substituting a new one is a more common practice. To change the secondary data source from currencies.xml to commoncurs.xml, do the following:

26

1. Make a backup copy of ChangeOrder.xsn in case you encounter a problem.

2. Open ChangeOrder.xsn in design mode, and choose Tools, Secondary Data Sources to open the dialog of the same name.
3. With currencies selected, click the Remove button and confirm your choice.
4. Click Add to open the Data Source Setup Wizard and accept the Default XML Data File option. Click Next.
5. In the second Wizard dialog, click Browse, select the commoncurs.xml file, and click Next.
6. In the third Wizard dialog, and change the name of the data source from commoncurs to **currency**, which is the name of the data source for the Currency list (see Figure 26.17). Verify that the Connect to This Secondary Data Source When the Form Is Opened check box is marked, and click Finish.

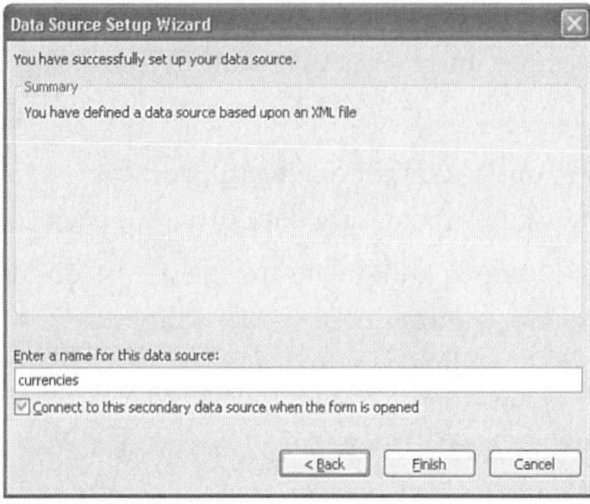

Figure 26.17
By default, the Data Source Setup Wizard uses the source XML document's filename as the Data Source name. Changing the name to that of the original data source retains the list's binding.

TIP

> When changing a control's secondary data source, always use the original data source name to avoid unexpected results. You can avoid step 4 by clicking Modify in step 3 and selecting the new .xml file to replace the original.
>
> If you don't change the data source name to currency, you must right-click the Currency list, choose Drop-Down List Box Properties to open the properties dialog, and select commoncurs in the Data Source list.

7. Click Yes to add the file to the form template file.
8. Click OK to close the Secondary Data Source dialog.
9. Click Preview Form and open the Currencies list to verify the change (see Figure 26.18).

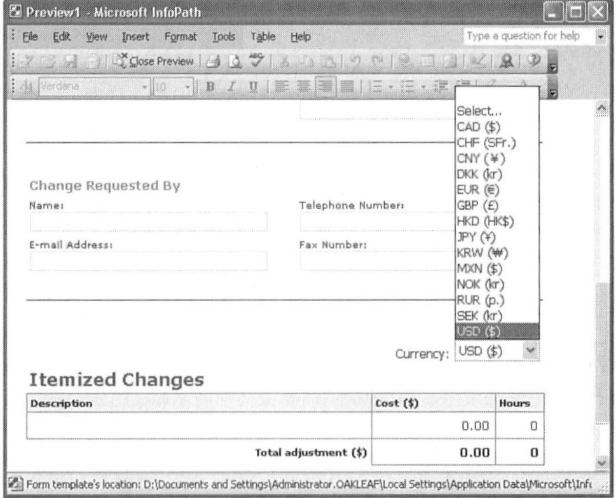

Figure 26.18
Opening the list in form preview mode confirms the secondary data source change.

10. Click Close Preview and press Ctrl+S to save your changes.

Unfortunately, changing the primary data source for a form isn't as simple as a secondary data source.

➔ To learn how to alter the primary data source, **see** "Changing a Form's Primary Data Source," **p. 1134**.

DESIGNING AN INFOPATH QUERY AND DATA EDITING FORM

InfoPath has a set of built-in operations for database query and editing operations. When you specify a database table or query as the primary data source for the form, InfoPath automatically generates a form with two views of the data. The query view is remarkably similar to Access's Filter by Form feature. You type one or more exact values to match in the view's text boxes; the query view doesn't accept wildcards. Data entry view displays records that match the query values. You can restrict the data entry view to display a single record or deliver multiple records to a repeating section. If the data source is updatable, you can add new records to the table(s) in data entry view.

InfoPath lets you save query and data entry views locally in the form's XML document. Local storage lets users work with the data while they're offline, edit the data, and then submit the changes when they reconnect to the network. In this respect, InfoPath data editing process emulates ADO's batch-optimistic updating feature.

➔ For more information on batch-optimistic updates, **see** "Taking Advantage of Disconnected `Recordsets`," **p. 1312**.

InfoPath offers the following three pre-defined command buttons for database operations:

- **Run Query** applies the filter you define in query view text boxes to the ADO Recordset and returns the filtered result set to the data view.
- **New Record** generates a data entry view with an empty form for adding a record to the table(s).
- **Submit** sends edits to existing data or a new record to the record source's table(s). InfoPath applies local validation rules to the entries. Submission fails if the database rejects the changes.
- **Delete & Submit** deletes the current record if deletion doesn't violate referential integrity or table/field validation constraints.

Figure 26.19 shows the InfoPath form similar to the one you create in the following sections. The form connects to Northwind.mdb's Customers table and lets users perform `UPDATE`, `INSERT`, and `DELETE` operations. The form is restricted to operating on a single record, so query and data entry operations appear in a single view. Using a single view simplifies use of the form.

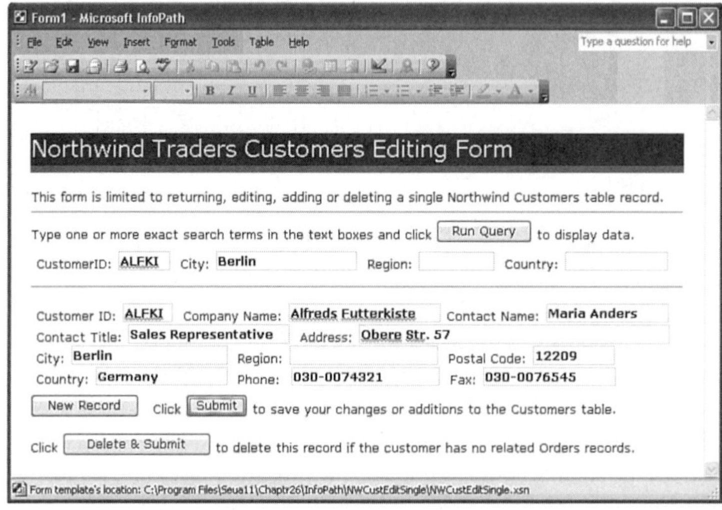

Figure 26.19
This data editing form combines query and data editing operations in a single view. Spell checking is enabled by default for InfoPath query and data entry views.

NOTE

The completed Northwind Traders Customers Editing Form template and its associated files are located in the \Seua11\Chaptr26\NWCustEditSingle folder of the accompanying CD-ROM. The NWCustEditSingle.xsn template expects Northwind.mdb to be in the default C:\Program Files\Microsoft Office\Office11\Samples folder and will fail if the database is located elsewhere.

If you encounter an "InfoPath cannot create a new, blank form" error when you attempt to open see the "Changing the Publishing Point of an InfoPath Template" topic of the "Troubleshooting" section near the end of this chapter.

26

Creating a Dual-View Template from the Primary Data Source

Generating the initial form template from an Access or SQL Server 2000 database is a simple, Wizard-based process. Before you modify Northwind.mdb's Customers table with InfoPath, make a backup copy of the table.

TIP

Be especially careful to follow the exact instructions for setting up the primary data source. Unlike secondary data sources, there's no simple method for changing the primary data source or its properties once you complete the process.

To create the standard query view for the Customers table, do the following:

1. Open InfoPath and click the Design a Form link in the task pane's default Fill Out a Form pane.
2. Click the New from Data Source link of the Design a Form pane to start the Data Source Setup Wizard.

3. Select the Database (Microsoft SQL Server or Microsoft Access Only) option, and click Next.
4. In the second Wizard dialog, click Select Database to open the Select Database dialog, navigate to ...\Office11\Samples, and double-click Northwind.mdb to open the Select Table dialog, which also displays Access queries.
5. Scroll to and double-click the Customers table to return to the Wizard dialog, which displays the table's field list with all fields selected for inclusion in the query and data views (see Figure 26.20).

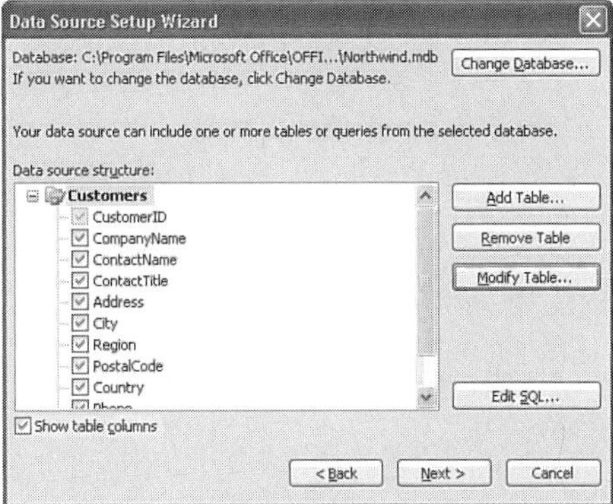

Figure 26.20
The second Data Source Setup Wizard dialog lets you select fields for the views and modify the SQL statement that generates the primary data source.

6. Click Modify Table to open the Sort Order dialog. You don't need to sort the table, but returning a single record is important to the design of the form. Clear the Allow Multiple Records from This Table to be Displayed in the Form check box (see Figure 26.21). Click Finish.

Figure 26.21
The Sort Order dialog also includes the check box that you clear to limit the query result set to a single record.

7. Click Edit SQL to view the SQL statement that InfoPath uses to generate the XML schemas for the two views. When you click Test SQL Statement, a message indicates that the query satisfies InfoPath's requirements (see Figure 26.22). Click OK twice to return to the Wizard, and then click Next.

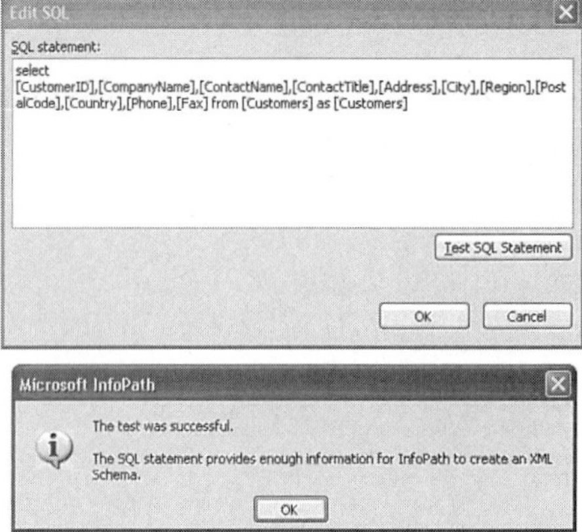

Figure 26.22
The SQL statement doesn't include the expected SELECT TOP 1 statement to limit the query to a single record. InfoPath uses the query to generate schemas only.

8. The third Wizard dialog confirms your choices, except the single-record restriction. By default, the Wizard generates the query view first (see Figure 26.23).

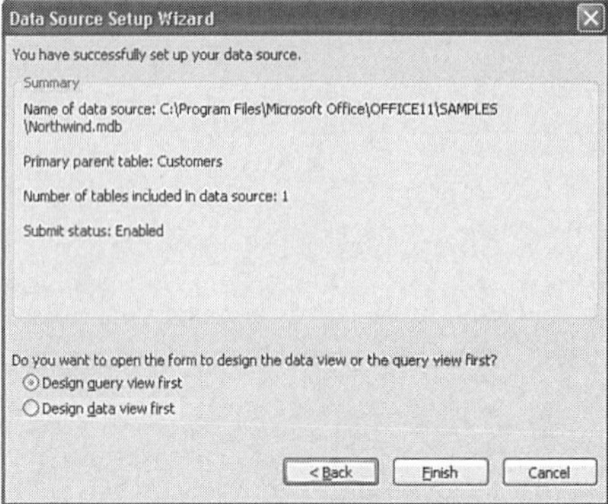

Figure 26.23
You can specify the sequence of view generation in the final Wizard dialog.

26

9. Click Finish to generate and display the query view in design mode. Expand the nodes in the Data Source task pane to display the `queryFields` and `dataFields` members. Mark the Show Details check box to display the XML Schema (XSD) data type of the fields (see Figure 26.24).

The query view has a New Record button at the top of the form and a Run Query button at the bottom, but the Wizard doesn't add a section with edit controls to the default data entry view. Why the Microsoft developers didn't populate the default entry view is a mystery.

You must add a temporary editing section to data entry view and run a sample query to test your database connection and verify that query view behaves as expected.

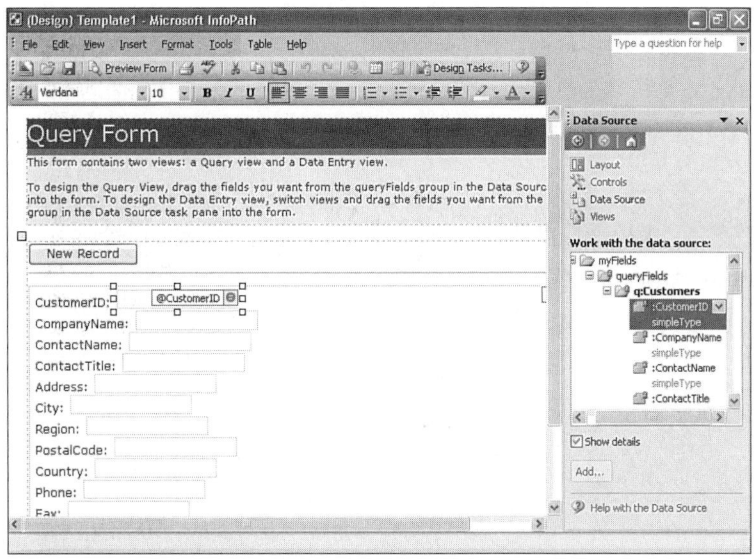

Figure 26.24 The Wizard generates a query view with all fields in one cell of a single-column table contained in the Customers section.

To add a data editing section to the temporary data entry view, do this:

1. Choose View, Manage Views to display the Views task pane, and click Data Entry (default) to open an empty view.
2. In the Views task pane, click the Data Source link, and scroll to the dataFields node.
3. Drag the d:Customers node to the empty view, release the mouse button, and select Section with Controls from the context menu to create a section that's identical to query view (see Figure 26.25). Unlike query view, labels in data entry view display the field's Caption property value, not the field name.

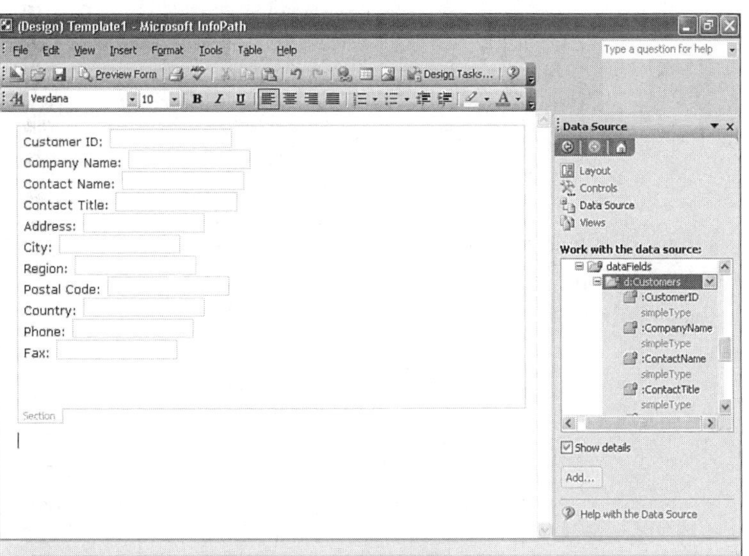

Figure 26.25 The Wizard generates a query view with all fields in one cell of a single-column table contained in the Customers section.

4. Click Preview Form, choose View, Query and type a valid CustomerID value, such as **ALFKI**, in the text box.
5. Scroll to the bottom of the form and click Run Query. Data for the selected record appears in the section controls you added in step 4 (see Figure 26.26).

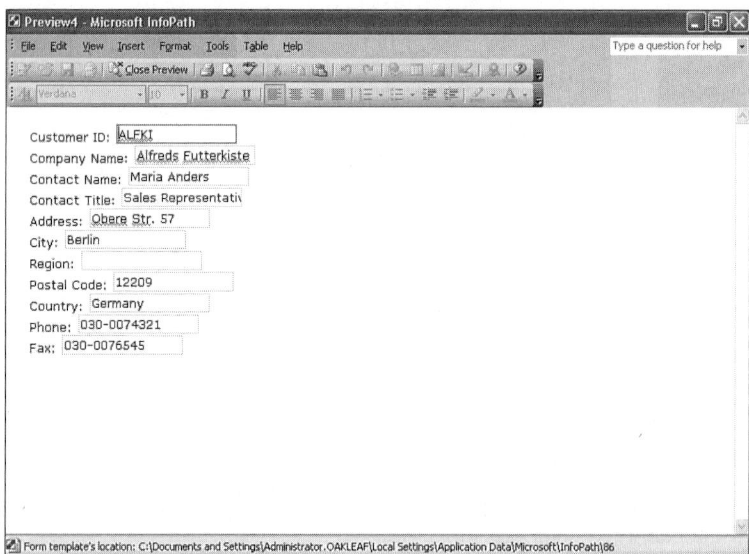

Figure 26.26
This data entry view is temporary. You use it to test the connection to the database and query (filter) execution only.

6. Choose View, Query to return to query view and click New Record to verify that the data entry view opens with empty text boxes.
7. Click Close Preview to return to design mode.

NOTE

If you click Run Query with no filter values or with a filter that returns more than one record, you receive an "InfoPath cannot run the specified query" error message. Supplying a filter value that doesn't match a record displays a "The specified query did not return any data" message.

Combining Query and Data Entry Operations in a Single View

The design and form completion processes for a dual-view data entry form aren't intuitive, to be generous. For example, the data entry view should include auto-generated Submit and Query View buttons. Submit is a built-in button that you can add to the form easily, but Query View isn't. Thus most data form designers probably will choose a single-view approach.

NOTE

> Adding a Query View button requires writing a JScript or VBA event handler to change the view.

Single views require compact query and data entry sections to minimize scrolling when editing data. Compact presentation is especially important for forms that display multiple records. The lack of wild-card support for queries makes many fields, such as Company Name, inappropriate for searching because you must type the search term exactly (other than case). CustomerID, City, Region, and Country should satisfy most users' query requirements.

To remove the data entry view and redesign the form to a compact, single-view version, do the following:

1. In the Views task pane, right-click Data Entry (default), choose Delete, and acknowledge the warning message. Query becomes the default view.
2. Replace Query Form with an appropriate title, in this case **Northwind Traders Customers Data Entry Form** or the like. Select and delete the table row under the title row.
3. Select the CompanyName, ContactName, ContactTitle, and Address labels and text boxes and delete them. Do the same for PostalCode and Phone and Fax.
4. Delete the line feed after each text box and add a space between the text box and the adjacent label.

TIP

> If you want to increase the width of the form to permit wider text boxes, right-click each table and section, choose properties, and change the width from the default 625 px to **700** px or greater.

5. Adjust the width of the text boxes to accommodate common filter values. The objective is to reduce the query section's table to a single row of labels and text boxes.
6. Click the Data Source link to display the Data Source task pane, select the `d:Customers` node under the `dataFields` node, drag the node to the right of the Run Query button, release the mouse, and select Section with Controls from the menu. Remove the extra line feeds at the bottom of the new section (see Figure 26.27).
7. Click the Preview Form button to display the Query view, type a filter parameter or two, and click Run Query to test your work so far (see Figure 26.28).

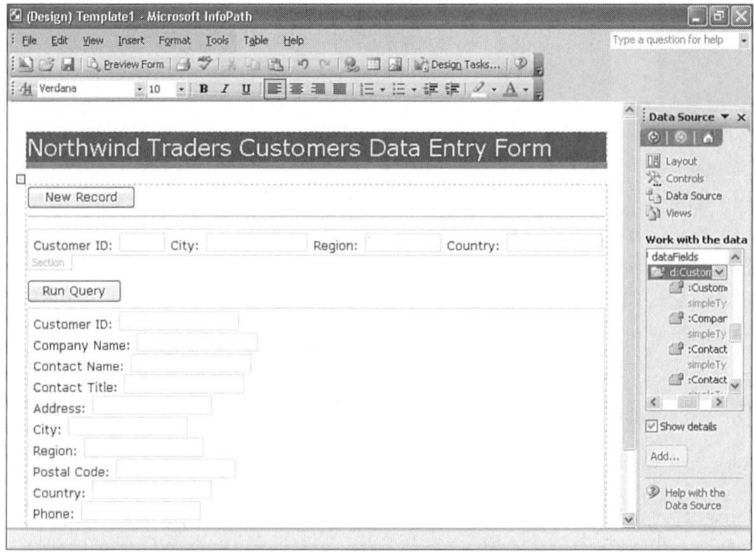

Figure 26.27
Removing unneeded filter parameters and rearranging the controls increases the region available for the data entry section.

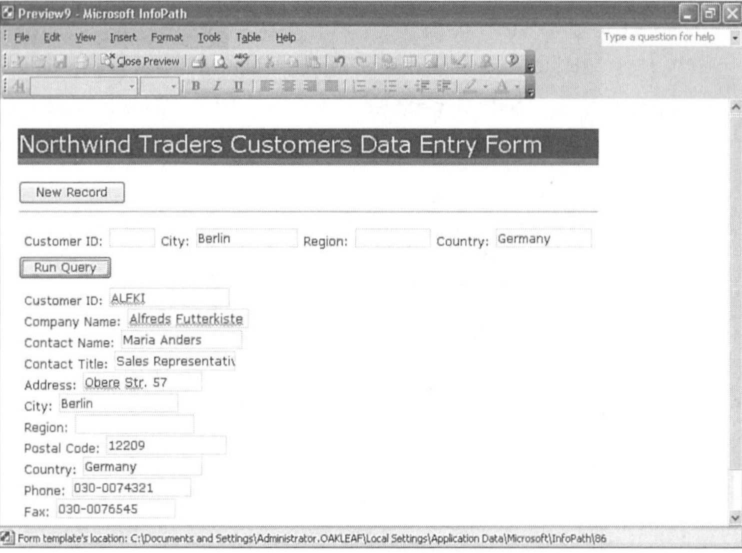

Figure 26.28
Running a query in form preview mode demonstrates that the data entry section of query view works as expected.

8. Return to design mode and repeat steps 4 and 5 for the fields in the data entry section to reduce its height. You can eliminate unneeded words in the field labels to conserve space.
9. Buttons for data entry operations should be located adjacent to the data entry section, so exchange the location of the Run Query and New Record buttons.

10. Save your template with a descriptive name in a folder of its own. If you save multiple forms in the same folder, extracting the individual template files overwrites those of other templates in the folder.

ADDING PRE-BUILT BUTTONS TO THE FORM

The InfoPath toolbox has a collection of conventional HTML elements, such as text, check, list, and drop-down list boxes, button, option button, text lists of various types, hyperlink, and picture. InfoPath-specific elements consist of a rich text box, various types of sections, repeating table, and expression box.

To make date entry operations function, you must add at least a Submit button to update the form's underlying table(s) with edits or new records. Adding a Delete & Submit button is optional. Adding buttons demonstrates how you set the buttons to perform pre-built data entry actions.

To add both buttons to your template, do the following:

1. In design mode, click the Controls link on the task pane to display the Insert Controls list.
2. Scroll to the Button control and drag it to the right of the New Record button.
3. Right-click the new button, and choose Properties to open the Button Properties dialog (see Figure 26.29). The default action for the button is to create a JScript `onClick` event handler.

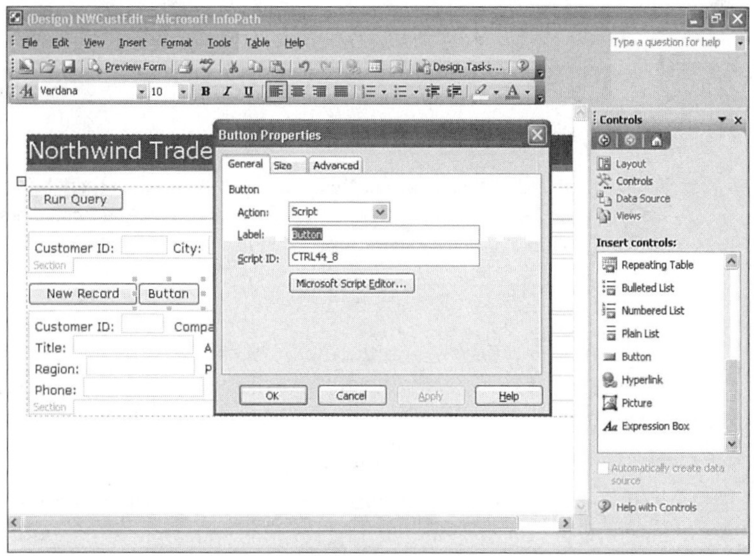

Figure 26.29 The Button Properties dialog lets you specify the action that occurs when the user clicks the button.

CAUTION

> Be careful not to select Script when modifying the button. With Script selected, clicking OK or Microsoft Script Editor creates an `onClick` event handler for the button, which attaches script.js to your project. Deleting the button doesn't remove the event handler, so attempts to preview the form throw a script error. To eliminate the error, you must open the Script Editor and delete the `onClick` function manually.

4. Select Submit from the Action list to open the Submitting Forms dialog, which lets you specify what happens after the user submits the form. You can select the submission method from the Submit list; the default, Submit to a Database applies to this example. Be sure that the Enable the Submit Menu Item on the File Menu check box is marked (see Figure 26.30).

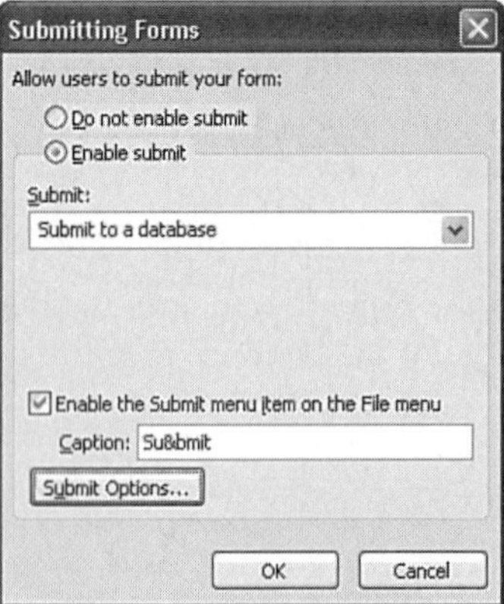

Figure 26.30 The Submitting Forms dialog lets you customize the submit operation.

26

TIP

> If the Enable the Submit Menu Item on the File Menu check box is cleared, you receive an "InfoPath cannot submit the form data because the form template does not support submit" error. This error occurs despite your having selected the Enable Submit option.

5. Click Submit Options to open the dialog of the same name that lets you choose what happens to the form after successful submission and specify custom success and failure messages (see Figure 26.31).
6. Click OK three times to close the dialogs.
7. Repeat steps 2 and 3, but add the new button to the right of Submit and select Delete & Submit from the Action list. The settings you apply in the Submitting Forms and Submit Options dialogs to the Submit built-in button also apply to the Submit & Delete button.

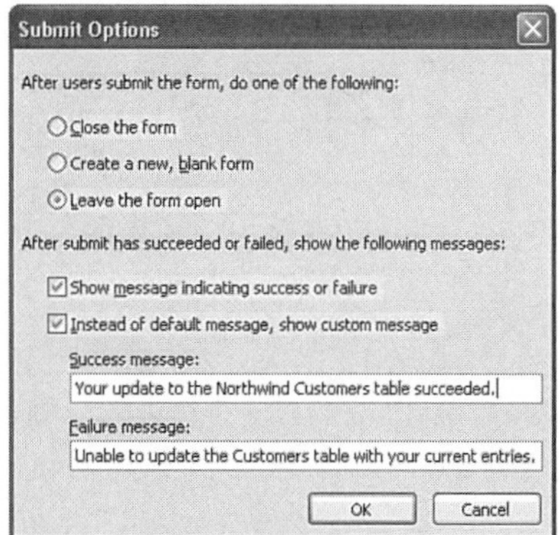

Figure 26.31
The Submit Options dialog enables further customization of the submittal operation.

8. Add some spaces between the three buttons and choose Preview Form to test submission of edits and new records (see Figure 26.32). A message box requests conformation of each submittal request.
9. Press Ctrl+S to save your changes.

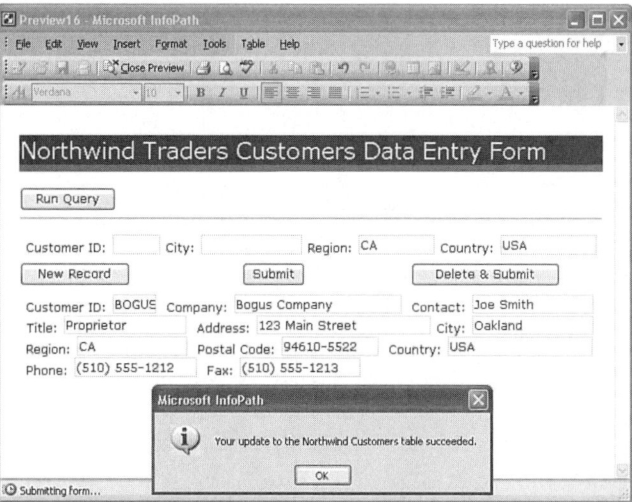

Figure 26.32
This example of adding a new Customers record demonstrates the custom success message shown in Figure 26.31.

You must add a new record to enable testing Delete & Submit, because all sample Customers records have dependent Orders records. If you submit an invalid update request, InfoPath returns an error message; in some cases, the errors originate from the database server. Some error messages have a Details button to open a text box that displays full text of the InfoPath or ADO error message.

The NWCustEdit.xsn template file is located in the \Seua11\Chaptr26\NWCustEdit folder of the accompanying CD-ROM. This template connects to Northwind.mdb in its default location—C:\Program Files\Microsoft Office\Office11\Samples.

If you encounter an "InfoPath cannot create a new, blank form" error when you attempt to open a form, see the "Changing the Publishing Point of an InfoPath Template" topic of the "Troubleshooting" section near the end of this chapter.

DISABLING SPELL-CHECKING OF TEXT BOX VALUES

Spell-checking fields whose values aren't likely to appear in Office 2003's dictionary—such as CustomerID and CompanyName—is likely to distract users of your forms.

To turn off spell-checking for a text box control, open the Properties dialog for the control, click the Display tab, and clear the Enable Spelling Checker and Enable Auto-complete check boxes (see Figure 26.33). Unlike Access, you can't multi-select InfoPath controls and change a common property value; you must alter the property value for each control on the form.

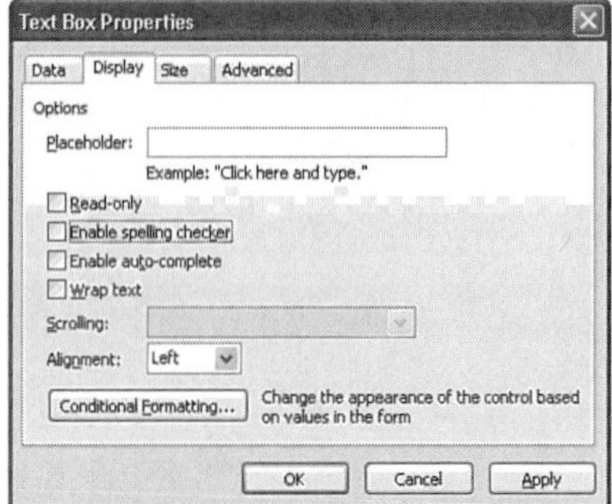

Figure 26.33
Disable spell-checking of text box values by clearing the Enable Spelling Checker check box on the Display page. Disabling auto-complete also is a good practice for data entry forms.

TIP

Click the Advanced tab of the text box's Properties dialog to add a screen tip to or change the tab order of the text box.

APPLYING ADVANCED INFOPATH TECHNIQUES

The data editing form you created in the preceding sections is adequate for use by experienced users, but adding data entry validation and lookup lists for queries makes the form easier to use. You also are likely to be faced with the need to change the primary data source for the form. The following sections cover these three topics.

SETTING LOCAL DATA VALIDATION RULES

If the schema for your form specifies XSD built-in datatypes of elements, such as `decimal`, `int`, `boolean`, `date`, or `dateTime`, InfoPath tests your query filter and data entry values for conformance to the requirements of the World Wide Web Consortium (W3C) XML Schema Part 2: Datatypes recommendation. XSD schema also can apply constraints to data values by facets, such as `length`, `minLength`, and `maxLength` for the `string` data type. Each datatype has its own set of facets. The built-in primitive and derived data types handle almost all Jet and SQL Server 2000 datatypes. (Jet's Hyperlink field data type is an exception; Jet Currency and SQL Server money fields convert to the `decimal` datatype.)

NOTE

You can read the W3C XML Schema Part 2: Datatypes recommendation at `http://www.w3.org/TR/xmlschema-2/`.

InfoPath doesn't attempt to determine the `dataType` or other constraints, other than `maxLength` of `queryFields` and `dataFields` subelements. You could alter the schema(s) for your form to add `dataType`, but the process isn't simple. ADO Recordsets use attribute-centric, not element-centric, XML. The nodes that appear to be elements under the `q:customers` and `d:customers` nodes in the Data Source list are attribute name/value pairs. If you mark the Show Details check box, InfoPath reports the data type as `simpleType`, which corresponds to XSD's `anySimpleType` datatype. Schema1.xml (for `q:customers`) and Schema2.xml (for `d:customers`) specify `string` as the data type of all fields.

→ To review the differences between element- and attribute-centric XML, **see** "Gaining an XML Vocabulary," **p. 944**.

InfoPath uses XML Path Language (XPath) 1.0 expressions to apply validation constraints to controls. Fortunately, you don't need to learn XPath syntax to add simple constraints, such as Jet's Required = Yes or Allow Zero Length = No. Adding constraints to numeric values is equally simple.

As an example, do the following to require CustomerID and CompanyName values for new Customers records:

1. Right-click the data entry section's Customer ID field, and choose Text Box Properties to open the Properties dialog.
2. Click the Data Validation button to open the Data Validation (*FieldName*) dialog, and click Add to display an expanded version of the dialog.
3. Select Is Blank from the middle (condition) list (see Figure 26.34).
4. Type a screen tip to appear when the text box value doesn't comply with the validation rule, and add an optional message box that contains an alternate or more descriptive validation error message (see Figure 26.35).

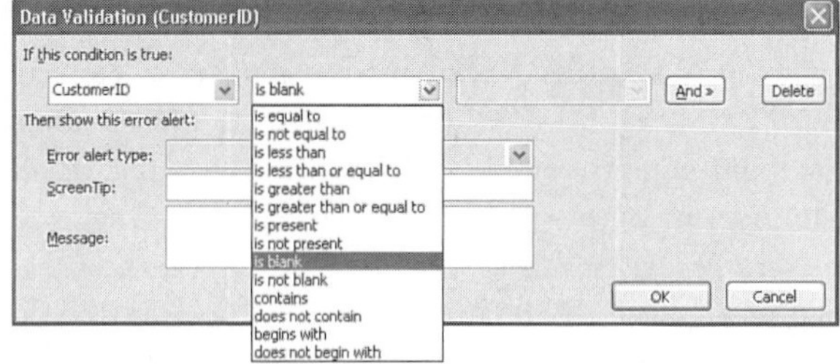

Figure 26.34
To prevent users from submitting a form with an empty field value, add the Is Blank validation rule to the field's text box.

Figure 26.35
Add screen tip and, optionally, message box text to describe the validation rule violation.

5. Accept the default Inline Alert, and click OK three times to close the dialogs.
6. Select the Company Name field and repeat steps 1 through 5, but change text in step 4 to require a company name.
7. Preview the form. Text boxes whose values don't conform to validation rules display a red underline and the screen tip.
8. Right-click the text box and choose Full Error Description to display the message box (see Figure 26.36).

26

Figure 26.36
Text boxes with values that don't meet validation rules gain a red underline. Attempting to submit a form with a validation error displays an error message and draws a red rectangle around the control.

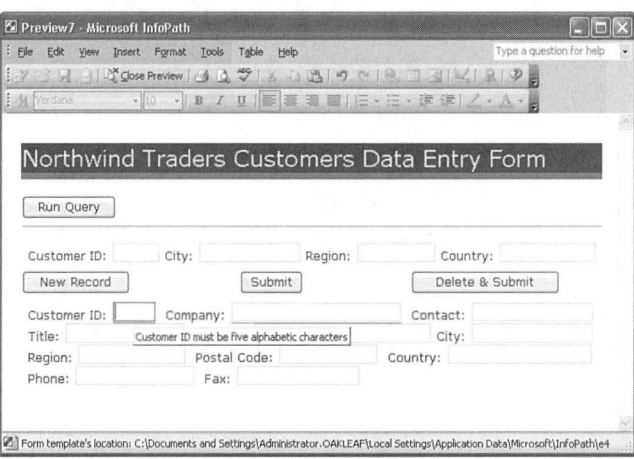

9. Return to template design mode, and press Ctrl+S to save your changes.

If you attempt to submit a form with a value that violates a validation rule, you receive an "InfoPath cannot submit the form because it has errors" message and a red dashed outline surrounds the offending text box or other control.

The Data Validation dialog lets you create compound validation rules that are similar to Access's table-level validation. You can combine validation rules for the same or different fields with and/or logic by clicking the And button and selecting And or Or in the right-most list (see Figure 26.37).

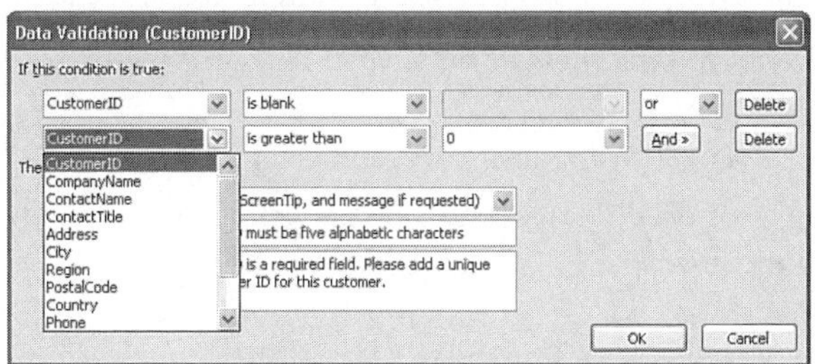

Figure 26.37 The Data Validation dialog lets you design compound validation rules that are similar to Access's table-level validation rules.

TIP

Open the Section Properties dialog for a section, click the Display tab, click the Conditional Formatting button, and then click the Add button to open the Conditional Formatting version of the Data Validation dialog. This dialog lets you change the background color of the section, the font color of the control, and other display attributes when users violate a validation rule.

Changing a Text Box to a Bound Drop-down List

InfoPath controls have a Change To context menu choice that emulates Access's Change To feature. You can change a bound text box to one of nine bound InfoPath controls. The most common change is from a text box to a drop-down list or date picker control for `date` or `dateTime` fields.

At the risk of creating an extraordinarily long list, you can change the CustomerID text box of the query field to a drop-down list of CustomerID values populated by a secondary data source. HTML lists don't have the flexibility of Access combo boxes, so you can't type a value into the list's text element. However, InfoPath thoughtfully adds an empty value at the top of the list, so users can apply a query filter without specifying a CustomerID value.

Creating the Secondary Data Source

Creating a secondary data source from a database is almost identical to creating the primary data source. For a drop-down list, you usually add only the field to which the text box is bound.

To add the CustomerID field as a secondary data source for a drop-down list on the form, do this:

1. In design mode, choose Tools, Secondary Data Sources to open the Secondary Data Sources dialog and click Add to start the Data Source Wizard.

> **TIP**
>
> Refer to steps 2 through 8 of the earlier "Creating a Dual-View Template from the Primary Data Source" section for a more detailed description of the following steps.

2. Choose the Database option in the First Wizard dialog and click Next.
3. Click Select Database, navigate to the ...\Samples folder, and double-click Northwind.mdb.
4. Clear all but the CustomerID check box and click Next.
5. In the final Wizard dialog, replace Customers with a more descriptive name, such as **CustIDLookup**, and click Finish and Close.

REPLACING A TEXT BOX WITH A DROP-DOWN LIST

To replace the CustomerID text box of the query section with the drop-down list and specify the list's row source, do the following.

1. Right-click the query section's text box, choose Change To, and select Drop-Down List, which fills a line.
2. Adjust the width of the list to accommodate five characters.
3. Right-click the list and choose Drop-Down List Properties to open the dialog of the same name.
4. Select the Look up in a Database, Web Service or File option, which sets CustIDLookup as the value of the Data Source list.
5. Click the Select XPath button to the right of the Entries text box to open the Select Field or Group dialog (see Figure 26.38). Select either `d:Customers` (because the group has only one field) or `:CustomerID` and click OK.

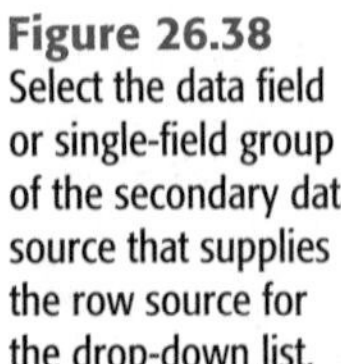

Figure 26.38
Select the data field or single-field group of the secondary data source that supplies the row source for the drop-down list.

6. Specifying `d:Customers` adds the XPath designation for the node and the `@CustomerID` XPath pointer to the single child node to the Value and Display Name text boxes (see Figure 26.39).

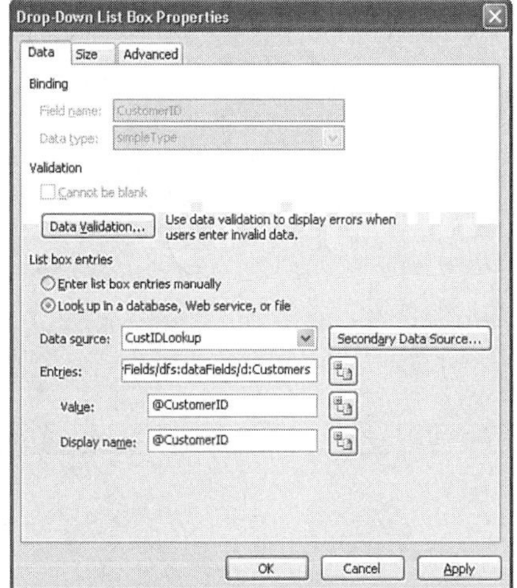

Figure 26.39
The Entries text box contains the XPath expression that points to the `d:Customers` node; `@CustomerID` is the child node that populates the drop-down list.

NOTE

> If you specify `:CustomerID` in step 5, Value and Display Name contain periods (`.`), the XPath self-reference.

7. Click OK to close the dialog, click Preview Form, and open the new list (see Figure 36.40).
8. If you want to retain the drop-down list, save your changes. Otherwise, exit InfoPath and don't save the changes.

The entire XPath expression for the list entries, which isn't visible fully in Figure 26.39, is `/dfs:myFields/dfs:dataFields/d:Customers`. The `dfs:` qualifier presumably represents "data field source."

TIP

> If you want to display values from another field, such as CompanyName, instead of the primary key value, include the field when you create the secondary data source. Change the XPath reference to the other field (@CompanyName) in the Drop-Down List Properties dialog's Display Name text box. You must increase the width of the list to make the company names readable.

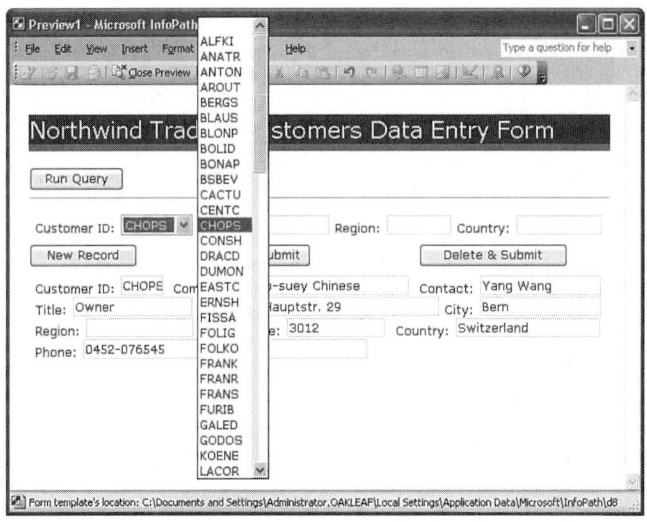

Figure 26.40 The new drop-down list lets users select from a long list of CustomerID values or an empty value that enables query filters based on City, Region, Country, or all three. This double-exposure shows the list to the right of the added drop-down list.

Changing a Form's Primary Data Source

As mentioned earlier in the chapter, changing an InfoPath 1.0 primary data source isn't as easy as changing secondary data sources. To change the path or filename for a Jet data source or change from the Jet to an SQL Server version of the data source, you must manually alter the manifest file in Notepad and then refresh the template file with the altered manifest file. The process is similar to the changes you made to the Currency data source in the earlier "Changing a Secondary Data Source" section.

To change the location of a Jet primary data source, do the following:

1. Make a backup copy of your template (.xsn) file.
2. In template design mode, choose File, Extract Form Files, and save the extracted files to the folder with the template file. Overwrite any existing files in the folder.
3. Close InfoPath.
4. Open the manifest.xsf file in Notepad with WordWrap on, and search for **.mdb** to locate the `<adoAdapter>` element. This element contains the ADO connect string, the query that generates the data source, and the `queryAllowed` and `submitAllowed` attributes (see Figure 26.41).
5. Edit the path and filename, as necessary, for each instance of the `<adoAdapter>` element. Each secondary data source adds an element.
6. Press Ctrl+S to save the file.
7. Right-click manifest.xsf and choose Design to open InfoPath from the manifest file.
8. Verify that queries and drop-down lists work correctly, and submit a temporary edit or new record to the table.

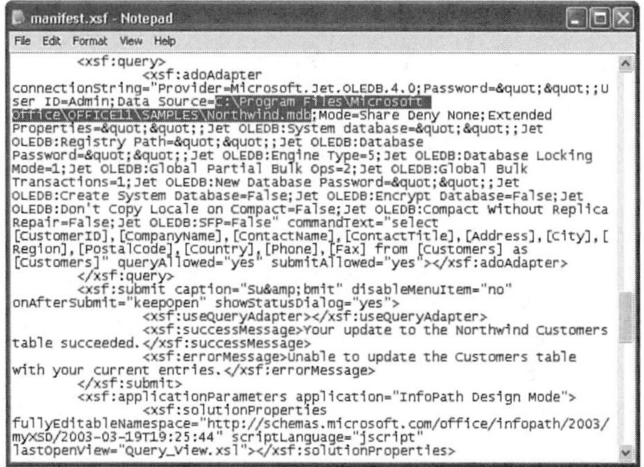

Figure 26.41
Manually edit in Notepad the path and, if necessary, name of the Jet .mdb file that contains the tables for the primary data source.

CAUTION

> Don't add a new record to a table with an AutoNumber field if you're concerned about auditability. Deleting the record will create a gap in the AutoNumber sequence.

9. Open the table and verify that the temporary update was successful.
10. Undo the change you made in step 8 by an InfoPath Submit or Delete & Submit operation, and verify the undo operation in the table.
11. Choose File, Save As, click the Save button, and overwrite the *TemplateName*.xsn file.
12. Repeat steps 8 through 10 with a form opened from the .xsn file to verify update of the template archive.

If you don't explicitly overwrite the *TemplateName*.xsn file, you might find that the changes you made to manifest.xsf aren't reflected in the template file.

26

TIP

> If you want to move the primary data source from Jet to an upgraded SQL Server 2000 database, create in a different folder a temporary template from the SQL Server data source and extract the manifest.xsf file. Copy the entire contents of each `<adoAdapter>` element and paste-replace the corresponding element in the original manifest.xsf file.

The NWCustEditCS.xsn template file, which uses the NorthwindCS SQL Server 2000 (local) database's Customers table for the two data sources, is located in the \Seua11\Chaptr26\NWCustEditCS folder of the accompanying CD-ROM. This form incorporates the features described in the "Applying Advanced InfoPath Techniques" sections.

If you encounter an "InfoPath cannot create a new, blank form" error when you attempt to open a form, see the "Changing the Publishing Point of an InfoPath Template" topic of the "Troubleshooting" section near the end of this chapter.

WORKING WITH WINDOWS SHAREPOINT SERVICES AND ACCESS

Windows SharePoint Services (WSS) is a workgroup portal server that uses Internet Information Services 6.0 to manage and display content and MSDE or SQL Server 2000 as its data store. WSS is intended for sharing documents, lists, InfoPath forms, Web pages, and images among portal users. WSS also offers newsgroup-style discussion boards, instant messaging, and survey features. Unlike its more powerful relative, SharePoint Portal Server, WSS doesn't require client licenses for users.

WSS is an add-in to Windows Server 2003 that you access with IE 5.0+. (Using browsers other than IE 5.0+ results in reduced functionality.) The examples of the following sections require that you have access to a WSS site on a local development computer, your organization's intranet, or from a third-party WSS hosting facility. You also need administrative privileges for the site. Limited experience administering a WSS site is helpful but not required.

TIP

Apptix On-Demand hosts WSS services as an application service provider (ASP). You can learn more about this program at `http://www.apptix.net/sharepoint.htm`.

26

NEW

Access 2003 lets you interact with WSS by importing or linking STS lists and exporting tables or queries to lists. WSS can export tables to Jet or SQL Server 2000 databases, host InfoPath templates, and store saved forms. You also can generate Access reports from WSS lists. The following sections describe how to use these data-related WSS features.

NOTE

The following sections' examples run WSS in a development environment. WSS is installed as the default Web site at `http://oakleaf-w2k3/`. OakLeaf-W2K3 is a Windows 2003 member server in the OAKLEAF Windows 2000 domain. Office System 2003 and InfoPath 2003 are installed on the member server, so `http://localhost/` opens the WSS home page in IE. If you have a different configuration, you might need to change the URL, security settings, or file paths to achieve the expected results.

EXPORTING TABLES OR QUERIES TO A SHAREPOINT LIST

The simplest interaction with WSS is exporting a Jet or SQL Server table or query as a WSS list. In this case, there is no connection between the list and your Jet or SQL Server database.

To export a table, such as the Northwind.mdb or NorthwindCS Customers table to the default WSS site, do the following:

1. Launch Access 2003 and select the Customers table in the Database window.
2. Right-click the table entry, choose Export, and select SharePoint Team Services in the Files of Type list to open the Export SharePoint Team Services Wizard.
3. Complete the URL to your WSS site (`http://localhost/` for this example), and modify the default list name and description, if you want (see Figure 26.42).

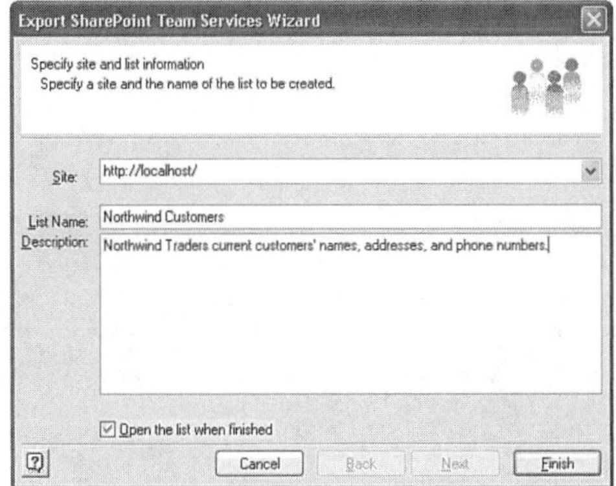

Figure 26.42
Type the URL for your WSS site and give the list a name and description in the first Wizard dialog.

4. With the Open This List When Finished check box marked, click Finish to export the list. After you acknowledge the "Finished exporting table '*listname*' to '*URL*'" message, the list opens in WSS datasheet view (see Figure 26.43).

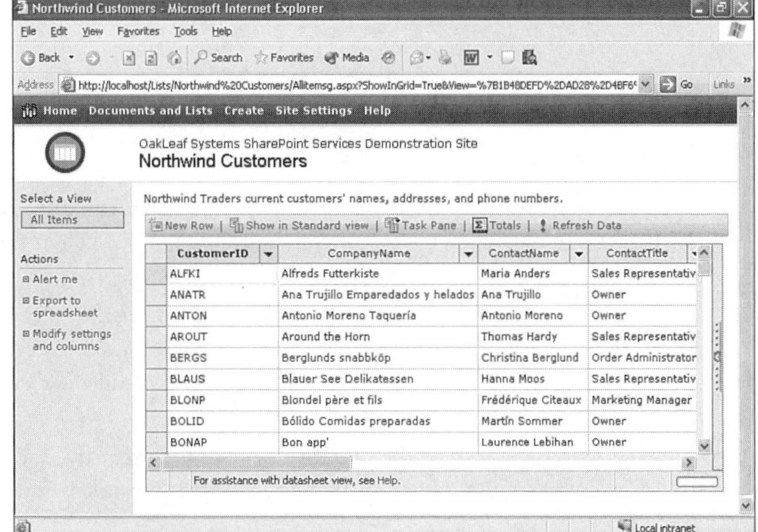

CustomerID	CompanyName	ContactName	ContactTitle
ALFKI	Alfreds Futterkiste	Maria Anders	Sales Representativ
ANATR	Ana Trujillo Emparedados y helados	Ana Trujillo	Owner
ANTON	Antonio Moreno Taquería	Antonio Moreno	Owner
AROUT	Around the Horn	Thomas Hardy	Sales Representativ
BERGS	Berglunds snabbköp	Christina Berglund	Order Administrator
BLAUS	Blauer See Delikatessen	Hanna Moos	Sales Representativ
BLONP	Blondel père et fils	Frédérique Citeaux	Marketing Manager
BOLID	Bólido Comidas preparadas	Martín Sommer	Owner
BONAP	Bon app'	Laurence Lebihan	Owner

Figure 26.43
The exported table appears as a list in WSS's data sheet view for users who have Office 2003 installed.

26

NOTE

> Users who don't have Office System 2003 installed see the list in standard view, because datasheet view requires Office Web Components 11.0 on the client. You can add a new item—but not edit existing entries—in standard view.

5. Right-click a column to display a context menu of operations you can perform on the column. For example, choosing Edit/Delete Column opens the Edit Column page that lets you add a default value, specify formatting for the data type, require a value for new items, and set the maximum number of characters.
6. Open a column's drop-down list to sort or add a filter in datasheet view. You can select Sort Ascending or Sort Descending, and then select an individual value or up to three custom sort conditions in the Custom Filter dialog (see Figure 26.44).

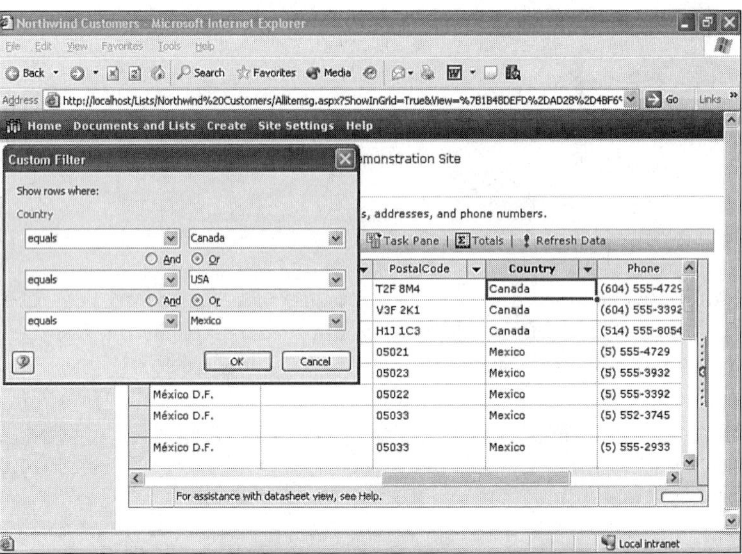

Figure 26.44
The Custom Filter dialog lets you apply up to three WHERE clause criteria to the list.

26

7. Open the list and select (Show All) to remove the filter. You can't remove the sort in this list; you're only choice is to sort on another column, such as the primary key (CustomerID).
8. Click the Task Pane button and click the Sort link to open Custom Sort dialog that lets you sort the list by a sequence of up to three columns. You can remove the sort you applied in the preceding step by opening the drop-down list and selecting the empty choice.
9. Click New Row to move to the tentative append record at the end of the list. Like Access, you don't add a record until you type values for at least the required fields.

If you encounter an error when exporting your table to a WSS list, see the "Table Column Name Conflicts with WSS Lists" topic of the "Troubleshooting" section near the end of this chapter.

Linking a WSS List to an Access Table

The most common reason to export Access data to WSS is to link a Jet table to the list. Linking makes edits to the table in Access or the list in WSS visible in both applications. This capability lets you establish relationships between the list and other tables, and use Access forms and VBA code to maintain the list.

NOTE

> You can't create a link from WSS to the SQL Server database of an Access Data Project. You receive a "Links can only be created between Microsoft Access database files" error message if you try.

To link a new Jet table to a WSS list using the Customers list you created in the preceding section as an example, do the following:

1. Click the Task Pane button to open the task pane and scroll down to expose the three Access options.
2. Click the Create Linked Table in Access link to open the Export dialog. Accept the default Existing Database option and click OK to display the Open dialog.
3. Navigate to Northwind.mdb or NorthwindCS.adp and double-click the filename to launch Access 2003 and add the link to the list's underlying MSDE database (see Figure 26.45). The table name is the list name with a colon-separated view name; by default, the view is All Items.

26

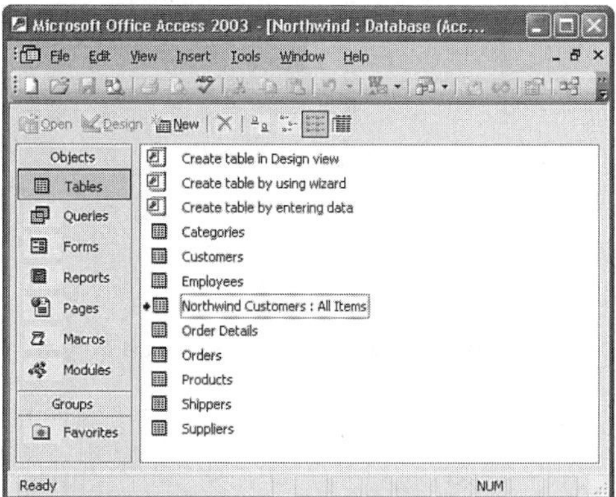

Figure 26.45
A combination of the list and view names creates the linked table's name.

TIP

> Rename the link to simplify Access references to the table—for example, **CustomersList**. Renaming the link doesn't affect the connection to the list.

4. Open the linked table in Access. Linking to a list adds an AutoNumber column for *row-level tracking*.
5. Add a temporary new record to the Access table, **BOGUS** and **Bogus Company** for this example.
6. Return to the WSS list, click the Refresh Data button to display the added record at the end of the list. You might need to reapply the sort instruction to the sorted column once or twice to reposition the new item to the correct location (see Figure 26.46).

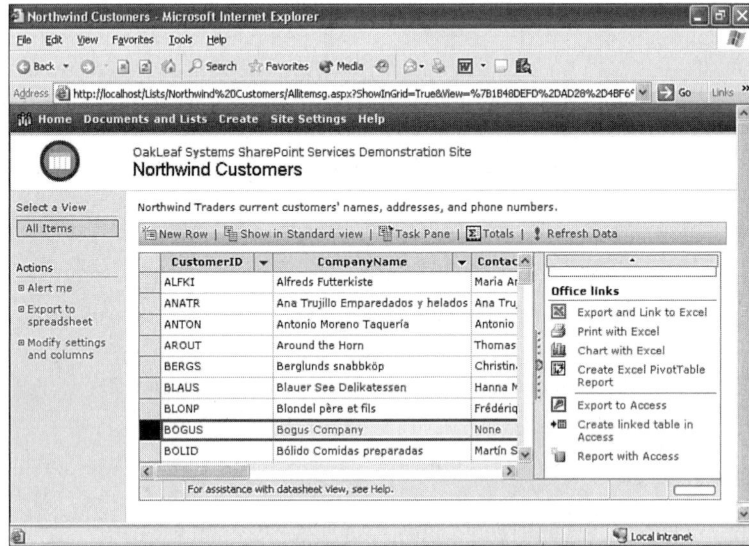

Figure 26.46
Inserting a new temporary record in Access adds the record to the end of the WSS list when you click Refresh Data. Reapply the sort to make the record appear at its correct position in the list.

7. Select the added record, press delete, and confirm the deletion to remove it from the list.
8. In Access, close and reopen the table to verify that the record has been deleted in the linked table. Choosing Records, Refresh doesn't indicate that the record has been deleted.
9. Verify updates propagate from the list to Access by clicking New Record, adding a temporary new record, and opening the table in Access.
10. Delete the record in Access, return to WSS, click Refresh Records, and verify the temporary record is gone.

LINKING AN ACCESS TABLE TO A WSS LIST

An alternative to creating a link from WSS to an Access table or query is using Access's linked Jet tables feature to create a link to the data underlying the WSS list. You can't create a usable link to WSS's named MSDE instance—*COMPUTERNAME*\SharePoint. The table linked from Access to a WSS list has a different structure than that from a link you establish in the reverse direction.

To export another WSS list and link to it in Access 2003, do the following:

1. Open Access and export another Jet or SQL Server table, such as Suppliers to your SBS site. (Refer to the earlier "Exporting Tables or Queries to a SharePoint List" section for the detailed steps.)
2. If you export the Jet Suppliers table, check the HomePage column of the list to confirm that WSS supports the Jet Hyperlink field data type.
3. Return to Access and choose File, Get External Data, Link Tables to open the Link dialog.
4. Choose SharePoint Team Services in the Files of Type list to open the first Link SharePoint Team Services Wizard. Select or type the URL to your WSS site, and click Next to open the Select Lists dialog.
5. Select the list to link, Northwind Suppliers for this example, select the Link to One or More Lists option, and clear the Retrieve IDs for Lookup Columns, because this list has no lookup columns (see Figure 26.47).

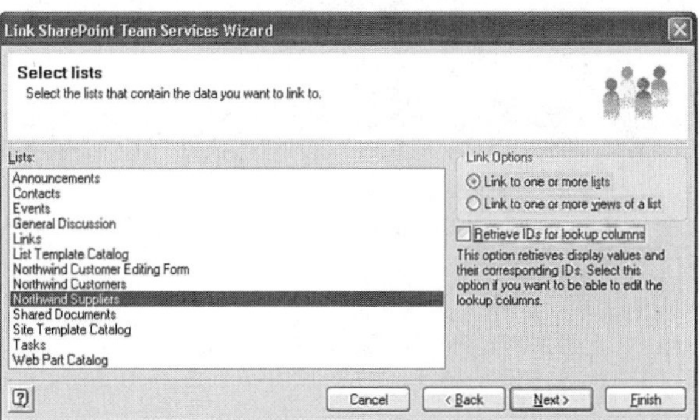

Figure 26.47 Access's Link SharePoint Team Services Wizard lets you create one or more links to every list in your WSS site.

6. Click Finish to create the link. When you open the link, it's obvious that linking from Access to WSS generates a table structure that differs dramatically from that created by linking from WSS to Access (see Figure 26.48).
7. Click a hyperlink in the Edit column to open a WSS editing form for the record you select. A red asterisk indicates a required field (see Figure 26.49).
8. Test the ability of Access to add a new record to the list by clicking the new record button, typing the next SupplierID value, and adding at least the required CompanyName value.
9. Move the record pointer to add an Edit hyperlink to the record. You can edit the record either in Access or in the WSS form.
10. Return to WSS, open the Northwind Suppliers list, if necessary, click Refresh Data, and verify presence of the record at the end of the list.
11. Delete the record. As was the case in the preceding example, you must close and reopen the table to verify deletion.

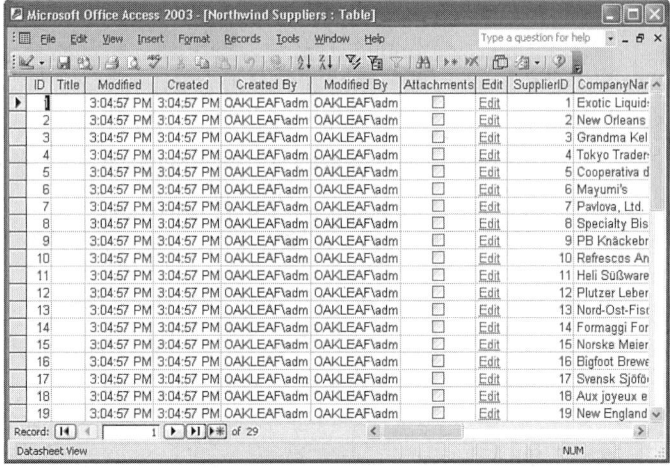

Figure 26.48 Linking a Jet table to a WSS list from Access adds list management fields to the table. These fields don't appear when you create the link from WSS.

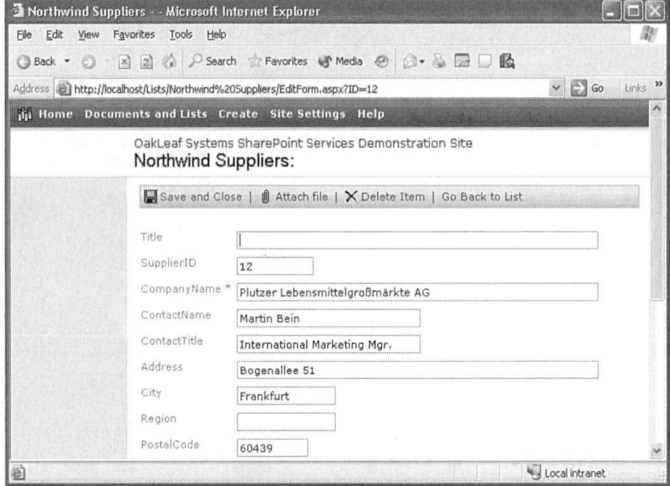

Figure 26.49 Linking from Access creates a hyperlink to WSS that lets you edit the record in an WSS form. You also can edit the list in Access's Datasheet view.

Publishing Data-Bound InfoPath Templates to WSS

You can share InfoPath templates and forms with WSS users by publishing the *TemplateName*.xsn file to a document library of a WSS site. It's a good practice to create a new form library for each template. The library stores each form that users generate and save.

To publish the NWCustEdit.xsn template you created in the earlier "Designing an InfoPath Query and Data Editing Form" section or one the sample templates from your Program Files\Seua11\Chaptr26 folder, do the following:

1. Open the *TemplateName*.xsn template in InfoPath design mode.
2. Choose File, Publish to start the InfoPath Publishing Wizard. Click Next.
3. In the second Wizard dialog, select the To a SharePoint Form Library option, and click Next.
4. In the third dialog, accept the Create a New Form Library option, and click Next.
5. Type in the fourth dialog the URL for your WSS site, **http://localhost** for this example, and click Next.
6. Type the name and a brief description of the template in the fifth dialog, and click Next.
7. The sixth dialog lets you specify query or data columns as column names on the WSS site. This feature isn't required, so click Next to publish the template.
8. The seventh dialog lets you send email announcements to users about the new form's availability. Mark the Open This Form from Its Published Location check box, and click Close to dismiss the Wizard and open the new form library page.
9. Click the Fill Out This Form button, and acknowledge the two "ADO Warning" messages to open an empty form. For this example, execute a query to populate the form.

TIP

Reset IE's Security options for the Intranet Zone to Low if you want to prevent the two "ADO Warning" messages from appearing each time you click the Fill Out This Form button or open a form.

10. Press Ctrl+S to open the Save As dialog, which incorporates parts of the form library page (see Figure 26.50).

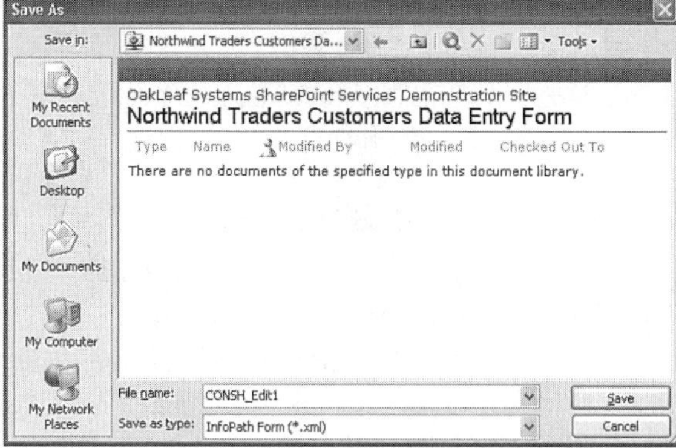

Figure 26.50
Type a filename for the form in the Save As window.

11. Click Save to add the form to library and click the All Forms link to refresh the list.
12. Open the drop-down list for the form to display the available WSS form operations (see Figure 26.51).

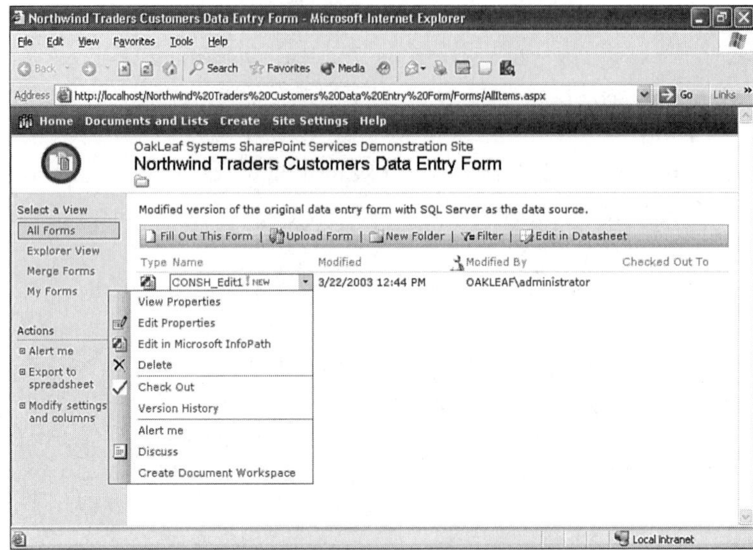

Figure 26.51
After you click the All Forms link to refresh the form library, the form you saved appears in the list.

Troubleshooting

Changing the Publishing Point of an InfoPath Template

When I try to open a TemplateName.xsn file, I receive an "InfoPath cannot create a new, blank form" message because the publishing location has changed.

Publishing an InfoPath template generates a reference to the folder in which you saved the *TemplateName*.xsn file. When you publish a template and then copy or move the file, you can't create a form from the relocated or copied template. To solve this problem, right-click the *TemplateName*.xsn file and choose Design to open the file in InfoPath design mode. Choose File, Save As and overwrite the existing *TemplateName*.xsn file. Alternatively, publish the form to the new location. In either case, XML data files you copy to the new location open in the original template, not the template in the new location. If the original template is missing, you can't open the copied data files.

Table Column Name Conflicts with WSS Lists

When I try to export an Access or SQL Server table to a WSS list, I receive an error message, the list is missing some of the table columns, or both.

WSS lists have several internal columns for list management that don't appear in datasheet or standard view. Figure 26.48 shows these columns: ID, Title, Modified, Created, Created By, Modified By, Attachments, and Edit. Tables having columns with any of these names cause problems during the export process. You must rename conflicting table columns or substitute a query with column name aliases to export the table data successfully.

IN THE REAL WORLD—DATA-CENTRIC COLLABORATION

Collaboration is the watchword of Office System 2003 and its members. A Google search of the `microsoft.com` site returns about 15,100 instances of the word. Similarly, Bill Gates and Microsoft marketing folk use phrases such as "knowledge workers without limits" and "empower[ing] knowledge workers." More than 800 `microsoft.com` pages contain both "collaboration" and "knowledge worker." Most of this book's readers probably are knowledge workers or persons responsible for assisting knowledge workers.

The role of corporate knowledge workers is to produce information that's useful to other organization members, customers, suppliers, other "business partners," or all of these groups. The usefulness of the information is related directly to the workers' knowledge and skill set. The problem is that most such information—whether generated by computer or handwritten on a business form—is unstructured or—at best—semi-structured. Some analysts suggest that more information resides in Excel worksheet files than in all the world's databases. If you add Word document files to the mix, the conclusion is undoubtedly correct. Business email contains an enormous amount of unstructured information, especially if your organization is required to archive messages for several years.

The goal of Office Systems 2003's XML feature set is to enable generating human-readable, *structured information* from the productivity applications running on 90% or more of today's PCs. Creating structured information requires adherence to a standardized XML schema (.xsd file) for identical or similar documents. Another requirement is separating presentation of information from the underlying data; formatting for viewing or printing is the province of XSL, XSLT, and XML Formatting Objects (XML-FO). InfoPath achieves this objective by generating a validated XML document from an XSD schema, which you provide or InfoPath generates for you. An auto-generated XSLT transform (.xsl file) writes the HTML code that's required to display the form in IE. You can open and edit the InfoPath XML file in Word or Excel 2003. If you extract and apply the .xsl file for the form in Word, you can view—but not edit—the form. Predictable and consistent document structure is critical to sharing data between applications as well as your colleagues.

One of the most useful capabilities of InfoPath is email routing of forms, such as expense reports or purchase requisitions, through the workflow process. Recipients with InfoPath can edit the form and add digital signatures to authenticate specific actions. Those without InfoPath can add text and digitally sign the forwarded message. Over the next few years, an increasing percentage of business and governmental email messages will originate from XML form editing applications. The benefits of structured messages to the information gathering and analysis process will far outweigh the added cost of storing the XML documents in databases. The next version of SQL Server, code-named Yukon when this book was written, has a native XML data type that enables SQL-like queries against XML documents.

Windows SharePoint Services, SharePoint Portal Server, and Exchange Server are Microsoft's primary offerings for information sharing. WSS is the logical portal candidate for small- and medium-sized organizations (SMOs) because it's easy to set up and manage, and WSS client access licenses (CALs) aren't required. Shared InfoPath form libraries can emulate a small-scale document database. For example, the library can contain forms for all changes or the latest change to the a query/data entry form's table(s). Lists make the contents of linked Access tables or queries accessible to any authorized WSS user on an intranet or via the Internet. You can control whether users have read-only, read-write, or no access to data-centric forms and lists by their WSS group membership.

Consider collaboration when you design your Access databases and applications, even if InfoPath, SharePoint, or both aren't on your immediate horizon. Collaboration by sharing structured data—primarily in the form of XML documents with associated XSD schema—is in the early-adopter stage today, but its momentum is increasing. It won't be long until forms-based XML editors, such as InfoPath, become as common as Microsoft Word on users' desktops and entry-level portals, such as WSS, become the central information source for teams, workgroups, and departments.

Programming and Converting Access Applications

CHAPTER 27

Learning Visual Basic for Applications

In this chapter

UNDERSTANDING THE ROLE OF VBA IN ACCESS

Historically, productivity applications—such as the members of Microsoft Office—have used macros (short for macroinstructions) to automate repetitive operations. Microsoft Word and Excel, for instance, let you capture a sequence of menu choices, mouse clicks, and keyboard operations. You save the captured sequence as a macro that you subsequently execute from a menu choice or a shortcut-key combination. The macros in recent versions of Word and Excel consist of Visual Basic for Applications (VBA) code, but you don't need to understand VBA programming to create and execute Word and Excel macros. Unfortunately, the keyboard and mouse actions you use with Access applications don't translate to a usable macro. For better or worse, automation of Access applications requires programming.

Simple Access applications require you to write little or no VBA code. Most users of early versions of Access wrote Access macros, rather than various flavors of Access Basic to automate their applications. Access macros define actions, such as opening a form, that you assign to events, such as clicking a command button. Starting with Access 95, Microsoft recommended that you use VBA code instead of macros, with the clear implication that macros might not be supported in future versions of Access. (Access 2003 does support macro operations, but the Microsoft documentation states that it does so primarily for backward compatibility.)

This chapter describes VBA, introduces you to VBA modules and procedures that replace Access macros, shows you how to use the VBA editor to write and test VBA code, and helps you start writing user-defined functions. The chapter also includes examples of simple VBA programs.

There are no significant changes to VBA 6.0 in the upgrade from Access 2000 or 2002 to Access 2003. If you're migrating from Access 97 to 2003, following are the most important new VBA-related features added by Access 2000+ and the transition from VBA 5.0 to 6.0:

27

- *VBA editor*, which replaces the dedicated Access code editor of Access 97 and earlier, now is a common component that serves all Office 2000+ members.
- **`Decimal`** data type improves the accuracy of operations on numbers with decimal fractions.
- *Array functions*—**`Filter`**, **`Split`**, and **`Join`**—provide array search, string-to-array, and array-to-string capabilities, respectively.
- *String functions*—**`Replace`**, **`StrReverse`**, and **`InstrRev`**—enhance VBA's character manipulation features.
- **`Round`** rounds numbers with decimal fractions to a specified number of decimal places.
- **`MonthName`** and **`WeekDayName`** return the localized name of the month and day from a **`Date`** argument.
- **`FileSystemObject`** provides an object model for disk drives.
- **`Assert`**, when set to **`False`**, causes execution of code to halt and enter break mode.
- **`Event`** and **`RaiseEvent`** let you declare and fire events in class modules.

- **`Friend`** members of class modules have **`Public`** scope within an Access project (application), but aren't accessible from other projects.
- **`Implements`** lets class modules share property and method declarations.
- **`AddressOf`** supports callbacks in Windows API functions by providing the address of the calling VBA function or subprocedure.
- **`Enum`** lets you define custom enumerations for, as an example, sets of named constants that supply property values.

The items in the preceding list aren't of great significance to beginning VBA programmers. Advanced VBA coders, however, appreciate the incremental improvements to the language that occur with every upgrade.

NOTE

> Version 6.0 is Microsoft's *last* upgrade to VBA. Visual Basic .NET isn't an upgrade—it's a complete makeover of the venerable Visual Basic language that's required for compatibility with the .NET Framework's Common Language Runtime (CLR) environment.

➔ For more commentary on the VBA versus Visual Basic .NET issue as it relates to Access, **see** "In the Real World—Macro Schizophrenia," **p. 1188**.

GETTING ACQUAINTED WITH VBA 6.0

VBA is a real programming language, not a macro language. You create the preferred equivalent of macros with VBA functions and subprocedures. Although you can execute VBA subprocedures directly from an open code module, you more typically execute VBA subprocedures from user-initiated events, such as clicking a command button or changing the current record of a bound form. (Chapter 28, "Handling Events with VBA 6.0," explains how to use VBA subprocedures as event-handlers.) You execute VBA functions by calling them from calculated controls in forms and reports, from the Validation Rule property value of a field or table, or from within a VBA subprocedure.

WHERE YOU USE VBA CODE

Short VBA procedures using the `DoCmd` object usually are sufficient to provide the methods needed by simple applications to run queries, display forms, and print reports. The Access-specific `DoCmd` object lets you run any macro action from VBA as a method of the `DoCmd` object. For example, executing `DoCmd.OpenForm("`*`FormName`*`")` opens the *`FormName`* form.

The built-in functions of Access allow you to perform complex calculations in Jet queries, but not in Transact-SQL (T-SQL) queries. You might want or need to use VBA code for any of the following reasons:

- To create user-defined functions (UDFs) that substitute for complex expressions you use repeatedly to validate input data, compute values for text boxes, and perform other duties. Creating a UDF that you refer to by a short name minimizes potential typing errors and lets you document the way your expressions work.
- To write query expressions that include more complex decision structures than allowed by Jet's inline `IIf` function (in an **`If...Then...Else...End If`** structure, for example), or to write expressions that need loops for repetitive operations.

> **NOTE**
>
> You can't incorporate VBA in T-SQL queries, so queries that include VBA user-defined functions won't upsize to SQL Server 2000 databases.

- To write and execute `SELECT` queries with `WHERE` clauses or other SQL elements whose values come from controls on forms, such as list or combo boxes.
- To execute transaction processing SQL statements with `BEGIN TRANSACTION`, `COMMIT TRANSACTION`, and `ROLLBACK TRANSACTION` key words against Jet or SQL Server databases.
- To manipulate ActiveX controls and other applications' objects with Automation code.
- To open more than one database in a Jet application where attaching a table or using the Jet SQL `IN` statement isn't sufficient for your application.
- To provide hard-copy documentation for your application. If you execute actions from VBA code, you can print the code to improve the documentation for your application.
- To provide graceful error handling if something goes wrong in your application. With VBA code, you can closely control how your application responds to errors such as missing data, incorrect values entered by a user, and other problems. One of the shortcomings of Access macros is their inability to respond appropriately to execution errors.

27

Typographic and Naming Conventions Used for VBA

This book uses a special set of typographic conventions for references to VBA keywords and object variable names in VBA examples:

- `Monospace` type is used for all VBA code in the examples, as in `lngItemCounter`.
- **`Bold monospace`** type is used for all VBA reserved words and type-declaration symbols, as in **`Dim`** and `%`. (Type-declaration symbols aren't used in this book; instead, your VBA code defines the data type of each variable prior to use.) Standard function names in VBA, such as those as described in Chapter 10, "Understanding Jet Operators and Expressions," also are set in bold type so that reserved words, standard function names, and reserved symbols stand out from variable names, function names, and values you assign to variables. Keywords incorporated by reference in Access, such as `DoCmd` (an Access-specific object) or `Recordset` (a data-specific object), are not set in bold type.

→ To review some of the VBA functions and their descriptions, **see** "Functions for Date and Time," **p. 370** and "Text-Manipulation Functions," **p. 373**.

- *`Italic monospace`* type indicates a replaceable item, also called a placeholder, as in **`Dim`** *`DataItem`* **`As String`**. *`DataItem`* is replaced by a name that you supply.
- ***`Bold-italic monospace`*** type indicates a replaceable reserved word, such as a data type, as in **`Dim`** *`DataItem`* **`As`** ***`DataType`***; ***`DataType`*** is replaced by a VBA reserved word corresponding to the desired VBA data type, such as **`String`** or **`Object`**.
- Names of variables that refer to Jet and Access objects, such as queries, forms or reports, use a three-letter prefix derived from the object name, as in `qry`*`FormName`*, `frm`*`FormName`* and `rpt`*`ReportName`*. SQL Server objects use two-letter prefixes for views, functions, and stored procedures—`vw`*`ViewName`*, `fn`*`FunctionName`*, `sp`*`ProcedureName`*. With a few exceptions, this book doesn't use prefixes for table or field names.

TIP

> Most of the three-letter prefixes used in this book correspond to those recommended by Microsoft or the "Leszynski Naming Conventions for Access," a white paper published by Stan Leszynski of Kwery Corporation. You can order copies of the standards in the form of help files or white papers at `http://www.kwery.com/`.

- Names of all other variables are preceded by a three-letter data type identifier, such as `var`*`VariantVariable`* (**`Variant`**) and `int`*`IntegerVariable`* (**`Integer`**). Variables representing instances of objects use an arbitrary three-letter prefix, such as `cht`*`Object`* for a PivotChart.
- Optional elements appear in the text within square brackets, as in `[`*`OptionItem`*`]`. If you add the optional element, you don't type the brackets. Square brackets also enclose object names that contain spaces or special punctuation symbols for compatibility with Jet SQL and T-SQL. In this case, your code must contain the square brackets.
- Elements requiring you to choose from a set of alternatives are enclosed with French braces and separated by pipe symbols, as in **`Do {While|Until}`** *`Expression`*`...`**`Loop`**.
- An ellipsis (...) substitutes for code that isn't shown in syntax and code examples, as in **`If...Then...Else...End If`**.

27

Modules, Functions, and Subprocedures

A *module* is a container for VBA code, just as a form is a container for control objects. Access 2003 provides the following four types of modules:

- **Access modules**—You create an Access module to contain your VBA code the same way that you create any other new database object: Click the Module button in the Database window and then click the New button. Alternatively, you can click the New Object button on the toolbar and choose Module from the drop-down menu. Figure 27.1 shows the `IsLoaded()` function of the Utility Functions module of Northwind.mdb. Access modules are also called *standard modules*.

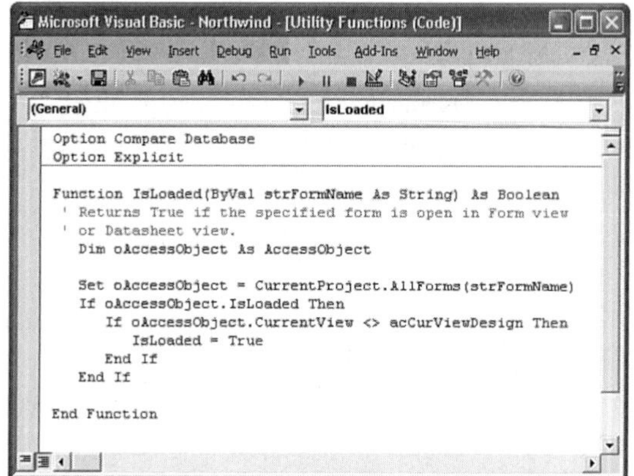

Figure 27.1
The VBA editor displays the `IsLoaded()` function of the Utility Functions module.

- **Form modules**—Form modules contain code to respond to events triggered by forms or controls on forms. Essentially, when you add VBA code to a form object, you create a new class of object in the database. The event-handling procedures you create for the form are its new class's methods, hence the term class module for the code module associated with a particular form. You open a form module by clicking the Code button of the toolbar in Form Design view. Alternatively, choose View, Code. Either of these methods opens a module that Access automatically names `Form_`*`FormName`*, where *`FormName`* is the name of the selected form. Forms in Access 2002 have a `HasModule` property. If this read-only property is set to Yes, then the form has a class module; otherwise, it doesn't.

TIP

Another method of opening a form module is to click the Builder button for one of the event properties for a form or a control object on a form. Selecting Code Builder from the Choose Builder dialog displays the `Form_`*`FormName`* module with a procedure stub, **`Private Sub`** *`ObjectName_EventName`*`()...`**`End Sub`**, written for you. Access 2003 adds the VBA **`Private`** prefix by default. Figure 27.2 shows the VBA code for the `CustomerID_AfterUpdate` and part of the `CustomerID_BeforeUpdate` event-handling subprocedures of Northwind.mdb's Orders form.

- **Report modules**—Report modules contain code for responding to events triggered by reports, sections of reports, or group headers and footers. (Control objects on reports don't trigger events.) You open a report's class module the same way you open a form's class module. Report class modules are named `Report_`*`ReportName`* automatically. Like forms, if an Access 2003 report has a class module, the Has Module property value is set to Yes (`HasModule =` **`True`**).

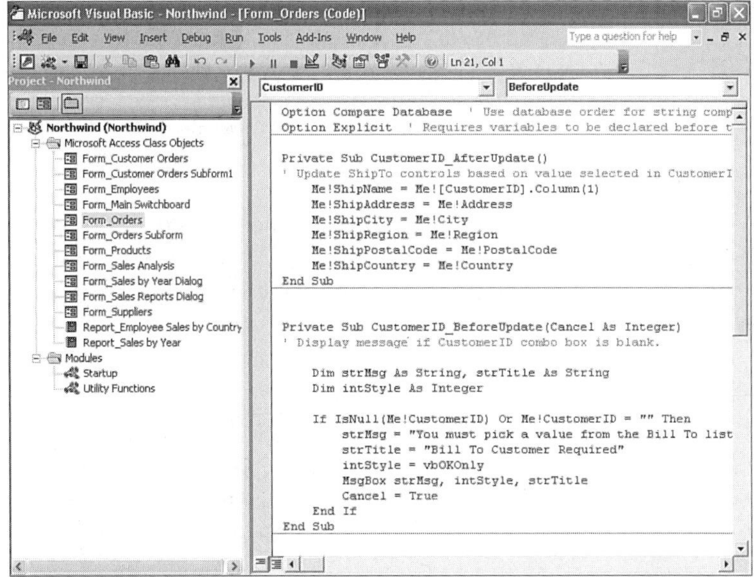

Figure 27.2 The `CustomerID_AfterUpdate` subprocedure is a typical event-handler for a combo list. The code executes when you select a CustomerID value in the Order form's Bill To combo box.

- **Class modules**—A class module not associated with a form or report lets you define your own custom objects, together with their properties and methods. Writing unassociated class modules is beyond the scope of this book.

ELEMENTS OF MODULES

A module consists of a Declarations section and usually one or more procedures (interchangeably called subprocedures) or functions. As the name suggests, the Declarations section of a module is used to declare items (usually variables and constants, the subjects of following sections) used by the procedures and functions contained in the module. You can use a module without functions or procedures to declare **`Public`** variables and constants that can be used by any function or procedure in any module of the database or project.

27

PROCEDURES

Procedures are typically defined as subprograms referred to by name in another program. Referring to a procedure by name calls or invokes the procedure; the code in the procedure executes, and then the sequence of execution returns to the program that called the procedure. Another name for a procedure is subroutine. Procedures are defined by beginning (**`Sub`**) and end (**`End Sub`**) reserved words with an optional **`Public`**, **`Private`**, or **`Static`** prefix, as in the following example:

```
Private Sub ProcName
    [Start of procedure code]
    ...
    [End of procedure code]
End Sub
```

TIP

> You can refer to the procedure name to invoke the procedure, but VBA provides a keyword, `Call`, that explicitly invokes a procedure. Prefixing the procedure name with `Call` is good programming practice because this keyword identifies the name that follows as the name of a procedure rather than a variable.

VBA introduces another class of procedure called property procedures that use the **`{Property Let¦Property Get¦Property Set}...End Property`** structure to create custom properties for Access objects, such as forms or controls. A discussion of property procedures is beyond the scope of this book.

PROCEDURES

Functions are a class of procedures that return values to their names, as explained in Chapter 10. C programmers would argue that procedures are a class of functions, called *void functions*, which don't return values. Regardless of how you view the difference between functions and subprocedures, keep the following points in mind:

- Access macros require that you write VBA functions (not subprocedures) to act in place of macro actions when using the RunCode macro action. Macros ignore the value returned by the function, if a return value is specified.
- Form and report class modules use subprocedures (not functions) to respond to events. Using form-level and report-level subprocedures for Access event-handling code mimics Visual Basic's approach for events triggered by forms, controls on forms, and other objects.
- A *custom subprocedure* is a subprocedure that isn't assigned to an event. The only way you can call a custom subprocedure in a VBA module is from a VBA function or another subprocedure. You can't directly execute a subprocedure in an Access module from any Access database object.
- Function names in Access modules are global in scope with respect to Access modules unless they are declared **`Private`**. Thus, you cannot have duplicate **`Public`** function names in any Access module in your application. However, form and report class modules can have a function with the same name as a **`Public`** function in a standard module because form and report function and procedure names have form-level or report-level scope. A function in a form module with the same name as a function in an Access module takes priority over the Access module version. Therefore, if you include the `IsLoaded()` function in a form module and call the `IsLoaded()` function from a procedure in the form module, the `IsLoaded()` function in the form module executes.

Functions are created within a structure similar to procedures, as in the following example:

```
Private Function FunctionName([Argument As DataType]) _
    As ReturnType
    [Start of function code]
    ...
```

```
    [End of function code]
    FunctionName = 123
End Function
```

In the preceding example, the *FunctionName* = 123 statement returns the value 123 to intReturnValue. In this case, the ***ReturnType*** data type must be a numeric data type, such as **Integer**. Most functions return **True** or **False** (**Boolean**), a numeric value (**Integer**, **Long**, **Single**, **Double**, or **Decimal**), or a set of characters (**String**).

To execute a VBA function in VBA code, you ordinarily use the function in an expression, such as

```
intReturnValue = FunctionName([Argument])
```

when the function returns a value. You can ignore the return value by calling the function with subprocedure syntax.

References to VBA and Access Modules

Access 2003 uses *references* to make Component Object Model (COM) objects available for programming by module code. A reference points to a COM dynamic link library (.dll), object library (.olb), or type library (.tlb) file installed on your computer with an entry in the Registry. To view the default references, open a new module in a new database, and then choose Tools, References to open the References dialog (see Figure 27.3). Current references are indicated by a mark in the adjacent check box. You add references by scrolling the list, and marking the check box of the new reference. When you click OK to close the References dialog and then reopen it, the new reference appears below the last of the original references.

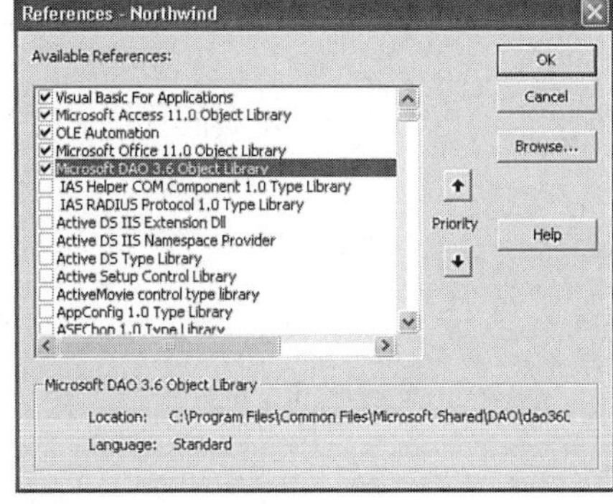

Figure 27.3 A new database created in Access 2000 format has the four standard references shown here. The Microsoft Access 11.0 Object Library enables programming of Access-specific objects, such as DoCmd.

27

TIP

You can't add a reference to more than one version of the same COM object. Attempting to do this results in a "Name conflicts with existing module, project, or object library" message. For example, if the Microsoft ActiveX Data Objects 2.1 Library is selected, you must clear its check box before adding a reference to the Microsoft ActiveX Data Objects 2.7 Library.

Microsoft Data Access Components (MDAC 2.7), which includes the ActiveX Data Objects 2.7 Library (ADO 2.7) is the current version installed by Office 2003. Running MSDE setup from the Office 2003 distribution CD-ROM installs MDAC 2.7 with ADO 2.7, which includes components specifically designed to support SQL Server 2000. The default reference for new Jet databases or Access data projects that you create in Access 2000 format, however, is ADO 2.1—the same version used by Access 2000. Creating a new Access database or data access project in Access 2002 format adds a reference to ADO 2.5. Converting a project from Access 2000 to 2002 format doesn't update the ADO reference from version 2.1 to 2.5. ADO 2.x is the subject of Chapter 30, "Understanding Universal Data Access, OLE DB, and ADO." If you open a database created with Access 2000 or earlier, the Microsoft DAO 3.6 Library (DAO 3.6) is the default data object reference.

TIP

> Always use the latest version of ADO for applications that don't require full backward compatibility with earlier versions of Access. If you intend to distribute runtime applications, the Windows Installer package includes the version of the MDAC type library–which includes ADO–that you specify as a reference to update users' computers. Be sure to specify ADO 2.7 as a reference if you're distributing Access Data Projects (ADP). All versions of ADO are backward compatible. (DAO 3.6 is backward compatible with DAO 3.5 and 3.0, but not DAO 2.5 and earlier.)

THE OBJECT BROWSER

Referenced objects appear in the Project/Library drop-down list of the Object Browser. To view the Object Browser, open a module and press F2, click the Object Browser button on the toolbar, or choose View, Object Browser. <All Libraries> is the default selection in the Project/Library list. Figure 27.4 shows a few of the references to Form, Report, and Module objects of Northwind.mdb in the Classes list. Only objects that can act as VBA containers appear in the Classes list; tables, queries, and macros don't qualify.

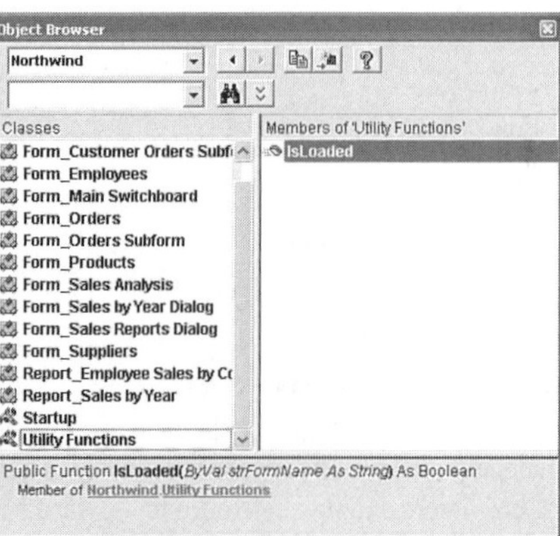

Figure 27.4
The Object Browser window displays classes of the object you choose in the top list (the Northwind database) in the Classes list and members of the class in the Members list. The bottom pane shows the calling syntax for the function.

When you select a function or subprocedure name in a module, the function or subprocedure name and arguments, if any, appear in the window at the bottom of the Object Browser dialog. You can get help on Access, VBA, and other objects by clicking the help (?) button, which ignores user-defined functions and the event-handling subprocedures you write. The next chapter describes object classes and the use of the Object Browser in detail.

DATA TYPES AND DATABASE OBJECTS IN VBA

When you create Jet tables, all data types that you use to assign field data types and sizes (except for OLE Object and Memo field data types) have data type counterparts in VBA. With the exception of the `Variant` and `Currency` data types, VBA data types are represented in most other dialects of BASIC, such as Microsoft's early QuickBASIC and the QBasic interpreter supplied with MS-DOS 5 and later.

Traditional BASIC dialects use a punctuation symbol called the type-declaration character, such as **$** for the String data type, to designate the data type. The VBA data types, the type-declaration characters, the corresponding field data types, and the ranges of values are shown in the VBA Type, Symbol, Field Type, Minimum Value, and Maximum Value columns, respectively, of Table 27.1. The Field Types `Byte`, `Integer`, `Long Integer`, `Single`, and `Double` correspond to the Field Size property of the Number data type in tables, queries, forms, and reports. VBA adds the `Byte` and `Boolean` data types to support the 8-bit Byte and 1-bit Yes/No field data types.

TABLE 27.1 VBA AND CORRESPONDING FIELD DATA TYPES

VBA	Symbol	Field Type	Minimum Value	Maximum Value
`Byte`	None	Byte	0	255
`Integer`	%	Integer	–32,768	32,767
`Boolean`	None	Yes/No	`True`	`False`
`Long`	&	Long Integer, AutoNumber	–2,147,483,648	2,147,483,647
`Single`	!	Single	–3.402823E38 1.401298E–45	–1.401298E–45 3.402823E38
`Double`	#	Double	–1.7200069313486232E308 4.94065645841247E–324	4.94065645841247E–324 1.7200069313486232E308
`Currency`	@	Currency	–922,337,203,685, 477.5808	922,337,203,685, 477.5807
`String`	$	Text or Memo	0 characters	Approximately 2 billion characters
`Date`	None	Date/Time	January 1, 100	December 31, 9999
`Variant`	None	All	Any of the preceding	Any of the preceding

27

TIP

> All data returned from fields of tables or queries is of the **Variant** data type by default. Variables of the **Variant** data type can hold any type of data listed in Table 27.1. If you assign the field value to a conventional data type, such as **Integer**, the data type is said to be *coerced*.

You can dispense with the type-declaration character if you explicitly declare your variables with the {**Dim**|**Private**|**Public**} typ*VarName* **As *DataType*** statement, discussed later in this section. If you don't explicitly declare the variables' data type or use a symbol to define an implicit data type, VBA variables default to the **Variant** data type.

TIP

> Using the **Variant** data type causes VBA code to execute more slowly than when you assign variables an explicit data type with the {**Dim**|**Private**|**Public**} typ*VarName* **As *DataType*** statement.

The # sign is also used to enclose values specified as dates, as in `varNewYear = #1/1/2001#`. In this case, bold type isn't used for the enclosing # signs because these symbols aren't intended for the purpose of the **#** reserved symbol that indicates the **Double** data type.

Jet database objects—such as databases, tables, and queries—and application objects (forms and reports), all of which you used in prior chapters, also have corresponding object data types in VBA. These object data types are defined by the object (also called type or class) library references. The most commonly used object data types and the object library that includes the objects are listed in Table 27.2. The `Database`, `QueryDef`, and `TableDef` object types are specific to Jet and DAO, and aren't available in ADP.

TABLE 27.2 THE MOST COMMON JET DATABASE OBJECT DATA TYPES SUPPORTED BY VBA

Object Data Type	Library	Corresponding Database Object Type
`Database`	DAO 3.6	Databases opened by the Jet database engine when using DAO
`Connection`	ADO 2.x	ADO replacement for DAO.Database object
`Form`	Access 11.0	Forms, including subforms
`Report`	Access 11.0	Reports, including subreports
`DataAccessPage`	Access 11.0	Definition of a link to a Data Access Page
`Control`	Access 11.0	Controls on forms, subforms, reports, and subreports
`QueryDef`	DAO 3.6	Jet query definitions (SQL statement equivalents) when using DAO
`Command`	ADO 2.x	ADO replacement for `DAO.QueryDef` object

Object Data Type	Library	Corresponding Database Object Type
`TableDef`	DAO 3.6	Jet table definitions (structure, indexes, and other table properties)
`DAO.Recordset`	DAO 3.6	A virtual representation of a Jet table or the result set of a Jet query created by DAO
`ADODB.Recordset`	ADO 2.x	ADO replacement for the `DAO.Recordset` object

NOTE

> OLE DB is Microsoft's current COM-based database connectivity architecture. OLE DB is the foundation of Microsoft's Universal Data Access initiative, which is described in Chapter 30. ADO is an "Automation wrapper" over OLE DB, which makes OLE DB objects accessible to Access and all other applications that support Automation through VBA. `Recordset` is an object that's common to both DAO and ADO, so it's good programming practice to prefix `Recordset` with its source class identifier, as in `DAO.Recordset` or `ADODB.Recordset`. You must specify the prefix if you include references to DAO 3.6 and ADO 2.x in your application. You can use ADO with both Jet and SQL Server databases; DAO is restricted to Jet databases only.
>
> The .NET framework's ADO.NET substitutes for OLE DB and ADO and currently offers an ADO.NET managed data provider for SQL Server databases. .NET adds a COM interop(erability) wrapper to ADO and OLE DB for handling connections to Jet and other databases that don't have managed data providers. COM interop ensures that your Jet databases won't become obsolete when Visual Studio .NET becomes the primary Windows programming environment.

VARIABLES AND NAMING CONVENTIONS

Variables are named placeholders for values of a specified data type that change when your VBA code is executed. You give variables names as you name fields, but the names of variables cannot include spaces or any other punctuation except the underscore character (_). The other restriction is that a variable cannot use a VBA keyword by itself as a name; keywords are called reserved words for this reason. The same rules apply to giving names to functions and procedures. Variable names in VBA typically use a combination of uppercase and lowercase letters to make them more readable.

27

IMPLICIT VARIABLES

You can create variables by assigning a value to a variable name, as in the following example:

```
NewVar = 1234
```

A statement of this type declares a variable, which means to create a new variable with a name you choose. The statement in the example creates a new implicit variable, `NewVar`, of the **`Variant`** data type with a value of `1234`. (`NewVar` would be more appropriately named `varNewVar`.) When you don't specify a data type for an implicit variable by appending one of the type-declaration characters to the variable name, the **Variant** data type is assigned by default. The following statement uses the % type identifier to create a variable of the **Integer** data type:

```
NewVar% = 1234
```

Explicit Variables

It's a better programming practice to declare your variables and assign those variables a data type before you give variables a value. The most common method of declaring variables is by using the **Dim** typ*VarName* **As** ***Datatype*** structure, in which **As** specifies the data type. This method declares explicit variables. An example follows:

```
Dim intNewVar As Integer
```

If you don't add the **As Integer** keywords, intNewVar is assigned the **Variant** data type by default.

You can require that all variables be explicitly declared before their use by adding the statement **Option** Explicit in the Declarations section of a module. The advantage of using **Option** Explicit is that the VBA compiler detects misspelled variable names and displays an error message when misspellings are encountered. If you don't use **Option** Explicit and you misspell a variable name, the VBA interpreter creates a new implicit variable with the misspelled name. The resulting errors in your code's execution can be difficult to diagnose. The VBA editor automatically adds an **Option** Explicit statement to the Declarations section of each module if you select the Require Variable Declaration option in the VBA editor's Options dialog, which you open by choosing Tools, Options (see Figure 27.5).

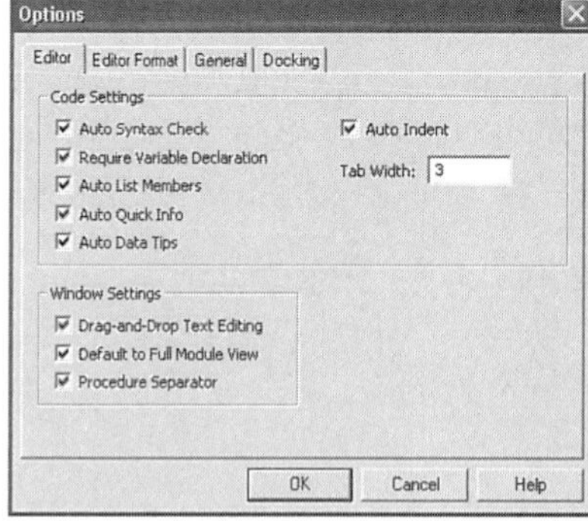

Figure 27.5 Mark the Require Variable Declaration check box on the Editor page of the VBA editor's Options dialog. Despite many requests from Access developers, this feature isn't enabled by default.

27

Scope and Duration of Variables

Variables have a characteristic called *scope*, which determines when the variables appear and disappear in your VBA code. Variables appear the first time you declare them and then disappear and reappear on the basis of the scope you assign to them. When a variable appears, it is said to be visible—meaning that you can assign the variable a value, change its value, and use it in expressions. Otherwise, the variable is invisible. If you use a variable's name while it's invisible, you instead create a new variable with the same name, if you haven't specified the Required Variable Declaration feature.

The following lists the four scope levels in VBA:

- **Local (procedure-level) scope**—The variable is visible only during the time when the procedure in which the variable is declared is running. Variables that you declare, with or without using **`Dim`** *`typVarName`* **`As`** ***`DataType`*** in a procedure or function, are local in scope.
- **Form-level and report-level scope**—The variable is visible only when the form or report in which it's declared is open. You declare form-level and report-level variables in the Declarations section of form and report modules with **`Private`** *`typVarName`* **`As`** ***`DataType`***. (**`Dim`** *`typVarName`* **`As`** ***`DataType`*** also works, but **`Private`** is the preferred scope identifier.)
- **Module-level scope**—The variable is visible to all procedures and functions contained in the module in which the variable was declared. (Modules open when you open the database.) You declare variables with module scope in the Declarations section of the module with the same syntax as form-level and report-level variables.
- **Global or public scope**—The variable is visible to all procedures and functions within all modules. You declare variables with global scope in the Declarations section of a module using **`Public`** *`typVarName`* `As` ***`DataType`***. The Public scope identifier is available only in Access modules.

The scope and visibility of variables declared in two different Access modules of the same database, both with two procedures, are illustrated by the diagram in Figure 27.6. In each procedure, variables declared with different scopes are used to assign values to variables declared within the procedure. Invalid assignment statements are shown crossed out in the figure. These assignment statements are invalid because the variable used to assign the value to the variable declared in the procedure isn't visible in the procedure.

Variables also have an attribute called duration, or lifetime. The duration of a variable is your code's execution time between the first appearance of the variable (its declaration) and its disappearance. Each time a procedure or function is called, local variables declared with the **`Dim`** *`typVarName`* **`As`** ***`DataType`*** statement are set to default values—`0` for numeric data types and the empty string (`""`) for string variables. The duration of these local variables is usually equal to the lifetime of the function or procedure—from the time the function or procedure is called until the **`End Function`** or **`End Sub`** statement is encountered.

27

To preserve the values of local variables between occurrences (called instances) of a procedure or function, you substitute the reserved word **`Static`** for **`Dim`**. **`Static`** variables have a duration of your Access application, but their scope is determined by where you declare them. **`Static`** variables are useful when you want to count the number of occurrences of an event. You can make all variables in a function or procedure static variables by preceding **`Function`** or **`Sub`** with the **`Static`** keyword.

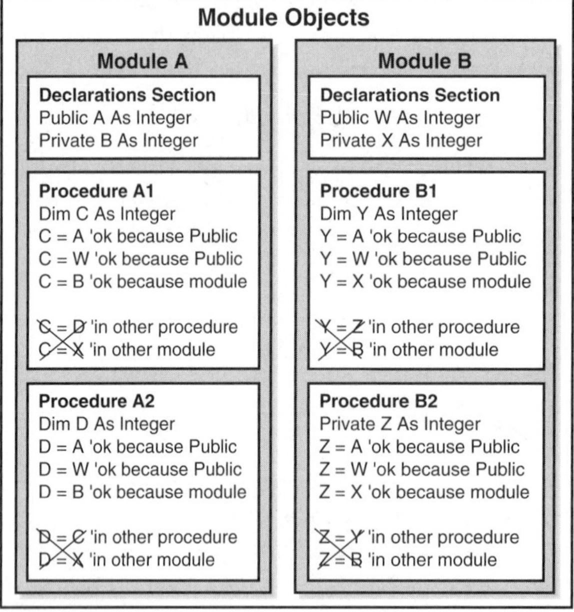

Figure 27.6
This diagram illustrates valid and invalid assignment for variables of different scopes.

TIP

Minimize the number of local variables that you declare **`Static`**. Local variables don't consume memory when they aren't visible. This characteristic of local variables is especially important in the case of arrays, discussed in the "VBA Arrays" section that follows shortly, because arrays are often very large.

User-Defined Data Types

You can create your own data type that consists of one or more Access data types. User-defined data types are discussed in this section pertaining to variables because you need to know what a variable is before you can declare a user-defined data type. You declare a user-defined data type between the **`Type...End Type`** keywords, as in the following example:

```
Type tagDupRec
    lngField1 As Long
    strField2 As String * 20
    sngField3 As Single
    dblField4 As Double
End Type
```

User-defined data types are particularly useful when you create a variable to hold the values of one or more records of a table that uses fields of different data types. The **`String * 20`** statement defines `lngField2` of the user-defined data type as a fixed-length string of 20 characters, usually corresponding to the Size property of the Text field data type. String variables in user-defined data types traditionally have a fixed length, but VBA 6.0 lets you use variable-length strings. You must declare your user-defined data type (called a record or structure in other programming languages) in the Declarations section of a module.

You must explicitly declare variables to be of the user-defined type with the **`Dim`**, **`Private`**, **`Public`**, or **`Static`** keywords because no reserved symbol exists to declare a user-defined data type, as in `Dim usrCurrentRec As tagDupRec`. To assign a value to a field of a variable with a user-defined data type, you specify the name of the variable and the field name, separating the names with a period, as in `usrCurrentRec.lngField1 = 2048`.

VBA ARRAYS

Arrays are variables that consist of a collection of values, called elements of the array, of a single data type in a regularly ordered structure. Implicitly declared arrays aren't allowed in VBA. You declare an array with the **`Dim`** statement, adding the number of elements in parentheses to the variable name for the array, as in the following example:

```
Dim astrNewArray(20) As String
```

This statement creates an array of 21 elements, each of which is a conventional, variable-length string variable. You create 21 elements because the first element of an array is the 0 (zero) element, unless you specify otherwise by adding the **`To`** modifier, as in the following example:

```
Dim astrNewArray(1 To 20) As String
```

The preceding statement creates an array with 20 elements.

You can create multidimensional arrays by adding more values separated by commas. The statement

```
Dim alngNewArray(9, 9, 9) As Long
```

creates a three-dimensional array of 10 elements per dimension. This array, when visible, occupies 4,000 bytes of memory (10×10×10×4 bytes/long integer).

You can create a dynamic array by declaring the array using **`Dim`** without specifying the number of elements and then using the **`ReDim`** reserved word to determine the number of elements the array contains. You can **`ReDim`** an array as many times as you want. Each time you do so, the values stored in the array are reinitialized to their default values, determined by the data type, unless you follow **`ReDim`** with the reserved word, **`Preserve`**. The following sample statements create a dynamic array:

27

```
Dim alngNewArray() As Long               'In Declarations sections
ReDim Preserve alngNewArray(9, 9, 9)     'In procedure, preserves prior values
ReDim alngNewArray(9, 9, 9)              'In procedure, reinitializes all
```

Dynamic arrays are useful when you don't know how many elements an array requires when you declare it. You can **`ReDim`** a dynamic array to zero elements when you no longer need the values it contains; this tactic lets you recover the memory that the array consumes while it's visible. Alternatively, you can use the **`Erase`** reserved word followed by a dynamic array's name to remove all the array's elements from memory. (**Erase** used on an array with fixed dimensions merely reinitializes the array to its condition before you assigned any values to it.) Arrays declared with **Dim** can have up to 60 dimensions. You can only use the **ReDim** statement to alter the size of the last dimension in a multidimensional array.

Scope, duration rules, and keywords apply to arrays in the same way in which they apply to conventional variables. You can declare dynamic arrays with global and module-level scope by adding the **Public** or **Private** statement to the Declarations section of a module and then using the **ReDim** statement by itself in a procedure. If you declare an array with **Static**, rather than **Dim**, the array retains its values between instances of a procedure.

TIP

> Don't use the **Option** Base keywords to change the default initial element of arrays from 0 to 1. **Option** Base is included in VBA for compatibility with earlier BASIC dialects. Many arrays you create from VBA objects must begin with element 0. If you're concerned about the memory occupied by an unused zero element of an array, use the **Dim** *ArrayName*(1 **To** *N*) **As** ***DataType*** declaration. In most cases, you can disregard the zero element.

NAMED DATABASE OBJECTS AS VARIABLES IN VBA CODE

Properties of database objects you create with Access can be treated as variables and assigned values within VBA code. For example, you can assign a new value to the text box that contains the address information for a customer by name with the following statement:

```
Forms!Customers!Address = "123 Elm St."
```

The collection name Forms defines the type of object. The exclamation point (called the bang symbol by programmers) separates the name of the form and the name of the control object. The ! symbol is analogous to the \ path separator that you use when you're dealing with folder and file names. If the name of the form or the control object contains a space or other punctuation, you must enclose the name within square brackets, as in the following statement:

```
Forms!Customers![Contact Name] = "Joe Hill"
```

27

Alternatively, you can use the **Set** keyword to create your own named variable for the control object. This procedure is convenient when you need to refer to the control object several times. It's more convenient to type txtContact rather than the full "path" to the control object—in this case, a text box.

```
Dim txtContact As Control
Set txtContact = Forms!Customers![Contact Name]
txtContact.Value = "Joe Hill"
```

TIP

> Specifying the Value property when assigning a value to a control isn't required because `Value` is the default property of controls and fields of `Recordset` objects. It's good programming practice, however, to do so. Adding the `Value` property when manipulating `ADODB.Recordset` objects with VBA results in improved performance. Specifying the Value property is important for code you might upgrade to Visual Basic .NET, because Visual Basic .NET doesn't support default properties of objects.

You can assign any database object to a variable name by declaring the variable as the object type and using the **`Set`** statement to assign the object to the variable. You don't create a copy of the object in memory when you assign it a variable name; the variable refers to the object in memory. Referring to an object in memory is often called *pointing* to an object; many languages have a pointer data type that holds the address of the location in memory where the variable is stored. VBA has no direct support for pointers . The next chapter deals with creating variables that point to the Access 2002 database objects supplied by ADO 2.x.

OBJECT PROPERTIES AND THE `With...End With` STRUCTURE

VBA provides the **`With...End With`** structure that offers a shorthand method of setting the values of object properties, such as the dimensions and other characteristics of a form. The **`With...End With`** structure also lets you set the values of fields of a user-defined data type without repeating the variable name in each instance. To use the **`With...End With`** structure to set object property values, you must first declare and set an object variable, as in the following example:

```
Dim frmFormName As Form
Set frmFormName = Forms!FormName
With frmFormName
    .Top = 1000
    .Left = 1000
    .Width = 5000
    .Height = 4000
End With
```

When using the **`With...End With`** structure with user-defined data types, you don't use the **`Set`** statement. Names of properties or fields within the structure are preceded by periods.

SYMBOLIC CONSTANTS

Symbolic constants are named placeholders for values of a specified data type that don't change when executing your VBA code. You precede the name of a symbolic constant with the keyword **`Const`**, as in **`Const`** `sngPI` **`As Single`** `= 3.1416`. You declare symbolic constants in the Declarations section of a module or within a function or procedure. Precede **Const** with the **Public** keyword if you want to create a global constant that's visible to all modules, as in **`Public Const`** `gsngPI = 3.1416`. The `g` prefix of the variable name is an abbreviation for **`Global`**, which most programmers prefer to `p` for **`Public`**. Public constants can be declared only in the Declarations section of a VBA module.

You don't need to specify a data type for constants explicitly because VBA chooses the data type that stores the data most efficiently. VBA can make this choice because it knows the value of the data when it "compiles" your code. It's a better programming practice, however, to specify the data type of constants.

NOTE

> Office 2003's VBA is an interpreted language, so the term compile in a VBA context is a misnomer. When you "compile" the VBA source code that you write in a code-editing window, the VBA editor creates a tokenized, binary version of the code (called *pseudo-code*, or *p-code*) stored in an.mdb or .adp file. Only Visual Basic 6.0 compiles VBA 6.0 code to create an executable (.exe) file. Visual Basic .NET is similar to Office 2003's VBA; programs written in Visual Basic .NET create p-code that the Common Language Runtime (CLR) executes.

ACCESS SYSTEM-DEFINED CONSTANTS

VBA includes seven system-defined constants—**`True`**, **`False`**, `Yes`, `No`, `On`, `Off`, and **`Null`**—that are created by the VBA and Access type libraries when launched. Of these seven, you can use **`True`**, **`False`**, and **`Null`**, which are declared by the VBA library, in VBA code. The remaining four are declared by the Access type library and are valid for use with all database objects except modules. When the system-defined constants **`True`**, **`False`**, and **`Null`** are used in VBA code examples in this book, they appear in bold monospace type. This book doesn't use the Access-defined `Yes`, `No`, `On`, and `Off` constants; don't use them in the code you write.

ACCESS INTRINSIC CONSTANTS

VBA provides a number of predeclared, intrinsic, symbolic constants that are primarily for use as arguments of Access `DoCmd.`*`ActionName`* statements. These statements let you execute standard database actions in VBA (such as opening forms, printing reports, applying sorts or filters, and so on). Access 2003 intrinsic constants carry the prefix `ac`, as in `acExportMerge`. You can display the list of Access intrinsic constants in the Object Browser by selecting Access in the Project/Library list and then selecting Globals in the Classes list.

27

When you select a constant in the Members Of list, its numeric value appears at the bottom of the Object Browser window (see Figure 27.7). A good programming practice is to use constant names rather than their numeric values when applicable to make your code more readable. You can't use any of these intrinsic constants' names as names for constants or variables that you define.

VBA INTRINSIC CONSTANTS

VBA has many of its own constants, in addition to the three mentioned in the earlier "Access System-Defined Constants" section. These constants carry a `vb` prefix. To see a list of the VBA constants, select VBA in Object Browsers top combo list, accept the default <globals> class, and scroll to the `vb...` entries. One of the most commonly used VBA intrinsic constants is `vbCrLf`, which inserts a (carriage) return and line feed into a string.

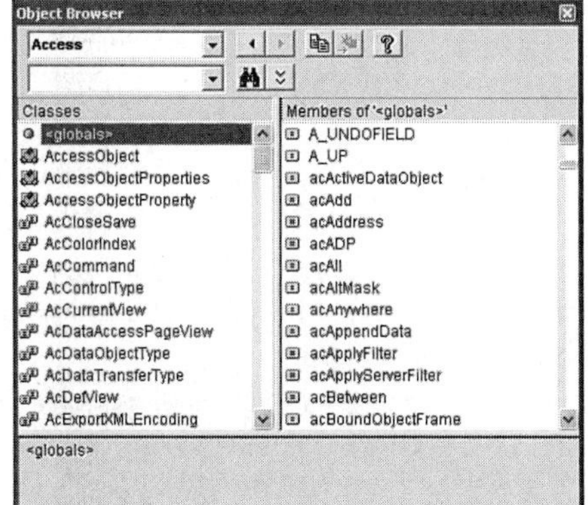

Figure 27.7 Access has hundreds of intrinsic constants defined by the Microsoft Access 11.0 Object Library. Constants with the prefix `A_` are included for backward compatibility with the Access Basic language used by Access 2.0 and earlier.

VBA Named and Optional Arguments

Procedures often have one or more arguments that pass values from the calling statement to the called procedure. Traditionally, you must pass all the values required by the procedure in your calling statement. As an example, if a procedure accepts four arguments, *Arg1...Arg4*, your calling statement must provide values for *Arg1...Arg4*, as in the following example:

```
Sub CallingProc()
    ...
    Call CalledProc(100000, 200000, 300000, 400000)
    ...
End Sub

Sub CalledProc(Arg1 As Long, Arg2 As Long, _
               Arg3 As Long, Arg4 As Long)
    [Subprocedure code]
End Sub
```

NOTE

> The space followed by an underscore following `Arg2 As Long` in the preceding subprocedure is called the *code-continuation character* (CCC or 3C). VBA interprets instructions on a line-by-line basis. The CCC lets you continue a statement on the next line. Using the CCC lets you format your code for easier readability.

VBA 6.0 lets you declare the arguments of the subprocedure to be **Optional**, eliminating the need to pass every parameter to the procedure. You use named arguments to pass values to specific arguments, as in the following example:

```
Sub CallingProc()
    ...
    Call CalledProc(Arg2:=200000, Arg3:=300000)
    ...
End Sub
```

```
Sub CalledProc(Optional Arg1 As Long, Optional Arg2 As Long,
               Optional Arg3 As Long, Optional Arg4 As Long)
    [Subprocedure code]
End Sub
```

The `:=` operator specifies that the preceding element is the name of an argument; named arguments need not be entered in the order that the arguments appear in the called procedure. However, if you want to omit an argument or arguments, the corresponding argument name(s) of the called procedure must be preceded by the keyword **Optional**. Missing arguments return **Null** values to subprocedure code, but you can supply a default argument value in the subprocedure. If you omit the **As *Datatype*** modifier of an argument in the called procedure, the argument assumes the default **Variant** data type.

CONTROLLING PROGRAM FLOW

Useful procedures must be able to make decisions based on the values of variables and then take specified actions based on those decisions. Blocks of code, for example, might need to be repeated until a specified condition occurs. Statements used to make decisions and repeat blocks of code are the fundamental elements that control program flow in VBA and all other programming languages.

All programming languages require methods of executing different algorithms based on the results of one or more comparison operations. You can control the flow of any program in any programming language with just three types of statements: conditional execution (**If...Then...End If**), repetition (**Do While...Loop** and related structures), and termination (**End...** and **Exit**). Additional flow control statements in VBA and other programming languages make writing code more straightforward.

BRANCHING AND LABELS

When BASIC was first developed, the only method of controlling program flow was through its GOTO *LineNumber* and GOSUB *LineNumber* statements. Every line in the program required a number that could be used as a substitute for a label. GOTO *LineNumber* caused the interpreter to skip to the designated line and continue executing the program from that point. GOSUB *LineNumber* caused the program to follow that same branch, but when the BASIC interpreter that executed the code encountered a RETURN statement, program execution jumped back to the line following the GOSUB statement and continued executing at that point.

27

VBA's **GoTo** *Label* statement causes your code to branch to the location named *Label*: and continue from that point. Note the colon following *Label*:, which identifies the single word you assigned as a label. However, the colon isn't required after the label name following the **GoTo**. In fact, if you add the colon, you get a "Label not found" error message.

A label name must begin in the leftmost column (1) of your code. This positioning often interferes with the orderly indenting of your code (explained in the next section), which is just one more reason, in addition to those following, for not using **GoTo**.

The **GoTo** statement is required for only one purpose in VBA: to handle errors with the **On Error GoTo** *Label* statement. Although VBA supports BASIC's ON...GOTO and ON...GOSUB statements, using those statements is not considered good programming practice. You can eliminate most GoTo statements in form and report modules by using Access's Error event and the DAO and ADO Errors collection. The Error event is described in the "Handling Runtime Errors" section later in this chapter, and the Errors collection is explained in the next chapter.

NOTE

> Visual Basic .NET finally dispenses with **On Error GoTo** *Label* statements by incorporating structured error handling similar to that provided by C/C++ and Java. Visual Basic .NET provides the **Try...Catch...Finally...End Try** structure to eliminate the need for **On Error GoTo** *Label* and the traditional *Label*: statement that identifies the beginning of error-handling code.

CONDITIONAL STATEMENTS

A conditional statement executes the statements between its occurrence and the terminating statement if the result of the relational operator is true. Statements that consist of or require more than one statement for completion are called structured statements, control structures, or just structures.

THE If...Then...End If STRUCTURE

The syntax of the primary conditional statement of VBA is as follows:

```
If blnCondition1 [= True] Then
    Statements to be executed if Condition1 is true
 [Else[If blnCondition2[ = True] Then]]
     Optional statements to be executed if blnCondition1
     is false [and blnCondition2 is true]
End If
```

The = **True** elements of the preceding conditional statement are optional and typically not included when you write actual code. **If** bln*Condition1* **Then** and **If** bln*Condition1* = **True Then** produce the same result when bln*Condition1* is **True**.

You can add a second condition with the **ElseIf** keyword. The **ElseIf** condition must be true to execute the statements that are executed if bln*Condition1* is not **True** (**False**). Note that no space is used between **Else** and **If**. An **If...End If** structure that incorporates an **ElseIf** statement is the simplified equivalent of the following:

```
If blnCondition1 Then
    Statements to be executed if Expression1 is true
Else
    If blnCondition2 Then
        Statements to be executed if Condition1% is
        false and blnCondition2 is true]
    End If
End If
```

A statement is executed based on the evaluation of the immediately preceding expression. Expressions that include **If...End If** or other flow-control structures within other **If...End If** structures are said to be nested, as in the preceding example. The number, or depth, of **If...End If** structures that can be nested within one another is unlimited.

Note that the code between the individual keywords that make up the flow-control structure is indented. Indentation makes code within structures easier to read. You usually use the Tab key to create indentation.

To evaluate whether a character is a letter and to determine its case, you can use the following code:

```
If Asc(strChar) > 63 And Asc(strChar) < 91 Then
   strCharType = "Uppercase Letter"
ElseIf Asc(strChar) > 96 And Asc(strChar) < 123 Then
   strCharType = "Lowercase Letter"
Else
   strCharType = "Not a Letter"
End If
```

You use the **If...End If** structure more often than any other flow control statement.

TIP

> For a list of the ASCII numeric codes for alphabetic, numeric, and special characters, type **ascii** in the Ask a Question text box of the VBA editor, and click the Character Set (0 - 127) item. Character Set (128 - 255) contains special characters.

THE Select Case...End Select CONSTRUCT

When you must choose among many alternatives, **If...End If** structures can become very complex and deeply nested. The **Select Case...End Select** construct was added to procedural BASIC to overcome this complexity. In addition to testing whether an expression evaluates to True or False, **Select Case** can evaluate variables to determine whether those variables fall within specified ranges. The generalized syntax is in the following example:

```
Select Case VarName
    Case Expression1[, Expressions, ...]
        (Statements executed if the value of VarName
         = Expression1 or Expressions)
   [Case Expression2 To Expression3
        (Statements executed if the value of VarName
         is in the range of Expression2 to Expression3)]
   [Case Is RelationalExpression
        (Statements executed if the value of
         VarName = RelationalExpression)]
   [Case Else
        (Statements executed if none of the
         above cases is met)]
End Select
```

27

Select Case evaluates *VarName*, which can be a string, a numeric variable, or an expression. It then tests each **Case** expression in sequence. **Case** expressions can take one of the following four forms:

- A single value or list of values to which to compare the value of *VarName*. Successive members of the list are separated from their predecessors by commas.
- A range of values separated by the keyword **To**. The value of the first member of the range limits must be less than the value of the second. Each string is compared by the ASCII value of its first character.
- The keyword **Is** followed by a relational operator, such as `<>`, `<`, `<=`, `=`, `>=`, or `>`, and a variable or literal value.
- The keyword **Else**. Expressions following **Case Else** are executed if no prior **Case** condition is satisfied.

The code associated with the first matching **Case** condition is executed. If no match is found and the **Case Else** statement is present, the code following the statement is executed. Program execution then continues at the line of code following the **End Select** terminating statement.

If *VarName* is a numeric type, all **Case** expressions that use *VarName* are forced to the same data type.

The following example is of **Select Case** using a numeric variable, `curSales`:

```
Select Case curSales
    Case 10000 To 49999.99
        intClass = 1
    Case 50000 To 100000
        intClass = 2
    Case Is < 10000
        intClass = 0
    Case Else
        intClass = 3
End Select
```

Note that because `curSales` is of the **Currency** type, all the comparison literals also are treated as **Currency** values for the purpose of comparison.

27

A more complex example that evaluates a single character follows:

```
Select Case strChar
    Case "A" To "Z"
        strCharType = "Upper Case"
    Case "a" To "z"
        strCharType = "Lower Case"
    Case "0" To "9"
        strCharType = "Number"
    Case "!", "?", ".", ",", ";"
        strCharType = "Punctuation"
    Case ""
        strCharType = "Empty String"
```

```
    Case < 32
        strCharType = "Special Character"
    Case Else
        strCharType = "Unknown Character"
End Select
```

This example demonstrates that **`Select Case`**, when used with strings, evaluates the ASCII value of the first character of the string—either as the variable being tested or the expressions following **`Case`** statements. Thus, **`Case`** `< 32` is a valid test, although `strChar` is a string variable.

REPETITIVE OPERATIONS: LOOPING

In many instances, you must repeat an operation until a given condition is satisfied, whereupon the repetitions terminate. You might want to examine each character in a word, sentence, or document, or you might want to assign values to an array with many elements. Loops are used for these and many other purposes.

USING THE `For...Next` STATEMENT

VBA's **`For...Next`** statement lets you repeat a block of code for a specified number of times, as shown in the following example:

```
For intCounter = intStartValue To intEndValue [Step intIncrement]
    Statements to be executed
    [Conditional statement
    Exit For
    End of conditional statement]
Next [intCounter]
```

The block of statements between the **`For`** and **`Next`** keywords is executed `(intEndValue - intStartValue + 1) / intIncrement)` times. As an example, if `intStartValue = 5`, `intEndValue = 10`, and `intIncrement = 1`, the execution of the statement block is repeated six times. You need not add the keyword **`Step`** in this case—the default increment is `1`. Although **`Integer`** data types are shown, you can use **`Long`** (integer) values. The use of real numbers (**`Single`** or **`Double`** data types) as values for counters and increments is possible but uncommon because decimal rounding errors can cause unexpected results.

The dividend of the previous expression must always be a positive number if the execution of the internal statement block is to occur. If `intEndValue` is less than `intStartValue`, `intIncrement` must be negative; otherwise, the **`For...Next`** statement is ignored by the VBA interpreter.

The optional **`Exit For`** statement is provided so that you can prematurely terminate the loop using a surrounding **`If...Then...End If`** conditional statement. Changing the value of the counter variable within the loop itself to terminate its operation is discouraged as a dangerous programming practice. You might make a change that would cause an infinite statement loop.

USING For...Next LOOPS TO ASSIGN VALUES TO ARRAY ELEMENTS

One of the most common applications of the **For...Next** loop is to assign successive values to the elements of an array. If you've declared a 26-element array named astrAlphabet, the following example assigns the capital letters A through Z to its elements:

```
For intLetter = 1 To 26
    strAlphabet(intLetter) = Chr$(intLetter + 64)
Next intLetter
```

The preceding example assigns 26 of the array's 27 elements if you used **Dim** strAlphabet(26) **As String** rather than **Dim** strAlphabet(1 **To** 26) **As String**. 64 is added to intLetter because the ASCII value of the letter A is 65, and the initial value of intLetter is 1. The VBA **Chr$**() function converts the ordinal position of intLetter in the ASCII character set to a **String** value. Using **Chr**() returns a **Variant** value that the interpreter must coerce to a **String** value.

> **TIP**
>
> VBA offers two versions of each function that returns a **String** value. Always use the version with the **$** data type identifier when returning values to a variable declared **As String**. Complex string expressions execute much faster if the compiler doesn't need to coerce **Variants** to **Strings**.

A special case of the **For...Next** loop, **For Each** *objName* **In** *colName*...**Next** *objName*, loop iterates each object (*objName*) in a collection (*colName*).

→ For statement an example of using a For Each...Next loop, **see** "Customizing Applications with CommandBar Objects," **p. 1213**.

UNDERSTANDING Do While...Loop AND Do Until...Loop

A more general form of the loop structure is **Do While...Loop**, which uses the following syntax:

```
Do While blnCondition [= True]
    Statements to be executed
    [Conditional statement
    Exit Do
    End of conditional statement]
Loop
```

This loop structure executes the intervening statements only if *blnCondition* equals **True** (**Not False**, a value other than 0) and continues to do so until *blnCondition* becomes **False** (0) or the optional **Exit Do** statement executes.

From the preceding syntax, you can duplicate the previous **For...Next** array assignment example with the following structure:

```
intLetter = 1
Do While intLetter <= 27
    astrAlphabet(intLetter) = Chr$(intLetter + 64)
    intLetter = intLetter + 1
Loop
```

Another example of a **Do** loop is the **Do Until...Loop** structure, which loops as long as the condition isn't satisfied, as in the following example:

```
Do Until {blnCondition <> True¦Not blnCondition}
    Statements to be executed
    [Conditional statement
    Exit Do
    End of conditional statement]
Loop
```

The **Not** blnCondition expression is more commonly used than blnCondition <> **True**, but either is acceptable.

VBA also supports the **While...Wend** loop, which is identical to the **Do While...Loop** structure, but you can't use the **Exit Do** statement within **While...Wend**. The **While...Wend** structure is provided for compatibility with earlier versions of BASIC and should be abandoned in favor of **Do {While¦Until}...Loop** in VBA.

Making Sure Statements in a Loop Occur at Least Once

You might have observed that the statements within a **Do While...Loop** structure are never executed if intCondition is false when the structure is encountered in your application. You can also use a structure in which the conditional statement that causes loop termination is associated with the **Loop** statement. The syntax of this format is in the following example:

```
Do
    Statements to be executed
    [Conditional statement then
    Exit Do
    End of conditional statement]
Loop While intCondition[ = True]
```

A similar structure is available for the **Do Until...** Loop:

```
Do
    Statements to be executed
    [Conditional statement
    Exit Do
    End of conditional statement]
Loop Until intCondition[ = False]
```

27

These structures ensure that the loop executes at least once before the condition is tested.

Handling Runtime Errors

No matter how thoroughly you test and debug your code, runtime errors appear eventually. Runtime errors are errors that occur when Access executes your VBA code. Use the **On Error GoTo** instruction to control what happens in your application when a runtime error occurs. **On Error** isn't a very sophisticated instruction, but it's your first choice for error processing in Access modules until Access supports Visual Basic .NET. You can branch to a label or ignore the error. The general syntax of **On Error...** follows:

```
On Error GoTo LabelName
On Error Resume Next
On Error GoTo 0
```

On Error GoTo *LabelName* branches to that part of your code that begins with the label *LabelName*:. *LabelName* must be a label; it can't be the name of a procedure. The code following *LabelName*, however, can (and often does) include a procedure call to an error-handling procedure, such as *ErrorProc*, as in the following:

```
On Error GoTo ErrHandler
...
[RepeatCode:
(Code using ErrProc to handle errors)]
...
GoTo SkipHandler
ErrHandler:
Call ErrorProc
[GoTo RepeatCode]
SkipHandler:
...
(Additional code)
```

In this example, the **On Error GoTo** instruction causes program flow to branch to the *ErrHandler* label that executes the error-handling procedure *ErrorProc*. Ordinarily, the error-handler code is located at the end of the procedure. If you have more than one error handler or if the error handler is in the middle of a group of instructions, you must bypass it if the preceding code is error-free. Use the **GoTo** *SkipHandler* statement that bypasses *ErrHandler*: instructions. To repeat the code that generated the error after *ErrorProc* has completed its job, add a label such as *RepeatCode*: at the beginning of the repeated code, and then branch to the code in the *ErrHandler*: code. Alternatively, you can add the keyword **Resume** at the end of your code to resume processing at the line that created the error.

On Error Resume Next disregards the error and continues processing the succeeding instructions.

After an **On Error GoTo** statement executes, it remains in effect for all succeeding errors until execution encounters another **On Error GoTo** instruction or you turn off error processing with the **On Error GoTo 0** form of the statement.

If you don't trap errors with an **On Error GoTo** statement or if you've turned error trapping off with **On Error GoTo 0**, a runtime error message appears when an error is encountered. Clicking Debug opens the VBA Editor at the offending line. If you correct the error at this point, press F5 to continue code execution. Otherwise, your only option is to click End to halt code execution.

TIP

Always include error-handling code in runtime applications. If you don't provide at least one error-handling routine in your VBA code for runtime Access applications you distribute with the MOD, your application quits abruptly when the error occurs.

DETECTING THE TYPE OF ERROR WITH THE Err OBJECT

The VBA **Err** object replaces the **Err** function of earlier versions of Access. The default property, **Err**.Number, returns an integer representing the code of the last error or returns 0 if no error occurs. This property ordinarily is used within a **Select Case** structure to determine the action to take in the error handler based on the type of error incurred. Use the **Err**.Description property, which replaces the **Error** function, to return the text name of the error number specified as its argument, as in the following example:

```
strErrorName = Err.Description
Select Case Err.Number
    Case 58 To 76
        Call FileError 'procedure for handling file errors
    Case 340 To 344
        Call ArrayError 'procedure for control array errors
    Case 281 To 22000
        Call DDEError 'procedure for handling DDE errors
End Select
Err.Clear
```

TIP

The preceding code example illustrate use of comments in VBA code. You create a comment be preceding text with an apostrophe ('). Adding explanatory comments to your code assists others in understanding the purpose of procedures and how the code within the procedures works–or is supposed to work.

You can substitute the actual error-processing code for the **Call** instructions shown in the preceding example, but using individual procedures for error handling is the recommended approach. **Err**.Number sets the error code to a specific integer. Use the **Err**.Clear method to reset the error code to 0 after your error handler has completed its operation, as shown in the preceding example.

The **Error** and **RaiseError** statements simulate an error so that you can test any error handlers you write. You can specify any of the valid integer error codes or create a user-defined error code by selecting an integer that's not included in the list. A user-defined error code returns "User-defined error" to **Error**.Description.

27

USING THE ERROR EVENT IN FORM AND REPORT MODULES

Access has an event, Error, that's triggered when an error occurs on a form or report. You can use an event-handling procedure in a form or report to process the error, or you can assign a generic error-handling function in an Access module to the Error event with an *=ErrorHandler()* entry to call the *ErrorHandler()* function.

When you invoke an error-handling function from the Error event, you must use the **Err** object to detect the error that occurred and take corrective action, as described in the preceding section.

Exploring the VBA Editor

You write VBA functions and procedures in the VBA editor. To open the VBA editor, click the Module shortcut of the Database window, and then double-click the name of the module you want to display. To open a new VBA module, click the New button; the VBA editor window appears with default Options set, as shown in Figure 27.8. The VBA editor window incorporates a text editor, similar to Windows Notepad, in which you type your VBA code. VBA color-codes keywords and comments. By default, the VBA editor opens with all of its windows docked.

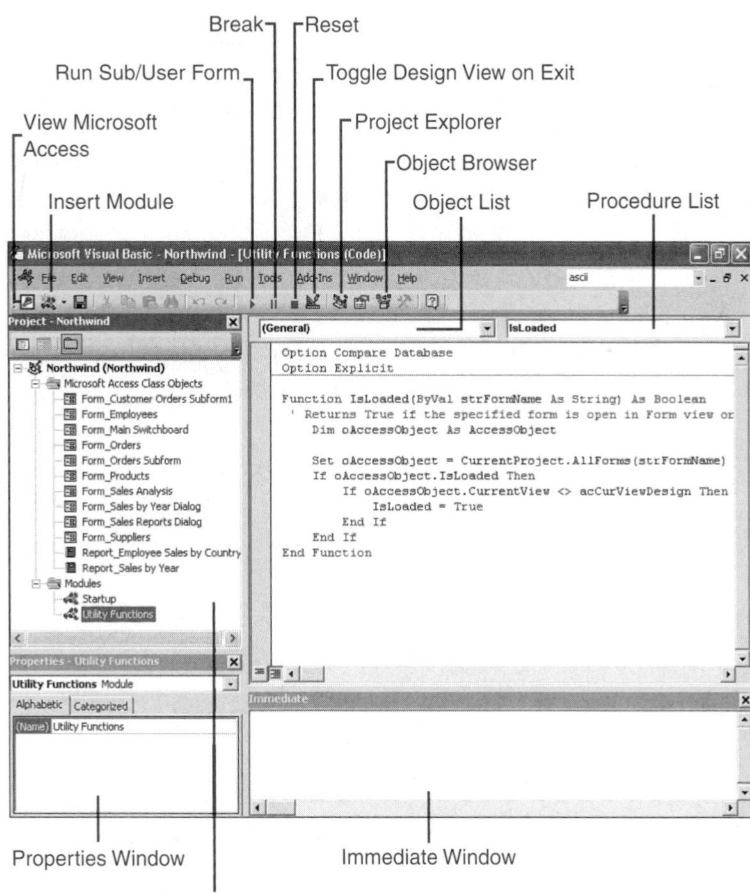

Figure 27.8 The VBA editor window opens with the Project Explorer, Properties, and Immediate windows docked as shown here.

The Toolbar of the Module Window

Table 27.3 lists the purpose of each item in the toolbar of the Module window (refer to Figure 27.8) and the menu commands and key combinations that you can substitute for toolbar components. Buttons marked with an asterisk (*) in the Item column were changed by Access 2000. There are no Access 2003 changes to the editor other than the appearance of active toolbar buttons, elimination of the Office Assistant barrier to obtaining online help for VBA, and the addition of the Ask a Question text box.

TABLE 27.3 VBA-SPECIFIC ELEMENTS OF THE VBA EDITOR'S TOOLBAR AND CODE-EDITING WINDOW

Button	Item	Alternative Method	Purpose
	View Micro-Access*	View, Microsoft Access or press Alt+F11	Displays the Access 2003 window.
	Insert Module	Insert, Module	Creates a new, empty module. Click the down arrow next to this button to create a new class module or to insert a new procedure or function.
	Find	Edit, Find or press Ctrl+F	Similar to the Find feature used in Table or Form view; allows you to search for a specific word or phrase in a module.
	Undo	Edit, Undo or press Ctrl+Z	Rescinds the last keyboard or mouse operation performed, if possible.
	Redo	Edit, Redo	Rescinds the last undo operation, if possible.
	Run Sub/* UserForm	Run, Run Sub/ User/Form or press F5	Starts the execution of the current procedure, or continues executing a procedure after its execution has been halted by a break condition. If the code-editing window doesn't have thefocus, this button is called Run Macro and opens the Macros dialog in which to select the macro to run, if any.
	Break*	Run, Break or press Ctrl+Break	Halts execution of a procedure.
	Reset Shift+F5	Run, Reset or press execution of a VBA procedure and reinitializes all variables to their default values.	Terminates

Button	Item	Alternative Method	Purpose
	Design mode	Run, Design Mode	Toggles design mode for UserForms.
	Project Explorer or	View, Project Explorer window.	Opens the Project Explorer press Ctrl+R
	Properties Window	View, Properties Window or press F4	Opens the Properties window for the object selected in the Project Explorer.
	Object Browser	View, Object Browser or press F2	Opens the Object Browser window.
	Toolbox	View, Toolbox	Shows the Toolbox for adding controls to UserForms.
	VBA Help	Help, Microsoft Visual Basic Help	Opens the Welcome topic of VBA online help.
N/A	Object List	None	Displays a list of objects in form or report modules. Only (General) appears for Access modules.
N/A	Procedure List	None	Displays a function or procedure in a module. Select the procedure or event name from the drop-down list. Procedures are listed in alphabetical order by name.

Module Shortcut Keys

Additional shortcut keys and key combinations listed in Table 27.4 can help you as you write and edit VBA code. Only the most commonly used shortcut keys are listed in Table 27.4.

Table 27.4 Primary Key Combinations for Entering and Editing VBA Code

Key Combination	Purpose
F3	Finds next occurrence of a search string
Shift+F3	Finds previous occurrence of a search string
F9	Sets or clears a breakpoint on the current line
Ctrl+Shift+F9	Clears all breakpoints
Tab	Indents single or multiple lines of code by four (default value) characters
Shift+Tab	Outdents single or multiple lines of code by four characters
Ctrl+Y	Deletes the line on which the cursor is located

You can change the default indentation of four characters per tab stop by choosing Tools, Options. Click the Editor tab and then enter the desired number of characters in the Tab Width text box.

THE VBA HELP SYSTEM

Microsoft provides an extensive, multilevel Help system to help you learn and use VBA. The majority of the help topics for VBA are supplied by a generic VBA help file that's applicable to all flavors of VBA. If you place the cursor on a keyword or select a keyword and then press the F1 key, for example, a help window for the keyword appears (see Figure 27.9). If you click the "Example" hot spot under the name of the keyword, the window displays VBA sample code (see Figure 27.10).

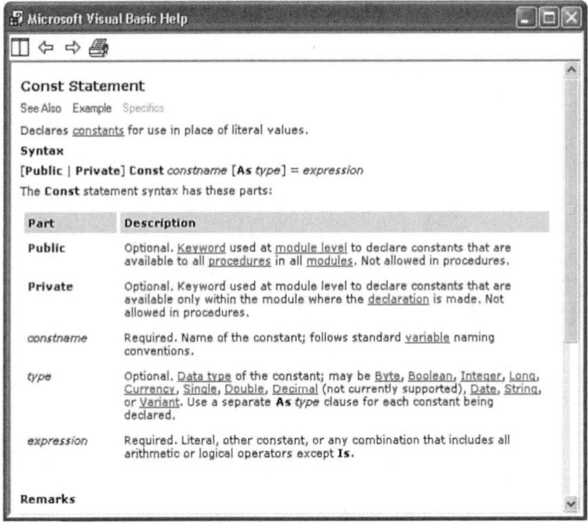

Figure 27.9
Placing the cursor on a keyword, such as `Const`, and pressing F1 opens the Microsoft Visual Basic Help window with the topic for the keyword.

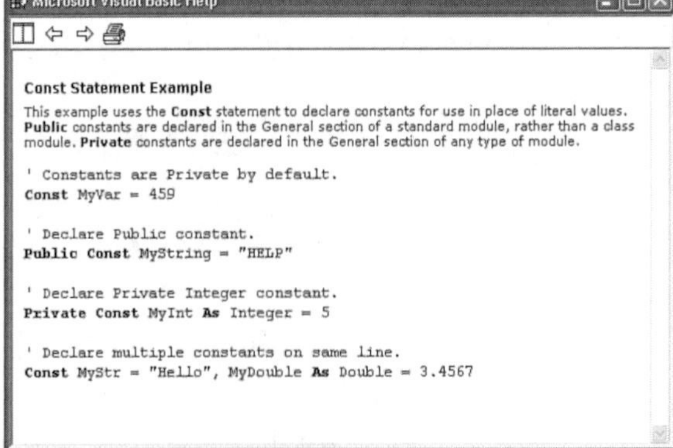

Figure 27.10
Clicking the Example link in the help window for a keyword opens a help window with VBA example code for the keyword.

EXAMINING THE UTILITY FUNCTIONS MODULE

One recommended way to learn a new programming language is to examine simple examples of code and analyze the statements used in the example.

The sections that follow show how to open a module, display a function in the Module window, add a breakpoint to the code, and then use the Immediate window to execute the function.

ADDING A BREAKPOINT TO THE `IsLoaded()` FUNCTION

When you examine the execution of VBA code written by others, and when you debug your own application, breakpoints are very useful. This section explains how to add a breakpoint to the `IsLoaded()` function so that the Suppliers form stops executing when the Suppliers form's On Current event calls the `Form_Current` event handler, which in turn calls the `IsLoaded()` function and Access displays the code in the Module window.

TIP

> To see how form events call event handlers in a class module, change to Design view, open the Properties window, and click the Event tab. Click the Builder button of the On Current event, which has [Event Procedure] in its text box, to open the VBA editor with the corresponding event-handling subprocedure in the code window.

To add a breakpoint to the `IsLoaded()` function, follow these steps:

1. If you have the VBA editor open with Northwind as the current database, double-click Utility Functions in the Project Explorer. Otherwise, display the Database window, click the Modules shortcut, and double-click the Utility Functions module to open the VBA editor with Utility Functions active.
2. Place the cursor on the line that begins with **`If`** `oAccessObject = ...` and press F9. The breakpoint you create is indicated by changing the display of the line to reverse red and by the placement of a red dot in the margin indicator at the left of the window (see Figure 27.11, which has a line break added).

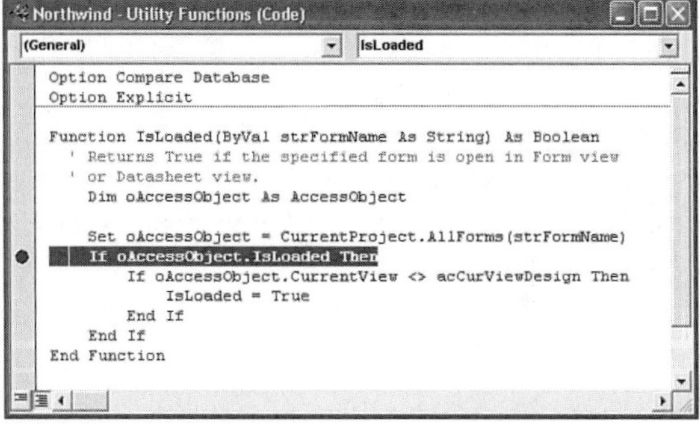

Figure 27.11 Adding a breakpoint to an instruction with a CCC highlights the entire instruction and adds a red dot for each line of the instruction.

3. Click the View Microsoft Access button and open the Suppliers form to execute the `Form_Current` procedure attached to the On Current event of the form. When the Suppliers form's `Form_Current` procedure calls the `IsLoaded()` function, the execution of `IsLoaded()` begins with the **Set** `oAccessObject = CurrentProject.AllForms(strFormName)`line and halts at the line with the breakpoint. When execution encounters a breakpoint, the module containing the breakpoint opens automatically. The line with the breakpoint turns yellow (see Figure 27.12).

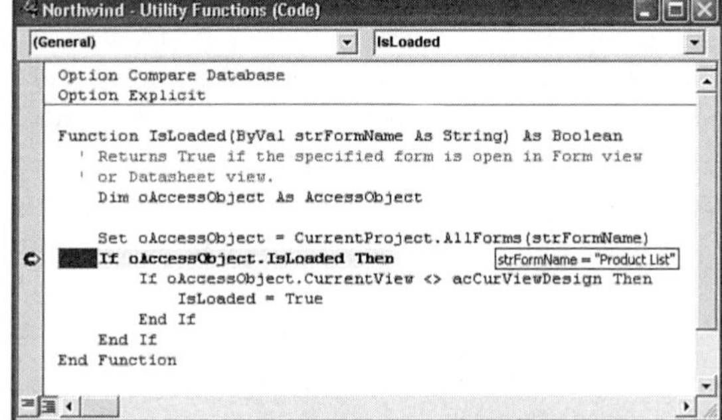

Figure 27.12 When VBA execution encounters a breakpoint, the interpreter stops before executing the instruction. The code of the breakpoint line turns yellow. Passing the cursor over a variable displays its value in a Data Tips window.

TIP

Data Tips, which are similar in appearance to ToolTips or ScreenTips, display the name and value of variables in break mode. When you pass the mouse pointer over the `strFormName` argument, a DataTips window displays the value.

4. Press F5 or click the Run Sub/UserForm button to resume execution of the VBA code. Alternatively, press F8 to step through the remaining lines of code. Access displays the Suppliers form.
5. Close the Suppliers form to execute the `Form_Close` procedure that's attached to the form's On Close event. When the Suppliers form's `Form_Close` procedure calls the `IsLoaded()` function, execution occurs as described in step 3, and the `IsLoaded()` function again halts at the line with the breakpoint. In this case, `IsLoaded` returns **`False`**.
6. Place the cursor on one of the highlighted lines, and press F9 to toggle the breakpoint off.

The **`Set`** `oAccessObject = CurrentProject.AllForms(strFormName)` instruction returns a pointer to the member of the `AllForms` collection specified by `strFormName`. If `strFormName` isn't a member of the collection, you receive a runtime error, because the `IsLoaded()` function doesn't include error-handling code.

PRINTING TO THE IMMEDIATE WINDOW WITH THE DEBUG OBJECT

Previous chapters of this book introduced you to the VBA editor's Immediate window and showed you how to obtain the values of variables with **?** *VarName* statements. When you want to view the values of several variables, you can use the `Print` method of the **`Debug`** object to automate printing to the Immediate window. If you add the **`Debug`** object to a function that tests the names of each open form, you can create a list in the Immediate window of all the forms that are open.

The `Forms` and `AllForms` collections contain a `Form` or `AccessObject` member for each form in the project. You can use a **`For`** `...` **`Next`** loop with a counter to obtain the form name or a **`For Each`** *`ObjectName`* **`In`** *`CollectionName`* `...` **`Next`** loop to avoid declaring a counter variable and specify the counter value as the `Item` index. You must declare a `Form` or `AccessObject` variable, however, to use **`For Each`**.

To create a `WhatsLoaded()` function to list all open forms, follow these steps:

1. Load three or more forms. The Customers, Categories, Employees, and Main Switchboard forms are good choices because these forms load quickly.
2. In the Utility Functions module, type **Private Sub WhatsLoaded()** below the **`End Function`** line of the `IsLoaded()` function. The VBA interpreter adds the **`End Sub`** statement for you automatically.
3. Type the following code between the **`Private Sub`**`...` and **`End Sub`** lines:

```
Dim intCtr As Integer
For intCtr = 0 To Forms.Count - 1
    Debug.Print intCtr & " = " & Forms(intCtr).FormName
Next intCtr
```

   The **`For`**`...`**`Next`** loop iterates the `Forms` collection. The **`Debug`**`.Print` statement prints the name of each open form in the Immediate window.

NOTE

> The VBA editor includes a powerful feature called statement autocompletion to help you write VBA code. The interpreter monitors each line of code as you type it in. When you type variable declarations, use built-in Access and VBA functions, or use object methods and properties in your code, the interpreter displays a pop-up window to help you select appropriate values.
>
> Figure 27.13 shows the pop-up list window that appears after you type the **`As`** keyword in the first **`Dim`** statement of the code you enter in step 3. For procedures, functions, and methods, the pop-up help window lists all the arguments for the procedure, function, or method, so you don't have to remember all the possible arguments. You can turn this feature on and off by choosing Tools, Options and then selecting or clearing the Auto List Members check box on the Editor tab of the Options dialog.

27

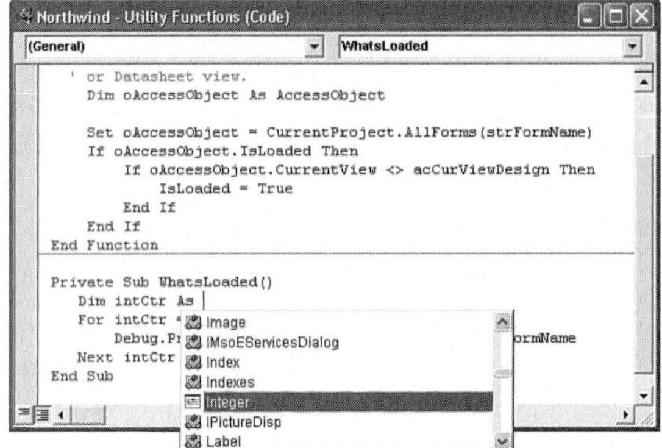

Figure 27.13
As you type VBA code in the editor window, an autocompletion list opens to provide a list of keywords, constants, or objects that are candidates for the following entry. As you add letters, the list displays items whose names start with those letters.

4. Place the cursor anywhere within the `WhatsLoaded` code you typed and press F5 or click the Run Sub/UserForm button. If the Immediate window isn't open, press Ctrl+G to open it. (The G shortcut comes from the windows prior name—Debug.) The name of each form is added to the Immediate window by the **`Debug`**`.Print` statement (see Figure 27.14).

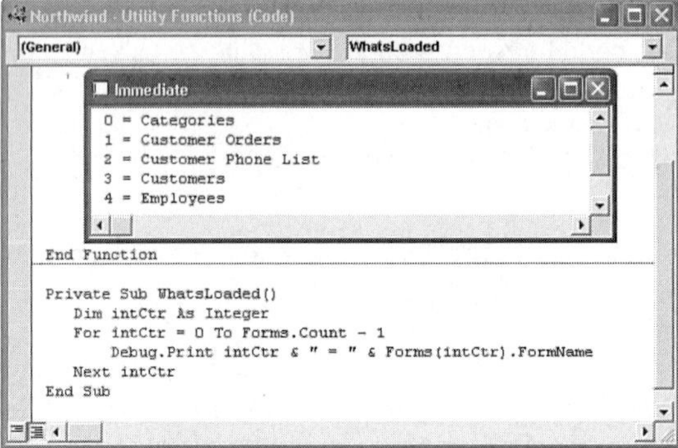

Figure 27.14
Executing the `WhatsLoaded` subprocedure prints a list of the forms open in Access.

5. Close and don't save changes to the Utility Function module. Then close the other forms you opened for this example.

The **`Debug`**`.Print` statement is particularly useful for displaying the values of variables that change when you execute a loop. When you've completed the testing of your procedure, you delete the Debug statements.

To create a list of all forms and their loaded state, add the following code to the module:

```
Private Sub FormState()
   Dim accForm As AccessObject
   For Each accForm In CurrentProject.AllForms
```

```
      Debug.Print accForm.Name & _
         " Open = " & accForm.IsLoaded
   Next accForm
End Sub
```

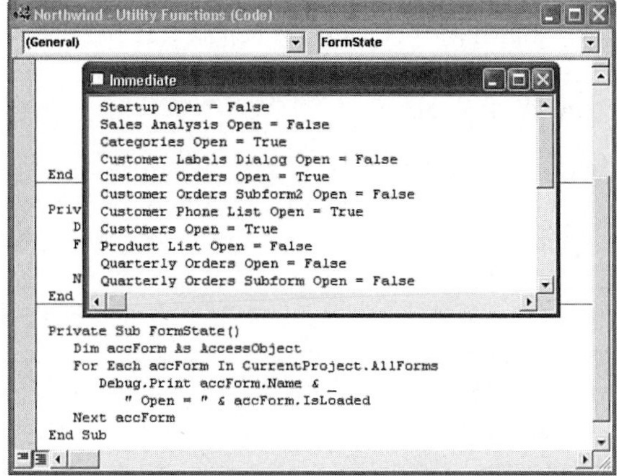

Figure 27.15
The FormState subprocedure lists all forms in the database and indicates if the form is open.

With the cursor on a line in the subprocedure, press F5 to execute the function. The Immediate window displays a list of all forms in the current project (see Figure 27.15).

Using Text Comparison Options

Tests of text data in fields of tables, query result sets, and `Recordset` objects against **`String`** or **`Variant`** text data in modules depends on the value of the **`Option Compare`**`...` statement, which appears in the Declarations section of the Utility Functions module. To determine how text comparisons are made in the module, you can use any of the following statements:

- **`Option Compare`** `Binary` comparisons are case sensitive. Lowercase letters are not equivalent to uppercase letters. To determine the sort order of characters, Access uses the character value assigned by the Windows ANSI character set.
- **`Option Compare`** `Text` comparisons are not case sensitive. Lowercase letters are treated as the equivalent of uppercase letters. For most North American users, the sort order is the same as **`Option Compare`** `Binary`, ANSI. Unless you have a reason to specify a different comparison method, use **`Option Compare`** `Text`.
- **`Option Compare`** `Database` comparisons are case sensitive, and the sort order is that specified for the database.

Access adds **`Option Compare`** `Database` to the Declarations section when you create a new module, overriding the default. `Binary` and `Database` are keywords in VBA, but these words don't have the same meaning when used in the **`Option Compare`**`...` statement. For compatibility with changes in possible future releases of Access, you should not use `Compare` or `Text` as names of variables.

27

IN THE REAL WORLD—MACRO SCHIZOPHRENIA

Macros have been a common add-on to productivity applications since the early days of WordPerfect, Lotus 1-2-3, and other popular DOS word processing and spreadsheet applications. Each application took a different approach to automating repetitive operations, which resulted in a Tower of Macro Language Babel. WordPerfect 4.x and 5.x for DOS, in particular, had an arcane set of macro commands and peculiar program structure that frustrated thousands of erstwhile programmers.

About 12 years ago, Bill Gates decided that all Microsoft applications using macros would share a common macro language built on BASIC. BASIC is the acronym for Beginners All-Purpose Symbolic Instruction Code, an interpreted language developed at Dartmouth College. The intended application for BASIC was programming on terminal-based (usually Teletype) time-sharing computers. Gates' choice of BASIC for a macro language isn't surprising when you consider that Microsoft Corporation was built on the foundation of Gates' BASIC interpreter that ran in the 8KB (not MB) of RAM common to the early predecessors of the PC, such as the Altair microcomputer. Gates reiterated his desire for a common macro language in an article that appeared in a late 1991 issue of the now-extinct *One-to-One with Microsoft* magazine.

NOTE

> A few years ago, Bill Gates gave a speech in which he mentioned a subscription model for licensing productivity software, thereby creating an "Office Annuity" for Microsoft Corporation. Microsoft abandoned the subscription model proposed for Office XP. But Microsoft's new Software Assurance and Licensing 6.0 terms, which most analysts and IT managers contend increases software costs substantially, is tantamount to a "Windows Annuity" for Office, operating systems, and server products. John Connors, Microsoft's chief financial officer, stated on January 24, 2003, that the company plans to establish a "financing group," presumably to deliver "easy monthly license payments" for small- and medium-size businesses.

27

Prior to Access 1.0, the only Microsoft application with a BASIC-like macro language was Word. WordBASIC, later Word Basic, was far more versatile, easy to understand, and useful than the competitors' pidgin-like languages. Access 1.0 offered Embedded Basic (EB)—later to become Access Basic—as its programming language. Apparently Microsoft believed that Access Basic would be incomprehensible to average Access users, so Microsoft's product team tacked on a simplified macro language. Thus, Access became saddled with two "macro" languages.

Visual Basic 3.0 was the most popular Windows programming tool by the time Microsoft released Access 1.0. Visual Basic, Access, and Word each had their own Basic flavor. Microsoft touted Visual Basic as a programming language, while Access Basic and Word Basic retained the macro terminology. Excel was the next Microsoft application to gain Basic as a macro language, this time in the guise of Visual Basic, Applications Edition, also known as Visual Basic for Applications. Microsoft's goal was to unify all three Visual Basic dialects under the VBA umbrella. Microsoft finally achieved Gates' objective with the release of Visual Basic 6.0 and Office 2000. There's a common aphorism that "after a few releases, Microsoft usually gets it right." But 10 years is a long time, even by Microsoft standards.

Macro and script traditionally have been synonyms for code that automates operations in productivity applications, but Visual Basic, Scripting Edition, also known as VBScript, ends that tradition. VBScript, a lightweight variant of VBA designed to compete with Netscape's JavaScript, appears primarily in Web-based applications. VBScript also can be used to automate repetitive operating system activities when run under the Windows Scripting Host (WSH). Access 2003 includes the Microsoft Script Editor—described in Chapter 24, "Designing and Deploying Data Access Pages"—to aid in adding VBScript subprocedures to DAP. So Access 2003 now offers macro, script, and programming languages.

Calling VBA a macro language is undeserved damnation by faint praise. VBA is a true programming language and, because of its integration with Microsoft Office, is undoubtedly the most widely used of all programming languages—including C/C++, COBOL, and Java. VBA is easier to learn than Java and is an order of magnitude less difficult to master than C++ or COBOL. Although VBA doesn't qualify as a truly object-oriented (OO) programming language—it lacks inheritance and some other OO niceties—VBA is sufficiently object-enabled to handle virtually all common database-related programming chores. Visual Basic. NET adds the missing OO features that developers have been requesting since the release of Visual Basic 1.0.

After you gain experience with VBA in Access, you can leverage your programming skills in Visual Basic 6.0 or Visual Basic .NET. A good foundation in VBA makes the transition to VBScript a snap, but mastering Visual Basic .NET involves a steep learning curve. Even if you're an accomplished Access macro writer, use Access's Macro converter to automate the process of moving to VBA. Click Tools, Macros, and then choose Convert Macros to Visual Basic, Create Menu from Macro, Create Toolbar from Macro, or Create Shortcut Menu from Macro to bring your existing applications to current Access development standards.

CHAPTER 28

HANDLING EVENTS WITH VBA 6.0

In this chapter

INTRODUCING EVENT-DRIVEN PROGRAMMING

All Windows applications are event-driven, which means that an event, such as a mouse click on a command button or a change in the position of a record pointer, executes individual blocks of application programming code. Thus, the majority of the VBA code you write consists of event-handling subprocedures—also called event procedures or event handlers—that are contained within `[{Public¦Private}] Sub {Form¦Report}_[ObjectName_]EventName...End Sub` structures of class modules. Class module is the VBA term that replaces Access 2.0's and Access 95's use of code-behind-forms (CBF) to describe Access Basic or Access-specific VBA code embedded within a `Form` or `Report` container. This chapter describes how to write Access VBA event-handling code in `Form` and `Report` class modules to automate your Access 2003 applications.

Early versions of Access emphasized the use of Access macros to respond to events. Microsoft promoted Access macros as a simplified programming language for users with little or no programming experience. The original repertoire of about 40 Access macro actions proved adequate to automate relatively simple applications. One of the major drawbacks of Access macros is the inability to handle errors gracefully. Thus, virtually all Access power users and developers have abandoned macros in favor of programming. There's no guarantee that future versions of Access will continue to support Access macros.

UNDERSTANDING THE ROLE OF CLASS MODULES

Class modules are containers for VBA code that relate to a particular class of objects. Access 2003 defines two classes (collections)—`Forms` and `Reports`—that contain VBA code for a particular instance of the class: a `Form` or `Report` object. In object-oriented programming terms, class modules *encapsulate* VBA code within a `Form` or `Report` object. Code encapsulation lets you create reusable objects. For example, when you copy a form from one Access database to another, the copy you make includes the code in the form's class module.

Access's `Form` and `Report` class modules differ from conventional modules in that a `Form` or `Report` object is integral to the code and contributes the object's visible properties (appearance). Conventional modules, such as Northwind.mdb's Utility Functions, appear in the Modules page of the Database window. Your event-handling code creates a custom set of methods (behavior) that are applicable to the object. When you open a form or report, you create the default instance of the corresponding `Form` or `Report` object. The default instance of the object appears in the Forms or Reports page of the Database window. VBA 6.0 also lets you create additional temporary, nondefault instances of `Form` and `Report` objects with the `New` reserved word. You don't need to add an explicit reference to the associated form or report in your code, although it's good programming practice to use the **`Me`** self-reference to specify the current instance of the `Form` or `Report` object.

NOTE

Access 9x called the window that displays class module code the Class Module window. The Class Module window was integrated with other Access windows. Access 2000+ uses the VBA Integrated Design Environment (IDE), which this book calls the *VBA editor*.

→ For help navigating through this integrated window, **see** "Exploring the VBA Editor," **p. 1179**.

THE MAIN SWITCHBOARD CLASS MODULE

The Northwind Traders Main Switchboard form is a good starting point for gaining an understanding of class modules and simple event-handling code. The Main Switchboard form contains two event-handling subprocedures: one each for the Display Database Window and Exit Microsoft Access command buttons, plus a single `OpenForms` function that services the Categories, Suppliers, Products, Orders, and Print Sales Reports command buttons. Figure 28.1 illustrates the relationships between the command buttons and the function or subprocedure that executes when you click the button.

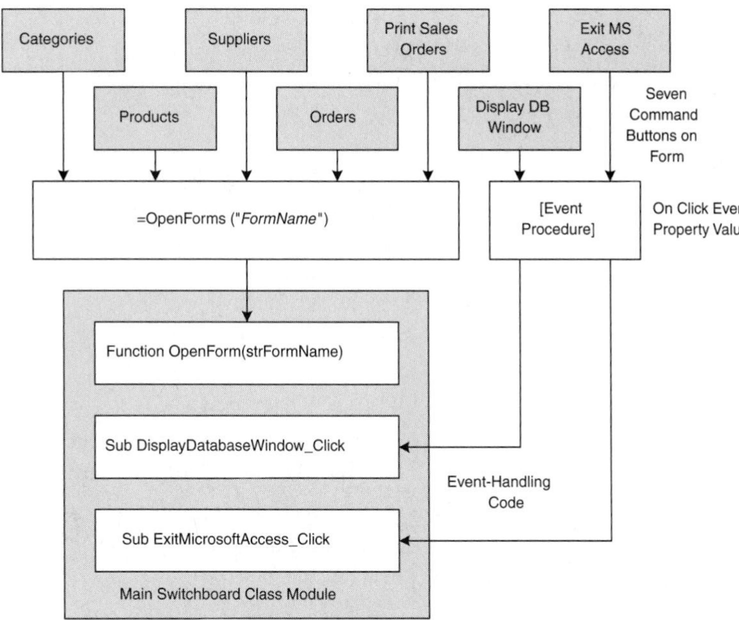

Figure 28.1 This diagram illustrates relationships between command buttons and event-handling code for the Main Switchboard form.

To view the event-handling code in the Main Switchboard form, follow these steps:

1. Select the Main Switchboard form in the Database window.

2. Click the Code button of the toolbar to open the VBA editor window, `Form_Main Switchboard (Code)`, for the Main Switchboard form. By default, the editor window opens with the Declarations section at the top of the window.

28

3. Open the left drop-down list, which Microsoft calls the Object box, to display a list of the control objects of the form, plus the `Form` object (see Figure 28.2).

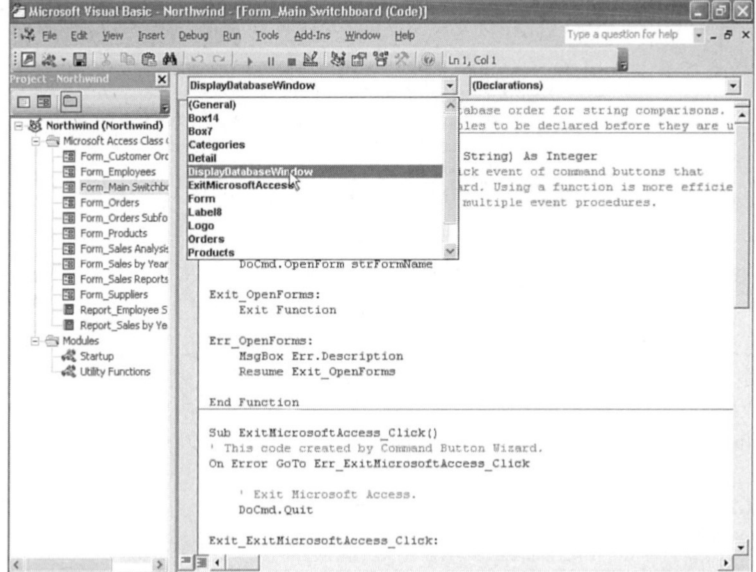

Figure 28.2
The lefthand list of a `Form` object contains items representing the form and its controls. Controls on the Main Switchboard form don't use the recommended VBA naming conventions, such as a `cmd` prefix for command buttons.

TIP

> Undocking and closing unused components of the VBA editor and maximizing the code window makes it easier to view and write code. To undock the individual VBA editor windows, choose Tools, Options, click the Docking tab, and clear the appropriate check boxes. Docking the Project Explorer window, however, makes it easier to switch between class modules of the forms and reports in your project.

4. Select one of the command buttons, such as `DisplayDatabaseWindow`, from the Object list to display the subprocedure—`Sub _DisplayDatabaseWindow_Click`—for the On Click event of the Display Database Window command button (see Figure 28.3).
5. Open the right drop-down list, which Microsoft calls the Procedure box, to display a list of events applicable to the selection in the Object box. The `Click` event appears in bold type because the `DisplayDatabaseWindows_Click` event subprocedure contains VBA code. When you select an event, such as `DblClick`, without an existing subprocedure, Access creates a subprocedure stub. A subprocedure stub in a class module consists only of the **`Private Sub`** `[`*`ObjectName_`*`]`*`EventName`*...**`End Sub`** entries (see Figure 28.4).

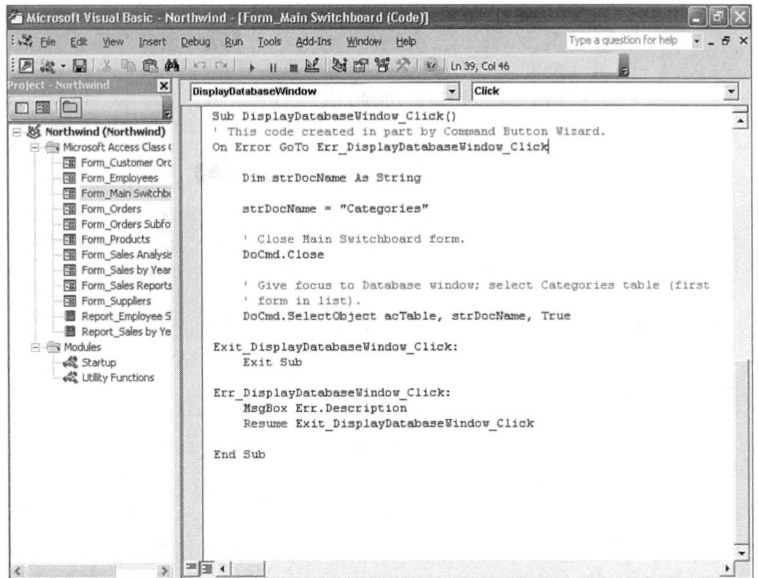

Figure 28.3 Selecting a control or the `Form` object in the left-hand list positions the beginning of the event-handler code for the object at the top of the editor window, if an event handler exists.

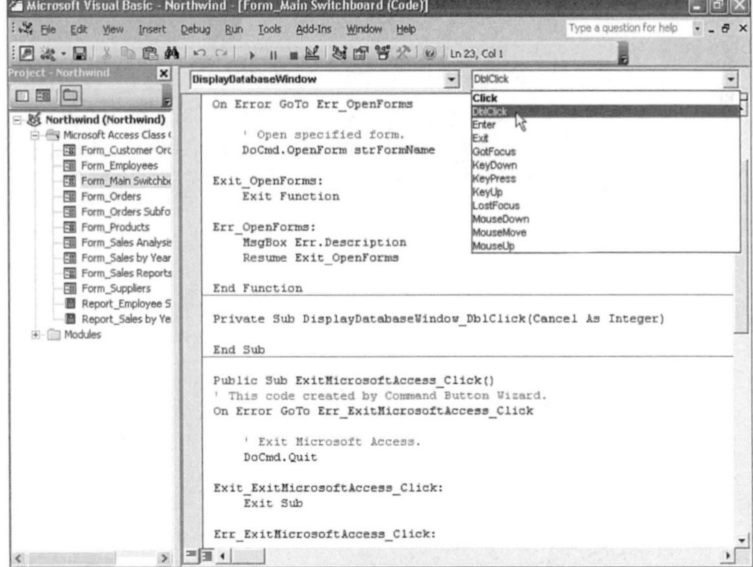

Figure 28.4 Selecting an event without a handler in the right-hand list creates a new `Private Sub` *`ControlName_EventName`* or `Private Sub Form_`*`EventName`* subprocedure stub.

28

TIP

All VBA procedures and functions in Access class modules have **`Public`** scope unless you specify otherwise; procedures that you declare with **`Sub`**, **`Function`**, **`Public Sub`**, or **`Public Function`** are visible to all other class modules and conventional code

continues

continued

> modules. For example, you can execute the Main Switchboard form's `ExitMicrosoftAccess_Click` procedure from the Utility Functions module with a `[Form_Main Switchboard].ExitMicrosoftAccess_Click` instruction. When you create a procedure stub in a class module, Access adds the **`Private`** modifier. **`Private`** subprocedures and functions have slightly less overhead than **`Public`** subprocedures and functions and improve performance in large Access applications. The function and subprocedures of the `Form_Main Switchboard` class module are declared without the default **`Private`** modifier, which is not a good programming practice for event handlers.

EVENT-HANDLING CODE IN THE MAIN SWITCHBOARD FORM

Listing 28.1 shows all the code contained in the `Form_Main Switchboard` class module. Each of the procedures includes standard error-handling code consisting of **`On Error GoTo`** `Err_`*`Lable`*...**`Resume`** `Exit_`*`Label`*...**`Exit`** `{`**`Function`**`¦`**`Sub`**`}` statements. Adding error handling to every procedure you write is a good VBA programming practice.

→ For details on use of the `On Error` statement, **see** "Handling Runtime Errors," **p. 1176**.

LISTING 28.1 EVENT-HANDLING CODE OF THE `Form_Main Switchboard` CLASS MODULE

```
Option Compare Database  'Use database order for string comparisons.
Option Explicit 'Requires variables to be declared before they are used.

Function OpenForms(strFormName As String) As Integer
'This function is used in the Click event of command buttons that
'open forms on the Main Switchboard. Using a function is more efficient
'than repeating the same code in multiple event procedures.
On Error GoTo Err_OpenForms

    'Open specified form.
    DoCmd.OpenForm strFormName

Exit_OpenForms:
    Exit Function

Err_OpenForms:
    MsgBox Err.Description
    Resume Exit_OpenForms
End Function

Sub ExitMicrosoftAccess_Click()
'This code created by Command Button Wizard.
On Error GoTo Err_ExitMicrosoftAccess_Click

    'Exit Microsoft Access.
    DoCmd.Quit
```

28

```
Exit_ExitMicrosoftAccess_Click:
    Exit Sub

Err_ExitMicrosoftAccess_Click:
    MsgBox Err.Description
    Resume Exit_ExitMicrosoftAccess_Click
End Sub

Sub DisplayDatabaseWindow_Click()
'This code created in part by Command Button Wizard.
On Error GoTo Err_DisplayDatabaseWindow_Click

    Dim strDocName As String
    strDocName = "Categories"

   'Close Main Switchboard form.
    DoCmd.Close

   'Give focus to Database window; select Categories table (first
   'form in list).
    DoCmd.SelectObject acTable, strDocName, True

Exit_DisplayDatabaseWindow_Click:
    Exit Sub

Err_DisplayDatabaseWindow_Click:
    MsgBox Err.Description
    Resume Exit_DisplayDatabaseWindow_Click
End Sub
```

TIP

> The Default to Full Module view and Procedure Separator settings on the Editor page of the Options properties sheet make reading VBA code easier. By default, all the procedures in the class module appear after the Declarations section of the class module in the alphabetical order of the procedure name, separated by a horizontal gray line. With Full Module view specified, you can use the scroll bars to view all the procedures within a module.

Access 2003's `DoCmd` object is the key to manipulating Access application objects with VBA. `DoCmd` lets a VBA statement execute the equivalent of an Access macro, such as OpenForm or Quit. Application-specific reserved words, such as `DoCmd`, preclude a common set of VBA objects for all members of Office; thus, `DoCmd` is an Access-specific object, not a reserved word.

→ To learn more about the DoCmd object, **see** "Working with Access 2003's `DoCmd` Methods," **p. 1209.**

Examining Project Class Module Members in Object Browser and Project Explorer

Each `Form` and `Report` object in the current database that has a class module appears in the Classes list when you select the project name of the current database in the Project/Library (upper) drop-down list of Object Browser. By default, the project name for an Access database is the file name of the database without a file extension; thus, the project name for Northwind.mdb is Northwind. The default <globals> object displays all the procedures in conventional Access modules of the current database in the right-hand Members Of '<globals>' list. These procedures also appear in Members Of '*ModuleName*' entries for each module in the project.

TIP

To launch Object Browser, select a form or report in the Database window, click the Code button to display the class module for the form, and then press F2 or choose View, Object Browser.

When you select a `Form` or `Report` object, items representing properties of the `Form` or `Report` object and each of the control objects added to the `Form` or `Report` object appear in the Members Of '*ObjectName*' list. Each procedure also appears (in bold type) in the list. Figure 28.5 shows the list item for OpenForms function; the syntax required to call the function appears in the bottom pane. Object Browser adds the **`Public`** prefix to functions and subprocedures that aren't declared **`Private`**. If you double-click a subprocedure or function item, the editor window displays its code.

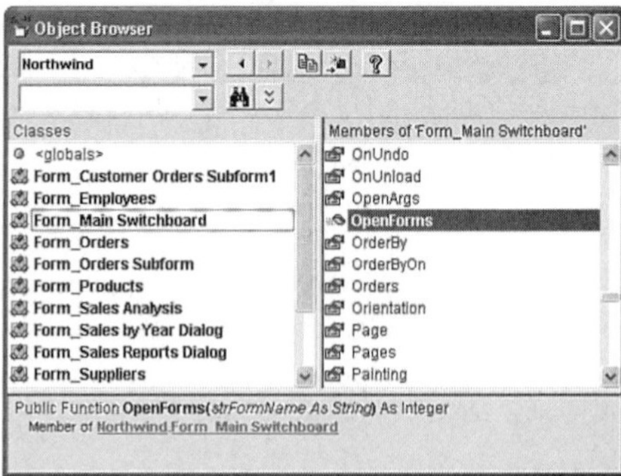

Figure 28.5 Selecting the `OpenForms` function in Object Browser displays a replica of its header in the bottom pane. If the function header doesn't include a scope prefix, Object Browser adds `Public`.

NOTE

VBA 6.0 lets you define your own classes and write custom class modules. Custom class modules give you the opportunity to define a set of properties and methods for the object class you create. Custom class modules appear in Object Browser's Classes list, and the properties and methods you define appear in the Members Of '*ObjectName*' list. Writing custom class modules is beyond the scope of this book.

The default reference to the Microsoft Access 11.0 Object library (Msacc.olb) enables programming of Access-specific objects, such as the `DoCmd` object described in the preceding section. To display Access-specific objects, select Access in Object Browser's Project/Library list. Scroll to and select the `DoCmd` object to display a list of its methods (see Figure 28.6). Object Browser's bottom pane displays the required and optional arguments of the method.

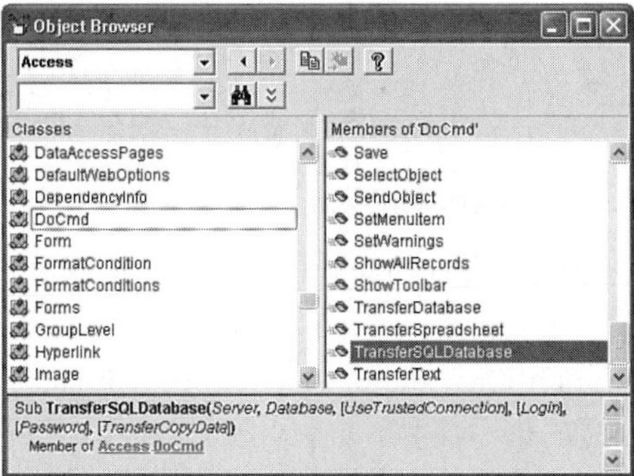

Figure 28.6 The Access `DoCmd` object has many methods, but no properties. The `TransferSQLDatabase` method lets you emulate the Tools, Database Utilities, Transfer Database menu command of Access Data Projects (ADP).

The Project Explorer window displays all `Form` and `Report` Microsoft Access Class Objects, plus modules that contain global code accessible to all class modules. Double-clicking a list item opens a new editor window. You can change the project name and add an optional project description by right-clicking the Project node and choosing *ProjectName* Properties to open the updated *ProjectName* - Project Properties window (see Figure 28.7). Independent (also called standalone) Class Objects have an `Instancing` property; `Form` and `Report` Class Objects don't have properties.

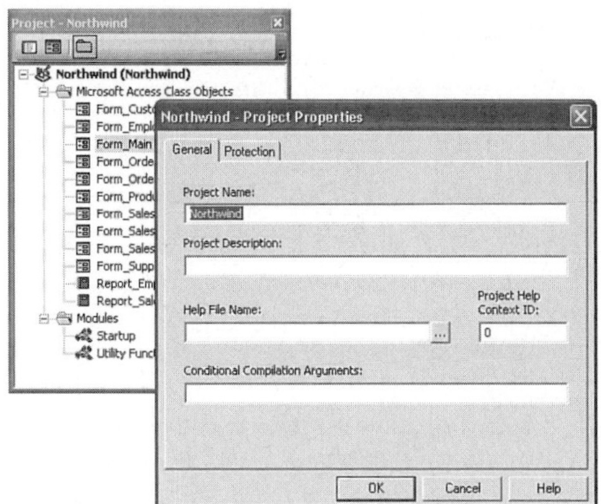

Figure 28.7 The General page of the Project Properties window lets you rename a project and add a description. The Protection page offers the option to hide your VBA code from others and password-protect the code.

ADDING EVENT-HANDLING CODE WITH THE COMMAND BUTTON WIZARD

Event-handling subprocedures represent the most common approach to handling events that are generated by control objects and `Recordset` objects bound to forms and reports. Command buttons are the most common control object to initiate user-generated events. The easiest way to create a simple VBA event-handling subprocedure is to add a command button to a form with the Command Button Wizard. The Command Button Wizard writes most or all the code for the most commonly used `...Click` event handlers.

DESIGNING A BUTTON TO OPEN ANOTHER FORM

To add a command button and its associated event-handling code for opening the Customers form, follow these steps:

1. Open Northwind.mdb, if necessary, and open a new form in Design view.
2. Click the Toolbox button, if necessary, to display the Toolbox.

3. Make sure the Control Wizard toggle button is depressed, and then click the Command Button tool and add a small button on the form. The first dialog of the Command Button Wizard opens.
4. Select Form Operations in the Categories list and Open Form in the Actions list (see Figure 28.8). Selecting Form Operations displays a sample button with a small form icon. Click Next.

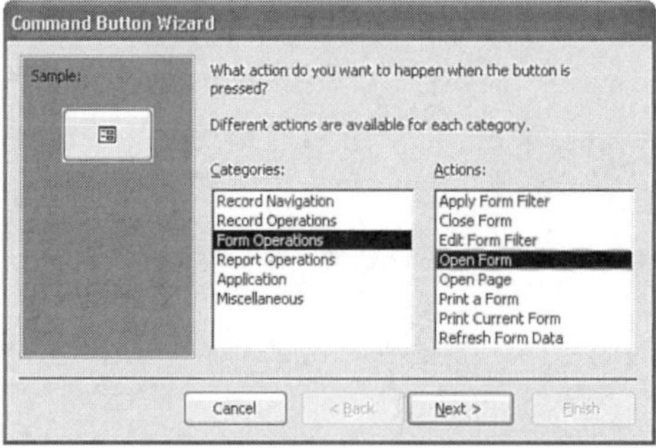

Figure 28.8 Select the category and action for the command button in the first Command Button Wizard dialog.

5. Select Customers (or another form) in the What Form Would You Like the Command Button to Open? list (see Figure 28.9), and click Next.
6. If the form to open is bound to a table or query, you can allow the form to display all records or add a filter to display only a single record based on the value of a field in your new form. The next section describes how to apply a filter. For this example, accept the Open the Form and Show All the Records option (see Figure 28.10), and click Next.

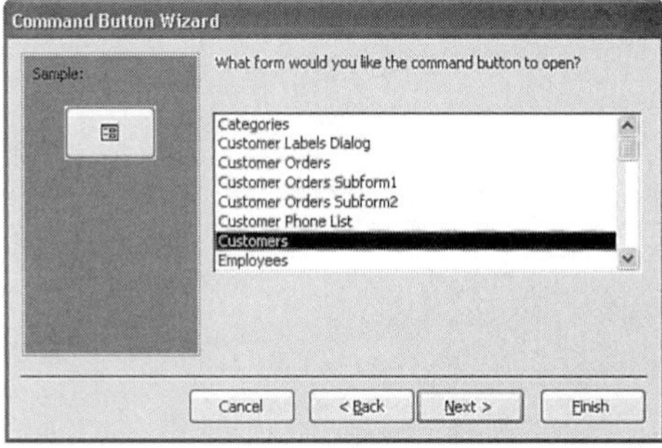

Figure 28.9
Select the name of the form to open in the second Wizard dialog.

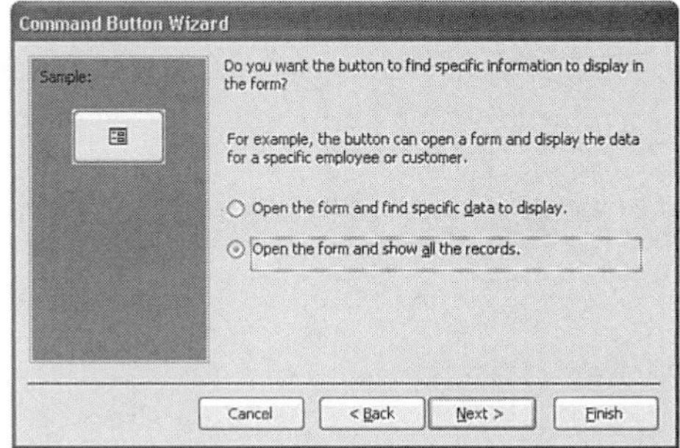

Figure 28.10
In the third Wizard dialog, select whether to apply a filter to the form's Recordset.

7. You can select from a variety of bitmapped icons for the button by marking the Show All Pictures check box. Alternatively, select the Text option button and type a caption—such as **Open Customers Form**—for the command button in the text box (see Figure 28.11). Click Next.

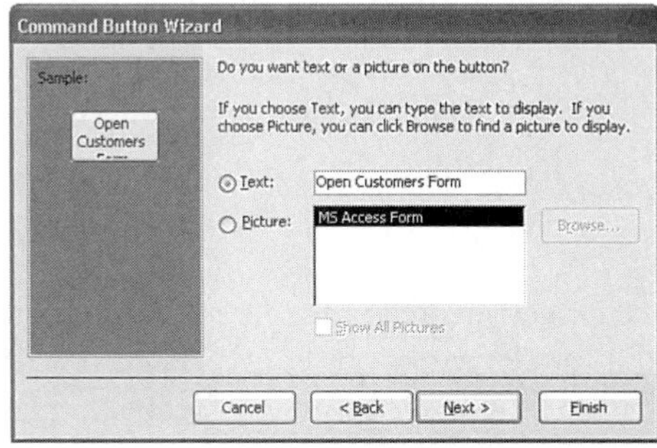

Figure 28.11
The fourth Wizard dialog lets you select between a text caption or a bitmap image for the command button.

8. Replace the default Command0 with a name for the command button that's related to the purpose of the button, such as **cmdOpenCustomersForm**, in the text box (see Figure 28.12). The `cmd` prefix is the naming convention for command buttons. Click Finish to add the event-handling code to the class module for the new form and close the last Command Button Wizard dialog.

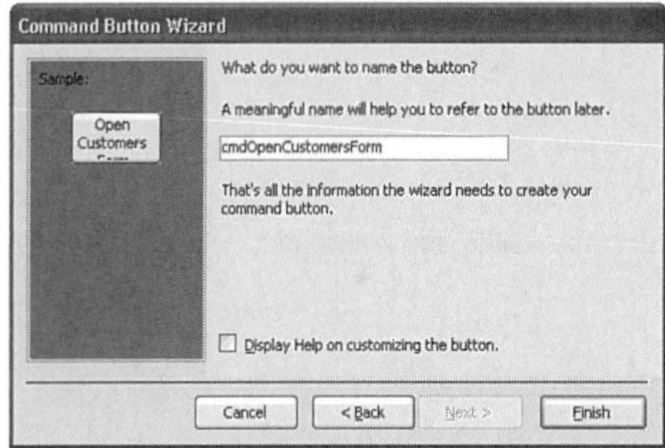

Figure 28.12
The last Wizard dialog prompts you for the Name property of the new command button.

9. Click the Code button to display the class module for your new form. Figure 28.13 shows the subprocedure added to the module by the Control Wizard. Click the View Microsoft Access button to return to your new form in Design view.

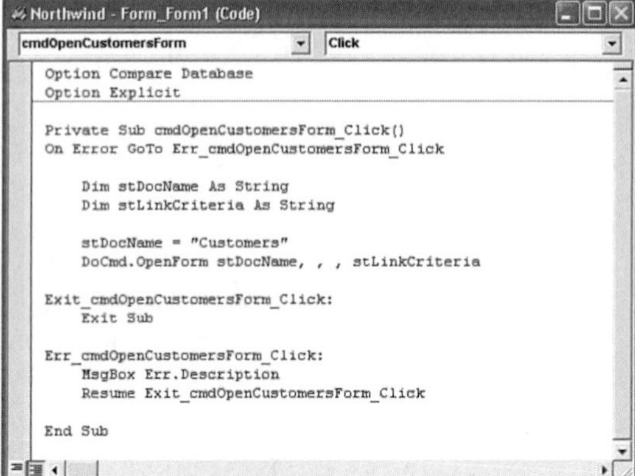

Figure 28.13
The Wizard generates the code shown here for the cmdOpenCustomers-Form command button you designed.

10. Click the Save button and save your form as **frmCommandWiz** or the like.
11. Close or minimize the Visual Basic Editor, change to Form view, and test the button's action.

The event-handling subprocedure you created in the preceding steps is bound to the On Click event of the cmdOpenCustomers button. In Form Design view, select the command button, click the Properties button on the toolbar to display the properties sheet for the button, and click the Event tab. The [Event Procedure] entry for the On Click event property specifies the `cmdOpenCustomers_Click` event handler. When you open the drop-down list for the On Click event, [Event Procedure] and the names of all the macros, if any, in your database appear (see Figure 28.14).

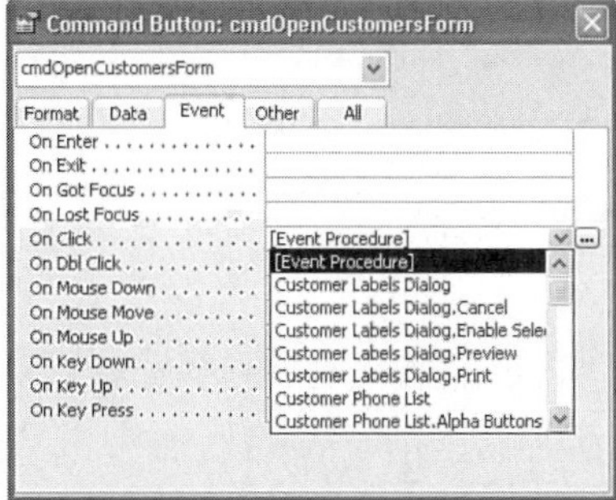

Figure 28.14
Select between a new or existing event-handling procedure or an existing Access macro to respond to an event.

NOTE

You can create a simple event-handling subprocedure stub for any event of an existing control by clicking the Builder button for the event and then double-clicking the Code Builder item in the Choose Builder list. In this case, it's up to you to fill in the code to handle the event. You can bypass the Choose Builder step and go directly to the Editor window by marking the Always Use Event Procedures check box in the Forms/Reports page of the Options dialog.

Adding a Button to Display a Specific Record on Another Form

The example of the preceding section simply opens the Customers form. In many cases, you need to open a form to display data based on the selected (current) record of the form with the command button—frmCommandWiz from the preceding section for this example. Applying a filter to the Recordset of the form you want to open (Customers) requires a link between a field of the Record Source of frmCommandWiz and the corresponding field of the Customers form. For this example, the link is the CustomerID field.

To add a filter (`WHERE`) criterion as the value of the `stLinkCriteria` argument of the `DoCmd.OpenForm` method, do this:

1. With frmCommandWiz in Design view, select the form, open the Properties dialog, click the Data tab, and select the Orders table as the value of the Record Source property, which opens the table's field list.
2. Drag the OrderID and CustomerID fields to the form to add a text box and combo list.
3. Follow steps 2–5 of the preceding section.
4. In the third Wizard dialog, select the Open the Form and Find Specific Data to Display option. Click Next.
5. In the added Wizard dialog that didn't appear in the preceding section's steps, select CustomerID in the left and right lists (see Figure 28.15). Click Next.
6. Continue with steps 7–11 of the preceding section, but specify **Display Customer Data** as the button caption, specify **cmdDisplayCustomerData** as the name of the button, and click Finish. Figure 28.16 shows the Customers form with a filter applied by the CustomerID value of the first Orders record.

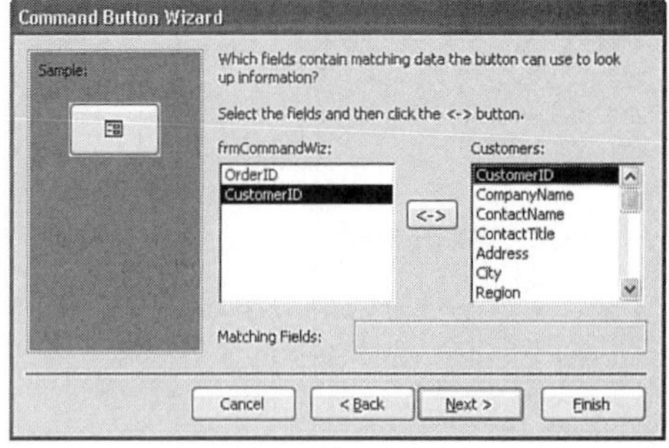

Figure 28.15 When you specify a filter on the Recordset of the form to open, this Command Button Wizard dialog lets you specify the field on which to link the two forms.

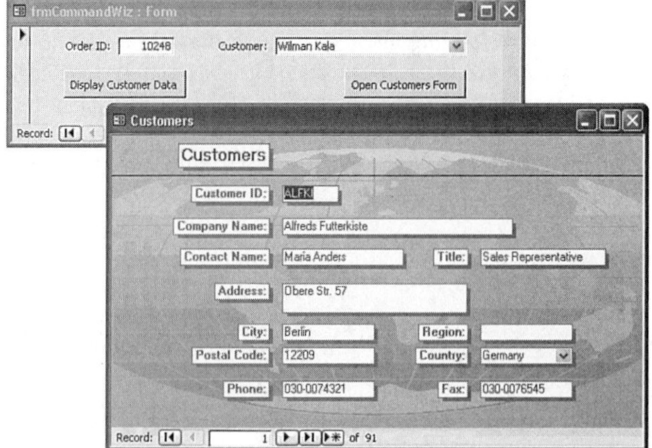

Figure 28.16 The Customers form displays the record specified by the frmCommandWiz form.

The Command Button Wizard generates the value of the filter argument and assigns it as the value of the `stLinkCriteria` variable with the following statement:

```
stLinkCriteria = "[CustomerID]=" & "'" & Me![CustomerID] & "'"
```

What the Wizard doesn't do is lock the opened form to prevent editing the customer data or adding a new record. To open the form in read-only mode, add **acFormReadOnly** as the last argument value of the `OpenForm` method:

```
DoCmd.OpenForm strDocName, , , strLinkCriteria, acFormReadOnly
```

→ For more information on the syntax of the `DoCmd.OpenForm` method, **see** "Arguments of `DoCmd` Methods," **p. 1212**.

28

TIP

Don't let users change values of records in the source table(s) when you bind a navigation form to a table or query. Set the Allow Edits, Allow Deletions, and Allow Deletions properties on the Data page of the form's Properties window to No. Doing this prevents inadvertent changes to the Orders table by selecting a another customer in the CustomerID combo box. Another way to prevent users from making changes in combo boxes is to set the List Rows property value to 1 on the Format page.

NOTE

The frmCommandWiz form is included in the Events28.mdb sample database located in the \Seua11\Chaptr28 folder of the accompanying CD-ROM.

USING FUNCTIONS TO RESPOND TO EVENTS

You can create your own Main Switchboard form by adding additional command buttons to the form for opening other forms. It's much more efficient, however, to use a single procedure to perform a set of identical tasks in which only the name of the form changes. Minimizing the amount of code in a form speeds opening of the form and minimizes the size of your database file.

Access lets you call a function and pass one or more parameter (argument) values to the function in response to events. A function (not a subprocedure) is required, despite the fact that Access disregards the return value, if the function returns a value. Control Wizards won't write the function code for you, nor will the Code Builder create a function stub. You must write the function yourself before calling it from an event. The `OpenForms` function in preceding Listing 28.1 is an example of using a function as an event handler.

You can easily change code written by the Command Button Wizard into a general-purpose function that opens any form whose name you pass as an argument. Figure 28.17 shows a simple modification of the `cmdOpenCustomers_Click` subprocedure (refer to Figure 28.13) to substitute a user-defined function for the event handler. When you replace **`Sub`** with **`Function`** in the first line, the VBA interpreter automatically changes **`Exit Sub`** to **`Exit Function`** and **`End Sub`** to **`End Function`**. You change the name of the function, add the `strFormName` parameter (the variable the Wizard adds to identify the form), pass the value of the `strFormName` parameter to the `OpenForm` action, and eliminate code that's not needed for the function, such as **`Dim`** `stDocName` **`As String`**.

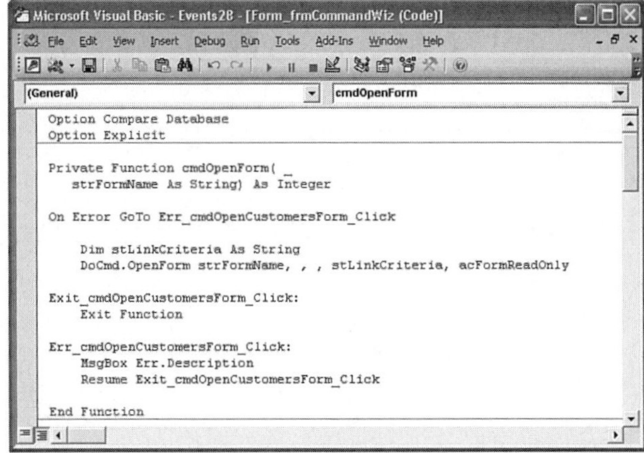

Figure 28.17
A few changes to the code of the `cmdOpenCustomers_Click` subprocedure converts it to a function that opens the form that you specify in the On Click event property value of the command button.

TIP

> If you don't change the name of the subprocedure or pass the cursor through the line containing the `Function` reserved word when converting from a subprocedure to a function, you receive a compile error. The VBA interpreter holds the existing subprocedure name in memory until the line is reinterpreted. Thus, creating a function of the same name results in a duplicate procedure name in the same class module if you press the Enter key when making the change. Duplicate procedure names aren't permitted within in the same module, nor are duplicate names of `Public` procedures permitted within the same project.

If you encounter compilation errors after changing the type or name of a function or procedure, see the "Calling Procedures and Functions in Class Modules" topic of the "Troubleshooting" section near the end of this chapter.

The syntax to enter in the event text box for executing a function is as follows:

```
=FunctionName([Argument1[, Argument2[, ...]]])
```

The arguments are optional, but unless you pass an argument value, such as a form name, there's no advantage to using a function call as an event handler. Arguments must be passed as literal values, such as "*FormName*" or a numeric value. Figure 28.18 shows the entry you type in the On Click text box to open the Customers form, **=cmdOpenForm("Customers")**. To add buttons to open other forms, copy the command button to the Clipboard, paste the copy to your form, and change the Customers caption to the name of the form you want to open.

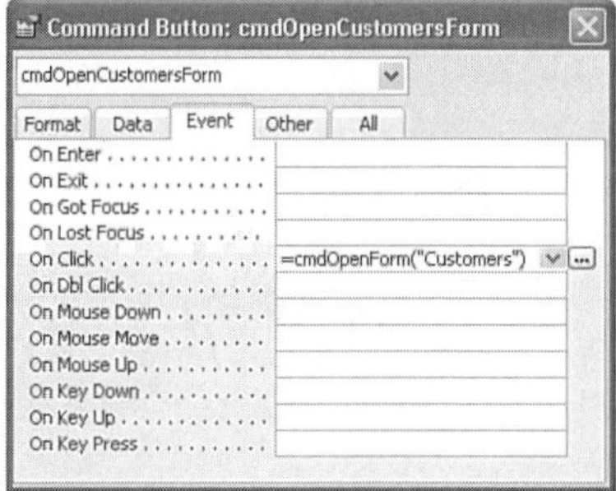

Figure 28.18 Replacing a subprocedure with a function requires the explicit calling syntax shown here for the On Click event.

UNDERSTANDING ACCESS 2003'S EVENT REPERTOIRE

When you interact with an object by using the keyboard or the mouse, you can change the object's state. The object's state is stored with the other data about the object. Access makes some of the changes in the object's state available as opportunities to interrupt normal processing. These special changes in an object's state are called events. An event is a change in the state of an object at which you can interrupt normal processing and define a response.

The best way to understand events is to categorize each by the type of action that causes the event to occur. There are 11 categories:

- *Mouse events* are triggered when you click form objects.
- *Keyboard events* are triggered by forms and form controls when you type or send keystrokes with the `SendKeys` action while the `Form` object has the focus.
- *Window events* are triggered by opening or closing forms or reports.
- *Focus events* are triggered when a form or form control gains or loses the focus or when a form or report becomes active or inactive.
- *Data events* are triggered by forms and form controls when you change data in controls or records, or by forms when the record pointer moves from one record to another.
- *Filter events* are triggered by forms when you apply or remove filters.
- *Print events* are triggered by reports and report sections when you print or preview a report.
- *Error events* are triggered by a form or report that has the focus when an error occurs.
- *Timing events* are triggered by forms when a specified time interval passes.
- *Class module* events fire when you open or close an instance of a class. You use the `With Events` qualifier to intercept events from ActiveX Data Objects (ADO) and the `RaiseEvent` command to define custom events.
- *Reference events* fire when you add or remove a reference to an object or type library in the `References` collection.

Table 28.1 groups Access 2003's events according to their source.

TABLE 28.1 EVENTS GROUPED BY CAUSE

Event Category	Source	Events

Mouse	The user creating mouse actions	`Click`
		`DblClick`
		`MouseDown`
		`MouseUp`
		`MouseMove`
		`MouseWheel`

Keyboard	The user typing on the keyboard or `SendKeys` sending keystrokes	`KeyDown`
		`KeyUp`
		`KeyPress`

Window	Opening, closing, or resizing a window	`Open`
		`Load`
		`Unload`
		`Close`
		`Resize`

28

continues

TABLE 28.1 CONTINUED

Event Category	Source	Events

Focus	An object losing or gaining the focus, or a form or report becoming active or inactive	`Enter`
		`GotFocus`
		`Exit`
		`LostFocus`
		`Activate`
		`Deactivate`

Data	Making changes to a control's data, displaying records in a form, or moving the focus from one record to another in a form	`Current`
		`BeforeInsert`
		`AfterInsert`
		`Delete`
		`BeforeDelConfirm`
		`AfterDelConfirm`
		`BeforeUpdate`
		`AfterUpdate`
		`Change`
		`Updated`
		`Dirty`
		`NotInList`
		`Undo*`

Filter	Opening or closing a filter window, or applying or removing a filter	`Filter` `ApplyFilter`

Print	Selecting or arranging data for printing	`Format`
		`Print`
		`Retreat`
		`NoData`
		`Page`

Error	Generating an error	`Error`
Timing	A specified period of time expiring	`Timer`
Class Module	Opening a new instance of *class module* or terminating an instance of *class module*	`Initialize` `Terminate`
Reference	Adding or removing a reference to an object or type library	`ItemAdded` `ItemRemoved`

28

Access 2000 added the `Dirty` event (and `Dirty` property) of bound forms. The `Dirty` event fires and the `Dirty` property is set to `True` when you change underlying data by typing in a bound text box or combo box, or change a page by clicking a Tab control. The `Dirty` event doesn't fire if you change a value with code, nor does it fire for any action on an unbound form. Moving the mouse wheel repeatedly triggers Access 2003's `MouseWheel` event. The `Undo` event is the reverse of the `Dirty` event; returning data in the form to its original, unmodified state fires the `Undo` event.

Each event that an object triggers has a corresponding event property listed in a separate category of the object's property sheet. Usually the corresponding event property is the event name preceded by the word "On"; for example, the `Click` event triggered by a command button becomes the On Click property in the button's property sheet. Figure 28.19 shows the Event page of the property sheet for a text box displaying the 17 events that the text box control can trigger. Notice that all event properties—except the Before Update and After Update data event properties—follow the pattern of preceding the event name with "On". Access 2002 added the On Dirty and On Undo events for controls.

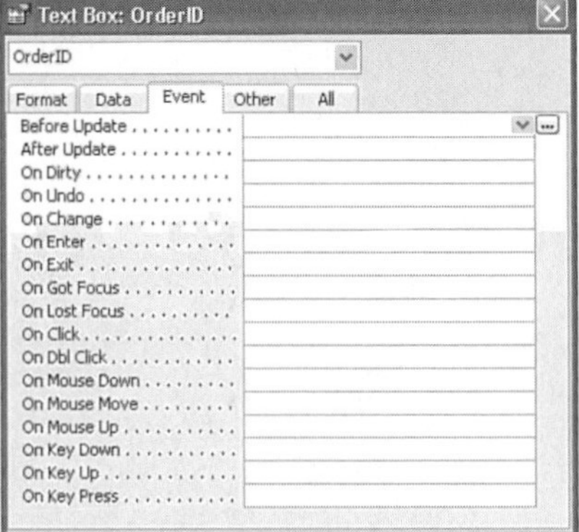

Figure 28.19 Text boxes fire 17 events. Access 2002 added the On Dirty and On Undo events to bound controls. The On MouseWheel event doesn't apply to text boxes.

NOTE

Events for PivotCharts and PivotTables arrived with Access 2002. These 17 new events appear at the end of the Events page of the Form properties window, and apply only to PivotChart and PivotTable views. Two of the events, On Connect and On Disconnect, retain the "On" prefix in their event handler names, `OnConnect` and `OnDisconnect`, which is inconsistent with other events.

Working with Access 2003's DoCmd Methods

Some of the `DoCmd` methods duplicate menu commands, such as Print, Close, and Apply Filter/Sort. Other methods substitute for mouse actions. For example, you can use the `SelectObject` method to select a database object in the same way that you select an open window by clicking it or select a database object in the Database window by clicking the object's name. Other `DoCmd` methods provide capabilities that aren't available through menu commands, such as `Beep`, which emits a beep sound, or `MsgBox`, which displays a custom message. It's a better practice, however, to execute **Beep** and **MsgBox** directly with VBA statements.

DoCmd METHODS BY TASK

Table 28.2 lists available DoCmd methods grouped by task. Access 2.0 provided 47 macro actions; Access 95 added 2 new DoCmd methods: Save and SetMenuItem. Access 2000 replaced the DoMenuItem action or method with the RunCommand method, which lets you execute any native menu choice or standard toolbar button. The AddMenu item in the Method column of Table 28.2 is an Access 95 and earlier macro action; it's not a method of the DoCmd object and can't be executed from Access VBA code.

TABLE 28.2 DoCmd METHODS GROUPED BY TASK

Task by Category	Method
Manipulating	
Copy or rename a database object	CopyObject, Rename
Delete a database object	DeleteObject
Open a table, query, form, report, module	OpenTable, OpenQuery, OpenForm, OpenReport, OpenModule
Open one of the new Access objects	OpenDataAccessPage OpenDiagram OpenStoredProcedure OpenView
Close a database object	Close
Save a database object	Save
Print the current database object	PrintOut,
Select a database window object	SelectObject
Copy or rename an object	CopyObject, Rename
Update data or update the screen	RepaintObject, Requery, ShowAllRecords
Set the value of a field, control, or property	SetValue
Executing	
Carry out a menu command	RunCommand
Run a query	OpenQuery, RunSQL

28

Task by Category	Method
Executing	
Run a macro or a VBA procedure	RunMacro, RunCode
Run another Windows or DOS application	RunApp
Stop execution of a macro	StopMacro, StopAllMacros
Stop execution of Access	Quit
Stop execution following an event	CancelEvent
Working with Data in Forms and Reports	
Select or sort records	ApplyFilter
Find a record	FindRecord, FindNext
Move to a particular location	GoToControl, GoToRecord, GoToPage
Importing and Exporting Data	
Output data from a table, query, exporting data form, report, or module in .xls, .rtf, or .txt formats	OutputAs
Include in an email message data from a table, query, form, report, or module in .xls, .rtf, or .txt format	SendObject
Transfer data between Access and other data formats	TransferDatabase, TransferSpreadsheet, TransferText, TransferSQLDatabase, CopyDatabaseFile
Miscellaneous	
Create a custom menubar	AddMenu, SetMenuItem
Sound a beep	Beep
Display or hide a toolbar	ShowToolbar
Send keystrokes to Access or a Windows application	SendKeys
Display an hourglass	Hourglass
Display or hide system information	Echo, SetWarnings
Display custom messages	MsgBox

NOTE

> Methods applicable to macros—such as `RunMacro`, `RunCode`, `StopMacro`, and `StopAllMacros`—are obsolete in Access 2003; these `DoCmd` methods are included for backward compatibility only.

ARGUMENTS OF DoCmd METHODS

Most `DoCmd` methods require additional information as arguments to specify how the method works. For example, when you use the `OpenForm` method, you must specify the name of the form to open as the `strFormName` argument. Also, to specify whether you want to display the Form, Design, Print Preview, or Datasheet view, you must use the `intView` argument. To specify whether you want to allow editing or adding new records, you must use the `intDataMode` argument. Finally, to specify whether you want the form to be hidden, behave like a dialog, or be in normal mode, you must use the `intWindowMode` argument. You specify the values of arguments of the `Integer` data type by substituting Access intrinsic constants, which use the `ac` prefix, as in

```
DoCmd.OpenForm strFormName, acNormal, strFilterName, strCriterion, acEdit,
acDialog, strOpenArg
```

The `acNormal`, `acEdit`, and `acDialog` argument values are Access intrinsic constant values for the `int`*`View`*, `int`*`DataMode`*, and `int`*`WindowMode`* arguments, respectively. You can also specify the numeric value of the constant, but there's no guarantee that the numeric values of Access 2003 constants will remain the same in future versions of Access. Thus, using the names of Access intrinsic constants is better programming practice than supplying numeric values for method arguments. When you type `DoCmd` in the Visual Basic Editor, the statement auto-completion feature lists the Access constants that are applicable to each argument of the method.

The `DoCmd.RunCommand` method lets you execute any Access menu choice. The method requires a single `acCmd`*`MenuChoiceName`* Access command constant argument, such as `acCmdApplyFilterSort`, to specify the action to perform. To see the list (called an *enumeration* or *enum*) of all command-related constants, select acCommand in Object Browser's Classes list.

The `OutputTo`, `TransferDatabase`, `TransferSpreadsheet`, and `TransferText` methods deserve special attention by application developers. These bulk transfer methods greatly simplify the data interchange between Access and other Office 2003 applications, such as Excel and Word. The more complex `DoCmd` methods, together with Access 2003's flexible report generation capabilities, are often the deciding factor when choosing between Visual Basic 6+ or Access 2003 for developing database front ends. Visual Basic doesn't offer equivalents of the bulk transfer Access methods.

The new `TransferSQLDatabase` and `CopyDatabaseFile` methods only apply to ADP and SQL Server databases.

Customizing Applications with CommandBar Objects

Office 2003 applications use CommandBar objects to create menubars, pop-up menus, toolbar buttons, and toolbar combo boxes. To gain VBA programming access to CommandBar objects, your database must include a reference to the Microsoft Office 11.0 Object Library, Mso11.dll. Northwind.mdb includes a reference to Mso11.dll. If it's missing from your VBA project, choose Tools, References, scroll to the Microsoft Office 11.0 Object Library entry, and mark the check box (see Figure 28.20).

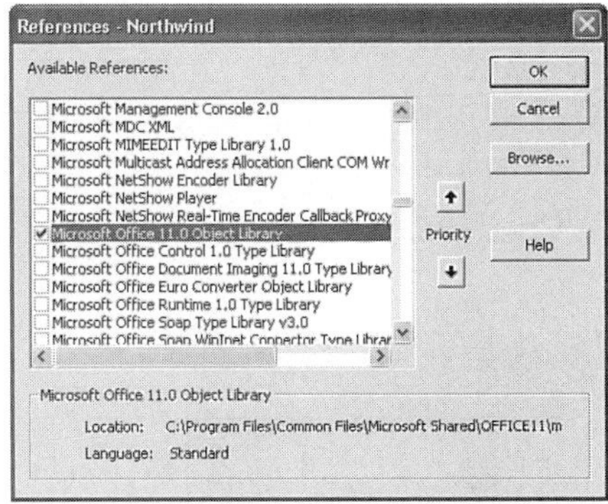

Figure 28.20 Add a reference to Mso11.dll to enable use of the CommandBar object in your VBA project.

Mso11.dll includes other objects that are common to Office 2003, such as the Balloon object of the Office Assistant object and the DocumentProperty object for files. Figure 28.21 shows the Microsoft Office Objects help topic that displays some of the collections and objects exposed by Mso11.dll, which differ considerably from the Office 2000 model. (Type **Microsoft Office Objects** in the Visual Basic Editor's Ask a Question box and click the Microsoft Office Objects link to display the help topic.)

With a reference to Mso11.dll, Office 2003 object classes appear in Object Browser's window when you select the Office library (see Figure 28.22). Selecting a class or member of the class and then clicking Object Browser's Help (?) button displays the Microsoft Office Visual Basic Help topic for most selections. Using Object Browser's Help button is the easiest way to obtain the VBA syntax for programming specific Office objects.

The Immediate window is useful for gaining familiarity with programming Office objects. Figure 28.23 shows how to obtain property values of the CommandBars collection, CommandBar objects, and the Control objects of CommandBars. The Access 2003 version of Northwind.mdb has 178 CommandBars, an increase from 173 in Access 2002, 141 in Access 2000, and 104 in Access 97. Unlike most other Access collections that begin with an index value of 0, the first member of Office collections has an index value of 1. The first CommandBar of Office XP members is the TaskPane. The Application preface in the first statement of Figure 28.23 is optional; the Application object is assumed when referring to top-level Access objects.

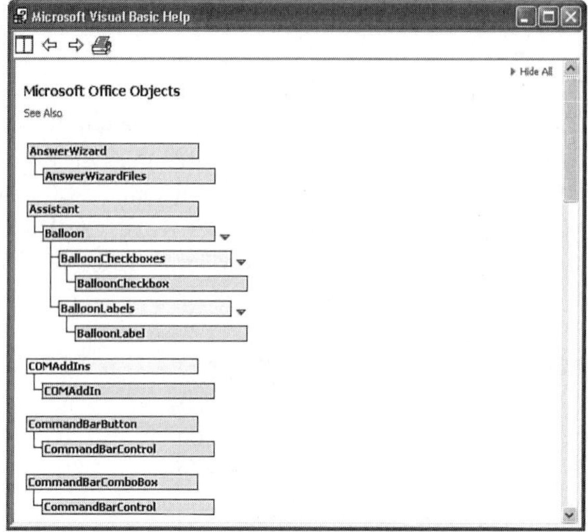

Figure 28.21
The Office 2003 object model includes objects for all Office members, such as the `OfficeDataSourceObject`. The `CommandBars` collection is missing from the Help topic, but it appears in Object Browser.

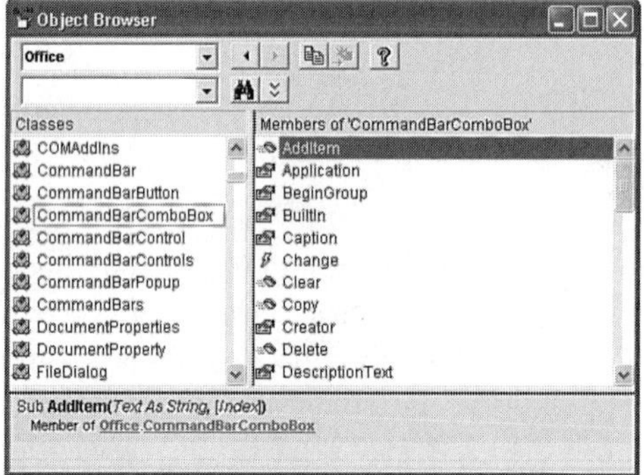

Figure 28.22
Adding a reference to Mso11.dll adds an Office entry to Object Browser's Project/Library list. Office classes include application objects common to Office 2003 members.

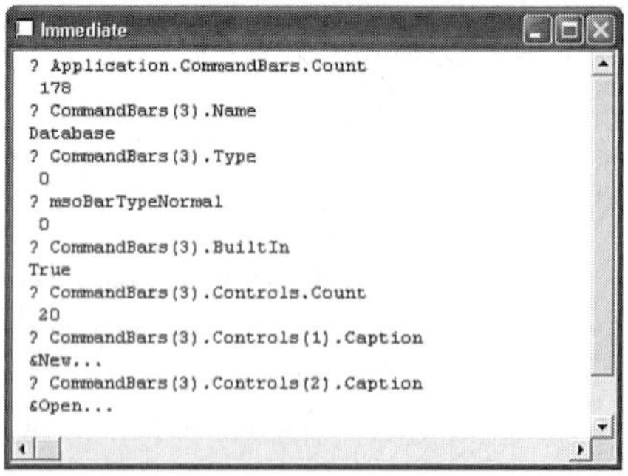

```
Immediate
? Application.CommandBars.Count
 178
? CommandBars(3).Name
Database
? CommandBars(3).Type
 0
? msoBarTypeNormal
 0
? CommandBars(3).BuiltIn
True
? CommandBars(3).Controls.Count
 20
? CommandBars(3).Controls(1).Caption
&New...
? CommandBars(3).Controls(2).Caption
&Open...
```

Figure 28.23
The Immediate window lets you explore the properties of Access 2003's built-in toolbars and menu bars. The second `CommandBar` is the toolbar that appears when the Database window has the focus.

NOTE

The Northwind.mdb database of Access 2000 and earlier specified a custom menu bar (NorthwindCustomMenuBar), which added a Show Me command to the main menu. Access 2003 dispenses with the custom menubar and it's associated help topic.

TIP

To view the members of the Access `Application` class, open the Access library in Object Browser and select Application in the Classes list.

The following simple VBA subprocedure, added to a temporary new module, Module1, iterates the `CommandBars` collection and prints the `Name` and `Visible` property values of each `CommandBar` in the Immediate window:

```
Sub PrintCommandBars()
   Dim msoBar As CommandBar
   For Each msoBar In CommandBars
      Debug.Print msoBar.Name, msoBar.Visible
   Next msoBar
End Sub
```

Figure 28.24 shows the preceding subprocedure and the first 15 built-in `CommandBars` of Access 2003.

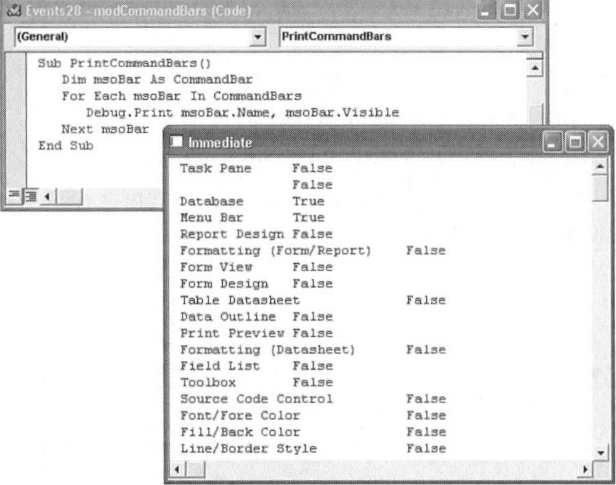

Figure 28.24 The Immediate window displays the `Name` and `Visible` property values of the built-in `CommandBar` objects.

You add a new `CommandBar` object by applying the `Add` method to the `CommandBars` collection, setting the properties of the new `CommandBar` object, and adding members to the `CommandBar` object's `Controls` collection. For example, the code in Listing 28.2 adds a command button to the Form View command bar when you open the frmCommandWiz form of the Events28.mdb sample database.

LISTING 28.2 ADD A COMMAND BUTTON AS A MEMBER OF THE Controls COLLECTION OF THE FORM VIEW CommandBar OBJECT

```
Private Sub Form_Load()
   'Add a button that opens the Customers form to the
   'Form View toolbar at the right of the View menu
   Dim cmbFormView As CommandBar
   Dim cbcCustData As CommandBarControl
   Dim intCtr As Integer

   'Create the CommandBar object
   Set cmbFormView = CommandBars("Form View")

   'Test to see if the button exists
   For intCtr = 1 To cmbFormView.Controls.Count
      Set cbcCustData = cmbFormView.Controls(intCtr)
      If cbcCustData.Caption = "Customer Data" Then
         'The control already exists, don't add another
         Exit Sub
      End If
   Next intCtr

   'If the button isn't present, add it in position 2
   Set cbcCustData = cmbFormView.Controls.Add(msoControlButton, , , 2)
   With cbcCustData
      .Caption = "Customer Data"
      .FaceId = 209
      .OnAction = "=DisplayCustomerData"
      .TooltipText = "Click to display customer data"
   End With
End Sub
```

The `OnAction` property of the cbcCustData command button calls the `DisplayCustomerData` function, which must have **`Public`** scope. The code of the `DisplayCustomerData` function is identical to that of the `subDisplayCustomerData_Click` subprocedure, which is described in the earlier "Adding a Button to Display a Specific Record on Another Form" section. Figure 28.25 shows the new button added to the right of the View button with its ToolTip activated.

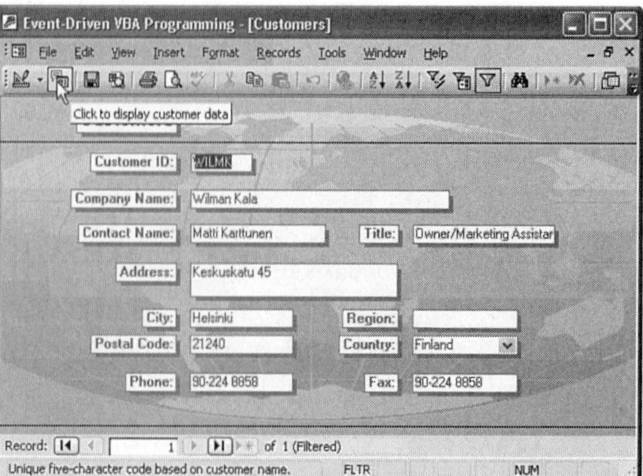

Figure 28.25 Clicking the added command button of the Form View toolbar performs the same task as clicking the Display Customer Data button of frmCommandWiz.

TIP

> To remove the added button from the Form View toolbar, choose View, Toolbars, Customize, drag the button off the command bar, and drop it anywhere.

A full exposition of VBA programming of custom `CommandBar` objects is beyond the scope of this book. Most of the developer-level books for Access 2003 listed in the "Bibliography" section of the Introduction to this book cover custom `CommandBar` programming in detail.

Specifying Database Startup Properties

The Startup dialog lets you assign an application title to the database, specify a form to open when the application starts, and specify the name of a custom `CommandBar` as Access's main menubar. To set Startup properties, follow these steps:

1. Make the Database window active and choose Tools, Startup to open the Startup dialog.
2. Type a name for your application in the Application Title text box; the application name replaces Access's default title bar caption. If you have a special icon file (*Filename*.ico), you can specify the icon file in the Application Icon text box.
3. If you've created a custom `CommandBar` for your application, select the `CommandBar` in the drop-down Menu Bar list.
4. Open the Display Form/Page list and select the form that you want to appear when you open the database (see Figure 28.26). You can elect to hide the Database window and the status bar by clearing the Display Database Window and Display Status Bar check boxes.

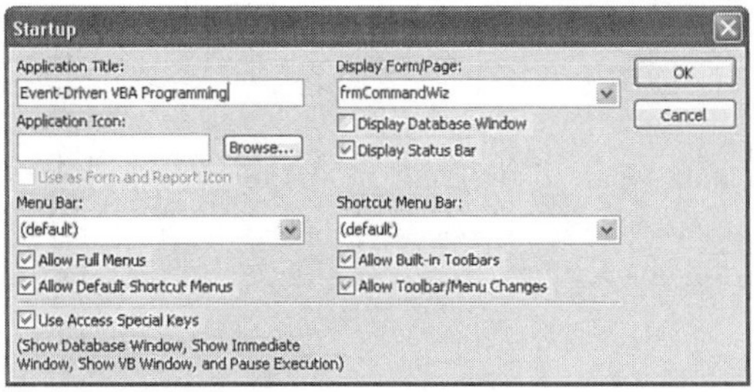

Figure 28.26
The Startup dialog lets you customize behavior of your application when it opens. The settings shown here are applied to the Events28.mdb sample application.

5. The remaining check boxes let you limit use of your application's menubars, shortcut menus, and toolbars. You can also disable Access's special key combinations.

TIP

> Don't clear any of the Startup dialog's check boxes until you're ready to release your application to users. Limiting Access's built-in menu, toolbar, and code-viewing feature set is likely to impede your development activities.

6. Click OK to assign the changes you made and close the Startup dialog.

REFERRING TO ACCESS OBJECTS WITH VBA

One of the reasons for occasional use of the term *Access VBA* in this book is that Access defines its own set of objects and uses specialized VBA syntax to refer to many Access objects. Although `Form` objects are common to most Office 2000+ members as well as Visual Basic, a subform (a form embedded in a form) is unique to Access. You find `Report` objects and subreports only in Access. The syntax for referring to a subform or subreport and for referring to controls contained in a subform or subreport is unique to Access. Even if you're an experienced Visual Basic programmer, you must become acquainted with the object reference syntax to write VBA code and refer to objects that are unique to Access.

REFERRING TO OPEN FORMS OR REPORTS AND THEIR PROPERTIES

You can refer to a form or report only if it's open. Access uses the `Forms` and `Reports` collections to keep track of which forms and reports are open. The `Forms` collection is the set of open forms, and the `Reports` collection is the set of open reports. Because Access lets you use the same name for a form and a report, you must distinguish between the two by specifying the collection. The syntax for the reference is the collection name followed by the exclamation point operator (`!`), more commonly called the bang operator, and the name of the form or report:

```
Forms![Form Name]
Reports![Report Name]
```

Use the bang operator (`!`) to separate the collection name from the name of an object in the collection. You need to use the square brackets (`[...]`) to enclose object names that include spaces or other punctuation that's illegal in VBA statements or object names that duplicate VBA reserved words.

A `Form` or `Report` object has properties that define its characteristics. The general syntax for referring to a property is the object name followed by the dot (.) operator and the name of the property:

```
Forms![Form Name].PropertyName
Reports![Report Name].PropertyName
```

Use the dot operator to separate the object's name from the name of one of its properties. For example, `Forms!frmProducts.RecordSource` refers to the `RecordSource` property of the open `frmProducts` form. You can get or set the value of the `RecordSource` property with the following two VBA statements:

```
strSource = Forms!frmProducts.RecordSource
Forms!frmProducts.RecordSource = strSource
```

If you add the `.Value` qualifier to RecordSource, you receive an "Invalid Qualifier" error.

To get or set the value of a form property in the form's own *class module*, you use the **`Me`** self-identifier, as in:

```
strSource = Me.RecordSource
Me.RecordSource = strSource
```

The **`Me`** self-reference is valid only for the instance of the form open in Form view. Thus, you can't use the two preceding statements in the Immediate window unless you create a breakpoint in your code, open the form in Form view, and then execute the procedure that contains the breakpoint. Figure 28.27 shows the Immediate window opened by a breakpoint and set at the first active line of code of the `ReviewProducts_Click` subprocedure of Northwind.mdb's Suppliers form. In Break mode, typing **? Me.RecordSource** returns Suppliers—the name of the table to which the Suppliers form is bound. If you press F8 repeatedly to step through the code, after you pass the `DoCmd.OpenForm...` statement for the Product List form, you can use the `Forms!...` syntax described in the next section to test the property values of control objects on the Product List form.

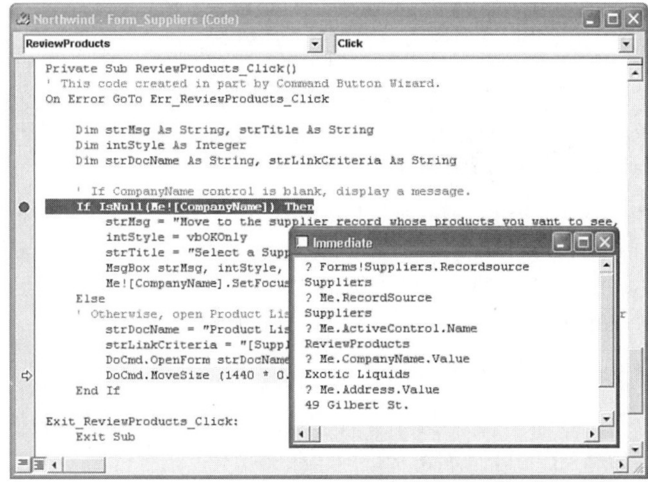

Figure 28.27 When VBA code execution reaches the breakpoint line, the VBA editor window opens in break mode with the breakpoint instruction highlighted. Pressing F5 continues code execution and returns the focus to the currently open form.

→ For detailed instructions on using breakpoints, **see** "Adding a Breakpoint to the `IsLoaded` Function," **p. 1183**.

A form's properties window lists the form properties that you can set in Design view. Forms also have properties that you can't set in Design view and that don't appear in the property window, such as the default `Form` property. The `Form` property refers to the collection of controls on a form. Similarly, a report's default `Report` property refers to the collection of controls in a report.

REFERRING TO CONTROLS AND THEIR PROPERTIES

The following is the general syntax for referring to a control on a form or report:

```
Forms![FormName].Form![ControlName]
```

```
Reports![ReportName].Report![ControlName]
```

As before, the bang operator separates the collection name from the object name. The `Form` property is the default property that Access assumes for a form; therefore, you need not include the `Form` property explicitly in the reference.

The following expression is the short-form identifier syntax for a form control:

```
Forms![FormName]![ControlName]
```

Similarly, the following is the full identifier syntax for a report control:

```
Reports![ReportName]![ControlName]
```

For example, `Forms!frmProducts!ProductName` refers to the `ProductName` control on the open `frmProducts` form.

The syntax for referring to a control's property value includes the reference to the control, followed by the dot operator, and then followed by the property name:

```
Forms![FormName]![ControlName].[PropertyName]
```

```
Reports![ReportName]![ControlName].[PropertyName]
```

For example, `Forms!frmProducts!ProductName.Visible` refers to the value of the `ProductName` control's `Visible` property.

A control also has a default property. The default property of a text box is the `Text` property. To refer to the value in the `ProductName` text box control in the last example, you could use any of the following equivalent references:

```
Forms!frmProducts.Form!ProductName.Text
```

```
Forms!frmProducts!ProductName.Text
```

```
Forms!frmProducts.Form!ProductName
```

```
Forms!frmProducts!ProductName
```

28

NOTE

> Notice that the last two expressions refer both to the control's text value and to the control itself. The `.Text` qualifier isn't required, but adding the name of the default property is a good programming practice and complies with VBA.NET programming rules.

When you refer to a control on the active form or report, you can use a shorter version of the reference and refer to the control as follows:

```
[ControlName]
```

Likewise, you can refer to the control property as follows:

```
[ControlName].PropertyName
```

Normally, you can use either the short or full syntax to refer to a control on the active form or report. However, in some cases, you must use the short syntax. For example, the `GoToControl` action's `ControlName` argument requires the short syntax. You can explicitly refer to a control on the form of the *class module* with **`Me`**`!ControlName` statements. When you refer to a control on a form or report that's not the active object, you usually must use the full identifier syntax.

REFERRING TO CONTROLS ON A SUBFORM OR THE MAIN FORM

The key to understanding the syntax for referring to a control on a subform is to realize that the subform is a form that's bound to a subform control on the main form. The subform control has the usual attribute properties that control its display behavior, such as size and visibility, as well as linking properties that relate the records in the subform to records in the form, including the `SourceObject`, `LinkChildFields`, and `LinkMasterFields` properties. In addition, the subform control has the `Form` property. A subform control's `Form` property refers to the controls contained on the subform.

The following is the syntax for referring to the subform control:

```
Forms![FormName]![SubformControlName]
```

The syntax for referring to a control on a subform bound to a subform control is as follows:

```
Forms![FormName]![SubformControlName]![ControlName].PropertyName
```

When the form is active, the following short syntax refers to a control on a subform of the active form:

```
[SubformControlName]![ControlName]
```

The `Form` property of the subform, required in Access 95 and earlier when referring to controls on a subform, now is the subform control's default property, so you don't need to include it in the reference. Normally, you use the subform's name as the name of the subform control. For example, if `sbfSuppliers` is the name of a form bound to a subform control also named `sbfSuppliers` on the `frmProducts` form, the following is the full syntax for referring to the `SupplierName` control on the subform:

```
Forms!frmProducts!sbfSuppliers[.Form]!SupplierName
```

28

The short syntax is as follows:

```
sbfSuppliers[.Form]!SupplierName
```

When the focus is in a subform's control, you can refer to a control on the main form by using the control's `Parent` property. The `Parent` property refers to the collection of controls on the main form. In the previous example, to refer to the `ProductName` control on the main form from VBA code in the *class module* of a subform, use the following syntax:

```
Parent!ProductName
```

All the preceding syntax examples in this section apply to reports and subreports; just change `Forms` to `Reports` and `Form` to `Report`.

Using Alternative Collection Syntax

An alternative to the *`CollectionName!ObjectName`* syntax is to specify *`CollectionName`* and supply *`ObjectName`* as an argument value:

```
Forms("frmProducts")!sbfSuppliers!SupplierName
```

The advantage of the argument method is that you can substitute a `String` variable for the literal argument value:

```
Forms(strFormName)!sbfSuppliers!SupplierName
```

You also can pass a 0-based `Long` value to specify the ordinal (position) of the object in the collection:

```
Forms(2)!sbfSuppliers!SupplierName
```

Passing the ordinal value, however, isn't a safe programming practice because the ordinal position of objects in a collection change as you add or delete members.

Responding to Data Events Triggered by Forms and Controls

`Recordsets` underlying forms and reports trigger data events when you move the record pointer or change the value in one or more cells of the `Recordset`. The two most important of these events are `BeforeUpdate` and `OnCurrent`. The following two sections illustrate use of these two data-related events of bound forms.

Validating Data Entry in a `BeforeUpdate` Event Handler

The most common use of data events is to validate updates to the `Recordset`; you add validation code to the event-handling subprocedure for the `BeforeUpdate` event. The use of code, instead of setting field-level or table-level `ValidationRule` property values, is that VBA provides a much more flexible method of ensuring data consistency. Validation rules you write in VBA commonly are called business rules. Business rules often are quite complex and require access to multiple lookup tables—some of which might be located in other databases.

28

→ For information on enforcing business rules, see "Validating Data Entry," **p. 227**.

Listing 28.3 shows an example of a set of validation rules for postal codes in the Suppliers table of Northwind.mdb, the `Recordset` of which is bound to the Suppliers form. The

BeforeUpdate event, which triggers before a change is made to the Recordset, includes a predefined Cancel argument. If you set Cancel = **True** in your event-handling code, the proposed update to the Recordset doesn't occur.

LISTING 28.3 A VBA VALIDATION SUBPROCEDURE FOR SOME INTERNATIONAL POSTAL CODES

```
Private Sub Form_BeforeUpdate(Cancel As Integer)
' If number of digits entered in PostalCode text box is
' incorrect for value in Country text box, display message
' and undo PostalCode value.

   Select Case Me!Country
      Case IsNull(Me![Country])
         Exit Sub
      Case "France", "Italy", "Spain"
         If Len(Me![PostalCode]) <> 5 Then
            MsgBox "Postal Code must be 5 characters", 0, _
               "Postal Code Error"
            Cancel = True
            Me![PostalCode].SetFocus
         End If
      Case "Australia", "Singapore"
         If Len(Me![PostalCode]) <> 4 Then
            MsgBox "Postal Code must be 4 characters", 0, _
               "Postal Code Error"
            Cancel = True
            Me![PostalCode].SetFocus
         End If
      Case "Canada"
         If Not Me![PostalCode] Like _
            "[A-Z][0-9][A-Z] [0-9][A-Z][0-9]" Then
            MsgBox "Postal Code not valid. " & _
               "Example of Canadian code: H1J 1C3", _
               0, "Postal Code Error"
            Cancel = True
            Me![PostalCode].SetFocus
         End If
   End Select
End Sub
```

USING THE ON CURRENT EVENT TO SET LINKED PIVOTCHART PROPERTIES

The "Persisting Linked PivotChart Properties with VBA Code" section of Chapter 18 describes the need to update formatting and other PivotChart properties when moving to a new record in the Recordset that supplies values for linked graphs. The code required to set the properties must execute each time you use the navigation buttons to change the current record. The On Current event fires immediately after a new record becomes the current record, so the VBA code is contained in the **Private Sub** Form_Current event handler of the frm1997SalesPCLinked form of the Charts18.mdb sample database.

→ To review how to create linked PivotChart graphs, **see** "Working with PivotChart Forms," **p. 726**.

`Form_Current`'s code illustrates the use of `Forms!...` references to objects in subforms, sbf1997SalesPCLinked for this example. The sbf1997SalesPCLinked form contains only a PivotChart and is restricted to PivotChart view. Although you can use VBA code to create a PivotChart from scratch, using the Office Web Components (OWC) 11 design tools grafted to Access 2003's Form View toolbar is *much* easier.

ADDING A REFERENCE TO THE MICROSOFT OFFICE XP WEB CONTROLS

Gaining programmatic access to OWC requires adding a VBA reference to OWC11.dll manually. Versions 10.0 and 11.0 of the PivotChart, PivotTable, Spreadsheet, Data Source, Expand, and Record Navigation controls—both of which are provided by OWC11.dll—appear individually in Access 2003's Insert ActiveX Control list. Adding an individual Web control to a form and then adding a reference to OWC10.dll can cause conflicts.

TIP

> **Adding a PivotChart (or any other OWC) control to a form from the Insert Object dialog adds a reference to the individual control, so you don't need to add a reference to OWC11.dll.**

To add the required reference to OWC11.dll and explore PivotChart objects in Object Browser, do the following:

1. Open the form in which you intend to write event-handling code for a PivotChart (or PivotTable) in Form Design view or select the form in the Database window and click the Code button to open the VBA editor.
2. Choose Tools, References to open the References dialog, which doesn't contain a reference to the Microsoft Office Web Components 11.0 in the Available References list.
3. Click the Browse button to open the Add Reference dialog, navigate to the \Program Files\Common Files\Microsoft Shared\Web Components\11 folder, and click to select OWC10.dll (see Figure 28.28).

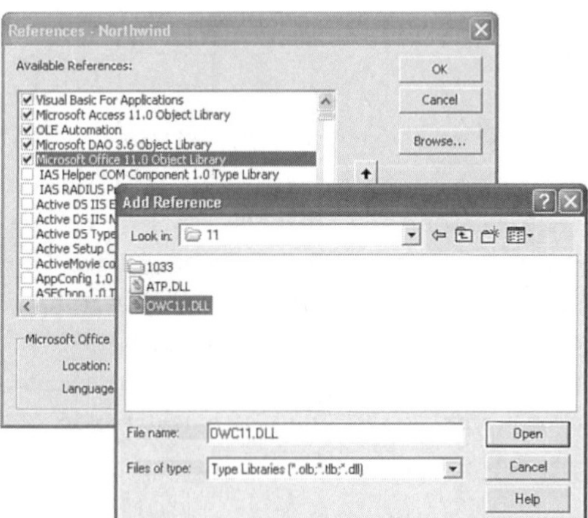

Figure 28.28
The VBA editor's References dialog doesn't include Microsoft Office Web Components 11.0 in the Available References list, so you must add the reference to OWC11.dll manually.

28

4. Click Open to add the Microsoft Office Web Components 11.0 reference to the end of the Available References list (see Figure 28.29). Verify that the new reference's check box is marked, and click OK to close the dialog and add the reference to your VBA project.

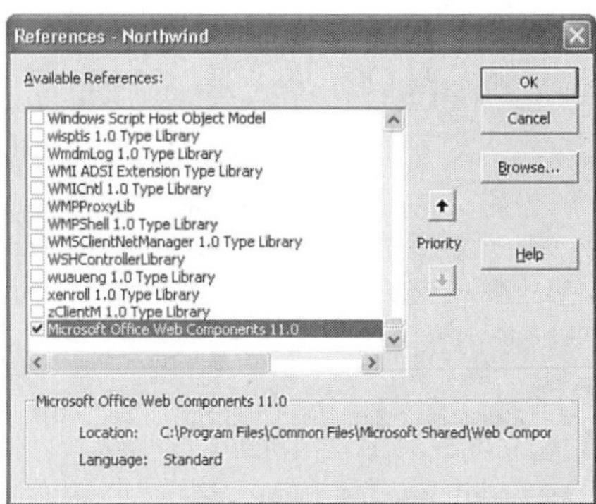

Figure 28.29 Manually adding a reference to an object (.olb), type (.tlb), or dynamic link (.dll) library file adds the reference to the bottom of the Available References list and enables the reference.

5. Press F2 to open Object Browser, and select OWC11 in the Project/Library list. Scroll to the PivotChart objects, which have names with a `Ch...` prefix (see Figure 28.30).

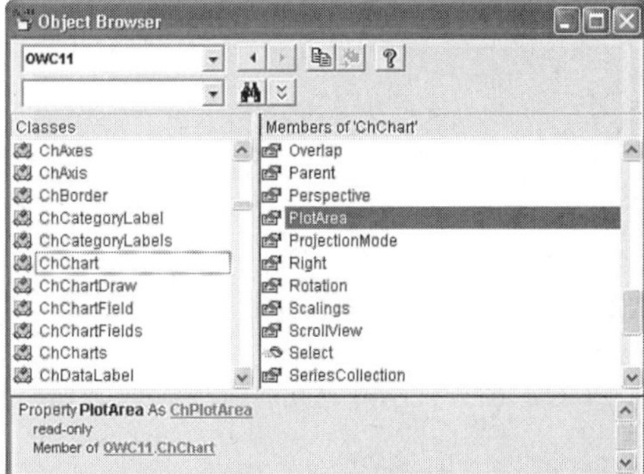

Figure 28.30 Object Browser's Classes list for the OWC11 library displays all objects exposed by OWC11.dll. PivotChart objects begin with `Ch...`. PivotTable objects have a `Pivot...` prefix.

6. To obtain programming help for PivotChart objects and their properties and methods, select the object in the Classes list and click the Help (?) button to open the VBA help topic for the object (see Figure 28.31). Many topics have simple VBA programming examples for the object.

Writing VBA Code to Apply Non-Persistent Property Values to Charts

After you've created a reference to OWC11.dll, you declare `ChartSpace` (all charts or graphs), `ChChart` (the current graph), `ChSeries` (the graph's line), and if your graph includes a trend line, `ChTrendline` object variables. The `Form_Current` event handler begins with a series of **`Set`** statements to create a pointer to each of these objects when you move to a new record (see Listing 28.4). The remaining `Form_Current` code sets custom property values of the `ChChart`, `ChSeries`, and `ChTrendline` objects. You can modify the code of Listing 28.4 to apply special properties to any line chart, not just linked charts. If your line chart isn't linked, change the subprocedure name to `Form_Load` to apply the property values when the form opens.

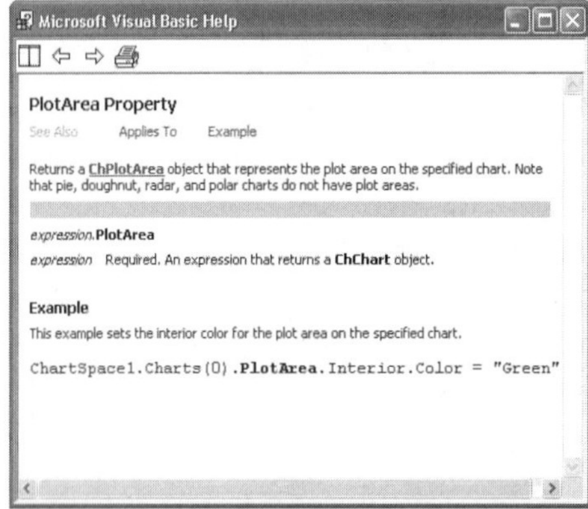

Figure 28.31 Click the Help button of the Object Browser to display the help topic for a Web component.

Listing 28.4 VBA Code to Set Non-Persistent Properties of Linked PivotCharts

```
Option Compare Database
Option Explicit

'Declare the required OWC object variables for PivotCharts
Private chtSpace As OWC11.ChartSpace
Private chtChart As OWC11.ChChart
Private chtSeries As OWC11.ChSeries
Private chtTrendLine As OWC11.ChTrendline

Private Sub Form_Current()
   'Update non-persistent linked PivotChart properties

   'Specify the subform's ChartSpace object
   Set chtSpace = Me.sbf1997SalesPivotChart.Form.ChartSpace
   'Specify the first (and only) chart in the Charts collection
   Set chtChart = chtSpace.Charts(0)
   'Specify the first (and only) series for the line graph
   Set chtSeries = chtChart.SeriesCollection(0)

   'Change the number format to remove the decimal digits
   chtChart.Axes(1).NumberFormat = "$#,##0"

   'Maintain the scale for all graphs
   chtChart.Scalings(chDimValues).Maximum = 25000
   chtChart.Scalings(chDimValues).Minimum = 0

   'Set the line weight to thick
   chtSeries.Line.Weight = owcLineWeightThick
```

28

```
    'If there are no trend lines, add one
    If chtSeries.Trendlines.Count = 0 Then
       Set chtTrendLine = chtSeries.Trendlines.Add()
    Else
       'The first graph has a trend line
       Set chtTrendLine = chtSeries.Trendlines(0)
    End If
    With chtTrendLine
       'Hide the equation and RSquared values
       .IsDisplayingEquation = False
       .IsDisplayingRSquared = False
       'Change the color and weight
       .Line.Color = "Red"
       .Line.Weight = owcLineWeightThick
    End With
End Sub
```

TROUBLESHOOTING

CALLING PROCEDURES AND FUNCTIONS IN CLASS MODULES

After adding test code to a form class module, I encounter a "Compile Error - Sub or Function not defined" error message when running the code from the Immediate window.

To execute subprocedures or functions in *class modules* from the Immediate window, you must preface the name of the subprocedure or function with the name of the *class module*. For example, if you add the `PrintCommandBars` function to the Main Switchboard form's *class module*, and type `PrintCommandBars` in the Immediate window, you get the error message. You must preface the command with the *class module* name, as in `[Form_Main Switchboard].PrintCommandBars`. (Add the square brackets only if the form name contains a space.) You also must add the class name prefix when calling with code subprocedures or functions from another *class module* or conventional module. You don't need to add the form name prefix to call public functions in conventional modules.

MISSING OBJECTS IN COLLECTIONS

"Object not found in this collection" errors occur with explicit object names or values passed as argument values.

You misspelled the object name or failed to assign a value to an argument variable. To check the names of objects, especially those with long or convoluted names, type **?** ***CollectionName*(0)** in the Immediate window to return the name of the first collection. If you receive an error or don't obtain the expected name, replace 0 with increasing values.

IN THE REAL WORLD—DEALING WITH EVENT-DRIVEN PROGRAMMING

Beginning programmers and Web page designers often find that understanding Windows' event-driven programming model to be quite difficult. The same problem befalls many programmers experienced in conventional procedural languages, such as assembly, COBOL, Pascal, and xBase. With a very few exceptions, VBA code in an Access application or script in a DHTML page executes only in response to a predefined event. (The primary exceptions are variable and Windows function prototype declarations that precede VBA subprocedure and function code in modules.)

The first Office data object model that fired events was Access 97's ODBCDirect, an object wrapper over Visual Basic 4.0 Enterprise Edition's Remote Data Object (RDO) 1.0. Being able to intercept data-related events, such as when making a connection or starting and ending query execution, enables you to handle connection errors and asynchronous data operations. An asynchronous data operation is one in which control returns to your program after query execution starts. When the query completes, the corresponding event lets you write code to process the resulting `Recordset`. Your application isn't in a state of suspended animation while waiting for a "query from hell" to complete.

OLE DB and ActiveX Data Objects (ADO), however, provide a much richer (more granular) event model than ODBCDirect, as demonstrated by the event-related sections of Chapter 30, "Understanding Universal Data Access, OLE DB, and ADO." For optimum front-end VBA programming simplicity and flexibility, it's hard to beat ADO's event model. The .NET Framework's ADO.NET replacement for COM-based ADO, which emphasizes XML representation of `DataTable` and `DataSet` objects, dooms ADO and OLE DB to "legacy" status. It's unlikely that you'll see any significant upgrades to the current version, ADO 2.7, that's included in Microsoft Data Access Components (MDAC) 2.7.

The VBA code examples in this chapter cover only the basics of using VBA 6.0 for responding to events triggered by forms, controls, and Recordsets bound to forms or reports. A full course in VBA database programming exceeds both the scope and the publishing limitations of this book. Many of the examples in this chapter are drawn from the sample databases supplied with Access 2003. You can adapt the techniques illustrated in the event-handling subprocedures of the sample databases to custom applications you create.

To become an expert in VBA programming requires study, experimentation, and perseverance. Periodicals, books, and Web sites, such as those listed in the "Other Sources of Information for Access" section of the introduction to this book, are likely to satisfy the studious reader. There's no substitute, however, for experimentation. Writing and testing code is the only sure way to become proficient in Access VBA programming.

CHAPTER 29

Programming Combo and List Boxes

In this chapter

Streamlining Decision Support Front Ends

Decision-support applications deliver information used by executive management to analyze business trends and by-line managers to analyze day-to-day performance of their business area and its staff. Most executives and line managers prefer graphs and charts to display trends, but deviations from expected results require display of detail data to pinpoint problem areas. Supervisors need more targeted data for monitoring employees' activities, such as reviewing order entry operations for accuracy and timeliness.

Decision-support applications involve read-only access to data, so you aren't limited to datasheet or form/subform views of queries. Access list boxes offer faster performance and easier multi-record navigation than forms and subforms, which are intended primarily for data entry. Combo boxes are the ideal control for letting users make ad hoc choices of the information they need to see.

NOTE

> Online-data entry applications also can take advantage of list boxes for applications such as finding a specific customer and displaying the customer's orders. The A11Oltp.mdb application described in Chapter 14, "Creating and Using Access Forms," takes advantage of list boxes to display all historical customer and order data.

This chapter shows you how to combine combo boxes and list boxes with VBA code to create an interactive form for a simple decision-support application that includes a drill-down feature. You also learn how to generate Jet SQL and Transact-SQL (T-SQL) queries from selections made in list and combo boxes.

Constraining Query Choices with Combo Boxes

Users of decision-support applications, especially managers, aren't likely to be able to or want to use Access's graphical Query Design window. Instead, most users prefer to pick criteria (`SELECT` query `WHERE` clause elements) from one or more lists of available options. One primary advantage of offering users a set of choices to construct a query is the ability to prevent execution of ad hoc queries that return an excessive number of rows. Accidentally returning thousands of rows or—even worse—a Cartesian product of a million rows or more can bring a multiuser application or the entire network to its knees. Network and database administrators call such events "queries from hell."

TIP

> Combo boxes are the better choice for generating `WHERE` clause criteria because they occupy less room on forms than list boxes. Also, you can navigate quickly to a combo box item by typing the first few characters of the item in the combo box's text box element.

The following sections describe how to create an unbound form with two combo boxes that displays a list of orders from a specified country that include a particular product.

DESIGNING THE DECISION-SUPPORT QUERY

Query design is one of the most important elements of decision-support applications. One primary objective of decision-support systems is fast response time. To return selected information quickly, the query design should be as simple as possible. Include in the query only those fields needed to display necessary information, plus the foreign key fields to be selected in the combo boxes.

Follow these steps to create the minimal query for the customer-product-order information to be returned from the combo box selections:

1. Open the Northwind sample database or your working copy of Northwind.mdb.
2. Create a new query in Design view and add the Customers, Orders, and Order Details tables.
3. Drag the CompanyName and Country fields of the Customers table, the OrderID and ShippedDate fields of the Orders table, and the ProductID of the Order Details table to the Query Design grid (see Figure 29.1).

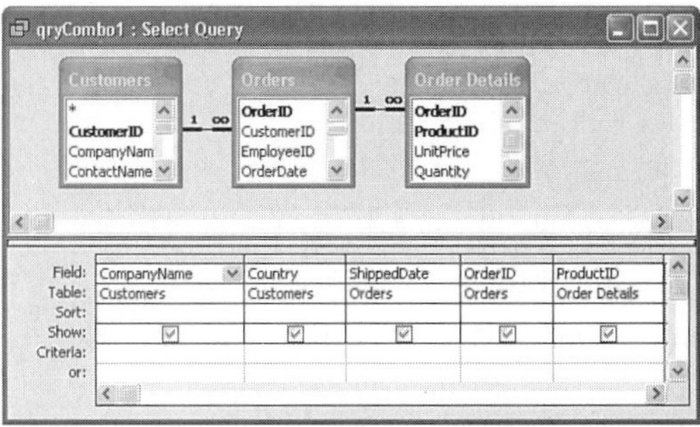

Figure 29.1 This query design delivers the data required to populate combo and list boxes.

4. Click Run to test your query, and then close and save your query as **qryCombo1**.

CREATING THE FORM AND ADDING A LIST BOX

An Access list box is the most efficient control for displaying the read-only query result sets of decision-support applications. List boxes consume fewer computer resources than subforms, are easier for users to navigate, and have the properties and events needed to give your application drill-down capabilities. Drill down is the process of providing users with more detailed information about a specific item in the list. Later, the section "Drilling Down from a List Box Selection" shows you how to add drill-down capabilities to the form you create here.

→ For list and combo box basics, **see** "Adding Combo and List Boxes," **p. 596**.

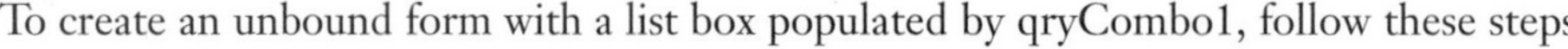

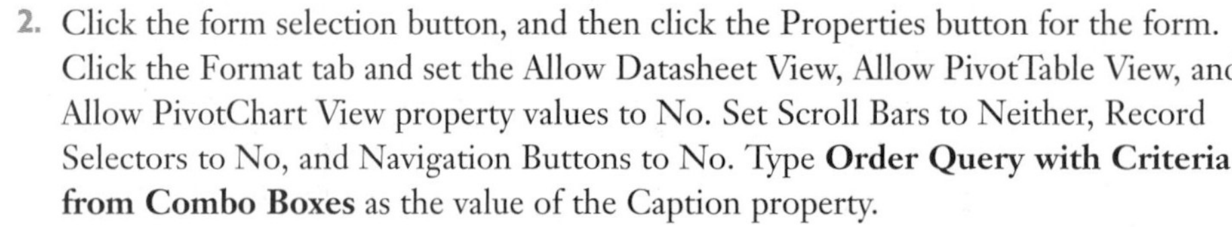

To create an unbound form with a list box populated by qryCombo1, follow these steps:

1. Create a new unbound form in Design view. (Don't specify a Record Source for the form.) Adjust the size of the form to about 4.5 inches wide by 2.5 inches deep.
2. Click the form selection button, and then click the Properties button for the form. Click the Format tab and set the Allow Datasheet View, Allow PivotTable View, and Allow PivotChart View property values to No. Set Scroll Bars to Neither, Record Selectors to No, and Navigation Buttons to No. Type **Order Query with Criteria from Combo Boxes** as the value of the Caption property.
3. With the Control Wizards button depressed, add a list box from the Toolbox to the form. Adding the list box opens the first dialog of the List Box Wizard.
4. Select the I Want the List Box to Look Up the Values in a Table or Query option, and click Next.
5. Select the Queries option in the View frame, select qryCombo1 (created in the preceding section) from the list, and click Next.
6. Select the CompanyName field in the Available Fields list and click the > button to add the field to the Selected Fields list. Repeat the process for the OrderID and ShippedDate fields, and then click Next twice to bypass the sort dialog.

NOTE

> You don't display the Country or Product ID in the list box because these fields are specified by combo box selection.

7. Adjust the widths of the columns to suit the list headers and data. Click Next.
8. Select OrderID as the column to uniquely identify the row. Click Next.
9. Type **Orders by Country and Product** as the caption for the list box's label, and click Finish to add the list box to the form.
10. Move the label to the top of the list box, click the Bold button on the toolbar to make the label's caption more visible, and adjust the width of the label.
11. Select the list box label, open the Properties window, click the Other tab, and change the value of its Name property to **lblList**.
12. Select the list box, click the All tab and change the Name property value of the combo box to **lstOrders**. Set Yes as the value of the Column Heads property and set Bound Column to 2 (see Figure 29.2).
13. Click the Form View button to check the layout of the list box. Choose Windows, Size to Fit Form to set the dimensions of the form window. Your form appears as shown in Figure 29.3.
14. Press Ctrl+S to save the form and name it **frmCombo1**.

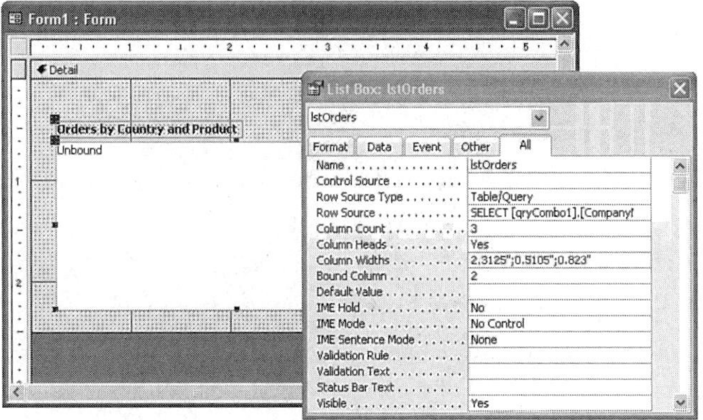

Figure 29.2 Setting OrderID (column 2) as the Bound Column property value prepares the form for later addition of the drill-down feature.

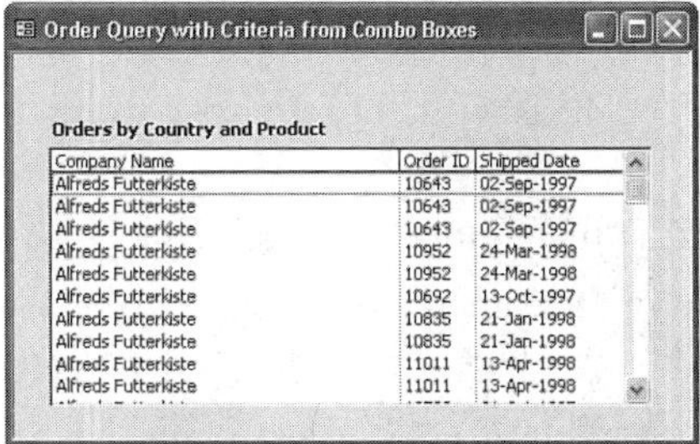

Figure 29.3 The lstOrders list box displays all rows of the query at this point.

Adding the Query Combo Boxes to the Form

You need one combo box to select the country and another to select the product. Northwind.mdb doesn't have a Countries table, so the data source for the country combo box is the Country field of the Customers table. The data source for the product combo box is the Products table.

➔ For detailed combo box instructions, **see** "Using the Combo Box Wizard," **p. 596**.

To add the country and product combo boxes to the form, follow these steps:

1. Change to Design mode and add a combo box to the upper left of the form; the first dialog of the Combo Box Wizard opens.
2. Select the I Want the Combo Box to Look Up the Values in a Table or Query and click Next.
3. With the Tables option selected, select Customers from the list and click Next.
4. Select Country in the Available Fields list and click the > button to move Country to the Selected Fields list. Click Next.
5. Open the first sort list and select Country. Click Next.
6. Adjust the width of the Country column and click Next.
7. Accept Country as the caption for the label and click Finish to add the combo box to the form.

8. Select the Country label, click the Bold button, and adjust the position and size of the label (look ahead to Figure 29.4).
9. Select the combo box, click the Data tab of the Properties window, and verify that the value of the Limit to List property is Yes.
10. Click the Other tab of the Properties window and type **cboCountry** as the value of the Name property.
11. Repeat steps 1 and 2.
12. With the Tables option selected, select Products from the list and click Next.
13. Select ProductID in the Available Fields list and click the > button to move ProductID to the Selected Fields list. Do the same for ProductName, and then click Next.
14. Select ProductName as the sort order, and click Next.
15. Adjust the width of the ProductName column to accommodate long product names, and click Next.
16. Type **Product** as the caption for the label, and click Finish to add the combo box to the form.
17. Click the Bold button and adjust the position and size of the label.
18. With the text box component of the combo control selected, click the Other tab of the Properties window, and type **cboProduct** as the value of the Name property (see Figure 29.4).

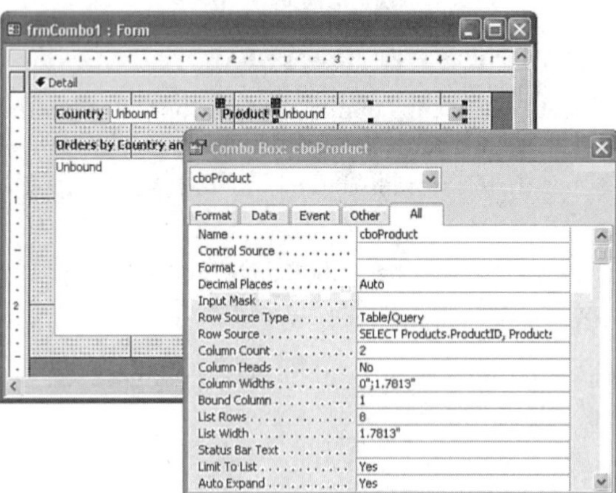

Figure 29.4
The final form design has the two combo boxes you use to select the country and product to populate the orders list box.

19. Choose View, Tab Order to open the Tab Order dialog. Click the Auto Order button to set a cboCountry, cboProduct, lstOrders sequence. Click OK to close the dialog.
20. Click the Form View button and test both combo boxes (see Figure 29.5).

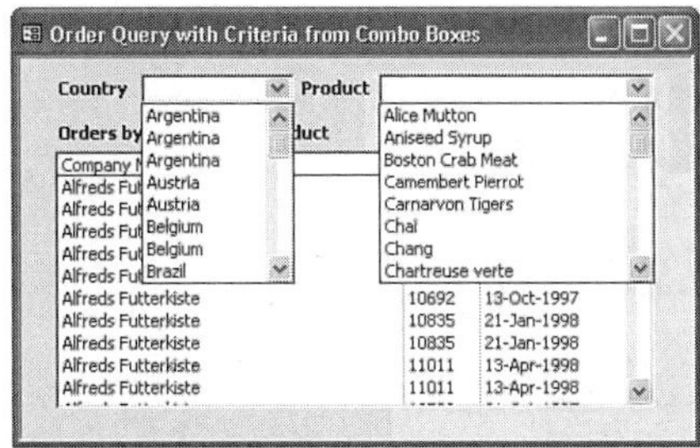

Figure 29.5
At this point, the Country combo box has a row for each customer, instead of a row for each country.

NOTE

Figure 29.5 is a double exposure created from two display captures. You can't open both combo boxes simultaneously.

21. Press Ctrl+S to save the changes to frmCombo1.

The Country combo box in Figure 29.5 has an obvious defect: multiple instances of country names. These problems arise from the SQL statement that the Combo Box Wizard creates as the value of the combo box's Row Source property:

```
SELECT Customers.CustomerID, Customers.Country
   FROM Customers ORDER BY [Country];
```

The Combo Box Wizard automatically includes the primary-key field of the table (CustomerID) as the bound column, so you must remove the `Customers.CustomerID` column from the SQL statement and modify cboCountry's properties to accommodate this change. ANSI SQL's `DISTINCT` or Access SQL's `DISTINCTROW` qualifier solves the duplication problem.

➔ For the differences between the two `SELECT` qualifiers, **see** "Writing `SELECT` Queries in SQL," **p. 857**.

To make the required changes to the Country combo box, do the following:

1. Select the cboCountry combo box, and click the Properties button. Access 2003 lets you change most of the properties of combo boxes in Form view.
2. Click the Data tab, and then edit the value of the Row Source property to the following:

   ```
   SELECT DISTINCT Country FROM Customers ORDER BY Country;
   ```

   The table name prefix for field names isn't needed because the query includes just one table.

NOTE

Make sure the Row/Source Type property value remains set to Table/Query after you make the change.

3. Click the All tab and change the value of the Column Count property from 2 to 1.
4. Remove the first 0"; element of the Column Widths property value, and set the Limit to List property value to Yes (see Figure 29.6).

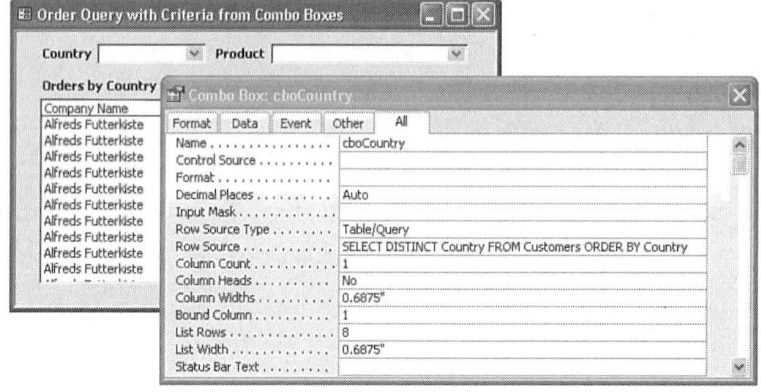

Figure 29.6
Change the Row Source to a `SELECT` query with the `DISTINCT` qualifier, change the list to display a single column, and set the Limit to List property value to Yes.

NOTE

> If you don't change the Column Count and Column Widths property values in steps 3 and 4, cboCountry displays an empty list.

5. Open the modified combo box. As shown in Figure 29.7, the duplicates are removed and the country names are in alphabetical order. Close the form and save your changes.

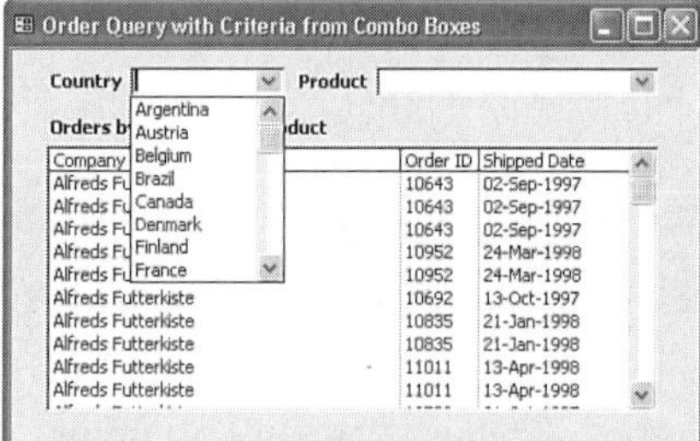

Figure 29.7
The Country list displays a single row for each country in alphabetical order.

ADDING CODE TO CREATE THE QUERY'S SQL STATEMENT

Selections you make in the combo boxes return the values required for the `WHERE` clause criteria of the query that serves as the Row Source property of the lstOrders list box. Selecting an item in the combo list returns the value of the bound column to the combo box's Value property. The Row Source property value of the lstOrders list box created by the List Box Wizard is as follows:

```
SELECT qryCombo1.CompanyName,
     qryCombo1.OrderID, qryCombo1.ShippedDate
   FROM qryCombo1;
```

A model SQL statement that simplifies the query syntax, uses the combo box values, and sorts the rows in reverse date order (newest orders first) is this:

```
SELECT CompanyName, OrderID, ShippedDate
   FROM qryCombo1
   WHERE Country = cboCountry.Value AND
      ProductID = cboProduct.Value
   ORDER by ShippedDate DESC;
```

To write the VBA code to create the `SELECT` query based on combo box values and add instructions for the user, follow these steps:

1. Select frmCombo1 in the Database window and then click the Code button to display the Class Module for the frmCombo1 form in the VBA editor and add the following constant and variable declarations for the SQL statement to the Declarations section, immediately below `Option Explicit`:

```
Private Const strSQL1 = "SELECT CompanyName, OrderID, ShippedDate " & _
   "FROM qryCombo1 WHERE Country = '"
Private Const strSQL2 = "' AND ProductID = "
Private Const strSQL3 = " ORDER BY ShippedDate DESC;"
Private strSQL As String
```

TIP

The single quotation marks (') are required to set off String values within SQL statements. Numeric values don't require quotation marks.

2. Add the following code for messages to the Declarations section:

```
Private Const strMsg1 = "Select a product from the list"
Private Const strMsg2 = "Select a country from the list"
```

3. Type **Private Sub FillList** and press Enter to create a subprocedure stub to fill the list box.

4. Add the following code to the `FillList` stub to create the SQL statement for the list box's `RowSource` property, refresh the list box by applying the `Requery` method, and change the caption of the list box label to display the `WHERE` clause criteria:

```
strSQL = strSQL1 & Me!cboCountry.Value & _
   strSQL2 & Me!cboProduct.Value & strSQL3
Me!lstOrders.RowSource = strSQL
Me!lstOrders.Requery
Me!lblList.Caption = "Orders from " & _
Me!cboCountry.Value & " for " & _
Me!cboProduct.Column(1)
If Me!lstOrders.ListCount = 0 Then
   Me!lblList.Caption = "No " & Me!lblList.Caption
End If
```

NOTE

A combo box or list box's Column(*n*) property returns the value of the specified column. The first column (*n* = `0`) of `cboProduct` is ProductID; the second (*n* = `1`) is ProductName.

5. Select cboCountry from the Object list and select AfterUpdate from the Procedure list to create the **Private Sub** `cboCountry_AfterUpdate()` event-handler stub.
6. Add the following code to the `AfterUpdate()` stub to alter the caption of the list box label:

```
If Me!cboProduct.Value > 0 Then
   Call FillList
Else
   Me!lblList.Caption = strMsg1
End If
```

7. Repeat steps 5 and 6 for the `cboProduct` combo box, but change the code for step 6 as follows:

```
If Me!cboCountry.Value <> "" Then
   Call FillList
Else
   Me!lblList.Caption = strMsg2
End If
```

8. Select Form from the Object list and Activate from the Procedure list to create a `Form_Activate` event-handling stub.
9. Add the following code to `Form_Activate` to generate the list from persisted country and product selections:

```
If Me!cboCountry.Value <> "" And Me!cboProduct.Value > 0 Then
   Call FillList
Else
   Me!lblList.Caption = strMsg2
End If
```

10. Choose Debug, Compile *ProjectName* to verify the VBA code you added. If compilation errors occur, check your code against Listing 29.1.

11. Click the View Microsoft Access button to return to Form Design view, select the lstOrders list box, click the Data tab of the Properties window, and delete the default Row Source value so that the full result set of qryCombo1 doesn't appear when you open the form.
12. Increase the width of lblList to match the width of the list box.
13. Change to Form view to run the code. If you previously selected country and product criteria, the form displays the query result set.

Listing 29.1 contains all code added in the preceding steps. If error messages arise when compiling your code or displaying the form, compare it with this listing.

LISTING 29.1 VBA CODE FOR THE FRMCOMBO1 CLASS MODULE AS IT APPEARS IN THE EDITING WINDOW

```
Option Compare Database
Option Explicit

Private Const strSQL1 = "SELECT CompanyName, OrderID, ShippedDate " & _
   "FROM qryCombo1 WHERE Country = '"
```

```
Private Const strSQL2 = "' AND ProductID = "
Private Const strSQL3 = " ORDER BY ShippedDate DESC;"
Private strSQL As String

Private Const strMsg1 = "Select a product from the list"
Private Const strMsg2 = "Select a country from the list"

Private Sub cboCountry_AfterUpdate()
   If Me!cboProduct.Value > 0 Then
      Call FillList
   Else
      Me!lblList.Caption = strMsg2
   End If
End Sub

Private Sub cboProduct_AfterUpdate()
   If Me!cboCountry.Value <> "" Then
      Call FillList
   Else
      Me!lblList.Caption = strMsg1
   End If
End Sub

Private Sub FillList()
      strSQL = strSQL1 & Me!cboCountry.Value & _
         strSQL2 & Me!cboProduct.Value & strSQL3
      Me!lstOrders.RowSource = strSQL
      Me!lstOrders.Requery
      Me!lblList.Caption = "Orders from " & _
         Me!cboCountry.Value & " for " & _
         Me!cboProduct.Column(1)
      If Me!lstOrders.ListCount = 0 Then
         Me!lblList.Caption = "No " & Me!lblList.Caption
   End If
End Sub

Private Sub Form_Activate()
   If Me!cboCountry.Value <> "" And Me!cboProduct.Value > 0 Then
      Call FillList
   Else
      Me!lblList.Caption = strMsg2
   End If
End Sub
```

Save your form, and then test your work by selecting values from the Country and Product combo boxes to display the query result set (see Figure 29.8). You can type a few letters in the Country or Product list boxes, and then press Enter to fire the `AfterUpdate` event for the closest matching item.

If you encounter errors when you test your form, see the "Run-Time Error '2465'" and "Spurious Parameter Messages" topics of the "Troubleshooting" section near the end of this chapter.

The completed frmCombo1 form is included in VBACombo.mdb, located in the \Seua11\Chaptr29 folder of the accompanying CD-ROM.

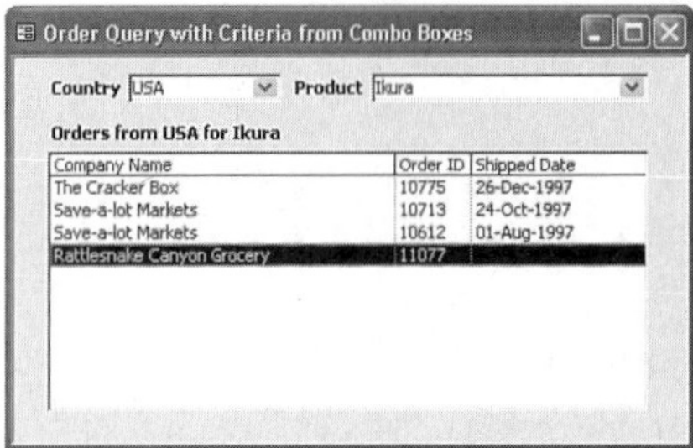

Figure 29.8
Settings of the two combo boxes determine the contents of the orders list box.

DRILLING DOWN FROM A LIST BOX SELECTION

The most common use of a drill-down form that displays a list of orders is to present the line items of a particular order. It's relatively easy to add and program a line items list box, based on the Order Details table, to the form you created in the preceding sections. An additional use of a line items list box is to verify that the cboProduct combo box correctly performs its assigned role.

CREATING THE DRILL-DOWN QUERY AND ADDING THE LIST BOX

Create the query and add the list box with the following steps:

1. Open frmCombo1 or select it in the Database window, and save it as **frmDrillDown**.
2. Create a new query and add the Order Details and Products tables.
3. Drag the Product Name field of the Products table and the OrderID, UnitPrice, Quantity, and Discount fields of the Order Details table to the Query Design grid. Move the OrderID field to the first column of the query. OrderID doesn't appear in the line items list box; it's used to link to the OrderID column of lstOrders.
4. Add a calculated field defined by typing the following expression in the sixth column of the Field row:

```
Extended: CCur(Format([Order Details].[UnitPrice]*
[Quantity]*(1-[Discount]),"$#,###.00"))
```

Figure 29.9 illustrates the design of the query.

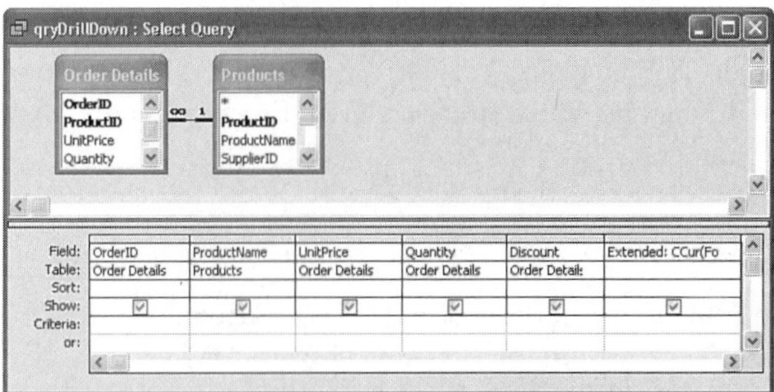

Figure 29.9
The query of this design populates a list box of order line items.

5. Run the query to verify your design, and then close it, saving it as **qryDrillDown**.

6. Open frmDrillDown in Design view, increase the height of frmDrillDown to about 3.75 inches. and add a list box with the same width as lstOrders and a height of about 1 inch at the bottom of the form.
7. Select the Table or Query option in the first Wizard dialog, accept the default, and click Next.
8. Select Queries and qryDrillDown, and then click Next.
9. Click the >> button to add all query columns to the Selected Fields list and then select the OrderID field and click < to remove it. Click Next twice.
10. Adjust the widths of the columns to fit the size of the data in the fields. Click Next.
11. Accept the default ProductName column for the default value of the list box. Click Next.
12. Replace the default caption of the label for the combo box with **Line Items**. Click Finish.

13. Move the label to a spot above the new list box, and click the Bold button.

14. Select the new list box, click the Format tab of the Properties window, and change the value of the Column Heads property to Yes.
15. Change the Caption property value of the form to **Orders and Line Items by Country and Product**.

16. Change to Form view to check your design (see Figure 29.10) and press Ctrl+S to save your changes.

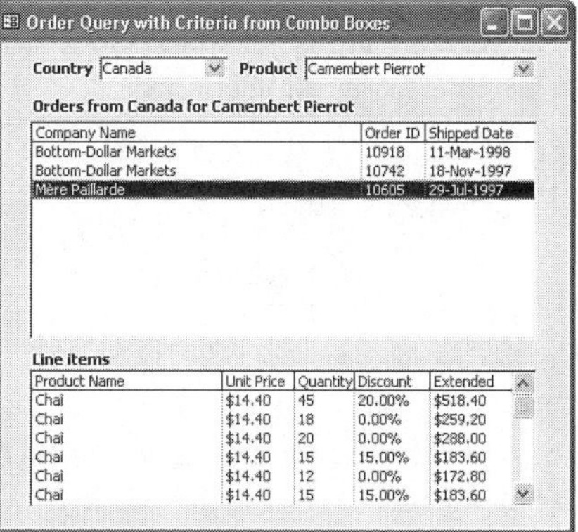

Figure 29.10 The list box for the drill-down query in Form view displays the first few rows of the entire Order Details table.

PROGRAMMING THE DRILL-DOWN LIST BOX

The List Box Wizard supplies the following SQL statement as the Row Source property of the new list box:

```
SELECT qryDrillDown.ProductName,
      qryDrillDown.UnitPrice, qryDrillDown.Quantity,
      qryDrillDown.Discount, qryDrillDown.Extended
   FROM qryDrillDown;
```

The simplified Jet SQL statement used to populate the Line Items list box from an order selected in the `lstOrders` list box is as follows:

```
SELECT ProductName, UnitPrice, Quantity, Discount, Extended
   FROM qryDrillDown
   WHERE OrderID = lstOrders.Value;
```

The following steps complete the modification of the list box and add VBA code to execute the preceding query:

1. Return to Form Design view, select the drill-down list box, click the Other tab of the Properties window, and change the value of the Name property to **lstLineItems**.
2. Select the label for lstLineItems and change the value of its Name property to **lblLineItems**.

3. Click the Code button and add the following string constants to the Declarations section of the frmDrillDown Class Module:

```
Private Const strSQL4 = "SELECT ProductName, UnitPrice, Quantity, " & _
   "Discount, Extended FROM qryDrillDown WHERE OrderID = "

Private Const strMsg3 = "Double-click an order to display line items"
Private Const strMsg4 = "Line items for order "
Private Const strMsg5 = "Line items"
```

4. Select lstOrders from the Object list and DblClick from the Procedures list to add a `lstOrders_DblClick` subprocedure stub.
5. Add the following code to the `lstOrders_DblClick` stub to set the value of the `RowSource` property of the list box and requery the control:

```
If Me!lstOrders.Value <> "" Then
   With Me!lstLineItems
      strSQL = strSQL4 & Me!lstOrders.Value & ";"
      .RowSource = strSQL
      .Requery
   End With
   Me!lblLineItems.Caption = strMsg4 & Me!lstOrders.Value
End If
```

6. Add the following lines to the end of the `Form_Activate`, `cboCountry_AfterUpdate`, and `cboProduct_AfterUpdate` event handlers to clear the list box and change the label caption when opening the form or setting new query criteria:

```
With Me!lstLineItems
   .RowSource = ""
   .Requery
End With
Me!lblLineItems.Caption = strMsg5
```

7. Add the following lines to the end of the `Form_Activate` event handler to clear the persisted values in the lstLineItem list:

```
With Me!lstLineItems
    .RowSource = ""
    .Requery
End With
```

8. Add the following line above the **End If** line of the FillList subprocedure to change the Line Item list box label's caption:

```
Me!lblLineItems.Caption = strMsg3
```

9. Return to Access and change to Form view. Double-click one of the order items to populate lstLineItems (see Figure 29.11).

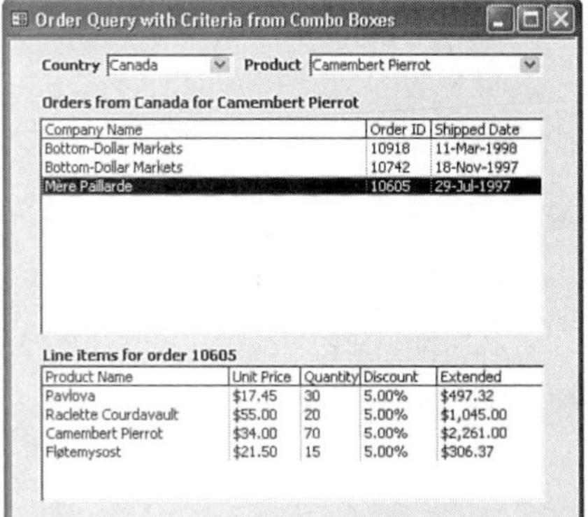

Figure 29.11
The Line Items list box displays Order Details records for the order you double-clicked in the Orders list box.

Adding New Features to List and Combo Boxes

List and combo boxes offer various properties and methods that are accessible only through VBA code. The next two sections describe programming techniques that take advantage of additional list and combo box features.

Iterating List Box Items and Selecting an Item

Access list boxes share many common properties with the native ListBox control of Visual Basic 5.0 and earlier. The `ListCount` property returns the number of items in the list, the `ItemData` or `Column` property returns a value from the list, and the `Selected` property sets or returns whether the row is selected. This example emphasizes a product in the Line Items list box by automatically selecting the row corresponding to the `cboProduct` selection. The `Column` property is more versatile than the `ItemData` property; `ItemData` is restricted to values in the bound column.

Follow these steps to add the code required to automatically select a product in the `lstLineItems` list box:

1. Add this statement to the Declarations section of the frmDrillDown Class Module:

```
Private intCtr As Integer
```

2. Add these lines immediately above the **End If** statement of the lstOrders_DblClick event handler:

```
With Me!lstLineItems
   For intCtr = 0 To .ListCount - 1
      If .Column(0, intCtr) = Me!cboProduct.Column(1) Then
         .Selected(intCtr) = True
         Exit For
      End If
   Next intCtr
End With
```

The optional second argument of the Column property specifies the row. The **If...Then** statement determines a match between the text values of the ProductName columns of lstLineItems and cboProduct.

3. Open the form in Form view. Double-click one of the order items to fill lstLineItems and automatically select the specified product (see Figure 29.12).

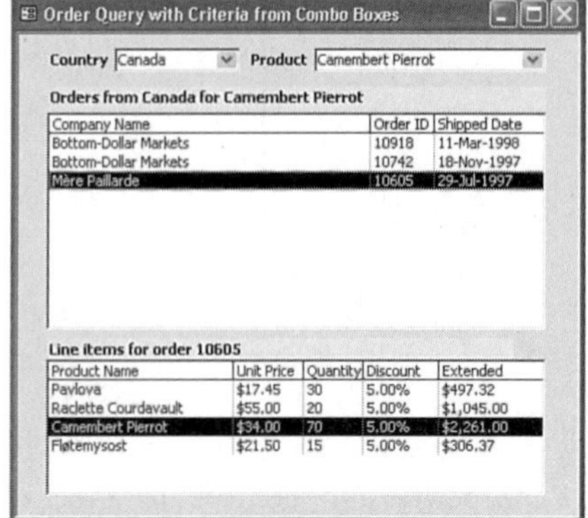

Figure 29.12 Adding a few lines of VBA code automatically highlights the Order Details record for the selected product in the Line Items list.

TIP

> You can use code similar to what's in this example to emulate a SELECT query against the content of any list box or combo box. Selecting a list box item ensures that the item is visible in the text box, regardless of its location in the list.

ADDING AN OPTION TO SELECT ALL COUNTRIES OR PRODUCTS

It's often useful to give users the option to pick all items represented by combo box selections. In this chapter's example, selecting all countries or all products (but not both) represents an enhancement to the application. How you add an "(All)" choice to cboCountry and cboProduct and write the code for the appropriate SELECT query to fill lstOrders isn't obvious, at best.

NOTE

Access 2002 finally added the `AddItem` method of Visual Basic list and combo boxes for populating these controls with VBA code. Unfortunately, you can't take advantage of this new feature, because you must specify Value List as the Row Source Type property of the Access list and combo boxes to use `AddItem`.

A `UNION` query is the most straightforward way to add custom rows to a combo or list box populated by an SQL statement. You specify your own values for each column returned by the `SELECT` query to which the `UNION` clause applies. The Jet `UNION` query to populate `cboCountry` is as follows:

```
SELECT Country FROM Customers
   UNION SELECT '(All)' FROM Customers ORDER BY Country;
```

You don't need the `DISTINCT` modifier of the original `SELECT` statement because UNION queries don't return duplicate rows. The `'(All)'` custom item is surrounded with parentheses because `(` sorts before numerals and letters, making (All) the first item in the list. The Customers table has no (All) record, but all `UNION` queries require a `FROM` *`TableName`* clause.

→ For UNION query syntax, **see** "Using UNION Queries and Subqueries," **p. 452**.

Similarly, the `UNION` query to fill `cboProduct` is as follows:

```
SELECT ProductID, ProductName FROM Products
   UNION SELECT 0, '(All)' FROM Products ORDER BY ProductName;
```

Here you must supply a numeric value—in this case 0—for the first column of the query (ProductID) and the `'(All)'` string value for the second column (ProductName). `UNION` queries require that both `SELECT` statements return the same number of columns, and all rows of each column must be of the same field data type. ProductID is an AutoNumber field, which starts with 1 unless you make the effort to begin autonumbering with a higher value.

In addition to adding the (All) item to the combo boxes, you must alter your `SELECT` queries to populate `lstOrders` when you select (All). In the all-countries case, the Jet `SELECT` query is as follows:

```
SELECT CompanyName, OrderID, ShippedDate
   FROM qryCombo1
   WHERE ProductID = cboProduct.Value
   ORDER by ShippedDate DESC;
```

For the all-products situation, the Jet query is the following:

```
SELECT CompanyName, OrderID, ShippedDate
   FROM qryCombo1
   WHERE Country = cboCountry.Value
   ORDER by ShippedDate DESC;
```

The preceding changes require you to add logic to detect when you select (All) and change the assembly of the SQL statement to suit. The following steps add the (All) selection to both combo boxes:

1. Make a copy of frmDrillDown as **frmDrillDownAll**, and open the copy in Form Design view.
2. Select cboCountry, and change its Row Source property value to the following:

```
SELECT Country FROM Customers UNION SELECT '(All)'
FROM Customers ORDER BY Country;
```

3. Select cboProduct and change its Row Source property value to the following:

```
SELECT ProductID, ProductName FROM Products
UNION SELECT 0, '(All)' FROM Products ORDER BY ProductName;
```

4. Click the Code button, and add the following lines to the Declarations section to create the SQL statement that populates the lstOrder list and to prevent returning all orders:

```
Private Const strSQL5 = "SELECT Customers.CompanyName, " & _
   "Orders.OrderID, Orders.ShippedDate FROM (Customers " & _
   "INNER JOIN Orders ON Customers.CustomerID = Orders.CustomerID) " & _
   "INNER JOIN [Order Details] ON Orders.OrderID = " & _
   "[Order Details].OrderID "
Private Const strSQL6 = "WHERE Country = '"
Private Const strSQL7 = "WHERE ProductID = "


Private Const strMsg6 = "You can't select (All) countries and products"
```

5. Replace the `If...End If` code at the beginning (and before the `With`) of the `cboCountry_AfterUpdate` event handler as follows to indicate that you can't execute a query that returns all orders:

```
If Me!cboProduct.Value > 0 Then
   Me!lblList.Caption = strMsg1
   Call FillList
Else
   If Me!cboCountry.Value = "(All)" Then
      MsgBox strMsg6
   Else
      Me!lblList.Caption = strMsg2
      Call FillList
   End If
End If
```

6. Replace the `If...End If` code at the beginning (and before the `With`) of the cboProduct_AfterUpdate event handler to the following:

```
If Me!cboCountry.Value <> "" Then
   If Me!cboCountry.Value = "(All)" And _
         Me!cboProduct.Value = 0 Then
      MsgBox strMsg6
   Else
      Me!lblList.Caption = strMsg1
      Call FillList
   End If
Else
   Me!lblList.Caption = strMsg2
   Call FillList
End If
```

7. Replace the first two lines of the `FillList` subprocedure (above the `Me!lstOrders.RowSource = strSQL` line) with the following:

```
If Me!cboProduct.Value = 0 Then
   strSQL = strSQL5 & strSQL6 & Me!cboCountry.Value & _
      "'" & strSQL3
ElseIf Me!cboCountry.Value = "(All)" Then
   strSQL = strSQL5 & strSQL7 & Me!cboProduct.Value & _
      strSQL3
Else
   strSQL = strSQL1 & Me!cboCountry.Value & _
      strSQL2 & Me!cboProduct.Value & strSQL3
End If
```

8. Choose Debug, Compile to check your code and fix any VBA statements that won't compile.

9. Return to Access, close the form, and reopen it in Form view. Select a product in cboProduct and (All) in cboCountry to verify your additions, and double-click lstOrders (see Figure 29.13). Reverse the process, by selecting a country, and then selecting (All) products.

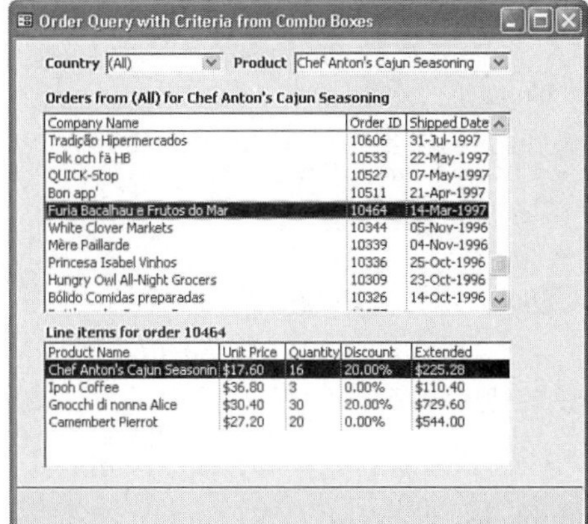

Figure 29.13
Select a product and then (All) to display all orders shipped that include the specified product.

If your orders or line items list boxes don't display expected rows, see the "Problems with SQL Statements as Row Source Property Values" topic of the "Troubleshooting" section near the end of this chapter.

CONVERTING YOUR COMBO BOX FORM TO AN ACCESS DATA PROJECT

Access 2003 and 2002's Upsizing Wizard (AUW) does a much better job of converting Jet applications to Access data projects (ADP) than the Access 2000 version. In most cases, however, the AUW can't upsize complex forms that are operable in ADP. For instance, the AUW doesn't translate to Transact-SQL (T-SQL), the Jet-specific SQL statements that serve as the Record Source property of bound forms and reports, and the Row Source property value of controls. The forms you created in the preceding sections provide good examples of the problems you encounter when upsizing forms to ADP.

→ For an explanation of some of the limitations of the AUW, **see** "Upsizing with the Trial and Error Approach," **p. 889**.

Upsizing VBACombo.mdb isn't practical, so the sections that follow show you how to manually upsize forms imported to the project from VBACombo.mdb. You can't import Jet queries to ADP, so you create SQL Server views based on the Jet SQL of VBACombo.mdb's queries.

NOTE

> The NorthwindCS SQL Server database for NorthwindCS.adp must be installed to execute the code in the following example.
> If you created the copy of the NorthwindCS database as Northwind (or any other name) for use with the AddOrders.adp project described in Chapter 30, "Understanding Universal Data Access, OLE DB, and ADO," you can use AddOrders.adp to add a large number of records to the Orders and Order Details tables to test the performance of combo and list boxes with databases that are more representative of production applications.

→ If you haven't created NorthwindCS, **see** "Exploring the NorthwindCS Sample Project," **p. 808**.

→ To use AddOrders.adp with a copy of NorthwindCS, **see** "Exploring the AddOrder.adp Sample Project," **p. 1327**.

IMPORTING AND TESTING THE COMBO BOX FORMS

To import the three forms you created in the preceding sections to an .adp file and test them against a local instance of MSDE, do the following:

1. Start MSDE with SQL Service Manager, if MSDE isn't running.
2. Open the task pane and double-click Project (Existing Data) to open the File New Database dialog.
3. Type **VBACombo.adp** as the File Name, and click Create to close the dialog and open the Data Link Properties dialog.
4. Type **(local)** or your computer for the Server Name, and select the Use Windows NT Integrated Security option.
5. Select NorthwindCS from the drop-down list, and click the Test Connection button to check the Data Link properties you specified (see Figure 29.14).
6. Click OK twice to return to the Database window for the new project.

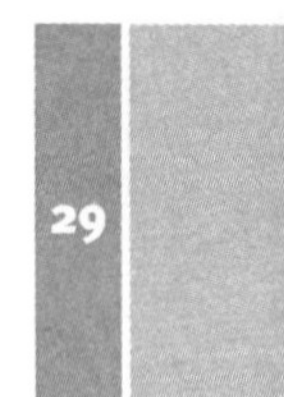

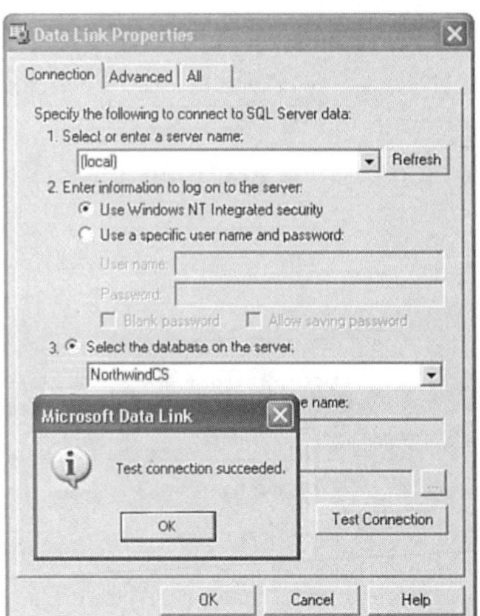

Figure 29.14
Establish a connection to the NorthwindCS sample database on your machine.

7. Choose File, Get External Data, Import to open the Import dialog. (You can import the three forms from the sample file, VBACombo.mdb or your working copy of Northwind.mdb, if you created those forms earlier.) Click the Forms tab and click Select All if you're importing from VBACombo.mdb. If you're importing from Northwind, select the three forms—frmCombo1, frmDrillDown, and frmDrillDownAll—and then click OK to import the three forms to the project.
8. Open the frmCombo1 form. The Country and Product combo boxes work, but no records appear in the Orders list box, despite the fact that combo box selections generate the correct label caption text. (Populating the Orders list box depends on the missing qryCombo1 query.) Close the form.
9. Open the frmDrillDown form. You receive two error messages stating that the Jet qryCombo1 and qryDrillDown queries don't exist. Close the form.

REPLACING THE JET QRYCOMBO1 QUERY WITH AN SQL SERVER VIEW

One approach to upsizing Row Source property values from Jet queries to SQL Server databases is to substitute T-SQL statements for the queries. A simpler method is to create SQL Server 2000 views that duplicate the Jet queries.

To create a view to replace qryCombo1, do this:

1. Open another instance of Access 2003, open VBACombo.mdb or Northwind.mdb (if you created the forms earlier), and open qryCombo1.
2. Select SQL View to open the SQL window, select the SQL statement, and press Ctrl+C to copy the text to the Clipboard.
3. Return to the project, select Queries in the Database window, and double-click the Create View in Designer item to open the project designer.

4. Close the Add Table dialog, and click the SQL button to open the designer's SQL pane.
5. Select the `SELECT` and `FROM` lines, press Ctrl+V to replace the lines with the qryCombo1 SQL statement, and delete the trailing semicolon.
6. Change the `Orders.ShippedDate` field list item to **Orders.OrderDate**. (AddOrders.adp doesn't add ShippedDate values.)
7. Click the Run button, save your view as vwCombo1, and verify that the query executes correctly. Figure 29.15 shows the design of the view.

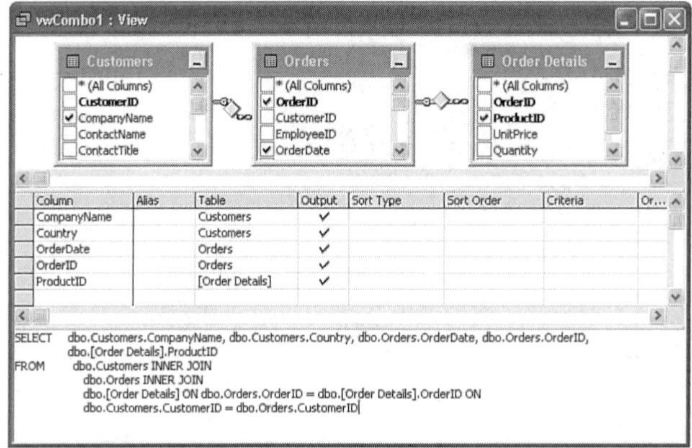

Figure 29.15 This SQL Server view replaces the Jet qryCombo1 query in the three imported forms of VBACombo.adp.

8. Select frmCombo1 in the Database window and click the Code button to open the VBA editor. Replace `qryCombo1` with **vwCombo1**, `ShippedDate` with **OrderDate** in the declaration of strSQL1, and `ShippedDate` with **OrderDate** in strSQL3 (see Figure 29.16).

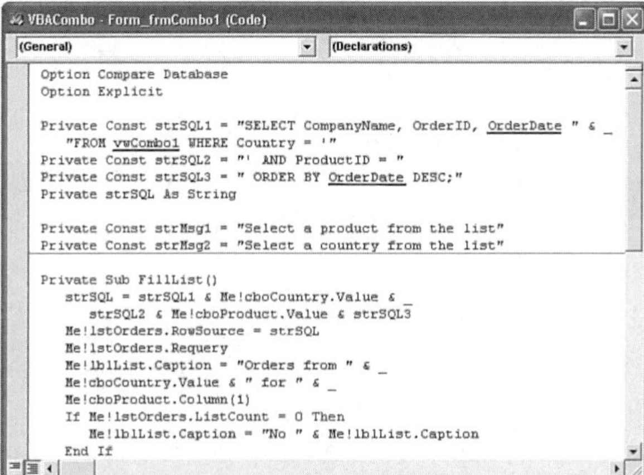

Figure 29.16 Change `qryCombo1` to `vwCombo1` and `ShippedDate` to `OrderDate` in the Class Module for each form.

9. Change to Form view, test the form with a few combinations of Country and Product selections, close the form, and save your changes.
10. Repeat steps 8 and 9 for the frmDrillDown and frmDrillDownAll forms. In frmDrillDownAll, also change `Orders.ShippedDate` to **Orders.OrderDate** in the declaration of `strSQL5`. Acknowledge the error messages when you open frmDrillDown for testing. (The lstLineItems list isn't operable at this point.)

CONFORMING THE JET SQL OF QRYDRILLDOWN TO T-SQL SYNTAX

The Jet SQL statement for qryDrillDown includes the VBA **`CCur`** and **`Format`** functions that T-SQL doesn't support, and has the Percent format applied to the Discount column. Thus, you must substitute the T-SQL `CONVERT` function for the **`CCur`** and **`Format`** combination. The `CONVERT` function and an added % symbol solve the formatting problem with the Discount column.

→ For another example of using the CONVERT function, **see** "Exploring SQL Server Views," **p. 819**.

To create a view that emulates the formatting of the original Jet query, do the following:

1. Copy the Jet SQL statement for the qryDrillDown query to a new SQL Server view by the method described in steps 2–5 of the preceding section.
2. Click Run, save the query as vwDrillDown, and acknowledge the error message caused by the VBA functions in qryDrillDown's SQL statement.
3. Replace the `CCur(Format(…)) AS Extended` line with the following:

```
(dbo.[Order Details].UnitPrice * dbo.[Order Details].Quantity) *
(1 - dbo.[Order Details].Discount) AS Extended
```

4. Run the query again to check your initial changes to conform to T-SQL syntax.
5. Return to Design view, and edit the line you changed in step 3 to add the `CONVERT` function as follows:

```
CONVERT(money, (dbo.[Order Details].UnitPrice * dbo.[Order Details].Quantity)
*
(1 - dbo.[Order Details].Discount)) AS Extended
```

6. Rerun the query to check your change. The Extended column now has currency formatting.
7. In Design view, replace `dbo.[Order Details].Discount,` with this expression to multiply by 100, add two decimal places, convert to a string, and add the % symbol:

```
CONVERT(varchar, CONVERT(decimal(5,2), dbo.[Order Details].Discount * 100))
   + '%' AS Discount,
```

8. Run the query again to verify the format changes (see Figure 29.17, which illustrates the effect of inflation on the price of Alice Mutton). Figure 29.18 shows the query design.

Figure 29.17
The result set of the modified vwDrillDown view duplicates the formatting of the Jet qryDrillDown query. The Discount column is left-justified because Discount has the `varchar` datatype.

vwDrillDown : View

OrderID	ProductName	Quantity	UnitPrice	Discount	Extended
10265	Alice Mutton	30	$31.20	0.00%	$936.00
10279	Alice Mutton	15	$31.20	25.00%	$351.00
10294	Alice Mutton	15	$31.20	0.00%	$468.00
10302	Alice Mutton	40	$31.20	0.00%	$1,248.00
10319	Alice Mutton	8	$31.20	0.00%	$249.60
10338	Alice Mutton	20	$31.20	0.00%	$624.00
10339	Alice Mutton	70	$31.20	5.00%	$2,074.80
10346	Alice Mutton	36	$31.20	10.00%	$1,010.88
10415	Alice Mutton	2	$31.20	0.00%	$62.40
10430	Alice Mutton	45	$31.20	20.00%	$1,123.20
10431	Alice Mutton	50	$31.20	25.00%	$1,170.00
10444	Alice Mutton	10	$31.20	0.00%	$312.00
10523	Alice Mutton	25	$39.00	10.00%	$877.50
10530	Alice Mutton	40	$39.00	0.00%	$1,560.00
10550	Alice Mutton	8	$39.00	10.00%	$280.80
10564	Alice Mutton	16	$39.00	5.00%	$592.80
10573	Alice Mutton	18	$39.00	0.00%	$702.00
10607	Alice Mutton	100	$39.00	0.00%	$3,900.00

Record: 13 of 2155

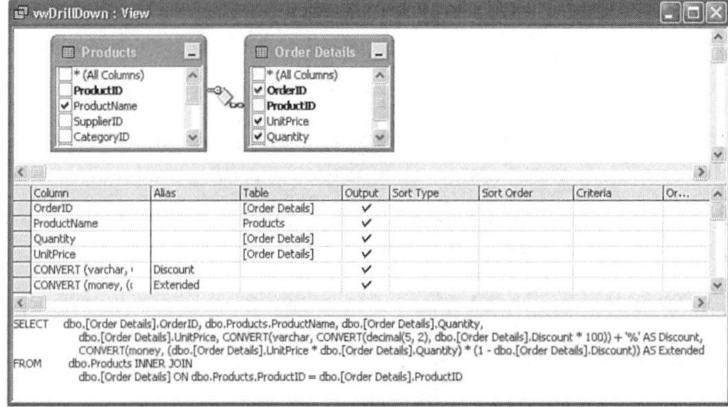

Figure 29.18
The Design view of vwDrillDown has been modified here to improve readability of the T-SQL statements.

9. Close the view, select frmDrillDown in the Database window, and click the Code button to open the VBA editor.
10. In the Declarations section, change `qryDrillDown` to **vwDrillDown** in the declaration of `strSQL4`, and save your change.

11. In Form Design view, select lstOrders, open the Properties window, click the Data tab, and delete the persisted Row Source value, if present. Select lstLineItems, and delete its Row Source value.

12. Run the form and verify your changes.
13. Repeat steps 9–12 for the frmDrillDownAll form. When testing this form, verify that (All) products and (All) countries deliver the expected result.

NOTE

The VBACombo.adp sample project has two versions of each form. Form names with a (View) suffix are intended to operate with two SQL Server views that are equivalent to the queries you created in this and the preceding section. Forms without the suffix send T-SQL statements to the server, so you don't need to create the views to test these forms.

You can use Chapter 30's AddOrders.adp to add a few thousand new orders to the Orders and Order Details tables of a copy of NorthwindCS and connect to the copy, the time to fill lstOrders increases (as expected). The time required to retrieve the line items for an order, however, doesn't increase perceptively. Figure 29.19 shows the result of a frmDrillDownAll selection against tables with 10,830 orders and 113,865 line items. The sample forms without the suffix have two added features—when you click lstOrders, the code adds the number of orders in lstOrders to lblList's caption and adds the total amount of the order to lblLineItems' caption.

Figure 29.19 The sample frmDrillDownAll form displays a few of the 2,021 orders from the USA for a database with 10,830 orders added by the AddOrders.adp sample project.

TIP

> If your list-based application runs against tables with a large number of rows, consider adding a `WHERE` clause criterion to eliminate unneeded rows. For this example, you might add a date-based criterion to limit the Orders query to OrderDate values within the last year, quarter, or month. Alternatively, add a `TOP 500` or `TOP 25 PERCENT` modifier to your select statement.

TROUBLESHOOTING

RUN-TIME ERROR '2465'

I receive a "Run-Time Error '2465'" message in Form view.

The most likely cause of this error is failure to change the default Name property value of a combo box or list box to cboCountry, cboProduct, or lblList. Alternatively, you might have misspelled one of the names. Check the Object list for Combo#, Label#, or List# control names. Alternatively, select the Other page of the Properties sheet and select each control object to make sure the Name property value is correct.

Spurious Parameter Messages

A "Parameter" message appears in Form view.

One field name in your SQL statement doesn't correspond to a field name of qryCombo1. Double-check your values of the strSQL1, strSQL2, and strSQL3 constants against the field names included in qryCombo1.

Problems with SQL Statements as Row Source Property Values

My list box doesn't display rows after I make valid selections in the Country and Product lists.

The SQL syntax for the query that populates the list box is incorrect or no orders meet your criteria. If you believe the query should return rows with the criteria you specify, set a breakpoint on the line that sets the `RowSource` property value of the list box. Repeat the operation that failed and, when the VBA editor opens, press Ctrl+G to open the Immediate window. Type ? and the name of the variable you use to assign the `RowSource` value to print the value. Break long statements by pressing Ctrl+Enter (see Figure 29.20).

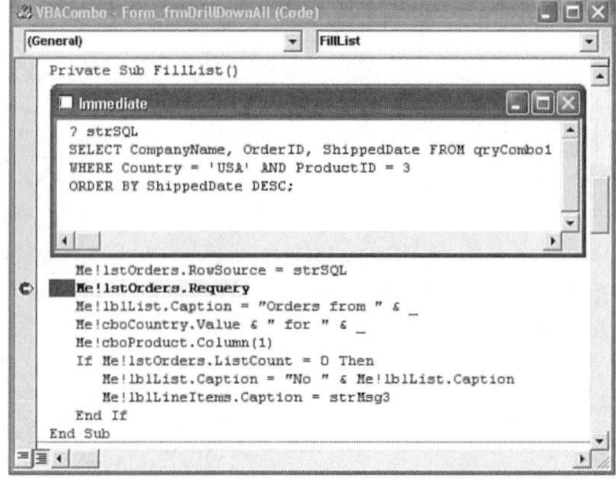

Figure 29.20 Adding a breakpoint and displaying the SQL statement that provides the `RowSource` property of a list or combo box lets you debug the statement in the Immediate window.

If you can't determine the source of the problem, copy the SQL Statement to the Clipboard, and then paste it into the SQL window of a Jet Query or the SQL pane of an SQL Server view to test execution. The resulting error message *might* lead you to the source of the problem.

In the Real World—Access Combo and List Boxes

Access's bound combo and list boxes offer many advantages over corresponding native controls available to Visual Basic programmers. Automatic multi-field capability in both combo and list boxes, and semi-formatted columns in Access list boxes are just two of the advantages of the Access version. When you migrate to ADP, another advantage of Access combo and list boxes becomes evident. As the frmDrillDown and frmDrillDownAll forms of the sample VBACombo.adp file demonstrate, you can populate combo and list boxes from Transact-SQL statements sent to the server as an alternative to creating SQL Server views.

The downside of sending SQL statements to SQL Server is that performance suffers because SQL Server optimizes and compiles the query before execution. Sending long SQL statements to a remote server also contributes to list-box latency. Compare the time required to first populate the Line Items list box using a connection to MSDE's NorthwindCS database on your PC to that for Jet's Northwind; Jet is significantly faster. (The performance difference is accentuated on a slower PC or one having 256MB or less RAM.) After you run the query once, however, the performance difference is minimal because SQL Server stores the compiled version in memory. When you re-execute the query, SQL Server 2000 checks to see whether it's in memory; if so, it executes the copy without recompilation. If you alter `WHERE` clause criteria, SQL Server must recompile the query on each execution.

Views and stored procedures optimize combo and list box performance by eliminating the initial optimization and compilation step. The view-based examples of this chapter minimize recompilation time by specifying only `WHERE` criteria and the `ORDER BY` clause for each query. If your query is complex—and especially if it requires multiple joins between large tables—substitute a parameterized stored procedure to return the Recordset that populates list and combo boxes. Stored procedures return read-only Recordsets that have forward-only (Microsoft calls them firehose) cursors, which provide better performance than the default dynamic cursor.

Access multi-column list boxes still have a few warts that need attention in future versions. For instance, you can't specify the alignment of individual columns; numeric values (including currency) and dates should right-align. A long-standing complaint of Access 97 developers was the lack of the simple syntax for adding items to VBA combo boxes—the `AddItem` method. The callback method of programmatically adding items to Access combo and list boxes was gruesome, and writing code to generate a value list was almost as bad. Access 2003 combo and list boxes have an `AddItem` method. Developers also complained about the 2KB limit on the length of the SQL statement used as the `RowSource` property of combo and list boxes, as well as the `RecordSource` property of forms in Access 2000 and earlier. The maximum length of Access 2003's RowSource and RecordSource property values is 64KB (32KB Unicode characters).

Regardless of their column format shortcomings, Access's native combo and list boxes are effective tools for both decision support and online transaction processing front ends. Consider replacing all read-only subforms with multicolumn list boxes, even if doing so requires some extra VBA code. Your customers—the users of your application—will appreciate their speedy response and space-saving format. You also gain the respect of DBAs when you substitute views and stored procedures for ad hoc queries against production databases.

CHAPTER 30

Understanding Universal Data Access, OLE DB, and ADO

In this chapter

Gaining a Perspective on Microsoft Data Access Components

Integrated data management is the key to Access's success in the desktop RDBMS and client/server front-end market. Access and its wizards let you create basic data-bound forms, reports, and pages with minimal effort and little or no VBA programming. Linked tables provide dynamic access to a wide range of data sources. As your Access applications grow larger and more complex, automation with VBA code in class and public modules becomes essential. When networked Access applications gain more users, performance may suffer as a result of Jet record-locking issues or multiple connections to client/server back ends. Decreasing performance with increasing user load is a symptom of lack of *scalability*. Achieving scalability requires VBA code to manage your application's database connections. This advanced chapter shows you how to write the VBA code that's required to improve the scalability of Access front ends. You also learn how to use the `Stream` object to generate XML data documents from SQL Server 2000's `FOR XML AUTO` queries.

Access 2003 continues Microsoft's emphasis on "Universal Data Access" for VBA and Visual Basic 6.0 programmers. Microsoft wants Access developers to abandon Jet's Data Access Objects (DAO), Access 97's ODBCDirect, and the venerable Open Database Connectivity (ODBC) Application Programming Interface (API) in favor of a collection of Component Object Model (COM) interfaces called OLE DB and ActiveX Data Objects (ADO). To encourage Access power users and developers to adopt OLE DB and ADO, all traditional Microsoft database technologies (referred to by Microsoft as *downlevel* or *legacy*, synonyms for "obsolete") are destined for maintenance mode. Maintenance mode is a technological purgatory in which Microsoft fixes only the worst bugs and upgrades occur infrequently, if ever. In 1999, OLE DB, ADO, and, for Jet programmers, ActiveX Data Object Extensions (ADOX), became Microsoft's mainstream data access technologies.

Microsoft's primary goals for Universal Data Access were to

- Provide the capability to accommodate less common data types unsuited to SQL queries, such as directory services (specifically Active Directory), spreadsheets, email messages, and file systems
- Minimize the size and memory consumption of the dynamic link libraries (DLLs) required to support data access on Internet and intranet clients
- Reduce development and support costs for the multiplicity of Windows-based data access architectures in common use today
- Extend the influence of COM in competition with other object models, primarily Common Object Request Broker Architecture (CORBA) and its derivatives

This chapter introduces you to the fundamentals of Universal Data Access and Microsoft Data Access Components (MDAC). MDAC makes connecting to databases with OLE DB practical for Access users and developers. MDAC includes ADO and ADOX for conventional relational data, plus ADOMD for multidimensional expressions (MDX) to create and manipulate data cubes.

NOTE

Microsoft SQL Server Analysis Services (formerly OLAP Services) generates data cubes from online sources, such as transactional databases. Office 2003 installs Msadomd.dll and other supporting files for MDX and data cubes. Microsoft provides OLE DB for OLAP and the PivotTable Service to enable Excel 2003 PivotTables to manipulate data cubes. MDX and PivotTable services are beyond the scope of this book.

REDESIGNING FROM THE BOTTOM UP WITH OLE DB

To accommodate the widest variety of data sources, as well as to spread the gospel of COM and Windows XP/2000+'s COM+, Microsoft's data architects came up with a new approach to data connectivity—OLE DB. OLE DB consists of three basic elements:

- *Data providers* that abstract information contained in data sources into a tabular (row-column) format called a *rowset*. Microsoft currently offers native OLE DB data providers for Jet, SQL Server, IBM DB2, IBM AS/400 and ISAM, and Oracle databases, plus ODBC data sources. (Only Microsoft SNA Server installs the providers for IBM data sources.) Other Microsoft OLE DB providers include an OLE DB Simple Provider for delimited text files, the MSPersist provider for saving and opening Recordsets to files (called *persisted Recordsets*), and the MSDataShape provider for creating hierarchical data sets. The MSDataShape provider also plays an important role in ADP and when using VBA to manipulate the Recordset of Access forms and reports.

TIP

To see the list of OLE DB data sources installed on your computer, open the NorthwindCS.adp project, and choose File, Get External Data, Link Tables to start the Link Table Wizard. With the Linked Server option selected in the first dialog, click Next to open the Select Data Source dialog, and double-click the +Connect to New Data Source.odc file to open the second Wizard dialog. With the Other/Advanced item selected in the data source list, click Next to open the Data Link Properties dialog. The Providers page lists all currently installed OLE DB data providers. Click Cancel three times to return to the Database window.

- *Data consumers* that display and/or manipulate rowsets, such as Access application objects or OLE DB service providers. `Rowset` is the OLE DB object that ADO converts to a `Recordset` object.
- *Data services* (usually called *OLE DB service providers*) that consume data from providers and, in turn, provide data to consumers. Examples of data services are SQL query processors and cursor engines, which can create scrollable rowsets from forward-only rowsets. A scrollable cursor lets you move the record pointer forward and backward in the Datasheet view of a Jet or SQL Server query.

Figure 30.1 illustrates the relationship between OLE DB data providers, data consumers, and data services within Microsoft's Universal Data Access architecture. You should understand the relationships between these objects, because Microsoft commonly refers to them in ADO documentation, help files, and Knowledge Base articles. Database front ends written in C++ can connect directly to the OLE DB interfaces. High-level languages, such as VBA, use ADO as an intermediary to connect to OLE DB's COM interfaces. Msado15.dll, which implements ADO 2.x, has a memory footprint of about 327KB, about 60% of Dao360.dll's 547KB.

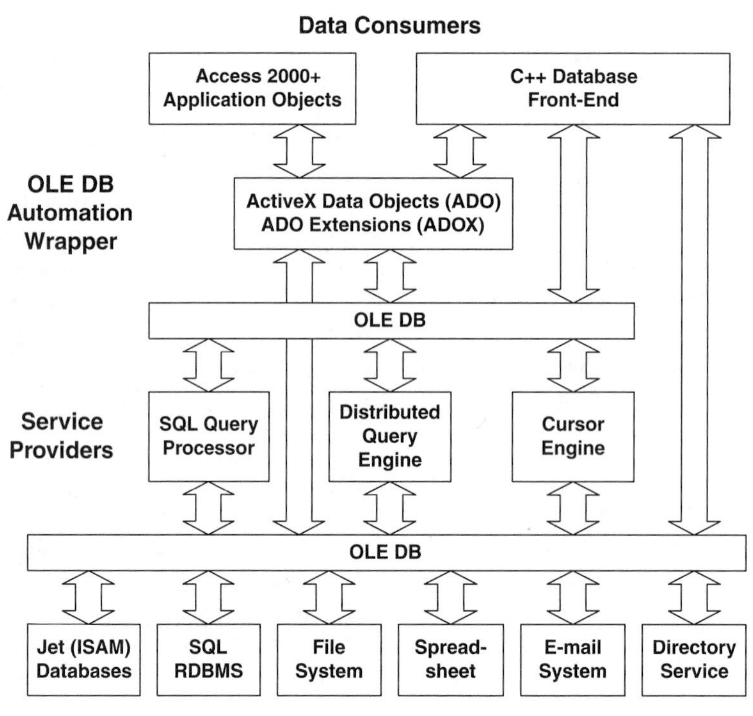

Figure 30.1 This diagram shows the relationships between front-end applications, ADO and ADOX, and OLE DB service and data providers.

ADO support files install in your \Program Files\System\Ado folder. If you're running Windows XP/2000+, the ADO support files are subject to Windows File Protection (WFP), which places a copy of the file in the DLL cache and prevents you from permanently deleting or moving the ADO support files. WFP also prevents unruly installation programs from overwriting the ADO support files with an earlier or corrupt (hacked) version.

Some ADO 2.x support file names have a 1.5 version number, as in Msado15.dll; the strange versioning of these files is required for backward compatibility with applications that used very early versions of ADO.

NOTE

> MDAC 2.x also supports Remote Data Services (RDS, formerly Advanced Database Connector, or ADC). RDS handles lightweight `ADOR.Recordsets` for browser-based applications; RDS, which commonly is used for three-tier, Web-based applications, is required to make Data Access Pages (DAP) accessible safely over the Internet.

→ For more information on the use of RDS with DAP, **see** "Enabling Private or Public Internet Access," **p. 1058**.

MAPPING OLE DB INTERFACES TO ADO

You need to know the names and relationships of OLE DB interfaces to ADO objects, because Microsoft includes references to these interfaces in its technical and white papers on OLE DB and ADO. Figure 30.2 illustrates the correspondence between OLE DB interfaces and the highest levels of the ADO hierarchy.

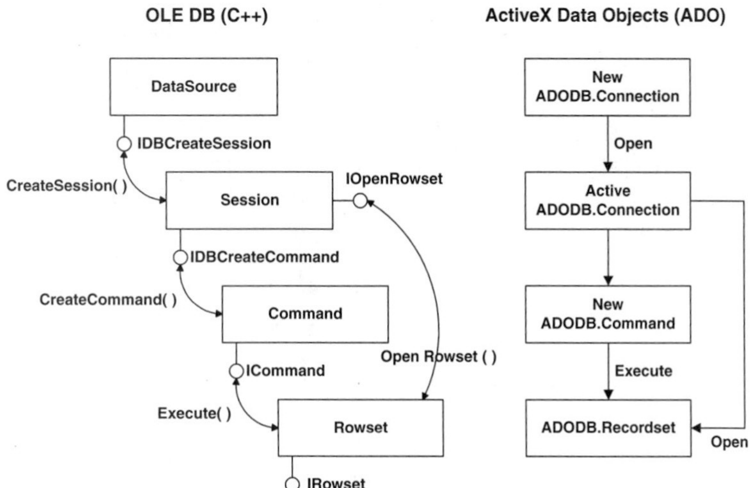

Figure 30.2 This diagram illustrates the correspondence between OLE DB interfaces and ADO Automation objects.

The OLE DB specification defines a set of interfaces to the following objects:

- `DataSource` objects provide a set of functions to identify a particular OLE DB data provider, such as the Jet or SQL Server provider, and determine whether the caller has the required security permissions for the provider. If the provider is found and authentication succeeds, a connection to the data source results.
- `Session` objects provide an environment for creating rowsets and isolating transactions, especially with Microsoft Transaction Server (MTS), which runs under Windows NT. The COM+ components of Windows 2000+ provide MTS services.
- `Command` objects include sets of functions to handle queries, usually (but not necessarily) in the form of SQL statements or names of stored procedures.

- `Rowset` objects can be created directly from `Session` objects or as the result of execution of `Command` objects. `Rowset` objects deliver data to the consumer through the `IRowset` interface.

ADO maps the four OLE DB objects to the following three top-level Automation objects that are familiar to Access programmers who've used ODBCDirect:

- `Connection` objects combine OLE DB's `DataSource` and `Session` objects to specify the OLE DB data provider, establish a connection to the data source, and isolate transactions to a specific connection. The `Execute` method of the `ADODB.Connection` object can return a forward-only `ADODB.Recordset` object.
- `Command` objects are directly analogous to OLE DB's `Command` object. `ADODB.Command` objects accept an SQL statement, the name of a table, or the name of a stored procedure. `Command` objects are used primarily for executing SQL `UPDATE`, `INSERT`, `DELETE`, and SQL Data Definition Language (DDL) queries that don't return records. You also can return an `ADODB.Recordset` by executing an `ADODB.Command` object.
- `Recordset` objects correspond to OLE DB's `Rowset` objects and have properties and methods similar to Access 97's ODBCDirect `Recordset`. A `Recordset` is an in-memory image of a table or a query result set.

The `ADODB` prefix, the short name of the ADO type library, explicitly identifies ADO objects that share object names with DAO (`Recordset`) and DAO's ODBCDirect (`Connection` and `Recordset`). For clarity, all ADO code examples in this book use the `ADODB` prefix.

TIP

> To make ADOX 2.7 accessible to VBA, you must add a reference to Microsoft ADO Ext. 2.7 for DDL and Security to your application. Access 2003 doesn't add the ADOX reference automatically to new projects.

Comparing ADO and DAO Objects

Figure 30.3 is a diagram that compares the ADO and DAO object hierarchies. The ADO object hierarchy, which can consist of nothing more than an `ADODB.Connection` object, is much simpler than the collection-based object hierarchy of DAO. To obtain a scrollable, updatable `Recordset` (dynaset), you must open an `ADODB.Recordset` object on an active `ADODB.Connection` object.

Access VBA provides a DAO shortcut, `Set dbName = CurrentDB()`, to bypass the first two collection layers and open the current database, but `CurrentDB()` isn't available in VBA code for other members of Office 2003 or Visual Basic 6.0.

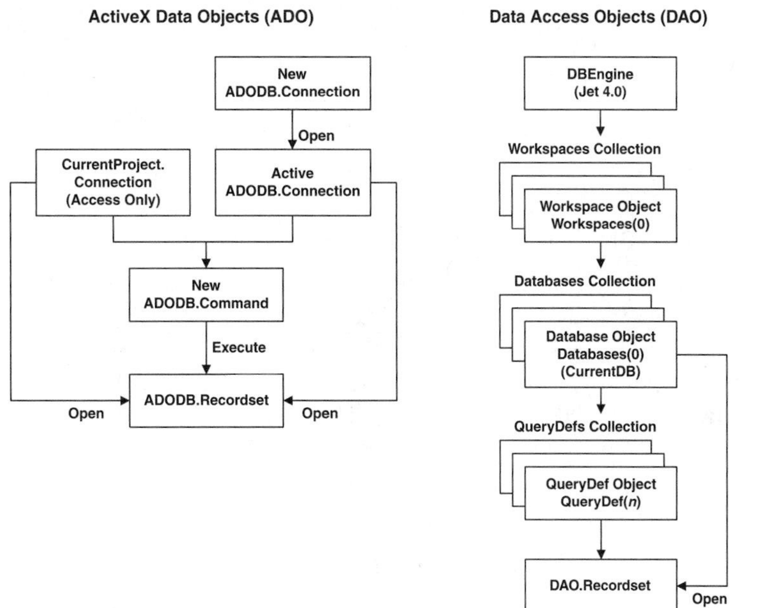

Figure 30.3 This diagram compares the ADO and DAO object hierarchies.

NOTE

> Access VBA provides a similar ADO shortcut, `CurrentProject.Connection`, which points to a default `ADODB.Connection` object with the Jet OLE DB Service Provider for the current database. Unlike `CurrentDB()`, which is optional, you must use `CurrentProject.Connection` as the `ADODB.Connection` to the currently open database. If you try to open a new `ADODB.Connection` to the current database, you receive a runtime error stating that the database is locked.

Unlike DAO objects, most of which are members of collections, you use the **`New`** reserved word with the **`Set`** instruction to create and the `Close` method, the **`Set`** *`ObjectName`* `=` **`Nothing`**, or both statements to remove instances of `ADODB.Connection`, `ADODB.Command`, and `ADODB.Recordset` objects independently of one another. The **`Set`** *`ObjectName`* `=` **`Nothing`** instruction releases memory consumed by the object.

DAO supports a variety of Jet collections, such as Users and Groups, and Jet SQL Data Definition Language (DDL) operations that ADO 2.7 alone doesn't handle. ADOX 2.7 defines Jet-specific collections and objects that aren't included in ADO 2.x. The "Provider-Specific Properties and Their Values" section later in the chapter describes how to roll your own cross-reference table to aid in migrating your DAO code to ADO.

The most important functional difference between DAO and ADO is that ADO supports Web-based applications and DAO doesn't. Thus, DAP bind to `ADODB.Recordset` objects. The continuing trend toward Internet-enabling everything means that Windows database programmers must make the transition from ODBC, ODBCDirect, RDO, and DAO technologies to ADO and OLE DB, so this book covers VBA programming of ADO, not DAO, objects. ADO supports ODBC connections to shared-file and client/server RDBMSs with the Microsoft OLE DB Provider for ODBC (more commonly called by its beta code name, *Kagera*). ODBC introduces another layer into the database connection, so it's less efficient than OLE DB. The examples of this chapter use only native OLE DB providers.

Upgrading from ADO 2.5 and Earlier to Version 2.6+

ADO 2.x in this chapter refers collectively to ADO 2.1, 2.5, 2.6, and 2.7. Windows XP and Office 2003 install ADO 2.7, which includes type libraries for ADO 2.0, 2.1, 2.5, 2.6 for backward compatibility. Windows 2000 Service Pack (SP) 1 or later installs ADO 2.5 SP1, which includes type libraries for for prior versions. Installing the SQL Server 2000 Desktop Engine (MSDE2000) from the Office 2003 distribution CD-ROM—or any other version of SQL Server 2000—upgrades Windows 2000's ADO 2.5 to 2.6. Version 2.7 is required only to support Intel's 64-bit Itanium processors. Upgrading from ADO 2.6 to 2.7 doesn't add new features or alter existing features.

NOTE

As mentioned in Chapter 27, "Learning Visual Basic for Applications," the default VBA reference for new ADP is ADO 2.1 for Access 2000 database format. If you change the default database version to Access 2002 in the Options dialog, the reference changes to ADO 2.5. Use of non-current references is required for backward compatibility with Access 2000 and 2002 ADP.

→ To review use of the VBA editor's References dialog, **see** "References to VBA and Access Modules," **p. 1157**.

Following are the new or altered ADO objects, properties, and methods in ADO 2.6+:

- `Record` objects can contain fields defined as `Recordsets`, `Streams` of binary or text data, and child records of hierarchical `Recordset` objects. Use of `Record` objects is beyond the scope of this book.
- `Stream` objects can send T-SQL `FOR XML` queries to SQL Server 2000 and return result sets as XML documents. `Stream` objects also are used with the `Record` object to return binary data from URL queries executed on file systems, Exchange 2000 Web Folders, and email messages. The "Programming `Stream` Objects" section, near the end of the chapter, provides a simple example of the use of a `Stream` object to return XML data from a `FOR XML` T-SQL query to a text box.

- Command objects gain new CommandStream and Dialect properties to support Stream objects, and a NamedParameters property that applies to the Parameters collection.
- Group and User ADOX objects add a Properties collection that contains Jet-specific Property objects. This chapter doesn't cover ADOX programming with VBA, because ADOX applies only to Jet databases.

TIP

If you're interested in learning more about ADOX, open the VBA Editor, type **adox** in the Ask a Question text box, select the ADOX methods option, click See Also in the "ADOX Methods" help page, and select ADOX API Reference in the list.

30

CREATING ADODB.Recordset OBJECTS

The concept of database object independence is new to Access. The best way of demonstrating this feature is to compare DAO and ADO code to create a Recordset object from an SQL statement. DAO syntax uses successive instantiation of each object in the DAO hierarchy: DBEngine, Workspace, Database, and Recordset, as in the following example:

```
Dim wsName As DAO.Workspace
Dim dbName As DAO.Database
Dim rstName As DAO.Recordset

Set wsName = DBEngine.Workspaces(0)
Set dbName = wsName.OpenDatabase ("DatabaseName.mdb")
Set rstName = dbName.OpenRecordset ("SQL Statement")
```

As you descend through the hierarchy, you open new child objects with methods of the parent object.

The most common approach with ADO is to create one or more independent, reusable instances of each object in the Declarations section of a form or module:

```
Private cnnName As New ADODB.Connection
Private cmmName As New ADODB.Command
Private rstName As New ADODB.Recordset
```

NOTE

This book uses cnn as the object type prefix for Connection, cmm for Command, and rst for Recordset. The cmm prefix is used because the cmd prefix traditionally identifies a command button control and the com prefix identifies the MSComm ActiveX control (Microsoft Comm Control 6.0).

Although you're likely to find references to DAO.Recordset dynasets and snapshots in the Access documentation, these terms don't apply to ADODB.Recordset objects. See the CursorType property of the ADODB.Recordset object in the "Recordset Properties" section later in this chapter for the CursorType equivalents of dynasets and snapshots.

After the initial declarations, you set the properties of the new object instances and apply methods—`Open` for `Connections` and `Recordsets`, or `Execute` for `Commands`—to activate the object. Invoking the `Open` method of the `ADODB.Recordset` object, rather than the `OpenRecordset` method of the `DAO.Database` object, makes ADO objects independent of one another. Object independence and batch-optimistic locking, for instance, let you close the `ADODB.Recordset`'s `ADODB.Connection` object, make changes to the `Recordset`, and then reopen the `Connection` to send only the changes to the underlying tables. Minimizing the number of open database connections conserves valuable server resources. The examples that follow illustrate the independence of top-level ADO members.

30

DESIGNING A FORM BOUND TO AN `ADODB.Recordset` OBJECT

NEW 2002 Access 2000+ forms have a property, `Recordset`, which lets you assign an `ADODB.Recordset` object as the `RecordSource` for one or more forms. The `Recordset` property of a form is an important addition, because you can assign the same `Recordset` to multiple forms. All forms connected to the `Recordset` synchronize to the same current record. Access developers have been requesting this feature since version 1.0. Access 2002 delivered updatable `ADODB.Recordsets` for Jet, SQL Server, and Oracle data sources that you can assign to the `Recordset` property value of forms and reports.

To create a simple form that uses VBA code to bind a form to a Jet `ADODB.Recordset` object, follow these steps:

1. Open a new database in Access 2000 format named **ADOTest.mdb** or the like in your ...\Office11\Samples folder. Add a new form in design mode and save it as **frmADO_Jet**.
2. Click the Code button on the toolbar to open the VBA editor, and choose Tools, References to open the References dialog.

3. Clear the check box for the reference to the Microsoft ActiveX Data Objects 2.1 Library, scroll to the Microsoft ActiveX Data Objects 2.7 Library, and mark the check box. Close and reopen the References dialog to verify that the new reference has percolated to the select region of the list (see Figure 30.4). Close the References dialog.

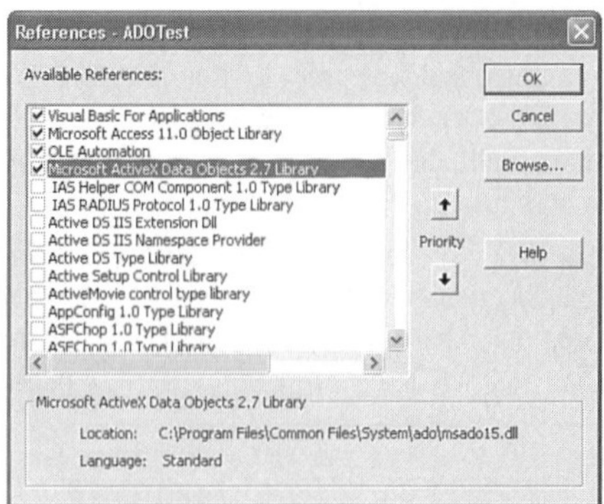

Figure 30.4
If you don't need backward compatibility with Access 2000 and 2002 applications, specify the latest version of ADO (2.7 for this example) as the reference.

4. Add the following code to the Declarations section of the `frmADO_Jet` Class Module:

```
Private strSQL As String
Private cnnNwind As New ADODB.Connection
Private rstNwind As New ADODB.Recordset
```

5. Add the following code to create the `Form_Load` event handler:

```
Private Sub Form_Load()
    'Specify the OLE DB provider and open the connection
    With cnnNwind
        .Provider = "Microsoft.Jet.OLEDB.4.0"
        .Open CurrentProject.Path & "\Northwind.mdb", "Admin"
    End With

    strSQL = "SELECT * FROM Customers"
    With rstNwind
        Set .ActiveConnection = cnnNwind
        .CursorType = adOpenKeyset
        .CursorLocation = adUseClient
        .LockType = adLockOptimistic
        .Open strSQL
    End With

    'Assign rstNwind as the Recordset for the form
    Set Me.Recordset = rstNwind

End Sub
```

NOTE

> The preceding code includes several properties that this chapter hasn't discussed yet. The objective of this and the following sections is to get you started with a quick demonstration of the `Form.Recordset` property. Properties and methods of the `Connection` and `Recordset` objects are the subject of the "Exploring Top-Level ADO Properties, Methods, and Events" section that follows shortly.

6. Return to Access and change to Form view to execute the preceding code. Then open the Properties window and click the Data tab. Your form appears as shown in Figure 30.5, with the first of 91 records selected by the navigation buttons.

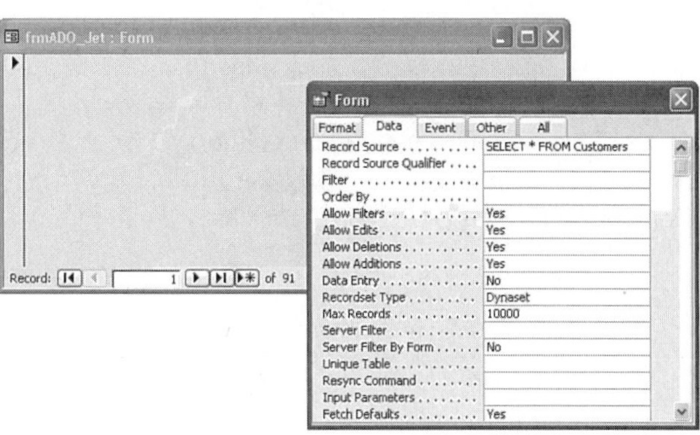

Figure 30.5
The frmADOTest form has its Recordset property set to an `ADODB.Recordset` object opened on the Northwind.mdb Customers table.

NOTE

> The form's Record Source property value is the SQL statement specified as the argument of the `Recordset` object's `Open` method. The Recordset Type property value appears as Dynaset, which isn't a valid `ADODB.Recordset` type. The enabled Add New Record navigation button confirms that the form is updatable.

30

BINDING CONTROLS TO A `Recordset` OBJECT WITH CODE

Adding the equivalent of bound controls to a form whose Record Source is an `ADODB.Recordset` object requires that you first add unbound controls and then bind the controls to the form's underlying `Recordset` with code. To create a simple data display form for the Customers table, do the following:

1. Return to Design view, display the Toolbox, and add seven unbound text boxes to the form. Name the text boxes **txtCustomerID**, **txtCompanyName**, **txtAddress**, **txtCity**, **txtRegion**, **txtPostalCode**, and **txtCountry**. Change the width of the text boxes to reflect approximately the number of characters in each of the Customer table's fields.
2. Change the label captions to **CustID:**, **Name:**, **Address:**, **City:**, **Region:**, **Postal Code:**, and **Country:**, respectively. Apply the Bold attribute to the labels for readability (see Figure 30.6).

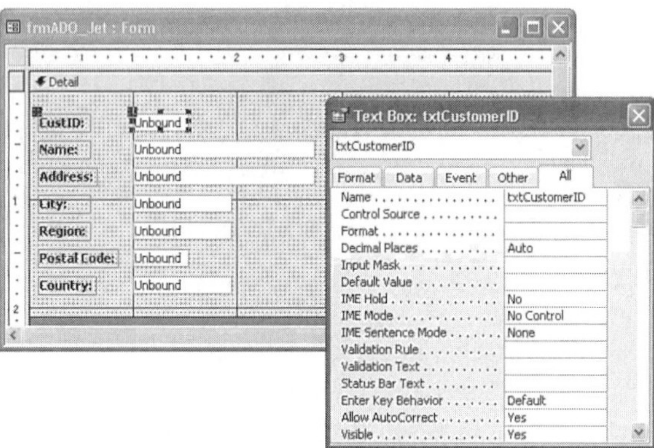

Figure 30.6
Add seven unbound text boxes to the frmADO_Jet form.

3. To bind the Control Source property of each text box to the appropriate field of the Customers table, click the Code button and add the following lines of code immediately after the `Set Me.Recordset = rstNwind` line:

```
Me.txtCustomerID.ControlSource = "CustomerID"
Me.txtCompanyName.ControlSource = "CompanyName"
Me.txtAddress.ControlSource = "Address"
Me.txtCity.ControlSource = "City"
Me.txtRegion.ControlSource = "Region"
Me.txtPostalCode.ControlSource = "PostalCode"
Me.txtCountry.ControlSource = "Country"
```

4. Choose Form view and navigate the Recordset (see Figure 30.7). The Control Source property value of the text boxes displays the field name you specified in the preceding code.

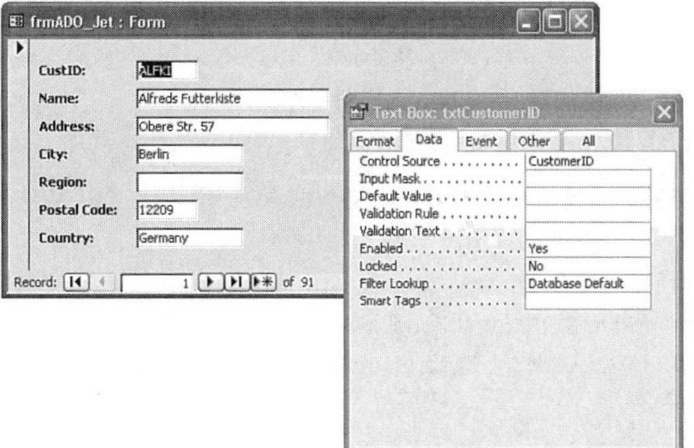

Figure 30.7 Form view displays field values in the unbound text boxes. The Data page of the Properties window of the txtCustomerID text box shows CustomerID as the Control Source property value.

5. Choose Datasheet view. The seven fields of the text boxes provide data to the columns of the datasheet, and the label captions serve as column headers.

6. Edit one of the CustID values; for example, change BLONP to BONX. If Cascade Update Related Fields for the join between the Customers and Orders tables isn't enabled, a message box states that you can't edit the field (see Figure 30.8).

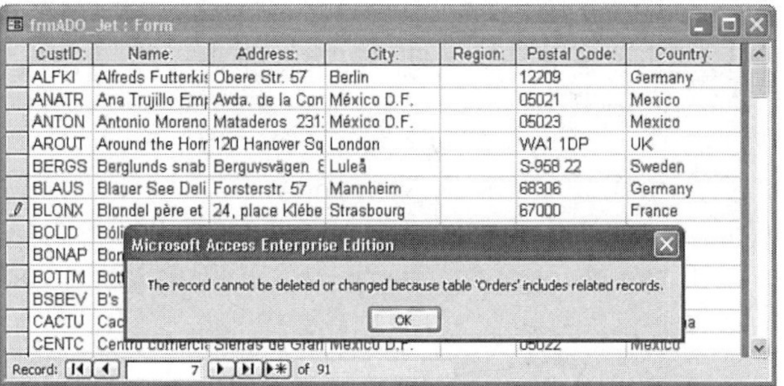

Figure 30.8 Datasheet view of the form displays only the fields of the Customers table that have associated text boxes. Changing the value of the primary key without cascading updates displays the error message shown here.

TIP

To emulate a table Datasheet view with code, add to the form text boxes for every field of the table. To open a table-type `ADODB.Recordset` object, substitute the table name for the SQL statement as the argument of the `rstName.Open` statement. You also can specify the name of an SQL Server view or Jet QueryDef object.

CONNECTING TO THE NORTHWINDCS MSDE DATABASE

Creating an `ADODB.Recordset` object with VBA code lets you connect to SQL Server and other client/server RDBMSs in a Jet database or Access project. To substitute the MSDE version of the Northwind sample database for Northwind.mdb, do the following:

1. Start your local MSDE2000 server if it isn't already running.

2. Make a copy of frmADO_Jet as **frmADO_MSDE**, open frmADO_MSDE in Design view, and open the VBA Editor for frmADO_MSDE.
3. Delete the `.Provider = "Microsoft.Jet.OLEDB.4.0"` line. For this example, the `Open` method's argument specifies the OLE DB data provider
4. MSDE uses integrated Windows security by default, so change the `.Open CurrentProject.Path & "\Northwind.mdb", "Admin"` line to

```
.Open "Provider=SQLOLEDB.1;Data Source=(local);" & _
   "Integrated Security=SSPI;Initial Catalog=NorthwindCS"
```

   (`SSPI` is an abbreviation for Security Support Provider, Integrated.)
5. Add the following statement after the `Set Me.Recordset = rstNwind` line:

```
Me.UniqueTable = "Customers"
```

TIP

> Even if your query returns data from a single table only, you should specify the table as unique. For updatable result sets from Transact-SQL (T-SQL) queries with joins, you must set the `UniqueTable` property value to specify the "most-many" table. As an example, if your query returns values from one-to-many joins between the Customers, Orders, and Order Details table, Order Details is the "most-many" table. Fields of the Order Details table contribute the uniqueness to the rows of the query result set.

6. Run frmADO_MSDE in Datasheet view and verify that the form is updatable by temporarily editing any cell except primary-key values of the CustID field. You receive a constraint conflict error if you attempt to change a CustomerID value (see Figure 30.9).

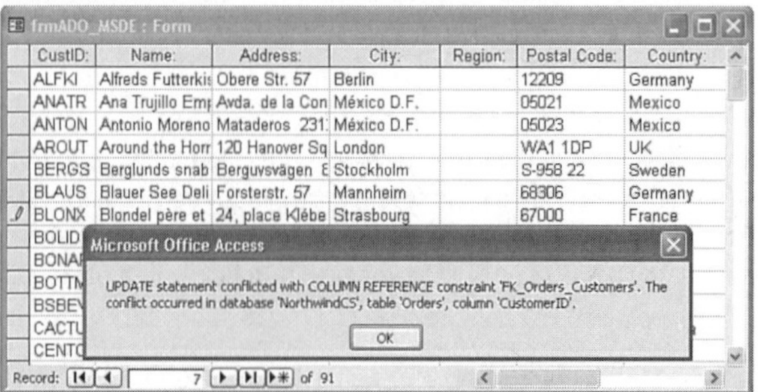

Figure 30.9
When you attempt to edit a primary-key value on which other records depend, you receive the SQL Server message shown here.

NOTE

> The ADOTest.mdb database and ADOTest.adp project in the \SEUA11\Chaptr30 folder of the accompanying CD-ROM contain the frmADO_Jet and frmADO_MSDE forms described in the preceding two sections. This folder contains a copy of the tables of Northwind.mdb.

USING THE OBJECT BROWSER TO DISPLAY ADO PROPERTIES, METHODS, AND EVENTS

At this point in your ADO learning curve, a detailed list of properties, enumerations of constant values, methods, and events of ADO components might appear premature. Understanding the capabilities and benefits of ADO, however, requires familiarity with ADO's repertoire of properties, methods, and events. To get the most out of ADP and to program DAP you must have a working knowledge of ADO programming techniques.

DAO objects don't fire events; ADO objects do. Access objects offer fine-grained events, but don't provide programmers with a lower-level event model for basic operations, such as connecting to a database and executing queries. Access 97's ODBCDirect offered an event model, but you couldn't bind ODBCDirect Recordsets to forms. ADO offers a complete and very fine-grained event model.

Object Browser is the most useful tool for becoming acquainted with the properties, methods, and events of ADODB objects. Object Browser also is the most convenient method for obtaining help with the syntax and usage of ADO objects, methods, and events.

NOTE

> The examples and tabular list of properties, methods, and events of ADO objects in this and other related chapters are for ADO 2.6. Objects, methods, and events that are added by ADO 2.5+ are identified by the new in Access 2002 icon. (Access 2003's ADO 2.7 doesn't add any new elements.) If your .mdb or .adp file has a reference to ADO 2.1 or 2.5, your results for this chapter's examples might differ or fail to execute.

To use Object Browser with ADO objects, follow these steps:

1. Open in design mode one of the forms of ADOTest.mdb that you created in the preceding sections, and then open the VBA Editor for its code. Alternatively, open the sample ADOTest.mdb or ADOTest.adp file.

2. Press F2 to open Object Browser.
3. Select ADODB in the library (upper) list.
4. Select one of the top-level components, such as `Connection`, in the Classes (left) pane.
5. Select a property, event, or method, such as Open, in the Members of '*ObjectName*' (right) pane. A short-form version of the syntax for the selected method or event appears in Object Browser's lower pane (see Figure 30.10).

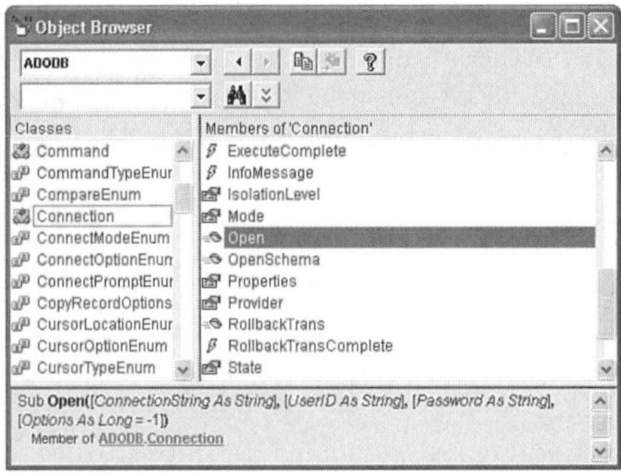

Figure 30.10
Object Browser displays in the status pane the syntax of the object class member you select in the Members of '*ObjectName*' pane.

30

6. Click the Help button to open the help topic for the selected object, property, method, or event. Figure 30.11 shows the help topic for `ADODB.Connection.Open`.

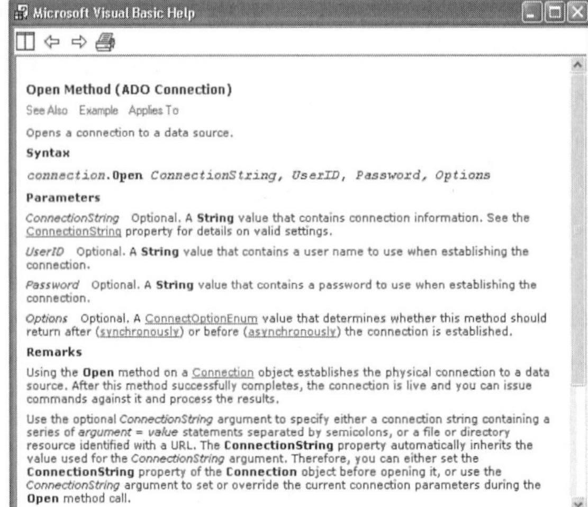

Figure 30.11
The Object Browser's help button opens the online VBA help topic for the selected ADODB object, method, property, or event. The See Also link leads to related help topics. If enabled, the Example link opens a sample VBA subprocedure. The Applies To link opens a list of objects that share the method, property, or event.

ADO type libraries also include enumerations (lists) of numeric (usually **`Long`**) constant values with an `ad` prefix. These constant enumerations are specific to one or more properties. Figure 30.12 shows Object Browser displaying the members of the `ConnectModeEnum` enumeration for the `Mode` property of an `ADODB.Connection` object. The lower pane displays the **`Long`** value of the constant.

TIP

> You can substitute the numeric value of enumerated constants for the constant name in VBA, but doing so isn't considered a good programming practice. Numeric values of the constants might change in subsequent ADO versions, causing unexpected results when upgrading applications to a new ADO release.

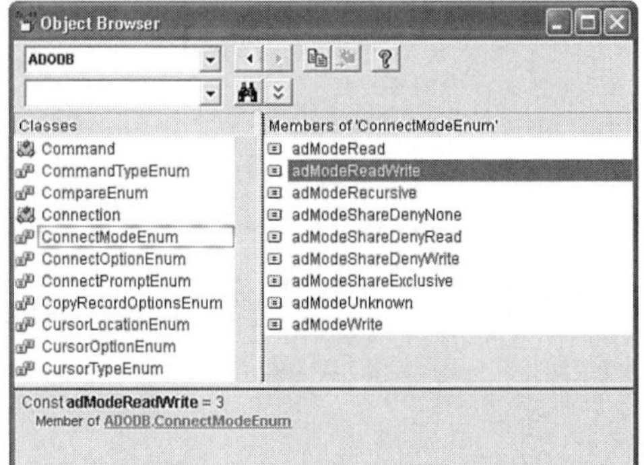

Figure 30.12 Object Browser displays in the status pane the numeric value of members of ADO enumerations, which are a collection of related ADO constant values.

WORKING WITH THE ADODB.Connection OBJECT

The `Connection` object is the primary top-level ADO component. You must successfully open a `Connection` object to a data source before you can use associated `Command` or `Recordset` objects.

CONNECTION PROPERTIES

Table 30.1 lists the names and descriptions of the properties of the `ADODB.Connection` object.

TABLE 30.1 PROPERTIES OF THE ADODB.Connection OBJECT

Property Name	Data Type and Purpose
`Attributes`	A **`Long`** read/write value that specifies use of retaining transactions by the sum of two constant values. The `adXactCommitRetaining` constant starts a new transaction when calling the `CommitTrans` method; `adXactAbortRetaining` starts a new transaction when calling the `RollbackTrans` method. The default value is `0`, don't use retaining trans actions.
`CommandTimeout`	A **`Long`** read/write value that determines the time in seconds before terminating an `Execute` call against an associated `Command` object. The default value is `30` seconds.
`ConnectionString`	A **`String`** read/write variable that supplies specific information required by a data or service provider to open a connection to the data source.
`ConnectionTimeout`	A **`Long`** read/write value that determines the number of seconds before terminating an unsuccessful `Connection.Open` method call. The default value is `15` seconds.

continues

TABLE 30.1 CONTINUED

Property Name	Data Type and Purpose
`CursorLocation`	A **`Long`** read/write value that determines whether the client-side (`adUseClient`) or the server-side (`adUseServer`) cursor engine is used. The default is `adUseServer`.
`DefaultDatabase`	A **`String`** read/write variable that specifies the name of the database to use if not specified in the `ConnectionString`. For SQL Server examples, the value is the default Initial Catalog.
`Errors`	A pointer to the `Errors` collection for the connection that contains one or more `Error` objects if an error is encountered when attempting the connection. The later "`Errors` Collection and `Error` Objects" section describes this property.
`IsolationLevel`	A **`Long`** read/write value that determines the behavior or transactions that interact with other simultaneous transactions (see Table 30.2).
`Mode`	A **`Long`** value that determines read and write permissions for `Connection` objects (see Table 30.3).
`Properties`	A pointer to the OLE DB provider-specific (also called dynamic) `Properties` collection of the `Connection` object. Jet 4.0 databases have 94 `Property` objects and SQL Server databases have 93. The next section shows you how to enumerate provider-specific properties.
`Provider`	A **`String`** read/write value that specifies the name of the OLE DB data or service provider if not specified in the `ConnectionString` value. The default value is MSDASQL, the Microsoft OLE DB Provider for ODBC. The most common providers used in the programming chapters of this book are Microsoft.Jet.OLEDB.4.0, more commonly known by its code name, "Jolt 4," and SQLOLEDB, the OLE DB provider for SQL Server.
`State`	A **`Long`** read-only value that specifies whether the connection to the database is open, closed, or in an intermediate state (see Table 30.4).
`Version`	A **`String`** read-only value that returns the ADO version number.

NOTE

Most property values identified in Table 30.1 as being read/write are writable only when the connection is in the closed state. Some provider-specific properties are read/write, but most are read-only.

PROVIDER-SPECIFIC PROPERTIES AND THEIR VALUES

When you're tracking down problems with `Connection`, `Command`, `Recordset`, or `Record` objects, you might need to provide the values of some provider-specific properties to a Microsoft or another database vendor's technical service representative. To display the names and values of provider-specific `ADODB.Property` objects for an `ADODB.Connection` to a Jet database in the Immediate window, do the following:

1. In the declarations section of the VBA code for the frmADO_Jet or frmADO_MSDE form, add the following object variable declaration:

```
Private prpProp As ADODB.Property
```

   `Property` objects exist in the `Properties` collection, so you don't add the **`New`** keyword in this case.

2. After the **`End With`** statement for cnnNwind, add the following instructions to print the property names and values:

```
Debug.Print cnnNwind.Properties.Count & _
   " {SQL Server¦Jet} Connection Properties"
For Each prpProp In cnnNwind.Properties
   Debug.Print prpProp.Name & " = " & prpProp.Value
Next prpProp
```

3. Press Ctrl+G to open the Immediate window and delete its contents.
4. Reopen the form in Datasheet view to execute the `Form_Load` event handler, and return to the VBA editor to view the result in the Immediate window (see Figure 30.13).

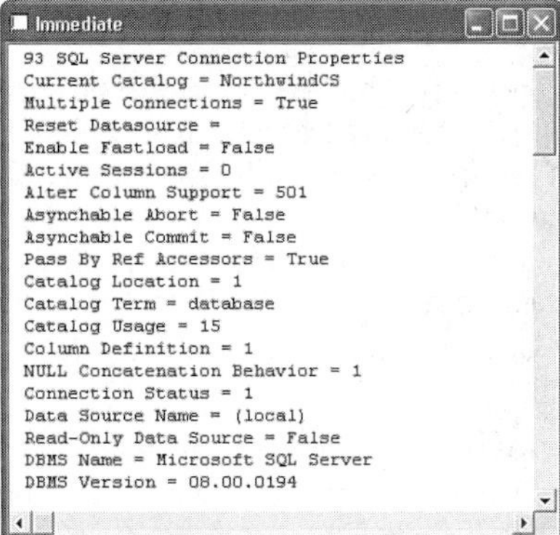

Immediate
93 SQL Server Connection Properties
Current Catalog = NorthwindCS
Multiple Connections = True
Reset Datasource =
Enable Fastload = False
Active Sessions = 0
Alter Column Support = 501
Asynchable Abort = False
Asynchable Commit = False
Pass By Ref Accessors = True
Catalog Location = 1
Catalog Term = database
Catalog Usage = 15
Column Definition = 1
NULL Concatenation Behavior = 1
Connection Status = 1
Data Source Name = (local)
Read-Only Data Source = False
DBMS Name = Microsoft SQL Server
DBMS Version = 08.00.0194

Figure 30.13
The Immediate window displays the first 19 of the 93 provider-specific properties for a connection to SQL Server 2000.

5. To find a definition of a provider-specific property of Jet or SQL Server data sources, connect to the Microsoft Web site, copy or type the name of the property in the Search For text box, add double quotes (") to the beginning and end of the term, and click Search. Click the appropriate link (usually the first) to display the definition of the property (see Figure 30.14).
6. After you've satisfied your curiosity about provider-specific properties and their values, comment out or delete the added code. Sending a significant amount of data to the Immediate window delays opening the form.

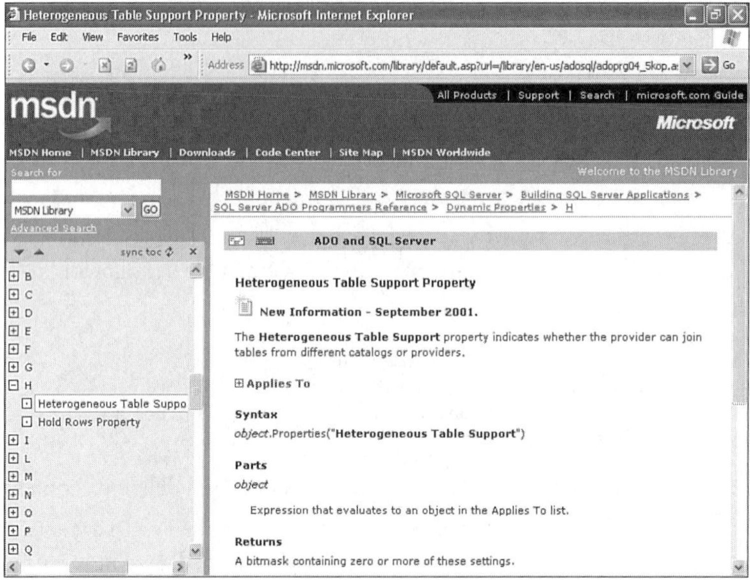

Figure 30.14
Most Jet and SQL Server provider-specific properties have pages in the Microsoft Developer Network (MSDN) library for the Platform SDK (psdk). Click Show TOC to find your relative location within the library.

30

NOTE

Pages that define SQL Server-specific properties specify values by reference to `DBPROPVAL_...` constants whose values aren't included in the table. Many searches for Jet-specific `Property` object definitions lead to the "Appendix C: Microsoft Jet 4.0 OLE DB Provider-Defined Property Values" page (`http://msdn.microsoft.com/library/techart/daotoadoupdate_topic15.htm`), which provides a set of constant values that you can add to an Access module.

Some of the SQL Server provider-specific properties appear in a list on the All page of the Data Link Properties dialog for a project's connection. To view these properties and their values, when set, open the NorthwindCS project, choose File, Connection to open the Data Link Properties dialog, and click the All tab (see Figure 30.15).

TIP

The "Appendix A: DAO to ADO Quick Reference" page (`http://msdn.microsoft.com/library/techart/daotoadoupdate_topic13.htm`) of the "Migrating from DAO to ADO" white paper contains a table that translates DAO objects and properties to ADO objects, properties, and provider-specific Jet properties. To create an easily searchable version, copy the table to the clipboard, paste it into a Word document and save the file in both .doc and .htm formats. Importing the .htm table to a Jet or SQL Server table lets you view the contents in a searchable datasheet (see Figure 30.16). Contents of the Microsoft Web site are copyrighted, so the table isn't included in this chapter's example databases.

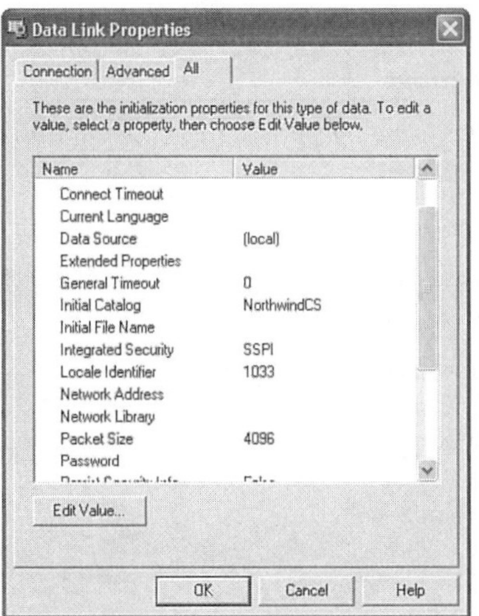

Figure 30.15 The All page of the Data Link Properties dialog for the NorthwindCS connection to MSDE displays a few of the 93 provider-specific properties of the OLE DB Provider for SQL Server (SQLOLEDB).

DAO to ADO Cross Reference : Table

ID	DAO Object	DAO Property/Method	ADO/ADOX/JRO	Object	ADO Property/Method
1	DBEngine	DefaultType1	N/A	N/A	N/A
2	DBEngine	DefaultPassword1	N/A	N/A	N/A
3	DBEngine	DefaultUser1	N/A	N/A	N/A
4	DBEngine	IniPath	ADO	Connection	Jet OLEDB:Registry Path2
5	DBEngine	LoginTimeout	ADO	Connection	ConnectionTimeout
6	DBEngine	SystemDB	ADO	Connection	Jet OLEDB:System Database2
7	DBEngine	Version	ADO	Connection	Version
8	DBEngine	BeginTrans	ADO	Connection	BeginTrans
9	DBEngine	CommitTrans	ADO	Connection	CommitTrans
10	DBEngine	Rollback	ADO	Connection	RollbackTrans
11	DBEngine	CompactDatabase	JRO	JetEngine	CompactDatabase
12	DBEngine	CreateDatabase	ADOX	Catalog	Create
13	DBEngine	CreateWorkspace	ADO	Connection	Open
14	DBEngine	Idle	JRO	JetEngine	RefreshCache
15	DBEngine	OpenDatabase	ADO	Connection	Open
16	DBEngine	RegisterDatabase1	N/A	N/A	N/A
17	DBEngine	RepairDatabase1	N/A	N/A	N/A
18	DBEngine	SetOption	ADO	Connection	Properties3
19	Workspace	IsolateODBCTrans	ADO	Connection	Isolation Levels2
20	Workspace	LoginTimeout	ADO	Connection	ConnectionTimeout
21	Workspace	Name1	N/A	N/A	N/A

Record: 1 of 198

Figure 30.16 This Jet table was created by importing a copy of the HTML table of the "DAO to ADO Cross Reference" page from the Microsoft Web site. Property or method names with number suffixes, such as DefaultType1, refer to footnotes in the source Web page.

TRANSACTION ISOLATION LEVELS

The ability to specify the transaction isolation level applies only when you use the `BeginTrans`, `CommitTrans`, and `RollbackTrans` methods (see Table 30.6 later in this chapter) to perform a transaction on a `Connection` object. If multiple database users simultaneously execute transactions, your application should specify how it responds to other transactions in-process. Table 30.2 lists the options for the degree of your application's isolation from other simultaneous transactions.

30

TABLE 30.2 CONSTANT ENUMERATION FOR THE `IsolationLevel` PROPERTY

`IsolationLevelEnum`	Description
`adXactCursorStability`	Allows reading only committed changes in other transactions (default value).
`adXactBrowse`	Allows reading uncommitted changes in other transactions.
`adXactChaos`	The transaction won't overwrite changes made to transaction(s) at a higher isolation level.
`adXactIsolated`	All transactions are independent of (isolated from) other transactions.
`adXactReadCommitted`	Same as `adXactCursorStability`.
`adXactReadUncommitted`	Same as `adXactBrowse`.
`adXactRepeatableRead`	Prohibits reading changes in other transactions.
`adXactSerializable`	Same as `adXactIsolated`.
`adXactUnspecified`	The transaction level of the provider can't be determined.

NOTE

Enumeration tables in this book list the default value first, followed by the remaining constants in alphabetical order. Where two members of Table 30.2 represent the same isolation level, one of the members is included for backward compatibility.

THE `Connection.Mode` PROPERTY

Unless you have a specific reason to specify a particular `ADODB.Connection.Mode` value, the default `adModeUnknown` is adequate. The Jet OLE DB provider defaults to `adModeShareDenyNone`. The Access Permissions list on the Advanced page of the Data Link properties page for SQLOLEDB is disabled, but you can set the `Mode` property with code. Table 30.3 lists all the constants for the `Mode` property.

TABLE 30.3 CONSTANT ENUMERATION FOR THE `Mode` PROPERTY

`ConnectModeEnum`	Description
`adModeUnknown`	No connection permissions have been set on the data source (default value).
`adModeRead`	Connect with read-only permission.
`adModeReadWrite`	Connect with read/write permissions.
`adModeRecursive`	If an `adModeShareDeny...` flag is specified, applies the mode to child records of a chaptered (hierarchical) `Recordset` object.

TABLE 30.3 CONTINUED

ConnectModeEnum	Description
adoModeRecursive	Used in conjunction with the Record objects, which this chapter doesn't cover.
adModeShareDenyNone	Don't deny other users read or write access.
adModeShareDenyRead	Deny others permission to open a read connection to the data source.
adModeShareDenyWrite	Deny others permission to open a write connection to the data source.
adModeShareExclusive	Open the data source for exclusive use.
adModeWrite	Connect with write-only permission.

TIP

You often can improve performance of client/server decision-support applications by opening the connection as read only (adModeRead). Modifying the structure of a database with SQL's DDL usually requires exclusive access to the database (adModeShareExclusive).

THE Connection.State PROPERTY

Table 30.4 lists the constants that return the state of the Connection object. These constants also are applicable to the State property of the Command and Recordset objects.

It's common to open and close connections as needed to reduce the connection load on the database. (Each open connection to a client/server database consumes a block of memory.) In many cases, you must test whether the Connection object is open or closed before applying the Close or Open method, or changing Connection property values, which are read-only when the connection is open.

TABLE 30.4 CONSTANT ENUMERATION FOR THE State PROPERTY

ObjectStateEnum	Description
adStateClosed	The Connection (or other object) is closed (default value).
adStateConnecting	A connection to the data source is in progress.
adStateExecuting	The Execute method of a Connection or Command object has been called.
adStateFetching	Rows are returning to a Recordset object.
adStateOpen	The Connection (or other object) is open (active).

Errors COLLECTION AND Error OBJECTS

Figure 30.17 illustrates the relationship between top-level ADO components and their collections. The dependent Errors collection is a property of the Connection object, and if errors are encountered with any operation on the connection, contains one or more Error objects. The Errors collection has one property, Count, which you test to determine whether an error has occurred after executing a method call on Connection and Recordset objects. A collection is required, because it's possible for an object to generate several errors.

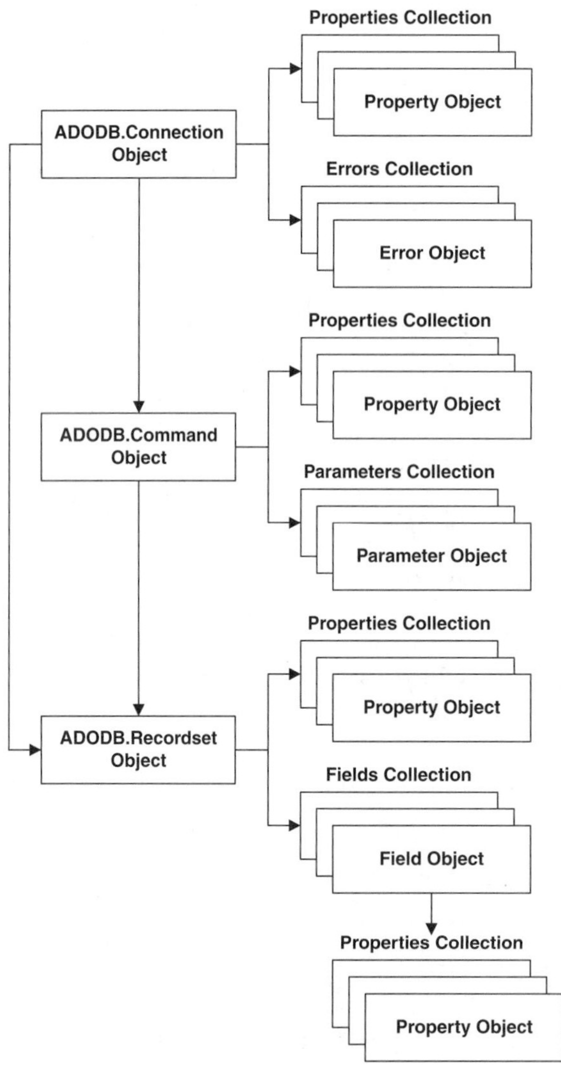

Figure 30.17 The Connection, Command, and Recordset objects have Properties and Errors collections. The Command object also has a Parameters collection and the Recordset object has a Fields Collection. The new Record object isn't included in this diagram.

The Errors collection has two methods, Clear and Item. The Clear method deletes all current Error objects in the collection, resetting the value of Count to 0. The Item method, which is the default method of the `Errors` and other collections, returns an object reference (pointer) to an `Error` object. The syntax for explicit and default use of the `Item` method is

```
Set errName = cnnName.Errors.Index({strName¦intIndex})
Set errName = cnnName.Errors({strName¦intIndex})
```

The `Error` object has the seven read-only properties listed in Table 30.5. `Error` objects have no methods or events. The `InfoMessage` event of the `Connection` object, described in the "Connection Events" section later in this chapter, fires when an `Error` object is added to the `Errors` collection and supplies a pointer to the newly added `Error` object.

30

TABLE 30.5 PROPERTY NAMES AND DESCRIPTIONS OF THE `Error` OBJECT

Property Name	Description
`Description`	A **`String`** value containing a brief text description of the error
`HelpContext`	A **`Long`** value specifying the error's context ID in a Windows Help file
`HelpFile`	A **`String`** value specifying the full path to and name of the Windows Help file, usually for the data provider
`NativeError`	A **`Long`** value specifying a provider-specific error code
`Number`	A **`Long`** value specifying the number assigned to the error by the provider or data source
`Source`	A **`String`** value containing the name of the object that generated the error, `ADODB.`*`ObjectName`* for ADO errors
`SQLState`	A **`String`** value (`SQLSTATE`) containing a five-letter code specified by the ANSI/ISO SQL-92 standard, consisting of two characters specifying Condition, followed by three characters for Subcondition

➔ For the basics of error handling in VBA, **see** "Handling Runtime Errors," **p. 1176**.

NOTE

Unfortunately, not all RDBMS vendors implement `SQLSTATE` in the same way. If you test the `SQLState` property value, make sure to follow the vendor-specific specifications for Condition and Subcondition values.

Listing 30.1 is an example of code to open a `Connection` (`cnnNwind`) and a `Recordset` (`rstCusts`) with conventional error handling; `rstCusts` supplies the `Recordset` property of the form. The "Non-existent" table name generates a "Syntax error in FROM clause" error in the Immediate window. The **`Set`** *`ObjectName`* `=` **`Nothing`** statements in the error handler recover the memory consumed by the objects.

30

Listing 30.1 VBA Code That Writes Error Properties to the Immediate Window

```
Private Sub Form_Load
   Dim cnnNwind As New ADODB.Connection
   Dim rstCusts As New ADODB.Recordset

   On Error GoTo CatchErrors
   cnnNwind.Provider = "Microsoft.Jet.OLEDB.4.0"
   cnnNwind.Open CurrentProject.Path & "\Northwind.mdb", "Admin"
   With rstCusts
      Set .ActiveConnection = cnnNwind
      .CursorType = adOpenKeyset
      .LockType = adLockBatchOptimistic
      .Open "SELECT * FROM Non-existent"
   End With
   Set Me.Recordset = rstCusts
   Exit Sub

CatchErrors:
   Dim colErrors As Errors
   Dim errNwind As Error
   Set colErrors = cnnNwind.Errors
   For Each errNwind In colErrors
      Debug.Print "Description:  " & errNwind.Description
      Debug.Print "Native Error: " & errNwind.NativeError; ""
      Debug.Print "SQL State:    " & errNwind.SQLState
      Debug.Print vbCrLf
   Next errNwind
   Set colErrors = Nothing
   Set errNwind = Nothing
   Set rstCusts = Nothing
   Set cnnNwind = Nothing
   Exit Sub
End Sub
```

NOTE

The frmErrors form of ADOTest.mdb and ADOTest.adp incorporates the preceding code. Open the form to execute the code, change to Design view, open the VBA editor, and press Ctrl+G to read the error message in the Immediate window.

Connection Methods

Table 30.6 lists the methods of the `ADODB.Connection` object. Only the `Execute`, `Open`, and `OpenSchema` methods accept argument values. The `OpenSchema` method is of interest primarily for creating database diagrams, data transformation for data warehouses and marts, and online analytical processing (OLAP) applications.

TABLE 30.6 METHODS OF THE ADODB.Connection OBJECT

Method	Description
BeginTrans	Initiates a transaction; must be followed by CommitTrans and/or RollbackTrans.
Close	Closes the connection.
CommitTrans	Commits a transaction, making changes to the data source permanent. (Requires a prior call to the BeginTrans method.)
Execute	Returns a forward-only Recordset object from a SELECT SQL statement. Also used to execute statements that don't return Recordset objects, such as INSERT, UPDATE, and DELETE queries or DDL statements. You use this method to execute T-SQL stored procedures, regardless of whether they return a Recordset.
Open	Opens a connection based on a connection string.
OpenSchema	Returns a Recordset object that provides information on the structure of the data source, called metadata.
RollbackTrans	Cancels a transaction, reversing any temporary changes made to the data source. (Requires a prior call to the BeginTrans method.)

THE Connection.Open AND Connection.OpenSchema METHODS

You must open a connection before you can execute a statement on it. The syntax of the Open method is

```
cnnName.Open [strConnect[, strUID[, strPwd, lngOptions]]]]
```

Alternatively, you can assign the connection string values to the Connection object's Provider and ConnectionString properties. The following example, similar to that for the Recordset object examples early in the chapter, is for a connection to Northwind.mdb in the same folder as the application .mdb:

```
With cnnNwind
   .Provider = "Microsoft.Jet.OLEDB.4.0"
   .ConnectionString = CurrentProject.Path & "\Northwind.mdb"
   .Open
End With
```

In this case, all the information required to open a connection to Northwind.mdb is provided as property values, so the Open method needs no argument values.

If you're creating a data dictionary or designing a generic query processor for a client/server RDBMS, the OpenSchema method is likely to be of interest to you. Otherwise, you might want to skip the details of the OpenSchema method, which is included here for completeness. Schema information is called *metadata*, data that describes the structure of data.

TIP

> ADOX 2.7 defines a `Catalog` object for Jet 4.0 databases that's more useful for Jet databases than the generic `OpenSchema` method, which is intended primarily for use with client/server RDBMs. The `Catalog` object includes `Groups`, `Users`, `Tables`, `Views`, and `Procedures` collections.

30

THE `Connection.Execute` METHOD

The syntax of the `Connection.Execute` method to return a reference to a forward-only `ADODB.Recordset` object is

```
Set rstName = cnnName.Execute (strCommand, [lngRowsAffected[, lngOptions]])
```

Alternatively, you can use named arguments for all ADO methods. Named arguments, however, require considerably more typing than conventional comma-separated argument syntax. The named argument equivalent of the preceding **`Set`** statement is

```
Set rstName = cnnName.Execute (Command:=strCommand, _
   RowsAffected:=lngRowsAffected, Options:=lngOptions)
```

If `strCommand` doesn't return a `Recordset`, the syntax is

```
cnnName.Execute strCommand, [lngRowsAffected[, lngOptions]]
```

The value of `strCommand` can be an SQL statement, a table name, the name of a stored procedure, or an arbitrary text string acceptable to the data provider.

TIP

> For best performance, specify a value for the `lngOptions` argument (see Table 30.7) so the provider doesn't need to interpret the statement to determine its type. The optional `lngRowsAffected` argument returns the number of rows affected by an `INSERT`, `UPDATE`, or `DELETE` query; these types of queries return a closed `Recordset` object. A `SELECT` query returns `0` to `lngRowsAffected` and an open, forward-only `Recordset` with 0 or more rows. The value of `lngRowsAffected` is `0` for T-SQL updates queries and stored procedures that include the `SET NOCOUNT ON` statement.

TABLE 30.7 CONSTANT ENUMERATION FOR THE `lngOptions` ARGUMENT OF THE `Execute` METHOD FOR `Connection` AND `Command` OBJECTS

CommandTypeEnum	Description
`adCmdUnknown`	The type of command isn't specified (default). The data provider determines the syntax of the command.
`adCmdFile`	The command is the name of a file in a format appropriate to the object type.
`adCmdStoredProc`	The command is the name of a stored procedure.
`adCmdTable`	The command is a table name, which generates an internal `SELECT * FROM TableName` query.

CommandTypeEnum	Description
adCmdTableDirect	The command is a table name, which retrieves rows directly from the table
adCmdText	The command is an SQL statement.

Forward-only Recordset objects, created by what's called a firehose cursor, provide the best performance and minimum network traffic in a client/server environment. However, forward-only Recordsets are limited to manipulation by VBA code. If you set the RecordSource property of a form to a forward-only Recordset, controls on the form don't display field values.

CONNECTION EVENTS

Events are useful for trapping errors, eliminating the need to poll the values of properties, such as State, and performing asynchronous database operations. To expose the ADODB.Connection events to your application, you must use the **WithEvents** reserved word (without **New**) to declare the ADODB.Connection object in the Declarations section of a class or form module and then use a **Set** statement with **New** to create an instance of the object, as shown in the following example:

```
Private WithEvents cnnName As ADODB.Connection

Private Sub Form_Load
   Set cnnName = New ADODB.Connection
   ...
   Code using the Connection object
   ...
   cnnName.Close
End Sub
```

The preceding syntax is required for most Automation objects that source (expose) events. Event-handling subprocedures for Automation events often are called event sinks. Source and sink terminology derives from the early days of transistors; the source (emitter) supplies electrons and the sink (collector) accumulates electrons.

Table 30.8 lists the events that appear in the Procedures list of the code-editing window for the cnn*Name* Connection object and gives a description of when the events fire.

TABLE 30.8 EVENTS FIRED BY THE ADODB.Connection OBJECT

Event Name	When Fired
BeginTransComplete	After the BeginTrans method executes
CommitTransComplete	After the CommitTrans method executes
ConnectComplete	After a Connection to the data source succeeds
Disconnect	After a Connection is closed

continues

30

Table 30.8 Continued

Event Name	When Fired
`ExecuteComplete`	On completion of the `Connection.Execute` or `Command.Execute` method call
`InfoMessage`	When an `Error` object is added to the `ADODB.`*`Connection`*`.Errors` collection
`RollbackTransComplete`	After the `RollbackTrans` method executes
`WillConnect`	On calling the `Connection.Open` method but before the connection is made
`WillExecute`	On calling the `Connection.Execute` or `Command.Execute` method, just before the command executes a connection

TIP

Take full advantage of ADO events in your VBA data-handling code. Relatively few developers currently use event-handling code in ordinary database front ends. ADO's event model will be of primary interest to developers migrating from Access 97's RDO to ADO. Developers of data warehousing and OLAP applications, which often involve very long-running queries, are most likely to use events in conjunction with asynchronous query operations.

Using the ADODB.Command Object

The primary purpose of the `Command` object is to execute parameterized stored procedures, either in the form of the default temporary prepared statements or persistent, precompiled T-SQL statements in SQL Server databases. MSDE and SQL Server create temporary prepared statements that exist only for the lifetime of the current client connection. Precompiled SQL statements are procedures stored in the database file; their more common name is stored procedure. When creating `Recordset` objects from ad hoc SQL statements, the more efficient approach is to bypass the `Command` object and use the `Recordset.Open` method.

Command Properties

The `Command` object has relatively few properties, many of which duplicate those of the `Connection` object. Table 30.9 lists the names and descriptions of the `Command` object's properties. Like the `Connection` object, the `Command` object has its own provider-specific `Properties` collection, which you can print to the Immediate window using statements similar to those for `Command` objects described in the earlier "Provider-Specific Properties and Their Values" section.

TIP

> The Command object is required to take advantage of ADO 2.6+'s Stream object, which contains data in the form of a continuous stream of binary data or text. Text streams often contain XML documents or document fragments returned from SQL Server 2000 XML AUTO queries. The Microsoft OLE DB Provider for Internet Publishing (MSDAIPP) enables Connection, Recordset, Record, and Stream objects to bind to a URL and retrieve data into a Stream object. Windows XP/2000+'s Internet Information Server (IIS) 5.0+ adds the MSDAIPP provider.

30

Table 30.9 Properties of the Command Object

Property Name	Description
ActiveConnection	A pointer to the Connection object associated with the Command. Use **Set** cmm*Name*.ActiveConnection = cnn*Name* for an existing open Connection. Alternatively, you can use a valid connection string to create a new connection without associating a named Connection object. The default value is **Null**.
NEW 2002 CommandStream	A **Variant** read/write value that contains the input stream used to specify the output stream.
CommandText	A **String** read/write value that specifies an SQL statement, table name, stored procedure name, or an arbitrary string acceptable to the provider of the ActiveConnection. The value of the CommandType property determines the format of the CommandText value. The default value is an empty string, "". CommandText and CommandStream are mutually exclusive. You can't specify a CommandStream and a CommandText value for the same Command object.
CommandTimeout	A **Long** read/write value that determines the time in seconds before terminating a Command.Execute call. This value overrides the Connection.CommandTimeout setting. The default value is 30 seconds.
CommandType	A **Long** read/write value that specifies how the data provider interprets the value of the CommandText property. (CommandType is the equivalent of the optional lng*CommandType* argument of the Connection.Execute method, described earlier in the chapter (refer to Table 30.7). The default value is adCmdUnknown.

continues

TABLE 30.9 CONTINUED

Property Name	Description
NEW 2002 Dialect	A **String** read/write value that accepts one of four globally unique ID (GUID) values specifying the type of CommandStream object. Valid settings are DBGUID_DEFAULT (the provider decides how to handle the CommandStream value), DBGUID_SQL (an SQL statement), DBGUID_MSSQLXML (an SQL Server XML AUTO query), and DBGUID_XPATH (an SQL Server XPath query). The values of these constants are defined in the "Programming Stream Objects" section near the end of this chapter.
Name	A **String** read/write value specifying the name of the command, such as cmmNwind.
NEW 2002 NamedParameters	A **Boolean** read/write value that, when set to **True**, specifies that the names of members of the Parameters collection be used, rather than their sequence, when passing parameter values to and from SQL Server functions and stored procedures, or accepting return or output values from stored procedures.
Prepared	A **Boolean** read/write value that determines whether the data source compiles the CommandText SQL statement as a prepared statement (a temporary stored procedure). The prepared statement exists only for the lifetime of the Command object's ActiveConnection. Many client/server RDBMSs, including Microsoft SQL Server, support prepared statements. If the data source doesn't support prepared statements, setting Prepared to **True** results in a trappable error.
Properties	Same as the Properties collection of the Connection object.
State	A **Long** read/write value specifying the status of the Command. Refer to Table 30.4 for ObjectStateEnum constant values.

TIP

Always set the CommandType property to the appropriate adCmd... constant value. If you accept the default adCmdUnknown value, the data provider must test the value of CommandText to determine whether it is the name of a stored procedure, a table, or an SQL statement before executing the query. If the targeted database contains a large number of objects, testing the CommandText value for each Command object you execute can significantly reduce performance.

The initial execution of a prepared statement often is slower than for a conventional SQL query because some data sources must compile, rather than interpret, the statement. Thus, you should limit use of prepared statements to parameterized queries in which the query is executed multiple times with differing parameter values.

Parameters Collection

To supply and accept parameter values, the Command object uses the Parameters collection, which is similar to the DAO and ODBCDirect Parameters collections. ADODB.Parameters is independent of its parent, ADODB.Command, but you must associate the Parameters collection with a Command object before defining or using Parameter objects.

The Parameters collection has a read-only **Long** property, Count, an Item property that returns a Parameter object, and the methods listed in Table 30.10. The syntax for the Count and Item properties property is


```
lngNumParms = cmmName.Parameters.Count
prmParamName = cmmName.Parameters.Item(lngIndex)
```

Table 30.10 Method Names, Descriptions, and Calling Syntax for the Parameters Collection

Method Name	Description and VBA Calling Syntax
Append	Appends a Parameter object created by the cmmName.CreateParameter method, described in the "Command Methods" section, to the collection. The calling syntax is Parameters.Append prmName.
Delete	Deletes a Parameter object from the collection. The calling syntax is cmmName.Parameters.Delete {strName¦intIndex}, where strName is the name of the Parameter or intIndex is the 0-based ordinal position (index) of the Parameter in the collection.
Refresh	Retrieves the properties of the current set of parameters for the stored procedure or query specified as the value of the CommandText property. The calling syntax is cmmName.Parameters.Refresh. If you don't specify your own members of the Parameters collection with the CreateParameter method, accessing any member of the Parameters collection automatically calls the Refresh method. If you apply the Refresh method to a data source that doesn't support stored procedures, prepared statements, or parameterized queries, the Parameters collection is empty (cmmName.Parameters.Count = 0).

You gain a performance improvement for the initial execution of your stored procedure or query if you use the cmmName.CreateParameter method to predefine the required Parameter objects. The Refresh method makes a round-trip to the server to retrieve the properties of each Parameter.

Parameter Object

One Parameter object must exist in the Parameters collection for each parameter of the stored procedure, prepared statement, or parameterized query. Table 30.11 lists the property names and descriptions of the Parameter object. The syntax for getting and setting Parameter property values is

```
typPropValue = cmmName.Parameters({strName¦lngIndex}).PropertyName
cmmName.Parameters({strName¦lngIndex}).PropertyName = typPropValue
```

You don't need to use the `Index` property of the Parameters collection; `Index` is the default property of `Parameters`.

TABLE 30.11 PROPERTY NAMES AND DESCRIPTIONS FOR `Parameter` OBJECTS

Property Name	Description
`Attributes`	A **`Long`** read/write value representing the sum of the `adParam...` constants listed in Table 30.12.
`Direction`	A **`Long`** read/write value representing one of the `adParam...` constants listed in Table 30.13.
`Name`	A **`String`** read/write value containing the name of the `Parameter` object, such as `prmStartDate`. The name of the `Parameter` object need not (and usually does not) correspond to the name of the corresponding parameter variable of the stored procedure. After the `Parameter` is appended to the `Parameters` collection, the `Name` property value is read-only.
`NumericScale`	A **`Byte`** read/write value specifying the number of decimal places for numeric values.
`Precision`	A **`Byte`** read/write value specifying the total number of digits (including decimal digits) for numeric values.
`Size`	A **`Long`** read/write value specifying the maximum length of variable-length data types supplied as the `Value` property. You must set the `Size` property value before setting the `Value` property to variable-length data.
`Type`	A **`Long`** read/write value representing a valid OLE DB 2+ data type, the most common of which are listed in Table 30.14.
`Value`	The value of the parameter having a data type corresponding to the value of the `Type` property.

TABLE 30.12 CONSTANT VALUES FOR THE `Attributes` PROPERTY OF THE `Parameter` OBJECT

`ParameterAttributesEnum`	Description
`adParamSigned`	The `Parameter` accepts signed values (default).
`adParamNullable`	The `Parameter` accepts **`Null`** values.
`adParamLong`	The `Parameter` accepts long binary data.

TABLE 30.13 CONSTANT VALUES FOR THE Direction PROPERTY OF THE Parameter OBJECT

ParameterDirectionEnum	Description
adParamInput	Specifies an input parameter (default).
adParamOutput	Specifies an output parameter.
adParamInputOutput	Specifies an input/output parameter.
adParamReturnValue	Specifies the return value of a stored procedure.
adParamUnknown	The parameter direction is unknown.

The `Type` property has the largest collection of constants of any ADO enumeration; you can review the entire list of data types by selecting the `DataTypeEnum` class in Object Browser. Most of the data types aren't available to VBA programmers, so Table 30.14 shows only the most commonly used `DataTypeEnum` constants. In most cases, you only need to choose among `adChar` (for **String** values), `adInteger` (for **Long** values), and `adCurrency` (for **Currency** values). You use the `adDate` data type to pass Date/Time parameter values to Jet databases, but not to most stored procedures. Stored procedures generally accept `datetime` parameter values as the `adChar` data type, with a format, such as mm/dd/yyyy, acceptable to the RDBMS.

TABLE 30.14 COMMON CONSTANT VALUES FOR THE Type PROPERTY OF THE Parameter AND Field OBJECTS

DataTypeEnum	Description of Data Type
adBinary	**Binary** value.
adBoolean	**Boolean** value.
adChar	**String** value.
adCurrency	**Currency** values are fixed-point numbers with four decimal digits stored in an 8-byte, signed integer, which is scaled (divided) by 10,000.
adDate	**Date** values are stored as a **Double** value, the integer part being the number of days since December 30, 1899, and the decimal part being the fraction of a day.
adDecimal	Exact numeric value with a specified precision and scale.
adDouble	**Double**-precision floating-point value.
adInteger	4-byte signed **Long** integer.
adLongVarBinary	Long binary value (`Parameter` objects only).
adLongVarChar	**String** value greater than 225 characters (`Parameter` objects only).

continues

TABLE 30.14 CONTINUED

DataTypeEnum	Description of Data Type
adNumeric	Exact numeric value with a specified precision and scale.
adSingle	**Single**-precision floating-point value.
adSmallInt	2-byte signed **Integer**.
adTinyInt	**Byte** (1-byte signed integer).
adVarBinary	Binary value for Jet OLE Object and SQL Server image fields (Parameter objects only).
adVarChar	**String** value for Jet Memo and SQL Server text fields (Parameter objects only).

NOTE

The values for the Type property in the preceding table are valid for the Type property of the Field object, discussed later in the chapter, except for those data types in which "Parameter objects only" appears in the Description of Data Type column. The members of DataTypeEnum are designed to accommodate the widest possible range of desktop and client/server RDBMSs, but the ad... constant names are closely related to those for the field data types of Microsoft SQL Server 2000 and MSDE, which support Unicode strings.

For a complete list with descriptions of DataTypeEnum constants, go to http://msdn.microsoft.com/library/en-us/ado270/htm/mdcstdatatypeenum.asp.

The Parameter object has a single method, AppendChunk, which you use to append long text (adLongText) or long binary (adLongVarBinary) **Variant** data as a parameter value. The syntax of the AppendChunk method call is

```
cmmName.Parameters({strName¦lngIndex}).AppendChunk = varChunk
```

The adParamLong flag of the prm*Name*.Attributes property must be set to apply the AppendChunk method. If you call AppendChunk more than once on a single Parameter, the second and later calls append the current value of var*Chunk* to the parameter value.

Command METHODS

Command objects have only three methods: Cancel, CreateParameter and Execute. Executing Command.Cancel terminates an asynchronous command opened with the adAsyncConnect, adAsyncExecute, or adAsyncFetch option.

You must declare an ADODB.Parameter object, prm*Name*, prior to executing CreateParameter. The syntax of the CreateParameter method call is

```
Set prmName = cmmName.CreateParameter [strName[, lngType[, _
   lngDirection[, lngSize[, varValue]]]]]
cmmName.Parameters.Append prmName
```

The arguments of CreateParameter are optional only if you subsequently set the required Parameter property values before executing the Command. For example, if you supply only the str*Name* argument, you must set the remaining properties, as in the following example:

```
Set prmName = cmmName.CreateParameter strName
cmmName.Parameters.Append prmName
With prmName
   .Type = adChar
   .Direction = adParamInput
   .Size = Len(varValue)
   .Value = varValue
End With
```


The syntax of the Command.Execute method is similar to that for the Connection.Execute method except for the argument list. The following syntax is for Command objects that return Recordset objects:

```
Set rstName = cmmName.Execute([lngRowsAffected[, _
   avarParameters[, lngOptions]]])
```

For Command objects that don't return rows, use this form:

```
cmmName.Execute [lngRowsAffected[, avarParameters[, lngOptions]]]
```

All the arguments of the Execute method are optional if you set the required Command property values before applying the Execute method. Listing 30.2 later in this chapter gives an example of the use of the Command.Execute method without arguments.

TIP

Presetting all property values of the Command object, rather than supplying argument values to the Execute method, makes your VBA code easier for others to comprehend.

Like the Connection.Execute method, the returned value of lng*RowsAffected* is 0 for SELECT and DDL queries and the number of rows modified by execution of INSERT, UPDATE, and DELETE queries. (For SQL Server, lng*RowsAffected* is 0 if the SQL statement includes SET NOCOUNT ON.) The avar*Parameters* argument is an optional **Variant** array of parameter values. Using the Parameters collection is a better practice than using the avar*Parameters* argument because output parameters don't return correct values to the array. For lng*Options* constant values, refer to Table 30.7.

Code to Pass Parameter Values to a Stored Procedure

Most stored procedures that return Recordset objects require input parameters to supply values to WHERE clause criteria to limit the number of rows returned. The code of Listing 30.2 executes a simple SQL Server 2000 stored procedure with a Command object. The Sales by Year stored procedure of the NorthwindCS project has two datetime input parameters, @Beginning_Date and @Ending_Date, the values for which are supplied by strBegDate and strEndDate, respectively. The stored procedure, whose SQL statement follows, returns the ShippedDate and OrderID columns of the Orders table, the Subtotal column of the Order

Subtotals view, and a calculated Year value. The stored procedure returns rows for values of the OrderDate field between `strBegDate` and `strEndDate`.

```
ALTER PROCEDURE "Sales by Year"
  @Beginning_Date datetime,
  @Ending_Date datetime
  AS SELECT Orders.ShippedDate, Orders.OrderID,
     "Order Subtotals".Subtotal,
     DATENAME(yy,ShippedDate) AS Year
  FROM Orders INNER JOIN "Order Subtotals"
     ON Orders.OrderID = "Order Subtotals".OrderID
  WHERE Orders.ShippedDate Between @Beginning_Date And @Ending_Date
```


LISTING 30.2 CODE USING A `Command` OBJECT TO EXECUTE A PARAMETERIZED STORED PROCEDURE

```
Option Explicit
Option Compare Database

Private cnnOrders As New ADODB.Connection
Private cmmOrders As New ADODB.Command
Private prmBegDate As New ADODB.Parameter
Private prmEndDate As New ADODB.Parameter
Private rstOrders As New ADODB.Recordset

Private Sub Form_Load()
   Dim strBegDate As String
   Dim strEndDate As String
   Dim strFile As String

   strBegDate = "1/1/1997"
   strEndDate = "12/31/1997"
   strFile = CurrentProject.Path & "Orders.rst"

   'Specify the OLE DB provider and open the connection
   With cnnOrders
      .Provider = "SQLOLEDB.1"
      On Error Resume Next
      .Open "Data Source=(local);" & _
         "UID=sa;PWD=;Initial Catalog=NorthwindCS"
      If Err.Number Then
         .Open "Data Source=(local);" & _
            "Integrated Security=SSPI;Initial Catalog=NorthwindCS"
      End if
      On Error GoTo 0
   End With

   With cmmOrders
      'Create and append the BeginningDate parameter
      Set prmBegDate = .CreateParameter("BegDate", adChar, _
         adParamInput, Len(strBegDate), strBegDate)
      .Parameters.Append prmBegDate
      'Create and append the endingDate parameter
      Set prmEndDate = .CreateParameter("EndDate", adChar, _
         adParamInput, Len(strEndDate), strEndDate)
      .Parameters.Append prmEndDate
```

```
        Set .ActiveConnection = cnnOrders
        'Specify a stored procedure
        .CommandType = adCmdStoredProc
        'Brackets must surround stored procedure names with spaces
        .CommandText = "[Sales By Year]"
        'Receive the Recordset
        Set rstOrders = .Execute  'returns a "firehose" Recordset
    End With

    With rstOrders
        'Save (persist) the forward-only Recordset to a file
        On Error Resume Next
        'Delete the file, if it exists
        Kill strFile
        On Error GoTo 0
        .Save strFile
        .Close
        .Open strFile, "Provider=MSPersist", , , adCmdFile
    End With

    'Assign rstOrders to the Recordset of the form
    Set Me.Recordset = rstOrders

    Me.txtShippedDate.ControlSource = "ShippedDate"
    Me.txtOrderID.ControlSource = "OrderID"
    Me.txtSubtotal.ControlSource = "Subtotal"
    Me.txtYear.ControlSource = "Year"
End Sub
```


CAUTION

When used in ADO code, you must enclose names of stored procedures and views having spaces with square brackets. Including spaces in database object names, especially in client/server environments, isn't a recommended practice. Microsoft developers insist on adding spaces in names of views and stored procedures, perhaps because SQL Server 2000 supports this dubious feature. Use underscores to make object names more readable if necessary.

NOTE

The code of Listing 30.2 uses an ADO 2.5+ feature, persisted (saved) `Recordset` objects. Stored procedures return forward-only ("firehose") `Recordset` objects, which you can't assign to the `Recordset` property of a form. To create a `Recordset` with a cursor acceptable to Access forms, you must persist the `Recordset` as a file and then close and reopen the `Recordset` with the MSPersist OLE DB provider as the `ActiveConnection` property value. The "Recordset Methods" section, later in the chapter, provides the complete syntax for the `Save` and `Open` methods of the `Recordset` object.

Figure 30.18 shows the result of executing the code of Listing 30.2. The frmParams form that contains the code is included in the ADOTest.mdb and ADOTest.adp files described earlier in the chapter. The AddOrders.adp project, described in the "Exploring the AddOrders.adp Sample Project" section near the end of the chapter, also includes code for setting stored procedure parameter values.

frmParams : Form

Ship Date	Order ID	Subtotal	Year
1/16/1997	10380	$1,313.82	1997
1/1/1997	10392	$1,440.00	1997
1/3/1997	10393	$2,556.95	1997
1/3/1997	10394	$442.00	1997
1/3/1997	10395	$2,122.92	1997
1/6/1997	10396	$1,903.80	1997
1/2/1997	10397	$716.72	1997
1/9/1997	10398	$2,505.60	1997
1/8/1997	10399	$1,765.60	1997
1/16/1997	10400	$3,063.00	1997
1/10/1997	10401	$3,868.60	1997
1/10/1997	10402	$2,713.50	1997
1/9/1997	10403	$855.02	1997
1/8/1997	10404	$1,591.25	1997
1/22/1997	10405	$400.00	1997
1/13/1997	10406	$1,830.78	1997
1/30/1997	10407	$1,194.00	1997

Record: 1 of 398

Figure 30.18
This Datasheet view of the read-only Recordset returned by the Sales By Year stored procedure displays the value of each order received in 1997.

UNDERSTANDING THE ADODB.Recordset OBJECT

Creating, viewing, and updating `Recordset` objects is the ultimate objective of most Access database front ends. Opening an independent `ADODB.Recordset` object offers a myriad of cursor, locking, and other options. You must explicitly open a `Recordset` with a scrollable cursor if you want to use code to create the `Recordset` for assignment to the `Form.Recordset` property. Unlike Jet and ODBCDirect `Recordset` objects, `ADODB.Recordset` objects expose a number of events that are especially useful for validating `Recordset` updates.

Recordset PROPERTIES

Microsoft attempted to make `ADODB.Recordset` objects backward compatible with `DAO.Recordset` objects to minimize the amount of code you must change to migrate existing applications from DAO to ADO. Unfortunately, the attempt at backward compatibility for code-intensive database applications didn't fully succeed. You must make substantial changes in DAO code to accommodate ADO's updated `Recordset` object. Thus, most Access developers choose ADO for new Access front-end applications and stick with DAO when maintaining existing Jet projects.

Table 30.15 lists the names and descriptions of the standard property set of `ADODB.Recordset` objects. `ADODB.Recordset` objects have substantially fewer properties than `DAO.Recordset` objects have. The standard properties of `ADODB.Recordset` objects are those that are supported by the most common OLE DB data providers for relational databases.

TABLE 30.15 PROPERTY NAMES AND DESCRIPTIONS FOR ADODB.Recordset OBJECTS

Property Name	Description
AbsolutePage	A **Long** read/write value that sets or returns the number of the page in which the current record is located or one of the constant values of PositionEnum (see Table 30.16). You must set the PageSize property value before getting or setting the value of AbsolutePage. AbsolutePage is 1 based; if the current record is in the first page, AbsolutePage returns 1. Setting the value of AbsolutePage causes the current record to be set to the first record of the specified page.
AbsolutePosition	A **Long** read/write value (1 based) that sets or returns the position of the current record. The maximum value of AbsolutePosition is the value of the RecordCount property.
ActiveCommand	A **Variant** read-only value specifying the name of a previously opened Command object with which the Recordset is associated.
ActiveConnection	A pointer to a previously opened Connection object with which the Recordset is associated or a fully qualified ConnectionString value.
BOF	A **Boolean** read-only value that, when True, indicates that the record pointer is positioned before the first row of the Recordset and there is no current record.
Bookmark	A **Variant** read/write value that returns a reference to a specific record or uses a Bookmark value to set the record pointer to a specific record.
CacheSize	A **Long** read/write value that specifies the number of records stored in local (cache) memory. The minimum (default) value is 1. Increasing the value of CacheSize minimizes round trips to the server to obtain additional rows when scrolling through Recordset objects.
CursorLocation	A **Long** read/write value that specifies the location of a scrollable cursor, subject to the availability of the specified CursorType on the client or server (see Table 30.17). The default is to use a cursor supplied by the OLE DB data source (called a *server-side* cursor).
CursorType	A **Long** read/write value that specifies the type of Recordset cursor (see Table 30.18). The default is a forward-only (fire hose) cursor.
DataMember	Returns a pointer to an associated Command object created by Visual Basic's Data Environment Designer.
DataSource	Returns a pointer to an associated Connection object.
EditMode	A **Long** read-only value that returns the status of editing of the current record (see Table 30.19).

continues

TABLE 30.15 CONTINUED

Property Name	Description
EOF	A **Boolean** read-only value that, when True, indicates that the record pointer is beyond the last row of the Recordset and there is no current record.
Fields	A pointer to the Fields collection of Field objects of the Recordset.
Filter	A **Variant** read/write value that can be a criteria string (a valid SQL WHERE clause without the WHERE reserved word), an array of Bookmark values specifying a particular set of records, or a constant value from FilterGroupEnum (see Table 30.20).
Index	A **String** read/write value that sets or returns the name of an existing index on the base table of the Recordset. The Recordset must be closed to set the Index value to the name of an index. The Index property is used primarily in conjunction with the Recordset.Seek method.
LockType	A **Long** read/write value that specifies the record-locking method employed when opening the Recordset (see Table 30.21). The default is read-only, corresponding to the read-only characteristic of forward-only cursors.
MarshalOptions	A **Long** read/write value that specifies which set of records is returned to the server after client-side modification. The MarshallOptions property applies only to the lightweight ADOR.Recordset object, a member of RDS.
MaxRecords	A **Long** read/write value that specifies the maximum number of records to be returned by a SELECT query or stored procedure. The default value is 0, all records.
PageCount	A **Long** read-only value that returns the number of pages in a Recordset. You must set the PageSize value to cause PageCount to return a meaningful value. If the Recordset doesn't support the PageCount property, the value is -1.
PageSize	A **Long** read/write value that sets or returns the number of records in a logical page. You use logical pages to break large Recordsets into easily manageable chunks. PageSize isn't related to the size of table pages used for locking in Jet (2KB) or SQL Server (2KB in version 6.5 and earlier, 8KB in version 7+) databases.

Property Name	Description
PersistFormat	A **Long** read/write value that sets or returns the format of Recordset files created by calling the Save method. The two constant values of PersistFormatEnum are adPersistADTG (the default format, Advanced Data TableGram or ADTG) and adPersistXML, which saves the Recordset as almost-readable XML. The XML schema, rowset, is a variation of the XML Data Reduced (XDR) schema, a Microsoft-only attribute-centric namespace that isn't compatible with Access's XSD (XML Schema) format.
Properties	A pointer to the Properties collection of provider-specific Property values of the Recordset.
RecordCount	A **Long** read-only value that returns the number of records in Recordset objects with scrollable cursors if the Recordset supports approximate positioning or Bookmarks. (See the Recordset.Supports method later in this chapter.) If not, you must apply the MoveLast method to obtain an accurate RecordCount value, which retrieves and counts all records. If a forward-only Recordset has one or more records, RecordCount returns -1 (**True**). An empty Recordset of any type returns 0 (**False**).
Sort	A **String** read/write value, consisting of a valid SQL ORDER BY clause without the ORDER BY reserved words, which specifies the sort order of the Recordset.
Source	A **String** read/write value that can be an SQL statement, a table name, a stored procedure name, or the name of an associated Command object. If you supply the name of a Command object, the Source property returns the value of the Command.CommandText property as text. Use the lng*Options* argument of the Open method to specify the type of the value supplied to the Source property.
State	A **Long** read/write value representing one of the constant values of ObjectStateEnum (refer to Table 30.4).
Status	A **Long** read-only value that indicates the status of batch operations or other multiple-record (bulk) operations on the Recordset (see Table 30.22).
 StayInSync	A **Boolean** read/write value, which, if set to **True**, updates references to child (chapter) rows when the parent row changes. StayInSync applies only to hierarchical Recordset objects.

The most obvious omission in the preceding table is the `DAO.Recordset`'s `NoMatch` property value used to test whether applying one of the `DAO.Recordset.Find...` methods or the `DAO.Recordset.Seek` method succeeds. The new `ADODB.Recordset.Find` method, listed in the "Recordset Methods" section later in this chapter, substitutes for DAO's `FindFirst`, `FindNext`, `FindPrevious`, and `FindLast` methods. The `Find` method uses the `EOF` property value for testing the existence of one or more records matching the `Find` criteria.

Another omission in the `ADODB.Recordset` object's preceding property list is the `PercentPosition` property. The workaround, however, is easy:


```
rstName.AbsolutePostion = Int(intPercentPosition * rstName.RecordCount / 100)
```

Tables 30.16 through 30.22 enumerate the valid constant values for the `AbsolutePage`, `CursorLocation`, `CursorType`, `EditMode`, `Filter`, `LockType`, and `Status` properties. Default values appear first, if defined; the list of remaining enumeration members is ordered by frequency of use in Access applications.

TABLE 30.16 CONSTANT VALUES FOR THE `AbsolutePage` PROPERTY

AbsolutePageEnum	**Description**
`adPosUnknown`	The data provider doesn't support pages, the `Recordset` is empty, or the data provider can't determine the page number.
`adPosBOF`	The record pointer is positioned at the beginning of the file. (The `BOF` property is **`True`**.)
`adPosEOF`	The record pointer is positioned at the end of the file. (The `EOF` property is **`True`**.)

TABLE 30.17 CONSTANT VALUES FOR THE `CursorLocation` PROPERTY

CursorLocationEnum	**Description**
`adUseClient`	Use cursor(s) provided by a cursor library located on the client. The `ADOR.Recordset` (RDS) requires a client-side cursor.
`adUseServer`	Use cursor(s) supplied by the data source, usually (but not necessarily) located on a server (default value).

TABLE 30.18 CONSTANT VALUES FOR THE CursorType PROPERTY

CursorLocationEnum	Description
adOpenForwardOnly	Provides only unidirectional cursor movement and a read-only Recordset (default value).
adOpenDynamic	Provides a scrollable cursor that displays all changes, including new records, which other users make to the Recordset.
adOpenKeyset	Provides a scrollable cursor that hides only records added or deleted by other users; similar to a DAO.Recordset of the dynaset type.
adOpenStatic	Provides a scrollable cursor over a static copy of the Recordset. Similar to a DAO.Recordset of the snapshot type, but the Recordset is updatable.

TABLE 30.19 CONSTANT VALUES FOR THE EditMode PROPERTY

EditModeEnum	Description
adEditNone	No editing operation is in progress (default value).
adEditAdd	A tentative append record has been added, but not saved to the database table(s).
adEditDelete	The current record has been deleted.
adEditInProgress	Data in the current record has been modified, but not saved to the database table(s).

TABLE 30.20 CONSTANT VALUES FOR THE Filter PROPERTY

FilterGroupEnum	Description
adFilterNone	Removes an existing filter and exposes all records of the Recordset (equivalent to setting the Filter property to an empty string, the default value).
adFilterAffectedRecords	View only records affected by the last execution of the CancelBatch, Delete, Resync, or UpdateBatch method.
adFilterFetchedRecords	View only records in the current cache. The number of records is set by the CacheSize property.
adFilterConflictingRecords	View only records that failed to update during the last batch update operation.
adFilterPendingRecords	View only records that have been modified but not yet processed by the data source (for Batch Update mode only).

30

TABLE 30.21 CONSTANT VALUES FOR THE LockType PROPERTY

LockTypeEnum	Description
adLockReadOnly	Specifies read-only access (default value).
adLockBatchOptimistic	Use Batch Update mode instead of the default Immediate Update mode.
adLockOptimistic	Use optimistic locking (lock the record or page only during the table update process).
adLockPessimistic	Use pessimistic locking (lock the record or page during editing and the updated process).
adLockUnspecified	No lock type specified. (Use this constant only for Recordset clones.)

TABLE 30.22 CONSTANT VALUES FOR THE Status PROPERTY (APPLIES TO BATCH OR BULK Recordset OPERATIONS ONLY)

RecordStatusEnum	Description of Record Status
adRecOK	Updated successfully
adRecNew	Added successfully
adRecModified	Modified successfully
adRecDeleted	Deleted successfully
adRecUnmodified	Not modified
adRecInvalid	Not saved; the Bookmark property is invalid
adRecMultipleChanges	Not saved; saving would affect other records
adRecPendingChanges	Not saved; the record refers to a pending insert operation)
adRecCanceled	Not saved; the operation was canceled
adRecCantRelease	Not saved; existing record locks prevented saving
adRecConcurrencyViolation	Not saved; an optimistic concurrency locking problem occurred
adRecIntegrityViolation	Not saved; the operation would violate integrity constraints
adRecMaxChangesExceeded	Not saved; an excessive number of pending changes exist
adRecObjectOpen	Not saved; a conflict with an open storage object occurred
adRecOutOfMemory	Not saved; the machine is out of memory
adRecPermissionDenied	Not saved; the user doesn't have required permissions
adRecSchemaViolation	Not saved; the record structure doesn't match the database schema
adRecDBDeleted	Not saved or deleted; the record was previously deleted

Fields COLLECTION AND Field OBJECTS

Like DAO's Fields collection, ADO's dependent Fields collection is a property of the Recordset object, making the columns of the Recordset accessible to VBA code and bound controls. The Fields collection has one property, Count, and only two methods, Item and Refresh. You can't append new Field objects to the Fields collection, unless you're creating a persisted Recordset from scratch or you use ADOX's ALTER TABLE DDL command to add a new field.

All but one (Value) of the property values of Field objects are read-only, because the values of the Field properties are derived from the database schema. The Value property is read-only in forward-only Recordsets and Recordsets opened with read-only locking. Table 30.23 gives the names and descriptions of the properties of the Field object.

TABLE 30.23 PROPERTY NAMES AND DESCRIPTIONS OF THE Field OBJECT

Field Property	Description
ActualSize	A **Long** read-only value representing the length of the Field's value by char acter count.
Attributes	A **Long** read-only value that represents the sum of the constants (flags) included in FieldAttributeEnum (see Table 30.24).
DefinedSize	A **Long** read-only value specifying the maximum length of the Field's value by character count.
Name	A **String** read-only value that returns the field (column) name.
NumericScale	A **Byte** read-only value specifying the number of decimal places for numeric values.
OriginalValue	A **Variant** read-only value that represents the Value property of the field before applying the Update method to the Recordset. (The CancelUpdate method uses OriginalValue to replace a changed Value property.)
Precision	A **Byte** read-only value specifying the total number of digits (including decimal digits) for numeric values.
Properties	A collection of provider-specific Property objects. SQL Server 2000's extended properties are an example Properties collection members for the SQL Server OLE DB provider.
Status	An undocumented **Long** read-only value.
Type	A **Long** read-only value specifying the data type of the field. Refer to Table 30.14 for Type constant values.
UnderlyingValue	A **Variant** read-only value representing the current value of the field in the database table(s). You can compare the values of OriginalValue and UnderlyingValue to determine whether a persistent change has been made to the database, perhaps by another user.
Value	A **Variant** read/write value of a subtype appropriate to the value of the Type property for the field. If the Recordset isn't updatable, the Value property is read-only.

`Value` is the default property of the `Field` object, but it's a good programming practice to set and return field values by explicit use of the `Value` property name in VBA code. In most cases, using `varName = rstName.Fields(n).Value` instead of `varName = rstName.Fields(n)` results in a slight performance improvement.

TABLE 30.24 CONSTANT VALUES AND DESCRIPTIONS FOR THE ATTRIBUTES PROPERTY OF THE `Field` OBJECT

FieldAttributeEnum	Description
`adFldCacheDeferred`	The provider caches field values. Multiple reads are made on the cached value, not the database table.
`adFieldDefaultStream`	The field contains a stream of bytes. For example, the field might contain the HTML stream from a Web page specified by a field whose `adFldIsRowURL` attribute is **`True`**.
`adFldFixed`	The field contains fixed-length data with the length determined by the data type or field specification.
`adFldIsChapter`	The field is a member of a chaptered recordset and contains a child recordset of this field.
`adFldIsCollection`	The field contains a reference to a collection of resources, rather than a single resource.
`adFldIsNullable`	The field accepts **`Null`** values.
`adFldIsRowURL`	The field contains a URL for a resource such as a Web page.
`adFldKeyColumn`	The field is the primary key field of a table.
`adFldLong`	The field has a long binary data type, which permits the use of the `AppendChunk` and `GetChunk` methods.
`adFldMayBeNull`	The field can return **`Null`** values.
`adFldMayDefer`	The field is deferrable, meaning that `Values` are retrieved from the data source only when explicitly requested.
`adFldNegativeScale`	The field contains data from a column that supports negative `Scale` values.
`adFldRowID`	The field is a row identifier (typically an `identity`, AutoIncrement, or GUID data type).
`adFldRowVersion`	The field contains a timestamp or similar value for determining the time of the last update.
`adFldUpdatable`	The field is read/write (updatable).
`adFldUnknownUpdatable`	The data provider can't determine whether the field is updatable. Your only recourse is to attempt an update and trap the error that occurs if the field isn't updatable.

The Field object has two methods, AppendChunk and GetChunk, which are applicable only to fields of various long binary data types, indicated by an adFldLong flag in the Attributes property of the field. The AppendChunk method is discussed in the "Parameter Object" section earlier in this chapter. The syntax for the AppendChunk method call, which writes **Variant** data to a long binary field (fld*Name*), is

```
fldName.AppendChunk varData
```


NOTE

ADO 2.x doesn't support the Access OLE Object field data type, which adds a proprietary object wrapper around the data (such as a bitmap) to identify the OLE server that created the object (for bitmaps, usually Windows Paint).

The GetChunk method enables you to read long binary data in blocks of the size you specify. Following is the syntax for the GetChunk method:

```
varName = fldName.GetChunk(lngSize)
```

A common practice is to place AppendChunk and GetChunk method calls within **Do Until...Loop** structures to break up the long binary value into chunks of manageable size. In the case of the **GetChunk** method, if you set the value of lng*Size* to less than the value of the field's ActualSize property, the first GetChunk call retrieves lng*Size* bytes. Successive GetChunk calls retrieve lng*Size* bytes beginning at the next byte after the end of the preceding call. If the remaining number of bytes is less than lng*Size*, only the remaining bytes appear in var*Name*. After you retrieve the field's bytes, or if the field is empty, GetChunk returns **Null**.

NOTE

Changing the position of the record pointer of the field's Recordset resets GetChunk's byte pointer. Accessing a different Recordset and moving its record pointer doesn't affect the other Recordset's GetChunk record pointer.

Recordset METHODS

ADODB.Recordset methods are an amalgam of the DAO.Recordset and rdoResultset methods. Table 30.25 gives the names, descriptions, and calling syntax for Recordset methods. OLE DB data providers aren't required to support all the methods of the Recordset object. If you don't know which methods the data provider supports, you must use the Supports method with the appropriate constant from CursorOptionEnum, listed in Table 30.28 later in this chapter, to test for support of methods that are provider dependent. Provider-dependent methods are indicated by an asterisk after the method name in Table 30.25.

30

Table 30.25 Names and Descriptions of Methods of the Recordset Object

Method Name	Description and Calling Syntax
AddNew	Adds a new record to an updatable Recordset. The calling syntax is rst*Name*.AddNew [{var*Field*¦avar*Fields*}, {var*Value*¦avar*Values*}], where var*Field* is a single field name, avar*Fields* is an array of field names, var*Value* is single value, and avar*Values* is an array of values for the columns defined by the members of avar*Fields*. Calling the Update method adds the new record to the database table(s). If you add a new record to a Recordset having a primary-key field that isn't the first field of the Recordset, you must supply the name and value of the primary-key field in the AddNew statement.
Cancel	Cancels execution of an asynchronous query and terminates creation of multiple Recordsets from stored procedures or compound SQL statements. The calling syntax is rst*Name*.Cancel.
CancelBatch	Cancels a pending batch update operation on a Recordset whose LockEdits property value is adBatchOptimistic. The calling syntax is rst*Name*.CancelBatch [lng*AffectRecords*]. The optional lng*AffectRecords* argument is one of the constants of AffectEnum (see Table 30.26).
CancelUpdate	Cancels a pending change to the table(s) underlying the Recordset before applying the Update method. The calling syntax is rst*Name*.CancelUpdate.
Clone	Creates a duplicate Recordset object with an independent record pointer. The calling syntax is **Set** rstDupe = rst*Name*.Clone().
Close	Closes a Recordset object, allowing reuse of the Recordset variable by setting new Recordset property values and applying the Open method. The calling syntax is rst*Name*.Close.
NEW 2002 CompareBookmarks	Returns the relative value of two bookmarks in the same Recordset or a Recordset and its clone. The calling syntax is lng*Result* = rst*Name*.CompareBookmarks(var*Bookmark1*, var*Bookmark2*).
Delete	Deletes the current record immediately from the Recordset and the underlying tables, unless the LockEdits property value of the Recordset is set to adLockBatchOptimistic. The calling syntax is rst*Name*.Delete.

Method Name	Description and Calling Syntax
`Find`	Searches for a record based on criteria you supply. The calling syntax is `rstName.Find strCriteria[, lngSkipRecords, lngSearchDirection[, lngStart]]`, where `strCriteria` is a valid SQL `WHERE` clause without the `WHERE` keyword, the optional `lngSkipRecords` value is the number of records to skip before applying `Find`, `lngSearchDirection` specifies the search direction (`adSearchForward`, the default, or `adSearchBackward`), and the optional `varStart` value specifies the `Bookmark` value of the record at which to start the search or one of the members of `BookmarkEnum` (see Table 30.27). If `Find` succeeds, the `EOF` property returns **`False`**; otherwise, `EOF` returns **`True`**.
`GetRows`	Returns a two-dimensional (row, column) **`Variant`** array of records. The calling syntax is `avarName = rstName.GetRows(lngRows[, varStart[, {strFieldName¦lngFieldIndex¦avarFieldNames¦ avarFieldIndexes}]]])`, where `lngRows` is the number of rows to return, `varStart` specifies a `Bookmark` value of the record at which to start the search or one of the members of `BookmarkEnum` (see Table 30.27), and the third optional argument is the name or index of a single column, or a **`Variant`** array of column names or indexes. If you don't specify a value of the third argument, `GetRows` returns all columns of the `Recordset`.
`GetString`	By default, returns a tab-separated **`String`** value for a specified number of records, with records separated by return codes. The calling syntax is `strClip = rstName.GetString (lngRows[, strColumnDelimiter[, strRowDelimiter, [strNullExpr]]])`, where `lngRows` is the number of rows to return, `strColumnDelimiter` is an optional column-separation character (`vbTab` is the default), `strRowDelimiter` is an optional row-separation character (`vbCR` is the default), and `strNullExpr` is an optional value to substitute when enco untering **`Null`** values (an empty string, `""`, is the default value).
`Move`	Moves the record pointer from the current record. The calling syntax is `rstName.Move lngNumRecords[, varStart]`, where `lngNumRecords` is the number of records by which to move the record pointer and the optional `varStart` value specifies the `Bookmark` of the record at which to start the search or one of the members of `BookmarkEnum` (see Table 30.27).

continues

30

TABLE 30.25 CONTINUED

Method Name	Description and Calling Syntax
`MoveFirst`	Moves the record pointer to the first record. The calling syntax is `rstName.MoveFirst`.
`MoveLast`	Moves the record pointer to the last record. The calling syntax is `rstName.MoveLast`.
`MoveNext`	Moves the record pointer to the next record. The calling syntax is `rstName.MoveNext`. The `MoveNext` method is the only `Move...` method that you can apply to a forward-only `Recordset`.
`MovePrevious`	Moves the record pointer to the previous record. The calling syntax is `rstName.MovePrevious`.
`NextRecordset`	Returns additional `Recordset` objects generated by a com pound Jet SQL statement, such as `SELECT * FROM Orders; SELECT * FROM Customers`, or a T-SQL stored procedure that returns multiple `Recordsets`. The calling syntax is `rstNext = rstName.NextRecordset [(lngRecordsAffected)]`, where `lngRecordsAffected` is an optional return value that specifies the number of records in `rstNext`, if `SET NOCOUNT ON` isn't included in the SQL statement or stored procedure code. If no additional `Recordset` exists, `rstNext` is set to **`Nothing`**.
`Open`	Opens a `Recordset` on an active `Command` or `Connection` object. The calling syntax is `rstName.Open [varSource[, varActiveConnection[, lngCursorType[, lngLockType[, lngOptions]]]]]`. The `Open` arguments are optional if you set the equivalent `Recordset` property values, which is the practice recommended in this book. For valid values, refer to the Source, `ActiveConnection`, `CursorType`, and `LockType` properties in Table 30.15 earlier in this chapter and to the `CommandTypeEnum` values listed in Table 30.7 earlier in this chapter for the `lngOptions` property.
`Requery`	Refreshes the content of the `Recordset` from the underlying table(s), the equivalent of calling `Close` and then `Open`. `Requery` is a very resource-intensive operation. The calling syntax is `rstName.Requery`.
`Resync`	Refreshes a specified subset of the `Recordset` from the underlying table(s). The calling syntax is `rstName.Resync [lngAffectRecords]`, where `lngAffectRecords` is one of the members of `AffectEnum` (see Table 30.26). If you select `adAffectCurrent` or `adAffectGroup` as the value of `lngAffectRecords`, you reduce the required resources in comparison with `adAffectAll` (the default).

Method Name	Description and Calling Syntax
Save	Creates a file containing a persistent copy of the Recordset. The calling syntax is rst*Name*.Save str*FileName*, where str*FileName* is the path to and the name of the file. You open a Recordset from a file with a rst*Name*.Open strFileName, Options:=adCmdFile statement. This book uses .rst as the extension for persistent Recordsets in the ADTG format and .xml for XML formats.
Seek	Performs a high-speed search on the field whose index name is specified as the value of the Recordset.Index property. The calling syntax is rst*Name*.Seek avar*KeyValues*[, lng*Option*], where avar*KeyValues* is a **Variant** array of search values for each field of the index. The optional lng*Option* argument is one of the members of the SeekEnum (see Table 30.29) constant enumeration; the default value is adSeekFirstEQ (find the first equal value). You can't specify adUseClient as the CursorLocation property value when applying the Seek method; Seek requires a server-side (adUseServer) cursor.
Supports	Returns **True** if the Recordset's data provider supports a specified cursor-dependent method; otherwise, Supports returns **False**. The calling syntax is bln*Supported* = rst*Name*.Supports(lng*CursorOptions*). Table 30.28 lists the names and descriptions of the CursorOptionEnum values.
Update	Applies the result of modifications to the Recordset to the underlying table(s) of the data source. For batch operations, Update applies the modifications only to the local (cached) Recordset. The calling syntax is rst*Name*.Update.
UpdateBatch	Applies the result of all modifications made to a batch-type Recordset (LockType property set to adBatchOptimistic, CursorType property set to adOpenKeyset or adOpenStatic, and CursorLocation property set to adUseClient) to the underlying table(s) of the data source. The calling syntax is rst*Name*.UpdateBatch [lng*AffectRecords*], where lng*AffectRecords* is a member of AffectEnum (see Table 30.26).

The "Code to Pass Parameter Values to a Stored Procedure" section, earlier in the chapter, illustrates use of the Save and Open methods with persisted Recordsets of the ADTG type.

30

TIP

The `Edit` method of `DAO.Recordset` objects is missing from Table 30.25. To change the value of one or more fields of the current record of an `ADODB.Recordset` object, execute `rstName.Fields(n).Value = varValue` for each field whose value you want to change and then execute `rstName.Update`. `ADODB.Recordset` objects don't support the `Edit` method.

To improve the performance of `Recordset` objects opened on `Connection` objects, set the required property values of the `Recordset` object and then use a named argument to specify the `intOptions` value of the `Open` method, as in `rstName.Open Options:=adCmdText`. This syntax is easier to read and less prone to error than the alternative, `rstName.Open , , , , adCmdText`.

TABLE 30.26 NAMES AND DESCRIPTIONS OF CONSTANTS FOR THE `CancelBatch` METHOD'S `lngAffectRecords` ARGUMENT

AffectEnum	Description
adAffectAll	Include all records in the `Recordset` object, including any records hidden by the `Filter` property value (the default)
adAffectAllChapters	Include all chapter fields in a chaptered recordset, including any records hidden by the `Filter` property value.
adAffectCurrent	Include only the current record
adAffectGroup	Include only those records that meet the current Filter criteria

TABLE 30.27 NAMES AND DESCRIPTIONS OF `Bookmark` CONSTANTS FOR THE `Find` METHOD'S `varStart` ARGUMENT

BookmarkEnum	Description
adBookmarkCurrent	Start at the current record (the default value)
adBookmarkFirst	Start at the first record
adBookmarkLast	Start at the last record

TABLE 30.28 NAMES AND DESCRIPTIONS OF CONSTANTS FOR THE `Supports` METHOD

CursorOptionEnum	Permits
adAddNew	Applying the `AddNew` method
adApproxPosition	Setting and getting `AbsolutePosition` and `AbsolutePage` property values
adBookmark	Setting and getting the `Bookmark` property value
adDelete	Applying the `Delete` method

CursorOptionEnum	Permits
adFind	Applying the Find method
adHoldRecords	Retrieving additional records or changing the retrieval record pointer position without committing pending changes
adIndex	Use of the Index property
adMovePrevious	Applying the GetRows, Move, MoveFirst, and MovePrevious methods (indicates a bidirectional scrollable cursor)
adNotify	Use of Recordset events
adResync	Applying the Resync method
adSeek	Applying the Seek method
adUpdate	Applying the Update method
adUpdateBatch	Applying the UpdateBatch and CancelBatch methods

Table 30.29 lists the SeekEnum constants for the optional lng*SeekOptions* argument of the Seek method. Unfortunately, the syntax for the ADODB.Recordset.Seek method isn't even close to being backward-compatible with the DAO.Recordset.Seek method.

TABLE 30.29 NAMES AND DESCRIPTIONS OF CONSTANTS FOR THE Seek METHOD'S lng*SeekOptions* ARGUMENT

SeekEnum	Finds
adSeekFirstEQ	The first equal value (the default value)
adSeekAfterEQ	The first equal value or the next record after which a match would have occurred (logical equivalent of >=)
adSeekAfter	The first record after which an equal match would have occurred (logical equivalent of >)
adSeekBeforeEQ	The first equal value or the previous record before which a match would have occurred (logical equivalent of <=)
adSeekBefore	The first record previous to where an equal match would have occurred (logical equivalent of <)
adSeekLastEQ	The last record having an equal value

TIP

Use the Find method for searches unless you are working with a table having an extremely large number of records. Find takes advantage of index(es), if present, but Find's search algorithm isn't quite as efficient as Seek's. You'll probably encounter the threshold for considering substituting Seek for Find in the range of 500,000 to 1,000,000 records. Tests on a large version the Oakmont.mdb Jet and Oakmont SQL Server Students table (50,000) rows show imperceptible performance differences between Seek and Find operations.

Recordset EVENTS

Recordset events are new to users of DAO. Table 30.30 names the Recordset events and gives the condition under which the event fires.

TABLE 30.30 NAMES AND OCCURRENCE OF RECORDSET EVENTS

Event Name	When Fired
EndOfRecordset	When the record pointer attempts to move beyond the last record
FetchComplete	When all records have been retrieved asynchronously
FetchProgress	During asynchronous retrieval, periodically reports the number of records returned
FieldChangeComplete	After a change to the value of a field
MoveComplete	After execution of the Move or Move... methods
RecordChangeComplete	After an edit to a single record
RecordsetChangeComplete	After cached changes are applied to the underlying tables
WillChangeField	Before a change to a field value
WillChangeRecord	Before an edit to a single record
WillChangeRecordset	Before cached changes are applied to the underlying tables
WillMove	Before execution of the Move or Move... methods

TAKING ADVANTAGE OF DISCONNECTED Recordsets

If you set the value of the Recordset's LockEdits property to adBatchOptimistic and the CursorType property to adKeyset or adStatic, you create a batch-type Recordset object that you can disconnect from the data source. You can then edit the Recordset object offline with a client-side cursor, reopen the Connection object, and send the updates to the data source over the new connection. A Recordset without an active connection is called a *disconnected Recordset*. The advantage of a disconnected Recordset is that you eliminate the need for an active server connection during extended editing sessions. Batch updates solve the Access front-end scalability issues mentioned at the beginning of the chapter.

NOTE

Unfortunately, you can't assign a disconnected Recordset to the Recordset property of a form or subform and take advantage of batch updates. Bound forms require an active connection to the database. You must write VBA code to handle updating, adding, and deleting records.

To learn more about updatability issues with disconnected Recordsets and the Client Data Manager (CDM) added by Access 2002, open Microsoft Knowledge Base article Q301987, "Using ADO in Microsoft Access 2002" and download the white paper.

Batch updates with disconnected Recordsets are stateless and resemble the interaction of Web browsers and servers when displaying conventional Web pages. The term *stateless* means that the current interaction between the client application and the server isn't dependent on the outcome of previous interactions. For example, you can make local updates to a disconnected Recordset, go to lunch, make additional updates as needed, and then send the entire batch to the server. A properly designed batch update application lets you close the application or shut down the client computer, and then resume the updating process when you restart the application.

TIP

Disconnected Recordsets minimize the effect of MSDE "five-user tuning" on the performance of Access online transaction processing (OLTP) applications. Batch updates execute very quickly, so most user connections remain open for a second or less.

Transaction processing with stored procedures or T-SQL statements that incorporate `BEGIN TRANS...COMMIT TRANS...ROLLBACK TRANS` statements are the better choice for OLTP operations on multiple tables, such as order-entry systems. It's possible for batch updates to succeed partially, which might result in a missing line item. You can use the `Errors` collection to analyze and potentially correct such problems, but doing so requires high-level VBA coding skills.

THE BASICS OF DISCONNECTING AND RECONNECTING RECORDSETS

Following is an example of VBA pseudocode that creates and operates on a disconnected `Recordset` and then uses the `UpdateBatch` method to persist the changes in the data source:

```
Set rstName = New ADODB.Recordset
With rstName
   .ActiveConnection = cnnName
   .CursorType = adKeyset
   .CursorLocation = adUseClient
   .LockEdits = adBatchOptimistic
   .Open "SELECT * FROM TableName WHERE Criteria", Options:=adCmdText
   Set .ActiveConnection = Nothing 'Disconnect the Recordset
   'Close the connection to the server, if desired
   'Edit the field values of multiple records here
   'You also can append and delete records
   'Reopen the server connection, if closed
   Set .ActiveConnection = cnnName
   .UpdateBatch  'Send all changes to the data source
End With
rstName.Close
```

If calling the `UpdateBatch` method causes conflicts with other users' modifications to the underlying table(s), you receive a trappable error and the `Errors` collection contains `Error` object(s) that identify the conflict(s). Unlike transactions, which require all attempted modifications to succeed or all to be rolled back, `Recordset` batch modifications that don't cause conflicts are made permanent in the data source.

An Example Batch Update Application

The frmBatchUpdate form of the ADOTest.mdb application and ADOTest.adp project demonstrates the effectiveness of batch updates with MSDE. For example, you can edit data, persist the edited disconnected `Recordset` as an ADTG or XML file, close the form (or Access), and then reopen the form and submit the changes to the server. A subform, sbfBatchUpdate, which is similar to the frmADO_Jet and frmADO_MSDE forms you created early in the chapter, displays the original and updated data. The subform is read-only; VBA code simulates user updates to the data. The example also demonstrates how to use VBA code to display the XML representation of a `Recordset` object in Internet Explorer (IE) 5+.

To give frmBatchUpdate a trial run, do this:

1. If you haven't installed the entire set of sample applications, copy ADOTest.mdb, ADOTest.adp, or both from the \Seua11\Chaptr30 folder of the accompanying CD-ROM to a ...\Program Files\Seua11\Chapter30 folder.
2. Verify that your local MSDE instance is running, and then open frmBatchUpdate, which connects to the NorthwindCS database, opens a Recordset, saves it in a local file named Batch.rst, and closes the connection. The subform displays the first 10 rows of seven fields of the Customers table by opening a Recordset from the local Batch.rst file (see Figure 30.19).

Figure 30.19 Opening frmBatchUpdate displays a disconnected Recordset opened on the Customers table for batch updates and saves the initial Recordset as Batch.xml.

3. Click the Update Disconnected Recordset button to replace `NULL` values in the Region cells with 123. The button caption changes to Restore Disconnected Recordset and the Send Batch Updates to Server button is enabled. The new values don't appear in the datasheet because the `UpdateBatch` method hasn't been applied at this point.
4. Click the Send Batch Updates to Server button to reopen the connection, execute the `UpdateBatch` method, and close the connection. The datasheet displays the updated Recordset returned by the server (see Figure 30.20).

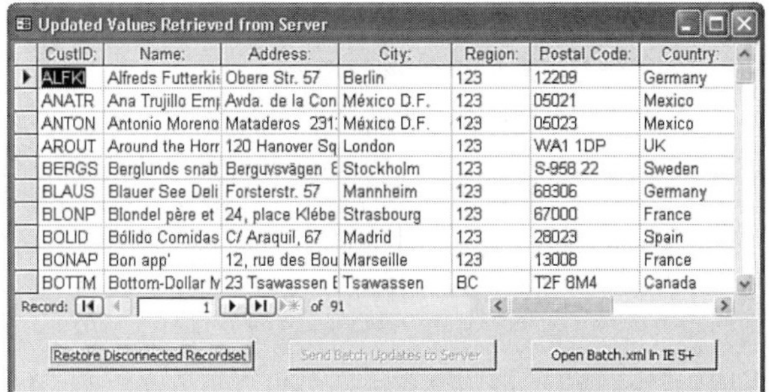

CustID:	Name:	Address:	City:	Region:	Postal Code:	Country:
ALFKI	Alfreds Futterkis	Obere Str. 57	Berlin	123	12209	Germany
ANATR	Ana Trujillo Emp	Avda. de la Con	México D.F.	123	05021	Mexico
ANTON	Antonio Moreno	Mataderos 231	México D.F.	123	05023	Mexico
AROUT	Around the Horr	120 Hanover Sq	London	123	WA1 1DP	UK
BERGS	Berglunds snab	Berguvsvägen 8	Stockholm	123	S-958 22	Sweden
BLAUS	Blauer See Deli	Forsterstr. 57	Mannheim	123	68306	Germany
BLONP	Blondel père et	24, place Klébe	Strasbourg	123	67000	France
BOLID	Bólido Comidas	C/ Araquil, 67	Madrid	123	28023	Spain
BONAP	Bon app'	12, rue des Bou	Marseille	123	13008	France
BOTTM	Bottom-Dollar M	23 Tsawassen E	Tsawassen	BC	T2F 8M4	Canada

Figure 30.20 Clicking Send Batch Updates to Server updates the server table and then retrieves the updated Recordset by opening and then closing another connection.

5. Click Restore Disconnected Recordset and Send Batch Updates to Server to return the Customers table to its original state. (Clicking Update and Restore Disconnected Recordset toggles the Region values in the local Recordset.)
6. Click the Open Batch.xml in IE 5+ button to launch IE with `file://path/Batch.xml` as the URL. IE 5+'s XML parser formats the attribute-centric document and color-codes XML tags (see Figure 30.21).

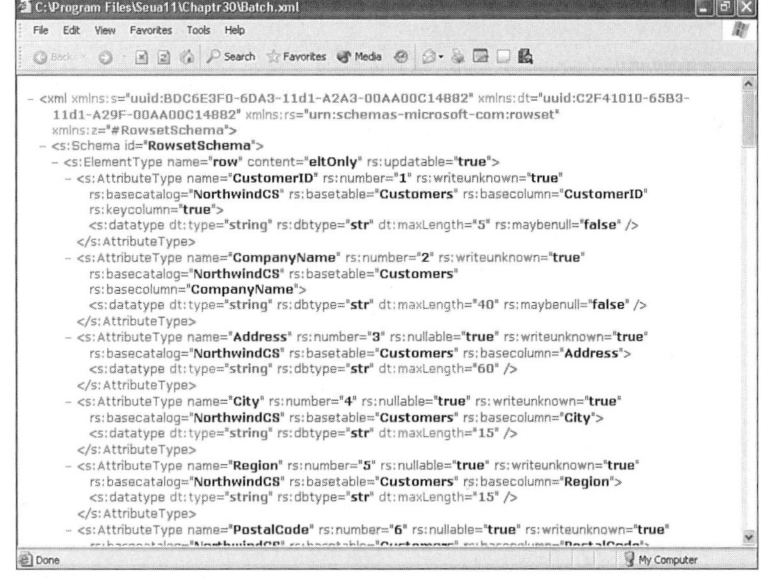


```
- <xml xmlns:s="uuid:BDC6E3F0-6DA3-11d1-A2A3-00AA00C14882" xmlns:dt="uuid:C2F41010-65B3-
  11d1-A29F-00AA00C14882" xmlns:rs="urn:schemas-microsoft-com:rowset"
  xmlns:z="#RowsetSchema">
 - <s:Schema id="RowsetSchema">
  - <s:ElementType name="row" content="eltOnly" rs:updatable="true">
   - <s:AttributeType name="CustomerID" rs:number="1" rs:writeunknown="true"
      rs:basecatalog="NorthwindCS" rs:basetable="Customers" rs:basecolumn="CustomerID"
      rs:keycolumn="true">
      <s:datatype dt:type="string" rs:dbtype="str" dt:maxLength="5" rs:maybenull="false" />
    </s:AttributeType>
   - <s:AttributeType name="CompanyName" rs:number="2" rs:writeunknown="true"
      rs:basecatalog="NorthwindCS" rs:basetable="Customers"
      rs:basecolumn="CompanyName">
      <s:datatype dt:type="string" rs:dbtype="str" dt:maxLength="40" rs:maybenull="false" />
    </s:AttributeType>
   - <s:AttributeType name="Address" rs:number="3" rs:nullable="true" rs:writeunknown="true"
      rs:basecatalog="NorthwindCS" rs:basetable="Customers" rs:basecolumn="Address">
      <s:datatype dt:type="string" rs:dbtype="str" dt:maxLength="60" />
    </s:AttributeType>
   - <s:AttributeType name="City" rs:number="4" rs:nullable="true" rs:writeunknown="true"
      rs:basecatalog="NorthwindCS" rs:basetable="Customers" rs:basecolumn="City">
      <s:datatype dt:type="string" rs:dbtype="str" dt:maxLength="15" />
    </s:AttributeType>
   - <s:AttributeType name="Region" rs:number="5" rs:nullable="true" rs:writeunknown="true"
      rs:basecatalog="NorthwindCS" rs:basetable="Customers" rs:basecolumn="Region">
      <s:datatype dt:type="string" rs:dbtype="str" dt:maxLength="15" />
    </s:AttributeType>
   - <s:AttributeType name="PostalCode" rs:number="6" rs:nullable="true" rs:writeunknown="true"
```

Figure 30.21 IE 5+'s XML parser formats the XML document saved as Batch.xml. This example shows the `Schema` elements collapsed and the `data` elements expanded. (The `Region` attribute of the `row` element is in the updated state.)

If you update the local copy of the Recordset and don't send the changes to the server, you receive a message reminding you that changes are pending when you close the form. If you don't save the changes to the server and reopen the form, a message asks if you want to send the changes to the server before proceeding.

VBA Code in the frmBatchUpdate Class Module

The VBA code of the event-handling and supporting subprocedures of the `frmBatchUpdate` Class Module illustrates how to program many of the ADO properties and methods described in the preceding sections devoted to the `Connection` and `Recordset` objects. The `Command` object isn't used in this example, because the form opens `Recordset` objects on a temporary `Connection` object or from a copy of a `Recordset` persisted to a local file in ADTG format.

30

The Form_Load Event Handler

Listing 30.3 shows the VBA code for the `Form_Load` event handler. The first operation uses the VBA **`Dir`** function to determine whether the Batch.rst file exists; if so, response to the message specified by the **`MsgBox`** function determines whether existing updates are processed by the `cmdUpdate_Click` subprocedure or discarded.

Listing 30.3 Code for Saving the Initial Recordset Object

```
Private Sub Form_Load()
   'Open the connection, and create and display the Recordset

   blnUseJet = False 'Set True to use the Jet provider

   'Test for presence of the saved Recordset
   If Dir(CurrentProject.Path & "\Batch.rst") <> "" Then
      'File is present so updates are pending
      If MsgBox("Do you want to send your changes to the server?", vbQuestion +
vbYesNo, _
            "Updates Are Pending for the Server") = vbYes Then
         Call cmdUpdate_Click
         Exit Sub
      Else
         Kill CurrentProject.Path & "\Batch.rst"
      End If
   End If

   'Create a Form object variable for the subform
   Set sbfBatch = Forms!frmBatchUpdate!sbfBatchUpdate.Form
   Me.cmdBulkUpdate.SetFocus
   Me.cmdUpdate.Enabled = False
   Me.cmdOpenXML.Enabled = False

   'Open a connection to the server
   Call OpenConnection

   'Create a Recordset for Batch Updates
   strSQL = "SELECT CustomerID, CompanyName, Address, City, Region, PostalCode,
Country FROM Customers"
   With rstBatch
      Set .ActiveConnection = cnnBatch
      .CursorType = adOpenStatic
      .CursorLocation = adUseClient
```

```
      .LockType = adLockBatchOptimistic
      .Open strSQL

      'Save the Recordset to a file
      .Save CurrentProject.Path & "\Batch.rst", adPersistADTG

      'Save an XML version
      On Error Resume Next
      Kill CurrentProject.Path & "\Batch.xml"
      .Save CurrentProject.Path & "\Batch.xml", adPersistXML
      On Error GoTo 0
      Me.cmdOpenXML.Enabled = True

      'Disconnect the Recordset
      Set .ActiveConnection = Nothing

      If .Fields("Region").Value = "123" Then
         Me.cmdBulkUpdate.Caption = "Restore Disconnected Recordset"
      Else
         Me.cmdBulkUpdate.Caption = "Update Disconnected Recordset"
      End If
   End With

   'Destroy the connection
   cnnBatch.Close
   Set cnnBatch = Nothing

   'Open a local Recordset from the saved file
   Call OpenRstFromFile

   'Delete the source of the file Recordset
   Kill CurrentProject.Path & "\Batch.rst"
   Me.Caption = "Datasheet Contains Values from Server (Disconnected Recordset)"
End Sub
```

NOTE

In a real-world application, you probably wouldn't delete a saved Recordset that contains updates. Instead of deleting the file with a `Kill` instruction, you would open the saved Recordset to permit continued editing.

The **Set** `sbfBatch = Forms!frmBatchUpdate!sbfBatchUpdate.Form` statement creates a `Form` object for the subform, so you can set property values for the sbfBatchUpdate subform by code of the frmBatchUpdate form in the `OpenRstFromFile` subprocedure. Combining the VBA code for forms and subforms in a single Class Module makes the code more readable.

➔ For more information on the strange syntax to point to another `Form` or `Report` object, **see** "Referring to Access Objects with VBA," **p. 1218**.

After disabling the Send Updates to Server and Open Batch.xml in IE 5+ buttons, the code calls the `OpenConnection` subprocedure to create a temporary `Connection` object, creates a

Recordset object with batch-optimistic locking, saves the Recordset to Batch.rst and Batch.xml, and disconnects the Recordset from the connection with the **Set .ActiveConnection = Nothing** statement. Finally the code closes the Connection, releases it from memory, calls the OpenRstFromFile subprocedure, and deletes the Batch.rst file.

THE OpenConnection SUBPROCEDURE

The OpenConnection subprocedure (see Listing 30.4) accommodates a Jet database by setting the value of blnUseJet to True in the Form_Load event handler. By default, the code attempts to open the connection with integrated Windows security. If this attempt fails, the code attempts to use SQL Server security with the sa logon ID (UID=sa) and no password. (If you've secured the sa account, add the password for the account to PWD=.)

30

LISTING 30.4 CONNECTING TO A JET DATABASE OR USE SQL SERVER OR INTEGRATED WINDOWS SECURITY TO CONNECT TO THE LOCAL MSDE INSTANCE

```
Private Sub OpenConnection()
   'Specify the OLE DB provider and open the connection
   With cnnBatch
      If blnUseJet Then
         .Provider = "Microsoft.Jet.OLEDB.4.0"
         .Open CurrentProject.Path & "\Northwind.mdb", "Admin"
      Else
         On Error Resume Next
         'Try integrated Windows security first
         .Open "Provider=SQLOLEDB.1;Data Source=(local);" & _
             "Integrated Security=SSPI;Initial Catalog=NorthwindCS"
         If Err.Number Then
             Err.Clear
             On Error GoTo 0
            'Now try SQL Server security
            .Open "Provider=SQLOLEDB.1;Data Source=(local);" & _
                "UID=sa;PWD=;Initial Catalog=NorthwindCS"
         End If
      End If
   End With
End Sub
```

THE OpenRstFromFile SUBPROCEDURE

The code for the OpenRstFromFile Subprocedure derives from that behind the frmADO_Jet and frmADO_MSDE forms. The primary difference in the code of Listing 30.5 is that the Recordset.Open method specifies the temporary Batch.rst file as its data source.

LISTING 30.5 OPENING A SAVED Recordset OBJECT AND ASSIGNING IT TO THE Recordset PROPERTY OF THE SUBFORM

```
Private Sub OpenRstFromFile()
   If rstBatch.State = adStateOpen Then
      rstBatch.Close
   End If
```

```
    rstBatch.Open CurrentProject.Path & "\Batch.rst", , adOpenStatic, _
       adLockBatchOptimistic, adCmdFile
    With sbfBatch
       'Assign rstBatch as the Recordset for the subform
       Set .Recordset = rstBatch
       .UniqueTable = "Customers"
       .txtCustomerID.ControlSource = "CustomerID"
       .txtCompanyName.ControlSource = "CompanyName"
       .txtAddress.ControlSource = "Address"
       .txtCity.ControlSource = "City"
       .txtRegion.ControlSource = "Region"
       .txtPostalCode.ControlSource = "PostalCode"
       .txtCountry.ControlSource = "Country"
    End With
End Sub
```

30

THE cmdBulkUpdate EVENT HANDLER

Clicking the Update Disconnected Recordset/Restore Disconnected Recordset button executes the `cmdBulkUpdate` event-handler (see Listing 30.6). The **`Set`** `sbfBatch.Recordset =` **`Nothing`** statement prevents flashing of the subform during edits performed in the **`Do While Not`** `.EOF...`**`Loop`** process. This loop traverses the `Recordset` and changes the values of unused Region cells from `NULL` to `123` or vice-versa. After the loop completes, the form hooks back up to the edited `Recordset`. The call to the `Form_Load` subprocedure displays the updated Customers table fields in the subform.

> **NOTE**
>
> Real-world applications use an unbound form and unbound text boxes to edit the Recordset. The form requires command buttons to navigate the Recordset by invoking `Move...` methods. The event handler for an Update Record button makes the changes to the field values of the local Recordset.

LISTING 30.6 THE cmdBulkUpdate EVENT HANDLER USES A LOOP TO EMULATE MULTIPLE RECORDSET EDITING OPERATIONS

```
Private Sub cmdBulkUpdate_Click()
   Dim blnUpdate As Boolean
   Dim strCapSuffix As String

   'Housekeeping for form and button captions
   strCapSuffix = " While Disconnected (Updates Are Pending)"
   If Me.cmdBulkUpdate.Caption = "Update Disconnected Recordset" Then
      Me.Caption = "Changing Empty Region Values to 123" & strCapSuffix
      blnUpdate = True
      Me.cmdBulkUpdate.Caption = "Restore Disconnected Recordset"
   Else
      Me.Caption = "Returning Region Values from 123 to Null" & strCapSuffix
      blnUpdate = False
      Me.cmdBulkUpdate.Caption = "Update Disconnected Recordset"
   End If
```

continues

```
    'If you don't execute the following instruction, the subform
    'datasheet can cause flutter vertigo during updates
    Set sbfBatch.Recordset = Nothing

    'Set the Field variable (improves performance)
    Set fldRegion = rstBatch.Fields("Region")

    'Now update or restore Region values
    With rstBatch
       .MoveFirst
       Do While Not .EOF
          If blnUpdate Then
             If IsNull(fldRegion.Value) Then
                fldRegion.Value = "123"
             End If
          Else
             'Restore the original Null value
             If fldRegion.Value = "123" Then
                fldRegion.Value = Null
             End If
          End If
          .MoveNext
       Loop
       On Error Resume Next
       'For safety
       Kill CurrentProject.Path & "\Batch.rst"
       On Error GoTo 0
       .Save CurrentProject.Path & "\Batch.rst", adPersistADTG
    End With

    'Now restore the subform's Recordset property
    Set sbfBatch.Recordset = rstBatch
    Me.cmdUpdate.Enabled = True
End Sub
```

TIP

Create a `Field` variable (`fldRegion`), instead of using a `Recordset.Fields(str`*`FieldName`*`).Value = var`*`Value`* instruction. Specifying a `Field` variable improves performance, especially if the `Recordset` has many fields.

THE `cmdUpdate` EVENT HANDLER

Clicking the Send Updates to Server button executes the `cmdUpdate` event handler and the `UpdateBatch` method to update the server tables (see Listing 30.7). Before executing the update, `Debug.Print` statements record the `OriginalValue` and `Value` property values for the first row in the Immediate window.

LISTING 30.7 UPDATING THE SERVER TABLES RECONNECTS THE Recordset TO THE DATA SOURCE, EXECUTES THE UpdateBatch METHOD, AND CLOSES THE Connection

```
Private Sub cmdUpdate_Click()
   'Recreate the connection
   Call OpenConnection

   'Reopen the Recordset from the file
   With rstBatch
      If .State = adStateOpen Then
         .Close
      End If
      Set rstBatch.ActiveConnection = cnnBatch
      .Open CurrentProject.Path & "\Batch.rst", , adOpenStatic, _
      adLockBatchOptimistic, adCmdFile

      'To demonstrate these two properties
      Debug.Print "Original Value: " & .Fields("Region").OriginalValue
      Debug.Print "Updated Value:  " & .Fields("Region").Value

      'Send the updates to the server
      .UpdateBatch
      .Close
   End With

   'Clean up
   Set rstBatch = Nothing
   cnnBatch.Close
   Set cnnBatch = Nothing
   Kill CurrentProject.Path & "\Batch.rst"

   'Load the subform datasheet from the server
   Call Form_Load
   Me.Caption = "Updated Values Retrieved from Server"
End Sub
```

THE cmdOpenXML EVENT HANDLER

The `cmdOpenXML` event handler for the Open Batch.rst in IE 5+ button demonstrates use of the VBA **`Shell`** function to launch another application (see Listing 30.8). The argument of the **`Shell`** function is identical to the instruction you type in the Run dialog's Open text box to launch an application manually. If successful, the **`Shell`** function returns the task ID value of the running application; if not, the function returns an empty **`Variant`** value.

LISTING 30.8 OPENING A PERSISTENT Recordset OBJECT SAVED AS AN XML FILE IN IE 5+

```
Private Sub cmdOpenXML_Click()
   'Launch IE 5+ with Batch.xml as the source URL
   Dim strURL As String
   Dim strShell As String
   Dim varShell As Variant
```

continues

LISTING 30.8 CONTINUED

```
   strURL = "file://" & CurrentProject.Path & "\Batch.xml"
   strShell = "\Program Files\Internet Explorer\Iexplore.exe " & strURL
   varShell = Shell(strShell, vbNormalFocus)
   If IsEmpty(varShell) Then
      MsgBox "Can't open Internet Explorer", vbOKOnly + vbExclamation, _
         "Unable to Display Batch.xml"
   End If
End Sub
```

THE Form_Unload EVENT HANDLER

Variables in form Class Modules disappear (go out of scope) when the form closes. However, it's a good programming practice to "clean up" all object variables before closing a form. In addition to cleanup operations, this event handler (see Listing 30.9) detects the presence of unsent updates in Batch.rst. Setting the `intCancel` argument to **`True`** cancels the unload operation.

LISTING 30.9 THE Form_Unload EVENT HANDLER CHECKS FOR UNSENT UPDATES AND, IF THE USER CLICKS YES IN THE MESSAGE BOX, CLOSES OPEN OBJECTS AND SETS THEM TO **Nothing**

```
Private Sub Form_Unload(intCancel As Integer)
   'Check for pending updates before unloading
   If Dir(CurrentProject.Path & "\Batch.rst") <> "" Then
      If MsgBox("Are you sure you want to quit now?", vbQuestion + vbYesNo, _
            "Updates Are Pending for the Server") = vbNo Then
         intCancel = True
         Exit Sub
      End If
   End If
   'Clean up objects
   If rstBatch.State = adStateOpen Then
      rstBatch.Close
   End If
   Set rstBatch = Nothing
   If cnnBatch.State = adStateOpen Then
      cnnBatch.Close
   End If
   Set cnnBatch = Nothing
   'If you don't execute the following instruction,
   'you receive an error when opening the form
   Set sbfBatch.Recordset = Nothing
End Sub
```

TIP

> Unlike Visual Basic forms, values you assign with VBA code to Access `Form`, `Report`, and `Control` objects persist after closing the object and exiting the Access application. In some cases, reopening the object results in an error message. Executing the **`Set`** `sbfBatch.Recordset =` **`Nothing`** instruction before closing the form and its subform prevents the possibility of an error on reopening the form, because the source value of the `Recordset` property isn't present before the `Form_Load` event handler executes.

PROGRAMMING Stream OBJECTS

For Access programmers, `Stream` objects primarily are of interest for returning attribute-centric XML data documents from SQL Server 2000. The T-SQL statement for the query must terminate with the `FOR XML AUTO` or `FOR XML RAW` option. Both options return a well-formed XML document using Microsoft's `xml-sql` schema. Unlike the .xml files saved from `Recordset` objects with the `adPersistXML` option, the stream doesn't include the schema elements. Like the `rowset` schema, `xml-sql` isn't compatible with Access 2003's native XML schema. SQL Server HTTP template queries, which can return HTML tables to Web browsers from `FOR XML AUTO` queries, require the `xml-sql` schema.

→ For an example of using the FOR XML AUTO option in SQL Server HTTP template queries, **see** "Using SQL Server 2000's HTTP Query Features," **p. 976**.

EXECUTING FOR XML AUTO QUERIES WITH THE FRMSTREAM FORM

The frmStream form has unbound text boxes to display a default T-SQL `FOR XML AUTO` query, the modifications to the query syntax needed to return a well-formed XML document, and the XML document resulting from execution of the `Command` object that specifies MSSQLXML as the query dialect. To test the frmStream form, do this:

1. Open ADOTest.mdb's or ADOTest.adp's frmStream form. The default query is a simple T-SQL query, similar to that used by the frmBatchUpdate form, with the `FOR XML AUTO` modifier added. SQL Server's default rowset document style is attribute-centric. Mark the Element-Centric check box to add `ELEMENTS` to the modifier and return an element-centric document.
2. Click the Execute FOR XML Query button to display the XML query wrapper required by SQL Server 2000 to return a well-formed XML data document. A `Command` object returns a `Stream` object that contains an XML data document, which opens in the bottom text box. The `Stream` object is saved to Stream.xml in the folder that contains ADOTest.mdb.
3. Click the Open Stream.xml in IE 5+ button to launch IE with `file://`*`path`*`/Stream.xml` as the URL. IE's XML parser makes it easier to read the XML document.

4. Mark the Multi-Table Query check box to replace the simple query with a T-SQL query against the Customers and Orders tables. Making a change to the T-SQL FOR XML Query text box clears the other two text boxes.
5. Click Execute FOR XML Query again to display the resulting XML document (see Figure 30.22).

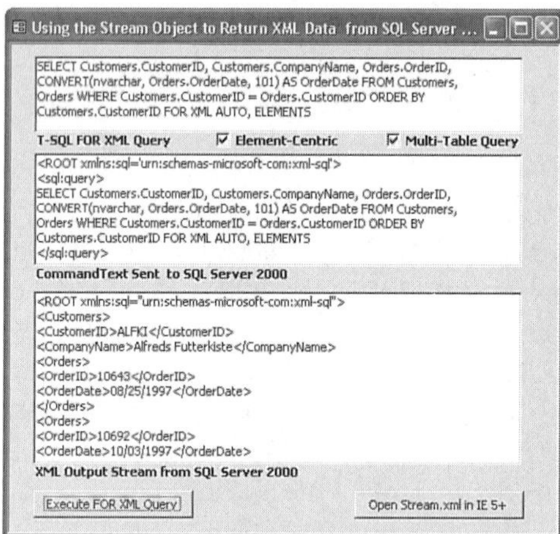

Figure 30.22
The multi-table query with the `FOR XML AUTO, ELEMENTS` option returns elements from the Orders table nested within Customers table elements.

6. Click Open Stream.xml in IE 5+. The nesting of Orders elements within the Customers is more evident in IE's presentation (see Figure 30.23).

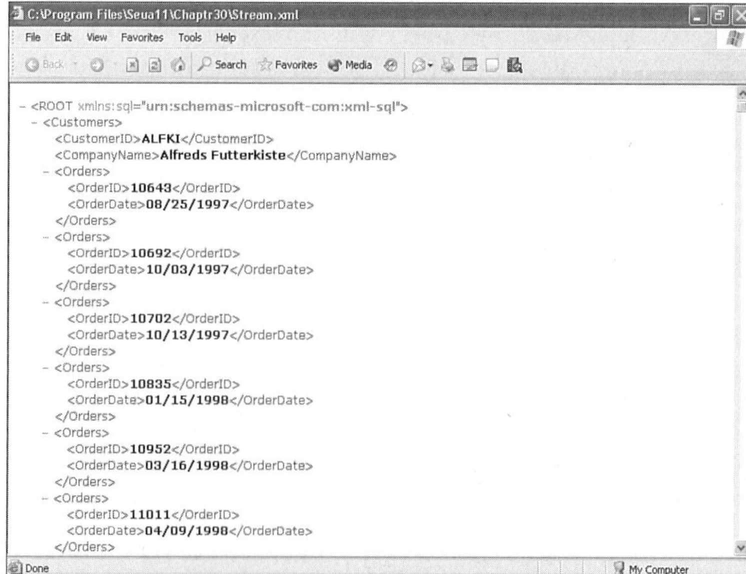

Figure 30.23
IE 5+'s XML parser formats the document to make nesting of table elements readily apparent.

7. To see the effect of the `FOR XML RAW` modifier, replace `AUTO` with **`RAW`** in the T-SQL query, execute the command, and open the query in IE 5+ (see Figure 30.24).

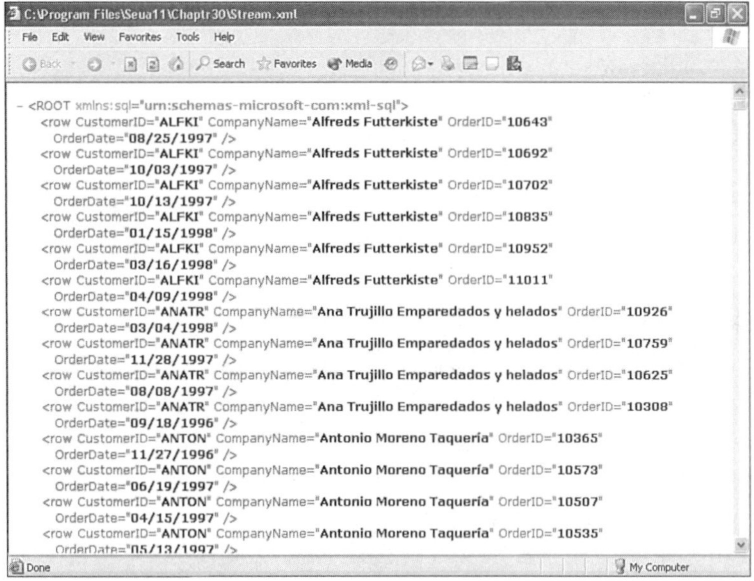

Figure 30.24
The `FOR XML RAW` modifier combines all attribute values for a query row in a single, generic `row` element.

NOTE

> Changing the `ORDER BY` clause from `Customers.CustomerID` to `Orders.OrderID` generates a very different XML document strcture. In this case, most Customers elements contain a single nested order; only consecutive orders for a particular customer appear as multiple nested order elements. (See the entry for ROMEY as the first example.)

EXPLORING THE VBA CODE TO CREATE A Stream OBJECT

Most of the event handlers and subprocedures used by the VBA code for the frmStream form derive from those of the frmBatch form described earlier. The two important code elements behind frmStream are the Declarations section, which declares the `ADODB.Command` and `ADODB.Stream` object variables, and constants for the currently allowable GUID values of the `Command.Dialect` property, and the `cmdExecute_Click` event handler (see Listing 30.10).

LISTING 30.10 CREATING A STREAM OBJECT FROM AN SQL SERVER `FOR XML AUTO` QUERY AND DISPLAYING THE STREAM IN A TEXT BOX

```
Option Compare Database
Option Explicit
```

continues

LISTING 30.10 CONTINUED

```
Private cnnStream As New ADODB.Connection
Private cmmStream As New ADODB.Command
Private stmQuery As ADODB.Stream

'GUID constants for Stream.Dialect
Private Const DBGUID_DEFAULT As String = _
   "{C8B521FB-5CF3-11CE-ADE5-00AA0044773D}"
Private Const DBGUID_SQL As String = _
   "{C8B522D7-5CF3-11CE-ADE5-00AA0044773D}"
Private Const DBGUID_MSSQLXML As String = _
   "{5D531CB2-E6Ed-11D2-B252-00C04F681B71}"
Private Const DBGUID_XPATH As String = _
   "{ec2a4293-e898-11d2-b1b7-00c04f680c56}"

'Constants for XML query prefix and suffix
Private Const strXML_SQLPrefix As String = _
   "<ROOT xmlns:sql='urn:schemas-microsoft-com:xml-sql'>" & vbCrLf & "<sql:query>"
Private Const strXML_SQLSuffix As String = "</sql:query>" & vbCrLf & "</ROOT>"

Private Sub cmdExecute_Click()
   'Use Command and Stream objects to return XML as text
   Dim strXMLQuery As String
   Dim strXML As String
   Dim lngCtr As Long

   On Error GoTo errGetXMLStream
   strXMLQuery = Me.txtQuery.Value

   'Add the XML namespace and <ROOT...> and </ROOT> tags to the query text
   strXMLQuery = strXML_SQLPrefix & vbCrLf & strXMLQuery & vbCrLf &
strXML_SQLSuffix

   'Display the CommandText property value
   Me.txtXMLQuery.Value = strXMLQuery
   DoEvents

   'Create a new Stream for each execution
   Set stmQuery = New ADODB.Stream
   stmQuery.Open

   'Set and execute the command to return a stream
   With cmmStream
      Set .ActiveConnection = cnnStream
      'Query text is used here, not an input stream
      .CommandText = strXMLQuery
      'Specify an SQL Server FOR XML query
      .Dialect = DBGUID_MSSQLXML
      'Specify the stream to receive the output
      .Properties("Output Stream") = stmQuery
      .Execute , , adExecuteStream
   End With

   'Reset the stream position
   stmQuery.Position = 0
```

```
    'Save the stream to a local file
    stmQuery.SaveToFile CurrentProject.Path & "\Stream.xml", adSaveCreateOverWrite
    cmdOpenXML.Enabled = True

    'Extract the text from the stream
    strXML = stmQuery.ReadText

    'Make the XML more readable with line feeds, if it isn't too long
    If Len(strXML) < 15000 Then
       Me.txtXML.Value = Replace(strXML, "><", ">" & vbCrLf & "<")
    Else
       If Len(strXML) > 32000 Then
          'Limit the display to capacity of text box
          Me.txtXML.Value = Left$(strXML, 30000)
       Else
          Me.txtXML.Value = strXML
       End If
    End If
    Exit Sub

errGetXMLStream:
    MsgBox Err.Description, vbOKOnly + vbExclamation, "Error Returning XML Stream"
    Exit Sub
End Sub
```


This form only uses the `DBGUID_MSSQLXML` constant; the other three `GUID` constants are for reference only. ADO 2.6+'s type library doesn't have a "`DialectGUIDEnum`" or similar enumeration, so you must declare at least the `DBGUID_MSSQLXML` constant to request SQL Server to return XML data documents in the `xml-sql` dialect. Comments in the body of the code of the `cmdExecute_Click` event handler describe the purpose of each `Stream`-related statement.

EXPLORING THE ADDORDER.ADP SAMPLE PROJECT

The AddOrders.adp sample project in the \Seua11\Chaptr30 folder of the accompanying CD-ROM demonstrates practical application for this chapter's example of the programming of ADO objects, methods, and properties. The primary purpose of the AddOrders project is to add a large number of records to the Orders and Order Details tables of a copy of the NorthwindCS SQL Server database. Working with test tables having a large number of rows lets you debug online transaction processing (OLTP) applications with real-world data. The code uses random record numbers to specify the CustomerID for each added order and the ProductID for order line items.

The AddOrders project also lets you compare the performance difference between sending SQL statements to the server and using stored procedures to add, edit, and delete Orders and Order Details records. Code in the frmAddNorthwindOrders Class Module creates the required stored procedures.

To give the AddOrders.adp project a test drive, do the following:

1. Open NorthwindCS.adp, choose Tools, Database Tools, Transfer Database and create a copy of NorthwindCS as NorthwindSQL or any other name you prefer in your (local) SQL Server instance.
2. Open AddOrders.adp, choose File, Connection, and specify the server, authentication method, and name of the database copy. When you add a connection to AddOrders.adp, you have the option of using the project's connection or specifying a connection to another server or database.
3. Click Connect and click Yes when the message box asks if you want to use the current connection to the new database. If you specified SQL Server security, type your login ID and password in the two text boxes. You receive the message about the OrderID field's `Identity` attribute shown in Figure 30.25.

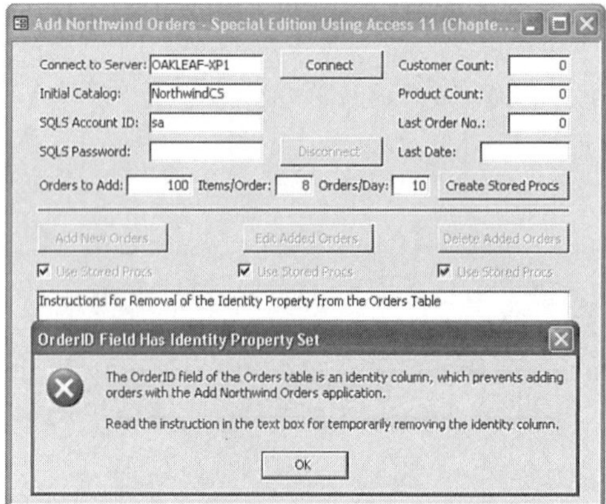

Figure 30.25
Opening NorthwindCS or a copy of NorthwindCS displays the warning message shown here.

NOTE

The `Identity` attribute must be removed from the Orders table to permit deleting added records and then adding new records with numbers that are consective with the orginal OrderID numbers (10248–11077).

4. Acknowledge the message, open the Orders table in Design view, and select the OrderID column. In the Columns property page, select Identity and change the value from Yes to No (see Figure 30.26). Close the table and save the changes.

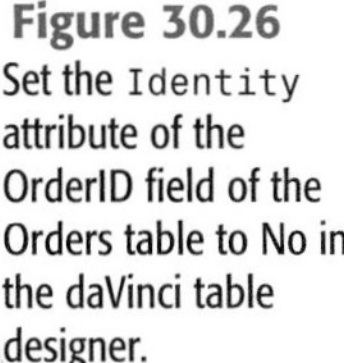

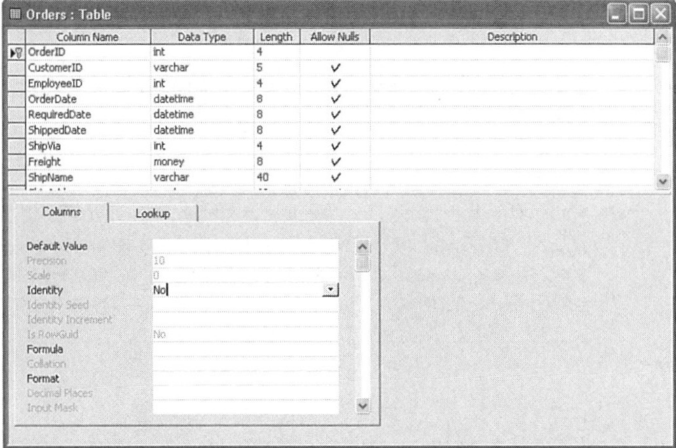

Figure 30.26
Set the `Identity` attribute of the OrderID field of the Orders table to No in the daVinci table designer.

TIP

> You also can change the design in SQL Server Enterprise Manager, but using Access's Table Design view is easier.

5. In the form, click the Clear Report Text button, click Connect to open the connection to the database, and click the Create Stored Procs button to add three stored procedures to the database. Adding the procedures enables the three Use Stored Procs check boxes.
6. Change the Orders to Add, Items/Order, and Orders/Day values, if you want, and click Add New Orders. The number of Orders and Order Details records added and the time required for addition appears in the text box.
7. Mark the Use Stored Procs check box under the Add New Orders button to compare the speed of order addition with a stored procedure. Depending on your hardware configuration, you might gain about a 10% performance improvement by using a stored procedure instead of sending `INSERT` statements to the database (see Figure 30.27).

Figure 30.27
Adding, editing, or delecting records adds the number of records affected and timing data to the text box.

8. Repeat steps 6 and 7, but click the Edit Added Orders button to change the Quantity values of all Order Details records you've added.
9. Click the Delete Added Orders button to restore the tables to their original number of records. A message box lets you choose between bulk and individual order deletion.

NOTE

> The code in the form's Class Module originated in a Visual Basic 6.0 program for testing SQL Server 7.0 and 2000 OLTP performance in a variety of server hardware configurations. Only a few code changes were necessary to the Visual Basic 6.0 code that was copied to the Access form.

TROUBLESHOOTING

SPACES IN ADO OBJECT NAMES

When I attempt to open a Command object on the views, functions, or stored procedures of NorthwindCS, I receive a "Syntax error or access violation" message.

SQL Server 7.0+ (unfortunately) supports spaces in object names, such as views and stored procedures. However, SQL Server wants these names enclosed within double quotes. Sending double quotes in an object name string is a pain in VBA, but surrounding the object name with square brackets also solves the problem. For example, `cnnName.CommandText = "Sales By Year"` fails but `cnnName.CommandText = "[Sales By Year]"` works. Using square brackets for otherwise-illegal object identifiers is the better programming practice.

IN THE REAL WORLD—WHY LEARN ADO PROGRAMMING?

As observed in Chapter 4, "Exploring Relational Database Theory and Practice," "Everything has to be somewhere" is a popular corollary of the Law of Conservation of Matter. So just about everything you need to know about ADO 2.x and OLE DB is concentrated in this chapter. The problem with this "laundry list" approach to describing a set of data-related objects is that readers are likely to doze off in mid-chapter. If you've gotten this far (and have at least scanned the intervening code and tables), you probably surmised that ADO is more than just a replacement for DAO—it's a relatively new and expansive approach to database connectivity.

The most important reason to become an accomplished ADO programmer is to create Web-based database applications. Microsoft designed OLE DB and ADO expressly for HTML- and XML-based applications, such as DAP—the subject of the three chapters of Part VI, "Publishing Data to Intranets and the Internet." You can use VBScript or JScript (Microsoft's variant of ECMAScript) to open and manipulate ADO `Connection`, `Command`,

and `Recordset` objects on Web pages. With DAO, you're stuck with conventional Access applications that require users to have a copy of Office 2003 or you to supply runtime versions of your Access 2003 applications.

Another incentive for becoming ADO-proficient is migrating from Jet 4.0 to ADP and SQL Server back ends. When SQL Server marketing honchos say that SQL Server is Microsoft's "strategic database direction," believe them. Jet still isn't dead, but the handwriting is on the wall; ultimately SQL Server will replace Jet in all but the most trivial database applications. The ADO 2.7 documentation on MSDN states that "Microsoft has deprecated the Microsoft Jet Engine, and plans no new releases or service packs for this component." SQL Server 2000 Standard Edition and MSDE 2000 dominate the "sweet spot" of the client/server RDBMS market—small- to mid-size firms—plus division-level intranets of the Fortune 1000. SQL Server Enterprise and DataCenter editions are making inroads on Oracle's and IBM's share of the enterprise RDBMS market.

NOTE

> Microsoft's intention might have been to release no new service packs (SPs) for Jet 4.0, but Access 2003 required a new Jet 4.0 SP7 to support macro security and "sandbox" mode.

Microsoft released .NET Framework 1.0 and Visual Studio .NET on February 13, 2002. ADO.NET now is Microsoft's strategic data access approach. Word and Excel are the only members of Office 2003 to integrate Visual Basic .NET, C#, J#, and other .NET Common Language Runtime-compliant programming languages as alternatives to VBA. As mentioned in earlier chapters, moving from VBA to object-oriented programming with Visual Basic .NET is challenging for most Office developers and overwhelming for Access power users. It's a good bet that VBA will dominate Office-related programming for at least the next five years.

.NET Framework 1.0 and 1.1 include managed (native) .NET data providers only for SQL Server and Oracle 7.3x databases, and managed wrappers for OLE DB and ODBC. (The Oracle provider offers "limited support for Oracle 8x.") IBM offers a .NET managed provider for DB2. Until other RDBMS vendors—such as MySQL AB and Sybase—write native .NET providers for their databases, Visual Studio .NET programmers must rely on OLE DB, ADO and .NET's COM interoperability (COM interop) layer to connect to other popular RDBMSs. Thus, OLE DB and ADO are likely to remain in widespread use through at least the first decade of the twentieth century.

The ultimate answer to "Why learn ADO programming?", however, is "Microsoft wants YOU to use ADO until you move to .NET." Like the proverbial one-ton gorilla, Microsoft usually gets what it wants, but it will take more than chest-thumping and bellowing to convince today's VBA programmers to take on the challenge of Visual Basic .NET and ADO.NET.

CHAPTER 31

Consuming and Providing XML Web Services

In this chapter

Integrating Access 2003 with XML Web Services

Prior to its release, there was widespread speculation that most Microsoft Office System 2003 members would include native support for XML Web services. As mentioned in Chapter 1's "Support for XML Web Services" section, this didn't happen; only InfoPath 2003 has out-of-the-box support for retrieving and updating SQL Server and Jet data with XML Web services. The initial reaction of most Access power users and developers to this omission is likely to be "So what?" When this book was written, XML Web services were in the "early adopter" stage. Major players in the RDBMS market—IBM, Microsoft, and, to a lesser degree, Sun Microsystems and Oracle—have invested many millions of dollars to integrate XML Web services with their data-related development tools. Microsoft emphasizes support for XML Web services as a key incentive for migrating to Windows Server 2003 and Visual Studio .NET.

31

NOTE

> Microsoft uses the term *XML Web services* to differentiate the subject of this chapter from conventional Web services, such as search services, electronic commerce applications, portals, and the like. Most other development tool and application server vendors, such as BEA Systems, Borland, IBM, Oracle, and Sun Microsystems drop the *XML* prefix. The *XML* prefix applies to all instances of the term Web *service(s)* in this chapter.

The benefits of Web services assure their ultimate adoption as the *lingua franca* of interoperable software components of distributed applications. Unlike Microsoft's Component Object Model (COM and COM+), Web services are platform- and operating system-agnostic. Conventional Web services use HTTP (TCP port 80) or Secure HTTP (HTTPS, TCP port 443) as the transport protocol for XML text messages. Few firewalls block text content on these ports, so you can connect to public Web services over the Internet. HTTPS currently is the most common method for securing confidential messages by encrypting the human-readable XML content.

A Microsoft Office Web Services Toolkit enables your Access applications to connect to and utilize most basic Web services written in any programming language and running on Linux, Unix, or Windows servers. The key to Web services' interoperability is adherence to a set of public standards and specifications developed by the World Wide Web Consortium (W3C), the Organization for the Advancement of Structured Information Standards (OASIS), and the Web Services Interoperability (WS-I) Organization.

NOTE

> WS-I doesn't purport to be an official standards organization. WS-I's charter is to establish a common set of specifications for implementing existing Web service standards. WS-I published its first recommendation, Basic Profile Version 1.0, in early 2003. WS-I also provides tools for testing Web service conformance to the recommendations. Links to all WS-I specifications are at `http://www.ws-i.org`.

The Office XP Web Services Toolkit 2.0, which Microsoft released in July 2002, was the current version when this book was published. You can expect Microsoft to release updated versions periodically. The Toolkit adds the Web Service References Tool (WSR) 2.0 to the Visual Basic Editor's Tools menu. WSR automatically generates almost all the VBA code you need to consume simple and complex Web services. The Toolkit also includes useful documentation and sample Web service consumer applications.

This advanced chapter shows you how to take advantage of WSR with typical public Web services and describes a simple approach to delivering rowsets from SQL Server stored procedures as Web services. The chapter also includes instructions for installing and using Microsoft's .NET WebService Studio, which is an exceptionally useful tool for learning Web service technology and message structure.

GAINING A WEB SERVICES VOCABULARY

Web services exchange messages between a *consumer* (client or sender) and *provider* (server or receiver). The provider and consumer are called *endpoints*. The consumer initiates the exchange with an XML *request* document; the provider ordinarily returns an XML *response* document that contains the requested information. If the request message is malformed or the provider can't supply the requested information, a *fault* occurs.

Like other Web-related technologies, Web services are, by definition, *loosely coupled*. Loosely coupled means that Web services don't rely on a permanent connection between the consumer and provider. Providers listen for incoming SOAP request messages and respond in ad hoc fashion. Windows XP/2000+ use Internet Information Server (IIS) 5.0+ and an Internet Services Application Programming Interface (ISAPI) filter to listen for incoming request messages and route the messages to the appropriate service. Thus, you can set up your own public or private services that run on Windows XP or 2000 Professional, as well as Windows 2000+ server.

WEB SERVICE STANDARDS AND SPECIFICATIONS

Much of the vocabulary of Web services is defined in the following three standards that apply to Web services and the messages they exchange:

- *SOAP* (originally Simple Object Access Protocol) is the basic specification that covers the structure of XML request and response messages. SOAP 1.1, the version in common use when this book was published, isn't a W3C recommendation; it's a W3C note that's been adopted as a *de facto* industry standard. The SOAP 1.2 recommendation consists of three parts—Part 0: Primer (`http://www.w3.org/TR/soap12-part0/`) is a SOAP tutorial; Part 1: Messaging Framework (`http://www.w3.org/TR/soap12-part1/`) is the basic SOAP 1.2 specification; and Part 2: Adjuncts (`http://www.w3.org/TR/soap12-part2/`) provides recommendations for SOAP 1.2 implementations.
- *Web Services Description Language* (WSDL, pronounced "wizdle") is the specification for an XML document that defines the structure and content of SOAP request and

response documents for a particular Web service. A WSDL document serves as a contract between the provider and consumer. If the consumer submits a request message that conforms to the WSDL document's requirements, the provider agrees to respond in a WSDL-defined fashion. Office 2003's WSR and Visual Studio .NET's Add Web Reference feature automatically generate custom classes from WSDL documents. Like SOAP 1.1, WSDL 1.1 is a W3C note; the current W3C specification for WSDL 1.2 is at `http://www.w3.org/TR/wsdl12/`.

NOTE

> The term *WSDL document* includes static WSDL files (*ServiceName*.wsdl) and the dynamic WSDL documents generated by Microsoft's ASP.NET Web services.

31

- *Universal Description, Discovery, and Integration (UDDI)* specifications define methods for locating endpoints and WSDL documents for Web services on private intranets or the Internet. IBM, Microsoft, and SAP are operators of public UDDI Business Registries (UBRs) where providers can advertise their Web services. Potential consumers can search the UBRs by provider name, service name, or industrial and geographical classifications. UBRs replicate registrations frequently, so each UBR delivers identical information. WSR2 defaults to the Microsoft UBR for Web service discovery. OASIS maintains the UDDI 2.0 and 3.0 standards. You can learn more about UBRs at `http://www.uddi.org/faqs.html`. Windows Server 2003 includes a private UDDI 2.0 registry for deployment on intranets.

Fortunately, you don't need a thorough understanding of the Web services standards and specifications to consume or provide them. WSR automates VBA code generation for Access 2003 Web service consumers. The Microsoft SOAP Toolkit 3.0+ installs an ISAPI SOAP listener for IIS 5.0+ to enable providing Web services. This Toolkit also creates SOAP 1.1 wrappers and generates WSDL files for Visual Basic 6.0 ActiveX components automatically.

SOAP MESSAGE FORMATS

SOAP messages consist of an *envelope* that contains a *body* and optional *header* elements. The body contains the request or response message. Header elements typically provide message routing and security-related information for advanced Web services. Most public Web services don't include header elements; if they do, processing the header usually is optional. WSR2 can't handle mandatory headers, so this chapter's examples don't include them.

Following is an example of a simplified SOAP 1.1 request message to ZipCodeResolver, a public address-correction Web service provided by EraServer.NET:

```
<?xml version="1.0" encoding="utf-8"?>
<soap:Envelope
    xmlns:soap="http://schemas.xmlsoap.org/soap/envelope/"
    xmlns:xsi="http://www.w3.org/2001/XMLSchema-instance"
    xmlns:xsd="http://www.w3.org/2001/XMLSchema">
```

```
  <soap:Body>
    <CorrectedAddressXml
        xmlns="http://webservices.eraserver.net/">
      <accessCode>9999</accessCode>
      <address>1000 Broadway</address>
      <city>Oakland</city>
      <state>CA</state>
    </CorrectedAddressXml>
  </soap:Body>
<soap:Envelope>
```

The request message invokes a `CorrectedAddressXml` function (called a *Web service method* or *Web method*) that returns the address in standard US Postal Service format with five-digit and ZIP+4 ZIP codes. The Web method sends an HTTP GET request with the address, city, and state to the USPS Web site, which delivers a page that contains the corrected address in an HTML table. The service extracts the required data from the page to a public class (user-defined type) named `USPSAddress`, which has `Street`, `City`, `State`, `ShortZIP` and `FullZIP` members. The process of extracting specific pieces of data from Web pages is known as *screen scraping*. Transforming an instance of a class to an XML document fragment is called *serialization*; the reverse is *deserialization*.

31

Following is the `CorrectedAddressXML` method's SOAP 1.1 response message:

```
<?xml version="1.0" encoding="utf-8"?>
<soap:Envelope
    xmlns:soap="http://schemas.xmlsoap.org/soap/envelope/"
    xmlns:xsi="http://www.w3.org/2001/XMLSchema-instance"
    xmlns:xsd="http://www.w3.org/2001/XMLSchema">
  <soap:Body>
    <CorrectedAddressXmlResponse
        xmlns="http://webservices.eraserver.net/">
      <CorrectedAddressXmlResult>
        <Street>1200 BROADWAY</Street>
        <City>OAKLAND</City>
        <State>CA</State>
        <ShortZIP>94612</ShortZIP>
        <FullZIP>94612-1802</FullZIP>
      </CorrectedAddressXmlResult>
    </CorrectedAddressXmlResponse>
  </soap:Body>
</soap:Envelope>
```

A WSDL document defines the format of the SOAP request and response messages, and specifies the Web service's URL. There are two widely used Web service message formats—*rpc/encoded* and *document/literal*. The first element (rpc or document) specifies the SOAP body's `use` and the second determines the message `style`. You determine the format of the request and response messages by inspecting the `<operation>` node(s) of the WSDL document, as illustrated by the following excerpt for the document/literal `CorrectedAddressXml` method:

```
<operation name="CorrectedAddressXml">
  <soap:operation
    soapAction="http://webservices.eraserver.net/CorrectedAddressXml"
    style="document" />
```

```
    <input>
      <soap:body use="literal" />
    </input>
    <output>
      <soap:body use="literal" />
    </output>
  </operation>
```

NOTE

The WSDL document for ZipCodeResolver is 20KB in size and far too large to be reproduced here. Typical request and response messages, and ZipCodeResolver.wsdl are located in the \Seua11\Chaptr31\ZipCodeResolver folder of the accompanying CD-ROM.

31

Most early Web services employed the rpc/encoded format, which emulates a remote procedure call by encoding specific message data types in accordance with section 5 "SOAP Encoding" of the SOAP 1.1 specification. It turned out to be very difficult to assure service interoperability with the rpc/encoded format, so WS-I's Basic Profile 1.0 specification precludes its use by requiring `literal` as the value of the `use` attribute. The `literal` value requires that message data types conform to the W3C's XML Schema Part 2: Datatypes recommendation.

The Basic Profile 1.0 permits two message formats—document/literal and rpc/literal. The document/literal format is much more popular; only a few SOAP toolkits support rpc/literal messages. WSDL files for document/literal—often abbreviated *doc/lit*—services define the messages, not just datatypes, by XML schemas (XSD). All but one of this chapter's examples are document/literal.

EXECUTING ASP.NET WEB SERVICES FROM INTERNET EXPLORER

The .NET Framework's ASP.NET Web services default to document/literal format; .NET doesn't support rpc/literal format directly. ZipCodeResolver is an ASP.NET Web service developed with Visual Studio .NET that includes documentation for each Web method. ASP.NET automatically generates a Web service help page when you open a file with an .asmx extension in a browser. As an example, `http://webservices.eraserver.net/zipcoderesolver/zipcoderesolver.asmx` displays the help page shown in Figure 31.1. Web service help pages let you determine quickly whether the service is operational and has the potential to fulfill your needs.

NOTE

The .asmx file extension identifies an ASP.NET Web service; ASP.NET Web pages use the .aspx extension.

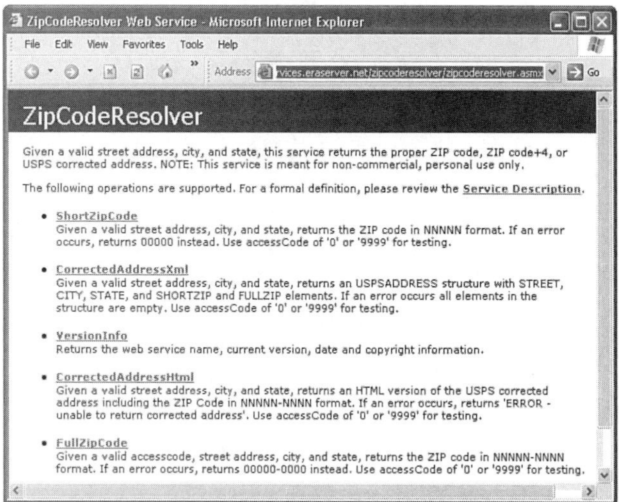

Figure 31.1
ASP.NET Web services created with Visual Studio .NET provide Web service help pages with a list of Web methods and optional service documentation.

If the Web method has simple parameters, clicking a Web method link opens a page with a test form in which you type required parameter values. ZipCodeResolver has five Web methods, each of which opens a test form. The `VersionInfo` method doesn't require parameters, so its test form only has an Invoke button. The other services require the parameters shown in Figure 31.2. When you click the Invoke button, an HTTP `GET` operation returns the SOAP body elements to IE (see Figure 31.3).

Figure 31.2
This test form for the ZipCodeResolver's `CorrectedAddressXML` method lets you send required parameters to a service that supports the HTTP `GET` protocol.

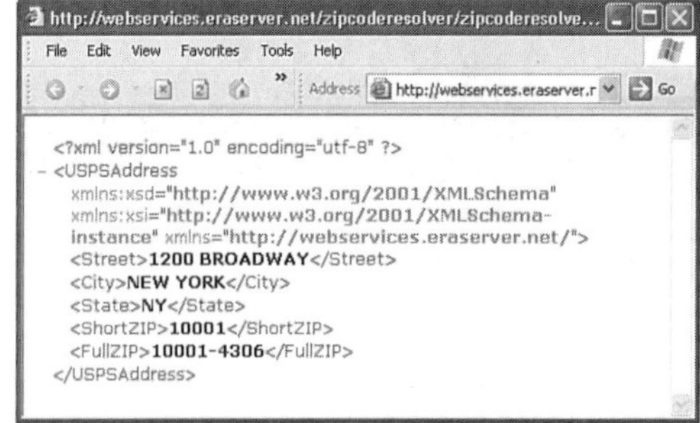

Figure 31.3
The response message from a service port that implements HTTP GET contains the inner XML elements of the SOAP response message.

By default, ASP.NET 1.0 WSDL documents include HTTP GET and POST as well as SOAP operations (called *ports*). Following is the <service> node of ZipCodeResolver's WSDL document that defines the three ports:

```
<service name="ZipCodeResolver">
  <documentation>Given a valid street address, city,
    and state, this service returns the proper ZIP code,
    ZIP code+4, or USPS corrected address. NOTE: This
    service is meant for non-commercial, personal use only.
  </documentation>
  <port name="ZipCodeResolverSoap"
      binding="s0:ZipCodeResolverSoap">
    <soap:address location="http://webservices.eraserver.net/
      zipcoderesolver/zipcoderesolver.asmx" />
  </port>
  <port name="ZipCodeResolverHttpGet"
      binding="s0:ZipCodeResolverHttpGet">
    <http:address location="http://.../zipcoderesolver.asmx" />
  </port>
  <port name="ZipCodeResolverHttpPost"
      binding="s0:ZipCodeResolverHttpPost">
    <http:address location="http://... /zipcoderesolver.asmx" />
  </port>
</service>
```

XMethods operates one of the earliest and most popular public Web services lists at http://www.xmethods.net. About a third of the listed services are ASP.NET document/literal and provide Web service help pages. For the complete list of services, click the FULL LIST link.

NOTE

> ASP.NET Web services whose request messages include complex types don't support test forms. Developers of commercial Web services often remove the HTTP GET and POST entries from their services' WSDL files. Thus, you might find that some of the ASP.NET Web services you explore don't provide a test form.

Downloading and Installing the Office Web Services Toolkit

The Microsoft Office Developer Downloads page (`http://msdn.microsoft.com/library/default.asp?url=/downloads/list/officedev.asp`) has a link to the current version(s) of the Web Services Toolkit. The following instructions apply to the Office XP Web Services Toolkit 2.0, but might apply to later versions also:

1. Click the Toolkit link to open the download page, click the Download link, and save Offwstk.exe to a temporary folder, \Temp for this example.
2. Double-click Offwstk.exe to start the installation process, accept the default location (\Temp\Office XP Web Services Toolkit 2.0 Downloaded Files) in which to expand the archived files, and click Unzip.
3. In the ...Downloaded Files folder, click Offwstk.msi, click Next on the installer's Welcome page, click Next on Readme Information page, accept the default destination folder, click Next two more times to install the files, and click Finish.
4. Choose Programs, Office XP Web Services Toolkit, Office XP Web Services Toolkit Overview to open the Office XP Web Services Toolkit 2.0 installation dialog (see Figure 31.4).

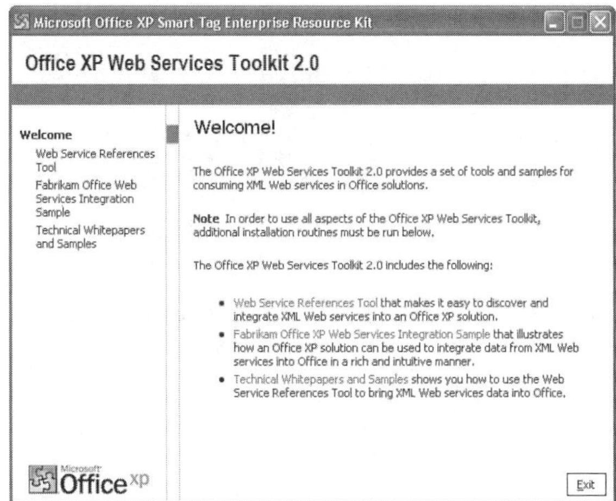

Figure 31.4 You must install at least the Web Services Reference Tool; installing the Fabrikam sample and Technical Whitepapers and Samples is optional. (Disregard the erroneous "Microsoft Office XP Smart Tag Enterprise Resource Kit" title.)

5. Click the Web Services Reference Tool link to open the Web References Tool dialog (see Figure 31.5). Click the WSR2ReadMe link to review system requirements, and then click the Setup.exe link to open the File Download dialog.

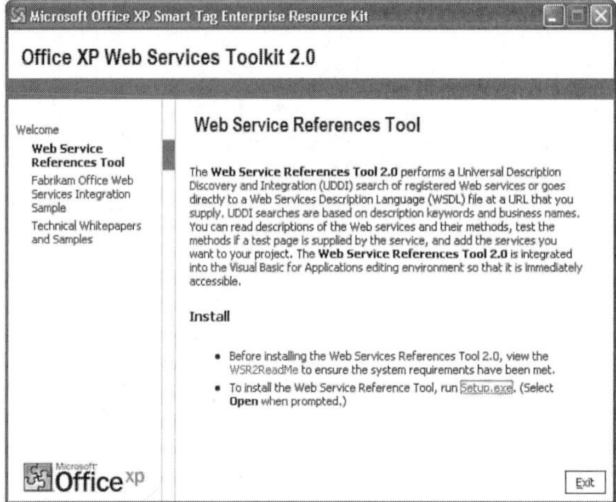

Figure 31.5
Clicking the Setup.exe link starts the installation process for WSR 2.0.

6. Click Open to install WSR 2.0. Accept the End-User License Agreement, and click Install. Click Finish when installation completes. Installing WSR copies Access, Excel, and Word sample application subfolders to the ...\Whitepapers\Samples folder.
7. Optionally, click the Technical Whitepapers and Samples link to copy the Toolkit documentation.

Later Toolkit versions probably will simplify this convoluted installation process.

Creating an Access Web Service Consumer

WSR makes it easy to integrate Web services into Access applications. Following are the basic steps:

1. Design a form with controls to supply the Web method's parameter values and display the SOAP response message's content. For ASP.NET services, the test form and its response message usually provide an indication of the type of control required. Text boxes work for most services; use list boxes to display response messages containing arrays.
2. Run WSR to generate the Web service class(es) from the service's WSDL document. Services that return simple datatypes generate a single class module—`clsws_ServiceName`, which is called a *Web service proxy*. Services whose request, response, or both messages contain complex datatypes generate a `clsof_Factory_ServiceName` class module and a `struct_ClassName` module for each type.
3. Add code to the form's class module to invoke the Web service proxy's Web method with the required parameter(s) and populate the response controls.

This example uses \Program Files\Seua11\Chaptr31\ZipCodeResolver\AddressCorrector.mdb, which contains a pre-built form for the ZipCodeResolver service.

The form is derived from the Office XP Web Services Toolkit 2.0's ComplexTypesDemo.mdb application.

GENERATING THE WEB SERVICE PROXY AND USPSADDRESS CLASSES

The Web service proxy is an Access class module that creates an instance of the `SoapClient30` object and generates a WSML document to handle complex types, if required by the service. The `SoapClient30` instance uses the `SoapConnectorFactory` to create a `SoapConnector30` instance for the WSDL documents's `<port>` element that specifies SOAP binding.

Following is the WSML document generated by WSR for the ZipCodeResolver service's `USPSAddress` type:

```
<servicemapping>
  <service name='ZipCodeResolver'>
    <using PROGID='MSSOAP.GenericCustomTypeMapper30'
      cachable='0' ID='GCTM'/>
    <types>
      <type name='USPSAddress'
        targetNamespace='http://webservices.eraserver.net/'
        uses='GCTM' targetClassName='struct_USPSAddress'/>
    </types>
  </service>
</servicemapping>
```

The `MSSOAP.GenericCustomTypeMapper30` is responsible for populating the four string elements of the `USPSAddress` type: `Street`, `City`, `State`, `ShortZIP`, and `FullZip`.

TIP

> Make at least one copy of AddressCorrector.mdb before you add the Web service reference. If you need to change the service name or location, it's easier to start over from scratch than to remove the existing classes from a modified version of the database.

To add the required classes to consume a Web service, using the ZipCodeResolver service as an example, do the following:

1. Open AddressCorrector.mdb, close the form, select Modules in the Database window, and click the New Module button to create a temporary Module1 and open it in the Visual Basic Editor.
2. Choose Tools, Web Service References to open the Web Services Reference Tool 2.0 dialog.
3. Select the Web Service URL option and type the URL for the Web service to return the WSDL document. (WSR doesn't require adding `?wsdl` to return the WSDL document. For this example, the URL is **`http://webservices.eraserver.net/zipcoderesolver/zipcoderesolver.asmx`**.
4. Click Search to display the Web service name in the Search Result list, mark the ZipCodeResolver check box to select the service, and expand the node to display the service's Web methods.

TIP

> If you don't receive a response with step 3's URL within a few seconds, substitute **`www.oakleaf.ws`** for `webservices.eraserver.net`. The OakLeaf version is derived from the EraServer service, but has several additional complex type methods.

5. Select a method to return its documentation, if present (see Figure 31.6). Clicking Test opens the Web service help page (refer to Figure 31.1).

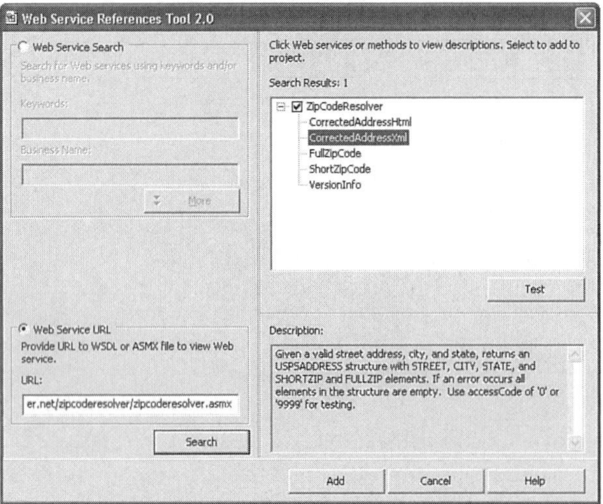

Figure 31.6 When you type a URL for an accessible .asmx or .wsdl file, WSR opens a tree view list with the name of the service and its Web methods. Selecting a method displays its documentation, if present.

6. Click Add to generate the VBA code for the Web service proxy, class factory, and type class modules (see Figure 31.7).
7. Close the database, and save the added class modules with their assigned names; don't save Module1. Then reopen the database.
8. In frmAddressCorrector, type a valid U.S. address in the text boxes or accept the default values, and click the Correct Address button to execute the service's `CorrectedAddressXML` method and populate the five text boxes with the data (see Figure 31.8). Code behind frmAddressCorrector separates the building name from the street address. (Very few US addresses have building names.)

NOTE

> If the Web service or the USPS ZIP+4 Web site isn't accessible, the service times out in 30 seconds. Occasionally, attempts to consume the service might freeze the application. If you don't receive a response in a minute or two, use Task Manager to end the Access process and try again.

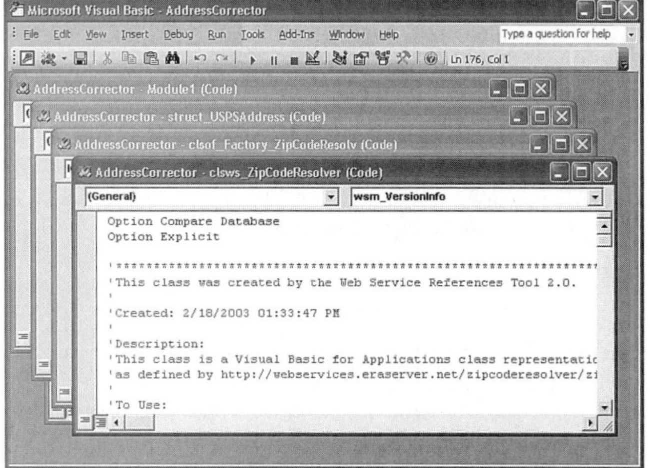

Figure 31.7 WSR adds multiple classes for Web methods that return complex types. If the method returns simple types, WSR generates a single `clsws_Service-Name` class.

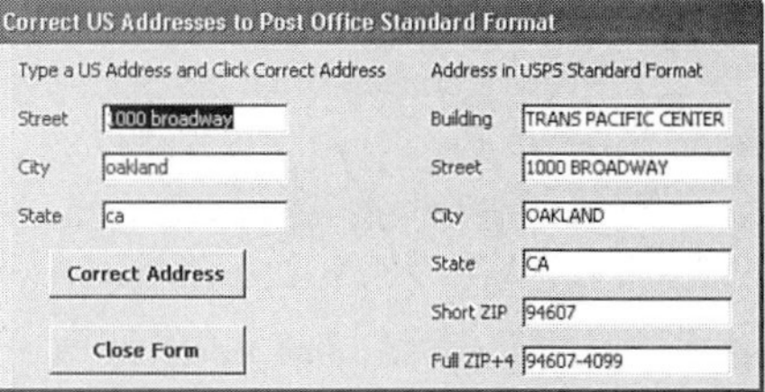

Figure 31.8 This simple form sends a U.S. address as arguments of the ZipCodeResolver's CorrectedAddressXML method and displays the address in USPS standard format.

FOLLOWING PROXY CODE EXECUTION

You can gain insight into the service consumption process by stepping through the code in the class modules. If you didn't add the classes to AddressCorrector.mdb, the completed version is CorrectAddress.mdb in your \Program Files\Seua11\Chaptr31\ZipCodeResolver\ folder.

Do the following to trace execution of the `CorrectedAddressXml` Web method:

1. Open frmAddressCorrector's class module, navigate to the `Set prxResolver = New clsws_ZipCodeResolver` line, and press F9 to add a breakpoint.

2. Return to Form view and click Correct Address to open the Visual Basic Editor. Press F8 to move to the `clsws_ZipCodeResolver`'s `Class_Initialize` event handler (called a *constructor*).
3. Step through the code that generates the WSML document. The `Set sc_ZipCodeResolver = New SoapClient30` statement creates the required `SoapClient30` instance. This object handles serialization and transmission of the SOAP request message, interception of the response message, and, with help from other classes, deserialization of the response message to an instance of the USPS class.

4. Step to the next line. The `sc_ZipCodeResolver.MSSoapInit2` method specifies the URL for the WSDL document (the service's endpoint URL, plus the `?wsdl` suffix), the local WSML document content, service name, SOAP port name (`ZipCodeResolverSoap`), and the service namespace (`http://webservices.eraserver.net`).

> **NOTE**
>
> The alternative `MSSoapInit` method only requires the URL for the WSDL document; the remaining four arguments are optional.

> **TIP**
>
> Retrieving the WSDL document from the service provider requires an extra round trip. If it's unlikely that the WSDL document will undergo frequent changes, you can save a local copy as a *ServiceName*.wsdl file. In this case, replace the value of the `c_WSDL_URL` constant with `d:/Path/ServiceName.wsdl`.

5. Step through the next two lines, which enable the client to communicate through a proxy server, if required. The third active statement creates an instance of the `cls_of_Factory_ZipCodeResolv` class for the `struct_USPS` class.
6. Step to return to the form class. The `Set ObjUSPSAddress = New struct_USPSAddress` creates an instance of the USPSClass to receive the deserialized response message values.
7. Step through the Set `objUSPSAddress = prxResolver.wsm_CorrectedAddressXml(...)` call to execute the `wsm_CorrectedAddressXml` function, which finally invokes the Web method.
8. Continue stepping until you reach the `IGCTMObjectFactory_CreateObject(...)` which extracts the `targetClassName` value (`struct_USPSAddress`) from the WSML document, and then creates and returns a new instance of the `struct_USPSAddress` object with its members populated by the response data.
9. Continue stepping until you return to the form class module, which populates the text boxes with the `struct_USPSAddress` instance's member values.

Finally, the **clsws_ZipCodeResolver**'s `Class_Terminate` event handler (called a *destructor*) sets the `sc_ZipCodeResolver` instance to **`Nothing`**, which releases its resources.

> **NOTE**
>
> The execution process for Web services that return simple types—such as strings, integers, or both—is much simpler than the preceding example.

SOLVING WSR CLASS GENERATION PROBLEMS

WSR tries to create classes for any valid WSDL documents. If WSR determines the WSDL document isn't valid or WSR can't process it, the Search Result text box displays a "Your search returned no results" message. In rare cases, you receive an error message when you click WSR's Add button. Some WSDL documents generate classes that won't compile. As an example, the WSDL documents that Microsoft SQLXML 3.0 generates for Web services created from SQL Server 2000 stored procedures produce VBA classes that generate compilation errors. This is an important issue, because SQLXML 3.0 makes providing data-driven Web services a quick and easy process. A typical application for SQL Server 2000 Web services is delivering up-to-date product catalogs or similar reference data via the Internet to Access order processing applications designed for sales agents or customers.

NOTE

> Future versions of SQLXML, WSR, or both might correct the problem you solve in the following sections. The techniques you learn, however, let you—rather than WSR—manage the processing of any SOAP response message by writing relatively simple VBA procedures.

If the capability to consume problematic Web services is important to your Access application, you must modify the code of WSR-generated classes. Following are the typical steps to handle defective WSR classes for complex types:

1. Comment the statement(s) that prevent compilation. In most cases, removing the statements causes execution of one or more Web methods to fail.
2. Add code to the form's class module to create a Web service proxy and invoke one of the methods you plan to use.
3. Execute the Web method. If you encounter runtime errors or the service doesn't return the data you expected, the problem is likely to be deserializing the soap response message to one or more of the custom types specified in the WSML file.

NOTE

> If WSR doesn't interpret the WSDL document correctly or can't generate a VBA-compliant type, the offending `struct_`*`ClassName`* class module often contains members of the `MSXML2.IXMLDOMNodeList` type. `IXMLDOMNodeList` is the default type returned by the `SoapClient30` object.

4. Delete or comment all `str_WSDL = ...` lines to return an empty string, and delete all WSR classes except `clsws_`*`ServiceName`*.
5. Determine the type returned by `clsws_`*`ServiceName`*'s **`Public Function`** `wsm_`*`FunctionName`*`(`*`Parameters...`*`)` **`As`** *`Type`*. If *`Type`* isn't `[MSXML2.]IXMLDOMNodeList`, change it to this value. (Adding the `MSXML2` type library name is optional).
6. Compile the code and remove statements that generate compile errors.

Completing the preceding steps disables WSR's complex type handling features and requires writing VBA code to process the response message that's contained in the

IXMLDOMNodeList instance. You can handle any complex SOAP response message, regardless of its structure, with the IXMLDOMNodeList class.

UNDERSTANDING THE XML DOCUMENT OBJECT MODEL

Working with the IXMLDOMNodeList object requires some familiarity with the XML Document Object Model (XML DOM). The XML DOM represents any well-formed XML document as a set of elements (*nodes*) that contain information (text), other nodes (called *child nodes*), or both. You extract the document's text values to populate controls or tables with an XML *parser*. The MSXML2 library (Microsoft XML v5.0, Msxml5.dll), which Office 2003 installs in your \Program Files\Common Files\Microsoft Shared\Office11 folder, was Microsoft's latest COM-based XML parser when this book was written.

NOTE

> MSXML2 is best suited for processing relatively small XML documents, because it loads at least one copy of the entire document into memory. Other XML parsers, such as the Simple API for XML (SAX), don't require loading the document into memory but have a more complex, event-driven programming model.

As its name implies, the IXMLDOMNodeList class provides access (a pointer) to XML DOM nodes in a document from a list. Each node is a member of the IXMLDOMNode class. You iterate the list in a set of nested **For...Next** loops that return IXMLDOMNode members at each level of the document's hierarchy. The IXMLDOMNode.text property at the lowest level of the hierarchy returns individual data values.

Following is an abbreviated example of a SOAP response message returned by a demonstration Web service (Alpha) that's generated from one of four SQL Server stored procedures exposed as Web methods:

```
<?xml version="1.0" encoding="utf-8"?>
<SOAP-ENV:Envelope xmlns:xsd="http://www.w3.org/2001/XMLSchema"
  xmlns:xsi="http://www.w3.org/2001/XMLSchema-instance"
  xmlns:SOAP-ENV="http://schemas.xmlsoap.org/soap/envelope/"
  xmlns:sqltypes=".../SQLServer/2001/12/SOAP/types"
  xmlns:sqlmessage=".../SQLServer/2001/12/SOAP/types/SqlMessage"
  xmlns:sqlresultstream=".../SQLServer/2001/12/SOAP/types/SqlResultStream"
  xmlns:tns="http://www.oakleaf.ws/SQLXML/Alpha">
  <SOAP-ENV:Body>
    <tns:GetTop10Response>
      <tns:GetTop10Result xsi:type="sqlresultstream:SqlResultStream">
        <sqlresultstream:SqlXml xsi:type="sqltypes:SqlXml"
            sqltypes:IsNested="false">
          <SqlXml>
            <row>
              <SKU>DVDP0345</SKU>
              <Category>DVD Players</Category>
              <Brand>Onkyo</Brand>
              <Model>DV-S939</Model>
              <Description>
                DVD-Audio/Video/CD Player with Progressive
              </Description>
```

```
            <NetPrice>1275</NetPrice>
            <Quantity>516</Quantity>
          </row>
          <!-- Eight rows not shown -->
          <row>
            <SKU>DVDP0009</SKU>
            <Category>DVD Players</Category>
            <Brand>Aiwa</Brand>
            <Model>XD-DW5</Model>
            <Description>
              Portable DVD player with 5.8-inch Color Screen
            </Description>
            <NetPrice>375</NetPrice>
            <Quantity>514</Quantity>
          </row>
        </SqlXml>
      </sqlresultstream:SqlXml>
      <sqlresultstream:SqlResultCode
           xsi:type="sqltypes:SqlResultCode"
           sqltypes:IsNested="false">
         0
       </sqlresultstream:SqlResultCode>
    </tns:GetTop10Result>
  </tns:GetTop10Response>
 </SOAP-ENV:Body>
</SOAP-ENV:Envelope>
```

31

The Alpha Web service delivers a catalog from Alpha Electronics, Inc., a fictitious consumer electronics distributor. The `GetTop10Result` Web method returns a list of Alpha's 10 most expensive consumer electronics products in one or more of six categories as an `sqlresultstream` message, which contains first-level `SqlXml` and `SqlResultCode` child nodes. The `SqlXml` node contains a collection (array) of second-level child `row` nodes, which contain the third-level data elements. The `SqlResultCode` node has a value of `0` if the request is successful or an error number if it isn't. In the event of an SQL Server error, the response message includes a serialized `sqlmessage` object, which contains a detailed description of the problem.

Navigating the `IXMLDOMNodeList`

Before you can write the VBA code necessary to populate a list box or table with data, it's a good practice to perform a test iteration of the `IXMLDOMNodeList` object to determine the level in the hierarchy at which you obtain a useful representation of the data. "Walking the nodes" also lets you explore the structure of XML data in a SOAP response message when you can't infer the structure from the WSDL document's schema.

NOTE

The size of the WSDL document for the SQLXML's Alpha service exceeds reasonable publishing limitations. The complete document for the GetTop25 method–GetTop25.wsdl.xml– is in your \Project Files\Seua11\Chaptr31\Alpha folder.

You can view the WSDL document in IE at `http://www.oakleaf.ws/sqlxml/alpha?wsdl`. Web services generated by SQL Server stored procedures don't use an .asmx file, so you specify the service name and omit the .asmx suffix in the URL.

Listing 31.1 is the VBA code for a general-purpose subprocedure that prints to the Immediate window the level, `nodeName`, and `text` properties of an `IXMLDomNodeList` object you pass as a parameter. You can use this code as a model for the procedures you write to populate controls or tables from the SOAP response message, as illustrated in the next section. You can add additional **For...Next** loops if the message contains more than three levels of child nodes.

31

Listing 31.1 This VBA subprocedure lets you use the Immediate window to explore SOAP response message structure and data.

```
Public Sub PrintNodeList(nodList As MSXML2.IXMLDOMNodeList)
  'Generates an indented list of node names and
  'values in the Immediate window
  'This procedure is limited to three levels of child nodes
  Dim intNodes As Integer
  Dim intMaxNodes As Integer
  Dim intMaxLength As Integer
  Dim intChild1 As Integer
  Dim intChild2 As Integer
  Dim intChild3 As Integer
  Dim domNode As MSXML2.IXMLDOMNode
  Dim domChild1 As MSXML2.IXMLDOMNode
  Dim domChild2 As MSXML2.IXMLDOMNode
  Dim domChild3 As MSXML2.IXMLDOMNode

  'Set the maximum number of child nodes printed at each level
  intMaxNodes = 6
  'Set the maximum length of node text strings
  intMaxLength = 100

  With nodList
    'The parent node
    If .length > 0 Then
      For intNodes = 0 To .length - 1
        'List nodes (level 0)
        Set domNode = .Item(intNodes)
        With domNode
          Debug.Print "Level 0: nodeName(" & intNodes & ") = " _
             & .nodeName
          Debug.Print "Level 0: text(" & intNodes & ") = " _
             & Left$(.Text, intMaxLength)
          If .hasChildNodes Then
            'First-level child nodes
            For intChild1 = 0 To .childNodes.length - 1
              If intChild1 > intMaxNodes Then
                Exit For
              End If
              Set domChild1 = .childNodes(intChild1)
              With domChild1
                Debug.Print "  Level 1: nodeName(" & intChild1 & ") = " _
                   & .nodeName
                Debug.Print "  Level 1: text(" & intChild1 & ") = " _
                   & Left$(.Text, intMaxLength)
                If .hasChildNodes Then
                  'Second-level child nodes
```

```
                    For intChild2 = 0 To .childNodes.length - 1
                      If intChild2 > intMaxNodes Then
                        Exit For
                      End If
                      Set domChild2 = .childNodes(intChild2)
                      With domChild2
                        Debug.Print "   Level 2: nodeName(" & intChild2 & ") = " _
                           & .nodeName
                        Debug.Print "   Level 2: text(" & intChild2 & ") = " _
                           & Left$(.Text, intMaxLength)
                        If .hasChildNodes Then
                          'Third-level child nodes
                          For intChild3 = 0 To .childNodes.length - 1
                            If intChild3 > intMaxNodes Then
                              Exit For
                            End If
                            Set domChild3 = .childNodes(intChild3)
                            With domChild3
                             Debug.Print "Level 3: nodeName(" & intChild3 & ") = " _
                                 & .nodeName
                              Debug.Print "Level 3: text(" & intChild3 & ") = " _
                                 & Left$(.Text, intMaxLength)
                            End With
                          Next intChild3
                        End If
                      End With
                    Next intChild2
                  End If
                End With
              Next intChild1
            End If
          End With
        Next intNodes
      Else
        'There's nothing in the node list
      End If
    End With
  End Sub
```

The `hasChildNodes` property returns **True** if the current node contains child nodes, and the `length` property returns the number of child nodes. The `length` property is the counterpart of the `Count` property for collections. The `nodeName` property value returns the type (class) or element name, and the `text` property returns the element value. At the lowest level of the hierarchy, `nodeNames` are data element tag names and `text` returns the data values.

Following is the abbreviated result of passing the `IXMLDOMNodeList` object generated by the `SQLXML.GetTop10` method to the `PrintNodeList` procedure:

```
Level 0: nodeName(0) = xsi:type
Level 0: text(0) = sqlresultstream:SqlResultStream
  Level 1: nodeName(0) = #text
  Level 1: text(0) = sqlresultstream:SqlResultStream
Level 0: nodeName(1) = sqlresultstream:SqlXml
Level 0: text(1) = AMPL0692AmplifiersSonyTA-N9000ES...
```

```
  Level 1: nodeName(0) = SqlXml
  Level 1: text(0) = AMPL0692AmplifiersSonyTA-N9000...
    Level 2: nodeName(0) = row
    Level 2: text(0) = AMPL0692AmplifiersSonyTA-N9000ES...
      Level 3: nodeName(0) = SKU
      Level 3: text(0) = AMPL0692
      Level 3: nodeName(1) = Category
      Level 3: text(1) = Amplifiers
      Level 3: nodeName(2) = Brand
      Level 3: text(2) = Sony
      Level 3: nodeName(3) = Model
      Level 3: text(3) = TA-N9000ES
      Level 3: nodeName(4) = Description
      Level 3: text(4) = Five-channel Amplifier (ES)
      Level 3: nodeName(5) = NetPrice
      Level 3: text(5) = 1000
      Level 3: nodeName(6) = Quantity
      Level 3: text(6) = 503
    Level 2: nodeName(1) = row
    Level 2: text(1) = AMPL0697AmplifiersNilesSI-1230...
      Level 3: nodeName(0) = SKU
      Level 3: text(0) = AMPL0697
      Level 3: nodeName(1) = Category
      Level 3: text(1) = Amplifiers
      Level 3: nodeName(2) = Brand
      Level 3: text(2) = Niles
      Level 3: nodeName(3) = Model
      Level 3: text(3) = SI-1230 FG00737
      Level 3: nodeName(4) = Description
      Level 3: text(4) = Multi-room 12 x 30-Watt Amplifier
      Level 3: nodeName(5) = NetPrice
      Level 3: text(5) = 750
      Level 3: nodeName(6) = Quantity
      Level 3: text(6) = 511
   'Remaining row nodes omitted for brevity
Level 0: nodeName(2) = sqlresultstream:SqlResultCode
Level 0: text(2) = 0
  Level 1: nodeName(0) = #text
  Level 1: text(0) = 0
```

The preceding sample output demonstrates that the data you need to populate a list box or table is contained in the third-level child nodes.

POPULATING A LIST BOX WITH XML DATA

The AlphaTest.mdb sample application in your \Program Files\Seua11\Chaptr31\Alpha folder executes the Alpha service's four Web methods to populate a list box with 10, 25, 50, or 100 items (see Figure 31.9). The products in the list are real, but the prices are fictitious. AlphaTest.mdb has five WSR-generated classes, but uses the `clsws_Alpha` class only. The AlphaCopy.mdb example doesn't include unneeded class modules.

Figure 31.9
The frmAlphaTest form of the AlphaTest.mdb application consumes the four methods of the online Alpha Web service and displays the data in an Access list box.

> **TIP**
>
> If you can't connect to the public Alpha Web service at `http://www.oakleaf.ws/sqlxml/alpha[?wsdl]`, the "Creating and Consuming a Local Alpha Web Service" section, near the end of the chapter, shows you how to provide the service from your computer.

The following event handler generates the SOAP request message for the `GetTop10` Web method:

```
Private Sub cmdGetTop10_Click()
    'Event handler for Alpha SQLXML 3.0 stored procedure XML Web services
    Me.Caption = "Alpha Electronics, Inc. - Top 10 Amplifiers by Net Price"
    Dim wsAlpha As New clsws_Alpha
    Set objResponse = wsAlpha.wsm_GetTop10("AMPL", "XXXX", _
       "XXXX", "XXXX", "XXXX", "XXXX")
    Call PrintNodeList(objResponse)
    Call IterateNodes
End Sub
```

The other three event handlers replace `XXXX` with valid category codes, such as `DVDP` (DVD players), `TVRC` (TV receivers), and `CDPL` (CD players). The event-handler invokes the `PrintNodeList` procedure, which is contained in the modNodeList module.

Listing 31.2 demonstrates a simple approach to iterating the `<row>` nodes and adding data items to a list box. In this case, you add a list box item with a semicolon-separated string that contains multiple child element data (`text`) values. This approach for filling multicolumn list boxes requires you to replace commas and semicolons in the returned values with another character, such as a hyphen.

LISTING 31.2 THE ITERATENODES SUBPROCEDURE TESTS THE VALIDITY OF THE SOAP RESPONSE MESSAGE AND ADDS AN ITEM TO THE LIST BOX FOR EACH `<row>` ELEMENT.

```
Private Sub IterateNodes()
   'Iterate nodes and display results in a list box
   Dim nodXml As MSXML2.IXMLDOMNode
```

continues

LISTING 31.2 CONTINUED

```
Dim nodRow As MSXML2.IXMLDOMNode
Dim intRows As Integer
Dim intRow As Integer
Dim intCol As Integer
Dim strItem As String
Dim strTemp As String

intRows = lstData.ListCount - 1
On Error Resume Next
For intRow = 0 To intRows
   'Clear the list box
   lstData.RemoveItem (0)
Next intRow
On Error GoTo 0
With objResponse
   If .length = 3 Then
     'Test sqlResultStream:SqlResultCode
     If .Item(2).Text = "0" Then
        'sqlResultStream:SqlXml is second item
        Set nodXml = objResponse.Item(1).childNodes(0)
     Else
        MsgBox "SQL Server returned an error.", _
          vbOKOnly + vbExclamation, "Request Failed"
        Exit Sub
     End If
   Else
     MsgBox "Incorrect node list length ( " & _
       .length & "); should be 3.", _
       vbOKOnly + vbExclamation, "Request Failed"
     Exit Sub
   End If
End With
With nodXml
   'Iterate by row
   For intRow = 0 To nodXml.childNodes.length - 1
     Set nodRow = nodXml.childNodes.Item(intRow)
     strItem = ""
     With nodRow
        'Iterate by column to generate the list entry
        'with semicolon-separated values
        For intCol = 0 To nodRow.childNodes.length - 1
           'Replace , and ; with -
           strTemp = Replace(nodRow.childNodes.Item(intCol).Text, ",", "-")
           strTemp = Replace(strTemp, ";", "-")
           If intCol = 5 Then
             'Add currency format
             strTemp = Format$(CSng(strTemp), "$0.00")
           End If
           strItem = strItem + strTemp + ";"
        Next intCol
     End With
     strItem = Left$(strItem, Len(strItem) - 1)
     'Add the row to the Access list box
     lstData.AddItem strItem
```

```
        Next intRow
    End With
End Sub
```

The `Set nodXml = objResponse.Item(1).childNodes(0)` statement retrieves the `SqlXml` node. `SqlXml`'s child nodes are `<row>` elements assigned to the `nodRow` variable, which represents a list box item, in the first **`For...Next`** loop. The second **`For...Next`** loop generates the semicolon-separated item string.

FILLING A TABLE WITH A COMPLEX SOAP RESPONSE MESSAGE

Populating local Jet or SQL Server tables with data from Internet-accessible Web services lets you update remote Access applications with new reference information. As an example, you can provide customers, sales agents, distributors, and others in the supply chain with up-to-date information on new or discontinued products, price changes, inventory levels, and related product information. The process is similar to one-way Access briefcase replication or SQL Server merge replication. Many firewalls block binary replication traffic; using a Web service makes the updates available to anyone with an Internet connection. Usernames and passwords in the SOAP request message can authenticate service consumers. HTTPS provides security by encrypting the SOAP request and response messages between endpoints.

31

SQLXML3Alpha.mdb is a sample Web service consumer that's similar to AlphaTest.mdb (see Figure 31.10). The application's unbound form and bound subform design are based on a demonstration ASP.NET Web service consumer page at `http://www.oakleaf.ws/SQLXML3/` (see Figure 31.11). Both consumers have option buttons to select one of the four `GetTop###` stored procedures and check boxes to determine the product categories included in the list. The primary difference between the two projects is the ASP.NET page's substitution of a Visual Studio .NET DataGrid, which the SOAP response message's XML payload populates directly, for the Access version's table and bound subform.

Alpha Distributors, Inc. Consumer Electronic Products Ranked by Net Selling Price

Top How Many?
- Top 10
- Top 50
- Top 25 (selected)
- Top100

Get Data
Close Form

IncludeThese Categories in the List
- [x] Amplifiers (AMPL)
- [ ] Receivers - Home (RCVH)
- [ ] DV Camcorders (CAMC)
- [ ] Speakers - Floor (SPKF)
- [x] DVD Players (DVDP)
- [ ] TV Sets - All (TVRC)

SKU	Category	Brand	Model	Description	Net Price	Quan.
DVDP0345	DVD Players	Onkyo	DV-S939	DVD-Audio/Video/CD Player with P	$1,275.00	516
DVDP0583	DVD Players	Sony	DVP-FX1	Portable DVD/CD Player with Scree	$1,125.00	508
DVDP0602	DVD Players	Sony	DVP-S9000ES	Progressive Scan DVD/CD/SACD F	$1,125.00	505
AMPL0692	Amplifiers	Sony	TA-N9000ES	Five-channel Amplifier (ES)	$1,000.00	503
AMPL0697	Amplifiers	Niles	SI-1230 FG0073;	Multi-room 12 x 30-Watt Amplifier	$750.00	511
DVDP0418	DVD Players	Pioneer	DVL-919	DVD/CD/Laserdisc Player	$750.00	511
DVDP0371	DVD Players	Panasonic	DVD-LV70	Portable DVD/CD Player with Scree	$675.00	524
AMPL0695	Amplifiers	NHT	SA-3	250-Watt Mono Subwoofer Amplifier	$562.50	439
DVDP0370	DVD Players	Panasonic	DVD-LV60	Portable DVD Player with 5.8-inch S	$525.00	511
DVDP0417	DVD Players	Pioneer	DV-F727	300+1 disc DVD/CD Changer	$450.00	508
DVDP0102	DVD Players	Harman Karc	DVD 50	5 Disc Progressive Scan DVD Playe	$450.00	502
DVDP0581	DVD Players	Sony	DVP-CX860	DVD/CD Player	$450.00	513
DVDP0009	DVD Players	Aiwa	XD-DW5	Portable DVD player with 5.8-inch C	$375.00	514

Figure 31.10 The SQLXML3Alpha.mdb application's frmTopNProducts form has controls to select the number of records and categories. The bound sbfTopN subform displays the records added to its record source, tblTopNProducts.

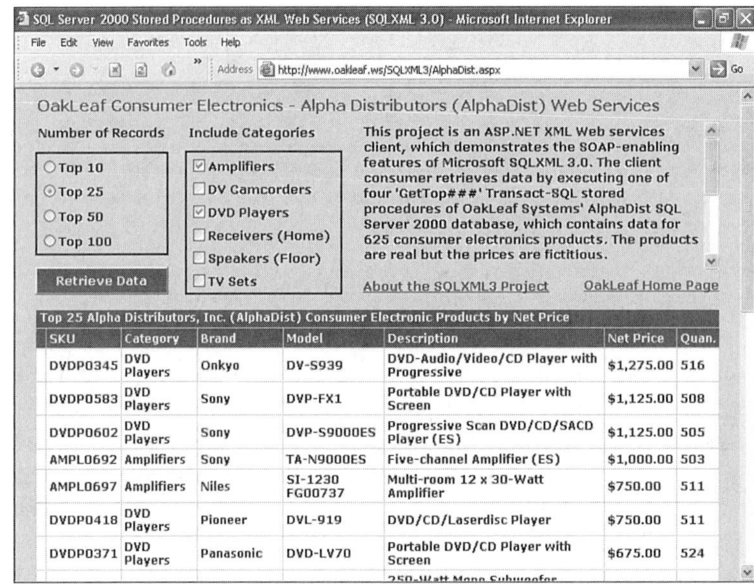

Figure 31.11 The original version of frmTopNProducts is this ASP.NET Web form that displays the product information in a DataGrid control, which expands vertically to display all returned rows.

Code to populate a table from an IXMLDomNodeList object is similar to that of the preceding section's `IterateNodes` subprocedure. Listing 31.3 is the VBA code to add records to the tblTopNProducts table. Code for adding rows to or updating the table is simpler than that for adding items to a list box.

LISTING 31.3 THE `PopulateTable` SUBPROCEDURE IS A SIMPLIFIED VERSION OF ALPHATEST.MDB'S `IterateNodes` CODE.

```
Private Sub PopulateSubform(objResponse As _
    MSXML2.IXMLDOMNodeList)
  'Iterate nodes and display results in a subform
  Dim nodXml As MSXML2.IXMLDOMNode
  Dim nodRow As MSXML2.IXMLDOMNode
  Dim intRows As Integer
  Dim intRow As Integer
  Dim intCol As Integer
  Dim strData As String

  With objResponse
    If .length = 3 Then
      'Test sqlResultStream:SqlResultCode
      If .Item(2).Text = "0" Then
         'sqlResultStream:SqlXml is second item
         Set nodXml = objResponse.Item(1).childNodes(0)
      Else
        DoCmd.Hourglass False
        MsgBox "SQL Server returned an error.",
          vbOKOnly + vbExclamation, "Request Failed"
        Exit Sub
      End If
```

```
    Else
      DoCmd.Hourglass False
      MsgBox "Incorrect node list length ( " & .length & _
          "); should be 3.", _
        vbOKOnly + vbExclamation, "Request Failed"
      Exit Sub
    End If
  End With
  Me.sbfTopN.Form.AllowAdditions = True
  With Me.sbfTopN.Form.Recordset
    'Iterate by row
    For intRow = 0 To nodXml.childNodes.length - 1
      'New row
      .AddNew
      Set nodRow = nodXml.childNodes.Item(intRow)
      'Add data to table by column
      For intCol = 0 To nodRow.childNodes.length - 1
        strData = nodRow.childNodes.Item(intCol).Text
        .Fields(intCol).Value = strData
      Next intCol
      .Update
    Next intRow
  End With
  Me.sbfTopN.Form.AllowAdditions = False
End Sub
```


The table defines the data type for each column, so you don't need to use the **CCur** or **CInt** functions to change the **String** datatype to **Currency** or Integer for the **NetPrice** and **Inventory** fields. VBA handles the **Variant** type change, which developers call *Evil Type Coercion (ETC)*, automatically.

EXPLORING XML WEB SERVICES WITH .NET WEBSERVICE STUDIO

Microsoft's .NET WebService Studio (WSS) is an extraordinarily useful application for testing your own and others' Web services. The primary reason that this section is located midway through the chapter is the time and effort to prepare for its use if you haven't installed the prerequisites to run .NET applications. Another reason is WSS's capability to display the IXMLDOMNode property values that are described in the four preceding sections. Basic knowledge of the IXMLDOMNodeList and IXMLDOMNodes objects makes WSS's SOAP response data display meaningful.

WSS consists of a single tabbed .NET Windows form that lets you send SOAP request messages to a service, inspect the full text of the request and response messages, view the service's WSDL document, and read the C# proxy code. Like WSR, WSS generates the client proxy for the service. WSS, however, provides text boxes to supply the service's parameter values.

TIP

> WSS is an essential tool for testing SQLXML Web services that you develop in the following sections. If you intend to make your SQL Server data accessible to Web services consumers, your investment to install WSS will be well rewarded.

INSTALLING .NET WEBSERVICE STUDIO AND ITS PREREQUISITES

Following are the steps required to install and run WSS:

1. Install the latest service pack (SP) and security upgrades for your operating system and IIS 5.1+ from the Windows Update site at `http://v4.windowsupdate.microsoft.com/en/default.asp`. You might not be able to install or use the .NET Framework if you haven't installed the latest SP or current security patches are missing.
2. If you don't have the .NET Framework 1.0 or 1.1 installed on your machine, download and install the .NET Framework 1.1 Redistributable or SDK version from `http://msdn.microsoft.com/netframework/`.

NOTE

> The Redistributable version is about a 20MB download; the SDK version, which includes documentation, sample applications, and command-line tools, is 270MB.
>
> If you encounter a run-time error when you start WSS under .NET Framework 1.1, install the .NET Framework 1.0 redistributable version from the same page. The two versions run side by side.

3. Create a \Program Files\WebService Studio folder in which to install the application (WebServiceStudio.exe).
4. Download and install .NET WebService Studio from `http://www.gotdotnet.com/team/tools/web_svc/default.aspx`. Be sure to download the original .NET Web Service Studio version, *not* version 2.0. Version 2.0 includes additional features that are beyond the scope of this book.
5. If you want to learn more than this section offers about WSS, open and save the Readme file (`http://www.gotdotnet.com/team/tools/Web_svc/readme.rtf`) in your installation folder.

TIP

> Microsoft's GotDotNet site offers several additional tools for Web service development, plus XML utilities. One of the most interesting XML utilities is an online XSD schema inference engine at `http://apps.gotdotnet.com/xmltools/xsdinference/`. Supply the path to an XML file and Microsoft XSD Inference 1.0 generates its XSD schema. You can read more about XSD Inference 1.0 at `http://www.fawcette.com/xmlmag/2002_11/online/xml_rjennings_11_11_02/`.

RUNNING WSS WITH A PUBLIC WEB SERVICE

Here's how to give WSS a test drive, using the Alpha service as an example:

1. Run WebServiceStudio.exe from your installation folder.
2. Type the URL for a public Web service's WSDL file in the WSDL EndPoint text box. Alternatively, you can browse for a local copy of a WSDL file. For this example, type **`http://www.oakleaf.ws/SQLXML/alpha?wsdl`**.
3. Click the Get button to connect to the WSDL document. WSS generates and compiles the C# client proxy code for the service. WSS displays the parameter datatypes and names in the Input list, if the service has parameters.
4. Select one of the service's Web methods in the Invoke list (look ahead to Figure 31.12).
5. Select a parameter and type an appropriate entry in the Value text box of the Value list—**AMPL** for the Alpha service.
6. Repeat step 5 for each required parameter. Additional parameters for Alpha's `GetTop###` methods are optional, so add **DVDP** only.
7. Click the Invoke button to consume the service and populate the lower Output and Value lists with data from the SOAP response message. Items in the Output tree view correspond to `IXMLDOMNode` elements from the `IXMLDOMNodeList` object returned by the proxy.
8. Scroll the Output list to display the data elements at the lowest level of the hierarchy. Select a `TextValue` element to display its contents in the Value list (see Figure 31.12).

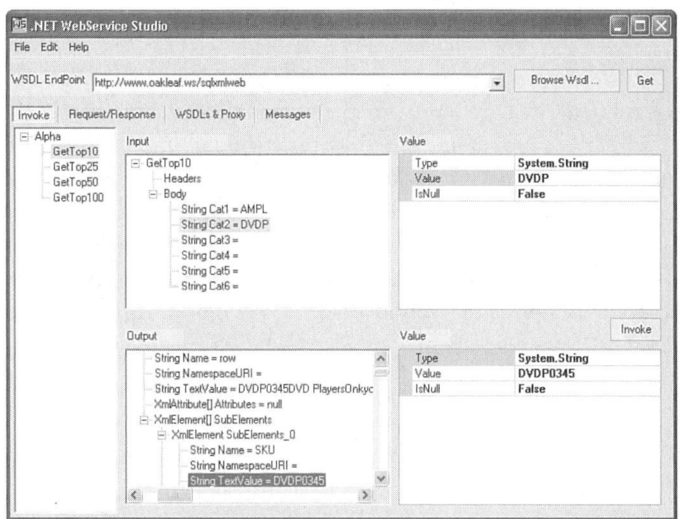

Figure 31.12
WSS uses the IXMLDOMNodeList to generate a tree view of the contents of each IXMLDOMNode of the SOAP response message in the Output list.

Clicking the Request/Response tab displays the full text of the SOAP request and response messages in two text boxes (see Figure 31.13). If the Web service requires Basic (clear-text) authentication, provide the credentials in the BasicAuthPassword and BasicAuthUserName text boxes. For services on an intranet that require Windows (NTLM) authentication, you can pass your logon credentials to the service by changing UseDefaultCredential's value to True. To use NTLM authentication, you also must set the AutoRedirect and KeepAlive HTTP properties to True.

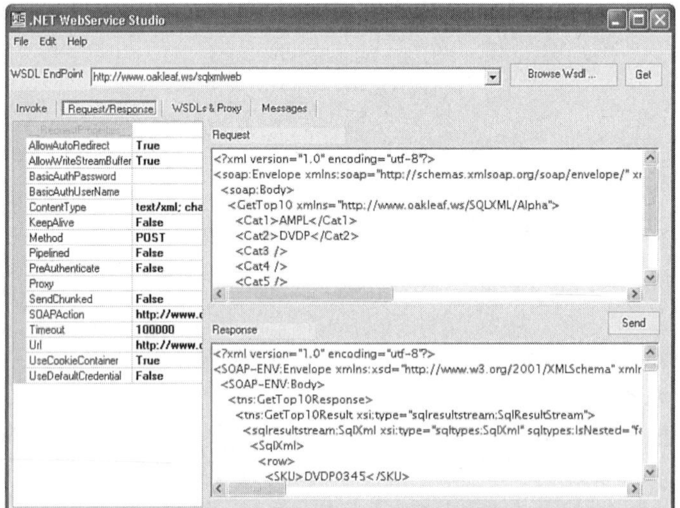

Figure 31.13 Code behind WSS's form intercepts the serialized SOAP request and response messages and displays the XML contents in two text boxes.

The WSDLs & Proxy page has a tree view list that lets you display the contents of the WSDL document, XSD schemas for the response document, if present, and the C# code for the Web service proxy, and WSS's client code that invokes the proxy. Selecting the Proxy and scrolling to the proxy for the first Web method lets you compare the C# code for invoking the method with the WSR `clsws_`*`ServiceName`*'s `wsm_`*`FunctionName`*`(`*`Parameters...`*`)` **`As`** `MSXML2.IXMLDOMNodeList` VBA function (see Figure 31.14). WSS returns the `SqlRowSet` object as a .NET `System.Data.DataSet` type, which simplifies populating a DataGrid control in a .NET Windows or Web form (refer to Figure 31.11). The `System.Xml.XmlNode` type for `SqlXml` rows corresponds to `MSXML2`'s `IXMLDOMNode` type.

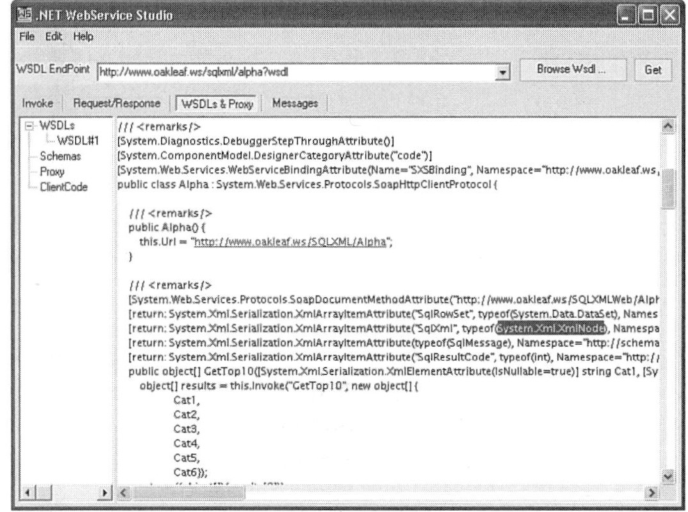

Figure 31.14
The C# code for the Alpha Web service proxy is much more complex than that generated by WSR. The WSS proxy works, however, while the original WSR proxy fails.

PROVIDING SQLXML WEB SERVICES

Visual Basic 6.0 programmers can use the Microsoft SOAP Toolkit 3.0+ to generate SOAP wrappers and WSDL files for ActiveX components. Visual Studio .NET 1.0+ automates the process for creating ASP.NET XML Web services. Access 2003 developers have only one option for delivering data with Web services—SQL Server 2000 stored procedures delivered from virtual directories you create with Microsoft's SQLXML 3.0+ Web release.

The first two versions of SQLXML extended SQL Server/MSDE 2000's built-in XML feature set with additional XML capabilities, such as updategrams and support for XSD schemas in addition to Microsoft's original (and proprietary) XML Data Reduced (XDR) annotated schemas. SQLXML 3.0 adds the Web service feature, which automates the process of exposing stored procedures as document/literal Web services. The following sections describe how to install SQLXML, and create and test a simple Web service from NorthwindSQL's Sales by Year stored procedure.

NOTE

SQLXML 3.0 SP 1 was current when this book was written. It's likely that Microsoft will continue to issue service packs and add features to SQLXML 3.0, at least until releasing the next version of SQL Server, codenamed "Yukon." Successive versions of SQLXML have proven to be backwardly compatible, so the following examples should apply to later SQLXML releases.

If you're running Windows Server 2003, SQLXML 3.0 requires running IIS 6.0+ in IIS 5 Emulation mode. Some applications, such as Windows SharePoint Services, won't run in IIS 5 Emulation mode. Microsoft probably will remove this SQLXML 3.0 limitation in future SQLXML Web releases.

Downloading and Installing SQLXML

SQLXML requires installation of the SQL Server Client Tools, which are included with the 120-day evaluation version of SQL Server 2000. You can obtain a CD-ROM containing the SQL Server 2000 Trial Software Release A at `http://www.microsoft.com/sql/evaluation/trial/`. Alternatively, you can purchase the SQL Server 2000 Developer Edition for $49. Neither version's Client Tools are licensed for production applications, but you don't need to use the Tools with SQLXML 3.0+—they need only be present during SQLXML 3.0 installation or removal.

→ For more information on the SQL Server Client Tools, **see** "Exporting Live Web Reports," **p. 967**.

NOTE

> SQL Server Trial Version Release A includes SQL Server SP3, which immunizes the product from effects of the "Slammer" worm.

CAUTION

> Don't install SQL Server 2000 from Developer or evaluation editions. Although you can add either edition as a named SQL Server instance, you take the chance of overwriting or disabling your current MSDE 2000 installation. During installation, select the Client Tools Only option.

If you're running Windows 2000, you must download and install the current version of the Microsoft SOAP Toolkit—3.0 when this book was written—from MSDN to make SQLXML 3.0+'s Web service features operational. To find the latest version, go to `http://msdn.microsoft.com/downloads/` and search for **"SOAP Toolkit"** in Downloads Only.

After you've installed the SQL Server 2000 Client Tools (and installed the SOAP Toolkit, if necessary), download and run the current version of SQLXML (Sqlxml.msi) from the link at `http://www.microsoft.com/sql/`. Installation adds a SQLXML 3.0 or later choice to your Programs menu with Configure IIS Support, SQLXML (3.0) Documentation, and SQLXML (3.0) Readme items.

NOTE

> The IIS Virtual Directory Management for SQLXML 3.0 snap-in installs side-by-side with the Client Tools' IIS Virtual Directory Management. You must use SQLXML version 3.0 or later to take advantage of SQLXML's Web service features.

Creating a Simple Web Service

NorthwindSQL's Sales by Year stored procedure is a good candidate for an initial trial of SQLXML's capabilities, because it requires `Beginning_Date` and `Ending_Date` parameter values. The XSD schema for document/literal SOAP messages requires SQL Server `datetime` datatypes to conform to the XML Schema Part 2: Datatypes specification's `dateTime` datatype, which is based on the ISO 8601 standard.

NOTE

> The ISO8601 format is *CCYY-MM-DDThh:mm:ss[.##...]*. *CC* represents the century, *YY* the year, *MM* the two-digit month and *DD* the two-digit day. *hh*, *mm*, and *ss* represent two-digit hours (24-hour clock), minutes, and seconds, which can have additional fractional digits (`.##...`).
>
> An additional option is a trailing Universal Coordinated Time (UTC, Greenwich Mean Time, or Zulu) code (`Z`) or offset, expressed as {+|-}hh:mm. Thus the UTC `dateTime` value for 1:20:00 PM on June 20, 2003 is Pacific Standard Time, which is 8 hours behind UTC, is `2003-06-20T13:20:00-08:00`.

To create a SalesByYearWS Web service, do the following:

1. Add a folder to contain the WSDL and supporting files for the service. For this example the location is \Inetpub\SalesByYear.
2. Choose Programs, SQLXML (3.0), Configure IIS Support to open the IIS Virtual Directory Management for SQLXML 3.0 snap-in.
3. Expand the nodes in the tree view, right-click the Default Web Site item, and choose New, Virtual Directory to open the General Page of the New Virtual Directory Properties dialog.
4. Replace New Virtual Directory with the virtual directory alias name—**SalesByYear** for this example.
5. Type the folder name you added in step 1 in the Local Path dialog (see Figure 31.15). Click Apply.

31

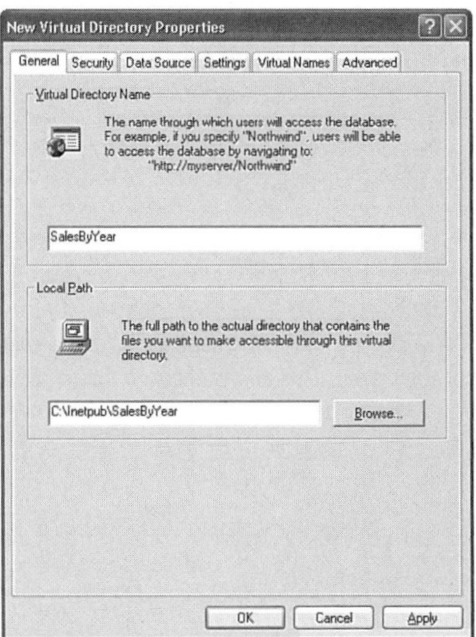

Figure 31.15
Specify the virtual directory alias name and the folder for the WSDL and supporting files in the General page of the New Virtual Directory Properties dialog.

6. Click the Security tab and select the Use Windows Integrated Authentication option to use your Administrator account for MSDE 2000. Click Apply.

➔ For alternative security choices, **see** "Setting Up the IIS Virtual Directory for the Database," **p. 968**.

7. Click the Data Source tab, accept (local) as the SQL Server instance, clear the Use Default Database for Current Login check box, and select NorthwindSQL as the active database. Click Apply.
8. Click the Settings tab, mark the Allow POST check box, and click Apply.
9. Click the Virtual Names tab, which selects the <New Virtual Name> item in the Defined Virtual Names list, type the virtual name—**SalesByYearWS**—in the Name text box, select SOAP in the Type list, specify the path to folder you added in step 1, and type the virtual name in the Web Service Name text box. Accept your computer's NetBIOS name as the domain name (see Figure 31.16).

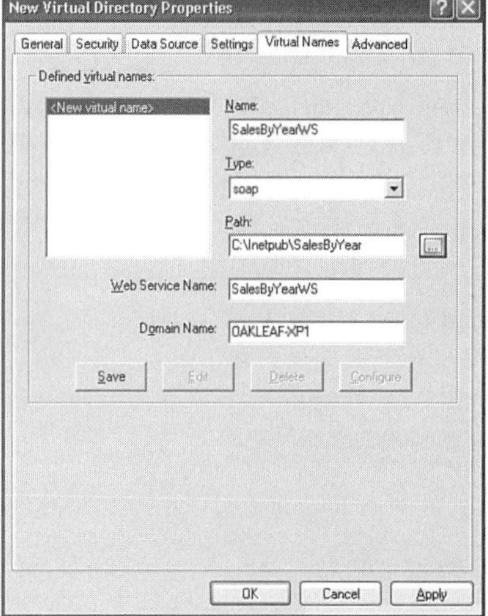

Figure 31.16 Specify the virtual name, type (soap), path to the virtual name folder, Web service name, and computer name on the Virtual Names page.

NOTE

> Microsoft developers appear to have "SOAP schizophrenia." "SOAP," "Soap," and "soap" appear throughout SQLXML and other Microsoft Web service-related applications. *SOAP* is the official name of the protocol, so all instances of the name are capitalized in this and other chapters.

10. Click Save to save your virtual name settings and add the virtual name to the list, which enables the Edit, Delete, and Configure buttons.

11. Click Configure to open the SOAP Virtual Name Configuration dialog with <New Method Mapping> selected, accept the SP type option, and click the button to the right of the SP/Template text box to open the SOAP Stored Procedure Mapping dialog.
12. Select the Sales by Year stored procedure and click OK to return to the SOAP Virtual Name Configuration Dialog. Change the Method Name from `Sales_by_Year` to **`SalesByYear`**, and accept the default Raw and XML Objects options and Return Errors as SOAP Faults (see Figure 31.17).

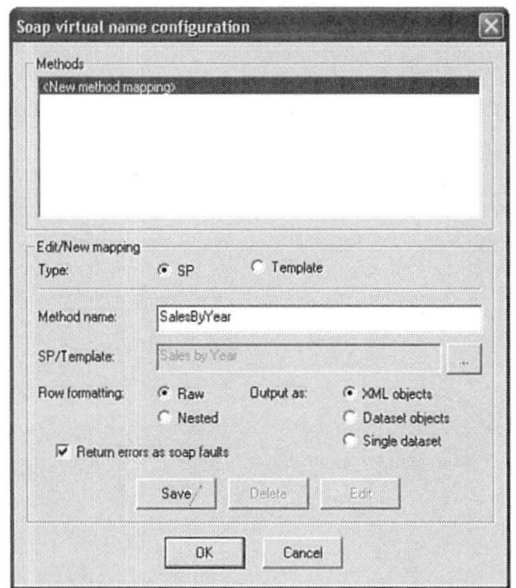

Figure 31.17
Select the stored procedure for the Web service, and specify the method name and structure of the SOAP response message in the Soap Virtual Name Configuration dialog.

13. Click save to add the `SalesByYear` method to the Methods list and click OK to return to the Virtual Names page. Click Apply and OK to close the dialog, save the *ServiceName*.wsdl and *ServiceName*.ssc (SQL Server configuration) files, and return to IIS Virtual Directory Management for SQLXML (3.0), which displays the new virtual directory in its list (see Figure 31.18). Close the snap-in.

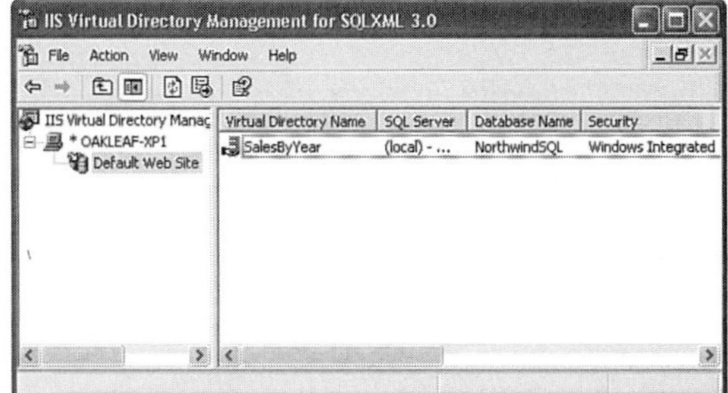

Figure 31.18
IIS Virtual Directory Management for SQLXML 3.0 adds a 3 icon to the IIS virtual directories you create. The icon is important because it distinguishes SQLXML virtual directories from those you create with the snap-in that's included with the SQL Server 2000 Client Tools.

Your \Program Files\Seuall\Chaptr31\SalesByYearWS folder contains a copy of SalesByYearWS.wsdl and SalesByYearWS.ssc. Following is a very abbreviated version of SalesByYearWS.wsdl's XML content:

```
<?xml version="1.0"?>
<wsdl:definitions name="SalesByYearWS" ...>
<!-- Namespace and schema definitions omitted for brevity -->
  <wsdl:message name="SalesByYearIn">
    <wsdl:part name="parameters" element="tns:SalesByYear"/>
  </wsdl:message>
  <wsdl:message name="SalesByYearOut">
    <wsdl:part name="parameters"
      element="tns:SalesByYearResponse"/>
  </wsdl:message>
  <wsdl:portType name="SXSPort">
    <wsdl:operation name="SalesByYear">
      <wsdl:input message="tns:SalesByYearIn"/>
      <wsdl:output message="tns:SalesByYearOut"/>
    </wsdl:operation>
  </wsdl:portType>
  <wsdl:binding name="SXSBinding" type="tns:SXSPort">
    <soap:binding style="document"
      transport="http://schemas.xmlsoap.org/soap/http"/>
    <wsdl:operation name="SalesByYear">
      <soap:operation
        soapAction="http://OAKLEAF-XP1/SalesByYear/SalesByYearWS/SalesByYear"
        style="document"/>
      <wsdl:input>
        <soap:body use="literal"/>
      </wsdl:input>
      <wsdl:output>
        <soap:body use="literal"/>
      </wsdl:output>
    </wsdl:operation>
  </wsdl:binding>
  <wsdl:service name="SalesByYearWS">
    <wsdl:port name="SXSPort" binding="tns:SXSBinding">
      <soap:address location="http://OAKLEAF-XP1/SalesByYear/SalesByYearWS"/>
    </wsdl:port>
  </wsdl:service>
</wsdl:definitions>
```

The most important element in SalesByYearWS.wsdl is the value of the `location` attribute, which combines the domain, virtual directory, and Web service names you specify to create a URL that points to the service's virtual name and location of the WSDL document.

SQLXML Web services require a *ServiceName*.ssc file to map stored procedure parameters, their datatypes, direction, and other attributes to Web service input/output parameters. Following is the reformatted content of SalesByYearWS.ssc:

```
<?xml version="1.0"?>
<sxs:methods name="SalesByYearWS" domain="OAKLEAF-XP1"
    url="http://OAKLEAF-XP1/SalesByYear/SalesByYearWS"
    xmlns:sxs="http://schemas.microsoft.com/SQLServer/2001/12/SOAPxml">
  <sxs:method name="SalesByYear" type="storedproc"
      spname="[Sales by Year]" format="raw" output="xmlobject"
```

```
      faults="true">
    <parameter name="@RETURN_VALUE" type="3" paramSize="4" precision="10"
      input="false" output="true" is-="false"/>
    <parameter name="@Beginning_Date" type="135" paramSize="16" precision="23"
      scale="3" input="true" output="false" is-="false"/>
    <parameter name="@Ending_Date" type="135" paramSize="16" precision="23"
      scale="3" input="true" output="false" is-="false"/>
  </sxs:method>
</sxs:methods>
```

SalesByYearWS.ssc defined one output and two input SQL Server parameters. SQLXML3 ignores the `@RETURN_VALUE integer (type="3")` output parameter, which is present for backward compatibility with prior SQLXML3 versions. The `@Beginning_Date` and `@Ending_Date` input parameters require SQL Server `datetime` (type="135") data types. Unfortunately, SQL Server Books Online doesn't include a cross reference between numeric `type` values and SQL Server datatypes.

31

TESTING THE SERVICE WITH .NET WEBSERVICE STUDIO

It's usually not worth the effort to create an Access consumer application for a test service, especially when you can verify operability and read the SOAP request and response messages with WSS.

Follow these steps to test drive SalesByYearWS's `SalesByYear` Web method with Windows (NTLM) authentication:

1. Open WSS, type **http://*computername*/salesbyyear/salesbyyearws?wsdl**" in the WSDL EndPoint text box, and click get to generate the Web service client proxy.

> **TIP**
>
> If you encounter an error with the preceding URL, click Continue to dismiss the error dialog, click Browse, and select the SalesByYearWS.wsdl file in your \IntetPub\SalesByYearSales folder.

2. Click the Request/Response tab and set the AllowRedirect, KeepAlive, and UseDefaultCredential HTTP properties to True (look ahead to Figure 31.20).
3. Return to the Invoke page, select the `Beginning_Date` parameter, and type **1/1/1998** as its value. Do the same for `Ending_Date`, but substitute a later date, and click Invoke to consume the Web service.

If you encounter an error when you attempt to invoke your local Web service, see the "Problems with WSS Security Settings" topic of the "Troubleshooting" section near the end of the chapter.

4. Scroll the Output list to reveal the four child node values of the `row` node: `ShippedDate`, `OrderID`, `Subtotal`, and `Year` (see Figure 31.19).

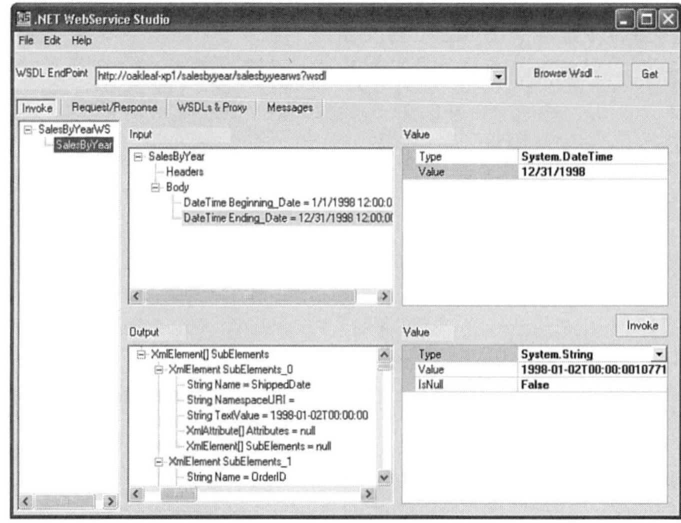

Figure 31.19 SalesByYearWS's `SalesByYear` method returns a hierarchy of `XMLDOMNodes`, which is similar in structure to that created by Alpha's `GetTop###` methods.

5. Click Request/Response to read the SOAP request and response messages (see Figure 31.20). WSS transforms the parameter's date value to XSD `dateTime` values, which have seven fractional time digits and the UTC offset for your time zone. (Your computer's time zone setting establishes the offset value.)

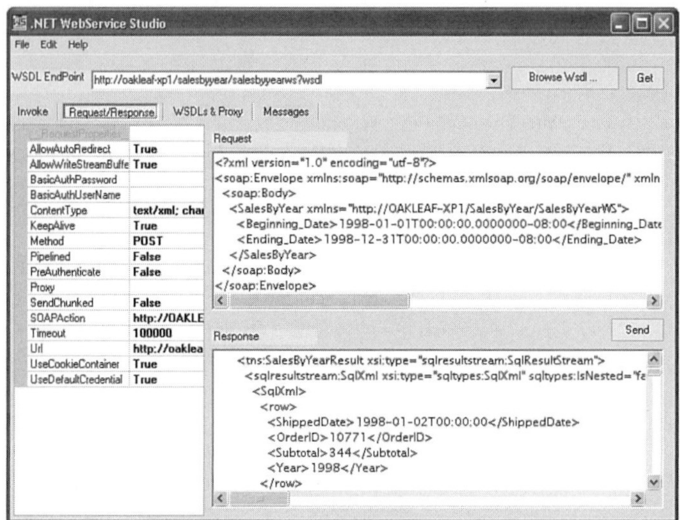

Figure 31.20 WSS's display of SOAP request and response messages illustrates the full and minimal ISO 8601 `dateTime` formats.

Creating and Consuming a Local Alpha Web Service

Your \Program Files\Seua11\Chaptr31\AlphaDist folder contains a duplicate of the AlphaDist.mdf MSDE 2000 database that serves as the data source for the online Alpha Web service. Attaching the database to your local SQL Server 2000 instance is easy, and so is modifying the AlphaTest.mdb or SQLXML3 consumers to run from your computer rather than the OakLeaf site. Testing the new service requires installing WSS, as described in the earlier "Exploring XML Web Services with .NET WebService Studio" section.

Setting Up and Testing the Local Alpha Web Service

Following is the drill to attach the AlphaDist to SQL Server and expose AlphaDist's four stored procedures as Web methods of a local Alpha service:

1. Create a new Access data project using existing data named AlphaDist.mdb.
2. On the Connection page of the DataLink Properties dialog, select (local) or your computer name as the server, select the use Windows Integrated Security option, and select the Attach a Database File as a Database Name option.
3. In the text box under the selected option, type **AlphaDist**, click the Browse button, navigate to your \Program Files\Seua11\Chaptr31\AlphaDist folder and double-click AlphaDist.mdf to attach the database and close the Select SQL Server Database dialog (see Figure 31.21).

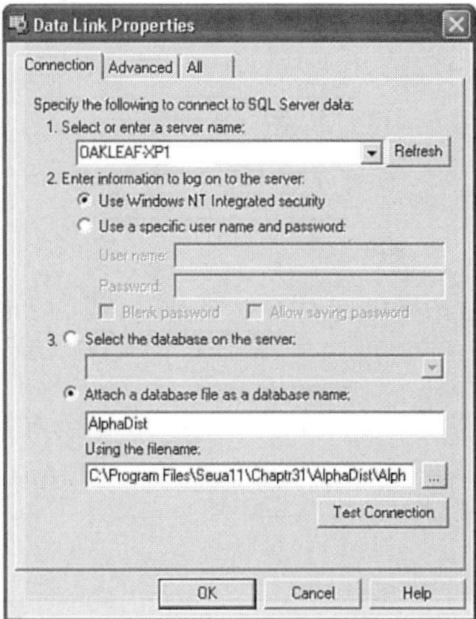

Figure 31.21 These settings attach the AlphaDist.mdf sample database to your local instance of SQL Server2000 and create a new AlphaDist_log.ldf log file.

4. Click Test Connection to verify that attaching succeeded, dismiss the dialog, and click OK to close the DataLink Properties dialog.

5. Open the Products table to verify that you have access to the new database as a member of the local BUILTIN\Administrators group.
6. Open one of the `GetTop###` queries; each query returns a result set for all products because the stored procedures have default values for the six parameters. Close AlphaDist.adp.

NOTE

Opening the stored procedures in Query Design view doesn't display the parameter values in the SQL pane. If you open the procedures, don't save changes.

TIP

The following accelerated steps assume that you completed (or at least read) the earlier "Creating a Simple Web Service" section. If you didn't, review that section's steps and figures before proceeding.

7. Create an \Inetpub\SQLXML folder for the new virtual directory, and open the IIS Virtual Directory Management for SQLXML (3.0) snap-in.
8. Add a virtual directory named **SQLXML** that points to the new subfolder, specify the Use Windows Integrated authentication option on the Security page, select (local) as the server and AlphaDist as the database on the Datasource page, mark the Allow POST checkbox on the Settings page, and click the Virtual Names tab.
9. On the Virtual Names page specify **Alpha** as the Name, **SOAP** as the type, and set the Path to \Intetpub**SQLXML**. Click Save and Configure to open the SOAP Virtual Name Configuration dialog.
10. Click the Browse button to open the SOAP Stored Procedure Mapping dialog, select GetTop10 from the list, and click OK to close the dialog.
11. Accept the SOAP Virtual Name Configuration page's defaults, and click Save to Add the method to the Methods list.
12. With the <New Method Mapping> item selected, repeat steps 8 and 9 for the GetTop25, GetTop50, and GetTop100 procedures. Click OK twice to close both dialogs and add the **SQLXML** virtual directory.

Give your new Web service a quick test with WSS by following the instructions in the earlier "Running WSS with a Public Web Service" section. In step 2, type **http://*computername*/sqlxml/alpha?wsdl** in the WSDL EndPoint text box. Alternatively, substitute `localhost` for your computer's NetBIOS name.

MODIFYING THE SAMPLE CONSUMERS TO USE THE LOCAL SERVICE

Moving from the public Web service at `http://www.oakleaf.ws/sqlxml/alpha` to your locally hosted service is simple. The only changes you need to make to Web service consumer applications are the WSDL document location (`c_WSDL_URL`) and namespace (c_SERVICE_NAMESPACE) constant values in the clsws_*ServiceName* class's Declarations section.

CAUTION

When changing c_WSDL_URL and c_SERVICE_NAMESPACE values, make sure the new values are *identical* to the values you specified for the domain, virtual directory, and service name. Namespaces are case sensitive, and you receive an error message if the c_SERVICE_NAMESPACE doesn't match exactly. WSDL URLs aren't case sensitive, but it's a good practice to use identical URL and namespace values.

Follow these steps to change consuming applications' Web service providers, using the Alpha service as an example:

1. Create a copy of AlphaTest.mdb and, optionally, SQLXML3Alpha.mdb in the same or another directory.
2. Open the clsws_*ServiceName* class module, clsws_Alpha for this example, and replace all instances of the original service location (www.oakleaf.ws) with the new domain name, usually your *COMPUTERNAME*. OAKLEAF-XP1 is the domain name for this chapter's examples.

TIP

If you changed the name or capitalization of the virtual directory, Web service, or both, you must replace additional elements of the c_SERVICE_NAMESPACE and c_WSDL_URL values.

3. Compile your code and test the application with the new service.

If you encounter an error message when attempting to consume the Web service from the new location, verify that the changes you made to c_SERVICE_NAMESPACE are identical to the targetNamespace attribute value in the second line of the service's WSDL document.

TIP

If you want to give other users in your Windows 2000+ domain access to your service, you must add SQL Server logins and user accounts for the database. Alternatively, you can specify Anonymous Access to the virtual directory with the built-in IUSR_*COMPUTERNAME* Windows guest account. In either case, you must grant the account at least sp_datareader privileges for the server or specific privileges for the database.

Troubleshooting

Problems with WSS Security Settings

I receive an "access denied" message when attempting to consume a local Web service with .NET WebService Studio.

The `SoapClient30` object that `clsws_ServiceName` creates for each Web method automatically uses your Windows logon credentials when invoking a Web method, but WSS doesn't. The most likely cause of "access denied" errors when invoking a service, is failure to set the AllowAutoRedirect, KeepAlive, and UseDefaultCredential properties to True on the Request/Response page.

If setting the preceding property values doesn't work, you probably have a problem with your server login. You must be logged on to your computer as the local Administrator or a member of the BUILTIN\Administrators account for the Web service to gain access to the database.

In the Real World—Why Web Services Are Important

The introduction to this chapter observed that Web services were in the "early adopter" stage when Microsoft released Office 2003. Most organizations' information technology (IT) groups are conducting internal pilot deployments of Web services for enterprise application integration (EAI) projects. EIA is a catch-all term for making packaged and custom software from multiple vendors—often running under different operating systems—communicate with one another. EIA consumes much of the programming effort and IT budgets of medium to large organizations. Web services promise to reduce EIA costs dramatically by breaking away from proprietary interapplication communication methods and moving to standards-based messaging with XML and SOAP.

Business-to-business (B2B) communication over the Internet is another promising application for Web services. The first commercial B2B Web service implementations are likely to involve supply-chain management (SCM). SCM enables organizations to automate purchasing and contracting operations with "business partners." Many standards bodies are involved in establishing a common XML vocabulary for B2B services. OASIS's electronic business XML (ebXML) is an example of a standardized XML business document format intended to replace costly and complex Electronic Document Interchange (EDI) programs with XML Web services.

One of the primary reasons that Web services are important to Access power users and developers is Microsoft's implementation of XML Web service interfaces in almost all new products. As examples, InfoPath is a Web service consumer, and SQL Server Reporting Services, which Microsoft announced in February 2003, is a Web service provider. Yukon, the codename for the next version of SQL Server, adds built-in service provider capability to eliminate the need for IIS as a participant in the SOAP message chain. Windows SharePoint Services also offers Web service connectivity. It wouldn't surprise anyone if a future XBox version turns out to be a Web service consumer.

Word and Excel 2003's integration of the .NET Common Language Runtime lets Visual Studio .NET developers take full advantage of complex commercial Web services. Despite WSR's limitations, such as the inability to handle SOAP headers, you can take advantage of free, public Web services in your Access applications today. An Oakland, California publisher of a scholarly journal uses EraServer's AddressCorrector service daily to verify U.S. addresses in a 15,000-row Access subscriber database. Ultimately, the USPS probably will provide a public XML Web service for this purpose, eliminating AddressCorrector as a middleman. Amazon.com provides a Web service interface to its product catalogs and Google offers a SOAP-enabled search service. Other major players in related markets are sure to follow suite.

Delivering data from your ADP's MSDE 2000 stored procedures as XML Web services might strike you as "new technology for technology's sake," but SQLXML 3.0+ makes the process so easy that it's almost trivial. This capability extends Access's reach to department-level and even enterprise-wide projects. If your current or future employment plans involve database development or administration, a basic understanding of XML Web services is—or soon will become—essential.

CHAPTER 32

Upgrading Access 97 and 2000/2002 Applications to Access 2003

In this chapter

Understanding the .mdb File Upgrade Process

Access 2003 is the first Access release that doesn't introduce a new Jet database format. Prior to Access 2003, each version of Access—1.0, 1.1, 2.0, 95, 97, 2000, and 2002—had a different database file structure at the binary (byte) level. The differences between 16-bit .mdb files created with versions 1.0 and 1.1 were relatively minor; thus you could use the Compact feature of Access to convert version 1.0 .mdbs to version 1.1, or vice versa. The file formats of later versions of Jet databases are sufficiently different to require, with the exception of the Access 2000 and 2002 formats, one-way conversion during the upgrade process.

TIP

> Access 2003 uses the 2000 and 2002 version of Jet 4.0 files interchangeably. Only very large Access front-end applications benefit by upgrading from the default Access 2000 (version 9.0) .mdb structure and the 2002 version (10.0). Version 10.0 supports a few VBA-related properties and methods that aren't available in version 9.0.
>
> Unless you encounter slow compilation of VBA code in the Access 2000 version or need to use version 10.0's VBA extensions, there's no reason to change the .mdb format to 10.0. The term *Access 2003* in this chapter means the application version, not the .mdb or .adp file format. *Access 2002+* refers to features that remain the same in Access 2002 and 2003. *Jet 4.0* means either Access 2000 or 2002 file format.

32

Access 2002 lets you convert data .mdbs from Jet 4.0 to Access 97 (Jet 3.5x) format, which makes them accessible by Access 97 front-end applications. You also can down-convert Jet 4.0 application .mdbs that don't contain objects—such as Data Access Pages (DAP)—or references to objects—ActiveX Data Objects (ADO and ADOX) or Data Access Objects (DAO) 3.6—that are missing in Access 97. After you downgrade a front end to Jet 3.51, you must make all design changes in Access 97. Downgrading a complex Jet 4.0 front end to Access 97's Jet 3.51 isn't a piece of cake, especially if the application uses libraries. Expect to spend a few hours (or days) fixing references and tracking code compilation errors.

CAUTION

> Don't upgrade shared data (back-end) .mdb files or workgroup .mdw files to Jet 4.0 format until all users who connect to these files have upgraded their application .mdb (front-end) files to Jet 4.0. Prior versions of Access can't link to Jet 4.0 tables; you receive an "Unrecognized data format" error message if you attempt to link an Access 9x front end to Jet 4.0 .mdb or .mdw files.

Access 2002 and 2003 save ordinary forms, reports, and modules in compound document files (DocFiles), which are stored within application .mdb files. This change supports Access Data Projects (ADP), which save application objects in .adp DocFiles, not in conventional .mdb files. The "Upgrading from MSDE 1.0 to the SQL Server 2000 Desktop Engine" section later in this chapter covers issues you encounter when moving to the new MSDE 2000 version.

CONVERTING UNSECURED FILES FROM ACCESS 9X TO JET 4.0

The definition of an unsecured Access 9x file is an .mdb file containing data objects, application objects, or both that you or others created with Access's default Admin account, with or without Access 97's database-level password protection. In this case, the Admin account has Administrator privileges and is the owner of all objects in the .mdb file(s).

NOTE

> The following sections don't apply to .mdb files you create as the Admin user with password protection for the Admin account. If the Admin user has a password, the .mdb file is secure. The later "Converting Secure Access 9x Files" section covers conversion of files with an Admin password.

UPGRADING ON FIRST OPENING THE FILE IN ACCESS 2003

Conversion of unsecured Access 9x .mdb files to Jet 4.0 is straightforward. If you're opening the Access 9x .mdb file for the first time in Access 2002, do the following:

32

1. Make sure you have sufficient disk space to accommodate the new .mdb file. The size of the Access 2000 version will be about 10 percent to 15 percent larger than the Access 9x version.
2.  If the Access 9x .mdb file contains VBA code, open the code editor window and compile the code in Access 9x. Compiling all code in the source .mdb file minimizes the likelihood of errors during the upgrade process.
3. Compact the file in Access 9x. Compacting the file immediately before conversion often speeds the conversion process and ensures against problems during conversion.
4. Close the Access 9x .mdb file if it's open. You must have exclusive access to the file for conversion to proceed.
5. Open the Access 9x .mdb file in Access 2003, which displays the Convert/Open Database dialog (see Figure 32.1). By default, the conversion is to Access 2000 format. If the database is password-protected, you must type the password to open the .mdb file.

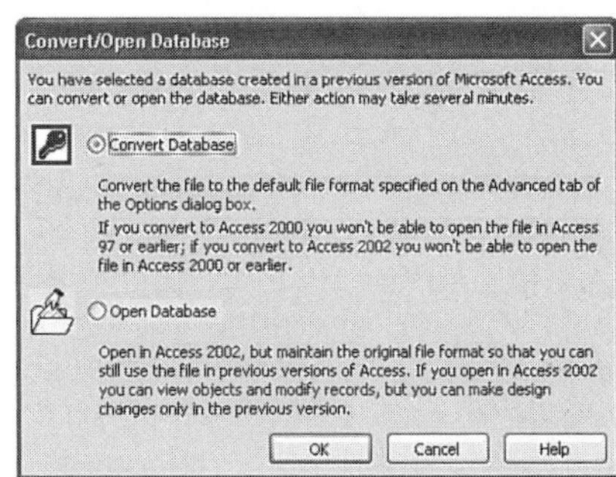

Figure 32.1 The Convert/Open Database dialog appears when you open an Access 9x .mdb file in Access 2003.

6. Accept the default Convert Database option and click OK to open the Convert Database Into dialog.
7. Replace the default db1.mdb with a new file name for the converted file (see Figure 32.2). Unlike the compact/repair process, you can't use the original file name and overwrite the Access 9x file.

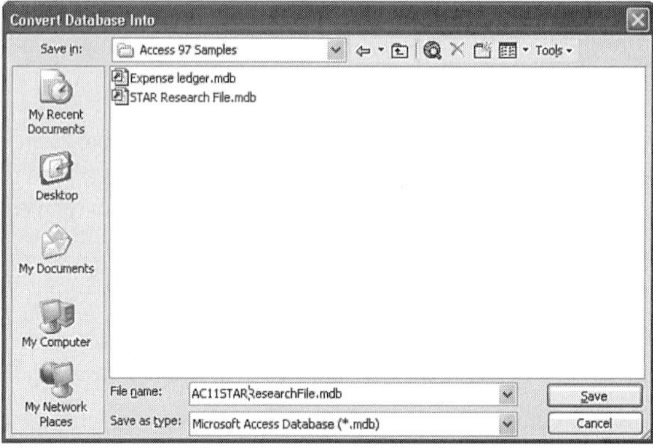

Figure 32.2
You must specify a different location or file name when converting an .mdb file from Access 9x to Jet 4.0.

TIP

> Keep a backup copy of your Access 9x .mdb files after conversion in a different folder or on removable media. You might find it necessary to restore your backup in the event you discover unexpected changes in your application caused by conversion artifacts. After you move the Access 9x file(s) to a new location, you can rename the converted file(s) to the original name(s).

8. Click Save to close the dialog and perform the conversion. After a few seconds—or minutes, if the file is large—the message shown in Figure 32.3 appears. Click OK to open your newly converted file in the Database window.

Figure 32.3
You receive this message after converting an Access 9x .mdb to Access 2000 format.

TIP

> You don't need to convert the existing default workgroup information file, System.mdw, which Access 9x installs in your \Windows\System or \Winnt\System32 folder. If your application is secure, however, you must first compact the Access 97 workgroup file in Access 2003, and then use Workgroup Administrator to join the workgroup defined by your Access 9x System.mdw. (You can't compact the Access 9x workgroup file if a user is connected to it.) Compacting the workgroup information file in Access 2003 doesn't change its version.

You can't open or convert Access 97 .mde files in Access 2003. When you attempt to open an .mde file, the terse message shown in Figure 32.4 appears. This restriction makes it impossible to run demonstration versions of commercial Access 97 applications under Access 2003. If you don't have Access 97 installed, you must wait for the upgraded version from the publisher.

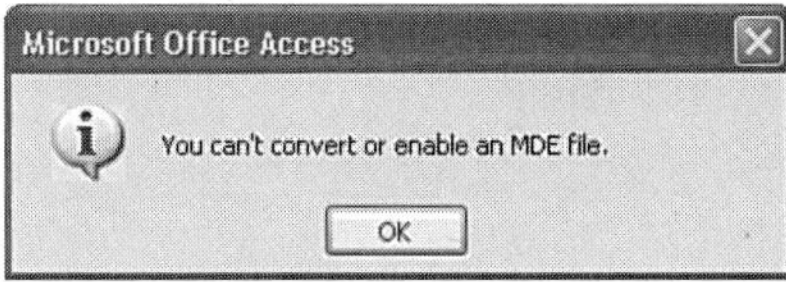

Figure 32.4
You receive this message if you attempt to open an Access 9x .mde file in Access 2003.

NOTE

> Secure .mde and .ade files you've created with Access 2000 don't require modification to run under Access 2003.

Upgrading After Opening the File in Access 2002

When you elect to open an unsecured Access 9x file in Access 2003, you can't change the design of any Access object. If you've previously opened an Access 9x file in Access 2003 and selected the Open Database option in the Convert/Open Database dialog, the Convert/Open Database dialog doesn't appear on successive open operations. You receive the message shown in Figure 32.5 the first time you open an Access 9x database in Access 2003.

32

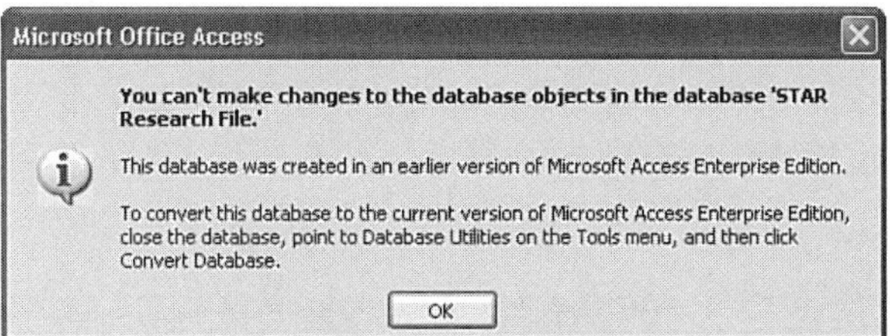

Figure 32.5
When you open an Access 9x .mdb file in Access 2003, you receive this message.

You can't save changes to the design of any object in an Access 9x database opened in Access 2003; you receive the message shown in Figure 32.5 when you open an object in Design view. The New button of the Database window's toolbar is disabled, and no Create... shortcuts appear in the Database window list for any object class.

NOTE

> You can open Access 9x objects in Design view, and even make changes to the design. However, you can't save (persist) the design changes.

If you want to take advantage of Access 2003 features—such as converting forms to DAP—or make changes to the design of existing objects, do the following to convert a previously opened database to the Jet 4.0 format:

1. Compile the VBA code and compact the file to be converted in Access 9x.
2. For this example, launch Access 2002 without opening a current database.
3. Choose Tools, Database Utilities, Convert Database, To Access 2000 File Format to open the Database to Convert From dialog.
4. Navigate to and select the Access 9x database to convert (see Figure 32.6).

Figure 32.6 When you convert an Access 9x database without opening it in Access 2003, select the source .mdb file in the Database to Convert From dialog.

32

5. Click Convert to open the Convert Database Into dialog.
6. Replace the default db1.mdb with a new file name for the converted file (refer to Figure 32.2).
7. Click Save to close the dialog and save the file in Access 2000 format.
8. Acknowledge the warning message, and then open the file in Access 2003.

Converting Secure Access 9x Files

Converting secure Access 9x files is a complex process that requires advance planning. Multiuser networked applications are the most common environment for secure Access files. To upgrade either the front-end or back-end .mdb file(s), you must open the files exclusively under an account that has Modify Design or Administer permission for all objects in the .mdb file. Alternatively, you must be the owner (creator) of all the database's objects. All users must close their front-end applications for you to obtain exclusive-open access to the back-end .mdb file.

TIP

> VBA code in secured forms and modules becomes unsecured when converting to Jet 4.0 because the change to the VBA Integrated Design Environment results in a different storage mechanism for your code. After you convert secured front-end .mdbs containing any VBA code, you must use the VBA IDE to password protect the code.

➔ To review System.mdw basics, **see** "Jet Workgroup Information Files," **p. 153**.

➔ For instruction on how to use the Workgroup Administrator tool, **see** "Establishing Your Own Admins Name, Password, and PID," **p. 783**.

Upgrading in a Mixed Access 9x and 2000 Environment

If you have many database users or several shared databases in operation, it's unlikely that you can upgrade all database users at one time without incurring excessive downtime. In this case, you must perform the following sequence of operations:

1. Make a backup copy of your Access 9x System.mdw file.
2. Launch Access 2003 and choose Tools, Database Utilities, Compact and Repair Database to open the Database to Compact From dialog. Choose Workgroup Files (*.mdw) in the Files of Type list and navigate to and select the shared workgroup file, usually System.mdw, and compact it with the same name. Click Cancel to close the Convert/Open Database dialog.
3. Open the Access 97 version of the front-end .mdb file in Access 97 to verify that the compacted System.mdw file opens with your Admins account, and you have design permissions for front-end objects. Verify that members of groups other than Admins don't have design permissions.
4. Choose Tools, Security, Workgroup Administrator, and join the workgroup you updated in step 2. Close and reopen Access 2002.
5. Open and convert the secure front-end .mdb file to Access 2000 format.
6. Thoroughly test the Jet 4.0 version of the secure application .mdb file with the existing Access 97 data .mdb file(s) and the compacted Access 97 System.mdw file.
7. Convert and distribute the upgraded front-end .mdb file to users.

Upgrading the Back-End Database and Workgroup File

After you've upgraded all your client .mdbs, you can upgrade the back-end (data) .mdb file, if you have a compelling reason to do so. If you decide to upgrade the back-end database and—optionally—the workgroup file, complete the upgrade process as follows:

1. Compact the shared data .mdb file with a new name so that you can convert the file to a new version with the same name as the old version.
2. Upgrade the data .mdb file to Jet 4.0.

CAUTION

> Don't delete the original .mdb file. You might need to revert to the original files in case you encounter conversion problems.

3. Create a local copy of the existing shared workgroup file and join the local workgroup so you can compact the original workgroup file.
4. Compact the shared workgroup file with a new name and then convert it to Jet 4.0 with the original name.

CAUTION

> Don't delete the original .mdw file. You might need it as conversion insurance.

5. After testing the new configuration, request each user to open Workgroup Administrator and rejoin the workgroup with the new workgroup file.

Converting Data Access Pages from Access 2000 or 2002 to 2003

DAP are an exception to the transparency between Access 2000 and 2002 file formats, and application object compatibility between Access 2002 and 2003. DAP store page design in .htm files, not in .mdb or .adp files; .mdb and .adp files store only links to the .htm files. When you open a page created by Access 2000 or 2002 in Page Design view, you receive the first message shown in Figure 32.7. After you convert the .htm file to Access 2003 format, the second message appears to advise you that upgrading created a backup file.

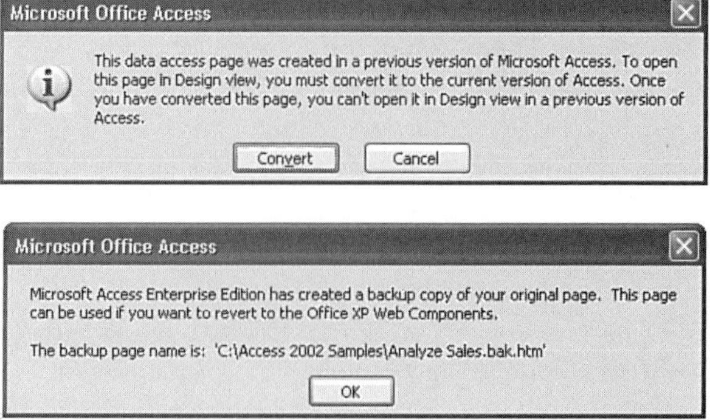

Figure 32.7 You receive the upper warning message when you open in Access 2003 DAP created in Access 2000. After you convert the page, the lower message appears.

Access 2003 automatically creates a backup of the page named *FileName*.bak.htm and updates the *FileName*.htm file from version 9.0 (Access 2000) or 10.0 (Access 2002) to 11.0. Users must have Office 2003 and Office Web Components (OWC) 11.0 to view and update data in the upgraded DAP. If your DAP must support Office 2000 or XP users, create a new virtual directory on your Web server to hold the Office 2003 versions, move the upgraded files to the new virtual directory, and rename the backup copies from *FileName*.bak.htm to *FileName*.htm in the original virtual directory.

Moving from MSDE 1.0 to the SQL Server 2000 Desktop Engine

When you upgrade from Office 2000 to 2003, your existing MSDE 1.0 installation remains intact, and your existing ADP, DAP, and linked Jet databases continue to connect to the local instance of MSDE 1.0 installed by Office 2000 or the remote server specified by the front-end application's ODBC or OLE DB/ADO connection string. When you open the Access 2003 version of NorthwindCS.adp, however, you receive the message shown in Figure 32.8. The Access 2000 version of the NorthwindCS database's Employees table stores bitmaps in the Photo field; the Access 2003 version has links to nine EmpID*x*.bmp files in the ...\Office11\Samples folder.

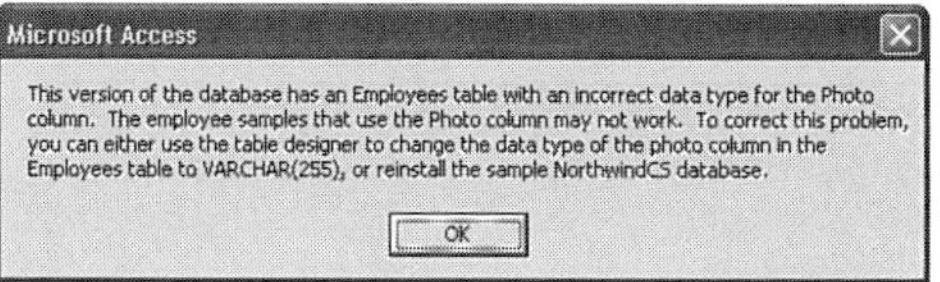

Figure 32.8
This message appears when you open Access 2003's NorthwindCS.adp sample application connected to the MSDE 1.0 version of the NorthwindCS sample database.

32

You can continue to use MSDE 1.0 with Access 2003, but doing so prevents you from taking advantage of the many new and important features of SQL Server 2000, such as full support for declarative referential integrity (DRI), linked servers, and extended properties that support Access 2002+ features—such as lookup fields, subdatasheets, and input masks.

Microsoft recommends that you remove MSDE 1.0 before installing the Desktop Edition. This recommendation applies only if *none* of the following three statements are true:

- You have a substantial investment in customizing SQL Server 7.0 features, such as publish/subscribe replication, database roles, and other management options.
- You have many individual server login and database user accounts to which you have granted specific database roles or individual database object permissions.
- You're using SQL Server authentication for MSDE 1.0 login and database user accounts. Office 2003 installs MSDE 2000 with integrated Windows (NTLM) authentication only.

If none of the preceding three conditions apply to you, skip to the "Removing MSDE 1.0 and Installing SQL Server 2000" section. Otherwise, choose one of the upgrade options described in the following two sections.

UPGRADING FROM MSDE 1.0 TO SQL SERVER 2000

NEW The version of MSDE 2000 on the Office 2003 installation disk is SQL Server 2000 Service Pack (SP) 3. SP3 removes earlier versions' vulnerability to the infamous "Slammer" worm. MSDE 2000's new Setup.exe program doesn't open dialogs to let you choose installation options. Instead, you supply command line parameters to tell Setup.exe that you want to upgrade—rather than replace—MSDE 1.0. Upgrading an instance of MSDE 1.0 to SQL Server 2000 SP3 is very similar to that for installing a new version of MSDE 2000.

→ To review the installation process for a new MSDE 2000 instance, **see** "Running the MSDE Setup Program," **p. 48**.

CAUTION

If you're running MSDE 1.0 under Windows XP or 2000+ and you've specified Windows integrated and SQL Server (mixed) security, you lose SQL Server security during the upgrade to MSDE 2000. You can change the security settings with SQL Server Enterprise Manager, if installed, to re-enable SQL Server security.

32

To upgrade MSDE 1.0 to MSDE 2000 SP3, do the following:

1. Log on as an administrative user, and use SQL Server Service Manager to stop MSDE 1.0.
2. Navigate to the \MSDE2000 folder of the Office System 2003 distribution CD-ROM or a network installation share.
3. Double-click Msde2ks3.exe to open the License Agreement dialog, and click I Agree.
4. In the Installation Folder dialog, accept the default location, C:\Sql2ksp3, to extract and copy the installation files to the folder. Click Yes to create the folder. Extracting the files takes about a minute.
5. Choose Start, Run, type **cmd** in the Open text box, and click OK to open a Command window.
6. Type **cd \sql2ksp3\msde** and press Enter.

TIP

If you want to learn more about SQL Server 2000 SP3, open Sp3readme.htm in your \Sql2ksp3\MSDE folder before proceeding.

7. Type **setup.exe upgrade=1 blanksapwd=1** and press Enter. The installation process takes a few minutes.

8. Reboot your computer to restart SQL Server Service manager.
9. Follow the instructions for resetting the blank sa password in the next section.

NOTE

> The following Microsoft Knowledge Base articles contain information on upgrading MSDE 1.0 to MSDE 2000: Q282017, "PRB: SQL Server 2000 Help File Contains Confusing Information About the Desktop Engine Setup"; Q290627, "ACC2002: Microsoft SQL Server 2000 Desktop Engine Is Not Installed by Office XP Setup;" and Q271887, "PRB: Desktop Engine Upgrade of MSDE 1.0 Fails." If you encounter a problem upgrading MSDE 1.0 to 2000, check article Q271887 for instructions to generate an installation log file. Q301413, "Configuring SQL Server 2000 Desktop Engine," has a link to download a white paper on MSDE 2000 configuration. The information in the articles, which were written for Access 2002, also applies to Access 2003.

SETTING OR RESETTING A SYSTEM ADMINISTRATOR PASSWORD

A empty (blank) sa password poses a serious security risk, because anyone with access to your computer can gain full administrative control over your databases. Access 2003 includes a feature that permits members of the local Administrators group to enable the sysadmin (sa) account with an empty password. You change the password in a second operation.

32

NOTE

> Adding a password to the sa account is important, even if you install MSDE 2000 with Windows authentication only. A determined person with access to your computer might be able to change a Registry setting to enable SQL Server security.

To add the sa account for SQL Server security, do the following:

1. Open an Access data project that connects to a server that doesn't have SQL Server security enabled. You must run Access 2003 on the machine that hosts the SQL Server instance to change the sa password.
2. Choose View, Server Properties to open the Server Properties dialog.
3. Mark the Enable System Administrator (SA) User Name check box (see Figure 32.9), and click OK to close the dialog. (If the sa account exists, the check box is disabled. In this case click Cancel.)
4. Acknowledge the message that recommends changing the system administrator password. After a few seconds, the Logon dialog opens.
5. Accept the default sa login ID and empty password, and click OK to log in with SQL Server security.

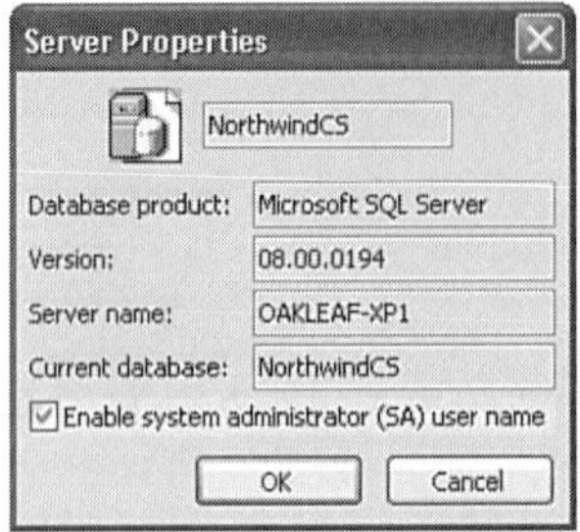

Figure 32.9
Enable SQL Server security for the sa account in Access 2003's Server Properties dialog.

Adding the sa account and logging in to MSDE 2000 changes the selected security option of the DataLink Properties dialog from Windows NT to SQL Server security with sa as the username and an empty password.

To set or reset the password, follow these steps:

1. Choose Tools, Security, Set Login Password to open the Change Password dialog.
2. If the sa password is empty, accept the default (empty) value in the Old Password text box. Otherwise, type the password you want to reset.
3. Type and confirm the new password in the New Password and Verify text boxes (see Figure 32.10) and click OK.

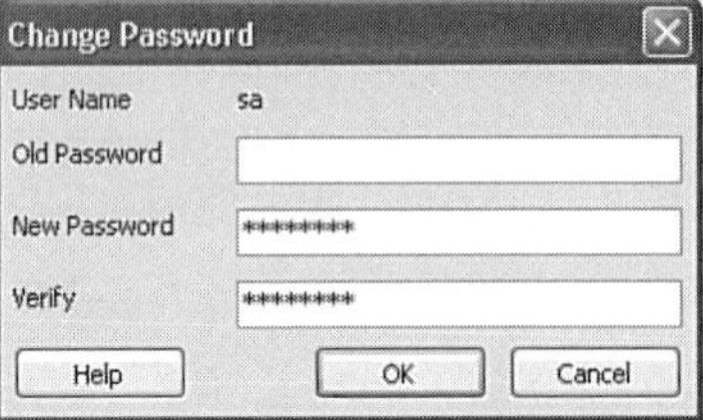

Figure 32.10
Use the Change Password dialog to add or change a password for the system administrator (sa) account.

4. If you used the Server Properties dialog to add the sa account, open the DataLink Properties dialog, select the Use Windows NT Integrated Security option, and click OK.

Changing an existing password affects all ADP that rely on SQL Server security. In this case, you must open each project's DataLink Properties dialog and change to the new password.

Installing a Named Instance of SQL Server 2000

SQL Server 7.0 doesn't support named instances, so MSDE 1.0 remains the primary instance of SQL Server on your computer. You can create a side-by-side installation of the two versions, but doing so requires creating a named instance of MSDE 2000 on the machine. Connecting to a named instance of MSDE 2000 requires substituting the computer's NetBIOS name and server instance name, as in `ServerName\InstanceName`, wherever you ordinarily specify *ServerName*.

TIP

> Access 2003's "Install and configure SQL Server 2000 Desktop Engine" online Help topic contains the following note: "Be sure to read the Readme.txt file in the \MSDE2000 folder for late-breaking information." Much of the information regarding MSDE in the Readme.txt file applies to the conventional installation from SQL Server CD-ROMs, not the "no options" installation of SP3 from the \MSDE2000 folder of the distribution CD-ROM.

To add a named instance of MSDE 2000—MSDE2K for this example—to a computer with MSDE 1.0 installed, do the following:

1. Perform steps 1–5 of the earlier "Upgrading from MSDE 1.0 to SQL Server 2000" section.
2. Type **setup.exe instancename=MSDE2K blanksapwd=1** and press Enter. The installation process takes a few minutes.

   You can substitute another short name for *MSDE2K*, if you want, but don't include spaces or punctuation symbols in the name.
3. After installation completes, click OK to acknowledge the message, and reboot your computer.
4. Verify installation of the new instance in Windows XP/2000+ by opening Control Panel's Administrative Tools\Services tool and scrolling to find MSSQL$MSDE2K (see Figure 32.11). Alternatively, right-click My Computer, choose Manage to open the Computer Management snap-in, expand the Services and Applications node, and click Services to display the list.

32

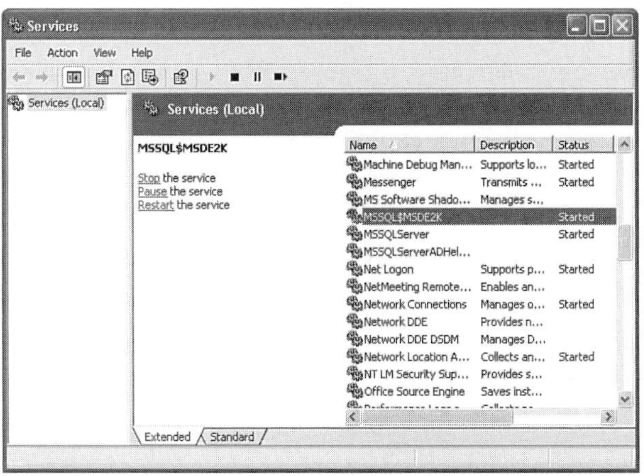

Figure 32.11 Windows XP displays the new instance of MSDE 2000, which runs under the LocalSystem account by default. In the SQL Server service, a dollar sign ($) separates the server and instance name.

5. Double-click the MSSQL$*MSDE2K* item to open the MSSQL$*MSDE2K* Properties (Local Computer) dialog. Click the Logon tab, select the This Account option, and type the name of a local Administrators account (usually Administrator), the password, and the password confirmation (see Figure 32.12). Click OK to change the logon account for the instance, and acknowledge the two message boxes. (You don't need to stop and start the service before completing the remaining steps of this procedure.)

MSSQL$MSDE2K Properties (Local Computer)
General | Log On | Recovery | Dependencies
Log on as:
Local System account
Allow service to interact with desktop
This account: Administrator [Browse...]
Password: ••••••••••
Confirm password: ••••••••••
You can enable or disable this service for the hardware profiles listed below:
Hardware Profile | Service
Profile 1 | Enabled
[Enable] [Disable]
[OK] [Cancel] [Apply]

Figure 32.12 Change the logon account for the new SQL Server 2000 instance to an account with membership in the local Administrators group.

6. Repeat step 4 for the SQLAgent$*MSDE2K* service, and close the Services tool.
7. Test the new SQL Server 2000 instance by launching Access 2003, if necessary, and opening a project with a connection to the MSDE 1.0 database, such as the upgraded NorthwindCS project.
8. Choose Tools, Database Utilities, Transfer Database to start the Transfer Database tool.
9. In the first dialog, select the SQL Server instance (OAKLEAF-XP1\MSDE2K for this example) in the What SQL Server Would You Like... list and type the name for the new database in the text box (see Figure 32.13). Alternatively, clear the check box, and type your login ID and password in the two text boxes for SQL Server security.

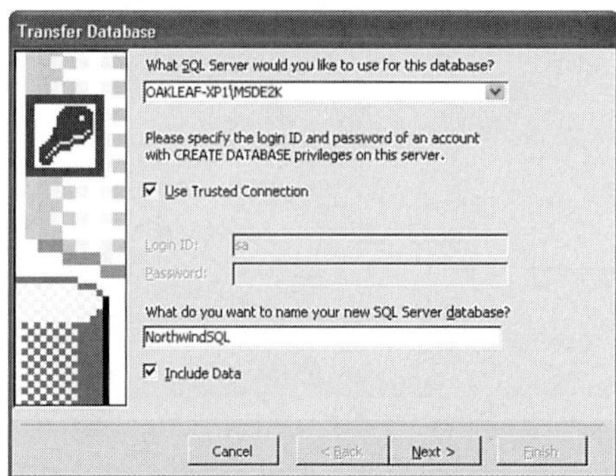

Figure 32.13 Test the new SQL Server 2000 instance by copying an SQL Server 7.0 database and its objects with the Transfer Database tool.

10. Click Next, and then click Finish to start the transfer process. Transferring the database creates a copy in the destination instance.
11. In the current or a new Access project, choose File, Connection to open the Connection page of the Data Link Properties dialog.
12. In the Select or Enter a Server Name list, select the new SQL Server 2000 instance (see Figure 32.14), and click OK.

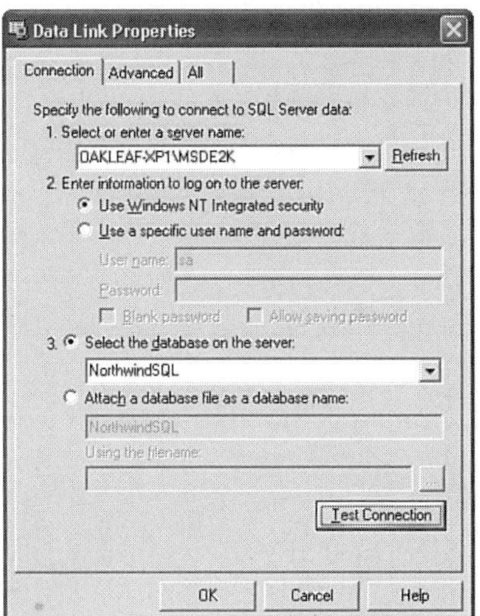

Figure 32.14 Installing a new instance adds the instance name to the Select or Enter a Server Name list. Select the new instance for testing with the Access project.

13. Verify that your current Access 2003 project behaves as expected with the new data source, and then return to the original server connection, if you want.

Any ADP you connect to databases in the new server instance can take advantage of Access 2003-specific extended properties, but you must set the property values manually in Table Design view in the da Vinci toolset.

➔ To review using the da Vinci table designer, **see** "Working with SQL Server Tables in the Project Designer," **p. 810**.

Removing MSDE 1.0 and Installing SQL Server 2000

If you've made a significant investment in customizing MSDE 1.0, the better choice is to retain your MSDE 1.0 instance and install a named instance of SQL Server 2000. If you decide to migrate your ADP to SQL Server 2000, do the following before removing MSDE:

1. Back up your data (.mdf) and log (.ldf) files, plus at least master.mdf, mastlog.ldf, msdbdata.mdf, and msdblog.ldf. Removing MSDE 1.0 doesn't delete production .mdf and .ldf files, but it does delete the existing master, msdb, model, and tempdb database and log files. Loss of the model and tempdb databases isn't important.

2. If you've added custom settings for MSDE 1.0 features, such as publish/subscribe replication, server roles, SQL Server logins, and the like, make sure you document them thoroughly. You must manually reestablish your server-wide MSDE 1.0 settings in SQL Server 2000.

Removing MSDE 1.0 isn't as simple as the "Install and configure SQL Server Desktop Engine" online Help topic suggests. Do the following to remove MSDE and all its components, including SQL Service Manager from your computer:

1. Open SQL Server Service Manager and clear the Auto-start Service when OS Starts check box for MSSQLServer and SQLServerAgent.
2. Delete the shortcut to Service Manager in your ...\Start Menu\Programs\Startup folder(s). The location of the Service Manager shortcut depends on your operating system. Use Search to search for **service manager**, and delete *all* Service Manager shortcuts you find.
3. Reboot your computer and verify that the Service Manager icon no longer appears in the tray.
4. Choose Start, Programs, MSDE, Uninstall MSDE to start the uninstall process. Click Yes to confirm you want to continue with removal, click OK when uninstallation completes, and reboot your computer.
5. Perform a new installation of MSDE 2000 SP3 as described in Chapter 1's "Running the MSDE Setup Program" section.
6. Reboot your computer when setup completes.
7. For additional security, add and password-protect the sa account, as described in the earlier "Setting or Resetting a System Administrator Password" section.

Removing MSDE deletes the Programs, MSDE menu; MSDE 2000 doesn't add a menu. Other SQL Server 2000 editions add a Microsoft SQL Server menu to replace the MSDE menu.

Reattaching and Upgrading MSDE 1.0 Databases

ADP and ODBC-linked Jet front ends lose their connections to existing MSDE 1.0 databases when you migrate to SQL Server 2000, so you must reattach the databases to your front-end applications. When you attach the MSDE 1.0 .mdf file, SQL Server upgrades the database to the SQL Server 2000 version. This process is not reversible; the upgraded database files no longer are operable with MSDE 1.0.

Access Data Projects

To reattach and upgrade the MSDE 1.0 files for ADP, do this:

1. Open the .adp file in Access 2003. The project displays "Disconnected" in the Database window's title bar.

2. Choose File, Connection to open the Data Link Properties dialog.
3. Accept (local) or select the server name in the Select or Enter a Server Name list.
4. Select the Attach a Database File as a Database Name option, and type the database name for your project in the first text box.
5.  Click the Browse button to open the Select SQL Server Database File dialog and navigate to the folder that holds the MSDE 1.0 .mdf file for the database. The default location of MSDE 1.0 .mdf and .ldf files is C:\MSSQL7\Data. Select the file and click Open to add the file name to the Using the Filename text box (see Figure 32.15).

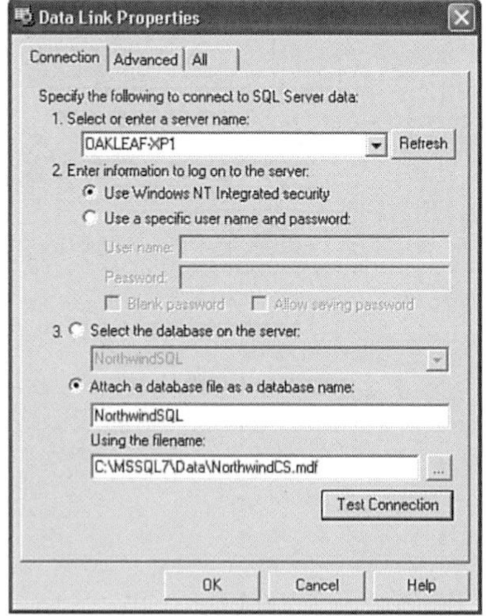

Figure 32.15 Specify the database name and .mdf file to upgrade MSDE 1.0 databases to MSDE 2000 and attach them to ADP.

6. Click Test Connection to upgrade the attached file, which takes a few seconds or more, depending on the size of the database.
7. Click OK to close the Data Link Properties dialog, and verify that your project works correctly with the upgraded database.
8. Repeat steps 1 through 7 for each project having an upgraded database.

NOTE

Attaching the files moves the .mdf and .ldf files from their original location–normally \MSSQL7\Data–to the standard location for SQL Server 2000 file–\Program Files\Microsoft SQL Server\MSSQL\Data.

After you've attached the upgraded tables, they appear in the Select the Database on the Server List. If you maintained the original database name and security option, you don't need to modify the Data Link Properties entries for other front ends that connect to the upgraded database.

JET FRONT ENDS LINKED WITH ODBC

ODBC DSNs that link Jet front ends to MSDE 1.0 databases fail after migrating to SQL Server 2000. If the Jet front ends share SQL Server 2000 databases you've upgraded for ADP, the upgrade process of the preceding section makes the DSNs operable. You must attach and upgrade other MSDE 1.0 databases to enable connectivity with existing ODBC DSNs.

If you have SQL Server Enterprise Manager, you can attach and upgrade the MSDE 1.0 files by doing this:

1. Open Enterprise Manager, and expand the SQL Server Group node to display the server list.
2. Right-click the Databases node of the migrated server, and choose All Tasks, Attach Database to open the Attach Database - *ServerName* dialog.
3. Click the browse button to open the Browse for Existing File - *ServerName* dialog, select the .mdf file to attach, and click OK.
4. Accept or change the database name in the Attach As text box (see Figure 32.16).

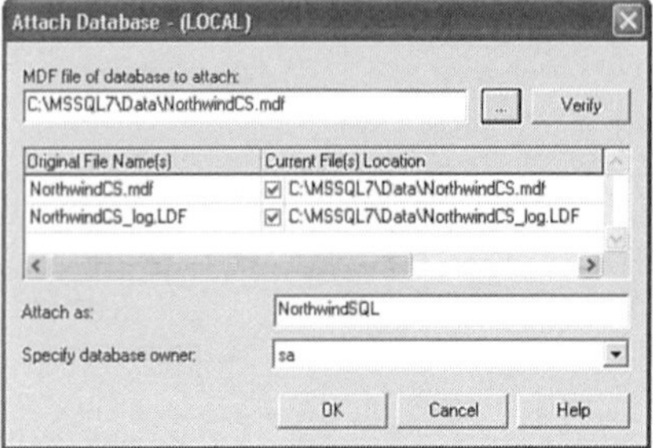

Figure 32.16 Use Enterprise Manager's Attach Database tool to reattach and upgrade MSDE 1.0 databases you connect to Jet front ends with ODBC.

5. Click OK to attach the database and click OK again to acknowledge the "success" message.

If you don't have SQL Server Enterprise Manager, you can attach and upgrade MSDE files by creating a temporary project—typically Adp1.adp—and performing the steps in the preceding "Access Data Projects" section for each database you need to upgrade.

TROUBLESHOOTING

MISSING LIBRARY OR PROJECT MESSAGE

I get a "The expression EventName you entered as the event property setting produced the following error: Can't find project or library" message when attempting to open or convert an Access 97 application .mdb.

The most common cause of this error message results from use of Access 97's Microsoft DAO 2.5/3.5 Compatibility Library, which permits compiling code with the remnants of Access 2.0's VBA code conventions that are incompatible with DAO 3.5+. You must update the code to DAO 3.5x standards in Access 97, and then convert the Access 97 version to Jet 4.0. To do so, substitute a reference to the Microsoft DAO 3.51 Object Library for the Microsoft DAO 2.5/3.5 Compatibility Library. Correct the unsupported syntax by repeatedly compiling the code until all modules compile and the application runs properly. Then convert the .mdb file to Access 2000 format.

In the Real World—The Access Upgrade Blues

Previous upgrades to Access (except the 1.0 to 1.1 transition) undoubtedly increased the market for mood-altering substances—both legal and illegal—among Access developers. Migrating from Access 97 to Access 2003 isn't a piece of cake. The larger and more complex your Access application, the more taxing the process. Access Basic detritus from Version 2.0 or earlier plagues the conversion of mature Access applications. (Many developers didn't upgrade Access 2.0 applications to Access 95 because of performance issues.) Thus, the more history behind your code, the greater the chance that it breaks when upgrading.

The obvious temptation is not to upgrade any Access 9x application to Access 2002. This approach is viable only for applications you distribute as self-contained runtime versions generated by the Office 9x Developer Edition's Setup Wizard. Access 97 runtime versions install roughly 50MB of Access 97, Jet 3.51, DAO 3.51, and other obsolete dependency files on Office 2003 users' PCs. The Access 97 runtime baggage probably won't be a problem for today's desktop PCs, but road warriors' older laptops often have much less available disk space than modern desktops.

If you avoid temptation and bite the upgrade bullet, take the opportunity to optimize your VBA code. Make sure that the first line in every module is `Option Explicit`, substitute variable declarations for explicit references to objects used more than once in your code, and minimize use of the `Variant` data type. Add `.Value` instead of using the default property value of Access and Jet objects. Search for all instances of `CreateObject`, which results in late binding, and replace the call with a referenced object variable declaration, such as `Private objName As ObjectLibrary.ObjectName`, for a class member to force early binding. When you complete the optimization process, your Access 2002 application might execute as quickly as its 16-bit Access 2.0 predecessor. (But don't count on it.)

After you've converted your application to Jet 4.0 and DAO 3.6, and then gone through an exhaustive testing process, your next decision is whether to move from DAO to ADO and ADOX 2.1. OLE DB, and ADO are Microsoft's current recommendations for database connectivity, but surfing the current ADO/ADOX versions demonstrates no significant performance improvement or other benefits that justify the time and effort required for conversion. ADO/ADOX 2.x don't offer full parity with DAO 3.6 for Jet databases, and many workarounds for missing DAO features are inelegant, at best.

Don't let the preceding admonition discourage you from adopting ADO for new Access projects. DAO 3.6 is Microsoft's last iteration of this venerable object model. Microsoft is directing virtually all of its data connectivity investment to improving and expanding the capabilities of OLE DB, ADO, and especially the .NET Framework's ADO.NET. You can expect upgrades to ADO on a less frequent basis than new Office or Visual Studio versions because of Microsoft's emphasis on .NET technologies.

Web-based applications require OLE DB and ADO to support scripting, DHTML, and XML; DAO is extra baggage for ADP. If you employ object-oriented programming methodology, your classes must use ADO to assure object compatibility across all Access application types. Take the time to learn OLE DB fundamentals and gain expertise in ADO. The ADO learning curve isn't as steep as you might think. Your investment will pay handsome dividends when a later version of Access adopts the .NET Framework's Common Language Runtime (CLR) as an alternative to VBA 6.0.

Finally, make the transition from Jet to SQL Server 2000 and its successors. The limitations of Jet 4.0 are here to stay. SQL Server 2000 delivers industrial-strength reliability and scalability to your Access 2003 applications.

Appendix

APPENDIX A

GLOSSARY

A

.NET Microsoft's strategy, announced in June 2000, to reorient its operating systems, developer tools, and productivity applications from the Component Object Model (COM) to the .NET Framework and its Common Language Runtime (CLR). The CLR supports multiple programming languages, such as Microsoft's Visual C#, Visual Basic .NET, and Visual J#. Much of Microsoft's marketing campaign for the .NET Framework and Visual Studio .NET focuses on support for Internet-enabled XML Web services. Microsoft Office 2003 installs version 1.1 of the .NET framework to support Excel 2003 and Word 2003. The .NET Framework is a reincarnation of *Next Generation Windows Services* (*NGWS*), the follow-up to Microsoft's earlier *Distributed iNternet Architecture* (*Windows DNA*). See also *CLR*, *COM*, *SOAP*, and *XML Web services*.

Access 2003 Developer Extensions The replacement for the Access related components of the Microsoft Office Developer edition (MOD). The extensions include a license for distribution of the runtime versions of MSAccess.exe and MSGraph.exe, a Package Wizard for creating Microsoft Installer packages (.msi files) for runtime applications, and two add-ins—Property Scanner and Custom Startup Wizard—for Access developers. See also *MOD* and *VST*.

Access Data Project See *ADP*.

Access SQL Former name of Jet SQL, a dialect of ANSI SQL-92. See also *ANSI*, *Jet SQL*, *SQL*, and *Transact-SQL*.

Active Server Pages See *ASP* and *ASP+*.

ActiveX A Microsoft trademark for a collection of technologies based on the Common Object Model (COM) and Distributed Common Object Model (DCOM). See also *COM*, *COM+*, and *DCOM*.

ActiveX components A replacement term for OLE Automation mini-servers and in-process servers, also called Automation servers. See also *Automation*.

ActiveX controls Insertable objects supplied in the form of .ocx files that, in addition to offering a collection of properties and methods, also fire events. ActiveX controls are lightweight versions of earlier OLE controls that also use the .ocx file extension.

ActiveX Data Objects See *ADO*.

ActiveX Data Object Extensions See *ADOX*.

ActiveX documents Files such as those created by Microsoft Excel 7+ and Word 7+ that can be displayed in their native format in Internet Explorer 3+. ActiveX documents originally were called Document Objects or DocObjects.

ActiveX scripting Another name for Visual Basic, Scripting Edition (VBScript), a simplified version of VBA designed for client- and server-side automation of Web pages.

ADC An abbreviation for Advanced Data Control, the predecessor to Remote Data Service. See also *RDS*.

add-in Wizards and other programming aids, usually in the form of Access libraries, that help Access programmers create and deploy applications. You use Access's Add-In Manager to install Microsoft and third-party add-ins. COM add-ins are a class of add-in objects introduced in Office 2000. See also *COM* and *Builder*.

ADO An abbreviation for ActiveX Data Objects, which are similar in concept to the Data Access Object (DAO) and Remote Data Object (RDO). ADO uses Microsoft's OLE Database (OLE DB) technology to access data from various data sources, including text files and mainframe databases. ADO is a member of the Microsoft Data Access Components (MDAC.) ADO 2.7 is the preferred database connectivity method for Access 2003. See also *MDAC*, *MSDE*, and *OLE DB*.

ADO MD An abbreviation for ADO Multidimensional (Expressions), the Automation library that provides access to CubeDef and Cellset objects created with the PivotTable Service or Microsoft SQL Server Analysis Services (formerly Microsoft Decision Support Services, MSDSS, and OLAP Services). See also *Cellset*, *CubeDef*, *MDX*, *OLAP*, and *PivotTable Service*.

ADODB An abbreviation and object library name for ADO 2.x. ADODB is used as an object prefix to specify the source of an ADO data object, as in `ADODB.Recordset`.

ADOX An abbreviation for ActiveX Data Object Extensions, a set of extensions to ADO 2.1+ that support Jet 4.0's new SQL Data Definition Language reserved words, such as `CREATE GROUP` and `ALTER USER`. See also *data definition*.

ADP An abbreviation for Access data projects, an alternative to conventional Access client/server applications that store application objects (forms and reports) in Jet .mdb files. ADP requires an ADO 2.1+ connection to one of the five versions of SQL Server 7.0 or 2000 (Desktop or MSDE, Personal, Developer, Standard, Enterprise, or DataCenter editions). ADP stores application objects in OLE docfiles having an .adp or .ade (encrypted) extension. See also *ADO*, *application object*, *docfile*, and *MSDE*.

ADTG An abbreviation for Advanced Data TableGram, a Microsoft-proprietary MIME format used by Remote Data Services (RDS) to marshal Recordsets between client and server via the HTTP protocol. By default, ADO `Recordsets` saved to files use the ADTG format. See also *ADO*, *HTTP*, *MIME*, and *RDS*.

Advanced Data TableGram See *ADTG*.

aggregate functions The ANSI SQL functions `AVG()`, `SUM()`, `MIN()`, `MAX()`, and `COUNT()`, and Jet SQL functions `StDev()`, `Var()`, `First()`, and `Last()`. Aggregate functions calculate summary values from a group of values in a specified column and are usually associated with `GROUP BY` and `HAVING` clauses. See also *domain aggregate functions*.

A

alias A temporary name assigned to a table in a self-join, to a column of a query, or to rename a table, implemented by the `AS` reserved word in ANSI SQL. You can use `AS` to rename any field or table with Jet SQL or SQL Server's Transact-SQL. `Alias` is also an embedded keyword option for the VBA `Declare` statement. The `Alias` keyword is used to register prototypes of DLL functions so that the function can be called from programs by another name. Aliasing the ANSI versions of 32-bit Windows API functions to function names without the A suffix is common when converting Access 97 and earlier applications to Access 2003, which uses Unicode for text data.

ANSI An acronym for the American National Standards Institute. ANSI in the Windows context refers to the ANSI character set that Microsoft decided to use for Windows (rather than the IBM PC character set that includes special characters such as those used for line drawing, called the OEM character set). The most common character set is ASCII (American Standard Code for Information Interchange), which for English alphabetic and numeric characters is the same as ANSI. Windows 98 and Windows NT include ANSI (suffix A) and Unicode (suffix W) versions of Windows API functions. ANSI also is the standards body responsible for the definition of SQL. The latest ANSI standard is SQL-99 (also called SQL:1999 and SQL3); most of today's RDBMSs support the previous version, SQL-92. See also *ASCII*, *SQL*, and *Unicode*.

application object Any object in a database application that doesn't contain or define data (data objects). Access forms, pages, reports, macros, and modules are examples of application objects. Production Access applications usually store application objects separately from data objects. See also *data object*.

argument A piece of data supplied to a function that the function uses or acts on to perform its task. Arguments are enclosed in parentheses. Additional arguments, if any, are separated by commas. Arguments passed to procedures usually are called parameters.

array An ordered sequence of values (elements) stored within a single named variable, accessed by referring to the variable name with the number of the element (index or subscript) in parentheses, as in `strValue = strArray(3)`. VBA arrays can have more than one dimension, in which case access to the value includes indexes for each dimension, as in `strValue = strArray(3,3)`.

ASCII An acronym for the American Standard Code for Information Interchange. A set of standard numerical values for printable, control, and special characters used by PCs and most other computers. Other commonly used codes for character sets are ANSI (used by Windows 3.1+), Unicode (used by Windows 98 and Windows NT), and EBCDIC (Extended Binary-Coded Decimal Interchange Code, used by IBM for mainframe computers). See also *ANSI* and *Unicode*.

ASP An acronym for Active Server Pages, Microsoft's server-side technology for dynamically creating standard HTML (Internet) Web pages. Conventional ASP uses VBScript or ECMAScript to manipulate ASP objects. Access 2003 lets you export tables, queries, and forms in ASP format for Web deployment. Exported .asp files send data in HTML tables to client browsers. ASP.NET is the successor to ASP. See also *ECMAScript*.

ASP.NET An .NET upgrade to ASP that supports the Simple Object Access Protocol (SOAP), managed code compiled by the Common Language Runtime (CLR) and Web Forms, a new methodology for designing interactive HTML forms. ASP.NET also supports the creation of XML Web services. See also *.NET*, *CLR*, *SOAP*, and *XML Web services*.

assign To give a value to a named variable.

asynchronous A process that can occur at any time, regardless of the status of the operating system or running applications.

attached table A table that's not stored in the currently open Jet database (a native table), but which you can manipulate as though the table were a native table. In Jet 3+ terminology, an attached table is a linked table. See also *linked table*.

authentication The process of verifying a user's identity, most commonly by a login ID and password.

Automation An ActiveX and OLE 2+ term that refers to a means of manipulating another application's objects.

Automation client An ActiveX- or OLE 2–compliant Windows application with an application programming (macro) language, such as VBA, that can reference and manipulate objects exposed by (OLE) Automation servers.

Automation server Technically, any COM-compliant Windows application that supports Automation operations by exposing a set of objects for manipulation by Automation client applications. This book restricts the term Automation server to applications that expose application objects, but aren't ActiveX full servers. The members of Office 2003 are examples of full Automation servers.

AutoNumber A Jet 3+ replacement for the Counter field data type of Jet 2.0, Access 1.x, and Access 2.0. AutoNumber fields can be of the Increment or Random type. Fields of the Increment AutoNumber field data type usually are used to create primary keys when a unique primary key can't be created easily from data in the table.

base date A date used as a reference from which other date values are calculated. In the case of VBA and SQL Server, the base date is January 1, 1900, 12:00 AM. Dates earlier than the base date are negative.

base tables The permanent tables from which a query is created, usually acting as the one side of a one-to-many relationship. Jet documentation also uses the term *base table* to refer to a table in the current database in contrast to a linked (attached) table. See also *linked table*.

batch A group of statements or database operations processed as an entity. Execution of DOS batch files, such as AUTOEXEC.BAT, and SQL statements are examples of batch processes.

A

batch update A process in which multiple update operations on a Recordset are conducted on a locally cached copy of the Recordset. When all updates are completed, calling the `UpdateBatch` method attempts to make permanent (persist) all changes to the underlying tables in a single operation. Access 2003's ADP and DAP support batch updates without the need to write VBA code.

binary string A string consisting of binary, not text, data that contains bytes outside the range of ANSI or ASCII values for printable characters or don't correspond to Unicode characters. Access 2003 requires that you store binary strings as arrays of the Byte data type to avoid problems with Unicode/ANSI conversion.

binding The process of connecting one object to another through interfaces. In Access 2003, local object binding is accomplished by COM interfaces and remote object binding by DCOM interfaces. See also *COM*, *COM+*, *DCOM*, and *data binding*.

bitwise A process that evaluates each bit of a combination, such as a byte or word, rather than process the combination as a single element. Logical operations and masks use bitwise procedures.

Boolean A type of arithmetic in which all digits are bits—that is, the numbers can have only two states: on (true or 1) or off (false or 0). Widely used in set theory and computer programming, Boolean, named after the mathematician George Boole, also is used to describe a VBA data type that can have only two states: true or false. In VBA, true is represented by **`&HFF`** (all bits of an 8-bit byte set to 1) and false by **`&H0`** (all bits set to 0). **`Boolean`** is a VBA data type.

bound A term commonly used in Access applications to identify form, report, and control objects that are connected to and can receive values from data objects. See also *binding*.

breakpoint A designated statement that causes VBA program execution to halt after executing the statement preceding it. To toggle breakpoints on or off, press F9 on the line of code in Access's VBA editor before which you want execution to halt.

Briefcase replication A feature of Jet 3+ running under Windows 98 or Windows NT 4.0/2000 that permits the creation of Jet replication sets stored in Briefcase folders, which can be updated by mobile users. ADO 2.1+ supports Jet replication. See also *design-master* replica.

Builder A component that provides assistance in defining new objects, writing SQL statements, or creating expressions. Buttons with an ellipsis symbol commonly open Access Builders.

built-in functions Functions that are included in a computer language and don't need to be created by the programmer as user-defined functions. VBA has hundreds of built-in functions, many of which you can use in Jet queries.

business rules A set of rules for adding or altering data in a database that are specific to an enterprise's method of conducting its operations. Business rules are in addition to rules for maintaining the domain and referential integrity of tables in a database. Business rules most commonly are implemented in the middle-tier of a three-tier client/server database environment. See also *middle tier* and *three-tier*.

A

cache A block of memory reserved for temporary storage. Caches usually store data from disk files in memory to speed access to the data. Access Recordset objects, which store in memory an image of data in tables or returned by queries are typical cached objects.

CAL An acronym for Client Access License, which are required for client PCs connecting to Microsoft server products, such as Windows 2000+/NT, SQL Server 2000, and Exchange 2000. With the exception of bundled server products, such as Small Business Server 2000+ and BackOffice 2000+, separate CALs are required for each server product. CALs aren't required for local installation of or connections to MSDE, which is covered by an Office XP license. You do, however, require a CAL if a local copy of MSDE connects to SQL Server 2000, such as occurs with SQL Server merge replication. See *MSDE.*

Cartesian product Named for Ren[as]e Descartes, a French mathematician. The term describes `JOIN` operations that return all possible combinations of rows and columns from each table in a database. The number of rows in a Cartesian product is equal to the number of rows in table 1 times that in table 2 times that in table 3, and so on. Cartesian rows that don't satisfy the `JOIN` condition are disregarded.

cascading deletion A process that deletes data from one table based on a deletion from another table to maintain referential integrity. Triggers and declarative referential integrity (DRI) are two means of implementing cascading deletions. DRI or triggers usually are used to delete detail data (such as invoice items) when the master record (invoice) is deleted. Jet 2+ and SQL Server 7.0+ provide cascading deletion as an optional element of its referential integrity features. See also *DRI* and *referential integrity*.

cascading update A process that automatically changes foreign key values to correspond to altered values of a primary key. DRI or triggers implement cascading updates, which are another optional referential integrity element.

Cellset The multidimensional equivalent of an ADO Recordset. See also *ADO MD*, *CubeDef*, *OLAP*, and *PivotTable Service*.

chaptered Recordset See *hierarchical Recordset.*

child In Access, a reference to the table or query that serves as the record source for a subform, subreport, or subdatasheet. Also used in computer programming in general to describe an object that's related to but lower in hierarchical level than a parent object.

class identifier See *CLSID*.

clause The portion of an SQL statement beginning with a keyword that names a basic operation to be performed.

client The device or application that receives data from or manipulates a server device or application. The data might be in the form of a file received from a network file server, an object from an ActiveX component or Automation server, or values from a DDE server assigned to client variables. See also *Automation client*.

A

client tier A logical entity that represents a networked computer where an Access application interacts with a client/server database or a browser displays a Web page from a remote data source. The client tier often is called the *presentation tier*. See also *middle tier* and *data source* tier.

CLR The abbreviation for Common Language Runtime, the unifying components of the .NET Framework to support intercommunication of components written in different programming languages, such as Visual Basic .NET, managed Visual C++, and Visual C#. Excel 2003 and Word 2003 support the CLR as a macro language, in addition to VBA; Microsoft chose not to support CLR programming for Access 2003 and Outlook 2003.

CLSID An identification tag that's associated with an Automation object created by a specific server. CLSID values appear in the Registry and must be unique for each ActiveX component or Automation server and for each type of object that the server can create. See also *Registry*.

clustered index An index in which the physical record order and index order of a table are the same. SQL Server offers the option of using a clustered (recommended) or nonclustered index on the primary key of a table.

coercion The process of forcing a change from one data type to another, such as `Integer` to `String`. VBA supports type coercion; Visual Basic .NET coerces data types unless explicitly instructed not to by adding an `Option Strict On` instruction prior to the first line of code.

collection A group of objects of the same class that are contained within another object. Collections are named as the plural of their object class—for example, the `Parameters` collection is a group of `Parameter` objects contained in a `Command` object.

COM An acronym for Component Object Model, the name of Microsoft's design strategy to implement ActiveX. Distributed COM (DCOM) allows networked and cross-platform implementation of ActiveX and Automation. See also *DCOM*.

COM+ A feature of Windows 2000 and later Windows server operating systems that integrates COM, DCOM, and elements of MSMQ into the operating system. COM+ adds event services, load balancing, asynchronous queuing services with MSMQ, and an in-memory database for the MTS catalog. See also *COM*, *DCOM*, *MSMQ*, and *MTS*.

comment Explanatory material within source code not designed to be interpreted or compiled into the final application. In VBA, comments are usually preceded by an apostrophe (`'`) but can also be created by preceding them with the `Rem` keyword.

common dialog A standardized dialog, provided by Windows, that can be created by a Windows API function call to functions contained in Cmdlg32.dll and its successors. Common dialogs include File Open, File Save, Print and Printer Setup, ColorPalette, Font, and Search and Replace. Access 2003 provides the `Application.FileDialog` object as a simpler alternative to the File Open and File Save common dialogs.

comparison operators See *operator*.

A

compile To create an executable or object (machine-language) file from source (readable) code. In Access, compile means to create pseudocode (tokenized code), not native code, from the VBA source code you write in the code-editing window. The .NET Framework's CLR compiles source code to an intermediate language (IL) which executes on a specified processor class, such as Intel's x86 or Itanium processors.

Component Object Model See *COM*.

composite key or index A key or index based on the values in two or more columns. See also *index* and *key or key field*.

compound In computer programming, a set of instructions or statements that requires more than one keyword or group of related keywords to complete. **`Select Case...Case...End Select`** is an example of a compound statement in VBA.

concatenation Combining two expressions, usually strings, to form a longer expression. The concatenation operator is **`&`** in Jet SQL and VBA, although VBA also permits and Transact-SQL requires the + symbol to be used to concatenate strings.

concurrency The condition when more than one user has access to a specific set of records or files at the same time. Also used to describe the capability of a database management system to handle simultaneous and potentially conflicting update queries against a single set of tables.

container An object or application that can create or manipulate compound documents or host ActiveX controls.

CORBA An acronym for Common Object Request Broker Architecture, the primary competitor to Microsoft's COM- and DCOM-based technologies. See also *COM*, *COM+*, and *DCOM*.

correlated subquery A subquery that can't be evaluated independently. Subqueries depend on an outer query for their result. See also *subquery* and *nested query*.

counter A special field data type of Access 1.x and 2.0, and Jet 2.0 tables that numbers each new record consecutively; called an AutoNumber field in Jet 3+. See also *AutoNumber*.

CubeDef An ADO MD object that provides the metadata for multidimensional data, such as that provided by Microsoft SQL Server Analysis or PivotTable Services. See also *ADO MD*, *Cellset*, *OLAP*, and *PivotTable Service*.

current database The database opened in Access by choosing File, Open Database (or the equivalent) that contains the objects of an Access application.

current record The record in a `Recordset` object whose values are available to bound forms, reports, and controls. The current record supplies values of the record's data cells to control objects that are bound to the table's fields. The current record is specified by a record pointer.

DAP An abbreviation for data access pages, a Web-based technology introduced in Access 2000 for generating data-bound Dynamic HTML pages for use on intranets. DAP use the Data Source Control (DSC) for data binding and other ActiveX Controls, such as the Office Web Components (OWC), for displaying and manipulating data. See also *DHTML*, *DSC*, and *OWC*.

Data Access Object The original container for all database objects in Access, often abbreviated DAO. The top member of the Jet DAO hierarchy is the `DBEngine` object, which contains `Workspace`, `User`, and `Group` objects in collections. Database objects are contained in `Workspace` objects. ADO 2.7 is the preferred alternative to DAO 3.6 in Access 2003, although ADO 2.1–2.6 are supported for backward compatibility. See also *ADO*.

Data access pages See *DAP*.

data binding Connecting two or more data-related objects, usually a data consumer to a data provider, to pass a `Recordset` or other data object between objects. Access 2003 has the capability to bind a variety of OLE DB data providers to OLE DB data consumers via ADO. See also *ADO*, *data consumer*, *data object*, and *data provider*.

data consumer An OLE DB term for an object that presents and/or manipulates data. All Access 2003 data-bound controls are capable of being OLE DB data consumers.

data definition The process of describing databases and database objects such as tables, indexes, views, procedures, rules, default values, triggers, and other characteristics. SQL's Data Definition Language (DDL) defines the components of SQL-compliant databases.

data dictionary The result of the data definition process. Also used to describe a set of database system tables that contain the data definitions of database objects, often called metadata.

data element The value contained in a data cell, also called a data item or simply an element. A piece of data that describes a single property of a data entity, such as a person's first name, last name, Social Security number, age, sex, or hair color. In this case, the person is the data entity.

data entity A distinguishable set of objects that is the subject of a data table and usually has at least one unique data element. A data entity might be a person (unique Social Security number), an invoice (unique invoice number), or a vehicle (unique vehicle ID number, because license plates aren't necessarily unique across state lines).

data integrity The maintenance of rules that prevent inadvertent or intentional modifications to the content of a database that would compromise its accuracy or reliability. See also *domain integrity* and *referential integrity*.

data object A component of a database. Data objects include tables, views, indexes, stored procedures, columns, rules, triggers, database diagrams, and defaults. See also *application object*.

data provider An OLE DB term for an object that connects to a database or other source of persistent data and supplies data to a data consumer. The SQLOLEDB OLE DB data provider for SQL Server is an example of a native OLE DB provider. MSDASQL, the OLE DB data provider for ODBC, is a nonnative (indirect) data provider.

data shaping The process of creating a hierarchical (also called chaptered) `Recordset` object using `SHAPE` syntax. See also *hierarchical Recordset* and `SHAPE` *statements*.

data sharing The feature that allows more than one user to access information stored in a database from the same or a different application. Multiuser Access applications that use Jet databases employ data sharing.

data source A database or other form of persistent (file) data storage. Data source commonly is used to describe an ODBC data source name (DSN). In Access 2003, a data source is a named OLE DB data provider or service provider.

Data Source Control See *DSC*.

data source tier A logical entity that represents a server running a client/server RDBMS, such as SQL Server, also called the data services tier. See also *client tier*, *middle tier*, and *three-tier*.

data type The description of how the computer is to interpret a particular item of data. Data types are generally divided into three families: strings that usually have text or readable content, numeric data, and objects. The types of numeric data supported vary with the compiler or interpreter. Most programming languages support a user-defined record or structure data type that can contain multiple data types within it. Field data types, which define the data types of values in Jet and SQL Server database tables, are distinguished from VBA data types in this book.

database A set of related data tables and other database objects, such as a data dictionary or database diagram, that are organized as a group.

database administrator The individual(s) responsible for the administrative functions of client/server databases. The database administrator (DBA) has privileges (permissions) for all commands that might be executed by the RDBMS and is ordinarily responsible, directly or indirectly, for maintaining system security, including access by users to the RDBMS itself and performing backup and restoration functions.

database device A file in which databases and related information, such as transaction logs, are stored. Database devices usually have physical names (such as a filename) and a logical name (the parameter of the `USE` statement). In SQL Server 6.5 and earlier, database devices use the .dat file extension. SQL Server 7.0+ dispenses with database devices and stores databases and logs in conventional operating system files with .mdf and .ldf extensions, respectively.

database owner The user who originally created a database. The database owner has control over all the objects in the database but can delegate control to other users. Access calls the database owner the creator. The database owner is identified by the prefix `dbo` in SQL Server.

date function A function that provides date and time information or manipulates date and time values.

DCOM An acronym for Distributed Common Object Model. Allows communication and manipulation of objects over a network connection. Windows NT 4.0 was the first Microsoft operating system to support DCOM (formerly called NetworkOLE). Microsoft's goal for its .NET technologies is to replace DCCOM with XML Web services. See also *COM*, *COM+*, and *XML Web services*.

DDE An abbreviation for dynamic data exchange. DDE is a method that early versions of Windows and OS/2 use to transfer data between different applications. Automation implemented by ActiveX components provides a more robust method for communication between applications or components of applications. DDE is obsolete.

deadlock A condition that occurs when two users with a lock on one data item attempt to lock the other's data item. Most RDBMSs detect this condition, prevent its occurrence, and advise both users of the potential deadlock situation.

debug The act of removing errors in the source code for an application.

declaration A statement that creates a user-defined data type, names a variable, creates a symbolic constant, or registers the prototypes of functions incorporated within dynamic link libraries.

declarations section A section of a VBA module reserved for statements containing declarations, such as **`Public`** or **`Private`** variables.

declarative referential integrity See *DRI*.

declare In text and not as a keyword, to create a user-defined data holder for a variable or constant. As a VBA keyword, to register a function contained in a dynamic link library in the declarations section of a module.

default A value assigned or an option chosen when no value is specified by the user or assigned by a program statement.

default database The logical name of the database assigned to a user when logging in to the database application.

dependent A condition in which master data in a table (such as invoices) is associated with detail data in a subsidiary table (invoice items). In this case, invoice items are dependent on invoices.

design-master replica The member of a Jet replica set that allows changes in the design of objects, such as tables. The design-master replica usually (but not necessarily) is the .mdb file that is updated by briefcase replicas of the file. See also *Briefcase replication*.

Design mode One of two modes of operation of Access, also called design time or Design view. Design mode lets you create and modify database objects and write VBA code. The other mode is Run mode, also called runtime (when the application is executing).

DHTML An abbreviation for Dynamic HTML, an extension of HTML 4.0 that permits client-side scripting to modify the appearance and/or content of a Web page without requiring repeated round trips to the Web server. Early Web browsers implemented DHTML differently, so DHTML was suitable only for intranets on which all clients run a single browser. Most current browsers have very similar DHTML interpreters, which makes DHTML practical for Internet use.

disconnected Recordset A `Recordset` object that is cached on the client and doesn't have an active connection to its source database. After editing the data in an updatable disconnected Recordset, reconnecting to the server updates the database. Use of disconnected Recordsets, which requires VBA code, minimizes the number of simultaneous connections to the database. Access 2003's ADP support disconnected Recordsets. See also *Recordset.*

distributed database A database, usually of the client/server type, that's located on more than one database server, often at widely separated locations. Synchronization of data contained in distributed databases is most commonly accomplished by the two-phase commit or replication methods. See also *replication* and *two-phase commit.*

Distributed Transaction Coordinator See *DTC.*

DLL An abbreviation for dynamic link library, a file containing a collection of Windows functions designed to perform a specific class of operations. Most DLLs carry the .dll extension, but some Windows DLLs, such as Gdi32.exe, use the .exe extension. Applications call (invoke) functions within DLLs, as necessary, to perform the desired operation.

docfile The file format for creating persistent OLE objects, now called ActiveX documents. ADP use docfiles to store application objects.Docfiles include file property values derived from the File menu's Properties command. See also *ActiveX documents* and *ADP.*

domain aggregate functions A set of functions, identical to the SQL aggregate functions, such as `Sum` or `Max` that you can incorporate within Jet queries. See also *aggregate functions.*

domain integrity The process of assuring that values added to fields of a table comply with a set of rules for reasonableness and other constraints. For example, domain integrity is violated if you enter a ship date value that's earlier than an order date. Jet maintains domain integrity by field-level and table-level validation rules. See also *business rules.*

DRI An abbreviation for declarative referential integrity, a set of SQL-92 SQL keywords, including `CONSTRAINT`, `FOREIGN KEY`, `REFERENCES`, and `CASCADE`, which, when included in the `CREATE TABLE` statement, enforce referential integrity rules for the table. Jet enforces referential integrity by an internal programming mechanism. SQL Server 7.0+ supports DRI; earlier versions used triggers to handle referential integrity violations. See also *referential integrity* and *trigger.*

DSC An abbreviation for Data Source Control, one of the four Office Web Components (OWC). The DSC provides data binding for Data access pages. See also *DAP* and *OWC*.

DTC An abbreviation for Microsoft's Distributed Transaction Coordinator, a feature of SQL Server required to support distributed transactions and Microsoft Transaction Server (MTS). See also *distributed database* and *MTS*.

dynamic data exchange See *DDE*.

dynamic link library See *DLL*.

dynaset A set of rows and columns in your computer's memory that represent the values in an attached table, a table with a filter applied, or a query result set. You can update the values of the fields of the underlying table(s) by changing the values of the data cells of an updatable dynaset object. In Jet 2+, `Dynaset` is a type of `Recordset` object. See also *Recordset*.

ECMAScript The official name for Netscape's JavaScript, now that standardization of JavaScript is under the aegis of the European Computer Manufacturers Association (ECMA). Microsoft's version of ECMAScript is JScript.

empty A condition of a VBA **`Variant`** variable that has been declared but hasn't been assigned a value. Empty is not the same as the **`Null`** value, nor is it equal to the empty or zero-length string (`""`). Assigning an empty **`Variant`** to a **`String`** variable, however, results in a zero-length string.

enabled The capability of a control object to respond to user actions such as a mouse click, expressed as the **`True`** or **`False`** value of the `Enabled` property of the control.

equi-join A `JOIN` in which the values in the columns being joined are compared for equality. Only those rows with matching column values appear in the query result set. Access queries default to equi-joins—also called inner joins. See also *outer join*, and *self-join*.

error trapping A procedure by which errors generated during the execution of an application are rerouted to a designated group of code lines (called an *error handler*) that performs a predefined operation, such as ignoring the error. If errors aren't trapped in VBA, the standard modal message dialog with the text message for the error that occurred appears.

event The occurrence of an action taken by the user and recognized by one of the object's event properties, such as VBA's `Click` and `DblClick` event handlers for most controls. Events are usually related to mouse movements and keyboard actions; however, events also can be generated by code with the Timer control object and during manipulation of database objects. ADO `Connection`, `Command`, and `Recordset` objects trigger many data-related events.

exclusive lock A lock that prevents others from locking data items until the exclusive lock is cleared. Exclusive locks are placed on data items by update operations, such as SQL's `INSERT`, `UPDATE`, and `DELETE`. Jet and SQL Server 6.5 use page locking. SQL Server 6.5 provides row locking for `INSERT` operations, and SQL Server 7.0+ provides both `INSERT` and `UPDATE` row locking.

exponent The second element of a number expressed in scientific notation, the power of 10 by which the first element, the mantissa, is multiplied to obtain the actual number. For +1.23E3, the exponent is 3, so you multiply 1.23 by 1,000 (10 to the third power) to obtain the result 1,230.

expression A combination of variable names, values, functions, and operators that return a result, usually assigned to a variable name. `Result = 1 + 1` is an expression that returns `2` to the variable named `Result`. `DiffVar = LargeVar-SmallVar` returns the difference between the two variables to `DiffVar`. Functions can be used in expressions, and the expression can return the value determined by the function to the same variable as that of the argument. `strVar = Mid$(strVar, 2, 3)` replaces the value of `strVar` with three of its characters, starting at the second character.

extended properties A new feature of SQL Server 2000, which supports properties previously restricted to Jet databases, such as lookup fields, subdatasheets, master-child table relationships, text for data validation messages, data-entry masks, and column formatting.

facts table The table of a multidimensional database, also called a measures table, that stores numeric data (metrics). The facts table is related to the dimension tables. See also *ADO MD*, *metrics*, *PivotTable Service*, *star schema*, and *snowflake schema*.

field Synonym for a column that contains attribute values. Also, a single item of information in a record or row.

fifth normal form The rule for relational databases requiring that a table that has been divided into multiple tables must be capable of being reconstructed to its exact original structure by one or more `JOIN` statements.

first normal form The rule for relational databases which dictates that tables must be flat. Flat tables can contain only one data value set per row. Members of the data value set, called data cells, are contained in one column of the row and must have only one value.

flag A variable, usually **`Boolean`** (**`True`**/**`False`**), which is used to determine the status of a particular condition within an application. The term *set* is often used to indicate turning a flag from **`False`** to **`True`**, and *reset* for the reverse.

flow control In general usage, conditional expressions that control the execution sequence of instructions or statements in the source code of an application. **`If...Then...End If`** is a flow-control statement.

foreign key A column or combination of columns whose value must match a primary key in another table when joined with it. Foreign keys need not be unique for each record or row. See also *primary key*.

form In this book, an Access Form object contains the control objects that appear on its surface and the code associated with the events, methods, and properties applicable to the form and its control objects.

form level Variables that are declared in the Declarations section of an Access form. These variables are said to have form-level scope and aren't visible to procedures outside the `Form` object in which the variables are declared.

fourth normal form The rule for relational databases which requires that only related data entities be included in a single table and that tables cannot contain data related to more than one data entity when many-to-one relationships exist among the entities.

front end When used with database management systems, an application used to access and view database records, as well as add to, edit, or delete them.

function A subprogram called from within an expression in which a value is computed and returned to the program that called it through its name. Functions are classified as internal to the application language when their names are keywords. You can create your own user-defined functions in VBA by adding code between **`Function`** *`FunctionName`*`...`**`End Function`** statements.

function (SQL Server) A new SQL Server 2000 feature, which substitutes for views and stored procedures that return a single Recordset. Unlike views, you can specify the name of a user-defined function as the data source for a `SELECT` query. Functions enable ADP to execute the equivalent of nested Jet queries (a query against a `SELECT` query's Recordset). Functions also can return numeric and character (scalar) values.

global Pertaining to the program as a whole. Global variables and constants are accessible to, and global variables can be modified by, code at the form, module, and procedure level. VBA uses the reserved word **`Public`** to create or refer to global variables.

globally-unique identifier See *GUID*.

group In reports, one or more records that are collected into a single category, usually for the purpose of totaling. Database security systems use the term group to identify a collection of database users with common permissions. See also *permissions*.

GUID An acronym for globally-unique identifier, pronounced "goo-id." GUIDs consist of 32 hexadecimal characters surrounded by French braces, as in {00000535-0000-0010-8000-00AA006D2EA4}, which the operating system creates from a combination of numeric values, including PC-specific values. COM makes extensive use of GUIDs to identify objects, interfaces, and other COM elements. Jet 4.0 and SQL Server 7.0+ have a GUID data type, primarily used to uniquely identify rows in a table for replication purposes.

handle An unsigned **`Long`** integer assigned by Windows to uniquely identify an instance (occurrence) of a module (application, `hModule`), task (`hTask`), window (`hWnd`), or device context (`hDC`) of a graphic object. Handles in 32-bit Windows applications are 32-bit unsigned long integers (dw, or double words). Also used to identify the sizing elements of control objects in Design mode. See also *sizing handle*.

hierarchical Recordset A Recordset that contains detail records in the form of a **`Variant`** array. Hierarchical Recordsets are more efficient than conventional Recordsets for displaying one-to-many query result sets, because cells of the one side aren't repeated. The

PivotTable component is capable of displaying hierarchical Recordsets in Access's PivotTable view and DAP. See also *Cellset*, *CubeDef*, *MDX*, *OLAP*, and *PivotTable Service*.

A

host Any computer on a network running an Internet Protocol (IP). See also *IP* and *IP address*.

HTTP An abbreviation for Hypertext Transport Protocol, the transport protocol used by the World Wide Web and private intranets.

identifier A synonym for name or symbol, usually applied to variable and constant names.

index For arrays, the position of the particular element with respect to others, usually beginning with 0 as the first element. In the context of database files or tables, index refers to a lookup table, usually in the form of a file or component of a file, that relates the value of a field in the indexed file to its record or page number and location in the page (if pages are used).

InfoPath—A new Microsoft form design and development tool—codenamed XDocs during its early beta period—for displaying and manipulating XML data. InfoPath uses XML schemas to validate data entry and XSLT to create form-based views of the data. The primary data sources for InfoPath forms are XML document files and XML Web services. Alternatively, InfoPath can use ADO to connect to Jet and SQL Server databases directly. The official name of InfoPath 1.0 is Microsoft Office InfoPath 2003. InfoPath can substitute for Access 2003's ADP for many applications. See also *ADP*, *ADO*, *XML Schema*, *XML Web services*, and *XSLT*.

initialize In programming, setting all variables to their default values and resetting the point of execution to the first executable line of code. Initialization is accomplished automatically in VBA when you start an application.

inner query Synonym for subquery. See also *subquery*.

in-process A term applied to Automation servers, also called ActiveX DLLs, that operate within the same process space (memory allocation) of the Automation client. In-process servers commonly are called InProc servers.

instance (SQL Server) A named SQL Server running on a Windows 2000/NT server. The default instance is the server's computer name. All versions of SQL Server 2000 except MSDE and the Personal Edition permit running multiple, independent instances of SQL Server on a single server. Instances other than the default instance are called *named instances*.

integer A whole number. In most programming languages, an integer is a data type that occupies two bytes (16 bits). Integers can have signs (as in the VBA **`Integer`** data type), taking on values from –32,768 to +32,767, or be unsigned. In the latter case, integers can represent numbers up to 65,535. SQL Server's `integer` datatype is a 32-bit bit value, which corresponds to VBA's **`Long`** datatype.

intersection The group of data elements included in both tables that participate in a `JOIN` operation.

intranet A private network that uses Internet protocols and common Internet applications (such as Web browsers) to emulate the public Internet. Intranets on LANs and high-speed WANs provide increased privacy and improved performance compared with today's Internet.

invoke To cause execution of a block of code, particularly a procedure or subprocedure. Invoke also indicates application of a method to an object.

IP An abbreviation for Internet Protocol, the basic network transmission protocol of the Internet.

IP address The 32-bit hexadecimal address of a host, gateway, or router on an IP network. For convenience, IP addresses are specified as the decimal value of the four address bytes, separated by periods, as in `124.33.15.1`. Addresses are classified as types A, B, and C, depending on the subnet mask applied. See also *subnet mask*.

JDBC An abbreviation for Java Database Connector, despite Sun Microsystems' insistence that JDBC "doesn't stand for anything." JDBC is Java's purportedly platform-agnostic version of ODBC, which it closely resembles.

Jet Microsoft's name for the database engine native to Access and Visual Basic. The name Jet came from the acronym for Joint Engine Technology, an early predecessor of Jet 4.0 used by Access 2003.

Jet SQL The dialect of ANSI SQL used by the Data Access Object and by all versions of Microsoft Access. For the most part, Access SQL complies with ANSI SQL-92. Jet SQL offers additional features, such as the capability to include user-defined functions within queries. See also *Transact-SQL*.

join A basic operation, initiated by the SQL `JOIN` statement, which links the rows or records of two or more tables by one or more columns in each table. See also *equi-join*, *outer join*, and *self-join*.

key or key field A field that identifies a record by its value, also called a *primary key* [field]. Access automatically creates an index on primary key fields, which must consist of unique values. See also *primary key* and *foreign key*.

key value A value of a key field included in an index.

keyword A word that has specific meaning to the interpreter or compiler in use and causes predefined events to occur when encountered in source code. Keywords and reserved words are not exactly the same. You can use keywords as variable, procedure, or function names, but you can't use reserved words as variable or constant names. Using keywords for this purpose, however, isn't a good programming practice.

label In VBA programming, a name given to a target line in the source code at which execution results on the prior execution of a **`GoTo`** *`LabelName`* instruction. A label also is an Access control object that displays, but can't update, character values.

LAN An acronym for local area network, a system comprising multiple computers that are physically interconnected through network adapter cards and cabling. LANs allow one computer to share specified resources, such as disk drives, printers, and modems, with other computers on the LAN.

leaf level The lowest level of an index. Indexes derive the names of their elements from the objects found on trees, such as trunks, limbs, and leaves.

library A collection of functions, compiled as a group and accessible to applications by calling the function name and any required arguments. DLLs are one type of library; those used by compilers to provide built-in functions are another type.

library database An Access database that's automatically attached to Access when you launch it. Access library databases usually have the extension .mda; compiled libraries, which hide the original source code, use the extension .mde. Attachment of library databases to Access is controlled by Registry entries.

linked table A table that's not stored in the currently open Access database (native table), but which you can manipulate as though it were a native table. Linked tables were called attached tables in Access 1.x and 2.0, and Jet 2.0.

livelock A request for an exclusive lock on a data item that's repeatedly denied because of shared locks imposed by other users.

local The scope of a variable declared within a procedure, rather than at the form, module, or global level. Local variables are visible (defined) only within the procedure in which they were declared. VBA uses the prefix `Private` to define functions, subprocedures, and variable of local scope.

local area network See *LAN*.

lock A restriction of access to a table, portion of a table, or data item imposed to maintain data integrity of a database. Locks can be shared, in which case more than one user can access the locked element(s), or exclusive, in which the user with the exclusive lock prevents other users from creating simultaneous shared or exclusive locks on the element(s). Jet classifies locks as optimistic (a lock applied only when physically changing table data) and pessimistic (a lock applied for the duration of the user's editing operation.) Access 2003 uses page locks (8KB of the .mdb file), which can lock several adjacent records; earlier versions of Access used 2KB pages. Some RDBMSs provide row locks that lock only a single record. SQL Server 6.5 uses row locking for `INSERT` operations and page locking for `UPDATE` and `DELETE` operations. SQL Server 7.0+ offers row locking for all three operations.

logical A synonym for Boolean, a data type that can have true or false values only. Logical is also used to define a class of operators whose result is only True or False. VBA includes a `Boolean` data type.

loop A compound program flow-control structure that causes statements contained between the instructions that designate the beginning and end of the structure to be repeatedly executed until a given condition is satisfied. When the condition is satisfied, program execution continues at the source code line after the loop termination statement.

mantissa The first element of a number expressed in scientific notation that's multiplied by the power of 10 given in the exponent to obtain the actual number. For +1.23E3, the exponent is 3, so you multiply the mantissa, 1.23, by 1,000 (10 to the third power) to obtain the result: 1,230.

master database A database that controls user access to other databases, usually in a client/server system.

master table A table containing data on which detail data in another table depends. Master tables have a primary key that's matched to a foreign key in a detail table and often have a one-to-many relationship with detail tables. Master tables usually are called base tables.

MDAC An abbreviation for Microsoft Data Access Components, a collection of the files required to implement Microsoft's Universal Data Access strategy. MDAC includes ActiveX Data Objects (ADO), Remote Data Services (RDS), OLE DB, and ODBC. Office 2003 installs MDAC version 2.7, plus support for Jet databases. See also *ADO*, *ODBC*, *OLE DB*, *RDS*, and *Universal Data Access*.

MDX An acronym for Multidimensional Expressions, an SQL-like language for creating and manipulating multidimensional data (cubes) created by Microsoft SQL Server Analytical Services. See also *ADO MD*, *Cellset*, *CubeDef*, *OLAP*, and *PivotTable Service*.

Memo A Jet field data type that can store text with a length of up to about 64,000 bytes. (The length of Jet's Text field data type is limited to 255 bytes.)

metadata Data that describes the structure, organization, and/or location of data. Metadata commonly is called "data about data."

method One characteristic of an object and a classification of keywords in VBA. Methods are the procedures that apply to an Access object. Methods that apply to a class of objects are inherited by other objects of the same class and can be modified to suit the requirements of the object by a characteristic of an object.

metrics Numeric data, also called measures, contained within a facts table of a multidimensional database. See also *facts table*.

Microsoft Data Engine The desktop version of SQL Server 7.0 included with Access 2000, often called MSDE 1.0. See *MSDE*.

Microsoft SQL Server Desktop Edition See *MSDE*.

Microsoft Transaction Server See *MTS*.

middle tier A logical entity that connects a data source tier to a client tier and implements business rules or performs other data-related services. See also *business rule*, *client tier*, *data source tier*, and *three-tier*.

MIME An acronym for Multipurpose Internet Mail Extensions, an Internet standard that lets binary data be published and read on the Internet or intranets. The header of a file containing binary data exposes the MIME type of the data. Recordsets transported by RDS use a special MIME data type called the Advanced Data TableGram protocol (ADTG). See also *ADTG* and *RDS*.

mission critical A cliché used in software and hardware advertising to describe the need to use the promoted product if you want to create a reliable database system.

MOD An acronym for Microsoft Office Developer Edition, which includes a royalty-free license to distribute Msaccess.exe for runtime use, the runtime version of Microsoft Chart, additional ActiveX controls, and other distributable components of Access 97, 2000, and 2002. The Access 2003 Developer Extensions, which are part of the Visual Studio Tools (VST) for Microsoft Office System 2003, replace MOD. See also *Access 2003 Developer Extensions and VST*.

modal A window or dialog that must be closed before users can take further action within the application.

modeless A window or dialog that users can close or minimize without taking any other action; the opposite of modal.

module A block of code, consisting of one or more procedures, for which the source code is stored in a single location (a form or report class module, or public `Module` object in Access). In a compiled language, a code module is compiled to a single object file.

module level Variables and constants that are declared in the Declarations section of a VBA module, such as an Access `Module` object. These variables have module-level scope and are visible (defined) to all procedures contained within the module, unless declared **`Public`**, in which case the variables are visible to all procedures.

MSDE An acronym for Microsoft [SQL Server] Desktop Edition, a special version of Microsoft SQL Server 2000 that is included with Office 2003 but not installed by default. ADP use MSDE or other SQL Server versions as their only data source; DAP offer the option of connecting to MSDE. See also *ADP* and *DAP*.

MSMQ An acronym for Microsoft Message Queue Server, a middle-tier component (similar to Microsoft Transaction Server) that uses messaging techniques to permit execution of transactions over unreliable network connections. See also *middle tier*.

MTS An acronym for Microsoft Transaction Server, a component-based transaction monitor (TM) and object request broker (ORB) for developing, deploying, and managing the middle tier of component-based applications. Access 2003 applications can connect to MTS objects using VBA code. MTS is an integral component of COM+. See also *COM+*, *middle tier*, *ORB*, *three-tier*, and *TM*.

Multidimensional Expressions See *MDX*.

multiuser Concurrent use of a single computer by more than one user, usually through by way remote terminals. UNIX is inherently a multiuser operating system. Jet uses the term multiuser to refer to front-end database applications that share a common back-end .mdb file on a network file server.

Named Pipes A method of interprocess communication, originally developed for OS/2, that provides a secure channel for network communication. Named Pipes is one of the methods of connecting to an SQL Server database, but TCP/IP connections are more common.

natural join An SQL `JOIN` operation in which the values of the columns engaged in the join are compared, with all columns of each table in the join that don't duplicate other columns being included in the result. Same as an equi-join except that the joined columns aren't duplicated in the result. See also *equi-join*.

nested query An SQL `SELECT` statement that contains subqueries. See also *subquery*. An Access query that uses one or more queries—rather than tables—as it data source is called a nested query also.

newline pair A combination of a carriage return, the Enter key (CR or `Chr(13)`), and line feed (LF or `Chr(10)`) used to terminate a line of text onscreen or within a text file. Other characters or combinations can be substituted for the CR/LF pair to indicate the type of newline character (soft, hard, deletable, and so on). The VBA newline constant is `vbCrLf`.

nonclustered index An index that stores key values and pointers to data based on these values. In this case, the leaf level points to data pages rather than to the data itself, as is the case for a clustered index. Equivalent to `SET INDEX TO field_name` in xBase. See also *clustered index*.

normal forms A set of five rules, the first three originally defined by Dr. E.F. Cobb, that are used to design relational databases. Five normal forms are generally accepted in the creation of relational databases. See also *first normal form*, *second normal form*, *third normal form*, *fourth normal form*, and *fifth normal form*.

normalization Creation of a database according to the five generally accepted rules of normal forms. See also *normal forms*.

not-equal join A `JOIN` statement that specifies that the columns engaged in the join don't equal one another. In Access, you must specify a not-equal join by using the SQL `WHERE field1 <> field2` clause.

null A variable of no value or of unknown value. The default values—0 for numeric variables and an empty string ("") for string variables—aren't the same as the `Null` value. The `NULL` value in SQL statements specifies a data cell with no value assigned to the cell.

object In programming, elements that combine data (properties) and behavior (methods) in a single container of code called an object. Objects inherit their properties and methods from the classes above them in the hierarchy and can modify the properties and methods to suit their own purposes. The code container can be part of the language itself, or you can define your own objects in source code.

object library A file with the extension .olb that contains information on the objects, properties, and methods exposed by an .exe or .dll file of the same filename that supports Automation. See also *type library*.

object permissions Permissions granted by the database administrator for others to view and modify the values of database objects, including data in tables.

object request broker See *ORB*.

ODBC An abbreviation for the Microsoft Open Database Connectivity API, a set of functions that provide access to client/server RDBMSs, desktop database files, text files, and Excel worksheet files through ODBC drivers. ODBC most commonly is used to connect to client/server databases, such as Microsoft SQL Server, Sybase, IBM DB2/Informix, and Oracle. Microsoft intends for OLE DB to replace ODBC and won't provide significant enhancements for ODBC. See *ADO* and *OLE DB*.

ODBCDirect A feature of Access 97 and the Jet 3.5+ database engine that lets you use ODBC to access client/server databases without needing to load all of Jet 3.6. ODBCDirect conserves client resources if you need to connect only to SQL Server or another client/server RDBMS. ADO 2.1+ provides client/server features equivalent to ODBCDirect, so ODBCDirect is obsolete.

offset The number of bytes from a reference point, usually the beginning of a file, to the particular byte of interest. The first byte in a file, when offset is used to specify location, is always 0.

Office Web Components See *OWC*.

OLAP An acronym for online analytical processing, a technology that operates on nonrelational, multidimensional databases (data cubes). Microsoft SQL Server Analytical Services, a component of SQL Server 2000, enables the creation, manipulation, and distribution of multidimensional data. Analytical Services were called OLAP Services in SQL Server 7.0. See also *ADO MD*, *PivotTable Service*, *snowflake schema*, and *star schema*.

OLE DB A Microsoft framework for providing a uniform interface to data from various sources, including text files and mainframe databases. OLE DB replaces ODBC as a means of database access, but includes an ODBC provider that takes the place of the ODBC driver manager. ADO is an Automation wrapper for OLE DB. See also *ADO* and *ODBC*.

online analytical processing See *OLAP*.

OLTP An abbreviation for online transaction processing. OLTP most commonly refers to database applications that update multiple tables, such as order-entry and reservation systems, which use transaction processing to assure data integrity. See also *transaction*.

operand One variable or constant on which an operator acts. In `1 + 2 = 3`, `1` and `2` are operands, `+` and `=` are the operators. See also *operator*.

operator A keyword or reserved symbol that, in its unary form, acts on a single variable, or otherwise acts on two variables, to give a result. Operators can be of the conventional mathematics type such as + (add), – (subtract), / (divide), and * (multiply), as well as logical, such as **`And`** or **`Not`**. The unary minus (-), when applied to a single variable in a statement such as `intVar = -intVar`, inverts the sign of `intVar` from - to + or from + to -.

optimistic locking A method of locking a record or page of a table that makes the assumption that the probability of other users locking the same record or page is low. With optimistic locking, the record or page is locked only when the data is updated, not during the editing process (`LockType` property set to `adLockOptimistic`). See also *pessimistic locking*.

ORB An acronym for object request broker, a server-based application that provides a means for client applications to locate and instantiate middle-tier objects in three-tier applications. See also *middle tier*, *MTS*, and *three-tier*.

outer join An SQL `JOIN` operation in which all rows of the joined tables are returned, whether or not a match is made between columns. SQL database managers that don't support the `OUTER JOIN` reserved words use the `*=` (`LEFT JOIN`) operator to specify that all the rows in the preceding table return and the `=*` (`RIGHT JOIN`) to return all the rows in the succeeding table.

outer query A synonym for the primary query in a statement that includes a subquery. See also *subquery*.

OWC The abbreviation for Microsoft Office Web Components, which consist of the following four ActiveX Controls: Data Source (DSC), PivotChart, PivotTable, and Spreadsheet. The DSC is used only with DAP; the remaining three controls can be embedded in forms. Office 2003 installs OWC versions 10 and 11; upgrading ADP created in Access 2000 (OWC 9.0) and 2002 (OWC 10.0) changes the version to 11.0). OWC have special licensing restrictions for users of Access 2003 runtime applications who don't have Office 2003 licenses. See also *Access 2003 Developer Extensions*, *DAP*, *DSC*, *PivotChart*, *PivotTable*, and *Spreadsheet Control*.

page In tables of client/server RDBMSs, such as Microsoft SQL Server 7.0+, and Jet 3.6+ databases, a 8KB block that contains records of tables. Client/server and Jet databases lock pages, whereas other desktop databases usually lock individual records. Most RDBMSs require page locking when variable-length records are used in tables.

parameter The equivalent of an argument, but associated with the procedure that receives the value of an argument from the calling function. The terms *parameter* and *argument*, however, are often used interchangeably. An ADO `Parameter` object provides or returns a value to or from a query or a stored procedure.

permissions Authority given by the system administrator, database administrator, or database owner to perform operations on a network or on data objects in a database. Permissions also are called user rights.

persistent An object that's stored in the form of a file or an element of a file, rather than only in memory. Jet `Table` and `QueryDef` objects are persistent because they're stored in .mdb files. `Recordset` objects, on the other hand, usually are stored in memory. Such objects are called temporal or impersistent objects. ADO 2.x lets you persist `Recordset` objects as files.

pessimistic locking A method of locking a record or page of a table that makes the assumption that the probability of other users locking the same record or page is high. With pessimistic locking, the record or page is locked during the editing and updating process (`LockType` property set to `adLockPessimistic`). See also *optimistic locking*.

PivotChart An ActiveX Control that displays charts or graphs derived from data displayed by a PivotTable control. Access 2003 adds a new PivotChart view for tables, queries, and forms. The PivotChart control is a member of the Office Web Components (OWC). See also *OWC*.

PivotTable An ActiveX Control that displays data in spreadsheet format in which the user can expand or contract the level of detail displayed and interchange the axes of the data presentation. Access 2003 offers a PivotTable view of tables, queries, and forms. The PivotTable control is a member of the Office Web Components (OWC). See also *OWC*.

PivotTable Service A Microsoft-trademarked desktop OLAP implementation that used ADO MD to operate on persistent (file-based) multidimensional data cubes created by a subset of Microsoft SQL Server Analytical Services. The PivotTable service delivers hierarchical Recordsets to PivotTables. See also *ADO MD*, *Cellset*, *CubeDef*, *hierarchical Recordsets*, and *OLAP*.

point In typography, the unit of measurement of the vertical dimension of a font, about 1/72 of an inch. The point is also a unit of measurement in Windows, where it represents exactly 1/72 of a logical inch, or 20 twips. Unless otherwise specified, all distance measurements in VBA are in twips.

precedence The sequence of execution of operators in statements that contain more than one operator.

primary key The column or columns whose individual or combined values (in the case of a composite primary key) uniquely identify a row in a table.

procedure A self-contained collection of source code statements, executable as an entity. All VBA procedures begin with the reserved word **`Sub`** or **`Function`** (which can be preceded by the **`Public`**, **`Private`**, **`Static`**, or **`Property`** reserved words) and terminate with **`End Sub`** or **`End Function`**.

programmable object An object exposed by an Automation server with a set of properties and methods applicable to the object. The application programming language of an Automation client application can manipulate the exposed object.

projection A projection identifies the desired subset of the columns contained in a table. You create a projection with a query that defines the fields of the table you want to display but without criteria that limit the records that are displayed.

property One of two principal characteristics of objects (the other is methods). Properties define the manifestation of the object—for example, its appearance. Properties might be defined for an object or for the class of objects to which the particular object belongs, in which case they are said to be inherited.

proxy An object that supplies parameter marshaling and communication methods required by a client to instantiate an Automation component running in another execution environment, such as on a server. The proxy is located on the client PC and communicates with a corresponding stub on the server. The Office Web Services Toolkit's Web Service Reference tool automatically creates client proxies for XML Web services. See also *three-tier*, *WSR*, and *XML Web services*.

qualification A search condition that data values must meet to be included in the result of the search.

qualified To precede the name of a database object with the name of the database and the object's owner, or to precede the name of a file with its drive designator and the path to the directory in which the file is stored. The terms well-qualified path and well-formed path to a file appear often in documentation.

query A request to retrieve data from a database with the SQL `SELECT` instruction (select query) or to modify data in the database, called an action query by Access.

QueryDef A persistent Jet object that stores the Jet SQL statements that define a query. `QueryDef` objects are optimized, when applicable, by the Jet database engine's query optimizer and stored in a special format in the .mdb file.

RDBMS An abbreviation for relational database management system. An RDBMS is an application that can create, organize, and edit databases; display data through user-selected views; and, in some cases, print formatted reports. Most RDBMSs include at least a macro language, and most provide a system programming language. Access, dBASE, Paradox, and FoxPro are desktop RDBMSs. SQL Server and Oracle are typical client/server RDBMSs.

RDS An acronym for Remote Data Service, a lightweight version of ADO 2.x that provides transport for Recordset objects via DCOM or HTTP over intranets.

record A single element of a relational database table that contains a cell for each field defined for the table. A record is the logical equivalent of a row of a spreadsheet. This book uses *record* when referring to table data and *row* for query result sets.

Recordset A temporary local image of a table or a query result set stored in the PC's memory or virtual memory. Recordset objects are the primary means for manipulating data with VBA.

reference In VBA, the incorporation of pointers to specific sets of programmable objects exposed by Automation servers in a type library and manipulated by VBA code in the Automation client. You create a VBA reference to a set of objects exposed by an Automation component in the References dialog that's accessible by choosing Tools, References when a code module is the active Access object. After you declare a reference to the set of objects, the VBA interpreter checks the syntax of your code against the syntax specified for the referenced object. You also can use predefined intrinsic constants for the referenced objects in your VBA code. See also *type library*.

referential integrity Rules governing the relationships between primary keys and foreign keys of tables within a relational database that determine data consistency. Referential integrity requires the values of every foreign key in every table be matched by the value of a primary key in another table. Jet 2+ includes features for maintaining referential integrity, such as cascading updates and cascading deletions. SQL Server 7.0+ uses triggers or SQL's declarative referential integrity (DRI) keywords to maintain referential integrity. See also *DRI* and *trigger*.

refresh To redisplay records in Access's Datasheet views or in a form or report so as to reflect changes others in a multiuser environment have made to the records.

Registry A database that contains information required for the operation of 32-bit Windows The Registry also includes user information, such as user IDs, encrypted passwords, and permissions. Windows 98 and Windows XP/2003+/NT include Regedit.exe for editing the Registry. ActiveX components add entries to the Registry to specify the location of their .exe files. Automation servers add Registry entries for each object they expose.

relation Synonym for a table or a data table in an RDBMS.

relational database See *RDBMS*.

relational operators Operators such as `>`, `<`, `<>`, and `=` that compare the values of two operands and return `True` or `False` depending on the values compared. They are sometimes called comparison operators.

Remote Data Object (RDO) A substitute for Access 97's Jet 3.6 Data Access Object that provides a more direct connection to the ODBC API. ADO 2.1+ replaces RDO, which is now obsolete.

Remote Data Service See *RDS*.

replication The process of duplicating database objects (usually tables) in more than one location, including a method of periodically rationalizing (synchronizing) updates to the objects. Database replication is an alternative to the two-phase commit process. Microsoft SQL Server 7.0+ supports replication of databases across multiple Windows 2000+/NT servers. See also *Briefcase replication* and *two-phase commit*.

A

ReportML Microsoft's XML representation of the design of Access forms and reports that is used as an intermediary when saving Access 2003 forms and reports as XML files or converting forms and reports to DAP.

reserved word A word that's reserved for specific use by the programming language. You can't assign a reserved word as the name of a constant, variable, function, or subprocedure. Although the terms reserved word and keyword often are used interchangeably, they don't describe an identical set of words. VBA reserved words are set in **`bold monospace type`** in this book. See also *keyword.*

restriction A query statement that defines a subset of the rows of a table based on the value of one or more of its columns. A restriction more commonly is called a criterion.

rollback In transaction processing, the cancellation of a proposed transaction that modifies one or more tables and undoes changes, if any, made by the transaction before a `COMMIT` or `COMMIT TRANSACTION` SQL statement.

routine A synonym for procedure.

row A set of related columns that describe a specific data entity. Row is a synonym for record. This book uses *row* when referring to query result sets and *record* for data in tables.

row aggregation functions See *aggregate functions*.

rowset An OLE DB term for a set of rows returned by a fetch with a block cursor. ADO creates Recordsets from rowsets.

rule A specification that determines the data type and data value that can be entered in a column of a table. Rules are classified as validation rules and business rules. See also *business rules*.

Run mode The mode when Access 2003 is executing your application. Run mode is called runtime by Microsoft; however, the term runtime normally is used to describe the distributable version of Access (*runtime Access*) applications. See also *Access 2003 Developer Extensions*.

scope In programming, the extent of visibility (definition) of a variable. VBA has global (**`Public`**, visible to all objects and procedures in the application), form/report (**`Private`**, visible to all objects and procedures within a single form or report), module (visible to all procedures in a single module file), and local (**`Dim`**, visible only within the procedure in which declared) scope. The scope of a variable depends on where it's declared. See also *form level*, *global*, *local*, and *module level*.

second normal form The rule for relational databases requiring that columns that aren't key fields each be related to the key field—that is, a row might not contain values in data cells that don't pertain to the value of the key field. In an invoice item table, for instance, the columns of each row must pertain solely to the value of the invoice number key field.

seek To locate a specific byte, record, or chunk within a disk file. The `Seek` method of Access VBA can be used only with DAO `Recordset` objects of the `Table` type and requires that the table be indexed. ADO 2.1+ has a `Seek` method; previous versions of ADO didn't offer `Seek`.

select list The list of column names, separated by commas, that specify the columns to be included in the result of a `SELECT` statement.

self-join An SQL `JOIN` operation used to compare values within the columns of one table. Self-joins join a table with itself, requiring that the table be assigned two different names, one of which must be an alias.

separator A reserved symbol used to distinguish one item from another, as exemplified by the use of the exclamation point (`!`, bang character) in Access to separate the name of an object class from a specific object of the class, and an object contained within a specified object. The period separator (`.`, dot) separates the names of objects and their methods or properties.

sequential access file A file in which one record follows another in the sequence applicable to the application. Text files, for the most part, are sequential.

service provider An OLE DB term for an object that is both a data consumer and a data provider to another data consumer. OLE DB service providers include query engines and other intermediaries, such as the Remote Provider for enabling ADO 2.0+ data sources to use Remote Data Service. See also *RDS*.

session In DAO, an instance of the Jet database engine for a single user represented by the `Workspace` object. You can establish multiple sessions that become members of the `Workspaces` collection. With ADO, a `Connection` object represents a session. In RDBMS terminology, the period between the time that a user opens a connection to a database and the time that the connection to the database is closed.

`SHAPE` statements An SQL-like language for defining parent-child relationships within hierarchical Recordsets. See also *hierarchical Recordsets*.

shared lock A lock created by read-only operations that doesn't allow the user who creates the shared lock to modify the data. Other users can place shared locks on data so they can read it, but none can apply an exclusive lock on the data while any shared locks are in effect.

SID An acronym for security ID, a numeric value that identifies a logged-in user who has been authenticated by Windows NT or a user group. Access workgroup files use SIDs to authenticate users of secured Jet databases.

single-stepping A debugging process by which the source code is executed one line at a time to allow you to inspect the value of variables, find infinite loops, or remove other types of bugs.

sizing handle The small black rectangles on the perimeter of control objects that appear on the surface of the form or report in Design mode when the object is selected. You drag the handles of the rectangles to shrink or enlarge the size of control objects.

snowflake schema An alternative to the star schema for multidimensional data. Snowflake schema store dimension definitions in a set of hierarchical tables, rather than the star schema's individual tables. See also *ADO MD*, *facts table*, *PivotTable Service*, and *star schema*.

SOAP Originally an acronym for Simple Object Access Protocol, an XML-based messaging protocol for exchanging information between applications, usually over a network. SOAP is one of the primary enablers of XML Web services. SOAP has three parts: an envelope that describes and incorporates the message's content; rules for encoding and decoding the content; and methods for processing XML messages or to represent remote procedure calls (RPCs) and responses to RPCs. Office 2003 members and SQL Server 2000 support SOAP 1.1, which isn't a W3C standard. The May 8, 2000 SOAP 1.1 note is at `http://www.w3.org/TR/2000/NOTE-SOAP-20000508/`. The latest version of the W3C' SOAP 1.2 standard is at `http://www.w3.org/TR/soap12-part0/`. See also *WSDL* and *XML Web services*.

SOAP tookit—A set of components or libraries designed to simplify the process of encoding conventional data or objects as SOAP messages. Office 2003 installs elements of the Microsoft SOAP Toolkit 3.0 to enable writing VBA code that consumes XML Web services. SOAP Toolkit 3.0 also provides the Internet Services API (ISAPI) extensions needed to host (provide) Web services and filters to listen for incoming SOAP messages. See also *XML Web services*.

Spreadsheet Control An ActiveX Control that emulates an Excel worksheet. The Office 2003 version of the control can be bound to data. The Spreadsheet control is one of the Office Web Components (OWC). See also *OWC*.

SQL An acronym, pronounced "S-Q-L", for Structured Query Language, a language developed by IBM Corporation for processing data contained in mainframe computer databases. (Sequel is the name of a language, similar to SQL, developed by IBM but no longer in use.) SQL has now been institutionalized by the creation of an ANSI standard for the language.

SQL aggregate functions See *aggregate functions*.

star schema The most common schema (database design) for multidimensional data. Multiple base tables storing dimension definitions form the points of a star. The body of the star is the dependent facts table. See also *ADO MD*, *facts table*, *PivotTable Service*, and *snowflake schema*.

statement A syntactically acceptable (to the interpreter or compiler of the chosen language) combination of instructions or keywords and symbols, constants, and variables. A VBA statement must appear on a single line or use the line-continuation pair (a space followed by an underscore) to permit multiple-line statements.

static When referring to a variable, a variable that retains its last value until another is assigned, even though the procedure in which it is defined has completed execution. All global variables are static. VBA variables declared as **`Static`** are similar to global variables, but their visibility is limited to their declared scope. The term is also used to distinguish between statically linked (conventional) executable files and those that use DLLs.

stored procedure A set of SQL statements (and with those RDBMSs that support them, flow-control statements) that are stored under a procedure name so that the statements can be executed as a group by the database server. Some RDBMSs, such as Microsoft SQL Server, precompile stored procedures so that they execute more rapidly.

string A data type used to contain textual material, such as alphabetic characters and punctuation symbols. Numbers can be included in or constitute the value of string variables, but can't be manipulated by mathematical operators.

structure Two or more keywords used together to create an instruction, which is usually conditional in nature. In C, C#, and C++ programming, a user-defined data type. See also *compound*.

Structured Query Language See *SQL*.

stub A procedure or user-defined function that, in VBA, consists only of **`Sub`** *`SubName`*`...`**`End Sub`** or **`Function`** *`FnName`*`...`**`End Function`** lines with no intervening code. Access automatically creates stubs for subprocedures for event-handling code stored in `Form` and `Report` objects. Stubs block out the procedures required by the application that can be called by the main program. The intervening code statements are filled in during the programming process.

subform An Access form contained within another form, which commonly has a link to the data source for the parent form.

subnet mask A local bit mask (set of flags) that specifies which bits of the IP address specify a particular IP network or a host within a subnetwork. An IP address of `128.66.12.1` with a subnet mask of `255.255.255.0` specifies host `1` on subnet `128.66.12.0`. The subnet mask determines the maximum number of hosts on a subnetwork.

subprocedure A procedure called by a procedure other than the main procedure (`WinMain` in Windows). In Access, all procedures except functions are subprocedures because Msaccess.exe implements the `WinMain` function.

subquery An SQL `SELECT` statement that's included (nested) within another `SELECT`, `INSERT`, `UPDATE`, or `DELETE` statement or nested within another subquery.

subreport An Access report contained within another report.

syntax The set of rules governing the expression of a language, often called grammar. As with English, Spanish, Esperanto, or Swahili, programming languages each have their own syntax. Some languages allow much more latitude (irregular forms) in their syntax. VBA has a relatively rigid syntax, whereas C provides more flexibility at the expense of complexity. The syntax of SQL is defined by ANSI, but most RDBMS vendors add proprietary extensions to SQL. See also *ANSI*.

system administrator The individual(s) responsible for the administrative functions for all applications on a LAN or users of a UNIX cluster or network, usually including supervision of all databases on servers attached to the LAN. If the system administrator's (sa's) responsibility is limited to databases, the term database administrator (DBA) is ordinarily assigned.

system databases Databases that control access to databases on a server or across a LAN. Microsoft SQL Server has four system databases: the master database, which controls user databases; tempdb, which holds temporary tables; msdbdata for data relating to management tasks, and model, which is used as the skeleton to create new user databases. Any database that's not a user database is a system database.

system function Functions that return data about the database (metadata) rather than from the content of the database.

system object An object defined by Access rather than by the user. Examples of Access system objects are the `Application`, **`Screen`** and **`Debug`** objects.

system table A data dictionary table that maintains information on users of the database manager and each database under the control by the system. Jet system tables carry the prefix MSys and are hidden.

tab order The order in which the focus is assigned to multiple control objects within a form or dialog with successive pressing of the Tab key.

table A database object consisting of a group of records (rows) divided into fields (columns) that contain data or Null values. A table, which also is called a *relation*, is treated as a database object.

text file A disk file containing characters with values ordinarily ranging from `Chr(1)` through `Chr(127)` in which lines of text are separated from one another with newline pairs (`Chr(13) & Chr(10)`).

theta join An SQL `JOIN` operation that uses comparison or relational operators in the `JOIN` statement. See also *operator*.

third normal form The rule for relational databases which imposes the requirement that a column that's not a key column can't depend on another column that's not a key column. The third normal form is generally considered the most important because it's the first in the series that isn't intuitive.

three-tier The architecture of a database application, usually involving a client/server RDBSM, where the front-end application is separated from the back-end RDBMS by a middle-tier application. In Access applications, the middle tier usually is implemented as an ActiveX (Automation) component, which implements the database connection, enforces business rules, and handles transfer of data to and from databases of the RDBMS. See also *business rules*.

time stamp The date and time data attributes applied to a disk file when created or edited. SQL Server supports the `timestamp` field data type to resolve concurrency issues when updating tables.

timer A native Access form property that's invisible in Run mode and used to trigger a `Timer` event at preselected intervals.

TM An abbreviation for transaction monitor, an application that manages database transactions, usually between more than one database, to assure data consistency during `INSERT` and `UPDATE` operations. See also *MTS*.

toggle A property of an object, such as a check box, that alternates its state when repeatedly clicked or activated by a shortcut key combination.

transaction A group of processing steps that are treated as a single activity to perform a desired result. A transaction might entail all the steps necessary to modify the values in or add records to each table involved when a new invoice is created. RDBMSs that can process transactions must include the capability to cancel the transaction by a rollback instruction or to cause it to become a permanent part of the tables with the `COMMIT` or `COMMIT TRANSACTION` statement. See also *rollback*.

transaction monitor A synonym for transaction manager. See also *TM*.

Transact-SQL A superset of ANSI SQL-92 used by Microsoft SQL Server. Transact-SQL (T-SQL) includes flow-control instructions and the capability to define and use stored procedures that include conditional execution and looping.

trigger A stored procedure that executes automatically when a user or query executes an instruction that might affect the referential integrity of a database. Triggers usually occur before the execution of `INSERT`, `DELETE`, or `UPDATE` statements so that the effect of the statement on referential integrity can be examined by a stored procedure before execution. See also *stored procedure*.

twip The smallest unit of measurement in Windows and the default unit of measurement of VBA. The twip is 1/20 of a point, or 1/1440 of a logical inch.

two-phase commit A process applicable to updates to multiple (distributed) databases that prevents a transaction from completing until all the distributed databases acknowledge that the transaction can be completed. The replication process has supplanted two-phase commit in most of today's distributed client/server RDBMSs. See also *replication*.

type See *data type*.

type library A file with the extension .tlb that provides information about the types of objects exposed by an ActiveX component or Automation server. See also *object library*.

unary See *operator*.

A

UNC An abbreviation for Uniform Naming Convention, the method of identifying the location of files on a remote server. UNC names begin with \\. All 32-bit Windows applications support UNC.

Unicode A replacement for the 7- or 8-bit ASCII and ANSI representations of characters with a 16-bit model that allows a wider variety of characters to be used. Windows Me/98 and Windows XP/2000+/NT support Unicode. Access 95 and later support Unicode data.

unique index An index in which no two key fields or combinations of key fields on which the index is created can have the same value.

Universal Data Access Microsoft's all-encompassing database strategy based on COM, DCOM, OLE DB, ADO, MTS, Internet Information Server, ASP, and other proprietary Windows technologies. See also *ADO*, *ASP*, *COM*, *DCOM*, *MTS*, and *OLE DB*.

update A permanent change to data values in one or more data tables. An update occurs when the `INSERT`, `DELETE`, `UPDATE`, or `TRUNCATE TABLE` SQL commands are executed.

user defined A data type, also called a record, that's specified in your VBA source code by a **`Type...End Type`** declaration statement in the Declarations section of a module. The elements of the user-defined record type can be any data type valid for the language and can include other user-defined types.

user-defined transaction A group of instructions combined under a single name and executed as a block when the name is invoked in a statement executed by the user.

validation The process of determining whether an update to a value in a table's data cell is within a preestablished range or is a member of a set of allowable values. Validation rules establish the range or set of allowable values. Access 2+ supports validation rules at the field and table levels.

variable The name given to a symbol that represents or substitutes for a number (numeric), letter, or combination of letters (string).

VBA An abbreviation for Visual Basic for Applications, the official name of which is Visual Basic, Applications Edition. VBA is Microsoft's common application programming (macro) language for members of Microsoft Office and Visual Basic 6.0. Each application has its own "flavor" of VBA as a result of automatically created references to the application's object hierarchy in VBA code.

VDT An abbreviation for Visual Data Tools, which comprises the Query Designer and Database Designer for SQL Server. VDT (commonly called the da Vinci toolset) lets you create views, modify data structures, and add tables to Microsoft SQL Server databases. Access Data Projects use a subset of the VDT to create new tables, modify table structure, and add data to tables.

view The method by which data is presented for review by users, usually onscreen, or supplied to intermediary applications. Views can be created from subsets of columns from one or more tables by implementing the SQL `CREATE VIEW` instruction. A Jet select query is equivalent to an SQL Server view.

Visual Basic for Applications See *VBA.*

Visual Data Tools See *VDT.*

VST An abbreviation for Visual Studio Tools for Microsoft Office System 2003. VST includes the Access 2003 Developer Extensions and the SQL Server 2000 Developer Edition, which adds SQL Server 2000 management tools—SQL Server Enterprise Manager, Query Analyzer, Books Online, and the other database management components missing from MSDE 2000. VST also provides Visual Studio .NET templates for extending Microsoft Word and Excel 2003 macros with .NET managed code. See also *Access 2003 Developer Extensions.*

W3C An abbreviation for the World Wide Web Consortium, which "develops interoperable technologies (specifications, guidelines, software, and tools) to lead the Web to its full potential." W3C's home page is at `http://www.w3.org/`.

Web Services Interoperability Organization—A vendor-supported consortium (WS-I.org) dedicated to developing recommendations to make Web services created by different SOAP toolkits and hosted by common application servers interoperate with one another. Go to `http://www.ws-i.org` for additional information about WS-I's activities.

Web services See *XML Web services.*

Web Services Reference See *WSR.*

wildcard A character that substitutes for and allows a match by any character or set of characters in its place. The DOS ? and * wildcards are used in Jet expressions; SQL uses _ and `%` as wildcards.

WSDL An acronym (pronounced "wizdle") for Web Service Description Language, an XML dialect that describes the capabilities, data structure, and location of an XML Web service. Like SOAP 1.1, WSDL 1.1 isn't a W3C standard; the WSDL 1.1 W3C Note of March 15, 2001 is at `http://www.w3c.org/TR/wsdl`. The current version of the W3C specification for WSDL 1.2 is at `http://www.w3.org/TR/wsdl12/`.

NEW **WSR** An abbreviation for the Web Services Reference 2.0 tool, a COM add-in for the VBA Editor that's installed by the Office Web Services Toolkit. WSR uses an XML Web service's WSDL 1.1 file to generate the VBA code for an XML Web service proxy. WSR simplifies the VBA code for enabling an Access application to consume an XML Web service. See *SOAP toolkit*, *WSR*, and *XML Web services.*

xBase Any language interpreter or compiler or a database manager built on the dBASE III+ model and incorporating all dBASE III+ commands and functions. Microsoft's Visual FoxPro and Computer Associates' CA-Clipper are xBase dialects.

NEW **XDocs** The codename for Microsoft InfoPath during its beta period. See *InfoPath.*

XDR An abbreviation for XML Data Reduced, Microsoft's proprietary (non-standard) implementation of an XML-based schema definition of data structures for interpreting classes of data-related XML documents. ADO Recordsets saved to XML files use the XDR schema. W3C's XML Schema 1.0 specification has replaced XDR, which is obsolete except for some early XML features of SQL Server 2000. See also *XML Schema*.

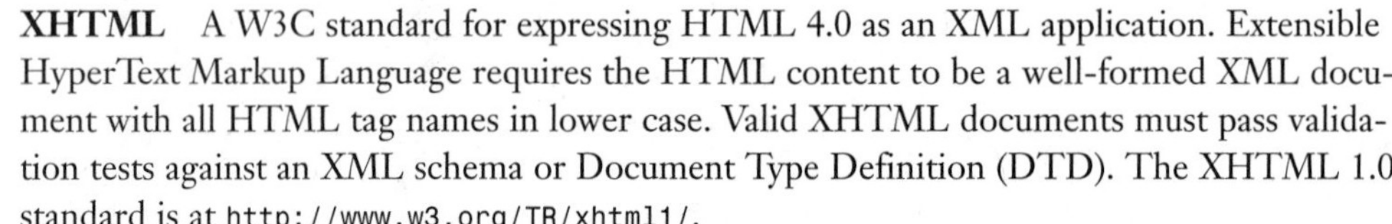

XHTML A W3C standard for expressing HTML 4.0 as an XML application. Extensible HyperText Markup Language requires the HTML content to be a well-formed XML document with all HTML tag names in lower case. Valid XHTML documents must pass validation tests against an XML schema or Document Type Definition (DTD). The XHTML 1.0 standard is at `http://www.w3.org/TR/xhtml1/`.

XML Infoset A W3C standard for XML Information Set, a set of definitions for 11 different types of information items—and their properties—that can make up a conforming XML document. All but three information items (Document, Element, and Namespace) are optional. Adherence to XML Infoset definitions is especially important for authoring data-related XML documents that interoperate with multiple XML parsers and schema validators. XML documents exported by Access conform to the XML Infoset definitions. W3C's XML Information Set recommendation is at `http://www.w3.org/TR/xml-infoset/`.

XML An abbreviation for Extensible Markup Language, a derivative of SGML (Standardized General Markup Language), that permits definition of custom markup tags. XML is especially useful for displaying and manipulating data when using the Internet HTTP protocol. XML documents carry an .xml extension. Data-related variations of XML include XML Query and XML Schema. The World Wide Web Consortium (W3C, `http://www.w3.org/`) maintains the XML standards, called recommendations. The second edition of the XML 1.0 standard (October 6, 2000) is at `http://www.w3.org/TR/REC-xml`.

XML Schema A standardized XML document type (`xsd` XML namespace) for describing the structure of documents and data. Most XML schema documents have an .xsd extension. XML Schema was a W3C candidate recommendation when this books was written. Access 2003's XML import/export features use the XSD namespace; some SQL Server 2000 XML features use XDR. A primer for XML Schema, which uses a purchase order as the model, is available at `http://www.w3.org/TR/xmlschema-0/`. See also *XDR*.

XML Web services Software components that reside on Web servers and use SOAP as the protocol and XML as the message format to communicate with one another—usually by HTTP or secure HTTP (HTTPS)—through corporate and personal firewalls. Microsoft uses the XML prefix to distinguish SOAP-based Web services from conventional Web-based services, such as search engines, portals, and e-commerce. W3C's Web Services Activity (`http://www.w3.org/2002/ws/`) coordinates development of basic XML Web services specifications. See also *SOAP*, *WSDL*, and *XML*.

XSL An abbreviation for Extensible Stylesheet Language, which specifies how the contents of an XML document are formatted for presentation to the user with XML Formatting Objects. XSL documents use the .xsl extension. The October 15 2001 XSL 1.0 recommendation is at `http://www.w3.org/TR/xsl/`.

XSLT An abbreviation for XSL Transformations, part of the XSL standard but maintained by a different W3C working group (WG). XSLT is a language for transforming an XML document into other XML documents or XHTML pages. XSLT documents also use the .xsl extension. Access 2003 makes extensive use of XSLT in conjunction with the use of ReportML for exporting Access application objects to XML/XSL files and DAP. The W3C recommendation for XSLT 1.0 (November 16, 1999) is at `http://www.w3.org/TR/xslt/`. A working draft of XSLT 1.1 and a requirements document for XSLT 2.0 also are available from the W3C Web site. See also *ReportML*.

Yes/No field A field of a table whose allowable values are Yes (True) or No (False). Yes/No fields were called logical or Boolean fields by Access 95 and earlier.

INDEX

B

How can we make this index more useful? Email us at indexes@quepublishing.com

C

G

H

I

M

N

O

P

Q

R

U

V

W

X

Y-Z

What's on the CD-ROM

The companion CD-ROM contains Woody's Office POWER Pack (WOPR) 2003, book examples, additional software, Web resources, and a graphics library.

Windows Installation Instructions

1. Insert the disc into your CD-ROM drive.
2. From the Windows desktop, double-click the My Computer icon.
3. Double-click the icon representing your CD-ROM drive.
4. Double-click on `start.exe`. Follow the on-screen prompts to access the CD content.

NOTE

> If you have the AutoPlay feature enabled, `start.exe` will be launched automatically whenever you insert the disc into your CD-ROM drive.

License Agreement

By opening this package, you are also agreeing to be bound by the following agreement:

You may not copy or redistribute the entire CD-ROM as a whole. Copying and redistribution of individual software programs on the CD-ROM is governed by terms set by individual copyright holders.

The installer and code from the author are copyrighted by the publisher and the author. Individual programs and other items on the CD-ROM are copyrighted or are under an Open Source license by their various authors or other copyright holders.

This software is sold as-is without warranty of any kind, either expressed or implied, including but not limited to the implied warranties of merchantability and fitness for a particular purpose. Neither the publisher nor its dealers or distributors assumes any liability for any alleged or actual damages arising from the use of this program. (Some states do not allow for the exclusion of implied warranties, so the exclusion may not apply to you.)